Savings Certificate

YES! Send me the next issue of ESPN The Magazine, **RISK-FREE!** If I like it, I'll get 22 more issues (23 in all) for just $11.97 – $103 savings off the newsstand price!

ESPN The Magazine - Get coverage on all the major sports including: MLB, NBA, NHL and NFL in every issue.

NO OBLIGATION: If I decide ESPN The Magazine is not for me, I'll return your bill marked "cancel." The **Risk-Free** issue is mine to keep.

Save $103

Name

Address   Apt. No.

City   State   Zip

E Mail Address   S3LW2A

By providing my e-mail address, I am indicating I'd like to receive information about my subscription and special offers from ESPN The Magazine and carefully selected partners via e-mail.
26 issues is one year. 23 issue newsstand price $114.77.
Canada and foreign add $19. © ESPN, Inc.

Order now: 1-877-503-6026

Subscribe online: www.sub14.espnmag.com

Savings Certificate

YES! Send me the next issue of ESPN The Magazine, **RISK-FREE!** If I like it, I'll get 22 more issues (23 in all) for just $11.97 – $103 savings off the newsstand price!

ESPN The Magazine - Get coverage on all the major sports including: MLB, NBA, NHL and NFL in every issue.

NO OBL...   ...t for
me, I'll re...   ...e is
mine to k...   ...103

Name

D1374238

Address   No.

City   State   Zip

E Mail Address   S3LW2A

By providing my e-mail address, I am indicating I'd like to receive information about my subscription and special offers from ESPN The Magazine and carefully selected partners via e-mail.
26 issues is one year. 23 issue newsstand price $114.77.
Canada and foreign add $19. © ESPN, Inc.

Order now: 1-877-503-6026

Subscribe online: www.sub14.espnmag.com

For up-to-the-minute scores, news and information, visit *ESPN.com*

NO POSTAGE
NECESSARY
IF MAILED
IN THE
UNITED STATES

BUSINESS REPLY MAIL
FIRST-CLASS MAIL PERMIT NO. 200 BOONE, IA

POSTAGE WILL BE PAID BY ADDRESSEE

ESPN®
THE MAGAZINE
PO Box 37325
Boone, IA 50037-2325

2004
ESPN
SPORTS
ALMANAC

With Exclusive Year in Review Commentary from ESPN Anchors and Analysts

Chris Berman
on Pro Football

Dan Patrick
on Top Personalities

Steve Levy
on Hockey

Linda Cohn
on Top Personalities

Stuart Scott
on Top Moments

Karl Ravech
*on Baseball
& Golf*

Chris Fowler
*on College Football
& College Basketball*

Trey Wingo
on Top Moments

Also Contributing

Dick Vitale
on College Basketball

Lee Corso
on College Football

Jerry Bembry
on Pro Basketball

The Champions of 2003

Auto Racing
For all the statistics, see the Auto Racing section.

NASCAR Circuit
Daytona 500	Michael Waltrip
Coca-Cola 600	Jimmie Johnson
Brickyard 400	Kevin Harvick
Mountain Dew Southern 500	Terry Labonte
EA Sports 500	Michael Waltrip
Winston Cup Points Leader	Matt Kenseth, 4548 pts (through Oct. 19)

CART Circuit
CART Championship	Paul Tracy, 226 pts (through Oct. 19)

Indy Racing League Circuit
Indianapolis 500	Gil de Ferran
IRL Championship	Scott Dixon, 507 pts

Formula One Circuit
U.S. Grand Prix	Michael Schumacher
World Driving Champion	Michael Schumacher, 93 pts

Baseball
For all the statistics, see the Baseball section.

World Series	Florida def. NY Yankees, 4 games to 2
MVP	Josh Beckett, Florida, P
ALCS	New York def. Boston, 4 games to 3
NLCS	Florida def. Chicago, 4 games to 3
All-Star Game	American League 7, National League 6
MVP	Garret Anderson, AL (Anaheim), LF
College World Series	Rice 14, Stanford 2
MVP	John Hudgins, Stanford, P

College Basketball
For all the statistics, see the College Basketball section.

Men's NCAA Tournament
Championship	Syracuse 81, Kansas 78
MVP	Carmelo Anthony, Syracuse, G

Women's NCAA Tournament
Championship	Connecticut 73, Tennessee 68
MVP	Diana Taurasi, Connecticut, G

Pro Basketball
For all the statistics, see the Pro Basketball section.

NBA Finals	San Antonio def. New Jersey, 4 games to 2
MVP	Tim Duncan, San Antonio, F/C
Eastern Final	New Jersey def. Detroit, 4 games to 0
Western Final	San Antonio def. Dallas, 4 games to 2
All-Star Game	West 155, East 145 2OT
MVP	Kevin Garnett, West (Minnesota), F

Bowling
For all the statistics, see the Bowling section.

Men's Major Championships
PBA World Championship	Walter Ray Williams, Jr.
Tournament of Champions (2002)	Jason Couch
ABC Masters	Bryon Smith
U.S. Open	Walter Ray Williams, Jr.

Women's Major Championships
WIBC Queens	Wendy Macpherson
U.S. Open	Kelly Kulick

College Football (2002)
For all the statistics, see the College Football section.

National Champions
AP	Ohio State (14-0)
ESPN/USA Today Coaches'	Ohio State (14-0)

Major Bowls
Rose	Oklahoma 34, Washington St. 14
Fiesta	Ohio St. 31, Miami-FL 24 2OT
Orange	USC 38, Iowa 17
Sugar	Georgia 26, Florida St. 13
Heisman Trophy	Carson Palmer, USC, QB

Pro Football (2002)
For all the statistics, see the Pro Football section.

Super Bowl XXXVII	Tampa Bay 48, Oakland 21
MVP	Dexter Jackson, Tampa Bay, S
AFC Championship	Oakland 41, Tennessee 24
NFC Championship	Tampa Bay 27, Philadelphia 10
Pro Bowl	AFC 45, NFC 20
MVP	Ricky Williams, Miami, RB
CFL Grey Cup Final	Montreal 25, Edmonton 16
MVP	Anthony Cavillo, Montreal, QB

Golf
For all the statistics, see the Golf section.

Men's Major Championships
Masters	Mike Weir
U.S. Open	Jim Furyk
British Open	Ben Curtis
PGA Championship	Shaun Micheel

Champions (Seniors) Major Championships
The Tradition	Tom Watson
PGA Seniors	John Jacobs
U.S. Senior Open	Bruce Lietzke
Senior Players Championship	Craig Stadler
Senior British Open	Tom Watson

Women's Major Championships
Nabisco Championship	Patricia Meunier-Lebouc
LPGA Championship	Annika Sorenstam
U.S. Women's Open	Hilary Lunke
Women's British Open	Annika Sorenstam

National Team Competition
Solheim Cup	Europe 17½, United States 10½

Hockey
For all the statistics, see the Hockey section.

Stanley Cup	New Jersey def. Anaheim, 4 games to 3
MVP	Jean-Sebastien Giguere, Anaheim, G
Eastern Final	New Jersey def. Ottawa, 4 games to 3
Western Final	Anaheim def. Minnesota, 4 games to 0
All-Star Game	West 6, East 5 (SO, 3-1)
MVP	Dany Heatley, Atlanta, RW

Horse Racing
For all the statistics, see the Horse Racing section.

Triple Crown Champions
Kentucky Derby	Funny Cide (Jose Santos)
Preakness Stakes	Funny Cide (Jose Santos)
Belmont Stakes	Empire Maker (Jerry Bailey)

Harness Racing
Hambletonian	Amigo Hall (Mike Lachance)
Little Brown Jug	No Pan Intended (David Miller)
Messenger Stakes	No Pan Intended (David Miller)

Soccer
For all the statistics, see the Soccer section.

Women's World Cup Final	Germany 2, Sweden 1 OT
MVP	Birgit Prinz, Germany, F

Tennis
For all the statistics, see the Tennis section.

Men's Grand Slam Championships
Australian Open	Andre Agassi
French Open	Juan Carlos Ferrero
Wimbledon	Roger Federer
U.S. Open	Andy Roddick

Women's Grand Slam Championships
Australian Open	Serena Williams
French Open	Justine Henin-Hardenne
Wimbledon	Serena Williams
U.S. Open	Justine Henin-Hardenne

Miscellaneous Champions
For more, see the Miscellaneous Sports section.

Little League World Series	Tokyo, Japan
Tour de France	Lance Armstrong (USA)
Iditarod	Robert Sorlie
World Series of Poker	Chris Moneymaker

2004 ESPN® SPORTS ALMANAC

Gerry Brown
Michael Morrison
EDITORS

HYPERION
ESPN®
BOOKS

12.99

1/2/03

040001

Editors
Gerry Brown
Michael Morrison

Technical Support
Sean Dessureau
Mike Leary
Adam Polgreen

Conversion Diva
Susan Hyde

Comments and suggestions from readers are invited. Because of the many letters received, however, it is not possible to respond personally to every correspondent. Nevertheless, all letters are welcome and each will be carefully considered. The **ESPN Sports Almanac** does not rule on bets or wagers. Address all correspondence to: Sports Almanac, Inc., P.O. Box 542281, Lake Worth, FL 33454-2281. Email: sportsalmanac@mac.com.

ISBN 0–7868–8716–8

FIRST EDITION

10 9 8 7 6 5 4 3 2 1

CONTENTS 5

CONTENTS

Wow. It's been an interesting off-season to say the least. Despite several changes in ownership and a myriad of changes in business environments the book carries on through the rough seas. Its an obvious testament to the quality of the product not to mention all the sweating and swearing that has gone into it since founding editor Mike Meserole launched this ship over a decade and a half ago. She's still racing ahead, unlike Team New Zealand's broken down boat that lost the America's Cup to a land-locked country this year. That's kind of like losing the Kentucky Derby to a gelding from Upstate New York or the World Series to an expansion franchise. Oh, wait.

To continue with obvious, and bad, sports metaphors, we've had to develop a whole new set of tools and didn't have as much of a spring training as we'd like but if you're reading this, then something good happened. It was most likely in spite of us and due to the help and guidance from the all the great people listed on this page. We want to take this opportunity to say THANK YOU in case we failed to during the past year. It was a busy one for us.

At ESPN, thanks to John Hassan for saving the day on a regular basis, Russell Baxter, Mary Moore and all the essay and list contributors. Thanks also to our friends in the Meadowlands: Rick Sommers of Command Web and Rob Conte and Paul Morgan from SCI for their incredible patience with the technically ignorant.

As always, thanks to Gretchen Young, Natalie Kaire and David Lott at Hyperion. A giant tip of the cap to Almanac Editor Emeritus Mike Meserole for continuing to care so much.

Also, Ed Macedo and Paul Kinney from ESPN research, Barbara Zidovsky from Nielsen Media Research, Paul Michinard from Getty Images and Yvette Reyes from AP/Wide World Photos.

Thanks again to Matthew Byrd and Byron Laws from TechBooks for a super job on the big conversion project.

Salutations to all our former colleagues, most especially John Gettings.

Big thank yous go out to Bill Trippe, Liz Kubik, Susan Hyde, George Kane, Jess Brallier, Mike Rozett and Steve Lewers for all the great advice along the way.

We couldn't have done it without the invaluable technical advice from the likes of Adam Polgreen, Sean Dessureau and Mike Leary.

Thanks once again to Rick Campbell and Gary Johnson at the NCAA, U.S. Trotting's Paul Ramlow, the PBA Tour's Russ Twoey, Kathi Reichert from CART and Cadillac Bill Magrath from the *Sports Business Daily.*

Also, our gratitude goes out to the numbingly numerous pro and college sports media relations folks from coast to coast that answered our calls and emails. Thanks also to money player Jay Lind at Miller Wachman and to expert proof-reader Rick Reilly.

The famous saying goes "what fails to kill you makes you stronger." Well, after the past year, not to mention Game 7 of the 2003 ALCS, we must be ready for anything. Look for us late night on "World's Strongest Man." But most of all, look back (in the following pages) and then forward, as we always do, to another great year of sports.

Lastly, we can't forget our wives, Lisa and Lori, for their unending support. We obviously married out of our conference.

Gerry Brown
Michael Morrison

October 28, 2003

Major League Cities & Teams

As of Oct. 31, 2003, there were 132 major league teams playing or scheduled to play men's baseball, men's basketball, NFL football, hockey and men's soccer in 52 cities in the United States, Canada and Puerto Rico. Listed below are the cities and the teams that play there.

Anaheim
AL	Angels
NHL	Mighty Ducks of Anaheim

Atlanta
NL	Braves
NBA	Hawks
NFL	Falcons
NHL	Thrashers

Baltimore
AL	Orioles
NFL	Ravens

Boston
AL	Red Sox
NBA	Celtics
NFL	N.E. Patriots (Foxboro)
NHL	Bruins
MLS	N.E. Revolution (Foxboro)

Buffalo
NFL	Bills (Orchard Park)
NHL	Sabres

Calgary
NHL	Flames

Charlotte
NBA	Bobcats (2004-05)
NFL	Carolina Panthers

Chicago
AL	White Sox
NL	Cubs
NBA	Bulls
NFL	Bears
NHL	Blackhawks
MLS	Fire

Cincinnati
NL	Reds
NFL	Bengals

Cleveland
AL	Indians
NBA	Cavaliers
NFL	Browns

Columbus
NHL	Blue Jackets
MLS	Crew

Dallas
AL	Texas Rangers (Arlington)
NBA	Mavericks
NFL	Cowboys (Irving)
NHL	Stars
MLS	Burn

Denver
NL	Colorado Rockies
NBA	Nuggets
NFL	Broncos
NHL	Colorado Avalanche
MLS	Colorado Rapids

Detroit
AL	Tigers
NBA	Pistons (Auburn Hills)
NFL	Lions
NHL	Red Wings

East Rutherford
NBA	New Jersey Nets
NFL	New York Giants
NFL	New York Jets
NHL	New Jersey Devils
MLS	MetroStars

Edmonton
NHL	Oilers

Green Bay
NFL	Packers

Houston
NL	Astros
NBA	Rockets
NFL	Texans

Indianapolis
NBA	Indiana Pacers
NFL	Colts

Jacksonville
NFL	Jaguars

Kansas City
AL	Royals
NFL	Chiefs
MLS	Wizards

Los Angeles
NL	Dodgers
NBA	Clippers
NBA	Lakers
NHL	Kings
MLS	Galaxy

Memphis
NBA	Grizzlies

Miami
NL	Florida Marlins
NBA	Heat
NFL	Dolphins
NHL	Florida Panthers (Sunrise)

Milwaukee
NL	Brewers
NBA	Bucks

Minneapolis
AL	Minnesota Twins
NBA	Minnesota Timberwolves
NFL	Minnesota Vikings

Montreal
NL	Expos
NHL	Canadiens

Nashville
NFL	Tennessee Titans
NHL	Predators

New Orleans
NBA	Hornets
NFL	Saints

New York
AL	Yankees
NL	Mets (Flushing)
NBA	Knicks
NHL	Rangers
NHL	Islanders (Uniondale)

Oakland
AL	Athletics
NBA	Golden St. Warriors
NFL	Raiders

Orlando
NBA	Magic

Ottawa
NHL	Senators (Kanata)

Philadelphia
NL	Phillies
NBA	76ers
NFL	Eagles
NHL	Flyers

Phoenix
NL	Arizona Diamondbacks
NBA	Suns
NFL	Arizona Cardinals (Tempe)
NHL	Coyotes

Pittsburgh
NL	Pirates
NFL	Steelers
NHL	Penguins

Portland
NBA	Trail Blazers

Raleigh
NHL	Carolina Hurricanes

Sacramento
NBA	Kings

St. Louis
NL	Cardinals
NFL	Rams
NHL	Blues

St. Paul
NHL	Minnesota Wild

Salt Lake City
NBA	Utah Jazz

San Antonio
NBA	Spurs

San Diego
NL	Padres
NFL	Chargers

San Francisco
NL	Giants
NFL	49ers

San Jose
NHL	Sharks
MLS	Earthquakes

San Juan, Puerto Rico
MLB	Expos

Seattle
AL	Mariners
NBA	SuperSonics
NFL	Seahawks

Tampa
AL	T.B. Devil Rays (St. Petersburg)
NFL	T.B. Buccaneers
NHL	T.B. Lightning

Toronto
AL	Blue Jays
NBA	Raptors
NHL	Maple Leafs

Vancouver
NHL	Canucks

Washington
NBA	Wizards
NFL	Redskins (Raljon, Md.)
NHL	Capitals
MLS	D.C. United

Updates

Trainer **Richard Mandella** and jockey **Alex Solis** celebrate Mandella's history-making four wins at the 2003 Breeders' Cup at Santa Anita.

AP/Wide World Photos

10 UPDATES

AUTO RACING
Late 2003 Results
NASCAR

Date	Event	Location	Winner (Pos)	Avg.mph	Earnings	Pole	Qual.mph
Oct. 19	Subway 500	Martinsville	Jeff Gordon (1)	67.658	$183,018	J. Gordon	93.650
Oct. 27	Bass Pro Shops MBNA 500*Atlanta		Jeff Gordon (19)	127.769	249,978	R. Newman	194.295

*The Bass Pro Shops MBNA 500, scheduled for Oct. 26, was interrupted after 39 of 325 laps and completed on Monday, Oct. 27.
Winning Cars: CHEVROLET (2)—Gordon 2.
Remaining Races (3): Checker Auto Parts 500 in Phoenix (Nov. 2); Pop Secret Microwave 400 in Rockingham (Nov. 9); Ford 400 in Homestead-Miami (Nov. 16).

CART

Date	Event	Location	Winner	Time	Avg.mph	Pole	Qual.mph
Oct. 26	Lexmark Indy 300* . .	Queensland	Ryan Hunter-Reay	1:49:02.803	72.280	S. Bourdais	109.706

*The Lexmark Indy 300 was shortened from 65 laps to 47 due to thunderstorms.
Winning Cars: FORD/REYNARD (1)—Hunter-Reay.
Remaining Race: The 500 in Fontana, Calif. (Nov. 2)

NHRA

Date	Event	Winner	Time	MPH	2nd Place	Time	MPH
Oct. 26 Las Vegas Nationals	Top Fuel	Kenny Bernstein	4.545	326.87	T. Schumacher	5.436	174.68
	Funny Car	Tony Pedregon	5.135	273.39	W. Bazemore	5.183	266.64
	Pro Stock	Greg Anderson	6.837	201.73	K. Johnson	6.878	200.56

Remaining Event (1): Automobile Club of Southern California NHRA Finals in Pomona, Cal. (Nov. 6-9).

GOLF
Late 2003 Tournament Results
PGA Tour

Last Rd Tournament	Winner	Earnings	Runner-Up
Oct. 12 Las Vegas Invitational.	Stuart Appleby (328)*	$720,000	S. McCarron (328)
Oct. 19 Chrysler Classic of Greensboro.	Shigeki Maruyama (266)	810,000	B. Faxon (271)
Oct. 26 Funai Classic at Walt Disney World . . .	Vijay Singh (265)	720,000	3-way tie (269)

*Playoffs: Las Vegas—Appleby won on the 1st hole.
Second place ties (three players or more): **Funai** (S. Verplank, T. Woods, S. Cink).
Remaining Events (10): Chrysler Championship (Oct. 27-Nov. 2); The Tour Championship (Nov. 6-9); World Golf Championships: EMC World Cup (Nov. 13-16); Franklin Templeton Shootout (Nov. 13-16); The Presidents Cup (Nov. 21-23); ConAgra Foods Skins Game (Nov. 29-30); Team Matches (Dec. 6-7); UBS Warburg Cup (Dec. 6-7); Target World Challenge (Dec. 11-14); Wendy's Three-Tour Challenge (Dec. 21).
Note: The Tour Championship (Nov. 6-9) is the final official PGA Tour event of 2003.

European PGA Tour

Last Rd Tournament	Winner	Earnings	Runner-Up
Oct. 12 Dutch Open	Maarten Lafeber (267)	E 166,660	S. Hansen & M. Gronberg (268)
Oct. 19 World Match Play Championship	Ernie Els (4&3)	£1,000,000	T. Bjorn
Oct. 19 Turespaña Mallorca Classic	Miguel A. Jimenez (204)	E 66,660	J.M. Olazabal (205)
Oct. 26 Telefonica Open de Madrid	Ricardo Gonzalez (270)	E 233,330	Four-way tie (271)

Second place ties (three players or more): **Madrid** (P. Casey, P. Harrington, M. Olander, N. O'Hern).
Remaining Events (3): Volvo Masters Andalucia (Oct. 30-Nov. 2); The Seve Trophy (Nov. 6-9); World Golf Championships: EMC World Cup (Nov. 13-16).

Champions Tour
(formerly Senior PGA Tour)

Last Rd Tournament	Winner	Earnings	Runner-Up
Oct. 12 Turtle Bay Championship	Hale Irwin (208)	$225,000	T. Kite (210)
Oct. 19 SBC Championship	Craig Stadler (198)	225,000	B. Gilder (202)
Oct. 26 Charles Schwab Cup Championship . . .	Jim Thorpe (268)	440,000	T. Watson (271)

Remaining Events (3): UBS Warburg Cup (Nov. 21-23); Office Depot Father-Son Challenge (Dec. 6-7); Wendy's Three-Tour Challenge (Dec. 21).

LPGA Tour

Last Rd Tournament	Winner	Earnings	Runner-Up
Oct. 12 Samsung World Championship.	Sophie Gustafson (274)	$200,000	R. Teske & B. Daniel (276)

Remaining Events (5): Sports Today CJ Nine Bridges Classic (Oct. 31-Nov. 2); Mizuno Classic (Nov. 7-9); Mobile LPGA Tournament of Champions (Nov. 13-16); ADT Championship (Nov. 20-23); Wendy's Three-Tour Challenge (Dec. 21).

TENNIS

Late 2003 Tournament Results

Men's Tour

Finals	Tournament	Winner	Earnings	Loser	Score
Oct. 5	Japan Open (Tokyo)	Rainer Schuettler	$118,000	S. Grosjean	76 62
Oct. 5	Kremlin Cup (Moscow)	Taylor Dent	142,000	S. Sargsian	76 64
Oct. 5	Open De Moselle (Metz)	Arnaud Clement	E 52,000	F. Gonzalez	63 16 63
Oct. 12	CA Tennis Trophy (Vienna)	Roger Federer	$151,135	C. Moya	63 63 63
Oct. 12	Grand Prix of Tennis (Lyon)	Rainer Schuettler	113,000	A. Clement	75 63
Oct. 19	TMS—Madrid	Juan Carlos Ferrero	540,000	N. Massu	63 64 63
Oct. 26	St. Petersburg Open	Gustavo Kuerten	142,000	S. Sargsian	64 63
Oct. 26	Stockholm Open	Mardy Fish	E 91,000	R. Soderling	75 36 76
Oct. 26	Swiss Indoors (Basel)	Guillermo Coria	E 142,000	D. Nalbandian	walkover

Remaining Events (4): BNP Paribas Master (Nov. 2); ATP Tour World Doubles Championship (Nov. 9); Tennis Masters Cup Houston (Nov. 23); Davis Cup Final (Nov. 30).

Women's Tour

Finals	Tournament	Winner	Earnings	Loser	Score
Oct. 5	Kremlin Cup (Moscow)	Anastasia Myskina	$189,000	A. Mauresmo	62 64
Oct. 5	Japan Open (Tokyo)	Maria Sharapova	27,000	A. Kapros	26 62 76
Oct. 12	Porsche Tennis Grand Prix (Filderstadt)	Kim Clijsters	98,500	J. Henin-Hardenne	57 64 62
Oct. 12	Tashkent Open (Uzbekistan)	Virginia Ruano Pascual	22,000	S. Obata	62 76
Oct. 19	Swisscom Challenge (Zurich)	Justine Henin-Hardenne	189,000	J. Dokic	60 64
Oct. 26	Generali Open (Linz)	Ai Sugiyama	93,000	N. Petrova	75 64
Oct. 26	Seat Open (Luxembourg)	Kim Clijsters	35,000	C. Rubin	62 75

Remaining Events (3): Advanta Championships (Nov. 2); Bell Challenge (Nov. 2); Volvo Open (Nov. 9); Bank of America Tour Championships (Nov. 10); Fed Cup Final (Nov. 23).

THOROUGHBRED RACING

Late 2003 Major Stakes Races

Date	Race	Location	Miles	Winner	Jockey	Purse
Sept. 27	Vosburgh Stakes	Belmont	6½ F	Ghostzapper	Javier Castellano	$500,000
Sept. 27	Flower Bowl Invitational	Belmont	1¼ (T)	Dimitrova	Jerry Bailey	750,000
Sept. 27	Turf Classic Invitational	Belmont	1½ (T)	Sulamani (IRE)	Jerry Bailey	750,000
Sept. 27	Jockey Club Gold Cup	Belmont	1¼	Mineshaft	Robby Albarado	1,000,000
Sept. 28	Lady's Secret BC Handicap	Santa Anita	1 1/16	Got Koko	Alex Solis	300,000
Sept. 28	Yellow Ribbon Stakes	Santa Anita	1¼ (T)	Tates Creek	Patrick Valenzuela	500,000
Sept. 28	Oak Leaf Stakes	Santa Anita	1 1/16	Halfbridled	Julie Krone	200,000
Sept. 28	Clement L. Hirsch Turf Championship Stakes	Santa Anita	1¼ (T)	Storming Home (GB)	Gary Stevens	245,000
Oct. 5	Norfolk Stakes	Santa Anita	1 1/16	Ruler's Court	Alex Solis	200,000
Oct. 4	Frizette Stakes	Belmont	1 1/16	Society Selection	Ray Ganpath	500,000
Oct. 4	Champagne Stakes	Belmont	1 1/16	Birdstone	Jerry Bailey	500,000
Oct. 4	Lane's End Futurity Stakes	Keeneland	1 1/16	Eurosilver	Javier Castellano	400,000
Oct. 4	Shadwell Turf Mile	Keeneland	1 (T)	Perfect Soul (IRE)	Edgar Prado	600,000
Oct. 5	WinStar Galaxy Stakes	Keeneland	1 3/16	Bien Nicole	Donald Pettinger	500,000
Oct. 5	Beldame Stakes	Belmont	1 1/8	Sightseek	Jerry Bailey	750,000
Oct. 5	Kelso Handicap	Belmont	1 (T)	Freefourinternet	Jose Espinoza	347,000
Oct. 5	Ancient Title B.C. Handicap	Santa Anita	6 F	Avanzado (ARG)	Tyler Baze	156,625
Oct. 5	Oak Tree B.C. Mile	Santa Anita	1 (T)	Designed for Luck	Patrick Valenzuela	300,000
Oct. 4	Goodwood B.C. Handicap	Santa Anita	1 1/8	Pleasantly Perfect	Alex Solis	482,000
Oct. 5	Spinster Stakes	Keeneland	1 1/8	Take Charge Lady	Edgar Prado	500,000
Oct. 5	Prix de l'Arc de Triomphe*	Longchamp	1½ (T)	Dalakhani (IRE)	Christophe Soumillon	E 1,600,000
Oct. 12	My Dear Girl Stakes	Calder	1 1/16	Chatter Chatter	Jerry Bailey	400,000
Oct. 12	Calder Oaks	Calder	1 1/8 T	Lover String	Gary Wilbert Bain	200,000
Oct. 12	In Reality Stakes	Calder	1 1/16	Sir Oscar	Julio Garcia	400,000
Oct. 11	QE II Challenge Cup	Keeneland	1 1/8 (T)	Film Maker	Edgar Prado	500,000
Oct. 12	TC of America Stakes	Keeneland	6 F	Summer Mis	Rene Douglas	125,000
Oct. 13	Oak Tree Derby	Santa Anita	1 1/8	Devious Boy (GB)	Julie Krone	150,000
Oct. 18	Empire Classic Handicap	Belmont	1 1/8	Well Fancied	Edgar Prado	250,000
Oct. 19	E.P. Taylor Stakes	Woodbine	1¼ (T)	Volga (IRE)	Richard Migliore	750,000
Oct. 19	Canadian International*	Woodbine	1½ (T)	Phoenix Reach (IRE)	Martin Dwyer	1,500,000

Thoroughbred Racing (Cont.)

Date	Race	Location	Miles	Winner	Jockey	Purse
Oct. 25	Breeders' Cup - Distaff.....	Santa Anita	1⅛	Adoration	Patrick Valenzuela	1,834,000
Oct. 25	Breeders' Cup - Juv. Fillies ..	Santa Anita	1¹⁄₁₆	Halfbridled	Julie Krone	917,000
Oct. 25	Breeders' Cup - Mile	Santa Anita	1 (T)	Six Perfections	Jerry Bailey	1,375,000
Oct. 25	Breeders' Cup - Sprint	Santa Anita	6 F	Cajun Beat	Cornelio Velasquez	1,082,060
Oct. 25	Breeders' Cup - F&M Turf...	Santa Anita	1¼ (T)	Islington (IRE)	Kieren Fallon	972,020
Oct. 25	Breeders' Cup - Juvenile...	Santa Anita	1⅛	Action This Day	David Flores	1,375,500
Oct. 25	Breeders' Cup - Turf*......	Santa Anita	1½ (T)	High Chaparral (IRE) Johar	Michael Kinane Alex Solis	1,944,040
Oct. 25	Breeders' Cup - Classic* ...	Santa Anita	1¼	Pleasantly Perfect	Alex Solis	4,000,000

*World Series Racing Championship race.

Note: The 2003 Breeders' Cup Turf (Oct. 25) ended in a dead heat.

Mandella's Four Wins is Top Story at Breeders' Cup

Trainer Richard Mandella made history at the 2003 Breeders' Cup World Thoroughbred Championships at Santa Anita. Running his horses at their home track, Mandella won four of the day's eight races, a feat never matched in the 20-year history of the event. His record win total included an historic victory in the Juvenille Fillies by Hall of Fame and recently un-retired jockey Julie Krone aboard *Halfbridled*. Krone became the first female to ride a Breeders' Cup champion with the win.

Mandella's other winners were *Johar*, who shared the winner's circle in the Turf with High Chapparal due to the first ever Breeders' Cup dead heat, *Action This Day* in the Juvenile and *Pleasantly Perfect* in the day's biggest race, the $4 million Classic. Mandella became only the third trainer (D. Wayne Lukas and Patrick Byrne) to win both races for 2-year-olds in the same year at the Breeders' Cup, setting himself up for a pontentially big year in 2004.

HARNESS RACING
Late 2003 Major Stakes Races

Date	Race	Raceway	Winner	Driver	Purse
Sept. 27	**Kentucky Futurity**......	Lexington	Mr. Muscleman	Ron Pierce	$526,000
Oct. 18	**Messenger Stakes**	The Meadows	No Pan Intended	Dave Miller	270,000

Note: *No Pan Intended* became the tenth pacer in history, and first since Blissful Hall in 1999, to win the Triple Crown, following wins in the Cane Pace and Little Brown Jug with the victory in the Messenger Stakes.

BOWLING
Late 2003 Results
PBA

Final	Event	Winner	Earnings	Final	Runner-Up
Sept. 15	Deam Bowl	Walter Ray Williams Jr.	$25,000	445-421	Yasuyuki Sadamatsu
Sept. 21	Japan Cup.	Chris Barnes	40,000	210-179	Tommy Jones
Oct. 12	PBA Banquet Open	Robert Smith	40,000	244-187	Michael Machuga
Oct. 19	Greater Kansas City Classic	Norm Duke	40,000	197-194	Mika Koivuniemi
Oct. 26	PBA Miller High Life Open	Brian Himmler	40,000	230-215	Mika Koivuniemi

Remaining 2003 Events: see the 2003-04 PBA Tour schedule on page 769.

Personalities

Sammy Sosa made more headlines in 2003 with this groundout than with his 40 homers.

Top 20 Sports Personalities of 2003

Dan and Linda salute their top newsmakers of the year.

by **Dan Patrick** and **Linda Cohn**

Michael Vick

If there were any disbelievers out there, surely they had to be swayed on Dec. 1, 2002. With his team already on a seven-game unbeaten streak, Michael Vick led the Falcons into the Metrodome to take on the Vikings. His cannon arm was misfiring that day, so Vick relied on his other weapons – his legs. Vick ran for an NFL record (since the 1970 merger) 173 yards on ten carries, including a 46-yard touchdown run to win the game in overtime that had half of the Vikings defense falling at his feet. He pushed the Falcons into the playoffs where they would achieve the unthinkable, winning at Lambeau Field.

Pete Sampras

I know what you're thinking. The guy didn't play one game of tennis in 2003. So how can he make this list? This was the year Sampras walked away from the game, officially announcing his retirement at an emotional ceremony on the opening day of the U.S. Open, where just a year earlier he won his record 14th grand slam event. Some might say he's boring. I say he's classy. His friendly rivalry with Andre Agassi provided a decade-long shot in the arm for American tennis not seen since the somewhat less friendly rivalry of Jimmy Connors and John McEnroe. He'll be missed.

The Buccaneers D

This is meant as no slight to Brad Johnson, Mike Alstott and the rest of the offense, but the Bucs' defense in 2002-03 may go down as one of the greatest

Dan Patrick is a co-anchor on ESPN's SportsCenter and hosts The Dan Patrick Show from 1-4 p.m. EST, M-F, on ESPN Radio.

AP/Wide World Photos

Michael Vick scampers for a 46-yard touchdown run in overtime on a record-setting day against the Minnesota Vikings on Dec. 1, 2002.

ever. Defensive coordinator Monte Kiffin's unit was the first since the 1985 Bears to lead the NFL in fewest yards per game, fewest points per game and interceptions. Simeon Rice, Warren Sapp (whose taunting and pre-game skipping sometimes overshadows his performance) and defensive player of the year Derrick Brooks highlight a group that tormented quarterbacks all season, especially Rich Gannon in Super Bowl XXXVII. The Steel Curtain and the Doomsday Defense had nothing on them. Now all they need is a nickname.

LeBron James

Even Michael Jordan never had as much hype as this high school phenom from Ohio. Before he was even drafted by an NBA team, Nike had given him a $90-plus million contract, and reportedly, they didn't even have the highest offer. St. Vincent-St. Mary games sold out in minutes. His home games were sold on pay-per-view, and his game against Oak Hill Academy in December was watched by 1.5 million people, the second-highest rated event ever on ESPN2. A high school game!

AP/Wide World Photos

Tim Duncan celebrates his second NBA title and second Finals MVP award.

Alex Zanardi

The two-time CART driving champion had his legs amputated after a crash in Sept., 2001 that left him lucky to be alive. Two years later, he was back behind the wheel, competing in the final event of the FIA European Touring Car Championship in Italy in October. His BMW was modified to allow him to brake with his thigh and control the clutch and accelerator with his hands. As if his heart wasn't beating fast enough, on the first turn after the start Zanardi was involved in a six-car pileup that ended the race after just a half-mile. In his second race he finished seventh. Victory.

Dave Bliss

In the wake of the murder of Baylor basketball player Patrick Dennehy, head coach Dave Bliss outwardly did all the right things. He grieved along with the family at the funeral and offered to help in any way he could. Secretly, however, it was a different story. As it turned out, Bliss had been paying part of Dennehy's tuition, just one of many NCAA violations occurring within the Baylor program. In order to make it seem that Dennehy could afford the payments himself, Bliss tried to coax some of his assistant coaches and players into portraying Dennehy as a drug dealer.

What he didn't know was that one of his assistants was taping the whole thing. Bliss resigned days later. It was yet another example of a Division I coach losing his job over unethical behavior. But this example was truly pathetic.

Maurice Clarett

It was quite an eventful year for Maurice Clarett. He began 2003 by scoring two touchdowns in the Fiesta Bowl to lead his Ohio State Buckeyes to their first national football title since 1968. Then things went downhill. In April he filed a police report saying his car was stolen, and along with it, the contents inside – a couple of TV's, thousands of dollars of CD's and stereo equipment, and about $800 in cash. As you might expect, the NCAA infractions committee took notice. Clarett later said the car was borrowed and the value of its content was exaggerated. Too late. And when reports also came out that he walked out of a midterm and passed the course by taking an oral exam, he was suspended for the 2003 season by his school. By the fall, he sued the NFL with the hopes of making him eligible for the 2004 draft.

Sammy Sosa

Sammy's ubiquitous smile disappeared for a while in the late spring. Mired in a prolonged slump, Sosa reached into the bat rack, picked one out and stepped to the plate against the Devil Rays. His bat splintered as he grounded out, exposing a row of cork in the center. He was immediately ejected and later suspended for eight games (reduced to seven). He claimed he used the bat for batting practice and grabbed it during the game by mistake. Only he knows the truth. For what it's worth, 76 more of Sosa's bats were tested and all came back clean. Either way, his golden reputation took a hit. It was another 40-home run season for Sosa, but it was one groundout that caused the most stir.

Tim Duncan

There's not much glitz. There's not much flashiness. And quite honestly there's just not a whole lot of "wow" from Tim Duncan. But here's what there is a lot of: class, effort, awards...and NBA Championship rings. Duncan led San Antonio to its second title in the last five years and was named NBA regular season and Finals MVP for the second time in his career. In Game 6 against the Nets, he was unstoppable, recording 21 points, 20 rebounds and ten assists. His eight blocks left him two short of a quadruple-double. Ask Spurs fans if they need more glitz.

Josh Beckett

In the end, the whole "three-days rest" controversy didn't matter one bit. Josh Beckett could have thrown on one-day's rest. After allowing three hits over $7\frac{1}{3}$ innings in Game 3, the cocky 23-year-old Texan with the "mentality of a burglar" took to the mound in arguably the most intimidating baseball venue in the world, with the World Series at stake, and simply blew away the New York Yankees. Nine innings, five hits, nine strikeouts and most importantly...no runs. Manager Jack McKeon summed things up after the game, in what may be the understatement of the year. "This guy is going to be something special."

Carmelo Anthony

While LeBron-mania was capturing the headlines, all Syracuse freshman Carmelo Anthony was doing was leading Syracuse to its first NCAA basketball championship – ever. In the championship game against Kansas, the kid from the tough streets of Baltimore scored 20 points, hauled in 10 rebounds and dished out seven assists, all while nursing a sore back. Syracuse fans hoped he'd stay, even for one more year, but had to know the chances were slim. Weeks later, after he left his mark at Syracuse, he left for the NBA.

Andy Roddick

Fittingly, the 2003 U.S. Open began with Pete Sampras' retirement ceremony and ended with America's next great hope, Andy Roddick celebrating his first grand slam title. With a booming serve that neared 150 m.p.h., Roddick registered 23 aces in taking down Juan Carlos Ferrero in straight sets for the title. And then he cried. For a cocky, fist-pumping 21-year-old often accused of being too demonstrative on the court, he showed humility and maturity beyond his years.

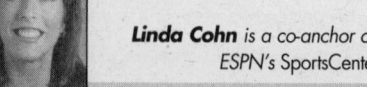

Linda Cohn *is a co-anchor on ESPN's SportsCenter*

Lance Armstrong

You know what's most impressive about Lance Armstrong? He basically made us forget that he had cancer a few years ago that left him with a 50 percent chance to live. Remember that? Now we just seem to take him for granted. Ho-hum, another Tour de France win. If he doesn't win the 2004 race, we'll wonder what's wrong. That's how good he is. His win in 2003 was the most grueling of all. He overcame the flu. He wiped out twice. And he avoided another spill by going off-roading across a French field. But in the end it was Lance in his familiar yellow jersey, sipping champagne. Again.

Serena Williams

By beating her sister Venus in the finals of the 2003 Australian Open, Serena Williams became the ninth woman in history to win all four grand slam events, and just the fifth to win four majors in a row, something she dubbed the "Serena Slam." After being upset by Belgian Justine Henin-Hardenne in the semis of the French Open, she returned to the winner's circle at Wimbledon, defeating her big sister in the finals yet again. Unfortunately that would be her final match of the year, as a knee injury accomplished what no one on the court could, knocking her from the WTA Tour's No. 1 ranking.

AP/Wide World Photos

His Mighty Ducks of Anaheim may have fallen one game shy of a Stanley Cup, but at least goaltender **Jean-Sebastien Giguere** *spent some quality time with Jay Leno in 2003.*

Kobe Bryant

As a star player for the Lakers, Kobe Bryant has attracted his share of attention over the past several years. In 2003, however, the attention was for all the wrong reasons. In early July, Bryant, who had always been viewed as one of the NBA's "good guys," was charged with sexually assaulting a 19-year-old woman at a hotel in Eagle, Colo. At a press conference following the initial reports, Bryant sat with his wife and admitted he had sex with the woman but denied forcing her to do anything. At best, Bryant committed adultery and destroyed his sterling reputation. At worst, he committed a violent act. In any case, neither he nor the alleged victim will ever be the same.

Funny Cide

OK, so he didn't win the Triple Crown. So what else is new? What made this horse and this story so special was that so few people had even heard of him heading into the Kentucky Derby. His pedigree wasn't much to speak of. His owner and trainer weren't very well known in the racing world. He was a 12-to-1 long shot! But Funny Cide prevailed over other horses that were "supposed" to win. By doing so he turned normal everyday sports fans into horse racing fans, if only for a few weeks.

Annika Sorenstam

She won five LPGA tournaments through October, including the fifth and sixth majors of her career. In October she was inducted into the LPGA and World Golf Halls of Fame. And we all know that's not the story here. In late May at the Colonial, Annika Sorenstam became the first woman since Babe Zaharias in 1945 to play in a PGA event. Ultimately she failed to make the cut, shooting 5-over par for 36 holes. But she succeeded in so many other ways. While her accuracy and ball-striking ability impressed the rest of the field, it was her emotion and positive attitude amidst a glaring spotlight that won over the public and provided an immeasurable boost to the LPGA.

Rich Gannon

After the Patriots selected Rich Gannon in the fourth-round of the 1987 draft, team officials had thoughts of him being a defensive back. Fortunately for the Raiders, that little experiment didn't work. Gannon had quite a year in 2002-03, leading the NFL in passing yards and setting a record with 418 completions. He was everything a leader should be, willing the Raiders to the Super Bowl where he met up with an unforgiving Tampa Bay defense. It was a horrible day for Gannon and the rest of the Raiders, but it doesn't take away his MVP season.

Jim Boeheim

Finally Jim Boeheim can erase the memory of Indiana's Keith Smart's baseline jumper in the 1987 championship game. After three years as a player, then 27 years and 653 wins as a coach, Boeheim brought a national basketball title to Syracuse. He can now be removed from the list of best coaches without a national title. So does that make him a better coach than he was before his title? Not according to Boeheim. "I don't feel any smarter yet," he said after the win. "Maybe tomorrow."

Jean-Sebastien Giguere

In 2003 the Mighty Ducks of Anaheim came within one game of winning the Stanley Cup. They went 15-6 in the playoffs, sweeping the defending champion Red Wings, taking out the powerful Dallas Stars, and then sweeping the Wild before their Cup Finals meeting with the Devils. Now consider this: over those 21 games, they averaged a meager 2.1 goals per game. So how did they get as far as they did? They got "Giggy." Their goalie Jean-Sebastien Giguere was, as they say in the hockey world, "standing on his head." With five playoff shutouts, including three in a row against Minnesota, he was awarded the Conn Smythe Award. As a kid Giguere used to imitate his idol Patrick Roy. Now a pro, it seems he's still imitating him.

Moments

Annika Sorenstam takes a moment to think during her historic appearance on the PGA Tour at the 2003 Colonial.

AP/Wide World Photos

Top 20 Sports Moments of 2003

by **Stuart Scott** and **Trey Wingo**

Interesting. A year when some of the biggest sports stories were the ones that occurred OFF the field. Not one off-the-field scandal, or two, but several. Plural. A lot. It makes our job less SportsCenter and more Peter Jennings World News Tonight.

Don't get us wrong. Sports is still sports. The highlights still thrill us, the emotional and physical hurdles these athletes leap still drop our jaws. There will always be the highlights, but in 2003, along with the highlights, there were "life-lights," events that reminded us that athletes are human too. In their egos, their insecurities, their frailties. So, as Trey Wingo and I delve into the top 20 moments from 2003 understand some will make us smile, others will make us wistful and a few might just make us wanna cry.

Stuart Scott
is an anchor/reporter on
ESPN's SportsCenter.

Stuart Scott and Trey Wingo give us their picks for the biggest moments of the year in sports.

Ohio State Fiesta

The 'Canes came in undefeated, not just this season but for the last two. Miami quarterback Ken Dorsey didn't know how to lose and few thought Ohio State would teach him. But in one of the best college football games ever played, with more sheer stomach-twisting moments than anyone could ask for, the Buckeyes used two overtimes, a questionable pass interference call, and all the drama of a Dickinson novel to claim the national title. Ohio State's first since 1968.

Roy Steps Up

His only problem for most of his career has been that there's been no one to fight. Possessing maybe the best combination of speed and power since Sugar Ray Leonard, Roy Jones Jr. decided to climb one more mountain. The mountain. The heavyweight variety. True, the heavyweight division is a splinter of alphabet soup. WBC. WBA. W-whatever else. But to beat John Ruiz and beat him soundly to grab one of the heavyweight crowns, Roy proved once again that he is in a class all his own.

AP/Wide World Photos

Roy Jones Jr. *provided one of the moments of the year with his historic heavyweight title bout victory over John Ruiz in March. Promoter Don King had promised to cut his famous hair should Ruiz lose, but apparently King exaggerated.*

Outhouse to Penthouse

Some time ago the Tampa Bay Bucs were not only the laughingstock of football, but all of professional sports. Who else starts their life 0-26? Who else is called the "Yucks?" Now, call those old Yucks "champions" as Tampa Bay crushed Oakland in Super Bowl XXXVII. With a defense that flat out dominated like few before, with a quiet confidence (see Derrick Brooks and John Lynch) and a loud arrogance (see Warren Sapp), they took new coach Jon Gruden's snarl and turned into a smile. A smile that somehow still looked like a snarl. As for the Raiders, who let Gruden go to the Bucs...they just looked old.

And a Youngster shall lead Them

While his former high school rival stole all the headlines with his jump to the NBA, freshman forward Carmelo Anthony silently made Syracuse's satisfying run to the national championship all his. It was clear that 'Melo man was only going to be big man on campus one year before making his own jump. But he made it count: scoring, passing, rebounding and *leading* as the Orangemen and longtime head coach Jim Boeheim won their first NCAA title.

AP/Wide World Photos

*In his national television debut, the mega-hyped high-schooler **LeBron James** drew high praise from the crowds of experienced basketball observers in attendance.*

Crimson-faced Tide

Bear Bryant wasn't just turning in his grave. He was doing calisthenics. Legendary Alabama needed a new football coach when Dennis Franchione bolted the program for Texas A&M. So they hired Mike Price from Washington State but, apparently, the Price wasn't right, except for the hotel mini-bar tab, a strip club and a party in his hotel room. And before Price even coached one game for the Crimson Tide, he was fired.

World Cup half-empty

The U.S. Women's National Team was supposed to win its second straight World Cup. They were supposed to be crowned the best in the world, again. Mia and her teammates were supposed to wave goodbye from the top of the mountain. But a not-so-funny thing happened. We never even made it to the finals. The German squad came up big and sent the American women packing in the semifinals. Fortunately, the Olympics are less than a year away and the team veterans will get a chance for a proper farewell.

Out of the Blocks

Memo to the world: In about 20 years or so, somebody real, real fast is going to be breaking all kinds of sprinting world records, that is if there's a gene for speed. Marion Jones, the fastest woman in the world, and her boyfriend Tim Montgomery, the fastest man in the world, had a baby together in June. The boy, named Tim Jr., is already pretty quick. He arrived several weeks early.

Spurs Dig In

There were no asterisks this time. There was just a pure, classic throttling. The San Antonio Spurs beat Los Angeles coach Phil Jackson (who said the Spurs' 1999 title should have an asterisk because they won it in a shortened season) and his Lakers in the playoffs then took apart the New Jersey Nets in the Finals. Some people called it a boring Finals. They said nobody could shoot. Really?? Looked to me like it was two tough defensive teams cloaking each other like thick wool blankets. When the dust cleared Tim Duncan had been outstanding. His points, assists, rebounds and blocks were statistically loud and dominating. The way he did it was quietly ruthless and efficient. Duncan, now a two-time NBA regular season and Finals MVP, has earned the right to be called one of the best of all-time.

Curses!

The Curses of the Bambino and of the billy goat continue. The Boston Red Sox had not won the World Series since 1918 and the Chicago Cubs hadn't won one since 1908. The Red Sox hadn't even made it since 1986. And the Cubs? Don't ask. But both teams finally looked to be on the fast track in 2003. Think about it. Both the Cubs and Red Sox were just five outs away from making The Series...and *both* lost in Game 7 of the LCS. From Fall Classic to classic fall. Oh the humanity! As a public service, counselors are available for those who need to talk.

In Court, Not On Court

A preliminary hearing that took two days...but set six days apart. A hearing about an alleged rape involving one of the brightest stars in the NBA. A hearing where the language is graphic and the sexual content, explicit. Words that aren't usually heard in the world of sports, at least outside the locker room, hang heavily in the air. And once again, this was just Kobe Bryant's preliminary hearing. What can we expect to hear as the trial begins next year?

That's my 10 this year...once again there were plenty of them to go around. Trey, now it's your chance...

Thanks again, Stu. Here are my picks...

LeBron Arrives

LeBron's national television debut. Yes. It was just a high school game, against clearly inferior opposition. But in LeBron's United States coming out party—as seen on ESPN2—King James showed in a hurry that he was worth the hype. A monster dunk and a few "Magic-esque" passes made you realize right away. James is going to build upon, and not be beaten down by, the hype machine that preceded his pro career.

Big Mess on Campus

The inexcusable actions by former Baylor head basketball coach Dave Bliss was the cherry on the sundae for perhaps the single worst six months in the history of college sports. St. Bonaventure's basketball team quits. Larry Eustachy leaves Iowa State, Mike Price gets dumped from Alabama. Rick Neuheisel is fired at Washington and the mess made by Maurice Clarett at Ohio State leaves a dark stain on the college game.

Tiger Bomb

For the first time I can remember Tiger Woods makes a mental mistake in a major. Having closed to within three strokes of the lead on Sunday at the Masters, Woods confers with caddy Steve Williams and ultimately decides to go with the driver on the short third hole, a 350-

Trey Wingo *is a co-anchor on ESPN's SportsCenter*

yard par 4. A five iron would have left him a wedge shot away from the green. But Tiger went for it, lost it right, into the pine needles, made double bogey and golf's unpredictable summer began.

Annika

No, she didn't make the cut. But she cut through a lot of B.S. Annika Sorenstam's two rounds at the Colonial was the most interesting 36 holes in golf this summer. And don't buy the good 'ole boy argument that by getting in on a sponsor's exemption she didn't earn her way. Why shouldn't the best female player on the planet be given one over some schmo from the Nationwide Tour?

Emmitt Goes to the Desert

Emmitt Smith signs with Arizona. The NFL's all-time leading rusher goes to the NFL's all-time woeful franchise. And the Cardinals fans respond in typical fashion. Emmitt was signed to help increase ticket sales. How did it work? There were more than 50,000 seats unused for the Cards home opener. Oops.

Torch Passed

A few years ago the marketing slogan of men's professional tennis was "new balls please," showcasing the young, up-and-coming talent. Andy Roddick no longer qualifies as up and coming. He arrived with a splash, literally, at the wettest U.S. Open on record. Sampras said goodbye and Andre will someday as well. But all of that is OK. With Roddick, the future of U.S. men's tennis is in pretty good shape.

AP/Wide World Photos

*Former Cowboy **Emmit Smith**, the NFL's all-time leading rusher, moved to Arizona in the off-season but made a return to the field, this time from the visitor's sideline, at Texas Stadium.*

Say it ain't Sosa!

Sammy Sosa's corked bat bust gave baseball yet another black eye. While further tests found no additional cork in any of his remaining lumber, the idea that Sammy used a bogus bat at least once makes us all look a little harder at the man who had become baseball's goodwill ambassador. Even the chance that the loveable Cub could have been using a secret weapon in 1998's thrilling home run battle with St. Louis slugger Mark McGwire raised questions that nobody wants to think about.

WUSA shuts doors

What timing! The Women's United Soccer Association (WUSA) ceases operations just five days before the Women's World Cup, the tournament that got it off the ground to begin with, opens at stadiums across the United States. Soccer moms may be still taking their kids to play games down at the park, but apparently not enough are willing to pay to watch the kids play when they're all grown up.

AP/Wide World Photos

*American cyclist **Lance Armstrong** joined the ranks of five-time Tour de France winners with his gutty win in 2003. Armstrong hopes to make a return to Moments of the Year in 2004 with a record-breaking sixth Tour title.*

Bonds bonds

It was Barry Bonds' summer of discontent. Begrudgingly showing his humanity, the greatest slugger in baseball finally found a way to America's heart. Playing through the pain of his father's death, Barry gave us all he had before...and after...winning game after game and finally public opinion with dramatic home runs.

Lance in France Again

The record-tying fifth win was easily the hardest. But the bottom line is he still reigns supreme. American-in-Paris Lance Armstrong may never be the fan favorite in France but that's not always a bad thing. The bottom line is that no one's won the Tour de France more times than Lance and in 2004 he'll go for an unprecedented sixth straight. As they say in Paris..."Merde!"

Calendar

*It was a tumultuous offseason for **Kobe Bryant**, who was charged with sexual assault in July.*

AP/Wide World Photos

November 2002

Sun	Mon	Tue	Wed	Thu	Fri	Sat
					1	2
3	4	5	6	7	8	9
10	11	12	13	14	15	16
17	18	19	20	21	22	23
24	25	26	27	28	29	30

Quote of the Month

"I'm embarrassed for all mothers all over the world...I mean, my church group! I'm a born again Christian and this is not going to help."

Jackie Hurlbut, mother of Tim Hurlbut, the 21-year-old man who climbed over the glass a Calgary Flames game wearing nothing but red socks. He then fell onto the ice, knocked himself out cold and was carried off on a stretcher.

Bulging Offense

It sure didn't take St. Louis quarterback Marc Bulger very long to get accustomed to running the Rams offense. After taking over for the injured Kurt Warner in late Oct., 2002, Bulger rolled through November, winning five in a row and throwing for the most yards ever for a quarterback's first five starts.

	Team	Yards
Marc Bulger	St. Louis	1,496
Jeff Blake	Cincinnati	1,410
Gary Hogeboom	Dallas	1,400
Elvis Grbac	San Francisco	1,376
Vinny Testaverde	Tampa Bay	1,358

The State(s) of Bowling

According to *Strike Ten Entertainment*, here are the five states in the country with the most bowling centers.

State	Centers
Pennsylvania	422
New York	412
Ohio	392
Wisconsin	392
Michigan	381

2 **On "Upset Saturday,"** Boston College stuns No. 4-ranked Notre Dame, 14-7, in South Bend, handing the Irish their first loss under coach Ty Willingham. Also, Pitt beats No. 3 Virginia Tech, 28-21, and Florida beats No. 5 Georgia, 20-13.

New York outpolls San Francisco and is named the United States candidate to host the 2012 Olympic Games.

3 **Kenya's Rodgers Rop** (2:08:07) and Joyce Chepchumba (2:25:56) win the men's and women's divisions, respectively, of the New York Marathon. American Marla Runyan, who is legally blind, is the fifth-fastest woman (2:27:10).

Buffalo Bills quarterback Drew Bledsoe's first meeting against his old team, the New England Patriots, is a nightmare as the Bills are walloped, 38-7.

Johnny Benson wins his first-ever NASCAR race in his 226th career start, taking the checkered flag at the Pop Secret 400 in Rockingham.

4 **Longtime St. Louis Blues** star Bernie Federko, Islanders power forward Clark Gillies, defensive stalwart Rod Langway and coach Roger Neilson are inducted into the Hockey Hall of Fame.

Colorado Rockies hurler Jason Jennings and Toronto third baseman Eric Hinske are selected major league baseball's rookies of the year.

Michigan State football coach Bobby Williams is fired two days after his team's 49-3 loss to Michigan, its worst loss in 55 years.

5 **Randy Johnson outduels** Arizona teammate Curt Schilling for the N.L. Cy Young Award, his record-tying fourth consecutive and fifth overall.

6 **Less than two weeks after** losing Game 7 of the World Series to the Anaheim Angels, manager Dusty Baker parts ways with the San Francisco Giants after ten years with the club.

World Series champ Mike Scioscia of Anaheim and St. Louis' Tony La Russa are named A.L. and N.L. managers of the year, respectively. La Russa becomes the award's first four-time winner.

Hall of fame high school basketball coach Morgan Wootten announces his retirement after 46 years and 1,274 wins at DeMatha Catholic High School in Maryland.

7 **Oakland A's lefty** Barry Zito outdistances Boston's Pedro Martinez and Derek Lowe to win his first A.L. Cy Young Award.

Michigan announces self-imposed sanctions on its men's basketball program due to various violations in the 90's. The punishment includes forfeiting five seasons worth of wins, a 2003 postseason ban, and the removal of their Final Four banners from 1992-93.

9 **Top-ranked Oklahoma** is upset by Texas A&M, 30-26, at College Station, all but ruining the Sooners' chance to play for a national title.

10 **Annika Sorenstam cards** a final-round 67 at the Mizuno Classic in Japan to capture her tenth LPGA title of the year. She is the tour's first ten-time winner in 34 years.

For the first time in NFL history, the NFL has two 450-yard passers on the same day as Pittsburgh's Tommy Maddox throws for 473 against the Atlanta Falcons and St. Louis' Mark Bulger goes for 453 against the San Diego Chargers.

The Atlanta Falcons and Pittsburgh Steelers battle to a 34-34 tie, the NFL's first since 1997.

Olympic wrestling hero Rulon Gardner returns to the mat for the first time since losing a toe to frostbite. He soundly defeats Sweden's Eddy Bengtsson at the Kurt Angle Classic in New Orleans.

AP/Wide World Photos

*High school basketball coaching legend **Morgan Wootten** announces his retirement after 46 seasons at the helm of DeMatha Catholic High School in Hyattsville, Md. He leaves the game as the winningest coach with a record of 1,274-192.*

11 Giants slugger Barry Bonds unanimously wins the N.L. MVP award, becoming the majors' first five-time winner.

12 Oakland A's shortstop Miguel Tejada is named A.L. MVP, outpacing runner-up Alex Rodriguez.

Miami-OH defensive coordinator Jon Wauford is taken away in handcuffs and charged with battery after an altercation with a Marshall fan who ran onto the field following Marshall's 36-34 win.

Sidney Lowe resigns as coach of the 0-8 Memphis Grizzlies and is replaced by 69-year-old TNT broadcaster Hubie Brown.

Spanish tennis star Arantxa Sanchez Vicario retires at age 30 after a 17-year career that included 29 wins and four grand slam singles titles.

13 Felipe Alou is hired as manager of the N.L. champion San Francisco Giants.

17 Australian Lleyton Hewitt needs five sets to defeat Juan Carlos Ferrero in the Tennis Masters Cup, the final event on the men's ATP Tour.

Kurt Busch wins NASCAR's season-ending Ford 400 in Miami, his third win in the last five races. Tony Stewart finishes 18th, which is enough for him to clinch the overall Winston Cup points race by just 38 points over Mark Martin.

20 A computer programmer at Autotote, pleads guilty to wire fraud conspiracy and money laundering in connection with a suspicious winning Pick-Six bet on the Breeders' Cup that returned $3 million. Chris Harn also implicated two of his Drexel University fraternity brothers in the scheme.

Fernando Vargas is suspended for nine months and fined $100,000 by the Nevada State Athletic Commission for testing positive for steroids following his September loss to Oscar De La Hoya.

22 Shaquille O'Neal returns to the Lakers lineup following toe surgery scoring 17 points in limited minutes in Los Angeles' 86-73 win over Chicago. In Houston Yao Ming, in his first NBA start scores 18 points and blocks three shots.

The Buffalo Sabres end their month-long 12-game winless streak, holding on for a 5-4 win over Columbus.

23 Ohio State beats rival Michigan, 14-9, to secure a Big Ten title, undefeated regular season and a spot in the Fiesta Bowl to play for the national championship.

Arturo Gatti wins his highly anticipated rematch with Micky Ward on 10-round unanimous decision setting the stage for a rubber match between the two throwback junior welterweight brawlers.

24 Annika Sorenstam wins the season-ending ADT Championships for her 11th win of 2003, capping the best LPGA season in 38 years.

Anthony Calvillo throws for 260 yards and two touchdowns to lead the Montreal Alouettes to a 25-16 win over Edmonton in the 90th Grey Cup.

Falbrav, ridden by jockey Frankie Dettori, wins the prestigious $4 million Japan Cup, the penultimate event in thoroughbred racing's World Series Racing Championship.

25 Theo Epstein, 28, is named general manager of Boston Red Sox, becoming the youngest GM in baseball history

28 The Dallas Mavericks suffer their first loss in 15 games, falling to Indiana 110-98, and one game short of matching the NBA record for best start to a season.

In the annual Thanksgiving Day NFL matchups, the Dallas Cowboys storm back from a 20-10 third-quarter deficit to beat the Washington Redskins, 27-20, and the Detroit Lions lose to the New England Patriots, 20-12.

DECEMBER 2002

Sun	Mon	Tue	Wed	Thu	Fri	Sat
1	2	3	4	5	6	7
8	9	10	11	12	13	14
15	16	17	18	19	20	21
22	23	24	25	26	27	28
29	30	31				

Quote of the Month

"The evil empire extends its tentacles even into Latin America."

Larry Lucchino, president of the Boston Red Sox after long-time Red Sox rivals the New York Yankees win the Jose Contreras sweepstakes by signing the highly coveted Cuban pitcher to a four year contract.

Tuck it and Run

Atlanta Falcon Michael Vick set an NFL record for quarterbacks with 173 yards rushing on Dec. 1. Vick's total included the 46-yard game-winning touchdown run in overtime.

Yards	Player	Season
173	Michael Vick, Atlanta	2002
150	Tobin Rote, Green Bay	1951
131	Billy Kilmer, San Francisco	1961
131	Tobin Rote, Green Bay	1951
129	Jack Concannon, Phila.	1966
127	Bobby Douglass, Chicago	1972
125	Donovan McNabb, Phi	2000

Heisman U.

Trojans quarterback Carson Palmer won the 2002 Heisman Trophy, giving Southern Cal five of the 68 Heismans ever awarded. But that is only good for third place on the list of schools with the most Heisman Trophies.

School	Heisman Trophies
Notre Dame	7
Ohio St.	6
USC	5
Michigan	3
Army	3
Oklahoma	3
Nebraska	3

Note: OSU's Archie Griffin won it twice.

1 **The slumping San Jose Sharks fire** coach Darryl Sutter as well as assistants Lorne Molleken and Rich Preston following an 8-12-2-2 record to start the season.

Atlanta's Michael Vick rushes for an NFL quarterback-record 173 yards, including a 46-yard run for the winning touchdown in overtime at Minnesota.

2 **Free agent slugger Jim Thome signs** a 6-year, $87.5 million contract with the Philadelphia Phillies.

Oakland receiver Tim Brown became the third player in NFL history with 1,000 catches in a 26-20 Raiders win over the New York Jets.

3 **A's Closer Billy Koch is traded** to the Chicago White Sox as part of a 6-player deal, the A's receive closer Keith Foulke two other players and cash in exchange for Koch and two minor-leaguers.

The last-place Calgary Flames relieve head coach Greg Gilbert of his duties, firing him and assistant Brad McCrimmon after winning just one of the past 12 games.

4 **Veteran NHL coach Ron Wilson is hired** to replace Darryl Sutter as head coach of the San Jose Sharks.

5 **Long-time Braves pitcher Tom Glavine** signs a three-year deal with the New York Mets worth a reported $35 million.

6 **The top-ranked Miami Hurricanes secure** an undefeated regular season and their spot in the BCS title game at the Fiesta Bowl with a 56-45 win over No. 18 Virginia Tech.

8 **Former Patriots QB Drew Bledsoe** returns to New England for the first time as a member of the Buffalo Bills following his off-season trade and is intercepted four times as the Pats beat the Bills, 27-17.

Oakland's Rich Gannon sets an NFL record with his 10th 300-yard passing game of the season, throwing for 328 yards in a 27-7 Raiders win over San Diego.

9 **Miami's Ricky Williams joins** Earl Campbell and O.J. Simpson as the only running backs in NFL history to rush for 200 yards in back-to-back games in a 27-9 win over the Bears on Monday Night Football.

11 **Colorado captain Joe Sakic scores** the 500th goal of his NHL career with a second-period wrister in a 3-1 loss in Vancouver.

12 **High school star LeBron James makes** his national television debut on ESPN2 finishing with 31 points, 13 rebounds and six assists as he led St. Vincent-St. Mary's to an upset win over the nation's top prep team Oak Hill Academy.

14 **USC quarterback Carson Palmer** is named the 68th winner of the Heisman Trophy, becoming the fifth Trojan to earn college football's most prestigious award.

Chris Byrd earns a unanimous decision over four-time heavyweight champion Evander Holyfield for the vacant IBF heavyweight title.

16 **Yankees bullpen stalwart Mike Stanton** moves across town, signing a three-year, $9 million free agent contract with the Mets.

18 **Washington State's Mike Price is hired** by Alabama to replaced outgoing head football coach Dennis Franchione.

The under-achieving Colorado Avalanche fire head coach Bob Hartley, just two seasons after he led them to the Stanley Cup. Assistant Tony Granato was tabbed as his replacement.

Billionaire Robert Johnson is awarded the NBA's Charlotte expansion franchise set to begin play for the 2004-05 season. Johnson becomes the first African-American majority owner in major pro sports.

AP/Wide World Photos

*Billionaire founder of Black Entertainment Television, **Robert Johnson**, was awarded the NBA's newest Charlotte expansion franchise in December 2002. The team, scheduled to begin play for the 2004-05 season replaces the Hornets, who were relocated to New Orleans following the 2001-2002 season.*

19 Godzilla is coming! The New York Yankees reach an agreement to sign Japanese MVP Hideki Matsui for a reported $21 million over three years.

20 Western Kentucky beats McNeese St., 34-14, for the NCAA Div. 1-AA football national championship behind 159 rushing yards and a pair of touchdowns from running back Jon Frazier.

Free agent slugger Cliff Floyd signs a four-year $26 million contract with the New York Mets.

In a salary dump, the Atlanta Braves trade right-handed pitcher Kevin Millwood to their National League East rivals the Philadelphia Phillies for catcher Johnny Estrada.

22 American skier Bode Miller wins his first World Cup race of the season, taking first in the giant slalom event at Alta Badia in Italy. It's the fifth World Cup win of his career and moves him into second place on the overall season standings.

24 The New York Yankees win the battle for free-agent pitcher and Cuban defector Jose Contreras, signing him to a four-year, $32 million deal.

25 New Mexico's Katie Hnida became the first woman to play in a Division 1-A college football game when she attempts an extra-point kick in the Las Vegas Bowl. The kick was blocked and New Mexico lost the game to UCLA 27-13.

26 It's cut-down day in Atlanta as AOL Time Warner, owner of the NBA's Hawks and NHL's Thrashers, do some downsizing and fire both team's head coaches on the same day. Hawks coach Lon Kruger and assistant Gar Heard lose their jobs after the team starts 11-16. Hawks assistant Terry Stotts is tabbed as interim coach. The Thrashers' Curt Fraser and assistant Tim Bothwell gets shown the door after compiling a 8-20-1-4 mark in 2002 and Thrashers GM Don Waddell named himself the interim replacement.

Cyclist Lance Armstrong is named Associated Press Male Athlete of the Year for winning his fourth straight Tour de France, edging out second-place finisher and 2001 winner Barry Bonds.

27 Tennis superstar Serena Williams wins the Associated Press Female Athlete of the Year award. Williams won three of the four tennis Grand Slam events in 2002. Golfer Annika Sorenstam places a distant second.

28 Darryl Sutter, recently fired by the San Jose Sharks (see Dec. 1), is named head coach of the Calgary Flames, replacing the recently fired Greg Gilbert (see Dec. 3).

29 On the NFL's final regular-season Sunday, the defending Super Bowl champion New England Patriots finish 9-7 but are eliminated from the playoffs on a tiebreaker.

30 Cowboys head coach Dave Campo is fired by Dallas following the team's third straight 5-11 season and amid speculation that veteran NFL coach and proven winner Bill Parcells will be named as his replacement.

The Jacksonville Jaguars fire the only head coach in franchise history, Tom Coughlin, after eight years and a 72-64 record with the Jaguars, but only 19-29 the last three.

31 Mike Holmgren announces that he is stepping down as Seattle Seahawks general manager but will continue to serves as the team's head coach.

JANUARY 2003

Sun	Mon	Tue	Wed	Thu	Fri	Sat
			1	2	3	4
5	6	7	8	9	10	11
12	13	14	15	16	17	18
19	20	21	22	23	24	25
26	27	28	29	30	31	

Quote of the Month

"Martina said earlier today that she won her first Grand Slam in 1973. I was born in that year."

Leander Paes, mixed doubles partner of 46-year-old Martina Navratilova following their win Jan. 26 at the Australian Open. It is Navraliova's 57th Grand Slam title (who actually won her first Grand Slam title in 1974) and she becomes the oldest player to win a Grand Slam event.

From Way Back

San Francisco's shocking come-from-way-behind win over the New York Giants in the NFC wild card game on Jan. 5 ranks as the second biggest postseason comeback in NFL history.

Deficit	Game	Playoff Round
32	Buffalo vs. Houston, 1/3/93	AFC WC
24	S.F. vs. NYG, 1/5/03	NFC WC
20	Detroit vs. S.F., 12/22/57	NFL div.
18	Dallas vs. S.F., 12/23/72	NFC div.
18	Miami vs. Cleveland, 1/4/85	AFC div.

Yo. Yao. Yo.

At 7-foot-5, Houston's rookie center Yao Ming is one of the tallest players in NBA history. But the Rockets hope that his career reaches heights not seen in the careers of the league's other really big men.

Height	Name	Career PPG	RPG
7'7"	Manute Bol	2.6	4.2
7'7"	Gheorghe Muresan	9.8	6.4
7'6"	Shawn Bradley*	9.2	7.1
7'5"	Yao Ming*	13.5	8.2
7'5"	Chuck Nevitt	1.6	1.5

*active players. Career averages are through the 2002-03 season.

1 **Bill Parcells confirms the speculation** that he will shortly be named head coach of the Dallas Cowboys when he tells ESPN that he will be leaving the network that he worked for the past season to go to Dallas.

Oklahoma wins the Rose Bowl, beating Washington State, 34-14, in Pasadena. The loss sends outgoing Cougars coach Mike Price, who has been hired at Alabama, with a loss in his final game at Washington State.

Oakland quarterback Rich Gannon earns the NFL's MVP award for his record-setting season with the Raiders. Gannon completed a record 418 passes in 2002.

2 **The Dallas Cowboys officially introduce** Bill Parcells as the franchise's sixth head coach after signing him to a four-year, $17.1 million contract.

USC and its newly minted Heisman Trophy winner Carson Palmer thump Iowa and its Heisman Trophy runner-up Brad Banks, 38-17, at the Orange Bowl.

3 **The Ohio State Buckeyes beat** Miami, 31-24, in two overtimes to win their fifth national championship and first since 1968. The loss ended Miami's 34-game winning streak.

Longtime college hoops coach Lefty Driesell retired after 41 seasons at four different schools, most recently at Georgia State and most famously at Maryland. Driesell retires with 786 wins, fifth most in NCAA Division 1 history.

4 **The New York Jets destroy** the Indianapolis Colts, 41-0, and Michael Vick and the Atlanta Falcons upset the Green Bay Packers, 27-7, handing them their first postseason home loss in team history, opening wild card weekend in the NFL.

Skier Bode Miller wins his second straight World Cup giant slalom and takes the lead in the overall season standings, becoming the first American to do so since Phil Mahre in 1983.

Michael Jordan scores a season-high 41 points in a 107-104, double overtime Washington win over Indiana.

5 **The San Francisco 49ers stage** the second biggest comeback in NFL playoff history coming from 24 points down to beat the New York Giants, 39-38, in the NFC wild card game. The game ended on a botched game-winning field goal attempt by the Giants with six seconds left. Replays later revealed that off-setting penalties should have been called, giving the Giants another attempt.

8 **NFL Commissioner Paul Tagliabue** announces the league will immediately implement several officiating changes, including the arrangement of officials during field goal attempts, in the aftermath of the San Francisco-New York game-ending missed call (see Jan. 5).

Tampa Bay linebacker Derrick Brooks is named the AP NFL Defensive Player of the Year topping runner up Miami Dolphin and NFL sack leader Jason Taylor.

9 **The first-place but financially strapped** Ottawa Senators file for bankruptcy protection joining the Pittsburgh Penguins and Los Angeles Kings as the only franchises in the four major professional sports leagues to do so.

11 **The Tennessee Titans outlast** the Pittsburgh Steelers, 34-31, in overtime to advance to the AFC Championship Game. Kicker Joe Nedney converted the game-winning field goal after three tries, the first of which was good, but called back because someone had called timeout and the second of which missed but was negated on a roughing the kicker penalty. In the day's other game, Philadelphia eliminates Atlanta, 20-6.

12 **Tampa Bay crushes San Francisco**, 31-6, advancing to face Philadelphia in the NFC Championship Game. Oakland beats the New York Jets, 30-10, advancing to face Tennessee in the AFC Championship Game.

Ronald Martinez/Getty Images

Dallas Cowboys owner/general manager and notorious meddler Jerry Jones named proven-winner and notorious control freak **Bill Parcells** *as the franchise's sixth head coach in January 2003.*

14 **World's greatest skier Hermann Maier** returns to the World Cup ski circuit for the first time since nearly losing his right leg in a motorcycle crash 18 months ago. He fails to qualify for the second run of the giant slalom event.

The Atlanta Thrashers hire Bob Hartley as head coach replacing interim coach and general manager Don Waddell. Hartley, who won a Stanley Cup with Colorado in 2001 but had recently been fired by the Avalanche.

The Cincinnati Bengals hire longtime NFL assistant Marvin Lewis as their new head coach. Lewis becomes the NFL's third black coach in the NFL, joining Indianapolis' Tony Dungy and the New York Jets' Herman Edwards.

The Buffalo Sabres join the Ottawa Senators in bankruptcy (see Jan. 9) as the team files for protection from its creditors.

15 **San Francisco 49ers fire** head coach Steve Mariucci despite their fourth playoff season in six years.

16 **MLB owners vote** to award the winning league in baseball's All-Star Game the home-field advantage in that season's World Series. They also decide to adopt a minimum age of 14 years old for bat boys, meaning that former Giants bat boy Darren Baker (son of Dusty), who had a close call at home plate during the 2002 playoffs, will have to wait 10 more years before getting his job back.

17 **Yao Ming blocks Shaquille O'Neal's** first three shots and the Rockets beat the Lakers in overtime, 108-104, in the highly anticipated first meeting between the two Western Conference centers. Shaq finishes the game with the better stat line with 31 points, 13 rebounds and 4 assists to Ming's 10 points, 10 rebounds and 6 blocks.

18 **Michael Weiss comes from** fourth place to win the U.S. figure skating crown in a bizarre men's final. Michelle Kwan win her sixth straight U.S. title in the women's final

19 **Tampa Bay beats** Philadelphia, 27-10 in the NFC Championship Game and will face the Oakland Raiders and ex-coach Jon Gruden, in Super Bowl XXXVII following Oakland's 41-24 win over Tennessee in the AFC Championship.

20 **John Lucas is fired** as head coach of the Cleveland Cavaliers following an NBA-worst 8-34 start. The Cavs promote assistant Keith Smart to the top job.

22 **All-Star catcher Ivan Rodriguez** signs a one-year, $10 million free agent contract with the Florida Marlins.

24 **Serena Williams beats sister Venus**, 7-6, 3-6. 6-4. for her fourth straight Grand Slam victory at the Australian Open.

25 **Thirty-two-year-old Andre Agassi wins** his eighth Grand Slam singles title with his straight-set win over Rainer Schuettler at the Australian Open.

26 **Tampa Bay upsets Oakland**, 48-21, at Super Bowl XXXVII at Qualcomm Stadium in San Diego intercepting Oakland QB and NFL MVP Rich Gannon five times, as Bucs coach Jon Gruden gets the upper hand on his former team.

27 **Marty Mornhinweg is fired** by the Detroit Lions following a 3-13 season and a two-year record of 5-27 as head coach.

29 **The last-place New York Rangers** fire first-year coach Bryan Trottier after compiling a 21-26-6-1 record.

31 **High school basketball player LeBron James** is ruled ineligible for the remainder of the season by the Ohio state athletic board for accepting a gift of two throwback jerseys (Gale Sayers and Wes Unseld).

FEBRUARY 2003

Sun	Mon	Tue	Wed	Thu	Fri	Sat
						1
2	3	4	5	6	7	8
9	10	11	12	13	14	15
16	17	18	19	20	21	22
23	24	25	26	27	28	

Quote of the Month

"As of this writing, 15 men in the history of baseball have ever thrown a perfect game. Only one of those men did it half-drunk, with bloodshot eyes, monster breath and a raging hangover. That would be me."

David Wells, New York Yankees pitcher, in an excerpt from his autobiography released in February.

Over 40 Club

Los Angeles Lakers star Kobe Bryant scored 40 or more points in nine straight games in February 2003. Only Hall of Fame center Wilt Chamberlain had a longer such streak (actually three) in the history of the NBA.

Player	Season	Games
Wilt Chamberlain	1961-62	14
Wilt Chamberlain	1961-62	14
Wilt Chamberlain	1962-63	10
Michael Jordan	1986-87	9
Kobe Bryant	2002-03	9

Note: Chamberlain had two separate streaks of 14 games during the 1961-62 season. A season in which he averaged 50.4 points over 80 games.

Quick Results

Mike Tyson knocked out Clifford "The Black Rhino" Etienne 49 seconds into their Feb. 22 heavyweight fight. It was only the sixth-fastest knockout in Iron Mike's destructive career.

Opponent	Year	Seconds to KO
Marvis Frazier	1986	30
Robert Colay	1985	37
Lou Savarese	2000	38
Rick Spain	1985	39
Michael Johnson	1985	39
Clifford Ettiene	2003	49
Mark Young	1985	50

1 **American runner Regina Jacobs breaks** the world indoor record in the 1,500 meters with her time of 3:59.98 in Boston.

Washington's Michael Jordan scores a season-high 45 points in a 109-104 home win over the New Orleans Hornets

Canadian Olympic hockey star Hayley Wickenheiser becomes the first woman to score a goal in a men's professional game in a Finnish league game in Helsinki, knocking in a backhander in the first period. She also assisted on a goal in the second period but her team, Salamat, lost to Titaanit, 5-4.

2 **The West beats the East** in a shootout in the NHL All-Star Game despite four goals from Atlanta's Dany Heatley who wins the game's MVP trophy.

Miami's Ricky Williams scores two touchdowns in his first Pro Bowl as the AFC beat the NFC, 45-20. Williams wins the game's MVP award.

4 **USOC president Marty Mankamyer** resigns from her post before the executive committee can take a no-confidence vote against her in wake of allegations of conflict-of-interest business dealings. Michigan AD William Martin, the USOC's vice president-secretariat was automatically elevated to replace Mankamyer on an interim basis.

Washington's Jaromir Jagr scores his 500th career goal as part of a hat trick, becoming the 33rd player in NHL history to reach the 500-goal plateau in a 5-1 Capitals win over Tampa Bay.

Recently fired 49ers coach Steve Mariucci (see Jan. 15) is hired as head coach of the Detroit Lions, a week after the team dismissed Marty Mornhinweg (see Jan. 27).

5 **Ohio high schooler LeBron James** is allowed to play basketball again, at least temporarily, after a judge blocks a ruling that determined he was ineligible for accepting two throwback jerseys.

6 **American skiing phenom Bode Miller** wins the gold medal in the men's combined at the World Alpine Championships in St. Mortiz, Switzerland.

8 **LeBron James** returns to his high school team after temporary eligibility issues (see Feb 5). St. Vincent-St. Mary and scores a career-high 52 points in a 78-52 win.

USOC CEO Lloyd Ward keeps his job but loses his considerable year-end bonus as a penalty for an ethical violation involving conflict of interest issues in a 16-1 vote of confidence by the USOC's executive committee.

At NBA All-Star Saturday, Sacramento's Peja Stojakovic wins the three-point shootout in a tiebreaker over Wesley Person and Golden State's Jason Richardson successfully defends his title in the slam-dunk contest, beating Seattle Desmond Mason in the final round.

9 **The West beats the East 155-145** in double overtime at the NBA All-Star Game. Vince Carter, voted as an East starter by fan ballot, gives up his spot in the starting five for Michael Jordan, making his final All-Star game appearance. Minnesota's Kevin Garnett scores 37 points and wins the game's MVP trophy.

10 **Jeff Green, 41, wins his first** Daytona 500 pole with a qualifying lap of 186.606 miles per hour, edging out Dale Earnhardt Jr.

Detroit's Brett Hull scores the 700th goal of his career, becoming just the sixth player to reach the milestone as the Red Wings beat the San Jose Sharks, 5-4.

11 **Dennis Erickson is hired** by the San Francisco 49ers to replace fired head coach Steve Mariucci. Erickson, the head coach of Oregon State the last four seasons, is the former head coach of the Seattle Seahawks.

Agence Zoom/Getty Images

Bode Miller, of Franconia Notch, N.H., won gold medals in the men's combined and giant slalom events and a silver medal in the Super G at the World Alpine Championships in St. Moritz, Switzerland in February 2003.

12 **The U.S. Ski Team adds** to a wildly successful run at the World Alpine Championship in St. Moritz, with three more medals including a come-from-behind gold by Bode Miller in the men's giant slalom.

13 **Tennessee State Athletic Director Teresa Phillips** becomes the first woman to coach a men's Division1 basketball team when she filled in for interim head coach Hosea Lewis who was serving a one-game suspension for a benches-clearing brawl against Eastern Kentucky earlier in the week. Tennessee State lost to Austin Peay, 71-56.

14 **Mark Martin ties Al Unser Jr.** and Dale Earnhardt for the most career wins in the International Race of Champions (IROC) with his 11th victory at the series opener at Daytona.

Team New Zealand's 10-race win streak in America's Cup races comes to a crashing halt as the two-time defending champions lose their best-of-nine series opener against the Swiss boat Alinghi, captained by former Kiwi skipper Russell Coutts, when their boat breaks down twice on the race's first leg.

16 **Michael Waltrip wins his second** Daytona 500 in a race that was halted by rain with 91 laps remaining. The first time Waltrip won the Winston Cup's biggest race was in 2001 but his win was spoiled by the last-lap crash that killed his car-owner and racing legend Dale Earnhardt.

Tiger Woods makes his 2003 debut returning from rehab after knee surgery and wins the Buick Invitational at Torrey Pines by four strokes over Carl Petterson.

17 **Baltimore Orioles pitching prospect** Steve Bechler, 23, falls ill from heatstroke following a spring training workout and dies at Fort Lauderdale hospital.

Atlanta pitching ace Greg Maddux signs a record-setting one-year deal, worth $14.75 million, to stay with the Braves.

20 **In a blockbuster NBA trade,** Ray Allen and two other players, are sent to the Seattle SuperSonics from the Milwaukee Bucks in exchange for Gary Payton and Desmond Mason. The Sonics got Kevin Ollie and Ronald Murray and a draft pick as part of the deal.

22 **Mike Tyson knocks out** Clifford Etienne in 49 seconds in their heavyweight non-title bout at The Pyramid in Memphis.

23 **Los Angeles Laker Kobe Bryant** scores 41 points, in a 106-101 win over the Seattle SuperSonics. The game marks the ninth straight that he's scored at least 40 points. Its the fourth-longest such streak in NBA history, five games short of Wilt Chamberlain's all-time record.

26 **The Chicago Bears release** long-time QB Kordell Stewart in a move to get under the salary cap. Top running back Stephen Davis becomes another salary cap casualty when he is released by the Washington Redskins.

27 **The NFL's all-time leading rusher**, Emmitt Smith, is released by the Dallas Cowboys and new head coach Bill Parcells due to salary cap restrictions. Smith, who helped lead the Cowboys to three Super Bowl titles, says he is not ready to retire and plans to play two more seasons with another team.

28 **The University of Georgia suspends** assistant basketball coach Jim Harrick Jr. after a former Bulldog player levels accusations of NCAA violations and academic fraud.

MARCH 2003

Sun	Mon	Tue	Wed	Thu	Fri	Sat
						1
2	3	4	5	6	7	8
9	10	11	12	13	14	15
16	17	18	19	20	21	22
23	24	25	26	27	28	29
30	31					

Quote of the Month

"I can't imagine what you'd do if you tried to give a Pekingese a face lift. I suppose you could implant a tooth, but then when the dog opened its mouth you'd see a big blue thing flashing back at you."

Tom Bradley, Westminster Dog Show Chairman, while discussing a claim made by British tabloid, *The Sun*, that a dog who won best in show at a British dog show had a face lift.

Familiar Rings

The Food City 500 won by Kurt Busch on Mar. 23 was the 2,000th race in NASCAR Winston Cup history and the 85th at Bristol (Tenn.) Motor Speedway. Bristol is seventh on the list of tracks to host the most Winston Cup races.

Track	Races
Darlington Raceway	100
Martinsville Speedway	95
Richmond International Raceway	93
Daytona International Speedway	89
Atlanta Motor Speedway	87
Lowe's Motor Speedway	86
Bristol Motor Speedway	85

Source: USA Today.

Super Streakers

Connecticut's women's basketball team lost for the first time in two years on Mar. 10, ending a 70-game winning streak. Although impressive, the streak was not the longest in NCAA Div. 1 sports history.

School, sport	Years	Wins
N. Carolina women's soccer	1990-94	92
UCLA men's basketball	1971-74	88
UConn women's basketball	2001-03	70
Oklahoma football	1953-57	47
Arizona softball	1996-97	47
Penn St. women's volleyball	1990	44

1 **USOC CEO Lloyd Ward announces** his resignation from the embattled organization following two months of swirling controversy.

Switzerland becomes the first European country to win the 152-year-old America's Cup as Team Alinghi and skipper Russell Coutts complete their five-race sweep of two-time defending champions Team New Zealand.

Roy Jones Jr. wins the WBA heavyweight title, despite being out-weighed by 33 pounds, with a unanimous 12-round decision over John Ruiz. With the win Jones becomes only the second former middleweight champion in history to win the heavyweight crown.

A.J. Foyt IV, 18, becomes the youngest driver in the Indy Racing League's eight-year history to qualify for a race and will start 17th in the Toyota Indy 300.

Tiger Woods beats David Toms, 2 and 1 to win the WGC-Accenture Match Play Championship at La Costa Resort and Spa in Carlsbad, Calif.

3 **The Los Angeles Clippers fire** head coach Alvin Gentry after an 89-133 record over 2½ years and promote assistant Dennis Johnson to the top job on an interim basis. Johnson becomes the 24th head coach in the franchise's 33 year history.

5 **Georgia fires assistant** basketball coach Jim Harrick Jr. amid allegations of NCAA violations and academic fraud.

9 **St. Bonaventure University President** Robert Wickenheiser resigns after the men's basketball team refused to play the final two games of the season. The team was forced to forfeit six games and was disqualified from the Atlantic 10 tournament for using an ineligible player whose transfer to St. Bonaventure was approved by Wickenheiser.

10 **No. 22 Georgia forfeits** the remainder of its men's basketball schedule, removes itself from NCAA tournament consideration and suspends head coach Jim Harrick Sr. following an internal investigation that uncovered "unethical conduct" within the program.

Outfielder Damian Costantino of Div. III Salve Regina (R.I.) extends his hit streak to 59 games with a single against Mt. Union (Ohio), breaking the NCAA record set by New York Yankee Robin Ventura in 1987 when he played for Oklahoma St.

UConn's record 70-game win streak in women's basketball is snapped by Villanova, 52-48, in the Big East Tournament championship game.

13 **Robert Sorlie of Norway wins** the Iditarod Trail Sled Dog Race, fighting through intense winds to finish the 1,125-mile course in nine days, 15 hours and 47 minutes.

Billionaire B. Thomas Golisano agrees to buy the bankrupt Buffalo Sabres for $92 million, securing the troubled team's future in Buffalo.

16 **Kentucky, Arizona, Texas and Oklahoma** are the four top-seeds on the NCAA men's basketball tournament's Selection Sunday.

In one of the closest finishes in NASCAR history, Ricky Craven edges out Kurt Busch by just inches, and two-thousandths of a second, at the Carolina Dodge Dealers 400 at Darlington. It is the smallest margin of victory since NASCAR first introduced electronic timing in 1983.

17 **UCLA fires** head basketball coach Steve Lavin after the school's first losing season in 55 years.

18 **Major League Baseball cancels** its planned season-opening series in Tokyo scheduled for March 25-26 between the Oakland A's and Seattle Mariners due to concerns regarding a presumed impending invasion of Iraq by U.S. forces.

AP/Wide World Photos

*Norwegian firefighter **Robert Sorlie** celebrates his win in the 2003 Iditarod Trail Sled Dog Race on March 13 with his lead dogs Takk, left, and Blue. In just his second Iditarod appearance, Sorlie became the second non-Alaskan (Doug Swingley) to win the famous race.*

North Carolina-Asheville beats Texas Southern, 92-84, in the NCAA tournament play-in game to advance to play top-seed Texas in the tournament's first round

19 Cleveland's Ricky Davis is fined by the Cavaliers for attempting to pad his stats during a 122-95 win over Utah on Mar. 16. Davis, in an attempt to earn his first career triple-double intentionally misses a shot late in the game in order to get his 10th rebound Davis finished the game with 28 points, 9 rebounds and 12 assists.

The Boston Bruins fire head coach Robbie Ftorek and assistant Jim Hughes after a 33-28-8-4 start to the season that has the team in seventh place in the Eastern Conference. Boston general manager Mick O'Connell names himself as the replacement.

20 Insane Thursday starts a somewhat subdued version of March Madness that played out amid the backdrop of a U.S.-led invasion of Iraq.

22 Top-seed Arizona edges perennial giant-killers Gonzaga, 96-95, in double overtime, to advance to the Sweet 16 in one of the greatest games in NCAA tournament history.

23 Tiger Woods becomes the first golfer in 73 years to win the same event in four straight years with his dominating 11-shot win at the Bay Hill Invitational in Orlando. Woods overcomes a case of food poisoning to join Gene Sarazen and Walter Hagen as the only players to four-peat in an event.

Minnesota-Duluth wins its third consecutive NCAA women's ice hockey title, beating Harvard, 4-3, in double overtime.

24 Barry Sanders and Joe Theismann headline a group of 11 players selected to the College Football Hall of Fame.

The Yakima Sun Kings beat Grand Rapids, 117-107, to win their third Continental Basketball Association title.

26 LeBron James leads the East over the West, 122-107 at the McDonald's All-American game earning MVP honors with 27 points, 7 rebounds and 7 assists.

27 Russia's Evgeny Plushenko wins the men's title at the World Figure Skating Championship in Washington, D.C. American Timothy Goebel, bronze medallist at the 2002 Winter Olympics, takes second place.

29 Michelle Kwan wins the fifth World Figure Skating title of her career, beat Russian Elena Sokolova in Washington, D.C.

30 Davis Love III shoots an 8-under 64 to win the Players Championship at Sawgrass and the $1,170,000 first prize by six strokes.

Texas becomes the lone top-seed to advance to the Final Four with an 85-76 win over Michigan State, joining Syracuse, Marquette and Kansas in New Orleans.

The defending World Series champion Anaheim Angels open the 2003 Major League Baseball season with a 6-3 loss to the Texas Rangers.

Frenchwoman Patricia Meunier-Lebouc holds off two-time defending champion Annika Sorenstam to win the first LPGA major of the season, and her career, at the Kraft Nabisco Championship.

April 2003

Sun	Mon	Tue	Wed	Thu	Fri	Sat
		1	2	3	4	5
6	7	8	9	10	11	12
13	14	15	16	17	18	19
20	21	22	23	24	25	26
27	28	29	30			

Quote of the Month

"I Was a Tar Heel born. When I die, I'll be a Tar Heel dead. But in the middle, I have been Tar Heel and Jayhawk bred, and I am so, so happy and proud of that."

Roy Williams, upon leaving Kansas after 15 successful seasons (albeit without a national title) to become the head basketball coach at North Carolina.

Major Pain

Cincinnati's Ken Griffey Jr. just can't seem to escape the injury bug. His first stint on the disabled list began April 5. Here are Junior's career injuries.

Years	Dates Missed	Injury
1989	7/25-8/20	broken finger
1992	6/9-6/24	sprained wrist
1995	5/25-8/15	broken wrist
1996	6/19-7/13	broken hamate
2000	9/11-end of season	torn hamstring
2001	4/29-6/15	strained hamstring
2002	4/6-5/25	torn knee tendon
2002	6/24-7/22	strained hamstring
2003	4/6-5/15	dislocated shoulder
2003	7/17-end of season	ruptured ankle tendon

Long Division Authorities

The Colorado Avalanche won their ninth consecutive division title in 2002-03, the longest such streak in NHL history. Listed are the top five streaks in pro sports.

	Years	Division Titles
Atlanta Braves	1991–	12*
Los Angeles Lakers	1982-90	9
Boston Celtics	1957-65	9
Colorado Avalanche	1994–	9
Montreal Canadiens	1975-82	8

*The Braves won their 12th straight in Sept., 2003.

1 **Matt Doherty resigns** under pressure after three seasons as coach of North Carolina's men's basketball team.

Yankees shortstop Derek Jeter goes on the disabled list with a separated shoulder suffered against the Blue Jays on March 31.

Toronto Raptors head coach Lenny Wilkens, already the all-time NBA wins leader, loses his 1,106th game to become the all-time leader in that category as well.

2 **The Atlanta Hawks fire** general manager Pete Babcock and name Billy Knight his successor.

At 27 years, 249 days, Texas shortstop Alex Rodriguez becomes the youngest player in major league history to reach the 300 home run plateau.

3 **Hall of famer Kirby Puckett** is cleared of all charges in his sexual assault case.

Indiana Pacers' Ron Artest is fined $20,000 for making an obscene gesture to fans at Cleveland's Gund Arena in an April 2 game against the Cavaliers. He has now been fined $65,000 for the season.

4 **Sammy Sosa lines** a pitch from Reds reliever Scott Sullivan into the right field seats at Cincinnati's Great American Ballpark for his 500th career home run.

5 **Syracuse defeats Texas,** 95-84, and Kansas crushes Marquette, 94-61, to set up the NCAA men's basketball final game matchup.

Cincinnati center fielder Ken Griffey Jr. suffers yet another serious injury, dislocating his right shoulder while diving for a ball in a 9-7 loss to the Chicago Cubs.

6 **Dale Earnhardt Jr.** wins the Aaron's 499 and is the first driver to win four consecutive races at Talladega (Ala.) Superspeedway. It is a controversial win, however, as he appears to pass race leader Matt Kenseth below the yellow out-of-bounds line with four laps to go.

7 **Syracuse freshmen Carmelo Anthony** and Gerry McNamara score 20 and 18 points, respectively, to give Jim Boeheim his first national title with an 81-78 win over Kansas. Orangeman Hakim Warrick swats Kansas' Michael Lee's game-tying attempt in the final seconds. Anthony is named most outstanding player of the Final Four.

Chicago Bulls GM Jerry Krause resigns from his post, citing health problems.

8 **Connecticut beats Tennessee,** 73-68 to win its second consecutive Division I women's basketball championship and its fourth in the last nine years. The win improves the Huskies' record to 37-1. Player of the year Diana Taurasi scores 28 points to lead all scorers and is named most outstanding player of the Final Four.

9 **On the day before** the start of the 67th Masters tournament, Hootie Johnson and Martha Burk continue to spar in the press about Augusta National's all-male membership policy.

Kansas fires athletic director Al Bohl, resumable paving the way for the arrival of Kansas coach Roy Williams.

Baseball Hall of Fame president Dale Petroskey, a former White House assistant under Ronald Reagan, cancels a ceremony to honor the 15-year anniversary of the movie *Bull Durham*, blaming the anti-war views of actors Tim Robbins and Susan Sarandon.

10 **The NHL approves the sale** of the bankrupt Buffalo Sabres to B. Thomas Golisano for $92 million.

11 **After a rain-soaked Thursday,** Masters officials try to jam the first two rounds of golf into one day. Canadian Mike Weir opens with a 70 to take the first round lead but only makes it through 12 holes of the second round.

The Montreal Expos slam the NY Mets, 10-0, in their first of 22 games played in Puerto Rico.

12 **The Minnesota Gophers** grab their second straight NCAA hockey title with a 5-1 win over New Hampshire.

AP/Wide World Photos

The Buffalo Bills made Miami-FL running back **Willis McGahee**, *left, their first-round pick in the NFL Draft on April 26, much to the delight of his agent,* **Drew Rosenhaus**. *The two were actually speaking to each other on their cell phones to make it seem like other teams were in contact.*

Hallelujah! After nine straight losses to start the season, the Detroit Tigers beat the Chicago White Sox, 4-3, at Comerica Park to break into the win column.

13 Mike Weir defeats Len Mattiace on the first sudden-death playoff hole to win his first major at the Masters. He is the first left-hander to win the green jacket. Defending champ Tiger Woods finishes nine strokes back.

Great Britain's Paula Radcliffe shatters her own world record by winning the London Marathon with a time of 2:15:25. Deena Drossin (2:21:16) breaks Joan Benoit's American record.

Paul Tracy becomes the first driver in CART's 25-year history to win the first three races of the season.

14 Roy Williams makes it official, leaving Kansas to become basketball coach of his alma mater, North Carolina.

15 Another idiot fan jumps out of the stands at Chicago's U.S. Cellular Field to attack someone on the field. This time first base umpire Laz Diaz is attacked at the end of the eighth inning before security and players rush to his aid. The assailant is the fourth fan to run onto the field that night.

Michael Jordan scores 15 points in the final game of his career, a 107-87 Wizard loss to the 76ers in Philadelphia. His final shot is a free throw. And of course, it's good.

16 The Mighty Ducks of Anaheim complete their unlikely first-round sweep of the defending champion Detroit Red Wings with a 3-2 overtime win in Game 4.

17 St. Bonaventure fires coach Jan van Breda Kolff and accepts the resignation of athletic director Gothard Lane, weeks after the basketball team boycotts its remaining games in protest of sanctions levied for using an ineligible player.

18 The WNBA and its players' union agree to a five-year deal that will save the 2003 season.

20 Sammy Sosa takes a Salomon Torres fastball to the head in the Cubs 8-2 loss to the Pirates. The ball smashes Sosa's helmet but he is relatively unhurt.

21 Kenyan Robert Cheriyot wins the 107th Boston Marathon with a time of 2:10:11. Svetlana Zakharova of Russia wins the women's event in 2:25:20.

22 Kansas hires Illinois basketball coach Bill Self to replace the departed Roy Williams.

24 Syracuse hoops hero Carmelo Anthony declares his intentions to leave the school and make himself eligible for the NBA draft.

Phoenix Suns forward Amare Stoudemire wins the NBA Rookie of the Year award over Houston's Yao Ming.

25 The Mighty Ducks beat the Dallas Stars, 4-3, in five overtimes in the fourth-longest playoff game in the history of the NHL. The game lasts five hours and 52 minutes but finally ends on a goal by Petr Sykora.

26 The Cincinnati Bengals make Heisman Trophy winner Carson Palmer the No. 1 pick in the NFL Draft. Wide receivers Charles Rogers (Detroit) and Andre Johnson (Houston) go 2nd and 3rd overall. The biggest surprise in the first round is Buffalo's selection of Miami-FL running back Willis McGahee, still recovering from a torn ACL.

27 Phillies pitcher Kevin Millwood throws a no-hitter in beating the San Francisco Giants, 1-0, in Philadelphia. Millwood whiffs 10 and walks three.

The St. Louis Cardinals beat the Florida Marlins, 7-6, in 20 innings, the longest game in the majors since the Twins beat the Indians in 22 innings in 1993.

29 All-time winningest jockey Laffit Pincay is forced to retire with 9,530 victories after breaking his neck in a race in March.

May 2003

Sun	Mon	Tue	Wed	Thu	Fri	Sat
				1	2	3
4	5	6	7	8	9	10
11	12	13	14	15	16	17
18	19	20	21	22	23	24
25	26	27	28	29	30	31

Quote of the Month

"[Batting] average is a bothersome stat. It can go up and it can go down. RBI and home runs can never go down. They can only go up."

Scott Rolen, St. Louis Cardinals third baseman, on May 4 after his team's 6-2 win over Montreal. At the time Rolen was batting just .245 but ranked fifth in the National League in RBI.

Fourth Time's a Charm

After getting win no. 299 on May 21, it took Roger Clemens four more starts before finally reaching the elusive 300-win plateau. Listed are the 300-game winners since 1950 and the amount of starts they needed after 299.

	300th win	Starts
Warren Spahn	Aug. 11, 1961	1
Early Wynn	July 13, 1963	8
Gaylord Perry	May 6, 1982	1
Steve Carlton	Sept. 23, 1983	1
Tom Seaver	Aug. 4, 1985	1
Phil Niekro	Oct. 6, 1985	5
Don Sutton	June 18, 1986	2
Nolan Ryan	July 31, 1990	2
Roger Clemens	June 13, 2003	4

A Duck With Goose Eggs

Mighty Ducks goalie Jean-Sebastien Giguere stonewalled the Minnesota Wild for three straight games (including one that went to double OT) in the Western Conference Final. Listed are the six goalies who have recorded three straight playoff shutouts, and the result in their bid for a fourth.

Year		Result
1926	Clint Benedict, Montreal	3-2 loss
1929	John Ross Roach, NY Rangers	2-1 win
1945	Frank McCool, Toronto	5-3 loss
2002	Brent Johnson, St. Louis	5-3 win
2002	Patrick Lalime, Ottawa	2-1 win
2003	Jean-Sebastien Giguere, Ana.	2-1 win

Source: *USA Today* research

2 **NASCAR Winston Cup driver** Jerry Nadeau is critically injured after crashing in a practice run at Richmond International Speedway.

3 **Funny Cide**, a 12-to-1 long shot, upsets favorite Empire Maker to become the first gelding since 1929 to win the Kentucky Derby. Empire Maker finishes in second while Peace Rules places third.

Alabama football coach Mike Price is fired after details emerge about his behavior on a Florida golfing trip. Price reportedly spent time at topless bar and had a $1,000 hotel room service bill charged to his credit card by an unknown woman.

The upcoming Women's World Cup soccer tournament is moved from China (eventually to the United States) due to the SARS outbreak in Asia.

Oscar De La Hoya knocks out outmatched Yory Boy Campos in the seventh round as a tuneup for his Sept. rematch with Sugar Shane Mosely.

5 **Iowa State basketball coach** Larry Eustachy accepts a cash settlement and resigns a week after photos are published showing him partying with college students after a game at the University of Missouri.

6 **Prominent** *Boston Globe* **sportswriter** Bob Ryan is suspended without pay for one month for what he later called an "inappropriate and offensive remark" about Jason Kidd's wife, Joumana.

7 **Portland Trail Blazers** president and general manager Bob Whitsitt resigns as head of the franchise after yet another season plagued with off-the-court troubles.

9 **Sam Lacy**, longtime sports editor for *The Afro-American Newspaper* and former Red Smith Award winner, dies at 99.

11 **Jeff Torborg is fired** by the Florida Marlins after a 16-22 start to the season and replaced by 72-year-old Jack McKeon.

12 **Jose Santos**, the jockey who rode Funny Cide to victory at the Kentucky Derby, is cleared of any wrongdoing after a photo taken just after the finish line raises questions whether Santos was using an electrical buzzer.

PGA Tour veteran Vijay Singh comments that Annika Sorenstam, scheduled to play in a PGA event later in the month, has no business playing in a men's tournament and would withdraw if he was paired up with her. He later claims it wasn't meant to be a personal attack and refines his comment by saying, "I don't want to have a woman beat me."

13 **The Atlantic Coast Conference** votes to expand its membership from its current nine, and immediately targets three Big East teams—Miami-FL, Boston College and Syracuse.

14 **Dave DeBusschere**, the former New York Knicks great and commissioner of the ABA, dies of a heart attack at the age of 62.

15 **The Los Angeles Lakers**, three-time defending NBA champions, are ousted from the playoffs in resounding fashion, losing Game 6 of their Western Conference quarterfinal series with the San Antonio Spurs, 110-82, in Los Angeles.

Mexican-American businessman Arturo Moreno becomes the first Hispanic owner of a professional United States sports franchise when his purchase of the world champion Anaheim Angels is unanimously approved by league owners.

16 **New York Mets catcher Mike Piazza** tears a groin muscle while trying to avoid being hit by a Jason Schmidt fastball against the Giants. He will not need surgery, but will miss at least six weeks.

17 **Funny Cide becomes** the fifth horse in the last seven years to win both the Kentucky Derby and the Preakness with an amazing 9¾-length romp at Pimlico.

*England's **Dan Wheldon** goes airborne after hitting the wall in the third turn on lap 186 of 200 at the Indianapolis 500 on May 25. Wheldon landed upside down, but walked away with no serious injuries.*

The bright side for the Minnesota Wild is that they finally score their first goal against Anaheim goalie Jean-Sebastien Giguere in the Western Conference Finals. The bad news? They're swept in four games by the Ducks.

18 Vijay Singh wins the EDS Byron Nelson Championship, then promptly withdraws from next week's Colonial, removing any chance of him being paired up with Annika Sorenstam.

Martina Navratilova, still going strong at age 46, wins the 170th doubles championship of her career, in the Italian Open.

19 Michael Schumacher has to drive through a fire that breaks out during a pit stop, but still goes on to win the Austrian Grand Prix, his third straight Formula One victory.

21 LeBron James becomes a multi-millionaire before even being drafted by an NBA team. He signs a $1 million deal to sponsor Upper Deck trading cards, and then the biggie, a reported $90 million deal with Nike.

Former Yankees shortstop Bucky Dent, hated by Red Sox fans everywhere, watches Roger Clemens win his 299th game from atop Fenway Park's Green Monster, where he deposited a Mike Torrez pitch in a 1978 playoff game.

22 Annika Sorenstam cards a one-over-par 71 in her historic first round of the PGA Bank of America Colonial. She is in 73rd place out of the 113-player field, seven shots off the leader. Her driving accuracy is as impressive as any player in the tournament, but her putting is among the worst.

The ping-pong balls bounce the right way for the Cleveland Cavaliers, who win the 2003 NBA Draft Lottery for the right to draft hometown hero LeBron James.

23 The New Jersey Devils advance to the Stanley Cup Finals with their 3-2 win over Ottawa in Game 7 of their series.

Five bogeys and one birdie add up to a four-over-par 74 for Annika Sorenstam in round two of the Colonial. Her 36-hole total of 145 is 13 shots back of the leaders and not good enough to make the cut. Sorenstam is disappointed in her score but still thrilled at the way she hits the ball and handles the immense pressure.

Rudy Tomjanovich steps down from his position as head coach of the Houston Rockets after 12 seasons and two NBA titles.

25 Brazilian Gil de Ferran overcomes a painful shoulder injury to become the ninth Roger Penske team driver and third consecutive (Helio Castroneves in 2001-02) to win the Indianapolis 500. Polesitter Castroneves finishes in second, while Tony Kanaan comes in third.

Jimmie Johnson wins the rain-shortened Coca-Cola 600, normally the longest race on the NASCAR circuit. Robby Gordon, who raced in the Indy 500 earlier in the day (but didn't finish), ends up in 17th place.

26 Thirteen-year-old soccer star Freddy Adu signs a $1 million deal with Nike.

27 Colorado goaltender Patrick Roy, the NHL all-time leader in wins and games, announces his retirement after 18 seasons.

28 Italy's AC Milan defeats Juventus, 3-2, in a shootout after a 0-0 tie, to win its sixth Champions Cup soccer title in Manchester, England.

29 Desperate for bullpen help, the Boston Red Sox trade third baseman Shea Hillenbrand to the Arizona Diamondbacks for pitcher Byung-Hyun Kim.

30 The San Antonio Spurs, buoyed by a 23-0 run, eliminate the Dallas Mavericks, 90-78, and advance to the NBA Finals against the New Jersey Nets.

June 2003

Sun	Mon	Tue	Wed	Thu	Fri	Sat
1	2	3	4	5	6	7
8	9	10	11	12	13	14
15	16	17	18	19	20	21
22	23	24	25	26	27	28
29	30					

Quote of the Month

"The process doesn't work. QuesTec itself, the actual machines, I'm sure they work. But machines don't call balls and strikes. Umpires do."

Curt Schilling, Arizona Diamondbacks pitcher, after being fined for destroying a camera used for the QuesTec Umpire Evaluation System. The cameras are used in 13 of the 30 major league parks to make sure umps are making the proper calls on balls and strikes.

They Put a Cork in It

On June 11, Sammy Sosa had his eight-game suspension for using an illegally-corked bat reduced down to seven. He is the sixth major league player to be issued a corked-bat suspension.

	Team	Year	Games
Craig Nettles	Yankees	1974	0
Billy Hatcher	Astros	1987	10
Albert Belle	Indians	1994	7
Chris Sabo	Reds	1996	7
Wilton Guerrero	Dodgers	1997	8
Sammy Sosa	Cubs	2003	7

Note: Nettles was caught with superballs in his bat.

Naturally

On June 24 Montreal Expos outfielder Brad Wilkerson became just the 13th player to hit for a natural cycle, meaning a single, double, triple and homer in sequential order. Below are the natural cycles since 1950.

	Team	Date
Jim Hickman	Mets	8/7/63
Ken Boyer	Cardinals	6/16/64
Billy Williams	Cubs	7/17/66
Tim Foli	Expos	4/22/76
Bob Watson	Red Sox	9/15/79
John Mabry	Cardinals	5/18/96
Jose Valentin	White Sox	4/27/00
Brad Wilkerson	Expos	6/24/03

1 **Annika Sorenstam** is triumphant in the Kellogg-Keebler Classic, her first LPGA tournament after competing in the PGA's Bank of America Colonial.

2 **Larry Brown** is named head coach of the Detroit Pistons, a week after resigning as coach and vice president of the Philadelphia 76ers. Paul Silas signs a multi-year deal to coach the Cleveland Cavaliers.

Curt Schilling is fined a reported $15,000 by Major League Baseball for destroying a camera used as part of the new QuesTec Umpire Evaluation System. He is upset that umpires are changing the way they call balls and strikes to comply with the system.

3 **Sammy Sosa splinters his bat** while grounding out in the first inning against the Tampa Bay Devil Rays, and umpires discover a row of cork in the bat. Sosa is immediately ejected and the run that scores on the play is sent back to third base. Sosa claims he occasionally used the bat to impress fans during batting practice, and simply grabbed the wrong one during the game.

Outfielder Delmon Young, out of Camarillo High School in Calif., is selected first overall by the Tampa Bay Devil Rays in the 2003 Major League Baseball First-Year Player Draft. The 17-year-old is the brother of Detroit Tigers outfielder Dmitri Young.

4 **Seventy-six of Sammy Sosa's** bats are examined by Major League Baseball and determined to be free of cork.

University of Washington football coach Rick Neuheisel admits to participating in a college basketball gambling pool and winning over $12,000 over the past two years. He also asserts that he didn't know participating in a pool could jeopardize his job at the school.

6 **Sammy Sosa appeals** the eight-game suspension he is handed down by Major League Baseball for using a corked bat.

NBC spends $2.201 billion for the television rights to the 2010 Winter and 2012 Summer Olympic Games.

7 **Empire Maker**, the runner-up in the Kentucky Derby, wins the 135th Belmont Stakes, crushing Funny Cide's bid to be the first horse since Affirmed in 1978 to win thoroughbred racing's Triple Crown. Ten Most Wanted places second while Funny Cide is third, five lengths behind the winner. The win is trainer Bobby Frankel's first in a Triple Crown event.

In an all-Belgian final, Justine Henin-Hardenne defeats Kim Clijsters, 6-0, 6-4, to win the French Open women's singles title.

Micky Ward and Arturo Gatti once again batter each other for ten rounds, with Gatti earning the decision in their junior welterweight bout in Atlantic City. It is Ward's final fight, prompting him to say, "Some retirement party."

Harvard crew beats Yale by a margin of roughly 16 boat lengths to win the 137th Harvard-Yale Regatta, the nation's oldest intercollegiate sporting event.

8 **Annika Sorenstam defeats Grace Park** on the first sudden death playoff hole to win the McDonald's LPGA Championship, her fifth major title.

Juan Carlos Ferrero beats unseeded Martin Verkerk, 6-1, 6-3, 6-2, in the most lopsided French Open men's singles final since 1978.

9 **Martin Brodeur shuts out** the Mighty Ducks of Anaheim, 3-0, in Game 7 of the Stanley Cup Finals as the Devils win their third Cup since 1995. It is Brodeur's seventh shutout of the 2003 playoffs. Ducks goalie Jean-Sebastien Giguere is awarded the Conn Smythe Trophy as playoff MVP.

Texas Longhorns baseball coach Augie Garrido gets win no. 1,428 to become the all-time NCAA leader.

Tim Floyd and Jeff Van Gundy are named coach of the New Orleans Hornets and Houston Rockets, respectively.

SAMMY SOSA'S HALL OF FAME BATS

| 500th Career HR | 1998 HR's 64-66 | 1998 HR's 59-62 | 1998 HR 57 | 1,998 HR 18 |

AP/Wide World Photos

All five of **Sammy Sosa's bats** *currently on display at the National Baseball Hall of Fame were x-rayed after the Cubs slugger was found to have used cork in his bat in a game against the Devil Rays on July 3. All were clean.*

10 Washington coach Rick Neuheisel is fired by AD Barbara Hedges for participating in NCAA basketball pools.

Spectacular Bid, winner of 26 of 30 career races including the 1979 Kentucky Derby and Preakness, dies of an apparent heart attack at age 27.

11 A record six Houston Astros pitchers combine to no-hit the New York Yankees, 8-0, in Yankee Stadium. Roy Oswalt, Pete Munro, Kirk Saarloos, winning pitcher Brad Lidge, Octavio Dotel and Billy Wagner all stymie the Yankees. It is the first no-hitter against the Yankees since 1958.

Sammy Sosa's suspension is reduced to seven games by MLB chief operating officer Bob DuPuy.

12 Steve Phillips is fired as GM of the New York Mets.

Colorado Avalanche center Peter Forsberg wins the Hart Trophy as the NHL's regular season MVP. Nicklas Lidstrom wins his third consecutive Norris Trophy and Martin Brodeur wins his first Vezina as best goaltender.

13 On his fourth try, Roger Clemens finally wins his 300th game, beating the St. Louis Cardinals, 5-2. During the game he also gets his 4,000th career strikeout, becoming only the third pitcher in history to reach that mark.

14 The Frankfurt Galaxy beat the Rhein Fire, 35-16, to win the World Bowl (NFL Europe's championship game), behind 126 rushing yards from MVP Jonas Lewis.

15 Tim Duncan is two blocks shy of a quadruple double and the Spurs put together a 19-0 run in the fourth quarter to beat the Nets and win their second NBA title. Duncan wins the Finals MVP award and David Robinson retires on top.

Jim Furyk shoots a record-tying 272 over 72 holes to win his first major at the 103rd U.S. Open at Olympia Fields. He defeats runner-up Stephen Leaney by three strokes.

Tom Kristensen, Rinaldo Capello and Guy Smith, driving a Bentley Speed 8, capture the 24 Hours at Le Mans, Kristensen's fourth in a row. It is the first title for Bentley since 1930.

17 David Beckham, who has been with Manchester United for the past 13 years, agrees to a deal that will send him to Spanish powerhouse Real Madrid.

18 Hall of famer Larry Doby, the American League's first black baseball player, dies after a long illness at 79.

19 NASCAR officially announces it has reached a deal with wireless communications company Nextel, to replace Winston and become title sponsor of what has been the Winston Cup Series since 1971.

Chicago Bulls guard Jay Williams is seriously injured in a motorcycle crash in Chicago.

21 Vitali Klitschko puts up a strong challenge but loses his bout with heavyweight champ Lennox Lewis thanks to a nasty gash across his left eye. Lewis wins by TKO in the sixth round.

The Pittsburgh Penguins make goaltender Marc-Andre Fleury the top selection in the 2003 NHL Draft.

Long-time NHL coach Roger Neilson loses his battle with cancer at age 69.

23 Rice crushes Stanford, 14-2, in the deciding game of the College Baseball World Series, for the school's first title.

24 The ACC makes its long-awaited decision, inviting Big East schools Miami-FL and Virginia Tech to join the conference in 2004. Both schools later accept the offer.

25 Lisa Guerrero is hired as the new sideline reporter for Monday Night Football.

26 To no one's surprise, LeBron James is the top pick in the NBA Draft by the Cleveland Cavaliers. European Darko Milicic (Detroit) and Syracuse's Carmelo Anthony (Denver) round out the top three.

July 2003

Sun	Mon	Tue	Wed	Thu	Fri	Sat
		1	2	3	4	5
6	7	8	9	10	11	12
13	14	15	16	17	18	19
20	21	22	23	24	25	26
27	28	29	30	31		

Quote of the Month

"I don't know where I'm going to keep her. Maybe it would be better to leave her in the mountains. She'll be happier there than in the streets of Basel."

Roger Federer, men's Wimbledon titlist, upon being awarded a 1,760-pound cow named Juliette by Swiss Open officials, for being the first Swiss man to win a Grand Slam event.

Young Guns

On July 3, the U.S. Women's Open began at Pumpkin Ridge Golf Club in Oregon with 14 teenagers in the field. Thirteen-year-old Michelle Wie grabbed most of the press with her 300-plus-yard drives, but it was 17-year-old University of Florida freshman Aree Song that finished just two shots back of the lead.

Name	Age	Finish
Sydney Burlison	13	Missed cut
Michelle Wie	13	T-39th
Morgan Pressel	15	52nd
Paula Creamer	16	Missed cut
Jane Park	16	T-30th
Aree Song	17	5th
Naree Song	17	Missed cut
Whitney Wade	17	Missed cut
Cindy Shin	18	Missed cut
Soo-Young Moon	18	Missed cut
Alice Kim	18	Missed cut
Irene Cho	18	58th
Elizabeth Janangelo	19	T-30th
Christina Kim	19	T-22nd

1 **The Chicago White Sox acquire** oft-traded second baseman Roberto Alomar from the Mets and centerfielder Carl Everett from the Rangers for their stretch run.

2 **The 2010 Winter Olympic Games** are awarded to Vancouver, British Columbia. They will be the first Olympics held in Canada since the 1988 Games in Calgary. Other finalists were Salzburg, Austria and Pyeongchang, South Korea.

3 **The U.S. Women's Open** golf tournament begins with 36-year-old Michelle Wie the most recognizable of 14 teenagers competing.

4 **Lakers star Kobe Bryant** turns himself in to the Eagle, Colo. Sheriffs Department after an arrest warrant was issued stemming from charges that he sexually assaulted a 19-year-old hotel employee while in Colorado for knee surgery.

Former Anaheim teammates Teemu Selanne and Paul Kariya are reunited in Colorado. Each takes a pay cut to join the already talent-rich Avalanche.

5 **Lance Armstrong begins** his quest for his record-tying fifth Tour de France victory with a five-mile prologue in Paris. Only 2,072 more miles until the finish line.

Serena Williams wins her second grand slam event of the year and sixth of her career, 4-6, 6-4, 6-2, over her sister, Venus, in the finals at Wimbledon. Venus puts up a valiant struggle but is overcome by a sore abdomen, a sore thigh and her sister's relentless play.

6 **Roger Federer defeats** Mark Philippoussis in straight sets, 7-6 (5), 6-2, 7-6 (3), in the men's finals at Wimbledon for his first grand slam win. Forty-six-year-old tennis legend Martina Navratilova wins her 20th Wimbledon title, 27 years after her first, pairing up with Leander Paes for the mixed doubles crown.

7 **Unheralded Hilary Lunke** wins a gripping three-way 18-hole playoff round with Angela Stanford and Kelly Robbins for her first LPGA title at the U.S. Women's Open. Lunke drains a 15-foot birdie putt on the 18th hole for the one-shot win just after Stanford sinks a 30-footer of her own.

8 **Six-time Vezina Trophy winner** and two-time league MVP Dominik Hasek comes out of retirement to play goaltender for the Detroit Red Wings.

9 **Pirates first baseman Randall Simon** playfully smacks a sausage mascot over the head with his bat at Miller Park during a "sausage race." The sausage, and more importantly the 18-year-old woman inside the costume, is knocked to the ground but is relatively unhurt. Simon is led away in handcuffs and later suspended for three games.

11 **Center Alonzo Mourning** leaves the Miami Heat after eight seasons to join the New Jersey Nets.

The Florida Marlins obtain American League saves leader Ugueth Urbina from Texas for former top pick Adrian Gonzalez and two other players.

Atlanta second baseman Marcus Giles and Chicago pitcher Mark Prior are involved in a nasty collision on the basepaths that leaves Giles with a concussion and Prior with an injured shoulder.

14 **Lance Armstrong averts** disaster by swerving across a grass field to avoid a fallen rider in Stage 9 of the Tour de France. Despite a previous crash, fatigue and sickness, Lance Armstrong is in the lead by 21 seconds.

Anaheim outfielder Garret Anderson defeats St. Louis' Albert Pujols, 9-8, in the finals of Major League Baseball's annual Home Run Derby.

ESPN hires Rush Limbaugh to deliver a weekly opinion feature on *Sunday NFL Countdown*.

Major League Soccer announces an expansion team to be based in Monterrey, Mexico to begin play in the 2003-04 season.

AP/Wide World Photos

The hot dog smokes the bratwurst at the sausage race at Miller Park on July 11. Two days earlier, the Pirates' Randall Simon whacked Guido the sausage over the head, causing the woman inside the costume to fall and take down another sausage with her. Both women are shown here holding the tape.

15 **Football visionary** and former Cowboys president and general manager Tex Schramm dies at the age of 83.

Texas Rangers third baseman Hank Blalock blasts a two-run, eighth inning homer off Dodgers' relief ace Eric Gagne to lead the American League over the National League, 7-6, in the Major League All-Star Game. Anaheim's Garret Anderson goes 3-for-4 and wins the MVP award, now known as the Ted Williams Award. The win gives the A.L. homefield advantage in the 2003 World Series.

16 **Serena Williams and Lance Armstrong** win Female and Male Athlete of the Year, respectively, at the 11th annual ESPY Awards in Los Angeles.

18 **Kobe Bryant is officially charged** with a Class 3 felony of sexual assault, carrying a penalty of anywhere from probation to life in prison, and a fine of between $3,000 and $750,000. He later conducts a press conference, with his wife sitting next to him, and admits to having sex with the 19-year-old hotel employee, but denies forcing her to do anything against her will.

19 **Thomas Bjorn** leads the British Open by a stroke over Davis Love III after three rounds. An eagle on the seventh hole boosts Tiger Woods into a five-way tie for third, two shots back.

Longtime Detroit Red Wing Sergei Fedorov signs a five-year, $40 million contract with the Western Conference champion Mighty Ducks of Anaheim.

20 **Playing in his first major,** unknown Ben Curtis, ranked 396th in the world, stuns the favorites to win the Claret Jug as British Open champion. The 26-year-old shoots a final round 69 to edge Thomas Bjorn and Vijay Singh by a stroke for the title.

Arenafootball2 player Julian Yearwood collapses and dies at the age of 31 while sitting on the sidelines.

21 **Lance Armstrong crashes** again, after catching his handlebar on a spectator's bag during Stage 15 of the Tour de France. He maintains his lead, which is now over a minute.

Ex-Baylor basketball player Carlton Dotson is charged with the murder of his former roommate and teammate Patrick Dennehy.

23 **Latrell Sprewell is dealt** from the Knicks to the Timberwolves in a four-team, six-player trade.

24 **Suzy Whaley**, the club pro who became the first woman to qualify for a PGA Tour event since 1945, shoots a 75 in the opening round of the Greater Hartford Open.

25 **The NFL fines** Detroit Lions president Matt Millen $200,000 for failing to interview any minority candidates before hiring Steve Mariucci in February.

26 **The body of Patrick Dennehy** is found in an abandoned gravel pit outside of Waco, Texas.

27 **Lance Armstrong cruises** down the Champs-Elysees in Paris for his fifth consecutive Tour de France win.

Catcher Gary Carter and first baseman Eddie Murray are inducted into the Baseball Hall of Fame. Announcer Bob Uecker wins the Ford Frick Award.

The World Swimming Championships come to a close with the U.S. grabbing 28 medals and 11 golds. Michael Phelps, 18, steals the show with three golds and five world records broken.

28 **The Cincinnati Reds clean house,** firing manager Bob Boone and general manager Jim Bowden.

31 **The Yankees acquire Aaron Boone** while the Giants grab coveted Orioles ace Sidney Ponson, highlighting six deals made on major league baseball's trade deadline day. The Red Sox hope to improve their rotation with the addition of Pittsburgh's Jeff Suppan

August 2003

Sun	Mon	Tue	Wed	Thu	Fri	Sat
					1	2
3	4	5	6	7	8	9
10	11	12	13	14	15	16
17	18	19	20	21	22	23
24/31	25	26	27	28	29	30

Quote of the Month

"He'll probably be effective, because those guys haven't seen a 68-mph fastball since Little League."

Paul Azinger, PGA Tour pro, after hearing about fellow golfer Phil Mickelson's ill-fated tryout with the Triple-A Toledo Mud Hens on Aug. 29.

Road Raging

The punch that Jimmy Spencer threw at Kurt Busch after the GFS Marketplace 400 was hardly the first incident between the two rivals. Listed below are some of the others.

Oct. 28, 2001
At the Phoenix International Raceway in Busch's rookie year, the two bump, causing Busch to drop from a top-ten finish down to 22nd. Busch would bring up the incident in an interview the following year.

March 24, 2002
With Spencer looking good for his first Winston Cup win since 1994, Busch makes contact with him with 45 laps to go in the Food City 500 at Bristol Motor Speedway. Busch ends up with *his* first win, edging Spencer by 1.556 seconds.

Aug. 4, 2002
At the Brickyard 400 at Indianapolis Motor Speedway, Spencer nips the back-rear corner of Busch's car, causing him to spin out and crash into the outside wall. Busch gets out of his damaged car, stands on the track and gestures at Spencer.

Aug. 18, 2003
After much bumping at Michigan International Speedway, Busch apparently runs out of gas in the garage area and is rammed by Spencer. Spencer then gets out of his car and punches Busch, who is still in his car.

Source: NASCAR.com

1 **WTA top-ranked Serena Williams** undergoes knee surgery that will keep her sidelined for the rest of the season, and keep her from defending her U.S. Open title.

2 **Heavyweight Mike Tyson**, whose fortune had once been estimated between $300-500 million, files for Chapter 11 protection in U.S. Bankruptcy Court.

Major League Soccer all-stars defeat Chivas de Guadalajara of Mexico, 3-1, in the eighth MLS All-Star Game. Los Angeles Galaxy star Carlos Ruiz scores the game-winner in the 68th minute.

Amigo Hall, a 27-1 long shot, is the surprise winner of the Hambletonian, harness racing's biggest race for trotters, at the Meadowlands.

3 **Annika Sorenstam** shoots a final-round 70 to edge Se Ri Pak by one stroke at the Weetabix Women's British Open. In doing so she wins her second major of the year and becomes the sixth woman to win the career Grand Slam.

Polesitter Kevin Harvick takes the lead on a restart with 15 laps remaining to win the Brickyard 400.

Five are inducted into the Pro Football Hall of Fame, including coach Hank Stram and running back Marcus Allen.

New Jersey native Michael Iaconelli hooks a 3¾-pound bass with mere minutes remaining to win the Citgo Bassmasters Classic in New Orleans.

4 **Arizona running back Emmitt Smith** issues a public apology for derogatory comments he made about his former Dallas teammates in a *Sports Illustrated* interview. Smith claimed he "felt like a diamond being surrounded by trash."

6 **Kobe Bryant makes** his first court appearance in his sexual assault case. The entire proceeding lasts seven minutes and Bryant utters two words—"No sir."

The Yankees give up on newly-acquired reliever Armando Benitez, shipping him to Seattle for Jeff Nelson.

6 **More than 300 people**, including Baylor president Robert Sloan Jr. and head coach Dave Bliss, attend the memorial service for murdered Baylor basketball player Patrick Dennehy.

8 **Baylor basketball coach Dave Bliss** and athletic director Tom Stanton resign after major violations in the Baylor program are uncovered following the death of Patrick Dennehy.

10 **Atlanta Braves shortstop Rafael Furcal** accomplishes one of the rarest feats in baseball, turning just the 13th unassisted triple play in major league history. In the fifth inning against the Cardinals, Furcal catches Woody Williams' liner, steps on second to double off Mike Matheny and then tags Orlando Palmeiro heading back to first.

11 **American hockey icon Herb Brooks** is killed in a car accident in Minnesota at the age of 66. Brooks coached four NHL teams and the U.S. Olympic hockey team in Salt Lake City, but will always be remembered as the coach of the U.S. "Miracle on Ice" team that won the gold medal in 1980.

12 **A** *Sports Illustrated* **article** is released containing grisly details about the current state of hall of famer Ted Williams' body. An employee from the cryogenics company, Alcor, claims Williams' head was separated from his body and cracked several times.

14 **Fourteen-year-old soccer prodigy** Freddy Adu scores three goals in the United States' rout of South Korea in the opening game of the Under-17 World Championship.

Cleveland first baseman Travis Hafner hits for the cycle in his first four at bats in the Indians' 8-3 win over Minnesota. He is the first Indian to hit for the cycle since 1978.

16 **Secret tape recordings** reveal Baylor head coach Dave Bliss plotting a scheme to portray slain player Patrick Dennehy as a drug dealer in order to hide the fact that Bliss had given him money for tuition and a car loan.

*United States sprinter **Jon Drummond** is shown a red card by a race official at the Track and Field World Championships in Paris on Aug. 24. After being disqualified for a false start in the men's 100-meter race, Drummond protested by lying down on the track and refusing to budge for several minutes.*

Jim Thorpe ties a Champions Tour record with his 10-under par 60 in the second round of the Long Island Classic.

The Atlanta Falcons are dealt a terrible blow when star quarterback Michael Vick breaks his right leg in an exhibition game against the Baltimore Ravens.

Jockey Gary Stevens is thrown from his horse, Storming Home, just past the finish line at the Arlington Million. He somehow avoids being trampled by other horses but still suffers a fractured vertebra and a collapsed lung. He would return to racing three weeks later.

17 Shaun Micheel wins the 85th PGA Championship by two strokes over Chad Campbell for his first major and first PGA Tour victory in 164 starts. Micheel clinches the win with an amazing 18th hole shot from the rough from 175 yards out that stops two inches from the cup.

18 NASCAR driver Jimmy Spencer is suspended, fined $25,000 and placed on probation after punching fellow driver Kurt Busch after the GFS Marketplace 400 in Michigan. The two had been involved in other incidents in the past, and bumped each other more than usual during the race.

20 The United States women's gymnastics team, led by alternate Chellsie Memmel, wins its first overall team title at the world championships in Anaheim. The American men claim the silver as China takes its fifth team title in the last six world championships. Paul Hamm would later become the first American man to win the overall individual title after a brilliant routine on the high bar.

22 Baylor announces the hiring of Valparaiso's Scott Drew to lead the basketball program reeling from the death of one of its players and the controversy surrounding its former coach. Drew's father Homer replaces him at Valpo.

St. Louis Cardinals Albert Pujols is hitless in five at bats against the Phillies, ending his 30-game hitting streak.

23 Ten Most Wanted wins the Travers Stakes in Saratoga, N.Y. in what was originally anticipated to be a rematch between Triple Crown rivals Funny Cide and Empire Maker. Both horses bow out in the week leading up to the race. Empire Maker was later retired do to a hoof injury, removing any possibility for another showdown.

Boynton Beach, Fla. hits four home runs while pitcher Cody Emerson allows four hits and strikes out nine to beat Saugus, Mass., 9-2, to advance to the Little League World Series Championship Game against Japan.

Laila Ali knocks out Christy Martin 48 seconds into the fourth round to improve her record to 16-0.

Bobby Bonds, father of Barry and former major league all-star who swatted 332 home runs and stole 461 bases, dies at the age of 57.

NY Jets quarterback Chad Pennington breaks his left wrist in a exhibition game against the Giants.

24 Abby Wambach's two goals lead the Washington Freedom to the WUSA title, beating the Atlanta Beat in Founders Cup III in San Diego.

Japan scores eight runs in the fourth inning and goes on to beat Boynton Beach, Fla., 10-1, in the Little League World Championship Game.

25 Pete Sampras officially announces his retirement at an emotional ceremony on center court before the start of the U.S. Open, where he won the last of his 14 majors.

28 In his first move as Indiana Pacers president, Larry Bird fires head coach and former rival Isiah Thomas.

September 2003

Sun	Mon	Tue	Wed	Thu	Fri	Sat
	1	2	3	4	5	6
7	8	9	10	11	12	13
14	15	16	17	18	19	20
21	22	23	24	25	26	27
28	29	30				

Quote of the Month

"Let's see how much Parcells wins this year. I'll make him pay when we play them...the homo."

Jeremy Shockey, NY Giants tight end, in an interview with *New York* magazine. The brash second-year player was apparently responding to comments new Dallas Cowboys head coach Bill Parcells made about him while working as an ESPN analyst in 2002. In Parcells' first meeting against the Giants on Sept. 15, the Cowboys won, 35-32.

Dropping the Ball

St. Louis Rams quarterback Kurt Warner fumbled six times on Sept. 7 in a 23-13 loss to the NY Giants, missing the all-time single-game record by one.

		Date
7	Len Dawson, KC vs. SD	11/15/64
6	Sam Etcheverry, St.L vs NYG	9/17/61
6	Dave Kreig, Sea. vs KC	11/5/89
6	Brett Favre, GB vs TB	12/7/98
6	Kurt Warner, St.L vs NYG	9/7/03
	Ten tied with five each.	

Source: NFL

American Dream

On Sept. 7 Andy Roddick became just the sixth American to win the U.S. Open men's singles title since the Open Era began in 1968.

Winner	Year(s)
Arthur Ashe	1968
Stan Smith	1971
Jimmy Connors	1974,76,78,82-83
John McEnroe	1979-81,84
Pete Sampras	1990,93,95-96,2002
Andre Agassi	1994,99
Andy Roddick	2003

Source: ATP Tour

2 **The NCAA releases** its annual report on graduation rates, which show Division I student-athletes graduating at a rate of 62 percent, three percent higher than non-athletes.

The New England Patriots release Pro Bowl safety Lawyer Milloy, just five days before their opening game against the Buffalo Bills. He is signed by Buffalo two days later.

3 **The Indiana Pacers** name 2002 Coach of the Year Rick Carlisle as their new head coach.

4 **The NFL kicks off** its 2003-04 regular season as four former Jets, dubbed "Jetskins," all contribute to the Redskins 16-13 win over the Jets.

NY Rangers goalie Mike Richter announces his retirement after 14 years and 301 victories.

5 **Robert Parish and James Worthy** highlight a list of seven people inducted into the National Basketball Hall of Fame in Springfield, Mass.

The Detroit Tigers lose, 8-6, to the Toronto Blue Jays, making hurler Mike Maroth the majors' first 20-game loser since Oakland's Brian Kingman in 1980.

6 **The third-ranked Miami Hurricanes** overcome a 33-10 deficit to beat No. 21 Florida, 38-33, at the Orange Bowl. Former Gator Brock Berlin throws for two TD's for Miami.

Justine Henin-Hardenne defeats fellow Belgian Kim Clijsters, 7-5, 6-1, to win her second grand slam event of the year.

7 **American 21-year-old Andy Roddick** wins the first major of his career, besting Juan Carlos Ferrero in straight sets, 6-3, 7-6 (2), 6-3, for the U.S. Open men's singles title.

8 **For the second time** in four days, an NHL Hall of Fame candidate hangs ups his skates, as feisty forward Doug Gilmour calls it a career after 20 season.

9 **Vanderbilt totally overhauls** its athletic department in what could be a sign of things to come for other NCAA programs. Under the new arrangement, the athletic department is folded into the school's central administration to be overseen by Chancellor Gordon Gee.

10 **Ohio State running back** Maurice Clarett is suspended by the school for the entire 2003 season for lying to investigators and accepting improper benefits.

13 **Sugar Shane Mosley** defeats Oscar De La Hoya for the second time in the last three years in a unanimous decision to win the WBA and WBC Super Welterweight titles. All three judges score the fight, 115-113, in favor of Mosley, but De La Hoya disagrees and demands an investigation, claiming, "I thought I won the fight. I didn't even think it was close."

Tonya Butler of Division II West Alabama becomes the first woman to kick a field goal in a college football game. Her 27-yarder propelled her team to a 24-17 win over Arkansas-Monticello.

Bill France Jr., 70, steps down as chairman and CEO of NASCAR and hands the reins to his son, Brian.

14 **Ravens running back Jamal Lewis** rushes for an all-time single-game record 295 yards in Baltimore's 33-13 win over the Cleveland Browns, breaking Corey Dillon's three-year old mark of 278. Three days earlier, he had predicted that he would break the record.

Venus and Serena Williams' half-sister, Yetunde Price, is shot to death in Compton, Calif. at the age of 31.

Japan and Georgia take the women's and men's team titles, respectively, at the World Freestyle Championships in New York. Kristie Marano wins the only gold medal for the United States. Cael Sanderson, perfect as a collegian at Iowa State, wins a silver.

Europe puts the finishing touches on its dominating Solheim Cup win over the United States, 17½-10½.

Michigan hands Notre Dame its worst football loss in 18 years with a 38-0 pasting in Ann Arbor.

Jon Bon Jovi, left, stands with Arena Football League commissioner David Baker, center, and Craig A. Spencer on Sept. 22 after their announcement that the rock star had become co-owner, along with Spencer, of the Philadelphia Soul, an expansion Arena League franchise to begin play at the Wachovia Center in 2004.

15 Women's United Soccer Association (WUSA) shuts down operations after three seasons amidst financial losses. The news comes just days before the start of the 2003 Women's World Cup.

Dallas kicker Billy Cundiff boots a record-tying seven field goals, including the game winner in OT as the Cowboys beat the NY Giants, 35-32, on Monday Night Football.

16 The NBA's Atlanta Hawks and the NHL's Thrashers are sold from AOL Time Warner to Atlanta Spirit, LLC, pending approval.

The Detroit Shock beat the Los Angeles Sparks, 83-78, to win their first WNBA Championship. Head coach Bill Laimbeer takes the Shock from the worst team in the league in 2002 to the best in 2003. Ruth Riley pumps in 27 for the Shock and is names Finals MVP.

17 Miami is awarded the 2007 Super Bowl, the ninth in history for the city and first since 1999.

18 San Jose State's Neil Parry plays in his first game for the Spartans since a freak injury in a game during the 2000 season caused the loss of his right leg from the knee down.

Michigan asks former Fab-Fiver and current NBA star Chris Webber to reimburse almost $700,000 for what the school claims was spent on legal fees and NCAA penalties caused by Webber.

The Atlanta Braves and San Francisco 49ers each clinch their respective division titles. For Atlanta it is their record 12th consecutive.

19 With safety in mind, NASCAR installs a new rule prohibiting drivers from racing back to the caution flag after an accident. The new rule forbids passing under caution.

20 Oklahoma State's Rashaun Woods sets an NCAA record with seven receiving touchdowns in the Cowboys' 52-6 pummeling of SMU.

21 The United States begins its defense of its 1999 Women's World Cup title with a 3-1 win over Sweden in front of over 34,000 fans in Washington D.C.

Atlanta pitcher Greg Maddux goes five innings in the Braves' 8-0 win over Florida to become the first pitcher in MLB history to win 15 games for 16 consecutive years.

22 Rock star Jon Bon Jovi announces he will be co-owner of the Philadelphia Soul, an expansion Arena Football League team beginning in 2004.

23 Ohio State running back Maurice Clarett sues the NFL to change a rule that prohibits players from being drafted until they have been out of high school for at least three years.

25 Toronto first baseman Carlos Delgado becomes the 15th player in major league history to hit four home runs in a game in the Blue Jays' 10-8 win over Tampa Bay.

Michigan wins its appeal to have its postseason NCAA basketball eligibility restored for the 2003-04 season.

28 Tennis pioneer Althea Gibson dies at the age of 76. She was the first African-American Wimbledon winner and recorded five grand slam singles titles in all.

The 2003 MLB regular season comes to a close, mercifully for the Detroit Tigers who finish 43-119, one loss shy of the tying the 1962 Mets record for futility.

Paul Tergat wins the Berlin Marathon in 2:04:55, shattering the world record by 43 seconds.

29 Baltimore's Mike Hargrove and the White Sox' Jerry Manuel are the first managers to be fired in the offseason.

October 2003

Sun	Mon	Tue	Wed	Thu	Fri	Sat
			1	2	3	4
5	6	7	8	9	10	11
12	13	14	15	16	17	18
19	20	21	22	23	24	25
26	27	28	29	30	31	

Quote of the Month

"To Moises Alou, the Chicago Cubs organization, Ron Santo, Ernie Banks and Cub fans everywhere, I am so truly sorry from the bottom of this Cub fan's broken heart."

Steve Bartman, in an emotional statement apologizing for any affect he may have had on the outcome of the Cubs' loss to the Marlins in Game 6 of the NLCS. Bartman reached for a foul ball headed his way that might have been caught by Moises Alou. Florida then scored eight runs in the inning.

Shoe Shines

Jockey Bill Shoemaker died on Oct. 12. As fellow hall of fame jockey Eddie Delahoussaye said, "For a man his size, wearing a size $2^1/_2$ shoe, he was a giant." Below are just some of his achievements.

- 42 years as a jockey
- 8,833 wins (2nd all-time)
- 40,350 mounts
- winner of 11 Triple Crown races (4 Kentucky Derbys, 2 Preaknesses, 5 Belmonts)
- oldest winner of Kentucky Derby (54 in 1986)
- $123,375,524 in career jockey earnings

Road Dogs

The Detroit Lions 24-16 loss to the Bears in Chicago on Oct. 26 extended their road losing streak to 20 games. The last Lions road win came on Dec. 17, 2000. Below are the longest NFL road losing streaks of all time (as of Oct. 26).

	Years	Streak
Houston Oilers	1981-84	23
Buffalo Bills	1983-86	22
Detroit Lions	2000–	20
T.B. Buccaneers	1983-85	19
Atlanta Falcons	1988-91	19

Source: NFL and *USA Today*

1 **Timberwolves forward Kevin Garnett** signs a five-year contract extension worth a reported $179 million.

ESPN *NFL Sunday Countdown* analyst Rush Limbaugh resigns three days after causing an uproar with his controversial comments about Donovan McNabb. He claimed that the Eagles quarterback was overrated by the media that wanted to see a black quarterback succeed.

2 **The Miami Hurricanes** avert a BCS disaster with a last-second 23-yd FG to defeat West Virginia, 22-20. News isn't all good, however, as running back and Heisman hopeful Frank Gore is lost for the season with a torn ACL.

Lee Seung-yeop of the Samsung Lions blasts his 56th homer of the year to break Sadaharu Oh's Asian single-season record.

4 **The underdog Florida Marlins** advance to the NLCS with a shocking 3-1 series win over San Francisco. The series clinching 7-6 win for the Marlins ends when catcher Ivan Rodriguez holds onto the ball after a collision at home plate with Giants first baseman J.T. Snow.

James Toney, making his debut as a heavyweight, knocks out 40-year-old Evander Holyfield at 1:42 of the ninth round in their bout in Las Vegas.

Texas Tech quarterback B.J. Symons throws a Big-12 record eight TD passes in a 59-28 win over Texas A&M.

5 **Goalkeeper Silke Rottenberg** stymies Mia Hamm, Brandi Chastain and Co., as Germany knocks out the United States, 3-0, in the semifinals of the Women's World Cup. The defending champion U.S. squad hadn't even trailed in a World Cup match since 1999.

Atlanta Thrashers' forward Dan Snyder dies of injuries sustained in a car crash six days earlier with teammate Dany Heatley.

Tiger Woods wins the American Express Championship by two strokes for his 39th career win and the 100th for caddie Steve Williams.

The Chicago Cubs win their first playoff series since 1908 with their Game 5 NLDS victory over the Atlanta Braves.

Emmitt Smith's return to Dallas is a rough one as his Arizona Cardinals are pounded by the Cowboys, 24-7. Smith gains minus-1 yards on six carries and leaves the game with a broken left shoulder blade.

6 **The Boston Red Sox** finalize their come-from-behind Divisional series win with a 4-3 victory over the Oakland Athletics, setting up an ALCS with rivals, the New York Yankees.

Down 35-14 with four minutes left in regulation, the Indianapolis Colts stage an improbable comeback to beat Tampa Bay, 38-35 in OT. Colts kicker Mike Vanderjagt gets a second chance at the game-winning FG in OT after Simeon Rice is penalized for "leaping."

6 **LeBron James scores** eight points and adds seven assists and three rebounds in his first pre-season game with the Cleveland Cavaliers.

9 **The preliminary hearing** in the Kobe Bryant case begins in Eagle, Colo. with graphic testimony by the prosecution.

LPGA's Jan Stephenson, in an interview with *Golf Magazine*, claims Asians are killing the tour with their lack of emotion and their refusal to speak English. She later apologizes.

Jacksonville punter Chris Hanson suffers a gash on his leg from chopping wood with an ax in the Jaguars locker room. It was supposed to be used as a motivational tool.

10 **New Corp. agrees** to sell the Los Angeles Dodgers to a group led by Boston real estate developer Frank McCourt. The sale now must be approved by MLB owners.

Annika Sorenstam qualifies for the LPGA Hall of Fame by completing 18 holes at the Samsung World Champ's.

Ohio State's 19-game football winning streak ends with their 17-10 loss to Wisconsin. Buckeye LB Robert Reynolds is later suspended for choking Wisconsin QB Jim Sorgi.

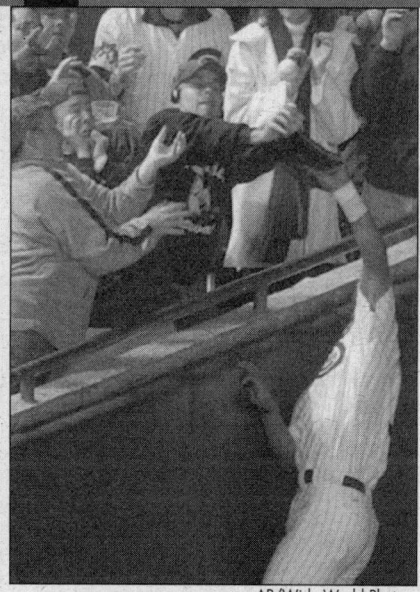

AP/Wide World Photos

*Bizarre incidents in the ALCS and NLCS took center stage as **Don Zimmer**, left, is laid out by Pedro Martinez, and Cubs fan **Steve Bartman** becomes more involved in Game 5 than he'd like.*

11 Game 3 of the ALCS takes an ugly turn when Boston ace Pedro Martinez hits Yankee OF Karim Garcia with a pitch. The incident leads to the benches emptying an inning later and Martinez throwing down 72-year-old Yankee coach Don Zimmer, who charged at him. The Yankees win 4-3.

12 Hall of Fame Jockey Bill Shoemaker, winner of 8,833 races and 11 Triple Crown events, dies in his sleep at the age of 72.

Germany wins the women's soccer World Cup with a 2-1 victory over Sweden. The U.S. beat Canada, 3-1, to take third place in the tournament.

Ferrari's Michael Schumacher finishes eighth at the Japanese Grand Prix which is enough for him to win his record sixth Formula One Driving Championship.

Boston College accepts an invitation to leave the Big East and join the ACC, creating a 12-member league.

In a race marred by a horrible crash that left Kenny Brack in serious condition, Gil de Ferran wins the final IRL event of the year, the Chevy 500, at the Texas Motor Speedway. Scott Dixon places second to win the season points title.

14 The Florida Marlins score eight runs in a wild eighth inning to beat the Cubs, 8-3, in Game 6 of the NLCS. Cub fan Steve Bartman feels the wrath of many after reaching for a foul ball that may have been caught by Cubs LF Moises Alou.

15 The Marlins win Game 7 of the NLCS, 9-6, to advance to the their second World Series in seven years.

16 The NBA's Charlotte Bobcats, who begin play in 2004-05, tab Bernie Bickerstaff as their head GM and coach.

Yankees 3B Aaron Boone launches an 11th-inning HR to beat the Red Sox in Game 7 of the ALCS, 6-5. Red Sox manager Grady Little takes the brunt of the blame for the Red Sox loss for leaving ace Pedro Martinez in for the eighth inning, when the Yankees rallied from a 5-2 deficit.

18 Canadians Peter Reid and Lori Bowden win the Ironman Triathlon championships in Hawaii.

19 Alex Zanardi, who had both legs amputated after a Sept. 2001 crash, returns to the track in Monza, Italy. He finishes the European Touring Car event in seventh in the day's second race, after being involved in a crash in the first.

20 Celtics all-star forward Antoine Walker is dealt to the Dallas Mavericks in a five-player deal.

22 Shortstop Alex Gonzalez hits a 12th-inning HR off Yankees' Jeff Weaver to give the Marlins a 4-3 win and tie the World Series at two games apiece.

Indy Racing League's Tony Renna is killed in a crash while tire testing at Indianapolis Motor Speedway.

23 The Western Athletic Conference announces that Utah St. and New Mexico St. will join them for the 2005-06 season, a week after they lost Tulsa, Rice and SMU to C-USA.

24 Miami Heat President Pat Riley relinquishes his head coaching duties and names Stan Van Gundy his successor.

25 Florida's Josh Beckett spins a five-hit shutout in Game 6 as the Marlins defeat the Yankees, 2-0, and win their second World Series in the last seven years.

Florida State defeats Wake Forest, 48-24, to give coach Bobby Bowden his 339th win, pushing him past Penn State's Joe Paterno for the all-time Division I-A lead.

Pleasantly Perfect wins the $4 million Classic at the Breeders' Cup, the fourth title of the day for trainer Richard Mandella. The day also sees the Cup's first dead heat, and jockey Julie Krone becoming the first woman to win a BC race.

26 Paul Tracy puts the finishing touches on his first CART points title as runner up Bruno Junqueira crashes.

27 Red Sox manager Grady Little is fired.

28 The 2003-04 NBA season tips off with Shaq and Kobe jawing with each other in the press like never before.

Preview 2004

A look at the sports world's major events and happenings in 2004.

AP/Wide World Photos

In July, American Lance Armstrong will go for an unprecedented sixth Tour de France victory.

AP/Wide World Photos

In August, the Olympics will make their return to the site of the first Games, Athens, Greece.

AP/Wide World Photos

In September, the United States will attempt to win back the Ryder Cup from Europe.

AP/Wide World Photos

There will be plenty of difficult moments on and off the court while the Kobe Bryant trial unfolds.

Baseball

Josh Beckett celebrates after shutting down the Yankees in Game 6 of the World Series.

AP/Wide World Photos

Fish Story

The Marlins, led by a 23-year-old pitcher and a 72-year-old manager, win their second World Series.

Karl Ravech
is an analyst for ESPN's baseball coverage.

Simply put the 2003 major league baseball season was the best, ever. You have to understand where baseball had been to comprehend the magnitude of the comeback the sport has made since it was read its last rights following the strike of 1994.

The idea that the Florida Marlins, left for dead following their own destruction after winning the 1997 World Series, could beat the New York Yankees, a team almost ten times older and certainly three times more expensive, left baseball observers of all ages shaking their heads.

For starters, both the Chicago Cubs and Boston Red Sox were in the playoffs. For a while many held out hope they'd eventually meet in the World Series. As fate would have it, or thanks to Grady Little's decision making, neither got there, but there will be more on that in a moment.

For closers, there was Eric Gagne of the Los Angeles Dodgers and John Smoltz of the Atlanta Braves. All these two men did was elevate the role of closer to a new level. The man called on in the bullpen to come in and put out any fires someone else had created. Gagne had a Cy Young-caliber season. He was called on 55 times to save games and he delivered every time. Smoltz pitched with an elbow that on the inside looked like spaghetti but on the outside held up like Kevlar. He saved 45 of 49 games with an ERA of 1.12 to lead the Braves to their 12th straight division title. Remarkable stuff for pitchers accustomed to pitching in a hitter's era.

The 2003 season also saw the comeback of the starting pitcher. How else do you explain that the two top strikeout artists in the National League both pitched for the loveable losers, the Chicago Cubs. Kerry Wood and Mark Prior had the entire city believing this was the year. In the end, they both had chances to get new manager Dusty Baker's team into the World Series. Neither could come through, however, as the Marlins beat them both in Games 6 and 7 of the League Championship Series, in Chicago no less.

AP/Wide World Photos

*When 72-year-old **Jack McKeon** took over the Florida Marlins on May 11, the team was tied for last place in the N.L. East. Here he is after leading the Marlins to the World Series title.*

Florida had a young gun of its own. His name was Josh Beckett. He carried a very modest 9-8 record into the postseason but by the end of October, Beckett had left no doubt that he too deserved to be mentioned in the same breath as the great young arms of the game.

Though it didn't really show on the mound, Roger Clemens, the workhorse of the New York Yankees and a sure fire first ballot hall of famer, apparently ran out of whatever fuel he had used over an illustrious 300 win, 4,000 strikeout career, and planned to retire after the 2003 season. He played a major role in the American League Championship Series, a memorable (and arguably the

greatest) League Championship Series of all time. It was a seven-game affair that had the Red Sox leading by three runs in the seventh game with only five outs to go and their ace Pedro Martinez pitching a gem.

But someone neglected to get the message to the manager of the Red Sox that Martinez was through. He had done his job and it was time for a much-maligned bullpen, albeit very successful in the postseason to get the call. Inexplicably as Little went to the mound in the eighth inning to check on Martinez, he opted to let his ace stay in the game. Bad idea. Martinez got pummeled the same way boxer Trevor Berbick used to—by any and all oppo-

AP/Wide World Photos

*Flamethrowing Texan **Roger Clemens** called it quits in 2003 after 20 seasons with the Red Sox, Blue Jays and Yankees.*

nents. When Little finally realized his mistake, it was too late. The Yankees tied it up in the eighth and went on to win in the 11th on Aaron Boone's homer, and Little's fate was sealed. He was fired two days after the World Series ended.

For many the World Series was anti-climactic. Chicago was out, so too was Boston. Atlanta had done its typical postseason fade and the San Francisco Giants were shut down by the solid play of the Florida Marlins of all teams. The same organization that had conducted a fire sale that would make any arsonist proud following the '97 title was back again. Back and younger, and older, than ever.

Led by 72-year-old manager Jack McKeon, who was hired only after the team limped out to a 16-22 start, the Marlins kept coming like a runaway locomotive.

The team was backboned by a catcher nobody wanted. Pudge Rodriguez was given a one-year contract for ten million dollars. He proved to be worth every bit. His game calling and handling of a young pitching staff was impeccable. His timely hitting and tenacious defense were emblematic of this ensemble that played in front of more empty seats than an NFL game in Los Angeles. Oh that's right, they don't play NFL games in Los Angeles. You get

continued on page 60 ▶

The Ten Biggest Stories
of the Year in Baseball

10   With 101 wins, the Atlanta Braves cruise to the National League East division title by 10 games. It is the 12th consecutive division title for the Braves, adding to their all-time major league record.

9   In just his third professional season, St. Louis Cardinals outfielder Albert Pujols makes a serious bid to win the Triple Crown. His .359 batting average leads the league but he finishes tied for fourth in both home runs and runs batted in.

8   Six Astros pitchers combine to no-hit the New York Yankees, 8-0, in Yankee Stadium on June 11. Roy Oswalt, Pete Munro, Kirk Saarloos, Brad Lidge, Octavio Dotel and Billy Wagner set the major league record for pitchers combining for a no-hitter.

7   Bobby Bonds dies at the age of 57 after his year-long battle with lung cancer and a brain tumor. He is one of only four major leaguers (son Barry is another) to steal 300 bases and hit 300 home runs.

6   The Detroit Tigers, under first-year manager Alan Trammell, lose 119 games, missing out on the not-so-coveted modern day major league record, 120, set by the Mets in 1962. Starter Mike Maroth becomes the first pitcher since 1980 to lose 20 games in a season.

5   Roger Clemens retires after 20 seasons that include two World Series rings and a major league record six Cy Young awards. He gets his long-awaited 300th win with a 5-2 victory over the Cardinals on June 13, and on the same night becomes the third player in history to record 4,000 career strikeouts.

4   Cubs slugger Sammy Sosa is ejected and later suspended for seven games for using a corked bat in a game against the Devil Rays on June 3. Seventy-six of his bats are subsequently proven to be clean but to many, the damage has already been done.

3   The Cubs win their first playoff series since 1908 and are five outs away from a World Series appearance when disaster strikes.

2   The Red Sox and Yankees wage an epic seven-game battle in the ALCS, finally won by the Yankees on an 11th-inning home run by Aaron Boone. Red Sox manager Grady Little is the scapegoat after leaving ace Pedro Martinez on the mound too long in Game 7.

1   The Florida Marlins win their second World Series title in the team's 11-year existence. Jack McKeon, 72, takes over as manager on May 11 and leads the team to a 91-win season. Fireballer Josh Beckett wins World Series MVP after shutting out the Yankees in Game 6.

the picture. McKeon proved genius when he opted to pitch the brash 23-year-old Beckett on three day's rest in Game 6 of the World Series. The good news for McKeon was that his Marlins were up three games to two. The bad news? Games 6 and 7 were to be played at Yankee Stadium.

No problem.

A young stud, Beckett never wavered and he never came out of the game. It was a complete game shutout of the vaunted Yankees. Once again the Marlins were world champions and the rest of the baseball world was left shaking its head, wondering if the season they had just witnessed could ever be duplicated. It was that special.

Boone-town

Aaron Boone's 11th inning home run to beat the Red Sox in Game 7 of the ALCS was just the fifth series-clinching "walk-off" home run in major league history.

			Clinched
2003	Aaron Boone*, NYY vs. Bos	ALCS	
1999	Todd Pratt*, NYM vs Ari	NLDS	
1993	Joe Carter, Tor vs Phi	WS	
1976	Chris Chambliss, NYY vs KC	ALCS	
1960	Bill Mazeroski, Pit vs NYY	WS	

*extra innings

Who Needs Social Security?

At 72, Florida's Jack McKeon became the oldest manager ever to bring his team to the postseason.

		Age
2003	Jack McKeon, Florida	72
1960	Casey Stengel, NY Yankees	70
1931	Connie Mack, Phila. A's	68
2003	Felipe Alou, San Francisco	68
1995	Tommy Lasorda, Los Angeles	68

Catching On

In 2003 Atlanta Brave Javy Lopez set the all-time major league home run mark by a catcher, breaking the record held since 1996 by Todd Hundley.

		Home runs
2003	Javy Lopez, Atlanta	42*
1996	Todd Hundley, NY Mets	41
1999	Mike Piazza, NY Mets	40
1997	Mike Piazza, Los Angeles	40
1953	Roy Campanella, Brooklyn	40

*also hit one HR as a pinch-hitter.

No Seventh Heaven

Yankees catcher Yogi Berra once said, "It's deja-vu all over again." That's certainly the case for the Boston Red Sox, whose last three Game 7 postseason losses look eerily familiar.

Series	Red Sox led	Final
2003 ALCS vs NYY	5-2 in 8th	L, 6-5*
1986 WS vs NYM	3-0 in 6th	L, 8-5
1975 WS vs Cin	3-0 in 6th	L, 4-3

*11th inning

2003
Season in Review

SPORTS ALMANAC

Final Major League Standings

Division champions (*) and Wild Card (†) winners are noted. Number of seasons listed after each manager refers to current tenure with club.

American League

East Division

	W	L	Pct	GB	Home	Road
*New York	101	61	.623	—	50-32	51-29
†Boston	95	67	.586	6	53-28	42-39
Toronto	86	76	.531	15	41-40	45-36
Baltimore	71	91	.438	30	40-40	31-51
Tampa Bay	63	99	.389	38	36-45	27-54

2003 Managers: NY–Joe Torre (8th season); **Bos**–Grady Little (2nd); **Tor**–Carlos Tosca (2nd); **Bal**–Mike Hargrove (4th); **TB**–Lou Piniella (1st).
2002 Standings: 1. New York (103-58); 2. Boston (93-69); 3. Toronto (78-84); 4. Baltimore (67-95); 5. Tampa Bay (55-106).

Central Division

	W	L	Pct	GB	Home	Road
*Minnesota	90	72	.556	—	48-33	42-39
Chicago	86	76	.531	4	51-30	35-46
Kansas City	83	79	.512	7	40-40	43-39
Cleveland	68	94	.420	22	38-43	30-51
Detroit	43	119	.265	47	23-58	20-61

2003 Managers: Min–Ron Gardenhire (2nd season); **Chi**–Jerry Manuel (6th); **KC**–Tony Pena (2nd); **Cle**–Eric Wedge (1st); **Det**–Alan Trammell (1st).
2002 Standings: 1. Minnesota (94-67); 2. Chicago (81-81); 3. Cleveland (74-88); 4. Kansas City (62-100); 5. Detroit (55-106).

West Division

	W	L	Pct	GB	Home	Road
*Oakland	96	66	.593	—	57-24	39-42
Seattle	93	69	.574	3	50-31	43-38
Anaheim	77	85	.475	19	45-37	32-48
Texas	71	91	.438	25	43-38	28-53

2003 Managers: Oak–Ken Macha (1st season); **Sea**–Bob Melvin (1st); **Ana**–Mike Scioscia (4th); **Tex**–Buck Showalter (1st).
2002 Standings: 1. Oakland (103-59); 2. Anaheim (99-63); 3. Seattle (93-69); 4. Texas (72-90).

National League

East Division

	W	L	Pct	GB	Home	Road
*Atlanta	101	61	.623	—	55-26	46-35
†Florida	91	71	.562	10	53-28	38-43
Philadelphia	86	76	.531	15	49-32	37-44
Montreal	83	79	.512	18	52-29	31-50
New York	66	95	.410	34½	34-46	32-49

2003 Managers: Atl–Bobby Cox (14th season); **Fla**–Jeff Torborg (2nd, 16-22) was fired on May 11 and replaced by Jack McKeon (75-49); **Phi**–Larry Bowa (3rd); **Mon**– Frank Robinson (2nd); **NY**–Art Howe (1st).
2002 Standings: 1. Atlanta (101-59); 2. Montreal (83-79); 3. Philadelphia (80-81); 4. Florida (79-83); 5. New York (75-86).

Central Division

	W	L	Pct	GB	Home	Road
*Chicago	88	74	.543	—	44-37	44-37
Houston	87	75	.537	1	48-33	39-42
St. Louis	85	77	.525	3	48-33	37-44
Pittsburgh	75	87	.463	13	39-42	36-45
Cincinnati	69	93	.426	19	35-46	34-47
Milwaukee	68	94	.420	20	31-50	37-44

2003 Managers: Chi–Dusty Baker (1st season); **Hou**–Jimy Williams (2nd); **St. L**–Tony La Russa (8th); **Pit**–Lloyd McClendon (3rd); **Cin**–Bob Boone (3rd, 46-58) was fired on July 28 and replaced by bench coach Ray Knight (1-0) and then Dave Miley (22-35); **Mil**–Ned Yost (1st).
2002 Standings: 1. St. Louis (97-65); 2. Houston (84-78); 3. Cincinnati (78-84); 4. Pittsburgh (72-89); 5. Chicago (67-95); 6. Milwaukee (56-106).

West Division

	W	L	Pct	GB	Home	Road
*San Francisco	100	61	.621	—	57-24	43-37
Los Angeles	85	77	.525	15½	46-35	39-42
Arizona	84	78	.519	16½	45-36	39-42
Colorado	74	88	.457	26½	49-32	25-56
San Diego	64	98	.395	36½	35-46	29-52

2003 Managers: SF–Felipe Alou (1st season); **LA**–Jim Tracy (3rd); **Ari**–Bob Brenly (3rd); **Col**– Clint Hurdle (2nd); **SD**–Bruce Bochy (9th).
2002 Standings: 1. Arizona (98-64); 2. San Francisco (95-66); 3. Los Angeles (92-70); 4. Colorado (73-89); 5. San Diego (66-96).

Interleague Play Standings

American League

	W-L	Pct		W-L	Pct
New York	13-5	.722	Oakland	9-9	.500
Boston	11-7	.611	Cleveland	6-12	.333
Anaheim	11-7	.611	Baltimore	5-13	.278
Toronto	10-8	.556	Detroit	4-14	.222
Minnesota	10-8	.556	Texas	4-14	.278
Chicago	10-8	.556	Tampa Bay	3-15	.167
Seattle	10-8	.556	**Totals**	**115-137**	**.456**
Kansas City	9-9	.500			

National League

	W-L	Pct		W-L	Pct
Arizona	11-4	.733	Philadelphia	8-7	.533
Atlanta	10-5	.667	Chicago	9-9	.500
Houston	11-7	.611	Montreal	9-9	.500
Los Angeles	11-7	.611	San Diego	8-10	.444
Florida	9-6	.600	Pittsburgh	5-7	.417
Colorado	9-6	.600	Milwaukee	5-7	.417
Cincinnati	7-5	.556	New York	5-10	.333
St. Louis	10-8	.556	**Totals**	**137-115**	**.544**
San Francisco	10-8	.556			

Boston Red Sox
Bill Mueller
Batting Avgerage

Texas Rangers
Alex Rodriguez
HR, Runs, Slg. Pct.

Boston Red Sox
Pedro Martinez
ERA, Opp. BA, WHIP

Toronto Blue Jays
Roy Halladay
Wins, Innings, ShO

American League Leaders

(*) indicates rookie.

Batting

	Bat	Gm	AB	R	H	Avg	TB	2B	3B	HR	RBI	BB	SO	SB	Slg Pct	OBP
Bill Mueller, Bos	S	146	524	85	171	**.326**	283	45	5	19	85	59	77	1	.540	.398
Manny Ramirez, Bos	R	154	569	117	185	**.325**	334	36	1	37	104	97	94	3	.587	.427
Derek Jeter, NY	R	119	482	87	156	**.324**	217	25	3	10	52	43	88	11	.450	.393
Vernon Wells, Tor	R	161	678	118	215	**.317**	373	49	5	33	117	42	80	4	.550	.359
Magglio Ordonez, Chi	R	160	606	95	192	**.317**	331	46	3	29	99	57	73	9	.546	.380
Garret Anderson, Ana	L	159	638	80	201	**.315**	345	49	4	29	116	31	83	6	.541	.345
Ichiro Suzuki, Sea	L	159	679	111	212	**.312**	296	29	8	13	62	36	69	34	.436	.352
A.J. Pierzynski, Min	L	137	487	63	152	**.312**	226	35	3	11	74	24	55	3	.464	.360
Aubrey Huff, TB	L	162	636	91	198	**.311**	353	47	3	34	107	53	80	2	.555	.367
Shannon Stewart, Tor-Min	R	136	573	90	176	**.307**	263	44	2	13	73	52	66	4	.459	.364
Carlos Beltran, KC	S	141	521	102	160	**.307**	272	14	10	26	100	72	81	41	.522	.389
Michael Young, Tex	R	160	666	106	204	**.306**	297	33	9	14	72	36	103	13	.446	.339
Trot Nixon, Bos	L	134	441	81	135	**.306**	255	24	6	28	87	65	96	4	.578	.396
Jacque Jones, Min	L	136	517	76	157	**.304**	240	33	1	16	69	21	105	13	.464	.333
Carlos Delgado, Tor	L	161	570	117	172	**.302**	338	38	1	42	145	109	137	0	.593	.426

Note: Batters must have 3.1 plate appearances per their team's games played to qualify.

Home Runs

Rodriguez, Tex	47
Thomas, Chi	42
Delgado, Tor	42
Giambi, NY	41
Palmeiro, Tex	38
Soriano, NY	38
Ramirez, Bos	37
Boone, Sea	35
Huff, TB	34
Wells, Tor	33

Triples

Guzman, Min	14
Garciaparra, Bos	13
Beltran, KC	10
Rivas, Min	9
Byrnes, Oak	9
Young, Tex	9
Crawford, TB	9

On Base Pct.

Ramirez, Bos	.427
Delgado, Tor	.426
Giambi, NY	.412
Martinez, Sea	.406
Posada, NY	.405
Mueller, Bos	.398
Nixon, Bos	.396
Rodriguez, Tex	.396

Runs Batted In

Delgado, Tor	145
Rodriguez, Tex	118
Boone, Sea	117
Wells, Tor	117
Anderson, Ana	116
Lee, Chi	113
Palmeiro, Tex	112
Giambi, NY	107
Huff, TB	107
Tejada, Oak	106
Matsui*, NY	106

Doubles

Anderson, Ana	49
Wells, Tor	49
Huff, TB	47
Ordonez, Chi	46
Mueller, Bos	45
Hinske, Tor	45
Stewart, Tor-Min	44

Slugging Pct.

Rodriguez, Tex	.600
Delgado, Tor	.593
Ortiz, Bos	.592
Ramirez, Bos	.587
Nixon, Bos	.578
Thomas, Chi	.562
Huff, TB	.555

Hits

Wells, Tor	215
Suzuki, Sea	212
Young, Tex	204
Anderson, Ana	201
Garciaparra, Bos	198
Soriano, NY	198
Huff, TB	198
Ordonez, Chi	192
Ramirez, Bos	185

Runs

Rodriguez, Tex	124
Garciaparra, Bos	120
Wells, Tor	118
Ramirez, Bos	117
Delgado, Tor	117
Soriano, NY	114
Boone, Sea	111
Suzuki, Sea	111

Walks

Giambi, NY	129
Delgado, Tor	109
Thomas, Chi	100
Durazo, Oak	100
Ramirez, Bos	97
Posada, NY	93
Martinez, Sea	92
Rodriguez, Tex	87

Stolen Bases

	SB	CS
Crawford, TB	55	10
Sanchez, Det	44	18
Beltran, KC	41	4
Soriano, NY	35	8
Suzuki, Sea	34	8
Damon, Bos	30	6
Baldelli*, TB	27	10

Total Bases

Wells, Tor	373
Rodriguez, Tex	364
Soriano, NY	358
Huff, TB	353
Anderson, Ana	345
Garciaparra, Bos	345
Delgado, Tor	338
Ramirez, Bos	334

Strikeouts

Giambi, NY	140
Cameron, Sea	137
Delgado, Tor	137
Young, Det	130
Soriano, NY	130
Baldelli*, TB	128
Rodriguez, Tex	126
Boone, Sea	125

Pitching

	Arm	W	L	ERA	Gm	GS	CG	ShO	Sv	IP	H	R	ER	HR	HB	BB	SO	WP
Pedro Martinez, Bos	R	14	4	2.22	29	29	3	0	0	186.2	147	52	46	7	9	47	206	5
Tim Hudson, Oak	R	16	7	2.70	34	34	3	2	0	240.0	197	84	72	15	10	61	162	6
Esteban Loaiza, Chi	R	21	9	2.90	34	34	1	0	0	226.1	196	75	73	17	10	56	207	3
Mark Mulder, Oak	L	15	9	3.13	26	26	9	2	0	186.2	180	66	65	15	2	40	128	7
Roy Halladay, Tor	R	22	7	3.25	36	36	9	2	0	266.0	253	111	96	26	9	32	204	6
Jamie Moyer, Sea	L	21	7	3.27	33	33	1	0	0	215.0	199	83	78	19	8	66	129	0
Barry Zito, Oak	L	14	12	3.30	35	35	4	1	0	231.2	186	.98	85	19	6	88	146	4
Mike Mussina, NY	R	17	8	3.40	31	31	2	1	0	214.2	192	86	81	21	3	40	195	4
Ryan Franklin, Sea	R	11	13	3.57	32	32	1	0	0	212.0	199	93	84	34	9	61	99	1
C.C. Sabathia, Cle	L	13	9	3.60	30	30	2	1	0	197.2	190	85	79	19	6	66	141	4
Darrell May, KC	L	10	8	3.77	35	32	1	2	0	210.0	197	98	88	31	2	53	115	5
Brian Anderson, Cle-KC . . .	L	14	11	3.78	32	31	1	0	0	197.2	212	110	83	27	4	43	87	3
Joel Pineiro, Sea	R	16	11	3.78	32	32	3	2	0	211.2	192	94	89	19	6	76	151	5
Bartolo Colon, Chi	R	15	13	3.87	34	34	9	0	0	242.0	223	107	104	30	5	67	173	8
Roger Clemens, NY	R	17	9	3.91	33	33	1	1	0	211.2	199	99	92	24	5	58	190	5

Note: Pitchers must have one inning pitched per their team's games played to qualify.

Wins

Halladay, Tor 22-7
Moyer, Sea 21-7
Pettitte, NY 21-8
Loaiza, Chi 21-9
Lowe, Bos 17-7
Mussina, NY 17-8
Clemens, NY 17-9
Hudson, Oak 16-7
Pineiro, Sea 16-11
Ortiz, Ana 16-13

Appearances

Miller, Tor 79
Walker, Det 78
Grimsley, KC 76
Ryan, Bal. 76
Hawkins, Min 74
Cordero, Tex 73
Romero, Min 73
Baez, Cle 73

Complete Games

Colon, Chi. 9
Halladay, Tor 9
Mulder, Oak 9
Wells, NY 4
Ponson, Bal 4
Zito, Oak 4
Six tied with 3 each.

Shutouts

Halladay, Tor 2
Hudson, Oak 2
Mulder, Oak 2
Pineiro, Sea. 2
Lackey, Ana 2
21 tied with 1 each.

Losses

Maroth, Det 9-21
Bonderman*, Det. . . 6-19
Cornejo, Det 6-17
Lackey, Ana 10-16
Washburn, Ana . . . 10-15
Lidle, Tor 12-15
Garcia, Sea 12-14
Thomson, Tex . . . 13-14
Buehrle, Chi 14-14
Five tied with 13 each.

Innings

Halladay, Tor 266.0
Colon, Chi 242.0
Hudson, Oak 240.0
Zito, Oak 231.2
Buehrle, Chi 230.1
Loaiza, Chi. 226.1
Thomson, Tex 217.0
Moyer, Sea 215.0
Mussina, NY 214.2
Wells, NY. 213.0

Saves

	SV	BS
Foulke, Oak	.43	5
Guardado, Min . . .	.41	4
Rivera, NY	.40	6
Julio, Bal	.36	8
Percival, Ana	.33	4
MacDougal*, KC . .	.27	8
Urbina, Tex	.26	4
Carter*, TB	.26	7
Baez, Cle	.25	10
Hasegawa, Sea . . .	.16	1
Kim, Bos	.16	3

Walks

Zambrano, TB 106
Zito, Oak 88
Johnson, Bal 80
Escobar, Tor 78
Pineiro, Sea 76
Garland, Chi 74
Lowe, Bos 72
Two tied with 71 each.

HRs Allowed

Washburn, Ana 34
Franklin, Sea 34
Maroth, Det 34
Radke, Min 32
May, KC 31
Garcia, Sea. 31
Lackey, Ana 31

Wild Pitches

Zambrano, TB 15
Bonderman*, Det . . . 12
Garcia, Sea. 11
Lackey, Ana 11
Lohse, Min 10
Lidle, Tor 9
Escobar, Tor 9
Romero, Min 9
Davis*, Cle 9

Hit Batters

Zambrano, TB 20
Wakefield, Bos. 12
Sele, Ana 12
Helling, Bal 12
Gonzalez, TB. 12
Ortiz, Ana. 12
Westbrook, Cle 12

Strikeouts

Loaiza, Chi 207
Martinez, Bos 206
Halladay, Tor 204
Mussina, NY 195
Clemens, NY 190
Pettitte, NY 180
Colon, Chi. 173
Wakefield, Bos. 169
Santana, Min. 169
Hudson, Oak 162

Opp. Batting Average

Martinez, Bos 215
Zito, Oak 219
Hudson, Oak. 223
Loaiza, Chi 233
Zambrano, TB 237
Mussina, NY 238
Pineiro, Sea. 241
May, KC 246
Moyer, Sea 246
Wakefield, Bos 246

WHIP

(Walks + Hits/IP)
Martinez, Bos 1.04
Halladay, Tor 1.07
Hudson, Oak 1.08
Mussina, NY. 1.08
Loaiza, Chi. 1.11
Mulder, Oak. 1.18
Zito, Oak 1.18
May, KC 1.19
Colon, Chi 1.20
Clemens, NY 1.21

Fielding

Put Outs

Delgado, Tor 1355
Lee, TB 1223
Hatteberg, Oak 1177
Pena, Det 1135
Olerud, Sea. 1096
Mientkiewicz, Min . . 1091
Conine, Bal 1061
Broussard*, Cle 957
Posada, NY. 933
Teixeira*, Tex. 931

Assists

Tejada, Oak 490
Hudson, Tor 477
Berroa*, KC 472
Young, Tex. 472
Rodriguez, Tex 464
Garciaparra, Bos . . . 456
Ellis, Oak 455
Soriano 445
Boone, Sea 426
Cruz, Bal. 409

OF Assists

Baldelli*, TB 15
Anderson, Ana. 14
Suzuki, Sea 12
Ramirez, Bos 11
Matsui*, NY 11
Beltran, KC 10
Crawford, TB 10
Gonzalez, Tex 10
Guiel, KC 9
Four tied with 8 each.

Errors

Berroa*, KC 24
Hinske, Tor 22
Tejada, Oak 21
Batista, Bal 20
Garciaparra, Bos 20
Valentin, Chi 20
Blake, Cle 19
Soriano, NY 19
Lugo, TB 17
Three tied with 16 each.

St. Louis Cardinals
Albert Pujols
BA, H, 2B, R, TB

San Francisco Giants
Barry Bonds
SLG, OBP, Walks

San Francisco Giants
Jason Schmidt
ERA, Opp. BA, WHIP
Shutouts

Los Angeles Dodgers
Eric Gagne
Saves

National League Leaders

(*) indicates rookie.

Batting

	Bat	Gm	AB	R	H	Avg	TB	2B	3B	HR	RBI	BB	SO	SB	Slg Pct	OBP
Albert Pujols, St.L.	R	157	591	137	212	**.359**	394	51	1	43	124	79	65	5	.667	.439
Todd Helton, Col	L	160	583	135	209	**.358**	367	49	5	33	117	111	72	0	.630	.458
Barry Bonds, SF	L	130	390	111	133	**.341**	292	22	1	45	90	148	58	7	.749	.529
Edgar Renteria, St.L	R	157	587	96	194	**.330**	282	47	1	13	100	65	54	34	.480	.394
Gary Sheffield, Atl.	R	155	574	126	190	**.330**	348	37	2	39	132	86	55	18	.604	.419
Jason Kendall, Pit	R	150	587	84	191	**.325**	244	29	3	6	58	49	40	8	.416	.399
Marcus Giles, Atl.	R	145	551	101	174	**.316**	290	49	2	21	69	59	80	14	.526	.390
Luis Castillo, Fla	S	152	595	99	187	**.314**	236	19	6	6	39	63	60	21	.397	.381
Mark Loretta, SD	R	154	589	74	185	**.314**	260	28	4	13	72	54	62	5	.441	.372
Mark Grudzielanek, Chi.	R	121	481	73	151	**.314**	200	38	1	3	38	30	64	6	.416	.366
Scott Podsednik*, Mil.	L	154	558	100	175	**.314**	247	29	8	9	58	56	91	43	.443	.379
Mike Lieberthal, Phi	R	131	508	68	159	**.313**	230	30	1	13	81	38	59	0	.453	.373
Jose Vidro, Mon	S	144	509	77	158	**.310**	239	36	0	15	65	69	50	3	.470	.397
Richard Hidalgo, Hou	R	141	514	91	159	**.309**	294	43	4	28	88	58	104	9	.572	.385
Juan Pierre, Fla	L	162	668	100	204	**.305**	249	28	7	1	41	55	35	65	.373	.361

Note: Batters must have 3.1 plate appearances per their team's games played to qualify.

Home Runs

Thome, Phi	47
Bonds, SF	45
Sexson, Mil	45
Lopez, Atl	43
Pujols, St.L	43
Sosa, Chi	40
Sheffield, Atl	39
Bagwell, Hou	39
Edmonds, St.L	39

Runs Batted In

Wilson, Col	141
Sheffield, Atl	132
Thome, Phi	131
Sexson, Mil	124
Pujols, St.L	124
Helton, Col	117
A. Jones, Atl	116
Lopez, Atl	109
C. Jones, Atl	106
Ramirez, Pit-Chi	106

Hits

Pujols, St.L	212
Helton, Col	209
Pierre, Fla	204
Renteria, St.L	194
Furcal, Atl	194
Kendall, Pit	191
Sheffield, Atl	190
Castillo, Fla	187
Cabrera, Mon	186

Stolen Bases

	SB	CS
Pierre, Fla	65	20
Podsednik*, Mil	43	10
Roberts, LA	40	14
Renteria, St.L	34	7
Lofton, Pit-Chi	30	9
Young, Mil-SF	28	12
Furcal, Atl	25	2
Cabrera, Mon	24	2

Triples

Finley, Ari	10
Furcal, Atl	10
Lofton, Pit-Chi	8
Podsednik*, Mil	8
Four tied with 7 each.	

Doubles

Pujols, St.L	51
Green, LA	49
Rolen, St.L	49
Helton, Col	49
Giles, Atl	49
Renteria, St.L	47
Cabrera, Mon	47

Runs

Pujols, St.L	137
Helton, Col	135
Furcal, Atl	130
Sheffield, Atl	126
Bonds, SF	111
Thome, Phi	111
Berkman, Hou	110
Bagwell, Hou	109

Total Bases

Pujols, St.L	394
Helton, Col	367
Sheffield, Atl	348
Sexson, Mil	332
Thome, Phi	331
Wilson, Col	322
Bagwell, Hou	317
Lopez, Atl	314

On Base Pct.

Bonds, SF	.529
Helton, Col	.458
Pujols, St.L	.439
Giles, Pit-SD	.427
Walker, Col	.422
Sheffield, Atl	.419
Berkman, Hou	.412
Abreu, Phi	.409
C. Jones, Atl	.402
L. Gonzalez, Ari	.402

Slugging Pct.

Bonds, SF	.749
Pujols, St.L	.667
Helton, Col	.630
Edmonds, St.L	.617
Sheffield, Atl	.604
Thome, Phi	.573
Hidalgo, Hou	.572

Walks

Bonds, SF	148
Thome, Phi	111
Helton, Col	111
Abreu, Phi	109
Berkman, Hou	107
Giles, Pit-SD	105
Cruz, SF	102

Strikeouts

Thome, Phi	182
Hernandez, Col-Chi-Pit.	177
Wilkerson, Mon	155
Sexson, Mil	151
Sosa, Chi	143
Burrell, Phi	142
Wilson, Col	139

Pitching

	Arm	W	L	ERA	Gm	GS	CG	ShO	Sv	IP	H	R	ER	HR	HB	BB	SO	WP
Jason Schmidt, SF	R	17	5	**2.34**	29	29	5	3	0	207.2	152	56	54	14	5	46	208	7
Kevin Brown, LA	R	14	9	**2.39**	32	32	0	0	0	211.0	184	67	56	11	5	56	185	5
Mark Prior, Chi	R	18	6	**2.43**	30	30	3	1	0	211.1	183	67	57	15	9	50	245	9
Brandon Webb*, Ari	R	10	9	**2.84**	29	28	1	1	0	180.2	140	65	57	12	13	68	172	9
Curt Schilling, Ari	R	8	9	**2.95**	24	24	3	2	0	168.0	144	58	55	17	3	32	194	4
Hideo Nomo, LA	R	16	13	**3.09**	33	33	2	2	0	218.1	175	82	75	24	1	98	177	11
Carlos Zambrano, Chi	R	13	11	**3.11**	32	32	3	1	0	214.0	188	88	74	9	10	94	168	6
Kerry Wood, Chi	R	14	11	**3.20**	32	32	4	2	0	211.0	152	77	75	24	21	100	266	10
Livan Hernandez, Mon	R	15	10	**3.20**	33	33	8	0	0	233.1	225	92	83	27	10	57	178	6
Javier Vazquez, Mon	R	13	12	**3.24**	34	34	4	1	0	230.2	198	93	83	28	4	57	241	11
Kip Wells, Pit	R	10	9	**3.28**	31	31	1	0	0	197.1	171	77	72	24	7	76	147	7
Miguel Batista, Ari	R	10	9	**3.54**	36	29	.2	1	0	193.1	197	85	76	13	8	60	142	7
Mark Redman, Fla	L	14	9	**3.59**	29	29	3	0	0	190.2	172	82	76	16	5	61	151	4
Vicente Padilla, Phi	R	14	12	**3.62**	32	32	1	1	0	208.2	196	94	84	22	16	62	133	3
Tim Redding, Hou	R	10	14	**3.68**	33	32	0	0	0	176.0	179	85	72	16	7	65	116	3

Note: Pitchers must have one inning pitched per their team's games played to qualify.

Wins

Ortiz, Atl 21-7
Prior, Chi 18-6
Williams, St.L 18-9
Schmidt, SF 17-5
Trachsel, NY 16-10
Wolf, Phi 16-10
Maddux, Atl 16-11
Nomo, LA 16-13
Three tied with 15 each.

Appearances

Quantrill, LA 89
Villarreal*, Ari 86
Martin, LA 80
King, Atl 80
Wagner, Hou 78
Kline, St.L 78
Nathan, SF 78
Lidge*, Hou 78

Complete Games

L. Hernandez, Mon 8
Schmidt, SF 5
Morris, St.L 5
Millwood, Phi 5
Vazquez, Mon 4
Wood, Chi 4

Shutouts

Schmidt, SF 3
Morris, St.L 3
Millwood, Phi 3
Seven tied with 2 each.

Losses

D'Amico, Pit 9-16
Graves, Cin 4-15
Lawrence, SD 10-15
Glavine, NY 9-14
Redding, Hou 10-14
Eight tied with 13 each.

Innings

L. Hernandez, Mon . 233.1
Vazquez, Mon 230.2
Millwood, Phi 222.0
Williams, St.L 220.2
Sheets, Mil 220.2
Maddux, Atl 218.1
Nomo, LA 218.1
Zambrano, Chi 214.0
Ortiz, Atl 212.1
Prior, Chi 211.1
Brown, LA 211.0
Wood, Chi 211.0

Saves

	SV	BS
Gagne, LA	.55	0
Smoltz, Atl	.45	4
Wagner, Hou	.44	3
Worrell, SF	.38	7
Biddle, Mon	.34	7
Borowski, Chi	.33	4
Mantei, Ari	.29	3
Williams, Pit-Phi	.28	7
Looper, Fla	.28	6
Mesa, Phi	.24	4
Isringhausen, St.L	.22	3

Walks

Ortiz, Atl 102
Ishii, LA 101
Wood, Chi 100
Nomo, LA 98
Leiter, NY 94
Franklin, Mil 94
Zambrano, Chi 94
Jennings, Col 88

HR Allowed

Franklin, Mil 36
Tomko, St.L 35
Peavy, SD 33
Graves, Cin 30
Stephenson, St.L 30
Sheets, Mil 29

Wild Pitches

Clement, Chi 13
Day*, Mon 13
Wright, SD-Atl 12
Silva, Phi 12
Foppert*, SF 12
Four tied with 11 each.

Hit Batters

Wood, Chi 21
Padilla, Phi 16
Clement, Chi 14
Stephenson, St.L 13
Webb*, Ari 13
Chacon, Col 12
Williams, St.L 11
Lawrence, SD 11

Strikeouts

Wood, Chi 266
Prior, Chi 245
Vazquez, Mon 241
Schmidt, SF 208
Schilling, Ari 194
Brown, LA 185
L. Hernandez, Mon . 178
Nomo, LA 177
Wolf, Phi 177
Webb*, Ari 172

Opp. Batting Average

Schmidt, SF 200
Wood, Chi 203
Webb*, Ari 212
Ortiz, Atl 223
Nomo, LA 223
Clement, Chi 227
Vazquez, Mon 229
Schilling, Ari 230
Prior, Chi 231
Wells, Pit 233

WHIP
(Walks + Hits/IP)

Schmidt, SF 0.95
Schilling, Ari 1.05
Prior, Chi 1.10
Vazquez, Mon 1.11
Brown, LA 1.14
Webb*, Ari 1.15
Morris, St.L 1.18
Maddux, Atl 1.18

Fielding

Put Outs

Helton, Col 1418
Thome, Phi 1373
Sexson, Mil 1362
Bagwell, Hou 1290
Lee, Fla 1279
Casey, Cin 1257
Cordero, Mon 1066
Martinez, St.L 1026
Lo Duca, LA 1014
Fick, Atl 1004

Assists

Izturis, LA 482
Furcal, Atl 481
Giles, Atl 471
Rollins, Phi 463
Cabrera, Mon 456
J. Wilson, Pit 454
Renteria, St.L 439
Castilllo, Fla 433
Gonzalez, Fla 426
Gonzalez, Chi 423

OF Assists

Hidalgo, Hou 22
Cruz, SF 18
Kotsay, SD 13
Edmonds, St.L 12
Nady*, SD 12
Jenkins, Mil 11
L. Gonzalez, Ari 10
Berkman, Hou 10
Guerrero, Mon 10
Six tied with 9 each.

Errors

Ramirez, Pit-Chi 33
Furcal, Atl 31
Beltre, LA 19
Castilla, Atl 19
Helms, Mil 19
Cabrera, Mon 18
J. Wilson, Pit 17
Everett*, Hou 17
Five tied with 16 each.

Team Batting Statistics

American League

Team	Avg	AB	R	H	HR	RBI	SB
Boston	.289	5769	961	1667	238	932	88
Toronto	.279	5661	894	1580	190	853	37
Minnesota	.277	5655	801	1567	155	755	94
Kansas City	.274	5568	836	1526	162	781	120
Seattle	.271	5561	795	1509	139	759	108
New York	.271	5605	877	1518	230	845	98
Anaheim	.268	5487	736	1473	150	687	129
Baltimore	.268	5665	743	1516	152	695	89
Texas	.266	5664	826	1506	239	799	65
Tampa Bay	.265	5654	715	1501	137	678	142
Chicago	.263	5487	791	1445	220	766	77
Oakland	.254	5497	768	1398	176	742	48
Cleveland	.254	5572	699	1413	158	660	86
Detroit	.240	5466	591	1312	153	553	98

National League

Team	Avg	AB	R	H	HR	RBI	SB
Atlanta	.284	5670	907	1608	235	872	68
St. Louis	.279	5672	876	1580	196	827	82
Pittsburgh	.267	5581	753	1492	163	711	86
Colorado	.267	5518	853	1472	198	814	63
Florida	.266	5490	751	1459	157	709	150
San Fran.	.264	5456	755	1440	180	713	52
Arizona	.263	5570	717	1467	152	696	76
Houston	.263	5583	805	1466	191	763	66
Philadelphia	.261	5543	791	1448	166	757	72
San Diego	.261	5531	678	1442	128	641	76
Chicago	.259	5519	724	1431	172	691	73
Montreal	.258	5437	771	1404	144	682	100
Milwaukee	.256	5548	714	1423	196	685	99
New York	.247	5341	642	1317	124	607	70
Cincinnati	.245	5509	694	1349	182	669	80
Los Angeles	.243	5458	574	1328	124	544	80

Team Pitching Statistics

American League

Team	ERA	W	Sv	CG	ShO	HR	BB	SO
Oakland	3.63	99	48	16	14	140	499	1018
Seattle	3.76	93	38	8	15	173	466	1001
New York	4.02	101	49	8	12	145	375	1119
Chicago	4.17	86	36	12	4	162	518	1056
Cleveland	4.21	68	34	5	7	179	501	943
Anaheim	4.28	77	39	5	9	190	486	980
Minnesota	4.41	90	45	7	8	187	402	997
Boston	4.48	95	36	5	6	153	488	1141
Toronto	4.69	86	36	14	6	184	485	984
Baltimore	4.76	71	41	9	3	198	526	981
Tampa Bay	4.93	63	30	7	7	196	639	877
Kansas City	5.05	83	36	7	10	190	566	865
Detroit	5.30	43	27	3	5	195	557	764
Texas	5.67	71	43	4	3	208	603	1009

National League

Team	ERA	W	Sv	CG	ShO	HR	BB	SO
Los Angeles	3.16	85	58	3	17	127	526	1289
San Fran.	3.73	100	43	7	10	136	546	1006
Chicago	3.83	88	36	13	14	143	617	1404
Arizona	3.84	84	42	7	11	150	526	1291
Houston	3.86	87	50	1	5	161	565	1139
Montreal	4.01	83	42	15	10	181	463	1028
Florida	4.04	91	36	7	11	128	530	1132
Philadelphia	4.04	86	33	9	13	142	536	1060
Atlanta	4.10	101	51	4	7	147	555	992
New York	4.48	66	38	3	10	168	576	907
St. Louis	4.60	85	41	9	10	210	508	969
Pittsburgh	4.64	75	44	7	10	178	502	926
San Diego	4.87	64	31	2	10	208	611	1091
Milwaukee	5.02	68	44	5	3	219	575	1034
Cincinnati	5.09	69	38	4	5	209	590	932
Colorado	5.20	74	34	3	4	200	552	866

Team Fielding Statistics

American League

Team	Pct	TC	E	PO	A	DP	TP
Seattle	.989	5839	65	4323	1451	159	0
Minnesota	.985	5954	87	4385	1482	114	0
Texas	.985	6097	94	4300	1703	168	0
Chicago	.984	5975	93	4293	1589	154	0
Baltimore	.983	6137	105	4349	1683	164	0
Tampa Bay	.983	5994	103	4310	1581	158	0
Oakland	.983	6211	107	4325	1779	145	0
Kansas City	.982	6128	108	4316	1704	143	0
Anaheim	.982	5914	105	4294	1515	138	0
Boston	.982	6186	113	4394	1679	130	0
New York	.981	6080	114	4386	1580	126	0
Toronto	.981	6162	117	4305	1740	161	0
Cleveland	.980	6285	126	4378	1781	178	0
Detroit	.978	6267	138	4316	1813	194	0

National League

Team	Pct	TC	E	PO	A	DP	TP
St. Louis	.987	6112	77	4391	1644	138	0
Florida	.987	6004	78	4336	1590	162	0
San Fran.	.987	6067	80	4312	1675	163	0
Houston	.985	6154	95	4350	1709	149	0
Philadelphia	.984	6122	97	4331	1694	146	0
Montreal	.983	6147	102	4313	1732	152	0
San Diego	.983	6030	102	4294	1634	141	0
Chicago	.983	6156	106	4369	1681	157	0
Arizona	.983	6167	107	4365	1695	132	0
Milwaukee	.981	6086	114	4356	1616	142	0
Colorado	.981	6161	116	4260	1785	165	1
Los Angeles	.981	6301	119	4373	1809	164	0
Atlanta	.981	6374	121	4369	1884	166	1
Pittsburgh	.980	6302	123	4333	1846	159	0
New York	.980	6012	118	4240	1654	158	0
Cincinnati	.977	6181	141	4339	1701	152	0

Pct—Fielding Percentage; **TC**—Total Chances; **E**—Errors; **PO**—Putouts; **A**—Assists; **DP**—Double Plays; **TP**—Triple Plays.

2003 All-Star Game

74th Baseball All-Star Game. **Date:** July 15 at U.S. Cellular Field, Chicago, Ill.; **Managers:** Mike Scioscia, Anaheim (AL) and Dusty Baker, Chicago (NL); **Ted Williams Award (MVP):** Garret Anderson, Anaheim (AL): 3-for-4 with HR and 2 RBI.

Note: For the first time in history, the league that won the All-Star Game also secured home-field advantage for the World Series.

National League

	AB	R	H	BI	BB	SO	Avg
Edgar Renteria, St.L, ss	2	0	0	0	0	1	.000
Rafael Furcal, Atl, ph-ss	3	1	1	0	0	1	.333
Jim Edmonds, St.L, cf	2	0	1	0	0	1	.500
Andruw Jones, Atl, ph-cf	2	2	2	3	0	0	1.000
Albert Pujols, St.L, lf	3	0	1	1	0	0	.333
Luis Gonzalez, Ari, lf	1	0	1	0	0	0	1.000
Barry Bonds, SF, dh	3	0	0	0	0	0	.000
Rondell White, SD, ph-dh	1	0	0	0	0	0	.000
Gary Sheffield, Atl, rf	1	1	0	1	0	0	.000
Preston Wilson, Col, rf	2	0	1	0	0	1	.500
Todd Helton, Col, 1b	2	1	1	2	0	1	.500
Richie Sexson, Mil, 1b	2	0	0	0	0	0	.000
Scott Rolen, St.L, 3b	2	1	1	0	0	0	.500
Mike Lowell, Fla, 3b	1	0	1	0	0	0	1.000
Aaron Boone, Cin, ph-3b	1	0	0	0	0	0	.000
Javy Lopez, Atl, c	2	0	0	0	0	0	.000
Paul Lo Duca, Atl, ph-c	2	0	1	0	0	0	.500
Jose Vidro, Mon, 2b	2	0	0	0	0	2	.000
Luis Castillo, Fla, 2b	2	0	0	0	0	0	.000
TOTALS	36	6	11	6	1	7	.306

American League

	AB	R	H	BI	BB	SO	Avg
Ichiro Suzuki, Sea, rf	1	1	0	0	2	0	.000
Magglio Ordonez, Chi, ph-rf	1	0	0	0	0	0	.000
Alfonso Soriano, NY, 2b	3	0	0	0	0	1	.000
Jason Giambi, NY, 1b	1	1	1	1	0	1	1.000
Carlos Delgado, Tor, 1b	3	0	1	1	0	1	.333
Ramon Hernandez, Oak, c	1	0	0	0	0	0	.000
Alex Rodriguez, Tex, ss	3	1	1	0	0	1	.333
Nomar Garciaparra, Bos, ss	1	0	0	0	0	0	.000
Garret Anderson, Ana, lf	4	1	3	2	0	1	.750
Melvin Mora, Bal, pr-lf	0	1	0	0	0	0	.000
Edgar Martinez, Sea, dh	2	0	0	0	2	0	.000
Carl Everett, Chi, ph-dh	1	0	0	0	0	0	.000
Hideki Matsui, NY, cf	2	0	1	0	0	0	.500
Vernon Wells, Tor, pr-cf	2	1	1	0	0	0	.500
Troy Glaus, Ana, 3b	3	0	0	0	0	2	.000
Hank Blalock, Tex, ph-3b	1	1	1	2	0	0	1.000
Jorge Posada, NY, c	2	0	0	0	0	2	.000
Bret Boone, Sea, 2b	2	0	0	0	0	1	.000
TOTALS	33	7	9	7	2	11	.273

	1	2	3	4	5	6	7	8	9		R	H	E
National League	0	0	1	0	5	0	1	0	0	–	6	11	1
American League	0	0	1	0	0	2	1	3	x	–	7	9	0

E—Furcal (NL). **LOB**—National 4, American 5. **2B**—Jones, Lowell (NL), Anderson, Wells (AL). **HR**—Helton (NL, off Hasegawa, 0 on); Jones (NL, off Mulder, 0 on), Anderson (AL, off Williams, 0 on), Giambi (AL, off Wagner, 0 on), Blalock (AL, off Gagne, 1 on). **SB**—none. **SF**—none. **GIDP**—Sexson, White (NL).

NL Pitching

	IP	H	R	ER	BB	SO
Jason Schmidt, SF	2.0	1	0	0	0	3
Randy Wolf, Phi	1.0	1	1	1	1	2
Kerry Wood, Chi	1.0	1	0	0	0	2
Russ Ortiz, Atl	1.0	0	0	0	1	2
Woody Williams, St.L	1.0	2	2	2	0	1
Billy Wagner, Hou	1.0	1	1	1	0	0
Eric Gagne, LA (L, 0-1)	1.0	3	3	3	0	1
TOTALS	8.0	9	7	7	2	11

AL Pitching

	IP	H	R	ER	BB	SO
Esteban Loaiza, Chi	2.0	1	0	0	0	1
Roger Clemens, NY	1.0	0	0	0	0	2
Jamie Moyer, Sea	1.0	0	0	0	0	1
Shigetoshi Hasegawa, Sea	0.2	3	4	4	1	1
Eddie Guardado, Min	0.1	2	1	1	0	0
Mark Mulder, Oak	2.0	5	1	1	0	1
B. Donnelly, Ana (W, 1-0)	1.0	0	0	0	0	1
Keith Foulke, Oak (S, 1)	1.0	0	0	0	0	0
TOTALS	9.0	11	6	6	1	7

HBP—by Schmidt (Martinez). **WP**—Wolf (NL). **Umpires**—Tim McClelland (plate); Larry Young (1b); Gary Darling (2b); Gary Cederstrom (3b); Mark Carlson (lf); Bill Welke (rf). **Attendance**—47,609. **Time**—2:38. **TV Rating**—9.5/17 share (FOX).

Home Attendance

Overall 2003 MLB regular season attendance (based on tickets sold) was 67,667,670 for an average per game crowd of 28,055, virtually equaling 2002 totals; numbers in parentheses indicate ranking in 2002; HD indicates home dates.

American League

	Attendance	HD	Average
1 New York (2)	3,465,660	81	42,785
2 Seattle (1)	3,268,509	81	40,351
3 Anaheim (7)	3,061,094	81	37,791
4 Boston (4)	2,724,165	81	33,631
5 Baltimore (3)	2,454,523	81	30,302
6 Oakland (8)	2,216,596	81	27,365
7 Texas (6)	2,094,394	81	25,856
8 Minnesota (9)	1,946,011	81	24,024
9 Chicago (10)	1,939,524	81	23,944
10 Kansas City (13)	1,779,895	78	22,819
11 Toronto (11)	1,799,458	81	22,215
12 Cleveland (5)	1,730,002	81	21,358
13 Detroit (12)	1,368,245	80	17,103
14 Tampa Bay (14)	1,058,695	81	13,070
TOTALS	30,906,771	1130	27,351

National League

	Attendance	HD	Average
1 San Francisco (1)	3,264,898	81	40,307
2 Los Angeles (3)	3,138,626	81	38,748
3 Chicago (6)	2,962,630	80	37,032
4 St. Louis (4)	2,910,386	81	35,930
5 Arizona (2)	2,805,542	81	34,636
6 Atlanta (8)	2,401,084	79	30,393
7 Houston (9)	2,454,241	81	30,299
8 Cincinnati (12)	2,355,259	81	29,077
9 Philadelphia (14)	2,259,948	78	28,973
10 Colorado (7)	2,334,085	81	28,815
11 New York (5)	2,140,599	76	28,165
12 San Diego (10)	2,030,084	81	25,062
13 Milwaukee (11)	1,700,354	81	20,992
14 Pittsburgh (13)	1,636,751	78	20,983
15 Florida (15)	1,303,215	80	16,290
16 Montreal (16)	1,025,639	81	12,662
TOTALS	36,723,341	1281	28,668

AL Team by Team Statistics

At least 135 at bats or 40 innings pitched during the regular season, unless otherwise indicated. Players who competed for more than one AL team are listed with their final club. Players traded from the NL are listed with AL team only if they have 135 AB or 40 IP. Note that (*) indicates rookie and PTBN indicates player to be named.

Anaheim Angels

Batting (135 AB)	Avg	AB	R	H	HR	RBI	SB
Garrett Anderson . . .	.315	638	80	201	29	116	6
Brad Fullmer	.306	206	32	63	9	35	5
Chone Figgins*	.296	240	34	71	0	27	13
Jeff DaVanon	.282	330	56	93	12	43	17
Bengie Molina	.281	409	37	115	14	71	1
Tim Salmon	.275	528	78	145	19	72	3
Eric Owens	.270	241	29	65	1	20	11
Adam Kennedy	.269	449	71	121	13	49	22
Scott Spiezio	.265	521	69	138	16	83	6
David Eckstein	.252	452	59	114	3	31	16
Darin Erstad	.252	258	35	65	4	17	9
Troy Glaus	.248	319	53	79	16	50	7
Shawn Wooten	.243	272	25	66	7	32	0

Acquired: P Glover and 2 minor leaguers from Chi-AL for P Scott Schoeneweis and a minor leaguer (July 29).

Pitching (40 IP)	ERA	W-L	Gm	IP	BB	SO
Brendan Donnelly . .	1.58	2-2	63	74.0	24	79
Ben Weber	2.69	5-1	62	80.1	22	46
Scot Shields	2.85	5-6	44	148.1	38	111
Francisco Rodriguez*	3.03	8-3	59	86.0	35	95
Troy Percival	3.47	0-5	52	49.1	23	48
Jarrod Washburn . . .	4.43	10-15	32	207.1	54	118
John Lackey	4.63	10-16	33	204.0	66	151
Gary Glover	4.74	2-0	42	62.2	22	37
Ramon Ortiz	5.20	16-13	32	180.0	63	94
Aaron Sele	5.77	7-11	25	121.2	58	53

Saves: Percival (33), Donnelly (3), F. Rodriguez (2), Shields (1). **Complete games:** Washburn and Lackey (2), Ortiz (1). **Shutouts:** Lackey (1).

Baltimore Orioles

Batting (165 AB)	Avg	AB	R	H	HR	RBI	SB
Melvin Mora	.317	344	68	109	15	48	6
Larry Bigbie	.303	287	43	87	9	31	7
Luis Matos	.303	439	70	133	13	45	15
B.J. Surhoff	.295	319	32	94	5	41	2
Jeff Conine	.290	493	75	143	15	80	5
Jay Gibbons	.277	625	80	173	23	100	0
Brook Fordyce	.273	348	28	95	6	31	2
Jerry Hairston Jr. . . .	.271	218	25	59	2	21	14
Brian Roberts	.270	460	65	124	5	41	23
David Segui	.263	224	26	59	5	25	1
Deivi Cruz	.250	548	61	137	14	65	1
Geronimo Gil	.237	169	22	40	3	16	0
Tony Batista	.235	631	76	148	26	99	4

Acquired: P Moss, P Kurt Ainsworth and a minor league P from SF for P Ponson (July 31). **Traded:** OF Conine to Fla. for 2 minor league pitchers (Aug. 31). **Waived:** P Helling (Aug. 15).

Pitching (50 IP)	ERA	W-L	Gm	IP	BB	SO
Kerry Ligtenberg . . .	3.34	4-2	68	59.1	14	47
B.J. Ryan	3.40	4-1	76	50.1	27	63
Sidney Ponson	3.77	14-6	21	148.0	43	100
Eric DuBose*	3.79	3-6	17	73.2	25	44
Pat Hentgen	4.09	7-8	28	160.2	58	100
Jason Johnson	4.18	10-10	32	189.2	80	118
Jorge Julio	4.38	0-7	64	61.2	34	52
Rick Bauer	4.55	0-0	35	61.1	24	43
Rick Helling	5.71	7-8	24	138.2	40	86
Rodrigo Lopez	5.82	7-10	26	147.0	43	103
Travis Driskill	6.00	3-5	20	48.0	9	33
Damian Moss	6.22	1-5	10	50.2	29	22
Omar Daal	6.34	4-11	19	93.2	30	53

Saves: Julio (36), Ligtenberg, Hentgen, Driskill, Buddy Groom and Hector Carrasco (1). **Complete games:** Ponson (4), Lopez (3), DuBose and Hentgen (1). **Shutouts:** Lopez (1).

Boston Red Sox

Batting (160 AB)	Avg	AB	R	H	HR	RBI	SB
Bill Mueller	.326	524	85	171	19	85	1
Manny Ramirez	.325	569	117	185	37	104	3
Trot Nixon	.306	441	81	135	28	87	4
Shea Hillenbrand . . .	.303	185	20	56	3	38	1
Nomar Garciaparra . .	.301	658	120	198	28	105	19
David Ortiz	.288	448	79	129	31	101	0
Todd Walker	.283	587	92	166	13	85	1
Kevin Millar	.276	544	83	150	25	96	3
Johnny Damon	.273	608	103	166	12	67	30
Jason Varitek	.273	451	63	123	25	85	3
Damian Jackson	.261	161	34	42	1	13	16
Doug Mirabelli	.258	163	23	42	9	28	0

Acquired: P Kim from Ari. for IF Hillenbrand (May 29); P Suppan from Pit. for IF Freddy Sanchez (July 31).

Pitching (40 IP)	ERA	W-L	Gm	IP	BB	SO
Pedro Martinez	2.22	14-4	29	186.2	47	206
Byung-Hyun Kim	3.18	8-5	49	79.1	18	69
Mike Timlin	3.55	6-4	72	83.2	9	65
Tim Wakefield	4.09	11-7	35	202.1	71	169
Brandon Lyon	4.12	4-6	49	59.0	19	50
Alan Embree	4.25	4-1	65	55.0	16	45
Derek Lowe	4.47	17-7	33	203.1	72	110
John Burkett	5.15	12-9	32	181.2	47	107
Casey Fossum	5.47	6-5	19	79.0	34	63
Jeff Suppan	5.57	3-4	11	63.0	20	32
Ramiro Mendoza . . .	6.75	3-5	37	66.2	20	36

Saves: Kim (16), Lyon (9), Chad Fox (3), Timlin (2), Wakefield, Embree, Fossum, Bronson Arroyo, Robert Person and Jason Shiell (1). **Complete games:** Martinez (3), Lowe and Burkett (1). **Shutouts:** none.

Chicago White Sox

Batting (200 AB)	Avg	AB	R	H	HR	RBI	SB
Magglio Ordonez . . .	.317	606	95	192	29	99	9
Carlos Lee	.291	623	100	181	31	113	18
Carl Everett	.287	526	93	151	28	92	8
Frank Thomas	.267	546	87	146	42	105	0
Joe Crede	.261	536	68	140	19	75	1
Tony Graffanino	.260	250	51	65	7	23	8
D'Angelo Jimenez . . .	.255	271	35	69	7	26	4
Roberto Alomar	.253	253	42	64	3	17	6
Miguel Olivo*	.237	317	37	75	6	27	6
Jose Valentin	.237	503	79	119	28	74	8
Paul Konerko	.234	444	49	104	18	65	0

Acquired: IF Alomar from NY-NL for 3 minor leaguers (July 1); OF Everett and cash from Tex. for 2 minor leaguers (July 1); P Schoeneweis and a minor leaguer from Ana. for P Gary Glover and 2 minor leaguers (July 29). **Traded:** IF Jimenez to Cin. for minor leaguer (July 7). **Waived:** P White (Aug. 12).

Pitching (40 IP)	ERA	W-L	Gm	IP	BB	SO
Damaso Marte	1.58	4-2	71	79.2	34	87
Esteban Loaiza	2.90	21-9	34	226.1	56	207
Tom Gordon	3.16	7-6	66	74.0	31	91
Bartolo Colon	3.87	15-13	34	242.0	67	173
Mark Buehrle	4.14	14-14	35	230.1	61	119
Scott Schoeneweis . .	4.18	3-2	59	64.2	19	56
Jon Garland	4.51	12-13	32	191.2	74	108
Billy Koch	5.77	5-5	55	53.0	28	42
Dan Wright	6.15	1-7	20	86.1	46	47
Rick White	6.61	1-2	34	47.2	13	37

Saves: Gordon (12), Marte and Koch (11), Wright and White (1). **Complete games:** Colon (9), Buehrle (2), Loaiza (1). **Shutouts:** none.

Cleveland Indians

Batting (165 AB)	Avg	AB	R	H	HR	RBI	SB
Milton Bradley	.321	377	61	121	10	56	17
Jody Gerut*	.279	480	66	134	22	75	4
Coco Crisp*	.266	414	55	110	3	27	15
Ellis Burks	.263	198	27	52	6	28	1
Casey Blake	.257	557	80	143	17	67	7
Travis Hafner*	.254	291	35	74	14	40	2
Ben Broussard*	.249	386	53	96	16	55	5
Matt Lawton	.249	374	57	93	15	53	10
Josh Bard*	.244	303	25	74	8	36	0
Omar Vizquel	.244	250	43	61	2	19	8
Jhonny Peralta*	.227	242	24	55	4	21	1
John McDonald	.215	214	21	46	1	14	3
Brandon Phillips*	.208	370	36	77	6	33	4

Claimed: P Bierbrodt off waivers from TB (June 11).

Pitching (40 IP)	ERA	W-L	Gm	IP	BB	SO
David Riske	2.29	2-2	68	74.2	20	82
Jack Cressend	2.51	2-1	33	43.0	9	28
C.C. Sabathia	3.60	13-9	30	197.2	66	141
Jason Stanford*	3.60	1-3	13	50.0	16	30
Cliff Lee*	3.61	3-3	9	52.1	20	44
Danys Baez	3.81	2-9	73	75.2	23	66
Jason Boyd	4.30	3-1	44	52.1	26	31
Jake Westbrook	4.33	7-10	34	133.0	56	58
Jason Davis*	4.68	8-11	27	165.1	47	85
Terry Mulholland	4.91	3-4	45	99.0	37	42
Billy Traber*	5.24	6-9	33	111.2	40	88
Nick Bierbrodt	9.14	0-2	18	43.1	27	29

Saves: Baez (25), Riske (8), Rafael Betancourt (1).
Complete games: Sabathia (2), Westbrook, Davis and Traber (1). **Shutouts:** Sabathia and Traber (1).

Detroit Tigers

Batting (140 AB)	Avg	AB	R	H	HR	RBI	SB
Dmitri Young	.297	562	78	167	29	85	2
Alex Sanchez	.289	394	43	114	1	22	44
Warren Morris	.272	346	37	94	6	37	4
Kevin Witt*	.263	270	25	71	10	26	1
Carlos Pena	.248	452	51	112	18	50	4
Craig Monroe*	.240	425	51	102	23	70	4
Eric Munson*	.240	313	28	75	18	50	3
Bobby Higginson	.235	469	61	110	14	52	8
Ramon Santiago	.225	444	41	100	2	29	10
Omar Infante*	.222	221	24	49	0	8	6
Andres Torres*	.220	168	23	37	1	9	5
Shane Halter	.217	360	33	78	12	30	2
Brandon Inge	.203	330	32	67	8	30	4

Acquired: OF Sanchez from Mil. for 2 minor leaguers (May 27). **Traded:** P Bernero to Col. for C Ben Petrick (July 13).

Pitching (40 IP)	ERA	W-L	Gm	IP	BB	SO
Jamie Walker	3.32	4-3	78	65.0	17	45
Nate Cornejo	4.67	6-17	32	194.2	58	46
Chris Spurling*	4.68	1-3	66	77.0	22	38
Nate Robertson*	5.44	1-2	8	44.2	23	33
Chris Mears*	5.44	1-3	29	41.1	11	21
Matt Roney*	5.45	1-9	45	100.2	48	47
Jeremy Bonderman*	5.56	6-19	33	162.0	58	108
Mike Maroth	5.73	9-21	33	193.1	50	87
Wilfredo Ledezma*	5.79	3-7	34	84.0	35	49
Gary Knotts*	6.04	3-8	20	95.1	47	51
Franklyn German*	6.04	2-4	45	44.2	45	41
Adam Bernero	6.08	1-12	18	100.2	41	54

Saves: Mears and German (5), Walker, Spurling, Matt Anderson, Danny Patterson and Fernando Rodney (3).
Complete games: Cornejo (2), Maroth (1). **Shutouts:** none.

Kansas City Royals

Batting (130 AB)	Avg	AB	R	H	HR	RBI	SB
Carlos Beltran	.307	521	102	160	26	100	41
Raul Ibanez	.294	608	95	179	18	90	8
Mike Sweeney	.293	392	62	115	16	83	3
Joe Randa	.291	502	80	146	16	72	1
Angel Berroa*	.287	567	92	163	17	73	21
Aaron Guiel	.277	354	63	98	15	52	3
Ken Harvey*	.266	485	50	129	13	64	2
Michael Tucker*	.262	389	61	102	13	55	8
Desi Relaford	.254	500	70	127	8	59	20
Mike DiFelice	.254	189	29	48	3	25	1
Brent Mayne	.245	372	39	91	6	36	0
Carlos Febles	.235	196	31	46	0	11	8
Dee Brown	.227	132	16	30	2	14	1

Acquired: P Levine from TB for cash (Aug. 1); P Anderson from Cle. for 2 minor leaguers (Aug. 25). **Signed:** P Appier off waivers from Ana. (Aug. 6).

Pitching (50 IP)	ERA	W-L	Gm	IP	BB	SO
Al Levine	2.79	3-6	54	71.0	29	30
Darrell May	3.77	10-8	35	210.0	53	115
Brian Anderson	3.78	14-11	32	197.2	43	87
Jeremy Affeldt	3.93	7-6	36	126.0	38	98
Mike MacDougal*	4.08	3-5	68	64.0	32	57
Jimmy Gobble*	4.61	4-5	9	52.2	15	31
Runelvys Hernandez	4.61	7-5	16	91.2	37	48
D.J. Carrasco*	4.82	6-5	50	80.1	40	57
Jose Lima	4.91	8-3	14	73.1	26	32
Jason Grimsley	5.16	2-6	76	75.0	36	58
Kyle Snyder*	5.17	1-6	15	85.1	21	39
Kris Wilson	5.33	6-3	29	72.2	16	42
Kevin Appier	5.40	8-9	23	111.2	43	55
Chris George	7.11	9-6	18	93.2	44	39

Saves: MacDougal (27), Affeldt (4), Carrasco and Curtis Leskanic (2), Levine (1). **Complete games:** May, Anderson and Jamey Wright (2), Miguel Asencio (1). **Shutouts:** May, Anderson and Wright (1).

Minnesota Twins

Batting (135 AB)	Avg	AB	R	H	HR	RBI	SB
A.J. Pierzynski	.312	487	63	152	11	74	3
Shannon Stewart	.307	573	90	176	13	73	4
Jacque Jones	.304	517	76	157	16	69	13
Doug Mientkiewicz	.300	487	67	146	11	65	4
Corey Koskie	.292	469	76	137	14	69	11
Matt LeCroy	.287	345	39	99	17	64	0
Cristian Guzman	.268	534	78	143	3	53	18
Luis Rivas	.259	475	69	123	8	43	17
Chris Gomez	.251	175	14	44	1	15	2
Dustan Mohr	.250	348	50	87	10	36	5
Torii Hunter	.250	581	83	145	26	102	6
Denny Hocking	.239	188	22	45	3	22	0

Acquired: OF Stewart and PTBN from Tor. for OF Bobby Kielty (July 16).

Pitching (40 IP)	ERA	W-L	Gm	IP	BB	SO
LaTroy Hawkins	1.86	9-3	74	77.1	15	75
Eddie Guardado	2.89	3-5	66	65.1	14	60
Johan Santana	3.07	12-3	45	158.1	47	169
Juan Rincon	3.68	5-6	58	85.2	38	63
Brad Radke	4.49	14-10	33	212.1	28	120
Kenny Rogers	4.57	13-8	33	195.0	50	116
Kyle Lohse	4.61	14-11	33	201.0	45	130
J.C. Romero	5.00	2-0	73	63.0	42	50
Rick Reed	5.07	6-12	27	135.0	29	71
Joe Mays	6.30	8-8	31	130.0	39	50

Saves: Guardado (41), Hawkins (2), James Baldwin and Mike Nakamura (1). **Complete games:** Radke (3), Lohse and Reed (2). **Shutouts:** Radke, Lohse and Reed (1).

New York Yankees

Batting (140 AB)	Avg	AB	R	H	HR	RBI	SB
Derek Jeter	.324	482	87	156	10	52	11
Alfonso Soriano	.290	682	114	198	38	91	35
Hideki Matsui*	.287	623	82	179	16	106	2
Nick Johnson	.284	324	60	92	14	47	5
Jorge Posada	.281	481	83	135	30	101	2
Ruben Sierra	.270	307	33	83	9	43	2
Juan Rivera*	.266	173	22	46	7	26	0
Bernie Williams	.263	445	77	117	15	64	5
Karim Garcia	.262	244	25	64	11	35	0
Raul Mondesi	.258	361	56	93	16	49	17
Aaron Boone	.254	189	31	48	6	31	8
Robin Ventura	.251	283	31	71	9	42	0
Jason Giambi	.250	535	97	134	41	107	2
Todd Zeile	.210	186	29	39	6	23	0

Acquired: OF Sierra from Tex. for a minor leaguer (June 6); OF Garcia and P Dan Miceli from Cle. for PTBN (June 25); IF Boone and P Gabe White from Cin. for 2 minor leaguers and cash (July 31); P Nelson from Sea. for P Armando Benitez (Aug. 6). **Traded:** OF Mondesi to Ari. for David Dellucci and 2 minor leaguers (July 29); IF Ventura for 2 minor leaguers (July 31). **Released:** Zeile (Aug. 17).

Pitching (50 IP)	ERA	W-L	Gm	IP	BB	SO
Mariano Rivera	1.66	5-2	64	70.2	10	63
Chris Hammond	2.86	3-2	62	63.0	11	45
Jose Contreras*	3.30	7-2	18	71.0	30	72
Mike Mussina	3.40	17-8	31	214.2	40	195
Antonio Osuna	3.73	2-5	48	50.2	20	47
Jeff Nelson	3.74	4-2	70	55.1	24	68
Roger Clemens	3.91	17-9	33	211.2	58	190
Andy Pettitte	4.02	21-8	33	208.1	50	180
David Wells	4.14	15-7	31	213.0	20	101
Jeff Weaver	5.99	7-9	32	159.1	47	93

Saves: Rivera (40), Nelson (8), Hammond and Dan Miceli (1). **Complete games:** Wells (4), Mussina (2), Clemens and Pettitte (1). **Shutouts:** Mussina, Clemens and Wells (1).

Oakland Athletics

Batting (135 AB)	Avg	AB	R	H	HR	RBI	SB
Eric Chavez	.282	588	94	166	29	101	8
Miguel Tejada	.278	636	98	177	27	106	10
Ramon Hernandez	.273	483	70	132	21	78	0
Billy McMillon	.268	153	15	41	6	26	0
Jose Guillen	.265	170	25	45	8	23	0
Eric Byrnes	.263	414	64	109	12	51	10
Erubiel Durazo	.259	537	92	139	21	77	1
Scott Hatteberg	.253	541	63	137	12	61	0
Mark Ellis	.248	553	78	137	9	52	6
Chris Singleton	.245	306	38	75	1	36	7
Terrence Long	.245	486	64	119	14	61	4
Jermaine Dye	.172	221	28	38	4	20	1

Acquired: OF Guillen from Cin. for P Aaron Harang and 2 minor leaguers (July 30). **Signed:** P Sparks off waivers from Det. (Aug. 30).

Pitching (40 IP)	ERA	W-L	Gm	IP	BB	SO
Keith Foulke	2.08	9-1	72	86.2	20	88
Tim Hudson	2.70	16-7	34	240.0	61	162
Chad Bradford	3.04	7-4	72	77.0	30	62
Mark Mulder	3.13	15-9	26	186.2	40	128
Ricardo Rincon	3.25	8-4	64	55.1	32	40
Barry Zito	3.30	14-12	35	231.2	88	146
Mike Neu*	3.64	0-0	32	42.0	26	20
John Halama	4.22	3-5	35	108.2	36	51
Ted Lilly	4.34	12-10	32	178.1	58	147
Rich Harden*	4.46	5-4	15	74.2	40	67
Steve Sparks	4.88	0-6	51	107.0	37	54

Saves: Foulke (43), Bradford and Sparks (2), Neu, Jim Mecir and Chad Harville (1). **Complete games:** Mulder (9), Zito (4), Hudson (3). **Shutouts:** Hudson and Mulder (2), Zito (1).

Seattle Mariners

Batting (135 AB)	Avg	AB	R	H	HR	RBI	SB
Ichiro Suzuki	.312	679	111	212	13	62	34
Randy Winn	.295	600	103	177	11	75	23
Bret Boone	.294	622	111	183	35	117	16
Rey Sanchez	.294	170	22	50	0	11	1
Edgar Martinez	.294	497	72	146	24	98	0
Carlos Guillen	.276	388	63	107	7	52	4
John Olerud	.269	539	64	145	10	83	0
Mike Cameron	.253	534	74	135	18	76	17
Willie Bloomquist*	.250	196	30	49	1	14	4
Dan Wilson	.241	316	32	76	4	43	0
Ben Davis	.236	246	25	58	6	42	0
Mark McLemore	.233	309	34	72	2	37	5
Jeff Cirillo	.205	258	24	53	2	23	1

Acquired: IF Sanchez from NY-NL for a minor leaguer (July 29).

Pitching (30 IP)	ERA	W-L	Gm	IP	BB	SO
Shigetoshi Hasegawa	1.48	2-4	63	73.0	18	32
Rafael Soriano*	1.53	3-0	40	53.0	12	68
Julio Mateo	3.15	4-0	50	85.2	13	71
Jamie Moyer	3.27	21-7	33	215.0	66	129
Ryan Franklin	3.57	11-13	32	212.0	61	99
Joel Pineiro	3.78	16-11	32	211.2	76	151
Kazuhiro Sasaki	4.05	1-2	35	33.1	15	29
Arthur Rhodes	4.17	3-3	67	54.0	18	48
Freddy Garcia	4.51	12-14	33	201.1	71	144
Gil Meche	4.59	15-13	32	186.1	63	130

Saves: Hasegawa (16), Sasaki (10), Rhodes (3), Soriano and Mateo (1). **Complete games:** Pineiro (3), Franklin (2), Moyer, Garcia and Meche (1). **Shutouts:** Pineiro (2), Franklin (1).

Tampa Bay Devil Rays

Batting (135 AB)	Avg	AB	R	H	HR	RBI	SB
Aubrey Huff	.311	636	91	198	34	107	2
Rocco Baldelli*	.289	637	89	184	11	78	27
Carl Crawford	.281	630	80	177	5	54	55
Travis Lee	.275	542	75	149	19	70	6
Julio Lugo	.275	433	58	119	15	53	10
Marlon Anderson	.270	482	59	130	6	67	19
Damian Rolls	.255	373	43	95	7	46	11
Toby Hall	.253	463	50	117	12	47	0
Al Martin	.252	238	19	60	3	26	2
Ben Grieve	.230	165	28	38	4	17	0
Javier Valentin	.222	135	13	30	3	15	0
Jared Sandberg	.213	136	15	29	6	23	0

Signed: IF Lugo (May 15).

Pitching (40 IP)	ERA	W-L	Gm	IP	BB	SO
Chad Gaudin	3.60	2-0	15	40.0	16	23
Travis Harper	3.77	4-8	61	93.0	31	64
Jeremi Gonzalez	3.91	6-11	25	156.1	69	97
Victor Zambrano	4.21	12-10	34	188.1	106	132
Lance Carter*	4.33	7-5	62	79.0	19	47
Jesus Colome	4.50	3-7	54	74.0	46	69
Jorge Sosa	4.62	5-12	29	128.2	60	72
Brandon Backe*	5.44	1-1	28	44.2	25	36
Rob Bell	5.52	5-4	19	101.0	39	44
Joe Kennedy	6.13	3-12	32	133.2	47	77
Steve Parris	6.18	0-3	10	43.2	13	14
Dewon Brazelton*	6.89	1-6	10	48.1	23	24

Saves: Carter (26), Colome (2), Harper and Kennedy (1). **Complete games:** Gonzalez (2), Zambrano, Sosa, Kennedy, Jason Standridge and Doug Waechter (1). **Shutouts:** Sosa, Kennedy and Waechter (1).

Texas Rangers

Batting (135 AB)

	Avg	AB	R	H	HR	RBI	SB
Michael Young	.306	666	106	204	14	72	13
Hank Blalock	.300	567	89	170	29	90	2
Alex Rodriguez	.298	607	124	181	47	118	17
Juan Gonzalez	.294	327	49	96	24	70	1
Doug Glanville	.272	195	22	53	4	14	4
Rafael Palmeiro	.260	561	92	146	38	112	2
Mark Teixeira*	.259	529	66	137	26	84	1
Einar Diaz	.257	334	30	86	4	35	3
Laynce Nix*	.255	184	25	47	8	30	3
Shane Spencer	.251	395	39	99	12	49	2
Todd Greene	.229	205	25	47	10	20	0
Ryan Christenson	.176	165	22	29	2	16	2

Acquired: OF Spencer and P Rodriguez from Cle. for OF Ryan Ludwick (July 18). **Traded:** OF Glanville to Chi-NL for aa minor leaguer and cash (July 30). **Signed:** P Callaway (Aug. 8).

Pitching (50 IP)

	ERA	W-L	Gm	IP	BB	SO
Francisco Cordero	2.94	5-8	73	72.2	38	90
Brian Shouse	3.10	0-1	62	61.0	14	40
John Thomson	4.85	13-14	35	217.0	49	136
R.A. Dickey*	5.09	9-8	38	116.2	38	94
Aaron Fultz	5.21	1-3	64	67.1	27	53
Joaquin Benoit	5.49	8-5	25	105.0	51	87
Ricardo Rodriguez*	5.73	3-9	15	81.2	28	41
Ismael Valdes	6.10	8-8	22	115.0	29	47
Mickey Callaway	6.68	1-7	23	60.2	24	41
Tony Mounce*	7.11	1-5	11	50.2	25	30
Colby Lewis*	7.30	10-9	26	127.0	70	88
Jay Powell	7.82	3-0	51	58.2	34	40

Saves: Ugueth Urbina (26), Cordero (15), Shouse and Dickey (1). **Complete games:** Thomson (3), Dickey (1). **Shutouts:** Thomson and Dickey (1).

Toronto Blue Jays

Batting (170 AB)

	Avg	AB	R	H	HR	RBI	SB
Vernon Wells	.317	678	118	215	33	117	4
Greg Myers	.307	329	51	101	15	52	0
Carlos Delgado	.302	570	117	172	42	145	0
Frank Catalanotto	.299	489	83	146	13	59	2
Reed Johnson*	.294	412	79	121	10	52	5
Mike Bordick	.274	343	39	94	5	54	3
Orlando Hudson	.268	474	54	127	9	57	5
Josh Phelps	.268	396	57	106	20	66	1
Chris Woodward	.261	349	49	91	7	45	1
Tom Wilson	.258	256	37	66	5	35	0
Bobby Kielty	.244	427	71	104	13	57	8
Eric Hinske	.243	449	74	109	12	63	12

Acquired: OF Kielty from Min. for OF Shannon Stewart and PTBN (July 16). **Claimed:** P Davis off waivers from Tex. (Apr. 30). **Released:** P Davis (July 13).

Pitching (50 IP)

	ERA	W-L	Gm	IP	BB	SO
Jason Kershner*	3.17	3-3	40	54.0	15	32
Roy Halladay	3.25	22-7	36	266.0	32	204
Aquilino Lopez*	3.42	1-3	72	73.2	34	64
Kelvim Escobar	4.29	13-9	41	180.1	78	159
Josh Towers	4.48	8-1	14	64.1	7	42
Trever Miller	4.61	2-2	79	52.2	28	44
Pete Walker	4.88	2-2	23	55.1	24	29
Doug Davis	5.37	4-6	13	57.0	30	27
Mark Hendrickson*	5.51	9-9	30	158.1	40	76
Cory Lidle	5.75	12-15	31	192.2	60	112
Tanyon Sturtze	5.94	7-6	40	89.1	43	54

Saves: Lopez (14), Cliff Politte (12), Juan Acevedo (6), Escobar and Miller (4), Towers and Jeff Tam (1). **Complete games:** Halladay (9), Lidle (2), Escobar, Towers and Hendrickson (1). **Shutouts:** Halladay (2), Escobar and Hendrickson (1).

Players Who Played in Both Leagues in 2003

While all individual major league statistics count for career records, players cannot transfer their stats from one league to the other if they are traded during the regular season. Here are the combined stats for batters with at least 400 at bats and pitchers with at least 110 innings pitched, who played in both leagues in 2003. Players listed alphabetically.

Batters (400 AB)

	Avg	AB	R	H	HR	RBI	SB
Roberto Alomar	.258	516	76	133	5	39	12
NY-NL	.262	263	34	69	2	22	6
CHI-AL	.253	253	42	64	3	17	6
Aaron Boone	.267	592	92	158	24	96	23
CIN	.273	403	61	110	18	65	15
NY-AL	.254	189	31	48	6	31	8
Jeff Conine	.282	577	88	163	20	95	5
BAL	.290	493	75	143	15	80	5
FLA	.238	84	13	20	5	15	0
Jose Guillen	.311	485	77	151	31	86	1
CIN	.337	315	52	106	23	63	1
OAK	.265	170	25	45	8	23	0
Shea Hillenbrand	.280	515	60	144	20	97	1
BOS	.303	185	20	56	3	38	1
ARI	.267	330	40	88	17	59	0
D'Angelo Jimenez	.273	561	69	153	14	57	11
CHI-AL	.255	271	35	69	7	26	4
CIN	.290	290	34	84	7	31	7
Julio Lugo	.271	498	64	135	15	55	12
HOU	.246	65	6	16	0	2	2
TB	.275	433	58	119	15	53	10
Gary Matthews Jr.	.248	468	71	116	6	42	12
BAL	.204	162	21	33	2	20	0
SD	.271	306	50	83	4	22	12
Raul Mondesi	.272	523	83	142	24	71	22
NY-AL	.258	361	56	93	16	49	17
ARI	.302	162	27	49	8	22	5
Alex Sanchez	.287	557	58	160	1	32	52
MIL	.282	163	15	46	0	10	8
DET	.289	394	43	114	1	22	44
Rondell White	.289	488	62	141	22	87	1
SD	.278	413	49	115	18	66	1
KC	.347	75	13	26	4	21	0

Pitchers (110 IP)

	ERA	W-L	Gm	IP	BB	SO
Adam Bernero	5.87	1-14	49	133.1	54	80
DET	6.08	1-12	18	100.2	41	54
COL	5.23	0-2	31	32.2	13	26
Rick Helling	5.17	8-8	35	155.0	45	98
BAL	5.71	7-8	24	138.2	40	86
FLA	0.55	1-0	11	16.1	5	12
Byung-Hyun Kim	3.31	9-10	56	122.1	33	102
ARI	3.56	1-5	7	43.0	15	33
BOS	3.18	8-5	49	79.1	18	69
Damian Moss	5.16	10-12	31	165.2	92	79
SF	4.70	9-7	21	115.0	63	57
BAL	6.22	1-5	10	50.2	29	22
Sidney Ponson	3.75	17-12	31	216.0	61	134
BAL	3.77	14-6	21	148.0	43	100
SF	3.71	3-6	10	68.0	18	34
Jeff Suppan	4.19	13-11	32	204.0	51	110
PIT	3.57	10-7	21	141.0	31	78
BOS	5.57	3-4	11	63.0	20	32

NL Team by Team Statistics

At least 135 at bats or 40 innings pitched during the regular season unless otherwise indicated. Players who competed for more than one NL team are listed with their final club. Players traded from the AL are listed with NL team only if they have 135 AB or 40 IP. Note that (*) indicates rookie and PTBN indicates player to be named.

Arizona Diamondbacks

Batting (170 AB)	Avg	AB	R	H	HR	RBI	SB
Carlos Baerga	.343	207	31	71	4	39	1
Alex Cintron	.317	448	70	142	13	51	2
Luis Gonzalez	.304	579	92	176	26	104	5
Steve Finley	.287	516	82	148	22	70	15
Robby Hammock*	.282	195	30	55	8	28	3
Lyle Overbay*	.276	254	23	70	4	28	1
Danny Bautista	.275	284	29	78	4	36	3
Chad Moeller	.268	239	29	64	7	29	1
Shea Hillenbrand	.267	330	40	88	17	59	0
Matt Kata*	.257	288	42	74	7	29	3
Junior Spivey	.255	365	52	93	13	50	4
Craig Counsell	.234	303	40	71	3	21	11
Quinton McCracken	.227	203	17	46	0	18	5
Rod Barajas	.218	220	19	48	3	28	0

Acquired: IF Hillenbrand from Bos. for P Kim (May 29).

Pitching (40 IP)	ERA	W-L	Gm	IP	BB	SO
Jose Valverde*	2.15	2-1	54	50.1	26	71
Oscar Villarreal	2.57	10-7	86	98.0	46	80
Matt Mantei	2.62	5-4	50	55.0	18	68
Brandon Webb*	2.84	10-9	29	180.2	68	172
Curt Schilling	2.95	8-9	24	168.0	32	194
Miguel Batista	3.54	10-9	36	193.1	60	142
Byung-Hyun Kim	3.56	1-5	7	43.0	15	33
Stephen Randolph*	4.05	8-1	50	60.0	43	50
Randy Johnson	4.26	6-8	18	114.0	27	125
Elmer Dessens	5.07	8-8	34	175.2	57	113
Andrew Good*	5.29	4-2	16	66.1	16	42
John Patterson*	6.05	1-4	16	55.0	30	43

Saves: Mantei (29), Valverde (10), Patterson, Brady Raggio and Scott Service (1). **Complete games:** Schilling (3), Batista (2), Johnson and Webb (1). **Shutouts:** Schilling (2); Batista, Johnson and Webb (1).

Atlanta Braves

Batting (135 AB)	Avg	AB	R	H	HR	RBI	SB
Gary Sheffield	.330	576	126	190	39	132	18
Javy Lopez	.328	457	89	150	43	109	0
Marcus Giles	.316	551	101	174	21	69	14
Chipper Jones	.305	555	103	169	27	106	2
Julio Franco	.294	197	28	58	5	31	0
Rafael Furcal	.292	664	130	194	15	61	25
Andruw Jones	.277	595	101	165	36	116	4
Vinny Castilla	.277	542	65	150	22	76	1
Robert Fick	.269	409	52	110	11	80	1
Mark DeRosa	.263	266	40	70	6	22	1
Darren Bragg	.241	162	21	39	0	9	2
Henry Blanco	.199	151	11	30	1	13	0

Acquired: P Mercker from Cin. for PTBN (Aug. 12). **Claimed:** P Wright off waivers from SD (Aug. 29).

Pitching (45 IP)	ERA	W-L	Gm	IP	BB	SO
John Smoltz	1.12	0-2	62	64.1	8	73
Kent Mercker	1.95	0-2	67	55.1	32	48
Ray King	3.51	3-4	80	59.0	27	43
Russ Ortiz	3.81	21-7	34	212.1	102	149
Mike Hampton	3.84	14-8	31	190.0	78	110
Greg Maddux	3.96	16-11	36	218.1	33	124
Horacio Ramirez*	4.00	12-4	29	182.1	72	100
Roberto Hernandez	4.35	5-3	66	60.0	43	45
Trey Hodges*	4.66	3-3	52	65.2	31	66
Jung Bong*	5.05	6-2	44	57.0	31	47
Shane Reynolds	5.43	11-9	30	167.1	59	94
Jaret Wright	7.35	2-5	20	56.1	31	50

Saves: Smoltz (45); Will Cunnane (3), Wright (2), Bong, Mercker and Jason Marquis (1). **Complete games:** Ortiz, Hampton, Maddux and Ramirez (1). **Shutouts:** Ortiz (1).

Chicago Cubs

Batting (190 AB)	Avg	AB	R	H	HR	RBI	SB
Mark Grudzielanek	.314	481	73	151	3	38	6
Corey Patterson	.298	329	49	98	13	55	16
Kenny Lofton	.296	547	97	162	12	46	30
Eric Karros	.286	336	37	96	12	40	1
Ramon Martinez	.283	293	30	83	3	34	0
Moises Alou	.280	565	83	158	22	91	3
Sammy Sosa	.279	517	99	144	40	103	0
Randall Simon	.276	410	47	113	16	72	0
Aramis Ramirez	.272	607	75	165	27	106	2
Damian Miller	.233	352	34	82	9	36	1
Alex Gonzalez	.228	536	71	122	20	59	3
Tony Womack	.226	349	43	79	2	22	13
Hee Seop Choi*	.218	202	31	44	8	28	1

Acquired: OF Lofton and IF Ramirez from Pit. for IF Jose Hernandez and 2 minor leaguers (July 22); IF Simon from Pit. for a minor leaguer (Aug. 16); IF Womack from Col. for a minor leaguer (Aug. 19).

Pitching (45 IP)	ERA	W-L	Gm	IP	BB	SO
Mark Prior	2.43	18-6	30	211.1	50	245
Joe Borowski	2.63	2-2	68	68.1	19	66
Carlos Zambrano	3.11	13-11	32	214.0	94	168
Kerry Wood	3.20	14-11	32	211.0	100	266
Kyle Farnsworth	3.30	3-2	77	76.1	36	92
Mike Remlinger	3.65	6-5	73	69.0	39	83
Matt Clement	4.11	14-12	32	201.2	79	171
Shawn Estes	5.73	8-11	29	152.1	83	103
Antonio Alfonseca	5.83	3-1	60	66.1	27	51
Juan Cruz	6.05	2-7	25	61.0	28	65

Saves: Borowski (33), Alan Benes, Dave Veres and Todd Wellemeyer (1). **Complete games:** Wood (4), Prior and Zambrano (3), Clement (2), Estes (1). **Shutouts:** Wood (2), Clement, Estes, Prior and Zambrano (1).

Cincinnati Reds

Batting (200 AB)	Avg	AB	R	H	HR	RBI	SB
Jose Guillen	.337	315	52	106	23	63	1
Sean Casey	.291	573	71	167	14	80	4
D'Angelo Jimenez	.290	290	34	84	7	31	7
Barry Larkin	.282	241	39	68	2	18	2
Aaron Boone	.273	403	61	110	18	65	15
Austin Kearns	.264	292	39	77	15	58	5
Juan Castro	.253	320	28	81	9	33	2
Ruben Mateo	.242	207	16	50	3	18	0
Ray Olmedo*	.239	230	24	55	0	17	1
Jason LaRue	.230	379	52	87	16	50	3
Adam Dunn	.215	381	70	82	27	57	8

Acquired: IF Jimenez from Chi-AL for a minor leaguer (July 7); P Harang and 2 minor leaguers from Oak. for OF Guillen (July 30). **Traded:** IF Boone and P Gabe White to NY-AL for 2 minor leaguers and cash (July 31); P Sullivan and cash to Chi-AL for PTBN (Aug. 21). **Waived:** P Heredia (Aug. 25).

Pitching (45 IP)	ERA	W-L	Gm	IP	BB	SO
Felix Heredia	3.00	5-2	57	72.0	28	41
Scott Sullivan	3.62	6-0	50	49.2	26	43
Brian Reith	4.11	2-3	42	61.1	36	39
Chris Reitsma	4.29	9-5	57	84.0	19	53
John Bale	4.47	1-2	10	46.1	12	37
Paul Wilson	4.64	8-10	28	166.2	50	93
John Riedling	4.90	2-3	55	101.0	47	65
Aaron Harang	5.28	4-3	9	46.0	10	27
Danny Graves	5.33	4-15	30	169.0	41	60
Jimmy Haynes	6.30	2-12	18	94.1	57	43
Ryan Dempster	6.54	3-7	22	115.2	70	84

Saves: Scott Williamson (21), Reitsma (12), Graves (2), Heredia, Reidling and Reith (1). **Complete games:** Graves (2), Haynes and Jose Acevedo (1). **Shutouts:** Graves (1).

Colorado Rockies

Batting (135 AB)	Avg	AB	R	H	HR	RBI	SB
Todd Helton	.358	583	135	209	33	117	0
Jay Payton	.302	600	93	181	28	89	6
Larry Walker	.284	454	86	129	16	79	7
Preston Wilson	.282	600	94	169	36	141	14
Ronnie Belliard	.277	447	73	124	8	50	7
Greg Norton	.263	179	19	47	6	31	2
Chris Stynes	.255	443	71	113	11	73	3
Juan Uribe	.253	316	45	80	10	33	7
Charles Johnson	.230	356	49	82	20	61	1
Gregg Zaun	.229	166	15	38	4	21	1
Mark Bellhorn	.221	249	27	55	2	26	5
Bobby Estalella	.200	140	17	28	7	21	2

Acquired: IF Bellhorn and a minor leaguer from Chi-NL for IF Jose Hernandez (June 19). **Signed:** C Zaun (Aug. 26).

Pitching (40 IP)	ERA	W-L	Gm	IP	BB	SO
Brian Fuentes	2.75	3-3	75	75.1	34	82
Steve Reed	3.27	5-3	67	63.1	26	39
Javier Lopez*	3.70	4-1	75	58.1	12	40
Justin Speier	4.05	3-1	72	73.1	23	66
Shawn Chacon	4.60	11-8	23	137.0	58	93
Darren Oliver	5.04	13-11	33	180.1	61	88
Jason Jennings	5.11	12-13	32	181.1	88	119
Jose Jimenez	5.22	2-10	63	101.2	32	45
Denny Stark	5.83	3-3	17	78.2	33	30
Chin-hui Tsao	6.02	3-3	9	43.1	20	29
Aaron Cook*	6.02	4-6	43	124.0	57	43
Scott Elarton	6.27	4-4	11	51.2	20	20
Nelson Cruz	7.21	3-5	20	53.2	11	38

Saves: Jimenez (20), Speier (9), Fuentes (4), Lopez (1).
Complete games: Oliver, Jennings and Cook (1).
Shutouts: none.

Florida Marlins

Batting (135 AB)	Avg	AB	R	H	HR	RBI	SB
Luis Castillo	.314	595	99	187	6	39	21
Juan Pierre	.305	668	100	204	1	41	65
Ivan Rodriguez	.297	511	90	152	16	85	10
Mike Lowell	.276	492	76	136	32	105	3
Derrek Lee	.271	539	91	146	31	92	21
Juan Encarnacion	.270	601	80	162	19	94	19
Miguel Cabrera*	.268	314	39	84	12	62	0
Alex Gonzalez	.256	528	52	135	18	77	0
Todd Hollandsworth	.254	228	32	58	3	20	2
Brian Banks	.235	149	14	35	4	23	2
Lenny Harris	.193	145	14	28	1	8	1

Acquired: P Urbina from Tex. for 3 minor leaguers (July 11). **Signed:** IF/OF Harris off waivers from Chi-NL (Aug. 8).

Pitching (35 IP)	ERA	W-L	Gm	IP	BB	SO
Ugueth Urbina	1.41	3-0	33	38.1	13	37
Josh Beckett	3.04	9-8	24	142.0	56	152
Dontrelle Willis*	3.30	14-6	27	160.2	58	142
Mark Redman	3.59	14-9	29	190.2	61	151
Braden Looper	3.68	6-4	74	80.2	29	56
Tommy Phelps*	4.00	3-2	27	63.0	23	43
Tim Spooneybarger	4.07	1-2	33	42.0	11	32
Brad Penny	4.13	14-10	32	196.1	56	138
Carl Pavano	4.30	12-13	33	201.0	49	133
Michael Tejera	4.67	3-4	50	81.0	36	58
Nate Bump*	4.71	4-0	32	36.1	20	17
Armando Almanza	6.08	4-5	51	50.1	25	49

Saves: Looper (28), Urbina (6), Tejera (2). **Complete games:** Redman (3), Pavano and Willis (2). **Shutouts:** Willis (2).

Houston Astros

Batting (135 AB)	Avg	AB	R	H	HR	RBI	SB
Richard Hidalgo	.309	514	91	159	28	88	9
Jeff Kent	.297	505	77	150	22	93	6
Morgan Ensberg	.291	385	69	112	25	60	7
Lance Berkman	.288	538	110	155	25	93	5
Jeff Bagwell	.278	605	109	168	39	100	11
Craig Biggio	.264	628	102	166	15	62	8
Geoff Blum	.262	420	51	110	10	52	0
Adam Everett*	.256	387	51	99	8	51	8
Jose Vizcaino	.249	189	14	47	3	26	0
Orlando Merced	.231	212	20	49	3	26	3
Brad Ausmus	.229	450	43	103	4	47	5

Acquired: P Miceli from NY-AL for PTBN or cash (July 30).

Pitchers (40 IP)	ERA	W-L	Gm	IP	BB	SO
Billy Wagner	1.78	1-4	78	86.0	23	105
Octavio Dotel	2.48	6-4	76	87.0	31	97
Roy Oswalt	2.97	10-5	21	127.1	29	108
Dan Miceli	3.55	1-3	37	50.2	16	38
Brad Lidge*	3.60	6-3	78	85.0	42	97
Tim Redding	3.68	10-14	33	176.0	65	116
Ricky Stone	3.69	6-4	65	83.0	31	47
Wade Miller	4.13	14-13	33	187.1	77	161
Ron Villone	4.13	6-6	19	106.2	48	91
Pete Munro	4.67	3-4	40	54.0	26	27
Kirk Saarloos	4.93	2-1	36	49.1	17	43
Jeriome Robertson*	5.10	15-9	32	160.2	64	99

Saves: Wagner (44); Dotel (4); Lidge and Stone (1).
Complete games: Miller (1). **Shutouts:** none.

Los Angeles Dodgers

Batting (120 AB)	Avg	AB	R	H	HR	RBI	SB
Brian Jordan	.299	224	28	67	6	28	1
Jolbert Cabrera	.282	347	43	98	6	37	6
Shawn Green	.280	611	84	171	19	85	6
Paul Lo Duca	.273	568	64	155	7	52	0
Dave Ross*	.258	124	19	32	10	18	0
Cesar Izturis	.251	558	47	140	1	40	10
Dave Roberts	.250	388	56	97	2	16	40
Alex Cora	.249	477	39	119	4	34	4
Fred McGriff	.249	297	32	74	13	40	0
Ron Coomer	.240	125	11	30	4	15	0
Adrian Beltre	.240	559	50	134	23	80	2
Jeromy Burnitz	.239	464	63	111	31	77	5
Mike Kinkade	.216	162	25	35	5	14	1

Acquired: OF Burnitz from NY-NL for 3 minor leaguers (July 14).

Pitching (40 IP)	ERA	W-L	Gm	IP	BB	SO
Eric Gagne	1.20	2-3	77	82.1	20	137
Paul Quantrill	1.75	2-5	89	77.1	15	44
Guillermo Mota	1.97	6-3	76	105.0	26	99
Wilson Alvarez	2.37	6-2	21	95.0	23	82
Kevin Brown	2.39	14-9	32	211.0	56	185
Paul Shuey	3.00	6-4	62	69.0	33	60
Hideo Nomo	3.09	16-13	33	218.1	98	177
Tom Martin	3.53	1-2	80	51.0	24	51
Kazuhisa Ishii	3.86	9-7	27	147.0	101	140
Darren Dreifort	4.03	4-4	10	60.1	25	67
Odalis Perez	4.52	12-12	30	185.1	46	141
Andy Ashby	5.18	3-10	21	73.0	17	41

Saves: Gagne (55); Quantrill, Mota and Alvarez (1). **Complete games:** Nomo (2), Alvarez (1). **Shutouts:** Nomo (2), Alvarez (1).

Milwaukee Brewers

Batting (135 AB)	Avg	AB	R	H	HR	RBI	SB
Scott Podsednik*	.314	558	100	175	9	58	43
Geoff Jenkins	.296	487	81	144	28	95	0
Alex Sanchez	.282	163	15	46	0	10	8
Brady Clark	.273	315	33	86	6	40	13
Richie Sexson	.272	606	97	165	45	124	2
Eddie Perez	.271	350	26	95	11	45	0
Bill Hall*	.261	142	23	37	5	20	1
Wes Helms	.261	476	56	124	23	67	0
Keith Ginter*	.257	358	51	92	14	44	1
John Vander Wal	.257	327	50	84	14	45	1
Keith Osik	.249	241	22	60	2	21	0
Royce Clayton	.228	483	49	110	11	39	5

Traded: OF Sanchez to Det. for 2 minor leaguers (May 27). **Signed:** P Davis (July 13).

Pitching (40 IP)	ERA	W-L	Gm	IP	BB	SO
Danny Kolb	1.96	1-2	37	41.1	19	39
Doug Davis	2.58	3-2	8	52.1	21	35
Dave Burba	3.53	1-1	17	43.1	19	35
Matt Ford*	4.33	0-3	25	43.2	21	26
Leo Estrella*	4.36	7-3	58	66.0	21	25
Ben Sheets	4.45	11-13	34	220.2	43	157
Wes Obermueller*	5.07	2-5	12	65.2	25	34
Matt Kinney	5.19	10-13	33	190.2	80	152
Brooks Kieschnick	5.26	1-1	42	53.0	13	39
Wayne Franklin	5.50	10-13	36	194.2	94	116
Luis Vizcaino	6.39	4-3	75	62.0	25	61
Glendon Rusch	6.42	1-12	32	123.1	45	93
Rubén Quevedo	6.75	1-4	9	42.2	23	19

Saves: Kolb (21), Estrella (3), Rusch (1). **Complete games:** Davis, Sheets, Kinney, Franklin and Rusch (1). **Shutouts:** Franklin (1).

New York Mets

Batting (140 AB)	Avg	AB	R	H	HR	RBI	SB
Jose Reyes*	.307	274	47	84	5	32	13
Jason Phillips*	.298	403	45	120	11	58	0
Cliff Floyd	.290	365	57	106	18	68	3
Mike Piazza	.286	234	37	67	11	34	0
Timo Perez	.269	346	32	93	4	42	5
Roger Cedeno	.267	484	70	129	7	37	14
Roberto Alomar	.262	263	34	69	2	22	6
Ty Wigginton*	.255	573	73	146	11	71	12
Vance Wilson	.242	269	28	65	8	39	1
Joe McEwing	.241	278	31	67	1	16	3
Tony Clark	.232	254	29	59	16	43	0
Raul Gonzalez*	.230	217	28	50	2	21	3
Rey Sanchez	.207	174	11	36	0	12	1

Traded: IF Alomar to Chi-AL for 3 minor leaguers (July 1); P Benitez to NY-AL for 3 minor leaguers (July 16); IF Sanchez to Sea. for a minor leaguer (July 29).

Pitching (40 IP)	ERA	W-L	Gm	IP	BB	SO
Dave Weathers	3.08	1-6	77	87.2	40	75
Armando Benitez	3.10	3-3	45	49.1	24	50
Pedro Feliciano*	3.30	0-0	23	48.1	21	43
Dan Wheeler	3.71	1-3	35	51.0	17	35
Steve Trachsel	3.78	16-10	33	204.2	65	111
Jae Weong Seo*	3.82	9-12	32	188.1	46	110
Al Leiter	3.99	15-9	30	180.2	94	139
Tom Glavine	4.52	9-14	32	183.1	66	82
Mike Stanton	4.57	2-7	50	45.1	19	34
Aaron Heilman*	6.75	2-7	14	65.1	41	51
Jeremy Griffiths*	7.02	1-4	9	41.0	19	25

Saves: Benitez (21), Weathers (7), Stanton (5), Wheeler and John Franco (2), Grant Roberts (1). **Complete games:** Trachsel (2), Leiter (1). **Shutouts:** Trachsel (2), Leiter (1).

Montreal Expos

Batting (145 AB)	Avg	AB	R	H	HR	RBI	SB
Vladimir Guerrero	.330	394	71	130	25	79	9
Jose Vidro	.310	509	77	158	15	65	3
Orlando Cabrera	.297	626	95	186	17	80	24
Wil Cordero	.278	436	57	121	16	71	1
Brad Wilkerson	.268	504	78	135	19	77	13
Jamey Carroll*	.260	227	31	59	1	10	5
Endy Chavez	.251	483	66	121	5	47	18
Henry Mateo	.240	154	29	37	0	7	11
Edwards Guzman	.240	146	15	35	1	14	0
Jose Macias	.239	272	31	65	4	22	4
Ron Calloway*	.238	340	36	81	9	52	9
Brian Schneider	.230	335	34	77	9	46	0
Michael Barrett	.208	226	33	47	10	30	0
Fernando Tatis	.194	175	15	34	2	15	2

Pitching (40 IP)	ERA	W-L	Gm	IP	BB	SO
Luis Ayala	2.92	10-3	65	71.0	13	46
Joey Eischen	3.06	2-2	70	53.0	13	40
Livan Hernandez	3.20	15-10	33	233.1	57	178
Javier Vazquez	3.24	13-12	34	230.2	57	241
Scott Stewart	3.98	3-1	51	43.0	13	29
Tomo Ohka	4.16	10-12	34	199.0	45	118
Zach Day*	4.18	9-8	23	131.1	59	61
Claudio Vargas*	4.34	6-8	23	114.0	41	62
Rocky Biddle	4.65	5-8	73	71.2	40	54
T.J. Tucker	4.73	2-3	45	80.0	20	47

Saves: Biddle (34), Ayala (5), Eischen, Julio Manon and Chad Cordero (1). **Complete games:** L. Hernandez (8), Vazquez (4), Ohka (2), Day (1). **Shutouts:** Vazquez and Day (1).

Philadelphia Phillies

Batting (135 AB)	Avg	AB	R	H	HR	RBI	SB
Mike Lieberthal	.313	508	68	159	13	81	0
Marlon Byrd*	.303	495	86	150	7	45	11
Bobby Abreu	.300	577	99	173	20	101	22
Placido Polanco	.289	492	87	142	14	63	14
Jim Thome	.266	578	111	154	47	131	0
Tomas Perez	.265	298	39	79	5	33	0
Jimmy Rollins	.263	628	85	165	8	62	20
Ricky Ledee	.247	255	37	63	13	46	0
Kelly Stinnett	.237	186	14	44	3	19	0
Pat Burrell	.209	522	57	109	21	64	0
David Bell	.195	297	32	58	4	37	0

Acquired: P Williams and cash from Pit. for a minor leaguer (July 20); C Stinnett from Cin. for PTBN (Aug. 31); P De Los Santos from Mil. for PTBN or cash (Sept. 2).

Pitchers (40 IP)	ERA	W-L	Gm	IP	BB	SO
Rheal Cormier	1.70	8-0	65	84.2	25	67
Terry Adams	2.65	1-4	66	68.0	23	51
Turk Wendell	3.38	3-3	56	64.0	28	27
Vicente Padilla	3.62	14-12	32	208.2	62	133
Amaury Telemaco	3.97	1-4	8	45.1	11	29
Kevin Millwood	4.01	14-12	35	222.0	68	169
Randy Wolf	4.23	16-10	33	200.0	78	177
Brett Myers	4.43	14-9	32	193.0	76	143
Carlos Silva	4.43	3-1	62	87.1	37	48
Valerio De Los Santos	4.50	4-3	51	52.0	25	39
Brandon Duckworth	4.94	4-7	24	93.0	44	68
Mike Williams	6.14	1-7	68	63.0	41	39
Jose Mesa	6.52	5-7	61	58.0	31	45

Saves: Williams (28), Mesa (24), Dan Plesac (2), Cormier, Wendell, Silva, De Los Santos and Hector Mercado (1). **Complete games:** Millwood (5), Wolf (2), Padilla and Myers (1). **Shutouts:** Millwood (3), Wolf (2), Padilla and Myers (1).

Pittsburgh Pirates

Batting (135 AB)	Avg	AB	R	H	HR	RBI	SB
Tike Redman	.330	230	36	76	3	19	7
Jason Kendall	.325	587	84	191	6	58	8
Matt Stairs	.292	305	49	89	20	57	0
Reggie Sanders	.285	453	74	129	31	87	15
Rob Mackowiak	.270	174	20	47	6	19	6
Craig Wilson	.262	309	49	81	18	48	3
Jack Wilson	.256	558	58	143	9	62	5
Abraham Nunez	.248	311	37	77	4	35	9
Jeff Reboulet	.241	261	37	63	3	25	2
Jose Hernandez	.225	519	58	117	13	57	2

Acquired: IF Hernandez and 2 minor leaguers from Chi-NL for OF Kenny Lofton and IF Aramis Ramirez (July 22); P Perez, OF Jason Bay and PTBN from SD for OF Brian Giles (Aug. 26). **Traded:** P Sauerbeck and a minor leaguer to Bos. for P Brandon Lyon and a minor leaguer (July 22) — deal later reworked due to an injury to Lyon; P Suppan to Bos. for IF Freddy Sanchez (July 31).

Pitching (40 IP)	ERA	W-L	Gm	IP	BB	SO
Kip Wells	3.29	10-9	31	197.1	76	147
Jeff Suppan	3.57	10-7	21	141.0	31	78
Julian Tavarez	3.66	3-3	64	83.2	27	39
Scott Sauerbeck	4.05	3-4	53	40.0	25	32
Brian Meadows	4.72	2-1	34	76.1	11	38
Salomon Torres	4.76	7-5	41	121.0	42	84
Jeff D'Amico	4.77	9-16	29	175.1	42	100
Kris Benson	4.97	5-9	18	105.0	36	68
Joe Beimel	5.05	1-3	69	62.1	33	42
Josh Fogg	5.26	10-9	26	142.0	40	71
Oliver Perez	5.47	4-10	24	126.2	77	141
Brian Boehringer	5.49	5-4	62	62.1	30	47

Saves: Tavarez (11), Mike Lincoln (5), Torres (2), Meadows (1). **Complete games:** Suppan (3), D'Amico (2), Wells and Fogg (1). **Shutouts:** Suppan (2), D'Amico (1).

St. Louis Cardinals

Batting (135 AB)	Avg	AB	R	H	HR	RBI	SB
Albert Pujols	.359	591	137	212	43	124	5
Edgar Renteria	.330	587	96	194	13	100	34
J.D. Drew	.289	287	60	83	15	42	2
Scott Rolen	.286	559	98	160	28	104	13
Eduardo Perez	.285	253	47	72	11	41	5
Bo Hart*	.277	296	46	82	4	28	3
Jim Edmonds	.275	447	89	123	39	89	1
Tino Martinez	.273	476	66	130	15	69	1
Orlando Palmeiro	.271	317	37	86	3	33	3
Mike Matheny	.252	441	43	111	8	47	1
Fernando Vina	.251	259	35	65	4	23	4
Kerry Robinson	.250	208	19	52	1	16	6
Miguel Cairo	.245	261	41	64	5	32	4

Acquired: P Yan and cash from Tex. for a minor leaguer (May 27); P DeJean from Mil. for 2 PTBN (Aug. 22).

Pitching (40 IP)	ERA	W-L	Gm	IP	BB	SO
Jason Isringhausen	2.36	0-1	40	42.0	18	41
Cal Eldred	3.74	7-4	62	67.1	31	67
Matt Morris	3.76	11-8	27	172.1	39	120
Steve Kline	3.82	5-5	78	63.2	30	31
Woody Williams	3.87	18-9	34	220.2	55	153
Garrett Stephenson	4.59	7-13	32	174.1	60	91
Mike DeJean	4.68	5-8	76	82.2	39	71
Dan Haren*	5.08	3-7	14	72.2	22	43
Brett Tomko	5.28	13-9	33	202.2	57	114
Jason Simontacchi	5.56	9-5	46	126.1	41	74
Jeff Fassero	5.68	1-7	62	77.2	34	55
Esteban Yan	6.02	2-0	39	43.1	16	28

Saves: Isringhausen (22); DeJean (19), Eldred (8), Kline and Fassero (3), Simontacchi, Yan and Kiko Calero (1). **Complete games:** Morris (5), Tomko (2), Stephenson and Simontacchi. **Shutouts:** Morris (3).

San Diego Padres

Batting (150 AB)	Avg	AB	R	H	HR	RBI	SB
Mark Loretta	.314	589	74	185	13	72	5
Brian Giles	.299	492	93	147	20	88	4
Sean Burroughs	.286	517	62	148	7	58	7
Phil Nevin	.279	226	30	63	13	46	2
Rondell White	.278	413	49	115	18	66	1
Lou Merloni	.272	151	20	41	1	17	2
Gary Matthews Jr.	.271	306	50	83	4	22	12
Xavier Nady*	.267	371	50	99	9	39	6
Mark Kotsay	.266	482	64	128	7	38	6
Brian Buchanan	.263	198	29	52	8	29	6
Ramon Vazquez	.261	422	56	110	3	30	10
Ryan Klesko	.252	397	47	100	21	67	2
Gary Bennett	.238	307	26	73	2	42	3

Acquired: OF Giles from Pit. for P Oliver Perez, OF Jason Bay and PTBN (Aug. 26). **Traded:** OF White to KC for 2 minor leaguers (Aug. 26); IF Merloni to Bos. for a minor leaguer (Aug. 29). **Claimed:** OF Matthews Jr. off waivers from Bal. (May 23); P Linebrink off waivers from Hou. (May 29); P Roa off waivers from Col. (July 23).

Pitching (40 IP)	ERA	W-L	Gm	IP	BB	SO
Scott Linebrink	3.31	5-2	92.1	36	68
Adam Eaton	4.08	9-12	31	183.0	68	146
Jake Peavy	4.11	12-11	32	194.2	82	156
Brian Lawrence	4.19	10-15	33	210.2	57	116
Brandon Villafuerte	4.20	0-2	31	40.2	26	34
Mike Matthews	4.45	6-4	77	64.2	29	44
Jay Witasick	4.53	3-7	46	45.2	25	42
Luther Hackman	5.17	2-2	65	76.2	36	48
Kevin Jarvis	5.87	4-8	16	92.0	32	49
Joe Roa	6.14	1-3	28	51.1	10	38

Saves: Rod Beck (20), Villafuerte, Witasick and Jesse Orosco (2). **Complete games:** Eaton and Lawrence (1). **Shutouts:** none.

San Francisco Giants

Batting (135 AB)	Avg	AB	R	H	HR	RBI	SB
Barry Bonds	.341	390	111	133	45	90	7
Andres Galarraga	.301	272	36	82	12	42	1
Marquis Grissom	.300	587	82	176	20	79	11
Ray Durham	.285	410	61	117	8	33	7
Benito Santiago	.279	401	53	112	11	56	0
Rich Aurilia	.277	505	65	140	13	58	2
J.T. Snow	.273	330	48	90	8	51	1
Yorvit Torrealba	.260	200	22	52	4	29	1
Edgardo Alfonzo	.259	514	56	133	13	81	5
Neifi Perez	.256	328	27	84	1	31	3
Eric Young	.251	475	80	119	15	34	27
Jose Cruz	.250	539	90	135	20	68	5
Pedro Feliz	.247	235	31	58	16	48	2

Acquired: P Herges from SD for a minor leaguer and PTBN (July 13); P Ponson from Bal. for P Moss, P Ainsworth and a minor league P (July 31); IF Young from Mil for a minor leaguer (Aug. 20). **Signed:** P Hermanson (July 11).

Pitching (50 IP)	ERA	W-L	Gm	IP	BB	SO
Jason Schmidt	2.34	17-5	29	207.2	46	208
Matt Herges	2.62	3-2	67	79.0	29	68
Tim Worrell	2.87	4-4	76	78.1	28	65
Joe Nathan	2.96	12-4	78	79.0	33	83
Felix Rodriguez	3.10	8-2	68	61.0	29	46
Jerome Williams*	3.30	7-5	21	131.0	49	88
Scott Eyre	3.32	2-1	74	57.0	26	35
Sidney Ponson	3.71	3-6	10	68.0	18	34
Kurt Ainsworth*	3.82	5-4	11	66.0	26	48
Jim Brower	3.96	8-5	51	100.0	39	65
Dustin Hermanson	4.06	3-3	38	68.2	24	39
Kirk Rueter	4.53	10-5	27	147.0	47	41
Damian Moss	4.70	9-7	21	115.0	63	57
Jesse Foppert*	5.03	8-9	23	111.0	69	101

Saves: Worrell (38), Herges (3), Rodriguez and Brower (2), Eyre and Hermanson (1). **Complete games:** Schmidt (5), Williams (2). **Shutouts:** Schmidt (3), Williams (1).

BASEBALL PLAYOFFS

DIVISIONAL SERIES	LCS	WORLD SERIES 100th ANNIVERSARY 2003	LCS	DIVISIONAL SERIES
†Boston 3	Boston 3			Chicago 3
Oakland 2			Chicago 3	Atlanta 2
	AMERICAN LEAGUE	Florida 4 New York 3	NATIONAL LEAGUE	
New York 3	New York 4		Florida 4	†Florida 3
Minnesota 1				San Fran. 1
†Wild Card Team				†Wild Card Team

Divisional Series Summaries
AMERICAN LEAGUE

Red Sox, 3-2

Date	Winner	Home Field
Oct. 1............	Athletics, 5-4 (12 inn.)	at Oakland
Oct. 2............	Athletics, 5-1	at Oakland
Oct. 4............	Red Sox, 3-1 (11 inn.)	at Boston
Oct. 5............	Red Sox, 5-4	at Boston
Oct. 6............	Red Sox, 4-3	at Oakland

Game 1
Wednesday, Oct. 1, at Oakland

	1 2 3	4 5 6	7 8 9	10 11 12	R	H	E
Boston	.1 0 0	0 1 0	2 0 0	0 0 0 -	4	12	2
Oakland	..0 0 3	0 0 0	0 0 1	0 0 1 -	5	8	0

Win: Harden, Oak. (1-0). **Loss:** Lowe, Bos. (0-1).
2B: Boston—Mueller (1); Oakland—Singleton (1), Durazo (1). **HR:** Boston—Walker 2 (2), Varitek (1). **RBI:** Boston—Walker 3 (3), Varitek (1); Oakland—Durazo 3 (3), Tejada (1), Hernandez (1). **SB:** Boston—Damon (1); Oakland—Singleton (1), Chavez (1). **E:** Boston—Martinez (1), Walker (1).
Attendance: 50,606 (43,662). **Time:** 4:37.

Game 2
Thursday, Oct. 2, at Oakland

	1 2 3	4 5 6	7 8 9	R	H	E
Boston	.....0 0 1	0 0 0	0 0 0 -	1	6	1
Oakland	....0 5 0	0 0 0	0 0 x -	5	6	0

Win: Zito, Oak. (1-0). **Loss:** Wakefield, Bos. (0-1).
2B: Boston—Mirabelli (1), Damon (1); Oakland—Byrnes (1). **RBI:** Boston—Damon (1); Oakland—Hernandez (2), Byrnes 2 (2). **E:** Boston—Walker (2).
Attendance: 36,305 (43,662). **Time:** 2:37.

Game 3
Saturday, Oct. 4, at Boston

	1 2 3	4 5 6	7 8 9	10 11	R	H	E
Oakland	...0 0 0	0 0 1	0 0 0	0 0 -1	6	4
Boston	.....0 1 0	0 0 0	0 0 0	0 2 -3	7	2

Win: Williamson, Bos. (1-0). **Loss:** Harden, Oak. (1-1).
2B: Boston—Damon (1). **HR:** Boston—Nixon (1). **RBI:** Boston—Nixon 2 (2), Varitek (1); Oakland—Byrnes (1); Boston—Garciaparra (1). **E:** Oakland—Tejada (1), Chavez 2 (2), Hernandez (1); Boston—Lowe (1), Garciaparra (1).
Attendance: 35,460 (33,991). **Time:** 3:42.

Game 4
Sunday, Oct. 5, at Boston

	1 2 3	4 5 6	7 8 9	R	H	E
Oakland	...0 1 0	0 0 3	0 0 0 -	4	11	1
Boston	......0 0 2	0 0 1	0 2 x -	5	7	0

Win: Williamson, Bos. (2-0). **Loss:** Foulke, Oak. (0-1).
2B: Oakland—Chavez (1); Boston—Garciaparra (1), Ortiz (1). **3B:** Oakland—Melhuse, Oak. (1). **HR:** Oakland—Dye (1); Boston—Damon (1), Walker (3). **RBI:** Oakland—Dye 3 (3), Melhuse (1); Boston—Damon 2 (3), Walker (4), Ortiz 2 (2). **E:** Oakland—Ellis (1).
Attendance: 35,048 (33,991). **Time:** 3:02.

Game 5
Monday, Oct. 6, at Oakland

	1 2 3	4 5 6	7 8 9	R	H	E
Boston	......0 0 0	4 0 0	0 0 0 -	4	6	0
Oakland	...0 0 0	1 0 1	0 1 0 -	3	7	0

Win: Martinez, Bos. (1-0). **Loss:** Zito, Oak. (1-1). **Save:** Lowe, Bos. (1).
2B: Oakland—Guillen (1), Durazo (2), Tejada (1), Singleton (2). **HR:** Boston—Varitek (2), Ramirez (1). **RBI:** Oakland—Guillen (1), Tejada (2), McMillon (1); Boston—Varitek (2), Ramirez 3 (3). **SB:** Boston—Damon (2).
Attendance: 49,397 (43,662). **Time:** 3:05.

Yankees, 3-1

Date	Winner	Home Field
Sept. 30	Twins, 3-1	at New York
Oct. 2	Yankees, 4-1	at New York
Oct. 4	Yankees, 3-1	at Minnesota
Oct. 5	Yankees, 8-1	at Minnesota

Game 1
Tuesday, Sept. 30, at New York

	1 2 3	4 5 6	7 8 9	R H E
Minnesota	0 0 1	0 0 2	0 0 0	- 3 8 0
New York	0 0 0	0 0 0	0 0 1	- 1 9 1

Win: Hawkins, Min. (1-0). **Loss:** Mussina, NY (0-1). **Save:** Guardado, Min. (1).
2B: Minnesota—Stewart (1), Koskie (1); New York—Soriano (1), Boone (1). **3B:** Minnesota—Hunter (1). **RBI:** Minnesota—Rivas (1), Hunter (1); New York—Soriano (1). **SB:** New York—Soriano (1). **E:** New York—Soriano (1). **Attendance:** 56,292 (57,478). **Time:** 3:18.

Game 2
Thursday, Oct. 2, at New York

	1 2 3	4 5 6	7 8 9	R H E
Minnesota	0 0 0	0 1 0	0 0 0	- 1 4 1
New York	1 0 0	0 0 0	3 0 0	- 4 8 1

Win: Pettitte, NY (1-0). **Loss:** Radke, Min. (0-1). **Save:** Rivera, NY (1).
2B: New York—Posada (1). **HR:** Minnesota—Hunter (1). **RBI:** Minnesota—Hunter (2); New York—Williams (1), Soriano (2), Giambi 2 (2). **SB:** New York—Jeter (1), Soriano (2). **E:** Minnesota—Hawkins (1); New York—Jeter (1). **Attendance:** 56,479 (57,478). **Time:** 3:07.

Game 3
Saturday, Oct. 4, at Minnesota

	1 2 3	4 5 6	7 8 9	R H E
New York	0 2 1	0 0 0	0 0 0	- 3 8 1
Minnesota	0 0 1	0 0 0	0 0 0	- 1 5 0

Win: Clemens, NY (1-0). **Loss:** Lohse, Min. (0-1). **Save:** Rivera, NY (2).
2B: New York—Williams (1). **HR:** New York—Matsui (1); Minnesota—Pierzynski (1). **RBI:** New York— Matsui 2 (2), Williams (2); Minnesota—Pierzynski (1). **SB:** Minnesota—Stewart (1). **E:** New York—Williams (1). **Attendance:** 55,915 (48,678). **Time:** 3:02.

Game 4
Sunday, Oct. 5, at Minnesota

	1 2 3	4 5 6	7 8 9	R H E
New York	0 0 0	6 0 0	0 1 1	- 8 13 0
Minnesota	0 0 0	1 0 0	0 0 0	- 1 9 1

Win: Wells, NY (1-0). **Loss:** Santana, Min. (0-1).
2B: New York—Giambi 2 (2), Williams (2), Matsui (1), Johnson (1); Minnesota—Stewart (2). **HR:** New York—Jeter (1). **RBI:** New York—Williams (3), Matsui (3), Johnson 2 (2), Soriano 2 (4), Jeter (1); Minnesota—Cuddyer (1). **SB:** New York—Boone (1). **E:** Minnesota—Hawkins (2). **Attendance:** 55,875 (48,678). **Time:** 2:49.

NATIONAL LEAGUE

Cubs, 3-2

Date	Winner	Home Field
Sept. 30	Cubs, 4-2	at Atlanta
Oct. 1	Braves, 5-3	at Atlanta
Oct. 3	Cubs, 3-1	at Chicago
Oct. 4	Braves, 6-4	at Chicago
Oct. 5	Cubs, 5-1	at Atlanta

Game 1
Tuesday, Sept. 30, at Atlanta

	1 2 3	4 5 6	7 8 9	R H E
Chicago	0 0 0	0 0 4	0 0 0	- 4 10 0
Atlanta	0 0 1	0 0 0	0 1 0	- 2 3 1

Win: Wood, Chi. (1-0). **Loss:** Ortiz, Atl. (0-1). **Save:** Borowski, Chi. (1).
2B: Chicago—Wood (1). **HR:** Atlanta—Giles (1). **RBI:** Chicago—Bako (1), Wood 2 (2), Lofton (1); Atlanta—Giles (1), C. Jones (1). **SB:** Chicago—Lofton (1), Sosa (1). **E:** Atlanta—Giles (1). **Attendance:** 52,043 (50,091). **Time:** 3:21.

Game 2
Wednesday, Oct. 1, at Atlanta

	1 2 3	4 5 6	7 8 9	R H E
Chicago	2 0 0	0 0 0	0 1 0	- 3 6 0
Atlanta	1 0 0	1 0 1	0 2 x	- 5 13 0

Win: Smoltz, Atl. (1-0). **Loss:** Veres, Chi. (0-1).
2B: Chicago—Sosa (1); Atlanta—DeRosa (1). **RBI:** Chicago—Sosa (1), Alou (1), Goodwin (1); Atlanta— C. Jones (2), A. Jones (1), Giles (2), DeRosa 2 (2). **Attendance:** 52,743 (50,091). **Time:** 3:07.

Game 3
Friday, Oct. 3, at Chicago

	1 2 3	4 5 6	7 8 9	R H E
Atlanta	0 0 0	0 0 0	0 1 0	- 1 2 4
Chicago	2 0 0	0 0 0	0 1 x	- 3 8 0

Win: Prior, Chi. (1-0). **Loss:** Maddux, Atl. (0-1). **2B:** Atlanta—DeRosa (2); Chicago—Ramirez (1). **RBI:** Atlanta—Giles (1); Chicago—Simon 2 (2), Ramirez (1). **SB:** Chicago—Lofton 2 (3), Alou (1). **E:** Atlanta—Lopez (1), Castilla (1), Furcal (1), A. Jones (1). **Attendance:** 39,982 (39,241). **Time:** 2:43.

Game 4
Saturday, Oct. 4, at Chicago

	1 2 3	4 5 6	7 8 9	R H E
Atlanta	0 0 0	1 3 0	0 2 0	- 6 12 0
Chicago	0 0 1	0 0 1	0 1 1	- 4 10 0

Win: Ortiz, Atl. (1-1). **Loss:** Clement, Chi. (0-1). **Save:** Smoltz, Atl. (1).
2B: Atlanta—Lopez (1); Chicago—Alou (1), Simon (1), Miller (1). **HR:** Atlanta—C. Jones 2 (2); Chicago—Karros 2 (2). **RBI:** Atlanta—Bragg (1), C. Jones 4 (6), Castilla (1); Chicago—Alou (2), Karros 2 (2), Miller (1). **SB:** Atlanta—Furcal (1). **Attendance:** 39,983 (39,241). **Time:** 3:40.

Game 5
Sunday, Oct. 5, at Atlanta

	1 2 3	4 5 6	7 8 9	R H E
Chicago	1 1 0	0 0 2	0 0 1	- 5 9 0
Atlanta	0 0 0	0 0 1	0 0 0	- 1 5 1

Win: Wood, Chi. (2-0). **Loss:** Hampton, Atl. (0-1).
2B: Chicago—Lofton (1), Goodwin (1); Atlanta—Lopez (2), J. Franco (1). **HR:** Chicago—Gonzalez (1), Ramirez (1). **RBI:** Chicago—Alou (3), Gonzalez (1), Ramirez 2 (3), Goodwin (2); Atlanta— Sheffield (1). **E:** Atlanta—Castilla (2). **Attendance:** 54,357 (50,091). **Time:** 2:50.

Divisional Series Summaries (Cont.)

Marlins, 3-1

Date	Winner	Home Field
Sept. 30	Giants, 2-0	at San Francisco
Oct. 1	Marlins, 9-5	at San Francisco
Oct. 3	Marlins, 4-3 (11 inn.)	at Florida
Oct. 4	Marlins, 7-6	at Florida

Game 1
Tuesday, Sept. 30, at San Francisco

	1 2 3	4 5 6	7 8 9	R H E
Florida	0 0 0	0 0'0	0 0 0	0 3 1
San Francisco	0 0 0	1 0 0	1 0 x	2 3 2

Win: Schmidt, SF (1-0). **Loss:** Beckett, Fla. (0-1).
2B: San Francisco—Alfonzo (1). **RBI:** San Francisco—Alfonzo (1). **SB:** San Francisco—Bonds (1). **E:** Florida—Cabrera (1); San Francisco—Snow (1).
Attendance: 43,704 (41,503). **Time:** 2:33.

Game 2
Wednesday, Oct. 1, at San Francisco

	1 2 3	4 5 6	7 8 9	R H E
Florida	1 0 0	0 3 3	1 1 0	9 14 0
San Francisco	1 0 0	3 1 0	0 0 0	5 8 2

Win: Pavano, Fla. (1-0). **Loss:** Nathan, SF (0-1).
2B: Florida—Pierre (1); San Francisco—Bonds (1), Alfonzo (2). **3B:** San Francisco—Feliz (1). **HR:** Florida—Encarnacion (1). **RBI:** Florida—Lee 2 (2), Pierre 3 (3), Castillo (1), Rodriguez (1), Encarnacion (1), Conine (1); San Francisco—Bonds (1), Alfonzo 2 (3), Grissom (1), Snow (1). **SB:** Florida—Pierre (1). **E:** San Francisco—Snow (2).
Attendance: 43,766 (41,503). **Time:** 3:06.

Game 3
Friday, Oct. 3, at Florida

	1 2 3 4 5 6 7 8 9 10 11	R H E
San Francisco	0 0 0 0 0 2 0 0 0 0 1	3 12 1
Florida	2 0 0 0 0 0 0 0 0 2	4 8 1

Win: Looper, Fla. (1-0). **Loss:** Worrell, SF (0-1).
2B: San Francisco—Alfonzo (3); Florida—Castillo 2 (2), Lee (1). **HR:** Florida—Rodriguez (1). **RBI:** San Francisco—Cruz (1), Feliz (1), Alfonzo (4); Florida—Rodriguez 4 (5). **SB:** Florida—Lee (1). **E:** San Francisco—Grissom (1); Florida—Gonzalez (1).
Attendance: 61,488 (36,331). **Time:** 4:11.

Game 4
Saturday, Oct. 4, at Florida

	1 2 3	4 5 6	7 8 9	R H E
San Francisco	0 1 0	0 0 4	0 0 1	6 9 2
Florida	0 1 2	2 0 0	0 2 x	7 12 0

Win: Pavano (2-0). **Loss:** Rodriguez, SF (0-1). **Loss:** Urbina, Fla. (1).
2B: San Francisco—Aurilia (1), Alfonzo (4), Perez (1); Florida—Castillo (2), Cabrera 2 (2), Rodriguez (1). **3B:** Florida—Willis (1). **RBI:** San Francisco—Torrealba (1), Aurilia (1), Bonds (2), Alfonzo (5), Snow 2 (3); Florida—Conine (2), Rodriguez (6), Lee (2), Cabrera 3 (3). **E:** San Francisco—Aurilia (2), Torrealba (1).
Attendance: 65,464 (36,331). **Time:** 3:19.

American League Championship Series

Yankees, 4-3

Date	Winner	Home Field
Oct. 8	Red Sox, 5-2	at New York
Oct. 9	Yankees, 6-2	at New York
Oct. 11	Yankees, 4-3	at Boston
Oct. 13	Red Sox, 3-2	at Boston
Oct. 14	Yankees, 4-2	at Boston
Oct. 15	Red Sox, 9-6	at New York
Oct. 16	Yankees, 6-5 (11 inn.)	at New York

Game 1
Wednesday, Oct. 8, at New York

	1 2 3	4 5 6	7 8 9	R H E
Boston	0 0 0	2 2 0	1 0 0	5 13 0
New York	0 0 0	0 0 0	2 0 0	2 3 0

Win: Wakefield, Bos. (1-1). **Loss:** Mussina, NY (0-2). **Save:** Williamson, Bos. (1).
2B: New York—Posada (4). **HR:** Boston—Ortiz (1), Walker (4), Ramirez (2). **RBI:** Boston—Ortiz 2 (4), Walker (5), Ramirez (4), Millar (1); New York—Posada (1), Matsui (1).
Attendance: 56,281 (57,478). **Time:** 3:20.

Game 2
Thursday, Oct. 9, at New York

	1 2 3	4 5 6	7 8 9	R H E
Boston	0 1 0	0 0 1	0 0 0	2 10 1
New York	0 2 1	0 2 0	x	6 8 0

Win: Pettitte, NY (2-0). **Loss:** Lowe, Bos. (0-2).
2B: Boston—Varitek (1); New York—Williams (3), Posada (3). **HR:** Boston—Varitek (1); New York—Johnson (1). **RBI:** Boston—Jackson (1), Varitek (3); New York—Johnson 2 (2), Williams (4), Matsui (5), Posada 2 (3). **SB:** Boston—Nixon (1); New York—Boone (2). **E:** Boston—Jackson (1).
Attendance: 56,295 (57,478). **Time:** 3:05.

Game 3
Saturday, Oct. 11, at Boston

	1 2 3	4 5 6	7 8 9	R H E
New York	0 1 1	2 0 0	0 0 0	4 7 0
Boston	2 0 0	0 0 0	1 0 0	3 6 0

Win: Clemens, NY (2-0). **Loss:** Martinez, Bos. (1-1). **Save:** Rivera, NY (3). **2B:** New York—Posada (4), Matsui (2); Boston—Walker (5). **HR:** New York—Jeter (2). **RBI:** New York—Garcia (1), Jeter (2), Matsui (6); Boston—Ramirez 2 (6).
Attendance: 34,209 (33,991). **Time:** 3:09.

Game 4
Monday, Oct. 13, at Boston

	1 2 3	4 5 6	7 8 9	R H E
New York . . .	0 0 0	0 1 0	0 0 1	2 6 1
Boston	0 0 0	1 1 0	1 0 x	3 6 0

Win: Wakefield, Bos. (2-1). **Loss:** Mussina, NY (0-3). **Save:** Williamson, Bos. (2).
2B: New York—Jeter (1); Boston—Nixon (1). **HR:** New York—Sierra (1); Boston—Walker (5). **RBI:** New York—Jeter (3), Sierra (1); Boston—Walker (6), Nixon (3), Varitek (4). **SB:** New York—Dellucci (1). **E:** New York—Boone (1).
Attendance: 34,599 (33,991). **Time:** 2:49.

Game 5
Tuesday, Oct. 14, at Boston

	1 2 3	4 5 6	7 8 9	R H E
New York . . .	0 3 0	0 0 0	0 1 0	4 7 1
Boston	0 0 0	1 0 0	1 0 x	2 6 0

Win: Wells, NY (2-0). **Loss:** Lowe, Bos. (0-3). **Save:** Rivera, NY (4). **3B:** Boston—Walker (1). **HR:** Boston—Ramirez (3). **RBI:** New York—Garcia 2 (3), Soriano (5), Matsui (7); Boston—Ramirez (7), Garciaparra (1). **E:** New York—Soriano (2); Boston—Millar (1).
Attendance: 34,619 (33,991). **Time:** 3:04.

Game 6
Wednesday, Oct. 15, at New York

	1 2 3	4 5 6	7 8 9	R	H	E
Boston	0 0 4	0 0 0	3 0 2	- 9	16	1
New York	1 0 0	4 1 0	0 0 0	- 6	12	2

Win: Embree, Bos. (1-0). **Loss:** Contreras, NY (0-1). **Save:** Williamson, Bos. (3).
2B: Boston—Mueller 2 (3), Ramirez (1), Damon (3); New York—Johnson (2), Soriano (2). **HR:** Boston—Varitek (4), Nixon (3); New York—Giambi (1), Posada (1). **RBI:** Boston—Varitek (5), Ortiz 3 (7), Millar (2), Damon (4), Nixon 2 (5); New York—Giambi (3), Johnson (5), Boone (1), Soriano 2 (7), Posada (4). **SB:** Boston—Damon (3); New York—Soriano 2 (4), Jeter (2). **E:** Boston—Garciaparra (2); New York—Boone (2), Matsui (1).
Attendance: 56,277 (57,478). **Time:** 3:57.

Game 7
Thursday, Oct. 16, at New York

	1 2 3	4 5 6	7 8 9	10 11	R	H	E
Boston	0 3 0	1 0 0	1 0 0	0 0	-5	11	0
New York	0 0 0	0 1 0	1 3 0	0 1	-6	11	1

Win: Rivera, NY (1-0). **Loss:** Wakefield, Bos. (2-2).
2B: Boston—Varitek (2), Ortiz (2); New York—Matsui 2 (4), Jeter (2), Posada (5). **HR:** Boston—Nixon (4), Millar (1), Ortiz (2); New York—Giambi 2 (3), Boone (1). **RBI:** Boston—Nixon 2 (7), Millar (3), Ortiz (8); New York—Giambi 2 (5), Williams (5), Posada 2 (6), Boone (2). **E:** New York—Wilson (1).
Attendance: 56,279 (57,478). **Time:** 3:56.

Most Valuable Player
Mariano Rivera, New York, P

ERA	W-L	Sv	IP	H	ER	BB	SO
1.13	1-0	2	8.0	5	1	0	6

ALCS Composite Box Score
New York Yankees

	LCS vs. Boston							Overall AL Playoffs							
Batting	Avg	AB	R	H	HR	RBI	BB	SO	Avg	AB	R	H	HR	RBI	BB	SO
Ruben Sierra	.500	2	1	1	1	1	1	0	.250	4	1	1	1	1	1	0
David Dellucci	.333	3	2	1	0	0	0	1	.333	3	2	1	0	0	0	1
Hideki Matsui	.308	26	3	8	0	4	1	3	.293	41	5	12	.1	7	3	6
Jorge Posada	.296	27	4	8	1	6	3	4	.250	44	6	11	1	6	3	10
Karim Garcia	.250	16	1	4	0	3	2	4	.250	16	1	4	0	3	2	4
Derek Jeter	.233	30	3	7	1	2	2	4	.295	44	5	13	2	3	6	6
Jason Giambi	.231	26	4	6	3	3	4	7	.238	42	5	10	3	5	6	12
Nick Johnson	.231	26	4	6	1	3	2	4	.179	39	6	7	1	5	5	6
Bernie Williams	.192	26	5	5	0	4	2	3	.268	41	8	11	0	5	6	5
Aaron Boone	.176	17	2	3	1	2	1	6	.188	32	3	6	1	2	1	9
Enrique Wilson	.143	7	0	1	0	0	0	1	.143	7	0	1	0	0	0	1
Alfonso Soriano	.133	30	0	4	0	3	1	11	.224	49	2	11	0	7	1	17
Juan Rivera	.000	2	0	0	0	0	0	1	.286	14	2	4	0	0	1	1
TOTALS	.227	238	30	54	8	29	21	49	.245	376	46	92	10	44	35	78

	LCS vs. Boston						Overall AL Playoffs						
Pitching	ERA	W-L	Sv	Gm	IP	H	BB	SO	ERA	W-L	Sv	Gm	IP	H	BB	SO
Mariano Rivera	1.13	1-0	2	4	8.0	5	0	6	0.75	1-0	4	6	12.0	5	0	10
David Wells	2.35	1-0	0	2	7.2	5	2	5	1.76	2-0	0	3	15.1	13	2	10
Felix Heredia	3.38	0-0	0	5	2.2	0	3	3	1.93	0-0	0	6	4.2	1	4	4
Mike Mussina	4.11	0-2	0	3	15.1	16	4	17	4.03	0-4	0	4	22.1	23	7	23
Gabe White	4.50	0-0	0	2	2.0	4	0	1	2.70	0-0	0	3	3.1	5	0	2
Andy Pettitte	4.63	1-0	0	2	11.2	17	4	10	3.38	2-0	0	3	18.2	21	7	20
Roger Clemens	5.00	1-0	0	2	9.0	11	2	8	3.38	2-0	0	3	16.0	16	3	14
Jose Contreras	5.79	0-1	0	4	4.2	6	2	7	5.79	0-1	0	4	4.2	6	2	7
Jeff Nelson	6.00	0-0	0	4	3.0	4	0	3	6.00	0-0	0	5	3.0	4	1	3
TOTALS	3.94	4-3	2	7	64.0	68	17	60	3.06	7-4	4	11	100.0	94	26	93

Boston Red Sox

	LCS vs. New York							Overall AL Playoffs							
Batting	Avg	AB	R	H	HR	RBI	BB	SO	Avg	AB	R	H	HR	RBI	BB	SO
Todd Walker	.370	27	5	10	2	2	1	2	.349	43	9	15	5	6	1	3
Damian Jackson	.333	3	0	1	0	1	0	1	.125	8	0	1	0	1	0	3
Trot Nixon	.333	24	3	8	3	7	4	7	.294	34	4	10	4	7	4	10
Manny Ramirez	.310	29	6	9	2	4	1	4	.265	49	8	13	3	7	4	11
Jason Varitek	.300	20	4	6	2	-3	1	5	.294	34	8	10	4	5	3	7
Doug Mirabelli	.286	7	0	2	0	0	0	2	.364	11	2	4	0	0	0	4
David Ortiz	.269	26	4	7	2	6	3	8	.191	47	4	9	2	8	5	15
Nomar Garciaparra	.241	29	2	7	0	1	2	8	.265	49	4	13	0	5	5	10
Kevin Millar	.241	29	3	7	1	3	1	9	.240	50	3	12	1	3	3	13
Bill Mueller	.222	27	1	6	0	0	2	7	.174	46	1	8	0	0	5	11
Johnny Damon	.200	20	1	4	0	1	3	3	.256	39	3	10	1	4	5	4
Gabe Kapler	.125	8	0	1	0	0	0	1	.059	17	0	1	0	0	0	6
Dave McCarty	.000	1	0	0	0	0	0	1	.000	1	0	0	0	0	0	1
Adrian Brown	.—	0	0	0	0	0	0	0	.000	0	0	0	0	0	0	0
TOTALS	.272	250	29	68	12	26	17	60	.247	430	46	106	20	42	35	99

ALCS Composite Box Score (Cont.)

Pitching	LCS vs. New York							Overall AL Playoffs						
	ERA	W-L	Sv	Gm	IP	H	BB	SO	ERA	W-L	Sv	Gm	IP	H	BB	SO
Alan Embree	0.00	1-0	0	5	4.2	3	0	1	0.00	1-0	0	8	6.2	4	0	1
Todd Jones	0.00	0-0	0	1	0.1	1	1	1	0.00	0-0	0	1	0.1	1	1	1
Scott Sauerbeck	0.00	0-0	0	1	0.1	1	1	0	0.00	0-0	0	1	0.1	1	1	0
Mike Timlin	0.00	0-0	0	5	5.1	1	2	6	0.00	0-0	0	8	9.2	1	2	11
Tim Wakefield	2.57	2-1	0	3	14.0	8	6	10	2.91	2-2	0	5	21.2	14	9	17
Bronson Arroyo	2.70	0-0	0	3	3.1	2	2	5	2.70	0-0	0	3	3.1	2	2	5
Scott Williamson	3.00	0-0	3	3	3.0	1	0	6	1.13	2-0	3	8	8.0	3	3	14
Pedro Martinez	5.65	0-1	0	2	14.1	16	2	14	4.76	1-1	0	4	28.1	29	7	23
Derek Lowe	6.43	0-2	0	2	14.0	14	7	5	4.18	0-3	1	5	23.2	21	14	11
John Burkett	7.36	0-0	0	1	3.2	7	0	1	7.00	0-0	0	2	9.0	16	2	2
Byung-Hyun Kim	—	0-0	0	1	63.0	0	0	49	13.50	0-0	0	1	0.2	0	1	1
TOTALS	4.00	3-4	3	7	63.0	54	21	49	3.47	6-6	4	12	111.2	92	42	86

Score by Innings

	1	2	3	4	5	6	7	8	9	10	11	R	H	E
Boston	2	4	0	9	3	1	6	2	2	0	0	–	29	68	3
New York	1	6	2	6	4	5	5	4	1	0	1	–	30	54	5

E: Boston—Garciaparra, Jackson, Millar; New York—Boone 2, Matsui, Soriano, Wilson. **2B:** Boston—Varitek 2, Mueller 2, Walker, Nixon, Ortiz, Damon; New York—Posada 4, Matsui 3, Jeter 2, Johnson, Williams, Soriano. **3B:** Boston—Walker, Garciaparra. **SB:** Boston—Damon, Nixon; New York—Soriano 2, Boone, Dellucci, Jeter. **CS:** Boston—Nixon 2, Jackson, Kapler, Ramirez; New York—Boone. **SF:** New York—Matsui. **PB:** Boston—Varitek 2, Mirabelli. **HBP:** by Wells (Nixon), by Nelson (Ortiz), by Heredia (Walker), by Lowe (Boone), by Wakefield (Dellucci), by Martinez (Garcia), by Arroyo (Soriano). **WP:** New York—Contreras 2, Heredia. **LOB:** Boston—46; New York—45.
Umpires: Tim McClelland, Terry Craft, Alfonso Marquez, Derryl Cousins, Joe West, Angel Hernandez.

National League Championship Series

Marlins, 4-3

Date	Winner	Home Field
Oct. 7	Marlins, 9-8 (11 inn.)	at Chicago
Oct. 8	Cubs, 12-3	at Chicago
Oct. 10	Cubs, 5-4 (11 inn.)	at Florida
Oct. 11	Cubs, 8-3	at Florida
Oct. 12	Marlins, 4-0	at Florida
Oct. 14	Marlins, 8-3	at Chicago
Oct. 15	Marlins, 9-6	at Chicago

Game 1

Tuesday, Oct. 7, at Chicago

	1	2	3	4	5	6	7	8	9	10	11	R	H	E
Florida	0	0	5	0	0	1	0	0	2	0	1	9	14	1
Chicago	4	0	0	0	0	2	0	0	2	0	0	8	11	1

Win: Urbina, Fla. (1-0). **Loss:** Guthrie, Chi. (0-1). **Save:** Looper, Fla. (1).
2B: Florida—Castillo (4), Hollandsworth (1); Chicago—Gonzalez (1), Simon (2), Miller (2), Lofton (2). **3B:** Florida—Conine (1), Pierre (1); Chicago—Grudzielanek (1), Ramirez (1). **HR:** Florida—Rodriguez (4), Cabrera (1), Encarnacion (2), Lowell (1); Chicago—Alou (1), Gonzalez (2), Sosa (1). **RBI:** Florida—Rodriguez 5 (11), Cabrera (4), Encarnacion (2), Conine (3), Lowell (1); Chicago—Grudzielanek (1), Alou 2 (5), Gonzalez 3 (4), Sosa 2 (3). **SB:** Florida—Castillo 2 (2). **E:** Florida—Gonzalez (2); Chicago—Grudzielanek (1).
Attendance: 39,567 (39,241). **Time:** 3:44.

Game 2

Wednesday, Oct. 8, at Chicago

	1	2	3	4	5	6	7	8	9	R	H	E
Florida	0	0	0	0	0	2	0	1	0	3	9	1
Chicago	2	3	3	0	3	1	0	0	x	12	16	1

Win: Prior, Chi. (2-0). **Loss:** Penny, Fla. (0-1).
2B: Florida—Encarnacion (1), Conine (1); Chicago—Bako (1), Simon (3), Grudzielanek (1). **HR:** Florida—Lee (1), Cabrera (2); Chicago—Sosa (2), Ramirez (1), Gonzalez 2 (4). **RBI:** Florida—Lee (3), Cabrera (5); Chicago— Simon 2 (4), Lofton 2 (3), Sosa 2 (5), Ramirez (4), Bako (2), Gonzalez 3 (7), Grudzielanek (2). **SB:** Chicago—Lofton (4). **E:** Florida—Conine (1); Chicago—Simon (1).
Attendance: 39,562 (39,241). **Time:** 3:02.

Game 3

Friday, Oct. 10, at Florida

	1	2	3	4	5	6	7	8	9	10	11	R	H	E
Chicago	1	1	0	0	0	0	0	0	1	0	1	5	12	0
Florida	0	1	0	0	0	0	2	1	0	0	0	4	10	0

Win: Borowski, Chi. (1-0). **Loss:** Tejera, Fla. (0-1). **Save:** Remlinger, Chi. (1).
2B: Chicago—Alou (2); Florida—Gonzalez (1). **3B:** Chicago—Goodwin (1), Glanville (1). **HR:** Chicago—Simon (1). **RBI:** Chicago—Sosa (6), Wood (3), Simon 2 (6), Glanville (1); Florida—Gonzalez (1), Castillo (2). Rodriguez (12), Hollandsworth (1). **SB:** Florida—Pierre (2).
Attendance: 65,115 (36,331). **Time:** 4:16.

Game 4

Saturday, Oct. 11, at Florida

	1	2	3	4	5	6	7	8	9	R	H	E
Chicago	4	0	2	1	0	0	1	0	0	8	8	0
Florida	0	0	0	0	2	0	0	1	0	3	6	1

Win: Clement, Chi. (1-1). **Loss:** Willis, Fla. (0-1).
2B: Florida—Rodriguez (2). **HR:** Chicago—Ramirez 2 (2). **RBI:** Chicago—Ramirez 6 (10), Gonzalez (8), Alou (6); Florida—Gonzalez (2), Hollandsworth (2), Rodriguez (13). **E:** Florida—Rodriguez (1).
Attendance: 65,829 (36,331). **Time:** 2:58.

Game 5

Sunday, Oct. 12, at Florida

	1	2	3	4	5	6	7	8	9	R	H	E
Chicago	0	0	0	0	0	0	0	0	0	0	2	0
Florida	0	0	0	0	2	0	1	1	x	4	8	0

Win: Beckett, Fla. (1-1). **Loss:** Zambrano, Chi. (0-1).
HR: Florida—Lowell (2), Rodriguez (3), Conine (4). **RBI:** Florida—Lowell 2 (3), Rodriguez (14), Conine (4).
Attendance: 65,279 (36,331). **Time:** 2:42.

Most Valuable Player

Ivan Rodriguez, Florida, C

AVG	AB	R	H	HR	RBI	BB
.321	28	5	9	2	10	5

Game 6
Tuesday, Oct. 14, at Chicago

	1 2 3	4 5 6	7 8 9	R H E
Florida	0 0 0	0 0 0	8 0 0 -	8 9 0
Chicago	1 0 0	0 0 1	1 0 0 -	3 10 2

Win: Fox, Fla. (1-0). **Loss:** Prior, Chi. (2-1).
2B: Florida—Pierre (2), Lee (2), Mordecai (1); Chicago—Sosa (2). **RBI:** Florida—Rodriguez (15), Lee 2 (5), Conine (5), Mordecai 3 (3), Pierre (4); Chicago—Sosa (7), Grudzielanek (3). **E:** Chicago—Grudzielanek (2), Gonzalez (1).
Attendance: 65,829 (36,331). **Time:** 2:58.

Game 7
Wednesday, Oct. 15, at Chicago

	1 2 3	4 5 6	7 8 9	R H E
Florida	3 0 0	0 0 3	1 2 0 0 -	9 12 0
Chicago	0 3 2	0 0 0	1 0 0 -	6 6 0

Win: Penny, Fla. (1-1). **Loss:** Wood, Chi. (2-1). **Save:** Urbina, Fla. (2). **2B:** Florida—Rodriguez (3), Gonzalez (2), Lee (3); Chicago—Gonzalez (2). **3B:** Florida—Pierre (1). **HR:** Florida—Cabrera (3); Chicago—Wood (1), Alou (2), O'Leary (1). **RBI:** Florida—Cabrera 4 (9), Rodriguez (1), Lee (6), Castillo (3), Gonzalez 2 (4); Chicago—Miller (2), Wood 2 (5), Alou 2 (8), O'Leary (1). **SB:** Florida—Lee (2).
Attendance: 39,574 (39,241). **Time:** 3:11.

NLCS Composite Box Score
Florida Marlins

Batting		LCS vs. Chicago								Overall NL Playoffs						
	Avg	AB	R	H	HR	RBI	BB	SO	Avg	AB	R	H	HR	RBI	BB	SO
Todd Hollandsworth	1.000	3	2	3	0	2	1	0	.667	6	3	4	0	2	1	2
Jeff Conine	.458	24	4	11	1	3	4	2	.385	39	6	15	1	5	6	3
Miguel Cabrera	.333	30	9	10	3	6	2	6	.318	44	10	14	3	9	3	12
Ivan Rodriguez	.321	28	5	9	2	10	5	7	.333	45	8	15	3	16	8	8
Juan Pierre	.303	33	5	10	0	1	2	1	.288	52	10	15	0	4	3	2
Juan Encarnacion	.250	12	1	3	1	1	0	4	.185	27	2	5	2	2	2	7
Josh Beckett	.250	8	0	2	0	0	1	3	.222	9	0	2	0	0	1	4
Luis Castillo	.214	28	3	6	0	2	5	2	.244	45	5	11	0	3	8	5
Mike Lowell	.200	20	5	4	2	3	3	4	.174	23	5	4	2	3	3	5
Mike Mordecai	.200	5	1	1	0	3	0	0	.200	5	1	1	0	3	0	0
Derrek Lee	.188	32	2	6	1	4	1	8	.208	48	4	10	1	6	2	10
Alex Gonzalez	.125	24	1	3	0	4	0	6	.100	40	3	4	0	4	1	9
Rick Helling	.000	1	0	0	0	0	0	0	.000	1	0	0	0	0	0	0
Brad Penny	.000	1	0	0	0	0	0	1	.500	2	0	1	0	0	0	1
Brian Banks	.000	1	1	0	0	0	1	0	.000	3	1	0	0	0	1	0
Lenny Harris	.000	2	0	0	0	0	0	1	.250	4	0	1	0	0	0	1
Carl Pavano	.000	2	0	0	0	0	0	0	.000	2	0	0	0	0	0	1
Mark Redman	.000	2	0	0	0	0	0	1	.000	4	0	0	0	0	1	1
Mike Redmond	—	0	1	0	0	0	0	0	—	0	1	0	0	0	0	0
Dontrelle Willis	—	0	0	0	0	0	0	0	1.000	3	1	3	0	0	0	0
TOTALS	.266	256	40	68	10	39	28	45	.247	402	60	105	12	57	42	70

Pitching																
	ERA	W-L	Sv	Gm	IP	H	BB	SO	ERA	W-L	Sv	Gm	IP	H	BB	SO
Braden Looper	0.00	0-0	0	2	1.2	1	1	1	0.00	1-0	0	4	3.1	2	3	1
Carl Pavano	2.35	0-0	0	3	7.2	8	1	8	1.74	2-0	0	6	10.1	9	2	9
Ugueth Urbina	2.57	1-0	1	4	7.0	2	0	10	2.70	1-0	2	7	10.0	6	1	12
Josh Beckett	3.26	1-0	0	3	19.1	11	2	19	2.73	1-1	0	4	26.1	13	7	28
Chad Fox	5.40	1-0	0	3	3.1	5	2	2	3.24	1-0	0	6	8.1	8	5	5
Nate Bump	6.00	0-0	0	2	3.0	3	0	3	6.00	0-0	0	2	3.0	3	0	3
Rick Helling	6.35	0-0	0	2	5.2	7	4	5	7.50	0-0	0	3	6.0	9	6	5
Mark Redman	6.52	0-0	0	2	9.2	13	4	4	5.17	0-0	0	3	15.2	20	7	8
Michael Tejera	6.75	0-1	0	2	1.1	2	0	1	6.75	0-1	0	2	1.1	2	0	1
Brad Penny	15.75	1-1	0	3	4.0	9	3	5	10.24	1-1	0	5	9.2	14	4	6
Dontrelle Willis	18.90	0-1	0	2	3.1	4	6	4	12.00	0-1	0	4	9.0	11	8	7
TOTALS	5.59	4-3	2	7	66.0	65	23	57	4.89	7-4	3	11	103.0	97	43	85

Chicago Cubs

Batting		LCS vs. Florida								Overall NL Playoffs						
	Avg	AB	R	H	HR	RBI	BB	SO	Avg	AB	R	H	HR	RBI	BB	SO
Doug Glanville	1.000	1	0	1	0	1	0	0	.500	2	1	1	0	1	0	0
Troy O'Leary	.333	3	1	1	1	1	0	0	.250	4	1	1	1	1	0	0
Kerry Wood	.333	3	1	1	1	3	0	0	.300	10	2	3	1	5	0	2
Kenny Lofton	.323	31	8	10	0	3	0	4	.308	52	11	16	0	3	5	6
Moises Alou	.310	29	4	9	2	5	2	1	.388	49	7	19	2	8	3	5
Sammy Sosa	.308	26	7	8	2	6	6	9	.262	42	8	11	2	7	12	13
Randall Simon	.294	17	3	5	1	4	0	3	.333	24	4	8	1	6	0	5
Alex Gonzalez	.286	28	5	8	3	7	2	7	.275	40	6	11	4	8	4	10
Paul Bako	.250	16	4	4	0	1	1	7	.200	20	4	4	0	2	4	9
Tom Goodwin	.250	4	1	1	0	0	0	3	.400	5	1	2	0	2	0	3
Aramis Ramirez	.231	26	4	6	3	7	5	6	.250	44	6	11	4	10	7	8
Eric Karros	.231	13	2	3	1	1	1	2	.310	29	6	9	2	2	2	6
Mark Grudzielanek	.200	30	2	6	0	3	0	5	.180	50	4	9	0	3	3	9
Damian Miller	.200	10	0	2	0	3	1	2	.143	21	0	3	0	4	1	4
Ramon Martinez	.000	4	0	0	0	0	0	0	.000	8	0	0	0	0	0	3
Mark Prior	.000	4	0	0	0	0	0	2	.000	7	0	0	0	0	0	2
Matt Clement	.000	4	0	0	0	0	0	2	.000	6	0	0	0	0	0	3
Carlos Zambrano	.000	3	0	0	0	0	0	0	.000	6	0	0	0	0	0	0
TOTALS	.258	252	42	65	13	40	13	57	.258	419	61	108	17	60	43	95

NLCS Composite Box Score (Cont.)

Pitching	ERA	W-L	Sv	Gm	IP	H	BB	SO	ERA	W-L	Sv	Gm	IP	H	BB	SO
	LCS vs. Florida								Overall NL Playoffs							
Antonio Alfonseca	0.00	0-0	0	3	2.1	2	2	0	0.00	0-0	0	4	3.1	3	2	0
Joe Borowski	1.59	1-0	0	3	5.2	5	3	1	1.17	1-0	1	5	7.2	6	3	6
Mike Remlinger	2.70	0-0	1	5	3.1	3	1	2	2.25	0-0	1	7	4.0	3	2	3
Dave Veres	3.00	0-0	0	3	3.0	4	1	0	6.23	0-1	0	5	4.1	6	3	0
Mark Prior	3.14	1-1	0	2	14.1	14	5	11	2.31	2-1	0	3	23.1	16	9	18
Matt Clement	3.52	1-0	0	1	7.2	5	2	3	5.11	1-1	0	2	12.1	13	6	6
Carlos Zambrano	5.73	0-1	0	2	11.0	14	5	8	5.40	0-1	0	3	16.2	25	5	12
Kerry Wood	7.30	0-1	0	2	12.1	14	7	13	4.23	2-1	0	4	27.2	21	14	31
Mark Guthrie	9.00	0-1	0	2	1.0	1	0	0	16.20	0-1	0	3	1.2	3	1	0
Kyle Farnsworth	10.13	0-0	0	5	5.1	6	2	7	6.75	0-0	0	8	8.0	7	3	9
Juan Cruz	—	0-0	0	0	0.0	0	0	0	0.00	0-0	0	1	1.0	0	1	2
TOTALS	4.36	3-4	1	7	66.0	68	28	45	3.85	6-6	2	12	110.0	103	49	87

Score by Innings

	1	2	3	4	5	6	7	8	9	10	11		R	H	E
Florida	3	1	5	0	7	4	5	12	2	0	1	–	40	68	3
Chicago	1	2	7	7	1	3	4	3	2	0	1	–	42	65	4

E: Florida—Conine, Gonzalez, Rodriguez; Chicago—Grudzielanek 2, Gonzalez, Simon. **2B:** Florida—Rodriguez 2, Lee 2, Gonzalez 2, Hollandsworth, Conine, Pierre, Encarnacion, Castillo, Mordecai; Chicago—Simon 2, Gonzalez 2, Lofton, Alou, Sosa, Bako, Grudzielanek, Miller. **3B:** Florida—Pierre 2, Conine; Chicago—Glanville, Goodwin, Ramirez, Grudzielanek. **SB:** Florida—Castillo 2, Lee, Pierre; Chicago—Lofton. **CS:** Florida—Pierre 3. **S:** Florida—Castillo, Mordecai, Pierre; Chicago—Prior 3, Grudzielanek 2, Lofton, Wood. **SF:** Florida—Conine 2; Chicago—Wood. **PB:** Chicago—Bako 2. **HBP:** by Zambrano (Cabrera), by Clement (Lee), by Urbina (Ramirez), by Redman (Sosa). **WP:** Florida—Helling 2, Bump, Willis; Chicago—Prior, Remlinger, Zambrano. **LOB:** Florida—49; Chicago—45.

Umpires: Jerry Crawford, Chuck Meriwether, Fieldin Culbreth, Mike Everitt, Larry Poncino, Mike Reilly.

WORLD SERIES

Marlins, 4-3

Date	Winner	Home Field	Date	Winner	Home Field
Oct. 18	Marlins, 3-2	at New York	Oct. 22	Marlins, 4-3 (12 inn.)	at Florida
Oct. 19	Yankees, 6-1	at New York	Oct. 23	Marlins, 6-4	at Florida
Oct. 21	Yankees, 6-1	at Florida	Oct. 25	Marlins, 2-0	at New York

Game 1
Saturday, Oct. 18, at New York

Florida	AB	R	H	RBI	New York	AB	R	H	RBI
Pierre, cf	3	1	2	2	Soriano, 2b	5	0	1	0
Castillo, 2b	5	0	1	0	Johnson, 1b	4	0	0	0
Rodriguez, c	3	0	0	1	Jeter, ss	4	0	1	1
Cabrera, lf	3	0	0	0	Williams, cf	4	1	2	1
Lee, 1b	4	0	1	0	Matsui, lf	4	0	3	0
Lowell, 3b	4	0	0	0	Posada, c	2	0	0	0
Conine, dh	2	1	1	0	Giambi, dh	3	0	0	0
Encarnacion, rf	4	1	2	0	Dellucci, pr	0	0	0	0
Gonzalez, ss	3	0	0	0	Boone, 3b	4	0	0	0
Goodwin, dh	1	0	0	0	Garcia, rf	2	1	2	0
					J. Rivera, ph-rf	1	0	0	0
					Sierra, ph	0	0	0	0
Totals	31	3	7	3	Totals	33	2	9	2

	R	H	E
Florida	100 020 000 —	3	7	1
New York	001 001 000 —	2	9	0

E: Florida—Cabrera (1). **HR:** New York—Williams (1). **BB:** Florida—Pierre, Cabrera, Conine 2; New York—Johnson, Posada 2, Giambi, Sierra. **S:** Florida—Gonzalez. **SF:** Florida—Rodriguez. **SB:** Florida—Castillo (1), Pierre (1); New York—Soriano (1), Posada (1).

Florida	IP	H	R	ER	BB	SO	HR	ERA
Penny (W, 1-0)	5⅓	7	2	2	3	3	1	3.37
Willis	2⅓	2	0	0	0	2	0	0.00
Urbina (S, 1)	1⅓	0	0	0	2	0	0	0.00
New York								
Wells (L, 0-1)	7	6	3	3	2	1	0	3.86
Nelson	1	1	0	0	1	0	0	0.00
Contreras	1	0	0	0	1	2	0	0.00

HBP: by Wells (Pierre).
Attendance: 55,769 (57,478). **Time:** 3:43.

Game 2
Sunday, Oct. 19, at New York

Florida	AB	R	H	RBI	New York	AB	R	H	RBI
Pierre, cf	4	0	1	0	Soriano, 2b	3	1	1	2
Castillo, 2b	4	1	2	0	Jeter, ss	4	0	1	0
Rodriguez, c	3	0	1	0	Giambi, dh	3	1	1	0
Redmond, c	1	0	0	0	Williams, cf	2	1	1	0
Cabrera, lf	4	0	1	1	Matsui, lf	4	1	1	3
Lee, 1b	4	0	1	0	Posada, c	3	0	0	0
Lowell, 3b	4	0	1	0	Boone, 3b	4	0	1	0
Conine, dh	3	0	0	0	Johnson, 1b	4	2	3	0
Encarnacion, rf	2	0	0	0	J. Rivera, rf	4	0	1	1
Gonzalez, ss	3	0	0	0					
Totals	32	1	6	1	Totals	31	6	10	6

	R	H	E
Florida	000 000 001 —	1	6	0
New York	310 200 00x —	6	10	2

E: New York—Boone 2 (2). **2B:** New York—J. Rivera (1), Johnson (1), Giambi (1). **HR:** New York—Matsui (1), Soriano (1). **BB:** Florida—Encarnacion; New York—Soriano, Williams 2, Posada. **CS:** Florida—Castillo (1); New York—Soriano (1), Posada (1).

Florida	IP	H	R	ER	BB	SO	HR	ERA
Redman (L, 0-1)	2⅓	5	4	4	2	2	1	15.43
Helling	2⅔	2	2	2	0	2	1	6.75
Fox	1	1	0	0	1	0	0	0.00
Pavano	1	1	0	0	1	2	0	0.00
Looper	1	1	0	0	0	2	0	0.00
New York								
Pettitte (W, 1-0)	8⅔	6	1	0	1	7	0	0.00
Contreras	⅓	0	0	0	0	0	0	0.00

WP: Redman. **HBP:** by Redman (Giambi).
Attendance: 55,750 (57,478). **Time:** 2:56.

Game 3
Tuesday, Oct. 21, at Florida

New York	AB	R	H	RBI		Florida	AB	R	H	RBI
Soriano, 2b	4	1	0	0		Pierre, cf	3	1	2	0
Jeter, ss	4	3	3	0		Castillo, 2b	4	0	0	0
Giambi, 1b	2	0	0	0		Rodriguez, c	4	0	1	0
Dellucci, pr-rf	1	0	0	0		Cabrera, rf	4	0	2	1
Williams, cf	5	1	1	3		Lee, 1b	4	0	0	0
Matsui, lf	3	0	1	1		Lowell, 3b	4	0	0	0
Posada, c	2	0	0	1		Conine, lf	4	0	2	0
Garcia, rf	3	0	0	0		Gonzalez, ss	3	0	1	0
Sierra, ph	1	0	0	0		Encarnacion, ph	1	0	0	0
M. Rivera, p	0	0	0	0		Beckett, p	2	0	0	0
Boone, 3b	4	1	1	1		Willis, p	0	0	0	0
Mussina, p	3	0	0	0		Fox, p	0	0	0	0
Johnson, 1b	1	0	0	0		Looper, p	0	0	0	0
						Hllndswrth, ph	1	0	0	0
Totals	**33**	**6**	**6**	**6**		**Totals**	**34**	**1**	**8**	**1**

		R	H	E
New York	000 100 014 —	6	6	1
Florida	100 000 000 —	1	8	0

E: New York—Boone (3). **2B:** New York—Jeter 2 (2); Florida—Pierre (1), Gonzalez (1), Rodriguez (1). **HR:** New York—Boone (1), Williams (2). **BB:** New York—Soriano, Giambi 2, Matsui, Posada 2; Florida—Pierre. **S:** Florida—Beckett. **CS:** Florida—Pierre (1). **PB:** New York—Posada.

New York	IP	H	R	ER	BB	SO	HR	ERA
Mussina (W, 1-0)	7	7	1	1	1	9	0	1.29
M. Rivera (S, 1)	2	1	0	0	0	2	0	0.00
Florida								
Beckett (L, 0-1)	7⅓	3	2	2	3	10	0	2.45
Willis	⅓	1	0	0	2	0	0	0.00
Fox	⅔	1	2	2	1	1	1	10.80
Looper	⅔	1	2	2	0	1	1	10.80

HBP: by Beckett (Matsui), by Looper (Jeter).
Attendance: 65,731 (36,331). **Time:** 3:21.

Game 4
Wednesday, Oct. 22, at Florida

New York	AB	R	H	RBI		Florida	AB	R	H	RBI
Soriano, 2b	6	0	1	0		Pierre, cf	4	0	0	0
Jeter, ss	6	0	1	0		Castillo, 2b	4	0	0	0
Giambi, 1b	6	0	2	0		Rodriguez, c	5	1	2	0
Williams, cf	6	2	4	0		Cabrera, rf	5	1	1	2
Matsui, lf	3	0	1	0		Looper, p	0	0	0	0
Posada c	4	0	1	0		Conine, lf	5	1	3	0
Dellucci, pr	0	1	0	0		Lowell, 3b	5	0	1	0
Garcia, rf	3	0	0	0		Lee, 1b	5	0	2	1
Sierra, ph	1	0	1	2		Gonzalez, ss	5	1	1	1
Contreras, p	0	0	0	0		Pavano, p	2	0	0	0
J. Rivera, p	0	0	0	0		Urbina, p	0	0	0	0
Weaver, p	0	0	0	0		Hllndswrth, ph	1	0	0	0
Boone, 3b	4	0	0	1		Fox, p	0	0	0	0
Clemens, p	2	0	1	0		Encarnacion, rf	0	0	0	0
Johnson, ph	1	0	0	0						
Nelson, p	0	0	0	0						
Flaherty, c	2	0	0	0						
Totals	**44**	**3**	**12**	**3**		**Totals**	**41**	**4**	**10**	**4**

		R	H	E
New York	010 000 002 000 —	3	12	0
Florida	300 000 000 001 —	4	10	0

2B: New York—Jeter (3), Williams (1); Florida—Rodriguez (1). **3B:** New York—Sierra (1). **HR:** Florida—Gonzalez (1), Cabrera (1). **BB:** New York—Matsui 2, J. Rivera 1; Florida—Pierre.

New York	IP	H	R	ER	BB	SO	HR	ERA
Clemens	7	8	3	3	0	5	1	3.86
Nelson	1	1	0	0	0	1	0	0.00
Contreras	2	0	0	0	1	4	0	0.00
Weaver (L, 0-1)	1	1	1	1	0	0	1	9.00
Florida								
Pavano	8	7	1	1	0	4	0	1.00
Urbina	1	2	2	2	1	0	0	7.71
Fox	1⅓	2	0	0	2	2	0	6.00
Looper (W, 1-0)	1⅔	1	0	0	0	1	0	5.40

Attendance: 65,934 (36,331). **Time:** 4:03.

AP/Wide World Photos

*Marlins shortstop **Alex Gonzalez** blasts a dramatic 12th-inning homer in Game 4 to give the Marlins a 4-3 win and a 2-2 series tie.*

World Series (Cont.)

Game 5
Thursday, Oct. 23, at Florida

New York	AB	R	H	RBI	Florida	AB	R	H	RBI
Jeter, ss	4	2	3	1	Pierre, cf	3	0	1	1
Wilson, 2b	4	0	2	1	Castillo, 2b	4	0	0	0
Williams, cf	4	0	1	1	Rodriguez, c	4	1	1	0
Matsui, lf	5	0	0	0	Cabrera, rf	4	0	1	0
Posada, c	4	0	1	0	Willis, p	0	0	0	0
Johnson, 1b	4	1	2	0	Looper, p	0	0	0	0
Garcia, rf	3	0	1	0	Urbina, p	0	0	0	0
Soriano, ph-rf	1	0	0	0	Conine, lf	3	1	1	0
Boone, 3b	4	0	1	0	Lowell, 3b	3	1	1	2
Wells, p	0	0	0	0	Lee, 1b	3	2	1	0
Dellucci, ph	1	0	0	0	Gonzalez, ss	4	1	2	1
Contreras, p	0	0	0	0	Penny, p	2	0	1	2
J. Rivera, ph	1	0	0	0	Encarnacion, rf	1	0	0	0
Hammond, p	0	0	0	0					
Sierra, ph	1	0	0	0					
Nelson, p	0	0	0	0					
Giambi, ph	1	1	1	1					
Totals	**37**	**4**	**12**	**4**	**Totals**	**31**	**6**	**9**	**6**

						R	H	E
New York	100	000	102	—		4	12	1
Florida	030	120	00x	—		6	9	1

E: New York—Wilson (1); Florida—Lee (1). **2B:** New York—Wilson (1); Florida—Pierre (2), Conine (1), Gonzalez (2). **HR:** New York—Giambi (1). **BB:** New York—Jeter, Wilson; Florida—Pierre, Conine, Lowell, Lee. **S:** Florida—Penny. **SF:** New York—Williams. **CS:** Florida—Gonzalez.

New York	IP	H	R	ER	BB	SO	HR	ERA
Wells	1	0	0	0	0	0	0	3.38
Contreras (L, 0-1)	3	5	4	4	3	4	0	5.68
Hammond	2	2	0	0	0	0	0	0.00
Nelson	2	2	0	0	1	4	0	0.00
Florida								
Penny (W, 2-0)	7	8	2	1	2	4	0	2.19
Willis	1	1	0	0	0	1	0	0.00
Looper	⅓	3	2	2	0	0	1	9.82
Urbina (S, 2)	⅔	0	0	0	0	0	0	6.00

Attendance: 65,975 (36,331). **Time:** 3:05.

Game 6
Saturday, Oct. 25, at New York

Florida	AB	R	H	RBI	New York	AB	R	H	RBI
Pierre, cf	4	0	1	0	Jeter, ss	4	0	0	0
Castillo, 2b	5	0	1	1	Johnson, 1b	3	0	0	0
Rodriguez, c	3	0	1	0	Williams, cf	4	0	1	0
Cabrera, lf	4	0	0	0	Matsui, lf	4	0	1	0
Conine, dh	4	1	0	0	Posada, c	4	0	1	0
Lowell, 3b	3	0	2	0	Giambi, dh	2	0	0	0
Lee, 1b	4	0	0	0	Garcia, rf	3	0	1	0
Encarnacion, rf3	0	0	1		Wilson, 3b	0	0	0	0
Gonzalez, ss	4	1	2	0	Boone, 3b	1	0	0	0
					Sierra, ph-rf	1	0	0	0
					Soriano, 2b	3	0	2	0
Totals	**34**	**2**	**7**	**2**	**Totals**	**29**	**0**	**5**	**0**

						R	H	E
Florida	000	011	000	—		2	7	0
New York	000	000	000	—		0	5	1

E: New York—Jeter (1). **2B:** Florida—Lowell (1); New York—Williams (2), Posada (1). **BB:** Florida—Pierre, Rodriguez, Lowell; New York—Johnson, Giambi. **S:** New York—Boone. **SF:** Florida—Encarnacion.

Florida	IP	H	R	ER	BB	SO	HR	ERA
Beckett (W, 1-1)	9	5	0	0	2	9	0	1.10

New York	IP	H	R	ER	BB	SO	HR	ERA
Pettitte (L, 1-1)	7	6	2	1	3	7	0	0.57
M. Rivera	2	1	0	0	0	2	0	0.00

Attendance: 55,773 (57,478). **Time:** 2:57.

Most Valuable Player
Josh Beckett, Florida, P

ERA	W-L	IP	H	ER	BB	K	ShO
1.10	1-1	16.1	8	2	5	19	1

World Series Composite Box Score
Florida Marlins

	WS vs. New York							Overall Playoffs						
Batting	Avg	AB	R	H	HR	RBI	BB	SO	Avg	AB	R	H	HR	RBI	BB	SO
Brad Penny	.500	2	0	1	0	2	0	0	.500	4	0	2	0	2	0	1
Jeff Conine	.333	21	4	7	0	0	3	2	.367	60	10	22	1	5	9	5
Juan Pierre	.333	21	2	7	0	3	5	2	.301	73	12	22	0	7	8	4
Alex Gonzalez	.273	22	3	6	1	2	0	7	.161	62	6	10	1	6	1	16
Ivan Rodriguez	.273	22	2	6	0	1	1	4	.313	67	10	21	3	17	9	12
Mike Lowell	.217	23	1	5	0	2	2	3	.196	46	6	9	2	5	5	8
Derrek Lee	.208	24	2	5	0	2	1	7	.208	72	6	15	1	8	3	17
Juan Encarnacion	.182	11	1	2	0	1	1	5	.184	38	3	7	2	3	3	12
Miguel Cabrera	.167	24	1	4	1	3	1	7	.265	68	11	18	4	12	4	19
Luis Castillo	.154	26	1	4	0	1	0	7	.211	71	6	15	0	4	8	12
Todd Hollandsworth	.000	2	0	0	0	0	1	0	.500	8	3	4	0	2	1	3
Carl Pavano	.000	2	0	0	0	0	0	1	.000	4	0	0	0	0	0	2
Josh Beckett	.000	2	0	0	0	0	0	1	.182	11	0	2	0	0	0	6
Mike Redmond	.000	1	0	0	0	0	0	0	.000	1	1	0	0	0	1	0
Mike Mordecai	—	0	0	0	0	0	0	0	.200	5	1	1	0	3	0	0
Lenny Harris	—	0	0	0	0	0	0	0	.250	4	0	1	0	0	0	1
Mark Redman	—	0	0	0	0	0	0	0	.000	4	0	0	0	0	1	1
Brian Banks	—	0	0	0	0	0	0	0	.000	1	0	0	0	0	1	0
Dontrelle Willis	—	0	0	0	0	0	0	0	1.000	3	1	3	0	0	0	0
Rick Helling	—	0	0	0	0	0	0	0	.000	1	0	0	0	0	0	0
TOTALS	.232	203	17	47	2	17	14	48	.251	605	77	152	14	74	56	118

WS vs. New York / Overall Playoffs

Pitching	ERA	W-L	Sv	Gm	IP	H	BB	SO	ERA	W-L	Sv	Gm	IP	H	BB	SO
ontrelle Willis	0.00	0-0	0	3	3.2	4	2	3	8.53	0-1	0	7	12.2	15	10	10
arl Pavano	1.00	0-0	0	2	9.0	8	1	6	1.40	2-0	0	8	19.1	17	3	15
sh Beckett	1.10	1-1	0	2	16.1	8	5	19	2.11	2-2	0	6	42.2	21	3	12
ad Penny	2.19	2-0	0	2	12.1	15	5	7	5.73	3-1	0	7	22.0	29	9	13
had Fox	6.00	0-0	0	3	3.0	4	4	4	3.97	1-0	0	9	11.1	12	9	9
gueth Urbina	6.00	0-0	2	3	3.0	2	3	2	3.46	1-0	4	10	13.0	8	4	14
ck Helling	6.75	0-0	0	1	2.2	2	0	2	7.27	0-0	0	4	8.2	11	6	7
aden Looper	9.82	1-0	0	4	3.2	6	0	4	5.14	2-0	1	8	7.0	8	3	5
ark Redman	15.43	0-1	0	1	2.1	5	2	2	6.50	0-1	0	4	18.0	25	9	10
ate Bump	—	0-0	0	0	0.0	0	0	0	6.00	0-0	0	2	3.0	3	0	3
ichael Tejera	—	0-0	0	0	0.0	0	0	0	6.75	0-1	0	2	1.1	2	0	1
OTALS	3.21	4-2	2	6	56.0	54	22	49	4.30	11-6	5	17	159.0	151	65	134

New York Yankees

WS vs. Florida / Overall Playoffs

Batting	Avg	AB	R	H	HR	RBI	BB	SO	Avg	AB	R	H	HR	RBI	BB	SO
nrique Wilson	.500	4	0	2	0	1	1	0	.273	11	0	3	0	1	1	1
oger Clemens	.500	2	0	1	0	0	0	0	.500	2	0	1	0	0	0	0
ernie Williams	.400	25	5	10	2	5	2	2	.318	66	13	21	2	10	8	7
erek Jeter	.346	26	5	9	0	2	1	7	.314	70	10	22	2	5	7	13
ick Johnson	.294	17	3	5	0	0	2	3	.214	56	9	12	1	5	7	9
arim Garcia	.286	14	1	4	0	0	0	3	.267	30	2	8	0	3	2	7
ideki Matsui	.261	23	1	6	1	4	3	2	.281	64	6	18	2	11	6	8
uben Sierra	.250	4	0	1	0	2	1	3	.250	8	1	2	1	3	2	3
ason Giambi	.235	17	2	4	1	1	4	3	.237	59	7	14	4	6	10	15
lfonso Soriano	.227	22	2	5	1	2	2	9	.225	71	4	16	1	9	3	26
van Rivera	.167	6	0	1	0	1	1	1	.250	20	2	5	0	1	2	2
orge Posada	.158	19	0	3	0	1	5	7	.222	63	6	14	1	7	8	17
aron Boone	.143	21	1	3	1	2	0	6	.170	53	4	9	2	4	1	15
ike Mussina	.000	3	0	0	0	0	0	0	.000	3	0	0	0	0	0	3
ohn Flaherty	.000	2	0	0	0	0	0	0	.000	2	0	0	0	0	0	0
avid Dellucci	.000	2	1	0	0	0	0	0	.200	5	3	1	0	0	0	1
OTALS	.261	207	21	54	6	21	22	49	.250	583	67	146	16	65	57	127

Pitching	ERA	W-L	Sv	Gm	IP	H	BB	SO	ERA	W-L	Sv	Gm	IP	H	BB	SO
eff Nelson	0.00	0-0	0	3	4.0	4	2	5	2.57	0-0	0	8	7.0	8	3	8
ariano Rivera	0.00	0-0	1	2	4.0	2	0	4	0.56	1-0	5	8	16.0	7	0	14
hris Hammond	0.00	0-0	0	1	2.0	2	0	0	0.00	0-0	0	1	2.0	2	0	0
ndy Pettitte	0.57	1-1	0	2	15.2	12	4	14	2.10	3-1	0	5	34.1	33	11	34
ike Mussina	1.29	1-0	0	1	7.0	7	1	9	3.38	1-3	0	5	29.1	30	8	32
avid Wells	3.38	0-1	0	2	8.0	6	2	1	2.31	2-1	0	5	23.1	19	4	11
oger Clemens	3.86	0-0	0	1	7.0	8	0	5	3.52	2-0	0	4	23.0	24	3	19
ose Contreras	5.68	0-1	0	4	6.1	5	5	10	5.73	0-2	0	8	11.0	11	7	17
eff Weaver	9.00	0-1	0	1	1.0	1	0	0	9.00	0-1	0	1	1.0	1	0	0
elix Heredia	—	0-0	0	0	0.0	0	0	0	1.93	0-0	0	6	4.2	1	4	4
abe White	—	0-0	0	0	0.0	0	0	0	2.70	0-0	0	3	3.1	5	0	2
OTALS	2.13	2-4	1	6	55.0	47	14	48	2.78	9-8	5	17	155.0	141	40	141

Score by Innings

	1	2	3	4	5	6	7	8	9	10	11	12		R	H	E
lorida	5	3	0	1	5	1	0	0	1	0	0	1	–	17	47	2
ew York	4	2	1	3	0	1	1	1	8	0	0	0	–	21	54	5

E: Florida—Cabrera, Lee; New York—Boone 3, Jeter, Wilson. 2B: Florida—Conine, Pierre 2, Gonzalez 2, Rodriguez 2, owell; New York—Wilson, Williams 2, Jeter 3, Johnson, Giambi, J. Rivera, Posada. 3B: New York—Sierra. SB: Florida—Castillo, Pierre; New York—Posada, Soriano. CS: Florida—Castillo, Gonzalez, Pierre; New York—Posada, Soriano. S: lorida—Beckett, Castillo, Gonzalez, Pavano, Penny; New York—Boone, Dellucci. SF: Florida—Encarnacion, Rodriguez; New ork—Boone, Williams. PB: New York—Posada. WP: Florida—Redman. HBP: by Wells (Pierre), by Redman (Giambi), by ooper (Jeter), by Beckett (Matsui). LOB: Florida—43; New York—47.
Umpires: Tim Welke, Randy Marsh, Larry Young, Gary Darling, Jeff Kellogg, Ed Rapuano.

COLLEGE

Final *Baseball America* Top 25

Final 2003 Division I Top 25, voted on by the editors of *Baseball America* and released after the NCAA CollegeWorld Seri
Given are final records (excluding ties) and winning percentage (including all postseason games); records in College Wo
Series and team eliminated by (DNP indicates team did not play in tourney); head coach (career years and four-year colle
record including 2003 postseason); preseason ranking and rank before start of CWS.

		Record	Pct	CWS Recap	Head Coach	Preseason Rank	Ra befo CV
1	Rice	58-12	.829	5-1	Wayne Graham (12 yrs: 536-224)	2	
2	Stanford	51-18	.739	5-3 (Rice)	Mark Marquess (27 yrs: 1144-551-5)	3	
3	CS-Fullerton	51-16	.761	2-2 (Stanford)	George Horton (7 yrs: 310-132-1)	13	
4	Texas	50-20	.714	2-2 (Rice)	Augie Garrido (35 yrs: 1430-686-8)	5	
5	Louisiana St.	45-22	.672	0-2 (S. Carolina)	Smoke Laval (9 yrs: 330-203)	9	
6	Florida State	54-13	.806		Mike Martin (24 yrs: 1293-429-4)	4	
7	Arizona St.	54-14	.794		Pat Murphy (19 yrs: 731-351-3)	8	
8	Miami-FL	45-17	.726	1-2 (Texas)	Jim Morris (22 yrs: 976-409-2)	NR	
9	Long Beach St	41-20	.672		Mike Weathers (4 yrs: 120-80)	16	
10	South Carolina	45-22	.672	1-2 (Stanford)	Ray Tanner (16 yrs: 714-308-3)	14	
11	Baylor	45-23	.662		Steve Smith (9 yrs: 343-203)	10	
12	North Carolina St.	45-18	.714		Elliott Avent (15 yrs: 486-382)	NR	
13	Nebraska	47-18	.723		Mike Anderson (1 yr: 47-18)	20	
14	Texas A&M	45-19	.703		Mark Johnson (19 yrs: 804-384-2)	NR	
15	Southern Mississippi	47-16	.746		Corky Palmer (6 yrs: 212-147)	NR	
16	SW Missouri St.	40-26	.606	0-2 (Miami)	Keith Guttin (21 yrs: 751-423)	NR	
17	Georgia Tech	44-18	.710		Danny Hall (16 yrs: 648-307)	1	
18	Auburn	42-21	.667		Steve Renfroe (3 yrs: 113-68)	21	
19	North Carolina	42-23	.646		Mike Fox (5 yrs: 203-105)	22	
20	UNLV	47-17	.734		Jim Schlossnagle (2 yrs: 77-47)	NR	
21	Ohio St.	44-21	.677		Bob Todd (20 yrs: 774-401)	NR	
22	Houston	37-30	.552		Rayner Noble (9 yrs: 331-224)	11	
23	Florida Atlantic	47-16	.746		Kevin Cooney (20 yrs: 704-412-9)	24	
24	Mississippi St.	42-20	.677		Ron Polk (30 yrs: 1199-578-2)	17	
25	Washington	42-18	.700		Ken Knutson (11 yrs: 389-253)	NR	

College World Series

CWS participants: CS-Fullerton (49-14); LSU (45-20);
Miami-FL (44-15); Rice (53-11); South Carolina (44-20); SW
Missouri St. (40-24); Stanford (46-15); Texas (48-18).

Bracket One

June 13—Stanford 8	South Carolina 0
June 13—CS-Fullerton 8	LSU 2
June 15—South Carolina 11	LSU 10 (out)
June 15—CS-Fullerton 6	Stanford 5
June 17—Stanford 13	South Carolina 6 (out)
June 18—Stanford 5	CS-Fullerton 2
June 19—Stanford 7	CS-Fullerton 5 (out)

Bracket Two

June 14—Rice 4	SW Missouri St. 2
June 14—Texas 13	Miami-FL 2
June 16—Miami-FL 7	SW Missouri St. 5 (out)
June 16—Rice 12	Texas 2
June 17—Texas 5	Miami-FL 1 (out)
June 18—Rice 5	Texas 4 (out)

Championship Series

June 21—Rice 4	Stanford 3
June 22—Stanford 8	Rice 3
June 23—Rice 14	Stanford 2 (out)

CWS Championship Game

Monday, June 23, at Rosenblatt Stadium in Omaha, Neb.

	1	2	3	4	5	6	7	8	9		R	H
Stanford	0	0	0	0	0	0	1	1	0	—	2	5
Rice	3	1	0	0	0	7	0	3	x	—	14	14

Win: RICE–Philip Humber (11-3). **Loss:** STAN–Mc
Romanczuk (12-2). **Save:** none. **Strikeouts:** RICE–Humb
4; STAN–Romanczuk, Matt Manship and Tim Cunningha
2B: RICE–Chris Kolkhorst 2, Paul Janish; STAN–Brian Hall
Ryan Garko. **HR:** none. **SB:** none.
Attendance: 18,484. **Time** 2:57.

Most Outstanding Player
John Hudgins, Stanford, P

IP	H	ER	BB	K	W-L	ER
24.0	17	5	6	15	3-0	1.8

All-Tournament Team

C–Ryan Garko, Stanford; **1B**–Curtis Thigpen, Texa
2B–Enrique Cruz, Rice; **3B**–Jonny Ash, Stanford; **SS**–Jus
Turner, CS-Fullerton; **OF**–Carlos Quentin, Stanford; Dan
Putnam, Stanford; Chris Kolkhorst, Rice; **DH**–P.J. Pillittere, C
Fullerton; **P**–John Hudgins, Stanford; Jeff Niemann, Rice.

Annual Awards

Chosen by *Baseball America*, *Collegiate Baseball*, National Collegiate Baseball Writers Association, American Baseball
Coaches Association and USA Baseball. The Rotary Smith award is chosen by college sports information directors.

Player of the Year

Rickie Weeks, Southern, 2B . . . . *BA*, *CB*, Dick Howser
(NCBWA), ABCA, Smith, Golden Spikes (USA Baseball)

Coach of the Year

Wayne Graham, Rice . . . . *CB*, ABCA
George Horton, CS-Fullerton . . . . *BA*

Consensus All-America Team

NCAA Division I players cited most frequently by the following four selectors: the American Baseball Coaches Assn. (ABCA), *Baseball America, Collegiate Baseball* and the National Collegiate Baseball Writers Assn. (NCBWA).

First Team

Pos		Cl	Avg	HR	RBI
C	Ryan Garko, Stanford	Sr.	.402	18	92
1B	Michael Aubrey, Tulane	Jr.	.420	18	79
2B	Rickie Weeks, Southern	Jr.	.479	17	73
SS	Dustin Pedroia, Arizona St.	So.	.404	4	52
3B	Jamie D'Antona, Wake Forest	Jr.	.360	21	82
OF	Brad Snyder, Ball St.	Jr.	.405	14	61
OF	Dustin Majewski, Texas	Sr.	.391	12	85
OF	David Murphy, Baylor	Jr.	.413	11	67
UT	Scott Beerer, Texas A&M	Jr.	.335	11	69

Pos		Cl	W-L	Sv	ERA
P	Jeff Niemann, Rice	So.	17-0	1	1.70
P	Jered Weaver, Long Beach St.	So.	14-4	0	1.96
P	David Marchbanks, S. Carol.	Jr.	15-3	0	2.73
P	Tim Stauffer, Richmond	Jr.	9-5	0	1.97
P	Scott Lewis, Ohio St.	So.	9-1	0	1.61
P	Huston Street, Texas	So.	8-1	15	1.33

Second Team

Pos		Cl	Avg	HR	RBI
C	Tony Richie, Florida St.	Jr.	.366	12	78
1B	Billy Becher, N. Mexico St.	Sr.	.420	32	118
2B	Luke Appert, Minnesota	Sr.	.373	4	45
SS	Aaron Hill, LSU	Jr.	.358	9	67
3B	Brian Snyder, Stetson	Jr.	.396	11	55
OF	Clint King, Southern Miss.	So.	.394	23	77
OF	Josh Anderson, Eastern Ky.	Jr.	.447	6	53
OF	Jeremy Cleveland, N. Carol.	Jr.	.410	19	65
UT	Mitch Maier, Toledo	Jr.	.448	9	61

Pos		Cl	W-L	Sv	ERA
P	Vern Sterry, N.C. St.	Jr.	11-0	0	3.25
P	Wade Townsend, Rice	So.	11-2	5	2.20
P	Abe Alvarez, Long Beach St.	Jr.	11-2	0	2.35
P	Justin Orenduff, VCU	So.	9-3	0	2.27
P	Trent Peterson, Florida St.	Jr.	10-1	0	2.70
P	Ryan Wagner, Houston	So.	6-5	15	1.93

NCAA Division I Leaders

Batting

Average

(At least 75 AB & 2.5/Gm)	Cl	Gm	AB	H	Avg
Rickie Weeks, Southern	Jr.	51	163	78	.479
Mitch Maier, Toledo	Jr.	51	194	87	.448
Josh Anderson, Eastern Ky.	Jr.	53	237	106	.447
Kelly Hunt, Bowling Green	Sr.	45	171	75	.439
Adrian Brown, Miss. Valley St.	Sr.	50	167	71	.425
Tim D'Aquila, Central Conn. St.	Jr.	50	186	79	.425
Michael Brown, Wm. & Mary	Sr.	51	201	85	.423
Ryan Roberts, Texas-Arlington	Sr.	62	230	97	.422
Jaime Landin, Tex. A&M Corp Ch.	So.	50	202	85	.421
Keith Brachold, Marist	So.	54	214	90	.421
John Gragg, Bethune-Cookman	Sr.	57	214	90	.421

Runs Batted In (per game)

(At least 50 RBI)	Cl	Gm	RBI	Avg
Billy Becher, New Mexico St.	Jr.	61	118	1.93
Neil Sellers, Eastern Ky.	Sr.	53	85	1.60
Chris Alexander, New Mexico	Sr.	58	93	1.60
Jamie D'Antona, Wake Forest	Jr.	53	82	1.55
Humberto Aguilar, Tex. A&M Corp Ch.	Sr.	48	74	1.54
Jeff Larish, Arizona St.	So.	65	95	1.46
Kelly Hunt, Bowling Green	Sr.	45	61	1.36
Ryan Garko, Stanford	Sr.	69	92	1.33
Beau Hearod, Alabama	Sr.	62	82	1.32
Kevin Vital, Southern	Sr.	50	66	1.32

Home Runs (per game)

(At least 15 HR)	Cl	Gm	HR	Avg
Billy Becher, New Mexico St.	Jr.	61	32	0.52
Chris Alexander, New Mexico	Sr.	58	25	0.43
Humberto Aguilar, Tex. A&M Corp Ch.	Sr.	48	20	0.42
Jamie D'Antona, Wake Forest	Jr.	53	21	0.40
Michael Brown, Wm. & Mary	Sr.	51	20	0.39
Chad Boudon, Washington	Jr.	57	22	0.39
Jeff Clement, USC	Fr.	56	21	0.38
Jeff Cook, Alabama St.	Sr.	63	23	0.37
Clint King, Southern Miss.	So.	63	23	0.37
Matt Hopper, Nebraska	Sr.	62	22	0.35

Stolen Bases (per game)

(At least 25)	Cl	Gm	SB	SBA	Avg
Josh Anderson, Eastern Ky.	Jr.	53	57	65	1.08
Sebastien Boucher, Beth.-Cook.	So.	56	48	52	0.86
Jonny Kaplan, Tulane	Sr.	62	48	56	0.77
Carl Loadenthal, Rider	Sr.	48	35	37	0.73
Ryan McGraw, Coastal Carol.	Jr.	63	45	57	0.71
Graig Badger, Rutgers	Jr.	59	41	48	0.69
Kenji Williams, Jackson St.	So.	39	27	27	0.69
Ryan Hubbard, Wake Forest	Sr.	51	35	40	0.69
Reggie Willits, Oklahoma	Sr.	54	37	44	0.69
Danny Figueroa, Miami-FL	So.	63	41	47	0.65

Pitching

Earned Run Avg.

(At least 50 inn.)	Cl	Gm	IP	ERA
Tom Mastny, Furman	Sr.	16	124.0	1.09
Cla Meredith, VCU	So.	29	60.1	1.19
Carlos Fernandez, Louisville	Sr.	32	59.1	1.21
Huston Street, Texas	So.	40	74.2	1.33
Aaron Sims, Alabama A&M	Sr.	8	51.0	1.41
Thomas Pauly, Princeton	Jr.	19	55.1	1.46
Jamie Merchant, Vermont	Sr.	11	75.0	1.56
Chuck Betchel, Marist	Sr.	13	85.0	1.59
Scott Lewis, Ohio St.	So.	12	83.2	1.61
Jeff Niemann, Rice	So.	22	137.1	1.70

Wins

	Cl	Gm	IP	W-L
Jeff Niemann, Rice	So.	22	137.1	17-0
David Marchbanks, S. Carolina	Jr.	21	135.1	15-3
Tim Alvarez, SE Missouri St.	Sr.	21	108.1	14-3
John Hudgins, Stanford	Jr.	22	165.1	14-3
Jered Weaver, Long Beach St.	So.	19	133.1	14-4
Randy Beam, Florida Atlantic	Jr.	17	101.2	13-2
Matt Lynch, Florida St.	Sr.	19	112.1	13-4
Brad Ziegler, SW Missouri St.	Sr.	17	106.2	12-1
Mark Romanczuk, Stanford	Fr.	23	112.1	12-2
Zac Cline, West Virginia	So.	16	125.2	12-3
Michael Rogers, N.C. State	Fr.	17	125.0	12-3

Strikeouts (per 9 inn.)

(At least 50 inn.)	Cl	IP	SO	Avg
Ryan Wagner, Houston	So.	79.1	148	16.8
Scott Lewis, Ohio St.	So.	83.2	127	13.7
Chris Schutt, Cornell	Jr.	62.0	89	12.9
Steve Schmoll, Maryland	Sr.	87.2	124	12.7
Thomas Diamond, New Orleans	So.	69.0	96	12.5
Casey Abrams, Wright St.	Jr.	114.1	158	12.4
Wade Townsend, Rice	So.	118.2	164	12.4
Thomas Pauly, Princeton	Jr.	55.1	74	12.0
Brad Cherry, Ark.-Little Rock	Jr.	82.1	108	11.8
Tim Stuaffer, Richmond	Jr.	114.0	146	11.5

Saves

	Cl	IP	ERA	Save
Steven Register, Auburn	So.	52.0	2.94	1
Ryan Wagner, Houston	So.	79.1	1.93	1
Huston Street, Texas	So.	74.2	1.33	1
Mike Dennison, Wichita St.	Sr.	40.2	3.10	1
Mark Badgley, Northern Illinois	Fr.	34.0	5.29	1
Matt Dalton, Virginia Tech	Sr.	35.2	0.76	1
Matt Davis, Ohio St.	So.	38.2	6.05	1
Joey Devine, N.C. State	Fr.	65.2	2.19	1
Seven tied with 13 each.				

Other College World Series
Participants' final records in parentheses.

NCAA Div. II
at Montgomery, Ala. (May 24-31)

Participants: Abilene Christian, Texas (45-20); Central Missouri State (51-7); Franklin Pierce, N.H. (32-17); Grand Valley St., Mich. (41-14-1); Kennesaw St., Geo. (40-18); Slippery Rock, Penn. (48-13); Tampa, Fla. (45-18); UC-Davis (36-24).

Championship: Central Missouri St. def. Tampa, 11-4.

NAIA
at Lewiston, Idaho (May 23-30)

Participants: Bellevue, Neb. (47-22); Biola, Calif. (41-17); Embry-Riddle, Fla. (48-16); Indiana Tech (42-20); Lewis-Clark St., Idaho (48-13); LSU-Shreveport (51-24); Ohio Dominican (40-18); Oklahoma City (63-8-1); Olivet Nazarene, Ill. (45-10); Spalding, Ky. (52-20).

Championship: Lewis-Clark def. Oklahoma City, 7-5.

NCAA Div. III
at Appleton, Wis. (May 23-27)

Participants: Anderson, Ind. (35-16); Chapman, Calif. (39-12); Christopher Newport, Va. (35-9); DeSales, Penn. (30-14); Eastern Connecticut St. (42-9); Emory, Geo. (37-15); Trinity, Conn. (27-12); Wisconsin-Oshkosh (37-7).

Championship: Chapman def. Christopher Newport, 15-7

NJCAA Div. I
at Grand Junction, Colo. (May 24-31)

Participants: Connors St., Okla. (46-17); Grayson County JC, Texas (55-15); Indian Hills CC, Iowa (38-23); Meridian CC, Miss. (39-19); Neosho County CC, Kan. (42-15); San Jacinto-North, Texas (52-13); Seminole CC, Fla. (42-21); CC of Southern Nevada (55-10); Spartanburg Methodist, S.C. (49-16); Walters St. CC, Tenn. (47-13).

Championship: CC of Southern Nevada def. San Jacinto North, 4-1.

2003 MLB First-Year Player Draft

First round selections at the 39th First-Year Player Draft held June 3-4, 2003 in New York. Clubs select in reverse order of their standing from the preceding season. The worst National League team selects first in even years and the worst American League team goes first in odd years. Leagues then alternate picks throughout the rounds. Note that picks 31-37 are supplemental compensatory selections.

First Round

No		Pos
1	Tampa Bay . Delmon Young, Camarillo (Calif.) HS	OF
2	Milwaukee . . . . Rickie Weeks, Southern U	2B
3	Detroit . . . . Kyle Sleeth, Wake Forest	RHP
4	San Diego . . . . Tim Stauffer, Richmond	RHP
5	Kansas City . . . Chris Lubanski, Kennedy-Kenrick HS, Schwenksville, Penn.	OF
6	Chicago-NL . . . . . Ryan Harvey, Dunedin HS Palm Harbor, Fla.	OF
7	Baltimore . . . . . Nick Markakis, Young Harris JC	LHP
8	Pittsburgh . . . . Paul Maholm, Mississippi St.	LHP
9	Texas . . . . . John Danks, Round Rock (Texas) HS	LHP
10	Colorado . . . . . . Ian Stewart, La Quinta HS Garden Grove, Calif.	3B
11	Cleveland . . . . Michael Aubrey, Tulane	1B
12	NY Mets . . . Lastings Milledge, Lakewood Ranch HS, Palmetto, Fla.	OF
13	Toronto . . . . Aaron Hill, LSU	SS
14	Cincinnati . . . . Ryan Wagner, Houston	RHP
15	Chicago-AL . . . . Brian Anderson, Arizona	OF
16	Florida . . . . . Jeff Allison, Veterans Memorial HS Peabody, Mass.	RHP
17	Boston . . . . David Murphy, Baylor	OF
18	**a**-Cleveland . . . . Brad Snyder, Ball St.	OF
19	**b**-Arizona . . . . . . Connor Jackson, California	3B
20	Montreal . . . . Chad Cordero, CS-Fullerton	RHP
21	Minnesota . . Matthew Moses, Mills Godwin HS Richmond, Va.	3B
22	**c**-San Francisco . . . . . . David Aardsma, Rice	RHP
23	Anaheim . . . . Richard Wood, Horizon HS Scottsdale, Ariz.	SS
24	Los Angeles . Chad Billingsley, Defiance (Ohio) HS	RHP
25	Oakland . . . . Bradley Sullivan, Houston	RHP
26	**d**-Oakland . . . . Brian Snyder, Stetson	3B
27	NY Yankees . . . . . Eric Duncan, Seton Hall Prep Florham Park, N.J.	3B
28	St. Louis . . . . Daric Barton, Marina HS Huntington Beach, Calif.	C
29	Arizona . . . . Carlos Quentin, Stanford	OF
30	**e**-Kansas City . . . . Mitch Maier, Toledo	C
31	**f**-Cleveland . Adam Miller, McKinney (Texas) HS	RHP
32	**g**-Boston . . . . . Matthew Murton, Georgia Tech	OF
33	**h**-Oakland . . . . . . Omar Quintanilla, Texas	SS
34	**i**-San Francisco Roger Whitaker, Lufkin (Texas) HS	RHP
35	**j**-Atlanta . . . . Luis Atilano Gabriela, Gabriela Mistral HS, San Juan, P.R.	RHP
36	**k**-Atlanta . . . Jarrod Saltalamacchia, Royal Palm Beach HS, West Palm Beach, Fla.	C
37	**l**-Seattle . . . . . . Adam Jones, Samuel Morse HS San Diego, Calif.	SS

Acquired picks: a-from Philadelphia for signing Jim Thome; **b**-from Seattle for signing Greg Colbrunn; **c**-from Houston for signing Jeff Kent; **d**-San Francisco for signing Ray Durham; **e**-from Atlanta for signing Paul Byrd; **f**-for Jim Thome; **g**-for Cliff Floyd; **h**-for Ray Durham; **i**-for Jeff Kent; **j**-for Tom Glavine; **k**-for Mike Remlinger; **l**-for John Mayberry.

1876-2003
Through the Years

The World Series

The World Series began in 1903 when Pittsburgh of the older National League (founded in 1876) invited Boston of the American League (founded in 1901) to play a best-of-9 game series to determine which of the two league champions was the best. Boston was the surprise winner, 5 games to 3. The 1904 NL champion New York Giants refused to play Boston the following year, so there was no Series. Giants' owner John T. Brush and his manager John McGraw both despised AL president Ban Johnson and considered the junior circuit to be a minor league. By the following year, however, Brush and Johnson had smoothed out their differences and the Giants agreed to play Philadelphia in a best-of-7 game series. Since then the World Series has been a best-of-7 format, except from 1919-21 when it returned to best-of-9.

After surviving two world wars and an earthquake in 1989, the World Series was cancelled for only the second time in 1994 due to the players' strike.

In the chart below, the National League teams are listed in CAPITAL letters. Also, each World Series champion's wins and losses are noted in parentheses after the Series score in games.

Multiple champions: New York Yankees (26); Philadelphia-Oakland A's and St. Louis Cardinals (9); Brooklyn-Los Angeles Dodgers (6); Boston Red Sox, Cincinnati Reds, New York-San Francisco Giants and Pittsburgh Pirates (5); Detroit Tigers (4); Baltimore Orioles, Boston-Milwaukee-Atlanta Braves and Washington Senators-Minnesota Twins (3); Chicago Cubs, Chicago White Sox, Cleveland Indians, Florida Marlins, New York Mets and Toronto Blue Jays (2).

Year	Winner	Manager	Series	Loser	Manager
1903	Boston Red Sox	Jimmy Collins	5-3 (LWLLWWWW)	PITTSBURGH	Fred Clarke
1904	Not held				
1905	NY GIANTS	John McGraw	4-1 (WLWWW)	Philadelphia A's	Connie Mack
1906	Chicago White Sox	Fielder Jones	4-2 (WLWLWW)	CHICAGO CUBS	Frank Chance
1907	CHICAGO CUBS	Frank Chance	4-0-1 (TWWWW)	Detroit	Hughie Jennings
1908	CHICAGO CUBS	Frank Chance	4-1 (WWLWW)	Detroit	Hughie Jennings
1909	PITTSBURGH	Fred Clarke	4-3 (WLWLWLW)	Detroit	Hughie Jennings
1910	Philadelphia A's	Connie Mack	4-1 (WWWLW)	CHICAGO CUBS	Frank Chance
1911	Philadelphia A's	Connie Mack	4-2 (LWWWLW)	NY GIANTS	John McGraw
1912	Boston Red Sox	Jake Stahl	4-3-1 (WTLWWLLW)	NY GIANTS	John McGraw
1913	Philadelphia A's	Connie Mack	4-1 (WLWWW)	NY GIANTS	John McGraw
1914	BOSTON BRAVES	George Stallings	4-0	Philadelphia A's	Connie Mack
1915	Boston Red Sox	Bill Carrigan	4-1 (LWWWW)	PHILA. PHILLIES	Pat Moran
1916	Boston Red Sox	Bill Carrigan	4-1 (WWWLW)	BROOKLYN	Wilbert Robinson
1917	Chicago White Sox	Pants Rowland	4-2 (WWLLWW)	NY GIANTS	John McGraw
1918	Boston Red Sox	Ed Barrow	4-2 (WLWWLW)	CHICAGO CUBS	Fred Mitchell
1919	CINCINNATI	Pat Moran	5-3 (WWLWWLLW)	Chicago White Sox	Kid Gleason
1920	Cleveland	Tris Speaker	5-2 (WLLWWWW)	BROOKLYN	Wilbert Robinson
1921	NY GIANTS	John McGraw	5-3 (LLWLWWWW)	NY Yankees	Miller Huggins
1922	NY GIANTS	John McGraw	4-0-1 (WTWWW)	NY Yankees	Miller Huggins
1923	NY Yankees	Miller Huggins	4-2 (LWLWWW)	NY GIANTS	John McGraw
1924	Washington	Bucky Harris	4-3 (LWLWLWW)	NY GIANTS	John McGraw
1925	PITTSBURGH	Bill McKechnie	4-3 (LWLLWWW)	Washington	Bucky Harris
1926	ST.L. CARDINALS	Rogers Hornsby	4-3 (LWWLLWW)	NY Yankees	Miller Huggins
1927	NY Yankees	Miller Huggins	4-0	PITTSBURGH	Donie Bush
1928	NY Yankees	Miller Huggins	4-0	ST.L. CARDINALS	Bill McKechnie
1929	Philadelphia A's	Connie Mack	4-1 (WWWLW)	CHICAGO CUBS	Joe McCarthy
1930	Philadelphia A's	Connie Mack	4-2 (WWLLWW)	ST.L. CARDINALS	Gabby Street
1931	ST.L. CARDINALS	Gabby Street	4-3 (LWWLWLW)	Philadelphia A's	Connie Mack
1932	NY Yankees	Joe McCarthy	4-0	CHICAGO CUBS	Charlie Grimm
1933	NY GIANTS	Bill Terry	4-1 (WWLWW)	Washington	Joe Cronin
1934	ST.L. CARDINALS	Frankie Frisch	4-3 (WLWLLWW)	Detroit	Mickey Cochrane
1935	Detroit	Mickey Cochrane	4-2 (LWWWLW)	CHICAGO CUBS	Charlie Grimm
1936	NY Yankees	Joe McCarthy	4-2 (LWWWLW)	NY GIANTS	Bill Terry
1937	NY Yankees	Joe McCarthy	4-1 (WWWLW)	NY GIANTS	Bill Terry
1938	NY Yankees	Joe McCarthy	4-0	CHICAGO CUBS	Gabby Hartnett
1939	NY Yankees	Joe McCarthy	4-0	CINCINNATI	Bill McKechnie
1940	CINCINNATI	Bill McKechnie	4-3 (LWLWLWW)	Detroit	Del Baker
1941	NY Yankees	Joe McCarthy	4-1(WLWWW)	BKLN. DODGERS	Leo Durocher
1942	ST.L. CARDINALS	Billy Southworth	4-1 (LWWWW)	NY Yankees	Joe McCarthy
1943	NY Yankees	Joe McCarthy	4-1 (WLWWW)	ST.L. CARDINALS	Billy Southworth
1944	ST.L. CARDINALS	Billy Southworth	4-2 (LWLWWW)	St. Louis Browns	Luke Sewell
1945	Detroit	Steve O'Neill	4-3 (LWLLWWW)	CHICAGO CUBS	Charlie Grimm
1946	ST.L. CARDINALS	Eddie Dyer	4-3 (LWLWLWW)	Boston Red Sox	Joe Cronin
1947	NY Yankees	Bucky Harris	4-3 (WWLLWLW)	BKLN. DODGERS	Burt Shotton

Year	Winner	Manager	Series	Loser	Manager
1948	Cleveland	Lou Boudreau	4-2 (LWWWLW)	BOSTON BRAVES	Billy Southworth
1949	NY Yankees	Casey Stengel	4-1 (WLWWW)	BKLN. DODGERS	Burt Shotton
1950	NY Yankees	Casey Stengel	4-0	PHILA. PHILLIES	Eddie Sawyer
1951	NY Yankees	Casey Stengel	4-2 (LWLWWW)	NY GIANTS	Leo Durocher
1952	NY Yankees	Casey Stengel	4-3 (LWWLWW)	BKLN. DODGERS	Charlie Dressen
1953	NY Yankees	Casey Stengel	4-2 (WWLLWW)	BKLN. DODGERS	Charlie Dressen
1954	NY GIANTS	Leo Durocher	4-0	Cleveland	Al Lopez
1955	BKLN. DODGERS	Walter Alston	4-3 (LLWWWLW)	NY Yankees	Casey Stengel
1956	NY Yankees	Casey Stengel	4-3 (LLWWWLW)	BKLN. DODGERS	Walter Alston
1957	MILW. BRAVES	Fred Haney	4-3 (LWLWWLW)	NY Yankees	Casey Stengel
1958	NY Yankees	Casey Stengel	4-3 (LLWWWWW)	MILW. BRAVES	Fred Haney
1959	LA DODGERS	Walter Alston	4-2 (LWWWLW)	Chicago White Sox	Al Lopez
1960	PITTSBURGH	Danny Murtaugh	4-3 (WLLWWLW)	NY Yankees	Casey Stengel
1961	NY Yankees	Ralph Houk	4-1 (WLWWW)	CINCINNATI	Fred Hutchinson
1962	NY Yankees	Ralph Houk	4-3 (WLWLWLW)	SF GIANTS	Alvin Dark
1963	LA DODGERS	Walter Alston	4-0	NY Yankees	Ralph Houk
1964	ST.L. CARDINALS	Johnny Keane	4-3 (WLWWLW)	NY Yankees	Yogi Berra
1965	LA DODGERS	Walter Alston	4-3 (LLWWWLW)	Minnesota	Sam Mele
1966	Baltimore	Hank Bauer	4-0	LA DODGERS	Walter Alston
1967	ST.L. CARDINALS	Red Schoendienst	4-3 (WLWWLLW)	Boston Red Sox	Dick Williams
1968	Detroit	Mayo Smith	4-3 (LWLLWWW)	ST.L. CARDINALS	Red Schoendienst
1969	NY METS	Gil Hodges	4-1 (LWWWW)	Baltimore	Earl Weaver
1970	Baltimore	Earl Weaver	4-1 (WWWLW)	CINCINNATI	Sparky Anderson
1971	PITTSBURGH	Danny Murtaugh	4-3 (LLWWWLW)	Baltimore	Earl Weaver
1972	Oakland A's	Dick Williams	4-3 (WWLWLLW)	CINCINNATI	Sparky Anderson
1973	Oakland A's	Dick Williams	4-3 (WLWLLWW)	NY METS	Yogi Berra
1974	Oakland A's	Alvin Dark	4-1 (WLWWW)	LA DODGERS	Walter Alston
1975	CINCINNATI	Sparky Anderson	4-3 (LWWLWLW)	Boston Red Sox	Darrell Johnson
1976	CINCINNATI	Sparky Anderson	4-0	NY Yankees	Billy Martin
1977	NY Yankees	Billy Martin	4-2 (WLWWLW)	LA DODGERS	Tommy Lasorda
1978	NY Yankees	Bob Lemon	4-2 (LLWWWW)	LA DODGERS	Tommy Lasorda
1979	PITTSBURGH	Chuck Tanner	4-3 (LWLLWWW)	Baltimore	Earl Weaver
1980	PHILA. PHILLIES	Dallas Green	4-2 (WWLLWW)	Kansas City	Jim Frey
1981	LA DODGERS	Tommy Lasorda	4-2 (LLWWWW)	NY Yankees	Bob Lemon
1982	ST.L. CARDINALS	Whitey Herzog	4-3 (LWWWLW)	Milwaukee Brewers	Harvey Kuenn
1983	Baltimore	Joe Altobelli	4-1 (LWWWW)	PHILA. PHILLIES	Paul Owens
1984	Detroit	Sparky Anderson	4-1 (WWWLW)	SAN DIEGO	Dick Williams
1985	Kansas City	Dick Howser	4-3 (LLWWLWW)	ST.L. CARDINALS	Whitey Herzog
1986	NY METS	Davey Johnson	4-3 (LLWWLWW)	Boston Red Sox	John McNamara
1987	Minnesota	Tom Kelly	4-3 (WWLLLWW)	ST.L. CARDINALS	Whitey Herzog
1988	LA DODGERS	Tommy Lasorda	4-1 (WWLWW)	Oakland A's	Tony La Russa
1989	Oakland A's	Tony La Russa	4-0	SF GIANTS	Roger Craig
1990	CINCINNATI	Lou Piniella	4-0	Oakland A's	Tony La Russa
1991	Minnesota	Tom Kelly	4-3 (WWLLLWW)	ATLANTA BRAVES	Bobby Cox
1992	Toronto	Cito Gaston	4-2 (LWWWLW)	ATLANTA BRAVES	Bobby Cox
1993	Toronto	Cito Gaston	4-2 (WLWWLW)	PHILA. PHILLIES	Jim Fregosi
1994	Not held				
1995	ATLANTA BRAVES	Bobby Cox	4-2 (WWLWLW)	Cleveland	Mike Hargrove
1996	NY Yankees	Joe Torre	4-2 (LLWWWW)	ATLANTA BRAVES	Bobby Cox
1997	FLORIDA	Jim Leyland	4-3 (WLWLWLW)	Cleveland	Mike Hargrove
1998	NY Yankees	Joe Torre	4-0	SAN DIEGO	Bruce Bochy
1999	NY Yankees	Joe Torre	4-0	ATLANTA BRAVES	Bobby Cox
2000	NY Yankees	Joe Torre	4-1 (WWLWW)	NY METS	Bobby Valentine
2001	ARIZONA	Bob Brenly	4-3 (WWLLLWW)	NY Yankees	Joe Torre
2002	Anaheim	Mike Scioscia	4-3 (LWWLLWW)	SF GIANTS	Dusty Baker
2003	FLORIDA	Jack McKeon	4-2 (WLLWWW)	NY Yankees	Joe Torre

Most Valuable Players

Currently selected by media panel and World Series official scorers. Presented by *Sport* magazine from 1955-88 and by Major League Baseball since 1989. Winner who did not play for World Series champions is in **bold** type.

Multiple winners: Bob Gibson, Reggie Jackson and Sandy Koufax (2).

Year	Year	Year
1955 Johnny Podres, Bklyn, P	1965 Sandy Koufax, LA, P	1975 Pete Rose, Cin., 3B
1956 Don Larsen, NY, P	1966 Frank Robinson, Bal., OF	1976 Johnny Bench, Cin., C
1957 Lew Burdette, Mil., P	1967 Bob Gibson, St.L., P	1977 Reggie Jackson, NY, OF
1958 Bob Turley, NY, P	1968 Mickey Lolich, Det., P	1978 Bucky Dent, NY, SS
1959 Larry Sherry, LA, P	1969 Donn Clendenon, NY, 1B	1979 Willie Stargell, Pit., 1B
1960 **Bobby Richardson**, NY, 2B	1970 Brooks Robinson, Bal., 3B	1980 Mike Schmidt, Phi., 3B
1961 Whitey Ford, NY, P	1971 Roberto Clemente, Pit., OF	1981 Pedro Guerrero, LA, OF;
1962 Ralph Terry, NY, P	1972 Gene Tenace, Oak., C	Ron Cey, LA, 3B;
1963 Sandy Koufax, LA, P	1973 Reggie Jackson, Oak., OF	& Steve Yeager, LA, C
1964 Bob Gibson, St.L., P	1974 Rollie Fingers, Oak., P	1982 Darrell Porter, St.L., C

Year	Year	Year
1983 Rick Dempsey, Bal., C	1991 Jack Morris, Min., P	1999 Mariano Rivera, NY, P
1984 Alan Trammell, Det., SS	1992 Pat Borders, Tor., C	2000 Derek Jeter, NY, SS
1985 Bret Saberhagen, KC, P	1993 Paul Molitor, Tor., DH/1B/3B	2001 Curt Schilling, Ari., P
1986 Ray Knight, NY, 3B	1994 Series not held.	& Randy Johnson, Ari., P
1987 Frank Viola, Min., P	1995 Tom Glavine, Atl., P	2002 Troy Glaus, Ana., 3B
1988 Orel Hershiser, LA, P	1996 John Wetteland, NY, P	2003 Josh Beckett, Fla., P
1989 Dave Stewart, Oak., P	1997 Livan Hernandez, Fla., P	
1990 Jose Rijo, Cin., P	1998 Scott Brosius, NY, 3B	

All-Time World Series Leaders
CAREER
World Series leaders through 2003. Years listed indicate number of World Series appearances.

Hitting

Games

	Yrs	Gm
Yogi Berra, NY Yankees	14	75
Mickey Mantle, NY Yankees	12	65
Elston Howard, NY Yankees—Boston	10	54
Hank Bauer, NY Yankees	9	53
Gil McDougald, NY Yankees	8	53

At Bats

	Yrs	AB
Yogi Berra, NY Yankees	14	259
Mickey Mantle, NY Yankees	12	230
Joe DiMaggio, NY Yankees	10	199
Frankie Frisch, NY Giants-St.L. Cards	8	197
Gil McDougald, NY Yankees	8	190

Batting Avg. (minimum 50 AB)

	AB	H	Avg
Pepper Martin, St.L. Cards	55	23	.418
Paul Molitor, Mil. Brewers-Tor. Blue Jays	55	23	.418
Lou Brock, St. Louis	87	34	.391
Marquis Grissom, Atl-Cle	77	30	.390
Thurman Munson, NY Yankees	67	25	.373
George Brett, Kansas City	51	19	.373
Hank Aaron, Milw. Braves	55	20	.364

Hits

	AB	H	Avg
Yogi Berra, NY Yankees	259	71	.274
Mickey Mantle, NY Yankees	230	59	.257
Frankie Frisch, NYG-St.L. Cards	197	58	.294
Joe DiMaggio, NY Yankees	199	54	.271
Hank Bauer, NY Yankees	188	46	.245
Pee Wee Reese, Brooklyn	169	46	.272

Runs

	Gm	R
Mickey Mantle, NY Yankees	65	42
Yogi Berra, NY Yankees	75	41
Babe Ruth, Boston Red Sox-NY Yankees	41	37
Lou Gehrig, NY Yankees	34	30
Joe DiMaggio, NY Yankees	51	27
Derek Jeter, NY Yankees	32	27

Home Runs

	AB	HR
Mickey Mantle, NY Yankees	230	18
Babe Ruth, Boston Red Sox-NY Yankees	129	15
Yogi Berra, NY Yankees	259	12
Duke Snider, Brooklyn-LA	133	11
Lou Gehrig, NY Yankees	119	10
Reggie Jackson, Oakland-NY Yankees	98	10

Runs Batted In

	Gm	RBI
Mickey Mantle, NY Yankees	65	40
Yogi Berra, NY Yankees	75	39
Lou Gehrig, NY Yankees	34	35
Babe Ruth, Boston Red Sox-NY Yankees	41	33
Joe DiMaggio, NY Yankees	51	30

World Series Appearances
In the 99 years that the World Series has been contested, American League teams have won 58 championships while National League teams have won 41.

The following teams are ranked by number of appearances through the 2003 World Series; (*) indicates AL teams.

	App	W	L	Pct.	Last Series	Last Title
NY Yankees*	39	26	13	.667	2003	2000
Bklyn/LA Dodgers	18	6	12	.333	1988	1988
NY/SF Giants	17	5	12	.294	2002	1954
St.L. Cardinals	15	9	6	.600	1987	1982
Phi/KC/Oak.A's*	14	9	5	.643	1990	1989
Chicago Cubs	10	2	8	.200	1945	1908
Boston Red Sox*	9	5	4	.556	1986	1918
Cincinnati Reds	9	5	4	.556	1990	1990
Detroit Tigers*	9	4	5	.444	1984	1984
Bos/Mil/Atl.Braves	9	3	6	.333	1999	1995
Pittsburgh Pirates	7	5	2	.714	1979	1979
St.L/Bal.Orioles*	7	3	4	.429	1983	1983
Wash/Min.Twins*	6	3	3	.500	1991	1991
Cle. Indians*	5	2	3	.400	1997	1948
Phi. Phillies	5	1	4	.200	1993	1980
Chi. White Sox*	4	2	2	.500	1959	1917
NY Mets	4	2	2	.500	2000	1986
Fla. Marlins	2	2	0	1.000	2003	2003
Tor. Blue Jays*	2	2	0	1.000	1993	1993
KC Royals*	2	1	1	.500	1985	1985
SD Padres	2	0	2	.000	1998	—
Anaheim Angels*	1	1	0	1.000	2002	2002
Ari. Diamondbacks	1	1	0	1.000	2001	2001
Sea/Mil.Brewers*	1	0	1	.000	1982	—

Stolen Bases

	Gm	SB
Lou Brock, St. Louis	21	14
Eddie Collins, Phi. A's-Chisox	34	14
Frank Chance, Chi. Cubs	20	10
Davey Lopes, Los Angeles	23	10
Phil Rizzuto, NY Yankees	52	10

Total Bases

	Gm	TB
Mickey Mantle, NY Yankees	65	123
Yogi Berra, NY Yankees	75	117
Babe Ruth, Boston Red Sox-NY Yankees	41	96
Lou Gehrig, NY Yankees	34	87
Joe DiMaggio, NY Yankees	51	84

Slugging Pct. (minimum 50 AB)

	AB	Pct
Reggie Jackson, Oakland-NY Yankees	98	.755
Babe Ruth, Boston Red Sox-NY Yankees	129	.744
Lou Gehrig, NY Yankees	119	.731
Al Simmons, Phi. A's-Cincinnati	73	.658
Lou Brock, St. Louis	87	.655

Pitching

Games

	Yrs	Gm
Whitey Ford, NY Yankees	11	22
Mike Stanton, Atlanta-NY Yankees	6	20
Mariano Rivera, NY Yankees	6	20
Rollie Fingers, Oakland	3	16
Allie Reynolds, NY Yankees	6	15
Bob Turley, NY Yankees	5	15
Clay Carroll, Cincinnati	3	14

Wins

	Gm	W-L
Whitey Ford, NY Yankees	22	10-8
Bob Gibson, St. Louis	9	7-2
Allie Reynolds, NY Yankees	15	7-2
Red Ruffing, NY Yankees	10	7-2
Lefty Gomez, NY Yankees	7	6-0
Chief Bender, Philadelphia A's	10	6-4
Waite Hoyt, NY Yankees-Phi. A's	12	6-4

ERA (minimum 25 IP)

	Gm	IP	ERA
Jack Billingham, Cincinnati	7	25.1	0.36
Harry Brecheen, St. Louis	7	32.2	0.83
Babe Ruth, Boston Red Sox	3	31.0	0.87
Sherry Smith, Brooklyn	3	30.1	0.89
Sandy Koufax, Los Angeles	8	57.0	0.95

Saves

	Gm	IP	Sv
Mariano Rivera, NY Yankees	20	31.0	9
Rollie Fingers, Oakland	16	33.1	6
Allie Reynolds, NY Yankees	15	77.1	4
Johnny Murphy, NY Yankees	8	16.1	4
John Wetteland, NY Yankees	5	4.1	4
Robb Nen, Florida-SF	7	7.2	4
Nine pitchers tied with 3 each.			

Shutouts

	GS	CG	ShO
Christy Mathewson, NY Giants	11	10	4
Three Finger Brown, Chi. Cubs	7	5	3
Whitey Ford, NY Yankees	22	7	3
Seven pitchers tied with 2 each.			

Innings Pitched

	Gm	IP
Whitey Ford, NY Yankees	22	146.0
Christy Mathewson, NY Giants	11	101.2
Red Ruffing, NY Yankees	10	85.2
Chief Bender, Philadelphia A's	10	85.0
Waite Hoyt, NY Yankees-Phi. A's	12	83.2

Complete Games

	GS	CG	W-L
Christy Mathewson, NY Giants	11	10	5-5
Chief Bender, Philadelphia A's	10	9	6-4
Bob Gibson, St. Louis	9	8	7-2
Whitey Ford, NY Yankees	22	7	10-8
Red Ruffing, NY Yankees	10	7	7-2

Strikeouts

	Gm	IP	SO
Whitey Ford, NY Yankees	22	146.0	94
Bob Gibson, St. Louis	9	81.0	92
Allie Reynolds, NY Yankees	15	77.1	62
Sandy Koufax, Los Angeles	8	57.0	61
Red Ruffing, NY Yankees	10	85.2	61

Losses

	Gm	W-L
Whitey Ford, NY Yankees	22	10-8
Christy Mathewson, NY Giants	11	5-5
Joe Bush, Phi. A's-Bosox-NY Yankees	9	2-5
Rube Marquard, NY Giants-Brooklyn	11	2-5
Eddie Plank, Philadelphia A's	7	2-5
Schoolboy Rowe, Detroit	8	2-5

League Championship Series

Division play came to the major leagues in 1969 when both the American and National Leagues expanded to 12 teams. With an East and West Division in each league, League Championship Series (LCS) became necessary to determine the NL and AL pennant winners. In 1994, teams were realigned into three divisions, the East, Central, and West with division winners and one wildcard team playing a best-of-5 League Divisional Series (see following pages for LDS results) to determine the LCS competitors. In the tables below, the East Division champions are noted by the letter E, the Central division champions by C and the West Division champions by W. Wildcard winners are noted by WC. Also, each playoff winner's wins and losses are noted in parentheses after the series score. The LCS changed from best-of-5 to best-of-7 in 1985. Each league's LCS was cancelled in 1994 due to the players' strike.

National League

Multiple champions: Atlanta, Cincinnati and LA Dodgers (5); NY Mets (4); Philadelphia and St. Louis (3); Florida, Pittsburgh, San Diego and San Francisco (2).

Year	Winner	Manager	Series		Loser	Manager
1969	E–New York	Gil Hodges	3-0		W–Atlanta	Lum Harris
1970	W–Cincinnati	Sparky Anderson	3-0		E–Pittsburgh	Danny Murtaugh
1971	E–Pittsburgh	Danny Murtaugh	3-1	(LWWW)	W–San Francisco	Charlie Fox
1972	W–Cincinnati	Sparky Anderson	3-2	(LWLWW)	E–Pittsburgh	Bill Virdon
1973	E–New York	Yogi Berra	3-2	(LWWLW)	W–Cincinnati	Sparky Anderson
1974	W–Los Angeles	Walter Alston	3-1	(WWLW)	E–Pittsburgh	Danny Murtaugh
1975	W–Cincinnati	Sparky Anderson	3-0		E–Pittsburgh	Danny Murtaugh
1976	W–Cincinnati	Sparky Anderson	3-0		E–Philadelphia	Danny Ozark
1977	W–Los Angeles	Tommy Lasorda	3-1	(LWWW)	E–Philadelphia	Danny Ozark
1978	W–Los Angeles	Tommy Lasorda	3-1	(WWLW)	E–Philadelphia	Danny Ozark
1979	E–Pittsburgh	Chuck Tanner	3-0		W–Cincinnati	John McNamara
1980	E–Philadelphia	Dallas Green	3-2	(WLLWW)	W–Houston	Bill Virdon
1981	W–Los Angeles	Tommy Lasorda	3-2	(WLLWW)	E–Montreal	Jim Fanning
1982	E–St. Louis	Whitey Herzog	3-0		W–Atlanta	Joe Torre
1983	E–Philadelphia	Paul Owens	3-1	(WLWW)	W–Los Angeles	Tommy Lasorda
1984	W–San Diego	Dick Williams	3-2	(LLWWW)	E–Chicago	Jim Frey
1985	E–St. Louis	Whitey Herzog	4-2	(LLWWWW)	W–Los Angeles	Tommy Lasorda
1986	E–New York	Davey Johnson	4-2	(LWWLWW)	W–Houston	Hal Lanier
1987	E–St. Louis	Whitey Herzog	4-3	(WLWLLWW)	W–San Francisco	Roger Craig
1988	W–Los Angeles	Tommy Lasorda	4-3	(LWLWWLW)	E–New York	Davey Johnson
1989	W–San Francisco	Roger Craig	4-1	(WLWWW)	E–Chicago	Don Zimmer

Year	Winner	Manager	Series	Loser	Manager
1990	W–Cincinnati	Lou Piniella	4-2 (LWWWLW)	E–Pittsburgh	Jim Leyland
1991	W–Atlanta	Bobby Cox	4-3 (LWWLLWW)	E–Pittsburgh	Jim Leyland
1992	W–Atlanta	Bobby Cox	4-3 (WWLLWLW)	E–Pittsburgh	Jim Leyland
1993	E–Philadelphia	Jim Fregosi	4-2 (WLLWWW)	W–Atlanta	Bobby Cox
1994	Not held				
1995	E–Atlanta	Bobby Cox	4-0	C–Cincinnati	Davey Johnson
1996	E–Atlanta	Bobby Cox	4-3 (WLLLWWW)	C–St. Louis	Tony La Russa
1997	WC–Florida	Jim Leyland	4-2 (WLWLWW)	E–Atlanta	Bobby Cox
1998	W–San Diego	Bruce Bochy	4-2 (WWWLLW)	E–Atlanta	Bobby Cox
1999	E–Atlanta	Bobby Cox	4-2 (WWWLLW)	WC–New York	Bobby Valentine
2000	WC–New York	Bobby Valentine	4-1 (WWLWW)	C–St. Louis	Tony La Russa
2001	W–Arizona	Bob Brenly	4-1 (WLWWW)	E–Atlanta	Bobby Cox
2002	WC–San Francisco	Dusty Baker	4-1 (WWLWW)	C–St. Louis	Tony La Russa
2003	WC–Florida	Jack McKeon	4-3 (WLLLWWW)	C–Chicago	Dusty Baker

NLCS Most Valuable Players

Winners who did not play for NLCS champions are in **bold** type.

Multiple winner: Steve Garvey (2).

Year		
1977 Dusty Baker, LA, OF	1987 **Jeff Leonard,** SF, OF	1996 Javy Lopez, Atl., C
1978 Steve Garvey, LA, 1B	1988 Orel Hershiser, LA, P	1997 Livan Hernandez, Fla., P
1979 Willie Stargell, Pit., 1B	1989 Will Clark, SF, 1B	1998 Sterling Hitchcock, SD, P
1980 Manny Trillo, Phi., 2B	1990 Rob Dibble, Cin., P	1999 Eddie Perez, Atl., C
1981 Burt Hooton, LA, P	& Randy Myers, Cin., P	2000 Mike Hampton, NY, P
1982 Darrell Porter, St.L., C	1991 Steve Avery, Atl., P	2001 Craig Counsell, Ari., 2B
1983 Gary Matthews, Phi., OF	1992 John Smoltz, Atl., P	2002 Benito Santiago, SF, C
1984 Steve Garvey, SD, 1B	1993 Curt Schilling, Phi., P	2003 Ivan Rodriguez, Fla., C
1985 Ozzie Smith, St.L., SS	1994 LCS not held.	
1986 **Mike Scott,** Hou., P	1995 Mike Devereaux, Atl., OF	

American League

Multiple champions: NY Yankees (10); Oakland (6); Baltimore (5); Boston, Cleveland, Kansas City, Minnesota and Toronto (2).

Year	Winner	Manager	Series	Loser	Manager
1969	E–Baltimore	Earl Weaver	3-0	W–Minnesota	Billy Martin
1970	E–Baltimore	Earl Weaver	3-0	W–Minnesota	Bill Rigney
1971	E–Baltimore	Earl Weaver	3-0	W–Oakland	Dick Williams
1972	W–Oakland	Dick Williams	3-2 (LLWWW)	E–Detroit	Billy Martin
1973	W–Oakland	Dick Williams	3-2 (LWWLW)	E–Baltimore	Earl Weaver
1974	W–Oakland	Alvin Dark	3-1 (LWWW)	E–Baltimore	Earl Weaver
1975	E–Boston	Darrell Johnson	3-0	W–Oakland	Alvin Dark
1976	E–New York	Billy Martin	3-2 (WLWLW)	W–Kansas City	Whitey Herzog
1977	E–New York	Billy Martin	3-2 (LWWLW)	W–Kansas City	Whitey Herzog
1978	E–New York	Bob Lemon	3-1 (WLWW)	W–Kansas City	Whitey Herzog
1979	E–Baltimore	Earl Weaver	3-1 (WWLW)	W–California	Jim Fregosi
1980	W–Kansas City	Jim Frey	3-0	E–New York	Dick Howser
1981	E–New York	Bob Lemon	3-0	W–Oakland	Billy Martin
1982	E–Milwaukee	Harvey Kuenn	3-2 (LLWWW)	W–California	Gene Mauch
1983	E–Baltimore	Joe Altobelli	3-1 (LWWW)	W–Chicago	Tony La Russa
1984	E–Detroit	Sparky Anderson	3-0	W–Kansas City	Dick Howser
1985	W–Kansas City	Dick Howser	4-3 (LLWWWW)	E–Toronto	Bobby Cox
1986	E–Boston	John McNamara	4-3 (LWWLLWW)	W–California	Gene Mauch
1987	W–Minnesota	Tom Kelly	4-1 (WWLWW)	E–Detroit	Sparky Anderson
1988	W–Oakland	Tony La Russa	4-0	E–Boston	Joe Morgan
1989	W–Oakland	Tony La Russa	4-1 (WWLWW)	E–Toronto	Cito Gaston
1990	W–Oakland	Tony La Russa	4-0	E–Boston	Joe Morgan
1991	W–Minnesota	Tom Kelly	4-1 (WLWWW)	E–Toronto	Cito Gaston
1992	E–Toronto	Cito Gaston	4-2 (LWWWLW)	W–Oakland	Tony La Russa
1993	E–Toronto	Cito Gaston	4-2 (WWLLWW)	W–Chicago	Gene Lamont
1994	Not held				
1995	C–Cleveland	Mike Hargrove	4-2 (LWLWWW)	W–Seattle	Lou Piniella
1996	E–New York	Joe Torre	4-1 (WLWWW)	WC–Baltimore	Davey Johnson
1997	C–Cleveland	Mike Hargrove	4-2 (WLWWLW)	E–Baltimore	Davey Johnson
1998	E–New York	Joe Torre	4-2 (WLLWWW)	C–Cleveland	Mike Hargrove
1999	E–New York	Joe Torre	4-1 (WWLWW)	WC–Boston	Jimy Williams
2000	E–New York	Joe Torre	4-2 (LWWLWW)	WC–Seattle	Lou Piniella
2001	E–New York	Joe Torre	4-1 (WLWWW)	W–Seattle	Lou Piniella
2002	WC–Anaheim	Mike Scioscia	4-1 (LWWWW)	C–Minnesota	Ron Gardenhire
2003	E–New York	Joe Torre	4-3 (LWWLWLW)	WC–Boston	Grady Little

ALCS Most Valuable Players

Winner who did not play for ALCS champions is in **bold** type.

Multiple winner: Dave Stewart (2).

Year		
1980 Frank White, KC, 2B	1988 Dennis Eckersley, Oak., P	1996 Bernie Williams, NY, OF
1981 Graig Nettles, NY, 3B	1989 Rickey Henderson, Oak., OF	1997 Marquis Grissom, Cle., OF
1982 **Fred Lynn,** Cal., OF	1990 Dave Stewart, Oak., P	1998 David Wells, NY, P
1983 Mike Boddicker, Bal., P	1991 Kirby Puckett, Min., OF	1999 Orlando Hernandez, NY, P
1984 Kirk Gibson, Det., OF	1992 Roberto Alomar, Tor., 2B	2000 Dave Justice, NY, OF
1985 George Brett, KC, 3B	1993 Dave Stewart, Tor., P	2001 Andy Pettitte, NY, P
1986 Marty Barrett, Bos., 2B	1994 LCS not held.	2002 Adam Kennedy, Ana., 2B
1987 Gary Gaetti, Min., 3B	1995 Orel Hershiser, Cle., P	2003 Mariano Rivera, NY, P

League Divisional Series

In 1994, leagues were realigned into three divisions, the East, Central, and West with division winners and one wildcard team playing a best-of-5 League Divisional Series to determine the LCS competitors. In the tables below, the East Division champions are noted by the letter E, the Central division champions by C and the West Division champions by W. Wildcard winners are noted by WC. Also, each playoff winner's wins and losses are noted in parentheses after the series score. Each league's LDS was cancelled in 1994 due to the players' strike.

National League

Multiple champions: Atlanta (6); St. Louis (3); Florida and NY Mets (2).

Year	Winner	Manager	Series		Loser	Manager
1995	E–Atlanta	Bobby Cox	3-1 (WWLW)		WC–Colorado	Don Baylor
	C–Cincinnati	Davey Johnson	3-0		W–Los Angeles	Tommy Lasorda
1996	E–Atlanta	Bobby Cox	3-0		WC–Los Angeles	Bill Russell
	C–St. Louis	Tony La Russa	3-0		W–San Diego	Bruce Bochy
1997	E–Atlanta	Bobby Cox	3-0		C–Houston	Larry Dierker
	WC–Florida	Jim Leyland	3-0		W–San Francisco	Dusty Baker
1998	E–Atlanta	Bobby Cox	3-0		WC–Chicago	Jim Riggleman
	W–San Diego	Bruce Bochy	3-1 (WLWW)		C–Houston	Larry Dierker
1999	E–Atlanta	Bobby Cox	3-1 (LWWW)		C–Houston	Larry Dierker
	WC–New York	Bobby Valentine	3-1 (WLWW)		W–Arizona	Buck Showalter
2000	C–St. Louis	Tony La Russa	3-0		E–Atlanta	Bobby Cox
	WC–New York	Bobby Valentine	3-1 (LWWW)		W–San Francisco	Dusty Baker
2001	E–Atlanta	Bobby Cox	3-0		C–Houston	Larry Dierker
	W–Arizona	Bob Brenly	3-2 (WLWLW)		WC–St. Louis	Tony La Russa
2002	WC–San Francisco	Dusty Baker	3-2 (WLLWW)		E–Atlanta	Bobby Cox
	C–St. Louis	Tony La Russa	3-0		W–Arizona	Bob Brenly
2003	C–Chicago	Dusty Baker	3-2 (WLWLW)		E–Atlanta	Bobby Cox
	WC–Florida	Jack McKeon	3-1 (LWWW)		W–San Francisco	Felipe Alou

American League

Multiple champions: NY Yankees (5); Cleveland and Seattle (3); Baltimore (2).

Year	Winner	Manager	Series		Loser	Manager
1995	C–Cleveland	Mike Hargrove	3-0		E–Boston	Kevin Kennedy
	W–Seattle	Lou Piniella	3-2 (LLWWW)		WC–New York	Buck Showalter
1996	E–New York	Joe Torre	3-1 (LWWW)		W–Texas	Johnny Oates
	WC–Baltimore	Davey Johnson	3-1 (WWLW)		C–Cleveland	Mike Hargrove
1997	E–Baltimore	Davey Johnson	3-1 (WWLW)		W–Seattle	Lou Piniella
	C–Cleveland	Mike Hargrove	3-2 (LWLWW)		WC–New York	Joe Torre
1998	E–New York	Joe Torre	3-0		W–Texas	Johnny Oates
	C–Cleveland	Mike Hargrove	3-1 (LWWW)		WC–Boston	Jimy Williams
1999	E–New York	Joe Torre	3-0		W–Texas	Johnny Oates
	WC–Boston	Jimy Williams	3-2 (LLWWW)		C–Cleveland	Mike Hargrove
2000	E–New York	Joe Torre	3-2 (LVWWLW)		W–Oakland	Art Howe
	WC–Seattle	Lou Piniella	3-0		C–Chicago	Jerry Manuel
2001	E–New York	Joe Torre	3-2 (LLWWW)		WC–Oakland	Art Howe
	W–Seattle	Lou Piniella	3-2 (LWLWW)		C–Cleveland	Charlie Manuel
2002	WC–Anaheim	Mike Scioscia	3-1 (LWWW)		E–New York	Joe Torre
	C–Minnesota	Ron Gardenhire	3-2 (WLLWW)		W–Oakland	Art Howe
2003	E–New York	Joe Torre	3-1 (LWWW)		C–Minnesota	Ron Gardenhire
	WC–Boston	Grady Little	3-2 (LLWWW)		W–Oakland	Ken Macha

Other Playoffs

Ten times since 1946, playoffs have been necessary to decide league or division championships or wild card berths when two teams were tied at the end of the regular season. Additionally, in the strike year of 1981 there were playoffs between the first and second half-season champions in both leagues.

National League

Year	NL	W	L	Manager	Year	NL	W	L	Manager
1946	Brooklyn	96	58	Leo Durocher	1959	Milwaukee	86	68	Fred Haney
	St. Louis	96	58	Eddie Dyer		Los Angeles	86	68	Walter Alston
	Playoff: (Best-of-3) St. Louis, 2-0					Playoff: (Best-of-3) Los Angeles, 2-0			

	NL	W	L	Manager		NL	W	L	Manager
1951	Brooklyn	96	58	Charlie Dressen	1962	Los Angeles	101	61	Walter Alston
	New York	96	58	Leo Durocher		San Francisco	101	61	Alvin Dark
	Playoff: (Best-of-3) New York, 2-1 (WLW)					Playoff: (Best-of-3) San Francisco, 2-1 (WLW)			

Year	NL West	W	L	Manager
1980	Houston	92	70	Bill Virdon
	Los Angeles	92	70	Tommy Lasorda

Playoff: (1 game) Houston, 7-1 (at LA)

Year	NL East	W	L	Manager
1981	(1st Half) Philadelphia	34	21	Dallas Green
	(2nd Half) Montreal	.30	23	Jim Fanning

Playoff: (Best-of-5) Montreal, 3-2 (WWLLW)

Year	NL West	W	L	Manager
1981	(1st Half) Los Angeles	.36	21	Tommy Lasorda
	(2nd Half) Houston	.33	20	Bill Virdon

Playoff: (Best-of-5) Los Angeles, 3-2 (LLWWW)

Year	NL Wild Card	W	L	Manager
1998	Chicago	89	73	Jim Riggleman
	San Francisco	89	73	Dusty Baker

Playoff: (1 game) Chicago, 5-3 (at Chicago)

Year	NL Wild Card	W	L	Manager
1999	Cincinnati	96	66	Jack McKeon
	New York	96	66	Bobby Valentine

Playoff: (1 game) New York, 5-0 (at Cincinnati)

American League

Year	AL	W	L	Manager
1948	Boston	96	58	Joe McCarthy
	Cleveland	96	58	Lou Boudreau

Playoff: (1 game) Cleveland, 8-3 (at Boston)

Year	AL East	W	L	Manager
1978	Boston	99	63	Don Zimmer
	New York	99	63	Bob Lemon

Playoff: (1 game) New York, 5-4 (at Boston)

Year	AL East	W	L	Manager
1981	(1st Half) N.Y.	.34	22	Bob Lemon
	(2nd Half) Milw	.31	22	Buck Rodgers

Playoff: (Best-of-5) New York, 3-2 (WWLLW)

Year	AL West	W	L	Manager
1981	(1st Half) Oakland	.37	23	Billy Martin
	(2nd Half) Kan. City	.30	23	Jim Frey

Playoff: (Best-of-5), Oakland, 3-0

Year	AL West	W	L	Manager
1995	Seattle	78	66	Lou Piniella
	California	78	66	M. Lachemann

Playoff: (1 game) Seattle, 9-1 (at Seattle)

Regular Season League & Division Winners

Regular season National and American League pennant winners from 1900-68, as well as West and East divisional champions from 1969-93. In 1994, both leagues went to three divisions, West, Central and East, and each league also sent a wild card (WC) team to the playoffs. Note that (*) indicates 1994 divisional champion is unofficial (due to the players' strike). Note that **GA** column indicates games ahead of the second place club.

National League

Year	Team	W	L	Pct	GA
1900	Brooklyn	82	54	.603	4½
1901	Pittsburgh	90	49	.647	7½
1902	Pittsburgh	103	36	.741	27½
1903	Pittsburgh	91	49	.650	6½
1904	New York	106	47	.693	13
1905	New York	105	48	.686	9
1906	Chicago	116	36	.763	20
1907	Chicago	107	45	.704	17
1908	Chicago	99	55	.643	1
1909	Pittsburgh	110	42	.724	6½
1910	Chicago	104	50	.675	13
1911	New York	99	54	.647	7½
1912	New York	103	48	.682	10
1913	New York	101	51	.664	12½
1914	Boston	94	59	.614	10½
1915	Philadelphia	90	62	.592	7
1916	Brooklyn	94	60	.610	2½
1917	New York	98	56	.636	10
1918	Chicago	84	45	.651	10½
1919	Cincinnati	96	44	.686	9
1920	Brooklyn	93	61	.604	7
1921	New York	94	59	.614	4
1922	New York	93	61	.604	7
1923	New York	95	58	.621	4½
1924	New York	93	60	.608	1½
1925	Pittsburgh	95	58	.621	8½
1926	St. Louis	89	65	.578	2
1927	Pittsburgh	94	60	.610	1½
1928	St. Louis	95	59	.617	2
1929	Chicago	98	54	.645	10½
1930	St. Louis	92	62	.597	2
1931	St. Louis	101	53	.656	13
1932	Chicago	90	64	.584	4
1933	New York	91	61	.599	5
1934	St. Louis	95	58	.621	2
1935	Chicago	100	54	.649	4
1936	New York	92	62	.597	5
1937	New York	95	57	.625	3
1938	Chicago	89	63	.586	2
1939	Cincinnati	97	57	.630	4½
1940	Cincinnati	100	53	.654	12
1941	Brooklyn	100	54	.649	2½
1942	St. Louis	106	48	.688	2
1943	St. Louis	105	49	.682	18
1944	St. Louis	105	49	.682	14½
1945	Chicago	98	56	.636	3
1946	St. Louis†	98	58	.628	2
1947	Brooklyn	94	60	.610	5
1948	Boston	91	62	.595	6½
1949	Brooklyn	97	57	.630	1
1950	Philadelphia	91	63	.591	2
1951	New York†	98	59	.624	1
1952	Brooklyn	96	57	.627	4½
1953	Brooklyn	105	49	.682	13
1954	New York	97	57	.630	5
1955	Brooklyn	98	55	.641	13½
1956	Brooklyn	93	61	.604	1
1957	Milwaukee	95	59	.617	8
1958	Milwaukee	92	62	.597	8
1959	Los Angeles†	88	68	.564	2
1960	Pittsburgh	95	59	.617	7
1961	Cincinnati	93	61	.604	4
1962	San Francisco†	103	62	.624	1
1963	Los Angeles	99	63	.611	6
1964	St. Louis	93	69	.574	1
1965	Los Angeles	97	65	.599	2
1966	Los Angeles	95	67	.586	1½
1967	St. Louis	101	60	.627	10½
1968	St. Louis	97	65	.599	9
1969	West—Atlanta	93	69	.574	3
	East—N.Y. Mets	100	62	.617	8
1970	West—Cincinnati	102	60	.630	14½
	East—Pittsburgh	89	73	.549	5
1971	West—San Francisco	90	72	.556	1
	East—Pittsburgh	97	65	.599	7
1972	West—Cincinnati	95	59	.617	10½
	East—Pittsburgh	96	59	.619	11

Year		W	L	Pct	GA
1973	West—Cincinnati	99	63	.611	3½
	East—N.Y. Mets	82	79	.509	1½
1974	West—Los Angeles	102	60	.630	4
	East—Pittsburgh	88	74	.543	1½
1975	West—Cincinnati	108	54	.667	20
	East—Pittsburgh	92	69	.571	6½
1976	West—Cincinnati	102	60	.630	10
	East—Philadelphia	101	61	.623	9
1977	West—Los Angeles	98	64	.605	10
	East—Philadelphia	101	61	.623	5
1978	West—Los Angeles	95	67	.586	2½
	East—Philadelphia	90	72	.556	1½
1979	West—Cincinnati	90	71	.559	1½
	East—Pittsburgh	98	64	.605	2
1980	West—Houston†	93	70	.571	1
	East—Philadelphia	91	71	.562	1
1981	West—Los Angeles$	63	47	.573	—
	East—Montreal$	60	48	.556	—
1982	West—Atlanta	89	73	.549	1
	East—St. Louis	92	70	.568	3
1983	West—Los Angeles	91	71	.562	3
	East—Philadelphia	90	72	.556	6
1984	West—San Diego	92	70	.568	12
	East—Chicago	96	65	.596	6½
1985	West—Los Angeles	95	67	.586	5½
	East—St. Louis	101	61	.623	3
1986	West—Houston	96	66	.593	10
	East—N.Y. Mets	108	54	.667	21½
1987	West—San Francisco	90	72	.556	6
	East—St. Louis	95	67	.586	3
1988	West—Los Angeles	94	67	.584	7
	East—N.Y. Mets	100	60	.625	15
1989	West—San Francisco	92	70	.568	3
	East—Chicago	93	69	.574	6
1990	West—Cincinnati	91	71	.562	5
	East—Pittsburgh	95	67	.586	4
1991	West—Atlanta	94	68	.580	1
	East—Pittsburgh	98	64	.605	14
1992	West—Atlanta	98	64	.605	8
	East—Pittsburgh	96	66	.593	9
1993	West—Atlanta	104	58	.642	1
	East—Philadelphia	97	65	.599	3
1994	West—Los Angeles*	58	56	.509	3½
	Central—Cincinnati*	66	48	.579	½
	East—Montreal*	74	40	.649	6
1995	West—Los Angeles	78	66	.542	1
	Central—Cincinnati	85	59	.590	9
	East—Atlanta	90	54	.625	21
	WC—Colorado	77	67	.535	—
1996	West—San Diego	91	71	.562	1
	Central—St. Louis	88	74	.543	6
	East—Atlanta	96	66	.593	8
	WC—Los Angeles	90	72	.556	—
1997	West—San Francisco	90	72	.556	2
	Central—Houston	84	78	.519	5
	East—Atlanta	101	61	.623	9
	WC—Florida	92	70	.568	—
1998	West—San Diego	98	64	.605	9½
	Central—Houston	102	60	.630	12½
	East—Atlanta	106	56	.654	18
	WC—Chicago†	90	73	.552	—
1999	West—Arizona	100	62	.617	14
	Central—Houston	97	65	.599	1½
	East—Atlanta	103	59	.636	6½
	WC—N.Y. Mets†	97	66	.595	—
2000	West—San Francisco	97	65	.599	11
	Central—St. Louis	95	67	.586	10
	East—Atlanta	95	67	.586	1
	WC—N.Y. Mets	94	68	.580	—
2001	West—Arizona	92	70	.568	2
	Central—Houston@	93	69	.574	—
	East—Atlanta	88	74	.543	2
	WC—St. Louis	93	69	.574	—
2002	West—Arizona	98	64	.605	2½
	Central—St. Louis	97	65	.599	13
	East—Atlanta	101	59	.631	19
	WC—San Francisco	95	66	.590	—
2003	West—San Francisco	100	61	.621	15½
	Central—Chicago	88	74	.543	1
	East—Atlanta	101	59	.623	10
	WC—Florida	91	71	.562	—

†**Regular season playoffs:** See "Other Playoffs" on pages 94-95 for details.
$**Divisional playoffs:** See "Other Playoffs" on pages 94-95 for details.
@Houston (93-69) won the division over St. Louis (93-69) due to a better head-to-head record.

American League

Year		W	L	Pct	GA
1901	Chicago	83	53	.610	4
1902	Philadelphia	83	53	.610	5
1903	Boston	91	47	.659	14½
1904	Boston	95	59	.617	1½
1905	Philadelphia	92	56	.622	2
1906	Chicago	93	58	.616	3
1907	Detroit	92	58	.613	1½
1908	Detroit	90	63	.588	½
1909	Detroit	98	54	.645	3½
1910	Philadelphia	102	48	.680	14½
1911	Philadelphia	101	50	.669	13½
1912	Boston	105	47	.691	14
1913	Philadelphia	96	57	.627	6½
1914	Philadelphia	99	53	.651	8½
1915	Boston	101	50	.669	2½
1916	Boston	91	63	.591	2
1917	Chicago	100	54	.649	9
1918	Boston	75	51	.595	2½
1919	Chicago	88	52	.629	3½
1920	Cleveland	98	56	.636	2
1921	New York	98	55	.641	4½
1922	New York	94	60	.610	1
1923	New York	98	54	.645	16
1924	Washington	92	62	.597	2
1925	Washington	96	55	.636	8½
1926	New York	91	63	.591	3
1927	New York	110	44	.714	19
1928	New York	101	53	.656	2½
1929	Philadelphia	104	46	.693	18
1930	Philadelphia	102	52	.662	8
1931	Philadelphia	107	45	.704	13½
1932	New York	107	47	.695	13
1933	Washington	99	53	.651	7
1934	Detroit	101	53	.656	7
1935	Detroit	93	58	.616	3
1936	New York	102	51	.667	19½
1937	New York	102	52	.662	13
1938	New York	99	53	.651	9½
1939	New York	106	45	.702	17
1940	Detroit	90	64	.584	1
1941	New York	101	53	.656	17
1942	New York	103	51	.669	9
1943	New York	98	56	.636	13½
1944	St. Louis	89	65	.578	1
1945	Detroit	88	65	.575	1½
1946	Boston	104	50	.675	12
1947	New York	97	57	.630	12
1948	Cleveland†	97	58	.626	1
1949	New York	97	57	.630	1
1950	New York	98	56	.636	3
1951	New York	98	56	.636	5
1952	New York	95	59	.617	2
1953	New York	99	52	.656	8½
1954	Cleveland	111	43	.721	8

Year		W	L	Pct	GA
1955	New York	96	58	.623	3
1956	New York	97	57	.630	9
1957	New York	98	56	.636	8
1958	New York	92	62	.597	10
1959	Chicago	94	60	.610	5
1960	New York	97	57	.630	8
1961	New York	109	53	.673	8
1962	New York	96	66	.593	5
1963	New York	104	57	.646	10½
1964	New York	99	63	.611	1
1965	Minnesota	102	60	.630	7
1966	Baltimore	97	63	.606	9
1967	Boston	92	70	.568	1
1968	Detroit	103	59	.636	12
1969	West—Minnesota	97	65	.599	9
	East—Baltimore	109	53	.673	19
1970	West—Minnesota	98	64	.605	9
	East—Baltimore	108	54	.667	15
1971	West—Oakland	101	60	.627	16
	East—Baltimore	101	57	.639	12
1972	West—Oakland	93	62	.600	5½
	East—Detroit	86	70	.551	½
1973	West—Oakland	94	68	.580	6
	East—Baltimore	97	65	.599	8
1974	West—Oakland	90	72	.556	5
	East—Baltimore	91	71	.562	2
1975	West—Oakland	98	64	.605	7
	East—Boston	95	65	.594	4½
1976	West—KansasCity	90	72	.556	2½
	East—New York	97	62	.610	10½
1977	West—Kansas City	102	60	.630	8
	East—New York	100	62	.617	2½
1978	West—Kansas City	92	70	.568	5
	East—New York†	100	63	.613	1
1979	West—California	88	74	.543	3
	East—Baltimore	102	57	.642	8
1980	West—Kansas City	97	65	.599	14
	East—New York	103	59	.636	3
1981	West—Oakland$	64	45	.587	—
	East—New York$	59	48	.551	—
1982	West—California	93	69	.574	3
	East—Milwaukee	95	67	.586	1
1983	West—Chicago	99	63	.611	20
	East—Baltimore	98	64	.605	6
1984	West—Kansas City	84	78	.519	3
	East—Detroit	104	58	.642	15
1985	West—Kansas City	91	71	.562	1
	East—Toronto	99	62	.615	2
1986	West—California	92	70	.568	5
	East—Boston	95	66	.590	5½
1987	West—Minnesota	85	77	.525	2
	East—Detroit	98	64	.605	2

Year		W	L	Pct	GA
1988	West—Oakland	104	58	.642	13
	East—Boston	89	73	.549	1
1989	West—Oakland	99	63	.611	7
	East—Toronto	89	73	.549	2
1990	West—Oakland	103	59	.636	9
	East—Boston	88	74	.543	2
1991	West—Minnesota	95	67	.586	8
	East—Toronto	91	71	.562	7
1992	West—Oakland	96	66	.593	6
	East—Toronto	96	66	.593	4
1993	West—Chicago	94	68	.580	8
	East—Toronto	95	67	.586	7
1994	West—Texas*	52	62	.456	1
	Central—Chicago*	67	46	.593	1
	East—New York*	70	43	.619	6½
1995	West—Seattle†	79	66	.545	1
	Central—Cleveland	100	44	.694	30
	East—Boston	86	58	.597	7
	WC—New York	79	65	.549	—
1996	West—Texas	90	72	.556	4½
	Central—Cleveland	99	62	.615	14½
	East—New York	92	70	.568	4
	WC—Baltimore	88	74	.543	—
1997	West—Seattle	90	72	.556	6
	Central—Cleveland	86	75	.534	6
	East—Baltimore	98	64	.605	2
	WC—New York	96	66	.593	—
1998	West—Texas	88	74	.543	3
	Central—Cleveland	89	73	.549	9
	East—New York	114	48	.704	22
	WC—Boston	92	70	.568	—
1999	West—Texas	95	67	.586	8
	Central—Cleveland	97	65	.599	21½
	East—New York	98	64	.605	4
	WC—Boston	94	68	.580	—
2000	West—Oakland	91	70	.565	½
	Central—Chicago	95	67	.586	5
	East—New York	87	74	.540	2½
	WC—Seattle	91	71	.562	—
2001	West—Seattle	116	46	.716	14
	Central—Cleveland	91	71	.562	6
	East—New York	95	65	.594	13½
	WC—Oakland	102	60	.630	—
2002	West—Oakland	103	59	.636	4
	Central—Minnesota	94	67	.584	13½
	East—New York	103	58	.640	10½
	WC—Anaheim	99	63	.611	—
2003	West—Oakland	96	66	.593	3
	Central—Minnesota	90	72	.556	4
	East—New York	101	61	.623	6
	WC—Boston	95	67	.586	—

†**Regular season playoffs:** See "Other Playoffs" on pages 94-95 for details.
$**Divisional playoffs:** See "Other Playoffs" on pages 94-95 for details.

The All-Star Game

Baseball's first All-Star Game was held on July 6, 1933, before 47,595 at Comiskey Park in Chicago. From that year on, the All-Star Game has matched the best players in the American League against the best in the National. From 1959-62, two All-Star Games were played. The only year an All-Star Game wasn't played was 1945, when World War II travel restrictions made it necessary to cancel the meeting. The NL leads the series, 40-32-2. In the chart below, the American League is listed in **bold** type.

Since 2002, the game's MVP award has been named the Ted Williams Award, after the Red Sox Hall of Famer. Beginning in 2003, the league that wins the All-Star Game receives home-field advantage in that season's World Series.

MVP Multiple winners: Gary Carter, Steve Garvey, Willie Mays and Cal Ripken Jr. (2).

Year		Host	AL Manager	NL Manager	MVP
1933	**American, 4-2**	Chicago (AL)	Connie Mack	John McGraw	No award
1934	**American, 9-7**	New York (NL)	Joe Cronin	Bill Terry	No award
1935	**American, 4-1**	Cleveland	Mickey Cochrane	Frankie Frisch	No award
1936	National, 4-3	Boston (NL)	Joe McCarthy	Charlie Grimm	No award
1937	**American, 8-3**	Washington	Joe McCarthy	Bill Terry	No award
1938	National, 4-1	Cincinnati	Joe McCarthy	Bill Terry	No award
1939	**American, 3-1**	New York (AL)	Joe McCarthy	Gabby Hartnett	No award
1940	National, 4-0	St. Louis (NL)	Joe Cronin	Bill McKechnie	No award
1941	**American, 7-5**	Detroit	Del Baker	Bill McKechnie	No award

The All-Star Game (Cont.)

Year		Host	AL Manager	NL Manager	MVP
1942	**American,** 3-1	New York (NL)	Joe McCarthy	Leo Durocher	No award
1943	**American,** 5-3	Philadelphia (AL)	Joe McCarthy	Billy Southworth	No award
1944	National, 7-1	Pittsburgh	Joe McCarthy	Billy Southworth	No award
1945	Not held				
1946	**American,** 12-0	Boston (AL)	Steve O'Neill	Charlie Grimm	No award
1947	**American,** 2-1	Chicago (NL)	Joe Cronin	Eddie Dyer	No award
1948	**American,** 5-2	St. Louis (AL)	Bucky Harris	Leo Durocher	No award
1949	**American,** 11-7	Brooklyn	Lou Boudreau	Billy Southworth	No award
1950	National, 4-3 (14)	Chicago (AL)	Casey Stengel	Burt Shotton	No award
1951	National, 8-3	Detroit	Casey Stengel	Eddie Sawyer	No award
1952	National, 3-2 (5, rain)	Philadelphia (NL)	Casey Stengel	Leo Durocher	No award
1953	National, 5-1	Cincinnati	Casey Stengel	Charlie Dressen	No award
1954	**American,** 11-9	Cleveland	Casey Stengel	Walter Alston	No award
1955	National, 6-5 (12)	Milwaukee	Al Lopez	Leo Durocher	No award
1956	National, 7-3	Washington	Casey Stengel	Walter Alston	No award
1957	**American,** 6-5	St. Louis	Casey Stengel	Walter Alston	No award
1958	**American,** 4-3	Baltimore	Casey Stengel	Fred Haney	No award
1959-a	National, 5-4	Pittsburgh	Casey Stengel	Fred Haney	No award
1959-b	**American,** 5-3	Los Angeles	Casey Stengel	Fred Haney	No award
1960-a	National, 5-3	Kansas City	Al Lopez	Walter Alston	No award
1960-b	National, 6-0	New York	Al Lopez	Walter Alston	No award
1961-a	National, 5-4 (10)	San Francisco	Paul Richards	Danny Murtaugh	No award
1961-b	TIE, 1-1 (9, rain)	Boston	Paul Richards	Danny Murtaugh	No award
1962-a	National, 3-1	Washington	Ralph Houk	Fred Hutchinson	Maury Wills, LA (NL), SS
1962-b	**American,** 9-4	Chicago (NL)	Ralph Houk	Fred Hutchinson	Leon Wagner, LA (AL), OF
1963	National, 5-3	Cleveland	Ralph Houk	Alvin Dark	Willie Mays, SF, OF
1964	National, 7-4	New York (NL)	Al Lopez	Walter Alston	Johnny Callison, Phi., OF
1965	National, 6-5	Minnesota	Al Lopez	Gene Mauch	Juan Marichal, SF, P
1966	National, 2-1 (10)	St. Louis	Sam Mele	Walter Alston	Brooks Robinson, Bal., 3B
1967	National, 2-1 (15)	California	Hank Bauer	Walter Alston	Tony Perez, Cin., 3B
1968	National, 1-0	Houston	Dick Williams	Red Schoendienst	Willie Mays, SF, OF
1969	National, 9-3	Washington	Mayo Smith	Red Schoendienst	Willie McCovey, SF, 1B
1970	National, 5-4 (12)	Cincinnati	Earl Weaver	Gil Hodges	Carl Yastrzemski, Bos., OF
1971	**American,** 6-4	Detroit	Earl Weaver	Sparky Anderson	Frank Robinson, Bal., OF
1972	National, 4-3 (10)	Atlanta	Earl Weaver	Danny Murtaugh	Joe Morgan, Con., 2B
1973	National, 7-1	Kansas	Dick Williams	Sparky Anderson	Bobby Bonds, SF, OF
1974	National, 7-2	Pittsburgh	Dick Williams	Yogi Berra	Steve Garvey, LA, 1B
1975	National, 6-3	Milwaukee	Alvin Dark	Walter Alston	Bill Madlock, Chi. (NL), 3B & Jon Matlack, NY (NL), P
1976	National, 7-1	Philadelphia	Darrell Johnson	Sparky Anderson	George Foster, Cin., OF
1977	National, 7-5	New York (AL)	Billy Martin	Sparky Anderson	Don Sutton, LA, P
1978	National, 7-3	San Diego	Billy Martin	Tommy Lasorda	Steve Garvey, LA, 1B
1979	National, 7-6	Seattle	Bob Lemon	Tommy Lasorda	Dave Parker, Pit, OF
1980	National, 4-2	Los Angeles	Earl Weaver	Chuck Tanner	Ken Griffey, Cin., OF
1981	National, 5-4	Cleveland	Jim Frey	Dallas Green	Gary Carter, Mon., C
1982	National, 4-1	Montreal	Billy Martin	Tommy Lasorda	Dave Concepcion, Cin., SS
1983	**American,** 13-3	Chicago (AL)	Harvey Kuenn	Whitey Herzog	Fred Lynn, Cal., OF
1984	National, 3-1	San Francisco	Joe Altobelli	Paul Owens	Gary Carter, Mon., C
1985	National, 6-1	Minnesota	Sparky Anderson	Dick Williams	LaMarr Hoyt, SD, P
1986	**American,** 3-2	Houston	Dick Howser	Whitey Herzog	Roger Clemens, Bos., P
1987	National, 2-0 (13)	Oakland	John McNamara	Davey Johnson	Tim Raines, Mon., OF
1988	**American,** 2-1	Cincinnati	Tom Kelly	Whitey Herzog	Terry Steinbach, Oak., C
1989	**American,** 5-3	California	Tony La Russa	Tommy Lasorda	Bo Jackson, KC, OF
1990	**American,** 2-0	Chicago (NL)	Tony La Russa	Roger Craig	Julio Franco, Tex., 2B
1991	**American,** 4-2	Toronto	Tony La Russa	Lou Piniella	Cal Ripken Jr., Bal., SS
1992	**American,** 13-6	San Diego	Tom Kelly	Bobby Cox	Ken Griffey Jr., Sea., OF
1993	**American,** 9-3	Baltimore	Cito Gaston	Bobby Cox	Kirby Puckett, Min., OF
1994	National, 8-7 (10)	Pittsburgh	Cito Gaston	Jim Fregosi	Fred McGriff, Atl., 1B
1995	National, 3-2	Texas	Buck Showalter	Felipe Alou	Jeff Conine, Fla., PH
1996	National, 6-0	Philadelphia	Mike Hargrove	Bobby Cox	Mike Piazza, LA, C
1997	**American,** 3-1	Cleveland	Joe Torre	Bobby Cox	Sandy Alomar Jr., Cle., C
1998	**American,** 13-8	Colorado	Mike Hargrove	Jim Leyland	Roberto Alomar, Bal., 2B
1999	**American,** 4-1	Boston	Joe Torre	Bruce Bochy	Pedro Martinez, Bos., P
2000	**American,** 6-3	Atlanta	Joe Torre	Bobby Cox	Derek Jeter, NY (AL), SS
2001	**American,** 4-1	Seattle	Joe Torre	Bobby Valentine	Cal Ripken Jr., Bal., SS-3B
2002	TIE, 7-7 (11 inn.) *	Milwaukee	Joe Torre	Bob Brenly	No award
2003	**American,** 7-6	Chicago (AL)	Mike Scioscia	Dusty Baker	Garret Anderson, Ana., OF

* Due to the depletion of both the AL and NL rosters, the 2002 game was called a tie after 11 innings.

Major League Franchise Origins

Here is what the current 30 teams in Major League Baseball have to show for the years they have put in as members of the National League (NL) and American League (AL). Pennants and World Series championships are since 1901.

National League

	1st Year	Pennants & World Series	Franchise Stops
Arizona Diamondbacks	..1998	1 NL (2001) 1 WS (2001)	• Phoenix (1998–)
Atlanta Braves	1876	9 NL (1914,48,57-58,91-92,95,96,99) 3 WS (1914,57,95)	• Boston (1876–1952) Milwaukee (1953–65) Atlanta (1966–)
Chicago Cubs	1876	10 NL (1906-08,10,18,29,32,35,38,45) 2 WS (1907-08)	• Chicago (1876–)
Cincinnati Reds	1876	9 NL (1919,39-40,61,70,72,75-76,90) 5 WS (1919,40,75-76,90)	• Cincinnati (1876–80) Cincinnati (1890–)
Colorado Rockies	1993	None	• Denver (1993–)
Florida Marlins	1993	2 NL (1997, 2003) 2 WS (1997, 2003)	• Miami (1993–)
Houston Astros	1962	None	• Houston (1962–)
Los Angeles Dodgers	1890	18 NL (1916,20,41,47,49,52-53,55-56, 59,63, 65-66,74,77-78, 81,88) 6 WS (1955,59,63,65,81,88)	• Brooklyn (1890-1957) Los Angeles (1958–)
Milwaukee Brewers	1969	1 AL (1982)	• Seattle (1969) Milwaukee (1970–)
Montreal Expos	1969	None	• Montreal (1969–)
New York Mets	1962	4 NL (1969,73,86,00) 2 WS (1969,86)	• New York (1962–)
Philadelphia Phillies	1883	5 NL (1915,50,80,83,93) 1 WS (1980)	• Philadelphia (1883–)
Pittsburgh Pirates	1887	7 NL (1903,09,25,27,60,71,79) 5 WS (1909,25,60,71,79)	• Pittsburgh (1887–)
St. Louis Cardinals	1892	15 NL (1926,28,30-31,34,42-44,46,64, 67-68,82,85,87) 9 WS (1926,31,34,42,44,46,64,67,82)	• St. Louis (1892–)
San Diego Padres	1969	2 NL (1984,98)	• San Diego (1969–)
San Francisco Giants	1883	17 NL (1905,11-13,17,21-24,33,36-37,51, 54,62,89,2002) 5 WS (1905,21-22,33,54)	• New York (1883–1957) San Francisco (1958–)

American League

	1st Year	Pennants & World Series	Franchise Stops
Anaheim Angels	1961	1 AL (2002) 1 WS (2002)	• Los Angeles (1961–65) Anaheim, CA (1966–)
Baltimore Orioles	1901	7 AL (1944,66,69-71,79,83) 3 WS (1966,70,83)	• Milwaukee (1901) St. Louis (1902–53) Baltimore (1954–)
Boston Red Sox	1901	9 AL (1903,12,15-16,18,46,67,75,86) 5 WS (1903,12,15-16,18)	• Boston (1901–)
Chicago White Sox	1901	4 AL (1906,17,19,59) 2 WS (1906,17)	• Chicago (1901–)
Cleveland Indians	1901	5 AL (1920,48,54,95,97) 2 WS (1920,48)	• Cleveland (1901–)
Detroit Tigers	1901	9 AL (1907-09,34-35,40,45,68,84) 4 WS (1935,45,68,84)	• Detroit (1901–)
Kansas City Royals	1969	2 AL (1980,85) 1 WS (1985)	• Kansas City (1969–)
Minnesota Twins	1901	6 AL (1924-25,33,65,87,91) 3 WS (1924,87,91)	• Washington, DC (1901–60) Bloomington, MN (1961–81) Minneapolis (1982–)
New York Yankees	1901	39 AL (1921-23,26-28,32,36-39,41-43,47, 49-53,55-58,60-64,76-78,81,96,98-01,03) 26 WS (1923,27-28,32,36-39,41,43,47, 49-53,56,58,61-62,77-78,96,98-00)	• Baltimore (1901–02) New York (1903–)
Oakland Athletics	1901	14 AL (1905,10-11,13-14,29-31,72-74, 88-90) 9 WS (1910-11,13,29-30,72-74,89)	• Philadelphia (1901-54) Kansas City (1955–67) Oakland (1968–)
Seattle Mariners	1977	None	• Seattle (1977–)
Tampa Bay Devil Rays	...1998	None	• Tampa Bay (1998–)
Texas Rangers	1961	None	• Washington, DC (1961–71) Arlington, TX (1972–)
Toronto Blue Jays	1977	2 AL (1992-93) 2 WS (1992-93)	• Toronto (1977–)

The Growth of Major League Baseball

The National League (founded in 1876) and the American League (founded in 1901) were both eight-team circuits at the turn of the century and remained that way until expansion finally came to Major League Baseball in the 1960s. The AL added two teams in 1961 and the NL did the same a year later. Both leagues went to 12 teams and split into two divisions in 1969. The AL then grew by two more teams to 14 in 1977, but the NL didn't follow suit until adding its 13th and 14th clubs in 1993. The NL added two teams (making it 16) in 1998 when the expansion Arizona Diamondbacks entered the league and the Milwaukee Brewers moved over from the AL. The Tampa Bay Devil Rays joined the AL in 1998, keeping the AL at 14 teams.

Expansion Timetable (Since 1901)

1961—Los Angeles Angels (now Anaheim) and Washington Senators (now Texas Rangers) join AL; **1962**—Houston Colt .45s (now Astros) and New York Mets join NL; **1969**—Kansas City Royals and Seattle Pilots (now Milwaukee Brewers) join AL, while Montreal Expos and San Diego Padres join NL; **1977**—Seattle Mariners and Toronto Blue Jays join AL; **1993**—Colorado Rockies and Florida Marlins join NL; **1998**—Arizona Diamondbacks join NL and Tampa Bay Devil Rays join AL.

City and Nickname Changes
National League

1953—Boston Braves move to Milwaukee; **1958**—Brooklyn Dodgers move to Los Angeles and New York Giants move to San Francisco; **1965**—Houston Colt .45s renamed Astros; **1966**—Milwaukee Braves move to Atlanta.

Other nicknames: Boston (Beaneaters and Doves through 1908, and Bees from 1936-40); **Brooklyn** (Superbas through 1926, then Robins from 1927-31; then Dodgers from 1932-57); **Cincinnati** (Red Legs from 1944-45, then Redlegs from 1954-60, then Reds since 1961); **Philadelphia** (Blue Jays from 1943-44).

American League

1902—Milwaukee Brewers move to St. Louis and become Browns; **1903**—Baltimore Orioles move to New York and become Highlanders; **1913**—NY Highlanders renamed Yankees; **1954**—St. Louis Browns move to Baltimore and become Orioles; **1955**—Philadelphia Athletics move to Kansas City; **1961**—Washington Senators move to Bloomington, Minn., and become Minnesota Twins; **1965**—LA Angels renamed California Angels; **1966**—California Angels move to Anaheim; **1968**—KC Athletics move to Oakland and become A's; **1970**—Seattle Pilots move to Milwaukee and become Brewers; **1972**—Washington Senators move to Arlington, Texas, and become Rangers; **1982**—Minnesota Twins move to Minneapolis; **1987**—Oakland A's renamed Athletics; **1997**—California Angels renamed Anaheim Angels.

Other nicknames: Boston (Pilgrims, Puritans, Plymouth Rocks and Somersets through 1906); **Cleveland** (Broncos, Blues, Naps and Molly McGuires through 1914); **Washington** (Senators through 1904, then Nationals from 1905-44, then Senators again from 1945-60).

National League Pennant Winners from 1876-99

Founded in 1876, the National League played 24 seasons before the turn of the century and its eventual rivalry with the younger American League.

Multiple winners: Boston (8); Chicago (6); Baltimore (3); Brooklyn, New York and Providence (2).

Year		Year		Year		Year	
1876	Chicago	1882	Chicago	1888	New York	1894	Baltimore
1877	Boston	1883	Boston	1889	New York	1895	Baltimore
1878	Boston	1884	Providence	1890	Brooklyn	1896	Baltimore
1879	Providence	1885	Chicago	1891	Boston	1897	Boston
1880	Chicago	1886	Chicago	1892	Boston	1898	Boston
1881	Chicago	1887	Detroit	1893	Boston	1899	Brooklyn

Champions of Leagues That No Longer Exist

A Special Baseball Records Committee appointed by the commissioner found in 1968 that four extinct leagues qualified for major league status—the American Association (1882-91), the Union Association (1884), the Players' League (1890) and the Federal League (1914-15). The first years of the American League (1900) and Federal League (1913) were not recognized.

American Association

Year	Champion	Manager	Year	Champion	Manager	Year	Champion	Manager
1882	Cincinnati	Pop Snyder	1886	St. Louis	Charlie Comiskey	1890	Louisville	Jack Chapman
1883	Philadelphia	Lew Simmons	1887	St. Louis	Charlie Comiskey	1891	Boston	Arthur Irwin
1884	New York	Jim Mutrie	1888	St. Louis	Charlie Comiskey			
1885	St. Louis	Charlie Comiskey	1889	Brooklyn	Bill McGunnigle			

Union Association

Year	Champion	Manager
1884	St. Louis	Henry Lucas

Players' League

Year	Champion	Manager
1890	Boston	King Kelly

Federal League

Year	Champion	Manager
1914	Indianapolis	Bill Phillips
1915	Chicago	Joe Tinker

Annual Batting Leaders (since 1900)
Batting Average
National League

Multiple winners: Tony Gwynn and Honus Wagner (8); Rogers Hornsby and Stan Musial (7); Roberto Clemente and Bill Madlock (4); Pete Rose, Larry Walker and Paul Waner (3); Hank Aaron, Richie Ashburn, Jake Daubert, Tommy Davis, Ernie Lombardi, Willie McGee, Lefty O'Doul, Dave Parker and Edd Roush (2).

Year		Avg	Year		Avg	Year		Avg
1900	Honus Wagner, Pit	.381	1935	Arky Vaughan, Pit	.385	1970	Rico Carty, Atl	.366
1901	Jesse Burkett, St.L	.382	1936	Paul Waner, Pit	.373	1971	Joe Torre, St.L	.363
1902	Ginger Beaumont, Pit	.357	1937	Joe Medwick, St.L	.374	1972	Billy Williams, Chi	.333
1903	Honus Wagner, Pit	.355	1938	Ernie Lombardi, Cin	.342	1973	Pete Rose, Cin	.338
1904	Honus Wagner, Pit	.349	1939	Johnny Mize, St.L	.349	1974	Ralph Garr, Atl	.353
1905	Cy Seymour, Cin	.377	1940	Debs Garms, Pit	.355	1975	Bill Madlock, Chi	.354
1906	George Stone, St.L	.339	1941	Pete Reiser, Bklyn	.343	1976	Bill Madlock, Chi	.339
1907	Honus Wagner, Pit	.350	1942	Ernie Lombardi, Bos	.330	1977	Dave Parker, Pit	.338
1908	Honus Wagner, Pit	.354	1943	Stan Musial, St.L	.357	1978	Dave Parker, Pit	.334
1909	Honus Wagner, Pit	.339	1944	Dixie Walker, Bklyn	.357	1979	Keith Hernandez, St.L	.344
1910	Sherry Magee, Phi	.331	1945	Phil Cavarretta, Chi	.355	1980	Bill Buckner, Chi	.324
1911	Honus Wagner, Pit	.334	1946	Stan Musial, St.L	.365	1981	Bill Madlock, Pit	.341
1912	Heinie Zimmerman, Chi.	.372	1947	Harry Walker, St.L-Phi	.363	1982	Al Oliver, Mon	.331
1913	Jake Daubert, Bklyn	.350	1948	Stan Musial, St.L	.376	1983	Bill Madlock, Pit	.323
1914	Jake Daubert, Bklyn	.329	1949	Jackie Robinson, Bklyn	.342	1984	Tony Gwynn, SD	.351
1915	Larry Doyle, NY	.320	1950	Stan Musial, St.L	.346	1985	Willie McGee, St.t	.353
1916	Hal Chase, Cin.	.339	1951	Stan Musial, St.L	.355	1986	Tim Raines, Mon	.334
1917	Edd Roush, Cin.	.341	1952	Stan Musial, St.L	.336	1987	Tony Gwynn, SD	.370
1918	Zack Wheat, Bklyn	.335	1953	Carl Furillo, Bklyn	.344	1988	Tony Gwynn, SD	.313
1919	Edd Roush, Cin.	.321	1954	Willie Mays, NY.	.345	1989	Tony Gwynn, SD	.336
1920	Rogers Hornsby, St.L	.370	1955	Richie Ashburn, Phi	.338	1990	Willie McGee, St.L	.335
1921	Rogers Hornsby, St.L	.397	1956	Hank Aaron, Mil.	.328	1991	Terry Pendleton, Atl	.319
1922	Rogers Hornsby, St.L	.401	1957	Stan Musial, St.L	.351	1992	Gary Sheffield, SD	.330
1923	Rogers Hornsby, St.L	.384	1958	Richie Ashburn, Phi	.350	1993	Andres Galarraga, Col	.370
1924	Rogers Hornsby, St.L	.424	1959	Hank Aaron, Mil.	.355	1994	Tony Gwynn, SD	.394
1925	Rogers Hornsby, St.L	.403	1960	Dick Groat, Pit	.325	1995	Tony Gwynn, SD	.368
1926	Bubbles Hargrave, Cin	.353	1961	Roberto Clemente, Pit	.351	1996	Tony Gwynn, SD	.353
1927	Paul Waner, Pit.	.380	1962	Tommy Davis, LA	.346	1997	Tony Gwynn, SD	.372
1928	Rogers Hornsby, Bos	.387	1963	Tommy Davis, LA	.326	1998	Larry Walker, Col.	.363
1929	Lefty O'Doul, Phi.	.398	1964	Roberto Clemente, Pit	.339	1999	Larry Walker, Col.	.379
1930	Bill Terry, NY	.401	1965	Roberto Clemente, Pit	.329	2000	Todd Helton, Col.	.372
1931	Chick Hafey, St.L	.349	1966	Matty Alou, Pit	.342	2001	Larry Walker, Col.	.350
1932	Lefty O'Doul, Bklyn	.368	1967	Roberto Clemente, Pit	.357	2002	Barry Bonds, SF	.370
1933	Chuck Klein, Phi	.368	1968	Pete Rose, Cin	.335	2003	Albert Pujols, St.L	.359
1934	Paul Waner, Pit.	.362	1969	Pete Rose, Cin	.348			

American League

Multiple winners: Ty Cobb (12); Rod Carew (7); Ted Williams (6); Wade Boggs (5); Harry Heilmann (4); George Brett, Nap Lajoie, Tony Oliva and Carl Yastrzemski (3); Luke Appling, Joe DiMaggio, Ferris Fain, Jimmie Foxx, Nomar Garciaparra, Edgar Martinez, Pete Runnels, Al Simmons, George Sisler and Mickey Vernon (2).

Year		Avg	Year		Avg	Year		Avg
1901	Nap Lajoie, Phi.	.422	1924	Babe Ruth, NY	.378	1947	Ted Williams, Bos	.343
1902	Ed Delahanty, Wash.	.376	1925	Harry Heilmann, Det	.393	1948	Ted Williams, Bos	.369
1903	Nap Lajoie, Cle	.355	1926	Heinie Manush, Det	.378	1949	George Kell, Det.	.343
1904	Nap Lajoie, Cle	.381	1927	Harry Heilmann, Det.	.398	1950	Billy Goodman, Bos	.354
1905	Elmer Flick, Cle.	.306	1928	Goose Goslin, Wash.	.379	1951	Ferris Fain, Phi	.344
1906	George Stone, St.L	.358	1929	Lew Fonseca, Cle	.369	1952	Ferris Fain, Phi	.327
1907	Ty Cobb, Det	.350	1930	Al Simmons, Phi	.381	1953	Mickey Vernon, Wash.	.337
1908	Ty Cobb, Det	.324	1931	Al Simmons, Phi	.390	1954	Bobby Avila, Clev.	.341
1909	Ty Cobb, Det	.377	1932	Dale Alexander, Det-Bos	.367	1955	Al Kaline, Det.	.340
1910	Ty Cobb, Det	.385	1933	Jimmie Foxx, Phi	.356	1956	Mickey Mantle, NY	.353
1911	Ty Cobb, Det	.420	1934	Lou Gehrig, NY.	.363	1957	Ted Williams, Bos	.388
1912	Ty Cobb, Det	.410	1935	Buddy Myer, Wash.	.349	1958	Ted Williams, Bos	.328
1913	Ty Cobb, Det	.390	1936	Luke Appling, Chi.	.388	1959	Harvey Kuenn, Det	.353
1914	Ty Cobb, Det	.368	1937	Charlie Gehringer, Det	.371	1960	Pete Runnels, Bos	.320
1915	Ty Cobb, Det	.369	1938	Jimmie Foxx, Bos.	.349	1961	Norm Cash, Det	.361*
1916	Tris Speaker, Cle.	.386	1939	Joe DiMaggio, NY	.381	1962	Pete Runnels, Bos	.326
1917	Ty Cobb, Det	.383	1940	Joe DiMaggio, NY	.352	1963	Carl Yastrzemski, Bos.	.321
1918	Ty Cobb, Det	.382	1941	Ted Williams, Bos	.406	1964	Tony Oliva, Min	.323
1919	Ty Cobb, Det	.384	1942	Ted Williams, Bos	.356	1965	Tony Oliva, Min	.321
1920	George Sisler, St.L	.407	1943	Luke Appling, Chi.	.328	1966	Frank Robinson, Bal	.316
1921	Harry Heilmann, Det.	.394	1944	Lou Boudreau, Clev.	.327	1967	Carl Yastrzemski, Bos.	.326
1922	George Sisler, St.L	.420	1945	Snuffy Stirnweiss, NY.	.309	1968	Carl Yastrzemski, Bos.	.301
1923	Harry Heilmann, Det.	.403	1946	Mickey Vernon, Wash.	.353	1969	Rod Carew, Min	.332

Batting Average (Cont.)

Year		Avg	Year		Avg	Year		Avg
1970	Alex Johnson, Cal.	.329	1983	Wade Boggs, Bos.	.361	1996	Alex Rodriguez, Sea	.358
1971	Tony Oliva, Min	.337	1984	Don Mattingly, NY	.343	1997	Frank Thomas, Chi	.347
1972	Rod Carew, Min	.318	1985	Wade Boggs, Bos.	.368	1998	Bernie Williams, NY.	.339
1973	Rod Carew, Min	.350	1986	Wade Boggs, Bos.	.357	1999	Nomar Garciaparra,	.357
1974	Rod Carew, Min	.364	1987	Wade Boggs, Bos.	.363	2000	Nomar Garciaparra, Bos.	.372
1975	Rod Carew, Min	.359	1988	Wade Boggs, Bos.	.366	2001	Ichiro Suzuki, Sea.	.350
1976	George Brett, KC	.333	1989	Kirby Puckett, Min.	.339	2002	Manny Ramirez, Bos.	.349
1977	Rod Carew, Min	.388	1990	George Brett, KC	.329	2003	Bill Mueller, Bos	.326
1978	Rod Carew, Min	.333	1991	Julio Franco, Tex	.341			
1979	Fred Lynn, Bos	.333	1992	Edgar Martinez, Sea.	.343	*Norm Cash later admitted to using a		
1980	George Brett, KC	.390	1993	John Olerud, Tor	.363	corked bat the entire season. He		
1981	Carney Lansford, Bos.	.336	1994	Paul O'Neill, NY	.359	played 16 other seasons and never hit		
1982	Willie Wilson, KC.	.332	1995	Edgar Martinez, Sea.	.356	better than .286.		

Home Runs
National League

Multiple winners: Mike Schmidt (8); Ralph Kiner (7); Gavvy Cravath and Mel Ott (6); Hank Aaron, Chuck Klein, Willie Mays, Johnny Mize, CyWilliams and HackWilson (4);Willie McCovey (3); Ernie Banks, Johnny Bench, Barry Bonds, George Foster, Rogers Hornsby, Tim Jordan, Dave Kingman, Eddie Mathews, Mark McGwire, Dale Murphy, Bill Nicholson, Dave Robertson, Wildfire Schulte, Sammy Sosa and Willie Stargell (2).

Year		HR	Year		HR	Year		HR
1900	Herman Long, Bos	12	1933	Chuck Klein, Phi	28	1966	Hank Aaron, Atl	44
1901	Sam Crawford, Cin	16	1934	Rip Collins, St.L	35	1967	Hank Aaron, Atl	39
1902	Tommy Leach, Pit	6		& Mel Ott, NY.	35	1968	Willie McCovey, SF	36
1903	Jimmy Sheckard, Bklyn	9	1935	Wally Berger, Bos.	34	1969	Willie McCovey, SF	45
1904	Harry Lumley, Bklyn	9	1936	Mel Ott, NY.	33	1970	Johnny Bench, Cin	45
1905	Fred Odwell, Cin.	9	1937	Joe Medwick, St.L.	31	1971	Willie Stargell, Pit.	48
1906	Tim Jordan, Bklyn	12		& Mel Ott, NY.	31	1972	Johnny Bench, Cin	40
1907	Dave Brain, Bos	10	1938	Mel Ott, NY.	36	1973	Willie Stargell, Pit.	44
1908	Tim Jordan, Bklyn	12	1939	Johnny Mize, St.L	28	1974	Mike Schmidt, Phi.	36
1909	Red Murray, NY	7	1940	Johnny Mize, St.L	43	1975	Mike Schmidt, Phi.	38
1910	Fred Beck, Bos.	10	1941	Dolph Camilli, Bklyn.	34	1976	Mike Schmidt, Phi.	38
	& Wildfire Schulte, Chi	10	1942	Mel Ott, NY.	30	1977	George Foster, Cin	52
1911	Wildfire Schulte, Chi.	21	1943	Bill Nicholson, Chi	29	1978	George Foster, Cin	40
1912	Heinie Zimmerman, Chi.	14	1944	Bill Nicholson, Chi	33	1979	Dave Kingman, Chi	48
1913	Gavvy Cravath, Phi.	19	1945	Tommy Holmes, Bos	28	1980	Mike Schmidt, Phi.	48
1914	Gavvy Cravath, Phi.	19	1946	Ralph Kiner, Pit.	23	1981	Mike Schmidt, Phi.	31
1915	Gavvy Cravath, Phi.	24	1947	Ralph Kiner, Pit.	51	1982	Dave Kingman, NY.	37
1916	Cy Williams, Chi	12		& Johnny Mize, NY	51	1983	Mike Schmidt, Phi.	40
	& Dave Robertson, NY.	12	1948	Ralph Kiner, Pit.	40	1984	Dale Murphy, Atl.	36
1917	Gavvy Cravath, Phi.	12		& Johnny Mize, NY	40		& Mike Schmidt, Phi.	36
	& Dave Robertson, NY.	12	1949	Ralph Kiner, Pit.	54	1985	Dale Murphy, Atl.	37
1918	Gavvy Cravath, Phi.	8	1950	Ralph Kiner, Pit.	47	1986	Mike Schmidt, Phi.	37
1919	Gavvy Cravath, Phi.	12	1951	Ralph Kiner, Pit.	42	1987	Andre Dawson, Chi	49
1920	Cy Williams, Phi.	15	1952	Ralph Kiner, Pit.	37	1988	Darryl Strawberry, NY.	39
1921	George Kelly, NY	23		& Hank Sauer, Chi	37	1989	Kevin Mitchell, SF	47
1922	Rogers Hornsby, St.L.	42	1953	Eddie Mathews, Mil	47	1990	Ryne Sandberg, Chi	40
1923	Cy Williams, Phi.	41	1954	Ted Kluszewski, Cin	49	1991	Howard Johnson, NY.	38
1924	Jack Fournier, Bklyn	27	1955	Willie Mays, NY.	51	1992	Fred McGriff, SD	35
1925	Rogers Hornsby, St.L.	39	1956	Duke Snider, Bklyn	43	1993	Barry Bonds, SF	46
1926	Hack Wilson, Chi	21	1957	Hank Aaron, Mil.	44	1994	Matt Williams, SF	43
1927	Cy Williams, Phi.	30	1958	Ernie Banks, Chi	47	1995	Dante Bichette, Col.	40
	& Hack Wilson, Chi	30	1959	Eddie Mathews, Mil	46	1996	Andres Galarraga, Col	47
1928	Jim Bottomley, St.L.	31	1960	Ernie Banks, Chi	41	1997	Larry Walker, Col	49
	& Hack Wilson, Chi	31	1961	Orlando Cepeda, SF.	46	1998	Mark McGwire, St.L	70
1929	Chuck Klein, Phi	43	1962	Willie Mays, SF	49	1999	Mark McGwire, St.L	65
1930	Hack Wilson, Chi	56	1963	Hank Aaron, Mil.	44	2000	Sammy Sosa, Chi	50
1931	Chuck Klein, Phi	31		& Willie McCovey, SF	44	2001	Barry Bonds, SF	73
1932	Chuck Klein, Phi	38	1964	Willie Mays, SF	47	2002	Sammy Sosa, Chi	49
	& Mel Ott, NY.	38	1965	Willie Mays, SF	52	2003	Jim Thome, Phi	47

American League

Multiple winners: Babe Ruth (12); Harmon Killebrew (6); Home Run Baker, Harry Davis, Jimmie Foxx, Hank Greenberg, Ken Griffey Jr., Reggie Jackson, Mickey Mantle and Ted Williams (4); Lou Gehrig, Jim Rice and Alex Rodriguez (3); Dick Allen, Tony Armas, Jose Canseco, Joe DiMaggio, Larry Doby, Cecil Fielder, Juan Gonzalez, Mark McGwire, Wally Pipp, Al Rosen and Gorman Thomas (2).

Year		HR	Year		HR	Year		HR
1901	Nap Lajoie, Phi	14	1905	Harry Davis, Phi	8	1909	Ty Cobb, Det	9
1902	Socks Seybold, Phi	16	1906	Harry Davis, Phi	12	1910	Jake Stahl, Bos	10
1903	Buck Freeman, Bos	13	1907	Harry Davis, Phi	8	1911	Home Run Baker, Phi.	11
1904	Harry Davis, Phi	10	1908	Sam Crawford, Det.	7			

Year	HR	Year	HR	Year	HR
1912 Home Run Baker, Phi	10	1944 Nick Etten, NY	22	1977 Jim Rice, Bos	39
& Tris Speaker, Bos	10	1945 Vern Stephens, St.L	24	1978 Jim Rice, Bos	46
1913 Home Run Baker, Phi	12	1946 Hank Greenberg, Det	44	1979 Gorman Thomas, Mil	45
1914 Home Run Baker, Phi	9	1947 Ted Williams, Bos	32	1980 Reggie Jackson, NY	41
1915 Braggo Roth, Chi-Cle	7	1948 Joe DiMaggio, NY	39	& Ben Oglivie, Mil	41
1916 Wally Pipp, NY	12	1949 Ted Williams, Bos	43	1981 Tony Armas, Oak	22
1917 Wally Pipp, NY	9	1950 Al Rosen, Cle	37	Dwight Evans, Bos	22
1918 Babe Ruth, Bos	11	1951 Gus Zernial, Chi-Phi	33	Bobby Grich, Cal	22
& Tilly Walker, Phi	11	1952 Larry Doby, Cle	32	& Eddie Murray, Bal	22
1919 Babe Ruth, Bos	29	1953 Al Rosen, Cle	43	1982 Reggie Jackson, Cal	39
1920 Babe Ruth, NY	54	1954 Larry Doby, Cle	32	& Gorman Thomas, Mil	39
1921 Babe Ruth, NY	59	1955 Mickey Mantle, NY	37	1983 Jim Rice, Bos	39
1922 Ken Williams, St.L	39	1956 Mickey Mantle, NY	52	1984 Tony Armas, Bos	43
1923 Babe Ruth, NY	41	1957 Roy Sievers, Wash	42	1985 Darrell Evans, Det	40
1924 Babe Ruth, NY	46	1958 Mickey Mantle, NY	42	1986 Jesse Barfield, Tor	40
1925 Bob Meusel, NY	33	1959 Rocky Colavito, Cle	42	1987 Mark McGwire, Oak	49
1926 Babe Ruth, NY	47	& Harmon Killebrew, Wash	42	1988 Jose Canseco, Oak	42
1927 Babe Ruth, NY	60	1960 Mickey Mantle, NY	40	1989 Fred McGriff, Tor	36
1928 Babe Ruth, NY	54	1961 Roger Maris, NY	61	1990 Cecil Fielder, Det	51
1929 Babe Ruth, NY	46	1962 Harmon Killebrew, Min	48	1991 Jose Canseco, Oak	44
1930 Babe Ruth, NY	49	1963 Harmon Killebrew, Min	45	& Cecil Fielder, Det	44
1931 Lou Gehrig, NY	46	1964 Harmon Killebrew, Min	49	1992 Juan Gonzalez, Tex	43
& Babe Ruth, NY	46	1965 Tony Conigliaro, Bos	32	1993 Juan Gonzalez, Tex	46
1932 Jimmie Foxx, Phi	58	1966 Frank Robinson, Bal	49	1994 Ken Griffey Jr., Sea	40
1933 Jimmie Foxx, Phi	48	1967 Harmon Killebrew, Min	44	1995 Albert Belle, Cle	50
1934 Lou Gehrig, NY	49	& Carl Yastrzemski, Bos	44	1996 Mark McGwire, Oak	52
1935 Jimmie Foxx, Phi	36	1968 Frank Howard, Wash	44	1997 Ken Griffey Jr., Sea	56
& Hank Greenberg, Det	36	1969 Harmon Killebrew, Min	49	1998 Ken Griffey Jr., Sea	56
1936 Lou Gehrig, NY	49	1970 Frank Howard, Wash	44	1999 Ken Griffey Jr., Sea	48
1937 Joe DiMaggio, NY	46	1971 Bill Melton, Chi	33	2000 Troy Glaus, Ana	47
1938 Hank Greenberg, Det	58	1972 Dick Allen, Chi	37	2001 Alex Rodriguez, Tex	52
1939 Jimmie Foxx, Bos	35	1973 Reggie Jackson, Oak	32	2002 Alex Rodriguez, Tex	57
1940 Hank Greenberg, Det	41	1974 Dick Allen, Chi	32	2003 Alex Rodriguez, Tex	47
1941 Ted Williams, Bos	37	1975 Reggie Jackson, Oak	36		
1942 Ted Williams, Bos	36	& George Scott, Mil	36		
1943 Rudy York, Det	34	1976 Graig Nettles, NY	32		

Runs Batted In
National League

Multiple winners: Hank Aaron, Rogers Hornsby, Sherry Magee, Mike Schmidt and Honus Wagner (4); Johnny Bench, George Foster, Joe Medwick, Johnny Mize and Heinie Zimmerman (3); Ernie Banks, Jim Bottomley, Orlando Cepeda, Gavvy Cravath, Andres Galarraga, George Kelly, Chuck Klein, Willie McCovey, Dale Murphy, Stan Musial, Bill Nicholson, Sammy Sosa and Hack Wilson (2).

Year	RBI	Year	RBI	Year	RBI
1900 Elmer Flick, Phi	110	1925 Rogers Hornsby, St.L	143	1952 Hank Sauer, Chi	121
1901 Honus Wagner, Pit	126	1926 Jim Bottomley, St.L	120	1953 Roy Campanella, Bklyn	142
1902 Honus Wagner, Pit	91	1927 Paul Waner, Pit	131	1954 Ted Kluszewski, Cin	141
1903 Sam Mertes, NY	104	1928 Jim Bottomley, St.L	136	1955 Duke Snider, Bklyn	136
1904 Bill Dahlen, NY	80	1929 Hack Wilson, Chi	159	1956 Stan Musial, St.L	109
1905 Cy Seymour, Cin	121	1930 Hack Wilson, Chi	191	1957 Hank Aaron, Mil	132
1906 Jim Nealon, Pit	83	1931 Chuck Klein, Phi	121	1958 Ernie Banks, Chi	129
& Harry Steinfeldt, Chi	83	1932 Don Hurst, Phi	143	1959 Ernie Banks, Chi	143
1907 Sherry Magee, Phi	85	1933 Chuck Klein, Phi	120	1960 Hank Aaron, Mil	126
1908 Honus Wagner, Pit	109	1934 Mel Ott, NY	135	1961 Orlando Cepeda, SF	142
1909 Honus Wagner, Pit	100	1935 Wally Berger, Bos	130	1962 Tommy Davis, LA	153
1910 Sherry Magee, Phi	123	1936 Joe Medwick, St.L	138	1963 Hank Aaron, Mil	130
1911 Wildfire Schulte, Chi	121	1937 Joe Medwick, St.L	154	1964 Ken Boyer, St.L	119
1912 Heinie Zimmerman, Chi	103	1938 Joe Medwick, St.L	122	1965 Deron Johnson, Cin	130
1913 Gavvy Cravath, Phi	128	1939 Frank McCormick, Cin	128	1966 Hank Aaron, Atl	127
1914 Sherry Magee, Phi	103	1940 Johnny Mize, St.L	137	1967 Orlando Cepeda, St.L	111
1915 Gavvy Cravath, Phi	115	1941 Dolph Camilli, Bklyn	120	1968 Willie McCovey, SF	105
1916 Heinie Zimmerman, Chi-NY	83	1942 Johnny Mize, NY	110	1969 Willie McCovey, SF	126
1917 Heinie Zimmerman, NY	102	1943 Bill Nicholson, Chi	128	1970 Johnny Bench, Cin	148
1918 Sherry Magee, Cin	76	1944 Bill Nicholson, Chi	122	1971 Joe Torre, St.L	137
1919 Hy Myers, Bklyn	73	1945 Dixie Walker, Bklyn	124	1972 Johnny Bench, Cin	125
1920 Rogers Hornsby, St.L	94	1946 Enos Slaughter, St.L	130	1973 Willie Stargell, Pit	119
& George Kelly, NY	94	1947 Johnny Mize, NY	138	1974 Johnny Bench, Cin	129
1921 Rogers Hornsby, St.L	126	1948 Stan Musial, St.L	131	1975 Greg Luzinski, Phi	120
1922 Rogers Hornsby, St.L	152	1949 Ralph Kiner, Pit	127	1976 George Foster, Cin	121
1923 Irish Meusel, NY	125	1950 Del Ennis, Phi	126	1977 George Foster, Cin	149
1924 George Kelly, NY	136	1951 Monte Irvin, NY	121	1978 George Foster, Cin	120

Runs Batted In (Cont.)

Year		RBI	Year		RBI	Year		RBI
1979	Dave Winfield, SD	118	1986	Mike Schmidt, Phi.	119	1995	Dante Bichette, Col	128
1980	Mike Schmidt, Phi.	121	1987	Andre Dawson, Chi	137	1996	Andres Galarraga, Col	150
1981	Mike Schmidt, Phi.	91	1988	Will Clark, SF	109	1997	Andres Galarraga, Col	140
1982	Dale Murphy, Atl	109	1989	Kevin Mitchell, SF.	125	1998	Sammy Sosa, Chi.	158
	& Al Oliver, Mon	109	1990	Matt Williams, SF.	122	1999	Mark McGwire, St.L.	147
1983	Dale Murphy, Atl	121	1991	Howard Johnson, NY	117	2000	Todd Helton, Col	147
1984	Gary Carter, Mon.	106	1992	Darren Daulton, Phi.	109	2001	Sammy Sosa, Chi.	160
	& Mike Schmidt, Phi.	106	1993	Barry Bonds, SF	123	2002	Lance Berkman, Hou	128
1985	Dave Parker, Cin	125	1994	Jeff Bagwell, Hou	116	2003	Preston Wilson, Col	141

American League

Multiple winners: Babe Ruth (6); Lou Gehrig (5); Ty Cobb, Hank Greenberg and Ted Williams (4); Albert Belle, Sam Crawford, Cecil Fielder, Jimmie Foxx, Jackie Jensen, Harmon Killebrew, Vern Stephens and Bobby Veach (3); Home Run Baker, Cecil Cooper, Harry Davis, Joe DiMaggio, Buck Freeman, Nap Lajoie, Roger Maris, Jim Rice, Al Rosen, and Bobby Veach (2).

Year		RBI	Year		RBI	Year		RBI
1901	Nap Lajoie, Phi.	125	1936	Hal Trosky, Cle.	162	1970	Frank Howard, Wash	126
1902	Buck Freeman, Bos.	121	1937	Hank Greenberg, Det	183	1971	Harmon Killebrew, Min	119
1903	Buck Freeman, Bos.	104	1938	Jimmie Foxx, Bos	175	1972	Dick Allen, Chi	113
1904	Nap Lajoie, Cle	102	1939	Ted Williams, Bos.	145	1973	Reggie Jackson, Oak.	117
1905	Harry Davis, Phi.	83	1940	Hank Greenberg, Det	150	1974	Jeff Burroughs, Tex	118
1906	Harry Davis, Phi.	96	1941	Joe DiMaggio, NY.	125	1975	George Scott, Mil.	109
1907	Ty Cobb, Det.	116	1942	Ted Williams, Bos.	137	1976	Lee May, Bal	109
1908	Ty Cobb, Det.	108	1943	Rudy York, Det	118	1977	Larry Hisle, Min	119
1909	Ty Cobb, Det.	107	1944	Vern Stephens, St.L.	109	1978	Jim Rice, Bos	139
1910	Sam Crawford, Det.	120	1945	Nick Etten, NY.	111	1979	Don Baylor, Cal	139
1911	Ty Cobb, Det.	144	1946	Hank Greenberg, Det	127	1980	Cecil Cooper, Mil.	122
1912	Home Run Baker, Phi.	133	1947	Ted Williams, Bos.	114	1981	Eddie Murray, Bal.	78
1913	Home Run Baker, Phi.	126	1948	Joe DiMaggio, NY.	155	1982	Hal McRae, KC.	133
1914	Sam Crawford, Det.	104	1949	Ted Williams, Bos.	159	1983	Cecil Cooper, Mil.	126
1915	Sam Crawford, Det.	112		& Vern Stephens, Bos.	159		& Jim Rice, Bos.	126
	& Bobby Veach, Det	112	1950	Walt Dropo, Bos.	144	1984	Tony Armas, Bos.	123
1916	Del Pratt, St.L.	103		& Vern Stephens, Bos.	144	1985	Don Mattingly, NY	145
1917	Bobby Veach, Det.	103	1951	Gus Zernial, Chi-Phi.	129	1986	Joe Carter, Cle	121
1918	Bobby Veach, Det.	78	1952	Al Rosen, Cle.	105	1987	George Bell, Tor	134
1919	Babe Ruth, Bos.	114	1953	Al Rosen, Cle.	145	1988	Jose Canseco, Oak.	124
1920	Babe Ruth, NY.	137	1954	Larry Doby, Cle.	126	1989	Ruben Sierra, Tex	119
1921	Babe Ruth, NY.	171	1955	Ray Boone, Det.	116	1990	Cecil Fielder, Det	132
1922	Ken Williams, St.L.	155		& Jackie Jensen, Bos.	116	1991	Cecil Fielder, Det	133
1923	Babe Ruth, NY.	131	1956	Mickey Mantle, NY.	130	1992	Cecil Fielder, Det	124
1924	Goose Goslin, Wash.	129	1957	Roy Sievers, Wash	114	1993	Albert Belle, Cle.	129
1925	Bob Meusel, NY.	138	1958	Jackie Jensen, Bos.	122	1994	Kirby Puckett, Min.	112
1926	Babe Ruth, NY.	145	1959	Jackie Jensen, Bos.	112	1995	Albert Belle, Cle.	126
1927	Lou Gehrig, NY	175	1960	Roger Maris, NY.	112		& Mo Vaughn, Bos.	126
1928	Lou Gehrig, NY	142	1961	Roger Maris, NY.	142	1996	Albert Belle, Cle.	148
	& Babe Ruth, NY	142	1962	Harmon Killebrew, Min	126	1997	Ken Griffey Jr., Sea.	147
1929	Al Simmons, Phi	157	1963	Dick Stuart, Bos	118	1998	Juan Gonzalez, Tex.	157
1930	Lou Gehrig, NY	174	1964	Brooks Robinson, Bal	118	1999	Manny Ramirez, Cle.	165
1931	Lou Gehrig, NY	184	1965	Rocky Colavito, Cle	108	2000	Edgar Martinez, Sea.	145
1932	Jimmie Foxx, Phi.	169	1966	Frank Robinson, Bal	122	2001	Bret Boone, Sea	141
1933	Jimmie Foxx, Phi.	163	1967	Carl Yastrzemski, Bos	121	2002	Alex Rodriguez, Tex.	142
1934	Lou Gehrig, NY	165	1968	Ken Harrelson, Bos.	109	2003	Carlos Delgado, Tor	145
1935	Hank Greenberg, Det	170	1969	Harmon Killebrew, Min	140			

Batting Triple Crown Winners

Players who led either league in Batting Average, Home Runs and Runs Batted In over a single season.

National League

	Year	Avg	HR	RBI
Paul Hines, Providence	1878	.358	4	50
Hugh Duffy, Boston	1894	.438	18	145
Heinie Zimmerman, Chicago	1912	.372	14	103
Rogers Hornsby, St. Louis	1922	.401	42	152
Rogers Hornsby, St. Louis	1925	.403	39	143
Chuck Klein, Philadelphia	1933	.368	28	120
Joe Medwick, St. Louis	1937	.374	31*	154

*Tied for league lead in HRs with Mel Ott, NY.

American League

	Year	Avg	HR	RBI
Nap Lajoie, Philadelphia	1901	.422	14	125
Ty Cobb, Detroit.	1909	.377	9	115
Jimmie Foxx, Philadelphia	1933	.356	48	163
Lou Gehrig, New York	1934	.363	49	165
Ted Williams, Boston	1942	.356	36	137
Ted Williams, Boston	1947	.343	32	114
Mickey Mantle, New York	1956	.353	52	130
Frank Robinson, Baltimore	1966	.316	49	122
Carl Yastrzemski, Boston	1967	.326	44*	121

*Tied for league lead in HRs with Harmon Killebrew, Min.

Stolen Bases
National League

Multiple winners: Max Carey (10); Lou Brock (8); Vince Coleman and MauryWills (6); HonusWagner (5); Bob Bescher, Kiki Cuyler, Willie Mays and Tim Raines (4); Bill Bruton, Frankie Frisch, Pepper Martin and Tony Womack (3); George Burns, Luis Castillo, Frank Chance, Augie Galan, Marquis Grissom, Stan Hack, Sam Jethroe, Davey Lopes, Omar Moreno, Pete Reiser and Jackie Robinson (2).

Year		SB	Year		SB	Year		SB
1900	Patsy Donovan, St.L	45	1934	Pepper Martin, St.L.	23	1970	Bobby Tolan, Cin	57
	& George Van Haltren, NY.	45	1935	Augie Galan, Chi	22	1971	Lou Brock, St.L	64
1901	Honus Wagner, Pit	49	1936	Pepper Martin, St.L.	23	1972	Lou Brock, St.L	63
1902	Honus Wagner, Pit	42	1937	Augie Galan, Chi	23	1973	Lou Brock, St.L	70
1903	Frank Chance, Chi	67	1938	Stan Hack, Chi.	16	1974	Lou Brock, St.L.	118
	& Jimmy Sheckard, Bklyn.	67	1939	Stan Hack, Chi.	17	1975	Davey Lopes, LA.	77
1904	Honus Wagner, Pit	53		& Lee Handley, Pit	17	1976	Davey Lopes, LA.	63
1905	Art Devlin, NY.	59				1977	Frank Taveras, Pit	70
	& Billy Maloney, Chi	59	1940	Lonny Frey, Cin	22	1978	Omar Moreno, Pit.	71
1906	Frank Chance, Chi	57	1941	Danny Murtaugh, Phi	18	1979	Omar Moreno, Pit.	77
1907	Honus Wagner, Pit	61	1942	Pete Reiser, Bklyn	20			
1908	Honus Wagner, Pit	53	1943	Arky Vaughan, Bklyn.	20	1980	Ron LeFlore, Mon	97
1909	Bob Bescher, Cin	54	1944	Johnny Barrett, Pit.	28	1981	Tim Raines, Mon.	71
			1945	Red Schoendienst, St.L.	26	1982	Tim Raines, Mon.	78
1910	Bob Bescher, Cin	70	1946	Pete Reiser, Bklyn	34	1983	Tim Raines, Mon.	90
1911	Bob Bescher, Cin	81	1947	Jackie Robinson, Bklyn.	29	1984	Tim Raines, Mon.	75
1912	Bob Bescher, Cin	67	1948	Richie Ashburn, Phi.	32	1985	Vince Coleman, St.L.	110
1913	Max Carey, Pit	61	1949	Jackie Robinson, Bklyn.	37	1986	Vince Coleman, St.L.	107
1914	George Burns, NY	62				1987	Vince Coleman, St.L.	109
1915	Max Carey, Pit.	36	1950	Sam Jethroe, Bos.	35	1988	Vince Coleman, St.L	81
1916	Max Carey, Pit.	63	1951	Sam Jethroe, Bos.	35	1989	Vince Coleman, St.L	65
1917	Max Carey, Pit.	46	1952	Pee Wee Reese, Bklyn.	30			
1918	Max Carey, Pit.	58	1953	Bill Bruton, Mil.	26	1990	Vince Coleman, St.L	77
1919	George Burns, NY	40	1954	Bill Bruton, Mil.	34	1991	Marquis Grissom, Mon	76
			1955	Bill Bruton, Mil.	25	1992	Marquis Grissom, Mon	78
1920	Max Carey, Pit.	52	1956	Willie Mays, NY.	40	1993	Chuck Carr, Fla.	58
1921	Frankie Frisch, NY	49	1957	Willie Mays, NY.	38	1994	Craig Biggio, Hou	39
1922	Max Carey, Pit.	51	1958	Willie Mays, SF	31	1995	Quilvio Veras, Fla	56
1923	Max Carey, Pit.	51	1959	Willie Mays, SF	27	1996	Eric Young, Col	53
1924	Max Carey, Pit.	49	1960	Maury Wills, LA	50	1997	Tony Womack, Pit	60
1925	Max Carey, Pit.	46	1961	Maury Wills, LA	35	1998	Tony Womack, Pit.	58
1926	Kiki Cuyler, Pit.	35	1962	Maury Wills, LA	104	1999	Tony Womack, Ari	72
1927	Frankie Frisch, St.L	48	1963	Maury Wills, LA	40	2000	Luis Castillo, Fla	62
1928	Kiki Cuyler, Chi.	37	1964	Maury Wills, LA	53	2001	Juan Pierre, Col.	46
1929	Kiki Cuyler, Chi.	43	1965	Maury Wills, LA	94		& Jimmy Rollins, Phi	46
1930	Kiki Cuyler, Chi.	37	1966	Lou Brock, St.L	74	2002	Luis Castillo, Fla	48
1931	Frankie Frisch, St.L	28	1967	Lou Brock, St.L	52	2003	Juan Pierre, Fla.	65
1932	Chuck Klein, Phi	20	1968	Lou Brock, St.L	62			
1933	Pepper Martin, St.L.	26	1969	Lou Brock, St.L	53			

30 Homers & 30 Stolen Bases in One Season

National League

	Year	Gm	HR	SB
Willie Mays, NY Giants	1956	152	36	40
Willie Mays, NY Giants	1957	152	35	38
Hank Aaron, Milwaukee.	1963	161	44	31
Bobby Bonds, San Francisco	1969	158	32	45
Bobby Bonds, San Francisco	1973	160	39	43
Dale Murphy, Atlanta	1983	162	36	30
Eric Davis, Cincinnati	1987	129	37	50
Howard Johnson, NY Mets	1987	157	36	32
Darryl Strawberry, NY Mets	1987	154	39	36
Howard Johnson, NY Mets.	1989	153	36	41
Ron Gant, Atlanta	1990	152	32	33
Barry Bonds, Pittsburgh	1990	151	33	52
Ron Gant, Atlanta	1991	154	32	34
Howard Johnson, NY Mets.	1991	156	38	30
Barry Bonds, Pittsburgh	1992	140	34	39
Sammy Sosa, Chicago	1993	159	33	36
Barry Bonds, San Francisco	1995	144	33	31
Sammy Sosa, Chicago	1995	144	36	34
Barry Bonds, San Francisco	1996	158	42	40
Ellis Burks, Colorado	1996	156	40	32
Dante Bichette, Colorado	1996	159	31	31
Barry Larkin, Cincinnati.	1996	152	33	36
Larry Walker, Colorado	1997	153	49	33
Barry Bonds, San Francisco	1997	159	40	37
Raul Mondesi, Los Angeles.	1997	159	30	32
Jeff Bagwell, Houston	1997	162	43	31
Jeff Bagwell, Houston	1999	162	42	30
Raul Mondesi, Los Angeles.	1999	159	33	36
Preston Wilson, Florida	2000	161	31	36
Vladimir Guerrero, Montreal	2001	159	34	37
Bobby Abreu, Philadelphia.	2001	162	31	36
Vladimir Guerrero, Montreal	2002	161	39	40

American League

	Year	Gm	HR	SB
Kenny Williams, St. Louis	1922	153	39	37
Tommy Harper, Milwaukee.	1970	154	31	38
Bobby Bonds, New York.	1975	145	32	30
Bobby Bonds, California.	1977	158	37	41
Bobby Bonds, Chicago-Texas.	1978	156	31	43
Joe Carter, Cleveland	1987	149	32	31
Jose Canseco, Oakland	1988	158	42	40
Alex Rodriguez, Seattle.	1998	161	42	46
Shawn Green, Toronto	1998	158	35	35
Jose Cruz Jr., Toronto.	2001	146	34	32
Alfonso Soriano, New York	2002	156	39	41
Alfonso Soriano, New York	2003	156	38	35

Stolen Bases (Cont.)
American League

Multiple winners: Rickey Henderson (12); Luis Aparicio (9); Bert Campaneris, George Case and Ty Cobb (6); Kenny Lofton (5); Ben Chapman, Eddie Collins and George Sisler (4); Bob Dillinger, Minnie Minoso and Bill Werber (3); Elmer Flick, Tommy Harper, Brian Hunter, Clyde Milan, Johnny Mostil, Bill North and Snuffy Stirnweiss (2).

Year		SB	Year		SB	Year		SB
1901	Frank Isbell, Chi	52	1936	Lyn Lary, St.L	37	1970	Bert Campaneris, Oak.	42
1902	Topsy Hartsel, Phi	47	1937	Ben Chapman, Wash-Bos	35	1971	Amos Otis, KC	52
1903	Harry Bay, Cle	45		& Bill Werber, Phi	35	1972	Bert Campaneris, Oak.	52
1904	Elmer Flick, Cle	42	1938	Frank Crosetti, NY	27	1973	Tommy Harper, Bos.	54
1905	Danny Hoffman, Phi	46	1939	George Case, Wash	51	1974	Bill North, Oak.	54
1906	John Anderson, Wash	39	1940	George Case, Wash	35	1975	Mickey Rivers, CA	70
	& Elmer Flick, Cle	39	1941	George Case, Wash	33	1976	Bill North, Oak.	75
1907	Ty Cobb, Det	49	1942	George Case, Wash	44	1977	Freddie Patek, KC.	53
1908	Patsy Dougherty, Chi	47	1943	George Case, Wash	61	1978	Ron LeFlore, Det	68
1909	Ty Cobb, Det	76	1944	Snuffy Stirnweiss, NY.	55	1979	Willie Wilson, KC.	83
1910	Eddie Collins, Phi	81	1945	Snuffy Stirnweiss, NY.	33	1980	Rickey Henderson, Oak.	100
1911	Ty Cobb, Det	83	1946	George Case, Cle	28	1981	Rickey Henderson, Oak.	56
1912	Clyde Milan, Wash.	88	1947	Bob Dillinger, St.L	34	1982	Rickey Henderson, Oak.	130
1913	Clyde Milan, Wash.	75	1948	Bob Dillinger, St.L	28	1983	Rickey Henderson, Oak.	108
1914	Fritz Maisel, NY	74	1949	Bob Dillinger, St.L	20	1984	Rickey Henderson, Oak.	66
1915	Ty Cobb, Det	96	1950	Dom DiMaggio, Bos.	15	1985	Rickey Henderson, NY.	80
1916	Ty Cobb, Det	68	1951	Minnie Minoso, Cle-Chi.	31	1986	Rickey Henderson, NY.	87
1917	Ty Cobb, Det	55	1952	Minnie Minoso, Chi	22	1987	Harold Reynolds, Sea	60
1918	George Sisler, St.L	45	1953	Minnie Minoso, Chi	25	1988	Rickey Henderson, NY.	93
1919	Eddie Collins, Chi	33	1954	Jackie Jensen, Bos.	22	1989	R. Henderson, NY-Oak	77
1920	Sam Rice, Wash.	63	1955	Jim Rivera, Chi	25	1990	Rickey Henderson, Oak.	65
1921	George Sisler, Wash.	35	1956	Luis Aparicio, Chi	21	1991	Rickey Henderson, Oak.	58
1922	George Sisler, St.L	51	1957	Luis Aparicio, Chi	28	1992	Kenny Lofton, Cle	66
1923	Eddie Collins, Chi.	47	1958	Luis Aparicio, Chi	29	1993	Kenny Lofton, Cle	70
1924	Eddie Collins, Chi.	42	1959	Luis Aparicio, Chi	56	1994	Kenny Lofton, Cle	60
1925	Johnny Mostil, Chi	43	1960	Luis Aparicio, Chi	51	1995	Kenny Lofton, Cle	54
1926	Johnny Mostil, Chi	35	1961	Luis Aparicio, Chi	53	1996	Kenny Lofton, Cle	75
1927	George Sisler, St.L	27	1962	Luis Aparicio, Chi	31	1997	Brian Hunter, Det	74
1928	Buddy Myer, Bos.	30	1963	Luis Aparicio, Bal	40	1998	Rickey Henderson, Oak.	66
1929	Charlie Gehringer, Det.	28	1964	Luis Aparicio, Bal	57	1999	Brian Hunter, Det-Sea.	44
1930	Marty McManus, Det	23	1965	Bert Campaneris, KC	51	2000	Johnny Damon, KC.	46
1931	Ben Chapman, NY.	61	1966	Bert Campaneris, KC	52	2001	Ichiro Suzuki, Sea.	56
1932	Ben Chapman, NY.	38	1967	Bert Campaneris, KC	55	2002	Alfonso Soriano, NY.	41
1933	Ben Chapman, NY.	27	1968	Bert Campaneris, Oak.	62	2003	Carl Crawford, TB	55
1934	Bill Werber, Bos	40	1969	Tommy Harper, Sea	73			
1935	Bill Werber, Bos	29						

Consecutive Game Streaks
(Regular season games through 2003)

Games Played

Gm		Dates of Streak
2632	Cal Ripken Jr., Bal	5/30/82 to 9/19/98
2130	Lou Gehrig, NY	6/1/25 to 4/30/39
1307	Everett Scott, Bos-NY	6/20/16 to 5/5/25
1207	Steve Garvey, LA-SD.	9/3/75 to 7/29/83
1117	Billy Williams, Cubs	9/22/63 to 9/2/70
1103	Joe Sewell, Cle	9/13/22 to 4/30/30
895	Stan Musial, St.L	4/15/52 to 8/23/57
829	Eddie Yost, Wash	4/30/49 to 5/11/55
822	Gus Suhr, Pit	9/11/31 to 6/4/37
798	Nellie Fox, Chisox.	8/8/55 to 9/3/60
745	Pete Rose, Cin-Phi	9/2/78 to 8/23/83
740	Dale Murphy, Atl.	9/26/81 to 7/8/86
730	Richie Ashburn, Phi	6/7/50 to 4/13/55
717	Ernie Banks, Cubs.	8/28/56 to 6/22/61
678	Pete Rose, Cin	9/28/73 to 5/7/78

Others

Gm		Gm	
673	Earl Averill	565	Aaron Ward
652	Frank McCormick	546	Alex Rodriguez
648	Sandy Alomar Sr.	540	Candy LaChance
618	Eddie Brown	535	Buck Freeman
594	Miguel Tejada*	533	Fred Luderus
585	Roy McMillan	511	Clyde Milan
577	George Pinckney	511	Charlie Gehringer
574	Steve Brodie	508	Vada Pinson

* Current

Hitting

	Gm	Year
Joe DiMaggio, New York (AL)	56	1941
Willie Keeler, Baltimore (NL).	44	1897
Pete Rose, Cincinnati (NL)	44	1978
Bill Dahlen, Chicago (NL)	42	1894
George Sisler, St. Louis (AL)	41	1922
Ty Cobb, Detroit (AL)	40	1911
Paul Molitor, Milwaukee (AL)	39	1987
Tommy Holmes, Boston (NL)	37	1945
Billy Hamilton, Philadelphia (NL)	36	1894
Fred Clarke, Louisville (NL)	35	1895
Ty Cobb, Detroit (AL)	35	1917
Luis Castillo, Florida (NL).	35	2002
Ty Cobb, Detroit (AL)	34	1912
George Sisler, St. Louis (AL)	34	1925
George McQuinn, St. Louis (AL).	34	1938
Dom DiMaggio, Boston (AL)	34	1949
Benito Santiago, San Diego (NL)	34	1987
George Davis, New York (NL)	33	1893
Hal Chase, New York (AL)	33	1907
Rogers Hornsby, St. Louis (NL)	33	1922
Heinie Manush, Washington (AL).	33	1933
Ed Delahanty, Philadelphia (NL).	31	1899
Nap Lajoie, Cleveland (AL).	31	1906
Sam Rice, Washington, (AL)	31	1924
Willie Davis, Los Angeles (NL)	31	1969
Rico Carty, Atlanta (NL)	31	1970
Ken Landreaux, Minnesota (AL)	31	1980
Vladimir Guerrero, Montreal (NL).	31	1999

Annual Pitching Leaders (since 1900)
Winning Percentage
At least 15 wins, except in strike years of 1981 and 1994 (when the minimum was 10).

National League

Multiple winners: Ed Reulbach and Tom Seaver (3); Larry Benton, Harry Brecheen, Jack Chesbro, Paul Derringer, Freddie Fitzsimmons, Don Gullett, Claude Hendrix, Carl Hubbell, Randy Johnson, Sandy Koufax, Bill Lee, Greg Maddux, Christy Mathewson, Don Newcombe, Preacher Roe and John Smoltz (2).

Year		W-L	Pct	Year		W-L	Pct
1900	Jesse Tannehill, Pittsburgh	20-6	.769	1953	Carl Erskine, Brooklyn	20-6	.769
1901	Jack Chesbro, Pittsburgh	21-10	.677	1954	Johnny Antonelli, New York	21-7	.750
1902	Jack Chesbro, Pittsburgh	28-6	.824	1955	Don Newcombe, Brooklyn	20-5	.800
1903	Sam Leever, Pittsburgh	25-7	.781	1956	Don Newcombe, Brooklyn	27-7	.794
1904	Joe McGinnity, New York	35-8	.814	1957	Bob Buhl, Milwaukee	18-7	.720
1905	Christy Mathewson, New York	31-8	.795	1958	Warren Spahn, Milwaukee	22-11	.667
1906	Ed Reulbach, Chicago	19-4	.826		& Lew Burdette, Milwaukee	20-10	.667
1907	Ed Reulbach, Chicago	17-4	.810	1959	Roy Face, Pittsburgh	18-1	.947
1908	Ed Reulbach, Chicago	24-7	.774				
1909	Howie Camnitz, Pittsburgh	25-6	.806	1960	Ernie Broglio, St. Louis	21-9	.700
	& Christy Mathewson, New York	25-6	.806	1961	Johnny Podres, Los Angeles	18-5	.783
				1962	Bob Purkey, Cincinnati	23-5	.821
1910	King Cole, Chicago	20-4	.833	1963	Ron Perranoski, Los Angeles	16-3	.842
1911	Rube Marquard, New York	24-7	.774	1964	Sandy Koufax, Los Angeles	19-5	.792
1912	Claude Hendrix, Pittsburgh	24-9	.727	1965	Sandy Koufax, Los Angeles	26-8	.765
1913	Bert Humphries, Chicago	16-4	.800	1966	Juan Marichal, San Francisco	25-6	.806
1914	Bill James, Boston	26-7	.788	1967	Dick Hughes, St. Louis	16-6	.727
1915	Grover Alexander, Phila.	31-10	.756	1968	Steve Blass, Pittsburgh	18-6	.750
1916	Tom Hughes, Boston	16-3	.842	1969	Tom Seaver, New York	25-7	.781
1917	Ferdie Schupp, New York	21-7	.750				
1918	Claude Hendrix, Chicago	19-7	.731	1970	Bob Gibson, St. Louis	23-7	.767
1919	Dutch Ruether, Cincinnati	19-6	.760	1971	Don Gullett, Cincinnati	16-6	.727
				1972	Gary Nolan, Cincinnati	15-5	.750
1920	Burleigh Grimes, Brooklyn	23-11	.676	1973	Tommy John, Los Angeles	16-7	.696
1921	Bill Doak, St. Louis	15-6	.714	1974	Andy Messersmith, Los Angeles	20-6	.769
1922	Pete Donohue, Cincinnati	18-9	.667	1975	Don Gullett, Cincinnati	15-4	.789
1923	Dolf Luque, Cincinnati	27-8	.771	1976	Steve Carlton, Philadelphia	20-7	.741
1924	Emil Yde, Pittsburgh	16-3	.842	1977	John Candelaria, Pittsburgh	20-5	.800
1925	Bill Sherdel, St. Louis	15-6	.714	1978	Gaylord Perry, San Diego	21-6	.778
1926	Ray Kremer, Pittsburgh	20-6	.769	1979	Tom Seaver, Cincinnati	16-6	.727
1927	Larry Benton, Boston-NY	17-7	.708				
1928	Larry Benton, New York	25-9	.735	1980	Jim Bibby, Pittsburgh	19-6	.760
1929	Charlie Root, Chicago	19-6	.760	1981	Tom Seaver, Cincinnati	14-2	.875
				1982	Phil Niekro, Atlanta	17-4	.810
1930	Freddie Fitzsimmons, NY	19-7	.731	1983	John Denny, Philadelphia	19-6	.760
1931	Paul Derringer, St. Louis	18-8	.692	1984	Rick Sutcliffe, Chicago	16-1	.941
1932	Lon Warneke, Chicago	22-6	.786	1985	Orel Hershiser, Los Angeles	19-3	.864
1933	Ben Cantwell, Boston	20-10	.667	1986	Bob Ojeda, New York	18-5	.783
1934	Dizzy Dean, St. Louis	30-7	.811	1987	Dwight Gooden, New York	15-7	.682
1935	Bill Lee, Chicago	20-6	.769	1988	David Cone, New York	20-3	.870
1936	Carl Hubbell, New York	26-6	.813	1989	Mike Bielecki, Chicago	18-7	.720
1937	Carl Hubbell, New York	22-8	.733				
1938	Bill Lee, Chicago	22-9	.710	1990	Doug Drabek, Pittsburgh	22-6	.786
1939	Paul Derringer, Cincinnati	25-7	.781	1991	John Smiley, Pittsburgh	20-8	.714
					& Jose Rijo, Cincinnati	15-6	.714
1940	Freddie Fitzsimmons, Bklyn	16-2	.889	1992	Bob Tewksbury, St. Louis	16-5	.762
1941	Elmer Riddle, Cincinnati	19-4	.826	1993	Mark Portugal, Houston	18-4	.818
1942	Larry French, Brooklyn	15-4	.789	1994	Marvin Freeman, Colorado	10-2	.833
1943	Mort Cooper, St. Louis	21-8	.724	1995	Greg Maddux, Atlanta	19-2	.905
1944	Ted Wilks, St. Louis	17-4	.810	1996	John Smoltz, Atlanta	24-8	.750
1945	Harry Brecheen, St. Louis	14-4	.778	1997	Greg Maddux, Atlanta	19-4	.826
1946	Murray Dickson, St. Louis	15-6	.714	1998	John Smoltz, Atlanta	17-3	.850
1947	Larry Jansen, New York	21-5	.808	1999	Mike Hampton, Houston	22-4	.846
1948	Harry Brecheen, St. Louis	20-7	.741				
1949	Preacher Roe, Brooklyn	15-6	.714	2000	Randy Johnson, Arizona	19-7	.731
				2001	Curt Schilling, Arizona	22-6	.786
1950	Sal Maglie, New York	18-4	.818	2002	Randy Johnson, Arizona	24-5	.828
1951	Preacher Roe, Brooklyn	22-3	.880	2003	Jason Schmidt, San Francisco	17-5	.773
1952	Hoyt Wilhelm, New York	15-3	.833				

Note: In 1984, Sutcliffe was also 4-5 with Cleveland for a combined AL-NL record of 20-6 (.769).

Winning Percentage (Cont.)

American League

Multiple winners: Lefty Grove (5); Chief Bender, Roger Clemens and Whitey Ford (3); Johnny Allen, Eddie Cicotte, Mike Cuellar, Lefty Gomez, Ron Guidry, Catfish Hunter, Randy Johnson, Walter Johnson, Pedro Martinez, Jim Palmer, Pete Vuckovich and Smokey Joe Wood (2).

Year		W-L	Pct	Year		W-L	Pct
1901	Clark Griffith, Chicago	24-7	.774	1954	Sandy Consuegra, Chicago.	16-3	.842
1902	Bill Bernhard, Phila-Cleve	18-5	.783	1955	Tommy Byrne, New York.	16-5	.762
1903	Cy Young, Boston	28-9	.757	1956	Whitey Ford, New York	19-6	.760
1904	Jack Chesbro, New York	41-12	.774	1957	Dick Donovan, Chicago	16-6	.727
1905	Andy Coakley, Philadelphia	20-7	.741		& Tom Sturdivant, New York	16-6	.727
1906	Eddie Plank, Philadelphia.	19-6	.760	1958	Bob Turley, New York	21-7	.750
1907	Wild Bill Donovan, Detroit	25-4	.862	1959	Bob Shaw, Chicago	18-6	.750
1908	Ed Walsh, Chicago.	40-15	.727	1960	Jim Perry, Cleveland	18-10	.643
1909	George Mullin, Detroit	29-8	.784	1961	Whitey Ford, New York	25-4	.862
1910	Chief Bender, Philadelphia.	23-5	.821	1962	Ray Herbert, Chicago	20-9	.690
1911	Chief Bender, Philadelphia.	17-5	.773	1963	Whitey Ford, New York	24-7	.774
1912	Smokey Joe Wood, Boston.	34-5	.872	1964	Wally Bunker, Baltimore	19-5	.792
1913	Walter Johnson, Washington	36-7	.837	1965	Mudcat Grant, Minnesota	21-7	.750
1914	Chief Bender, Philadelphia.	17-3	.850	1966	Sonny Siebert, Cleveland	16-8	.667
1915	Smokey Joe Wood, Boston.	15-5	.750	1967	Joe Horlen, Chicago	19-7	.731
1916	Eddie Cicotte, Chicago.	15-7	.682	1968	Denny McLain, Detroit.	31-6	.838
1917	Reb Russell, Chicago.	15-5	.750	1969	Jim Palmer, Baltimore	16-4	.800
1918	Sad Sam Jones, Boston.	16-5	.762	1970	Mike Cuellar, Baltimore	24-8	.750
1919	Eddie Cicotte, Chicago.	29-7	.806	1971	Dave McNally, Baltimore	21-5	.808
1920	Jim Bagby, Cleveland	31-12	.721	1972	Catfish Hunter, Oakland.	21-7	.750
1921	Carl Mays, New York	27-9	.750	1973	Catfish Hunter, Oakland.	21-5	.808
1922	Joe Bush, New York.	26-7	.788	1974	Mike Cuellar, Baltimore	22-10	.688
1923	Herb Pennock, New York	19-6	.760	1975	Mike Torrez, Baltimore	20-9	.690
1924	Walter Johnson, Washington	23-7	.767	1976	Bill Campbell, Minnesota	17-5	.773
1925	Stan Coveleski, Washington	20-5	.800	1977	Paul Splittorff, Kansas City	16-6	.727
1926	George Uhle, Cleveland	27-11	.711	1978	Ron Guidry, New York	25-3	.893
1927	Waite Hoyt, New York	22-7	.759	1979	Mike Caldwell, Milwaukee	16-6	.727
1928	General Crowder, St. Louis	21-5	.808	1980	Steve Stone, Baltimore	25-7	.781
1929	Lefty Grove, Philadelphia	20-6	.769	1981	Pete Vuckovich, Milwaukee	14-4	.778
1930	Lefty Grove, Philadelphia.	28-5	.848	1982	Pete Vuckovich, Milwaukee	18-6	.750
1931	Lefty Grove, Philadelphia.	31-4	.886		& Jim Palmer, Baltimore	15-5	.750
1932	Johnny Allen, New York	17-4	.810	1983	Rich Dotson, Chicago	22-7	.759
1933	Lefty Grove, Philadelphia.	24-8	.750	1984	Doyle Alexander, Toronto	17-6	.739
1934	Lefty Gomez, New York	26-5	.839	1985	Ron Guidry, New York	22-6	.786
1935	Eldon Auker, Detroit	18-7	.720	1986	Roger Clemens, Boston	24-4	.857
1936	Monte Pearson, New York	19-7	.731	1987	Roger Clemens, Boston	20-9	.690
1937	Johnny Allen, Cleveland	15-1	.938	1988	Frank Viola, Minnesota.	24-7	.774
1938	Red Ruffing, New York	21-7	.750	1989	Bret Saberhagen, Kansas City	23-6	.793
1939	Lefty Grove, Boston	15-4	.789	1990	Bob Welch, Oakland	27-6	.818
1940	Schoolboy Rowe, Detroit	16-3	.842	1991	Scott Erickson, Minnesota.	20-8	.714
1941	Lefty Gomez, New York	15-5	.750	1992	Mike Mussina, Baltimore	18-5	.783
1942	Ernie Bonham, New York	21-5	.808	1993	Jimmy Key, New York	18-6	.750
1943	Spud Chandler, New York	20-4	.833	1994	Jason Bere, Chicago	12-2	.857
1944	Tex Hughson, Boston	18-5	.783	1995	Randy Johnson, Seattle	18-2	.900
1945	Hal Newhouser, Detroit	25-9	.735	1996	Charles Nagy, Cleveland	17-5	.773
1946	Boo Ferriss, Boston	25-6	.806	1997	Randy Johnson, Seattle	20-4	.833
1947	Allie Reynolds, New York	19-8	.704	1998	David Wells, New York.	18-4	.818
1948	Jack Kramer, Boston	18-5	.783	1999	Pedro Martinez, Boston	23-4	.852
1949	Ellis Kinder, Boston	23-6	.793	2000	Tim Hudson, Oakland	20-6	.769
1950	Vic Raschi, New York	21-8	.724	2001	Roger Clemens, New York	20-3	.870
1951	Bob Feller, Cleveland	22-8	.733	2002	Pedro Martinez, Boston	20-4	.833
1952	Bobby Shantz, Philadelphia.	24-7	.774	2003	Roy Halladay, Toronto	22-7	.759
1953	Ed Lopat, New York	16-4	.800				

Earned Run Average

Earned Run Averages were based on at least 10 complete games pitched (1900-49), at least 154 innings pitched (1950-60), and at least 162 innings pitched since 1961 in the AL and 1962 in the NL. In the strike years of 1981, '94 and '95, qualifiers had to pitch at least as many innings as the total number of games their team played that season.

National League

Multiple winners: Grover Alexander, Sandy Koufax and Christy Mathewson (5); Greg Maddux (4); Carl Hubbell, Randy Johnson, Tom Seaver, Warren Spahn and Dazzy Vance (3); Kevin Brown, Bill Doak, Ray Kremer, Dolf Luque, Howie Pollet, Nolan Ryan, Bill Walker and Bucky Walters (2).

Year		ERA	Year		ERA	Year		ERA
1900	Rube Waddell, Pit	2.37	1935	Cy Blanton, Pit	2.58	1970	Tom Seaver, NY	2.81
1901	Jesse Tannehill, Pit	2.18	1936	Carl Hubbell, NY	2.31	1971	Tom Seaver, NY	1.76
1902	Jack Taylor, Chi	1.33	1937	Jim Turner, Bos	2.38	1972	Steve Carlton, Phi	1.97
1903	Sam Leever, Pit	2.06	1938	Bill Lee, Chi	2.66	1973	Tom Seaver, NY	2.08
1904	Joe McGinnity, NY	1.61	1939	Bucky Walters, Cin	2.29	1974	Buzz Capra, Atl	2.28
1905	Christy Mathewson, NY	1.27	1940	Bucky Walters, Cin	2.48	1975	Randy Jones, SD	2.24
1906	Three Finger Brown, Chi	1.04	1941	Elmer Riddle, Cin	2.24	1976	John Denny, St.L	2.52
1907	Jack Pfiester, Chi	1.15	1942	Mort Cooper, St.L	1.78	1977	John Candelaria, Pit	2.34
1908	Christy Mathewson, NY	1.43	1943	Howie Pollet, St.L	1.75	1978	Craig Swan, NY	2.43
1909	Christy Mathewson, NY	1.14	1944	Ed Heusser, Cin	2.38	1979	J.R. Richard, Hou	2.71
1910	George McQuillan, Phi	1.60	1945	Hank Borowy, Chi	2.13	1980	Don Sutton, LA	2.21
1911	Christy Mathewson, NY	1.99	1946	Howie Pollet, St.L	2.10	1981	Nolan Ryan, Hou	1.69
1912	Jeff Tesreau, NY	1.96	1947	Warren Spahn, Bos	2.33	1982	Steve Rogers, Mon	2.40
1913	Christy Mathewson, NY	2.06	1948	Harry Brecheen, St.L	2.24	1983	Atlee Hammaker, SF	2.25
1914	Bill Doak, St.L	1.72	1949	Dave Koslo, NY	2.50	1984	Alejandro Peña, LA	2.48
1915	Grover Alexander, Phi	1.22	1950	Jim Hearn, St.L-NY	2.49	1985	Dwight Gooden, NY	1.53
1916	Grover Alexander, Phi	1.55	1951	Chet Nichols, Bos	2.88	1986	Mike Scott, Hou	2.22
1917	Grover Alexander, Phi	1.86	1952	Hoyt Wilhelm, NY	2.43	1987	Nolan Ryan, Hou	2.76
1918	Hippo Vaughn, Chi	1.74	1953	Warren Spahn, Mil	2.10	1988	Joe Magrane, St.L	2.18
1919	Grover Alexander, Chi	1.72	1954	Johnny Antonelli, NY	2.30	1989	Scott Garrelts, SF	2.28
1920	Grover Alexander, Chi	1.91	1955	Bob Friend, Pit	2.83	1990	Danny Darwin, Hou	2.21
1921	Bill Doak, St.L	2.59	1956	Lew Burdette, Mil	2.70	1991	Dennis Martinez, Mon	2.39
1922	Rosy Ryan, NY	3.01	1957	Johnny Podres, Bklyn	2.66	1992	Bill Swift, SF	2.08
1923	Dolf Luque, Cin	1.93	1958	Stu Miller, SF	2.47	1993	Greg Maddux, Atl	2.36
1924	Dazzy Vance, Bklyn	2.16	1959	Sam Jones, SF	2.83	1994	Greg Maddux, Atl	1.56
1925	Dolf Luque, Cin	2.63	1960	Mike McCormick, SF	2.70	1995	Greg Maddux, Atl	1.63
1926	Ray Kremer, Pit	2.61	1961	Warren Spahn, Mil	3.02	1996	Kevin Brown, Fla.	1.89
1927	Ray Kremer, Pit	2.47	1962	Sandy Koufax, LA	2.54	1997	Pedro Martinez, Mon	1.90
1928	Dazzy Vance, Bklyn	2.09	1963	Sandy Koufax, LA	1.88	1998	Greg Maddux, Atl	2.22
1929	Bill Walker, NY	3.09	1964	Sandy Koufax, LA	1.74	1999	Randy Johnson, Ari.	2.48
1930	Dazzy Vance, Bklyn	2.61	1965	Sandy Koufax, LA	2.04	2000	Kevin Brown, LA	2.58
1931	Bill Walker, NY	2.26	1966	Sandy Koufax, LA	1.73	2001	Randy Johnson, Ari.	2.49
1932	Lon Warneke, Chi	2.37	1967	Phil Niekro, Atl	1.87	2002	Randy Johnson, Ari.	2.32
1933	Carl Hubbell, NY	1.66	1968	Bob Gibson, St.L	1.12	2003	Jason Schmidt, SF	2.34
1934	Carl Hubbell, NY	2.30	1969	Juan Marichal, SF	2.10			

Note: In 1945, Borowy had a 3.13 ERA in 18 games with New York (AL) for a combined ERA of 2.65.

American League

Multiple winners: Lefty Grove (9); Roger Clemens (6); Walter Johnson (5); Pedro Martinez (4); Spud Chandler, Stan Coveleski, Red Faber, Whitey Ford, Lefty Gomez, Ron Guidry, Addie Joss, Hal Newhouser, Jim Palmer, Gary Peters, Luis Tiant and Ed Walsh (2).

Year		ERA	Year		ERA	Year		ERA
1901	Cy Young, Bos	1.62	1919	Walter Johnson, Wash	1.49	1937	Lefty Gomez, NY	2.33
1902	Ed Siever, Det	1.91	1920	Bob Shawkey, NY	2.45	1938	Lefty Grove, Bos	3.08
1903	Earl Moore, Cle	1.77	1921	Red Faber, Chi	2.48	1939	Lefty Grove, Bos	2.54
1904	Addie Joss, Cle	1.59	1922	Red Faber, Chi	2.80			
1905	Rube Waddell, Phi	1.48	1923	Stan Coveleski, Cle	2.76	1940	Ernie Bonham, NY	1.90
1906	Doc White, Chi	1.52	1924	Walter Johnson, Wash	2.72	1941	Thornton Lee, Chi	2.37
1907	Ed Walsh, Chi	1.60	1925	Stan Coveleski, Wash	2.84	1942	Ted Lyons, Chi	2.10
1908	Addie Joss, Cle	1.16	1926	Lefty Grove, Phi	2.51	1943	Spud Chandler, NY	1.64
1909	Harry Krause, Phi	1.39	1927	Wilcy Moore, NY	2.28	1944	Dizzy Trout, Det	2.12
			1928	Garland Braxton, Wash	2.51	1945	Hal Newhouser, Det	1.81
1910	Ed Walsh, Chi	1.27	1929	Lefty Grove, Phi	2.81	1946	Hal Newhouser, Det	1.94
1911	Vean Gregg, Cle	1.81				1947	Spud Chandler, NY	2.46
1912	Walter Johnson, Wash	1.39	1930	Lefty Grove, Phi.	2.54	1948	Gene Bearden, Cle	2.43
1913	Walter Johnson, Wash	1.09	1931	Lefty Grove, Phi.	2.06	1949	Mel Parnell, Bos	2.77
1914	Dutch Leonard, Bos	1.01	1932	Lefty Grove, Phi.	2.84			
1915	Smokey Joe Wood, Bos	1.49	1933	Monte Pearson, Cle	2.33	1950	Early Wynn, Cle	3.20
1916	Babe Ruth, Bos	1.75	1934	Lefty Gomez, NY	2.33	1951	Saul Rogovin, Det-Chi	2.78
1917	Eddie Cicotte, Chi	1.53	1935	Lefty Grove, Bos	2.70	1952	Allie Reynolds, NY	2.06
1918	Walter Johnson, Wash	1.27	1936	Lefty Grove, Bos	2.81	1953	Ed Lopat, NY	2.42
						1954	Mike Garcia, Cle	2.64

Earned Run Average (Cont.)

Year		ERA	Year		ERA	Year		ERA
1955	Billy Pierce, Chi	1.97	1972	Luis Tiant, Bos	1.91	1989	Bret Saberhagen, KC	2.16
1956	Whitey Ford, NY	2.47	1973	Jim Palmer, Bal	2.40	1990	Roger Clemens, Bos	1.93
1957	Bobby Shantz, NY	2.45	1974	Catfish Hunter, Oak	2.49	1991	Roger Clemens, Bos	2.62
1958	Whitey Ford, NY	2.01	1975	Jim Palmer, Bal	2.09	1992	Roger Clemens, Bos	2.41
1959	Hoyt Wilhelm, Bal.	2.19	1976	Mark Fidrych, Det.	2.34	1993	Kevin Appier, KC	2.56
1960	Frank Baumann, Chi	2.67	1977	Frank Tanana, Cal	2.54	1994	Steve Ontiveros, Oak	2.65
1961	Dick Donovan, Wash	2.40	1978	Ron Guidry, NY	1.74	1995	Randy Johnson, Sea	2.48
1962	Hank Aguirre, Det.	2.21	1979	Ron Guidry, NY	2.78	1996	Juan Guzman, Tor.	2.93
1963	Gary Peters, Chi	2.33	1980	Rudy May, NY	2.47	1997	Roger Clemens, Tor	2.05
1964	Dean Chance, LA	1.65	1981	Steve McCatty, Oak	2.32	1998	Roger Clemens, Tor	2.65
1965	Sam McDowell, Cle	2.18	1982	Rick Sutcliffe, Cle	2.96	1999	Pedro Martinez, Bos	2.07
1966	Gary Peters, Chi	1.98	1983	Rick Honeycutt, Tex	2.42			
1967	Joe Horlen, Chi	2.06	1984	Mike Boddicker, Bal	2.79	2000	Pedro Martinez, Bos	1.74
1968	Luis Tiant, Cle	1.60	1985	Dave Stieb, Tor	2.48	2001	Freddy Garcia, Sea	3.05
1969	Dick Bosman, Wash	2.19	1986	Roger Clemens, Bos	2.48	2002	Pedro Martinez, Bos	2.26
1970	Diego Segui, Oak.	2.56	1987	Jimmy Key, Tor	2.76	2003	Pedro Martinez, Bos	2.22
1971	Vida Blue, Oak	1.82	1988	Allan Anderson, Min	2.45			

Strikeouts

National League

Multiple winners: Dazzy Vance (7); Grover Alexander (6); Steve Carlton, Christy Mathewson and Tom Seaver (5); Dizzy Dean, Randy Johnson, Sandy Koufax and Warren Spahn (4); Don Drysdale, Sam Jones and Johnny Vander Meer (3); David Cone, Dwight Gooden, Bill Hallahan, J.R. Richard, Robin Roberts, Nolan Ryan, Curt Schilling, John Smoltz and Hippo Vaughn (2).

Year		SO	Year		SO	Year		SO
1900	Rube Waddell, Pit	130	1936	Van Lingle Mungo, Bklyn	238	1970	Tom Seaver, NY	283
1901	Noodles Hahn, Cin	239	1937	Carl Hubbell, NY	159	1971	Tom Seaver, NY	289
1902	Vic Willis, Bos	225	1938	Clay Bryant, Chi	135	1972	Steve Carlton, Phi	310
1903	Christy Mathewson, NY	267	1939	Claude Passeau, Phi-Chi	137	1973	Tom Seaver, NY	251
1904	Christy Mathewson, NY	212		& Bucky Walters, Cin	137	1974	Steve Carlton, Phi	240
1905	Christy Mathewson, NY	206	1940	Kirby Higbe, Phi	137	1975	Tom Seaver, NY	243
1906	Fred Beebe, Chi-St.L	171	1941	John Vander Meer, Cin	202	1976	Tom Seaver, NY	235
1907	Christy Mathewson, NY	178	1942	John Vander Meer, Cin	186	1977	Phil Niekro, Atl	262
1908	Christy Mathewson, NY	259	1943	John Vander Meer, Cin	174	1978	J.R. Richard, Hou	303
1909	Orval Overall, Chi	205	1944	Bill Voiselle, NY	161	1979	J.R. Richard, Hou	313
1910	Earl Moore, Phi	185	1945	Preacher Roe, Pit	148	1980	Steve Carlton, Phi	286
1911	Rube Marquard, NY	237	1946	Johnny Schmitz, Chi	135	1981	F. Valenzuela, LA	180
1912	Grover Alexander, Phi	195	1947	Ewell Blackwell, Cin.	193	1982	Steve Carlton, Phi	286
1913	Tom Seaton, Phi	168	1948	Harry Brecheen, St.L	149	1983	Steve Carlton, Phi	275
1914	Grover Alexander, Phi	214	1949	Warren Spahn, Bos	151	1984	Dwight Gooden, NY	276
1915	Grover Alexander, Phi	241	1950	Warren Spahn, Bos	191	1985	Dwight Gooden, NY	268
1916	Grover Alexander, Phi	167	1951	Don Newcombe, Bklyn	164	1986	Mike Scott, Hou	306
1917	Grover Alexander, Phi	201		& Warren Spahn, Bos	164	1987	Nolan Ryan, Hou	270
1918	Hippo Vaughn, Chi	148	1952	Warren Spahn, Bos	183	1988	Nolan Ryan, Hou	228
1919	Hippo Vaughn, Chi	141	1953	Robin Roberts, Phi	198	1989	Jose DeLeon, St.L	201
1920	Grover Alexander, Chi	173	1954	Robin Roberts, Phi	185	1990	David Cone, NY	233
1921	Burleigh Grimes, Bklyn	136	1955	Sam Jones, Chi	198	1991	David Cone, NY	241
1922	Dazzy Vance, Bklyn	134	1956	Sam Jones, Chi	176	1992	John Smoltz, Atl.	215
1923	Dazzy Vance, Bklyn	197	1957	Jack Sanford, Phi	188	1993	Jose Rijo, Cin	227
1924	Dazzy Vance, Bklyn	262	1958	Sam Jones, St.L	225	1994	Andy Benes, SD	189
1925	Dazzy Vance, Bklyn	221	1959	Don Drysdale, LA	242	1995	Hideo Nomo, LA	236
1926	Dazzy Vance, Bklyn	140	1960	Don Drysdale, LA	246	1996	John Smoltz, Atl	276
1927	Dazzy Vance, Bklyn	184	1961	Sandy Koufax, LA	269	1997	Curt Schilling, Phi	319
1928	Dazzy Vance, Bklyn	200	1962	Don Drysdale, LA	232	1998	Curt Schilling, Phi	300
1929	Pat Malone, Chi	166	1963	Sandy Koufax, LA	306	1999	Randy Johnson, Ari	364
1930	Bill Hallahan, St.L	177	1964	Bob Veale, Pit	250	2000	Randy Johnson, Ari	347
1931	Bill Hallahan, St.L	159	1965	Sandy Koufax, LA	382	2001	Randy Johnson, Ari	372
1932	Dizzy Dean, St.L	191	1966	Sandy Koufax, LA	317	2002	Randy Johnson, Ari	334
1933	Dizzy Dean, St.L	199	1967	Jim Bunning, Phi	253	2003	Kerry Wood, Chi	266
1934	Dizzy Dean, St.L	195	1968	Bob Gibson, St.L	268			
1935	Dizzy Dean, St.L	190	1969	Ferguson Jenkins, Chi	273			

American League

Multiple winners: Walter Johnson (12); Nolan Ryan (9); Bob Feller and Lefty Grove (7); Rube Waddell (6); Roger Clemens and Sam McDowell (5); Randy Johnson (4); Lefty Gomez, Mark Langston, Pedro Martinez and Camilo Pascual (3); Len Barker, Tommy Bridges, Jim Bunning, Hal Newhouser, Allie Reynolds, Herb Score, Ed Walsh and Early Wynn (2).

Year		SO	Year		SO	Year		SO
1901	Cy Young, Bos	158	1937	Lefty Gomez, NY	194	1971	Mickey Lolich, Det	308
1902	Rube Waddell, Phi	210	1938	Bob Feller, Cle	240	1972	Nolan Ryan, Cal	329
1903	Rube Waddell, Phi	302	1939	Bob Feller, Cle	246	1973	Nolan Ryan, Cal	383
1904	Rube Waddell, Phi	349	1940	Bob Feller, Cle	261	1974	Nolan Ryan, Cal	367
1905	Rube Waddell, Phi	287	1941	Bob Feller, Cle	260	1975	Frank Tanana, Cal	269
1906	Rube Waddell, Phi	196	1942	Tex Hughson, Bos	113	1976	Nolan Ryan, Cal	327
1907	Rube Waddell, Phi	232		& Bobo Newsom, Wash	113	1977	Nolan Ryan, Cal	341
1908	Ed Walsh, Chi	269	1943	Allie Reynolds, Cle	151	1978	Nolan Ryan, Cal	260
1909	Frank Smith, Chi	177	1944	Hal Newhouser, Det	187	1979	Nolan Ryan, Cal	223
1910	Walter Johnson, Wash	313	1945	Hal Newhouser, Det	212	1980	Len Barker, Cle	187
1911	Ed Walsh, Chi	255	1946	Bob Feller, Cle	348	1981	Len Barker, Cle	127
1912	Walter Johnson, Wash	303	1947	Bob Feller, Cle	196	1982	Floyd Bannister, Sea	209
1913	Walter Johnson, Wash	243	1948	Bob Feller, Cle	164	1983	Jack Morris, Det	232
1914	Walter Johnson, Wash	225	1949	Virgil Trucks, Det	153	1984	Mark Langston, Sea	204
1915	Walter Johnson, Wash	203	1950	Bob Lemon, Cle	170	1985	Bert Blyleven, Cle-Min	206
1916	Walter Johnson, Wash	228	1951	Vic Raschi, NY	164	1986	Mark Langston, Sea	245
1917	Walter Johnson, Wash	188	1952	Allie Reynolds, NY	160	1987	Mark Langston, Sea	262
1918	Walter Johnson, Wash	162	1953	Billy Pierce, Chi	186	1988	Roger Clemens, Bos	291
1919	Walter Johnson, Wash	147	1954	Bob Turley, Bal	185	1989	Nolan Ryan, Tex	301
1920	Stan Coveleski, Cle	133	1955	Herb Score, Cle	245	1990	Nolan Ryan, Tex	232
1921	Walter Johnson, Wash	143	1956	Herb Score, Cle	263	1991	Roger Clemens, Bos	241
1922	Urban Shocker, St.L	149	1957	Early Wynn, Cle	184	1992	Randy Johnson, Sea	241
1923	Walter Johnson, Wash	130	1958	Early Wynn, Chi	179	1993	Randy Johnson, Sea	308
1924	Walter Johnson, Wash	158	1959	Jim Bunning, Det	201	1994	Randy Johnson, Sea	204
1925	Lefty Grove, Phi	116	1960	Jim Bunning, Det	201	1995	Randy Johnson, Sea	294
1926	Lefty Grove, Phi	194	1961	Camilo Pascual, Min	221	1996	Roger Clemens, Bos	257
1927	Lefty Grove, Phi	174	1962	Camilo Pascual, Min	206	1997	Roger Clemens, Tor	292
1928	Lefty Grove, Phi	183	1963	Camilo Pascual, Min	202	1998	Roger Clemens, Tor	271
1929	Lefty Grove, Phi	170	1964	Al Downing, NY	217	1999	Pedro Martinez, Bos	313
1930	Lefty Grove, Phi	209	1965	Sam McDowell, Cle	325	2000	Pedro Martinez, Bos	284
1931	Lefty Grove, Phi	175	1966	Sam McDowell, Cle	225	2001	Hideo Nomo, Bos	220
1932	Red Ruffing, NY	190	1967	Jim Lonborg, Bos	246	2002	Pedro Martinez, Bos	239
1933	Lefty Gomez, NY	163	1968	Sam McDowell, Cle	283	2003	Esteban Loaiza, Chi	207
1934	Lefty Gomez, NY	158	1969	Sam McDowell, Cle	279			
1935	Tommy Bridges, Det	163	1970	Sam McDowell, Cle	304			
1936	Tommy Bridges, Det	175						

Pitching Triple Crown Winners

Pitchers who led either league in Earned Run Average, Wins and Strikeouts over a single season.

National League

	Year	ERA	W-L	SO
Tommy Bond, Bos	1877	2.11	40-17	170
Hoss Radbourn, Prov	1884	1.38	60-12	441
Tim Keefe, NY	1888	1.74	35-12	333
John Clarkson, Bos	1889	2.73	49-19	284
Amos Rusie, NY	1894	2.78	36-13	195
Christy Mathewson, NY	1905	1.27	31-8	206
Christy Mathewson, NY	1908	1.43	37-11	259
Grover Alexander, Phi	1915	1.22	31-10	241
Grover Alexander, Phi	1916	1.55	33-12	167
Grover Alexander, Phi	1917	1.86	30-13	201
Hippo Vaughn, Chi	1918	1.74	22-10	148
Grover Alexander, Chi	1920	1.91	27-14	173
Dazzy Vance, Bklyn	1924	2.16	28-6	262
Bucky Walters, Cin	1939	2.29	27-11	137
Sandy Koufax, LA	1963	1.88	25-5	306
Sandy Koufax, LA	1965	2.04	26-8	382
Sandy Koufax, LA	1966	1.73	27-9	317
Steve Carlton, Phi	1972	1.97	27-10	310
Dwight Gooden, NY	1985	1.53	24-4	268
Randy Johnson, Ari	2002	2.32	24-5	334

Ties: In 1894, Rusie tied for league lead in wins with Jouett Meekin, NY (36-10); in 1939, Walters tied for league lead in strikeouts with Claude Passeau, Phi-Chi; in 1963, Koufax tied for the league lead in wins with Juan Marichal, SF.

American League

	Year	ERA	W-L	SO
Cy Young, Bos	1901	1.62	33-10	158
Rube Waddell, Phi.	1905	1.48	26-11	287
Walter Johnson, Wash	1913	1.09	36-7	243
Walter Johnson, Wash	1918	1.27	23-13	162
Walter Johnson, Wash	1924	2.72	23-7	158
Lefty Grove, Phi	1930	2.54	28-5	209
Lefty Grove, Phi	1931	2.06	31-4	175
Lefty Gomez, NY	1934	2.33	26-5	158
Lefty Gomez, NY	1937	2.33	21-11	194
Hal Newhouser, Det	1945	1.81	25-9	212
Roger Clemens, Tor	1997	2.05	21-7	292
Roger Clemens, Tor	1998	2.65	20-6	271
Pedro Martinez, Bos	1999	2.07	23-4	313

Ties: In 1998, Clemens tied for league lead in wins with David Cone, NY (20-7) and Rick Helling, Tex (20-7).

Saves

The "save" was created by Chicago baseball writer Jerome Holtzman in the 1960's and accepted as an official statistic by the Official Rules Committee of Major League Baseball in 1969. From 1969-72, a save was credited to a pitcher who finished a game his team won. From 1973-74, a save was credited to a pitcher who finished a game his team won with the tying or winning run on base or at bat. Since 1975 a pitcher has been credited with a save when he meets all three of the following conditions:

(1) He is the finishing pitcher in a game won by his club; (2) He is not the winning pitcher; (3) He qualifies under one of the following conditions: (a) He enters the game with a lead of no more than three runs and pitches for at least one inning; (b) He enters the game, regardless of the count, with the potential tying run either on base, or at bat, or on deck (that is, the potential tying run is either already on base or is one of the first two batsmen he faces); (c) He pitches effectively for at least three innings. No more than one save may be credited in each game.

National League

Multiple winners: Bruce Sutter (5); John Franco and Lee Smith (3); Rawly Eastwick, Rollie Fingers, Mike Marshall, Randy Myers and Todd Worrell (2).

Year		Svs	Year		Svs	Year		Svs
1969	Fred Gladding, Hou	.29	1981	Bruce Sutter, St.L	.25	1994	John Franco, NY	.30
1970	Wayne Granger, Cin	.35	1982	Bruce Sutter, St.L	.36	1995	Randy Myers, Chi	.38
1971	Dave Giusti, Pit	.30	1983	Lee Smith, Chi	.29	1996	Jeff Brantley, Cin	.44
1972	Clay Carroll, Cin	.37	1984	Bruce Sutter, St.L	.45		& Todd Worrell, LA	.44
1973	Mike Marshall, Mon.	.31	1985	Jeff Reardon, Mon	.41	1997	Jeff Shaw, Cin	.42
1974	Mike Marshall, LA	.21	1986	Todd Worrell, St.L	.36	1998	Trevor Hoffman, SD	.53
1975	Rawly Eastwick, Cin	.22	1987	Steve Bedrosian, Phi.	.40	1999	Ugueth Urbina, Mon	.41
	& Al Hrabosky, St.L	.22	1988	John Franco, Cin	.39	2000	Antonio Alfonseca, Fla	.45
1976	Rawly Eastwick, Cin	.26	1989	Mark Davis, SD.	.44	2001	Robb Nen, SF	.45
1977	Rollie Fingers, SD	.35	1990	John Franco, NY	.33	2002	John Smoltz, Atl	.55
1978	Rollie Fingers, SD	.37	1991	Lee Smith, St.L	.47	2003	Eric Gagne, LA	.55
1979	Bruce Sutter, Chi	.37	1992	Lee Smith, St.L	.43			
1980	Bruce Sutter, Chi	.28	1993	Randy Myers, Chi	.53			

American League

Multiple winners: Dan Quisenberry (5); Rich Gossage (3); Dennis Eckersley, Sparky Lyle, Ron Perranoski and Mariano Rivera (2).

Year		Svs	Year		Svs	Year		Svs
1969	Ron Perranoski, Min	.31	1981	Rollie Fingers, Mil	.28	1993	Jeff Montgomery, KC	.45
1970	Ron Perranoski, Min	.34	1982	Dan Quisenberry, KC	.35		& Duane Ward, Tor	.45
1971	Ken Sanders, Mil.	.31	1983	Dan Quisenberry, KC.	.45	1994	Lee Smith, Bal	.33
1972	Sparky Lyle, NY.	.35	1984	Dan Quisenberry, KC.	.44	1995	Jose Mesa, Cle	.46
1973	John Hiller, Det	.38	1985	Dan Quisenberry, KC.	.37	1996	John Wetteland, NY	.43
1974	Terry Forster, Chi	.24	1986	Dave Righetti, NY	.46	1997	Randy Myers, Bal	.45
1975	Rich Gossage, Chi	.26	1987	Tom Henke, Tor	.34	1998	Tom Gordon, Bos	.46
1976	Sparky Lyle, NY.	.23	1988	Dennis Eckersley, Oak	.45	1999	Mariano Rivera, NY	.45
1977	Bill Campbell, Bos	.31	1989	Jeff Russell, Tex	.38	2000	Todd Jones, Det.	.42
1978	Rich Gossage, NY	.27	1990	Bobby Thigpen, Chi	.57		& Derek Lowe, Bos	.42
1979	Mike Marshall, Min	.32	1991	Bryan Harvey, Cal	.46	2001	Mariano Rivera, NY.	.50
1980	Rich Gossage, NY	.33	1992	Dennis Eckersley, Oak	.51	2002	Eddie Guardado, Min	.45
	& Dan Quisenberry, KC	.33				2003	Keith Foulke, Oak	.43

Perfect Games

Seventeen pitchers have thrown perfect games (27 up, 27 down) in major league history. However, the game pitched by Ernie Shore is not considered to be official.

National League

	Game	Date	Score
Lee Richmond	Wor. vs Cle.	6/12/1880	1-0
Monte Ward	Prov. vs Bos.	6/17/1880	5-0
Jim Bunning	Phi. at NY	6/21/1964	6-0
Sandy Koufax	LA vs Chi.	9/9/1965	1-0
Tom Browning	Cin. vs LA	9/16/1988	1-0
Dennis Martinez	Mon. at LA	7/28/1991	2-0

Note: Pittsburgh's Harvey Haddix pitched 12 perfect innings against the Milwaukee Braves on May 26, 1959 before losing, 1-0, in the 13th. Braves' lead-off batter Felix Mantilla reached on a throwing error by Pirates 3B Don Hoak, Eddie Mathews sacrificed Mantilla to 2nd, Hank Aaron was walked intentionally, and Joe Adcock hit a 3-run HR. Adcock, however, passed Aaron on the bases and was only credited with a 1-run double.

Note: Montreal's Pedro Martinez pitched nine perfect innings against the San Diego Padres on June 3, 1995 before surrendering a leadoff double to Bip Roberts in the 10th. He was then relieved by Mel Rojas, who finished the game, which Montreal won, 1-0.

American League

	Game	Date	Score
Cy Young	Bos. vs Phi.	5/5/1904	3-0
Addie Joss	Cle. vs Chi.	10/2/1908	1-0
Ernie Shore	Bos. vs Wash.	6/23/1917	4-0*
Charlie Robertson	Chi. at Det.	4/30/1922	2-0
Catfish Hunter	Oak. vs Min.	5/8/1968	4-0
Len Barker	Cle. vs Tor.	5/15/1981	3-0
Mike Witt	Cal. at Tex.	9/30/1984	1-0
Kenny Rogers	Tex. vs Cal.	7/28/1994	4-0
David Wells	NY vs Min.	5/17/1998	4-0
David Cone	NY vs Mon.	7/18/1999	6-0

*Babe Ruth started for Boston, walking Senators' lead-off batter Ray Morgan, then was thrown out of game by umpire Brick Owens for arguing the call. Shore came on in relief. Morgan was caught stealing and Shore retired the next 26 batters in a row. While technically not a perfect game—since he didn't start—Shore gets credit anyway.

World Series

Pitcher	Game	Date	Score
Don Larsen	NY vs Bklyn	10/8/1956	2-0

No-Hit Games

Nine innings or more, including perfect games, since 1876. Losing pitchers in **bold** type. **Multiple no-hitters:** Nolan Ryan (7); Sandy Koufax (4); Larry Cocoran, Bob Feller and Cy Young (3); Jim Bunning, Steve Busby, Carl Erskine, Bob Forsch, Pud Galvin, Ken Holtzman, Addie Joss, Hub Leonard, Jim Maloney, Christy Mathewson, Hideo Nomo, Allie Reynolds, Warren Spahn, Bill Stoneham, Virgil Trucks, Johnny Vander Meer and Don Wilson (2).

National League

Year	Date	Pitcher	Result
1876	7/15	George Bradley	St.L vs Har, 2-0
1880	6/12	Lee Richmond	Wor vs Cle, 1-0 (perfect game)
	6/17	Monte Ward	Prov vs Buf, 5-0 (perfect game)
	8/19	Larry Corcoran	Chi vs Bos, 6-0
	8/20	Pud Galvin	Buf at Wor, 1-0
1882	9/20	Larry Corcoran	Chi vs Wor, 1-0
1883	7/25	Old Hoss Radbourn	Prov at Cle, 8-0
	9/13	Hugh Daily	Cle at Phi, 1-0
1884	6/27	Larry Cocoran	Chi vs Prov, 6-0
	8/4	Pud Galvin	Buf at Det, 18-0
1885	7/27	John Clarkson	Chi vs Prov, 4-0
	8/29	Charlie Ferguson	Phi vs Prov, 1-0
1891	6/22	Tom Lovett	Bklyn vs NY, 4-0
	7/31	Amos Rusie	NY vs Bklyn, 11-0
1892	8/6	John Stivetts	Bos vs Bklyn, 11-0
	8/22	Ben Sanders	Lou vs Bal, 6-2
	10/22	Bumpus Jones	Cin vs Pit, 7-1 (1st major league game)
1893	8/16	Bill Hawke	Bal vs Wash, 5-0
1897	9/18	Cy Young	Cle vs Cin, 6-0
1898	4/22	Ted Breitenstein	Cin vs Pit, 11-0
	4/22	Jim Hughes	Bal vs Bos, 8-0
	7/8	Frank Donahue	Phi vs Bos, 5-0
	8/21	Walter Thornton	Chi vs Bklyn, 2-0
1899	5/25	Deacon Phillippe	Lou vs NY, 7-0
1900	7/12	Noodles Hahn	Cin vs Phi, 4-0
1901	7/15	Christy Mathewson	NY vs St.L, 5-0
1903	9/18	Chick Fraser	Phi at Chi, 10-0
1905	6/13	Christy Mathewson	NY at Chi, 1-0
1906	5/1	John Lush	Phi at Bklyn, 1-0
	7/20	Mal Eason	Bklyn at St.L, 2-0
1907	5/8	Frank Pfeffer	Bos vs Cin, 6-0
	9/20	Nick Maddox	Pit vs Bkn, 2-1
1908	7/4	Hooks Wiltse	NY vs Phi, 1-0 (10)
	9/5	Nap Rucker	Bklyn vs Bos, 6-0
1912	9/6	Jeff Tesreau	NY at Phi, 3-0
1914	9/9	George Davis	Bos vs Phi, 7-0
1915	4/15	Rube Marquard	NY vs Bklyn, 2-0
	8/31	Jimmy Lavender	Chi at N.Y, 2-0
1916	6/16	Tom Hughes	Bos vs. Pit, 2-0
1917	5/2	Fred Toney	Cin at Chi, 1-0 (10)
1919	5/11	Hod Eller	Cin at St.L, 6-0
1922	5/7	Jesse Barnes	NY vs Phi, 6-0
1924	7/17	Jesse Haines	St.L vs Bos, 5-0
1925	9/17	Dazzy Vance	Bklyn vs Phi, 10-1
1929	5/8	Carl Hubbell	NY vs Pit, 2-0
1934	9/21	Paul Dean	St.L vs Bklyn, 3-0
1938	6/11	Johnny Vander Meer	Cin vs Bos, 3-0
	6/15	Johnny Vander Meer	Cin at Bklyn, 6-0 (consecutive starts)
1940	4/30	Tex Carleton	Bklyn at Cin, 3-0
1941	8/30	Lon Warneke	St.L at Cin, 2-0
1944	4/27	Jim Tobin	Bos vs Bklyn, 2-0
	5/15	Clyde Shoun	Cin vs Bos, 1-0
1946	4/23	Ed Head	Bklyn at NY, 2-0
1947	6/18	Ewell Blackwell	Cin vs Bos, 6-0
1948	9/9	Rex Barney	Bklyn at NY, 2-0
1950	8/11	Vern Bickford	Bos vs Bklyn, 7-0
1951	5/6	Cliff Chambers	Pit at Bos, 3-0
1952	6/19	Carl Erskine	Bklyn vs Chi, 5-0
1954	6/12	Jim Wilson	Mil vs Phi, 2-0
1955	5/12	Sam Jones	Chi vs Pit, 4-0
1956	5/12	Carl Erskine	Bklyn vs NY, 3-0
	9/25	Sal Maglie	Bklyn vs Phi, 5-0
1960	5/15	Don Cardwell	Chi vs St.L, 4-0
	8/18	Lew Burdette	Mil vs Phi, 1-0
	9/16	Warren Spahn	Mil vs Phi, 4-0
1961	4/28	Warren Spahn	Mil vs SF, 1-0
1962	6/30	Sandy Koufax	LA vs NY, 5-0
1963	5/11	Sandy Koufax	LA vs SF, 1-0
	5/17	Don Nottebart	Hou vs Phi, 4-1
	6/15	Juan Marichal	SF vs Hou, 1-0
1964	4/23	**Ken Johnson**	Hou vs Cin, 0-1
	6/4	Sandy Koufax	LA at Phi, 3-0
	6/21	Jim Bunning	Phi at NY, 6-0 (perfect game)
1965	8/19	Jim Maloney	Cin at Chi, 1-0 (10)
	9/9	Sandy Koufax	LA vs Chi, 1-0 (perfect game)
1967	6/18	Don Wilson	Hou vs Atl, 2-0
1968	7/29	George Culver	Cin at Phi, 6-1
	9/17	Gaylord Perry	SF vs St.L, 1-0
	9/18	Ray Washburn	St.L at SF, 2-0 (next day, same park)
1969	4/17	Bill Stoneman	Mon at Phi, 7-0
	4/30	Jim Maloney	Cin vs Hou, 10-0
	5/1	Don Wilson	Hou at Cin, 4-0
	8/19	Ken Holtzman	Chi vs Atl, 3-0
	9/20	Bob Moose	Pit at NY, 4-0
1970	6/12	Dock Ellis	Pit at SD, 2-0
	7/20	Bill Singer	LA vs Phi, 5-0
1971	6/3	Ken Holtzman	Chi at Cin, 1-0
	6/23	Rick Wise	Phi at Cin, 4-0
	8/14	Bob Gibson	St.L at Pit, 11-0
1972	4/16	Burt Hooton	Chi vs Phi, 4-0
	9/2	Milt Pappas	Chi vs SD, 8-0
	10/2	Bill Stoneman	Mon vs NY, 7-0
1973	8/5	Phil Niekro	Atl vs SD, 9-0
1975	8/24	Ed Halicki	SF vs NY, 6-0
1976	7/9	Larry Dierker	Hou vs Mon, 6-0
	8/9	John Candelaria	Pit vs LA, 2-0
	9/29	John Montefusco	SF vs Atl, 9-0
1978	4/16	Bob Forsch	St.L vs Phi, 5-0
	6/16	Tom Seaver	Cin vs St.L, 4-0
1979	4/7	Ken Forsch	Hou vs Atl, 6-0
1980	6/27	Jerry Reuss	LA at SF, 4-0
1981	5/10	Charlie Lea	Mon vs SF, 4-0
	9/26	Nolan Ryan	Hou vs LA, 5-0
1983	9/26	Bob Forsch	St.L vs Mon, 3-0
1986	9/25	Mike Scott	Hou vs SF, 2-0
1988	9/16	Tom Browning	Cin vs LA, 1-0 (perfect game)
1990	6/29	Fernando Valenzuela	LA vs St.L, 6-0
	8/15	Terry Mulholland	Phi vs SF, 6-0
1991	5/23	Tommy Greene	Phi at Mon, 2-0
	7/28	Dennis Martinez	Mon at LA, 2-0 (perfect game)
	9/11	Kent Mercker (6), Mark Wohlers (2) & Alejandro Peña (1)	Atl vs SD, 1-0 (combined no-hitter)
1992	8/17	Kevin Gross	LA vs SF, 2-0
1993	9/8	Darryl Kile	Hou vs NY, 7-1
1994	4/8	Kent Mercker	Atl at LA, 6-0
1995	7/14	Ramon Martinez	LA vs Fla, 7-0
1996	5/11	Al Leiter	Fla vs Col, 11-0
	9/17	Hideo Nomo	LA at Col, 9-0
1997	6/10	Kevin Brown	Fla at SF, 9-0
	7/12	Francisco Cordova (9) Ricardo Rincon (1)	Pit vs. Hou, 3-0 (10 inn.) (combined no-hitter)
1999	6/25	Jose Jimenez	St.L vs Ari, 1-0
2001	5/12	A.J. Burnett	Fla at SD, 3-0
	9/3	Bud Smith	St.L at SD, 4-0
2003	4/27	Kevin Millwood	Phi vs SF, 1-0
	6/11	Oswalt (1), Munro (2⅔) Saarloos (1⅓), Lidge (2), Dotel (1) & Wagner (1)	Hou at NY-AL, 8-0 (combined no-hitter)

No-Hit Games (Cont.)
American League

Year	Date	Pitcher	Result
1902	9/20	Jimmy Callahan	Chi vs Det, 3-0
1904	5/5	Cy Young	Bos vs Phi, 3-0
			(perfect game)
	8/17	Jesse Tannehill	Bos vs Chi, 6-0
1905	7/22	Weldon Henley	Phi at St. L, 6-0
	9/6	Frank Smith	Chi at Det, 15-0
	9/27	Bill Dinneen	Bos vs Chi, 2-0
1908	6/30	Cy Young	Bos at NY, 8-0
	9/18	Dusty Rhoades	Cle vs Bos, 2-0
	9/20	Frank Smith	Chi vs Phi, 1-0
	10/2	Addie Joss	Cle vs Chi, 1-0
			(perfect game)
1910	4/20	Addie Joss	Cle at Chi, 1-0
	5/12	Chief Bender	Phi vs Cle, 4-0
1911	7/19	Smokey Joe	Wood Bos vs St. L, 5-0
	8/27	Ed Walsh	Chi vs Bos, 5-0
1912	7/4	George Mullin	Det vs St. L, 7-0
	8/30	Earl Hamilton	St. L at Det, 5-1
1914	5/31	Joe Benz	Chi vs Cle, 6-1
1916	6/16	Rube Foster	Bos vs NY, 2-0
	8/26	Joe Bush	Phi vs Cle, 5-0
	8/30	Hub Leonard	Bos vs St. L, 4-0
1917	4/14	Ed Cicotte	Chi at St. L, 11-0
	4/24	George Mogridge	NY at Bos, 2-1
	5/5	Ernie Koob	St. L vs Chi, 1-0
	5/6	Bob Groom	St. L vs Chi, 3-0
	6/23	Babe Ruth (0)	Bos vs Wash, 4-0
		& Ernie Shore (9)	(combined no-hitter)
1918	6/3	Hub Leonard	Bos at Det, 5-0
1919	9/10	Ray Caldwell	Cle at NY, 3-0
1920	7/1	Walter Johnson	Wash at Bos, 1-0
1922	4/30	Charlie Robertson	Chi at Det, 2-0
			(perfect game)
1923	9/4	Sam Jones	NY at Phi, 2-0
	9/7	Howard Ehmke	Bos at Phi, 4-0
1926	8/21	Ted Lyons	Chi at Bos, 6-0
1931	4/29	Wes Ferrell	Cle vs St. L, 9-0
	8/8	Bob Burke	Wash vs Bos, 5-0
1935	8/31	Vern Kennedy	Chi vs Cle, 5-0
1937	6/1	Bill Dietrich	Chi vs St. L, 8-0
1938	8/27	Monte Pearson	NY vs Cle, 13-0
1940	4/16	Bob Feller	Cle at Chi, 1-0
			(Opening Day)
1945	9/9	Dick Fowler	Phi vs St. L, 1-0
1946	4/30	Bob Feller	Cle vs NY, 1-0
1947	7/10	Don Black	Cle vs Phi, 3-0
	9/3	Bill McCahan	Phi vs Wash, 3-0
1948	6/30	Bob Lemon	Cle at Det, 2-0
1951	7/1	Bob Feller	Cle vs Det, 2-1
	7/12	Allie Reynolds	NY vs Cle, 1-0
	9/28	Allie Reynolds	NY vs Bos, 8-0
1952	5/15	Virgil Trucks	Det vs Wash, 1-0
	8/25	Virgil Trucks	Det at NY, 1-0
1953	5/6	Bobo Holloman	St. L vs Phi, 6-0
			(first major league start)
1956	7/14	Mel Parnell	Bos vs Chi, 4-0
	10/8	Don Larsen	NY vs Bklyn, 2-0
			(perfect W. Series game)
1957	8/20	Bob Keegan	Chi vs Wash, 6-0
1958	7/20	Jim Bunning	Det at Bos, 3-0
	9/20	Hoyt Wilhelm	Bal vs NY, 1-0
1962	5/5	Bo Belinsky	LA vs Bal, 2-0
	6/26	Earl Wilson	Bos vs LA, 2-0
	8/1	Bill Monbouquette	Bos at Chi, 1-0
	8/26	Jack Kralick	Min vs KC, 1-0
1965	9/16	Dave Morehead	Bos vs Cle, 2-0
1966	6/10	Sonny Siebert	Cle vs Wash, 2-0
1967	4/30	**Steve Barber** (8⅔)	Bal vs Det, 1-2
		& **Stu Miller** (⅓)	(combined no-hitter)
	8/25	Dean Chance	Min at Cle, 2-1
	9/10	Joel Horlen	Chi vs Det, 6-0
1968	4/27	Tom Phoebus	Bal vs Bos, 6-0
	5/8	Catfish Hunter	Oak vs Min, 4-0
			(perfect game)
1969	8/13	Jim Palmer	Bal vs Oak, 8-0
1970	7/3	Clyde Wright	Cal vs Oak, 4-0
	9/21	Vida Blue	Oak vs Min, 6-0
1973	4/27	Steve Busby	KC at Det, 3-0
	5/15	Nolan Ryan	Cal at KC, 3-0
	7/15	Nolan Ryan	Cal at Det, 6-0
	7/30	Jim Bibby	Tex at Oak, 6-0
1974	6/19	Steve Busby	KC at Mil, 2-0
	7/19	Dick Bosman	Cle at Oak, 4-0
	9/28	Nolan Ryan	Cal at Min, 4-0
1975	6/1	Nolan Ryan	Cal vs Bal, 1-0
	9/28	Vida Blue (5),	Oak vs Cal, 5-0
		Glenn Abbott (1),	(combined no-hitter)
		Paul Lindblad (1),	
		& Rollie Fingers (2)	
1976	7/28	John Odom (5) &	Chi at Oak, 2-1
		Francisco Barrios (4)	(combined no-hitter)
1977	5/14	Jim Colborn	KC vs Tex, 6-0
	5/30	Dennis Eckersley	Cle vs Cal, 1-0
	9/22	Bert Blyleven	Tex at Cal, 6-0
1981	5/15	Len Barker	Cle vs Tor, 3-0
			(perfect game)
1983	7/4	Dave Righetti	NY vs Bos, 4-0
	9/29	Mike Warren	Oak vs Chi, 3-0
1984	4/7	Jack Morris	Det at Chi, 4-0
	9/30	Mike Witt	Cal at Tex, 1-0
			(perfect game)
1986	9/19	Joe Cowley	Chi at Cal, 7-1
1987	4/15	Juan Nieves	Mil at Bal, 7-0
1990	4/11	Mark Langston (7)	Cal vs Sea, 1-0
		& Mike Witt (2)	(combined no-hitter)
	6/2	Randy Johnson	Sea vs Det, 2-0
	6/11	Nolan Ryan	Tex at Oak, 5-0
	6/29	Dave Stewart	Oak at Tor, 5-0
	9/2	Dave Stieb	Tor at Cle, 3-0
1991	5/1	Nolan Ryan	Tex vs Tor, 3-0
	7/13	Bob Milacki (6),	Bal at Oak, 2-0
		Mike Flanagan (1),	(combined no-hitter)
		Mark Williamson (1)	
		& Gregg Olson (1)	
	8/11	Wilson Alvarez	Chi at Bal, 7-0
	8/26	Bret Saberhagen	KC vs Chi, 7-0
1993	4/22	Chris Bosio	Sea vs Bos, 7-0
	9/4	Jim Abbott	NY vs Cle, 4-0
1994	4/27	Scott Erickson	Min vs Mil, 6-0
	7/28	Kenny Rogers	Tex vs Cal, 4-0
			(perfect game)
1996	5/14	Dwight Gooden	NY vs Sea, 2-0
1998	5/17	David Wells	NY vs Min, 4-0
			(perfect game)
1999	7/18	David Cone	NY vs Mon, 6-0
			(perfect game)
	9/11	Eric Milton	Min vs Ana, 7-0
2001	4/4	Hideo Nomo	Bos at Bal, 3-0
2002	4/27	Derek Lowe	Bos vs TB, 10-0

All-Time Major League Leaders

Based on statistics compiled by *The Baseball Encyclopedia* (9th ed.); through 2003 regular season.

CAREER

Players active in 2003 in **bold** type.

Batting

Note that (*) indicates left-handed hitter and (†) indicates switch-hitter.

Batting Average

(Minimum 3,000 AB)

		Yrs	AB	H	Avg
1	Ty Cobb*	.24	11,434	4189	.366
2	Rogers Hornsby	.23	8,173	2930	.358
3	Joe Jackson*	.13	4,981	1772	.356
4	Ed Delahanty	.16	7,505	2596	.346
5	Tris Speaker*	.22	10,195	3514	.345
6	Ted Williams*	.19	7,706	2654	.344
7	Billy Hamilton*	.14	6,269	2159	.344
8	Dan Brouthers*	.19	6,711	2296	.342
9	Babe Ruth*	.22	8,399	2873	.342
10	Harry Heilmann	.17	7,787	2660	.342
11	Pete Browning	.13	4,820	1646	.341
12	Willie Keeler*	.19	8,591	2932	.341
13	Bill Terry*	.14	6,428	2193	.341
14	George Sisler*	.15	8,267	2812	.340
15	Lou Gehrig*	.17	8,001	2721	.340
16	Jesse Burkett*	.16	8,421	2850	.338
17	Tony Gwynn*	.20	9,288	3141	.338
18	Nap Lajoie	.21	9,589	3242	.338
19	**Todd Helton***	.7	3,504	1182	.337
20	Riggs Stephenson	.14	4,508	1515	.336
21	Al Simmons	.20	8,759	2927	.334
22	Paul Waner*	.20	9,459	3152	.333
23	Eddie Collins*	.25	9,949	3315	.333
24	Stan Musial*	.22	10,972	3630	.331
25	Sam Thompson*	.14	5,984	1979	.331

Hits

		Yrs	AB	H	Avg
1	Pete Rose†	.24	14,053	**4256**	.303
2	Ty Cobb*	.24	11,434	**4189**	.366
3	Hank Aaron	.23	12,364	**3771**	.305
4	Stan Musial*	.22	10,972	**3630**	.331
5	Tris Speaker*	.22	10,195	**3514**	.345
6	Carl Yastrzemski*	.23	11,988	**3419**	.285
7	Honus Wagner	.21	10,430	**3415**	.327
8	Paul Molitor	.21	10,835	**3319**	.306
9	Eddie Collins*	.25	9,949	**3315**	.333
10	Willie Mays	.22	10,881	**3283**	.302
11	Eddie Murray†	.21	11,336	**3255**	.287
12	Nap Lajoie	.21	9,589	**3242**	.338
13	Cal Ripken Jr	.21	11,551	**3184**	.276
14	George Brett*	.21	10,349	**3154**	.305
15	Paul Waner*	.20	9,459	**3152**	.333
16	Robin Yount	.20	11,008	**3142**	.285
17	Tony Gwynn*	.20	9,288	**3141**	.338
18	Dave Winfield	.22	11,003	**3110**	.283
19	**Rickey Henderson**	.25	10,961	**3055**	.279
20	Rod Carew*	.19	9,315	**3053**	.328
21	Lou Brock*	.19	10,332	**3023**	.293
22	Wade Boggs*	.18	9,180	**3010**	.328
23	Al Kaline	.22	10,116	**3007**	.297
24	Cap Anson	.22	9,108	**3000**	.329
	Roberto Clemente	.18	9,454	**3000**	.317

Players Active in 2003

		Yrs	AB	H	Avg
1	Todd Helton*	.7	3,504	1182	.337
2	Nomar Garciaparra	.8	3,812	1231	.323
3	Vladimir Guerrero	.8	3,763	1215	.323
4	Mike Piazza	.12	5,350	1708	.319
5	Derek Jeter	.9	4,870	1546	.317
6	Manny Ramirez	.11	5,004	1585	.317
7	Edgar Martinez	.17	6,727	2119	.315
8	Larry Walker*	.15	6,334	1992	.314
9	Frank Thomas	.14	6,611	2048	.310
10	Chipper Jones†	.10	5,144	1588	.309
11	Alex Rodriguez	.10	4,989	1535	.308
12	Magglio Ordonez	.7	3,605	1108	.307
13	Bobby Abreu*	.8	3,566	1091	.306

Players Active in 2003

		Yrs	AB	H	Avg
1	Rickey Henderson	.25	10,961	**3055**	.279
2	Rafael Palmeiro*	.18	9,553	**2780**	.291
3	Roberto Alomar†	.16	8,902	**2679**	.301
4	Barry Bonds*	.18	8,725	**2595**	.297
5	Fred McGriff*	.18	8,685	**2477**	.285
6	Craig Biggio	.16	8,588	**2461**	.287
7	Mark Grace*	.16	8,065	**2445**	.303
8	Julio Franco	.19	7,869	**2358**	.300
9	Andres Galarraga	.18	8,086	**2330**	.288
10	Barry Larkin	.18	7,591	**2240**	.295
11	Steve Finley*	.15	7,843	**2166**	.276
12	B.J. Surhoff	.17	7,612	**2142**	.281
13	Jeff Bagwell	.13	7,125	**2137**	.300

Games Played

1	Pete Rose	.3562
2	Carl Yastrzemski	.3308
3	Hank Aaron	.3298
4	**Rickey Henderson**	.3081
5	Ty Cobb	.3035
6	Stan Musial	.3026
	Eddie Murray	.3026
8	Cal Ripken Jr.	.3001
9	Willie Mays	.2992
10	Dave Winfield	.2973
11	Rusty Staub	.2951
12	Brooks Robinson	.2896
13	Robin Yount	.2856
14	Al Kaline	.2834
15	Harold Baines	.2830
16	Eddie Collins	.2826
17	Reggie Jackson	.2820
18	Frank Robinson	.2808
19	Honus Wagner	.2792
20	Tris Speaker	.2789

At Bats

1	Pete Rose	.14,053
2	Hank Aaron	.12,364
3	Carl Yastrzemski	.11,988
4	Cal Ripken Jr.	.11,551
5	Ty Cobb	.11,434
6	Eddie Murray	.11,336
7	Robin Yount	.11,008
8	Dave Winfield	.11,003
9	Stan Musial	.10,972
10	**Rickey Henderson**	.10,961
11	Willie Mays	.10,881
12	Paul Molitor	.10,835
13	Brooks Robinson	.10,654
14	Honus Wagner	.10,430
15	George Brett	.10,349
16	Lou Brock	.10,332
17	Luis Aparicio	.10,230
18	Tris Speaker	.10,195
19	Al Kaline	.10,116
20	Rabbit Maranville	.10,078

Total Bases

1	Hank Aaron	.6856
2	Stan Musial	.6134
3	Willie Mays	.6066
4	Ty Cobb	.5854
5	Babe Ruth	.5793
6	Pete Rose	.5752
7	Carl Yastrzemski	.5539
8	Eddie Murray	.5397
9	Frank Robinson	.5373
10	**Barry Bonds**	.5253
11	Dave Winfield	.5221
12	Cal Ripken Jr.	.5168
13	Tris Speaker	.5101
14	Lou Gehrig	.5060
15	George Brett	.5044
16	Mel Ott	.5041
17	**Rafael Palmeiro**	.4983
18	Jimmie Foxx	.4956
19	Ted Williams	.4884
20	Honus Wagner	.4862

Home Runs

		Yrs	AB	HR	AB/HR
1	Hank Aaron	.23	12,364	**755**	16.4
2	Babe Ruth*	.22	8,399	**714**	11.8
3	Willie Mays	.22	10,881	**660**	16.5
4	**Barry Bonds***	.18	8,725	**658**	13.3
5	Frank Robinson	.21	10,006	**586**	17.1
6	Mark McGwire	.16	6,187	**583**	10.6
7	Harmon Killebrew	.22	8,147	**573**	14.2
8	Reggie Jackson*	.21	9,864	**563**	17.5
9	Mike Schmidt	.18	8,352	**548**	15.2
10	**Sammy Sosa**	.15	7,543	**539**	14.0
11	Mickey Mantle†	.18	8,102	**536**	15.1
12	Jimmie Foxx	.20	8,134	**534**	15.2
13	**Rafael Palmeiro***	.18	9,553	**528**	18.1
14	Ted Williams*	.19	7,706	**521**	14.8
	Willie McCovey*	.22	8,197	**521**	15.7
16	Eddie Mathews*	.17	8,537	**512**	16.7
	Ernie Banks	.19	9,421	**512**	18.4
18	Mel Ott*	.22	9,456	**511**	18.5
19	Eddie Murray†	.21	11,336	**504**	22.5
20	Lou Gehrig*	.17	8,001	**493**	16.2
21	**Fred McGriff***	.18	8,685	**491**	17.7
22	**Ken Griffey Jr.***	.15	7,079	**481**	14.7
23	Willie Stargell*	.21	7,927	**475**	16.7
	Stan Musial*	.22	10,972	**475**	23.1
25	Dave Winfield	.22	11,003	**465**	23.7

Runs Batted In

		Yrs	Gm	RBI	P/G
1	Hank Aaron	.23	3298	**2297**	.70
2	Babe Ruth*	.22	2503	**2213**	.88
3	Lou Gehrig*	.17	2164	**1995**	.92
4	Stan Musial*	.22	3026	**1951**	.64
5	Ty Cobb*	.24	3034	**1938**	.64
6	Jimmie Foxx	.20	2317	**1922**	.83
7	Eddie Murray†	.21	2980	**1917**	.64
8	Willie Mays	.22	2992	**1903**	.64
9	Mel Ott*	.22	2730	**1860**	.68
10	Carl Yastrzemski*	.23	3308	**1844**	.56
11	Ted Williams*	.19	2292	**1839**	.80
12	Dave Winfield	.22	2973	**1833**	.62
13	Al Simmons	.20	2215	**1827**	.82
14	Frank Robinson	.21	2808	**1812**	.65
15	**Barry Bonds***	.18	2569	**1742**	.68
16	Honus Wagner	.21	2792	**1732**	.62
17	Cap Anson	.22	2276	**1715**	.75
18	Reggie Jackson*	.21	2820	**1702**	.60
19	Cal Ripken Jr.	.21	3001	**1695**	.56
20	**Rafael Palmeiro***	.18	2567	**1687**	.66
21	Tony Perez	.23	2777	**1652**	.59
22	Ernie Banks	.19	2528	**1636**	.65
23	Harold Baines*	.22	2830	**1628**	.58
24	Goose Goslin*	.18	2287	**1609**	.70
25	Nap Lajoie	.21	2480	**1599**	.64

Players Active in 2003

		Yrs	AB	HR	AB/HR
1	Barry Bonds*	.18	8,725	**658**	13.3
2	Sammy Sosa	.15	7,543	**539**	14.0
3	Rafael Palmeiro*	.18	9,553	**528**	18.1
4	Fred McGriff*	.18	8,685	**491**	17.7
5	Ken Griffey Jr.*	.15	7,079	**481**	14.7
6	Juan Gonzalez	.15	6,428	**429**	15.0
7	Jeff Bagwell	.13	7,125	**419**	17.0
8	Frank Thomas	.14	6,611	**418**	15.8
9	Andres Galarraga	.18	8,086	**398**	20.3
10	Jim Thome*	.13	5,218	**381**	13.7
11	Gary Sheffield	.16	6,729	**379**	17.8
12	Matt Williams	.17	7,000	**378**	18.5
13	Mike Piazza	.15	5,350	**358**	14.9
14	Greg Vaughn	.15	6,103	**355**	17.2
15	Ellis Burks	.17	7,199	**351**	20.5
	Larry Walker*	.15	6,334	**351**	18.0

Players Active in 2003

		Yrs	Gm	RBI	P/G
1	Barry Bonds*	.18	2569	**1742**	.68
2	Rafael Palmeiro*	.18	2567	**1687**	.66
3	Fred McGriff*	.18	2433	**1543**	.63
4	Sammy Sosa	.15	2012	**1450**	.72
5	Andres Galarraga	.18	2250	**1423**	.63
6	Jeff Bagwell	.13	1955	**1421**	.73
7	Frank Thomas	.14	1851	**1390**	.75
8	Juan Gonzalez	.15	1655	**1387**	.84
9	Ken Griffey Jr.*	.15	1914	**1384**	.72
10	Gary Sheffield	.16	1882	**1232**	.65
11	Ruben Sierra†	.17	2004	**1224**	.61
12	Matt Williams	.17	1866	**1218**	.65
13	Larry Walker*	.15	1806	**1212**	.67
14	Ellis Burks	.17	1989	**1205**	.61
15	Edgar Martinez	.17	1914	**1198**	.63

Runs

1	**Rickey Henderson**	.2295
2	Ty Cobb	.2246
3	Babe Ruth	.2174
	Hank Aaron	.2174
5	Pete Rose	.2165
6	Willie Mays	.2062
7	Stan Musial	.1949
8	**Barry Bonds**	.1941
9	Lou Gehrig	.1888
10	Tris Speaker	.1882
11	Mel Ott	.1859
12	Frank Robinson	.1829
13	Eddie Collins	.1821
14	Carl Yastrzemski	.1816
15	Ted Williams	.1798
16	Paul Molitor	.1782
17	Charlie Gehringer	.1774
18	Jimmie Foxx	.1751
19	Honus Wagner	.1736
20	Willie Keeler	.1727

Extra Base Hits

1	Hank Aaron	.1477
2	Stan Musial	.1377
3	Babe Ruth	.1356
4	Willie Mays	.1323
5	**Barry Bonds**	.1268
6	Lou Gehrig	.1190
7	Frank Robinson	.1186
8	Carl Yastrzemski	.1157
9	Ty Cobb	.1136
10	Tris Speaker	.1131
11	George Brett	.1119
12	Ted Williams	.1117
	Jimmie Foxx	.1117
14	**Rafael Palmeiro**	.1109
15	Eddie Murray	.1099
16	Dave Winfield	.1093
17	Cal Ripken Jr.	.1078
18	Reggie Jackson	.1075
19	Mel Ott	.1071
20	Pete Rose	.1041

Slugging Percentage

(Minimum 3,000 AB)

1	Babe Ruth	.690
2	Ted Williams	.634
3	Lou Gehrig	.632
4	**Todd Helton**	.616
5	Jimmie Foxx	.609
6	Hank Greenberg	.605
7	**Barry Bonds**	.602
8	**Manny Ramirez**	.598
9	Mark McGwire	.588
10	**Vladimir Guerrero**	.588
11	**Alex Rodriguez**	.581
12	Joe DiMaggio	.579
13	Rogers Hornsby	.577
14	**Mike Piazza**	.572
15	**Jim Thome**	.568
16	Frank Thomas	.568
17	**Larry Walker**	.567
18	Albert Belle	.564
19	**Juan Gonzalez**	.563
20	**Brian Giles**	.563

Stolen Bases

1	Rickey Henderson	1406
2	Lou Brock	938
3	Billy Hamilton	912
4	Ty Cobb	892
5	Tim Raines	808
6	Vince Coleman	752
7	Eddie Collins	745
8	Max Carey	738
9	Honus Wagner	722
10	Joe Morgan	689
11	Arlie Latham	679
12	Willie Wilson	668
13	Bert Campaneris	649
14	Tom Brown	627
15	Otis Nixon	620
16	George Davis	616
17	Dummy Hoy	594
18	Maury Wills	586
19	George Van Haltren	583
20	Ozzie Smith	580

Walks

1	Rickey Henderson	2190
2	Babe Ruth	2062
3	Ted Williams	2019
4	Barry Bonds	2070
5	Joe Morgan	1865
6	Carl Yastrzemski	1845
7	Mickey Mantle	1733
8	Mel Ott	1708
9	Eddie Yost	1614
10	Darrell Evans	1605
11	Stan Musial	1599
12	Pete Rose	1566
13	Harmon Killebrew	1559
14	Lou Gehrig	1508
15	Mike Schmidt	1507
16	Eddie Collins	1499
17	Willie Mays	1464
18	Jimmie Foxx	1452
19	Eddie Mathews	1444
20	Frank Robinson	1420

Strikeouts

1	Reggie Jackson	2597
2	Andres Galarraga	2000
3	Sammy Sosa	1977
4	Jose Canseco	1942
5	Willie Stargell	1936
6	Mike Schmidt	1883
7	Tony Perez	1867
8	Fred McGriff	1863
9	Dave Kingman	1816
10	Bobby Bonds	1757
11	Dale Murphy	1748
12	Lou Brock	1730
13	Mickey Mantle	1710
14	Harmon Killebrew	1699
15	Chili Davis	1698
16	Dwight Evans	1697
17	Rickey Henderson	1694
18	Dave Winfield	1686
19	Gary Gaetti	1602
20	Mark McGwire	1596

Pitching

Note that (*) indicates left-handed pitcher. Active pitching leaders are listed for wins and strikeouts.

Wins

		Yrs	GS	W	L	Pct
1	Cy Young	22	815	511	316	.618
2	Walter Johnson	21	666	417	279	.599
3	Christy Mathewson	17	551	373	188	.665
	Grover Alexander	20	598	373	208	.642
5	Pud Galvin	15	688	365	310	.541
6	Warren Spahn*	21	665	363	245	.597
7	Kid Nichols	15	561	361	208	.634
8	Tim Keefe	14	594	342	225	.603
9	Steve Carlton*	24	709	329	244	.574
10	John Clarkson	12	518	328	178	.648
11	Eddie Plank*	17	529	326	194	.627
12	Don Sutton	23	756	324	256	.559
	Nolan Ryan	27	773	324	292	.526
14	Phil Niekro	24	716	318	274	.537
15	Gaylord Perry	22	690	314	265	.542
16	Tom Seaver	20	647	311	205	.603
17	Roger Clemens	20	606	310	160	.660
18	Old Hoss Radbourn	12	503	309	195	.613
19	Mickey Welch	13	549	307	210	.594
20	Lefty Grove*	17	456	300	141	.680
	Early Wynn*	23	612	300	244	.551
22	Bobby Mathews	15	568	297	248	.545
23	Greg Maddux	18	571	289	163	.639
24	Tommy John*	26	700	288	231	.555
25	Bert Blyleven	22	685	287	250	.534
26	Robin Roberts	19	609	286	245	.539
27	Tony Mullane	13	504	284	220	.563
	Ferguson Jenkins	19	594	284	226	.557
29	Jim Kaat*	25	625	283	237	.544
30	Red Ruffing	22	536	273	225	.548

Strikeouts

		Yrs	IP	SO	P/9
1	Nolan Ryan	27	5386.0	5714	9.55
2	Steve Carlton*	24	5217.1	4136	7.13
3	Roger Clemens	20	4278.2	4099	8.62
4	Randy Johnson*	16	3122.1	3871	11.16
5	Bert Blyleven	22	4970.0	3701	6.70
6	Tom Seaver	20	4782.2	3640	6.85
7	Don Sutton	23	5282.1	3574	6.09
8	Gaylord Perry	22	5350.1	3534	5.94
9	Walter Johnson	21	5914.1	3508	5.34
10	Phil Niekro	24	5404.1	3342	5.57
11	Ferguson Jenkins	19	4500.2	3192	6.38
12	Bob Gibson	17	3884.1	3117	7.22
13	Jim Bunning	17	3760.1	2855	6.83
14	Mickey Lolich*	16	3638.1	2832	7.01
15	Cy Young	22	7356.0	2803	3.43
16	Frank Tanana*	21	4186.2	2773	5.96
17	Greg Maddux	18	3968.2	2765	6.27
18	David Cone	17	2898.2	2668	8.28
19	Chuck Finley*	17	3197.1	2610	7.35
20	Warren Spahn*	21	5243.2	2583	4.43
21	Bob Feller	18	3827.0	2581	6.07
22	Tim Keefe	14	5049.2	2564	4.57
23	Jerry Koosman*	19	3839.1	2556	5.99
24	Curt Schilling	16	2586.0	2542	8.85
25	Christy Mathewson	17	4781.0	2502	4.71
26	Don Drysdale	17	3432.0	2486	6.52
27	Jack Morris	18	3824.2	2478	5.83
28	Mark Langston*	16	2962.2	2464	7.49
29	Jim Kaat*	25	4530.1	2461	4.89
30	Sam McDowell*	15	2492.1	2453	8.86

Pitchers Active in 2003

		Yrs	GS	W	L	Pct
1	Roger Clemens	20	606	310	160	.660
2	Greg Maddux	18	571	289	163	.639
3	Tom Glavine*	17	537	251	157	.615
4	Randy Johnson*	16	444	230	114	.669
5	David Wells*	17	386	200	128	.610
6	Mike Mussina	13	386	199	110	.644
7	Kevin Brown	17	441	197	131	.601
8	David Cone	17	419	194	126	.606
9	Jamie Moyer*	17	420	185	132	.584
10	Kevin Appier	15	400	169	136	.554

Pitchers Active in 2003

		Yrs	IP	SO	P/9
1	Roger Clemens	20	4278.2	4099	8.62
2	Randy Johnson*	16	3122.1	3871	11.16
3	Greg Maddux	18	3968.2	2765	6.27
4	David Cone	17	2898.2	2668	8.28
5	Curt Schilling	16	2586.0	2542	8.85
6	Pedro Martinez	12	2079.0	2426	10.50
7	John Smoltz	16	2618.0	2313	7.95
8	Kevin Brown	17	3051.0	2264	6.68
9	Tom Glavine*	17	3528.1	2136	5.45
10	Mike Mussina	13	2668.2	2126	7.17

Winning Pct.
(Minimum 100 wins)

		Yrs	W-L	Pct
1	Al Spalding	.7	252-65	.795
2	Spud Chandler	.11	109-43	.717
3	**Pedro Martinez**	.12	166-67	.712
4	Dave Foutz	.11	147-66	.690
5	Whitey Ford*	.16	236-106	.690
6	Bob Caruthers	.9	218-99	.688
7	Don Gullett*	.9	109-50	.686
8	Lefty Grove*	.17	300-141	.680
9	Joe Wood	.11	117-57	.672
10	**Randy Johnson***	.16	230-114	.669
11	Vic Raschi	.10	132-66	.667
12	Larry Corcoran	.8	177-89	.665
13	Christy Mathewson	.17	373-188	.665
14	Sam Leever	.13	194-100	.660
15	**Roger Clemens**	.20	310-160	.660

Losses

		Yrs	GS	W	L	Pct
1	Cy Young	.22	815	511	**316**	.618
2	Pud Galvin	.15	688	365	**310**	.541
3	Nolan Ryan	.27	773	324	**292**	.526
4	Walter Johnson	.21	666	417	**279**	.599
5	Phil Niekro	.24	716	318	**274**	.537
6	Gaylord Perry	.22	690	314	**265**	.542
7	Don Sutton	.23	756	324	**256**	.559
8	Jack Powell	.16	516	245	**254**	.491
9	Eppa Rixey*	.21	552	266	**251**	.515
10	Bert Blyleven	.22	685	287	**250**	.534
11	Bobby Mathews	.15	568	297	**248**	.545
12	Robin Roberts*	.19	609	286	**245**	.539
	Warren Spahn*	.21	665	363	**245**	.597
14	Early Wynn	.23	612	300	**244**	.551
	Steve Carlton*	.24	709	329	**244**	.574

Appearances

1	**Jesse Orosco**	1252
2	Dennis Eckersley	1071
3	Hoyt Wilhelm	1070
4	**Dan Plesac**	1064
5	Kent Tekulve	1050
6	**John Franco**	1036
7	Lee Smith	1022
8	Rich Gossage	1002
9	Lindy McDaniel	987
10	Mike Jackson	960
11	Rollie Fingers	944
12	Gene Garber	931
13	Cy Young	906
14	Sparky Lyle	899
15	Jim Kaat	898

Innings Pitched

1	Cy Young	7356.0
2	Pud Galvin	6003.1
3	Walter Johnson	5914.1
4	Phil Niekro	5404.1
5	Nolan Ryan	5386.0
6	Gaylord Perry	5350.1
7	Don Sutton	5282.1
8	Warren Spahn	5243.2
9	Steve Carlton	5217.1
10	Grover Alexander	5190.0
11	Kid Nichols	5056.1
12	Tim Keefe	5049.2
13	Bert Blyleven	4970.0
14	Bobby Mathews	4956.0
15	Mickey Welch	4802.0

Earned Run Avg.
(Minimum 1500 IP)

1	Ed Walsh	1.82
2	Addie Joss	1.89
3	Al Spalding	2.04
4	Three Finger Brown	2.06
5	Monte Ward	2.10
6	Christy Mathewson	2.13
7	Rube Waddell	2.16
8	Walter Johnson	2.17
9	Orval Overall	2.23
10	Tommy Bond	2.25
11	Will White	2.28
12	Ed Reulbach	2.28
13	Jim Scott	2.30
14	Eddie Plank	2.35
15	Larry Corcoran	2.36

Shutouts

1	Walter Johnson	110
2	Grover Alexander	90
3	Christy Mathewson	79
4	Cy Young	76
5	Eddie Plank	69
6	Warren Spahn	63
7	Nolan Ryan	61
	Tom Seaver	61
9	Bert Blyleven	60
10	Don Sutton	58
11	Pud Galvin	57
	Ed Walsh	57
13	Bob Gibson	56
14	Three Finger Brown	55
	Steve Carlton	55

Walks Allowed

1	Nolan Ryan	2795
2	Steve Carlton	1833
3	Phil Niekro	1809
4	Early Wynn	1775
5	Bob Feller	1764
6	Bobo Newsom	1732
7	Amos Rusie	1704
8	Charlie Hough	1665
9	Gus Weyhing	1566
10	Red Ruffing	1541
11	Bump Hadley	1442
12	Warren Spahn	1434
13	Earl Whitehill	1431
14	Tony Mullane	1408
15	Sad Sam Jones	1396

HRs Allowed

1	Robin Roberts	505
2	Ferguson Jenkins	484
3	Phil Niekro	482
4	Don Sutton	472
5	Frank Tanana	448
6	Warren Spahn	434
7	Bert Blyleven	430
8	Steve Carlton	414
9	Gaylord Perry	399
10	Jim Kaat	395
11	Jack Morris	389
12	Charlie Hough	383
13	Tom Seaver	380
14	Catfish Hunter	374
15	Jim Bunning	372
	Dennis Martinez	372

Saves

1	Lee Smith	478
2	John Franco	422
3	Dennis Eckersley	390
4	Jeff Reardon	367
5	**Trevor Hoffman**	352
6	Randy Myers	347
7	Rollie Fingers	341
8	John Wetteland	330
9	**Roberto Hernandez**	320
10	Rick Aguilera	318
11	**Robb Nen**	314
12	Tom Henke	311
13	Rich Gossage	310
14	Jeff Montgomery	304
15	Doug Jones	303
16	Bruce Sutter	300
17	**Rod Beck**	286
18	**Troy Percival**	283
	Mariano Rivera	283
20	Todd Worrell	256
21	Dave Righetti	252
22	**Jose Mesa**	249
23	Dan Quisenberry	244
24	Sparky Lyle	238
25	Hoyt Wilhelm	227
26	**Billy Wagner**	225
27	Gene Garber	218
28	Gregg Olson	217
29	Dave Smith	216
30	**Ugueth Urbina**	206

SINGLE SEASON
Through 2003 regular season.
Batting

Home Runs

		Year	Gm	AB	HR
1	Barry Bonds, SF	2001	153	476	73
2	Mark McGwire, St.L	1998	155	509	70
3	Sammy Sosa, Chi-NL	1998	159	643	66
4	Mark McGwire, St.L	1999	153	521	65
5	Sammy Sosa, Chi-NL	2001	160	577	64
6	Sammy Sosa, Chi-NL	1999	162	625	63
7	Roger Maris, NY-AL	1961	162	590	61
8	Babe Ruth, NY-AL	1927	151	540	60
9	Babe Ruth, NY-AL	1921	152	540	59
10	Mark McGwire, Oak-St.L	1997	156	540	58
	Hank Greenberg, Det	1938	155	556	58
	Jimmie Foxx, Phi-AL	1932	154	585	58
13	Alex Rodriguez, Tex	2002	162	624	57
	Luis Gonzalez, Ari	2001	162	609	57
15	Hack Wilson, Chi-NL	1930	155	585	56
	Ken Griffey Jr., Sea	1997	157	608	56
	Ken Griffey Jr., Sea	1998	161	633	56
18	Babe Ruth, NY-AL	1920	142	458	54
	Mickey Mantle, NY-AL	1961	153	514	54
	Babe Ruth, NY-AL	1928	154	536	54
	Ralph Kiner, Pit	1949	152	549	54

Hits

		Year	AB	H	Avg
1	George Sisler, Stl-AL	1920	631	257	.407
2	Bill Terry, NY-NL	1930	633	254	.401
	Lefty O'Doul, Phi-NL	1929	638	254	.398
4	Al Simmons, Phi-AL	1925	658	253	.384
5	Rogers Hornsby, Stl-NL	1922	623	250	.401
	Chuck Klein, Phi-NL	1930	648	250	.386
7	Ty Cobb, Det	1911	591	248	.420
8	George Sisler, Stl-AL	1922	586	246	.420
9	Ichiro Suzuki, Sea	2001	692	242	.350
10	Babe Herman, Bklyn	1930	614	241	.393
	Heinie Manush, Stl-AL	1928	638	241	.378
12	Wade Boggs, Bos	1985	653	240	.368
	Darin Erstad, Ana	2000	676	240	.355
14	Rod Carew, Min	1977	616	239	.388
15	Don Mattingly, NY-AL	1986	677	238	.352
16	Harry Heilmann, Det	1921	602	237	.394
	Paul Waner, Pit	1927	623	237	.380
	Joe Medwick, Stl-NL	1937	633	237	.374
19	Jack Tobin, Stl-AL	1921	671	236	.352
20	Rogers Hornsby, Stl-NL	1921	592	235	.397

Batting Average

From 1900-49

		Year	AB	H	Avg
1	Rogers Hornsby, Stl-NL	1924	536	227	.424
2	Nap Lajoie, Phi-AL	1901	543	229	.422
3	George Sisler, Stl-AL	1922	586	246	.420
4	Ty Cobb, Det	1911	591	248	.420
5	Ty Cobb, Det	1912	533	227	.410
6	Joe Jackson, Cle	1911	571	233	.408
7	George Sisler, Stl-AL	1920	631	257	.407
8	Ted Williams, Bos-AL	1941	456	185	.406
9	Rogers Hornsby, Stl-NL	1925	504	203	.403
10	Harry Heilmann, Det	1923	524	211	.403

Since 1950

		Year	AB	H	Avg
1	Tony Gwynn, SD	1994	419	175	.394
2	George Brett, KC	1980	449	175	.390
3	Ted Williams, Bos	1957	420	163	.388
4	Rod Carew, Min	1977	616	239	.388
5	Larry Walker, Col	1999	438	166	.379
6	Todd Helton, Col	2000	580	216	.372
7	Nomar Garciaparra, Bos	2000	529	197	.372
8	Tony Gwynn, SD	1997	592	220	.372
9	Andres Galarraga, Col	1993	470	174	.370
10	Tony Gwynn, SD	1987	589	218	.370

Total Bases

From 1900-49

		Year	TB
1	Babe Ruth, New York-AL	1921	457
2	Rogers Hornsby, St. Louis-NL	1922	450
3	Lou Gehrig, New York-AL	1927	447
4	Chuck Klein, Philadelphia-NL	1930	445
5	Jimmie Foxx, Philadelphia-AL	1932	438
6	Stan Musial, St. Louis-NL	1948	429
7	Hack Wilson, Chicago-NL	1930	423
8	Chuck Klein, Philadelphia-NL	1932	420
9	Lou Gehrig, New York-AL	1930	419
10	Joe DiMaggio, New York-AL	1937	418

Since 1950

		Year	TB
1	Sammy Sosa, Chicago-NL	2001	425
2	Luis Gonzalez, Arizona	2001	419
3	Sammy Sosa, Chicago-NL	1998	416
4	Barry Bonds, San Francisco	2001	411
5	Larry Walker, Colorado	1997	409
6	Jim Rice, Boston	1978	406
7	Todd Helton, Colorado	2000	405
8	Todd Helton, Colorado	2001	402
9	Hank Aaron, Milwaukee	1959	400
10	Albert Belle, Chicago-AL	1998	399

Runs Batted In

From 1900-49

		Year	Avg	HR	RBI
1	Hack Wilson, Chi-NL	1930	.356	56	191
2	Lou Gehrig, NY-AL	1931	.341	46	184
3	Hank Greenberg, Det	1937	.337	40	183
4	Lou Gehrig, NY-AL	1927	.373	47	175
	Jimmie Foxx, Bos-AL	1938	.349	50	175
6	Lou Gehrig, NY-AL	1930	.379	41	174
7	Babe Ruth, NY-AL	1921	.378	59	171
8	Chuck Klein, Phi-NL	1930	.386	40	170
	Hank Greenberg, Det	1935	.328	36	170
10	Jimmie Foxx, Phi-AL	1932	.364	58	169

Since 1950

		Year	Avg	HR	RBI
1	Manny Ramirez, Cle	1999	.333	44	165
2	Sammy Sosa, Chi-NL	2001	.328	64	160
3	Sammy Sosa, Chi-NL	1998	.308	66	158
4	Juan Gonzalez, Tex	1998	.318	45	157
5	Tommy Davis, LA-NL	1962	.346	27	153
6	Albert Belle, Chi-AL	1998	.328	49	152
7	Andres Galarraga, Col	1996	.304	47	150
8	George Foster, Cin	1977	.320	52	149
9	Rafael Palmeiro, Tex	1999	.324	47	148
	Johnny Bench, Cin	1970	.293	45	148
	Albert Belle, Cle	1996	.311	48	148

Runs

		Year	Runs
1	Babe Ruth, New York-AL	1921	177
2	Lou Gehrig, New York-AL	1936	167
3	Babe Ruth, New York-AL	1928	163
	Lou Gehrig, New York-AL	1931	163
5	Babe Ruth, New York-AL	1920	158
	Babe Ruth, New York-AL	1927	158
	Chuck Klein, Philadelphia-NL	1930	158
8	Rogers Hornsby, Chicago-NL	1929	156
9	Kiki Cuyler, Chicago-NL	1930	155
10	Lefty O'Doul, Philadelphia-NL	1929	152
	Woody English, Chicago-NL	1930	152
	Al Simmons, Philadelphia-NL	1930	152
	Chuck Klein, Philadelphia-NL	1932	152
	Jeff Bagwell, Houston	2000	152
15	Babe Ruth, New York-AL	1923	151
	Jimmie Foxx, Philadelphia-AL	1932	151
	Joe DiMaggio, New York-AL	1937	151
18	Babe Ruth, New York-AL	1930	150
	Ted Williams, Boston-AL	1949	150
20	Lou Gehrig, New York-AL	1927	149
	Babe Ruth, New York-AL	1931	149

Walks

		Year	BB
1	Barry Bonds, San Francisco	2002	198
2	Barry Bonds, San Francisco	2001	177
3	Babe Ruth, New York-AL	1923	170
4	Ted Williams, Boston-AL	1947	162
	Ted Williams, Boston-AL	1949	162
	Mark McGwire, St. Louis	1998	162
7	Ted Williams, Boston-AL	1946	156
8	Barry Bonds, San Francisco	1996	151
	Eddie Yost, Washington	1956	151
10	Jeff Bagwell, Houston	1999	149
	Eddie Joost, Philadelphia-AL	1949	149

Extra Base Hits

		Year	EBH
1	Babe Ruth, New York-AL	1921	119
2	Lou Gehrig, New York-AL	1927	117
3	Chuck Klein, Philadelphia-NL	1930	107
	Barry Bonds, San Francisco	2001	107
5	Todd Helton, Colorado	2001	105
6	Chuck Klein, Philadelphia-NL	1932	103
	Hank Greenberg, Detroit	1937	103
	Stan Musial, St. Louis-NL	1948	103
	Albert Belle, Cleveland	1995	103
	Todd Helton, Colorado	2000	103
	Sammy Sosa, Chicago-NL	2001	103

Slugging Percentage
From 1900-49

		Year	Pct
1	Babe Ruth, New York-AL	1920	.847
2	Babe Ruth, New York-AL	1921	.846
3	Babe Ruth, New York-AL	1927	.772
4	Lou Gehrig, New York-AL	1927	.765
5	Babe Ruth, New York-AL	1923	.764
6	Rogers Hornsby, St. Louis-NL	1925	.756
7	Jimmie Foxx, Philadelphia-AL	1932	.749
8	Babe Ruth, New York-AL	1924	.739
9	Babe Ruth, New York-AL	1926	.737
10	Ted Williams, Boston-AL	1941	.735

Since 1950

		Year	Pct
1	Barry Bonds, San Francisco	2001	.863
2	Barry Bonds, San Francisco	2002	.799
3	Mark McGwire, St. Louis	1998	.752
4	Jeff Bagwell, Houston	1994	.750
5	**Barry Bonds**, San Francisco	2003	.749
6	Sammy Sosa, Chicago-NL	2001	.737
7	Ted Williams, Boston	1957	.731
8	Mark McGwire, Oakland	1996	.730
9	Frank Thomas, Chicago-AL	1994	.729
10	Larry Walker, Colorado	1997	.720

Doubles

		Year	2B
1	Earl Webb, Boston-AL	1931	67
2	George Burns, Cleveland	1926	64
	Joe Medwick, St. Louis-NL	1936	64
4	Hank Greenberg, Detroit	1934	63
5	Paul Waner, Pittsburgh	1932	62
6	Charlie Gehringer, Detroit	1936	60
7	Tris Speaker, Cleveland	1923	59
	Chuck Klein, Philadelphia-NL	1930	59
	Todd Helton, Colorado	2000	59
10	Three tied with 57 each.		

Triples
From 1900-49

		Year	3B
1	Chief Wilson, Pittsburgh	1912	36
2	Joe Jackson, Cleveland	1912	26
3	Sam Crawford, Detroit	1914	26
4	Kiki Cuyler, Pittsburgh	1925	26
5	Three tied with 25 each.		

Since 1950

		Year	3B
1	Willie Wilson, Kansas City	1985	21
	Lance Johnson, New York-NL	1996	21
3	Willie Mays, New York-NL	1957	20
	George Brett, Kansas City	1979	20
	Cristian Guzman, Minnesota	2000	20

Stolen Bases

		Year	SB
1	Rickey Henderson, Oakland	1982	130
2	Lou Brock, St. Louis	1974	118
3	Vince Coleman, St. Louis	1985	110
4	Vince Coleman, St. Louis	1987	109
5	Rickey Henderson, Oakland	1983	108
6	Vince Coleman, St. Louis	1986	107
7	Maury Wills, Los Angeles-NL	1962	104
8	Rickey Henderson, Oakland	1980	100
9	Ron LeFlore, Montreal	1980	97
10	Ty Cobb, Detroit	1915	96
	Omar Moreno, Pittsburgh	1980	96
12	Maury Wills, Los Angeles	1965	94
13	Rickey Henderson, New York-AL	1988	93
14	Tim Raines, Montreal	1983	90
15	Clyde Milan, Washington	1912	88

Strikeouts

		Year	SO
1	Bobby Bonds, San Francisco	1970	189
2	Jose Hernandez, Milwaukee	2002	188
3	Bobby Bonds, San Francisco	1969	187
	Preston Wilson, Florida	2000	187
5	Rob Deer, Milwaukee	1987	186
6	Pete Incaviglia, Texas	1986	185
	Jose Hernandez, Milwaukee	2001	185
	Jim Thome, Cleveland	2001	185
9	Cecil Fielder, Detroit	1990	182
	Jim Thome, Philadelphia	2003	182

Pinch Hits
Career pinch hits in parentheses.

		Year	PH	
1	John Vander Wal, Colorado	1995	28	(123)
2	Lenny Harris, Col-Ari	1999	26	(181)
3	Jose Morales, Montreal	1976	25	(123)
4	Dave Philley, Baltimore	1961	24	(93)
	Vic Davalillo, St. Louis	1970	24	(95)
	Rusty Staub, New York-NL	1983	24	(100)
	Gerald Perry, St. Louis	1993	24	(95)

Note: Harris (181) is the career leader.

Pitching
Wins

From 1900-49

		Year	W	L	Pct
1	Jack Chesbro, NY-AL	1904	41	12	.774
2	Ed Walsh, Chi-AL	1908	40	15	.727
3	Christy Mathewson, NY-NL	1908	37	11	.771
4	Walter Johnson, Wash	1913	36	7	.837
5	Joe McGinnity, NY-NL	1904	35	8	.814
6	Smokey Joe Wood, Bos-AL	1912	34	5	.872
7	Cy Young, Bos-AL	1901	33	10	.767
	Grover Alexander, Phi-NL	1916	33	12	.733
	Christy Mathewson, NY-NL	1904	33	12	.733
10	Cy Young, Bos-AL	1902	32	11	.744

Since 1950

		Year	W	L	Pct
1	Denny McLain, Det	1968	31	6	.838
2	Robin Roberts, Phi-NL	1952	28	7	.800
3	Bob Welch, Oak	1990	27	6	.818
	Don Newcombe, Bklyn	1956	27	7	.794
	Sandy Koufax, LA	1966	27	9	.750
	Steve Carlton, Phi	1972	27	10	.730
7	Sandy Koufax, LA	1965	26	8	.765
	Juan Marichal, SF	1968	26	9	.743

Note: 11 pitchers tied with 25 wins, including Marichal twice.

Earned Run Average

From 1900-49

		Year	ShO	ERA
1	Dutch Leonard, Bos-AL	1914	7	1.01
2	Three Finger Brown, Chi-NL	1906	10	1.04
3	Walter Johnson, Wash	1913	11	1.09
4	Christy Mathewson, NY-NL	1909	8	1.14
5	Jack Pfiester, Chi-NL	1907	3	1.15
6	Addie Joss, Cle	1908	9	1.16
7	Carl Lundgren, Chi-NL	1907	7	1.17
8	Grover Alexander, Phi-NL	1915	12	1.22
9	Cy Young, Bos-AL	1908	3	1.26
10	Three pitchers tied at 1.27			

Since 1950

		Year	ShO	ERA
1	Bob Gibson, St.L	1968	13	1.12
2	Dwight Gooden, NY-NL	1985	8	1.53
3	Greg Maddux, Atl	1994	3	1.56
4	Luis Tiant, Cle	1968	9	1.60
5	Greg Maddux, Atl	1995	3	1.63
6	Dean Chance, LA-AL	1964	11	1.65
7	Nolan Ryan, Cal	1981	3	1.69
8	Sandy Koufax, LA	1966	5	1.73
9	Sandy Koufax, LA	1964	7	1.74
10	Pedro Martinez, Bos	2000	4	1.74

Note: Koufax's ERA in 1964 was 1.735. Martinez' ERA in 2000 was 1.742. The Yankees' Ron Guidry narrowly missed the top 10 list with an ERA of 1.743 in 1978.

Winning Pct.

		Year	W-L	Pct
1	Roy Face, Pit	1959	18-1	.947
2	Rick Sutcliffe, Chi-NL*	1984	16-1	.941
3	Johnny Allen, Cle	1937	15-1	.938
4	Greg Maddux, Atl	1995	19-2	.904
5	Randy Johnson, Sea	1995	18-2	.900
6	Ron Guidry, NY-AL	1978	25-3	.893
7	Freddie Fitzsimmons, Bklyn	1940	16-2	.889
8	Lefty Grove, Phi-AL	1931	31-4	.886
9	Bob Stanley, Bos	1978	15-2	.882
10	Preacher Roe, Bklyn	1951	22-3	.880

*Sutcliffe began 1984 with Cleveland and was 4-5 before being traded to the Cubs; his overall winning pct. was .769 (20-6).

Strikeouts

		Year	SO	P/9
1	Nolan Ryan, Cal	1973	383	10.57
2	Sandy Koufax, LA	1965	382	10.24
3	Randy Johnson, Ari	2001	372	13.41
4	Nolan Ryan, Cal	1974	367	9.93
5	Randy Johnson, Ari	1999	364	12.06
6	Rube Waddell, Phi-AL	1904	349	8.20
7	Bob Feller, Cle	1946	348	8.43
8	Randy Johnson, Ari	2000	347	12.56
9	Nolan Ryan, Cal	1977	341	10.26
10	Randy Johnson, Ari	2002	334	11.56

Appearances

		Year	App	Sv
1	Mike Marshall, LA	1974	106	21
2	Kent Tekulve, Pit	1979	94	31
3	Mike Marshall, LA	1973	92	31
4	Kent Tekulve, Pit	1978	91	31
5	Wayne Granger, Cin	1969	90	27
	Mike Marshall, Min	1979	90	32
	Kent Tekulve, Phi	1987	90	3

Saves

		Year	App	Sv
1	Bobby Thigpen, Chi-AL	1990	77	57
2	John Smoltz, Atl	2002	75	55
	Eric Gagne, LA	2003	77	55
4	Randy Myers, Chi-NL	1993	73	53
	Trevor Hoffman, SD	1998	66	53
6	Eric Gagne, LA	2002	77	52
7	Dennis Eckersley, Oak	1992	69	51
	Rod Beck, Chi-NL	1998	81	51
9	Mariano Rivera, NY-AL	2001	71	50
10	Three tied with 48 each.			

Innings Pitched (since 1920)

		Year	IP	W-L
1	Wilbur Wood, Chi-AL	1972	376.2	24-17
2	Mickey Lolich, Det	1971	376.0	25-14
3	Bob Feller, Cle	1946	371.1	26-15
4	Grover Alexander, Chi-NL	1920	363.1	27-14
5	Wilbur Wood, Chi-AL	1973	359.1	24-20

Shutouts

		Year	ShO	ERA
1	Grover Alexander, Phi-NL	1916	16	1.55
2	Jack Coombs, Phi-AL	1910	13	1.30
	Bob Gibson, St.L	1968	13	1.12
4	Christy Mathewson, NY-NL	1908	12	1.43
	Grover Alexander, Phi-NL	1915	12	1.22

Walks Allowed (since 1920)

		Year	BB	SO
1	Bob Feller, Cle	1938	208	240
2	Nolan Ryan, Cal	1977	204	341
3	Nolan Ryan, Cal	1974	202	367
4	Bob Feller, Cle	1941	194	260
5	Bobo Newsom, St.L-AL	1938	192	226

Home Runs Allowed

		Year	HRs
1	Bert Blyleven, Minnesota	1986	50
2	Jose Lima, Houston	2000	48
3	Robin Roberts, Philadelphia	1956	46
	Bert Blyleven, Minnesota	1987	46
5	Pedro Ramos, Washington	1957	43

SINGLE GAME
Through 2003 regular season.

Batting

Home Runs

No		Date	Inn
4	Bobby Lowe, Boston-NL	5/30/1894	9
	Ed Delahanty, Philadelphia-NL	7/13/1896	9
	Lou Gehrig, New York-AL	6/3/1932	9
	Chuck Klein, Philadelphia-NL	7/10/1936	10
	Pat Seerey, Chicago-AL	7/18/1948	11
	Gil Hodges, Brooklyn	8/31/1950	9
	Joe Adcock, Milwaukee	7/31/1954	9
	Rocky Colavito, Cleveland	6/10/1959	9
	Willie Mays, San Francisco	4/30/1961	9
	Mike Schmidt, Philadelphia	4/17/1976	10
	Bob Horner, Atlanta	7/6/1986	9
	Mark Whiten, St. Louis	9/7/1993	9
	Mike Cameron, Seattle	5/2/2002	9
	Shawn Green, Los Angeles	5/23/2002	9
	Carlos Delgado, Toronto	9/25/2003	9

Runs

No		Date	Inn
7	Guy Hecker, Louisville	8/15/1886	9

Hits

No		Date	Inn
9	Johnny Burnett, Cleveland (9-for-11)	7/10/1932	18
7	Wilbert Robinson, Baltimore (7-for-7)	6/10/1892	9
	Rennie Stennett, Pittsburgh (7-for-7)	9/16/1975	9
	Cesar Gutierrez, Detroit (7-for-7)	6/21/1970	12
	Rocky Colavito, Detroit (7-for-10)	6/24/1962	22

Runs Batted In

No		Date	Inn
12	Jim Bottomley, St. Louis-NL	9/16/1924	9
	Mark Whiten, St. Louis	9/7/1993	9

Pitching

Strikeouts

No		Date	Inn
21	Tom Cheney, Washington	9/12/1962	16
20	Roger Clemens, Boston	4/29/1986	9
	Roger Clemens, Boston	9/18/1996	9
	Kerry Wood, Chicago-NL	5/6/1998	9
	Randy Johnson, Arizona	5/8/2001	9*

*Johnson struck out 20 in nine innings and was removed with the game tied, 1-1. Arizona beat Cincinnati, 4-3, in 11 innings.

Innings Pitched

No		Date
26	Leon Cadore, Brooklyn (tie, 1-1)	5/1/1920
	Joe Oeschger, Boston-NL (tie, 1-1)	5/1/1920

Unassisted Triple Plays

One of the rarest feats in baseball, the unassisted triple play has been accomplished only 12 times in major league history. Ironically, in what can only be described as a statistic anomaly, the trick was turned twice in two days in May of 1927.

Player, Position, Team	Date	Opponent
Paul Hines, OF, Providence	May 8, 1878	Boston-NL
Neal Ball, SS, Cleveland	July 19, 1909	Boston-AL
Bill Wambganss, 2B, Cleveland*	Oct. 10, 1920	Brooklyn
George Burns, 1B, Boston-AL	Sept. 14, 1923	Cleveland
Ernie Padgett, SS, Boston-NL	Oct. 6, 1923	Philadelphia
Glenn Wright, SS, Pittsburgh	May 7, 1925	St.Louis-NL
Jimmy Cooney, SS, Chicago-NL	May 30, 1927	Pittsburgh
Johnny Neun, 1B, Detroit	May 31, 1927	Cleveland
Ron Hansen, SS, Washington	July 30, 1968	Cleveland
Mickey Morandini, 2B, Philadelphia	Sept. 20, 1992	Pittsburgh
John Valentin, SS, Boston	July 8, 1994	Seattle
Randy Velarde, 2B, Oakland	May 29, 2000	NY Yankees
Rafael Furcal, SS, Atlanta	Aug. 10, 2003	St. Louis

* World Series game

Most Gold Gloves (by position)

Gold Gloves have been awarded since the 1957 season by Rawlings Sporting Goods to superior major league fielders at each position in both leagues. Voting has been conducted by a panel of sportswriters appointed by *The Sporting News* publisher J.G. Taylor Spink (1957), major league players (1958-1964) and managers and coaches (1965-present). Top 5 in each position are listed, through the 2002 season.

Pitchers	No	Catchers	No	First Basemen	No	Second Basemen	No
1 Jim Kaat	16	1 Johnny Bench	10	1 Keith Hernandez	11	1 Roberto Alomar	10
2 Greg Maddux	13	Ivan Rodriguez	10	2 Don Mattingly	9	2 Ryne Sandberg	9
3 Bob Gibson	9	3 Bob Boone	7	3 George Scott	8	3 Bill Mazeroski	8
4 Bobby Shantz	8	4 Jim Sundberg	6	4 Vic Power	7	Frank White	8
5 Mark Langston	7	5 Bill Freehan	5	Bill White	7	5 Joe Morgan	5
						Bobby Richardson	5

Third Basemen	No	Shortstops	No	Outfielders	No
1 Brooks Robinson	16	1 Ozzie Smith	13	1 Roberto Clemente	12
2 Mike Schmidt	10	2 Luis Aparicio	9	Willie Mays	12
3 Buddy Bell	6	Omar Vizquel	9	3 Ken Griffey Jr.	10
4 Robin Ventura	6	4 Mark Belanger	8	Al Kaline	10
5 Three tied with 5 each.		5 Dave Concepcion	5	5 Five tied with 8 each	

All-Time Winningest Managers

Top 20 Major League career victories through the 2003 season. Career, regular season and postseason (playoffs and World Series) records are noted along with AL and NL pennants and World Series titles won. Managers active during 2003 season in **bold** type.

			Career			Regular Season			Postseason			
		Yrs	W	L	Pct	W	L	Pct	W	L	Pct	Titles
1	Connie Mack	53	**3755**	3967	.486	3731	3948	.486	24	19	.558	9 AL, 5 WS
2	John McGraw	33	**2866**	2012	.588	2840	1984	.589	26	28	.482	10 NL, 3 WS
3	Sparky Anderson	26	**2228**	1855	.545	2194	1834	.545	34	21	.618	4 NL, 1 AL, 3 WS
4	Bucky Harris	29	**2168**	2228	.493	2157	2218	.493	11	10	.524	3 AL, 2 WS
5	Joe McCarthy	24	**2155**	1346	.616	2125	1333	.615	30	13	.698	1 NL, 8 AL, 7 WS
6	Walter Alston	23	**2063**	1634	.558	2040	1613	.558	23	21	.523	7 NL, 4 WS
7	**Tony La Russa**	25	**2045**	1820	.529	2009	1789	.529	36	31	.537	3 AL, 1 WS
8	Leo Durocher	24	**2015**	1717	.540	2008	1709	.540	7	8	.467	3 NL, 1 WS
9	**Bobby Cox**	22	**1969**	1524	.564	1906	1465	.565	63	59	.516	5 NL, 1 WS
10	Casey Stengel	25	**1942**	1868	.510	1905	1842	.508	37	26	.587	10 AL, 7 WS
11	Gene Mauch	26	**1907**	2044	.483	1902	2037	.483	5	7	.417	—None—
12	Bill McKechnie	25	**1904**	1737	.523	1896	1723	.524	8	14	.364	4 NL, 2 WS
13	**Joe Torre**	22	**1746**	1545	.531	1680	1509	.527	66	36	.647	6 AL, 4 WS
14	Tommy Lasorda	21	**1630**	1469	.526	1599	1439	.526	31	30	.508	4 NL, 2 WS
15	Ralph Houk	20	**1627**	1539	.514	1619	1531	.514	8	8	.500	3 AL, 2 WS
16	Fred Clarke	19	**1609**	1189	.575	1602	1181	.576	7	8	.467	4 NL, 1 WS
17	Dick Williams	21	**1592**	1474	.519	1571	1451	.520	21	23	.477	3 AL, 1 NL, 2 WS
18	Earl Weaver	17	**1506**	1080	.582	1480	1060	.583	26	20	.565	4 AL, 1 WS
19	Clark Griffith	20	**1491**	1367	.522	1491	1367	.522	0	0	.000	1 AL (1901)
20	Miller Huggins	17	**1431**	1149	.555	1413	1134	.555	18	15	.545	6 AL, 3 WS

Notes: John McGraw's postseason record also includes two World Series tie games (1912/'22); Miller Huggins postseason record also includes one World Series tie game (1922).

Where They Managed

Alston—Brooklyn/Los Angeles NL (1954-76); **Anderson**—Cincinnati NL (1970-78), Detroit AL (1979-95); **Clarke**—Louisville NL (1897-99), Pittsburgh NL (1900-15); **Cox**—Atlanta (1978-81, 1990–), Toronto (1982-85); **Durocher**—Brooklyn NL (1939-46,48), New York NL (1948-55), Chicago NL (1966-72), Houston NL (1972-73); **Griffith**—Chicago AL (1901-02), New York NL (1903-08), Cincinnati NL (1909-11), Washington AL (1912-20); **Harris**—Washington AL (1924-28,35-42,50-54), Detroit AL (1929-33,55-56), Boston AL (1934), Philadelphia NL (1943), New York AL (1947-48); **Houk**—New York AL (1961-63,66-73), Detroit AL (1974-78), Boston AL (1981-84); **Huggins**—St. Louis NL (1913-17), New York AL (1918-29); **La Russa**—Chicago AL (1979-86), Oakland (1986-95); St. Louis (1996–) **Lasorda**—Los Angeles NL (1976-96); **Mack**—Pittsburgh NL (1894-96), Philadelphia AL (1901-50). **Mauch**—Philadelphia NL (1960-68), Montreal NL (1969-75), Minnesota AL (1976-80), California AL (1981-82,85-87); **McCarthy**—Chicago NL (1926-30), New York AL (1931-46), Boston AL (1948-50); **McGraw**—Baltimore AL (1899), Baltimore AL (1901-02), New York NL (1902-32); **McKechnie**—Newark FL (1915), Pittsburgh NL (1922-26), St. Louis NL (1928-29), Boston NL (1930-37), Cincinnati NL (1938-46); **Stengel**—Brooklyn NL (1934-36), Boston NL (1938-43), New York AL (1949-60), New York NL (1962-65); **Torre**—New York NL (1977-81), Atlanta (1982-84), St. Louis (1990-95), New York AL (1996–); **Weaver**—Baltimore AL (1968-82,85-86); **Williams**—Boston AL (1967-69), Oakland AL (1971-73), California AL (1974-76), Montreal NL (1977-81), San Diego NL (1982-85), Seattle AL (1986-88).

Regular Season Winning Pct.

Minimum of 750 victories.

		Yrs	W	L	Pct	Pen
1	Joe McCarthy	24	2125	1333	**.615**	9
2	Charlie Comiskey	12	838	541	**.608**	4
3	Frank Selee	16	1284	862	**.598**	5
4	Billy Southworth	13	1044	704	**.597**	4
5	Frank Chance	11	946	648	**.593**	4
6	John McGraw	33	2840	1984	**.589**	10
7	Al Lopez	17	1410	1004	**.584**	2
8	Earl Weaver	17	1480	1060	**.583**	4
9	Cap Anson	20	1296	947	**.578**	5
10	Fred Clarke	19	1602	1181	**.576**	4
11	Davey Johnson	14	1148	888	**.564**	1
12	**Bobby Cox**	22	1906	1465	**.565**	5
13	Steve O'Neill	14	1040	821	**.559**	1
14	Walter Alston	23	2040	1613	**.558**	7
15	Bill Terry	10	823	661	**.555**	3
16	Miller Huggins	17	1413	1134	**.555**	6
17	Billy Martin	16	1253	1013	**.553**	2
18	Harry Wright	18	1000	825	**.548**	3
19	Charlie Grimm	19	1287	1067	**.547**	3
20	Sparky Anderson	26	2194	1834	**.545**	5

World Series Victories

		App	W	L	T	Pct	WS
1	Casey Stengel	10	**37**	26	0	.587	7
2	Joe McCarthy	9	**30**	13	0	.698	7
3	John McGraw	9	**26**	28	2	.482	3
4	Connie Mack	8	**24**	19	0	.558	5
5	**Joe Torre**	6	**21**	11	0	.656	4
6	Walter Alston	7	**20**	20	0	.500	4
7	Miller Huggins	6	**18**	15	1	.544	3
8	Sparky Anderson	5	**16**	12	0	.571	3
9	Tommy Lasorda	4	**12**	11	0	.522	2
	Dick Williams	4	**12**	14	0	.462	2
11	Frank Chance	4	**11**	9	1	.548	2
	Bucky Harris	3	**11**	10	0	.524	2
	Billy Southworth	4	**11**	11	0	.500	2
	Earl Weaver	4	**11**	13	0	.458	1
	Bobby Cox	5	**11**	18	0	.379	1
16	Whitey Herzog	3	**10**	11	0	.476	1
17	Bill Carrigan	2	**8**	2	0	.800	2
	Danny Murtaugh	2	**8**	6	0	.571	2
	Cito Gaston	2	**8**	6	0	.571	2
	Tom Kelly	2	**8**	6	0	.571	2
	Ralph Houk	3	**8**	8	0	.500	2
	Bill McKechnie	4	**8**	14	0	.364	2

Active Managers' Records
Regular season games only; through 2003 (updated as of Oct. 22).

National League

		Yrs	W	L	Pct
1	Tony La Russa, St.L.	.25	**2009**	1789	.529
2	Bobby Cox, Atl.	.22	**1906**	1465	.565
3	Art Howe, NY	.12	**1058**	1046	.503
4	Dusty Baker, Chi	.11	**928**	789	.540
5	Jimy Williams, Hou.	.11	**866**	746	.537
6	Frank Robinson, Mon.	.13	**846**	909	.482
7	Jack McKeon, Fla.	.13	**845**	782	.519
8	Felipe Alou, SF	.11	**791**	778	.504
9	Bruce Bochy, SD	.9	**694**	746	.482
10	Larry Bowa, Phi.	.5	**333**	360	.481
11	Bob Brenly, Ari	.3	**274**	212	.564
12	Jim Tracy, LA	.3	**263**	223	.541
13	Lloyd McClendon, Pit.	.3	**209**	276	.431
14	Clint Hurdle, Col	.2	**141**	161	.467
15	Ned Yost, Mil	.1	**68**	94	.420
	Cincinnati				

American League

		Yrs	W	L	Pct
1	Joe Torre, NY	.22	**1680**	1509	.527
2	Lou Piniella, TB	.17	**1382**	1234	.528
3	Buck Showalter, Tex.	.8	**634**	595	.516
4	Mike Scioscia, Ana.	.4	**333**	315	.514
5	Grady Little, Bos.	.2	**188**	136	.580
6	Ron Gardenhire, Min.	.2	**184**	139	.570
7	Carlos Tosca, Tor.	.2	**144**	127	.531
8	Tony Pena, KC	.2	**132**	156	.458
9	Ken Macha, Oak	.1	**96**	66	.593
10	Bob Melvin, Sea	.1	**93**	69	.574
11	Eric Wedge, Cle.	.1	**68**	94	.420
12	Alan Trammell, Det.	.1	**43**	119	.265
	Baltimore				
	Chicago				

Annual Awards

MOST VALUABLE PLAYER

There have been three different Most Valuable Player awards in baseball since 1911—the Chalmers Award (1911-14), presented by the Detroit-based automobile company; the League Award (1922-29), presented by the National and American Leagues; and the Baseball Writers' Award (since 1931), presented by the Baseball Writers' Association of America. Statistics for winning players are provided below. Stats for winning pitchers before advent of Cy Young Award are in MVP Pitchers' Statistics table.

Multiple winners: NL—Barry Bonds (5); Roy Campanella, Stan Musial and Mike Schmidt (3); Ernie Banks, Johnny Bench, Rogers Hornsby, Carl Hubbell, Willie Mays, Joe Morgan and Dale Murphy (2). **AL**—Yogi Berra, Joe DiMaggio, Jimmie Foxx and Mickey Mantle (3); Mickey Cochrane, Lou Gehrig, Juan Gonzalez, Hank Greenberg, Walter Johnson, Roger Maris, Hal Newhouser, Cal Ripken Jr., Frank Thomas, Ted Williams and Robin Yount (2). **NL & AL**—Frank Robinson (2, one in each).

Chalmers Award

National League

Year		Pos	HR	RBI	Avg
1911	Wildfire Schulte, Chi	.OF	21	121	.300
1912	Larry Doyle, NY	.2B	10	90	.330
1913	Jake Daubert, Bklyn	.1B	2	52	.350
1914	Johnny Evers, Bos	.2B	1	40	.279

American League

Year		Pos	HR	RBI	Avg
1911	Ty Cobb, Det	.OF	8	144	.420
1912	Tris Speaker, Bos	.OF	10	98	.383
1913	Walter Johnson, Wash	.P	—	—	—
1914	Eddie Collins, Phi	.2B	2	85	.344

League Award

National League

Year		Pos	HR	RBI	Avg
1922	No selection				
1923	No selection				
1924	Dazzy Vance, Bklyn	.P	—	—	—
1925	Rogers Hornsby, St.L	.2B-Mgr	39	143	.403
1926	Bob O'Farrell, St.L	.C	7	68	.293
1927	Paul Waner, Pit	.OF	9	131	.380
1928	Jim Bottomley, St.L	.1B	31	136	.325
1929	Rogers Hornsby, Chi	.2B	39	149	.380

American League

Year		Pos	HR	RBI	Avg
1922	George Sisler, St.L	.1B	8	105	.420
1923	Babe Ruth, NY	.OF	41	131	.393
1924	Walter Johnson, Wash	.P	—	—	—
1925	Roger Peckinpaugh, Wash	.SS	4	64	.294
1926	George Burns, Cle	.1B	4	114	.358
1927	Lou Gehrig, NY	.1B	47	175	.373
1928	Mickey Cochrane, Phi	.C	10	57	.293
1929	No selection				

Most Valuable Player
National League

Year		Pos	HR	RBI	Avg	Year		Pos	HR	RBI	Avg
1931	Frankie Frisch, St.L	.2B	4	82	.311	1950	Jim Konstanty, Phi	.P	—	—	—
1932	Chuck Klein, Phi	.OF	38	137	.348	1951	Roy Campanella, Bklyn	.C	33	108	.325
1933	Carl Hubbell, NY	.P	—	—	—	1952	Hank Sauer, Chi	.OF	37	121	.270
1934	Dizzy Dean, St.L	.P	—	—	—	1953	Roy Campanella, Bklyn	.C	41	142	.312
1935	Gabby Hartnett, Chi	.C	13	91	.344	1954	Willie Mays, NY	.OF	41	110	.345
1936	Carl Hubbell, NY	.P	—	—	—	1955	Roy Campanella, Bklyn	.C	32	107	.318
1937	Joe Medwick, St.L	.OF	31	154	.374	1956	Don Newcombe, Bklyn	.P	—	—	—
1938	Ernie Lombardi, Cin	.C	19	95	.342	1957	Hank Aaron, Mil	.OF	44	132	.322
1939	Bucky Walters, Cin	.P	—	—	—	1958	Ernie Banks, Chi	.SS	47	129	.313
1940	Frank McCormick, Cin	.1B	19	127	.309	1959	Ernie Banks, Chi	.SS	45	143	.304
1941	Dolf Camilli, Bklyn	.1B	34	120	.285	1960	Dick Groat, Pit	.SS	2	50	.325
1942	Mort Cooper, St.L	.P	—	—	—	1961	Frank Robinson, Cin	.OF	37	124	.323
1943	Stan Musial, St.L	.OF	13	81	.357	1962	Maury Wills, LA	.SS	6	48	.299
1944	Marty Marion, St.L	.SS	6	63	.267	1963	Sandy Koufax, LA	.P	—	—	—
1945	Phil Cavarretta, Chi	.1B	6	97	.355	1964	Ken Boyer, St.L	.3B	24	119	.295
1946	Stan Musial, St.L	.1B-OF	16	103	.365	1965	Willie Mays, SF	.OF	52	112	.317
1947	Bob Elliott, Bos	.3B	22	113	.317	1966	Roberto Clemente, Pit	.OF	29	119	.317
1948	Stan Musial, St.L	.OF	39	131	.376	1967	Orlando Cepeda, St.L	.1B	25	111	.325
1949	Jackie Robinson, Bklyn	.2B	16	124	.342	1968	Bob Gibson, St.L	.P	—	—	—

Year		Pos	HR	RBI	Avg
1969	Willie McCovey, SF	1B	45	126	.320
1970	Johnny Bench, Cin	C	45	148	.293
1971	Joe Torre, St.L	3B	24	137	.363
1972	Johnny Bench, Cin	C	40	125	.270
1973	Pete Rose, Cin	OF	5	64	.338
1974	Steve Garvey, LA	1B	21	111	.312
1975	Joe Morgan, Cin	2B	17	94	.327
1976	Joe Morgan, Cin	2B	27	111	.320
1977	George Foster, Cin	OF	52	149	.320
1978	Dave Parker, Pit	OF	30	117	.334
1979	Keith Hernandez, St.L	1B	11	105	.344
	Willie Stargell, Pit	1B	32	82	.281
1980	Mike Schmidt, Phi	3B	48	121	.286
1981	Mike Schmidt, Phi	3B	31	91	.316
1982	Dale Murphy, Atl	OF	36	109	.281
1983	Dale Murphy, Atl	OF	36	121	.302
1984	Ryne Sandberg, Chi	2B	19	84	.314
1985	Willie McGee, St.L	OF	10	82	.353
1986	Mike Schmidt, Phi	3B	37	119	.290
1987	Andre Dawson, Chi	OF	49	137	.287
1988	Kirk Gibson, LA	OF	25	76	.290
1989	Kevin Mitchell, SF	OF	47	125	.291
1990	Barry Bonds, Pit	OF	33	114	.301
1991	Terry Pendleton, Atl	3B	22	86	.319
1992	Barry Bonds, Pit	OF	34	103	.311
1993	Barry Bonds, SF	OF	46	123	.336
1994	Jeff Bagwell, Hou	1B	39	116	.368
1995	Barry Larkin,	SS	15	66	.319
1996	Ken Caminiti, SD	3B	40	130	.326
1997	Larry Walker, Col	OF	49	130	.366
1998	Sammy Sosa, Chi	OF	66	158	.308
1999	Chipper Jones, Atl	3B	45	110	.319
2000	Jeff Kent, SF	2B	33	125	.334
2001	Barry Bonds, SF	OF	73	137	.328
2002	Barry Bonds, SF	OF	46	110	.370

American League

Year		Pos	HR	RBI	Avg
1931	Lefty Grove, Phi	P	—	—	—
1932	Jimmie Foxx, Phi	1B	58	169	.364
1933	Jimmie Foxx, Phi	1B	48	163	.356
1934	Mickey Cochrane, Det	C-Mgr	2	76	.320
1935	Hank Greenberg, Det	1B	36	170	.328
1936	Lou Gehrig, NY	1B	49	152	.354
1937	Charlie Gehringer, Det	2B	14	96	.371
1938	Jimmie Foxx, Bos	1B	50	175	.349
1939	Joe DiMaggio, NY	OF	30	126	.381
1940	Hank Greenberg, Det	OF	41	150	.340
1941	Joe DiMaggio, NY	OF	30	125	.357
1942	Joe Gordon, NY	2B	18	103	.322
1943	Spud Chandler, NY	P	—	—	—
1944	Hal Hewhouser, Det	P	—	—	—
1945	Hal Newhouser, Det	P	—	—	—
1946	Ted Williams, Bos	OF	38	123	.342
1947	Joe DiMaggio, NY	OF	20	97	.315
1948	Lou Boudreau, Cle	SS-Mgr	18	106	.355
1949	Ted Williams, Bos	OF	43	159	.343
1950	Phil Rizzuto, NY	SS	7	66	.324
1951	Yogi Berra, NY	C	27	88	.294
1952	Bobby Shantz, Phi	P	—	—	—
1953	Al Rosen, Cle	3B	43	145	.336
1954	Yogi Berra, NY	C	22	125	.307
1955	Yogi Berra, NY	C	27	108	.272
1956	Mickey Mantle, NY	OF	52	130	.353
1957	Mickey Mantle, NY	OF	34	94	.365
1958	Jackie Jensen, Bos	OF	35	122	.286
1959	Nellie Fox, Chi	2B	2	70	.306
1960	Roger Maris, NY	OF	39	112	.283
1961	Roger Maris, NY	OF	61	142	.269
1962	Mickey Mantle, NY	OF	30	89	.321
1963	Elston Howard, NY	C	28	85	.287
1964	Brooks Robinson, Bal	3B	28	118	.317
1965	Zoilo Versalles, Min	SS	19	77	.273
1966	Frank Robinson, Bal	OF	49	122	.316
1967	Carl Yastrzemski, Bos	OF	44	121	.326
1968	Denny McLain, Det	P	—	—	—
1969	Harmon Killebrew, Min	3B-1B	49	140	.276
1970	Boog Powell, Bal	1B	35	114	.297
1971	Vida Blue, Oak	P	—	—	—
1972	Dick Allen, Chi	1B	37	113	.308
1973	Reggie Jackson, Oak	OF	32	117	.293
1974	Jeff Burroughs, Tex	OF	25	118	.301
1975	Fred Lynn, Bos	OF	21	105	.331
1976	Thurman Munson, NY	C	17	105	.302
1977	Rod Carew, Min	1B	14	100	.388
1978	Jim Rice, Bos	OF-DH	46	139	.315
1979	Don Baylor, Cal	OF-DH	36	139	.296
1980	George Brett, KC	3B	24	118	.390
1981	Rollie Fingers, Mil	P	—	—	—
1982	Robin Yount, Mil	SS	29	114	.331
1983	Cal Ripken Jr., Bal	SS	27	102	.318
1984	Willie Hernandez, Det	P	—	—	—
1985	Don Mattingly, NY	1B	35	145	.324
1986	Roger Clemens, Bos	P	—	—	—
1987	George Bell, Tor	OF	47	134	.308
1988	Jose Canseco, Oak	OF	42	124	.307
1989	Robin Yount, Mil	OF	21	103	.318
1990	Rickey Henderson, Oak	OF	28	61	.325
1991	Cal Ripken Jr., Bal	SS	34	114	.323
1992	Dennis Eckersley, Oak	P	—	—	—
1993	Frank Thomas, Chi	1B	41	128	.317
1994	Frank Thomas, Chi	1B	38	101	.353
1995	Mo Vaughn, Bos	1B	39	126	.300
1996	Juan Gonzalez, Tex	OF-DH	47	144	.314
1997	Ken Griffey Jr., Sea	OF	56	147	.304
1998	Juan Gonzalez, Tex	OF	45	157	.318
1999	Ivan Rodriguez, Tex	C	35	113	.332
2000	Jason Giambi, Oak	1B	43	137	.333
2001	Ichiro Suzuki, Sea	OF	8	69	.350
2002	Miguel Tejada, Oak	SS	34	131	.308

MVP Pitchers' Statistics

Pitchers have been named Most Valuable Player on 23 occasions, 10 times in the NL and 13 in the AL. Four have been relief pitchers—Jim Konstanty, Rollie Fingers, Willie Hernandez and Dennis Eckersley. For statistics of MVP pitchers since 1956, see the Cy Young Award tables on following page.

National League

Year		Gm	W-L	SV	ERA
1924	Dazzy Vance, Bklyn	.35	28-6	0	2.16
1933	Carl Hubbell, NY	.45	23-12	5	1.66
1934	Dizzy Dean, St.L	.50	30-7	7	2.66
1936	Carl Hubbell, NY	.42	26-6	3	2.31
1939	Bucky Walters, Cin	.39	27-11	0	2.29
1942	Mort Cooper, St.L	.37	22-7	0	1.78
1950	Jim Konstanty, Phi	.74	16-7	22	2.66

American League

Year		Gm	W-L	SV	ERA
1913	Walter Johnson, Wash	.47	36-7	2	1.09
1924	Walter Johnson, Wash	.38	23-7	0	2.72
1931	Lefty Grove, Phi	.41	31-4	5	2.06
1943	Spud Chandler, NY	.30	20-4	0	1.64
1944	Hal Hewhouser, Det	.47	29-9	2	2.22
1945	Hal Newhouser, Det	.40	25-9	2	1.81
1952	Bobby Shantz, Phi	.33	24-7	0	2.48

CY YOUNG AWARD

Voted on by the Baseball Writers Association of America. One award was presented from 1956-66, two since 1967. Pitchers who won the MVP and Cy Young awards in the same season are in **bold** type.

Multiple winners: NL—Steve Carlton, Greg Maddux and Randy Johnson (4); Sandy Koufax and Tom Seaver (3); Bob Gibson and Tom Glavine (2). **AL**—Roger Clemens (6); Jim Palmer (3); Pedro Martinez and Denny McLain (2). **NL & AL**—Randy Johnson (5, four in NL, one in AL), Pedro Martinez (3, two in AL, one in NL) and Gaylord Perry (2, one in each).

NL and AL Combined

Year	National League	Gm	W-L	SV	ERA	Year	American League	Gm	W-L	SV	ERA
1956	**Don Newcombe**, Bklyn	38	27-7	0	3.06	1958	Bob Turley, NY	33	21-7	1	2.97
1957	Warren Spahn, Mil	39	21-11	3	2.69	1959	Early Wynn, Chi	37	22-10	0	3.17
1960	Vernon Law, Pit	35	20-9	0	3.08	1961	Whitey Ford, NY	39	25-4	0	3.21
1962	Don Drysdale, LA	43	25-9	1	2.83	1964	Dean Chance, LA	46	20-9	4	1.65
1963	**Sandy Koufax**, LA	40	25-5	0	1.88						
1965	Sandy Koufax, LA	43	26-8	2	2.04						
1966	Sandy Koufax, LA	41	27-9	0	1.73						

Separate League Awards

National League / American League

Year	National League	Gm	W-L	SV	ERA	Year	American League	Gm	W-L	SV	ERA
1967	Mike McCormick, SF	40	22-10	0	2.85	1967	Jim Lonborg, Bos	39	22-9	0	3.16
1968	**Bob Gibson**, St.L	34	22-9	0	1.12	1968	**Denny McLain**, Det	41	31-6	0	1.96
1969	Tom Seaver, NY	36	25-7	0	2.21	1969	Denny McLain, Det	42	24-9	0	2.80
1970	Bob Gibson, St.L	34	23-7	0	3.12		Mike Cuellar, Bal	39	23-11	0	2.38
1971	Ferguson Jenkins, Chi	39	24-13	0	2.77	1970	Jim Perry, Min	40	24-12	0	3.03
1972	Steve Carlton, Phi	41	27-10	0	1.97	1971	**Vida Blue**, Oak	39	24-8	0	1.82
1973	Tom Seaver, NY	36	19-10	0	2.08	1972	Gaylord Perry, Cle	41	24-16	1	1.92
1974	Mike Marshall, LA	106	15-12	21	2.42	1973	Jim Palmer, Bal	38	22-9	1	2.40
1975	Tom Seaver, NY	36	22-9	0	2.38	1974	Catfish Hunter, Oak	41	25-12	0	2.49
1976	Randy Jones, SD	40	22-14	0	2.74	1975	Jim Palmer, Bal	39	23-11	1	2.09
1977	Steve Carlton, Phi	36	23-10	0	2.64	1976	Jim Palmer, Bal	40	22-13	0	2.51
1978	Gaylord Perry, SD	37	21-6	0	2.72	1977	Sparky Lyle, NY	72	13-5	26	2.17
1979	Bruce Sutter, Chi	62	6-6	37	2.23	1978	Ron Guidry, NY	35	25-3	0	1.74
1980	Steve Carlton, Phi	38	24-9	0	2.34	1979	Mike Flanagan, Bal	39	23-9	0	3.08
1981	Fernando Valenzuela, LA	25	13-7	0	2.48	1980	Steve Stone, Bal	37	25-7	0	3.23
1982	Steve Carlton, Phi	38	23-11	0	3.10	1981	**Rollie Fingers**, Mil	47	6-3	28	1.04
1983	John Denny, Phi	36	19-6	0	2.37	1982	Pete Vuckovich, Mil	30	18-6	0	3.34
1984	Rick Sutcliffe, Chi	20*	16-1	0	2.69	1983	LaMarr Hoyt, Chi	36	24-10	0	3.66
1985	Dwight Gooden, NY	35	24-4	0	1.53	1984	**Willie Hernandez**, Det	80	9-3	32	1.92
1986	Mike Scott, Hou	37	18-10	0	2.22	1985	Bret Saberhagen, KC	32	20-6	0	2.87
1987	Steve Bedrosian, Phi	65	5-3	40	2.83	1986	**Roger Clemens**, Bos	33	24-4	0	2.48
1988	Orel Hershiser, LA	35	23-8	1	2.26	1987	Roger Clemens, Bos	36	20-9	0	2.97
1989	Mark Davis, SD	70	4-3	44	1.85	1988	Frank Viola, Min	35	24-7	0	2.64
1990	Doug Drabek, Pit	33	22-6	0	2.76	1989	Bret Saberhagen, KC	36	23-6	0	2.16
1991	Tom Glavine, Atl	34	20-11	0	2.55	1990	Bob Welch, Oak	35	27-6	0	2.95
1992	Greg Maddux, Chi	35	20-11	0	2.18	1991	Roger Clemens, Bos	35	18-10	0	2.62
1993	Greg Maddux, Atl	36	20-10	0	2.36	1992	**Dennis Eckersley**, Oak	69	7-1	51	1.91
1994	Greg Maddux, Atl	25	16-6	0	1.56	1993	Jack McDowell, Chi	34	22-10	0	3.37
1995	Greg Maddux, Atl	28	19-2	0	1.63	1994	David Cone, KC	23	16-5	0	2.94
1996	John Smoltz, Atl	35	24-8	0	2.94	1995	Randy Johnson, Sea	30	18-2	0	2.48
1997	Pedro Martinez, Mon	31	17-8	0	1.90	1996	Pat Hentgen, Tor	35	20-10	0	3.22
1998	Tom Glavine, Atl	33	20-6	0	2.47	1997	Roger Clemens, Tor	34	21-7	0	2.05
1999	Randy Johnson, Ari	35	17-9	0	2.48	1998	Roger Clemens, Tor	33	20-6	0	2.65
2000	Randy Johnson, Ari	35	19-7	0	2.64	1999	Pedro Martinez, Bos	31	23-4	0	2.07
2001	Randy Johnson, Ari	35	21-6	0	2.49	2000	Pedro Martinez, Bos	29	18-6	0	1.74
2002	Randy Johnson, Ari	35	24-5	0	2.32	2001	Roger Clemens, NY	33	20-3	0	3.51
						2002	Barry Zito, Oak	35	23-5	0	2.75

*NL games only, Sutcliffe pitched 15 games with Cleveland before being traded to the Cubs.

ROOKIE OF THE YEAR

Voted on by the Baseball Writers Assn. of America. One award was presented from 1947-48. Two awards (one for each league) have been presented since 1949. Winners who were also named MVP in the same season are in **bold** type.

NL and AL Combined

Year		Pos	Year		Pos
1947	Jackie Robinson, Brooklyn	1B	1948	Alvin Dark, Boston-NL	SS

National League

Year		Pos	Year		Pos	Year		Pos
1949	Don Newcombe, Bklyn	P	1952	Joe Black, Bklyn	P	1955	Bill Virdon, St.L	OF
1950	Sam Jethroe, Bos	OF	1953	Jim Gilliam, Bklyn	2B	1956	Frank Robinson, Cin	OF
1951	Willie Mays, NY	OF	1954	Wally Moon, St.L	OF	1957	Jack Sanford, Phi	P

Year		Pos	Year		Pos	Year		Pos
1958	Orlando Cepeda, SF	1B	1974	Bake McBride, St.L	OF	1989	Jerome Walton, Chi	OF
1959	Willie McCovey, SF	1B	1975	John Montefusco, SF	P	1990	David Justice, Atl	OF
1960	Frank Howard, LA	OF	1976	Butch Metzger, SD	P	1991	Jeff Bagwell, Hou.	1B
1961	Billy Williams, Chi	OF		& Pat Zachry, Cin	P	1992	Eric Karros, LA	1B
1962	Ken Hubbs, Chi	2B	1977	Andre Dawson, Mon	OF	1993	Mike Piazza, LA	C
1963	Pete Rose, Cin	2B	1978	Bob Horner, Atl	3B	1994	Raul Mondesi, LA	OF
1964	Richie Allen, Phi	3B	1979	Rick Sutcliffe, LA	P	1995	Hideo Nomo, LA	P
1965	Jim Lefebvre, LA	2B	1980	Steve Howe, LA	P	1996	Todd Hollandsworth, LA	OF
1966	Tommy Helms, Cin	3B	1981	Fernando Valenzuela, LA	P	1997	Scott Rolen, Phi	3B
1967	Tom Seaver, NY	P	1982	Steve Sax, LA	2B	1998	Kerry Wood, Chi	P
1968	Johnny Bench, Cin	C	1983	Darryl Strawberry, NY	OF	1999	Scott Williamson, Cin	P
1969	Ted Sizemore, LA	2B	1984	Dwight Gooden, NY	P			
1970	Carl Morton, Mon	P	1985	Vince Coleman, St.L	OF	2000	Rafael Furcal, Atl	SS
1971	Earl Williams, Atl	C	1986	Todd Worrell, St.L	P	2001	Albert Pujols, St.L	OF-3B
1972	Jon Matlack, NY	P	1987	Benito Santiago, SD	C	2002	Jason Jennings, Col	P
1973	Gary Matthews, SF	OF	1988	Chris Sabo, Cin	3B			

American League

Year		Pos	Year		Pos	Year		Pos
1949	Roy Sievers, St.L	OF	1968	Stan Bahnsen, NY	P	1986	Jose Canseco, Oak	OF
1950	Walt Dropo, Bos	1B	1969	Lou Piniella, KC	OF	1987	Mark McGwire, Oak	1B
1951	Gil McDougald, NY	3B	1970	Thurman Munson, NY	C	1988	Walt Weiss, Oak	SS
1952	Harry Byrd, Phi	P	1971	Chris Chambliss, Cle	1B	1989	Gregg Olson, Bal	P
1953	Harvey Kuenn, Det	SS	1972	Carlton Fisk, Bos	C	1990	Sandy Alomar Jr., Cle	C
1954	Bob Grim, NY	P	1973	Al Bumbry, Bal	OF	1991	Chuck Knoblauch, Min	2B
1955	Herb Score, Cle	P	1974	Mike Hargrove, Tex	1B	1992	Pat Listach, Mil	SS
1956	Luis Aparicio, Chi	SS	1975	**Fred Lynn**, Bos	OF	1993	Tim Salmon, Cal	OF
1957	Tony Kubek, NY	INF-OF	1976	Mark Fidrych, Det	P	1994	Bob Hamelin, KC	DH
1958	Albie Pearson, Wash	OF	1977	Eddie Murray, Bal	DH-1B	1995	Marty Cordova, Min	OF
1959	Bob Allison, Wash	OF	1978	Lou Whitaker, Det	2B	1996	Derek Jeter, NY	SS
1960	Ron Hansen, Bal	SS	1979	John Castino, Min	3B	1997	Nomar Garciaparra, Bos	SS
1961	Don Schwall, Bos	P		& Alfredo Griffin, Tor	SS	1998	Ben Grieve, Oak	OF
1962	Tom Tresh, NY	SS-OF	1980	Joe Charboneau, Cle	OF-DH	1999	Carlos Beltran, KC	OF
1963	Gary Peters, Chi	P	1981	Dave Righetti, NY	P			
1964	Tony Oliva, Min	OF	1982	Cal Ripken Jr., Bal	SS-3B	2000	Kazuhiro Sasaki, Sea	P
1965	Curt Blefary, Bal	OF	1983	Ron Kittle, Chi	OF	2001	**Ichiro Suzuki**, Sea	OF
1966	Tommie Agee, Chi	OF	1984	Alvin Davis, Sea	1B	2002	Eric Hinske, Tor	3B
1967	Rod Carew, Min	2B	1985	Ozzie Guillen, Chi	SS			

MANAGER OF THE YEAR

Voted on by the Baseball Writers Association of America. Two awards (one for each league) presented since 1983. Note that (*) indicates manager's team won division championship and (†) indicates unofficial division won in 1994.

Multiple winners: Tony La Russa (4); Dusty Baker (3); Sparky Anderson, Bobby Cox, Tommy Lasorda, Jim Leyland, Lou Piniella and Joe Torre (2).

National League

Year		Improvement	
1983	Tommy Lasorda, LA	88-74 to	91-71*
1984	Jim Frey, Chi	71-91 to	96-75*
1985	Whitey Herzog, St. L	84-78 to	101-61*
1986	Hal Lanier, Hou	83-79 to	96-66*
1987	Buck Rodgers, Mon	78-83 to	91-71
1988	Tommy Lasorda, LA	73-89 to	94-67*
1989	Don Zimmer, Chi	77-85 to	93-69*
1990	Jim Leyland, Pit	74-88 to	95-67*
1991	Bobby Cox, Atl	65-97 to	94-68*
1992	Jim Leyland, Pit	98-64* to	96-66*
1993	Dusty Baker, SF	72-90 to	103-59
1994	Felipe Alou, Mon	94-68 to	74-40†
1995	Don Baylor, Col	53-64 to	77-67
1996	Bruce Bochy, SD	70-74 to	91-71*
1997	Dusty Baker, SF	68-94 to	90-72
1998	Larry Dierker, Hou	84-78 to	102-60*
1999	Jack McKeon, Cin	77-85 to	96-67
2000	Dusty Baker, SF	86-76 to	97-65*
2001	Larry Bowa, Phi	65-97 to	86-76
2002	Tony La Russa, St.L	93-69 to	97-65*

American League

Year		Improvement	
1983	Tony La Russa, Chi	87-75 to	99-63*
1984	Sparky Anderson, Det	92-70 to	104-58*
1985	Bobby Cox, Tor	89-73 to	99-62*
1986	John McNamara, Bos	81-81 to	95-66*
1987	Sparky Anderson, Det	87-75 to	98-64*
1988	Tony La Russa, Oak	81-81 to	104-58*
1989	Frank Robinson, Bal	54-107 to	87-75
1990	Jeff Torborg, Chi	69-92 to	94-68
1991	Tom Kelly, Min	74-88 to	95-67*
1992	Tony La Russa, Oak	84-78 to	96-66*
1993	Gene Lamont, Chi	86-76 to	94-68*
1994	Buck Showalter, NY	88-74 to	70-43†
1995	Lou Piniella, Sea	49-63 to	79-66*
1996	Joe Torre, NY	79-65 to	92-70
	& Johnny Oates, Tex	74-70 to	90-72
1997	Davey Johnson, Bal	88-74 to	98-64
1998	Joe Torre, NY	96-66 to	114-48*
1999	Jimy Williams, Bos	92-70 to	94-68
2000	Jerry Manuel, Chi	75-86 to	95-67*
2001	Lou Piniella, Sea	91-71 to	116-46*
2002	Mike Scioscia, Ana	75-87 to	99-63

COLLEGE BASEBALL

College World Series

The NCAA Division I College World Series has been held in Kalamazoo, Mich. (1947-48), Wichita, Kan. (1949) and Omaha, Neb. (since 1950).

Multiple winners: USC (12); Arizona St., LSU and Texas (5); Miami-FL (4); Arizona, CS-Fullerton and Minnesota (3); California, Michigan, Oklahoma and Stanford (2).

Year	Winner	Coach	Score	Runner-up	Year	Winner	Coach	Score	Runner-up
1947	California	Clint Evans	8-7	Yale	1976	Arizona	Jerry Kindall	7-1	E. Michigan
1948	USC	Sam Barry	9-2	Yale	1977	Arizona St.	Jim Brock	2-1	S. Carolina
1949	Texas	Bibb Falk	10-3	W. Forest	1978	USC	Rod Dedeaux	10-3	Ariz. St.
1950	Texas	Bibb Falk	3-0	Wash. St.	1979	CS-Fullerton	Augie Garrido	2-1	Arkansas
1951	Oklahoma	Jack Baer	3-2	Tennessee	1980	Arizona	Jerry Kindall	5-3	Hawaii
1952	Holy Cross	Jack Barry	8-4	Missouri	1981	Arizona St.	Jim Brock	7-4	Okla. St.
1953	Michigan	Ray Fisher	7-5	Texas	1982	Miami-FL	Ron Fraser	9-3	Wichita St.
1954	Missouri	Hi Simmons	4-1	Rollins	1983	Texas	Cliff Gustafson	4-3	Alabama
1955	Wake Forest	Taylor Sanford	7-6	W. Mich.	1984	CS-Fullerton	Augie Garrido	3-1	Texas
1956	Minnesota	Dick Siebert	12-1	Arizona	1985	Miami-FL	Ron Fraser	10-6	Texas
1957	California	Geo. Wolfman	1-0	Penn St.	1986	Arizona	Jerry Kindall	10-2	Fla. St.
1958	USC	Rod Dedeaux	8-7	Missouri	1987	Stanford	M. Marquess	9-5	Okla. St.
1959	Oklahoma St.	Toby Greene	5-3	Arizona	1988	Stanford	M. Marquess	9-4	Ariz. St.
1960	Minnesota	Dick Siebert	2-1	USC	1989	Wichita St.	G. Stephenson	5-3	Texas
1961	USC	Rod Dedeaux	1-0	Okla. St.	1990	Georgia	Steve Webber	2-1	Okla. St.
1962	Michigan	Don Lund	5-4	S. Clara	1991	LSU	Skip Bertman	6-3	Wichita St.
1963	USC	Rod Dedeaux	5-2	Arizona	1992	Pepperdine	Andy Lopez	3-2	CS-Fullerton
1964	Minnesota	Dick Siebert	5-1	Missouri	1993	LSU	Skip Bertman	8-0	Wichita St.
1965	Arizona St.	Bobby Winkles	2-1	Ohio St.	1994	Oklahoma	Larry Cochell	13-5	Ga. Tech
1966	Ohio St.	Marty Karow	8-2	Okla. St.	1995	CS-Fullerton	Augie Garrido	11-5	USC
1967	Arizona St.	Bobby Winkles	11-2	Houston	1996	LSU	Skip Bertman	9-8	Miami-FL
1968	USC	Rod Dedeaux	4-3	So. Ill.	1997	LSU	Skip Bertman	13-6	Alabama
1969	Arizona St.	Bobby Winkles	10-1	Tulsa	1998	USC	Mike Gillespie	21-14	Arizona St.
1970	USC	Rod Dedeaux	2-1	Fla. St.	1999	Miami-FL	Jim Morris	6-5	Fla. St.
1971	USC	Rod Dedeaux	7-2	So. Ill.	2000	LSU	Skip Bertman	6-5	Stanford
1972	USC	Rod Dedeaux	1-0	Ariz. St.	2001	Miami-FL	Jim Morris	12-1	Stanford
1973	USC	Rod Dedeaux	4-3	Ariz. St.	2002	Texas	Augie Garrido	12-6	S.Carolina
1974	USC	Rod Dedeaux	7-3	Miami-FL	2003	Rice	Wayne Graham	14-2	Stanford
1975	Texas	Cliff Gustafson	5-1	S. Carolina					

Most Outstanding Player

The Most Outstanding Player has been selected every year of the College World Series since 1949. Winners who did not play for the CWS champion are listed in **bold** type. No player has won the award more than once.

Year		Year		Year	
1949	**Charles Teague,** W. Forest, 2B	1968	Bill Seinsoth, USC, 1B	1987	Paul Carey, Stanford, RF
1950	**Ray VanCleef,** Rutgers, CF	1969	John Dolinsek, Ariz. St., LF	1988	Lee Plemel, Stanford, P
1951	**Sidney Hatfield,** Tenn., P-1B	1970	**Gene Ammann,** Fla. St., P	1989	Greg Brummett, Wich. St., P
1952	James O'Neill, Holy Cross, P	1971	**Jerry Tabb,** Tulsa, 1B	1990	Mike Rebhan, Georgia, P
1953	**J.L. Smith,** Texas, P	1972	Russ McQueen, USC, P	1991	Gary Hymel, LSU, C
1954	**Tom Yewcic,** Mich. St., C	1973	**Dave Winfield,** Minn., P-OF	1992	**Phil Nevin,** CS-Fullerton, 3B
1955	**Tom Borland,** Okla. St., P	1974	George Milke, USC, P	1993	Todd Walker, LSU, 2B
1956	Jerry Thomas, Minn., P	1975	Mickey Reichenbach, Texas, 1B	1994	Chip Glass, Oklahoma, OF
1957	**Cal Emery,** Penn St., P-1B	1976	Steve Powers, Arizona, P-DH	1995	Mark Kotsay, CS-Fullerton, OF
1958	Bill Thom, USC, P	1977	Bob Horner, Ariz. St., 3B	1996	**Pat Burrell,** Miami-FL, 3B
1959	Jim Dobson, Okla. St., 3B	1978	Rod Boxberger, USC, P	1997	Brandon Larson, LSU, SS
1960	John Erickson, Minn., 2B	1979	Tony Hudson, CS-Fullerton, P	1998	Wes Rachels, USC, 2B
1961	**Littleton Fowler,** Okla. St., P	1980	Terry Francona, Arizona, LF	1999	**Marshall McDougall,** Fla. St., 2B
1962	**Bob Garibaldi,** Santa Clara, P	1981	Stan Holmes, Ariz. St., LF	2000	Trey Hodges, LSU, P
1963	Bud Hollowell, USC, C	1982	Dan Smith, Miami-FL, P	2001	Charlton Jimerson, Miami-FL, CF
1964	**Joe Ferris,** Maine, P	1983	Calvin Schiraldi, Texas, P	2002	Huston Street, Texas, P
1965	Sal Bando, Ariz. St., P	1984	John Fishel, CS-Fullerton, LF	2003	**John Hudgins,** Stanford, P
1966	Steve Arlin, Ohio St., P	1985	Greg Ellena, Miami-FL, LF		
1967	Ron Davini, Ariz. St., C	1986	Mike Senne, Arizona, DH		

Annual Awards
Golden Spikes Award

First presented in 1978 by USA Baseball, honoring the nation's best amateur player; sponsored by the Major League Baseball Players Association. Alex Fernandez, the 1990 winner, has been the only junior college player chosen.

Year		Year		Year	
1978	Bob Horner, Ariz. St, 2B	1987	Jim Abbott, Michigan, P	1996	Travis Lee, San Diego St., 1B
1979	Tim Wallach, CS-Fullerton, 1B	1988	Robin Ventura, Okla. St., 3B	1997	J.D. Drew, Florida St., OF
1980	Terry Francona, Arizona, OF	1989	Ben McDonald, LSU, P	1998	Pat Burrell, Miami-FL, 3B
1981	Mike Fuentes, Fla. St., OF	1990	Alex Fernandez, Miami-Dade, P	1999	Jason Jennings, Baylor, DH/P
1982	Augie Schmidt, N. Orleans, SS	1991	Mike Kelly, Ariz. St., OF	2000	Kip Bouknight, South Carolina, P
1983	Dave Magadan, Alabama, 1B	1992	Phil Nevin, CS-Fullerton, 3B	2001	Mark Prior, USC, P
1984	Oddibe McDowell, Ariz. St., OF	1993	Darren Dreifort, Wichita St., P	2002	Khalil Greene, Clemson, SS
1985	Will Clark, Miss. St., 1B	1994	Jason Varitek, Ga. Tech, C	2003	Rickie Weeks, Southern, 2B
1986	Mike Loynd, Fla. St., P	1995	Mark Kotsay, CS-Fullerton, OF		

Baseball America Player of the Year

Presented to the College Player of the Year since 1981 by *Baseball America*.

Year		Year		Year	
1981	Mike Sodders, Ariz. St., 3B	1989	Ben McDonald, LSU, P	1997	J.D. Drew, Florida St., OF
1982	Jeff Ledbetter, Fla. St., OF/P	1990	Mike Kelly, Ariz. St., OF	1998	Jeff Austin, Stanford, P
1983	Dave Magadan, Alabama, 1B	1991	David McCarty, Stanford, 1B	1999	Jason Jennings, Baylor, DH/P
1984	Oddibe McDowell, Ariz. St., OF	1992	Phil Nevin, CS-Fullerton, 3B	2000	Mark Teixeira, Ga. Tech, 3B
1985	Pete Incaviglia, Okla. St., OF	1993	Brooks Kieschnick, Texas, DH/P	2001	Mark Prior, USC, P
1986	Casey Close, Michigan, OF	1994	Jason Varitek, Ga. Tech, C	2002	Khalil Greene, Clemson, SS
1987	Robin Ventura, Okla. St., 3B	1995	Todd Helton, Tenn., 1B/P	2003	Rickie Weeks, Southern, 2B
1988	John Olerud, Wash. St., 1B/P	1996	Kris Benson, Clemson, P		

Dick Howser Trophy

Presented to the College Player of the Year since 1987, by the American Baseball Coaches Association (ABCA) from 1987-98 and the National Collegiate Baseball Writers Association (NCBWA) beginning in 1999. Founded and owned by the St. Petersburg (Fla.) Area Chamber of Commerce. Named after the late two-time All-America shortstop and college coach at Florida State. Howser was also a major league manager with Kansas City and the New York Yankees.

Multiple winner: Brooks Kieschnick (2).

Year		Year		Year	
1987	Mike Fiore, Miami-FL, OF	1993	Brooks Kieschnick, Texas, DH/P	1999	Jason Jennings, Baylor, DH/P
1988	Robin Ventura, Okla. St., 3B	1994	Jason Varitek, Ga. Tech, C	2000	Mark Teixeira, Ga. Tech, 3B
1989	Scott Bryant, Texas, DH	1995	Todd Helton, Tenn., 1B/P	2001	Mark Prior, USC, P
1990	Paul Ellis, UCLA, C	1996	Kris Benson, Clemson, P	2002	Khalil Greene, Clemson, SS
1991	Bobby Jones, Fresno St., P	1997	J.D. Drew, Florida St., OF	2003	Rickie Weeks, Southern, 2B
1992	Brooks Kieschnick, Texas, DH/P	1998	Eddie Furniss, LSU, 1B		

Baseball America Coach of the Year

Presented to the College Coach of the Year since 1981 by *Baseball America*.

Multiple winners: Skip Bertman, Augie Garrido, Dave Snow and Gene Stephenson (2).

Year		Year		Year	
1981	Ron Fraser, Miami-FL	1988	Jim Brock, Arizona St.	1996	Skip Bertman, LSU
1982	Gene Stephenson, Wichita St.	1989	Dave Snow, Long Beach St.	1997	Jim Wells, Alabama
1983	Barry Shollenberger, Alabama	1990	Steve Webber, Georgia	1998	Pat Murphy, Arizona St.
1984	Augie Garrido, CS-Fullerton	1991	Jim Hendry, Creighton	1999	Wayne Graham, Rice
1985	Ron Polk, Mississippi St.	1992	Andy Lopez, Pepperdine	2000	Ray Tanner, S. Carolina
1986	Skip Bertman, LSU	1993	Gene Stephenson, Wichita St.	2001	Dave Van Horn, Nebraska
	& Dave Snow, Loyola-CA	1994	Jim Morris, Miami-FL	2002	Augie Garrido, Texas
1987	Mark Marquess, Stanford	1995	Rod Delmonico, Tennessee	2003	George Horton, CS-Fullerton

All-Time Winningest Coaches

Coaches active in 2003 are in **bold** type. Records given are for four-year colleges only. For winning percentage, a minimum 10 years in Division I is required.

Top 25 Winning Percentage

		Yrs	W	L	T	Pct
1	John Barry	.40	619	147	6	.806
2	W.J. Disch	.29	465	115	0	.802
3	Cliff Gustafson	.29	1427	373	2	.792
4	Harry Carlson	.17	143	41	0	.777
5	**Gene Stephenson**	.26	1406	449	3	.758
6	George Jacobs	.11	76	25	0	.752
7	Bobby Winkles	.13	524	173	0	.752
8	**Mike Martin**	.24	1293	429	3	.750
9	Frank Sancet	.23	831	283	8	.744
10	Ron Fraser	.30	1271	438	9	.742
11	Bob Wren	.23	464	160	4	.742
12	Bibb Falk	.25	435	152	0	.741
13	Gary Ward	.21	1022	361	1	.739
14	Skip Bertman	.18	870	330	3	.724
15	Bud Middaugh	.22	821	319	1	.720
16	J.F. "Pop" McKale	.30	302	118	7	.715
17	Jim Brock	.28	1100	440	0	.714
18	Toby Green	.21	318	132	0	.707
19	**Wayne Graham**	.12	536	224	0	.705
20	Joe Arnold	.18	750	313	2	.705
21	**Jim Morris**	.22	976	409	4	.704
22	Joe Bedenk	.32	380	159	3	.701
23	Rod Dedeaux	.45	1332	571	11	.699
24	**Ray Tanner**	.16	714	308	3	.698
25	Enos Semore	.22	851	370	1	.697

Top 25 Victories

		Yrs	W	L	T	Pct
1	**Augie Garrido**	.35	**1430**	686	8	.675
2	Cliff Gustafson	.29	**1427**	373	2	.792
3	**Gene Stephenson**	.26	**1406**	449	3	.758
4	**Chuck Hartman**	.44	**1372**	728	8	.653
5	**Larry Hays**	.33	**1350**	731	2	.649
6	Rod Dedeaux	.45	**1332**	571	11	.699
7	Bob Bennett	.34	**1300**	757	8	.631
8	**Mike Martin**	.24	**1293**	429	4	.750
9	Ron Fraser	.30	**1271**	438	9	.742
10	**Larry Cochell**	.37	**1269**	770	3	.622
11	Jack Stallings	.39	**1258**	796	5	.612
12	Jim Dietz	.31	**1230**	751	18	.620
13	Al Ogletree	.41	**1217**	713	1	.631
14	**Ron Polk**	.30	**1199**	578	2	.675
15	**Richard Jones**	.37	**1187**	696	5	.630
16	Chuck Brayton	.33	**1162**	523	8	.689
17	Bill Wilhelm	.36	**1161**	536	10	.683
	Norm DeBriyn	.33	**1161**	650	6	.641
19	**Mark Marquess**	.27	**1144**	551	5	.674
20	**Gary Adams**	.34	**1137**	863	12	.568
21	Jim Brock	.23	**1100**	440	0	.714
22	Les Murakami	.30	**1077**	570	4	.654
23	Bob Hannah	.36	**1054**	463	6	.694
24	**Jay Bergman**	.27	**1044**	587	3	.640
25	Gary Ward	.21	**1022**	361	1	.739

Other NCAA Champions
Division II

Multiple winners: Florida Southern (8); Cal Poly Pomona and Tampa (3); Central Missouri St., CS-Chico, CS-Northridge, Jacksonville St., Troy St., UC-Irvine and UC-Riverside (2).

Year		Year		Year		Year	
1968	Chapman, CA	1977	UC-Riverside	1986	Troy St., AL	1995	Florida Southern
1969	Illinois St.	1978	Florida Southern	1987	Troy St., AL	1996	Kennesaw St., GA
1970	CS-Northridge	1979	Valdosta St., GA	1988	Florida Southern	1997	CS-Chico
1971	Florida Southern	1980	Cal Poly Pomona	1989	Cal Poly SLO	1998	Tampa
1972	Florida Southern	1981	Florida Southern	1990	Jacksonville St., AL	1999	CS-Chico
1973	UC-Irvine	1982	UC-Riverside	1991	Jacksonville St., AL	2000	Southeastern Okla.
1974	UC-Irvine	1983	Cal Poly Pomona	1992	Tampa	2001	St. Mary's, TX
1975	Florida Southern	1984	CS-Northridge	1993	Tampa	2002	Columbus St., GA
1976	Cal Poly Pomona	1985	Florida Southern	1994	Central Missouri St.	2003	Central Missouri St.

Division III

Multiple winners: Eastern Conn. St. (4); Marietta and Montclair St. (3); CS-Stanislaus, Glassboro St., Ithaca, NC-Wesleyan, Southern Maine and Wm. Paterson, NJ (2).

Year		Year		Year		Year	
1976	CS-Stanislaus	1983	Marietta, OH	1990	Eastern Conn. St.	1997	Southern Maine
1977	CS-Stanislaus	1984	Ramapo, NJ	1991	Southern Maine	1998	Eastern Conn. St.
1978	Glassboro St., NJ	1985	Wisconsin-Oshkosh	1992	Wm. Paterson, NJ	1999	NC-Wesleyan
1979	Glassboro St., NJ	1986	Marietta, OH	1993	Montclair St., NJ	2000	Montclair St., NJ
1980	Ithaca, NY	1987	Monclair St., NJ	1994	Wisconsin-Oshkosh	2001	St. Thomas, MN
1981	Marietta, OH	1988	Ithaca, NY	1995	La Verne, CA	2002	Eastern Conn. St.
1982	Eastern Conn. St.	1989	NC-Wesleyan	1996	Wm. Paterson, NJ	2003	Chapman, CA

Major League Number One Draft Picks

The Major League First-Year Player Draft has been held every year since 1965. Clubs select in reverse order of their won-loss records from the previous regular season with National League and American League teams alternating. AL teams select first in odd-numbered years while NL teams go first in even-numbered years. The pool of draftees consists of graduated high school players, junior or senior college players, Junior college players and anyone over the age of 21. Listed are the top selections from each draft.

Year		Pos	Team	Year		Pos	Team
1965	Rick Monday	OF	Kansas City Athletics	1985	B.J. Surhoff	C	Milwaukee Brewers
1966	Steve Chilcott	C	New York Mets	1986	Jeff King	IF	Pittsburgh Pirates
1967	Rom Blomberg	1B	New York Yankees	1987	Ken Griffey Jr.	OF	Seattle Mariners
1968	Tim Foli	IF	New York Mets	1988	Andy Benes	P	San Diego Padres
1969	Jeff Burroughs	OF	Washington Senators	1989	Ben McDonald	P	Baltimore Orioles
1970	Mike Ivie	C	San Diego Padres	1990	Chipper Jones	SS	Atlanta Braves
1971	Danny Goodwin	C	Chicago White Sox	1991	Brien Taylor	P	New York Yankees
1972	Dave Roberts	IF	San Diego Padres	1992	Phil Nevin	3B	Houston Astros
1973	David Clyde	P	Texas Rangers	1993	Alex Rodriguez	SS	Seattle Mariners
1974	Bill Almon	IF	San Diego Padres	1994	Paul Wilson	P	New York Mets
1975	Danny Goodwin	C	California Angels	1995	Darin Erstad	OF/P	California Angels
1976	Floyd Bannister	P	Houston Astros	1996	Kris Benson	P	Pittsburgh Pirates
1977	Harold Baines	OF	Chicago White Sox	1997	Matt Anderson	P	Detroit Tigers
1978	Bob Horner	3B	Atlanta Braves	1998	Pat Burrell	3B	Philadelphia Phillies
1979	Al Chambers	OF	Seattle Mariners	1999	Josh Hamilton	OF	T.B. Devil Rays
1980	Darryl Strawberry	OF	New York Mets	2000	Adrian Gonzalez	1B	Florida Marlins
1981	Mike Moore	P	Seattle Mariners	2001	Joe Mauer	C	Minnesota Twins
1982	Shawon Dunston	SS	Chicago Cubs	2002	Bryan Bullington	P	Pittsburgh Pirates
1983	Tim Belcher	P	Minnesota Twins	2003	Delmon Young	OF	T.B. Devil Rays
1984	Shawn Abner	OF	New York Mets				

Straight to the Majors

Since Major League baseball began its First-Year Player Draft in 1965, 19 selections have advanced directly to the major leagues without first playing in the minors

Draft		Pos	Team	Draft		Pos	Team
1967	Mike Adamson, USC	P	Baltimore	1978	Tim Conroy, Gateway HS (Pa.)	P	Oakland
1969	Steve Dunning, Stanford	P	Cleveland		Bob Horner, Arizona St.	3B	Atlanta
1971	Pete Broberg, Dartmouth	P	Washington		Brian Milner, Southwest HS (Tex.)	C	Toronto
	Rob Ellis, Michigan St.	OF	Milwaukee		Mike Morgan, Valley HS (Nev.)	P	Oakland
	Burt Hooton, Texas	P	Chicago-NL	1985	Pete Incaviglia, Oklahoma St.	OF	Montreal
1972	Dave Roberts, Oregon	3B	San Diego	1988	Jim Abbott, Michigan	P	California
1973	Dick Ruthven, Fresno St.	P	Philadelphia	1989	John Olerud, Washington St.	1B	Toronto
	David Clyde, Westchester HS (Tex.)	P	Texas	1995	Ariel Prieto, Fajardo U (Cuba)	P	Oakland
	Dave Winfield, Minnesota	OF	San Diego	2000	Xavier Nady, California	3B	San Diego
	Eddie Bane, Arizona St.	P	Minnesota				

College Football

Ohio State got a second chance when Miami's Glenn Sharpe wrapped up Chris Gamble during OT at the Fiesta Bowl, resulting in a controversial call.

Plucky Buckeyes

Ohio State upsets defending national champion Miami in overtime to win its first national title since 1968.

Chris Fowler
is the host of ESPN's College GameDay

For three seconds, the Miami Hurricanes felt like national champions again. A fourth down pass by Ohio State's Craig Krenzel had caromed incomplete in the end zone. A winning streak spanning three seasons would seal this program's status as a modern day dynasty worthy of Rockne's Irish or Wilkinson's Sooners.

Jubilant Canes streamed off the bench. The small fraction of fans in Sun Devil Stadium not wearing Scarlet and Grey jumped around. A Miami helmet went sailing up into the night sky of Tempe, Ariz.

But wait. A penalty flag was spotted amidst the chaos, and now the crew of Big Twelve zebras was huddling. Pass interference, Miami. First and goal, Ohio State.

The most suspenseful championship game ever would continue, thereby becoming also the most controversial. Standing on Miami's sideline (the one nearer our set) the emotional swing was astounding.

Did Hurricane freshman Glenn Sharpe interfere with OSU's Chris Gamble? Yes. A little bit. His timing was just off and he was a little

aggressive with his left arm. But it was stunning to see a flag fly on a borderline play in overtime of a national title game. Most officials would have kept the hanky in their pocket.

Miami, to a man, refused to blame the painful defeat on the call. That is to their eternal credit. I'll remember it as a classy footnote to an amazing 34-game run. The Hurricanes had been outplayed, out-coached, and out-lasted. And they knew it. Kellen Winslow, Jr. admitted OSU "deserved to win."

After all, in the decisive second overtime, Miami had first and goal from the two and failed on four plays.

All night, the Buckeyes' defense had backed up a tough guy confidence that had simmered since the heavy underdogs hit Arizona soil. They dogged and drilled Ken Dorsey, sacking him four times, destroying the passing game's timing, and forcing five turnovers.

Most of the time, the "Silver Bullets" smothered Willis McGahee. The Canes' extraordinary back was just beginning to find some cracks, when his knee was shattered on a clean tackle. To see a true college football soldier crying in agony, career over, is a sickening memory I will not soon forget.

AP/Wide World Photos

*Ohio State and first year head coach **Jim Tressel** handed Miami its first loss in three years at the Fiesta Bowl to win its first national championship in 35 years.*

Dorsey shed postgame tears, too, in the arms of his mother. Not for himself. But because he believed he had let teammates down, after just his second loss in 40 career starts. It was not the preferred postscript for a superb career. But you can't really pity Dorsey. Exactly a year earlier, he had known the joy felt that night by Krenzel.

The admittedly dull but certainly brainy quarterback had completed just five passes. But his toughness and game management were typically solid. It was Krenzel who had provided the miracle that propelled Ohio State to the Big Ten title, improvising a fourth and one bomb to Michael Jenkins for the game winning TD at Purdue. More than any other, that play shaped the 2003 championship race.

All season, Krenzel had been over-

shadowed in his own backfield, as the icy Yin to the fiery Yang of Maurice Clarett. The Bucks' prodigy had dominated recent headlines and sound bytes by blasting his own school's administration for refusing his request to fly home for a murdered friend's funeral. But then, Clarett seems to gain strength and focus from chaos.

What can you say about an 18-year-old who lectured seniors on commitment, talked back to his coaches, often decided when he would or would not come off the field, and a couple months into his career even hinted he might challenge NFL rules against entering the draft as a freshman?

Well, you can say a lot of things, and folks have. But you cannot question the heart or talent of this new age star. More than anything else, Clarett

AP/Wide World Photos

*USC quarterback **Carson Palmer** overcame any perceived or actual East coast bias to win the 2002 Heisman Trophy. Palmer became the first West coast player to win the trophy since fellow Trojan Marcus Allen captured the award in 1981.*

seemed humbled after victory. The speed of Miami's D had greatly limited his impact. Afterwards, he was quiet... relieved. He just wanted to get home.

After a rocky two weeks, Clarett would return a champion, but his off-field troubles were just beginning.

Jim Tressel had been a national champion three times before, at 1-AA Youngstown State. But this was different. In delivering Ohio State's first title in two generations, he was now king of college football's highest hill, along the way making corny homespun sayings and sweater vests cool.

Tressel had dusted off the old school blueprint that Ohio State had followed religiously to almost all of its' 14 victories: take very few chances on offense, rely on a stout defense and superb kicking game.

The philosophy carries a slim margin for error, and created margins of victory of a touchdown or less in more than half the Buckeyes' games. But every stressed out OSU fan knew that somewhere, Woody approved.

Besides the fateful flag, the epic left us with another issue to debate over the years. Was this the best national championship game ever?

In the afterglow, many proclaimed it just that. It's certainly the most dramatic I've witnessed, and I've been ringside for the last 14. How do you top a big upset in double OT, decided by a goal line stand, wrapped in controversy?

I'll always defer to my colleague Beano Cook on the relative merits of the pre-Eisenhower title battles, but I doubt I'll see a finer college football finale in my lifetime.

Lee Corso's Ten Biggest Stories of the Year in College Football

10 The Georgia Bulldogs win their first Southeastern Conference championship in 20 seasons and finish the season at 13-1.

9 Following a disappointing 6-6 season, Texas A&M fires head coach R.C. Slocum, who never had a losing season in his 14-year career at College Station.

8 Strong-armed quarterback Byron Leftwich carries Marshall to another Mid-American Conference crown while his teammates carry him. A late-season leg injury so bad that two of his offensive linemen have to carry him downfield at times, and that's a lot of quarterback to move. Leftwich is 6-feet-5, 240 pounds, but one leg is apparently enough to throw off of and he gets his fifth 400-yard passing game of the season in the MAC title game against Toledo.

7 Southern Cal, led by their Heisman Trophy-winning quarterback Carson Palmer, makes a return to glory with an 11-2 record and a win in the Orange Bowl.

6 Florida State takes another Atlantic Coast Conference title despite an un-FSU-like record of 9-5. It's the Seminoles' worst record since 1961 when they went 6-5.

5 Nebraska finishes at 7-7, ending the Cornhuskers' record streak of 33 seasons with at least nine wins.

4 Alabama head coach Dennis Franchione leaves Tuscaloosa after just two seasons to succeed R.C. Slocum at Texas A&M. The Crimson Tide hire Mike Price to replace Franchione but the school fires him just months later for his behavior on an April trip to Florida, saying Price failed to live his "personal and professional life in a manner consistent with university policies." Former Tide quarterback Mike Shula, son of NFL coaching legend Don Shula, becomes Bama's third head coach in six months on May 8.

3 Tyrone Willingham, the first African-American to coach any sport at Notre Dame, rekindles the program's pride with an 8-0 start to the season. The Irish finish with a final record of 10-3, their best mark in nine years.

2 The Miami Hurricanes run their impressive winning streak to 34 games before finally falling to Ohio State on a controversial pass interference call in the end zone during double overtime of the national championship game.

1 Ohio State, led by record-breaking freshman tailback Maurice Clarett, wins its first national championship since 1968. The Buckeyes beat Miami, 31-24, in double overtime at the Fiesta Bowl.

Drought Over

The Ohio State Buckeyes won their first national championship in 35 years at the 2003 Fiesta Bowl. Here's a look at the longest stretches between national titles in Div. 1A college football history since 1936.

Team	Seasons	Years
Michigan	49	1948-97
Tennessee	47	1951-98
Ohio State	34	1968-2002
Nebraska	23	1971-94
Oklahoma	18	1956-74

Nine Times, Nine Times

The Nebraska Cornhuskers ended their amazing streak of 33 straight seasons with nine or more wins in 2002. In fact, Nebraska wasn't the only team to have a streak of nine-win seasons come to a close last year. Florida had 12 straight seasons with nine wins in the books before stumbling in 2002. Here's a look at the longest such streaks in Div. 1A college football history: .

Years	Team	Seasons
1969-2001	Nebraska	33
1987-2000	Florida St.	14
1990-2001	Florida	12
1971-1981	Alabama	11
1985-1994	Miami-FL	10

Beginner's Luck?

Miami Hurricanes head coach Larry Coker finally lost the first game of his career after 24 straight wins when his team fell to Ohio State at the 2003 Fiesta Bowl. Coker had the second best start in college football coaching history. Here's a look at the list of most wins to start a coaching career:

Coach, School	Seasons	Wins
Walter Camp, Yale	1888-89	28
Larry Coker, Miami-FL	2001-02	24
George Woodruff, Penn	1892	13
Carroll Widdoes, Ohio St.	1944-45	12
Dan McGugin, Vanderbilt	1904-05	11
Bennie Oosterbaan, Mich.	1948-49	11

Look At Those Streaks!

Miami's 34-game win streak was ended by Ohio State at the 2003 Fiesta Bowl. Here's a side-by-side comparison of Miami's run and Oklahoma's NCAA record 47-game win streak.

	Mia	Okla
W vs team with winning rec.	23	18
W vs team with 2 wins or less	2	10
W vs team with 3 wins or less	5	1
Opp. combined win pct.	62.1	52.2
Avg. margin of victory	28.1	28.7
W over ranked teams	12	10
W over top ten teams	6	3
Games decided by single digits	4	9
Games decided by 20+	25	31
1st round draft picks during streak	9	3

2002-2003
Season in Review

ESPN
SPORTS ALMANAC

Final AP Top 25 Poll

Voted on by panel of 71 sportswriters & broadcasters and released on Jan. 4, 2003, following the Fiesta Bowl: winning team receives the Bear Bryant Trophy, given since 1983; first place votes in parentheses, records, total points (based on 25 for 1st, 24 for 2nd, etc.) bowl game result, head coach and career record, preseason rank (released Aug. 10, 2002) and final regular season rank (released Dec. 8, 2002).

	Final Record	Points	Bowl Game	Head Coach	Aug. 10 Rank	Dec. 8 Rank
1 Ohio St. (71)	14-0	1,775	won Fiesta	Jim Tressel (17 yrs: 156-62-2)	10	2
2 Miami-FL	12-1	1,693	lost Fiesta	Larry Coker (2 yrs: 24-1)	1	1
3 Georgia	13-1	1,598	won Sugar	Mark Richt (2 yrs: 21-5)	8	4
4 USC	11-2	1,590	won Orange	Pete Carroll (2 yrs: 17-8)	20	5
5 Oklahoma	12-2	1,476	won Rose	Bob Stoops (4 yrs: 43-9)	2	8
6 Texas	11-2	1,363	won Cotton	Mack Brown (19 yrs: 135-89-1)	3	9
7 Kansas St.	11-2	1,356	won Holiday	Bill Snyder (14 yrs: 116-51-1)	NR	6
8 Iowa	11-2	1,334	lost Orange	Kirk Ferentz (4 yrs: 34-47)	NR	3
9 Michigan	10-3	1,182	won Outback	Lloyd Carr (8 yrs: 76-23)	13	12
10 Washington St.	10-3	1,085	lost Rose	Mike Price (22 yrs: 129-122)	12	7
11 Alabama	10-3	988	no bowl	Dennis Franchione (2 yrs: 17-8)	NR	13
12 N.C. State	11-3	943	won Gator	Chuck Amato (3 yrs: 26-12)	25	17
13 Maryland	11-3	844	won Peach	Ralph Friedgen (2 yrs: 21-5)	21	20
14 Auburn	9-4	821	won Capital One	Tommy Tuberville (8 yrs: 55-39)	NR	19
15 Boise St.	12-1	692	won Humanitarian	Dan Hawkins (7 yrs: 59-16-1)	NR	18
16 Penn St.	9-4	675	lost Capital One	Joe Paterno (37 yrs: 336-101-3)	24	10
17 Notre Dame	10-3	657	lost Gator	Tyrone Willingham (8 yrs: 54-39-1)	NR	11
18 Virginia Tech	10-4	544	won San Francisco	Frank Beamer (22 yrs: 159-92-4)	16	21
19 Pittsburgh	9-4	520	won Insight	Walt Harris (9 yrs: 47-59)	NR	24
20 Colorado	9-5	307	lost Alamo	Gary Barnett (13 yrs: 72-77-2)	7	14
21 Florida St.	9-5	291	lost Sugar	Bobby Bowden (37 yrs: 332-96-4)	5	16
22 Virginia	9-5	250	won Cont. Tire	Al Groh (8 yrs: 40-51)	NR	NR
23 TCU	10-2	231	won Liberty	Gary Patterson (2 yrs: 16-9)	NR	NR
24 Marshall	11-2	201	won GMAC	Bob Pruett (7 yrs: 80-13)	19	NR
25 West Virginia	9-4	195	lost Cont. Tire	Rich Rodriguez (10 yrs: 57-48-2)	NR	15

Other teams receiving votes: 26. **Florida** (8-5, lost Outback Bowl, 120 points); 27. **Texas Tech** (9-5, won Tangerine, 80 pts); 28. **Oklahoma State** (8-5, won Houston Bowl, 73 pts); 29. **Boston College** (9-4, won Motor City Bowl, 52 pts); 30. **Colorado State** (10-4, lost Liberty Bowl, 44 pts); 31. **LSU** (8-5, lost Cotton Bowl, 38 pts); 32. **South Florida** (9-2, no bowl, 37 pts); 33. **Wisconsin** (8-6, won Alamo Bowl, 15 pts); 34. **Minnesota** (8-5, won Music City Bowl, 4 pts); 35. **Arkansas** (9-5, lost Music City Bowl, 3 pts); 36. **Air Force** (8-5, lost San Francisco Bowl, 2 pts), **Hawaii** (10-4, lost Hawaii Bowl, 2 pts) and **Purdue** (7-6, won Sun Bowl, 2 pts), 39. **Fresno State** (9-5, won Silicon Valley Classic, 1 pt) and **North Texas** (8-5, won New Orleans Bowl, 1 pt).

AP Preseason and Final Regular Season Polls

First place votes in parentheses.

Top 25
(Aug. 10, 2002)

		Pts			Pts
1	Miami-FL (27)	1,746	14	LSU	832
2	Oklahoma (21)	1,732	15	Oregon	736
3	Florida St. (10)	1,683	16	Virginia Tech	583
4	Texas (13)	1,682	17	Louisville	574
5	Tennessee (3)	1,601	18	Michigan St.	468
6	Florida	1,313	19	Marshall	433
7	Colorado	1,291	20	USC	420
8	Georgia	1,179	21	Maryland	318
9	Washington	1,133	22	South Carolina	268
10	Nebraska	1,131	23	Texas A&M	247
11	Washington St.	1,096	24	Penn St.	221
12	Michigan	1,061	25	Wisconsin	193
13	Ohio St.	1,092			

Top 25
(Dec. 8, 2002)

		Pts			Pts
1	Miami-FL (74)	1,850	14	Colorado	758
2	Ohio St.	1,773	15	West Virginia	706
3	Iowa	1,678	16	Florida St.	661
4	Georgia	1,627	17	N.C. State	570
5	USC	1,559	18	Boise St.	505
6	Kansas St.	1,397	19	Auburn	483
7	Washington St.	1,388	20	Maryland	446
8	Oklahoma	1,371	21	Virginia Tech	409
9	Texas	1,297	22	Florida	309
10	Penn St.	1,107	23	Colorado St.	277
11	Notre Dame	1,104	24	Pittsburgh	255
12	Michigan	1,061	25	Arkansas	160
13	Alabama	984			

2002-2003 Bowl Games

Listed by bowls matching highest-ranked teams as of final regular season AP poll (released Dec. 8, 2002). Attendance figures indicate tickets sold.

Bowl		Winner	Regular Season		Loser	Regular Season	Score	Date	Attendance
Fiesta	#2	Ohio St.	13-0	#1	Miami-FL	12-0	31-24 (2 OT)	Jan. 3	77,502
Orange	#5	USC	10-2	#3	Iowa	11-1	38-17	Jan. 2	75,971
Sugar	#4	Georgia	12-1	#16	Florida St.	10-3	26-13	Jan. 1	74,269
Holiday	#6	Kansas St.	10-2		Arizona St.	8-5	34-27	Dec. 27	58,717
Rose	#8	Oklahoma	11-2	#7	Washington St.	9-3	34-14	Jan. 1	86,848
Cotton	#9	Texas	10-2		LSU	8-4	35-20	Jan. 1	70,817
Capital One	#19	Auburn	8-4	#10	Penn St.	9-3	13-9	Jan. 1	66,334
Gator	#17	N.C. State	10-3	#11	Notre Dame	9-3	28-6	Jan. 1	73,491
Outback	#12	Michigan	9-3	#22	Florida	8-4	38-30	Jan. 1	65,101
Alamo		Wisconsin	7-6	#14	Colorado	9-4	31-28 (OT)	Dec. 28	50,690
Continental Tire		Virginia	8-5	#15	West Virginia	9-3	48-22	Dec. 28	72,202
Humanitarian	#18	Boise St.	11-1		Iowa St.	7-6	34-16	Dec. 31	30,446
Peach	#20	Maryland	10-3		Tennessee	8-4	30-3	Dec. 31	68,330
San Francisco	#21	Virginia Tech	9-4		Air Force	8-4	20-13	Dec. 31	25,966
Liberty		TCU	9-2	#23	Colorado St.	10-3	17-3	Dec. 31	55,207
Insight	#24	Pittsburgh	8-4		Oregon St.	7-4	38-13	Dec. 26	40,533
Music City		Minnesota	7-5	#25	Arkansas	7-4	29-14	Dec. 30	39,183
Silicon Valley Classic . .		Fresno St.	8-5		Georgia Tech	7-5	30-21	Dec. 31	10,142
Sun		Purdue	6-6		Washington	7-5	34-24	Dec. 31	48,917
Seattle		Wake Forest	6-6		Oregon	7-5	38-17	Dec. 30	38,241
Houston		Oklahoma St.	7-5		Southern Miss.	7-5	33-23	Dec. 27	44,687
Independence		Mississippi	6-6		Nebraska	7-6	27-23	Dec. 27	46,096
Motor City		Boston College	8-4		Toledo	9-4	51-25	Dec. 26	51,872
Las Vegas		UCLA	7-5		New Mexico	7-6	27-13	Dec. 25	30,324
Hawaii		Tulane	7-5		Hawaii	10-3	36-28	Dec. 25	35,513
Tangerine		Texas Tech	8-5		Clemson	7-5	55-15	Dec. 23	21,689
GMAC		Marshall	10-2		Louisville	7-5	38-15	Dec. 18	40,646
New Orleans		North Texas	7-5		Cincinnati	7-6	24-19	Dec. 17	19,024

FAVORITES: Fiesta (Miami by 11½); **Orange** (USC by 6); **Sugar** (Georgia by 8); **Holiday** (Kansas St. by 18); **Rose** (Oklahoma by 6½); **Cotton** (Texas by 10½); **Capital One** (Penn St. by 6½); **Gator** (Even); **Outback** (Florida by 1½); **Alamo** (Colorado by 7); **Continental Tire** (West Virginia by 5); **Humanitarian** (Boise St. by 11½); **Peach** (Even); **San Francisco** (Virginia Tech by 11½); **Liberty** (Colorado St. by 5); **Insight** (Oregon St. by 2½); **Music City** (Arkansas by 7½); **Silicon Valley** (Georgia Tech by 6½); **Sun** (Washington by 3); **Seattle** (Oregon by 7); **Houston** (Oklahoma St. by 8); **Independence** (Nebraska by 6); **Motor City** (Boston College by 4); **Las Vegas** (UCLA by 10½); **Hawaii** (Hawaii by 12); **Tangerine** (Texas Tech by 5); **GMAC** (Marshall by 2½); **New Orleans** (Cincinnati by 7½).

Final BCS Rankings

The Bowl Championship Series rankings were used for the first time during the 1998 season to determine BCS bowl match-ups and revised slightly for the 1999, 2001 and 2002 seasons. The final rankings were released Dec. 8, 2002. Note that S-rank refers to schedule rank and L refers to games lost.

	Polls		Computer Rankings										Sub	Quality	
	AP	ESPN	A&H	R.B.	C.M.	K.M.	NYT	Sag.	P.W.	Avg.	Sched.	S-rank	L	Total	wins	Total
1 Miami-FL	1	1	2	1	1	1	1	1	2	1.17	19	0.76	0	2.93	0.0	2.93
2 Ohio St.	2	2	1	2	2	2	3	2	1	1.67	20	0.80	0	4.47	-0.5	3.97
3 Georgia	4	4	3	3	4	4	3	3	3	3.17	5	0.20	1	8.37	0.0	8.37
4 USC	5	5	5	6	4	3	2	4	4	3.67	1	0.04	2	10.71	-0.2	10.51
5 Iowa	3	3	4	5	5	8	5	5	5	4.83	49	1.96	1	10.79	0.0	10.79
6 Washington St.	7	7	8	9	8	5	10	6	6	7.00	21	0.84	2	16.84	-0.7	16.14
7 Oklahoma	8	8	7	4	7	6	8	7	7	6.33	14	0.56	2	16.89	-0.1	16.79
8 Kansas St.	6	6	15	11	13	10	8	12	10	10.67	54	2.16	2	20.83	-0.7	20.13
9 Notre Dame . .	11	12	6	8	6	6	14.5	7	8	6.83	15	0.60	2	20.93	0.0	20.93
10 Texas	9	9	10	7	9	11	12	9	11	9.50	22	0.88	2	21.38	-0.3	21.08
11 Michigan	12	11	9	16	10	9	9	10	9	9.33	2	0.08	3	23.91	0.0	23.91
12 Penn St.	10	10	12	14	14	15	11	16	14	13.33	16	0.64	3	26.97	0.0	26.97
13 Colorado	14	14	14	23	16	14	17	14	16	15.17	10	0.40	4	33.57	-0.3	33.27
14 Florida St. . . .	16	16	13	24	12	13	19	13	13	15.83	3	0.12	4	33.95	0.0	33.95
15 West Virginia .	15	13	19	15	17	19	16	19	18	17.33	41	1.64	3	35.97	0.0	35.97

Explanation Key
Computer Rankings—A&H refers to Anderson & Hester, R.B. refers to Richard Billingsley, C.M. refers to Colley Matrix, K.M. refers to Kenneth Massey, NYT refers to New York Times, Sag. refers to Jeff Sagarin, P.W. refers to Peter Wolfe, Avg. refers to the teams average position in the computer rankings.
Schedule Rank—Rank of schedule strength compared to other Division I-A teams divided by 25. This component is calculated by determining the cumulative won/loss records of the team's opponents (66.6 percent) and the cumulative won/loss record of the team's opponents' opponents (33.3 percent).
Quality Wins—This component will reward teams that defeat opponents ranked among the top 10 in the weekly standings. The scale will range from 1.0 points for a win over the top ranked team to 0.1 for a win over the 10th-ranked BCS team. The final BCS Standings determine final quality win points. If a team beats a team more than once during the regular season, quality points will be awarded just once.

National Championship Game

Miami and Ohio State were ranked first and second, respectively, in the final Bowl Championship Series rankings (released Dec. 8, 2002) and according to the BCS plan met in the so-called National Championship Game at the Fiesta Bowl on Jan. 3. Opponents' records and AP rank listed below are day of game. Final statistics listed below include the Fiesta Bowl.

Miami Hurricanes (12-0)

Date	AP Rank	Opponent	Result
Aug. 31	#1	Florida A&M (0-0)	W, 63-17
Sept. 7	#1	at #6 Florida (1-0)	W, 41-16
Sept. 14	#1	at Temple (1-1)	W, 44-21
Sept. 21	#1	Boston College (2-0)	W, 38-6
Oct. 5	#1	Connecticut (2-3)	W, 48-14
Oct. 12	#1	#9 Florida St. (5-1)	W, 28-27
Oct. 26	#1	at West Virginia (5-2)	W, 40-23
Nov. 2	#1	at Rutgers (1-7)	W, 42-17
Nov. 9	#2	at Tennessee (5-3)	W, 26-3
Nov. 21	#1	#17 Pittsburgh (8-2)	W, 28-21
Nov. 30	#1	at Syracuse (4-7)	W, 49-7
Dec. 7	#1	#18 Virginia Tech (9-3)	W, 56-45

Final Statistics

Passing (5 Att)	Att	Cmp	Pct.	Yds	TD	Rate
Ken Dorsey	.393	222	56.5	3369	28	145.9
Derrick Crudup	.26	15	57.7	226	2	156.1
Marc Guillon	.5	3	60.0	53	1	215.0

Interceptions: Dorsey 12.

Top Receivers	No	Yds	Avg	Long	TD
Kellen Winslow	.57	726	12.7	58	8
Andre Johnson	.52	1092	21.0	68	9
Willis McGahee	.27	355	13.1	77	0
Kevin Beard	.23	262	11.4	32	4
Ethenic Sands	.21	312	14.9	53	4
Roscoe Parrish	.19	340	17.9	58	2
Quadtrine Hill	.15	192	12.8	42	0

Top Rushers	Car	Yds	Avg	Long	TD
Willis McGahee	.282	1753	6.2	69	28
Jason Geathers	.68	398	5.9	62	3
Jarrett Payton	.50	223	4.5	37	0
Roscoe Parrish	.4	69	17.2	46	1
Quadtrine Hill	.6	16	2.7	5	1
Jeff Malley	.1	5	5.0	5	0

Most Touchdowns	TD	Run	Rec	Ret	Pts
Willis McGahee	.28	28	0	0	168
Andre Johnson	.9	0	9	0	54
Kellen Winslow	.8	0	8	0	48
Jason Geathers	.5	3	2	0	30
Ethenic Sands	.4	0	4	0	24
Kevin Beard	.4	0	4	0	24

2-Pt. Conversions: none.

Kicking	FG/Att	Lg	PAT/Att	Pts
Todd Sievers	.13/22	53	66/69	105

Punting	No	Yds	Long	Blkd	Avg
Freddie Capshaw	.54	2225	59	3	41.2
Jon Peattie	.3	133	53	0	44.3
Todd Sievers	.2	38	23	0	19.0

Most Interceptions		Most Sacks	
Sean Taylor	.4	Jamaal Green	.10.0
Maurice Sikes	.3	Jerome McDougle	.7.0
Five tied at	.1	Vince Wilfork	.7.0

Ohio State Buckeyes (13-0)

Date	AP Rank	Opponent	Result
Aug. 24	#10	Texas Tech (0-0)	W, 45-21
Sept. 7	#8	Kent St. (1-0)	W, 51-17
Sept. 14	#6	#10 Washington St. (2-0)	W, 25-7
Sept. 21	#6	at Cincinnati (1-1)	W, 23-19
Sept. 28	#6	Indiana (2-2)	W, 45-17
Oct. 5	#5	at Northwestern (2-3)	W, 27-16
Oct. 12	#5	San Jose St. (4-2)	W, 50-7
Oct. 19	#4	at Wisconsin (5-2)	W, 19-14
Oct. 26	#4	#17 Penn St. (5-2)	W, 13-7
Nov. 2	#6	#19 Minnesota (7-1)	W, 34-3
Nov. 9	#3	at Purdue (4-5)	W, 10-6
Nov. 16	#2	at Illinois (4-6)	W, 23-16 (OT)
Nov. 23	#2	#9 Michigan (9-2)	W, 14-9

Final Statistics

Passing (5 Att)	Att	Cmp	Pct.	Yds	TD	Rate
Craig Krenzel	.249	148	59.4	2110	12	140.9
Scott McMullen	.31	25	80.6	315	2	187.2

Interceptions: Krenzel 7.

Top Receivers	No	Yds	Avg	Long	TD
Michael Jenkins	.61	1076	17.6	50	6
Chris Gamble	.31	499	16.1	57	0
Ben Hartsock	.17	137	8.1	20	2
Chris Vance	.13	178	13.7	37	3
Maurice Clarett	.12	104	8.7	26	2
Drew Carter	.10	147	14.7	28	0
Lydell Ross	.10	75	7.5	28	0

Top Rushers	Car	Yds	Avg	Long	TD
Maurice Clarett	.222	1237	5.6	59	16
Lydell Ross	.166	619	3.7	36	6
Maurice Hall	.78	370	4.7	28	4
Craig Krenzel	.125	368	2.9	29	3
Chris Gamble	.3	49	16.3	43	1
JaJa Riley	.12	44	3.7	10	0
Donnie Nickey	.1	28	28.0	28	0

Most Touchdowns	TD	Run	Rec	Ret	Pts
Maurice Clarett	.18	16	2	0	108
Michael Jenkins	.6	0	6	0	36
Lydell Ross	.6	6	0	0	36
Maurice Hall	.4	4	0	0	24
Craig Krenzel	.3	3	0	0	18
Chris Vance	.3	0	3	0	18

2-Pt. Conversions: none.

Kicking	FG/Att	Lg	PAT/Att	Pts
Mike Nugent	.25/28	51	45/46	120

Punting	No	Yds	Long	Blkd	Avg
Andy Groom	.60	2697	74	1	45.0

Most Interceptions		Most Sacks	
Chris Gamble	.4	Darrion Scott	.8.5
Dustin Fox	.3	Kenny Peterson	.6.0
		Will Smith	.5.5

Fiesta Bowl

Friday, Jan. 3, 2003 at Sun Devil Stadium, Tempe, Ariz.

	1	2	3	4	OT	2OT	F
#2 Ohio St. (Big Ten)	..0	14	3	0	7	7	31
#1 Miami-FL (Big East)	.7	0	7	3	7	0	24

1st: 4:09; **Miami**— Roscoe Parrish 25-yd pass from Ken Dorsey (Todd Sievers kick).
2nd: 2:28; **OSU**— Craig Krenzel 1-yd run (Mike Nugent kick). 1:10; **OSU**— Maurice Clarett 7-yd run (Nugent kick).
3rd: 8:33; **OSU**— Nugent 44-yd FG. 2:11; **Miami**— Willis McGahee 9-yd run (Sievers kick).
4th: 0:00; **Miami**— Sievers 40-yd FG.
OT: 15:00; **Miami**— Kellen Winslow 7-yd pass from Dorsey (Sievers kick); 15:00; **OSU**— Krenzel 1-yd run (Nugent kick). 15:00; **OSU**— Clarett 5-yd run (Nugent kick)

Favorite: Miami by 11½   **Attendance:** 77,502
Field: Grass   **Weather:** Beautiful
Time: 3:56   **TV Rating:** 17.2/29 (ABC)
MVPs: OFF-Craig Krenzel, Ohio St., QB; DEF-Mike Doss, Ohio St., S

Team Statistics

	OSU	Mia
First downs	14	19
Rushing	7	3
Passing	6	14
Penalty	1	2
Total Plays	73	77
Total Net Yards	267	369
Average gain per play	3.7	4.8
Carries/yards (includ. sacks)	52/145	33/65
Passing yards	122	304
Completions/attempts	7/21	29/44
Had intercepted	2	2
Fumbles/lost	0/0	3/3
Penalties/yards	9/49	6/30
Punts/average	6/47.7	4/43.2
3rd down conversions	6/18	6/18
4th down conversions	2/3	1/2
Red-Zone scores/chances	2/4	2/2
Sacks by/yards	4/18	1/4
Time of possession	46:27	28:33

INDIVIDUAL STATISTICS

Ohio St. Buckeyes

Passing (5 Att)	Att	Cmp	Pct.	Yds	TD	Int
Craig Krenzel	21	7	33.3	122	0	2

Rushing	Car	Yds	Avg	Long	TD
Craig Krenzel	19	81	4.3	11	2
Maurice Clarett	23	47	2.0	10	2
Lydell Ross	9	17	1.9	9	0
Andy Groom	1	0	0.0	0	0
TOTALS	52	145	2.8	11	4

Receiving	No	Yds	Avg	Long	TD
Michael Jenkins	4	45	11.3	17	0
Chris Gamble	2	69	34.5	57	0
Chris Vance	1	8	8.0	8	0
TOTALS	7	122	17.4	57	0

Field Goals	20-29	30-39	40-49	50-59	Total
Mike Nugent	0-0	0-0	1-2	0-0	1-2

Punting	No	Yds	Long	Blkd	Avg
Andy Groom	6	286	63	0	47.7

Punt Returns	No	Yds	Long	Avg	TD
Chris Gamble	1	1	1	1.0	0

Kickoff Returns	No	Yds	Long	Avg	TD
Maurice Hall	1	15	15	15.0	0

Sacks
Kenny Peterson 2.0
Will Smith 1.0
Simon Fraser 1.0

Interceptions
Mike Doss 1
Dustin Fox 1

Miami Hurricanes

Passing (5 Att)	Att	Cmp	Pct.	Yds	TD	Int
Ken Dorsey	43	28	65.1	296	2	2

Rushing	Car	Yds	Avg	Long	TD
Willis McGahee	20	67	-3.3	10	1
Jarrett Payton	8	17	2.1	8	0
Quadtrine Hill	1	0	0.0	0	0
Ken Dorsey	4	-19	-4.8	0	0
TOTALS	33	65	2.0	10	1

Receiving	No	Yds	Avg	Long	TD
Kellen Winslow	11	122	11.1	28	1
Roscoe Parrish	5	70	14.0	26	1
Andre Johnson	4	54	13.5	20	0
Ethenic Sands	3	34	11.3	14	0
Willis McGahee	3	5	1.7	5	0
Quadtrine Hill	1	8	8.0	8	0
Jarrett Payton	1	7	7.0	7	0
Jason Geathers	1	4	4.0	4	0
TOTALS	29	304	10.5	28	2

Field Goals	20-29	30-39	40-49	50-59	Total
Todd Sievers	0-0	0-0	1-1	0-1	1-2

Punting	No	Yds	Long	Blkd	Avg
Freddie Capshaw	3	130	44	0	43.3
Derrick Crudup	1	43	43	0	43.0
TOTALS	4	173	44	0	43.2

Punt Returns	No	Yds	Long	Avg	TD
Roscoe Parrish	2	56	50	28.0	0

Kickoff Returns	No	Yds	Long	Avg	TD
Andre Johnson	1	39	39	39.0	0

Sacks
Jamal Green 1.0

Interceptions
Sean Taylor 2

Other Final Division I-A Polls
USA Today/ESPN Coaches' Poll

Voted on by panel of 61 Division I-A head coaches; winning team receives the Sears Trophy (originally the McDonald's Trophy, 1991-93); first place votes in parentheses with total points (based on 25 for 1st, 24 for 2nd, etc.).

	Pts		Pts		Pts		Pts
1 Ohio St. (61)	1,525	8 Iowa	1,105	15 Penn St.	619	22 TCU	274
2 Miami-FL	1,451	9 Michigan	1,011	16 Auburn	579	23 Florida St.	219
3 Georgia	1,378	10 Washington St.	932	17 Notre Dame	525	24 Florida	145
4 USC	1,362	11 N.C. State	876	18 Pittsburgh	486	25 Virginia	141
5 Oklahoma	1,244	12 Boise St.	808	19 Marshall	333		
6 Kansas St.	1,230	13 Maryland	803	20 West Virginia	297		
7 Texas	1,140	14 Virginia Tech	644	21 Colorado	291		

Other teams receiving votes: 26. Boston College (129 points), 27. Colorado St. (100), 28. Texas Tech (60), 29. South Florida (28), 30. LSU (25), 31. Fresno St. (19), 32. Oklahoma St. (17), 33. Hawaii (8), 34. Minnesota (6), 35. Air Force and Wisconsin (4), 37. Bowling Green, North Texas and Tennessee (2), 40. UCLA (1).

AP Weekly Ratings

The Associated Press Top 25 college football polls on a weekly basis are listed below. The table starts with the preseason and progresses through the season.

	Pre	Sep 1	7	14	21	28	Oct 5	12	19	26	Nov 2	10	16	23	30	Dec 7	Jan 3
Miami-FL	1	1	1	1	1	1	1	1	1	1	2	1	1	1	1	1	2
Oklahoma	2	2	2	2	2	3	2	2	2	2	1	4	4	3	8	8	5
Texas	3	3	3	3	3	2	3	8	7	7	4	4	11	10	9	9	6
Tennessee	4	4	4	4	11	10	16	16	25	-	-	-	-	-	-	-	-
Florida St.	5	5	5	5	4	11	9	12	11	18	17	15	14	23	16	16	21
Florida	6	6	12	10	7	6	14	-	-	-	23	20	19	15	23	22	-
Colorado	7	17	18	-	-	-	-	23	21	13	18	17	16	13	12	14	20
Georgia	8	10	9	8	8	7	6	5	5	5	7	7	6	5	4	4	3
Nebraska	9	9	8	18	20	-	-	-	-	-	-	-	-	-	-	-	-
Ohio St.	10	8	6	6	6	5	5	4	4	6	3	2	2	2	2	2	1
Washington	11	14	14	13	13	12	22	22	-	-	-	-	-	-	-	-	-
Washington St.	12	11	10	16	16	17	12	10	9	8	5	3	3	9	7	7	10
Michigan	13	7	7	14	14	14	13	11	8	15	13	12	12	12	13	12	9
LSU	14	24	25	24	22	21	18	14	10	17	16	14	21	18	-	-	-
Oregon	15	13	13	9	9	8	7	6	14	19	15	23	-	-	-	-	-
Virginia Tech	16	12	11	7	5	4	4	3	3	3	8	13	13	22	18	21	18
Louisville	17	-	-	-	-	-	-	-	-	-	-	-	-	-	-	-	-
Michigan St.	18	15	15	-	-	-	-	-	-	-	-	-	-	-	-	-	-
Marshall	19	16	16	-	-	-	-	-	-	-	-	-	-	-	-	-	24
USC	20	18	17	11	18	18	20	19	15	11	10	8	7	6	5	5	4
Maryland	21	-	-	-	-	-	-	-	-	-	-	19	18	25	21	20	13
South Carolina	22	22	-	-	-	-	-	-	-	-	-	-	-	-	-	-	-
Texas A&M	23	20	21	19	24	23	-	-	-	-	-	-	-	-	-	-	-
Penn St.	24	-	-	15	12	20	15	20	18	20	19	16	15	11	10	10	16
N.C. State	25	21	19	17	17	16	14	13	12	10	14	22	-	21	17	17	12
Colorado St.	-	19	24	-	25	25	-	-	-	24	24	21	20	16	24	23	-
Notre Dame	-	23	20	12	10	9	8	7	6	4	9	9	8	7	11	11	17
Wisconsin	-	25	22	22	21	19	23	-	-	-	-	-	-	-	-	-	-
UCLA	-	-	23	20	-	-	-	-	-	-	-	25	-	-	-	-	-
Iowa St.	-	-	-	21	19	15	11	9	17	22	21	-	-	-	-	-	-
California	-	-	23	-	-	-	-	-	-	-	-	-	-	-	-	-	-
Kansas St.	-	-	-	25	15	13	19	17	20	14	12	11	10	8	6	6	7
Oregon	-	-	-	-	23	-	-	-	-	-	-	-	-	-	-	-	-
Alabama	-	-	-	-	22	-	24	19	12	11	11	10	9	14	14	13	11
Iowa	-	-	-	-	-	24	17	15	13	9	6	6	5	4	3	3	8
Air Force	-	-	-	-	-	-	21	18	22	-	-	-	-	-	-	-	-
Auburn	-	-	-	-	-	-	24	-	-	-	-	24	-	20	20	19	14
Mississippi	-	-	-	-	-	-	25	21	-	-	-	-	-	-	-	-	-
Bowling Green	-	-	-	-	-	-	-	25	24	21	20	-	-	-	-	-	-
Arizona St.	-	-	-	-	-	-	-	-	23	16	8	-	-	-	-	-	-
Minnesota	-	-	-	-	-	-	-	-	25	23	-	-	-	-	-	-	-
Pittsburgh	-	-	-	-	-	-	-	-	-	-	22	18	17	17	17	24	19
TCU	-	-	-	-	-	-	-	-	-	-	25	22	-	-	-	-	23
Boise St.	-	-	-	-	-	-	-	-	-	-	-	-	23	19	19	18	15
Texas Tech	-	-	-	-	-	-	-	-	-	-	24	-	-	-	-	-	-
West Virginia	-	-	-	-	-	-	-	-	-	-	-	-	-	24	15	15	25
Arkansas	-	-	-	-	-	-	-	-	-	-	-	-	-	-	22	25	-
Virginia	-	-	-	-	-	-	-	-	-	-	-	-	-	-	-	-	22

NCAA Division I-A Final Standings

Standings based on conference games only; overall records include postseason games.

Atlantic Coast Conference

	Conference				Overall		
	W	L	PF	PA	W	L	PF	PA
*Florida St.	7	1	275	141	9	5	428	301
*Maryland	6	2	247	161	11	3	451	228
*Virginia	6	2	220	185	9	5	402	348
*N.C. State	5	3	192	127	11	3	460	238
*Clemson	4	4	197	223	7	6	330	349
*Georgia Tech	4	4	148	150	7	6	180	267
Wake Forest	3	5	196	198	7	6	356	327
North Carolina	1	7	113	285	3	9	223	421
Duke	0	8	137	254	2	10	227	353

Bowls (4-3): Florida St. (lost Sugar); Maryland (won Peach); Virginia (won Continental Tire); N.C. State (won Gator); Clemson (lost Tangerine); Georgia Tech (lost Silicon Valley Classic); Wake Forest (won Seattle).

Big East Conference

	Conference				Overall		
	W	L	PF	PA	W	L	PF	PA
*Miami-FL	7	0	297	140	12	1	527	248
*West Virginia	6	1	212	116	9	4	396	302
*Pittsburgh	5	2	185	138	9	4	331	232
*Virginia Tech	3	4	209	202	10	4	429	263
*Boston College	3	4	180	157	9	4	392	253
Temple	2	5	124	208	4	8	242	351
Syracuse	2	5	169	245	4	8	347	406
Rutgers	0	7	79	249	1	11	167	397

Bowls (3-2): Miami-FL (lost Fiesta); West Virginia (lost Continental Tire); Pittsburgh (won Insight); Virginia Tech (won San Francisco); Boston College (won Motor City).

Big Ten Conference

	Conference				Overall		
	W	L	PF	PA	W	L	PF	PA
*Ohio St.	8	0	185	88	14	0	410	183
*Iowa	8	0	302	130	11	2	484	256
*Michigan	6	2	224	162	10	3	361	265
*Penn St.	5	3	286	152	9	4	446	227
*Purdue	4	4	235	182	7	6	386	288
Illinois	4	4	212	206	5	7	346	307
*Minnesota	3	5	198	256	8	5	376	319
*Wisconsin	2	6	202	218	8	6	372	322
Michigan St.	2	6	194	314	4	8	316	398
Indiana	1	7	164	332	3	9	258	445
Northwestern	1	7	170	332	3	9	272	498

Bowls (5-2): Ohio St. (won Fiesta); Iowa (lost Orange); Michigan (won Outback); Penn St. (lost Capital One); Purdue (won Sun); Minnesota (won Music City); Wisconsin (won Alamo).

I-A Independents

	W	L	PF	PA
Notre Dame	10	3	290	217
Connecticut	6	6	373	270
Troy State	4	8	218	252
Navy	2	10	290	436

Big 12 Conference

	Conference				Overall		
North	W	L	PF	PA	W	L	PF	PA
*Colorado	7	1	281	175	9	5	398	325
*Kansas St.	6	2	342	91	11	2	582	154
*Iowa St.	4	4	201	238	7	7	404	396
*Nebraska	3	5	192	215	7	7	383	335
Missouri	2	6	214	268	5	7	360	352
Kansas	0	8	125	380	2	10	248	507

	Conference				Overall		
South	W	L	PF	PA	W	L	PF	PA
*Oklahoma	6	2	305	154	12	2	541	216
*Texas	6	2	235	160	11	2	439	212
*Texas Tech	5	3	298	286	9	5	537	439
*Oklahoma St.	5	3	256	230	8	5	446	356
Texas A&M	3	5	266	245	6	6	345	280
Baylor	1	7	93	366	3	9	202	496

Big 12 championship game: Oklahoma 29, Colorado 7 (Dec. 7, 2002).

Bowls (5-3): Colorado (lost Alamo); Kansas St. (won Holiday); Iowa St. (lost Humanitarian); Nebraska (lost Independence); Oklahoma (won Rose); Texas (won Cotton); Texas Tech (won Tangerine); Oklahoma St. (won Houston).

Conference USA

	Conference				Overall		
	W	L	PF	PA	W	L	PF	PA
*TCU	6	2	263	179	10	2	361	222
*Cincinnati	6	2	259	174	7	7	409	329
*Southern Miss	5	3	161	142	7	6	282	238
*Louisville	5	3	243	200	7	6	371	319
*Tulane	4	4	185	147	8	5	361	282
UAB	4	4	218	232	5	7	268	370
East Carolina	4	4	250	266	4	8	335	399
Houston	3	5	235	293	5	7	320	393
Memphis	2	6	190	223	3	9	303	327
Army	1	7	158	300	1	11	226	491

Bowls (2-3): TCU (won Liberty); Cincinnati (lost New Orleans); Southern Miss (lost Houston); Louisville (lost GMAC); Tulane (won Hawaii).

Mid-American Conference

	Conference				Overall		
East	W	L	PF	PA	W	L	PF	PA
*Marshall	7	1	275	184	11	2	457	315
Central Florida	6	2	271	187	7	5	391	315
Miami-OH	5	3	295	216	7	5	384	325
Ohio	4	4	260	245	4	8	299	374
Akron	3	5	212	209	4	8	325	379
Kent St.	1	7	93	269	3	9	202	424
Buffalo	0	8	134	303	1	11	214	416

	Conference				Overall		
West	W	L	PF	PA	W	L	PF	PA
Northern Illinois	7	1	280	167	8	4	375	298
*Toledo	7	1	303	173	9	5	495	378
Bowling Green	6	2	352	224	9	3	490	304
Ball St.	4	4	218	220	6	6	278	333
Western Michigan	3	5	219	220	4	8	303	330
Central Michigan	2	6	172	272	4	8	267	384
Eastern Michigan	1	7	193	388	3	9	286	566

MAC championship game: Marshall 49, Toledo 45 (Dec. 7, 2002).

Bowls (1-1): Marshall (won GMAC); Toledo (lost Motor City).

Mountain West Conference

	Conference				Overall			
	W	L	PF	PA	W	L	PF	PA
*Colorado State	.6	1	244	149	10	4	418	332
*New Mexico	...5	2	196	155	7	7	341	358
*Air Force	4	3	241	201	8	5	440	303
San Diego St.	...4	3	168	190	4	9	309	411
Utah	3	4	162	177	5	6	249	226
UNLV	3	4	195	217	5	7	292	366
BYU	2	5	113	187	5	7	272	333
Wyoming	1	6	207	250	2	10	288	432

Bowls (0-3): Colorado St. (lost Liberty); New Mexico (lost Las Vegas); Air Force (lost San Francisco).

Pacific 10 Conference

	Conference				Overall			
	W	L	PF	PA	W	L	PF	PA
*Washington St.	.7	1	285	188	10	3	431	296
*USC	7	1	299	163	11	2	456	240
*Arizona St.	5	3	257	244	8	6	452	407
*UCLA	4	4	232	232	8	5	387	326
*Oregon St.	4	4	211	180	8	5	414	267
California	4	4	256	238	7	5	427	318
*Washington	4	4	232	233	7	6	398	342
*Oregon	3	5	237	266	7	6	417	362
Arizona	1	7	143	250	4	8	227	310
Stanford	1	7	128	286	2	9	225	377

Bowls (2-5): Washington St. (lost Rose); USC (won Orange); Arizona St. (lost Holiday); UCLA (won Las Vegas); Oregon St. (lost Insight); Washington (lost Sun); Oregon (lost Seattle).

Southeastern Conference

	Conference				Overall			
Eastern	W	L	PF	PA	W	L	PF	PA
*Georgia	7	1	226	144	13	1	450	212
*Florida	6	2	191	160	8	5	336	279
*Tennessee	5	3	182	147	8	5	296	227
Kentucky	3	5	215	228	7	5	385	301
South Carolina	.3	5	108	156	5	7	225	262
Vanderbilt	0	8	121	260	2	10	221	368

	Conference				Overall			
Western	W	L	PF	PA	W	L	PF	PA
Alabama	6	2	227	99	10	3	377	200
*Arkansas	5	3	223	184	9	5	370	277
*Auburn	5	3	213	150	9	4	388	231
*LSU	5	3	179	160	8	5	323	238
*Mississippi	3	5	175	230	7	6	351	331
Mississippi St.	..0	8	123	265	3	9	227	339

SEC championship game: Georgia 30, Arkansas 3 (Dec. 7, 2002).

Bowls (3-4): Georgia (won Sugar); Florida (lost Outback); Tennessee (lost Peach); Arkansas (lost Music City); Auburn (won Capital One); LSU (lost Cotton); Mississippi (won Independence).

Note: Kentucky and Alabama were ineligible for SEC title.

Sun Belt Conference

	Conference				Overall			
	W	L	PF	PA	W	L	PF	PA
*North Texas	6	0	159	59	8	5	249	192
New Mexico St	.5	1	177	160	7	5	327	328
Arkansas St.	3	3	125	109	6	7	259	361
Middle Tenn. St.	.2	4	158	151	4	8	297	332
LA-Monroe	2	4	140	176	3	9	236	451
LA-Lafayette	2	4	117	178	3	9	203	352
Idaho	1	5	123	166	2	10	285	428

Bowl (1-0): North Texas (won New Orleans).

Western Athletic Conference

	Conference				Overall			
	W	L	PF	PA	W	L	PF	PA
*Boise St.	8	0	409	111	12	1	593	240
*Hawaii	7	1	304	202	10	4	502	389
*Fresno St.	6	2	236	204	9	5	378	379
San Jose St.	4	4	262	271	6	7	376	467
Nevada	4	4	248	259	5	7	331	371
Rice	3	5	216	235	4	7	253	296
La. Tech	3	5	248	277	4	8	320	426
SMU	3	5	164	247	3	9	207	378
UTEP	1	7	147	305	2	10	220	511
Tulsa	1	7	156	279	1	11	233	417

Bowls (2-1): Boise St. (won Humanitarian); Hawaii (lost Hawaii); Fresno St. (won Silicon Valley Classic).

NCAA Division I-A Individual Leaders

Total Offense

		Rushing				Passing		Total Offense			
	Cl	Car	Gain	Loss	Net	Att	Yds	Plays	Yds	YdsPP	YdsPG
Byron Leftwich, Marshall	.......Sr.	37	93	94	-1	491	4268	528	4267	8.08	355.6
Kliff Kingsbury, Texas Tech	.....Sr.	102	221	335	-114	712	5017	814	4903	6.02	350.2
Cody Pickett, Washington	.......Jr.	86	154	339	-185	612	4458	698	4273	6.12	328.7
Timmy Chang, Hawaii	........So.	39	120	137	-17	624	4474	663	4457	6.72	318.4
Ryan Schneider, C. Florida	.....Jr.	37	44	133	-89	430	3770	467	3681	7.88	306.8
Luke McCown, La. Tech	........Jr.	61	220	190	30	505	3539	566	3569	6.31	297.4
Zack Threadgill, Nevada	.....Sr.	62	229	113	116	451	3418	513	3534	6.89	294.5
Carson Palmer, USC	........Sr.	50	105	227	-122	489	3942	539	3820	7.09	293.8
Jose Fuentes, Utah St.	........Sr.	57	112	216	-104	454	3268	511	3164	6.19	287.6
Adam Hall, San Diego St.	.....Jr.	64	128	238	-110	452	3253	516	3143	6.09	285.7

All-Purpose Yards

	Cl	Gm	Rush	Rec	PR	KOR	Total Yds	YdsPG
Larry Johnson, Penn St.	.......Sr.	13	2087	349	0	219	2655	204.23
Michael Turner, N. Illinois	...Jr.	12	1915	100	0	269	2284	190.33
Robbie Micon, C. Michigan	...Sr.	12	1361	253	0	524	2138	178.17
Jason Wright, Northwestern	...Jr.	12	1234	266	0	513	2013	167.75
Brock Forsey, Boise St.	......Sr.	13	1611	282	0	234	2127	163.62
Domanick Davis, LSU	......Sr.	13	931	130	499	560	2120	163.08
Bobby Wade, Arizona	......Sr.	12	4	1389	224	332	1949	162.42
Willis McGahee, Miami-FL	...So.	13	1753	355	0	0	2108	162.15
Charles Pauley, San Jose St.	..Sr.	13	67	804	237	978	2086	160.46
Derek Abney, Kentucky	......Jr.	13	5	569	544	804	1922	160.17

Iowa   Marshall   Nevada   Penn St.

Brad Banks — Passing Efficiency   **Byron Leftwich** — Total Offense   **Nate Burleson** — Receptions   **Larry Johnson** — Rushing

Passing Efficiency
(Minimum 15 attempts per game)

	Cl	Gm	Att	Cmp	Cmp Pct	Int	Int Pct	Yds	Yds/Att	TD	TD Pct	Rating Points
Brad Banks, Iowa	Sr.	13	294	170	57.82	5	1.70	2573	8.75	26	8.84	157.1
Byron Leftwich, Marshall	Sr.	12	491	331	67.41	10	2.04	4268	8.69	30	6.11	156.5
Brian Jones, Toledo	Sr.	14	423	297	70.21	9	2.13	3446	8.15	23	5.44	153.2
Ryan Schneider, C. Florida	Jr.	12	430	265	61.63	16	3.72	3770	8.77	31	7.21	151.6
Carson Palmer, USC	Sr.	13	489	309	63.19	10	2.04	3942	8.06	33	6.75	149.1
Matt Schaub, Virginia	Jr.	14	418	288	68.90	7	1.67	2976	7.12	28	6.70	147.5
Jason Gesser, Washington St.	Sr.	13	402	236	58.71	13	3.23	3408	8.48	28	6.97	146.4
Ken Dorsey, Miami-FL	Sr.	13	393	222	56.49	12	3.05	3369	8.57	28	7.12	145.9
Kliff Kingsbury, Texas Tech	Sr.	14	712	479	67.28	13	1.83	5017	7.05	45	6.32	143.7
Bryan Randall, Virginia Tech	So.	14	248	158	63.71	11	4.44	2134	8.60	12	4.84	143.1
Chris Simms, Texas	Sr.	13	396	235	59.34	12	3.03	3207	8.10	26	6.57	143.0
Scott McBrien, Maryland	Jr.	14	284	162	57.04	10	3.52	2497	8.79	15	5.28	141.3
Philip Rivers, N.C. State	Jr.	14	418	262	62.68	10	2.39	3353	8.02	20	4.78	141.1
Craig Krenzel, Ohio St.	Sr.	14	249	148	59.44	7	2.81	2110	8.47	12	4.82	140.9
Josh Fields, Oklahoma St.	So.	13	408	226	55.39	10	2.45	3145	7.71	31	7.60	140.3

Rushing

	Cl	Car	Yds	TD	YdsPG
Larry Johnson, Penn St.	Sr.	271	2087	20	160.54
Michael Turner, N. Illinois	Jr.	338	1915	19	159.58
Chris Brown, Colorado	Jr.	303	1841	19	153.42
Willis McGahee, Miami-FL	So.	282	1753	28	134.85
Marcus Merriweather, Ball St.	Sr.	332	1618	12	134.83
Quentin Griffin, Oklahoma	Sr.	287	1884	15	134.57
Avon Cobourne, West Va.	Sr.	335	1710	17	131.54
Steven Jackson, Oregon St.	So.	319	1690	15	130.00
Joffrey Reynolds, Houston	Sr.	316	1545	11	128.75
Terry Caulley, Connecticut	Fr.	220	1247	15	124.70
Brock Forsey, Boise St.	Sr.	295	1611	26	123.92
Anthony Davis, Wisconsin	So.	300	1555	13	119.62

Games: All played 13, except Turner, Brown, Merriweather, Reynolds (12), Griffin (14) and Caulley (10).

Field Goals

	Cl	FG/Att	Pct	P/Gm
Nick Browne, TCU	Jr.	23/30	.767	1.92
Billy Bennett, Georgia	Jr.	26/33	.788	1.86
Mike Nugent, Ohio St.	So.	25/28	.893	1.79
Sandro Sciortino, Boston Coll.	Jr.	23/32	.719	1.77
Nick Novak, Maryland	So.	24/28	.857	1.71
Jeff Babcock, Colorado St.	So.	24/32	.750	1.71
John Anderson, Washington	Sr.	22/34	.647	1.69
Drew Dunning, Washington St.	Jr.	22/33	.667	1.69
Mike Barth, Arizona St.	Sr.	23/33	.697	1.64
Asen Asparuhov, Fresno St.	Sr.	23/30	.767	1.64

Games: All played 14, except Browne (12), Sciortino, Anderson and Dunning (13).

Longest FGs of season: 59 yds by Jared Siegel, Oregon vs. UCLA (Nov. 15) and Keith Robinson, UTEP vs. Rice (Oct. 19).

Receptions

	Cl	No	Yds	TD	P/Gm
Nate Burleson, Nevada	Sr.	138	1629	12	11.50
J.R. Tolver, San Diego St.	Sr.	128	1785	13	9.85
Kassim Osgood, San Diego St.	Sr.	108	1552	8	8.31
Rashaun Woods, Oklahoma St.	Jr.	107	1695	17	8.23
Kevin Walter, E. Michigan	Sr.	93	1368	9	7.75
Bobby Wade, Arizona	Sr.	93	1389	4	7.75
Taylor Stubblefield, Purdue	So.	77	789	0	7.70
Reggie Williams, Washington	So.	94	1454	11	7.23
Taurean Henderson, Tex. Tech	Fr.	98	633	6	7.00
Robert Redd, Bowling Green	Sr.	83	973	9	6.92
Justin Gage, Missouri	Sr.	82	1074	9	6.83
Kevin Curtis, Utah St.	Sr.	74	1258	9	6.73
Denero Marriott, Marshall	Sr.	86	993	8	6.62
Mack Vincent, La-Monroe	Jr.	79	1198	7	6.58

Games: All played 12, except Tolver, Osgood, Woods, Williams, Marriott (13), Stubblefield (10), Henderson (14) and Curtis (11).

Interceptions

	Cl	No	Yds	TD	P/Gm
Jim Leonhard, Wisconsin	So.	11	115	0	.79
Jason David, Washington St.	Jr.	7	101	0	.70
Gerald Jones, San Jose St.	Jr.	8	116	1	.67
Jason Goss, TCU	Sr.	8	27	0	.67
Gabe Franklin, Boise St.	So.	8	70	0	.62
Lynaris Elpheage, Tulane	Jr.	8	133	1	.62
Justin Miller, Clemson	Fr.	8	70	0	.62
Randee Drew, Northern Ill.	Jr.	7	103	0	.58
Vince Thompson, Northern Ill.	Sr.	5	4	0	.56

Games: All played 13 except, Leonhard (14), David (10), Jones, Goss, Drew (12) and Thompson (9).

Scoring

Non-Kickers

	Cl	TD	Pts	P/Gm
Brock Forsey, Boise St.	Sr.	32	192	14.77
Willis McGahee, Miami-FL	So.	28	168	12.92
Josh Harris, Bowling Green	Jr.	22	134*	11.17
Larry Johnson, Penn St.	Sr.	23	140*	10.77
Lee Suggs, Virginia Tech	Sr.	24	144	10.29
Art Brown, E. Carolina	Jr.	17	102	10.20
Chance Harridge, Air Force	Jr.	22	132	10.15
Michael Turner, N. Illinois	Jr.	20	120	10.00
Maurice Clarett, Ohio St.	Fr.	18	108	9.82
Terry Caulley, Connecticut	Fr.	16	96	9.60
Chris Brown, Colorado	Jr.	19	114	9.50
Zack Abron, Missouri	Jr.	17	102	9.27

Games: All played 13, except Harris, Turner (12), Suggs (14), Brown (10) and Clarett (11).
*includes one two-point conversion.

Kickers

	FG/Att	PAT/Att	Pts	P/Gm
Nick Calaycay, Boise St.	11/13	63/66	96	9.60
Billy Bennett, Georgia	26/33	52/52	130	9.29
Nate Kaeding, Iowa	21/24	57/58	120	9.23
Nick Novak, Maryland	24/28	53/54	125	8.93
Mark-Christian Jensen, Cal.	19/27	50/51	107	8.92
Nick Browne, TCU	23/30	36/38	105	8.75
Drew Dunning, Wash. St.	22/33	47/49	113	8.69
Mike Nugent, Ohio St.	25/28	45/46	120	8.57
Mike Barth, Arizona St.	23/33	49/49	118	8.43
Jeff Babcock, Colorado St.	24/32	40/44	118*	8.43
Jared Siegel, Oregon	22/24	49/50	109	8.38
John Anderson, Washington	22/34	42/44	108	8.31

Games: All played 13, Calaycay (10), Bennett, Novak, Nugent, Barth, Babcock (14), Jensen and Browne (12).
*includes one touchdown.

Punting

(Minimum of 3.6 per game)

	Cl	No	Yds	Avg
Matt Payne, BYU	So.	51	2427	47.59
Mark Mariscal, Colorado	Sr.	67	3186	47.55
Glenn Pakulak, Kentucky	Sr.	66	3008	45.58
Andy Groom, Ohio St.	Sr.	60	2697	44.95
Donnie Jones, LSU	Jr.	64	2813	43.95
Greg Johnson, Vanderbilt	Sr.	66	2892	43.82
Cody Scates, Texas A&M	Jr.	67	2931	43.75
Dusty Colquitt, Tennessee	So.	65	2833	43.58

Punt Returns

(Minimum of 1.2 per game)

	Cl	No	Yds	TD	Avg
Dan Sheldon, N. Illinois	So.	21	477	3	22.71
Aris Comeaux, Army	Sr.	12	233	2	19.42
Cody Cardwell, SMU	Sr.	27	467	1	17.30
DeJuan Groce, Nebraska	Sr.	43	732	4	17.02
Lynaris Elpheage, Tulane	Jr.	28	463	1	16.54
Dexter Wynn, Colorado St.	Jr.	35	567	1	16.20
DeAngelo Hall, Virginia Tech	So.	22	352	2	16.00
Craig Bragg, UCLA	So.	16	256	1	16.00

Kickoff Returns

(Minimum of 1.2 per game)

	Cl	No	Yds	TD	Avg
Charles Pauley, San Jose St.	Jr.	31	978	2	31.55
Broderick Clark, Louisville	Fr.	31	897	2	28.94
LaShaun Ward, California	Sr.	28	809	1	28.89
Jason Wright, Northwestern	Jr.	18	513	1	28.50
Nathan Jones, Rutgers	Jr.	26	736	2	28.31
LaTarence Dunbar, TCU	Sr.	18	501	1	27.83
Jerome Dennis, Utah St.	So.	14	388	0	27.71
Vontez Duff, Notre Dame	Jr.	19	526	1	27.68
Makonnen Fenton, Temple	Jr.	14	380	1	27.14

NCAA Division I-A Team Leaders

Scoring Offense

	Gm	Record	Pts	Avg
Boise St.	13	12-1	593	45.62
Kansas St.	13	11-2	582	44.77
Bowling Green	12	9-3	490	40.83
Miami-FL	13	12-1	527	40.54
Oklahoma	14	12-2	541	38.64
Texas Tech	14	9-5	541	38.36
Iowa	13	11-2	484	37.23
Hawaii	14	10-4	502	35.86
USC	13	11-2	465	35.77
California	12	7-5	427	35.58

Total Offense

	Gm	Plays	Yds	Avg	TD	YdsPG
Boise St.	13	950	6519	6.86	79	501.46
Hawaii	14	1039	6939	6.68	66	495.64
Marshall	13	991	6439	6.50	59	495.31
Texas Tech	14	1155	6835	5.92	71	488.21
Toledo	14	1033	6611	6.40	66	472.21
Miami-FL	13	887	6056	6.83	70	465.85
Purdue	13	1034	5879	5.69	51	452.23
USC	13	1009	5840	5.79	60	449.23
Bowling Green	12	898	5387	6.00	65	448.92
Illinois	12	915	5356	5.85	43	446.33

Note: Touchdowns scored by rushing and passing only.

Scoring Defense

	Gm	Record	Pts	Avg
Kansas St.	13	11-2	154	11.8
Ohio St.	14	14-0	183	13.1
North Texas	13	8-5	192	14.8
Georgia	14	13-1	212	15.1
Alabama	13	10-3	200	15.4
Oklahoma	14	12-2	216	15.4
Maryland	14	11-3	228	16.3
Texas	13	11-2	212	16.3
Notre Dame	13	10-3	217	16.7
N.C. State	14	11-3	238	17.0

Total Defense

	Gm	Plays	Yds	Avg	TD	YdsPG
TCU	12	799	2883	3.61	27	240.25
Kansas St.	13	864	3237	3.75	19	249.00
Alabama	13	764	3345	4.38	24	257.31
Troy St.	12	784	3322	4.24	31	276.83
Tennessee	13	840	3703	4.41	24	284.85
USC	13	842	3704	4.40	27	284.92
Miami-FL	13	935	3705	3.96	31	285.00
LSU	13	825	3728	4.52	30	286.77
North Texas	13	870	3778	4.34	23	290.62
Oklahoma	14	928	4104	4.42	27	293.14

Note: Opponents' TDs scored by rushing and passing only.

Single Game Highs

INDIVIDUAL

Rushing Yards

Yds	
377	Robbie Mixon, C. Mich. vs. E. Mich. (Nov. 2)
327	Larry Johnson, Penn St. vs. Indiana (Nov.16)
309	Chris Brown, Colorado vs. Kansas (Oct. 12)
301	Anthony Davis, Wisconsin vs. Minnesota (Nov. 23)
300	Joffrey Reynolds, Houston vs. E. Carolina (Nov. 9)

Total Offense

Yds	
508	Andrew Walter, Arizona St. vs. Oregon (Oct. 19)
501	Kliff Kingsbury, Texas Tech vs. Missouri (Oct. 19)

Passing Yards

Yds	
536	Andrew Walter, Arizona St. vs. Oregon (Oct. 19)
525	Ben Roethlisberger, Miami-OH vs. N. Ill. (Oct. 12)
516	Adam Hall, San Diego St. vs. Ariz. St. (Sept. 14)

Passes Completed

No	
49	Kliff Kingsbury, Texas Tech vs. Missouri (Oct. 19)
49	Kliff Kingsbury, Texas Tech vs. Texas A&M (Oct. 5)
42	Eli Manning, Mississippi vs. Arkansas (Oct. 26)

Receptions

No	
19	Nate Burleson, Nevada vs. UTEP (Nov. 9)
18	J.R. Tolver, San Diego St. vs. Hawaii (Dec. 7)

Receiving Yards

Yds	
296	J.R. Tolver, San Diego St. vs. Ariz. St. (Sept. 14)
283	J.R. Tolver, San Diego St. vs. Hawaii (Dec. 7)
279	Ernest Wilford, Virginia Tech vs. Syracuse (Nov. 9)
264	Josh Davis, Marshall vs. Appalachian St. (Aug. 31)
246	Taylor Jacobs, Florida vs. UAB (Aug. 31)

TEAM

Total Offense Yards Gained

Yds	
733	Marshall vs. Buffalo (Oct. 12)
692	Bowling Green vs. Ohio (Oct. 5)

Total Defense Yards Allowed

Yds	
60	Oklahoma vs. Iowa St. (Oct. 19)
61	USC vs. Colorado (Sept. 14)

Annual Awards

Player of the Year

Carson Palmer, USC, QB . . . . .Heisman
Larry Johnson, Penn St., RB . . . . .Camp, Maxwell
Brad Banks, Iowa, QB . . . . .AP

Payton Award (IAA) . . . . .Tony Romo, E. Illinois, QB
Hill Trophy (Div. II) . . . . . . .Curt Anes, Grand Valley St., QB
Melberger Award (Div. III) . . . . . .Dan Pincelli, Hartwick, QB

Position Players of the Year

O'Brien Award (Quarterback) . . . . .Brad Banks, Iowa
Walker Award (Running Back) . . . . .Larry Johnson, Penn St.
Biletnikoff Award (Receiver) . . .Charles Rogers, Michigan St.
Outland Trophy (Interior Lineman) . .Rien Long, Wash. St., OL
Lombardi Award (Lineman) . . . . .Terrell Suggs, Ariz. St., DL
Butkus Award (Linebacker) . . . . . .E.J. Henderson, Maryland
Thorpe Award (Defensive Back) . .Terence Newman, Kan. St.
Nagurski Award (Defensive Player) Terrell Suggs, Ariz. St., DL
Groza Award (Kicker) . . . . .Nate Kaeding, Iowa
Ray Guy Award (Punter) . . . . . . .Mark Mariscal, Colorado
Mackey Award (Tight End) . . . . .Dallas Clark, Iowa

Coach of the Year

Jim Tressel, Ohio St. . . . . .AFCA, Dodd, FWAA
Kirk Ferentz, Iowa . . . . .AP, Camp

Heisman Trophy Vote

Presented since 1935 by the Downtown Athletic Club of New York City and named after former college coach and DAC athletic director John W. Heisman. Voting done by national media and former Heisman winners. Each ballot allows for three names (points based on 3 for 1st, 2 for 2nd and 1 for 3rd).

Top 10 Vote-Getters

	Pos	1st	2nd	3rd	Pts
Carson Palmer, USC	QB	242	224	154	1328
Brad Banks, Iowa	QB	199	173	152	1095
Larry Johnson, Penn St.	RB	108	130	142	726
Willis McGahee, Miami-FL . .	RB	101	118	121	660
Ken Dorsey, Miami-FL	QB	122	89	99	643
Byron Leftwich, Marshall . . .	QB	22	26	34	125
Jason Gesser, Wash. St. . . .	QB	5	22	15	74
Chris Brown, Colorado	RB	5	11	11	48
Kliff Kingsbury, Texas Tech . .	QB	6	2	11	33
Quentin Griffin, Oklahoma . .	RB	1	8	9	28

Consensus All-America Team

NCAA Division I-A players cited most frequently by the following selectors: AFCA, AP, and Walter Camp Foundation. (*) indicates unanimous selection. Maryland's E.J. Henderson was the lone holdover from the 2001 team.

Offense

	Player	Class	Ht	Wt
WR	Charles Rogers*, Michigan St.	Jr..	6-4	205
WR	Nate Burleson, Nevada	Sr.	6-2	187
TE	Dallas Clark*, Iowa	Sr.	6-4	244
C	Brett Romberg*, Miami-FL	Sr.	6-3	290
OL	Eric Steinbach*, Iowa	Sr.	6-7	284
OL	Jordan Gross, Utah	Sr.	6-5	306
OL	Derrick Dockery, Texas	Sr.	6-6	345
OL	Shawn Anders, Arkansas	So.	6-5	345
QB	Ken Dorsey, Miami-FL	Sr.	6-5	200
RB	Larry Johnson*, Penn St.	Sr.	6-2	222
RB	Willis McGahee, Miami-FL	So.	6-1	224
K	Mike Nugent*, Ohio St.	So.	5-10	170

Defense

	Player	Class	Ht	Wt
DL	Tommie Harris*, Oklahoma	So.	6-3	280
DL	Terrell Suggs*, Arizona St.	Jr.	6-3	251
DL	Rien Long, Washington St.	Jr.	6-6	287
DL	Calvin Pace, Wake Forest	Sr.	6-6	260
LB	E.J. Henderson*, Maryland	Sr.	6-2	243
LB	Boss Bailey, Georgia	Sr.	6-3	229
LB	Teddy Lehman, Oklahoma	Jr.	6-3	235
DB	Terence Newman*, Kansas St.	Sr.	5-11	185
DB	Mike Doss, Ohio St.	Sr.	5-11	204
DB	Shane Walton*, Notre Dame	Sr.	5-11	185
DB	Troy Polamalu, USC	Sr.	5-10	215
P	Mark Mariscal*, Colorado	Sr.	6-2	200

Underclassmen who declared for the 2003 draft

Forty-five players forfeited the remainder of their college eligibility and declared for the NFL draft in 2003. NFL teams drafted 31 underclassmen. Players listed in alphabetical order; first round selections in **bold** type.

	Pos	Drafted by	Overall Pick
Santonio Beard, Alabama	RB	Not Drafted	—
Anquan Boldin, Florida	WR	Arizona	54
Chris Brown, Colorado	RB	Tennessee	93
Peter Christofilakos, Illinois	K	Not Drafted	—
Dallas Clark, Iowa	TE	Indianapolis	24
Chris Clemons, Georgia	LB	Not Drafted	—
J.P. Comella, Boston College	FB	Not Drafted	—
Brennan Curtin, Notre Dame	OT	Green Bay	212
Reggie Duncan, Kansas	RB	Not Drafted	—
Dante Ellington, Alabama	OT	Not Drafted	—
Lynaris Elpheage, Tulane	DB	Not Drafted	—
Bret Engemann, BYU	QB	Not Drafted	—
Jeff Faine, Notre Dame	C	Cleveland	21
Brandon George, Temple	C	Not Drafted	—
Rex Grossman, Florida	QB	Chicgao	22
Ken Hamlin, Arkansas	DB	Seattle	42
Kwame Harris, Stanford	OT	San Francisco	26
Wayne Hunter, Hawaii	OT	Seattle	73
Andre Johnson, Miami-FL	WR	Houston	3
Robert Johnson, Auburn	TE	Not Drafted	—
Teyo Johnson, Stanford	WR	Oakland	63
Derek Jones, West Va.	QB/WR	Not Drafted	—
Reshard Lee, Mid. Tennessee	RB	Not Drafted	—

	Pos	Drafted by	Overall Pick
Brandon Lloyd, Illinois	WR	San Francisco	124
Rien Long, Washington St.	DT	Tennessee	126
James Lynch, Maryland	FB	Not Drafted	—
Shaun McDonald, Ariz. St.	WR	St. Louis	106
Willis McGahee, Miami-FL	RB	Buffalo	23
Clint Mitchell, Florida	DE	Denver	227
Shantee Orr, Michigan	DE	Not Drafted	—
Terry Pierce, Kansas St.	LB	Denver	51
Shurron Pierson, South Florida	DE	Oakland	129
Dewayne Robertson, Ky.	DT	NY Jets	4
Charles Rogers, Mich. St.	WR	Detroit	2
Ian Scott, Florida	DT	Chicago	116
Musa Smith, Georgia	RB	Baltimore	77
Onterrio Smith, Oregon	RB	Minnesota	105
Terrell Suggs, Arizona St.	DE	Baltimore	10
Johnathan Sullivan, Ga.	DT	New Orleans	6
LaBrandon Toefield, LSU	RB	Jacksonville	132
Kelley Washington, Tennessee	WR	Cincinnati	65
Dewayne White, Louisville	DE	Tampa Bay	64
Jimmy Wilkerson, Oklahoma	DE	Kansas City	189
Jason Witten, Tennessee	TE	Dallas	69
George Wrighster, Oregon	TE	Jacksonville	104

NCAA Division I-AA Final Standings

Standings based on conference games only; overall records include postseason games.

Atlantic 10 Conference

	Conference W	L	PF	PA	Overall W	L	PF	PA
*Northeastern	7	2	283	165	10	3	403	208
*Maine	7	2	195	150	11	3	343	216
*Villanova	6	3	277	169	11	4	448	278
Massachusetts	6	3	209	178	8	4	327	250
William & Mary	5	4	247	228	6	5	326	284
Delaware	5	4	218	174	6	6	291	227
Hofstra	4	5	211	218	6	6	270	255
Richmond	4	5	185	151	6	6	199	202
James Madison	3	6	152	228	5	7	196	272
New Hampshire	2	7	163	285	3	8	199	345
Rhode Island	1	8	104	298	3	9	187	389

Playoffs (3-3): Northeastern (0-1), Maine (1-1), Villanova (2-1).

Big Sky Conference

	Conference W	L	PF	PA	Overall W	L	PF	PA
*Montana	5	2	173	125	11	3	441	260
Idaho St.	5	2	184	112	8	3	331	188
*Montana St.	5	2	169	125	7	6	298	282
Eastern Wash.	3	4	209	198	6	5	365	276
Northern Arizona	3	4	154	197	6	5	252	284
Portland St.	3	4	166	161	6	5	236	245
Sacramento St.	3	4	211	228	5	7	325	380
Weber St.	1	6	116	236	3	8	266	309

Playoffs (1-2): Montana (1-1), Montana St. (0-1).

Big South Conference

	Conference W	L	PF	PA	Overall W	L	PF	PA
Gardner-Webb	3	0	126	63	9	1	288	204
Elon	2	1	104	86	4	7	230	301
Liberty	1	2	87	104	2	9	227	332
Charleston So.	0	3	45	109	4	8	192	324

Playoffs: No teams invited.

Gateway Athletic Conference

	Conference W	L	PF	PA	Overall W	L	PF	PA
*Western Ill.	6	1	222	127	11	2	470	241
*Western Ky.	6	1	156	63	12	3	432	246
Youngstown St.	3	114	113	7	4	215	201
Illinois St.	4	3	150	121	6	5	249	250
Indiana St.	3	4	121	180	5	7	226	318
Northern Iowa	2	5	123	191	5	6	227	286
Southern Ill.	2	5	177	228	4	8	414	360
SW Missouri St.	1	6	149	189	4	7	255	294

Playoffs (5-1): Western Ill. (1-1), Western Ky. (4-0).

Ivy League

	Conference W	L	PF	PA	Overall W	L	PF	PA
Pennsylvania	7	0	284	73	9	1	363	132
Harvard	6	1	190	154	7	3	267	230
Princeton	4	3	154	176	6	4	226	236
Yale	4	3	173	141	6	4	257	188
Cornell	3	4	119	205	4	6	216	281
Dartmouth	2	5	151	200	3	7	247	295
Brown	2	5	135	160	2	8	223	279
Columbia	0	7	115	223	1	9	161	295

Playoffs: League does not play postseason games.

Metro Atlantic Athletic Conference

	Conference W	L	PF	PA	Overall W	L	PF	PA
Duquesne	8	0	304	27	11	1	397	115
Fairfield	5	3	181	170	5	6	210	266
St. Peter's	5	3	207	118	6	5	234	207
Marist	5	3	196	163	7	4	282	230
Iona	4	4	130	160	5	6	156	243
Siena	3	5	109	148	3	7	112	194
St. John's	2	6	167	258	2	8	184	308
Canisius	2	6	86	201	2	9	113	329
La Salle	2	6	162	297	2	9	200	388

Playoffs: No teams invited.

NCAA Division I-AA Final Standings (Cont.)

Mid-Eastern Athletic Conference

	Conference				Overall		
	W	L	PF	PA	W	L	PF	PA
*Bethune-Cookman	7	1	263	133	11	2	407	200
Florida A&M	5	3	196	202	7	5	321	319
Hampton	5	3	276	167	7	5	405	250
Morgan St.	5	3	235	207	7	5	364	345
S. Carolina St.	4	4	187	166	7	5	321	212
Howard	4	4	148	198	6	5	243	286
Norfolk St.	2	6	111	240	5	6	209	286
N. Carolina A&T	2	6	155	159	4	8	281	271
Delaware St.	2	6	134	233	4	8	218	313

*Playoffs (0-1): Bethune-Cookman (0-1).

Northeast Conference

	Conference				Overall		
	W	L	PF	PA	W	L	PF	PA
Albany	6	1	214	102	8	4	357	245
Stony Brook	5	2	142	102	8	2	232	118
Sacred Heart	5	2	152	85	7	3	241	129
Wagner	4	3	98	89	7	4	232	134
Central Conn.	3	4	87	112	5	6	139	251
Robert Morris	2	5	56	142	3	7	128	227
Monmouth (N.J.)	2	5	66	92	2	8	115	177
St. Francis (Pa.)	1	6	59	150	2	8	101	229

Playoffs: No teams invited.

Ohio Valley Conference

	Conference				Overall		
	W	L	PF	PA	W	L	PF	PA
*Eastern Ill.	5	1	248	207	8	4	424	414
*Murray St.	5	1	206	141	7	5	382	351
SE Missouri St.	4	2	228	193	8	4	416	353
Eastern Ky.	4	2	198	90	8	4	383	220
Tennessee Tech	2	4	160	142	5	7	328	333
Tennessee St.	1	5	160	227	2	10	308	403
Tenn.-Martin	0	6	99	299	2	10	186	459

*Playoffs (0-2): Eastern Illinois (0-1), Murray St. (0-1).

Patriot League

	Conference				Overall		
	W	L	PF	PA	W	L	PF	PA
*Fordham	6	1	250	141	10	3	418	225
Colgate	6	1	177	138	9	3	301	216
Lafayette	5	2	183	111	7	5	303	270
Lehigh	4	3	180	100	8	4	319	216
Towson	3	4	129	136	6	5	285	245
Georgetown	2	5	118	277	5	6	190	345
Holy Cross	2	5	161	201	4	8	293	344
Bucknell	0	7	86	177	2	9	163	254

*Playoffs (1-1): Fordham (1-1).

Pioneer Football League

North	Conference				Overall		
	W	L	PF	PA	W	L	PF	PA
Dayton	4	0	155	27	11	1	423	118
San Diego	3	1	162	126	5	5	297	309
Butler	2	2	126	142	4	6	294	374
Drake	1	3	149	169	5	6	355	435
Valparaiso	0	4	87	215	1	10	268	498

South	Conference				Overall		
	W	L	PF	PA	W	L	PF	PA
Morehead St.	3	0	132	46	9	3	347	218
Davidson	2	1	84	77	7	3	320	227
Austin Peay	1	2	73	110	7	5	287	333
Jacksonville	0	3	40	96	3	7	185	314

PFL Championship Game: Dayton 28, Morehead St. 0
Playoffs: No teams invited.

Southern Conference

	Conference				Overall		
	W	L	PF	PA	W	L	PF	PA
*Ga. Southern	7	1	284	127	11	3	493	190
Wofford	6	2	201	145	9	3	298	197
*Furman	6	2	235	147	8	4	365	255
*Appalachian St.	6	2	219	159	8	4	314	273
VMI	3	5	177	299	6	6	314	415
W. Carolina	3	5	209	232	5	6	279	294
E. Tenn St.	2	6	106	214	4	8	167	286
Tenn.-Chattanooga	2	6	175	241	2	10	232	377
The Citadel	1	7	188	230	3	9	305	338

*Playoffs (2-3): Ga. Southern (2-1), Furman (0-1), Appalachian St. (0-1).

Southland Conference

	Conference				Overall		
	W	L	PF	PA	W	L	PF	PA
*McNeese St.	6	0	224	74	13	2	477	273
*Northwestern St.	4	2	154	132	9	4	359	283
Nicholls St.	3	3	121	114	7	4	289	195
Stephen F. Austin	3	3	138	157	6	5	322	245
Jacksonville St.	2	4	121	137	5	5	226	257
Sam Houston St.	2	4	89	168	4	7	197	313
SW Texas St.	1	5	117	182	4	7	211	290

*Playoffs (3-2): McNeese St. (3-1), Northwestern St. (0-1).

Southwestern Athletic Conference

Eastern	Conference				Overall		
	W	L	PF	PA	W	L	PF	PA
Alabama A&M	6	2	191	141	8	4	261	217
Jackson St.	5	2	214	142	7	4	330	267
Alcorn St.	3	4	124	137	6	5	280	283
Miss. Valley St.	3	4	124	137	5	6	241	260
Alabama St.	2	5	181	202	6	6	337	276

Western	Conference				Overall		
	W	L	PF	PA	W	L	PF	PA
Grambling St.	7	1	313	210	11	2	506	355
Southern	5	2	179	165	6	6	279	296
Texas Southern	3	4	219	188	4	7	314	277
Ark.-Pine Bluff	2	5	167	209	3	8	284	368
Prairie View A&M	0	7	81	272	1	10	123	413

SWAC Championship Game: Grambling St. 31, Alabama A&M 19.
Playoffs: No teams invited.

NCAA I-AA Independents

	W	L	PF	PA
St. Mary's (Ca.)	6	6	318	267
Florida International	5	6	241	228
Samford	4	7	285	385
Cal Poly-SLO	3	8	247	302
Florida Atlantic	2	9	176	339
Savannah St.	1	9	106	341
Southern Utah	1	10	202	427
Morris Brown	1	11	225	431

Playoffs: No teams invited.

San Diego
Eric Rasmussen
Passing Efficiency

Austin Peay
Jay Bailey
Rushing

Morgan St.
T.J. Stallings
Scoring

Brown
Chas Gessner
Receptions

NCAA Division I-AA Leaders
INDIVIDUAL
Passing Efficiency
(Minimum 15 attempts per game)

	Cl	Gm	Att	Cmp	Cmp Pct	Int	Int Pct	Yds	Yds/ Att	TD	TD Pct	Rating Points
Eric Rasmussen, San Diego	Jr.	10	279	170	60.93	1	0.36	2473	8.86	25	8.96	164.2
Billy Napier, Furman	Sr.	12	276	189	68.48	8	2.90	2475	8.97	16	5.80	157.1
Ira Vandever, Drake	Sr.	11	361	205	56.79	11	3.05	3239	8.97	32	8.86	155.3
Russ Michna, Western Ill.	Jr.	13	330	189	57.27	5	1.52	3037	9.20	23	6.97	154.5
Jack Tomco, SE Missouri St. . . .	Jr.	12	372	242	65.05	16	4.30	3132	8.42	29	7.80	152.9
David Paulus, Georgetown	Sr.	11	182	107	58.79	4	2.20	1438	7.90	17	9.34	151.6
Robert Kent, Jackson St.	Jr.	11	395	232	58.73	12	3.04	3386	8.57	31	7.85	150.6
Tony Romo, Eastern Ill.	Sr.	12	407	258	63.39	16	3.93	3165	7.78	34	8.35	148.4
Josh Blankenship, Eastern Wash.	Sr.	11	418	250	59.81	7	1.67	3243	7.76	30	7.18	145.3
David Splithoff, Princeton	Jr.	8	142	85	59.86	4	2.82	1223	8.61	8	5.63	145.2
Ryan Fitzpatrick, Harvard	So.	10	150	94	62.67	0	0.00	1155	7.70	8	5.33	144.9
Brett Gordon, Villanova	Sr.	15	578	385	66.61	14	2.42	4305	7.45	36	6.23	144.9

Total Offense

	Cl	Rush	Pass	Yds	YdsPG
Bruce Eugene, Grambling . .	So.	535	4483	5018	386.0
Ira Vandever, Drake	Sr.	415	3239	3654	332.2
Brian Mann, Dartmouth	Sr.	393	2913	3306	330.6
Robert Kent, Jackson St. . . .	Jr.	179	3386	3565	324.1
David Macchi, Valparaiso . .	Jr.	223	3326	3549	322.6
David Caudill, Morehead St. .	Sr.	533	2979	3512	292.7
Josh Blankenship, E. Wash. .	Sr.	-96	3243	3147	286.1
Brett Gordon, Villanova	Sr.	-150	4305	4155	277.0
Doug Baughman, Idaho St. . .	Sr.	72	2936	3008	273.5
Mike Mitchell, Pennsylvania .	Sr.	-74	2803	2729	272.9
Tony Romo, Eastern Ill.	Sr.	-16	3165	3149	262.4
Kyle Slager, Brown	Jr.	-27	2609	2582	258.2

Games: All played 11, except Eugene (13), Mann, Mitchell, Slager (10), Caudill, Romo (12) and Gordon (15).

Rushing

	Cl	Car	Yds	TD	YdsPG
Jay Bailey, Austin Peay	Sr.	319	1687	18	140.58
J.R. Taylor, Eastern Ill.	Sr.	254	1522	18	126.83
Gary Jones, Albany	Jr.	231	1509	22	125.75
Veronde Barnes, Liberty	So.	221	1304	5	118.55
P.J. Mays, Youngstown St. . . .	Sr.	255	1284	11	116.73
Ryan Fuqua, Portland St.	So.	305	1283	10	116.64
Derek Clayton, St. Peter's . . .	Jr.	233	1277	9	116.09
Joe McCourt, Lafayette	So.	314	1393	13	116.08
Kirwin Watson, Fordham	Jr.	285	1467	18	112.85
Jermaine Pugh, Lehigh	Jr.	263	1339	11	111.58
Mike Hilliard, Duquesne	Jr.	303	1310	14	109.17
Christopher Price, Marist	Sr.	230	1196	9	108.73

Games: All played 12, except Barnes, Mays, Fuqua, Clayton, Price (11) and Watson (13).

Receptions

	Cl	No	Yds	TD	P/Gm
Chas Gessner, Brown	Sr.	114	1166	11	11.40
Carl Morris, Harvard	Sr.	90	1288	8	9.00
Rob Milanese, Pennsylvania . .	Sr.	85	1112	8	8.50
Aryvia Holmes, Samford	Sr.	84	1158	9	8.40
Jay Barnard, Dartmouth	Jr.	83	899	8	8.30
Tramon Douglas, Grambling . .	Jr.	92	1704	18	7.67
Willie Ponder, SE Missouri St. .	Sr.	87	1453	15	7.25
Casey Cramer, Dartmouth . . .	Jr.	72	1017	7	7.20
Keith Ferguson, Cornell	Sr.	69	844	2	6.90
Chisom Opara, Princeton	Sr.	57	772	3	6.33
Aaron Overton, Drake	Sr.	68	1180	12	6.18
Tim Manning, Jackson St.	Jr.	66	1077	7	6.00
Korea McKay, Ark.-Pine Bluff .	Jr.	66	1009	7	6.00
Jon Turner, Jacksonville	Sr.	60	890	6	6.00
Jeremy Conley, Duquesne . . .	Sr.	72	1216	14	6.00

Games: All played 10, except Douglas, Ponder, Conley (12), Opara (9), Overton, Manning and McKay (11).

Interceptions

	Cl	No	Yds	TD	Int/Gm
Rashean Mathis, Bet-Cookman	Sr.	14	455	3	1.08
Mark Kasmer, Dayton	Sr.	11	157	2	0.92
Antwan Hill, Alabama St.	So.	10	199	1	0.83
Corey Oaks, Robert Morris . . .	Sr.	7	130	2	0.70
Chris Blackshear, C. Conn. St.	So.	7	204	1	0.70
Chad King, Stony Brook	Jr.	7	109	1	0.70
Mike Devore, St. John's	Jr.	7	45	0	0.70
Ricky Brown, Florida A&M . . .	Sr.	8	38	0	0.67

Games: All played 10, except Mathis (13), Kasmer, Hill and Brown (12).

NCAA Division I-AA Leaders (Cont.)

Scoring

(ranked by points per game)

Non-Kickers

	Cl	TD	XPt	Pts	P/Gm
T. J. Stallings, Morgan St.	.Sr.	23	6	144	12.00
Dale Jennings, Butler	.Sr.	20	0	120	12.00
Chaz Williams, Ga. Southern	.So.	27	0	162	11.57
Gary Jones, Albany	.Jr.	23	0	138	11.50
J.R. Taylor, Eastern Ill.	.Sr.	18	4	112	9.33
Tramon Douglas, Grambling	.Jr.	18	0	108	9.00
Jay Bailey, Austin Peay	.Sr.	18	0	108	9.00
Kirwin Watson, Fordham	.Jr.	19	0	114	8.77
Billy Blanchard, Murray St.	.Sr.	16	0	96	8.73
Lee Davis, SW Texas St.	.Sr.	14	0	84	8.40

Games: All played 12, except Jennings, Davis (10), Williams (14), and Watson (13).

Kickers

	Cl	FG/Att	PAT/Att	Pts
Justin Langan, Western Ill.	.So.	20/27	56/58	116
Mac Hoambrecker, N. Iowa	.Sr.	25/28	18/19	93
Jesse Obert, Dayton	.Sr.	17/23	48/50	99
Peter Veldman, Pennsylvania	.Jr.	12/15	43/43	79
Chris Snyder, Montana	.Jr.	19/32	50/50	107
Matt Fordyce, Fordham	.Sr.	18/26	44/51	98
Greg Kuehn, Wm. & Mary	.So.	14/21	36/39	78

Games: All played 13, except Hoambrecker, Kuehn (11), Obert (12), Veldman (10) and Snyder (14).

Field Goals

	Cl	FG/Att	Pct	P/Gm
Mac Hoambrecker, N. Iowa	.Sr.	25/28	.893	2.27
Justin Langan, Western Ill.	.So.	20/27	.741	1.54
Jesse Obert, Dayton	.Sr.	17/23	.739	1.42
Matt Fordyce, Fordham	.Sr.	18/26	.692	1.38
Chris Snyder, Montana	.Jr.	19/32	.594	1.36
Martin Brecht, Lafayette	.Sr.	16/26	.615	1.33
Stephen Carroll, Illinois St.	.So.	13/19	.684	1.30

Games: All played 12, except Hoambrecker (11), Langan, Fordyce (13), Snyder (14) and Carroll (10).
Longest FG of season: 59 yds by Mac Hoambrecker, N. Iowa vs. SW Missouri St. (Nov. 16)

Punt/Kickoff Leaders

Punting	Cl	No	Yds	Avg
Mark Gould, Northern Ariz.	.Jr.	62	2987	48.18
Mike Scifres, Western Ill.	.Sr.	53	2545	48.02
Brent Barth, VMI	.Sr.	64	3032	47.38

Punt Returns	Cl	No	Yds	TD	Avg
Zuriel Smith, Hampton	.Sr.	27	500	1	18.52
Toby Ziegler, Northwestern St.	.Fr.	24	392	1	16.33
Aryvia Holmes, Samford	.Sr.	16	250	0	15.63

Kickoff Returns	Cl	No	Yds	TD	Avg
Corey Alexander, TX-Southern	.So.	19	615	1	32.37
Cortland Finnegan, Samford	.Fr.	23	741	2	32.22
William Sherman, Morgan St.	.Sr.	15	452	0	30.13

TEAM

Scoring Offense

	Gm	Record	Pts	Avg
Grambling	13	11-2	506	38.92
Pennsylvania	10	9-1	363	36.30
Western Illinois	13	11-2	470	36.15
Eastern Illinois	12	8-4	424	35.33
Dayton	12	11-1	423	35.25
Ga. Southern	14	11-3	493	35.21
SE Missouri St.	12	8-4	416	34.67
Southern Illinois	12	4-8	414	34.50
Hampton	12	7-5	405	33.75
Eastern Washington	11	6-5	365	33.18
Duquesne	12	11-1	397	33.08
Drake	10	5-5	355	35.50
Fordham	13	10-3	418	32.15
Davidson	10	7-3	320	32.00
Eastern Ky.	12	8-4	383	31.92
McNeese St.	15	13-2	478	31.87

Scoring Defense

	Gm	Record	Pts	Avg
Duquesne	12	11-1	115	9.6
Dayton	12	11-1	118	9.8
Stony Brook	10	8-2	118	11.8
Wagner	11	7-4	134	12.2
Sacred Heart	10	7-3	129	12.9
Pennsylvania	10	9-1	132	13.2
Ga. Southern	14	11-3	190	13.6
Bethune-Cookman	13	11-2	200	15.4
Maine	14	11-3	216	15.4
Northeastern	13	10-3	208	16.0
Western Ky.	15	12-3	246	16.4
Wofford	12	9-3	197	16.4
Idaho St.	11	8-3	188	17.1
Fordham	13	10-3	225	17.3
South Carolina St.	12	7-5	212	17.7
Monmouth	10	2-8	177	17.7

Total Offense

	Record	Plays	Yds	Avg
Jackson St.	7-4	869	5340	485.45
Grambling	11-2	969	6217	478.23
Ga. Southern	11-3	981	6575	469.64
Drake	5-5	764	5070	460.91
Eastern Illinois	8-4	888	5431	452.58
Eastern Washington	6-5	766	4923	447.55
SE Missouri St.	8-4	886	5368	447.33
Harvard	7-3	758	4267	426.70
Morehead St.	9-3	889	5108	425.67
Dartmouth	3-7	767	4166	416.60
Gardner-Webb	9-1	739	4149	414.90
Furman	8-4	842	4966	413.83
Idaho St.	8-3	789	4534	412.18
Villanova	11-4	1116	6146	409.73
Pennsylvania	9-1	749	4084	408.40
Cal St. Sacramento	5-7	904	4893	407.75

Total Defense

	Record	Plays	Yds	Avg
Duquesne	11-1	724	2256	188.00
Wagner	7-4	628	2192	199.27
Sacred Heart	7-3	678	2063	206.30
Marist	7-4	671	2731	248.27
St. Francis (Pa.)	2-8	623	2508	250.80
Stony Brook	8-2	693	2570	257.00
Robert Morris	3-7	619	2616	261.60
Siena	3-7	636	2645	264.50
Maine	11-3	908	3747	267.64
Iona	5-6	726	2947	267.91
Wofford	9-3	752	3245	270.42
Pennsylvania	9-1	689	2756	275.60
Bethune-Cookman	11-2	829	3584	275.69
Morehead St.	9-3	758	3311	275.92
Northwestern St.	9-4	817	3596	276.62
Monmouth	2-8	655	2769	276.90

NCAA Playoffs

Division I-AA

First Round (Nov. 30)
at McNeese St. 21 . . . . .Montana St. 14
at Montana 45 . . . . .Northwestern St. 14
at Villanova 45 . . . . .Furman 38
Fordham 29 . . . . .at Northeastern 24
at Ga. Southern 34 . . . . .Bethune-Cookman 0
Maine 14 . . . . .at Appalachian St. 13
at Western Ky. 59 . . . . .Murray St. 20
at Western Ill. 48 . . . . .Eastern Ill. 9

Quarterfinals (Dec. 7)
at McNeese St. 24 . . . . .Montana 20
at Villanova 24 . . . . .Fordham 10
at Ga. Southern 31 . . . . .Maine 7
Western Ky. 31 . . . . .at Western Ill. 28

Semifinals (Dec. 14)
at McNeese St. 39 . . . . .Villanova 28
Western Ky. 31 . . . . .at Ga. Southern 28

Championship Game
Dec. 20 at Chattanooga, Tenn. (Att: 12,360)

Western Ky. 34 . . . . .McNeese St. 14
(12-3)   (13-2)

Division II

First Round (Nov. 23)
at Valdosta St. 24 . . . . .Catawba 7
at Carson-Newman 40 . . . . .Fayetteville St. 27
UC-Davis 24 . . . . .at Central Washington 6
Texas A&M-Kingsville 58 . . . . . . .at Nebraska-Kearney 40
at Grand Valley St. 62 . . . . .C.W. Post 13
at Indiana (Pa.) 27 . . . . .Saginaw Valley 23
at Northwest Missouri St. 45 . . . . . .Minnesota Duluth 41
at Northern Colorado 49 . . . . . . .Central Missouri St. 28

Quarterfinals (Nov. 30)
at Valdosta St. 31 . . . . .Carson-Newman 28
at Tex. A&M-Kingsville 27 . . .OT . . . . .UC-Davis 20
at Grand Valley St. 62 . . . . .Indiana 21
Northern Colorado 23 . . . . . .at Northwest Missouri St. 12

Semifinals (Dec. 7)
at Valdosta St. 21 . . . . .Tex. A&M-Kingsville 12
at Grand Valley St. 44 . . . . .Northern Colorado 7

Championship Game
Dec. 14 at Florence, Ala. (Att: 9,738)

Grand Valley St. 31 . . . . .Valdosta St. 24
(13-0)   (13-1)

Division I-AA, II and III Awards

AFCA Coaches of the Year
NCAA Div. I-AA . . . . Jack Harbaugh, Western Ky.
College Div. II/NAIA . . . .Brian Kelly, Grand Valley St.
NCAA Div. III . . . . .Larry Kehres, Mt. Union

Players of the Year
NCAA I-AA . . . . .Tony Romo, Eastern Ill., QB
NCAA II . . . . .Curt Anes, Grand Valley St., QB
NCAA III . . . . .Dan Pincelli, Hartwick, QB
NAIA . . . . .Nick Kortan, Sioux Falls (S.D.), RB

Division III

First Round (Nov. 23)
Wheaton (Ill.) 42 . . . . .at Alma 14
Wittenberg 34 . . . . .at Hanover 33
at Wabash 42 . . . . .MacMurray 7
at Brockport St. 16 . . . . .Springfield 0
John Carroll 27 . . . . .at Hobart 7
at Muhlenberg 56 . . . . .UMass-Dartmouth 6
at Wartburg 45 . . . . .Lake Forest 0
at Coe 21 . . . . .Wisconsin-La Crosse 18
at St. John's (Minn.) 31 . . . . .Redlands 24
at King's (Pa.) 28 . . . . .Salisbury 0
at Washington & Jefferson 24 . . .Christopher Newport 10
at Trinity (Texas) 48 . . . . . . .Mary Hardin-Baylor 38

Second Round (Nov. 30)
at Mount Union 42 . . . . .Wheaton (Ill.) 21
at Wabash 25 . . . . .Wittenberg 14
Brockport St. 15 . . . . .Rowan 12
John Carroll 21 . . . . .at Muhlenberg 10
at Linfield 52 . . . . .Wartburg 15
at St. John's 45 .Coe 14
at Bridgewater (Va.) 19 . . . . .King's (Pa.) 17
at Trinity 45 . . . . .Washington & Jefferson 10

Quarterfinals (Dec. 7)
at Mount Union 45 . . . . .Wabash 16
John Carroll 16 . . . . .OT . . . . .at Brockport St. 10
St. John's 21 . . . . .at Linfield 14
Trinity 38 . . . . .at Bridgewater 17

Semifinals (Dec. 14)
at Mount Union 57 . . . . .John Carroll 19
at Trinity 41 .St. John's 34

Amos Alonzo Stagg Bowl
Dec. 21 at Salem, Va. (Att: 4,389)

Mount Union 48 . . . . .Trinity 7
(15-0)   (14-1)

NAIA Playoffs

Division I

First Round (Nov. 23)
at Sioux Falls (S.D.) 45 . . . . .Kansas Wesleyan 7
at Mary (N.D.) 21 . . . . .Minot St. (N.D.) 18
at NW Oklahoma St. 22 . . . . .Benedictine (Kan.) 7
at Georgetown (Ky.) 35 . . . . .St. Ambrose (Iowa) 14
at St. Francis (Ind.) 34 . . . . .St. Xavier (Ill.) 30
at McKendree (Ill.) 21 . . .MidAmerica Nazarene (Kan.) 13
at Carroll (Mont.) 42 . . . . .Dickinson St. (N.D.) 23
at Southern Oregon 30 . . . . .Montana-Western 12

Quarterfinals (Nov. 30)
at Georgetown 24 . . . . .St. Francis 0
Sioux Falls 13 . . . . .at Mary 10
McKendree 32 . . . . .at NW Oklahoma St. 27
at Carroll 24 . . . . .Southern Oregon 31

Semifinals (Dec. 7)
at Georgetown 35 . . . . .McKendree 19
at Carroll 20 . . . . .Sioux Falls 17

Championship
Dec. 21 at Savannah, Tenn. (Att: 5,878)

Carroll 28 . . . . .Georgetown 7
(12-2)   (12-2)

1869-2003
Through the Years

SPORTS ALMANAC

National Champions

Over the last 132 years, there have been 25 major selectors of national champions by way of polls (11), mathematical rating systems (10) and historical research (4). The best-known and most widely circulated of these surveys, the Associated Press poll of sportswriters and broadcasters, first appeared during the 1936 season. Champions prior to 1936 have been determined by retro polls, ratings and historical research.

The Early Years (1869-1935)

National champions based on the Dickinson mathematical system (DS) and three historical retro polls taken by the College Football Researchers Association (CFRA), the National Championship Foundation (NCF) and the Helms Athletic Foundation (HF). The CFRA and NCF polls start in 1869, college football's inaugural year, while the Helms poll begins in 1883, the first season the game adopted a point system for scoring. Frank Dickinson, an economics professor at Illinois, introduced his system in 1926 and retro-picked winners in 1924 and '25. Bowl game results were counted in the Helms selections, but not in the other three.

Multiple champions: Yale (18); Princeton (17); Harvard (9); Michigan (7); Notre Dame and Penn (4); Alabama, California, Cornell, Illinois, Pittsburgh and USC (3); Georgia Tech, Minnesota and Penn St. (2).

Year		Record	Year		Record	Year		Record
1869	Princeton	1-1-0	1880	Yale (CFRA)	4-0-1	1891	Yale	13-0-0
1870	Princeton	1-0-0		& Princeton (NCF)	4-0-1	1892	Yale	13-0-0
1871	No games played		1881	Yale	5-0-1	1893	Princeton	11-0-0
1872	Princeton	1-0-0	1882	Yale	8-0-0	1894	Yale	16-0-0
1873	Princeton	1-0-0	1883	Yale	8-0-0	1895	Penn	14-0-0
1874	Yale	3-0-0	1884	Yale	8-0-1	1896	Princeton (CFRA)	10-0-1
1875	Princeton (CFRA)	2-0-0	1885	Princeton	9-0-0		& Lafayette (NCF)	11-0-1
	& Harvard (NCF)	4-0-0	1886	Yale	9-0-1	1897	Penn	15-0-0
1876	Yale	3-0-0	1887	Yale	9-0-0	1898	Harvard	11-0-0
1877	Yale	3-0-1	1888	Yale	13-0-0	1899	Princeton (CFRA)	12-1-0
1878	Princeton	6-0-0	1889	Princeton	10-0-0		& Harvard (NCF, HF)	10-0-1
1879	Princeton	4-0-1	1890	Harvard	11-0-0			

Year		Record	Bowl Game	Head Coach	Outstanding Player
1900	Yale	12-0-0	No bowl	Malcolm McBride	Perry Hale, HB
1901	Harvard (CFRA)	12-0-0	No bowl	Bill Reid	Bob Kernan, HB
	& Michigan (NCF, HF)	11-0-0	Won Rose	Hurry Up Yost	Neil Snow, E
1902	Michigan	11-0-0	No bowl	Hurry Up Yost	Boss Weeks, QB
1903	Princeton	11-0-0	No bowl	Art Hillebrand	John DeWitt, G
1904	Penn (CFRA, HF)	12-0-0	No bowl	Carl Williams	Andy Smith, FB
	& Michigan (NCF)	10-0-0	No bowl	Hurry Up Yost	Willie Heston, HB
1905	Chicago	10-0-0	No bowl	Amos Alonzo Stagg	Walter Eckersall, QB
1906	Princeton	9-0-1	No bowl	Bill Roper	Cap Wister, E
1907	Yale	9-0-1	No bowl	Bill Knox	Tad Jones, HB
1908	Penn (CFRA, HF)	11-0-1	No bowl	Sol Metzger	Hunter Scarlett, E
	& LSU (NCF)	10-0-0	No bowl	Edgar Wingard	Doc Fenton, QB
1909	Yale	12-1-0	No bowl	Howard Jones	Ted Coy, FB
1910	Harvard (CFRA, HF)	8-0-1	No bowl	Percy Haughton	Percy Wendell, HB
	& Pittsburgh (NCF)	9-0-0	No bowl	Joe Thompson	Ralph Galvin, C
1911	Princeton (CFRA, HF)	8-0-2	No bowl	Bill Roper	Sam White, E
	& Penn St. (NCF)	8-0-1	No bowl	Bill Hollenback	Dexter Very, E
1912	Harvard (CFRA, HF)	9-0-0	No bowl	Percy Haughton	Charley Brickley, HB
	& Penn St. (NCF)	8-0-0	No bowl	Bill Hollenback	Dexter Very, E
1913	Harvard	9-0-0	No bowl	Percy Haughton	Eddie Mahan, FB
1914	Army	9-0-0	No bowl	Charley Daly	John McEwan, C
1915	Cornell	9-0-0	No bowl	Al Sharpe	Charley Barrett, QB
1916	Pittsburgh	8-0-0	No bowl	Pop Warner	Bob Peck, C
1917	Georgia Tech	9-0-0	No bowl	John Heisman	Ev Strupper, HB
1918	Pittsburgh (CFRA, HF)	4-1-0	No bowl	Pop Warner	Tom Davies, HB
	& Michigan (NCF)	5-0-0	No bowl	Hurry Up Yost	Frank Steketee, FB
1919	Harvard-tie, HF)	9-0-1	Won Rose	Bob Fisher	Eddie Casey, HB
	Illinois (CFRA-tie)	6-1-0	No bowl	Bob Zuppke	Chuck Carney, E
	& Notre Dame (NCF)	9-0-0	No bowl	Knute Rockne	George Gipp, HB
1920	California	9-0-0	Won Rose	Andy Smith	Dan McMillan, T
1921	California (CFRA)	9-0-1	Tied Rose	Andy Smith	Brick Muller, E
	& Cornell (NCF, HF)	8-0-0	No bowl	Gil Dobie	Eddie Kaw, HB
1922	Princeton (CFRA)	8-0-0	No bowl	Bill Roper	Herb Treat, T
	California (NCF)	9-0-0	No bowl	Andy Smith	Brick Muller, E
	& Cornell (HF)	8-0-0	No bowl	Gil Dobie	Eddie Kaw, HB

Year		Record	Bowl Game	Head Coach	Outstanding Player
1923	**Illinois** (CFRA, HF)	8-0-0	No bowl	Bob Zuppke	Red Grange, HB
	& Michigan (NCF)	8-0-0	No bowl	Hurry Up Yost	Jack Blott, C
1924	**Notre Dame**	10-0-0	Won Rose	Knute Rockne	"The Four Horsemen"*
1925	**Alabama** (CFRA, HF)	10-0-0	Won Rose	Wallace Wade	Johnny Mack Brown, HB
	& Dartmouth (DS)	8-0-0	No bowl	Jesse Hawley	Swede Oberlander, HB
1926	**Alabama** (CFRA, HF)	9-0-1	Tied Rose	Wallace Wade	Hoyt Winslett, E
	& Stanford (DS)	10-0-1	Tied Rose	Pop Warner	Ted Shipkey, E
1927	**Yale** (CFRA)	7-1-0	No bowl	Tad Jones	Bill Webster, G
	& Illinois (NCF, HF, DS)	7-0-1	No bowl	Bob Zuppke	Bob Reitsch, C
1928	**Georgia Tech** (CFRA, NCF, HF)	10-0-0	Won Rose	Bill Alexander	Pete Pund, C
	& USC (DS)	9-0-1	No bowl	Howard Jones	Jesse Hibbs, T
1929	**Notre Dame**	9-0-0	No bowl	Knute Rockne	Frank Carideo, QB
1930	**Alabama** (CFRA)	10-0-0	Won Rose	Wallace Wade	Fred Sington, T
	& Notre Dame (NCF, HF, DS)	10-0-0	No bowl	Knute Rockne	Marchy Schwartz, HB
1931	**USC**	10-1-0	Won Rose	Howard Jones	John Baker, G
1932	**USC** (CFRA, NCF, HF)	10-0-0	Won Rose	Howard Jones	Ernie Smith, T
	& Michigan (DS)	8-0-0	No bowl	Harry Kipke	Harry Newman, QB
1933	**Michigan**	8-0-0	No bowl	Harry Kipke	Chuck Bernard, C
1934	**Minnesota**	8-0-0	No bowl	Bernie Bierman	Pug Lund, HB
1935	**Minnesota** (CFRA, NCF, HF)	8-0-0	No bowl	Bernie Bierman	Dick Smith, T
	& SMU (DS)	12-1-0	Lost Rose	Matty Bell	Bobby Wilson, HB

*Notre Dame's Four Horsemen were Harry Stuhldreher (QB), Jim Crowley (HB), Don Miller (HB-P) and Elmer Layden (FB).

The Media Poll Years (since 1936)

National champions according to seven media and coaches' polls: Associated Press (since 1936), United Press (1950-57), International News Service (1952-57), United Press International (1958-92), Football Writers Association of America (since 1954), National Football Foundation and Hall of Fame (since 1959) and USA Today/CNN (since 1991). In 1991, the American Football Coaches Association switched outlets for its poll from UPI to USA Today/CNN and then to USA Today/ESPN in 1997.

After 29 years of releasing its final Top 20 poll in early December, AP named its 1965 national champion following that season's bowl games. AP returned to a pre-bowls final vote in 1966 and '67, but has polled its writers and broadcasters after the bowl games since the 1968 season. The FWAA has selected its champion after the bowl games since the 1955 season, the NFF-Hall of Fame since 1971, UPI after 1974, USA Today/CNN 1991-96, and USA Today/ESPN since 1997.

The Associated Press changed the name of its national championship award from the AP trophy to the Bear Bryant Trophy after the legendary Alabama coach's death in 1983. The FootballWriters' trophy is called the Grantland Rice Award (after the celebrated sportswriter) and the NFF-Hall of Fame trophy is called the MacArthur Bowl (in honor of Gen. Douglas MacArthur).

Multiple champions: Notre Dame (9); Alabama, Ohio St. and Oklahoma (7); Miami-FL, Nebraska and USC (5); Minnesota (4); Michigan St. and Texas (3); Army, Florida St., Georgia Tech, Michigan, Penn St., Pittsburgh and Tennessee (2).

Year		Record	Bowl Game	Head Coach	Outstanding Player
1936	**Minnesota**	7-1-0	No bowl	Bernie Bierman	Ed Widseth, T
1937	**Pittsburgh**	9-0-1	No bowl	Jock Sutherland	Marshall Goldberg, HB
1938	**TCU**	11-0-0	Won Sugar	Dutch Meyer	Davey O'Brien, QB
1939	**Texas A&M**	11-0-0	Won Sugar	Homer Norton	John Kimbrough, FB
1940	**Minnesota**	8-0-0	No Bowl	Bernie Bierman	George Franck, HB
1941	**Minnesota**	8-0-0	No bowl	Bernie Bierman	Bruce Smith, HB
1942	**Ohio St.**	9-1-0	No bowl	Paul Brown	Gene Fekete, FB
1943	**Notre Dame**	9-1-0	No bowl	Frank Leahy	Angelo Bertelli, QB
1944	**Army**	9-0-0	No bowl	Red Blaik	Glenn Davis, HB
1945	**Army**	9-0-0	No bowl	Red Blaik	Doc Blanchard, FB
1946	**Notre Dame**	8-0-1	No bowl	Frank Leahy	Johnny Lujack, QB
1947	**Notre Dame**	9-0-0	No bowl	Frank Leahy	Johnny Lujack, QB
1948	**Michigan**	9-0-0	No bowl	Bennie Oosterbaan	Dick Rifenburg, E
1949	**Notre Dame**	10-0-0	No bowl	Frank Leahy	Leon Hart, E
1950	**Oklahoma**	10-1-0	Lost Sugar	Bud Wilkinson	Leon Heath, FB
1951	**Tennessee**	10-0-0	Lost Sugar	Bob Neyland	Hank Lauricella, TB
1952	**Michigan St.** (AP, UP)	9-0-0	No bowl	Biggie Munn	Don McAuliffe, HB
	& Georgia Tech (INS)	12-0-0	Won Sugar	Bobby Dodd	Hal Miller, T
1953	**Maryland**	10-1-0	Lost Orange	Jim Tatum	Bernie Faloney, QB
1954	**Ohio St.** (AP, INS)	10-0-0	Won Rose	Woody Hayes	Howard Cassady, HB
	& UCLA (UP, FW)	9-0-0	No bowl	Red Sanders	Jack Ellena, T
1955	**Oklahoma**	11-0-0	Won Orange	Bud Wilkinson	Jerry Tubbs, C
1956	**Oklahoma**	10-0-0	No bowl	Bud Wilkinson	Tommy McDonald, HB
1957	**Auburn** (AP)	10-0-0	No bowl	Shug Jordan	Jimmy Phillips, E
	& Ohio St. (UP, FW, INS)	9-1-0	Won Rose	Woody Hayes	Bob White, FB
1958	**LSU** (AP, UPI)	11-0-0	Won Sugar	Paul Dietzel	Billy Cannon, HB
	& Iowa (FW)	8-1-1	Won Rose	Forest Evashevski	Randy Duncan, QB
1959	**Syracuse**	11-0-0	Won Cotton	Ben Schwartzwalder	Ernie Davis, HB
1960	**Minnesota** (AP, UPI, NFF)	8-2-0	Lost Rose	Murray Warmath	Tom Brown, G
	& Mississippi (FW)	10-0-1	Won Sugar	Johnny Vaught	Jake Gibbs, QB
1961	**Alabama** (AP, UPI, NFF)	11-0-0	Won Sugar	Bear Bryant	Billy Neighbors, T
	& Ohio St. (FW)	8-0-1	No bowl	Woody Hayes	Bob Ferguson, HB
1962	**USC**	11-0-0	Won Rose	John McKay	Hal Bedsole, E
1963	**Texas**	11-0-0	Won Cotton	Darrell Royal	Scott Appleton, T

National Champions (Cont.)

Year	Record	Bowl Game	Head Coach	Outstanding Player
1964	**Alabama** (AP, UPI), ...10-1-0	Lost Orange	Bear Bryant	Joe Namath, QB
	Arkansas (FW) 11-0-0	Won Cotton	Frank Broyles	Ronnie Caveness, LB
	& **Notre Dame** (NFF) 9-1-0	No bowl	Ara Parseghian	John Huarte, QB
1965	**Alabama** (AP, FW-tie) 9-1-1	Won Orange	Bear Bryant	Paul Crane, C
	& **Michigan St.** (UPI, NFF, FW-tie) .10-1-0	Lost Rose	Duffy Daugherty	George Webster, LB
1966	**Notre Dame** (AP, UPI, FW, NFF-tie) .9-0-1	No bowl	Ara Parseghian	Jim Lynch, LB
	& **Michigan St.** (NFF-tie) 9-0-1	No bowl	Duffy Daugherty	Bubba Smith, DE
1967	**USC** 10-1-0	Won Rose	John McKay	O.J. Simpson, HB
1968	**Ohio St.** 10-0-0	Won Rose	Woody Hayes	Rex Kern, QB
1969	**Texas** 11-0-0	Won Cotton	Darrell Royal	James Street, QB
1970	**Nebraska** (AP, FW) 11-0-1	Won Orange	Bob Devaney	Jerry Tagge, QB
	Texas (UPI, NFF-tie), ...10-1-0	Lost Cotton	Darrell Royal	Steve Worster, RB
	& **Ohio St.** (NFF-tie) 9-1-0	Lost Rose	Woody Hayes	Jim Stillwagon, MG
1971	**Nebraska** 13-0-0	Won Orange	Bob Devaney	Johnny Rodgers, WR
1972	**USC** 12-0-0	Won Rose	John McKay	Charles Young, TE
1973	**Notre Dame** (AP, FW, NFF) 11-0-0	Won Sugar	Ara Parseghian	Mike Townsend, DB
	& **Alabama** (UPI) 11-1-0	Lost Sugar	Bear Bryant	Buddy Brown, OT
1974	**Oklahoma** (AP) 11-0-0	No bowl	Barry Switzer	Joe Washington, RB
	& **USC** (UPI, FW, NFF) 10-1-1	Won Rose	John McKay	Anthony Davis, RB
1975	**Oklahoma** 11-1-0	Won Orange	Barry Switzer	Lee Roy Selmon, DT
1976	**Pittsburgh** 12-0-0	Won Sugar	Johnny Majors	Tony Dorsett, RB
1977	**Notre Dame** 11-1-0	Won Cotton	Dan Devine	Ross Browner, DE
1978	**Alabama** (AP, FW, NFF) 11-1-0	Won Sugar	Bear Bryant	Marty Lyons, DT
	& **USC** (UPI) 12-1-0	Won Rose	John Robinson	Charles White, RB
1979	**Alabama** 12-0-0	Won Sugar	Bear Bryant	Jim Bunch, OT
1980	**Georgia** 12-0-0	Won Sugar	Vince Dooley	Herschel Walker, RB
1981	**Clemson** 12-0-0	Won Orange	Danny Ford	Jeff Davis, LB
1982	**Penn St.** 11-1-0	Won Sugar	Joe Paterno	Todd Blackledge, QB
1983	**Miami-FL** 11-1-0	Won Orange	H. Schnellenberger	Bernie Kosar, QB
1984	**BYU** 13-0-0	Won Holiday	LaVell Edwards	Robbie Bosco, QB
1985	**Oklahoma** 11-1-0	Won Orange	Barry Switzer	Brian Bosworth, LB
1986	**Penn St.** 12-0-0	Won Fiesta	Joe Paterno	D.J. Dozier, RB
1987	**Miami-FL** 12-0-0	Won Orange	Jimmy Johnson	Steve Walsh, QB
1988	**Notre Dame** 12-0-0	Won Fiesta	Lou Holtz	Tony Rice, QB
1989	**Miami-FL** 11-1-0	Won Sugar	Dennis Erickson	Craig Erickson, QB
1990	**Colorado** (AP, FW, NFF) 11-1-1	Won Orange	Bill McCartney	Eric Bieniemy, RB
	& **Georgia Tech** (UP) 11-0-1	Won Citrus	Bobby Ross	Shawn Jones, QB
1991	**Miami-FL** (AP) 12-0-0	Won Orange	Dennis Erickson	Gino Torretta, QB
	& **Washington** (USA, FW, NFF) . .12-0-0	Won Rose	Don James	Steve Emtman, DT
1992	**Alabama** 13-0-0	Won Sugar	Gene Stallings	Eric Curry, DE
1993	**Florida St.** 12-1-0	Won Orange	Bobby Bowden	Charlie Ward, QB
1994	**Nebraska** 13-0-0	Won Orange	Tom Osborne	Zach Wiegert, OT
1995	**Nebraska** 12-0-0	Won Fiesta	Tom Osborne	Tommie Frazier, QB
1996	**Florida** 12-1*	Won Sugar	Steve Spurrier	Danny Wuerffel, QB
1997	**Michigan** (AP, FW, NFF) 12-0	Won Rose	Lloyd Carr	Charles Woodson, DB
	& **Nebraska** (ESPN/USA) 13-0	Won Orange	Tom Osborne	Ahman Green, RB
1998	**Tennessee** 13-0	Won Fiesta	Phillip Fulmer	Peerless Price, WR
1999	**Florida St.** 12-0	Won Sugar	Bobby Bowden	Peter Warrick, WR
2000	**Oklahoma** 13-0	Won Orange	Bob Stoops	Josh Heupel, QB
2001	**Miami-FL** 12-0	Won Rose	Larry Coker	Ken Dorsey, QB
2002	**Ohio St.** 14-0	Won Fiesta	Jim Tressel	Craig Krenzler, QB

*The NCAA instituted overtime for regular season games in 1996.

Number 1 vs. Number 2

Since the Associated Press writers poll started keeping track of such things in 1936, the No. 1 and No. 2 ranked teams in the country have met 33 times; 20 during the regular season and 13 in bowl games. Since the first showdown in 1943, the No. 1 team has beaten the No. 2 team 21 times, lost 10 and there have been two ties. Each showdown is listed below with the date, the match-up, each team's record going into the game, the final score, the stadium and site.

Date		Match-up		Stadium
Oct. 9 1943	#1	Notre Dame (2-0) . . .35	Michigan (Ann Arbor)	Michigan
	#2	Michigan (3-0) 12		
Nov. 20 1943	#1	Notre Dame (8-0) . . .14	Notre Dame (South Bend)	Notre Dame
	#2	Iowa Pre-Flight (8-0) .13		
Dec. 2 1944	#1	Army (8-0) 23	Municipal (Baltimore)	Municipal
	#2	Navy (6-2) 7		
Nov. 10 1945	#1	Army (6-0) 48	Yankee (New York)	Yankee
	#2	Notre Dame (5-0-1) . .0		

Date		Match-up		Stadium
Dec. 1 1945	#1	Army (8-0) 32	Municipal (Philadelphia)	Municipal
	#2	Navy (7-0-1) 13		
Nov. 9 1946	#1	Army (7-0) 0	Yankee (New York)	Yankee
	#2	Notre Dame (5-0) 0		
Jan. 1 1963	#1	USC (10-0) 42	ROSE BOWL (Pasadena)	ROSE BOWL
	#2	Wisconsin (8-1) 37		
Oct. 12 1963	#2	Texas (3-0) 28	Cotton Bowl (Dallas)	Cotton Bowl
	#1	Oklahoma (2-0) 7		

Date	Match-up		Stadium	Date	Match-up		Stadium
Jan. 1	#1	Texas (10-0) 28	COTTON BOWL	Nov. 21	#2	Oklahoma (10-0) ...17	Memorial
1964	#2	Navy (9-1) 6	(Dallas)	1987	#1	Nebraska (10-0) 7	(Lincoln)
Nov. 19	#1	Notre Dame (8-0) ..10	Spartan	Jan. 1	#2	Miami-FL (11-0) 20	ORANGE BOWL
1966	#2	Michigan St. (9-0) ...10	(East Lansing)	1988	#1	Oklahoma (11-0) ...14	(Miami)
Sept. 28	#1	Purdue (1-0) 37	Notre Dame	Nov. 26	#1	Notre Dame (10-0) ..27	Coliseum
1968	#2	Notre Dame (1-0) ..22	(South Bend)	1988	#2	USC (10-0) 10	(Los Angeles)
Jan. 1	#1	Ohio St. (9-0) 27	ROSE BOWL	Sept. 16	#1	Notre Dame (1-0) ..24	Michigan
1969	#2	USC (9-0-1) 16	(Pasadena)	1989	#2	Michigan (0-0) 19	(Ann Arbor)
Dec. 6	#1	Texas (9-0) 15	Razorback	Nov. 16	#2	Miami-FL (8-0) 17	Doak Campbell
1969	#2	Arkansas (9-0) 14	(Fayetteville)	1991	#1	Florida St. (10-0) ...16	(Tallahassee)
Nov. 25	#1	Nebraska (10-0) 35	Owen Field	Jan. 1	#2	Alabama (12-0) 34	SUGAR BOWL
1971	#2	Oklahoma (9-0) 31	(Norman)	1993	#1	Miami-FL (11-0) 13	(New Orleans)
Jan. 1	#1	Nebraska (12-0) 38	ORANGE BOWL	Nov. 13	#2	Notre Dame (9-0) ...31	Notre Dame
1972	#2	Alabama (11-0) 6	(Miami)	1993	#1	Florida St. (9-0) ...24	(South Bend)
Jan. 1	#2	Alabama (10-1) 14	SUGAR BOWL	Jan. 1	#1	Florida St. (11-1) ...18	ORANGE BOWL
1979	#1	Penn St. (11-0) 7	(New Orleans)	1994	#2	Nebraska (11-0) 16	(Miami)
Sept. 26	#1	USC (2-0) 28	Coliseum	Jan. 2	#1	Nebraska (11-0) ...62	FIESTA BOWL
1981	#2	Oklahoma (1-0) 24	(Los Angeles)	1996	#2	Florida (12-0) 24	(Tempe)
Jan. 1	#2	Penn St. (10-1) 27	SUGAR BOWL	Nov. 30	#2	Florida St. (10-0) ...24	Doak Campbell
1983	#1	Georgia (11-0) 23	(New Orleans)	1996	#1	Florida (10-1) 21	(Tallahassee)
Oct. 19	#1	Iowa (5-0) 12	Kinnick	Jan. 4	#1	Tennessee (12-0) ...23	FIESTA BOWL
1985	#2	Michigan (5-0) 10	(Iowa City)	1999	#2	Florida St. (11-1) ..16	(Tempe)
Sept. 27	#2	Miami-FL (3-0) 28	Orange Bowl	Jan. 4	#1	Florida St. (11-0) ...46	SUGAR BOWL
1986	#1	Oklahoma (2-0) 16	(Miami)	2000	#2	Virginia Tech (11-0) .29	(New Orleans)
Jan. 2	#2	Penn St. (11-0) 14	FIESTA BOWL	Jan. 3	#2	Ohio St. (13-0) 31	FIESTA BOWL
1987	#1	Miami-FL (11-0) 10	(Tempe)	2003	#1	Miami-FL (12-0) .2OT 24	(Tempe)

Note: Bowl games are listed in CAPITAL letters.

Top 50 Rivalries

Top Division I-A and I-AA series records, including games through the 2002 season. All rivalries listed below are renewed annually with the following exceptions. **Nebraska-Oklahoma** now play only when matched up as part of the rotating Big 12 schedule.
RECENTLY DISCONTINUED SERIES: **Penn State vs Pitt** in 2001 after 96 games (Penn State ahead 50-42-4), **Baylor vs TCU** in 1995 after 102 games (Baylor ahead 48-47-7); **Florida vs Miami-FL** in 1991 after 49 games (Florida ahead, 25-24); **Miami-FL vs Notre Dame** in 1990 after 23 games (ND ahead, 15-7-1). Note that Miami beat Florida in the 2000 Sugar Bowl.

	Gm	Series Leader		Gm	Series Leader
Air Force-Army	.37	Air Force (24-12-1)	**Michigan-Michigan St.**	.95	Michigan (62-28-5)
Air Force-Navy	.35	Air Force (25-10-0)	**Michigan-Notre Dame**	.30	Michigan (17-12-1)
Alabama-Auburn	.67	Alabama (38-28-1)	**Michigan-Ohio St.**	.99	Michigan (56-37-6)
Alabama-Tennessee	.85	Alabama (43-35-7)	**Minnesota-Wisconsin**	.112	Minnesota (58-46-8)
Arizona-Arizona St.	.76	Arizona (43-32-1)	**Mississippi-Miss. St.**	.99	Ole Miss (56-37-6)
Army-Navy	.103	Army (49-47-7)	**Missouri-Kansas**	.111	Missouri (52-50-9)
Auburn-Georgia	.106	Auburn (51-47-8)	**Nebraska-Oklahoma**	.80	Oklahoma (40-37-3)
California-Stanford	.105	Stanford (54-40-11)	**N. Mexico-N. Mexico St.**	.92	New Mexico (59-28-5)
The Citadel-VMI	.62	Tied (30-30-2)	**N. Carolina-N.C. State**	.92	N. Carolina (60-26-6)
Clemson-S. Carolina	.100	Clemson (60-36-4)	**Notre Dame-Purdue**	.74	Notre Dame (49-23-2)
Colorado-Nebraska	.61	Nebraska (43-16-2)	**Notre Dame-USC**	.74	Notre Dame (42-27-5)
Colo. St.-Wyoming	.92	Colorado St. (49-38-5)	**Oklahoma-Okla. St.**	.97	Oklahoma (74-16-7)
Duke-N. Carolina	.88	N. Carolina (49-36-4)*	**Oregon-Oregon St.**	.106	Oregon (53-43-10)
Florida-Florida St.	.47	Florida (27-18-2)	**Penn-Cornell**	.109	Penn (63-41-5)
Florida-Georgia	.81	Georgia (46-33-2)	**Pittsburgh-West Va**	.95	Pitt (57-35-3)
Florida St.-Miami,FL	.46	Miami (26-20-0)	**Princeton-Yale**	.125	Yale (67-48-10)
Georgia-Georgia Tech	.97	Georgia (54-38-5)*	**Purdue-Indiana**	.105	Purdue (64-35-6)
Grambling-Southern	.51	Southern (27-24-0)	**Richmond-Wm. & Mary**	.112	Wm. & Mary (57-50-5)
Harvard-Yale	.119	Yale (64-47-8)	**Tennessee-Vanderbilt**	.96	Tennessee (65-26-5)
Iowa-Iowa St.	.50	Iowa (33-17-0)	**Texas-Oklahoma**	.97	Texas (56-36-5)
Kansas-Kansas St.	.100	Kansas (61-34-5)	**Texas-Texas A&M**	.109	Texas (70-34-5)
Kentucky-Tennessee	.98	Tennessee (66-23-9)	**UCLA-USC**	.72	USC (38-27-7)
Lafayette-Lehigh	.138	Lafayette (72-61-5)	**Utah-BYU**	.78	Utah (46-28-4)*
LSU-Tulane	.94	LSU (65-22-7)*	**Utah-Utah St.**	.100	Utah (67-29-4)
Miami,OH-Cincinnati	.107	Miami (57-43-7)	**Washington-Wash. St.**	.95	Washington (63-26-6)

*Disputed series records: UNC claims lead of 50-35-4; Georgia claims lead of 54-36-5; Tulane claims LSU leads 62-23-7; Utah claims lead of 49-31-4

Associated Press Final Polls

The Associated Press introduced its weekly college football poll of sportswriters (later, sportswriters and broadcasters) in 1936. The final AP poll was released at the end of the regular season until 1965, when bowl results were included for one year. After a two-year return to regular season games only, the final poll has come out after the bowls since 1968. Starting in 1989, the AP Poll has ranked 25 teams.

1936

Final poll released Nov. 30. Top 20 regular season results after that: **Dec. 5**–#8 Notre Dame tied USC, 13-13; #17 Tennessee tied Ole Miss, 0-0; #18 Arkansas over Texas, 6-0. **Dec. 12**–#16 TCU over #6 Santa Clara, 9-0.

		As of Nov. 30	Head Coach	After Bowls
1	Minnesota	7-1-0	Bernie Bierman	same
2	LSU	9-0-1	Bernie Moore	9-1-1
3	Pittsburgh	7-1-1	Jock Sutherland	8-1-1
4	Alabama	8-0-1	Frank Thomas	same
5	Washington	7-1-1	Jimmy Phelan	7-2-1
6	Santa Clara	7-0-0	Buck Shaw	8-1-0
7	Northwestern	7-1-0	Pappy Waldorf	same
8	Notre Dame	6-2-0	Elmer Layden	6-2-1
9	Nebraska	7-2-0	Dana X. Bible	same
10	Penn	7-1-0	Harvey Harman	same
11	Duke	9-1-0	Wallace Wade	same
12	Yale	7-1-0	Ducky Pond	same
13	Dartmouth	7-1-1	Red Blaik	same
14	Duquesne	7-2-0	John Smith	8-2-0
15	Fordham	5-1-2	Jim Crowley	same
16	TCU	7-2-2	Dutch Meyer	9-2-2
17	Tennessee	6-2-1	Bob Neyland	6-2-2
18	Arkansas	6-3-0	Fred Thomsen	7-3-0
	Navy	6-3-0	Tom Hamilton	same
20	Marquette	7-1-0	Frank Murray	7-2-0

Key Bowl Games

Sugar–#6 Santa Clara over #2 LSU, 21-14; **Rose**–#3 Pitt over #5 Washington, 21-0; **Orange**–#14 Duquesne over Mississippi St., 13-12; **Cotton**–#16 TCU over #20 Marquette, 16-6.

1937

Final poll released Nov. 29. Top 20 regular season results after that: **Dec. 4**–#18 Rice over SMU, 15-7.

		As of Nov. 29	Head Coach	After Bowls
1	Pittsburgh	9-0-1	Jock Sutherland	same
2	California	9-0-1	Stub Allison	10-0-1
3	Fordham	7-0-1	Jim Crowley	same
4	Alabama	9-0-0	Frank Thomas	9-1-0
5	Minnesota	6-2-0	Bernie Bierman	same
6	Villanova	8-0-1	Clipper Smith	same
7	Dartmouth	7-0-2	Red Blaik	same
8	LSU	9-1-0	Bernie Moore	9-2-0
9	Notre Dame	6-2-1	Elmer Layden	same
	Santa Clara	8-0-0	Buck Shaw	9-0-0
11	Nebraska	6-1-2	Biff Jones	same
12	Yale	6-1-1	Ducky Pond	same
13	Ohio St.	6-2-0	Francis Schmidt	same
14	Holy Cross	8-0-2	Eddie Anderson	same
	Arkansas	6-2-2	Fred Thomsen	same
16	TCU	4-2-2	Dutch Meyer	same
17	Colorado	8-0-0	Bunnie Oakes	8-1-0
18	Rice	4-3-2	Jimmy Kitts	6-3-2
19	North Carolina	7-1-1	Ray Wolf	same
20	Duke	7-1-0	Wallace Wade	same

Key Bowl Games

Rose–#2 Cal over #4 Alabama, 13-0; **Sugar**–#9 Santa Clara over #8 LSU, 6-0; **Cotton**–#18 Rice over #17 Colorado, 28-14; **Orange**–Auburn over Michigan St., 6-0.

1938

Final poll released Dec. 5. Top 20 regular season results after that: **Dec. 26**–#14 Cal over Georgia Tech, 13-7.

		As of Dec. 5	Head Coach	After Bowls
1	TCU	10-0-0	Dutch Meyer	11-0-0
2	Tennessee	10-0-0	Bob Neyland	11-0-0
3	Duke	9-0-0	Wallace Wade	9-1-0
4	Oklahoma	10-0-0	Tom Stidham	10-1-0
5	Notre Dame	8-1-0	Elmer Layden	same
6	Carnegie Tech	7-1-0	Bill Kern	7-2-0
7	USC	8-2-0	Howard Jones	9-2-0
8	Pittsburgh	8-2-0	Jock Sutherland	same
9	Holy Cross	8-1-0	Eddie Anderson	same
10	Minnesota	6-2-0	Bernie Bierman	same
11	Texas Tech	10-0-0	Pete Cawthon	10-1-0
12	Cornell	5-1-1	Carl Snavely	same
13	Alabama	7-1-1	Frank Thomas	same
14	California	9-1-0	Stub Allison	10-1-0
15	Fordham	6-1-2	Jim Crowley	same
16	Michigan	6-1-1	Fritz Crisler	same
17	Northwestern	4-2-2	Pappy Waldorf	same
18	Villanova	8-0-1	Clipper Smith	same
19	Tulane	7-2-1	Red Dawson	same
20	Dartmouth	7-2-0	Red Blaik	same

Key Bowl Games

Sugar–#1 TCU over #6 Carnegie Tech, 15-7; **Orange**–#2 Tennessee over #4 Oklahoma, 17-0; **Rose**–#7 USC over #3 Duke, 7-3; **Cotton**–St. Mary's over #11 Texas Tech 20-13.

1939

Final poll released Dec. 11. Top 20 regular season results after that: None.

		As of Dec. 11	Head Coach	After Bowls
1	Texas A&M	10-0-0	Homer Norton	11-0-0
2	Tennessee	10-0-0	Bob Neyland	10-1-0
3	USC	7-0-2	Howard Jones	8-0-2
4	Cornell	8-0-0	Carl Snavely	same
5	Tulane	8-0-1	Red Dawson	8-1-1
6	Missouri	8-1-0	Don Faurot	8-2-0
7	UCLA	6-0-4	Babe Horrell	same
8	Duke	8-1-0	Wallace Wade	same
9	Iowa	6-1-1	Eddie Anderson	same
10	Duquesne	8-0-1	Buff Donelli	same
11	Boston College	9-1-0	Frank Leahy	9-2-0
12	Clemson	8-1-0	Jess Neely	9-1-0
13	Notre Dame	7-2-0	Elmer Layden	same
14	Santa Clara	5-1-3	Buck Shaw	same
15	Ohio St.	6-2-0	Francis Schmidt	same
16	Georgia Tech	7-2-0	Bill Alexander	8-2-0
17	Fordham	6-2-0	Jim Crowley	same
18	Nebraska	7-1-1	Biff Jones	same
19	Oklahoma	6-2-1	Tom Stidham	same
20	Michigan	6-2-0	Fritz Crisler	same

Key Bowl Games

Sugar–#1 Texas A&M over #5 Tulane, 14-13; **Rose**–#3 USC over #2 Tennessee, 14-0; **Orange**–#16 Georgia Tech over #6 Missouri, 21-7; **Cotton**–#12 Clemson over #11 Boston College, 6-3.

1940

Final poll released Dec. 2. Top 20 regular season results after that: **Dec. 7**–#16 SMU over Rice, 7-6.

			As of Dec. 2	Head Coach	After Bowls
1	Minnesota	8-0-0		Bernie Bierman	same
2	Stanford	9-0-0		Clark Shaughnessy	10-0-0
3	Michigan	7-1-0		Fritz Crisler	same
4	Tennessee	10-0-0		Bob Neyland	10-1-0
5	Boston College	..10-0-0		Frank Leahy	11-0-0
6	Texas A&M	8-1-0		Homer Norton	9-1-0
7	Nebraska	8-1-0		Biff Jones	8-2-0
8	Northwestern	6-2-0		Pappy Waldorf	same
9	Mississippi St.	9-0-1		Allyn McKeen	10-0-1
10	Washington	7-2-0		Jimmy Phelan	same
11	Santa Clara	6-1-1		Buck Shaw	same
12	Fordham	7-1-0		Jim Crowley	7-2-0
13	Georgetown	8-1-0		Jack Hagerty	8-2-0
14	Penn	6-1-1		George Munger	same
15	Cornell	6-2-0		Carl Snavely	same
16	SMU	7-1-1		Matty Bell	8-1-1
17	Hardin-Simmons	..9-0-0		Warren Woodson	same
18	Duke	7-2-0		Wallace Wade	same
19	Lafayette	9-0-0		Hooks Mylin	same
20	–				

Note: Only 19 teams ranked.

Key Bowl Games

Rose–#2 Stanford over #7 Nebraska, 21-13; **Sugar**– #5 Boston College over #4 Tennessee, 19-13; **Cotton**–#6 Texas A&M over #12 Fordham, 13-12; **Orange**–#9 Mississippi St. over #13 Georgetown, 14-7.

1941

Final poll released Dec. 1. Top 20 regular season results after that: **Dec. 6**–#4 Texas over Oregon, 71-7; #9 Texas A&M over #19 Washington St., 7-0; #16 Mississippi St. over San Francisco, 26-13.

			As of Dec. 1	Head Coach	After Bowls
1	Minnesota	8-0-0		Bernie Bierman	same
2	Duke	9-0-0		Wallace Wade	9-1-0
3	Notre Dame	8-0-1		Frank Leahy	same
4	Texas	7-1-1		Dana X. Bible	8-1-1
5	Michigan	6-1-1		Fritz Crisler	same
6	Fordham	7-1-0		Jim Crowley	8-1-0
7	Missouri	8-1-0		Don Faurot	8-2-0
8	Duquesne	8-0-0		Buff Donelli	same
9	Texas A&M	8-1-0		Homer Norton	9-2-0
10	Navy	7-1-1		Swede Larson	same
11	Northwestern	5-3-0		Pappy Waldorf	same
12	Oregon St.	7-2-0		Lon Stiner	8-2-0
13	Ohio St.	6-1-1		Paul Brown	same
14	Georgia	6-1-1		Wally Butts	9-1-1
15	Penn	7-1-1		George Munger	same
16	Mississippi St.	7-1-1		Allyn McKeen	8-1-1
17	Mississippi	6-2-1		Harry Mehre	same
18	Tennessee	8-1-1		John Barnhill	same
19	Washington St.	...6-3-0		Babe Hollingbery	6-4-0
20	Alabama	8-2-0		Frank Thomas	9-2-0

Note: 1942 Rose Bowl moved to Durham, N.C., for one year after outbreak of World War II.

Key Bowl Games

Rose–#12 Oregon St. over #2 Duke, 20-16; **Sugar**–#6 Fordham over #7 Missouri, 2-0; **Cotton**–#20 Alabama over #9 Texas A&M, 29-21; **Orange**–#14 Georgia over TCU, 40-26.

1942

Final poll released Nov. 30. Top 20 regular season results after that: **Dec. 5**–#6 Notre Dame tied Great Lakes Naval Station, 13-13; #13 UCLA over Idaho, 40-13; #14 William & Mary over Oklahoma, 14-7; #17 Washington St. lost to Texas A&M, 21-0; #18 Mississippi St. over San Francisco, 19-7. **Dec. 12**–#13 UCLA over USC, 14-7.

			As of Nov. 30	Head Coach	After Bowls
1	Ohio St.	9-1-0		Paul Brown	same
2	Georgia	10-1-0		Wally Butts	11-1-0
3	Wisconsin	8-1-1		Harry Stuhldreher	same
4	Tulsa	10-0-0		Henry Frnka	10-1-0
5	Georgia Tech	...9-1-0		Bill Alexander	9-2-0
6	Notre Dame	7-2-1		Frank Leahy	7-2-2
7	Tennessee	8-1-1		John Barnhill	9-1-1
8	Boston College	..8-1-0		Denny Myers	8-2-0
9	Michigan	7-3-0		Fritz Crisler	same
10	Alabama	7-3-0		Frank Thomas	8-3-0
11	Texas	8-2-0		Dana X. Bible	9-2-0
12	Stanford	6-4-0		Marchy Schwartz	same
13	UCLA	5-3-0		Babe Horrell	7-4-0
14	William & Mary	.8-1-1		Carl Voyles	9-1-1
15	Santa Clara	7-2-0		Buck Shaw	same
16	Auburn	6-4-1		Jack Meagher	same
17	Washington St.	...6-1-2		Babe Hollingbery	6-2-2
18	Mississippi St.	7-2-0		Allyn McKeen	8-2-0
19	Minnesota	5-4-0		George Hauser	same
	Holy Cross	5-4-1		Ank Scanlon	same
	Penn St.	6-1-1		Bob Higgins	same

Key Bowl Games

Rose–#2 Georgia over #13 UCLA, 9-0; **Sugar**–#7 Tennessee over #4 Tulsa, 14-7; **Cotton**–#11 Texas over #5 Georgia Tech, 14-7; **Orange**–#10 Alabama over #8 Boston College, 37-21.

1943

Final poll released Nov. 29. Top 20 regular season results after that: **Dec.11**–#10 March Field over #19 Pacific, 19-0.

			As of Nov. 29	Head Coach	After Bowls
1	Notre Dame	9-1-0		Frank Leahy	same
2	Iowa Pre-Flight	..9-1-0		Don Faurot	same
3	Michigan	8-1-0		Fritz Crisler	same
4	Navy	8-1-0		Billick Whelchel	same
5	Purdue	9-0-0		Elmer Burnham	same
6	Great Lakes Naval Station	...10-2-0		Tony Hinkle	same
7	Duke	8-1-0		Eddie Cameron	same
8	DelMonte Pre-Flight	7-1-0		Bill Kern	same
9	Northwestern	6-2-0		Pappy Waldorf	same
10	March Field	8-1-0		Paul Schissler	9-1-0
11	Army	7-2-1		Red Blaik	same
12	Washington	4-0-0		Ralph Welch	4-1-0
13	Georgia Tech	...7-3-0		Bill Alexander	8-3-0
14	Texas	7-1-0		Dana X. Bible	7-1-1
15	Tulsa	6-0-1		Henry Frnka	6-1-1
16	Dartmouth	6-1-0		Earl Brown	same
17	Bainbridge Navy Training School	...7-0-0		Joe Maniaci	same
18	Colorado College	.7-0-0		Hal White	same
19	Pacific	7-1-0		Amos A. Stagg	7-2-0
20	Penn	6-2-1		George Munger	same

Key Bowl Games

Rose–USC over #12 Washington, 29-0; **Sugar**–#13 Georgia Tech over #15 Tulsa, 20-18; **Cotton**–#14 Texas tied Randolph Field, 7-7; **Orange**–LSU over Texas A&M, 19-14.

Associated Press Final Polls (Cont.)

1944

Final poll released Dec. 4. Top 20 regular season results after that: **Dec. 10**–#3 Randolph Field over #10 March Field, 20-7; #18 Fort Pierce over Kessler Field, 34-7; Morris Field over #20 Second Air Force, 14-7.

	As of Dec. 4	Head Coach	After Bowls
1 Army	.9-0-0	Red Blaik	same
2 Ohio St.	.9-0-0	Carroll Widdoes	same
3 Randolph Field	.10-0-0	Frank Tritico	12-0-0
4 Navy	.6-3-0	Oscar Hagberg	same
5 Bainbridge Navy Training School	.10-0-0	Joe Maniaci	same
6 Iowa Pre-Flight	.10-1-0	Jack Meagher	same
7 USC	.7-0-2	Jeff Cravath	8-0-2
8 Michigan	.8-2-0	Fritz Crisler	same
9 Notre Dame	.8-2-0	Ed McKeever	same
10 March Field	.7-0-2	Paul Schissler	7-1-2
11 Duke	.5-4-0	Eddie Cameron	6-4-0
12 Tennessee	.7-0-1	John Barnhill	7-1-1
13 Georgia Tech	.8-2-0	Bill Alexander	8-3-0
14 Norman Pre-Flight	.6-0-0	John Gregg	same
15 Illinois	.5-4-1	Ray Eliot	same
16 El Toro Marines	.8-1-0	Dick Hanley	same
17 Great Lakes Naval Station	.9-2-1	Paul Brown	same
18 Fort Pierce	.8-0-0	Hamp Pool	9-0-0
19 St. Mary's Pre-Flight	.4-4-0	Jules Sikes	same
20 Second Air Force	.10-2-1	Bill Reese	10-4-1

Key Bowl Games
Treasury–#3 Randolph Field over #20 Second Air Force, 13-6; **Rose**–#7 USC over #12 Tennessee, 25-0; **Sugar**–#11 Duke over Alabama, 29-26; **Orange**–Tulsa over #13 Georgia Tech, 26-12; **Cotton**–Oklahoma A&M over TCU, 34-0.

1945

Final poll released Dec. 3. Top 20 regular season results after that: None.

	As of Dec. 3	Head Coach	After Bowls
1 Army	.9-0-0	Red Blaik	same
2 Alabama	.9-0-0	Frank Thomas	10-0-0
3 Navy	.7-1-1	Oscar Hagberg	same
4 Indiana	.9-0-1	Bo McMillan	same
5 Oklahoma A&M	.8-0-0	Jim Lookabaugh	9-0-0
6 Michigan	.7-3-0	Fritz Crisler	same
7 St. Mary's-CA	.7-1-0	Jimmy Phelan	7-2-0
8 Penn	.6-2-0	George Munger	same
9 Notre Dame	.7-2-1	Hugh Devore	same
10 Texas	.9-1-0	Dana X. Bible	10-1-0
11 USC	.7-3-0	Jeff Cravath	7-4-0
12 Ohio St.	.7-2-0	Carroll Widdoes	same
13 Duke	.6-2-0	Eddie Cameron	same
14 Tennessee	.8-1-0	John Barnhill	same
15 LSU	.7-2-0	Bernie Moore	same
16 Holy Cross	.8-1-0	John DeGrosa	8-2-0
17 Tulsa	.8-2-0	Henry Frnka	8-3-0
18 Georgia	.8-2-0	Wally Butts	9-2-0
19 Wake Forest	.4-3-1	Peahead Walker	5-3-1
20 Columbia	.8-1-0	Lou Little	same

Key Bowl Games
Rose–#2 Alabama over #11 USC, 34-14; **Sugar**–#5 Oklahoma A&M over #7 St. Mary's, 33-13; **Cotton**–#10 Texas over Missouri, 40-27; **Orange**–Miami-FL over #16 Holy Cross, 13-6.

1946

Final poll released Dec. 2. Top 20 regular season results after that: None.

	As of Dec. 2	Head Coach	After Bowls
1 Notre Dame	.8-0-1	Frank Leahy	same
2 Army	.9-0-1	Red Blaik	same
3 Georgia	.10-0-0	Wally Butts	11-0-0
4 UCLA	.10-0-0	Bert LaBrucherie	10-1-0
5 Illinois	.7-2-0	Ray Eliot	8-2-0
6 Michigan	.6-2-1	Fritz Crisler	same
7 Tennessee	.9-1-0	Bob Neyland	9-2-0
8 LSU	.9-1-0	Bernie Moore	9-1-1
9 North Carolina	.8-1-1	Carl Snavely	8-2-1
10 Rice	.8-2-0	Jess Neely	9-2-0
11 Georgia Tech	.8-2-0	Bobby Dodd	9-2-0
12 Yale	.7-1-1	Howard Odell	same
13 Penn	.6-2-0	George Munger	same
14 Oklahoma	.7-3-0	Jim Tatum	8-3-0
15 Texas	.8-2-0	Dana X. Bible	same
16 Arkansas	.6-3-1	John Barnhill	6-3-2
17 Tulsa	.9-1-0	J.O. Brothers	same
18 N.C. State	.8-2-0	Beattie Feathers	8-3-0
19 Delaware	.9-0-0	Bill Murray	10-0-0
20 Indiana	.6-3-0	Bo McMillan	same

Key Bowl Games
Sugar–#3 Georgia over #9 N. Carolina, 20-10; **Rose**–#5 Illinois over #4 UCLA, 45-14; **Orange**–#10 Rice over #7 Tennessee, 8-0; **Cotton**–#8 LSU tied #16 Arkansas, 0-0.

1947

Final poll released Dec. 8. Top 20 regular season results after that: None.

	As of Dec. 8	Head Coach	After Bowls
1 Notre Dame	.9-0-0	Frank Leahy	same
2 Michigan	.9-0-0	Fritz Crisler	10-0-0
3 SMU	.9-0-1	Matty Bell	9-0-2
4 Penn St.	.9-0-0	Bob Higgins	9-0-1
5 Texas	.9-1-0	Blair Cherry	10-1-0
6 Alabama	.8-2-0	Red Drew	8-3-0
7 Penn	.7-0-1	George Munger	same
8 USC	.7-1-1	Jeff Cravath	7-2-1
9 North Carolina	.8-2-0	Carl Snavely	same
10 Georgia Tech	.9-1-0	Bobby Dodd	10-1-0
11 Army	.5-2-2	Red Blaik	same
12 Kansas	.8-0-2	George Sauer	8-1-2
13 Mississippi	.8-2-0	Johnny Vaught	9-2-0
14 William & Mary	.9-1-0	Rube McCray	9-2-0
15 California	.9-1-0	Pappy Waldorf	same
16 Oklahoma	.7-2-1	Bud Wilkinson	same
17 N.C. State	.5-3-1	Beattie Feathers	same
18 Rice	.6-3-1	Jess Neely	same
19 Duke	.4-3-2	Wallace Wade	same
20 Columbia	.7-2-0	Lou Little	same

Key Bowl Games
Rose–#2 Michigan over #8 USC, 49-0; **Cotton**–#3 SMU tied #4 Penn St., 13-13; **Sugar**–#5 Texas over #6 Alabama, 27-7; **Orange**–#10 Georgia Tech over #12 Kansas, 20-14.
Note: An unprecedented "Who's No. 1?" poll was conducted by AP after the Rose Bowl game, pitting Notre Dame against Michigan. The Wolverines won the vote, 226-119, but AP ruled that the Irish would be the No. 1 team of record.

1948

Final poll released Nov. 29. Top 20 regular season results after that: **Dec. 3**–#12 Vanderbilt over Miami-FL, 33-6. **Dec. 4**–#2 Notre Dame tied USC, 14-14; #11 Clemson over The Citadel, 20-0.

	As of Nov. 29	Head Coach	After Bowls
1	Michigan 9-0-0	Bennie Oosterbaan	same
2	Notre Dame 9-0-0	Frank Leahy	9-0-1
3	North Carolina . . .9-0-1	Carl Snavely	9-1-1
4	California 10-0-0	Pappy Waldorf	10-1-0
5	Oklahoma 9-1-0	Bud Wilkinson	10-1-0
6	Army 8-0-1	Red Blaik	same
7	Northwestern . . .7-2-0	Bob Voigts	8-2-0
8	Georgia 9-1-0	Wally Butts	9-2-0
9	Oregon 9-1-0	Jim Aiken	9-2-0
10	SMU 8-1-1	Matty Bell	9-1-1
11	Clemson 9-0-0	Frank Howard	11-0-0
12	Vanderbilt 7-2-1	Red Sanders	8-2-1
13	Tulane 9-1-0	Henry Frnka	same
14	Michigan St. 6-2-2	Biggie Munn	same
15	Mississippi 8-1-0	Johnny Vaught	same
16	Minnesota 7-2-0	Bernie Bierman	same
17	William & Mary . .6-2-2	Rube McCray	7-2-2
18	Penn St. 7-1-1	Bob Higgins	same
19	Cornell 8-1-0	Lefty James	same
20	Wake Forest 6-3-0	Peahead Walker	6-4-0

Note: Big Nine "no-repeat" rule kept Michigan from Rose Bowl.

Key Bowl Games

Sugar–#5 Oklahoma over #3 North Carolina, 14-6; **Rose**–#7 Northwestern over #4 Cal, 20-14; **Orange**– Texas over #8 Georgia, 41-28; **Cotton**–#10 SMU over #9 Oregon, 21-13.

1949

Final poll released Nov. 28. Top 20 regular season results after that: **Dec. 2**–#14 Maryland over Miami-FL, 13-0. **Dec. 3**–#1 Notre Dame over SMU, 27-20; #10 Pacific over Hawaii, 75-0.

	As of Nov. 28	Head Coach	After Bowls
1	Notre Dame 9-0-0	Frank Leahy	10-0-0
2	Oklahoma 10-0-0	Bud Wilkinson	11-0-0
3	California 10-0-0	Pappy Waldorf	10-1-0
4	Army 9-0-0	Red Blaik	same
5	Rice 9-1-0	Jess Neely	10-1-0
6	Ohio St. 6-1-2	Wes Fesler	7-1-2
7	Michigan 6-2-1	Bennie Oosterbaan	same
8	Minnesota 7-2-0	Bernie Bierman	same
9	LSU 8-2-0	Gaynell Tinsley	8-3-0
10	Pacific 10-0-0	Larry Siemering	11-0-0
11	Kentucky 9-2-0	Bear Bryant	9-3-0
12	Cornell 8-1-0	Lefty James	same
13	Villanova 8-1-0	Jim Leonard	same
14	Maryland 7-1-0	Jim Tatum	9-1-0
15	Santa Clara 7-2-1	Len Casanova	8-2-1
16	North Carolina . .7-3-0	Carl Snavely	7-4-0
17	Tennessee 7-2-1	Bob Neyland	same
18	Princeton 6-3-0	Charlie Caldwell	same
19	Michigan St. 6-3-0	Biggie Munn	same
20	Missouri 7-3-0	Don Faurot	7-4-0
	Baylor 8-2-0	Bob Woodruff	same

Key Bowl Games

Sugar–#2 Oklahoma over #9 LSU, 35-0; **Rose**–#6 Ohio St. over #3 Cal, 17-14; **Cotton**–#5 Rice over #16 North Carolina, 27-13; **Orange**–#15 Santa Clara over #11 Kentucky, 21-13.

1950

Final poll released Nov. 27. Top 20 regular season results after that: **Nov. 30**–#3 Texas over Texas A&M, 17-0. **Dec. 1**–#15 Miami-FL over Missouri, 27–9. **Dec. 2**–#1 Oklahoma over Okla. A&M, 41-14; Navy over #2 Army, 14-2; #4 Tennessee over Vanderbilt, 43-0; #16 Alabama over Auburn, 34-0; #19 Tulsa over Houston, 28-21; #20 Tulane tied LSU, 14-14. **Dec. 9**–#3 Texas over LSU, 21-6.

	As of Nov. 27	Head Coach	After Bowls
1	Oklahoma 9-0-0	Bud Wilkinson	10-1-0
2	Army 8-0-0	Red Blaik	8-1-0
3	Texas 7-1-0	Blair Cherry	9-2-0
4	Tennessee 9-1-0	Bob Neyland	11-1-0
5	California 9-0-1	Pappy Waldorf	9-1-1
6	Princeton 9-0-0	Charlie Caldwell	same
7	Kentucky 10-1-0	Bear Bryant	11-1-0
8	Michigan St. 8-1-0	Biggie Munn	same
9	Michigan 5-3-1	Bennie Oosterbaan	6-3-1
10	Clemson 8-0-1	Frank Howard	9-0-1
11	Washington 8-2-0	Howard Odell	same
12	Wyoming 9-0-0	Bowden Wyatt	10-0-0
13	Illinois 7-2-0	Ray Eliot	same
14	Ohio St. 6-3-0	Wes Fesler	same
15	Miami-FL 8-0-1	Andy Gustafson	9-1-1
16	Alabama 8-2-0	Red Drew	9-2-0
17	Nebraska 6-2-1	Bill Glassford	same
18	Wash. & Lee 8-2-0	George Barclay	8-3-0
19	Tulsa 8-1-1	J.O. Brothers	9-1-1
20	Tulane 6-2-0	Henry Frnka	6-2-1

Key Bowl Games

Sugar–#7 Kentucky over #1 Oklahoma, 13-7; **Cotton**–#4 Tennessee over #3 Texas, 20-14; **Rose**–#9 Michigan over #5 Cal, 14-6; **Orange**–#10 Clemson over #15 Miami-FL, 15-14.

1951

Final poll released Dec. 3. Top 20 regular season results after that: None.

	As of Dec. 3	Head Coach	After Bowls
1	Tennessee 10-0-0	Bob Neyland	10-1-0
2	Michigan St. 9-0-0	Biggie Munn	same
3	Maryland 9-0-0	Jim Tatum	10-0-0
4	Illinois 8-0-1	Ray Eliot	9-0-1
5	Georgia Tech . . .10-0-1	Bobby Dodd	11-0-1
6	Princeton 9-0-0	Charlie Caldwell	same
7	Stanford 9-1-0	Chuck Taylor	9-2-0
8	Wisconsin 7-1-1	Ivy Williamson	same
9	Baylor 8-1-1	George Sauer	8-2-1
10	Oklahoma 8-2-0	Bud Wilkinson	same
11	TCU 6-4-0	Dutch Meyer	6-5-0
12	California 8-2-0	Pappy Waldorf	same
13	Virginia 8-1-0	Art Guepe	same
14	San Francisco . . .9-0-0	Joe Kuharich	same
15	Kentucky 7-4-0	Bear Bryant	8-4-0
16	Boston Univ. 6-4-0	Buff Donelli	same
17	UCLA 5-3-1	Red Sanders	same
18	Washington St. . . .7-3-0	Forest Evashevski	same
19	Holy Cross 8-2-0	Eddie Anderson	same
20	Clemson 7-2-0	Frank Howard	7-3-0

Key Bowl Games

Sugar–#3 Maryland over #1 Tennessee, 28-13; **Rose**–#4 Illinois over #7 Stanford, 40-7; **Orange**–#5 Georgia Tech over #9 Baylor, 17-14; **Cotton**–#15 Kentucky over #11 TCU, 20-7.

Associated Press Final Polls (Cont.)

1952

Final poll released Dec. 1. Top 20 regular season results after that: **Dec. 6**–#15 Florida over #20 Kentucky, 27-20.

		As of Dec. 1	Head Coach	After Bowls
1	Michigan St.	.9-0-0	Biggie Munn	same
2	Georgia Tech	.11-0-0	Bobby Dodd	12-0-0
3	Notre Dame	.7-2-1	Frank Leahy	same
4	Oklahoma	.8-1-1	Bud Wilkinson	same
5	USC	.9-1-0	Jess Hill	10-1-0
6	UCLA	.8-1-0	Red Sanders	same
7	Mississippi	.8-0-2	Johnny Vaught	8-1-2
8	Tennessee	.8-1-1	Bob Neyland	8-2-1
9	Alabama	.9-2-0	Red Drew	10-2-0
10	Texas	.8-2-0	Ed Price	9-2-0
11	Wisconsin	.6-2-1	Ivy Williamson	6-3-1
12	Tulsa	.8-1-1	J.O. Brothers	8-2-1
13	Maryland	.7-2-0	Jim Tatum	same
14	Syracuse	.7-2-0	Ben Schwartzwalder	7-3-0
15	Florida	.6-3-0	Bob Woodruff	8-3-0
16	Duke	.8-2-0	Bill Murray	same
17	Ohio St.	.6-3-0	Woody Hayes	same
18	Purdue	.4-3-2	Stu Holcomb	same
19	Princeton	.8-1-0	Charlie Caldwell	same
20	Kentucky	.5-3-2	Bear Bryant	5-4-2

Note: Michigan St. would officially join Big Ten in 1953.

Key Bowl Games

Sugar–#2 Georgia Tech over #7 Ole Miss, 24-7; **Rose**–#5 USC over #11 Wisconsin, 7-0; **Cotton**–#10 Texas over #8 Tennessee, 16-0; **Orange**–#9 Alabama over #14 Syracuse, 61-6.

1953

Final poll released Nov. 30. Top 20 regular season results after that: **Dec. 5**–#2 Notre Dame over SMU, 40-14.

		As of Nov. 30	Head Coach	After Bowls
1	Maryland	.10-0-0	Jim Tatum	10-1-0
2	Notre Dame	.8-0-1	Frank Leahy	9-0-1
3	Michigan St.	.8-1-0	Biggie Munn	9-1-0
4	Oklahoma	.8-1-1	Bud Wilkinson	9-1-1
5	UCLA	.8-1-0	Red Sanders	8-2-0
6	Rice	.8-2-0	Jess Neely	9-2-0
7	Illinois	.7-1-1	Ray Eliot	same
8	Georgia Tech	.8-2-1	Bobby Dodd	9-2-1
9	Iowa	.5-3-1	Forest Evashevski	same
10	West Virginia	.8-1-0	Art Lewis	8-2-0
11	Texas	.7-3-0	Ed Price	same
12	Texas Tech	.10-1-0	DeWitt Weaver	11-1-0
13	Alabama	.6-2-3	Red Drew	6-3-3
14	Army	.7-1-1	Red Blaik	same
15	Wisconsin	.6-2-1	Ivy Williamson	same
16	Kentucky	.7-2-1	Bear Bryant	same
17	Auburn	.7-2-1	Shug Jordan	7-3-1
18	Duke	.7-2-1	Bill Murray	same
19	Stanford	.6-3-1	Chuck Taylor	same
20	Michigan	.6-3-0	Bennie Oosterbaan	same

Key Bowl Games

Orange–#4 Oklahoma over #1 Maryland, 7-0; **Rose**–#3 Michigan St. over #5 UCLA, 28-20; **Cotton**–#6 Rice over #13 Alabama, 28-6; **Sugar**–#8 Georgia Tech over #10 West Virginia, 42-19.

1954

Final poll released Nov. 29. Top 20 regular season results after that: **Dec. 4**–#4 Notre Dame over SMU, 26-14.

		As of Nov. 29	Head Coach	After Bowls
1	Ohio St.	.9-0-0	Woody Hayes	10-0-0
2	UCLA	.9-0-0	Red Sanders	same
3	Oklahoma	.10-0-0	Bud Wilkinson	same
4	Notre Dame	.8-1-0	Terry Brennan	9-1-0
5	Navy	.7-2-0	Eddie Erdelatz	8-2-0
6	Mississippi	.9-1-0	Johnny Vaught	9-2-0
7	Army	.7-2-0	Red Blaik	same
8	Maryland	.7-2-1	Jim Tatum	same
9	Wisconsin	.7-2-0	Ivy Williamson	same
10	Arkansas	.8-2-0	Bowden Wyatt	8-3-0
11	Miami-FL	.8-1-0	Andy Gustafson	same
12	West Virginia	.8-1-0	Art Lewis	same
13	Auburn	.7-3-0	Shug Jordan	8-3-0
14	Duke	.7-2-1	Bill Murray	8-2-1
15	Michigan	.6-3-0	Bennie Oosterbaan	same
16	Virginia Tech	.8-0-1	Frank Moseley	same
17	USC	.8-3-0	Jess Hill	8-4-0
18	Baylor	.7-3-0	George Sauer	7-4-0
19	Rice	.7-3-0	Jess Neely	same
20	Penn St.	.7-2-0	Rip Engle	same

Note: PCC and Big Seven "no-repeat" rules kept UCLA and Oklahoma from Rose and Orange bowls, respectively.

Key Bowl Games

Rose–#1 Ohio St. over #17 USC, 20-7; **Sugar**–#5 Navy over #6 Ole Miss, 21-0; **Cotton**–Georgia Tech over #10 Arkansas, 14-6; **Orange**–#14 Duke over Nebraska, 34-7.

1955

Final poll released Nov. 28. Top 20 regular season results after that: None.

		As of Nov. 28	Head Coach	After Bowls
1	Oklahoma	.10-0-0	Bud Wilkinson	11-0-0
2	Michigan St.	.8-1-0	Duffy Daugherty	9-1-0
3	Maryland	.10-0-0	Jim Tatum	10-1-0
4	UCLA	.9-1-0	Red Sanders	9-2-0
5	Ohio St.	.7-2-0	Woody Hayes	same
6	TCU	.9-1-0	Abe Martin	9-2-0
7	Georgia Tech	.8-1-1	Bobby Dodd	9-1-1
8	Auburn	.8-1-1	Shug Jordan	8-2-1
9	Notre Dame	.8-2-0	Terry Brennan	same
10	Mississippi	.9-1-0	Johnny Vaught	10-1-0
11	Pittsburgh	.7-3-0	John Michelosen	7-4-0
12	Michigan	.7-2-0	Bennie Oosterbaan	same
13	USC	.6-4-0	Jess Hill	same
14	Miami-FL	.6-3-0	Andy Gustafson	same
15	Miami-OH	.9-0-0	Ara Parseghian	same
16	Stanford	.6-3-1	Chuck Taylor	same
17	Texas A&M	.7-2-1	Bear Bryant	same
18	Navy	.6-2-1	Eddie Erdelatz	same
19	West Virginia	.8-2-0	Art Lewis	same
20	Army	.6-3-0	Red Blaik	same

Note: Big Ten "no-repeat" rule kept Ohio St. from Rose Bowl.

Key Bowl Games

Orange–#1 Oklahoma over #3 Maryland, 20-6; **Rose**–#2 Michigan St. over #4 UCLA, 17-14; **Cotton**–#10 Ole Miss over #6 TCU, 14-13; **Sugar**–#7 Georgia Tech over #11 Pitt, 7-0; **Gator**–Vanderbilt over #8 Auburn, 25-13.

1956

Final poll released Dec. 3. Top 20 regular season results after that: **Dec. 8**–#13 Pitt over #6 Miami-FL, 14-7.

	As of Dec. 3	Head Coach	After Bowls
1	Oklahoma 10-0-0	Bud Wilkinson	same
2	Tennessee 10-0-0	Bowden Wyatt	10-1-0
3	Iowa 8-1-0	Forest Evashevski	9-1-0
4	Georgia Tech . . .9-1-0	Bobby Dodd	10-1-0
5	Texas A&M 9-0-1	Bear Bryant	same
6	Miami-FL 8-0-1	Andy Gustafson	8-1-1
7	Michigan 7-2-0	Bennie Oosterbaan	same
8	Syracuse 7-1-0	Ben Schwartzwalder	7-2-0
9	Michigan St. . . .7-2-0	Duffy Daugherty	same
10	Oregon St. 7-2-1	Tommy Prothro	7-3-1
11	Baylor 8-2-0	Sam Boyd	9-2-0
12	Minnesota 6-1-2	Murray Warmath	same
13	Pittsburgh 6-2-1	John Michelosen	7-3-1
14	TCU 7-3-0	Abe Martin	8-3-0
15	Ohio St. 6-3-0	Woody Hayes	same
16	Navy 6-1-2	Eddie Erdelatz	same
17	G. Washington . .7-1-1	Gene Sherman	8-1-1
18	USC 8-2-0	Jess Hill	same
19	Clemson 7-1-2	Frank Howard	7-2-2
20	Colorado 7-2-1	Dallas Ward	8-2-1

Note: Big Seven "no-repeat" rule kept Oklahoma from Orange Bowl and Texas A&M on probation.

Key Bowl Games

Sugar–#11 Baylor over #2 Tennessee, 13-7; **Rose**–#3 Iowa over #10 Oregon St., 35-19; **Gator**–#4 Georgia Tech over #13 Pitt, 21-14; **Cotton**–#14 TCU over #8 Syracuse, 28-27; **Orange**–#20 Colorado over #19 Clemson, 27-21.

1957

Final poll released Dec. 2. Top 20 regular season results after that: **Dec. 7**–#10 Notre Dame over SMU, 54-21.

	As of Dec. 2	Head Coach	After Bowls
1	Auburn 10-0-0	Shug Jordan	same
2	Ohio St. 8-1-0	Woody Hayes	9-1-0
3	Michigan St. . . .8-1-0	Duffy Daugherty	same
4	Oklahoma 9-1-0	Bud Wilkinson	10-1-0
5	Navy 8-1-1	Eddie Erdelatz	9-1-1
6	Iowa 7-1-1	Forest Evashevski	9-1-1
7	Mississippi 8-1-1	Johnny Vaught	9-1-1
8	Rice 7-3-0	Jess Neely	7-4-0
9	Texas A&M 8-2-0	Bear Bryant	8-3-0
10	Notre Dame . . .6-3-0	Terry Brennan	7-3-0
11	Texas 6-3-1	Darrell Royal	6-4-1
12	Arizona St. 10-0-0	Dan Devine	same
13	Tennessee 7-3-0	Bowden Wyatt	8-3-0
14	Mississippi St. . . .6-2-1	Wade Walker	same
15	N.C. State 7-1-2	Earle Edwards	same
16	Duke 6-2-2	Bill Murray	6-3-2
17	Florida 6-2-1	Bob Woodruff	same
18	Army 7-2-0	Red Blaik	same
19	Wisconsin 6-3-0	Milt Bruhn	same
20	VMI 9-0-1	John McKenna	same

Note: Auburn on probation, ineligible for bowl game.

Key Bowl Games

Rose–#2 Ohio St. over Oregon, 10-7; **Orange**–#4 Oklahoma over #16 Duke, 48-21; **Cotton**–#5 Navy over #8 Rice, 20-7; **Sugar**–#7 Ole Miss over #11 Texas, 39-7; **Gator**–#13 Tennessee over #9 Texas A&M, 3-0.

1958

Final poll released Dec. 1. Top 20 regular season results after that: None.

	As of Dec. 1	Head Coach	After Bowls
1	LSU 10-0-0	Paul Dietzel	11-0-0
2	Iowa 7-1-1	Forest Evashevski	8-1-1
3	Army 8-0-1	Red Blaik	same
4	Auburn 9-0-1	Shug Jordan	same
5	Oklahoma 9-1-0	Bud Wilkinson	10-1-0
6	Air Force 9-0-1	Ben Martin	9-0-2
7	Wisconsin 7-1-1	Milt Bruhn	same
8	Ohio St. 6-1-2	Woody Hayes	same
9	Syracuse 8-1-0	Ben Schwartzwalder	8-2-0
10	TCU 8-2-0	Abe Martin	8-2-1
11	Mississippi 8-2-0	Johnny Vaught	9-2-0
12	Clemson 8-2-0	Frank Howard	8-3-0
13	Purdue 6-1-2	Jack Mollenkopf	same
14	Florida 6-3-1	Bob Woodruff	6-4-1
15	South Carolina . .7-3-0	Warren Giese	same
16	California 7-3-0	Pete Elliott	7-4-0
17	Notre Dame . . .6-4-0	Terry Brennan	same
18	SMU 6-4-0	Bill Meek	same
19	Oklahoma St. . . .7-3-0	Cliff Speegle	8-3-0
20	Rutgers 8-1-0	John Stiegman	same

Key Bowl Games

Sugar–#1 LSU over #12 Clemson, 7-0; **Rose**–#2 Iowa over #16 Cal, 38-12; **Orange**–#5 Oklahoma over #9 Syracuse, 21-6; **Cotton**–#6 Air Force tied #10 TCU, 0-0.

1959

Final poll released Dec. 7. Top 20 regular season results after that: None.

	As of Dec. 7	Head Coach	After Bowls
1	Syracuse 10-0-0	Ben Schwartzwalder	11-0-0
2	Mississippi 9-1-0	Johnny Vaught	10-1-0
3	LSU 9-1-0	Paul Dietzel	9-2-0
4	Texas 9-1-0	Darrell Royal	9-2-0
5	Georgia 9-1-0	Wally Butts	10-1-0
6	Wisconsin 7-2-0	Milt Bruhn	7-3-0
7	TCU 8-2-0	Abe Martin	8-3-0
8	Washington 9-1-0	Jim Owens	10-1-0
9	Arkansas 8-2-0	Frank Broyles	9-2-0
10	Alabama 7-1-2	Bear Bryant	7-2-2
11	Clemson 8-2-0	Frank Howard	9-2-0
12	Penn St. 8-2-0	Rip Engle	9-2-0
13	Illinois 5-3-1	Ray Eliot	same
14	USC 8-2-0	Don Clark	same
15	Oklahoma 7-3-0	Bud Wilkinson	same
16	Wyoming 9-1-0	Bob Devaney	same
17	Notre Dame . . .5-5-0	Joe Kuharich	same
18	Missouri 6-4-0	Dan Devine	6-5-0
19	Florida 5-4-1	Bob Woodruff	same
20	Pittsburgh 6-4-0	John Michelosen	same

Note: Big Seven "no-repeat" rule kept Oklahoma from Orange Bowl.

Key Bowl Games

Cotton–#1 Syracuse over #4 Texas, 23-14; **Sugar**–#2 Ole Miss over #3 LSU, 21-0; **Orange**–#5 Georgia over #18 Missouri, 14-0; **Rose**–#8 Washington over #6 Wisconsin, 44-8; **Bluebonnet**–#11 Clemson over #7 TCU, 23-7; **Gator**–#9 Arkansas over Georgia Tech, 14-7; **Liberty**–#12 Penn St. over #10 Alabama, 7-0.

Associated Press Final Polls (Cont.)

1960

Final poll released Nov. 28. Top 20 regular season results after that: **Dec. 3**–UCLA over #10 Duke, 27-6.

		As of Nov. 28	Head Coach	After Bowls
1	Minnesota	8-1-0	Murray Warmath	8-2-0
2	Mississippi	9-0-1	Johnny Vaught	10-0-1
3	Iowa	8-1-0	Forest Evashevski	same
4	Navy	9-1-0	Wayne Hardin	9-2-0
5	Missouri	9-1-0	Dan Devine	10-1-0
6	Washington	9-1-0	Jim Owens	10-1-0
7	Arkansas	8-2-0	Frank Broyles	8-3-0
8	Ohio St.	7-2-0	Woody Hayes	same
9	Alabama	8-1-1	Bear Bryant	8-1-2
10	Duke	7-2-0	Bill Murray	8-3-0
11	Kansas	7-2-1	Jack Mitchell	same
12	Baylor	8-2-0	John Bridgers	8-3-0
13	Auburn	8-2-0	Shug Jordan	same
14	Yale	9-0-0	Jordan Olivar	same
15	Michigan St.	6-2-1	Duffy Daugherty	same
16	Penn St.	6-3-0	Rip Engle	7-3-0
17	New Mexico St.	10-0-0	Warren Woodson	11-0-0
18	Florida	8-2-0	Ray Graves	9-2-0
19	Syracuse	7-2-0	Ben Schwartzwalder	same
	Purdue	4-4-1	Jack Mollenkopf	same

Key Bowl Games

Rose–#6 Washington over #1 Minnesota, 17-7; **Sugar**–#2 Ole Miss over Rice, 14-6; **Orange**–#5 Missouri over #4 Navy, 21-14; **Cotton**–#10 Duke over #7 Arkansas, 7-6; **Bluebonnet**–#9 Alabama tied Texas, 3-3.

1961

Final poll released Dec. 4. Top 20 regular season results after that: None.

		As of Dec. 4	Head Coach	After Bowls
1	Alabama	10-0-0	Bear Bryant	11-0-0
2	Ohio St.	8-0-1	Woody Hayes	same
3	Texas	9-1-0	Darrell Royal	10-1-0
4	LSU	9-1-0	Paul Dietzel	10-1-0
5	Mississippi	9-1-0	Johnny Vaught	9-2-0
6	Minnesota	7-2-0	Murray Warmath	8-2-0
7	Colorado	9-1-0	Sonny Grandelius	9-2-0
8	Michigan St.	7-2-0	Duffy Daugherty	same
9	Arkansas	8-2-0	Frank Broyles	8-3-0
10	Utah St.	9-0-1	John Ralston	9-1-1
11	Missouri	7-2-1	Dan Devine	same
12	Purdue	6-3-0	Jack Mollenkopf	same
13	Georgia Tech	7-3-0	Bobby Dodd	7-4-0
14	Syracuse	7-3-0	Ben Schwartzwalder	8-3-0
15	Rutgers	9-0-0	John Bateman	same
16	UCLA	7-3-0	Bill Barnes	7-4-0
17	Rice	7-3-0	Jess Neely	7-4-0
	Penn St.	7-3-0	Rip Engle	8-3-0
	Arizona	8-1-1	Jim LaRue	same
20	Duke	7-3-0	Bill Murray	same

Note: Ohio St. faculty council turned down Rose Bowl invitation citing concern with OSU's overemphasis on sports.

Key Bowl Games

Sugar–#1 Alabama over #9 Arkansas, 10-3; **Cotton**–#3 Texas over #5 Ole Miss, 12-7; **Orange**–#4 LSU over #7 Colorado, 25-7; **Rose**–#6 Minnesota over #16 UCLA, 21-3; **Gotham**–Baylor over #10 Utah St., 24-9.

1962

Final poll released Dec. 3. Top 10 regular season results after that: None.

		As of Dec. 3	Head Coach	After Bowls
1	USC	10-0-0	John McKay	11-0-0
2	Wisconsin	8-1-0	Milt Bruhn	8-2-0
3	Mississippi	9-0-0	Johnny Vaught	10-0-0
4	Texas	9-0-1	Darrell Royal	9-1-1
5	Alabama	9-1-0	Bear Bryant	10-1-0
6	Arkansas	9-1-0	Frank Broyles	9-2-0
7	LSU	8-1-1	Charlie McClendon	9-1-1
8	Oklahoma	8-2-0	Bud Wilkinson	8-3-0
9	Penn St.	9-1-0	Rip Engle	9-2-0
10	Minnesota	6-2-1	Murray Warmath	same

Key Bowl Games

Rose–#1 USC over #2 Wisconsin, 42-37; **Sugar**–#3 Ole Miss over #6 Arkansas, 17-13; **Cotton**–#7 LSU over #4 Texas, 13-0; **Orange**–#5 Alabama over #8 Oklahoma, 17-0; **Gator**–Florida over #9 Penn St.,17-7.

1963

Final poll released Dec. 9. Top 10 regular season results after that: **Dec.14**–#8 Alabama over Miami-FL, 17-12.

		As of Dec. 9	Head Coach	After Bowls
1	Texas	10-0-0	Darrell Royal	11-0-0
2	Navy	9-1-0	Wayne Hardin	9-2-0
3	Illinois	7-1-1	Pete Elliott	8-1-1
4	Pittsburgh	9-1-0	John Michelosen	same
5	Auburn	9-1-0	Shug Jordan	9-2-0
6	Nebraska	9-1-0	Bob Devaney	10-1-0
7	Mississippi	7-0-2	Johnny Vaught	7-1-2
8	Alabama	7-2-0	Bear Bryant	9-2-0
9	Michigan St.	6-2-1	Duffy Daugherty	same
10	Oklahoma	8-2-0	Bud Wilkinson	same

Key Bowl Games

Cotton–#1 Texas over #2 Navy, 28-6; **Rose**–#3 Illinois over Washington, 17-7; **Orange**–#6 Nebraska over #5 Auburn, 13-7; **Sugar**–#8 Alabama over #7 Ole Miss, 12-7.

1964

Final poll released Nov. 30. Top 10 regular season results after that: **Dec. 5**–Florida over #7 LSU, 20-6.

		As of Nov. 30	Head Coach	After Bowls
1	Alabama	10-0-0	Bear Bryant	10-1-0
2	Arkansas	10-0-0	Frank Broyles	11-0-0
3	Notre Dame	9-1-0	Ara Parseghian	same
4	Michigan	8-1-0	Bump Elliott	9-1-0
5	Texas	9-1-0	Darrell Royal	10-1-0
6	Nebraska	9-1-0	Bob Devaney	9-2-0
7	LSU	7-1-1	Charlie McClendon	8-2-1
8	Oregon St.	8-2-0	Tommy Prothro	8-3-0
9	Ohio St.	7-2-0	Woody Hayes	same
10	USC	7-3-0	John McKay	same

Key Bowl Games

Orange–#5 Texas over #1 Alabama, 21-17; **Cotton**–#2 Arkansas over #6 Nebraska, 10-7; **Rose**–#4 Michigan over #8 Oregon St., 34-7; **Sugar**–#7 LSU over Syracuse, 13-10.

1965
Final poll taken after bowl games for the first time.

		Head Coach	After Bowls	Regular Season
1	Alabama	Bear Bryant	9-1-1	8-1-1
2	Michigan St	Duffy Daugherty	10-1-0	10-0-0
3	Arkansas	Frank Broyles	10-1-0	10-0-0
4	UCLA	Tommy Prothro	8-2-1	7-1-1
5	Nebraska	Bob Devaney	10-1-0	10-0-0
6	Missouri	Dan Devine	8-2-1	7-2-1
7	Tennessee	Doug Dickey	8-1-2	6-1-2
8	LSU	Charlie McClendon	8-3-0	7-3-0
9	Notre Dame	Ara Parseghian	7-2-1	same
10	USC	John McKay	7-2-1	same

Key Bowl Games
Rankings below reflect final regular season poll, released Nov. 29. No bowls for then #8 USC or #9 Notre Dame. **Rose**–#5 UCLA over #1 Michigan St., 14-12; **Cotton**–LSU over #2 Arkansas, 14-7; **Orange**–#4 Alabama over #3 Nebraska, 39-28; **Sugar**–#6 Missouri over Florida, 20-18; **Bluebonnet**–#7 Tennessee over Tulsa, 27-6; **Gator**–Georgia Tech over #10 Texas Tech, 31-21.

1966
Final poll released Dec. 5, returning to pre-bowl status. Top 10 regular season results after that: None.

		As of Dec. 5	Head Coach	After Bowls
1	Notre Dame	9-0-1	Ara Parseghian	same
2	Michigan St	9-0-1	Duffy Daugherty	same
3	Alabama	10-0-0	Bear Bryant	11-0-0
4	Georgia	9-1-0	Vince Dooley	10-1-0
5	UCLA	9-1-0	Tommy Prothro	same
6	Nebraska	9-1-0	Bob Devaney	9-2-0
7	Purdue	8-2-0	Jack Mollenkopf	9-2-0
8	Georgia Tech	9-1-0	Bobby Dodd	9-2-0
9	Miami-FL	7-2-1	Charlie Tate	8-2-1
10	SMU	8-2-0	Hayden Fry	8-3-0

Key Bowl Games
Sugar–#3 Alabama over #6 Nebraska, 34-7; **Cotton**–#4 Georgia over #10 SMU, 24-9; **Rose**–#7 Purdue over USC, 14-13; **Orange**–Florida over #8 Georgia Tech, 27-12; **Liberty**–#9 Miami-FL over Virginia Tech, 14-7.

1967
Final poll released Nov. 27. Top 10 regular season results after that: **Dec. 2**–#2 Tennessee over Vanderbilt, 41-14; #3 Oklahoma over Oklahoma St., 38-14; #8 Alabama over Auburn, 7-3.

		As of Nov. 27	Head Coach	After Bowls
1	USC	9-1-0	John McKay	10-1-0
2	Tennessee	8-1-0	Doug Dickey	9-2-0
3	Oklahoma	8-1-0	Chuck Fairbanks	10-1-0
4	Indiana	9-1-0	John Pont	9-2-0
5	Notre Dame	8-2-0	Ara Parseghian	same
6	Wyoming	10-0-0	Lloyd Eaton	10-1-0
7	Oregon St.	7-2-1	Dee Andros	same
8	Alabama	7-1-1	Bear Bryant	8-2-1
9	Purdue	8-2-0	Jack Mollenkopf	same
10	Penn St.	8-2-0	Joe Paterno	8-2-1

Key Bowl Games
Rose–#1 USC over #4 Indiana, 14-3; **Orange**–#3 Oklahoma over #2 Tennessee, 26-24; **Sugar**–LSU over #6 Wyoming, 20-13; **Cotton**–Texas A&M over #8 Alabama, 20-16; **Gator**–#10 Penn St. tied Florida St. 17-17.

1968
Final poll taken after bowl games for first time since close of 1965 season.

		After Bowls	Head Coach	Regular Season
1	Ohio St.	10-0-0	Woody Hayes	9-0-0
2	Penn St.	11-0-0	Joe Paterno	10-0-0
3	Texas	9-1-1	Darrell Royal	8-1-1
4	USC	9-1-1	John McKay	9-0-1
5	Notre Dame	7-2-1	Ara Parseghian	same
6	Arkansas	10-1-0	Frank Broyles	9-1-0
7	Kansas	9-2-0	Pepper Rodgers	9-1-0
8	Georgia	8-1-2	Vince Dooley	8-0-2
9	Missouri	8-3-0	Dan Devine	7-3-0
10	Purdue	8-2-0	Jack Mollenkopf	same
11	Oklahoma	7-4-0	Chuck Fairbanks	7-3-0
12	Michigan	8-2-0	Bump Elliott	same
13	Tennessee	8-2-1	Doug Dickey	8-1-1
14	SMU	8-3-0	Hayden Fry	7-3-0
15	Oregon St.	7-3-0	Dee Andros	same
16	Auburn	7-4-0	Shug Jordan	6-4-0
17	Alabama	8-3-0	Bear Bryant	8-2-0
18	Houston	6-2-2	Bill Yeoman	same
19	LSU	8-3-0	Charlie McClendon	7-3-0
20	Ohio Univ	10-1-0	Bill Hess	10-0-0

Key Bowl Games
Rankings below reflect final regular season poll, released Dec. 2. No bowls for then #7 Notre Dame and #11 Pudue. **Rose**–#1 Ohio St. over #2 USC, 27-16; **Orange**–#3 Penn St. over #6 Kansas, 15-14; **Sugar**–#9 Arkansas over #4 Georgia, 16-2; **Cotton**–#5 Texas over #8 Tennessee, 36-13; **Bluebonnet**–#20 SMU over #10 Oklahoma, 28-27; **Gator**–#16 Missouri over #12 Alabama, 35-10.

1969
Final poll taken after bowl games.

		After Bowls	Head Coach	Regular Season
1	Texas	11-0-0	Darrell Royal	10-0-0
2	Penn St	11-0-0	Joe Paterno	10-0-0
3	USC	10-0-1	John McKay	9-0-1
4	Ohio St.	8-1-0	Woody Hayes	same
5	Notre Dame	8-2-1	Ara Parseghian	8-1-1
6	Missouri	9-2-0	Dan Devine	9-1-0
7	Arkansas	9-2-0	Frank Broyles	9-1-0
8	Mississippi	8-3-0	Johnny Vaught	7-3-0
9	Michigan	8-3-0	Bo Schembechler	8-2-0
10	LSU	9-1-0	Charlie McClendon	same
11	Nebraska	9-2-0	Bob Devaney	8-2-0
12	Houston	9-2-0	Bill Yeoman	8-2-0
13	UCLA	8-1-1	Tommy Prothro	same
14	Florida	9-1-1	Ray Graves	8-1-1
15	Tennessee	9-2-0	Doug Dickey	9-1-0
16	Colorado	8-3-0	Eddie Crowder	7-3-0
17	West Virginia	10-1-0	Jim Carlen	9-1-0
18	Purdue	8-2-0	Jack Mollenkopf	same
19	Stanford	7-2-1	John Ralston	same
20	Auburn	8-3-0	Shug Jordan	8-2-0

Key Bowl Games
Rankings below reflect final regular season poll, released Dec. 8. No bowls for then #4 Ohio St., #8 LSU and #10 UCLA. **Cotton**–#1 Texas over #9 Notre Dame, 21-17; **Orange**–#2 Penn St. over #6 Missouri, 10-3; **Sugar**–#13 Ole Miss over #3 Arkansas, 27-22; **Rose**–#5 USC over #7 Michigan, 10-3.

Associated Press Final Polls (Cont.)

1970

		After Bowls	Head Coach	Regular Season
1	Nebraska	11-0-1	Bob Devaney	10-0-1
2	Notre Dame	10-1-0	Ara Parseghian	9-0-1
3	Texas	10-1-0	Darrell Royal	10-0-0
4	Tennessee	11-1-0	Bill Battle	10-1-0
5	Ohio St.	9-1-0	Woody Hayes	9-0-0
6	Arizona St.	11-0-0	Frank Kush	10-0-0
7	LSU	9-3-0	Charlie McClendon	9-2-0
8	Stanford	9-3-0	John Ralston	8-3-0
9	Michigan	9-1-0	Bo Schembechler	same
10	Auburn	9-2-0	Shug Jordan	8-2-0
11	Arkansas	9-2-0	Frank Broyles	same
12	Toledo	12-0-0	Frank Lauterbur	11-0-0
13	Georgia Tech	9-3-0	Bud Carson	8-3-0
14	Dartmouth	9-0-0	Bob Blackman	same
15	USC	6-4-1	John McKay	same
16	Air Force	9-3-0	Ben Martin	9-2-0
17	Tulane	8-4-0	Jim Pittman	7-4-0
18	Penn St.	7-3-0	Joe Paterno	same
19	Houston	8-3-0	Bill Yeoman	same
20	Oklahoma	7-4-1	Chuck Fairbanks	7-4-0
	Mississippi	7-4-0	Johnny Vaught	7-3-0

Key Bowl Games

Rankings below reflect final regular season poll, released Dec. 7. No bowls for then #4 Arkansas and #7 Michigan. **Cotton**–#6 Notre Dame over #1 Texas, 24-11; **Rose**–#12 Stanford over #2 Ohio St., 27-17; **Orange**–#3 Nebraska over #8 LSU, 17-12; **Sugar**–#5 Tennessee over #11 Air Force, 34-13; **Peach**–#9 Ariz. St. over N. Carolina, 48-26.

1972

		After Bowls	Head Coach	Regular Season
1	USC	12-0-0	John McKay	11-0-0
2	Oklahoma	11-1-0	Chuck Fairbanks	10-1-0
3	Texas	10-1-0	Darrell Royal	9-1-0
4	Nebraska	9-2-1	Bob Devaney	8-2-1
5	Auburn	10-1-0	Shug Jordan	9-1-0
6	Michigan	10-1-0	Bo Schembechler	same
7	Alabama	10-2-0	Bear Bryant	10-1-0
8	Tennessee	10-2-0	Bill Battle	9-2-0
9	Ohio St.	9-2-0	Woody Hayes	9-1-0
10	Penn St.	10-2-0	Joe Paterno	10-1-0
11	LSU	9-2-1	Charlie McClendon	9-1-1
12	North Carolina	11-1-0	Bill Dooley	10-1-0
13	Arizona St.	10-2-0	Frank Kush	9-2-0
14	Notre Dame	8-3-0	Ara Parseghian	8-2-0
15	UCLA	8-3-0	Pepper Rodgers	same
16	Colorado	8-4-0	Eddie Crowder	8-3-0
17	N.C. State	8-3-1	Lou Holtz	7-3-1
18	Louisville	9-1-0	Lee Corso	same
19	Washington St.	7-4-0	Jim Sweeney	same
20	Georgia Tech	7-4-1	Bill Fulcher	6-4-1

Key Bowl Games

Rankings below reflect final regular season poll, released Dec. 4. No bowl for then #8 Michigan. **Rose**–#1 USC over #3 Ohio St., 42-17; **Sugar**–#2 Oklahoma over #5 Penn St., 14-0; **Cotton**–#7 Texas over #4 Alabama, 17-13; **Orange**–#9 Nebraska over #12 Notre Dame, 40-6; **Gator**–#6 Auburn over #13 Colorado, 24-3; **Bluebonnet**–#11 Tennessee over #10 LSU, 24-17.

1971

		After Bowls	Head Coach	Regular Season
1	Nebraska	13-0-0	Bob Devaney	12-0-0
2	Oklahoma	11-1-0	Chuck Fairbanks	10-1-0
3	Colorado	10-2-0	Eddie Crowder	9-2-0
4	Alabama	11-1-0	Bear Bryant	11-0-0
5	Penn St.	11-1-0	Joe Paterno	10-1-0
6	Michigan	11-1-0	Bo Schembechler	11-0-0
7	Georgia	11-1-0	Vince Dooley	10-1-0
8	Arizona St.	11-1-0	Frank Kush	10-1-0
9	Tennessee	10-2-0	Bill Battle	9-2-0
10	Stanford	9-3-0	John Ralston	8-3-0
11	LSU	9-3-0	Charlie McClendon	8-3-0
12	Auburn	9-2-0	Shug Jordan	9-1-0
13	Notre Dame	8-2-0	Ara Parseghian	same
14	Toledo	12-0-0	John Murphy	11-0-0
15	Mississippi	10-2-0	Billy Kinard	9-2-0
16	Arkansas	8-3-1	Frank Broyles	8-2-1
17	Houston	9-3-0	Bill Yeoman	9-2-0
18	Texas	8-3-0	Darrell Royal	8-2-0
19	Washington	8-3-0	Jim Owens	same
20	USC	6-4-1	John McKay	same

Key Bowl Games

Rankings below reflect final regular season poll, released Dec. 6. **Orange**–#1 Nebraska over #2 Alabama, 38-6; **Sugar**–#3 Oklahoma over #5 Auburn, 40-22; **Rose**–#16 Stanford over #4 Michigan, 13-12; **Gator**–#6 Georgia over N. Carolina, 7-3; **Bluebonnet**–#7 Colorado over #15 Houston, 29-17; **Fiesta**–#8 Ariz. St. over Florida St., 45-38; **Cotton**–#10 Penn St. over #12 Texas, 30-6.

1973

		After Bowls	Head Coach	Regular Season
1	Notre Dame	11-0-0	Ara Parseghian	10-0-0
2	Ohio St.	10-0-1	Woody Hayes	9-0-1
3	Oklahoma	10-0-1	Barry Switzer	same
4	Alabama	11-1-0	Bear Bryant	11-0-0
5	Penn St.	12-0-0	Joe Paterno	11-0-0
6	Michigan	10-0-1	Bo Schembechler	same
7	Nebraska	9-2-1	Tom Osborne	8-2-1
8	USC	9-2-1	John McKay	9-1-1
9	Arizona St.	11-1-0	Frank Kush	10-1-0
	Houston	11-1-0	Bill Yeoman	10-1-0
11	Texas Tech	11-1-0	Jim Carlen	10-1-0
12	UCLA	9-2-0	Pepper Rodgers	same
13	LSU	9-3-0	Charlie McClendon	9-2-0
14	Texas	8-3-0	Darrell Royal	8-2-0
15	Miami-OH	11-0-0	Bill Mallory	10-0-0
16	N.C. State	9-3-0	Lou Holtz	8-3-0
17	Missouri	8-4-0	Al Onofrio	7-4-0
18	Kansas	7-4-1	Don Fambrough	7-3-1
19	Tennessee	8-4-0	Bill Battle	8-3-0
20	Maryland	8-4-0	Jerry Claiborne	8-3-0
	Tulane	9-3-0	Bennie Ellender	9-2-0

Key Bowl Games

Rankings below reflect final regular season poll, released Dec. 3. No bowls for then #2 Oklahoma (probation), #5 Michigan and #9 UCLA. **Sugar**–#3 Notre Dame over #1 Alabama, 24-23; **Rose**–#4 Ohio St. over #7 USC, 42-17; **Orange**–#6 Penn St. over #13 LSU, 16-9; **Cotton**–#12 Nebraska over #8 Texas, 19-3; **Fiesta**–#10 Ariz. St. over Pitt, 28-7; **Bluebonnet**–#14 Houston over #17 Tulane, 47-7.

1974

		After Bowls	Head Coach	Regular Season
1	Oklahoma	11-0-0	Barry Switzer	same
2	USC	10-1-1	John McKay	9-1-1
3	Michigan	10-1-0	Bo Schembechler	same
4	Ohio St.	10-2-0	Woody Hayes	10-1-0
5	Alabama	11-1-0	Bear Bryant	11-0-0
6	Notre Dame	10-2-0	Ara Parseghian	9-2-0
7	Penn St.	10-2-0	Joe Paterno	9-2-0
8	Auburn	10-2-0	Shug Jordan	9-2-0
9	Nebraska	9-3-0	Tom Osborne	8-3-0
10	Miami-OH	10-0-1	Dick Crum	9-0-1
11	N.C. State	9-2-1	Lou Holtz	9-2-0
12	Michigan St.	7-3-1	Denny Stolz	same
13	Maryland	8-4-0	Jerry Claiborne	8-3-0
14	Baylor	8-4-0	Grant Teaff	8-3-0
15	Florida	8-4-0	Doug Dickey	8-3-0
16	Texas A&M	8-3-0	Emory Ballard	same
17	Mississippi St.	9-3-0	Bob Tyler	8-3-0
	Texas	8-4-0	Darrell Royal	8-3-0
19	Houston	8-3-1	Bill Yeoman	8-3-0
20	Tennessee	7-3-2	Bill Battle	6-3-2

Key Bowl Games

Rankings below reflect final regular season poll, released Dec. 2. No bowls for #1 Oklahoma (probation) and then #4 Michigan.

Orange–#9 Notre Dame over #2 Alabama, 13-11; **Rose**–#5 USC over #3 Ohio St., 18-17; **Gator**–#6 Auburn over #11 Texas, 27-3; **Cotton**–#7 Penn St. over #12 Baylor, 41-20; **Sugar**–#8 Nebraska over #18 Florida, 13-10; **Liberty**–Tennessee over #10 Maryland, 7-3.

1975

		After Bowls	Head Coach	Regular Season
1	Oklahoma	11-1-0	Barry Switzer	10-1-0
2	Arizona St.	12-0-0	Frank Kush	11-0-0
3	Alabama	11-1-0	Bear Bryant	10-1-0
4	Ohio St.	11-1-0	Woody Hayes	11-0-0
5	UCLA	9-2-1	Dick Vermeil	8-2-1
6	Texas	10-2-0	Darrell Royal	9-2-0
7	Arkansas	10-2-0	Frank Broyles	9-2-0
8	Michigan	8-2-2	Bo Schembechler	8-1-2
9	Nebraska	10-2-0	Tom Osborne	10-1-0
10	Penn St.	9-3-0	Joe Paterno	9-2-0
11	Texas A&M	10-2-0	Emory Bellard	10-1-0
12	Miami-OH	11-1-0	Dick Crum	10-1-0
13	Maryland	9-2-1	Jerry Claiborne	8-2-1
14	California	8-3-0	Mike White	same
15	Pittsburgh	8-4-0	Johnny Majors	7-4-0
16	Colorado	9-3-0	Bill Mallory	9-2-0
17	USC	8-4-0	John McKay	7-4-0
18	Arizona	9-2-0	Jim Young	same
19	Georgia	9-3-0	Vince Dooley	9-2-0
20	West Virginia	9-3-0	Bobby Bowden	8-3-0

Key Bowl Games

Rankings below reflect final regular season poll, released Dec. 1. Texas A&M was unbeaten and ranked 2nd in that poll, but lost to #18 Arkansas, 31-6, in its final regular season game on Dec.6.

Rose–#11 UCLA over #1 Ohio St., 23-10; **Liberty**–#17 USC over #2 Texas A&M, 20-0; **Orange**–#3 Oklahoma over #5 Michigan, 14-6; **Sugar**–#4 Alabama over #8 Penn St., 13-6; **Fiesta**–#7 Ariz. St. over #6 Nebraska, 17-14; **Bluebonnet**–#9 Texas over #10 Colorado, 38-21; **Cotton**–#18 Arkansas over #12 Georgia, 31-10.

1976

		After Bowls	Head Coach	Regular Season
1	Pittsburgh	12-0-0	Johnny Majors	11-0-0
2	USC	11-1-0	John Robinson	10-1-0
3	Michigan	10-2-0	Bo Schembechler	10-1-0
4	Houston	10-2-0	Bill Yeoman	9-2-0
5	Oklahoma	9-2-1	Barry Switzer	8-2-1
6	Ohio St.	9-2-1	Woody Hayes	8-2-1
7	Texas A&M	10-2-0	Emory Bellard	9-2-0
8	Maryland	11-1-0	Jerry Claiborne	11-0-0
9	Nebraska	9-3-1	Tom Osborne	8-3-1
10	Georgia	10-2-0	Vince Dooley	10-1-0
11	Alabama	9-3-0	Bear Bryant	8-3-0
12	Notre Dame	9-3-0	Dan Devine	8-3-0
13	Texas Tech	10-2-0	Steve Sloan	10-1-0
14	Oklahoma St.	9-3-0	Jim Stanley	8-3-0
15	UCLA	9-2-1	Terry Donahue	9-1-1
16	Colorado	8-4-0	Bill Mallory	8-3-0
17	Rutgers	11-0-0	Frank Burns	same
18	Kentucky	8-4-0	Fran Curci	7-4-0
19	Iowa St.	8-3-0	Earle Bruce	same
20	Mississippi St.	9-2-0	Bob Tyler	same

Key Bowl Games

Rankings below reflect final regular season poll, released Nov. 29. No bowl for then #20 Miss. St. (probation).

Sugar–#1 Pitt over #5 Georgia, 27-3; **Rose**–#3 USC over #2 Michigan, 14-6; **Cotton**–#6 Houston over #4 Maryland, 30-21; **Liberty**–#16 Alabama over #7 UCLA, 36-6; **Fiesta**–#8 Oklahoma over Wyoming, 41-7; **Bluebonnet**–#13 Nebraska over #9 Texas Tech, 27-24; **Sun**–#10 Texas A&M over Florida, 37-14; **Orange**–#11 Ohio St. over #12 Colorado, 27-10.

1977

		After Bowls	Head Coach	Regular Season
1	Notre Dame	11-1-0	Dan Devine	10-1-0
2	Alabama	11-1-0	Bear Bryant	10-1-0
3	Arkansas	11-1-0	Lou Holtz	10-1-0
4	Texas	11-1-0	Fred Akers	11-0-0
5	Penn St.	11-1-0	Joe Paterno	10-1-0
6	Kentucky	10-1-0	Fran Curci	same
7	Oklahoma	10-2-0	Barry Switzer	10-1-0
8	Pittsburgh	9-2-1	Jackie Sherrill	8-2-1
9	Michigan	10-2-0	Bo Schembechler	10-1-0
10	Washington	8-4-0	Don James	7-4-0
11	Ohio St.	9-3-0	Woody Hayes	9-2-0
12	Nebraska	9-3-0	Tom Osborne	8-3-0
13	USC	8-4-0	John Robinson	7-4-0
14	Florida St.	10-2-0	Bobby Bowden	9-2-0
15	Stanford	9-3-0	Bill Walsh	8-3-0
16	San Diego St.	10-1-0	Claude Gilbert	same
17	North Carolina	8-3-1	Bill Dooley	8-2-1
18	Arizona St.	9-3-0	Frank Kush	9-2-0
19	Clemson	8-3-1	Charley Pell	8-2-1
20	BYU	9-2-0	LaVell Edwards	same

Key Bowl Games

Rankings below reflect final regular season poll, released Nov. 28. No bowl for then #7 Kentucky (probation).

Cotton–#5 Notre Dame over #1 Texas, 38-10; **Orange**–#6 Arkansas over #2 Oklahoma, 31-6; **Sugar**–#3 Alabama over #9 Ohio St., 35-6; **Rose**–#13 Washington over #4 Michigan, 27-20; **Fiesta**–#8 Penn St. over #15 Ariz. St., 42-30; **Gator**–#10 Pitt over #11 Clemson, 34-3.

Associated Press Final Polls (Cont.)

1978

		After Bowls	Head Coach	Regular Season
1	Alabama	11-1-0	Bear Bryant	10-1-0
2	USC	12-1-0	John Robinson	11-1-0
3	Oklahoma	11-1-0	Barry Switzer	10-1-0
4	Penn St.	11-1-0	Joe Paterno	11-0-0
5	Michigan	10-2-0	Bo Schembechler	10-1-0
6	Clemson	11-1-0	Charley Pell	10-1-0
7	Notre Dame	9-3-0	Dan Devine	8-3-0
8	Nebraska	9-3-0	Tom Osborne	9-2-0
9	Texas	9-3-0	Fred Akers	8-3-0
10	Houston	9-3-0	Bill Yeoman	9-2-0
11	Arkansas	9-2-1	Lou Holtz	9-2-0
12	Michigan St.	8-3-0	Darryl Rogers	same
13	Purdue	9-2-1	Jim Young	8-2-1
14	UCLA	8-3-1	Terry Donahue	8-3-0
15	Missouri	8-4-0	Warren Powers	7-4-0
16	Georgia	9-2-1	Vince Dooley	9-1-1
17	Stanford	8-4-0	Bill Walsh	7-4-0
18	N.C. State	9-3-0	Bo Rein	8-3-0
19	Texas A&M	8-4-0	Emory Bellard (4-2) & Tom Wilson (4-2)	7-4-0
20	Maryland	9-3-0	Jerry Claiborne	9-2-0

Key Bowl Games

Rankings below reflect final regular season poll, released Dec. 4. No bowl for then #12 Michigan St. (probation).

Sugar–#2 Alabama over #1 Penn St., 14-7; **Rose**–#3 USC over #5 Michigan, 17-10; **Orange**–#4 Oklahoma over #6 Nebraska, 31-24; **Gator**–#7 Clemson over #20 Ohio St., 17-15; **Fiesta**–#8 Arkansas tied #15 UCLA, 10-10; **Cotton**–#10 Notre Dame over #9 Houston, 35-34.

1979

		After Bowls	Head Coach	Regular Season
1	Alabama	12-0-0	Bear Bryant	11-0-0
2	USC	11-0-1	John Robinson	10-0-1
3	Oklahoma	11-1-0	Barry Switzer	10-1-0
4	Ohio St.	11-1-0	Earle Bruce	11-0-0
5	Houston	11-1-0	Bill Yeoman	10-1-0
6	Florida St.	11-1-0	Bobby Bowden	11-0-0
7	Pittsburgh	11-1-0	Jackie Sherrill	10-1-0
8	Arkansas	10-2-0	Lou Holtz	10-1-0
9	Nebraska	10-2-0	Tom Osborne	10-1-0
10	Purdue	10-2-0	Jim Young	9-2-0
11	Washington	9-3-0	Don James	8-3-0
12	Texas	9-3-0	Fred Akers	9-2-0
13	BYU	11-1-0	LaVell Edwards	11-0-0
14	Baylor	8-4-0	Grant Teaff	7-4-0
15	North Carolina	8-3-1	Dick Crum	7-3-1
16	Auburn	8-3-0	Doug Barfield	same
17	Temple	10-2-0	Wayne Hardin	9-2-0
18	Michigan	8-4-0	Bo Schembechler	8-3-0
19	Indiana	8-4-0	Lee Corso	7-4-0
20	Penn St.	8-4-0	Joe Paterno	7-4-0

Key Bowl Games

Rankings below reflect final regular season poll, released Dec. 3. No bowl for then #17 Auburn (probation).

Sugar–#2 Alabama over #6 Arkansas, 24-9; **Rose**–#3 USC over #1 Ohio St., 17-16; **Orange**–#5 Oklahoma over #4 Florida St., 24-7; **Sun**–#13 Washington over #11 Texas, 14-7; **Cotton**–#8 Houston over #7 Nebraska, 17-14; **Fiesta**–#10 Pitt over Arizona, 16-10.

1980

		After Bowls	Head Coach	Regular Season
1	Georgia	12-0-0	Vince Dooley	11-0-0
2	Pittsburgh	11-1-0	Jackie Sherrill	10-1-0
3	Oklahoma	10-2-0	Barry Switzer	9-2-0
4	Michigan	10-2-0	Bo Schembechler	9-2-0
5	Florida St.	10-2-0	Bobby Bowden	10-1-0
6	Alabama	10-2-0	Bear Bryant	9-2-0
7	Nebraska	10-2-0	Tom Osborne	9-2-0
8	Penn St.	10-2-0	Joe Paterno	9-2-0
9	Notre Dame	9-2-1	Dan Devine	9-1-1
10	North Carolina	11-1-0	Dick Crum	10-1-0
11	USC	8-2-1	John Robinson	same
12	BYU	12-1-0	LaVell Edwards	11-1-0
13	UCLA	9-2-0	Terry Donahue	same
14	Baylor	10-2-0	Grant Teaff	10-1-0
15	Ohio St.	9-3-0	Earle Bruce	9-2-0
16	Washington	9-3-0	Don James	9-2-0
17	Purdue	9-3-0	Jim Young	8-3-0
18	Miami-FL	9-3-0	H. Schnellenberger	8-3-0
19	Mississippi St.	9-3-0	Emory Bellard	9-2-0
20	SMU	8-4-0	Ron Meyer	8-3-0

Key Bowl Games

Rankings below reflect final regular season poll, released Dec. 8.

Sugar–#1 Georgia over #7 Notre Dame, 17-10; **Orange**–#4 Oklahoma over #2 Florida St., 18-17; **Gator**–#3 Pitt over #18 S. Carolina, 37-9; **Rose**–#5 Michigan over # 16 Washington, 23-6; **Cotton**–#9 Alabama over #6 Baylor, 30-2; **Sun**–#8 Nebraska over #17 Miss. St., 31-17; **Fiesta**–#10 Penn St. over #11 Ohio St., 31-19; **Bluebonnet**–#13 N. Carolina over Texas, 16-7.

1981

		After Bowls	Head Coach	Regular Season
1	Clemson	12-0-0	Danny Ford	11-0-0
2	Texas	10-1-1	Fred Akers	9-1-1
3	Penn St.	10-2-0	Joe Paterno	9-2-0
4	Pittsburgh	11-1-0	Jackie Sherrill	10-1-0
5	SMU	10-1-0	Ron Meyer	same
6	Georgia	10-2-0	Vince Dooley	10-1-0
7	Alabama	9-2-1	Bear Bryant	9-1-1
8	Miami-FL	9-2-0	H. Schnellenberger	same
9	North Carolina	10-2-0	Dick Crum	9-2-0
10	Washington	10-2-0	Don James	9-2-0
11	Nebraska	9-3-0	Tom Osborne	9-2-0
12	Michigan	9-3-0	Bo Schembechler	8-3-0
13	BYU	11-2-0	LaVell Edwards	10-2-0
14	USC	9-3-0	John Robinson	9-2-0
15	Ohio St.	9-3-0	Earle Bruce	8-3-0
16	Arizona St.	9-2-0	Darryl Rogers	same
17	West Virginia	9-3-0	Don Nehlen	8-3-0
18	Iowa	8-4-0	Hayden Fry	8-3-0
19	Missouri	8-4-0	Warren Powers	7-4-0
20	Oklahoma	7-4-1	Barry Switzer	6-4-1

Key Bowl Games

Rankings below reflect final regular season poll, released Nov. 30. No bowl for then #5 SMU (probation), #9 Miami-FL (probation), and #17 Ariz. St. (probation).

Orange–#1 Clemson over #4 Nebraska, 22-15; **Sugar**–#10 Pitt over #2 Georgia, 24-20; **Cotton**–#6 Texas over #3 Alabama, 14-12; **Fiesta**–#7 Penn St. over #8 USC, 26-10; **Gator**–#11 N. Carolina over Arkansas, 31-27; **Rose**–#12 Washington over #13 Iowa, 28-0.

1982

		After Bowls	Head Coach	Regular Season
1	Penn St.	11-1-0	Joe Paterno	10-1-0
2	SMU	11-0-1	Bobby Collins	10-0-1
3	Nebraska	12-1-0	Tom Osborne	11-1-0
4	Georgia	11-1-0	Vince Dooley	11-0-0
5	UCLA	10-1-1	Terry Donahue	9-1-1
6	Arizona St.	10-2-0	Darryl Rogers	9-2-0
7	Washington	10-2-0	Don James	9-2-0
8	Clemson	9-1-1	Danny Ford	same
9	Arkansas	9-2-1	Lou Holtz	8-2-1
10	Pittsburgh	9-3-0	Foge Fazio	9-2-0
11	LSU	8-3-1	Jerry Stovall	8-2-1
12	Ohio St.	9-3-0	Earle Bruce	8-3-0
13	Florida St.	9-3-0	Bobby Bowden	8-3-0
14	Auburn	9-3-0	Pat Dye	8-3-0
15	USC	8-3-0	John Robinson	same
16	Oklahoma	8-4-0	Barry Switzer	8-3-0
17	Texas	9-3-0	Fred Akers	9-2-0
18	North Carolina	8-4-0	Dick Crum	7-4-0
19	West Virginia	9-3-0	Don Nehlen	9-2-0
20	Maryland	8-4-0	Bobby Ross	8-3-0

Key Bowl Games

Rankings below reflect final regular season poll, released Dec. 6. No bowl for then #7 Clemson (probation) and #15 USC (probation).

Sugar–#2 Penn St. over #1 Georgia, 27-23; **Orange**–#3 Nebraska over #13 LSU, 21-20; **Cotton**–#4 SMU over #6 Pitt, 7-3; **Rose**–#5 UCLA over #19 Michigan, 24-14; **Aloha**–#9 Washington over #16 Maryland, 21-20; **Fiesta**–#11 Ariz. St. over #12 Oklahoma, 32-21; **Bluebonnet**–#14 Arkansas over Florida, 28-24.

1984

		After Bowls	Head Coach	Regular Season
1	BYU	13-0-0	LaVell Edwards	12-0-0
2	Washington	11-1-0	Don James	10-1-0
3	Florida	9-1-1	Charley Pell (0-1-1) & Galen Hall (9-0)	same
4	Nebraska	10-2-0	Tom Osborne	9-2-0
5	Boston College	10-2-0	Jack Bicknell	9-2-0
6	Oklahoma	9-2-1	Barry Switzer	9-1-1
7	Oklahoma St.	10-2-0	Pat Jones	9-2-0
8	SMU	10-2-0	Bobby Collins	9-2-0
9	UCLA	9-3-0	Terry Donahue	8-3-0
10	USC	9-3-0	Ted Tollner	8-3-0
11	South Carolina	10-2-0	Joe Morrison	10-1-0
12	Maryland	9-3-0	Bobby Ross	8-3-0
13	Ohio St.	9-3-0	Earle Bruce	9-2-0
14	Auburn	9-4-0	Pat Dye	8-4-0
15	LSU	8-3-1	Bill Arnsparger	8-2-1
16	Iowa	8-4-1	Hayden Fry	7-4-1
17	Florida St.	7-3-2	Bobby Bowden	7-3-1
18	Miami-FL	8-5-0	Jimmy Johnson	8-4-0
19	Kentucky	9-3-0	Jerry Claiborne	8-3-0
20	Virginia	8-2-2	George Welsh	7-2-2

Key Bowl Games

Rankings below reflect final regular season poll, released Dec. 3. No bowl for then #3 Florida (probation).

Holiday–#1 BYU over Michigan, 24-17;
Orange–#4 Washington over #2 Oklahoma, 28-17; **Sugar**–#5 Nebraska over #11 LSU, 28-10; **Rose**–#18 USC over #6 Ohio St., 20-17; **Gator**–#9 Okla. St. over #7 S. Carolina, 21-14; **Cotton**–#8 BC over Houston, 45-28; **Aloha**–#10 SMU over #17 Notre Dame, 27-20.

1983

		After Bowls	Head Coach	Regular Season
1	Miami-FL	11-1-0	H. Schnellenberger	10-1-0
2	Nebraska	12-1-0	Tom Osborne	12-0-0
3	Auburn	11-1-0	Pat Dye	10-1-0
4	Georgia	10-1-1	Vince Dooley	9-1-1
5	Texas	11-1-0	Fred Akers	11-0-0
6	Florida	9-2-1	Charley Pell	8-2-1
7	BYU	11-1-0	LaVell Edwards	10-1-0
8	Michigan	9-3-0	Bo Schembechler	9-2-0
9	Ohio St.	9-3-0	Earle Bruce	8-3-0
10	Illinois	10-2-0	Mike White	10-1-0
11	Clemson	9-1-1	Danny Ford	same
12	SMU	10-2-0	Bobby Collins	10-1-0
13	Air Force	10-2-0	Ken Hatfield	9-2-0
14	Iowa	9-3-0	Hayden Fry	9-2-0
15	Alabama	8-4-0	Ray Perkins	7-4-0
16	West Virginia	9-3-0	Don Nehlen	8-3-0
17	UCLA	7-4-1	Terry Donahue	6-4-1
18	Pittsburgh	8-3-1	Foge Fazio	8-2-1
19	Boston College	9-3-0	Jack Bicknell	9-2-0
20	East Carolina	8-3-0	Ed Emory	same

Key Bowl Games

Rankings below reflect final regular season poll, released Dec. 5. No bowl for then #12 Clemson (probation).

Orange–#5 Miami-FL over #1 Nebraska, 31-30; **Cotton**–#7 Georgia over #2 Texas, 10-9; **Sugar**–#3 Auburn over #8 Michigan, 9-7; **Rose**–UCLA over #4 Illinois, 45-9; **Holiday**–#9 BYU over Missouri, 21-17; **Gator**–#11 Florida over #10 Iowa, 14-6; **Fiesta**–#14 Ohio St. over #15 Pitt, 28-23.

1985

		After Bowls	Head Coach	Regular Season
1	Oklahoma	11-1-0	Barry Switzer	10-1-0
2	Michigan	10-1-1	Bo Schembechler	9-1-1
3	Penn St.	11-1-0	Joe Paterno	11-0-0
4	Tennessee	9-1-2	Johnny Majors	8-1-2
5	Florida	9-1-1	Galen Hall	same
6	Texas A&M	10-2-0	Jackie Sherrill	9-2-0
7	UCLA	9-2-1	Terry Donahue	8-2-1
8	Air Force	12-1-0	Fisher DeBerry	11-1-0
9	Miami-FL	10-2-0	Jimmy Johnson	10-1-0
10	Iowa	10-2-0	Hayden Fry	10-1-0
11	Nebraska	9-3-0	Tom Osborne	9-2-0
12	Arkansas	10-2-0	Ken Hatfield	9-2-0
13	Alabama	9-2-1	Ray Perkins	8-2-1
14	Ohio St.	9-3-0	Earle Bruce	8-3-0
15	Florida St.	9-3-0	Bobby Bowden	8-3-0
16	BYU	11-3-0	LaVell Edwards	11-2-0
17	Baylor	9-3-0	Grant Teaff	8-3-0
18	Maryland	9-3-0	Bobby Ross	8-3-0
19	Georgia Tech	9-2-1	Bill Curry	8-2-1
20	LSU	9-2-1	Bill Arnsparger	9-1-1

Key Bowl Games

Rankings below reflect final regular season poll, released Dec. 9. No bowl for then #6 Florida (probation).

Orange–#3 Oklahoma over #1 Penn St., 25-10; **Sugar**–#8 Tennessee over #2 Miami-FL, 35-7; **Rose**–#13 UCLA over #4 Iowa, 45-28; **Fiesta**–#5 Michigan over #7 Nebraska, 27-23; **Bluebonnet**–#10 Air Force over Texas, 24-16; **Cotton**–#11 Texas A&M over #16 Auburn, 36-16.

Associated Press Final Polls (Cont.)

1986

		After Bowls	Head Coach	Regular Season
1	Penn St.	12-0-0	Joe Paterno	11-0-0
2	Miami-FL	11-1-0	Jimmy Johnson	11-0-0
3	Oklahoma	11-1-0	Barry Switzer	10-1-0
4	Arizona St.	10-1-1	John Cooper	9-1-1
5	Nebraska	10-2-0	Tom Osborne	9-2-0
6	Auburn	10-2-0	Pat Dye	9-2-0
7	Ohio St.	10-3-0	Earle Bruce	9-3-0
8	Michigan	11-2-0	Bo Schembechler	11-1-0
9	Alabama	10-3-0	Ray Perkins	9-3-0
10	LSU	9-3-0	Bill Arnsparger	9-2-0
11	Arizona	9-3-0	Larry Smith	8-3-0
12	Baylor	9-3-0	Grant Teaff	8-3-0
13	Texas A&M	9-3-0	Jackie Sherrill	9-2-0
14	UCLA	8-3-1	Terry Donahue	7-3-1
15	Arkansas	9-3-0	Ken Hatfield	9-2-0
16	Iowa	9-3-0	Hayden Fry	8-3-0
17	Clemson	8-2-2	Danny Ford	7-2-2
18	Washington	8-3-1	Don James	8-2-1
19	Boston College	9-3-0	Jack Bicknell	8-3-0
20	Virginia Tech	9-2-1	Bill Dooley	8-2-1

Key Bowl Games

Rankings below reflect final regular season poll, released Dec. 1.

Fiesta—#2 Penn St. over #1 Miami-FL, 14-10; **Orange**—#3 Oklahoma over #9 Arkansas, 42-8; **Rose**—#7 Ariz. St. over #4 Michigan, 22-15; **Sugar**—#6 Nebraska over #5 LSU, 30-15; **Cotton**—#11 Ohio St. over #8 Texas A&M, 28-12; **Citrus**—#10 Auburn over USC, 16-7; **Sun**—#13 Alabama over #12 Washington, 28-6.

1987

		After Bowls	Head Coach	Regular Season
1	Miami-FL	12-0-0	Jimmy Johnson	11-0-0
2	Florida St.	11-1-0	Bobby Bowden	10-1-0
3	Oklahoma	11-1-0	Barry Switzer	11-0-0
4	Syracuse	11-0-1	Dick MacPherson	11-0-0
5	LSU	10-1-1	Mike Archer	9-1-1
6	Nebraska	10-2-0	Tom Osborne	10-1-0
7	Auburn	9-1-2	Pat Dye	9-1-1
8	Michigan St.	9-2-1	George Perles	8-2-1
9	UCLA	10-2-0	Terry Donahue	9-2-0
10	Texas A&M	10-2-0	Jackie Sherrill	9-2-0
11	Oklahoma St.	10-2-0	Pat Jones	9-2-0
12	Clemson	10-2-0	Danny Ford	9-2-0
13	Georgia	9-3-0	Vince Dooley	8-3-0
14	Tennessee	10-2-1	Johnny Majors	9-2-1
15	South Carolina	8-4-0	Joe Morrison	8-3-0
16	Iowa	10-3-0	Hayden Fry	9-3-0
17	Notre Dame	8-4-0	Lou Holtz	8-3-0
18	USC	8-4-0	Larry Smith	8-3-0
19	Michigan	8-4-0	Bo Schembechler	7-4-0
20	Arizona St.	7-4-1	John Cooper	6-4-1

Key Bowl Games

Rankings below reflect final regular season poll, released Dec. 7.

Orange—#2 Miami-FL over #1 Oklahoma, 20-14; **Fiesta**—#3 Florida St. over #5 Nebraska, 31-28; **Sugar**—#4 Syracuse tied #6 Auburn, 16-16; **Gator**—#7 LSU over #9 S. Carolina, 30-13; **Rose**—#8 Mich. St. over #16 USC, 20-17; **Aloha**—#10 UCLA over Florida, 20-16; **Cotton**—#13 Texas A&M over #12 Notre Dame, 35-10.

1988

		After Bowls	Head Coach	Regular Season
1	Notre Dame	12-0-0	Lou Holtz	11-0-0
2	Miami-FL	11-1-0	Jimmy Johnson	10-1-0
3	Florida St.	11-1-0	Bobby Bowden	10-1-0
4	Michigan	9-2-1	Bo Schembechler	8-2-1
5	West Virginia	11-1-0	Don Nehlen	11-0-0
6	UCLA	10-2-0	Terry Donahue	9-2-0
7	USC	10-2-0	Larry Smith	10-1-0
8	Auburn	10-2-0	Pat Dye	10-1-0
9	Clemson	10-2-0	Danny Ford	9-2-0
10	Nebraska	11-2-0	Tom Osborne	11-1-0
11	Oklahoma St.	10-2-0	Pat Jones	9-2-0
12	Arkansas	10-2-0	Ken Hatfield	10-1-0
13	Syracuse	10-2-0	Dick MacPherson	9-2-0
14	Oklahoma	9-3-0	Barry Switzer	9-2-0
15	Georgia	9-3-0	Vince Dooley	8-3-0
16	Washington St.	9-3-0	Dennis Erickson	8-3-0
17	Alabama	9-3-0	Bill Curry	8-3-0
18	Houston	9-3-0	Jack Pardee	9-2-0
19	LSU	8-4-0	Mike Archer	8-3-0
20	Indiana	8-3-1	Bill Mallory	7-3-1

Key Bowl Games

Rankings below reflect final regular season poll, released Dec. 5.

Fiesta—#1 Notre Dame over #3 West Va., 34-21; **Orange**—#2 Miami-FL over #6 Nebraska, 23-3; **Sugar**—#4 Florida St. over #7 Auburn, 13-7; **Rose**—#11 Michigan over #5 USC, 22-14; **Cotton**—#9 UCLA over #8 Arkansas, 17-3; **Citrus**—#13 Clemson over #10 Oklahoma, 13-6.

1989

		After Bowls	Head Coach	Regular Season
1	Miami-FL	11-1-0	Dennis Erickson	10-1-0
2	Notre Dame	12-1-0	Lou Holtz	11-1-0
3	Florida St.	10-2-0	Bobby Bowden	9-2-0
4	Colorado	11-1-0	Bill McCartney	11-0-0
5	Tennessee	11-1-0	Johnny Majors	10-1-0
6	Auburn	10-2-0	Pat Dye	9-2-0
7	Michigan	10-2-0	Bo Schembechler	10-1-0
8	USC	9-2-1	Larry Smith	8-2-1
9	Alabama	10-2-0	Bill Curry	10-1-0
10	Illinois	10-2-0	John Mackovic	9-2-0
11	Nebraska	10-2-0	Tom Osborne	10-1-0
12	Clemson	10-2-0	Danny Ford	9-2-0
13	Arkansas	10-2-0	Ken Hatfield	10-1-0
14	Houston	9-2-0	Jack Pardee	same
15	Penn St.	8-3-1	Joe Paterno	7-3-1
16	Michigan St.	8-4-0	George Perles	7-4-0
17	Pittsburgh	8-3-1	Mike Gottfried (7-3-1) & Paul Hackett (1-0)	7-3-1
18	Virginia	10-3-0	George Welsh	10-2-0
19	Texas Tech	9-3-0	Spike Dykes	8-3-0
20	Texas A&M	8-4-0	R.C. Slocum	8-3-0
21	West Virginia	8-3-1	Don Nehlen	8-2-1
22	BYU	10-3-0	LaVell Edwards	10-2-0
23	Washington	8-4-0	Don James	7-4-0
24	Ohio St.	8-4-0	John Cooper	8-3-0
25	Arizona	8-4-0	Dick Tomey	7-4-0

Key Bowl Games

Rankings below reflect final regular season poll, released Dec. 11. No bowl for then #13 Houston (probation).

Orange—#4 Notre Dame over #1 Colorado, 21-6; **Sugar**—#2 Miami-FL over #7 Alabama, 33-25; **Rose**—#12 USC over #3 Michigan, 17-10; **Fiesta**—#5 Florida St. over #6 Nebraska, 41-17; **Cotton**—#8 Tennessee over #10 Arkansas, 31-27; **Hall of Fame**—#9 Auburn over #21 Ohio St., 31-14; **Citrus**—#11 Illinois over #15 Virginia, 31-21.

1990

		Head Coach	Regular Season
	After Bowls		
1	Colorado 11-1-1	Bill McCartney	10-1-1
2	Georgia Tech . .11-0-1	Bobby Ross	10-0-1
3	Miami-FL 10-2-0	Dennis Erickson	9-2-0
4	Florida St. 10-2-0	Bobby Bowden	9-2-0
5	Washington . . .10-2-0	Don James	9-2-0
6	Notre Dame 9-3-0	Lou Holtz	9-2-0
7	Michigan 9-3-0	Gary Moeller	8-3-0
8	Tennessee 9-2-2	Johnny Majors	8-2-2
9	Clemson 10-2-0	Ken Hatfield	9-2-0
10	Houston 10-1-0	John Jenkins	same
11	Penn St. 9-3-0	Joe Paterno	9-2-0
12	Texas 10-2-0	David McWilliams	10-1-0
13	Florida 9-2-0	Steve Spurrier	same
14	Louisville 10-1-1	H. Schnellenberger	9-1-1
15	Texas A&M 9-3-1	R.C. Slocum	8-3-1
16	Michigan St. 8-3-1	George Perles	7-3-1
17	Oklahoma 8-3-0	Gary Gibbs	same
18	Iowa 8-4-0	Hayden Fry	8-3-0
19	Auburn 8-3-1	Pat Dye	7-3-1
20	USC 8-4-1	Larry Smith	8-3-1
21	Mississippi 9-3-0	Billy Brewer	9-2-0
22	BYU 10-3-0	LaVell Edwards	10-2-0
23	Virginia 8-4-0	George Welsh	8-3-0
24	Nebraska 9-3-0	Tom Osborne	9-2-0
25	Illinois 8-4-0	John Mackovic	8-3-0

Key Bowl Games

Rankings below reflect final regular season poll, released Dec. 3. No bowl for then #9 Houston (probation), #11 Florida (probation) and #20 Oklahoma (probation).

Orange–#1 Colorado over #5 Notre Dame, 10-9; **Citrus**–#2 Ga. Tech over #19 Nebraska, 45-21; **Cotton** –#4 Miami-FL over #3 Texas, 46-3; **Blockbuster**–#6 Florida St. over #7 Penn St., 24-17; **Rose**–#8 Washington over #17 Iowa, 46-34; **Sugar**–#10 Tennessee over Virginia, 23-22; **Gator**–#12 Michigan over #25 Ole Miss, 35-3.

1991

		Head Coach	Regular Season
	After Bowls		
1	Miami-FL 12-0-0	Dennis Erickson	11-0-0
2	Washington 12-0-0	Don James	11-0-0
3	Penn St. 11-2-0	Joe Paterno	10-2-0
4	Florida St. 11-2-0	Bobby Bowden	10-2-0
5	Alabama 11-1-0	Gene Stallings	10-1-0
6	Michigan 10-2-0	Gary Moeller	10-1-0
7	Florida 10-2-0	Steve Spurrier	10-1-0
8	California 10-2-0	Bruce Snyder	9-2-0
9	East Carolina . . .11-1-0	Bill Lewis	10-1-0
10	Iowa 10-1-1	Hayden Fry	10-1-0
11	Syracuse 10-2-0	Paul Pasqualoni	9-2-0
12	Texas A&M 10-2-0	R.C. Slocum	10-1-0
13	Notre Dame 10-3-0	Lou Holtz	9-3-0
14	Tennessee 9-3-0	Johnny Majors	9-2-0
15	Nebraska 9-2-1	Tom Osborne	9-1-1
16	Oklahoma 9-3-0	Gary Gibbs	8-3-0
17	Georgia 9-3-0	Ray Goff	8-3-0
18	Clemson 9-2-1	Ken Hatfield	9-1-1
19	UCLA 9-3-0	Terry Donahue	8-3-0
20	Colorado 8-3-1	Bill McCartney	8-2-1
21	Tulsa 10-2-0	David Rader	9-2-0
22	Stanford 8-4-0	Dennis Green	8-3-0
23	BYU 8-3-2	LaVell Edwards	8-3-1
24	N.C. State 9-3-0	Dick Sheridan	9-2-0
25	Air Force 10-3-0	Fisher DeBerry	9-3-0

Key Bowl Games

Rankings below reflect final regular season poll, taken Dec. 2.

Orange–#1 Miami-FL over #11 Nebraska, 22-0; **Rose**–#2 Washington over #4 Michigan, 34-14; **Sugar**–#18 Notre Dame over #3 Florida, 39-28; **Cotton**–#5 Florida St. over #9 Texas A&M, 10-2; **Fiesta**–#6 Penn St. over #10 Tennessee, 42-17; **Holiday**–#7 Iowa tied BYU, 13-13; **Blockbuster**–#8 Alabama over #15 Colorado, 30-25; **Citrus**–#14 California over #13 Clemson, 37-13; **Peach**– #12 East Carolina over #21 N.C. State, 37-34.

1992

		Head Coach	Regular Season
	After Bowls		
1	Alabama 13-0-0	Gene Stallings	12-0-0
2	Florida St. 11-1-0	Bobby Bowden	10-1-0
3	Miami-FL 11-1-0	Dennis Erickson	11-0-0
4	Notre Dame 10-1-1	Lou Holtz	9-1-1
5	Michigan 9-0-3	Gary Moeller	8-0-3
6	Syracuse 10-2-0	Paul Pasqualoni	9-2-0
7	Texas A&M 12-1-0	R.C. Slocum	12-0-0
8	Georgia 10-2-0	Ray Goff	9-2-0
9	Stanford 10-3-0	Bill Walsh	9-3-0
10	Florida 9-4-0	Steve Spurrier	8-4-0
11	Washington 9-3-0	Don James	9-2-0
12	Tennessee 9-3-0	Johnny Majors (5-3) & Phillip Fulmer (4-0)	8-3-0
13	Colorado 9-2-1	Bill McCartney	9-1-1
14	Nebraska 9-3-0	Tom Osborne	9-2-0
15	Washington St. . . .9-3-0	Mike Price	8-3-0
16	Mississippi 9-3-0	Billy Brewer	8-3-0
17	N.C. State 9-3-1	Dick Sheridan	9-2-1
18	Ohio St. 8-3-1	John Cooper	8-2-1
19	North Carolina . . .9-3-0	Mack Brown	8-3-0
20	Hawaii 11-2-0	Bob Wagner	10-2-0
21	Boston College . . .8-3-1	Tom Coughlin	8-2-1
22	Kansas 8-4-0	Glen Mason	7-4-0
23	Mississippi St. 7-5-0	Jackie Sherrill	7-4-0
24	Fresno St. 9-4-0	Jim Sweeney	9-3-0
25	Wake Forest 8-4-0	Bill Dooley	7-4-0

Key Bowl Games

Rankings below reflect final regular season poll, taken Dec. 5. **Sugar**–#2 Alabama over #1 Miami-FL, 34-13; **Orange**–#3 Florida St. over #11 Nebraska, 27-14; **Cotton**–#5 Notre Dame over #4 Texas A&M, 28-3; **Fiesta**–#6 Syracuse over #10 Colorado, 26-22; **Rose**–#7 Michigan over #9 Washington, 38-31; **Citrus**–#8 Georgia over #15 Ohio St., 21-14.

All-Time AP Top 20

The composite AP Top 20 from the 1936 season through the 2002 season, based on the final rankings of each year. The final AP poll has been taken after the bowl games in 1965 and since 1968. Team point totals are based on 20 points for all 1st place finishes, 19 for each 2nd, etc. Also listed are the number of times each team has been named national champion by AP and times ranked in the final Top 10 and Top 20.

		Pts	No.1	Top 10	Top 20
1	Notre Dame 636		8	34	46
2	Michigan 614		2	35	50
3	Oklahoma 609		7	32	44
4	Alabama 574		6	31	43
5	Nebraska 546		4	29	41
6	Ohio St 538		4	25	42
7	Tennessee 450		2	22	37
8	Texas 446		2	21	35
9	USC 431		3	21	37
10	Penn St 408		2	21	36
11	Miami-FL 329		5	16	26
12	UCLA 322		0	16	29
13	Florida St 320		2	16	21
14	LSU 291		1	15	26
	Auburn 291		1	14	28
16	Georgia 280		1	15	25
17	Arkansas 267		0	13	25
18	Florida 257		1	13	22
19	Michigan St 252		1	13	20
20	Washington 222		0	11	21

Associated Press Final Polls (Cont.)

1993

		After Bowls	Head Coach	Regular Season
1	Florida St	12-1-0	Bobby Bowden	11-1-0
2	Notre Dame	11-1-0	Lou Holtz	10-1-0
3	Nebraska	11-1-0	Tom Osborne	11-0-0
4	Auburn	11-0-0	Terry Bowden	11-0-0
5	Florida	11-2-0	Steve Spurrier	10-2-0
6	Wisconsin	10-1-1	Barry Alvarez	9-1-1
7	West Virginia	11-1-0	Don Nehlen	11-0-0
8	Penn St	10-2-0	Joe Paterno	9-2-0
9	Texas A&M	10-2-0	R.C. Slocum	10-1-0
10	Arizona	10-2-0	Dick Tomey	9-2-0
11	Ohio St	10-1-1	John Cooper	9-1-1
12	Tennessee	9-2-1	Phillip Fulmer	9-1-1
13	Boston College	9-3-0	Tom Coughlin	8-3-0
14	Alabama	9-3-1	Gene Stallings	8-3-1
15	Miami-FL	9-3-0	Dennis Erickson	9-2-0
16	Colorado	8-3-1	Bill McCartney	7-3-1
17	Oklahoma	9-3-0	Gary Gibbs	8-3-0
18	UCLA	8-4-0	Terry Donahue	8-3-0
19	North Carolina	10-3-0	Mack Brown	10-2-0
20	Kansas St	9-2-1	Bill Snyder	8-2-1
21	Michigan	8-4-0	Gary Moeller	7-4-0
22	Va. Tech	9-3-0	Frank Beamer	9-2-0
23	Clemson	9-3-0	Ken Hatfield (8-3) & Tommy West (1-0)	8-3-0
24	Louisville	9-3-0	H. Schnellenberger	8-3-0
25	California	9-4-0	Keith Gilbertson	8-4-0

Key Bowl Games

Rankings below reflect final regular season poll, taken Dec. 5. No bowl for then #5 Auburn (probation). **Orange**–#1 Florida St. over #2 Nebraska, 18-16; **Sugar**–#8 Florida over #3 West Virginia, 41-7; **Cotton**–#4 Notre Dame over #7 Texas A&M, 24-21; **Citrus**–#13 Penn St. over #6 Tennessee, 31-13; **Rose**–#9 Wisconsin over #14 UCLA, 21-16; **Fiesta**–#16 Arizona over #10 Miami-FL, 29-0;

1994

		After Bowls	Head Coach	Regular Season
1	Nebraska	13-0-0	Tom Osborne	12-0-0
2	Penn St	12-0-0	Joe Paterno	11-0-0
3	Colorado	11-1-0	Bill McCartney	10-1-0
4	Florida St	10-1-1	Bobby Bowden	9-1-1
5	Alabama	12-1-0	Gene Stallings	11-1-0
6	Miami-FL	10-2-0	Dennis Erickson	10-1-0
7	Florida	10-2-1	Steve Spurrier	10-1-1
8	Texas A&M	10-0-1	R.C. Slocum	same
9	Auburn	9-1-1	Terry Bowden	same
10	Utah	10-2-0	Ron McBride	9-2-0
11	Oregon	9-4-0	Rich Brooks	9-3-0
12	Michigan	8-4-0	Gary Moeller	7-4-0
13	USC	8-3-1	John Robinson	7-3-1
14	Ohio St	9-4-0	John Cooper	9-3-0
15	Virginia	9-3-0	George Welsh	8-3-0
16	Colorado St	10-2-0	Sonny Lubick	10-1-0
17	N.C. State	9-3-0	Mike O'Cain	8-3-0
18	BYU	10-3-0	LaVell Edwards	9-3-0
19	Kansas St	9-3-0	Bill Snyder	9-2-0
20	Arizona	8-4-0	Dick Tomey	8-3-0
21	Washington St	8-4-0	Mike Price	7-4-0
22	Tennessee	8-4-0	Phillip Fulmer	7-4-0
23	Boston College	7-4-1	Dan Henning	6-4-1
24	Mississippi St	8-4-0	Jackie Sherrill	8-3-0
25	Texas	8-4-0	John Mackovic	7-4-0

Key Bowl Games

Rankings below reflect final regular season poll, taken Dec. 4. No bowls for then #8 Texas A&M (probation) and #9 Auburn (probation). **Orange**–#1 Nebraska over #3 Miami-FL, 24-17; **Rose**–#2 Penn St. over #12 Oregon, 38-20; **Fiesta**–#4 Colorado over Notre Dame, 41-24; **Sugar**–#7 Florida St. over #5 Florida, 23-17; **Citrus**–#6 Alabama over #13 Ohio St., 24-17; **Freedom**–#14 Utah over #15 Arizona, 16-13.

1995

		After Bowls	Head Coach	Regular Season
1	Nebraska	12-0-0	Tom Osborne	11-0-0
2	Florida	12-1-0	Steve Spurrier	12-0-0
3	Tennessee	11-1-0	Phillip Fulmer	10-1-0
4	Florida St	10-2-0	Bobby Bowden	9-2-0
5	Colorado	10-2-0	Rick Neuheisel	9-2-0
6	Ohio St	11-2-0	John Cooper	11-1-0
7	Kansas St	10-2-0	Bill Snyder	9-2-0
8	Northwestern	10-2-0	Gary Barnett	10-1-0
9	Kansas	10-2-0	Glen Mason	9-2-0
10	Va. Tech	10-2-0	Frank Beamer	9-2-0
11	Notre Dame	9-3-0	Lou Holtz	9-2-0
12	USC	9-2-1	John Robinson	8-2-1
13	Penn St	9-3-0	Joe Paterno	8-3-0
14	Texas	10-2-1	John Mackovic	10-1-1
15	Texas A&M	9-3-0	R.C. Slocum	8-3-0
16	Virginia	9-4-0	George Welsh	8-4-0
17	Michigan	9-4-0	Lloyd Carr	9-3-0
18	Oregon	9-3-0	Mike Bellotti	9-2-0
19	Syracuse	9-3-0	Paul Pasqualoni	8-3-0
20	Miami-FL	8-3-0	Butch Davis	same
21	Alabama	8-3-0	Gene Stallings	same
22	Auburn	8-4-0	Terry Bowden	8-3-0
23	Texas Tech	9-3-0	Spike Dykes	8-3-0
24	Toledo	11-0-1	Gary Pinkel	10-0-1
25	Iowa	8-4-0	Hayden Fry	7-4-0

Key Bowl Games

Rankings below reflect final regular season poll, taken Dec. 3. No bowl for then #21 Ala. (probation) and #22 Miami-FL (probation). **Fiesta**–#1 Neb. over #2 Fla., 62-24; **Rose**–#17 USC over #3 Northwestern, 41-32; **Citrus**–#4t Tenn. over #4t Ohio St., 20-14; **Orange**–#8 Fla. St. over #6 N. Dame, 31-26; **Cotton**–#7 Colo. over #12 Oregon, 38-6; **Sugar**–#13 Va. Tech over #9 Texas, 28-10.

1996

		After Bowls	Head Coach	Regular Season
1	Florida	12-1	Steve Spurrier	11-1
2	Ohio St.	11-1	John Cooper	10-1
3	Florida St	11-1	Bobby Bowden	11-0
4	Arizona St	11-1	Bruce Snyder	11-0
5	BYU	14-1	LaVell Edwards	13-1
6	Nebraska	11-2	Tom Osborne	10-2
7	Penn St.	11-2	Joe Paterno	10-2
8	Colorado	10-2	Rick Neuheisel	9-2
9	Tennessee	10-2	Phillip Fulmer	9-2
10	North Carolina	10-2	Mack Brown	9-2
11	Alabama	10-3	Gene Stallings	9-3
12	LSU	10-2	Gerry DiNardo	9-2
13	Virginia Tech	10-2	Frank Beamer	10-1
14	Miami-FL	9-3	Butch Davis	8-3
15	Northwestern	9-3	Gary Barnett	9-2
16	Washington	9-3	Jim Lambright	9-2
17	Kansas St.	9-3	Bill Snyder	9-2
18	Iowa	9-3	Hayden Fry	8-3
19	Notre Dame	8-3	Lou Holtz	same
20	Michigan	8-4	Lloyd Carr	8-3
21	Syracuse	9-3	Paul Pasqualoni	8-3
22	Wyoming	10-2	Joe Tiller	same
23	Texas	8-5	John Mackovic	8-4
24	Auburn	8-4	Terry Bowden	7-4
25	Army	10-2	Bob Sutton	10-1

Key Bowl Games

Rankings below reflect final regular season poll, taken Dec. 8. No bowl for then #18 N. Dame and #22 Wyoming. **Sugar**–#3 Fla. over #1 Fla. St., 52-20; **Rose**–#4 Ohio St. over #2 Ariz. St., 20-17; **Fiesta**–#7 Penn St. over #20 Texas, 38-15; **Cotton**–#5 BYU over #14 Kansas St., 19-15; **Citrus**–#9 Tenn. over #11 Northwestern, 48-28; **Orange**–#6 Neb. over #10 Va. Tech, 41-21.

1997

		After Bowls	Head Coach	Regular Season
1	Michigan	12-0	Lloyd Carr	11-0
2	Nebraska	13-0	Tom Osborne	12-0
3	Florida St	11-1	Bobby Bowden	10-1
4	Florida	10-2	Steve Spurrier	9-2
5	UCLA	10-2	Bob Toledo	9-2
6	North Carolina	11-1	Mack Brown (10-1) & Carl Torbush	10-1 (1-0)
7	Tennessee	11-2	Phillip Fulmer	11-1
8	Kansas St	11-1	Bill Snyder	10-1
9	Washington St.	10-2	Mike Price	10-1
10	Georgia	10-2	Jim Donnan	9-2
11	Auburn	10-3	Terry Bowden	9-3
12	Ohio St.	10-3	John Cooper	10-2
13	LSU	9-3	Gerry DiNardo	8-3
14	Arizona St.	8-3	Bruce Snyder	7-3
15	Purdue	9-3	Joe Tiller	8-3
16	Penn St.	9-3	Joe Paterno	9-2
17	Colorado St.	11-2	Sonny Lubick	10-2
18	Washington	8-4	Jim Lambright	7-4
19	So. Mississippi	9-3	Jeff Bower	8-3
20	Texas A&M	9-4	R.C. Slocum	9-3
21	Syracuse	9-4	Paul Pasqualoni	9-3
22	Mississippi	8-4	Tommy Tuberville	7-4
23	Missouri	7-5	Larry Smith	6-5
24	Oklahoma St.	8-4	Bobby Simmons	8-3
25	Georgia Tech	7-5	George O'Leary	6-5

Key Bowl Games

Rankings below reflect final regular season poll, taken Dec. 7. **Rose**–#1 Michigan over #7 Washington St., 21-16; **Orange**–#2 Nebraska over #3 Tennessee, 42-17; **Sugar**–#4 Florida St. over #10 Ohio St., 31-14; **Gator**–#5 North Carolina over Virginia Tech, 42-3; **Cotton**–#6 UCLA over #19 Texas A&M, 29-23; **Citrus**–#8 Florida over #12 Penn St., 21-6; **Fiesta**–#9 Kansas St. over #14 Syracuse, 35-18.

1998

		After Bowls	Head Coach	Regular Season
1	Tennessee	13-0	Phillip Fulmer	12-0
2	Ohio St.	11-1	John Cooper	10-1
3	Florida St.	11-2	Bobby Bowden	11-1
4	Arizona	12-1	Dick Tomey	11-1
5	Florida	10-2	Steve Spurrier	9-2
6	Wisconsin	11-1	Barry Alvarez	10-1
7	Tulane	12-0	Tommy Bowden	11-0
8	UCLA	10-2	Bob Toledo	10-1
9	Georgia Tech	10-2	George O'Leary	9-2
10	Kansas St.	11-2	Bill Snyder	11-1
11	Texas A&M	11-3	R.C. Slocum	11-2
12	Michigan	10-3	Lloyd Carr	9-3
13	Air Force	12-1	Fisher DeBerry	11-1
14	Georgia	9-3	Jim Donnan	8-3
15	Texas	9-3	Mack Brown	8-3
16	Arkansas	9-3	Houston Nutt	9-2
17	Penn St.	9-3	Joe Paterno	8-3
18	Virginia	9-3	George Welsh	9-2
19	Nebraska	9-4	Frank Solich	9-3
20	Miami-FL	9-3	Butch Davis	8-3
21	Missouri	8-4	Larry Smith	7-4
22	Notre Dame	9-3	Bob Davie	9-2
23	Va. Tech	9-3	Frank Beamer	8-3
24	Purdue	9-4	Joe Tiller	8-4
25	Syracuse	8-4	Paul Pasqualoni	8-3

Key Bowl Games

Rankings below reflect final regular season poll, taken Dec. 6. **Fiesta**– #1 Tennessee over #2 Florida St., 23-16; **Sugar**–#3 Ohio St. over #8 Texas A&M, 24-14; **Orange**–#7 Florida over #18 Syracuse, 31-10; **Rose**–#9 Wisconsin over #6 UCLA, 38-31; **Holiday**–#5 Arizona over #14 Nebraska, 23-20; **Alamo**–Purdue over #4 Kansas St., 37-34.

1999

		After Bowls	Head Coach	Regular Season
1	Florida St.	12-0	Bobby Bowden	11-0
2	Va. Tech	11-1	Frank Beamer	11-0
3	Nebraska	12-1	Frank Solich	11-1
4	Wisconsin	10-2	Barry Alvarez	9-2
5	Michigan	10-2	Lloyd Carr	9-2
6	Kansas St	11-1	Bill Snyder	10-1
7	Michigan St.	10-2	Nick Saban (9-2) & B. Williams (1-0)	9-2
8	Alabama	10-3	Mike DuBose	10-2
9	Tennessee	9-3	Phillip Fulmer	8-3
10	Marshall	13-0	Bob Pruett	12-0
11	Penn St.	10-3	Joe Paterno	9-3
12	Florida	9-4	Steve Spurrier	9-3
13	Mississippi St.	10-2	Jackie Sherrill	9-2
14	Southern Miss.	9-3	Jeff Bower	8-3
15	Miami-FL	9-4	Butch Davis	8-4
16	Georgia	8-4	Jim Donnan	7-4
17	Arkansas	8-4	Houston Nutt	7-4
18	Minnesota	8-4	Glen Mason	8-3
19	Oregon	9-3	Mike Bellotti	8-3
20	Georgia Tech	8-4	George O'Leary	8-3
21	Texas	9-5	Mack Brown	9-4
22	Mississippi	8-4	David Cutcliffe	7-4
23	Texas A&M	8-4	R.C. Slocum	8-3
24	Illinois	8-4	Ron Turner	7-4
25	Purdue	7-5	Joe Tiller	7-4

Key Bowl Games

Rankings below reflect final regular season poll, taken Dec. 5. **Sugar**–#1 Florida St. over #2 Va. Tech, 46-29; **Fiesta**–#3 Nebraska over #6 Tennessee, 31-21; **Rose**–#4 Wisconsin over #22 Stanford, 17-9; **Orange**–#8 Michigan over #5 Alabama, 35-34; **Holiday**–#7 Kansas St. over Washington, 24-20; **Citrus**–#9 Michigan St. over #10 Florida, 37-34.

2000

		After Bowls	Head Coach	Regular Season
1	Oklahoma	13-0	Bob Stoops	12-0
2	Miami-FL	11-1	Butch Davis	10-1
3	Washington	11-1	Rick Neuheisel	10-1
4	Oregon St.	11-1	Dennis Erickson	10-1
5	Florida St.	11-2	Bobby Bowden	11-1
6	Va. Tech	11-1	Frank Beamer	10-1
7	Oregon	10-2	Mike Bellotti	9-2
8	Nebraska	10-2	Frank Solich	9-2
9	Kansas St.	11-3	Bill Snyder	10-3
10	Florida	10-3	Steve Spurrier	10-2
11	Michigan	9-3	Lloyd Carr	8-3
12	Texas	9-3	Mack Brown	9-2
13	Purdue	8-4	Joe Tiller	8-3
14	Colorado St.	10-2	Sonny Lubick	9-2
15	Notre Dame	9-3	Bob Davie	9-2
16	Clemson	9-3	Tommy Bowden	9-2
17	Georgia Tech	9-3	George O'Leary	9-2
18	Auburn	9-4	Tommy Tuberville	9-3
19	South Carolina	8-4	Lou Holtz	7-4
20	Georgia	8-4	Jim Donnan	7-4
21	TCU	10-2	D. Franchione (10-1) & G. Patterson (0-1)	10-1
22	LSU	8-4	Nick Saban	7-4
23	Wisconsin	9-4	Barry Alvarez	8-4
24	Mississippi St.	8-4	Jackie Sherrill	7-4
25	Iowa St.	9-3	Dan McCarney	8-3

Key Bowl Games

Rankings below reflect final regular season poll, taken Dec. 4. **Orange**–#1 Oklahoma over #3 Florida St., 13-2; **Sugar**–#2 Miami-FL over #7 Florida, 37-20; **Rose**–#4 Washington over #14 Purdue, 34-24; **Fiesta**–#5 Oregon St. over #10 Notre Dame, 41-9; **Gator**–#6 Virginia Tech over #16 Clemson, 41-20; **Holiday**–#8 Oregon over #12 Texas, 35-30; **Alamo**–#9 Nebraska over #18 Northwestern, 66-17.

Associated Press Final Polls (Cont.)

2001

		After Bowls	Head Coach	Regular Season
1	Miami-FL	12-0	Larry Coker	11-0
2	Oregon	11-1	Mike Bellotti	10-1
3	Florida	10-2	Steve Spurrier	9-2
4	Tennessee	11-2	Phillip Fullmer	10-2
5	Texas	11-2	Mack Brown	10-2
6	Oklahoma	11-2	Bob Stoops	10-2
7	LSU	10-3	Nick Saban	9-3
8	Nebraska	11-2	Frank Solich	11-1
9	Colorado	10-3	Gary Barnett	10-2
10	Washington St.	10-2	Mike Price	9-2
11	Maryland	10-2	Ralph Friedgen	10-1
12	Illinois	10-2	Ron Turner	10-1
13	South Carolina	9-3	Lou Holtz	8-3
14	Syracuse	10-3	Paul Pasqualoni	9-3
15	Florida St.	8-4	Bobby Bowden	7-4
16	Stanford	9-3	Tyrone Willingham	9-2
17	Louisville	11-2	John L. Smith	10-2
18	Va. Tech	8-4	Frank Beamer	8-3
19	Washington	8-4	Rick Neuheisel	8-3
20	Michigan	8-4	Lloyd Carr	8-3
21	Boston College	8-4	Tom O'Brien	7-4
22	Georgia	8-4	Mark Richt	8-3
23	Toledo	10-2	Tom Amstutz	9-2
24	Georgia Tech	8-5	George O'Leary (7-5) & Mac McWhorter (1-0)	7-5
25	BYU	12-2	Gary Crowton	12-1

Key Bowl Games

Rankings below reflect final regular season poll, taken Dec. 9. **Rose**–#1 Miami-FL over #4 Nebraska, 37-14; **Fiesta**–#2 Oregon over #3 Colorado, 38-16; **Orange**–#5 Florida over #6 Maryland, 56-23; **Sugar**–#12 LSU over #7 Illinois 47-34; **Citrus**–#8 Tennessee over #17 Michigan, 45-17; **Holiday**–#9 Texas over #21 Washington, 47-43; **Cotton**–#10 Oklahoma over #14 Arkansas, 10-3; **Seattle**–Georgia Tech over #11 Stanford, 24-14; **Sun**–#13 Washington St. over Purdue, 33-27; **Outback**–#14 South Carolina over #22 Ohio St., 31-28; **Gator**–#24 Florida St. over #15 Virginia Tech, 30-17; **Music City**–Boston College over #16 Georgia 20-16; **Liberty**–#23 Louisville over #19 BYU, 28-10; **Insight.com**–#18 Syracuse over Kansas St., 26-3.

2002

		After Bowls	Head Coach	Regular Season
1	Ohio St.	14-0	Jim Tressel	13-0
2	Miami-FL	12-1	Larry Coker	12-0
3	Georgia	13-1	Mark Richt	12-1
4	USC	11-2	Pete Carroll	10-2
5	Oklahoma	12-2	Bob Stoops	11-2
6	Texas	11-2	Mack Brown	10-2
7	Kansas St.	11-2	Bill Snyder	10-2
8	Iowa	11-2	Kirk Ferentz	11-1
9	Michigan	10-3	Lloyd Carr	9-3
10	Washington St.	10-3	Mike Price	10-2
11	Alabama	10-3	Dennis Franchione	10-3
12	N.C. State	11-3	Chuck Amato	10-3
13	Maryland	11-3	Ralph Friedgen	10-3
14	Auburn	9-4	Tommy Tuberville	8-4
15	Boise St.	12-1	Dan Hawkins	11-1
16	Penn St.	9-4	Joe Paterno	9-2
17	Notre Dame	10-3	Tyrone Willingham	10-2
18	Va. Tech	10-4	Frank Beamer	9-4
19	Pittsburgh	9-4	Walt Harris	8-4
20	Colorado	9-5	Gary Barnett	9-4
21	Florida St.	9-5	Bobby Bowden	9-4
22	Virginia	9-5	Al Groh	8-5
23	TCU	10-2	Gary Patterson	9-2
24	Marshall	11-2	Bob Pruett	10-2
25	West Virginia	9-4	Rich Rodriguez	9-3

Key Bowl Games

Rankings below reflect final regular season poll, taken Dec. 8. No bowl for then #13 Alabama (probation).

Fiesta–#2 Ohio St. over #1 Miami-FL, 31-24 (2OT); **Orange**–#5 USC over #3 Iowa, 38-17; **Sugar**–#4 Georgia over #16 Florida St. 26-13; **Holiday**–#6 Kansas St. over Arizona St., 34-27; **Rose**–#8 Oklahoma over #7 Washington St., 34-14; **Cotton**–#9 Texas over LSU, 35-20; **Capital One**–#19 Auburn over #10 Penn St., 13-9; **Gator**–#17 N.C. State over #11 Notre Dame, 28-6; **Outback**–#12 Michigan over #22 Florida, 38-30; **Alamo**–Wisconsin over #14 Colorado, 31-28; **Continental Tire**–Virginia over #15 West Va., 48-22; **Humanitarian**–#18 Boise St. over Iowa St., 34-16; **Peach**– #20 Maryland over Tennessee, 30-3; **San Francisco**–#21 Va. Tech over Air Force, 20-13.

The Special Election That Didn't Count

There was one No. 1 vs. No. 2 confrontation not noted in the Number 1 vs. Number 2 table on pages 156-157. It came in a special election or re-vote of Associated Press selectors following the 1948 Rose Bowl. Here's what happened: Unbeaten Notre Dame was declared 1947 national champion by the AP on Dec. 8, two days after closing out an undefeated season with a 38-7 rout of then third-ranked USC in Los Angeles. Twenty-four days later, however, unbeaten Michigan, AP's final No. 2 team, clobbered now eighth-ranked USC, 49-0, in the Rose Bowl. An immediate cry went up for an unprecedented two-team "Who's No. 1?" ballot and the AP gave in. Michigan won the election 226-119, with 12 voters calling it even. However, AP ruled that the Dec. 8 final poll vote won by Notre Dame would be the poll of record.

Bowl Games

From Jan. 1, 1902 through Jan. 3, 2003. Please note that the Bowl selection process is now dominated by the Bowl Championship Series (which includes the Fiesta, Orange, Rose and Sugar bowls) and the following non-BCS bowls' so called "automatic berths" are contingent upon several factors, including the leftovers from the BCS, Notre Dame's record and the record of their designated choices.

Rose Bowl

City: Pasadena, Calif. **Stadium:** Rose Bowl. **Capacity:** 102,083. **Playing surface:** Grass. **First game:** Jan. 1, 1902. **Playing sites:** Tournament Park (1902, 1916-22), Rose Bowl (1923-41 and since 1943) and Duke Stadium in Durham, N.C. (1942, due to wartime restrictions following Japan's attack on Pearl Harbor on Dec. 7, 1941). **Corporate sponsors:** AT&T (1998-2002) and Sony Playstation 2 (2003).

Automatic berths: Pacific Coast Conference champion vs. opponent selected by PCC (1924-45 seasons); Big Ten champion vs. Pac-10 champion (1946-97); Bowl Championship Series: Big Ten champion vs. Pac-10 champion, if available (1998-2000, 2002-05 seasons) and #1 vs. #2 in Jan. 2002 and Jan. 2006.

Multiple wins: USC (20); Michigan (8); Washington (7); Ohio St. (6); Stanford and UCLA (5); Alabama (4); Illinois, Michigan St. and Wisconsin (3); California and Iowa (2).

Year		Year		Year	
1902*	Michigan 49, Stanford 0	1945	USC 25, Tennessee 0	1975	USC 18, Ohio St. 17
1916	Washington St. 14, Brown 0	1946	Alabama 34, USC 14	1976	UCLA 23, Ohio St. 10
1917	Oregon 14, Penn 0	1947	Illinois 45, UCLA 14	1977	USC 14, Michigan 6
1918	Mare Island 19, Camp Lewis 7	1948	Michigan 49, USC 0	1978	Washington 27, Michigan 20
1919	Great Lakes 17, Mare Island 0	1949	Northwestern 20, California 14	1979	USC 17, Michigan 10
1920	Harvard 7, Oregon 6	1950	Ohio St. 17, California 14	1980	USC 17, Ohio St. 16
1921	California 28, Ohio St. 0	1951	Michigan 14, California 6	1981	Michigan 23, Washington 6
1922	0-0, California vs Wash. & Jeff.	1952	Illinois 40, Stanford 7	1982	Washington 28, Iowa 0
1923	USC 14, Penn St. 0	1953	USC 7, Wisconsin 0	1983	UCLA 24, Michigan 14
1924	14-14, Navy vs Washington	1954	Michigan St. 28, UCLA 20	1984	UCLA 45, Illinois 9
1925	Notre Dame 27, Stanford 10	1955	Ohio St. 20, USC 7	1985	USC 20, Ohio St. 17
1926	Alabama 20, Washington 19	1956	Michigan St. 17, UCLA 14	1986	UCLA 45, Iowa 28
1927	7-7, Alabama vs Stanford	1957	Iowa 35, Oregon St. 19	1987	Arizona St. 22, Michigan 15
1928	Stanford 7, Pittsburgh 6	1958	Ohio St. 10, Oregon 7	1988	Michigan St. 20, USC 17
1929	Georgia Tech 8, California 7	1959	Iowa 38, California 12	1989	Michigan 22, USC 14
1930	USC 47, Pittsburgh 14	1960	Washington 44, Wisconsin 8	1990	USC 17, Michigan 10
1931	Alabama 24, Washington St. 0	1961	Washington 17, Minnesota 7	1991	Washington 46, Iowa 34
1932	USC 21, Tulane 12	1962	Minnesota 21, UCLA 3	1992	Washington 34, Michigan 14
1933	USC 35, Pittsburgh 0	1963	USC 42, Wisconsin 37	1993	Michigan 38, Washington 31
1934	Columbia 7, Stanford 0	1964	Illinois 17, Washington 7	1994	Wisconsin 21, UCLA 16
1935	Alabama 29, Stanford 13	1965	Michigan 34, Oregon St. 7	1995	Penn St. 38, Oregon 20
1936	Stanford 7, SMU 0	1966	UCLA 14, Michigan St. 12	1996	USC 41, Northwestern 32
1937	Pittsburgh 21, Washington 0	1967	Purdue 14, USC 13	1997	Ohio St. 20, Arizona St. 17
1938	California 13, Alabama 0	1968	USC 14, Indiana 3	1998	Michigan 21, Washington St. 16
1939	USC 7, Duke 3	1969	Ohio St. 27, USC 16	1999	Wisconsin 38, UCLA 31
1940	USC 14, Tennessee 0	1970	USC 10, Michigan 3	2000	Wisconsin 17, Stanford 9
1941	Stanford 21, Nebraska 13	1971	Stanford 27, Ohio St. 17	2001	Washington 34, Purdue 24
1942	Oregon St. 20, Duke 16	1972	Stanford 13, Michigan 12	2002	Miami-FL 37, Nebraska 14
1943	Georgia 9, UCLA 0	1973	USC 42, Ohio St. 17	2003	Oklahoma 34, Washington St. 14
1944	USC 29, Washington 0	1974	Ohio St. 42, USC 21		* January game since 1902.

Fiesta Bowl

City: Tempe, Ariz. **Stadium:** Sun Devil. **Capacity:** 73,656. **Playing surface:** Grass. **First game:** Dec. 27, 1971. **Playing site:** Sun Devil Stadium (since 1971). **Corporate title sponsors:** Sunkist Citrus Growers (1986-91), IBM OS/2 (1993-95) and Frito-Lay Tostitos chips (since 1996).

Automatic berths: Western Athletic Conference champion vs. at-large opponent (1971-79 seasons); Two of first five picks from 8-team Bowl Coalition pool (1992-94). Bowl Alliance (#1 vs. #2 on Jan. 2, 1996; #3 vs. #5 on Jan. 1, 1997; and #4 vs. #6 on Dec. 31, 1997); Big 12 champion vs. next best team in pool (New Bowl Alliance 1995-1997 seasons); Bowl Championship Series: #1 vs. #2 on Jan. 4, 1999 and Jan., 2003 and Big 12 champion, if available, vs. at-large (1999-2001 and 2003-05 seasons).

Multiple wins: Penn St. (6); Arizona St. (5); Florida St., Nebraska and Ohio St. (2).

Year		Year		Year	
1971†	Arizona St. 45, Florida St. 38	1984	Ohio St. 28, Pittsburgh 23	1996	Nebraska 62, Florida 24
1972	Arizona St. 49, Missouri 35	1985	UCLA 39, Miami-FL 37	1997	Penn St. 38, Texas 15
1973	Arizona St. 28, Pittsburgh 7	1986	Michigan 27, Nebraska 23	1997†	Kansas St. 35, Syracuse 18
1974	Oklahoma St. 16, BYU 6	1987	Penn St. 14, Miami-FL 10	1999	Tennessee 23, Florida St. 16
1975	Arizona St. 17, Nebraska 14	1988	Florida St. 31, Nebraska 28		
1976	Oklahoma 41, Wyoming 7	1989	Notre Dame 34, West Va. 21	2000	Nebraska 31, Tennessee 21
1977	Penn St. 42, Arizona St. 30			2001	Oregon St. 41, Notre Dame 9
1978	10-10, Arkansas vs UCLA	1990	Florida St. 41, Nebraska 17	2002	Oregon 38, Colorado 16
1979	Pittsburgh 16, Arizona 10	1991	Louisville 34, Alabama 7	2003	Ohio St. 31, Miami-FL 24 (2OT)
		1992	Penn St. 42, Tennessee 17		
1980	Penn St. 31, Ohio St. 19	1993	Syracuse 26, Colorado 22	†December game from 1971-80 and
1982*	Penn St. 26, USC 10	1994	Arizona 29, Miami-FL 0	in '97.
1983	Arizona St. 32, Oklahoma 21	1995	Colorado 41, Notre Dame 24	*January game since 1982.

Bowl Games (Cont.)
Sugar Bowl

City: New Orleans, La. **Stadium:** Louisiana Superdome. **Capacity:** 77,446. **Playing surface:** Turf. **First game:** Jan. 1, 1935. **Playing sites:** Tulane Stadium (1935-74) and Superdome (since 1975). **Corporate title sponsors:** USF&G Financial Services (1987-95) and Nokia (starting in 1995).

Automatic berths: SEC champion vs. at-large opponent (1976-91 seasons); SEC champion vs. one of first five picks from 8-team Bowl Coalition pool (1992-94 seasons); #4 vs. #6 on Dec. 31, 1995; #1 vs. #2 on Jan. 2, 1997; and #3 vs. #5 on Jan. 1, 1998; Bowl Championship Series: SEC champion, if available, vs. at-large (1998-99, 2000-02, 2004-05 seasons) and #1 vs. #2 on Jan. 4, 2000 and Jan. 2004.

Multiple wins: Alabama (8); Mississippi (5); Florida St., Georgia Tech, LSU, Oklahoma and Tennessee (4); Georgia and Nebraska (3); Florida, Miami-FL, Notre Dame, Pittsburgh, Santa Clara and TCU (2).

Year		Year		Year	
1935*	Tulane 20, Temple 14	1960	Mississippi 21, LSU 0	1985	Nebraska 28, LSU 10
1936	TCU 3, LSU 2	1961	Mississippi 14, Rice 6	1986	Tennessee 35, Miami-FL 7
1937	Santa Clara 21, LSU 14	1962	Alabama 10, Arkansas 3	1987	Nebraska 30, LSU 15
1938	Santa Clara 6, LSU 0	1963	Mississippi 17, Arkansas 13	1988	16-16, Syracuse vs Auburn
1939	TCU 15, Carnegie Tech 7	1964	Alabama 12, Mississippi 7	1989	Florida St. 13, Auburn 7
1940	Texas A&M 14, Tulane 13	1965	LSU 13, Syracuse 10	1990	Miami-FL 33, Alabama 25
1941	Boston College 19, Tennessee 13	1966	Missouri 20, Florida 18	1991	Tennessee 23, Virginia 22
1942	Fordham 2, Missouri 0	1967	Alabama 34, Nebraska 7	1992	Notre Dame 39, Florida 28
1943	Tennessee 14, Tulsa 7	1968	LSU 20, Wyoming 13	1993	Alabama 34, Miami-FL 13
1944	Georgia Tech 20, Tulsa 18	1969	Arkansas 16, Georgia 2	1994	Florida 41, West Va. 7
1945	Duke 29, Alabama 26	1970	Mississippi 27, Arkansas 22	1995	Florida St. 23, Florida 17
1946	Okla. A&M 33, St.Mary's 13	1971	Tennessee 34, Air Force 13	1995†	Va. Tech 28, Texas 10
1947	Georgia 20, N. Carolina 10	1972	Oklahoma 40, Auburn 22	1997	Florida 52, Florida St. 20
1948	Texas 27, Alabama 7	1972†	Oklahoma 14, Penn St. 0	1998	Florida St. 31, Ohio St. 14
1949	Oklahoma 14, N. Carolina 6	1973	Notre Dame 24, Alabama 23	1999	Ohio St. 24, Texas A&M 14
1950	Oklahoma 35, LSU 0	1974	Nebraska 13, Florida 10	2000	Florida St. 46, Va. Tech 29
1951	Kentucky 13, Oklahoma 7	1975	Alabama 13, Penn St. 6	2001	Miami-FL 37, Florida 20
1952	Maryland 28, Tennessee 13	1977*	Pittsburgh 27, Georgia 3	2002	LSU 47, Illinois 34
1953	Georgia Tech 24, Mississippi 7	1978	Alabama 35, Ohio St. 6	2003	Georgia 26, Florida St. 13
1954	Georgia Tech 42, West Va. 19	1979	Alabama 14, Penn St. 7		
1955	Navy 21, Mississippi 0	1980	Alabama 24, Arkansas 9	* January game from 1935-72 and
1956	Georgia Tech 7, Pittsburgh 0	1981	Georgia 17, Notre Dame 10	since 1977 (except in 1995).
1957	Baylor 13, Tennessee 7	1982	Pittsburgh 24, Georgia 20	† Game played on Dec. 31 from
1958	Mississippi 39, Texas 7	1983	Penn St. 27, Georgia 23	1972-75 and in 1995.
1959	LSU 7, Clemson 0	1984	Auburn 9, Michigan 7		

Orange Bowl

City: Miami, Fla. **Stadium:** Pro Player. **Capacity:** 74,916. **Playing surface:** Grass. **First game:** Jan. 1, 1935. **Playing sites:** Orange Bowl (1935-95); Pro Player Stadium (since 1996). **Corporate title sponsor:** Federal Express (since 1989).

Automatic berths: Big 8 champion vs. Atlantic Coast Conference champion (1953-57 seasons); Big 8 champion vs. at-large opponent (1958-63 seasons and 1975-91 seasons); Big 8 champion vs. one of first five picks from 8-team Bowl Coalition pool (1992-94 seasons); #3 vs. #5 on Jan. 1, 1996; #4 vs. #6 on Dec. 31, 1996; and #1 vs. #2 on Jan. 2, 1998 (New Bowl Alliance 1995-97 seasons); Bowl Championship Series: Big East or ACC champion, if available, vs. at-large (1998-99, 2001-03, 2005 seasons) and #1 vs. #2 Jan. 3, 2001 and Jan. 2005.

Multiple wins: Oklahoma (12); Nebraska (6); Miami-FL (5); Alabama (4); Florida, Florida State, Georgia Tech and Penn St. (3); Clemson, Colorado, Georgia, LSU, Notre Dame and Texas (2).

Year		Year		Year	
1935*	Bucknell 26, Miami-FL 0	1955	Duke 34, Nebraska 7	1975	Notre Dame 13, Alabama 11
1936	Catholic U. 20, Mississippi 19	1956	Oklahoma 20, Maryland 6	1976	Oklahoma 14, Michigan 6
1937	Duquesne 13, Mississippi St. 12	1957	Colorado 27, Clemson 21	1977	Ohio St. 27, Colorado 10
1938	Auburn 6, Michigan St. 0	1958	Oklahoma 48, Duke 21	1978	Arkansas 31, Oklahoma 6
1939	Tennessee 17, Oklahoma 0	1959	Oklahoma 21, Syracuse 6	1979	Oklahoma 31, Nebraska 24
1940	Georgia Tech 21, Missouri 7	1960	Georgia 14, Missouri 0	1980	Oklahoma 24, Florida St. 7
1941	Mississippi St. 14, Georgetown 7	1961	Missouri 21, Navy 14	1981	Oklahoma 18, Florida St. 17
1942	Georgia 40, TCU 26	1962	LSU 25, Colorado 7	1982	Clemson 22, Nebraska 15
1943	Alabama 37, Boston College 21	1963	Alabama 17, Oklahoma 0	1983	Nebraska 21, LSU 20
1944	LSU 19, Texas A&M 14	1964	Nebraska 13, Auburn 7	1984	Miami-FL 31, Nebraska 30
1945	Tulsa 26, Georgia Tech 12	1965†	Texas 21, Alabama 17	1985	Washington 28, Oklahoma 17
1946	Miami-FL 13, Holy Cross 6	1966	Alabama 39, Nebraska 28	1986	Oklahoma 25, Penn St. 10
1947	Rice 8, Tennessee 0	1967	Florida 27, Georgia Tech 12	1987	Oklahoma 42, Arkansas 8
1948	Georgia Tech 20, Kansas 14	1968	Oklahoma 26, Tennessee 24	1988	Miami-FL 20, Oklahoma 14
1949	Texas 41, Georgia 28	1969	Penn St. 15, Kansas 14	1989	Miami-FL 23, Nebraska 3
1950	Santa Clara 21, Kentucky 13	1970	Penn St. 10, Missouri 3	1990	Notre Dame, 21, Colorado 6
1951	Clemson 15, Miami-FL 14	1971	Nebraska 17, LSU 12	1991	Colorado 10, Notre Dame 9
1952	Georgia Tech 17, Baylor 14	1972	Nebraska 38, Alabama 6	1992	Miami-FL 22, Nebraska 0
1953	Alabama 61, Syracuse 6	1973	Nebraska 40, Notre Dame 6	1993	Florida St. 27, Nebraska 14
1954	Oklahoma 7, Maryland 0	1974	Penn St. 16, LSU 9	1994	Florida St. 18, Nebraska 16

Year		Year		
1995	Nebraska 24, Miami-FL 17	2000	Michigan 35, Alabama 34	* January game 1935-1996 and since
1996	Florida St. 31, Notre Dame 26	2001	Oklahoma 13, Florida St. 2	'98.
1996**	Nebraska 41, Virginia Tech 21	2002	Florida 56, Maryland 23	** December game in 1996
1998*	Nebraska 42, Tennessee 21	2003	USC 38, Iowa 17	† Night game since 1965.
1999	Florida 31, Syracuse 10			

Cotton Bowl

City: Dallas, Tex. **Stadium:** Cotton Bowl. **Capacity:** 68,252. **Playing surface:** Grass. **First game:** Jan 1, 1937. **Playing sites:** Fair Park Stadium (1937) and Cotton Bowl (since 1938). **Corporate title sponsor:** Mobil Corporation (1988-95), SBC Communications Inc., previously Southwestern Bell, (since 1997).

Automatic berths: SWC champion vs. at-large opponent (1941-91 seasons); SWC champion vs. one of first five picks from 8-team Bowl Coalition pool (1992-1994 seasons); second pick from Big 12 vs. first choice of WAC champion or second pick from Pac-10 (1995-97 seasons); Big 12 vs. SEC (since 1998).

Multiple wins: Texas (11); Notre Dame (5); Texas A&M (4); Arkansas and Rice (3); Alabama, Georgia, Houston, LSU, Penn St., SMU, Tennessee, TCU and UCLA (2).

Year		Year		Year	
1937*	TCU 16, Marquette 6	1960	Syracuse 23, Texas 14	1983	SMU 7, Pittsburgh 3
1938	Rice 28, Colorado 14	1961	Duke 7, Arkansas 6	1984	Georgia 10, Texas 9
1939	St. Mary's 20, Texas Tech 13	1962	Texas 12, Mississippi 7	1985	Boston College 45, Houston 28
1940	Clemson 6, Boston College 3	1963	LSU 13, Texas 0	1986	Texas A&M 36, Auburn 16
1941	Texas A&M 13, Fordham 12	1964	Texas 28, Navy 6	1987	Ohio St. 28, Texas A&M 12
1942	Alabama 29, Texas A&M 21	1965	Arkansas 10, Nebraska 7	1988	Texas A&M 35, Notre Dame 10
1943	Texas 14, Georgia Tech 7	1966	LSU 14, Arkansas 7	1989	UCLA 17, Arkansas 3
1944	7-7, Texas vs Randolph Field	1966†	Georgia 24, SMU 9	1990	Tennessee 31, Arkansas 27
1945	Oklahoma A&M 34, TCU 0	1968*	Texas A&M 20, Alabama 16	1991	Miami-FL 46, Texas 3
1946	Texas 40, Missouri 27	1969	Texas 36, Tennessee 13	1992	Florida St. 10, Texas A&M 2
1947	0-0, Arkansas vs LSU	1970	Texas 21, Notre Dame 17	1993	Notre Dame 28, Texas A&M 3
1948	13-13, SMU vs Penn St.	1971	Notre Dame 24, Texas 11	1994	Notre Dame 24, Texas A&M 21
1949	SMU 21, Oregon 13	1972	Penn St. 30, Texas 6	1995	USC 55, Texas Tech 14
1950	Rice 27, N. Carolina 13	1973	Texas 17, Alabama 13	1996	Colorado 38, Oregon 6
1951	Tennessee 20, Texas 14	1974	Nebraska 19, Texas 3	1997	BYU 19, Kansas St. 15
1952	Kentucky 20, TCU 7	1975	Penn St. 41, Baylor 20	1998	UCLA 29, Texas A&M 23
1953	Texas 16, Tennessee 0	1976	Arkansas 31, Georgia 10	1999	Texas 38, Mississippi St. 11
1954	Rice 28, Alabama 6	1977	Houston 30, Maryland 21	2000	Arkansas 27, Texas 6
1955	Georgia Tech 14, Arkansas 6	1978	Notre Dame 38, Texas 10	2001	Kansas St. 35, Tennessee 21
1956	Mississippi 14, TCU 13	1979	Notre Dame 35, Houston 34	2002	Oklahoma 10, Arkansas 3
1957	TCU 28, Syracuse 27	1980	Houston 17, Nebraska 14	2003	Texas 35, LSU 20
1958	Navy 20, Rice 7	1981	Alabama 30, Baylor 2	* January game from 1937-66 and
1959	0-0, TCU vs Air Force	1982	Texas 14, Alabama 12	since 1968.
				† Game played on Dec. 31, 1966.	

Capital One Bowl

City: Orlando, Fla. **Stadium:** Florida Citrus Bowl. **Capacity:** 70,188. **Playing surface:** Grass. **First game:** Jan. 1, 1947. **Name change:** Tangerine Bowl (1947-82), Florida Citrus Bowl (1983-2002) and Capital One Bowl (since 2003). **Playing sites:** Tangerine Bowl (1947-72, 1974-82), Florida Field in Gainesville (1973), Orlando Stadium (1983-85) and Florida Citrus Bowl (since 1986). The Tangerine Bowl, Orlando Stadium and Florida Citrus Bowl are all the same stadium. **Corporate title sponsors:** Florida Department of Citrus (1983-2002), CompUSA (1992-99), Ourhouse.com (2000) and Capital One (since 2001).

Automatic berths: Championship game of Atlantic Coast Regional Conference (1964-67 seasons); Mid-American Conference champion vs. Southern Conference champion (1968-71 seasons); ACC champion vs. at-large opponent (1988-91 seasons); second pick from SEC, if available, vs. second pick from Big 10, if available (since 1992 season).

Multiple wins: Tennessee (4); Auburn, East Texas St., Miami-OH and Toledo (3); Catawba, Clemson, East Carolina, Florida and Michigan (2).

Year		Year		Year	
1947*	Catawba 31, Maryville 6	1966	Morgan St. 14, West Chester 6	1987*	Auburn 16, USC 7
1948	Catawba 7, Marshall 0	1967	Tenn-Martin 25, West Chester 8	1988	Clemson 35, Penn St. 10
1949	21-21, Murray St. vs Sul Ross St.	1968	Richmond 49, Ohio U. 42	1989	Clemson 13, Oklahoma 6
1950	St. Vincent 7, Emory & Henry 6	1969	Toledo 56, Davidson 33	1990	Illinois 31, Virginia 21
1951	M. Harvey 35, Emory & Henry 14	1970	Toledo 40, Wm. & Mary 12	1991	Georgia Tech 45, Nebraska 21
1952	Stetson 35, Arkansas St. 20	1971	Toledo 28, Richmond 3	1992	California 37, Clemson 13
1953	E. Texas St. 33, Tenn. Tech 0	1972	Tampa 21, Kent St. 18	1993	Georgia 21, Ohio St. 14
1954	7-7, E. Texas St. vs Arkansas St.	1973	Miami-OH 16, Florida 7	1994	Penn St. 31, Tennessee 13
1955	Neb.-Omaha 7, Eastern Ky. 6	1974	Miami-OH 21, Georgia 10	1995	Alabama 24, Ohio St. 17
1956	6-6, Juniata vs Missouri Valley	1975	Miami-OH 20, S. Carolina 7	1996	Tennessee 20, Ohio St. 14
1957	W. Texas St. 20, So. Miss. 13	1976	Oklahoma 49, BYU 21	1997	Tennessee 48, Northwestern 28
1958	E. Texas St. 10, So. Miss. 9	1977	Florida St. 40, Texas Tech 17	1998	Florida 21, Penn St. 6
1958†	E. Texas St. 26, Mo. Valley 7	1978	N.C. State 30, Pittsburgh 17	1999	Michigan 45, Arkansas 31
1960*	Mid. Tenn. 21, Presbyterian 12	1979	LSU 34, Wake Forest 10	2000	Michigan St. 37, Florida 34
1960†	Citadel 27, Tenn. Tech 0	1980	Florida 35, Maryland 20	2001	Michigan 31, Auburn 28
1961	Lamar 21, Middle Tenn. 14	1981	Missouri 19, Southern Miss. 17	2002	Tennessee 45, Michigan 17
1962	Houston 49, Miami-OH 21	1982	Auburn 33, Boston College 26	2003	Auburn 13, Penn St. 9
1963	Western Ky. 27, Coast Guard 0	1983	Tennessee 30, Maryland 23	*January game from 1947-58, in 1960
1964	E. Carolina 14, Massachusetts 13	1984	17-17, Florida St. vs Georgia	and since 1987.
1965	E. Carolina 31, Maine 0	1985	Ohio St. 10, BYU 7	†December game in 1958, 1960-85.

Bowl Games (Cont.)
Gator Bowl

City: Jacksonville, Fla. **Stadium:** ALLTEL Stadium. **Capacity:** 73,000. **Playing surface:** Grass. **First game:** Jan. 1, 1946. **Playing sites:** Gator Bowl (1946-93), Florida Field in Gainesville (1994) and New Gator Bowl (since 1995). Name was changed to ALLTEL Stadium in 1997. **Corporate title sponsors:** Mazda Motors of America, Inc. (1986-91), Outback Steakhouse, Inc. (1992-94) and Toyota Motor Co. (since 1995).

Automatic berths: Third pick from SEC vs. sixth pick from 8-team Bowl Coalition pool (1992-94 seasons); second pick from ACC, if available, vs. second pick from Big East or Notre Dame, if available (since 1995 season).

Multiple wins: Florida (6); North Carolina (5); Auburn, Clemson and Florida St. (4); Georgia Tech and Tennessee (3); Georgia, Maryland, Miami-FL, Oklahoma, Pittsburgh, and Texas Tech (2).

Year		Year		Year	
1946*	Wake Forest 26, S. Carolina 14	1966	Tennessee 18, Syracuse 12	1987	LSU 30, S. Carolina 13
1947	Oklahoma 34, N.C. State 13	1967	17-17, Florida St. vs Penn St.	1989*	Georgia 34, Michigan St. 27
1948	20-20, Maryland vs Georgia	1968	Missouri 35, Alabama 10	1989†	Clemson 27, West Va. 7
1949	Clemson 24, Missouri 23	1969	Florida 14, Tennessee 13	1991*	Michigan 35, Mississippi 3
1950	Maryland 20, Missouri 7	1971*	Auburn 35, Mississippi 28	1991†	Oklahoma 48, Virginia 14
1951	Wyoming 20, Wash. & Lee 7	1971†	Georgia 7, N. Carolina 3	1992	Florida 27, N.C. State 10
1952	Miami-FL 14, Clemson 0	1972	Auburn 24, Colorado 3	1993	Alabama 24, N. Carolina 10
1953	Florida 14, Tulsa 13	1973	Texas Tech 28, Tennessee 19	1994	Tennessee 45, Va. Tech 23
1954	Texas Tech 35, Auburn 13	1974	Auburn 27, Texas 3	1996*	Syracuse 41, Clemson 0
1954†	Auburn 33, Baylor 13	1975	Maryland 13, Florida 0	1997	N. Carolina 20, West Va. 13
1955	Vanderbilt 25, Auburn 13	1976	Notre Dame 20, Penn St. 9	1998	N. Carolina 42, Va. Tech 3
1956	Georgia Tech 21, Pittsburgh 14	1977	Pittsburgh 34, Clemson 3	1999	Ga. Tech 35, Notre Dame 28
1957	Tennessee 3, Texas A&M 0	1978	Clemson 17, Ohio St. 15	2000	Miami-FL 28, Ga. Tech 13
1958	Mississippi 7, Florida 3	1979	N. Carolina 17, Michigan 15	2001	Va. Tech 41, Clemson 20
1960*	Arkansas 14, Georgia Tech 7	1980	Pittsburgh 37, S. Carolina 9	2002	Florida St. 30, Va. Tech 17
1960†	Florida 13, Baylor 12	1981	N. Carolina 31, Arkansas 27	2003	N.C. State 28, Notre Dame 6
1961	Penn St. 30, Georgia 15	1982	Florida St. 31, West Va. 12	*January game from 1946-54, 1960,
1962	Florida 17, Penn St. 7	1983	Florida 14, Iowa 6	1965, 1971, 1989, 1991 and since
1963	N. Carolina 35, Air Force 0	1984	Oklahoma St. 21, S. Carolina 14	1996.
1965*	Florida St. 36, Oklahoma 19	1985	Florida St. 34, Oklahoma St. 23	†December game from 1954-58, 1960-
1965†	Georgia Tech 31, Texas Tech 21	1986	Clemson 27, Stanford 21	63, 1965-69, 1971-87, 1989 and
					1991-94.

Holiday Bowl

City: San Diego, Calif. **Stadium:** Qualcomm. **Capacity:** 71,000. **Playing surface:** Grass. **First game:** Dec. 22, 1978. **Playing site:** San Diego/Jack Murphy Stadium (since 1978). Name changed to Qualcomm Stadium in 1997. **Corporate title sponsors:** SeaWorld (1986-90), Thrifty Car Rental (1991-94), Chrysler-Plymouth Division of Chrysler Corp. (1995-97), U.S. Filter/Culligan Water Tech. (1998-2001) and Pacific Life Insurance Co. (since 2002).

Automatic berths: WAC champion vs. at-large opponent (1978-84, 1986-90 seasons); WAC champ vs. second pick from Big 10 (1991 season); WAC champ vs. third pick from Big 10 (1992-94 seasons); choice of WAC champion, if available, or second pick from Pac-10, if available vs. third pick from Big 12, if available (1995-99); second pick from Pac-10 vs. third pick from Big 12 (since 2000).

Multiple wins: BYU (4); Kansas St. (3) Iowa and Ohio St. (2).

Year		Year		Year	
1978†	Navy 23, BYU 16	1987	Iowa 20, Wyoming 19	1996	Colorado 33, Washington 21
1979	Indiana 38, BYU 37	1988	Oklahoma St. 62, Wyoming 14	1997	Colorado St. 35, Missouri 24
1980	BYU 46, SMU 45	1989	Penn St. 50, BYU 39	1998	Arizona 23, Nebraska 20
1981	BYU 38, Washington St. 36			1999	Kansas St. 24, Washington 20
1982	Ohio St. 47, BYU 17	1990	Texas A&M 65, BYU 14		
1983	BYU 21, Missouri 17	1991	13-13, Iowa vs BYU	2000	Oregon 35, Texas 30
1984	BYU 24, Michigan 17	1992	Hawaii 27, Illinois 17	2001	Texas 47, Washington 43
1985	Arkansas 18, Arizona St. 17	1993	Ohio St. 28, BYU 21	2002	Kansas St. 34, Arizona St. 27
1986	Iowa 39, San Diego St. 38	1994	Michigan 24, Colo. St. 14	†December game since 1978.
		1995	Kansas St. 54, Colorado St. 21		

Outback Bowl

City: Tampa, Fla. **Stadium:** Raymond James. **Capacity:** 66,005. **Playing surface:** Grass. **First game:** Dec. 23, 1986. **Name change:** Hall of Fame Bowl (1986-95) and Outback Bowl (since 1995). **Playing sites:** Tampa/Houlihan's Stadium (1986-98) and Raymond James Stadium (since 1999). **Corporate title sponsor:** Outback Steakhouse, Inc. (since 1995).

Automatic berths: Fourth pick from ACC vs. fourth pick from Big 10 (1993-94 seasons); third pick from Big 10, if available, vs. third pick from SEC, if available (1995-99); fourth pick from Big 10 vs. third pick from SEC (2000 season).

Multiple wins: Michigan (3); Georgia, Penn St., South Carolina and Syracuse (2).

Year		Year		Year	
1986†	Boston College 27, Georgia 24	1994	Michigan 42, N.C. State 7	2000	Georgia 28, Purdue 25
1988*	Michigan 28, Alabama 24	1995	Wisconsin 34, Duke 20	2001	S. Carolina 24, Ohio St. 7
1989	Syracuse 23, LSU 10	1996	Penn St. 43, Auburn 14	2002	S. Carolina 31, Ohio St. 28
1990	Auburn 31, Ohio St. 14	1997	Alabama 17, Michigan 14	2003	Michigan 38, Florida 30
1991	Clemson 30, Illinois 0	1998	Georgia 33, Wisconsin 6	†December game in 1986.
1992	Syracuse 24, Ohio St. 17	1999	Penn St. 26, Kentucky 14	*January game since 1988.
1993	Tennessee 38, Boston Col. 23				

Peach Bowl

City: Atlanta, Ga. **Stadium:** Georgia Dome. **Capacity:** 71,228. **Playing surface:** Turf. **First game:** Dec. 30, 1968. **Playing sites:** Grant Field (1968-70), Atlanta-Fulton County Stadium (1971-92) and Georgia Dome (since 1993). **Corporate title sponsor:** Chick-fil-A (since 1998).

Automatic berths: Third pick from ACC vs. at-large opponent (1992 season); third pick from ACC vs. fourth pick from SEC (1993-94 seasons); third pick from ACC, if available, vs. fourth pick from SEC, if available (since 1995 season).

Multiple wins: N.C. State (4); LSU and West Virginia (3); Auburn, Georgia, North Carolina and Virginia (2).

Year		Year		Year	
1968†	LSU 31, Florida St. 27	1982	Iowa 28, Tennessee 22	1996	LSU 10, Clemson 7
1969	West Va. 14, S. Carolina 3	1983	Florida St. 28, N. Carolina 3	1998*	Auburn 21, Clemson 17
1970	Arizona St. 48, N. Carolina 26	1984	Virginia 27, Purdue 24	1998†	Georgia 35, Virginia 33
1971	Mississippi 41, Georgia Tech 18	1985	Army 31, Illinois 29	1999	Mississippi St. 17, Clemson 7
1972	N.C. State 49, West Va. 13	1986	Va. Tech 25, N.C. State 24	2000	LSU 28, Ga. Tech 14
1973	Georgia 17, Maryland 16	1988*	Tennessee 27, Indiana 22	2001	N. Carolina 16, Auburn 10
1974	6-6, Vanderbilt vs Texas Tech	1988†	N.C. State 28, Iowa 23	2002	Maryland 30, Tennessee 3
1975	West Va. 13, N.C. State 10	1989	Syracuse 19, Georgia 18		
1976	Kentucky 21, N. Carolina 0	1990	Auburn 27, Indiana 23	†December game from 1968-79,	
1977	N.C. State 24, Iowa St. 14	1992*	E. Carolina 37, N.C. State 34	1981-86, 1988-90, 1993, 1995,	
1978	Purdue 41, Georgia Tech 21	1993	N. Carolina 21, Miss. St. 17	1996, 1998 and since 1999.	
1979	Baylor 24, Clemson 18	1993†	Clemson 14, Kentucky 13	*January game in 1981, 1988, 1992-	
1981*	Miami-FL 20, Va. Tech 10	1995*	N.C. State 24, Miss. St. 24	93, 1995 and 1998.	
1981†	West Va. 26, Florida 6	1995†	Virginia 34, Georgia 27		

Alamo Bowl

City: San Antonio, Tex. **Stadium:** Alamodome. **Capacity:** 65,000. **Playing surface:** Turf. **First game:** Dec. 31, 1993. **Playing site:** Alamodome (since 1993). **Corporate title sponsor:** Builders Square (1993-98) and Sylvania (1999-2001).

Automatic berths: third pick from SWC vs. fourth pick from Pac-10 (1993-94 seasons); fourth pick from Big 10, if available vs. fourth pick from Big 12, if available (1995-99 seasons); fourth pick from Big 12 vs. third pick from Big 10 (2000 season).

Multiple wins: Iowa and Purdue (2).

Year		Year		Year	
1993†	California 37, Iowa 3	1997	Purdue 33, Oklahoma St. 20	2001	Iowa 19, Texas Tech 16
1994	Washington St. 10, Baylor 3	1998	Purdue 37, Kansas St. 34	2002	Wisconsin 31, Colorado 28 (OT)
1995	Texas A&M 22, Michigan 20	1999	Penn St. 24, Texas A&M 0		
1996	Iowa 27, Texas Tech 0	2000	Nebraska 66, Northwestern 17	†December game since 1993.	

Sun Bowl

City: El Paso, Tex. **Stadium:** Sun Bowl. **Capacity:** 52,000. **Playing surface:** Turf. **First game:** Jan. 1, 1936. **Name changes:** Sun Bowl (1936-85), John Hancock Sun Bowl (1986-88), John Hancock Bowl (1989-93) and Sun Bowl (since 1994). **Playing sites:** Kidd Field (1936-62) and Sun Bowl (since 1963). **Corporate title sponsors:** John Hancock Financial Services (1986-93), Norwest Bank (1996-98), Wells Fargo (since 1999).

Automatic berths: Eighth pick from 8-team Bowl Coalition pool vs. at-large opponent (1992); Seventh and eighth picks from 8-team Bowl Coalition pool (1993-94 seasons); third pick from Pac-10, if available, vs. fifth pick from Big 10, if available (since 1995 season).

Multiple wins: Texas Western/UTEP (5); Alabama and Wyoming (3); Nebraska, New Mexico St., North Carolina, Oklahoma, Oregon, Pittsburgh, Southwestern, Stanford, Texas, West Texas St. and West Virginia (2).

Year		Year		Year	
1936*	14-14, Hardin-Simmons vs New Mexico St.	1958†	Wyoming 14, Hardin-Simmons 6	1983	Alabama 28, SMU 7
		1959	New Mexico St. 28, N. Texas 8	1984	Maryland 28, Tennessee 27
1937	Hardin-Simmons 34, Texas Mines 6	1960	New Mexico St. 20, Utah St. 13	1985	13-13, Georgia vs Arizona
1938	West Va. 7, Texas Tech 6	1961	Villanova 17, Wichita 9	1986	Alabama 28, Washington 6
1939	Utah 26, New Mexico 0	1962	West Texas 15, Ohio U. 14	1987	Oklahoma St. 35, West Va. 33
1940	0-0, Catholic U. vs Arizona St.	1963	Oregon 21, SMU 14	1988	Alabama 29, Army 28
1941	W. Reserve 26, Arizona St. 13	1964	Georgia 7, Texas Tech 0	1989	Pittsburgh 31, Texas A&M 28
1942	Tulsa 6, Texas Tech 0	1965	Texas Western 13, TCU 12	1990	Michigan St. 17, USC 16
1943	Second Air Force 13, Hardin-Simmons 7	1966	Wyoming 28, Florida St. 20	1991	UCLA 6, Illinois 3
1944	Southwestern 7, New Mexico 0	1967	UTEP 14, Mississippi 7	1992	Baylor 20, Arizona 15
1945	Southwestern 35, U. of Mexico 0	1968	Auburn 34, Arizona 10	1993	Oklahoma 41, Texas Tech 10
1946	New Mexico 34, Denver 24	1969	Nebraska 45, Georgia 6	1994	Texas 35, N. Carolina 31
1947	Cincinnati 18, Va. Tech 6	1970	Georgia Tech 17, Texas Tech 9	1995	Iowa 38, Washington 18
1948	Miami-OH 13, Texas Tech 12	1971	LSU 33, Iowa St. 15	1996	Stanford 38, Michigan St. 0
1949	West Va. 21, Texas Mines 12	1972	N. Carolina 32, Texas Tech 28	1997	Arizona St. 17, Iowa 7
1950	Tex. Western 33, Georgetown 20	1973	Missouri 34, Auburn 17	1998	TCU 28, USC 19
1951	West Texas 14, Cincinnati 13	1974	Miss. St. 26, N. Carolina 24	1999	Oregon 24, Minnesota 20
1952	Texas Tech 25, Pacific 14	1975	Pittsburgh 33, Kansas 19	2000	Wisconsin 21, UCLA 20
1953	Pacific 26, Southern Miss. 7	1977*	Texas A&M 37, Florida 14	2001	Washington St. 33, Purdue 27
1954	Tex. Western 37, So. Miss. 14	1977†	Stanford 24, LSU 14	2002	Purdue 34, Washington 24
1955	Tex. Western 47, Florida St. 20	1978	Texas 42, Maryland 0	*January game from 1936-58 and in 1977.	
1956	Wyoming 21, Texas Tech 14	1979	Washington 14, Texas 7	†December game from 1958-75 and since 1977.	
1957	Geo. Wash. 13, Tex. Western 0	1980	Nebraska 31, Miss. St. 17		
1958*	Louisville 34, Drake 20	1981	Oklahoma 40, Houston 14		
		1982	N. Carolina 26, Texas 10		

Bowl Games (Cont.)

Insight Bowl

City: Phoenix, Ariz. **Stadium:** Bank One Ballpark. **Capacity:** 42,915. **Playing surface:** Grass. **First game:** Dec. 31, 1989. **Name change:** Copper Bowl (1989-1996), Insight.com Bowl (1997-2001) and Insight Bowl (since 2002). **Playing sites:** Arizona Stadium (1989-2000) and Bank One Ballpark (since 2000). **Corporate title sponsors:** Domino's Pizza (1990-91), Weiser Lock (1992-1996) and Insight Enterprises (since 1997).

    Automatic berths: Third pick from WAC vs. at-large opponent (1992 season); third pick from WAC vs. fourth pick from Big Eight (1993-94 seasons); second pick from WAC vs. sixth pick from Big 12 (1995-97); third pick from Big East or Notre Dame, if available vs. fifth pick from Big 12, if available (since 1998 season).

    Multiple wins: Arizona (2).

Year		Year		Year	
1989†	Arizona 17, N.C. State 10	1994	BYU 31, Oklahoma 6	1999	Colorado 62, Boston College 28
1990	California 17, Wyoming 15	1995	Texas Tech 55, Air Force 41	2000	Iowa St. 37, Pittsburgh 29
1991	Indiana 24, Baylor 0	1996	Wisconsin 38, Utah 10	2001	Syracuse 26, Kansas St. 3
1992	Washington St. 31, Utah 28	1997	Arizona 20, New Mexico 14	2002	Pittsburgh 38, Oregon St. 13
1993	Kansas St. 52, Wyoming 17	1998	Missouri 34, W. Virginia 31		
				†December game since 1989.	

Liberty Bowl

City: Memphis, Tenn. **Stadium:** Liberty Bowl Memorial. **Capacity:** 62,380. **Playing surface:** Grass. **First game:** Dec. 19, 1959. **Playing sites:** Municipal Stadium in Philadelphia (1959-63), Convention Hall in Atlantic City, N.J. (1964), Memphis Memorial Stadium (1965-75) and Liberty Bowl Memorial Stadium (since 1976). Memphis Memorial Stadium renamed Liberty Bowl Memorial in 1976. **Corporate title sponsors:** St. Jude's Hospital (since 1993), AXA/Equitable (since 1997).

    Automatic berths: Commander-in-Chief's Trophy winner (Army, Navy or Air Force) vs. at-large opponent (1989-92 seasons); none (1993 season); first pick from independent group of Cincinnati, East Carolina, Memphis, Southern Miss. and Tulane vs. at-large opponent (for 1994 and '95 seasons); Conference USA champion vs. fourth pick from the Big East (1996-97 seasons); Conference USA champion, if available, vs. fifth, sixth or seventh pick or at-large from SEC (1998-99 seasons); Mountain West champion vs. Conference USA champion, if available (2000 season).

    Multiple wins: Mississippi (4); Penn St. and Tennessee (3); Air Force, Alabama, Louisville, N.C. State, Southern Miss., Syracuse and Tulane (2).

Year		Year		Year	
1959†	Penn St. 7, Alabama 0	1975	USC 20, Texas A&M 0	1991	Air Force 38, Mississippi St. 15
1960	Penn St. 41, Oregon 12	1976	Alabama 36, UCLA 6	1992	Mississippi 13, Air Force 0
1961	Syracuse 15, Miami-FL 14	1977	Nebraska 21, N. Carolina 17	1993	Louisville 18, Michigan St. 7
1962	Oregon St. 6, Villanova 0	1978	Missouri 20, LSU 15	1994	Illinois 30, E. Carolina 0
1963	Mississippi St. 16, N.C. State 12	1979	Penn St. 9, Tulane 6	1995	E. Carolina 19, Stanford 13
1964	Utah 32, West Virginia 6	1980	Purdue 28, Missouri 25	1996	Syracuse 30, Houston 17
1965	Mississippi 13, Auburn 7	1981	Ohio St. 31, Navy 28	1997	Southern Miss. 41, Pittsburgh 7
1966	Miami-FL 14, Virginia Tech 7	1982	Alabama 21, Illinois 15	1998	Tulane 41, BYU 27
1967	N.C. State 14, Georgia 7	1983	Notre Dame 19, Boston Col. 18	1999	Southern Miss. 23, Colorado St. 17
1968	Mississippi 34, Virginia Tech 17	1984	Auburn 21, Arkansas 15		
1969	Colorado 47, Alabama 33	1985	Baylor 21, LSU 7	2000	Colorado St. 22, Louisville 17
1970	Tulane 17, Colorado 3	1986	Tennessee 21, Minnesota 14	2001	Louisville 28, BYU 10
1971	Tennessee 14, Arkansas 13	1987	Georgia 20, Arkansas 17	2002	TCU 17, Colorado St. 3
1972	Georgia Tech 31, Iowa St. 30	1988	Indiana 34, S. Carolina 10		
1973	N.C. State 31, Kansas 18	1989	Mississippi 42, Air Force 29	† December game since 1959.	
1974	Tennessee 7, Maryland 3	1990	Air Force 23, Ohio St. 11		

Tangerine Bowl

City: Orlando, Fla. **Stadium:** Florida Citrus. **Capacity:** 65,525. **Playing surface:** Grass. **First game:** Dec. 28, 1990. **Name change:** Blockbuster Bowl (1990-93), Carquest Bowl (1994-97), Micron PC Bowl (1998), MicronPC.com Bowl (1999-2000) and Tangerine Bowl (since 2001). The game was called the Sunshine Football Classic for a short time in the offseason after Carquest Auto Parts dropped its sponsorship and before Micron signed on. Also, this game should not be confused with the Tangerine Bowl that became the Citrus Bowl in 1982. **Playing sites:** Joe Robbie Stadium (1990-2000). Name changed to Pro Player Stadium in 1996. **Corporate title sponsors:** Blockbuster Video (1990-93), Carquest Auto Parts (1993-97), Micron Electronics (1998-2000) and Mazda (since 2002).

    Automatic berths: Penn St. vs. seventh pick from 8-team Bowl Coalition pool (1992 season); third pick from Big East vs. fifth pick from SEC (1993-94 seasons); third pick from Big East vs. fifth pick from SEC (1995 season); third pick from Big East vs. fourth pick from ACC (1996-97 seasons); sixth pick from Big Ten, if available, vs. fourth pick from ACC, if available (1998-2000 seasons); fifth pick from ACC vs. fifth pick from Big East (2001).

    Multiple wins: Miami-FL (2).

Year		Year		Year	
1990†	Florida St. 24, Penn St. 17	1996	Miami-FL 31, Virginia 21	2002	Texas Tech 55, Clemson 15
1991	Alabama 30, Colorado 25	1997	Ga. Tech 35, W. Virginia 30		
1993*	Stanford 24, Penn St. 3	1998	Miami-FL 46, N.C. State 23	†December game from 1990-91 and	
1994	Boston College 31, Virginia 13	1999	Illinois 63, Virginia 21	since 1995.	
1995	S. Carolina 24, West Va. 21	2000	N.C. State 38, Minnesota 30	*January game 1993-95.	
1995†	N. Carolina 20, Arkansas 10	2001	Pittsburgh 34, N.C. State 19		

Seattle Bowl

City: Seattle, Wash. **Stadium:** Safeco Field. **Capacity:** 47,116 (for baseball). **Playing surface:** Grass. **First game:** Dec. 25, 1998. **Name change:** Oahu Bowl (1998-2000); Seattle Bowl (since 2001). **Playing sites:** Aloha Stadium (1998-2000), Safeco Field (2001), new Seahawks stadium (2002-). **Corporate title sponsor:** Jeep Eagle Division of Chrysler (1998-2000), 989 Sports (2001).

Automatic berths: second or third pick from WAC, if available, vs. fifth pick from Pac-10, if available (1998-99 seasons); fourth or fifth pick from Pac-10 vs. fourth or fifth pick from Big East or fourth pick from ACC (2000 season).

Year		Year		Year	
1998†	Air Force 45, Washington 25	2000	Georgia 37, Virginia 14	2002	Wake Forest 38, Oregon 17
1999	Hawaii 23, Oregon St. 17	2001	Georgia Tech 24, Stanford 14		†December game since 1998.

Humanitarian Bowl

City: Boise, Idaho. **Stadium:** Bronco. **Capacity:** 30,000. **Playing surface:** Turf. **First game:** Dec. 29, 1997. **Playing sites:** Bronco Stadium (since 1997). **Corporate title sponsor:** World Sports Humanitarian Hall of Fame (since 1997) and Crucial.com (since 1999).

Automatic berths: Big West champion, if available, vs. at-large (since 1997 season).

Multiple wins: Boise St. (3).

Year		Year		Year	
1997†	Cincinnati 35, Utah St. 19	1999	Boise St. 34, Louisville 31	2001	Clemson 49, La. Tech 24
1998	Idaho 42, Southern Miss. 35	2000	Boise St. 38, UTEP 23	2002	Boise St. 34, Iowa St. 16
					†December game since 1997.

Las Vegas Bowl

City: Las Vegas, Nev. **Stadium:** Sam Boyd. **Capacity:** 40,000. **Playing surface:** Turf. **First game:** Dec. 18, 1992. **Playing site:** Sam Boyd Stadium (since 1992). **Corporate title sponsor:** EA Sports (1999-2000) Sega Sports (since 2001).

Automatic berths: Mid-American champion vs. Big West champion (1992-96 season); none (1997 season); second or third pick from WAC, if available vs. at-large (since 1998 season).

Multiple wins: Fresno St. (4); UNLV (3); Bowling Green, San Jose St., Toledo and Utah (2).

Year		Year		Year	
1981†	Toledo 27, San Jose St. 25	1990	San Jose St. 48, C. Michigan 24	1999	Utah 17, Fresno St. 16
1982	Fresno St. 29, Bowling Green 28	1991	Bowling Green 28, Fresno St. 21	2000	UNLV 31, Arkansas 14
1983	Northern Ill. 20, CS-Fullerton 13	1992	Bowling Green 35, Nevada 34	2001	Utah 10, USC 6
1984*	UNLV 30, Toledo 13	1993	Utah St. 42, Ball St. 33	2002	UCLA 27, New Mexico 13
1985	Fresno St. 51, Bowling Green 7	1994	UNLV 52, C. Michigan 24		
1986	San Jose St. 37, Miami-OH 7	1995	Toledo 40, Nevada 37 (OT)		†December game since 1981.
1987	E. Michigan 30, San Jose St. 27	1996	Nevada 18, Ball St. 15		
1988	Fresno St. 35, W. Michigan 30	1997	Oregon 41, Air Force 13		*Toledo later ruled winner of 1984
1989	Fresno St. 27, Ball St. 6	1998	N. Carolina 20, San Diego St. 13		game by forfeit because UNLV used ineligible players.

Note: The MAC and Big West champs met in a bowl game from 1981 to 1996, originally in Fresno at the California Bowl (1981-88, 1992) and California Raisin Bowl (1989-91). The results from 1981-91 are included below.

Independence Bowl

City: Shreveport, La. **Stadium:** Independence. **Capacity:** 50,832. **Playing surface:** Grass. **First game:** Dec. 13, 1976. **Playing site:** Independence Stadium (since 1976). **Corporate title sponsors:** Poulan/Weed Eater (1990-97), Sanford (1998-2000) and Mainstay (since 2001). **Automatic berths:** Southland Conference champion vs. at-large opponent (1976-81 seasons); none (1982-95 seasons); fifth pick from SEC, if available, vs. at-large (1995-97 seasons); fifth, sixth or seventh pick from SEC, if available, vs. at-large (1998-99 season); sixth pick from Big 12 vs. SEC (2000 season).

Multiple wins: Mississippi (3); Air Force, LSU and Southern Miss (2).

Year		Year		Year	
1976†	McNeese St. 20, Tulsa 16	1985	Minnesota 20, Clemson 13	1994	Virginia 20, TCU 10
1977	La. Tech 24, Louisville 14	1986	Mississippi 20, Texas Tech 17	1995	LSU 45, Michigan St. 26
1978	E. Carolina 35, La. Tech 13	1987	Washington 24, Tulane 12	1996	Auburn 32, Army 29
1979	Syracuse 31, McNeese St. 7	1988	Southern Miss 38, UTEP 18	1997	LSU 27, Notre Dame 9
1980	Southern Miss 16, McNeese St. 14	1989	Oregon 27, Tulsa 24	1998	Mississippi 35, Texas Tech 18
1981	Texas A&M 33, Oklahoma St. 16	1990	34-34, La. Tech vs Maryland	1999	Mississippi 27, Oklahoma 25
1982	Wisconsin 14, Kansas St. 3	1991	Georgia 24, Arkansas 15	2000	Mississippi St. 43, Texas A&M 41
1983	Air Force 9, Mississippi 3	1992	Wake Forest 39, Oregon 35	2001	Alabama 14, Iowa St. 13
1984	Air Force 23, Va. Tech 7	1993	Va. Tech 45, Indiana 20	2002	Mississippi 27, Nebraska 23
					†December game since 1976.

Motor City Bowl

City: Detroit, Mich. **Stadium:** Ford Field. **Capacity:** 65,000. **Playing surface:** Turf. **First game:** Dec. 26, 1997. **Playing site:** Pontiac Silverdome (1997-2001) and Ford Field (since 2002). **Corporate title sponsor:** Ford Division of Ford Motor Company (since 1997), Daimler Chrysler and General Motors (since 2002). **Automatic berths:** Mid-American champions vs at-large (1997-99 season); Mid-American champions vs. fourth pick from Conference USA (2000 season).

Multiple wins: Marshall (3).

Year		Year			
1997†	Mississippi 34, Marshall 31	2000	Marshall 25, Cincinnati 14		
1998	Marshall 48, Louisville 29	2001	Toledo 23, Cincinnati 16		
1999	Marshall 21, BYU 3	2002	Boston College 51, Toledo 25		†December game since 1997.

Bowl Games (Cont.)

Music City Bowl

City: Nashville, Tenn. **Stadium:** Adelphia Coliseum. **Capacity:** 67,000. **Playing surface:** Grass. **First game:** Dec. 29, 1998. **Playing sites:** Vanderbilt Stadium (1998) and Adelphia Coliseum (since 1999). **Corporate title sponsors:** American General (1998), HomePoint.com (1999-2000) and Gaylord Hotels (since 2002). **Automatic berths:** sixth choice from the SEC, if available, vs. at-large (1998-99 season); fourth pick from Big East, if available vs. SEC (2000 season).

Year		Year		Year	
1998†	Va. Tech 38, Alabama 7	2000	West Va. 49, Mississippi 38	2002	Minnesota 29, Arkansas 14
1999	Syracuse 20, Kentucky 13	2001	Boston College 20, Georgia 16		†December game since 1998.

GMAC Bowl

City: Mobile, Ala. **Stadium:** Ladd-Peebles. **Capacity:** 40,646. **Playing surface:** Grass. **First game:** Dec. 22, 1999. **Name change:** Mobile Bowl (1999-2000), GMAC Bowl (since 2001). **Playing sites:** Ladd-Peebles Stadium (since 1999). **Corporate title sponsors:** GMAC Financial Services (since 2001). **Automatic berths:** WAC champions (if team is from the east) or second pick from WAC vs. second pick from Conference USA, if available (2000 season). **Multiple wins:** Marshall (2).

Year		Year		
1999†	TCU 28, E. Carolina 14	2001	Marshall 64, East Carolina 61	†December game since 1999.
2000	So. Miss 28, TCU 21	2002	Marshall 38, Louisville 15	

Houston Bowl

City: Houston, Tex. **Stadium:** Reliant. **Capacity:** 69,500. **Playing surface:** Turf. **First game:** Dec. 27, 2000. **Name change:** GalleryFurniture.com Bowl (2000-01), Houston Bowl (2002) and EV1.net Houston Bowl (since 2003). **Playing sites:** Astrodome (2000-2002), Reliant Stadium (since 2003). **Corporate title sponsors:** GalleryFurniture.com (2000-2002) and EV1 (since 2003). **Automatic berths:** Big 12 vs. Conference USA.

Year		Year		
2000†	E. Carolina 40, Tex. Tech 27	2002	Oklahoma St. 33, So. Miss. 23	†December game since 2000.
2001	Texas A&M 28, TCU 9			

Silicon Valley Classic

City: San Jose, Calif. **Stadium:** Spartan. **Capacity:** 30,578. **Playing surface:** Grass. **First game:** Dec. 31, 2000. **Playing sites:** Spartan Stadium (since 2000). **Corporate title sponsors:** none. **Automatic berths:** WAC vs. at-large

Year		Year		
2000†	Air Force 37, Fresno St. 34	2002	Fresno St. 30, Ga. Tech 21	†December game since 2000.
2001	Michigan St. 44, Fresno St. 35			

New Orleans Bowl

City: New Orleans, La. **Stadium:** Louisiana Superdome. **Capacity:** 70,200. **Playing surface:** Turf. **First game:** Dec. 18, 2001. **Playing sites:** Louisiana Superdome (since 2001). **Corporate title sponsors:** none. **Automatic berths:** Sun Belt champion vs. Conference USA (since 2002).

Year		
2001†	Colorado St. 45, North Texas 20	
2002	North Texas 24, Cincinnati 19	†December game since 2001.

San Francisco Bowl

City: San Francisco, Calif. **Stadium:** Pacific Bell Park. **Capacity:** 37,00. **Playing surface:** Grass. **First game:** Dec. 31, 2002. **Playing sites:** Pacific Bell Park (since 2002). **Corporate title sponsors:** Diamond Walnut (since 2002). **Automatic berths:** Mountain West vs. Big East or Notre Dame (since 2002).

Year	
2002†	Virginia Tech 20, Air Force 13

†December game since 2002.

Continental Tire Bowl

City: Charlotte, N.C. **Stadium:** Ericsson Stadium. **Capacity:** 73,367. **Playing surface:** Grass. **First game:** Dec. 28, 2002. **Playing sites:** Ericsson Stadium (since 2002). **Corporate title sponsors:** Continental Tire North America (since 2002). **Automatic berths:** ACC vs. Big East or Notre Dame (since 2002).

Year	
2002†	Virginia 48, West Va. 22

†December game since 2002.

Hawaii Bowl

City: Honolulu, Hi. **Stadium:** Aloha Bowl. **Capacity:** 50,000. **Playing surface:** Turf. **First game:** Dec. 25, 2002. **Playing sites:** Aloha Bowl (since 2002). **Corporate title sponsors:** ConAgra Foods (since 2002). **Automatic berths:** Hawaii (if bowl eligible) otherwise another WAC shcool vs. Conference USA (since 2002).

Year	
2002†	Tulane 36, Hawaii 28

†December game since 2002.

All-Time Winningest Division I-A Teams

Schools classified as Division I-A for at least 10 years; through 2002 season (including bowl games).

Top 25 Winning Percentage

		Yrs	Gm	W	L	T	Pct	Bowls App	Record	2002 Season Bowl	Record
1	Notre Dame	114	1083	791	250	42	.750	25	13-12-0	lost Gator	10-3
2	Michigan	123	1128	823	269	36	.746	34	18-16-0	won Outback	10-3
3	Alabama*	108	1081	754	284	43	.717	51	29-19-3	none	10-3
4	Oklahoma	108	1060	725	282	53	.709	36	23-12-1	won Rose	12-2
5	Texas	110	1105	766	306	33	.708	42	20-20-2	won Cotton	11-2
6	Ohio St.	113	1090	745	292	53	.708	34	15-19-0	won Fiesta	14-0
7	Nebraska	113	1119	771	308	40	.707	41	20-21-0	lost Independence	7-7
8	Tennessee*	106	1077	726	299	52	.698	43	23-20-0	lost Peach	8-5
9	Penn St.	116	1116	753	322	41	.693	37	23-12-2	lost Capital One	9-4
10	USC	110	1045	695	296	54	.691	41	26-15-0	won Orange	11-2
11	Florida St.*	56	620	409	194	17	.673	31	18-11-2	lost Sugar	9-5
12	Washington*	113	1029	632	347	50	.638	29	14-14-1	lost Sun	7-6
13	Georgia	109	1083	649	367	54	.636	38	20-15-3	won Sugar	13-1
14	Miami-OH*	114	997	611	342	44	.635	7	5-2-0	none	7-5
15	Miami-FL	76	798	496	283	19	.633	27	15-12-0	lost Fiesta	12-1
16	LSU*	109	1051	636	368	47	.627	34	16-17-1	lost Cotton	8-5
17	Auburn*	110	1047	626	374	47	.620	28	14-12-2	lost Peach	7-5
18	Arizona St.	90	829	502	303	24	.620	20	10-9-1	lost Holiday	8-6
19	Central Michigan	102	872	519	317	36	.616	2	0-2-0	none	4-8
20	Colorado*	113	1050	630	384	36	.617	25	11-14-0	lost Alamo	9-5
21	Florida	96	976	582	354	40	.617	30	14-16-0	lost Outback	8-5
22	Army	113	1066	622	393	51	.607	4	2-2-0	none	1-11
23	Texas A&M	108	1067	623	396	48	.606	27	13-14-0	none	6-6
24	UCLA	84	859	499	323	37	.602	24	12-11-1	won Las Vegas	8-5
25	Syracuse	113	1123	622	422	49	.602	21	12-8-1	none	4-8

*Includes games forfeited following rulings by the NCAA Executive Council and/or the Committee on Infractions.

Top 50 Victories

		Wins				Wins				Wins
1	Michigan	.823	18	Army	.622	35	Rutgers	.553		
2	Notre Dame	.791	19	Georgia Tech	.616		Boston College	.553		
3	Nebraska	.771	20	West Virginia	.615	37	Missouri	.549		
4	Texas	.766	21	Pittsburgh	.612		Wisconsin	.549		
5	Alabama	.754	22	North Carolina	.611	39	Illinois	.541		
6	Penn St	.753		Miami-OH	.611	40	Utah	.537		
7	Ohio St	.745	24	Arkansas	.610	41	Vanderbilt	.529		
8	Tennessee	.726	25	Minnesota	.599		Stanford	.529		
9	Oklahoma	.725	26	Virginia Tech	.597		Purdue	.529		
10	USC	.695	27	Clemson	.585	44	Kentucky	.528		
11	Georgia	.662	28	Florida	.582	45	Kansas	.520		
12	Syracuse	.652	29	Navy	.581	46	Central Michigan	.519		
13	LSU	.636	30	Mississippi	.573		Iowa	.519		
14	Washington	.632	31	Michigan St	.572	48	Arizona	.517		
15	Colorado	.630	32	Virginia	.570	49	Oregon	.509		
16	Auburn	.626	33	California	.566	50	Louisiana Tech	.505		
17	Texas A&M	.623	34	Maryland	.556					

Top 30 Bowl Appearances

		App	Record			App	Record			App	Record
1	Alabama	51	29-19-3	12	Arkansas	33	10-20-3	23	Notre Dame	25	13-12-0
2	Tennessee	43	23-20-0	13	Georgia Tech	31	20-11-0		Colorado	25	11-14-0
3	Texas	42	20-20-2		Florida St	31	18-11-2	25	North Carolina	24	12-12-0
4	USC	41	26-15-0	15	Mississippi	30	18-12-0		UCLA	24	12-11-1
	Nebraska	41	20-21-0		Florida	30	14-16-0	27	BYU	23	7-15-1
6	Georgia	38	20-15-3	17	Auburn	29	15-12-2	28	Pittsburgh	22	10-12-0
7	Penn St	37	23-12-2		Washington	29	14-14-1		West Virginia	22	9-13-0
8	Oklahoma	36	23-12-1	19	Texas A&M	27	13-14-0	30	Missouri	21	9-12-0
9	LSU	34	16-17-1		Miami-FL	27	15-12-0		Syracuse	21	12-8-1
	Ohio St	34	15-19-0	21	Texas Tech	26	6-19-1				
	Michigan	34	18-16-0		Clemson	26	13-13-0				

Major Conference Champions
Atlantic Coast Conference

Founded in 1953 when charter members all left Southern Conference to form ACC. **Charter members** (7): Clemson, Duke, Maryland, North Carolina, N.C. State, South Carolina and Wake Forest. **Admitted later** (3): Virginia in 1953 (began play in '54), Georgia Tech in 1979 (began play in '83); Florida St. in 1990 (began play in '92). **Withdrew later** (1): South Carolina in 1971 (became an independent after '70 season).

2003 playing membership (9): Clemson, Duke, Florida St., Georgia Tech, Maryland, North Carolina, N.C. State, Virginia and Wake Forest.

Multiple titles: Clemson (13); Florida St. (10); Maryland (9); Duke and N.C. State (7); North Carolina (5); Georgia Tech & Virginia (2).

Year		Year		Year		Year	
1953	Duke (4-0)	1965	Clemson (5-2)	1980	North Carolina (6-0)	1994	Florida St. (8-0)
	& Maryland (3-0)		& N.C. State (5-2)	1981	Clemson (6-0)	1995	Virginia (7-1)
1954	Duke (4-0)	1966	Clemson (6-1)	1982	Clemson (6-0)		& Florida St. (7-1)
1955	Maryland (4-0)	1967	Clemson (6-0)	1983	Clemson (7-0) †	1996	Florida St. (8-0)
	& Duke (4-0)	1968	N.C. State (6-1)		& Maryland (5-0)	1997	Florida St. (8-0)
1956	Clemson (4-0-1)	1969	South Carolina (6-0)	1984	Maryland (5-0)	1998	Florida St. (7-1)
1957	N.C. State (5-0-1)	1970	Wake Forest (5-1)	1985	Maryland (6-0)		& Georgia Tech (7-1)
1958	Clemson (5-1)	1971	North Carolina (6-0)	1986	Clemson (5-1-1)	1999	Florida St. (8-0)
1959	Clemson (6-1)	1972	North Carolina (6-0)	1987	Clemson (6-1)	2000	Florida St. (8-0)
1960	Duke (5-1)	1973	N.C. State (6-0)	1988	Clemson (6-1)	2001	Maryland (7-1)
1961	Duke (5-1)	1974	Maryland (6-0)	1989	Virginia (6-1)	2002	Florida St. (7-1)
1962	Duke (6-0)	1975	Maryland (5-0)		& Duke (6-1)		
1963	North Carolina (6-1)	1976	Maryland (5-0)	1990	Georgia Tech (6-0-1)	†On probation, ineligible	
	& N.C. State (6-1)	1977	North Carolina (5-0-1)	1991	Clemson (6-0-1)		for championship.
1964	N.C. State (5-2)	1978	Clemson (6-0)	1992	Florida St. (8-0)		
		1979	N.C. State (5-1)	1993	Florida St. (8-0)		

Big East Conference

Founded in 1991 when charter members gave up independent football status to form Big East. **Charter members** (8): Boston College, Miami-FL, Pittsburgh, Rutgers, Syracuse, Temple, Virginia Tech and West Virginia. **Note:** Temple and Virginia Tech are Big East members in football only.

2003 playing membership (8): Boston College, Miami-FL, Pittsburgh, Rutgers, Syracuse, Temple, Virginia Tech and West Virginia.

Conference champion: Member schools needed two years to adjust their regular season schedules in order to begin round-robin conference play in 1993. In the meantime, the 1991 and '92 Big East titles went to the highest-ranked member in the final regular season USA Today/CNN coaches' poll.

Multiple titles: Miami-FL (8); Syracuse (4); Virginia Tech (3).

Year		Year		Year		Year	
1991	Miami-FL (2-0, #1)	1995	Virginia Tech (6-1)	1997	Syracuse (6-1)	2002	Miami-FL (7-0)
	& Syracuse (5-0, #16)		& Miami-FL (6-1)	1998	Syracuse (6-1)		
1992	Miami-FL (4-0, #1)	1996	Virginia Tech (6-1),	1999	Virginia Tech (7-0)		
1993	West Virginia (7-0)		Miami-FL (6-1)	2000	Miami-FL (7-0)		
1994	Miami-FL (7-0)		& Syracuse (6-1)	2001	Miami-FL (7-0)		

Big Ten Conference

Originally founded in 1895 as the Intercollegiate Conference of Faculty Representatives, better known as the Western Conference. **Charter members** (7): Chicago, Illinois, Michigan, Minnesota, Northwestern, Purdue and Wisconsin. **Admitted later** (5): Indiana and Iowa in 1899; Ohio St. in 1912; Michigan St. in 1950 (began play in '53); Penn St. in 1990 (began play in '93). **Withdrew later** (2): Michigan in 1907 (rejoined in '17); Chicago in 1940 (dropped football after '39 season). **Note:** Iowa belonged to both the Western and Missouri Valley conferences from 1907-10.

Unofficially called the **Big Ten** from 1912 until Chicago's withdrawal in 1939, then the **Big Nine** from 1940 until Michigan St. began conference play in 1953. Formally named the **Big Ten** in 1984 and has kept the name even after adding Penn St. as its 11th member in 1990.

2003 playing membership (11): Illinois, Indiana, Iowa, Michigan, Michigan St., Minnesota, Northwestern, Ohio St., Penn St., Purdue and Wisconsin.

Multiple titles: Michigan (40); Ohio St. (29); Minnesota (18); Illinois (15); Wisconsin (11); Iowa (10); Purdue and Northwestern (8); Chicago and Michigan St. (6); Indiana (2).

Year		Year		Year		Year	
1896	Wisconsin (2-0-1)	1906	Wisconsin (3-0),	1917	Ohio St. (4-0)	1927	Illinois (5-0)
1897	Wisconsin (3-0)		Minnesota (2-0)	1918	Illinois (4-0),		& Minnesota (3-0-1)
1898	Michigan (3-0)		& Michigan (1-0)		Michigan (2-0)	1928	Illinois (4-1)
1899	Chicago (4-0)	1907	Chicago (4-0)		& Purdue (1-0)	1929	Purdue (5-0)
1900	Iowa (3-0-1)	1908	Chicago (5-0)	1919	Illinois (6-1)	1930	Michigan (5-0)
	& Minnesota (3-0-1)	1909	Minnesota (3-0)	1920	Ohio St. (5-0)		& Northwestern (5-0)
1901	Michigan (4-0)	1910	Illinois (4-0)	1921	Iowa (5-0)	1931	Purdue (5-1),
	& Wisconsin (2-0)		& Minnesota (2-0)	1922	Iowa (5-0)		Michigan (5-1)
1902	Michigan (5-0)	1911	Minnesota (3-0-1)		& Michigan (4-0)		& Northwestern (5-1)
1903	Michigan (3-0-1),	1912	Wisconsin (6-0)	1923	Illinois (5-0)	1932	Michigan (6-0)
	Minnesota (3-0-1)	1913	Chicago (7-0)		& Michigan (4-0)		& Purdue (5-0-1)
	& Northwestern (1-0-2)	1914	Illinois (6-0)	1924	Chicago (3-0-3)	1933	Michigan (5-0-1)
1904	Minnesota (3-0)	1915	Minnesota (3-0-1)	1925	Michigan (5-1)		& Minnesota (2-0-4)
	& Michigan (2-0)		& Illinois (3-0-2)	1926	Michigan (5-0)	1934	Minnesota (5-0)
1905	Chicago (7-0)	1916	Ohio St. (4-0)		& Northwestern (5-0)	1935	Minnesota (5-0)
							& Ohio St. (5-0)

Year		Year		Year		Year	
1936	Northwestern (6-0)	1957	Ohio St. (7-0)	1975	Ohio St. (8-0)	1992	Michigan (6-0-2)
1937	Minnesota (5-0)	1958	Iowa (5-1)	1976	Michigan (7-1) & Ohio St. (7-1)	1993	Wisconsin (6-1-1) & Ohio St. (6-1-1)
1938	Minnesota (4-1)	1959	Wisconsin (5-2)	1977	Michigan (7-1) & Ohio St. (7-1)	1994	Penn St. (8-0)
1939	Ohio St. (5-1)	1960	Minnesota (5-1) & Iowa (5-1)	1978	Michigan (7-1) & Michigan St. (7-1)	1995	Northwestern (8-0)
1940	Minnesota (6-0)	1961	Ohio St. (6-0)	1979	Ohio St. (8-0)	1996	Ohio St. (7-1) & Northwestern (7-1)
1941	Minnesota (5-0)	1962	Wisconsin (6-1)	1980	Michigan (8-0)	1997	Michigan (8-0)
1942	Ohio St. (5-1)	1963	Illinois (5-1-1)	1981	Iowa (6-2) & Ohio St. (6-2)	1998	Ohio St. (7-0), Wisconsin (7-1) & Michigan (7-1)
1943	Purdue (6-0) & Michigan (6-0)	1964	Michigan (6-1)	1982	Michigan (8-1)	1999	Wisconsin (7-1)
1944	Ohio St. (6-0)	1965	Michigan St. (7-0)	1983	Illinois (9-0)	2000	Purdue (6-2), Michigan (6-2) & Northwestern (6-2)
1945	Indiana (5-0-1)	1966	Michigan St. (7-0)	1984	Ohio St. (7-2)	2001	Illinois (7-1)
1946	Illinois (6-1)	1967	Indiana (6-1), Purdue (6-1) & Minnesota (6-1)	1985	Iowa (7-1)	2002	Ohio St. (8-0) & Iowa (8-0)
1947	Michigan (6-0)	1968	Ohio St. (7-0)	1986	Michigan (7-1) & Ohio St. (7-1)		
1948	Michigan (6-0)	1969	Ohio St. (6-1) & Michigan (6-1)	1987	Michigan St. (7-0-1)		
1949	Ohio St. (4-1-1) & Michigan (4-1-1)	1970	Ohio St. (7-0)	1988	Michigan (7-0-1)		
1950	Michigan (4-1-1)	1971	Michigan (8-0)	1989	Michigan (8-0)		
1951	Illinois (5-0-1)	1972	Ohio St. (7-1) & Michigan (7-1)	1990	Iowa (6-2), Michigan (6-2), Michigan St. (6-2) & Illinois (6-2)		
1952	Wisconsin (4-1-1) & Purdue (4-1-1)	1973	Ohio St. (7-0-1) & Michigan (7-0-1)	1991	Michigan (8-.90)		
1953	Michigan St. (5-1) & Illinois (5-1)	1974	Ohio St. (7-1) & Michigan (7-1)				
1954	Ohio St. (7-0)						
1955	Ohio St. (6-0)						
1956	Iowa (5-1)						

Big Eight Conference (1907-1996)

Originally founded in 1907 as the Missouri Valley Intercollegiate Athletic Assn. **Charter members** (5): Iowa, Kansas, Missouri, Nebraska and Washington University of St. Louis. **Admitted later** (11): Drake and Iowa St. (then Ames College) in 1908; Kansas St. (then Kansas College of Applied Science and Agriculture) in 1913; Grinnell (Iowa) College in 1919; Oklahoma in 1920; Oklahoma A&M (now Oklahoma St.) in 1925; Colorado in 1947 (began play in '48).

Withdrew later (9): Iowa in 1911 (left for Big Ten after 1910 season); Colorado, Iowa St., Kansas, Kansas St. Missouri, Nebraska, Oklahoma and Oklahoma St. in 1996 (left for Big 12 after 1995 season); **Excluded later** (4): Drake, Grinnell, Oklahoma A&M and Washington-MO (left out when MVIAA cut membership to six teams in 1928).

Streamlined MVIAA unofficially called **Big Six** from 1928-47 with surviving members Iowa St., Kansas, Kansas St., Missouri, Nebraska and Oklahoma. Became the **Big Seven** after 1947 season when Colorado came over from the Skyline Conference, and then the **Big Eight** with the return of Oklahoma A&M in 1957. A&M, which resumed conference play in '60, became Oklahoma St. on July 10, 1957. The MVIAA was officially renamed the Big Eight in 1964. The league folded in 1996 when the existing members formed the newly created Big 12 along with four schools from the Southwest Conference.

Multiple titles: Nebraska (43); Oklahoma (34); Missouri (12); Colorado and Kansas (5); Iowa St. and Oklahoma St. (2).

Year		Year		Year		Year	
1907	Iowa (1-0) & Nebraska (1-0)	1928	Nebraska (4-0)	1952	Oklahoma (5-0-1)	1976	Colorado (5-2), Oklahoma (5-2) & Oklahoma St. (5-2)
1908	Kansas (4-0)	1929	Nebraska (3-0-2)	1953	Oklahoma (6-0)		
1909	Missouri (4-0-1)	1930	Kansas (4-1)	1954	Oklahoma (6-0)	1977	Oklahoma (7-0)
1910	Nebraska (2-0)	1931	Nebraska (5-0)	1955	Oklahoma (6-0)	1978	Nebraska (6-1) & Oklahoma (6-1)
1911	Iowa St. (2-0-1) & Nebraska (2-0-1)	1932	Nebraska (5-0)	1956	Oklahoma (6-0)	1979	Oklahoma (7-0)
1912	Iowa St. (2-0) & Nebraska (2-0)	1933	Nebraska (5-0)	1957	Oklahoma (6-0)	1980	Oklahoma (7-0)
1913	Missouri (4-0) & Nebraska (3-0)	1934	Kansas St. (5-0)	1958	Oklahoma (6-0)	1981	Nebraska (7-0)
1914	Nebraska (3-0)	1935	Nebraska (4-0-1)	1959	Oklahoma (5-1)	1982	Nebraska (7-0)
1915	Nebraska (4-0)	1936	Nebraska (5-0)	1960	Missouri (7-0)	1983	Nebraska (7-0)
1916	Nebraska (3-1)	1937	Nebraska (3-0-2)	1961	Colorado (7-0)	1984	Oklahoma (6-1) & Nebraska (6-1)
1917	Nebraska (2-0)	1938	Oklahoma (5-0)	1962	Oklahoma (7-0)	1985	Oklahoma (7-0)
1918	Vacant (WW I)	1939	Missouri (5-0)	1963	Nebraska (7-0)	1986	Oklahoma (7-0)
1919	Missouri (4-0-1)	1940	Nebraska (5-0)	1964	Nebraska (6-1)	1987	Oklahoma (7-0)
1920	Oklahoma (4-0-1)	1941	Missouri (5-0)	1965	Nebraska (7-0)	1988	Nebraska (7-0)
1921	Nebraska (3-0)	1942	Missouri (4-0-1)	1966	Nebraska (6-1)	1989	Colorado (7-0)
1922	Nebraska (5-0)	1943	Oklahoma (5-0)	1967	Oklahoma (7-0)	1990	Colorado (7-0)
1923	Nebraska (3-0-2) & Kansas (3-0-3)	1944	Oklahoma (4-0-1)	1968	Kansas (6-1) & Oklahoma (6-1)	1991	Nebraska (6-0-1) & Colorado (6-0-1)
1924	Missouri (5-1)	1945	Missouri (5-0)	1969	Missouri (6-1) & Nebraska (6-1)	1992	Nebraska (6-1)
1925	Missouri (5-1)	1946	Oklahoma (4-1) & Kansas (4-1)	1970	Nebraska (7-0)	1993	Nebraska (7-0)
1926	Okla. A&M (3-0-1)	1947	Kansas (4-0-1) & Oklahoma (4-0-1)	1971	Nebraska (7-0)	1994	Nebraska (7-0)
1927	Missouri (5-1)	1948	Oklahoma (5-0)	1972	Nebraska (5-1-1)*	1995	Nebraska (7-0)
		1949	Oklahoma (5-0)	1973	Oklahoma (7-0)		
		1950	Oklahoma (6-0)	1974	Oklahoma (7-0)		
		1951	Oklahoma (6-0)	1975	Nebraska (6-1) & Oklahoma (6-1)		

*Oklahoma (6-1) forfeited title in 1972 after a player was ruled ineligible.

Major Conference Champions (Cont.)
Big 12 Conference

Originally founded in 1996 by the former teams of the Big Eight and four schools from the Southwest Conference. The league stages a conference championship game between the two division winners on the first Saturday in December. **Playing sites:** Trans World Dome in St. Louis (1996, 1998), the Alamodome in San Antonio (1997, 1999), Arrowhead Stadium in Kansas City, Mo. (2000) and Texas Stadium in Irving, Texas (2001). The 2002 game is set for Houston's Reliant Stadium and the game returns to Arrowhead Stadium in 2003.

2003 playing membership: (12) NORTH—Colorado, Iowa St., Kansas, Kansas St., Missouri and Nebraska; SOUTH—Baylor, Oklahoma, Oklahoma St., Texas, Texas A&M and Texas Tech.

Multiple titles: Nebraska and Oklahoma (2).

Year		Year		Year	
1996	Texas 37, Nebraska 27	1999	Nebraska 22, Texas 6	2002	Oklahoma 29, Colorado 7
1997	Nebraska 54, Texas A&M 15	2000	Oklahoma 27, Kansas St. 24		
1998	Texas A&M 36, Kansas St. 33	2001	Colorado 39, Texas 37		

Big West Conference (1969-2000)

Originally founded in 1969 as Pacific Coast Athletic Assn. **Charter members** (7): CS-Los Angeles, Fresno St., Long Beach St., Pacific, San Diego St., San Jose St. and UC-Santa Barbara. **Admitted later** (12): CS-Fullerton in 1974; Utah St. in 1977 (began play in '78); UNLV in 1982; New Mexico St. in 1983 (began play in '84); Nevada in 1991 (began play in '92); Arkansas St., Louisiana Tech, Northern Illinois and SW Louisiana in 1992 (all four began play in football only in '93); Boise St., Idaho and North Texas in 1994 (all three began play in '96); Arkansas St. rejoined in 1999 (in football only). **Withdrew later** (14): CS-Los Angeles and UC-Santa Barbara in 1972 (both dropped football after '71 season); San Diego St. in 1975 (became an independent after '75 season); Fresno St. in 1991 (left for WAC after '91 season); Long Beach St. in 1991 (dropped football after '91 season); CS-Fullerton in 1992 (dropped football after '92 season); San Jose St. and UNLV in 1994 (left for WAC after '95 season); Pacific in 1995 (dropped football after '95 season); Arkansas St., Louisiana Tech, Northern Illinois and SW Louisiana in 1995 (all four returned to independent football status after '95 season); Nevada in 2000 (left for WAC after '99 season). **Conference renamed** Big West in 1988.

Multiple titles: San Jose St. (8); Fresno St. (6); Nevada, San Diego St. and Utah St. (5); Long Beach St., Boise St., CS-Fullerton and SW Louisiana (2).

Year		Year		Year	
1969	San Diego St. (6-0)	1982	Fresno St. (6-0)	1994	UNLV (5-1),
1970	Long Beach St. (5-1)	1983	CS-Fullerton (5-1)		Nevada (5-1),
	& San Diego St. (5-1)	1984	CS-Fullerton (6-1)†		& SW Louisiana (5-1)
1971	Long Beach St. (5-1)	1985	Fresno St. (7-0)	1995	Nevada (6-0)
1972	San Diego St. (4-0)	1986	San Jose St. (7-0)	1996	Nevada (4-1)
1973	San Diego St. (3-0-1)	1987	San Jose St. (7-0)		& Utah St. (4-1)
1974	San Diego St. (4-0)	1988	Fresno St. (7-0)	1997	Utah St. (4-1)
1975	San Jose St. (5-0)	1989	Fresno St. (7-0)		& Nevada (4-1)
1976	San Jose St. (4-0)	1990	San Jose St. (7-0)	1998	Idaho (4-1)
1977	Fresno St. (4-0)	1991	Fresno St. (6-1)	1999	Boise St. (5-1)
1978	San Jose St. (4-1)		& San Jose St. (6-1)	2000	Boise St. (5-0)
	& Utah St. (4-1)	1992	Nevada (5-1)	*San Jose St. (4-0-1) forfeited share of
1979	Utah St. (4-0-1)*	1993	Utah St. (5-1)	1979 title for using ineligible player.
1980	Long Beach St. (5-0)		& SW Louisiana (5-1)	†UNLV (7-0) forfeited title in 1984 for
1981	San Jose St. (5-0)			use of ineligible players.

Conference USA

Founded in 1994 by six independent football schools which began play as a conference in 1996. **Charter members** (6): Cincinnati, Houston, Louisville, Memphis, Southern Mississippi and Tulane. **Admitted later** (4): East Carolina in 1997, Army in 1998, Univ. of Alabama-Birmingham in 1999, Texas Christian Univ. in 2001, South Florida in 2003;
2003 playing members (11): Alabama-Birmingham, Army, Cincinnati, East Carolina, Houston, Louisville, Memphis, South Florida, Southern Mississippi, TCU and Tulane.

Multiple titles: Southern Mississippi (3), Louisville (2).

Year		Year		Year	
1996	Southern Mississippi (4-1)	1998	Tulane (6-0)	2001	Louisville (6-1)
	& Houston (4-1)	1999	Southern Mississippi (6-0)	2002	TCU (6-2)
1997	Southern Mississippi (6-0)	2000	Louisville (6-1)		& Cincinnati (6-2)

Mid-American Conference

Founded in 1946. **Charter members** (6): Butler, Cincinnati, Miami-OH, Ohio University, Western Michigan and Western Reserve (Miami and WMU began play in '48). **Admitted later** (12): Kent St. (now Kent) and Toledo in 1951 (Toledo began play in '52); Bowling Green in 1952; Marshall in 1954; Central Michigan and Eastern Michigan in 1972 (CMU began play in '75 and EMU in '76); Ball St. and Northern Illinois in 1973 (both began play in '75); Akron in 1991 (began play in '92); Marshall and Northern Illinois in 1995 (both resumed play in '97); Buffalo in 1995 (resumed play in '99); Central Florida in 2002. **Withdrew later** (5): Butler in 1950 (left for the Indiana Collegiate Conference); Cincinnati in 1953 (went independent); Western Reserve (now Case Western) in 1955 (left for President's Athletic Conference); Marshall in 1969 (went independent); and Northern Illinois in 1986 (went independent).

2003 playing membership (14): EAST—Akron, Buffalo, Central Florida, Kent St., Marshall, Miami-OH and Ohio University; WEST—Ball St., Bowling Green, Central Michigan, Eastern Michigan, Northern Illinois, Toledo and Western Michigan.

Multiple titles: Miami-OH (13); Bowling Green (10); Toledo (8); Ball St., Marshall and Ohio University (5); Central Michigan, Cincinnati (4); Western Michigan (2).

Year		Year		Year		Year	
1947	Cincinnati (3-1)	1960	Ohio Univ. (6-0)	1972	Kent St. (4-1)	1987	Eastern Mich. (7-1)
1948	Miami-OH (4-0)	1961	Bowling Green (5-1)	1973	Miami-OH (5-0)	1988	Western Mich. (7-1)
1949	Cincinnati (4-0)	1962	Bowling Green (5-0-1)	1974	Miami-OH (5-0)	1989	Ball St. (6-1-1)
1950	Miami-OH (4-0)	1963	Ohio Univ. (5-1)	1975	Miami-OH (6-0)	1990	Central Mich. (7-1)
1951	Cincinnati (3-0)	1964	Bowling Green (5-1)	1976	Ball St. (4-1)		& Toledo (7-1)
1952	Cincinnati (3-0)	1965	Bowling Green (5-1)	1977	Miami-OH (5-0)	1991	Bowling Green (8-0)
1953	Ohio Univ. (5-0-1)		& Miami-OH (5-1)	1978	Ball St. (8-0)	1992	Bowling Green (8-0)
	& Miami-OH (3-0-1)	1966	Miami-OH (5-1)	1979	Central Mich. (8-0-1)	1993	Ball St. (7-0-1)
1954	Miami-OH (4-0)		& Western Mich. (5-1)	1980	Central Mich. (7-2)	1994	Central Mich. (8-1)
1955	Miami-OH (5-0)	1967	Toledo (5-1)	1981	Toledo (8-1)	1995	Toledo (7-0-1)
1956	Bowling Green (5-0-1)		& Ohio Univ. (5-1)	1982	Bowling Green (7-2)	1996	Ball St. (7-1)
	& Miami-OH (4-0-1)	1968	Ohio Univ. (6-0)	1983	Northern Ill. (8-1)		
1957	Miami-OH (5-0)	1969	Toledo (5-0)	1984	Toledo (7-1-1)		
1958	Miami-OH (5-0)	1970	Toledo (5-0)	1985	Bowling Green (9-0)		
1959	Bowling Green (6-0)	1971	Toledo (5-0)	1986	Miami-OH (6-2)		

MAC Championship Game

After expanding to 12 teams (and then 13 in 1999 with the addition of Buffalo) and splitting into two divisions in 1997, the MAC now stages a conference championship game between the two division winners on the first Saturday in December. The game was played at Marshall Stadium in Huntington, W.V. (1997-2000, 2002) and Glass Bowl Stadium in Toledo, Ohio (2001).

Year		Year		Year	
1997	Marshall 34, Toledo 13	1999	Marshall 34, W. Michigan 30	2001	Toledo 41, Marshall 36
1998	Marshall 23, Toledo 17	2000	Marshall 19, W. Michigan 14	2002	Marshall 49, Toledo 45

Mountain West Conference

Founded in 1999. **Charter members** (8): Air Force, Brigham Young, Colorado St., New Mexico, Nevada-Las Vegas, San Diego St., Utah and Wyoming.

2003 playing membership (8): Air Force, Brigham Young, Colorado St., New Mexico, Nevada-Las Vegas, San Diego St., Utah and Wyoming. **Multiple titles:** Colorado St. (3), BYU (2).

Year		Year		Year	
1999	BYU (5-2),	2000	Colorado St. (6-1)	2002	Colorado St. (6-1)
	Colorado St. (5-2)	2001	BYU (7-0)		
	& Utah (5-2)				

Pacific-10 Conference

Originally founded in 1915 as Pacific Coast Conference. **Charter members** (4): California, Oregon, Oregon St. and Washington. **Admitted later** (6): Washington St. in 1917; Stanford in 1918; Idaho and USC (Southern Cal) in 1922; Montana in 1924; and UCLA in 1928. **Withdrew later** (1): Montana in 1950 (left for the Mountain States Conf.).

The **PCC** dissolved in 1959 and the **AAWU** (Athletic Assn. of Western Universities) was founded. **Charter members** (5): California, Stanford, UCLA, USC and Washington. **Admitted later** (5): Washington St. in 1962; Oregon and Oregon St. in 1964; Arizona and Arizona St. in 1978. **Conference renamed** Pacific-8 in 1968 and Pacific-10 in 1978.

2002 playing membership (10): Arizona, Arizona St., California, Oregon, Oregon St., Stanford, UCLA, USC, Washington and Washington St.

Multiple titles: USC (32); UCLA (17); Washington (15); California (13); Stanford (12); Oregon (7); Oregon St. (5); Washington St. (4); Arizona St. (2).

Year		Year		Year		Year	
1916	Washington (3-0-1)	1938	USC (6-1)	1960	Washington (4-0)	1986	Arizona St. (5-1-1)
1917	Washington St. (3-0)		& California (6-1)	1961	UCLA (3-1)	1987	USC (7-1)
1918	California (3-0)	1939	USC (5-0-2)	1962	USC (4-0)		& UCLA (7-1)
1919	Oregon (2-1)		& UCLA (5-0-3)	1963	Washington (4-1)	1988	USC (8-0)
	& Washington (2-1)	1940	Stanford (7-0)	1964	Oregon St. (3-1)	1989	USC (6-0-1)
1920	California (3-0)	1941	Oregon St. (7-2)		& USC (3-1)	1990	Washington (7-1)
1921	California (5-0)	1942	UCLA (6-1)	1965	UCLA (4-0)	1991	Washington (8-0)
1922	California (3-0)	1943	USC (4-0)	1966	USC (4-1)	1992	Washington (6-2)
1923	California (5-0)	1944	USC (3-0-2)	1967	USC (6-1)		& Stanford (6-2)
1924	Stanford (3-0-1)	1945	USC (5-1)	1968	USC (6-0)	1993	UCLA (6-2),
1925	Washington (5-0)	1946	UCLA (7-0)	1969	USC (6-0)		Arizona (6-2)
1926	Stanford (4-0)	1947	USC (6-0)	1970	Stanford (6-1)		& USC (6-2)
1927	USC (4-0-1)	1948	California (6-0)	1971	Stanford (6-1)	1994	Oregon (7-1)
	& Stanford (4-0-1)		& Oregon (6-0)	1972	USC (7-0)	1995	USC (6-1-1)
1928	USC (4-0-1)	1949	California (7-0)	1973	USC (7-0)		& Washington (6-1-1)
1929	USC (6-1)	1950	California (5-0-1)	1974	USC (6-0-1)	1996	Arizona St. (8-0)
1930	Washington St. (6-0)	1951	Stanford (6-1)	1975	UCLA (6-1)	1997	Washington St. (7-1)
1931	USC (7-0)	1952	USC (6-0)		& California (6-1)		& UCLA (7-1)
1932	USC (6-0)	1953	UCLA (6-1)	1976	USC (7-0)	1998	UCLA (8-0)
1933	Oregon (4-1)	1954	UCLA (6-0)	1977	Washington (6-1)	1999	Stanford (7-1)
	& Stanford (4-1)	1955	UCLA (6-0)	1978	USC (6-1)	2000	Washington (7-1),
1934	Stanford (5-0)	1956	Oregon St. (6-1-1)	1979	USC (6-0-1)		Oregon St. (7-1)
1935	California (4-1),	1957	Oregon (6-2)	1980	Washington (6-1)		& Oregon (7-1)
	Stanford (4-1)		& Oregon St. (6-2)	1981	Washington (6-2)	2001	Oregon (7-1)
	& UCLA (4-1)	1958	California (6-1)	1982	UCLA (5-1-1)	2002	Washington St. (7-1)
1936	Washington (6-0-1)	1959	Washington (3-1),	1983	UCLA (6-1-1)		& USC (7-1)
1937	California (6-0-1)		USC (3-1)	1984	USC (7-1)		
			& UCLA (3-1)	1985	UCLA (6-2)		

Major Conference Champions (Cont.)
Southeastern Conference

Founded in 1933 when charter members all left Southern Conference to form SEC. **Charter members** (13): Alabama, Auburn, Florida, Georgia, Georgia Tech, Kentucky, LSU (Louisiana St.), Mississippi, Mississippi St., Sewanee, Tennessee, Tulane and Vanderbilt. **Admitted later** (2): Arkansas and South Carolina in 1990 (both began play in '92). **Withdrew later** (3): Sewanee in 1940; Georgia Tech in 1964; and Tulane in 1966.

2003 playing membership (12): Alabama, Arkansas, Auburn, Florida, Georgia, Kentucky, LSU, Mississippi, Mississippi St., South Carolina, Tennessee and Vanderbilt. **Note:** Conference title decided by championship game between Western and Eastern division winners since 1992.

Multiple titles: Alabama (21); Tennessee (13); Georgia (11); Florida (9); LSU (8); Mississippi (6); Auburn and Georgia Tech (5); Kentucky and Tulane (3).

Year		Year		Year		Year	
1933	Alabama (5-0-1)	1950	Kentucky (5-1)	1968	Georgia (5-0-1)	1985	Florida (5-1)†
1934	Tulane (8-0)	1951	Georgia Tech (7-0)	1969	Tennessee (5-1)		& Tennessee (5-1)
	& Alabama (7-0)		& Tennessee (5-0)	1970	LSU (5-0)	1986	LSU (5-1)
1935	LSU (5-0)	1952	Georgia Tech (6-0)	1971	Alabama (7-0)	1987	Auburn (5-0-1)
1936	LSU (6-0)	1953	Alabama (4-0-3)	1972	Alabama (7-1)	1988	Auburn (6-1)
1937	Alabama (6-0)	1954	Mississippi (6-0)	1973	Alabama (8-0)		& LSU (6-1)
1938	Tennessee (7-0)	1955	Mississippi (5-1)	1974	Alabama (6-0)	1989	Alabama (6-1),
1939	Tennessee (6-0),	1956	Tennessee (6-0)	1975	Alabama (6-0)		Tennessee (6-1)
	Georgia Tech (6-0)	1957	Auburn (7-0)	1976	Georgia (5-1)		& Auburn (6-1)
	& Tulane (5-0)	1958	LSU (6-0)		& Kentucky (5-1)	1990	Florida (6-1)†
1940	Tennessee (5-0)	1959	Georgia (7-0)	1977	Alabama (7-0)		& Tennessee (5-1-1)
1941	Mississippi St. (4-0-1)	1960	Mississippi (5-0-1)		& Kentucky (6-0)	1991	Florida (7-0)
1942	Georgia (6-1)	1961	Alabama (7-0)	1978	Alabama (6-0)		
1943	Georgia Tech (3-0)		& LSU (6-0)	1979	Alabama (6-0)	*Title vacated.	
1944	Georgia Tech (4-0)	1962	Mississippi (6-0)	1980	Georgia (6-0)	†On probation, ineligible	
1945	Alabama (6-0)	1963	Mississippi (5-0-1)	1981	Georgia (6-0)	for championship.	
1946	Georgia (5-0)	1964	Alabama (8-0)		& Alabama (6-0)		
	& Tennessee (5-0)	1965	Alabama (6-1-1)	1982	Georgia (6-0)		
1947	Mississippi (6-1)	1966	Alabama (6-0)	1983	Auburn (6-0)		
1948	Georgia (6-0)		& Georgia (6-0)	1984	Florida (5-0-1)*		
1949	Tulane (5-1)	1967	Tennessee (6-0)				

Southwest Conference (1914-95)

Founded in 1914 as Southwest Intercollegiate Athletic Conference. **Charter members** (8): Arkansas, Baylor, Oklahoma, Oklahoma A&M (now Oklahoma St.), Rice, Southwestern, Texas and Texas A&M. **Admitted later** (5): SMU (Southern Methodist) in 1918; Phillips University in 1920; TCU (Texas Christian) in 1923; Texas Tech in 1956 (began play in '60); Houston in 1971 (began play in '76). **Withdrew later** (13): Southwestern in 1917 (went independent); Oklahoma in 1920 (left for Missouri Valley after '19 season); Phillips in 1921; Oklahoma A&M (now Oklahoma St.) in 1925 (left for Big Six); Arkansas in 1990 (left for SEC after '91 season); Baylor, Texas, Texas A&M and Texas Tech in 1994 (all four left for Big 12 after '95 season); Rice, SMU and TCU in 1994 (all three left for WAC after '95 season); Houston in 1994 (left for Conference USA after '95 season). Conference folded on June 30, 1996.

Multiple titles: Texas (25); Texas A&M (17); Arkansas (13); SMU (9); TCU (9); Rice (7); Baylor (5); Houston (4); Texas Tech (2).

Year		Year		Year		Year	
1914	No champion	1940	Texas A&M (5-1)	1961	Texas (6-1)	1981	SMU (7-1)
1915	Oklahoma (3-0)	1941	Texas A&M (5-1)		& Arkansas (6-1)	1982	SMU (7-0-1)
1916	No champion	1942	Texas (5-1)	1962	Texas (6-0-1)	1983	Texas (8-0)
1917	Texas A&M (2-0)	1943	Texas (5-0)	1963	Texas (7-0)	*1984	SMU (6-2)
1918	No champion	1944	TCU (3-1-1)	1964	Arkansas (7-0)		& Houston (6-2)
1919	Texas A&M (4-0)	1945	Texas (5-1)	1965	Arkansas (7-0)	1985	Texas A&M (7-1)
1920	Texas (5-0)	1946	Rice (5-1)	1966	SMU (6-1)	1986	Texas A&M (7-1)
1921	Texas A&M (3-0-2)		& Arkansas (5-1)	1967	Texas A&M (6-1)	1987	Texas A&M (6-1)
1922	Baylor (5-0)	1947	SMU (5-0-1)	1968	Arkansas (6-1)	1988	Arkansas (7-0)
1923	SMU (5-0)	1948	SMU (5-0-1)		& Texas (6-1)	1989	Arkansas (7-1)
1924	Baylor (4-0-1)	1949	Rice (6-0)	1969	Texas (7-0)	1990	Texas (8-0)
1925	Texas A&M (4-1)	1950	Texas (6-0)	1970	Texas (7-0)	1991	Texas A&M (8-0)
1926	SMU (5-0)	1951	TCU (5-1)	1971	Texas (6-1)	1992	Texas A&M (7-0)
1927	Texas A&M (4-0-1)	1952	Texas (6-0)	1972	Texas (7-0)	1993	Texas A&M (7-0)
1928	Texas (5-1)	1953	Rice (5-1)	1973	Texas (7-0)	1994	Baylor, Rice, TCU,
1929	TCU (4-0-1)		& Texas (5-1)	1974	Baylor (6-1)		Texas and Texas Tech†
1930	Texas (4-1)	1954	Arkansas (5-1)	1975	Arkansas (6-1),		(4-3)
1931	SMU (5-0-1)	1955	TCU (5-1)		Texas (6-1)	1995	Texas (7-0)
1932	TCU (6-0)	1956	Texas A&M (6-0)		& Texas A&M (6-1)		
1933	Arkansas (4-1)*	1957	Rice (5-1)	1976	Houston (7-1)	*Arkansas (4-1) forced to	
1934	Rice (5-1)	1958	TCU (5-1)		& Texas Tech (7-1)	vacate 1933 title for use of	
1935	SMU (6-0)	1959	Texas (5-1),	1977	Texas (8-0)	ineligible player.	
1936	Arkansas (5-1)		TCU (5-1)	1978	Houston (7-1)	†Texas A&M had the best	
1937	Rice (4-1-1)		& Arkansas (5-1)	1979	Houston (7-1)	record (6-0-1) in 1994 but	
1938	TCU (6-0)	1960	Arkansas (6-1)		& Arkansas (7-1)	was on probation and	
1939	Texas A&M (6-0)			1980	Baylor (8-0)	therefore ineligible for the	
						Southwest championship.	

SEC Championship Game

Since expanding to 12 teams and splitting into two divisions in 1992, the SEC has staged a conference championship game between the two division winners on the first Saturday in December. The game has been played at Legion Field in Birmingham, Ala., (1992-93) and the Georgia Dome in Atlanta (since 1994). The divisions: EAST— Florida, Georgia, Kentucky, South Carolina, Tennessee and Vanderbilt; WEST— Alabama, Arkansas, Auburn, LSU, Mississippi and Mississippi St.

Year		Year		Year	
1992	Alabama 28, Florida 21	1996	Florida 45, Alabama 30	2000	Florida 28, Auburn 6
1993	Florida 28, Alabama 23	1997	Tennessee 30, Auburn 29	2001	LSU 31, Tennessee 20
1994	Florida 24, Alabama 23	1998	Tennessee 24, Miss. St. 14	2002	Georgia 30, Arkansas 3
1995	Florida 34, Arkansas 3	1999	Alabama 34, Florida 7		

Sun Belt Conference

Founded in 2001 when the Sun Belt Conference sponsored football for the first time. **Charter members** (7): Arkansas State, Idaho, Louisiana-Lafayette, Louisiana-Monroe, Middle Tennessee State, New Mexico State and North Texas. **2003 playing members** (8): same plus Utah St which was added in 2003. **Multiple titles:** North Texas (2)

Year		Year	
2001	North Texas (5-1) & Mid. Tenn. St. (5-1)	2002	North Texas (6-0)

Western Athletic Conference

Founded in 1962 when charter members left the Skyline and Border conferences to form theWAC. **Charter members** (6): Arizona and Arizona St. from Border; BYU (Brigham Young), New Mexico, Utah and Wyoming from Skyline. **Admitted later** (15): Colorado St. and UTEP (Texas-El Paso) in 1967 (both began play in '68); San Diego St. in 1978; Hawaii in 1979; Air Force in 1980; Fresno St. in 1991 (began play in '92); Rice, San Jose St., SMU , TCU , Tulsa and UNLV in 1994 (all began play in '96); Nevada in 2000; Boise St. and Louisiana Tech in 2001. **Withdrew later** (11): Arizona and Arizona St. in 1978 (left for Pac-10 after '77 season); Air Force, BYU, Colorado St., New Mexico, San Diego St., UNLV, Utah and Wyoming (left to form Mountain West conference in '99); TCU in 2000 (left for Conference USA after 2000 season).

2003 playing membership (10): Boise St., Fresno St., Hawaii, Louisiana Tech, Nevada, Rice, San Jose St., SMU, Tulsa and UTEP.

Multiple titles: BYU (19); Arizona St. and Wyoming (7); Air Force, Fresno St., New Mexico and Colorado St. (3); Arizona, Hawaii, TCU and Utah (2).

Year		Year		Year		Year	
1962	New Mexico (2-1-1)	1974	BYU (6-0-1)	1986	San Diego St. (7-1)	1995	Colorado St. (6-2), Air Force (6-2), BYU (6-2) & Utah (6-2)
1963	New Mexico (3-1)	1975	Arizona St. (7-0)	1987	Wyoming (8-0)		
1964	Utah (3-1), New Mexico (3-1) & Arizona (3-1)	1976	BYU (6-1) & Wyoming (6-1)	1988	Wyoming (8-0)		
				1989	BYU (7-1)		
		1977	Arizona St. (6-1) & BYU (6-1)	1990	BYU (7-1)	1999	Fresno St. (5-2), Hawaii (7-2) & TCU (7-2)
1965	BYU (4-1)			1991	BYU (7-0-1)		
1966	Wyoming (5-0)	1978	BYU (5-1)	1992	Hawaii (6-2), BYU (6-2) & Fresno St. (6-2)	2000	TCU (7-1) & UTEP (7-1)
1967	Wyoming (5-0)	1979	BYU (7-0)			
1968	Wyoming (6-1)	1980	BYU (6-1)			2001	La. Tech (7-1)
1969	Arizona St. (6-1)	1981	BYU (7-1)	1993	BYU (6-2), Fresno St. (6-2) & Wyoming (6-2)	2002	Boise St. (8-0)
1970	Arizona St. (7-0)	1982	BYU (7-1)1983 BYU (7-0)			
1971	Arizona St. (7-0)					
1972	Arizona St. (5-1)	1984	BYU (8-0)	1994	Colorado St. (7-1)		
1973	Arizona St. (6-1) & Arizona (6-1)	1985	Air Force (7-1) & BYU (7-1)				

Longest Division I Streaks

Winning Streaks
(Including bowl games)

No		Seasons	Spoiler	Score
47	Oklahoma	1953-57	Notre Dame	7-0
39	Washington	1908-14	Oregon St.	0-0
37	Yale	1890-93	Princeton	6-0
37	Yale	1887-89	Princeton	10-0
35	Toledo	1969-71	Tampa	21-0
34	Miami-FL	2000-02	Ohio St.	31-24*
34	Penn	1894-96	Lafayette	6-4
31	Oklahoma	1948-50	Kentucky	13-7*
31	Pittsburgh	1914-18	Cleve. Naval	10-9
31	Penn	1896-98	Harvard	10-0
30	Texas	1968-70	Notre Dame	24-11*
29	Miami-FL	1990-93	Alabama	34-13
29	Michigan	1901-03	Minnesota	6-6
28	Alabama†	1991-93	Tennessee	17-17
28	Alabama	1978-80	Mississippi St.	6-3
28	Oklahoma	1973-75	Kansas	23-3
28	Michigan St.	1950-53	Purdue	6-0
27	Nebraska	1901-04	Colorado	6-0

*Ohio St. beat Miami in 2003 Fiesta Bowl in double overtime. Kentucky beat Oklahoma in 1951 Sugar Bowl and Notre Dame beat Texas in 1971 Cotton Bowl.

†Alabama was forced to forfeit eight victories and one tie in 1993 by the NCAA Committee on Infractions.

Unbeaten Streaks
(Including bowl games)

No	W-T		Seasons	Spoiler	Score
63	59-4	Washington	1907-17	California	27-0
56	55-1	Michigan	1901-05	Chicago	2-0
50	46-4	California	1920-25	Olympic Club	15-0
48	47-1	Oklahoma	1953-57	N. Dame	7-0
48	47-1	Yale	1885-89	Princeton	10-0
47	42-5	Yale	1879-85	Princeton	6-5
44	42-2	Yale	1894-96	Princeton	24-6
42	39-3	Yale	1904-08	Harvard	4-0
39	37-2	N. Dame	1946-50	Purdue	28-14
37	36-1	Oklahoma	1972-75	Kansas	23-3
37	37-0	Yale	1890-93	Princeton	6-0
35	35-0	Toledo	1967-71	Tampa	21-0
35	34-1	Minnesota	1903-05	Wisconsin	16-12

Losing Streaks

No		Seasons	Victim	Score
80	Prairie View	1989-98	Langston	14-12
44	Columbia	1983-88	Princeton	16-14
34	Northwestern	1979-82	No. Illinois	31-6
28	Virginia	1958-60	Wm. & Mary	21-6
28	Kansas St	1944-48	Arkansas St.	37-6

Note: Virginia ended its losing streak in the opening game of the 1961 season.

Major Conference Champions (Cont.)

WAC Championship Game

In addition to expanding to 16 teams and splitting into two divisions in 1996, the WAC staged a conference championship game between the two division winners on the first Saturday in December at Sam Boyd Stadium in Las Vegas until eight teams split off and formed the Mountain West Conference in 1999. The divisions: PACIFIC—BYU, Fresno St., Hawaii, New Mexico, San Diego St., San Jose St., UTEP, Utah; MOUNTAIN—Air Force, Colorado St., Rice, SMU, TCU, Tulsa, UNLV, Wyoming.

Year	Year	Year
1996 BYU 28, Wyoming 25 (OT)	1997 Colorado St. 41, New Mexico 13	1998 Air Force 20, BYU 13

Annual NCAA Division I-A Leaders

Note that Oklahoma A&M is now Oklahoma St. and Texas Mines is now UTEP.

Rushing

Individual championship decided on Rushing Yards (1937-69), and on Yards Per Game (since 1970).

Multiple winners: Troy Davis, Marshall Faulk, Art Luppino, Ed Marinaro, Rudy Mobley, Jim Pilot, O.J. Simpson, LaDainian Tomlinson and Ricky Williams (2).

Year		Car	Yards	Year		Car	Yards	P/Gm
1937	Byron (Whizzer) White, Colorado	181	1121	1970	Ed Marinaro, Cornell	285	1425	158.3
1938	Len Eshmont, Fordham	132	831	1971	Ed Marinaro, Cornell	356	1881	209.0
1939	John Polanski, Wake Forest	137	882	1972	Pete VanValkenburg, BYU	232	1386	138.6
1940	Al Ghesquiere, Detroit	146	957	1973	Mark Kellar, Northern Ill	291	1719	156.3
1941	Frank Sinkwich, Georgia	209	1103	1974	Louie Giammona, Utah St.	329	1534	153.4
1942	Rudy Mobley, Hardin-Simmons	187	1281	1975	Ricky Bell, USC	357	1875	170.5
1943	Creighton Miller, Notre Dame	151	911	1976	Tony Dorsett, Pittsburgh	338	1948	177.1
1944	Red Williams, Minnesota	136	911	1977	Earl Campbell, Texas	267	1744	158.5
1945	Bob Fenimore, Oklahoma A&M	142	1048	1978	Billy Sims, Oklahoma	231	1762	160.2
1946	Rudy Mobley, Hardin-Simmons	227	1262	1979	Charles White, USC.	293	1803	180.3
1947	Wilton Davis, Hardin-Simmons	193	1173	1980	George Rogers, S. Carolina	297	1781	161.9
1948	Fred Wendt, Texas Mines	184	1570	1981	Marcus Allen, USC.	403	2342	212.9
1949	John Dottley, Ole Miss	208	1312	1982	Ernest Anderson, Okla. St.	353	1877	170.6
1950	Wilford White, Arizona St	199	1502	1983	Mike Rozier, Nebraska	275	2148	179.0
1951	Ollie Matson, San Francisco	245	1566	1984	Keith Byars, Ohio St.	313	1655	150.5
1952	Howie Waugh, Tulsa	164	1372	1985	Lorenzo White, Mich. St.	386	1908	173.5
1953	J.C. Caroline, Illinois	194	1256	1986	Paul Palmer, Temple	346	1866	169.6
1954	Art Luppino, Arizona	179	1359	1987	Ickey Woods, UNLV	259	1658	150.7
1955	Art Luppino, Arizona	209	1313	1988	Barry Sanders, Okla. St.	344	2628	238.9
1956	Jim Crawford, Wyoming	200	1104	1989	Anthony Thompson, Ind	358	1793	163.0
1957	Leon Burton, Arizona St	117	1126	1990	Gerald Hudson, Okla. St.	279	1642	149.3
1958	Dick Bass, Pacific	205	1361	1991	Marshall Faulk, S. Diego St.	201	1429	158.8
1959	Pervis Atkins, New Mexico St	130	971	1992	Marshall Faulk, S. Diego St.	265	1630	163.0
1960	Bob Gaiters, New Mexico St	197	1338	1993	LeShon Johnson, No. Ill.	327	1976	179.6
1961	Jim Pilot, New Mexico St	191	1278	1994	Rashaan Salaam, Colorado	298	2055	186.8
1962	Jim Pilot, New Mexico St	208	1247	1995	Troy Davis, Iowa St.	345	2010	182.7
1963	Dave Casinelli, Memphis St	219	1016	1996	Troy Davis, Iowa St.	402	2185	198.6
1964	Brian Piccolo, Wake Forest	252	1044	1997	Ricky Williams, Texas.	279	1893	172.1
1965	Mike Garrett, USC	267	1440	1998	Ricky Williams, Texas.	361	2124	193.1
1966	Ray McDonald, Idaho	259	1329	1999	LaDainian Tomlinson, TCU	268	1850	168.2
1967	O.J. Simpson, USC.	266	1415	2000	LaDainian Tomlinson, TCU	369	2158	196.2
1968	O.J. Simpson, USC.	355	1709	2001	Chance Kretschmer, Nevada	302	1732	157.5
1969	Steve Owens, Oklahoma	358	1523	2002	Larry Johnson, Penn St.	271	2087	160.5

All-Purpose Yardage

Multiple winners: Marcus Allen, Pervis Atkins, Ryan Benjamin, Troy Davis, Troy Edwards, Louie Giammona, Tom Harmon, Art Luppino, Napolean McCallum, O.J. Simpson, Charles White and Gary Wood (2).

Year		Yards	P/Gm	Year		Yards	P/Gm
1937	Byron (Whizzer) White, Colorado	1970	246.3	1953	J.C. Caroline, Illinois	1470	163.3
1938	Parker Hall, Ole Miss	1420	129.1	1954	Art Luppino, Arizona	2193	219.3
1939	Tom Harmon, Michigan.	1208	151.0	1955	Jim Swink, TCU	1702	170.2
1940	Tom Harmon, Michigan.	1312	164.0		& Art Luppino, Arizona	1702	170.2
1941	Bill Dudley, Virginia	1674	186.0	1956	Jack Hill, Utah St	1691	169.1
1942	Complete records not available			1957	Overton Curtis, Utah St	1608	160.8
1943	Stan Koslowski, Holy Cross	1411	176.4	1958	Dick Bass, Pacific	1878	187.8
1944	Red Williams, Minnesota	1467	163.0	1959	Pervis Atkins, New Mexico St	1800	180.0
1945	Bob Fenimore, Oklahoma A&M	1577	197.1	1960	Pervis Atkins, New Mexico St	1613	161.3
1946	Rudy Mobley, Hardin-Simmons	1765	176.5	1961	Jim Pilot, New Mexico St	1606	160.6
1947	Wilton Davis, Hardin-Simmons	1798	179.8	1962	Gary Wood, Cornell	1395	155.0
1948	Lou Kusserow, Columbia	1737	193.0	1963	Gary Wood, Cornell	1508	167.6
1949	Johnny Papit, Virginia	1611	179.0	1964	Donny Anderson, Texas Tech	1710	171.0
1950	Wilford White, Arizona St.	2065	206.5	1965	Floyd Little, Syracuse	1990	199.0
1951	Ollie Matson, San Francisco	2037	226.3	1966	Frank Quayle, Virginia	1616	161.6
1952	Billy Vessels, Oklahoma	1512	151.2	1967	O.J. Simpson, USC	1700	188.9

Year		Yards	P/Gm	Year		Yards	P/Gm
1968	O.J. Simpson, USC.	1966	196.6	1986	Paul Palmer, Temple	2633	239.4
1969	Lynn Moore, Army	1795	179.5	1987	Eric Wilkerson, Kent St.	2074	188.6
1970	Don McCauley, North Carolina	2021	183.7	1988	Barry Sanders, Oklahoma St.	3250	295.5
1971	Ed Marinaro, Cornell	1932	214.7	1989	Mike Pringle, CS-Fullerton	2690	244.6
1972	Howard Stevens, Louisville.	2132	213.2	1990	Glyn Milburn, Stanford	2222	202.0
1973	Willard Harrell, Pacific	1777	177.7	1991	Ryan Benjamin, Pacific.	2995	249.6
1974	Louie Giammona, Utah St	1984	198.4	1992	Ryan Benjamin, Pacific.	2597	236.1
1975	Louie Giammona, Utah St	2045	185.9	1993	LeShon Johnson, Northern Ill.	2082	189.3
1976	Tony Dorsett, Pittsburgh	2021	183.7	1994	Rashaan Salaam, Colorado	2349	213.5
1977	Earl Campbell, Texas	1855	168.6	1995	Troy Davis, Iowa St.	2466	224.2
1978	Charles White, USC.	2096	174.7	1996	Troy Davis, Iowa St.	2364	214.9
1979	Charles White, USC.	1941	194.1	1997	Troy Edwards, La. Tech	2144	194.9
1980	Marcus Allen, USC.	1794	179.4	1998	Troy Edwards, La. Tech	2784	232.0
1981	Marcus Allen, USC.	2559	232.6	1999	Trevor Insley, Nevada	2176	197.8
1982	Carl Monroe, Utah	2036	185.1	2000	Emmett White, Utah St.	2628	238.9
1983	Napoleon McCallum, Navy	2385	216.8	2001	Levron Williams, Indiana	2201	200.1
1984	Keith Byars, Ohio St	2284	207.6	2002	Larry Johnson, Penn St.	2655	204.2
1985	Napoleon McCallum, Navy	2330	211.8				

Total Offense

Individual championship decided on Total Yards (1937-69) and on Yards Per Game (since 1970).

Multiple winners: Tim Rattay (3); Johnny Bright, Bob Fenimore, Mike Maxwell and Jim McMahon (2).

Year		Plays	Yards	Year		Plays	Yards	P/Gm
1937	Byron (Whizzer) White, Colorado.	224	1596	1970	Pat Sullivan, Auburn.	333	2856	285.6
1938	Davey O'Brien, TCU	291	1847	1971	Gary Huff, Florida St	386	2653	241.2
1939	Kenny Washington, UCLA	259	1370	1972	Don Strock, Va. Tech	480	3170	288.2
1940	Johnny Knolla, Creighton	298	1420	1973	Jesse Freitas, San Diego St.	410	2901	263.7
1941	Bud Schwenk, Washington-MO	354	1928	1974	Steve Joachim, Temple	331	2227	222.7
1942	Frank Sinkwich, Georgia.	341	2187	1975	Gene Swick, Toledo	490	2706	246.0
1943	Bob Hoernschemeyer, Indiana	355	1648	1976	Tommy Kramer, Rice.	562	3272	297.5
1944	Bob Fenimore, Oklahoma A&M.	241	1758	1977	Doug Williams, Gambling .	377	3229	293.5
1945	Bob Fenimore, Oklahoma A&M.	203	1641	1978	Mike Ford, SMU	459	2957	268.8
1946	Travis Bidwell, Auburn	339	1715	1979	Marc Wilson, BYU	488	3580	325.5
1947	Fred Enke, Arizona	329	1941	1980	Jim McMahon, BYU	540	4627	385.6
1948	Stan Heath, Nevada-Reno.	233	1992	1981	Jim McMahon, BYU	487	3458	345.8
1949	Johnny Bright, Drake	275	1950	1982	Todd Dillon, Long Beach St	585	3587	326.1
1950	Johnny Bright, Drake	320	2400	1983	Steve Young, BYU.	531	4346	395.1
1951	Dick Kazmaier, Princeton	272	1827	1984	Robbie Bosco, BYU	543	3932	327.7
1952	Ted Marchibroda, Detroit	305	1813	1985	Jim Everett, Purdue	518	3589	326.3
1953	Paul Larson, California.	262	1572	1986	Mike Perez, San Jose St.	425	2969	329.9
1954	George Shaw, Oregon	276	1536	1987	Todd Santos, San Diego St.	562	3688	307.3
1955	George Welsh, Navy.	203	1348	1988	Scott Mitchell, Utah	589	4299	390.8
1956	John Brodie, Stanford.	295	1642	1989	Andre Ware, Houston	628	4661	423.7
1957	Bob Newman, Washington St	263	1444	1990	David Klingler, Houston.	704	5221	474.6
1958	Dick Bass, Pacific	218	1440	1991	Ty Detmer, BYU	478	4001	333.4
1959	Dick Norman, Stanford	319	2018	1992	Jimmy Klingler, Houston.	544	3768	342.6
1960	Billy Kilmer, UCLA.	292	1889	1993	Chris Vargas, Nevada.	535	4332	393.8
1961	Dave Hoppmann, Iowa St.	320	1638	1994	Mike Maxwell, Nevada.	477	3498	318.0
1962	Terry Baker, Oregon St	318	2276	1995	Mike Maxwell, Nevada.	443	3623	402.6
1963	George Mira, Miami-FL	394	2318	1996	Josh Wallwork, Wyoming	525	4209	350.8
1964	Jerry Rhome, Tulsa	470	3128	1997	Tim Rattay, La. Tech	541	3968	360.7
1965	Bill Anderson, Tulsa	580	3343	1998	Tim Rattay, La. Tech	602	4840	403.3
1966	Virgil Carter, BYU.	388	2545	1999	Tim Rattay, La. Tech	562	3810	381.0
1967	Sal Olivas, New Mexico St.	368	2184	2000	Drew Brees, Purdue	564	3939	358.1
1968	Greg Cook Cincinnati	507	3210	2001	Rex Grossman, Florida	429	3904	354.9
1969	Dennis Shaw, San Diego St	388	3197	2002	Byron Leftwich, Marshall	528	4267	355.6

Passing

Individual championship decided on Completions (1937-69), on Completions Per Game (1970-78) and on Passing Efficiency rating points (since 1979).

Multiple winners: Elvis Grbac, Don Heinrich, Jim McMahon, Davey O'Brien and Don Trull (2).

Year		Cmp	Pct	TD	Yds	Year		Cmp	Pct	TD	Yds
1937	Davey O'Brien, TCU.	94	.402	–	969	1949	Adrian Burk, Baylor	110	.576	14	1428
1938	Davey O'Brien, TCU.	93	.557	1	1457	1950	Don Heinrich, Washington	134	.606	14	1846
1939	Kay Eakin, Arkansas.	78	.404	–	962	1951	Don Klosterman, Loyola-CA	159	.505	9	1843
1940	Billy Sewell, Wash. St	86	.494	–	1023	1952	Don Heinrich, Washington	137	.507	13	1647
1941	Bud Schwenk, Wash.-MO	114	.487	1	1457	1953	Bob Garrett, Stanford	118	.576	17	1637
1942	Ray Evans, Kansas	101	.505	–	1117	1954	Paul Larson, California	125	.641	10	1537
1943	Johnny Cook, Georgia.	73	.465	1	1007	1955	George Welsh, Navy.	94	.627	8	1319
1944	Paul Rickards, Pittsburgh	84	.472	–	997	1956	John Brodie, Stanford	139	.579	12	1633
1945	Al Dekdebrun, Cornell	90	.464	–	1227	1957	Ken Ford, H-Simmons	115	.561	14	1254
1946	Travis Tidwell, Auburn	79	.500	5	943	1958	Buddy Humphrey, Baylor	112	.574	7	1316
1947	Charlie Conerly, Ole Miss	133	.571	18	1367	1959	Dick Norman, Stanford	152	.578	11	1963
1948	Stan Heath, Nev-Reno	126	.568	22	2005	1960	Harold Stephens, H-Simm	145	.566	3	1254

Annual NCAA Division I-A Leaders (Cont.)

Year		Cmp	Pct	TD	Yds
1961	Chon Gallegos, S. Jose St	.117	.594	14	1480
1962	Don Trull, Baylor	.125	.546	11	1627
1963	Don Trull, Baylor	.174	.565	12	2157
1964	Jerry Rhome, Tulsa	.224	.687	32	2870
1965	Bill Anderson, Tulsa	.296	.582	30	3464
1966	John Eckman, Wichita St	.195	.426	7	2339
1967	Terry Stone, N. Mexico	.160	.476	9	1946
1968	Chuck Hixson, SMU	.265	.566	21	3103
1969	John Reaves, Florida	.222	.561	24	2896

Year		CmpP/Gm	TD	Yds
1970	Sonny Sixkiller, Wash	.186	18.6	15	2303
1971	Brian Sipe, S. Diego St	.196	17.8	17	2532
1972	Don Strock, Va. Tech	.228	20.7	16	3243
1973	Jesse Freitas, S. Diego St.	.227	20.6	21	2993
1974	Steve Bartkowski, Cal	.182	16.5	12	2580
1975	Craig Penrose, S. Diego St.	.198	18.0	15	2660
1976	Tommy Kramer, Rice.	.269	24.5	21	3317
1977	Guy Benjamin, Stanford	.208	20.8	19	2521
1978	Steve Dils, Stanford	.247	22.5	22	2943

Year		Cmp	TD	Yds	Rating
1979	Turk Schonert, Stanford	.148	19	1922	163.0
1980	Jim McMahon, BYU	.284	47	4571	176.9
1981	Jim McMahon, BYU	.272	30	3555	155.0
1982	Tom Ramsey, UCLA.	.191	21	2824	153.5
1983	Steve Young, BYU.	.306	33	3902	168.5
1984	Doug Flutie, BC.	.233	27	3454	152.9
1985	Jim Harbaugh, Michigan.	.139	18	1913	163.7
1986	Vinny Testaverde, Miami-FL	.175	26	2557	165.8
1987	Don McPherson, Syracuse.	.129	22	2341	164.3
1988	Timm Rosenbach, Wash. St.	199	23	2791	162.0
1989	Ty Detmer, BYU	.265	32	4560	175.6
1990	Shawn Moore, Virginia	.144	21	2262	160.7
1991	Elvis Grbac, Michigan	.152	24	1955	169.0
1992	Elvis Grbac, Michigan	.112	15	1465	154.2
1993	Trent Dilfer, Fresno St.	.217	28	3276	173.1
1994	Kerry Collins, Penn St.	.176	21	2679	172.9
1995	Danny Wuerffel, Florida	.210	35	3266	178.4
1996	Steve Sarkisian, BYU	.278	33	4027	173.6
1997	Cade McNown, UCLA.	.173	22	2877	168.6
1998	Shaun King, Tulane	.223	36	3232	183.3
1999	Michael Vick, Va. Tech.	.90	12	1840	180.4
2000	Bart Hendricks, Boise St.	.210	35	3364	170.6
2001	Rex Grossman, Florida	.259	34	3896	170.8
2002	Brad Banks, Iowa	.170	26	2573	157.1

Receptions

Championship decided on Passes Caught (1937-69) and on Catches Per Game (since 1970). Touchdown totals unavailable in 1939 and 1941-45.

Multiple winners: Neil Armstrong, Hugh Campbell, Manny Hazard, Reid Moseley, Jason Phillips, Howard Twilley and Alex Van Dyke (2).

Year		No	TD	Yds
1937	Jim Benton, Arkansas	.47	7	754
1938	Sam Boyd, Baylor	.32	5	537
1939	Ken Kavanaugh, LSU	.30	–	467
1940	Eddie Bryant, Virginia	.30	2	222
1941	Hank Stanton, Arizona	.50	–	820
1942	Bill Rogers, Texas A&M	.39	–	432
1943	Neil Armstrong, Okla. A&M	.39	–	317
1944	Reid Moseley, Georgia	.32	–	506
1945	Reid Moseley, Georgia	.31	–	662
1946	Neil Armstrong, Okla. A&M	.32	1	479
1947	Barney Poole, Ole Miss	.52	8	513
1948	Red O'Quinn, Wake Forest	.39	7	605
1949	Art Weiner, N. Carolina	.52	7	762
1950	Gordon Cooper, Denver	.46	8	569
1951	Dewey McConnell, Wyoming	.47	9	725
1952	Ed Brown, Fordham	.57	6	774
1953	John Carson, Georgia	.45	4	663
1954	Jim Hanifan, California	.44	7	569
1955	Hank Burnine, Missouri	.44	2	594
1956	Art Powell, San Jose St	.40	5	583
1957	Stuart Vaughan, Utah	.53	5	756
1958	Dave Hibbert, Arizona	.61	4	606
1959	Chris Burford, Stanford	.61	6	756
1960	Hugh Campbell, Wash. St	.66	10	881
1961	Hugh Campbell, Wash. St	.53	5	723
1962	Vern Burke, Oregon St	.69	10	1007
1963	Lawrence Elkins, Baylor	.70	8	873
1964	Howard Twilley, Tulsa	.95	13	1178
1965	Howard Twilley, Tulsa	.134	16	1779
1966	Glenn Meltzer, Wichita St	.91	4	1115
1967	Bob Goodridge, Vanderbilt	.79	6	1114
1968	Ron Sellers, Florida St	.86	12	1496
1969	Jerry Hendren, Idaho	.95	12	1452

Year		No	P/Gm	TD	Yds
1970	Mike Mikolayunas, Davidson	87	8.7	8	1128
1971	Tom Reynolds, San Diego St	.67	6.7	7	1070
1972	Tom Forzani, Utah St	.85	7.7	8	1169
1973	Jay Miller, BYU	.100	9.1	8	1181
1974	D. McDonald, San Diego St	.86	7.8	7	1157
1975	Bob Farnham, Brown	.56	6.2	2	701
1976	Billy Ryckman, La. Tech	.77	7.0	10	1382
1977	W. Tolleson, W. Carolina	.73	6.6	7	1101
1978	Dave Petzke, Northern Ill	.91	8.3	11	1217
1979	Rick Beasley, Appalach. St	.74	6.7	12	1205
1980	Dave Young, Purdue	.67	6.1	8	917
1981	Pete Harvey, N. Texas St	.57	6.3	3	743
1982	Vincent White, Stanford.	.68	6.8	8	677
1983	Keith Edwards, Vanderbilt	.97	8.8	8	909
1984	David Williams, Illinois	.101	9.2	8	1278
1985	Rodney Carter, Purdue	.98	8.9	4	1099
1986	Mark Templeton, L. Beach St	.99	9.0	2	688
1987	Jason Phillips, Houston	.99	9.0	3	875
1988	Jason Phillips, Houston.	.108	9.8	15	1444
1989	Manny Hazard, Houston.	.142	12.9	22	1689
1990	Manny Hazard, Houston	.78	7.8	9	946
1991	Fred Gilbert, Houston.	.106	9.6	7	957
1992	Sherman Smith, Houston	.103	9.4	6	923
1993	Chris Penn, Tulsa	.105	9.6	12	1578
1994	Alex Van Dyke, Nevada	.98	8.9	10	1246
1995	Alex Van Dyke, Nevada	.129	11.7	16	1854
1996	Damond Wilkins, Nevada	.114	10.4	4	1121
1997	Eugene Baker, Kent	.103	9.4	18	1549
1998	Troy Edwards, La. Tech	.140	11.7	27	1996
1999	Trevor Insley, Nevada	.134	12.2	13	2060
2000	James Jordan, La. Tech	.109	9.1	4	1003
2001	Kevin Curtis, Utah St.	.100	9.1	10	1531
2002	Nate Burleson, Nevada	.138	11.5	12	1629

Scoring

Championship decided on Total Points (1937-69) and on Points Per Game (since 1970).

Multiple winners: Tom Harmon and Billy Sims (2).

Year		TD	XP	FG	Pts	Year		TD	XP	FG	Pts	P/Gm
1937	Byron (Whizzer) White, Colo	16	23	1	122	1970	Brian Bream, Air Force	20	0	0	120	12.0
1938	Parker Hall, Ole Miss	11	7	0	73		& Gary Kosins, Dayton	18	0	0	108	12.0
1939	Tom Harmon, Michigan	14	15	1	102	1971	Ed Marinaro, Cornell	24	4	0	148	16.4
1940	Tom Harmon, Michigan	16	18	1	117	1972	Harold Henson, Ohio St	20	0	0	120	12.0
1941	Bill Dudley, Virginia	18	23	1	134	1973	Jim Jennings, Rutgers	21	2	0	128	11.6
1942	Bob Steuber, Missouri	18	13	0	121	1974	Bill Marek, Wisconsin	19	0	0	114	12.7
1943	Steve Van Buren, LSU	14	14	0	98	1975	Pete Johnson, Ohio St	25	0	0	150	13.6
1944	Glenn Davis, Army	20	0	0	120	1976	Tony Dorsett, Pitt	22	2	0	134	12.2
1945	Doc Blanchard, Army	19	1	0	115	1977	Earl Campbell, Texas	19	0	0	114	10.4
1946	Gene Roberts, Tenn-Chatt.	18	9	0	117	1978	Billy Sims, Oklahoma	20	0	0	120	10.9
1947	Lou Gambino, Maryland	16	0	0	96	1979	Billy Sims, Oklahoma	22	0	0	132	12.0
1948	Fred Wendt, Texas Mines	20	32	0	152	1980	Sammy Winder, So. Miss	20	0	0	120	10.9
1949	George Thomas, Oklahoma	19	3	0	117	1981	Marcus Allen, USC	23	0	0	138	12.5
1950	Bobby Reynolds, Nebraska	22	25	0	157	1982	Greg Allen, Fla. St	21	0	0	126	11.5
1951	Ollie Matson, San Francisco	21	0	0	126	1983	Mike Rozier, Nebraska	29	0	0	174	14.5
1952	Jackie Parker, Miss. St.	16	24	0	120	1984	Keith Byars, Ohio St	24	0	0	144	13.1
1953	Earl Lindley, Utah St.	13	3	0	81	1985	Bernard White, B. Green.	19	0	0	114	10.4
1954	Art Luppino, Arizona	24	22	0	166	1986	Steve Bartalo, Colo. St	19	0	0	114	10.4
1955	Jim Swink, TCU	20	5	0	125	1987	Paul Hewitt, S. Diego St	24	0	0	144	12.0
1956	Clendon Thomas, Oklahoma	18	0	0	108	1988	Barry Sanders, Okla.St.	39	0	0	234	21.3
1957	Leon Burton, Ariz. St.	16	0	0	96	1989	Anthony Thompson, Ind	25	4	0	154	14.0
1958	Dick Bass, Pacific	18	8	0	116	1990	Stacey Robinson, No. Ill.	19	6	0	120	10.9
1959	Pervis Atkins, N. Mexico St.	17	5	0	107	1991	Marshall Faulk, S.D. St.	23	2	0	140	15.6
1960	Bob Gaiters, N. Mexico St.	23	7	0	145	1992	Garrison Hearst, Georgia	21	0	0	126	11.5
1961	Jim Pilot, N. Mexico St.	21	12	0	138	1993	Bam Morris, Texas Tech	22	2	0	134	12.2
1962	Jerry Logan, W. Texas St.	13	32	0	110	1994	Rashaan Salaam, Colo	24	0	0	144	13.1
1963	Cosmo Iacavazzi, Princeton	14	0	0	84	1995	Eddie George, Ohio St.	24	0	0	144	12.0
	& Dave Casinelli, Memphis St.	14	0	0	84	1996	Corey Dillon, Washington	23	0	0	138	12.6
1964	Brian Piccolo, Wake Forest	17	9	0	111	1997	Ricky Williams, Texas	25	2	0	152	13.8
1965	Howard Twilley, Tulsa	16	31	0	127	1998	Troy Edwards, La. Tech	31	2	0	188	15.7
1966	Ken Hebert, Houston	11	41	2	113	1999	Shaun Alexander, Alabama	24	0	0	144	13.1
1967	Leroy Keyes, Purdue	19	0	0	114	2000	Lee Suggs, Va. Tech	28	0	0	168	15.3
1968	Jim O'Brien, Cincinnati	12	31	13	142	2001	Luke Staley, BYU	28	2	0	170	15.5
1969	Steve Owens, Oklahoma	23	0	0	138	2002	Brock Forsey, Boise St.	32	0	0	192	14.8

All-Time NCAA Division I-A Leaders

Through the 2002 regular season. The NCAA does not recognize active players among career Per Game leaders.

CAREER

Passing

(Minimum 500 Completions)

Passing Efficiency	Years	Rating
1 Danny Wuerffel, Florida	1993-96	163.6
2 Ty Detmer, BYU	1988-91	162.7
3 Steve Sarkisian, BYU	1995-96	162.0
4 Billy Blanton, San Diego St.	1993-96	157.1
5 Jim McMahon, BYU	1977-78, 80-81	156.9

Yards Gained	Years	Yards
1 Ty Detmer, BYU	1988-91	15,031
2 Tim Rattay, La. Tech	1997-99	12,746
3 Chris Redman, Louisville	1996-99	12,541
4 Kliff Kingsbury, Texas Tech	1999-02	12,429
5 Todd Santos, San Diego St	1984-87	11,425

Completions	Years	No
1 Kliff Kingsbury, Texas Tech	1999-02	1231
2 Chris Redman, Louisville	1996-99	1031
3 Tim Rattay, La. Tech	1997-99	1015
4 Ty Detmer, BYU	1988-91	958
5 Drew Brees, Purdue	1997-00	942

Receptions

Catches	Years	No
1 Arnold Jackson, Louisville	1997-00	300
2 Trevor Insley, Nevada	1996-99	298
3 Geoff Noisy, Nevada	1995-98	295
4 Troy Edwards, La. Tech	1996-98	280
5 Aaron Turner, Pacific	1989-92	266

Catches Per Game	Years	No	P/Gm
1 Manny Hazard, Houston	1989-90	220	10.5
2 Alex Van Dyke, Nevada	1994-95	227	10.3
3 Howard Twilley, Tulsa	1963-65	261	10.0
4 Jason Phillips, Houston	1987-88	207	9.4
5 Troy Edwards, La. Tech	1996-98	280	8.2

Yards Gained	Years	No	Yards
1 Trevor Insley, Nevada	1996-99	298	5005
2 Marcus Harris, Wyoming	1993-96	259	4518
3 Ryan Yarborough, Wyoming	1990-93	229	4357
4 Troy Edwards, La. Tech	1996-98	280	4352
5 Aaron Turner, Pacific	1989-92	266	4345

Rushing

Yards Gained	Years	Yards
1 Ron Dayne, Wisconsin	1996-99	6397
2 Ricky Williams, Texas	1995-98	6279
3 Tony Dorsett, Pittsburgh	1973-76	6082
4 Charles White, USC	1976-79	5598
5 Travis Prentice, Miami-OH	1996-99	5596

Yards Per Game	Years	Yards	P/Gm
1 Ed Marinaro, Cornell	1969-71	4715	174.6
2 O.J. Simpson, USC	1967-68	3124	164.4
3 Herschel Walker, Georgia	1980-82	5259	159.4
4 LeShon Johnson, No. Ill.	1992-93	3314	150.6
5 Ron Dayne, Wisconsin	1996-99	6397	148.8

All-Time NCAA Division I-A Leaders (Cont.)
Total Offense

Yards Gained	Years	Yards
1 Ty Detmer, BYU	1988-91	14,665
2 Tim Rattay, La. Tech	1997-99	12,689
3 Kliff Kingsbury, Texas Tech	1999-02	12,263
4 Chris Redman, Louisville	1996-99	12,129
5 Drew Brees, Purdue	1997-00	11,815

Yards Per Game	Years	Yards P/Gm
1 Tim Rattay, La. Tech	1997-99	12,689 382.4
2 Chris Vargas, Nevada	1992-93	6,417 320.9
3 Ty Detmer, BYU	1988-91	14,665 318.8
4 Daunte Culpepper*, C. Fla.	1996-98	10,344 313.5
5 Mike Perez, San Jose St	1986-87	6,182 309.1
*Culpepper played I-AA with Central Florida in 1995.		

All-Purpose Yardage

Yards Gained	Years	Yards
1 Ricky Williams, Texas	1995-98	7206
2 Napoleon McCallum, Navy	1981-85	7172
3 Darrin Nelson, Stanford	1977-78, 80-81	6885
4 Kevin Faulk, LSU	1995-98	6833
5 Ron Dayne, Wisconsin	1996-99	6701

Yards Per Game	Years	Yards P/Gm
1 Ryan Benjamin, Pacific	1990-92	5706 237.8
2 Sheldon Canley, S. Jose St.	1988-90	5146 205.8
3 Howard Stevens, Louisville	1971-72	3873 193.7
4 O.J. Simpson, USC	1967-68	3666 192.9
5 Alex Van Dyke, Nevada	1994-95	4146 188.5

Miscellaneous

Interceptions	Years	No
1 Al Brosky, Illinois	1950-52	29
2 John Provost, Holy Cross	1972-74	27
Martin Bayless, Bowling Green	1980-83	27
4 Tom Curtis, Michigan	1967-69	25
Tony Thurman, Boston College	1981-84	25
Tracy Saul, Texas Tech.	1989-92	25

Punting Average*	Years	Avg
1 Todd Sauerbrun, West Va.	1991-94	46.3
2 Reggie Roby, Iowa	1979-82	45.6
3 Greg Montgomery, Mich. St	1985-87	45.4
4 Tom Tupa, Ohio St.	1984-87	45.2
5 Barry Helton, Colorado.	1984-87	44.9
*At least 150 punts.		

Punt Return Average*	Years	Avg
1 Jack Mitchell, Oklahoma.	1946-48	23.6
2 Gene Gibson, Cincinnati	1949-50	20.5
3 Eddie Macon, Pacific.	1949-51	18.9
4 Jackie Robinson, UCLA	1939-40	18.8
5 Mike Fuller, Auburn	1972-74	17.7
* Minimum 1.2 punt returns per game and 30 career returns.		

Kickoff Return Average*	Years	Avg
1 Anthony Davis, USC	1972-74	35.1
2 Eric Booth, So. Miss.	1994-97	32.4
3 Overton Curtis, Utah St	1957-58	31.0
4 Fred Montgomery, New Mexico St.	1991-92	30.5
5 Altie Taylor, Utah St.	1966-68	29.3
*Minimum 1.2 kickoff returns per game and 30 career returns.		

Scoring
Non-kickers

Points	Years	TD	Xpt	FG	Pts
1 Travis Prentice, Miami-OH	1996-99	78	0	0	468
2 Ricky Williams, Texas	1995-98	75	2	0	452
3 Brock Forsey, Boise St.	1999-02	68	0	0	408
4 Anthony Thompson, Ind.	1986-89	65	4	0	394
5 Ron Dayne, Wisconsin	1996-99	63	0	0	378

Points Per Game	Years	Pts	P/Gm
1 Marshall Faulk, S. Diego St.	1991-93	376	12.1
2 Ed Marinaro, Cornell.	1969-71	318	11.8
3 Bill Burnett, Arkansas	1968-70	294	11.3
4 Steve Owens, Oklahoma	1967-69	336	11.2
5 Eddie Talboom, Wyoming	1948-50	303	10.8

Touchdowns Rushing	Years	No
1 Travis Prentice, Miami-OH	1996-99	73
2 Ricky Williams, Texas	1995-98	72
3 Anthony Thompson, Indiana.	1986-89	64
4 Ron Dayne, Wisconsin	1996-99	63
5 Eric Crouch, Nebraska	1998-01	59

Touchdowns Passing	Years	No
1 Ty Detmer, BYU.	1988-91	121
2 Tim Rattay, La. Tech	1997-99	115
3 Danny Wuerffel, Florida	1993-96	114
4 Chad Pennington, Marshall	1997-99	100
5 Kliff Kingsbury, Texas Tech.	1999-02	95

Touchdown Catches	Years	No
1 Troy Edwards, La. Tech	1996-98	50
2 Aaron Turner, Pacific	1989-92	43
3 Ryan Yarborough, Wyoming	1990-93	42
4 Clarkston Hines, Duke	1986-89	38
Marcus Harris, Wyoming	1993-96	38
6 Terance Mathis, New Mexico	1985-87, 89	36

Kickers

Points	Years	FG	XP	Pts
1 Roman Anderson, Hou	1988-91	70	213	423
2 Carlos Huerta, Mia-FL	1988-91	73	178	397
3 Jason Elam, Hawaii	1988-89, 91-92	79	158	395
4 Derek Schmidt, Fla. St	1984-87	73	174	393
5 Kris Brown, Nebraska	1995-98	57	217	388

Field Goals	Years	No
1 Jeff Jaeger, Washington	1983-86	80
2 John Lee, UCLA	1982-85	79
Jason Elam, Hawaii.	1988-89, 91-92	79
4 Philip Doyle, Alabama	1987-90	78
Luis Zendejas, Arizona St	1981-84	78

SINGLE SEASON
Rushing

Yards Gained	Year	Gm	Car	Yards
Barry Sanders, Okla. St	1988	11	344	2628
Marcus Allen, USC	1981	11	403	2342
Troy Davis, Iowa St.	1996	11	402	2185
LaDainian Tomlinson, TCU	2000	11	369	2158
Mike Rozier, Nebraska	1983	12	275	2148

Yards Per Game	Year	Gm	Yards	P/Gm
Barry Sanders, Okla. St	1988	11	2628	238.9
Marcus Allen, USC	1981	11	2342	212.9
Ed Marinaro, Cornell.	1971	9	1881	209.0
Troy Davis, Iowa St.	1996	11	2185	198.6
LaDainian Tomlinson, TCU	2000	11	2158	196.2

Passing
(Minimum 15 Attempts Per Game)

Passing Efficiency	Year	Rating
Shaun King, Tulane	1998	183.3
Michael Vick, Va. Tech	1999	180.4
Danny Wuerffel, Florida	1995	178.4
Jim McMahon, BYU	1980	176.9
Ty Detmer, BYU	1989	175.6

Yards Gained	Year	Yards
Ty Detmer, BYU	1990	5188
David Klingler, Houston	1990	5140
Kliff Kingsbury, Texas Tech	2002	5017
Tim Rattay, La. Tech	1998	4943
Andre Ware, Houston	1989	4699

Completions	Year	Att	No
Kliff Kingsbury, Texas Tech	2002	712	479
Tim Rattay, La. Tech	1998	559	380
David Klingler, Houston	1990	643	374
Andre Ware, Houston	1989	578	365
Kliff Kingsbury, Texas Tech	2001	528	364

Receptions

Catches	Year	Gm	No
Manny Hazard, Houston	1989	11	142
Troy Edwards, La. Tech	1998	12	140
Nate Burleson, Nevada	2002	12	138
Howard Twilley, Tulsa	1965	10	134
Trevor Insley, Nevada	1999	11	134

Catches Per Game	Year	No	P/Gm
Howard Twilley, Tulsa	1965	134	13.4
Manny Hazard, Houston	1989	142	12.9
Trevor Insley, Nevada	1999	134	12.2
Alex Van Dyke, Nevada	1995	129	11.7
Troy Edwards, La. Tech	1998	140	11.7

Yards Gained	Year	No	Yards
Trevor Insley, Nevada	1999	134	2060
Troy Edwards, La. Tech	1998	140	1996
Alex Van Dyke, Nevada	1995	129	1854
J.R. Tolver, San Diego St.	2002	128	1785
Howard Twilley, Tulsa	1965	134	1779
Josh Reed, LSU	2001	94	1740

Total Offense

Yards Gained	Year	Gm	Plays	Yards
David Klingler, Houston	1990	11	704	5221
Ty Detmer, BYU	1990	12	635	5022
Kliff Kingsbury, Texas Tech	2002	14	814	4903
Tim Rattay, La. Tech	1998	12	602	4840
Andre Ware, Houston	1989	11	628	4661

Yards Per Game	Year	Gm	Yards	P/Gm
David Klingler, Houston	1990	11	5221	474.6
Andre Ware, Houston	1989	11	4661	423.7
Ty Detmer, BYU	1990	12	5022	418.5
Tim Rattay, La. Tech	1998	12	4840	403.3
Mike Maxwell, Nevada	1995	9	3623	402.6

All-Purpose Yardage

Yards Gained	Year	Yards
Barry Sanders, Okla. St	1988	3250
Ryan Benjamin, Pacific	1991	2995
Troy Edwards, La. Tech	1998	2784
Mike Pringle, CS-Fullerton	1989	2690
Larry Johnson, Penn St.	2002	2655

Yards Per Game	Year	Yards	P/Gm
Barry Sanders, Okla. St	1988	3250	295.5
Ryan Benjamin, Pacific	1991	2995	249.6
Byron (Whizzer) White, Colo	1937	1970	246.3
Mike Pringle, CS-Fullerton	1989	2690	244.6
Paul Palmer, Temple	1986	2633	239.4

Scoring

Points	Year	TD	Xpt	FG	Pts
Barry Sanders, Okla. St	1988	39	0	0	234
Brock Forsey, Boise St.	2002	32	0	0	192
Troy Edwards, La. Tech	1998	31	2	0	188
Mike Rozier, Nebraska	1983	29	0	0	174
Lydell Mitchell, Penn St	1971	29	0	0	174

Touchdowns Passing	Year	No
David Klingler, Houston	1990	54
Jim McMahon, BYU	1980	47
Andre Ware, Houston	1989	46
Tim Rattay, La. Tech	1998	46
Kliff Kingsbury, Texas Tech	2002	45

Points Per Game	Year	Pts	P/Gm
Barry Sanders, Okla. St	1988	234	21.3
Bobby Reynolds, Nebraska	1950	157	17.4
Art Luppino, Arizona	1954	166	16.6
Ed Marinaro, Cornell	1971	148	16.4
Lydell Mitchell, Penn St	1971	174	15.8

Touchdown Catches	Year	No
Troy Edwards, La. Tech	1998	27
Randy Moss, Marshall	1997	25
Manny Hazard, Houston	1989	22
Desmond Howard, Michigan	1991	19
Ashley Lelie, Hawaii	2001	19

Touchdowns Rushing	Year	No
Barry Sanders, Okla. St	1988	37
Mike Rozier, Nebraska	1983	29
Willis McGahee, Miami-FL	2002	28
Ricky Williams, Texas	1998	27
Lee Suggs, Va. Tech	2000	27
Brock Forsey, Boise St.	2002	26

Field Goals	Year	No
John Lee, UCLA	1984	29
Paul Woodside, West Virginia	1982	28
Luis Zendejas, Arizona St	1983	28
Fuad Reveiz, Tennessee	1982	27
Sebastian Janikowski, FSU	1998	27

Miscellaneous

Interceptions	Year	No
Al Worley, Washington	1968	14
George Shaw, Oregon	1951	13
Eight tied with 12 each.		

Punting Average*	Year	Avg
Chad Kessler, LSU	1997	50.3
Reggie Roby, Iowa	1981	49.8
Kirk Wilson, UCLA	1956	49.3
Todd Sauerbrun, West Virginia	1994	48.4
Travis Dorsch, Purdue	2001	48.4

*Qualifiers for championship.

Punt Return Average*	Year	Avg
Bill Blackstock, Tennessee	1951	25.9
George Sims, Baylor	1948	25.0
Gene Derricotte, Michigan	1947	24.8

*At least 1.2 returns per game.

Kickoff Return Average*	Year	Avg
Paul Allen, BYU	1961	40.1
Tremain Mack, Miami-FL	1996	39.5
Leeland McElroy, Texas A&M	1993	39.3
Forrest Hall, San Francisco	1946	38.2
Tony Ball, Tenn-Chattanooga	1977	36.4

*At least 1.2 kickoff returns per game.

All-Time NCAA Division I-A Leaders (Cont.)
SINGLE GAME

Rushing

Yards Gained	Opponent	Year	Yds
LaDainian Tomlinson, TCU	UTEP	1999	406
Tony Sands, Kansas	Missouri	1991	396
Marshall Faulk, San Diego St	Pacific	1991	386
Troy Davis, Iowa St.	Missouri	1996	378
Anthony Thompson, Indiana	Wisconsin	1989	377
Robbie Mixon, C. Michigan	E. Michigan	2002	377

Passing

Yards Gained	Opponent	Year	Yds
David Klingler, Houston	Arizona St.	1990	716
Matt Vogler, TCU	Houston	1990	690
Brian Lindgren, Idaho	Mid. Tenn. St.	2001	637
Scott Mitchell, Utah	Air Force	1988	631
Jeremy Leach, New Mexico	Utah	1989	622

Completions	Opponent	Year	No
Drew Brees, Purdue	Wisconsin	1998	55
Rusty LaRue, Wake Forest	Duke	1995	55
Rusty LaRue, Wake Forest	N.C. St.	1995	50
Brian Lindgren, Idaho	Mid. Tenn. St.	2001	49
Kliff Kingsbury, Texas Tech	Missouri	2002	49
Kliff Kingsbury, Texas Tech	Texas A&M	2002	49

Scoring

Points	Opponent	Year	Pts
Howard Griffith, Illinois	So. Ill.	1990	48
Marshall Faulk, S. Diego St	Pacific	1991	44
Jim Brown, Syracuse	Colgate	1956	43
Showboat Boykin, Ole Miss	Miss. St.	1951	42
Fred Wendt, UTEP*	N. Mex. St.	1948	42

*UTEP was Texas Mines in 1948.

Touchdowns Rushing	Opponent	Year	No
Howard Griffith, Illinois	So. Ill	1990	8
Showboat Boykin, Ole Miss	Miss. St.	1951	7

Note: Griffith's TD runs (5-51-7-41-5-18-5-3).

Touchdowns Passing	Opponent	Year	No
David Klingler, Houston	E.Wash.	1990	11
Dennis Shaw, San Diego St	N. Mex. St.	1969	9

Note: Klingler's TD passes (5-48-29-7-3-7-40-8-7-8-51).

Total Offense

Yards Gained	Opponent	Year	Yds
David Klingler, Houston	Arizona St.	1990	732
Matt Vogler, TCU	Houston	1990	696
David Klingler, Houston	TCU	1990	625
Scott Mitchell, Utah	Air Force	1988	625
Jimmy Klingler, Houston	Rice	1992	612

Receiving

Catches	Opponent	Year	No
Randy Gatewood, UNLV.	Idaho	1994	23
Jay Miller, BYU	New Mexico	1973	22
Troy Edwards, La. Tech	Nebraska	1998	21
Chris Daniels, Purdue.	Mich. St.	1999	21

Two tied with 20 each.

Yards Gained	Opponent	Year	Yds
Troy Edwards, La. Tech	Nebraska	1998	405
Randy Gatewood, UNLV.	Idaho	1994	363
Chuck Hughes, UTEP*	N. Texas St.	1965	349
Nate Burleson, Nevada	San Jose St.	2001	326
Rick Eber, Tulsa.	Idaho St.	1967	322

*UTEP was Texas Western in 1965.

Touchdown Catches	Opponent	Year	No
Tim Delaney, S. Diego St	N. Mex. St.	1969	6

Note: Delaney's TD catches (2-22-34-31-30-9).

Field Goals	Opponent	Year	No
Dale Klein, Nebraska	Missouri	1985	7
Mike Prindle, W. Mich	Marshall	1984	7

Note: Klein's FGs (32-22-43-44-29-43-43); Prindle's FGs (32-44-42-23-48-41-27).

Extra Points (Kick)	Opponent	Year	No
Terry Leiweke, Houston	Tulsa	1968	13
Derek Mahoney, Fresno St	New Mexico	1991	13

Longest Plays (since 1941)

Rushing

Rushing	Opponent	Year	Yds
Gale Sayers, Kansas	Nebraska	1963	99
Max Anderson, Ariz. St	Wyoming	1967	99
Ralph Thompson, W. Texas St	Wich. St.	1970	99
Kelsey Finch, Tennessee	Florida	1977	99
Eric Vann, Kansas	Oklahoma	1997	99

Eleven tied at 98 each.

Passing	Opponent	Year	Yds
Fred Owens to Jack Ford, Portland	St. Mary's	1947	99
Bo Burris to Warren McVea, Houston	Wash. St.	1966	99
Colin Clapton to Eddie Jenkins, Holy Cross	Boston U.	1970	99
Terry Peel to Robert Ford, Houston	Syracuse	1970	99
Terry Peel to Robert Ford, Houston	S. Diego St.	1972	99
Cris Collinsworth to Derrick Gaffney, Florida	Rice	1977	99

Passing	Opponent	Year	Yds
Scott Ankrom to James Maness, TCU	Rice	1984	99
Gino Torretta to Horace Copeland, Miami-FL	Ark.	1991	99
John Paci to Thomas Lewis, Indiana	Penn St.	1993	99
Drew Brees to Vinny Sutherland, Purdue	Northwestern	1999	99

Field Goals	Opponent	Year	Yds
Steve Little, Arkansas	Texas	1977	67
Russell Erxleben, Texas.	Rice	1977	67
Joe Williams, Wichita St	So. Ill.	1978	67
Tony Franklin, Tex. A&M	Baylor	1976	65
Martin Gramatica, Kan. St.	No. Ill.	1998	65

Annual Awards
Heisman Trophy

Originally presented in 1935 as the DAC Trophy by the Downtown Athletic Club of New York City to the best college football player east of the Mississippi. In 1936, players across the country were eligible and the award was renamed the Heisman Trophy following the death of former college coach and DAC athletic director John W. Heisman.

Multiple winner: Archie Griffin (2).

Winners in junior year (13): Doc Blanchard (1945), Ty Detmer (1990); Archie Griffin (1974), Desmond Howard (1991), Vic Janowicz (1950), Rashaan Salaam (1994), Barry Sanders (1988), Billy Sims (1978), Roger Staubach (1963), Doak Walker (1948), Herschel Walker (1982), Andre Ware (1989) and Charles Woodson (1997).

Winners on AP national champions (10): Angelo Bertelli (Notre Dame, 1943); Doc Blanchard (Army, 1945); Tony Dorsett (Pittsburgh, 1976); Leon Hart (Notre Dame, 1949); Johnny Lujack (Notre Dame, 1947); Davey O'Brien (TCU, 1938); Bruce Smith (Minnesota, 1941); CharlieWard (Florida St., 1993); DannyWuerffel (Florida, 1996); and CharlesWoodson (Michigan, 1997).

Year		Points
1935	**Jay Berwanger,** Chicago, HB	.84
	2nd–Monk Meyer, Army, HB	.29
	3rd–Bill Shakespeare, Notre Dame, HB	.23
	4th–Pepper Constable, Princeton, FB	.20
1936	**Larry Kelley,** Yale, E	.219
	2nd–Sam Francis, Nebraska, FB	.47
	3rd–Ray Buivid, Marquette, HB	.43
	4th–Sammy Baugh, TCU, HB	.39
1937	**Clint Frank,** Yale, HB	.524
	2nd–Byron (Whizzer) White, Colo., HB	.264
	3rd–Marshall Goldberg, Pitt, HB	.211
	4th–Alex Wojciechowicz, Fordham, C	.85
1938	**Davey O'Brien,** TCU, QB	.519
	2nd–Marshall Goldberg, Pitt, HB	.294
	3rd–Sid Luckman, Columbia, QB	.154
	4th–Bob MacLeod, Dartmouth, HB	.78
1939	**Nile Kinnick,** Iowa, HB	.651
	2nd–Tom Harmon, Michigan, HB	.405
	3rd–Paul Christman, Missouri, QB	.391
	4th–George Cafego, Tennessee, QB	.296
1940	**Tom Harmon,** Michigan, HB	.1303
	2nd–John Kimbrough, Texas A&M, FB	.841
	3rd–George Franck, Minnesota, HB	.102
	4th–Frankie Albert, Stanford, QB	.90
1941	**Bruce Smith,** Minnesota, HB	.554
	2nd–Angelo Bertelli, Notre Dame, QB	.345
	3rd–Frankie Albert, Stanford, QB	.336
	4th–Frank Sinkwich, Georgia, HB	.249
1942	**Frank Sinkwich,** Georgia, TB	.1059
	2nd–Paul Governali, Columbia, QB	.218
	3rd–Clint Castleberry, Ga. Tech, HB	.99
	4th–Mike Holovak, Boston College, FB	.95
1943	**Angelo Bertelli,** Notre Dame, QB	.648
	2nd–Bob Odell, Penn, HB	.177
	3rd–Otto Graham, Northwestern, HB	.140
	4th–Creighton Miller, Notre Dame, HB	.134
1944	**Les Horvath,** Ohio St., TB-QB	.412
	2nd–Glenn Davis, Army, HB	.287
	3rd–Doc Blanchard, Army, FB	.237
	4th–Don Whitmire, Navy, T	.115
1945	**Doc Blanchard,** Army, FB	.860
	2nd–Glenn Davis, Army, HB	.638
	3rd–Bob Fenimore, Oklahoma A&M, HB	.187
	4th–Herman Wedemeyer, St. Mary's, HB	.152
1946	**Glenn Davis,** Army, HB	.792
	2nd–Charlie Trippi, Georgia, HB	.435
	3rd–Johnny Lujack, Notre Dame, QB	.379
	4th–Doc Blanchard, Army, FB	.267
1947	**Johnny Lujack,** Notre Dame, QB	.742
	2nd–Bob Chappuis, Michigan, HB	.555
	3rd–Doak Walker, SMU, HB	.196
	4th–Charlie Conerly, Mississippi, QB	.186
1948	**Doak Walker,** SMU, HB	.778
	2nd–Charlie Justice, N. Carolina, HB	.443
	3rd–Chuck Bednarik, Penn, C	.336
	4th–Jackie Jensen, California, HB	.143
1949	**Leon Hart,** Notre Dame, E	.995
	2nd–Charlie Justice, N. Carolina, HB	.272
	3rd–Doak Walker, SMU, HB	.229
	4th–Arnold Galiffa, Army QB	.196
1950	**Vic Janowicz,** Ohio St., HB	.633
	2nd–Kyle Rote, SMU, HB	.280
	3rd–Reds Bagnell, Penn, HB	.231
	4th–Babe Parilli, Kentucky, QB	.214
1951	**Dick Kazmaier,** Princeton, TB	.1777
	2nd–Hank Lauricella, Tennessee, HB	.424
	3rd–Babe Parilli, Kentucky, QB	.344
	4th–Bill McColl, Stanford, E	.313
1952	**Billy Vessels,** Oklahoma, HB	.525
	2nd–Jack Scarbath, Maryland, QB	.367
	3rd–Paul Giel, Minnesota, HB	.329
	4th–Donn Moomaw, UCLA, C	.257
1953	**Johnny Lattner,** Notre Dame, HB	.1850
	2nd–Paul Giel, Minnesota, HB	.1794
	3rd–Paul Cameron, UCLA, HB	.444
	4th–Bernie Faloney, Maryland, QB	.258

Year		Points
1954	**Alan Ameche,** Wisconsin, FB	.1068
	2nd–Kurt Burris, Oklahoma, C	.838
	3rd–Howard Cassady, Ohio St., HB	.810
	4th–Ralph Guglielmi, Notre Dame, QB	.691
1955	**Howard Cassady,** Ohio St., HB	.2219
	2nd–Jim Swink, TCU, HB	.742
	3rd–George Welsh, Navy, QB	.383
	4th–Earl Morrall, Michigan St., QB	.323
1956	**Paul Hornung,** Notre Dame, QB	.1066
	2nd–Johnny Majors, Tennessee, HB	.994
	3rd–Tommy McDonald, Oklahoma, HB	.973
	4th–Jerry Tubbs, Oklahoma, C	.724
1957	**John David Crow,** Texas A&M, HB	.1183
	2nd–Alex Karras, Iowa, T	.693
	3rd–Walt Kowalczyk, Mich. St., HB	.630
	4th–Lou Michaels, Kentucky, T	.330
1958	**Pete Dawkins,** Army, HB	.1394
	2nd–Randy Duncan, Iowa, QB	.1021
	3rd–Billy Cannon, LSU, HB	.975
	4th–Bob White, Ohio St., FB	.365
1959	**Billy Cannon,** LSU, HB	.1929
	2nd–Richie Lucas, Penn St., QB	.613
	3rd–Don Meredith, SMU, QB	.286
	4th–Bill Burrell, Illinois, G	.196
1960	**Joe Bellino,** Navy, HB	.1793
	2nd–Tom Brown, Minnesota, G	.731
	3rd–Jake Gibbs, Mississippi, QB	.453
	4th–Ed Dyas, Auburn, HB	.319
1961	**Ernie Davis,** Syracuse, HB	.824
	2nd–Bob Ferguson, Ohio St., HB	.771
	3rd–Jimmy Saxton, Texas, HB	.551
	4th–Sandy Stephens, Minnesota, QB	.543
1962	**Terry Baker,** Oregon St., QB	.707
	2nd–Jerry Stovall, LSU, HB	.618
	3rd–Bobby Bell, Minnesota, T	.429
	4th–Lee Roy Jordan, Alabama, C	.321
1963	**Roger Staubach,** Navy, QB	.1860
	2nd–Billy Lothridge, Ga. Tech, QB	.504
	3rd–Sherman Lewis, Mich. St., HB	.369
	4th–Don Trull, Baylor, QB	.253
1964	**John Huarte,** Notre Dame, QB	.1026
	2nd–Jerry Rhome, Tulsa, QB	.952
	3rd–Dick Butkus, Illinois, C	.505
	4th–Bob Timberlake, Michigan, QB	.361
1965	**Mike Garrett,** USC, HB	.926
	2nd–Howard Twilley, Tulsa, E	.528
	3rd–Jim Grabowski, Illinois, FB	.481
	4th–Donny Anderson, Texas Tech, HB	.408
1966	**Steve Spurrier,** Florida, QB	.1679
	2nd–Bob Griese, Purdue, QB	.816
	3rd–Nick Eddy, Notre Dame, HB	.456
	4th–Gary Beban, UCLA, QB	.318
1967	**Gary Beban,** UCLA, QB	.1968
	2nd–O.J. Simpson, USC, HB	.1722
	3rd–Leroy Keyes, Purdue, HB	.1366
	4th–Larry Csonka, Syracuse, FB	.136
1968	**O.J. Simpson,** USC, HB	.2853
	2nd–Leroy Keyes, Purdue, HB	.1103
	3rd–Terry Hanratty, Notre Dame, QB	.387
	4th–Ted Kwalick, Penn St., TE	.254
1969	**Steve Owens,** Oklahoma, HB	.1488
	2nd–Mike Phipps, Purdue, QB	.1344
	3rd–Rex Kern, Ohio St., QB	.856
	4th–Archie Manning, Mississippi, QB	.582
1970	**Jim Plunkett,** Stanford, QB	.2229
	2nd–Joe Theismann, Notre Dame, QB	.1410
	3rd–Archie Manning, Mississippi, QB	.849
	4th–Steve Worster, Texas, RB	398
1971	**Pat Sullivan,** Auburn, QB	.1597
	2nd–Ed Marinaro, Cornell, RB	.1445
	3rd–Greg Pruitt, Oklahoma, RB	.586
	4th–Johnny Musso, Alabama, RB	.365
1972	**Johnny Rodgers,** Nebraska, FL	.1310
	2nd–Greg Pruitt, Oklahoma, RB	.966
	3rd–Rich Glover, Nebraska, MG	.652
	4th–Bert Jones, LSU, QB	.351

Annual Awards (Cont.)

Year		Points
1973	**John Cappelletti,** Penn St., RB	.1057
	2nd–John Hicks, Ohio St., OT	.524
	3rd–Roosevelt Leaks, Texas, RB	.482
	4th–David Jaynes, Kansas, QB	.394
1974	**Archie Griffin,** Ohio St., RB	.1920
	2nd–Anthony Davis, USC, RB	.819
	3rd–Joe Washington, Oklahoma, RB	.661
	4th–Tom Clements, Notre Dame, QB	.244
1975	**Archie Griffin,** Ohio St., RB	.1800
	2nd–Chuck Muncie, California, RB	.730
	3rd–Ricky Bell, USC, RB	.708
	4th–Tony Dorsett, Pitt, RB	.616
1976	**Tony Dorsett,** Pittsburgh, RB	.2357
	2nd–Ricky Bell, USC, RB	.1346
	3rd–Rob Lytle, Michigan, RB	.413
	4th–Terry Miller, Oklahoma St., RB	.197
1977	**Earl Campbell,** Texas, RB	.1547
	2nd–Terry Miller, Oklahoma St., RB	.812
	3rd–Ken MacAfee, Notre Dame, TE	.343
	4th–Doug Williams, Grambling, QB	.266
1978	**Billy Sims,** Oklahoma, RB	.827
	2nd–Chuck Fusina, Penn St., QB	.750
	3rd–Rick Leach, Michigan, QB	.435
	4th–Charles White, USC, RB	.354
1979	**Charles White,** USC, RB	.1695
	2nd–Billy Sims, Oklahoma, RB	.773
	3rd–Marc Wilson, BYU, QB	.589
	4th–Art Schlichter, Ohio St., QB	.251
1980	**George Rogers,** South Carolina, RB	.1128
	2nd–Hugh Green, Pittsburgh, DE	.861
	3rd–Herschel Walker, Georgia, RB	.683
	4th–Mark Herrmann, Purdue, QB	.405
1981	**Marcus Allen,** USC, RB	.1797
	2nd–Herschel Walker, Georgia, RB	.1199
	3rd–Jim McMahon, BYU, QB	.706
	4th–Dan Marino, Pitt, QB	.256
1982	**Herschel Walker,** Georgia, RB	.1926
	2nd–John Elway, Stanford, QB	.1231
	3rd–Eric Dickerson, SMU, RB	.465
	4th–Anthony Carter, Michigan, WR	.142
1983	**Mike Rozier,** Nebraska, RB	.1801
	2nd–Steve Young, BYU, QB	.1172
	3rd–Doug Flutie, Boston College, QB	.253
	4th–Turner Gill, Nebraska, QB	.190
1984	**Doug Flutie,** Boston College, QB	.2240
	2nd–Keith Byars, Ohio St., RB	.1251
	3rd–Robbie Bosco, BYU, QB	.443
	4th–Bernie Kosar, Miami-FL, QB	.320
1985	**Bo Jackson,** Auburn, RB	.1509
	2nd–Chuck Long, Iowa, QB	.1464
	3rd–Robbie Bosco, BYU, QB	.459
	4th–Lorenzo White, Michigan St., RB	.391
1986	**Vinny Testaverde,** Miami-FL, QB	.2213
	2nd–Paul Palmer, Temple, RB	.672
	3rd–Jim Harbaugh, Michigan, QB	.458
	4th–Brian Bosworth, Oklahoma, LB	.395
1987	**Tim Brown,** Notre Dame, WR	.1442
	2nd–Don McPherson, Syracuse, QB	.831
	3rd–Gordie Lockbaum, Holy Cross, WR-DB	.657
	4th–Lorenzo White, Michigan St., RB	.632

Year		Points
1988	**Barry Sanders,** Oklahoma St., RB	.1878
	2nd–Rodney Peete, USC, QB	.912
	3rd–Troy Aikman, UCLA, QB	.582
	4th–Steve Walsh, Miami-FL, QB	.341
1989	**Andre Ware,** Houston, QB	.1073
	2nd–Anthony Thompson, Ind., RB	.1003
	3rd–Major Harris, West Va., QB	.709
	4th–Tony Rice, Notre Dame, QB	.523
1990	**Ty Detmer,** BYU, QB	.1482
	2nd–Rocket Ismail, Notre Dame, FL	.1177
	3rd–Eric Bieniemy, Colorado, RB	.798
	4th–Shawn Moore, Virginia, QB	.465
1991	**Desmond Howard,** Michigan, WR	.2077
	2nd–Casey Weldon, Florida St., QB	.503
	3rd–Ty Detmer, BYU, QB	.445
	4th–Steve Emtman, Washington, DT	.357
1992	**Gino Torretta,** Miami-FL, QB	.1400
	2nd–Marshall Faulk, San Diego St., RB	.1080
	3rd–Garrison Hearst, Georgia, RB	.982
	4th–Marvin Jones, Florida St., LB	.392
1993	**Charlie Ward,** Florida St., QB	.2310
	2nd–Heath Shuler, Tennessee, QB	.688
	3rd–David Palmer, Alabama, RB	.292
	4th–Marshall Faulk, S. Diego St., RB	.250
1994	**Rashaan Salaam,** Colorado, RB	.1743
	2nd–Ki-Jana Carter, Penn St., RB	.901
	3rd–Steve McNair, Alcorn St., QB	.655
	4th–Kerry Collins, Penn St., QB	.639
1995	**Eddie George,** Ohio St., RB	.1460
	2nd–Tommie Frazier, Nebraska, QB	.1196
	3rd–Danny Wuerffel, Florida, QB	.987
	4th–Darnell Autry, Northwestern, RB	.535
1996	**Danny Wuerffel,** Florida, QB	.1363
	2nd–Troy Davis, Iowa St., RB	.1174
	3rd–Jake Plummer, Arizona St., QB	.685
	4th–Orlando Pace, Ohio St., OT	.599
1997	**Charles Woodson,** Michigan, DB-WR	.1815
	2nd–Peyton Manning, Tennessee, QB	.1543
	3rd–Ryan Leaf, Washington St., QB	.861
	4th–Randy Moss, Marshall, WR	.253
1998	**Ricky Williams,** Texas, RB	.2355
	2nd–Michael Bishop, Kansas St., QB	.792
	3rd–Cade McNown, UCLA, QB	.696
	4th–Tim Couch, Kentucky, QB	.527
1999	**Ron Dayne,** Wisconsin, RB	.2042
	2nd–Joe Hamilton, Ga. Tech, QB	.994
	3rd–Michael Vick, Va. Tech, QB	.319
	4th–Drew Brees, Purdue, QB	.308
2000	**Chris Weinke,** Florida St., QB	.1628
	2nd–Josh Heupel, Oklahoma, QB	.1552
	3rd–Drew Brees, Purdue, QB	.619
	4th–LaDainian Tomlinson, TCU, RB	.566
2001	**Eric Crouch,** Nebraska, QB	.770
	2nd–Rex Grossman, Florida, QB	.708
	3rd–Ken Dorsey, Miami-FL, QB	.638
	4th–Joey Harrington, Oregon, QB	.364
2002	**Carson Palmer,** USC, QB	.1328
	2nd–Brad Banks, Iowa, QB	.1095
	3rd–Larry Johnson, Penn St., RB	.726
	4th–Willis McGahee, Miami-FL, RB	.660

Maxwell Award

First presented in 1937   by the Maxwell Memorial Football Club of Philadelphia, the award is named after Robert (Tiny) Maxwell, a Philadelphia native who was a standout lineman at the University of Chicago at the turn of the century. Like the Heisman, the Maxwell is given to the outstanding college player in the nation. Both awards have gone to the same player in the same season 34 times. Those players are preceded by (#). Glenn Davis of Army and Doak Walker of SMU won both but in different years.

Multiple winner: Johnny Lattner (2).

Year		Year		Year	
1937	#Clint Frank, Yale, HB	1960	#Joe Bellino, Navy, HB	1983	#Mike Rozier, Nebraska, RB
1938	#Davey O'Brien, TCU, QB	1961	Bob Ferguson, Ohio St., HB	1984	#Doug Flutie, Boston Col., QB
1939	#Nile Kinnick, Iowa, HB	1962	#Terry Baker, Oregon St., QB	1985	Chuck Long, Iowa, QB
1940	#Tom Harmon, Michigan, HB	1963	#Roger Staubach, Navy, QB	1986	#V. Testaverde, Miami-FL, QB
1941	Bill Dudley, Virginia, HB	1964	Glenn Ressler, Penn St., G	1987	Don McPherson, Syracuse, QB
1942	Paul Governali, Columbia, QB	1965	Tommy Nobis, Texas, LB	1988	#Barry Sanders, Okla. St., RB
1943	Bob Odell, Penn, HB	1966	Jim Lynch, Notre Dame, LB	1989	Anthony Thompson, Indiana, RB
1944	Glenn Davis, Army, HB	1967	#Gary Beban, UCLA, QB	1990	#Ty Detmer, BYU, QB
1945	#Doc Blanchard, Army, FB	1968	#O.J. Simpson, USC, HB	1991	#Desmond Howard, Mich., WR
1946	Charley Trippi, Georgia, HB	1969	Mike Reid, Penn St., DT	1992	#Gino Torretta, Miami-FL, QB
1947	Doak Walker, SMU, HB	1970	#Jim Plunkett, Stanford, QB	1993	#Charlie Ward, Florida St., QB
1948	Chuck Bednarik, Penn, C	1971	Ed Marinaro, Cornell, RB	1994	Kerry Collins, Penn St., QB
1949	#Leon Hart, Notre Dame, E	1972	Brad Van Pelt, Michigan St., DB	1995	#Eddie George, Ohio St., RB
1950	Reds Bagnell, Penn, HB	1973	#John Cappelletti, Penn St., RB	1996	#Danny Wuerffel, Florida, QB
1951	#Dick Kazmaier, Princeton, TB	1974	Steve Joachim, Temple, QB	1997	Peyton Manning, Tennessee, QB
1952	Johnny Lattner, Notre Dame, HB	1975	#Archie Griffin, Ohio St., RB	1998	#Ricky Williams, Texas, RB
1953	#Johnny Lattner, N. Dame, HB	1976	#Tony Dorsett, Pitt, RB	1999	#Ron Dayne, Wisconsin, RB
1954	Ron Beagle, Navy, E	1977	Ross Browner, Notre Dame, DE	2000	Drew Brees, Purdue, QB
1955	#Howard Cassady, Ohio St., HB	1978	Chuck Fusina, Penn St., QB	2001	Ken Dorsey, Miami-FL, QB
1956	Tommy McDonald, Okla., HB	1979	#Charles White, USC, RB	2002	Larry Johnson, Penn St., RB
1957	Bob Reifsnyder, Navy, T	1980	Hugh Green, Pitt, DE		
1958	#Pete Dawkins, Army, HB	1981	#Marcus Allen, USC, RB		
1959	Rich Lucas, Penn St., QB	1982	#Herschel Walker, Georgia, RB		

Outland Trophy

First presented in 1946 by the Football Writers Association of America, honoring the nation's outstanding interior lineman. The award is named after its benefactor, Dr. John H. Outland (Kansas, Class of 1898). Players listed in **bold** type helped lead their team to a national championship (according to AP).

Multiple winner: Dave Rimington (2). **Winners in junior year:** Ross Browner (1976), Steve Emtman (1991), Rien Long (2002), Orlando Pace (1996) and Rimington (1981).

Year		Year		Year	
1946	**George Connor,** N. Dame, T	1966	Loyd Phillips, Arkansas, T	1986	Jason Buck, BYU, DT
1947	Joe Steffy, Army, G	1967	**Ron Yary,** USC, T	1987	Chad Hennings, Air Force, DT
1948	Bill Fischer, Notre Dame, G	1968	Bill Stanfill, Georgia, T	1988	Tracy Rocker, Auburn, DT
1949	Ed Bagdon, Michigan St., G	1969	Mike Reid, Penn St., DT	1989	Mohammed Elewonibi, BYU, G
1950	Bob Gain, Kentucky, T	1970	Jim Stillwagon, Ohio St., MG	1990	Russell Maryland, Miami-FL, NT
1951	Jim Weatherall, Oklahoma, T	1971	**Larry Jacobson,** Neb., DT	1991	Steve Emtman, Washington, DT
1952	Dick Modzelewski, Maryland, T	1972	Rich Glover, Nebraska, MG	1992	Will Shields, Nebraska, G
1953	J.D. Roberts, Oklahoma, G	1973	John Hicks, Ohio St., OT	1993	Rob Waldrop, Arizona, NG
1954	Bill Brooks, Arkansas, T	1974	Randy White, Maryland, DT	1994	**Zach Wiegert,** Nebraska, OT
1955	Calvin Jones, Iowa, G	1975	**Lee Roy Selmon,** Okla., DT	1995	Jonathan Ogden, UCLA, OT
1956	Jim Parker, Ohio St., G	1976	Ross Browner, Notre Dame, DE	1996	Orlando Pace, Ohio St., OT
1957	Alex Karras, Iowa, T	1977	Brad Shearer, Texas, DT	1997	Aaron Taylor, Nebraska, G
1958	Zeke Smith, Auburn, G	1978	Greg Roberts, Oklahoma, G	1998	Kris Farris, UCLA, OT
1959	Mike McGee, Duke, T	1979	Jim Richter, N.C. State, C	1999	Chris Samuels, Alabama, OT
1960	**Tom Brown,** Minnesota, G	1980	Mark May, Pittsburgh, OT	2000	John Henderson, Tennessee, DT
1961	Merlin Olsen, Utah St., T	1981	Dave Rimington, Nebraska, C	2001	**Bryant McKinnie,** Miami-FL, OT
1962	Bobby Bell, Minnesota, T	1982	Dave Rimington, Nebraska, C	2002	Rien Long, Washington St., DT
1963	**Scott Appleton,** Texas, T	1983	Dean Steinkuhler, Nebraska, G		
1964	Steve DeLong, Tennessee, T	1984	Bruce Smith, Virginia Tech, DT		
1965	Tommy Nobis, Texas, G	1985	Mike Ruth, Boston College, NG		

Butkus Award

First presented in 1985 by the Downtown Athletic Club of Orlando, Fla., to honor the nation's outstanding linebacker. The award is named after Dick Butkus, two-time consensus All-America at Illinois and six-time All-Pro with the Chicago Bears.

Multiple winner: Brian Bosworth (2).

Year		Year		Year	
1985	Brian Bosworth, Oklahoma	1991	Erick Anderson, Michigan	1997	Andy Katzenmoyer, Ohio St.
1986	Brian Bosworth, Oklahoma	1992	Marvin Jones, Florida St.	1998	Chris Claiborne, USC
1987	Paul McGowan, Florida St.	1993	Trev Alberts, Nebraska	1999	LaVar Arrington, Penn St.
1988	Derrick Thomas, Alabama	1994	Dana Howard, Illinois	2000	Dan Morgan, Miami-FL
1989	Percy Snow, Michigan St.	1995	Kevin Hardy, Illinois	2001	Rocky Calmus, Oklahoma
1990	Alfred Williams, Colorado	1996	Matt Russell, Colorado	2002	E.J. Henderson, Maryland

Lombardi Award

First presented in 1970 by the Rotary Club of Houston, honoring the nation's best lineman. The award is named after pro football coach Vince Lombardi, who, as a guard, was a member of the famous "Seven Blocks of Granite" at Fordham in the 1930s. The Lombardi and Outland awards have gone to the same player in the same year ten times. Those players are preceded by (#). Ross Browner of Notre Dame won both, but in different years.

Multiple winner: Orlando Pace (2).

Year		Year		Year	
1970	#Jim Stillwagon, Ohio St., MG	1972	#Rich Glover, Nebraska, MG	1974	#Randy White, Maryland, DT
1971	Walt Patulski, Notre Dame, DE	1973	#John Hicks, Ohio St., OT	1975	#Lee Roy Selmon, Okla., DT

Annual Awards (Cont.)

Year		Year		Year	
1976	Wilson Whitley, Houston, DT	1985	Tony Casillas, Oklahoma, NG	1994	Warren Sapp, Miami-FL, DT
1977	Ross Browner, Notre Dame, DE	1986	Cornelius Bennett, Alabama, LB	1995	Orlando Pace, Ohio St., OT
1978	Bruce Clark, Penn St., DT	1987	Chris Spielman, Ohio St., LB	1996	#Orlando Pace, Ohio St., OT
1979	Brad Budde, USC, G	1988	#Tracy Rocker, Auburn, DT	1997	Grant Wistrom, Nebraska, DE
1980	Hugh Green, Pitt, DE	1989	Percy Snow, Michigan St., LB	1998	Dat Nguyen, Tex. A&M, LB
1981	Kenneth Sims, Texas, DT	1990	Chris Zorich, Notre Dame, NT	1999	Corey Moore, Va. Tech, DE
1982	#Dave Rimington, Neb., C	1991	#Steve Emtman, Wash., DT	2000	Jamal Reynolds, Florida St., DE
1983	#Dean Steinkuhler, Neb., G	1992	Marvin Jones, Florida St., LB	2001	Julius Peppers, N. Carolina, DE
1984	Tony Degrate, Texas, DT	1993	Aaron Taylor, Notre Dame, OT	2002	Terrell Suggs, Arizona St., DE

O'Brien Quarterback Award

First presented in 1977 as the O'Brien Memorial Trophy, the award went to the outstanding player in the Southwest. In 1981, however, the Davey O'Brien Educational and Charitable Trust of Ft. Worth renamed the prize the O'Brien National Quarterback Award and now honors the nation's best quarterback. The award is named after 1938 Heisman Trophy-winning QB Davey O'Brien of Texas Christian.

Multiple winners: Ty Detmer, Mike Singletary and Danny Wuerffel (2).

Memorial Trophy

Year		Year	
1977	Earl Campbell, Texas, RB	1979	Mike Singletary, Baylor, LB
1978	Billy Sims, Oklahoma, RB	1980	Mike Singletary, Baylor, LB

National QB Award

Year		Year		Year	
1981	Jim McMahon, BYU	1989	Andre Ware, Houston	1997	Peyton Manning, Tennessee
1982	Todd Blackledge, Penn St.	1990	Ty Detmer, BYU	1998	Michael Bishop, Kansas St.
1983	Steve Young, BYU	1991	Ty Detmer, BYU	1999	Joe Hamilton, Ga. Tech
1984	Doug Flutie, Boston College	1992	Gino Torretta, Miami-FL	2000	Chris Weinke, Florida St.
1985	Chuck Long, Iowa	1993	Charlie Ward, Florida St.	2001	Eric Crouch, Nebraska
1986	Vinny Testaverde, Miami, FL	1994	Kerry Collins, Penn St.	2002	Brad Banks, Iowa
1987	Don McPherson, Syracuse	1995	Danny Wuerffel, Florida		
1988	Troy Aikman, UCLA	1996	Danny Wuerffel, Florida		

Thorpe Award

First presented in 1986 by the Jim Thorpe Athletic Club of Oklahoma City to honor the nation's outstanding defensive back. The award is named after Jim Thorpe–Olympic champion and two-time consensus All-America halfback at Carlisle.

Year		Year		Year	
1986	Thomas Everett, Baylor	1991	Terrell Buckley, Florida St.	1997	Charles Woodson, Michigan
1987	Bennie Blades, Miami-FL	1992	Deon Figures, Colorado	1998	Antoine Winfield, Ohio St.
	& Rickey Dixon, Oklahoma	1993	Antonio Langham, Alabama	1999	Tyrone Carter, Minnesota
1988	Deion Sanders, Florida St.	1994	Chris Hudson, Colorado	2000	Jamar Fletcher, Wisconsin
1989	Mike Carrier, USC	1995	Greg Myers, Colorado St.	2001	Roy Williams, Oklahoma
1990	Darryl Lewis, Arizona	1996	Lawrence Wright, Florida	2002	Terence Newman, Kansas St.

Payton Award

First presented in 1987 by the Sports Network and Division I-AA sports information directors to honor the nation's outstanding Division I-AA player. The award is named after Walter Payton, the NFL's all-time leading rusher who was an All-America running back at Jackson St.

Year		Year		Year	
1987	Kenny Gamble, Colgate, RB	1993	Doug Nussmeier, Idaho, QB	1999	Adrian Peterson, Ga. Southern, RB
1988	Dave Meggett, Towson St., RB	1994	Steve McNair, Alcorn St., QB	2000	Louis Ivory, Furman, RB
1989	John Friesz, Idaho, QB	1995	Dave Dickenson, Montana, QB	2001	Brian Westbrook, Villanova, RB
1990	Walter Dean, Grambling, RB	1996	Archie Amerson, N. Arizona, RB	2002	Tony Romo, Eastern Illinois, QB
1991	Jamie Martin, Weber St., QB	1997	Brian Finneran, Villanova, WR		
1992	Michael Payton, Marshall, QB	1998	Jerry Azumah, N. Hampshire, RB		

Hill Trophy

First presented in 1986 by the Harlon Hill Awards Committee in Florence, Ala., to honor the nation's outstanding Division II player. The award is named after three-time NFL All-Pro Harlon Hill, who played college ball at North Alabama.

Multiple winners: Johnny Bailey (3), Dusty Bonner (2).

Year		Year		Year	
1986	Jeff Bentrim, N. Dakota St., QB	1992	Ronald Moore, Pittsburg St., RB	1998	Brian Shay, Emporia St., RB
1987	Johnny Bailey, Texas A&I, RB	1993	Roger Graham, New Haven, RB	1999	Corte McGuffet, N. Colo., QB
1988	Johnny Bailey, Texas A&I, RB	1994	Chris Hatcher, Valdosta St., QB	2000	Dusty Bonner, Valdosta St., QB
1989	Johnny Bailey, Texas A&I, RB	1995	Ronald McKinnon, N. Alabama, LB	2001	Dusty Bonner, Valdosta St., QB
1990	Chris Simdorn, N. Dakota St., QB	1996	Jarrett Anderson, Truman St., RB	2002	Curt Anes, Grand Valley St., QB
1991	Ronnie West, Pittsburg St., WR	1997	Irv Sigler, Bloomsburg, RB		

All-Time Winningest Division I-A Coaches

Minimum of 10 years in Division I-A through 2002 season. Regular season and bowl games included. Coaches active in 2002 in **bold** type.

Top 25 Winning Percentage

		Yrs	W	L	T	Pct
1	Knute Rockne	13	105	12	5	.881
2	Frank Leahy	13	107	13	9	.864
3	George Woodruff	12	142	25	2	.846
4	Barry Switzer	16	157	29	4	.837
5	Tom Osborne	25	255	49	3	.836
6	Percy Haughton	13	96	17	6	.832
7	Bob Neyland	21	173	31	12	.829
8	Hurry Up Yost	29	196	36	12	.828
9	Bud Wilkinson	17	145	29	4	.826
10	Jock Sutherland	20	144	28	14	.812
11	Bob Devaney	16	136	30	7	.806
12	**Phillip Fulmer**	11	103	25	0	.805
13	Frank Thomas	19	141	33	9	.795
14	Henry Williams	23	141	34	12	.786
15	Gil Dobie	33	180	45	15	.781
16	Bear Bryant	38	323	85	17	.780
17	Fred Folsom	19	106	28	6	.779
18	Steve Spurrier	15	142	40	2	.777
19	Bo Schembechler	27	234	65	8	.775
20	**Bobby Bowden**	37	332	96	4	.773
21	Fritz Crisler	18	116	32	9	.768
22	**Joe Paterno**	37	336	101	3	.767
23	Charley Moran	18	122	33	12	.766
24	Wallace Wade	24	171	49	10	.765
25	Frank Kush	22	176	54	1	.764

Top 25 Victories

		Yrs	W	L	T	Pct
1	**Joe Paterno**	37	336	101	3	.767
2	**Bobby Bowden**	37	332	96	4	.773
3	Bear Bryant	38	323	85	17	.780
4	Pop Warner	44	319	106	32	.733
5	Amos Alonzo Stagg	57	314	199	35	.605
6	LaVell Edwards	29	257	101	3	.722
7	Tom Osborne	25	255	49	3	.836
8	Woody Hayes	33	238	72	10	.759
9	**Lou Holtz**	31	238	120	7	.662
10	Bo Schembechler	27	234	65	8	.775
11	Hayden Fry	37	232	178	10	.564
12	Jess Neely	40	207	176	19	.539
13	Warren Woodson	31	203	95	14	.673
14	Don Nehlen	30	202	128	8	.609
15	Vince Dooley	25	201	77	10	.715
	Eddie Anderson	39	201	128	15	.606
17	Jim Sweeney	32	200	154	4	.564
18	Dana X. Bible	33	198	72	23	.715
19	Dan McGugin	30	197	55	19	.762
20	Hurry Up Yost	29	196	36	12	.828
21	Howard Jones	29	194	64	21	.733
22	John Cooper	24	192	84	6	.691
23	Johnny Vaught	25	190	61	12	.745
24	George Welsh	28	189	132	4	.588
25	John Heisman	36	185	70	17	.711
	Johnny Majors	29	185	137	10	.572

Note: Eddie Robinson of Division I-AA Grambling St. (1941-42, 1945-97) is the all-time NCAA leader in coaching wins with a 408-165-15 record and 708 winning pct. over 55 seasons.

Where They Coached

Anderson–Loras (1922-24), DePaul (1925-31), Holy Cross (1933-38), Iowa (1939-42), Holy Cross (1950-64); **Bible**– Mississippi College (1913-15), LSU (1916), Texas A&M (1917,1919-28), Nebraska (1929-36), Texas (1937-46); **Bowden**–Samford (1959-62), West Virginia (1970-75), Florida St. (1976–); **Bryant**–Maryland (1945), Kentucky (1946-53), Texas A&M (1954-57), Alabama (1958-82); **Cooper**– Tulsa (1977-84), Arizona St. (1985-87), Ohio St. (1988-2000); **Crisler**–Minnesota (1930-31), Princeton (1932-37), Michigan (1938-47); **Devaney**–Wyoming (1957-61), Nebraska (1962-72); **Dobie**–North Dakota St. (1906-07), Washington (1908-16), Navy (1917-19), Cornell (1920-35), Boston College (1936-38); **V. Dooley**–Georgia (1964-88); **Edwards**–BYU (1972-2000); **Folsom**–Colorado (1895-99, 1901-02), Dartmouth (1903-06), Colorado (1908-15); **Fry**–SMU (1962-72), North Texas (1973-78), Iowa (1979-98); **Fulmer**–Tennessee (1992–).

   Haughton–Cornell (1899-1900), Harvard (1908-16), Columbia (1923-24); **Hayes**–Denison (1946-48), Miami-OH (1949-50), Ohio St. (1951-78); **Heisman**–Oberlin (1892), Akron (1893), Oberlin (1894), Auburn (1895-99), Clemson (1900-03), Georgia Tech (1904-19), Penn (1920-22), Washington & Jefferson (1923), Rice (1924-27); **Holtz**–William & Mary (1969-71), N.C. State (1972-75), Arkansas (1977-83), Minnesota (1984-85), Notre Dame (1986-96), South Carolina (1999–); **Jones**–Syracuse (1908), Yale (1909), Ohio St. (1910), Yale (1913), Iowa (1916-23), Duke (1924), USC (1925-40); **Kush**–Arizona St. (1958-79); **Leahy**–Boston College (1939-40), Notre Dame (1941-43, 1946-53); **Majors**–Iowa St. (1968-72), Pittsburgh (1973-76, 93-96), Tennessee (1977-92); **Moran**–Texas A&M (1909-14), Centre (1919-23), Bucknell (1924-26), Catawba (1930-33).

   Neely–Rhodes (1924-27), Clemson (1931-39), Rice (1940-66); **Nehlen**–Bowling Green (1968-76), West Virginia (1980-2000); **Neyland**–Tennessee (1926-34, 1936-40, 1946-52); **Osborne**–Nebraska (1973-97); **Paterno**–Penn St. (1966–); Rockne–Notre Dame (1918-30); **Schembechler**–Miami-OH (1963-68), Michigan (1969-89); **Spurrier**–Duke (1987-89), Florida (1990-2001); **Stagg**–Springfield College (1890-91), Chicago (1892-1932), Pacific (1933-46); **Sutherland**–Lafayette (1919-23), Pittsburgh (1924-38); **Sweeney**–Montana St. (1963-67), Washington St. (1968-75), Fresno St. (1976-96); **Switzer**–Oklahoma (1973-88).

   Thomas–Chattanooga (1925-28), Alabama (1931-42, 1944-46); **Vaught**–Mississippi (1947-70); **Wade**–Alabama (1923-30), Duke (1931-41, 1946-50); **Warner**–Georgia (1895-96), Cornell (1897-98), Carlisle (1899-1903), Cornell (1904-06), Carlisle (1907-13), Pittsburgh (1915-23), Stanford (1924-32), Temple (1933-38); **Welsh**–Navy (1973-81), Virginia (1982-2000); **Wilkinson**–Oklahoma (1947-63); **Williams**–Army (1891), Minnesota (1900-21); **Woodruff**–Penn (1892-1901), Illinois (1903), Carlisle (1905); **Woodson**–Central Arkansas (1935-39), Hardin-Simmons (1941-42, 1946-51), Arizona (1952-56), New Mexico St. (1958-67), Trinity-TX (1972-73); **Yost**–Ohio Wesleyan (1897), Nebraska (1898), Kansas (1899), Stanford (1900), Michigan (1901-23, 1925-26).

All-Time Winningest Division I-A Coaches (Cont.)

All-Time Bowl Appearances
Coaches active in 2002 in **bold** type.

		App	W	L	T
1	**Joe Paterno**	31	20	10	1
2	Bear Bryant	29	15	12	2
3	**Bobby Bowden**	26	18	7	1
4	Tom Osborne	25	12	13	0
5	LaVell Edwards	22	7	14	1
	Lou Holtz	22	12	8	2
7	Vince Dooley	20	8	10	2
8	Johnny Vaught	18	10	8	0
9	Hayden Fry	17	7	9	1
	Bo Schembechler	17	5	12	0
11	Johnny Majors	16	9	7	0
	Darrell Royal	16	8	7	1
13	Don James	15	10	5	0
	George Welsh	15	5	10	0
15	John Cooper	14	5	9	0
	Jackie Sherrill	14	8	6	0
17	Bobby Dodd	13	9	4	0
	Terry Donahue	13	8	4	1
	Barry Switzer	13	8	5	0
	Charlie McClendon	13	7	6	0
	Don Nehlen	13	4	9	0

Active Coaches' Victories
(Minimum 5 years in Division I-A.)

		Yrs	W	L	T	Pct
1	Joe Paterno, Penn St	37	336	101	3	.767
2	Bobby Bowden, Fla. St	37	332	96	4	.773
3	Lou Holtz, South Carolina	31	238	120	7	.662
4	Jackie Sherrill, Miss. St	24	178	110	4	.616
5	Ken Hatfield, Rice	23	159	115	4	.579
	Frank Beamer, Va. Tech	22	159	92	4	.631
7	Dennis Franchione, Tex. A&M	19	155	74	2	.675
8	Fisher DeBerry, Air Force	19	149	83	1	.642
9	Mack Brown, Texas	19	135	89	1	.602
10	Paul Pasqualoni, Syracuse	17	129	64	1	.668
11	John Robinson, UNLV	16	124	62	4	.663
12	Bill Snyder, Kansas St.	14	116	51	1	.693
13	John L. Smith, Michigan St.	14	110	60	0	.647
14	Sonny Lubick, Colorado St.	14	105	57	0	.648
15	Phillip Fulmer, Tennessee	11	103	25	0	.805
16	John Mackovic, Arizona	15	94	78	3	.546
17	Glen Mason, Minnesota	17	93	101	1	.479
18	Barry Alvarez, Wisconsin	13	92	61	4	.599
19	Mike Bellotti, Oregon	13	88	54	2	.618
20	Joe Tiller, Purdue	12	85	58	1	.594

AFCA Coach of the Year
First presented in 1935 by the American Football Coaches Association.

Multiple winners: Joe Paterno (4), Bear Bryant (3), John McKay and Darrell Royal (2).

Year		Year		Year	
1935	Pappy Waldorf, Northwestern	1960	Murray Warmath, Minnesota	1983	Ken Hatfield, Air Force
1936	Dick Harlow, Harvard	1961	Bear Bryant, Alabama	1984	LaVell Edwards, BYU
1937	Hooks Mylin, Lafayette	1962	John McKay, USC	1985	Fisher DeBerry, Air Force
1938	Bill Kern, Carnegie Tech	1963	Darrell Royal, Texas	1986	Joe Paterno, Penn St.
1939	Eddie Anderson, Iowa	1964	Frank Broyles, Arkansas	1987	Dick MacPherson, Syracuse
1940	Clark Shaughnessy, Stanford		& Ara Parseghian, Notre Dame	1988	Don Nehlen, West Virginia
1941	Frank Leahy, Notre Dame	1965	Tommy Prothro, UCLA	1989	Bill McCartney, Colorado
1942	Bill Alexander, Georgia Tech	1966	Tom Cahill, Army	1990	Bobby Ross, Georgia Tech
1943	Amos Alonzo Stagg, Pacific	1967	John Pont, Indiana	1991	Bill Lewis, East Carolina
1944	Carroll Widdoes, Ohio St.	1968	Joe Paterno, Penn St.	1992	Gene Stallings, Alabama
1945	Bo McMillin, Indiana	1969	Bo Schembechler, Michigan	1993	Barry Alvarez, Wisconsin
1946	Red Blaik, Army	1970	Charlie McClendon, LSU	1994	Tom Osborne, Nebraska
1947	Fritz Crisler, Michigan		& Darrell Royal, Texas	1995	Gary Barnett, Northwestern
1948	Bennie Oosterbaan, Michigan	1971	Bear Bryant, Alabama	1996	Bruce Snyder, Arizona St.
1949	Bud Wilkinson, Oklahoma	1972	John McKay, USC	1997	Lloyd Carr, Michigan
1950	Charlie Caldwell, Princeton	1973	Bear Bryant, Alabama	1998	Phillip Fulmer, Tennessee
1951	Chuck Taylor, Stanford	1974	Grant Teaff, Baylor	1999	Frank Beamer, Va. Tech
1952	Biggie Munn, Michigan St.	1975	Frank Kush, Arizona St.	2000	Bob Stoops, Oklahoma
1953	Jim Tatum, Maryland	1976	Johnny Majors, Pittsburgh	2001	Ralph Friedgen, Maryland
1954	Red Sanders, UCLA	1977	Don James, Washington		& Larry Coker, Miami-FL
1955	Duffy Daugherty, Michigan St.	1978	Joe Paterno, Penn St.	2002	Jim Tressel, Ohio St.
1956	Bowden Wyatt, Tennessee	1979	Earle Bruce, Ohio St.		
1957	Woody Hayes, Ohio St.	1980	Vince Dooley, Georgia		
1958	Paul Dietzel, LSU	1981	Danny Ford, Clemson		
1959	Ben Schwartzwalder, Syracuse	1982	Joe Paterno, Penn St.		

FWAA Coach of the Year
First presented in 1957 by the Football Writers Association of America. The FWAA and AFCA awards have both gone to the same coach in the same season 32 times. Those double winners are preceded by (#).

Multiple winners: Woody Hayes and Joe Paterno (3); Lou Holtz, Johnny Majors and John McKay (2).

Year		Year		Year	
1957	#Woody Hayes, Ohio St.	1966	#Tom Cahill, Army	1975	Woody Hayes, Ohio St.
1958	#Paul Dietzel, LSU	1967	#John Pont, Indiana	1976	#Johnny Majors, Pitt
1959	#Ben Schwartzwalder, Syracuse	1968	Woody Hayes, Ohio St.	1977	Lou Holtz, Arkansas
1960	Murray Warmath, Minnesota	1969	#Bo Schembechler, Michigan	1978	#Joe Paterno, Penn St.
1961	Darrell Royal, Texas	1970	Alex Agase, Northwestern	1979	#Earle Bruce, Ohio St.
1962	#John McKay, USC	1971	Bob Devaney, Nebraska	1980	#Vince Dooley, Georgia
1963	#Darrell Royal, Texas	1972	#John McKay, USC	1981	#Danny Ford, Clemson
1964	#Ara Parseghian, Notre Dame	1973	Johnny Majors, Pitt	1982	#Joe Paterno, Penn St.
1965	Duffy Daugherty, Michigan St.	1974	#Grant Teaff, Baylor	1983	Howard Schnellenberger, Miami-FL

Year		Year		Year	
1984	#LaVell Edwards, BYU	1992	#Gene Stallings, Alabama	2000	#Bob Stoops, Oklahoma
1985	#Fisher DeBerry, Air Force	1993	Terry Bowden, Auburn	2001	#Ralph Friedgen, Maryland
1986	#Joe Paterno, Penn St.	1994	Rich Brooks, Oregon	2002	#Jim Tressel, Ohio St.
1987	#Dick MacPherson, Syracuse	1995	#Gary Barnett, Northwestern		
1988	Lou Holtz, Notre Dame	1996	#Bruce Snyder, Arizona St.		
1989	#Bill McCartney, Colorado	1997	Mike Price, Washington St.		
1990	#Bobby Ross, Georgia Tech	1998	#Phillip Fulmer, Tennessee		
1991	Don James, Washington	1999	#Frank Beamer, Va. Tech		

All-Time NCAA Division I-AA Leaders
CAREER

Total Offense

	Yards Gained	Years	Yards
1	Steve McNair, Alcorn St.	1991-94	16,823
2	Marcus Brady, CS-Northridge	1998-01	13,095
3	Willie Totten, Miss. Valley	1982-85	13,007
4	Jamie Martin, Weber St.	1989-92	12,287
5	Doug Nussmeier, Idaho	1990-93	12,054

	Yards per Game	Years	Yards	P/Gm
1	Steve McNair, Alcorn St.	1991-94	16,823	400.5
2	Neil Lomax, Portland St.	1978-80	11,647	352.9
3	Aaron Flowers, CS-N'ridge	1996-97	6,754	337.7
4	Chris Sanders, Chatt.	1999-00	7,247	329.4
5	Dave Dickenson, Montana	1992-95	11,523	329.2

Passing
(Minimum 500 Completions)

	Passing Efficiency	Years	Rating
1	Shawn Knight, William & Mary	1991-94	170.8
2	Dave Dickenson, Montana	1992-95	166.3
3	Drew Miller, Montana	1999-00	160.5
4	Doug Nussmeier, Idaho	1990-93	154.4
5	Mark Washington, Jackson St.	1996-99	153.5

	Yards Gained	Years	Yards
1	Steve McNair, Alcorn St.	1991-94	14,496
2	Willie Totten, Miss. Valley	1982-85	12,711
3	Marcus Brady, CS-Northridge	1998-01	12,479
4	Jamie Martin, Weber St.	1989-92	12,207
5	Neil Lomax, Portland St.	1978-80	11,550

Receiving

	Catches	Years	No
1	Jacquay Nunnally, Fla. A&M	1997-00	317
2	Stephen Campbell, Brown	1997-00	305
3	Jerry Rice, Miss. Valley	1981-84	301
4	Chas Gessner, Brown	1999-02	292
5	Kasey Dunn, Idaho	1988-91	268

	Yards Gained	Years	No	Yards
1	Jerry Rice, Miss. Valley	1981-84	301	4693
2	Jacquay Nunnally, Fla. A&M	1997-00	317	4239
3	Cedric Ward, N. Iowa	1993-96	176	3876
4	Sean Morey, Brown	1995-98	251	3850
5	Kasey Dunn, Idaho	1988-91	268	3847

Rushing

	Yards Gained	Years	Yards
1	Adrian Peterson, Ga. So.	1998-01	6559
2	Charles Roberts, CS-Sac.	1997-00	6553
3	Jerry Azumah, N. Hampshire.	1995-98	6193
4	Matt Cannon, S. Utah	1997-00	5489
5	Reggie Greene, Siena	1994-97	5415

	Yards per Game	Years	Yards	P/Gm
1	Arnold Mickens, Butler	1994-95	3813	190.7
2	Adrian Peterson, Ga. So.	1998-01	6559	156.2
3	Aaron Stecker, W. Ill.	1997-98	3081	154.1
4	Tim Hall, Robert Morris	1994-95	2908	153.1
5	Jerry Azumah, N. Hampshire	1995-98	6193	151.0

Miscellaneous

	Interceptions	Years	No
1	Rashean Mathis, Bethune-Cookman	1999-02	31
2	Dave Murphy, Holy Cross	1986-89	28
3	Cedric Walker, S.F. Austin	1990-93	25
4	Issiac Holt, Alcorn St.	1981-84	24
	Bill McGovern, Holy Cross	1981-84	24
	Darren Sharper, Wm. & Mary	1993-96	24

	Punting Average	Years	Avg
1	Pumpy Tudors, Tenn.-Chatt.	1989-91	44.4
2	Case de Brujin, Idaho St.	1978-81	43.7
3	Mike Scifres, Western Illinois	1999-02	43.6
4	Terry Belden, Northern Ariz.	1990-93	43.4
5	Chad Stanley, SF Austin	1996-98	43.3

	Punt Return Average*	Years	Avg
1	Willie Ware, Miss. Valley	1982-85	16.4
2	Buck Phillips, Western Ill.	1994-95	16.4
3	Tim Egerton, Delaware St.	1986-89	16.1
4	Mark Orlando, Towson St.	1991-94	15.7
5	Joseph Jefferson, Western Ky.	1998-01	15.3

	Kickoff Return Average*	Years	Avg
1	Lamont Brightful, E. Wash.	1998-01	30.0
2	Troy Brown, Marshall	1991-92	29.7
3	Charles Swann, Indiana St.	1989-91	29.3
4	Craig Richardson, Eastern Wash.	1983-86	28.5
5	Ramondo North, N.C. A&T	1998-00	28.3
*(Minimum 1.2 returns per game)

Scoring
NON-KICKERS

	Points	Years	TD	XP	Pts
1	B. Westbrook, Villanova	1997-98,00-01	89	10	544
2	Adrian Peterson, Ga. Southern	1998-01	87	2	524
3	Matt Cannon, S. Utah	1997-00	69	6	420
4	Jerry Azumah, New Hampshire.	1995-98	69	4	418
5	David Dinkins, Morehead St.	1997-00	63	6	384

	Touchdowns Passing	Years	No
1	Willie Totten, Miss. Valley	1982-85	139
2	Steve McNair, Alcorn St.	1991-94	119
3	Marcus Brady, CS-Northridge	1998-01	109
4	Dave Dickenson, Montana	1992-95	96
5	Chris Boden, Villanova	1996-99	93

	Touchdowns Rushing	Years	No
1	Adrian Peterson, Ga. Southern	1998-01	84
2	Matt Cannon, S. Utah	1997-00	69
3	David Dinkins, Morehead St.	1997-00	63
4	Jerry Azumah, New Hampshire.	1995-98	60
5	Charles Roberts, CS-Sacramento	1997-00	56

	Touchdown Catches	Years	No
1	Jerry Rice, Miss. Valley	1981-84	50
2	Rennie Benn, Lehigh	1982-85	44
3	Dedric Ward, N. Iowa	1993-96	41
4	Sean Morey, Brown	1995-98	39
	Gharun Hester, Georgetown	1997-00	39

All-Time NCAA Division I-AA leaders (Cont.)

KICKERS

Points	Years	FG	XP	Pts		Field Goals	Years	No
1 Marty Zendejas, Nevada	...1984-87	72	169	385		1 Marty Zendejas, Nevada	1984-87	72
2 Dave Ettinger, Hofstra	1994-97	62	140	326		2 Kirk Roach, Western Carolina	1984-87	71
3 B. Mitchell, Marshall/N.Iowa	1987,89-91	64	130	322		3 Tony Zendejas, Nevada.	1981-83	70
Scott Shields, Weber St.	...1995-98	67	109	322		4 Scott Shields, Weber St.	1995-98	67
5 Thayne Doyle, Idaho	1988-91	49	160	307		5 Brian Mitchell, Marshall/N. Iowa	...1987,89-91	64

Note: Scott Shields's point total includes 2 touchdowns.

All-Time NCAA Division I-AA leaders (Cont.)

Includes record at a senior college only, minimum of 20 seasons of competition. Bowl and playoff games are included.

Top 20 Winning Percentage

		Yrs	Gm	W	L	T	Pct.	Playoffs W-L-T
1	Yale	.130	1181	815	311	55	.713	0-0-0
2	Grambling St.	.60	646	451	180	15	.710	9-7-0
3	Florida A&M	.70	715	497	200	18	.708	5-8-0
4	Tennessee St.	.75	706	471	205	30	.688	8-4-1
5	Princeton	.133	1133	749	334	50	.683	0-0-0
6	Harvard	.128	1162	750	362	50	.667	1-0-0
7	Georgia Southern	.34	391	255	129	7	.661	38-8-0
8	Jackson St.	.57	588	376	199	13	.651	1-11-1
9	Eastern Kentucky	.79	789	486	276	27	.633	17-17-0
10	Pennsylvania	.126	1233	758	433	42	.632	0-1-0
11	Southern.	.81	793	488	280	25	.631	6-1-0
12	Fordham	.104	1161	706	402	53	.631	3-4-0
13	Dayton	.95	904	554	324	26	.627	16-11-0
14	Hofstra	.62	603	371	221	11	.624	4-12-0
15	Dartmouth	.121	1049	630	373	46	.623	6-1-0
16	McNeese St.	.52	568	347	207	14	.623	14-13-0
17	Appalachian St.	.73	773	465	279	29	.620	9-16-0
18	Albany	.30	300	185	115	0	.617	0-0-0
19	S. Carolina St.	.75	700	414	259	27	.611	6-5-0
20	Youngstown St.	.62	635	376	242	17	.606	26-9-0

Top 50 Victories

		Wins			Wins			Wins
1	Yale	.815	18 Villanova	.507	35 Maine	.447
2	Pennsylvania	.758	19 Drake	.506	34 Georgetown	.446
3	Harvard	.750	20 Furman.	.502	37 Western Ill.	.445
4	Princeton	.749	21 Florida A&M	.497	38 Howard	.439
5	Fordham	.706	22 Southern	.488	39 VMI.	.437
6	Dartmouth	.630	William & Mary	.488	40 Richmond.	.435
7	Lafayette	.599	24 Massachusetts	.486	41 SW Texas St.	.433
8	Cornell	.592	E. Kentucky	.486	42 The Citadel	.422
9	Lehigh.	.584	26 Tennessee St.	.471	43 Eastern Ill.	.421
10	Delaware	.581	W. Kentucky	.471	44 Idaho St.	.420
11	Dayton	.554	28 Hampton	.468	45 Murray St.	.416
12	Holy Cross	.552	29 Appalachian St.	.465	46 S. Carolina St.	.414
13	Colgate	.537	30 Northwestern St.	.458	47 Wofford	.409
14	N. Iowa	.536	31 Tenn-Chat	.453	48 E. Washington	.408
15	Bucknell	.531	32 Grambling St.	.451	49 SW Missouri St.	.406
16	Brown	.529	33 Montana	.450	50 N.C. A&T	.405
17	Butler	.511	34 New Hampshire	.449		

Top 10 Playoff Game Appearances

Ranked by NCAA Division 1-AA playoff games played from 1978-2002. CH refers to championships won.

		Years	Games	Record	CH			Years	Games	Record	CH
1	Georgia Southern	14	46	38-8	6	6 Furman	12	25	14-11	1
2	Eastern Ky.	17	31	16-15	2	7 Delaware	11	22	11-11	0
3	Montana.	13	30	19-11	2	8 Northern Iowa	10	21	11-10	0
4	Marshall*	8	29	23-6	2	McNeese St.	10	21	11-10	0
	Youngstown St.	10	29	23-6	4	10 Appalachian St.	12	20	8-12	0

*Marshall moved up to I-A in 1997.

Active Division I-AA Coaches
Minimum of 5 years as a Division I-A and/or Division I-AA through 2002 season.

Top 10 Winning Percentage

		Yrs	W	L	T	Pct
1	Mike Kelly, Dayton	22	206	41	1	.833
2	Al Bagnoli, Pennsylvania	21	162	51	0	.761
3	Pete Richardson, Southern	15	126	47	1	.727
4	Greg Gattuso, Duquesne	10	82	26	0	.759
5	Joe Walton, Robert Morris	9	61	28	1	.683
6	Joe Gardi, Hofstra	13	105	42	2	.711
7	Billy Joe, Florida A&M	29	228	94	4	.706
8	Joe Taylor, Hampton	20	153	64	4	.701
9	Walt Hameline, Wagner	22	157	71	2	.687
10	Dick Biddle, Colgate	7	54	26	0	.675

Top 10 Victories

		Yrs	W	L	T	Pct
1	Billy Joe, Florida A&M	29	228	94	4	.706
2	Mike Kelly, Dayton	20	206	41	1	.833
3	Ron Randleman, Sam Houston St.	34	205	155	6	.575
4	Al Bagnoli, Pennsylvania	21	162	51	0	.761
5	Walt Hameline, Wagner	22	157	71	2	.687
6	Jimmye Laycock, Wm. & Mary	23	154	105	2	.594
7	Joe Taylor, Hampton	20	153	64	4	.701
8	Andy Talley, Villanova	23	152	91	2	.624
9	Rob Ash, Drake	23	145	85	5	.628
10	Jerry Moore, Appalachian St.	21	142	103	2	.579

Note: Eddie Robinson of Grambling State (1941-42, 1945-97) retired following the 1997 season as the all-time NCAA leader in coaching wins with a 408-165-15 record and a .707 winning percentage over 55 seasons.

Division I-AA Coach of the Year
First presented in 1983 by the American Football Coaches Association.

Multiple winners: Mark Duffner, Paul Johnson and Erk Russell (2).

Year		Year		Year	
1983	Rey Dempsey, Southern Ill.	1990	Tim Stowers, Ga. Southern	1997	Andy Talley, Villanova
1984	Dave Arnold, Montana St.	1991	Mark Duffner, Holy Cross	1998	Mark Whipple, Massachusetts
1985	Dick Sheridan, Furman	1992	Charlie Taafe, Citadel	1999	Paul Johnson, Ga. Southern
1986	Erk Russell, Ga. Southern	1993	Dan Allen, Boston Univ.	2000	Paul Johnson, Ga. Southern
1987	Mark Duffner, Holy Cross	1994	Jim Tressel, Youngstown St.	2001	Bobby Johnson, Furman
1988	Jimmy Satterfield, Furman	1995	Don Read, Montana	2002	Jack Harbaugh, E. Kentucky
1989	Erk Russell, Ga. Southern	1996	Ray Tellier, Columbia		

NCAA Playoffs

Division I-AA

Established in 1978 as a four-team playoff. Tournament field increased to eight teams in 1981, 12 teams in 1982 and 16 teams in 1986. Automatic berths are awarded to champions of the Big Sky, Gateway, Mid-Eastern Athletic, Ohio Valley, Patriot, Southern, Southland and Atlantic 10 (formerly Yankee) conferences.

Multiple winners: Georgia Southern (6); Youngstown St. (4); Eastern Kentucky, Marshall and Montana (2).

Year	Winner	Score	Loser	Year	Winner	Score	Loser
1978	Florida A&M	35-28	Massachusetts	1991	Youngstown St., OH	25-17	Marshall
1979	Eastern Kentucky	30-7	Lehigh, PA	1992	Marshall	31-28	Youngstown St.
1980	Boise St., ID	31-29	Eastern Kentucky	1993	Youngstown St.	17-5	Marshall
1981	Idaho St.	34-23	Eastern Kentucky	1994	Youngstown St.	28-14	Boise St.
1982	Eastern Kentucky	17-14	Delaware	1995	Montana	22-20	Marshall
1983	Southern Illinois	43-7	Western Carolina	1996	Marshall	49-29	Montana
1984	Montana St.	19-6	Louisiana Tech	1997	Youngstown St.	10-9	McNeese St.
1985	Georgia Southern	44-42	Furman, SC	1998	Massachusetts	55-43	Georgia Southern
1986	Georgia Southern	48-21	Arkansas St.	1999	Georgia Southern	59-24	Youngstown St.
1987	NE Louisiana	43-42	Marshall, WV	2000	Georgia Southern	27-25	Montana
1988	Furman, SC	17-12	Georgia Southern	2001	Montana	13-6	Furman
1989	Georgia Southern	37-34	S.F. Austin St.	2002	Western Kentucky	34-14	McNeese St.
1990	Georgia Southern	36-13	Nevada-Reno				

Division II

Established in 1973 as an eight-team playoff. Tournament field increased to 16 teams in 1988. From 1964-72, eight qualifying NCAA College Division member institutions competed in four regional bowl games, but there was no tournament and no national championship until 1973.

Multiple winners: North Dakota St. (5); North Alabama (3); Northern Colorado, Northwest Missouri St., Southwest Texas St. and Troy St. (2).

Year	Winner	Score	Loser	Year	Winner	Score	Loser
1973	Louisiana Tech	34-0	Western Kentucky	1988	North Dakota St	35-21	Portland St., OR
1974	Central Michigan	54-14	Delaware	1989	Mississippi Col.	3-0	Jacksonville St., AL
1975	Northern Michigan	16-14	Western Kentucky	1990	North Dakota St.	51-11	Indiana, PA
1976	Montana St.	24-13	Akron, OH	1991	Pittsburg St., KS	23-6	Jacksonville St., AL
1977	Lehigh, PA	33-0	Jacksonville St., AL	1992	Jacksonville St., AL	17-13	Pittsburg St., KS
1978	Eastern Illinois	10-9	Delaware	1993	North Alabama	41-34	Indiana, PA
1979	Delaware	38-21	Youngstown St., OH	1994	North Alabama	16-10	Tex. A&M (Kings.)
1980	Cal Poly-SLO	21-13	Eastern Illinois	1995	North Alabama	22-7	Pittsburg St., KS
1981	SW Texas St.	42-13	North Dakota St.	1996	Northern Colorado	23-14	Carson-Newman
1982	SW Texas St.	34-9	UC-Davis	1997	Northern Colorado	51-0	New Haven
1983	North Dakota St.	41-21	Central St., OH	1998	NW Missouri St.	24-6	Carson-Newman
1984	Troy St., AL	18-17	North Dakota St.	1999	NW Missouri St.	58-52*	Carson-Newman
1985	North Dakota St.	35-7	North Alabama	2000	Delta St., MS	63-34	Bloomsburg, PA
1986	North Dakota St.	27-7	South Dakota	2001	North Dakota	17-14	Grand Valley St.
1987	Troy St., AL	31-17	Portland St., OR	2002	Grand Valley St., OH	31-24	Valdosta St., GA
				*Four overtimes			

Division III

Established in 1973 as a four-team playoff. Tournament field increased to eight teams in 1975, 16 teams in 1985 and 28 teams in 1999. From 1969-72, four qualifying NCAA College Division member institutions competed in two regional bowl games, but there was no tournament and no national championship until 1973. (*) denotes overtime.

Multiple winners: Mt. Union (7); Augustana (4); Ithaca (3); Dayton, Widener, WI-La Crosse and Wittenberg (2).

Year	Winner	Score	Loser	Year	Winner	Score	Loser
1973	Wittenberg, OH	41-0	Juniata, PA	1988	Ithaca, NY	39-24	Central, IA
1974	Central, IA	10-8	Ithaca, NY	1989	Dayton, OH	17-7	Union, NY
1975	Wittenberg, OH	28-0	Ithaca, NY	1990	Allegheny, PA	21-14*	Lycoming, PA
1976	St. John's, MN	31-28	Towson St., MD	1991	Ithaca, NY	34-20	Dayton, OH
1977	Widener, PA	39-36	Wabash, IN	1992	WI-La Crosse	16-12	Wash. & Jeff., PA
1978	Baldwin-Wallace	24-10	Wittenberg, OH	1993	Mt. Union, OH	34-24	Rowan, NJ
1979	Ithaca, NY	14-10	Wittenberg, OH	1994	Albion, MI	38-15	Wash. & Jeff.
1980	Dayton, OH	63-0	Ithaca, NY	1995	WI-La Crosse	36-7	Rowan, NJ
1981	Widener, PA	17-10	Dayton, OH	1996	Mt. Union, OH	56-24	Rowan, NJ
1982	West Georgia	14-0	Augustana, IL	1997	Mt. Union, OH	61-12	Lycoming
1983	Augustana, IL	21-17	Union, NY	1998	Mt. Union, OH	44-24	Rowan, NJ
1984	Augustana, IL	21-12	Central, IA	1999	Pacific Lutheran	42-13	Rowan, NJ
1985	Augustana, IL	20-7	Ithaca	2000	Mt. Union, OH	10-7	St. John's, MN
1986	Augustana, IL	31-3	Salisbury St., MD	2001	Mt. Union, OH	30-27	Bridgewater, VA
1987	Wagner, NY	19-3	Dayton, OH	2002	Mt. Union, OH	48-7	Trinity, TX

NAIA Playoffs

Division I

Established in 1956 as two-team playoff. Tournament field increased to four teams in 1958, eight teams in 1978 and 16 teams in 1987 before cutting back to eight teams in 1989. NAIA went back to a single division 16-team playoff in 1997. The title game has ended in a tie four times (1956, '64, '84 and '85). Note that Northeastern St., OK was called NE Oklahoma in 1958.

Multiple winners: Texas A&I (7); Carson-Newman (5); Central Arkansas and Central St-OH (3); Abilene Christian, Central St-OK, Elon, Georgetown-KY, Northeastern St-OK, Pittsburg St. and St. John's-MN (2).

Year	Winner	Score	Loser	Year	Winner	Score	Loser
1956	Montana St.	0-0	St. Joseph's, IN	1980	Elon, NC	17-10	NE Oklahoma
1957	Pittsburg St., KS	27-26	Hillsdale, MI	1981	Elon, NC	3-0	Pittsburg St., KS
1958	NE Oklahoma	19-13	Northern Arizona	1982	Central St., OK	14-11	Mesa, CO
1959	Texas A&I	20-7	Lenoir-Rhyne, NC	1983	Car-Newman, TN	36-28	Mesa, CO
1960	Lenoir-Rhyne, NC	15-14	Humboldt St., CA	1984	Car-Newman, TN	19-19	Central Arkansas
1961	Pittsburg St., KS	12-7	Linfield, OR	1985	Hillsdale, MI	10-10	Central Arkansas
1962	Central St., OK	28-13	Lenoir-Rhyne, NC	1986	Car-Newman, TN	17-0	Cameron, OK
1963	St. John's, MN	33-27	Prairie View, TX	1987	Cameron, OK	30-2	Car-Newman, TN
1964	Concordia, MN	7-7	Sam Houston, TX	1988	Car-Newman, TN	56-21	Adams St., CO
1965	St. John's, MN	33-0	Linfield, OR	1989	Car-Newman, TN	34-20	Emporia St., KS
1966	Waynesburg, PA	42-21	WI-Whitewater	1990	Central St., OH	38-16	Mesa, CO
1967	Fairmont St., WV	28-21	Eastern Wash.	1991	Central Arkansas	19-16	Central St., OH
1968	Troy St., AL	43-35	Texas A&I	1992	Central St., OH	19-16	Gardner-Webb, NC
1969	Texas A&I	32-7	Concordia, MN	1993	E. Central, OK	49-35	Glenville St., WV
1970	Texas A&I	48-7	Wofford, SC	1994	N'eastern St., OK	13-12	Ark-Pine Bluff
1971	Livingston, AL	14-12	Arkansas Tech	1995	Central St., OH	37-7	N'eastern St., OK
1972	East Texas St.	21-18	Car-Newman, TN	1996	SW Oklahoma St.	33-31	Montana Tech
1973	Abilene Christian	42-14	Elon, NC	1997	Findlay, OH	14-7	Willamette, ORE
1974	Texas A&I	34-23	Henderson St., AR	1998	Azusa Pacific, CA	17-14	Olivet Nazarene, IL
1975	Texas A&I	37-0	Salem, WV	1999	NW Oklahoma St.	34-26	Georgetown, KY
1976	Texas A&I	26-0	Central Arkansas	2000	Georgetown, KY	20-0	NW Oklahoma St.
1977	Abilene Christian	24-7	SW Oklahoma	2001	Georgetown, KY	49-27	Sioux Falls, S.D.
1978	Angelo St., TX	34-14	Elon, NC	2002	Carroll, MT	28-7	Georgetown, KY
1979	Texas A&I	20-14	Central St., OK				

Division II

Established in 1970 as four-team playoff. Tournament field increased to eight teams in 1978 and 16 teams in 1987. NAIA went back to a single division playoff in 1997. The title game has ended in a tie twice (1981 and '87).

Multiple winners: Westminster (6); Findlay, Linfield and Pacific Lutheran (3); Concordia-MN, Northwestern-IA and Texas Lutheran (2).

Year	Winner	Score	Loser	Year	Winner	Score	Loser
1970	Westminster, PA	21-16	Anderson, IN	1984	Linfield, OR	33-22	Northwestern, IA
1971	Calif. Lutheran	20-14	Westminster, PA	1985	WI-La Crosse	24-7	Pacific Lutheran
1972	Missouri Southern	21-14	Northwestern, IA	1986	Linfield, OR	17-0	Baker, KS
1973	Northwestern, IA	10-3	Glenville St., WV	1987	Pacific Lutheran	16-16	WI-Stevens Pt.*
1974	Texas Lutheran	42-0	Missouri Valley	1988	Westminster, PA	21-14	WI-La Crosse
1975	Texas Lutheran	34-8	Calif. Lutheran	1989	Westminster, PA	51-30	WI-La Crosse
1976	Westminster, PA	20-13	Redlands, CA	1990	Peru St., NE	17-7	Westminster, PA
1977	Westminster, PA	17-9	Calif. Lutheran	1991	Georgetown, KY	28-20	Pacific Lutheran
1978	Concordia, MN	7-0	Findlay, OH	1992	Findlay, OH	26-13	Linfield, OR
1979	Findlay, OH	51-6	Northwestern, IA	1993	Pacific Lutheran	50-20	Westminster, PA
1980	Pacific Lutheran	38-10	Wilmington, OH	1994	Westminster, PA	27-7	Pacific Lutheran
1981	Austin College, TX	24-24	Concordia, MN	1995	Findlay, OH	21-21	Central Wash.
1982	Linfield, OR	33-15	Wm. Jewell, MO	1996	Sioux Falls, S.D.	47-25	W. Washington
1983	Northwestern, IA	25-21	Pacific Lutheran				

*Wisconsin-Stevens Point forfeited its entire 1987 schedule due to its use of an ineligible player.

Pro Football

Buccaneers owner Malcolm Glazer, right, made a shrewd move hiring coach **Jon Gruden**.

Loveable Losers No Longer

Behind Jon Gruden's fiery leadership and a stifling defense, the Bucs run away with Super Bowl XXXVII.

Chris Berman
is the host of ESPN's NFL Prime Time.

The Tampa Bay Buccaneers are Super Bowl champions. It still has an odd sound to it, doesn't it?

But it's true...finally...and with a little irony as well.

After taking 27 games to win AT all, the Bucs took 27 years to win IT all. It was a long time coming for a franchise synonymous with tangerine uniforms and football follies.

But for all of the organization's waiting, it took new head coach Jon Gruden just one season with the team for it to reach its potential. The Buccaneers paid a heavy price in the form of draft choices and cash to get him from the Raiders, and not only did he lead the club to a franchise-record 12 wins, but a great season became even more incredible when Gruden's new team bested his old one, 48-21, in Super Bowl XXXVII in San Diego. But it was hardly a fluke as Tampa Bay rolled both the 49ers and the Eagles (playing their final game at the Vet) en route to the Big Game.

The Buccaneers' win was the latest installment of what the modern NFL has become. For the fifth time in six seasons, a team that had never won a Super Bowl came away with a championship. The new NFL has teams grabbing Lombardi trophies like they're available on e-bay.

Not that the Bucs were a major surprise. The only team to make the playoffs the last four seasons, it finally all came together for a club which cut its teeth under Tony Dungy (who gave way to Gruden and wound up leading the Colts to the playoffs) and matured under Gruden. Well-traveled quarterback Brad Johnson overcame a slow start and was one of the league's hottest passers from November on, while Defensive Player of the Year Derrick Brooks led an experienced unit that gave up the fewest yards and points in the league.

Brian Bahr/Getty Images

Rich Gannon and the Raiders offensive line had a tough time with the stellar Tampa Bay defense in Super Bowl XXXVII. Gannon was sacked five times and had five passes picked off.

Perhaps it was only fitting that a team known more for being the "Yucks" than the Bucs emerged the winner in one of the wildest seasons in recent memories. Armed with an unprecedented 32 teams and eight divisions, the 2002 campaign started with a bang and ended with nearly every team in the playoff chase entering the final weekend. But when the smoke cleared, many of the 12 clubs in the postseason parade were surprises in one way or another.

The Jets (thanks mainly to quarterback Chad Pennington) and Titans rebounded from 1-4 starts to win division titles. The Steelers lost three of their first four games but still captured the AFC North.

The Falcons opened 1-3 and the Browns began 2-4, and both reached the playoffs. On the other hand, seven teams got off to 3-0 or better starts, but only one parlayed it into a postseason appearance.

That would be the Raiders, who proved that putting age before beauty pays off, as they reached the Super Bowl for the first time since the Los Angeles Raiders humbled the Redskins nearly two decades earlier. Rich Gannon earned league MVP honors while commanding the league's best offense, assisted by future Hall of Fame wideouts Jerry Rice and Tim Brown, as well as versatile runner Charlie Garner.

AP/Wide World Photos

*Giants lineman **Rich Seubert** is hauled down while trying to catch a pass from holder Matt Allen in the controversial waning seconds of the 49ers 39-38 playoff win.*

Sadly their quest for a title became over-shadowed by teammate Barret Robbins, who went AWOL Super Bowl weekend.

But there were a plethora of memorable moments during the NFL's 83rd season. Falcons' second-year quarterback Michael Vick electrified audiences with his strong arm and fast feet and led Atlanta to one of the biggest wins in league history as Dan Reeves' team humbled the Packers in the playoffs at Lambeau Field, the first home postseason loss for the league's most storied franchise. And the next day, the Steelers and 49ers rallied from 17 and 24 points down, respectively, to stun the Browns and Giants.

Running back Ricky Williams' first season with Miami proved to be a smashing success individually, although the Dolphins inexplicably missed the playoffs for the first time in six years. Pittsburgh's Tommy Maddox became the ultimate Comeback Player of the Year, rejuvenating his NFL career and recovering from being temporary paralyzed to lead the Steelers into the playoffs.

There was flamboyant 49er Terrell Owens and his Sharpie, Colts' wide receiver Marvin Harrison and his amazing record-setting 143 receptions and quarterback Drew Bledsoe reviving his

continued on page 210 ▶

The Ten Biggest Stories
of the Year in Pro Football

10   The New York Jets limp out to a disappointing 1-4 start, but turn their season around behind the accurate passing of Chad Pennington. The Marshall product leads the NFL in passing efficiency and takes the Jets into the second round of the playoffs.

9   In part two of "new quarterbacks injecting life into their team," Tommy Maddox takes over for the ineffective Kordell Stewart and leads the Steelers into the playoffs. Maddox makes an inspirational return to the team after a scary injury in mid-November that left him temporarily paralyzed.

8   Kansas City running back Priest Holmes scores 24 touchdowns and leads the AFC in all-purpose yards despite missing the final two weeks of the season with a hip injury. He rushes for 100 yards in nine of his 14 games.

7   The NFL (and especially the Dallas Cowboys) welcomes the Houston Texans as the league's 32nd team. The Texans stun the Cowboys, 19-10, in Week 1 to become the second expansion team in history (joining the 1961 Minnesota Vikings) to win its first game.

6   In one of the tightest playoff races in recent memory, 14 of the 16 AFC teams enter Week 16 with a chance to make the postseason. Two teams with 9-7 records (the Jets and Browns) make the playoffs while three others don't.

5   Michael Vick truly arrives, and carries the Falcons into the playoffs and an upset win over Green Bay in Lambeau Field. His most memorable performance comes in a 30-24 victory over the Vikings, in which he rushes for 173 yards including a dazzling 46-yard TD run to win the game in overtime.

4   The 49ers stage an amazing 24-point comeback in the first round of the playoffs to defeat the Giants, 39-38. The game ends on a controversial non-pass interference call after a botched Giants field goal attempt.

3   With an 11-yard run against Seattle in Week 8, Dallas' Emmitt Smith breaks Walter Payton's career rushing record. Payton had held the record (16,726 yards) for almost two decades.

2   First-year coach Bill Callahan and MVP quarterback Rich Gannon lead the Raiders to the Super Bowl for the first time since 1984 when the team was in Los Angeles. Gannon sets an NFL record with ten 300-yard passing games.

1   The Tampa Bay Buccaneers throttle the favored Raiders, 48-21, in Super Bowl XXXVII. Tampa Bay's defense, among the greatest ever, picks off Rich Gannon five time and returns three of those for touchdowns. The win is especially sweet for coach Jon Gruden, who wins it all in his first year with the Bucs, beating his former team in the process.

career in Buffalo. There were huge seasons by workhorse runners Priest Holmes and LaDainian Tomlinson, although Kansas City and San Diego failed to take advantage. Tight end Jeremy Shockey (Giants), running back Clinton Portis (Broncos) and defensive end Julius Peppers (Panthers) made splashes as rookies, the former helping his team to the playoffs after a sluggish start. Cinderella quarterback Tom Brady led the league with 28 touchdown passes, but neither his Patriots nor Marshall Faulk and his battered Rams made it back to the postseason, much less the Super Bowl.

But when the smoke cleared, it was those Tampa Bay Buccaneers. A team that became familiar with finishing last finally emerged as the last team standing.

Fire those cannons!

Colossal Comebacks

The thrilling 2002 postseason saw two of the largest deficits overcome to win a playoff game in NFL history.

	Opp.	Points
1992 Buffalo	Houston	32
2002 San Francisco	NY Giants	24
1957 Detroit	San Francisco	20
1985 Miami	Cleveland	18
1972 Dallas	San Francisco	18
2002 Pittsburgh	Cleveland	17

Workhorses

Along with Emmitt Smith's many other NFL records, he holds the mark for consecutive seasons with at least 250 carries.

		Seasons
Emmitt Smith	1991-2002	12
Curtis Martin	1995-2002	8
Thurman Thomas	1989-1996	8
Eddie George	1996-2002	7
Eric Dickerson	1983-1989	7

Overboard on Overtimes

There have been 342 regular season overtime games in the NFL since the OT rule was established in 1974. The 2002 season had more than any other year.

Season	OT Games
2002	25
1995	21
2001	17
1997	17
1994	16
1986	16

Source: NFL Media.

Raising Arizona?

In the offseason, longtime Cowboy Emmitt Smith joined the Arizona Cardinals, a team he has single-handedly outperformed over his career.

	E. Smith	Cardinals
Rushing Yards	17,162	16,912
Rushing TDs	153	110
100-yd games	76	22

2002-2003
Season in Review

SPORTS ALMANAC

Final NFL Standings

Division champions (*) and wild card playoff qualifiers (†) are noted; division champions with two best records received first round byes. Number of seasons listed after each head coach refers to latest tenure with club through 2002 season.

American Football Conference

East Division

	W	L	T	PF	PA	vs Div	vs AFC
*NY Jets	9	7	0	359	336	4-2	6-6
New England	9	7	0	381	346	4-2	6-6
Miami	9	7	0	378	301	2-4	7-5
Buffalo	8	8	0	379	397	2-4	5-7

2002 Head Coaches: NY—Herman Edwards (2nd season); **NE**—Bill Belichick (3rd); **Mia**—Dave Wannstedt (3rd); **Buf**—Gregg Williams (2nd).

North Division

	W	L	T	PF	PA	vs Div	vs AFC
*Pittsburgh	10	5	1	390	345	6-0	8-4
†Cleveland	9	7	0	344	320	3-3	7-5
Baltimore	7	9	0	316	354	3-3	7-5
Cincinnati	2	14	0	279	456	0-6	1-11

2002 Head Coaches: Pit—Bill Cowher (11th season); **Cle**—Butch Davis (2nd); **Bal**—Brian Billick (4th); **Cin**—Dick LeBeau (3rd).

South Division

	W	L	T	PF	PA	vs Div	vs AFC
*Tennessee	11	5	0	367	324	6-0	9-3
†Indianapolis	10	6	0	349	313	4-2	8-4
Jacksonville	6	10	0	328	315	1-5	4-8
Houston	4	12	0	213	356	1-5	2-10

2002 Head Coaches: Ten—Jeff Fisher (9th season); **Ind**—Tony Dungy (1st); **Jax**—Tom Coughlin (8th); **Hou**—Dom Capers (1st).

West Division

	W	L	T	PF	PA	vs Div	vs AFC
*Oakland	11	5	0	450	304	4-2	9-3
Denver	9	7	0	392	344	3-3	5-7
San Diego	8	8	0	333	367	3-3	6-6
Kansas City	8	8	0	467	399	2-4	6-6

2002 Head Coaches: Oak—Bill Callahan (1st season); **Den**—Mike Shanahan (8th); **SD**—Marty Schottenheimer (1st); **KC**—Dick Vermeil (2nd).

National Football Conference

East Division

	W	L	T	PF	PA	vs Div	vs NFC
*Philadelphia	12	4	0	415	241	5-1	11-1
†NY Giants	10	6	0	320	279	5-1	8-4
Washington	7	9	0	307	365	1-5	4-8
Dallas	5	11	0	217	329	1-5	3-9

2002 Head Coaches: Phi—Andy Reid (4th season); **NY**—Jim Fassel (6th); **Wash**—Steve Spurrier (1st); **Dal**—Dave Campo (3rd).

North Division

	W	L	T	PF	PA	vs Div	vs NFC
*Green Bay	12	4	0	398	328	5-1	9-3
Minnesota	6	10	0	390	442	4-2	5-7
Chicago	4	12	0	281	379	2-4	3-9
Detroit	3	13	0	306	451	1-5	3-9

2002 Head Coaches: GB—Mike Sherman (3rd season); **Min**—Mike Tice (2nd); **Chi**—Dick Jauron (4th); **Det**—Marty Mornhinweg (2nd).

South Division

	W	L	T	PF	PA	vs Div	vs NFC
*Tampa Bay	12	4	0	346	196	4-2	9-3
†Atlanta	9	6	1	402	314	4-2	7-5
New Orleans	9	7	0	432	388	3-3	7-5
Carolina	7	9	0	258	302	1-5	4-8

2002 Head Coaches: TB—Jon Gruden (1st season); **Atl**—Dan Reeves (6th); **NO**—Jim Haslett (3rd); **Car**—John Fox (1st).

West Division

	W	L	T	PF	PA	vs Div	vs NFC
*San Francisco	10	6	0	367	351	5-1	8-4
St. Louis	7	9	0	316	369	4-2	5-7
Seattle	7	9	0	355	369	2-4	5-7
Arizona	5	11	0	262	417	1-5	5-7

2002 Head Coaches: SF—Steve Mariucci (6th season); **St.L**—Mike Martz (3rd); **Sea**—Mike Holmgren (4th); **Ariz**—Dave McGinnis (3rd).

Playoff Tiebreakers

Division Championship—AFC: NY Jets (9-7) qualified over New England (9-7) due to a better record in common games (8-4 to 7-5). The Jets qualified over Miami (9-7) due to a better division record (4-2 to 2-4). New England finished in second place over Miami due to a better division record (4-2 to 2-4).

Wildcard Berths—AFC: Cleveland (9-7) qualified over Denver (9-7) and New England (9-7) due to a better conference record (7-5 to Denver's 5-7 and New England's 6-6). Since Miami finished behind New England in East division, they were eliminated.

NFL Regular Season Individual Leaders
(* indicates rookies)

Passing Efficiency
(Minimum of 224 attempts)

AFC	Att	Cmp	Cmp Pct	Yds	Yds/ Att	TD	Long	Int	Sack/Lost	Rating Points
Chad Pennington, NYJ	399	275	68.9	3120	7.82	22	47	6	22/135	104.2
Rich Gannon, Oak	618	418	67.6	4689	7.59	26	75	10	36/214	97.3
Trent Green, KC	470	287	61.1	3690	7.85	26	99-td	13	26/141	92.6
Peyton Manning, Ind	591	392	66.3	4200	7.11	27	69	19	23/145	88.8
Drew Bledsoe, Buf	610	375	61.5	4359	7.15	24	73-td	15	54/369	86.0
Tom Brady, NE	601	373	62.1	3764	6.26	28	49-td	14	31/190	85.7
Mark Brunell, Jax	416	245	58.9	2788	6.70	17	79-td	7	34/210	85.7
Brian Griese, Den	436	291	66.7	3214	7.37	15	82-td	15	34/237	85.6
Jay Fiedler, Mia	292	179	61.3	2024	6.93	14	59-td	9	13/89	85.2
Tommy Maddox, Pit	377	234	62.1	2836	7.52	20	72-td	16	26/148	85.2
Steve McNair, Ten	492	301	61.2	3387	6.88	22	55	15	21/121	84.0
Jon Kitna, Cin	473	294	62.2	3178	6.72	16	72-td	16	24/159	79.1
Jeff Blake, Bal	295	165	55.9	2084	7.06	13	77-td	11	30/203	77.3
Drew Brees, SD	526	320	60.8	3284	6.24	17	52-td	16	24/180	76.9
Tim Couch, Cle	443	273	61.6	2842	6.42	18	78-td	18	30/213	76.8

NFC	Att	Cmp	Cmp Pct	Yds	Yds/ Att	TD	Long	Int	Sack/Lost	Rating Points
Brad Johnson, TB	451	281	62.3	3049	6.76	22	76-td	6	21/121	92.9
Matt Hasselbeck, Sea	419	267	63.7	3075	7.34	15	49	10	26/143	87.8
Donovan McNabb, Phi	361	211	58.4	2289	6.34	17	59-td	6	28/166	86.0
Jeff Garcia, SF	528	328	62.1	3344	6.33	21	76-td	10	17/93	85.6
Brett Favre, GB	551	341	61.9	3658	6.64	27	85-td	16	26/188	85.6
Kerry Collins, NYG	545	335	61.5	4073	7.47	19	82-td	14	24/152	85.4
Michael Vick, Atl	421	231	54.9	2936	6.97	16	74-td	8	33/206	81.6
Aaron Brooks, NO	528	283	53.6	3572	6.77	27	64	15	37/239	80.1
Jim Miller, Chi	314	180	57.3	1944	6.19	13	54	9	16/101	77.5
Rodney Peete, Car	381	223	58.5	2630	6.90	15	69	14	31/192	77.4
Daunte Culpepper, Min	549	333	60.7	3853	7.02	18	61	23	47/244	75.3
Shane Matthews, Wash	237	124	52.3	1251	5.28	11	43-td	6	9/54	72.6
Patrick Ramsey*, Wash	227	117	51.5	1539	6.78	9	62-td	8	18/132	71.8
Chad Hutchinson*, Dal	250	127	50.8	1555	6.22	7	58	8	34/265	66.3

Receptions

AFC	No	Yds	Avg	Long	TD
Marvin Harrison, Ind	143	1722	12.0	69	11
Hines Ward, Pit	112	1329	11.9	72-td	12
Eric Moulds, Buf	100	1292	12.9	70-td	10
Troy Brown, NE	97	890	9.2	38	3
Peerless Price, Buf	94	1252	13.3	73-td	9
Jerry Rice, Oak	92	1211	13.2	75	7
Charlie Garner, Oak	91	941	10.3	69-td	4
Laveranues Coles, NYJ	89	1264	14.2	43	5
Rod Smith, Den	89	1027	11.5	46	5
Tim Brown, Oak	81	930	11.5	45	2
Jimmy Smith, Jax	80	1027	12.8	47	7
Derrick Mason, Ten	79	1012	12.8	40	5
LaDainian Tomlinson, SD	79	489	6.2	30	1
Plaxico Burress, Pit	78	1325	17.0	62-td	7
Preist Holmes, KC	70	672	9.6	64-td	3

NFC	No	Yds	Avg	Long	TD
Randy Moss, Min	106	1347	12.7	60	7
Terrell Owens, SF	100	1300	13.0	76-td	13
Marty Booker, Chi	97	1189	12.3	54	6
Torry Holt, St.L	91	1302	14.3	58	7
Joe Horn, NO	88	1312	14.9	63	7
Amani Toomer, NYG	82	1343	16.4	82-td	8
Marshall Faulk, St.L	80	537	6.7	40	2
Isaac Bruce, St.L	79	1075	13.6	34-td	7
Koren Robinson, Sea	78	1240	15.9	83	5
Keyshawn Johnson, TB	76	1088	14.3	76-td	5
Jeremy Shockey*, NYG	74	894	12.1	30	2
Tai Streets, SF	72	756	10.5	47-td	5
Rod Gardner, Wash	71	1006	14.2	43-td	8
Donald Driver, GB	70	1064	15.2	85-td	9

Rushing Yards

AFC	Att	Yds	Avg	Long	TD
Ricky Williams, Mia	383	1853	4.8	63-td	16
LaDainian Tomlinson, SD	372	1683	4.5	76	14
Priest Holmes, KC	313	1615	5.2	56	21
Clinton Portis*, Den	273	1508	5.5	59	15
Travis Henry, Buf	325	1438	4.4	34	13
Jamal Lewis, Bal	308	1327	4.3	75	6
Fred Taylor, Jax	287	1314	4.6	63-td	8
Corey Dillon, Cin	314	1311	4.2	67-td	7
Eddie George, Ten	343	1165	3.4	35	12
Curtis Martin, NYJ	261	1094	4.2	35	7
Edgerrin James, Ind	277	989	3.6	20	2
Antowain Smith, NE	252	982	3.9	42-td	6
Charlie Garner, Oak	182	962	5.3	36-td	7
William Green*, Cle	243	887	3.7	64-td	6
Amos Zereoue, Pit	193	762	3.9	42	4

NFC	Att	Yds	Avg	Long	TD
Deuce McAllister, NO	325	1388	4.3	62	13
Tiki Barber, NYG	304	1387	4.6	70	11
Michael Bennett, Min	255	1296	5.1	85-td	5
Ahman Green, GB	286	1240	4.3	43	7
Shaun Alexander, Sea	295	1175	4.0	58	16
Duce Staley, Phi	269	1029	3.8	57	5
James Stewart, Det	231	1021	4.4	56	4
Emmitt Smith, Dal	254	975	3.8	30-td	5
Garrison Hearst, SF	215	972	4.5	40	8
Marshall Faulk, St.L	212	953	4.5	44	8
Warrick Dunn, Atl	230	927	4.0	59-td	7
Marcel Shipp, Ari	188	834	4.4	56	6
Stephen Davis, Wash	207	820	4.0	33	7
Michael Vick, Atl	113	777	6.9	46-td	8

New York Jets
Chad Pennington
Passing Efficiency

Indianapolis Colts
Marvin Harrison
Receptions

Kansas City Chiefs
Priest Holmes
Scoring

Miami Dolphins
Jason Taylor
Sacks

All-Purpose Yardage

AFC	Rush	Rec	Ret	Total	NFC	Rush	Rec	Ret	Total
Priest Holmes, KC	1615	672	0	2287	Michael Lewis, NO	15	200	2432	2647
Ricky Williams, Mia	1853	363	0	2216	Tiki Barber, NYG	1387	597	5	1989
LaDainian Tomlinson, SD	1683	489	0	2172	Steve Smith, Car	-4	872	1041	1909
Dante Hall, KC	54	322	1744	2120	Deuce McAllister, NO	1388	352	0	1740
Charlie Garner, Oak	962	941	0	1903	Brian Mitchell, Phi	0	0	1738	1738
Clinton Portis*, Den	1508	364	0	1872	Michael Bennett, Min	1296	351	0	1647
Jamal Lewis, Bal	1327	442	0	1769	Shaun Alexander, Sea	1175	460	0	1635
Travis Henry, Buf	1438	309	0	1747	Ahman Green, GB	1240	393	0	1633
Marvin Harrison, Ind	10	1722	0	1732	Duce Staley, Phi	1029	541	0	1570
Fred Taylor, Jax	1314	408	0	1722	Kevin Kasper, Den-Sea-Ari	19	180	1300	1499
Troy Walters, Ind	33	207	1420	1660	Marshall Faulk, St.L	953	537	0	1490
Antwaan Randle El*, Pit	134	489	990	1613	Allen Rossum, Atl	0	0	1452	1452
Corey Dillon, Cin	1311	298	0	1609	Randy Moss, Min	51	1347	11	1409
Chad Morton, NYJ	8	19	1560	1587	Terrence Wilkins, St.L	56	31	1316	1403
Andre' Davis*, Cle	7	420	1101	1528	Terrell Owens, SF	79	1300	0	1379

Ret column indicates all kickoff, punt, fumble and interception returns.

Scoring

Touchdowns

AFC	TD	Rush	Rec	Ret	Pts
Priest Holmes, KC	24	21	3	0	144
Clinton Portis*, Den	17	15	2	0	102
Ricky Williams, Mia	17	16	1	0	102
LaDainian Tomlinson, SD	15	14	1	0	90
Eddie George, Ten	14	12	2	0	86†
Travis Henry, Buf	14	13	1	0	84
Hines Ward, Pit	12	0	12	0	78†
Marvin Harrison, Ind	11	0	11	0	68†
Charlie Garner, Oak	11	7	4	0	66
Eric Moulds, Buf	10	0	10	0	60
Jerry Porter, Oak	9	0	9	0	58†
Four tied with 9 TD for 54 pts.					

NFC	TD	Rush	Rec	Ret	Pts
Shaun Alexander, Sea	18	16	2	0	108
Deuce McAllister, NO	16	13	3	0	96
Terrell Owens, SF	14	1	13	0	84
Tiki Barber, NYG	11	11	0	0	66
Moe Williams, Min	11	11	0	0	66
Daunte Culpepper, Min	10	10	0	0	62†
Marshall Faulk, St.L	10	8	2	0	60
Garrison Hearst, SF	9	8	1	0	56†
Donald Driver, GB	9	0	9	0	54
Warrick Dunn, Atl	9	7	2	0	54
Ahman Green, GB	9	7	2	0	54
Marcel Shipp, Ari	9	6	3	0	54

† Two-point conversions: Ward (3), Porter (2), George, Harrison, Culpepper and Hearst (1).

Kickers

AFC	PAT	FG	Long	Pts
Sebastien Janikowski, Oak	50/50	26/33	51	128
Jason Elam, Den	42/43	26/36	55	120
Morten Andersen, KC	51/51	22/26	50	117
Adam Vinatieri, NE	36/36	27/30	57	117
Mike Hollis, Buf	40/40	25/33	54	115
Olindo Mare, Mia	42/43	24/31	53	114
Joe Nedney, Ten	36/36	25/31	53	111
John Hall, NYJ	35/37	24/31	46	107
Mike Vanderjagt, Ind	34/34	23/31	54	103
Phil Dawson, Cle	34/35	22/28	52	100
Matt Stover, Bal	33/33	21/25	51	96
Steve Christie, SD	35/36	18/26	53	89
Neil Rackers, Cin	30/32	15/18	54	75

NFC	PAT	FG	Long	Pts
Jay Feely, Atl	42/43	32/40	52	138
David Akers, Phi	43/43	30/34	51	133
John Carney, NO	37/37	31/35	48	130
Martin Gramatica, TB	32/32	32/39	53	128
Ryan Longwell, GB	44/44	28/34	49	128
Matt Bryant*, NYG	30/32	26/32	47	108
Rian Lindell, Sea	38/38	23/29	52	107
Jose Cortez, SF-Wash	34/34	23/32	45	103
Jason Hanson, Det	31/31	23/28	49	100
Paul Edinger, Chi	29/29	22/28	53	95
Jeff Wilkins, St.L	37/37	19/25	47	94
Gary Anderson, Min	36/37	18/23	53	90
Bill Gramatica, Ari	29/29	15/21	50	74
Bill Cundiff*, Dal	25/25	12/19	48	61

NFL Regular Season Individual Leaders (Cont.)

Interceptions

AFC

	No	Yds	Long	TD
Rod Woodson, Oak.	8	225	98-td	2
Greg Wesley, KC	6	170	50	0
Marlon McCree, Jax	6	129	53	0
Nate Clements, Buf	6	82	42	1
Patrick Surtain, Mia	6	79	40-td	1
Lance Schulters, Ten	6	56	28	0

NFC

	No	Yds	Long	TD
Brian Kelly, TB	8	68	31	0
Darren Sharper, GB	7	233	89-td	1
Tony Parrish, SF	7	204	60	0
Seven tied with 5 int's each.				

Sacks

AFC

	No
Jason Taylor, Mia	18.5
Dwight Freeney*, Ind.	13.0
Roderick Coleman, Oak.	11.0
Two tied with 10.0 each.	

NFC

	No
Simeon Rice, TB	15.5
Andre Carter, SF	12.5
Hugh Douglas, Phi.	12.5
Kabeer Gbaja-Biamila, GB.	12.0
Leonard Little, St.L.	12.0
Julius Peppers*, Car	12.0

Punting

AFC

	No	Yds	Lg	Avg	In20
Chris Hanson, Jax	81	3583	64	44.2	27
Brian Moorman, Buf	66	2844	84	43.1	18
Tom Rouen, Den-NYG-Pit	44	1888	63	42.9	8
Shane Lechler, Oak	53	2251	70	42.5	18
Craig Hentrich, Ten	65	2725	56	41.9	28

NFC

	No	Yds	Lg	Avg	In20
Todd Sauerbrun, Car	104	4735	67	45.5	31
Scott Player, Ari	88	3864	58	43.9	28
Sean Landeta, Phi	52	2229	63	42.9	19
Tom Tupa, TB	90	3856	71	42.8	30
Brad Maynard, Chi	87	3679	75	42.3	26

Punt Returns

(Minimum of 20 returns)

AFC

	No	Yds	Avg	Long	TD
Santana Moss, NYJ	25	413	16.5	63-td	2
Dennis Northcutt, Cle	25	367	14.7	87-td	2
Dante Hall, KC	29	390	13.4	90-td	2
Bobby Shaw, Jax	25	310	12.4	69-td	1
Deltha O'Neal, Den	30	251	8.4	53	0

NFC

	No	Yds	Avg	Long	TD
Jimmy Williams, SF	20	336	16.8	89-td	1
Michael Lewis, NO	44	625	14.2	83-td	1
Brian Mitchell, Phi	46	567	12.3	76-td	1
Allen Rossum, Atl	24	288	12.0	36	0
Bobby Engram, Sea	21	224	10.7	61-td	1

Kickoff Returns

(Minimum of 20 returns)

AFC

	No	Yds	Avg	Long	TD
Kevin Faulk, NE	26	1725	27.9	87-td	2
Chad Morton, NYJ	58	1509	26.0	98-td	2
Reuben Droughns, Den	20	516	25.8	53	0
Brandon Bennett, Cin	49	1231	25.1	94-td	1
Marcus Knight, Oak	29	705	24.3	65	0

NFC

	No	Yds	Avg	Long	TD
MarTay Jenkins, Ari	20	559	28.0	95-td	1
Brian Mitchell, Phi	43	1162	27.0	57	0
Eddie Drummond*, Det	40	1039	26.0	91	0
Michael Lewis, NO	70	1807	25.8	97-td	2
Aaron Stecker, TB	37	934	25.2	67	0

Single Game Highs

Passing Yards

AFC

	Cmp/Att	Yds	TD
Tommy Maddox, Pit vs. Atl (11/10, OT)	28/41	473	4
Drew Bledsoe, Buf vs. Min (9/15, OT)	35/49	463	4
Drew Bledsoe, Buf vs. Oak (10/6)	32/53	417	2
Tom Brady, NE vs. KC (9/22, OT)	39/54	410	4
Rich Gannon, Oak vs. Pit (9/15)	43/64	403	1

NFC

	Cmp/Att	Yds	TD
Marc Bulger, St.L vs. SD (11/10)	36/48	453	4
M. Hasselbeck, Sea vs. SD (12/29, OT)	36/53	449	2
Matt Hasselbeck, Sea vs. SF (12/1)	30/55	427	3
Kerry Collins, NYG vs. Ind (12/22)	23/29	366	4
Matt Hasselbeck, Sea vs. KC (11/24)	25/36	362	3

Rushing Yards

AFC

	Car	Yds	TD
Ricky Williams, Mia vs. Buf (12/1)	27	228	2
Clinton Portis*, Den vs. Ari (12/29)	24	228	2
LaDainian Tomlinson, SD vs. Den (12/1, OT)	37	220	3
LaDainian Tomlinson, SD vs. NE (9/29)	27	217	2
Ricky Williams, Mia vs. Chi (12/9)	31	216	1

NFC

	Car	Yds	TD
Tiki Barber, NYG vs. Phi (12/28, OT)	32	203	0
Marshall Faulk, St.L vs. Sea (10/20)	32	183	3
Marshall Faulk, St.L vs. Ari (11/3)	27	178	1
Michael Vick, Atl vs. Min (12/1, OT)	10	173	2
Terry Jones, Ari vs. Sea (9/15)	24	173	1

Receiving Yards

AFC

	Ct	Yds	TD
Plaxico Burress, Pit vs. Atl (11/10, OT)	9	253	2
Shannon Sharpe, Den vs. KC (10/20, OT)	12	214	2
Peerless Price, Buf vs. Min (9/15, OT)	13	185	2
Troy Brown, NE vs. KC (9/22, OT)	16	176	1
Marvin Harrison, Ind vs. Cle (12/15)	9	172	2

NFC

	Ct	Yds	TD
Amani Toomer, NYG vs. Ind (12/22)	10	204	3
Marty Booker, Chi vs. Min (9/8)	8	198	1
Terrell Owens, SF vs. Oak (11/3, OT)	12	191	0
Quentin McCord, Atl vs. Det (12/22)	7	182	1
Darrell Jackson, Sea vs. Ari (9/15)	10	174	0

NFL Bests

Longest Field Goal
57 yds . . . . Adam Vinatieri, NE vs. Chi (11/10)

Longest Run from Scrimmage
85 yds . . . . Michael Bennett, Min vs. TB (11/3) TD

Longest Pass Play
99 yds . . . . Trent Green to Marc Boerigter*, KC vs. SD (12/22) TD

Longest Interception Return
102 yds . . . . Artrell Hawkins, Cin vs. Hou (11/3) TD

Longest Punt Return
95 yds . . . . Lamont Brightful*, Bal vs. Cin (11/10) TD

Longest Kickoff Return
100 yds . . . . Reggie Swinton, Dal vs. Phi (9/22) TD

NFL Regular Season Team Leaders

Offense

AFC	Points For	Avg	Rush	Pass	Total	Avg
Oakland	450	28.1	1762	4475	6237	389.8
Denver	392	24.5	2266	3824	6090	380.6
Kansas City	467	29.2	2378	3622	6000	375.0
Pittsburgh	390	24.4	2120	3832	5952	372.0
Indianapolis	349	21.8	1561	4055	5616	351.0
Buffalo	379	23.7	1596	3995	5591	349.4
Miami	378	23.6	2502	2890	5392	337.0
San Diego	333	20.8	2137	3188	5325	332.8
Tennessee	367	22.9	1952	3320	5272	329.5
Cincinnati	279	17.4	1730	3476	5206	325.4
New England	381	23.8	1508	3577	5085	317.8
NY Jets	359	22.4	1618	3418	5036	314.8
Cleveland	344	21.5	1615	3412	5027	314.2
Jacksonville	328	20.5	2089	2762	4851	303.2
Baltimore	316	19.8	1792	2847	4639	289.9
Houston	213	13.3	1347	2225	3572	223.3

NFC	Points For	Avg	Rush	Pass	Total	Avg
Minnesota	390	24.4	2507	3685	6192	387.0
NY Giants	320	20.0	1875	3951	5826	364.1
Seattle	355	22.2	1740	4078	5818	363.6
San Francisco	367	22.9	2244	3457	5701	356.3
Philadelphia	415	25.9	2220	3384	5604	350.3
Green Bay	398	24.9	1933	3627	5560	347.5
St. Louis	316	19.8	1405	4154	5559	347.4
Atlanta	402	25.1	2368	3167	5535	345.9
New Orleans	432	27.0	1764	3441	5205	325.3
Washington	307	19.2	1889	3254	5143	321.4
Tampa Bay	346	21.6	1557	3445	5002	312.6
Arizona	262	16.4	1823	2740	4563	285.2
Detroit	306	19.1	1477	2994	4471	279.4
Chicago	281	17.6	1344	3051	4395	274.7
Dallas	217	13.6	1754	2621	4375	273.4
Carolina	258	16.1	1586	2694	4280	267.5

Defense

AFC	Points Opp	Avg	Rush	Pass	Total	Avg
Miami	301	18.8	1554	3102	4656	291.0
Denver	344	21.5	1489	3337	4826	301.6
Pittsburgh	345	21.6	1375	3460	4835	302.2
Indianapolis	313	19.6	1992	2917	4909	306.8
Tennessee	324	20.3	1424	3540	4964	310.3
Oakland	304	19.0	1453	3526	4979	311.2
Buffalo	397	24.8	2122	3067	5189	324.3
Houston	356	22.3	2089	3141	5230	326.9
Cincinnati	456	28.5	2003	3262	5265	329.1
Jacksonville	315	19.7	2071	3264	5335	333.4
Cleveland	320	20.0	2079	3269	5348	334.3
Baltimore	354	22.1	1762	3591	5353	334.6
New England	346	21.6	2198	3179	5377	336.1
NY Jets	336	21.0	1973	3490	5463	341.4
San Diego	367	22.9	1739	4295	6034	377.1
Kansas City	399	24.9	2067	4181	6248	390.5

NFC	Points Opp	Avg	Rush	Pass	Total	Avg
Tampa Bay	196	12.3	1554	2490	4044	252.8
Carolina	302	18.9	1653	2993	4646	290.4
Philadelphia	241	15.1	1660	3094	4754	297.1
Washington	365	22.8	1754	3033	4787	299.2
NY Giants	279	17.4	1830	3119	4949	309.3
Green Bay	328	20.5	1998	2987	4985	311.6
St. Louis	369	23.1	1816	3209	5025	314.1
San Francisco	351	21.9	1652	3506	5158	322.4
Dallas	329	20.6	1818	3449	5267	329.2
Atlanta	314	19.6	2047	3287	5334	333.4
Chicago	379	23.7	2076	3530	5606	350.4
Minnesota	442	27.6	1666	4103	5769	360.6
New Orleans	388	24.3	1991	3805	5796	362.3
Seattle	369	23.1	2441	3411	5852	365.8
Arizona	417	26.1	2146	3874	6020	376.3
Detroit	451	28.2	1967	4150	6117	382.3

Overall Club Rankings

Combined AFC and NFC rankings by yards gained on offense and yards given up on defense. Teams are ranked by offense, with AFC teams in *italics*.

	Offense Rush	Pass	Rank	Defense Rush	Pass	Rank
Oakland	18	1	1	3	23	11
Minnesota	1	9	2	10	29	26
Denver	5	8	3	4	17	6
Kansas City	3	11	4	24	31	32
Pittsburgh	9	7	5	1	20	7
NY Giants	14	6	6	16	9	9
Seattle	20	3	7	32	18	28
San Francisco	6	14	8	7	22	14
Indianapolis	26	4	9	20	2	8
Philadelphia	7	19	10	9	7	4
Buffalo	24	5	11	29	6	15
Green Bay	12	10	12	21	3	12
St. Louis	30	2	13	14	12	13
Atlanta	4	23	14	23	16	19
Miami	2	26	15	5t	8	3
San Diego	8	22	16	11	32	30

	Offense Rush	Pass	Rank	Defense Rush	Pass	Rank
Tennessee	11	20	17	2	25	10
Cincinnati	21	13	18	22	13	17
New Orleans	17	16	19	27	27	27
Washington	13	21	20	12	5	5
New England	28	12	21	31	11	23
NY Jets	22	17	22	18	21	24
Cleveland	23	18	23	27	15	21
Tampa Bay	27	15	24	5t	1	1
Jacksonville	10	28	25	25	14	20
Baltimore	16	27	26	13	26	22
Arizona	15	29	27	30	28	29
Detroit	29	25	28	17	30	31
Chicago	32	24	29	26	24	25
Dallas	19	31	30	15	19	18
Carolina	25	30	31	8	4	2
Houston	31	32	32	28	10	16

AFC Team by Team Results

(*) indicates an overtime game. Note: the NFL set a single-season record in 2002 with 25 overtime games.

Baltimore Ravens (7-9)

at Carolina	L, 7-10
Tampa Bay	L, 0-25
OPEN	—
Denver	W, 34-23
at Cleveland	W, 26-21
at Indianapolis	L, 20-22
Jacksonville	W, 17-10
Pittsburgh	L, 18-31
at Atlanta	L, 17-20
Cincinnati	W, 38-27
at Miami	L, 7-26
Tennessee	W, 13-12
at Cincinnati	W, 27-23
New Orleans	L, 25-37
at Houston	W, 23-19
Cleveland	L, 13-14
at Pittsburgh	L, 31-34

Buffalo Bills (8-8)

NY Jets	L, 31-37*
at Minnesota	W, 45-39*
at Denver	L, 23-28
Chicago	W, 33-27*
Oakland	L, 31-49
at Houston	W, 31-24
at Miami	W, 23-10
Detroit	W, 24-17
N. England	L, 7-38
OPEN	—
at Kansas City	L, 16-17
at NY Jets	L, 13-31
Miami	W, 38-21
at N. England	L, 17-27
San Diego	W, 20-13
at Green Bay	L, 0-10
Cincinnati	W, 27-9

Cincinnati Bengals (2-14)

San Diego	L, 6-34
at Cleveland	L, 7-20
at Atlanta	L, 3-30
Tampa Bay	L, 7-35
at Indianapolis	L, 21-28
Pittsburgh	L, 7-34
OPEN	—
Tennessee	L, 24-30
at Houston	W, 38-3
at Baltimore	L, 27-38
Cleveland	L, 20-27
at Pittsburgh	L, 21-29
Baltimore	L, 23-27
at Carolina	L, 31-52
Jacksonville	L, 15-29
New Orleans	W, 20-13
at Buffalo	L, 9-27

Cleveland Browns (9-7)

Kansas City	L, 39-40
Cincinnati	W, 20-7
at Tennessee	W, 31-28*
at Pittsburgh	L, 13-16*
Baltimore	L, 21-26
at Tampa Bay	L, 3-17
Houston	W, 34-17
at NY Jets	W, 24-21
Pittsburgh	L, 20-23
OPEN	—
at Cincinnati	W, 27-20
at N. Orleans	W, 24-15
Carolina	L, 6-13
at Jacksonville	W, 21-20
Indianapolis	L, 23-28
at Baltimore	W, 14-13
Atlanta	W, 24-16

Denver Broncos (9-7)

St. Louis	W, 23-16
at San Fran.	W, 24-14
Buffalo	W, 28-23
at Baltimore	L, 23-34
San Diego	W, 26-9
Miami	L, 22-24
at Kansas City	W, 37-34*
at N. England	W, 24-16
OPEN	—
Oakland	L, 10-34
at Seattle	W, 31-9
Indianapolis	L, 20-23*
at San Diego	L, 27-30*
at NY Jets	L, 13-19
Kansas City	W, 31-24
at Oakland	L, 16-28
Arizona	W, 37-7

Houston Texans (4-12)

Dallas	W, 19-10
at San Diego	L, 3-24
Indianapolis	L, 3-23
at Philadelphia	L, 17-35
OPEN	—
Buffalo	L, 24-31
at Cleveland	L, 17-34
at Jacksonville	W, 21-19
Cincinnati	L, 3-38
at Tennessee	L, 10-17
Jacksonville	L, 21-24
NY Giants	W, 16-14
at Indianapolis	L, 3-19
at Pittsburgh	W, 24-6
Baltimore	L, 19-23
at Washington	L, 10-26
Tennessee	L, 3-13

Indianapolis Colts (10-6)

at Jacksonville	W, 28-25
Miami	L, 13-21
at Houston	W, 23-3
OPEN	—
Cincinnati	W, 28-21
Baltimore	W, 22-20
at Pittsburgh	L, 10-28
at Washington	L, 21-26
Tennessee	L, 15-23
at Philadelphia	W, 35-13
Dallas	W, 20-3
at Denver	W, 23-20*
Houston	W, 19-3
at Tennessee	L, 17-27
at Cleveland	W, 28-23
NY Giants	L, 27-44
Jacksonville	L, 20-13

Jacksonville Jaguars (6-10)

Indianapolis	L, 25-28
at Kansas City	W, 23-16
OPEN	—
NY Jets	W, 28-3
Philadelphia	W, 28-25
at Tennessee	L, 14-23
at Baltimore	L, 10-17
Houston	L, 19-21
at NY Giants	L, 17-24
Washington	W, 26-7
at Houston	W, 24-21
at Dallas	L, 19-21
Pittsburgh	L, 23-25
Cleveland	L, 20-21
at Cincinnati	W, 29-15
Tennessee	L, 10-28
at Indianapolis	L, 13-20

Kansas City Chiefs (8-8)

at Cleveland	W, 40-39
Jacksonville	L, 16-23
at N. England	L, 38-41*
Miami	W, 48-30
at NY Jets	W, 29-25
at San Diego	L, 34-35
Denver	L, 34-37*
Oakland	W, 20-10
OPEN	—
at San Fran.	L, 13-17
Buffalo	W, 17-16
at Seattle	L, 32-39
Arizona	W, 49-0
St. Louis	W, 49-10
at Denver	L, 24-31
San Diego	W, 24-22
at Oakland	L, 0-24

Miami Dolphins (9-7)

Detroit	W, 49-21
at Indianapolis	W, 21-13
NY Jets	W, 30-3
at Kansas City	L, 30-48
N. England	W, 26-13
at Denver	W, 24-22
Buffalo	L, 10-23
OPEN	—
at Green Bay	L, 10-24
at NY Jets	L, 10-13
Baltimore	W, 26-7
San Diego	W, 30-3
at Buffalo	L, 21-38
Chicago	W, 27-9
Oakland	W, 23-17
at Minnesota	L, 17-20
at N. England	L, 24-27*

New England Patriots (9-7)

Pittsburgh	W, 30-14
at NY Jets	W, 44-7
Kansas City	W, 41-38*
at San Diego	L, 14-21
at Miami	L, 13-26
Green Bay	L, 10-28
OPEN	—
Denver	L, 16-24
at Buffalo	W, 38-7
at Chicago	W, 33-30
at Oakland	L, 20-27
Minnesota	W, 24-17
at Detroit	W, 20-12
Buffalo	W, 27-17
at Tennessee	L, 7-24
NY Jets	L, 17-30
Miami	W, 27-24*

New York Jets (9-7)

at Buffalo	W, 37-31*
N. England	L, 7-44
at Miami	L, 3-30
at Jacksonville	L, 3-28
Kansas City	L, 25-29
OPEN	—
Minnesota	W, 20-7
Cleveland	L, 21-24
at San Diego	W, 44-13
Miami	W, 13-10
at Detroit	W, 31-14
Buffalo	W, 31-13
at Oakland	L, 20-26
Denver	W, 19-13
at Chicago	L, 13-20
at N. England	W, 30-17
Green Bay	W, 42-17

Oakland Raiders (11-5)

Seattle	W, 31-17
at Pittsburgh	W, 30-17
OPEN	—
Tennessee	W, 52-25
at Buffalo	W, 49-31
at St. Louis	L, 13-28
San Diego	L, 21-27*
at Kansas City	L, 10-20
San Fran.	L, 20-23*
at Denver	W, 34-10
N. England	W, 27-20
at Arizona	W, 41-20
NY Jets	W, 26-20
at San Diego	W, 27-7
at Miami	L, 17-23
Denver	W, 28-16
Kansas City	W, 24-0

Pittsburgh Steelers (10-5-1)

at N. England	L, 14-30
Oakland	L, 17-30
OPEN	—
Cleveland	W, 16-13*
at New Orleans	L, 29-32
at Cincinnati	W, 34-7
Indianapolis	W, 28-10
at Baltimore	W, 31-18
at Cleveland	W, 23-20
Atlanta	T, 34-34*
at Tennessee	L, 23-31
Cincinnati	W, 29-21
at Jacksonville	W, 25-23
Houston	L, 6-24
Carolina	W, 30-14
at Tampa Bay	W, 17-7
Baltimore	W, 34-31

San Diego Chargers (8-8)

at Cincinnati	W, 34-6
Houston	W, 24-3
at Arizona	W, 23-15
N. England	W, 21-14
at Denver	L, 9-26
Kansas City	W, 35-34
at Oakland	W, 27-21*
OPEN	—
NY Jets	L, 13-44
at St. Louis	L, 24-28
San Fran.	W, 20-17*
at Miami	L, 3-30
Denver	W, 30-27*
Oakland	L, 7-27
at Buffalo	L, 13-20
at Kansas City	L, 22-24
Seattle	L, 28-31*

Tennessee Titans (11-5)

Philadelphia	W, 27-24
at Dallas	L, 13-21
Cleveland	L, 28-31*
at Oakland	L, 25-52
Washington	L, 14-31
Jacksonville	W, 23-14
OPEN	—
at Cincinnati	W, 30-24
at Indianapolis	W, 23-15
Houston	W, 17-10
Pittsburgh	W, 31-23
at Baltimore	L, 12-13
at NY Giants	W, 32-29*
Indianapolis	W, 27-17
N. England	W, 24-7
at Jacksonville	W, 28-10
at Houston	W, 13-3

NFC Team by Team Results

(*) indicates overtime game

Arizona Cardinals (5-11)

at Washington	L, 23-31
at Seattle	W, 24-13
San Diego	L, 15-23
NY Giants	W, 21-7
at Carolina	W, 16-13
OPEN	—
Dallas	W, 9-6*
at San Fran.	L, 28-38
St. Louis	L, 14-27
Seattle	L, 6-27
at Philadelphia	L, 14-38
Oakland	L, 20-41
at Kansas City	L, 0-49
Detroit	W, 23-20*
at St. Louis	L, 28-30
San Fran.	L, 14-17
at Denver	L, 7-37

Atlanta Falcons (9-6-1)

at Green Bay	L, 34-37*
Chicago	L, 13-14
Cincinnati	W, 30-3
OPEN	—
Tampa Bay	L, 6-20
at NY Giants	W, 17-10
Carolina	W, 30-0
at New Orleans	W, 37-35
Baltimore	W, 20-17
at Pittsburgh	T, 34-34*
New Orleans	W, 24-17
at Carolina	W, 41-0
at Minnesota	W, 30-24*
at Tampa Bay	L, 10-34
Seattle	L, 24-30*
Detroit	W, 36-15
at Cleveland	L, 16-24

Carolina Panthers (7-9)

Baltimore	W, 10-7
Detroit	W, 31-7
at Minnesota	W, 21-14
at Green Bay	L, 14-17
Arizona	L, 13-16
at Dallas	L, 13-14
at Atlanta	L, 0-30
Tampa Bay	L, 9-12
OPEN	—
New Orleans	L, 24-34
at Tampa Bay	L, 10-23
Atlanta	L, 0-41
at Cleveland	W, 13-6
Cincinnati	W, 52-31
at Pittsburgh	L, 14-30
Chicago	W, 24-14
at New Orleans	W, 10-6

Chicago Bears (4-12)

Minnesota	W, 27-23
at Atlanta	W, 14-13
New Orleans	L, 23-29
at Buffalo	L, 27-33*
Green Bay	L, 21-34
OPEN	—
at Detroit	L, 20-23*
at Minnesota	L, 7-25
Philadelphia	L, 13-19
N. England	L, 30-33
at St. Louis	L, 16-21
Detroit	W, 20-17*
at Green Bay	L, 20-30
at Miami	L, 9-27
NY Jets	L, 20-13
at Carolina	L, 14-24
Tampa Bay	L, 0-15

Dallas Cowboys (5-11)

at Houston	L, 10-19
Tennessee	W, 21-13
at Philadelphia	L, 13-44
at St. Louis	W, 13-10
NY Giants	L, 17-21
Carolina	W, 14-13
at Arizona	L, 6-9*
Seattle	L, 14-17
at Detroit	L, 7-9
OPEN	—
at Indianapolis	L, 3-20
Jacksonville	W, 21-19
Washington	W, 27-20
San Fran.	L, 27-31
at NY Giants	L, 7-37
Philadelphia	L, 3-27
at Washington	L, 14-20

Detroit Lions (3-13)

at Miami	L, 21-49
at Carolina	L, 7-31
Green Bay	L, 31-37
New Orleans	W, 26-21
OPEN	—
at Minnesota	L, 24-31
Chicago	W, 23-20*
at Buffalo	L, 17-24
Dallas	W, 9-7
at Green Bay	L, 14-40
NY Jets	L, 14-31
at Chicago	L, 17-20*
N. England	L, 12-20
at Arizona	L, 20-23*
Tampa Bay	L, 20-23
at Atlanta	L, 15-36
Minnesota	L, 36-38

Green Bay Packers (12-4)

Atlanta	W, 37-34*
at New Orleans	L, 20-35
at Detroit	W, 37-31
Carolina	W, 17-14
at Chicago	W, 34-21
at N. England	W, 28-10
Washington	W, 30-9
OPEN	—
Miami	W, 24-10
Detroit	W, 40-14
at Minnesota	L, 21-31
at Tampa Bay	L, 7-21
Chicago	W, 30-20
Minnesota	W, 26-22
at San Fran.	W, 20-14
Buffalo	W, 10-0
at NY Jets	L, 17-42

Minnesota Vikings (6-10)

at Chicago	L, 23-27
Buffalo	L, 39-45*
Carolina	L, 14-21
at Seattle	L, 23-48
OPEN	—
Detroit	W, 31-24
at NY Jets	L, 7-20
Chicago	W, 25-7
at Tampa Bay	L, 24-38
NY Giants	L, 20-27
Green Bay	W, 31-21
at N. England	L, 17-24
Atlanta	L, 24-30*
at Green Bay	L, 22-26
at New Orleans	W, 32-31
Miami	W, 20-17
at Detroit	W, 38-36

NFC Team by Team Results (Cont.)

New Orleans Saints (9-7)

at Tampa Bay	W, 26-20*
Green Bay	W, 35-20
at Chicago	W, 29-23
at Detroit	L, 21-26
Pittsburgh	W, 32-29
at Washington	W, 43-27
San Fran.	W, 35-27
Atlanta	L, 35-37
OPEN	—
at Carolina	W, 34-24
at Atlanta	L, 17-24
Cleveland	L, 15-24
Tampa Bay	W, 23-20
at Baltimore	W, 37-25
Minnesota	L, 31-32
at Cincinnati	L, 13-20
Carolina	L, 6-10

New York Giants (10-6)

San Fran.	L, 13-16
at St. Louis	W, 26-21
Seattle	W, 9-6
at Arizona	L, 7-21
at Dallas	W, 21-17
Atlanta	L, 10-17
OPEN	—
at Philadelphia	L, 3-17
Jacksonville	W, 24-17
at Minnesota	W, 27-20
Washington	W, 19-17
at Houston	L, 14-16
Tennessee	L, 29-32*
at Washington	W, 27-21
Dallas	W, 37-7
at Indianapolis	W, 44-27
Philadelphia	W, 10-7*

Philadelphia Eagles (12-4)

at Tennessee	L, 24-27
at Washington	W, 37-7
Dallas	W, 44-13
Houston	W, 35-17
at Jacksonville	L, 25-28
OPEN	—
Tampa Bay	W, 20-10
NY Giants	W, 17-3
at Chicago	W, 19-13
Indianapolis	L, 13-35
Arizona	W, 38-14
at San Fran.	W, 38-17
St. Louis	W, 10-3
at Seattle	W, 27-20
Washington	W, 34-21
at Dallas	W, 27-3
at NY Giants	L, 7-10*

St. Louis Rams (7-9)

at Denver	L, 16-23
NY Giants	L, 21-26
at Tampa Bay	L, 14-26
Dallas	L, 10-13
at San Fran.	L, 13-37
Oakland	W, 28-13
Seattle	W, 37-20
OPEN	—
at Arizona	W, 27-14
San Diego	W, 28-24
Chicago	W, 21-16
at Washington	L, 17-20
at Philadelphia	L, 3-10
at Kansas City	L, 10-49
Arizona	W, 30-28
at Seattle	L, 10-30
San Fran.	W, 31-20

San Francisco 49ers (10-6)

at NY Giants	W, 16-13
Denver	L, 14-24
Washington	W, 20-10
OPEN	—
St. Louis	W, 37-13
at Seattle	W, 28-21
at New Orleans	L, 27-35
Arizona	W, 38-28
at Oakland	W, 23-20*
Kansas City	W, 17-13
at San Diego	L, 17-20*
Philadelphia	L, 17-38
Seattle	W, 31-24
at Dallas	W, 31-27
Green Bay	L, 14-20
at Arizona	W, 17-14
at St. Louis	L, 20-31

Seattle Seahawks (7-9)

at Oakland	L, 17-31
Arizona	L, 13-24
at NY Giants	L, 6-9
Minnesota	W, 48-23
OPEN	—
San Fran.	L, 21-28
at St. Louis	L, 20-37
at Dallas	W, 17-14
Washington	L, 3-14
at Arizona	W, 27-6
Denver	L, 9-31
Kansas City	W, 39-32
at San Fran.	L, 24-31
Philadelphia	L, 20-27
at Atlanta	W, 30-24*
St. Louis	W, 30-10
at San Diego	W, 31-28*

Tampa Bay Buccaneers (12-4)

New Orleans	L, 20-26*
at Baltimore	W, 25-0
St. Louis	W, 26-14
at Cincinnati	W, 35-7
at Atlanta	W, 20-6
Cleveland	W, 17-3
at Philadelphia	L, 10-20
at Carolina	W, 12-9
Minnesota	W, 38-24
OPEN	—
Carolina	W, 23-10
Green Bay	W, 21-7
at New Orleans	L, 20-23
Atlanta	W, 34-10
at Detroit	W, 23-20
Pittsburgh	L, 7-17
at Chicago	W, 15-0

Washington Redskins (7-9)

Arizona	W, 31-23
Philadelphia	L, 7-37
at San Fran.	L, 10-20
OPEN	—
at Tennessee	W, 31-14
New Orleans	L, 27-43
at Green Bay	L, 9-30
Indianapolis	W, 26-21
at Seattle	W, 14-3
at Jacksonville	L, 7-26
at NY Giants	L, 17-19
St. Louis	W, 20-17
at Dallas	L, 20-27
NY Giants	L, 21-27
at Philadelphia	L, 21-34
Houston	W, 26-10
Dallas	W, 20-14

Takeaways/Giveaways

AFC	Takeaways Int	Fum	Total	Giveaways Int	Fum	Total	Net Diff
Kansas City	18	13	31	13	2	15	+16
Jacksonville	14	13	27	9	6	15	+12
Oakland	21	10	31	10	9	19	+12
New England	18	11	29	14	10	24	+5
NY Jets	15	8	23	10	9	19	+4
Tennessee	18	11	29	15	10	25	+4
San Diego	17	10	27	16	8	24	+3
Miami	21	9	30	15	15	30	0
Pittsburgh	19	17	36	22	14	36	0
Baltimore	25	6	31	14	18	32	-1
Cleveland	17	12	29	22	9	31	-2
Denver	9	13	22	20	7	27	-5
Indianapolis	10	17	27	19	13	32	-5
Houston	10	11	21	15	14	29	-8
Buffalo	10	9	19	15	16	31	-12
Cincinnati	9	11	20	22	13	35	-15
TOTALS	251	181	432	251	173	424	+8

NFC	Takeaways Int	Fum	Total	Giveaways Int	Fum	Total	Net Diff
Green Bay	24	21	45	16	12	28	+17
Tampa Bay	31	7	38	10	11	21	+17
Philadelphia	15	23	38	11	13	24	+14
Atlanta	24	15	39	12	15	27	+12
San Francisco	19	8	27	10	7	17	+10
New Orleans	20	18	38	15	15	30	+8
Seattle	19	11	30	16	12	28	+2
NY Giants	11	14	25	14	13	27	-2
Dallas	19	11	30	16	18	34	-4
Carolina	17	16	33	22	18	40	-7
Chicago	9	19	28	18	17	35	-7
Detroit	10	14	24	25	6	31	-7
Arizona	17	8	25	22	13	35	-10
Washington	14	12	26	20	20	40	-14
Minnesota	16	7	23	23	18	41	-18
St. Louis	12	14	26	27	18	45	-19
TOTALS	277	218	495	277	226	503	-8

AFC Team by Team Statistics

Players with more than one team during the regular season are listed with club they ended season with; (*) indicates rookies.

Baltimore Ravens

Passing (5 Att)

	Att	Cmp	Pct	Yds	TD	Rate
Jeff Blake	.295	165	55.9	2084	13	77.3
Chris Redman	.182	97	55.3	1034	7	76.1

Interceptions: Blake 11, Redman 3.

Top Receivers

	No	Yds	Avg	Long	TD
Todd Heap	.68	836	12.3	43	6
Travis Taylor	.61	869	14.2	64	6
Jamal Lewis	.47	442	9.4	77-td	1
Brandon Stokley	.24	357	14.9	35-td	2
Chester Taylor*	.14	129	9.2	20-td	2
Terry Jones*	.11	106	9.6	27	1

Top Rushers

	Car	Yds	Avg	Long	TD
Jamal Lewis	.308	1327	4.3	75	6
Chester Taylor*	.33	122	3.7	17	0
Jeff Blake	.39	106	2.7	17	1
Travis Taylor	.11	105	9.5	39	0
Alan Ricard	.14	58	4.1	19-td	2

Most Touchdowns

	TD	Run	Rec	Ret	Pts
Jamal Lewis	.7	6	1	0	42
Todd Heap	.6	0	6	0	38
Travis Taylor	.6	0	6	0	36
Alan Ricard	.3	2	0	1	18

Three tied with 2 TD each.

2-Pt. Conversions: (2-3) Heap, C. Taylor.

Kicking

	PAT/Att	FG/Att	Lg	Pts
Matt Stover	.33/33	21/25	51	96
J.R. Jenkins*	.0/0	0/1	—	0

Punts (10 or more)

	No	Yds	Long	Avg	In20
Dave Zastudil*	.81	3368	61	41.6	31

Most Interceptions
Edward Reed* 5

Most Sacks
Peter Boulware 7

Buffalo Bills

Passing (5 Att)

	Att	Cmp	Pct	Yds	TD	Rate
Drew Bledsoe	.610	375	61.5	4359	24	86.0

Interceptions: Bledsoe 15.

Top Receivers

	No	Yds	Avg	Long	TD
Eric Moulds	.100	1287	12.9	70-td	10
Peerless Price	.94	1252	13.3	73-td	9
Larry Centers	.43	388	9.0	25	0
Travis Henry	.43	309	7.2	26-td	1
Josh Reed*	.37	514	13.9	42	2
Jay Riemersma	.32	350	10.9	29	0

Top Rushers

	Car	Yds	Avg	Long	TD
Travis Henry	.325	1438	4.4	34	13
Drew Bledsoe	.27	67	2.5	11	2
Larry Centers	.11	56	5.1	13	2
Shawn Bryson	.13	35	2.7	10	0

Most Touchdowns

	TD	Run	Rec	Ret	Pts
Travis Henry	.14	13	1	0	84
Eric Moulds	.10	0	10	0	60
Peerless Price	.9	0	9	0	54
Drew Bledsoe	.2	2	0	0	12
Larry Centers	.2	2	0	0	12
Dave Moore	.2	0	2	0	12
Josh Reed*	.2	0	2	0	12

2-Pt. Conversions: (0-2).

Kicking

	PAT/Att	FG/Att	Lg	Pts
Mike Hollis	.40/40	25/33	54	115

Punts (10 or more)

	No	Yds	Long	Avg	In20
Brian Moorman	.66	2844	84	43.1	18

Most Interceptions
Nate Clements 6

Most Sacks
Aaron Schobel 8.5

Cincinnati Bengals

Passing (5 Att)

	Att	Cmp	Pct	Yds	TD	Rate
Jon Kitna	.473	294	62.2	3178	16	79.1
Gus Frerotte	.85	44	51.8	437	1	46.1
Akili Smith	.33	12	36.4	117	0	34.5

Interceptions: Kitna 16, Frerotte 5, Smith 1.

Top Receivers

	No	Yds	Avg	Long	TD
Chad Johnson	.69	1166	16.9	72-td	5
Peter Warrick	.53	606	11.4	37-td	6
Ron Dugans	.47	421	9.0	31	0
Corey Dillon	.43	298	6.9	19	0
T.J. Houshmandzadeh	.41	492	12.0	31	1
Matt Schobel	.27	212	7.9	20-td	2

Top Rushers

	Car	Yds	Avg	Long	TD
Corey Dillon	.314	1311	4.2	67-td	7
Brandon Bennett	.33	155	4.7	29	0
Rudi Johnson	.17	67	3.9	13	0
Nicolas Luchey	.12	59	4.9	10	2

Most Touchdowns

	TD	Run	Rec	Ret	Pts
Corey Dillon	.7	7	0	0	42
Peter Warrick	.6	0	6	0	36
Chad Johnson	.5	0	5	0	30
John Kitna	.4	4	0	0	24

Three tied with 2 TD each.

2-Pt. Conversions: (0-2).

Kicking

	PAT/Att	FG/Att	Lg	Pts
Neil Rackers	.30/32	15/18	54	75

Punts (10 or more)

	No	Yds	Long	Avg	In20
Nick Harris	.65	2608	57	40.1	11

Most Interceptions
Kevin Kaesviharn 2
Artrell Hawkins

Most Sacks
Justin Smith 6.5

Cleveland Browns

Passing (5 Att)

	Att	Cmp	Pct	Yds	TD	Rate
Tim Couch	.443	273	61.6	2842	18	76.8
Kelly Holcomb	.106	64	60.4	790	8	92.9

Interceptions: Couch 18, Holcomb 4.

Top Receivers

	No	Yds	Avg	Long	TD
Kevin Johnson	.67	703	10.5	30-td	4
Jamel White	.63	452	7.2	33	0
Quincy Morgan	.56	964	17.2	78-td	7
Dennis Northcutt	.38	601	15.8	43-td	5
Andre' Davis*	.37	420	11.4	31	6
Mark Campbell	.25	179	7.2	26	3

Top Rushers

	Car	Yds	Avg	Long	TD
William Green*	.243	887	3.7	64-td	6
Jamel White	.106	470	4.4	54	3
Dennis Northcutt	.8	104	13.0	36-td	1
Tim Couch	.23	77	3.3	14	0

Most Touchdowns

	TD	Run	Rec	Ret	Pts
Dennis Northcutt	.8	1	5	2	50
Quincy Morgan	.7	0	7	0	44
Andre' Davis*	.7	0	6	1	42
William Green*	.6	6	0	0	36
Kevin Johnson	.4	0	4	0	24

Two tied with 3 TD each.

2-Pt. Conversions: (2-5) Northcutt, Morgan.

Kicking

	PAT/Att	FG/Att	Lg	Pts
Phil Dawson	.34/35	22/28	52	100

Punts (10 or more)

	No	Yds	Long	Avg	In20
Chris Gardocki	.81	3388	59	41.8	27

Most Interceptions
Earl Little 4

Most Sacks
Mark Word 8

Denver Broncos

Passing (5 Att)

	Att	Cmp	Pct	Yds	TD	Rate
Brian Griese	.436	291	66.7	3214	15	85.6
Steve Beuerlein	...117	68	58.1	925	6	82.7

Interceptions: Griese 15, Beuerlein 5.

Top Receivers

	No	Yds	Avg	Long	TD
Rod Smith	.89	1027	11.5	46	5
Ed McCaffrey	.69	903	13.1	69-td	2
Shannon Sharpe	61	686	11.2	82-td	3
Ashley Lelie	.35	525	15.0	48	2
Clinton Portis*	33	364	11.0	66-td	2
Dwayne Carswell	21	189	9.0	19	1

Top Rushers

	Car	Yds	Avg	Long	TD
Clinton Portis*	273	1508	5.5	59	15
Mike Anderson	.84	386	4.6	32	2
Olandis Gary	37	147	4.0	26	1
Brian Griese	37	107	2.9	13	1

Most Touchdowns

	TD	Run	Rec	Ret	Pts
Clinton Portis*	.17	15	2	0	102
Rod Smith	.5	0	5	0	30
Mike Anderson	.4	2	2	0	24
Shannon Sharpe	.3	0	3	0	18

Five tied with 2 TD each.

2-Pt. Conversions: (0-2).

Kicking

	PAT/Att	FG/Att	Lg	Pts
Jason Elam	.42/43	26/36	55	120

Punts (10 or more)

	No	Yds	Long	Avg	In20
Micah Knorr	71	2834	59	39.9	19
DAL	.47	1928	56	41.0	11
DEN	.24	906	59	37.8	8

Signed: Knorr on Oct. 29.

Released: Tom Rouen on Oct. 29 (see Pit.)

Most Interceptions — Deltha O'Neal 5

Most Sacks — Trevor Pryce.........9

Houston Texans

Passing (5 Att)

	Att	Cmp	Pct	Yds	TD	Rate
David Carr	444	233	52.5	2592	9	62.8

Interceptions: Carr 15.

Top Receivers

	No	Yds	Avg	Long	TD
Billy Miller	51	613	12.0	42	3
James Allen	47	302	6.4	21	0
Corey Bradford	.45	697	15.5	81	6
Jabar Gaffney*	41	483	11.8	27	1
JaJuan Dawson	21	286	13.6	28	0
Jonathan Wells*	9	48	5.3	9	0

Top Rushers

	Car	Yds	Avg	Long	TD
Jonathan Wells*	197	529	2.7	37	3
James Allen	155	519	3.3	32	0
David Carr*	.59	282	4.8	20	3
Jarrod Baxter*	7	-14	2.0	6	0

Most Touchdowns

	TD	Run	Rec	Ret	Pts
Corey Bradford	6	0	6	0	36
David Carr*	.3	3	0	0	18
Billy Miller	.3	0	3	0	18
Jonathan Wells*	.3	3	0	0	18
Aaron Glenn	.2	0	0	2	12

2-Pt. Conversions: (2-2) Allen, Gaffney.

Kicking

	PAT/Att	FG/Att	Lg	Pts
Kris Brown	.20/20	17/24	51	71

Punts (10 or more)

	No	Yds	Long	Avg	In20
Chad Stanley	.114	4720	62	41.4	36

Most Interceptions — Aaron Glenn 5

Most Sacks — Jeff Posey...........8

Indianapolis Colts

Passing (5 Att)

	Att	Cmp	Pct	Yds	TD	Rate
Peyton Manning	...591	392	66.3	4200	27	88.8

Interceptions: Manning 19.

Top Receivers

	No	Yds	Avg	Long	TD
Marvin Harrison	143	1722	12.0	69	11
Edgerrin James	61	354	5.8	23	1
Reggie Wayne	49	716	14.6	49	4
Qadry Ismail	44	462	10.5	42-td	3
Marcus Pollard	43	478	11.1	41-td	6

Top Rushers

	Car	Yds	Avg	Long	TD
Edgerrin James	277	989	3.6	20	2
James Mungro*	97	336	3.5	49	8
Peyton Manning	38	148	3.9	13	2
Ricky Williams*	11	35	3.2	10	0

Most Touchdowns

	TD	Run	Rec	Ret	Pts
Marvin Harrison	.11	0	11	0	68
James Mungro*	.8	8	0	0	48
Marcus Pollard	.6	0	6	0	38
Reggie Wayne	.4	0	4	0	24
Edgerrin James	.3	2	1	0	20
Qadry Ismail	.3	0	3	0	18

2-Pt. Conversions: (3-6) Harrison, James, Pollard.

Kicking

	PAT/Att	FG/Att	Lg	Pts
Mike Vanderjagt	.......34/34	23/31	54	103

Punts (10 or more)

	No	Yds	Long	Avg	In20
Hunter Smith	.66	2672	69	40.5	26

Most Interceptions — Mike Peterson 3

Most Sacks — Dwight Freeney* 13

Jacksonville Jaguars

Passing (5 Att)

	Att	Cmp	Pct	Yds	TD	Rate
Mark Brunell	416	245	58.9	2788	17	85.7
David Garrard*	46	23	50.0	231	1	53.8

Interceptions: Brunell 7, Garrard 2.

Top Receivers

	No	Yds	Avg	Long	TD
Jimmy Smith	.80	1027	12.8	47	7
Fred Taylor	49	408	8.3	72	0
Bobby Shaw	44	525	11.9	48	1
Kyle Brady	43	461	10.7	42-td	4

Top Rushers

	Car	Yds	Avg	Long	TD
Fred Taylor	287	1314	4.6	63-td	8
Stacey Mack	98	436	4.4	23	9
Mark Brunell	43	207	4.8	27	0
David Garrard*	25	139	5.6	41-td	2

Most Touchdowns

	TD	Run	Rec	Ret	Pts
Stacey Mack	.9	9	0	0	54
Fred Taylor	.8	8	0	0	52
Jimmy Smith	.7	0	7	0	44
Kyle Brady	.4	0	4	0	24
Kevin Lockett	.4	0	4	0	24
WASH	.2	0	2	0	12
JAX	.2	0	2	0	12

2-Pt. Conversions: (3-5) Taylor 2, Smith.

Signed: Lockett off waivers from Wash. (11/2).

Kicking

	PAT/Att	FG/Att	Lg	Pts
Tim Seder	.11/11	8/12	43	35
Danny Boyd*	.7/7	5/5	33	22
Richie Cunningham	.......2/2	1/1	23	5

Released: Hayden Epstein on Oct. 22 (see Min.).

Punts (10 or more)

	No	Yds	Long	Avg	In20
Chris Hanson	.81	3583	64	44.2	27

Most Interceptions — Marlon McCree 6

Most Sacks — John Henderson* ......6.5 / Marcus Stroud.......6.5

Kansas City Chiefs

Passing (5 Att)	Att	Cmp	Pct	Yds	TD	Rate
Trent Green	.470	287	61.1	3690	26	92.6
Todd Collins	.6	5	83.3	73	1	156.9

Interceptions: Green 13.

Top Receivers	No	Yds	Avg	Long	TD
Priest Holmes	.70	672	9.6	64-td	3
Tony Gonzalez	.63	773	12.3	42-td	7
Eddie Kennison	.53	906	17.1	64	2
Johnnie Morton	.29	397	13.7	30	1
Marc Boerigter*	.20	420	21.0	99-td	8
Dante Hall	.20	322	16.1	75-td	3
Tony Richardson	.18	125	6.9	23	1

Top Rushers	Car	Yds	Avg	Long	TD
Priest Holmes	.313	1615	5.2	56	21
Trent Green	.31	225	7.3	24	1
Johnnie Morton	.10	124	12.4	36	0
Mike Cloud	.49	115	2.3	9	2
Tony Richardson	.22	81	3.7	14-td	2

Most Touchdowns	TD	Run	Rec	Ret	Pts
Priest Holmes	.24	21	3	0	144
Marc Boerigter*	.8	0	8	0	48
Tony Gonzalez	.7	0	7	0	42
Dante Hall	.6	0	3	3	36
Tony Richardson	.3	2	1	0	18

2-Pt. Conversions: (1-3) Green.

Kicking	PAT/Att	FG/Att	Lg	Pts
Morten Andersen	.51/51	22/26	50	117
Michael Husted	.3/3	1/1	38	6

Punts (10 or more)	No	Yds	Long	Avg	In20
Dan Stryzinski	.64	2422	56	37.8	15

Most Interceptions		Most Sacks	
Greg Wesley	.6	Eric Hicks	.9

Miami Dolphins

Passing (5 Att)	Att	Cmp	Pct	Yds	TD	Rate
Jay Fiedler	.292	179	61.3	2024	14	85.2
Ray Lucas	.160	92	57.5	1045	4	69.9

Interceptions: Fiedler 9, Lucas 6.

Top Receivers	No	Yds	Avg	Long	TD
Chris Chambers	.52	734	14.1	59-td	3
Ricky Williams	.47	363	7.7	52	1
Randy McMichael*	.39	485	12.4	45	4
Rob Konrad	.34	233	6.9	19	3
James McKnight	.29	528	18.2	77	2
Dedric Ward	.19	172	9.1	22	0

Top Rushers	Car	Yds	Avg	Long	TD
Ricky Williams	.383	1853	4.8	63-td	16
Travis Minor	.44	180	4.1	23	2
Ray Lucas	.36	126	3.5	17	2
Robert Edwards	.20	107	5.4	19	1

Most Touchdowns	TD	Run	Rec	Ret	Pts
Ricky Williams	.17	16	1	0	102
Randy McMichael*	.4	0	4	0	24
Chris Chambers	.3	0	3	0	18
Jay Fiedler	.3	3	0	0	18
Rob Konrad	.3	0	3	0	18
Jed Weaver	.3	0	3	0	18

2-Pt. Conversions: (0-1).

Kicking	PAT/Att	FG/Att	Lg	Pts
Olindo Mare	.42/43	24/31	53	114

Punts (10 or more)	No	Yds	Long	Avg	In20
Mark Royals	.69	2772	56	40.2	15

Most Interceptions		Most Sacks	
Patrick Surtain	.6	Jason Taylor	.18.5

New England Patriots

Passing (5 Att)	Att	Cmp	Pct	Yds	TD	Rate
Tom Brady	.601	373	62.1	3764	28	85.7

Interceptions: Brady 14.

Top Receivers	No	Yds	Avg	Long	TD
Troy Brown	.97	890	9.2	38	3
David Patten	.61	824	13.5	39	5
Deion Branch*	.43	489	11.4	49-td	2
Kevin Faulk	.37	379	10.2	36-td	3
Antowain Smith	.31	243	7.8	35	2
Christian Fauria	.27	253	9.4	33	7
Marc Edwards	.23	196	8.5	27	0

Top Rushers	Car	Yds	Avg	Long	TD
Antowain Smith	.252	982	3.9	42-td	6
Kevin Faulk	.52	271	5.2	45-td	2
Tom Brady	.42	110	2.6	15	1
Marc Edwards	.31	96	3.1	17	0

Most Touchdowns	TD	Run	Rec	Ret	Pts
Antowain Smith	.8	6	2	0	50
Christian Fauria	.7	0	7	0	44
Kevin Faulk	.7	2	3	2	42
David Patten	.5	0	5	0	30
Troy Brown	.3	0	3	0	20

Three tied with 2 TD each.

2-Pt. Conversions: (3-7) Brown, Fauria, A. Smith.

Kicking	PAT/Att	FG/Att	Lg	Pts
Adam Vinatieri	.36/36	27/30	57	117

Punts (10 or more)	No	Yds	Long	Avg	In20
Ken Walter	.70	2723	55	38.9	19

Most Interceptions		Most Sacks	
Terrell Buckley	.4	Willie McGinest	.5.5
Ty Law	.4	Richard Seymour	.5.5

New York Jets

Passing (5 Att)	Att	Cmp	Pct	Yds	TD	Rate
Chad Pennington	.399	275	68.9	3120	22	104.2
Vinny Testaverde	.83	54	65.1	499	3	78.3

Interceptions: Pennington 6, Testaverde 3.

Top Receivers	No	Yds	Avg	Long	TD
Laveranues Coles	.89	1264	14.2	43	5
Wayne Chrebet	.51	691	13.5	37	9
Curtis Martin	.49	362	7.4	28	0
Richie Anderson	.45	257	5.7	15	1
Santana Moss	.30	433	14.4	47	4
Anthony Becht	.28	243	8.7	21	5
LaMont Jordan	.17	160	9.4	27	0

Top Rushers	No	Yds	Avg	Long	TD
Curtis Martin	.261	1094	4.2	35	7
LaMont Jordan	.84	316	3.8	61-td	3
Chad Pennington	.29	49	1.7	14	2
Santana Moss	.7	48	6.9	14	0

Most Touchdowns	TD	Run	Rec	Ret	Pts
Wayne Chrebet	.9	0	9	0	54
Curtis Martin	.7	7	0	0	44
Santana Moss	.6	0	4	2	36
Anthony Becht	.5	0	5	0	32
Laveranues Coles	.5	0	5	0	32
LaMont Jordan	.3	3	0	0	18

2-Pt. Conversions: (3-3) Martin, Becht, Coles.

Kicking	PAT/Att	FG/Att	Lg	Pts
John Hall	.35/37	24/31	46	107

Punts (10 or more)	No	Yds	Long	Avg	In20
Matt Turk	.63	2584	65	41.0	13

Most Interceptions		Most Sacks	
Donnie Abraham	.4	John Abraham	.10

Oakland Raiders

Passing (5 Att)

	Att	Cmp	Pct	Yds	TD	Rate
Rich Gannon	.618	418	67.6	4689	26	97.3

Interceptions: Gannon 10.

Top Receivers

	No	Yds	Avg	Long	TD
Jerry Rice	.92	1211	13.2	75	7
Charlie Garner	.91	941	10.3	69-td	4
Tim Brown	.81	930	11.5	45	2
Jerry Porter	.51	688	13.5	36	9
Doug Jolley*	.32	409	12.8	33	2
Roland Williams	.27	213	7.9	19	0

Top Rushers

	Car	Yds	Avg	Long	TD
Charlie Garner	.182	962	5.3	36-td	7
Tyrone Wheatley . . .	.108	419	3.9	36	2
Rich Gannon	.50	156	3.1	24	3
Zack Crockett	.40	118	3.0	33	8

Most Touchdowns

	TD	Run	Rec	Ret	Pts
Charlie Garner	.11	7	4	0	66
Jerry Porter	.9	0	9	0	58
Zack Crockett	.8	8	0	0	48
Jerry Rice	.7	0	7	0	42

Two tied with 3 TD each.

2-Pt. Conversions: (2-3) Porter 2.

Kicking

	PAT/Att	FG/Att	Lg	Pts
Sebastian Janikowski	.50/50	26/33	51	128

Punts (10 or more)

	No	Yds	Long	Avg	In20
Shane Lechler	.53	2251	70	42.5	18

Most Interceptions
Rod Woodson 8

Most Sacks
Rod Coleman 11

Pittsburgh Steelers

Passing (5 Att)

	Att	Cmp	Pct	Yds	TD	Rate
Tommy Maddox . . .	.377	234	62.1	2836	20	85.2
Kordell Stewart . . .	.166	109	65.7	1155	6	82.8
Antwaan Randle El* .	.8	7	87.5	45	0	90.1

Interceptions: Maddox 16, Stewart 6.

Top Receivers

	No	Yds	Avg	Long	TD
Hines Ward	.112	1329	11.9	72-td	12
Plaxico Burress	.78	1325	17.0	62-td	7
Antwaan Randle El* . .	.47	489	10.4	36	2
Amos Zereoue	.42	341	8.1	54	0
Terance Mathis	.23	218	9.5	22	2

Top Rushers

	Car	Yds	Avg	Long	TD
Amos Zereoue	.193	762	3.9	42	4
Jerome Bettis	.187	666	3.6	41-td	9
Kordell Stewart	.43	191	4.4	28-td	2
Hines Ward	.12	142	11.8	39	0
Antwaan Randle El* . .	.19	134	7.1	24	0

Most Touchdowns

	TD	Run	Rec	Ret	Pts
Hines Ward	.12	0	12	0	78
Jerome Bettis	.9	9	0	0	54
Plaxico Burress	.7	0	7	0	44
Amos Zereoue	.4	4	0	0	24

2-Pt. Conversions: (5-6) Ward 3, Burress, Dan Kreider.

Kicking

	PAT/Att	FG/Att	Lg	Pts
Todd Peterson	.25/26	12/21	46	61
Jeff Reed*	.10/11	17/19	50	61

Punts (10 or more)

	No	Yds	Long	Avg	In20
Josh Miller	.55	2267	62	41.2	14
Tom Rouen	.44	1888	63	42.9	8
DEN	.29	1239	63	42.7	6
NYG	.8	333	55	41.6	1
PIT	.7	316	55	38.7	1

Most Interceptions
Joey Porter 4
Brent Alexander 4

Most Sacks
Jason Gildon 9
Joey Porter 9

San Diego Chargers

Passing (5 Att)

	Att	Cmp	Pct	Yds	TD	Rate
Drew Brees	.526	320	60.8	3284	17	76.9
Doug Flutie	.11	3	27.3	64	0	51.3

Interceptions: Brees 16.

Top Receivers

	No	Yds	Avg	Long	TD
LaDainian Tomlinson . .	.79	489	6.2	30	1
Curtis Conway	.57	852	14.9	52-td	5
Tim Dwight	.50	623	12.5	42	2
Stephen Alexander . .	.45	510	11.3	32	1
Reche Caldwell*	.22	208	9.5	26	3
Fred McCrary	.22	96	4.4	25	3
Eric Parker*	.17	268	15.8	31-td	1
Josh Norman*	.16	201	12.6	29	1

Top Rushers

	No	Yds	Avg	Long	TD
LaDainian Tomlinson . .	.372	1683	4.5	76	14
Drew Brees	.38	130	3.4	15	1
Terrell Fletcher	.26	128	4.9	15	1
Tim Dwight	.12	108	9.0	20	1

Most Touchdowns

	TD	Run	Rec	Ret	Pts
LaDainian Tomlinson . .	.15	14	1	0	90
Curtis Conway	.7	2	5	0	42
Reche Caldwell*	.3	0	3	0	20
Tim Dwight	.3	1	2	0	18
Fred McCrary	.3	0	3	0	18

2-Pt. Conversions: (1-3) Caldwell.

Kicking

	PAT/Att	FG/Att	Lg	Pts
Steve Christie	.35/36	18/26	53	89

Punts (10 or more)

	No	Yds	Long	Avg	In20
Darren Bennett	.87	3540	63	40.7	31

Most Interceptions
Donnie Edwards 5

Most Sacks
Raylee Johnson 6.5

Tennessee Titans

Passing (5 Att)

	Att	Cmp	Pct	Yds	TD	Rate
Steve McNair . .	.492	301	61.2	3387	22	84.0
Neil O'Donnell	.5	3	60.0	24	0	72.1

Interceptions: McNair 15.

Top Receivers

	No	Yds	Avg	Long	TD
Derrick Mason	.79	1012	12.8	40	5
Kevin Dyson	.41	460	11.2	40	4
Frank Wycheck	.40	346	8.7	19	2
Eddie George	.36	255	7.1	14-td	2
Drew Bennett	.33	478	14.5	53	2
Justin McCareins . . .	.19	301	15.8	55	2
John Simon*	.16	167	10.4	42-td	3

Top Rushers

	Car	Yds	Avg	Long	TD
Eddie George	.343	1165	3.4	35	12
Steve McNair	.82	440	5.4	26	3
Robert Holcombe . . .	.47	242	5.1	39	0
Mike Green	.21	71	3.4	12	0

Most Touchdowns

	TD	Run	Rec	Ret	Pts
Eddie George	.14	12	2	0	86
Derrick Mason	.5	0	5	0	30
Kevin Dyson	.4	0	4	0	24
John Simon*	.4	1	3	0	24
Steve McNair	.3	3	0	0	20

Three tied with 2 TD each.

2-Pt. Conversions: (2-6) George, McNair.

Kicking

	PAT/Att	FG/Att	Lg	Pts
Joe Nedney	.36/36	25/31	53	111

Punts (10 or more)

	No	Yds	Long	Avg	In20
Craig Hentrich	.65	2725	56	41.9	28

Most Interceptions
Lance Schulters 6

Most Sacks
Kevin Carter 10

NFC Team by Team Statistics

Players with more than one team during the regular season are listed with club they ended season with; (*) indicates rookies.

Arizona Cardinals

Passing (5 Att)	Att	Cmp	Pct	Yds	TD	Rate
Jake Plummer	530	284	53.6	2972	18	65.7
Josh McCown*	18	7	38.9	66	0	10.2

Interceptions: Plummer 20, McCown 2.

Top Receivers	No	Yds	Avg	Long	TD
Freddie Jones	44	358	8.1	24	1
Marcel Shipp	38	413	10.9	80-td	3
Frank Sanders	34	400	11.8	37	2
David Boston	32	512	16.0	34	1
Jason McAddley*	25	362	14.5	42	1
MarTay Jenkins	21	250	11.9	65-td	1

Top Rushers	Car	Yds	Avg	Long	TD
Marcel Shipp	188	834	4.4	56	6
Thomas Jones	138	511	3.7	58-td	2
Jake Plummer	46	283	6.2	34-td	2
Damien Anderson*	24	65	2.7	14	0

Most Touchdowns	TD	Run	Rec	Ret	Pts
Marcel Shipp	9	6	3	0	54
Kevin Kasper	3	0	3	0	18
DEN	0	0	0	0	0
SEA	0	0	0	0	0
ARI	3	0	3	0	18
Joel Mackovicka	3	0	3	0	18

2-Pt. Conversions: (1-2) Sanders.
Signed: Kasper off waivers from Sea. (Nov. 22).

Kicking	PAT/Att	FG/Att	Lg	Pts
Bill Gramatica	29/29	15/21	50	74

Punts (10 or more)	No	Yds	Long	Avg	In20
Scott Player	88	3864	58	43.9	28

Most Interceptions		Most Sacks	
Adrian Wilson	4	Kyle Vanden Bosch	3.5

Atlanta Falcons

Passing (5 Att)	Att	Cmp	Pct	Yds	TD	Rate
Michael Vick	421	231	54.9	2936	16	81.6
Doug Johnson	57	37	64.9	448	2	78.7

Interceptions: Vick 8, Johnson 3.

Top Receivers	No	Yds	Avg	Long	TD
Brian Finneran	56	838	15.0	47	6
Warrick Dunn	50	377	7.5	31-td	2
Alge Crumpler	36	455	12.6	33	5
Shawn Jefferson	27	394	14.6	63	1
Trevor Gaylor	25	385	15.4	74-td	3

Top Rushers	Car	Yds	Avg	Long	TD
Warrick Dunn	230	927	4.0	59-td	7
Michael Vick	113	777	6.9	46-td	8
T.J. Duckett*	130	507	3.9	33	4
Bob Christian	31	119	3.8	16	3

Most Touchdowns	TD	Run	Rec	Ret	Pts
Warrick Dunn	9	7	2	0	54
Michael Vick	8	8	0	0	48
Brian Finneran	6	0	6	0	36
Alge Crumpler	5	0	5	0	30
T.J. Duckett*	4	4	0	0	24

2-Pt. Conversions: (0-0).

Kicking	PAT/Att	FG/Att	Lg	Pts
Jay Feely	42/43	32/40	52	138

Punts (10 or more)	No	Yds	Long	Avg	In20
Chris Mohr	67	2804	59	41.9	21

Most Interceptions		Most Sacks	
Keion Carpenter	4	Patrick Kerney	10.5
Juran Bolden	4		

Carolina Panthers

Passing (5 Att)	Att	Cmp	Pct	Yds	TD	Rate
Rodney Peete	381	223	58.5	2630	15	77.4
Randy Fasani*	44	15	34.1	171	0	8.8
Chris Weinke	38	17	44.7	180	0	26.2

Interceptions: Peete 14, Fasani 4, Weinke 3.

Top Receivers	No	Yds	Avg	Long	TD
Muhsin Muhammad	63	823	13.1	42	3
Steve Smith	54	872	16.1	69	3
Lamar Smith	20	167	8.4	58	0
Wesley Walls	19	241	12.7	27	4

Top Rushers	Car	Yds	Avg	Long	TD
Lamar Smith	209	737	3.5	59	7
Dee Brown	102	360	3.5	24	4
Nick Goings	50	188	3.8	20	0
Brad Hoover	31	129	4.2	11	0

Most Touchdowns	TD	Run	Rec	Ret	Pts
Lamar Smith	7	7	0	0	42
Dee Brown	5	4	1	0	30
Steve Smith	5	0	3	2	30
Wesley Walls	4	0	4	0	24

2-Pt. Conversions: (1-1) Goings.

Kicking	PAT/Att	FG/Att	Lg	Pts
Shayne Graham	21/21	13/18	50	60
John Kasay	5/5	2/5	27	11
Jon Hilbert	3/3	0/2	—	3

Signed: Hilbert (Sept. 21). Graham (Sept. 27).
Released: Hilbert (Sept. 27).

Punts (10 or more)	No	Yds	Long	Avg	In20
Todd Sauerbrun	104	4735	67	45.5	31

Most Interceptions		Most Sacks	
Mike Minter	4	Julius Peppers*	12

Chicago Bears

Passing (10 Att)	Att	Cmp	Pct	Yds	TD	Rate
Jim Miller	314	180	57.3	1944	13	77.5
Chris Chandler	161	103	64.0	1023	4	79.8
Henry Burris	51	18	35.3	207	3	28.4

Interceptions: Miller 19, Burris 5, Chandler 4.

Top Receivers	No	Yds	Avg	Long	TD
Marty Booker	97	1183	12.2	54	6
Dez White	51	656	12.9	76-td	4
Anthony Thomas	24	163	6.8	19	0
Marcus Robinson	21	244	11.6	45-td	3
John Davis	20	193	9.7	37	3

Top Rushers	Car	Yds	Avg	Long	TD
Anthony Thomas	214	721	3.4	34	6
Leon Johnson	103	329	3.2	23	1
Henry Burris	15	104	6.9	17	0
Adrian Peterson*	19	101	5.3	14	1

Most Touchdowns	TD	Run	Rec	Ret	Pts
Marty Booker	6	0	6	0	36
Anthony Thomas	6	6	0	0	36
Dez White	4	0	4	0	24

Three tied with 2 TD each.
2-Pt. Conversions: (0-2).

Kicking	PAT/Att	FG/Att	Lg	Pts
Paul Edinger	29/29	22/28	53	95

Punts (10 or more)	No	Yds	Long	Avg	In20
Brad Maynard	87	3679	75	42.3	26

Most Interceptions		Most Sacks	
Mike Brown	3	Rosevelt Colvin	10.5

Dallas Cowboys

Passing (10 Att)	Att	Cmp	Pct	Yds	TD	Rate
Chad Hutchinson*	.250	127	50.8	1555	7	66.3
Quincy Carter	.221	125	56.6	1465	7	72.3

Interceptions: Hutchinson 8, Carter 8.

Top Receivers	No	Yds	Avg	Long	TD
Joey Galloway	.61	908	14.9	80-td	6
Antonio Bryant*	.44	733	16.7	78-td	6
Tony McGee	.23	294	12.8	58	1
Darnay Scott	.22	218	9.9	17-td	1
Troy Hambrick	.21	99	4.7	14	0
James Whalen	.17	152	8.9	33	0
Emmitt Smith	.16	89	5.6	17	0

Top Rushers	Car	Yds	Avg	Long	TD
Emmitt Smith	.254	975	3.8	30-td	5
Troy Hambrick	.79	317	4.0	18	1
Michael Wiley	.22	168	7.6	46-td	1
Quincy Carter	.27	91	3.4	16	0

Most Touchdowns	TD	Run	Rec	Ret	Pts
Antonio Bryant*	.6	0	6	0	36
Joey Galloway	.6	0	6	0	36
Emmitt Smith	.5	5	0	0	30
Roy Williams*	.2	0	0	2	12

2-Pt. Conversions: (0-1).

Kicking	PAT/Att	FG/Att	Lg	Pts
Bill Cundiff*	.25/25	12/19	48	61

Punts (10 or more)	No	Yds	Long	Avg	In20
Filip Filipovic*	.65	2640	60	40.6	14

Released: Micah Knorr on Oct. 22 (see Den.).

Most Interceptions		**Most Sacks**
Roy Williams*	.5	Greg Ellis	.7.5
Derek Ross	.5	

Detroit Lions

Passing (5 Att)	Att	Cmp	Pct	Yds	TD	Rate
Joey Harrington*	.429	215	50.1	2294	12	59.9
Mike McMahon	.147	62	42.2	874	7	52.4

Interceptions: Harrington 16, McMahon 9.

Top Receivers	No	Yds	Avg	Long	TD
James Stewart	.46	333	7.2	52-td	2
Az-Zahir Hakim	.37	541	14.6	64-td	3
Bill Schroeder	.36	595	16.5	46	5
Cory Schlesinger	.35	263	7.5	43	0
Mikhael Ricks	.27	339	12.6	49	3
Scotty Anderson	.25	322	12.9	34	1
Germane Crowell	.22	201	9.1	22	1

Top Rushers	Car	Yds	Avg	Long	TD
James Stewart	.231	1021	4.4	56	4
Cory Schlesinger	.49	139	2.8	17	2
Aveion Cason	.26	107	4.1	40	0
Mike McMahon	.14	96	6.9	22	3
Rafael Cooper*	.12	57	4.8	18	0

Most Touchdowns	TD	Run	Rec	Ret	Pts
James Stewart	.6	4	2	0	36
Bill Schroeder	.5	0	5	0	32
Az-Zahir Hakim	.4	0	3	1	24
Mike McMahon	.3	3	0	0	18
Mikhael Ricks	.3	0	3	0	18

2-Pt. Conversions: (1-3) Schroeder.

Kicking	PAT/Att	FG/Att	Lg	Pts
Jason Hanson	.31/31	23/28	49	100

Punts (10 or more)	No	Yds	Long	Avg	In20
John Jett	.91	3838	57	42.2	29

Most Interceptions		**Most Sacks**
Chris Claiborne	.3	Kalimba Edwards*	.6.5

Green Bay Packers

Passing (5 Att)	Att	Cmp	Pct	Yds	TD	Rate
Brett Favre	.551	341	61.9	3658	27	85.6
Doug Pederson	.28	19	67.9	134	1	90.5

Interceptions: Favre 16.

Top Receivers	No	Yds	Avg	Long	TD
Donald Driver	.70	1064	15.2	85-td	9
Ahman Green	.57	393	6.9	23-td	2
Terry Glenn	.56	817	14.6	49	2
Bubba Franks	.54	442	8.2	20-td	7
William Henderson	.26	168	6.5	17	3
Javon Walker*	.23	319	13.9	30	1

Top Rushers	Car	Yds	Avg	Long	TD
Ahman Green	.286	1240	4.3	43	7
Tony Fisher*	.70	283	4.0	28	2
Najeh Davenport*	.39	184	4.7	43	1
Brett Favre	.25	73	2.9	17	0

Most Touchdowns	TD	Run	Rec	Ret	Pts
Donald Driver	.9	0	9	0	54
Ahman Green	.9	7	2	0	54
Bubba Franks	.7	0	7	0	42
William Henderson	.4	1	3	0	24
Robert Ferguson	.3	0	3	0	18

2-Pt. Conversions: (0-1).

Kicking	PAT/Att	FG/Att	Lg	Pts
Ryan Longwell	.44/44	28/34	49	128

Punts (10 or more)	No	Yds	Long	Avg	In20
Josh Bidwell	.79	3296	57	41.7	26

Most Interceptions		**Most Sacks**
Darren Sharper	.7	Kabeer Gbaja-Biamila	.12

Minnesota Vikings

Passing (5 Att)	Att	Cmp	Pct	Yds	TD	Rate
Daunte Culpepper	.549	333	60.7	3853	18	75.3
Todd Bouman	.6	3	50.0	85	0	95.8

Interceptions: Culpepper 23.

Top Receivers	No	Yds	Avg	Long	TD
Randy Moss	.106	1347	12.7	60	7
D'Wayne Bates	.50	689	13.8	59	4
Jim Kleinsasser	.37	393	10.6	39	1
Michael Bennett	.37	351	9.5	45-td	1
Byron Chamberlain	.34	389	11.4	61	0

Top Rushers	Car	Yds	Avg	Long	TD
Michael Bennett	.255	1296	5.1	85-td	5
Daunte Culpepper	.106	609	5.7	38	10
Moe Williams	.84	414	4.9	44	11

Most Touchdowns	TD	Run	Rec	Ret	Pts
Moe Williams	.11	11	0	0	66
Daunte Culpepper	.10	10	0	0	62
Randy Moss	.7	0	7	0	42
Michael Bennett*	.6	5	1	0	36

2-Pt. Conversions: (1-2) Culpepper.

Kicking	PAT/Att	FG/Att	Lg	Pts
Gary Anderson	.36/37	18/23	53	90
Hayden Epstein	.13/13	5/9	34	28
JAX	.13/13	5/9	34	28
MIN	.0	0	0	0
Doug Brien	.5/7	5/6	42	20

Released: Brien on Oct. 23. **Signed:** Epstein off waivers from Jax on Oct. 23.

Punts (10 or more)	No	Yds	Long	Avg	In20
Kyle Richardson	.62	2474	59	39.9	21

Most Interceptions		**Most Sacks**
Greg Biekert	.4	Lance Johnstone	.7

New Orleans Saints

Passing (5 Att)	Att	Cmp	Pct	Yds	TD	Rate
Aaron Brooks	.528	283	53.6	3572	27	80.1
Jake Delhomme	.10	8	80.0	113	0	113.8

Interceptions: Brooks 15.

Top Receivers	No	Yds	Avg	Long	TD
Joe Horn	.88	1312	14.9	63	7
Deuce McAllister	.47	352	7.5	30	3
Jerome Pathon	.43	523	12.2	64	4
Donte' Stallworth	.42	594	14.1	57-td	8
Jake Reed	.21	360	17.1	54	3
Boo Williams	.13	143	11.0	32-td	2
David Sloan	.12	127	10.6	29	0

Top Rushers	Car	Yds	Avg	Long	TD
Deuce McAllister	.325	1388	4.3	62	13
Aaron Brooks	.62	253	4.1	21	2
James Fenderson	.13	65	5.0	17-td	1

Most Touchdowns	TD	Run	Rec	Ret	Pts
Deuce McAllister	.16	13	3	0	96
Donte' Stallworth	.8	0	8	0	48
Joe Horn	.7	0	7	0	44
Jerome Pathon	.4	0	4	0	24
Michael Lewis	.3	0	0	3	18
Jake Reed	.3	0	3	0	18

2-Pt. Conversions: (4-11) Brooks 2, Horn, Williams.

Kicking	PAT/Att	FG/Att	Lg	Pts
John Carney	.37/37	31/35	48	130

Punts (10 or more)	No	Yds	Long	Avg	In20
Toby Gowin	.61	2553	59	41.9	15

Most Interceptions		Most Sacks	
Fred Thomas	.5	Darren Howard	.8
Sammy Knight	.5		

New York Giants

Passing (5 Att)	Att	Cmp	Pct	Yds	TD	Rate
Kerry Collins	.545	335	61.5	4073	19	85.4

Interceptions: Collins 14.

Top Receivers	No	Yds	Avg	Long	TD
Amani Toomer	.82	1343	16.4	82-td	8
Jeremy Shockey*	.74	894	12.1	30	2
Tiki Barber	.69	597	8.7	38	0
Ike Hilliard	.27	386	14.3	38	2
Ron Dixon	.22	377	17.1	33	2
Daniel Campbell	.22	175	8.0	27	1
Charles Stackhouse*	.13	88	6.8	18-td	3

Top Rushers	Car	Yds	Avg	Long	TD
Tiki Barber	.304	1387	4.6	70	11
Ron Dayne	.125	428	3.4	30-td	3
Tim Carter*	.3	28	9.3	13	0

Most Touchdowns	TD	Run	Rec	Ret	Pts
Tiki Barber	.11	11	0	0	66
Amani Toomer	.8	0	8	0	48
Ron Dayne	.3	3	0	0	18
Charles Stackhouse*	.3	0	3	0	18

Three tied with 2 TD each.

2-Pt. Conversions: (1-3) Marcellus Rivers.

Kicking	PAT/Att	FG/Att	Lg	Pts
Matt Bryant*	.30/32	26/32	47	108

Punts (10 or more)	No	Yds	Long	Avg	In20
Matt Allen*	.63	2326	65	36.9	20

Most Interceptions		Most Sacks	
Jason Sehorn	.2	Michael Strahan	.11
Will Peterson	.2		
Shaun Williams	.2		

Philadelphia Eagles

Passing (5 Att)	Att	Cmp	Pct	Yds	TD	Rate
Donovan McNabb	.361	211	58.4	2289	17	86.0
A.J. Feeley	.154	86	55.8	1011	6	75.4
Koy Detmer	.28	19	67.9	224	2	115.8

Interceptions: McNabb 6, Feeley 5.

Top Receivers	No	Yds	Avg	Long	TD
Todd Pinkston	.60	798	13.3	42-td	7
James Thrash	.52	635	12.2	39-td	6
Duce Staley	.51	541	10.6	45	3
Antonio Freeman	.46	600	13.0	59-td	4
Chad Lewis	.42	398	9.5	30	3

Top Rushers	Car	Yds	Avg	Long	TD
Duce Staley	.269	1029	3.8	57	5
Donovan McNabb	.63	460	7.3	40-td	6
Dorsey Levens	.75	411	5.5	47-td	1
Brian Westbrook*	.46	193	4.2	18	0

Most Touchdowns	TD	Run	Rec	Ret	Pts
Duce Staley	.8	5	3	0	50
James Thrash	.8	2	6	0	48
Todd Pinkston	.7	0	7	0	42
Donovan McNabb	.6	6	0	0	36
Antonio Freeman	.4	0	4	0	24

2-Pt. Conversions: (3-3) C. Lewis 2, Staley.

Kicking	PAT/Att	FG/Att	Lg	Pts
David Akers	.43/43	30/34	51	133

Punts (15 or more)	No	Yds	Long	Avg	In20
Jason Baker	.55	2133	51	38.8	14
SF	.42	1688	51	40.2	12
PHI	.13	445	44	34.2	2
Sean Landeta	.52	2229	63	42.9	19

Signed: Baker on Dec. 3. **Released:** Baker on Dec. 16.

Most Interceptions		Most Sacks	
Bobby Taylor	.5	Hugh Douglas	.12.5

St. Louis Rams

Passing (10 Att)	Att	Cmp	Pct	Yds	TD	Rate
Kurt Warner	.220	144	65.5	1431	3	67.4
Marc Bulger	.214	138	64.5	1826	14	101.5
Jamie Martin	.195	124	63.6	1216	7	71.7

Interceptions: Warner 11, Martin 10, Bulger 6.

Top Receivers	No	Yds	Avg	Long	TD
Torry Holt	.91	1302	14.3	58	4
Marshall Faulk	.80	537	6.7	40	2
Isaac Bruce	.79	1075	13.6	34-td	7
Ricky Proehl	.43	466	10.8	33	4
Ernie Conwell	.34	419	12.3	52	2
Lamar Gordon*	.30	278	9.3	25	2

Top Rushers	Car	Yds	Avg	Long	TD
Marshall Faulk	.212	953	4.5	44	8
Lamar Gordon*	.65	228	3.5	29	1
Terrence Wilkins	.6	56	9.3	18	0

Most Touchdowns	TD	Run	Rec	Ret	PTS
Marshall Faulk	.10	8	2	0	60
Isaac Bruce	.7	0	7	0	42
Torry Holt	.4	0	4	0	24
Ricky Proehl	.4	0	4	0	24

Two tied with 3 TD each.

2-Pt. Conversions: (0-0).

Kicking	PAT/Att	FG/Att	Lg	Pts
Jeff Wilkins	.37/37	19/25	47	94

Punts (10 or more)	No	Yds	Long	Avg	In20
Mitch Berger	.72	3020	64	41.9	26

Most Interceptions		Most Sacks	
Kim Herring	.3	Leonard Little	.12

San Francisco 49ers

Passing (5 Att)	Att	Cmp	Pct	Yds	TD	Rate
Jeff Garcia	.528	328	62.1	3344	21	85.6
Tim Rattay	.43	26	60.5	232	2	90.5

Interceptions: Garcia 10.

Top Receivers	No	Yds	Avg	Long	TD
Terrell Owens	100	1300	13.0	76-td	13
Tai Streets	.72	756	10.5	47-td	5
Garrison Hearst	.48	317	6.6	16	1
Eric Johnson	.36	321	8.9	38	0
J.J. Stokes	.32	332	10.4	51	1
Fred Beasley	.22	152	6.9	25-td	1

Top Rushers	Car	Yds	Avg	Long	TD
Garrison Hearst	.215	972	4.5	40	8
Kevan Barlow	.145	675	4.7	35	4
Jeff Garcia	.73	353	4.8	21-td	3
Paul Smith	.18	90	5.0	16	0

Most Touchdowns	TD	Run	Rec	Ret	Pts
Terrell Owens	14	1	13	0	84
Garrison Hearst	.9	8	1	0	56
Kevan Barlow	.5	4	1	0	30
Tai Streets	.5	0	5	0	30
Jeff Garcia	.3	3	0	0	20

2-Pt. Conversions: (2-2) Hearst, Garcia.

Kicking	PAT/Att	FG/Att	Lg	Pts
Jeff Chandler*	14/14	8/12	47	38

Released: Jose Cortez on Nov. 26 (see Wash.).

Punts (10 or more)	No	Yds	Long	Avg	In20
Billy LaFleur*	.22	805	60	36.6	5

Released: Jason Baker on Nov. 26 (see Phi.).
Signed: LaFleur on Nov. 27.

Most Interceptions		Most Sacks	
Tony Parrish	.7	Andre Carter	12.5

Seattle Seahawks

Passing (5 Att)	Att	Cmp	Pct	Yds	TD	Rate
Matt Hasselbeck	.419	267	63.7	3075	15	87.8
Trent Dilfer	.168	94	56.0	1182	4	71.1

Interceptions: Hasselbeck 10, Dilfer 6.

Top Receivers	No	Yds	Avg	Long	TD
Koren Robinson	.78	1240	15.9	83	5
Darrell Jackson	.62	877	14.1	48	4
Shaun Alexander	.59	460	7.8	80-td	2
Bobby Engram	.50	619	12.4	38	0
Itula Mili	.43	508	11.8	49	2
Jerramy Stevens*	.26	252	9.7	29	3
Mack Strong	.22	120	5.5	12	2

Top Rushers	Car	Yds	Avg	Long	TD
Shaun Alexander	.295	1175	4.0	58	16
Matt Hasselbeck	.40	202	5.1	21	1
Maurice Morris*	.32	153	4.8	24	0
Mack Strong	.23	94	4.1	9	0

Most Touchdowns	TD	Run	Rec	Ret	Pts
Shaun Alexander	18	16	2	0	108
Koren Robinson	.5	0	5	0	30
Darrell Jackson	.4	0	4	0	24
Jerramy Stevens*	.3	0	3	0	18
Itula Mili	.2	0	2	0	12
Mack Strong	.2	0	2	0	12

2-Pt. Conversions: (1-2) Hasselbeck.

Kicking	PAT/Att	FG/Att	Lg	Pts
Rian Lindell	.38/38	23/29	52	107

Punts (10 or more)	No	Yds	Long	Avg	In20
Jeff Feagles	.61	2542	58	41.7	22

Most Interceptions		Most Sacks	
Reggie Tongue	.5	John Randle	.7

Tampa Bay Buccaneers

Passing (5 Att)	Att	Cmp	Pct	Yds	TD	Rate
Brad Johnson	.451	281	62.3	3049	22	92.9
Rob Johnson	.88	57	64.8	536	1	75.8
Shaun King	.27	10	37.0	80	0	30.0

Interceptions: B. Johnson 6, R. Johnson 2, King 1.

Top Receivers	No	Yds	Avg	Long	TD
Keyshawn Johnson	.76	1088	14.3	76-td	5
Keenan McCardell	.61	670	11.0	65-td	6
Michael Pittman	.59	477	8.1	64	0
Joe Jurevicius	.37	423	11.4	26	4
Mike Alstott	.35	242	6.9	44-td	2
Ken Dilger	.34	329	9.7	40	2

Top Rushers	Car	Yds	Avg	Long	TD
Michael Pittman	.204	718	3.5	21	1
Mike Alstott	.146	548	3.8	32	5
Aaron Stecker	.28	174	6.2	59	0

Most Touchdowns	TD	Run	Rec	Ret	Pts
Mike Alstott	.7	5	2	0	42
Keenan McCardell	.6	0	6	0	36
Keyshawn Johnson	.5	0	5	0	34
Derrick Brooks	.4	0	0	4	24
Joe Jurevicius	.4	0	4	0	24

2-Pt. Conversions: (2-3) K. Johnson 2.

Kicking	PAT/Att	FG/Att	Lg	Pts
Martin Gramatica	.32/32	32/39	53	128

Punts (10 or more)	No	Yds	Long	Avg	In20
Tom Tupa	.90	3856	71	42.8	30

Most Interceptions		Most Sacks	
Brian Kelly	.8	Simeon Rice	15.5

Washington Redskins

Passing (5 Att)	Att	Cmp	Pct	Yds	TD	Rate
Shane Matthews	.237	124	52.3	1251	11	72.6
Patrick Ramsey*	.227	117	51.5	1539	9	71.8
Danny Wuerffel	.92	58	63.0	719	3	70.9

Interceptions: Ramsey 8, Matthews and Wuerffel 6.

Top Receivers	No	Yds	Avg	Long	TD
Rod Gardner	.71	1006	14.2	43-td	8
Derrius Thompson	.53	773	14.6	47	4
Kenny Watson	.32	253	7.9	62-td	1
Willie Jackson	.25	257	10.3	29	1
ATL	.18	199	11.1	29	0
WASH	.7	58	8.3	19	1

Signed: Jackson (Oct. 31). **Released:** Jackson (Dec. 13).

Top Rushers	Car	Yds	Avg	Long	TD
Stephen Davis	.207	820	4.0	33	7
Kenny Watson	.116	534	4.6	24	1
Ladell Betts*	.65	307	4.7	27	1

Most Touchdowns	TD	Run	Rec	Ret	Pts
Stephen Davis	.8	7	1	0	48
Rod Gardner	.8	0	8	0	48
Derrius Thompson	.4	0	4	0	24

2-Pt. Conversions: (1-3) Chris Doering.

Top Kickers	PAT/Att	FG/Att	Lg	Pts
Jose Cortez	.34/34	23/32	45	103
SF	.25/25	18/24	45	79
WASH	.9/9	5/8	44	24
James Tuthill	.20/21	10/16	53	50

Signed: Cortez (Dec. 2). **Released:** Tuthill (Dec. 2).

Punts (10 or more)	No	Yds	Long	Avg	In20
Bryan Barker	.48	1924	63	40.1	13
Craig Jarrett*	.20	771	74	38.6	5

Signed: Jarrett on Dec. 2

Most Interceptions		Most Sacks	
Fred Smoot	.4	LaVar Arrington	.11

NFL Playoffs

| 1ST ROUND | SEMIFINALS | FINAL | | FINAL | SEMIFINALS | 1ST ROUND |

†Cleveland 33
Pittsburgh 36
   Pittsburgh 31
   (OT)
   Tennessee 34
     Tennessee 24

†Indianapolis 0
NY Jets 41
   NY Jets 10
   Oakland 41
   Oakland 30

AFC

Oakland 21
Tampa Bay 48

NFC

San Fran. 6
San Fran. 39   †NY Giants 38

Tampa Bay 27
Tampa Bay 31

Atlanta 6
Philadelphia 10
Philadelphia 20

Atlanta 27
Green Bay 7   †Atlanta

Jan. 26, 2003
Qualcomm Stadium, San Diego

†Wild Card Team   †Wild Card Team

Playoff Game Summaries

Team records listed in parentheses indicate records before game.

WILD CARD ROUND

AFC

Jets, 41-0

Indianapolis (10-6) 0   0   0   0— **0**
NY Jets (9-7) 7   17   10   7— **41**
  Date—Jan. 4. **Att**—78,524. **Time**—2:48.
  1st Quarter: NYJ—Richie Anderson 56-yd pass from Chad Pennington (John Hall kick), 10:50.
  2nd Quarter: NYJ—Hall 41-yd FG, 14:08; NYJ—Lamont Jordan 1-yd run (Hall kick), 9:41; NYJ—Santana Moss 4-yd pass from Pennington (Hall kick), 0:37.
  3rd Quarter: NYJ—Hall 39-yd FG, 13:28; NYJ—Chris Baker 3-yd pass from Pennington (Hall kick), 1:44.
  4th Quarter: NYJ—Jordan 1-yd run (Hall kick), 4:59.

Steelers, 36-33

Cleveland (9-7) 7   10   7   9— **33**
Pittsburgh (10-5-1) 0   7   7   22— **36**
  Date—Jan. 5. **Att**—62,595. **Time**—3:39.
  1st Quarter: CLE—William Green 1-yd run (Phil Dawson kick), 13:44.
  2nd Quarter: CLE—Dennis Northcutt 32-yd pass from Kelly Holcomb (Dawson kick), 14:38; PIT—Antwaan Randle El 66-yd punt return (Jeff Reed kick), 9:35; CLE—Dawson 31-yd FG, 0:49.
  3rd Quarter: CLE—Northcutt 15-yd pass from Holcomb (Dawson kick), 12:11; PIT—Plaxico Burress 6-yd pass from Tommy Maddox (Reed kick), 3:50.
  4th Quarter: CLE—Dawson 24-yd FG, 14:52; PIT—Jerame Tuman 3-yd pass from Maddox (Reed kick), 12:28; CLE—Andre' Davis 22-yd pass from Holcomb (2-pt conversion failed), 10:17; PIT—Hines Ward 5-yd pass from Maddox (Reed kick), 3:06; PIT—Chris Fuamatu-Ma'afala 3-yd run (Tuman pass from Randle El), 0:54.

NFC

Falcons, 27-7

Atlanta (9-6-1) 14   10   3   0— **27**
Green Bay (12-4) 0   0   7   0— **7**
  Date—Jan. 4. **Att**—65,358. **Time**—2:57.
  1st Quarter: ATL—Shawn Jefferson 10-yd pass from Michael Vick (Jay Feely kick), 9:17; ATL—Artie Ulmer 1-yd return of blocked punt (Feely kick), 6:38.
  2nd Quarter: ATL—T.J. Duckett 6-yd run (Feely kick), 12:06; ATL—Feely 22-yd FG, 0:00.
  3rd Quarter: GB—Donald Driver 14-yd pass from Brett Favre (Ryan Longwell kick), 10:26; ATL—Feely 23-yd FG, 3:43.

49ers, 39-38

NY Giants (10-6) 7   21   10   0— **38**
San Francisco (10-6) 7   7   8   17— **39**
  Date—Jan. 5. **Att**—66,318. **Time**—3:22.
  1st Quarter: SF—Terrell Owens 76-yd pass from Jeff Garcia (Jeff Chandler kick), 9:59; NYG—Amani Toomer 12-yd pass from Kerry Collins (Matt Bryant kick), 0:18.
  2nd Quarter: NYG—Jeremy Shockey 2-yd pass from Collins (Bryant kick), 12:19; SF—Kevan Barlow 1-yd run (Chandler kick), 6:05; NYG—Toomer 8-yd pass from Collins (Bryant kick), 2:49; NYG—Toomer 24-yd pass from Collins (Bryant kick), 0:10.
  3rd Quarter: NYG—Tiki Barber 6-yd run (Bryant kick), 9:53; NYG—Bryant 21-yd FG, 4:27; SF—Owens 26-yd pass from Garcia (Owens pass from Garcia), 2:03.
  4th Quarter: SF—Garcia 14-yd run (Owens pass from Garcia), 14:55; SF—Chandler 25-yd FG, 7:49; SF—Tai Streets 13-yd pass from Garcia (2-pt conversion failed), 1:00.

NFL Playoffs (Cont.)
DIVISIONAL PLAYOFFS

AFC

Titans, 34-31 (OT)

Pittsburgh (11-5-1) . . . . .0 13 7 11   0— **31**
Tennessee (11-5) 14   0.14 3   3— **34**
   Date—Jan. 11. **Att**—68,809. **Time**—3:50.

   1st Quarter: TEN—Steve McNair 8-yd run (Joe Nedney kick), 11:01; TEN—Eddie George 1-yd run (Nedney kick), 0:17.

   2nd Quarter: PIT—Hines Ward 8-yd pass from Tommy Maddox (Jeff Reed kick), 9:29; PIT—Reed 30-yd FG, 6:47; PIT—Reed 39-yd FG, 0:00.

   3rd Quarter: PIT—Amos Zereoue 31-yd run (Reed kick), 14:37; TEN—Frank Wycheck 7-yd pass from McNair (Nedney kick), 9:37; TEN—Erron Kinney 2-yd pass from McNair (Nedney kick), 4:38.

   4th Quarter: PIT—Ward 21-yd pass from Maddox (Burress pass from Ward), 10:09; PIT—Reed 40-yd FG, 8:30; TEN—Nedney 42-yd FG, 5:40.

   Overtime: TEN—Nedney 26-yd FG, 12:45.

Raiders, 30-10

NY Jets (10-7) 3   7 0   0— **10**
Oakland (11-5) 3   7 7 13— **30**
   Date—Jan. 12. **Att**—62,207. **Time**—3:19.

   1st Quarter: NYJ—John Hall 38-yd FG, 10:58; OAK—Sebastian Janikowski 29-yd FG, 5:48.

   2nd Quarter: OAK—Zack Crockett 1-yd run (Janikowski kick), 13:44; NYJ—Jerald Sowell 1-yd pass from Chad Pennington (Hall kick), 0:22.

   3rd Quarter: OAK—Jerry Porter 29-yd pass from Rich Gannon (Janikowski kick), 4:24.

   4th Quarter: OAK—Jerry Rice 9-yd pass from Gannon (Janikowski kick), 14:15; OAK—Janikowski 34-yd FG, 7:55; OAK—Janikowski 31-yd FG, 2:42.

NFC

Eagles, 20-6

Atlanta (10-6-1) 0   6 0   0— **6**
Philadelphia (12-4) 10   3 0   7— **20**
   Date—Jan. 11. **Att**—66,452. **Time**—3:22.

   1st Quarter: PHI—Bobby Taylor 39-yd interception return (David Akers kick), 7:58; PHI—Akers 34-yd FG, 3:47.

   2nd Quarter: PHI—Akers 39-yd FG, 10:05; ATL—Jay Feely 34-yd FG, 4:10; ATL—Feely 52-yd FG, 0:00.

   4th Quarter: PHI—James Thrash 35-yd pass from Donovan McNabb (Akers kick), 6:26.

Buccaneers, 31-6

San Francisco (11-6) 3   3 0   0— **6**
Tampa Bay (12-4) . . . . .7 21 3   0— **31**
   Date—Jan. 12. **Att**—65,599. **Time**—3:10.

   1st Quarter: TB—Mike Alstott 2-yd run (Martin Gramatica kick), 6:34; SF—Jeff Chandler 24-yd FG, 0:17.

   2nd Quarter: TB—Joe Jurevicius 20-yd pass from Brad Johnson (Gramatica kick), 9:27; SF—Chandler 40-yd FG, 8:31; TB—Rickey Dudley 12-yd pass from B. Johnson (Gramatica kick), 7:24; TB—Alstott 2-yd run (Gramatica kick), 0:50.

   3rd Quarter: TB—Gramatica 19-yd FG, 8:28.

CONFERENCE CHAMPIONSHIPS

AFC

Raiders, 41-24

Tennessee (12-5) . . . . .7 10 7   0— **24**
Oakland (12-5) . . . . .14 10 3 14— **41**
   Date—Jan. 19. **Att**—62,544. **Time**—3:34.

   1st Quarter: OAK—Jerry Porter 3-yd pass from Rich Gannon (Sebastian Janikowski kick), 10:59; TEN—Drew Bennett 33-yd pass from Steve McNair (Joe Nedney kick), 5:59; OAK—Charlie Garner 12-yd pass from Gannon (Janikowski kick), 2:47.

   2nd Quarter: TEN—Nedney 29-yd FG, 12:39; TEN—McNair 9-yd run (Nedney kick), 2:47; OAK—Doug Jolley 1-yd pass from Gannon (Janikowski kick), 1:00; OAK—Janikowski 43-yd FG, 0:00.

   3rd Quarter: OAK—Janikowski 32-yd FG, 4:29; TEN—McNair 13-yd run (Craig Hentrich kick), 0:31.

   4th Quarter: OAK—Gannon 2-yd run (Janikowski kick), 11:27; OAK—Zack Crockett 7-yd run (Janikowski kick), 3:25.

NFC

Buccaneers, 27-10

Tampa Bay (13-4) 10   7 3   7— **27**
Philadelphia (13-4) 7   3 0   0— **10**
   Date—Jan. 19. **Att**—66,713. **Time**—3:19.

   1st Quarter: PHI—Duce Staley 20-yd run (David Akers kick), 14:08; TB—Martin Gramatica 48-yd FG, 9:58; TB—Mike Alstott 1-yd run (Gramatica kick), 0:40.

   2nd Quarter: PHI—Akers 30-yd FG, 8:04; TB—Keyshawn Johnson 9-yd pass from Brad Johnson (Gramatica kick), 2:28.

   3rd Quarter: TB—Gramatica 27-yd FG, 1:02.

   4th Quarter: TB—Ronde Barber 92-yd interception return (Gramatica kick), 3:12.

Super Bowl XXXVII

Sunday, Jan. 26, 2003 at Qualcomm Stadium in San Diego, California

Oakland (13-5) 3   0   6   12—   **21**
Tampa Bay (14-4) 3   17   14   14—   **48**

1st: OAK—Sebastian Janikowski 40-yd FG, 10:40. Drive: 14 yards in 7 plays. Key play: Charles Woodson 12-yd int. return of Brad Johnson pass to TB 36. **TB**—Martin Gramatica 31-yd FG, 7:51. Drive: 58 yards in 9 plays. Key play: Michael Pittman 23-yd run to OAK 14.

2nd: TB—Gramatica 43-yd FG, 11:16. Drive: 26 yards in 9 plays. Key play: Dexter Jackson 9-yd int. return of Rich Gannon pass to TB 49. **TB**—Mike Alstott 2-yd run (Gramatica kick), 6:24. Drive: 27 yards in 4 plays. Key play: Karl Williams 25-yd punt return to OAK 27. **TB**—Keenan McCardell 5-yd pass from B. Johnson (Gramatica kick), 0:30. Drive: 77 yards in 3 plays. Key play: Alstott 16-yd pass from B. Johnson to OAK 42.

3rd: TB—McCardell 8-yd pass from B. Johnson (Gramatica kick), 5:30. Drive: 89 yards in 14 plays. Key play: Joe Jurevicius 33-yd pass from B. Johnson to OAK 14. **TB**—Dwight Smith 44-yd int. return (Gramatica kick), 4:47. **OAK**—Jerry Porter 39-yd pass from Gannon (2-pt conversion failed), 2:14. Drive: 82 yards in 8 plays.

4th: OAK—Eric Johnson 13-yd return of blocked punt (2-pt conversion failed), 14:16. **OAK**—Jerry Rice 48-yd pass from Gannon (2-pt conversion failed), 6:06. Drive: 78 yards in 8 plays. **TB**—Derrick Brooks 44-yd int. return (Gramatica kick), 1:18. **TB**—Dwight Smith 50-yd int. return (Gramatica kick), 0:02.

Favorite: Raiders by 3½ **Attendance:** 67,603
Time: 3:50   **TV Rating:** 40.7/61 share - ABC
MVP—Dexter Jackson, Tampa Bay safety

Team Statistics

	Raiders	Buccaneers
First downs	11	24
Rushing	1	6
Passing	9	15
Penalty	1	3
3rd down efficiency	7/16	6/15
4th down efficiency	0/0	0/1
Total offense (net yards)	269	365
Plays	60	76
Average gain	4.5	4.8
Rushes/yards	11/19	42/150
Yards per rush	1.7	3.6
Passing yards (net)	250	215
Times sacked/yards lost	5/22	0/0
Passing yards (gross)	272	215
Completions/attempts	24/44	18/34
Yards per pass	5.1	6.3
Times intercepted	5	1
Return yardage	190	287
Punt returns/yards	3/29	1/25
Kickoff returns/yards	9/149	4/90
Interceptions/yards	1/12	5/172
Fumbles/lost	1/0	1/0
Penalties/yards	7/51	5/41
Punts/average	5/39.0	5/31.0
Punts blocked	0	1
Field Goals made/attempted	1/1	2/2
Time of possession	22:46	37:14

Individual Statistics

Oakland Raiders

Passing	Att	Cmp	Pct.	Yds	TD	Int
Rich Gannon	44	24	54.5	272	2	5

Receiving	No	Yds	Avg	Long	TD
Charlie Garner	7	51	7.3	9	0
Jerry Rice	5	77	15.4	48	1
Doug Jolley	5	59	11.8	25	0
Jerry Porter	4	62	15.5	39	1
Tim Brown	1	9	9.0	9	0
Jon Ritchie	1	7	7.0	7	0
Tyrone Wheatley	1	7	7.0	7	0
TOTAL	24	272	11.3	48	2

Rushing	Car	Yds	Avg	Long	TD
Charlie Garner	7	10	1.4	4	0
Zack Crockett	2	6	3.0	4	0
Rich Gannon	2	3	1.5	2	0
TOTAL	11	19	1.7	4	0

Field Goals	20-29	30-39	40-49	50-59	Total
S. Janikowski	0-0	0-0	1-1	0-0	1-1

Punting	No	Yds	Avg	Long	In20	Blk
Shane Lechler	5	195	39.0	53	2	0

Punt Returns	Ret	Yds	Long	Avg	FC	TD
Darrien Gordon	3	29	17	9.7	0	0
Tim Brown	0	0	0	0.0	1	0

Kickoff Returns	Ret	Yds	Long	Avg	FC	TD
Marcus Knight	8	143	29	17.9	0	0
Chris Cooper	1	6	6	6.0	0	0
TOTAL	9	149	29	16.6	0	0

Interceptions	No	Yds	Long	Avg	TD
Charles Woodson	1	12	12	12.0	0

Sacks
none

Most Tackles (solo)
Eric Barton 8
Charles Woodson 8

Tampa Bay Buccaneers

Passing	Att	Cmp	Pct.	Yds	TD	Int
Brad Johnson	34	18	52.9	215	2	1

Receiving	No	Yds	Avg	Long	TD
Keyshawn Johnson	6	69	11.5	18	0
Mike Alstott	5	43	8.6	16	0
Joe Jurevicius	4	78	19.5	33	0
Keenan McCardell	2	13	6.5	8	2
Ken Dilger	1	12	12.0	12	0
TOTAL	18	215	11.9	33	2

Rushing	Car	Yds	Avg	Long	TD
Michael Pittman	29	124	4.3	24	0
Mike Alstott	10	15	1.5	5	1
Brad Johnson	1	10	10.0	10	0
Aaron Stecker	1	1	1.0	1	0
Tom Tupa	1	0	0.0	0	0
TOTAL	42	150	3.6	24	1

Field Goals	20-29	30-39	40-49	50-59	Total
Martin Gramatica	0-0	1-1	1-1	0-0	2-2

Punting	No	Yds	Avg	Long	In20	Blk
Tom Tupa	5	155	31.0	43	1	1

Punt Returns	Ret	Yds	Long	Avg	FC	TD
Karl Williams	1	25	25	25.0	4	0

Kickoff Returns	Ret	Yds	Long	Avg	FC	TD
Aaron Stecker	3	67	27	22.3	0	0
Dwight Smith	1	23	23	23.0	0	0
TOTAL	4	90	27	22.5	0	0

Interceptions	No	Yds	Long	Avg	TD
Dwight Smith	2	94	50	47.0	2
Dexter Jackson	2	34	25	17.0	0
Derrick Brooks	1	44	44	44.0	1
TOTAL	5	172	50	34.4	3

Most Sacks
Simeon Rice 2

Most Tackles (solo)
Shelton Quarles 7

Super Bowl Finalists' Playoff Statistics

Oakland Raiders (2-1)

Passing	Att	Cmp	Pct.	Yds	TD	Rating
Rich Gannon	115	73	63.5	841	7	84.0

Interceptions: Gannon 6.

Top Receivers	No	Yds	Avg	Long	TD
Charlie Garner	17	132	7.8	20	1
Jerry Porter	14	237	16.9	50	3
Jerry Rice	14	203	14.5	48	2
Tim Brown	13	134	10.3	27	0
Doug Jolley	11	93	8.5	25	1

Top Rushers	Car	Yds	Avg	Long	TD
Charlie Garner	35	139	4.0	18	0
Rich Gannon	13	41	3.2	14	1
Tyrone Wheatley	5	35	7.0	24	0
Zack Crockett	5	20	4.0	7	2

Touchdowns	TD	Run	Rec	Ret	Pts
Jerry Porter	3	0	3	0	18
Zack Crockett	2	2	0	0	12
Jerry Rice	2	0	2	0	12

Four tied with 1 TD each.

Kicking	PAT/Att	FG/Att	Lg	Pts
Sebastian Janikowski	8/8	6/7	43	26

Punts	No	Yds	Avg	Long	In20
Shane Lechler	11	423	38.5	53	5

Most Interceptions		Most Sacks	
Charles Woodson	1	Rod Coleman	1.5
Eric Barton	1	Six tied with 1 each.	
Tory James	1		

Tampa Bay Buccaneers (3-0)

Passing	Att	Cmp	Pct.	Yds	TD	Rating
Brad Johnson	98	53	54.1	670	5	79.9
Rob Johnson	1	1	100.0	21	0	118.8

Interceptions: B. Johnson 3.

Top Receivers	No	Yds	Avg	Long	TD
Keyshawn Johnson	14	194	13.9	28	1
Joe Jurevicius	8	197	24.6	71	1
Mike Alstott	8	70	8.8	17	0
Ken Dilger	7	88	12.6	21	0
Keenan McCardell	7	50	7.1	11	2

Top Rushers	Car	Yds	Avg	Long	TD
Michael Pittman	54	182	3.4	24	0
Mike Alstott	44	100	2.3	20	4
Aaron Stecker	4	18	4.5	9	0

Touchdowns	TD	Run	Rec	Ret	Pts
Mike Alstott	4	4	0	0	24
Keenan McCardell	2	0	2	0	12
Dwight Smith	2	0	0	2	12

Five tied with 1 TD each.

Kicking	PAT/Att	FG/Att	Lg	Pts
Martin Gramatica	13/13	5/6	48	28

Punts	No	Yds	Avg	Long	In20
Tom Tupa	15	598	39.9	52	3

Most Interceptions		Most Sacks	
Dwight Smith	3	Simeon Rice	4
Three tied with 2 each.		Greg Spires	2

NFL Playoff Leaders

Passing Efficiency
(Minimum of 25 attempts)

	Gm	Att	Cmp	Cmp%	Yards	Avg Gain	TD	TD%	Int	Int%	Rating
Kerry Collins, NYG	1	43	29	67.4	342	7.95	4	9.3	1	2.3	112.7
Kelly Holcomb, Cle	1	43	26	60.5	429	9.98	3	7.0	1	2.3	107.6
Tommy Maddox, Pit	2	89	51	57.3	633	7.11	5	5.6	3	3.4	84.2
Rich Gannon, Oak	3	115	73	63.5	841	7.31	7	6.1	6	5.2	84.0
Steve McNair, Ten	2	80	48	60.0	532	6.65	3	3.8	2	2.5	81.9

Receptions

	No	Yds	Avg	Long	TD
Hines Ward, Pit	18	186	10.3	21-td	3
Charlie Garner, Oak	17	132	7.8	20	1
Jerry Porter, Oak	14	237	16.9	50	3
Jerry Rice, Oak	14	203	14.5	48-td	2
Keyshawn Johnson, TB	14	194	13.9	28	1
Frank Wycheck, Ten	14	164	11.7	39	1

Rushing

	No	Yds	Avg	Long	TD
Michael Pittman, TB	54	182	3.4	24	0
Curtis Martin, NYJ	31	141	4.5	15	0
Charlie Garner, Oak	35	139	4.0	18	0
Amos Zereoue, Pit	27	122	4.5	36	1
Duce Staley, Phi	31	121	3.9	20-td	1

Touchdowns

	TD	Rush	Rec	Ret	Pts
Mike Alstott, TB	4	4	0	0	24
Amani Toomer, NYG	3	0	3	0	18
Steve McNair, Ten	3	3	0	0	18
Jerry Porter, Oak	3	0	3	0	18
Hines Ward, Pit	3	0	3	0	18

Kicking

	PAT	FG	Long	Pts
Martin Gramatica, TB	13/13	5/6	48	28
Sebastian Janikowski, Oak	8/8	6/7	43	26
Jay Feely, Atl	3/3	4/7	52	15
John Hall, NYJ	6/6	3/4	41	15
Joe Nedney, Ten	6/6	3/4	42	15
Jeff Reed, Pit	6/6	3/5	40	15

Interceptions

	No	Yds	Long	TD
Dwight Smith, TB	3	100	50-td	2
Ronde Barber, TB	2	117	92-td	1
Derrick Brooks, TB	2	44	44-td	1
Daylon McCutcheon, Cle	2	41	28	0
Bobby Taylor, Phi	2	40	39-td	1
Dexter Jackson, TB	2	34	25	0
Damien Robinson, NYJ	2	24	24	0
Keion Carpenter, Atl	2	5	3	0

Sacks

	No
Simeon Rice, TB	4

Four tied with 2 each.

NFL Pro Bowl

53rd NFL Pro Bowl Game and 33rd AFC-NFC contest (AFC leads,17-16). **Date:** Feb. 2, 2003 at Aloha Stadium in Honolulu. **Coaches:** Jeff Fisher, Ten. (AFC) and Andy Reid, Phi. (NFC). **Most Valuable Player:** RB Ricky Williams, Mia. (11 rushes for 56 yds and 2 TD).

NFC	3	3	0	14—	**20**
AFC	14	14	3	14—	**45**

1st: AFC—Ricky Williams 1-yd run (Adam Vinatieri kick), 12:15; NFC—David Akers 45-yd FG, 9:16; AFC—Tony Gonzalez 11-yd pass from Rich Gannon (Vinatieri kick), 5:06.

2nd: AFC—Travis Henry 13-yd pass from Gannon (Vinatieri kick), 10:20; NFC—Akers 53-yd FG, 4:27; AFC—Williams 1-yd run (Vinatieri kick), 0:47.

3rd: AFC—Vinatieri 20-yd FG, 10:41.

4th: AFC—Ty Law 43-yd interception return (Vinatieri kick), 11:52; AFC—Hines Ward 32-yd pass from Peyton Manning (Vinatieri kick), 7:31; NFC—Joe Horn 12-yd pass from Brad Johnson (Akers kick), 5:01; NFC—Mike Alstott 4-yd pass from Johnson (Akers kick), 2:04.

Attendance— 50,125. **TV Rating**— 6.9/11 share (ABC). **Time**— 3:14.

STARTING LINEUPS

As voted on by NFL players, coaches, and fans. (*) denotes injured and unable to play.

American Conference

Pos	Offense	Pos	Defense
WR	Marvin Harrison, Ind.	E	Trevor Pryce, Den.
WR	Jerry Rice, Oak.	E	Jason Taylor, Mia.
TE	Tony Gonzalez, KC	T	Richard Seymour, NE
T	Willie Roaf, KC	T	Gary Walker, Hou.
T	Jonathan Ogden, Bal.	LB	Joey Porter, Pit.
G	Alan Faneca, Pit.	LB	Peter Boulware, Bal.
G	Will Shields, KC	LB	Zach Thomas, Mia.
C	Kevin Mawae, NYJ	CB	Aaron Glenn, Hou.
QB	Rich Gannon, Oak.	CB	Ty Law, NE
RB	Ricky Williams, Mia.	SS	Lawyer Milloy, NE
FB	Lorenzo Neal, Cin.	FS	Rod Woodson, Oak.
K	Adam Vinatieri, NE	P	Chris Hanson, Jax
KR	Dante Hall, KC	ST	Larry Izzo, NE

Reserves

Offense: WR—Eric Moulds, Buf. and Hines Ward, Pit.; **TE**—Todd Heap, Bal.; **T**—Lincoln Kennedy, Oak.; **G**—Ruben Brown, Buf.; **C**—Barrett Robbins*, Oak.; **QB**—Drew Bledsoe, Buf. and Peyton Manning, Ind.; **RB**—LaDainian Tomlinson, SD and Priest Holmes*, KC.

Defense: E—John Abraham, NYJ and Kevin Carter, Ten.; **T**—Tim Bowens, Mia.; **LB**—Junior Seau*, SD and Al Wilson*, Den.; **CB**—Patrick Surtain*, Mia.; **FS**—Brock Marion, Mia.

Replacements: OFFENSE—C Damien Woody, NE for Robbins; RB Travis Henry, Buf. for Holmes. DEFENSE—LB Jason Gildon, Pit. for Seau; LB Donnie Edwards, SD for Wilson; CB Sam Madison, Mia. for Surtain.

National Conference

Pos	Offense	Pos	Defense
WR	Joe Horn, NO	E	Simeon Rice, TB
WR	Terrell Owens, SF	E	Michael Strahan, NYG
TE	Bubba Franks, GB	T	La'Roi Glover, Dal.
T	Walter Jones*, Sea.	T	Bryant Young, SF
T	Tra Thomas, Phi.	LB	LaVar Arrington, Wash.
G	Jermane Mayberry, Phi.	LB	Derrick Brooks, TB
G	Ron Stone, SF	LB	Brian Urlacher, Chi.
C	Olin Kreutz, Chi.	CB	Champ Bailey, Wash.
QB	Jeff Garcia, SF	CB	Troy Vincent, Phi.
RB	Deuce McAllister, NO	SS	John Lynch, TB
FB	Mike Alstott, TB	FS	Darren Sharper, GB
K	David Akers, Phi.	P	Todd Sauerbrun, Car.
KR	Michael Lewis, NO	ST	Fred McAfee, NO

Reserves

Offense: WR—Marty Booker, Chi. and Randy Moss*, Min.; **TE**—Jeremy Shockey, NYG and Chad Lewis, Phi.; **T**—Orlando Pace*, St.L; **G**—Marco Rivera, GB; **C**—Jeremy Newberry, SF; **QB**—Brett Favre*, GB and Michael Vick*, Atl.; **RB**—Marshall Faulk, St.L and Ahman Green*, GB.

Defense: E—Hugh Douglas, Phi.; **T**—Warren Sapp*, TB; **LB**—Julian Peterson, SF and Keith Brooking*, Atl.; **CB**—Bobby Taylor, Phi.; **FS**—Brian Dawkins, Phi.

Replacements: OFFENSE—WR Donald Driver, GB for Moss; T Chris Samuels, Wash. for Jones; T Jon Runyan, Phi. for Pace; QB Donovan McNabb, Phi. for Favre; QB Brad Johnson, TB for Vick; RB Michael Bennett, Min. for Green. DEFENSE—T Kris Jenkins, Car. for Sapp; LB Shelton Quarles, TB for Brooking.

Annual Awards

The NFL does not sanction any of the major postseason awards for players and coaches, but many are given out. Among the presenters for the 2002 regular season were AP, The Maxwell Football Club of Philadelphia (Bert Bell Award for player; Greasy Neale Award for coach), *The Sporting News* and the Pro Football Writers of America/*Pro Football Weekly*.

Most Valuable Player

Rich Gannon, Oakland, QB . . . . . . .AP, PFWA, *TSN*, Bell

Offensive Players of the Year

Priest Holmes, Kansas City, RB . . . . .AP
Rich Gannon, Oakland, QB . . . . .PFWA

Defensive Player of the Year

Derrick Brooks, Tampa Bay, LB . . . . .AP, PFWA

Rookies of the Year

NFL	Clinton Portis, Denver, RB	*TSN*
Offense	Clinton Portis, Denver, RB	AP, PFWA
Defense	Julius Peppers, Carolina, DE	AP, PFWA

Coach of the Year

Andy Reid, Philadelphia . . . . .AP, *TSN*, Neale, PFWA

2002 All-NFL Team

The 2002 All-NFL team combining the All-Pro selections of the Associated Press, *The Sporting News* (TSN) and the Pro Football Writers of America/*Pro Football Weekly* (PFWA). Holdovers from the 2001 All-NFL Team in **bold** type.

Offense

Pos		Selectors
WR—	Marvin Harrison, Indianapolis	AP, *TSN*, PFWA
WR—	**Terrell Owens**, San Francisco	AP, *TSN*, PFWA
TE—	**Tony Gonzalez**, Kansas City	*TSN*, PFWA
TE—	Jeremy Shockey, NY Giants	AP
T—	**Jonathan Ogden**, Baltimore	AP, *TSN*, PFWA
T—	Lincoln Kennedy, Oakland	AP
T—	Tra Thomas, Philadelphia	*TSN*
T—	**Walter Jones**, Seattle	PFWA
G—	**Alan Faneca**, Pittsburgh	AP, *TSN*, PFWA
G—	Will Shields, Kansas City	AP, *TSN*, PFWA
C—	**Kevin Mawae**, NY Jets	*TSN*, PFWA
C—	Barret Robbins, Oakland	AP
QB—	Rich Gannon, Oakland	AP, *TSN*, PFWA
RB—	**Priest Holmes**, Kansas City	AP, *TSN*, PFWA
RB—	Ricky Williams, Miami	AP, *TSN*, PFWA

Defense

Pos		Selectors
DE—	Simeon Rice, Tampa Bay	AP, *TSN*, PFWA
DE—	Jason Taylor, Miami	AP, *TSN*, PFWA
DT—	**Warren Sapp**, Tampa Bay	AP, *TSN*, PFWA
DT—	La'Roi Glover, Dallas	*TSN*, PFWA
DT—	Kris Jenkins, Carolina	AP
LB—	Derrick Brooks, Tampa Bay	AP, *TSN*, PFWA
LB—	Joey Porter, Pittsburgh	AP, *TSN*, PFWA
LB—	**Brian Urlacher**, Chicago	AP, *TSN*, PFWA
LB—	Zach Thomas, Miami	AP
CB—	Patrick Surtain, Miami	AP, *TSN*, PFWA
CB—	Aaron Glenn, Houston	*TSN*
CB—	Troy Vincent, Philadelphia	AP
CB—	Bobby Taylor, Philadelphia	PFWA
S—	**Brian Dawkins**, Philadelphia	AP, *TSN*, PFWA
S—	Rod Woodson, Oakland	AP, PFWA
S—	Darren Sharper, Green Bay	*TSN*

Specialists

Pos		Selectors
K—	**David Akers**, Philadelphia	*TSN*
K—	Adam Vinatieri, New England	AP, PFWA
P—	**Todd Sauerbrun**, Carolina	AP, *TSN*, PFWA

Pos		Selectors
KR—	Michael Lewis, New Orleans	AP, *TSN*, PFWA
PR—	Santana Moss, NY Jets	*TSN*, PFWA
ST—	Fred McAfee, New Orleans	PFWA

2003 College Draft

First and second round selections at the 68th annual NFL College Draft held April 26-27, 2003, in New York City. Fifteen underclassmen were among the first 64 players chosen and are listed in capital LETTERS.

First Round

No	Team		Pos
1	Cincinnati	Carson Palmer, USC	QB
2	Detroit	CHARLES ROGERS, Michigan St.	WR
3	Houston	ANDRE JOHNSON, Miami-FL	WR
4	NY Jets	DEWAYNE ROBERTSON, Kentucky	DT
5	Dallas	Terence Newman, Kansas St.	CB
6	N. Orleans	JOHNATHAN SULLIVAN, Georgia	DT
7	Jacksonville	Byron Leftwich, Marshall	QB
8	Carolina	Jordan Gross, Utah	OT
9	Minnesota	Kevin Williams, Oklahoma St.	DT
10	Baltimore	TERRELL SUGGS, Arizona St.	DE
11	Seattle	Marcus Trufant, Washington St.	CB
12	St. Louis	Jimmy Kennedy, Penn St.	DT
13	New England	Ty Warren, Texas A&M	DT
14	Chicago	Michael Haynes, Penn St.	DE
15	Philadelphia	Jerome McDougle, Miami-FL	DE
16	Pittsburgh	Troy Polamalu, USC	SS
17	Arizona	Bryant Johnson, Penn St.	WR
18	Arizona	Calvin Pace, Wake Forest	DE
19	Baltimore	Kyle Boller, California	QB
20	Denver	George Foster, Georgia	OT
21	Cleveland	JEFF FAINE, Notre Dame	C
22	Chicago	REX GROSSMAN, Florida	QB
23	Buffalo	WILLIS MCGAHEE, Miami-FL	RB
24	Indianapolis	DALLAS CLARK, Iowa	TE
25	NY Giants	William Joseph, Miami-FL	DT
26	San Francisco	KWAME HARRIS, Stanford	OT
27	Kansas City	Larry Johnson, Penn St.	RB
28	Tennessee	Andre Woolfolk, Oklahoma	CB
29	Green Bay	Nick Barnett, Oregon St.	LB
30	San Diego	Sammy Davis, Texas A&M	CB
31	Oakland	Nnamdi Asomugha, California	CB
32	Oakland	Tyler Brayton, Colorado	DE

Second Round

No	Team		Pos
33	Cincinnati	Eric Steinbach, Iowa	G
34	Detroit	Boss Bailey, Georgia	LB
35	Chicago	Charles Tillman, LA-Lafayette	DB
36	New England	Eugene Wilson, Illinois	CB
37	New Orleans	Jon Stinchcomb, Georgia	OT
38	Dallas	Al Johnson, Wisconsin	C
39	Jacksonville	Rashean Mathis, Beth. Cookman	FS
40	Minnesota	E.J. Henderson, Maryland	LB
41	Houston	Bennie Joppru, Michigan	TE
42	Seattle	KEN HAMLIN, Arkansas	FS
43	St. Louis	Pisa Tinoisamoa, Hawaii	LB
44	Washington	Taylor Jacobs, Florida	WR
45	New England	Bethel Johnson, Texas A&M	WR
46	San Diego	Drayton Florence, Tuskegee	CB
47	Kansas City	Kawika Mitchell, South Florida	LB
48	Buffalo	Chris Kelsay, Nebraska	DE
49	Miami	Eddie Moore, Tennessee	LB
50	Carolina	Bruce Nelson, Iowa	C
51	Denver	TERRY PIERCE, Kansas St.	LB
52	Cleveland	Chaun Thompson, W. Texas A&M	LB
53	NY Jets	Victor Hobson, Michigan	LB
54	Arizona	ANQUAN BOLDIN, Florida St.	WR
55	Atlanta	Bryan Scott, Penn St.	SS
56	NY Giants	Osi Umenyiora, Troy St.	DE
57	San Francisco	Anthony Adams, Penn St.	DT
58	Indianapolis	Mike Doss, Ohio St.	SS
59	Pittsburgh	Alonzo Jackson, Florida St.	DE
60	Tennessee	Tyrone Calico, Middle Tenn. St.	WR
61	Philadelphia	L.J. Smith, Rutgers	TE
62	San Diego	Terrence Kiel, Texas A&M	FS
63	Oakland	TEYO JOHNSON, Stanford	WR
64	Tampa Bay	DEWAYNE WHITE, Louisville	DE

NFL Europe

Final 2003 Standings

	W	L	T	Pct.	PF	PA
*Frankfurt	6	4	0	.600	252	182
*Rhein	6	4	0	.600	189	188
Scotland	6	4	0	.600	303	190
F.C. Barcelona	5	5	0	.500	150	221
Amsterdam	4	6	0	.400	230	273
Berlin	3	7	0	.200	248	318

*The teams with the top two records after the regular season play in the World Bowl. Frankfurt (6-4) and Rhein (6-4) advanced over Scotland (6-4) due to better records in games amongst themsleves.

World Bowl XI

June 14, 2003 at Hampden Park, Glasgow, Scotland (Att: 28,138)

Rhein (6-4)	3	6	0	7—	**16**
Frankfurt (6-4)	11	14	7	3—	**35**

MVP: Jonas Lewis, Frankfurt, RB (16 carries for 126 yards and 1 TD)

Regular Season Individual Leaders

Passing Efficiency
(Min. 140 pass attempts)

	Att	Cmp	Cmp Pct	Yds	Yds/ Att	TD	TDPct	Long	Int	IntPct	Rating
Craig Nall, Sco	258	151	58.5	2050	7.95	18	7.0	52	7	2.7	95.9
Phil Stambaugh, Ber	254	169	66.5	1759	6.93	13	5.1	80-td	6	2.4	93.6
Shaun Hill, Ams	356	220	61.8	2256	6.34	13	3.7	56	5	1.4	86.3
Seth Burford, Bar	175	102	58.3	1054	6.02	8	4.6	59-td	3	1.7	83.8
James Brown, Fra	196	112	57.1	1402	7.15	5	2.6	43	5	2.6	77.4

Scoring

Touchdowns	TD	Rus	Rec	Ret	Pts
Ken Simonton, Sco	10	8	2	0	60
Jonas Lewis, Fra	9	8	1	0	54
Matthew Hatchette, Ams	8	0	7	1	48
Robert Baker, Fra	8	0	7	1	48
Sean Morey, Bar	7	0	7	0	42

Kicking	PAT	FG/FGA	Lg	Pts
Rob Hart, Sco	37/38	9/13	35	64
Ralf Kleinmann, Fra	22/23	10/14	34	52
Axel Kruse, Ber	28/29	6/7	31	46
Silvio Diliberto, Ams	20/22	6/7	33	38
Ingo Anderbrugge, Rhe	18/20	6/7	27	36

Rushing

	Car	Yards	Avg	Long	TD
Ken Simonton, Sco	162	871	5.4	70	8
Autry Denson, Rhe	128	725	5.7	31	3
Jonas Lewis, Fra	160	669	4.2	25	8
David Allen, Ber	102	635	6.2	39	3
Maurice Hicks, Sco	74	546	7.4	93-td	4

Receptions

	No	Yards	Avg	Long	TD
Matthew Hatchette, Ams	61	790	13.0	36	7
Marc Lester, Fra	45	678	15.1	61-td	6
Kirk McMullen, Ams	40	316	7.9	24	2
Ken Simonton, Sco	39	382	9.8	40	2
Elijah Thurmon, Ber	37	412	11.1	80-td	5
Justin Skaggs, Ams	37	401	10.8	35-td	5

Punting

	No	Yards	Avg	Long	In20
Nick Murphy, Bar	68	2886	42.4	68	15
Steve Cheek, Ber	43	1772	41.2	65	13
Tim Morgan, Fra	37	1522	41.1	58	9
Kevin Stemke, Sco	35	1382	39.5	54	10
Jeff Crowell, Ams	49	1893	38.6	60	10

Sacks

	No
Lamanzer Williams, Ber	10.5
Joey Evans, Fra	8.0
T.J. Bingham, Sco	7.0
Jonathan Brown, Ams	6.5
Bastian Lano, Rhe	6.5
Michael Landry, Sco	6.5

Interceptions

	No	Yds	Long	TD
Rashidi Barnes, Fra	4	60	16	0
Jeremy Unertl, Fra	4	52	35	0
Greg Brown, Rhe	3	78	41	0
Calvin Spears, Fra	3	28	28	0
Lemual Ligon, Rhe	3	18	18	0
Jason Waters, Bar	3	1	1	0

All-NFL Europe League Team

The All-NFL Europe League Team as selected by NFL Europe coaches, media and fans.

Offense
QB	Craig Nall, Sco	
WR	Robert Baker, Fra	
WR	Matthew Hatchette, Ams	
WR	Kendall Newson, Rhe	
RB	Ken Simonton, Sco	
TE	Ryan Collins, Ams	
T	David Costa, Sco	
G	Troy Andrew, Bar	
C	Luke Butkus, Rhe	
G	Michael Moore, Ams	
T	Justin Bland, Sco	

Defense
DE	Lamanzer Williams, Ber
DT	Luis Almanzer, Fra
DT	Michael Landry, Sco
DE	Jonathan Brown, Ams
LB	Tito Rodriguez, Bar
LB	Yubrenal Isabelle, Sco
LB	Idris Price, Fra
CB	Jason Waters, Bar
S	Rashidi Barnes, Fra
S	Calvin Spears, Fra
CB	Antuan Simmons, Bar

Special Teams
K	Rob Hart, Sco
P	Nick Murphy, Bar
Spec.	David Allen, Ber

Annual Awards

Offensive MVP	Ken Simonton, Scotland, RB
Defensive MVP	Rashidi Barnes, Frankfurt, S
Coach of the Year	Doug Graber, Frankfurt

Canadian Football League
Final 2002 Standings

Division champions (*) and playoff qualifiers (†) are noted. Wins are worth two points in the standings. Ties and overtime losses (OTL) are each worth one point. Overtime losses are included in the loss column.

East Division

	W	L	T	OTL	Pts	PF	PA
*Montreal	13	5	0	1	27	577	408
†Toronto	8	10	0	0	16	344	482
Hamilton	7	11	0	0	15	427	524
Ottawa	4	14	0	2	10	356	550

West Division

	W	L	T	OTL	Pts	PF	PA
*Edmonton	13	5	0	0	26	516	450
†Winnipeg	12	6	0	0	24	566	421
†Brit. Columbia	10	8	0	0	20	480	399
†Saskatchewan	8	10	0	2	18	435	393
Calgary	6	12	0	2	14	438	512

Playoffs

Division Semifinals (Nov. 10)

East: at Toronto 24 . . . . Saskatchewan 14
West: at Winnipeg 30 . . . . British Columbia 3

Division Finals (Nov. 17)

East: at Montreal 35 . . . . Toronto 18
West: at Edmonton 33 . . . . Winnipeg 30

90th Grey Cup Championship

November 24, 2002 at Commonwealth Stadium in Edmonton, Alberta

(Att: 62,531)

Montreal	1	10	0	14—	**25**
Edmonton	0	0	10	6—	**16**

MVP: Anthony Calvillo, Montreal, QB (11-31 for 260 yards, 2 TD, 0 INT)

Regular Season Individual Leaders
Passing Yards

	Att	Cmp	Cmp Pct	Yds	Yds/ Att	TD	TD Pct	Int	IntPct	Rating
Khari Jones, Win.	620	382	61.6	5334	8.6	46	7.4	29	4.7	94.3
Anthony Calvillo, Mon.	569	338	59.4	5013	8.8	27	4.7	10	1.8	96.4
Danny McManus, Ham.	604	318	52.6	4531	7.5	23	3.8	30	5.0	68.9
Marcus Crandell, Calg.	516	268	51.9	4072	7.9	26	5.0	20	3.9	78.6
Damon Allen, B.C.	474	268	56.5	3987	8.4	22	4.6	10	2.1	90.8

Scoring

Touchdowns	TD	Rus	Rec	Ret	Pts
Milt Stegall, Win	23	0	23	0	138
Sean Millington, B.C.	16	14	2	0	96
Derrell Mitchell, Tor.	14	0	13	1	84
Lawrence Phillips, Mon.	13	13	0	0	78
Arland Bruce, Win.	13	1	12	0	78

Kicking	PAT	FG	S*	Pts
Troy Westwood, Win.	57	45/62	12	204
Terry Baker, Mon.	61	36/54	16	185
Paul McCallum, Sask.	39	41/54	19	181
Paul Osbaldiston, Ham.	29	38/47	16	159
Sean Fleming, Edm.	51	32/37	10	157

*Singles (or Rouges)

Rushing

	Car	Yards	Avg	TD
John Avery, Edm.	229	1448	6.3	9
Charles Roberts, Win.	216	1162	5.4	5
Troy Davis, Ham.	230	1143	5.0	6
Kelvin Anderson, Calg.	221	1074	4.9	4
Lawrence Phillips, Mon.	187	1022	5.5	13

All-CFL Team

Offense		Defense	
WR	Derick Armstrong, Sask.	E	Joe Montford, Tor.
WR	Jason Tucker, Edm.	E	Elfrid Payton, Edm.
T	Uzooma Okeke, Mon.	T	Doug Brown, Win.
T	Dave Mudge, Win.	T	Denny Fortney, Win.
G	Jay McNeil, Calg.	LB	John Grace, Ott.
G	Scott Flory, Mon.	LB	Barrin Simpson, B.C.
C	Bryan Chiu, Mon.	LB	B. Ayanbadejo, B.C.
QB	Anthony Calvillo, Mon.	DB	Barron Miles, Mon.
RB	John Avery, Edm.	DB	Clifford Ivory, Tor.
RB	Charles Roberts, Win.	DB	Omar Morgan, Sask.
SB	Terry Vaughn, Edm.	DB	Eric Carter, B.C.
SB	Milt Stegall, Win.	S	Rob Hitchcock, Ham.

Specialists

K/P	Sean Fleming, Edm.	P	Noel Prefontaine, Tor.
Special Teams	Corey Holmes, Sask.		

Receptions

	No	Yards	Avg	TD
Milt Stegall, Win.	106	1896	17.9	23
Terry Vaughn, Edm.	94	1291	13.7	9
Jimmy Oliver, Ott.	82	1004	12.2	6
Ben Cahoon, Mon.	75	1060	14.1	6
Travis Moore, Calg.	70	1108	15.8	10
Derick Armstrong, Sask.	70	1104	15.8	5

Most Outstanding Awards

Player . . . . Milt Stegall, Winnipeg, SB	Rookie . . . . Jason Clermont, British Columbia, SB
Canadian . . . . Ben Cahoon, Montreal, SB	Tom Pate Award (Sportsmanship) . . Greg Frers, Calgary, S
Offensive Lineman . . . . Bryan Chiu, Montreal, C	Special Teams . . . . Corey Holmes, Saskatchewan, RB
Defensive Player . . . . Elfrid Payton, Edmonton, DE	Coach . . . . Don Matthews, Montreal

Arena Football
Final 2003 Standings

Division champions (*) and playoff qualifiers (†) are noted; top twelve teams advance to the playoffs, with top four receiving first-round byes.

American Conference
Central Division

	W	L	T	Pct.	PF	PA
*Dallas	10	6	0	.625	910	875
†Grand Rapids	8	8	0	.500	925	848
†Chicago	8	8	0	.500	785	754
Indiana	6	10	0	.375	774	831

Western Division

	W	L	T	Pct.	PF	PA
*San Jose	12	4	0	.750	966	781
†Los Angeles	11	5	0	.688	924	802
†Arizona	10	6	0	.625	917	842
Colorado	2	14	0	.125	748	958

National Conference
Eastern Division

	W	L	T	Pct.	PF	PA
*New York	8	8	0	.500	857	825
†Detroit	8	8	0	.500	799	819
†Las Vegas	8	8	0	.500	756	821
Buffalo	5	11	0	.313	554	751

Southern Division

	W	L	T	Pct.	PF	PA
*Tampa Bay	12	4	0	.750	849	689
†Orlando	12	4	0	.750	805	670
†Georgia	8	8	0	.500	731	701
Carolina	0	16	0	.000	553	886

Annual Awards

Ironman of the Year . . . . .Randy Gatewood, Arizona
Offensive Player of the Year . . .Chris Jackson, Los Angeles
Defensive Player of the Year . . . .Clevan Thomas, San Jose
Rookie of the Year . . . . .Travis McGriff, Orlando
Coach of the Year . . . . .Todd Shell, New York

ArenaBowl XVII

June 22, 2003 at St. Pete Times Forum in Tampa, Fla.
(Att: 20,496)

Arizona	10	6	6	7—	**29**
Tampa Bay	14	9	7	13—	**43**

MVP: Lawrence Samuels, Tampa Bay, WR/LB (5 catches for 109 yards and 3 TD.)

arenafootball2
Final 2003 Standings

Division champions (*) and playoff qualifiers (†) are noted; division champions with two best records received first round byes.

American Conference
Northeast Division

	W	L	T	Pct.	PF	PA
*Albany	13	3	0	.813	878	731
†Mohegan	10	6	0	.625	727	619
Wilkes-Barre/Scranton	6	10	0	.375	692	793
Rochester	3	13	0	.188	571	799

South Division

	W	L	T	Pct.	PF	PA
*Tennessee Valley	14	2	0	.875	845	669
†Florida	10	6	0	.625	731	627
†Macon	10	6	0	.625	788	675
Birmingham	7	9	0	.438	735	716
Columbus	4	12	0	.250	548	767

Atlantic Division

	W	L	T	Pct.	PF	PA
*Cape Fear	10	6	0	.625	819	713
Charleston	9	7	0	.563	749	652
Greensboro	9	7	0	.563	809	813
Norfolk	8	8	0	.500	727	693
Richmond	6	10	0	.375	629	761

National Conference
Midwest Division

	W	L	T	Pct.	PF	PA
*Quad City	14	2	0	.875	915	647
Cincinnati	7	9	0	.438	658	691
Louisville	5	11	0	.313	595	786
Peoria	5	11	0	.313	740	748
Green Bay	2	14	0	.125	547	760

Central Division

	W	L	T	Pct.	PF	PA
*Tulsa	13	3	0	.813	823	690
†Arkansas	9	7	0	.563	722	702
Memphis	6	10	0	.375	703	655
Bossier City	3	13	0	.188	631	840

West Division

	W	L	T	Pct.	PF	PA
*Hawaii	10	6	0	.625	737	747
†Wichita	8	7	1	.533	726	721
†Bakersfield	8	7	1	.533	697	663
San Diego	6	10	0	.375	688	752

Annual Awards

Ironman of the Year . .Bobby Sippio, Greensboro, WR/DB
Offensive Player of the Year . .Tony Zimmerman, Q.C., QB
Defensive Player of the Year . . .Kahlil Carter, Arkansas, DS
Lineman of the Year . . .Wes Stephens, Tenn. Valley, OL/DL
Rookie of the Year . . . . . .Johnny Turman, Charleston, QB
Coach of the Year . . . . .Kevin Guy, Tennessee Valley

ArenaCup 2003

August 23, 2003 at the Tulsa Convention Center.
(Att: 7,184)

Macon	7	0	13	20—	**40**
Tulsa	14	21	3	20—	**58**

MVP: Craig Strickland, Tulsa, QB (19-28 for 254 yards, 5 TD, 0 INT; 8 rushes for 19 yards, 2 TD)

1920-2003
Through the Years

SPORTS ALMANAC

The Super Bowl

The first AFL-NFL World Championship Game, as it was originally called, was played seven months after the two leagues agreed to merge in June of 1966. It became the Super Bowl (complete with roman numerals) by the third game in 1969. The Super Bowl winner has been presented the Vince Lombardi Trophy since 1971. Lombardi, whose Green Bay teams won the first two title games, died in 1970. NFL champions (1966-69) and NFC champions (since 1970) are listed in CAPITAL letters.

Multiple winners: Dallas and San Francisco (5); Pittsburgh (4); Green Bay, Oakland-LA Raiders and Washington (3); Denver, Miami and NY Giants (2).

Bowl	Date	Winner	Head Coach	Score	Loser	Head Coach	Site
I	1/15/67	GREEN BAY	Vince Lombardi	35-10	Kansas City	Hank Stram	Los Angeles
II	1/14/68	GREEN BAY	Vince Lombardi	33-14	Oakland	John Rauch	Miami
III	1/12/69	NY Jets	Weeb Ewbank	16- 7	BALT. COLTS	Don Shula	Miami
IV	1/11/70	Kansas City	Hank Stram	23- 7	MINNESOTA	Bud Grant	New Orleans
V	1/17/71	Balt. Colts	Don McCafferty	16-13	DALLAS	Tom Landry	Miami
VI	1/16/72	DALLAS	Tom Landry	24- 3	Miami	Don Shula	New Orleans
VII	1/14/73	Miami	Don Shula	14- 7	WASHINGTON	George Allen	Los Angeles
VIII	1/13/74	Miami	Don Shula	24- 7	MINNESOTA	Bud Grant	Houston
IX	1/12/75	Pittsburgh	Chuck Noll	16- 6	MINNESOTA	Bud Grant	New Orleans
X	1/18/76	Pittsburgh	Chuck Noll	21-17	DALLAS	Tom Landry	Miami
XI	1/ 9/77	Oakland	John Madden	32-14	MINNESOTA	Bud Grant	Pasadena
XII	1/15/78	DALLAS	Tom Landry	27-10	Denver	Red Miller	New Orleans
XIII	1/21/79	Pittsburgh	Chuck Noll	35-31	DALLAS	Tom Landry	Miami
XIV	1/20/80	Pittsburgh	Chuck Noll	31-19	LA RAMS	Ray Malavasi	Pasadena
XV	1/25/81	Oakland	Tom Flores	27-10	PHILADELPHIA	Dick Vermeil	New Orleans
XVI	1/24/82	SAN FRANCISCO	Bill Walsh	26-21	Cincinnati	Forrest Gregg	Pontiac, MI
XVII	1/30/83	WASHINGTON	Joe Gibbs	27-17	Miami	Don Shula	Pasadena
XVIII	1/22/84	LA Raiders	Tom Flores	38- 9	WASHINGTON	Joe Gibbs	Tampa
XIX	1/20/85	SAN FRANCISCO	Bill Walsh	38-16	Miami	Don Shula	Stanford
XX	1/26/86	CHICAGO	Mike Ditka	46-10	New England	Raymond Berry	New Orleans
XXI	1/25/87	NY GIANTS	Bill Parcells	39-20	Denver	Dan Reeves	Pasadena
XXII	1/31/88	WASHINGTON	Joe Gibbs	42-10	Denver	Dan Reeves	San Diego
XXIII	1/22/89	SAN FRANCISCO	Bill Walsh	20-16	Cincinnati	Sam Wyche	Miami
XXIV	1/28/90	SAN FRANCISCO	George Seifert	55-10	Denver	Dan Reeves	New Orleans
XXV	1/27/91	NY GIANTS	Bill Parcells	20-19	Buffalo	Marv Levy	Tampa
XXVI	1/26/92	WASHINGTON	Joe Gibbs	37-24	Buffalo	Marv Levy	Minneapolis
XXVII	1/31/93	DALLAS	Jimmy Johnson	52-17	Buffalo	Marv Levy	Pasadena
XXVIII	1/30/94	DALLAS	Jimmy Johnson	30-13	Buffalo	Marv Levy	Atlanta
XXIX	1/29/95	SAN FRANCISCO	George Seifert	49-26	San Diego	Bobby Ross	Miami
XXX	1/28/96	DALLAS	Barry Switzer	27-17	Pittsburgh	Bill Cowher	Tempe, AZ
XXXI	1/26/97	GREEN BAY	Mike Holmgren	35-21	New England	Bill Parcells	New Orleans
XXXII	1/25/98	Denver	Mike Shanahan	31-24	GREEN BAY	Mike Holmgren	San Diego
XXXIII	1/31/99	Denver	Mike Shanahan	34-19	ATLANTA	Dan Reeves	Miami
XXXIV	1/30/00	ST.L RAMS	Dick Vermeil	23-16	Tennessee	Jeff Fisher	Atlanta
XXXV	1/28/01	Balt. Ravens	Brian Billick	34- 7	NY GIANTS	Jim Fassel	Tampa
XXXVI	2/3/02	New England	Bill Belichick	20-17	ST.L RAMS	Mike Martz	New Orleans
XXXVII	1/26/03	TAMPA BAY	Jon Gruden	48-21	Oakland	Bill Callahan	San Diego

Super Bowl Appearances

App		W	L	Pct	PF	PA	App		W	L	Pct	PF	PA
8	Dallas	5	3	.625	221	132	3	New England	1	2	.333	51	98
6	Denver	2	4	.333	115	206	2	Baltimore Colts	1	1	.500	23	29
5	San Francisco	5	0	1.000	188	89	2	Kansas City	1	1	.500	33	42
5	Pittsburgh	4	1	.800	120	100	2	Cincinnati	0	2	.000	37	46
5	Oak/LA Raiders	3	2	.600	132	114	1	Baltimore Ravens	1	0	1.000	34	7
5	Washington	3	2	.600	122	103	1	Chicago	1	0	1.000	46	10
5	Miami	2	3	.400	74	103	1	NY Jets	1	0	1.000	16	7
4	Green Bay	3	1	.750	127	76	1	Tampa Bay	1	0	1.000	48	21
4	Buffalo	0	4	.000	73	139	1	Atlanta	0	1	.000	19	34
4	Minnesota	0	4	.000	34	95	1	Philadelphia	0	1	.000	10	27
3	NY Giants	2	1	.667	66	73	1	San Diego	0	1	.000	26	49
3	LA/St.L Rams	1	2	.333	59	67	1	Tennessee	0	1	.000	16	23

Pete Rozelle Award (MVP)

The Most Valuable Player in the Super Bowl. Currently selected by a 15-member panel made up of national pro football writers and broadcasters chosen by the NFL (80 percent) and fans voting via the internet (20 percent). Presented by *Sport* magazine from 1967-89 and by the NFL since 1990. Named after former NFL commissioner Pete Rozelle in 1990. Winner who did not play for Super Bowl champion in **bold** type.

Multiple winners: Joe Montana (3); Terry Bradshaw and Bart Starr (2).

Bowl		Bowl		Bowl	
I	Bart Starr, Green Bay, QB	XIII	Terry Bradshaw, Pittsburgh, QB	XXVI	Mark Rypien, Washington, QB
II	Bart Starr, Green Bay, QB	XIV	Terry Bradshaw, Pittsburgh, QB	XXVII	Troy Aikman, Dallas, QB
III	Joe Namath, NY Jets, QB	XV	Jim Plunkett, Oakland, QB	XXVIII	Emmitt Smith, Dallas, RB
IV	Len Dawson, Kansas City, QB	XVI	Joe Montana, San Francisco, QB	XXIX	Steve Young, San Fran., QB
V	Chuck Howley, Dallas, LB	XVII	John Riggins, Washington, RB	XXX	Larry Brown, Dallas, CB
VI	Roger Staubach, Dallas, QB	XVIII	Marcus Allen, LA Raiders, RB	XXXI	Desmond Howard, Gr. Bay, KR
VII	Jake Scott, Miami, S	XIX	Joe Montana, San Francisco, QB	XXXII	Terrell Davis, Denver, RB
VIII	Larry Csonka, Miami, RB	XX	Richard Dent, Chicago, DE	XXXIII	John Elway, Denver, QB
IX	Franco Harris, Pittsburgh, RB	XXI	Phil Simms, NY Giants, QB	XXXIV	Kurt Warner, St. Louis, QB
X	Lynn Swann, Pittsburgh, WR	XXII	Doug Williams, Washington, QB	XXXV	Ray Lewis, Baltimore, LB
XI	Fred Biletnikoff, Oakland, WR	XXIII	Jerry Rice, San Francisco, WR	XXXVI	Tom Brady, New England, QB
XII	Harvey Martin, Dallas, DE	XXIV	Joe Montana, San Francisco, QB	XXXVII	Dexter Jackson, Tampa Bay, S
	& Randy White, Dallas, DT	XXV	Ottis Anderson, NY Giants, RB		

All-Time Super Bowl Leaders

Through 2003; participants in Super Bowl XXXVII in **bold** type.

CAREER

Passing Efficiency

		Gm	Att	Cmp	Cmp%	Yards	Avg Gain	TD	TD%	Int	Int%	Rating
1	Phil Simms, NYG	1	25	22	88.0	268	10.72	3	12.0	0	0.0	150.9
2	Steve Young, SF	2	39	26	66.7	345	8.85	6	15.4	0	0.0	134.1
3	Doug Williams, Wash	1	29	18	62.1	340	11.72	4	13.8	1	3.4	128.1
4	Joe Montana, SF	4	122	83	68.0	1142	9.36	11	9.0	0	0.0	127.8
5	Jim Plunkett, Raiders	2	46	29	63.0	433	9.41	4	8.7	0	0.0	122.8
6	Terry Bradshaw, Pit	4	84	49	58.3	932	11.10	9	10.7	4	4.8	112.8
7	Troy Aikman, Dal	3	80	56	70.0	689	8.61	5	6.3	1	1.3	111.9
8	Bart Starr, GB	2	47	29	61.7	452	9.62	3	6.4	1	2.1	106.0
9	Brett Favre, GB	2	69	39	56.5	502	7.28	5	7.2	1	1.4	97.6
10	Roger Staubach, Dal	4	98	61	62.2	734	7.49	8	8.2	4	4.1	95.4

Ratings based on performance standards established for completion percentage, average gain, touchdown percentage and interception percentage. Quarterbacks are allocated points according to how their statistics measure up to those standards. Minimum 25 passing attempts.

Passing Yards

		Gm	Att	Cmp	Pct	Yds
1	Joe Montana, SF	4	122	83	68.0	1142
2	John Elway, Den	5	152	76	50.0	1128
3	Terry Bradshaw, Pit	4	84	49	58.3	932
4	Jim Kelly, Buf	4	145	81	55.9	829
5	Kurt Warner, St.L	2	89	52	58.4	779
6	Roger Staubach, Dal	4	98	61	62.2	734
7	Troy Aikman, Dal	3	80	56	70.0	689
8	Brett Favre, GB	2	69	39	56.5	502
9	Fran Tarkenton, Min	3	89	46	51.7	489
10	Bart Starr, GB	2	47	29	61.7	452
11	Jim Plunkett, Raiders	2	46	29	63.0	433
12	Joe Theismann, Wash	2	58	31	53.4	386
13	Len Dawson, KC	2	44	28	63.6	353
14	Steve Young, SF	2	39	26	66.7	345
15	Doug Williams, Wash	1	29	18	62.1	340

Receptions

		Gm	No	Yds	Avg	TD
1	**Jerry Rice**, SF-Oak	4	33	589	17.8	8
2	Andre Reed, Buf	4	27	323	12.0	0
3	Roger Craig, SF	3	20	212	10.6	2
	Thurman Thomas, Buf	4	20	144	7.2	0
5	Jay Novacek, Dal	3	17	148	8.7	2
6	Lynn Swann, Pit	4	16	364	22.8	3
7	Michael Irvin, Dal	3	16	256	16.0	2
8	Chuck Foreman, Min	3	15	139	9.3	0
9	Cliff Branch, Raiders	3	14	181	12.9	3
10	Don Beebe, Buf	3	12	171	14.3	2
	Torry Holt, St.L	2	12	158	13.2	1
	Preston Pearson, Bal-Pit-Dal	5	12	105	8.8	0
	Kenneth Davis, Buf	4	12	72	6.0	0
	Antonio Freeman, GB	2	12	231	19.3	3
15	John Stallworth, Pit	4	11	268	24.4	3
	Isaac Bruce, St.L	2	11	218	19.8	1
	Dan Ross, Cin	1	11	104	9.5	2

Rushing

		Gm	Car	Yds	Avg	TD
1	Franco Harris, Pit	4	101	354	3.5	4
2	Larry Csonka, Mia	3	57	297	5.2	2
3	Emmitt Smith, Dal	3	70	289	4.1	5
4	Terrell Davis, Den	2	55	259	4.7	3
5	John Riggins, Wash	2	64	230	3.6	2
6	Timmy Smith, Wash	1	22	204	9.3	2
	Thurman Thomas, Buf	4	52	204	3.9	4
8	Roger Craig, SF	3	52	201	3.9	2
9	Marcus Allen, Raiders	1	20	191	9.5	2
10	Tony Dorsett, Dal	2	31	162	5.2	1

All-Purpose Yards

		Gm	Rush	Rec	Ret	Total
1	**Jerry Rice**, SF-Oak	4	15	589	0	604
2	Franco Harris, Pit	4	354	114	0	468
3	Roger Craig, SF	3	201	212	0	413
4	Lynn Swann, Pit	4	-7	364	34	391
5	Thurman Thomas, Buf	4	204	144	0	348
6	Emmitt Smith, Dal	3	289	56	0	345
7	Antonio Freeman, GB	2	0	231	104	335
8	Andre Reed, Buf	4	0	323	0	323
9	Terrell Davis, Den.	2	259	58	0	317
10	Larry Csonka, Mia	3	297	17	0	314

All-Time Super Bowl Leaders (Cont.)
Scoring

Points

	Gm	TD	FG	PAT	Pts
1 **Jerry Rice**, SF-Oak	4	8	0	0	48
2 Emmitt Smith, Dal	3	5	0	0	30
3 Roger Craig, SF	3	4	0	0	24
Franco Harris, Pit	4	4	0	0	24
Thurman Thomas, Buf	4	4	0	0	24
John Elway, Den	5	4	0	0	24
7 Ray Wersching, SF	2	0	5	7	22
8 Don Chandler, GB	2	0	4	8	20
9 Cliff Branch, Raiders	3	3	0	0	18
John Stallworth, Pit	4	3	0	0	18
Lynn Swann, Pit	4	3	0	0	18
Ricky Watters, SF	1	3	0	0	18
Terrell Davis, Den	2	3	0	0	18
Antonio Freeman, GB	2	3	0	0	18
15 Chris Bahr, Raiders	2	0	3	8	17
Jason Elam, Den	2	0	3	8	17

Punting

(Minimum 10 Punts)	Gm	No	Yds	Avg.
1 Jerrel Wilson, KC	2	11	511	46.5
2 **Tom Tupa**, NE-TB	2	12	516	43.0
Kyle Richardson, Bal	1	10	430	43.0
4 Ray Guy, Raiders	3	14	587	41.9
5 Larry Seiple, Mia	3	15	620	41.3

Punt Returns

(Minimum 4 Returns)	Gm	No	Yds	Avg.	TD
1 John Taylor, SF	3	6	94	15.7	0
2 Desmond Howard, GB	1	6	90	15.0	0
3 Neal Colzie, Raiders	1	4	43	10.8	0
4 Dana McLemore, SF	1	5	51	10.2	0
5 Mike Fuller, Cin	1	4	35	8.8	0

Kickoff Returns

(Minimum 4 Returns)	Gm	No	Yds	Avg.	TD
1 Tim Dwight, Atl	1	5	210	42.0	1
2 Desmond Howard, GB	1	4	154	38.5	1
3 Fulton Walker, Mia	2	8	283	35.4	1
4 Andre Coleman, SD	1	8	242	30.3	1
5 Larry Anderson, Pit	2	8	207	25.9	0

Touchdowns

	Gm	Rush	Rec	Ret	TD
1 **Jerry Rice**, SF-Oak	4	0	8	0	8
2 Emmitt Smith, Dal	3	5	0	0	5
3 Roger Craig, SF	3	2	2	0	4
Franco Harris, Pit	4	4	0	0	4
John Elway, Den	5	4	0	0	4
Thurman Thomas, Buf	4	4	0	0	4
7 Cliff Branch, Raiders	3	0	3	0	3
John Stallworth, Pit	4	0	3	0	3
Lynn Swann, Pit	4	0	3	0	3
Ricky Watters, SF	1	1	2	0	3
Terrell Davis, Den	2	3	0	0	3
Antonio Freeman, GB	2	0	3	0	3
13 Twenty-six tied with 2 TDs each.					

Interceptions

	Gm	No	Yds	TD
1 Larry Brown, Dal	3	3	77	0
Chuck Howley, Dal	2	3	63	0
Rod Martin, Raiders	2	3	44	0
4 Randy Beverly, NYJ	1	2	0	0
Mel Blount, Pit	4	2	23	0
Brad Edwards, Wash	1	2	56	0
Thomas Everett, Dal	2	2	22	0
Darrien Gordon, SD-Den-Oak	4	2	108	0
Dexter Jackson, TB	1	2	34	0
Jake Scott, Mia	3	2	63	0
Dwight Smith, TB	1	2	94	2
Mike Wagner, Pit	3	2	45	0
James Washington, Dal	2	2	25	0
Barry Wilburn, Wash	1	2	11	0
Eric Wright, SF	4	2	25	0

Sacks

	Gm	No
1 Charles Haley, SF-Dal	5	4.5
2 Reggie White, GB	2	3
Leonard Marshall, NYG	2	3
Danny Stubbs, SF	2	3
Jeff Wright, Buf	4	3

Four or More Super Bowl Wins
Dallas Cowboys (5)

Year	Bowl	Head Coach	Quarterback	MVP	Opponent	Score	Site
1972	VI	Tom Landry	Roger Staubach	Staubach	Miami	24-3	New Orleans
1978	XII	Tom Landry	Roger Staubach	Harvey Martin & Randy White	Denver	27-10	New Orleans
1993	XXVII	Jimmy Johnson	Troy Aikman	Aikman	Buffalo	52-17	Pasadena
1994	XXVIII	Jimmy Johnson	Troy Aikman	Emmitt Smith	Buffalo	30-13	Atlanta
1996	XXX	Barry Switzer	Troy Aikman	Larry Brown	Pittsburgh	27-17	Tempe

San Francisco 49ers (5)

Year	Bowl	Head Coach	Quarterback	MVP	Opponent	Score	Site
1982	XVI	Bill Walsh	Joe Montana	Montana	Cincinnati	26-21	Pontiac
1985	XIX	Bill Walsh	Joe Montana	Montana	Miami	38-16	Stanford
1989	XXIII	Bill Walsh	Joe Montana	Jerry Rice	Cincinnati	20-16	Miami
1990	XXIV	George Seifert	Joe Montana	Montana	Denver	55-10	New Orleans
1995	XXIX	George Seifert	Steve Young	Young	San Diego	49-26	Miami

Pittsburgh Steelers (4)

Year	Bowl	Head Coach	Quarterback	MVP	Opponent	Score	Site
1975	IX	Chuck Noll	Terry Bradshaw	Franco Harris	Minnesota	16-6	New Orleans
1976	X	Chuck Noll	Terry Bradshaw	Lynn Swann	Dallas	21-17	Miami
1979	XIII	Chuck Noll	Terry Bradshaw	Bradshaw	Dallas	35-31	Miami
1980	XIV	Chuck Noll	Terry Bradshaw	Bradshaw	LA Rams	31-19	Pasadena

SINGLE GAME

Passing

Yards Gained

		Year	Att/Cmp	Yds
1	Kurt Warner, St.L vs Ten	2000	45/24	414
2	Kurt Warner, St.L vs NE	2002	44/28	365
3	Joe Montana, SF vs Cin	1989	36/23	357
4	Doug Williams, Wash vs Den	1988	29/18	340
5	John Elway, Den vs Atl	1999	29/18	336
6	Joe Montana, SF vs Mia	1985	35/24	331
7	Steve Young, SF vs SD	1995	36/24	325
8	Terry Bradshaw, Pit vs Dal	1979	30/17	318
	Dan Marino, Mia vs SF	1985	50/29	318
10	Terry Bradshaw, Pit vs Rams	1980	21/14	309

Touchdown Passes

		Year	TD	Int
1	Steve Young, SF vs SD	1995	6	0
2	Joe Montana, SF vs Den	1990	5	0
3	Terry Bradshaw, Pit vs Dal	1979	4	1
	Doug Williams, Wash vs Den	1988	4	1
	Troy Aikman, Dal vs Buf	1993	4	0
6	Roger Staubach, Dal vs Pit	1979	3	1
	Jim Plunkett, Raiders vs Phi	1981	3	0
	Joe Montana, SF vs Mia	1985	3	0
	Phil Simms, NYG vs Den	1987	3	0
	Brett Favre, GB vs Den	1998	3	1

Receiving

Catches

		Year	No	Yds	TD
1	Dan Ross, Cin vs SF	1982	11	104	2
	Jerry Rice, SF vs Cin	1989	11	215	1
3	Tony Nathan, Mia vs SF	1985	10	83	0
	Jerry Rice, SF vs SD	1995	10	149	3
	Andre Hastings, Pit vs Ind	1996	10	98	0
6	Ricky Sanders, Wash vs Den	1988	9	193	2
	Antonio Freeman, GB vs Den	1998	9	126	2

Five tied with 8 each, including twice by Andre Reed.

Yards Gained

		Year	No	Yds	TD
1	Jerry Rice, SF vs Cin	1989	11	215	1
2	Ricky Sanders, Wash vs Den	1988	9	193	2
3	Isaac Bruce, St.L vs Ten	2000	6	162	1
4	Lynn Swann, Pit vs Dal	1976	4	161	1
5	Andre Reed, Buf vs Dal	1993	8	152	0
	Rod Smith, Den vs Atl	1999	5	152	1
7	Jerry Rice, SF vs SD	1995	10	149	3
8	Jerry Rice, SF vs Den	1990	7	148	3
9	Max McGee, GB vs KC	1967	7	138	2
10	George Sauer, NYJ vs Bal	1969	8	133	0

Rushing

Yards Gained

		Year	Car	Yds	TD
1	Timmy Smith, Wash vs Den	1988	22	204	2
2	Marcus Allen, Raiders vs Wash	1984	20	191	2
3	John Riggins, Wash vs Mia	1983	38	166	1
4	Franco Harris, Pit vs Min	1975	34	158	1
5	Terrell Davis, Den vs GB	1998	30	157	3
6	Larry Csonka, Mia vs Min	1974	33	145	2
7	Clarence Davis, Raiders vs Min.	1977	16	137	0
8	Thurman Thomas, Buf vs NYG	1991	15	135	1
9	Emmitt Smith, Dal vs Buf	1994	30	132	2
10	**Michael Pittman**, TB vs Oak	2003	29	124	0
11	Matt Snell, NYJ vs Bal	1969	30	121	1
12	Tom Matte, Bal vs NYJ	1969	11	116	0
13	Larry Csonka, Mia vs Wash	1973	15	112	1
14	Emmitt Smith, Dal vs Buf	1993	22	108	1
15	Ottis Anderson, NYG vs Buf	1991	21	102	1
	Terrell Davis, Den vs Atl	1999	25	102	0
	Jamal Lewis, Bal vs NYG	2001	27	102	1

Scoring

Points

		Year	TD	FG	PAT	Pts
1	Roger Craig, SF vs Mia	1985	3	0	0	18
	Jerry Rice, SF vs Den	1990	3	0	0	18
	Jerry Rice, SF vs SD	1995	3	0	0	18
	Ricky Watters, SF vs SD	1995	3	0	0	18
	Terrell Davis, Den vs GB	1998	3	0	0	18
6	Don Chandler, GB vs Raiders	1968	0	4	3	15

Touchdowns

		Year	TD	Rush	Rec
1	Roger Craig, SF vs Mia	1985	3	1	2
	Jerry Rice, SF vs Den	1990	3	0	3
	Jerry Rice, SF vs SD	1995	3	0	3
	Ricky Watters, SF vs SD	1995	3	1	2
	Terrell Davis, Den vs GB	1998	3	3	0

Punt Returns

(Minimum 3 returns)

		Year	No	Yds	Avg
1	John Taylor, SF vs Cin	1989	3	56	18.7
2	Desmond Howard, GB vs NE	1997	6	90	15.0
3	John Taylor, SF vs Den	1990	3	38	12.7
4	Kelvin Martin, Dal vs Buf	1993	3	35	11.7

All-Purpose Yards

Yards Gained

		Year	Run	Rec	Tot
1	Desmond Howard, GB vs NE	1997	0	0	244
2	Andre Coleman, SD vs SF	1995	0	0	242
3	Ricky Sanders, Wash vs Den	1988	193	-4	235
4	Antonio Freeman, GB vs Den	1998	0	126	230
5	Jerry Rice, SF vs Cin	1989	5	215	220
6	Tim Dwight, Atl vs Den	1999	5	0	215
7	Timmy Smith, Wash vs Den	1988	204	9	213
8	Marcus Allen, Raiders vs Wash	1984	191	18	209
9	Stephen Starring, NE vs Chi	1986	0	39	192
10	Fulton Walker, Mia vs Wash	1983	0	0	190
	Thurman Thomas, Buf vs NYG	1991	135	55	190

Return Yardage: Howard 244, Coleman 242, Sanders 46, Freeman 104, Dwight 210, Starring 153, Walker 190.

Interceptions

		Year	No	Yds	TD
1	Rod Martin, Raiders vs Phi	1981	3	44	0

Ten tied with 2 each.

Punting

(Minimum 4 punts)

		Year	No	Yds	Avg
1	Bryan Wagner, SD vs SF	1995	4	195	48.8
2	Jerrel Wilson, KC vs Min	1970	4	194	48.5
3	Jim Miller, SF vs Cin	1982	4	185	46.3

Kickoff Returns

(Minimum 3 returns)

		Year	No	Yds	Avg
1	Fulton Walker, Mia vs Wash	1983	4	190	47.5
2	Tim Dwight, Atl vs Den	1999	5	210	42.0
3	Desmond Howard, GB vs NE	1997	4	154	38.5
4	Larry Anderson, Pit vs Rams	1980	5	162	32.4
5	Rick Upchurch, Den vs Dal	1978	3	94	31.3

Super Bowl Playoffs

The Super Bowl forced the NFL to set up pro football's first guaranteed multiple-game playoff format. Over the years, the NFL-AFL merger, the creation of two conferences comprised of four divisions each and the proliferation of wild card entries has seen the postseason field grow from four teams (1966), to six (1967-68), to eight (1969-77), to 10 (1978-81, 1983-89), to the present 12 (since1990).

In 1968, there was a special playoff between Oakland and Kansas City which were both 12-2 and tied for first in the AFL's Western Division. In 1982, when a 57-day players' strike shortened the regular season to just nine games, playoff berths were extended to 16 teams (eight from each conference) and a 15-game tournament was played.

. Note that in the following year-by-year summary, records of finalists include all games leading up to the Super Bowl; (*) indicates non-division winners or wild card teams.

1966 SEASON

AFL Playoffs

Championship . . . . .Kansas City 31, at Buffalo 7

NFL Playoffs

Championship . . . . .Green Bay 34, at Dallas 27

Super Bowl I
Jan. 15, 1967
Memorial Coliseum, Los Angeles
Favorite: Packers by 14—Attendance: 61,946

Kansas City (12-2-1) . . . . .0 10 0 0 **—10**
Green Bay (13-2) 7   7 14 7 **—35**
MVP: Green Bay QB Bart Starr (16 for 23, 250 yds, 2 TD, 1 Int)

1967 SEASON

AFL Playoffs

Championship . . . . .at Oakland 40, Houston 7

NFL Playoffs

Eastern Conference . . . . .at Dallas 52, Cleveland 14
Western Conference . . . . . . .at Green Bay 28, LA Rams 7
Championship . . . . .at Green Bay 21, Dallas 17

Super Bowl II
Jan. 14, 1968
Orange Bowl, Miami
Favorite: Packers by 13½—Attendance: 75,546

Green Bay (11-4-1) . . . . .3 13 10 7 **—33**
Oakland (14-1) 0   7 0 7 **—14**
MVP: Green Bay QB Bart Starr (13 for 24, 202 yds,1 TD)

1968 SEASON

AFL Playoffs

Western Div. Playoff . . . . . .at Oakland 41, Kansas City 6
AFL Championship . . . . .at NY Jets 27, Oakland 23

NFL Playoffs

Eastern Conference . . . . .at Cleveland 31, Dallas 20
Western Conference . . . . . .at Baltimore 24, Minnesota 14
NFL Championship . . . . .Baltimore 34, at Cleveland 0

Super Bowl III
Jan. 12, 1969
Orange Bowl, Miami
Favorite: Colts by 18—Attendance: 75,389

NY Jets (12-3) 0   7 6 3 **—16**
Baltimore (15-1) 0   0 0 7 **—7**
MVP: NY Jets QB Joe Namath (17 for 28, 206 yds)

1969 SEASON

AFL Playoffs

Inter-Division . . . .*Kansas City 13, at NY Jets 6
at Oakland 56, *Houston 7
AFL Championship . . . . . . .Kansas City 17, at Oakland 7

NFL Playoffs

Eastern Conference . . . . .Cleveland 38, at Dallas 14
Western Conference . . . . . .at Minnesota 23, LA Rams 20
NFL Championship . . . . . .at Minnesota 27, Cleveland 7

Super Bowl IV
Jan. 11, 1970
Tulane Stadium, New Orleans
Favorite: Vikings by 12—Attendance: 80,562

Minnesota (14-2) 0   0 7 0 **—7**
Kansas City (13-3) . . . . .3 13 7 0 **—23**
MVP: KC QB Len Dawson (12 for 17, 142 yds, 1 TD, 1Int)

1970 SEASON

AFC Playoffs

First Round . . . . .at Baltimore 17, Cincinnati 0
at Oakland 21,*Miami 14
Championship . . . . .at Baltimore 27, Oakland 17

NFC Playoffs

First Round. . . . . .at Dallas 5, *Detroit 0
San Francisco 17, at Minnesota 14
Championship . . . . .Dallas 17, at San Francisco 10

Super Bowl V
Jan. 17, 1971
Orange Bowl, Miami
Favorite: Cowboys by 2½—Attendance: 79,204

Baltimore (13-2-1) 0   6 0 10 **—16**
Dallas (12-4) . . . . .3 10 0 0 **—13**
MVP: Dallas LB Chuck Howley (2 interceptions for 22 yds)

1971 SEASON

AFC Playoffs

First Round . . . . .Miami 27, at Kansas City 24 (OT)
*Baltimore 20, at Cleveland 3
Championship . . . . .at Miami 21, Baltimore 0

NFC Playoffs

First Round . . . . .Dallas 20, at Minnesota 12
at San Francisco 24,*Washington 20
Championship . . . . .at Dallas 14, San Francisco 3

Super Bowl VI
Jan. 16, 1972
Tulane Stadium, New Orleans
Favorite: Cowboys by 6—Attendance: 81,023

Dallas (13-3) 3   7 7 7 **—24**
Miami (12-3-1) 0   3 0 0 **—3**
MVP: Dallas QB Roger Staubach (12 for 19, 119 yds, 2 TD)

1972 SEASON

AFC Playoffs

First Round . . . . .at Pittsburgh 13, Oakland 7
at Miami 20, *Cleveland 14
Championship . . . . .Miami 21, at Pittsburgh 17

NFC Playoffs

First Round . . . .*Dallas 30, at San Francisco 28
at Washington 16, Green Bay 3
Championship . . . . .at Washington 26, Dallas 3

Super Bowl VII
Jan. 14, 1973
Memorial Coliseum, Los Angeles
Favorite: Redskins by 1½—Attendance: 90,182

Miami (16-0) . . . . .7 7 0 0 **—14**
Washington (13-3) . . . . .0 0 0 7 **—7**
MVP: Miami safety Jake Scott (2 Interceptions for 63 yds)

1973 SEASON

AFC Playoffs

First Round . . . . .at Oakland 33, *Pittsburgh 14
at Miami 34, Cincinnati 16
Championship . . . . .at Miami 27, Oakland 10

NFC Playoffs

First Round . . . . .at Minnesota 27, *Washington 20
at Dallas 27, LA Rams 16
Championship . . . . .Minnesota 27, at Dallas 10

Super Bowl VIII
Jan. 13, 1974
Rice Stadium, Houston
Favorite: Dolphins by 6½—Attendance: 71,882

Minnesota (14-2) . . . . .0 0 0 7 **—7**
Miami (12-4) . . . . .14 3 7 0 **—24**
MVP: Miami FB Larry Csonka (33 carries, 145 yds, 2 TD)

1974 SEASON

AFC Playoffs

First Round . . . . .at Oakland 28, Miami 26
at Pittsburgh 32, *Buffalo 14
Championship . . . . .Pittsburgh 24, at Oakland 13

NFC Playoffs

First Round . . . . .at Minnesota 30, St. Louis 14
at LA Rams 19, *Washington 10
Championship . . . . .at Minnesota 14, LA Rams 10

Super Bowl IX
Jan. 12, 1975
Tulane Stadium, New Orleans
Favorite: Steelers by 3—Attendance: 80,997

Pittsburgh (12-3-1) . . . . .0 2 7 7 **—16**
Minnesota (12-4) . . . . .0 0 0 6 **—6**
MVP: Pittsburgh RB Franco Harris (34 carries, 158 yds, 1 TD)

1975 SEASON

AFC Playoffs

First Round . . . . .at Pittsburgh 28, Baltimore 10
at Oakland 31, *Cincinnati 28
Championship . . . . .at Pittsburgh 16, Oakland 10

NFC Playoffs

First Round . . . . .at LA Rams 35, St. Louis 23
*Dallas 17, at Minnesota 14
Championship . . . . .Dallas 37, at LA Rams 7

Super Bowl X
Jan. 18, 1976
Orange Bowl, Miami
Favorite: Steelers by 6½—Attendance: 80,187

Dallas (12-4) . . . . .7 3 0 7 **—17**
Pittsburgh (14-2) . . . . .7 0 0 14 **—21**
MVP: Pittsburgh WR Lynn Swann (4 catches, 161 yds, 1 TD)

1976 SEASON

AFC Playoffs

First Round . . . . .at Oakland 24, *New England 21
Pittsburgh 40, at Baltimore 14
Championship . . . . .at Oakland 24, Pittsburgh 7

NFC Playoffs

First Round . . . . .at Minnesota 35, *Washington 20
LA Rams 14, at Dallas 12
Championship . . . . .at Minnesota 24, LA Rams 13

Super Bowl XI
Jan. 9, 1977
Rose Bowl, Pasadena
Favorite: Raiders by 4½—Attendance: 103,438

Oakland (15-1) . . . . .0 16 3 13 **—32**
Minnesota (13-2-1) . . . . .0 0 7 7 **—14**
MVP: Oakland WR Fred Biletnikoff (4 catches, 79 yds)

1977 SEASON

AFC Playoffs

First Round . . . . .at Denver 34, Pittsburgh 21
*Oakland 37, at Baltimore 31 (OT)
Championship . . . . .at Denver 20, Oakland 17

NFC Playoffs

First Round . . . . .at Dallas 37, *Chicago 7
Minnesota 14, at LA Rams 7
Championship . . . . .at Dallas 23, Minnesota 6

Super Bowl XII
Jan. 15, 1978
Louisiana Superdome, New Orleans
Favorite: Cowboys by 6—Attendance: 75,583

Dallas (14-2) . . . . .10 3 7 7 **—27**
Denver (14-2) . . . . .0 0 10 0 **—10**
MVPs: Dallas DE Harvey Martin and DT Randy White
(Cowboys' defense forced 8 turnovers)

1978 SEASON

AFC Playoffs

First Round . . . .*Houston 17, at *Miami 9
Second Round . . . . .Houston 31, at New England 14
at Pittsburgh 33, Denver 10
Championship . . . . .at Pittsburgh 34, Houston 5

NFC Playoffs

First Round . . . . .at *Atlanta 14, *Philadelphia 13
Second Round . . . . .at Dallas 27, Atlanta 20
at LA Rams 34, Minnesota 10
Championship . . . . .Dallas 28, at LA Rams 0

Super Bowl XIII
Jan. 21, 1979
Orange Bowl, Miami
Favorite: Steelers by 4—Attendance: 79,484

Pittsburgh (16-2) . . . . .7 14 0 14 **—35**
Dallas (14-4) . . . . .7 7 3 14 **—31**
MVP: Pittsburgh QB Terry Bradshaw (17 for 30, 318 yds, 4 TD, 1 Int)

Super Bowl Playoffs (Cont.)

1979 SEASON

AFC Playoffs

First Round . . . . .at *Houston 13, *Denver 7
Second Round . . . . .Houston 17, at San Diego 14
                at Pittsburgh 34, Miami 14
Championship . . . . .at Pittsburgh 27, Houston 13

NFC Playoffs

First Round . . . . .at *Philadelphia 27, *Chicago 17
Second Round . . . . . . .at Tampa Bay 24, Philadelphia 17
                LA Rams 21, at Dallas 19
Championship . . . . .LA Rams 9,at Tampa Bay 0

Super Bowl XIV

Jan. 20, 1980
Rose Bowl, Pasadena
Favorite: Steelers by 10½—Attendance: 103,985

LA Rams (11-7) 7   6   6   0—**19**
Pittsburgh (14-4) 3   7   7   14—**31**
MVP: Pittsburgh QB Terry Bradshaw (14 for 21, 309 yds, 2 TD, 3 Int)

1980 SEASON

AFC Playoffs

First Round . . . . .at *Oakland 27, *Houston 7
Second Round . . . . .at San Diego 20, Buffalo 14
                Oakland 14, at Cleveland 12
Championship . . . . .Oakland 34, at San Diego 27

NFC Playoffs

First Round . . . . .at *Dallas 34, *LA Rams 13
Second Round . . . . .at Philadelphia 31, Minnesota 16
                Dallas 30, at Atlanta 27
Championship . . . . .at Philadelphia 20, Dallas 7

Super Bowl XV

Jan. 25, 1981
Louisiana Superdome, New Orleans
Favorite: Eagles by 3—Attendance: 76,135

Oakland (14-5) 14   0   10   3 —**27**
Philadelphia (14-4) 0   3   0   7 —**10**
MVP: Oakland QB Jim Plunkett (13 for 21, 261 yds, 3 TD)

1981 SEASON

AFC Playoffs

First Round . . . .*Buffalo 31, at *NY Jets 27
Second Round . . . . . . .San Diego 41, at Miami 38 (OT)
                at Cincinnati 28, Buffalo 21
Championship . . . . .at Cincinnati 27, San Diego 7

NFC Playoffs

First Round . . . .*NY Giants 27, at *Philadelphia 21
Second Round . . . . .at Dallas 38, Tampa Bay 0
                at San Francisco 38, NY Giants 24
Championship . . . . .at San Francisco 28, Dallas 27

Super Bowl XVI

Jan. 24, 1982
Pontiac Silverdome, Pontiac, Mich.
Favorite: Pick'em—Attendance: 81,270

San Francisco (15-3) 7   13   0   6 —**26**
Cincinnati (14-4) 0   0   7   14 —**21**
MVP: San Francisco QB Joe Montana (14 for 22, 157 yds, 1 TD; 6 carries, 18 yds, 1 TD)

1982 SEASON

A 57-day players' strike shortened the regular season from 16 games to nine. The playoff format was changed to a 16-team tournament open to the top eight teams in each conference.

AFC Playoffs

First Round . . . . .at LA Raiders 27, Cleveland 10
                at Miami 28, New England 13
                NY Jets 44, at Cincinnati 17
                San Diego 31, at Pittsburgh 28
Second Round . . . . .NY Jets 17, at LA Raiders 14
                at Miami 34, San Diego 13
Championship . . . . .at Miami 14, NY Jets 0

NFC Playoffs

First Round . . . . .at Washington 31, Detroit 7
                at Dallas 30, Tampa Bay 17
                at Green Bay 41, St. Louis 16
                at Minnesota 30, Atlanta 24
Second Round . . . . .at Washington 21, Minnesota 7
                at Dallas 37, Green Bay 26
Championship . . . . .at Washington 31, Dallas 17

Super Bowl XVII

Jan. 30, 1983
Rose Bowl, Pasadena
Favorite: Dolphins by 3—Attendance: 103,667

Miami (10-2) 7   10   0   0 —**17**
Washington (11-1) 0   10   3   14 —**27**
MVP: Washington RB John Riggins (38 carries, 166 yds, 1 TD; 1 catch, 15 yds)

1983 SEASON

AFC Playoffs

First Round . . . . .at *Seattle 31, *Denver 7
Second Round . . . . .Seattle 27, at Miami 20
                at LA Raiders 38, Pittsburgh 10
Championship . . . . .at LA Raiders 30, Seattle 14

NFC Playoffs

First Round . . . .*LA Rams 24, at *Dallas 17
Second Round . . . . .at San Francisco 24, Detroit 23
                at Washington 51, LA Rams 7
Championship . . . . . .at Washington 24, San Francisco 21

Super Bowl XVIII

Jan. 22, 1984
Tampa Stadium, Tampa
Favorite: Redskins by 3—Attendance: 72,920

Washington (16-2) 0   3   6   0 —**9**
LA Raiders (14-4) 7   14   14   3 —**38**
MVP: LA Raiders RB Marcus Allen (20 carries, 191 yds, 2 TD; 2 catches, 18 yds)

Most Popular Playing Sites

Stadiums hosting more than one Super Bowl.

No		Years
6	Superdome (N. Orleans)	1978, 81, 86, 90, 97, 2002
5	Orange Bowl (Miami)	1968-69, 71, 76, 79
5	Rose Bowl (Pasadena)	1977, 80, 83, 87, 93
3	Tulane Stadium (N. Orleans)	1970, 72, 75
3	Joe Robbie/Pro Player Stadium (Miami)	1989, 95, 99
3	Jack Murphy/Qualcomm Stadium (San Diego)	1988, 98, 2003
2	LA Memorial Coliseum	1967, 73
2	Tampa Stadium	1984, 91
2	Georgia Dome (Atlanta)	1994, 2000

1984 SEASON

AFC Playoffs

First Round . . . . .at *Seattle 13, *LA Raiders 7
Second Round . . . . .at Miami 31, Seattle 10
Pittsburgh 24, at Denver 17
Championship . . . . .at Miami 45, Pittsburgh 28

NFC Playoffs

First Round . . . .*NY Giants 16, at *LA Rams 13
Second Round . . . . . . .at San Francisco 21, NY Giants 10
Chicago 23, at Washington 19
Championship . . . . .at San Francisco 23, Chicago 0

Super Bowl XIX
Jan. 20, 1985
Stanford Stadium, Stanford, Calif.
Favorite: 49ers by 3—Attendance: 84,059

Miami (16-2)	10	6	0	0	**—16**
San Francisco (17-1)	7	21	10	0	**—38**

MVP: San Francisco QB Joe Montana (24 for 35, 331 yds, 2 TD; 5 carries, 59 yards, 1 TD)

1985 SEASON

AFC Playoffs

First Round . . . .*New England 26, at *NY Jets 14
Second Round . . . . .at Miami 24, Cleveland 21
New England 27, at LA Raiders 20
Championship . . . . .New England 31, at Miami 14

NFC Playoffs

First Round . . . . . . .at *NY Giants 17, *San Francisco 3
Second Round . . . . .at LA Rams 20, Dallas 0
at Chicago 21, NY Giants 0
Championship . . . . .at Chicago 24, LA Rams 0

Super Bowl XX
Jan. 26, 1986
Louisiana Superdome, New Orleans
Favorite: Bears by 10—Attendance: 73,818

Chicago Bears (17-1)	13	10	21	2	**—46**
New England (14-5)	3	0	0	7	**—10**

MVP: Chicago DE Richard Dent (Bears defense: 7 sacks, 6 turnovers, 1 safety and gave up just 123 total yards)

1986 SEASON

AFC Playoffs

First Round . . . . .at *NY Jets 35, *Kansas City 15
Second Round . . . . . . .at Cleveland 23, NY Jets 20 (OT)
at Denver 22, New England 17
Championship . . . . . . .Denver 23, at Cleveland 20 (OT)

NFC Playoffs

First Round . . . . .at *Washington 19, *LA Rams 7
Second Round . . . . .Washington 27, at Chicago 13
at NY Giants 49, San Francisco 3
Championship . . . . .at NY Giants 17, Washington 0

Super Bowl XXI
Jan. 25, 1987
Rose Bowl, Pasadena
Favorite: Giants by 9½—Attendance: 101,063

Denver (13-5)	10	0	0	10	**—20**
NY Giants (16-2)	7	2	17	13	**—39**

MVP: NY Giants QB Phil Simms (22 for 25, 268 yds, 3 TD; 3 carries, 25 yds)

1987 SEASON

A 24-day players' strike shortened the regular season to 15 games with replacement teams playing for three weeks.

AFC Playoffs

First Round . . . . .at *Houston 23, *Seattle 20 (OT)
Second Round . . . . . . .at Cleveland 38, Indianapolis 21
at Denver 34, Houston 10
Championship . . . . .at Denver 38, Cleveland 33

NFC Playoffs

First Round . . . .*Minnesota 44, at *New Orleans 10
Second Round . . . . . .Minnesota 36, at San Francisco 24
Washington 21, at Chicago 17
Championship . . . . .at Washington 17, Minnesota 10

Super Bowl XXII
Jan. 31, 1988
San Diego/Jack Murphy Stadium
Favorite: Broncos by 3½—Attendance: 73,302

Washington (13-4)	0	35	0	7	**—42**
Denver (12-4-1)	10	0	0	0	**—10**

MVP: Washington QB Doug Williams (18 for 29, 340 yds, 4 TD, 1 Int)

1988 SEASON

AFC Playoffs

First Round . . . .*Houston 24, at *Cleveland 23
Second Round . . . . .at Buffalo 17, Houston 10
at Cincinnati 21, Seattle 13
Championship . . . . .at Cincinnati 21, Buffalo 10

NFC Playoffs

First Round . . . . .at *Minnesota 28, *LA Rams 17
Second Round . . . . .at San Francisco 34, Minnesota 9
at Chicago 20, Philadelphia 12
Championship . . . . .San Francisco 28, at Chicago 3

Super Bowl XXIII
Jan. 22, 1989
Joe Robbie Stadium, Miami
Favorite: 49ers by 7—Attendance: 75,129

Cincinnati (14-4)	0	3	10	3	**—16**
San Francisco (12-6)	3	0	3	14	**—20**

MVP: San Francisco WR Jerry Rice (11 catches, 215 yds, 1 TD; 1 carry, 5 yds)

1989 SEASON

AFC Playoffs

First Round . . . .*Pittsburgh 26, at *Houston 23
Second Round . . . . .at Cleveland 34, Buffalo 30
at Denver 24, Pittsburgh 23
Championship . . . . .at Denver 37, Cleveland 21

NFC Playoffs

First Round . . . .*LA Rams 21, at *Philadelphia 7
Second Round . . . . .LA Rams 19, NY Giants 13 (OT)
at San Francisco 41, Minnesota 13
Championship . . . . .at San Francisco 30, LA Rams 3

Super Bowl XXIV
Jan. 28, 1990
Louisiana Superdome, New Orleans
Favorite: 49ers by 12½—Attendance: 72,919

San Francisco (17-2)	13	14	14	14	**—55**
Denver (13-6)	3	0	7	0	**—10**

MVP: San Francisco QB Joe Montana (22 for 29, 297 yds, 5 TD)

Super Bowl Playoffs (Cont.)

1990 SEASON

AFC Playoffs

First Round . . . . .at *Miami 17, *Kansas City 16
    at Cincinnati 41, *Houston 14
Second Round . . . . .at Buffalo 44, Miami 34
    at LA Raiders 20, Cincinnati 10
Championship . . . . .at Buffalo 51, LA Raiders 3

NFC Playoffs

First Round . . . .*Washington 20, at *Philadelphia 6
    at Chicago 16, *New Orleans 6
Second Round . . . . . .at San Francisco 28, Washington 10
    at NY Giants 31, Chicago 3
Championship . . . . . . .NY Giants 15, at San Francisco 13

Super Bowl XXV
Jan. 27, 1991
Tampa Stadium, Tampa
Favorite: Bills by 7—Attendance: 73,813

Buffalo (15-4) . . . . .3 9 0 7 **—19**
NY Giants (16-3) . . . . .3 7 7 3 **—20**
MVP: NY Giants RB Ottis Anderson (21 carries, 102 yds, 1 TD; 1 catch, 7 yds)

1991 SEASON

AFC Playoffs

First Round . . . . .at *Kansas City 10, *LA Raiders 6
    at Houston 17, *NY Jets 10
Second Round . . . . .at Denver 26, Houston 24
    at Buffalo 37, Kansas City 14
Championship . . . . .at Buffalo 10, Denver 7

NFC Playoffs

First Round . . . .*Atlanta 27, at New Orleans 20
    +*Dallas 17, at *Chicago 13
Second Round . . . . .at Washington 24, Atlanta 7
    at Detroit 38, Dallas 6
Championship . . . . .at Washington 41, Detroit 10

Super Bowl XXVI
Jan. 26, 1992
Hubert Humphrey Metrodome, Minneapolis
Favorite: Redskins by 7—Attendance: 63,130

Washington (16-2) . . . . .0 17 14 6 **—37**
Buffalo (15-3) . . . . .0 0 10 14 **—24**
MVP: Washington QB Mark Rypien (18 for 33, 292 yds, 2 TD, 1 Int)

1992 SEASON

AFC Playoffs

First Round . . . . .at *Buffalo 41, *Houston 38 (OT)
    at San Diego 17, *Kansas City 0
Second Round . . . . .Buffalo 24, at Pittsburgh 3
    at Miami 31, San Diego 0
Championship . . . . .Buffalo 29, at Miami 10

NFC Playoffs

First Round . . . .*Washington 24, at Minnesota 7
    *Philadelphia 36, at *New Orleans 20
Second Round . . . . . .at San Francisco 20, Washington 13
    at Dallas 34, Philadelphia 10
Championship . . . . .Dallas 30, at San Francisco 20

Super Bowl XXVII
Jan. 31, 1993
Rose Bowl, Pasadena
Favorite: Cowboys by 7—Attendance: 98,374

Buffalo (14-5) . . . . .7 3 7 0 **—17**
Dallas (15-3) . . . . .14 14 3 21 **—52**
MVP: Dallas QB Troy Aikman (22 for 30, 273 yds, 4 TD)

1993 SEASON

AFC Playoffs

First Round . . . . . .at Kansas City 27, *Pittsburgh 24 (OT)
    at *LA Raiders 42, *Denver 24
Second Round . . . . .at Buffalo 29, LA Raiders 23
    Kansas City 28, at Houston 20
Championship . . . . .at Buffalo 30, Kansas City 13

NFC Playoffs

First Round . . . .*Green Bay 28, at Detroit 24
    at *NY Giants 17, *Minnesota 10
Second Round . . . . . . .at San Francisco 44, NY Giants 3
    at Dallas 27, Green Bay 17
Championship . . . . .at Dallas 38, San Francisco 21

Super Bowl XXVIII
Jan. 30, 1994
Georgia Dome, Atlanta
Favorite: Cowboys by 10½—Attendance: 72,817

Dallas (15-4) . . . . .6 0 14 10 **—30**
Buffalo (14-5) . . . . .3 10 0 0 **—13**
MVP: Dallas RB Emmitt Smith (30 carries, 132 yds, 2 TDs; 4 catches, 26 yds)

1994 SEASON

AFC Playoffs

First Round . . . . .at Miami 27, *Kansas City 17
    at *Cleveland 20, *New England 13
Second Round . . . . .at Pittsburgh 29, Cleveland 9
    at San Diego 22, Miami 21
Championship . . . . .San Diego 17, at Pittsburgh 13

NFC Playoffs

First Round . . . . .at *Green Bay 16, *Detroit 12
    *Chicago 25, at Minnesota 18
Second Round . . . . .at San Francisco 44, Chicago 15
    at Dallas 35, Green Bay 9
Championship . . . . . . .at San Francisco 38, Dallas 28

Super Bowl XXIX
Jan. 29, 1995
Joe Robbie Stadium, Miami
Favorite: 49ers by 18 —Attendance: 74,107

San Diego (13-5) . . . . .7 3 8 8 **—26**
San Francisco (15-3) . . . . .14 14 14 7 **—49**
MVP: San Francisco QB Steve Young (24 for 36, 325 yds, 6 TD)

1995 SEASON

AFC Playoffs

First Round . . . . .at Buffalo 37, *Miami 22
    *Indianapolis 35, at *San Diego 20
Second Round . . . . .at Pittsburgh 40, Buffalo 21
    Indianapolis 10, at Kansas City 7
Championship . . . . .at Pittsburgh 20, Indianapolis 16

NFC Playoffs

First Round . . . . .at *Philadelphia 58, *Detroit 37
    at Green Bay 37, *Atlanta 20
Second Round . . . . . .Green Bay 27, at San Francisco 17
    at Dallas 30, Philadelphia 11
Championship . . . . .at Dallas 38, Green Bay 27

Super Bowl XXX
Jan. 28, 1996
Sun Devil Stadium, Tempe, Ariz.
Favorite: Cowboys by 13½—Attendance: 76,347

Dallas (14-4) . . . . .10 3 7 7 **—27**
Pittsburgh (13-5) . . . . .0 7 0 10 **—17**
MVP: Dallas CB Larry Brown (2 interceptions for 77 yds)

1996 SEASON

AFC Playoffs

First Round . . . .*Jacksonville 30, at *Buffalo 27
at Pittsburgh 42, *Indianapolis 14
Second Round . . . . Jacksonville 30, at Denver 27
at New England 28, Pittsburgh 3
Championship . . . . . . .at New England 20, Jacksonville 6

NFC Playoffs

First Round . . . . at Dallas 40, *Minnesota 15
at *San Francisco 14, *Philadelphia 0
Second Round . . . . . . at Green Bay 35, San Francisco 14
at Carolina 26, Dallas 17
Championship . . . . at Green Bay 30, Carolina 13

Super Bowl XXXI

Jan. 26, 1997
Louisiana Superdome, New Orleans
Favorite: Packers by 14—Attendance: 72,301

New England (13-5) . . . . .14 0 7 0 **—21**
Green Bay (15-3) . . . . .10 17 8 0 **—35**
MVP: Green Bay KR Desmond Howard (4 kickoff returns for
154 yds and 1 TD, also 6 punt returns for 90 yds)

1997 SEASON

AFC Playoffs

First Round . . . . .at *Denver 42, *Jacksonville 17
at New England 17, *Miami 3
Second Round . . . . .at Pittsburgh 7, New England 6
Denver 14, at Kansas City 10
Championship . . . . Denver 24, at Pittsburgh 21

NFC Playoffs

First Round . . . .*Minnesota 23, at NY Giants 22
at *Tampa Bay 20, *Detroit 10
Second Round . . . . . . .at San Francisco 38, Minnesota 22
at Green Bay 21, Tampa Bay 7
Championship . . . . . .Green Bay 23, at San Francisco 10

Super Bowl XXXII

Jan. 25, 1998
Qualcomm Stadium, San Diego
Favorite: Packers by 11½—Attendance: 68,912

Green Bay (15-3) . . . . .7 7 3 7 **—24**
Denver (15-4) . . . . .7 10 7 7 **—31**
MVP: Denver RB Terrell Davis (30 carries, 157 yds, 3 TDs; 2
catches, 8 yds)

1998 SEASON

AFC Playoffs

First Round . . . . .at *Miami 24, *Buffalo 17
at Jacksonville 25, *New England 10
Second Round . . . . .at NY Jets 34, Jacksonville 24
at Denver 38, Miami 3
Championship . . . . at Denver 23, NY Jets 10

NFC Playoffs

First Round . . . . . . .at *San Francisco 30, *Green Bay 27
*Arizona 20, at Dallas 7
Second Round . . . . .at Atlanta 20, San Francisco 18
at Minnesota 41, Arizona 21
Championship . . . . . . .Atlanta 30, at Minnesota 27 (OT)

Super Bowl XXXIII

Jan. 31, 1999
Pro Player Stadium, Miami
Favorite: Broncos by 7½—Attendance: 74,803

Denver (16-2) . . . . .7 10 0 17 **—34**
Atlanta (16-2) . . . . .3 3 0 13 **—19**
MVP: Denver QB John Elway (18 for 29, 336 yds, 1 TD, 1
Int and 1 rushing TD)

1999 SEASON

AFC Playoffs

First Round . . . . .at *Tennessee 22, *Buffalo 16
*Miami 20, at Seattle 17
Second Round . . . . .at Jacksonville 62, Miami 7
Tennessee 19, at Indianapolis 16
Championship . . . . .Tennessee 33, at Jacksonville 14

NFC Playoffs

First Round . . . . .at Washington 27, *Detroit 13
at *Minnesota 27, *Dallas 10
Second Round . . . . .at Tampa Bay 14, Washington 13
at St. Louis 49, Minnesota 37
Championship . . . . .at St. Louis 11, Tampa Bay 6

Super Bowl XXXIV

Jan. 30, 2000
Georgia Dome, Atlanta
Favorite: Rams by 7—Attendance: 72,625

St. Louis (15-3) . . . . .3 6 7 7 **—23**
Tennessee (16-3) . . . . .0 0 6 10 **—16**
MVP: St. Louis QB Kurt Warner (24 for 45, 414 yds, 2 TD)

2000 SEASON

AFC Playoffs

First Round . . . . .at Miami 23, *Indianapolis 17 (OT)
at *Baltimore 21, *Denver 3
Second Round . . . . .at Oakland 27, Miami 0
Baltimore 24, at Tennessee 10
Championship . . . . .Baltimore 16, at Oakland 3

NFC Playoffs

First Round . . . . .at New Orleans 31, *St. Louis 28
at *Philadelphia 21, *Tampa Bay 3
Second Round . . . . . . .at Minnesota 34, New Orleans 16
at NY Giants 20, Philadelphia 10
Championship . . . . .at NY Giants 41, Minnesota 0

Super Bowl XXXV

Jan. 28, 2001
Raymond James Stadium, Tampa
Favorite: Ravens by 3—Attendance: 71,921

Baltimore (15-4) . . . . .7 3 14 10 **—34**
NY Giants (14-4) . . . . .0 0 7 0 **—7**
MVP: Baltimore LB Ray Lewis (5 tackles, 4 passes defended)

2001 SEASON

AFC Playoffs

First Round . . . . .at Oakland 38, *NY Jets 24
*Baltimore 20, at *Miami 3
Second Round . . . .at New England 16, Oakland 13 (OT)
at Pittsburgh 27, Baltimore 10
Championship . . . . New England 24, at Pittsburgh 17

NFC Playoffs

First Round . . . . .at Philadelphia 31, *Tampa Bay 9
at *Green Bay 25, *San Francisco 15
Second Round . . . . .Philadelphia 33, at Chicago 19
at St. Louis 45, Green Bay 17
Championship . . . . .at St. Louis 29, Philadelphia 24

Super Bowl XXXVI

Feb. 3, 2002
Louisiana Superdome, New Orleans
Favorite: Rams by 14—Attendance: 72,922

St. Louis (16-2) . . . . .3 0 0 14 **—17**
New England (13-5) . . . . .0 14 3 3 **—20**
MVP: New England QB Tom Brady (16 for 27, 145 yds, 1
TD)

Super Bowl Playoffs (Cont.)

2002 SEASON

AFC Playoffs

First Round . . . . .at NY Jets 41, *Indianapolis 0
at Pittsburgh 36, *Cleveland 33
Second Round . . . . .at Tennessee 34, Pittsburgh 31 (OT)
at Oakland 30, NY Jets 10
Championship . . . . at Oakland 41, Tennessee 24

NFC Playoffs

First Round . . . .*Atlanta 27, at Green Bay 7
at San Francisco 39, *NY Giants 38
Second Round . . . . .at Philadelphia 20, Atlanta 6
at Tampa Bay 31, San Francisco 6
Championship . . . . . . Tampa Bay 27, at Philadelphia 10

Super Bowl XXXVII

Jan. 26, 2003
Qualcomm Stadium, San Diego
Favorite: Raiders by 3½ Attendance: 67,603

Oakland (13-5)	3	0	6	12—	**21**
Tampa Bay (14-4)	3	17	14	14—	**48**

MVP: Tampa Bay S Dexter Jackson (2 interceptions for 34 yards)

Before the Super Bowl

The first NFL champion was the Akron Pros in 1920, when the league was called the American Professional Football Association (APFA) and the title went to the team with the best regular season record. The APFA changed its name to the National Football League in 1922.

The first playoff game with the championship at stake came in 1932, when the Chicago Bears (6-1-6) and Portsmouth (Ohio) Spartans (6-1-4) ended the regular season tied for first place. The Bears won the subsequent playoff, 9-0. Due to a snowstorm and cold weather, the game was moved from Wrigley Field to an improvised 80-yard dirt field at Chicago Stadium, making it the first indoor title game as well.

The NFL Championship Game decided the league title until the NFL merged with the AFL and the first Super Bowl was played following the 1966 season.

NFL Champions, 1920-32

Winning player-coaches noted by position.
Multiple winners: Canton-Cleveland Bulldogs and Green Bay (3); Chicago Staleys/Bears (2).

Year	Champion	Head Coach	Year	Champion	Head Coach
1920	Akron Pros	Fritz Pollard, HB & Elgie Tobin, QB	1927	New York Giants	Earl Potteiger, QB
			1928	Providence Steam Roller	Jimmy Conzelman, HB
1921	Chicago Staleys	George Halas, E	1929	Green Bay Packers	Curly Lambeau, QB
1922	Canton Bulldogs	Guy Chamberlin, E	1930	Green Bay Packers	Curly Lambeau
1923	Canton Bulldogs	Guy Chamberlin, E	1931	Green Bay Packers	Curly Lambeau
1924	Cleveland Bulldogs	Guy Chamberlin, E	1932	Chicago Bears	Ralph Jones
1925	Chicago Cardinals	Norm Barry			
1926	Frankford Yellow Jackets	Guy Chamberlin, E	(Bears beat Portsmouth-OH in playoff, 9-0)		

NFL-NFC Championship Game

NFL Championship games from 1933-69 and NFC Championship games since the completion of the NFL-AFL merger following the 1969 season.

Multiple winners: Green Bay (10); Dallas (8); Chicago Bears and Washington (7); NY Giants (6); San Francisco and Cle-LA-St.L Rams (5); Cleveland Browns, Detroit, Minnesota, and Philadelphia (4); Baltimore Colts (3).

Season	Winner	Head Coach	Score	Loser	Head Coach	Site
1933	Chicago Bears	George Halas	23-21	New York	Steve Owen	Chicago
1934	New York	Steve Owen	30-13	Chicago Bears	George Halas	New York
1935	Detroit	Potsy Clark	26- 7	New York	Steve Owen	Detroit
1936	Green Bay	Curly Lambeau	21- 6	Boston Redskins	Ray Flaherty	New York
1937	Washington Redskins	Ray Flaherty	28-21	Chicago Bears	George Halas	Chicago
1938	New York	Steve Owen	23-17	Green Bay	Curly Lambeau	New York
1939	Green Bay	Curly Lambeau	27-0	New York	Steve Owen	Milwaukee
1940	Chicago Bears	George Halas	73- 0	Washington	Ray Flaherty	Washington
1941	Chicago Bears	George Halas	37-9	New York	Steve Owen	Chicago
1942	Washington	Ray Flaherty	14- 6	Chicago Bears	Hunk Anderson & Luke Johnsos	Washington
1943	Chicago Bears	Hunk Anderson & Luke Johnsos	41-21	Washington	Arthur Bergman	Chicago
1944	Green Bay	Curly Lambeau	14- 7	New York	Steve Owen	New York
1945	Cleveland Rams	Adam Walsh	15-14	Washington	Dudley DeGroot	Cleveland
1946	Chicago Bears	George Halas	24-14	New York	Steve Owen	New York
1947	Chicago Cardinals	Jimmy Conzelman	28-21	Philadelphia	Greasy Neale	Chicago
1948	Philadelphia	Greasy Neale	7- 0	Chicago Cardinals	Jimmy Conzelman	Philadelphia
1949	Philadelphia	Greasy Neale	14- 0	Los Angeles Rams	Clark Shaughnessy	Los Angeles
1950	Cleveland Browns	Paul Brown	30-28	Los Angeles	Joe Stydahar	Cleveland
1951	Los Angeles	Joe Stydahar	24-17	Cleveland	Paul Brown	Los Angeles
1952	Detroit	Buddy Parker	17- 7	Cleveland	Paul Brown	Cleveland
1953	Detroit	Buddy Parker	17-16	Cleveland	Paul Brown	Detroit
1954	Cleveland	Paul Brown	56-10	Detroit	Buddy Parker	Cleveland

Season	Winner	Head Coach	Score	Loser	Head Coach	Site
1955	Cleveland	Paul Brown	38-14	Los Angeles	Sid Gillman	Los Angeles
1956	New York	Jim Lee Howell	47- 7	Chicago Bears	Paddy Driscoll	New York
1957	Detroit	George Wilson	59-14	Cleveland	Paul Brown	Detroit
1958	Balt. Colts	Weeb Ewbank	23-17*	New York	Jim Lee Howell	New York
1959	Balt. Colts	Weeb Ewbank	31-16	New York	Jim Lee Howell	Baltimore
1960	Philadelphia	Buck Shaw	17-13	Green Bay	Vince Lombardi	Philadelphia
1961	Green Bay	Vince Lombardi	37- 0	New York	Allie Sherman	Green Bay
1962	Green Bay	Vince Lombardi	16- 7	New York	Allie Sherman	New York
1963	Chicago	George Halas	14-10	New York	Allie Sherman	Chicago
1964	Cleveland	Blanton Collier	27- 0	Balt. Colts	Don Shula	Cleveland
1965	Green Bay	Vince Lombardi	23-12	Cleveland	Blanton Collier	Green Bay
1966	Green Bay	Vince Lombardi	34-27	Dallas	Tom Landry	Dallas
1967	Green Bay	Vince Lombardi	21-17	Dallas	Tom Landry	Green Bay
1968	Balt. Colts	Don Shula	34- 0	Cleveland	Blanton Collier	Cleveland
1969	Minnesota	Bud Grant	27- 7	Cleveland	Blanton Collier	Minnesota
1970	Dallas	Tom Landry	17-10	San Francisco	Dick Nolan	San Francisco
1971	Dallas	Tom Landry	14- 3	SanFrancisco	Dick Nolan	Dallas
1972	Washington	George Allen	26- 3	Dallas	Tom Landry	Washington
1973	Minnesota	Bud Grant	27-10	Dallas	Tom Landry	Dallas
1974	Minnesota	Bud Grant	14-10	Los Angeles	Chuck Knox	Minnesota
1975	Dallas	Tom Landry	37- 7	Los Angeles	Chuck Knox	Los Angeles
1976	Minnesota	Bud Grant	24-13	Los Angeles	Chuck Knox	Minnesota
1977	Dallas	Tom Landry	23- 6	Minnesota	Bud Grant	Dallas
1978	Dallas	Tom Landry	28- 0	Los Angeles	Ray Malavasi	Los Angele
1979	Los Angeles	Ray Malavasi	9- 0	Tampa Bay	John McKay	Tampa Bay
1980	Philadelphia	Dick Vermeil	20- 7	Dallas	Tom Landry	Philadelphia
1981	San Francisco	Bill Walsh	28-27	Dallas	Tom Landry	San Francisco
1982	Washington	Joe Gibbs	31-17	Dallas	Tom Landry	Washington
1983	Washington	Joe Gibbs	24-21	San Francisco	Bill Walsh	Washington
1984	San Francisco	Bill Walsh	23- 0	Chicago	Mike Ditka	San Francisco
1985	Chicago	Mike Ditka	24- 0	Los Angeles	John Robinson	Chicago
1986	New York	Bill Parcells	17- 0	Washington	Joe Gibbs	New York
1987	Washington	Joe Gibbs	17-10	Minnesota	Jerry Burns	Washington
1988	San Francisco	Bill Walsh	28- 3	Chicago	Mike Ditka	Chicago
1989	San Francisco	George Seifert	30- 3	Los Angeles	John Robinson	San Francisco
1990	New York	Bill Parcells	15-13	San Francisco	George Seifert	San Francisco
1991	Washington	Joe Gibbs	41-10	Detroit	Wayne Fontes	Washington
1992	Dallas	Jimmy Johnson	30-20	San Francisco	George Seifert	San Francisco
1993	Dallas	Jimmy Johnson	38-21	San Francisco	George Seifert	Dallas
1994	San Francisco	George Seifert	38-28	Dallas	Barry Switzer	San Francisco
1995	Dallas	Barry Switzer	38-27	Green Bay	Mike Holmgren	Dallas
1996	Green Bay	Mike Holmgren	30-13	Carolina	Dom Capers	Green Bay
1997	Green Bay	Mike Holmgren	23-10	San Francisco	Steve Mariucci	San Francisco
1998	Atlanta	Dan Reeves	30-27*	Minnesota	Dennis Green	Minnesota
1999	St. Louis	Dick Vermeil	11-6	Tampa Bay	Tony Dungy	St. Louis
2000	New York	Jim Fassel	41-0	Minnesota	Dennis Green	New York
2001	St. Louis	Mike Martz	29-24	Philadelphia	Andy Reid	St. Louis
2002	Tampa Bay	Jon Gruden	27-10	Philadelphia	Andy Reid	Philadelphia

*Sudden death overtime

NFL-NFC Championship Game Appearances

App		W	L	Pct	PF	PA	App		W	L	Pct	PF	PA
17	NY Giants	6	11	.353	281	322	8	Minnesota	4	4	.500	135	151
16	Dallas Cowboys	8	8	.500	361	319	7	Philadelphia	4	3	.571	113	104
14	Cle-LA-St.L Rams	5	9	.357	163	300	6	Detroit	4	2	.667	139	141
13	Green Bay Packers	10	3	.769	303	177	4	Baltimore Colts	3	1	.750	88	60
13	Chicago Bears	7	6	.538	286	245	3	Tampa Bay	1	2	.333	33	30
12	Boston-Wash. Redskins	7	5	.583	222	255	2	Chicago Cardinals	1	1	.500	28	28
12	San Francisco	5	7	.417	245	222	1	Atlanta	1	0	1.000	30	27
11	Cleveland Browns	4	7	.364	224	253	1	Carolina	0	1	.000	13	30

AFL-AFC Championship Game

AFL Championship games from 1960-69 and AFC Championship games since the completion of the NFL-AFL merger following the 1969 season.

Multiple winners: Buffalo and Denver (6); Miami, Oakland-LA Raiders and Pittsburgh (5); Dallas Texans-KC Chiefs, Houston Oilers-Tennessee Titans and New England (3); Cincinnati, Jacksonville and San Diego (2).

Season	Winner	Head Coach	Score	Loser	Head Coach	Site
1960	Houston	Lou Rymkus	24-16	LA Chargers	Sid Gillman	Houston
1961	Houston	Wally Lemm	10- 3	SD Chargers	Sid Gillman	San Diego
1962	Dallas	Hank Stram	20-17*	Houston	Pop Ivy	Houston

AFL-AFC Championship Game (Cont.)

Season	Winner	Head Coach	Score	Loser	Head Coach	Site
1963	San Diego	Sid Gillman	51-10	Boston Patriots	Mike Holovak	San Diego
1964	Buffalo	Lou Saban	20- 7	SanDiego	Sid Gillman	Buffalo
1965	Buffalo	Lou Saban	23- 0	San Diego	Sid Gillman	San Diego
1966	Kansas City	Hank Stram	31- 7	Buffalo	Joel Collier	Buffalo
1967	Oakland	John Rauch	40- 7	Houston	Wally Lemm	Oakland
1968	NY Jets	Weeb Ewbank	27-23	Oakland	John Rauch	New York
1969	Kansas City	Hank Stram	17- 7	Oakland	John Madden	Oakland
1970	Balt. Colts	Don McCafferty	27-17	Oakland	John Madden	Baltimore
1971	Miami	Don Shula	21- 0	Balt. Colts	Don McCafferty	Miami
1972	Miami	Don Shula	21-17	Pittsburgh	Chuck Noll	Pittsburgh
1973	Miami	Don Shula	27-10	Oakland	John Madden	Miami
1974	Pittsburgh	Chuck Noll	24-13	Oakland	John Madden	Oakland
1975	Pittsburgh	Chuck Noll	16-10	Oakland	John Madden	Pittsburgh
1976	Oakland	John Madden	24- 7	Pittsburgh	Chuck Noll	Oakland
1977	Denver	Red Miller	20-17	Oakland	John Madden	Denver
1978	Pittsburgh	Chuck Noll	34- 5	Houston	Bum Phillips	Pittsburgh
1979	Pittsburgh	Chuck Noll	27-13	Houston	Bum Phillips	Pittsburgh
1980	Oakland	Tom Flores	34-27	San Diego	Don Coryell	San Diego
1981	Cincinnati	Forrest Gregg	27- 7	San Diego	Don Coryell	Cincinnati
1982	Miami	Don Shula	14- 0	NYJets	Walt Michaels	Miami
1983	LA Raiders	Tom Flores	30-14	Seattle	Chuck Knox	Los Angeles
1984	Miami	Don Shula	45-28	Pittsburgh	Chuck Noll	Miami
1985	New England	Raymond Berry	31-14	Miami	Don Shula	Miami
1986	Denver	Dan Reeves	23-20*	Cleveland	Marty Schottenheimer	Cleveland
1987	Denver	Dan Reeves	38-33	Cleveland	Marty Schottenheimer	Denver
1988	Cincinnati	Sam Wyche	21-10	Buffalo	Marv Levy	Cincinnati
1989	Denver	Dan Reeves	37-21	Cleveland	Bud Carson	Denver
1990	Buffalo	Marv Levy	51-3	LA Raiders	Art Shell	Buffalo
1991	Buffalo	Marv Levy	10- 7	Denver	Dan Reeves	Buffalo
1992	Buffalo	Marv Levy	29-10	Miami	Don Shula	Miami
1993	Buffalo	Marv Levy	30-13	Kansas City	Marty Schottenheimer	Buffalo
1994	San Diego	Bobby Ross	17-13	Pittsburgh	Bill Cowher	Pittsburgh
1995	Pittsburgh	Bill Cowher	20-16	Indianapolis	Ted Marchibroda	Pittsburgh
1996	New England	Bill Parcells	20-6	Jacksonville	Tom Coughlin	New England
1997	Denver	Mike Shanahan	24-21	Pittsburgh	Bill Cowher	Pittsburgh
1998	Denver	Mike Shanahan	23-10	NY Jets	Bill Parcells	Denver
1999	Tennessee	Jeff Fisher	33-14	Jacksonville	Tom Coughlin	Jacksonville
2000	Balt. Ravens	Brian Billick	16-3	Oakland	Jon Gruden	Oakland
2001	New England	Bill Belichick	24-17	Pittsburgh	Bill Cowher	Pittsburgh
2002	Oakland	Bill Callahan	41-24	Tennessee	Jeff Fisher	Oakland

*Sudden death overtime

AFL-AFC Championship Game Appearances

App		W	L	Pct	PF	PA	App		W	L	Pct	PF	PA
14	Oakland-LA Raiders	5	9	.357	272	304	4	Boston-NE Patriots	3	1	.750	85	88
11	Pittsburgh	6	5	.455	224	212	3	Baltimore-Indy Colts	1	2	.333	43	58
8	Buffalo	6	2	.750	180	92	3	NY Jets	1	2	.333	37	60
8	Houston Oilers/Ten. Titans	3	5	.375	133	195	3	Cleveland	0	3	.000	74	98
8	LA-San Diego Chargers	2	6	.250	128	161	2	Cincinnati	2	0	1.000	48	17
7	Denver	6	1	.857	172	132	2	Jacksonville	0	2	.000	20	53
7	Miami	5	2	.714	152	115	1	Baltimore Ravens	1	0	1.000	16	3
4	Dallas Texans/KC Chiefs	3	1	.750	81	61	1	Seattle	0	1	.000	14	30

NFL Divisional Champions

The NFL adopted divisional play for the first time in 1967, splitting both conferences into two four-team divisions—the Capitol and Century divisions in the East and the Central and Coastal divisions in the West. A merger with the AFL in 1970 increased NFL membership to 26 teams and made it necessary for realignment. These 13-team conferences—the AFC and NFC—were formed by moving established NFL clubs in Baltimore, Cleveland and Pittsburgh to the AFC and rearranging both conferences into Eastern, Central and Western divisions. Expansion has since increased the league to 32 teams (beginning in 2002) with four NFC divisions and four AFC divisions, all with four teams each.

Division champions are listed below; teams that went on to win the Super Bowl are in **bold** type. Note that in the 1980 season, Oakland won the Super Bowl as a wild card team, as did Denver in 1997 and Baltimore in 2000; and in 1982, the players' strike shortened the regular season to nine games and eliminated divisional play for one season.

Multiple champions (since 1970): **AFC**—Pittsburgh (16); Miami and Oakland-LA Raiders (12); Denver (9); Buffalo (7); Baltimore-Indianapolis Colts and Cleveland (6); Cincinnati, New England and San Diego (5); Houston Oilers-Tennessee Titans and Kansas City (4); Jacksonville, NY Jets and Seattle (2). **NFC**—San Francisco (17); Dallas (15); Minnesota (14); LA-St. Louis Rams (10); Chicago (7); Washington (6); Green Bay and NY Giants (5); Philadelphia and Tampa Bay (4); Detroit (3); Atlanta, New Orleans and St. Louis Cardinals (2).

	American Football League				National Football League	
Season	East	West		Season	East	West
1966	Buffalo	Kansas City		1966	Dallas	**Green Bay**

Season	East	West		Season	Capitol	Century	Central	Coastal
1967	Houston	Oakland		1967	Dallas	Cleveland	**Green Bay**	LA Rams
1968	**NY Jets**	Oakland		1968	Dallas	Cleveland	Minnesota	Baltimore
1969	NY Jets	Oakland		1969	Dallas	Cleveland	Minnesota	LA Rams

Note: Kansas City, an AFL second-place team, won the Super Bowl in the 1969 season.

	American Football Conference				National Football Conference		
Season	East	Central	West	Season	East	Central	West
1970	**Balt. Colts**	Cincinnati	Oakland	1970	Dallas	Minnesota	San Francisco
1971	Miami	Cleveland	Kansas City	1971	**Dallas**	Minnesota	San Francisco
1972	**Miami**	Pittsburgh	Oakland	1972	Washington	Green Bay	San Francisco
1973	**Miami**	Cincinnati	Oakland	1973	Dallas	Minnesota	LA Rams
1974	Miami	**Pittsburgh**	Oakland	1974	St. Louis	Minnesota	LA Rams
1975	Balt.Colts	**Pittsburgh**	Oakland	1975	St. Louis	Minnesota	LA Rams
1976	Balt.Colts	Pittsburgh	**Oakland**	1976	Dallas	Minnesota	LA Rams
1977	Balt.Colts	Pittsburgh	Denver	1977	**Dallas**	Minnesota	LA Rams
1978	New England	**Pittsburgh**	Denver	1978	Dallas	Minnesota	LA Rams
1979	Miami	**Pittsburgh**	San Diego	1979	Dallas	Tampa Bay	LA Rams
1980	Buffalo	Cleveland	San Diego	1980	Philadelphia	Minnesota	Atlanta
1981	Miami	Cincinnati	San Diego	1981	Dallas	Tampa Bay	**San Francisco**
1982	—	—	—	1982	—	—	—
1983	Miami	Pittsburgh	**LA Raiders**	1983	Washington	Detroit	San Francisco
1984	Miami	Pittsburgh	Denver	1984	Washington	Chicago	**San Francisco**
1985	Miami	Cleveland	LA Raiders	1985	Dallas	**Chicago**	LA Rams
1986	New England	Cleveland	Denver	1986	**NY Giants**	Chicago	San Francisco
1987	Indianapolis	Cleveland	Denver	1987	**Washington**	Chicago	San Francisco
1988	Buffalo	Cincinnati	Seattle	1988	Philadelphia	Chicago	**San Francisco**
1989	Buffalo	Cleveland	Denver	1989	NY Giants	Minnesota	**San Francisco**
1990	Buffalo	Cincinnati	LA Raiders	1990	**NY Giants**	Chicago	San Francisco
1991	Buffalo	Houston	Denver	1991	**Washington**	Detroit	New Orleans
1992	Miami	Pittsburgh	San Diego	1992	**Dallas**	Minnesota	San Francisco
1993	Buffalo	Houston	Kansas City	1993	**Dallas**	Detroit	San Francisco
1994	Miami	Pittsburgh	San Diego	1994	Dallas	Minnesota	**San Francisco**
1995	Buffalo	Pittsburgh	Kansas City	1995	**Dallas**	Green Bay	San Francisco
1996	New England	Pittsburgh	Denver	1996	Dallas	**Green Bay**	Carolina
1997	New England	Pittsburgh	Kansas City	1997	NY Giants	Green Bay	San Francisco
1998	NY Jets	Jacksonville	**Denver**	1998	Dallas	Minnesota	Atlanta
1999	Indianapolis	Jacksonville	Seattle	1999	Washington	Tampa Bay	**St. Louis**
2000	Miami	Tennessee	Oakland	2000	NY Giants	Minnesota	New Orleans
2001	**New England**	Pittsburgh	Oakland	2001	Philadelphia	Chicago	St. Louis

Season	East	North	South	West	Season	East	North	South	West
2002	NY Jets	Pittsburgh	Tennessee	Oakland	2002	Philadelphia	Green Bay	Tampa Bay	San Fran.

Overall Postseason Games

The postseason records of all NFL teams, ranked by number of playoff games participated in from 1933–2002.

Gm		W	L	Pct	PF	PA	Gm		W	L	Pct	PF	PA
53	Dallas Cowboys	32	21	.604	1271	979	23	Balt-Indianapolis Colts	10	13	.435	393	472
43	Oakland-LA Raiders	25	18	.581	1028	797	20	Boston-NE Patriots	10	10	.500	370	404
42	San Francisco 49ers	25	17	.595	1044	853	19	Dallas Texans/KC Chiefs	8	11	.421	301	384
40	Pittsburgh Steelers	23	17	.575	912	808	18	LA-San Diego Chargers	7	11	.389	332	428
40	Cle-LA-St.L Rams	18	22	.450	703	848	17	Detroit Lions	7	10	.412	365	404
40	Minnesota Vikings	17	23	.425	779	913	16	New York Jets	7	9	.438	335	315
39	Miami Dolphins	20	19	.513	780	848	13	Tampa Bay Buccaneers	6	7	.462	206	238
37	Boston-Wash. Redskins	22	15	.595	778	642	12	Cincinnati Bengals	5	7	.417	246	257
37	New York Giants	16	21	.432	647	699	12	Atlanta Falcons	5	7	.417	241	287
35	Green Bay Packers	23	12	.657	821	645	8	Jacksonville Jaguars	4	4	.500	208	200
31	Cleveland Browns	11	20	.355	629	728	8	Seattle Seahawks	3	5	.375	145	159
29	Buffalo Bills	14	15	.483	681	658	7	Chi-St.L-Ari. Cardinals	2	5	.286	122	182
29	Chicago Bears	14	15	.483	598	585	6	Baltimore Ravens	5	1	.833	125	53
29	Houston Oilers/Ten. Titans	13	16	.448	529	698	6	New Orleans Saints	1	5	.167	103	185
28	Denver Broncos	16	12	.571	616	657	2	Carolina Panthers	1	1	.500	39	47
27	Philadelphia Eagles	13	14	.481	508	482							

Champions of Leagues That No Longer Exist

No professional league in American sports has had to contend with more pretenders to the throne than the NFL. Eight times in nine decades, a rival league has risen up to challenge the NFL and seven of them (including the XFL) went under in less than five seasons. Only the fourth American Football League (1960-69) succeeded, forcing the older league to sue for peace and a full partnership in 1966.

Of the seven leagues that didn't make it, only the All-America Football Conference (1946-49) lives on—the Cleveland Browns and San Francisco 49ers joined the NFL after the AAFC folded in 1949. The champions of leagues past are listed below.

American Football League I

Year		Head Coach
1926	Philadelphia Quakers (8-2)	Bob Folwell

Note: Philadelphia was challenged to a postseason game by the 7th place New York Giants (8-4-1) of the NFL. The Giants won, 31-0, in a snowstorm.

American Football League II

Year		Head Coach
1936	Boston Shamrocks (8-3)	George Kenneally
1937	Los Angeles Bulldogs (9-0)	Gus Henderson

Note: Boston was scheduled to play 2nd place Cleveland (5-2-2) in the '36 championship game, but the Shamrock players refused to participate because they were owed pay for past games.

American Football League III

Year		Head Coach
1940	Columbus Bullies (8-1-1)	Phil Bucklew
1941	Columbus Bullies (5-1-2)	Phil Bucklew

All-America Football Conference

Year	Winner	Head Coach	Score	Loser	Head Coach	Site
1946	Cleveland Browns	Paul Brown	14-9	NY Yankees	Ray Flaherty	Cleveland
1947	Cleveland Browns	Paul Brown	14-3	NY Yankees	Ray Flaherty	New York
1948	Cleveland Browns	Paul Brown	49-7	Buffalo Bills	Red Dawson	Cleveland
1949	Cleveland Browns	Paul Brown	21-7	S.F. 49ers	Buck Shaw	Cleveland

World Football League

Year	Winner	Head Coach	Score	Loser	Head Coach	Site
1974	Birmingham Americans	Jack Gotta	22-21	Florida Blazers	Jack Pardee	Birmingham

United States Football League

Year	Winner	Head Coach	Score	Loser	Head Coach	Site
1983	Michigan Panthers	Jim Stanley	24-22	Philadelphia Stars	Jim Mora	Denver
1984	Philadelphia Stars	Jim Mora	23-3	Arizona Wranglers	George Allen	Tampa
1985	Baltimore Stars	Jim Mora	28-24	Oakland Invaders	Charlie Sumner	E. Rutherford

XFL

Year	Winner	Head Coach	Score	Loser	Head Coach	Site
2001	Los Angeles Xtreme	Al Luginbill	38-6	San Fran. Demons	Jim Skipper	Los Angeles

Defunct Leagues

AFL I (1926): Boston Bulldogs, Brooklyn Horseman, Chicago Bulls, Cleveland Panthers, Los Angeles Wildcats, New York Yankees, Newark Bears, Philadelphia Quakers, Rock Island Independents.

AFL II (1936-37): Boston Shamrocks (1936-37); Brooklyn Tigers (1936); Cincinnati Bengals (1937); Cleveland Rams (1936); Los Angeles Bulldogs (1937); New York Yankees (1936-37); Pittsburgh Americans (1936-37); Rochester Tigers (1936-37).

AFL III (1940-41): Boston Bears (1940); Buffalo Indians (1940-41); Cincinnati Bengals (1940-41); Columbus Bullies (1940-41); Milwaukee Chiefs (1940-41); New York Yankees (1940) renamed Americans (1941).

AAFC (1946-49): Brooklyn Dodgers (1946-48) merged to become Brooklyn-New York Yankees (1949); Buffalo Bisons (1946) renamed Bills (1947-49); Chicago Rockets (1946-48) renamed Hornets (1949); Cleveland Browns (1946-49); Los Angeles Dons (1946-49); Miami Seahawks (1946) became Baltimore Colts (1947-49); New York Yankees (1946-48) merged to become Brooklyn-New York Yankees (1949); San Francisco 49ers (1946-49).

WFL (1974-75): Birmingham Americans (1974) renamed Vulcans (1975); Chicago Fire (1974) renamed Winds (1975); Detroit Wheels (1974); Florida Blazers (1974) became San Antonio Wings (1975); The Hawaiians (1974-75); Houston Texans (1974) became Shreveport (La.) Steamer (1974-75); Jacksonville Sharks (1974) renamed Express (1975); Memphis Southmen (1974) also known as Grizzlies (1975); New York Stars (1974) became Charlotte Hornets (1974-75); Philadelphia Bell (1974-75); Portland Storm (1974) renamed Thunder (1975); Southern California Sun (1974-75).

USFL (1983-85): Arizona Wranglers (1983-84) merged with Oklahoma to become Arizona Outlaws (1985); Birmingham Stallions (1983-85); Boston Breakers (1983) became New Orleans Breakers (1984) and then Portland Breakers (1985); Chicago Blitz (1983-84); Denver Gold (1983-85); Houston Gamblers (1984-85); Jacksonville Bulls (1984-85); Los Angeles Express (1983-85); Memphis Showboats (1984-85).
Michigan Panthers (1983-84) merged with Oakland (1985); New Jersey Generals (1983-85); Oakland Invaders (1983-85); Oklahoma Outlaws (1984) merged with Arizona to become Arizona Outlaws (1985); Philadelphia Stars (1983-84) became Baltimore Stars (1985); Pittsburgh Maulers (1984); San Antonio Gunslingers (1984-85); Tampa Bay Bandits (1983-85); Washington Federals (1983-84) became Orlando Renegades (1985).

XFL (2001): Birmingham Thunderbolts, Chicago Enforcers, Las Vegas Outlaws, Los Angeles Xtreme, Memphis Maniax, New York New Jersey Hitmen, Orlando Rage, San Francisco Demons.

NFL Pro Bowl

A postseason All-Star game between the new league champion and a team of professional all-stars was added to the NFL schedule in 1939. In the first game at Wrigley Field in Los Angeles, the NY Giants beat a team made up of players from NFL teams and two independent clubs in Los Angeles (the LA Bulldogs and Hollywood Stars). An all-NFL All-Star team provided the opposition over the next four seasons, but the game was cancelled in 1943.

The Pro Bowl was revived in 1951 as a contest between conference all-star teams: American vs National (1951-53), Eastern vs Western (1954-70), and AFC vs NFC (since 1971). The AFC leads the current series, 17-16.

The MVP trophy was named the Dan McGuire Award in 1984 after the late SF 49ers publicist and *Honolulu Advertiser* sports columnist.

Year	Winner	Score	Loser
1939	NY Giants	13-10	All-Stars
1940	Green Bay	16-7	All-Stars
1940	Chicago Bears	28-14	All-Stars
1942	Chicago Bears	35-24	All-Stars
1942	All-Stars	17-14	Washington
1943-50	No game		

Year	Winner	MVP
1951	American, 28-27	Otto Graham, Cle., QB
1952	National, 30-13	Dan Towler, LA Rams, HB
1953	National, 27-7	Don Doll, Det., DB
1954	East, 20-9	Chuck Bednarik, Phi., LB
1955	West, 26-19	Billy Wilson, SF, E
1956	East, 31-30	Ollie Matson, Cards, HB
1957	West, 19-10	Back–Bert Rechichar, Bal.
		Line–Ernie Stautner, Pit.
1958	West, 26-7	Back–Hugh McElhenny, SF
		Line–Gene Brito, Wash.
1959	East, 28-21	Back–Frank Gifford, NY
		Line–Doug Atkins, Chi.
1960	West, 38-21	Back–Johnny Unitas, Bal.
		Line–Big Daddy Lipscomb, Pit.
1961	West, 35-31	Back–Johnny Unitas, Bal.
		Line–Sam Huff, NY
1962	West, 31-30	Back–Jim Brown, Cle.
		Line–Henry Jordan, GB
1963	East, 30-20	Back–Jim Brown, Cle.
		Line–Big Daddy Lipscomb, Pit.
1964	West, 31-17	Back–Johnny Unitas, Bal.
		Line–Gino Marchetti, Bal.
1965	West, 34-14	Back–Fran Tarkenton, Min.
		Line–Terry Barr, Det.
1966	East, 36-7	Back–Jim Brown, Cle.
		Line–Dale Meinhart, St. L.
1967	East, 20-10	Back–Gale Sayers, Chi.
		Line–Floyd Peters, Phi.
1968	West, 38-20	Back–Gale Sayers, Chi.
		Line–Dave Robinson, GB
1969	West, 10-7	Back–Roman Gabriel, LA Rams
		Line–Merlin Olsen, LA Rams
1970	West, 16-13	Back–Gale Sayers, Chi.
		Line–George Andrie, Dal.

Year	Winner	MVP
1971	NFC, 27-6	Back–Mel Renfro, Dal.
		Line–Fred Carr, GB
1972	AFC, 26-13	Off–Jan Stenerud, KC
		Def–Willie Lanier, KC
1973	AFC, 33-28	O.J. Simpson, Buf., RB
1974	AFC, 15-13	Garo Yepremian, Mia., PK
1975	NFC, 17-10	James Harris, LA Rams, QB
1976	NFC, 23-20	Billy Johnson, Hou., KR
1977	AFC, 24-14	Mel Blount, Pit., CB
1978	NFC, 14-13	Walter Payton, Chi., RB
1979	NFC, 13-7	Ahmad Rashad, Min., WR
1980	NFC, 37-27	Chuck Muncie, NO, RB
1981	NFC, 21-7	Eddie Murray, Det., PK
1982	AFC, 16-13	Kellen Winslow, SD, WR
		& Lee Roy Selmon, TB, DE
1983	NFC, 20-19	Dan Fouts, SD, QB
		& John Jefferson, GB, WR
1984	NFC, 45-3	Joe Theismann, Wash., QB
1985	AFC, 22-14	Mark Gastineau, NYJ, DE
1986	NFC, 28-24	Phil Simms, NYG, QB
1987	AFC, 10-6	Reggie White, Phi., DE
1988	AFC, 15-6	Bruce Smith, Buf., DE
1989	NFC, 34-3	Randall Cunningham, Phi., QB
1990	NFC, 27-21	Jerry Gray, LA Rams, CB
1991	AFC, 23-21	Jim Kelly, Buf., QB
1992	NFC, 21-15	Michael Irvin, Dal., WR
1993	AFC, 23-20 (OT)	Steve Tasker, Buf., Sp. Teams
1994	NFC, 17-3	Andre Rison, Atl., WR
1995	AFC, 41-13	Marshall Faulk, Ind., RB
1996	NFC, 20-13	Jerry Rice, SF, WR
1997	AFC, 26-23 (OT)	Mark Brunell, Jax, QB
1998	AFC, 29-24	Warren Moon, Sea., QB
1999	AFC, 23-10	Ty Law, NE, CB
		& Keyshawn Johnson, NYJ, WR
2000	NFC, 51-31	Randy Moss, Min., WR
2001	AFC, 38-17	Rich Gannon, Oak., QB
2002	AFC, 38-30	Rich Gannon, Oak., QB
2003	AFC, 45-20	Ricky Williams, Mia., RB

Playing sites: Wrigley Field in Los Angeles (1939); Gilmore Stadium in Los Angeles (1940–both games); Polo Grounds in New York (Jan., 1942); Shibe Park in Philadelphia (Dec., 1942); Memorial Coliseum in Los Angeles (1951-72 and 1979); Texas Stadium in Irving, TX (1973); Arrowhead Stadium in Kansas City (1974); Orange Bowl in Miami (1975); Superdome in New Orleans (1976); Kingdome in Seattle (1977); Tampa Stadium in Tampa (1978) and Aloha Stadium in Honolulu (since 1980).

AFL All-Star Game

The AFL did not play an All-Star game after its first season in 1960 but did stage All-Star games from 1962-70. All-Star teams from the Eastern and Western divisions played each other every year except 1966 with the West winning the series, 6-2. In 1966, the league champion Buffalo Bills met an elite squad made up of the best players from the league's other eight clubs and lost, 30-19.

Year	Winner	MVP
1962	West, 47-27	Cotton Davidson, Oak., QB
1963	West, 21-14	Off–Curtis McClinton, Dal.
		Def–Earl Faison, SD
1964	West, 27-24	Off–Keith Lincoln, SD
		Def–Archie Matsos, Oak.
1965	West, 38-14	Off–Keith Lincoln, SD
		Def–Willie Brown, Den.
1966	All-Stars 30	Off–Joe Namath, NY
	Buffalo 19	Def–Frank Buncom, SD

Year	Winner	MVP
1967	East, 30-23	Off–Babe Parilli, Bos.
		Def–Verlon Biggs, NY
1968	East, 25-24	Off–Joe Namath, NY
		& Don Maynard, NY
		Def–Speedy Duncan, SD
1969	West, 38-25	Off–Len Dawson, KC
		Def–George Webster, Hou.
1970	West, 26-3	John Hadl, SD, QB

Playing sites: Balboa Stadium in San Diego (1962-64); Jeppesen Stadium in Houston (1965); Rice Stadium in Houston (1966); Oakland Coliseum (1967); Gator Bowl in Jacksonville (1968-69) and Astrodome in Houston (1970).

NFL Franchise Origins

Here is what the current 32 teams in the National Football League have to show for the years they have put in as members of the American Professional Football Association (APFA), the NFL, the All-America Football Conference (AAFC) and the American Football League (AFL). Years given for league titles indicate seasons championships were won.

American Football Conference

	First Season	League Titles	Franchise Stops
Baltimore Ravens	1996 (NFL)	1 Super Bowl (2000)	• Baltimore (1996—)
Buffalo Bills	1960 (AFL)	2 AFL (1964-65)	• Buffalo (1960-72) Orchard Park, NY (1973—)
Cincinnati Bengals	1968 (AFL)	None	• Cincinnati (1968—)
Cleveland Browns	1946 (AAFC)	4 AAFC (1946-49) 4 NFL (1950,54-55,64)	• Cleveland (1946-95, 99—)
Denver Broncos	1960 (AFL)	2 Super Bowls (1997-98)	• Denver (1960—)
Houston Texans	2002 (NFL)	None	• Houston (2002—)
Indianapolis Colts	1953 (NFL)	3 NFL (1958-59,68) 1 Super Bowl (1970)	• Baltimore (1953-83) Indianapolis (1984—)
Jacksonville Jaguars	1995 (NFL)	None	• Jacksonville, FL (1995—)
Kansas City Chiefs	1960 (AFL)	3 AFL (1962,66,69) 1 Super Bowl (1969)	• Dallas (1960-62) Kansas City (1963—)
Miami Dolphins	1966 (AFL)	2 Super Bowls (1972-73)	• Miami (1966—)
New England Patriots	1960 (AFL)	1 Super Bowl (2001)	• Boston (1960-70) Foxboro, MA (1971—)
New York Jets	1960 (AFL)	1 AFL (1968) 1 Super Bowl (1968)	• New York (1960-83) E. Rutherford, NJ (1984—)
Oakland Raiders	1960 (AFL)	1 AFL (1967) 3 Super Bowls (1976,80,83)	• Oakland (1960-81, 1995—) Los Angeles (1982-94)
Pittsburgh Steelers	1933 (NFL)	4 Super Bowls (1974-75,78-79)	• Pittsburgh (1933—)
San Diego Chargers	1960 (AFL)	1 AFL (1963)	• Los Angeles (1960) San Diego (1961—)
Tennessee Titans	1960 (AFL)	2 AFL (1960-61)	• Houston (1960-96) Memphis (1997) Nashville (1998—)

National Football Conference

	First Season	League Titles	Franchise Stops
Arizona Cardinals	1920 (APFA)	2 NFL (1925,47)	• Chicago (1920-59) St. Louis (1960-87) Tempe, AZ (1988—)
Atlanta Falcons	1966 (NFL)	None	• Atlanta (1966—)
Carolina Panthers	1995 (NFL)	None	• Clemson, SC (1995) Charlotte, NC (1996—)
Chicago Bears	1920 (APFA)	8 NFL (1921, 32-33,40-41,43,46,63) 1 Super Bowl (1985)	• Decatur, IL (1920) Chicago (1921—)
Dallas Cowboys	1960 (NFL)	5 Super Bowls (1971,77,92-93,95)	• Dallas (1960-70) Irving, TX (1971—)
Detroit Lions	1930 (NFL)	4 NFL (1935,52-53,57)	• Portsmouth, OH (1930-33) Detroit (1934-74, 2002—) Pontiac, MI (1975-2001)
Green Bay Packers	1921 (APFA)	11 NFL (1929-31,36,39,44,61-62,65-67) 3 Super Bowls (1966-67,96)	• Green Bay (1921—)
Minnesota Vikings	1961 (NFL)	1 NFL (1969)	• Bloomington, MN (1961-81) Minneapolis, MN (1982—)
New Orleans Saints	1967 (NFL)	None	• New Orleans (1967—)
New York Giants	1925 (NFL)	4 NFL (1927,34,38,56) 2 Super Bowls (1986,90)	• New York (1925-73,75) New Haven, CT (1973-74) E. Rutherford, NJ (1976—)
Philadelphia Eagles	1933 (NFL)	3 NFL (1948-49,60)	• Philadelphia (1933—)
St. Louis Rams	1937 (NFL)	2 NFL (1945,51) 1 Super Bowl (1999)	• Cleveland (1937-45) Los Angeles (1946-79) Anaheim (1980-94) St. Louis (1995—)
San Francisco 49ers	1946 (AAFC)	5 Super Bowls (1981,84,88-89,94)	• San Francisco (1946—)
Seattle Seahawks	1976 (NFL)	None	• Seattle (1976—)
Tampa Bay Buccaneers	1976 (NFL)	1 Super Bowl (2002)	• Tampa, FL (1976—)
Washington Redskins	1932 (NFL)	2 NFL (1937,42) 3 Super Bowls (1982,87,91)	• Boston (1932-36) Washington, DC (1937-96) Raljon, MD (1997—)

The Growth of the NFL

Of the 14 franchises that comprised the American Professional Football Association in 1920, only two remain—the Arizona Cardinals (then the Chicago Cardinals) and the Chicago Bears (originally the Decatur-IL Staleys). Green Bay joined the APFC in 1921 and the league changed its name to the NFL in 1922. Since then, 54 NFL clubs have come and gone, six rival leagues have expired and two other leagues have been swallowed up.

The NFL merged with the **All-America Football Conference** (1946-49) following the 1949 season and adopted three of its seven clubs—the Baltimore Colts, Cleveland Browns and San Francisco 49ers. The four remaining AAFC teams—the Brooklyn/NY Yankees, Buffalo Bills, Chicago Hornets and Los Angeles Dons—did not survive. After the 1950 season, the financially troubled Colts were sold back to the NFL. The league folded the team and added its players to the 1951 college draft pool. A new Baltimore franchise, also named the Colts, joined the NFL in 1953.

The formation of the **American Football League** (1960-69) was announced in 1959 with ownership lined up in eight cities—Boston, Buffalo, Dallas, Denver, Houston, Los Angeles, Minneapolis and New York. Set to begin play in the autumn of 1960, the AFL was stunned early that year when Minneapolis withdrew to accept an offer to join the NFL as an expansion team in 1961. The new league responded by choosing Oakland to replace Minneapolis and inherit the departed team's draft picks. Since no AFL team actually played in Minneapolis, it is not considered the original home of the Oakland Raiders.

In 1966, the NFL and AFL agreed to a merger that resulted in the first Super Bowl (originally called the AFL-NFL World Championship Game) following the '66 league playoffs. In 1970, the now 10-member AFL officially joined the NFL, forming a 26-team league made up of two conferences of three divisions each. In 2002, the 32-team league was realigned into two conferences of four divisions each.

Expansion/Merger Timetable

For teams currently in NFL.

1921–Green Bay Packers; **1925**–New York Giants; **1930**–Portsmouth-OH Spartans (now Detroit Lions); **1932**–Boston Braves (now Washington Redskins); **1933**–Philadelphia Eagles and Pittsburgh Pirates (now Steelers); **1937**–Cleveland Rams (now St. Louis); **1950**–added AAFC's Cleveland Browns and San Francisco 49ers; **1953**–Baltimore Colts (now Indianapolis). **1960**–Dallas Cowboys; **1961**–Minnesota Vikings; **1966**–Atlanta Falcons; **1967**–New Orleans Saints; **1970**–added AFL's Boston Patriots (now New England), Buffalo Bills, Cincinnati Bengals (1968 expansion team), Denver Broncos, Houston Oilers (now Tennessee Titans), Kansas City Chiefs, Miami Dolphins (1966 expansion team), New York Jets, Oakland Raiders and San Diego Chargers (the AFL-NFL merger divided the league into two 13-team conferences with old-line NFL clubs Baltimore, Cleveland and Pittsburgh moving to the AFC); **1976**–Seattle Seahawks and Tampa Bay Buccaneers (Seattle was originally in the NFC West and Tampa Bay in the AFC West, but were switched to AFC West and NFC Central, respectively, in 1977); **1995**–Carolina Panthers and Jacksonville Jaguars; **1996**—Cleveland Browns move to Baltimore and become Ravens. City of Cleveland retains rights to team name, colors and all memorabilia; **1999**–Cleveland Browns return to the NFL. **2002**–Houston Texans. Seattle moves back to the NFC West.

City and Nickname Changes

1921—Decatur Staleys move to Chicago; **1922**—Chicago Staleys renamed Bears; **1933**—Boston Braves renamed Redskins; **1937**—Boston Redskins move to Washington; **1934**—Portsmouth (Ohio) Spartans move to Detroit and become Lions; **1941**—Pittsburgh Pirates renamed Steelers; **1943**—Philadelphia and Pittsburgh merge for one season and become Phil-Pitt, or the "Steagles;" **1944**—Chicago Cardinals and Pittsburgh merge for one season and become Card-Pitt; **1946**—Cleveland Rams move to Los Angeles.

1960—Chicago Cardinals move to St. Louis; **1961**—Los Angeles Chargers (AFL) move to San Diego; **1963**—New York Titans (AFL) renamed Jets and Dallas Texans (AFL) move to Kansas City and become Chiefs; **1971**—Boston Patriots become New England Patriots; **1982**—Oakland Raiders move to Los Angeles; **1984**—Baltimore Colts move to Indianapolis; **1988**—St. Louis Cardinals move to Phoenix; **1994**—Phoenix Cardinals become Arizona Cardinals; **1995**—L.A. Rams move to St. Louis and L.A. Raiders move back to Oakland; **1996**—Cleveland Browns move to Baltimore and become Ravens. City of Cleveland retains rights to team name, colors and all memorabilia; **1997**—Houston Oilers move to Memphis and become Tennessee Oilers; **1998**—Tennessee Oilers move to Nashville; **1999**—Tennessee Oilers renamed Titans.

Defunct NFL Teams

Teams that once played in the APFA and NFL, but no longer exist.

Akron-OH–Pros (1920-25) and Indians (1926); **Baltimore**–Colts (1950); **Boston**–Bulldogs (1926) and Yanks (1944-48); **Brooklyn**–Lions (1926), Dodgers (1930-43) and Tigers (1944); **Buffalo**–All-Americans (1920-23), Bisons (1924-25), Rangers (1926), Bisons (1927,1929); **Canton-OH**–Bulldogs (1920-23,1925-26); **Chicago**–Tigers (1920); **Cincinnati**–Celts (1921) and Reds (1933-34); **Cleveland**–Tigers (1920), Indians (1921), Indians (1923), Bulldogs (1924-25,1927) and Indians (1931); **Columbus-OH**–Panhandles (1920-22) and Tigers (1923-26); **Dallas**–Texans (1952); **Dayton-OH**–Triangles (1920-29).

Detroit–Heralds (1920-21), Panthers (1925-26) and Wolverines (1928); **Duluth-MN**–Kelleys (1923-25) and Eskimos (1926-27); **Evansville-IN**–Crimson Giants (1921-22); **Frankford-PA**–Yellow Jackets (1924-31); **Hammond-IN**–Pros (1920-26); **Hartford**–Blues (1926); **Kansas City**–Blues (1924) and Cowboys (1925-26); **Kenosha-WI**–Maroons (1924); **Los Angeles**–Buccaneers (1926); **Louisville**–Brecks (1921-23) and Colonels (1926); **Marion-OH**–Oorang Indians (1922-23); **Milwaukee**–Badgers (1922-26); **Minneapolis**–Marines (1922-24) and Red Jackets (1929-30); **Muncie-IN**–Flyers (1920-21).

New York–Giants (1921), Yankees (1927-28), Bulldogs (1949) and Yankees (1950-51); **Newark-NJ**–Tornadoes (1930); **Orange-NJ**–Tornadoes (1929); **Pottsville-PA**–Maroons (1925-28); **Providence-RI**–Steam Roller (1925-31); **Racine-WI**–Legion (1922-24) and Tornadoes (1926); **Rochester-NY**–Jeffersons (1920-25); **Rock Island-IL**–Independents (1920-26); **Staten Island-NY**–Stapletons (1929-32); **St. Louis**–All-Stars (1923) and Gunners (1934); **Toledo-OH**–Maroons (1922-23); **Tonawanda-NY**–Kardex (1921), also called Lumbermen; **Washington**–Senators (1921).

Annual NFL Leaders

Individual leaders in NFL (1932-69), NFC (since 1970), AFL (1960-69) and AFC (since 1970).

Passing

Since 1932, the NFL has used several formulas to determine passing leadership, from Total Yards alone (1932-37), to the current rating system—adopted in 1973—that takes Completions, Completion Percentage, Yards Gained, TD Passes, Interceptions, Interception Percentage and other factors into account. The quarterbacks listed below all led the league according to the system in use at the time.

NFL-NFC

Multiple winners: Sammy Baugh and Steve Young (6); Joe Montana and Roger Staubach (5); Arnie Herber, Sonny Jurgensen, Bart Starr and Norm Van Brocklin (3); Ed Danowski, Otto Graham, Cecil Isbell, Milt Plum, Kurt Warner and Bob Waterfield (2).

Year	Player	Att	Cmp	Yds	TD
1932	Arnie Herber, GB	101	37	639	9
1933	Harry Newman, NY	136	53	973	11
1934	Arnie Herber, GB	115	42	799	8
1935	Ed Danowski, NY	113	57	794	10
1936	Arnie Herber, GB	173	77	1239	11
1937	Sammy Baugh, Wash	171	81	1127	8
1938	Ed Danowski, NY	129	70	848	7
1939	Parker Hall, Cle. Rams	208	106	1227	9
1940	Sammy Baugh, Wash	177	111	1367	12
1941	Cecil Isbell, GB	206	117	1479	15
1942	Cecil Isbell, GB	268	146	2021	24
1943	Sammy Baugh, Wash	239	133	1754	23
1944	Frank Filchock, Wash	147	84	1139	13
1945	Sammy Baugh, Wash	182	128	1669	11
	& Sid Luckman, Chi. Bears	217	117	1725	14
1946	Bob Waterfield, LA	251	127	1747	18
1947	Sammy Baugh, Wash	354	210	2938	25
1948	Tommy Thompson, Phi	246	141	1965	25
1949	Sammy Baugh, Wash	255	145	1903	18
1950	Norm Van Brocklin, LA	233	127	2061	18
1951	Bob Waterfield, LA	176	88	1566	13
1952	Norm Van Brocklin, LA	205	113	1736	14
1953	Otto Graham, Cle	258	167	2722	11
1954	Norm Van Brocklin, LA	260	139	2637	13
1955	Otto Graham, Cle	185	98	1721	15
1956	Ed Brown, Chi. Bears	168	96	1667	11
1957	Tommy O'Connell, Cle	110	63	1229	9
1958	Eddie LeBaron, Wash	145	79	1365	11
1959	Charlie Conerly, NY	194	113	1706	14
1960	Milt Plum, Cle	250	151	2297	21
1961	Milt Plum, Cle	302	177	2416	16
1962	Bart Starr, GB	285	178	2438	12
1963	Y.A. Tittle, NY	367	221	3145	36
1964	Bart Starr, GB	272	163	2144	15
1965	Rudy Bukich, Chi	312	176	2641	20
1966	Bart Starr, GB	251	156	2257	14
1967	Sonny Jurgensen, Wash	508	288	3747	31
1968	Earl Morrall, Bal	317	182	2909	26
1969	Sonny Jurgensen, Wash	442	274	3102	22
1970	John Brodie, SF	378	223	2941	24
1971	Roger Staubach, Dal	211	126	1882	15
1972	Norm Snead, NY	325	196	2307	17
1973	Roger Staubach, Dal	286	179	2428	23
1974	Sonny Jurgensen, Wash	167	107	1185	11
1975	Fran Tarkenton, Min	425	273	2994	25
1976	James Harris, LA	158	91	1460	8
1977	Roger Staubach, Dal	361	210	2620	18
1978	Roger Staubach, Dal	413	231	3190	25
1979	Roger Staubach, Dal	461	267	3586	27
1980	Ron Jaworski, Phi	451	257	3529	27
1981	Joe Montana, SF	488	311	3565	19
1982	Joe Theismann, Wash	252	161	2033	13
1983	Steve Bartkowski, Atl	432	274	3167	22
1984	Joe Montana, SF	432	279	3630	28
1985	Joe Montana, SF	494	303	3653	27
1986	Tommy Kramer, Min	372	208	3000	24
1987	Joe Montana, SF	398	266	3054	31
1988	Wade Wilson, Min	332	204	2746	15
1989	Don Majkowski, GB	599	353	4318	27
1990	Joe Montana, SF	520	321	3944	26
1991	Steve Young, SF	279	180	2517	17
1992	Steve Young, SF	402	268	3465	25
1993	Steve Young, SF	462	314	4023	29
1994	Steve Young, SF	461	324	3969	35
1995	Brett Favre, GB	570	359	4413	38
1996	Steve Young, SF	316	214	2410	14
1997	Steve Young, SF	356	241	3029	19
1998	Randall Cunningham, Min	425	259	3704	34
1999	Kurt Warner, St.L	499	325	4353	41
2000	Trent Green, St.L	240	145	2063	16
2001	Kurt Warner, St.L	546	375	4830	36
2002	Brad Johnson, TB	451	281	3049	22

Note: In 1945, Sammy Baugh and Sid Luckman tied with 8 points on an inverse rating system.

AFL-AFC

Multiple winners: Dan Marino (5); Ken Anderson and Len Dawson (4); Bob Griese, Daryle Lamonica, Warren Moon and Ken Stabler (2).

Year	Player	Att	Cmp	Yds	TD
1960	Jack Kemp, LA	406	211	3018	20
1961	George Blanda, Hou	362	187	3330	36
1962	Len Dawson, Dal	310	189	2759	29
1963	Tobin Rote, SD	286	170	2510	20
1964	Len Dawson, KC	354	199	2879	30
1965	John Hadl, SD	348	174	2798	20
1966	Len Dawson, KC	284	159	2527	26
1967	Daryle Lamonica, Oak	425	220	3228	30
1968	Len Dawson, KC	224	131	2109	17
1969	Greg Cook, Cin	197	106	1854	15
1970	Daryle Lamonica, Oak	356	179	2516	22
1971	Bob Griese, Mia	263	145	2089	19
1972	Earl Morrall, Mia	150	83	1360	11
1973	Ken Stabler, Oak	260	163	1997	14
1974	Ken Anderson, Cin	328	213	2667	18
1975	Ken Anderson, Cin	377	228	3169	21
1976	Ken Stabler, Oak	291	194	2737	27
1977	Bob Griese, Mia	307	180	2252	22
1978	Terry Bradshaw, Pit	368	207	2915	28
1979	Dan Fouts, SD	530	332	4082	24
1980	Brian Sipe, Cle	554	337	4132	30
1981	Ken Anderson, Cin	479	300	3753	29
1982	Ken Anderson, Cin	309	218	2495	12
1983	Dan Marino, Mia	296	173	2210	20
1984	Dan Marino, Mia	564	362	5084	48
1985	Ken O'Brien, NY	488	297	3888	25
1986	Dan Marino, Mia	623	378	4746	44
1987	Bernie Kosar, Cle	389	241	3033	22
1988	Boomer Esiason, Cin	388	223	3572	28
1989	Warren Moon, Hou	550	308	3997	24
1990	Warren Moon, Hou	584	362	4689	33
1991	Jim Kelly, Buf	474	304	3844	33
1992	Warren Moon, Hou	346	224	2521	18
1993	John Elway, Den	551	348	4030	25
1994	Dan Marino, Mia	615	385	4453	30
1995	Jim Harbaugh, Ind	314	200	2575	17
1996	John Elway, Den	466	287	3328	26
1997	Mark Brunell, Jax	435	264	3281	18
1998	Vinny Testaverde, NYJ	421	259	3256	29
1999	Peyton Manning, Ind	533	331	4135	26
2000	Brian Griese, Den	336	216	2688	19
2001	Rich Gannon, Oak	549	361	3828	27
2002	Chad Pennington, NYJ	399	275	3120	22

Receptions
NFL-NFC

Multiple winners: Don Hutson (8); Raymond Berry, Tom Fears, Pete Pihos, Jerry Rice, Sterling Sharpe and Billy Wilson (3); Dwight Clark, Herman Moore, Muhsin Muhammad, Ahmad Rashad and Charley Taylor (2).

Year		No	Yds	Avg	TD	Year		No	Yds	Avg	TD
1932	Ray Flaherty, NY	21	350	16.7	3	1967	Charley Taylor, Wash	70	990	14.1	9
1933	Shipwreck Kelly, Bklyn	22	246	11.2	3	1968	Clifton McNeil, SF	71	994	14.0	7
1934	Joe Carter, Phi	16	238	14.9	4	1969	Dan Abramowicz, NO	73	1015	13.9	7
	& Red Badgro, NY	16	206	12.9	1	1970	Dick Gordon, Chi	71	1026	14.5	13
1935	Tod Goodwin, NY	26	432	16.6	4	1971	Bob Tucker, NY	59	791	13.4	4
1936	Don Hutson, GB	34	536	15.8	8	1972	Harold Jackson, Phi	62	1048	16.9	4
1937	Don Hutson, GB	41	552	13.5	7	1973	Harold Carmichael, Phi	67	1116	16.7	9
1938	Gaynell Tinsley, Chi. Cards	41	516	12.6	1	1974	Charles Young, Phi	63	696	11.0	3
1939	Don Hutson, GB	34	846	24.9	6	1975	Chuck Foreman, Min	73	691	9.5	9
1940	Don Looney, Phi	58	707	12.2	4	1976	Drew Pearson, Dal	58	806	13.9	6
1941	Don Hutson, GB	58	739	12.7	10	1977	Ahmad Rashad, Min	51	681	13.4	2
1942	Don Hutson, GB	74	1211	16.4	17	1978	Rickey Young, Min	88	704	8.0	5
1943	Don Hutson, GB	47	776	16.5	11	1979	Ahmad Rashad, Min	80	1156	14.5	9
1944	Don Hutson, GB	58	866	14.9	9	1980	Earl Cooper, SF	83	567	6.8	4
1945	Don Hutson, GB	47	834	17.7	9	1981	Dwight Clark, SF	85	1105	13.0	4
1946	Jim Benton, LA	63	981	15.6	6	1982	Dwight Clark, SF	60	913	12.2	5
1947	Jim Keane, Chi. Bears	64	910	14.2	10	1983	Roy Green, St. L	78	1227	15.7	14
1948	Tom Fears, LA	51	698	13.7	4		Charlie Brown, Wash	78	1225	15.7	8
1949	Tom Fears, LA	77	1013	13.2	9		& Earnest Gray, NY	78	1139	14.6	5
1950	Tom Fears, LA	84	1116	13.3	7	1984	Art Monk, Wash	106	1372	12.9	7
1951	Elroy Hirsch, LA	66	1495	22.7	17	1985	Roger Craig, SF	92	1016	11.0	6
1952	Mac Speedie, Cle	62	911	14.7	5	1986	Jerry Rice, SF	86	1570	18.3	15
1953	Pete Pihos, Phi	63	1049	16.7	10	1987	J.T. Smith, St. L	91	1117	12.3	8
1954	Pete Pihos, Phi	60	872	14.5	10	1988	Henry Ellard, LA	86	1414	16.4	10
	& Billy Wilson, SF	60	830	13.8	5	1989	Sterling Sharpe, GB	90	1423	15.8	12
1955	Pete Pihos, Phi	62	864	13.9	7	1990	Jerry Rice, SF	100	1502	15.0	13
1956	Billy Wilson, SF	60	889	14.8	5	1991	Michael Irvin, Dal	93	1523	16.4	8
1957	Billy Wilson, SF	52	757	14.6	6	1992	Sterling Sharpe, GB	108	1461	13.5	13
1958	Raymond Berry, Bal	56	794	14.2	9	1993	Sterling Sharpe, GB	112	1274	11.4	11
	& Pete Retzlaff, Phi	56	766	13.7	2	1994	Cris Carter, Min	122	1256	10.3	7
1959	Raymond Berry, Bal	66	959	14.5	14	1995	Herman Moore, Det	123	1686	13.7	14
1960	Raymond Berry, Bal	74	1298	17.5	10	1996	Jerry Rice, SF	108	1254	11.6	8
1961	Red Phillips, LA	78	1092	14.0	5	1997	Herman Moore, Det	104	1293	12.4	8
1962	Bobby Mitchell, Wash	72	1384	19.2	11	1998	Frank Sanders, Ari	89	1145	12.9	3
1963	Bobby Joe Conrad, St. L	73	967	13.2	10	1999	Muhsin Muhammad, Car	96	1253	13.1	8
1964	Johnny Morris, Chi. Bears	93	1200	12.9	10	2000	Muhsin Muhammad, Car	102	1183	11.6	6
1965	Dave Parks, SF	80	1344	16.8	12	2001	Keyshawn Johnson, TB	106	1266	11.9	1
1966	Charley Taylor, Wash	72	1119	15.5	12	2002	Randy Moss, Min	106	1347	12.7	7

AFL-AFC

Multiple winners: Lionel Taylor (5); Lance Alworth, Haywood Jeffires, Lydell Mitchell and Kellen Winslow (3); Fred Biletnikoff, Todd Christensen, Marvin Harrison, Carl Pickens and Al Toon (2).

Year		No	Yds	Avg	TD	Year		No	Yds	Avg	TD
1960	Lionel Taylor, Den	92	1235	13.4	12	1982	Kellen Winslow, SD	54	721	13.4	6
1961	Lionel Taylor, Den	100	1176	11.8	4	1983	Todd Christensen, LA	92	1247	13.6	12
1962	Lionel Taylor, Den	77	908	11.8	4	1984	Ozzie Newsome, Cle	89	1001	11.2	5
1963	Lionel Taylor, Den	78	1101	14.1	10	1985	Lionel James, SD	86	1027	11.9	6
1964	Charley Hennigan, Hou	101	1546	15.3	8	1986	Todd Christensen, LA	95	1153	12.1	8
1965	Lionel Taylor, Den	85	1131	13.3	6	1987	Al Toon, NY	68	976	14.4	5
1966	Lance Alworth, SD	73	1383	18.9	13	1988	Al Toon, NY	93	1067	11.5	5
1967	George Sauer, NY	75	1189	15.9	6	1989	Andre Reed, Buf	88	1312	14.9	9
1968	Lance Alworth, SD	68	1312	19.3	10	1990	Haywood Jeffires, Hou	74	1048	14.2	8
1969	Lance Alworth, SD	64	1003	15.7	4		& Drew Hill, Hou	74	1019	13.8	5
1970	Marlin Briscoe, Buf	57	1036	18.2	8	1991	Haywood Jeffires, Hou	100	1181	11.8	7
1971	Fred Biletnikoff, Oak	61	929	15.2	9	1992	Haywood Jeffires, Hou	90	913	10.1	9
1972	Fred Biletnikoff, Oak	58	802	13.8	7	1993	Reggie Langhorne, Ind	85	1038	12.2	3
1973	Fred Willis, Hou	57	371	6.5	1	1994	Ben Coates, NE	96	1174	12.2	7
1974	Lydell Mitchell, Bal	72	544	7.6	2	1995	Carl Pickens, Cin	99	1234	12.5	17
1975	Reggie Rucker, Cle	60	770	12.8	3	1996	Carl Pickens, Cin	100	1180	11.8	12
	& Lydell Mitchell, Bal	60	544	9.1	4	1997	Tim Brown, Oak	104	1408	13.5	5
1976	MacArthur Lane, KC	66	686	10.4	1	1998	O.J. McDuffie, Mia	90	1050	11.7	7
1977	Lydell Mitchell, Bal	71	620	8.7	4	1999	Jimmy Smith, Jax	116	1636	14.1	6
1978	Steve Largent, Sea	71	1168	16.5	8	2000	Marvin Harrison, Ind	102	1413	13.9	14
1979	Joe Washington, Bal	82	750	9.1	3	2001	Rod Smith, Den	113	1343	11.9	11
1980	Kellen Winslow, SD	89	1290	14.5	9	2002	Marvin Harrison, Ind	143	1722	12.0	11
1981	Kellen Winslow, SD	88	1075	12.2	10						

Annual NFL Leaders (Cont.)
Rushing
NFL-NFC

Multiple winners: Jim Brown (8); Walter Payton and Barry Sanders (5); Emmitt Smith and Steve Van Buren (4); Eric Dickerson (3); Cliff Battles, John Brockington, Larry Brown, Bill Dudley, Leroy Kelly, Bill Paschal, Joe Perry, Gale Sayers, Stephen Davis and Whizzer White (2).

Year		Car	Yds	Avg	TD	Year		Car	Yds	Avg	TD
1932	Cliff Battles, Bos	148	576	3.9	3	1968	Leroy Kelly, Cle	248	1239	5.0	16
1933	Jim Musick, Bos	173	809	4.7	5	1969	Gale Sayers, Chi	236	1032	4.4	8
1934	Beattie Feathers, Chi. Bears	119	1004	8.4	8	1970	Larry Brown, Wash	237	1125	4.7	5
1935	Doug Russell, Chi. Cards	140	499	3.6	0	1971	John Brockington, GB	216	1105	5.1	4
1936	Tuffy Leemans, NY	206	830	4.0	2	1972	Larry Brown, Wash	285	1216	4.3	8
1937	Cliff Battles, Wash	216	874	4.0	5	1973	John Brockington, GB	265	1144	4.3	3
1938	Whizzer White, Pit	152	567	3.7	4	1974	Lawrence McCutcheon, LA	236	1109	4.7	3
1939	Bill Osmanski, Chi. Bears	121	699	5.8	7	1975	Jim Otis, St.L	269	1076	4.0	5
1940	Whizzer White, Det	146	514	3.5	5	1976	Walter Payton, Chi	311	1390	4.5	13
1941	Pug Manders, Bklyn	111	486	4.4	5	1977	Walter Payton, Chi	339	1852	5.5	14
1942	Bill Dudley, Pit	162	696	4.3	5	1978	Walter Payton, Chi	333	1395	4.2	11
1943	Bill Paschal, NY	147	572	3.9	10	1979	Walter Payton, Chi	369	1610	4.4	14
1944	Bill Paschal, NY	196	737	3.8	9	1980	Walter Payton, Chi	317	1460	4.6	6
1945	Steve Van Buren, Phi	143	832	5.8	15	1981	George Rogers, NO	378	1674	4.4	13
1946	Bill Dudley, Pit	146	604	4.1	3	1982	Tony Dorsett, Dal	177	745	4.2	5
1947	Steve Van Buren, Phi	217	1008	4.6	13	1983	Eric Dickerson, LA	390	1808	4.6	18
1948	Steve Van Buren, Phi	201	945	4.7	10	1984	Eric Dickerson, LA	379	2105	5.6	14
1949	Steve Van Buren, Phi	263	1146	4.4	11	1985	Gerald Riggs, Atl	397	1719	4.3	10
1950	Marion Motley, Cle	140	810	5.8	3	1986	Eric Dickerson, LA	404	1821	4.5	11
1951	Eddie Price, NY Giants	271	971	3.6	7	1987	Charles White, LA	324	1374	4.2	11
1952	Dan Towler, LA	156	894	5.7	10	1988	Herschel Walker, Dal	361	1514	4.2	5
1953	Joe Perry, SF	192	1018	5.3	10	1989	Barry Sanders, Det	280	1470	5.3	14
1954	Joe Perry, SF	173	1049	6.1	8	1990	Barry Sanders, Det	255	1304	5.1	13
1955	Alan Ameche, Bal	213	961	4.5	9	1991	Emmitt Smith, Dal	365	1563	4.3	12
1956	Rick Casares, Chi. Bears	234	1126	4.8	12	1992	Emmitt Smith, Dal	373	1713	4.6	18
1957	Jim Brown, Cle	202	942	4.7	9	1993	Emmitt Smith, Dal	283	1486	5.3	9
1958	Jim Brown, Cle	257	1527	5.9	17	1994	Barry Sanders, Det	331	1883	5.7	7
1959	Jim Brown, Cle	290	1329	4.6	14	1995	Emmitt Smith, Dal	377	1773	4.7	25
1960	Jim Brown, Cle	215	1257	5.8	9	1996	Barry Sanders, Det	307	1553	5.1	11
1961	Jim Brown, Cle	305	1408	4.6	8	1997	Barry Sanders, Det	335	2053	6.1	11
1962	Jim Taylor, GB	272	1474	5.4	19	1998	Jamal Anderson, Atl	410	1846	4.5	14
1963	Jim Brown, Cle	291	1863	6.4	12	1999	Stephen Davis, Wash	290	1405	4.8	17
1964	Jim Brown, Cle	280	1446	5.2	7	2000	Robert Smith, Min	295	1521	5.2	7
1965	Jim Brown, Cle	289	1544	5.3	17	2001	Stephen Davis, Wash	356	1432	4.0	5
1966	Gale Sayers, Chi	229	1231	5.4	8	2002	Deuce McAllister, NO	325	1388	4.3	13
1967	Leroy Kelly, Cle	235	1205	5.1	11						

Note: Jim Brown led the NFL in rushing eight of his nine years in the league. The one season he didn't win (1962) he finished fourth (996 yds) behind Jim Taylor, John Henry Johnson of Pittsburgh (1,141 yds) and Dick Bass of the LA Rams (1,033 yds).

AFL-AFC

Multiple winners: Earl Campbell and O.J. Simpson (4); Terrell Davis and Thurman Thomas (3); Eric Dickerson, Cookie Gilchrist, Edgerrin James, Floyd Little, Jim Nance and Curt Warner (2).

Year		Car	Yds	Avg	TD	Year		Car	Yds	Avg	TD
1960	Abner Haynes, Dal	157	875	5.6	9	1982	Freeman McNeil, NY	151	786	5.2	6
1961	Billy Cannon, Hou	200	948	4.7	6	1983	Curt Warner, Sea	335	1449	4.3	13
1962	Cookie Gilchrist, Buf	214	1096	5.1	13	1984	Earnest Jackson, SD	296	1179	4.0	8
1963	Clem Daniels, Oak	215	1099	5.1	3	1985	Marcus Allen, LA	380	1759	4.6	11
1964	Cookie Gilchrist, Buf	230	981	4.3	6	1986	Curt Warner, Sea	319	1481	4.6	13
1965	Paul Lowe, SD	222	1121	5.0	7	1987	Eric Dickerson, Ind	223	1011	4.5	5
1966	Jim Nance, Bos	299	1458	4.9	11	1988	Eric Dickerson, Ind	388	1659	4.3	14
1967	Jim Nance, Bos	269	1216	4.5	7	1989	Christian Okoye, KC	370	1480	4.0	12
1968	Paul Robinson, Cin	238	1023	4.3	8	1990	Thurman Thomas, Buf	271	1297	4.8	11
1969	Dickie Post, SD	182	873	4.8	6	1991	Thurman Thomas, Buf	288	1407	4.9	7
1970	Floyd Little, Den	209	901	4.3	3	1992	Barry Foster, Pit	390	1690	4.3	11
1971	Floyd Little, Den	284	1133	4.0	6	1993	Thurman Thomas, Buf	355	1315	3.7	6
1972	O.J. Simpson, Buf	292	1251	4.3	6	1994	Chris Warren, Sea	333	1545	4.6	9
1973	O.J. Simpson, Buf	332	2003	6.0	12	1995	Curtis Martin, NE	368	1487	4.0	14
1974	Otis Armstrong, Den	263	1407	5.3	9	1996	Terrell Davis, Den	345	1538	4.5	13
1975	O.J. Simpson, Buf	329	1817	5.5	16	1997	Terrell Davis, Den	369	1750	4.7	15
1976	O.J. Simpson, Buf	290	1503	5.2	8	1998	Terrell Davis, Den	392	2008	5.1	21
1977	Mark van Eeghen, Oak	324	1273	3.9	7	1999	Edgerrin James, Ind	369	1553	4.2	13
1978	Earl Campbell, Hou	302	1450	4.8	13	2000	Edgerrin James, Ind	387	1709	4.4	13
1979	Earl Campbell, Hou	368	1697	4.6	19	2001	Priest Holmes, KC	327	1555	4.8	8
1980	Earl Campbell, Hou	373	1934	5.2	13	2002	Ricky Williams, Mia	383	1853	4.8	16
1981	Earl Campbell, Hou	361	1376	3.8	10						

Note: Eric Dickerson was traded to Indianapolis from the NFC's LA Rams during the 1987 season. In three games with the Rams, he carried the ball 60 times for 277 yds, a 4.6 avg and 1 TD. His official AFC statistics above came in nine games with the Colts.

Scoring

NFL-NFC

Multiple winners: Don Hutson (5); Dutch Clark, Pat Harder, Paul Hornung, Chip Lohmiller and Mark Moseley (3); Kevin Butler, Mike Cofer, Fred Cox, Marshall Faulk, Jack Manders, Chester Marcol, Eddie Murray, Emmitt Smith, Gordy Soltau and Doak Walker (2).

Year		TD	FG	PAT	Pts
1932	Dutch Clark, Portsmouth	6	3	10	55
1933	Glenn Presnell, Portsmouth	6	6	10	64
	& Ken Strong, NY	6	5	13	64
1934	Jack Manders, Chi. Bears	3	10	31	79
1935	Dutch Clark, Det	6	1	16	55
1936	Dutch Clark, Det	7	4	19	73
1937	Jack Manders, Chi. Bears	5	8	15	69
1938	Clarke Hinkle, GB	7	3	7	58
1939	Andy Farkas, Wash	11	0	2	68
1940	Don Hutson, GB	7	0	15	57
1941	Don Hutson, GB	12	1	20	95
1942	Don Hutson, GB	17	1	33	138
1943	Don Hutson, GB	12	3	26	117
1944	Don Hutson, GB	9	0	31	85
1945	Steve Van Buren, Phi	18	0	2	110
1946	Ted Fritsch, GB	10	9	13	100
1947	Pat Harder, Chi. Cards	7	7	39	102
1948	Pat Harder, Chi. Cards	6	7	53	110
1949	Gene Roberts, NY Giants	17	0	0	102
	& Pat Harder, Chi. Cards	8	3	45	102
1950	Doak Walker, Det	11	8	38	128
1951	Elroy Hirsch, LA	17	0	0	102
1952	Gordy Soltau, SF	7	6	34	94
1953	Gordy Soltau, SF	6	10	48	114
1954	Bobby Walston, Phi	11	4	36	114
1955	Doak Walker, Det	7	9	27	96
1956	Bobby Layne, Det	5	12	33	99
1957	Sam Baker, Wash	1	14	29	77
	& Lou Groza, Cle	0	15	32	77
1958	Jim Brown, Cle	18	0	0	108
1959	Paul Hornung, GB	7	7	31	94
1960	Paul Hornung, GB	15	15	41	176
1961	Paul Hornung, GB	10	15	41	146
1962	Jim Taylor, GB	19	0	0	114
1963	Don Chandler, NY	0	18	52	106
1964	Lenny Moore, Bal	20	0	0	120
1965	Gale Sayers, Chi	22	0	0	132
1966	Bruce Gossett, LA	0	28	29	113
1967	Jim Bakken, St.L	0	27	36	117
1968	Leroy Kelly, Cle	20	0	0	120
1969	Fred Cox, Min	0	26	43	121
1970	Fred Cox, Min	0	30	35	125
1971	Curt Knight, Wash	0	29	27	114
1972	Chester Marcol, GB	0	33	29	128
1973	David Ray, LA	0	30	40	130
1974	Chester Marcol, GB	0	25	19	94
1975	Chuck Foreman, Min	22	0	0	132
1976	Mark Moseley, Wash	0	22	31	97
1977	Walter Payton, Chi	16	0	0	96
1978	Frank Corral, LA	0	29	31	118
1979	Mark Moseley, Wash	0	25	39	114
1980	Eddie Murray, Det	0	27	35	116
1981	Rafael Septien, Dal	0	27	40	121
	& Eddie Murray, Det	0	25	46	121
1982	Wendell Tyler, LA	13	0	0	78
1983	Mark Moseley, Wash	0	33	62	161
1984	Ray Wersching, SF	0	25	56	131
1985	Kevin Butler, Chi	0	31	51	144
1986	Kevin Butler, Chi	0	28	36	120
1987	Jerry Rice, SF	23	0	0	138
1988	Mike Cofer, SF	0	27	40	121
1989	Mike Cofer, SF	0	29	49	136
1990	Chip Lohmiller, Wash	0	30	41	131
1991	Chip Lohmiller, Wash	0	31	56	149
1992	Chip Lohmiller, Wash	0	30	30	120
	& Morten Andersen, NO	0	29	33	120
1993	Jason Hanson, Det	0	34	28	130
1994	Emmitt Smith, Dal	22	0	0	132
	& Fuad Reveiz, Min	0	34	30	132
1995	Emmitt Smith, Dal	25	0	0	150
1996	John Kasay, Car.	0	37	34	145
1997	Richie Cunningham, Dal	0	34	24	126
1998	Gary Anderson, Min	0	35	59	164
1999	Jeff Wilkins, St.L	0	20	64	124
2000	Marshall Faulk, St.L	26	0	4	160
2001	Marshall Faulk, St.L	21	0	2	128
2002	Jay Feely, Atl	0	32	42	138

AFL-AFC

Multiple winners: Gino Cappelletti (5); Gary Anderson (3); Jim Breech, Roy Gerela, Gene Mingo, Nick Lowery, John Smith, Pete Stoyanovich, Jim Turner and Mike Vanderjagt (2).

Year		TD	FG	PAT	Pts
1960	Gene Mingo, Den	6	18	33	123
1961	Gino Cappelletti, Bos	8	17	48	147
1962	Gene Mingo, Den	4	27	32	137
1963	Gino Cappelletti, Bos	2	22	35	113
1964	Gino Cappelletti, Bos	7	25	36	155
1965	Gino Cappelletti, Bos	9	17	27	132
1966	Gino Cappelletti, Bos	6	16	35	119
1967	George Blanda, Oak	0	20	56	116
1968	Jim Turner, NY	0	34	43	145
1969	Jim Turner, NY	0	32	33	129
1970	Jan Stenerud, KC	0	30	26	116
1971	Garo Yepremian, Mia	0	28	33	117
1972	Bobby Howfield, NY	0	27	40	121
1973	Roy Gerela, Pit	0	29	36	123
1974	Roy Gerela, Pit	0	20	33	93
1975	O.J. Simpson, Buf	23	0	0	138
1976	Toni Linhart, Bal	0	20	49	109
1977	Errol Mann, Oak	0	20	39	99
1978	Pat Leahy, NY	0	22	41	107
1979	John Smith, NE	0	23	46	115
1980	John Smith, NE	0	26	51	129
1981	Nick Lowery, KC	0	26	37	115
	& Jim Breech, Cin	0	22	49	115
1982	Marcus Allen, LA	14	0	0	84
1983	Gary Anderson, Pit	0	27	38	119
1984	Gary Anderson, Pit	0	24	45	117
1985	Gary Anderson, Pit	0	33	40	139
1986	Tony Franklin, NE	0	32	44	140
1987	Jim Breech Cin	0	24	25	97
1988	Scott Norwood, Buf	0	32	33	129
1989	David Treadwell, Den	0	27	39	120
1990	Nick Lowery, KC	0	34	37	139
1991	Pete Stoyanovich, Mia	0	31	28	121
1992	Pete Stoyanovich, Mia	0	30	34	124
1993	Jeff Jaeger, LA	0	35	27	132
1994	John Carney, SD	0	34	33	135
1995	Norm Johnson, Pit	0	34	39	141
1996	Cary Blanchard, Ind	0	36	27	135
1997	Mike Hollis, Jax	0	31	41	134
1998	Steve Christie, Buf	0	33	41	140
1999	Mike Vanderjagt, Ind	0	34	43	145
2000	Matt Stover, Bal	0	35	30	135
2001	Mike Vanderjagt, Ind	0	28	41	125
2002	Priest Holmes, KC	24	0	0	144

All-Time NFL Leaders
Through 2002 regular season.

CAREER
Players active in 2002 in **bold** type.

Passing Efficiency

Ratings based on performance standards established for completion percentage, average gain, touchdown percentage and interception percentage. Quarterbacks are allocated points according to how their statistics measure up to those standards. Minimum 1500 passing attempts.

		Yrs	Att	Cmp	Cmp%	Yards	Avg Gain	TD	TD%	Int	Int%	Rating
1	**Kurt Warner**	5	1623	1083	66.7	14,082	8.68	101	6.2	64	3.9	98.2
2	Steve Young	15	4149	2667	64.3	33,124	7.98	232	5.6	107	2.6	96.8
3	Joe Montana	15	5391	3409	63.2	40,551	7.52	273	5.1	139	2.6	92.3
4	**Jeff Garcia**	4	1968	1224	62.2	13,704	6.96	95	4.8	43	2.2	89.9
5	**Brett Favre**	12	5993	3652	60.9	42,285	7.06	314	5.2	188	3.1	86.7
6	Dan Marino	17	8358	4967	59.4	61,361	7.34	420	5.0	252	3.0	86.4
7	**Peyton Manning**	5	2817	1749	62.1	20,618	7.32	138	4.9	100	3.5	85.9
8	**Rich Gannon**	14	3913	2367	60.5	26,945	6.89	171	4.4	98	2.5	85.3
9	**Mark Brunell**	9	3561	2142	60.2	25,309	7.11	142	4.0	86	2.4	85.1
10	**Brad Johnson**	11	2831	1747	61.7	19,428	6.86	114	4.0	74	2.6	84.6
11	Jim Kelly	11	4779	2874	60.1	35,467	7.42	237	5.0	175	3.7	84.4
12	**Trent Green**	5	1743	1006	57.7	12,977	7.45	82	4.7	53	3.0	84.2
13	**Brian Griese**	5	1678	1044	62.2	11,763	7.01	71	4.2	53	3.2	84.1
14	Roger Staubach	11	2958	1685	57.0	22,700	7.67	153	5.2	109	3.7	83.4
15	Neil Lomax	8	3153	1817	57.6	22,771	7.22	136	4.3	90	2.9	82.7
16	Sonny Jurgensen	18	4262	2433	57.1	32,224	7.56	255	6.0	189	4.4	82.625
17	Len Dawson	19	3741	2136	57.1	28,711	7.67	239	6.4	183	4.9	82.555
18	Ken Anderson	16	4475	2654	59.3	32,838	7.34	197	4.4	160	3.6	81.9
19	Bernie Kosar	12	3365	1994	59.3	23,301	6.92	124	3.7	87	2.6	81.8
20	**Steve McNair**	8	2780	1634	58.8	19,422	6.99	108	3.9	76	2.7	81.733
21	Danny White	13	2950	1761	59.7	21,959	7.44	155	5.3	132	4.5	81.715
22	**Neil O'Donnell**	13	3202	1847	57.7	21,458	6.70	118	3.7	67	2.1	81.640
23	Troy Aikman	12	4715	2898	61.5	32,942	6.99	165	3.5	141	3.0	81.619
24	Dave Krieg	19	5311	3105	58.5	38,147	7.18	261	4.9	199	3.7	81.499
25	Randall Cunningham	17	4289	2429	56.6	29,979	6.99	207	4.8	134	3.1	81.471

Note: The NFL does not recognize records from the All-American Football Conference (1946-49). If it did, **Otto Graham** would rank 6th (after Favre) with the following stats: 10 Yrs; 2,626 Att; 1,464 Comp; 55.8 Comp Pct; 23,584 Yards; 8.98 Avg Gain; 174 TD; 6.6 TD Pct; 135 Int; 5.1 Int Pct; and 86.6 Rating Pts.

Touchdown Passes

		No			No			No
1	Dan Marino	420	16	George Blanda	236	31	Ken Stabler	194
2	Fran Tarkenton	342	17	Steve Young	232	32	Bob Griese	192
3	**Brett Favre**	314	18	John Brodie	214	33	**Drew Bledsoe**	190
4	John Elway	300	19	Terry Bradshaw	212	34	Sammy Baugh	187
5	Warren Moon	291		Y.A. Tittle	212	35	Craig Morton	183
6	Johnny Unitas	290	21	Jim Hart	209	36	Steve Grogan	182
7	Joe Montana	273	22	Randall Cunningham	207	37	Ron Jaworski	179
8	Dave Krieg	261	23	Jim Everett	203	38	Babe Parilli	178
9	Sonny Jurgensen	255	24	Roman Gabriel	201	39	Charlie Conerly	173
10	Dan Fouts	254	25	Phil Simms	199		Joe Namath	173
11	Boomer Esiason	247	26	Ken Anderson	197		Norm Van Brocklin	173
12	John Hadl	244	27	Joe Ferguson	196	42	**Rich Gannon**	171
	Vinny Testaverde	244		Bobby Layne	196	43	Charley Johnson	170
14	Len Dawson	239		Steve DeBerg	196	44	Troy Aikman	165
15	Jim Kelly	237		Norm Snead	196		**Chris Chandler**	165

Note: The NFL does not recognize records from the All-American Football Conference (1946-49). If it did, **Y.A. Tittle** would move up from 19th to 14th (after Hadl and Testaverde) with 242 TDs and **Otto Graham** would rank 39th (after Parilli) with 174 TDs.

Passes Intercepted

		No			No			No
1	George Blanda	277	10	Warren Moon	233	19	Joe Ferguson	209
2	John Hadl	268		**Vinny Testaverde**	233	20	Steve Grogan	208
3	Fran Tarkenton	266	12	John Elway	226	21	Steve DeBerg	204
4	Norm Snead	257	13	John Brodie	224	22	Sammy Baugh	203
5	Johnny Unitas	253	14	Ken Stabler	222	23	Dave Krieg	199
6	Dan Marino	252	15	Y.A. Tittle	221	24	Jim Plunkett	198
7	Jim Hart	247	16	Joe Namath	220	25	Tobin Rote	191
8	Bobby Layne	245		Babe Parilli	220			
9	Dan Fouts	242	18	Terry Bradshaw	210			

Passing Yards

		Yrs	Att	Comp	Pct	Yards
1	Dan Marino	17	8358	4967	59.4	61,361
2	John Elway	16	7250	4123	56.9	51,475
3	Warren Moon	17	6823	3988	58.5	49,325
4	Fran Tarkenton	18	6467	3686	57.0	47,003
5	Dan Fouts	15	5604	3297	58.8	43,040
6	**Brett Favre**	12	5993	3652	60.9	42,285
7	Joe Montana	15	5391	3409	63.2	40,551
8	Johnny Unitas	18	5186	2830	54.6	40,239
9	**Vinny Testaverde**	16	5727	3211	56.1	39,558
10	Dave Krieg	19	5311	3105	58.5	38,147
11	Boomer Esiason	14	5205	2969	57.0	37,920
12	Jim Kelly	11	4779	2874	60.1	35,467
13	Jim Everett	12	4923	2841	57.7	34,837
14	Jim Hart	19	5076	2593	51.1	34,665
15	Steve DeBerg	17	5024	2874	57.2	34,241
16	**Drew Bledsoe**	10	5128	2919	56.9	34,016
17	John Hadl	16	4687	2363	50.4	33,503
18	Phil Simms	14	4647	2576	55.4	33,462
19	Steve Young	15	4149	2667	64.3	33,124
20	Troy Aikman	12	4715	2898	61.5	32,942
21	Ken Anderson	16	4475	2654	59.3	32,838
22	Sonny Jurgensen	18	4262	2433	57.1	32,224
23	John Brodie	17	4491	2469	55.0	31,548
24	Norm Snead	15	4353	2276	52.3	30,797
25	Randall Cunningham	17	4289	2429	56.6	29,979

Note: The NFL does not recognize records from the All-American Football Conference (1946-49). If it did, **Y.A. Tittle** would rank 20th (after Young) with the following stats: 17 Yrs; 4,395 Att; 2,427 Comp; 55.2 Pct; and 33,070 Yards.

Receptions

		Yrs	No	Yards	Avg	TD
1	**Jerry Rice**	18	1456	21,597	14.8	192
2	**Cris Carter**	16	1101	13,899	12.6	130
3	**Tim Brown**	15	1018	14,167	13.9	97
4	Andre Reed	16	951	13,198	13.9	87
5	Art Monk	16	940	12,721	13.5	68
6	Irving Fryar	17	851	12,785	15.0	84
7	Steve Largent	14	819	13,089	16.0	100
8	Henry Ellard	16	814	13,777	16.9	65
9	**Larry Centers**	13	808	6,691	8.3	27
10	James Lofton	16	764	14,004	18.3	75
11	**Shannon Sharpe**	13	753	9,290	12.3	54
12	Charlie Joiner	18	750	12,146	16.2	65
	Michael Irvin	12	750	11,904	15.9	65
14	Andre Rison	12	743	10,205	13.7	84
15	Gary Clark	11	699	10,856	15.5	65
16	**Terance Mathis**	13	689	8,809	12.8	63
17	**Herman Moore**	12	670	9,174	13.7	62
18	**Marvin Harrison**	7	665	8,800	13.2	73
19	**Jimmy Smith**	9	664	9,287	14.0	51
20	Ozzie Newsome	13	662	7,980	12.1	47
21	Charley Taylor	13	649	9,110	14.0	79
22	**Keenan McCardell**	11	640	8,196	12.8	44
23	Drew Hill	15	634	9,831	15.5	60
24	Don Maynard	15	633	11,834	18.7	88
25	Raymond Berry	13	631	9,275	14.7	68

Rushing

		Yrs	Car	Yards	Avg	TD
1	**Emmitt Smith**	13	4052	17,162	4.2	153
2	Walter Payton	13	3838	16,726	4.4	110
3	Barry Sanders	10	3062	15,269	5.0	99
4	Eric Dickerson	11	2996	13,259	4.4	90
5	Tony Dorsett	12	2936	12,739	4.3	77
6	Jim Brown	9	2359	12,312	5.2	106
7	Marcus Allen	16	3022	12,243	4.1	123
8	Franco Harris	13	2949	12,120	4.1	91
9	Thurman Thomas	13	2877	12,074	4.2	65
10	**Jerome Bettis**	10	2873	11,542	4.0	62
11	John Riggins	14	2916	11,352	3.9	104
12	O.J. Simpson	11	2404	11,236	4.7	61
13	Ricky Watters	10	2622	10,643	4.1	78
14	**Marshall Faulk**	9	2367	10,395	4.4	87
15	**Curtis Martin**	8	2604	10,361	4.0	71
16	Ottis Anderson	14	2562	10,273	4.0	81
17	Earl Campbell	8	2187	9,407	4.3	74
18	**Eddie George**	7	2421	8,978	3.7	59
19	Terry Allen	10	2152	8,614	4.0	73
20	Jim Taylor	10	1941	8,597	4.4	83
21	Joe Perry	14	1737	8,378	4.8	53
22	Ernest Byner	14	2095	8,261	3.9	56
23	Herschel Walker	12	1954	8,225	4.2	61
24	Roger Craig	11	1991	8,189	4.1	56
25	Gerald Riggs	10	1989	8,188	4.1	69

Note: The NFL does not recognize records from the All-American Football Conference (1946-49). If it did, **Joe Perry** would move up from 21st to 17th (after Anderson) with the following stats: 16 Yrs; 1,929 Att; 9,723 Yards; 5.0 Avg; and 71 TD.

All-Purpose Yards

		Rush	Rec	Ret	Total
1	**Jerry Rice**	645	21,597	6	22,248
2	**Brian Mitchell**	1,947	2,298	17,756	22,001
3	Walter Payton	16,726	4,538	539	21,803
4	**Emmitt Smith**	17,162	3,012	0	20,174
5	**Tim Brown**	190	14,167	4,510	18,867
6	Barry Sanders	15,269	2,921	118	18,308
7	Herschel Walker	8,225	4,859	5,084	18,168
8	Marcus Allen	12,243	5,411	-6	17,648
9	**Eric Metcalf**	2,392	5,572	9,266	17,230
10	Thurman Thomas	12,074	4,458	0	16,532
11	**Marshall Faulk**	10,395	5,984	36	16,415
12	Tony Dorsett	12,739	3,554	33	16,326
13	Henry Ellard	50	13,777	1,891	15,718
14	Irving Fryar	242	12,785	2,567	15,594
15	Jim Brown	12,312	2,499	648	15,459
16	Eric Dickerson	13,259	2,137	15	15,411
17	Glyn Milburn	817	1,322	12,772	14,911
18	James Brooks	7,962	3,621	3,327	14,910
19	Ricky Watters	10,643	4,248	0	14,891
20	Franco Harris	12,120	2,287	215	14,622
21	O.J. Simpson	11,236	2,142	990	14,368
22	James Lofton	246	14,004	27	14,277
23	**Cris Carter**	41	13,899	244	14,184
24	Bobby Mitchell	2,735	7,954	3,389	14,078
25	Dave Meggett	1,684	3,038	9,274	13,996

Years played: Allen (16), Brooks (12), J. Brown (9), T. Brown (15), Carter (16), Dickerson (11), Dorsett (12), Ellard (16), Faulk (9), Fryar (17), Harris (13), Lofton (16), Meggett (10), Metcalf (13), Milburn (9), Bri. Mitchell (13), Bo. Mitchell (11), Payton (13), Rice (18), Sanders (10), Simpson (11), Smith (13), Thomas (13), Walker (12) and Watters (10).

All-Time NFL Leaders (Cont.)
Scoring

Points

		Yrs	TD	FG	PAT	Total
1	**Gary Anderson**	.21	0	494	741	2223
2	**Morten Andersen**	21	0	486	695	2153
3	George Blanda	26	9	335	943	2002
4	Norm Johnson	.18	0	366	638	1736
5	Nick Lowery	18	0	383	562	1711
6	Jan Stenerud	19	0	373	580	1699
7	Eddie Murray	19	0	352	538	1594
8	Al Del Greco	.17	0	347	543	1584
9	Pat Leahy	.18	0	304	558	1470
10	Jim Turner	16	1	304	521	1439
11	Matt Bahr	.17	0	300	522	1422
12	Mark Moseley	.'....16	0	300	482	1382
13	Jim Bakken	17	0	282	534	1380
14	Fred Cox	15	0	282	519	1365
15	Lou Groza	.17	1	234	641	1349
16	**John Carney**	15	.0	321	368	1331
17	**Steve Christie**	.13	0	299	399	1296
18	Jim Breech	.14	0	243	517	1246
19	Pete Stoyanovich	12	0	272	420	1236
20	**Matt Stover**	12	0	288	366	1230
21	**Jerry Rice**	18	203	0	0	1226†
22	Chris Bahr	.14	0	241	490	1213
23	Kevin Butler	13	0	265	413	1208
24	**Jason Elam**	10	0	261	410	1193
25	Jason Hanson	11	.0	262	358	1144

†Rice's total includes four 2-point conversions.
Note: The NFL does not recognize records from the All-American Football Conference (1946-49). If it did, **Lou Groza** would move up from 15th to 7th (after Stenerud) with the following stats: 21 Yrs; 264 FG, 810 PAT; 1,608 Pts.

Interceptions

		Yrs	No	Yards	TD
1	Paul Krause	16	81	1185	3
2	Emlen Tunnell	14	79	1282	4
3	**Rod Woodson**	16	69	1465	12
4	Dick (Night Train) Lane	14	68	1207	5
5	Ken Riley	15	65	596	5

Sacks

		Yrs	No
1	Reggie White	15	198
2	**Bruce Smith**	18	195
3	Kevin Greene	15	160
4	Chris Doleman	15	150.5
5	Richard Dent	15	137.5

Note: The NFL did not begin officially compiling sacks until 1982. Deacon Jones, who played with the Rams, Chargers and Redskins from 1961-74, is often credited with 173½ sacks. Jack Youngblood and Alan Page are unofficially credited with 150½ and 148, respectively. Also, Lawrence Taylor has 142 career sacks if you count his rookie year of 1981, the year before sacks became an official stat.

Safeties

		Yrs	No
1	Ted Hendricks	15	4
	Doug English	10	4
3	Seventeen players tied with 3 each.		

Touchdowns

		Yrs	Rush	Rec	Ret	Total
1	**Jerry Rice**	18	10	192	1	203
2	**Emmitt Smith**	13	153	11	0	164
3	Marcus Allen	16	123	21	1	145
4	**Cris Carter**	16	0	130	1	131
5	Jim Brown	9	106	20	0	126
6	Walter Payton	13	110	15	0	125
7	**Marshall Faulk**	9	87	33	0	120
8	John Riggins	14	104	12	0	116
9	Lenny Moore	12	63	48	2	113
10	Barry Sanders	10	99	10	0	109
11	Don Hutson	11	3	99	3	105
12	**Tim Brown**	15	1	97	4	102
13	Steve Largent	14	1	100	0	101
14	Franco Harris	13	91	9	0	100
15	Eric Dickerson	11	90	6	0	96
16	Jim Taylor	10	83	10	0	93
17	Tony Dorsett	12	77	13	1	91
	Bobby Mitchell	11	18	65	8	91
	Ricky Watters	10	78	13	0	91
20	Leroy Kelly	10	74	13	3	90
	Charley Taylor	13	11	79	0	90
22	Irving Fryar	17	1	84	3	88
	Don Maynard	15	0	88	0	88
	Andre Reed	16	1	87	0	88
	Thurman Thomas	13	65	23	0	88

Kickoff Returns
Minimum 75 returns.

		Yrs	No	Yards	Avg	TD
1	Gale Sayers	7	91	2781	30.6	6
2	Lynn Chandnois	7	92	2720	29.6	3
3	Abe Woodson	9	193	5538	28.7	5
4	Buddy Young	6	90	2514	27.9	2
5	Travis Williams	5	102	2801	27.5	6

Punting
Minimum 300 punts.

		Yrs	No	Yards	Avg
1	Sammy Baugh	16	338	15,245	45.1
2	Tommy Davis	11	511	22,833	44.7
3	Yale Lary	11	503	22,279	44.3
4	**Darren Bennett**	8	689	30,340	44.0
5	**Todd Sauerbrun**	8	607	26,659	43.9

Punt Returns
Minimum 75 returns.

		Yrs	No	Yards	Avg	TD
1	George McAfee	8	112	1431	12.8	2
2	Jack Christiansen	.8	85	1084	12.8	8
3	Claude Gibson	5	110	1381	12.6	3
4	Bill Dudley	9	124	1515	12.2	3
5	Rick Upchurch	9	248	3008	12.1	8

Long-Playing Records

	Seasons			Games			Consecutive Games	
		No			No			No
1	George Blanda, QB-K	.26	1	George Blanda, QB-K	...340	1	Jim Marshall, DE	282
2	Earl Morrall, QB	21	2	**Gary Anderson**, K	323	2	**Morten Andersen**, K	248
	Gary Anderson, K	21	3	**Morten Andersen**, K	322	3	Mick Tingelhoff, C	240
	Morten Andersen, K	21	4	Bruce Matthews, OL	...296	4	Jim Bakken, K	234
5	Four tied with 20 each.		5	**Darrell Green**, DB	295		**Gary Anderson**, K	234

SINGLE SEASON
Passing

Yards Gained	Year	Att	Cmp	Pct	Yds
Dan Marino, Mia	1984	564	362	64.2	5084
Kurt Warner, St.L	2001	546	375	68.7	4830
Dan Fouts, SD	1981	609	360	59.1	4802
Dan Marino, Mia	1986	623	378	60.7	4746
Dan Fouts, SD	1980	589	348	59.1	4715
Warren Moon, Hou	1991	655	404	61.7	4690
Rich Gannon, Oak	2002	618	418	67.6	4689
Warren Moon, Hou	1990	584	362	62.0	4689
Neil Lomax, St.L	1984	560	345	61.6	4614
Drew Bledsoe, NE	1994	691	400	57.9	4555

Efficiency	Year	Att/Cmp	TD	Rtg
Steve Young, SF	1994	461/324	35	112.8
Joe Montana, SF	1989	386/271	26	112.4
Milt Plum, Cle	1960	250/151	21	110.4
Sammy Baugh, Wash	1945	182/128	11	109.9
Kurt Warner, St.L	1999	499/325	41	109.2
Dan Marino, Mia	1984	564/362	48	108.9
Sid Luckman, Bears	1943	202/110	28	107.5
Steve Young, SF	1992	402/268	25	107.0
Randall Cunningham, Min	1998	425/259	34	106.0
Bart Starr, GB	1966	251/156	14	105.0

Receptions

Catches	Year	No	Yds
Marvin Harrison, Ind	2002	143	1722
Herman Moore, Det	1995	123	1686
Jerry Rice, SF	1995	122	1848
Cris Carter, Min	1995	122	1371
Cris Carter, Min	1994	122	1256
Isaac Bruce, St.L	1995	119	1781
Jimmy Smith, Jax	1999	116	1636
Marvin Harrison, Ind	1999	115	1663
Rod Smith, Den	2001	113	1343
Hines Ward, Pit	2002	112	1329
Jimmy Smith, Jax	2001	112	1373
Jerry Rice, SF	1994	112	1499
Sterling Sharpe, GB	1993	112	1274

Rushing

Yards Gained	Year	Car	Yds	Avg
Eric Dickerson, LA Rams	1984	379	2105	5.6
Barry Sanders, Det	1997	335	2053	6.1
Terrell Davis, Den	1998	392	2008	5.1
O.J. Simpson, Buf	1973	332	2003	6.0
Earl Campbell, Hou	1980	373	1934	5.2
Barry Sanders, Det	1994	331	1883	5.7
Jim Brown, Cle	1963	291	1863	6.4
Ricky Williams, Mia	2002	383	1853	4.8
Walter Payton, Chi	1977	339	1852	5.5
Jamal Anderson, Atl	1998	410	1846	4.5
Eric Dickerson, LA Rams	1986	404	1821	4.5
O.J. Simpson, Buf	1975	329	1817	5.5
Eric Dickerson, LA Rams	1983	390	1808	4.6

Scoring
Points

	Year	TD	PAT	FG	Pts
Paul Hornung, GB	1960	15	41	15	176
Gary Anderson, Min	1998	0	59	35	164
Mark Moseley, Wash	1983	0	62	33	161
Marshall Faulk, St.L	2000	26	4	0	160
Gino Cappelletti, Bos	1964	7	38	25	155
Emmitt Smith, Dal	1995	25	0	0	150
Chip Lohmiller, Wash	1991	0	56	31	149
Gino Cappelletti, Bos	1961	8	48	17	147
Paul Hornung, GB	1961	10	41	15	146
Jim Turner, Jets	1968	0	43	34	145
John Kasay, Car.	1996	0	34	37	145
Mike Vanderjagt, Ind	1999	0	43	34	145
John Riggins, Wash	1983	24	0	0	144
Kevin Butler, Chi	1985	0	51	31	144
Olindo Mare, Mia	1999	0	27	39	144
Priest Holmes, KC	2002	24	0	0	144

Touchdowns

	Year	Rush	Rec	Ret	Total
Marshall Faulk, St.L	2000	18	8	0	26
Emmitt Smith, Dal	1995	25	0	0	25
John Riggins, Wash	1983	24	0	0	24
Priest Holmes, KC	2002	21	3	0	24
Terrell Davis, Den	1998	21	2	0	23
O.J. Simpson, Buf	1975	16	7	0	23
Jerry Rice, SF	1987	1	22	0	23
Gale Sayers, Chi	1966	14	6	2	22
Chuck Foreman, Min	1975	13	9	0	22
Emmitt Smith, Dal	1994	21	1	0	22
Jim Brown, Cle	1965	17	4	0	21
Joe Morris, NY Giants	1985	21	0	0	21
Terry Allen, Wash	1996	21	0	0	21
Marshall Faulk, St.L	2001	12	9	0	21
Lenny Moore, Bal	1964	16	3	1	20
Leroy Kelly, Cle	1968	16	4	0	20
Eric Dickerson, LA Rams	1983	18	2	0	20

Note: The NFL regular season schedule grew from 12 games (1947-60) to 14 (1961-77) to 16 (1978-present). The AFL regular season schedule was always 14 games (1960-69).

Touchdowns Passing

	Year	No
Dan Marino, Miami	1984	48
Dan Marino, Miami	1986	44
Kurt Warner, St. Louis	1999	41
Brett Favre, Green Bay	1996	39
Brett Favre, Green Bay	1995	38
George Blanda, Houston	1961	36
Y.A. Tittle, NY Giants	1963	36
Steve Young, San Francisco	1998	36
Steve Beuerlein, Carolina	1999	36
Kurt Warner, St. Louis	2001	36
Brett Favre, Green Bay	1997	35
Steve Young, San Francisco	1994	35
Randall Cunningham, Minnesota	1998	34

Nine tied with 33 each, incl. Warren Moon twice.

Touchdowns Receiving

	Year	No
Jerry Rice, San Francisco	1987	22
Mark Clayton, Miami	1984	18
Sterling Sharpe, Green Bay	1994	18
Don Hutson, Green Bay	1942	17
Elroy (Crazylegs) Hirsch, LA Rams	1951	17
Bill Groman, Houston	1961	17
Jerry Rice, San Francisco	1989	17
Cris Carter, Minnesota	1995	17
Carl Pickens, Cincinnati	1995	17
Randy Moss, Minnesota	1998	17
Art Powell, Oakland	1963	16
Terrell Owens, SF	2001	16

Eight tied with 15 each, incl. Rice three times.

All-Time NFL Leaders (Cont.)

Touchdowns Rushing

	Year	No
Emmitt Smith, Dallas	1995	25
John Riggins, Washington	1983	24
Joe Morris, NY Giants	1985	21
Emmitt Smith, Dallas	1994	21
Terry Allen, Washington	1996	21
Terrell Davis, Denver	1998	21
Priest Holmes, Kansas City	2002	21
Jim Taylor, Green Bay	1962	19
Earl Campbell, Houston	1979	19
Chuck Muncie, San Diego	1981	19
Eric Dickerson, LA Rams	1983	18
George Rogers, Washington	1986	18
Emmitt Smith, Dallas	1992	18
Marshall Faulk, St. Louis	2000	18
Jim Brown, Cleveland	1958	17
Jim Brown, Cleveland	1965	17
Stephen Davis, Washington	1999	17

Field Goals

	Year	Att	No
Olindo Mare, Miami	1999	46	39
John Kasay, Carolina	1996	45	37
Cary Blanchard, Indianapolis	1996	40	36
Al Del Greco, Tennessee	1998	39	36
Ali Haji-Sheikh, NY Giants	1983	42	35
Jeff Jaeger, LA Raiders	1993	44	35
Gary Anderson, Minnesota	1998	35	35
Matt Stover, Baltimore	2000	39	35
Jim Turner, NY Jets	1968	46	34
Nick Lowery, Kansas City	1990	37	34
Jason Hanson, Detroit	1993	43	34
John Carney, San Diego	1994	38	34
Fuad Reveiz, Minnesota	1994	39	34
Norm Johnson, Pittsburgh	1995	41	34
Richie Cunningham, Dallas	1997	37	34
Mike Vanderjagt, Indianapolis	1999	38	34
Todd Peterson, Seattle	1999	40	34
Joe Nedney, Den.-Car.	2000	38	34

Interceptions

	Year	No
Dick (Night Train) Lane, Detroit	1952	14
Dan Sandifer, Washington	1948	13
Spec Sanders, NY Yanks	1950	13
Lester Hayes, Oakland	1980	13

Punting

Qualifiers	Year	Avg
Sammy Baugh, Washington	1940	51.4
Yale Lary, Detroit	1963	48.9
Sammy Baugh, Washington	1941	48.7
Yale Lary, Detroit	1961	48.4

Kickoff Returns

	Year	Avg
Travis Williams, Green Bay	1967	41.1
Gale Sayers, Chicago Bears	1967	37.7
Ollie Matson, Chicago Cards	1958	35.5

Punt Returns

	Year	Avg
Herb Rich, Baltimore	1950	23.0
Jack Christiansen, Detroit	1952	21.5
Dick Christy, NY Titans	1961	21.3
Bob Hayes, Dallas	1968	20.8

Sacks

	Year	No		Year	No
Michael Strahan, NY Giants	2001	22.5	Chris Doleman, Minnesota	1989	21
Mark Gastineau, NY Jets	1984	22	Lawrence Taylor, NY Giants	1986	20.5
Reggie White, Philadelphia	1987	21	Derrick Thomas, Kansas City	1990	20

Note: The NFL did not begin officially compiling sacks until 1982. Cincinnati's Coy Bacon is widely, although not officially, credited with 26 sacks during the 1976 season.

SINGLE GAME

Passing

Yards Gained	Date	Yds
Norm Van Brocklin, LA vs NY Yanks	9/28/51	554
Warren Moon, Hou vs KC	12/16/90	527
Boomer Esiason, Ariz vs Wash.	11/10/96	522
Dan Marino, Mia vs NYJ	10/23/88	521
Phil Simms, NYG vs Cin	10/13/85	513

Completions	Date	No
Drew Bledsoe, NE vs Min	11/13/94	45
Rich Gannon, Oak vs Pit	9/15/02	43
Richard Todd, NYJ vs SF	9/21/80	42
Vinny Testaverde, NYJ vs Sea	12/6/98	42
Warren Moon, Hou vs Dal	11/10/91	41
Three tied with 40 each.		

Receiving

Catches	Date	No
Terrell Owens, SF vs Chi	12/17/00	20
Tom Fears, LA vs GB	12/3/50	18
Clark Gaines, NYJ vs SF	9/21/80	17
Four tied with 16 each.		

Yards Gained	Date	Yds
Flipper Anderson, LA Rams vs NO	11/26/89	336
Stephone Paige, KC vs SD	12/22/85	309
Jim Benton, Cle vs Det	11/22/45	303
Cloyce Box, Det vs Bal	12/3/50	302
Jimmy Smith, Jax vs Bal	9/10/00	291
Jerry Rice, SF vs Det	9/25/95	289

Rushing

Yards Gained	Date	Yds
Corey Dillon, Cin vs Den	10/22/00	278
Walter Payton, Chi vs Min	11/20/77	275
O.J. Simpson, Buf vs Det	11/25/76	273
Shaun Alexander, Sea vs Oak	11/11/01	266
Mike Anderson, Den vs NO	12/3/00	251
O.J. Simpson, Buf vs NE	9/16/73	250
Willie Ellison, LA Rams vs NO	12/5/71	247
Corey Dillon, Cin vs Ten	12/4/97	246

All-Purpose Yards

	Date	Yds
Glyn Milburn, Den vs Sea	12/10/95	404
Billy Cannon, Hou vs NY Titans	12/10/61	373
Michael Lewis, NO vs Wash	10/13/02	356
Tyrone Hughes, NO vs LA Rams	10/23/94	347
Lionel James, SD vs Raiders	11/10/85	345
Timmy Brown, Phi vs St.L	12/16/62	341
Gale Sayers, Chi vs Min	12/18/66	339
Gale Sayers, Chi vs SF	12/12/65	336
Flipper Anderson, LA Rams vs NO	11/26/89	336

Scoring

Points

	Date	Pts
Ernie Nevers, Chi. Cards vs Chi. Bears	11/28/29	40
Dub Jones, Cle vs Chi. Bears	11/25/51	36
Gale Sayers, Chi vs SF	12/12/65	36
Paul Hornung, GB vs Bal	10/8/61	33
Bob Shaw, Chi. Cards vs Bal	10/2/50	30
Jim Brown, Cle vs Bal	11/1/59	30
Abner Haynes, Dal. Texans vs Oak	11/26/61	30
Billy Cannon, Hou vs NY Titans	12/10/61	30
Cookie Gilchrist, Buf vs NY Jets	12/8/63	30
Kellen Winslow, SD vs Oak	11/22/81	30
Jerry Rice, SF vs Atl	10/14/90	30
James Stewart, Jax vs Phi.	10/12/97	30
Shaun Alexander, Sea vs Min.	9/29/02	30

Note: Nevers celebrated Thanksgiving, 1929, by scoring all of the Chicago Cardinals' points on six rushing TDs and four PATs. The Cards beat Red Grange and the Chicago Bears, 40-6.

Touchdowns Passing

	Date	No
Sid Luckman, Chi. Bears vs NYG	11/14/43	7
Adrian Burk, Phi vs Wash	10/17/54	7
George Blanda, Hou vs NY Titans	11/19/61	7
Y.A. Tittle, NYG vs Wash	10/28/62	7
Joe Kapp, Min vs Bal	9/28/69	7

Touchdowns Receiving

	Date	No
Bob Shaw, Chi. Cards vs Bal	10/2/50	5
Kellen Winslow, SD vs Oak	11/22/81	5
Jerry Rice, SF vs Atl	10/14/90	5

Touchdowns Rushing

	Date	No
Ernie Nevers, Chi. Cards vs Chi. Bears	11/28/29	6
Jim Brown, Cle vs Bal	11/1/59	5
Cookie Gilchrist, Buf vs NY Jets	12/8/63	5
James Stewart, Jax vs Phi.	10/12/97	5

Field Goals

	Date	No
Jim Bakken, St.L vs Pit	9/24/67	7
Chris Boniol, Dal vs GB	11/18/96	7
Rich Karlis, Min vs LA Rams	11/5/89	7

Eighteen players tied with 6 each, incl. Gary Anderson and John Carney twice.

Note: Bakken was 7-for-9, Boniol and Karlis 7-for-7.

Extra Point Kicks

	Date	No
Pat Harder, Cards vs NYG	10/17/48	9
Bob Waterfield, LA Rams vs Bal	10/22/50	9
Charlie Gogolak, Wash vs NYG	11/27/66	9

Interceptions

	No
By 18 players	4

Sacks

	Date	No
Derrick Thomas, KC vs Sea	11/11/90	7
Fred Dean, SF vs NO	11/13/83	6
Derrick Thomas, KC vs Oak	9/6/98	6
William Gay, Det vs TB	9/4/83	5.5

Longest Plays

Passing (all for TDs)	Date	Yds
Frank Filchock to Andy Farkas, Wash vs Pit	10/15/39	99
George Izo to Bobby Mitchell, Wash vs Cle	9/15/63	99
Karl Sweetan to Pat Studstill, Det vs Bal	10/16/66	99
Sonny Jurgensen to Gerry Allen, Wash vs Chi	9/15/68	99
Jim Plunkett to Cliff Branch, LA Raiders vs Wash	10/2/83	99
Ron Jaworski to Mike Quick, Phi vs Atl	11/10/85	99
Stan Humphries to Tony Martin, SD vs Sea	9/18/94	99
Brett Favre to Robert Brooks, GB vs Chi	9/11/95	99
Trent Green to **Marc Boerigter**, KC vs SD	12/22/02	99

Runs from Scrimmage (all for TDs)	Date	Yds
Tony Dorsett, Dal vs Min	1/3/83	99
Andy Uram, GB vs Chi. Cards	10/8/39	97
Bob Gage, Pit vs Bears	12/4/49	97
Jim Spavital, Balt. Colts vs GB	11/5/50	96
Bob Hoernschemeyer, Det vs NY Yanks	11/23/50	96
Garrison Hearst, SF vs NYJ	9/6/98	96
Corey Dillon, Cin vs Det	10/28/01	96

Punts	Date	Yds
Steve O'Neal, NYJ vs Den	9/21/69	98
Joe Lintzenich, Chi. Bears vs NYG	11/15/31	94
Shawn McCarthy, NE vs Buf	11/3/91	93

Field Goals	Date	Yds
Tom Dempsey, NO vs Det	11/8/70	63
Jason Elam, Den vs Jax	10/25/98	63
Steve Cox, Cle vs Cin	10/21/84	60
Morten Andersen, NO vs Chi	10/27/91	60
Tony Franklin, Phi vs Dal	11/12/79	59
Pete Stoyanovich, Mia vs NYJ	11/12/89	59
Steve Christie, Buf vs Mia	9/26/93	59
Morten Andersen, Atl vs SF	12/24/95	59

Punt Returns (all for TDs)	Date	Yds
Robert Bailey, Rams vs NO	10/23/94	103
Gil LeFebvre, Cin vs Bklyn	12/3/33	98
Charlie West, Min vs Wash	11/3/68	98
Dennis Morgan, Dal vs St.L	10/13/74	98
Terance Mathis, NYJ vs Dal	11/4/90	98
Greg Pruitt, LA Raiders vs Wash.	10/2/83	97

Kickoff Returns (all for TDs)	Date	Yds
Al Carmichael, GB vs Chi. Bears	10/7/56	106
Noland Smith, KC vs Den	12/17/67	106
Roy Green, St.L vs Dal	10/21/79	106

Interception Returns (all for TDs)	Date	Yds
James Willis (14 yds) lateral to Troy Vincent (90 yds), Phi vs Dal	11/3/96	104
Vencie Glenn, SD vs Den	11/29/87	103
Louis Oliver, Mia vs Buf	10/4/92	103

Seven players tied with 102-yd returns.

Note: On 9/30/02 Baltimore's Chris McAlister returned a missed FG 107 yards, the longest play in NFL history.

Chicago College All-Star Game

On Aug. 31, 1934, a year after sponsoring Major League Baseball's first All-Star Game, *Chicago Tribune* sports editor Arch Ward presented the first Chicago College All-Star Game at Soldier Field. A crowd of 79,432 turned out to see an all-star team of graduated college seniors battle the 1933 NFL champion Chicago Bears to a scoreless tie. The preseason game was played at Soldier Field and pitted the College All-Stars against the defending NFL champions (1933-1966) or Super Bowl champions (1967-75) every year except 1935 until it was cancelled in 1977. The NFL champs won the series, 31-9-1.

Year		Year		Year	
1934	Chi. Bears 0, All-Stars 0	1949	Philadelphia 38, All-Stars 0	1964	Chi. Bears 28, All-Stars 17
1935	Chi. Bears 5, All-Stars 0			1965	Cleveland 24, All-Stars 16
1936	Detroit 7, All-Stars 0	1950	All-Stars 17, Philadelphia 7	1966	Green Bay 38, All-Stars 0
1937	All-Stars 6, Green Bay 0	1951	Cleveland 33, All-Stars 0	1967	Green Bay 27, All-Stars 0
1938	All-Stars 28, Washington 16	1952	LA Rams 10, All-Stars 7	1968	Green Bay 34, All-Stars 17
1939	NY Giants 9, All-Stars 0	1953	Detroit 24, All-Stars 10	1969	NY Jets 26, All-Stars 24
		1954	Detroit 31, All-Stars 0		
1940	Green Bay 45, All-Stars 28	1955	All-Stars 30, Cleveland 27	1970	Kansas City 24, All-Stars 3
1941	Chi. Bears 37, All-Stars 13	1956	Cleveland 26, All-Stars 0	1971	Baltimore 24, All-Stars 17
1942	Chi. Bears 21, All-Stars 0	1957	NY Giants 22, All-Stars 12	1972	Dallas 20, All-Stars 7
1943	All-Stars 27, Washington 7	1958	All-Stars 35, Detroit 19	1973	Miami 14, All-Stars 3
1944	Chi. Bears 24, All-Stars 21	1959	Baltimore 29, All-Stars 0	1974	No Game (NFLPA Strike)
1945	Green Bay 19, All-Stars 7			1975	Pittsburgh 21, All-Stars 14
1946	All-Stars 16, LA Rams 0	1960	Baltimore 32, All-Stars 7	1976	Pittsburgh 24, All-Stars 0*
1947	All-Stars 16, Chi. Bears 0	1961	Philadelphia 28, All-Stars 14		
1948	Chi. Cards 28, All-Stars 0	1962	Green Bay 42, All-Stars 20	*Downpour flooded field, game called
		1963	All-Stars 20, Green Bay 17	with 1:22 left in 3rd quarter.

Number One Draft Choices

In an effort to blunt the dominance of the Chicago Bears and New York Giants in the 1930s and distribute talent more evenly throughout the league, the NFL established the college draft in 1936. The first player chosen in the first draft was Jay Berwanger, who was also college football's first Heisman Trophy winner. In all, 17 Heisman winners have also been the NFL's No. 1 draft choice. They are noted in **bold** type. The American Football League (formed in 1960) held its own draft for six years before agreeing to merge with the NFL and select players in a common draft starting in 1967.

Year	Team	
1936	Philadelphia	**Jay Berwanger**, HB, Chicago
1937	Philadelphia	Sam Francis, FB, Nebraska
1938	Cleveland Rams	Corbett Davis, FB, Indiana
1939	Chicago Cards	Ki Aldrich, C, TCU
1940	Chicago Cards	George Cafego, HB, Tennessee
1941	Chicago Bears	**Tom Harmon**, HB, Michigan
1942	Pittsburgh	Bill Dudley, HB, Virginia
1943	Detroit	**Frank Sinkwich**, HB, Georgia
1944	Boston Yanks	**Angelo Bertelli**, QB, N. Dame
1945	Chicago Cards	Charley Trippi, HB, Georgia
1946	Boston Yanks	Frank Dancewicz, QB, N. Dame
1947	Chicago Bears	Bob Fenimore, HB, Okla. A&M
1948	Washington	Harry Gilmer, QB, Alabama
1949	Philadelphia	Chuck Bednarik, C, Penn
1950	Detroit	**Leon Hart**, E, Notre Dame
1951	NY Giants	Kyle Rote, HB, SMU
1952	LA Rams	Bill Wade, QB, Vanderbilt
1953	San Francisco	Harry Babcock, E, Georgia
1954	Cleveland	Bobby Garrett, QB, Stanford
1955	Baltimore	George Shaw, QB, Oregon
1956	Pittsburgh	Gary Glick, DB, Colo. A&M
1957	Green Bay	**Paul Hornung**, QB, N. Dame
1958	Chicago Cards	King Hill, QB, Rice
1959	Green Bay	Randy Duncan, QB, Iowa
1960	NFL–LA Rams	**Billy Cannon**, HB, LSU
	AFL–No choice	
1961	NFL–Minnesota	Tommy Mason, HB, Tulane
	AFL–Buffalo	Ken Rice, G, Auburn
1962	NFL–Washington	**Ernie Davis**, HB, Syracuse
	AFL–Oakland	Roman Gabriel, QB, N.C. State
1963	NFL–LA Rams	**Terry Baker**, QB, Oregon St.
	AFL–Kan.City	Buck Buchanan, DT, Grambling
1964	NFL–San Fran	Dave Parks, E, Texas Tech
	AFL–Boston	Jack Concannon, QB, Boston Col.
1965	NFL–NY Giants	Tucker Frederickson, FB, Auburn
	AFL–Houston	Lawrence Elkins, E, Baylor
1966	NFL–Atlanta	Tommy Nobis, LB, Texas
	AFL–Miami	Jim Grabowski, FB, Illinois

Year	Team	
1967	Baltimore	Bubba Smith, DT, Michigan St.
1968	Minnesota	Ron Yary, T, USC
1969	Buffalo	**O.J. Simpson**, RB, USC
1970	Pittsburgh	Terry Bradshaw, QB, La.Tech
1971	New England	**Jim Plunkett**, QB, Stanford
1972	Buffalo	Walt Patulski, DE, Notre Dame
1973	Houston	John Matuszak, DE, Tampa
1974	Dallas	Ed (Too Tall) Jones, DE, Tenn. St.
1975	Atlanta	Steve Bartkowski, QB, Calif.
1976	Tampa Bay	Lee Roy Selmon, DE, Oklahoma
1977	Tampa Bay	Ricky Bell, RB, USC
1978	Houston	**Earl Campbell**, RB, Texas
1979	Buffalo	Tom Cousineau, LB, Ohio St.
1980	Detroit	**Billy Sims**, RB, Oklahoma
1981	New Orleans	**George Rogers**, RB, S. Carolina
1982	New England	Kenneth Sims, DT, Texas
1983	Baltimore	John Elway, QB, Stanford
1984	New England	Irving Fryar, WR, Nebraska
1985	Buffalo	Bruce Smith, DE, Va. Tech
1986	Tampa Bay	**Bo Jackson**, RB, Auburn
1987	Tampa Bay	**V. Testaverde**, QB, Miami-FL
1988	Atlanta	Aundray Bruce, LB, Auburn
1989	Dallas	Troy Aikman, QB, UCLA
1990	Indianapolis	Jeff George, QB, Illinois
1991	Dallas	Russell Maryland, DT, Miami-FL
1992	Indianapolis	Steve Emtman, DT, Washington
1993	New England	Drew Bledsoe, QB, Washington St.
1994	Cincinnati	Dan Wilkinson, DT, Ohio St.
1995	Cincinnati	Ki-Jana Carter, RB, Penn St.
1996	NY Jets	Keyshawn Johnson, WR, USC
1997	St. Louis	Orlando Pace, OT, Ohio St.
1998	Indianapolis	Peyton Manning, QB, Tennessee
1999	Cleveland	Tim Couch, QB, Kentucky
2000	Cleveland	Courtney Brown, DE, Penn St.
2001	Atlanta	Michael Vick, QB, Va. Tech
2002	Houston	David Carr, QB, Fresno St.
2003	Cincinnati	**Carson Palmer**, QB, USC

AP/Wide World Photos
Don Shula

NFL Media
Dan Reeves

NFL Media
Bill Parcells

NFL Media
Bill Cowher

All-Time Winningest NFL Coaches

NFL career victories through the 2002 season. Career, regular season and playoff records are noted along with NFL, AFL and Super Bowl titles won. Coaches active during 2002 season in **bold** type.

			Career			Regular Season				Playoffs			
		Yrs	W	L	T	Pct	W	L	T	Pct	W	L	Pct.	League Titles
1	Don Shula	33	347	173	6	.665	328	156	6	.676	19	17	.528	2 Super Bowls and 1 NFL
2	George Halas	40	324	151	31	.671	318	148	31	.671	6	3	.667	5 NFL
3	Tom Landry	29	270	178	6	.601	250	162	6	.605	20	16	.556	2 Super Bowls
4	Curly Lambeau	33	229	134	22	.623	226	132	22	.624	3	2	.600	6 NFL
5	Chuck Noll	23	209	156	1	.572	193	148	1	.566	16	8	.667	4 Super Bowls
6	**Dan Reeves**	22	198	164	2	.547	187	155	2	.547	11	9	.550	—None—
7	Chuck Knox	22	193	158	1	.550	186	147	1	.558	7	11	.389	—None—
8	Paul Brown	21	170	108	6	.609	166	100	6	.621	4	8	.333	3 NFL
9	Bud Grant	18	168	108	5	.607	158	96	5	.620	10	12	.455	1 NFL
10	**M. Schottenheimer**	17	166	112	1	.597	161	101	1	.614	5	11	.313	—None—
11	Marv Levy	17	154	120	0	.562	143	112	0	.561	11	8	.579	—None—
12	Steve Owen	23	153	108	17	.581	151	100	17	.595	2	8	.200	2 NFL
13	Bill Parcells	15	149	106	1	.584	138	100	1	.579	11	6	.647	2 Super Bowls
14	Joe Gibbs	12	140	65	0	.683	124	60	0	.674	16	5	.762	3 Super Bowls
15	Hank Stram	17	136	100	10	.573	131	97	10	.571	5	3	.625	1 Super Bowl and 3 AFL
16	Weeb Ewbank	20	134	130	7	.507	130	129	7	.502	4	1	.800	1 Super Bowl, 2 NFL, and 1 AFL
17	Mike Ditka	14	127	101	0	.557	121	95	0	.560	6	6	.500	1 Super Bowl
18	Jim Mora	15	125	112	0	.527	125	106	0	.541	0	6	.000	—None—
19	George Seifert	11	124	67	0	.649	114	62	0	.648	10	5	.667	2 Super Bowls
20	Sid Gillman	18	123	104	7	.541	122	99	7	.550	1	5	.167	1 AFL
21	George Allen	12	118	54	5	.681	116	47	5	.705	2	7	.222	—None—
22	**Bill Cowher**	11	116	74	1	.610	109	66	1	.622	7	8	.467	—None—
23	**Mike Holmgren**	11	115	76	0	.602	106	70	0	.602	9	6	.600	1 Super Bowl
24	Don Coryell	14	114	89	1	.561	111	83	1	.572	3	6	.333	—None—
25	John Madden	10	112	39	7	.731	103	32	7	.750	9	7	.563	1 Super Bowl

Notes: The NFL does not recognize records from the All-American Football Conference (1946-49). If it did, **Paul Brown** (52-4-3 in four AAFC seasons) would move up from 8th to 5th on the all-time list with the following career stats— 25 Yrs; 222 Wins; 112 Losses; 9 Ties; .660 Pct; 9-8 playoff record; and 4 AAFC titles.

The NFL also considers the Playoff Bowl or "Runner-up Bowl" (officially: the Bert Bell Benefit Bowl) as a postseason exhibition game. The Playoff Bowl was contested every year from 1960-69 in Miami between Eastern and Western Conference second place teams. While the games did not count, six of the coaches above went to the Playoff Bowl at least once and came away with the following records— Allen (2-0), Brown (0-1), Grant (0-1), Landry (1-2), Lombardi (1-1) and Shula (2-0).

Where They Coached

Allen—LA Rams (1966-70), Washington (1971-77); **Brown**—Cleveland (1950-62), Cincinnati (1968-75); **Coryell**—St. Louis (1973-77), San Diego (1978-86); **Cowher**—Pittsburgh (1992—); **Ditka**— Chicago (1982-92), New Orleans (1997-99); **Ewbank**— Baltimore (1954-62), NY Jets (1963-73); **Gibbs**—Washington (1981-92); **Gillman**—LA Rams (1955-59), LA-San Diego Chargers (1960-69), Houston (1973-74).

Grant—Minnesota (1967-83, 1985); **Halas**—Chicago Bears (1920-29,33-42,46-55,58-67); **Holmgren**—Green Bay (1992-98), Seattle (1999—); **Knox**— LA Rams (1973-77, 1992-94); Buffalo (1978-82), Seattle (1983-91); **Lambeau**— Green Bay (1921-49), Chicago Cards (1950-51), Washington (1952-53); **Landry**—Dallas (1960-88); **Levy**— Kansas City (1978-82), Buffalo (1986-97); **Madden**—Oakland (1969-78); **Mora**—New Orleans (1986-1995), Indianapolis (1998-2001).

Noll—Pittsburgh (1969-91); **Owen**—NY Giants (1931-53); **Parcells**— NY Giants (1983-90), New England (1993-97), NY Jets (1997-99), Dallas (2003—); **Reeves**— Denver (1981-92), NY Giants (1993-96), Atlanta (1997—); **Schottenheimer**— Cleveland (1984-88), Kansas City (1989-98), Washington (2001), San Diego (2002—); **Seifert**—San Francisco (1989-96), Carolina (1999-2001); **Shula**—Baltimore (1963-69), Miami (1970-95); **Stram**—Dallas-Kansas City (1960-74), New Orleans (1976-77).

Top Winning Percentages

Minimum of 85 NFL victories, including playoffs.

		Yrs	W	L	T	Pct
1	Vince Lombardi	10	105	35	6	**.740**
2	John Madden	10	112	39	7	**.731**
3	Joe Gibbs	12	140	65	0	**.683**
4	George Allen	12	118	54	5	**.681**
5	George Halas	40	324	151	31	**.671**
6	Don Shula	33	347	173	6	**.665**
7	George Seifert	11	124	67	0	**.649**
8	Curly Lambeau	33	229	134	22	**.623**
9	Bill Walsh	10	102	63	1	**.617**
11	**Mike Shanahan**	10	96	61	0	**.611**
13	**Bill Cowher**	11	116	74	1	**.610**
12	Paul Brown	21	170	108	6	**.609**
14	Bud Grant	18	168	108	5	**.607**
10	**Mike Holmgren**	11	115	76	0	**.602**
16	Tom Landry	29	270	178	6	**.601**
15	**Marty Schottenheimer**	17	166	112	1	**.597**
17	Dennis Green	10	101	70	0	**.591**
18	Bill Parcells	15	149	106	1	**.584**
19	Steve Owen	23	153	108	17	**.581**
20	Buddy Parker	15	107	76	9	**.581**
21	Hank Stram	17	136	100	10	**.573**
22	Chuck Noll	23	209	156	1	**.572**
23	Jimmy Johnson	9	89	68	0	**.567**
24	Marv Levy	17	154	120	0	**.562**
25	Don Coryell	14	114	89	1	**.561**

Note: If AAFC records are included, **Paul Brown** moves from 12th to 7th with a percentage of .660 (25 yrs, 222-112-9) and **Buck Shaw** would be 11th at .619 (8 yrs, 91-55-5).

Active Coaches' Victories

Through 2002 season, including playoffs.

		Yrs	W	L	T	Pct
1	Dan Reeves, Atlanta	22	**198**	164	2	.547
2	Marty Schottenheimer, SD	17	**166**	112	1	.597
3	Bill Parcells, Dallas	15	**149**	106	1	.584
4	Bill Cowher, Pittsburgh	11	**116**	74	1	.610
5	Mike Holmgren, Seattle	11	**115**	76	0	.602
6	Mike Shanahan, Denver	10	**96**	61	0	.611
	Dick Vermeil, KC	12	**96**	95	0	.503
8	Jeff Fisher, Tennessee	9	**80**	61	0	.567
9	Dave Wannstedt, Miami	9	**73**	76	0	.490
10	Tony Dungy, Indianapolis	7	**66**	53	0	.555
11	Bill Belichick, New England	8	**65**	68	0	.489
12	Steve Mariucci, Detroit	6	**60**	43	0	.583
13	Jim Fassel, NY Giants	6	**56**	44	1	.559
14	Jon Gruden, Tampa Bay	5	**55**	32	0	.632
15	Andy Reid, Philadelphia	4	**43**	28	0	.606
16	Brian Billick, Baltimore	4	**42**	28	0	.600
17	Dom Capers, Houston	5	**35**	47	0	.427
18	Mike Sherman, Green Bay	3	**34**	17	0	.667
19	Mike Martz, St. Louis	3	**33**	19	0	.635
20	Dennis Erickson, San Fran.	4	**31**	33	0	.484
21	Dick Jauron, Chicago	4	**28**	37	0	.431
22	Jim Haslett, New Orleans	3	**27**	23	0	.540
23	Herman Edwards, NY Jets	2	**20**	15	0	.571
24	Butch Davis, Cleveland	2	**16**	17	0	.485
25	Bill Callahan, Oakland	1	**13**	6	0	.684
	Dave McGinnis, Arizona	3	**13**	28	0	.317
27	Gregg Williams, Buffalo	2	**11**	21	0	.344
28	John Fox, Carolina	1	**7**	9	0	.438
	Steve Spurrier, Washington	1	**7**	9	0	.438
30	Mike Tice, Minnesota	2	**6**	11	0	.353
31	Jack Del Rio, Jacksonville	0	**0**	0	0	.000
	Marvin Lewis, Cincinnati	0	**0**	0	0	.000

Annual Awards
Most Valuable Player

Currently, the NFL does not sanction an official MVP award. It awarded the Joe F. Carr Trophy (Carr was NFL president from 1921-39) to the league MVP from 1938 to 1946. Since then, four principal MVP awards have been given out throughout the years and are noted below: UPI (1953-69), AP (since 1957), the Maxwell Club of Philadelphia's Bert Bell Trophy (since 1959) and the Pro Football Writers Assn. (since 1976). UPI switched to AFC and NFC Player of the Year awards in 1970 and then discontinued its awards in 1997.

Multiple winners (more than one season): Jim Brown (4); Randall Cunningham, Brett Favre, Johnny Unitas and Y.A. Tittle (3); Earl Campbell, Marshall Faulk, Rich Gannon, Otto Graham, Don Hutson, Joe Montana, Walter Payton, Barry Sanders, Ken Stabler, Joe Theismann, Kurt Warner and Steve Young (2).

Year	Awards
1938 Mel Hein, NY Giants, C	Carr
1939 Parker Hall, Cleveland Rams, HB	Carr
1940 Ace Parker, Brooklyn, HB	Carr
1941 Don Hutson, Green Bay, E	Carr
1942 Don Hutson, Green Bay, E	Carr
1943 Sid Luckman, Chicago Bears, QB	Carr
1944 Frank Sinkwich, Detroit, HB	Carr
1945 Bob Waterfield, Cleveland Rams, QB	Carr
1946 Bill Dudley, Pittsburgh, HB	Carr
1947-52 No award	
1953 Otto Graham, Cleveland Browns, QB	UPI
1954 Joe Perry, San Francisco, FB	UPI
1955 Otto Graham, Cleveland, QB	UPI
1956 Frank Gifford, NY Giants, HB	UPI
1957 Y.A. Tittle, San Francisco, QB	UPI
& Jim Brown, Cleveland, FB	AP
1958 Jim Brown, Cleveland, FB	UPI
& Gino Marchetti, Baltimore, DE	AP
1959 Johnny Unitas, Baltimore, QB	UPI, Bell
& Charley Conerly, NY Giants, QB	AP
1960 Norm Van Brocklin, Phi., QB	UPI, AP (tie), Bell
& Joe Schmidt, Detroit, LB	AP (tie)
1961 Paul Hornung, Green Bay, HB	UPI, AP, Bell
1962 Y.A. Tittle, NY Giants, QB	UPI
Jim Taylor,Green Bay, FB	AP
& Andy Robustelli, NY Giants,DE	Bell
1963 Jim Brown, Cleveland, FB	UPI, AP
& Y.A. Tittle, NY Giants, QB	AP
1964 Johnny Unitas, Baltimore, QB	UPI, AP, Bell
1965 Jim Brown, Cleveland, FB	UPI, AP
& Pete Retzlaff, Philadelphia, TE	Bell
1966 Bart Starr, Green Bay, QB	UPI, AP
& Don Meredith, Dallas, QB	Bell
1967 Johnny Unitas, Baltimore, QB	UPI, AP, Bell
1968 Earl Morrall, Baltimore, QB	UPI, AP, Bell
& Leroy Kelly, Cleveland, RB	Bell
1969 Roman Gabriel, LA Rams, QB	UPI, AP, Bell
1970 John Brodie, San Francisco, QB	AP
& George Blanda, Oakland, QB-PK	Bell
1971 Alan Page, Minnesota,DT	AP
& Roger Staubach, Dallas, QB	Bell
1972 Larry Brown, Washington, RB	AP, Bell
1973 O.J. Simpson, Buffalo, RB	AP, Bell
1974 Ken Stabler, Oakland, QB	AP
& Merlin Olsen, LA Rams, DT	Bell
1975 Fran Tarkenton, Minnesota, QB	AP, Bell
1976 Bert Jones, Baltimore, QB	AP, PFWA
& Ken Stabler, Oakland, QB	Bell
1977 Walter Payton, Chicago, RB	AP, PFWA
& Bob Griese, Miami, QB	Bell
1978 Terry Bradshaw, Pittsburgh, QB	AP, Bell
& Earl Campbell, Houston, RB	PFWA
1979 Earl Campbell, Houston, RB	AP, Bell, PFWA
1980 Brian Sipe, Cleveland, QB	AP, PFWA
& Ron Jaworski, Philadelphia, QB	Bell
1981 Ken Anderson, Cincinnati, QB	AP, Bell, PFWA

Year	Awards	Year	Awards
1982 Mark Moseley, Washington, PK	AP	1992 Steve Young, San Francisco, QB	AP, Bell, PFWA
Joe Theismann, Washington, QB	Bell	1993 Emmitt Smith, Dallas, RB	AP, Bell, PFWA
& Dan Fouts, San Diego, QB	PFWA	1994 Steve Young, San Francisco, QB	AP, Bell, PFWA
1983 Joe Theismann, Washington, QB	AP, PFWA	1995 Brett Favre, Green Bay, QB	AP, Bell, PFWA
& John Riggins, Washington, RB	Bell	1996 Brett Favre, Green Bay, QB	AP, Bell, PFWA
1984 Dan Marino, Miami, QB	AP, Bell, PFWA	1997 Barry Sanders, Detroit, RB	AP, Bell, PFWA
1985 Marcus Allen, LA Raiders, RB	AP, PFWA	& Brett Favre, Green Bay, QB	AP
& Walter Payton, Chicago, RB	Bell	1998 Terrell Davis, Denver, RB	AP, PFWA
1986 Lawrence Taylor, NY Giants, LB	AP, Bell, PFWA	& Randall Cunningham, Minnesota, QB	Bell
1987 Jerry Rice, San Francisco, WR	Bell, PFWA	1999 Kurt Warner, St. Louis, QB	AP, Bell, PFWA
& John Elway, Denver, QB	AP	2000 Marshall Faulk, St. Louis, RB	AP, PFWA
1988 Boomer Esiason, Cincinnati, QB	AP, PFWA &	& Rich Gannon, Oakland, QB	Bell
Randall Cunningham, Phila., QB	Bell	2001 Kurt Warner, St. Louis, QB	AP
1989 Joe Montana, San Francisco, QB	AP, Bell, PFWA	& Marshall Faulk, St. Louis, RB	Bell, PFWA
1990 Randall Cunningham, Phila., QB	Bell, PFWA	2002 Rich Gannon, Oakland, QB	AP, Bell, PFWA
& Joe Montana, San Francisco, QB	AP		
1991 Thurman Thomas, Buffalo, RB	AP, PFWA		
& Barry Sanders, Detroit, RB	Bell		

AP Offensive Player of the Year

Selected by The Associated Press in balloting by a nationwide media panel. Given out since 1972. Rookie winners are in **bold** type.
Multiple winners: Earl Campbell and Marshall Faulk (3); Terrell Davis, Jerry Rice and Barry Sanders (2).

Year	Pos	Year	Pos	Year	Pos
1972 Larry Brown, Was	RB	1983 Joe Theismann, Was	QB	1994 Barry Sanders, Det	RB
1973 O.J. Simpson, Buf	RB	1984 Dan Marino, Mia	QB	1995 Brett Favre, GB	QB
1974 Ken Stabler, Oak	QB	1985 Marcus Allen, Raiders	RB	1996 Terrell Davis, Den	RB
1975 Fran Tarkenton, Min	QB	1986 Eric Dickerson, Rams	RB	1997 Barry Sanders, Det	RB
1976 Bert Jones, Bal	QB	1987 Jerry Rice, SF	WR	1998 Terrell Davis, Den	RB
1977 Walter Payton, Chi	RB	1988 Roger Craig, SF	RB	1999 Marshall Faulk, St.L	RB
1978 **Earl Campbell**, Hou	RB	1989 Joe Montana, SF	QB	2000 Marshall Faulk, St.L	RB
1979 Earl Campbell, Hou	RB	1990 Warren Moon, Hou	QB	2001 Marshall Faulk, St.L	RB
1980 Earl Campbell, Hou	RB	1991 Thurman Thomas, Buf	RB	2002 Priest Holmes, KC	RB
1981 Ken Anderson, Cin	QB	1992 Steve Young, SF	QB		
1982 Dan Fouts, SD	QB	1993 Jerry Rice, SF	WR		

AP Defensive Player of the Year

Selected by The Associated Press in balloting by a nationwide media panel. Given out since 1971. Rookie winners are in **bold** type.
Multiple winners: Lawrence Taylor (3); Joe Greene, Mike Singletary, Bruce Smith and Reggie White (2).

Year	Pos	Year	Pos	Year	Pos
1971 Alan Page, Min	DT	1982 Lawrence Taylor, NYG	LB	1993 Rod Woodson, Pit	CB
1972 Joe Greene, Pit	DT	1983 Doug Betters, Mia	DE	1994 Deion Sanders, SF	CB
1973 Dick Anderson, Mia	S	1984 Kenny Easley, Sea	S	1995 Bryce Paup, Buf	LB
1974 Joe Greene, Pit	DT	1985 Mike Singletary, Chi	LB	1996 Bruce Smith, Buf	DE
1975 Mel Blount, Pit	CB	1986 Lawrence Taylor, NYG	LB	1997 Dana Stubblefield, SF	DT
1976 Jack Lambert, Pit	LB	1987 Reggie White, Phi	DE	1998 Reggie White, GB	DE
1977 Harvey Martin, Dal	DE	1988 Mike Singletary, Chi	LB	1999 Warren Sapp, TB	DT
1978 Randy Gradishar, Den	LB	1989 Keith Millard, Min	DT	2000 Ray Lewis, Bal	LB
1979 Lee Roy Selmon, TB	DE	1990 Bruce Smith, Buf	DE	2001 Michael Strahan, NYG	DE
1980 Lester Hayes, Oak	CB	1991 Pat Swilling, NO	LB	2002 Derrick Brooks, TB	LB
1981 **Lawrence Taylor**, NYG	LB	1992 Cortez Kennedy, Sea	DT		

UPI NFC Player of the Year

Given out by UPI from 1970-96. Offensive and defensive players honored since 1983. Rookie winners are in **bold** type.
Multiple winners: Eric Dickerson, Reggie White and Mike Singletary (3); Brett Favre, Charles Haley, Walter Payton, Lawrence Taylor and Steve Young (2).

Year	Pos	Year	Pos	Year	Pos
1970 John Brodie, SF	QB	1984 Off–Eric Dickerson, Rams	RB	1991 Off–Mark Rypien, Was	QB
1971 Alan Page, Min	DT	Def–Mike Singletary, Chi	LB	Def–Reggie White, Phi	DE
1972 Larry Brown, Was	RB	1985 Off–Walter Payton, Chi	RB	1992 Off–Steve Young, SF	QB
1973 John Hadl, Rams	QB	Def–Mike Singletary, Chi	LB	Def–Chris Doleman, Min	DE
1974 Jim Hart, St.L	QB	1986 Off–Eric Dickerson, Rams	RB	1993 Off–Emmitt Smith, Dal	RB
1975 Fran Tarkenton, Min	QB	Def–Lawrence Taylor, NYG	LB	Def–Eric Allen, Phi	CB
1976 Chuck Foreman, Min	RB	1987 Off–Jerry Rice, SF	WR	1994 Off–Steve Young, SF	QB
1977 Walter Payton, Chi	RB	Def–Reggie White, Phi	DE	Def–Charles Haley, Dal	DE
1978 Archie Manning, NO	QB	1988 Off–Roger Craig, SF	RB	1995 Off–Brett Favre, GB	QB
1979 Ottis Anderson, St.L	RB	Def–Mike Singletary, Chi	LB	Def–Reggie White, GB	DE
1980 Ron Jaworski, Phi	QB	1989 Off–Joe Montana, SF	QB	1996 Off–Brett Favre, GB	QB
1981 Tony Dorsett, Dal	RB	Def–Keith Millard, Min	DT	Def–Kevin Greene, Car	LB
1982 Mark Moseley, Was	PK	1990 Off–Randall Cunningham, Phi.	QB	1997 Award discontinued.	
1983 Off–Eric Dickerson, Rams	RB	Def–Charles Haley, SF	LB		
Def–Lawrence Taylor, NYG	LB				

Annual Awards (Cont.)

UPI AFL-AFC Player of the Year

Presented by UPI to the top player in the AFL (1960-69) and AFC (1970-96). Offensive and defensive players have been honored since 1983. Rookie winners are in **bold** type.

Multiple winners: Bruce Smith (4); O.J. Simpson (3); Cornelius Bennett, George Blanda, John Elway, Dan Fouts, Daryle Lamonica, Dan Marino and Curt Warner (2).

Year		Pos	Year		Pos	Year		Pos
1960	**Abner Haynes**, Dal	HB	1978	**Earl Campbell**, Hou	RB	1989	Off–Christian Okoye, KC	RB
1961	George Blanda, Hou	QB	1979	Dan Fouts, SD	QB		Def–Michael Dean Perry,Cle	NT
1962	Cookie Gilchrist, Buf	FB	1980	Brian Sipe, Cle	QB	1990	Off–Warren Moon, Hou	QB
1963	Lance Alworth, SD	FL	1981	Ken Anderson, Cin	QB		Def–Bruce Smith,Buf	DE
1964	Gino Cappelletti, Bos	FL-PK	1982	Dan Fouts, SD	QB	1991	Off–Thurman Thomas, Buf	RB
1965	Paul Lowe, SD	HB	1983	Off–**Curt Warner**, Sea	RB		Def–Cornelius Bennett, Buf	LB
1966	Jim Nance, Bos	FB		Def–Rod Martin, Raiders	LB	1992	Off–Barry Foster, Pit	RB
1967	Daryle Lamonica, Raiders	QB	1984	Off–Dan Marino, Mia	QB		Def–Junior Seau, SD	LB
1968	Joe Namath, NYJ	QB		Def–Mark Gastineau, NYJ	DE	1993	Off–John Elway, Den	QB
1969	Daryle Lamonica, Raiders	QB	1985	Off–Marcus Allen, Raiders	RB		Def–Rod Woodson, Pit	CB
1970	George Blanda, Raiders	QB-PK		Def–Andre Tippett, NE	LB	1994	Off–Dan Marino, Mia	QB
1971	Otis Taylor, KC	WR	1986	Off–Curt Warner, Sea	RB		Def–Greg Lloyd, Pit	LB
1972	O.J. Simpson, Buf	RB		Def–Rulon Jones, Den	DE	1995	Off–Jim Harbaugh, Ind	QB
1973	O.J. Simpson, Buf	RB	1987	Off–John Elway, Den	QB		Def–Bryce Paup, Buf	LB
1974	Ken Stabler, Raiders	QB		Def–Bruce Smith, Buf	DE	1996	Off–Terrell Davis, Den	RB
1975	O.J. Simpson, Buf	RB	1988	Off–Boomer Esiason, Cin	QB		Def–Bruce Smith, Buf	DE
1976	Bert Jones, Bal	QB		Def–Bruce Smith, Buf	DE	1997	Award discontinued.	
1977	Craig Morton, Den	QB		& Cornelius Bennett, Buf	LB			

UPI NFL-NFC Rookie of the Year

Presented by UPI to the top rookie in the NFL (1955-69) and NFC (1970-96). Players who were the overall first pick in the NFL draft are in **bold** type.

Year		Pos	Year		Pos	Year		Pos
1955	Alan Ameche, Bal	FB	1970	Bruce Taylor, SF	DB	1985	Jerry Rice, SF	WR
1956	Lenny Moore, Bal	HB	1971	John Brockington, GB	RB	1986	Reuben Mayes, NO	RB
1957	Jim Brown, Cle	FB	1972	Chester Marcol, GB	PK	1987	Robert Awalt, St.L	TE
1958	Jimmy Orr, Pit	FL	1973	Charle Young, Phi	TE	1988	Keith Jackson, Phi	TE
1959	Boyd Dowler, GB	FL	1974	John Hicks, NY	G	1989	Barry Sanders, Det	RB
1960	Gail Cogdill, Det	FL	1975	Mike Thomas, Wash	RB	1990	Mark Carrier, Chi	S
1961	Mike Ditka, Chi	TE	1976	Sammy White, Min	WR	1991	Lawrence Dawsey, TB	WR
1962	Ronnie Bull, Chi	FB	1977	Tony Dorsett, Dal	RB	1992	Robert Jones, Dal	LB
1963	Paul Flatley, Min	FL	1978	Bubba Baker, Det	DE	1993	Jerome Bettis, LA	RB
1964	Charley Taylor, Wash	HB	1979	Ottis Anderson, St.L	RB	1994	Bryant Young, SF	DT
1965	Gale Sayers, Chi	HB	1980	**Billy Sims**, Det	RB	1995	Rashaan Salaam, Chi	RB
1966	Johnny Roland, St.L	HB	1981	**George Rogers**, NO	RB	1996	Simeon Rice, Ari.	DE
1967	Mel Farr, Det	RB	1982	Jim McMahon, Chi	QB	1997	Award discontinued.	
1968	Earl McCullough, Det	FL	1983	Eric Dickerson, LA	RB			
1969	Calvin Hill, Dal	RB	1984	Paul McFadden, Phi	PK			

UPI AFL-AFC Rookie of the Year

Presented by UPI to the top rookie in the AFL (1960-69) and AFC (1970-96). Players who were the overall first pick in the AFL or NFL draft are in **bold** type.

Year		Pos	Year		Pos	Year		Pos
1960	Abner Haynes, Dal	HB	1973	Bobbie Clark, Cin	RB	1986	Leslie O'Neal, SD	DE
1961	Earl Faison, SD	DE	1974	Don Woods, SD	RB	1987	Shane Conlan, Buf	LB
1962	Curtis McClinton, Dal	FB	1975	Robert Brazile, Hou	LB	1988	John Stephens, NE	RB
1963	Billy Joe, Den	FB	1976	Mike Haynes, NE	DB	1989	Derrick Thomas, KC	LB
1964	Matt Snell, NY	FB	1977	A.J. Duhe, Mia	DE	1990	Richmond Webb, Mia	OT
1965	Joe Namath, NY	QB	1978	**Earl Campbell**, Hou	RB	1991	Mike Croel, Den	LB
1966	Bobby Burnett, Buf	HB	1979	Jerry Butler, Buf	WR	1992	Dale Carter, KC	CB
1967	George Webster, Hou	LB	1980	Joe Cribbs, Buf	RB	1993	Rick Mirer, Sea	QB
1968	Paul Robinson, Cin	RB	1981	Joe Delaney, KC	RB	1994	Marshall Faulk, Ind	RB
1969	Greg Cook, Cin	QB	1982	Marcus Allen, LA	RB	1995	Curtis Martin, NE	RB
1970	Dennis Shaw, Buf	QB	1983	Curt Warner, Sea	RB	1996	Terry Glenn, NE	WR
1971	**Jim Plunkett**, NE	QB	1984	Louis Lipps, Pit	WR	1997	Award discontinued.	
1972	Franco Harris, Pit	RB	1985	Kevin Mack, Cle	RB			

AP Offensive Rookie of the Year

Selected by The Associated Press in balloting by a nationwide media panel. Given out since 1967.

Year		Pos	Year		Pos	Year		Pos
1967	Mel Farr, Det	RB	1979	Ottis Anderson, St.L	RB	1991	Leonard Russell, NE	RB
1968	Earl McCullouch, Det	OE	1980	Billy Sims, Det	RB	1992	Carl Pickens, Cin	WR
1969	Calvin Hill, Dal	RB	1981	George Rogers, NO	RB	1993	Jerome Bettis, Rams	RB
1970	Dennis Shaw, Buf	QB	1982	Marcus Allen, Raiders	RB	1994	Marshall Faulk, Ind	RB
1971	John Brockington, GB	RB	1983	Eric Dickerson, Rams	RB	1995	Curtis Martin, NE	RB
1972	Franco Harris, Pit	RB	1984	Louis Lipps, Pit	WR	1996	Eddie George, Hou	RB
1973	Chuck Foreman, Min	RB	1985	Eddie Brown, Cin	WR	1997	Warrick Dunn, TB	RB
1974	Don Woods, SD	RB	1986	Reuben Mayes, NO	RB	1998	Randy Moss, Min	WR
1975	Mike Thomas, Was	RB	1987	Troy Stradford, Mia	RB	1999	Edgerrin James, Ind	RB
1976	Sammy White, Min	WR	1988	John Stephens, NE	RB	2000	Mike Anderson, Den	RB
1977	Tony Dorsett, Dal	RB	1989	Barry Sanders, Det	RB	2001	Anthony Thomas, Chi	RB
1978	Earl Campbell, Hou	RB	1990	Emmitt Smith, Dal	RB	2002	Clinton Portis, Den	RB

AP Defensive Rookie of the Year

Selected by The Associated Press in balloting by a nationwide media panel. Given out since 1967.

Year		Pos	Year		Pos	Year		Pos
1967	Lem Barney, Det	CB	1980	Buddy Curry, Atl	LB	1992	Dale Carter, KC	CB
1968	Claude Humphrey, Atl	DE		& Al Richardson, Atl	LB	1993	Dana Stubblefield, SF	DT
1969	Joe Greene, Pit	DT	1981	Lawrence Taylor, NYG	LB	1994	Tim Bowens, Mia	DT
1970	Bruce Taylor, SF	CB	1982	Chip Banks, Cle	LB	1995	Hugh Douglas, NYJ	DE
1971	Isiah Robertson, Rams	LB	1983	Vernon Maxwell, Bal	LB	1996	Simeon Rice, Ari	DE
1972	Willie Buchanon, GB	CB	1984	Bill Maas, KC	DT	1997	Peter Boulware, Bal	LB
1973	Wally Chambers, Chi	DT	1985	Duane Bickett, Ind	LB	1998	Charles Woodson, Raiders	CB
1974	Jack Lambert, Pit	LB	1986	Leslie O'Neal, SD	DE	1999	Jevon Kearse, Ten	DE
1975	Robert Brazile, Hou	LB	1987	Shane Conlan, Buf	LB	2000	Brian Urlacher, Chi	LB
1976	Mike Haynes, NE	CB	1988	Erik McMillan, NYJ	S	2001	Kendrell Bell, Pit	LB
1977	A.J. Duhe, Mia	DE	1989	Derrick Thomas, KC	LB	2002	Julius Peppers, Car	DE
1978	Al Baker, Det	DE	1990	Mark Carrier, Chi	S			
1979	Jim Haslett, Buf	LB	1991	Mike Croel, Den	LB			

Coach of the Year

Presented by UPI to the top coach in the AFL-NFL (1955-69) and AFC-NFC (1970-96). In 1997, the UPI awards were discontinued. Awards beginning in 1997 are the consensus selections from presenters such as AP, The Maxwell Football Club of Philadelphia, *The Sporting News* and the Pro Football Writers Association. Records indicate the team's change in record from the previous season.

Multiple winners: Dan Reeves (4); Paul Brown, Chuck Knox and Don Shula (3); George Allen, Leeman Bennett, Mike Ditka, George Halas, Tom Landry, Marv Levy, Bill Parcells, Jack Pardee, Sam Rutigliano, Lou Saban, Allie Sherman, Marty Schottenheimer, Dick Vermeil and Bill Walsh (2).

Year		Improvement	Year		Improvement
1955	NFL–Joe Kuharich, Washington	3-9 to 8-4	1974	NFC–Don Coryell, St. Louis	4-9-1 to 10-4
1956	NFL–Buddy Parker, Detroit	3-9 to 9-3		AFC–Sid Gillman, Houston	1-13 to 7-7
1957	NFL–Paul Brown, Cleveland	5-7 to 9-2-1	1975	NFC–Tom Landry, Dallas	8-6 to 10-4
1958	NFL–Weeb Ewbank, Baltimore	7-5 to 9-3		AFC–Ted Marchibroda, Baltimore	2-12 to 10-4
1959	NFL–Vince Lombardi, Green Bay	1-10-1 to 7-5	1976	NFC–Jack Pardee, Chicago	4-10 to 7-7
1960	NFL–Buck Shaw, Philadelphia	7-5 to 10-2		AFC–Chuck Fairbanks, New England	3-11 to 11 3
	AFL–Lou Rymkus, Houston	10-4	1977	NFC–Leeman Bennett, Atlanta	4-10 to 7-7
1961	NFL–Allie Sherman, New York	6-4-2 to 10-3-1		AFC–Red Miller, Denver	9-5 to 12-2
	AFL–Wally Lemm, Houston	10-4 to 10-3-1	1978	NFC–Dick Vermeil, Philadelphia	5-9 to 9-7
1962	NFL–Allie Sherman, New York	10-3-1 to 12-2		AFC–Walt Michaels, New York	3-11 to 8-8
	AFL–Jack Faulkner, Denver	3-11 to 7-7	1979	NFC–Jack Pardee, Washington	8-8 to 10-6
1963	NFL–George Halas, Chicago	9-5 to 11-1-2		AFC–Sam Rutigliano, Cleveland	8-8 to 9-7
	AFL–Al Davis, Oakland	1-13 to 10-4	1980	NFC–Leeman Bennett, Atlanta	6-10 to 12-4
1964	NFL–Don Shula, Baltimore	8-6 to 12-2		AFC–Sam Rutigliano, Cleveland	9-7 to 11-5
	AFL–Lou Saban, Buffalo	7-6-1 to 12-2	1981	NFC–Bill Walsh, San Francisco	6-10 to 13-3
1965	NFL–George Halas, Chicago	5-9 to 9-5		AFC–Forrest Gregg, Cincinnati	6-10 to 12-4
	AFL–Lou Saban, Buffalo	12-2 to 10-3-1	1982	NFC–Joe Gibbs, Washington	8-8 to 8-1
1966	NFL–Tom Landry, Dallas	7-7 to 10-3-1		AFC–Tom Flores, Los Angeles	7-9 to 8-1
	AFL–Mike Holovak, Boston	4-8-2 to 8-4-2	1983	NFC–John Robinson, Los Angeles	2-7 to 9-7
1967	NFL–George Allen, Los Angeles	8-6 to 11-1-2		AFC–Chuck Knox, Seattle	4-5 to 9-7
	AFL–John Rauch, Oakland	8-5-1 to 13-1	1984	NFC–Bill Walsh, San Francisco	10-6 to 15-1
1968	NFL–Don Shula, Baltimore	11-1-2 to 13-1		AFC–Chuck Knox, Seattle	9-7 to 12-4
	AFL–Hank Stram, Kansas City	9-5 to 12-2	1985	NFC–Mike Ditka, Chicago	10-6 to 15-1
1969	NFL–Bud Grant, Minnesota	8-6 to 12-2		AFC–Raymond Berry, New England	9-7 to 11-5
	AFL–Paul Brown, Cincinnati	3-11 to 4-9-1	1986	NFC–Bill Parcells, New York	10-6 to 14-2
1970	NFC–Alex Webster, New York	6-8 to 9-5		AFC–Marty Schottenheimer, Cleveland	8-8 to 12-4
	AFC–Paul Brown, Cincinnati	4-9-1 to 8-6	1987	NFC–Jim Mora, New Orleans	7-9 to 12-3
1971	NFC–George Allen, Washington	6-8 to 9-4-1		AFC–Ron Meyer, Indianapolis	3-13 to 9-6
	AFC–Don Shula, Miami	10-4 to 10-3-1	1988	NFC–Mike Ditka, Chicago	11-4 to 12-4
1972	NFC–Dan Devine, Green Bay	4-8-2 to 10-4		AFC–Marv Levy, Buffalo	7-8 to 12-4
	AFC–Chuck Noll, Pittsburgh	6-8 to 11-3	1989	NFC–Lindy Infante, Green Bay	4-12 to 10-6
1973	NFC–Chuck Knox, Los Angeles	6-7-1 to 12-2		AFC–Dan Reeves, Denver	8-8 to 11-5
	AFC–John Ralston, Denver	5-9 to 7-5-2			

Annual Awards (Cont.)

Year		Improvement
1990	NFC–Jimmy Johnson, Dallas	.1-15 to 7-9
	AFC–Art Shell, Los Angeles	.8-8 to 12-4
1991	NFC–Wayne Fontes, Detroit	.6-10 to 12-4
	AFC–Dan Reeves, Denver	.5-11 to 12-4
1992	NFC–Dennis Green, Minnesota	.8-8 to 11-5
	AFC–Bobby Ross, San Diego	.4-12 to 11-5
1993	NFC–Dan Reeves, New York	.6-10 to 11-5
	AFC–Marv Levy, Buffalo	.11-5 to 12-4
1994	NFC–Dave Wannstedt, Chicago	.7-9 to 9-7
	AFC–Bill Parcells, New England	.5-11 to 10-6

Year		Improvement
1995	NFC–Ray Rhodes, Philadelphia	.7-9 to 10-6
	AFC–Marty Schottenheimer, Kansas City	.9-7 to 13-3
1996	NFC–Dom Capers, Carolina	.7-9 to 12-4
	AFC–Tom Coughlin, Jacksonville	.4-12 to 9-7
1997	NFL–Jim Fassel, NY Giants	.6-10 to 10-5-1
1998	NFL–Dan Reeves, Atlanta	.7-9 to 14-2
1999	NFL–Dick Vermeil, St. Louis	.4-12 to 13-3
2000	NFL–Jim Haslett, New Orleans	.3-13 to 10-6
2001	NFL–Dick Jauron, Chicago	.5-11 to 13-3
2002	NFL–Andy Reid, Philadelphia	.11-5 to 12-4

CANADIAN FOOTBALL

The Grey Cup

Earl Grey, the Governor-General of Canada (1904-11), donated a trophy in 1909 for the Rugby Football Championship of Canada. The trophy, which later became known as the Grey Cup, was originally open to competition for teams registered with the Canada Rugby Union. Since 1954, the Cup has gone to the champion of the Canadian Football League (CFL).

Overall multiple winners: Toronto Argonauts (14); Edmonton Eskimos (11); Winnipeg Blue Bombers (9); Hamilton Tiger-Cats (8); Ottawa Rough Riders (7); Calgary Stampeders, Hamilton Tigers and Montreal Alouettes (5); B.C. Lions and University of Toronto (4); Queen's University (3); Ottawa Senators, Sarnia Imperials, Saskatchewan Roughriders and Toronto Balmy Beach (2).

CFL multiple winners (since 1954): Edmonton (11); Hamilton and Winnipeg (7); Ottawa (5); B.C. Lions, Calgary, Montreal and Toronto (4); Saskatchewan (2).

Year Cup Final
1909 Univ. of Toronto 26, Toronto Parkdale 6
1910 Univ. of Toronto 16, Hamilton Tigers 7
1911 Univ. of Toronto 14, Toronto Argonauts 7
1912 Hamilton Alerts 11, Toronto Argonauts 4
1913 Hamilton Tigers 44, Toronto Parkdale 2
1914 Toronto Argonauts 14, Univ. of Toronto 2
1915 Hamilton Tigers 13, Toronto Rowing 7
1916-19 Not held (WWI)

1920 Univ. of Toronto 16, Toronto Argonauts 3
1921 Toronto Argonauts 23, Edmonton Eskimos 0
1922 Queens Univ. 13, Edmonton Elks 1
1923 Queens Univ. 54, Regina Roughriders 0
1924 Queens Univ. 11, Toronto Balmy Beach 3
1925 Ottawa Senators 24, Winnipeg Tigers 1
1926 Ottawa Senators 10, Univ. of Toronto 7
1927 Toronto Balmy Beach 9, Hamilton Tigers 6
1928 Hamilton Tigers 30, Regina Roughriders 0
1929 Hamilton Tigers 14, Regina Roughriders 3

1930 Toronto Balmy Beach 11, Regina Roughriders 6
1931 Montreal AAA 22, Regina Roughriders 0
1932 Hamilton Tigers 25, Regina Roughriders 6
1933 Toronto Argonauts 4, Sarnia Imperials 3

Year Cup Final
1934 Sarnia Imperials 20, Regina Roughriders 12
1935 Winnipeg 'Pegs 18, Hamilton Tigers 12
1936 Sarnia Imperials 26, Ottawa Rough Riders 20
1937 Toronto Argonauts 4, Winnipeg Blue Bombers 3
1938 Toronto Argonauts 30, Winnipeg Blue Bombers 7
1939 Winnipeg Blue Bombers 8, Ottawa Rough Riders 7

1940 Gm 1: Ottawa Rough Riders 8, Toronto B-Beach 2
     Gm 2: Toronto Rough Riders 12, Toronto B-Beach 4
1941 Winnipeg Blue Bombers 18, Ottawa Rough Riders 16
1942 Toronto RACF 8, Winnipeg RACF 5
1943 Hamilton Wildcats 23, Winnipeg RACF 14
1944 Montreal HMCS 7, Hamilton Wildcats 6
1945 Toronto Argonauts 35, Winnipeg Blue Bombers 0
1946 Toronto Argonauts 28, Winnipeg Blue Bombers 6
1947 Toronto Argonauts 10, Winnipeg Blue Bombers 9
1948 Calgary Stampeders 12, Ottawa Rough Riders 7
1949 Montreal Alouettes 28, Calgary Stampeders 15

1950 Toronto Argonauts 13, Winnipeg Blue Bombers 0
1951 Ottawa Rough Riders 21, Saskatch. Roughriders 14
1952 Toronto Argonauts 21, Edmonton Eskimos 11
1953 Hamilton Tiger-Cats 12, Winnipeg Blue Bombers 6

Year	Winner	Head Coach	Score	Loser	Head Coach	Site
1954	Edmonton	Frank (Pop) Ivy	26-25	Montreal	Doug Walker	Toronto
1955	Edmonton	Frank (Pop) Ivy	34-19	Montreal	Doug Walker	Vancouver
1956	Edmonton	Frank (Pop) Ivy	50-27	Montreal	Doug Walker	Toronto
1957	Hamilton	Jim Trimble	32-7	Winnipeg	Bud Grant	Toronto
1958	Winnipeg	Bud Grant	35-28	Hamilton	Jim Trimble	Vancouver
1959	Winnipeg	Bud Grant	21-7	Hamilton	Jim Trimble	Toronto
1960	Ottawa	Frank Clair	16-6	Edmonton	Eagle Keys	Vancouver
1961	Winnipeg	Bud Grant	21-14(OT)	Hamilton	Jim Trimble	Toronto
1962	Winnipeg	Bud Grant	28-27*	Hamilton	Jim Trimble	Toronto
1963	Hamilton	Ralph Sazio	21-10	B.C. Lions	Dave Skrien	Vancouver
1964	B.C. Lions	Dave Skrien	34-24	Hamilton	Ralph Sazio	Toronto
1965	Hamilton	Ralph Sazio	22-16	Winnipeg	Bud Grant	Toronto
1966	Saskatchewan	Eagle Keys	29-14	Ottawa	Frank Clair	Vancouver
1967	Hamilton	Ralph Sazio	24-1	Saskatchewan	Eagle Keys	Ottawa
1968	Ottawa	Frank Clair	24-21	Calgary	Jerry Williams	Toronto
1969	Ottawa	Frank Clair	29-11	Saskatchewan	Eagle Keys	Montreal
1970	Montreal	Sam Etcheverry	23-10	Calgary	Jim Duncan	Toronto
1971	Calgary	Jim Duncan	14-11	Toronto	Leo Cahill	Vancouver
1972	Hamilton	Jerry Williams	13-10	Saskatchewan	Dave Skrien	Hamilton
1973	Ottawa	Jack Gotta	22-18	Edmonton	Ray Jauch	Toronto
1974	Montreal	Marv Levy	20-7	Edmonton	Ray Jauch	Vancouver

Year	Winner	Head Coach	Score	Loser	Head Coach	Site
1975	Edmonton	Ray Jauch	9-8	Montreal	Marv Levy	Calgary
1976	Ottawa	George Brancato	23-20	Saskatchewan	John Payne	Toronto
1977	Montreal	Marv Levy	41-6	Edmonton	Hugh Campbell	Montreal
1978	Edmonton	Hugh Campbell	20-13	Montreal	Joe Scannella	Toronto
1979	Edmonton	Hugh Campbell	17-9	Montreal	Joe Scannella	Montreal
1980	Edmonton	Hugh Campbell	48-10	Hamilton	John Payne	Toronto
1981	Edmonton	Hugh Campbell	26-23	Ottawa	George Brancato	Montreal
1982	Edmonton	Hugh Campbell	32-16	Toronto	Bob O'Billovich	Toronto
1983	Toronto	Bob O'Billovich	18-17	B.C. Lions	Don Matthews	Vancouver
1984	Winnipeg	Cal Murphy	47-17	Hamilton	Al Bruno	Edmonton
1985	B.C. Lions	Don Matthews	37-24	Hamilton	Al Bruno	Montreal
1986	Hamilton	Al Bruno	39-15	Edmonton	Jack Parker	Vancouver
1987	Edmonton	Joe Faragalli	38-36	Toronto	Bob O'Billovich	Vancouver
1988	Winnipeg	Mike Riley	22-21	B.C. Lions	Larry Donovan	Ottawa
1989	Saskatchewan	John Gregory	43-40	Hamilton	Al Bruno	Toronto
1990	Winnipeg	Mike Riley	50-11	Edmonton	Joe Faragalli	Vancouver
1991	Toronto	Adam Rita	36-21	Calgary	Wally Buono	Winnipeg
1992	Calgary	Wally Buono	24-10	Winnipeg	Urban Bowman	Toronto
1993	Edmonton	Ron Lancaster	33-23	Winnipeg	Cal Murphy	Calgary
1994	B.C. Lions	Dave Ritchie	26-23	Baltimore	Don Matthews	Vancouver
1995	Baltimore	Don Matthews	37-20	Calgary	Wally Buono	Regina
1996	Toronto	Don Matthews	43-37	Edmonton	Ron Lancaster	Hamilton
1997	Toronto	Don Matthews	47-23	Saskatchewan	Jim Daley	Edmonton
1998	Calgary	Wally Buono	26-24	Hamilton	Ron Lancaster	Winnipeg
1999	Hamilton	Ron Lancaster	32-21	Calgary	Wally Buono	Vancouver
2000	B.C. Lions	Steve Buratto	28-26	Montreal	Charlie Taaffe	Calgary
2001	Calgary	Wally Buono	27-19	Winnipeg	Dave Ritchie	Montreal
2002	Montreal	Don Matthews	25-16	Edmonton	Tom Higgins	Edmonton

*Halted by fog in 4th quarter, final 9:29 played the following day.

CFL Most Outstanding Player

Regular season Player of the Year as selected by The Football Reporters of Canada since 1953.

Multiple winners: Doug Flutie (6); Russ Jackson and Jackie Parker (3); Dieter Brock, Ron Lancaster and Mike Pringle (2).

Year		Year		Year	
1953	Billy Vessels, Edmonton, RB	1970	Ron Lancaster, Saskatch., QB	1987	Tom Clements, Winnipeg, QB
1954	Sam Etcheverry, Montreal, QB	1971	Don Jonas, Winnipeg, QB	1988	David Williams, B.C. Lions, WR
1955	Pat Abbruzzi, Montreal, RB	1972	Garney Henley, Hamilton, WR	1989	Tracy Ham, Edmonton, QB
1956	Hal Patterson, Montreal, E-DB	1973	Geo. McGowan, Edmonton, WR	1990	Mike Clemons, Toronto, RB
1957	Jackie Parker, Edmonton, QB	1974	Tom Wilkinson, Edmonton, QB	1991	Doug Flutie, B.C. Lions, QB
1958	Jackie Parker, Edmonton, QB	1975	Willie Burden, Calgary, RB	1992	Doug Flutie, Calgary, QB
1959	Johnny Bright, Edmonton, RB	1976	Ron Lancaster, Saskatch., QB	1993	Doug Flutie, Calgary, QB
1960	Jackie Parker, Edmonton, QB	1977	Jimmy Edwards, Hamilton, RB	1994	Doug Flutie, Calgary, QB
1961	Bernie Faloney, Hamilton, QB	1978	Tony Gabriel, Ottawa, TE	1995	Mike Pringle, Baltimore, RB
1962	George Dixon, Montreal, RB	1979	David Green, Montreal, RB	1996	Doug Flutie, Toronto, QB
1963	Russ Jackson, Ottawa, QB	1980	Dieter Brock, Winnipeg, QB	1997	Doug Flutie, Toronto, QB
1964	Lovell Coleman, Calgary, RB	1981	Dieter Brock, Winnipeg, QB	1998	Mike Pringle, Montreal, RB
1965	George Reed, Saskatchewan, RB	1982	Condredge Holloway, Tor., QB	1999	Danny McManus, Hamilton, QB
1966	Russ Jackson, Ottawa, QB	1983	Warren Moon, Edmonton, QB	2000	Dave Dickenson, Calgary, QB
1967	Peter Liske, Calgary, QB	1984	Willard Reaves, Winnipeg, RB	2001	Khari Jones, Winnipeg, QB
1968	Bill Symons, Toronto, RB	1985	Merv Fernandez, B.C. Lions, WR	2002	Milt Stegall, Winnipeg, SB
1969	Russ Jackson, Ottawa, QB	1986	James Murphy, Winnipeg, WR		

All-Time CFL Leaders

Through the 2002 season. Players active in 2002 are in **bold** type.

Passing Yards

		Yrs	Att	Cmp	Yards	Cmp Pct	Avg Gain	TD	Int	Rating
1	**Damon Allen**	18	7425	4107	58,407	55.3	14.2	317	238	81.8
2	Ron Lancaster	19	6233	3384	50,535	54.3	14.9	333	396	72.4
3	Matt Dunigan	14	5476	3057	43,857	55.8	14.3	306	211	84.5
4	**Danny McManus**	13	5291	2869	42,528	54.2	14.8	209	215	77.0
5	Doug Flutie	8	4854	2975	41,355	61.3	13.9	270	155	93.9

Rushing Yards

		Yrs	Car	Yards	Avg	TD
1	George Reed	13	3243	16,116	5.0	134
2	**Mike Pringle**	11	2430	13,907	5.7	104
3	Johnny Bright	13	1969	10,909	5.5	69
4	**Damon Allen**	18	1536	10,468	6.8	82
5	Normie Kwong	13	1745	9,022	5.2	78

Receiving Yards

		Yrs	Ct	Yards	Avg	TD
1	Allen Pitts	11	966	14,891	15.4	117
2	**Darren Flutie**	12	972	14,359	14.8	66
3	Ray Elgaard	14	830	13,198	15.9	78
4	Don Narcisse	13	919	12,366	13.5	75
5	Brian Kelly	9	575	11,169	19.4	97

NFL EUROPE

The World League of American Football was formed in 1991 with hopes of expanding the popularity of the NFL to overseas markets. Funded by the NFL, the inaugural league in 1991 consisted of three European teams (London, Barcelona and Frankfurt), and seven North American teams (New York/New Jersey, Orlando, Montreal, Raleigh-Durham, Birmingham, Sacramento and San Antonio). The second season used the same format with Columbus, Ohio, replacing Raleigh-Durham.

In the fall of 1992, the NFL and WLAF Board of Directors voted to restructure the league to include more European teams. Play was subsequently suspended. In 1993, NFL clubs approved a six-team European-only league to resume play in 1995 with teams in Amsterdam, Barcelona, Frankfurt, London, Rhein and Scotland. In January 1998, the name of the league was changed to NFL Europe. Berlin was added for the 1999 season and London was disbanded.

The World Bowl

In 1991 and 1992, when the league consisted of three divisions, the top team from each division and one wild-card team advanced to the playoffs, with the winners of each game advancing to the World Bowl. There was no game played in 1993 or 1994. Since 1995, the top two regular season teams advance directly to the World Bowl.

Multiple Winners: Frankfurt (3); Berlin and Rhein (2).

Year	Winner	Head Coach	Score	Loser	Head Coach	Site
1991	London	Larry Kennan	21-0	Barcelona	Jack Bicknell	London
1992	Sacramento	Kay Stephenson	21-17	Orlando	Galen Hall	Montreal
1995	Frankfurt	Ernie Stautner	26-22	Amsterdam	Al Luginbill	Amsterdam
1996	Scotland	Jim Criner	32-27	Frankfurt	Ernie Stautner	Edinburgh, Scot.
1997	Barcelona	Jack Bicknell	38-24	Rhein	Galen Hall	Barcelona
1998	Rhein	Galen Hall	34-10	Frankfurt	Dick Curl	Frankfurt
1999	Frankfurt	Dick Curl	38-24	Barcelona	Jack Bicknell	Dusseldorf
2000	Rhein	Galen Hall	13-10	Scotland	Jim Criner	Frankfurt
2001	Berlin	Peter Vaas	24-17	Barcelona	Jack Bicknell	Amsterdam
2002	Berlin	Peter Vaas	26-20	Rhein	Pete Kuharchek	Dusseldorf
2003	Frankfurt	Doug Graber	35-16	Rhein	Pete Kuharchek	Glasgow

World Bowl MVP

Year		Year		Year	
1991	Dan Crossman, London, S	1997	Jon Kitna, Barcelona, QB	2001	Jonathan Quinn, Berlin, QB
1992	Davis Archer, Sacramento, QB	1998	Jim Arellanes, Rhein, QB	2002	Dane Looker, Berlin, WR
1995	Paul Justin, Frankfurt, QB	1999	Andy McCullough, Frankfurt, WR	2003	Jonas Lewis, Frankfurt, RB
1996	Yo Murphy, Scotland, WR	2000	Aaron Stecker, Scotland, RB		

ARENA FOOTBALL

The Arena Football League debuted in June of 1987 with four teams in Chicago, Denver, Pittsburgh and Washington D.C. Currently there are 16 teams in the league, divided into two conferences and four divisions.

ArenaBowl

Multiple Winners: Tampa Bay (5); Detroit (4); Arizona and Orlando (2).

Bowl	Year	Winner	Head Coach	Score	Loser	Head Coach	Site
I	1987	Denver	Tim Marcum	45-16	Pittsburgh	Joe Haering	Pittsburgh
II	1988	Detroit	Tim Marcum	24-13	Chicago	Perry Moss	Chicago
III	1989	Detroit	Tim Marcum	39-26	Pittsburgh	Joe Haering	Detroit
IV	1990	Detroit	Perry Moss	51-27	Dallas	Ernie Stautner	Detroit
V	1991	Tampa Bay	Fran Curci	48-42	Detroit	Tim Marcum	Detroit
VI	1992	Detroit	Tim Marcum	56-38	Orlando	Perry Moss	Orlando
VII	1993	Tampa Bay	Lary Kuharich	51-31	Detroit	Tim Marcum	Detroit
VIII	1994	Arizona	Danny White	36-31	Orlando	Perry Moss	Orlando
IX	1995	Tampa Bay	Tim Marcum	48-35	Orlando	Perry Moss	St. Petersburg
X	1996	Tampa Bay	Tim Marcum	42-38	Iowa	John Gregory	Des Moines
XI	1997	Arizona	Danny White	55-33	Iowa	John Gregory	Phoenix
XII	1998	Orlando	Jay Gruden	62-31	Tampa Bay	Tim Marcum	Tampa
XIII	1999	Albany	Mike Dailey	59-48	Orlando	Jay Gruden	Albany
XIV	2000	Orlando	Jay Gruden	41-38	Nashville	Pat Sperduto	Orlando
XV	2001	Grand Rapids	Michael Trigg	64-42	Nashville	Pat Sperduto	Grand Rapids
XVI	2002	San Jose	Darren Arbet	52-14	Arizona	Danny White	San Jose
XVII	2003	Tampa Bay	Tim Marcum	43-29	Arizona	Danny White	Tampa

ArenaBowl MVP

Multiple Winners: George LaFrance (3); Jay Gruden (2).

Year		Year		Year	
1987	Gary Mullen, Denver, WR	1993	Jay Gruden, Tampa Bay, QB	1999	Eddie Brown, Albany, OS
1988	Steve Griffin, Detroit, WR/DB	1994	Sherdrick Bonner, Arizona, QB	2000	Connell Maynor, Orlando, QB
1989	George LaFrance, Detroit, WR/DB	1995	George LaFrance, Tampa Bay, OS	2001	Terrill Shaw, Grand Rapids, OS
1990	Art Schlichter, Detroit, QB	1996	Stevie Thomas, Tampa Bay, WR/LB	2002	John Dutton, San Jose, QB
1991	Jay Gruden, Tampa Bay, QB	1997	Donnie Davis, Arizona, QB	2003	Lawrence Samuels, Tampa Bay, WR/LB
1992	George LaFrance, Detroit, OS	1998	Rick Hamilton, Orlando, FB/LB		

College Basketball

Jim Phelan got win 830 in the final game of his 49-year coaching career at Mt. St. Mary's.

Orange County

Syracuse head coach Jim Boeheim, behind freshman star Carmelo Anthony, finally finds that elusive national title in the Big Easy.

Chris Fowler
is the host of ESPN's College GameDay

There's something about the unlikely marriage of the Final Four and the city of New Orleans that produces Monday night magic. The NCAA's image of wholesome Americana doesn't quite match the carefree party atmosphere of the Big Easy and there may not be a worse place to actually try to watch a basketball game than the cavernous Superdome. But Final Fours at the French Quarter always equal high drama.

In 1982, a freshman named Michael Jordan hit the biggest shot in North Carolina's triumph over Georgetown. Dean Smith's first national title was aided by that infamous pass from Hoya Freddie Brown right in to the hands of surprised Tar Heel James Worthy.

Eleven years later, Chris Webber's time out gaffe helped seal another Tar Heel title.

But as the 2003 Final Four unfolded, the championship classic most often recalled was the one labeled "The Keith Smart game." The little jumper from the wing by Bob Knight's first JUCO transfer remained one of the most vivid Final Four images.

Had it really been 16 years? For Jim Boeheim, it seemed like last night. How much different would the ensuing years have been for the often maligned coach if Derrick Coleman had just sealed the win with his free throws...or if Smart's shot had bounced off iron? Unfairly, legacies of a three-decade career are sometimes defined by the arc of a single jump shot.

Boeheim had handled the inevitable questions admirably. Having the ultimate trophy snatched away in the final seconds? He refused to label it a "low point." It was just the opposite, he claimed.

But as Boeheim brought one of the youngest team's in Final Four history on to the Superdome court for the championship game against Kansas, history hardly seemed relevant. The current Orangemen, which included three freshman and four sophomores in the nine-man rotation, were in diapers when Smart drained that jumper. They had proven throughout the season, and particularly in the NCAA run, that nothing could phase or frighten them.

Twelve times Syracuse had rallied from second half deficits to win. In an

Getty Images/Craig Jones

*After 22 tries **Jim Boeheim** and Syracuse finally finished the NCAA Tournament on top.*

NCAA second round game, they were under an Oklahoma State avalanche, down 25-8 just twelve minutes in. Boeheim admitted his mind had drifted to tee times. Fab freshmen Carmelo Anthony and Gerry McNamara, who had carried the team all season, were out of mulligans after a combined 0-12 in the first half.

But Boeheim's shift from his trademark zone to an aggressive press sparked a run. Finally, the shots started falling. The most memorable came from McNamara, the tough Irish kid from Scranton. Slamming heads with a Cowboy, McNamara had cut open his head. As blood rolled down into his eye, he nailed a three-pointer, then headed to the locker room to get patched up. After returning, he nailed three more threes. Syracuse was moving on and McNamara was headed to the

hospital for a half dozen stitches. The comeback answered all questions about the team's toughness or lack of seasoning.

Still, Syracuse's journey to Monday night's big game had been overshadowed. The entire NCAA tournament had played out during the early days of the war in Iraq. How you could you keep your eyes on basketball, when the nightly pictures of bombs exploding in Baghdad signaled a frightening new chapter in history, and still more unease about domestic security?

On the courts, the headline had been the 14-point regional final loss by Kentucky, the biggest pre-tournament favorite since UNLV in 1991. Once the media assembled in New Orleans, the feeding frenzy centered on Roy Williams' impending but unannounced move to North Carolina and Anthony's

AP/Wide World Photos

Connecticut's *women's program, led by Player of the Year* ***Diana Taurasi*** *(left, with hand raised), won its second straight national championship and the third in the last four seasons.*

unstated intentions to turn pro. In fact, the brilliance of the prodigy from Baltimore's mean streets had been eclipsed all season by another prodigy, from Ohio.

"LeBron in Suspended!" "LeBron is Back!" "LeBron Scores Fifty!" "LeBron to be the Top Pick!" Every move the high school kid made was news. The fuss over Anthony, who had passed on the draft a year earlier, was muted by the bling-bling buzz of LeBron James' world.

But Final Four weekend belonged to the man called "Melo." Syracuse dismantled Oklahoma in the semis and Kansas smothered the brilliant Dwayne Wade, routing Marquette. It set up a couldn't lose final for sentimental storylines. Either Williams or Boeheim would finally be rewarded for sustained excellence with a climb up the ladder to cut out a piece of championship game net.

In the first half, it was Syracuse shredding the nets from long distance. McNamara connected on six of the Orangemen's 10 treys in the first 20 minutes, four from almost the same spot on the left wing. It was a breathtaking display of pressure shooting. Fifteen minutes in, the Orange had rolled to an 18-point lead.

Besides McNamara's barrage, what I will never forget about the night, was the news coming from the ear piece connected to my tiny radio: a house believed to contain Saddam Hussein and his two sons had been hit with 2000 pound bombs. Was he dead? Reports were fuzzy. I looked behind the press table, to see empty seats where the CBS executives had been seated.

Would the second half of the final be pre-empted by Dan Rather with historic
continued on page 278

Dick Vitale's Ten Biggest Stories of the Year in College Basketball

10 Coaching Greats say farewell. Lefty Driesell, a character on the sidelines, says bye-bye to the profession he loves after becoming the only coach to win at least 100 games at four different schools (Davidson, Maryland, James Madison and Georgia State) and Jim Phelan, after 49 years and 830 wins at Mount St. Mary's, walks off the court for the final time.

9 No ACC team in the Final Four. The proud league, a regular participant at the Final Four, is shutout from the big party in New Orleans in 2003. It's just the third time since 1985 that the ACC hasn't seen the national semis.

8 Butler makes Sweet 16. After being left out of the big dance the year before, the Bulldogs make a statement for all mid-majors by advancing to the Sweet 16, beating Mississippi State and Louisville along the way.

7 UCLA struggles and Steve Lavin is gone. The Bruins stumble big time, finishing the season at 10-19. Coach Lavin, under the microscope since day one, gets the ziggy.

6 Scandals rock college hoops. Troubles at Georgia, St. Bonaventure, Fresno State and Baylor make headlines and cast a dark cloud on college basketball.

5 Roy Williams says so-long to Kansas. He leaves the Jayhawks and returns to his alma mater, North Carolina. Williams hopes to get the Tar Heels back that Carolina pride.

4 Matt Doherty struggles at North Carolina and loses his job. The Tar Heels, despite a solid start, struggle and fail to make the NCAA tournament, costing coach Doherty his job.

3 Kentucky dominates the SEC. Consensus Coach of the Year Tubby Smith and his Wildcats go unblemished in the tough SEC. You don't see that happen too often in major conferences these days.

2 Marquette makes the Final Four. There is a new star on the coaching horizon in Tom Crean. He leads the Golden Eagles on a magical Final Four run, with All-America junior guard Dwayne Wade and company shocking favorite Kentucky in the NCAA tournament.

1 Syracuse wins it all. Jimmy Boeheim finally does it and shocks America as the underdog Orangemen win the gold trophy, beating Kansas, 81-78, in the national championship game. Diaper dandy Carmelo Anthony is super, scintillating and sensational for the 'Cuse.

continued from page 276

news? It was hard to focus on the floor.

Suddenly, though, Kansas was finding its focus. Five minutes into the second half, Kirk Hinrich's three-point play cut the lead to three. KU was in the game to stay. The margin was still three when KU's Michael Lee rose up on the wing for a three-pointer in the final seconds. After fighting from behind all night...after all the misses, would this be the shot to give the Jayhawks new life in overtime? Would the unlikely Lee become another Keith Smart?

No. Thanks to "the helicopter."

To watch Hakim Warrick play is to understand his nickname. Long, spidery arms that whirl in the face of shooters and a quick elevation to snag rebounds. From nowhere, Warrick swooped toward Lee and swatted his game-tying attempt into the seats. Seconds before, Warrick had clanged a couple of free throws that would have iced the game. This was redemption.

But wait. There was one final chance for KU...1.3 seconds...One last three pointer. It hit nothing but air. The Syracuse celebration erupted onto center court.

At the bottom of the pile, a team manager could be spotted planting a kiss on Anthony, who lay squashed flat on his back. Boeheim and Williams met for a handshake, the subtext of which perhaps only coaches could understand.

For better or worse, the arc of a basketball had defined personal legacies once again.

Frosh Frolic

Carmelo Anthony's 33 points in Syracuse's national semifinal win over Texas set a record for most points scored by a freshman in a Final Four Game. Here's a look at the top scoring performances by freshman in the Final Four since they became eligible in 1973.

Year	Player	Points
2003	Carmelo Anthony, Syracuse	33
1997	Mike O'Koren, UNC	31
1995	Toby Bailey, UCLA	26
1985	Pervis Ellison, Louisville	25
1975	Jack Givens, Kentucky	24

Delisted and Delighted

Entering the season, Jim Boeheim was atop the list of coaches with the most NCAA tournament wins without a national title. Boeheim not only got off the list in 2003, he kept two men on it. Roy Williams and Eddie Sutton both lost to Boeheim's Syracuse squad in this year's tourney. Here's a look at the list entering the 2002-03 season.

Coach	Wins
Jim Boeheim	32
Eddie Sutton	32
Roy Williams	29
Guy Lewis	26
John Chaney	23

Note: Roy Williams has 34 tournament wins and Eddie Sutton has 33 tournament wins entering the 2003-04 season.

2002-2003
Season in Review

SPORTS ALMANAC

Final Regular Season AP Men's Top 25 Poll
Taken **before** start of NCAA tournament.

The sportswriters & broadcasters poll: first place votes in parentheses; records through Monday, March 17, 2003; total points (based on 25 for 1st, 24 for 2nd, etc.); record in NCAA tourney and team lost to; head coach (career years and record including 2003 postseason), and preseason ranking. Teams in **bold** type went on to reach NCAA Final Four. Indiana, which did not make the final regular-season Top 25, was the other Final Four team.

		Mar. 17 Record	Points	NCAA Recap	Head Coach	Preseason Rank
1	Kentucky (70)	29-3	1774	3-1 (Marquette)	Tubby Smith (13 yrs: 288-109)	17
2	Arizona (1)	25-3	1686	3-1 (Kansas)	Lute Olson (30 yrs: 690-240)	1
3	Oklahoma	24-6	1589	3-1 (Syracuse)	Kelvin Sampson (19 yrs: 391-228)	3
4	Pittsburgh	26-4	1539	2-1 (Marquette)	Ben Howland (9 yrs: 168-99)	5
5	**Texas**	22-6	1498	4-1 (Syracuse)	Rick Barnes (16 yrs: 318-184)	4
6	**Kansas**	25-7	1450	5-1 (Syracuse)	Roy Williams (15 yrs: 417-100)	2
7	Duke	24-6	1224	2-1 (Kansas)	Mike Krzyzewski (28 yrs: 663-233)	6
8	Wake Forest	24-5	1160	1-1 (Auburn)	Skip Prosser (10 yrs: 211-97)	NR
9	**Marquette**	23-5	1147	4-1 (Kansas)	Tom Crean (4 yrs: 83-41)	18
10	Florida	24-7	1141	1-1 (Michigan St.)	Billy Donovan (9 yrs: 184-93)	7
11	Illinois	24-6	1101	1-1 (Notre Dame)	Bill Self (10 yrs: 208-104)	NR
12	Xavier	25-5	1006	1-1 (Maryland)	Thad Matta (3 yrs: 76-20)	10
13	**Syracuse**	24-5	968	6-0	Jim Boeheim (27 yrs: 653-226)	NR
14	Louisville	24-6	826	1-1 (Butler)	Rick Pitino (17 yrs: 396-144)	NR
15	Creighton	29-4	605	0-1 (C. Michigan)	Dana Altman (14 yrs: 258-167)	NR
16	Dayton	25-5	584	0-1 (Tulsa)	Oliver Purnell (15 yrs: 256-191)	NR
17	Maryland	19-9	580	3-1 (Michigan St.)	Gary Williams (25 yrs: 502-281)	13
18	Stanford	23-8	539	1-1 (Connecticut)	Mike Montgomery (25 yrs: 517-242)	NR
19	Memphis	23-6	468	0-1 (Arizona St.)	John Calipari (11 yrs: 264-102)	NR
20	Mississippi St.	21-9	372	0-1 (Butler)	Rick Stansbury (5 yrs: 100-60)	12
21	Wisconsin	22-7	369	2-1 (Kentucky)	Bo Ryan (19 yrs: 426-124)	NR
22	Notre Dame	22-9	313	2-1 (Arizona)	Mike Brey (8 yrs: 165-83)	NR
23	Connecticut	21-9	225	2-1 (Texas)	Jim Calhoun (31 yrs: 646-296)	15
24	Missouri	21-10	199	1-1 (Marquette)	Quin Snyder (4 yrs: 84-49)	19
25	Georgia	19-8	141	did not play	Jim Harrick (23 yrs: 471-234)	16

Others receiving votes: 26. **St. Joseph's** (23-6) 107 points; 27. **Oklahoma St.** (21-9) 100; 28. **Oregon** (23-9) 83; 29. **California** (21-8) 64; 30. **Weber St.** (26-5) 33; 31. **Utah** (24-7) 31; 32. **Butler** (25-5) and **LSU** (21-10) 27; 34. **Southern Illinois** (24-6) 23; 35. **N.C. State** (19-15) 18; 36. **Central Michigan** (24-6) 12; 37. **Kent St.** (21-10) 8; 38. **Holy Cross** (26-4) 7; 39. **BYU** (23-8), **Pennsylvania** (22-5) and **Western Kentucky** (24-8); 42. **Troy St.** (26-5) 4; 43. **Manhattan** (23-6); 44. **Michigan St.** (19-12) 2, 45. **NC-Wilmington** (24-6), **Tulsa** (22-9) and **Wisc-Milwaukee** (24-7).

NCAA Men's Division I Tournament Seeds

	WEST		MIDWEST		SOUTH		EAST
1	Arizona (25-3)	1	Kentucky (29-3)	1	Texas (22-6)	1	Oklahoma (24-6)
2	Kansas (25-7)	2	Pittsburgh (26-4)	2	Florida (24-7)	2	Wake Forest (24-5)
3	Duke (24-6)	3	Marquette (23-5)	3	Xavier (25-5)	3	Syracuse (24-5)
4	Illinois (24-6)	4	Dayton (25-5)	4	Stanford (23-8)	4	Louisville (24-6)
5	Notre Dame (22-9)	5	Wisconsin (22-7)	5	Connecticut (21-9)	5	Mississippi St. (21-9)
6	Creighton (29-4)	6	Missouri (21-10)	6	Maryland (19-9)	6	Oklahoma St. (21-9)
7	Memphis (23-6)	7	Indiana (20-12)	7	Michigan St. (19-12)	7	St. Joseph's (23-6)
8	Cincinnati (17-11)	8	Oregon (23-9)	8	LSU (21-10)	8	California (21-8)
9	Gonzaga (23-8)	9	Utah (24-7)	9	Purdue (18-10)	9	N.C. State (18-12)
10	Arizona St. (19-11)	10	Alabama (17-11)	10	Colorado (20-11)	10	Auburn (21-9)
11	C. Michigan (24-6)	11	So. Illinois (24-6)	11	NC-Wilmington (24-6)	11	Pennsylvania (22-5)
12	Wisc-Milwaukee (24-7)	12	Weber St. (26-5)	12	BYU (23-8)	12	Butler (25-5)
13	Western Kentucky (24-8)	13	Tulsa (22-9)	13	San Diego (18-11)	13	Austin Peay (23-7)
14	Colorado St. (19-13)	14	Holy Cross (26-4)	14	Troy St. (26-5)	14	Manhattan (23-6)
15	Utah St. (24-8)	15	Wagner (21-10)	15	Sam Houston St. (23-6)	15	E. Tennessee St. (20-10)
16	Vermont (21-11)	16	IUPUI (20-13)	16	NC-Asheville* (15-16)	16	So. Carolina St. (20-10)

*NC-Asheville defeated Texas Southern, 92-84, in the NCAA Tournament play-in game for a berth in the field of 64.

2003 NCAA Tournament Men's Division

Rounds: 1st ROUND March 20-21 · 2nd ROUND March 22-23 · SWEET 16 March 27-28 · ELITE EIGHT March 29-30 · FINAL FOUR April 5 · NATIONAL CHAMPIONSHIP · FINAL FOUR April 5 · ELITE EIGHT March 29-30 · SWEET 16 March 27-28 · 2nd ROUND March 22-23 · 1st ROUND March 20-21

SOUTH

1st Round
- (1) Texas 82 / (16) NC-Asheville 61
- (8) LSU 56 / (9) Purdue 80
- (5) Connecticut 58 / (12) BYU 53
- (4) Stanford 77 / (13) San Diego 69
- (6) Maryland 75 / (11) NC-Wilmin. 73
- (3) Xavier 59 / (14) Troy St. 71
- (7) Michigan St. 79 / (10) Colorado 64
- (2) Florida 85 / (15) Sam Hou 55
- NC-Asheville (ot) 92 / Texas Southern 84
- Play-in Game to South (16) seed

2nd Round: Texas 77, Purdue 67, Connecticut 85, Stanford 74, Maryland 77, Xavier 64, Michigan St. 68, Florida 46

Sweet 16: Texas 82, Connecticut 78, Maryland 58, Michigan St. 60

Elite Eight: Texas 85, Michigan St. 76

Final Four: Texas 84

EAST

1st Round
- (1) Oklahoma 71 / (16) S. Carolina St. 54
- (8) California 76 / (9) N.C. State 74
- (5) Miss. St. 46 / (12) Butler 47
- (4) Louisville 86 / (13) Austin Peay 64
- (6) Okla. St. 77 / (11) Penn 63
- (3) Syracuse 76 / (14) Manhattan 65
- (7) St. Joseph's 63 / (10) Auburn (ot) 65
- (2) Wake Forest 76 / (15) E. Tenn. St. 73

2nd Round: Oklahoma 74, California 65, Butler 79, Louisville 71, Oklahoma St. 56, Syracuse 68, Auburn 68, Wake Forest 78

Sweet 16: Oklahoma 65, Butler 54, Syracuse 79, Auburn 78

Elite Eight: Oklahoma 47, Syracuse 63

Final Four: Syracuse 95

MIDWEST

1st Round
- (1) Kentucky 95 / (16) IUPUI 64
- (8) Oregon 58 / (9) Utah 60
- (5) Wisconsin 81 / (12) Weber St. 74
- (4) Dayton 84 / (13) Tulsa
- (1) Missouri 72 / So. Illinois 71
- (3) Marquette 72 / (14) Holy Cross 68
- (7) Indiana 67 / (10) Alabama 62
- (2) Pittsburgh 87 / (15) Wagner 61

2nd Round: Kentucky 74, Utah 54, Wisconsin 61, Tulsa 60, Missouri 92, Marquette (ot) 101, Indiana 52, Pittsburgh 74

Sweet 16: Kentucky 63, Wisconsin 57, Marquette 77, Pittsburgh 74

Elite Eight: Kentucky 69, Marquette 83

Final Four: Marquette 61

WEST

1st Round
- (1) Arizona 80 / (16) Vermont 51
- (8) Cincinnati 69 / (9) Gonzaga 74
- (5) Notre Dame 70 / (12) WI-Milw. 69
- (4) Illinois 65 / (13) W. Kentucky 60
- (6) Creighton 73 / (11) C. Michigan 79
- (3) Duke 67 / (14) Colorado St. 57
- (7) Memphis 71 / (10) Arizona St. 84
- (2) Kansas 64 / (15) Utah St. 61

2nd Round: Arizona (2ot) 96, Gonzaga 95, Notre Dame 68, Illinois 60, C. Michigan 60, Duke 86, Arizona St. 76, Kansas 108

Sweet 16: Arizona 88, Notre Dame 71, Duke 65, Kansas 69

Elite Eight: Arizona 75, Kansas 78

Final Four: Kansas 94

NATIONAL CHAMPIONSHIP

Syracuse 81
Kansas 78

New Orleans

The Superdome
New Orleans, Louisiana
Monday, April 7, 2003

NCAA FINAL FOUR 2003

NCAA Men's Championship Game

65th NCAA Division I Championship Game. **Date:** Monday, April 7, at the Superdome in New Orleans. **Coaches:** Jim Boeheim of Syracuse and Roy Williams of Kansas. **Favorite:** Kansas by 4½.
Attendance: 54,524; **Officials:** Gerald Boudreaux, Reginald Cofer, Dick Cartmell; **TV Rating:** 12.6/19 share (CBS).

Syracuse 81

	Min	FG M-A	FT M-A	Pts	Reb O-T	A	PF
Hakim Warrick	.31	2-4	2-4	6	0-2	1	3
Carmelo Anthony	.37	7-16	3-4	20	4-10	7	2
Craig Forth	.24	3-4	0-1	6	1-3	0	5
Gerry McNamara	.34	6-13	0-0	18	0-0	1	2
Kueth Duany	.13	4-6	1-2	11	3-4	0	3
Josh Pace	.21	4-9	0-0	8	1-8	2	2
Billy Edelin	.27	4-10	4-6	12	0-2	2	1
Jeremy McNeil	.13	0-1	0-0	0	2-5	0	4
TOTALS	.200	30-63	10-17	81	11-34	13	22

Three-point FG: 11-18 (Anthony 3-5, McNamara 6-10, Duany 2-3); **Team Rebounds:** 2; **Blocked Shots:** 7 (Forth 4, McNeil 2, Warrick 2); **Turnovers:** 17 (Warrick 3, Anthony 3, McNamara 3, Duany 2, Edelin 2, McNeil 2, Pace 2); **Steals:** 10 (Pace 3, Edelin 2, Duany, Anthony, McNamara, Forth); **Percentages:** 2-Pt FG (.422), 3-Pt FG (.611), Total FG (.476), Free Throws (.588).

Kansas 78

	Min	FG M-A	FT M-A	Pts	Reb O-T	A	PF
Nick Collison	.40	8-14	3-10	19	8-21	3	5
Keith Langford	.23	7-9	5-10	19	2-2	0	5
Jeff Graves	.37	7-13	2-7	16	11-16	3	2
Kirk Hinrich	.38	6-20	1-1	16	1-2	4	1
Aaron Miles	.34	1-5	0-0	2	1-6	7	1
Michael Lee	.23	2-8	0-0	5	1-1	1	1
Bryant Nash	.5	0-2	1-2	1	0-1	0	1
TOTALS	.200	31-71	12-30	78	24-49	18	16

Three-point FGs: 4-20 (Langford 0-1, Hinrich 3-12, Miles 0-2, Lee 1-5); **Team Rebounds:** 3; **Blocked Shots:** 4 (Collison 3, Hinrich); **Turnovers:** 18 (Collison 5, Miles 4, Hinrich 3, Langford 3, Graves 2, Lee); **Steals:** 9 (Collison 3, Lee 2, Hinrich, Graves, Langford, Miles). **Percentages:** 2-Pt FG (.443), 3-Pt FG (.200), Total FG (.437), Free Throws (.588).

Syracuse (Big East)	53 28 —	**81**
Kansas (Big 12)	42 36 —	**78**

Final ESPN/USA Today Coaches' Poll

Taken **after** NCAA Tournament.
Voted on by a panel of 31 Division I head coaches following the NCAA tournament: first place votes in parentheses with total points (based on 25 for 1st, 24 for 2nd, etc.). Schools on major probation are ineligible to be ranked.

		W-L	Pts	Before NCAAs W-L	Rank
1	Syracuse (31)	30-5	775	24-5	12
2	Kansas	30-8	742	25-7	6
3	Texas	26-7	694	22-6	5
4	Kentucky	32-4	666	29-3	1
5	Arizona	28-4	654	25-3	2
6	Marquette	27-6	626	23-5	11
7	Oklahoma	27-7	595	24-6	3
8	Pittsburgh	28-5	559	26-4	4
9	Duke	26-7	493	24-6	7
10	Maryland	21-10	384	19-9	17
11	Connecticut	23-10	371	21-9	24
12	Wake Forest	25-6	361	24-5	9
13	Wisconsin	24-8	345	22-7	19
	Illinois	25-7	345	24-6	10
15	Notre Dame	24-10	333	22-9	20
16	Florida	25-8	309	24-7	8
17	Xavier	26-6	253	25-5	14
18	Michigan St.	22-13	252	19-12	NR
19	Louisville	25-7	244	24-6	13
20	Stanford	24-9	164	23-8	16
21	Butler	27-6	133	25-5	NR
22	Missouri	22-11	122	21-10	25
23	Creighton	29-5	121	29-4	15
24	Oklahoma St.	22-10	94	21-9	23
25	Dayton	25-6	81	24-5	18

Others receiving votes: 26. **Gonzaga** (73 pts); 27. **Auburn** (65); 28. **Mississippi St.** (59); 29. **Memphis** (45); 30. **California** (41); 31. **St. Joseph's** (20); 32. **Utah** (14); 33. **N.C. State** (9); 34. **Purdue** and **So. Illinois** (8); 36. **Oregon** (6); 37. **St. John's** and **Tulsa** (4); 39. **Arizona St., Central Michigan** and **Georgetown** (1).

THE FINAL FOUR

at the Superdome in New Orleans.
(April 5-7, 2003).

Semifinal — Game One

West Regional champ Kansas vs. Midwest Regional champ Marquette; Saturday, Apr. 5 (6:07 p.m. tipoff). **Coaches:** Roy Williams, Kansas and Tom Crean, Marquette. **Favorite:** Kansas by 4½.

Marquette (Conference USA)	30	31—	**61**
Kansas (Big 12)	59	34—	**94**

High scorers— Dwyane Wade, Marquette (19) and Keith Langford, Kansas (23); **Att—** 54,432; **TV rating—**6.3/13 share (CBS).

Semifinal — Game Two

East Regional champion Syracuse vs. South Regional champ Texas; Saturday, Apr. 5 (8:47 p.m. tipoff). **Coaches:** Jim Boeheim, Syracuse and Rick Barnes, Texas. **Favorite:** Texas by 3.

Syracuse (Big East)	48	47—	**95**
Texas (Big 12)	45	39—	**84**

High scorers— Carmelo Anthony, Syracuse (33) and Brandon Mouton, Texas (25); **Att—** 54,432; **TV rating—**7.9/14 share (CBS).

Most Outstanding Player

Carmelo Anthony, Syracuse freshman forward. SEMIFINAL—37 minutes, 33 points, 14 rebounds, 1 assist, 3 steals; FINAL—37 minutes, 20 points, 10 rebounds, 7 assists, 1 steal.

All-Final Four Team

Carmelo Anthony and freshman guard Gerry McNamara of Syracuse, senior forward Nick Collison, senior guard Kirk Hinrich and sophomore guard Keith Langford of Kansas.

NCAA Finalists' Tournament and Season Statistics
At least 10 games played during the overall season.

Syracuse (30-5)

	NCAA Tournament						Overall Season				
				—Per Game—						—Per Game—	
	Gm	FG %	TPts	Pts	Reb	Ast	Gm	FG %	TPts	Pts	Reb	Ast
Carmelo Athony 6	.475	121	20.2	9.8	2.5	35	.453	778	22.2	10.0	2.2
Hakim Warrick 6	.520	73	12.2	5.5	2.3	35	.541	518	14.8	8.5	1.6
Gerry McNamara 6	.429	80	13.3	1.8	3.5	35	.401	467	13.3	2.3	4.4
Kueth Duany 6	.483	44	7.3	3.8	0.8	35	.439	386	11.0	3.7	2.0
Billy Edelin 6	.537	66	11.0	3.8	2.7	23	.548	208	9.0	3.4	2.5
Josh Pace 6	.639	48	8.0	3.7	1.8	32	.525	138	4.3	2.7	1.9
Craig Forth 6	.400	10	1.7	2.7	1.0	35	.487	132	3.8	3.3	0.9
Jeremy McNeil 6	.643	20	3.3	4.3	0.2	35	.667	117	3.3	4.2	0.2
SYRACUSE 6	.503	462	77.0	38.3	14.8	35	.475	2785	79.6	40.7	14.9
OPPONENTS 6	.388	408	68.0	38.2	15.8	35	.390	2435	69.6	38.1	15.9

Three-pointers: NCAA TOURNAMENT—McNamara (18-44), Anthony (10-21), Duany (6-15), Team (34-80 for .425 pct.); OVERALL—McNamara (85-238), Anthony (56-166), Duany (43-123), Pace (0-2), Edelin (0-2), Warrick (0-1), Forth (0-1), Team 186-540 for .344 pct.).

Kansas (30-8)

	NCAA Tournament						Overall Season				
				—Per Game—						—Per Game—	
	Gm	FG %	TPts	Pts	Reb	Ast	Gm	FG %	TPts	Pts	Reb	Ast
Nick Collison 6	.649	112	18.7	81	22	38	.554	702	18.5	380	84
Keith Langford 6	.529	109	18.2	27	8	38	.530	603	15.9	185	75
Kirk Hinrich 6	.407	96	16.0	19	18	37	.475	641	17.3	139	130
Aaron Miles 6	.439	53	8.8	22	37	38	.408	340	8.9	3.3	244
Jeff Graves 6	.622	52	8.7	58	8	38	.509	227	6.0	6.8	35
Michael Lee 6	.438	41	6.8	16	8	37	.492	182	4.9	2.3	37
Bryant Nash 6	.529	21	3.5	10	2	38	.406	112	2.9	92	17
Moulaye Niang 3	.400	4	1.3	3	0	28	.361	34	1.2	17	13
Brett Olson 2	.000	2	1.0	2	0	21	.182	8	0.4	7	0
Stephen Vinson 2	.000	1	0.5	1	1	22	.150	13	0.6	6	4
Christian Moody 2	.000	0	0.0	3	0	21	.167	7	0.3	10	4
Jeff Hawkins 3	.000	0	0.0	0	0	29	.205	34	1.2	17	13
KANSAS 6	.505	491	81.8	42.5	17.3	38	.494	3141	82.7	41.8	17.2
OPPONENTS 6	.400	417	69.5	35.0	14.2	38	.402	2541	66.9	33.9	12.0

Three-pointers: NCAA TOURNAMENT— Hinrich (17-49), Lee (6-11), Miles (5-15), Lanford (0-11), Hawkins (0-3), Collison (0-1), Nash (0-1), Vinson (0-1), Team (28-92 for .304 pct.); OVERALL— Hinrich (89-219), Miles (24-98), Langford (22-76), Lee (21-42), Collison (13-38), Hawkins (7-27), Nash (6-30), Vinson (1-14), Olson (0-2), Team (183-546 for .335 pct.).

Syracuse's Schedule

Reg. Season
(23-4)

L	Memphis	.63-70
W	Valparaiso	.81-66
W	Colgate	.98-68
W	Cornell	.85-62
W	NC-Greensboro .	.92-65
W	Binghamton	.94-58
W	Georgia Tech . . .	.92-65
W	Albany	.109-79
W	Canisius	.87-69
W	at Seton Hall . . .	.70-66
W	Boston College . .	.82-74
W	Missouri	.76-69
L	at Pittsburgh . . .	.60-73
W	Seton Hall	.83-65
W	at Miami	.54-49
L	at Rutgers	.65-68
W	Pittsburgh	.67-65
W	Georgetown	.88-80
W	at West Virginia .	.94-80
L	at Connecticut . .	.61-75
W	Notre Dame	.82-80
W	St. John's	.66-60
W	at Michigan St. . .	.76-75
W	West Virginia . . .	.89-51
W	at Georgetown . .	.74-69
W	at Notre Dame . .	.92-88
W	Rutgers	.83-74

Big East Tourney
(1-1)

W	Georgetown	.74-69
L	Connecticut	.67-80

NCAA Tourney
(6-0)

W	Manhattan	.76-65
W	Oklahoma St. . . .	.68-56
W	Auburn	.79-78
W	Oklahoma	.63-47
W	Texas	.95-84
W	Kansas	.81-78

Kansas's Schedule

Reg. Season
(24-6)

W	Holy Cross	.81-57
W	NC-Greensboro	105-66
L	North Carolina .	.56-67
L	Florida	.73-83
W	C. Missouri St. . .	.97-70
L	Oregon	.78-84
W	at Tulsa	.89-80
W	Emporia St. . . .	.113-61
W	UCLA	.87-70
W	California	.80-67
W	NC-Asheville . .	.102-50
W	UMKC	.100-46
W	at Iowa St.	.83-54
W	Nebraska	.92-59
W	Wyoming	.98-70
W	Kansas St.	.81-64
L	at Colorado . . .	.59-60
L	Arizona	.74-91
W	Texas	.90-87
W	at Nebraska . . .	.81-51
W	Missouri	.76-70
W	at Kansas St. . . .	.82-64
W	at Baylor	.79-58
W	Iowa St.	.70-51
W	Colorado	.94-87
L	at Oklahoma . . .	.70-77
W	Texas A&M	.85-45
W	Oklahoma St. . .	.79-61
W	at Texas Tech . .	.65-56
W	at Missouri	.79-74

Big 12 Tourney
(1-1)

W	Iowa St.	.89-74
L	Missouri	.63-68

NCAA Tourney
(5-1)

W	Utah St. . . .	.64-61
W	Arizona St. . .	.108-76
W	Duke	.69-65
W	Arizona	.78-75
W	Marquette	.94-61
L	Syracuse	.78-81

Final NCAA Men's Division I Standings

Conference records include regular season games only. Overall records include all postseason tournament games.

America East Conference

Team	Conference			Overall		
	W	L	Pct	W	L	Pct
†Boston University	13	3	.812	20	11	.645
*Vermont	11	5	.688	21	12	.636
Hartford	10	6	.625	16	13	.552
Binghamton	9	7	.562	14	13	.519
Northeastern	8	8	.500	16	15	.516
Maine	8	8	.500	14	16	.467
Stony Brook	7	9	.438	13	15	.464
Albany	3	13	.188	7	21	.250
New Hampshire	3	13	.188	5	23	.179

Conf. Tourney Final: Vermont 56, Boston University 55.
***NCAA Tourney (0-1):** Vermont (0-1).
†**NIT (0-1):** Boston University (0-1).

Atlantic Coast Conference

Team	Conference			Overall		
	W	L	Pct	W	L	Pct
*Wake Forest	13	3	.813	25	6	.806
*Maryland	11	5	.688	21	10	.677
*Duke	11	5	.688	26	7	.787
*N.C. State	9	7	.563	18	13	.581
†Georgia Tech	7	9	.438	16	15	.516
†Virginia	6	10	.375	16	16	.500
†North Carolina	6	10	.375	19	16	.543
Clemson	5	11	.313	15	13	.536
Florida St	4	12	.250	14	15	.483

Conf. Tourney Final: Duke 84, N.C. State 77.
***NCAA Tourney (5-4):** Maryland (2-1), Duke (2-1), Wake Forest (1-1), N.C. State (0-1).
†**NIT (5-3):** Ga. Tech (2-1), N. Carolina (2-1), Virginia (1-1).

Atlantic Sun Conference

North	Conference			Overall		
	W	L	Pct	W	L	Pct
Belmont	12	4	.750	17	12	.586
Jacksonville St.	10	6	.625	20	10	.667
Samford	9	7	.562	13	15	.464
Georgia St.	8	8	.500	14	15	.483
Gardner-Webb	2	14	.125	5	24	.172
Campbell	1	15	.062	5	22	.185
South	W	L	Pct	W	L	Pct
*Troy St.	14	2	.875	26	6	.812
Mercer	14	2	.875	23	6	.793
Central Florida	11	5	.688	21	11	.656
Jacksonville	8	8	.500	13	16	.448
Stetson	4	12	.250	6	20	.231
Florida Atlantic	3	13	.188	7	21	.250

Conf. Tourney Final: Troy St. 80, Central Florida 69
***NCAA Tourney (0-1):** Troy St. (0-1).

Atlantic 10 Conference

East	Conference			Overall		
	W	L	Pct	W	L	Pct
*St. Joseph's	12	4	.750	23	7	.763
†Temple	10	6	.625	18	16	.529
†Rhode Island	10	6	.625	19	12	.613
Massachusetts	6	10	.375	11	18	.379
Fordham	3	13	.188	2	26	.071
St. Bonaventure	1	15	.063	13	14	.481
West	W	L	Pct	W	L	Pct
*Xavier	15	1	.938	26	6	.813
*Dayton	14	2	.875	24	6	.800
†Richmond	10	6	.625	15	14	.517
La Salle	6	10	.375	12	17	.414
Geo. Washington	5	11	.313	12	17	.414
Duquesne	4	12	.250	9	21	.300

Conf. Tourney Final: Dayton 79, Temple 72.
***NCAA Tourney (1-3):** Xavier (1-1), St. Joseph's (0-1), Dayton (0-1).
†**NIT (9-5):** Temple (3-1), Richmond (0-1), Rhode Island (1-1).

Big East Conference

East	Conference			Overall		
	W	L	Pct	W	L	Pct
†Boston College	10	6	.625	19	12	.613
*Connecticut	10	6	.625	23	10	.697
†Providence	8	8	.500	18	14	.563
†Villanova	8	8	.500	15	16	.484
†St. John's	7	9	.438	21	13	.618
Miami-FL	4	12	.250	11	17	.393
Virginia Tech	4	12	.250	11	18	.379
West	W	L	Pct	W	L	Pct
*Syracuse	13	3	.813	30	5	.857
*Pittsburgh	13	3	.813	28	5	.848
†Seton Hall	10	6	.625	17	13	.567
*Notre Dame	10	6	.625	24	10	.706
†Georgetown	6	10	.375	19	15	.559
West Virginia	5	11	.313	14	15	.483
Rutgers	4	12	.250	12	16	.429

Conf. Tourney Final: Pittsburgh 74, Connecticut 56.
***NCAA Tourney (12-3):** Syracuse (6-0), Connecticut (2-1), Pittsburgh (2-1), Notre Dame (2-1).
†**NIT (12-5):** St. John's (5-0), Providence (2-1), Georgetown (4-1), Boston College (1-1), Villanova (0-1), Seton Hall (0-1).

Big Sky Conference

Team	Conference			Overall		
	W	L	Pct	W	L	Pct
*Weber St	14	0	1.000	26	6	.813
†Eastern Washington	9	5	.643	18	13	.581
Montana	7	7	.500	13	17	.433
Idaho St	7	7	.500	14	14	.517
Northern Arizona	6	8	.429	15	13	.536
Sacramento St.	5	9	.357	12	17	.414
Montana St	5	9	.357	11	16	.407
Portland St.	3	11	.214	5	22	.185

Conf. Tourney Final: Weber St. 60, E. Washington 57.
***NCAA Tourney (0-1):** Weber St. (0-1).
†**NIT (0-1):** Eastern Washington (0-1).

Big South Conference

Team	Conference			Overall		
	W	L	Pct	W	L	Pct
Winthrop	11	3	.786	20	10	.667
Liberty	8	6	.571	14	15	.483
Charleston Southern	8	6	.571	14	14	.500
Elon	8	6	.571	12	15	.444
*NC-Asheville	7	7	.500	15	17	.469
Radford	6	8	.429	10	19	.345
Coastal Carolina	5	9	.357	13	15	.464
High Point	3	11	.273	7	20	.259
Birmingham-Southern	0	0	.000	19	9	.679

Conf. Tourney Final: NC-Asheville 85, Radford 71.
***NCAA Tourney (1-1):** NC-Asheville (1-1).

Big Ten Conference

Team	Conference			Overall		
	W	L	Pct	W	L	Pct
*Wisconsin	12	4	.750	24	8	.750
*Illinois	11	5	.688	25	7	.781
*Michigan St	10	6	.625	22	13	.629
*Purdue	10	6	.625	19	11	.633
Michigan	10	6	.625	17	13	.567
†Indiana	8	8	.500	21	13	.618
†Minnesota	8	8	.500	19	14	.576
†Iowa	7	9	.438	17	14	.548
†Ohio St	7	9	.438	17	15	.531
Northwestern	3	13	.188	12	17	.414
Penn St	2	14	.125	7	21	.250

Conf. Tourney Final: Illinois 72, Ohio St. 59.
***NCAA Tourney (8-5):** Indiana (1-1), Illinois (1-1), Wisconsin (2-1), Michigan State (3-1), Purdue (1-1).
†**NIT (5-4):** Ohio St. (0-1), Minnesota (3-2), Iowa (2-1).

COLLEGE BASKETBALL

Final NCAA Men's Division I Standings (Cont.)

Big 12 Conference

	Conference			Overall		
Team	W	L	Pct	W	L	Pct
*Kansas	14	2	.875	30	8	.789
*Texas	13	3	.813	26	7	.788
*Oklahoma	12	4	.750	27	7	.794
*Oklahoma St.	10	6	.625	22	10	.688
*Missouri	9	7	.563	22	11	.667
*Colorado	9	7	.563	20	12	.625
†Texas Tech	6	10	.375	21	12	.636
Texas A&M	6	10	.375	14	14	.500
†Iowa St.	5	11	.312	17	14	.548
Baylor	5	11	.312	14	14	.500
Kansas St	4	12	.250	13	17	.433
Nebraska	3	13	.187	11	19	.367

Conf. Tourney Final: Oklahoma 49, Missouri 47.
***NCAA Tourney (14-6):** Kansas (5-1), Texas (4-1), Oklahoma (3-1), Oklahoma St. (1-1), Missouri (1-1), Colorado (0-1).
†NIT (5-2): Texas Tech (4-1), Iowa St. (1-1).

Big West Conference

	Conference			Overall		
Team	W	L	Pct	W	L	Pct
†UC-Santa Barbara	14	4	.778	18	14	.563
UC-Irvine	13	5	.722	20	9	.690
*Utah St	12	6	.667	24	9	.727
Cal Poly	10	8	.556	16	14	.533
Idaho	9	9	.500	13	15	.464
Cal St.-Fullerton	8	10	.444	10	19	.345
Cal St.-Northridge	8	10	.444	14	15	.483
Pacific	7	11	.389	12	16	.429
UC-Riverside	5	13	.278	6	18	.250
Long Beach St	4	14	.222	5	22	.185

Conf. Tourney Final: Utah St. 57, Cal Poly 54.
***NCAA Tourney (0-1):** Utah St. (0-1).
†NIT (0-1): UC-Santa Barbara (0-1).

Colonial Athletic Association

	Conference			Overall		
Team	W	L	Pct	W	L	Pct
*NC-Wilmington	15	3	.883	24	7	.774
Va. Commonwealth	12	6	.667	18	10	.643
†Drexel	12	6	.667	19	12	.613
George Mason	11	7	.611	16	12	.571
Delaware	9	9	.500	15	14	.517
Old Dominion	9	9	.500	12	15	.444
James Madison	8	10	.444	13	17	.433
William & Mary	7	11	.389	12	16	.429
Hofstra	6	12	.333	8	21	.276
Towson	1	17	.056	4	24	.143

Conf. Tourney Final: NC-Wilmington 70, Drexel 62.
***NCAA Tourney (0-1):** NC-Wilmington (0-1).
†NIT (0-1): Drexel (0-1).

Conference USA

	Conference			Overall		
American Division	W	L	Pct	W	L	Pct
*Marquette	14	2	.875	27	6	.844
*Louisville	11	5	.688	25	7	.781
†Saint Louis	9	7	.563	16	14	.533
*Cincinnati	9	7	.563	17	12	.586
†De Paul	8	8	.500	13	16	.448
Charlotte	8	8	.500	13	16	.448
East Carolina	3	13	.188	12	15	.444

	Conference			Overall		
National Division	W	L	Pct	W	L	Pct
*Memphis	13	3	.813	23	7	.767
Tulane	8	8	.500	16	15	.516
†Ala-Birmingham	8	8	.500	21	13	.618
So. Florida	7	9	.438	15	14	.517
Houston	6	10	.375	8	20	.286
So. Mississippi	5	11	.313	13	16	.448
Texas Christian	3	13	.188	9	19	.321

Conf. Tourney Final: Louisville 83, Ala-Birmingham 78.
***NCAA Tourney (5-4):** Marquette (4-1), Louisville (1-1), Cincinnati (0-1), Memphis (0-1).
†NIT (2-3): Ala-Birmingham (2-1), Saint Louis (0-1), De Paul (0-1).

Horizon League

	Conference			Overall		
Team	W	L	Pct	W	L	Pct
*Butler	14	2	.875	27	6	.818
*WI-Milwaukee	13	3	.812	24	8	.750
†Illinois-Chicago	12	4	.750	21	9	.700
Detroit	9	7	.562	18	12	.600
Loyola-IL	9	7	.562	15	16	.484
Wright St	4	12	.250	10	18	.357
WI-Green Bay	4	12	.250	10	20	.333
Youngstown St.	4	12	.250	9	20	.310
Cleveland St.	3	13	.188	8	22	.267

Conf. Tourney Final: WI-Milwaukee 69, Butler 52.
***NCAA Tourney (2-2):** Butler (2-1), WI-Milwaukee (0-1).
†NIT Tourney (0-1): Illinois-Chicago (0-1).

Ivy League

	Conference			Overall		
Team	W	L	Pct	W	L	Pct
*Pennsylvania	14	0	1.000	22	6	.786
†Brown	12	2	.857	17	12	.586
Princeton	10	4	.714	16	11	.593
Yale	8	6	.571	14	13	.519
Harvard	4	10	.286	12	15	.444
Cornell	4	10	.286	9	18	.333
Dartmouth	4	10	.286	8	19	.296
Columbia	0	14	.000	2	25	.074

Conf. Tourney Final: Ivy League has no tournament.
***NCAA Tourney (0-1):** Pennsylvania (0-1).
†NIT (0-1): Brown (0-1).

Metro Atlantic Athletic Conference

	Conference			Overall		
Team	W	L	Pct	W	L	Pct
*Manhattan	14	4	.778	23	7	.767
†Fairfield	13	5	.722	19	12	.613
†Siena	12	6	.667	21	11	.656
Niagara	12	6	.667	17	12	.586
Iona	11	7	.611	17	12	.586
Marist	8	10	.444	13	16	.448
Rider	7	11	.389	12	16	.429
Saint Peter's	6	12	.333	10	19	.345
Canisius	6	12	.333	10	18	.357
Loyola	1	17	.056	4	22	.143

Conf. Tourney Final: Manhattan 69, Fairfield 54.
***NCAA Tourney (0-1):** Manhattan (0-1).
†NIT (2-2): Siena (2-1), Fairfield (0-1).

Mid-American Conference

East	Conference			Overall		
	W	L	Pct	W	L	Pct
Kent St.	12	6	.667	21	10	.677
Miami-OH	11	7	.611	13	15	.464
Akron	9	9	.500	14	14	.500
Marshall	9	9	.500	14	15	.483
Ohio	8	10	.444	14	16	.467
Buffalo	2	16	.111	5	23	.179
West	**W**	**L**	**Pct**	**W**	**L**	**Pct**
*Central Mich	14	4	.778	25	7	.781
N. Illinois	11	7	.611	17	14	.548
†Western Mich	10	8	.556	20	11	.645
Eastern Mich	8	10	.444	14	14	.500
Bowling Green	8	10	.444	13	16	.448
Ball St.	8	10	.444	13	17	.433
Toledo	7	11	.389	13	16	.448

Conf. Tourney Final: Central Michigan 77, Kent St. 67.
*NCAA Tourney (1-1): Central Michigan (1-1).
†NIT (0-1): Western Michigan (0-1).

Mid-Continent Conference

Team	Conference			Overall		
	W	L	Pct	W	L	Pct
†Valparaiso	12	2	.857	20	11	.645
*IUPUI	10	4	.714	20	14	.588
Oakland	10	4	.714	17	11	.607
Oral Roberts	10	4	.714	18	10	.643
Missouri-KC	7	7	.500	9	20	.310
Southern Utah	5	9	.357	11	17	.393
Western Illinois	3	11	.231	7	21	.250
Chicago St.	0	14	.000	3	27	.100

Conf. Tourney Final: Valparaiso 88, Indiana-Purdue 55.
*NCAA Tourney (0-1): IUPUI (0-1).
†NIT (0-1): Valparaiso (0-1).

Mid-Eastern Athletic Conference

Team	Conference			Overall		
	W	L	Pct	W	L	Pct
*S.C. State	15	3	.833	20	11	.645
Hampton	13	5	.722	19	11	.633
Delaware St.	13	5	.722	15	12	.556
Florida A&M	11	7	.611	17	12	.586
Coppin St.	11	7	.611	11	17	.393
Norfolk St.	10	8	.556	14	15	.483
Howard	9	9	.500	13	17	.433
Morgan St.	6	12	.333	7	22	.241
Bethune-Cookman	5	13	.278	8	22	.267
MD-Eastern Shore	5	13	.278	5	23	.179
N. Carolina A&T	1	17	.056	1	26	.037

Conf. Tourney Final: S.C. State 72, Hampton 67.
*NCAA Tourney (0-1): S.C. State (0-1).

Missouri Valley Conference

Team	Conference			Overall		
	W	L	Pct	W	L	Pct
*Southern Illinois	16	2	.889	24	7	.774
*Creighton	15	3	.833	29	5	.853
†Wichita St.	12	6	.667	18	12	.600
SW Missouri St.	12	6	.667	17	12	.586
Evansville	8	10	.444	12	16	.429
Bradley	8	10	.444	12	18	.400
Northern Iowa	7	11	.389	11	17	.393
Drake	5	13	.278	10	20	.333
Illinois St.	5	13	.278	8	21	.276
Indiana St.	2	16	.111	7	24	.226

Conf. Tourney Final: Creighton 80, Southern Illinois 56.
*NCAA Tourney (0-2): Creighton (0-1), Southern Illinois (0-1).
†NIT (0-1): Wichita St. (0-1).

Mountain West Conference

Team	Conference			Overall		
	W	L	Pct	W	L	Pct
*Utah	11	3	.786	25	8	.758
*BYU	11	3	.786	23	9	.719
†UNLV	8	6	.571	21	11	.656
†Wyoming	8	6	.571	21	11	.656
†San Diego St.	6	8	.429	16	14	.533
*Colorado St.	5	9	.357	19	14	.576
New Mexico	4	10	.286	10	18	.357
Air Force	3	11	.214	12	16	.429

Conf. Tourney Final: Colorado St. 62, UNLV 61.
*NCAA Tourney (1-3): Utah (1-1), BYU (0-1), Colorado St. (0-1).
†NIT (2-3): Wyoming (1-1), UNLV (0-1), San Diego St. (1-1).

Northeast Conference

Team	Conference			Overall		
	W	L	Pct	W	L	Pct
*Wagner	14	4	.778	21	11	.656
Monmouth	13	5	.722	15	13	.536
Central Connecticut St. . .	12	6	.667	15	13	.536
Quinnipiac	10	8	.556	17	12	.586
St. Francis-PA	10	8	.556	14	14	.500
Fairleigh Dickinson	9	9	.500	15	14	.517
St. Francis-NY	9	9	.500	14	16	.467
LIU Brooklyn	7	11	.389	9	19	.321
Robert Morris	7	11	.389	10	17	.370
Mt. St. Mary's	6	12	.333	11	16	.407
Sacred Heart	6	12	.333	8	21	.276
MD-Baltimore County . . .	5	13	.278	7	20	.259

Conf. Tourney Final: Wagner 78, St. Francis-NY 61.
*NCAA Tourney (0-1): Wagner (0-1).

Ohio Valley Conference

Team	Conference			Overall		
	W	L	Pct	W	L	Pct
*Austin Peay	13	3	.812	23	8	.742
Morehead St	13	3	.812	20	9	.690
Tennessee Tech	11	5	.688	20	12	.625
Murray St	9	7	.562	17	12	.586
Eastern Illinois	9	7	.562	14	15	.483
Tennessee-Martin	7	9	.438	14	14	.500
Eastern Kentucky	5	11	.312	11	17	.393
SE Missouri St	5	11	.312	11	19	.367
Tennessee St	0	16	.000	2	25	.074

Conf. Tourney Final: Austin Peay 63, Tennessee Tech 57.
*NCAA Tourney (0-1): Austin Peay (0-1).

Pacific-10 Conference

Team	Conference			Overall		
	W	L	Pct	W	L	Pct
*Arizona	17	1	.944	28	4	.875
*Stanford	14	4	.778	24	9	.727
*California	13	5	.722	22	9	.710
*Arizona St	11	7	.611	20	12	.625
*Oregon	10	8	.556	23	10	.697
Oregon St	6	12	.333	13	15	.464
USC	6	12	.333	13	17	.433
UCLA	6	12	.333	10	19	.345
Washington	5	13	.278	10	17	.370
Washington St	2	16	.111	7	20	.259

Conf. Tourney Final: Oregon 74, USC 66.
*NCAA Tourney (6-5): Arizona (3-1), Stanford (1-1), California (1-1), Arizona St. (1-1), Oregon (0-1).

Final NCAA Men's Division I Standings (Cont.)

Patriot League

Team	Conference W	L	Pct	Overall W	L	Pct
*Holy Cross	13	1	.929	26	5	.839
American	9	5	.643	16	14	.533
Colgate	9	5	.643	14	14	.500
Lehigh	8	6	.571	16	12	.571
Bucknell	7	7	.500	14	15	.483
Lafayette	6	8	.429	13	16	.448
Navy	4	10	.286	8	20	.286
Army	0	14	.000	5	22	.185

Conf. Tourney Final: Holy Cross 72, American 64.
***NCAA Tourney (0-1):** Holy Cross (0-1).

Southeastern Conference

Eastern Div.	Conference W	L	Pct	Overall W	L	Pct
*Kentucky	16	0	1.000	32	4	.889
*Florida	12	4	.750	25	8	.758
Georgia	11	5	.688	19	8	.704
†Tennessee	9	7	.563	17	12	.586
South Carolina	5	11	.313	12	16	.429
Vanderbilt	3	13	.188	11	18	.380

Western Div.	Conference W	L	Pct	Overall W	L	Pct
*Mississippi St	9	7	.563	21	10	.677
*Auburn	8	8	.500	22	12	.647
*LSU	8	8	.500	21	11	.656
*Alabama	7	9	.438	17	12	.586
Arkansas	4	12	.250	9	19	.321
Mississippi	4	12	.250	14	15	.483

Conf. Tourney Final: Kentucky 64, Mississippi St. 57.
***NCAA Tourney (7-6):** Kentucky (4-1), Auburn (2-1), Florida (1-1), Alabama (0-1), Mississippi St. (0-1), LSU (0-1).
†NIT (0-1): Tennessee (0-1).

Southern Conference

North Div.	Conference W	L	Pct	Overall W	L	Pct
Appalachian St	11	5	.688	19	10	.655
*East Tennessee St	11	5	.688	20	11	.645
Davidson	11	5	.688	17	10	.630
W. Carolina	6	10	.375	9	19	.321
Virginia Military	3	13	.188	10	20	.333
NC-Greensboro	3	13	.188	7	22	.241

South Div.	Conference W	L	Pct	Overall W	L	Pct
†College of Charleston	13	3	.812	25	8	.758
Chattanooga	11	5	.688	21	9	.700
Georgia Southern	8	8	.500	16	13	.552
Wofford	8	8	.500	14	15	.483
Furman	8	8	.500	14	17	.452
The Citadel	3	13	.188	8	20	.286

Conf. Tourney Final: East Tennessee St. 97, Chattanooga 90.
***NCAA Tourney (0-1):** East Tennessee St. (0-1).
†NIT (1-1): College of Charleston (1-1).

Southland Conference

Team	Conference W	L	Pct	Overall W	L	Pct
*Sam Houston St	17	3	.850	23	7	.767
Stephen F. Austin	16	4	.800	21	8	.724
Texas-Arlington	13	7	.650	16	13	.552
SW Texas St.	11	9	.550	17	12	.586
McNeese St	10	10	.500	15	14	.517
Lamar	10	10	.500	13	14	.481
Louisiana-Monroe	10	10	.500	12	16	.429
SE Louisiana	9	11	.450	11	16	.407
Texas-San Antonio	7	13	.350	10	17	.370
Northwestern St.	6	14	.300	6	21	.222
Nicholls St	1	19	.050	3	25	.107

Conf. Tourney Final: Sam Houston St. 69, Stephen F. Austin 66 (OT).
***NCAA Tourney (0-1):** Sam Houston St. (0-1).

Southwestern Athletic Conference

Team	Conference W	L	Pct	Overall W	L	Pct
Prairie View A&M	14	4	.778	17	12	.586
Miss. Valley St	13	5	.722	15	14	.517
*Texas Southern	11	7	.611	18	13	.581
Alabama St	11	7	.611	14	15	.483
Alcorn St.	10	8	.556	14	19	.424
Grambling	9	9	.500	12	18	.400
Jackson St	9	9	.500	10	18	.357
Southern	5	13	.278	9	20	.310
Alabama A&M	4	14	.222	8	19	.296
Ark-Pine Bluff	4	14	.222	4	24	.143

Conf. Tourney Final: Texas Southern 77, Alcorn St. 68.
***NCAA Tourney (0-1):** Texas Southern (0-1).

Sun Belt Conference

East Div.	Conference W	L	Pct	Overall W	L	Pct
*Western Kentucky	12	2	.857	24	9	.727
Middle Tennessee	9	5	.643	16	14	.533
Arkansas-Little Rock	8	6	.571	18	12	.600
Arkansas St	6	8	.429	13	15	.464
Florida International	1	13	.071	8	21	.276

West Div.	Conference W	L	Pct	Overall W	L	Pct
†Louisiana-Lafayette	12	3	.800	20	10	.667
New Mexico St.	9	6	.600	20	9	.690
South Alabama	7	8	.467	14	14	.500
New Orleans	7	8	.467	15	14	.517
Denver	7	8	.467	17	15	.531
North Texas	2	13	.133	7	21	.250

Conf. Tourney Final: Western Kentucky 64, Middle Tennessee 52.
***NCAA Tourney (0-1):** Western Kentucky (0-1).
†NIT (0-1): Louisiana-Lafayette (0-1).

West Coast Conference

Team	Conference W	L	Pct	Overall W	L	Pct
*Gonzaga	12	2	.857	24	9	.727
*San Diego	10	5	.714	18	12	.600
San Francisco	9	6	.643	15	14	.517
Pepperdine	7	7	.500	15	13	.536
St. Mary's-CA	6	8	.429	15	15	.500
Santa Clara	4	10	.286	13	15	.464
Portland	4	10	.286	11	17	.393
Loyola Marymount	4	10	.286	11	20	.355

Conf. Tourney Final: San Diego 72, Gonzaga 63.
***NCAA Tourney (1-2):** Gonzaga (1-1), San Diego (0-1).

Western Athletic Conference

Team	Conference			Overall		
	W	L	Pct	W	L	Pct
Fresno St. 13	13	5	.722	20	8	.714
*Tulsa 12	12	6	.667	23	10	.697
SMU 11	11	7	.611	17	13	.567
†Nevada 11	11	7	.611	18	14	.563
Rice 11	11	7	.611	19	10	.655
†Hawaii 9	9	9	.500	19	12	.613
Louisiana Tech 9	9	9	.500	12	15	.444
Boise St. 7	7	11	.389	13	16	.448
San Jose St 4	4	14	.222	7	21	.250
UTEP 3	3	15	.167	6	24	.200

Conf. Tourney Final: Tulsa 75, Nevada 64.
*NCAA Tourney (1-1): Tulsa (1-1).
†NIT (1-2): Nevada (0-1), Hawaii (1-1).

Division I Independents

Team	Overall		
	W	L	Pct
Centenary 14	14	14	.500
Texas A&M-Corpus Christi 14	14	15	.483
Texas-Pan American 10	10	20	.333
IPFW 9	9	21	.300
David Lipscomb .8	8	20	.286
Morris Brown 8	8	20	.286
Savannah St. 3	3	24	.111

Annual Awards

Players of the Year

T.J. Ford, Texas, G . . . . .Naismith, Wooden
David West, Xavier, F . . . . AP, USBWA
Nick Collison, Kansas, F .NABC

Wooden Award Voting

Presented since 1977 by the Los Angeles Athletic Club and named after the former Purdue All-America and UCLA coach John Wooden. Voting done by 1,047-member panel of national media; candidates must have a cumulative college grade point average of 2.0 (out of 4.0) and be making progress toward graduation.

		Cl	Pos	Pts
1	T.J. Ford, Texas	So.	G	4418
2	David West, Xavier	Sr.	F	3572
3	Hollis Price, Oklahoma	Sr.	G	3311
4	Nick Collison, Kansas	Sr.	F	3264
5	Dwayne Wade, Marquette	Jr.	G	2522
6	Josh Howard, Wake Forest	Sr.	F	—
7	Jason Gardner, Arizona	Sr.	G	—
8	Kirk Hinrich, Kansas	Sr.	G	—
9	Brandin Knight, Pittsburgh	Sr.	G	—
10	Emeka Okafor, Connecticut	So.	F/C	—

Note: Only the points totals of the top 5 finishers are released.

Defensive Player of the Year

Formerly the Henry Iba Award, for defensive skills, sportsmanship and dedication; first presented by the Rotary Club of River Oaks in Houston in 1987 and named after the late Oklahoma State and U.S. Olympic team coach. Voting done by the National Association of Basketball Coaches.

Emeka Okafor, Connecticut, F/C

Div. II and III Annual Awards

Awarded by the National Association of Basketball Coaches.

Players of the Year
Div. II . . . . .Marlon Parmer, Ky. Wesleyan
Div. III . . . . .Bryan Nelson, Williams
Coaches of the Year
Div. II . . . . .Larry Gipson, Northeastern St.
Div. III . . . . .David Paulsen, Williams
NAIA . . . . .Joe O'Brien, Southeastern CC
JuCo . . . . .Ken Ammann, Concordia

Coach of the Year

Tubby Smith, Kentucky . . . . .AP, USBWA, Naismith, NABC

Consensus All-America Teams

The NCAA Division I players cited most frequently by the following All-America selectors: Associated Press, U.S. Basketball Writers, National Association of Basketball Coaches and Wooden Award Committee. (*) indicates unanimous first team selection. There were no holdovers from the 2002-03 first team.

First Team

	Class	Hgt	Pos
David West*, Xavier	Sr.	6-9	F
T.J. Ford*, Texas	So.	5-10	G
Nick Collison*, Kansas	Sr.	6-9	F
Dwayne Wade, Marquette	Jr.	6-4	G
Hollis Price, Oklahoma	Sr.	6-1	G

Second Team

	Class	Hgt	Pos
Josh Howard, Wake Forest	Sr.	6-6	F
Jason Gardner, Arizona	Jr.	5-10	G
Carmelo Anthony, Syracuse	Fr.	6-8	F
Kyle Korver, Creighton	Sr.	6-7	F
Troy Bell, Boston College	Sr.	6-1	G

Third Team

	Class	Hgt	Pos
Keith Bogans, Kentucky	Sr.	6-5	G
Kirk Hinrich, Kansas	Sr.	6-3	G
Brian Cook, Illinois	Sr.	6-10	C
Reece Gaines, Louisville	Sr.	6-6	G
Emeka Okafor, Connecticut	So.	6-9	F/C

Players also named: Mike Sweetney, Georgetown; Brandin Knight, Pittsburgh; Ron Slay, Tennessee.

NCAA Men's Division I Leaders

Includes games through NCAA and NIT tourneys.

INDIVIDUAL

Scoring

	Cl	Gm	FG%	3FG/Att	FT%	Reb	Ast	Stl	Blk	Pts	Avg	Hi
Ruben Douglas, New Mexico	Sr.	28	.397	94/238	.841	185	58	35	8	783	28.0	43
Henry Domercant, E. Illinois	Sr.	29	.458	84/198	.844	199	81	40	15	810	27.9	46
Mike Helms, Oakland	Jr.	28	.452	74/195	.745	111	56	40	7	752	26.9	43
Michael Watson, UMKC	Jr.	29	.377	118/337	.753	108	109	41	6	740	25.5	54
Troy Bell, Boston College	Sr.	31	.441	106/264	.847	142	115	70	6	781	25.2	48
Keydren Clark, St. Peter's	Fr.	29	.396	109/278	.853	95	121	41	6	722	24.9	48
Luis Flores, Manhattan	Jr.	30	.455	56/145	.902	169	87	58	11	739	24.6	44
Chris Williams, Ball St.	Sr.	30	.429	64/196	.859	102	65	38	2	736	24.5	48
Mike Sweetney, Georgetown	Jr.	34	.547	0/3	.738	352	66	50	109	776	22.8	38
Kevin Martin, W. Carolina	So.	24	.424	50/160	.883	91	43	33	12	546	22.8	46
Willie Green, Detroit	Sr.	30	.490	37/99	.805	148	75	40	13	678	22.6	43
Ricky Minard, Morehead St.	Jr.	29	.516	54/147	.837	181	117	63	17	653	22.5	43
Chris Kaman, C. Michigan	Jr.	31	.622	0/0	.749	373	39	19	98	394	22.4	43
Seth Doliboa, Wright St.	Sr.	28	.446	67/176	.765	211	37	32	33	625	22.3	38
Marcus Hatten, St. John's	Sr.	34	.424	56/185	.730	189	138	100	16	756	22.2	44
Carmelo Anthony, Syracuse	Fr.	35	.453	56/166	.706	349	77	55	30	778	22.2	33
Andrew Wisniewski, Centenary	Jr.	28	.504	53/147	.833	70	124	72	3	617	22.0	31
Andre Emmett, Texas Tech	Jr.	34	.499	11/38	.712	226	63	64	16	741	21.8	34
Ron Williamson, Howard	Sr.	30	.412	104/237	.864	85	70	44	1	650	21.7	52
Julius Jenkins, Ga. Southern	Sr.	27	.454	74/177	.718	132	91	29	6	584	21.6	37

Rebounding

	Cl	Gm	No	Avg
Brandon Hunter, Ohio	Sr.	30	378	12.6
Amien Hicks, Morris Brown	Sr.	24	298	12.4
Adam Sonn, Belmont	Sr.	29	352	12.1
Chris Kaman, C. Michigan	Jr.	31	373	12.0
David West, Xavier	Sr.	32	379	11.8
Louis Truscott, Houston	Sr.	28	315	11.3
Emeka Okafor, Connecticut	So.	33	370	11.2
Kenny Adeleke, Hofstra	So.	29	320	11.0
James Singleton, Murray St.	Sr.	29	320	11.0
James Thomas, Texas	Jr.	33	363	11.0
Chris Massie, Memphis	Sr.	23	249	10.8
Brandon Griffin, SE Missouri St.	Jr.	30	314	10.5
Lawrence Roberts, Baylor	So.	26	271	10.4
Travis Watson, Virginia	Sr.	31	321	10.4
Mike Sweetney, Georgetown	Jr.	34	352	10.4
Kirby Lemons, Louisiana-Monroe	Sr.	28	285	10.2
Marcus Smallwood, No. Illinois	Jr.	31	313	10.1
Nick Collison, Kansas	Sr.	38	380	10.0
Carmelo Athony, Syracuse	Fr.	35	349	10.0
Chris Jackson, New Mexico St.	Sr.	23	229	10.0

Assists

	Cl	Gm	No	Avg
Martell Bailey, Illinois-Chicago	Jr.	30	244	8.1
Marques Green, St. Bonaventure	Jr.	27	216	8.0
T. J Ford, Texas	So.	33	254	7.7
Elliott Prasse-Freeman, Harvard	Sr.	27	207	7.7
Antawn Dobie, Long Island	Sr.	26	193	7.4
Richard Little, VMI	Jr.	30	216	7.2
Steve Blake, Maryland	Sr.	31	221	7.1
Chris Thomas, Notre Dame	So.	34	236	6.9
Raymond Felton, North Carolina	Fr.	35	236	6.7
Luke Ridnour, Oregon	Jr.	33	218	6.6
Chris Duhon, Duke	Jr.	33	212	6.4
Aaron Miles, Kansas	So.	38	244	6.4
Jay Collins, Southern Utah	Sr.	28	178	6.4
Brandin Knight, Pittsburgh	Sr.	33	209	6.3
Jave Meade, Holy Cross	Jr.	31	193	6.2
Reggie Kohn, South Florida	Sr.	29	180	6.2
Mark Campbell, Hawaii	Sr.	31	192	6.2
Kevin Roberts, SE Missouri St.	Sr.	29	179	6.2
Mike Slattery, Delaware	So.	29	179	6.2
T.J. Thompson, George Washington	So.	29	177	6.1

Field Goal Percentage

Minimum 5 Field Goals made per game.

	Cl	Gm	FG	FGA	Pct
Adam Mark, Belmont	Jr.	28	199	297	67.0
Rickey White, Maine	Sr.	24	131	198	66.2
Matt Nelson, Colorado St.	So.	31	205	319	64.3
Armond Williams, Ill-Chicago	Jr.	30	168	263	63.9
Michael Harris, Rice	So.	28	172	276	62.3
Chris Kaman, Central Michigan	Jr.	31	244	392	62.2
David Gruber, Northern Iowa	Jr.	28	141	231	61.0
Ike Diogu, Arizona St.	Fr.	32	209	344	60.8
Omar Barlett, Jacksonville St.	Sr.	30	178	293	60.8
Jason Keep, San Diego	Sr.	30	195	323	60.4
Craig Smith, Boston College	Fr.	31	241	400	60.3
Juan Mendez, Niagara	So.	29	207	344	60.2
Chris Massie, Memphis	Sr.	23	151	251	60.2
Steve Smith, Iona	Jr.	28	147	245	60.0
Jackie Rogers, Massachusetts	Sr.	29	148	247	59.9

Free Throw Percentage

Minimum 2.5 Free Throws made per game.

	Cl	Gm	FT	FTA	Pct
Steve Drabyn, Belmont	Jr.	29	78	82	95.1
Matt Logie, Lehigh	Sr.	28	91	96	94.8
Hollis Price, Oklahoma	Sr.	34	130	140	92.9
Brian Dux, Canisius	Sr.	28	115	125	92.0
J.J. Redick, Duke	Fr.	33	102	111	91.9
Tim Parker, Chattanooga	Sr.	30	78	85	91.8
Dwayne Byfield, Monmouth	So.	28	72	79	91.1
Gerry McNamara, Syracuse	Fr.	35	90	99	90.9
Kyle Korver, Creighton	Sr.	34	109	120	90.8
Jeb Ivey, Portland St.	Sr.	27	69	76	90.8
Luis Flores, Manhattan	Jr.	30	221	245	90.2
David Bennett, Marist	Sr.	28	117	130	90.0
Tevoris Thompson, Arkansas St.	Jr.	28	71	79	89.9
Tori Harris, Alcorn St.	Sr.	28	88	99	88.9
Ronald Blackshear, Marshall	Jr.	29	111	125	88.8

New Mexico	Ohio	Illinois-Chicago	Connecticut
Ruben Douglas	**Brandon Hunter**	**Martell Bailey**	**Emeka Okafor**
Scoring	Rebounds	Assists	Blocked Shots

3-Pt Field Goal Percentage

Minimum 2.5 Three-Point FGs made per game.

	Cl	Gm	FG	FGA	Pct
Jeff Schiffner, Pennsylvania	Jr.	28	74	150	49.3
Kyle Korver, Creighton	Sr.	34	129	269	48.0
Terrence Woods, Florida A&M	Jr.	28	139	304	45.7
Chez Marks, Morehead St.	Sr.	29	82	180	45.6
Tyson Dorsey, Samford	Jr.	27	75	165	45.5
Tim Keller, Air Force	So.	28	78	173	45.1
Pat Carroll, St. Joseph's	So.	30	76	169	45.0
Dedrick Dye, Wagner	Jr.	32	96	217	44.2
Jimmy Boykin, Coppin St.	Jr.	28	72	163	44.2
Brett Blizzard, NC-Wilmington	Sr.	31	109	247	44.1
Ron Williamson, Howard	Sr.	30	104	237	43.9

3-Pt Field Goals Per Game

	Cl	Gm	No	Avg
Terrence Woods, Florida A&M	Jr.	28	139	5.0
Demon Brown, Charlotte	Jr.	29	137	4.7
Michael Watson, UMKC	Jr.	29	118	4.1
Brad Boyd, Louisiana-Lafayette	Jr.	27	104	3.9
Kyle Korver, Creighton	Sr.	34	129	3.8
Keydren Clark, St. Peter's	Fr.	29	109	3.8
Shawn Hall, Appalachian St.	Sr.	28	103	3.7
Chris Young, South Alabama	Jr.	28	99	3.5
Brett Blizzard, NC-Wilmington	Sr.	31	109	3.5
Earl Bullock, Tennessee-Martin	Jr.	28	98	3.5
Marques Green, St. Bonaventure	Jr.	27	94	3.5

Blocked Shots

	Cl	Gm	No	Avg
Emeka Okafor, Connecticut	So.	33	156	4.7
Nick Billings, Binghampton	So.	27	117	4.3
Justin Rowe, Maine	Sr.	25	105	4.2
Deng Gai, Fairfield	So.	25	96	3.8
Robert Battle, Drexel	Sr.	31	116	3.7
Kyle Davis, Auburn	Jr.	34	124	3.6
Kendrick Moore, Oral Roberts	Sr.	28	94	3.4
David Harrison, Colorado	So.	32	106	3.3
Mike Sweetney, Georgetown	Jr.	34	109	3.2
Chris Kaman, Central Michigan	Jr.	31	98	3.2
Marcus Douthit, Providence	Jr.	32	97	3.0
Herve Lamizana, Rutgers	Jr.	28	83	3.0

Steals

	Cl	Gm	No	Avg
Alexis McMillan, Stetson	Sr.	22	87	4.0
Zakee Wadood, E. Tennessee St.	Jr.	29	93	3.2
Jay Heard, Jacksonville St.	Sr.	30	95	3.2
Eric Bush, UAB	Sr.	34	106	3.1
Marcus Hatten, St. John's	Sr.	34	100	2.9
Rawle Marshall, Oakland	So.	28	80	2.9
Marcus Banks, UNLV	Sr.	32	91	2.8
Tim Pickett, Florida St.	Jr.	29	82	2.8
Demetrice Williams, South Alabama	Sr.	28	76	2.7
Robby Collum, Western Michigan	Sr.	31	83	2.7
Edward O'Neil, Charleston Southern	Jr.	25	66	2.6

Single Game Highs

Points

No		Opponent	Date
54	Michael Watson, UMKC	Oral Roberts	Feb. 22
53	Antawn Dobie, LIU	St. Francis-NY	Feb. 22
52	Ron Williamson, Howard	N.C. A&T	Jan. 21

Rebounds

No		Opponent	Date
26	Brandon Hunter, Ohio	Akron	Jan. 8
24	Erroyl Bing, E. Carolina	South Florida	Jan. 25
24	Brandon Hunter, Ohio	St. Bonaventure	Dec. 31

Assists

No		Opponent	Date
17	Antawn Dobie, LIU	St. Francis-NY	Dec. 15
17	Zakee Smith, CS-Fullerton	Pepperdine	Dec. 4
16	Malcolm Campbell, Ala. St.	Miss. Valley	Feb. 10
16	Blake Stepp, Gonzaga	Long Beach St.	Dec. 20

Blocks

No		Opponent	Date
11	David Harrison, Colorado	Nebraska	Mar. 8
11	Jordan Cornette, Notre Dame	Belmont	Nov. 17
10	Four tied.		

Steals

No		Opponent	Date
10	Marcus Hatten, St. John's	Syracuse	Feb. 18
10	Joseph Frazier, CS-Northridge	Bethany	Dec. 7
10	Rawle Marshall, Oakland	Texas A&M	Dec. 2

3-point FGs

No		Opponent	Date
12	Terrence Woods, Fla. A&M	Coppin St.	Mar. 1
11	Terrence Woods, Fla. A&M	N.C. A&T	Feb. 1
11	Ron Williamson, Howard	N.C. A&T	Jan. 21
10	Three tied.		

NCAA Men's Division I Leaders (Cont.)
TEAM

Scoring Offense

	Gm	W-L	Pts	Avg
Arizona	32	28-4	2725	85.2
Appalachian St.	29	19-10	2434	83.9
Kansas	38	30-8	3141	82.7
E. Tennessee St.	31	20-11	2543	82.0
Louisville	32	25-7	2612	81.6
Oregon	33	23-10	2689	81.5
Morehead St.	29	20-9	2355	81.2
Chattanooga	30	21-9	2435	81.2
Duke	33	26-7	2677	81.1
Davidson	27	17-10	2180	80.7
Troy St.	32	26-6	2556	79.9
Central Michigan	32	25-7	2553	79.8
Maryland	31	21-10	2472	79.7
Syracuse	35	30-5	2785	79.6
St. Bonaventure	27	13-14	2146	79.5
Connecticut	33	23-10	2622	79.5
Boston College	31	19-12	2462	79.4
Texas	33	26-7	2618	79.3
Georgia	27	19-8	2138	79.2
Notre Dame	34	24-10	2692	79.2

Won-Lost Percentage

	W	L	Pct
Kentucky	32	4	88.9
Arizona	28	4	87.5
Syracuse	30	5	85.7
Creighton	29	5	85.3
Pittsburgh	28	5	84.8
Holy Cross	26	5	83.9
Butler	27	6	81.8
Marquette	27	6	81.8
Troy St.	26	6	81.3
Weber St.	26	6	81.3
Xavier	26	6	81.3
Wake Forest	25	6	80.6
Dayton	24	6	80.0
Oklahoma	27	7	79.4
Mercer	23	6	79.3
Kansas	30	8	78.9
Duke	26	7	78.8
Texas	26	7	78.8
Pennsylvania	22	6	78.6
Three schools tied	25	7	78.1

Scoring Defense

	Gm	W-L	Pts	Avg
Air Force	28	12-16	1596	57.0
Miami-OH	28	13-15	1643	58.7
Holy Cross	31	26-5	1821	58.7
Bucknell	29	14-15	1706	58.8
Pittsburgh	33	28-5	1955	59.2
Wisconsin	32	24-8	1899	59.3
St. Joseph's	30	23-7	1784	59.5
Mississippi St.	31	21-10	1852	59.7
Utah St.	33	24-9	1979	60.0
Oklahoma	34	27-7	2041	60.0
Pennsylvania	28	22-6	1681	60.0
NC-Wilmington	31	24-7	1863	60.1
Butler	33	27-6	1986	60.2
Utah	33	25-8	1991	60.3
UC-Santa Barbara	32	18-14	1931	60.3
George Mason	28	16-12	1694	60.5
St. Louis	30	16-14	1822	60.7
Michigan St.	35	22-13	2143	61.2
SW Missouri St.	29	17-12	1782	61.4
Illinois	32	25-7	1970	61.6

Field Goal Percentage

	FG	FGA	Pct
Morehead St.	854	1674	51.0
Pittsburgh	893	1766	50.6
Colorado St.	876	1733	50.5
Central Michigan	864	1714	50.4
Creighton	974	1956	49.8
Kansas	1182	2393	49.4
Stephen F. Austin	753	1534	49.1
Kentucky	1026	2102	48.8
Maine	827	1697	48.7
Akron	761	1567	48.7
Kent St.	848	1741	48.7
Chattanooga	846	1750	48.3
Evansville	670	1386	48.3
Arizona St.	886	1838	48.2
LSU	851	1767	48.2
Marquette	901	1871	48.2
Tennessee Tech	839	1743	48.1
Air Force	536	1114	48.1
Detroit	798	1662	48.0
Illinois	859	1793	47.9

Scoring Margin

	Off	Def	Mar
Kansas	82.7	66.9	15.8
Pittsburgh	74.9	59.2	15.7
Arizona	85.2	70.7	14.5
Creighton	79.1	64.8	14.3
Kentucky	77.3	64.1	13.1
Illinois	74.6	61.6	13.1
Maryland	79.7	66.7	13.0
Louisville	81.6	68.7	13.0
Holy Cross	70.3	58.7	11.6
Duke	81.1	69.6	11.5
Xavier	77.6	66.1	11.5
NC-Wilmington	71.4	60.1	11.3
Wisconsin	70.3	59.3	11.0
St. Joseph's	70.4	59.5	10.9
Florida	75.3	64.5	10.8
Oklahoma	70.4	60.0	10.3
Syracuse	79.6	69.6	10.0
Wake Forest	77.8	67.8	10.0
Pennsylvania	69.9	60.0	9.9
Mississippi St.	69.4	59.7	9.6

Field Goal Percentage Defense

	FG	FGA	Pct
St. Joseph's	609	1639	37.2
Illinois	657	1741	37.7
Maryland	704	1864	37.8
Connecticut	817	2157	37.9
Syracuse	878	2253	39.0
Pittsburgh	682	1750	39.0
Florida St.	650	1662	39.1
Sam Houston St.	676	1727	39.1
Lamar	621	1577	39.4
Oklahoma St.	699	1775	39.4
Wake Forest	734	1849	39.7
Davidson	673	1694	39.7
Tulsa	771	1940	39.7
Virginia Commonwealth	685	1723	39.8
South Florida	696	1744	39.9
Mississippi St.	670	1672	40.1
Cincinnati	615	1534	40.1
Kansas St.	689	1718	40.1
Kansas	937	2332	40.2
Colorado	813	2020	40.2

Rebound Margin

	Off	Def	Mar
Wake Forest	41.7	32.0	9.6
Kansas	41.8	33.9	7.9
Holy Cross	36.5	28.6	7.9
Vermont	39.2	31.9	7.4
Utah St.	35.0	28.0	7.0
Texas	42.0	35.1	6.9
DePaul	37.1	30.2	6.9
Davidson	41.1	34.3	6.8
Mercer	40.4	33.7	6.7
Pittsburgh	36.5	29.8	6.6
Arizona	42.9	36.5	6.4
Siena	39.7	33.4	6.3
Tennessee Tech	37.4	31.2	6.2
Mississippi St.	37.0	30.9	6.2
Hofstra	40.6	34.5	6.1
Murray St.	37.8	31.7	6.1

Free Throw Percentage

	FT	FTA	Pct
Manhattan	.560	711	78.8
Providence	.496	637	77.9
Marist	.442	568	77.8
Davidson	.413	531	77.8
Oregon	.530	685	77.4
Marquette	.585	759	77.1
N.C. State	.488	634	77.0
Marshall	.468	609	76.8
Eastern Illinois	.453	590	76.8
Central Michigan	.601	789	76.2
NC-Asheville	.506	665	76.1
Notre Dame	.575	756	76.1
Centenary	.518	682	76.0
St. Bonaventure	.369	486	75.9
Chattanooga	.517	683	75.7

3-point FG Percentage

	3PT	3PTA	Pct
Illinois St.	.188	427	44.0
Davidson	.269	645	41.7
Pennsylvania	.251	608	41.3
Illinois-Chicago	.187	463	40.4
SE Missouri St.	.212	529	40.1
Marquette	.202	508	39.8
New Orleans	.159	400	39.8
Arkansas St.	.241	611	39.4
Morehead St.	.179	454	39.4
Kent St.	.229	582	39.3
Butler	.274	699	39.2
Oklahoma	.250	638	39.2
Evansville	.164	419	39.1
Florida	.287	735	39.0
College of Charleston	.308	789	39.0

3-point FG Made Per Game

	Gm	No	Avg
Mississippi Valley St.	29	299	10.3
St. Bonaventure	27	271	10.0
Davidson	27	269	10.0
Troy St.	32	312	9.8
UMKC	29	272	9.4
College of Charleston	33	308	9.3
Samford	28	258	9.2
Baylor	28	254	9.1
Pennsylvania	28	251	9.0
Oregon	33	291	8.8
American	30	263	8.8
Florida	33	287	8.7
Arkansas St.	28	241	8.6
Toledo	29	248	8.6
Washington St.	27	230	8.5

Underclassmen in NBA Draft

Seventeen division I players (10 juniors, 4 sophomores and 3 freshmen), 2 div. II players, 1 div. III player, 1 NAIA player, 3 jr. college players, 5 high school seniors, and 17 international players forfeited their college eligibility and declared for the 2003 NBA Draft which took place at Madison Square Garden in New York City on June 26. First round selections in **bold** type, high school players in *italics*.

	Cl	Drafted by	Overall Pick
Chris Alexander, Iowa St.	Jr.	not drafted	—
Carmelo Anthony, Syracuse	Fr.	Denver	3
Mario Austin, Mississippi St.	Jr.	Chicago	36
Malick Badiane, Langen (Germany)		Houston	44
Leandro Barbosa, Bauru Tilibra (Brazil)		San Antonio	28
Ronald Blackshear, W. Virginia	Jr.	not drafted	—
Chris Bosh, Georgia Tech	Fr.	Toronto	4
Lamar Castile, Community College of Beaver Countty (PA)	So.	not drafted	—
Carlos Delfino, Skipper Bologna (Italy)		Detroit	25
Boris Diaw-Riffiod, Pau Orthez (France)		Atlanta	21
Ndubi Ebi, Westbury Christian	HS	Minnesota	26
Rod Edwards, Ouachita Baptist	Jr.	not drafted	—
Carl English, Hawaii		not drafted	—
T.J. Ford, Texas	So.	Milwaukee	8
Zac Fray, Santa Ana College	So.	not drafted	—
David Hamilton, Salem Int'l	Jr.	not drafted	—
Jonathan Hargett, West Virginia	Fr.	not drafted	—
Jarvis Hayes, Georgia	Jr.	Washington	10
Maurice Jackson, TX-Permian-Bas.	Jr.	not drafted	—
LeBron James, St. Vincent-St. Mary (OH) HS	HS	Cleveland	1
Richard Jeter, Atlanta Metro.	So.	not drafted	—
Chris Kaman, Central Michigan	Jr.	L.A. Clippers	6
Maciej Lampe, Universidad Complutense (Spain)		New York	30
James Lang, Central Park Christian (AL) HS	HS	New Orleans	48
Darko Milicic, Hemofarm Vrsac (Serbia/Montenegro)		Detroit	2
Travis Outlaw, Starkville (MS) HS		Portland	23
Zaur Pachulia, Ulker (Turkey)		Orlando	42
Aleksandar Pavlovic, Buducnost (Serbia/Montenegro)		Utah	19
Kendrick Perkins, Clifton J. Ozen (TX) HS	HS	Memphis	27
Michael Pietrus, Pau Orthez (France)		not drafted	—
Zoran Planinic, Cibona Zagreb (Croatia)		New Jersey	22
Josh Powell, N.C. State	So.	not drafted	—
Rick Rickert, Minnesota	So.	Minnesota	55
Luke Ridnour, Oregon	Jr.	Seattle	14
Sofoklis Schortsanitis, Iraklis (Greece)		L.A. Clippers	34
Nedzad Sinanovic, Zenica Celik (Bosnia-Herzegovina)		Portland	54
Robert Smith, North Carolina Wesleyan	Jr.	not drafted	—
Jon Stefansson, TBB Trier (Germany)		not drafted	—
Mike Sweetney, Georgetown	Jr.	New York	9
Szymon Szewczyk, Braunschweig (Germany)		Milwaukee	35
Remon Van de Hare, F.C. Barcelona (Spain)		Toronto	52
Slavko Vranes, Buducnost (Serbia/Montenegro)		New York	39
Dwyane Wade, Marquette	Jr.	not drafted	—
Maurice Williams, Alabama	So.	Utah	47
Doug Wrenn, Washington	Jr.	not drafted	—
Xue Yuyang, Hong Kong Flying Dragons (China)		Dallas	57

Note: Twenty-seven American and International players who initially declared themselves eligible for the 2003 NBA Draft withdrew their names before the June 19 deadline.

Other 2003 Men's Tournaments

NIT Tournament

The 66th annual National Invitation Tournament had a 40-team field. First three rounds played on home courts of higher seeded teams. Semifinal, Third Place and Championship games played April 1-3 at Madison Square Garden in New York City.

Opening Round

at Iowa 62	. . . .	Valparaiso 60
at Siena 74	. . . .	Villanova 59
at Temple 68	. . . .	Drexel 59
Boston College 90	. . . .	at Fairfield 78
at Western Michigan 63	. . . .	Illinois-Chicago 62
at Iowa State 76	. . . .	Wichita State 65
College of Charleston 71	. . . . .	at Kent State 66
Providence 67	. . . .	at Richmond 49

1st Round

Georgetown 70	. . . .	at Tennessee 60
at North Carolina 83	. . . .	DePaul 72
at Georgia Tech 72	. . . .	Ohio State 58
at St. John's 62	. . . . . .	Boston University 57
at Rhode Island 61	. . . .	Seton Hall 60
at Virginia 89	. . . .	Brown 73
at UAB 82	. . . .	Lousiana-Lafayette 80
Minnesota 62	. . . .	at St. Louis 52
at Texas Tech 66	. . . .	Nevada 54
at San Diego St. 67	. . . . OT . . .	UC-Santa Barbara 62
Hawaii 85	. . . .	at UNLV 68
at Wyoming 78	. . . . . .	Eastern Washington 71
at Temple 75	. . . .	Boston College 62
at Iowa 54	. . . .	Iowa St. 53
at Providence 69	. . . .	College of Charleston 64
at Siena 68	. . . .	Western Michigan 62

2nd Round

at Texas Tech 57	. . . .	San Diego St. 48
at St. John's 73	. . . .	Virginia 63
Georgetown 67	. . . .	at Providence 58
at Minnesota 84	. . . .	Hawaii 70
at North Carolina 90	. . . .	Wyoming 74
Georgia Tech 79	. . . .	at Iowa 78
UAB 80	. . . .	at Siena 71
Temple 61	. . . .	at Rhode Island 53

Quarterfinals

Georgetown 79	. . . . .	at North Carolina 74
at Texas Tech 80	. . . . .	Georgia Tech 72
Minnesota 63	. . . . OT . . .	at Temple 58
at St. John's 79	. . . .	UAB 71

Semifinals

Georgetown 88	. . . .	Minnesota 74
St. John's 64	. . . .	Texas Tech 63

Third Place

Texas Tech 71	. . . .	Minnesota 61

Championship

St. John's 70	. . . .	Georgetown 67

Most Valuable Players

NIT
Marcus Hatten, St. John's guard

NCAA Division II
Darnell Hinson, Northeastern St. guard

NCAA Division III
Benjamin Coffin, Williams forward

NAIA Division I
Reynardo Curry, Mountain St. guard

NAIA Division II
Brandon Woudstra, Northwestern guard

NCAA Division II

The eight regional winners of the 48-team field: NORTHEAST—UMass-Lowell (27-4); EAST—Queens, NC (28-3); SOUTH ATLANTIC—Bowie St. (29-4); SOUTH—Eckerd (25-6); SOUTH CENTRAL—Northeastern St., OK (29-3); GREAT LAKES—Kentucky Wesleyan (29-3); NORTH CENTRAL—Nebraska-Kearney (30-2); WEST—Cal Poly Pomona (23-7).

The Elite Eight was played March 26-29, at Lakeland, Fla. There was no Third Place game.

Quarterfinals

Bowie St. 72	. . . .	UMass-Lowell 62
Ky. Wesleyan 85	. . . . . .	Cal Poly Pomona 60
Northeastern St. 94	. . . . .	Nebraska-Kearney 75
Queens 99	. . . .	Eckerd 78

Semifinals

Ky. Wesleyan 84	. . . .	Bowie St. 64
Northeastern St. 84	. . . . . .	Queens 69

Championship

Northeastern St. 75	. . . . . .	Ky. Wesleyan 64

NCAA Division III

The four regional winners of the 48-team field: Hampden-Sydney (28-2), Gustavus Adolphus (25-6), Williams (29-1), Wooster (29-2).

The Final Four was played March 21-22, at Salem Civic Center in Salem, Va.

Semifinals

Gustavus Adolphus 79	. . . . .	Hampden-Sydney 68
Williams 74	. . . . . OT . . .	Wooster 72

Third Place

Wooster 78	. . . .	Hampden-Sydney 74

Championship

Williams 67	. . . .	Gustavus Adolphus 65

NAIA Division I

The quarterfinalists, in alphabetical order, after two rounds of the 32-team NAIA tournament: Barber-Scotia, NC (27-9); Concordia, CA (34-4); Georgetown, KY. (32-5); Lee, TN (27-8); McKendree, IL (34-3); Mountain St., WV (31-6); Oklahoma Baptist (26-6); Olivet Nazarene, IL (23-14).

All tournament games played, March 29-April 1, at the Municipal Auditorium, Kansas City, Mo. There was no Third Place game.

Quarterfinals: Georgetown def. Lee, 71-58; Mountain St. def. Oklahoma Baptist, 108-106 OT; Concordia def. Barber-Scotia, 64-52; McKendree def. Olivet Nazarene, 64-62.

Semifinals: Mountain St. def. Georgetown, 106-89; Concordia def. McKendree, 81-58.

Championship: Concordia def. Mountain St., 88-84 OT.

NAIA Division II

The quarterfinalists, in alphabetical order, after two rounds of the 32-team NAIA tournament: Bellevue, Neb. (32-5), Bethany, Kan. (25-9), Concordia, Neb. (25-9), Cornerstone, Mich. (29-5); Huntington, Ind. (29-8); Jamestown, N.D. (29-4); Northwestern, Iowa (31-2); Warner Southern, Fla. (25-8).

All tournament games played, March 15-18, at Point Lookout, Missouri. There was no Third Place game.

Quarterfinals: Northwestern def. Huntington, 74-60; Cornerstone def. Bellevue, 84-75; Warner-Southern def. Jamestown, 76-71; Bethany def. Concordia, 77-72.

Semifinals: Northwestern def. Cornerstone, 104-92; Bethany def. Warner Southern, 74-69.

Championship: Northwestern def. Bethany, 77-57.

Final Regular Season AP Women's Top 25 Poll

Taken **before** start of NCAA tournament.

The sportswriters & broadcasters poll: first place votes in parentheses; records through Sunday, March 16, 2003; total points (based on 25 for 1st, 24 for 2nd, etc.); record in NCAA tourney and team lost to; head coach (career years and career record including 2003 postseason), and preseason ranking. Teams in **bold** type went on to reach the NCAA Final Four.

		Mar. 16 Record	Points	NCAA Recap	Head Coach	Preseason Rank
1	**Connecticut** (21)	31-1	1,074	6-0	Geno Auriemma (18 yrs: 501-99)	4
2	**Duke** (19)	31-1	1,070	4-1 (Tennessee)	Gail Goestenkors (11 yrs: 272-84)	1
3	LSU (4)	27-3	1,018	3-1 (Texas)	Sue Gunter (33 yrs: 681-300)	3
4	**Tennessee**	28-4	945	4-1 (Connecticut)	Pat Summitt (29 yrs: 821-163)	2
5	**Texas**	25-5	939	4-1 (Connecticut)	Jody Conradt (34 yrs: 817-264)	11
6	Louisiana Tech	29-2	824	2-1 (LSU)	Kurt Budke (1 yr: 31-3)	16
7	Texas Tech	26-5	806	3-1 (Duke)	Marsha Sharp (21 yrs: 507-159)	7
8	Kansas St.	28-4	757	1-1 (Notre Dame)	Deb Patterson (7 yrs: 126-89)	5
9	Stanford	26-4	753	1-1 (Minnesota)	Tara VanDerveer (24 yrs: 575-161)	6
10	Purdue	26-5	722	3-1 (Connecticut)	Kristy Curry (4 yrs: 107-27)	8
11	Villanova	25-5	646	3-1 (Tennessee)	Harry Perretta (24 yrs: 445-251)	NR
12	North Carolina	27-5	629	1-1 (Colorado)	Sylvia Hatchell (28 yrs: 630-255)	13
13	Mississippi St.	23-7	623	1-1 (New Mexico)	Sharon Fanning (27 yrs: 443-312)	24
14	Vanderbilt	21-9	487	1-1 (Boston College)	Melanie Balcomb (10 yrs: 185-114)	12
15	Penn St.	24-8	456	2-1 (Tennessee)	Rene Portland (27 yrs: 621-216)	14
16	South Carolina	22-7	385	1-1 (Penn St.)	Susan Walvius (12 yrs: 194-179)	NR
17	Minnesota	23-5	383	2-1 (Texas)	Pam Borton (5 yrs: 94-36)	15
18	Santa Barbara	26-4	353	1-1 (Texas Tech)	Mark French (24 yrs: 430-262)	25
19	Georgia	19-9	253	2-1 (Duke)	Andy Landers (24 yrs: 585-179)	9
20	Ohio St.	21-9	249	1-1 (La. Tech)	Jim Foster (25 yrs: 526-235)	NR
21	Wisc-Green Bay	27-3	226	1-1 (LSU)	Kevin Borseth (17 yrs: 365-165)	NR
22	Arizona	22-8	203	0-1 (Notre Dame)	Joan Bonvicini (24 yrs: 540-211)	NR
23	Rutgers	20-7	147	1-1 (Georgia)	Vivian Stringer (32 yrs: 674-227)	NR
24	Arkansas	21-10	100	1-1 (Texas)	Gary Blair (18 yrs: 408-163)	17
25	Boston College	20-8	66	2-1 (Connecticut)	Cathy Inglese (17 yrs: 291-196)	20
	George Washington	24-6	66	1-1 (Villanova)	Joe McKeown (16 yrs: 179-47)	21

Others receiving votes: 26. **Colorado** (22-7, 24 points); 27. **TCU** (19-13, 19); 28. **DePaul** (22-9) and **New Mexico** (22-8, 16); 30. **Liberty** (26-3) and **Utah** (23-6, 9); 32. **Washington** (22-7, 8); 33. **Chattanooga** (26-4, 6); 34. **Virginia Tech** (21-9, 5); 35. **Austin Peay** (27-3, 4); 36. **Harvard** (22-4), **Holy Cross** (24-7), **St. Francis-PA** (23-7) and **Western Kentucky** (22-8, 1).

NCAA Women's Division I Tournament Seeds

	WEST		MIDWEST		MIDEAST		EAST
1	LSU (27-3)	1	Duke (31-1)	1	Tennessee (28-4)	1	Connecticut (31-1)
2	Texas (25-5)	2	Texas Tech (26-5)	2	Villanova (25-5)	2	Purdue (26-5)
3	Stanford (26-4)	3	Mississippi St. (23-7)	3	North Carolina (27-5)	3	Kansas St. (28-4)
4	Ohio St. (21-9)	4	Rutgers (20-7)	4	Penn St. (24-8)	4	Vanderbilt (21-9)
5	Louisiana Tech (29-2)	5	Georgia (19-9)	5	South Carolina (22-7)	5	Boston College (20-8)
6	Minnesota (23-5)	6	New Mexico (22-8)	6	Colorado (22-7)	6	Arizona (22-8)
7	Arkansas (21-10)	7	Santa Barbara (26-4)	7	Geo. Washington (24-6)	7	Virginia Tech (21-9)
8	Wisc-Green Bay (27-3)	8	Utah (23-6)	8	Virginia (16-13)	8	Michigan St. (17-11)
9	Washington (22-7)	9	DePaul (22-9)	9	Illinois (17-11)	9	TCU (19-13)
10	Cincinnati (23-7)	10	Xavier (20-9)	10	Oklahoma (19-12)	10	Georgia Tech (20-10)
11	Tulane (19-9)	11	Miami-FL (18-12)	11	BYU (19-11)	11	Notre Dame (19-10)
12	Pepperdine (22-7)	12	Charlotte (21-8)	12	Chattanooga (26-4)	12	Old Dominion (21-10)
13	Weber St. (21-8)	13	Western Ky. (22-8)	13	Holy Cross (24-7)	13	Liberty (26-3)
14	W. Michigan (20-11)	14	Manhattan (20-9)	14	Austin Peay (27-3)	14	Harvard (22-4)
15	Hampton (23-8)	15	SW Missouri St. (18-12)	15	St. Francis-PA (23-7)	15	Valparaiso (18-12)
16	SW Texas St. (18-13)	16	Georgia St. (20-10)	16	Alabama St. (20-10)	16	Boston University (16-14)

2003 NCAA Tournament Women's Division

EAST

1st ROUND — March 22-23
- (1) Connecticut 91
- (16) Boston Univ. 44
- (9) Michigan St. 47
- (8) TCU 50
- (5) Boston College 73
- (12) Old Dominion 72
- (4) Vanderbilt 54
- (13) Liberty 44
- (6) Arizona 47
- (11) Notre Dame 59
- (3) Kansas St. 79
- (14) Harvard 69
- (7) Virginia Tech 61
- (10) Ga. Tech 59
- (2) Purdue 66
- (15) Valparaiso 51

2nd ROUND — March 24-25
- Connecticut 81
- TCU 66
- Boston College (ot) 86
- Vanderbilt 85
- Notre Dame 59
- Kansas St. 53
- Virginia Tech 62
- Purdue 80

SWEET 16 — March 30
- Connecticut 70
- Boston College 49
- Notre Dame 47
- Purdue 66

ELITE EIGHT — April 1
- Connecticut 73
- Purdue 64

FINAL FOUR — April 6
- Connecticut 71

WEST

1st ROUND — March 22-23
- (1) LSU 86
- (16) SW Tex. St. 50
- (9) WI-Green Bay 78
- (8) Washington 65
- (5) La. Tech 94
- (12) Pepperdine 60
- (4) Ohio St. 66
- (13) Weber St. 44
- (6) Minnesota 68
- (11) Tulane 48
- (3) Stanford 82
- (14) W. Michigan 66
- (7) Arkansas 71
- (10) Cincinnati 57
- (2) Texas 90
- (15) Hampton 46

2nd ROUND — March 24-25
- LSU 80
- WI-Green Bay 69
- Louisiana Tech 74
- Ohio St. 61
- Minnesota 68
- Stanford 56
- Arkansas 50
- Texas 67

SWEET 16 — March 30
- LSU 69
- Louisiana Tech 63
- Minnesota 60
- Texas 73

ELITE EIGHT — April 1
- LSU 60
- Texas 78

FINAL FOUR — April 6
- Texas 69

NATIONAL CHAMPIONSHIP
- Connecticut 73
- Tennessee 68

NCAA WOMEN'S FINAL FOUR — ATLANTA

Georgia Dome
Atlanta, Georgia
Tuesday, April 8, 2003

MIDEAST

1st ROUND — March 22-23
- (1) Tennessee 95
- (16) Alabama St. 43
- (8) Virginia 72
- (9) Illinois 56
- (5) So. Carolina 68
- (12) Chattanooga 54
- (4) Penn St. 64
- (13) Holy Cross 33
- (6) Colorado 84
- (11) BYU 45
- (3) No. Carolina 72
- (14) Austin Peay 70
- (7) Geo. Wash. 71
- (10) Oklahoma 61
- (2) Villanova 51
- (15) St.Francis-PA 36

2nd ROUND — March 24-25
- Tennessee 81
- Virginia 51
- So. Carolina 67
- Penn St. 77
- Colorado 86
- North Carolina 67
- Geo. Washington 57
- Villanova 70

SWEET 16 — March 29
- Tennessee 86
- Penn St. 58
- Colorado 51
- Villanova 53

ELITE EIGHT — March 31
- Tennessee 73
- Villanova 49

FINAL FOUR — April 6
- Tennessee 66

MIDWEST

1st ROUND — March 22-23
- (1) Duke 66
- (16) Georgia St. 48
- (8) Utah 73
- (9) DePaul 64
- (5) Georgia 80
- (12) Charlotte 61
- (4) Rutgers 64
- (13) W. Kentucky 52
- (6) New Mexico 91
- (11) Miami-FL (ot) 85
- (3) Mississippi St.73
- (14) Manhattan 47
- (7) UC-Santa Barb. 62
- (10) Xavier 62
- (2) Texas Tech 67
- (15) SW Mo. St. 59

2nd ROUND — March 24-25
- Duke 65
- Utah 54
- Georgia 74
- Rutgers 64
- New Mexico 73
- Mississippi St. 61
- UC-Santa Barbara 68
- Texas Tech 72

SWEET 16 — March 29
- Duke 66
- Georgia 63
- New Mexico 48
- Texas Tech 71

ELITE EIGHT — March 31
- Duke 57
- Texas Tech 51

FINAL FOUR — April 6
- Duke 56

NCAA Championship Game
Tennessee 68

	Min	FG M-A	FT M-A	Pts	Reb O-T	A	PF
Tasha Butts	17	2-4	0-0	4	1-1	2	3
Gwen Jackson	35	6-14	3-6	15	6-9	4	3
Kara Lawson	40	5-13	5-5	18	1-5	5	1
Loree Moore	25	2-4	0-0	5	1-2	1	1
Shyra Ely	25	3-6	0-0	6	0-2	0	1
Shanna Zolman	11	0-0	0-0	0	1-2	0	2
Brittany Jackson	20	4-10	2-2	13	1-5	0	3
Ashley Robinson	17	1-2	1-6	3	4-8	1	8
Courtney McDaniel	6	1-3	0-0	2	1-2	0	2
Tye'sha Fluker	4	1-1	0-0	2	1-1	0	0
TOTALS	200	25-57	11-19	68	20-40	13	18

Three-point FG: 7-18 (B. Jackson 3-7, Lawson 3-8, Moore 1-1, G. Jackson 0-2); **Team Rebounds:** 3; **Blocked Shots:** 1 (G. Jackson); **Turnovers:** 15 (B. Jackson 3, K. Lawson 3, G. Jackson 2, Ely 2, Butts, Moore, Zolman, Robinson, Team); **Steals:** 7 (Moore 3, Butts, Lawson, Ely, Zolman); **Percentages:** 2-Pt FG (.462); 3-Pt FG (.389); Total FG (.439); Free Throws (.579).

Connecticut 73

	Min	FG M-A	FT M-A	Pts	Reb O-T	A	PF
Diana Taurasi	37	8-15	8-8	28	1-4	1	2
Maria Conlon	39	3-7	2-4	11	0-4	6	2
Jessica Moore	35	2-5	0-0	4	1-4	3	2
Barbara Turner	21	5-7	0-0	10	1-1	1	3
Ann Strother	32	6-11	2-2	17	0-3	3	2
Ashley Battle	12	0-3	0-0	0	0-0	1	0
Willnett Crockett	24	1-1	1-2	3	2-6	0	5
TOTALS	200	25-49	13-16	73	5-22	15	16

Three-point FG: 10-21 (Taurasi 4-9, Conlon 3-5, Strother 3-7); **Team Rebounds:** 0; **Blocked Shots:** 1 (Taurasi); **Turnovers:** 11 (Taurasi 3, Moore 3, Turner 2, Strother, Battle, Crockett); **Steals:** 4 (Conlon, Battle); **Percentages:** 2-Pt FG (.536); 3-Pt FG (.476); Total FG (.510); Free Throws (.813).

Tennessee (SEC)	30	38—	**68**
Connecticut (Big East)	35	38—	**73**

Technical Fouls: None. **Officials:** Lisa Mattingly, Melissa Barlow, Wesley Dean. **Attendance:** 28,210. **TV Rating:** 3.49 (ESPN).

Final *ESPN/USA Today* Coaches' Poll
Taken **after** NCAA tournament.

Voted on by panel of 40 women's coaches and media following the NCAA tournament: first place votes in parentheses.

	Pts		Pts
1 Connecticut (40)	1,000	13 Minnesota	.465
2 Tennessee	.958	14 Stanford	.427
3 Texas	.908	15 North Carolina	.394
4 Duke	.893	16 Mississippi St.	.362
5 LSU	.829	17 Boston College	.331
6 Texas Tech	.768	18 South Carolina	.262
7 Purdue	.725	19 Colorado	.239
8 Villanova	.699	20 Vanderbilt	.236
9 Louisiana Tech	.617	21 Notre Dame	.213
10 Kansas St.	.544	22 Santa Barbara	.200
11 Georgia	.492	23 New Mexico	.162
12 Penn St.	.475	24 Wisconsin-GB	.132
		25 Arkansas	.115

WOMEN'S FINAL FOUR
at Atlanta, Georgia (April 6-8).
Semifinals
Connecticut 71 ....Texas 69
Tennessee 66 ....Duke 56
Championship
Connecticut 73 ....Tennessee 68

Final Records: Connecticut (37-1), Tennessee (33-5), Texas (29-6), Duke (35-2).

Most Outstanding Player: Diana Taurasi, Connecticut forward. SEMIFINAL—38 minutes, 26 points, 4 rebounds, 4 assists; FINAL—37 minutes, 28 points, 4 rebounds, 1 block.

All-Tournament Team: Taurasi and guard Ann Strother of Connecticut, guard/forward Alana Beard of Duke and center/forward Gwen Jackson and guard Kara Lawson of Tennessee.

Annual Awards
Player of the Year
Diana Taurasi, Connecticut ....AP, Broderick, Wade USBWA, Naismith
Coach of the Year
Geno Auriemma, Connecticut ....AP, USBWA
Gail Goestenkors, Duke ....Naismith, WBCA

Consensus All-America Team
The NCAA Division I players cited most frequently by the Associated Press, US Basketball Writers Association and the Women's Basketball Coaches Association. Holdovers from 2001-02 All-America first team in **bold** type; (*) indicates unanimous first team selection.

First Team
	Class	Hgt	Pos
Diana Taurasi*, Connecticut	Jr.	6-0	G/F
Alana Beard, Duke*	Jr.	5-11	G/F
LaToya Thomas, Miss. St.*	Sr.	6-2	F
Kelly Mazzante*, Penn St.	Jr.	6-0	G
Nicole Ohlde*, Kansas St.	Jr.	6-4	C

Second Team
	Class	Hgt	Pos
Chantelle Anderson, Vanderbilt	Sr.	6-6	C
Kara Lawson, Tennessee	Sr.	5-8	G
Nicole Powell, Stanford	Jr.	6-2	F
Lindsay Whalen, Minnesota	Jr.	5-8	G
Jocelyn Penn, South Carolina	Sr.	6-0	F

Other Women's Tournaments
WNIT (April 4 at Waco, Tex.): Final— Auburn def. Baylor, 64-63.
NCAA Division II (Mar. 29 at St. Joseph, Missouri): Final— South Dakota St. def. Northern Kentucky, 65-50.
NCAA Division III (Mar. 22 at Terre Haute, Ind.): Final— Trinity def. East Connecticut St., 60-58.
NAIA Division I (Mar. 25 at Jackson, Tenn.): Final— Southern Nazarene (Okla.) def. Oklahoma City, 71-70.
NAIA Division II (Mar. 18 at Sioux City, Iowa): Final— Hastings (Neb.) def. Dakota Wesleyan (S.D.), 59–53.

NCAA Women's Division I Leaders

Includes games through NCAA and NIT tourneys.

INDIVIDUAL

Scoring

	Cl	Gm	Pts	Avg
Chandi Jones, Houston	Jr.	28	770	27.5
Molly Creamer, Bucknell	Sr.	31	759	27.1
LaToya Thomas, Miss. St.	Sr.	31	794	25.6
Tiffany Webb, Wright St.	So.	28	674	24.1
Kelly Mazzante, Penn St.	Jr.	35	837	23.9
Jocelyn Penn, South Carolina	Sr.	30	716	23.9
Alison Curtin, Tulsa	Jr.	30	692	23.1
Alana Beard, Duke	Jr.	37	813	22.0
Shanika Freeman, Jacksonville St.	So.	29	629	21.7
Hana Peljito, Harvard	Jr.	24	510	21.3
Shalayna Johnson, UMBC	Sr.	23	483	21.0
Tamara James, Miami-FL	Fr.	31	650	21.0
Nikki Reddick, Coastal Carolina	Jr.	27	560	20.7
Lindsay Whalen, Minnesota	Jr.	31	639	20.6
Tamara Bowie, Ball St.	Sr.	30	618	20.6
Jenel Stevens, Canisius	Jr.	30	615	20.5
Cricket Williams, San Jose St.	Jr.	28	571	20.4
Constance Jinks, UNLV	Sr.	29	585	20.2
Heather Ernest, Maine	Jr.	28	559	20.0
Katie Wolfe, Oakland	Sr.	28	557	19.9

Assists

	Cl	Gm	No	Avg
La'Terrica Dobin, Northwestern St.	Jr.	29	298	10.6
Latesha Lee, Jackson St.	Jr.	29	214	7.4
Laura Ingham, Nevada	Sr.	29	212	7.3
Ashley McElhiney, Vanderbilt	Sr.	30	219	7.3
Ivelina Vrancheva, Florida Int'l	Jr.	30	217	7.2
Yolanda Paige, West Virginia	So.	28	199	7.1
Jess Cichowicz, James Madison	Sr.	28	194	6.9
Sara Nord, Louisville	Jr.	29	199	6.9
Cricket Williams, San Jose St.	Jr.	28	192	6.9
Cristina Ciocan, South Carolina	Jr.	31	207	6.7
Mandie Vinck, Tex. A&M-CC	Sr.	27	179	6.6
Shiri Sharon, Duquesne	Jr.	29	192	6.6
Nancy Bowden, Butler	Jr.	29	191	6.6
Lisa Faulkner, UC-Irvine	So.	29	189	6.5
Erin Grant, Texas Tech	Fr.	35	228	6.5

Rebounding

	Cl	Gm	No	Avg
Jennifer Butler, Massachusetts	Sr.	28	412	14.7
Angela Buckner, Wichita St.	Jr.	28	366	13.1
Cheryl Ford, La. Tech	Sr.	34	438	12.9
Ashlee Kelly, Quinnipiac	Jr.	28	338	12.1
Tori Talbert, SW Texas St.	So.	32	385	12.0
Alex Cook, Northern Iowa	So.	30	360	12.0
Rosalee Mason, Manhattan	Jr.	30	342	11.4
Amie Williams, Jackson St.	Jr.	29	318	11.0
Jamie Gray, Evansville	Jr.	27	296	11.0
Shawntinice Polk, Arizona	Fr.	31	335	10.8
Jaysie Chambers, Illinois-Chicago	Sr.	27	291	10.8
Kristine Austgulen, Va. Comm.	Sr.	23	247	10.7
Rebekkah Brunson, Georgetown	Jr.	29	311	10.7
Katie Macfarlane, Army	Jr.	31	330	10.6
Shanika Freeman, Jacksonville St.	So.	29	302	10.4
Kim Watson, Florida A&M	Sr.	29	302	10.4

Blocked Shots

	Cl	Gm	No	Avg
Amie Williams, Jackson St.	Jr.	29	152	5.2
Sandora Irvin, TCU	So.	33	128	3.9
Christen Roper, Hawaii	Sr.	30	110	3.7
Amy Collins, S.F. Austin	Sr.	28	91	3.3
Alyssa Shriver, Tulsa	Sr.	30	96	3.2

Steals

	Cl	Gm	No	Avg
Teresa McNair, Eastern Ky.	Sr.	29	131	4.5
Toccara Williams, Texas A&M	Jr.	27	117	4.3
Maria Jilian, Western Mich.	So.	32	124	3.9
Melanie Boeglin, Indiana St.	Fr.	31	117	3.8
Jocelyn Penn, South Carolina	Sr.	30	112	3.7

High-Point Games

Pts		Opponent	Date
51	Jocelyn Penn, South Carolina	Stetson	Jan. 4
50	Jocelyn Penn, South Carolina	Wofford	Dec. 4
49	Tiffany Webb, Wright St.	Butler	Jan. 16

TEAM

Scoring Offense

	Gm	W-L	Pts	Avg
Indiana St.	31	22-9	2480	80.0
Tennessee	38	33-5	3037	79.9
Ball St.	31	21-10	2474	79.8
Duke	37	35-2	2922	79.0
Western Michigan	32	20-12	2523	78.8
Louisiana Tech	34	31-3	2666	78.4
Eastern Ky.	29	18-11	2268	78.2
Wisconsin-Green Bay	32	28-4	2502	78.2
Minnesota	31	25-6	2412	77.8
Georgia	31	21-10	2381	76.8

High-Point Games

Pts		Opponent	Date
136	Tennessee	P.R.-Mayaguez	Nov. 29
128	Duke	Howard	Dec. 6
119	Coastal Carolina	Southern Virginia	Feb. 26
116	Minnesota	IPFW	Nov. 23
115	Western Michigan	IPFW	Dec. 22
115	Kansas St.	Arkansas-Pine Bluff	Dec. 2
114	West Virginia	Robert Morris	Dec. 7

Scoring Defense

	Gm	W-L	Pts	Avg
Utah	31	24-7	1582	51.0
Villanova	34	28-6	1794	52.8
Connecticut	38	37-1	2032	53.5
Delaware	31	22-9	1658	53.5
Duke	37	35-2	1998	54.0
Texas-San Antonio	29	18-11	1570	54.1
NC-Wilmington	28	22-6	1517	54.2
Liberty	30	26-4	1641	54.7
Jackson St.	29	23-6	1594	55.0
UMBC	30	14-16	1656	55.2

Scoring Margin

	Off	Def	Mar
Duke	79.0	54.0	25.0
Tennessee	79.9	58.5	21.4
Connecticut	74.8	53.5	21.3
Louisiana Tech	78.4	57.6	20.9
Texas	74.5	55.8	18.7
Wisconsin-Green Bay	78.2	59.5	18.7
LSU	76.3	58.9	17.4
Kansas St.	74.7	57.5	17.2
UC-Santa Barbara	74.0	57.6	16.4

1901-2003
Through the Years

SPORTS ALMANAC

National Champions and NCAA Final Four

The Helms Foundation of Los Angeles, under the direction of founder Bill Schroeder, selected national college basketball champions from 1942-82 and researched retroactive picks from 1901-41. The first NIT tournament and then the NCAA tournament have settled the national championship since 1938, but there are four years (1939, '40, '44 and '54) where the Helms selections differ. In 1939, Helms picked undefeated LIU-Brooklyn (24-0), winners of the NIT. In 1940, Helms picked USC (20-3) although they were beaten by Kansas in the West Regionals of the NCAA tourney. In 1944, Helms picked unbeaten Army (15-0). Army did not lift its policy barring postseason play until the 1961 NIT. In 1954, Helms chose unbeaten Kentucky (25-0), even though Kentucky refused its NCAA bid after seniors Cliff Hagan, Frank Ramsey and Lou Tsioropoulos were declared ineligible.

Multiple champions (1901-37): Chicago, Columbia and Wisconsin (3); Kansas, Minnesota, Notre Dame, Penn, Pittsburgh, Syracuse and Yale (2). **Multiple champions (since 1938):** UCLA (11); Kentucky (7); Indiana (5); Duke and North Carolina (3); Cincinnati, Kansas, Louisville, Michigan St., N.C. State, Oklahoma A&M (now Oklahoma St.) and San Francisco (2).

Year	Champion	Record	Head Coach	Outstanding Player
1901	Yale	10-4	No coach	G.M. Clark, F
1902	Minnesota	11-0	Louis Cooke	W.C. Deering, F
1903	Yale	15-1	W.H. Murphy	R.B. Hyatt,F
1904	Columbia	17-1	No coach	Harry Fisher, F
1905	Columbia	19-1	No coach	Harry Fisher, F
1906	Dartmouth	16-2	No coach	George Grebenstein, F
1907	Chicago	22-2	Joseph Raycroft	John Schommer, C
1908	Chicago	21-2	Joseph Raycroft	John Schommer, C
1909	Chicago	12-0	Joseph Raycroft	John Schommer, C
1910	Columbia	11-1	Harry Fisher	Ted Kiendl, F
1911	St. John's-NY	14-0	Claude Allen	John Keenan, F/C
1912	Wisconsin	15-0	Doc Meanwell	Otto Stangel, F
1913	Navy	9-0	Louis Wenzell	Laurence Wild, F
1914	Wisconsin	15-0	Doc Meanwell	Gene Van Gent, C
1915	Illinois	16-0	Ralph Jones	Ray Woods, G
1916	Wisconsin	20-1	Doc Meanwell	George Levis, F
1917	Washington St	25-1	Doc Bohler	Roy Bohler, G
1918	Syracuse	16-1	Edmund Dollard	Joe Schwarzer, G
1919	Minnesota	13-0	Louis Cooke	Arnold Oss, F
1920	Penn	22-1	Lon Jourdet	George Sweeney, F
1921	Penn	21-2	Edward McNichol	Danny McNichol, G
1922	Kansas	16-2	Phog Allen	Paul Endacott, G
1923	Kansas	17-1	Phog Allen	Paul Endacott, G
1924	North Carolina	25-0	Bo Shepard	Jack Cobb, F
1925	Princeton	21-2	Al Wittmer	Art Loeb, G
1926	Syracuse	19-1	Lew Andreas	Vic Hanson, F
1927	Notre Dame	19-1	George Keogan	John Nyikos, C
1928	Pittsburgh	21-0	Doc Carlson	Chuck Hyatt, F
1929	Montana St.	36-2	Schubert Dyche	John (Cat) Thompson, F
1930	Pittsburgh	23-2	Doc Carlson	Chuck Hyatt, F
1931	Northwestern	16-1	Dutch Lonborg	Joe Reiff, C
1932	Purdue	17-1	Piggy Lambert	John Wooden, G
1933	Kentucky	20-3	Adolph Rupp	Forest Sale, F
1934	Wyoming	26-3	Willard Witte	Les Witte, G
1935	NYU	19-1	Howard Cann	Sid Gross, F
1936	Notre Dame	22-2-1	George Keogan	John Moir, F
1937	Stanford	25-2	John Bunn	Hank Luisetti, F

Year	Champion			Record	Winner	Head Coach	Outstanding Player
1938	Temple			23-2	NIT	James Usilton	Meyer Bloom, G

Year	Champion	Runner-up	Score	Final Two	Head Coach	Third Place
1939	Oregon	Ohio St.	46-33	@ Evanston, IL	Oklahoma	Villanova
1940	Indiana	Kansas	60-42	@ Kansas City	Duquesne	USC
1941	Wisconsin	Washington St.	39-34	@ Kansas City	Arkansas	Pittsburgh
1942	Stanford	Dartmouth	53-38	@ Kansas City	Colorado	Kentucky
1943	Wyoming	Georgetown	46-34	@ New York	DePaul	Texas
1944	Utah	Dartmouth	42-40 (OT)	@ New York	Iowa St.	Ohio St.
1945	Oklahoma A&M	NYU	49-45	@ New York	Arkansas	Ohio St.

Year	Champion	Runner-up	Score	Final Two	Third Place	Fourth Place
1946	Oklahoma A&M	North Carolina	43-40	@ New York	Ohio St.	California
1947	Holy Cross	Oklahoma	58-47	@ New York	Texas	CCNY
1948	Kentucky	Baylor	58-42	@ New York	Holy Cross	Kansas St.
1949	Kentucky	Oklahoma A&M	46-36	@ Seattle	Illinois	Oregon St.
1950	CCNY	Bradley	71-68	@ New York	N.C. State	Baylor
1951	Kentucky	Kansas St.	68-58	@ Minneapolis	Illinois	Oklahoma A&M

Year	Champion	Runner-up	Score	Third Place	Fourth Place	Final Four
1952	Kansas	St. John's	80-63	Illinois	Santa Clara	@ Seattle
1953	Indiana	Kansas	69-68	Washington	LSU	@ Kansas City
1954	La Salle	Bradley	92-76	Penn St.	USC	@ Kansas City
1955	San Francisco	La Salle	77-63	Colorado	Iowa	@ Kansas City
1956	San Francisco	Iowa	83-71	Temple	SMU	@ Evanston, IL
1957	North Carolina	Kansas	54-53 (3OT)	San Francisco	Michigan St.	@ Kansas City
1958	Kentucky	Seattle	84-72	Temple	Kansas St.	@ Louisville
1959	California	West Virginia	71-70	Cincinnati	Louisville	@ Louisville
1960	Ohio St.	California	75-55	Cincinnati	NYU	@ San Francisco
1961	Cincinnati	Ohio St.	70-65 (OT)	St. Joseph's-PA	Utah	@ Kansas City
1962	Cincinnati	Ohio St.	71-59	Wake Forest	UCLA	@ Louisville
1963	Loyola-IL	Cincinnati	60-58 (OT)	Duke	Oregon St.	@ Louisville
1964	UCLA	Duke	98-83	Michigan	Kansas St.	@ Kansas City
1965	UCLA	Michigan	91-80	Princeton	Wichita St.	@ Portland, OR
1966	Texas Western	Kentucky	72-65	Duke	Utah	@ College Park, MD
1967	UCLA	Dayton	79-64	Houston	North Carolina	@ Louisville
1968	UCLA	North Carolina	78-55	Ohio St.	Houston	@ Los Angeles
1969	UCLA	Purdue	92-72	Drake	North Carolina	@ Louisville
1970	UCLA	Jacksonville	80-69	New Mexico St.	St. Bonaventure	@ College Park, MD
1971	UCLA	Villanova	68-62	Western Ky.	Kansas	@ Houston
1972	UCLA	Florida St.	81-76	North Carolina	Louisville	@ Los Angeles
1973	UCLA	Memphis St.	87-66	Indiana	Providence	@ St. Louis
1974	N.C. State	Marquette	76-64	UCLA	Kansas	@ Greensboro, NC
1975	UCLA	Kentucky	92-85	Louisville	Syracuse	@ San Diego
1976	Indiana	Michigan	86-68	UCLA	Rutgers	@ Philadelphia
1977	Marquette	North Carolina	67-59	UNLV	NC-Charlotte	@ Atlanta
1978	Kentucky	Duke	94-88	Arkansas	Notre Dame	@ St. Louis
1979	Michigan St.	Indiana St.	75-64	DePaul	Penn	@ Salt Lake City
1980	Louisville	UCLA	59-54	Purdue	Iowa	@ Indianapolis
1981	Indiana	North Carolina	63-50	Virginia	LSU	@ Philadelphia

Year	Champion	Runner-up	Score	——Third Place——		Final Four
1982	North Carolina	Georgetown	63-62	Houston	Louisville	@ New Orleans
1983	N.C. State	Houston	54-52	Georgia	Louisville	@ Albuquerque
1984	Georgetown	Houston	84-75	Kentucky	Virginia	@ Seattle
1985	Villanova	Georgetown	66-64	Memphis St.	St. John's	@ Lexington
1986	Louisville	Duke	72-69	Kansas	LSU	@ Dallas
1987	Indiana	Syracuse	74-73	Providence	UNLV	@ New Orleans
1988	Kansas	Oklahoma	83-79	Arizona	Duke	@ Kansas City
1989	Michigan	Seton Hall	80-79 (OT)	Duke	Illinois	@ Seattle
1990	UNLV	Duke	103-73	Arkansas	Georgia Tech	@ Denver
1991	Duke	Kansas	72-65	North Carolina	UNLV	@ Indianapolis
1992	Duke	Michigan	71-51	Cincinnati	Indiana	@ Minneapolis
1993	North Carolina	Michigan	77-71	Kansas	Kentucky	@ New Orleans
1994	Arkansas	Duke	76-72	Arizona	Florida	@ Charlotte
1995	UCLA	Arkansas	89-78	North Carolina	Oklahoma St.	@ Seattle
1996	Kentucky	Syracuse	76-67	UMass	Mississippi St.	@ E. Rutherford, NJ
1997	Arizona	Kentucky	84-79 (OT)	Minnesota	North Carolina	@ Indianapolis
1998	Kentucky	Utah	78-69	Stanford	North Carolina	@ San Antonio
1999	Connecticut	Duke	77-74	Michigan St.	Ohio St.	@ St. Petersburg, FL
2000	Michigan St.	Florida	89-76	Wisconsin	North Carolina	@ Indianapolis
2001	Duke	Arizona	82-72	Michigan St.	Maryland	@ Minneapolis
2002	Maryland	Indiana	64-52	Oklahoma	Kansas	@ Atlanta
2003	Syracuse	Kansas	81-78	Marquette	Texas	@ New Orleans

Note: Six teams have had their standing in the Final Four vacated for using ineligible players: 1961–St. Joseph's-PA (3rd place); 1971–Villanova (Runner-up) and Western Kentucky (3rd); 1980–UCLA (Runner-up); 1985–Memphis St. (3rd); 1996–UMass (3rd)

The Red Cross Benefit Games, 1943-45

For three seasons during World War II, the NCAA and NIT champions met in a benefit game at Madison Square Garden in New York to raise money for the Red Cross. The NCAA champs won all three games.

Year	Winner	Score	Loser
1943	Wyoming (NCAA)	52-47	St. John's (NIT)
1944	Utah (NCAA)	43-36	St. John's (NIT)
1945	Oklahoma A&M (NCAA)	52-44	DePaul (NIT)

Most Outstanding Player

A Most Outstanding Player has been selected every year of the NCAA tournament. Winners who did not play for the tournament champion are listed in **bold** type. The 1939 and 1951 winners are unofficial and not recognized by the NCAA. Statistics listed are for Final Four games only.

Multiple winners: Lew Alcindor (3); Alex Groza, Bob Kurland, Jerry Lucas and Bill Walton (2).

Year		Gm	FGM	Pct	3PTM	3PTA	FTM	Pct	Reb	Ast	Blk	Stl	PPG
1939	**Jimmy Hull**, Ohio St.	2	15	—	—	—	10	.833	—	—	—	—	20.0
1940	Marv Huffman, Indiana	2	7	—	—	—	4	—	—	—	—	—	9.0
1941	John Kotz, Wisconsin	2	8	—	—	—	6	—	—	—	—	—	11.0
1942	Howie Dallmar, Stanford	2	8	—	—	—	4	.667	—	—	—	—	10.0
1943	Kenny Sailors, Wyoming	2	10	—	—	—	8	.727	—	—	—	—	14.0
1944	Arnie Ferrin, Utah	2	11	—	—	—	6	—	—	—	—	—	14.0
1945	Bob Kurland, Okla. A&M	2	16	—	—	—	5	—	—	—	—	—	18.5
1946	Bob Kurland, Okla. A&M	2	21	—	—	—	10	.667	—	—	—	—	26.0
1947	George Kaftan, Holy Cross	2	18	—	—	—	12	.706	—	—	—	—	24.0
1948	Alex Groza, Kentucky	2	16	—	—	—	5	—	—	—	—	—	18.5
1949	Alex Groza, Kentucky	2	19	—	—	—	14	—	—	—	—	—	26.0
1950	Irwin Dambrot, CCNY	2	12	.429	—	—	4	.500	—	—	—	—	14.0
1951	Bill Spivey, Kentucky	2	20	.400	—	—	10	.625	37	—	—	—	25.0
1952	Clyde Lovellette, Kansas	2	24	—	—	—	18	—	—	—	—	—	33.0
1953	**B.H. Born**, Kansas	2	17	—	—	—	17	—	—	—	—	—	25.5
1954	Tom Gola, La Salle	2	12	—	—	—	14	—	—	—	—	—	19.0
1955	Bill Russell, San Francisco	2	19	—	—	—	9	—	—	—	—	—	23.5
1956	**Hal Lear**, Temple	2	32	—	—	—	16	—	—	—	—	—	40.0
1957	**Wilt Chamberlain**, Kansas	2	18	.514	—	—	19	.704	25	—	—	—	32.5
1958	**Elgin Baylor**, Seattle	2	18	.340	—	—	12	.750	41	—	—	—	24.0
1959	**Jerry West**, West Virginia	2	22	.667	—	—	22	.688	25	—	—	—	33.0
1960	Jerry Lucas, Ohio St.	2	16	.667	—	—	3	1.000	23	—	—	—	17.5
1961	**Jerry Lucas**, Ohio St.	2	20	.714	—	—	16	.941	25	—	—	—	28.0
1962	Paul Hogue, Cincinnati	2	23	.639	—	—	12	.632	38	—	—	—	29.0
1963	**Art Heyman**, Duke	2	18	.409	—	—	15	.682	19	—	—	—	25.5
1964	Walt Hazzard, UCLA	2	11	.550	—	—	8	.667	10	—	—	—	15.0
1965	**Bill Bradley**, Princeton	2	34	.630	—	—	19	.950	24	—	—	—	43.5
1966	**Jerry Chambers**, Utah	2	25	.532	—	—	20	.833	35	—	—	—	35.0
1967	Lew Alcindor, UCLA	2	14	.609	—	—	11	.458	38	—	—	—	19.5
1968	Lew Alcindor, UCLA	2	22	.629	—	—	9	.900	34	—	—	—	26.5
1969	Lew Alcindor, UCLA	2	23	.676	—	—	16	.640	41	—	—	—	31.0
1970	Sidney Wicks, UCLA	2	15	.714	—	—	9	.600	34	—	—	—	19.5
1971	**Howard Porter**, Villanova	2	20	.488	—	—	7	.778	24	—	—	—	23.5
1972	Bill Walton, UCLA	2	20	.690	—	—	17	.739	41	—	—	—	28.5
1973	Bill Walton, UCLA	2	28	.824	—	—	2	.400	30	—	—	—	29.0
1974	David Thompson, N.C. State	2	19	.514	—	—	11	.786	17	—	—	—	24.5
1975	Richard Washington, UCLA	2	23	.548	—	—	8	.727	20	—	—	—	27.0
1976	Kent Benson, Indiana	2	17	.500	—	—	7	.636	18	—	—	—	20.5
1977	Butch Lee, Marquette	2	11	.344	—	—	8	1.000	6	2	1	1	15.0
1978	Jack Givens, Kentucky	2	28	.651	—	—	8	.667	17	4	1	3	32.0
1979	Magic Johnson, Michigan St.	2	17	.680	—	—	19	.864	17	3	0	2	26.5
1980	Darrell Griffith, Louisville	2	23	.622	—	—	11	.688	7	15	0	2	28.5
1981	Isiah Thomas, Indiana	2	14	.560	—	—	9	.818	4	9	3	4	18.5
1982	James Worthy, N. Carolina	2	20	.741	—	—	2	.286	8	9	0	4	21.0
1983	**Akeem Olajuwon**, Houston	2	16	.552	—	—	9	.643	40	3	2	5	20.5
1984	Patrick Ewing, Georgetown	2	8	.571	—	—	2	1.000	18	1	15	1	9.0
1985	Ed Pinckney, Villanova	2	8	.571	—	—	12	.750	15	6	3	0	14.0
1986	Pervis Ellison, Louisville	2	15	.600	—	—	6	.750	24	2	3	1	18.0
1987	Keith Smart, Indiana	2	14	.636	0	1	7	.778	7	7	0	2	17.5
1988	Danny Manning, Kansas	2	25	.556	0	1	6	.667	17	4	8	9	28.0
1989	Glen Rice, Michigan	2	24	.490	7	16	4	1.000	16	1	0	3	29.5
1990	Anderson Hunt, UNLV	2	19	.613	9	16	2	.500	4	9	1	1	24.5
1991	Christian Laettner, Duke	2	12	.545	1	1	21	.913	17	2	1	2	23.0
1992	Bobby Hurley, Duke	2	10	.417	7	12	8	.800	3	11	0	3	17.5
1993	Donald Williams, N. Carolina	2	15	.652	10	14	10	1.000	4	1	0	2	25.0
1994	Corliss Williamson, Arkansas	2	21	.500	0	0	10	.714	21	8	3	4	26.0
1995	Ed O'Bannon, UCLA	2	16	.457	3	8	10	.769	25	3	1	7	22.5
1996	Tony Delk, Kentucky	2	15	.417	8	16	6	.546	9	2	3	2	22.0
1997	Miles Simon, Arizona	2	17	.459	3	10	17	.773	8	6	0	1	27.0
1998	Jeff Sheppard, Kentucky	2	16	.552	4	10	7	.778	10	7	0	4	21.5
1999	Richard Hamilton, Connecticut	2	20	.513	3	7	8	.727	12	4	1	2	25.5
2000	Mateen Cleaves, Michigan St.	2	8	.444	3	10	10	.833	6	5	0	2	14.5
2001	Shane Battier, Duke	2	13	.464	5	12	12	.706	19	8	6	2	21.5
2002	Juan Dixon, Maryland	2	16	.593	7	15	12	.800	8	5	0	7	25.5
2003	Carmelo Anthony, Syracuse	2	19	.543	6	9	9	.818	24	8	0	4	26.5

Final Four All-Decade Teams

To celebrate the 50th anniversary of the NCAA tournament in 1989, five All-Decade teams were selected by a blue ribbon panel of coaches and administrators. An All-Time Final Four team was also chosen. Selections were actually made prior to the 1988 tournament.

Selection panel: Vic Bubas, Denny Crum, Wayne Duke, Dave Gavitt, Joe B. Hall, Jud Heathcote, Hank Iba, Pete Newell, Dean Smith, John Thompson and John Wooden.

All-1950s

	Years
Elgin Baylor, Seattle	1958
Wilt Chamberlain, Kansas	1957
Tom Gola, La Salle	1954
K.C. Jones, San Francisco	1955
Clyde Lovellette, Kansas	1952
Oscar Robertson, Cinn.	1959-60
Guy Rodgers, Temple	1958
Lennie Rosenbluth, N. Carolina	1957
Bill Russell, San Francisco	1955-56
Jerry West, West Virginia	1959

All-1970s

	Years
Kent Benson, Indiana	1976
Larry Bird, Indiana St	1979
Jack Givens, Kentucky	1978
Magic Johnson, Mich. St	1979
Marques Johnson, UCLA	1975-76
Scott May, Indiana	1976
David Thompson, N.C. State	1974
Bill Walton, UCLA	1972-74
Sidney Wicks, UCLA	1969-71
Keith Wilkes, UCLA	1972-74

All-Time Team

	Years
Lew Alcindor, UCLA	1967-69
Larry Bird, Indiana St.	1979
Wilt Chamberlain, Kansas	1957
Magic Johnson, Mich. St	1979
Michael Jordan, N. Carolina	1982

All-1940s

	Years
Ralph Beard, Kentucky	1948-49
Howie Dallmar, Stanford	1942
Dwight Eddleman, Illinois	1949
Arnie Ferrin, Utah	1944
Alex Groza, Kentucky	1948-49
George Kaftan, Holy Cross	1947
Bob Kurland, Okla. A&M	1945-46
Jim Pollard, Stanford	1942
Kenny Sailors, Wyoming	1943
Gerry Tucker, Oklahoma	1947

All-1960s

	Years
Lew Alcindor, UCLA	1967-69
Bill Bradley, Princeton	1965
Gail Goodrich, UCLA	1964-65
John Havlicek, Ohio St	1961-62
Elvin Hayes, Houston	1967
Walt Hazzard, UCLA	1964
Jerry Lucas, Ohio St	1960-61
Jeff Mullins, Duke	1964
Cazzie Russell, Michigan	1965
Charlie Scott, N. Carolina	1968-69

All-1980s

	Years
Steve Alford, Indiana	1987
Johnny Dawkins, Duke	1986
Patrick Ewing, Georgetown	1982-84
Darrell Griffith, Louisville	1980
Michael Jordan, N. Carolina	1982
Rodney McCray, Louisville	1980
Akeem Olajuwon, Houston	1983-84
Ed Pinckney, Villanova	1985
Isiah Thomas, Indiana	1981
James Worthy, N. Carolina	1982

Note: Lew Alcindor later changed his name to Kareem Abdul-Jabbar; Keith Wilkes later changed his first name to Jamaal; and Akeem Olajuwon later changed the spelling of his first name to Hakeem.

Seeds at the Final Four

NCAA champions in **bold** type.

Year Seeds (Total)	Teams
1979 1,2,2,9 (14)	Indiana St., **Mich. St.**, DePaul, Penn.
1980 2,5,6,8 (21)	**Louisville**, Iowa, Purdue, UCLA
1981 1,1,2,3 (7)	Virginia, LSU, N. Carolina, **Indiana**
1982 1,1,3,6 (11)	**N. Carolina**, Georgetown, Louisville, Houston
1983 1,1,4,6 (12)	Houston, Louisville, Georgia, **N.C. State**
1984 1,1,2,7 (11)	Kentucky, **Georgetown**, Houston, Virginia
1985 1,1,2,8 (12)	St. John's, Georgetown, Memphis, **Villanova**
1986 1,1,2,11 (15)	Duke, Kansas, **Louisville**, LSU
1987 1,1,2,6 (10)	UNLV, **Indiana**, Syracuse, Providence
1988 1,1,2,6 (10)	Arizona, Oklahoma, Duke, **Kansas**
1989 1,2,3,3 (9)	Illinois, Duke, Seton Hall, **Michigan**
1990 1,3,4,4 (12)	**UNLV**, Duke, Ga. Tech, Arkansas
1991 1,1,2,3 (7)	UNLV, N. Carolina, **Duke**, Kansas
1992 1,2,4,6 (13)	**Duke**, Indiana, Cincinnati, Michigan
1993 1,1,1,2 (5)	**N. Carolina**, Kentucky, Michigan, Kansas
1994 1,2,2,3 (8)	**Arkansas**, Arizona, Duke, Florida
1995 1,2,2,4 (9)	**UCLA**, Arkansas, N. Carolina, Okla. St.
1996 1,1,4,5 (11)	**Kentucky**, UMass, Syracuse, Miss. St.
1997 1,1,1,4 (7)	Kentucky, N. Carolina, Minnesota, **Arizona**
1998 1,2,3,3 (9)	N. Carolina, **Kentucky**, Stanford, Utah
1999 1,1,1,4 (7)	**Connecticut**, Duke, Michigan St., Ohio St.
2000 1,5,8,8 (22)	**Michigan St.**, Florida, Wisconsin, N. Carolina
2001 1,2,2,3 (7)	**Duke**, Michigan St., Arizona, Maryland
2002 1,1,2,5 (9)	**Maryland**, Kansas, Oklahoma, Indiana
2003 1,2,3,3 (9)	Texas, Kansas, **Syracuse**, Marquette

Note: teams were not seeded before 1979.

All-Time Seeds Records

All-time records of NCAA tournament seeds since tourney began seeding teams in 1979. Records are through the 2003 NCAA Tournament. Note that 1st refers to championships. 2nd refers to runners-up and FF refers to Final Four appearances not including 1st and 2nd place finishes.

Seed	W	L	Pct.	1st	2nd	FF
1	306	88	.777	13	9	20
2	220	95	.698	5	6	10
3	157	97	.618	3	4	5
4	136	99	.579	1	1	6
5	117	101	.537	0	2	2
6	134	98	.578	2	1	3
7	81	100	.448	0	0	1
8	76	99	.434	1	1	2
9	58	101	.365	0	0	1
10	70	100	.412	0	0	0
11	43	96	.309	0	0	1
12	41	96	.299	0	0	0
13	19	76	.200	0	0	0
14	15	76	.165	0	0	0
15	4	76	.050	0	0	0
16	0	76	.000	0	0	0

Collegiate Commissioners Association Tournament

The Collegiate Commissioners Association staged an eight-team tournament for teams that didn't make the NCAA tournament in 1974 and '75.

Most Valuable Players: 1974–Kent Benson, Indiana; 1975–Bob Elliot, Arizona.

Year	Winner	Score	Loser	Site
1974	Indiana	85-60	USC	St. Louis
1975	Drake	83-76	Arizona	Louisville

NCAA Tournament Appearances

App		W-L	F4	Championships		App		W-L	F4	Championships
45	Kentucky	94-40	13	7 (1948-49, 51, 58, 78, 96, 98)		22	Ohio St.	37-21	9	1 (1960)
38	UCLA	85-31	15	11 (1964-65,67-73,75,95)		22	Arizona	37-21	3	1 (1997)
35	N. Carolina	81-35	15	3 (1957,82,93)		22	Cincinnati	38-21	6	2 (1961-62)
32	Indiana	58-27	8	5 (1940,53,76,81,87)		22	Oklahoma	30-22	4	None
31	Kansas	65-31	11	2 (1952,88)		21	Texas	23-24	3	None
30	Louisville	49-32	7	2 (1980,86)		21	DePaul	20-24	2	None
28	Syracuse	46-28	4	1 (2003)		21	Missouri	18-21	0	None
27	Duke	77-24	13	3 (1991-92, 2001)		20	Michigan	41-19	6	1 (1989)
27	St. John's	27-29	2	None		20	Iowa	27-22	3	None
27	Notre Dame	29-31	1	None		20	Purdue	27-20	2	None
26	Arkansas	39-26	6	1 (1994)		20	BYU	11-23	0	None
25	Villanova	37-25	3	1 (1985)		20	Oklahoma St.	31-19	5	2 (1945-46)
25	Temple	31-25	2	None		20	Maryland	34-19	2	1 (2002)
24	Connecticut	32-24	1	1 (1999)		20	Pennsylvania	13-22	1	None
24	Utah	33-27	4	1 (1944)		19	N.C. State	28-18	3	2 (1974,83)
23	Marquette	32-24	3	1 (1977)		19	Western Ky.	15-20	1	None
23	Illinois	30-23	4	None		18	Houston	26-23	5	None
22	Kansas St.	27-26	4	None		18	Wake Forest	24-18	1	None
22	Georgetown	38-21	4	1 (1984)		18	West Virginia	13-18	1	None
22	Princeton	13-26	1	None						

Note: Although all NCAA tournament appearances are included above, the NCAA has officially voided the records of Villanova (4-1) and Western Ky. (4-1) in 1971; UCLA (5-1) in 1980 and again (0-1) in 1999; Oregon St. (2-3) from 1980-82; Memphis (9-5) from 1982-86; DePaul (6-4) from 1986-89; N.C. State (0-2) from 1987-88; Kentucky (2-1) and Maryland (1-1) in 1988; Missouri (3-1) in 1994; Connecticut (2-1) and Purdue (1-1) in 1996; Arizona (0-1) in 1999.

All-Time NCAA Division I Tournament Leaders

Through 2003; minimum of six games; **Last** column indicates final year played.

CAREER

Scoring

Points

		Yrs	Last	Gm	Pts
1	Christian Laettner, Duke	4	1992	23	407
2	Elvin Hayes, Houston	3	1968	13	358
3	Danny Manning, Kansas	4	1988	16	328
4	Oscar Robertson, Cincinnati	3	1960	10	324
5	Glen Rice, Michigan	4	1989	13	308
6	Lew Alcindor, UCLA	3	1969	12	304
7	Bill Bradley, Princeton	3	1965	9	303
	Corliss Williamson, Arkansas	3	1995	15	303
9	Juan Dixon, Maryland	4	2002	16	294
10	Austin Carr, Notre Dame	3	1971	7	289

Average

		Yrs	Last	Pts	Avg
1	Austin Carr, Notre Dame	3	1971	289	41.3
2	Bill Bradley, Princeton	3	1965	303	33.7
3	Oscar Robertson, Cincinnati	3	1960	324	32.4
4	Jerry West, West Virginia	3	1960	275	30.6
5	Bob Pettit, LSU	2	1954	183	30.5
6	Dan Issel, Kentucky	3	1970	176	29.3
	Jim McDaniels, Western Ky.	2	1971	176	29.3
8	Dwight Lamar, SW Louisiana	2	1973	175	29.2
9	Bo Kimble, Loyola-CA	3	1990	204	29.1
10	David Robinson, Navy	3	1987	200	28.6

Rebounds

Total

		Yrs	Last	Gm	No
1	Elvin Hayes, Houston	3	1968	13	222
2	Lew Alcindor, UCLA	3	1969	12	201
3	Jerry Lucas, Ohio St.	3	1962	12	197
4	Bill Walton, UCLA	3	1974	12	176
5	Christian Laettner, Duke	4	1992	23	169
6	Tim Duncan, Wake Forest	4	1997	11	165
7	Paul Hogue, Cincinnati	3	1962	12	160
8	Sam Lacey, New Mexico St.	3	1970	11	157
9	Derrick Coleman, Syracuse	4	1990	14	155
10	Akeem Olajuwon, Houston	3	1984	15	153

Average

		Yrs	Last	Reb	Avg
1	Johnny Green, Michigan St.	2	1959	118	19.7
2	Artis Gilmore, Jacksonville	2	1971	115	19.2
3	Paul Silas, Creighton	3	1964	111	18.5
4	Len Chappell, Wake Forest	2	1962	137	17.1
5	Elvin Hayes, Houston	3	1968	222	17.1
6	Lew Alcindor, UCLA	3	1969	201	16.8
7	Jerry Lucas, Ohio St.	3	1962	197	16.4
8	Tim Duncan, Wake Forest	4	1997	165	15.0
9	Bill Walton, UCLA	3	1974	176	14.7
10	Sam Lacey, New Mexico St.	3	1970	157	14.3

3-Pt Field Goals

Total

		Yrs	Last	Gm	No
1	Bobby Hurley, Duke	4	1993	20	42
2	Tony Delk, Kentucky	4	1996	17	40
3	Jeff Fryer, Loyola-CA	3	1990	7	38
	Donald Williams, North Carolina	4	1995	15	38
	Juan Dixon, Maryland	4	2002	16	38

Assists

Total

		Yrs	Last	Gm	No
1	Bobby Hurley, Duke	4	1993	20	145
2	Sherman Douglas, Syracuse	4	1989	14	106
3	Greg Anthony, UNLV	3	1991	15	100
4	Mark Wade, UNLV	2	1987	8	93
	Rumeal Robinson, Michigan	3	1990	11	93
	Jacque Vaughn, Kansas	4	1997	13	93
	Anthony Epps, Kentucky	4	1997	18	93

SINGLE TOURNAMENT

Scoring

Points

		Year	Gm	Pts
1	Glen Rice, Michigan	1989	6	184
2	Bill Bradley, Princeton	1965	5	177
3	Elvin Hayes, Houston	1968	5	167
4	Danny Manning, Kansas	1988	6	163
5	Hal Lear, Temple	1956	5	160
	Jerry West, West Virginia	1959	5	160

Average

		Year	Gm	Pts	Avg
1	Austin Carr, Notre Dame	1970	3	158	52.7
2	Austin Carr, Notre Dame	1971	3	125	41.7
3	Jerry Chambers, Utah	1966	4	143	35.8
	Bo Kimble, Loyola-CA	1990	4	143	35.8
5	Bill Bradley, Princeton	1965	5	177	35.4
6	Clyde Lovellette, Kansas	1952	4	141	35.3

Rebounds

Total	Year	Gm	No	Avg
1 Elvin Hayes, Houston	1968	5	**97**	19.4
2 Artis Gilmore, Jacksonville	1970	5	**93**	18.6
3 Elgin Baylor, Seattle	1958	5	**91**	18.2
4 Sam Lacey, New Mexico St.	1970	5	**90**	18.0
5 Clarence Glover, Western Ky	1971	5	**89**	17.8
6 Len Chappell, Wake Forest	1962	5	**86**	17.2

Assists

Total	Year	Gm	No	Avg
1 Mark Wade, UNLV	1987	5	**61**	12.2
2 Rumeal Robinson, Michigan	1989	6	**56**	9.3
3 T.J. Ford, Texas	2003	5	**51**	10.2
4 Sherman Douglas, Syracuse	1987	6	**49**	8.2
5 Bobby Hurley, Duke	1992	6	**47**	7.8
6 Lazarus Sims, Syracuse	1996	6	**46**	7.7

SINGLE GAME

Scoring

Points	Year	Pts
1 Austin Carr, Notre Dame vs Ohio Univ	1970	61
2 Bill Bradley, Princeton vs Wichita St.	1965	58
3 Oscar Robertson, Cincinnati vs Arkansas	1958	56
4 Austin Carr, Notre Dame vs Kentucky	1970	52
Austin Carr, Notre Dame vs TCU	1971	52
6 David Robinson, Navy vs Michigan	1987	50
7 Elvin Hayes, Houston vs Loyola-IL	1968	49
8 Hal Lear, Temple vs SMU	1956	48
9 Austin Carr, Notre Dame vs Houston	1971	47
10 Dave Corzine, DePaul vs Louisville	1978	46
11 Bob Houbregs, Washington vs Seattle	1953	45
Austin Carr, Notre Dame vs Iowa	1970	45
Bo Kimble, Loyola-CA vs New Mexico St.	1990	45
14 Seven players tied with 44 each.		

Rebounds

Total	Year	No
1 Fred Cohen, Temple vs UConn	1956	34
2 Nate Thurmond, Bowl. Green vs Miss. St.	1963	31
3 Jerry Lucas, Ohio St. vs Kentucky	1961	30
4 Toby Kimball, UConn vs St. Joseph's-PA	1965	29
5 Elvin Hayes, Houston vs Pacific	1966	28
6 Four players tied with 27 each.		

Assists

Total	Year	No
1 Mark Wade, UNLV vs Indiana	1987	18
2 Sam Crawford, N. Mexico St. vs Nebraska	1993	16
3 Kenny Patterson, DePaul vs Syracuse	1985	15
Keith Smart, Indiana vs Auburn	1987	15
5 Six players tied with 14 each.		

SINGLE FINAL FOUR GAME

Letters in the **Year** column indicate the following: C for Consolation Game, F for Final and S for Semifinal.

Scoring

Points	Year	Pts
1 Bill Bradley, Princeton vs Wichita St	1965-C	58
2 Hal Lear, Temple vs SMU	1956-C	48
3 Bill Walton, UCLA vs Memphis St	1973-F	44
4 Bob Houbregs, Washington vs LSU	1953-C	42
Jack Egan, St. Joseph's-PA vs Utah	1961-C	42*
Gail Goodrich, UCLA vs Michigan	1965-C	42
7 Jack Givens, Kentucky vs Duke	1978-F	41
8 Oscar Robertson, Cincinnati vs L'ville	1959-C	39
Al Wood, N. Carolina vs Virginia	1981-S	39
10 Jerry West, West Va. vs Louisville	1959-S	38
Jerry Chambers, Utah vs Texas Western	1966-S	38
Freddie Banks, UNLV vs Indiana	1987-S	38

*Four overtimes.

Rebounds

Total	Year	No
1 Bill Russell, San Francisco vs Iowa	1956-F	27
2 Elvin Hayes, Houston vs UCLA	1967-S	24
3 Bill Russell, San Francisco vs SMU	1956-S	23
4 Elgin Baylor, Seattle vs Kansas St.	1958-S	22
Tom Sanders, NYU vs Ohio St.	1960-S	22
Larry Kenon, Memphis vs Providence	1973-S	22
Akeem Olajuwon, Houston vs Louisville	1983-S	22
8 Bill Spivey, Kentucky vs Kansas St.	1951-C	21
Lew Alcindor, UCLA vs Drake	1969-C	21
Artis Gilmore, Jacksonville vs St. Bonaventure	1970-S	21
Bill Walton, UCLA vs Louisville	1972-S	21
Nick Collison, Kansas vs Syracuse	2003-C	21

Assists

Total	Year	No
1 Mark Wade, UNLV vs Indiana	1987-S	18
2 T.J. Ford, Texas vs. Syracuse	2003-C	13
3 Rumeal Robinson, Michigan vs Illinois	1989-S	12
Edgar Padilla, UMass vs. Ky.	1996-S	12
5 Michael Jackson, G'town vs St. John's	1985-S	11
Milt Wagner, Louisville vs LSU	1986-S	11
Rumeal Robinson, Mich. vs Seton Hall	1989-F	11*
Steve Blake, Maryland vs. Kansas	2002-S	11

*Overtime.

Blocked Shots

Total	Year	No
1 Danny Manning, Kansas vs Duke	1988-S	6
Marcus Camby, UMass vs Kentucky	1996-S	6
3 Six players tied with 4 each.		

Steals

Total	Year	No
1 Tommy Amaker, Duke vs. Louisville	1986-C	7
Mookie Blaylock, Oklahoma vs. Kansas	1988-C	7
3 Gilbert Arenas, Arizona vs Michigan St.	2001-S	6
4 Five players tied with 5 each.		

Teams in Both NCAA and NIT

Fourteen teams played in both the NCAA and NIT tournaments from 1940-52. Colorado (1940), Utah (1944), Kentucky (1949) and BYU (1951) won one of the titles, while CCNY won two in 1950, beating Bradley in both championship games.

Year		NIT	NCAA
1940	Colorado	**Won Final**	Lost 1st Rd
	Duquesne	Lost Final	Lost 2nd Rd
1944	Utah	Lost 1st Rd	**Won Final**
1949	Kentucky	Lost 2nd Rd	**Won Final**
1950	CCNY	**Won Final**	**Won Final**
	Bradley	Lost Final	Lost Final
1951	BYU	**Won Final**	Lost 2nd Rd
	St. John's	Lost 3rd Rd	Lost 2nd Rd
	N.C. State	Lost 2nd Rd	Lost 2nd Rd
	Arizona	Lost 2nd Rd	Lost 1st Rd
1952	St. John's	Lost 2nd Rd	Lost Final
	Dayton	Lost Final	Lost 1st Rd
	Duquesne	Lost 3rd Rd	Lost 2nd Rd
	Saint Louis	Lost 2nd Rd	Lost 2nd Rd

NIT Championship

The National Invitation Tournament began under the sponsorship of the Metropolitan New York Basketball Writers Association in 1938. The NIT is now administered by the Metropolitan Intercollegiate Basketball Association. All championship games have been played at Madison Square Garden.

Multiple winners: St. John's (6); Bradley (4); BYU, Dayton, Kentucky, LIU-Brooklyn, Michigan, Minnesota, Providence, Temple, Tulsa, Virginia and Virginia Tech (2).

Year	Winner	Score	Loser	Year	Winner	Score	Loser
1938	Temple	60-36	Colorado	1971	North Carolina	84-66	Georgia Tech
1939	LIU-Brooklyn	44-32	Loyola-IL	1972	Maryland	100-69	Niagara
1940	Colorado	51-40	Duquesne	1973	Virginia Tech	92-91 (OT)	Notre Dame
1941	LIU-Brooklyn	56-42	Ohio Univ.	1974	Purdue	97-81	Utah
1942	West Virginia	47-45	Western Ky.	1975	Princeton	80-69	Providence
1943	St. John's	48-27	Toledo	1976	Kentucky	71-67	NC-Charlotte
1944	St. John's	47-39	DePaul	1977	St. Bonaventure	94-91	Houston
1945	DePaul	71-54	Bowling Green	1978	Texas	101-93	N.C. State
1946	Kentucky	46-45	Rhode Island	1979	Indiana	53-52	Purdue
1947	Utah	49-45	Kentucky	1980	Virginia	58-55	Minnesota
1948	Saint Louis	65-52	NYU	1981	Tulsa	86-84 (OT)	Syracuse
1949	San Francisco	48-47	Loyola-IL	1982	Bradley	67-58	Purdue
1950	CCNY	69-61	Bradley	1983	Fresno St.	69-60	DePaul
1951	BYU	62-43	Dayton	1984	Michigan	83-63	Notre Dame
1952	La Salle	75-64	Dayton	1985	UCLA	65-62	Indiana
1953	Seton Hall	58-46	St. John's	1986	Ohio St.	73-63	Wyoming
1954	Holy Cross	71-62	Duquesne	1987	Southern Miss.	84-80	La Salle
1955	Duquesne	70-58	Dayton	1988	Connecticut	72-67	Ohio St.
1956	Louisville	93-80	Dayton	1989	St. John's	73-65	Saint Louis
1957	Bradley	84-83	Memphis St.	1990	Vanderbilt	74-72	Saint Louis
1958	Xavier-OH	78-74 (OT)	Dayton	1991	Stanford	78-72	Oklahoma
1959	St. John's	76-71 (OT)	Bradley	1992	Virginia	81-76 (OT)	Notre Dame
1960	Bradley	88-72	Providence	1993	Minnesota	62-61	Georgetown
1961	Providence	62-59	Saint Louis	1994	Villanova	80-73	Vanderbilt
1962	Dayton	73-67	St. John's	1995	Virginia Tech	65-64 (OT)	Marquette
1963	Providence	81-66	Canisius	1996	Nebraska	60-56	St. Joseph's
1964	Bradley	86-54	New Mexico	1997	Michigan	82-72	Florida St.
1965	St. John's	55-51	Villanova	1998	Minnesota	79-72	Penn St.
1966	BYU	97-84	NYU	1999	California	61-60	Clemson
1967	Southern Illinois	71-56	Marquette	2000	Wake Forest	71-61	Notre Dame
1968	Dayton	61-48	Kansas	2001	Tulsa	79-60	Alabama
1969	Temple	89-76	Boston Coll.	2002	Memphis	72-62	South Carolina
1970	Marquette	65-53	St. John's	2003	St. John's	70-67	Georgetown

Most Valuable Player

A Most Valuable Player has been selected every year of the NIT tournament. Winners who did not play for the tournament champion are listed in **bold** type.

Multiple winners: None. However, Tom Gola of La Salle is the only player to be named MVP in the NIT (1952) and Most Outstanding Player of the NCAA tournament (1954).

Year
- 1938 Don Shields, Temple
- 1939 **Bill Lloyd**, St. John's
- 1940 Bob Doll, Colorado
- 1941 **Frank Baumholtz**, Ohio U.
- 1942 Rudy Baric, West Virginia
- 1943 Harry Boykoff, St. John's
- 1944 Bill Kotsores, St. John's
- 1945 George Mikan, DePaul
- 1946 **Ernie Calverley**, Rhode Island
- 1947 Vern Gardner, Utah
- 1948 Ed Macauley, Saint Louis
- 1949 Don Lofgan, San Francisco
- 1950 Ed Warner, CCNY
- 1951 Roland Minson, BYU
- 1952 Tom Gola, La Salle
  & Norm Grekin, La Salle
- 1953 Walter Dukes, Seton Hall
- 1954 Togo Palazzi, Holy Cross
- 1955 **Maurice Stokes**, St. Francis-PA
- 1956 Charlie Tyra, Louisville
- 1957 **Win Wilfong**, Memphis St.
- 1958 Hank Stein, Xavier-OH
- 1959 Tony Jackson, St. John's
- 1960 **Lenny Wilkens**, Providence
- 1961 Vinny Ernst, Providence
- 1962 Bill Chmielewski, Dayton
- 1963 Ray Flynn, Providence

Year
- 1964 Lavern Tart, Bradley
- 1965 Ken McIntyre, St. John's
- 1966 **Bill Melchionni**, Villanova
- 1967 Walt Frazier, So. Illinois
- 1968 Don May, Dayton
- 1969 **Terry Driscoll**, Boston College
- 1970 Dean Meminger, Marquette
- 1971 Bill Chamberlain, N. Carolina
- 1972 Tom McMillen, Maryland
- 1973 **John Shumate**, Notre Dame
- 1974 **Mike Sojourner**, Utah
- 1975 **Ron Lee**, Oregon
- 1976 **Cedric Maxwell**, NC-Charlotte
- 1977 Greg Sanders, St. Bonaventure
- 1978 Ron Baxter, Texas
  & Jim Krivacs, Texas
- 1979 Clarence Carter, Indiana
  & Ray Tolbert, Indiana
- 1980 Ralph Sampson, Virginia
- 1981 Greg Stewart, Tulsa
- 1982 Mitchell Anderson, Bradley
- 1983 Ron Anderson, Fresno St.
- 1984 Tim McCormick, Michigan
- 1985 Reggie Miller, UCLA
- 1986 Brad Sellers, Ohio St.
- 1987 Randolph Keys, So. Miss.
- 1988 Phil Gamble, Connecticut

Year
- 1989 Jayson Williams, St. John's
- 1990 Scott Draud, Vanderbilt
- 1991 Adam Keefe, Stanford
- 1992 Bryant Stith, Virginia
- 1993 Voshon Lenard, Minnesota
- 1994 **Doremus Bennerman**, Siena
- 1995 Shawn Smith, Va. Tech
- 1996 Erick Strickland, Nebraska
- 1997 Robert Traylor, Michigan
- 1998 Kevin Clark, Minnesota
- 1999 Sean Lampley, California
- 2000 Robert O'Kelley, Wake Forest
- 2001 Marcus Hill, Tulsa
- 2002 Dajuan Wagner, Memphis
- 2003 Marcus Hatten, St. John's

All-Time NIT Team

As selected by a media panel (Mar. 15, 1997).

Walt Frazier, S. Illinois
George Mikan, DePaul
Tom Gola, La Salle
Maurice Stokes, St. Francis-PA
Ralph Beard, Kentucky

All-Time Winningest Division I Teams
Top 25 Winning Percentage

Division I schools with best winning percentages through 2002-03 season (including tournament games). Years in Division I only; minimum 20 years. NCAA tournament columns indicate years in tournament, record and number of championships.

		First Year	Yrs	Games	Won	Lost	Tied	Pct	NCAA Tourney Yrs	W-L	Titles
1	Kentucky	1903	100	2422	1849	572	1	**.764**	45	94-40	7
2	North Carolina	1911	93	2474	1808	666	0	**.731**	35	81-35	3
3	UNLV	1959	45	1291	928	363	0	**.719**	14	30-13	1
4	Kansas	1899	105	2552	1800	752	0	**.705**	32	70-32	2
5	UCLA	1920	84	2192	1520	672	0	**.693**	38	85-31	11
6	Duke	1906	98	2481	1706	775	0	**.688**	26	75-23	3
7	St. John's	1908	96	2425	1662	763	0	**.685**	27	27-29	0
8	Syracuse	1901	102	2339	1602	737	0	**.685**	28	46-28	1
9	Western Kentucky	1915	84	2189	1466	723	0	**.670**	19	15-20	0
10	Utah	1909	95	2267	1492	775	0	**.658**	24	33-27	1
11	Indiana	1901	103	2365	1540	825	0	**.651**	32	58-27	5
12	Arkansas	1924	80	2119	1377	742	0	**.650**	26	39-26	1
13	Temple	1895	107	2482	1608	874	0	**.648**	25	31-25	0
14	Louisville	1912	89	2209	1431	778	0	**.648**	30	49-32	2
15	Illinois	1906	98	2256	1460	798	0	**.647**	23	30-24	0
16	Weber St.	1963	41	1168	755	413	0	**.646**	13	6-14	0
17	Arizona	1905	98	2226	1438	788	0	**.646**	22	37-21	1
18	Notre Dame	1898	98	2368	1529	838	1	**.646**	27	29-31	0
19	Pennsylvania	1897	103	2433	1555	876	2	**.640**	20	13-22	0
20	DePaul	1924	80	1974	1258	716	0	**.637**	21	20-24	0
21	Villanova	1921	83	2149	1361	788	0	**.633**	25	37-25	1
22	Cincinnati	1902	102	2275	1440	835	0	**.633**	22	38-21	2
23	Murray St.	1926	78	2017	1274	744	0	**.632**	11	1-11	0
24	Purdue	1897	105	2302	1453	849	0	**.631**	20	27-20	0
25	Connecticut	1901	100	2134	1341	793	0	**.628**	24	32-24	1

Top 35 All-Time Victories

Division I schools with most victories through 2002-03 (including postseason tournaments). Minimum 20 years in Division I.

	Wins			Wins			Wins			Wins
1 Kentucky	1849	10 Notre Dame	1529	19 Cincinnati	1440	28 Fordham	1367
2 North Carolina	1808	11 UCLA	1520	20 Arizona	1438	29 Alabama	1365
3 Kansas	1800	12 Oregon St.	1517	21 Louisville	1431	30 Oklahoma	1364
4 Duke	1706	13 Utah	1492	22 N.C. State	1419	31 Villanova	1361
5 St. John's	1662	14 Princeton	1475	23 West Virginia	1412	32 Montana St.	1360
6 Temple	1608	15 Western Ky.	1466	Texas	1412	33 Iowa	1358
7 Syracuse	1602	16 Illinois	1460	25 Bradley	1409	34 St. Joseph's	1353
8 Penn	1555	17 Purdue	1453	26 Arkansas	1377	35 Washington St.	1352
9 Indiana	1540	18 Washington	1444	27 Ohio St	1375		

Top 30 Single-Season Victories

Division I schools with most victories in a season through 2002-03 (including postseason tournaments). NCAA champions in **bold** type.

		Year	Record		Year	Record		Year	Record
1	UNLV	1987	37-2	Kentucky	1947	34-3	Duke	1998	32-4
	Duke	1999	37-2	**Georgetown**	1984	34-3	Louisville	1983	32-4
	Duke	1986	37-3	Arkansas	1991	34-4	Kentucky	1986	32-4
4	**Kentucky**	1948	36-3	**N. Carolina**	1993	34-4	N. Carolina	1987	32-4
5	**Massachusetts***	1996	35-2	N. Carolina	1998	34-4	Temple	1987	32-4
	Georgetown	1985	35-3	25 Indiana St	1979	33-1	Kentucky	2003	32-4
	Arizona	1988	35-3	**Louisville**	1980	33-3	**Maryland**	2002	32-4
	Duke	2001	35-4	Kansas	2002	33-4	Bradley	1950	32-5
	Kansas	1986	35-4	Michigan St.	1999	33-5	Connecticut	1998	32-5
	Kansas	1998	35-4	UNLV	1986	33-5	Tulsa	2000	32-5
	Kentucky	1998	35-4	30 **N. Carolina**	1957	32-0	Iowa St.	2000	32-5
	Oklahoma	1988	35-4	**Indiana**	1976	32-0	Marshall	1947	32-5
	UNLV	1990	35-5	**Kentucky**	1949	32-2	Houston	1984	32-5
	Kentucky	1997	35-5	**Kentucky**	1951	32-2	Bradley	1951	32-6
15	UNLV	1991	34-1	**N. Carolina**	1982	32-2	**Louisville**	1986	32-7
	Connecticut	1999	34-2	Temple	1988	32-2	**Duke**	1991	32-7
	Duke	1992	34-2	Arkansas	1978	32-3	Arkansas	1995	32-7
	Kentucky	1996	34-2	Bradley	1986	32-3	**Michigan St.**	2000	32-7
	Kansas	1997	34-2	Connecticut*	1996	32-3			

*NCAA later stripped UMass of its four 1996 tournament victories after learning that center Marcus Camby accepted gifts from an agent. UConn was stripped of its two 1996 tournament victories because two players illegally accepted plane tickets.

Associated Press Final Polls

Taken before NCAA, NIT and Collegiate Commissioner's Association (1974-75) tournaments.

The Associated Press introduced its weekly college basketball poll of sportswriters (later, sportswriters and broadcasters) during the 1948-49 season.

Since the NCAA Division I tournament has determined the national champion since 1939, the final AP poll ranks the nation's best teams through the regular season and conference tournaments.

Except for four seasons (see AP Post-Tournament Final Polls), the final AP poll has been released prior to the NCAA and NIT tournaments and has gone from a Top 10 (1949 and 1963-67) to a Top 20 (1950-62 and 1968-89) to a Top 25 (since 1990). Tournament champions are in **bold** type.

1949

	Before Tourns	Head Coach	Final Record
1	**Kentucky** 29-1	Adolph Rupp	32-2
2	Oklahoma A&M .21-4	Hank Iba	23-5
3	Saint Louis 22-3	Eddie Hickey	22-4
4	Illinois 19-3	Harry Combes	21-4
5	Western Ky. 25-3	Ed Diddle	25-4
6	Minnesota 18-3	Ozzie Cowles	same
7	Bradley 25-6	Forddy Anderson	27-8
8	**San Francisco** .21-5	Pete Newell	25-5
9	Tulane 24-4	Cliff Wells	same
10	Bowling Green .21-6	Harold Anderson	24-7

NCAA Final Four (at Edmundson Pavilion, Seattle): **Third Place**—Illinois 57, Oregon St. 53. **Championship**—Kentucky 46, Oklahoma A&M 36.

NIT Final Four (at Madison Square Garden): **Semifinals**—San Francisco 49, Bowling Green 39; Loyola-IL 55, Bradley 50. **Third Place**—Bowling Green 82, Bradley 77. **Championship**—San Francisco 48, Loyola-IL 47.

1950

	Before Tourns	Head Coach	Final Record
1	Bradley 28-3	Forddy Anderson	32-5
2	Ohio St. 21-3	Tippy Dye	22-4
3	Kentucky 25-4	Adolph Rupp	25-5
4	Holy Cross 27-2	Buster Sheary	27-4
5	N.C. State 25-5	Everett Case	27-6
6	Duquesne 22-5	Dudey Moore	23-6
7	UCLA 24-5	John Wooden	24-7
8	Western Ky. 24-5	Ed Diddle	25-6
9	St. John's 23-4	Frank McGuire	24-5
10	La Salle 20-3	Ken Loeffler	21-4
11	Villanova 25-4	Al Severance	same
12	San Francisco . . .19-6	Pete Newell	19-7
13	LIU-Brooklyn . . .20-4	Clair Bee	20-5
14	Kansas St. 17-7	Jack Gardner	same
15	Arizona 26-4	Fred Enke	26-5
16	Wisconsin 17-5	Bud Foster	same
17	San Jose St. 21-7	Walter McPherson	same
18	Washington St. .19-13	Jack Friel	same
19	Kansas 14-11	Phog Allen	same
20	Indiana 17-5	Branch McCracken	same

Note: Unranked **CCNY**, coached by Nat Holman, won both the NCAAs and NIT. The Beavers entered the postseason at 17-5 and had a final record of 24-5.

NCAA Final Four (at Madison Square Garden): **Third Place**—N. Carolina St. 53, Baylor 41. **Championship**—CCNY 71, Bradley 68.

NIT Final Four (at Madison Square Garden): **Semifinals**—Bradley 83, St. John's 72; CCNY 62, Duquesne 52. **Third Place**—St. John's 69, Duquesne 67 (OT). **Championship**—CCNY 69, Bradley 61.

1951

	Before Tourns	Head Coach	Final Record
1	**Kentucky** 28-2	Adolph Rupp	32-2
2	Oklahoma A&M .27-4	Hank Iba	29-6
3	Columbia 22-0	Lou Rossini	22-1
4	Kansas St. 22-3	Jack Gardner	25-4
5	Illinois 19-4	Harry Combes	22-5
6	Bradley 32-6	Forddy Anderson	same
7	Indiana 19-3	Branch McCracken	same
8	N.C. State 29-4	Everett Case	30-7
9	St. John's 22-3	Frank McGuire	26-5
10	Saint Louis 21-7	Eddie Hickey	22-8
11	**BYU** 22-8	Stan Watts	26-10
12	Arizona 24-4	Fred Enke	24-6
13	Dayton 24-4	Tom Blackburn	27-5
14	Toledo 23-8	Jerry Bush	same
15	Washington 22-5	Tippy Dye	24-6
16	Murray St. 21-6	Harlan Hodges	same
17	Cincinnati 18-3	John Wiethe	18-4
18	Siena 19-8	Dan Cunha	same
19	USC 21-6	Forrest Twogood	same
20	Villanova 25-6	Al Severance	same

NCAA Final Four (at Williams Arena, Minneapolis): **Third Place**—Illinois 61, Oklahoma St. 46. **Championship**—Kentucky 68, Kansas St. 58.

NIT Final Four (at Madison Sq. Garden): **Semifinals**—Dayton 69, St. John's 62 (OT); BYU 69, Seton Hall 59. **Third Place**—St. John's 70, Seton Hall 68 (2 OT). **Championship**—BYU 62, Dayton 43.

1952

	Before Tourns	Head Coach	Final Record
1	Kentucky 28-2	Adolph Rupp	29-3
2	Illinois 19-3	Harry Combes	22-4
3	Kansas St. 19-5	Jack Gardner	same
4	Duquesne 21-1	Dudey Moore	23-4
5	Saint Louis 22-6	Eddie Hickey	23-8
6	Washington 25-6	Tippy Dye	same
7	Iowa 19-3	Bucky O'Connor	same
8	**Kansas** 24-3	Phog Allen	28-3
9	West Virginia . . .23-4	Red Brown	same
10	St. John's 22-3	Frank McGuire	25-5
11	Dayton 24-3	Tom Blackburn	28-5
12	Duke 24-6	Harold Bradley	same
13	Holy Cross 23-3	Buster Sheary	24-4
14	Seton Hall 25-2	Honey Russell	25-3
15	St. Bonaventure .19-5	Ed Melvin	21-6
16	Wyoming 27-6	Everett Shelton	28-7
17	Louisville 20-5	Peck Hickman	20-6
18	Seattle · 29-7	Al Brightman	29-8
19	UCLA 19-10	John Wooden	19-12
20	SW Texas St. . . .30-1	Milton Jowers	same

Note: Unranked La Salle, coached by Ken Loeffler, won the NIT. The Explorers entered the postseason at 21-7 and had a final record of 25-7.

NCAA Final Four (at Edmundson Pavillion, Seattle): **Semifinals**—St. John's 61, Illinois 59; Kansas 74, Santa Clara 59. **Third Place**—Illinois 67, Santa Clara 64. **Championship**—Kansas 80, St. John's 63.

NIT Final Four (at Madison Sq. Garden): **Semifinals**—La Salle 59, Duquesne 46; Dayton 69, St. Bonaventure 62. **Third Place**—St. Bonaventure 48, Duquesne 34. **Championship**—La Salle 75, Dayton 64.

Associated Press Final Polls (Cont.)

1953

		Before Tourns	Head Coach	Final Record
1	**Indiana**	18-3	Branch McCracken	23-3
2	La Salle	25-2	Ken Loeffler	25-3
3	**Seton Hall**	28-2	Honey Russell	31-2
4	Washington	27-2	Tippy Dye	30-3
5	LSU	22-1	Harry Rabenhorst	24-3
6	Kansas	16-5	Phog Allen	19-6
7	Oklahoma A&M	22-6	Hank Iba	23-7
	Kansas St.	17-4	Jack Gardner	same
9	Western Ky.	25-5	Ed Diddle	25-6
10	Illinois	18-4	Harry Combes	same
11	Oklahoma City	18-4	Doyle Parrick	18-6
12	N.C. State	26-6	Everett Case	same
13	Notre Dame	17-4	John Jordan	19-5
14	Louisville	21-5	Peck Hickman	22-6
	Seattle	27-3	Al Brightman	29-4
16	Miami-OH	17-5	Bill Rohr	17-6
17	Eastern Ky.	16-8	Paul McBrayer	16-9
18	Duquesne	18-7	Dudey Moore	21-8
	Navy	16-4	Ben Carnevale	16-5
20	Holy Cross	18-5	Buster Sheary	20-6

NCAA Final Four (at Municipal Auditorium, Kansas City): **Semifinals**—Indiana 80, LSU 67; Kansas 79, Washington 53. **Third Place**—Washington 88, LSU 69. **Championship**—Indiana 69, Kansas 68.

NIT Final Four (at Madison Sq. Garden): **Semifinals**—Seton Hall 74, Manhattan 56; St. John's 64, Duquesne 55. **Third Place**—Duquesne 81, Manhattan 67. **Championship**—Seton Hall 58, St. John's 46.

1954

		Before Tourns	Head Coach	Final Record
1	Kentucky	25-0	Adolph Rupp	same*
2	Indiana	19-3	Branch McCracken	20-4
3	Duquesne	24-2	Dudey Moore	26-3
4	Western Ky.	28-1	Ed Diddle	29-3
5	Oklahoma A&M	23-4	Hank Iba	24-5
6	Notre Dame	20-2	John Jordan	22-3
7	Kansas	16-5	Phog Allen	same
8	**Holy Cross**	23-2	Buster Sheary	26-2
9	LSU	21-3	Harry Rabenhorst	21-5
10	**La Salle**	21-4	Ken Loeffler	26-4
11	Iowa	17-5	Bucky O'Connor	same
12	Duke	22-6	Harold Bradley	same
13	Colorado A&M	22-5	Bill Strannigan	22-7
14	Illinois	17-5	Harry Combes	same
15	Wichita	27-3	Ralph Miller	27-4
16	Seattle	26-1	Al Brightman	26-2
17	N.C. State	26-6	Everett Case	28-7
18	Dayton	24-6	Tom Blackburn	25-7
	Minnesota	17-5	Ozzie Cowles	same
20	Oregon St.	19-10	Slats Gill	same
	UCLA	18-7	John Wooden	same
	USC	17-12	Forrest Twogood	19-14

*Kentucky turned down invitation to NCAA tournament after NCAA declared seniors Cliff Hagan, Frank Ramsey and Lou Tsioropoulos ineligible for postseason play.

NCAA Final Four (at Municipal Auditorium, Kansas City): **Semifinals**—La Salle 69, Penn St. 54; Bradley 74, USC 72. **Third Place**—Penn St. 70, USC 61. **Championship**—La Salle 92, Bradley 76.

NIT Final Four (at Madison Square Garden): **Semifinals**—Duquesne 66, Niagara 51; Holy Cross 75, Western Ky. 69. **Third Place**—Niagara 71, Western Ky. 65. **Championship**—Holy Cross 71, Duquesne 62.

1955

		Before Tourns	Head Coach	Final Record
1	**San Francisco**	23-1	Phil Woolpert	28-1
2	Kentucky	22-2	Adolph Rupp	23-3
3	La Salle	22-4	Ken Loeffler	26-5
4	N.C. State	28-4	Everett Case	same
5	Iowa	17-5	Bucky O'Connor	19-7
6	**Duquesne**	19-4	Dudey Moore	22-4
7	Utah	23-3	Jack Gardner	24-4
8	Marquette	22-2	Jack Nagle	24-3
9	Dayton	23-3	Tom Blackburn	25-4
10	Oregon St.	21-7	Slats Gill	22-8
11	Minnesota	15-7	Ozzie Cowles	same
12	Alabama	19-5	Johnny Dee	same
13	UCLA	21-5	John Wooden	same
14	G. Washington	24-6	Bill Reinhart	same
15	Colorado	16-5	Bebe Lee	19-6
16	Tulsa	20-6	Clarence Iba	21-7
17	Vanderbilt	16-6	Bob Polk	same
18	Illinois	17-5	Harry Combes	same
19	West Virginia	19-10	Fred Schaus	19-11
20	Saint Louis	19-7	Eddie Hickey	20-8

NCAA Final Four (at Municipal Auditorium, Kansas City): **Semifinals**—La Salle 76, Iowa 73; San Francisco 62, Colorado 50. **Third Place**—Colorado 75, Iowa 74. **Championship**—San Francisco 77, La Salle 63.

NIT Final Four (at Madison Square Garden): **Semifinals**—Dayton 79, St. Francis-PA 73 (OT); Duquesne 65, Cincinnati 51. **Third Place**—Cincinnati 96, St. Francis-PA 91 (OT). **Championship**—Duquesne 70, Dayton 58.

1956

		Before Tourns	Head Coach	Final Record
1	**San Francisco**	25-0	Phil Woolpert	29-0
2	N.C. State	24-3	Everett Case	24-4
3	Dayton	23-3	Tom Blackburn	25-4
4	Iowa	17-5	Bucky O'Connor	20-6
5	Alabama	21-3	Johnny Dee	same
6	**Louisville**	23-3	Peck Hickman	26-3
7	SMU	22-2	Doc Hayes	25-4
8	UCLA	21-5	John Wooden	22-6
9	Kentucky	19-5	Adolph Rupp	20-6
10	Illinois	18-4	Harry Combes	same
11	Oklahoma City	18-6	Abe Lemons	20-7
12	Vanderbilt	19-4	Bob Polk	same
13	North Carolina	18-5	Frank McGuire	same
14	Holy Cross	22-4	Roy Leenig	22-5
15	Temple	23-3	Harry Litwack	27-4
16	Wake Forest	19-9	Murray Greason	same
17	Duke	19-7	Harold Bradley	same
18	Utah	21-5	Jack Gardner	22-6
19	Oklahoma A&M	18-8	Hank Iba	18-9
20	West Virginia	21-8	Fred Schaus	21-9

NCAA Final Four (at McGaw Hall, Evanston, IL): **Semifinals**—Iowa 83, Temple 76; San Francisco 86, SMU 68. **Third Place**—Temple 90, SMU 81. **Championship**—San Francisco 83, Iowa 71.

NIT Final Four (at Madison Square Garden): **Semifinals**—Dayton 89, St. Francis-NY 58; Louisville 89, St. Joseph's-PA 79. **Third Place**—St. Joseph's-PA 93, St. Francis-NY 82. **Championship**—Louisville 93, Dayton 80.

1957

	Before Tourns	Head Coach	Final Record
1	**N. Carolina** ...27-0	Frank McGuire	32-0
2	Kansas ...21-2	Dick Harp	24-3
3	Kentucky ...22-4	Adolph Rupp	23-5
4	SMU ...21-3	Doc Hayes	22-4
5	Seattle ...24-2	John Castellani	24-3
6	Louisville ...21-5	Peck Hickman	same
7	West Va. ...25-4	Fred Schaus	25-5
8	Vanderbilt ...17-5	Bob Polk	same
9	Oklahoma City ...17-8	Abe Lemons	19-9
10	Saint Louis ...19-7	Eddie Hickey	19-9
11	Michigan St. ...14-8	Forddy Anderson	16-10
12	Memphis St. ...21-5	Bob Vanatta	24-6
13	California ...20-4	Pete Newell	21-5
14	UCLA ...22-4	John Wooden	same
15	Mississippi St. ...17-8	Babe McCarthy	same
16	Idaho St. ...24-2	John Grayson	25-4
17	Notre Dame ...18-7	John Jordan	20-8
18	Wake Forest ...19-9	Murray Greason	same
19	Canisius ...20-5	Joe Curran	22-6
20	Oklahoma A&M ...17-9	Hank Iba	same

Note: Unranked **Bradley**, coached by Chuck Orsborn, won the NIT. The Braves entered the tourney at 19-7 and had a final record of 22-7.

NCAA Final Four (at Municipal Auditorium, Kansas City): **Semifinals**—North Carolina 74, Michigan St. 70 (3 OT); Kansas 80, San Francisco 56. **Third Place**—San Francisco 67, Michigan St. 60. **Championship**—North Carolina 54, Kansas 53 (3 OT).

NIT Final Four (at Madison Square Garden): **Semifinals**—Memphis St. 80, St. Bonaventure 78; Bradley 78, Temple 66. **Third Place**—Temple 67, St. Bonaventure 50. **Championship**—Bradley 84, Memphis St. 83.

1958

	Before Tourns	Head Coach	Final Record
1	West Virginia ...26-1	Fred Schaus	26-2
2	Cincinnati ...24-2	George Smith	25-3
3	Kansas St. ...20-3	Tex Winter	22-5
4	San Francisco ...24-1	Phil Woolpert	25-2
5	Temple ...24-2	Harry Litwack	27-3
6	Maryland ...20-6	Bud Millikan	22-7
7	Kansas ...18-5	Dick Harp	same
8	Notre Dame ...22-4	John Jordan	24-5
9	**Kentucky** ...19-6	Adolph Rupp	23-6
10	Duke ...18-7	Harold Bradley	same
11	Dayton ...23-3	Tom Blackburn	25-4
12	Indiana ...12-10	Branch McCracken	13-11
13	North Carolina ...19-7	Frank McGuire	same
14	Bradley ...20-6	Chuck Orsborn	20-7
15	Mississippi St. ...20-5	Babe McCarthy	same
16	Auburn ...16-6	Joel Eaves	same
17	Michigan St. ...16-6	Forddy Anderson	same
18	Seattle ...20-6	John Castellani	24-7
19	Oklahoma St. ...19-7	Hank Iba	21-8
20	N.C. State ...18-6	Everett Case	same

Note: Unranked **Xavier-OH**, coached by Jim McCafferty, won the NIT. The Musketeers entered the tourney at 15-11 and had a final record of 19-11.

NCAA Final Four (at Freedom Hall, Louisville): **Semifinals**—Kentucky 61, Temple 60; Seattle 73, Kansas St. 51. **Third Place**—Temple 67, Kansas St. 57. **Championship**—Kentucky 84, Seattle 72.

NIT Final Four (at Madison Square Garden): **Semifinals**—Dayton 80, St. John's 56; Xavier-OH 72, St. Bonaventure 53. **Third Place**—St. Bonaventure 84, St. John's 69. **Championship**—Xavier-OH 78, Dayton 74 (OT).

1959

	Before Tourns	Head Coach	Final Record
1	Kansas St. ...24-1	Tex Winter	25-2
2	Kentucky ...23-2	Adolph Rupp	24-3
3	Mississippi St. ...24-1	Babe McCarthy	same*
4	Bradley ...23-3	Chuck Orsborn	25-4
5	Cincinnati ...23-3	George Smith	26-4
6	N.C. State ...22-4	Everett Case	same
7	Michigan St. ...18-3	Forddy Anderson	19-4
8	Auburn ...20-2	Joel Eaves	same
9	North Carolina ...20-4	Frank McGuire	20-5
10	West Virginia ...25-4	Fred Schaus	29-5
11	**California** ...21-4	Pete Newell	25-4
12	Saint Louis ...20-5	John Benington	20-6
13	Seattle ...23-6	Vince Cazzetta	same
14	St. Joseph's-PA ...22-3	Jack Ramsay	22-5
15	St. Mary's-CA ...18-5	Jim Weaver	19-6
16	TCU ...19-5	Buster Brannon	20-6
17	Oklahoma City ...20-6	Abe Lemons	20-7
18	Utah ...21-5	Jack Gardner	21-7
19	St. Bonaventure ...20-2	Eddie Donovan	20-3
20	Marquette ...22-4	Eddie Hickey	23-6

*Mississippi St. turned down invitation to NCAA tournament because it was an integrated event.

Note: Unranked **St. John's**, coached by Joe Lapchick, won the NIT. The Redmen entered the tourney at 16-6 and had a final record of 20-6.

NCAA Final Four (at Freedom Hall, Louisville): **Semifinals**—West Virginia 94, Louisville 79; California 64, Cincinnati 58. **Third Place**—Cincinnati 98, Louisville 85. **Championship**—California 71, West Virginia 70.

NIT Final Four (at Madison Square Garden): **Semifinals**—Bradley 59, NYU 57; St. John's 76, Providence 55. **Third Place**—NYU 71, Providence 57. **Championship**—St. John's 76, Bradley 71 (OT).

1960

	Before Tourns	Head Coach	Final Record
1	Cincinnati ...25-1	George Smith	28-2
2	California ...24-1	Pete Newell	28-2
3	**Ohio St.** ...21-3	Fred Taylor	25-3
4	**Bradley** ...24-2	Chuck Orsborn	27-2
5	West Virginia ...24-4	Fred Schaus	26-5
6	Utah ...24-2	Jack Gardner	26-3
7	Indiana ...20-4	Branch McCracken	same
8	Utah St. ...22-4	Cecil Baker	24-5
9	St. Bonaventure ...19-3	Eddie Donovan	21-5
10	Miami-FL ...23-3	Bruce Hale	23-4
11	Auburn ...19-3	Joel Eaves	same
12	NYU ...19-4	Lou Rossini	22-5
13	Georgia Tech ...21-5	Whack Hyder	22-6
14	Providence ...21-4	Joe Mullaney	24-5
15	Saint Louis ...19-7	John Benington	19-8
16	Holy Cross ...20-5	Roy Leenig	20-6
17	Villanova ...19-5	Al Severance	20-6
18	Duke ...15-10	Vic Bubas	17-11
19	Wake Forest ...21-7	Bones McKinney	same
20	St. John's ...17-7	Joe Lapchick	17-8

NCAA Final Four (at the Cow Palace, San Fran.): **Semifinals**—Ohio St. 76, NYU 54; California 77, Cincinnati 69. **Third Place**—Cincinnati 95, NYU 71. **Championship**—Ohio St. 75, California 55.

NIT Final Four (at Madison Square Garden): **Semifinals**—Bradley 82, St. Bonaventure 71; Providence 68, Utah St. 62. **Third Place**—Utah St. 99, St. Bonaventure 93. **Championship**—Bradley 88, Providence 72.

Associated Press Final Polls (Cont.)

1961

		Before Tourns	Head Coach	Final Record
1	Ohio St.	.24-0	Fred Taylor	27-1
2	**Cincinnati**	.23-3	Ed Jucker	27-3
3	St. Bonaventure	.22-3	Eddie Donovan	24-4
4	Kansas St.	.22-3	Tex Winter	23-4
5	North Carolina	.19-4	Frank McGuire	same
6	Bradley	.21-5	Chuck Orsborn	same
7	USC	.20-6	Forrest Twogood	21-8
8	Iowa	.18-6	S. Scheuerman	same
9	West Virginia	.23-4	George King	same
10	Duke	.22-6	Vic Bubas	same
11	Utah	.21-6	Jack Gardner	23-8
12	Texas Tech	.14-9	Polk Robison	15-10
13	Niagara	.16-4	Taps Gallagher	16-5
14	Memphis St.	.20-2	Bob Vanatta	20-3
15	Wake Forest	.17-10	Bones McKinney	19-11
16	St. John's	.20-4	Joe Lapchick	20-5
17	St. Joseph's-PA	.22-4	Jack Ramsay	25-5
18	Drake	.19-7	Maury John	same
19	Holy Cross	.19-4	Roy Leenig	22-5
20	Kentucky	.18-8	Adolph Rupp	19-9

Note: Unranked **Providence**, coached by Joe Mullaney, won the NIT. The Friars entered the tourney at 20-5 and had a final record of 24-5.

NCAA Final Four (at Municipal Auditorium, Kansas City): **Semifinals**–Ohio St. 95, St. Joseph's-PA 69; Cincinnati 82, Utah 67. **Third Place**–St. Joseph's-PA 127, Utah 120 (4 OT). **Championship**–Cincinnati 70, Ohio St. 65 (OT).

NIT Final Four (at Madison Square Garden) **Semifinals**–St. Louis 67, Dayton 60; Providence 90, Holy Cross 83 (OT). **Third Place**–Holy Cross 85, Dayton 67. **Championship**–Providence 62, St. Louis 59.

1962

		Before Tourns	Head Coach	Final Record
1	Ohio St.	.23-1	Fred Taylor	26-2
2	**Cincinnati**	.25-2	Ed Jucker	29-2
3	Kentucky	.22-2	Adolph Rupp	23-3
4	Mississippi St.	.19-6	Babe McCarthy	same
5	Bradley	.21-6	Chuck Orsborn	21-7
6	Kansas St.	.22-3	Tex Winter	same
7	Utah	.23-3	Jack Gardner	same
8	Bowling Green	.21-3	Harold Anderson	same
9	Colorado	.18-6	Sox Walseth	19-7
10	Duke	.20-5	Vic Bubas	same
11	Loyola-IL	.21-3	George Ireland	23-4
12	St. John's	.19-4	Joe Lapchick	21-5
13	Wake Forest	.18-8	Bones McKinney	22-9
14	Oregon St.	.22-4	Slats Gill	24-5
15	West Virginia	.24-5	George King	24-6
16	Arizona St.	.23-3	Ned Wulk	23-4
17	Duquesne	.20-5	Red Manning	22-7
18	Utah St.	.21-5	Ladell Andersen	22-7
19	UCLA	.16-9	John Wooden	18-11
20	Villanova	.19-6	Jack Kraft	21-7

Note: Unranked **Dayton**, coached by Tom Blackburn, won the NIT. The Flyers entered the tourney at 20-6 and had a final record of 24-6.

NCAA Final Four (at Freedom Hall, Louisville): **Semifinals**–Ohio St. 84, Wake Forest 68; Cincinnati 72, UCLA 70. **Third Place**–Wake Forest 82, UCLA 80. **Championship**–Cincinnati 71, Ohio St. 59.

NIT Final Four (at Madison Square Garden): **Semifinals**–Dayton 98, Loyola-IL 82; St. John's 76, Duquesne 65. **Third Place**–Loyola-IL 95, Duquesne 84. **Championship**–Dayton 73, St. John's 67.

1963

AP ranked only 10 teams from the 1962-63 season through 1967-68.

		Before Tourns	Head Coach	Final Record
1	Cincinnati	.23-1	Ed Jucker	26-2
2	Duke	.24-2	Vic Bubas	27-3
3	**Loyola-IL**	.24-2	George Ireland	29-2
4	Arizona St.	.24-2	Ned Wulk	26-3
5	Wichita	.19-7	Ralph Miller	19-8
6	Mississippi St.	.21-5	Babe McCarthy	22-6
7	Ohio St.	.20-4	Fred Taylor	same
8	Illinois	.19-5	Harry Combes	20-6
9	NYU	.17-3	Lou Rossini	18-5
10	Colorado	.18-6	Sox Walseth	19-7

Note: Unranked **Providence**, coached by Joe Mullaney, won the NIT. The Friars entered the tourney at 21-4 and had a final record of 24-4.

NCAA Final Four (at Freedom Hall, Louisville): **Semifinals**–Loyola-IL 94, Duke 75; Cincinnati 80, Oregon St. 46. **Third Place**–Duke 85, Oregon St. 63. **Championship**–Loyola-IL 60, Cincinnati 58 (OT).

NIT Final Four (at Madison Square Garden): **Semifinals**–Providence 70, Marquette 66; Canisius 61, Villanova 46. **Third Place**–Marquette 66, Villanova 58. **Championship**–Providence 81, Canisius 66.

1964

AP ranked only 10 teams from the 1962-63 season through 1967-68.

		Before Tourns	Head Coach	Final Record
1	**UCLA**	.26-0	John Wooden	30-0
2	Michigan	.20-4	Dave Strack	23-5
3	Duke	.23-4	Vic Bubas	26-5
4	Kentucky	.21-4	Adolph Rupp	21-6
5	Wichita St.	.22-5	Ralph Miller	23-6
6	Oregon St.	.25-3	Slats Gill	25-4
7	Villanova	.22-3	Jack Kraft	24-4
8	Loyola-IL	.20-5	George Ireland	22-6
9	DePaul	.21-3	Ray Meyer	21-4
10	Davidson	.22-4	Lefty Driesell	22-4

Note: Unranked **Bradley**, coached by Chuck Orsborn, won the NIT. The Braves entered the tourney at 20-6 and finished with a record of 23-6.

NCAA Final Four (at Municipal Auditorium, Kansas City): **Semifinals**–Duke 91, Michigan 80; UCLA 90, Kansas St. 84. **Third Place**–Michigan 100, Kansas St. 90. **Championship**–UCLA 98, Duke 83.

NIT Final Four (at Madison Square Garden): **Semifinals**–New Mexico 72, NYU 65; Bradley 67, Army 52. **Third Place**–Army 60, NYU 59. **Championship**–Bradley 86, New Mexico 54.

Undefeated National Champions

Seven NCAA seasons have ended with an undefeated national champion. UCLA has accomplished the feat four times.

Year		W-L
1956	San Francisco	29-0
1957	North Carolina	32-0
1964	UCLA	30-0
1967	UCLA	30-0
1972	UCLA	30-0
1973	UCLA	30-0
1976	Indiana	32-0

1965

AP ranked only 10 teams from the 1962-63 season through 1967-68.

		Before Tourns	Head Coach	Final Record
1	Michigan	21-3	Dave Strack	24-4
2	**UCLA**	24-2	John Wooden	28-2
3	St. Joseph's-PA	25-1	Jack Ramsay	26-3
4	Providence	22-1	Joe Mullaney	24-2
5	Vanderbilt	23-3	Roy Skinner	24-4
6	Davidson	24-2	Lefty Driesell	same
7	Minnesota	19-5	John Kundla	same
8	Villanova	21-4	Jack Kraft	23-5
9	BYU	21-5	Stan Watts	21-7
10	Duke	20-5	Vic Bubas	same

Note: Unranked **St. John's**, coached by Joe Lapchick, won the NIT. The Redmen entered the tourney at 17-8 and finished with a record of 21-8.
NCAA Final Four (at Memorial Coliseum, Portland, OR): **Semifinals**–Michigan 93, Princeton 76; UCLA 108, Wichita St. 89. **Third Place**–Princeton 118, Wichita St. 82. **Championship**–UCLA 91, Michigan 80.
NIT Final Four (at Madison Square Garden): **Semifinals**–Villanova 91, NYU 69; St. John's 67, Army 60. **Third Place**–Army 75, NYU 74. **Championship**– St. John's 55, Villanova 51.

1966

AP ranked only 10 teams from the 1962-63 season through 1967-68.

		Before Tourns	Head Coach	Final Record
1	Kentucky	24-1	Adolph Rupp	27-2
2	Duke	23-3	Vic Bubas	26-4
3	**Texas Western**	23-1	Don Haskins	28-1
4	Kansas	22-3	Ted Owens	23-4
5	St. Joseph's-PA	22-4	Jack Ramsay	24-5
6	Loyola-IL	22-2	George Ireland	22-3
7	Cincinnati	21-5	Tay Baker	21-7
8	Vanderbilt	22-4	Roy Skinner	same
9	Michigan	17-7	Dave Strack	18-8
10	Western Ky.	23-2	Johnny Oldham	25-3

Note: Unranked **BYU**, coached by Stan Watts, won the NIT. The Cougars entered the tourney at 17-5 and had a final record of 20-5.
NCAA Final Four (at Cole Fieldhouse, College Park, MD): **Semifinals**–Kentucky 83, Duke 79; Texas Western 85, Utah 78. **Third Place**–Duke 79, Utah 77. **Championship**–Texas Western 72, Kentucky 65.
NIT Final Four (at Madison Square Garden): **Semifinals**–BYU 66, Army 60; NYU 69, Villanova 63. **Third Place**–Villanova 76, Army 65. **Championship**–BYU 97, NYU 84.

1967

AP ranked only 10 teams from the 1962-63 season through 1967-68.

		Before Tourns	Head Coach	Final Record
1	**UCLA**	26-0	John Wooden	30-0
2	Louisville	23-3	Peck Hickman	23-5
3	Kansas	22-3	Ted Owens	23-4
4	North Carolina	24-4	Dean Smith	26-6
5	Princeton	23-2	B. van Breda Kolff	25-3
6	Western Ky.	23-2	Johnny Oldham	23-3
7	Houston	23-3	Guy Lewis	27-4
8	Tennessee	21-5	Ray Mears	21-7
9	Boston College	19-2	Bob Cousy	21-3
10	Texas Western	20-5	Don Haskins	22-6

Note: Unranked **Southern Illinois**, coached by Jack Hartman, won the NIT. The Salukis entered the tourney at 20-2 and had a final record of 24-2.
NCAA Final Four (at Freedom Hall, Louisville): **Semifinals**–Dayton 76, N. Carolina 62; UCLA 73, Houston 58. **Third Place**–Houston 84, N. Carolina 62. **Championship**–UCLA 79, Dayton 64.
NIT Final Four (at Madison Square Garden): **Semifinals**–Marquette 83, Marshall 78; Southern Ill. 79, Rutgers 70. **Third Place**–Rutgers 93, Marshall 76. **Championship**–Southern Ill. 71, Marquette 56.

1968

AP ranked only 10 teams from the 1962-63 season through 1967-68.

		Before Tourns	Head Coach	Final Record
1	Houston	28-0	Guy Lewis	31-2
2	**UCLA**	25-1	John Wooden	29-1
3	St. Bonaventure	22-0	Larry Weise	23-2
4	North Carolina	25-3	Dean Smith	28-4
5	Kentucky	21-4	Adolph Rupp	22-5
6	New Mexico	23-3	Bob King	23-5
7	Columbia	21-4	Jack Rohan	23-5
8	Davidson	22-4	Lefty Driesell	24-5
9	Louisville	20-6	John Dromo	21-7
10	Duke	21-5	Vic Bubas	22-6

Note: Unranked **Dayton**, coached by Don Donoher, won the NIT. The Flyers entered the tourney at 17-9 and had a final record of 21-9.
NCAA Final Four (at the Sports Arena, Los Angeles): **Semifinals**–N. Carolina 80, Ohio St. 66; UCLA 101, Houston 69. **Third Place**–Ohio St. 89, Houston 85. **Championship**–UCLA 78, N. Carolina 55.
NIT Final Four (at Madison Square Garden): **Semifinals**–Dayton 76, Notre Dame 74 (OT); Kansas 58, St. Peter's 46. **Third Place**–Notre Dame 81, St.Peter's 78. **Championship**–Dayton 61, Kansas 48.

All-Time AP Top 20

The composite AP Top 20 from the 1948-49 season through 2002-03, based on the final regular season rankings of each year. The final AP poll has been taken before the NCAA and NIT tournaments each season since 1949 except in 1953 and '54 and again in 1974 and '75 when the final poll came out after the postseason. Team point totals are based on 20 points for all 1st place finishes, 19 for each 2nd, etc. Also listed are the number of times ranked No.1 by AP going into the tournaments, and times ranked in the pre-tournament Top 10 and Top 20.

		Pts	No.1	Top 10	Top 20			Pts	No.1	Top10	Top 20
1	Kentucky	639	8	36	43	11	Illinois	199	0	9	21
2	North Carolina	510	5	28	36	12	Notre Dame	190	0	12	18
3	UCLA	449	7	22	35	13	Marquette	187	0	12	17
4	Duke	429	6	24	33	14	N.C. State	176	1	9	16
5	Kansas	355	1	19	27		Ohio St.	176	2	10	13
6	Indiana	293	4	16	24	16	UNLV	173	2	8	13
7	Cincinnati	249	2	13	18	17	Syracuse	168	0	9	18
8	Louisville	240	0	11	23	18	Arkansas	166	0	9	15
9	Arizona	233	1	11	19	19	Maryland	158	0	8	16
10	Michigan	200	2	10	15	20	Oklahoma	153	1	7	12

Associated Press Final Polls (Cont.)

1969

		Before Tours	Head Coach	Final Record
1	**UCLA**	.25-1	John Wooden	29-1
2	La Salle	.23-1	Tom Gola	same*
3	Santa Clara	.26-1	Dick Garibaldi	27-2
4	North Carolina	.25-3	Dean Smith	27-5
5	Davidson	.24-2	Lefty Driesell	26-3
6	Purdue	.20-4	George King	23-5
7	Kentucky	.22-4	Adolph Rupp	23-5
8	St. John's	.22-4	Lou Carnesecca	23-6
9	Duquesne	.19-4	Red Manning	21-5
10	Villanova	.21-4	Jack Kraft	21-5
11	Drake	.23-4	Maury John	26-5
12	New Mexico St.	.23-3	Lou Henson	24-5
13	South Carolina	.20-6	Frank McGuire	21-7
14	Marquette	.22-4	Al McGuire	24-5
15	Louisville	.20-5	John Dromo	21-6
16	Boston College	.21-3	Bob Cousy	24-4
17	Notre Dame	.20-6	Johnny Dee	20-7
18	Colorado	.20-6	Sox Walseth	21-7
19	Kansas	.20-6	Ted Owens	20-7
20	Illinois	.19-5	Harvey Schmidt	same

*On probation

Note: Unranked **Temple**, coached by Harry Litwack, won the NIT. The Owls entered the tourney at 18-8 and finished with a record of 22-8.

NCAA Final Four (at Freedom Hall, Louisville): **Semifinals**—Purdue 92, N. Carolina 65; UCLA 85, Drake 82. **Third Place**—Drake 104, N. Carolina 84. **Championship**—UCLA 92, Purdue 72.

NIT Final Four (at Madison Square Garden): **Semifinals**—Temple 63, Tennessee 58; Boston College 73, Army 61. **Third Place**—Tennessee 64, Army 52. **Championship**—Temple 89, Boston College 76.

1971

		Before Tours	Head Coach	Final Record
1	**UCLA**	.25-1	John Wooden	29-1
2	Marquette	.26-0	Al McGuire	28-1
3	Penn	.26-0	Dick Harter	28-1
4	Kansas	.25-1	Ted Owens	27-3
5	USC	.24-2	Bob Boyd	24-2
6	South Carolina	.23-4	Frank McGuire	23-6
7	Western Ky.	.20-5	John Oldham	24-6
8	Kentucky	.22-4	Adolph Rupp	22-6
9	Fordham	.25-1	Digger Phelps	26-3
10	Ohio St.	.19-5	Fred Taylor	20-6
11	Jacksonville	.22-3	Tom Wasdin	22-4
12	Notre Dame	.19-7	Johnny Dee	20-9
13	**N. Carolina**	.22-6	Dean Smith	26-6
14	Houston	.20-6	Guy Lewis	22-7
15	Duquesne	.21-3	Red Manning	21-4
16	Long Beach St.	.21-4	Jerry Tarkanian	23-5
17	Tennessee	.20-6	Ray Mears	21-7
18	Villanova	.19-5	Jack Kraft	23-6
19	Drake	.20-7	Maury John	21-8
20	BYU	.18-9	Stan Watts	18-11

NCAA Final Four (at the Astrodome, Houston): **Semifinals**—Villanova 92, Western Ky. 89 (2 OT); UCLA 68, Kansas 60. **Third Place**—Western Ky. 77, Kansas 75. **Championship**—UCLA 68, Villanova 62.

NIT Final Four (at Madison Square Garden): **Semifinals**—N. Carolina 73, Duke 69; Ga.Tech 76, St. Bonaventure 71 (2 OT). **Third Place**—St. Bonaventure 92, Duke 88 (OT). **Championship**—N. Carolina 84, Ga. Tech 66.

1970

		Before Tours	Head Coach	Final Record
1	Kentucky	.25-1	Adolph Rupp	26-2
2	**UCLA**	.24-2	John Wooden	28-2
3	St. Bonaventure	.22-1	Larry Weise	25-3
4	Jacksonville	.23-1	Joe Williams	27-2
5	New Mexico St.	.23-2	Lou Henson	27-3
6	South Carolina	.25-3	Frank McGuire	25-3
7	Iowa	.19-4	Ralph Miller	20-5
8	**Marquette**	.22-3	Al McGuire	26-3
9	Notre Dame	.20-6	Johnny Dee	21-8
10	N.C. State	.22-6	Norm Sloan	23-7
11	Florida St.	.23-3	Hugh Durham	23-3
12	Houston	.24-3	Guy Lewis	25-5
13	Penn	.25-1	Dick Harter	25-2
14	Drake	.21-6	Maury John	22-7
15	Davidson	.22-4	Terry Holland	22-5
16	Utah St.	.20-6	Ladell Andersen	22-7
17	Niagara	.21-5	Frank Layden	22-7
18	Western Ky.	.22-2	John Oldham	22-3
19	Long Beach St.	.23-3	Jerry Tarkanian	24-5
20	USC	.18-8	Bob Boyd	18-8

NCAA Final Four (at Cole Fieldhouse, College Park, MD): **Semifinals**—Jacksonville 91, St. Bonaventure 83; UCLA 93, New Mexico St. 77. **Third Place**—N. Mexico St. 79, St. Bonaventure 73. **Championship**—UCLA 80, Jacksonville 69.

NIT Final Four (at Madison Square Garden): **Semifinals**—St. John's 60, Army 59; Marquette 101, LSU 79. **Third Place**—Army 75, LSU 68. **Championship**—Marquette 65, St. John's 53.

1972

		Before Tours	Head Coach	Final Record
1	**UCLA**	.26-0	John Wooden	30-0
2	North Carolina	.23-4	Dean Smith	26-5
3	Penn	.23-2	Chuck Daly	25-3
4	Louisville	.23-4	Denny Crum	26-5
5	Long Beach St.	.23-3	Jerry Tarkanian	25-4
6	South Carolina	.22-4	Frank McGuire	24-5
7	Marquette	.24-2	Al McGuire	25-4
8	SW Louisiana	.23-3	Beryl Shipley	25-4
9	BYU	.21-4	Stan Watts	21-5
10	Florida St.	.23-5	Hugh Durham	27-6
11	Minnesota	.17-6	Bill Musselman	18-7
12	Marshall	.23-3	Carl Tacy	23-4
13	Memphis St.	.21-6	Gene Bartow	21-7
14	**Maryland**	.23-5	Lefty Driesell	27-5
15	Villanova	.19-6	Jack Kraft	20-8
16	Oral Roberts	.25-1	Ken Trickey	26-2
17	Indiana	.17-7	Bob Knight	17-8
18	Kentucky	.20-6	Adolph Rupp	21-7
19	Ohio St.	.18-6	Fred Taylor	same
20	Virginia	.21-6	Bill Gibson	21-7

NCAA Final Four (at the Sports Arena, Los Angeles): **Semifinals**—Florida St. 79, N. Carolina 75; UCLA 96, Louisville 77. **Third Place**—N. Carolina 105, Louisville 91. **Championship**—UCLA 81, Florida St. 76.

NIT Final Four (at Madison Square Garden): **Semifinals**—Maryland 91, Jacksonville 77; Niagara 69, St. John's 67. **Third Place**—Jacksonville 83, St. John's 80. **Championship**—Maryland 100, Niagara 69.

1973

		Before Tourns	Head Coach	Final Record
1	**UCLA**	26-0	John Wooden	30-0
2	N.C. State	27-0	Norm Sloan	same*
3	Long Beach St.	24-2	Jerry Tarkanian	26-3
4	Providence	24-2	Dave Gavitt	27-4
5	Marquette	23-3	Al McGuire	25-4
6	Indiana	19-5	Bob Knight	22-6
7	SW Louisiana	23-2	Beryl Shipley	24-5
8	Maryland	22-6	Lefty Driesell	23-7
9	Kansas St.	22-4	Jack Hartman	23-5
10	Minnesota	20-4	Bill Musselman	21-5
11	North Carolina	22-7	Dean Smith	25-8
12	Memphis St.	21-5	Gene Bartow	24-6
13	Houston	23-3	Guy Lewis	23-4
14	Syracuse	22-4	Roy Danforth	24-5
15	Missouri	21-5	Norm Stewart	21-6
16	Arizona St.	18-7	Ned Wulk	19-9
17	Kentucky	19-7	Joe B. Hall	20-8
18	Penn	20-5	Chuck Daly	21-7
19	Austin Peay	21-5	Lake Kelly	22-7
20	San Francisco	22-4	Bob Gaillard	23-5

*N.C. State was ineligible for NCAA tournament for using improper methods to recruit David Thompson.

Note: Unranked **Virginia Tech**, coached by Don DeVoe, won the NIT. The Hokies entered the tourney at 18-5 and finished with a record of 22-5.

NCAA Final Four (at The Arena, St. Louis): **Semifinals**—Memphis St. 98, Providence 85; UCLA 70, Indiana 59. **Third Place**—Indiana 97, Providence 79. **Championship**—UCLA 87, Memphis St. 66.

NIT Final Four (at Madison Square Garden): **Semifinals**—Va. Tech 74, Alabama 73; Notre Dame 78, N. Carolina 71. **Third Place**—N. Carolina 88, Alabama 69. **Championship**—Va. Tech 92, Notre Dame 91 (OT).

1974

		Before Tourns	Head Coach	Final Record
1	**N.C. State**	26-1	Norm Sloan	30-1
2	UCLA	23-3	John Wooden	26-4
3	Notre Dame	24-2	Digger Phelps	26-3
4	Maryland	23-5	Lefty Driesell	same
5	Providence	26-3	Dave Gavitt	28-4
6	Vanderbilt	23-3	Roy Skinner	23-5
7	Marquette	22-4	Al McGuire	26-5
8	North Carolina	22-5	Dean Smith	22-6
9	Long Beach St.	24-2	Lute Olson	same
10	**Indiana**	20-5	Bob Knight	23-5
11	Alabama	22-4	C.M. Newton	same
12	Michigan	21-4	Johnny Orr	22-5
13	Pittsburgh	22-3	Buzz Ridl	25-4
14	Kansas	21-5	Ted Owens	23-7
15	USC	22-4	Bob Boyd	24-5
16	Louisville	21-6	Denny Crum	21-7
17	New Mexico	21-6	Norm Ellenberger	22-7
18	South Carolina	22-4	Frank McGuire	22-5
19	Creighton	22-6	Eddie Sutton	23-7
20	Dayton	19-7	Don Donoher	20-9

NCAA Final Four (at Greensboro, NC, Coliseum): **Semifinals**—N.C. State 80, UCLA 77 (2 OT); Marquette 64, Kansas 51. **Third Place**—UCLA 78, Kansas 61. **Championship**—N.C. State 76, Marquette 64.

NIT Final Four (at Madison Square Garden): **Semifinals**—Purdue 78, Jacksonville 63; Utah 117, Boston Col. 93. **Third Place**—Boston Col. 87, Jacksonville 77. **Championship**—Purdue 87, Utah 81.

CCA Final Four (at The Arena, St. Louis): **Semifinals**—Indiana 73, Toledo 72; USC 74, Bradley 73. **Championship**—Indiana 85, USC 60.

1975

		Before Tourns	Head Coach	Final Record
1	Indiana	29-0	Bob Knight	31-1
2	**UCLA**	23-3	John Wooden	28-3
3	Louisville	24-2	Denny Crum	28-3
4	Maryland	22-4	Lefty Driesell	24-5
5	Kentucky	22-4	Joe B. Hall	26-5
6	North Carolina	21-7	Dean Smith	23-8
7	Arizona St.	23-3	Ned Wulk	25-4
8	N.C.State	22-6	Norm Sloan	22-6
9	Notre Dame	18-8	Digger Phelps	19-10
10	Marquette	23-3	Al McGuire	23-4
11	Alabama	22-4	C.M. Newton	22-5
12	Cincinnati	21-5	Gale Catlett	23-6
13	Oregon St.	18-10	Ralph Miller	19-12
14	**Drake**	16-10	Bob Ortegel	19-10
15	Penn	23-4	Chuck Daly	23-5
16	UNLV	22-4	Jerry Tarkanian	24-5
17	Kansas St.	18-8	Jack Hartman	20-9
18	USC	18-7	Bob Boyd	18-8
19	Centenary	25-4	Larry Little	same
20	Syracuse	20-7	Roy Danforth	23-9

NCAA Final Four (at San Diego Sports Arena): **Semifinals**—Kentucky 95, Syracuse 79; UCLA 75, Louisville 74 (OT). **Third Place**—Louisville 96, Syracuse 88 (OT). **Championship**—UCLA 92, Kentucky 85.

NIT Championship (at Madison Sq. Garden): Princeton 80, Providence 69. No Top 20 teams played in NIT.

CCA Championship (at Freedom Hall, Louisville): Drake 83, Arizona 76. No.14 Drake and No.18 USC were only Top 20 teams in CCA.

1976

		Before Tourns	Head Coach	Final Record
1	**Indiana**	27-0	Bob Knight	32-0
2	Marquette	25-1	Al McGuire	27-2
3	UNLV	28-1	Jerry Tarkanian	29-2
4	Rutgers	28-0	Tom Young	31-2
5	UCLA	24-3	Gene Bartow	28-4
6	Alabama	22-4	C.M. Newton	23-5
7	Notre Dame	22-5	Digger Phelps	23-6
8	North Carolina	25-3	Dean Smith	25-4
9	Michigan	21-6	Johnny Orr	25-7
10	Western Mich.	24-2	Eldon Miller	25-3
11	Maryland	22-6	Lefty Driesell	same
12	Cincinnati	25-5	Gale Catlett	25-6
13	Tennessee	21-5	Ray Mears	21-6
14	Missouri	24-4	Norm Stewart	26-5
15	Arizona	22-8	Fred Snowden	24-9
16	Texas Tech	24-5	Gerald Myers	25-6
17	DePaul	19-8	Ray Meyer	20-9
18	Virginia	18-11	Terry Holland	18-12
19	Centenary	22-5	Larry Little	same
20	Pepperdine	21-5	Gary Colson	22-6

NCAA Final Four (at the Spectrum, Phila.); **Semifinals**—Michigan 86, Rutgers 70; Indiana 65, UCLA 51. **Third Place**—UCLA 106, Rutgers 92. **Championship**—Indiana 86, Michigan 68.

NIT Championship (at Madison Square Garden): Kentucky 71, NC-Charlotte 67. No Top 20 teams played in NIT.

Associated Press Final Polls (Cont.)

1977

		Before Tours	Head Coach	Final Record
1	Michigan	24-3	Johnny Orr	26-4
2	UCLA	24-3	Gene Bartow	25-4
3	Kentucky	24-3	Joe B. Hall	26-4
4	UNLV	25-2	Jerry Tarkanian	29-3
5	North Carolina	24-4	Dean Smith	28-5
6	Syracuse	25-3	Jim Boeheim	26-4
7	**Marquette**	20-7	Al McGuire	25-7
8	San Francisco	29-1	Bob Gaillard	29-2
9	Wake Forest	20-7	Carl Tacy	22-8
10	Notre Dame	21-6	Digger Phelps	22-7
11	Alabama	23-4	C.M. Newton	25-6
12	Detroit	24-3	Dick Vitale	25-4
13	Minnesota	24-3	Jim Dutcher	same*
14	Utah	22-6	Jerry Pimm	23-7
15	Tennessee	22-5	Ray Mears	22-6
16	Kansas St.	23-6	Jack Hartman	24-7
17	NC-Charlotte	25-3	Lee Rose	28-5
18	Arkansas	26-1	Eddie Sutton	26-2
19	Louisville	21-6	Denny Crum	21-7
20	VMI	25-3	Charlie Schmaus	26-4

*On probation

NCAA Final Four (at the Omni, Atlanta): **Semifinals**—Marquette 51, NC-Charlotte, 49; N. Carolina 84, UNLV 83. **Third Place**—UNLV 106, NC-Charlotte 94. **Championship**—Marquette 67, N. Carolina 59.

NIT Championship (at Madison Square Garden): St. Bonaventure 94, Houston 91. No.11 Alabama was only Top 20 team in NIT.

1978

		Before Tours	Head Coach	Final Record
1	**Kentucky**	25-2	Joe B. Hall	30-2
2	UCLA	24-2	Gary Cunningham	25-3
3	DePaul	25-2	Ray Meyer	27-3
4	Michigan St.	23-4	Jud Heathcote	25-5
5	Arkansas	28-3	Eddie Sutton	32-3
6	Notre Dame	20-6	Digger Phelps	23-8
7	Duke	23-6	Bill Foster	27-7
8	Marquette	24-3	Hank Raymonds	24-4
9	Louisville	22-6	Denny Crum	23-7
10	Kansas	24-4	Ted Owens	24-5
11	San Francisco	22-5	Bob Gaillard	23-6
12	New Mexico	24-3	Norm Ellenberger	24-4
13	Indiana	20-7	Bob Knight	21-8
14	Utah	22-5	Jerry Pimm	23-6
15	Florida St.	23-5	Hugh Durham	23-6
16	North Carolina	23-7	Dean Smith	23-8
17	**Texas**	22-5	Abe Lemons	26-5
18	Detroit	24-3	Dave Gaines	25-4
19	Miami-OH	18-8	Darrell Hedric	19-9
20	Penn	19-7	Bob Weinhauer	20-8

NCAA Final Four (at the Checkerdome, St. Louis): **Semifinals**—Kentucky 64, Arkansas 59; Duke 90, Notre Dame 86. **Third Place**—Arkansas 71, Notre Dame 69. **Championship**—Kentucky 94, Duke 88.

NIT Championship (at Madison Square Garden): Texas 101, N.C. State 93. No. 17 Texas and No. 18 Detroit were only Top 20 teams in NIT.

1979

		Before Tours	Head Coach	Final Record
1	Indiana St.	29-0	Bill Hodges	33-1
2	UCLA	23-4	Gary Cunningham	25-5
3	**Michigan St.**	21-6	Jud Heathcote	26-6
4	Notre Dame	22-5	Digger Phelps	24-6
5	Arkansas	23-4	Eddie Sutton	25-5
6	DePaul	22-5	Ray Meyer	26-6
7	LSU	22-5	Dale Brown	23-6
8	Syracuse	25-3	Jim Boeheim	26-4
9	North Carolina	23-5	Dean Smith	23-6
10	Marquette	21-6	Hank Raymonds	22-7
11	Duke	22-7	Bill Foster	22-8
12	San Francisco	21-6	Dan Belluomini	22-7
13	Louisville	23-7	Denny Crum	24-8
14	Penn	21-5	Bob Weinhauer	25-7
15	Purdue	23-7	Lee Rose	27-8
16	Oklahoma	20-9	Dave Bliss	21-10
17	St. John's	18-10	Lou Carnesecca	21-11
18	Rutgers	21-8	Tom Young	22-9
19	Toledo	21-6	Bob Nichols	22-7
20	Iowa	20-7	Lute Olson	20-8

NCAA Final Four (at Special Events Center, Salt Lake City): **Semifinals**—Michigan St. 101; Penn 67; Indiana St. 76, DePaul 74; **Third Place**—DePaul 96, Penn 93; **Championship**—Michigan St. 75, Indiana St. 64.

NIT Championship (at Madison Square Garden): Indiana 53, Purdue 52. No. 15 Purdue was the only Top 20 team in NIT.

1980

		Before Tours	Head Coach	Final Record
1	DePaul	26-1	Ray Meyer	26-2
2	**Louisville**	28-3	Denny Crum	33-3
3	LSU	24-5	Dale Brown	26-6
4	Kentucky	28-5	Joe B. Hall	29-6
5	Oregon St.	26-3	Ralph Miller	26-4
6	Syracuse	25-3	Jim Boeheim	26-4
7	Indiana	20-7	Bob Knight	21-8
8	Maryland	23-6	Lefty Driesell	24-7
9	Notre Dame	20-7	Digger Phelps	20-8
10	Ohio St.	24-5	Eldon Miller	21-8
11	Georgetown	24-5	John Thompson	26-6
12	BYU	24-4	Frank Arnold	24-5
13	St. John's	24-4	Lou Carnesecca	24-5
14	Duke	22-8	Bill Foster	24-9
15	North Carolina	21-7	Dean Smith	21-8
16	Missouri	23-5	Norm Stewart	25-6
17	Weber St.	26-2	Neil McCarthy	26-3
18	Arizona St.	21-6	Ned Wulk	22-7
19	Iona	28-4	Jim Valvano	29-5
20	Purdue	19-9	Lee Rose	23-10

NCAA Final Four (at Market Square Arena, Indianapolis): **Semifinals**—Louisville 80, Iowa 72; UCLA 67, Purdue 62; **Championship**—Louisville 59, UCLA 54.

NIT Championship (at Madison Square Garden): Virginia 58, Minnesota 55. No Top 20 teams played in NIT.

1981

		Before Tourns	Head Coach	Final Record
1	DePaul	.27-1	Ray Meyer	27-2
2	Oregon St.	.26-1	Ralph Miller	26-2
3	Arizona St.	.24-3	Ned Wulk	24-4
4	LSU	.28-3	Dale Brown	31-5
5	Virginia	.25-3	Terry Holland	29-4
6	North Carolina	.25-7	Dean Smith	29-8
7	Notre Dame	.22-5	Digger Phelps	23-6
8	Kentucky	.22-5	Joe B. Hall	22-6
9	**Indiana**	.21-9	Bob Knight	26-9
10	UCLA	.20-6	Larry Brown	20-7
11	Wake Forest	.22-6	Carl Tacy	22-7
12	Louisville	.21-8	Denny Crum	21-9
13	Iowa	.21-6	Lute Olson	21-7
14	Utah	.24-4	Jerry Pimm	25-5
15	Tennessee	.20-7	Don DeVoe	21-8
16	BYU	.22-6	Frank Arnold	25-7
17	Wyoming	.23-5	Jim Brandenburg	24-6
18	Maryland	.20-9	Lefty Driesell	21-10
19	Illinois	.20-7	Lou Henson	21-8
20	Arkansas	.22-7	Eddie Sutton	24-8

NCAA Final Four (at the Spectrum, Phila.): **Semifinals**–N. Carolina 78, Virginia 65; Indiana 67, LSU 49. **Third Place**–Virginia 78, LSU 74. **Championship**–Indiana 63, N. Carolina 50.
NIT Championship (at Madison Square Garden): Tulsa 86, Syracuse 84. No Top 20 teams played in NIT.

1983

		Before Tourns	Head Coach	Final Record
1	Houston	.27-2	Guy Lewis	31-3
2	Louisville	.29-3	Denny Crum	32-4
3	St. John's	.27-4	Lou Carnesecca	28-5
4	Virginia	.27-4	Terry Holland	29-5
5	Indiana	.23-5	Bob Knight	24-6
6	UNLV	.28-2	Jerry Tarkanian	28-3
7	UCLA	.23-5	Larry Farmer	23-6
8	North Carolina	.26-7	Dean Smith	28-8
9	Arkansas	.25-3	Eddie Sutton	26-4
10	Missouri	.26-7	Norm Stewart	26-8
11	Boston College	.24-6	Gary Williams	25-7
12	Kentucky	.22-7	Joe B. Hall	23-8
13	Villanova	.22-7	Rollie Massimino	24-8
14	Wichita St.	.25-3	Gene Smithson	same*
15	Tenn-Chatt.	.26-3	Murray Arnold	26-4
16	**N.C. State**	.20-10	Jim Valvano	26-10
17	Memphis St.	.22-7	Dana Kirk	23-8
18	Georgia	.21-9	Hugh Durham	24-10
19	Oklahoma St.	.24-6	Paul Hansen	24-7
20	Georgetown	.21-9	John Thompson	22-10

*On probation
NCAA Final Four (at The Pit, Albuquerque, NM): **Semifinals**–N.C. State 67, Georgia 60; Louisville 81. **Championship**–N.C. State 54, Houston 52.
NIT Championship (at Madison Square Garden): Fresno St. 69, DePaul 60. No Top 20 teams played in NIT.

1982

		Before Tourns	Head Coach	Final Record
1	**N. Carolina**	.27-2	Dean Smith	32-2
2	DePaul	.26-1	Ray Meyer	26-2
3	Virginia	.29-3	Terry Holland	30-4
4	Oregon St.	.23-4	Ralph Miller	25-5
5	Missouri	.26-3	Norm Stewart	27-4
6	Georgetown	.26-6	John Thompson	30-7
7	Minnesota	.22-5	Jim Dutcher	23-6
8	Idaho	.26-2	Don Monson	27-3
9	Memphis St.	.23-4	Dana Kirk	24-5
10	Tulsa	.24-5	Nolan Richardson	24-6
11	Fresno St.	.26-2	Boyd Grant	27-3
12	Arkansas	.23-5	Eddie Sutton	23-6
13	Alabama	.23-6	Wimp Sanderson	24-7
14	West Virginia	.26-3	Gale Catlett	27-4
15	Kentucky	.22-7	Joe B. Hall	22-8
16	Iowa	.20-7	Lute Olson	21-8
17	Ala-Birmingham	.23-5	Gene Bartow	25-6
18	Wake Forest	.20-8	Carl Tacy	21-9
19	UCLA	.21-6	Larry Farmer	21-6
20	Louisville	.20-9	Denny Crum	23-10

NCAA Final Four (at the Superdome, New Orleans): **Semifinals**–N. Carolina 68, Houston 63; Georgetown 50, Louisville 46. **Championship**–N. Carolina 63, Georgetown 62.
NIT Championship (at Madison Square Garden): Bradley 67, Purdue 58. No Top 20 teams played in NIT.

1984

		Before Tourns	Head Coach	Final Record
1	North Carolina	.27-2	Dean Smith	28-3
2	**Georgetown**	.29-3	John Thompson	34-3
3	Kentucky	.26-4	Joe B. Hall	29-5
4	DePaul	.26-2	Ray Meyer	27-3
5	Houston	.28-4	Guy Lewis	32-5
6	Illinois	.24-4	Lou Henson	26-5
7	Oklahoma	.29-4	Billy Tubbs	29-5
8	Arkansas	.25-6	Eddie Sutton	25-7
9	UTEP	.27-3	Don Haskins	27-4
10	Purdue	.22-6	Gene Keady	22-7
11	Maryland	.23-7	Lefty Driesell	24-8
12	Tulsa	.27-3	Nolan Richardson	27-4
13	UNLV	.27-5	Jerry Tarkanian	29-6
14	Duke	.24-9	Mike Krzyzewski	24-10
15	Washington	.22-6	Marv Harshman	24-7
16	Memphis St.	.24-6	Dana Kirk	26-7
17	Oregon St.	.22-6	Ralph Miller	22-7
18	Syracuse	.22-8	Jim Boeheim	23-9
19	Wake Forest	.21-8	Carl Tacy	23-9
20	Temple	.25-4	John Chaney	26-5

NCAA Final Four (at the Kingdome, Seattle): **Semifinals**–Houston 49, Virginia 47 (OT); Georgetown 53, Kentucky 40. **Championship**–Georgetown 84, Houston 75.
NIT Championship (at Madison Square Garden): Michigan 83, Notre Dame 63. No Top 20 teams played in NIT.

Highest-Rated College Games on TV

The dozen highest-rated college basketball games seen on U.S. television have been NCAA tournament championship games, led by the 1979 Michigan State-Indiana State final that featured Magic Johnson and Larry Bird.

Listed below are the finalists (winning team first), date of game, TV network, and TV rating and audience share (according to Nielson Media Research).

		Date	Net	Rtg/Sh			Date	Net	Rtg/Sh
1	Michigan St.-Indiana St.	.3/26/79	NBC	24.1/38	7	N. Carolina-Georgetown	.3/29/82	CBS	21.6/31
2	Villanova-Georgetown	.4/1/85	CBS	23.3/33	8	UCLA-Kentucky	.3/31/75	NBC	21.3/33
3	Duke-Michigan	.4/6/92	CBS	22.7/35	9	Michigan-Seton Hall	.4/3/89	CBS	21.3/33
4	N.C. State-Houston	.4/4/83	CBS	22.3/32	10	Louisville-Duke	.3/31/86	CBS	20.7/31
5	N. Carolina-Michigan	.4/5/93	CBS	22.2/34	11	Indiana-N. Carolina	.3/30/81	NBC	20.7/29
6	Arkansas-Duke	.4/4/94	CBS	21.6/33	12	UCLA-Memphis St.	.3/26/73	NBC	20.5/32

Associated Press Final Polls (Cont.)

1985

		Before Tourns	Head Coach	Final Record
1	Georgetown	.30-2	John Thompson	35-3
2	Michigan	.25-3	Bill Frieder	26-4
3	St. John's	.27-3	Lou Carnesecca	31-4
4	Oklahoma	.28-5	Billy Tubbs	31-6
5	Memphis St.	.27-3	Dana Kirk	31-4
6	Georgia Tech	.24-7	Bobby Cremins	27-8
7	North Carolina	.24-8	Dean Smith	27-9
8	Louisiana Tech	.27-2	Andy Russo	29-3
9	UNLV	.27-3	Jerry Tarkanian	28-4
10	Duke	.22-7	Mike Krzyzewski	23-8
11	VCU	.25-5	J.D. Barnett	26-6
12	Illinois	.24-8	Lou Henson	26-9
13	Kansas	.25-7	Larry Brown	26-8
14	Loyola-IL	.25-5	Gene Sullivan	27-6
15	Syracuse	.21-8	Jim Boeheim	22-9
16	N.C. State	.20-9	Jim Valvano	23-10
17	Texas Tech	.23-7	Gerald Myers	23-8
18	Tulsa	.23-7	Nolan Richardson	23-8
19	Georgia	.21-8	Hugh Durham	22-9
20	LSU	.19-9	Dale Brown	19-10

Note: Unranked **Villanova**, coached by Rollie Massimino, won the NCAAs. The Wildcats entered the tourney at 19-10 and had a final record of 25-10.

NCAA Final Four (at Rupp Arena, Lexington, KY): **Semifinals**– Georgetown 77, St. John's 59; Villanova 52, Memphis St. 45. **Championship**–Villanova 66, Georgetown 64.

NIT Championship (at Madison Square Garden): UCLA 65, Indiana 62. No Top 20 teams played in NIT.

1986

		Before Tourns	Head Coach	Final Record
1	Duke	.32-2	Mike Krzyzewski	37-3
2	Kansas	.31-3	Larry Brown	35-4
3	Kentucky	.29-3	Eddie Sutton	32-4
4	St. John's	.30-4	Lou Carnesecca	31-5
5	Michigan	.27-4	Bill Frieder	28-5
6	Georgia Tech	.25-6	Bobby Cremins	27-7
7	**Louisville**	.26-7	Denny Crum	32-7
8	North Carolina	.26-5	Dean Smith	28-6
9	Syracuse	.24-5	Jim Boeheim	26-6
10	Notre Dame	.23-5	Digger Phelps	23-6
11	UNLV	.31-4	Jerry Tarkanian	33-5
12	Memphis St.	.25-5	Dana Kirk	28-6
13	Georgetown	.23-7	John Thompson	24-8
14	Bradley	.31-2	Dick Versace	32-3
15	Oklahoma	.25-8	Billy Tubbs	26-9
16	Indiana	.21-7	Bob Knight	21-8
17	Navy	.27-4	Paul Evans	30-5
18	Michigan St.	.21-7	Jud Heathcote	23-8
19	Illinois	.21-9	Lou Henson	22-10
20	UTEP	.27-5	Don Haskins	27-6

NCAA Final Four (at Reunion Arena, Dallas): **Semifinals**–Duke 71, Kansas 67; Louisville 88, LSU 77. **Championship**–Louisville 72, Duke 69.

NIT Championship (at Madison Square Garden): Ohio St. 73, Wyoming 63. No Top 20 teams played in NIT.

1987

		Before Tourns	Head Coach	Final Record
1	UNLV	.33-1	Jerry Tarkanian	37-2
2	North Carolina	.29-3	Dean Smith	32-4
3	**Indiana**	.24-4	Bob Knight	30-4
4	Georgetown	.26-4	John Thompson	29-5
5	DePaul	.26-2	Joey Meyer	28-3
6	Iowa	.27-4	Tom Davis	30-5
7	Purdue	.24-4	Gene Keady	25-5
8	Temple	.31-3	John Chaney	32-4
9	Alabama	.26-4	Wimp Sanderson	28-5
10	Syracuse	.26-6	Jim Boeheim	31-7
11	Illinois	.23-7	Lou Henson	23-8
12	Pittsburgh	.24-7	Paul Evans	25-8
13	Clemson	.25-5	Cliff Ellis	25-6
14	Missouri	.24-9	Norm Stewart	24-10
15	UCLA	.24-6	Walt Hazzard	25-7
16	New Orleans	.25-3	Benny Dees	26-4
17	Duke	.22-8	Mike Krzyzewski	24-9
18	Notre Dame	.22-7	Digger Phelps	24-8
19	TCU	.23-6	Jim Killingsworth	24-7
20	Kansas	.23-10	Larry Brown	25-11

NCAA Final Four (at the Superdome, New Orleans): **Semifinals**–Syracuse 77, Providence 63; Indiana 97, UNLV 93. **Championship**–Indiana 74, Syracuse 73.

NIT Championship (at Madison Square Garden): Southern Miss. 84, La Salle 80. No Top 20 teams played in NIT.

1988

		Before Tourns	Head Coach	Final Record
1	Temple	.29-1	John Chaney	32-2
2	Arizona	.31-2	Lute Olson	35-3
3	Purdue	.27-3	Gene Keady	29-4
4	Oklahoma	.30-3	Billy Tubbs	35-4
5	Duke	.24-6	Mike Krzyzewski	28-7
6	Kentucky	.25-5	Eddie Sutton	27-6
7	North Carolina	.24-6	Dean Smith	27-7
8	Pittsburgh	.23-6	Paul Evans	24-7
9	Syracuse	.25-8	Jim Boeheim	26-9
10	Michigan	.24-7	Bill Frieder	26-8
11	Bradley	.26-4	Stan Albeck	26-5
12	UNLV	.27-5	Jerry Tarkanian	28-6
13	Wyoming	.26-5	Benny Dees	26-6
14	N.C. State	.24-7	Jim Valvano	24-8
15	Loyola-CA	.27-3	Paul Westhead	28-4
16	Illinois	.22-9	Lou Henson	23-10
17	Iowa	.22-9	Tom Davis	24-10
18	Xavier-OH	.26-3	Pete Gillen	26-4
19	BYU	.25-5	Ladell Andersen	26-6
20	Kansas St.	.22-8	Lon Kruger	25-9

Note: Unranked **Kansas**, coached by Larry Brown, won the NCAAs. The Jayhawks entered the tourney at 21-11 and had a final record of 27-11.

NCAA Final Four (at Kemper Arena, Kansas City): **Semifinals**–Kansas 66, Duke 59; Oklahoma 86, Arizona 78. **Championship**–Kansas 83, Oklahoma 79.

NIT Championship (at Madison Square Garden): Connecticut 72, Ohio St. 67. No Top 20 teams played in NIT.

1989

		Before Tourns	Head Coach	Final Record
1	Arizona	27-3	Lute Olson	29-4
2	Georgetown	26-4	John Thompson	29-5
3	Illinois	27-4	Lou Henson	31-5
4	Oklahoma	28-5	Billy Tubbs	30-6
5	North Carolina	27-7	Dean Smith	29-8
6	Missouri	27-7	Norm Stewart & Rich Daly*	29-8
7	Syracuse	27-7	Jim Boeheim	30-8
8	Indiana	25-7	Bob Knight	27-8
9	Duke	24-7	Mike Krzyzewski	28-8
10	**Michigan**	24-7	Bill Frieder (24-7) & Steve Fisher (6-0)	30-7
11	Seton Hall	26-6	P.J. Carlesimo	31-7
12	Louisville	22-8	Denny Crum	24-9
13	Stanford	26-6	Mike Montgomery	26-7
14	Iowa	22-9	Tom Davis	23-10
15	UNLV	26-7	Jerry Tarkanian	29-8
16	Florida St.	22-7	Pat Kennedy	22-8
17	West Virginia	25-4	Gale Catlett	26-5
18	Ball State	28-2	Rick Majerus	29-3
19	N.C. State	20-8	Jim Valvano	22-9
20	Alabama	23-7	Wimp Sanderson	23-8

NCAA Final Four (at The Kingdome, Seattle): **Semifinals**–Seton Hall 95, Duke 78; Michigan 83, Illinois 81. **Championship**–Michigan 80, Seton Hall 79 (OT).
NIT Championship (at Madison Square Garden): St. John's 73, St. Louis 65. No Top 20 teams played in NIT.
*Norm Stewart's assistant Rich Daly temporarily took over for his ailing boss (Daly coached the final 14 games of the season) but returned to his role as an assistant when Stewart recovered before the start of the following season.

1990

		Before Tourns	Head Coach	Final Record
1	Oklahoma	26-4	Billy Tubbs	27-5
2	**UNLV**	29-5	Jerry Tarkanian	35-5
3	Connecticut	28-5	Jim Calhoun	31-6
4	Michigan St.	26-5	Jud Heathcote	28-6
5	Kansas	29-4	Roy Williams	30-5
6	Syracuse	24-6	Jim Boeheim	26-7
7	Arkansas	26-4	Nolan Richardson	30-5
8	Georgetown	23-6	John Thompson	24-7
9	Georgia Tech	24-6	Bobby Cremins	28-7
10	Purdue	21-7	Gene Keady	22-8
11	Missouri	26-5	Norm Stewart	26-6
12	La Salle	29-1	Speedy Morris	30-2
13	Michigan	22-7	Steve Fisher	23-8
14	Arizona	24-6	Lute Olson	25-7
15	Duke	24-8	Mike Krzyzewski	29-9
16	Louisville	26-7	Denny Crum	27-8
17	Clemson	24-8	Cliff Ellis	26-9
18	Illinois	21-7	Lou Henson	21-8
19	LSU	22-8	Dale Brown	23-9
20	Minnesota	20-8	Clem Haskins	23-9
21	Loyola-CA	23-5	Paul Westhead	26-6
22	Oregon St.	22-6	Jim Anderson	22-7
23	Alabama	24-8	Wimp Sanderson	26-9
24	New Mexico St.	26-4	Neil McCarthy	26-5
25	Xavier-OH	26-4	Pete Gillen	28-5

NCAA Final Four (at McNichols Sports Arena, Denver): **Semifinals**–Duke 97, Arkansas 83; UNLV 90, Georgia Tech 81. **Championship**–UNLV 103, Duke 73.
NIT Championship (at Madison Square Garden): Vanderbilt 74, St.Louis 72. No Top 25 teams played in NIT.

1991

		Before Tourns	Head Coach	Final Record
1	UNLV	30-0	Jerry Tarkanian	34-1
2	Arkansas	31-3	Nolan Richardson	34-4
3	Indiana	27-4	Bob Knight	29-5
4	North Carolina	25-5	Dean Smith	29-6
5	Ohio St.	25-3	Randy Ayers	27-4
6	**Duke**	26-7	Mike Krzyzewski	32-7
7	Syracuse	26-5	Jim Boeheim	26-6
8	Arizona	26-6	Lute Olson	28-7
9	Kentucky	22-6	Rick Pitino	same*
10	Utah	28-3	Rick Majerus	30-4
11	Nebraska	26-7	Danny Nee	26-8
12	Kansas	22-7	Roy Williams	27-8
13	Seton Hall	22-8	P.J. Carlesimo	25-9
14	Oklahoma St.	22-7	Eddie Sutton	24-8
15	New Mexico St.	23-5	Neil McCarthy	23-6
16	UCLA	23-8	Jim Harrick	23-9
17	E.Tennessee St.	24-4	Alan LaForce	28-5
18	Princeton	24-2	Pete Carril	24-3
19	Alabama	21-9	Wimp Sanderson	23-10
20	St. John's	20-8	Lou Carnesecca	23-9
21	Mississippi St.	20-8	Richard Williams	20-9
22	LSU	20-9	Dale Brown	20-10
23	Texas	22-8	Tom Penders	23-9
24	DePaul	20-8	Joey Meyer	20-9
25	Southern Miss.	21-7	M.K. Turk	21-8

*On probation
NCAA Final Four (at the Hoosier Dome, Indianapolis): **Semifinals**–Kansas 79, North Carolina 73; Duke 79, UNLV 77. **Championship**–Duke 72, Kansas 65.
NIT Championship (at Madison Square Garden): Stanford 78, Oklahoma 72. No Top 25 teams played in NIT.

1992

		Before Tourns	Head Coach	Final Record
1	**Duke**	28-2	Mike Krzyzewski	34-2
2	Kansas	26-4	Roy Williams	27-5
3	Ohio St.	23-5	Randy Ayers	26-6
4	UCLA	25-4	Jim Harrick	28-5
5	Indiana	23-6	Bob Knight	27-7
6	Kentucky	26-6	Rick Pitino	29-7
7	UNLV	26-2	Jerry Tarkanian	same*
8	USC	23-5	George Raveling	24-6
9	Arkansas	25-7	Nolan Richardson	26-8
10	Arizona	24-6	Lute Olson	24-7
11	Oklahoma St.	26-7	Eddie Sutton	28-8
12	Cincinnati	25-4	Bob Huggins	29-5
13	Alabama	25-8	Wimp Sanderson	26-9
14	Michigan St.	21-7	Jud Heathcote	22-8
15	Michigan	20-8	Steve Fisher	25-9
16	Missouri	20-8	Norm Stewart	21-9
17	Massachusetts	28-4	John Calipari	30-5
18	North Carolina	21-9	Dean Smith	23-10
19	Seton Hall	21-8	P.J. Carlesimo	23-9
20	Florida St.	20-9	Pat Kennedy	22-10
21	Syracuse	21-9	Jim Boeheim	22-10
22	Georgetown	21-9	John Thompson	22-10
23	Oklahoma	21-8	Billy Tubbs	21-9
24	DePaul	20-8	Joey Meyer	20-9
25	LSU	20-9	Dale Brown	21-10

*On probation
NCAA Final Four (at the Metrodome, Minneapolis): **Semifinals**–Michigan 76, Cincinnati 72; Duke 81, Indiana 78. **Championship**–Duke 71, Michigan 51.
NIT Championship (at Madison Square Garden): Virginia 81, Notre Dame 76 (OT). No Top 25 teams played in NIT.

Associated Press Final Polls (Cont.)

1993

		Before Tourns	Head Coach	Final Record
1	Indiana	28-3	Bob Knight	31-4
2	Kentucky	26-3	Rick Pitino	30-4
3	Michigan	26-4	Steve Fisher	31-5
4	**N. Carolina**	28-4	Dean Smith	34-4
5	Arizona	24-3	Lute Olson	24-4
6	Seton Hall	27-6	P.J. Carlesimo	28-7
7	Cincinnati	24-4	Bob Huggins	27-5
8	Vanderbilt	26-5	Eddie Fogler	28-6
9	Kansas	25-6	Roy Williams	29-7
10	Duke	23-7	Mike Krzyzewski	24-8
11	Florida St.	22-9	Pat Kennedy	25-10
12	Arkansas	20-8	Nolan Richardson	22-9
13	Iowa	22-8	Tom Davis	23-9
14	Massachusetts	23-6	John Calipari	24-7
15	Louisville	20-8	Denny Crum	22-9
16	Wake Forest	19-8	Dave Odom	21-9
17	New Orleans	26-3	Tim Floyd	26-4
18	Georgia Tech	19-10	Bobby Cremins	19-11
19	Utah	23-6	Rick Majerus	24-7
20	Western Ky.	24-5	Ralph Willard	26-6
21	New Mexico	24-6	Dave Bliss	24-7
22	Purdue	18-9	Gene Keady	18-10
23	Oklahoma St.	19-8	Eddie Sutton	20-9
24	New Mexico St.	25-7	Neil McCarthy	26-8
25	UNLV	21-7	Rollie Massimino	21-8

NCAA Final Four (at the Superdome, New Orleans): **Semifinals**–North Carolina 78, Kansas 68; Michigan 81, Kentucky 78 (OT). **Championship**–North Carolina 77, Michigan 71.
NIT Championship (at Madison Square Garden): Minnesota 62, Georgetown 61. No. 25 UNLV was the only Top 25 team that played in the NIT.

1994

		Before Tourns	Head Coach	Final Record
1	North Carolina	27-6	Dean Smith	28-7
2	**Arkansas**	25-3	Nolan Richardson	31-3
3	Purdue	26-4	Gene Keady	29-5
4	Connecticut	27-4	Jim Calhoun	29-5
5	Missouri	25-3	Norm Stewart	28-4
6	Duke	23-5	Mike Krzyzewski	28-6
7	Kentucky	26-6	Rick Pitino	27-7
8	Massachusetts	27-6	John Calipari	28-7
9	Arizona	25-5	Lute Olson	29-6
10	Louisville	26-5	Denny Crum	28-6
11	Michigan	21-7	Steve Fisher	24-8
12	Temple	22-7	John Chaney	23-8
13	Kansas	25-7	Roy Williams	27-8
14	Florida	25-7	Lon Kruger	29-8
15	Syracuse	21-6	Jim Boeheim	23-7
16	California	22-7	Todd Bozeman	22-8
17	UCLA	21-6	Jim Harrick	21-7
18	Indiana	19-8	Bob Knight	21-9
19	Oklahoma St.	23-9	Eddie Sutton	24-10
20	Texas	25-7	Tom Penders	26-8
21	Marquette	22-8	Kevin O'Neill	24-9
22	Nebraska	20-9	Danny Nee	20-10
23	Minnesota	20-11	Clem Haskins	21-12
24	Saint Louis	23-5	Charlie Spoonhour	23-6
25	Cincinnati	22-9	Bob Huggins	22-10

NCAA Final Four (at the Charlotte Coliseum): **Semifinals**– Arkansas 91, Arizona 82; Duke 70, Florida 65. **Championship**– Arkansas 76, Duke 72.
NIT Championship (at Madison Square Garden): Villanova 80, Vanderbilt 73. No top 25 teams played in NIT.

1995

		Before Tourns	Head Coach	Final Record
1	UCLA	25-2	Jim Harrick	31-2
2	Kentucky	25-4	Rick Pitino	28-5
3	Wake Forest	24-5	Dave Odom	26-6
4	North Carolina	24-5	Dean Smith	28-6
5	Kansas	23-5	Roy Williams	25-6
6	Arkansas	27-6	Nolan Richardson	32-7
7	Massachusetts	26-4	John Calipari	26-5
8	Connecticut	25-4	Jim Calhoun	28-5
9	Villanova	25-7	Steve Lappas	25-8
10	Maryland	24-7	Gary Williams	26-8
11	Michigan St.	22-5	Jud Heathcote	22-6
12	Purdue	24-6	Gene Keady	25-7
13	Virginia	22-8	Jeff Jones	25-9
14	Oklahoma St.	23-9	Eddie Sutton	27-10
15	Arizona	23-7	Lute Olson	23-8
16	Arizona St.	22-8	Bill Frieder	24-9
17	Oklahoma	23-8	Kelvin Sampson	23-9
18	Mississippi St.	20-7	Richard Williams	22-8
19	Utah	27-5	Rick Majerus	28-6
20	Alabama	22-9	David Hobbs	23-10
21	Western Ky.	26-3	Matt Kilcullen	27-4
22	Georgetown	19-9	John Thompson	21-10
23	Missouri	19-8	Norm Stewart	20-9
24	Iowa St.	22-10	Tim Floyd	23-11
25	Syracuse	19-9	Jim Boeheim	20-10

NCAA Final Four (at the Kingdome, Seattle): **Semifinals**– UCLA 74, Oklahoma St. 61; Arkansas 75, North Carolina 68. **Championship**– UCLA 89, Arkansas 78.
NIT Championship (at Madison Square Garden):Virginia Tech 65, Marquette 64 (OT). No top 25 teams played in NIT.

1996

		Before Tourns	Head Coach	Final Record
1	Massachusetts	31-1	John Calipari	35-2
2	**Kentucky**	28-2	Rick Pitino	34-2
3	Connecticut	30-2	Jim Calhoun	32-3
4	Georgetown	26-7	John Thompson	29-8
5	Kansas	26-4	Roy Williams	29-5
6	Purdue	25-5	Gene Keady	26-6
7	Cincinnati	25-4	Bob Huggins	28-5
8	Texas Tech	28-1	James Dickey	30-2
9	Wake Forest	23-5	Dave Odom	26-6
10	Villanova	25-6	Steve Lappas	26-7
11	Arizona	24-6	Lute Olson	26-7
12	Utah	25-6	Rick Majerus	27-7
13	Georgia Tech	22-11	Bobby Cremins	24-12
14	UCLA	23-7	Jim Harrick	23-8
15	Syracuse	24-8	Jim Boeheim	29-9
16	Memphis	22-7	Larry Finch	22-8
17	Iowa St.	23-8	Tim Floyd	24-9
18	Penn St.	21-6	Jerry Dunn	21-7
19	Mississippi St.	22-7	Richard Williams	26-8
20	Marquette	22-7	Mike Deane	23-8
21	Iowa	22-8	Tom Davis	23-9
22	Virginia Tech	22-5	Bill Foster	23-6
23	New Mexico	27-4	Dave Bliss	28-5
24	Louisville	20-11	Denny Crum	22-12
25	North Carolina	20-10	Dean Smith	21-11

NCAA Final Four (at the Meadowlands, E. Rutherford, N.J.): **Semifinals**– Kentucky 81, Massachusetts 74; Syracuse 77, Mississippi St. 69. **Championship**– Kentucky 76, Syracuse 67.
NIT Championship (at Madison Square Garden): Nebraska 60, St. Joseph's 56. No top 25 teams played in NIT.

1997

		Before Tourns	Head Coach	Final Record
1	Kansas	.32-1	Roy Williams	34-2
2	Utah	.26-3	Rick Majerus	29-4
3	Minnesota	.27-3	Clem Haskins	31-4
4	North Carolina	.24-6	Dean Smith	28-7
5	Kentucky	.30-4	Rick Pitino	35-5
6	South Carolina	.24-7	Eddie Fogler	24-8
7	UCLA	.21-7	Steve Lavin	24-8
8	Duke	.23-8	Mike Krzyzewski	24-9
9	Wake Forest	.23-6	Dave Odom	24-7
10	Cincinnati	.25-7	Bob Huggins	26-8
11	New Mexico	.24-7	Dave Bliss	25-8
12	St. Joseph's	.24-6	Phil Martelli	26-7
13	Xavier	.22-5	Skip Prosser	23-6
14	Clemson	.21-9	Rick Barnes	23-10
15	**Arizona**	.19-9	Lute Olson	25-9
16	Charleston	.28-2	John Kresse	29-3
17	Georgia	.24-8	Tubby Smith	24-9
18	Iowa St.	.20-8	Tim Floyd	22-9
19	Illinois	.21-9	Lon Kruger	22-10
20	Villanova	.23-9	Steve Lappas	24-10
21	Stanford	.20-7	Mike Montgomery	22-8
22	Maryland	.21-10	Gary Williams	21-11
23	Boston College	.21-8	Jim O'Brien	22-9
24	Colorado	.21-9	Ricardo Patton	22-10
25	Louisville	.23-8	Denny Crum	26-9

NCAA Final Four (at the RCA Dome, Indianapolis): **Semifinals–** Kentucky 78, Minnesota 69; Arizona 66, North Carolina 58. **Championship–** Arizona 84, Kentucky 79 (OT).
NIT Championship (at Madison Square Garden): Michigan 82, Florida St. 72. No top 25 teams played in NIT.

1998

		Before Tourns	Head Coach	Final Record
1	North Carolina	.30-3	Bill Guthridge	34-4
2	Kansas	.34-3	Roy Williams	35-4
3	Duke	.29-3	Mike Krzyzewski	32-4
4	Arizona	.27-4	Lute Olson	30-5
5	**Kentucky**	.29-4	Tubby Smith	35-4
6	Connecticut	.29-4	Jim Calhoun	32-5
7	Utah	.25-3	Rick Majerus	30-4
8	Princeton	.26-1	Bill Carmody	27-2
9	Cincinnati	.26-5	Bob Huggins	27-6
10	Stanford	.26-4	Mike Montgomery	30-5
11	Purdue	.26-7	Gene Keady	28-8
12	Michigan	.24-8	Brian Ellerbe	25-9
13	Mississippi	.22-6	Rob Evans	22-7
14	South Carolina	.23-7	Eddie Fogler	23-8
15	TCU	.27-5	Billy Tubbs	27-6
16	Michigan St.	.20-7	Tom Izzo	22-8
17	Arkansas	.23-8	Nolan Richardson	24-9
18	New Mexico	.23-7	Dave Bliss	24-8
19	UCLA	.22-8	Steve Lavin	24-9
20	Maryland	.19-10	Gary Williams	21-11
21	Syracuse	.24-8	Jim Boeheim	26-9
22	Illinois	.22-9	Lon Kruger	23-10
23	Xavier	.22-7	Skip Prosser	22-8
24	Temple	.21-8	John Chaney	21-9
25	Murray St.	.29-3	Mark Gottfried	29-4

NCAA Final Four (at the Alamodome, San Antonio): **Semifinals–** Kentucky 86, Stanford 85 (OT); Utah 65, North Carolina 59. **Championship–** Kentucky 78, Utah 69.
NIT Championship (at Madison Square Garden): Minnesota 79, Penn St. 72. No top 25 teams played in NIT.

AP Post-Tournament Final Polls

The final AP Top 20 poll has been released after the NCAA tournament and NIT four times– in 1953 and '54 and again in 1974 and '75. Those four polls are listed below; teams that were not included in the last regular season polls are in CAPITAL italic letters.

	1953	Final Record		1954	Final Record		1974	Final Record		1975	Final Record
1	Indiana	23-3	1	Kentucky	25-0	1	N.C. State	30-1	1	UCLA	28-3
2	Seton Hall	31-2	2	La Salle	26-4	2	UCLA	26-4	2	Kentucky	26-5
3	Kansas	19-6	3	Holy Cross	26-2	3	Marquette	26-5	3	Indiana	31-1
4	Washington	30-3	4	Indiana	20-4	4	Maryland	23-5	4	Louisville	28-3
5	LSU	24-3	5	Duquesne	26-3	5	Notre Dame	26-3	5	Maryland	24-5
6	La Salle	25-3	6	Notre Dame	22-3	6	Michigan	22-5	6	Syracuse	23-9
7	*ST. JOHN'S*	17-6	7	*BRADLEY*	19-13	7	Kansas	23-7	7	N.C. State	22-6
8	Okla. A&M	23-7	8	Western Ky.	29-3	8	Providence	28-4	8	Arizona St.	25-4
9	Duquesne	21-8	9	*PENN ST.*	18-6	9	Indiana	23-5	9	North Carolina	23-8
10	Notre Dame	19-5	10	Okla. A&M	24-5	10	Long Beach St.	24-2	10	Alabama	22-5
11	Illinois	18-4	11	USC	19-14	11	*PURDUE*	22-8	11	Marquette	23-4
12	Kansas St.	17-4	12	*GEO. WASH.*	23-3	12	North Carolina	22-6	12	*PRINCETON*	22-8
13	Holy Cross	20-6	13	Iowa	17-5	13	Vanderbilt	23-5	13	Cincinnati	23-6
14	Seattle	29-4	14	LSU	21-5	14	Alabama	22-4	14	Notre Dame	19-10
15	*WAKE FOREST*	22-7	15	Duke	22-6	15	*UTAH*	22-8	15	Kansas St.	20-9
16	*SANTA CLARA*	20-7	16	*NIAGARA*	24-6	16	Pittsburgh	25-4	16	Drake	19-10
17	Western Ky.	25-6	17	Seattle	26-2	17	USC	24-5	17	UNLV	24-5
18	N.C. State	26-6	18	Kansas	16-5	18	*ORAL ROBERTS*	23-6	18	Oregon St.	19-12
19	*DEPAUL*	19-9	19	Illinois	17-5	19	South Carolina	22-5	19	*MICHIGAN*	19-8
20	*SW MISSOURI*	24-4	20	*MARYLAND*	23-7	20	Dayton	20-9	20	Penn	23-5

Pre-Tournament Records

1953– St. John's (Al DeStefano, 14-5); Wake Forest (Murray Greason, 21-6); Santa Clara (Bob Feerick, 18-6); DePaul (Ray Meyer, 18-7); SW Missouri St. (Bob Vanatta, 19-4 before NAIA tourney). **1954–** Bradley (Forddy Anderson, 15-12); Penn St. (Elmer Gross, 14-5); George Washington (Bill Reinhart, 23-2); Niagara (Taps Gallagher, 22-5); Maryland (Bud Millikan, 23-7). **1974–** Purdue (Fred Schaus, 18-8); Utah (Bill Foster, 19-7); Oral Roberts (Ken Trickey, 21-5). **1975–** Princeton (Pete Carril, 18-8); Michigan (Johnny Orr, 19-7).

Associated Press Final Polls (Cont.)

1999

			Before Tourns	Head Coach	Final Record
1	Duke	. . . .	32-1	Mike Krzyzewski	37-2
2	Michigan St.	. . . .	29-4	Tom Izzo	33-5
3	**Connecticut**	. . .	28-2	Jim Calhoun	34-2
4	Auburn	. . . . . .	27-3	Cliff Ellis	29-4
5	Maryland	. . . . .	26-5	Gary Williams	28-6
6	Utah	. . . .	27-4	Rick Majerus	28-5
7	Stanford	. . . . .	25-6	Mike Montgomery	26-7
8	Kentucky	. . . .	25-8	Tubby Smith	28-9
9	St. John's	. . . .	25-8	Mike Jarvis	28-9
10	Miami-FL	. . . . .	22-6	Leonard Hamilton	23-7
11	Cincinnati	. . . .	26-5	Bob Huggins	27-6
12	Arizona	. . . . .	22-6	Lute Olson	22-7
13	North Carolina	. .	24-9	Bill Guthridge	24-10
14	Ohio St.	. . . . .	23-8	Jim O'Brien	27-9
15	UCLA	. . . .	22-8	Steve Lavin	22-9
16	College of Charleston	. .	28-2	John Kresse	28-3
17	Arkansas	. . . .	22-10	Nolan Richardson	23-11
18	Wisconsin	. . . .	22-9	Dick Bennett	22-10
19	Indiana	. . . . .	22-10	Bobby Knight	23-11
20	Tennessee	. . . .	20-8	Jerry Green	21-9
21	Iowa	. . . .	18-9	Tom Davis	20-10
22	Kansas	. . . . .	22-9	Roy Williams	23-10
23	Florida	. . . . .	20-8	Billy Donovan	22-9
24	NC-Charlotte	. .	22-10	Bob Lutz	23-11
25	New Mexico	. .	24-8	Dave Bliss	25-9

NCAA Final Four (at the Tropicana Field, St. Petersburg): **Semifinals**– Duke 68, Michigan St. 62; Connecticut 64, Ohio St. 58. **Championship**– Connecticut 77, Duke 74.

NIT Championship (at Madison Square Garden): California 61, Clemson 60. No top 25 teams played in NIT.

2000

			Before Tourns	Head Coach	Final Record
1	Duke	. . . .	27-4	Mike Krzyzewski	29-5
2	**Michigan St.**	. .	26-7	Tom Izzo	32-7
3	Stanford	. . . . .	26-3	Mike Montgomery	27-4
4	Arizona	. . . . .	26-6	Lute Olson	27-7
5	Temple	. . . . .	26-5	John Chaney	27-6
6	Iowa St.	. . . . .	29-4	Larry Eustachy	32-5
7	Cincinnati	. . . .	28-3	Bob Huggins	29-4
8	Ohio St.	. . . . .	22-6	Jim O'Brien	23-7
9	St. John's	. . . .	24-7	Mike Jarvis	25-8
10	LSU	. . . .	26-5	John Brady	28-6
11	Tennessee	. . . .	24-6	Jerry Green	26-7
12	Oklahoma	. . . .	26-6	Kelvin Sampson	27-7
13	Florida	. . . . .	24-7	Billy Donovan	29-8
14	Oklahoma St.	. .	24-6	Eddie Sutton	27-7
15	Texas	. . . . . .	23-8	Rick Barnes	24-9
16	Syracuse	. . . .	26-6	Jim Boeheim	26-6
17	Maryland	. . . .	24-9	Gary Williams	25-10
18	Tulsa	. . . . . .	29-4	Bill Self	32-5
19	Kentucky	. . . .	22-9	Tubby Smith	23-10
20	Connecticut	. . .	24-9	Jim Calhoun	25-10
21	Illinois	. . . . .	21-9	Lon Kruger	22-10
22	Indiana	. . . . .	20-8	Bobby Knight	20-9
23	Miami-FL	. . . .	21-10	Leonard Hamilton	23-11
24	Auburn	. . . . .	23-9	Cliff Ellis	24-10
25	Purdue	. . . . .	21-9	Gene Keady	24-10

NCAA Final Four (at the RCA Dome, Indianapolis): **Semifinals**– Michigan St. 53, Wisconsin 41; Florida 71, North Carolina 59. **Championship**– Michigan St. 89, Florida 76.

NIT Championship (at Madison Square Garden): Wake Forest 71, Notre Dame 61. No top 25 teams played in NIT.

2001

			Before Tourns	Head Coach	Final Record
1	**Duke**	. . . .	29-4	Mike Krzyzewski	35-4
2	Stanford	. . . . .	28-2	Mike Montgomery	31-3
3	Michigan St.	. . .	24-4	Tom Izzo	28-5
4	Illinois	. . . . .	24-7	Bill Self	27-8
5	Arizona	. . . . .	23-7	Lute Olson	28-8
6	North Carolina	.	25-6	Matt Doherty	26-7
7	Boston College	. .	26-4	Al Skinner	27-5
8	Florida	. . . . .	23-6	Billy Donovan	24-7
9	Kentucky	. . . .	22-9	Tubby Smith	24-10
10	Iowa St.	. . . . .	25-5	Larry Eustachy	25-6
11	Maryland	. . .	21-10	Gary Williams	25-11
12	Kansas	. . . . .	24-6	Roy Williams	26-7
13	Oklahoma	. . . .	26-6	Kelvin Sampson	26-7
14	Mississippi	. . .	25-7	Rod Barnes	27-8
15	UCLA	. . . . . .	21-8	Steve Lavin	23-9
16	Virginia	. . . . .	20-8	Pete Gillen	20-9
17	Syracuse	. . . .	24-8	Jim Boeheim	25-9
18	Texas	. . . . . .	25-8	Rick Barnes	25-9
19	Notre Dame	. . .	19-9	Mike Brey	20-10
20	Indiana	. . .	21-12	Mike Davis	21-13
21	Georgetown	. . .	23-7	Craig Esherick	25-8
22	St. Joseph's	. . .	25-6	Phil Martelli	26-7
23	Wake Forest	. .	19-10	Dave Odom	19-11
24	Iowa	. . . . .	22-11	Steve Alford	23-12
25	Wisconsin		18-10	Dick Bennett (2-1) & Brad Soderberg (16-10)	18-11

NCAA Final Four (at the HHH Metrodome, Minneapolis): **Semifinals**–Duke 95, Maryland 84; Arizona 80, Michigan St. 61. **Championship**–Duke 82, Arizona 72.

NIT Championship (at Madison Square Garden): Tulsa 79, Alabama 60. No top 25 teams played in NIT.

2002

			Before Tourns	Head Coach	Final Record
1	Duke	. . . .	29-3	Mike Krzyzewski	32-4
2	Kansas	. . . . .	29-3	Roy Williams	33-4
3	Oklahoma	. . . .	27-4	Kelvin Sampson	31-5
4	**Maryland**	. . . .	26-4	Gary Williams	32-4
5	Cincinnati	. . . .	30-3	Bob Huggins	31-4
6	Gonzaga	. . . . .	29-3	Mark Few	29-4
7	Arizona	. . . . .	22-9	Lute Olson	24-10
8	Alabama	. . . . .	26-7	Mark Gottfried	27-8
9	Pittsburgh	. . . .	27-5	Ben Howland	29-6
10	Connecticut	. . .	24-6	Jim Calhoun	27-7
11	Oregon	. . . . .	23-8	Ernie Kent	26-9
12	Marquette	. . . .	25-7	Tom Crean	25-8
13	Illinois	. . . . .	24-8	Bill Self	26-9
14	Ohio St.	. . . . .	23-7	Jim O'Brien	24-8
15	Florida	. . . . .	22-8	Billy Donovan	22-9
16	Kentucky	. . . .	20-9	Tubby Smith	22-10
17	Mississippi St.	. .	26-7	Rick Stansbury	27-8
18	USC	. . . .	22-9	Henry Bibby	22-10
19	Western Ky.	. . .	28-3	Dennis Felton	28-4
20	Oklahoma St.	. .	23-8	Eddie Sutton	23-9
21	Miami-FL	. . . .	24-7	Perry Clark	24-8
22	Xavier	. . . . .	25-5	Thad Matta	26-6
23	Georgia	. . . . .	21-9	Jim Harrick	22-10
24	Stanford	. . . . .	19-9	Mike Montgomery	20-10
25	Hawaii	. . . . .	27-5	Riley Wallace	27-6

NCAA Final Four (at the Georgia Dome, Atlanta): **Semifinals**–Maryland 97, Kansas 88; Indiana 73, Oklahoma 64. **Championship**–Maryland 64, Indiana 52.

NIT Championship (at Madison Square Garden): Memphis 72, South Carolina 62. No top 25 teams played in NIT.

2003

		Before Tourns	Head Coach	Final Record
1	Kentucky	29-3	Tubby Smith	32-4
2	Arizona	25-3	Lute Olson	28-4
3	Oklahoma	24-6	Kelvin Sampson	27-7
4	Pittsburgh	26-4	Ben Howland	28-5
5	Texas	22-6	Rick Barnes	26-7
6	Kansas	25-7	Roy Williams	30-8
7	Duke	24-6	Mike Krzyzewski	26-7
8	Wake Forest	24-5	Skip Prosser	25-6
9	Marquette	23-5	Tom Crean	27-6
10	Florida	24-7	Billy Donovan	25-8
11	Illinois	24-6	Bill Self	25-7
12	Xavier	25-5	Thad Matta	26-6
13	**Syracuse**	24-5	Jim Boeheim	30-5
14	Louisville	24-6	Rick Pitino	25-7
15	Creighton	29-4	Dana Altman	29-5
16	Dayton	25-5	Oliver Purnell	25-6
17	Maryland	19-9	Gary Williams	21-10
18	Stanford	23-8	Mike Montgomery	23-9
19	Memphis	23-6	John Calipari	23-7
20	Mississippi St.	21-9	Rick Stansbury	21-10
21	Wisconsin	22-7	Bo Ryan	24-8
22	Notre Dame	22-9	Mike Brey	24-10
23	Connecticut	21-9	Jim Calhoun	23-10
24	Missouri	21-10	Quin Snyder	22-11
25	Georgia	19-8	Jim Harrick	same*

*Georgia chose not to participate in any postseason tournaments due to an investigation into academic fraud.
NCAA Final Four (at the Superdome, New Orleans):
Semifinals—Syracuse 95, Texas 84; Kansas 94, Marquette 61. **Championship**—Syracuse 81, Kansas 78.
NIT Championship (at Madison Square Garden): St. John's 70, Georgetown 67. No top 25 teams played in NIT.

Division I Winning Streaks
Full Season
(including tournaments)

No		Seasons	Broken by	Score
88	UCLA	1971-74	Notre Dame	71-70
60	San Francisco	1955-57	Illinois	62-33
47	UCLA	1966-68	Houston	71-69
45	UNLV	1990-91	Duke	79-77
44	Texas	1913-17	Rice	24-18
43	Seton Hall	1939-41	LIU-Bklyn	49-26
43	LIU-Brooklyn	1935-37	Stanford	45-31
41	UCLA	1968-69	USC	46-44
39	Marquette	1970-71	Ohio St.	60-59
37	Cincinnati	1962-63	Wichita St.	65-64
37	North Carolina	1957-58	West Virginia	75-64
36	N.C. State	1974-75	Wake Forest	83-78
35	Arkansas	1927-29	Texas	26-25

Home Court

No		Seasons	Broken By	Score
129	Kentucky	1943-55	Georgia Tech	59-58
99	St. Bonaventure	1948-61	Detroit	77-70
98	UCLA	1970-76	Oregon	65-45
86	Cincinnati	1957-64	Kansas	51-47
81	Arizona	1945-51	Kansas St.	76-57
81	Marquette	1967-73	Notre Dame	71-69
80	Lamar	1978-84	Louisiana Tech	68-65
75	Long Beach St.	1968-74	San Francisco	94-84
72	UNLV	1974-78	New Mexico	102-98
71	Arizona	1987-92	UCLA	89-87

Annual NCAA Division I Leaders
Scoring

The NCAA did not begin keeping individual scoring records until the 1947-48 season. All averages include postseason games where applicable.

Multiple winners: Pete Maravich and Oscar Robertson (3); Darrell Floyd, Charles Jones, Harry Kelly, Frank Selvy and Freeman Williams (2).

Year		Gm	Pts	Avg
1948	Murray Wier, Iowa	19	399	21.0
1949	Tony Lavelli, Yale	30	671	22.4
1950	Paul Arizin, Villanova	29	735	25.3
1951	Bill Mlkvy, Temple	25	731	29.2
1952	Clyde Lovellette, Kansas	28	795	28.4
1953	Frank Selvy, Furman	25	738	29.5
1954	Frank Selvy, Furman	29	1209	41.7
1955	Darrell Floyd, Furman	25	897	35.9
1956	Darrell Floyd, Furman	28	946	33.8
1957	Grady Wallace, S. Carolina	29	906	31.2
1958	Oscar Robertson, Cincinnati	28	984	35.1
1959	Oscar Robertson, Cincinnati	30	978	32.6
1960	Oscar Robertson, Cincinnati	30	1011	33.7
1961	Frank Burgess, Gonzaga	26	842	32.4
1962	Billy McGill, Utah	26	1009	38.8
1963	Nick Werkman, Seton Hall	22	650	29.5
1964	Howie Komives, Bowling Green	23	844	36.7
1965	Rick Barry, Miami-FL	26	973	37.4
1966	Dave Schellhase, Purdue	24	781	32.5
1967	Jimmy Walker, Providence	28	851	30.4
1968	Pete Maravich, LSU	26	1138	43.8
1969	Pete Maravich, LSU	26	1148	44.2
1970	Pete Maravich, LSU	31	1381	44.5
1971	Johnny Neumann, Ole Miss	23	923	40.1
1972	Dwight Lamar, SW La	29	1054	36.3
1973	Bird Averitt, Pepperdine	25	848	33.9
1974	Larry Fogle, Canisius	25	835	33.4
1975	Bob McCurdy, Richmond	26	855	32.9
1976	Marshall Rodgers, Texas-Pan Am	25	919	36.8
1977	Freeman Williams, Portland St.	26	1010	38.8
1978	Freeman Williams, Portland St.	27	969	35.9
1979	Lawrence Butler, Idaho St.	27	812	30.1
1980	Tony Murphy, Southern-BR	29	932	32.1
1981	Zam Fredrick, S. Carolina	27	781	28.9
1982	Harry Kelly, Texas Southern	29	862	29.7
1983	Harry Kelly, Texas Southern	29	835	28.8
1984	Joe Jakubick, Akron	27	814	30.1
1985	Xavier McDaniel, Wichita St	31	844	27.2
1986	Terrance Bailey, Wagner	29	854	29.4
1987	Kevin Houston, Army	29	953	32.9
1988	Hersey Hawkins, Bradley	31	1125	36.3
1989	Hank Gathers, Loyola-CA	31	1015	32.7
1990	Bo Kimble, Loyola-CA	32	1131	35.3
1991	Kevin Bradshaw, US Int'l	28	1054	37.6
1992	Brett Roberts, Morehead St	29	815	28.1
1993	Greg Guy, Texas-Pan Am	19	556	29.3
1994	Glenn Robinson, Purdue	34	1030	30.3
1995	Kurt Thomas, TCU	27	781	28.9
1996	Kevin Granger, Texas Southern	24	648	27.0
1997	Charles Jones, LIU-Brooklyn	30	903	30.1
1998	Charles Jones, LIU-Brooklyn	30	869	29.0
1999	Alvin Young, Niagara	29	728	25.1
2000	Courtney Alexander, Fresno St.	27	669	24.8
2001	Ronnie McCollum, Centenary	27	787	29.1
2002	Jason Conley, VMI	28	820	29.3
2003	Ruben Douglas, New Mexico	28	783	28.0

Rebounds

The NCAA did not begin keeping individual rebounding records until the 1950-51 season. From 1956-62, the championship was decided on highest percentage of recoveries out of all rebounds made by both teams in all games. All averages include postseason games where applicable.

Multiple winners: Artis Gilmore, Jerry Lucas, Xavier McDaniel, Kermit Washington and Leroy Wright (2).

Year		Gm	No	Avg	Year		Gm	No	Avg
1951	Ernie Beck, Penn	27	556	20.6	1978	Ken Williams, N. Texas	28	411	14.7
1952	Bill Hannon, Army	17	355	20.9	1979	Monti Davis, Tennessee St.	26	421	16.2
1953	Ed Conlin, Fordham	26	612	23.5	1980	Larry Smith, Alcorn State	26	392	15.1
1954	Art Quimby, Connecticut	26	588	22.6	1981	Darryl Watson, Miss. Valley St.	27	379	14.0
1955	Charlie Slack, Marshall	21	538	25.6	1982	LaSalle Thompson, Texas	27	365	13.5
1956	Joe Holup, G. Washington	26	604	25.6	1983	Xavier McDaniel, Wichita St.	28	403	14.4
1957	Elgin Baylor, Seattle	25	508	23.5	1984	Akeem Olajuwon, Houston	37	500	13.5
1958	Alex Ellis, Niagara	25	536	26.2	1985	Xavier McDaniel, Wichita St.	31	460	14.8
1959	Leroy Wright, Pacific	26	652	23.8	1986	David Robinson, Navy	35	455	13.0
1960	Leroy Wright, Pacific	17	380	23.4	1987	Jerome Lane, Pittsburgh	33	444	13.5
1961	Jerry Lucas, Ohio St.	27	470	19.8	1988	Kenny Miller, Loyola-IL	29	395	13.6
1962	Jerry Lucas, Ohio St.	28	499	21.1	1989	Hank Gathers, Loyola-CA	31	426	13.7
1963	Paul Silas, Creighton	27	557	20.6	1990	Anthony Bonner, St. Louis	33	456	13.8
1964	Bob Pelkington, Xavier-OH	26	567	21.8	1991	Shaquille O'Neal, LSU	28	411	14.7
1965	Toby Kimball, Connecticut	23	483	21.0	1992	Popeye Jones, Murray St.	30	431	14.4
1966	Jim Ware, Oklahoma City	29	607	20.9	1993	Warren Kidd, Mid. Tenn. St.	26	386	14.8
1967	Dick Cunningham, Murray St.	22	479	21.8	1994	Jerome Lambert, Baylor	24	355	14.8
1968	Neal Walk, Florida	25	494	19.8	1995	Kurt Thomas, TCU	27	393	14.6
1969	Spencer Haywood, Detroit	22	472	21.5	1996	Marcus Mann, Miss. Valley St.	29	394	13.6
1970	Artis Gilmore, Jacksonville	28	621	22.2	1997	Tim Duncan, Wake Forest	31	457	14.7
1971	Artis Gilmore, Jacksonville	26	603	23.2	1998	Ryan Perryman, Dayton	33	412	12.5
1972	Kermit Washington, American	23	455	19.8	1999	Ian McGinnis, Dartmouth	26	317	12.2
1973	Kermit Washington, American	22	439	20.0	2000	Darren Phillip, Fairfield	29	405	14.0
1974	Marvin Barnes, Providence	32	597	18.7	2001	Chris Marcus, Western Ky.	31	374	12.1
1975	John Irving, Hofstra	21	323	15.4	2002	Jeremy Bishop, Quinnipiac	29	347	12.0
1976	Sam Pellom, Buffalo	26	420	16.2	2003	Brandon Hunter, Ohio	30	378	12.6
1977	Glenn Mosley, Seton Hall	29	473	16.3					

Note: Only three players have ever led the NCAA in scoring and rebounding in the same season: Xavier McDaniel of Wichita St. (1985), Hank Gathers of Loyola-Marymount (1989) and Kurt Thomas of TCU (1995).

Assists

The NCAA did not begin keeping individual assist records until the 1983-84 season. All averages include postseason games where applicable.

Multiple winner: Avery Johnson (2).

Year		Gm	No	Avg
1984	Craig Lathen, IL-Chicago	29	274	9.45
1985	Rob Weingard, Hofstra	24	228	9.50
1986	Mark Jackson, St. John's	36	328	9.11
1987	Avery Johnson, Southern-BR	31	333	10.74
1988	Avery Johnson, Southern-BR	30	399	13.30
1989	Glenn Williams, Holy Cross	28	278	9.93
1990	Todd Lehmann, Drexel	28	260	9.29
1991	Chris Corchiani, N.C. State	31	299	9.65
1992	Van Usher, Tennessee Tech	29	254	8.76
1993	Sam Crawford, N. Mexico St	34	310	9.12
1994	Jason Kidd, California	30	272	9.06
1995	Nelson Haggerty, Baylor	28	284	10.14
1996	Raimonds Miglinieks, UC-Irvine	27	230	8.52
1997	Kenny Mitchell, Dartmouth	26	203	7.81
1998	Ahlon Lewis, Arizona St.	32	294	9.19
1999	Doug Gottlieb, Oklahoma St.	34	299	8.79
2000	Mark Dickel, UNLV	31	280	9.03
2001	Markus Carr, CS-Northridge	32	286	8.94
2002	T.J. Ford, Texas	33	273	8.27
2003	Martell Bailey, Illinois-Chicago	30	244	8.13

Blocked Shots

The NCAA did not begin keeping individual blocked shots records until the 1985-86 season. All averages include postseason games where applicable.

Multiple winners: Keith Closs, David Robinson and Tarvis Williams (2).

Year		Gm	No	Avg
1986	David Robinson, Navy	35	207	5.91
1987	David Robinson, Navy	32	144	4.50
1988	Rodney Blake, St. Joe's-PA	29	116	4.00
1989	Alonzo Mourning, G'town	34	169	4.97
1990	Kenny Green, Rhode Island	26	124	4.77
1991	Shawn Bradley, BYU	34	177	5.21
1992	Shaquille O'Neal, LSU	30	157	5.23
1993	Theo Ratliff, Wyoming	28	124	4.43
1994	Grady Livingston, Howard	26	115	4.42
1995	Keith Closs, Cen. Conn. St.	26	139	5.35
1996	Keith Closs, Cen. Conn. St.	28	178	6.36
1997	Adonal Foyle, Colgate	28	180	6.43
1998	Jerome James, Florida A&M	27	125	4.63
1999	Tarvis Williams, Hampton	27	135	5.00
2000	Ken Johnson, Ohio St.	30	161	5.37
2001	Tarvis Williams, Hampton	32	147	4.59
2002	Wojciech Myrda, La-Monroe	32	172	5.38
2003	Emeka Okafor, Connecticut	33	156	4.73

All-Time NCAA Division I Individual Leaders

Through 2002-03; includes regular season and tournament games; **Last** column indicates final year played.

CAREER

Scoring

	Points	Yrs	Last	Gm	Pts
1	Pete Maravich, LSU	3	1970	83	3667
2	Freeman Williams, Port. St.	4	1978	106	3249
3	Lionel Simmons, La Salle	4	1990	131	3217
4	Alphonso Ford, Miss. Val. St.	4	1993	109	3165
5	Harry Kelly, Texas Southern	4	1983	110	3066
6	Hersey Hawkins, Bradley	4	1988	125	3008
7	Oscar Robertson, Cincinnati	3	1960	88	2973
8	Danny Manning, Kansas	4	1988	147	2951
9	Alfredrick Hughes, Loyola-IL	4	1985	120	2914
10	Elvin Hayes, Houston	3	1968	93	2884
11	Larry Bird, Indiana St.	3	1979	94	2850
12	Otis Birdsong, Houston	4	1977	116	2832
13	Kevin Bradshaw, Beth-Cook/US Int'l	4	1991	111	2804
14	Allan Houston, Tennessee	4	1993	128	2801
15	Hank Gathers, USC/Loyola-CA	4	1990	117	2723
16	Reggie Lewis, Northeastern	4	1987	122	2708
17	Daren Queenan, Lehigh	4	1988	118	2703
18	Byron Larkin, Xavier-OH	4	1988	121	2696
19	David Robinson, Navy	4	1987	127	2669
20	Wayman Tisdale, Oklahoma	3	1985	104	2661

	Average	Yrs	Last	Pts	Avg
1	Pete Maravich, LSU	3	1970	3667	44.2
2	Austin Carr, Notre Dame	3	1971	2560	34.6
3	Oscar Robertson, Cinn	3	1960	2973	33.8
4	Calvin Murphy, Niagara	3	1970	2548	33.1
5	Dwight Lamar, SW La	2	1973	1862	32.7
6	Frank Selvy, Furman	3	1954	2538	32.5
7	Rick Mount, Purdue	3	1970	2323	32.3
8	Darrell Floyd, Furman	3	1956	2281	32.1
9	Nick Werkman, Seton Hall	3	1964	2273	32.0
10	Willie Humes, Idaho St.	2	1971	1510	31.5
11	William Averitt, Pepperdine	2	1973	1541	31.4
12	Elgin Baylor, Idaho/Seattle	3	1958	2500	31.3
13	Elvin Hayes, Houston	3	1968	2884	31.0
14	Freeman Williams, Port. St.	4	1978	3249	30.7
15	Larry Bird, Indiana St.	3	1979	2850	30.3
16	Bill Bradley, Princeton	3	1965	2503	30.2
17	Rich Fuqua, Oral Roberts	2	1973	1617	29.9
18	Wilt Chamberlain, Kansas	2	1958	1433	29.9
19	Rick Barry, Miami-FL	3	1965	2298	29.8
20	Doug Collins, Illinois St.	3	1973	2240	29.1

	Field Goal Pct.	Yrs	Last	FG	FGA	Pct
1	Steve Johnson, Ore. St.	4	1981	828	1222	.678
2	Michael Bradley, Kentucky/ Villanova	3	2001	441	651	.677
3	Murray Brown, Fla. St.	4	1980	566	847	.668
4	Lee Campbell, M.Tenn St./ SW Mo.St.	3	1990	411	618	.665
5	Warren Kidd, M.Tenn.St.	3	1993	496	747	.664
6	Todd MacCulloch, Wash.	4	1999	702	1058	.664
7	Joe Senser, West Chester	4	1979	476	719	.662
8	Kevin Magee, UC-Irvine	2	1982	552	841	.656
9	Orlando Phillips, Pepperdine	2	1983	404	618	.654
10	Bill Walton, UCLA	3	1974	747	1147	.651

Note: minimum 400 FGs made and an average of four per game.

	Free Throw Pct.	Yrs	Last	FT	FTA	Pct
1	Gary Buchanan, Villanova	4	2003	324	355	.913
2	Greg Starrick, Ky/So.Ill	4	1972	341	375	.909
3	Jack Moore, Nebraska	4	1982	446	495	.901
4	Steve Henson, Kansas St.	4	1990	361	401	.900
5	Steve Alford, Indiana	4	1987	535	596	.898
6	Bob Lloyd, Rutgers	3	1967	543	605	.898
7	Jim Barton, Dartmouth	4	1989	394	440	.895
8	Tommy Boyer, Arkansas	3	1963	315	353	.892
9	Kyle Korver, Creighton	4	2003	312	350	.891
10	Brent Jolly, Tenn. Tech	4	2003	347	391	.887

Note: minimum 300 FTs made and an average of 2.5 per game.

	3-Pt Field Goals	Yrs	Last	Gm	3FG
1	Curtis Staples, Virginia	4	1998	122	413
2	Keith Veney, Lamar/Marshall	4	1997	111	409
3	Doug Day, Radford	4	1993	117	401
4	Ronnie Schmitz, Missouri-KC	4	1993	112	378
5	Mark Alberts, Akron	4	1993	107	375

	3-Pt Field Goals/Game	Yrs	Last	3FG	Avg
1	Timothy Pollard, Miss. Vall	2	1989	256	4.57
2	Sydney Grider, LA-Lafayette	2	1990	253	4.36
3	Brian Merriweather, TX-Pan Am	3	2001	332	3.95
4	Josh Heard, Tenn. Tech	2	2000	210	3.82
5	Kareem Townes, La Salle	3	1995	300	3.70

	3-Pt Field Goal Pct.	Yrs	Last	3FG	Att	Pct
1	Tony Bennett, Wisc-GB	4	1992	290	584	.497
2	David Olson, Eastern Ill.	4	1992	262	562	.466
3	Ross Land, N. Arizona	4	2000	308	664	.464
4	Dan Dickau, Washington/ Gonzaga	4	2002	215	465	.462
5	Sean Jackson, Ohio/ Princeton	4	1992	243	528	.460

Note: minimum 200 3FGs made and an average of two per game.

	Games Played	Yrs	Last	Gms
1	Wayne Turner, Kentucky	4	1999	151
2	Christian Laettner, Duke	4	1992	148
3	Danny Manning, Kansas	4	1988	147
4	Shane Battier, Duke	4	2001	146
5	Stacey Augmon, UNLV	4	1991	145
	Jamaal Magloire, Kentucky	4	2000	145

All-Time Highest Scoring Teams
SINGLE SEASON
Scoring Offense

Team	Season	Gm	Pts	Avg
Loyola-CA	1990	32	3918	122.4
Loyola-CA	1989	31	3486	112.5
UNLV	1976	31	3426	110.5
Loyola-CA	1988	32	3528	110.3
UNLV	1977	32	3426	107.1
Oral Roberts	1972	28	2943	105.1
Southern-BR	1991	28	2924	104.4
Loyola-CA	1991	31	3211	103.6
Oklahoma	1988	39	4012	102.9
Oklahoma	1989	36	3680	102.2

All-Time NCAA Division I Individual Leaders (Cont.)
Rebounds

	Total (before 1973)	Yrs	Last	Gm	No
1	Tom Gola, La Salle	4	1955	118	2201
2	Joe Holup, G. Washington	4	1956	104	2030
3	Charlie Slack, Marshall	4	1956	88	1916
4	Ed Conlin, Fordham	4	1955	102	1884
5	Dickie Hemric, Wake Forest	4	1955	104	1802
6	Paul Silas, Creighton	3	1964	81	1751
7	Art Quimby, Connecticut	4	1955	80	1716
8	Jerry Harper, Alabama	4	1956	93	1688
9	Jeff Cohen, Wm. & Mary	4	1961	103	1679
10	Steve Hamilton, Morehead St.	4	1958	102	1675

	Total (since 1973)	Yrs	Last	Gm	No
1	Tim Duncan, Wake Forest	4	1997	128	1570
2	Derrick Coleman, Syracuse	4	1990	143	1537
3	Malik Rose, Drexel	4	1996	120	1514
4	Ralph Sampson, Virginia	4	1983	132	1511
5	Pete Padgett, Nevada-Reno	4	1976	104	1464
6	Lionel Simmons, La Salle	4	1990	131	1429
7	Anthony Bonner, St. Louis	4	1990	133	1424
8	Tyrone Hill, Xavier-OH	4	1990	126	1380
9	Popeye Jones, Murray St.	4	1992	123	1374
10	Michael Brooks, La Salle	4	1980	114	1372

	Average (before 1973)	Yrs	Last	No	Avg
1	Artis Gilmore, Jacksonville	2	1971	1224	22.7
2	Charlie Slack, Marshall	4	1956	1916	21.8
3	Paul Silas, Creighton	3	1964	1751	21.6
4	Leroy Wright, Pacific	3	1960	1442	21.5
5	Art Quimby, Connecticut	4	1955	1716	21.5

Note: minimum 800 rebounds.

	Average (since 1973)	Yrs	Last	No	Avg
1	Glenn Mosley, Seton Hall	4	1977	1263	15.2
2	Bill Campion, Manhattan	3	1975	1070	14.2
3	Pete Padgett, Nevada-Reno	4	1976	1464	14.1
4	Bob Warner, Maine	4	1976	1304	13.6
5	Shaquille O'Neal, LSU	3	1992	1217	13.5

Note: minimum 650 rebounds.

Assists

	Total	Yrs	Last	Gm	No
1	Bobby Hurley, Duke	4	1993	140	1076
2	Chris Corchiani, N.C. State	4	1991	124	1038
3	Ed Cota, N. Carolina	4	2000	138	1030
4	Keith Jennings, E. Tenn. St.	4	1991	127	983
5	Steve Blake, Maryland	4	2003	138	972
6	Sherman Douglas, Syracuse	4	1989	138	960
7	Tony Miller, Marquette	4	1995	123	956
8	Greg Anthony, Portland/UNLV	4	1991	138	950
9	Doug Gottlieb, ND/Okla St.	4	2000	124	947
10	Gary Payton, Oregon St.	4	1990	120	938

	Average	Yrs	Last	No	Avg
1	Avery Johnson, Southern	2	1988	732	12.00
2	Sam Crawford, N. Mexico St.	2	1993	592	8.84
3	Mark Wade, Okla/UNLV	3	1987	693	8.77
4	Chris Corchiani, N.C. State	4	1991	1038	8.37
5	Taurence Chisholm, Delaware	4	1988	877	7.97
6	Van Usher, Tennessee Tech	3	1992	676	7.95
7	Anthony Manuel, Bradley	3	1989	855	7.92
8	Chico Fletcher, Ark. St.	4	2000	893	7.83
9	Gary Payton, Oregon St.	4	1990	938	7.82
10	Orlando Smart, San Francisco	4	1994	902	7.78

Note: minimum 550 assists.

Blocked Shots

	Average	Yrs	Last	No	Avg
1	Keith Closs, Cen. Conn. St.	2	1996	317	5.87
2	Adonal Foyle, Colgate	3	1997	492	5.66
3	David Robinson, Navy	2	1987	351	5.24
4	Wojciech Mydra, LA-Monroe	4	2002	535	4.65
5	Shaquille O'Neal, LSU	3	1992	412	4.58

Note: minimum 225 blocked shots.

Steals

	Average	Yrs	Last	No	Avg
1	Desmond Cambridge, Ala. A&M	3	2002	330	3.93
2	Mookie Blaylock, Oklahoma	2	1989	281	3.80
3	Ronn McMahon, Eastern Wash.	3	1990	225	3.52
4	Eric Murdock, Providence	4	1991	376	3.21
5	Van Usher, Tennessee Tech	3	1992	270	3.18

Note: minimum 225 steals.

2000 Points/1000 Rebounds
For a combined total of 4000 or more.

		Gm	Pts	Reb	Total
1	Tom Gola, La Salle	118	2462	2201	4663
2	Lionel Simmons, La Salle	131	3217	1429	4646
3	Elvin Hayes, Houston	93	2884	1602	4486
4	Dickie Hemric, W. Forest	104	2587	1802	4389
5	Oscar Robertson, Cinn.	88	2973	1338	4311
6	Joe Holup, G. Wash.	104	2226	2030	4256

		Gm	Pts	Reb	Total
7	Harry Kelly, TX-Southern	110	3066	1085	4151
8	Danny Manning, Kansas	147	2951	1187	4138
9	Larry Bird, Indiana St.	94	2850	1247	4097
10	Elgin Baylor, Col. Idaho/Seattle	80	2500	1559	4059
11	Michael Brooks, La Salle	114	2628	1372	4000

Years Played–Baylor (1956-58); **Bird** (1977-79); **Brooks** (1977-80); **Gola** (1952-55); **Hayes** (1966-68); **Hemric** (1952-55); **Holup** (1953-56); **Kelly** (1980-83); **Manning** (1985-88); **Robertson** (1958-60); **Simmons** (1987-90).

SINGLE SEASON
Scoring

	Points	Year	Gm	Pts
1	Pete Maravich, LSU	1970	31	1381
2	Elvin Hayes, Houston	1968	33	1214
3	Frank Selvy, Furman	1954	29	1209
4	Pete Maravich, LSU	1969	26	1148
5	Pete Maravich, LSU	1968	26	1138
6	Bo Kimble, Loyola-CA	1990	32	1131
7	Hersey Hawkins, Bradley	1988	31	1125
8	Austin Carr, Notre Dame	1970	29	1106
9	Austin Carr, Notre Dame	1971	29	1101
10	Otis Birdsong, Houston	1977	36	1090

	Average	Year	Gm	Pts	Avg
1	Pete Maravich, LSU	1970	31	1381	44.5
2	Pete Maravich, LSU	1969	26	1148	44.2
3	Pete Maravich, LSU	1968	26	1138	43.8
4	Frank Selvy, Furman	1954	29	1209	41.7
5	Johnny Neumann, Ole Miss	1971	23	923	40.1
6	Freeman Williams, Port. St.	1977	26	1010	38.8
7	Billy McGill, Utah	1962	26	1009	38.8
8	Calvin Murphy, Niagara	1968	24	916	38.2
9	Austin Carr, Notre Dame	1970	29	1106	38.1
10	Austin Carr, Notre Dame	1971	29	1101	38.0

Field Goal Pct.

		Year	FG	FGA	Pct
1	Steve Johnson, Oregon St.	1981	235	315	.746
2	Dwayne Davis, Florida	1989	179	248	.722
3	Keith Walker, Utica	1985	154	216	.713
4	Steve Johnson, Oregon St.	1980	211	297	.710
5	Adam Mark, Belmont	2002	150	212	.708

Free Throw Pct.

		Year	FT	FTA	Pct
1	Craig Collins, Penn St.	1985	94	98	.959
2	Rod Foster, UCLA	1982	95	100	.950
3	Clay McKnight, Pacific	2000	74	78	.949
4	Carlos Gibson, Marshall	1978	84	89	.944
5	Danny Basile, Marist	1994	84	89	.944

3-Pt Field Goal Pct.

		Year	3FG	Att	Pct
1	Glenn Tropf, Holy Cross	1988	52	82	.634
2	Sean Wightman, W. Mich.	1992	48	76	.632
3	Keith Jennings, E. Tenn. St.	1991	84	142	.592
4	Dave Calloway, Monmouth	1989	48	82	.585
5	Steve Kerr, Arizona	1988	114	199	.573

Assists

	Average	Year	Gm	No	Avg
1	Avery Johnson, Southern-BR	1988	30	399	13.3
2	Anthony Manuel, Bradley	1988	31	373	12.0
3	Avery Johnson, Southern-BR	1987	31	333	10.7
4	Mark Wade, UNLV	1987	38	406	10.7
5	Nelson Haggerty, Baylor	1995	28	284	10.1
6	Glenn Williams, Holy Cross	1989	28	278	9.9
7	Chris Corchiani, N.C. State	1991	31	299	9.7
8	Tony Fairley, Charleston-So.	1987	28	270	9.6
9	Tyrone Bogues, Wake Forest	1987	29	276	9.5
10	Ron Weingard, Hofstra	1985	24	228	9.5

Rebounds

	Average (before 1973)	Year	Gm	No	Avg
1	Charlie Slack, Marshall	1955	21	538	25.6
2	Leroy Wright, Pacific	1959	26	652	25.1
3	Art Quimby, Connecticut	1955	25	611	24.4
4	Charlie Slack, Marshall	1956	22	520	23.6
5	Ed Conlin, Fordham	1953	26	612	23.5

	Average (since 1973)	Year	Gm	No	Avg
1	Kermit Washington, American	1973	25	511	20.4
2	Marvin Barnes, Providence	1973	30	571	19.0
3	Marvin Barnes, Providence	1974	32	597	18.7
4	Pete Padgett, Nevada	1973	26	462	17.8
5	Jim Bradley, Northern Ill	1973	24	426	17.8

Blocked Shots

	Average	Year	Gm	No	Avg
1	Adonal Foyle, Colgate	1997	28	180	6.42
2	Keith Closs, Cen. Conn. St.	1996	28	178	6.36
3	David Robinson, Navy	1986	35	207	5.91
4	Wojciech Myrda, La-Monroe	2002	32	172	5.38
5	Ken Johnson, Ohio St.	2000	30	161	5.37

Steals

	Average	Year	Gm	No	Avg
1	Desmond Cambridge, Ala. A&M	2002	29	160	5.52
2	Darron Brittman, Chicago St.	1986	28	139	4.96
3	Aldwin Ware, Florida A&M	1988	29	142	4.90
4	John Linehan, Providence	2002	31	139	4.48
5	Ronn McMahon, East Wash.	1990	29	130	4.48

SINGLE GAME
Scoring

	Points vs Div. I Team	Year	Pts
1	Kevin Bradshaw, US Int'l vs Loyola-CA	1991	72
2	Pete Maravich, LSU vs Alabama	1970	69
3	Calvin Murphy, Niagara vs Syracuse	1969	68
4	Jay Handlan, Wash. & Lee vs Furman	1951	66
	Pete Maravich, LSU vs Tulane	1969	66
	Anthony Roberts, Oral Rbts vs N.C. A&T	1977	66
7	Anthony Roberts, Oral Rbts vs Ore	1977	65
	Scott Haffner, Evansville vs Dayton	1989	65
9	Pete Maravich, LSU vs Kentucky	1970	64
10	Johnny Neumann, Ole Miss vs LSU	1971	63
	Hersey Hawkins, Bradley vs Detroit	1988	63

	Points vs Non-Div. I Team	Year	Pts
1	Frank Selvy, Furman vs Newberry	1954	100
2	Paul Arizin, Villanova vs Phi. NAMC	1949	85
3	Freeman Williams, Port. St. vs Rocky Mt	1978	81
4	Bill Mlkvy, Temple vs Wilkes	1951	73
5	Freeman Williams, Port. St. vs So. Ore	1977	71
6	Darrell Floyd, Furman vs Morehead St.	1955	67

Note: Bevo Francis of Division II Rio Grande (Ohio) scored an overall collegiate record 113 points against Hillsdale in 1954. He also scored 84 against Alliance and 82 against Bluffton that same season.

Assists

		Year	No
1	Tony Fairley, Baptist vs Armstrong St.	1987	22
	Avery Johnson, Southern-BR vs TX-South	1988	22
	Sherman Douglas, Syracuse vs Providence	1989	22
4	Mark Wade, UNLV vs Navy	1986	21
	Kelvin Scarborough, N. Mexico vs Hawaii	1987	21
	Anthony Manuel, Bradley vs UC-Irvine	1987	21
	Avery Johnson, Southern-BR vs Ala. St.	1988	21
8	Eleven players tied with 20 each.		

3-Pt Field Goals

		Year	No
1	Keith Veney, Marshall vs Morehead St.	1996	15
2	Dave Jamerson, Ohio U. vs Charleston	1989	14
	Askia Jones, Kansas St. vs Fresno St.	1994	14
	Ronald Blackshear, Marshall vs. Akron	2002	14
5	Gary Bossert, Niagara vs Siena	1987	12
	Darrin Fitzgerald, Butler vs Detroit	1987	12
	Al Dillard, Arkansas vs Delaware St.	1993	12
	Mitch Taylor, South-BR vs La. Christian	1995	12
	David McMahan, Winthrop vs C. Carolina	1996	12
	Clarence Gilbert, Missouri vs Colorado	2002	12
	Terrence Woods, Fla. A&M vs Coppin St.	2003	12

Rebounds

	Total (before 1973)	Year	No
1	Bill Chambers, Wm. & Mary vs Virginia	1953	51
2	Charlie Slack, Marshall vs M. Harvey	1954	43
3	Tom Heinsohn, Holy Cross vs BC	1955	42
4	Art Quimby, UConn vs BU	1955	40
5	Three players tied with 39 each.		

	Total (since 1973)	Year	No
1	Larry Abney, Fresno St. vs SMU	2000	35
2	David Vaughn, Oral Roberts vs Brandeis	1973	34
3	Robert Parish, Centenary vs So. Miss	1973	33
4	Durand Macklin, LSU vs Tulane	1976	32
	Jervaughn Scales, South-BR vs Grambling	1994	32

Blocked Shots

		Year	No
1	David Robinson, Navy vs NC-Wilmington	1986	14
	Shawn Bradley, BYU vs Eastern Ky	1990	14
	Roy Rogers, Alabama vs Georgia	1996	14
	Loren Woods, Arizona vs Oregon	2000	14
5	Kevin Roberson, Vermont vs UNH	1992	13
	Jim McIlvaine, Marquette vs No. Ill	1993	13
	Keith Closs, C. Conn. St. vs St. Fran-PA	1994	13
	D'or Fischer, N'Western St. vs. SW Tex. St.	2001	13
	Wojciech Myrda, La-Monroe vs. Tx-SA	2002	13

All-Time NCAA Division I Individual Leaders (Cont.)
Steals

	Year	No			Year	No
1 Mookie Blaylock, Oklahoma vs Centenary	1987	13		Richard Duncan, Mid. Tenn St. vs E. Ky.	1999	12
Mookie Blaylock, Oklahoma vs Loyola-CA	1988	13		Greedy Daniels, TCU vs Ark-Pine Bluff	2001	12
3 Kenny Robertson, Cleve. St. vs Wagner	1988	12		Jehiel Lewis, Navy vs Bucknell	2002	12
Terry Evans, Oklahoma vs Florida A&M	1993	12				

Players of the Year and Top Draft Picks

Consensus College Players of the Year and first overall selections in NBA draft since the abolition of the NBA's territorial draft in 1966. Top draft picks who became Rookie of the Year are in **bold** type; (*) indicates top draft pick chosen as junior, (**) indicates top draft pick chosen as sophomore, (†) indicates top draft pick chosen as a high school senior.

Year	Player of the Year	Top Draft Pick	Year	Player of the Year	Top Draft Pick
1966	Cazzie Russell, Mich.	Cazzie Russell, NY	1987	David Robinson, Navy	**David Robinson**, SA
1967	Lew Alcindor, UCLA	Jimmy Walker, Det.	1988	Hersey Hawkins, Bradley	
1968	Elvin Hayes, Houston	Elvin Hayes, SD		& Danny Manning, Kan.	Danny Manning, LAC
1969	Lew Alcindor, UCLA	**Lew Alcindor**, Mil.	1989	Sean Elliott, Arizona	
1970	Pete Maravich, LSU	Bob Lanier, Det.		& Danny Ferry, Duke	Pervis Ellison, Sac.
1971	Sidney Wicks, UCLA	Austin Carr, Cle.	1990	Lionel Simmons, La Salle	**Derrick Coleman**, NJ
1972	Bill Walton, UCLA	LaRue Martin, Por.	1991	Larry Johnson, UNLV	
1973	Bill Walton, UCLA	Doug Collins, Phi.		& Shaquille O'Neal, LSU	**Larry Johnson**, Cha.
1974	Bill Walton, UCLA	Bill Walton, Por.	1992	Christian Laettner, Duke	**Shaquille O'Neal**, Orl.*
1975	David Thompson, N.C. St.	David Thompson, Atl.	1993	Calbert Cheaney, Ind.	**Chris Webber**, Orl.**
1976	Scott May, Indiana	John Lucas, Hou.	1994	Glenn Robinson, Purdue	**Glenn Robinson**, Mil.*
1977	Marques Johnson, UCLA	Kent Benson, Ind.	1995	Ed O'Bannon, UCLA	
1978	Butch Lee, Marquette			& Joe Smith, Maryland	Joe Smith, G. St.**
	& Phil Ford, N. Caro.	Mychal Thompson, Por.	1996	Marcus Camby, UMass	**Allen Iverson**, Phi.**
1979	Larry Bird, Indiana St.	Magic Johnson, LAL**	1997	Tim Duncan, Wake Forest	**Tim Duncan**, SA
1980	Mark Aguirre, DePaul	Joe Barry Carroll, G. St.	1998	Antawn Jamison, N. Caro.	M. Olowokandi, LAC
1981	Ralph Sampson, Va.		1999	Elton Brand, Duke	**Elton Brand**, Chi.**
	& Danny Ainge, BYU	Mark Aguirre, Dal.	2000	Kenyon Martin, Cincinnati	**Kenyon Martin**, NJ
1982	Ralph Sampson, Va.	James Worthy, LAL*	2001	Shane Battier, Duke	
1983	Ralph Sampson, Va.	**Ralph Sampson**, Hou.		& Jason Williams, Duke	Kwame Brown, Wash.†
1984	Michael Jordan, N. Caro.	Akeem Olajuwon, Hou.	2002	Jason Williams, Duke	
1985	Patrick Ewing, Georgetown			& Drew Gooden, Kansas	Yao Ming, Hou.
	& Chris Mullin, St. John's	**Patrick Ewing**, NY	2003	T.J. Ford, Texas	
1986	Walter Berry, St. John's	Brad Daugherty, Cle.		& David West, Xavier	LeBron James, Cle.†

Annual Awards

UPI picked the first national Division I Player of the Year in 1955. Since then, the U.S. Basketball Writers Assn. (1959), the Commonwealth Athletic Club of Kentucky's Adolph Rupp Trophy (1961), the Atlanta Tip-Off Club (1969), the National Assn. of Basketball Coaches (1975), and the LA Athletic Club's John Wooden Award (1977) have joined in. UPI discontinued its award in 1997. Since 1977, the first year all the following awards were given out, the same player has won all of them in the same season 13 times: Marques Johnson in 1977, Larry Bird in 1979, Ralph Sampson in both 1982 and '83, Michael Jordan in 1984, David Robinson in 1987, Lionel Simmons in 1990, Calbert Cheaney in 1993, Glenn Robinson in 1994, Tim Duncan in 1997, Antawn Jamison in 1998, Elton Brand in 1999 and Kenyon Martin in 2000.

United Press International

Voted on by a panel of UPI college basketball writers and first presented in 1955.
Multiple winners: Oscar Robertson, Ralph Sampson and Bill Walton (3); Lew Alcindor and Jerry Lucas (2).

Year		Year		Year	
1955	Tom Gola, La Salle	1970	Pete Maravich, LSU	1985	Chris Mullin, St. John's
1956	Bill Russell, San Francisco	1971	Austin Carr, Notre Dame	1986	Walter Berry, St. John's
1957	Chet Forte, Columbia	1972	Bill Walton, UCLA	1987	David Robinson, Navy
1958	Oscar Robertson, Cincinnati	1973	Bill Walton, UCLA	1988	Hersey Hawkins, Bradley
1959	Oscar Robertson, Cincinnati	1974	Bill Walton, UCLA	1989	Danny Ferry, Duke
1960	Oscar Robertson, Cincinnati	1975	David Thompson, N.C. State	1990	Lionel Simmons, La Salle
1961	Jerry Lucas, Ohio St.	1976	Scott May, Indiana	1991	Shaquille O'Neal, LSU
1962	Jerry Lucas, Ohio St.	1977	Marques Johnson, UCLA	1992	Jim Jackson, Ohio St.
1963	Art Heyman, Duke	1978	Butch Lee, Marquette	1993	Calbert Cheaney, Indiana
1964	Gary Bradds, Ohio St.	1979	Larry Bird, Indiana St.	1994	Glenn Robinson, Purdue
1965	Bill Bradley, Princeton	1980	Mark Aguirre, DePaul	1995	Joe Smith, Maryland
1966	Cazzie Russell, Michigan	1981	Ralph Sampson, Virginia	1996	Ray Allen, UConn
1967	Lew Alcindor, UCLA	1982	Ralph Sampson, Virginia	1997	award discontinued
1968	Elvin Hayes, Houston	1983	Ralph Sampson, Virginia		
1969	Lew Alcindor, UCLA	1984	Michael Jordan, N. Carolina		

U.S. Basketball Writers Association
Voted on by the USBWA and first presented in 1959.
Multiple winners: Ralph Sampson and Bill Walton (3); Lew Alcindor, Jerry Lucas and Oscar Robertson (2).

Year		Year		Year	
1959	Oscar Robertson, Cincinnati	1974	Bill Walton, UCLA	1989	Danny Ferry, Duke
1960	Oscar Robertson, Cincinnati	1975	David Thompson, N.C. State	1990	Lionel Simmons, La Salle
1961	Jerry Lucas, Ohio St.	1976	Adrian Dantley, Notre Dame	1991	Larry Johnson, UNLV
1962	Jerry Lucas, Ohio St.	1977	Marques Johnson, UCLA	1992	Christian Laettner, Duke
1963	Art Heyman, Duke	1978	Phil Ford, North Carolina	1993	Calbert Cheaney, Indiana
1964	Walt Hazzard, UCLA	1979	Larry Bird, Indiana St.	1994	Glenn Robinson, Purdue
1965	Bill Bradley, Princeton	1980	Mark Aguirre, DePaul	1995	Ed O'Bannon, UCLA
1966	Cazzie Russell, Michigan	1981	Ralph Sampson, Virginia	1996	Marcus Camby, UMass
1967	Lew Alcindor, UCLA	1982	Ralph Sampson, Virginia	1997	Tim Duncan, Wake Forest
1968	Elvin Hayes, Houston	1983	Ralph Sampson, Virginia	1998	Antawn Jamison, N. Carolina
1969	Lew Alcindor, UCLA	1984	Michael Jordan, N. Carolina	1999	Elton Brand, Duke
1970	Pete Maravich, LSU	1985	Chris Mullin, St. John's	2000	Kenyon Martin, Cincinnati
1971	Sidney Wicks, UCLA	1986	Walter Berry, St. John's	2001	Shane Battier, Duke
1972	Bill Walton, UCLA	1987	David Robinson, Navy	2002	Jason Williams, Duke
1973	Bill Walton, UCLA	1988	Hersey Hawkins, Bradley	2003	David West, Xavier

Rupp Trophy
Voted on by AP sportswriters and broadcasters and first presented in 1961 by the Commonwealth Athletic Club of Kentucky in the name of former University of Kentucky coach Adolph Rupp.
Multiple winners: Ralph Sampson (3); Lew Alcindor, Jerry Lucas, David Thompson and Bill Walton (2).

Year		Year		Year	
1961	Jerry Lucas, Ohio St.	1976	Scott May, Indiana	1991	Shaquille O'Neal, LSU
1962	Jerry Lucas, Ohio St.	1977	Marques Johnson, UCLA	1992	Christian Laettner, Duke
1963	Art Heyman, Duke	1978	Butch Lee, Marquette	1993	Calbert Cheaney, Indiana
1964	Gary Bradds, Ohio St.	1979	Larry Bird, Indiana St.	1994	Glenn Robinson, Purdue
1965	Bill Bradley, Princeton	1980	Mark Aguirre, DePaul	1995	Joe Smith, Maryland
1966	Cazzie Russell, Michigan	1981	Ralph Sampson, Virginia	1996	Marcus Camby, UMass
1967	Lew Alcindor, UCLA	1982	Ralph Sampson, Virginia	1997	Tim Duncan, Wake Forest
1968	Elvin Hayes, Houston	1983	Ralph Sampson, Virginia	1998	Antawn Jamison, N. Carolina
1969	Lew Alcindor, UCLA	1984	Michael Jordan, N. Carolina	1999	Elton Brand, Duke
1970	Pete Maravich, LSU	1985	Patrick Ewing, Georgetown	2000	Kenyon Martin, Cincinnati
1971	Austin Carr, Notre Dame	1986	Walter Berry, St. John's	2001	Shane Battier, Duke
1972	Bill Walton, UCLA	1987	David Robinson, Navy	2002	Jason Williams, Duke
1973	Bill Walton, UCLA	1988	Hersey Hawkins, Bradley	2003	David West, Xavier
1974	David Thompson, N.C. State	1989	Sean Elliott, Arizona		
1975	David Thompson, N.C. State	1990	Lionel Simmons, La Salle		

Naismith Award
Voted on by a panel of coaches, sportswriters and broadcasters and first presented in 1969 by the Atlanta Tip-Off Club in 1969 in the name of the inventor of basketball, Dr. James Naismith.
Multiple winners: Ralph Sampson and Bill Walton (3).

Year		Year		Year	
1969	Lew Alcindor, UCLA	1981	Ralph Sampson, Virginia	1993	Calbert Cheaney, Indiana
1970	Pete Maravich, LSU	1982	Ralph Sampson, Virginia	1994	Glenn Robinson, Purdue
1971	Austin Carr, Notre Dame	1983	Ralph Sampson, Virginia	1995	Joe Smith, Maryland
1972	Bill Walton, UCLA	1984	Michael Jordan, N. Carolina	1996	Marcus Camby, UMass
1973	Bill Walton, UCLA	1985	Patrick Ewing, Georgetown	1997	Tim Duncan, Wake Forest
1974	Bill Walton, UCLA	1986	Johnny Dawkins, Duke	1998	Antawn Jamison, N. Carolina
1975	David Thompson, N.C. State	1987	David Robinson, Navy	1999	Elton Brand, Duke
1976	Scott May, Indiana	1988	Danny Manning, Kansas	2000	Kenyon Martin, Cincinnati
1977	Marques Johnson, UCLA	1989	Danny Ferry, Duke	2001	Shane Battier, Duke
1978	Butch Lee, Marquette	1990	Lionel Simmons, La Salle	2002	Jason Williams, Duke
1979	Larry Bird, Indiana St.	1991	Larry Johnson, UNLV	2003	T.J. Ford, Texas
1980	Mark Aguirre, DePaul	1992	Christian Laettner, Duke		

National Association of Basketball Coaches
Voted on by the National Assn. of Basketball Coaches and presented by the Eastman Kodak Co. from 1975-94.
Multiple winners: Ralph Sampson and Jason Williams (2).

Year		Year		Year	
1975	David Thompson, N.C. State	1985	Patrick Ewing, Georgetown	1995	Shawn Respert, Mich. St.
1976	Scott May, Indiana	1986	Walter Berry, St. John's	1996	Marcus Camby, UMass
1977	Marques Johnson, UCLA	1987	David Robinson, Navy	1997	Tim Duncan, Wake Forest
1978	Phil Ford, North Carolina	1988	Danny Manning, Kansas	1998	Antawn Jamison, N. Carolina
1979	Larry Bird, Indiana St.	1989	Sean Elliott, Arizona	1999	Elton Brand, Duke
1980	Michael Brooks, La Salle	1990	Lionel Simmons, La Salle	2000	Kenyon Martin, Cincinnati
1981	Danny Ainge, BYU	1991	Larry Johnson, UNLV	2001	Jason Williams, Duke
1982	Ralph Sampson, Virginia	1992	Christian Laettner, Duke	2002	Jason Williams, Duke
1983	Ralph Sampson, Virginia	1993	Calbert Cheaney, Indiana		& Drew Gooden, Kansas
1984	Michael Jordan, N. Carolina	1994	Glenn Robinson, Purdue	2003	Nick Collison, Kansas

Wooden Award

Voted on by a panel of coaches, sportswriters and broadcasters and first presented in 1977 by the Los Angeles Athletic Club in the name of former Purdue All-American and UCLA coach John Wooden. Unlike the other five player of the year awards, candidates for the Wooden must have a minimum grade point average of 2.00 (out of 4.00).

Multiple winner: Ralph Sampson (2).

Year	Year	Year
1977 Marques Johnson, UCLA	1986 Walter Berry St. John's	1995 Ed O'Bannon, UCLA
1978 Phil Ford, North Carolina	1987 David Robinson, Navy	1996 Marcus Camby, UMass
1979 Larry Bird, Indiana St.	1988 Danny Manning, Kansas	1997 Tim Duncan, Wake Forest
1980 Darrell Griffith, Louisville	1989 Sean Elliott, Arizona	1998 Antawn Jamison, N. Carolina
1981 Danny Ainge, BYU	1990 Lionel Simmons, La Salle	1999 Elton Brand, Duke
1982 Ralph Sampson, Virginia	1991 Larry Johnson, UNLV	2000 Kenyon Martin, Cincinnati
1983 Ralph Sampson, Virginia	1992 Christian Laettner, Duke	2001 Shane Battier, Duke
1984 Michael Jordan, N. Carolina	1993 Calbert Cheaney, Indiana	2002 Jason Williams, Duke
1985 Chris Mullin, St. John's	1994 Glenn Robinson, Purdue	2003 T.J. Ford, Texas

All-Time Winningest Division I Coaches

Minimum of 10 seasons as Division I head coach; regular season and tournament games included; coaches active during 2002-03 in **bold** type.

Top 30 Winning Percentage

		Yrs	W	L	Pct
1	Clair Bee	21	412	87	.826
2	Adolph Rupp	41	876	190	.822
3	**Roy Williams**	15	417	100	.807
4	John Wooden	29	664	162	.804
5	John Kresse	23	560	143	.797
6	Jerry Tarkanian	31	778	202	.794
7	Dean Smith	36	879	254	.776
8	Harry Fisher	13	147	44	.770
9	Frank Keaney	27	387	117	.768
10	George Keogan	24	385	117	.767
11	Jack Ramsay	11	231	71	.765
12	Vic Bubas	10	213	67	.761
13	Chick Davies	21	314	106	.748
14	Ray Mears	21	399	135	.747
15	**Jim Boeheim**	27	653	226	.743
16	**Lute Olson**	30	690	240	.742
17	**Mike Krzyzewski**	28	663	233	.740
18	Al McGuire	20	405	143	.739
19	Everett Case	18	376	133	.739
20	Phog Allen	48	746	264	.739
21	**Bob Huggins**	22	517	184	.738
22	Walter Meanwell	22	280	101	.735
23	**Rick Pitino**	17	396	144	.733
24	**Rick Majerus**	19	422	154	.733
25	Lew Andreas	25	355	134	.726
26	**Tubby Smith**	12	288	109	.725
27	Lou Carnesecca	24	526	200	.725
28	Fred Schaus	12	251	96	.723
29	**Bob Knight**	37	808	311	.722
30	Cam Henderson	35	630	243	.722

Top 30 Victories

		Yrs	W	L	Pct
1	Dean Smith	36	879	254	.776
2	Adolph Rupp	41	876	190	.822
3	**Jim Phelan**	49	830	524	.613
4	**Bob Knight**	37	808	311	.722
5	**Lefty Driesell**	41	786	394	.666
6	**Lou Henson**	40	779	398	.667
7	Jerry Tarkanian	31	778	202	.794
8	Hank Iba	41	767	338	.694
9	Ed Diddle	42	759	302	.715
10	Phog Allen	48	746	264	.739
11	Norm Stewart	38	731	375	.661
12	Ray Meyer	42	724	354	.672
	Eddie Sutton	33	724	288	.715
14	Don Haskins	38	719	353	.671
15	John Chaney	31	693	269	.720
16	**Lute Olson**	30	690	240	.742
17	Denny Crum	30	675	295	.696
18	John Wooden	29	664	162	.804
19	**Mike Krzyzewski**	28	663	233	.740
20	Ralph Miller	38	657	382	.632
21	Marv Harshman	40	654	449	.593
22	**Jim Boeheim**	27	653	226	.743
23	Gene Bartow	34	647	353	.647
24	**Jim Calhoun**	31	646	296	.686
25	Cam Henderson	35	630	243	.722
26	Norm Sloan	37	624	393	.614
27	**Hugh Durham**	35	604	401	.601
28	Slats Gill	36	599	392	.604
29	Abe Lemons	34	597	344	.634
30	John Thompson	27	596	239	.714

Note: Clarence (Bighouse) Gaines of Division II Winston-Salem St. (1947-93) retired after the 1992-93 season to finish his 47-year career ranked No. 3 on the all-time NCAA list of all coaches regardless of division. His record is 828-446 with a .650 winning percentage.

Where They Coached

Allen–Baker (1906-08), Kansas (1908-09), Haskell (1909), Central Mo. St. (1913-19), Kansas (1920-56); **Andreas**–Syracuse (1925-43; 45-50); **Bartow**–Central Mo. St. (1962-64), Valparaiso (1965-70), Memphis St. (1971-74), Illinois (1975), UCLA (1976-77), UAB (1979-96); **Bee**–Rider (1929-31), LIU-Brooklyn (1932-45, 46-51); **Boeheim**–Syracuse (1977–); **Bubas**–Duke (1960-69); **Calhoun**–Northeastern (1973-86), Connecticut (1987–); **Carnesecca**–St. John's (1966-70, 74-92); **Case**–N.C. State (1947-64); **Chaney**–Cheyney St. (1973-82), Temple (1983–); **Crum**–Louisville (1972-01); **Davies**–Duquesne (1925-43, 47-48); **Diddle**–Western Ky. (1923-64); **Driesell**–Davidson (1961-69), Maryland (1970-86), J. Madison (1989-97), Georgia St. (1997-2003); **Durham**–Florida St. (1967-78), Georgia (1979-95), Jacksonville (1999–); **Fisher**–Columbia (1907-16), Army (1922-23, 25).
Gill–Oregon St. (1929-64); **Harshman**–Pacific Lutheran (1946-58), Wash. St. (1959-71), Washington (1972-85); **Haskins**–UTEP (1962-99); **Henderson**–Muskingum (1920-22), Davis & Elkins (1923-35), Marshall (1936-55); **Henson**–Hardin-Simmons (1963-66), N. Mexico St. (1967-75), Illinois (1976-96), N. Mexico St. (1997–); **Huggins**–Walsh (1981-83), Akron (1985-89), Cincinnati (1990–); **Iba**–NW Missouri St. (1930-33), Colorado (1934), Oklahoma St. (1935-70); **Keaney**–Rhode Island (1921-48); **Keogan**–St. Louis (1916), Allegheny (1919), Valparaiso (1920-21), Notre Dame (1924-43); **Knight**–Army (1966-71), Indiana (1972-00), Texas Tech (2001–); **Kresse**–Charleston (1979-2002); **Krzyzewski**–Army (1976-80), Duke (1981–).

Lemons–Okla. City (1956-73), Pan American (1974-76), Texas (1977-82), Okla. City (1984-90); **Majerus**–Marquette (1984-86), Ball St. (1988-89), Utah (1991–); **McGuire**–Belmont Abbey (1958-64), Marquette (1965-77); **Meanwell**–Wisconsin (1912-17, 21-34), Missouri (1918-20); **Mears**–Wittenberg (1957-62), Tennessee (1963-77); **Meyer**–DePaul (1943-84); **Miller**–Wichita St. (1952-64), Iowa (1965-70), Oregon St. (1971-89); **Olson**–Long Beach St. (1974), Iowa (1975-83), Arizona (1984–); **Phelan**– Mount St. Mary's (1955-2003); **Pitino**–Boston Univ. (1979-83), Providence (1986-87), Kentucky (1989-97), Louisville (2001–).

Ramsay–St. Joseph's-PA (1956-66); **Rupp**–Kentucky (1931-72); **Schaus**–West Va. (1955-60), Purdue (1973-78); **Sloan**–Presbyterian (1952-55), Citadel (1957-60), Florida (1961-66), N.C. State (1967-80), Florida (1981-89); **D. Smith**–North Carolina (1962-97); **T. Smith**–Tulsa (1992-95), Georgia (1996-97), Kentucky (1998–); **Stewart**–No. Iowa (1962-67), Missouri (1968-99); **Sutton**–Creighton (1970-74), Arkansas (1975-85), Kentucky (1986-89), Oklahoma St. (1991–); **Tarkanian**–Long Beach St. (1969-73), UNLV (1974-92), Fresno St. (1995-2002); **Thompson**–Georgetown (1973-99); **Williams**–Kansas (1989-2003), North Carolina (2003–); **Wooden**–Indiana St. (1947-48), UCLA (1949-75).

Most NCAA Tournaments

Through 2003; listed are number of appearances, overall tournament record, times reaching Final Four, and number of NCAA championships. (*) denotes that actual records are different from official NCAA records.

App		W-L	F4	Championships
27	Dean Smith	65-27	11	2 (1982, 93)
25	**Bob Knight**	42-21	5	3 (1976, 81, 87)
24	Lute Olson*	42-24	5	1 (1997)
24	**Eddie Sutton***	33-24	2	None
23	Denny Crum	42-23	6	2 (1980, 86)
22	**Jim Boeheim**	38-21	3	1 (2003)
20	Adolph Rupp	30-18	6	4 (1948-49, 51, 58)
20	John Thompson	34-19	3	1 (1984)
19	**Lou Henson**	19-20	2	None
19	**Mike Krzyzewski**	60-16	9	3 (1991-92, 2001)
18	Lou Carnesecca	17-20	1	None
18	Jerry Tarkanian	38-18	4	1 (1990)
18	**Gene Keady***	19-18	0	None
17	**John Chaney**	23-17	0	None
16	John Wooden	47-10	12	10 (1964-65, 67-73, 75)
16	Norm Stewart*	12-16	0	None
16	Nolan Richardson	26-15	3	1 (1994)
16	Jim Harrick	18-15	1	1 (1995)
16	**Jim Calhoun***	31-15	1	1 (1999)
15	Digger Phelps	17-17	1	None
14	Don Haskins	14-13	1	1 (1966)
14	Guy Lewis	26-18	5	None
14	**Roy Williams**	34-14	4	None

Active Coaches' Victories
Minimum five seasons in Division I.

		Yrs	W	L	Pct
1	Bob Knight, Texas Tech	37	808	311	.722
2	Lou Henson, N. Mexico St.	40	779	398	.667
3	Eddie Sutton, Okla. St.	33	724	288	.723
4	John Chaney, Temple	31	693	269	.720
5	Lute Olson, Arizona	30	690	240	.742
8	Mike Krzyzewski, Duke	28	663	233	.740
9	Jim Boeheim, Syracuse	27	653	226	.743
10	Jim Calhoun, UConn	31	646	296	.686
11	Hugh Durham, Jacksonville	35	604	401	.601
12	Billy Tubbs, Lamar	28	595	297	.667
13	Tom Davis, Drake	28	543	290	.652
14	Gene Keady, Purdue	25	526	254	.674
15	Cliff Ellis, Auburn	28	520	323	.617
16	Mike Montgomery, Stanford	25	517	242	.681
	Bob Huggins, Cincinnati	22	517	184	.738
18	Don DeVoe, Navy	30	507	366	.581
19	Gary Williams, Maryland	25	502	281	.641
20	Ben Braun, California	26	473	314	.601
21	Pat Douglass, UC-Irvine	22	471	195	.707
22	Dick Bennett, Washington St.	21	453	258	.637
23	Rick Majerus, Utah	19	422	154	.733
24	Roy Williams, North Carolina	15	417	100	.807
25	Pat Kennedy, Montana	23	406	293	.580
26	Rick Pitino, Louisville	17	396	144	.733
27	Kelvin Sampson, Oklahoma	20	391	228	.632
28	Danny Nee, Duquesne	23	386	319	.548
	John Beilein, West Virginia	21	386	230	.627
30	Mike Vining, Louisiana-Monroe	22	381	265	.590

Annual Awards
UPI picked the first national Division I Coach of the Year in 1955. Since then, the U.S. Basketball Writers Assn. (1959), AP (1967), the National Assn. of Basketball Coaches (1969), and the Atlanta Tip-Off Club (1987) have joined in. Since 1987, the first year all five awards were given out, no coach has won all of them in the same season.

United Press International
Voted on by a panel of UPI college basketball writers and first presented in 1955.
Multiple winners: John Wooden (6); Bob Knight, Ray Meyer, Adolph Rupp, Norm Stewart, Fred Taylor and Phil Woolpert (2).

Year
1955 Phil Woolpert, San Francisco
1956 Phil Woolpert, San Francisco
1957 Frank McGuire, North Carolina
1958 Tex Winter, Kansas St.
1959 Adolph Rupp, Kentucky
1960 Pete Newell, California
1961 Fred Taylor, Ohio St.
1962 Fred Taylor, Ohio St.
1963 Ed Jucker, Cincinnati
1964 John Wooden, UCLA
1965 Dave Strack, Michigan
1966 Adolph Rupp, Kentucky
1967 John Wooden, UCLA
1968 Guy Lewis, Houston
1969 John Wooden, UCLA

Year
1970 John Wooden, UCLA
1971 Al McGuire, Marquette
1972 John Wooden, UCLA
1973 John Wooden, UCLA
1974 Digger Phelps, Notre Dame
1975 Bob Knight, Indiana
1976 Tom Young, Rutgers
1977 Bob Gaillard, San Francisco
1978 Eddie Sutton, Arkansas
1979 Bill Hodges, Indiana St.
1980 Ray Meyer, DePaul
1981 Ralph Miller, Oregon St.
1982 Norm Stewart, Missouri
1983 Jerry Tarkanian, UNLV
1984 Ray Meyer, DePaul

Year
1985 Lou Carnesecca, St. John's
1986 Mike Krzyzewski, Duke
1987 John Thompson, Georgetown
1988 John Chaney, Temple
1989 Bob Knight, Indiana
1990 Jim Calhoun, Connecticut
1991 Rick Majerus, Utah
1992 Perry Clark, Tulane
1993 Eddie Fogler, Vanderbilt
1994 Norm Stewart, Missouri
1995 Leonard Hamilton, Miami-FL
1996 Gene Keady, Purdue
1997 award discontinued

Annual Awards (Cont.)
U.S. Basketball Writers Association
Voted on by the USBWA and first presented in 1959.

Multiple winners: John Wooden (5); Bob Knight (3); Lou Carnesecca, John Chaney, Ray Meyer and Fred Taylor (2).

Year	Year	Year
1959 Eddie Hickey, Marquette	1974 Norm Sloan, N.C. State	1989 Bob Knight, Indiana
1960 Pete Newell, California	1975 Bob Knight, Indiana	1990 Roy Williams, Kansas
1961 Fred Taylor, Ohio St.	1976 Bob Knight, Indiana	1991 Randy Ayers, Ohio St.
1962 Fred Taylor, Ohio St.	1977 Eddie Sutton, Arkansas	1992 Perry Clark, Tulane
1963 Ed Jucker, Cincinnati	1978 Ray Meyer, DePaul	1993 Eddie Fogler, Vanderbilt
1964 John Wooden, UCLA	1979 Dean Smith, North Carolina	1994 Charlie Spoonhour, St. Louis
1965 Butch van Breda Kolff, Princeton	1980 Ray Meyer, DePaul	1995 Kelvin Sampson, Oklahoma
1966 Adolph Rupp, Kentucky	1981 Ralph Miller, Oregon St.	1996 Gene Keady, Purdue
1967 John Wooden, UCLA	1982 John Thompson, Georgetown	1997 Clem Haskins, Minnesota
1968 Guy Lewis, Houston	1983 Lou Carnesecca, St. John's	1998 Tom Izzo, Michigan St.
1969 Maury John, Drake	1984 Gene Keady, Purdue	1999 Cliff Ellis, Auburn
1970 John Wooden, UCLA	1985 Lou Carnesecca, St. John's	2000 Larry Eustachy, Iowa St.
1971 Al McGuire, Marquette	1986 Dick Versace, Bradley	2001 Al Skinner, Boston College
1972 John Wooden, UCLA	1987 John Chaney, Temple	2002 Ben Howland, Pittsburgh
1973 John Wooden, UCLA	1988 John Chaney, Temple	2003 Tubby Smith, Kentucky

Associated Press
Voted on by AP sportswriters and broadcasters and first presented in 1967.

Multiple winners: John Wooden (5); Bob Knight (3); Guy Lewis, Ray Meyer, Ralph Miller and Eddie Sutton (2).

Year	Year	Year
1967 John Wooden, UCLA	1980 Ray Meyer, DePaul	1993 Eddie Fogler, Vanderbilt
1968 Guy Lewis, Houston	1981 Ralph Miller, Oregon St.	1994 Norm Stewart, Missouri
1969 John Wooden, UCLA	1982 Ralph Miller, Oregon St.	1995 Kelvin Sampson, Oklahoma
1970 John Wooden, UCLA	1983 Guy Lewis, Houston	1996 Gene Keady, Purdue
1971 Al McGuire, Marquette	1984 Ray Meyer, DePaul	1997 Clem Haskins, Minnesota
1972 John Wooden, UCLA	1985 Bill Frieder, Michigan	1998 Tom Izzo, Michigan St.
1973 John Wooden, UCLA	1986 Eddie Sutton, Kentucky	1999 Cliff Ellis, Auburn
1974 Norm Sloan, N.C. State	1987 Tom Davis, Iowa	2000 Larry Eustachy, Iowa St.
1975 Bob Knight, Indiana	1988 John Chaney, Temple	2001 Matt Doherty, North Carolina
1976 Bob Knight, Indiana	1989 Bob Knight, Indiana	2002 Ben Howland, Pittsburgh
1977 Bob Gaillard, San Francisco	1990 Jim Calhoun, Connecticut	2003 Tubby Smith, Kentucky
1978 Eddie Sutton, Arkansas	1991 Randy Ayers, Ohio St.	
1979 Bill Hodges, Indiana St.	1992 Roy Williams, Kansas	

National Association of Basketball Coaches
Voted on by NABC membership and first presented in 1969.

Multiple winners: John Wooden (3); Gene Keady and Mike Krzyzewski (2).

Year	Year	Year
1969 John Wooden, UCLA	1981 Ralph Miller, Oregon St.	1993 Eddie Fogler, Vanderbilt
1970 John Wooden, UCLA	& Jack Hartman, Kansas St.	1994 Nolan Richardson, Arkansas
1971 Jack Kraft, Villanova	1982 Don Monson, Idaho	& Gene Keady, Purdue
1972 John Wooden, UCLA	1983 Lou Carnesecca, St. John's	1995 Jim Harrick, UCLA
1973 Gene Bartow, Memphis St.	1984 Marv Harshman, Washington	1996 John Calipari, UMass
1974 Al McGuire, Marquette	1985 John Thompson, Georgetown	1997 Clem Haskins, Minnesota
1975 Bob Knight, Indiana	1986 Eddie Sutton, Kentucky	1998 Bill Guthridge, N. Carolina
1976 Johnny Orr, Michigan	1987 Rick Pitino, Providence	1999 Mike Krzyzewski, Duke
1977 Dean Smith, North Carolina	1988 John Chaney, Temple	& Jim O'Brien, Ohio St.
1978 Bill Foster, Duke	1989 P.J. Carlesimo, Seton Hall	2000 Gene Keady, Purdue
& Abe Lemons, Texas	1990 Jud Heathcote, Michigan St.	2001 Tom Izzo, Michigan St.
1979 Ray Meyer, DePaul	1991 Mike Krzyzewski, Duke	2002 Kelvin Sampson, Oklahoma
1980 Lute Olson, Iowa	1992 George Raveling, USC	2003 Tubby Smith, Kentucky

Naismith Award
Voted on by a panel of coaches, sportswriters and broadcasters and first presented by the Atlanta Tip-Off Club in 1987 in the name of the inventor of basketball, Dr. James Naismith.

Multiple winner: Mike Krzyzewski (3).

Year	Year	Year
1987 Bob Knight, Indiana	1993 Dean Smith, North Carolina	1999 Mike Krzyzewski, Duke
1988 Larry Brown, Kansas	1994 Nolan Richardson, Arkansas	2000 Mike Montgomery, Stanford
1989 Mike Krzyzewski, Duke	1995 Jim Harrick, UCLA	2001 Rod Barnes, Mississippi
1990 Bobby Cremins, Georgia Tech	1996 John Calipari, UMass	2002 Ben Howland, Pittsburgh
1991 Randy Ayers, Ohio St.	1997 Roy Williams, Kansas	2003 Tubby Smith, Kentucky
1992 Mike Krzyzewski, Duke	1998 Bill Guthridge, N. Carolina	

Player of the Year and NBA MVP

College Players of the Year who have gone on to win the NBA's Most Valuable Player award:

Bill Russell COLLEGE–San Francisco (1956); PROS–Boston Celtics (1958, 1961, 1962, 1963 and 1965).

Oscar Robertson COLLEGE–Cincinnati (1958, 1959 and 1960); PROS–Cincinnati Royals (1964).

Kareem Abdul-Jabbar COLLEGE–UCLA (1967 and 1969); PROS–Milwaukee Bucks (1971, 1972 and 1974) and LA Lakers (1976, 1977 and 1980).

Bill Walton COLLEGE–UCLA (1972, 1973 and 1974); PROS–Portland Trail Blazers (1978).

Larry Bird COLLEGE–Indiana St. (1979); PROS–Boston Celtics (1984, 1985, and 1986).

Michael Jordan COLLEGE–North Carolina (1984); PROS–Chicago Bulls (1988, 1991, 1992, 1996 and 1998).

David Robinson COLLEGE–Navy (1987); PROS–San Antonio Spurs (1995).

Shaquille O'Neal COLLEGE–LSU (1991); PROS–LA Lakers (2000).

Tim Duncan COLLEGE–Wake Forest (1997); PROS–San Antonio Spurs (2002, 2003).

Other Men's Champions

The NCAA has sanctioned national championship tournaments for Division II since 1957 and Division III since 1975. The NAIA sanctioned a single tournament from 1937-91, then split into two divisions in 1992.

NCAA Div. II Finals

Multiple winners: Kentucky Wesleyan (8); Evansville (5); CS-Bakersfield (3); Metropolitan State, North Alabama and Virginia Union (2).

Year	Winner	Score	Loser	Year	Winner	Score	Loser
1957	Wheaton, IL	89-65	Ky. Wesleyan	1981	Florida Southern	73-68	Mt. St. Mary's, MD
1958	South Dakota	75-53	St. Michael's, VT	1982	Dist. of Columbia	73-63	Florida Southern
1959	Evansville, IN	83-67	SW Missouri St.	1983	Wright St., OH	92-73	Dist. of Columbia
1960	Evansville	90-69	Chapman, CA	1984	Central Mo. St.	81-77	St. Augustine's, NC
1961	Wittenberg, OH	42-38	SE Missouri St.	1985	Jacksonville St.	74-73	South Dakota St.
1962	Mt. St. Mary's, MD	58-57*	CS-Sacramento	1986	Sacred Heart, CT	93-87	SE Missouri St.
1963	South Dakota St.	42-40	Wittenberg, OH	1987	Ky. Wesleyan	92-74	Gannon, PA
1964	Evansville	72-59	Akron, OH	1988	Lowell, MA	75-72	AK-Anchorage
1965	Evansville	85-82*	Southern Illinois	1989	N.C. Central	73-46	SE Missouri St.
1966	Ky. Wesleyan	54-51	Southern Illinois	1990	Ky. Wesleyan	93-79	CS-Bakersfield
1967	Winston-Salem, NC	77-74	SW Missouri St.	1991	North Alabama	79-72	Bridgeport, CT
1968	Ky. Wesleyan	63-52	Indiana St.	1992	Virginia Union	100-75	Bridgeport
1969	Ky. Wesleyan	75-71	SW Missouri St.	1993	CS-Bakersfield	85-72	Troy St., AL
1970	Phila. Textile	76-65	Tennessee St.	1994	CS-Bakersfield	92-86	Southern Ind.
1971	Evansville	97-82	Old Dominion, VA	1995	Southern Indiana	71-63	UC-Riverside
1972	Roanoke, VA	84-72	Akron, OH	1996	Fort Hays St.	70-63	N. Kentucky
1973	Ky. Wesleyan	78-76*	Tennessee St.	1997	CS-Bakersfield	57-56	N. Kentucky
1974	Morgan St., MD	67-52	SW Missouri St.	1998	UC-Davis	83-77	Ky. Wesleyan
1975	Old Dominion	76-74	New Orleans	1999	Ky. Wesleyan	75-60	Metropolitan St.
1976	Puget Sound, WA	83-74	Tennessee-Chatt.	2000	Metropolitan St.	97-79	Ky. Wesleyan
1977	Tennessee-Chatt.	71-62	Randolph-Macon	2001	Ky. Wesleyan	72-63	Washburn, KS
1978	Cheyney, PA	47-40	WI-Green Bay	2002	Metropolitan St.	80-72	Ky. Wesleyan
1979	North Alabama	64-50	WI-Green Bay	2003	Northeastern St., OK	75-64	Ky. Wesleyan
1980	Virginia Union	80-74	New York Tech		*Overtime		

NCAA Div. III Finals

Multiple winners: North Park (5); WI-Platteville (4); Calvin, Potsdam St., Scranton and WI-Whitewater (2).

Year	Winner	Score	Loser	Year	Winner	Score	Loser
1975	LeMoyne-Owen, TN	57-54	Glassboro St., NJ	1991	WI-Platteville	81-74	Franklin Marshall
1976	Scranton, PA	60-57	Wittenberg, OH	1992	Calvin, MI	62-49	Rochester, NY
1977	Wittenberg, OH	79-66	Oneonta St., NY	1993	Ohio Northern	71-68	Augustana, IL
1978	North Park, IL	69-57	Widener, PA	1994	Lebanon Valley, PA	66-59*	NYU
1979	North Park, IL	66-62	Potsdam St., NY	1995	WI-Platteville	69-55	Manchester, IN
1980	North Park, IL	83-76	Upsala, NJ	1996	Rowan, NJ	100-93	Hope, MI
1981	Potsdam St., NY	67-65*	Augustana, IL	1997	Illinois Wesleyan	89-86	Neb-Wesleyan
1982	Wabash, IN	83-62	Potsdam St., NY	1998	WI-Platteville	69-56	Hope, MI
1983	Scranton, PA	64-63	Wittenberg, OH	1999	WI-Platteville	76-75**	Hampden-Sydney
1984	WI-Whitewater	103-86	Clark, MA	2000	Calvin, MI	79-74	WI-Eau Claire
1985	North Park, IL	72-71	Potsdam St., NY	2001	Catholic, DC	76-62	Wm. Paterson
1986	Potsdam St., NY	76-73	LeMoyne-Owen, TN	2002	Otterbein	102-83	Elizabethtown
1987	North Park, IL	106-100	Clark, MA	2003	Williams, MA	67-65	Gustavus Adolphus
1988	Ohio Wesleyan	92-70	Scranton, PA		*Overtime		
1989	WI-Whitewater	94-86	Trenton St., NJ		**Double overtime		
1990	Rochester, NY	43-42	DePauw, IN				

COLLEGE BASKETBALL

NAIA Finals, 1937-91

Multiple winners: Grand Canyon, Hamline, Kentucky St. and Tennessee St. (3); Central Missouri, Central St., Fort Hays St. and SW Missouri St. (2).

Year	Winner	Score	Loser
1937	Central Missouri	35-24	Morningside, IA
1938	Central Missouri	45-30	Roanoke, VA
1939	Southwestern, KS	32-31	San Diego St.
1940	Tarkio, MO	52-31	San Diego St.
1941	San Diego St.	36-32	Murray St., KY
1942	Hamline, MN	33-31	SE Oklahoma
1943	SE Missouri St.	34-32	NW Missouri St.
1944	Not held		
1945	Loyola-LA	49-36	Pepperdine, CA
1946	Southern Illinois	49-40	Indiana St.
1947	Marshall, WV	73-59	Mankato St., MN
1948	Louisville, KY	82-70	Indiana St.
1949	Hamline, MN	57-46	Regis, CO
1950	Indiana St.	61-47	East Central, OK
1951	Hamline, MN	69-61	Millikin, IL
1952	SW Missouri St.	73-64	Murray St., KY
1953	SW Missouri St.	79-71	Hamline, MN
1954	St.Benedict's, KS	62-56	Western Illinois
1955	East Texas St.	71-54	SE Oklahoma
1956	McNeese St., LA	60-55	Texas Southern
1957	Tennessee St.	92-73	SE Oklahoma
1958	Tennessee St.	85-73	Western Illinois
1959	Tennessee St.	97-87	Pacific-Luth., WA
1960	SW Texas St.	66-44	Westminster, PA
1961	Grambling, LA	95-75	Georgetown, KY
1962	Prairie View, TX	62-53	Westminster, PA
1963	Pan American, TX	73-62	Western Carolina
1964	Rockhurst, MO	66-56	Pan American, TX
1965	Central St., OH	85-51	Oklahoma Baptist
1966	Oklahoma Baptist	88-59	Georgia Southern
1967	St.Benedict's, KS	71-65	Oklahoma Baptist
1968	Central St., OH	51-48	Fairmont St., WV
1969	Eastern N. Mex	99-76	MD-Eastern Shore
1970	Kentucky St.	79-71	Central Wash.
1971	Kentucky St.	102-82	Eastern Michigan
1972	Kentucky St.	71-62	WI-Eau Claire
1973	Guilford, NC	99-96	MD-Eastern Shore
1974	West Georgia	97-79	Alcorn St., MS

Year	Winner	Score	Loser
1975	Grand Canyon, AZ	65-54	M'western St., TX
1976	Coppin St., MD	96-91	Henderson St., AR
1977	Texas Southern	71-44	Campbell, NC
1978	Grand Canyon	79-75	Kearney St., NE
1979	Drury, MO	60-54	Henderson St., AR
1980	Cameron, OK	84-77	Alabama St.
1981	Beth. Nazarene, OK	86-85*	AL-Huntsville
1982	SC-Spartanburg	51-38	Biola, CA
1983	Charleston, SC	57-53	WV-Wesleyan
1984	Fort Hays St., KS	48-46*	WI-Stevens Pt.
1985	Fort Hays St.	82-80*	Wayland Bapt., TX
1986	David Lipscomb, TN	67-54	AR-Monticello
1987	Washburn, KS	79-77	West Virginia St.
1988	Grand Canyon	88-86*	Auburn-Montg, AL
1989	St.Mary's, TX	61-58	East Central, OK
1990	Birm-Southern, AL	88-80	WI-Eau Claire
1991	Oklahoma City	77-74	Central Arkansas
*Overtime

NAIA Div. I Finals
NAIA split tournament into two divisions in 1992.
Multiple winners: Life, GA and Oklahoma City (3).

Year	Winner	Score	Loser
1992	Oklahoma City	82-73*	Central Arkansas
1993	Hawaii Pacific	88-83	Okla. Baptist
1994	Oklahoma City	99-81	Life, GA
1995	Birm-Southern	92-76	Pfeiffer, NC
1996	Oklahoma City	86-80	Georgetown, KY
1997	Life, GA	73-64	Okla. Baptist
1998	Georgetown, KY	83-69	So. Nazarene
1999	Life, GA	63-60	Mobile, AL
2000	Life, GA	61-59	Georgetown, KY
2001	Faulkner, AL	63-59	Science & Arts, OK
2002	Science & Arts, OK	96-79	Okla. Baptist
2003	Concordia, CA	88-84*	Mountain St., WV
*Overtime

NAIA Div. II Finals
NAIA split tournament into two divisions in 1992.
Multiple winners: Bethel, IN (3), Northwestern, IA (2).

Year	Winner	Score	Loser
1992	Grace, IN	85-79*	Northwestern, IA
1993	Williamette, OR	63-56	Northern St., SD
1994	Eureka, IL	98-95*	Northern St.
1995	Bethel, IN	103-95*	NW Nazarene, ID
1996	Albertson, ID	81-72*	Whitworth, WA
1997	Bethel, IN	95-94	Siena Heights, MI
1998	Bethel, IN	89-87	Oregon Tech

Year	Winner	Score	Loser
1999	Cornerstone, MI	113-109	Bethel
2000	Embry-Riddle, FL	75-63	Ozarks, MO
2001	Northwestern, IA	82-78	Mid. Am. Nazarene, KS
2002	Evangel, MO	84-61	Robert Morris, IL
2003	Northwestern, IA	77-57	Bethany, KS
*Overtime

WOMEN

NCAA Final Four
Replaced the Association of Intercollegiate Athletics for Women (AIAW) tournament in 1982 as the official playoff for the national championship.
Multiple winners: Tennessee (6); Connecticut (4); Louisiana Tech, Stanford and USC.(2)

Year	Champion	Head Coach	Score	Runner-up		Third Place
1982	Louisiana Tech	Sonya Hogg	76-62	Cheyney	Maryland	Tennessee
1983	USC	Linda Sharp	69-67	Louisiana Tech	Georgia	Old Dominion
1984	USC	Linda Sharp	72-61	Tennessee	Cheyney	Louisiana Tech
1985	Old Dominion	Marianne Stanley	70-65	Georgia	NE Louisiana	Western Ky.
1986	Texas	Jody Conradt	97-81	USC	Tennessee	Western Ky.
1987	Tennessee	Pat Summitt	67-44	Louisiana Tech	Long Beach St.	Texas
1988	Louisiana Tech	Leon Barmore	56-54	Auburn	Long Beach St.	Tennessee
1989	Tennessee	Pat Summitt	76-60	Auburn	Louisiana Tech	Maryland
1990	Stanford	Tara VanDerveer	88-81	Auburn	Louisiana Tech	Virginia
1991	Tennessee	Pat Summitt	70-67 (OT)	Virginia	Connecticut	Stanford

Year	Champion	Head Coach	Score	Runner-up	—Third Place—	
1992	Stanford	Tara VanDerveer	78-62	Western Kentucky	SW Missouri St.	Virginia
1993	Texas Tech	Marsha Sharp	84-82	Ohio St.	Iowa	Vanderbilt
1994	N. Carolina	Sylvia Hatchell	60-59	Louisiana Tech	Alabama	Purdue
1995	Connecticut	Geno Auriemma	70-64	Tennessee	Georgia	Stanford
1996	Tennessee	Pat Summitt	83-65	Georgia	Connecticut	Stanford
1997	Tennessee	Pat Summitt	68-59	Old Dominion	Stanford	Notre Dame
1998	Tennessee	Pat Summitt	93-75	Louisiana Tech	Arkansas	N.C. State
1999	Purdue	Carolyn Peck	62-45	Duke	Louisiana Tech	Georgia
2000	Connecticut	Geno Auriemma	71-52	Tennessee	Penn St.	Rutgers
2001	Notre Dame	Muffet McGraw	68-66	Purdue	Connecticut	SW Missouri St.
2002	Connecticut	Geno Auriemma	82-70	Oklahoma	Tennessee	Duke
2003	Connecticut	Geno Auriemma	73-68	Tennessee	Texas	Duke

Final Four sites: 1982 (Norfolk, Va.), **1983** (Norfolk, Va.), **1984** (Los Angeles), **1985** (Austin), **1986** (Lexington), **1987** (Austin), **1988** (Tacoma), **1989** (Tacoma), **1990** (Knoxville), **1991** (New Orleans), **1992** (Los Angeles), **1993** (Atlanta), **1994** (Richmond), **1995** (Minneapolis), **1996** (Charlotte), **1997** (Cincinnati), **1998** (Kansas City), **1999** (San Jose), **2000** (Philadelphia), **2001** (St. Louis), **2002** (San Antonio), **2003** (Atlanta).

Most Outstanding Player

A Most Outstanding Player has been selected every year of the NCAA tournament. Winner who did not play for the tournament champion is listed in **bold,** type.
   Multiple winners: Chamique Holdsclaw and Cheryl Miller (2).

Year	Year	Year
1982 Janice Lawrence, La. Tech	1990 Jennifer Azzi, Stanford	1998 Chamique Holdsclaw, Tenn.
1983 Cheryl Miller, USC	1991 **Dawn Staley**, Virginia	1999 Ukari Figgs, Purdue
1984 Cheryl Miller, USC	1992 Molly Goodenbour, Stanford	2000 Shea Ralph, Connecticut
1985 Tracy Claxton, Old Dominion	1993 Sheryl Swoopes, Texas Tech	2001 Ruth Riley, Notre Dame
1986 Clarissa Davis, Texas	1994 Charlotte Smith, N. Carolina	2002 Swin Cash, Connecticut
1987 Tonya Edwards, Tennessee	1995 Rebecca Lobo, Connecticut	2003 Diana Taurasi, Connecticut
1988 Erica Westbrooks, La. Tech	1996 Michelle Marciniak, Tennessee	
1989 Bridgette Gordon, Tennessee	1997 Chamique Holdsclaw, Tenn.	

All-Time NCAA Division I Tournament Leaders

Through 2002-03; minimum of six games; **Last** column indicates final year played.

CAREER

Scoring

	Total Points	Yrs	Last	Pts	Avg
1	Chamique Holdsclaw, Tennessee	4	1999	**479**	21.8
2	Bridgette Gordon, Tenn	4	1989	**388**	21.6
3	Cheryl Miller, USC	4	1986	**333**	20.8
4	Janice Lawrence, La. Tech	3	1984	**312**	22.3
5	**Diana Taurasi**, Connecticut	3	active	**310**	18.2
6	Penny Toler, Long Beach St	4	1989	**291**	22.4
7	Ruth Riley, Notre Dame	4	2001	**274**	19.7
8	Dawn Staley, Virginia	4	1992	**274**	18.3
9	Tamika Catchings, Tennessee	3	2000	**269**	16.8
10	Cindy Brown, Long Beach St	4	1987	**263**	21.9
	Venus Lacy, La. Tech	3	1990	**263**	18.8
12	Clarissa Davis, Texas	3	1989	**261**	21.8
13	Sue Bird, Connecticut	3	2002	**260**	15.3
14	Janet Harris, Georgia	4	1985	**254**	19.5
15	Teresa Edwards, Georgia	4	1986	**249**	17.8
	Val Whiting, Stanford	4	1993	**249**	15.6

Rebounds

	Total Rebounds	Yrs	Last	No	Avg
1	Chamique Holdsclaw, Tennessee	4	1999	**196**	8.9
2	Cheryl Miller, USC	4	1986	**170**	10.6
3	Sheila Frost, Tennessee	4	1989	**162**	9.0
4	Val Whiting, Stanford	4	1993	**161**	10.1
5	Venus Lacy, La. Tech	3	1990	**148**	10.6
6	Bridgette Gordon, Tennessee	4	1989	**142**	7.9
	Tamika Catchings, Tennessee	3	2000	**142**	7.9
8	Kirsten Cummings, Long Beach St.	4	1985	**136**	10.5
9	Swin Cash, Connecticut	3	2002	**133**	6.7
10	Nora Lewis, La. Tech	3	1989	**130**	9.3
11	Pam McGee, USC	3	1984	**127**	9.8
12	Daedra Charles, Tennessee	3	1991	**125**	9.6
13	Paula McGee, USC	3	1984	**125**	9.6
14	Charlotte Smith, UNC	4	1995	**125**	10.4

SINGLE GAME

Scoring

		Year	Pts
1	Lorri Bauman, Drake vs Maryland	1982	50
2	Sheryl Swoopes, Texas Tech vs Ohio St	1993	47
3	Barbara Kennedy, Clemson vs Penn St	1982	43
4	Jackie Stiles, SW Mo. St. vs. Duke	2001	41
5	LaTaunya Pollard, L. Beach St. vs Howard	1982	40
	Cindy Brown, L. Beach St. vs Ohio St	1987	40
	Tamika Whitmore, Memphis vs. YSU	1998	40
	Tara Mitchem, SW Mo. St. vs. Toledo	2001	40

Rebounds

		Year	No
1	Cheryl Taylor, Tenn. Tech vs Georgia	1985	23
	Charlotte Smith, N. Car. vs La. Tech	1994	23
3	Daedra Charles, Tenn. vs SW Missouri	1991	22
4	Cherie Nelson, USC vs Western Ky	1987	21
5	Alison Lang, Oregon vs Missouri	1982	20
	Shelda Arceneaux, S.D. St. vs L. Beach St.	1984	20
	Tracy Claxton, ODU vs Georgia	1985	20
	Brigette Combs, West. Ky. vs West Va	1989	20
	Tandreia Green, West. Ky. vs West Va	1989	20

Associated Press Final Top 10 Polls

The Associated Press weekly women's college basketball poll was begun by Mel Greenberg of *The Philadelphia Inquirer* during the 1976-77 season. Although the poll was started as a Top 20 in 1977 and was expanded to a Top 25 in 1990, only the Top 10 from each poll are listed below due to space constraints. The Association of Intercollegiate Athletics for Women (AIAW) Tournament determined the Division I national champion from 1972-81. The NCAA began its women's Division I tournament in 1982. The final AP Polls were taken before the NCAA tournament. Eventual national champions are in **bold** type.

1977
1 **Delta St.**
2 Immaculata
3 St. Joseph's-PA
4 CS-Fullerton
5 Tennessee
6 Tennessee Tech
7 Wayland Baptist
8 Montclair St.
9 S.F. Austin St.
10 N.C. State

1978
1 Tennessee
2 Wayland Baptist
3 N.C. State
4 Montclair St.
5 **UCLA**
6 Maryland
7 Queens-NY
8 Valdosta St.
9 Delta St.
10 LSU

1979
1 **Old Dominion**
2 Louisiana Tech
3 Tennessee
4 Texas
5 S.F. Austin St.
6 UCLA
7 Rutgers
8 Maryland
9 Cheyney
10 Wayland Baptist

1980
1 **Old Dominion**
2 Tennessee
3 Louisiana Tech
4 South Carolina
5 S.F. Austin St.
6 Maryland
7 Texas
8 Rutgers
9 Long Beach St.
10 N.C. State

1981
1 **Louisiana Tech**
2 Tennessee
3 Old Dominion
4 USC
5 Cheyney
6 Long Beach St.
7 UCLA
8 Maryland
9 Rutgers
10 Kansas

1982
1 **Louisiana Tech**
2 Cheyney
3 Maryland
4 Tennessee
5 Texas
6 USC
7 Old Dominion
8 Rutgers
9 Long Beach St.
10 Penn St.

1983
1 **USC**
2 Louisiana Tech
3 Texas
4 Old Dominion
5 Cheyney
6 Long Beach St.
7 Maryland
8 Penn St.
9 Georgia
10 Tennessee

1984
1 Texas
2 Louisiana Tech
3 Georgia
4 Old Dominion
5 **USC**
6 Long Beach St.
7 Kansas St.
8 LSU
9 Cheyney
10 Mississippi

1985
1 Texas
2 NE Louisiana
3 Long Beach St.
4 Louisiana Tech
5 **Old Dominion**
6 Mississippi
7 Ohio St.
8 Georgia
9 Penn St.
10 Auburn

1986
1 **Texas**
2 Georgia
3 USC
4 Louisiana Tech
5 Western Ky.
6 Virginia
7 Auburn
8 Long Beach St.
9 LSU
10 Rutgers

1987
1 Texas
2 Auburn
3 Louisiana Tech
4 Long Beach St.
5 Rutgers
6 Georgia
7 **Tennessee**
8 Mississippi
9 Iowa
10 Ohio St.

1988
1 Tennessee
2 Iowa
3 Auburn
4 Texas
5 **Louisiana Tech**
6 Ohio St.
7 Long Beach St.
8 Rutgers
9 Maryland
10 Virginia

1989
1 **Tennessee**
2 Auburn
3 Louisiana Tech
4 Stanford
5 Maryland
6 Texas
7 Long Beach St.
8 Iowa
9 Colorado
10 Georgia

1990
1 Louisiana Tech
2 **Stanford**
3 Washington
4 Tennessee
5 UNLV
6 S.F. Austin St.
7 Georgia
8 Texas
9 Auburn
10 Iowa

1991
1 Penn St.
2 Virginia
3 Georgia
4 **Tennessee**
5 Purdue
6 Auburn
7 N.C. State
8 LSU
9 Arkansas
10 Western Ky.

1992
1 Virginia
2 Tennessee
3 **Stanford**
4 S.F. Austin St.
5 Mississippi
6 Miami-FL
7 Iowa
8 Maryland
9 Penn St.
10 SW Missouri St.

1993
1 Vanderbilt
2 Tennessee
3 Ohio St.
4 Iowa
5 **Texas Tech**
6 Stanford
7 Auburn
8 Penn St.
9 Virginia
10 Colorado

1994
1 Tennessee
2 Penn St.
3 Connecticut
4 **North Carolina**
5 Colorado
6 Louisiana Tech
7 USC
8 Purdue
9 Texas Tech
10 Virginia

1995
1 **Connecticut**
2 Colorado
3 Tennessee
4 Stanford
5 Texas Tech
6 Vanderbilt
7 Penn St.
8 Louisiana Tech
9 Western Ky.
10 Virginia

1996
1 Louisiana Tech
2 Connecticut
3 Stanford
4 **Tennessee**
5 Georgia
6 Old Dominion
7 Iowa
8 Penn St.
9 Texas Tech
10 Alabama

1997
1 Connecticut
2 Old Dominion
3 Stanford
4 North Carolina
5 Louisiana Tech
6 Georgia
7 Florida
8 Alabama
9 LSU
10 **Tennessee**

1998
1 **Tennessee**
2 Old Dominion
3 Connecticut
4 Louisiana Tech
5 Stanford
6 Texas Tech
7 North Carolina
8 Duke
9 Arizona
10 N.C. State

1999
1 **Purdue**
2 Tennessee
3 Louisiana Tech
4 Colorado St.
5 Old Dominion
6 Connecticut
7 Rutgers
8 Notre Dame
9 Texas Tech
10 Duke

2000
1 **Connecticut**
2 Tennessee
3 Louisiana Tech
4 Georgia
5 Notre Dame
6 Penn St.
7 Iowa St.
8 Rutgers
9 UC-Santa Barbara
10 Duke

2001
1 Connecticut
2 **Notre Dame**
3 Tennessee
4 Georgia
5 Duke
6 Louisiana Tech
7 Oklahoma
8 Iowa St.
9 Purdue
10 Vanderbilt

2002
1 **Connecticut**
2 Oklahoma
3 Duke
4 Vanderbilt
5 Stanford
6 Tennessee
7 Baylor
8 Louisiana Tech
9 Purdue
10 Iowa St.

2003
1 **Connecticut**
2 Duke
3 LSU
4 Tennessee
5 Texas
6 Louisiana Tech
7 Texas Tech
8 Kansas St.
9 Stanford
10 Purdue

All-Time AP Top 10

The composite AP Top 10 from the 1976-77 season through 2002-03, based on the final regular season rankings of each year. Team points are based on 10 points for all 1st place finishes, 9 for each 2nd, etc. Also listed are the number of times ranked No. 1 by AP going into the tournaments, and times ranked in the pre-tournament Top 10.

		Pts	No.1	Top 10			Pts	No.1	Top 10
1	Tennessee	189	5	25	6	Georgia	72	0	13
2	Louisiana Tech	169	4	23	7	Stanford	66	0	10
3	Connecticut	90	6	10	8	Penn St.	46	1	10
4	Texas	86	4	18	9	Long Beach St.	45	0	10
5	Old Dominion	81	2	11	10	Auburn	42	0	8

All-Time Winningest Division I Teams

Division I schools with best winning percentages (with a minimum of 350 victories) and most victories through 2002-03 (including postseason tournaments). Although official NCAA women's basketball records didn't begin until the 1981-82 season, results from previous seasons are included below.

Top 10 Winning Percentage

		Yrs	W	L	Pct
1	Louisiana Tech	29	824	136	.858
2	Tennessee	58	914	220	.806
3	Texas	29	738	219	.771
4	Stephen F. Austin St.	31	729	241	.752
5	Old Dominion	34	748	248	.751
6	Montana	29	607	216	.738
7	Utah	29	598	234	.719
8	Penn St.	39	665	263	.717
9	Virginia	30	624	255	.710
10	Auburn	32	642	263	.709
11	St. Peter's	36	626	257	.709
12	Mount St. Mary's*	29	556	230	.707
13	Stanford	29	599	248	.707
14	Texas Tech	28	640	269	.704
15	Tennessee Tech	33	709	300	.703

*Includes records prior to Division I.

Top 10 Victories

		Yrs	W	L	Pct
1	Tennessee	58	914	220	.806
2	Louisiana Tech	29	824	136	.858
3	Old Dominion	34	748	248	.751
4	Texas	29	738	219	.771
5	Stephen F. Austin St.	31	729	241	.752
6	James Madison	81	721	410	.637
7	Tennessee Tech	33	709	300	.703
8	Long Beach St.	41	706	311	.694
9	Penn St.	39	665	263	.717
10	Richmond	83	664	458	.592
11	Western Kentucky	41	652	320	.671
12	Auburn	32	642	263	.709
13	Texas Tech	28	640	269	.704
14	Kansas St.	35	629	392	.616
15	St. Peter's	36	626	257	.709

Annual NCAA Division I Leaders

All averages include postseason games

Scoring

Multiple winners: Cindy Blodgett, Andrea Congreaves and Jackie Stiles (2).

Year		Gm	Pts	Avg
1982	Barbara Kennedy, Clemson	31	908	29.3
1983	LaTaunya Pollard, L. Beach St	31	907	29.3
1984	Deborah Temple, Delta St	28	873	31.2
1985	Anucha Browne, Northwestern	28	855	30.5
1986	Wanda Ford, Drake	30	919	30.6
1987	Tresa Spaulding, BYU	28	810	28.9
1988	LeChandra LeDay, Grambling	28	850	30.4
1989	Patricia Hoskins, Miss. Valley	27	908	33.6
1990	Kim Perrot, SW Louisiana	28	839	30.0
1991	Jan Jensen, Drake	30	888	29.6
1992	Andrea Congreaves, Mercer	28	925	33.0
1993	Andrea Congreaves, Mercer	26	805	31.0
1994	Kristy Ryan, CS-Sacramento	26	727	28.0
1995	Koko Lahanas, CS-Fullerton	29	778	26.8
1996	Cindy Blodgett, Maine	32	889	27.8
1997	Cindy Blodgett, Maine	30	810	27.0
1998	Allison Feaster, Harvard	28	797	28.5
1999	Tamika Whitmore, Memphis	32	843	26.3
2000	Jackie Stiles, SW Missouri St.	32	890	27.8
2001	Jackie Stiles, SW Missouri St.	35	1062	30.3
2002	Kelly Mazzante, Penn St.	35	872	24.9
2003	Chandi Jones, Houston	28	770	27.5

Rebounds

Multiple winner: Patricia Hoskins (2).

Year		Gm	No	Avg
1982	Anne Donovan, Old Dominion	28	412	14.7
1983	Deborah Mitchell, Miss. Col	28	447	16.0
1984	Joy Kellog, Oklahoma City	23	373	16.2
1985	Rosina Pearson, Beth-Cookman	26	480	18.5
1986	Wanda Ford, Drake	30	506	16.9
1987	Patricia Hoskins, Miss. Valley St.	28	476	17.0
1988	Katie Beck, East Tenn. St.	25	441	17.6
1989	Patricia Hoskins, Miss. Valley St.	27	440	16.3
1990	Pam Hudson, Northwestern St	29	438	15.1
1991	Tarcha Hollis, Grambling	29	443	15.3
1992	Christy Greis, Evansville	28	383	13.7
1993	Ann Barry, Nevada	25	355	14.2
1994	DeShawne Blocker, E. Tenn. St.	26	450	17.3
1995	Tera Sheriff, Jackson St	29	401	13.8
1996	Dana Wynne, Seton Hall	29	372	12.8
1997	Etolia Mitchell, Georgia St.	25	330	13.2
1998	Alisha Hill, Howard	30	397	13.2
1999	Monica Logan, UMBC	27	364	13.5
2000	Malveata Johnson, N.C. A&T	27	363	13.4
2001	Andrea Gardner, Howard	31	439	14.2
2002	Mandi Carver, Idaho St.	27	336	12.4
2003	Jennifer Butler, Massachusetts	28	412	14.7

Note: Wanda Ford (1986) and Patricia Hoskins (1989) each led the country in scoring and rebounds in the same year.

All-Time NCAA Division I Individual Leaders

Through 2002-03; includes regular season and tournament games; Official NCAA women's basketball records began with 1981-82 season. Players who competed earlier than that are not included below; **Last** column indicates final year played.

CAREER

Scoring

Average	Yrs	Last	Pts	Avg
1 Patricia Hoskins, Miss. Valley St. . .4	1989	3122	28.4
2 Sandra Hodge, New Orleans 4	1984	2860	26.7
3 Jackie Stiles, SW Mo. St. 4	2001	3206	26.1
4 Lorri Bauman, Drake 4	1984	3115	26.0
5 Andrea Congreaves, Mercer 4	1993	2796	25.9
6 Cindy Blodgett, Maine 4	1998	3005	25.5
7 Valorie Whiteside, Aplach St. 4	1988	2944	25.4
8 Joyce Walker, LSU 4	1984	2906	24.8
9 Tarcha Hollis, Grambling 4	1991	2058	24.2
10 Korie Hlede, Duquesne 4	1998	2631	24.1

Rebounds

Average	Yrs	Last	Reb	Avg
1 Wanda Ford, Drake 4	1986	1887	16.1
2 Patricia Hoskins, Miss. Valley St. . .4	1989	1662	15.1
3 Tarcha Hollis, Grambling 4	1991	1185	13.9
4 Katie Beck, East Tenn. St. 4	1988	1404	13.4
5 Marilyn Stephens, Temple 4	1984	1519	13.0
6 Natalie Williams, UCLA 4	1994	1137	12.8
7 Cheryl Taylor, Tenn. Tech 4	1987	1532	12.8
8 DeShawne Blocker, E. Tenn. St. . .4	1995	1361	12.7
9 Olivia Bradley, West Virginia 4	1985	1484	12.7
10 Judy Mosley, Hawaii 4	1990	1441	12.6

SINGLE SEASON

Scoring

Average	Year	Gm	Pts	Avg
1 Patricia Hoskins, Miss.Valley St.	1989	27	908	33.6
2 Andrea Congreaves, Mercer . .	1992	28	925	33.0
3 Deborah Temple, Delta St.	1984	28	873	31.2
4 Andrea Congreaves, Mercer . .	1993	26	805	31.0
5 Wanda Ford, Drake	1986	30	919	30.6
6 Anucha Browne, Northwestern	1985	28	855	30.5
7 LeChandra LeDay, Grambling .	1988	28	850	30.4
8 Jackie Stiles, SW Mo. St.	2001	35	1062	30.3
9 Kim Perrot, SW Louisiana	1990	28	841	30.0
10 Tina Hutchinson, San Diego St.	1984	30	898	29.9

SINGLE GAME

Scoring

	Year	Pts
1 Cindy Brown, Long Beach St. vs San Jose St.	1987	60
2 Lorri Bauman, Drake vs SW Missouri St. . . .	1984	58
Kim Perrot, SW La. vs SE La	1990	58
4 Jackie Stiles, SW Mo. St. vs Evansville	2000	56
5 Patricia Hoskins, Miss.Valley St. vs South-BR	1989	55
Patricia Hoskins, Miss.Valley St. vs Ala. St.	1989	55
7 Wanda Ford, Drake vs SW Missouri St. . . .	1986	54
Anjinea Hopson, Grambling vs Jackson St.	1994	54
Mary Lowry, Baylor vs Texas	1994	54
10 Chris Starr, Nevada vs CS-Sacramento	1983	53
Felisha Edwards, NE La. vs Southern Miss	1991	53
Sheryl Swoopes, Texas Tech vs Texas	1993	53

Winningest Active Division I Coaches

Minimum of five seasons as Division I head coach; regular season and tournament games included.

Top 10 Winning Percentage

	Yrs	W	L	Pct
1 Geno Auriemma, Connecticut . . .18	501	99	**.835**
2 Pat Summitt, Tennessee 29	821	163	**.834**
3 Tara VanDerveer, Stanford . . .24	575	161	**.781**
4 Robin Selvig, Montana 25	575	168	**.774**
5 Andy Landers, Georgia 24	585	179	**.766**
6 Gail Goestenkors, Duke 11	272	84	**.764**
7 Marsha Sharp, Texas Tech 21	507	159	**.758**
8 Jody Conradt, Texas 34	817	264	**.756**
9 Wes Moore, Tenn-Chattanooga .14	309	100	**.756**
10 Vivian Stringer, Rutgers 31	674	227	**.748**

Top 10 Victories

	Yrs	W	L	Pct
1 Pat Summitt, Tennessee 29	**821**	163	.834
2 Jody Conradt, Texas 34	**817**	264	.756
3 Sue Gunter, LSU 33	**681**	300	.694
4 Vivian Stringer, Rutgers 31	**674**	227	.748
5 Kay Yow, N.C. State 32	**636**	285	.691
6 Sylvia Hatchell, N. Carolina 28	**630**	255	.712
7 Rene Portland, Penn St. 27	**621**	216	.742
8 Theresa Grentz, Illinois 29	**608**	252	.707
9 Mike Granelli, St. Peter's 31	**592**	234	.717
10 Andy Landers, Georgia 24	**585**	179	.766
Joe Ciampi, Auburn 26	**585**	204	.741

Annual Awards

The Broderick Award was first given out to the Women's Division I or Large School Player of the Year in 1977. Since then, the National Assn. for Girls and Women in Sports (1978), the Women's Basketball Coaches Assn. (1983), the Atlanta Tip-Off Club (1983) and the Associated Press (1995) have joined in.

Since 1983, the first year as many as four awards were given out, the same player has won all of them in the same season twice: Cheryl Miller of USC in 1985 and Rebecca Lobo of Connecticut in 1995.

Associated Press

Voted on by AP sportswriters and broadcasters and first presented in 1995.

Multiple winner: Chamique Holdsclaw (2).

Year	Year	Year
1995 Rebecca Lobo, Connecticut	1998 Chamique Holdsclaw, Tennessee	2001 Ruth Riley, Notre Dame
1996 Jennifer Rizzotti, Connecticut	1999 Chamique Holdsclaw, Tennessee	2002 Sue Bird, Connecticut
1997 Kara Wolters, Connecticut	2000 Tamika Catchings, Tennessee	2003 Diana Taurasi, Connecticut

Broderick Award

Voted on by a national panel of women's collegiate athletic directors and first presented by the late Thomas Broderick, an athletic outfitter, in 1977. Honda has presented the award since 1987. Basketball Player of the Year is one of 10 nominated for Collegiate Woman Athlete of the Year; (*) indicates player also won Athlete of the Year.

Multiple winners: Chamique Holdsclaw, Nancy Lieberman, Cheryl Miller and Dawn Staley (2).

Year	Year	Year
1977 Lucy Harris, Delta St.*	1979 Nancy Lieberman, Old Dominion*	1981 Lynette Woodard, Kansas
1978 Ann Meyers, UCLA*	1980 Nancy Lieberman, Old Dominion*	1982 Pam Kelly, La. Tech

Year	Year	Year
1983 Anne Donovan, Old Dominion	1990 Jennifer Azzi, Stanford	1997 Chamique Holdsclaw, Tennessee
1984 Cheryl Miller, USC*	1991 Dawn Staley, Virginia	1998 Chamique Holdsclaw,Tennessee*
1985 Cheryl Miller, USC	1992 Dawn Staley, Virginia	1999 Stephanie White-McCarty, Purdue
1986 Kamie Ethridge, Texas*	1993 Sheryl Swoopes, Texas Tech	2000 Shea Ralph, Connecticut
1987 Katrina McClain, Georgia	1994 Lisa Leslie, USC	2001 Jackie Stiles, SW Missouri St.*
1988 Teresa Weatherspoon, La. Tech*	1995 Rebecca Lobo, Connecticut	2002 Sue Bird, Connecticut
1989 Bridgette Gordon, Tennessee	1996 Jennifer Rizzotti, Connecticut	2003 Diana Taurasi, Connecticut

Wade Trophy

Originally voted on by the National Assn. for Girls and Women in Sports (NAGWS) and awarded for academics and community service as well as player performance. First presented in 1978 in the name of former Delta St. coach Lily Margaret Wade. Since 2002, the trophy has been awarded to the Women's Basketball Coaches Association player of the year.
   Multiple winner: Nancy Lieberman (2).

Year	Year	Year
1978 Carol Blazejowski, Montclair St.	1987 Shelly Pennefather, Villanova	1996 Jennifer Rizzotti, Connecticut
1979 Nancy Lieberman, Old Dominion	1988 Teresa Weatherspoon, La. Tech	1997 DeLisha Milton, Florida
1980 Nancy Lieberman, Old Dominion	1989 Clarissa Davis, Texas	1998 Ticha Penicheiro, Old Dominion
1981 Lynette Woodard, Kansas	1990 Jennifer Azzi, Stanford	1999 Stephanie White-McCarty, Purdue
1982 Pam Kelly, La. Tech	1991 Daedra Charles, Tennessee	2000 Edwina Brown, Texas
1983 LaTaunya Pollard, L. Beach St.	1992 Susan Robinson, Penn St.	2001 Jackie Stiles, SW Missouri St.
1984 Janice Lawrence, La. Tech	1993 Karen Jennings, Nebraska	2002 Sue Bird, Connecticut
1985 Cheryl Miller, USC	1994 Carol Ann Shudlick, Minnesota	2003 Diana Taurasi, Connecticut
1986 Kamie Ethridge, Texas	1995 Rebecca Lobo, Connecticut	

Naismith Trophy

Voted on by a panel of coaches, sportswriters and broadcasters and first presented in 1983 by the Atlanta Tip-Off Club in the name of the inventor of basketball, Dr. James Naismith.
   Multiple winners: Cheryl Miller (3); Clarissa Davis, Chamique Holdsclaw and Dawn Staley (2).

Year	Year	Year
1983 Anne Donovan, Old Dominion	1990 Jennifer Azzi, Stanford	1997 Kate Starbird, Stanford
1984 Cheryl Miller, USC	1991 Dawn Staley, Virgina	1998 Chamique Holdsclaw, Tennessee
1985 Cheryl Miller, USC	1992 Dawn Staley, Virginia	1999 Chamique Holdsclaw, Tennessee
1986 Cheryl Miller, USC	1993 Sheryl Swoopes, Texas Tech	2000 Tamika Catchings, Tennessee
1987 Clarissa Davis, Texas	1994 Lisa Leslie, USC	2001 Ruth Riley, Notre Dame
1988 Sue Wicks, Rutgers	1995 Rebecca Lobo, Connecticut	2002 Sue Bird, Connecticut
1989 Clarissa Davis, Texas	1996 Saudia Roundtree, Georgia	2003 Diana Taurasi, Connecticut

Women's Basketball Coaches Association

Voted on by the WBCA and first presented by Champion athletic outfitters in 1983.
   Multiple winners: Chamique Holdsclaw, Cheryl Miller and Dawn Staley (2).

Year	Year	Year
1983 Anne Donovan, Old Dominion	1990 Venus Lacy, La. Tech	1997 Kate Starbird, Stanford
1984 Janice Lawrence, La. Tech	1991 Dawn Staley, Virgina	1998 Chamique Holdsclaw, Tennessee
1985 Cheryl Miller, USC	1992 Dawn Staley, Virginia	1999 Chamique Holdsclaw, Tennessee
1986 Cheryl Miller, USC	1993 Sheryl Swoopes, Texas Tech	2000 Tamika Catchings, Tennessee
1987 Katrina McClain, Georgia	1994 Lisa Leslie, USC	2001 Ruth Riley, Notre Dame
1988 Michelle Edwards, Iowa	1995 Rebecca Lobo, Connecticut	2002 merged with Wade Trophy
1989 Clarissa Davis, Texas	1996 Saudia Roundtree, Georgia	

Coach of the Year Award

Voted on by the Women's Basketball Coaches Assn. and first presented by Converse athletic outfitters in 1983.
   Multiple winners: Geno Auriemma and Pat Summitt (3), Jody Conradt and Vivian Stringer (2).

Year	Year	Year
1983 Pat Summitt, Tennessee	1990 Kay Yow, N.C. State	1997 Geno Auriemma, Connecticut
1984 Jody Conradt, Texas	1991 Rene Portland, Penn St.	1998 Pat Summitt, Tennessee
1985 Jim Foster, St. Joseph's-PA	1992 Ferne Labati, Miami-FL	1999 Carolyn Peck, Purdue
1986 Jody Conradt, Texas	1993 Vivian Stringer, Iowa	2000 Geno Auriemma, Connecticut
1987 Theresa Grentz, Rutgers	1994 Marsha Sharp, Texas Tech	2001 Muffet McGraw, Notre Dame
1988 Vivian Stringer, Iowa	1995 Pat Summitt, Tennessee	2002 Geno Auriemma, Connecticut
1989 Tara VanDerveer, Stanford	1996 Leon Barmore, La. Tech	2003 Gail Goestenkors, Duke

Other Women's Champions

The NCAA has sanctioned national championship tournaments for Division II and Division III since 1982. The NAIA sanctioned a single tournament from 1981-91, then split in to two divisions in 1992.

NCAA Div. II Finals

Multiple winners: North Dakota St. and Cal Poly Pomona (5); Delta St. and North Dakota (3).

Year	Winner	Score	Loser
1982	Cal Poly Pomona	93-74	Tuskegee, AL
1983	Virginia Union	73-60	Cal Poly Pomona
1984	Central Mo.St.	80-73	Virginia Union
1985	Cal Poly Pomona	80-69	Central Mo.St.
1986	Cal Poly Pomona	70-63	North Dakota St.
1987	New Haven, CT	77-75	Cal Poly Pomona
1988	Hampton, VA	65-48	West Texas St.
1989	Delta St., MS	88-58	Cal Poly Pomona
1990	Delta St., MS	77-43	Bentley, MA
1991	North Dakota St.	81-74	SE Missouri St.
1992	Delta St., MS	65-63	North Dakota St.
1993	North Dakota St.	95-63	Delta St.
1994	North Dakota St.	89-56	CS-San Bernadino
1995	North Dakota St.	98-85	Portland St.
1996	North Dakota St.	104-78	Shippensburg, PA
1997	North Dakota	94-78	S. Indiana
1998	North Dakota	92-76	Emporia St.
1999	North Dakota	80-63	Arkansas Tech
2000	Northern Kentucky	71-62	North Dakota St.
2001	Cal Poly Pomona	87-80*	North Dakota
2002	Cal Poly Pomona	74-62	SE Oklahoma St.
2003	South Dakota St.	65-60	Northern Kentucky
*Overtime

NCAA Div. III Finals

Multiple winners: Washington (4); Capital, Elizabethtown and WI-Stevens Point (2).

Year	Winner	Score	Loser
1982	Elizabethtown, PA	67-66*	NC-Greensboro
1983	North Central, IL	83-71	Elizabethtown, PA
1984	Rust College, MS	51-49	Elizabethtown, PA
1985	Scranton, PA	68-59	New Rochelle, NY
1986	Salem St., MA	89-85	Bishop, TX
1987	WI-Stevens Pt.	81-74	Concordia, MN
1988	Concordia, MN	65-57	St. John Fisher, NY
1989	Elizabethtown, PA	66-65	CS-Stanislaus
1990	Hope, MI	65-63	St. John Fisher
1991	St. Thomas, MN	73-55	Muskingum, OH
1992	Alma, MI	79-75	Moravian, PA
1993	Central Iowa	71-63	Capital, OH
1994	Capital, OH	82-63	Washington, MO
1995	Capital, OH	59-55	WI-Oshkosh
1996	WI-Oshkosh	66-50	Mt. Union, OH
1997	NYU	72-70	WI-Eau Claire
1998	Washington, MO	77-69	So. Maine
1999	Washington, MO	74-65	Col.of St. Benedict, MN
2000	Washington, MO	79-33	So. Maine
2001	Washington, MO	67-45	Messiah, PA
2002	WI-Stevens Pt.	67-65	St. Lawrence, NY
2003	Trinity, TX	60-58	E. Connecticut St.
*Overtime

NAIA Finals

Multiple winners: One tournament–SW Oklahoma (4); Div. I tourney–Southern Nazarene (5), Oklahoma City (4); Arkansas Tech (2); Div. II tourney–Hastings, Northern St. and Western Oregon (2).

Year	Winner	Score	Loser
1981	Kentucky St.	73-67	Texas Southern
1982	SW Oklahoma	80-45	Mo. Southern
1983	SW Oklahoma	80-68	AL-Huntsville
1984	NC-Asheville	72-70*	Portland, OR
1985	SW Oklahoma	55-54	Saginaw Val., MI
1986	Francis Marion, SC	75-65	Wayland Baptist, TX
1987	SW Oklahoma	60-58	North Georgia
1988	Oklahoma City	113-95	Claflin, SC
1989	So. Nazarene, OK	98-96	Claflin, SC
1990	SW Oklahoma	82-75	AR-Monticello
1991	Ft. Hays St., KS	57-53	SW Oklahoma
1992	I– Arkansas Tech	84-68	Wayland Baptist, TX
	II– Northern St., SD	73-56	Tarleton St., TX
1993	I– Arkansas Tech	76-75	Union, TN
	II– No. Montana	71-68	Northern St., SD
1994	I– So. Nazarene	97-74	David Lipscomb, TN
	II– Northern St., SD	48-45	Western Oregon
1995	I– So. Nazarene	78-77	SE Oklahoma
	II– Western Oregon	75-67	NW Nazarene, ID

Year	Winner	Score	Loser
1996	I– So. Nazarene	80-79	SE Oklahoma
	II– Western Oregon	80-77	Huron, SD
1997	So. Nazarene	78-73	Union, TN
	II– NW Nazarene	64-46	Black Hills St., SD
1998	I– Union, TN	73-70	So. Nazarene
	II– Walsh, OH	73-66	Mary Hardin-Baylor
1999	I– Oklahoma City	72-55	Simon Fraser, B.C.
	II– Shawnee St., OH	80-65	St. Francis, IN
2000	I– Oklahoma City	64-55	Simon Fraser, B.C.
	II– Mary, N.D.	59-49	Northwestern, IA
2001	I– Oklahoma City	69-52	Auburn Montgomery, AL
	II– Northwestern, IA	77-50	Albertson, ID
2002	I– Oklahoma City	82-73	So. Nazarene
	II– Hastings, NE	73-69	Cornerstone, MI
2003	I–So. Nazarene	71-70	Oklahoma City
	II–Hastings, NE	59-53	Dakota Wesleyan
*Overtime

AIAW Finals

The Association of Intercollegiate Athletics for Women Large College tournament determined the women's national champion for 10 years until supplanted by the NCAA.

In 1982, most Division I teams entered the first NCAA tournament rather than the last one staged by the AIAW.

Year	Winner	Score	Loser
1972	Immaculata, PA	52-48	West Chester, PA
1973	Immaculata, PA	59-52	Queens College, NY
1974	Immaculata, PA	68-53	Mississippi College
1975	Delta St., MS	90-81	Immaculata, PA
1976	Delta St., MS	69-64	Immaculata, PA
1977	Delta St., MS	68-55	LSU

Year	Winner	Score	Loser
1978	UCLA	90-74	Maryland
1979	Old Dominion	75-65	Louisiana Tech
1980	Old Dominion	68-53	Tennessee
1981	Louisiana Tech	79-59	Tennessee
1982	Rutgers	83-77	Texas

Professional Basketball

Yao Ming *said hello to the NBA while* **Michael Jordan** *said goodbye in 2003.*

Spurs Net NBA Championship

Tim Duncan and David Robinson dethrone Shaq, Kobe and the Lakers then beat the Nets for the NBA title.

Jerry Bembry
is the NBA Editor for ESPN The Magazine.

He was Michael Jordan, scoring at will. He was Wilt Chamberlain, sucking up every rebound. He was Magic Johnson using the eyes in the back of his head to find every open man. And he was Bill Russell, swatting away every shot attempt.

When it counted most, he produced an especially gaudy stat line. One that just so happened to occur in the deciding game of the 2003 NBA Finals. The box score read 21 points, 20 rebounds, 10 assists, and eight blocks and left just one word to describe what Tim Duncan did to the New Jersey Nets.

Spectacular.

A spectacular player on the epitome of what a team should be, produced an NBA title for the Spurs, who dethroned the three-time defending NBA champion Lakers along the way. In leading the Spurs to victory over the Nets in the Finals—and David Robinson to a special ending to a special career—Duncan picked up his second straight regular season MVP award and then the Final

MVP trophy to boot. Duncan's accomplishments capped a 2002-03 NBA season that featured many milestones.

In Detroit, head coach Rick Carlisle led the Pistons to 50 wins to become just the second man in NBA history to have at least 50 wins in his first two coaching seasons.

The only other coach to achieve that? Pat Riley (with the Lakers), who reached a milestone of his own with the Heat, becoming the only coach in NBA history to lead two teams to 350 victories.

But enough about the coaches, this is a players' game, after all. And the players gave us plenty to talk about.

How about the scoring duel between the Lakers' Kobe Bryant and the Magic's Tracy McGrady? The two young guns went back and forth and in the end it was McGrady who won his first scoring title, averaging 32.1 points per game. It was also the first time two players averaged at least 30 points in the same season since Jordan and Utah's Karl Malone both did it in the 1989-90 season.

Getty Images

Tim Duncan, David Robinson and *Tony Parker* led the way as the Spurs knocked off *Shaquille O'Neal* and the 3-time defending champion Lakers on the way to the NBA title.

While Bryant missed out on his first scoring title, he did become the youngest player in NBA history to reach 10,000 points in his career and set a single-game record on Jan. 7, knocking down 12 of 18 three-pointers on his way to 45 points in a win over the Sonics.

It was also a season to pay homage to some of the NBA elders. In Utah, future hall of famer John Stockton fed Malone on the pick and roll one last time. The greatest assist man in NBA history called it quits without winning a title, retiring after 19 seasons.

There were special moments in Houston and New York City as well for some old foes as legendary big men Hakeem Olajuwon and Patrick Ewing had their jerseys raised to the rafters of the Compaq Center and Madison Square Garden, respectively.

Another big man, who looks to be on his way to a great career in Houston was 7-foot-5 rookie center Yao Ming, the overall top pick in the 2002 draft. In his first meeting with O'Neal, the Chinese import blocked Shaq's first three shots. Although his performance tailed off a bit in the second half of the season and he lost the Rookie of the Year award to Phoenix Sun forward Amare Stoudemire, Yao proved he will be a force in the West for years to come.

And Jordan, the greatest player of all-time, wearing the uniform of the Washington Wizards, played the last game of his legendary NBA career. For the third and final time. We hope.

AP/Wide World Photos

*The Cleveland Cavaliers won the **LeBron Derby,** also known as the NBA Draft Lottery, and shocked no one by selecting James, the most hyped NBA prospect in history with the top pick.*

Yes, it was a bit sad to see a player who once dominated with such ease, struggle in his attempt to prop up a floundering franchise. But Jordan still had moments, however brief, that reminded us of his former greatness. He retired with the highest scoring average in NBA history (30.12 ppg, just ahead of Chamberlain's 30.06 ppg).

Jordan also left the league as the top scorer in NBA All-Star Game history (251 points), getting the start in his 14th and final appearance when fellow North Carolina alum Vince Carter stepped aside in a gesture of respect. Jordan missed his first seven shots, but nearly won it for the East with an apparent game-winning shot with 4.8 seconds left in OT. The game went to dou-

ble OT (where the West won) when Bryant converted two of three last second free throws.

It sure would have been nice had the league extended an All-Star invitation to Robinson, who was in the final season of his hall-of-fame career. But when the Finals came to an end and Robinson was hoisting the championship trophy above his head, there were more people who wanted to be like David than be like Mike.

"My last game, streamers flying. How could you write a better script than this, man?" Robinson said. "I've had some ups and downs in my career, but I'm going to end on the highest of highs. I just praise God. This has been unbelievable."

Jerry Bembry's Ten Biggest Stories of the Year in Pro Basketball

10 FROM THE SIDELINES. Grant Hill was starting to look like Tracy McGrady's Pippen—then he was gone. Antonio McDyess was starting to give the Knicks a reason for hope—then *he* was gone. Chris Webber was hoping to duplicate his dominance over Dallas from the previous season, but a knee injury ended his season, as well as the Kings' title hopes. Too many falling stars, leaving too many voids.

9 LEBRON MANIA. While the Spurs, Kings and Nets were jockeying for positioning in their respective conferences, the Cavaliers and Nuggets were among the teams maneuvering to find a home for perhaps the most-hyped prospect in NBA history: LeBron James. The Cavs, uh, won and here's the result: the league's hottest jersey (James' number 23) and one of the most demanded tickets in the NBA.

8 CHANGE THE GAME. Remember those best-of-five opening rounds, with the long stretches between games to drag out the drama? David Stern put an end to that, giving the networks more games to televise and the fans some exciting opening round series. Memo to the commish: thanks.

7 STOCKTON TO MALONE. Sure, they were a hard team to watch. Sure, the networks shunned the Jazz. But for 18 years John Stockton and Karl Malone demonstrated how to win as a team, how to frustrate opponents by perfecting the simple pick-and-roll. Stockton, the NBA's all-time leader in assists and steals, retired after 19 years. Malone, who likely one day will become the league's all-time scoring leader, went to the Lakers. It's safe to say that Raul Lopez to Greg Ostertag won't have the same ring.

6 BOB'S A SAFE BET. That Bob Johnson became the first African-American majority owner of a major sports team had everything to do with color: the color of money. Bob's a billionaire and his bid to own the NBA's new Charlotte franchise compared to those of mere millionaires was no contest. A solid businessman, who made Black Entertainment Television the premier cable network aimed at African-Americans, Johnson is anxious to restore a strong NBA presence in Charlotte.

5 COACHING CAROUSEL. Rick Carlisle wins a conference title, becomes just the second coach in NBA history to win 50 games in his first two seasons—and gets fired. Paul Silas gets a near unanimous endorsement from his players—and gets fired. Of the top five teams in the East last season, four changed coaches and 10 teams in all changed coaches in the offseason.

4 THE YEAR OF YAO. Some suspected he'd be the new Shawn Bradley. Yet the moment Yao Ming manned up to Shaq for the first time, we knew the rookie from China was the real deal. Ultimately, the 7-foot-5 center ran out of gas and the Rockets failed to make the playoffs, but the fact that never in NBA history has there been this combination of size, coordination and desire raises the excitement level in Houston.

3   KOBE'S EXPLOSION. It was not the best Christmas in La-La land. The Lakers were 11-19 and the question around the league was not whether the Lakers would four-peat but whether they would even make the playoffs. Then Shaquille O'Neal got healthy and Kobe Bryant erupted in a scoring stretch not seen since the days of Wilt: nine straight games where he scored at least 40 points. In February, Bryant averaged 40.6 points, shot 47.2 percent from the field and 42.9 percent from three-point range. While the outburst proved not enough to get the Lakers homecourt advantage in the playoffs, it proved who is—outside of Shaq—the most dominant player in the league.

2   MJ LEAVES WITH A THUD. We were all excited to see Michael Jordan return. We thought he'd be able to dominate some games, that he could

regain most of the form that won him six NBA titles, that he could transform a perennial loser—Washington—into a playoff team. We liked the fact that he could still drop 45 points (Feb. 1 against the Hornets) and nearly gave us a special All-Star moment. But in failing to make the playoffs in the watered down East, it was clear that, in his older days, Air had definitely sprung a leak.

1   CLASS ACT, ULTIMATE REWARD. Individually, Tim Duncan was boring, David Robinson was old, Tony Parker was good—not exceptional—and the rest really didn't strike fear in anyone. Collectively, the Spurs were lethal. Duncan was the league's MVP again, Robinson played with tremendous desire in the playoffs, and Parker showed the poise of a vet. The result: the Spurs were NBA champs, survivors of the wild, wild West.

Hardware Store

In 2003, Tim Duncan became just the seventh player in NBA history to win multiple MVP awards and NBA titles during his career.

	MVPs	NBA Titles
Michael Jordan	5	6
Magic Johnson	3	5
Larry Bird	3	3
Kareem Abdul-Jabbar	6	6
Wilt Chamberlain	4	2
Bill Russell	5	11
Tim Duncan	2	2

Garden State Savior

Here's a look at how the New Jersey Nets have turned around the direction of the franchise ever since Jason Kidd arrived on the scene in a 2001 trade with the Phoenix Suns for Stephon Marbury.

	Kidd	Pre-Kidd
Avg. Wins	50.5	32.8
Division Titles	2	0
Playoff Series Wins	6	1
Playoff Game W-L	25-15	9-30

Note: The Pre-Kidd era average win total doesn't include the Nets record of 16-34 in the 1998-99 season because it was shortened due to a work stoppage.

2002-2003
Season in Review

Final NBA Standings

Division champions (*) and playoff qualifiers (†) are noted. Number of seasons listed after each head coach refers to current tenure with club.

Western Conference
Midwest Division

	W	L	Pct	GB	Per Game For	Opp
*San Antonio	60	22	.732	—	95.8	90.4
†Dallas	60	22	.732	—	103.0	95.2
†Minnesota	51	31	.622	9	98.1	96.0
†Utah	47	35	.573	13	94.7	92.3
Houston	43	39	.524	17	93.8	92.3
Memphis	28	54	.341	32	97.5	100.7
Denver	17	65	.207	43	84.2	92.4

Head Coaches: SA—Gregg Popovich (7th season); **Dal**—Don Nelson (6th); **Min**—Phil Saunders (8th); **Utah**—Jerry Sloan (15th); **Hou**—Rudy Tomjanovich (12th, 35-30) stepped down due to health reasons on Mar. 18, 2003 and was replaced by assistant Larry Smith (8-9) on an interim basis; **Mem**—Sidney Lowe (2nd, 0-8) fired on Nov. 12, 2002 and replaced by Hubie Brown (28-46); **Den**—Jeff Bzdelik (1st).

2001-02 Standings: 1. San Antonio (58-24); 2. Dallas (57-25); 3. Minnesota (50-32); Utah (44-38); 5. Houston (28-54); 6. Denver (27-55); 7. Memphis (23-59).

Pacific Division

	W	L	Pct	GB	Per Game For	Opp
*Sacramento	59	23	.720	—	101.7	95.2
†LA Lakers	50	32	.610	9	100.4	98.0
†Portland	50	32	.610	9	95.2	92.5
†Phoenix	44	38	.537	15	95.5	94.4
Seattle	40	42	.488	19	92.1	92.3
Golden St.	38	44	.463	21	102.4	103.6
LA Clippers	27	55	.329	32	93.8	97.9

Head Coaches: Sac—Rick Adelman (5th season); **LAL**—Phil Jackson (4th); **Port**—Maurice Cheeks (2nd); **Pho**—Frank Johnson (2nd); **Sea**—Nate McMillan (3rd); **G.St.**—Eric Musselman (1st); **LAC**—Alvin Gentry (3rd, 19-39) was fired on Mar. 2, 2003 and replaced by assistant Dennis Johnson (8-16) on an interim basis.

2001-02 Standings: 1. Sacramento (61-21); 2. LA Lakers (58-24); 3. Portland (49-33); 4. Seattle (45-37); 5. LA Clippers (39-43); 6. Phoenix (36-46); 7. Golden St. (21-61).

Eastern Conference
Atlantic Division

	W	L	Pct	GB	Per Game For	Opp
*New Jersey	49	33	.598	—	95.4	90.1
†Philadelphia	48	34	.585	1	96.8	94.5
†Boston	44	38	.537	5	92.7	93.1
†Orlando	42	40	.512	7	98.5	98.4
Washington	37	45	.451	12	91.5	92.5
New York	37	45	.451	12	95.9	97.2
Miami	25	57	.305	24	85.6	90.6

Head Coaches: NJ—Byron Scott (3rd season); **Phi**—Larry Brown (6th); **Bos**—Jim O'Brien (3rd); **Orl**—Doc Rivers (4th); **NY**—Don Chaney (2nd) **Mia**—Pat Riley (8th).

2001-02 Standings: 1. New Jersey (52-30); 2. Boston (49-33); 3. Orlando (44-38); 4. Philadelphia (43-39); 5. Washington (37-45); 6. Miami (36-46); 7. New York (30-52).

Central Division

	W	L	Pct	GB	Per Game For	Opp
*Detroit	50	32	.610	—	91.4	87.7
†Indiana	48	34	.585	2	96.8	93.3
†New Orleans	47	35	.573	3	93.9	91.8
†Milwaukee	42	40	.512	8	99.5	99.3
Atlanta	35	47	.427	15	94.1	97.6
Chicago	30	52	.366	20	95.0	100.1
Toronto	24	58	.293	26	90.9	96.8
Cleveland	17	65	.207	33	91.4	101.0

Head Coaches: Det—Rick Carlisle (2nd season); **Ind**—Isiah Thomas (3rd); **NO**—Paul Silas (5th); **Mil**—George Karl (5th); **Atl**—Lon Kruger (3rd, 11-16) was fired on Dec. 26, 2002 and replaced by assistant Terry Stotts (24-31) on an interim basis; **Chi**—Bill Cartwright (2nd); **Tor**—Lenny Wilkens (3rd); **Cle**—John Lucas (2nd, 8-34) was fired on Jan. 20, 2003 and replaced by assistant Keith Smart (9-31) on an interim basis.

2001-02 Standings: 1. Detroit (50-32); 2. Charlotte (44-38); 3. Toronto (42-40); 4. Indiana (42-40); 5. Milwaukee (41-41); 6. Atlanta (33-49); 7. Cleveland (29-53); 8. Chicago (21-61).

Overall Conference Standings

Sixteen teams—eight from each conference—qualify for the NBA Playoffs; (*) indicates division champions.

Western Conference

	W	L	Home	Away	Div	Conf
1 San Antonio*	60	22	33-8	27-14	17-7	36-16
2 Sacramento*	59	23	35-6	24-17	17-7	36-16
3 Dallas	60	22	33-8	27-14	18-6	34-18
4 Minnesota	51	31	33-8	18-23	15-9	33-19
5 LA Lakers	50	32	31-10	19-22	15-9	33-19
6 Portland	50	32	27-14	23-18	15-9	29-23
7 Utah	47	35	29-12	18-23	15-9	30-22
8 Phoenix	44	38	30-11	14-27	12-12	26-26
Houston	43	39	28-13	15-26	11-13	26-26
Seattle	40	42	25-16	15-26	11-13	26-26
Golden St.	38	44	24-17	14-27	8-16	19-33
Memphis	28	54	20-21	8-33	5-19	12-40
LA Clippers	27	55	16-25	11-30	6-18	16-36
Denver	17	65	13-28	4-37	3-21	8-44

Eastern Conference

	W	L	Home	Away	Div	Conf
1 Detroit*	50	32	30-11	20-21	19-9	35-19
2 New Jersey*	49	33	33-8	16-25	16-8	34-20
3 Indiana	48	34	32-9	16-25	19-9	35-19
4 Philadelphia	48	34	25-16	23-18	17-7	35-19
5 New Orleans	47	35	29-12	18-23	17-11	32-22
6 Boston	44	38	25-16	19-22	13-12	31-23
7 Milwaukee	42	40	25-16	17-24	16-12	32-22
8 Orlando	42	40	26-15	16-25	14-11	31-23
Washington	37	45	23-18	14-27	11-13	26-28
New York	37	45	24-17	13-28	9-15	23-31
Atlanta	35	47	26-15	9-32	14-14	24-30
Chicago	30	52	27-14	3-38	12-16	22-32
Miami	25	57	16-25	9-32	5-19	18-36
Toronto	24	58	15-26	9-32	10-18	18-36
Cleveland	17	65	14-27	3-38	5-23	9-45

2003 NBA All-Star Game
West, 155-145 (2 OT)

52nd NBA All-Star Game. **Date:** Feb. 9, at the Philips Arena in Atlanta; **Coaches:** Isiah Thomas, Indiana (East) and Rick Adelman, Sacramento (West); **MVP:** Kevin Garnett, Minnesota (37 points, 9 rebounds, 5 steals); Starters chosen by fan vote, (Los Angeles Laker Kobe Bryant was the leading vote-getter for the third consecutive year, receiving 1,474,386); bench chosen by conference coaches' vote. Note that Vince Carter was voted as an Eastern Conference starter but gave up his starting spot to Michael Jordan.

Western Conference

Pos	Starters	Min	FG M-A	Pts	Reb	A
G	Kobe Bryant, LAL	36	8-17	22	7	6
G	Steve Francis, Hou	32	9-12	20	2	9
F	Kevin Garnett, Min.	41	17-24	37	9	3
F	Tim Duncan, SA	40	8-18	19	15	4
C	Yao Ming, Hou	17	1-1	2	2	0
Bench						
C	Shaquille O'Neal	26	8-14	19	13	1
F	Shawn Marion	23	4-9	8	7	4
G	Steve Nash, Dal	16	1-3	5	3	3
F	Dirk Nowitzki, Dal	16	4-8	9	1	1
G	Gary Payton, Sea	15	4-6	8	1	2
G	Stephon Marbury	15	1-3	4	1	6
G	Peja Stojakovic, Sac	13	2-7	5	3	1
	TOTALS	290	67-122	155	66	40

Three-Point FG: 7-22 (Bryant 3-5, Francis 2-3, Nowitzki 1-4, Stojakovic 1-4, Marion 0-1, Payton 0-1, Nash 0-2, Marbury 0-2); **Free Throws:** 14-20 (Bryant 3-6, Garnett 3-3, Duncan 3-3, O'Neal 3-5, Marbury 2-2, Nash 0-1); **Percentages:** FG (.549), Three-Pt. FG (.318), Free Throws (.700); **Turnovers:** 30 (Bryant 5, Nash 4, Garnett 4, Francis 3, Duncan 3, O'Neal 3, Payton 3, Nowitzki 2, Marbury 2, Stojakovic); **Steals:** 16 (Garnett 5, Bryant 3, Marion 3, O'Neal 2, Duncan, Nash, Stojakovic); **Blocked Shots:** 5 (Bryant 2, Garnett, O'Neal, Marion); **Fouls:** 21 (Bryant 5, Garnett 3, Payton 3, O'Neal 3, Duncan 2, Francis, Ming, Marion, Nash, Nowitzki); **Team Rebounds:** 10.

Eastern Conference

Pos	Starters	Min	FG M-A	Pts	Reb	A
G	Allen Iverson, Phi	41	13-23	35	5	7
G	Tracy McGrady, Orl	36	10-17	29	5	2
F	Michael Jordan, Wash	36	9-27	20	5	2
F	Jermaine O'Neal, Ind	33	3-10	10	10	0
C	Ben Wallace, Det	24	1-2	2	6	0
Bench						
G	Jason Kidd, Pho	33	4-9	11	5	10
F	Vince Carter, Tor	25	4-9	9	1	2
G	Paul Pierce, Bos	18	4-11	8	2	3
C	Brad Miller, Ind	17	2-4	5	6	3
F	Jamal Mashburn, NO	14	4-7	10	4	2
F	Antoine Walker, Bos	9	2-4	6	1	0
C	Zydrunas Ilgauskas	4	0-1	0	0	0
	TOTALS	290	56-124	145	50	31

Three-Point FG: 10-27 (McGrady 4-7, Mashburn 2-2, Kidd 1-4, Walker 1-3, Iverson 1-3, Carter 1-1, Jordan 0-2, Pierce 0-5); **Free Throws:** 23-31 (Iverson 8-9, McGrady 5-6, O'Neal 4-6, Jordan 2-2, Kidd 2-2, Miller 1-2, Walker 0-2); **Percentages:** FG (.452), Three-Pt. FG (.370), Free Throws (.742); **Turnovers:** 22 (Iverson 6, Jordan 2, O'Neal 2, Wallace 2, Kidd 2, Pierce 2, Miller 2, McGrady, Carter, Walker, Ilgauskas); **Steals:** 22 (Iverson 5, Kidd 5, Pierce 4, Jordan 2, O'Neal 2, Wallace 2, Mashburn 2); **Blocked Shots:** 6 (O'Neal 4, Wallace 2); **Fouls:** 16 (Jordan 3, McGrady 3, Iverson 2, O'Neal 2, Miller 2, Carter, Pierce, Wallace, Ilgauskas); **Team Rebounds:** 11.

Halftime— West, 55-52; **Third Quarter—** East, 93-86; **Technical Fouls—** none; **Officials—** #16 Ted Bernhardt #6 Jim Clark, #8 Luis Grillo; **Attendance**—20,325; **Time—** 2:59; **TV Rating—** 6.6 (TNT).

	1	2	3	4	1OT	2OT	F
West	18	37	31	34	18	17	155
East	23	29	41	27	18	7	145

NBA 3-point Shootout

Six players are invited to compete in the annual three-point shooting contest held during All-Star Weekend, since 1986. Each shooter has 60 seconds to shoot the 25 balls in five racks outside the three-point line. Each ball is worth one point, except the last ball in each rack, which is worth two. Highest scores advance. First prize: $25,000.

First Round	Pts
Brent Barry, Seattle	19
Peja Stojakovic, Sac	19
Wesley Person, Mem	14

Failed to advance	Pts
Pat Garrity, Orlando	13
David Wesley, New Orleans	12
Antoine Walker, Boston	7

Finals	Pts
Peja Stojakovic	20*
Wesley Person	20
Brent Barry	17

*Stojakovic beat Person, 22-16, in a playoff. Stojakovic was allowed a rest period and a second chance when a buzzer mistakenly sounded 24 seconds into the one-minute playoff in which he scored just 13 points.

Slam Dunk Contest

Four players competed at the 2003 NBA Slam Dunk contest. The Dunk contest was held annually from 1984-97 before being replaced by the 2Ball competition. It made its return in 2000. The competitors are selected based on "the creativity and artistry they have displayed in dunking" over the course of the season. The first round consists of three dunks. The dunks are judged by five judges on a scale from six to ten. The top two scorers from the first round advance to the final round and attempt two dunks. The combined score of the two dunks determines the winner.

The 2003 Slam Dunk contest competitors were 2001 slam dunk champion Desmond Mason of the Seattle SuperSonics, defending champion Jason Richardson of the Golden State Warriors, rookie Amare Stoudemire of the Phoenix Suns and Richard Jefferson of the New Jersey Nets. First prize: $25,000.

First Round	Pts
Jason Richardson, Golden State	100
Desmond Mason, Seattle	90

Failed to advance	Pts
Amare Stoudemire, Phoenix	79
Richard Jefferson, New Jersey	74

Finals	Score
Jason Richardson def. Desmond Mason	96-93

	Orlando	Chicago	San Antonio	New Jersey
	Tracy McGrady	**Eddy Curry**	**Bruce Bowen**	**Jason Kidd**
	Scoring	Field Goal Pct.	3-pt FG Pct.	Assists

NBA Regular Season Individual Leaders

Scoring

(*indicates rookie)

	Gm	Min	FG	FG%	3pt/Att	FT	FT%	Reb	Ast	Stl	Blk	Pts	Avg	Hi
Tracy McGrady, Orl	75	2954	829	.457	173/448	576	.793	488	411	124	59	2407	**32.1**	52
Kobe Bryant, LAL	82	3401	868	.451	124/324	601	.843	564	481	181	67	2461	**30.0**	55
Allen Iverson, Phi	82	3485	804	.414	84/303	570	.774	344	454	225	13	2262	**27.6**	42
Shaquille O'Neal, LAL . .	67	2535	695	.574	0/0	451	.622	742	206	38	159	1841	**27.5**	48
Paul Pierce, Bos	79	3096	663	.416	118/391	604	.802	578	349	139	62	2048	**25.9**	46
Dirk Nowitzki, Dal	80	3117	690	.463	148/390	483	.881	791	239	111	82	2011	**25.1**	40
Tim Duncan, SA	81	3181	714	.513	6/22	450	.710	1043	316	55	237	1884	**23.3**	38
Chris Webber, Sac	67	2622	661	.461	5/21	215	.607	704	364	106	88	1542	**23.0**	36
Kevin Garnett, Min	82	3321	743	.502	20/71	377	.751	1102	495	113	129	1883	**23.0**	37
Ray Allen, Milw-Sea . . .	76	2880	598	.439	201/533	316	.916	381	334	103	14	1713	**22.5**	40
Allan Houston, NY	82	3108	652	.445	178/450	363	.919	231	220	54	7	1845	**22.5**	53
Stephon Marbury, Pho .	81	3240	671	.439	89/296	375	.803	263	654	108	20	1806	**22.3**	43
Antawn Jamison, G.St. .	81	3226	691	.470	65/209	375	.789	578	156	76	45	1822	**22.2**	41
Jalen Rose, Chi	82	3351	642	.406	133/359	399	.854	351	351	72	23	1816	**22.1**	38
Jamal Mashburn, NO . .	82	3321	670	.422	119/306	313	.848	498	462	83	17	1772	**21.6**	50
Jerry Stackhouse, Wash	70	2747	491	.409	71/245	455	.878	258	316	65	28	1508	**21.5**	38
Shawn Marion, Pho . . .	81	3373	662	.452	141/364	251	.851	773	198	185	95	1716	**21.2**	36
Steve Francis, Hou	81	3318	571	.435	85/240	476	.800	499	502	141	41	1703	**21.0**	44
Glenn Robinson, Atl . . .	69	2591	539	.432	90/263	268	.876	457	205	91	26	1436	**20.8**	37
Jermaine O'Neal, Ind . .	77	2864	610	.484	7/21	373	.731	796	155	66	178	1600	**20.8**	38
Ricky Davis, Cle	79	3131	602	.410	74/204	348	.748	390	436	125	36	1626	**20.6**	45
Karl Malone, Utah	81	2936	595	.462	3/14	474	.763	628	379	136	31	1667	**20.6**	40
Gary Payton, Sea-Milw .	80	3208	665	.454	54/182	250	.710	334	663	133	20	1634	**20.4**	40
Antoine Walker, Bos . . .	78	3235	603	.388	188/582	176	.615	563	373	116	31	1570	**20.1**	38
Michael Jordan, Wash . .	82	3031	679	.445	16/55	266	.821	497	311	123	39	1640	**20.0**	45
Shareef Abdur-Rahim, Atl	81	3087	566	.478	21/30	455	.841	677	242	87	38	1608	**19.9**	33
Sam Cassell, Milw	78	2700	546	.470	59/163	385	.861	341	450	88	14	1536	**19.7**	39
Richard Hamilton, Det . .	82	2640	570	.443	32/119	440	.833	318	208	64	13	1612	**19.7**	34
Predrag Stojakovic, Sac	72	2450	497	.481	155/406	231	.875	397	141	72	5	1380	**19.2**	37
Pau Gasol, Mem	82	2948	569	.510	1/10	416	.736	720	229	34	148	1555	**19.0**	32

Rebounds

	Gm	Off	Def	Tot	Avg
Ben Wallace, Det	73	293	833	1126	15.4
Kevin Garnett, Min	82	244	858	1102	13.4
Tim Duncan, SA	81	259	784	1043	12.9
Jermaine O'Neal, Ind . .	77	202	594	796	10.3
Brian Grant, Mia	82	241	596	837	10.2
Troy Murphy, G.St.	79	228	578	806	10.2
Dirk Nowitzki, Dal	80	81	710	791	9.9
Shawn Marion, Pho . . .	81	194	579	773	9.5
Jerome Williams, Tor . .	71	231	419	650	9.2
P.J. Brown, NO	78	243	458	701	9.0
Donyell Marshall, Chi . .	78	234	465	699	9.0
Jamaal Magloire, NO . .	82	260	464	724	8.8
Amare Stoudemire*, Pho	82	250	471	721	8.8
Pau Gasol, Mem	82	192	528	720	8.8
Shareef Abdur-Rahim, Atl	81	175	502	677	8.4

Assists

	Gm	Ast	Avg
Jason Kidd, NJ	80	711	8.9
Jason Williams, Mem	76	631	8.3
Gary Payton, Sea-Milw	80	663	8.3
Stephon Marbury, Pho	81	654	8.1
John Stockton, Utah	82	629	7.7
Jamaal Tinsley, Ind	73	548	7.5
Jason Terry, Atl	81	600	7.4
Steve Nash, Dal	82	634	7.7
Andre Miller, LAC	80	537	6.7
Eric Snow, Phi	82	544	6.6
Gilbert Arenas, G.St.	82	514	6.3
Steve Francis, Hou	81	502	6.2
Kevin Garnett, Min	82	495	6.0
Kobe Bryant, LAL	82	481	5.9
Sam Cassell, Milw	78	450	5.8

Field Goal Pct.

	Gm	FG	Att	Pct
Eddy Curry, Chi	.81	335	573	.585
Shaquille O'Neal, LAL	.67	695	1211	.574
Carlos Boozer*, Cle	.81	331	618	.536
P.J. Brown, NO	.78	319	601	.531
Radoslav Nesterovic, Min	.77	400	762	.525
Nene Hilario*, Den	.80	321	619	.519
Tim Duncan, SA	.81	714	1392	.513
Matt Harpring, Utah	.78	521	1020	.511
Pau Gasol, Mem	.82	569	1116	.510
Brian Grant, Mia	.82	344	676	.509
Kevin Garnett, Min	.82	743	1481	.502
Elton Brand, LAC	.62	451	899	.502

Free Throw Pct.

	Gm	FT	Att	Pct
Allan Houston, NY	.82	363	395	.919
Ray Allen, Milw-Sea	.76	316	345	.916
Steve Nash, Dal	.82	308	339	.909
Troy Hudson, Min	.79	208	231	.900
Reggie Miller, Ind	.70	207	230	.900
Jason Terry, Atl	.81	259	292	.887
Dirk Nowitzki, Dal	.80	483	548	.881
Chauncey Billups, Det	.74	318	362	.878
Jerry Stackhouse, Wash	.70	455	518	.878
Darrell Armstrong, Orl	.82	165	188	.878
Glenn Robinson, Atl	.69	268	306	.876
Predrag Stojakovic, Wash	.72	231	264	.875

3-Point Field Goal Pct.

	Gm	3FG	Att	Pct
Bruce Bowen, SA	.82	101	229	.441
Michael Redd, Milw	.82	182	416	.438
Wesley Person, Mem	.66	100	231	.433
David Wesley, NO	.73	134	316	.424
Wally Szczerbiak, Min	.52	61	145	.421
Steve Nash, Dal	.82	111	269	.413
Matt Harpring, Utah	.78	66	160	.413
Anthony Peeler, Min	.82	87	212	.410

High-Point Games

	Opp	Date	FG-FT-Pts
Kobe Bryant, LAL	vs Wash	3/28/03	15-16-55
Allan Houston, NY	at LAL	2/16/03	18-13-53
Kobe Bryant, LAL	vs Hou	2/18/03	19-11-52
Tracy McGrady, Orl	vs Chi	2/21/03	15-16-52
Kobe Bryant, LAL	at Den	2/12/03	15-18-51
Jamal Mashburn, NO	vs Mem	2/21/03	17-12-50
Allan Houston, NY	vs Milw	3/16/03	13-18-50
Tracy McGrady, Orl	vs Milw	3/5/03	17-8-48
Shaquille O'Neal, LAL	vs Bos	3/21/03	19-10-48
Tracy McGrady, Orl	at Milw	11/2/02	16-9-47

Blocked Shots

	Gm	Blk	Avg
Theo Ratliff, Atl	.81	262	3.23
Ben Wallace, Det	.73	230	3.15
Tim Duncan, SA	.81	237	2.93
Elton Brand, LAC	.62	158	2.55
Adonal Foyle, G. St	.82	205	2.50
Shaquille O'Neal, LAL	.67	159	2.37
Jermaine O'Neal, Ind	.77	178	2.31
Andrei Kirilenko, Utah	.80	175	2.19
Shawn Bradley, Dal	.81	170	2.10
Erick Dampier, G. St.	.82	154	1.88

Steals

	Gm	Stl	Avg
Allen Iverson, Phi	.82	225	2.74
Ron Artest, Ind	.69	159	2.30
Shawn Marion, Pho	.81	185	2.28
Doug Christie, Sac	.80	180	2.25
Jason Kidd, NJ	.80	179	2.24
Kobe Bryant, LAL	.82	181	2.21
Paul Pierce, Bos	.79	139	1.76
Caron Butler*, Mia	.78	137	1.76
Steve Francis, Hou	.81	141	1.74
Jamaal Tinsley, Ind	.73	125	1.71

Rookie Leaders

Scoring	Gm	FG	FT	Pts	Avg
Caron Butler, Mia	.78	429	309	1201	15.4
Amare Stoudemire, Pho	.82	392	320	1106	13.5
Yao Ming, Hou	.82	401	301	1104	13.5
Dajuan Wagner, Cle	.47	223	128	629	13.4
Drew Gooden, Mem-Orl	.70	355	151	875	12.5

Field Goal Pct.	Gm	FG	Att	Pct
Carlos Boozer, Cle	.81	331	618	.436
Nene Hilario, Den	.80	321	619	.519
Yao Ming, Hou	.82	401	805	.498
Amare Stoudemire, Pho	.82	392	830	.472
Drew Gooden, Mem-Orl	.70	355	777	.457

Rebounds	Gm	Off	Def	Tot	Avg
Amare Stoudemire, Pho	.82	250	471	721	8.8
Yao Ming, Hou	.82	196	479	675	8.2
Carlos Boozer, Cle	.81	202	407	609	7.5
Reggie Evans, Sea	.67	167	278	445	6.6
Drew Gooden, Mem-Orl	.70	163	292	455	6.5

Assists	Gm	No	Avg
Jay Williams, Chi	.75	350	4.7
Junior Harrington, Den	.82	277	3.4
Marko Jaric, LAC	.66	193	2.9
Dajuan Wagner, Cle	.47	130	2.8
Caron Butler, Mia	.78	213	2.7

Personal Fouls

Kurt Thomas, NY	.344
Brian Grant, Mia	.300
Nene Hilario*, Den	.295
Kenyon Martin, NJ	.294
Al Harrington, Ind	.280
Jermaine O'Neal, Ind	.277
Jamaal Magloire, NO	.276

Disqualifications

Kurt Thomas, NY	.12
Radoslav Nesterovic, Min	.9
Brian Grant, Mia	.8
Raef LaFrentz, Dal	.8
Ron Artest, Ind	.7
Keith Van Horm, Phi	.7
Lorenzen Wright, Mem	.7

Turnovers

Steve Francis, Hou	.299
Jason Kidd, NJ	.296
Gilbert Arenas, G.St.	.290
Kobe Bryant, LAL	.288
Paul Pierce, Bos	.288
Allen Iverson, Phi	.286
Jalen Rose, Chi	.285

Triple Doubles

Kevin Garnett, Min	.6
Kobe Bryant, LAL	.5
Jason Kidd, NJ	.4
Chris Webber, Sac	.3
Sam Cassell, Milw	.2
Jamal Mashburn, NO	.2
Antoine Walker, Bos	.2

Minutes Played

Allen Iverson, Phi	.3485
Kobe Bryant, LAL	.3401
Shawn Marion, Pho	.3373
Jalen Rose, Chi	.3351
Kevin Garnett, Min	.3321
Jamal Mashburn, NO	.3321
Steve Francis, Hou	.3318

Technical Fouls

Antoine Walker, Bos	.23
Steve Francis, Hou	.21
Kevin Garnett, Min	.17
Jermaine O'Neal, Ind	.17
Gary Payton, Mil	.17
Gilbert Arenas, G.St.	.14
Ron Artest, Ind	.14

Team by Team Statistics

Players who competed for more than one team during the regular season are listed with their final club; (*) indicates rookies.

Atlanta Hawks

	Gm	FG%	Tpts	PPG	RPG	APG
Glenn Robinson	.69	.432	1436	20.8	6.6	3.0
Shareef Abdur-Rahim	.81	.478	1608	19.9	8.4	3.0
Jason Terry	.81	.428	1395	17.2	3.4	7.4
Dion Glover	.76	.427	737	9.7	3.7	1.9
Theo Ratliff	.81	.464	706	8.7	7.5	0.9
Ira Newble	.73	.495	564	7.7	3.7	1.4
Alan Henderson	.82	.468	394	4.8	4.9	0.5
Chris Crawford	.5	.615	24	4.8	1.4	0.2
Nazr Mohammed	.35	.421	160	4.6	3.7	0.2
Corey Benjamin	.9	.302	40	4.4	3.4	1.1
Emanual Davis	.24	.364	88	3.7	1.8	1.5
Dan Dickau*	.50	.412	183	3.7	0.9	1.7
Darvin Ham	.75	.447	180	2.4	2.0	0.5
Jermaine Jackson	.53	.364	121	2.3	1.1	1.4
Mikki Moore	.8	.385	18	2.3	1.0	0.4
Matt Maloney	.14	.320	24	1.7	0.5	1.2
Antonio Harvey	.4	.400	4	1.0	1.5	0.0
Amal McCaskill	.11	.235	11	1.0	2.0	0.5
Brandon Williams	.6	.143	2	0.3	0.3	0.0
Paul Shirley	.2	.000	0	0.0	0.5	0.0

Triple Doubles: Terry (1). **3-pt FG leader:** Terry (160).
Steals leader: Terry (126). **Blocks leader:** Ratliff (262).
Signed: G Maloney (Nov. 21), C Shirley (Jan. 9), F Benjamin (Jan. 22); G Jackson (Jan. 30); F Williams (Feb. 21); C Moore (Mar. 24).

Boston Celtics

	Gm	FG%	Tpts	PPG	RPG	APG
Paul Pierce	.79	.416	2048	25.9	7.3	4.4
Antoine Walker	.78	.388	1570	20.1	7.2	4.8
Tony Delk	.67	.416	654	9.8	3.5	2.2
Eric Williams	.82	.442	746	9.1	4.7	1.7
J.R. Bremer*	.64	.369	528	8.3	2.3	2.6
Tony Battie	.67	.539	487	7.3	6.5	0.7
Walter McCarty	.82	.414	498	6.1	3.5	1.3
Vin Baker	.52	.478	270	5.2	3.8	0.6
Mark Blount	.81	.432	401	5.0	3.8	0.7
Bimbo Coles	.35	.333	154	4.4	1.7	2.1
Kedrick Brown	.51	.357	145	2.8	2.7	0.4
Grant Long	.41	.386	72	1.8	2.0	0.6
Bruno Sundov	.26	.250	32	1.2	1.1	0.3
Mark Bryant	.16	.263	13	0.8	1.3	0.3
Ruben Wolkowyski	.7	.500	5	0.7	0.1	0.1

Triple Doubles: Walker (2) and Pierce (1). **3-pt FG leader:** Walker (188). **Steals leaders:** Pierce (139). **Blocks leader:** Battie (81).
Signed: F Long (Jan. 16), G Coles (Mar. 8).
Acquired: C Blount and F Bryant from Denver for G Shammond Williams, a 2003 2nd round pick and cash. (Feb. 20).

Chicago Bulls

	Gm	FG%	Tpts	PPG	RPG	APG
Jalen Rose	.82	.406	1816	22.1	4.3	4.8
Donyell Marshall	.78	.459	1042	13.4	9.0	1.8
Marcus Fizer	.38	.465	445	11.7	5.7	1.3
Jamal Crawford	.80	.413	858	10.7	2.3	4.2
Eddy Curry	.81	.585	849	10.5	4.4	0.5
Jay Williams*	.75	.399	714	9.5	2.6	4.7
Tyson Chandler	.75	.531	691	9.2	6.9	1.0
Eddie Robinson	.64	.492	364	5.7	3.1	1.0
Lonny Baxter*	.55	.466	262	4.8	3.0	0.3
Trenton Hassell	.82	.367	342	4.2	3.1	1.8
Rick Brunson	.17	.460	60	3.5	1.1	2.1
Corie Blount	.50	.485	150	3.0	4.1	1.0
Fred Hoiberg	.63	.389	144	2.3	2.2	1.1
Dalibor Bagaric	.10	.308	19	1.9	2.0	0.4
Roger Mason*	.7	.355	30	1.8	0.7	0.7

Triple Doubles: Williams (1). **3-pt FG leader:** Rose (133).
Steals leader: Marshall (95). **Blocks leader:** Chandler (106).

Cleveland Cavaliers

	Gm	FG%	Tpts	PPG	RPG	APG
Ricky Davis	.79	.410	1626	20.6	4.9	5.5
Zydrunas Ilgauskas	.81	.441	1390	17.2	7.5	1.6
Dajuan Wagner*	.47	.369	629	13.4	1.7	2.8
Carlos Boozer*	.81	.536	810	10.0	7.5	1.3
Jumaine Jones	.80	.434	784	9.8	5.4	2.6
Darius Miles	.67	.410	618	9.2	5.4	2.6
Smush Parker*	.66	.402	408	6.2	1.8	2.5
Chris Mihm	.52	.404	308	5.9	4.4	0.5
Milt Palacio	.80	.418	397	5.0	2.9	3.2
Tierre Brown	.15	.458	65	4.3	2.0	2.6
DeSagana Diop	.80	.351	119	1.5	2.7	0.5
Michael Stewart	.47	.378	36	0.8	1.2	0.1

Triple Doubles: none. **3-pt FG leader:** Jones (111).
Steals leader: Davis (125). **Blocks leader:** Ilgauskas (152).
Signed: G Brown (Mar. 25).

Dallas Mavericks

	Gm	FG%	Tpts	PPG	RPG	APG
Dirk Nowitzki	.80	.463	2011	25.1	9.9	3.0
Michael Finley	.69	.425	1331	19.3	5.8	3.0
Steve Nash	.82	.465	1455	17.7	2.9	7.3
Nick Van Exel	.73	.412	912	12.5	2.8	4.3
Raef LaFrentz	.69	.518	639	9.3	4.8	0.8
Shawn Bradley	.81	.536	543	6.7	5.9	0.7
Eduardo Najera	.48	.558	320	6.7	4.6	1.0
Walt Williams	.66	.393	363	5.5	3.1	0.9
Adrian Griffin	.74	.433	325	4.4	3.6	1.4
Tariq Abdul-Wahad	.14	.466	57	4.1	2.9	1.5
Avery Johnson	.48	.420	156	3.3	0.6	1.3
Raja Bell	.75	.441	230	3.1	1.9	0.8
Popeye Jones	.26	.387	53	2.0	2.3	0.3
Antoine Rigaudeau	.11	.229	17	1.5	0.7	0.5
Evan Eschmeyer	.17	.368	17	1.0	1.7	0.4
Mark Strickland	.4	.400	17	1.0	1.8	0.0

Triple Doubles: none. **3-pt FG leader:** Nowitzki (148).
Steals leader: Nowitzki (111). **Blocks leader:** Bradley (170).
Signed: F Strickland (Nov. 17), G Rigaudeau (Jan. 18).

Denver Nuggets

	Gm	FG%	Tpts	PPG	RPG	APG
Juwan Howard	.77	.450	1418	18.4	7.6	3.0
Nene Hilario*	.80	.519	839	10.5	6.1	1.9
Rodney White	.72	.408	650	9.0	3.0	1.7
Shammond Williams	.78	.394	627	8.0	2.2	3.1
Donnell Harvey	.77	.446	611	7.9	5.3	1.3
Marcus Camby	.29	.410	221	7.6	7.2	1.6
Vincent Yarbrough*	.59	.393	406	6.9	2.7	2.2
Jeff Trepagnier	.8	.425	45	5.6	2.0	0.8
Chris Andersen	.59	.400	305	5.2	4.6	0.5
Junior Harrington*	.82	.362	418	5.1	3.0	3.4
Nikoloz Tskitishvili*	.81	.293	315	3.9	2.2	1.1
Ryan Bowen	.62	.492	223	3.6	2.5	0.9
John Crotty	.12	.341	41	3.4	1.3	2.4
Predrag Savovic*	.27	.312	83	3.1	0.9	0.8
Devin Brown	.10	.343	30	3.0	1.8	0.7
Adam Harrington	.19	.297	30	1.6	0.4	0.6

Triple Doubles: White (1). **3-pt FG leader:** Williams (93).
Steals leader: Hilario (127). **Blocks leader:** Hilario (65).
Signed: G Crotty (Jan. 9), G Trepagnier (Mar. 24).
Acquired: G Williams, a 2003 2nd round pick and cash from Boston for C Mark Blount and F Mark Bryant (Feb. 20).

Detroit Pistons

	Gm	FG%	Tpts	PPG	RPG	APG
Richard Hamilton	82	.443	1612	19.7	3.9	2.5
Chauncey Billups	74	.421	1199	16.2	3.7	3.9
Clifford Robinson	81	.398	992	12.2	3.9	3.3
Corliss Williamson	82	.453	987	12.0	4.4	1.3
Chucky Atkins	65	.361	462	7.1	1.5	2.7
Jon Barry	80	.450	555	6.9	2.3	2.6
Ben Wallace	73	.481	506	6.9	15.4	1.6
Mehmet Okur*	72	.426	494	6.9	4.7	1.0
Zeljko Rebraca	30	.552	198	6.6	3.1	0.3
Tayshaun Prince*	42	.449	137	3.3	1.1	0.6
Michael Curry	78	.402	236	3.0	1.6	1.3
Danny Manning	13	.406	34	2.6	1.4	0.5
Hubert Davis	43	.392	79	1.8	0.8	0.7
Don Reid	1	.000	1	1.0	0.0	0.0
Pepe Sanchez	9	.000	0	0.0	0.7	0.9

Triple Doubles: Wallace (1). **3-pt FG leader:** Billups (149).
Steals leader: Wallace (104). **Blocks leader:** Wallace (230).
Signed: F Manning (Feb. 6),

Golden St. Warriors

	Gm	FG%	Tpts	PPG	RPG	APG
Antawn Jamison	82	.470	1822	22.2	7.0	1.9
Gilbert Arenas	82	.431	1497	18.3	4.7	6.3
Jason Richardson	82	.410	1282	15.6	4.6	3.0
Troy Murphy	72	.451	923	11.7	10.2	1.3
Earl Boykins	68	.429	600	8.8	1.3	3.3
Erick Dampier	82	.496	673	8.2	6.6	0.7
Bob Sura	55	.412	401	7.3	3.0	3.2
Mike Dunleavy Jr.*	82	.403	466	5.7	2.6	1.3
Adonal Foyle	82	.536	440	5.4	6.0	0.5
Chris Mills	21	.368	101	4.8	2.4	1.0
Danny Fortson	17	.370	59	3.5	4.3	0.7
Oscar Torres	17	.444	53	3.1	0.7	0.2
Jiri Welsch*	37	.253	61	1.6	0.8	0.7
Dean Oliver	15	.241	22	6.2	1.5	1.1
A.J. Guyton	2	.000		0.0	0.0	1.0
Guy Rucker	3		0	0.0	0.3	0.3

Triple Doubles: none **3-pt FG leader:** Richardson (123).
Steals leader: Arenas (124). **Blocks leader:** Foyle (205).
Signed: F Rucker (Oct. 31), G Guyton (Nov. 19), G Boykins (Nov. 28)

Houston Rockets

	Gm	FG%	Tpts	PPG	RPG	APG
Steve Francis	81	.435	1703	21.0	6.2	6.2
Cuttino Mobley	73	.434	1280	17.5	4.2	2.8
Yao Ming*	82	.498	1104	13.5	8.2	1.7
James Posey	83	.411	893	10.8	5.1	2.2
Glen Rice	62	.429	556	9.0	2.5	1.0
Eddie Griffin	77	.400	664	8.6	6.0	1.1
Maurice Taylor	67	.432	562	8.4	3.6	1.0
Kelvin Cato	73	.520	332	4.5	5.9	0.3
Moochie Norris	82	.406	357	4.4	1.9	2.4
Terence Morris	49	.466	182	3.7	2.6	0.5
Jason Collier	13	.472	36	2.8	2.2	0.1
Juaquin Hawkins*	58	.385	134	2.3	1.3	0.8
Bostjan Nachbar*	14	.355	29	2.1	0.8	0.2
Tito Maddox*	9	.250	11	1.2	0.8	0.6

Triple Doubles: Francis and Posey (1). **3-pt FG leader:** Mobley (112). **Steals leader:** Francis (141). **Blocks leader:** Ming (147).
Acquired: G Posey from Denver and traded F Kenny Thomas to Philadelphia as part of three-team deal. (Dec. 19).

Indiana Pacers

	Gm	FG%	Tpts	PPG	RPG	APG
Jermaine O'Neal	77	.484	1600	20.8	10.3	2.0
Ron Artest	69	.428	1068	15.5	5.2	2.9
Brad Miller	73	.493	955	13.1	8.3	2.6
Reggie Miller	70	.441	882	12.6	2.5	2.4
Al Harrington	82	.434	1002	12.2	6.2	1.5
Jamaal Tinsley	73	.396	566	7.8	3.6	7.5
Ron Mercer	72	.409	556	7.7	2.1	1.6
Jonathan Bender	46	.441	303	6.6	2.9	0.9
Erick Strickland	71	.429	458	6.5	2.0	2.9
Austin Croshere	49	.411	252	5.1	3.2	1.1
Tim Hardaway	10	.367	49	4.9	1.5	2.4
Jamison Brewer	10	.529	22	2.2	0.9	1.8
Jeff Foster	77	.360	162	2.1	3.6	0.7
Primoz Brezec	22	.395	42	1.9	1.0	0.2
Fred Jones*	19	.375	23	1.2	0.5	0.3

Triple Doubles: O'Neal (1). **3-pt FG leader:** R. Miller (113).
Steals leader: Artest (159). **Blocks leader:** O'Neal (178).
Signed: G Hardaway (Mar. 27).

Los Angeles Clippers

	Gm	FG%	Tpts	PPG	RPG	APG
Elton Brand	62	.502	1146	18.5	11.3	2.5
Corey Maggette	64	.444	1073	16.8	5.0	1.9
Lamar Odom	49	.439	714	14.6	6.7	3.6
Andre Miller	80	.406	1088	13.6	4.0	6.7
Michael Olowokandi	36	.427	441	12.3	9.1	1.3
Eric Piatkowski	62	.471	601	9.7	2.5	1.1
Quentin Richardson	59	.372	552	9.4	4.8	0.9
Marko Jaric*	66	.401	490	7.4	2.4	2.9
Keyon Dooling	55	.389	350	6.4	1.3	1.6
Cherokee Parks	30	.503	188	6.3	4.4	0.7
Melvin Ely*	52	.495	236	4.5	3.3	0.3
Wang Zhi Zhi	41	.383	182	4.4	1.9	0.2
Tremaine Fowlkes	37	.438	164	4.4	2.8	0.6
Sean Rooks	70	.421	297	4.2	3.1	1.0
Chris Wilcox*	46	.521	171	3.7	2.3	0.5

Triple Doubles: Brand and Miller (1). **3-pt FG leader:** Piatkowski (80).
Steals leader: Miller (99). **Blocks leader:** Brand (158).

Los Angeles Lakers

	Gm	FG%	Tpts	PPG	RPG	APG
Kobe Bryant	82	.451	2461	30.0	6.9	5.9
Shaquille O'Neal	67	.574	1841	27.5	11.1	3.1
Derek Fisher	82	.437	863	10.5	2.9	3.6
Rick Fox	76	.422	681	9.0	4.3	3.3
Devean George	71	.390	492	6.9	4.0	1.3
Robert Horry	80	.387	522	6.5	6.4	2.9
Samaki Walker	67	.420	296	4.4	5.5	1.0
Slava Medvedenko	58	.434	255	4.4	2.4	0.3
Brian Shaw	72	.387	250	3.5	1.7	1.4
Mark Madsen	54	.423	174	3.2	2.9	0.7
Kareem Rush*	76	.393	227	3.0	1.2	0.9
Jannero Pargo*	34	.398	85	2.5	1.1	1.1
Tracy Murray	31	.324	61	2.0	0.7	0.4
Soumaila Samake	13	.417	22	1.7	1.8	0.3

Triple Doubles: Bryant (5). **3-pt FG leader:** Bryant (124).
Steals leader: Bryant (181). **Blocks leader:** O'Neal (159).

Memphis Grizzlies

	Gm	FG%	Tpts	PPG	RPG	APG
Pau Gasol	.82	.510	1555	19.0	8.8	2.8
Mike Miller	.65	.434	1011	15.6	5.2	2.6
Jason Williams	.76	.388	919	12.1	2.8	8.3
Lorenzen Wright	.70	.454	797	11.4	7.5	1.1
Wesley Person	.66	.456	727	11.0	2.9	1.7
Shane Battier	.78	.483	756	9.7	4.4	1.3
Stromile Swift	.67	.481	647	9.7	5.7	0.7
Mike Batiste*	.75	.422	481	6.4	3.4	0.7
Earl Watson	.79	.435	433	5.5	2.1	2.8
Michael Dickerson	.6	.417	29	4.8	1.0	1.3
Chris Owens	.1	.667	4	4.0	1.0	0.0
Brevin Knight	.55	.425	216	3.9	1.5	4.2
Ryan Humphrey*	.48	.292	93	1.9	2.1	0.2
Robert Archibald*	.32	.300	19	1.6	1.4	0.3
Cezary Trybanski*	.15	.250	14	0.9	0.9	0.1

Triple Doubles: none. **3-pt FG leader:** Williams (143).
Steals leader: Battier (102). **Blocks leader:** Gasol (148).
Acquired: F/G Miller, F Humphrey, a 2003 1st round pick and a 2004 2nd round pick from Orlando for F Drew Gooden, G Gordon Giricek and cash. (Feb. 19)

Miami Heat

	Gm	FG%	Tpts	PPG	RPG	APG
Eddie Jones	.47	.423	869	18.5	4.8	3.7
Caron Butler*	.78	.416	1201	15.4	5.1	2.7
Brian Grant	.82	.509	846	10.3	10.2	1.3
Malik Allen	.80	.424	767	9.6	5.3	0.7
Travis Best	.72	.396	603	8.4	2.0	3.5
Mike James	.78	.373	607	7.8	1.9	3.2
Rasual Butler*	.72	.362	540	7.5	2.6	1.3
Eddie House	.55	.387	411	7.5	1.8	1.6
Vladimir Stepania	.79	.433	441	5.6	7.0	0.3
LaPhonso Ellis	.55	.382	277	5.0	2.9	0.3
Sean Lampley*	.35	.434	169	4.8	2.4	0.9
Anthony Carter	.49	.356	199	4.1	1.7	4.1
Sean Marks	.23	.373	54	2.3	1.5	0.1
Ken Johnson	.16	.405	32	2.0	2.0	0.0

Triple Doubles: none. **3-pt FG leader:** Jones (98).
Steals leader: C. Butler (137). **Blocks leader:** Allen (78).

Milwaukee Bucks

	Gm	FG%	Tpts	PPG	RPG	APG
Gary Payton	.80	.454	1634	20.4	4.2	8.3
Sam Cassell	.78	.470	1536	19.7	4.4	5.8
Michael Redd	.82	.469	1241	15.1	4.5	1.4
Desmond Mason	.80	.449	1147	14.3	6.5	2.0
Tim Thomas	.80	.443	1066	13.3	4.9	1.3
Toni Kukoc	.63	.432	730	11.6	4.2	3.7
Anthony Mason	.65	.486	466	7.2	6.4	3.2
Jason Caffey	.51	.456	295	5.8	3.5	0.7
Marcus Haislip*	.39	.431	161	4.1	1.4	0.2
Dan Gadzuric*	.49	.483	169	3.4	4.0	0.2
Ervin Johnson	.69	.452	152	2.2	4.3	0.3
Joel Przybilla	.32	.391	48	1.5	4.5	0.4
Jamal Sampson*	.5	.000	0	0.0	0.4	0.2

Triple Doubles: Cassell (2). **3-pt FG leader:** Redd (182).
Steals leader: Payton (133). **Blocks leader:** Johnson (63).
Acquired: G Payton and G/F Mason from Seattle for G Ray Allen, G Kevin Ollie, G Ronald Murray and a conditional 1st round pick . (Feb. 20)

Minnesota Timberwolves

	Gm	FG%	Tpts	PPG	RPG	APG
Kevin Garnett	.82	.502	1883	23.0	13.4	6.0
Wally Szczerbiak	.52	.481	913	17.6	4.6	2.6
Troy Hudson	.79	.428	1123	14.2	2.3	5.7
Rasho Nesterovic	.77	.525	861	11.2	6.5	1.5
Kendall Gill	.82	.422	714	8.7	3.0	1.9
Anthony Peeler	.82	.414	630	7.7	2.9	3.0
Joe Smith	.54	.460	404	7.5	5.0	0.7
Rod Strickland	.47	.432	320	6.8	2.0	4.6
Gary Trent	.80	.535	476	6.0	3.6	1.0
Marc Jackson	.77	.438	421	5.5	2.9	0.5
Mike Wilks*	.46	.338	147	3.2	1.5	2.0
Reggie Slater	.26	.540	81	3.1	1.2	0.2
Loren Woods	.38	.382	80	2.1	2.5	0.5
Igor Rakocevic	.42	.379	78	1.9	0.4	0.8

Triple Doubles: Garnett (6). **3-pt FG leader:** Hudson (97).
Steals leader: Garnett (113). **Blocks leader:** Garnett (129).
Signed: G Wilks (Jan. 13).

New Jersey Nets

	Gm	FG%	Tpts	PPG	RPG	APG
Jason Kidd	.80	.414	1495	18.7	6.3	8.9
Kenyon Martin	.77	.470	1283	16.7	8.3	2.4
Richard Jefferson	.80	.501	1242	15.5	6.4	2.5
Kerry Kittles	.65	.467	848	13.0	3.9	2.6
Lucious Harris	.77	.413	795	10.3	3.0	2.0
Rodney Rogers	.68	.402	478	7.0	3.9	1.6
Aaron Williams	.81	.453	500	6.2	4.1	1.1
Dikembe Mutombo	.24	.374	138	5.8	6.4	0.8
Jason Collins	.81	.414	460	5.7	4.5	1.1
Anthony Johnson	.66	.446	270	4.1	1.2	1.3
Brian Scalabrine	.59	.402	180	3.1	2.4	0.8
Tamar Slay*	.36	.379	92	2.6	0.9	0.4
Brandon Armstrong	.17	.333	24	1.4	0.2	0.1
Chris Childs	.12	.300	15	1.3	0.4	1.3
Donny Marshall	.3	.000	0	0.0	1.0	0.0

Triple Doubles: Kidd (4). **3-pt FG leader:** Kidd (126).
Steals leader: Kidd (179). **Blocks leaders:** Martin (70).
Signed: F Marshall (Mar. 12).

New Orleans Hornets

	Gm	FG%	Tpts	PPG	RPG	APG
Jamal Mashburn	.82	.422	1772	21.6	6.1	5.6
Baron Davis	.50	.416	856	17.1	3.7	6.4
David Wesley	.73	.433	1217	16.7	2.4	3.4
P.J. Brown	.78	.531	832	10.7	9.0	1.9
Jamaal Magloire	.82	.480	841	10.3	8.8	1.1
Courtney Alexander	.66	.382	533	7.9	1.8	1.2
Kenny Anderson	.61	.427	372	6.1	2.2	3.2
Robert Pack	.28	.403	145	5.2	1.8	2.9
George Lynch	.81	.409	363	4.5	4.4	1.3
Jerome Moiso	.51	.520	205	4.0	3.5	0.4
Robert Traylor	.69	.443	268	3.9	3.8	0.7
Stacey Augmon	.70	.411	212	3.0	1.7	1.0
Randy Livingston	.2	.500	6	3.0	0.0	0.5
Bryce Drew	.13	.296	19	1.5	1.0	0.8
Kirk Haston	.12	.118	6	0.5	0.6	0.3

Triple Doubles: Mashburn (2). **3-pt FG leader:** Wesley (134).
Steals leader: Wesley (109). **Blocks leader:** Alexander (111).
Signed: G Pack (Jan. 11).
Acquired: G Anderson from Seattle for C Elden Campbell. (Feb. 20).

New York Knicks

	Gm	FG%	Tpts	PPG	RPG	APG
Allan Houston	.82	.445	1845	22.5	2.8	2.7
Latrell Sprewell	.74	.403	1215	16.4	3.9	4.5
Kurt Thomas	.81	.483	1134	14.0	7.9	2.0
Howard Eisley	.82	.417	744	9.1	2.3	5.4
Shandon Anderson	.82	.462	687	8.4	3.1	1.1
Othella Harrington	.74	.508	573	7.7	6.4	0.8
Charlie Ward	.66	.399	472	7.2	2.7	4.6
C. Weatherspoon	.79	.449	521	6.6	7.6	0.9
Lee Nailon	.38	.442	210	5.5	1.8	0.7
Michael Doleac	.75	.426	328	4.4	2.9	0.6
Lavor Postell	.12	.368	43	5.5	1.8	0.7
Travis Knight	.32	.385	60	1.9	1.9	0.4
Frank Williams*	.21	.273	28	1.3	0.9	1.6

Triple Doubles: Sprewell (1). **3-pt FG leader:** Houston (178).
Steals leader: Sprewell (102). **Blocks leader:** Thomas (97).

Orlando Magic

	Gm	FG%	Tpts	PPG	RPG	APG
Tracy McGrady	.75	.457	2407	32.1	6.5	5.5
Grant Hill	.29	.492	421	14.5	7.1	4.2
Drew Gooden*	.70	.457	875	12.5	6.5	1.2
Gordan Giricek*	.76	.436	935	12.3	6.5	1.2
Pat Garrity	.81	.419	868	10.7	3.8	1.5
Darrell Armstrong	.82	.409	769	9.4	3.6	3.9
Chris Whitney	.54	.355	355	7.0	1.3	2.8
Shawn Kemp	.79	.418	537	6.8	5.7	0.7
Jacque Vaughn	.80	.448	473	5.9	1.5	2.9
Horace Grant	.5	.520	26	5.2	1.6	1.4
Andrew DeClercq	.77	.534	365	4.7	4.4	0.7
Pat Burke*	.62	.382	267	4.3	2.4	0.4
Steven Hunter	.33	.544	130	3.9	2.8	0.2
Jeryl Sasser	.75	.309	194	2.6	2.5	0.9
Olumide Oyedeji	.27	.435	27	1.0	1.9	0.2

Triple Doubles: McGrady (1). **3-pt FG leader:** McGrady (173).
Steals leader: Armstrong (135). **Blocks leader:** McGrady (59).
Signed: G Whitney (Mar. 1).
Acquired: F Gooden, G Giricek and cash from Memphis for F/G Mike Miller, F Ryan Humphrey, a 2003 1st round pick and a 2004 2nd round pick. (Feb. 19).

Philadelphia 76ers

	Gm	FG%	Tpts	PPG	RPG	APG
Allen Iverson	.82	.414	2262	27.6	4.2	5.5
Keith Van Horn	.74	.482	1176	15.9	7.1	1.3
Eric Snow	.82	.452	1054	12.9	3.7	6.6
Kenny Thomas	.66	.465	667	10.1	8.0	1.7
Derrick Coleman	.64	.448	602	9.4	7.0	1.4
Aaron McKie	.80	.429	721	9.0	4.4	3.5
Todd MacCulloch	.42	.517	299	7.1	4.7	0.5
Greg Buckner	.75	.465	450	6.0	2.9	1.3
Brian Skinner	.77	.550	461	6.0	4.8	0.2
Tyrone Hill	.56	.422	312	5.6	7.0	0.7
Monty Williams	.21	.425	92	4.4	2.1	1.2
Kenny Satterfield	.39	.301	132	3.4	1.1	1.7
John Salmons*	.64	.414	132	2.1	0.9	0.7
Efthimios Rentzias*	.35	.339	52	1.5	0.7	0.2

Triple Doubles: Snow (1). **3-pt FG leader:** Iverson (84).
Steals leader: Iverson (225). **Blocks leader:** Coleman (69).
Claimed: G Satterfield off waivers from Denver. (Dec. 24).
Acquired: F Thomas from Houston for F Art Long, F Mark Bryant and a future 1st round pick. (Dec. 19).
Signed: F Hill (Mar. 4).

Phoenix Suns

	Gm	FG%	Tpts	PPG	RPG	APG
Stephon Marbury	.81	.439	1806	22.3	3.2	8.1
Shawn Marion	.81	.452	1716	21.2	9.5	2.4
Amare Stoudemire*	.82	.472	1106	13.5	8.8	1.0
Anfernee Hardaway	.58	.447	615	10.6	4.4	4.1
Joe Johnson	.82	.397	803	9.8	3.2	2.6
Casey Jacobsen*	.72	.373	368	5.1	1.2	1.0
Iakovos Tsakalidis	.33	.452	161	4.9	3.7	0.4
Tom Gugliotta	.27	.455	129	4.8	3.7	1.1
Bo Outlaw	.80	.550	378	4.7	4.6	1.4
Scott Williams	.69	.411	273	4.0	2.8	0.3
Jake Voskuhl	.65	.564	248	3.8	3.5	0.6
Dan Langhi	.60	.401	183	3.1	1.5	0.4
Randy Brown	.32	.372	41	1.3	0.8	1.1
Alton Ford	.11	.333	7	0.6	0.5	0.1

Triple Doubles: Hardaway (1). **3-pt FG leader:** Marion (141).
Steals leader: Marion (185). **Blocks leader:** Marion (95).

Portland Trailblazers

	Gm	FG%	Tpts	PPG	RPG	APG
Rasheed Wallace	.74	.471	1340	18.1	7.4	2.1
Bonzi Wells	.75	.441	1138	15.2	5.3	3.3
Derek Anderson	.76	.427	1057	13.9	3.5	4.3
Scottie Pippen	.64	.444	689	10.8	4.3	4.5
Zach Randolph	.77	.513	650	8.4	4.5	0.5
Ruben Patterson	.78	.492	649	8.3	3.4	1.3
Dale Davis	.78	.541	579	7.4	7.2	1.2
Damon Stoudamire	.59	.376	409	6.9	2.6	3.5
Arvydas Sabonis	.78	.476	476	6.1	4.3	1.8
Jeff McInnis	.75	.444	432	5.8	1.3	2.3
Antonio Daniels	.67	.452	251	3.7	1.1	1.3
Qyntel Woods*	.53	.500	128	2.4	1.0	0.2
Charles Smith	.3	.250	5	1.7	0.0	0.3
Ruben Boumtje-Boumtje	.2	.000	0	0.0	0.5	0.5
Chris Dudley	.3	.000	0	0.0	0.7	0.0

Triple Doubles: none. **3-pt FG leader:** Anderson (116).
Steals leader: Wells (123). **Blocks leader:** Wallace (77).

Sacramento Kings

	Gm	FG%	Tpts	PPG	RPG	APG
Chris Webber	.67	.461	1542	23.0	10.5	5.4
Predrag Stojakovic	.72	.481	1380	19.2	5.5	2.0
Mike Bibby	.55	.470	875	15.9	2.7	5.2
Bobby Jackson	.59	.464	895	15.2	3.7	3.1
Vlade Divac	.80	.466	795	9.9	7.2	3.4
Doug Christie	.80	.479	748	9.4	4.3	4.7
Jim Jackson	.63	.442	487	7.7	4.2	1.9
Keon Clark	.80	.501	536	6.7	5.6	1.0
Hidayet Turkoglu	.67	.422	447	6.7	2.8	1.3
Gerald Wallace	.47	.492	220	4.7	2.7	0.5
Damon Jones	.49	.381	224	4.6	1.4	1.6
Scot Pollard	.23	.460	103	4.5	4.6	0.3
Lawrence Funderburke	27	.444	74	2.7	2.0	0.3
Mateen Cleaves	.12	.261	16	1.3	0.7	0.8

Triple Doubles: Webber (3). **3-pt FG leader:** Stojakovic (155).
Steals leader: Christie (180). **Blocks leader:** Clark (150).

San Antonio Spurs

	Gm	FG%	Tpts	PPG	RPG	APG
Tim Duncan	.81	.513	1884	23.3	12.9	3.9
Tony Parker	.82	.464	1269	15.5	2.6	5.3
Stephen Jackson	.80	.435	946	11.8	3.6	2.3
Malik Rose	.79	.459	822	10.4	6.4	1.6
David Robinson	.64	.469	546	8.5	7.9	1.0
Emanuel Ginobili*	.69	.438	525	7.6	2.3	2.0
Bruce Bowen	.82	.466	583	7.1	2.9	1.4
Steve Smith	.53	.388	360	6.8	1.9	1.3
Speedy Claxton	.30	.462	173	5.8	1.9	2.5
Kevin Willis	.71	.479	297	4.2	3.2	0.3
Steve Kerr	.75	.430	299	4.0	0.8	0.9
Danny Ferry	.44	.355	119	1.9	1.2	0.3
Mengke Bateer	.12	.235	9	0.8	0.8	0.3

Triple Doubles: Duncan (1). **3-pt FG leader:** Bowen (101).
Steals leader: Jackson (125). **Blocks leader:** Duncan (237).

Seattle Supersonics

	Gm	FG%	Tpts	PPG	RPG	APG
Ray Allen	.76	.439	1713	22.5	5.0	4.4
Rashard Lewis	.77	.452	1396	18.1	6.5	1.7
Brent Barry	.75	.458	774	10.3	4.0	5.1
Vladimir Radmanovic	.72	.410	724	10.1	4.5	1.3
Predrag Drobnjak	.82	.412	771	9.4	3.9	1.0
Kevin Ollie	.82	.451	534	6.5	2.2	3.5
Elden Campbell	.56	.397	343	6.1	3.2	0.9
Jerome James	.51	.478	276	5.4	4.2	0.5
Vitaly Potapenko	.26	.441	104	4.0	3.4	0.2
Reggie Evans*	.67	.471	212	3.2	6.6	0.5
Calvin Booth	.47	.437	138	2.9	2.3	0.3
Ansu Sesay	.45	.383	94	2.1	1.6	0.5
Ronald Murray	.14	.355	27	1.9	0.3	0.4
Joseph Forte	.17	.286	24	1.4	0.6	0.6

Triple Doubles: Allen (1). **3-pt FG leader:** Allen (201).
Steals leader: Barry (113). **Blocks leader:** James (82).
Acquired: G Allen, G Ollie, G Murray and a conditional 1st round pick from Milwaukee for G Gary Payton, G/F Desmond Mason (Feb. 20). C Campbell from New Orleans for G Kenny Anderson. (Feb. 20).

Toronto Raptors

	Gm	FG%	Tpts	PPG	RPG	APG
Vince Carter	.43	.467	884	20.6	4.4	3.3
Voshon Lenard	.63	.402	898	14.3	3.4	2.3
Morris Peterson	.82	.392	1153	14.1	4.4	2.3
Antonio Davis	.53	.407	738	13.9	8.2	2.5
Alvin Williams	.78	.438	1027	13.2	3.1	5.3
Jerome Williams	.71	.499	691	9.7	9.2	1.3
Lindsey Hunter	.29	.351	280	9.7	2.0	2.4
Rafer Alston	.47	.415	366	7.8	2.3	4.1
Jelani McCoy	.67	.491	457	6.8	5.3	0.6
Damone Brown	.5	.314	28	5.6	3.0	0.6
Mamadou N'diaye	.22	.448	120	5.5	3.7	0.3
Michael Bradley	.67	.481	338	5.0	6.1	1.0
Greg Foster	.29	.385	121	4.2	3.5	0.4
Chris Jeffries	.51	.387	197	3.9	1.2	0.4
Nate Huffman*	.7	.360	23	3.3	3.3	0.7
Maceo Baston	.16	.600	40	2.5	1.4	0.0
Art Long	.26	.373	60	2.3	2.3	0.2
Zendon Hamilton	.4	.400	6	2.0	1.3	0.0

Triple Doubles: none. **3-pt FG leader:** Peterson (116).
Steals leader: J. Williams (116). **Blocks leader:** Davis (62).
Signed: C Foster (Nov. 7), G Alston and F Long (Jan. 8), F Brown (Jan. 14), F/C Hamilton (Jan. 27), F Baston (Feb. 10).

Utah Jazz

	Gm	FG%	Tpts	PPG	RPG	APG
Karl Malone	.81	.462	1667	20.6	7.8	4.7
Matt Harpring	.78	.511	1370	17.6	6.6	1.7
Andrei Kirilenko	.80	.491	963	12.0	5.3	1.7
John Stockton	.82	.483	884	10.8	2.5	7.7
Calbert Cheaney	.81	.499	700	8.6	3.5	2.0
Scott Padgett	.82	.402	466	5.7	3.3	1.0
Jarron Collins	.22	.442	120	5.5	2.7	0.6
Greg Ostertag	.81	.442	438	5.4	6.2	0.7
Tony Massenburg	.58	.448	273	4.7	2.7	0.3
Mark Johnson	.82	.398	382	4.7	2.1	4.6
DeShawn Stevenson	.61	.401	279	4.6	1.4	0.7
Carlos Arroyo	.44	.459	121	2.8	0.6	1.2
John Amaechi	.50	.314	99	2.0	1.5	0.4

Triple Doubles: none. **3-pt FG leader:** Harpring (66).
Steals leader: Stockton (137). **Blocks leader:** Kirilenko (175).

Washington Wizards

	Gm	FG%	Tpts	PPG	RPG	APG
Jerry Stackhouse	.70	.409	1508	21.5	3.7	4.5
Michael Jordan	.82	.445	1640	20.0	6.1	3.8
Larry Hughes	.67	.467	857	12.8	4.6	3.1
Tyronn Lue	.75	.433	647	8.6	2.0	3.5
Christian Laettner	.76	.494	632	8.3	6.6	3.1
Kwame Brown	.80	.446	593	7.4	5.3	0.7
Juan Dixon*	.47	.384	270	6.4	1.7	1.0
Brendan Haywood	.81	.510	501	6.2	5.0	0.4
Etan Thomas	.38	.492	182	4.8	4.3	0.1
Bryon Russell	.70	.353	315	4.5	3.0	1.0
Jahidi White	.16	.472	67	4.2	4.6	0.1
Jared Jeffries*	.20	.476	79	4.0	2.9	0.8
Bobby Simmons	.36	.393	120	3.3	2.1	0.6
Charles Oakley	.42	.418	74	1.8	2.5	1.0
Anthony Goldwire	.15	.360	25	1.7	0.4	0.3
Brian Cardinal	.5	.250	4	0.8	1.0	0.2

Triple Doubles: none. **3-pt FG leader:** Stackhouse (71).
Steals leader: Jordan (123). **Blocks leader:** Haywood (119).
Signed: G Goldwire (Mar. 2).

Individual Single Game Highs

Most Assists

18	Jason Kidd, NJ vs. Mem (3/22)
18	Gary Payton, Sea at Hou (11/5)

Most Rebounds

25	Tim Duncan, SA at Mia (2/1)

Most Blocks

10	Jermaine O'Neal, Ind vs Tor (1/22)
10	Ben Wallace, Det vs Mia (11/20)

Most Steals

9	Allen Iverson, Phi vs LAL (12/20)

Most Field Goals Made

19	Done five times, including twice by Kobe Bryant.

Most Field Goals Attempted

47	Kobe Bryant, LAL at Bos (11/7)

Most 3-pt Field Goals Made

12	Kobe Bryant, LAL vs Sea (1/7)

Most 3-pt Field Goals Attempted

18	Kobe Bryant, LAL vs Sea (1/7)

NBA Regular Season Team Leaders

OFFENSE

WEST	—Per Game— Pts	Reb	Ast	FG%	3Pt%	FT%
Dallas	103.0	42.1	22.4	.453	.381	.829
Golden State	102.4	46.7	20.9	.441	.344	.778
Sacramento	101.7	44.5	24.8	.464	.381	.746
LA Lakers	100.4	44.3	23.3	.451	.356	.734
Minnesota	98.1	43.6	25.2	.466	.368	.770
Memphis	97.5	41.6	23.1	.452	.365	.739
San Antonio	95.8	42.6	20.0	.462	.354	.725
Phoenix	95.5	42.6	21.0	.443	.343	.742
Portland	95.2	41.1	22.7	.460	.330	.745
Utah	94.7	41.5	25.6	.468	.349	.745
LA Clippers	93.8	42.3	19.6	.437	.331	.750
Houston	93.8	43.8	18.4	.440	.346	.768
Seattle	92.1	40.8	21.6	.437	.353	.744
Denver	84.2	42.4	21.2	.411	.278	.699

EAST	—Per Game— Pts	Reb	Ast	FG%	3Pt%	FT%
Milwaukee	99.5	39.6	22.2	.457	.383	.776
Orlando	98.5	40.9	20.4	.436	.357	.777
Indiana	96.8	44.2	23.3	.441	.339	.766
Philadelphia	96.8	42.2	21.6	.448	.311	.775
New York	95.9	39.2	21.6	.441	.383	.815
New Jersey	95.4	42.9	23.0	.441	.332	.757
Chicago	95.0	43.0	21.7	.445	.350	.722
Atlanta	94.1	42.6	20.5	.444	.352	.793
New Orleans	93.9	43.6	22.0	.435	.376	.768
Boston	92.7	40.5	19.2	.415	.334	.742
Washington	91.5	40.4	19.7	.440	.312	.779
Cleveland	91.4	44.6	20.9	.422	.327	.747
Detroit	91.4	40.6	19.8	.430	.358	.771
Toronto	90.9	41.2	19.3	.427	.343	.718
Miami	85.6	41.6	18.3	.412	.316	.765

DEFENSE

WEST	—Per Game— Pts	Reb	Ast	FG%	3Pt%	FT%
San Antonio	90.4	40.9	19.0	.427	.320	.768
Utah	92.3	38.2	19.5	.434	.349	.759
Houston	92.3	40.6	20.5	.433	.347	.775
Seattle	92.3	41.5	20.8	.447	.344	.742
Denver	92.4	40.3	21.5	.443	.370	.757
Portland	92.5	39.0	22.7	.450	.341	.764
Phoenix	94.4	42.9	22.2	.438	.320	.766
Dallas	95.2	45.5	21.7	.438	.340	.727
Sacramento	95.2	45.8	21.5	.420	.320	.741
Minnesota	96.0	41.7	22.8	.437	.347	.752
LA Clippers	97.9	42.8	22.4	.447	.365	.774
LA Lakers	98.0	42.1	21.4	.443	.380	.760
Memphis	100.7	44.9	24.3	.460	.363	.759
Golden State	103.6	43.8	23.6	.452	.372	.756

EAST	—Per Game— Pts	Reb	Ast	FG%	3Pt%	FT%
Detroit	87.7	41.3	18.3	.438	.344	.746
New Jersey	90.1	41.4	19.6	.427	.359	.749
Miami	90.6	42.2	18.1	.437	.353	.751
New Orleans	91.8	40.0	19.9	.438	.338	.766
Washington	92.5	41.4	21.7	.442	.362	.771
Boston	93.1	45.0	22.2	.435	.331	.749
Indiana	93.3	42.4	20.7	.428	.340	.767
Philadelphia	94.5	40.3	22.1	.452	.354	.760
Toronto	96.8	43.6	21.1	.461	.375	.759
New York	97.2	43.3	21.1	.457	.340	.771
Atlanta	97.6	42.6	21.6	.436	.359	.760
Orlando	98.4	43.5	22.4	.455	.334	.767
Milwaukee	99.3	43.4	23.1	.458	.375	.745
Chicago	100.1	45.0	23.8	.439	.323	.749
Cleveland	101.0	41.7	24.0	.453	.358	.722

Playoff Series Summaries

WESTERN CONFERENCE

FIRST ROUND (Best of 7)

San Antonio Spurs 4, Phoenix Suns 2

Date	Winner	Home Court
Apr. 19	Suns, 96-95 OT	at San Antonio
Apr. 21	Spurs, 84-76	at San Antonio
Apr. 25	Spurs, 99-86	at Phoenix
Apr. 27	Suns, 86-84	at Phoenix
Apr. 29	Spurs, 94-82	at San Antonio
May 1	Spurs 87-85	at San Antonio

Los Angeles Lakers 4, Minnesota Timberwolves 2

Date	Winner	Home Court
Apr. 20	Lakers, 117-98	at Minnesota
Apr. 22	Timberwolves, 119-91	at Minnesota
Apr. 24	Timberwolves, 114-110 OT	at Los Angeles
Apr. 27	Lakers, 102-97	at Los Angeles
Apr. 29	Lakers, 120-90	at Minnesota
May 1	Lakers, 101-85	at Los Angeles

Dallas Mavericks 4, Portland Trail Blazers 3

Date	Winner	Home Court
Apr. 19	Mavericks, 96-86	at Dallas
Apr. 23	Mavericks, 103-99	at Dallas
Apr. 25	Mavericks, 115-103	at Portland
Apr. 27	Trail Blazers, 98-79	at Portland
Apr. 30	Trail Blazers, 103-99	at Dallas
May 2	Trail Blazers, 125-103	at Portland
May 4	Mavericks, 107-95	at Dallas

Sacramento Kings 4, Utah Jazz 1

Date	Winner	Home Court
Apr. 19	Kings, 96-90	at Sacramento
Apr. 21	Kings, 108-95	at Sacramento
Apr. 26	Jazz, 107-104	at Utah
Apr. 28	Kings, 99-82	at Utah
Apr. 30	Kings, 111-91	at Sacramento

SEMIFINALS (Best of 7)

Dallas Mavericks 4, Sacramento Kings 3

Date	Winner	Home Court
May 6	Kings, 124-113	at Dallas
May 8	Mavericks, 132-110	at Dallas
May 10	Mavericks, 141-137 OT	at Sacramento
May 11	Kings, 99-83	at Sacramento
May 13	Mavericks, 112-93	at Dallas
May 15	Kings, 115-109	at Sacramento
May 17	Mavericks, 112-99	at Dallas

San Antonio Spurs 4, Los Angeles Lakers 2

Date	Winner	Home Court
May 5	Spurs, 87-82	at San Antonio
May 7	Spurs, 114-95	at San Antonio
May 9	Lakers, 110-95	at Los Angeles
May 11	Lakers, 99-95	at Los Angeles
May 13	Spurs, 96-94	at San Antonio
May 15	Spurs, 110-82	at Los Angeles

CHAMPIONSHIP (Best of 7)

San Antonio Spurs 4, Dallas Mavericks 2

Date	Winner	Home Court
May 19	Mavericks, 113-110	at San Antonio
May 21	Spurs, 119-106	at San Antonio
May 23	Spurs, 96-83	at Dallas
May 25	Spurs, 102-95	at Dallas
May 27	Mavericks, 103-91	at San Antonio
May 29	Spurs, 90-78	at Dallas

2003 NBA PLAYOFFS

| 1ST ROUND | SEMIFINALS | FINAL | | FINAL | SEMIFINALS | 1ST ROUND |

NBA FINALS 2003

(1) Detroit 4
(8) Orlando 3
— Detroit 4
(4) Philadelphia 4
(5) New Orleans 2
— Philadelphia 2
Detroit 0
EASTERN CONFERENCE
San Antonio 4
New Jersey 2
(3) Indiana 2
(6) Boston 4
— Boston 0
New Jersey 4
(2) New Jersey 4
(7) Milwaukee 2
— New Jersey 4

San Antonio 4
LA Lakers 2
Dallas 4
Sacramento 3
San Antonio 4
Dallas 2
WESTERN CONFERENCE

(1) San Antonio 4
(8) Phoenix 2
(4) Minnesota 2
(5) LA Lakers 4
(3) Dallas 4
(6) Portland 3
(2) Sacramento 4
(7) Utah 1

EASTERN CONFERENCE

FIRST ROUND (Best of 7)

New Jersey Nets 4, Milwaukee Bucks 2

Date	Winner	Home Court
Apr. 19	Nets, 109-96	at New Jersey
Apr. 22	Bucks, 88-85	at New Jersey
Apr. 24	Nets, 103-101	at Milwaukee
Apr. 26	Bucks, 119-114 OT	at Milwaukee
Apr. 29	Nets, 89-82	at New Jersey
May 1	Nets, 113-101	at Milwaukee

Detroit Pistons 4, Orlando Magic 3

Date	Winner	Home Court
Apr. 20	Magic, 99-94	at Detroit
Apr. 23	Pistons, 89-77	at Detroit
Apr. 25	Magic, 89-80	at Orlando
Apr. 27	Magic, 100-92	at Orland
Apr. 30	Pistons, 98-67	at Detroit
May 2	Pistons, 103-88	at Orlando
May 4	Pistons, 108-93	at Detroit

Philadelphia 76ers 4, New Orleans Hornets 2

Date	Winner	Home Court
Apr. 20	76ers, 98-90	at Philadelphia
Apr. 23	76ers, 90-85	at Philadelphia
Apr. 26	Hornets, 99-85	at New Orleans
Apr. 28	76ers, 96-87	at New Orleans
Apr. 30	Hornets, 93-91	at Philadelphia
May 2	76ers, 107-103	at New Orleans

Boston Celtics 4, Indiana Pacers 2

Date	Winner	Home Court
Apr. 19	Celtics, 103-100	at Indiana
Apr. 21	Pacers, 89-77	at Indiana
Apr. 24	Celtics, 101-83	at Boston
Apr. 27	Celtics, 102-92	at Boston
Apr. 29	Pacers, 93-88 OT	at Indiana
May 1	Celtics, 110-90	at Boston

SEMIFINALS (Best of 7)

New Jersey Nets 4, Boston Celtics 0

Date	Winner	Home Court
May 5	Nets, 97-93	at New Jersey
May 7	Nets, 104-95	at New Jersey
May 9	Nets, 94-76	at Boston
May 12	Nets, 110-101 (OT)	at Boston

Detroit Pistons 4, Philadelphia 76ers 2

Date	Winner	Home Court
May 6	Pistons, 98-87	at Detroit
May 8	Pistons, 104-97 OT	at Detroit
May 10	76ers, 93-83	at Philadelphia
May 11	76ers, 95-82	at Philadelphia
May 14	Pistons, 78-77	at Detroit
May 16	Pistons, 93-89 OT	at Philadelphia

CHAMPIONSHIP (Best of 7)

New Jersey Nets 4, Detroit Pitstons 0

Date	Winner	Home Court
May 18	Nets, 76-74	at Detroit
May 20	Nets, 88-86	at Detroit
May 22	Nets, 97-85	at New Jersey
May 24	Nets, 102-82	at New Jersey

NBA FINALS (Best of 7)

	W-L	Avg.	Leading Scorer
New Jersey	2-4	82.0	Kidd (19.7)
San Antonio	4-2	87.8	Duncan (24.2)

Date	Winner	Home Court
June 4	Spurs, 101-89	at San Antonio
June 6	Nets, 87-85	at San Antonio
June 8	Spurs, 84-79	at New Jersey
June 11	Nets, 77-76	at New Jersey
June 13	Spurs, 93-83	at New Jersey
June 15	Spurs, 88-77	at San Antonio

Finals MVP
Tim Duncan, San Antonio, F/C
24.2 ppg, 17.0 rpg, 5.3 apg, 5.3 bpg

NBA Finals Box Scores

Game 1

at San Antonio 101, New Jersey 89

Nets	Min	FG M-A	3PT M-A	FT M-A	Pts	Reb O-T	A	S	PF
J. Kidd	44	4-17	1-5	1-2	10	0-8	10	2	1
K. Kittles	30	2-7	1-3	3-4	8	2-3	2	0	1
R. Jefferson	36	5-10	0-0	5-6	15	0-4	1	2	3
K. Martin	33	10-25	0-1	1-2	21	4-12	2	1	6
J. Collins	31	1-4	0-0	3-4	5	4-9	3	0	4
L. Harris	24	4-10	1-2	6-7	15	0-4	1	0	1
R. Rogers	21	5-10	1-2	0-0	11	1-2	1	0	3
A. Williams	11	2-5	0-0	0-0	4	2-4	0	0	4
D. Mutombo	6	0-1	0-0	0-0	0	0-1	0	0	1
A. Johnson	4	0-1	0-0	0-0	0	0-0	0	0	1
TOTALS	240	33-89	4-13	19-25	89	13-45	19	5	26

Team Rebs: 11; **Blocks:** 5 (Martin 2, Kidd, Williams, Mutombo); **Turnovers:** 8 (Kidd 3, Jefferson 3, Kittles, Martin); **Pcts:** FG (.371), 3-Pt FG (.308), FT (.760);

Spurs	Min	FG M-A	3PT M-A	FT M-A	Pts	Reb O-T	A	S	PF
S. Jackson	42	5-15	0-4	2-5	12	1-3	5	2	3
T. Parker	40	6-14	1-2	3-4	16	0-3	5	1	0
T. Duncan	44	11-17	0-0	10-14	32	3-20	6	3	1
B. Bowen	26	2-3	2-2	0-0	6	0-2	1	0	4
D. Robinson	27	6-8	0-0	2-3	14	2-6	1	0	2
E. Ginobili	28	3-8	1-2	0-0	7	2-6	1	0	2
M. Rose	24	5-11	0-0	2-2	12	3-6	2	1	5
S. Claxton	8	1-3	0-0	0-0	2	0-1	1	0	2
D. Ferry	1	0-0	0-0	0-0	0	1-1	0	0	0
TOTALS	240	39-79	4-10	19-28	101	10-47	24	7	20

Team Rebs: 8; **Blocks:** 12 (Duncan 7, Robinson 4, Claxton); **Turnovers:** 12 (Jackson 3, Ginobili 3, Parker 2, Rose 2, Duncan, Bowen); **Pcts:** FG (.494), 3-Pt FG (.400), FT (.679)
Halftime: Tied, 42-42; **Attendance:** 18,797; **Time:** 2:32.

Game 2

New Jersey 87, at San Antonio 85

Nets	Min	FG M-A	3PT M-A	FT M-A	Pts	Reb O-T	A	S	PF
J. Kidd	42	11-24	2-4	6-8	30	4-7	3	0	1
K. Kittles	21	3-7	1-2	1-2	8	1-4	1	3	1
R. Jefferson	39	3-10	0-0	2-2	8	1-3	3	2	3
K. Martin	33	6-16	0-0	2-2	14	3-5	4	2	5
J. Collins	34	3-6	0-1	0-0	6	1-4	1	1	2
L. Harris	27	5-8	0-1	0-0	10	1-2	7	1	1
D. Mutombo	20	2-3	0-0	0-0	4	1-4	0	0	3
R. Rogers	18	2-8	1-3	2-2	7	2-5	2	0	4
A. Johnson	6	0-1	0-0	0-0	0	0-0	1	0	1
TOTALS	240	35-83	4-11	13-16	87	15-39	16	9	21

Team Rebs: 5; **Blocks:** 7 (Mutombo 3, Martin 2); **Turnovers:** 13 (Kidd 4, Jefferson 3, Kittles, Martin, Collins, Harris, Johnson); **Pcts:** FG (.422), 3-Pt FG (.364), FT (.813)

Spurs	Min	FG M-A	3PT M-A	FT M-A	Pts	Reb O-T	A	S	PF
T. Parker	41	9-17	0-2	3-4	21	1-5	5	0	3
S. Jackson	40	6-10	4-7	0-0	16	3-4	3	1	3
T. Duncan	43	8-19	0-1	3-10	19	2-12	3	0	3
B. Bowen	26	1-2	1-1	0-0	3	0-5	0	0	1
D. Robinson	33	3-6	0-0	4-6	10	2-6	0	1	4
E. Ginobili	29	1-6	0-2	2-2	4	4-6	3	1	4
M. Rose	19	3-4	0-0	1-1	7	2-3	1	1	1
S. Claxton	7	2-2	0-0	1-2	5	1-3	1	1	0
S. Kerr	1	0-1	0-0	0-0	0	0-0	1	0	2
K. Willis	1	0-1	0-0	0-0	0	1-2	0	0	0
TOTALS	240	33-68	5-13	14-25	85	14-43	17	6	16

Team Rebs: 10; **Blocks:** 7 (Duncan 3, Robinson 2, Parker, Jackson); **Turnovers:** 21 (Jackson 7, Duncan 4, Ginobili 3, Bowen 2, Rose 2, Parker, Robinson, Claxton); **Pcts:** FG (.484), 3-Pt FG (.385), FT (.560).
Halftime: Nets, 41-35; **Attendance:** 18,797; **Time:** 2:27.

Game 3

San Antonio 84, at New Jersey 79

Spurs	Min	FG M-A	3PT M-A	FT M-A	Pts	Reb O-T	A	S	PF
T. Parker	43	9-21	4-6	4-8	26	1-3	6	0	0
S. Jackson	36	2-7	1-2	1-2	7	0-6	2	1	3
T. Duncan	45	6-13	0-0	9-12	21	3-16	7	1	3
B. Bowen	32	0-5	0-2	0-0	0	1-4	0	1	3
D. Robinson	26	1-5	0-0	6-8	8	1-3	0	1	2
E. Ginobili	28	3-6	0-0	2-3	8	2-2	4	4	2
M. Rose	22	4-7	0-0	0-0	8	0-2	0	1	2
S. Claxton	5	2-2	0-0	0-0	4	0-1	0	1	1
K. Willis	3	1-1	0-0	0-0	2	1-1	0	0	1
TOTALS	240	28-67	5-10	23-35	84	9-38	19	10	17

Team Rebs: 15; **Blocks:** 8 (Duncan 3, Bowen 2, Ginobili 2, Rose); **Turnovers:** 17 (Duncan 5, Jackson 4, Rose 3, Parker, Bowen, Ginobili, Claxton, Willis); **Pcts:** FG (.418), 3-Pt FG (.500), FT (.657)

Nets	Min	FG M-A	3PT M-A	FT M-A	Pts	Reb O-T	A	S	PF
J. Kidd	42	6-19	0-5	0-0	12	2-3	11	2	3
K. Kittles	34	8-16	3-5	2-3	21	1-4	1	3	2
K. Martin	42	8-18	0-1	7-8	23	2-11	0	4	5
R. Jefferson	36	3-11	0-0	0-0	6	2-9	0	2	2
J. Collins	25	0-0	0-0	0-0	0	4-5	1	0	6
L. Harris	22	1-6	1-2	4-4	7	1-1	3	1	2
D. Mutombo	18	1-1	0-0	0-0	2	1-3	0	1	3
R. Rogers	11	0-3	0-0	0-0	0	0-3	0	0	0
A. Johnson	6	2-2	0-0	0-0	4	0-1	0	0	0
A. Williams	3	0-0	0-0	0-0	0	1-2	1	0	1
TOTALS	240	30-81	4-13	15-17	79	14-41	17	13	26

Team Rebs: 10; **Blocks:** 5 (Kittles 2, Martin 2, Collins); **Turnovers:** 13 (Kidd 4, Jefferson 3, Kittles, Martin, Collins, Harris, Rogers, Johnson); **Pcts:** FG (.370), 3-Pt FG (.308), FT (.882)
Halftime: Spurs, 33-30; **Attendance:** 19,280; **Time:** 2:33.

Game 4

at New Jersey 77, San Antonio 76

Spurs	Min	FG M-A	3PT M-A	FT M-A	Pts	Reb O-T	A	S	PF
T. Parker	31	1-12	0-2	1-2	3	0-4	3	0	3
S. Jackson	28	1-9	1-4	2-3	5	2-4	3	1	3
B. Bowen	40	2-9	1-5	0-0	5	1-7	1	2	2
T. Duncan	39	10-23	0-0	3-3	23	8-17	2	1	4
D. Robinson	24	4-5	0-0	3-3	14	3-7	1	1	6
E. Ginobili	28	3-10	2-6	2-3	10	1-2	4	1	1
S. Claxton	17	3-6	0-0	4-4	10	1-3	2	1	1
K. Willis	16	2-7	0-0	2-2	6	5-5	0	0	3
M. Rose	15	0-9	0-1	0-0	0	1-1	1	0	4
S. Kerr	1	0-0	0-0	0-0	0	0-0	1	0	1
D. Ferry	1	0-0	0-0	0-0	0	0-0	0	0	0
TOTALS	240	26-90	4-18	20-24	76	22-53	14	10	27

Team Rebs: 12; **Blocks:** 10 (Duncan 7, Jackson, Robinson, Willis); **Turnovers:** 11 (Ducan 3, Parker 2, Jackson 2, Willis 2, Jackson, Claxton); **Pcts:** FG (.289), 3-Pt FG (.222), FT (.833)

Nets	Min	FG M-A	3PT M-A	FT M-A	Pts	Reb O-T	A	S	PF
J. Kidd	47	5-18	0-4	6-6	16	3-8	9	0	3
K. Kittles	35	2-10	0-4	0-0	4	1-6	1	1	0
K. Martin	40	7-16	0-0	6-12	20	5-13	1	1	5
R. Jefferson	40	8-15	0-0	2-4	18	1-10	1	0	1
J. Collins	10	0-0	0-0	0-0	0	2-1	1	1	4
D. Mutombo	21	0-2	0-0	2-2	2	2-3	0	2	3
A. Williams	17	2-6	0-0	4-5	8	2-7	1	0	3
L. Harris	15	0-4	0-0	0-0	0	0-3	4	3	0
R. Rogers	11	2-5	0-0	0-0	4	0-0	0	0	2
A. Johnson	4	1-1	1-1	0-0	3	0-0	0	0	0
TOTALS	240	28-78	1-9	20-29	77	19-53	19	5	22

Team Rebs: 9; **Blocks:** 13 (Williams 4, Martin 3, Mutombo 3, Jefferson 2, Collins); **Turnovers:** 16 (Kidd 5, Martin 5, Jefferson 3, Harris, Rogers, Johnson); **Pcts:** FG (.359), 3-Pt FG (.111), FT (.690)
Halftime: Nets, 45-34; **Attendance:** 19,280; **Time:** 2:40.

Game 5
San Antonio 93, at New Jersey 83

Spurs	Min	FG M-A	3PT M-A	FT M-A	Pts	Reb O-T	A	S	PF
T. Parker	33	5-13	1-2	3-5	14	0-2	4	1	3
S. Jackson	32	2-7	1-4	0-0	5	1-7	3	0	2
T. Duncan	46	10-18	0-0	9-10	29	3-17	4	1	3
B. Bowen	29	1-4	0-2	2-2	4	0-1	1	0	4
D. Robinson	20	2-4	0-0	2-2	6	1-3	0	3	6
M. Rose	29	6-9	0-0	2-2	14	2-3	1	0	2
E. Ginobili	26	4-8	0-0	4-4	12	0-3	0	2	5
S. Claxton	15	1-4	0-0	1-2	3	0-1	2	2	4
S. Kerr	9	2-2	1-1	1-2	6	1-1	0	1	0
K. Willis	1	0-0	0-0	0-0	0	0-1	0	0	0
TOTALS	240	33-69	3-9	24-29	93	8-39	15	10	29

Team Rebs: 8; **Blocks:** 9 (Duncan 4, Robinson 2, Claxton 2, Ginobili); **Turnovers:** 15 (Duncan 6, Jackson 4, Parker 2, Robinson, Rose, Ginobili); **Pcts:** FG (.478), 3-Pt FG (.333), FT (.828)

Nets	Min	FG M-A	3PT M-A	FT M-A	Pts	Reb O-T	A	S	PF
J. Kidd	48	10-23	4-10	5-6	29	3-7	7	2	2
K. Kittles	34	3-9	0-3	2-2	8	1-4	1	1	3
K. Martin	38	2-8	0-1	0-0	4	1-9	3	1	5
R. Jefferson	37	5-11	0-0	9-11	19	2-6	4	2	4
J. Collins	26	1-3	0-0	5-6	7	4-5	0	1	5
A. Williams	23	4-9	0-0	2-3	10	4-7	0	0	4
L. Harris	22	1-7	0-0	3-4	5	0-1	0	0	0
D. Mutombo	7	0-1	0-0	0-0	0	0-0	0	0	2
R. Rogers	5	0-3	0-2	1-2	1	1	0	0	0
TOTALS	240	26-74	4-16	27-34	83	17-42	15	7	25

Team Rebs: 7; **Blocks:** 5 (Martin 3, Kittles, Williams); **Turnovers:** 16 (Martin 8, Kidd 2, Mutombo 2, Kittles, Jefferson, Harris, Rogers); **Pcts:** FG (.351), 3-Pt FG (.250), FT (.794).
Halftime: Spurs, 42-34; **Attendance:** 19,280; **Time:** 2:40.

Game 6
at San Antonio 88, New Jersey 77

Nets	Min	FG M-A	3PT M-A	FT M-A	Pts	Reb O-T	A	S	PF
J. Kidd	42	8-20	3-9	2-2	21	2-4	7	1	4
K. Kittles	34	5-12	2-6	4-4	16	0-4	2	3	2
R. Jefferson	41	6-15	0-1	1-1	13	2-7	2	0	5
K. Martin	39	3-23	0-2	0-0	6	0-10	1	1	3
J. Collins	25	2-5	0-0	0-0	4	0-3	0	1	4
A. Williams	16	2-4	0-0	0-0	4	1-1	2	1	4
L. Harris	15	0-1	0-1	2-4	2	1-2	0	0	1
D. Mutombo	10	1-1	0-0	2-2	4	2-3	0	0	1
R. Rogers	8	1-2	1-1	0-0	3	0-0	0	0	1
A. Johnson	8	2-4	0-1	0-0	4	0-0	1	0	0
T. Slay	1	0-0	0-0	0-0	0	0-0	0	0	0
B. Scalabrine	1	0-0	0-0	0-0	0	0-1	0	0	0
TOTALS	240	30-87	6-21	11-13	77	8-35	14	8	25

Team Rebs: 11; **Blocks:** 5 (Martin 2, Collins, Williams, Mutombo); **Turnovers:** 11 (Jefferson 3, Johnson 2, Martin 2, Collins, Williams, Harris, Mutombo); **Pcts:** FG (.345), 3-Pt FG (.286), FT (.846).

Spurs	Min	FG M-A	3PT M-A	FT M-A	Pts	Reb O-T	A	S	PF
S. Jackson	35	7-13	3-7	0-0	17	0-3	0	1	3
T. Parker	24	2-6	0-0	0-0	4	0-2	2	0	0
T. Duncan	46	9-19	0-1	3-5	21	4-20	10	0	2
B. Bowen	18	1-7	0-2	0-0	2	0-0	2	1	0
D. Robinson	31	6-8	0-0	1-4	13	4-17	1	0	2
E. Ginobili	33	2-8	0-4	7-9	11	1-7	1	2	3
S. Claxton	23	5-8	0-0	3-4	13	0-1	4	0	3
M. Rose	18	1-3	0-0	3-3	5	2-5	0	0	1
S. Kerr	9	1-1	0-0	0-0	2	0-0	0	0	0
D. Ferry	1	0-0	0-0	0-0	0	0-0	0	0	0
S. Smith	1	0-1	0-1	0-0	0	0-0	0	0	0
K. Willis	1	0-0	0-0	0-0	0	0-0	0	0	0
TOTALS	240	34-74	3-15	17-25	88	11-55	20	4	14

Team Rebs: 6; **Blocks:** 13 (Duncan 8, Robinson 2, Rose 2, Claxton 1); **Turnovers:** 19 (Jackson 6, Duncan 4, Parker 3, Claxton 2, Rose 2, Robinson, Ginobili); **Pcts:** FG (.459), 3-Pt FG (.200), FT (.680).
Halftime: Nets, 41-38; **Attendance:** 18,797; **Time:** 2:32.

NBA Finalists' Composite Box Scores
New Jersey Nets (14-6)

			Overall Playoffs		—Per Game—						Finals vs. San Antonio		—Per Game—		
	Gm	FG%	3PT-A	TPts	Pts	Reb	Ast	Gm	FG%	3PT-A	TPts	Pts	Reb	Ast
Jason Kidd	20	.402	34-104	402	20.1	7.7	8.2	6	.364	10-37	118	19.7	6.2	7.8
Kenyon Martin	20	.453	1-11	378	18.9	9.4	2.9	6	.343	0-5	44	14.7	10.0	2.2
Richard Jefferson	20	.476	0-3	281	14.1	6.4	2.4	6	.417	0-1	79	13.2	-6.5	1.8
Kerry Kittles	20	.395	26-63	216	10.8	3.5	2.0	6	.377	7-23	65	10.8	4.2	1.3
Lucious Harris	20	.391	11-33	155	7.8	2.6	1.6	6	.306	2-6	39	6.5	2.7	1.2
Rodney Rogers	20	.372	17-42	134	6.7	2.8	1.4	6	.323	3-8	28	4.7	1.7	0.5
Aaron Williams	19	.472	0-0	123	6.5	4.6	0.9	5	.423	0-0	28	5.6	4.2	0.8
Jason Collins	20	.363	0-2	117	5.9	6.3	0.9	6	.333	0-1	22	3.7	4.7	1.0
Anthony Johnson	17	.548	3-6	42	2.5	0.7	1.1	5	.556	1-2	11	4.7	0.2	0.2
Dikembe Mutombo	10	.467	0-0	18	1.8	2.7	0.6	6	.500	0-0	14	2.3	2.8	0.0
Brian Scalabrine	7	.500	0-1	4	0.6	0.6	0.0	1	.000	0-0	0	0.0	1.0	0.0
Tamar Slay	6	.250	1-1	3	0.5	0.0	0.0	1	.000	0-0	0	0.0	0.0	0.0
NETS	20	.425	93-266	1873	93.7	45.1	21.3	6	.370	23-83	492	82.0	42.5	16.7
OPPONENTS	20	.427	112-322	1806	90.3	39.8	19.2	6	.432	24-75	527	87.8	45.8	18.2

San Antonio Spurs (16-8)

			Overall Playoffs		—Per Game—						Finals vs. New Jersey		—Per Game—		
	Gm	FG%	3PT-A	TPts	Pts	Reb	Ast	Gm	FG%	3PT-A	TPts	Pts	Reb	Ast
Tim Duncan	24	.529	0-7	593	24.7	15.4	5.3	6	.495	0-2	145	24.2	17.0	5.3
Tony Parker	24	.403	15-56	352	14.7	2.8	3.5	6	.386	6-14	84	14.0	3.2	4.2
Stephen Jackson	24	.414	38-113	307	12.8	4.1	2.7	6	.377	10-28	62	10.3	4.2	2.7
Emanuel Ginobili	24	.386	28-73	226	9.4	3.8	2.9	6	.348	3-14	52	8.7	4.5	2.0
Malik Rose	24	.419	0-3	222	9.3	5.8	1.0	6	.442	0-1	46	7.7	3.8	0.7
David Robinson	23	.542	0-0	180	7.8	6.6	0.9	6	.611	0-0	65	10.8	7.3	0.7
Bruce Bowen	24	.372	35-80	166	6.9	2.9	1.6	6	.233	4-14	20	3.3	3.2	0.8
Speedy Claxton	24	.438	0-0	125	5.2	1.9	1.9	6	.560	0-0	37	6.2	1.0	1.5
Kevin Willis	18	.525	1-1	46	2.6	1.7	0.1	5	.333	0-0	8	1.6	1.8	0.0
Steve Kerr	10	.636	5-6	22	2.2	0.3	0.6	4	.750	1-1	8	2.0	0.3	0.5
Steve Smith	9	.208	4-14	20	1.8	0.8	0.7	1	.000	0-1	0	0.0	0.0	0.0
Danny Ferry	16	.286	2-12	16	1.3	1.4	0.4	3	.000	0-0	0	0.0	0.0	0.0
SPURS	24	.441	128-365	2275	94.8	45.5	20.7	6	.432	24-75	527	87.8	45.8	18.2
OPPONENTS	24	.404	139-420	2143	89.3	42.3	16.7	6	.370	23-83	492	82.0	42.5	16.7

Annual Awards

Most Valuable Player

The Maurice Podoloff Trophy; voting by 119-member panel of local and national pro basketball writers and broadcasters. Each ballot has five entries; points awarded on 10-7-5-3-1 basis.

	1st	2nd	3rd	4th	5th	Pts
Tim Duncan, San Antonio	33	38	18	2	0	962
Kevin Garnett, Minnesota	43	49	17	3	4	871
Kobe Bryant, LA Lakers	8	13	41	35	15	496
Tracy McGrady, Orlando	4	12	30	46	15	427
Shaquille O'Neal, LA Lakers	3	4	3	13	14	126
Allen Iverson, Philadelphia	0	2	3	9	27	83
Dirk Nowitzki, Dallas	0	1	2	2	20	43
Ben Wallace, Detroit	1	0	2	2	7	33
Jason Kidd, New Jersey	0	0	2	3	12	31
Chris Webber, Sacramento	0	0	1	4	2	19
Jamal Mashburn, N. Orleans	0	0	0	0	1	1
Steve Nash, Dallas	0	0	0	0	1	1
Paul Pierce, Boston	0	0	0	0	1	1

All-NBA Teams

Voting by a 122-member panel of local and national pro basketball writers and broadcasters. Each ballot has entries for three teams; points awarded on 5-3-1 basis. First Team repeaters from 2001-02 are in **bold** type.

Pos	First Team	1st	Pts
F	**Tim Duncan**, San Antonio	120	603
F	Kevin Garnett, Minnesota	115	596
C	**Shaquille O'Neal**, LA Lakers	112	593
G	**Tracy McGrady**, Orlando	107	578
G	**Kobe Bryant**, LA Lakers	118	599

Pos	Second Team	1st	Pts
F	Dirk Nowitzki, Dallas	5	360
F	Chris Webber, Sacramento	1	310
C	Ben Wallace, Detroit	5	307
G	Jason Kidd, New Jersey	16	355
G	Allen Iverson, Philadelphia	8	350

Pos	Third Team	1st	Pts
F	Paul Pierce, Boston	0	91
F	Jamal Mashburn, New Orleans	0	63
C/F	Jermaine O'Neal, Indiana	2	165
G	Stephon Marbury, Phoenix	1	141
G	Steve Nash, Dallas	0	85

All-Defensive Teams

Voting by NBA head coaches. Each ballot has entries for two teams; two points given for 1st team, one for 2nd. Coaches cannot vote for own players. First Team repeaters from 2001-02 are in **bold** type.

Pos	First Team	1st	Pts
F	**Tim Duncan**, San Antonio	18	44
F	**Kevin Garnett**, Minnesota	22	47
C	**Ben Wallace**, Detroit	27	55
G	Doug Christie, Sacramento	14	38
G	Kobe Bryant, LA Lakers	15	35

Pos	Second Team	1st	Pts
F	Ron Artest, Indiana	9	27
F	Bruce Bowen, San Antonio	8	24
C	Shaquille O'Neal, LA Lakers	1	12
G	Jason Kidd, New Jersey	15	37
G	Eric Snow, Philadelphia	3	16

Coach of the Year

The Red Auerbach Trophy; voting by a 121-member panel of local and national pro basketball writers and broadcasters.

	1st	2nd	3rd	Pts
Gregg Popovich, San Antonio	40	21	18	281
Eric Musselman, Golden St.	26	27	20	231
Jerry Sloan, Utah	18	14	11	143
Rick Carlisle, Detroit	8	21	14	117
Rich Adelman, Sacramento	8	161	13	71
Flip Saunders, Minnesota	5	6	14	57
Hubie Brown, Memphis	5	6	4	47
Don Nelson, Dallas	3	3	8	32
Larry Brown, Philadelphia	3	4	3	30
Maurice Cheeks, Portland	2	1	10	23
Frank Johnson, Phoenix	1	5	2	22
Paul Silas, New Orleans	1	3	3	17
Byron Scott, New Jersey	1	1	0	8
Phil Jackson, LA Lakers	0	1	1	4
Isiah Thomas, Indiana	0	1	0	3
Rudy Tomjanovich, Houston	0	1	0	3

Rookie of the Year

The Eddie Gottlieb Trophy; voting by 117-member panel of local and national pro basketball writers and broadcasters. Each ballot has entries for three players; points awarded on 5-3-1 basis.

	1st	2nd	3rd	Pts
Amare Stoudemire, Phoenix	59	53	4	458
Yao Ming, Houston	45	54	18	405
Caron Butler, Miami	13	9	87	179
Emanuel Ginobili, San Antonio	0	1	2	5
Drew Gooden, Mem-Orl	0	0	3	3
Nene Hilario, Denver	0	0	2	2
Carlos Boozer, Cleveland	0	0	1	1

All-Rookie Team

Voting by NBA's 29 head coaches, who cannot vote for players on their team. Each ballot has entries for two five-man teams, regardless of position; Coaches are not permitted to vote for players on their own team. two points given for 1st team, one for 2nd. First team votes in (parentheses).

First Team	College	Pts
Yao Ming, Houston (28)	—	56
Amare Stoudemire, Phoenix (28)	—	56
Caron Butler, Miami (27)	Connecticut	55
Drew Gooden, Mem-Orl. (17)	Kansas	45
Nene Hilario, Denver (13)	—	40

Second Team	College	Pts
Emanuel Ginobili, San Antonio (13)	—	38
Gordan Giricek, Mem-Orl. (7)	—	33
Carlos Boozer, Cleveland (5)	Duke	28
Jay Williams, Chicago (2)	Duke	28
J.R. Bremer, Boston (2)	St. Bonaventure	18

J. Walter Kennedy Citizenship Award

The award, named for the NBA's second commissioner, is presented annually by the Professional Basketball Writers Association to honor an NBA player or coach "for outstanding community service and commitment to serve and give of his time outside the arena." The other nominees for this season's award were Golden State's Adonal Foyle, Indiana's Reggie Miller, Boston's Walter McCarty and Washington's Jerry Stackhouse.

David Robinson, San Antonio

Sixth-Man Award

Voted on by a 118-member panel of local and national pro basketball writers and broadcasters. Each ballot has entries for three players; points awarded on 5-3-1 basis.

	1st	2nd	3rd	Pts
Bobby Jackson, Sacramento	.52	29	15	362
Michael Redd, Milwaukee	.33	25	17	257
Andrei Kirilenko, Utah	.10	18	23	127
Nick Van Exel, Dallas	.8	20	15	115
Corliss Williamson, Detroit	.5	14	20	87
Malik Rose, San Antonio	.6	5	12	57
Earl Boykins, Golden St.	.4	4	10	42
Al Harrington, Indiana	.0	2	1	7
Jon Barry, Detroit	.0	1	1	4
Toni Kukoc, Milwaukee	.0	1	0	3
Lucious Harris, New Jersey	.0	0	1	1
Keon Clark, Sacramento	.0	0	1	1
Joe Johnson, Phoenix	.0	0	1	1

Most Improved Player Award

Voted on by a 118-member panel of local and national pro basketball writers and broadcasters. Each ballot has entries for three players; points awarded on 5-3-1 basis.

	1st	2nd	3rd	Pts
Gilbert Arenas, Golden St.	41	24	11	288
Matt Harpring, Utah	29	24	17	234
Troy Murphy, Golden St.	18	13	15	144
Tony Parker, San Antonio	14	19	16	143
Ricky Davis, Cleveland	2	10	3	43
Chauncey Billips, Detroit	3	6	9	42
Jason Williams, Memphis	3	6	7	40

Defensive Player of the Year Award

Voted on by a 117-member panel of local and national pro basketball writers and broadcasters.

	1st	2nd	3rd	Pts
Ben Wallace, Detroit	.100	10	1	531
Ron Artest, Indiana	.2	30	22	122
Kevin Garnett, Minnesota	.8	21	18	121
Tim Duncan, San Antonio	.2	22	14	90
Doug Christie, Sacramento	.5	13	21	85
Allen Iverson, Philadelphia	.0	6	11	29
Bruce Bowen, San Antonio	.0	4	8	20
Kobe Bryant, LA Lakers	.0	3	7	16

Sportsmanship Award

Each of the 29 NBA teams nominated one player from their roster "who best represents the ideals of sportsmanship on the court," then a panel made up of former NBA players Walt Frazier, Mike Glenn, Tommy Heinsohn, Eddie Johnson, Gil McGregor and Ed Pinckney selected the four divisional winners from the pool of nominees. The award winner is chosen from the four divisional winners in vote by a 117-member panel of local and national pro basketball writers and broadcasters. The winner receives the Joe Dumars Trophy, named for the Detroit Pistons guard who won the inaugural sportsmanship award in 1996.

	1st	2nd	3rd	4th	Pts
Ray Allen, Seattle	.38	31	26	20	519
Allan Houston, New York	.30	36	22	29	485
P.J. Brown, New Orleans	.30	29	34	23	480
Michael Finley, Dallas	.18	20	34	44	372

2003 College Draft

First and second round picks at the 57th annual NBA College Draft held June 26, 2003 held in New York City at the Theatre at Madison Square Garden. The order of the first 13 positions were determined by a Draft Lottery held May 22, in Secaucus, N.J. Positions 14 through 29 reflect regular season records in reverse order. Underclassmen selected are noted in CAPITAL letters.

First Round

	Team		Pos
1	Cleveland	LEBRON JAMES, St Mary/St. Vincent	G/F
2	Detroit	Darko Milicic, Serbia	F
3	Denver	CARMELO ANTHONY, Syracuse	F
4	Toronto	CHRIS BOSH, Georgia Tech	F
5	Miami	DWYANE WADE, Marquette	G
6	L.A. Clippers	CHRIS KAMAN, C. Michigan	C
7	Chicago	Kirk Hinrich, Kansas	G
8	Milwaukee	T.J. FORD, Texas	G
9	New York	MICHAEL SWEETNEY, Georgetown	F
10	Washington	JARVIS HAYES, Georgia	G
11	Golden State	Michael Pietrus, France	G
12	Seattle	Nick Collison, Kansas	F
13	Memphis	Marcus Banks, UNLV	G
14	Seattle	LUKE RIDNOUR, Oregon	G
15	Orlando	Reece Gaines, Louisville	F
16	Boston	Troy Bell, Boston College	G
17	Phoenix	Zarko Cabarkapa, Serbia	F
18	New Orleans	David West, Xavier	F
19	Utah	Aleksandar Pavlovic, Serbia	F
20	Boston	Dahntay Jones, Duke	G
21	Atlanta	Boris Diaw, France	G
22	New Jersey	Zoran Planinic, Croatia	G
23	Portland	TRAVIS OUTLAW, Starkville (MS) HS	F
24	L.A. Lakers	Brian Cook, Illinois	F
25	Detroit	Carlos Delfino, Argentina	G
26	Minnesota	NDUBI EBI, Westbury Christ. (TX) HS	F
27	Memphis	KENDRICK PERKINS, Ozen (TX) HS	C
28	San Antonio	Leandrinho Barbosa, Brazil	G
29	Dallas	Josh Howard, Wake Forest	F

Second Round

	Team		Pos
30	New York	Maciej Lampe, Poland	C
31	Cleveland	Jason Kapono, UCLA	F
32	L.A. Lakers	Luke Walton, Arizona	F
33	Miami	Jerome Beasley, North Dakota	F
34	L.A. Clippers	Sofoklis Schortsanitis, Greece	C
35	Milwaukee	Szymon Szewczyk, Poland	F
36	Chicago	MARIO AUSTIN, Mississippi St.	F
37	Atlanta	Travis Hansen, BYU	G
38	Washington	Steve Blake, Maryland	G
39	New York	Slavko Vranes, Serbia	C
40	Golden St.	Derrick Zimmerman, Mississippi St.	G
41	Seattle	Willie Green, Detroit	G
42	Orlando	Zaur Pachulia, Georgia	F
43	Milwaukee	Keith Bogans, Kentucky	G
44	Houston	Malick Badiane, Senegal	F
45	Chicago	Matt Bonner, Florida	F
46	Denver	Sani Becirovic, Slovenia	G
47	Utah	MAURICE WILLIAMS, Alabama	G
48	New Orleans	JAMES LANG, C. Park Christ. (AL) HS	C
49	Indiana	James Jones, Miami-FL	F
50	Philadelphia	Paccelis Morlende, France	G
51	New Jersey	Kyle Korver, Creighton	G
52	Toronto	Remon Van de Hare, Spain	C
53	Chicago	Tommy Smith, Arizona St.	F
54	Portland	Nedzad Sinanovic, Bosnia	C
55	Minnesota	RICK RICKERT, Minnesota	F
56	Boston	Brandon Hunter, Ohio	F
57	Dallas	Xue Yuyang, China	C
58	Detroit	Andreas Gliniadakis, Greece	C

Continental Basketball Association
Final Standings

QW refers to quarters won. Teams get 3 points for a win, 1 point for each quarter won and $1/2$ point for any quarters tied. (*) denotes playoff qualifiers.

American Conference

	W	L	QW	Pts	Avg
*Rockford Lightning	32	16	112.5	208.5	4.3
*Grand Rapids Hoops	23	25	100.5	169.5	3.5
Gary Steelheads	25	23	93.5	168.5	3.5
Great Lakes Storm	19	29	80.5	137.5	2.9

National Conference

	W	L	QW	Pts	Avg
*Dakota Wizards	31	17	119.5	212.5	4.4
*Yakima Sun Kings	28	20	104.5	188.5	3.9
Idaho Stampede	17	31	87.5	138.5	2.9
Sioux Falls Skyforce	17	31	69.5	120.5	2.5

Playoffs
Semifinals

Rockford vs. Grand Rapids

Mar. 11 at Rockford 149 . . . . .OT . .Grand Rapids 146
Mar. 12 Grand Rapids 128 . . . . .at Rockford 120
Mar. 18 at Grand Rapids 116 . . . . .Rockford 108
Mar. 19 at Grand Rapids 127 . . . . .Rockford 124
Grand Rapids wins series, 3 games to 1

Dakota vs. Yakima

Mar. 11 at Dakota 100 . . . . .Yakima 98
Mar. 12 Yakima 110 . . . . .at Dakota 102
Mar. 16 at Yakima 109 . . . . .Dakota 102
Mar. 17 at Yakima 105 . . . . .Dakota 100
Yakima wins series, 3 games to 1

CBA Annual Awards

Most Valuable Player . . . . . . .Andy Panko, Dakota
Newcomer of the Year . .Damian Cantrell, Yakima
Rookie of the Year . .Immanuel McElroy, G. Rapids
Def. Player of the Year . . . . .Kevin Rice, Dakota
Coach of the Year . . . . .Chris Daleo, Rockford

Final

Mon., Mar. 24 at Yakima Valley SunDome, Yakima, Wash.
Attendance: 4,815.

	1	2	3	4	F
Grand Rapids Hoops	30	27	30	20	—107
Yakima Sun Kings	30	26	33	28	—117

Playoff MVP: Darrick Martin, Yakima, G (23.0 ppg, 5.8 apg)

CBA Regular Season Individual Leaders

Scoring

	Gm	Pts	Avg
Ronnie Fields, Rockford	48	1115	23.2
Andy Panko, Dakota	45	1025	22.8
Jerald Honeycutt, Grand Rapids	44	994	22.6
Albert White, Rockford	47	1035	22.0
Bryant Notree, Gary	48	1022	21.3
Alex Scales, Grand Rapids	46	907	19.7
Silas Mills, Gary	35	677	19.3
Kelley McClure, Sioux Falls	40	762	19.1

Field Goal Pct.

	FGM	FGA	Pct
Chianti Roberts, Idaho	120	183	.656
Livan Pyfrom, Rockford	171	278	.615
Shawn Daniels, Dakota	134	226	.593
Immanuel McElroy, Grand Rapids	212	358	.592
Victor Thomas, Sioux Falls	268	456	.588
Oliver Miller, Dakota	272	464	.586
Damien Cantrell, Yakima	221	392	.564
John Jackson, Rockford	122	217	.562

Rebounding

	Gm	Reb	Avg
Damien Cantrell, Yakima	34	434	12.8
Oliver Miller, Dakota	43	522	12.1
Olden Polynice, Grand Rapids	25	288	11.5
Kevin Simmons, Grand Rapids	47	459	9.8
Livan Pyfrom, Rockford	48	447	9.3
Andy Panko, Dakota	45	376	8.4
Galen Young, Gary	45	374	8.3
Antonio Harvey, Idaho	29	238	8.2

Assists

	Gm	Ast	Avg
Tyson Wheeler, Great Lakes	46	378	8.2
Jermeil Rich, Gary	48	358	7.5
Chris Garner, Idaho	48	341	7.1
Kelley McClure, Sioux Falls	40	237	5.9
Malik Dixon, Dakota	48	240	5.0
Michael Johnson, Idaho	36	178	4.9
Lazarus Sims, Grand Rapids	34	164	4.8
Tim Kisner, Grand Rapids	42	191	4.5

National Basketball Development League

The NBDL is a feeder league founded by the NBA in 2001. The individual teams do not have direct relationships with NBA clubs but players (and coaches) are called-up to the NBA occasionally. (*) denotes playoff qualifiers.

2003 Final Standings

	W	L	Pct	GB
*Fayetteville Patriots	32	18	.640	—
*North Charleston Lowgators	26	24	.520	6
*Mobile Revelers	26	24	.520	6
*Roanoke Dazzle	26	24	.520	6
Asheville Altitude	23	27	.460	9
Columbus Riverdragons	23	27	.460	9
Greenville Groove	22	28	.440	10
Huntsville Flight	22	28	.440	10

Annual Awards

Most Valuable Player . . . . . .Devin Brown, Fayetteville
Rookie of the Year . . . . .Devin Brown, Fayetteville
Def. Player of the Year . . . . .Mikki Moore, Roanoke
Sportsmanship . . . . .Billy Thomas, Greenville

All-NBDL Team

Pos		Team
F	Tang Hamilton	Columbus
F	Mikki Moore	Roanoke
G	Devin Brown	Fayetteville
G	Tierre Brown	North Charleston
G	Jeff Trepagnier	Asheville

Playoffs

Semifinals (Best of 3)

Fayetteville vs. Roanoke

Mar. 25 at Fayetteville 101 . . . . .Roanoke 88
Mar. 30 Fayetteville 78 . . . . .at Roanoke 77
Fayetteville wins series, 2 games to 0

Mobile vs. North Charleston

Mar. 28 Mobile 88 . . . . .at North Charleston 79
Mar. 30 at Mobile 81 . . . . .North Charleston 69
Mobile wins series, 2 games to 0

Finals (Best of 3)

Fayetteville vs. Mobile

Apr. 4 Mobile 92 . . . . .at Fayetteville 82
Apr. 9 Fayetteville 77 . . . . .at Mobile 71
Apr. 11 Mobile 75 . . . . .at Fayetteville 72

Mobile Revelers win series, 2 games to 1

Regular Season Individual Leaders

Scoring

	Gm	Pts	Avg
Nate Johnson, Columbus 49		955	19.5
Jeff Trepagnier, Asheville 48		850	17.7
Devin Brown, Fayetteville 44		742	16.9
Corey Benjamin, North Charleston . .38		632	16.6
Cory Alexander, Roanoke 50		827	16.5

Assists

	Gm	Ast	Avg
Cory Alexander, Roanoke 50		306	6.1
Omar Cook, Fayetteville 50		268	5.4
Eddie Gill, Asheville 35		182	5.2
Nate Green, Columbus 37		189	5.1
Terrell McIntyre, Fayetteville 50		255	5.1

Rebounds

	Gm	Reb	Avg
Tang Hamilton, Columbus 50		452	9.0
Mikki Moore, Roanoke 42		352	8.4
Derek Hood, Mobile 48		399	8.3
Rodney Bias, Huntsville 49		362	7.4
Soumaila Samake, Greenville 33		231	7.0

Women's National Basketball Association

Final WNBA Standings

Conference champions (*) and playoff qualifiers (†) are noted. GB refers to Games Behind leader. Number of seasons listed after each head coach refers to current tenure with club.

Eastern Conference

	W	L	Pct	GB	Home	Road
*Detroit 25		9	.735	—	13-4	12-5
†Charlotte 18		16	.529	7	12-12	13-4
†Connecticut 18		16	.529	7	10-7	8-9
†Cleveland 17		17	.500	8	11-6	6-11
Indiana 16		18	.471	9	11-6	5-12
New York 16		18	.471	9	11-6	5-12
Washington 9		25	.265	16	3-14	6-11

Head Coaches: Det–Bill Laimbeer (2nd season); **Cha**–Trudi Lacey (1st); **Conn**– Mike Thibault (1st); **Cle**–Dan Hughes (4th); **Ind**–Nell Fortner (3rd); **NY**–Richie Adubato (5th); **Wash**–Marianne Stanley (2nd).

2002 Standings: 1. New York (18-14); 2. Charlotte (18-14); 3. Washington (17-15); 4. Indiana (16-16); 5. Orlando (16-16); 6. Miami (15-17); 7. Cleveland (10-22); 8. Detroit (9-23).

Note: Prior to the 2003 season, two WNBA teams were relocated and two (Miami Sol and Portland Fire) were contracted. The Orlando Miracle moved to Uncasville, Conn. and became the Connecticut Sun. The Utah Starzz moved to San Antonio and became the San Antonio Silver Stars.

Western Conference

	W	L	Pct	GB	Home	Road
*Los Angeles 24		10	.706	—	11-6	13-4
†Houston 20		14	.588	4	14-3	6-11
†Sacramento 19		15	.559	5	12-5	7-10
†Minnesota 18		16	.529	6	11-6	7-10
Seattle 18		16	.529	6	13-4	5-12
San Antonio . . .12		22	.353	12	9-8	3-14
Phoenix 8		26	.235	16	6-11	2-15

Head Coaches: LA–Michael Cooper (4th season); **Hou**–Van Chancellor (7th); **Sac**–Maura McHugh (3rd, 7-11) was fired on July 9 and replaced by assistant general manager John Whisenant on an interim basis (12-4); **Min**–Suzie McConnell Serio (1st); **Sea**–Anne Donovan (1st); **SA**–Candi Harvey (2nd, 6-16) was fired on July 26 and replaced by assistant Shell Dailey (6-6) on an interim basis; **Pho**–John Shumate (1st).

2002 Standings: 1. Los Angeles (25-7); 2. Houston (24-8); 3. Utah (20-12); 4. Seattle (17-15); 5. Portland (16-16); 6. Sacramento (14-18); 7. Phoenix (11-21); 8. Minnesota (10-22).

WNBA Regular Season Individual Leaders

Scoring

	Gm	Pts	Avg
Lauren Jackson, Seattle 33		698	21.2
Chamique Holdsclaw, Washington . .27		554	20.5
Tamika Catchings, Indiana 34		671	19.7
Lisa Leslie, Los Angeles 23		424	18.4
Katie Smith, Minnesota 34		620	18.2
Tina Thompson, Houston 28		472	16.9
Swin Cash, Detroit 33		548	16.6
Nykesha Sales, Connecticut 34		548	16.1
Sheryl Swoopes, Houston 31		484	15.6
Marie Ferdinand, San Antonio 34		470	13.8
Yolanda Griffith, Sacramento 34		469	13.8
Mwadi Mabika, Los Angeles 32		441	13.8

Rebounding

	Gm	Reb	Avg
Chamique Holdsclaw, Washington . .27		294	10.9
Cheryl Ford, Detroit 32		334	10.4
Lisa Leslie, Los Angeles 23		231	10.0
Lauren Jackson, Seattle 33		307	9.3
Tari Phillips, New York 33		280	8.5
Tamika Catchings, Indiana 34		272	8.0
Michelle Snow, Houston 34		263	7.7
Natalie Williams, Indiana 34		255	7.5
Adrian Williams, Phoenix 34		252	7.4
Margo Dydek, San Antonio 34		251	7.4
Yolanda Griffith, Sacramento 34		248	7.3
DeLisha Milton, Los Angeles 31		220	7.1

Field Goal Pct.

	FGM	FGA	Pct
Tamika Williams, Minnesota	129	193	.668
Michelle Snow, Houston	126	253	.498
Ruth Riley, Detroit	115	231	.498
Yolanda Griffith, Sacramento	161	332	.485
Natalie Williams, Indiana	176	363	.485
Lauren Jackson, Seattle	254	526	.483
Chasity Melvin, Cleveland	159	333	.477
Kamila Vodichkova, Seattle	101	213	.474
Cheryl Ford, Detroit	128	270	.474
Kristen Rasmussen, Indiana	94	200	.470

Assists

	Gm	Ast	Avg
Ticha Penicheiro, Sacramento	34	229	6.7
Sue Bird, Seattle	34	221	6.5
Nikki Teasley, Los Angeles	34	214	6.3
Shannon Johnson, Connecticut	34	196	5.8
Dawn Staley, Charlotte	34	174	5.1
Teresa Weatherspoon, New York	34	148	4.4
Teresa Edwards, Minnesota	34	148	4.4
Tamicha Jackson, Phoenix	34	146	4.3
Elaine Powell, Detroit	33	129	3.9
Sheryl Swoopes, Houston	31	121	3.9

WNBA Annual Awards

Most Valuable Player . . . . . Lauren Jackson, Seattle	**Def. Player of the Year** . . Sheryl Swoopes, Houston
Rookie of the Year . . . . Cheryl Ford, Detroit	**Coach of the Year** . . . . Bill Laimbeer, Detroit
Most Improved . . . . Michelle Snow, Houston	**Sportsmanship Award** . . . . . Edna Campbell, Sac.

WNBA Playoffs

First Round (Best of 3)

East

Aug. 29   Detroit 76 . . . . at Cleveland 74
Aug. 31   Cleveland 66 . . . . at Detroit 59
Sept. 2   at Detroit 77 . . . . Cleveland 63

Detroit Shock win series, 2-1

Aug. 28   at Connecticut 68 . . . . Charlotte 66
Aug. 30   Connecticut 68 . . . . at Charlotte 62

Connecticut Sun win series, 2-0

West

Aug. 28   at Minnesota 74 . . . . Los Angeles 72
Aug. 30   at Los Angeles 80 . . . . Minnesota 69
Sept. 1   at Los Angeles 74 . . . . Minnesota 64

Los Angeles Sparks win series, 2-1

Aug. 29   at Sacramento 65 . . . . Houston 59
Aug. 31   at Houston 69 . . . . Sacramento 48
Sept. 2   Sacramento 70 . . . . at Houston 68

Sacramento Monarchs win series, 2-1

Conference Finals (Best of 3)

East

Sept. 5   Detroit 73 . . . . at Connecticut 63
Sept. 7   at Detroit 79 . . . . Connecticut 73

Detroit Shock win series, 2-0

West

Sept. 5   at Sacramento 77 . . . . Los Angeles 69
Sept. 7   at Los Angeles 79 . . . . Sacramento 54
Sept. 9   at Los Angeles 66 . . . . Sacramento 63

Los Angeles Sparks win series, 2-1

Championship Series (Best of 3)

Detroit Shock wins series, 2 games to 1

	W-L	Avg	Leading Scorer
Los Angeles	1-2	71.3	Milton (18.7)
Detroit	2-1	69.3	Nolan (15.3)

Date	Winner	Home Court
Sept. 12	Sparks, 75-63	at Los Angeles
Sept. 14	Shock, 62-61	at Detroit
Sept. 16	Shock, 83-78	at Detroit

Finals MVP: Ruth Riley, Detroit, C, (14.7 ppg, 5.0 rpg, 3.3 bpg)

WNBA 2003 Attendance

Attendance figures below are for the regular season and teams are listed in alphabetical order.

Team	Home Games	Total Attendance	Average Attendance
Charlotte Sting	17	120,061	7,062
Cleveland Rockers	17	125,793	7,400
Connecticut Sun	17	102,433	6,025
Detroit Shock	17	133,647	7,862
Houston Comets	17	150,199	8,835
Indiana Fever	17	141,778	8,340
Los Angeles Sparks	17	157,934	9,290
Minnesota Lynx	17	120,253	7,074
New York Liberty	17	212,346	12,491
Phoenix Mercury	17	144,511	8,501
Sacramento Monarchs	17	155,578	9,152
San Antonio Silver Stars	17	176,526	10,384
Seattle Storm	17	120,857	7,109
Washington Mystics	17	227,874	13,404
WNBA TOTALS	238	2,089,790	8,781

1938-2003
Through the Years

SPORTS ALMANAC

The NBA Finals

Although the National Basketball Association traces its first championship back to the 1946-47 season, the league was then called the Basketball Association of America (BAA). It did not become the NBA until after the 1948-49 season when the BAA and the National Basketball League (NBL) agreed to merge.

In the chart below, the Eastern finalists (representing the NBA Eastern Division from 1947-70, and the NBA Eastern Conference since 1971) are listed in CAPITAL letters. Also, each NBA champion's wins and losses are noted in parentheses after the series score.

Multiple winners: Boston (16); Minneapolis-LA Lakers (14); Chicago Bulls (6); Phi-SF-Golden St. Warriors and Syracuse Nationals-Phi. 76ers (3); Detroit, Houston, New York and San Antonio (2).

Year	Winner	Head Coach	Series	Loser	Head Coach
1947	PHILADELPHIA WARRIORS	Eddie Gottlieb	4-1 (WWWLW)	Chicago Stags	Harold Olsen
1948	Baltimore Bullets	Buddy Jeannette	4-2 (LWWWLW)	PHILA. WARRIORS	Eddie Gottlieb
1949	Minneapolis Lakers	John Kundla	4-2 (WWWLLW)	WASH. CAPITOLS	Red Auerbach
1950	Minneapolis Lakers	John Kundla	4-2 (WLWWLW)	SYRACUSE	Al Cervi
1951	Rochester	Les Harrison	4-3 (WWWLLLW)	NEW YORK	Joe Lapchick
1952	Minneapolis Lakers	John Kundla	4-3 (WLWLWLW)	NEW YORK	Joe Lapchick
1953	Minneapolis Lakers	John Kundla	4-1 (LWWWW)	NEW YORK	Joe Lapchick
1954	Minneapolis Lakers	John Kundla	4-3 (WWLWLW)	SYRACUSE	Al Cervi
1955	SYRACUSE	Al Cervi	4-3 (WWLLLWW)	Ft. Wayne Pistons	Charley Eckman
1956	PHILADELPHIA WARRIORS	George Senesky	4-1 (WLWWW)	Ft. Wayne Pistons	Charley Eckman
1957	BOSTON	Red Auerbach	4-3 (LWLWLWW)	St. Louis Hawks	Alex Hannum
1958	St. Louis Hawks	Alex Hannum	4-2 (WLWLWW)	BOSTON	Red Auerbach
1959	BOSTON	Red Auerbach	4-0	Mpls. Lakers	John Kundla
1960	BOSTON	Red Auerbach	4-3 (WLWLWLW)	St. Louis Hawks	Ed Macauley
1961	BOSTON	Red Auerbach	4-1 (WWLWW)	St. Louis Hawks	Paul Seymour
1962	BOSTON	Red Auerbach	4-3 (WLLWLWW)	LA Lakers	Fred Schaus
1963	BOSTON	Red Auerbach	4-2 (WWLWLW)	LA Lakers	Fred Schaus
1964	BOSTON	Red Auerbach	4-1 (WWLWW)	SF Warriors	Alex Hannum
1965	BOSTON	Red Auerbach	4-1 (WWLWW)	LA Lakers	Fred Schaus
1966	BOSTON	Red Auerbach	4-3 (LWWWLLW)	LA Lakers	Fred Schaus
1967	PHILADELPHIA 76ERS	Alex Hannum	4-2 (WWLWWW)	SF Warriors	Bill Sharman
1968	BOSTON	Bill Russell	4-2 (WLWLWW)	LA Lakers	B.van Breda Kolff
1969	BOSTON	Bill Russell	4-3 (LLWWLWW)	LA Lakers	B.van Breda Kolff
1970	NEW YORK	Red Holzman	4-3 (WLWLWLW)	LA Lakers	Joe Mullaney
1971	Milwaukee	Larry Costello	4-0	BALT. BULLETS	Gene Shue
1972	LA Lakers	Bill Sharman	4-1 (LWWWW)	NEW YORK	Red Holzman
1973	NEW YORK	Red Holzman	4-1 (LWWWW)	LA Lakers	Bill Sharman
1974	BOSTON	Tommy Heinsohn	4-3 (WLWLWLW)	Milwaukee	Larry Costello
1975	Golden St. Warriors	Al Attles	4-0	WASH. BULLETS	K.C. Jones
1976	BOSTON	Tommy Heinsohn	4-2 (WWLLWW)	Phoenix	John MacLeod
1977	Portland	Jack Ramsay	4-2 (LLWWWW)	PHILA. 76ERS	Gene Shue
1978	WASHINGTON BULLETS	Dick Motta	4-3 (LWLWLWW)	Seattle	Lenny Wilkens
1979	Seattle	Lenny Wilkens	4-1 (LWWWW)	WASH. BULLETS	Dick Motta
1980	LA Lakers	Paul Westhead	4-2 (WLWLWW)	PHILA. 76ERS	Billy Cunningham
1981	BOSTON	Bill Fitch	4-2 (WLWLWW)	Houston	Del Harris
1982	LA Lakers	Pat Riley	4-2 (WLWWLW)	PHILA. 76ERS	Billy Cunningham
1983	PHILADELPHIA 76ERS	Billy Cunningham	4-0	LA Lakers	Pat Riley
1984	BOSTON	K.C. Jones	4-3 (LWLWLWW)	LA Lakers	Pat Riley
1985	LA Lakers	Pat Riley	4-2 (LWWLWW)	BOSTON	K.C. Jones
1986	BOSTON	K.C. Jones	4-2 (WWWLWLW)	Houston	Bill Fitch
1987	LA Lakers	Pat Riley	4-2 (WWLWLW)	BOSTON	K.C. Jones
1988	LA Lakers	Pat Riley	4-3 (LWWLLWW)	DETROIT PISTONS	Chuck Daly
1989	DETROIT PISTONS	Chuck Daly	4-0	LA Lakers	Pat Riley
1990	DETROIT	Chuck Daly	4-1 (WLWWW)	Portland	Rick Adelman
1991	CHICAGO	Phil Jackson	4-1 (LWWWW)	LA Lakers	Mike Dunleavy
1992	CHICAGO	Phil Jackson	4-2 (WLWLWW)	Portland	Rick Adelman
1993	CHICAGO	Phil Jackson	4-2 (WWWLWLW)	Phoenix	Paul Westphal
1994	Houston	Rudy Tomjanovich	4-3 (WLWLLWW)	NEW YORK	Pat Riley
1995	Houston	Rudy Tomjanovich	4-0	ORLANDO	Brian Hill

Year	Winner	Head Coach	Series	Loser	Head Coach
1996	CHICAGO	Phil Jackson	4-2 (WWWLLW)	Seattle	George Karl
1997	CHICAGO	Phil Jackson	4-2 (WWLLWW)	Utah	Jerry Sloan
1998	CHICAGO	Phil Jackson	4-2 (LWWWLW)	Utah	Jerry Sloan
1999	San Antonio	Gregg Popovich	4-1 (WWLWW)	NEW YORK	Jeff Van Gundy
2000	LA Lakers	Phil Jackson	4-2 (WWWLLW)	INDIANA	Larry Bird
2001	LA Lakers	Phil Jackson	4-1 (LWWWW)	PHILA. 76ERS	Larry Brown
2002	LA Lakers	Phil Jackson	4-0	NEW JERSEY	Byron Scott
2003	San Antonio	Gregg Popovich	4-2 (WLWLWW)	NEW JERSEY	Byron Scott

Note: Four finalists were led by player-coaches: **1948**—Buddy Jeannette (guard) of Baltimore; **1950**—Al Cervi (guard) of Syracuse; **1968**—Bill Russell (center) of Boston; **1969**—Bill Russell (center) of Boston.

Most Valuable Player

Selected by an 11-member media panel. Winner who did not play for the NBA champion is in **bold** type.

Multiple winners: Michael Jordan (6); Magic Johnson and Shaquille O'Neal (3); Kareem Abdul-Jabbar, Larry Bird, Tim Duncan, Hakeem Olajuwon and Willis Reed (2).

Year		Year		Year	
1969	**Jerry West**, LA Lakers, G	1981	Cedric Maxwell, Boston, F	1993	Michael Jordan, Chicago, G
1970	Willis Reed, New York, C	1982	Magic Johnson, LA Lakers, G	1994	Hakeem Olajuwon, Houston, C
1971	Lew Alcindor, Milwaukee, C	1983	Moses Malone, Philadelphia, C	1995	Hakeem Olajuwon, Houston, C
1972	Wilt Chamberlain, LA Lakers, C	1984	Larry Bird, Boston, F	1996	Michael Jordan, Chicago, G
1973	Willis Reed, New York, C	1985	K. Abdul-Jabbar, LA Lakers, C	1997	Michael Jordan, Chicago, G
1974	John Havlicek, Boston, F	1986	Larry Bird, Boston, F	1998	Michael Jordan, Chicago, G
1975	Rick Barry, Golden State, F	1987	Magic Johnson, LA Lakers, G	1999	Tim Duncan, San Antonio, F/C
1976	Jo Jo White, Boston, G	1988	James Worthy, LA Lakers, F	2000	Shaquille O'Neal, LA Lakers, C
1977	Bill Walton, Portland, C	1989	Joe Dumars, Detroit, G	2001	Shaquille O'Neal, LA Lakers, C
1978	Wes Unseld, Washington, C	1990	Isiah Thomas, Detroit, G	2002	Shaquille O'Neal, LA Lakers, C
1979	Dennis Johnson, Seattle, G	1991	Michael Jordan, Chicago, G	2003	Tim Duncan, San Antonio, F/C
1980	Magic Johnson, LA Lakers, G/C	1992	Michael Jordan, Chicago, G		

Note: Lew Alcindor changed his name to Kareem Abdul-Jabbar after the 1970-71 season.

All-Time NBA Playoff Leaders

Through the 2003 playoffs.

CAREER

Years listed indicate number of playoff appearances. Players active in 2002 in **bold** type. DNP indicates player that was active in 2003 but did not participate in playoffs.

Points

		Yrs	Gm	Pts	Avg
1	**Michael Jordan** (DNP)	13	179	5987	33.4
2	Kareem Abdul-Jabbar	18	237	5762	24.3
3	**Karl Malone**	18	172	4519	26.3
4	Jerry West	13	153	4457	29.1
5	Larry Bird	12	164	3897	23.8
6	**Shaquille O'Neal**	10	136	3821	28.1
7	John Havlicek	13	172	3776	22.0
8	Hakeem Olajuwon	15	145	3755	25.9
9	Magic Johnson	13	190	3701	19.5
10	Elgin Baylor	12	134	3623	27.0
11	**Scottie Pippen**	16	208	3642	17.5
12	Wilt Chamberlain	13	160	3607	22.5
13	Kevin McHale	13	169	3182	18.8
14	Dennis Johnson	13	180	3116	17.3
15	Julius Erving	11	141	3088	21.9
16	James Worthy	9	143	3022	21.1
17	Clyde Drexler	15	145	2963	20.4
18	Sam Jones	12	154	2909	18.9
19	Charles Barkley	13	123	2833	23.0
20	Robert Parish	16	184	2820	15.3

Scoring Average

Minimum of 25 games or 700 points.

		Yrs	Gm	Pts	Avg
1	**Michael Jordan** (DNP)	13	179	5987	33.4
2	**Allen Iverson**	5	57	1743	30.6
3	Jerry West	13	153	4457	29.1
4	**Shaquille O'Neal**	10	136	3821	28.1
5	Elgin Baylor	12	134	3623	27.0
6	George Gervin	9	59	1592	27.0
7	**Karl Malone**	18	172	4519	26.3
8	Hakeem Olajuwon	15	145	3755	25.9
9	Dominique Wilkins	9	55	1421	25.8
10	Bob Pettit	9	88	2240	25.5
11	Rick Barry	7	74	1833	24.8
12	Bernard King	5	28	687	24.5
13	Alex English	10	68	1661	24.4
14	Kareem Abdul-Jabbar	18	237	5762	24.3
15	Paul Arizin	8	49	1186	24.2
16	**Tim Duncan**	5	72	1739	24.2
17	Larry Bird	12	164	3897	23.8
18	George Mikan	9	91	2141	23.5
19	Charles Barkley	13	123	2833	23.0
20	**Reggie Miller**	13	115	2618	22.8

Field Goals

		Yrs	FG	Att	Pct
1	Kareem Abdul-Jabbar	18	2356	4422	.533
2	**Michael Jordan** (DNP)	13	2188	4497	.487
3	Jerry West	13	1622	3460	.469
4	**Karl Malone**	18	1645	3550	.463
5	Hakeem Olajuwon	15	1504	2847	.528
6	**Shaquille O'Neal**	10	1476	2644	.558
7	Larry Bird	12	1458	3090	.472
8	John Havlicek	13	1451	3329	.436
9	Wilt Chamberlain	13	1425	2728	.522
10	Elgin Baylor	12	1388	3161	.439

Free Throws

		Yrs	FT	Att	Pct
1	**Michael Jordan** (DNP)	13	1463	1766	.828
2	**Karl Malone**	18	1223	1652	.740
3	Jerry West	13	1213	1507	.805
4	Kareem Abdul-Jabbar	18	1050	1419	.740
5	Magic Johnson	12	1040	1241	.838
6	Larry Bird	12	901	1012	.891
7	John Havlicek	13	874	1046	.836
8	**Shaquille O'Neal**	10	869	1635	.531
9	Elgin Baylor	12	847	1101	.769
10	**Scottie Pippen**	16	772	1067	.724

Assists

		Yrs	Gm	No	Avg
1	Magic Johnson	13	190	2346	12.3
2	John Stockton	19	182	1839	10.1
3	Larry Bird	12	164	1062	6.5
4	Scottie Pippen	16	208	1048	5.0
5	Michael Jordan (DNP)	13	179	1022	5.7

Rebounds

		Yrs	Gm	No	Avg
1	Bill Russell	13	165	4104	24.9
2	Wilt Chamberlain	13	160	3913	24.5
3	Kareem Abdul-Jabbar	237	2481	10.5	
4	Karl Malone	18	172	1877	10.9
5	Wes Unseld	12	119	1777	14.9

Appearances

	No		No
John Stockton	19	Sam Perkins	15
Kareem Abdul-Jabbar	18	Tree Rollins	15
Karl Malone	18	Dolph Schayes	15
Robert Parish	16	Charles Oakley	15
Scottie Pippen	16	Jerome Kersey	15
Terry Porter	16	Clyde Drexler	15

Games Played

	No		No
K. Abdul-Jabbar	237	Michael Jordan (DNP)	179
Scottie Pippen	208	Karl Malone	172
Danny Ainge	193	John Havlicek	172
Magic Johnson	190	Kevin McHale	169
Robert Parish	184	Michael Cooper	168
Byron Scott	183	Bill Russell	165
John Stockton	182	Larry Bird	164
Dennis Johnson	180	Paul Silas	163

SINGLE GAME

Points

	Date	FG-FT–Pts
Michael Jordan, Chi at Bos*	4/20/86	22-19–63
Elgin Baylor, LA at Bos	4/14/62	22-17–61
Wilt Chamberlain, Phi vs Syr	3/22/62	22-12–56
Michael Jordan, Chi at Mia	4/29/92	20-16–56
Charles Barkley, Pho vs G.St.	5/4/94	23-7–56
Rick Barry, SF vs Phi	4/18/67	22-11–55
Michael Jordan, Chi vs Cle	5/1/88	24-7–55
Michael Jordan, Chi vs Pho	4/16/93	21-13–55
Michael Jordan, Chi vs. Wash	4/27/97	22-10–55

*Double overtime.

Field Goals

	Date	FG	Att
Wilt Chamberlain, Phi vs Syr	3/14/60	24	42
John Havlicek, Bos vs Atl	4/1/73	24	36
Michael Jordan, Chi vs Cle	5/1/88	24	45

Eight tied with 22 each.

Miscellaneous

3-Pt Field Goals	Date	No
Rex Chapman, Pho at Sea	4/25/97	9
Dan Majerle, Pho vs Sea	6/1/93	8
Allen Iverson, Phi vs Tor	5/16/01	8

Eight tied with 7 each.

Assists	Date	No
Magic Johnson, LA vs Pho	5/15/84	24
John Stockton, Utah at LA Lakers	5/17/88	24
Magic Johnson, LA Lakers at Port	5/3/85	23
John Stockton, Utah vs Port	4/25/96	23
Doc Rivers, Atl vs Bos	5/16/88	22

Four tied with 21 each.

Rebounds	Date	No
Wilt Chamberlain, Phi vs Bos	4/5/67	41
Bill Russell, Bos vs Phi	3/23/58	40
Bill Russell, Bos vs St.L	3/29/60	40
Bill Russell, Bos vs LA*	4/18/62	40

Three tied with 39 each.
*Overtime.

Appearances in NBA Finals

Standings of all NBA teams that have reached the NBA Finals since 1947.

App		Titles	Last Won
27	Minneapolis-LA Lakers	14	2002
19	Boston Celtics	16	1986
9	Syracuse Nats-Phila. 76ers	3	1983
8	New York Knicks	2	1973
6	Chicago Bulls	6	1998
6	Phila-SF-Golden St. Warriors	3	1975
5	Ft. Wayne-Detroit Pistons	2	1990
4	Houston Rockets	2	1995
4	St. Louis Hawks	1	1958
4	Baltimore-Washington Bullets	1	1978
3	Portland Trail Blazers	1	1977
3	Seattle SuperSonics	1	1979
2	San Antonio Spurs	2	2003
2	Milwaukee Bucks	1	1971
2	New Jersey Nets	0	—
2	Phoenix Suns	0	—
2	Utah Jazz	0	—
1	Baltimore Bullets	1	1948
1	Rochester Royals	1	1951
1	Chicago Stags	0	—
1	Orlando Magic	0	—
1	Washington Capitols	0	—
1	Indiana Pacers	0	—

Change of address: The St. Louis Hawks now play in Atlanta and the Rochester Royals are now the Sacramento Kings.
Teams now defunct: Baltimore Bullets (1947-55), Chicago Stags (1946-50) and Washington Capitols (1946-51).

NBA FINALS
Points

Series		Year	Pts
4-Gm	Shaquille O'Neal, LAL vs NJ	2002	145
5-Gm	Allen Iverson, Phi vs LAL	2001	178
6-Gm	Michael Jordan, Chi vs Pho	1993	246
7-Gm	Elgin Baylor, LA vs Bos	1962	284

Field Goals

Series		Year	No
4-Gm	Hakeem Olajuwon, Hou vs Orl	1995	56
5-Gm	Allen Iverson, Phi vs LAL	2001	66
6-Gm	Michael Jordan, Chi vs Pho	1993	101
7-Gm	Elgin Baylor, LA vs Bos	1962	101

Assists

Series		Year	No
4-Gm	Bob Cousy, Bos vs Mpls	1959	51
5-Gm	Magic Johnson, LAL vs Chi	1991	62
6-Gm	Magic Johnson, LAL vs Bos	1985	84
7-Gm	Magic Johnson, LA vs Bos	1984	95

Rebounds

Series		Year	No
4-Gm	Bill Russell, Bos vs Mpls	1959	118
5-Gm	Bill Russell, Bos vs St.L	1961	144
6-Gm	Wilt Chamberlain, Phi vs SF	1967	171
7-Gm	Bill Russell, Bos vs LA	1962	189

The National Basketball League

The NBL started with 13 previously independent teams in 1937-38 and although GE, Firestone and Goodyear were gone by late 1942, ran 12 years before merging with the three-year-old Basketball Association of America in 1949 to form the NBA.
Multiple champions: Akron Firestone Non-Skids, Fort Wayne Zollner Pistons, Oshkosh All-Stars (2).

Year	Winner	Series	Loser	Year	Winner	Series	Loser
1938	Goodyear Wingfoots	2-1	Oshkosh All-Stars	1944	Ft. Wayne Pistons	3-0	Sheboygan Redskins
1939	Firestone Non-Skids	3-2	Oshkosh All-Stars	1945	Ft. Wayne Pistons	3-2	Sheboygan Redskins
1940	Firestone Non-Skids	3-2	Oshkosh All-Stars	1946	Rochester Royals	3-0	Sheboygan Redskins
1941	Oshkosh All-Stars	3-0	Sheboygan Redskins	1947	Chicago Gears	3-2	Rochester Royals
1942	Oshkosh All-Stars	2-1	Ft. Wayne Pistons	1948	Minneapolis Lakers	3-1	Rochester Royals
1943	Sheboygan Redskins	2-1	Ft. Wayne Pistons	1949	Anderson Packers	3-0	Oshkosh All-Stars

NBA All-Star Game

The NBA staged its first All-Star Game before 10,094 at Boston Garden on March 2, 1951. From that year on, the game has matched the best players in the East against the best in the West. Winning coaches are listed first. East leads series, 32-18.

Multiple MVP winners: Bob Pettit (4); Michael Jordan and Oscar Robertson (3); Bob Cousy, Julius Erving, Magic Johnson, Karl Malone and Isiah Thomas (2).

Year		Host	Coaches	Most Valuable Player
1951	East 111, West 94	Boston	Joe Lapchick, John Kundla	Ed Macauley, Boston
1952	East 108, West 91	Boston	Al Cervi, John Kundla	Paul Arizin, Philadelphia
1953	West 79, East 75	Ft. Wayne	John Kundla, Joe Lapchick	George Mikan, Minneapolis
1954	East 98, West 93 (OT)	New York	Joe Lapchick, John Kundla	Bob Cousy, Boston
1955	East 100, West 91	New York	Al Cervi, Charley Eckman	Bill Sharman, Boston
1956	West 108, East 94	Rochester	Charley Eckman, George Senesky	Bob Pettit, St. Louis
1957	East 109, West 97	Boston	Red Auerbach, Bobby Wanzer	Bob Cousy, Boston
1958	East 130, West 118	St. Louis	Red Auerbach, Alex Hannum	Bob Pettit, St. Louis
1959	West 124, East 108	Detroit	Ed Macauley, Red Auerbach	Bob Pettit, St. Louis
				& Elgin Baylor, Minneapolis
1960	East 125, West 115	Philadelphia	Red Auerbach, Ed Macauley	Wilt Chamberlain, Philadelphia
1961	West 153, East 131	Syracuse	Paul Seymour, Red Auerbach	Oscar Robertson, Cincinnati
1962	West 150, East 130	St. Louis	Fred Schaus, Red Auerbach	Bob Pettit, St. Louis
1963	East 115, West 108	Los Angeles	Red Auerbach, Fred Schaus	Bill Russell, Boston
1964	East 111, West 107	Boston	Red Auerbach, Fred Schaus	Oscar Robertson, Cincinnati
1965	East 124, West 123	St. Louis	Red Auerbach, Alex Hannum	Jerry Lucas, Cincinnati
1966	East 137, West 94	Cincinnati	Red Auerbach, Fred Schaus	Adrian Smith, Cincinnati
1967	West 135, East 120	San Francisco	Fred Schaus, Red Auerbach	Rick Barry, San Francisco
1968	East 144, West 124	New York	Alex Hannum, Bill Sharman	Hal Greer, Philadelphia
1969	East 123, West 112	Baltimore	Gene Shue, Richie Guerin	Oscar Robertson, Cincinnati
1970	East 142, West 135	Philadelphia	Red Holzman, Richie Guerin	Willis Reed, New York
1971	West 108, East 107	San Diego	Larry Costello, Red Holzman	Lenny Wilkens, Seattle
1972	West 112, East 110	Los Angeles	Bill Sharman, Tom Heinsohn	Jerry West, Los Angeles
1973	East 104, West 84	Chicago	Tom Heinsohn, Bill Sharman	Dave Cowens, Boston
1974	West 134, East 123	Seattle	Larry Costello, Tom Heinsohn	Bob Lanier, Detroit
1975	East 108, West 102	Phoenix	K.C. Jones, Al Attles	Walt Frazier, New York
1976	East 123, West 109	Philadelphia	Tom Heinsohn, Al Attles	Dave Bing, Washington
1977	West 125, East 124	Milwaukee	Larry Brown, Gene Shue	Julius Erving, Philadelphia
1978	East 133, West 125	Atlanta	Billy Cunningham, Jack Ramsay	Randy Smith, Buffalo
1979	West 134, East 129	Detroit	Lenny Wilkens, Dick Motta	David Thompson, Denver
1980	East 144, West 136 (OT)	Washington	Billy Cunningham, Lenny Wilkens	George Gervin, San Antonio
1981	East 123, West 120	Cleveland	Billy Cunningham, John MacLeod	Nate Archibald, Boston
1982	East 120, West 118	New Jersey	Bill Fitch, Pat Riley	Larry Bird, Boston
1983	East 132, West 123	Los Angeles	Billy Cunningham, Pat Riley	Julius Erving, Philadelphia
1984	East 154, West 145 (OT)	Denver	K.C. Jones, Frank Layden	Isiah Thomas, Detroit
1985	West 140, East 129	Indiana	Pat Riley, K.C. Jones	Ralph Sampson, Houston
1986	East 139, West 132	Dallas	K.C. Jones, Pat Riley	Isiah Thomas, Detroit
1987	West 154, East 149 (OT)	Seattle	Pat Riley, K.C. Jones	Tom Chambers, Seattle
1988	East 138, West 133	Chicago	Mike Fratello, Pat Riley	Michael Jordan, Chicago
1989	West 143, East 134	Houston	Pat Riley, Lenny Wilkens	Karl Malone, Utah
1990	East 130, West 113	Miami	Chuck Daly, Pat Riley	Magic Johnson, LA Lakers
1991	East 116, West 114	Charlotte	Chris Ford, Rick Adelman	Charles Barkley, Philadelphia
1992	West 153, East 113	Orlando	Don Nelson, Phil Jackson	Magic Johnson, LA Lakers
1993	West 135, East 132 (OT)	Salt Lake City	Paul Westphal, Pat Riley	Karl Malone, Utah
				& John Stockton, Utah
1994	East 127, West 118	Minneapolis	Lenny Wilkens, George Karl	Scottie Pippen, Chicago
1995	West 139, East 112	Phoenix	Paul Westphal, Brian Hill	Mitch Richmond, Sacramento
1996	East 129, West 118	San Antonio	Phil Jackson, George Karl	Michael Jordan, Chicago
1997	East 132, West 120	Cleveland	Doug Collins, Rudy Tomjanovich	Glen Rice, Charlotte
1998	East 135, West 114	New York	Larry Bird, George Karl	Michael Jordan, Chicago
1999	Not held—due to lockout			
2000	West 137, East 126	Oakland	Jeff Van Gundy, Phil Jackson	Tim Duncan, San Antonio
				& Shaquille O'Neal, LA Lakers
2001	East 111, West 110	Washington	Larry Brown, Rick Adelman	Allen Iverson, Philadelphia
2002	West 135, East 120	Philadelphia	Don Nelson, Byron Scott	Kobe Bryant, LA Lakers
2003	West 155, East 145 (2 OT)	Atlanta	Rick Adelman, Isiah Thomas	Kevin Garnett, Minnesota

NBA Franchise Origins

Here is what the current 30 teams in the National Basketball Association have to show for the years they have put in as members of the National Basketball League (NBL), Basketball Association of America (BAA), the NBA, and the American Basketball Association (ABA). League titles are noted by year won.

Western Conference

	First Season	League Titles	Franchise Stops
Dallas Mavericks	1980-81 (NBA)	None	•Dallas (1980–)
Denver Nuggets	1967-68 (ABA)	None	•Denver (1967–)
Golden St. Warriors	1946-47 (BAA)	1 BAA (1947)	•Philadelphia (1946-62)
		2 NBA (1956, 75)	San Francisco (1962-71)
			Oakland (1971–)
Houston Rockets	1967-68 (NBA)	2 NBA (1994-95)	•San Diego (1967-71)
			Houston (1971–)
Los Angeles Clippers	1970-71 (NBA)	None	•Buffalo (1970-78)
			San Diego (1978-84)
			Los Angeles (1984–)
Los Angeles Lakers	1947-48 (NBL)	1 NBL (1948)	•Minneapolis (1947-60)
		1 BAA (1949)	Los Angeles (1960-67)
		14 NBA (1950,52-54,72,	Inglewood, CA (1967-99)
		80,82,85,87-88,00-02)	Los Angeles (1999–)
Memphis Grizzlies	1995-96 (NBA)	None	•Vancouver (1995-01)
			Memphis, TN (2001–)
Minnesota Timberwolves	1989-90 (NBA)	None	•Minneapolis (1989–)
Phoenix Suns	1968-69 (NBA)	None	•Phoenix (1968–)
Portland Trail Blazers	1970-71 (NBA)	1 NBA (1977)	•Portland (1970–)
Sacramento Kings	1945-46 (NBL)	1 NBL (1946)	•Rochester, NY (1945-58)
		1 NBA (1951)	Cincinnati (1958-72)
			KC-Omaha (1972-75)
			Kansas City (1975-85)
			Sacramento (1985–)
San Antonio Spurs	1967-68 (ABA)	2 NBA (1999, 2003)	•Dallas (1967-73)
			San Antonio (1973–)
Seattle SuperSonics	1967-68 (NBA)	1 NBA (1979)	•Seattle (1967–)
Utah Jazz	1974-75 (NBA)	None	•New Orleans (1974-79)
			Salt Lake City (1979–)

Eastern Conference

	First Season	League Titles	Franchise Stops
Atlanta Hawks	1946-47 (NBL)	1 NBA (1958)	•Tri-Cities (1946-51)
			Milwaukee (1951-55)
			St. Louis (1955-68)
			Atlanta (1968–)
Boston Celtics	1946-47 (BAA)	16 NBA (1957,59-66,68-69	•Boston (1946–)
		74,76,81,84,86)	
Charlotte Bobcats	2004-05 (NBA)	None	•Charlotte (2004–)
Chicago Bulls	1966-67 (NBA)	6 NBA (1991-93,96-98)	•Chicago (1966–)
Cleveland Cavaliers	1970-71 (NBA)	None	•Cleveland (1970-74)
			Richfield, OH (1974-94)
			Cleveland (1994–)
Detroit Pistons	1941-42 (NBL)	2 NBL (1944-45)	•Ft. Wayne, IN (1941-57)
		2 NBA (1989-90)	Detroit (1957-78)
			Pontiac, MI (1978-88)
			Auburn Hills, MI (1988–)
Indiana Pacers	1967-68 (ABA)	3 ABA (1970,72-73)	•Indianapolis (1967–)
Miami Heat	1988-89 (NBA)	None	•Miami (1988–)
Milwaukee Bucks	1968-69 (NBA)	1 NBA (1971)	•Milwaukee (1968–)
New Jersey Nets	1967-68 (ABA)	2 ABA (1974,76)	•Teaneck, NJ (1967-68)
			Commack, NY (1968-69)
			W. Hempstead, NY (1969-71)
			Uniondale, NY (1971-77)
			Piscataway, NJ (1977-81)
			E. Rutherford, NJ (1981–)
New Orleans Hornets	1988-89 (NBA)	None	•Charlotte (1988-2002)
			New Orleans (2002–)
New York Knicks	1946-47 (BAA)	2 NBA (1970,73)	•New York (1946–)
Orlando Magic	1989-90 (NBA)	None	•Orlando, FL (1989–)
Philadelphia 76ers	1949-50 (NBA)	3 NBA (1955,67,83)	•Syracuse, NY (1949-63)
			Philadelphia (1963–)
Toronto Raptors	1995-96 (NBA)	None	•Toronto (1995–)
Washington Wizards	1961-62 (NBA)	1 NBA (1978)	•Chicago (1961-63)
			Baltimore (1963-73)
			Landover, MD (1973–)

Note: The Tri-Cities Blackhawks represented Moline and Rock Island, Ill., and Davenport, Iowa.

The Growth of the NBA

Of the 11 franchises that comprised the Basketball Association of America (BAA) at the start of the 1946-47 season, only three remain—the Boston Celtics, New York Knickerbockers and Golden State Warriors (originally Philadelphia Warriors).

Just before the start of the 1948-49 season, four teams from the more established **National Basketball League** (NBL)—the Ft. Wayne Pistons (now Detroit), Indianapolis Jets, Minneapolis Lakers (now Los Angeles) and Rochester Royals (now Sacramento Kings)—joined the BAA.

A year later, the six remaining NBL franchises—Anderson (Ind.), Denver, Sheboygan (Wisc.), the Syracuse Nationals (now Philadelphia 76ers), Tri-Cities Blackhawks (now Atlanta Hawks) and Waterloo (Iowa)—joined along with the new Indianapolis Olympians and the BAA became the 17-team **National Basketball Association**.

The NBA was down to 10 teams by the 1950-51 season and slipped to eight by 1954-55 with Boston, New York, Philadelphia and Syracuse in the Eastern Division, and Ft. Wayne, Milwaukee (formerly Tri-Cities), Minneapolis and Rochester in the West.

By 1960, five of those surviving eight teams had moved to other cities but by the end of the decade the NBA was a 14-team league. It also had a rival, the **American Basketball Association**, which began play in 1967 with a red, white and blue ball, a three-point line and 11 teams. After a nine-year run, the ABA merged four clubs—the Denver Nuggets, Indiana Pacers, New York Nets and San Antonio Spurs—with the NBA following the 1975-76 season. The NBA adopted the three-point shot in 1979-80.

Expansion/Merger Timetable

For teams currently in NBA.

1948—Added NBL's Ft. Wayne Pistons (now Detroit), Minneapolis Lakers (now Los Angeles) and Rochester Royals (now Sacramento Kings); **1949**—Syracuse Nationals (now Philadelphia 76ers) and Tri-Cities Blackhawks (now Atlanta Hawks).

1961—Chicago Packers (now Washington Wizards); **1966**—Chicago Bulls; **1967**—San Diego Rockets (now Houston) and Seattle SuperSonics; **1968**—Milwaukee Bucks and Phoenix Suns.

1970—Buffalo Braves (now Los Angeles Clippers), Cleveland Cavaliers and Portland Trail Blazers; **1974**—New Orleans Jazz (now Utah); **1976**—added ABA's Denver Nuggets, Indiana Pacers, New York Nets (now New Jersey) and San Antonio Spurs.

1980—Dallas Mavericks; **1988**—Charlotte Hornets and Miami Heat; **1989**—Minnesota Timberwolves and Orlando Magic.

1995—Toronto Raptors and Vancouver Grizzlies (Now Memphis).

2004—Charlotte Bobcats.

City and Nickname Changes

1951—Tri-Cities Blackhawks, who divided home games between Moline and Rock Island, Ill., and Davenport, Iowa, move to Milwaukee and become the Hawks; **1955**—Milwaukee Hawks move to St. Louis; **1957**—Ft. Wayne Pistons move to Detroit, while Rochester Royals move to Cincinnati.

1960—Minneapolis Lakers move to Los Angeles; **1962**—Chicago Packers renamed Zephyrs, while Philadelphia Warriors move to San Francisco; **1963**—Chicago Zephyrs move to Baltimore and become Bullets, while Syracuse Nationals move to Philadelphia and become the 76ers; **1968**—St. Louis Hawks move to Atlanta.

1971—San Diego Rockets move to Houston, while San Francisco Warriors move to Oakland and become Golden State Warriors; **1972**—Cincinnati Royals move to Midwest, divide home games between Kansas City, Mo., and Omaha, Neb., and become Kings; **1973**—Baltimore Bullets move to Landover, Md., outside Washington and become Capital Bullets; **1974**—Capital Bullets renamed Washington Bullets; **1975**—KC-Omaha Kings settle in Kansas City; **1977**—New York Nets move from Uniondale, N.Y., to Piscataway, N.J. (later East Rutherford) and become New Jersey Nets; **1978**—Buffalo Braves move to San Diego and become Clippers; **1979**—New Orleans Jazz move to Salt Lake City and become Utah Jazz.

1984—San Diego Clippers move to Los Angeles; **1985**—Kansas City Kings move to Sacramento.

1997—Washington Bullets become Washington Wizards.

2001—Vancouver Grizzlies move to Memphis, Tenn.; **2002**—Charlotte Hornets move to New Orleans.

Defunct NBA Teams·

Teams that once played in the BAA and NBA, but no longer exist.

Anderson (Ind.)—Packers (1949-50); **Baltimore**—Bullets (1947-55); **Chicago**—Stags (1946-50); **Cleveland**—Rebels (1946-47); **Denver**—Nuggets (1949-50); **Detroit**—Falcons (1946-47); **Indianapolis**—Jets (1948-49) and Olympians (1949-53); **Pittsburgh**—Ironmen (1946-47); **Providence**—Steamrollers (1946-49); **St. Louis**—Bombers (1946-50); **Sheboygan (Wisc.)**—Redskins (1949-50); **Toronto**—Huskies (1946-47); **Washington**—Capitols (1946-51); **Waterloo (Iowa)**—Hawks (1949-50).

ABA Teams (1967-76)

Anaheim—Amigos (1967-68, moved to LA); **Baltimore**—Claws (1975, never played); **Carolina**—Cougars (1969-74, moved to St. Louis); **Dallas**—Chaparrals (1967-73, called Texas Chaparrals in 1970-71, moved to San Antonio); **Denver**—Rockets (1967-76, renamed Nuggets in 1974-76); **Miami**—Floridians (1968-72, called simply Floridians from 1970-72).

Houston—Mavericks (1967-69, moved to North Carolina); **Indiana**—Pacers (1967-76); **Kentucky**—Colonels (1967-76); **Los Angeles**—Stars (1968-70, moved to Utah); **Memphis**—Pros (1970-75, renamed Tams in 1972 and Sounds in 1974, moved to Baltimore); **Minnesota**—Muskies (1967-68, moved to Miami) and Pipers (1968-69, moved back to Pittsburgh); **New Jersey**—Americans (1967-68, moved to New York).

New Orleans—Buccaneers (1967-70, moved to Memphis); **New York**—Nets (1968-76); **Oakland**—Oaks (1967-69, moved to Washington); **Pittsburgh**—Pipers (1967-68, moved to Minnesota), Pipers (1969-72, renamed Condors in 1970); **St. Louis**—Spirits of St. Louis (1974-76); **San Antonio**—Spurs (1973-76); **San Diego**—Conquistadors (1972-75, renamed Sails in 1975); **Utah**—Stars (1970-75); **Virginia**—Squires (1970-76); **Washington**—Caps (1969-70, moved to Virginia).

Annual NBA Leaders
Scoring

Decided by total points from 1947-69, and per game average since 1970. A lockout in 1999 shortened the regular season to 50 games.

Multiple winners: Michael Jordan (10); Wilt Chamberlain (7); George Gervin (4); Allen Iverson, Neil Johnston, Bob McAdoo and George Mikan (3); Kareem Abdul-Jabbar, Paul Arizin, Adrian Dantley, Shaquille O'Neal and Bob Pettit (2).

Year		Gm	Pts	Avg	Year		Gm	Pts	Avg
1947	Joe Fulks, Phi	.60	1389	23.2	1976	Bob McAdoo, Buf	.78	2427	31.1
1948	Max Zaslofsky, Chi	.48	1007	21.0	1977	Pete Maravich, NO	.73	2273	31.1
1949	George Mikan, Mpls	.60	1698	28.3	1978	George Gervin, SA	.82	2232	27.2
1950	George Mikan, Mpls	.68	1865	27.4	1979	George Gervin, SA	.80	2365	29.6
1951	George Mikan, Mpls	.68	1932	28.4	1980	George Gervin, SA	.78	2585	33.1
1952	Paul Arizin, Phi	.66	1674	25.4	1981	Adrian Dantley, Utah	.80	2452	30.7
1953	Neil Johnston, Phi	.70	1564	22.3	1982	George Gervin, SA	.79	2551	32.3
1954	Neil Johnston, Phi	.72	1759	24.4	1983	Alex English, Den	.82	2326	28.4
1955	Neil Johnston, Phi	.72	1631	22.7	1984	Adrian Dantley, Utah	.79	2418	30.6
1956	Bob Pettit, St.L	.72	1849	25.7	1985	Bernard King, NY	.55	1809	32.9
1957	Paul Arizin, Phi	.71	1817	25.6	1986	Dominique Wilkins, Atl	.78	2366	30.3
1958	George Yardley, Det	.72	2001	27.8	1987	Michael Jordan, Chi	.82	3041	37.1
1959	Bob Pettit, St.L	.72	2105	29.2	1988	Michael Jordan, Chi	.82	2868	35.0
1960	Wilt Chamberlain, Phi	.72	2707	37.6	1989	Michael Jordan, Chi	.81	2633	32.5
1961	Wilt Chamberlain, Phi	.79	3033	38.4	1990	Michael Jordan, Chi	.82	2753	33.6
1962	Wilt Chamberlain, Phi	.80	4029	50.4	1991	Michael Jordan, Chi	.82	2580	31.5
1963	Wilt Chamberlain, SF	.80	3586	44.8	1992	Michael Jordan, Chi	.80	2404	30.1
1964	Wilt Chamberlain, SF	.80	2948	36.9	1993	Michael Jordan, Chi	.78	2541	32.6
1965	Wilt Chamberlain, SF-Phi	.73	2534	34.7	1994	David Robinson, SA	.80	2383	29.8
1966	Wilt Chamberlain, Phi	.79	2649	33.5	1995	Shaquille O'Neal, Orl	.79	2315	29.3
1967	Rick Barry, SF	.78	2775	35.6	1996	Michael Jordan, Chi	.82	2491	30.4
1968	Dave Bing, Det	.79	2142	27.1	1997	Michael Jordan, Chi	.82	2431	29.7
1969	Elvin Hayes, SD	.82	2327	28.4	1998	Michael Jordan, Chi	.82	2357	28.7
1970	Jerry West, LA	.74	2309	31.2	1999	Allen Iverson, Phi	.48	1284	26.8
1971	Lew Alcindor, Mil	.82	2596	31.7	2000	Shaquille O'Neal, LAL	.79	2344	29.7
1972	Kareem Abdul-Jabbar, Mil	.81	2822	34.8	2001	Allen Iverson, Phi	.71	2207	31.1
1973	Nate Archibald, KC-Omaha	.80	2719	34.0	2002	Allen Iverson, Phi	.60	1883	31.4
1974	Bob McAdoo, Buf	.74	2261	30.6	2003	Tracy McGrady, Orl	.75	2407	32.1
1975	Bob McAdoo, Buf	.82	2831	34.5					

Note: Lew Alcindor changed his name to Kareem Abdul-Jabbar after the 1970-71 season.

Rebounds

Decided by total rebounds from 1951-69 and per game average since 1970.

Multiple winners: Wilt Chamberlain (11); Dennis Rodman (7); Moses Malone (6); Bill Russell (4); Elvin Hayes, Dikembe Mutombo, Hakeem Olajuwon and Ben Wallace (2).

Year		Gm	No	Avg	Year		Gm	No	Avg
1951	Dolph Schayes, Syr	.66	1080	16.4	1978	Len Robinson, NO	.82	1288	15.7
1952	Larry Foust, Ft. Wayne	.66	880	13.3	1979	Moses Malone, Hou	.82	1444	17.6
	& Mel Hutchins, Mil		880	13.3					
1953	George Mikan, Mpls	.70	1007	14.4	1980	Swen Nater, SD	.81	1216	15.0
1954	Harry Gallatin, NY	.72	1098	15.3	1981	Moses Malone, Hou	.80	1180	14.8
1955	Neil Johnston, Phi	.72	1085	15.1	1982	Moses Malone, Hou	.81	1188	14.7
1956	Bob Pettit, St.L	.72	1164	16.2	1983	Moses Malone, Phi	.78	1194	15.3
1957	Maurice Stokes, Roch	.72	1256	17.4	1984	Moses Malone, Phi	.71	950	13.4
1958	Bill Russell, Bos	.69	1564	22.7	1985	Moses Malone, Phi	.79	1031	13.1
1959	Bill Russell, Bos	.70	1612	23.0	1986	Bill Laimbeer, Det	.82	1075	13.1
1960	Wilt Chamberlain, Phi	.72	1941	27.0	1987	Charles Barkley, Phi	.68	994	14.6
1961	Wilt Chamberlain, Phi	.79	2149	27.2	1988	Michael Cage, LAC	.72	938	13.0
1962	Wilt Chamberlain, Phi	.80	2052	25.7	1989	Hakeem Olajuwon, Hou	.82	1105	13.5
1963	Wilt Chamberlain, SF	.80	1946	24.3	1990	Hakeem Olajuwon, Hou	.82	1149	14.0
1964	Bill Russell, Bos	.78	1930	24.7	1991	David Robinson, SA	.82	1063	13.0
1965	Bill Russell, Bos	.78	1878	24.1	1992	Dennis Rodman, Det	.82	1530	18.7
1966	Wilt Chamberlain, Phi	.79	1943	24.6	1993	Dennis Rodman, Det	.62	1232	18.3
1967	Wilt Chamberlain, Phi	.81	1957	24.2	1994	Dennis Rodman, SA	.79	1132	17.3
1968	Wilt Chamberlain, Phi	.82	1952	23.8	1995	Dennis Rodman, SA	.49	823	16.8
1969	Wilt Chamberlain, LA	.81	1712	21.1	1996	Dennis Rodman, Chi	.64	952	14.9
1970	Elvin Hayes, SD	.82	1386	16.9	1997	Dennis Rodman, Chi	.55	883	16.1
1971	Wilt Chamberlain, LA	.82	1493	18.2	1998	Dennis Rodman, Chi	.80	1201	15.0
1972	Wilt Chamberlain, LA	.82	1572	19.2	1999	Chris Webber, Sac	.42	545	13.0
1973	Wilt Chamberlain, LA	.82	1526	18.6					
1974	Elvin Hayes, Cap*	.81	1463	18.1	2000	Dikembe Mutombo, Atl	.82	1157	14.1
1975	Wes Unseld, Wash	.73	1077	14.8	2001	Dikembe Mutombo, Atl-Phi	.75	1015	13.5
1976	Kareem Abdul-Jabbar, LA	.82	1383	16.9	2002	Ben Wallace, Det	.80	1039	13.0
1977	Bill Walton, Port	.65	934	14.4	2003	Ben Wallace, Det	.73	1126	15.4

*The Baltimore Bullets moved to Landover, Md. in 1973-74 and became first the Capital Bullets, then the Washington Bullets in 1974-75.

Annual NBA Leaders (Cont.)
Assists

Decided by total assists from 1952-69 and per game average since 1970.

Multiple winners: John Stockton (9); Bob Cousy (8); Oscar Robertson (6); Magic Johnson, Jason Kidd and Kevin Porter (4); Andy Phillip and Guy Rodgers (2).

Year		No	Year		No	Year		No
1947	Ernie Calverly, Prov	202	1966	Oscar Robertson, Cin	847	1985	Isiah Thomas, Det	13.9
1948	Howie Dallmar, Phi	120	1967	Guy Rodgers, Chi	908	1986	Magic Johnson, LAL	12.6
1949	Bob Davies, Roch	321	1968	Wilt Chamberlain, Phi	702	1987	Magic Johnson, LAL	12.2
1950	Dick McGuire, NY	386	1969	Oscar Robertson, Cin	772	1988	John Stockton, Utah	13.8
1951	Andy Phillip, Phi	414	1970	Lenny Wilkens, Sea	9.1	1989	John Stockton, Utah	13.6
1952	Andy Phillip, Phi	539	1971	Norm Van Lier, Chi.	10.1	1990	John Stockton, Utah	14.5
1953	Bob Cousy, Bos	547	1972	Jerry West, LA	9.7	1991	John Stockton, Utah	14.2
1954	Bob Cousy, Bos	518	1973	Nate Archibald, KC-O	11.4	1992	John Stockton, Utah	13.7
1955	Bob Cousy, Bos	557	1974	Ernie DiGregorio, Buf	8.2	1993	John Stockton, Utah	12.0
1956	Bob Cousy, Bos	642	1975	Kevin Porter, Wash	8.0	1994	John Stockton, Utah	12.6
1957	Bob Cousy, Bos	478	1976	Slick Watts, Sea	8.1	1995	John Stockton, Utah	12.3
1958	Bob Cousy, Bos	463	1977	Don Buse, Ind	8.5	1996	John Stockton, Utah	11.2
1959	Bob Cousy, Bos	557	1978	Kevin Porter, Det-NJ	10.2	1997	Mark Jackson, Den-Ind	11.4
1960	Bob Cousy, Bos	715	1979	Kevin Porter, Det	13.4	1998	Rod Strickland, Wash	10.5
1961	Oscar Robertson, Cin	690	1980	M.R. Richardson, NY	10.1	1999	Jason Kidd, Pho	10.8
1962	Oscar Robertson, Cin	899	1981	Kevin Porter, Wash	9.1	2000	Jason Kidd, Pho	10.1
1963	Guy Rodgers, SF	825	1982	Johnny Moore, SA	9.6	2001	Jason Kidd, Pho	9.8
1964	Oscar Robertson, Cin	868	1983	Magic Johnson, LA	10.5	2002	Andre Miller, Cle	10.9
1965	Oscar Robertson, Cin	861	1984	Magic Johnson, LA	13.1	2003	Jason Kidd, NJ	8.9

Field Goal Percentage

Multiple winners: Wilt Chamberlain (9); Shaquille O'Neal (6); Artis Gilmore (4); Neil Johnston (3); Bob Feerick, Johnny Green, Alex Groza, Cedric Maxwell, Kevin McHale, Gheorghe Muresan, Kenny Sears and Buck Williams (2).

Year		Pct	Year		Pct	Year		Pct
1947	Bob Feerick, Wash	.401	1966	Wilt Chamberlain, Phi.	.540	1985	James Donaldson, LAC	.637
1948	Bob Feerick, Wash	.340	1967	Wilt Chamberlain, Phi.	.683	1986	Steve Johnson, SA	.632
1949	Arnie Risen, Roch	.423	1968	Wilt Chamberlain, Phi.	.595	1987	Kevin McHale, Bos	.604
1950	Alex Groza, Indpls	.478	1969	Wilt Chamberlain, LA	.583	1988	Kevin McHale, Bos	.604
1951	Alex Groza, Indpls	.470	1970	Johnny Green, Cin	.559	1989	Dennis Rodman, Det.	.595
1952	Paul Arizin, Phi	.448	1971	Johnny Green, Cin	.587	1990	Mark West, Pho.	.625
1953	Neil Johnston, Phi	.452	1972	Wilt Chamberlain, LA	.649	1991	Buck Williams, Port.	.602
1954	Ed Macauley, Bos	.486	1973	Wilt Chamberlain, LA	.727	1992	Buck Williams, Port.	.604
1955	Larry Foust, Ft.W	.487	1974	Bob McAdoo, Buf.	.547	1993	Cedric Ceballos, Pho	.576
1956	Neil Johnston, Phi	.457	1975	Don Nelson, Bos	.539	1994	Shaquille O'Neal, Orl.	.599
1957	Neil Johnston, Phi.	.447	1976	Wes Unseld, Wash	.561	1995	Chris Gatling, G.St.	.633
1958	Jack Twyman, Cin	.452	1977	K. Abdul-Jabbar, LA	.579	1996	Gheorghe Muresan, Wash.	.584
1959	Kenny Sears, NY	.490	1978	Bobby Jones, Den.	.578	1997	Gheorghe Muresan, Wash.	.604
1960	Kenny Sears, NY	.477	1979	Cedric Maxwell, Bos	.584	1998	Shaquille O'Neal, LAL	.584
1961	Wilt Chamberlain, Phi.	.509	1980	Cedric Maxwell, Bos	.609	1999	Shaquille O'Neal, LAL	.576
1962	Walt Bellamy, Chi.	.519	1981	Artis Gilmore, Chi.	.670	2000	Shaquille O'Neal, LAL	.574
1963	Wilt Chamberlain, SF	.528	1982	Artis Gilmore, Chi.	.652	2001	Shaquille O'Neal, LAL	.572
1964	Jerry Lucas, Cin	.527	1983	Artis Gilmore, SA	.626	2002	Shaquille O'Neal, LAL	.579
1965	W. Chamberlain, SF-Phi	.510	1984	Artis Gilmore, SA	.631	2003	Eddy Curry, Chi	.585

Free Throw Percentage

Multiple winners: Bill Sharman (7); Rick Barry (6); Larry Bird and Reggie Miller (4); Mark Price and Dolph Schayes (3); Mahmoud Abdul-Rauf, Larry Costello, Ernie DiGregorio, Bob Feerick, Kyle Macy, Calvin Murphy, Oscar Robertson and Larry Siegfried (2).

Year		Pct	Year		Pct	Year		Pct
1947	Fred Scolari, Wash	.811	1966	Larry Siegfried, Bos	.881	1985	Kyle Macy, Pho	.907
1948	Bob Feerick, Wash	.788	1967	Adrian Smith, Cin.	.903	1986	Larry Bird, Bos	.896
1949	Bob Feerick, Wash	.859	1968	Oscar Robertson, Cin	.873	1987	Larry Bird, Bos	.910
1950	Max Zaslofsky, Chi	.843	1969	Larry Siegfried, NY	.864	1988	Jack Sikma, Mil	.922
1951	Joe Fulks, Phi	.855	1970	Flynn Robinson, Mil	.898	1989	Magic Johnson, LAL	.911
1952	Bob Wanzer, Roch	.904	1971	Chet Walker, Chi	.859	1990	Larry Bird, Bos	.930
1953	Bill Sharman, Bos	.850	1972	Jack Marin, Bal	.894	1991	Reggie Miller, Ind	.918
1954	Bill Sharman, Bos	.844	1973	Rick Barry, G.St.	.902	1992	Mark Price, Cle	.947
1955	Bill Sharman, Bos	.897	1974	Ernie DiGregorio, Buf	.902	1993	Mark Price, Cle	.948
1956	Bill Sharman, Bos	.867	1975	Rick Barry, G.St.	.904	1994	M. Abdul-Rauf, Den	.956
1957	Bill Sharman, Bos	.905	1976	Rick Barry, G.St.	.923	1995	Spud Webb, Sac	.934
1958	Dolph Schayes, Syr	.904	1977	Ernie DiGregorio, Buf	.945	1996	M. Abdul-Rauf, Den	.930
1959	Bill Sharman, Bos	.932	1978	Rick Barry, G.St.	.924	1997	Mark Price, G.St.	.906
1960	Dolph Schayes, Syr	.892	1979	Rick Barry, Hou	.947	1998	Chris Mullin, Ind.	.939
1961	Bill Sharman, Bos	.921	1980	Rick Barry, Hou	.935	1999	Reggie Miller, Ind	.915
1962	Dolph Schayes, Syr	.896	1981	Calvin Murphy, Hou	.958	2000	Jeff Hornacek, Utah	.950
1963	Larry Costello, Syr	.881	1982	Kyle Macy, Pho	.899	2001	Reggie Miller, Ind	.928
1964	Oscar Robertson, Cin	.853	1983	Calvin Murphy, Hou	.920	2002	Reggie Miller, Ind	.911
1965	Larry Costello, Phi	.877	1984	Larry Bird, Bos	.888	2003	Allan Houston, NY	.919

Blocked Shots
Decided by per game average since 1973-74 season.

Multiple winners: Kareem Abdul-Jabbar and Mark Eaton (4); George Johnson, Dikembe Mutombo and Hakeem Olajuwon (3); Manute Bol, Alonzo Mourning and Theo Ratliff (2).

Year		Gm	No	Avg
1974	Elmore Smith, LA	.81	393	4.85
1975	Kareem Abdul-Jabbar, Mil	.65	212	3.26
1976	Kareem Abdul-Jabbar, LA	.82	338	4.12
1977	Bill Walton, Port	.65	211	3.25
1978	George Johnson, NJ	.81	274	3.38
1979	Kareem Abdul-Jabbar, LA	.80	316	3.95
1980	Kareem Abdul-Jabbar, LA	.82	280	3.41
1981	George Johnson, SA	.82	278	3.39
1982	George Johnson, SA	.75	234	3.12
1983	Tree Rollins, Atl	.80	343	4.29
1984	Mark Eaton, Utah	.82	351	4.28
1985	Mark Eaton, Utah	.82	456	5.56
1986	Manute Bol, Wash	.80	397	4.96
1987	Mark Eaton, Utah	.79	321	4.06
1988	Mark Eaton, Utah	.82	304	3.71
1989	Manute Bol, G.St.	.80	345	4.31
1990	Akeem Olajuwon, Hou	.82	376	4.59
1991	Hakeem Olajuwon, Hou	.56	221	3.95
1992	David Robinson, SA	.68	305	4.49
1993	Hakeem Olajuwon, Hou	.82	342	4.17
1994	Dikembe Mutombo, Den	.82	336	4.10
1995	Dikembe Mutombo, Den	.82	321	3.91
1996	Dikembe Mutombo, Den	.74	332	4.49
1997	Shawn Bradley, Dal-NJ	.73	248	3.40
1998	Marcus Camby, Tor.	.63	230	3.65
1999	Alonzo Mourning, Mia	.46	180	3.91
2000	Alonzo Mourning, Mia	.79	294	3.72
2001	Theo Ratliff, Phi-Atl	.50	187	3.74
2002	Ben Wallace, Det	.80	278	3.48
2003	Theo Ratliff, Atl	.81	262	3.23

Steals
Decided by per game average since 1973-74 season.

Multiple winners: Allen Iverson, Michael Jordan, Micheal Ray Richardson and Alvin Robertson (3); Mookie Blaylock, Magic Johnson and John Stockton (2).

Year		Gm	No	Avg
1974	Larry Steele, Port	.81	217	2.68
1975	Rick Barry, G.St.	.80	228	2.85
1976	Slick Watts, Sea	.82	261	3.18
1977	Don Buse, Ind	.81	281	3.47
1978	Ron Lee, Pho	.82	225	2.74
1979	M.L. Carr, Det	.80	197	2.46
1980	Micheal Ray Richardson, NY	.82	265	3.23
1981	Magic Johnson, LA	.37	127	3.43
1982	Magic Johnson, LA	.78	208	2.67
1983	Micheal Ray Richardson, G. ST-NJ	.64	182	2.84
1984	Rickey Green, Utah	.81	215	2.65
1985	Micheal Ray Richardson, NJ	.82	243	2.96
1986	Alvin Robertson, SA	.82	301	3.67
1987	Alvin Robertson, SA	.81	260	3.21
1988	Michael Jordan, Chi	.82	259	3.16
1989	John Stockton, Utah	.82	263	3.21
1990	Michael Jordan, Chi	.82	227	2.77
1991	Alvin Robertson, SA	.81	246	3.04
1992	John Stockton, Utah	.82	244	2.98
1993	Michael Jordan, Chi	.78	221	2.83
1994	Nate McMillan, Sea	.73	216	2.96
1995	Scottie Pippen, Chi	.79	232	2.94
1996	Gary Payton, Sea	.81	231	2.85
1997	Mookie Blaylock, Atl	.78	212	2.72
1998	Mookie Blaylock, Atl.	.70	183	2.61
1999	Kendall Gill, NJ	.50	134	2.68
2000	Eddie Jones, Cha	.72	192	2.67
2001	Allen Iverson, Phi.	.71	178	2.51
2002	Allen Iverson, Phi.	.60	168	2.80
2003	Allen Iverson, Phi	.82	225	2.74

Note: Akeem Olajuwon changed the spelling of his first name to Hakeem during the 1990-91 season.

All-Time NBA Regular Season Leaders
Through the 2002-03 regular season.

CAREER
Players active in 2002-03 in **bold** type.

Points

		Yrs	Gm	Pts	Avg
1	Kareem Abdul-Jabbar	20	1560	38,387	24.6
2	Karl Malone	18	1434	36,374	25.4
3	Michael Jordan	15	1072	32,292	30.1
4	Wilt Chamberlain	14	1045	31,419	30.1
5	Moses Malone	19	1329	27,409	20.6
6	Elvin Hayes	16	1303	27,313	21.0
7	Hakeem Olajuwon	18	1238	26,946	21.8
8	Oscar Robertson	14	1040	26,710	25.7
9	Dominique Wilkins	15	1074	26,668	24.8
10	John Havlicek	16	1270	26,395	20.8
11	Alex English	15	1193	25,613	21.5
12	Jerry West	14	932	25,192	27.0
13	Patrick Ewing	17	1183	24,815	21.0
14	Charles Barkley	16	1073	23,757	22.1
15	**Reggie Miller**	16	1243	23,505	18.9
16	Robert Parish	21	1611	23,334	14.5
17	Adrian Dantley	15	955	23,177	24.3
18	Elgin Baylor	14	846	23,149	27.4
19	Clyde Drexler	15	1086	22,195	20.4
20	Larry Bird	13	897	21,791	24.3
21	Hal Greer	15	1122	21,586	19.2
22	Walt Bellamy	14	1043	20,941	20.1
23	Bob Pettit	11	792	20,880	26.4
24	**David Robinson**	14	987	20,790	21.1
25	George Gervin	10	791	20,708	26.2
26	Mitch Richmond	14	976	20,497	21.0
27	**Shaquille O'Neal**	11	742	20,475	27.6
28	Tom Chambers	16	1107	20,049	18.1
29	**John Stockton**	19	1504	19,711	13.1
30	Bernard King	14	874	19,655	22.5

Scoring Average
Minimum of 400 games or 10,000 points.

		Yrs	Gm	Pts	Avg
1	**Michael Jordan**	15	1072	32,292	30.1
2	Wilt Chamberlain	14	1045	31,419	30.1
3	**Shaquille O'Neal**	11	742	20,475	27.6
4	Elgin Baylor	14	846	23,149	27.4
5	**Allen Iverson**	7	487	13,170	27.0
6	Jerry West	14	932	25,192	27.0
7	Bob Pettit	11	792	20,880	26.4
8	George Gervin	10	791	20,708	26.2
9	Oscar Robertson	14	1040	26,710	25.7
10	**Karl Malone**	18	1434	36,374	25.4
11	Dominique Wilkins	15	1074	26,668	24.8
12	Kareem Abdul-Jabbar	20	1560	38,387	24.6
13	Larry Bird	13	897	21,791	24.3
14	Adrian Dantley	15	955	23,177	24.3
15	Pete Maravich	10	658	15,948	24.2
16	Rick Barry	10	794	18,395	23.2
17	**Tim Duncan**	6	451	10,324	22.9
18	Paul Arizin	10	713	16,266	22.8
19	George Mikan	9	520	11,764	22.6
20	Bernard King	14	874	19,655	22.5
21	**Chris Webber**	10	596	13,209	22.2
22	David Thompson	8	509	11,264	22.1
23	Charles Barkley	16	1073	23,757	22.1
24	Bob McAdoo	14	852	18,787	22.1
25	Julius Erving	11	836	18,364	22.0
26	Geoff Petrie	6	446	9,732	21.8
27	Hakeem Olajuwon	18	1238	26,946	21.8
28	Kobe Bryant	7	496	10,658	21.5
29	Alex English	15	1193	25,613	21.5
30	**Jerry Stackhouse**	9	582	12,375	21.3

All-Time NBA Regular Season Leaders (Cont.)

NBA-ABA Top 20

Points

All-Time combined regular season scoring leaders, including ABA service (1968-76). NBA players with ABA experience are listed in CAPITAL letters. Players active during 2002-03 are in **bold** type.

		Yrs	Pts	Avg
1	Kareem Abdul-Jabbar	20	38,387	24.6
2	**Karl Malone**	18	36,374	25.4
3	Wilt Chamberlain	14	31,419	30.1
4	**Michael Jordan**	15	32,292	30.1
5	JULIUS ERVING	16	30,026	24.2
6	MOSES MALONE	21	29,580	20.3
7	DAN ISSEL	15	27,482	22.6
8	Elvin Hayes	16	27,313	21.0
9	Hakeem Olajuwon	18	26,946	21.8
10	Oscar Robertson	14	26,710	25.7
11	Dominique Wilkins	15	26,668	24.8
12	GEORGE GERVIN	14	26,595	25.1
13	John Havlicek	16	26,395	20.8
14	Alex English	15	25,613	21.5
15	RICK BARRY	14	25,279	24.8
16	Jerry West	14	25,192	27.0
17	ARTIS GILMORE	17	24,941	18.8
18	Patrick Ewing	17	24,815	21.0
19	Charles Barkley	16	23,757	22.1
20	**Reggie Miller**	16	23,505	18.9

ABA Totals: BARRY (4 yrs, 226 gm, 6884 pts, 30.5 avg); ERVING (5 yrs, 407 gm, 11,662 pts, 28.7 avg); GERVIN (4 yrs, 269 gm, 5887 pts, 21.9 avg); GILMORE (5 yrs, 420 gm, 9362 pts, 22.3 avg); ISSEL (6 yrs, 500 gm, 12,823 pts, 25.6 avg); MALONE (2 yrs, 126 gm, 2171 pts, 17.2 avg).

Field Goals

		Yrs	FG	Att	Pct
1	Kareem Abdul-Jabbar	20	15,837	28,307	.559
2	**Karl Malone**	18	13,335	25,810	.517
3	Wilt Chamberlain	14	12,681	23,497	.540
4	**Michael Jordan**	15	12,681	24,537	.497
5	Elvin Hayes	16	10,976	24,272	.452
6	Hakeem Olajuwon	18	10,749	20,991	.512
7	Alex English	15	10,659	21,036	.507
8	John Havlicek	16	10,513	23,930	.439
9	Dominique Wilkins	15	9,963	21,589	.461
10	Patrick Ewing	17	9,702	19,241	.504
11	Robert Parish	21	9,508	17,914	.537
12	Oscar Robertson	14	9,508	19,620	.485

Note: If field goals made in the ABA are included, consider these NBA-ABA totals: Julius Erving (11,818), Dan Issel (10,431), George Gervin (10,368), Moses Malone (10,277) and Rick Barry (9,695).

Free Throws

		Yrs	FT	Att	Pct
1	**Karl Malone**	18	9619	12,963	.742
2	Moses Malone	19	8531	11,090	.769
3	Oscar Robertson	14	7694	9,185	.838
4	**Michael Jordan**	15	7327	8,772	.835
5	Jerry West	14	7160	8,801	.814
6	Dolph Schayes	16	6979	8,273	.844
7	Adrian Dantley	15	6832	8,351	.818
8	Kareem Abdul-Jabbar	20	6712	9,304	.721
9	Charles Barkley	16	6349	8,643	.734
10	Bob Pettit	11	6182	8,119	.761
11	Wilt Chamberlain	14	6057	11,862	.511
12	**David Robinson**	14	6035	8,201	.736

Note: If free throws made in the ABA are included, consider these totals: Moses Malone (9,018), Dan Issel (6,591), and Julius Erving (6,256).

Assists

		Yrs	Gm	No	Avg
1	**John Stockton**	19	1504	15,806	10.5
2	**Mark Jackson**	16	1254	10,215	8.1
3	Magic Johnson	13	906	10,141	11.2
4	Oscar Robertson	14	1040	9,887	9.5
5	Isiah Thomas	13	979	9,061	9.3
6	**Rod Strickland**	15	1017	7,704	7.6
7	**Gary Payton**	13	1027	7,590	7.4
8	Maurice Cheeks	15	1101	7,392	6.7
9	Lenny Wilkens	15	1077	7,211	6.7
10	Terry Porter	17	1274	7,160	5.6

Rebounds

		Yrs	Gm	No	Avg
1	Wilt Chamberlain	14	1045	23,924	22.9
2	Bill Russell	13	963	21,620	22.5
3	Kareem Abdul-Jabbar	20	1560	17,440	11.2
4	Elvin Hayes	16	1303	16,279	12.5
5	Moses Malone	19	1329	16,212	12.2
6	Robert Parish	21	1611	14,715	9.1
7	**Karl Malone**	18	1434	14,601	10.2
8	Nate Thurmond	14	964	14,464	15.0
9	Walt Bellamy	14	1043	14,241	13.7
10	Wes Unseld	13	984	13,769	14.0

Note: If rebounds accumulated in the ABA are included, consider the following totals: Moses Malone (17,834) and Artis Gilmore (16,330).

Steals

		Yrs	Gm	No
1	**John Stockton**	19	1504	3265
2	**Michael Jordan**	15	1072	2514
3	Maurice Cheeks	15	1101	2310
4	**Scottie Pippen**	16	1155	2286
5	Clyde Drexler	15	1086	2207

Note: Steals have only been an official stat since the 1973-74 season.

Blocked Shots

		Yrs	Gm	No
1	Hakeem Olajuwon	18	1238	3830
2	Kareem Abdul-Jabbar	20	1560	3189
3	Mark Eaton	11	875	3064
4	**David Robinson**	14	987	2954
5	Patrick Ewing	17	1183	2894

Note: Blocked shots have only been an official stat since the 1973-74 season. Also, note that if ABA records are included, consider the following block totals: Artis Gilmore (3,178).

Games Played

		Yrs	Career	Gm
1	Robert Parish	21	1976-97	1611
2	Kareem Abdul-Jabbar	20	1970-89	1560
3	**John Stockton**	19	1984-03	1504
4	**Karl Malone**	18	1985-	1434
5	**Kevin Willis**	18	1985-	1342

Note: If ABA records are included, consider the following game totals: Moses Malone (1,455).

Personal Fouls

		Yrs	Gm	Fouls	DQ
1	Kareem Abdul-Jabbar	20	1560	4657	48
2	**Karl Malone**	18	1434	4462	27
3	Robert Parish	21	1611	4443	86
4	**Charles Oakley**	18	1275	4413	63
5	Hakeem Olajuwon	18	1238	4383	80

Note: If ABA records are included, consider the following personal foul totals: Artis Gilmore (4,529) and Caldwell Jones (4,436).

SINGLE SEASON

Scoring Average

		Season	Avg
1	Wilt Chamberlain, Phi	1961-62	50.4
2	Wilt Chamberlain, SF	1962-63	44.8
3	Wilt Chamberlain, Phi	1960-61	38.4
4	Elgin Baylor, LA	1961-62	38.3
5	Wilt Chamberlain, Phi	1959-60	37.6
6	Michael Jordan, Chi	1986-87	37.1
7	Wilt Chamberlain, SF	1963-64	36.9
8	Rick Barry, SF	1966-67	35.6
9	Michael Jordan, Chi	1987-88	35.0
10	Elgin Baylor, LA	1960-61	34.8
	Kareem Abdul-Jabbar, Mil	1971-72	34.8

Field Goal Pct.

		Season	Pct
1	Wilt Chamberlain, LA	1972-73	.727
2	Wilt Chamberlain, SF	1966-67	.683
3	Artis Gilmore, Chi	1980-81	.670
4	Artis Gilmore, Chi	1981-82	.652
5	Wilt Chamberlain, LA	1971-72	.649

Free Throw Pct.

		Season	Pct
1	Calvin Murphy, Hou	1980-81	.958
2	Mahmoud Abdul-Rauf, Den.	1993-94	.956
3	Mark Price, Cle	1992-93	.948
4	Mark Price, Cle	1991-92	.947
	Rick Barry, Hou	1978-79	.947

3-Pt Field Goal Pct.

		Season	Pct
1	Steve Kerr, Chi	1994-95	.524
2	Jon Sundvold, Mia	1988-89	.522
3	Tim Legler, Wash	1995-96	.522
4	Steve Kerr, Chi	1995-96	.515
5	Detlef Schrempf, Sea	1994-95	.514

Assists

		Season	Avg
1	John Stockton, Utah	1989-90	14.5
2	John Stockton, Utah	1990-91	14.2
3	Isiah Thomas, Det	1984-85	13.9
4	John Stockton, Utah	1987-88	13.8
5	John Stockton, Utah	1991-92	13.7
6	John Stockton, Utah	1988-89	13.6
7	Kevin Porter, Det	1978-79	13.4
8	Magic Johnson, LAL	1983-84	13.1
9	Magic Johnson, LAL	1988-89	12.8
10	Magic Johnson, LAL	1984-85	12.6
	John Stockton, Utah	1993-94	12.6

Rebounds

		Season	Avg
1	Wilt Chamberlain, Phi	1960-61	27.2
2	Wilt Chamberlain, Phi	1959-60	27.0
3	Wilt Chamberlain, Phi	1961-62	25.7
4	Bill Russell, Bos	1963-64	24.7
5	Wilt Chamberlain, Phi	1965-66	24.6

Blocked Shots

		Season	Avg
1	Mark Eaton, Utah	1984-85	5.56
2	Manute Bol, Wash	1985-86	4.96
3	Elmore Smith, LA	1973-74	4.85
4	Mark Eaton, Utah	1985-86	4.61
5	Hakeem Olajuwon, Hou	1989-90	4.59

Steals

		Season	Avg
1	Alvin Robertson, SA	1985-86	3.67
2	Don Buse, Ind	1976-77	3.47
3	Magic Johnson, LAL	1980-81	3.43
4	Micheal Ray Richardson, NY	1979-80	3.23
5	Alvin Robertson, SA	1986-87	3.21

SINGLE GAME

Points

	Date	FG-FT	Pts
Wilt Chamberlain, Phi vs NY	3/2/62	36-28–	100
Wilt Chamberlain, Phi vs LA***	12/8/61	31-16–	78
Wilt Chamberlain, Phi vs Chi	1/13/62	29-15–	73
Wilt Chamberlain, SF at NY	11/16/62	29-15–	73
David Thompson, Den at Det	4/9/78	28-17–	73
Wilt Chamberlain, SF at LA	11/3/62	29-14–	72
Elgin Baylor, LA at NY	11/15/60	28-15–	71
David Robinson, SA at LAC	4/24/94	26-18–	71
Wilt Chamberlain, SF at Syr	3/10/63	27-16–	70
Michael Jordan, Chi at Cle*	3/28/90	23-21–	69
Wilt Chamberlain, Phi at Chi	12/16/67	30-8–	68
Pete Maravich, NO vs NYK	2/25/77	26-16–	68
Wilt Chamberlain, Phi vs NY	3/9/61	27-13–	67
Wilt Chamberlain, Phi at St. L	2/17/62	26-15–	67
Wilt Chamberlain, Phi vs NY	2/25/62	25-17–	67
Wilt Chamberlain, SF vs LA	1/11/63	28-11–	67
Wilt Chamberlain, LA vs Pho	2/9/69	29-8–	66
Wilt Chamberlain, Phi at Cin	2/13/62	24-17–	65
Wilt Chamberlain, Phi at St. L	2/27/62	25-15–	65
Wilt Chamberlain, Phi vs LA	2/7/66	28-9–	65
Elgin Baylor, Mpls vs Bos	11/8/59	25-14–	64
Rick Barry, G.St. vs Port	3/26/74	30-4–	64
Michael Jordan, Chi vs Orl	1/16/93	27-9–	64

* Overtime
*** Triple overtime.
Note: Wilt Chamberlain's 100-point game vs New York was played at Hershey, Penn.

Field Goals

	Date	FG	Att
Wilt Chamberlain, Phi vs NY	3/2/62	36	63
Wilt Chamberlain, Phi vs LA***	12/8/61	31	62
Wilt Chamberlain, Phi at Chi	12/16/67	30	40
Rick Barry, G.St. vs Port	2/26/74	30	45

Wilt Chamberlain made 29 four times.
***Triple overtime.

Free Throws

	Date	FT	Att
Wilt Chamberlain, Phi vs NY	3/2/62	28	32
Adrian Dantley, Utah vs Hou	1/4/84	28	29
Adrian Dantley, Utah vs Den	11/25/83	27	31
Adrian Dantley, Utah vs Dal	10/31/80	26	29
Michael Jordan, Chi vs NJ	2/26/87	26	27

3-Pt Field Goals

	Date	No
Kobe Bryant, LAL vs Sea	1/7/03	12
Dennis Scott, Orl vs Atl	4/18/96	11
Ray Allen, Milw vs Char	4/14/02	10
Brian Shaw, Mia at Mil	4/8/93	10
Joe Dumars, Det vs Min	11/8/94	10
George McCloud, Dal vs Pho	12/16/95	10*

Many tied with 9 each
* Overtime

All-Time NBA Regular Season Leaders (Cont.)

Assists

	Date	No
Scott Skiles, Orl vs Den	12/30/90	30
Kevin Porter, NJ vs Hou	2/24/78	29
Bob Cousy, Bos vs Mpls	2/27/59	28
Guy Rodgers, SF vs St.L	3/14/63	28
John Stockton, Utah vs SA	1/15/91	28

Rebounds

	Date	No
Wilt Chamberlain, Phi vs Bos	11/24/60	55
Bill Russell, Bos vs Syr	2/5/60	51
Bill Russell, Bos vs Phi	11/16/57	49
Bill Russell, Bos vs Det	3/11/65	49
Wilt Chamberlain, Phi vs Syr	2/6/60	45
Wilt Chamberlain, Phi vs LA	1/21/61	45

Blocked Shots

	Date	No
Elmore Smith, LA vs Port	10/28/73	17
Manute Bol, Wash vs Atl	1/25/86	15
Manute Bol, Wash vs Ind	2/26/87	15
Shaquille O'Neal, Orl at NJ	11/20/93	15

Steals

	Date	No
Larry Kenon, San Antonio at KC	12/26/76	11
Kendall Gill, NJ vs Mia.	4/3/99	11

14 different players tied with 10 each, including Alvin Robertson, who had 10 steals in a game four times.

All-Time Winningest NBA Coaches

Top 25 NBA career victories through the 2002-03 season. Career, regular season and playoff records are noted along with NBA titles won. Coaches active during 2002-03 season in **bold** type.

		Career				Regular Season			Playoffs			
		Yrs	W	L	Pct	W	L	Pct	W	L	Pct	NBA Titles
1	**Lenny Wilkens**	30	**1372**	1208	.532	1292	1114	.537	80	94	.460	1 (1979)
2	**Pat Riley**	21	**1265**	669	.654	1110	569	.661	155	100	.608	4 (1982,85,87-88)
3	**Don Nelson**	25	**1165**	909	.562	1096	828	.570	69	81	.460	None
4	Red Auerbach	20	**1037**	548	.654	938	479	.662	99	69	.589	9 (1957, 59-66)
5	Bill Fitch	25	**999**	1160	.463	944	1106	.460	55	54	.505	1 (1981)
6	Dick Motta	25	**991**	1087	.477	935	1017	.479	56	70	.444	1 (1978)
7	**Jerry Sloan**	18	**953**	601	.613	875	521	.627	78	80	.494	None
8	**Larry Brown**	20	**948**	757	.556	879	685	.562	69	72	.489	None
9	**Phil Jackson**	13	**938**	350	.728	776	290	.728	162	60	.730	9 (1991-93,96-98,00-02)
10	Jack Ramsay	21	**908**	841	.519	864	783	.525	44	58	.431	1 (1977)
11	Cotton Fitzsimmons	21	**867**	824	.513	832	775	.518	35	49	.417	None
12	Gene Shue	22	**814**	908	.473	784	861	.477	30	47	.390	None
13	**George Karl**	16	**767**	56	.575	708	499	.587	59	67	.468	None
14	Red Holzman	18	**754**	652	.536	696	604	.535	58	48	.547	2 (1970, 73)
	John MacLeod	18	**754**	711	.515	707	657	.518	47	54	.465	None
16	Chuck Daly	14	**713**	488	.594	638	437	.593	75	51	.595	2 (1989-90)
17	Doug Moe	15	**661**	579	.533	628	529	.543	33	50	.398	None
18	K.C. Jones	10	**603**	309	.661	522	252	.674	81	57	.587	2 (1984,86)
19	**Rick Adelman**	13	**663**	439	.602	603	384	.611	60	55	.522	None
20	Del Harris	14	**594**	507	.540	556	457	.549	38	50	.432	None
21	Mike Fratello	14	**592**	499	.543	572	465	.552	20	34	.370	None
22	Al Attles	14	**588**	548	.518	557	518	.518	31	30	.508	1 (1975)
23	**Rudy Tomjanovich**	12	**546**	427	.561	495	388	.561	51	39	.567	2 (1994-95)
24	Billy Cunningham	8	**520**	235	.689	454	196	.698	66	39	.629	1 (1983)
25	Alex Hannum	12	**518**	446	.537	471	412	.533	47	34	.580	2 (1958, 67)

Note: The NBA does not recognize records from the National Basketball League (1937-49), the American Basketball League (1961-62) or the American Basketball Assn. (1968-76), so the following NBL, ABL and ABA overall coaching records are not included above: NBL—**John Kundla** (51-19 and a title in 1 year). ABA—**Larry Brown** (249-129 in 4 yrs), **Alex Hannum** (194-164 and one title in 4 yrs), **K.C. Jones** (30-58 in 1 yr), **Kevin Loughery** (189-95 and one title in 3 yrs).

Where They Coached

Adelman—Portland (1988-94), Golden State (1995-97), Sacramento (1998-); **Attles**—Golden St. (1970-80,80-83); **Auerbach**—Washington (1946-49), Tri-Cities (1949-50), Boston (1950-66); **Brown**—Denver (1976-79), New Jersey (1981-83), San Antonio (1988-92), LA Clippers (1992-93), Indiana (1993-97), Philadelphia (1997-2000), Detroit (2003-); **Cunningham**—Philadelphia (1977-85); **Daly**—Cleveland (1981-82), Detroit (1983-92), New Jersey (1992-94), Orlando (1997-99); **Fitch**—Cleveland (1970-79), Boston (1979-83), Houston (1983-88), New Jersey (1989-92), LA Clippers (1994-98); **Fitzsimmons**—Phoenix (1970-72), Atlanta (1972-76), Buffalo (1977-78), Kansas City (1978-84), San Antonio (1984-86), Phoenix (1988-92, 95-96); **Fratello**—Atlanta (1980-90), Cleveland (1993-99).

Hannum—St. Louis (1957-58), Syracuse (1960-63), San Francisco (1963-66), Phila. 76ers (1966-68), Houston (1970-71); **Harris**—Houston (1979-83), Milwaukee (1987-92), LA Lakers (1994-99); **Holzman**—Milwaukee-St. Louis Hawks (1954-57), NY Knicks (1968-77,78-82); **Jackson**—Chicago (1989-98), LA Lakers (1999-); **Jones**—Washington (1973-76), Boston (1983-88), Seattle (1990-92); **Karl**—Cleveland (1984-86), Golden St. (1986-88), Seattle (1991-98), Milwaukee (1999-); **MacLeod**—Phoenix (1973-87), Dallas (1987-89), NY Knicks (1990-91); **Moe**—San Antonio (1976-80), Denver (1981-90), Philadelphia (1992-93).

Motta—Chicago (1968-76), Washington (1976-80), Dallas (1980-87), Sacramento (1990-91), Dallas (1994-96), Denver (1997); **Nelson**—Milwaukee (1976-87), Golden St. (1988-95), New York (1995-96), Dallas (1997-); **Ramsay**—Philadelphia (1968-72), Buffalo (1972-76), Portland (1976-86), Indiana (1986-89); **Riley**—LA Lakers (1981-90), New York (1991-95), Miami (1995-); **Shue**—Baltimore (1967-73), Philadelphia (1973-77), San Diego Clippers (1978-80), Washington (1980-86), LA Clippers (1987-89); **Sloan**—Chicago (1979-82), Utah (1988-); **Tomjanovich**—Houston (1991-2003); **Wilkens**—Seattle (1969-72), Portland (1974-76), Seattle (1977-85), Cleveland (1986-93), Atlanta (1993-00), Toronto (2000-).

Top Winning Percentages

Minimum of 350 victories, including playoffs; coaches active during 2002-03 season in **bold** type.

		Yrs	W	L	Pct
1	Phil Jackson	13	938	350	**.728**
2	Billy Cunningham	8	520	235	**.689**
3	K.C. Jones	10	603	309	**.661**
4	Red Auerbach	20	1037	548	**.654**
5	**Pat Riley**	21	1265	669	**.654**
6	**Gregg Popovich**	7	386	215	**.642**
7	Tommy Heinsohn	9	474	296	**.616**
8	**Jerry Sloan**	18	953	601	**.613**
9	**Rick Adelman**	13	663	439	**.602**
10	Chuck Daly	14	713	488	**.594**
11	Larry Costello	10	467	323	**.591**
12	John Kundla	11	485	338	**.589**
13	Bill Sharman	7	368	267	**.580**
14	George Karl	16	767	566	**.575**
15	Al Cervi	9	359	267	**.573**
16	Joe Lapchick	9	356	277	**.562**
17	**Don Nelson**	25	1165	909	**.562**
18	**Rudy Tomjanovich**	12	546	427	**.561**
19	**Larry Brown**	20	948	757	**.556**
20	Mike Fratello	14	592	499	**.543**
21	Bill Russell	8	375	317	**.542**
22	Del Harris	14	594	507	**.540**
23	Alex Hannum	12	518	446	**.537**
24	Red Holzman	18	754	652	**.536**
25	Doug Moe	15	661	579	**.533**
26	**Lenny Wilkens**	30	1372	1208	**.532**
27	Richie Guerin	8	353	325	**.521**
28	Jack Ramsay	21	909	841	**.519**
29	Al Attles	14	588	548	**.518**
30	John MacLeod	18	754	711	**.515**

Active Coaches' Victories

Through 2002-03 season, including playoffs.

		Yrs	W	L	Pct
1	Pat Riley, Miami	21	1265	669	.654
2	Don Nelson, Dallas	25	1165	909	.562
3	Jerry Sloan, Utah	18	953	601	.613
4	Larry Brown, Detroit	20	948	757	.556
5	Phil Jackson, LA Lakers	13	938	350	.728
6	George Karl, Milwaukee	16	767	566	.575
7	Rick Adelman, Sacramento	13	663	439	.602
8	Mike Dunleavy, LA Clippers	10	429	418	.506
9	Gregg Popovich, San Antonio	7	386	215	.642
10	Hubie Brown, Memphis	11	383	476	.446
11	Phil Saunders, Minnesota	8	335	298	.529
12	Don Chaney, New York	11	324	479	.403
13	Paul Silas, Cleveland	9	299	339	.469
14	Jeff Van Gundy, Houston	7	285	204	.583
15	Doc Rivers, Orlando	4	175	168	.510
16	Byron Scott, New Jersey	3	152	134	.531
17	Jim O'Brien, Boston	3	130	108	.546
18	Nate McMillan, Seattle	3	125	111	.530
19	Rick Carlisle, Indiana	2	112	79	.586
20	Maurice Cheeks, Portland	2	102	72	.586
21	Frank Johnson, Phoenix	2	57	62	.479
22	Tim Floyd, New Orleans	4	49	190	.205
23	Bill Cartwright, Chicago	2	47	90	.343
24	Eric Musselman, Golden St.	1	38	44	.463
25	Eddie Jordan, Washington	2	33	64	.340
26	Terry Stotts, Atlanta	1	24	31	.436
27	Jeff Bzdelik, Denver	1	17	65	.207
28	Randy Ayers, Philadelphia	0	0	0	—
29	Kevin O'Neill, Toronto	0	0	0	—

Annual Awards
Most Valuable Player

The Maurice Podoloff Trophy for regular season MVP. Named after the first commissioner (then president) of the NBA. Winners first selected by the NBA players (1956-80) then a national panel of pro basketball writers and broadcasters (since 1981). Winners' scoring averages are provided; (*) indicates led league.

Multiple winners: Kareem Abdul-Jabbar (6); Michael Jordan and Bill Russell (5); Wilt Chamberlain (4); Larry Bird, Magic Johnson and Moses Malone (3); Tim Duncan, Karl Malone and Bob Pettit (2).

Year		Avg	Year		Avg
1956	Bob Pettit, St. Louis, F	25.7*	1980	Kareem Abdul-Jabbar, LA, C	24.8
1957	Bob Cousy, Boston, G	20.6	1981	Julius Erving, Philadelphia, F	24.6
1958	Bill Russell, Boston, C	16.6	1982	Moses Malone, Houston, C	31.1
1959	Bob Pettit, St. Louis, F	29.2*	1983	Moses Malone, Philadelphia, C	24.5
1960	Wilt Chamberlain, Philadelphia, C	37.6*	1984	Larry Bird, Boston, F	24.2
1961	Bill Russell, Boston, C	16.9	1985	Larry Bird, Boston, F	28.7
1962	Bill Russell, Boston, C	18.9	1986	Larry Bird, Boston, F	25.8
1963	Bill Russell, Boston, C	16.8	1987	Magic Johnson, LAL, G	23.9
1964	Oscar Robertson, Cincinnati, G	31.4	1988	Michael Jordan, Chicago, G	35.0*
1965	Bill Russell, Boston, C	14.1	1989	Magic Johnson, LAL, G	22.5
1966	Wilt Chamberlain, Philadelphia, C	33.5*	1990	Magic Johnson, LAL, G	22.3
1967	Wilt Chamberlain, Philadelphia, C	24.1	1991	Michael Jordan, Chicago, G	31.5*
1968	Wilt Chamberlain, Philadelphia, C	24.3	1992	Michael Jordan, Chicago, G	30.1*
1969	Wes Unseld, Baltimore, C	13.8	1993	Charles Barkley, Phoenix, F	25.6
1970	Willis Reed, New York, C	21.7	1994	Hakeem Olajuwon, Houston, C	27.3
1971	Lew Alcindor, Milwaukee, C	31.7*	1995	David Robinson, San Antonio, C	27.6
1972	Kareem Abdul-Jabbar, Milwaukee, C	34.8*	1996	Michael Jordan, Chicago, G	30.4*
1973	Dave Cowens, Boston, C	20.5	1997	Karl Malone, Utah, F	27.4
1974	Kareem Abdul-Jabbar, Milwaukee, C	27.0	1998	Michael Jordan, Chicago, G	28.7*
1975	Bob McAdoo, Buffalo, F	34.5*	1999	Karl Malone, Utah, F	23.8
1976	Kareem Abdul-Jabbar, LA, C	27.7	2000	Shaquille O'Neal, LAL, C	29.7*
1977	Kareem Abdul-Jabbar, LA, C	26.2	2001	Allen Iverson, Philadelphia, G	31.1*
1978	Bill Walton, Portland, C	18.9	2002	Tim Duncan, San Antonio, F/C	25.5
1979	Moses Malone, Houston, C	24.8	2003	Tim Duncan, San Antonio, F/C	23.3

Note: Lew Alcindor changed his name to Kareem Abdul-Jabbar after the 1970-71 season.

Annual Awards (Cont.)
Rookie of the Year

The Eddie Gottlieb Trophy for outstanding rookie of the regular season. Named after the pro basketball pioneer and owner-coach of the first NBA champion Philadelphia Warriors. Winners selected by a national panel of pro basketball writers and broadcasters. Winners' scoring averages provided; (*) indicates led league; winners who were also named MVP are in **bold** type.

Year		Avg	Year		Avg
1953	Don Meineke, Ft. Wayne, F	10.8	1979	Phil Ford, Kansas City, G	15.9
1954	Ray Felix, Baltimore, C	17.6	1980	Larry Bird, Boston, F	21.3
1955	Bob Pettit, Milwaukee Hawks, F	20.4	1981	Darrell Griffith, Utah, G	20.6
1956	Maurice Stokes, Rochester, F/C	16.8	1982	Buck Williams, New Jersey, F	15.5
1957	Tommy Heinsohn, Boston, F	16.2	1983	Terry Cummings, San Diego, F	23.7
1958	Woody Sauldsberry, Philadelphia, F/C	12.8	1984	Ralph Sampson, Houston, C	21.0
1959	Elgin Baylor, Minneapolis, F	24.9	1985	Michael Jordan, Chicago, G	28.2
1960	**Wilt Chamberlain, Philadelphia, C**	37.6*	1986	Patrick Ewing, New York, C	20.0
1961	Oscar Robertson, Cincinnati, G	30.5	1987	Chuck Person, Indiana, F	18.8
1962	Walt Bellamy, Chicago Packers, C	31.6	1988	Mark Jackson, New York, G	13.6
1963	Terry Dischinger, Chicago Zephyrs, F	25.5	1989	Mitch Richmond, Golden St., G	22.0
1964	Jerry Lucas, Cincinnati, F/C	17.7	1990	David Robinson, San Antonio, C	24.3
1965	Willis Reed, New York, C	19.5	1991	Derrick Coleman, New Jersey, F	18.4
1966	Rick Barry, San Francisco, F	25.7	1992	Larry Johnson, Charlotte, F	19.2*
1967	Dave Bing, Detroit, G	20.0	1993	Shaquille O'Neal, Orlando,C	23.4
1968	Earl Monroe, Baltimore, G	24.3	1994	Chris Webber, Golden St., F	17.5
1969	**Wes Unseld, Baltimore, C**	13.8	1995	Grant Hill, Detroit, F	19.9
1970	Lew Alcindor, Milwaukee Bucks, C	28.8		& Jason Kidd, Dallas, G	11.7
1971	Dave Cowens, Boston, C	17.0	1996	Damon Stoudamire, Toronto, G	19.0
	& Geoff Petrie, Portland, G	24.8	1997	Allen Iverson, Philadelphia, G	23.5
1972	Sidney Wicks, Portland, F	24.5	1998	Tim Duncan, San Antonio, F/C	21.6
1973	Bob McAdoo, Buffalo, C/F	18.0	1999	Vince Carter, Toronto, F	18.3
1974	Ernie DiGregorio, Buffalo, G	15.2	2000	Elton Brand, Chicago, F	20.1
1975	Keith Wilkes, Golden St., F	14.2		& Steve Francis, Houston, G	18.0
1976	Alvan Adams, Phoenix, C	19.0	2001	Mike Miller, Orlando, G/F	11.9
1977	Adrian Dantley, Buffalo, F	20.3	2002	Pau Gasol, Memphis, F	17.6
1978	Walter Davis, Phoenix, F	24.2	2003	Amare Stoudemire, Phoenix, F	13.5

Note: The Chicago Packers changed their name to the Zephyrs after 1961-62 season. Also, Lew Alcindor changed his name to Kareem Abdul-Jabbar after the 1970-71 season.

Number One Draft Choices

Overall first choices in the NBA draft since the abolition of the territorial draft in 1966. Players who became Rookie of the Year are in **bold** type. The draft lottery began in 1985.

Year		Overall 1st Pick	Year		Overall 1st Pick
1966	New York	Cazzie Russell, Michigan	1985	New York	**Patrick Ewing**, Georgetown
1967	Detroit	Jimmy Walker, Providence	1986	Cleveland	Brad Daugherty, N. Carolina
1968	San Diego	Elvin Hayes, Houston	1987	San Antonio	**David Robinson**, Navy
1969	Milwaukee	**Lew Alcindor**, UCLA	1988	LA Clippers	Danny Manning, Kansas
1970	Detroit	Bob Lanier, St. Bonaventure	1989	Sacramento	Pervis Ellison, Louisville
1971	Cleveland	Austin Carr, Notre Dame	1990	New Jersey	**Derrick Coleman**, Syracuse
1972	Portland	LaRue Martin, Loyola-Chicago	1991	Charlotte	**Larry Johnson**, UNLV
1973	Philadelphia	Doug Collins, Illinois St.	1992	Orlando	**Shaquille O'Neal**, LSU
1974	Portland	Bill Walton, UCLA	1993	Orlando	**Chris Webber**, Michigan
1975	Atlanta	David Thompson, N.C. State	1994	Milwaukee	Glenn Robinson, Purdue
1976	Houston	John Lucas, Maryland	1995	Golden St.	Joe Smith, Maryland
1977	Milwaukee	Kent Benson, Indiana	1996	Philadelphia	**Allen Iverson**, Georgetown
1978	Portland	Mychal Thompson, Minnesota	1997	San Antonio	**Tim Duncan**, Wake Forest
1979	LA Lakers	Magic Johnson, Michigan St.	1998	LA Clippers	Michael Olowokandi, Pacific
1980	Golden St	Joe Barry Carroll, Purdue	1999	Chicago	**Elton Brand**, Duke
1981	Dallas	Mark Aguirre, DePaul	2000	New Jersey	Kenyon Martin, Cincinnati
1982	LA Lakers	James Worthy, N. Carolina	2001	Washington	Kwame Brown, Glynn Acad.
1983	Houston	**Ralph Sampson**, Virginia	2002	Houston	Yao Ming, China
1984	Houston	Akeem Olajuwon, Houston	2003	Cleveland	LeBron James, St.Vincent/St.Mary

Note: Lew Alcindor changed his name to Kareem Abdul-Jabbar after the 1970-71 season; Akeem Olajuwon changed his first name to Hakeem in 1991; in 1975 David Thompson signed with Denver of the ABA and did not play for Atlanta; David Robinson joined NBA for 1989-90 season after fulfilling military obligation.

Sixth Man Award

Awarded to the Best Player Off the Bench for the regular season. Winners selected by a national panel of pro basketball writers and broadcasters.
Multiple winners: Kevin McHale, Ricky Pierce and Detlef Schrempf (2).

Year		Year		Year	
1983	Bobby Jones, Phi., F	1990	Ricky Pierce, Mil., G/F	1997	John Starks, NY, G
1984	Kevin McHale, Bos., F	1991	Detlef Schrempf, Ind., F	1998	Danny Manning, Pho., F
1985	Kevin McHale, Bos., F	1992	Detlef Schrempf, Ind., F	1999	Darrell Armstrong, Orl., G
1986	Bill Walton, Bos., F/C	1993	Cliff Robinson, Port., F	2000	Rodney Rogers, Pho., F
1987	Ricky Pierce, Mil., G/F	1994	Dell Curry, Char., G	2001	Aaron McKie, Phi., G
1988	Roy Tarpley, Dal., F	1995	Anthony Mason, NY, F	2002	Corliss Williamson, Det., F
1989	Eddie Johnson, Pho., F	1996	Toni Kukoc, Chi., F	2003	Bobby Jackson, Sac., G

Defensive Player of the Year

Awarded to the Best Defensive Player for the regular season. Winners selected by a national panel of pro basketball writers and broadcasters.
Multiple winners: Dikembe Mutombo (4); Mark Eaton, Sidney Moncrief, Alonzo Mourning, Hakeem Olajuwon, Dennis Rodman and Ben Wallace (2).

Year		Year		Year	
1983	Sidney Moncrief, Mil., G	1990	Dennis Rodman, Det., F	1997	Dikembe Mutombo, Atl., C
1984	Sidney Moncrief, Mil., G	1991	Dennis Rodman, Det., F	1998	Dikembe Mutombo, Atl., C
1985	Mark Eaton, Utah, C	1992	David Robinson, SA, C	1999	Alonzo Mourning, Mia., C
1986	Alvin Robertson, SA, G	1993	Hakeem Olajuwon, Hou., C	2000	Alonzo Mourning, Mia., C
1987	Michael Cooper, LAL, F	1994	Hakeem Olajuwon, Hou., C	2001	Dikembe Mutombo, Atl.-Phi., C
1988	Michael Jordan, Chi., G	1995	Dikembe Mutombo, Den., C	2002	Ben Wallace, Det., C/F
1989	Mark Eaton, Utah, C	1996	Gary Payton, Sea., G	2003	Ben Wallace, Det., C/F

Most Improved Player

Awarded to the Most Improved Player for the regular season. Winners selected by a national panel of pro basketball writers and broadcasters.

Year		Year		Year	
1986	Alvin Robertson, SA, G	1992	Pervis Ellison, Wash., C	1998	Alan Henderson, Atl., F
1987	Dale Ellis, Sea., G	1993	Mahmoud Abdul-Rauf, Den., G	1999	Darrell Armstrong, Orl., G
1988	Kevin Duckworth, Port., C	1994	Don MacLean, Wash., F	2000	Jalen Rose, Ind., G
1989	Kevin Johnson, Pho., G	1995	Dana Barros, Phi., G	2001	Tracy McGrady, Orl., F
1990	Rony Seikaly, Mia., C	1996	Gheorghe Muresan, Wash., C	2002	Jermaine O'Neal, Ind., F
1991	Scott Skiles, Orl., G	1997	Isaac Austin, Miami, C	2003	Gilbert Arenas, G.St., G

Coach of the Year

The Red Auerbach Trophy for outstanding coach of the year. Renamed in 1967 for the former Boston coach who led the Celtics to nine NBA titles. Winners selected by a national panel of pro basketball writers and broadcasters. Previous season and winning season records are provided; (*) indicates division title.
Multiple winners: Don Nelson and Pat Riley (3); Bill Fitch, Cotton Fitzsimmons and Gene Shue (2).

Year			Improvement	Year			Improvement
1963	Harry Gallatin, St. L	.29-51	to 48-32	1984	Frank Layden, Utah	.30-52	to 45-37*
1964	Alex Hannum, SF	.31-49	to 48-32*	1985	Don Nelson, Mil	.50-32*	to 59-23*
1965	Red Auerbach, Bos	.59-21*	to 61-18*	1986	Mike Fratello, Atl	.34-48	to 50-32
1966	Dolph Schayes, Phi	.40-40	to 55-25*	1987	Mike Schuler, Port	.40-42	to 49-33
1967	Johnny Kerr, Chi	Expan.	to 33-48	1988	Doug Moe, Den	.37-45	to 54-28*
1968	Richie Guerin, St. L	.39-42	to 56-26*	1989	Cotton Fitzsimmons, Pho	.28-54	to 55-27
1969	Gene Shue, Balt	.36-46	to 57-25*	1990	Pat Riley, LA Lakers	.57-25*	to 63-19*
1970	Red Holzman, NY	.54-28	to 60-22*	1991	Don Chaney, Hou	.41-41	to 52-30
1971	Dick Motta, Chi	.39-43	to 51-31	1992	Don Nelson, GS	.44-38	to 55-27
1972	Bill Sharman, LA	.48-34*	to 69-13*	1993	Pat Riley, NY	.51-31	to 60-22
1973	Tommy Heinsohn, Bos	.56-26*	to 68-14*	1994	Lenny Wilkens, Atl	.43-39	to 57-25*
1974	Ray Scott, Det	.40-42	to 52-30	1995	Del Harris, LA Lakers	.33-49	to 48-34
1975	Phil Johnson, KC-Omaha	.33-49	to 44-38	1996	Phil Jackson, Chi	.47-35	to 72-10*
1976	Bill Fitch, Cle	.40-42	to 49-33*	1997	Pat Riley, Mia	.42-40	to 61-21
1977	Tom Nissalke, Hou	.40-42	to 49-33*	1998	Larry Bird, Ind	.39-43	to 58-24
1978	Hubie Brown, Atl	.31-51	to 41-41	1999	Mike Dunleavy, Port.	.46-36	to 35-15*
1979	Cotton Fitzsimmons, KC	.31-51	to 48-34*	2000	Doc Rivers, Orlando	.33-17	to 41-41
1980	Bill Fitch, Bos	.29-53	to 61-21*	2001	Larry Brown, Phila.	.49-33	to 56-26*
1981	Jack McKinney, Ind	.37-45	to 44-38	2002	Rick Carlisle, Det	.32-50	to 50-32*
1982	Gene Shue, Wash	.39-43	to 43-39	2003	Gregg Popovich, SA	.58-24*	to 60-22*
1983	Don Nelson, Mil	.55-27*	to 51-31*				

World Championships

The World Basketball Championships for men and women have been played regularly at four-year intervals (give or take a year) since 1970. The men's tournament began in 1950 and the women's in 1953. The Federation Internationale de Basketball Amateur (FIBA), which governs the World and Olympic tournaments, was founded in 1932. FIBA first allowed professional players from the NBA to participate in 1994. A team of collegians represented the USA in 1998.

Men

Multiple wins: Yugoslavia (5); Soviet Union and USA (3); Brazil (2).

Year
1950 . . . .**Argentina**, United States, Chile
1954 . . . .**United States**, Brazil, Philippines
1959 . . . .**Brazil**, United States, Chile
1963 . . . .**Brazil**, Yugoslavia, Soviet Union
1967 . . . .**Soviet Union**, Yugoslavia, Brazil
1970 . . . .**Yugoslavia**, Brazil, Soviet Union
1974 . . : . . .**Soviet Union**, Yugoslavia, United States
1978 . . . .**Yugoslavia**, Soviet Union, Brazil
1982 . . . . . .**Soviet Union**, United States, Yugoslavia
1986 . . . . .**United States**, Soviet Union, Yugoslavia
1990 . . . .**Yugoslavia**, Soviet Union, United States
1994 . . . .**United States**, Russia, Croatia
1998 . . . .**Yugoslavia**, Russia, United States
2002 . . . .**Yugoslavia**, Argentina, Germany
2006 . . . . .at Japan

Women

Multiple wins: USA (7); Soviet Union (6).

Year
1953 . . . .**United States**, Chile, France
1957 . .**United States**, Soviet Union, Czechoslovakia
1959 . . . . .**Soviet Union**, Bulgaria, Czechoslovakia
1964 . . . . .**Soviet Union**, Czechoslovakia, Bulgaria
1967 . .**Soviet Union**, South Korea, Czechoslovakia
1971 . . . .**Soviet Union**, Czechoslovakia, Brazil
1975 . . . .**Soviet Union**, Japan, Czechoslovakia
1979 . . . .**United States**, South Korea, Canada
1983 . . . .**Soviet Union**, United States, China
1986 . . . .**United States**, Soviet Union, Canada
1990 . . . .**United States**, Yugoslavia, Cuba
1994 . . . .**Brazil**, China, United States
1998 . . . .**United States**, Russia, Australia
2002 . . . .**United States**, Russia, Australia
2006 . . . . .at Brazil

NBA's 50 Greatest Players

In October 1996, as part of its 50th anniversary celebration, the NBA named the 50 greatest players in league history. The voting was done by a league-approved panel of media, former players and coaches, current and former general managers and team executives. The players are listed alphabetically along with the dates of their professional careers and positions. Active players are in **bold** type.

Player	Pos	Player	Pos	Player	Pos
Kareem Abdul-Jabbar, 1969-89	C	George Gervin, 1972-86	G	Robert Parish, 1976-97.	C
Nate Archibald, 1970-84	G	Hal Greer, 1958-73	G	Bob Pettit, 1954-65	F/C
Paul Arizin, 1950-61	F/G	John Havlicek, 1962-78	F/G	**Scottie Pippen**, 1987—	F
Charles Barkley, 1984-00	F	Elvin Hayes, 1968-84	F/C	Willis Reed, 1964-74	C
Rick Barry, 1965-80	F	Magic Johnson, 1979-91, 96	G	Oscar Robertson, 1960-74	G
Elgin Baylor, 1958-72	F	Sam Jones, 1957-69	G	David Robinson, 1989-2003	C
Dave Bing, 1966-78	G	Michael Jordan, 1984-93,	G	Bill Russell, 1956-69	C
Larry Bird, 1979-92	F	95-98, 01-03		Dolph Schayes, 1948-64	F/C
Wilt Chamberlain, 1959-73	C	Jerry Lucas, 1963-74	F/C	Bill Sharman, 1950-61	G
Bob Cousy, 1950-63, 69-70	G	**Karl Malone**, 1985—	F	John Stockton, 1984-2003	G
Dave Cowens, 1970-80, 1982-83	C	Moses Malone, 1974-95	C	Isiah Thomas, 1981-94	G
Billy Cunningham, 1965-76	G	Pete Maravich, 1970-80	G	Nate Thurmond, 1963-77	C/F
Dave DeBusschere, 1962-74	F	Kevin McHale, 1980-93	F	Wes Unseld, 1968-81	C/F
Clyde Drexler, 1983-98	G	George Mikan, 1946-54, 55-56	C	Bill Walton, 1974-88	C
Julius Erving, 1971-87	F	Earl Monroe, 1967-80	G	Jerry West, 1960-74	G
Patrick Ewing, 1985-2002	C	Hakeem Olajuwon, 1984-2002	C	Lenny Wilkens, 1960-75	G
Walt Frazier, 1967-80	G	**Shaquille O'Neal**, 1992—	C	James Worthy, 1982-94	F

Note: Rick Barry, Billy Cunningham, Julius Erving, George Gervin and Moses Malone all played part of their pro careers in the ABA.

NBA's 10 Greatest Coaches

In December 1996, as part of its 50th anniversary celebration, the NBA named the 10 greatest coaches in league history. The voting was done by a league-approved panel of media. The coaches are listed alphabetically along with the dates of their professional coaching careers and overall records, including playoff games, and number of NBA titles won. Active coaches are in **bold** type.

Coach	W	L	Pct.	Titles	Coach	W	L	Pct.	Titles
Red Auerbach, 1946-66	1037	548	.654	9	**Don Nelson**, 1976-96, 97—	1165	909	.562	0
Chuck Daly, 1981-94, 97-99	713	488	.594	2	Jack Ramsay, 1968-89	908	841	.519	1
Bill Fitch, 1970-98	999	1160	.463	1	**Pat Riley**, 1981—	1265	669	.654	4
Red Holzman, 1953-82	754	652	.536	2	Lenny Wilkens, 1969-2003	1372	1208	.532	1
Phil Jackson, 1989-98, 99—	938	350	.728	9	TOTALS	9636	7163	.574	34
John Kundla, 1947-59	485	338	.589	5					

American Basketball Association
ABA Finals

The American Basketball Assn. began play in 1967-68 as a 10-team rival of the 21-year-old NBA. The ABA, which introduced the three-point basket, a multi-colored ball and the All-Star Game Slam Dunk Contest, lasted nine seasons before folding following the 1975-76 season. Four ABA teams–Denver, Indiana, New York and San Antonio–survived to enter the NBA in 1976-77. The NBA also adopted the three-point basket (in 1979-80) and the All-Star Game Slam Dunk Contest. The older league, however, refused to take in the ABA ball.

Multiple winners: Indiana (3); New York (2).

Year	Winner	Head Coach	Series	Loser	Head Coach
1968	Pittsburgh Pipers	Vince Cazzetta	4-3 (WLLWLWW)	New Orleans Bucs	Babe McCarthy
1969	Oakland Oaks	Alex Hannum	4-1 (WLWWW)	Indiana Pacers	Bob Leonard
1970	Indiana Pacers	Bob Leonard	4-2 (WWLWLW)	Los Angeles Stars	Bill Sharman
1971	Utah Stars	Bill Sharman	4-3 (WWLLWLW)	Kentucky Colonels	Frank Ramsey
1972	Indiana Pacers	Bob Leonard	4-2 (WLWLWW)	New York Nets	Lou Carnesecca
1973	Indiana Pacers	Bob Leonard	4-3 (WLLWLWW)	Kentucky Colonels	Joe Mullaney
1974	New York Nets	Kevin Loughery	4-1 (WWWLW)	Utah Stars	Joe Mullaney
1975	Kentucky Colonels	Hubie Brown	4-1 (WWLWW)	Indiana Pacers	Bob Leonard
1976	New York Nets	Kevin Loughery	4-2 (WLWWLW)	Denver Nuggets	Larry Brown

Most Valuable Player

Winners' scoring averages provided; (*) indicates led league.

Multiple winners: Julius Erving (3); Mel Daniels (2).

Year		Avg
1968	Connie Hawkins, Pittsburgh, C	.26.8*
1969	Mel Daniels, Indiana, C	24.0
1970	Spencer Haywood, Denver, C	30.0*
1971	Mel Daniels, Indiana, C	21.0
1972	Artis Gilmore, Kentucky, C	23.8
1973	Billy Cunningham, Carolina, F	24.1
1974	Julius Erving, New York, F	27.4*
1975	George McGinnis, Indiana, F	29.8*
	& Julius Erving, New York, F	27.9
1976	Julius Erving, New York, F	29.3*

Rookie of the Year

Winners' scoring averages provided; (*) indicates led league. Rookies who were also named Most Valuable Player are in **bold** type.

Year		Avg
1968	Mel Daniels, Minnesota, C	22.2
1969	Warren Armstrong, Oakland, G	21.5
1970	**Spencer Haywood**, Denver, C	30.0*
1971	Dan Issel, Kentucky, C	29.8*
	& Charlie Scott, Virginia, G	27.1
1972	**Artis Gilmore**, Kentucky, C	23.8
1973	Brian Taylor, New York, G	15.3
1974	Swen Nater, Virginia-SA, C	14.1
1975	Marvin Barnes, St. Louis, C	24.0
1976	David Thompson, Denver, F	26.0

Note: Warren Armstrong changed his name to Warren Jabali after the 1970-71 season.

Coach of the Year

Previous season and winning season records are provided; (*) indicates division title.

Multiple winner: Larry Brown (3).

Year		Improvement
1968	Vince Cazzetta, Pittsburgh	54-24*
1969	Alex Hannum, Oakland	.22-56 to 60-18*
1970	Joe Belmont, Denver	.44-34 to 51-33*
	& Bill Sharman, LA Stars	.33-45 to 43-41
1971	Al Bianchi, Virginia	.44-40 to 55-29*
1972	Tom Nissalke, Dallas	.30-54 to 42-42
1973	Larry Brown, Carolina	.35-49 to 57-27*
1974	Babe McCarthy, Kentucky	.56-28 to 53-31
	& Joe Mullaney, Utah	.55-29* to 51-33*
1975	Larry Brown, Denver	.37-47 to 65-19*
1976	Larry Brown, Denver	.65-19* to 60-24*

Scoring Leaders

Scoring championship decided by per game point average every season.

Multiple winner: Julius Erving (3).

Year		Gm	Avg	Pts
1968	Connie Hawkins, Pittsburgh	.70	1875	26.8
1969	Rick Barry, Oakland	.35	1190	34.0
1970	Spencer Haywood, Denver	.84	2519	30.0
1971	Dan Issel, Kentucky	.83	2480	29.8
1972	Charlie Scott, Virginia	.73	2524	34.6
1973	Julius Erving, Virginia	.71	2268	31.9
1974	Julius Erving, New York	.84	2299	27.4
1975	George McGinnis, Indiana	.79	2353	29.8
1976	Julius Erving, New York	.84	2462	29.3

ABA All-Star Game

The ABA All-Star Game was an Eastern Division vs. Western Division contest from 1968-75. League membership had dropped to seven teams by 1976, the ABA's last season, so the team in first place at the break (Denver) played an All-Star team made up from the other six clubs.

Series: East won 5, West 3 and Denver 1.

Year	Result	Host	Coaches	Most Valuable Player
1968	East 126, West 120	Indiana	Jim Pollard, Babe McCarthy	Larry Brown, New Orleans
1969	West 133, East 127	Louisville	Alex Hannum, Gene Rhodes	John Beasley, Dallas
1970	West 128, East 98	Indiana	Babe McCarthy, Bob Leonard	Spencer Haywood, Denver
1971	East 126, West 122	Carolina	Al Bianchi, Bill Sharman	Mel Daniels, Indiana
1972	East 142, West 115	Louisville	Joe Mullaney, Ladell Andersen	Dan Issel, Kentucky
1973	West 123, East 111	Utah	Ladell Andersen, Larry Brown	Warren Jabali, Denver
1974	East 128, West 112	Virginia	Babe McCarthy, Joe Mullaney	Artis Gilmore, Kentucky
1975	East 151, West 124	San Antonio	Kevin Loughery, Larry Brown	Freddie Lewis, St. Louis
1976	Denver 144, ABA 138	Denver	Larry Brown, Kevin Loughery	David Thompson, Denver

Continental Basketball Association

Originally named the Eastern Pennsylvania Basketball League when it formed on April 23, 1946, the league changed names several times before becoming known as the Eastern Basketball Association. In 1978, the EBA was redubbed the CBA. The CBA suspended operations following the 2000 season but reorganized for the 2001-02 season.

Multiple champions: Allentown and Wilkes-Barre (8); Scranton, Tampa Bay, Williamsport and Yakima (3); Albany, La Crosse, Pottsville, Rochester and Wilmington (2).

Year		Year		Year		Year	
1947	Wilkes-Barre Barons	1963	Allentown Jets	1977	Scranton Apollos	1992	La Crosse Catbirds
1948	Reading Keys	1964	Camden Bullets	1978	Wilkes-Barre Barons	1993	Omaha Racers
1949	Pottsville Packers	1965	Allentown Jets	1979	Rochester Zeniths	1994	Quad City Thunder
1950	Williamsport Billies	1966	Wilmington Blue Bombers	1980	Anchorage Northern Knights	1995	Yakima Sun Kings
1951	Sunbury Mercuries					1996	Sioux Falls Skyforce
1952	Pottsville Packers	1967	Wilmington Blue Bombers	1981	Rochester Zeniths	1997	Oklahoma City Calvary
1953	Williamsport Billies			1982	Lancaster Lightning		
1954	Williamsport Billies	1968	Allentown Jets	1983	Detroit Spirits	1998	Quad City Thunder
1955	Wilkes-Barre Barons	1969	Wilkes-Barre Barons	1984	Albany Patroons	1999	Connecticut Pride
1956	Wilkes-Barre Barons	1970	Allentown Jets	1985	Tampa Bay Thrillers	2000	Yakima Sun Kings
1957	Scranton Miners	1971	Scranton Apollos	1986	Tampa Bay Thrillers	2002	Dakota Wizards
1958	Wilkes-Barre Barons	1972	Allentown Jets	1987	Rapid City Thrillers*	2003	Yakima Sun Kings
1959	Wilkes-Barre Barons	1973	Wilkes-Barre Barons	1988	Albany Patroons		
1960	Easton Madisons	1974	Hartford Capitols	1989	Tulsa Fast Breakers	*The Tampa Bay Thrillers	
1961	Baltimore Bullets	1975	Allentown Jets	1990	La Crosse Catbirds	moved to Rapid City, S.D. at	
1962	Allentown Jets	1976	Allentown Jets	1991	Wichita Falls Texans	the end of the 1987 regular season.	

WOMEN
Women's National Basketball Association
League Champions

The WNBA, owned and operated by the NBA, began play in 1997 as an eight-team summer league. The league added two teams prior to its second season (1998), then added two more teams before its third season in 1999. Four additional teams were added before the 2000 season, bringing the total number of teams to 16. Prior to the 2003 season two franchises were relocated and two were contracted. The WNBA champion was determined by a single-game playoff between the winners of the semifinals in the league's 1997 inaugural season, before going to a best-of-three championship series in 1998.

Multiple winners: Houston (4); Los Angeles (2).

Year	Champions	Head Coach	Score	Runners-up	Head Coach
1997	Houston Comets	Van Chancellor	65-51	New York Liberty	Nancy Darsch
1998	Houston Comets	Van Chancellor	2-1 (LWW)	Phoenix Mercury	Cheryl Miller
1999	Houston Comets	Van Chancellor	2-1 (WLW)	New York Liberty	Richie Adubato
2000	Houston Comets	Van Chancellor	2-0	New York Liberty	Richie Adubato
2001	Los Angeles Sparks	Michael Cooper	2-0	Charlotte Sting	Anne Donovan
2002	Los Angeles Sparks	Michael Cooper	2-0	New York Liberty	Richie Adubato
2003	Detroit Shock	Bill Laimbeer	2-1 (LWW)	Los Angeles Sparks	Michael Cooper

Most Valuable Player

Winner's scoring averages provided; (*) indicates led league.

Multiple winners: Cynthia Cooper and Sheryl Swoopes (2).

Year		Avg
1997	Cynthia Cooper, Houston	22.2*
1998	Cynthia Cooper, Houston	22.7*
1999	Yolanda Griffith, Sacramento	18.8
2000	Sheryl Swoopes, Houston	20.7*
2001	Lisa Leslie, Los Angeles	19.5
2002	Sheryl Swoopes, Houston	18.5
2003	Lauren Jackson, Seattle	21.2*

Coach of the Year

Previous season and winning season's record are provided; (*) indicates division title.

Multiple winner: Van Chancellor (3).

Year		Improvement
1997	Van Chancellor, Houston	18-10*
1998	Van Chancellor, Houston	18-10 to 27-3*
1999	Van Chancellor, Houston	27-3 to 26-6*
2000	Michael Cooper, Los Angeles	20-12 to 28-4*
2001	Dan Hughes, Cleveland	17-15 to 22-10*
2002	Marianne Stanley, Washington	10-22 to 17-15
2003	Bill Laimbeer, Detroit	9-23 to 25-9*

American Basketball League (1997–98)
League Champions

The American Basketball League began play in 1996 as an eight-team league. Before the 1997-98 season the league added an expansion franchise in Long Beach, Calif. while the Richmond Rage was relocated to Philadelphia. In the spring of 1998, the league announced plans to dissolve an original franchise, the Atlanta Glory, and expand to Chicago and Nashville before the 1998-99 season, increasing the league's size to 10 teams. The ABL finals was a best of five series. Each ABL champion's wins and losses are noted in parentheses after the series score. The ABL folded before the 1999 season.

Multiple winner: Columbus (2).

Year	Champions	Head Coach	Series	Runners-up	Head Coach
1997	Columbus Quest	Brian Agler	3-2 (WLLWW)	Richmond Rage	Lisa Boyer
1998	Columbus Quest	Brian Agler	3-2 (LLWWW)	Long Beach StingRays	Maura McHugh

Most Valuable Player

Winner's scoring averages provided; (*) indicates led league.

Year		Avg
1997	Nikki McCray, Columbus	19.9
1998	Natalie Williams, Portland	21.9*

Coach of the Year

Previous season and winning season's record are provided; (*) indicates division title.

Year		Improvement
1997	Brian Agler, Columbus	31-9*
1998	Lin Dunn, Portland	14-26 to 27-17

Hockey

Martin Brodeur, *left*, and **Ken Daneyko** *have made a habit of lifting the Stanley Cup.*

Brian Bahr/Getty Images

Mighty Close

Unheralded J-S Giguere carried Anaheim to within one game of the cup, but the Devils prevailed—again.

Steve Levy *is a hockey play-by-play announcer and host of ESPN's National Hockey Night.*

Prior to Game 3 of the Stanley Cup finals in Anaheim, I was doing some last minute snooping outside the Mighty Ducks dressing room, looking for either Paul Kariya or Steve Rucchin, the two longest tenured Ducks.

I found Rucchin and asked him if during all the dark days and losing ways of the franchise, there was ever a time he thought any of this current success might be possible. He pointed to a 1997 first round playoff series against Phoenix. The Ducks won that series, 4-3, and many believed it would be the turning point in the franchise's history.

It was. But unfortunately it turned the wrong way. In the next series the team was swept by Detroit and hadn't been back to the playoffs since. Until this year. Now the entire hockey world had invaded Anaheim for the Stanley Cup Finals.

I was more surprised than Rucchin. In years past I had

done so many games in southern California that were, sadly, not in Los Angeles. To be honest, whenever my schedule came out and Anaheim was in the "home team" column, lets just say I wasn't exactly excited. Why should I have been? Almost no one in The Pond was excited either unless they were there to cheer for the visiting team.

This year, however, something very special happened. I had heard of Jean-Sebastien Giguere before the playoffs began, I just couldn't remember what I'd heard about him. I certainly didn't realize he was good enough to make 63 saves to win Game 1 (in triple overtime) of their first round series in Detroit. That game was supposed to be the wake-up call for the defending world champion Red Wings, just as they had awoken the year before, after losing Game 1 of the Finals on home ice to upstart Carolina. After that game, the Wings won the next four and the Cup. It had to be the same

*With five postseason shutouts, Anaheim goalie **Jean-Sebastien Giguere** grabbed the Conn Smythe Trophy as playoff MVP.*

deal here, right? Wrong. Mighty Detroit, one of the Original Six, couldn't get a single win and were swept by a team with a duck on their sweater.

For Anaheim it was onto Dallas. Most of the experts thought of the Ducks, "Hey, that's nice, now get ready to go home." But while the Stars and the rest of the teams still alive in the playoffs secretly cheered the fall of the Wings, they soon found out facing Detroit might have been easier. Hey at least the Stars won a game—two to be exact.

So the Western Conference Finals was set—the Wild vs. the Mighty Ducks. Huh? Could you imagine being over-seas for the first month of the playoffs and turning on ESPN International to find Anaheim and Minnesota competing for the right to play for Lord Stanley's cup? The hockey world had truly turned upside down.

The Wild were no match for the Ducks and Giguere, who blanked them for the first three games of the series, and they ultimately met the same fate as the Red Wings—out in four. Anaheim was going to the Stanley Cup Finals against...uhh, who was it again? Oh yeah. I'm 500 words into this and I'm just now mentioning the New Jersey Devils! Where's the love?

AP/Wide World Photos

*Mighty Ducks right wing **Paul Kariya** became Devils defenseman Scott Stevens' latest victim in Game 6. Moments later, Kariya would return to score his first goal of the series.*

For me, the lasting impression of the Finals is the brutal Scott Stevens hit on Paul Kariya, and then seeing Kariya return to the ice, fly down the left side and send a laser past Martin Brodeur. See, it just happened again! The Devils just don't capture anyone's imagination. All they capture are Stanley Cups - three of them in the last nine years to be exact. If they played eight miles away, either across the George Washington Bridge or through the Lincoln Tunnel, maybe we'd be going ga-ga over them and using words like "dynasty."

Despite having the best general manager in the game, if not all of sports, in Lou Lamoriello, the Devils don't get nearly the credit they deserve. In 2004, they'll be a favorite to win yet again.

When I think back to the postseason, I'll remember all the great new blood. Sure, a little old blood from New York City, Chicago or even Los Angeles, would have been nice, but Anaheim, Minnesota and Tampa Bay all coming to life made up for it.

continued on page 384 ▶

Steve Levy's Ten Biggest Stories of the Year in Hockey

10 Sens and Sabres are Saved— While part of me would like to see at least one franchise eliminated to let the players know that if owners are going to lose money, players are going to lose jobs, I'm glad it wasn't either of these franchises. Both are so woven into the fabric of their communities.

9 Offseason Changes out West — Despite its moving parts, it is still the power conference. Paul Kariya and Teemu Selanne are teammates again in Colorado... Dominik Hasek returns to Detroit and is joined by Derian Hatcher.

8 Postseason Battles—For all the abuse the NHL postseason absorbed for not being compelling enough, there were 22 overtime games, eight of them multi-overtime games. The five-overtime game between the Ducks and Stars was breathtaking (especially for Panger and I broadcasting the game).

7 Speed—Fast face offs and line changes had games averaging about two hours and twenty minutes. It's not so great for television (no time for instant replays) but great for the game.

6 All-Star Game Shootout—I'll never forget the crowd's reaction in Florida when it was announced the game was going to the shootout. It's time for the NHL to adopt it in the regular season after a ten minute 4-on-4 overtime. No one would leave the building early.

5 Comings and Goings—Mario Lemieux is coming back to save Pittsburgh (and his own investment) yet again. Patrick Roy says goodbye and Ken Daneyko (yes he belongs in this list) goes out a champion and everything that a hockey player should be.

4 Old Blood—There's no possible way that with all that talent and all that payroll the Rangers could miss the playoffs for a sixth straight season. They did. Do I hear seven?

3 The Devils!—New Jersey does everything right to win their third cup in nine years, and yet they continue to fight for attention and affection.

2 New Blood—The playoff runs of the Wild and Lightning were filled with excitement and their cities responded. We couldn't move in either St. Paul or Tampa without hearing constant hockey talk.

1 The Mighty Ducks—Anaheim didn't just give us the underdog we all crave but they showed they truly belonged by forcing a Game 7 in the Stanley Cup Finals. The sport needed this in a big way. Now can they repeat the feat?

P.S. This entry deserves its own category as it cannot be included in any top ten list. News of the death of Herb Brooks was absolutely devastating. I could fill the entire almanac with what he has meant to hockey in the U.S. He, and his achievements, will never be forgotten.

In addition, never again will I utter the phrase "a commanding 3-1 series lead." In 2003, 3-1 leads proved to be anything but commanding. St. Louis blew one to Vancouver, and Minnesota came back from a 3-1 deficit twice, first against Colorado and then Vancouver. Game 7 in that Colorado series was an overtime thriller that will be our last memory of the great Patrick Roy.

As we look ahead for surprises, lets first look back. Anaheim, Carolina, Buffalo and Washington have all represented their conferences in the past six years. The Ducks and Hurricanes were flat out shockers. They say these things happen in threes, so if the Blue Jackets or Predators represent the West in the Stanley Cup Finals in the near future, don't say you weren't warned.

Speaking of the near future, I remain an optimist and choose to see the (Stanley) cup as half full. So while there will be plenty of talk surrounding the end of NHL hockey as we know it, I'm counting on the owners and players getting together and working out their differences without any kind of work stoppage. They just couldn't possibly be foolish enough not to.

Too much R&R?

The Mighty Ducks had a full week and a half off between the Conference Finals and the Stanley Cup Finals, the longest lag since the NHL took control of the Stanley Cup in 1926. The Ducks, who were shut out in the first two games, are the only team in the following list to not win the Cup.

		Days off before Finals
2003	Anaheim Mighty Ducks	10
1966	Montreal Canadiens	9
1984	Edmonton Oilers	8
1952	Detroit Red Wings	8
1949	Toronto Maple Leafs	8

Gettin' Giggy

In 2003 Anaheim goalie Jean-Sebastien Giguere recorded the fifth-longest single-season playoff shutout streak in NHL history. He blanked Minnesota for the first three games of the Western Conference Finals and was finally scored on by Andrew Brunette, 4:37 into Game 4. The longest streaks are listed below.

		Min:Sec
1930	George Hainsworth, Mon.	270:08
1937	Dave Kerr, NYR	248:35
1936	Norm Smith, Det.	248:32
1951	Gerry McNeil, Mon.	218:42
2003	J-S Giguere, Ana.	217:54

2002-2003
Season in Review

ESPN SPORTS ALMANAC

Final NHL Standings

Division champions (*) and playoff qualifiers (†) are noted. OL signifies any game that was tied after regulation play but lost in overtime. Number of seasons listed after each head coach refers to current tenure with club through 2002-03 season.

Western Conference

Central Division

	W	L	T	OL	Pts	GF	GA
*Detroit	48	20	10	4	110	269	203
†St. Louis	41	24	11	6	99	253	222
Chicago	30	33	13	6	79	207	226
Nashville	27	35	13	7	74	183	206
Columbus	29	42	8	3	69	213	263

Head Coaches: Det—Dave Lewis (1st season); **St.L**—Joel Quenneville (7th); **Chi**—Brian Sutter (2nd); **Nash**—Barry Trotz (5th); **Clb**—Dave King (3rd, 14-20-4-2) was fired on Jan. 7 and replaced by GM Doug MacLean (15-22-4-1).

Northwest Division

	W	L	T	OL	Pts	GF	GA
*Colorado	42	19	13	8	105	251	194
†Vancouver	45	23	13	1	104	264	208
†Minnesota	42	29	10	1	95	198	178
†Edmonton	36	26	11	9	92	231	230
Calgary	29	36	13	4	75	186	228

Head Coaches: Col—Bob Hartley (5th season, 10-8-9-4) was fired on Dec. 18 and replaced by Tony Granato (32-11-4-4); **Van**—Marc Crawford (3rd); **Min**—Jacques Lemaire (3rd); **Edm**—Craig MacTavish (3rd); **Calg**—Greg Gilbert (3rd, 6-13-3-3) was fired on Dec. 3 and replaced by Al MacNeil (4-5-2-0), and then Darryl Sutter (19-18-8-1) on Dec. 28.

Pacific Division

	W	L	T	OL	Pts	GF	GA
*Dallas	46	17	15	4	111	245	169
†Anaheim	40	27	9	6	95	203	193
Los Angeles	33	37	6	6	78	203	221
Phoenix	31	35	11	5	78	204	230
San Jose	28	37	9	8	73	214	239

Head Coaches: Dal—Dave Tippett (1st season); **Ana**—Mike Babcock (1st); **LA**—Andy Murray (4th); **Pho**—Bob Francis (4th); **SJ**—Darryl Sutter (6th, 8-12-2-2) was fired on Dec. 1 and replaced by Cap Raeder (1-0-0-0) and then Ron Wilson (19-25-7-6) on Dec. 4.

Eastern Conference

Northeast Division

	W	L	T	OL	Pts	GF	GA
*Ottawa	52	21	8	1	113	263	182
†Toronto	44	28	7	3	98	236	208
†Boston	36	31	11	4	87	245	237
Montreal	30	35	8	9	77	206	234
Buffalo	27	37	10	8	72	190	219

Head Coaches: Ott—Jacques Martin (8th season); **Tor**—Pat Quinn (5th); **Bos**—Robbie Ftorek (2nd, 33-28-8-4) was fired on Mar. 19 and replaced by GM Mike O'Connell (3-3-3-0); **Mon**—Michel Therrien (3rd, 18-19-5-4) was fired on Jan. 17 and replaced by Claude Julien (12-16-3-5); **Buf**—Lindy Ruff (6th).

Atlantic Division

	W	L	T	OL	Pts	GF	GA
*New Jersey	46	20	10	6	108	216	166
†Philadelphia	45	20	13	4	107	211	166
†NY Islanders	35	34	11	2	83	224	231
NY Rangers	32	36	10	4	78	210	231
Pittsburgh	27	44	6	5	65	189	255

Head Coaches: NJ—Pat Burns (1st season); **Phi**—Ken Hitchcock (1st); **NYI**—Peter Laviolette (2nd); **NYR**—Brian Trottier (1st, 21-26-6-1) was fired on Jan. 29 and replaced by GM Glen Sather (11-10-4-3); **Pit**—Rick Kehoe (2nd).

Southeast Division

	W	L	T	OL	Pts	GF	GA
*Tampa Bay	36	25	16	5	93	219	210
†Washington	39	29	8	6	92	224	220
Atlanta	31	39	7	5	74	226	284
Florida	24	36	13	9	70	176	237
Carolina	22	43	11	6	61	171	240

Head Coaches: TB—John Tortorella (3rd season); **Wash**—Bruce Cassidy (1st); **Atl**—Curt Fraser (4th, 8-20-1-4) was fired on Dec. 26 and replaced by GM Don Waddell (4-5-1-0) and then Bob Hartley (19-14-5-1) on Jan. 14; **Fla**—Mike Keenan (2nd); **Car**—Paul Maurice (8th).

Home & Away, Division, Conference Records

Sixteen teams—eight from each conference—qualify for the Stanley Cup Playoffs; (*) indicates division champions.

Western Conference

		Pts	Home	Away	Div
1	Dallas*	111	28-5-6-2	18-12-9-2	14-3-3-0
2	Detroit*	110	28-6-5-2	20-14-5-2	14-3-2-1
3	Colorado*	105	21-9-8-3	21-10-5-5	8-5-4-3
4	Vancouver	104	22-13-6-0	23-10-7-1	10-6-4-0
5	St. Louis	99	23-11-4-3	18-13-7-3	7-8-3-2
6	Minnesota	95	25-13-3-0	17-16-7-1	7-8-4-1
7	Anaheim	95	22-10-7-2	18-17-2-4	8-9-3-0
8	Edmonton	92	20-12-5-4	16-14-6-5	7-7-2-4
	Chicago	79	17-15-7-2	13-18-6-4	11-3-3-3
	Los Angeles	78	19-19-2-1	14-18-4-5	10-9-1-0
	Phoenix	78	17-16-6-2	14-19-5-3	6-7-4-3
	Calgary	75	14-16-10-1	15-20-3-3	9-6-4-1
	Nashville	74	18-17-5-1	9-18-8-6	6-9-4-1
	San Jose	73	17-16-5-3	11-21-4-5	6-10-1-3
	Columbus	69	20-14-5-2	9-28-3-1	5-13-2-0

Eastern Conference

		Pts	Home	Away	Div
1	Ottawa*	113	28-9-3-1	24-12-5-0	14-4-1-1
2	New Jersey*	108	25-11-3-2	21-9-7-4	13-2-5-0
3	Tampa Bay*	93	22-9-7-3	14-16-9-2	10-4-5-1
4	Philadelphia	107	21-10-8-2	24-10-5-2	11-6-2-1
5	Toronto	98	24-13-4-0	20-15-3-3	9-10-1-0
6	Washington	92	24-13-2-2	15-16-6-4	14-4-2-0
7	Boston	87	23-11-5-2	13-20-6-2	9-9-1-1
8	NY Islanders	83	18-18-5-0	17-16-6-2	6-9-4-1
	NY Rangers	78	17-18-4-2	15-18-6-2	6-8-5-1
	Montreal	77	16-16-5-4	14-19-3-5	7-9-1-3
	Atlanta	74	15-19-4-3	16-20-3-2	7-7-3-3
	Buffalo	72	18-16-5-2	9-21-5-6	9-9-0-2
	Florida	70	8-21-7-5	16-15-6-4	7-7-3-3
	Pittsburgh	65	15-22-2-2	12-22-4-3	6-14-0-0
	Carolina	61	12-17-9-3	10-26-2-3	4-11-3-2

2003 NHL All-Star Game
Western 6, Eastern 5 (shootout)

53rd NHL All-Star Game. **Date:** Feb. 2 at Office Depot Center in Sunrise, Fla.; **Coaches:** Marc Crawford, Vancouver (Western) and Jacques Martin, Ottawa (Eastern); **MVP:** Dany Heatley, Atlanta right wing (Eastern)—four goals, one assist.

Starters were chosen by fan vote while reserves were selected by the NHL's Hockey Operations Department, after consultation with NHL general managers. Head coaches whose team had the best winning percentage in each conference on Jan. 8 were named all-star head coaches.

Centers Vincent Lecavalier and Olli Jokinen, right wing Miroslav Satan, defenseman Tom Poti and goaltender Patrick Lalime were added to the **Eastern Conference** team as injury replacements for Mario Lemieux, Saku Koivu, Mats Sundin, Brian Leetch and Ed Belfour, respectively. Jeremy Roenick and Scott Stevens replaced Lemieux and Leetch in the starting lineup.

Western Conference

Pos	Starters	G	A	Pts	PM
C	Mike Modano, Dallas	1	0	1	0
D	Nicklas Lidstrom, Detroit	0	1	1	0
W	Bill Guerin, Dallas	0	0	0	0
W	Teemu Selanne, San Jose	0	0	0	0
D	Rob Blake, Colorado	0	0	0	0
	Reserves				
W	Marian Gaborik, Minnesota	1	2	3	0
C	Sergei Fedorov, Detroit	0	2	2	0
D	Mathieu Schneider, Los Angeles	0	2	2	0
C	Peter Forsberg, Colorado	1	0	1	0
D	Ed Jovanovski, Vancouver	1	0	1	0
D	Al MacInnis, St. Louis	1	0	1	0
W	Marcus Naslund, Vancouver	0	1	1	0
W	Ray Whitney, Columbus	0	1	1	0
W	Jarome Iginla, Calgary	0	1	1	0
W	Todd Bertuzzi, Vancouver	0	0	0	0
D	Eric Brewer, Edmonton	0	0	0	0
W	Paul Kariya, Anaheim	0	0	0	0
C	Doug Weight, St. Louis	0	0	0	0
	TOTALS	5	10	15	0

Goaltenders	Mins	Shots	Saves	GA
Patrick Roy, Col.	20:00	11	9	2
Jocelyn Thibault, Chi.	20:00	12	10	2
Marty Turco, Dal. (W)	25:00	11	10	1
TOTALS	65:00	34	29	5

Eastern Conference

Pos	Starters	G	A	Pts	PM
W	Jaromir Jagr, Washington	0	3	3	0
W	Alexei Kovalev, Pittsburgh	0	0	0	0
D	Sandis Ozolinsh, Florida	0	0	0	0
C	Jeremy Roenick, Philadelphia	0	0	0	0
D	Scott Stevens, New Jersey	0	0	0	0
	Reserves				
W	Dany Heatley, Atlanta	4	1	5	0
C	Olli Jokinen, Florida	1	3	4	0
D	Roman Hamrlik, NY Islanders	0	1	1	0
D	Zdeno Chara, Ottawa	0	0	0	0
D	Sergei Gonchar, Washington	0	0	0	0
W	Marian Hossa, Ottawa	0	0	0	0
C	Vincent Lecavalier, Tampa Bay	0	0	0	0
W	Glen Murray, Boston	0	0	0	0
W	Jeff O'Neill, Carolina	0	0	0	0
D	Tom Poti, NY Rangers	0	0	0	0
W	Miroslav Satan, Buffalo	0	0	0	0
W	Martin St. Louis, Tampa Bay	0	0	0	0
C	Joe Thornton, Boston	0	0	0	0
	TOTALS	5	8	13	0

Goaltenders	Mins	Shots	Saves	GA
Nikolai Khabibulin, TB	20:00	14	11	3
Martin Brodeur, NJ	20:00	9	8	1
Patrick Lalime, Ott.	25:00	19	17	2
TOTALS	65:00	42	36	6

Score by Periods

	1	2	3	OT	2OT	Final
Western	3	1	1	0	1	— 6
Eastern	2	2	1	0	0	— 5

Power plays: Western—0/0; Eastern—0/0.
Officials: Dan O'Halloran and Dennis Larue (referees), Jean Morin and Tim Nowak (linesmen).
Attendance: 19,250.
TV Rating: 2.4/5 share (ABC).

Shootout

After a five-minute scoreless overtime, the game was settled by a shootout (for the first time in history). Each team was allowed five shooters and the team with the most goals was declared the winner. The Western Conference outscored the Eastern Conference, 3-1 in the shootout, but in the game stats it is officially viewed as one goal for the West.
Western (vs Lalime).—Fedorov (save), Naslund (score), Guerin (score), Kariya (score).
Eastern (vs Turco)—Kovalev (save), Heatley (score), Satan (save), Jokinen (save).

2003 NHL Skills Competition
Western, 15-9

Puck Control Relay
Team: Western (Weight, Lidstrom, Whitney)
Individual: Martin St. Louis (Eastern)
Fastest Skater
Team: Western (Avg.14.123 sec.: Gaborik, Fedorov, Guerin)
Individual: Marian Gaborik, Western (13.713 sec.)
Hardest Shot
Team: Western (Avg. 96.2 mph: Iginla, Blake, Fedorov, MacInnis)
Individual: Al MacInnis, Western (98.9 mph)

Shooting Accuracy (targets/shots)
Team: Eastern (15/28: O'Neill, Roenick, Murray, Thornton)
Individual: Jeremy Roenick, Eastern (4/6)
Pass and Score
Team: Western Conference wins, 3-1
Breakaway Relay
Team: Western Conference wins, 7-5
Goaltender Competition
(combined Pass and Score + Breakaway Relay)
Individual: Patrick Roy, Western

Colorado Avalanche
Peter Forsberg
Scoring, Assists, +/-

Colorado Avalanche
Milan Hejduk
Goals, Shooting Pct.

Dallas Stars
Marty Turco
GAA, Save Pct.

New Jersey Devils
Martin Brodeur
Wins, Shutouts

NHL Regular Season Individual Leaders
(*) indicates rookie eligible for Calder Trophy.

Scoring

	Pos	Gm	G	A	Pts	+/-	PM	PP	SH	GW	GT	Shots	Pct
Peter Forsberg, Colorado	C	75	29	77	**106**	52	70	8	0	2	0	166	17.5
Markus Naslund, Vancouver	L	82	48	56	**104**	6	52	24	0	12	1	294	16.3
Joe Thornton, Boston	C	77	36	65	**101**	12	109	12	2	4	1	196	18.4
Milan Hejduk, Colorado	R	82	50	48	**98**	52	32	18	0	4	1	244	20.5
Todd Bertuzzi, Vancouver	R	82	46	51	**97**	2	144	25	0	7	1	243	18.9
Pavol Demitra, St. Louis	C	78	36	57	**93**	0	32	11	0	4	1	205	17.6
Glen Murray, Boston	R	82	44	48	**92**	9	64	12	0	5	2	331	13.3
Mario Lemieux, Pittsburgh	C	67	28	63	**91**	-25	43	14	0	4	0	235	11.9
Dany Heatley, Atlanta	R	77	41	48	**89**	-8	58	19	1	6	0	252	16.3
Zigmund Palffy, Los Angeles	R	76	37	48	**85**	22	47	10	2	5	0	277	13.4
Mike Modano, Dallas	C	79	28	57	**85**	34	30	5	2	6	0	193	14.5
Sergei Fedorov, Detroit	C	80	36	47	**83**	15	52	10	2	11	0	281	12.8
Paul Kariya, Anaheim	L	82	25	56	**81**	-3	48	11	1	2	1	257	9.7
Marian Hossa, Ottawa	R	80	45	35	**80**	8	34	14	0	10	1	229	19.7
Alexander Mogilny, Toronto	R	73	33	46	**79**	4	12	5	3	9	0	165	20.0
Daniel Alfredsson, Ottawa	R	78	27	52	**79**	15	42	9	0	6	0	240	11.3
Vaclav Prospal, Tampa Bay	L	80	22	57	**79**	9	53	9	0	4	0	134	16.4
Vincent Lecavalier, Tampa Bay	C	80	33	45	**78**	0	39	11	2	3	1	275	12.0
Alexei Kovalev, Pit.-NYR	R	78	37	40	**77**	-9	70	11	0	3	1	271	13.7
Jaromir Jagr, Washington	R	75	36	41	**77**	5	38	13	2	9	0	290	12.4

Goals

Hejduk, Col. 50
Naslund, Van. 48
Bertuzzi, Van. 46
Hossa, Ott. 45
Murray, Bos. 44
Heatley, Atl. 41
Kovalchuk, Atl. 38
Sundin, Tor. 37
Palffy, LA 37
Kovalev, Pit.-NYR 37
Hull, Det. 37

Plus/Minus

Forsberg, Col. 52
Hejduk, Col. 52
Lidstrom, Det. 40
Lehtinen, Dal. 39
Hatcher, Dal. 37
Modano, Dal. 34
Tanguay, Col. 34
Foote, Col. 30
Desjardins, Phi. 30
Chara, Ott. 29
Boucher, Dal. 28

Assists

Forsberg, Col. 77
Thornton, Bos. 65
Lemieux, Pit. 63
Demitra, St.L 57
Modano, Dal. 57
Prospal, TB 57
Richards, TB 57
Kariya, Ana. 56
Naslund, Van. 56
Weight, St.L 52
MacInnis, St.L 52
Whitney, Clb. 52
Alfredsson, Ott. 52

Game Winning Goals

Naslund, Van. 12
Fedorov, Det. 11
Hossa Ott. 10
Mogilny, Tor. 9
Jagr, Wash. 9
Handzus, Phi. 9
Four tied with 8 each.

Defensemen Points

MacInnis, St.L 68
Gonchar, Wash. 67
Lidstrom, Det. 62
Zubov, Dal. 55
Boyle, TB 53
Schneider, LA-Det. 50
Morris, Col. 48
Poti, NYR 48
Kaberle, Tor. 47
Jovanovski, Van. 46
Four tied with 45 each.

Power Play Goals

Bertuzzi, Van. 25
Naslund, Van. 24
Heatley, Atl. 19
Hejduk, Col. 18
Sundin, Tor. 16
Sykora, Ana. 15
Sanderson, Clb. 15
Andreychuk, TB 15
Damphousse, SJ 15

Rookie Points

Zetterberg, Det. 44
Arnason, Chi. 39
Nash, Clb. 39
Kotalik, Buf. 35
Kapanen, Dal. 34
Frolov, LA 31
Chistov, Ana. 30
Hemsky, Edm. 30
Hall, Nash. 28
Radivojevic, Pho. 27
Bednar, LA-Fla. 27
Chimera, Edm. 23
Weinhandl, NYI 23

Short-Handed Goals

Bates, NYI 6
Rolston, Bos. 5
Brown, Buf. 4
Maltby, Det. 4
Rucinsky, St.L 4
Cooke, Van. 4
Fourteen tied with 3 each.

Shots

Murray, Bos.	.331
Iginla, Calg.	.316
O'Neill, Car.	.316
MacInnis, St.L.	.299
Sykora, Ana.	.299
Naslund, Van.	.294
Jagr, Wash.	.290
Sanderson, Clb.	.286
Fedorov, Det.	.281
Rolston, Bos.	.281
Gaborik, Min.	.280

Shooting Pct.
(Min. 70 shots)

Hejduk, Col.	.20.5
Mogilny, Tor.	.20.0
Morrow, Dal.	.20.0
Mellanby, St.L	.19.7
Hossa, Ott.	.19.7
Bertuzzi, Van.	.18.9
Boguniecki, St.L	.18.8
Brunette, Min.	.18.6
Thornton, Bos.	.18.4
Holmstrom, Det.	.18.3

Penalty Minutes

Shelley, Clb.	.249
Low, St.L	.234
Johnson, Min.	.201
Belak, Tor.	.196
Worrell, Fla.	.193
Jackman*, St.L	.190
Boulton, Buf.	.178
Mellanby, St.L	.176
Domi, Tor.	.171
Odgers, Atl.	.171
Three tied with 161 each.	

Minutes/Game
(Min. 50 Games)

Lidstrom, Det.	.29:20
Aucoin, NYI	.29:00
MacInnis, St.L	.26:54
Gonchar, Wash.	.26:34
Hamrlik, NYI	.26:34
Zhitnik, Buf.	.26:32
Blake, Col.	.26:21
Niinimaa, Edm.-NYI	26:09
Leetch, NYR	.26:05
Ozolinsh, Fla.-Ana.	.26:01

Goaltending
(Minimum 26 games)

	Gm	Min	GAA	GA	Shots	Sv%	EN	ShO	Record	G	A	Pts	PM
Marty Turco, Dallas	.55	3203	**1.72**	92	1359	.932	3	7	31-10-10	0	3	3	16
Roman Cechmanek, Philadelphia	.58	3350	**1.83**	102	1368	.925	2	6	33-15-10	0	0	0	8
Dwayne Roloson, Minnesota	.50	2945	**2.00**	98	1334	.927	1	4	23-16-8	0	1	1	4
Martin Brodeur, New Jersey	.73	4374	**2.02**	147	1706	.914	4	9	41-23-9	0	0	0	.10
Patrick Lalime, Ottawa	.67	3943	**2.16**	142	1591	.911	1	8	39-20-7	0	1	1	6
Patrick Roy, Colorado	.63	3769	**2.18**	137	1723	.920	3	5	35-15-13	0	0	0	20
Robert Esche, Philadelphia	.30	1638	**2.20**	60	647	.907	2	2	12-9-3	0	0	0	6
Tomas Vokoun, Nashville	.69	3974	**2.20**	146	1771	.918	5	3	25-31-11	0	1	1	28
Manny Fernandez, Minnesota	.35	1979	**2.24**	74	972	.924	0	2	19-13-2	0	1	1	6
Ed Belfour, Toronto	.62	3738	**2.26**	141	1816	.922	4	7	37-20-5	0	2	2	24
Jean-Sebastien Giguere, Anaheim	.65	3775	**2.30**	145	1820	.920	5	8	34-22-6	0	0	0	8
Garth Snow, NY Islanders	.43	2390	**2.31**	92	1120	.918	8	1	16-17-5	0	0	0	24
Jocelyn Thibault, Chicago	.62	3650	**2.37**	144	1690	.915	4	8	26-28-7	0	0	0	4
Olaf Kolzig, Washington	.66	3894	**2.40**	156	1925	.919	5	4	33-25-6	0	0	0	0
Dan Cloutier, Vancouver	.57	3376	**2.42**	136	1477	.908	6	2	33-16-7	0	3	3	24

Wins

Brodeur, NJ	.41
Lalime, Ott.	.39
Belfour, Tor.	.37
Roy, Col.	.35
Joseph, Det.	.34
Giguere, Ana.	.34
Cechmanek, Phi.	.33
Cloutier, Van.	.33
Kolzig, Wash.	.33
Turco, Dal.	.31
Khabibulin, TB	.30

Shutouts

Brodeur, NJ	.9
Lalime, Ott.	.8
Giguere, Ana.	.8
Thibault, Chi.	.8
Turco, Dal.	.7
Belfour, Tor.	.7
Cechmanek, Phi.	.6
Luongo, Fla.	.6
Five tied with 5 each.	

Save Pct.

Turco, Dal.	.932
Roloson, Min.	.927
Cechmanek, Phi.	.925
Fernandez, Min.	.924
Belfour, Tor.	.922
Roy, Col.	.920
Giguere, Ana.	.920
Kolzig, Wash.	.919
Luongo, Fla.	.918
Snow, NYI	.918
Vokoun, Nash.	.918

Losses

Denis, Clb.	.41
Luongo, Fla.	.34
Theodore, Mon.	.31
Vokoun, Nash.	.31
Turek, Calg.	.29
Biron, Buf.	.28
Nabokov, SJ	.28
Thibault, Chi.	.28
Salo, Edm.	.27
Dunham, Nash.-NYR	.26
Kolzig, Wash.	.25

Team Goaltending

WESTERN	GAA	Mins	GA	Shots	Sv%	EN	SO	EASTERN	GAA	Mins	GA	Shots	Sv%	EN	SO
Dallas	**2.02**	5020	169	2073	.918	3	11	New Jersey	**1.99**	5009	166	1933	.914	4	10
Minnesota	**2.14**	4997	178	2335	.924	1	6	Philadelphia	**1.99**	5005	166	2019	.918	4	8
Anaheim	**2.32**	4997	193	2377	.919	9	9	Ottawa	**2.19**	4977	182	2033	.910	1	8
Colorado	**2.32**	5026	194	2323	.916	7	6	Toronto	**2.50**	4987	208	2423	.914	4	7
Detroit	**2.44**	4993	203	2361	.914	4	5	Tampa Bay	**2.51**	5026	210	2298	.909	7	6
Nashville	**2.46**	5015	206	2252	.909	5	3	Buffalo	**2.63**	5002	219	2297	.905	8	6
Vancouver	**2.50**	4997	208	2185	.905	7	4	Washington	**2.64**	4995	220	2454	.910	7	4
Los Angeles	**2.66**	4986	221	2141	.897	9	7	NY Islanders	**2.78**	4992	231	2318	.900	13	3
St. Louis	**2.66**	5012	222	2047	.892	7	8	NY Rangers	**2.78**	4991	231	2426	.905	8	6
Chicago	**2.71**	5007	226	2345	.904	5	9	Montreal	**2.81**	4988	234	2678	.913	8	4
Calgary	**2.73**	5012	228	2222	.897	6	4	Florida	**2.83**	5021	237	2725	.913	7	7
Edmonton	**2.75**	5020	230	2248	.898	7	7	Boston	**2.85**	4993	237	2322	.898	3	2
Phoenix	**2.76**	5000	230	2458	.906	9	3	Carolina	**2.88**	5003	240	2332	.897	7	5
San Jose	**2.87**	4996	239	2392	.900	7	5	Pittsburgh	**3.08**	4972	255	2535	.899	8	4
Columbus	**3.17**	4984	263	2641	.900	4	5	Atlanta	**3.41**	4993	284	2593	.890	6	2

Power Play/Penalty Killing

Power play and penalty killing conversions. Power play: No—number of opportunities; GF—goals for; Pct—percentage. Penalty killing: No—number of times shorthanded; GA—goals against; Pct—percentage of penalties killed; SH—shorthanded goals for.

| WESTERN | —Power Play— | | | —Penalty Killing— | | | | EASTERN | —Power Play— | | | —Penalty Killing— | | | |
	No	GF	Pct	No	GA	Pct	SH		No	GF	Pct	No	GA	Pct	SH
Detroit	319	76	23.8	377	55	85.4	11	Ottawa	391	83	21.2	332	50	84.9	4
Vancouver	419	87	20.8	389	62	84.1	12	Pittsburgh	360	66	18.3	352	58	83.5	3
St. Louis	391	80	20.5	389	61	81.7	11	Boston	325	59	18.2	375	65	82.7	10
Dallas	327	62	19.0	346	50	85.5	9	Tampa Bay	391	70	17.9	316	55	82.6	6
Colorado	363	68	18.7	359	63	82.5	5	Toronto	359	63	17.5	426	56	86.9	11
San Jose	375	68	18.1	358	68	81.0	5	Atlanta	371	64	17.3	355	65	81.7	8
Columbus	410	71	17.3	409	60	85.3	12	Washington	331	57	17.2	384	72	81.3	8
Anaheim	348	56	16.1	333	42	87.4	8	NY Rangers	339	55	16.2	388	73	81.2	8
Los Angeles	354	52	14.7	371	62	83.3	8	NY Islanders	384	58	15.1	405	67	83.5	12
Edmonton	386	56	14.5	351	61	82.6	13	Buffalo	354	51	14.4	363	53	85.4	8
Phoenix	385	55	14.3	412	77	81.3	4	Philadelphia	328	47	14.3	338	50	85.2	8
Minnesota	366	52	14.2	308	43	86.0	9	Florida	347	49	14.1	356	66	81.5	7
Nashville	418	58	13.9	353	61	82.7	2	Montreal	315	44	14.0	317	58	81.7	2
Chicago	308	39	12.7	369	56	84.8	8	Carolina	420	58	13.8	392	71	81.9	6
Calgary	389	47	12.1	389	65	83.3	5	New Jersey	303	36	11.9	264	32	87.9	7

Single Game Highs

Goals		Opponent	Date
4	John LeClair, Philadelphia	Montreal	Oct. 15
4	Markus Naslund, Vancouver	Edmonton	Dec. 14
4	Marian Hossa, Ottawa	Atlanta	Jan. 2
4	Jarome Iginla, Calgary	Phoenix	Feb. 23
4	Scott Mellanby, St. Louis	Phoenix	Mar. 6
4	Alexei Yashin, NY Islanders	Chicago	Mar. 25
4	Geoff Sanderson, Columbus	Calgary	Mar. 29
4	Patrik Elias, New Jersey	NY Islanders	Mar. 30

Assists		Opponent	Date
5	Peter Forsberg, Colorado	Nashville	Jan. 1
5	Markus Naslund, Vancouver	Atlanta	Feb. 25
5	Peter Forsberg, Colorado	Chicago	Mar. 22
5	Scott Gomez, New Jersey	NY Islanders	Mar. 30

Points		Opponent	Date
7	Jaromir Jagr, Washington	Florida	Jan. 11

Saves		Opponent	Date
50	Ed Belfour, Toronto	New Jersey	Jan. 4

Team by Team Statistics

High scorers and goaltenders with at least ten games played. Players who competed for more than one team during the regular season are listed with their final club; (*) indicates rookies eligible for Calder Trophy.

Mighty Ducks of Anaheim

Top Scorers	Gm	G	A	Pts	+/-	PM	PP
Paul Kariya	82	25	56	81	-3	48	11
Petr Sykora	82	34	25	59	-7	24	15
Steve Rucchin	82	20	38	58	-14	12	6
Adam Oates	67	9	36	45	-1	16	4
Sandis Ozolinsh	82	12	32	44	-6	56	6
FLA	51	7	19	26	-16	40	5
ANA	31	5	13	28	10	16	1
Niclas Havelid	82	11	22	33	5	30	4
Steve Thomas	81	14	16	30	10	53	1
CHI	69	4	13	17	0	51	0
ANA	12	10	3	13	10	2	1
Stanislav Chistov*	79	12	18	30	4	54	3
Mike Leclerc	57	9	19	28	-8	34	1
Jason Krog	67	10	15	25	1	12	0
Rob Niedermayer	66	10	12	22	-10	57	3
CALG	54	8	10	18	-13	42	2
ANA	12	2	2	4	3	15	1
Keith Carney	81	4	18	22	8	65	0
Andy McDonald	46	10	11	21	-1	14	3
Patric Kjellberg	76	8	11	19	-9	16	2

Acquired: D Ozolinsh and D Lance Ward from Fla. for C Matt Cullen, D Pavel Trnka and a '03 4th-round pick (Jan. 30); RW Thomas from Chi. for a '03 5th-round pick (Mar. 11); LW Niedermayer from Calg. for D Mike Commodore and G J-F Damphousse (Mar. 11).

Goalies (10 Gm)	Gm	Min	GAA	Record	SV%
Martin Gerber	22	1203	1.95	6-11-3	.929
J-S Giguere	65	3775	2.30	34-22-6	.920
ANAHEIM	82	4997	2.32	40-33-9	.919

Shutouts: Giguere (8), Gerber (1). **Assists:** Gerber (1). **PM:** Giguere (8).

Atlanta Thrashers

Top Scorers	Gm	G	A	Pts	+/-	PM	PP
Dany Heatley	77	41	48	89	-8	58	19
Slava Kozlov	79	21	49	70	-10	66	9
Ilya Kovalchuk	81	38	29	67	-24	57	9
Marc Savard	67	17	33	50	-14	85	6
CALG	10	1	2	3	-3	8	0
ATL	57	16	31	47	-11	77	6
Patrik Stefan	71	13	21	34	-10	12	3
Yannick Tremblay	75	8	22	30	-27	32	5
Shawn McEachern	46	10	16	26	-27	28	4
Tony Hrkac	80	9	17	26	-16	14	2
Frantisek Kaberle	79	7	19	26	-19	32	3
Andy Sutton	53	3	18	21	4	114	1
Lubos Bartecko	37	7	9	16	3	8	0
Daniel Tjarnqvist	75	3	12	15	-20	26	1
Brad Tapper	35	10	4	14	2	23	1
Dan Snyder*	36	10	4	14	-4	34	0
Chris Tamer	72	1	9	10	-10	118	0
Jeff Cowan	66	3	5	8	-15	115	0
Per Svartvadet	62	1	7	8	-11	8	0
Mark Hartigan*	23	5	2	7	-8	6	1
Jeff Odgers	74	2	4	6	-13	171	0

Acquired: C Savard from Calg. for RW Ruslan Zainullin (Nov 15).

Goalies (10 Gm)	Gm	Min	GAA	Record	SV%
Pasi Nurminen	52	2856	2.88	21-19-5	.906
Milan Hnilicka	21	1097	3.56	4-13-1	.893
Byron Dafoe	17	895	4.36	5-11-1	.862
ATLANTA	82	4993	3.41	31-44-7	.890

Shutouts: Nurminen (2). **Assists:** Nurminen (3). **PM:** Nurminen (4), Hnilicka (2).

Boston Bruins

Top Scorers	Gm	G	A	Pts	+/-	PM	PP
Joe Thornton	.77	36	65	101	12	109	12
Glen Murray	.82	44	48	92	9	64	12
Mike Knuble	.75	30	29	59	18	45	9
Brian Rolston	.81	27	32	59	1	32	6
Jozef Stumpel	.78	14	37	51	0	12	4
Bryan Berard	.80	10	28	38	-4	64	4
P.J. Axelsson	.66	17	19	36	8	24	2
Nick Boynton	.78	7	17	24	8	99	0
Jonathan Girard	.73	6	16	22	4	21	2
Dan McGillis	.71	3	17	20	3	60	2
PHI	.24	0	3	3	7	20	0
SJ	.37	3	13	16	-6	30	2
BOS	.10	0	1	1	2	10	0
Michal Grosek	.63	2	18	20	2	71	0
Marty McInnis	.77	9	10	19	-11	38	0
Martin Lapointe	.59	8	10	18	-19	87	1
Ivan Huml*	.41	6	11	17	3	30	0
Hal Gill	.76	4	13	17	21	56	0
Rob Zamuner	.55	10	6	16	2	18	3
Sean O'Donnell	.70	1	15	16	8	76	0
Sergei Samsonov	.8	5	6	11	8	2	1
P.J. Stock	.71	1	9	10	-5	160	1

Acquired: G Hackett from Mon. and D Jeff Jillson from SJ in a 3-team deal that sent D Kyle McLaren and a '04 4th-round pick to SJ (Jan. 23); D McGillis from SJ for a '03 2nd-round pick (Mar. 11).

Goalies (10 Gm)	Gm	Min	GAA	Record	SV%
Steve Shields	.36	2112	2.76	12-13-9	.896
Jeff Hackett	.36	2054	2.86	15-17-2	.911
MON	.18	1063	2.54	7-8-2	.926
BOS	.18	991	3.21	8-9-0	.894
BOSTON	.82	4993	2.85	35-36-11	.898

Shutouts: Hackett (1). **Assists:** none. **PM:** Shields (8), Hackett (2).

Buffalo Sabres

Top Scorers	Gm	G	A	Pts	+/-	PM	PP
Miroslav Satan	.76	26	49	75	-3	20	11
Daniel Briere	.82	24	34	58	-20	62	9
PHO	.68	17	29	46	-21	50	4
BUF	.14	7	5	12	1	12	5
Ales Kotalik*	.68	21	14	35	-2	30	4
J.P. Dumont	.76	14	21	35	-14	44	2
Curtis Brown	.74	15	16	31	4	40	3
Taylor Pyatt	.78	14	14	28	-8	38	2
Jochen Hecht	.49	10	16	26	4	30	2
Tim Connolly	.80	12	13	25	-28	32	6
Dmitri Kalinin	.65	8	13	21	-7	57	3
Alexei Zhitnik	.70	3	18	21	-5	85	0
Brian Campbell	.65	2	17	19	-8	20	0
Adam Mair	.79	6	11	17	-4	146	0
James Patrick	.69	4	12	16	-3	26	2
Henrik Tallinder*	.46	3	10	13	-3	28	1
Maxim Afinogenov	.35	6	5	11	-12	21	2
Rhett Warrener	.50	0	9	9	1	63	0
Eric Boulton	.58	1	5	6	1	178	0
Jason Botterill	.17	1	4	5	1	14	1
Jay McKee	.59	0	5	5	-16	49	0
Chris Taylor	.11	1	3	4	-1	2	0
Rory Fitzpatrick	.36	1	3	4	-7	16	0

Acquired: C Briere and a '04 3rd-round pick from Pho. for C Chris Gratton and a '04 4th-round pick (Mar. 10).

Goalies (10 Gm)	Gm	Min	GAA	Record	Sv%
Mika Noronen*	.16	891	2.42	4-9-3	.912
Martin Biron	.54	3170	2.56	17-28-6	.908
Ryan Miller*	.15	912	2.63	6-8-1	.902
BUFFALO	.82	5002	2.63	27-45-10	.905

Shutouts: Biron (4), Noronen and Miller (1). **Assists:** Biron (1). **PM:** Biron (12).

Calgary Flames

Top Scorers	Gm	G	A	Pts	+/-	PM	PP
Jarome Iginla	.75	35	32	67	-10	49	11
Craig Conroy	.79	22	37	59	-4	36	5
Chris Drury	.80	23	30	53	-9	33	5
Martin Gelinas	.81	21	31	52	-3	51	6
Toni Lydman	.81	6	20	26	-7	28	3
Stephane Yelle	.82	10	15	25	-10	50	3
Oleg Saprykin	.52	8	15	23	5	46	1
Chris Clark	.81	10	12	22	-11	126	2
Dave Lowry	.34	5	14	19	4	22	1
Dean McAmmond	.41	10	8	18	1	10	2
COL	.41	10	8	18	1	10	2
Bob Boughner	.69	3	14	17	5	126	0
Jordan Leopold*	.58	4	10	14	-15	12	3
Shean Donovan	.65	5	7	12	-8	37	0
PIT	.52	4	5	9	-6	30	0
CALG	.13	1	2	3	-2	7	0
Denis Gauthier	.72	1	11	12	5	99	0
Robyn Regehr	.76	0	12	12	-9	87	0
Scott Nichol	.68	5	5	10	-7	149	0
Blake Sloan	.67	2	8	10	-5	28	0

Two tied with 8 points each.

Acquired: RW Donovan from Pit. for C Mathias Johansson and D Micki DuPont (Mar. 11); LW McAmmond from Col. for a '03 or '04 5th-round pick.

Goalies (10 Gm)	Gm	Min	GAA	Record	SV%
Roman Turek	.65	3822	2.57	27-29-9	.902
Jamie McLennan	.22	1165	2.99	2-11-4	.892
CALGARY	.82	5012	2.73	29-40-13	.897

Shutouts: Turek (4). **Assists:** Turek (4). **PM:** Turek and McLennan (14).

Carolina Hurricanes

Top Scorers	Gm	G	A	Pts	+/-	PM	PP
Jeff O'Neill	.82	30	31	61	-21	38	11
Ron Francis	.82	22	35	57	-22	30	8
Rod Brind'Amour	.48	14	23	37	-9	37	7
Radim Vrbata	.76	16	19	35	-7	18	6
COL	.66	11	19	30	0	16	3
CAR	.10	5	0	5	-7	2	3
Sean Hill	.82	5	24	29	4	141	1
Erik Cole	.53	14	13	27	1	72	6
Jan Hlavac	.61	10	16	26	-10	28	6
VAN	.9	1	1	2	-1	6	0
CAR	.52	9	15	24	-9	22	6
Josef Vasicek	.57	10	10	20	-19	33	4
Kevyn Adams	.77	9	9	18	-8	57	0
Craig Adams	.81	6	12	18	-11	71	1
Bret Hedican	.72	3	14	17	-24	75	1
Ryan Bayda*	.25	4	10	14	-5	16	0
Jaroslav Svoboda*	.48	3	11	14	-5	32	1
Pavel Brendl*	.50	5	8	13	5	6	1
PHI	.42	5	7	12	8	4	1
CAR	.8	0	1	1	-3	2	0
David Tanabe	.68	3	10	13	-27	24	2
Niclas Wallin	.77	2	8	10	-19	71	0
Aaron Ward	.77	3	6	9	-23	90	0

Acquired: LW Hlavac and C Harold Druken from Van. for D Marek Malik and LW Darren Langdon (Nov. 1); RW Brendl and D Bruno St. Jacques from Phi. for RW Sami Kapanen and D Ryan Bast (Feb. 7); LW Vrbata from Col. for LW Bates Battaglia (Mar. 11).

Goalies (10 Gm)	Gm	Min	GAA	Record	Sv%
Kevin Weekes	.51	2965	2.55	14-24-9	.912
Arturs Irbe	.34	1884	3.18	7-24-2	.877
CAROLINA	.82	5003	2.88	22-49-11	.897

Shutouts: Weekes (5). **Assists:** none. **PM:** Irbe (4), Weekes (2).

Chicago Blackhawks

Top Scorers	Gm	G	A	Pts	+/-	PM	PP
Steve Sullivan	.82	26	35	61	15	42	4
Alexei Zhamnov	.74	15	43	58	0	70	2
Eric Daze	.54	22	22	44	10	14	3
Kyle Calder	.82	15	27	42	-6	40	7
Tyler Arnason*	.82	19	20	39	7	20	3
Theo Fleury	.54	12	21	33	-7	77	1
Mark Bell	.82	14	15	29	0	113	0
Nathan Dempsey	.67	5	23	28	-7	26	1
Andrei Nikolishin	.60	6	15	21	-3	26	0
Chris Simon	.71	12	8	20	-7	148	2
WASH	.10	0	2	2	-3	23	0
CHI	.61	12	6	18	-4	125	2
Mike Eastwood	.70	3	13	16	-5	32	1
ST.L	.17	1	3	4	1	8	1
CHI	.53	2	10	12	-6	24	0
Jon Klemm	.70	2	14	16	-9	44	1
Alexander Karpovtsev	.40	4	10	14	-8	12	3
Steve Poapst	.75	2	11	13	14	50	0
Igor Korolev	.48	4	5	9	-1	30	1
Igor Radulov*	.7	5	0	5	-3	4	3
Jason Strudwick	.48	2	3	5	-4	87	0
Steve McCarthy	.57	1	4	5	-1	23	0

Acquired: LW Simon and C Nikolishin from Wash. for C Michael Nylander, a '03 3rd-round pick and a '04 conditional pick (Nov. 1); **Claimed:** C Eastwood off waivers from St.L (Dec. 11).

Goalies (10 Gm)	Gm	Min	GAA	Record	SV%
Jocelyn Thibault	.62	3650	2.37	26-28-7	.915
Steve Passmore	.11	617	3.70	2-5-2	.866
CHICAGO	.82	5007	2.71	30-39-13	.904

Shutouts: Thibault (8), Michael Leighton (1). **Assists:** none. **PM:** Thibault and Passmore (4).

Colorado Avalanche

Top Scorers	Gm	G	A	Pts	+/-	PM	PP
Peter Forsberg	.75	29	77	106	52	70	8
Milan Hejduk	.82	50	48	98	52	32	18
Alex Tanguay	.82	26	41	67	34	36	3
Joe Sakic	.58	26	32	58	4	24	8
Steve Reinprecht	.77	18	33	51	-6	18	2
Derek Morris	.75	11	37	48	16	68	9
Rob Blake	.79	17	28	45	20	57	8
Greg de Vries	.82	6	26	32	15	70	0
Adam Foote	.78	11	20	31	30	88	3
Bates Battaglia	.83	6	19	25	-19	100	.1
CAR	.70	5	14	19	-17	90	0
COL	.13	1	5	6	-2	10	1
Martin Skoula	.81	4	21	25	11	68	2
Eric Messier	.72	4	10	14	-2	16	0
Bryan Marchment	.81	2	12	14	2	141	0
SJ	.67	2	9	11	-3	108	0
COL	.14	0	3	3	4	33	0
Dan Hinote	.60	6	4	10	4	49	0
Mike Keane	.65	5	5	10	4	34	0
Serge Aubin	.66	4	6	10	-2	64	0
Vaclav Nedorost	.42	4	5	9	8	20	1
Jeff Shantz	.74	3	6	9	-12	35	0
Riku Hahl*	.42	3	4	7	3	12	0
Scott Parker	.43	1	3	4	6	82	0

Acquired: D Marchment from SJ for '03 3rd-round and 5th-round picks (Mar. 8); LW Battaglia from Car. for LW Radim Vrbata (Mar. 19).

Goalies (10 Gm)	Gm	Min	GAA	Record	SV%
Patrick Roy	.63	3769	2.18	35-15-13	.920
David Aebischer	.22	1235	2.43	7-12-0	.916
COLORADO	.82	5026	2.32	42-27-13	.916

Shutouts: Roy (5), Aebischer (1). **Assists:** none. **PM:** Roy (20), Aebischer (4).

Columbus Blue Jackets

Top Scorers	Gm	G	A	Pts	+/-	PM	PP
Ray Whitney	.81	24	52	76	-26	22	8
Andrew Cassels	.79	20	48	68	-4	30	9
Geoff Sanderson	.82	34	33	67	-4	34	15
David Vyborny	.79	20	26	46	12	16	4
Jaroslav Spacek	.81	9	36	45	-23	70	5
Mike Sillinger	.75	18	25	43	-21	52	9
Rick Nash*	.74	17	22	39	-27	78	6
Tyler Wright	.70	19	11	30	-25	113	3
Lasse Pirjeta	.51	11	10	21	-4	12	2
Derrick Walser*	.53	4	13	17	-9	34	3
Rostislav Klesla	.72	2	14	16	-22	71	0
Sean Pronger	.78	7	6	13	-26	72	1
Luke Richardson	.82	0	13	13	-16	73	0
Espen Knutsen	.31	5	4	9	-15	20	3
Matt Davidson*	.34	4	5	9	-12	18	0
Hannes Hyvonen	.36	4	5	9	-11	22	0
Duvie Westcott*	.39	0	7	7	-3	77	0
David Ling	.35	3	2	5	-6	86	0
Jody Shelley	.68	1	4	5	-5	249	0
Darren Van Impe	.14	1	1	2	-6	10	0

Signed: free agent D Van Impe (Jan. 20).

Goalies (10 Gm)	Gm	Min	GAA	Record	SV%
Marc Denis	.77	4511	3.09	27-41-8	.903
Jean-Francois Labbe	.11	451	3.59	2-4-0	.884
COLUMBUS	.82	4984	3.17	29-45-8	.900

Shutouts: Denis (5). **Assists:** none. **PM:** Denis (8), Labbe (2).

Dallas Stars

Top Scorers	Gm	G	A	Pts	+/-	PM	PP
Mike Modano	.79	28	57	85	34	30	5
Sergei Zubov	.82	11	44	55	21	26	8
Bill Guerin	.64	25	25	50	5	113	11
Jere Lehtinen	.80	31	17	48	39	20	5
Jason Arnott	.72	23	24	47	9	51	7
Brenden Morrow	.71	21	22	43	20	134	2
Scott Young	.79	23	19	42	24	30	5
Pierre Turgeon	.65	12	30	42	4	18	3
Stu Barnes	.81	13	26	39	-11	28	4
BUF	.68	11	21	32	-13	20	2
DAL	.13	2	5	7	2	8	2
Ulf Dahlen	.63	17	20	37	11	14	9
Darryl Sydor	.81	5	31	36	22	40	2
Niko Kapanen*	.82	5	29	34	25	44	0
Derian Hatcher	.82	8	22	30	37	106	1
Philippe Boucher	.68	7	20	27	28	94	1
Claude Lemieux	.68	8	12	20	-12	44	1
PHO	.36	6	8	14	-3	30	1
DAL	.32	2	4	6	-9	14	0
Rob DiMaio	.69	10	9	19	18	76	0
Lyle Odelein	.68	7	4	11	7	82	0
CHI	.65	7	4	11	7	76	0
DAL	.3	0	0	0	0	6	0
Manny Malhotra	.59	3	7	10	-2	42	0
Stephane Robidas	.76	3	7	10	15	35	0
Steve Ott*	.26	3	4	7	6	31	0
Kirk Muller	.55	1	5	6	-6	18	0
Richard Matvichuk	.68	1	5	6	1	58	0

Acquired: RW Lemieux from Pho. for LW Scott Pellerin and a '04 conditional pick (Jan. 17); D Odelein from Chi. for D Sami Helenius and a conditional pick (Mar. 10); LW Barnes from Buf. for F Mike Ryan and a '03 2nd-round pick (Mar. 10).

Goalies (10 Gm)	Gm	Min	GAA	Record	SV%
Marty Turco	.55	3203	1.72	31-10-10	.932
Ron Tugnutt	.31	1701	2.47	15-10-5	.896
DALLAS	.82	5020	2.02	46-21-15	.918

Shutouts: Turco (7), Tugnutt (4). **Assists:** Turco (3). **PM:** Turco (16).

Detroit Red Wings

Top Scorers

	Gm	G	A	Pts	+/-	PM	PP
Sergei Fedorov	80	36	47	83	15	52	10
Brett Hull	82	37	39	76	11	22	12
Brendan Shanahan	78	30	38	68	5	103	13
Nicklas Lidstrom	82	18	44	62	40	38	8
Pavel Datsyuk	64	12	39	51	20	16	1
Mathieu Schneider	78	16	34	50	2	73	11
LA	65	14	29	43	0	57	10
DET	13	2	5	7	2	16	1
Henrik Zetterberg*	79	22	22	44	6	8	5
Igor Larionov	74	10	33	43	-7	48	5
Tomas Holmstrom	74	20	20	40	11	62	12
Kirk Maltby	82	14	23	37	17	91	0
Kris Draper	82	14	21	35	6	82	0
Luc Robitaille	81	11	20	31	4	50	3
Jason Woolley	76	6	20	26	11	51	1
BUF	14	0	3	3	-1	29	0
DET	62	6	17	23	12	22	1
Darren McCarty	73	13	9	22	10	138	1
Mathieu Dandenault	74	4	15	19	25	64	1
Chris Chelios	66	2	17	19	4	78	0
Boyd Devereaux	61	3	9	12	4	16	0
Dmitri Bykov*	71	2	10	12	1	43	1
Steve Yzerman	16	2	6	8	6	8	1
Patrick Boileau	25	2	6	8	8	14	0

Acquired: D Woolley from Buf. for future considerations (Nov. 16); D Schneider from LA for C Sean Avery, D Maxim Kuznetsov, a '03 1st-round pick and a '04 2nd-round pick (Mar. 11).

Goalies (10 Gm)	Gm	Min	GAA	Record	Sv%
Manny Legace	25	1406	2.18	14-5-4	.925
Curtis Joseph	61	3566	2.49	34-19-6	.912
DETROIT	82	4993	2.44	48-24-10	.914

Shutouts: Joseph (5). **Assists:** Legace (1). **PM:** Joseph (4), Legace (2).

Florida Panthers

Top Scorers

	Gm	G	A	Pts	+/-	PM	PP
Olli Jokinen	81	36	29	65	-17	79	13
Viktor Kozlov	74	22	34	56	-8	18	7
Kristian Huselius	78	20	23	43	-6	20	3
Marcus Nilson	82	15	19	34	2	31	7
Matt Cullen	80	13	20	33	-8	34	3
ANA	50	7	14	21	-4	12	1
FLA	30	6	6	12	-4	22	2
Ivan Novoseltsev	78	10	17	27	-16	30	1
Jaroslav Bednar*	67	5	22	27	1	18	2
LA	15	0	9	9	3	4	0
FLA	52	5	13	18	-2	14	2
Niklas Hagman	80	8	15	23	-8	20	2
Stephen Weiss*	77	6	15	21	-13	17	0
Jay Bouwmeester*	82	4	12	16	-29	14	2
Andreas Lilja	73	4	11	15	13	70	0
LA	17	0	3	3	5	14	0
FLA	56	4	8	12	8	56	0
Ivan Majesky	82	4	8	12	-18	92	0
Pavel Trnka	46	3	9	12	1	30	1
ANA	24	3	6	9	2	6	1
FLA	22	0	3	3	-1	24	0
Mathieu Biron	34	1	8	9	-18	14	0
Stephane Matteau	52	4	4	8	-9	27	0
Denis Shvidki	23	4	2	6	-7	12	2

Acquired: RW Bednar and D Lilja from LA for D Dmitry Yushkevich (Nov. 26); C Cullen, D Trnka and a '03 4th-round pick from Ana. for D Sandis Ozolinsh and D Lance Ward (Jan. 30).

Goalies (10 Gm)	Gm	Min	GAA	Record	Sv%
Roberto Luongo	65	3627	2.71	20-34-7	.918
Jani Hurme	28	1376	2.88	4-11-6	.907
FLORIDA	82	5021	2.83	24-45-13	.913

Shutouts: Luongo (6), Hurme (1). **Assists:** none. **PM:** Luongo (4), Hurme (2).

Edmonton Oilers

Top Scorers

	Gm	G	A	Pts	+/-	PM	PP
Ryan Smyth	66	27	34	61	5	67	10
Todd Marchant	77	20	40	60	13	48	7
Mike York	71	22	29	51	-8	10	7
Mike Comrie	69	20	31	51	-18	90	8
Radek Dvorak	75	10	25	35	-6	30	3
NYR	63	6	21	27	-3	16	3
EDM	12	4	4	8	-3	14	1
Shawn Horcoff	78	12	21	33	10	55	2
Ethan Moreau	78	14	17	31	-7	112	2
Marty Reasoner	70	11	20	31	19	28	2
Ales Hemsky*	59	6	24	30	5	14	0
Eric Brewer	80	8	21	29	-11	45	1
Brad Isbister	66	13	15	28	-9	43	2
NYI	53	10	13	23	-9	34	2
EDM	13	3	2	5	0	9	0
Steve Staios	76	5	21	26	13	96	1
Jason Chimera*	66	14	9	23	-2	36	0
Dan Cleary	57	4	13	17	5	31	0
Fernando Pisani*	35	8	5	13	9	10	0
Georges Laraque	64	6	7	13	-4	110	0
Jason Smith	68	4	8	12	5	64	0
Brian Swanson	25	2	6	8	4	14	0

Acquired: RW Dvorak and D Cory Cross from NYR for RW Anson Carter and D Ales Pisa (Mar. 11); LW Isbister and LW Raffi Torres from NYI for D Janne Niinimaa and a '03 2nd-round pick (Mar. 11).

Goalies (10 Gm)	Gm	Min	GAA	Record	Sv%
Jussi Markkanen	22	1180	2.59	7-8-3	.904
Tommy Salo	65	3814	2.71	29-27-8	.899
EDMONTON	82	5020	2.75	36-35-11	.898

Shutouts: Salo (4), Markkanen (3). **Assists:** Markkanen (1). **PM:** Salo (4), Markkanen (2).

Los Angeles Kings

Top Scorers

	Gm	G	A	Pts	+/-	PM	PP
Zigmund Palffy	76	37	48	85	22	47	10
Jaroslav Modry	82	13	25	38	-13	68	8
Derek Armstrong	66	12	26	38	5	30	2
Eric Belanger	62	16	19	35	-5	26	0
Alexander Frolov*	79	14	17	31	12	34	1
Jason Allison	26	6	22	28	9	22	2
Lubomir Visnovsky	57	8	16	24	2	28	1
Ian Laperriere	73	7	12	19	-9	122	1
Adam Deadmarsh	20	13	4	17	2	21	4
Mikko Eloranta	75	5	12	17	-15	56	1
Erik Rasmussen	57	4	12	16	-1	28	0
Sean Avery	51	6	9	15	7	153	0
DET	39	5	6	11	7	120	0
LA	12	1	3	4	0	33	0
Brad Chartrand	62	8	6	14	-10	33	0
Steve Heinze	27	5	7	12	-5	12	1
Joe Corvo	50	5	7	12	2	14	2
Craig Johnson	70	3	6	9	-13	22	0
Michael Cammalleri*	28	5	3	8	-4	22	2
Brad Norton	53	3	3	6	1	97	0
Aaron Miller	49	0	6	6	-7	24	0
Mattias Norstrom	80	2	5	7	-6	49	0

Acquired: C Avery, D Maxim Kuznetsov, a '03 1st-round pick and a '04 2nd-round pick from Det. for D Mathieu Schneider (Mar. 11).

Goalies (10 Gm)	Gm	Min	GAA	Record	Sv%
Cristobal Huet	12	541	2.33	4-4-1	.913
Jamie Storr	39	2027	2.55	12-19-2	.905
Felix Potvin	42	2367	2.66	17-20-3	.894
LOS ANGELES	82	4986	2.66	33-43-6	.897

Shutouts: Storr and Potvin (3), Huet (1). **Assists:** Storr (1). **PM:** Storr (8), Potvin (4).

Minnesota Wild

Top Scorers	Gm	G	A	Pts	+/-	PM	PP
Marian Gaborik	.81	30	35	65	12	46	5
Pascal Dupuis	.80	20	28	48	17	44	6
Cliff Ronning	.80	17	31	48	-6	24	8
Andrew Brunette	.82	18	28	46	-10	30	9
Sergei Zholtok	.78	16	26	42	1	18	3
Wes Walz	.80	13	19	32	11	63	0
Antti Laaksonen	.82	15	16	31	4	26	1
Filip Kuba	.78	8	21	29	0	29	4
Jim Dowd	.78	8	17	25	-1	31	3
Richard Park	.81	14	10	24	-3	16	2
Pierre-Marc Bouchard*	.50	7	13	20	1	18	5
Andrei Zyuzin	.67	4	13	17	-8	36	2
NJ	.1	0	1	1	-1	2	0
MIN	.66	4	12	16	-7	34	2
Brad Bombardir	.58	1	14	15	15	16	1
Willie Mitchell	.69	2	12	14	13	84	0
Jeremy Stevenson	.32	5	6	11	6	69	1
Lubomir Sekeras	.60	2	9	11	-12	30	1
Nick Schultz	.75	3	7	10	11	23	0
Bill Muckalt	.8	5	3	8	5	6	0
Matt Johnson	.60	3	5	8	8	201	0
Darby Hendrickson	.28	5	2	7	-6	-3	8	0
Jason Marshall	.45	1	5	6	4	69	0
Stephane Veilleux*	.38	3	2	5	-6	23	1

Claimed: D Zyuzin off waivers from NJ (Nov. 2).

Goalies (10 Gm)	Gm	Min	GAA	Record	Sv%
Dwayne Roloson	.50	2945	2.00	23-16-8	.927
Manny Fernandez	.35	1979	2.24	19-13-2	.924
MINNESOTA	.82	4997	2.14	42-30-10	.924

Shutouts: Roloson (4), Fernandez (2). **Assists:** Roloson and Fernandez (1). **PM:** Fernandez (6), Roloson (4).

Montreal Canadiens

Top Scorers	Gm	G	A	Pts	+/-	PM	PP
Saku Koivu	.82	21	50	71	5	72	5
Richard Zednik	.80	31	19	50	4	79	9
Yanic Perreault	.73	24	22	46	-11	30	7
Jan Bulis	.82	16	24	40	9	30	0
Andrei Markov	.79	13	24	37	13	34	3
Patrice Brisebois	.73	4	25	29	-14	32	1
Niklas Sundstrom	.80	7	19	26	-1	30	0
SJ	.47	2	10	12	-4	22	0
MON	.33	5	9	14	3	8	0
Andreas Dackell	.73	7	18	25	-5	24	0
Donald Audette	.54	11	12	23	-7	19	4
Craig Rivet	.82	7	15	22	1	71	3
Joe Juneau	.72	6	16	22	-10	20	0
Randy McKay	.75	6	13	19	-14	72	2
Mike Ribeiro	.52	5	12	17	-3	6	2
Chad Kilger	.60	9	7	16	-4	21	0
Mariusz Czerkawski	.43	5	9	14	-7	16	1
Marcel Hossa*	.34	6	7	13	3	14	2
Patrick Traverse	.65	0	13	13	-9	24	0
Stephane Quintal	.67	5	5	10	-4	70	0
Jason Ward	.8	3	2	5	3	0	0
Karl Dykhuis	.65	1	4	5	-5	34	0
Francis Bouillon	.24	3	1	4	-2	4	0
NASH	.4	0	0	0	-1	2	0
MON	.20	3	1	4	-1	2	0
Bill Lindsay	.19	0	2	2	-1	23	0

Acquired: LW Sundstrom and a '04 3rd-round pick from SJ in a 3-team deal that sent G Jeff Hackett to Bos. (Jan. 23). **Claimed:** D Bouillon off waivers from Nash. (Oct. 25).

Goalies (10 Gm)	Gm	Min	GAA	Record	Sv%
Jose Theodore	.57	3419	2.90	20-31-6	.908
MONTREAL	.82	4988	2.81	30-44-8	.913

Shutouts: Theodore and Mathieu Garon (2). **Assists:** Theodore (2). **PM:** Theodore (6).

Nashville Predators

Top Scorers	Gm	G	A	Pts	+/-	PM	PP
David Legwand	.64	17	31	48	-2	34	3
Kimmo Timonen	.72	6	34	40	-3	46	4
Andreas Johansson	.56	20	17	37	-4	22	10
Denis Arkhipov	.79	11	24	35	-18	32	3
Andy Delmore	.71	18	16	34	-17	28	14
Scott Hartnell	.82	12	22	34	-3	101	2
Scott Walker	.60	15	18	33	2	58	7
Vladimir Orszagh	.78	16	16	32	-1	38	3
Rem Murray	.85	12	19	31	-2	22	2
NYR	.32	6	6	12	-3	4	1
NASH	.53	6	13	19	1	18	1
Adam Hall*	.79	16	12	28	-8	31	8
Oleg Petrov	.70	9	18	27	-6	18	2
MON	.53	7	16	23	-2	16	2
NASH	.17	2	2	4	-4	2	0
Vitali Yachmenev	.62	5	15	20	7	12	0
Jason York	.74	4	15	19	13	52	2
Greg Johnson	.38	8	9	17	7	22	0
Todd Warriner	.49	6	10	16	1	32	0
VAN	.30	4	6	10	0	22	0
PHI	.13	2	3	5	2	6	0
NASH	.6	0	1	1	-1	4	0
Clarke Wilm	.82	5	11	16	-11	36	0

Acquired: LW Murray, D Tomas Kloucek and D Marek Zidlicky from NYR for G Mike Dunham (Dec. 12); LW Petrov from Mon. for a '03 4th-round pick (Mar. 3). **Claimed:** LW Warriner off waivers from Phi. (Mar. 11).

Goalies (10 Gm)	Gm	Min	GAA	Record	Sv%
Tomas Vokoun	.69	3974	2.20	25-31-11	.918
NASHVILLE	.82	5015	2.46	27-42-13	.909

Shutouts: Vokoun (3). **Assists:** Vokoun and Wade Flaherty (1). **PM:** Vokoun (28).

New Jersey Devils

Top Scorers	Gm	G	A	Pts	+/-	PM	PP
Patrik Elias	.81	28	29	57	17	22	6
Jamie Langenbrunner	.78	22	33	55	17	65	5
Scott Gomez	.80	13	42	55	17	48	2
Jeff Friesen	.81	23	28	51	23	26	3
Joe Nieuwendyk	.80	17	28	45	10	56	3
John Madden	.80	19	22	41	13	26	2
Brian Rafalski	.79	3	37	40	18	14	2
Scott Niedermayer	.81	11	28	39	23	62	3
Grant Marshall	.76	9	23	32	-11	78	5
CLB	.66	8	20	28	-8	71	3
NJ	.10	1	3	4	-3	7	0
Brian Gionta	.58	12	13	25	5	23	2
Turner Stevenson	.77	7	13	20	7	115	0
Scott Stevens	.81	4	16	20	18	41	0
Sergei Brylin	.52	11	8	19	-2	16	3
Pascal Rheaume	.77	8	10	18	-5	32	0
ATL	.56	4	9	13	-8	24	0
NJ	.21	4	1	5	3	8	0
Jay Pandolfo	.68	6	11	17	12	23	0
Oleg Tverdovsky	.50	5	8	13	2	22	2
Colin White	.72	5	8	13	19	98	0
Richard Smehlik	.55	2	11	13	-5	16	0
ATL	.43	2	9	11	-4	16	0
NJ	.12	0	2	2	0	0	0

Acquired: C Rheaume from Atl. for a '04 conditional pick (Feb. 24); RW Marshall from Clb. for a '04 conditional pick (Mar. 10); D Smehlik and a '04 conditional pick from Atl. for a '03 4th-round pick (Mar. 10).

Goalies (10 Gm)	Gm	Min	GAA	Record	Sv%
Corey Schwab	.11	614	1.47	5-3-1	.933
Martin Brodeur	.73	4374	2.02	41-23-9	.914
NEW JERSEY	.82	5009	1.99	46-26-10	.914

Shutouts: Brodeur (9), Schwab (1). **Assists:** none. **PM:** Brodeur (10).

New York Islanders

Top Scorers

Top Scorers	Gm	G	A	Pts	+/-	PM	PP
Alexei Yashin	.81	26	39	65	-12	32	14
Jason Blake	.81	25	30	55	16	58	3
Mark Parrish	.81	23	25	48	-11	28	9
Dave Scatchard	.81	27	18	45	9	108	5
Michael Peca	.66	13	29	42	-4	43	4
Shawn Bates	.74	13	29	42	-9	52	1
Roman Hamrlik	.73	9	32	41	21	87	3
Adrian Aucoin	.73	8	27	35	-5	70	5
Arron Asham	.78	15	19	34	1	57	4
Janne Niinimaa	.76	5	29	34	-9	80	3
EDM	.63	4	24	28	-7	66	2
NYI	.13	1	5	6	-2	14	1
Jason Wiemer	.81	9	19	28	5	116	0
Oleg Kvasha	.69	12	14	26	4	44	0
Kenny Jonsson	.71	8	18	26	-8	24	3
Mattias Weinhandl	.47	6	17	23	-2	10	1
Randy Robitaille	.51	6	14	20	5	10	2
PIT	.41	5	12	17	5	8	1
NYI	.10	1	2	3	0	2	1
Mattias Timander	.80	3	13	16	-2	24	0
Radek Martinek	.66	2	11	13	15	26	0

Acquired: C Robitaille from Pit. for a '03 5th-round pick (Mar. 9); D Niinimaa and a '03 2nd-round pick from Edm. for LW Brad Isbister and LW Raffi Torres (Mar. 11).

Goalies (10 Gm)	Gm	Min	GAA	Record	Sv%
Garth Snow	.43	2390	2.31	16-17-5	.918
Rick DiPietro*	.10	585	2.97	2-5-2	.894
NY ISLANDERS	.82	4992	2.78	35-36-11	.900

Shutouts: Snow (1). **Assists:** none. **PM:** Snow (24), DiPietro (2).

New York Rangers

Top Scorers

Top Scorers	Gm	G	A	Pts	+/-	PM	PP
Alexei Kovalev	.78	37	40	77	-9	70	11
PIT	.54	27	37	64	-11	50	8
NYR	.24	10	3	13	2	20	3
Anson Carter	.79	26	34	60	-11	20	10
EDM	.68	25	30	55	-11	20	10
NYR	.11	1	4	5	0	0	0
Petr Nedved	.78	27	31	58	-4	64	8
Eric Lindros	.81	19	34	53	5	141	9
Tom Poti	.80	11	37	48	-6	60	3
Mark Messier	.78	18	22	40	-2	30	8
Matthew Barnaby	.79	14	22	36	9	142	0
Bobby Holik	.64	16	19	35	-1	50	3
Pavel Bure	.39	19	11	30	4	16	5
Brian Leetch	.51	12	18	30	-3	20	5
Jamie Lundmark*	.55	8	11	19	-3	16	0
Vladimir Malakhov	.71	3	14	17	-7	52	1
Boris Mironov	.56	6	10	16	2	56	2
CHI	.20	3	1	4	-1	22	1
NYR	.36	3	9	12	3	34	1
Sandy McCarthy	.82	6	9	15	-4	81	0
Ronald Petrovicky	.66	5	9	14	-12	77	2
Darius Kasparaitis	.80	3	11	14	5	85	0

Acquired: G Dunham from Nash. for LW Rem Murray, D Tomas Kloucek and D Marek Zidlicky (Dec. 12); D Mironov from Chi. for a '04 4th-round pick (Jan. 8); RW Kovalev, LW Dan LaCouture, D Janne Laukkanen and D Mike Wilson from Pit. for four players (Feb. 10); RW Carter and D Ales Pisa from Edm. for RW Radek Dvorak and D Cory Cross (Mar. 11).

Goalies (10 Gm)	Gm	Min	GAA	Record	SV%
Mike Dunham	.58	3286	2.50	21-26-7	.916
NASH	.15	819	3.15	2-9-2	.892
NYR	.43	2467	2.29	19-17-5	.924
Mike Richter	.13	694	2.94	5-6-1	.897
Dan Blackburn	.32	1762	3.17	8-16-4	.890
NY RANGERS	.82	4991	2.78	32-40-10	.905

Shutouts: Dunham (5), Blackburn (1). **Assists:** Dunham (1). **PM:** Blackburn (2).

Ottawa Senators

Top Scorers

Top Scorers	Gm	G	A	Pts	+/-	PM	PP
Marian Hossa	.80	45	35	80	8	34	14
Daniel Alfredsson	.78	27	52	79	15	42	9
Todd White	.80	25	35	60	19	28	8
Martin Havlat	.67	24	35	59	20	30	9
Radek Bonk	.70	22	32	54	6	36	11
Bryan Smolinski	.68	21	25	46	0	20	6
LA	.58	18	20	38	-1	18	6
OTT	.10	3	5	8	1	2	0
Wade Redden	.76	10	35	45	23	70	4
Zdeno Chara	.74	9	30	39	29	116	3
Mike Fisher	.74	18	20	38	13	54	5
Magnus Arvedson	.80	16	20	36	13	48	2
Shaun Van Allen	.78	12	20	32	17	66	2
Karel Rachunek	.58	4	25	29	23	30	3
Peter Schaefer	.75	6	17	23	11	32	0
Jason Spezza*	.33	7	14	21	-3	8	3
Petr Schastlivy	.33	9	10	19	3	4	5
Vaclav Varada	.55	9	10	19	1	31	2
BUF	.44	7	4	11	-2	23	1
OTT	.11	2	6	8	3	8	1
Chris Phillips	.78	3	16	19	7	71	2
Anton Volchenkov*	.57	3	13	16	-4	40	0

Acquired: RW Varada and a '03 5th-round pick from Buf. for C Jakub Klepis (Feb. 25); RW Smolinski from LA for D Tim Gleason and future considerations (Mar. 11).

Goalies (10 Gm)	Gm	Min	GAA	Record	Sv%
Patrick Lalime	.67	3943	2.16	39-20-7	.911
Martin Prusek	.18	935	2.37	12-2-1	.911
OTTAWA	.82	4977	2.19	52-22-8	.910

Shutouts: Lalime (8). **Assists:** Lalime (1). **PM:** Lalime (6).

Philadelphia Flyers

Top Scorers

Top Scorers	Gm	G	A	Pts	+/-	PM	PP
Jeremy Roenick	.79	27	32	59	20	75	8
Mark Recchi	.79	20	32	52	0	35	8
Tony Amonte	.72	20	31	51	0	28	7
PHO	.59	13	23	36	-12	26	6
PHI	.13	7	8	15	12	2	1
Keith Primeau	.80	19	27	46	4	93	6
Michal Handzus	.82	23	21	44	13	46	1
Kim Johnsson	.82	10	29	39	11	38	5
Eric Desjardins	.79	8	24	32	30	35	1
Sami Kapanen	.71	10	21	31	-18	18	5
CAR	.43	6	12	18	-17	12	3
PHI	.28	4	9	13	-1	6	2
John LeClair	.35	18	10	28	10	16	8
Simon Gagne	.46	9	18	27	20	16	1
Marty Murray	.76	11	15	26	-1	13	1
Donald Brashear	.80	8	17	25	5	161	0
Justin Williams	.41	8	16	24	15	22	0
Eric Weinrich	.81	2	18	20	16	40	1
Radovan Somik*	.60	8	10	18	9	10	0
Claude Lapointe	.80	8	8	16	2	36	0
NYI	.66	6	6	12	-3	20	0
PHI	.14	2	2	4	5	16	0
Marcus Ragnarsson	.68	3	13	16	7	62	1
SJ	.25	1	7	8	2	30	0
PHI	.43	2	6	8	5	32	1

Acquired: D Ragnarsson from SJ for D Dan McGillis (Dec. 6); RW Kapanen and D Ryan Bast from Car. for RW Pavel Brendl and D Bruno St. Jacques (Feb. 7); C Lapointe from NYI for a '03 5th-round pick (Mar. 9); RW Amonte from Pho. for F Guillaume Lefebvre, a '03 3rd-round pick and a '04 2nd-round pick (Mar. 10).

Goalies (10 Gm)	Gm	Min	GAA	Record	Sv%
Roman Cechmanek	.58	3350	1.83	33-15-10	.925
Robert Esche	.30	1638	2.20	12-9-3	.907
PHILADELPHIA	.82	5005	1.99	45-24-13	.918

Shutouts: Cechmanek (6), Esche (2). **Assists:** none. **PM:** Cechmanek (8), Esche (6).

Phoenix Coyotes

Top Scorers

Top Scorers	Gm	G	A	Pts	+/-	PM	PP
Mike Johnson	.82	23	40	63	9	47	8
Shane Doan	.82	21	37	58	3	86	7
Ladislav Nagy	.80	22	35	57	17	92	8
Daymond Langkow	.82	20	32	52	20	56	4
Chris Gratton	.80	15	30	45	-16	107	4
BUF	.66	15	29	44	-5	86	4
PHO	.14	0	1	1	-11	21	0
Jan Hrdina	.61	14	29	43	4	42	11
PIT	.57	14	25	39	1	34	11
PHO	.4	0	4	4	3	8	0
Teppo Numminen	.78	6	24	30	0	30	2
Branko Radivojevic*	.79	12	15	27	-2	63	1
Paul Mara	.73	10	15	25	-7	78	1
Danny Markov	.64	4	16	20	2	36	2
Deron Quint	.51	7	10	17	-5	20	2
Brian Savage	.43	6	10	16	-4	22	1
Landon Wilson	.31	6	8	14	1	26	0
Kelly Buchberger	.79	3	9	12	0	109	0
Paul Ranheim	.68	3	8	11	-8	16	0
PHI	.28	0	4	4	-4	6	0
PHO	.40	3	4	7	-4	10	0
Todd Simpson	.66	2	7	9	7	135	0
Ossi Vaananen	.67	2	7	9	1	82	0
Brad Ference	.75	2	7	9	-3	146	0
FLA	.60	2	6	8	2	118	0
PHO	.15	0	1	1	-5	28	0

Acquired: RW Ranheim from Phi. for a '04 conditional pick (Dec. 19); D Ference from Fla. for D Darcy Hordichuk and a '03 2nd-round pick (Mar. 8); C Gratton and a '04 4th-round pick from Buf. for C Daniel Briere and a '03 3rd-round pick (Mar. 10); LW Hrdina and D Francois Leroux for LW Ramzi Abid and 2 other players (Mar. 11).

Goalies (10 Gm)

Goalies (10 Gm)	Gm	Min	GAA	Record	Sv%
Sean Burke	.22	1248	2.12	12-6-2	.930
Zac Bierk	.16	884	2.17	4-9-1	.932
Brian Boucher	.45	2544	3.02	15-20-8	.894
PHOENIX	.82	5000	2.76	31-40-11	.906

Shutouts: Burke (2), Bierk (1). **Assists:** Boucher (1). **PM:** Burke (4), Bierk (2).

Pittsburgh Penguins

Top Scorers

Top Scorers	Gm	G	A	Pts	+/-	PM	PP
Mario Lemieux	.67	28	63	91	-25	43	14
Martin Straka	.60	18	28	46	-18	12	7
Dick Tarnstrom	.61	7	34	41	-11	50	3
Aleksey Morozov	.27	9	16	25	-3	16	6
Mikael Samuelsson	.80	10	14	24	-21	40	2
NYR	.58	8	14	22	0	32	1
PIT	.22	2	0	2	-21	8	1
Ville Nieminen	.75	9	12	21	-25	93	0
Rico Fata	.63	7	12	19	-7	16	0
NYR	.36	2	4	6	-1	6	0
PIT	.27	5	8	13	-6	10	0
Ramzi Abid*	.33	10	8	18	-4	32	4
PHO	.30	10	8	18	1	30	4
PIT	.3	0	0	0	-5	2	0
Mathias Johansson	.58	5	10	15	-14	16	2
CALG	.46	4	5	9	-15	12	1
PIT	.12	1	5	6	1	4	1
Joel Bouchard	.34	5	8	13	0	14	1
NYR	.27	5	7	12	6	14	1
PIT	.7	0	1	1	-6	0	0

Acquired: RW Samuelsson, LW Fata, D Bouchard and D Richard Lintner from NYR for RW Alexei Kovalev and 3 other players (Feb. 10); LW Abid and 2 other players from Pho. for LW Jan Hrdina and D Francois Leroux (Mar. 11); C Johansson and D Micki DuPont from Calg. for RW Shean Donovan (Mar. 11).

Goalies (10 Gm)

Goalies (10 Gm)	Gm	Min	GAA	Record	Sv%
Sebastien Caron*	.24	1408	2.64	7-14-2	.916
J-S Aubin	.21	1132	3.13	6-13-0	.900
Johan Hedberg	.41	2410	3.14	14-22-4	.895
PITTSBURGH	.82	4972	3.08	27-49-6	.899

Shutouts: Caron (2), Aubin and Hedberg (1). **Assists:** Hedberg (2), Aubin (1). **PM:** Hedberg (18), Caron (6), Aubin (2).

St. Louis Blues

Top Scorers

Top Scorers	Gm	G	A	Pts	+/-	PM	PP
Pavol Demitra	.78	36	57	93	0	32	11
Al MacInnis	.80	16	52	68	22	61	9
Cory Stillman	.79	24	43	67	12	56	6
Doug Weight	.70	15	52	67	-6	52	7
Scott Mellanby	.80	26	31	57	1	176	13
Keith Tkachuk	.56	31	24	55	1	139	14
Eric Boguniecki	.80	22	27	49	22	38	3
Petr Cajanek	.51	9	29	38	16	20	2
Alexander Khavanov	.81	8	25	33	-1	48	2
Dallas Drake	.80	20	10	30	-7	66	4
Martin Rucinsky	.61	16	14	30	-1	38	4
Valeri Bure	.51	5	23	28	-13	10	3
FLA	.46	5	21	26	-11	10	3
ST.L	.5	0	2	2	-2	0	0
Barret Jackman*	.82	3	16	19	23	190	0
Steve Martins	.42	5	6	11	-5	28	0
OTT	.14	2	3	5	3	10	0
ST.L	.28	3	3	6	-8	18	0
Shjon Podein	.68	4	6	10	7	28	1
Bryce Salvador	.71	2	8	10	7	95	1
Tyson Nash	.66	6	3	9	0	114	1
Christian Laflamme	.59	1	8	9	1	45	0

Acquired: RW Bure and a '04 conditional pick from Fla. for D Mike Van Ryn (Mar. 11); G Osgood and a '03 3rd-round pick from NYI for C Justin Papineau and a '03 2nd-round pick (Mar. 11). **Claimed:** Martins off waivers from Ott. (Jan. 15).

Goalies (10 Gm)

Goalies (10 Gm)	Gm	Min	GAA	Record	Sv%
Brent Johnson	.38	2042	2.47	16-13-5	.900
Fred Brathwaite	.30	1615	2.75	12-9-4	.883
Chris Osgood	.46	2525	2.95	21-17-6	.892
NYI	.37	1993	2.92	17-14-4	.894
ST.L	.9	532	3.05	4-3-2	.888
ST. LOUIS	.82	5012	2.66	41-30-11	.892

Shutouts: Osgood (4), Johnson and Brathwaite (2); Curtis Sanford and Tom Barrasso (1). **Assists:** Johnson (1). **PM:** Osgood (12), Johnson (2).

San Jose Sharks

Top Scorers

Top Scorers	Gm	G	A	Pts	+/-	PM	PP
Teemu Selanne	.82	28	36	64	-6	30	7
Vincent Damphousse	.82	23	38	61	-13	66	15
Patrick Marleau	.82	28	29	57	-10	33	8
Marco Sturm	.82	28	20	48	9	16	6
Mike Ricci	.75	11	23	34	-12	53	5
Mike Rathje	.82	7	22	29	-19	48	3
Alyn McCauley	.80	9	16	25	1	20	3
TOR	.64	6	9	15	3	16	0
SJ	.16	3	7	10	-2	4	3
Scott Hannan	.81	3	19	22	0	61	1
Scott Thornton	.41	9	12	21	-7	41	4
Jim Fahey*	.43	1	19	20	-3	33	0
Todd Harvey	.76	3	16	19	5	74	0
Adam Graves	.82	9	9	18	-14	32	1
Wayne Primeau	.77	6	12	18	-28	55	1
PIT	.70	5	11	16	-30	55	1
SJ	.7	1	1	2	2	0	0
Jonathan Cheechoo*	.66	9	7	16	-5	39	0
Mark Smith	.75	4	11	15	1	64	0
Brad Stuart	.36	4	10	14	-6	46	2
Niko Dimitrakos*	.21	6	7	13	-7	8	3

Acquired: C McCauley, C Brad Boyes and a '03 1st-round pick from Tor. for RW Owen Nolan (Mar. 5); C Primeau from Pit. for RW Matt Bradley (Mar. 11).

Goalies (10 Gm)

Goalies (10 Gm)	Gm	Min	GAA	Record	Sv%
Vesa Toskala*	.11	537	2.35	4-3-1	.927
Evgeni Nabokov	.55	3227	2.71	19-28-8	.906
Miikka Kiprusoff*	.22	1199	3.25	5-14-0	.879
SAN JOSE	.82	4996	2.87	28-45-9	.900

Shutouts: Nabokov (3), Toskala and Kiprusoff (1). **Assists:** none. **PM:** Nabokov (10).

Tampa Bay Lightning

Top Scorers	Gm	G	A	Pts	+/-	PM	PP
Vaclav Prospal	80	22	57	79	9	53	9
Vincent Lecavalier	80	33	45	78	0	39	11
Brad Richards	80	17	57	74	3	24	4
Martin St. Louis	82	33	37	70	10	32	12
Dan Boyle	77	13	40	53	9	44	8
Fredrik Modin	76	17	23	40	7	43	2
Dave Andreychuk	72	20	14	34	-12	34	15
Ruslan Fedotenko	76	19	13	32	-7	44	6
Pavel Kubina	75	3	19	22	-7	78	0
Ben Clymer	65	6	12	18	-2	57	1
Andre Roy	62	10	7	17	0	119	0
Brad Lukowich	70	1	14	15	4	46	0
Cory Sarich	82	5	9	14	-3	63	0
Tim Taylor	82	4	8	12	-13	38	0
Alexander Svitov*	63	4	4	8	-4	58	1
Janne Laukkanen	19	2	6	8	-2	8	0
PIT	17	1	6	7	-3	8	0
TB	2	1	0	1	1	0	0
Nolan Pratt	67	1	7	8	-6	35	0

Acquired: G Grahame from Bos. for a '04 4th-round pick (Jan. 13). Claimed: D Laukkanen off waivers from NYR (Mar. 11).

Goalies (10 Gm)	Gm	Min	GAA	Record	SV%
Nikolai Khabibulin	65	3787	2.47	30-22-11	.911
John Grahame	40	2266	2.52	17-14-6	.909
BOS	23	1352	2.71	11-9-2	.902
TB	17	914	2.23	6-5-4	.920
TAMPA BAY	82	5026	2.51	36-30-16	.909

Shutouts: Khabibulin (4), Grahame (3). **Assists:** Khabibulin (3), Grahame (2). **PM:** Grahame (11), Khabibulin (8), Kevin Hodson and Evgeny Konstantinov (2).

Toronto Maple Leafs

Top Scorers	Gm	G	A	Pts	+/-	PM	PP
Alexander Mogilny	73	33	46	79	4	12	5
Mats Sundin	75	37	35	72	1	58	16
Owen Nolan	75	29	25	54	-3	107	13
SJ	61	22	20	42	-5	91	8
TOR	14	7	5	12	2	16	5
Tomas Kaberle	82	11	36	47	20	30	4
Nik Antropov	72	16	29	45	11	124	2
Robert Svehla	82	7	38	45	13	46	2
Robert Reichel	81	12	30	42	7	26	1
Darcy Tucker	77	10	26	36	-7	119	4
Mikael Renberg	67	14	21	35	5	36	7
Jonas Hoglund	79	13	19	32	2	12	2
Doug Gilmour	62	11	19	30	-6	36	3
MON	61	11	19	30	-6	36	3
TOR	1	0	0	0	0	0	0
Tie Domi	79	15	14	29	-1	171	4
Phil Housley	58	6	23	29	6	26	2
CHI	57	6	23	29	7	24	2
TOR	1	0	0	0	-1	2	0
Travis Green	75	12	12	24	2	67	2
Bryan McCabe	75	6	18	24	9	135	3
Jyrki Lumme	73	6	11	17	10	46	1
Tom Fitzgerald	66	4	13	17	10	57	0
Shayne Corson	46	7	8	15	-5	49	0

Acquired: RW Nolan from SJ for C Alyn McCauley, C Brad Boyes and a '03 1st-round pick (Mar. 5); C Gilmour from Mon. for a '03 6th-round pick (Mar. 11); D Housley from Chi. for a conditional pick (Mar. 11).

Goalies (10 Gm)	Gm	Min	GAA	Record	Sv%
Ed Belfour	62	3738	2.26	37-20-5	.922
Trevor Kidd	19	1143	3.10	6-10-2	.896
TORONTO	82	4987	2.50	44-31-7	.914

Shutouts: Belfour (7). **Assists:** Belfour (2). **PM:** Belfour (24).

Vancouver Canucks

Top Scorers	Gm	G	A	Pts	+/-	PM	PP
Markus Naslund	82	48	56	104	6	52	24
Todd Bertuzzi	82	46	51	97	2	144	25
Brendan Morrison	82	25	46	71	18	36	6
Ed Jovanovski	67	6	40	46	19	113	2
Matt Cooke	82	15	27	42	21	82	1
Trevor Linden	71	19	22	41	-1	30	4
Henrik Sedin	78	8	31	39	9	38	4
Brent Sopel	81	7	30	37	-15	23	6
Daniel Sedin	79	14	17	31	8	34	4
Sami Salo	79	9	21	30	9	10	4
Trent Klatt	82	16	13	29	10	8	3
Mattias Ohlund	59	2	27	29	1	42	0
Trevor Letowski	78	11	14	25	8	36	1
Artem Chubarov	62	7	13	20	4	6	1
Marek Malik	79	7	13	20	20	68	1
CAR	10	0	2	2	-3	16	0
VAN	69	7	11	18	23	52	1
Mats Lindgren	54	5	9	14	-2	18	0
Bryan Allen	48	5	3	8	8	73	0
Brad May	23	3	4	7	4	42	0
PHO	20	3	4	7	3	32	0
VAN	3	0	0	0	1	10	0
Murray Baron	78	2	4	6	13	62	0

Acquired: D Malik and LW Darren Langdon from Car. for LW Jan Hlavac and C Harold Druken (Nov. 1); LW May from Pho. for a '03 conditional pick (Mar. 11). **Signed:** free agent C Mats Lindgren (Nov. 3).

Goalies (10 Gm)	Gm	Min	GAA	Record	SV%
Dan Cloutier	57	3376	2.42	33-16-7	.908
Peter Skudra	23	1192	2.72	9-5-6	.897
VANCOUVER	82	4997	2.50	45-24-13	.905

Shutouts: Cloutier (2), Skudra and Alex Auld (1). **Assists:** Cloutier (3), Skudra (1). **PM:** Cloutier (24).

Washington Capitals

Top Scorers	Gm	G	A	Pts	+/-	PM	PP
Jaromir Jagr	75	36	41	77	5	38	13
Robert Lang	82	22	47	69	12	22	10
Sergei Gonchar	82	18	49	67	13	52	7
Michael Nylander	80	17	43	60	3	40	7
CHI	9	0	4	4	0	4	0
WASH	71	17	39	56	3	36	7
Peter Bondra	76	30	26	56	-3	52	9
Kip Miller	72	12	38	50	-1	18	3
Sergei Berezin	75	23	17	40	7	12	5
CHI	66	18	13	31	-3	8	5
WASH	9	5	4	9	10	4	0
Dainius Zubrus	63	13	22	35	15	43	2
Jeff Halpern	82	13	21	34	6	88	1
Mike Grier	82	15	17	32	-14	36	2
Steve Konowalchuk	77	15	15	30	3	71	2
Ivan Ciernik	47	8	10	18	6	24	0
Ken Klee	70	1	16	17	22	89	0
Calle Johansson	82	3	12	15	9	22	1
Brendan Witt	69	2	9	11	12	106	0
Brian Sutherby*	72	2	9	11	7	93	0
Jason Doig	55	3	5	8	-3	108	0

Four tied with 5 points each.

Acquired: C Nylander, a '03 3rd-round pick and a '04 conditional pick from Chi. for LW Chris Simon and C Andrei Nikolishin (Nov. 1); LW Berezin from Chi. for a '04 4th-round pick (Mar. 11).

Goalies (10 Gm)	Gm	Min	GAA	Record	Sv%
Olaf Kolzig	66	3894	2.40	33-25-6	.919
Sebastien Charpentier*	17	859	2.79	5-7-1	.906
WASHINGTON	82	4995	2.64	39-35-8	.910

Shutouts: Kolzig (4). **Assists:** none. **PM:** none.

Stanley Cup Playoffs

| QUARTERFINALS | SEMIFINALS | FINAL | | FINAL | SEMIFINALS | QUARTERFINALS |

Dallas 4
Edmonton 2
— Dallas 2
Anaheim 4
Detroit 0
— Anaheim 4
Anaheim 4

WESTERN CONFERENCE

Minnesota 4
Colorado 3
— Minnesota 4
Minnesota 0
Vancouver 4
St. Louis 3
— Vancouver 3

New Jersey 4
Anaheim 3

Ottawa 3
New Jersey 4

EASTERN CONFERENCE

Ottawa 4
Philadelphia 2
— Ottawa 4

New Jersey 4
Tampa Bay 1
— New Jersey 4

Ottawa 4
NY Islanders 2
Philadelphia 4
Toronto 3
New Jersey 4
Boston 1
Tampa Bay 4
Washington 2

Stanley Cup Playoffs
Series Summaries

WESTERN CONFERENCE

FIRST ROUND (Best of 7)

	W-L	GF	Leading Scorers
Dallas 4-2		20	Modano (4-6–10)
			& Zubov (4-6–10)
Edmonton 2-4		11	Three tied with 4 pts.

Date	Winner	Home Ice
April 9	Oilers, 2-1	at Dallas
April 11	Stars, 6-1	at Dallas
April 13	Oilers, 3-2	at Edmonton
April 15	Stars, 3-1	at Edmonton
April 17	Stars, 5-2	at Dallas
April 19	Stars, 3-2	at Edmonton

	W-L	GF	Leading Scorers
Minnesota 4-3		16	Three tied with 6 pts.
Colorado 3-4		17	Sakic (6-3–9)

Date	Winner	Home Ice
April 10	Wild, 4-2	at Colorado
April 12	Avalanche, 3-2	at Colorado
April 14	Avalanche, 3-0	at Minnesota
April 16	Avalanche, 3-1	at Minnesota
April 19	Wild, 3-2	at Colorado
April 21	Wild, 3-2 (OT)	at Minnesota
April 22	Wild, 3-2 (OT)	at Colorado

Shutout: Roy, Colorado.

	W-L	GF	Leading Scorers
Anaheim 4-0		10	Niedermayer (0-3–3)
			& Chistov (1-2–3)
Detroit 0-4		6	Fedorov (1-2–3)

Date	Winner	Home Ice
April 10	Ducks, 2-1 (3OT)	at Detroit
April 12	Ducks, 3-2	at Detroit
April 14	Ducks, 2-1	at Anaheim
April 16	Ducks, 3-2 (OT)	at Anaheim

	W-L	GF	Leading Scorers
Vancouver 4-3		17	Naslund (4-3–7)
St. Louis. 3-4		21	Weight (5-8–13)

Date	Winner	Home Ice
April 10	Blues, 6-0	at Vancouver
April 12	Canucks, 2-1	at Vancouver
April 14	Blues, 3-1	at St. Louis
April 16	Blues, 4-1	at St. Louis
April 18	Canucks, 5-3	at Vancouver
April 20	Canucks, 4-3	at St. Louis
April 22	Canucks, 4-1	at Vancouver

Shutout: Osgood, St. Louis.

SEMIFINALS (Best of 7)

	W-L	GF	Leading Scorers
Anaheim 4-2		14	Leclerc (2-3–5)
Dallas 2-4		14	Kapanen (3-2–5)
			& Modano (1-4–5)

Date	Winner	Home Ice
April 24	Ducks, 4-3 (5OT)	at Dallas
April 26	Ducks, 3-2 (OT)	at Dallas
April 28	Stars, 2-1	at Anaheim
April 30	Ducks, 1-0	at Anaheim
May 3	Stars, 4-1	at Dallas
May 5	Ducks, 4-3	at Anaheim

Shutout: Giguere, Anaheim.

	W-L	GF	Leading Scorers
Minnesota 4-3		26	Gaborik (5-6–11)
Vancouver 3-4		17	Morrison (2-5–7)
			& Naslund (1-6–7)

Date	Winner	Home Ice
April 25	Canucks, 4-3 (OT)	at Vancouver
April 27	Wild, 3-2	at Vancouver
April 29	Canucks, 3-2	at Minnesota
May 2	Canucks, 3-2 (OT)	at Minnesota
May 5	Wild, 7-2	at Vancouver
May 7	Wild, 5-1	at Minnesota
May 8	Wild, 4-2	at Vancouver

CHAMPIONSHIP (Best of 7)

	W-L	GF	Leading Scorers
Anaheim	4-0	9	Oates (2-3–5)
Minnesota	0-4	1	Brunette (1-0–1), Ronning (0-1–1) & Bouchard (0-1–1)

Date	Winner	Home Ice
May 10	Ducks, 1-0 (2OT)	at Minnesota
May 12	Ducks, 2-0	at Minnesota
May 14	Ducks, 4-0	at Anaheim
May 16	Ducks, 2-1	at Anaheim

Shutouts: Giguere, Anaheim (3).

EASTERN CONFERENCE

FIRST ROUND (Best of 7)

	W-L	GF	Leading Scorers
Ottawa	4-1	13	Three tied with 4 pts.
NY Islanders	1-4	7	Yashin (2-2–4)

Date	Winner	Home Ice
April 9	Islanders, 3-0	at Ottawa
April 12	Senators, 3-0	at Ottawa
April 14	Senators, 3-2 (2OT)	at New York
April 16	Senators, 3-1	at New York
April 17	Senators, 4-1	at Ottawa

Shutouts: Snow, NY Islanders; Lalime, Ottawa.

	W-L	GF	Leading Scorers
Tampa Bay	4-2	14	St. Louis (5-4–9)
Washington	2-4	15	Jagr (2-5–7)

Date	Winner	Home Ice
April 10	Capitals, 3-0	at Tampa Bay
April 12	Capitals, 6-3	at Tampa Bay
April 15	Lightning, 4-3 (OT)	at Washington
April 16	Lightning, 3-1	at Washington
April 18	Lightning, 2-1	at Tampa Bay
April 20	Lightning, 2-1 (3OT)	at Washington

Shutout: Kolzig, Washington.

	W-L	GF	Leading Scorers
New Jersey	4-1	13	Madden (2-6–8)
Boston	1-4	8	McGillis (3-0–3) & Thornton (1-2–3)

Date	Winner	Home Ice
April 9	Devils, 2-1	at New Jersey
April 11	Devils, 4-2	at New Jersey
April 13	Devils, 3-0	at Boston
April 15	Bruins, 5-1	at Boston
April 17	Devils, 3-0	at New Jersey

Shutouts: Brodeur, New Jersey (2).

	W-L	GF	Leading Scorers
Philadelphia	4-3	24	Recchi (6-3–9)
Toronto	3-4	16	Mogilny (5-2–7)

Date	Winner	Home Ice
April 9	Maple Leafs, 5-3	at Philadelphia
April 11	Flyers, 4-1	at Philadelphia
April 14	Maple Leafs, 4-3 (2OT)	at Toronto
April 16	Flyers, 3-2 (3OT)	at Toronto
April 19	Flyers, 4-1	at Philadelphia
April 21	Maple Leafs, 2-1 (2OT)	at Toronto
April 22	Flyers, 6-1	at Philadelphia

SEMIFINALS (Best of 7)

	W-L	GF	Leading Scorers
Ottawa	4-2	17	Hossa (2-6–8)
Philadelphia	2-4	10	Handzus (2-2–4)

Date	Winner	Home Ice
April 25	Senators, 4-2	at Ottawa
April 27	Flyers, 2-0	at Ottawa
April 29	Senators, 3-2 (OT)	at Philadelphia
May 1	Flyers, 1-0	at Philadelphia
May 3	Senators, 5-2	at Ottawa
May 5	Senators, 5-1	at Philadelphia

Shutouts: Cechmanek, Philadelphia (2).

	W-L	GF	Leading Scorers
New Jersey	4-1	14	Gomez (1-6–7)
Tampa Bay	1-4	8	St. Louis (2-1–3) & Richards (0-3–3)

Date	Winner	Home Ice
April 24	Devils, 3-0	at New Jersey
April 26	Devils, 3-2 (OT)	at New Jersey
April 28	Lightning, 4-3	at Tampa Bay
April 30	Devils, 3-1	at Tampa Bay
May 2	Devils, 2-1 (3OT)	at New Jersey

Shutouts: Brodeur, New Jersey.

CHAMPIONSHIP (Best of 7)

	W-L	GF	Leading Scorers
New Jersey	4-3	17	Three tied with 5 pts.
Ottawa	3-4	13	Hossa (0-4–4)

Date	Winner	Home Ice
May 10	Senators, 3-2 (OT)	at Ottawa
May 13	Devils, 4-1	at Ottawa
May 15	Devils, 1-0	at New Jersey
May 17	Devils, 5-2	at New Jersey
May 19	Senators, 3-1	at Ottawa
May 21	Senators, 2-1 (OT)	at New Jersey
May 23	Devils, 3-2	at Ottawa

Shutouts: Brodeur, New Jersey.

STANLEY CUP FINAL (Best of 7)

	W-L	GF	Leading Scorers
New Jersey	4-3	19	Elias (3-4–7)
Anaheim	3-4	12	Sykora (2-3–5)

Date	Winner	Home Ice
May 27	Devils, 3-0	at New Jersey
May 29	Devils, 3-0	at New Jersey
May 31	Ducks, 3-2 (OT)	at Anaheim
June 2	Ducks, 1-0 (OT)	at Anaheim
June 5	Devils, 6-3	at New Jersey
June 7	Ducks, 5-2	at Anaheim
June 9	Devils, 3-0	at New Jersey

Shutouts: Brodeur, New Jersey (3), Giguere, Anaheim.

Conn Smythe Trophy (Playoff MVP)
Jean-Sebastien Giguere, Anaheim, G
15-6, 1.62 GAA, .945 save pct., 5 ShO

Stanley Cup Final Box Scores

Game 1

Tuesday, May 27, at New Jersey

Anaheim	.0	0	0	— **0**
New Jersey	.0	1	2	— **3**

2nd Period: NJ—Friesen 6 (Brylin, Gionta), 1:45.
3rd Period: NJ—Marshall 5 (Elias, Gomez), 5:34; NJ—Friesen 7 (White, Brodeur), 19:38 (en).
Shots on Goal: Anaheim—4-4-8—16; New Jersey—6-15-9—30. **Power plays:** Anaheim 0-2; New Jersey 0-1.
Goalies: Anaheim, Giguere (29 shots, 27 saves); New Jersey, Brodeur (16 shots, 16 saves). **Attendance:** 19,040. .

Game 2

Thursday, May 29, at New Jersey

Anaheim	.0	0	0	— **0**
New Jersey	.0	2	1	— **3**

2nd Period: NJ—Elias 3 (Tverdovsky, Gomez), 4:42 (pp); NJ—Gomez 2 (Tverdovsky, Elias), 12:11.
3rd Period: NJ—Friesen 8 (Gionta, Niedermayer), 4:22.
Shots on Goal: Anaheim—7-2-7—16; New Jersey—7-6-12—25. **Power plays:** Anaheim 0-3; New Jersey 1-4.
Goalies: Anaheim, Giguere (25 shots, 22 saves); New Jersey, Brodeur (16 shots, 16 saves). **Attendance:** 19,040.

Game 3

Saturday, May 31, at Anaheim

New Jersey	.0	1	0	0	— **2**
Anaheim	.0	2	0	1	— **3**

2nd Period: ANA—Chouinard 1 (Ozolinsh), 3:39; NJ—Elias 4 (Langenbrunner, Rafalski), 14:02; ANA—Ozolinsh 2 (Giguere), 14:47.
3rd Period: NJ—Gomez 3 (Marshall, Elias), 9:11.
Overtime: ANA—Salei 2 (Oates), 6:59.
Shots on Goal: New Jersey—8-12-8-3—31; Anaheim—9-9-10-5—33. **Power plays:** New Jersey 0-4; Anaheim 0-2.
Goalies: New Jersey, Brodeur (33 shots, 30 saves); Anaheim, Giguere (31 shots, 29 saves). **Attendance:** 17,174.

Game 4

Monday, June 2, at Anaheim

New Jersey	.0	0	0	0	— **0**
Anaheim	.0	0	0	1	— **1**

Overtime: ANA—Thomas 3 (Pahlsson, Ozolinsh), 0:39.
Shots on Goal: New Jersey—10-8-7-1—26; Anaheim—7-8-9-2—26. **Power plays:** New Jersey 0-3; Anaheim 0-1.
Goalies: New Jersey, Brodeur (26 shots, 25 saves); Anaheim, Giguere (26 shots, 26 saves). **Attendance:** 17,174.

Game 5

Thursday, June 5, at New Jersey

Anaheim	.2	1	0	— **3**
New Jersey	.2	2	2	— **6**

1st Period: ANA—Sykora 3 (Oates), 0:42; NJ—Rheaume 1 (Stevenson, Brylin), 3:35; NJ—Elias 5 (Rafalski, Gomez), 7:45 (pp); ANA—Rucchin 5 (Sykora, Kariya), 12:50.
2nd Period: NJ—Gionta 1 (Pandolfo, Niedermayer), 3:12; ANA—Pahlsson 2 (Niedermayer, Carney), 6:35; NJ—Pandolfo 5 (Gionta, Stevens), 9:02.
3rd Period: NJ—Langenbrunner 10 (Rupp, Niedermayer), 5:39; NJ—Langenbrunner 11 (Gionta), 12:52.
Shots on Goal: Anaheim—12-7-4—23; New Jersey—11-13-13—37. **Power plays:** Anaheim 0-1; New Jersey 1-4.
Goalies: Anaheim, Giguere (37 shots, 31 saves); New Jersey, Brodeur (23 shots, 20 saves). **Attendance:** 19,040.

Game 6

Saturday, June 7, at Anaheim

New Jersey	.0	1	1	— **2**
Anaheim	.3	1	1	— **5**

1st Period: ANA—Rucchin 6 (Kariya, Sykora), 4:26; ANA—Rucchin 7 (Leclerc, Niedermayer), 13:52; ANA—Thomas 4 (Kariya, Carney), 15:59 (pp).
2nd Period: NJ—Pandolfo 6 (Madden, Gionta), 2:18; ANA—Kariya 6 (Sykora, Oates), 17:15.
3rd Period: ANA—Sykora 4 (Chistov, Havelid), 3:51 (pp); NJ—Marshall 6 (Rafalski, Elias), 10:46 (pp).
Shots on Goal: New Jersey—9-10-9—28; Anaheim—9-10-5—24. **Power plays:** New Jersey 1-3; Anaheim 2-8.
Goalies: New Jersey, Brodeur (22 shots, 17 saves), Schwab (8:39 third, 2 shots, 2 saves); Anaheim, Giguere (28 shots, 26 saves). **Attendance:** 17,174.

Game 7

Monday, June 9, at New Jersey

Anaheim	.0	0	0	— **0**
New Jersey	.0	2	1	— **3**

2nd Period: NJ—Rupp 1 (Niedermayer, White), 2:22; NJ—Friesen 9 (Rupp, Niedermayer), 12:18.
3rd Period: NJ—Friesen 10 (Rupp, Stevens), 16:16.
Shots on Goal: Anaheim—5-9-10—24; New Jersey—7-12-6—25. **Power plays:** Anaheim 0-1; New Jersey 0-2.
Goalies: Anaheim, Giguere (25 shots, 22 saves); New Jersey, Brodeur (24 shots, 24 saves). **Attendance:** 19,040.

Stanley Cup Leaders

Scoring

	Gm	G	A	Pts	+/-	PM	PP
Jamie Langenbrunner, NJ	.24	11	7	**18**	11	16	1
Scott Niedermayer, NJ	.24	2	16	**18**	11	16	1
Marian Gaborik, Min	.18	9	8	**17**	2	6	4
John Madden, NJ	.24	6	10	**16**	10	2	2
Marian Hossa, Ott	.18	5	11	**16**	-1	6	3
Mike Modano, Dal	.12	5	10	**15**	2	4	1

Three tied with 14 pts. each.

Goaltending

(Minimum 390 minutes)

	Gm	Min	W-L	ShO	GAA
J-S Giguere, Ana	.21	1407	15-6	5	1.62
Martin Brodeur, NJ	.24	1491	16-8	7	1.65
Patrick Lalime, Ott	.18	1122	11-7	1	1.82
Marty Turco, Dal	.12	798	6-6	0	1.88
Manny Fernandez, Min	..9	552	3-4	0	1.96
Olaf Kolzig, Wash	..6	404	2-4	1	2.08

Final Stanley Cup Standings

				—Goals—		
	Gm	W	L	For	Opp	Dif
New Jersey	.24	16	8	63	41	+22
Anaheim	.21	15	6	45	40	+5
Ottawa	.18	11	7	43	34	+9
Minnesota	.18	8	10	43	43	—
Vancouver	.14	7	7	34	47	-13
Dallas	.12	6	6	34	25	+9
Philadelphia	.13	6	7	34	33	+1
Tampa Bay	.11	5	6	22	29	-7
St. Louis	..7	3	4	21	17	+4
Colorado	..7	3	4	17	16	+1
Toronto	..7	3	4	16	24	-8
Washington	..6	2	4	15	14	+1
Edmonton	..6	2	4	11	20	-9
Boston	..5	1	4	8	13	-5
NY Islanders	..5	1	4	7	13	-6
Detroit	.4	0	4	6	10	-4

Finalists' Composite Box Scores
New Jersey Devils (16-8)

Top Scorers	Pos	Gm	G	A	Pts	+/-	PM	PP	S	Gm	G	A	Pts	+/-	PM	PP	S
		Overall Playoffs								Finals vs Anaheim							
Jamie Langenbrunner	R	24	11	7	18	11	16	1	53	7	2	1	3	3	6	0	13
Scott Niedermayer	D	24	2	16	18	11	16	1	40	7	0	5	5	8	4	0	12
John Madden	C	24	6	10	16	10	2	2	77	7	0	1	1	0	0	0	21
Jeff Friesen	R	24	10	4	14	10	6	1	46	7	5	0	5	6	0	0	18
Patrik Elias	L	24	5	8	13	5	26	2	59	7	3	4	7	3	4	2	24
Jay Pandolfo	L	24	6	6	12	9	2	0	38	7	2	1	3	0	0	0	10
Scott Gomez	C	24	3	9	12	-3	2	0	56	7	2	3	5	2	0	0	19
Brian Rafalski	D	23	2	9	11	7	8	2	36	7	0	3	3	0	2	0	13
Joe Nieuwendyk	C	17	3	6	9	-2	4	1	24	0	0	0	0	0	0	0	0
Scott Stevens	D	24	3	6	9	14	14	1	33	7	0	2	2	2	2	0	6
Brian Gionta	R	24	1	8	9	5	6	0	59	7	1	5	6	3	2	0	21
Grant Marshall	R	24	6	2	8	3	8	2	47	7	2	1	3	3	4	1	8
Colin White	D	24	0	5	5	3	29	0	21	7	0	2	2	3	4	0	7
Michael Rupp*	C	4	1	3	4	4	0	0	2	4	1	3	4	4	0	0	2
Sergei Brylin	L	19	1	3	4	-4	8	0	25	7	0	2	2	0	2	0	9
Pascal Rheaume	C	24	1	2	3	-2	13	0	30	7	1	0	1	-3	2	0	8
Oleg Tverdovsky	D	15	0	3	3	-4	0	0	5	6	0	2	2	-2	0	0	1
Turner Stevenson	R	14	1	1	2	2	26	0	20	3	0	1	1	0	10	0	6
Tommy Albelin	D	16	1	0	1	3	2	0	6	0	0	0	0	0	0	0	3

Overtime goals—OVERALL (Langenbrunner, Marshall); FINALS (none). **Shorthanded goals**—OVERALL (Madden); FINALS (none). **Power Play conversions**—OVERALL (13 for 84, 15.5%); FINALS (3 for 21, 14.3%).

Goaltending	Gm	Min	GAA	GA	SA	Sv%	W-L	Gm	Min	GAA	GA	SA	Sv%	W-L
Corey Schwab	2	28	0.00	0	8	1.000	0-0	1	11	0.00	0	2	1.000	0-0
Martin Brodeur	24	1491	1.65	41	622	.934	16-8	7	416	1.73	12	160	.925	4-3
TOTAL	24	1520	1.62	41	630	.935	16-8	7	427	1.69	12	162	.926	4-3

Empty Net Goals—OVERALL (none), FINALS (none). **Shutouts**—OVERALL (Brodeur 7), FINALS (Brodeur 3). **Assists**—OVERALL (Brodeur), FINALS (Brodeur). **Penalty Minutes**—OVERALL (Brodeur 6), FINALS (none).

Mighty Ducks of Anaheim (15-6)

Top Scorers	Pos	Gm	G	A	Pts	+/-	PM	PP	S	Gm	G	A	Pts	+/-	PM	PP	S
		Overall Playoffs								Finals vs New Jersey							
Petr Sykora	R	21	4	9	13	3	12	1	58	7	2	3	5	-1	4	1	14
Adam Oates	C	21	4	9	13	2	6	3	18	7	0	3	3	-1	4	0	2
Paul Kariya	L	21	6	6	12	0	6	0	53	7	1	3	4	-1	2	0	10
Mike Leclerc	L	21	2	9	11	3	12	1	55	7	0	1	1	-5	8	0	20
Steve Rucchin	C	21	7	3	10	-2	2	1	46	7	3	0	3	-2	0	0	14
Rob Niedermayer	L	21	3	7	10	-5	18	0	41	7	0	2	2	-5	4	0	10
Steve Thomas	R	21	4	4	8	2	8	2	40	7	2	0	2	-4	4	1	12
Sandis Ozolinsh*	D	21	2	6	8	8	10	0	39	7	1	2	3	-1	0	0	14
Stanislav Chistov*	L	21	4	2	6	4	8	0	33	7	0	1	1	-3	2	0	6
Samuel Pahlsson	C	21	2	4	6	1	12	0	24	7	1	1	2	-3	4	0	5
Ruslan Salei	D	21	2	3	5	2	26	0	33	7	1	0	1	-2	8	0	13
Jason Krog	C	21	3	1	4	3	4	0	23	7	0	0	0	1	2	0	5
Niclas Havelid	D	21	0	4	4	0	2	0	29	7	0	1	1	-1	0	0	6
Keith Carney	D	21	0	4	4	3	16	0	26	7	0	2	2	-1	6	0	10
Kurt Sauer*	D	21	1	1	2	3	6	0	8	7	0	0	0	-4	2	0	3
Marc Chouinard	C	15	1	0	1	1	0	0	11	7	1	0	1	2	0	0	7
Dan Bylsma	R	11	0	1	1	3	2	0	12	7	0	0	0	2	2	0	8
Vitaly Vishnevski	D	21	0	1	1	-3	6	0	9	7	0	0	0	-3	0	0	3

Overtime goals—OVERALL (Sykora 2, Kariya, Leclerc, Rucchin, Thomas, Salei); FINALS (Thomas, Salei). **Shorthanded goals**—OVERALL (Niedermayer 2, Sauer); FINALS (none). **Power Play conversions**—OVERALL (8 for 70, 11.4%); FINALS (2 for 18, 11.1%).

Goaltending	Gm	Min	GAA	GA	SA	Sv%	W-L	Gm	Min	GAA	GA	SA	Sv%	W-L
Jean-Sebastien Giguere	21	1407	1.62	38	697	.945	15-6	7	426	2.54	18	201	.910	3-4
Martin Gerber	2	20	3.00	1	6	.833	0-0	0	0	0.00	0	0	—	0-0
TOTAL	21	1428	1.68	40	704	.943	15-6	7	427	2.67	19	202	.906	3-4

Empty Net Goals—OVERALL (1), FINALS (1). **Shutouts**—OVERALL (Giguere 5), FINALS (Giguere). **Assists**—OVERALL (Giguere), FINALS (Giguere). **Penalty Minutes**—OVERALL (none), FINALS (none).

Annual Awards

Voting for the Hart, Calder, Norris, Lady Byng, Selke, and Masterton Trophies is conducted after the regular season by the Professional Hockey Writers' Association. The Vezina Trophy is selected by the NHL general managers, while the Jack Adams Award is selected by NHL broadcasters. Points are awarded on 10–7–5–3–1 basis except for the Vezina Trophy and the Adams Award which are awarded 5–3–1.

Hart Trophy
For Most Valuable Player

	Pos	1st	2nd	3rd	4th	5th	Pts
Peter Forsberg, Col	...C	38	13	6	2	1—	508
Markus Naslund, Van	..L	5	26	17	7	4—	342
Martin Brodeur, NJ	...G	14	12	11	10	2—	311
Joe Thornton, Bos	C	0	6	6	15	14—	131
Todd Bertuzzi, Van	...R	2	2	7	7	10—	100

Calder Trophy
For Rookie of the Year

	Pos	1st	2nd	3rd	4th	5th	Pts
Barret Jackman, St.L	...D	39	15	1	2	0—	506
Henrik Zetterberg, Det	..L	18	33	9	2	0—	462
Rick Nash, Clb	L	2	3	19	15	9—	190
Tyler Arnason, Chi	C	1	3	13	11	17—	146
Ales Kotalik, Buf	......R	1	1	5	14	8—	92

Norris Trophy
For Best Defenseman

	1st	2nd	3rd	4th	5th	Pts
Nicklas Lidstrom, Det	.42	20	0	0	0—	560
Al MacInnis, St.L	20	38	4	0	0—	486
Derian Hatcher, Dal	...0	1	21	9	3—	142
Sergei Gonchar, Wash	.0	1	12	17	13—	131
Rob Blake, Col	0	0	8	5	7—	62

Vezina Trophy
For Outstanding Goaltender

	1st	2nd	3rd	Pts
Martin Brodeur, NJ	24	3	2—	131
Marty Turco, Dal	3	12	8—	59
Ed Belfour, Tor	2	5	3—	28
Patrick Roy, Col	1	2	6—	17
Patrick Lalime, Ott	0	3	1—	10

Lady Byng Trophy
For Sportsmanship and Gentlemanly Play

	Pos	1st	2nd	3rd	4th	5th	Pts
Alexander Mogilny, Tor	..R	10	5	6	11	2—	200
Nicklas Lidstrom, Det	..D	10	7	3	2	2—	172
Mike Modano, Dal	...C	6	4	3	7	6—	130
Milan Hejduk, Col	....R	3	6	3	3	2—	98
Marian Hossa, Ott	....R	4	3	3	4	3—	91

Selke Trophy
For Best Defensive Forward

	Pos	1st	2nd	3rd	4th	5th	Pts
Jere Lehtinen, Dal	....R	39	9	2	3	4—	476
John Madden, NJ	C	7	14	10	6	5—	241
Wes Walz, Min	C	2	8	6	7	3—	130
Peter Forsberg, Col	...C	5	5	5	2	5—	121
Michael Peca, NYI	C	2	6	6	5	11—	118

Adams Award
For Coach of the Year

	1st	2nd	3rd	Pts
Jacques Lemaire, Min	41	10	7—	242
John Tortorella, TB	8	18	13—	107
Jacques Martin, Ott	6	14	7—	79
Mike Babcock, Ana	3	10	13—	58
Dave Tippett, Dal	1	3	6—	20

AP/Wide World Photos
Colorado's **Peter Forsberg** made a triumphant return to the ice in 2002-03, grabbing the Art Ross and Hart Trophies.

Other Awards

Lester B. Pearson Award (NHL Players Assn. MVP)— Markus Naslund, Van.; **Jennings Trophy** (goaltenders with a minimum of 25 games played for team with fewest goals against)—(tie) Martin Brodeur, NJ and Roman Cechmanek/Robert Esche, Phi.; **Maurice "Rocket" Richard Trophy** (regular season goal-scoring leader)— Milan Hejduk, Col.; **Art Ross Trophy** (regular season points leader)—Peter Forsberg, Col.; **Masterton Trophy** (perseverance, sportsmanship, and dedication to hockey)—Steve Yzerman, Det.; **King Clancy Trophy** (leadership and humanitarian contributions to community)—Brendan Shanahan, Det.; **Lester Patrick Trophy** (outstanding service to hockey in the U.S.)—Willie O'Ree, Ray Bourque and Ron DeGregorio.

All-NHL Team

Voting by PHWA. Holdovers from 2001-02 first team in **bold**.

	First Team		Second Team
G	Martin Brodeur, NJ	G	Marty Turco, Dal
D	Al MacInnis, St.L	D	Derian Hatcher, Dal
D	**Nicklas Lidstrom**, Det	D	Sergei Gonchar, Wash
C	Peter Forsberg, Col	C	Joe Thornton, Bos
R	Todd Bertuzzi, Van	R	Milan Hejduk, Col
L	**Markus Naslund**, Van	L	Paul Kariya, Ana

All-Rookie Team

Voting by PHWA. Vote totals not released.

Pos		Pos	
G	Sebastien Caron, Pit	F	Tyler Arnason, Chi
D	Jay Bouwmeester, Fla	F	Rick Nash, Clb
D	Barret Jackman, St.L	F	Henrik Zetterberg, Det

2003 NHL Draft

First and second round selections at the 41st annual NHL Entry Draft held June 21-21, 2003, at Gaylord Entertainment Center in Nashville. The order of the first 14 positions were determined by a draft lottery of non-playoff teams held April 7 in New York City. Only the worst five teams from the 2002-03 regular season had the chance to win the first overall pick. No team could move up more than four spots in the draft order or drop more than one position. Positions 15 through 30 reflect regular season records in reverse order.

First Round

	Team	Player, Last Team	Pos
1	**a**-Pittsburgh	Marc-Andre Fleury, Cape Breton (QMJHL)	G
2	Carolina	Eric Staal, Peterborough (OHL)	C
3	**b**-Florida	Nathan Horton, Oshawa (OHL)	C
4	Columbus	Nikolai Zherdev, HC CSKA (Rus)	L
5	Buffalo	Thomas Vanek, Minnesota (WCHA)	L
6	San Jose	Milan Michalek, Budejovice (Cze)	R
7	Nashville	Ryan Suter, U.S. Nationall U-18	D
8	Atlanta	Braydon Coburn, Portland (WHL)	D
9	Calgary	Dion Phaneuf, Red Deer (WHL)	D
10	Montreal	Andrei Kastsitsyn, HC CSKA (Rus)	R
11	**c**-Philadelphia	Jeff Carter, Sault-Ste-Marie (OHL)	C
12	NY Rangers	Hugh Jessiman, Dartmouth (ECAC)	R
13	Los Angeles	Dustin Brown, Guelph (OHL)	R
14	Chicago	Brent Seabrook, Lethbridge (WHL)	D
15	NY Islanders	Robert Nilsson, Leksand (Swe)	C
16	**d**-San Jose	Steve Bernier, Moncton (QMJHL)	R
17	**e**-New Jersey	Zach Parise, North Dakota (WCHA)	C
18	Washington	Eric Fehr, Brandon (WHL)	R
19	Anaheim	Ryan Getzlaf, Calgary (WHL)	C
20	Minnesota	Brent Burns, Brampton (OHL)	R
21	**f**-Boston	Mark Stuart, Colorado Coll. (WCHA)	D
22	**g**-Edmonton	Marc-Antoine Pouliot, Rimouski (QMJHL)	C
23	Vancouver	Ryan Kesler, Ohio St. (CCHA)	C
24	Philadelphia	Mike Richards, Kitchener (OHL)	C
25	**h**-Florida	Anthony Stewart, Kingston (OHL)	R
26	**i**-Los Angeles	Brian Boyle, St. Sebastian's HS, Mass.	C
27	**j**-Los Angeles	Jeff Tambellini, Michigan (CCHA)	L
28	**k**-Anaheim	Corey Perry, London (OHL)	R
29	Ottawa	Patrick Eaves, Boston College (HE)	R
30	**l**-St. Louis	Shawn Belle, Tri-City (WHL)	D

Second Round

	Team	Player, Last Team	Pos
31	Carolina	Danny Richmond, Michigan (CCHA)	D
32	Pittsburgh	Ryan Stone, Brandon (WHL)	C
33	**m**-Dallas	Loui Eriksson, Frolunds Jr. (Swe)	L
34	**n**-Tampa Bay	Mike Egener, Calgary (WHL)	D
35	**o**-Nashville	Konstantin Glazachev, Yaroslavl (Rus)	L
36	**p**-Dallas	Vojtech Polak, Karlovy Vary (Cze)	L
37	Nashville	Kevin Klein, Tor. St. Michael's (OHL)	D
38	**q**-Florida	Kamil Kreps, Brampton (OHL)	C
39	Calgary	Tim Ramholt, Zurich (Swi)	D
40	Montreal	Cory Urquhart, Montreal (QMJHL)	C
41	**r**-Tampa Bay	Matt Smaby, Shatt. St. Mary's HS, Minn.	D
42	New Jersey	Peter Vrana, Halifax (QMJHL)	L
43	**s**-San Jose	Joshua Hennessy, Quebec (QMJHL)	C
44	Los Angeles	Konstantin Pushkaryov, Kamenogorsk (Kaz)	R
45	Boston	Patrice Bergeron, Acadia-Bathurst (QMJHL)	C
46	**t**-Columbus	Dan Fritsche, Sarnia (OHL)	C
47	**u**-San Jose	Matthew Carle, River City (USHL)	D
48	NY Islanders	Dimitri Chernykh, Chimik (Rus)	R
49	Nashville	Shea Weber, Kelowna (WHL)	D
50	**v**-NY Rangers	Ivan Baranka, Dubnica Jr. (Svk)	D
51	Edmonton	Colin McDonald, New England (EJHL)	R
52	Chicago	Corey Crawford, Moncton (QMJHL)	G
53	**w**-NY Rangers	Evgeni Tunik, Elektrostal (Rus)	C
54	**x**-Dallas	Brandon Crombeen, Barrie (OHL)	R
55	**y**-Florida	Stefan Meyer, Medicine Hat (WHL)	L
56	Minnesota	Patrick O'Sullivan, Mississauga (OHL)	C
57	Toronto	John Doherty, Phillips-Andover HS, Mass.	D
58	**z**-NY Islanders	Jeremy Colliton, Pr. Albert (WHL)	C
59	Chicago	Michal Barinka, Budejovice (Cze)	D
60	Vancouver	Marc-Andre Bernier, Halifax (QMJHL)	R
61	**aa**-Montreal	Maxim Lapierre, Montreal (QMJHL)	C
62	**bb**-St. Louis	David Backes, Lincoln (USHL)	C
63	Colorado	David Liffiton, Plymouth (OHL)	D
64	Detroit	James Howard, Maine (HE)	G
65	**cc**-Buffalo	Branislav Fabry, Bratislava Jr. (Svk)	R
66	**dd**-Boston	Masi Marjamaki, Red Deer (WHL)	L
67	Ottawa	Igor Mirnov, Dynamo (Rus)	R
68	**ee**-Edmonton	J-F Jacques, Baie Comeau (QMJHL)	L

Acquired picks: a—from Fla; **b**—from Pit; **c**—from Pho; **d**—from Bos; **e**—from TB; **f**—from Tor; **g**—from St.L; **h**—from Col; **i**—from Det; **j**—from Dal; **k**—from NJ; **m**—from Clb; **n**—from Fla; **o**—from Buf; **p**—from SJ; **q**—from Atl; **r**—from Pho; **s**—from NYR; **t**—from Chi; **u**—from Calg; **v**—from Bos; **w**—from Wash; **x**—from Ana; **y**—from Pit; **z**—from St.L; **aa**—from Phi; **bb**—from TB; **cc**—from Dal; **dd**—from SJ; **ee**—from NJ.

U.S. Division I College Hockey

Final regular season standings; overall records, including all postseason tournament games, in parentheses.

Central Collegiate Hockey Assn.

	W	L	T	Pts	GF	GA
*Ferris St. (31-10-1)	22	5	1	45	121	64
*Michigan (30-10-3)	18	7	3	39	111	72
*Ohio St. (25-13-5)	16	8	4	36	90	63
Michigan St. (23-14-2)	17	10	1	35	113	83
N. Michigan (22-17-2)	14	13	1	29	91	83
Miami-OH (21-17-3)	13	12	3	29	86	66
Notre Dame (17-17-6)	13	13	3	29	90	90
W. Michigan (15-21-2)	13	14	1	27	92	101
Alaska-Fairbanks (15-14-7)	10	11	7	27	78	104
Nebraska-Omaha (13-22-5)	9	17	2	20	64	97
Bowling Green (8-25-3)	5	20	3	13	71	116
Lake Superior (6-28-4)	3	24	1	7	40	108

Conf. Tourney Final: Michigan 5, Ferris St. 3.
*NCAA Tourney (3-3): Ferris St. (1-1), Michigan (2-1), Ohio St. (0-1).

College Hockey America

	W	L	T	Pts	GF	GA
Alab.-Huntsville (18-14-3)	13	5	2	28	88	59
Niagara (15-17-5)	11	4	5	27	77	60
*Wayne State (21-17-2)	11	7	2	24	62	56
Bemidji State (14-14-8)	10	6	4	24	58	46
Findlay (10-21-4)	3	13	4	10	41	77
Air Force (10-24-3)	2	15	3	7	45	73

Conf. Tourney Final: Wayne St. 3, Bemidji St. 2.
*NCAA Tourney (0-1): Wayne St. (0-1).
Note: For the first time in history, the winner of the CHA championship game earned an automatic bid to the NCAA tournament.

Eastern Collegiate Athletic Conf.

	W	L	T	Pts	GF	GA
*Cornell (30-5-1)	19	2	1	39	89	29
*Harvard (22-10-2)	17	4	1	35	94	47
Dartmouth (20-13-1)	13	9	0	26	77	71
Yale (18-14-0)	13	9	0	26	94	73
Brown (16-14-5)	10	8	4	24	65	54
Union (14-18-4)	10	10	2	22	62	68
Clarkson (12-20-3)	9	10	3	21	69	56
Colgate (17-19-4)	9	10	3	21	49	71
St. Lawrence (11-21-5)	7	12	3	17	65	80
Vermont (13-20-3)	8	14	0	16	58	85
Rensselaer (12-25-3)	4	15	3	11	49	84
Princeton (3-26-2)	2	18	2	6	46	99

Conf. Tourney Final: Cornell 3, Harvard 2 (OT).
*NCAA Tourney (2-2): Cornell (2-1), Harvard (0-1).

Hockey East Association

	W	L	T	Pts	GF	GA
*New Hampshire (28-8-6)	.15	5	4	34	84	55
*Boston College (24-11-4)	.16	6	2	34	97	55
*Maine (24-10-5)	.14	6	4	32	81	61
Providence (19-14-3)	.12	9	3	27	76	71
*Boston University (25-14-3)	.13	10	1	27	78	66
UMass-Amherst (19-17-1)	.10	14	0	20	60	80
Merrimack (12-18-6)	.7	13	4	18	59	80
UMass-Lowell (11-20-5)	.4	16	4	12	63	95
Northeastern (10-21-3)	.5	17	2	12	54	89

Conf. Tourney Final: New Hampshire 1, BU 0 (OT).
*NCAA Tourney (5-4): New Hampshire (3-1), Boston College (1-1), Boston University (1-1), Maine (0-1).

Metro Atlantic Athletic Conf.

	W	L	T	Pts	GF	GA
*Mercyhurst (22-13-2)	.19	5	2	40	105	73
Quinnipiac (22-13-1)	.18	7	1	37	109	72
Holy Cross (17-18-1)	.14	11	1	29	81	67
Sacred Heart (14-15-6)	.13	10	3	29	79	62
Army (15-16-0)	.13	13	0	26	67	72
Bentley (15-19-0)	.13	13	0	26	77	80
Canisius (12-21-4)	.11	13	2	24	66	71
Iona (11-22-2)	.11	14	1	23	80	80
American Int'l (10-20-2)	.9	16	1	19	66	105
Connecticut (8-23-3)	.7	16	3	17	74	102
Fairfield (8-23-2)	.7	17	2	16	67	87

Conf. Tourney Final: Mercyhurst 6, Quinnipiac 5.
*NCAA Tourney (0-1): Mercyhurst (0-1).

Western Collegiate Hockey Assn.

	W	L	T	Pts	GF	GA
*Colorado College (30-7-5)	.19	4	5	43	125	70
*Minnesota (28-8-9)	.15	6	7	37	106	81
*MSU-Mankato (20-11-10)	.15	6	7	37	116	104
*North Dakota (26-12-5)	.14	9	5	33	103	82
Minnesota-Duluth (22-15-5)	.14	10	4	32	95	80
*St. Cloud State (17-16-5)	.12	11	5	29	96	85
Denver (21-14-6)	.11	11	6	28	95	85
Wisconsin (13-23-4)	.7	17	4	18	61	101
Michigan Tech (10-24-4)	.7	18	3	17	77	116
Alaska-Anchorage (1-28-7)	.0	22	6	6	41	111

Conf. Tourney Final: Minnesota 4, Colorado College 2.
*NCAA Tourney (5-4): Minnesota (4-0), Colorado College (1-1), MSU-Mankato (0-1), N. Dakota (0-1), St. Cloud St. (0-1).

Hobey Baker Award

For College Hockey Player of the Year. Voting is done by a 25-member panel of college hockey personnel, national media, and pro scouts, plus a fan vote.

	Cl	Pos
Winner: Peter Sejna, Colorado College	Jr.	F

USA Today/American Hockey Magazine Coaches Poll

Taken after the NCAA Tournament. First place votes are in parentheses.

	League	W	L	T	Pts
1 Minnesota (17)	WCHA	28	8	9	255
2 New Hampshire	HE	28	8	6	238
3 Cornell	ECAC	30	5	1	218
4 Michigan	CCHA	30	10	3	207
5 Colorado College	WCHA	30	7	5	186
6 Ferris State	CCHA	31	10	1	158
7 Boston University	HE	25	14	3	152
8 Boston College	HE	24	11	4	150
9 Maine	HE	24	10	5	116
10 Harvard	ECAC	22	10	2	95

Scoring Leaders

Including postseason games; minimum 20 games.

	Cl	Gm	G	A	Pts	Avg
Peter Sejna, Colorado Col.	Jr.	42	36	46	82	**1.95**
Chris Kunitz, Ferris St.	Sr.	42	35	44	79	**1.88**
Noah Clarke, Colorado Col.	Sr.	42	21	49	70	**1.67**
Grant Stevenson, MSU-Mank.	So.	38	27	36	63	**1.66**
Joe Tallari, Niagara	Jr.	34	26	29	55	**1.62**

Goaltending Leaders

Including postseason games; minimum 15 games.

	Cl	Record	Sv%	GAA
Dave LeNeveu, Cornell	So.	28-3-1	.940	**1.20**
Frank Doyle, Maine	So.	10-4-5	.915	**2.14**
Mike Ayers, UNH	Jr.	27-8-6	.926	**2.18**
Matti Kaltiainen, BC	So.	18-9-3	.903	**2.21**
Mike Betz, Ohio St.	Jr.	20-11-5	.904	**2.24**

NCAA Division I Tournament

Regional seeds in parentheses

East Regional
Held in Providence, R.I., March 29-30.

First Round
(1) Cornell 5 . . . . (4) MSU-Mankato 2
(2) Boston College 1 . . . .(3) Ohio St. 0
Second Round
Cornell 2 . . . . .2OT . . . . .Boston College 1

Northeast Regional
Held in Worcester, Mass., March 28-29.

First Round
(1) New Hampshire 5 . . . . (4) St. Cloud St. 2
(2) Boston University 6 . . . .(3) Harvard 4
Second Round
New Hampshire 3 . . . . .Boston University 0

West Regional
Held in Minneapolis, Minn., March 28-29.

First Round
(1) Minnesota 9 . . . . (4) Mercyhurst 2
(2) Ferris St. 5 . . . .(3) North Dakota 2
Second Round
Minnesota 7 .Ferris St. 4

Midwest Regional
Held in Ann Arbor, Mich., March 29-30.

First Round
(1) Colorado College 4 . . . . (4) Wayne St. 2
(3) Michigan 2 . . . .(2) Maine 1
Second Round
Michigan 5 . . . . .Colorado College 3

THE FROZEN FOUR

Held at the HSBC Arena in Buffalo, N.Y., April 10 and April 12. Single elimination; no consolation game.

Semifinals

New Hampshire 3 . . . . .Cornell 2
Minnesota 3 . . . . .OT . . . . .Michigan 2

Championship Game

Minnesota, 5-1

New Hampshire (HE) . . . . .1 0 0 **—1**
Minnesota (WCHA) . . . . .1 0 4 **—5**
1st Period: MIN—Matt DeMarchi 8 (Garrett Smaagaard), 10:58; UNH—Sean Collins 22 (Nathan Martz, Justin Aikins), 19:41 (pp).
3rd Period: MIN—Thomas Vanek 31 (Matt Koalska), 8:14; MIN—Jon Waibel 9 (Vanek), 11:25; MIN—Barry Tallackson 8 (Gino Guyer, Chris Harrington), 13:34 (pp); MIN—Tallackson 9 (Grant Potulny), 18:31 (en).
Shots on Goal: New Hampshire—7-9-11—27; Minnesota—16-14-15—45. **Power plays:** New Hampshire 1-5; Minnesota 1-5.
Goalies: New Hampshire—Michael Ayers (44 shots, 40 saves); Minnesota—Travis Weber (27 shots, 26 saves). **Attendance:** 18,759.

Most Outstanding Player: Thomas Vanek, freshman forward; game-winning OT goal in semifinal game, game-winning goal in championship game, plus an assist in each.

All-Tournament Team: Vanek, defensemen Matt DeMarchi and Paul Martin and goalie Travis Weber of Minnesota; forwards Nathan Martz and Steve Saviano of New Hampshire.

Division I All-America

First team JOFA Division I All-Americans as chosen by the American Hockey Coaches Association. Holdover from 2001-02 All-America first team in **bold** type.

West Team

Pos		Yr	Hgt	Wgt
G	Mike Brown, Ferris St.	So	6-0	185
D	John-Michael Liles, Michigan St. . . .Sr		5-10	184
D	Tom Preissing, Colorado College . . .Sr		6-0	195
F	Noah Clarke, Colorado College . . .Sr		5-10	175
F	Chris Kunitz, Ferris St. . . . . .Sr		6-0	186
F	Peter Sejna, Colorado College . . . . Jr		5-11	200

East Team

Pos		Yr	Hgt	Wgt
G	David LeNeveu, Cornell . . . . .So		6-1	170
D	Freddy Meyer, Boston University . . .Sr		5-10	192
D	**Doug Murray**, Cornell . . . . .Sr		6-3	240
F	Ben Eaves, Boston College . . . . Jr		5-8	181
F	Chris Higgins, Yale . . . . .So		5-11	192
F	Dominic Moore, Harvard . . . . .Sr		6-1	190

Division III
Frozen Four

March 21-22 in Norwich, Vt.

Semifinals

Oswego St. (N.Y.) 6 . . . . .Middlebury (Vt.) 0
Norwich (Vt.) 6 . . . . .St. Norbert (Wisc.) 3

Championship

Norwich 2 . . . . .Oswego St. 1
Final records: Norwich (27-3-0); Oswego St. (25-7-1); St. Norbert (27-2-2); Middlebury (22-5-2).

Women's College Hockey

NCAA Division I Frozen Four

Held March 21 and 23 at the Duluth (Minn.) Entertainment Convention Center. Overall seeds in parentheses.

Semifinals

(1) Minnesota-Duluth 5 . . . .(4) Dartmouth 2
(2) Harvard 6 . . . .(3) Minnesota 1

Third Place

Dartmouth 4 . . . . .Minnesota 2

Championship

Minnesota-Duluth 4 . . . . .2OT . . . . .Harvard 3
Final records: Minnesota-Duluth (31-3-2); Harvard (30-3-1); Dartmouth (27-8-0); Minnesota (27-8-1).
Most Outstanding Player: Caroline Ouellette, Minnesota-Duluth sophomore forward; one goal and two assists in semifinal game, one goal in championship game.
All-Tournament Team: Ouellette, forwards Jenny Potter and Hanne Sikio of Minnesota-Duluth; defensemen Angela Ruggiero and forward Julie Chu of Harvard; goalie Amy Ferguson of Dartmouth.

NCAA Division III Championship

First round games held on campus sites of higher seed. Semifinals, finals and third place games held March 21-22 at the Murray Athletic Center in Elmira, N.Y. Overall seeds in parentheses.

First Round

at (4) Wisc.-River Falls 5 . . . . (5) St. Thomas (Minn.) 1
at (2) Manhattanville (N.Y.) 5 . . . . . .(7) Williams (Mass.) 1
at (3) Bowdoin (Maine) 3 . . . .(6) Middlebury (Vt.) 0

Semifinals

Manhattanville 4 .Bowdoin 1
(1) Elmira 2 .Wisc.-River Falls 1

Third Place

Bowdoin 4 . . . . .Wisc.-River Falls 2

Championship

Elmira 5 . . . . .Manhattanville 1
Final records: Elmira (23-4-2); Manhattanville (27-4-0); Bowdoin (23-2-3); Wisc.-River Falls (20-6-4).

Patty Kazmaier Award

For Women's College Hockey Player of the Year. Voting is done by a 13-member panel of national media, varsity college coaches, and one USA Hockey member.

		Cl	Pos
Winner: Jennifer Botterill, Harvard		Sr	F

MINOR LEAGUE HOCKEY

American Hockey League

Division champions (*) and playoff qualifiers (†) are noted. T denotes any game that was tied after regulation play and a five-minute overtime period. OL signifies any game that was tied after regulation play but lost in overtime. They are each worth one point in the standings.

Eastern Conference
East Division

Team (Affiliate)	W	L	T	OL	Pts	GF	GA
*Binghamton (Ott)	43	26	9	2	97	239	207
†Bridgeport (NYI)	40	26	11	3	94	219	198
†Hartford (NYR)	33	27	12	8	86	255	236
†Springfield (Pho/TB)	34	38	7	1	76	202	243
Albany (NJ)	25	37	11	7	68	197	235

North Division

Team (Affiliate)	W	L	T	OL	Pts	GF	GA
*Providence (Bos)	44	20	11	5	104	268	227
†Manchester (LA)	40	23	11	6	97	254	209
†Worcester (St.L)	35	27	15	3	88	235	220
†Portland (Wash)	33	28	13	6	85	221	195
Lowell (Car)	19	51	7	3	48	175	275

Canadian Division

Team (Affiliate)	W	L	T	OL	Pts	GF	GA
*Hamilton (Mon/Edm)	49	19	8	4	110	279	191
†Manitoba (Van)	37	33	8	2	84	229	228
St. John's (Tor)	32	40	6	2	72	236	285
Saint John (Calg)	32	41	6	1	71	203	223

Scoring Leaders

	Gm	G	A	Pts	PM
Steve Maltais, Chi.	79	30	56	86	86
Jean-Guy Trudel, Hou	79	31	54	85	85
Michel Picard, GR.	78	32	52	84	34
Mark Mowers, GR	78	34	47	81	47
Simon Gamache, Chi	76	35	42	77	37

Goaltending Leaders

(At least 1590 minutes)	GP	GAA	Sv%	Record
Craig Andersson, Nor	32	1.94	.923	15-11-5
Marc Lamothe, GR	60	2.13	.923	33-18-8
Rick DiPietro, Bri	34	2.14	.924	16-10-8

Western Conference
West Division

Team (Affiliate)	W	L	T	OL	Pts	GF	GA
*Houston (Min)	47	23	7	3	104	266	222
†Chicago (Atl)	43	25	8	4	98	276	237
†San Antonio (Fla)	36	29	11	4	87	235	226
†Milwaukee (Nash)	32	27	14	7	85	247	251
†Utah (Dal)	37	34	4	5	83	227	243

Central Division

Team (Affiliate)	W	L	T	OL	Pts	GF	GA
*Grand Rapids (Det)	48	22	8	2	106	240	177
†Rochester (Buf)	31	30	14	5	81	219	221
Cincinnati (Ana)	26	35	13	6	71	202	242
Syracuse (Clb)	27	41	8	4	66	201	256
Cleveland (SJ)	22	48	5	5	54	203	286

South Division

Team (Affiliate)	W	L	T	OL	Pts	GF	GA
*Norfolk (Chi)	37	26	12	5	91	201	187
†Hershey (Col)	36	27	14	3	89	217	209
†Wilkes-Barre (Pit)	36	32	7	5	84	245	248
Philadelphia (Phi)	33	33	6	8	80	198	212

Calder Cup Finals

	W-L	GF	Leading Scorers
Houston	4-3	18	Domenichelli (2-5–7)
Hamilton	3-4	15	Ward (3-2–5)

Date	Winner	Home Ice
May 28	Houston, 2-1	at Hamilton
May 30	Hamilton, 2-1 (4OT)	at Hamilton
June 4	Hamilton, 4-2	at Houston
June 6	Houston, 3-2 (OT)	at Houston
June 7	Houston, 6-4	at Houston
June 9	Hamilton, 2-1	at Hamilton
June 12	Houston, 3-0	at Chicago

East Coast Hockey League

Division champions (*) and playoff qualifiers (†) are noted. GF and GA refer to goals for and against.

Northern Conference
Northeast Division

Team	W	L	T	Pts	GF	GA
*Atlantic City	41	19	12	94	268	224
†Greensboro	42	21	9	93	235	211
†Roanoke	42	24	6	90	265	239
†Trenton	38	24	10	86	229	207
Charlotte	41	28	3	85	262	234
Richmond	35	31	6	76	240	239
Reading	32	35	5	69	261	303

Northwest Division

Team	W	L	T	Pts	GF	GA
*Toledo	47	15	10	104	248	196
†Peoria	48	17	7	103	241	181
†Cincinnati	36	29	7	79	257	236
†Lexington	34	31	7	75	188	212
Johnstown	28	33	11	67	214	243
Wheeling	28	41	3	59	193	261
Dayton	24	38	10	58	191	247

Southern Conference
Southeast Division

Team	W	L	T	Pts	GF	GA
*Columbia	47	23	2	96	265	202
†South Carolina	42	22	8	92	248	225
†Pee Dee	40	26	6	86	244	213
†Florida	35	23	14	84	239	243
†Greenville	28	36	8	64	217	262
Augusta	27	39	6	60	203	256
Columbus	25	39	8	58	197	270

Southwest Division

Team	W	L	T	Pts	GF	GA
*Mississippi	44	24	4	92	250	211
†Louisiana	40	20	12	92	249	210
†Arkansas	37	24	11	85	238	236
†Jackson	38	26	8	84	210	195
†Pensacola	33	30	9	75	228	241
Baton Rouge	20	43	9	49	184	266

MINOR LEAGUE HOCKEY (Cont.)

Scoring Leaders

	Gm	G	A	Pts	PM
Buddy Smith, Ark	72	30	74	104	28
Rejean Stringer, Cba	72	37	59	96	16
Brian McCullough, Rea	69	39	56	95	84
Shawn McNeil, Lou	72	40	51	91	58
Steffon Walby, Miss	59	42	47	89	51

Goaltending Leaders

(At least 1440 minutes)	GP	GAA	Sv%	Record
Alfie Michaud, Peo	30	2.10	.927	20-4-4-4
Patrick Couture, Cba	39	2.42	.917	27-11-0-1
Adam Hauser, Jack	34	2.46	.916	20-9-4-4

Kelly Cup Finals

	W-L	GF	Leading Scorers
Atlantic City	4-1	13	Caudron (4-2–6)
			& Colley (5-1–6)
Columbia	1-4	7	Carruthers (3-1–4)

Date	Winner	Home Ice
May 7	Atlantic City, 1-0	at Columbia
May 9	Atlantic City, 3-0	at Columbia
May 10	Columbia, 5-3	at Atlantic City
May 12	Atlantic City, 3-1	at Atlantic City
May 14	Atlantic City, 3-1	at Atlantic City

World Hockey Championships

MEN

The World Hockey Championships, held in Helsinki, Turku and Tampere, Finland from April 26-May 11, 2003. Top three teams (*) in each group after preliminary round-robin advance to the second round. Fourth-place teams play in a consolation round. Top four teams (*) from each group of the second round advance to the quarterfinals.

Final Round Robin Standings

GROUP A	W-L-T	Pts	GF	GA
*Slovakia	3-0-0	6	22	5
*Germany	2-1-0	4	9	8
*Ukraine	1-2-0	2	9	13
Japan	0-3-0	0	6	20

GROUP B	W-L-T	Pts	GF	GA
*Russia	3-0-0	6	14	5
*Switzerland	2-1-0	4	9	7
*Denmark	1-2-0	2	8	14
United States	0-3-0	0	4	9

GROUP C	W-L-T	Pts	GF	GA
*Canada	3-0-0	6	12	2
*Sweden	2-1-0	4	6	5
*Latvia	1-2-0	2	6	9
Belarus	0-3-0	0	1	9

GROUP D	W-L-T	Pts	GF	GA
*Czech Republic	3-0-0	6	15	4
*Finland	2-1-0	4	18	3
*Austria	1-2-0	2	8	15
Slovenia	0-3-0	0	4	23

Second Round

GROUP E	W-L-T	Pts	GF	GA
*Slovakia	5-0-1	11	37	10
*Czech Republic	5-0-1	11	32	9
*Finland	3-2-1	7	29	10
*Germany	3-2-1	7	16	15
Austria	2-4-0	4	15	29
Ukraine	1-5-0	2	11	27

GROUP F	W-L-T	Pts	GF	GA
*Canada	5-0-1	11	21	6
*Sweden	5-1-0	10	22	10
*Russia	3-3-0	6	19	16
*Switzerland	3-3-0	6	15	16
Latvia	3-3-0	6	14	16
Denmark	1-4-1	3	13	27

Note: Although they all finished the second round with six points, Russia and Switzerland advanced to the playoff round over Latvia due to a better goal differential.

Quarterfinals

Canada 3	OT	Germany 2
Sweden 6		Finland 5
Czech Republic 3		Russia 0
Slovakia 3		Switzerland 1

Semifinals

Canada 8	Czech Republic 4
Sweden 4	Slovakia 1

Bronze Medal Game

Slovakia 4	Czech Republic 2

Gold Medal Game

Canada 3	OT	Sweden 2

Scoring Leaders

	Gm	G	A	Pts	PM
Zigmund Palffy, Slovakia	9	7	8	15	18
Jozef Stumpel, Slovakia	9	4	11	15	0
Lubomir Visnovsky, Slovakia	9	4	8	12	2
Teemu Selanne, Finland	7	8	3	11	2
Saku Koivu, Finland	7	1	10	11	4

Four tied with 10 pts. each.

Goaltending Leaders

(At least 200 minutes)	Gm	Min	Sv%	GAA
Sean Burke, Canada	6	328	.955	1.28
Mikael Tellqvist, Sweden	7	393	.940	1.37
Marco Buhrer, Switzerland	5	297	.934	1.82
Jan Lasak, Slovakia	6	359	.935	1.84
Tomas Vokoun, Czech Republic	7	388	.925	2.16

Tournament All-Star Team
(Selected by media)

First team: G—Sean Burke, Canada; **D**—Lubomir Visnovsky, Slovakia; Jay Bouwmeester, Canada; **F**—Mats Sundin, Sweden (MVP); Dany Heatley, Canada; Peter Forsberg, Sweden.

Note: The 2003 IIHF Women's World Championship, scheduled for April 3-9 in Beijing, China, was cancelled due to risks surrounding the SARS virus.

1893-2003
Through the Years

SPORTS ALMANAC

The Stanley Cup

The Stanley Cup was originally donated to the Canadian Amateur Hockey Association by Sir Frederick Arthur Stanley, Lord Stanley of Preston and 16th Earl of Derby, who had become interested in the sport while Governor General of Canada from 1888 to 1893. Stanley wanted the trophy to be a challenge cup, contested for each year by the best amateur hockey teams in Canada.

In 1893, the Cup was presented without a challenge to the AHA champion Montreal Amateur Athletic Association team. Every year since, however, there has been a playoff. In 1914, Cup trustees limited the field challenging for the trophy to the champion of the eastern professional National Hockey Association (NHA, organized in 1910) and the western professional Pacific Coast Hockey Association (PCHA, organized in 1912).

The NHA disbanded in 1917 and the National Hockey League (NHL) was formed. From 1918 to 1926, the NHL and PCHA champions played for the Cup with the Western Canada Hockey League (WCHL) champion joining in a three-way challenge in 1923 and '24. The PCHA disbanded in 1924, while the WCHL became the Western Hockey League (WHL) for the 1925-26 season and folded the following year. The NHL playoffs have decided the winner of the Stanley Cup ever since.

Champions, 1893-1917

Multiple winners: Montreal Victorias and Montreal Wanderers (4); Montreal Amateur Athletic Association and Ottawa Silver Seven (3); Montreal Shamrocks, Ottawa Senators, Quebec Bulldogs and Winnipeg Victorias (2).

Year		Year		Year	
1893	Montreal AAA	1901	Winnipeg Victorias	1909	Ottawa Senators
1894	Montreal AAA	1902	Montreal AAA	1910	Montreal Wanderers
1895	Montreal Victorias	1903	Ottawa Silver Seven	1911	Ottawa Senators
1896	(Feb.) Winnipeg Victorias	1904	Ottawa Silver Seven	1912	Quebec Bulldogs
	(Dec.) Montreal Victorias	1905	Ottawa Silver Seven	1913	Quebec Bulldogs
1897	Montreal Victorias	1906	Montreal Wanderers	1914	Toronto Blueshirts (NHA)
1898	Montreal Victorias	1907	(Jan.) Kenora Thistles	1915	Vancouver Millionaires (PCHA)
1899	Montreal Shamrocks		(Mar.) Montreal Wanderers	1916	Montreal Canadiens (NHA)
1900	Montreal Shamrocks	1908	Montreal Wanderers	1917	Seattle Metropolitans (PCHA)

Champions Since 1918

Multiple winners: Montreal Canadiens (23); Toronto Arenas-St. Pats-Maple Leafs (13); Detroit Red Wings (10); Boston Bruins and Edmonton Oilers (5); NY Islanders, NY Rangers and Ottawa Senators (4); Chicago Blackhawks and New Jersey Devils (3); Colorado Avalanche, Montreal Maroons, Philadelphia Flyers and Pittsburgh Penguins (2).

Year	Winner	Head Coach	Series	Loser	Head Coach
1918	Toronto Arenas	Dick Carroll	3-2 (WLWLW)	Vancouver (PCHA)	Frank Patrick
1919	No Decision*				
1920	Ottawa	Pete Green	3-2 (WWLLW)	Seattle (PCHA)	Pete Muldoon
1921	Ottawa	Pete Green	3-2 (LWWLW)	Vancouver (PCHA)	Frank Patrick
1922	Toronto St. Pats	Eddie Powers	3-2 (LWLWW)	Vancouver (PCHA)	Frank Patrick
1923	Ottawa	Pete Green	3-1 (WLWW)	Vancouver (PCHA)	Frank Patrick
			2-0	Edmonton (WCHL)	K.C. McKenzie
1924	Montreal	Leo Dandurand	2-0	Vancouver (PCHA)	Frank Patrick
			2-0	Calgary (WCHL)	Eddie Oatman
1925	Victoria (WCHL)	Lester Patrick	3-1 (WWLW)	Montreal	Leo Dandurand
1926	Montreal Maroons	Eddie Gerard	3-1 (WWLW)	Victoria (WHL)	Lester Patrick
1927	Ottawa	Dave Gill	2-0-2 (TWTW)	Boston	Art Ross
1928	NY Rangers	Lester Patrick	3-2 (LWLWW)	Montreal Maroons	Eddie Gerard
1929	Boston	Cy Denneny	2-0	NY Rangers	Lester Patrick
1930	Montreal	Cecil Hart	2-0	Boston	Art Ross
1931	Montreal	Cecil Hart	3-2 (WLLWW)	Chicago	Art Duncan
1932	Toronto	Dick Irvin	3-0	NY Rangers	Lester Patrick
1933	NY Rangers	Lester Patrick	3-1 (WWLW)	Toronto	Dick Irvin
1934	Chicago	Tommy Gorman	3-1 (WWLW)	Detroit	Jack Adams
1935	Montreal Maroons	Tommy Gorman	3-0	Toronto	Dick Irvin
1936	Detroit	Jack Adams	3-1 (WWLW)	Toronto	Dick Irvin
1937	Detroit	Jack Adams	3-2 (LWLWW)	NY Rangers	Lester Patrick
1938	Chicago	Bill Stewart	3-1 (WLWW)	Toronto	Dick Irvin
1939	Boston	Art Ross	4-1 (WLWWW)	Toronto	Dick Irvin

* The 1919 finals were cancelled after five games due to an influenza epidemic with Montreal and Seattle (PCHA) tied at 2-2-1.

The Stanley Cup (Cont.)

Year	Winner	Head Coach	Series	Loser	Head Coach
1940	NY Rangers	Frank Boucher	4-2 (WWLLWW)	Toronto	Dick Irvin
1941	Boston	Cooney Weiland	4-0	Detroit	Jack Adams
1942	Toronto	Hap Day	4-3 (LLLWWWW)	Detroit	Jack Adams
1943	Detroit	Ebbie Goodfellow	4-0	Boston	Art Ross
1944	Montreal	Dick Irvin	4-0	Chicago	Paul Thompson
1945	Toronto	Hap Day	4-3 (WWWLLLW)	Detroit	Jack Adams
1946	Montreal	Dick Irvin	4-1 (WWWLW)	Boston	Dit Clapper
1947	Toronto	Hap Day	4-2 (LWWWLW)	Montreal	Dick Irvin
1948	Toronto	Hap Day	4-0	Detroit	Tommy Ivan
1949	Toronto	Hap Day	4-0	Detroit	Tommy Ivan
1950	Detroit	Tommy Ivan	4-3 (WLWLLWW)	NY Rangers	Lynn Patrick
1951	Toronto	Joe Primeau	4-1 (WLWWW)	Montreal	Dick Irvin
1952	Detroit	Tommy Ivan	4-0	Montreal	Dick Irvin
1953	Montreal	Dick Irvin	4-1 (WLWWW)	Boston	Lynn Patrick
1954	Detroit	Tommy Ivan	4-3 (WWLLWLW)	Montreal	Dick Irvin
1955	Detroit	Jimmy Skinner	4-3 (WWLLWLW)	Montreal	Dick Irvin
1956	Montreal	Toe Blake	4-1 (WWLWW)	Detroit	Jimmy Skinner
1957	Montreal	Toe Blake	4-1 (WWLWW)	Boston	Milt Schmidt
1958	Montreal	Toe Blake	4-2 (WLWLWW)	Boston	Milt Schmidt
1959	Montreal	Toe Blake	4-1 (WWLWW)	Toronto	Punch Imlach
1960	Montreal	Toe Blake	4-0	Toronto	Punch Imlach
1961	Chicago	Rudy Pilous	4-2 (WLWLWW)	Detroit	Sid Abel
1962	Toronto	Punch Imlach	4-2 (WWLLWW)	Chicago	Rudy Pilous
1963	Toronto	Punch Imlach	4-1 (WWLWW)	Detroit	Sid Abel
1964	Toronto	Punch Imlach	4-3 (WLLWLWW)	Detroit	Sid Abel
1965	Montreal	Toe Blake	4-3 (WWLLWLW)	Chicago	Billy Reay
1966	Montreal	Toe Blake	4-2 (LLWWWW)	Detroit	Sid Abel
1967	Toronto	Punch Imlach	4-2 (LWWLWW)	Montreal	Toe Blake
1968	Montreal	Toe Blake	4-0	St. Louis	Scotty Bowman
1969	Montreal	Claude Ruel	4-0	St. Louis	Scotty Bowman
1970	Boston	Harry Sinden	4-0	St. Louis	Scotty Bowman
1971	Montreal	Al MacNeil	4-3 (LLWWLWW)	Chicago	Billy Reay
1972	Boston	Tom Johnson	4-2 (WWLWLW)	NY Rangers	Emile Francis
1973	Montreal	Scotty Bowman	4-2 (WWLWLW)	Chicago	Billy Reay
1974	Philadelphia	Fred Shero	4-2 (LWWLWW)	Boston	Bep Guidolin
1975	Philadelphia	Fred Shero	4-2 (WWLLWW)	Buffalo	Floyd Smith
1976	Montreal	Scotty Bowman	4-0	Philadelphia	Fred Shero
1977	Montreal	Scotty Bowman	4-0	Boston	Don Cherry
1978	Montreal	Scotty Bowman	4-2 (WWLLWW)	Boston	Don Cherry
1979	Montreal	Scotty Bowman	4-1 (LWWWW)	NY Rangers	Fred Shero
1980	NY Islanders	Al Arbour	4-2 (WLWLWW)	Philadelphia	Pat Quinn
1981	NY Islanders	Al Arbour	4-1 (WWWLW)	Minnesota	Glen Sonmor
1982	NY Islanders	Al Arbour	4-0	Vancouver	Roger Neilson
1983	NY Islanders	Al Arbour	4-0	Edmonton	Glen Sather
1984	Edmonton	Glen Sather	4-1 (WLWWW)	NY Islanders	Al Arbour
1985	Edmonton	Glen Sather	4-1 (LWWWW)	Philadelphia	Mike Keenan
1986	Montreal	Jean Perron	4-1 (LWWWW)	Calgary	Bob Johnson
1987	Edmonton	Glen Sather	4-3 (WWLWLLW)	Philadelphia	Mike Keenan
1988	Edmonton	Glen Sather	4-0	Boston	Terry O'Reilly
1989	Calgary	Terry Crisp	4-2 (WLLLWW)	Montreal	Pat Burns
1990	Edmonton	John Muckler	4-1 (WWLWW)	Boston	Mike Milbury
1991	Pittsburgh	Bob Johnson	4-2 (LWLWWW)	Minnesota	Bob Gainey
1992	Pittsburgh	Scotty Bowman	4-0	Chicago	Mike Keenan
1993	Montreal	Jacques Demers	4-1 (LWWWW)	Los Angeles	Barry Melrose
1994	NY Rangers	Mike Keenan	4-3 (LWWWLLW)	Vancouver	Pat Quinn
1995	New Jersey	Jacques Lemaire	4-0	Detroit	Scotty Bowman
1996	Colorado	Marc Crawford	4-0	Florida	Doug MacLean
1997	Detroit	Scotty Bowman	4-0	Philadelphia	Terry Murray
1998	Detroit	Scotty Bowman	4-0	Washington	Ron Wilson
1999	Dallas	Ken Hitchcock	4-2 (LWWLWW)	Buffalo	Lindy Ruff
2000	New Jersey	Larry Robinson	4-2 (WLWWLW)	Dallas	Ken Hitchcock
2001	Colorado	Bob Hartley	4-3 (WLWLLWW)	New Jersey	Larry Robinson
2002	Detroit	Scotty Bowman	4-1 (LWWWW)	Carolina	Paul Maurice
2003	New Jersey	Pat Burns	4-3 (WWLLWLW)	Anaheim	Mike Babcock

M.J. O'Brien Trophy

Donated by Canadian mining magnate M.J. O'Brien, whose son Ambrose founded the National Hockey Association in 1910. Originally presented to the NHA champion until the league's demise in 1917, the trophy then passed to the NHL champion through 1927: It was awarded to the NHL's Canadian Division winner from 1927-38 and the Stanley Cup runner-up from 1939-50 before being retired in 1950.

NHA winners included the Montreal Wanderers (1910), original Ottawa Senators (1911 and '15), Quebec Bulldogs (1912 and '13), Toronto Blueshirts (1914) and Montreal Canadiens (1916 and '17).

Conn Smythe Trophy

The Most Valuable Player of the Stanley Cup Playoffs, as selected by the Pro Hockey Writers Association. Presented since 1965 by Maple Leaf Gardens Limited in the name of the former Toronto coach, GM and owner, Conn Smythe. Winners who did not play for the Cup champion are in **bold** type.

Multiple winners: Patrick Roy (3); Wayne Gretzky, Mario Lemieux, Bobby Orr and Bernie Parent (2).

Year		Year		Year	
1965	Jean Beliveau, Mon., C	1978	Larry Robinson, Mon., D	1991	Mario Lemieux, Pit., C
1966	**Roger Crozier**, Det., G	1979	Bob Gainey, Mon., LW	1992	Mario Lemieux, Pit., C
1967	Dave Keon, Tor., C	1980	Bryan Trottier, NYI, C	1993	Patrick Roy, Mon., G
1968	**Glenn Hall**, St.L., G	1981	Butch Goring, NYI, C	1994	Brian Leetch, NYR, D
1969	Serge Savard, Mon., D	1982	Mike Bossy, NYI, RW	1995	Claude Lemieux, NJ, RW
1970	Bobby Orr, Bos., D	1983	Billy Smith, NYI, G	1996	Joe Sakic, Col., C
1971	Ken Dryden, Mon., G	1984	Mark Messier, Edm., LW	1997	Mike Vernon, Det., G
1972	Bobby Orr, Bos., D	1985	Wayne Gretzky, Edm., C	1998	Steve Yzerman, Det., C
1973	Yvan Cournoyer, Mon., RW	1986	Patrick Roy, Mon., G	1999	Joe Nieuwendyk, Dal., C
1974	Bernie Parent, Phi., G	1987	**Ron Hextall**, Phi., G	2000	Scott Stevens, NJ, D
1975	Bernie Parent, Phi., G	1988	Wayne Gretzky, Edm., C	2001	Patrick Roy, Col., G
1976	**Reggie Leach**, Phi., RW	1989	Al MacInnis, Calg., D	2002	Nicklas Lidstrom, Det., D
1977	Guy Lafleur, Mon., RW	1990	Bill Ranford, Edm., G	2003	**J-S Giguere**, Ana., G

Note: Ken Dryden (1971) and Patrick Roy (1986) are the only players to win as rookies.

All-Time Stanley Cup Playoff Leaders
CAREER

Stanley Cup Playoff leaders through 2003. Years listed indicate number of playoff appearances. Players active in 2003 are in **bold** type; (DNP) indicates player that was active in 2003 but did not participate in playoffs.

Scoring

Points

		Yrs	Gm	G	A	Pts
1	Wayne Gretzky	16	208	122	260	382
2	**Mark Messier** (DNP)	17	236	109	186	295
3	Jari Kurri	14	200	106	127	233
4	Glenn Anderson	15	225	93	121	214
5	Paul Coffey	16	194	59	137	196
6	**Doug Gilmour** (DNP)	17	182	60	128	188
7	**Brett Hull**	18	190	100	85	185
8	Bryan Trottier	17	221	71	113	184
9	Ray Bourque	21	214	41	139	180
10	Jean Beliveau	17	162	79	97	176
	Steve Yzerman	18	181	67	109	176
12	Denis Savard	16	169	66	109	175
13	**Mario Lemieux** (DNP)	8	107	76	96	172
14	Denis Potvin	14	185	56	108	164
15	**Sergei Fedorov**	13	162	50	113	163
16	Mike Bossy	10	129	85	75	160
	Gordie Howe	20	157	68	92	160
	Bobby Smith	13	184	64	96	160
	Al MacInnis	19	177	39	121	160
20	**Claude Lemieux**	17	233	80	78	158
21	**Joe Sakic**	10	142	71	86	157
22	**Adam Oates**	15	163	42	114	156
23	**Jaromir Jagr**	12	146	67	87	154
24	Larry Murphy	20	215	37	115	152
25	Stan Mikita	18	155	59	91	150

Goals

		Yrs	Gm	G
1	Wayne Gretzky	16	208	122
2	**Mark Messier** (DNP)	17	236	109
3	Jari Kurri	14	200	106
4	**Brett Hull**	18	190	100
5	Glenn Anderson	15	225	93
6	Mike Bossy	10	129	85
7	Maurice Richard	15	133	82
8	**Claude Lemieux**	17	233	80
9	Jean Beliveau	17	162	79
10	**Mario Lemieux** (DNP)	8	107	76

Assists

		Yrs	Gm	A
1	Wayne Gretzky	16	208	260
2	**Mark Messier** (DNP)	17	236	186
3	Ray Bourque	21	214	139
4	Paul Coffey	16	194	137
5	**Doug Gilmour** (DNP)	17	182	128
6	Jari Kurri	15	200	127
7	Glenn Anderson	15	225	121
	Al MacInnis	19	177	121
9	Larry Robinson	20	227	116
10	Larry Murphy	20	215	115

The Stanley Cup (Cont.)

Goaltending
Wins

		Gm	W-L	Pct	GAA
1	**Patrick Roy**	247	151-94	.616	2.30
2	Grant Fuhr	150	92-50	.648	2.92
3	Billy Smith	132	88-36	.710	2.73
4	**Martin Brodeur**	139	83-56	.597	1.84
5	Ed Belfour	148	82-61	.573	2.17
6	Ken Dryden	112	80-32	.714	2.40
7	Mike Vernon	138	77-56	.579	2.68
8	Jacques Plante	112	71-37	.657	2.17
9	Andy Moog	132	68-57	.544	3.04
10	**Tom Barrasso** (DNP)	119	61-54	.530	3.01

Shutouts

		Gm	GAA	No
1	**Patrick Roy**	247	2.30	23
2	**Martin Brodeur**	139	1.84	20
3	Clint Benedict	48	1.80	15
	Jacques Plante	112	2.17	15
	Curtis Joseph	122	2.51	15

Appearances in Cup Finals

Standings of all teams that have reached the Stanley Cup championship round, since 1918.

App		Cup	Last Won
32	Montreal Canadiens	.23 *	1993
22	Detroit Red Wings	.10	2002
21	Toronto Maple Leafs	.13 †	1967
17	Boston Bruins	.5	1972
10	New York Rangers	.4	1994
10	Chicago Blackhawks	.3	1961
7	Philadelphia Flyers	.2	1975
6	Edmonton Oilers	.5	1990
5	New York Islanders	.4	1983
5	Vancouver Millionaires (PCHA)	.0	—
4	(original) Ottawa Senators	.4	1927
4	Minnesota/Dallas (North) Stars	.1	1999
4	New Jersey Devils	.3	2003
3	Montreal Maroons	.2	1935
3	St. Louis Blues	.0	—
2	Colorado Avalanche	.2	2001
2	Pittsburgh Penguins	.2	1992
2	Calgary Flames	.1	1989
2	Victoria Cougars (WCHL-WHL)	.1	1925
2	Buffalo Sabres	.0	—
2	Seattle Metropolitans (PCHA)	.0	—
2	Vancouver Canucks	.0	—
1	Mighty Ducks of Anaheim	.0	—
1	Calgary Tigers (WCHL)	.0	—
1	Carolina Hurricanes	.0	—
1	Edmonton Eskimos (WCHL)	.0	—
1	Florida Panthers	.0	—
1	Los Angeles Kings	.0	—
1	Washington Capitals	.0	—

*Les Canadiens also won the Cup in 1916 for a total of 24. Also, their final with Seattle in 1919 was cancelled due to an influenza epidemic that claimed the life of the Habs' Joe Hall.
†Toronto has won the Cup under three nicknames—Arenas (1918), St. Pats (1922) and Maple Leafs (1932,42,45,47-49,51,62-64,67).
Teams now defunct (7): Calgary Tigers, Edmonton Eskimos, Montreal Maroons, (original) Ottawa Senators, Seattle, Vancouver Millionaires and Victoria. Edmonton (1923) and Calgary (1924) represented the WCHL and later the WHL, while Vancouver (1918,1921-24) and Seattle (1919-20) played out of the PCHA.

Goals Against Average
Minimum of 50 games played

		Gm	Min	GA	GAA
1	**Martin Brodeur**	139	8702	267	1.84
2	George Hainsworth	52	3486	112	1.93
3	Turk Broda	101	6389	211	1.98
4	Dominik Hasek	97	5972	202	2.03
5	Jacques Plante	112	6652	240	2.16
6	**Ed Belfour**	148	9171	332	2.17
7	**Chris Osgood**	82	4798	178	2.23
8	**Patrick Roy**	247	15209	584	2.30
9	Ken Dryden	112	6846	274	2.40
10	Bernie Parent	71	4302	174	2.43

Note: Clint Benedict had an average of 1.80 but played in only 48 games.

Games Played

		Yrs	Gm
1	**Patrick Roy**, Mon-Col	17	247
2	Grant Fuhr, Edm-Buf-St.L	14	150
3	**Ed Belfour**, Chi-Dal-Tor	12	148
4	**Martin Brodeur**, New Jersey	11	139
5	Mike Vernon, Calg-Det-SJ-Fla	14	1,38

Miscellaneous
Championships

		Yrs	Cups
1	Henri Richard, Montreal	18	11
2	Yvan Cournoyer, Montreal	15	10
	Jean Beliveau, Montreal	17	10
4	Claude Provost, Montreal	14	9
5	Jacques Lemaire, Montreal	11	8
	Maurice Richard, Montreal	15	8
	Red Kelly, Detroit-Toronto	19	8

Years in Playoffs

		Yrs	Gm
1	Ray Bourque, Boston-Colorado	21	214
2	Gordie Howe, Detroit-Hartford	20	157
	Larry Robinson, Montreal-Los Angeles	20	227
	Larry Murphy, LA-Wash-Min-Pit-Tor-Det	20	215
	Scott Stevens, Wash-St.L-NJ	20	233

Games Played

		Yrs	Gm
1	**Mark Messier**, Edm-NYR-Van (DNP)	17	236
2	**Claude Lemieux**, Mon-NJ-Col-Pho-Dal	17	233
	Scott Stevens, Wash-St.L-NJ	20	233
4	Guy Carbonneau, Mon-St.L-Dal	17	231
5	Larry Robinson, Montreal-Los Angeles	20	227

Penalty Minutes

		Yrs	Gm	Min
1	Dale Hunter, Que-Wash-Col	18	186	729
2	Chris Nilan, Mon-NYR-Bos-Mon	12	111	541
3	**Claude Lemieux**, Mon-NJ-Col-Pho-Dal	17	233	529
4	Rick Tocchet, Phi-Pit-Bos-Pho	13	145	471
5	Willi Plett, Atl-Calg-Min-Bos	10	83	466

SINGLE SEASON
Scoring
Points

		Year	Gm	G	A	Pts
1	Wayne Gretzky, Edm	1985	18	17	30	47
2	Mario Lemieux, Pit	1991	23	16	28	44
3	Wayne Gretzky, Edm	1988	19	12	31	43
4	Wayne Gretzky, LA	1993	24	15	25	40
5	Wayne Gretzky, Edm	1983	16	12	26	38
6	Paul Coffey, Edm	1985	18	12	25	37
7	Mike Bossy, NYI	1981	18	17	18	35
	Wayne Gretzky, Edm	1984	19	13	22	35
	Doug Gilmour, Tor	1993	21	10	25	35
10	Six tied with 34 each.					

Goals

		Year	Gm	No
1	Reggie Leach, Philadelphia	1976	16	19
	Jari Kurri, Edmonton	1985	18	19
3	Joe Sakic, Colorado	1996	22	18
4	Seven tied with 17 each, incl. 3 times by Mike Bossy.			

Assists

		Year	Gm	No
1	Wayne Gretzky, Edmonton	1988	19	31
2	Wayne Gretzky, Edmonton	1985	18	30
3	Wayne Gretzky, Edmonton	1987	21	29
4	Mario Lemieux, Pittsburgh	1991	23	28
5	Wayne Gretzky, Edmonton	1983	16	26

Goaltending
Wins

1 15 tied with 16 each.

Shutouts

		Year	Gm	No
1	**Martin Brodeur**, New Jersey	2003	24	7
2	Dominik Hasek, Detroit	2002	23	6
3	**J-S Giguere**, Anaheim	2003	21	5

Goals Against Average

	(Min. 8 games played)	Year	Gm	Min	GA	GAA
1	Terry Sawchuk, Det.	1952	8	480	5	0.63
2	Clint Benedict, Mon-M	1928	9	555	8	0.89
3	Turk Broda, Tor.	1951	9	509	9	1.06
4	Dave Kerr, NYR	1937	9	553	10	1.11
5	Jacques Plante, Mon	1960	8	489	11	1.35

Note: Average determined by games played through 1942-43 season and by minutes played since then.

SINGLE SERIES
Points

	Year	Rd	G–A—Pts
Rick Middleton, Bos vs Buf	1983	DF	5-14—19
Wayne Gretzky, Edm vs Chi	1985	CF	4-14—18
Mario Lemieux, Pit vs Wash	1992	DSF	7-10—17
Barry Pedersen, Bos vs Buf	1983	DF	7-9—16
Doug Gilmour, Tor vs SJ	1994	CSF	3-13—16

Goals

	Year	Rd	No
Jari Kurri, Edm vs Chi	1985	CF	12
Newsy Lalonde, Mon vs Ott	1919	SF*	11
Tim Kerr, Phi vs Pit	1989	DF	10
Five tied with 9 each.			

*NHL final prior to Stanley Cup series with Seattle (PCHA).

Assists

	Year	Rd	No
Rick Middleton, Bos vs Buf	1983	DF	14
Wayne Gretzky, Edm vs Chi	1985	CF	14
Wayne Gretzky, Edm vs LA	1987	DSF	13
Doug Gilmour, Tor vs SJ	1994	CSF	13
Four tied with 11 each.			

SINGLE GAME
Points

	Date	G	A	Pts
Patrik Sundstrom, NJ vs Wash	4/22/88	3	5	8
Mario Lemieux, Pit vs Phi	4/25/89	5	3	8
Wayne Gretzky, Edm at Calg	4/17/83	4	3	7
Wayne Gretzky, Edm at Win	4/25/85	3	4	7
Wayne Gretzky, Edm vs LA	4/9/87	1	6	7

Goals

	Date	No
Newsy Lalonde, Mon vs Ott	3/1/19	5
Maurice Richard, Mon vs Tor	3/23/44	5
Darryl Sittler, Tor vs Phi	4/22/76	5
Reggie Leach, Phi vs Bos	5/6/76	5
Mario Lemieux, Pit vs Phi	4/25/89	5

Assists

	Date	No
Mikko Leinonen, NYR vs Phi	4/8/82	6
Wayne Gretzky, Edm vs LA	4/9/87	6
11 tied with 5 each.		

Five Longest Playoff Overtime Games

The 5 longest overtime games in Stanley Cup history. Note the following Series initials: SF (semifinals), CQF (conference quarterfinal), CSF (conference semifinal), DSF (division semifinal), QF (quarterfinal) and Final (Cup final). Series winners are in **bold** type; (*) indicates deciding game of series.

		OTs	Elapsed Time	Goal Scorer	Date	Series	Location
1	**Detroit** 1, Montreal Maroons 0	6	176:30	Mud Bruneteau	3/24/36	SF, Gm 1	Montreal
2	**Toronto** 1, Boston 0	6	164:46	Ken Doraty	4/3/33	SF, Gm 5	Toronto
3	**Philadelphia** 2, Pittsburgh 1	5	152:01	Keith Primeau	5/4/00	CSF, Gm 4	Pittsburgh
4	**Anaheim** 4, Dallas 3	5	140:48	Petr Sykora	4/24/03	CSF, Gm 1	Dallas
5	**Pittsburgh** 3 Washington 2	4	139:15	Petr Nedved	4/24/96	CQF, Gm 4	Washington

NHL All-Star Game

Three benefit NHL All-Star Games were staged in the 1930s for forward Ace Bailey and the families of Howie Morenz and Babe Siebert. Bailey, of Toronto, suffered a fractured skull on a career-ending check by Boston's Eddie Shore. Morenz, the Montreal Canadiens' legend, died of a heart attack at 35 after a severely broken leg ended his career. Siebert, who played with both Montreal teams, drowned at age 35.

The All-Star Game was revived at the start of the 1947-48 season as an annual exhibition match between the defending Stanley Cup champion and all-stars from the league's other five teams. The format has changed several times since then. The game was moved to midseason in 1966-67 and became an East vs. West contest in 1968-69. The Eastern (East, 1968-1974; Wales, 1975-93) Conference leads the series 18-8-1. From 1998-2002, the East-West format was abandoned for one pitting North America vs. the rest of the world (N. America leads that series 3-2). In 2003 the game returned to East vs. West.

NHL All-Star Game (Cont.)
Benefit Games

Date	Occasion		Host	Coaches
2/14/34	Ace Bailey Benefit	Toronto 7, All-Stars 3	Toronto	Dick Irvin, Lester Patrick
11/3/37	Howie Morenz Memorial	All-Stars 6, Montreals* 5	Montreal	Jack Adams, Ceil Hart
10/29/39	Babe Seibert Memorial	All-Stars 5, Canadiens 3	Montreal	Art Ross, Pit Lepine

*Combined squad of Montreal Canadiens and Montreal Maroons.

All-Star Games

Multiple MVP winners: Wayne Gretzky and Mario Lemieux (3); Bobby Hull and Frank Mahovlich (2).

Year		Host	Coaches	Most Valuable Player
1947	All-Stars 4, Toronto 3	Toronto	Dick Irvin, Hap Day	No award
1948	All-Stars 3, Toronto 1	Chicago	Tommy Ivan, Hap Day	No award
1949	All-Stars 3, Toronto 1	Toronto	Tommy Ivan, Hap Day	No award
1950	Detroit 7, All-Stars 1	Detroit	Tommy Ivan, Lynn Patrick	No award
1951	1st Team 2, 2nd Team 2	Toronto	Joe Primeau, Hap Day	No award
1952	1st Team 1, 2nd Team 1	Detroit	Tommy Ivan, Dick Irvin	No award
1953	All-Stars 3, Montreal 1	Montreal	Lynn Patrick, Dick Irvin	No award
1954	All-Stars 2, Detroit 2	Detroit	King Clancy, Jim Skinner	No award
1955	Detroit 3, All-Stars 1	Detroit	Jim Skinner, Dick Irvin	No award
1956	All-Stars 1, Montreal 1	Montreal	Jim Skinner, Toe Blake	No award
1957	All-Stars 5, Montreal 3	Montreal	Milt Schmidt, Toe Blake	No award
1958	Montreal 6, All-Stars 3	Montreal	Toe Blake, Milt Schmidt	No award
1959	Montreal 6, All-Stars 1	Montreal	Toe Blake, Punch Imlach	No award
1960	All-Stars 2, Montreal 1	Montreal	Punch Imlach, Toe Blake	No award
1961	All-Stars 3, Chicago 1	Chicago	Sid Abel, Rudy Pilous	No award
1962	Toronto 4, All-Stars 1	Toronto	Punch Imlach, Rudy Pilous	Eddie Shack, Tor., RW
1963	All-Stars 3, Toronto 3	Toronto	Sid Abel, Punch Imlach	Frank Mahovlich, Tor., LW
1964	All-Stars 3, Toronto 2	Toronto	Sid Abel, Punch Imlach	Jean Beliveau, Mon., C
1965	All-Stars 5, Montreal 2	Montreal	Billy Reay, Toe Blake	Gordie Howe, Det., RW
1966	No game (see below)			
1967	Montreal 3, All-Stars 0	Montreal	Toe Blake, Sid Abel	Henri Richard, Mon., C
1968	Toronto 4, All-Stars 3	Toronto	Punch Imlach, Toe Blake	Bruce Gamble, Tor., G
1969	West 3, East 3	Montreal	Scotty Bowman, Toe Blake	Frank Mahovlich, Det., LW
1970	East 4, West 1	St. Louis	Claude Ruel, Scotty Bowman	Bobby Hull, Chi., LW
1971	West 2, East 1	Boston	Scotty Bowman, Harry Sinden	Bobby Hull, Chi., LW
1972	East 3, West 2	Minnesota	Al MacNeil, Billy Reay	Bobby Orr, Bos., D
1973	East 5, West 4	NY Rangers	Tom Johnson, Billy Reay	Greg Polis, Pit., LW
1974	West 6, East 4	Chicago	Billy Reay, Scotty Bowman	Garry Unger, St.L., C
1975	Wales 7, Campbell 1	Montreal	Bep Guidolin, Fred Shero	Syl Apps Jr., Pit., C
1976	Wales 7, Campbell 5	Philadelphia	Floyd Smith, Fred Shero	Peter Mahovlich, Mon., C
1977	Wales 4, Campbell 3	Vancouver	Scotty Bowman, Fred Shero	Rick Martin, Buf., LW
1978	Wales 3, Campbell 2 (OT)	Buffalo	Scotty Bowman, Fred Shero	Billy Smith, NYI, G
1979	No game (see below)			
1980	Wales 6, Campbell 3	Detroit	Scotty Bowman, Al Arbour	Reggie Leach, Phi., RW
1981	Campbell 4, Wales 1	Los Angeles	Pat Quinn, Scotty Bowman	Mike Liut, St.L., G
1982	Wales 4, Campbell 2	Washington	Al Arbour, Glen Sonmor	Mike Bossy, NYI, RW
1983	Campbell 9, Wales 3	NY Islanders	Roger Neilson, Al Arbour	Wayne Gretzky, Edm., C
1984	Wales 7, Campbell 6	New Jersey	Al Arbour, Glen Sather	Don Maloney, NYR, LW
1985	Wales 6, Campbell 4	Calgary	Al Arbour, Glen Sather	Mario Lemieux, Pit., C
1986	Wales 4, Campbell 3 (OT)	Hartford	Mike Keenan, Glen Sather	Grant Fuhr, Edm., G
1987	No game (see below)			
1988	Wales 6, Campbell 5 (OT)	St. Louis	Mike Keenan, Glen Sather	Mario Lemieux, Pit., C
1989	Campbell 9, Wales 5	Edmonton	Glen Sather, Terry O'Reilly	Wayne Gretzky, LA, C
1990	Wales 12, Campbell 7	Pittsburgh	Pat Burns, Terry Crisp	Mario Lemieux, Pit., C
1991	Campbell 11, Wales 5	Chicago	John Muckler, Mike Milbury	Vincent Damphousse, Tor., LW
1992	Campbell 10, Wales 6	Philadelphia	Bob Gainey, Scotty Bowman	Brett Hull, St.L., RW
1993	Wales 16, Campbell 6	Montreal	Scotty Bowman, Mike Keenan	Mike Gartner, NYR, RW
1994	East 9, West 8	NY Rangers	Jacques Demers, Barry Melrose	Mike Richter, NYR, G
1995	No game (see below)			
1996	East 5, West 4	Boston	Doug MacLean, Scotty Bowman	Ray Bourque, Bos., D
1997	East 11, West 7	San Jose	Doug MacLean, Ken Hitchcock	Mark Recchi, Mon., RW
1998	North America 8, World 7	Vancouver	Jacques Lemaire, Ken Hitchcock	Teemu Selanne, Ana., RW
1999	North America 8, World 6	Tampa	Ken Hitchcock, Lindy Ruff	Wayne Gretzky, NYR, C
2000	World 9, North America 4	Toronto	Scotty Bowman, Pat Quinn	Pavel Bure, Fla., RW
2001	North America 14, World 12	Denver	Joel Quenneville, Jacques Martin	Bill Guerin, Bos., RW
2002	World 8, North America 5	Los Angeles	Scotty Bowman, Pat Quinn	Eric Daze, Chi., LW
2003	West 6, East 5 (OT)†	Florida	Marc Crawford, Jacques Martin	Dany Heatley, Atl., RW

†After a five-minute scoreless overtime, the game was settled by a shootout. The West outscored the East, 3-1.

No All-Star Game: in 1966 (moved from start of season to mid-season); in 1979 (replaced by Challenge Cup series with USSR); in 1987 (replaced by Rendez-Vous '87 series with USSR); and in 1995 (cancelled when NHL lockout shortened season to 48 games).

NHL Franchise Origins

Here is what the current 30 teams in the National Hockey League have to show for the years they have put in as members of the NHL, the early National Hockey Association (NHA) and the more recent World Hockey Association (WHA). League titles and Stanley Cup championships are noted by year won. The Stanley Cup has automatically gone to the NHL champion since the 1926-27 season. Following the 1992-93 season, the NHL renamed the Clarence Campbell Conference the Western Conference, while the Prince of Wales Conference became the Eastern Conference.

Western Conference

	First Season	League Titles	Franchise Stops
Anaheim, Mighty Ducks of	1993-94 (NHL)	None	•Anaheim, CA (1993—)
Calgary Flames	1972-73 (NHL)	1 Cup (1989)	•Atlanta (1972-80) Calgary (1980—)
Chicago Blackhawks	1926-27 (NHL)	3 Cups (1934,38,61)	•Chicago (1926—)
Colorado Avalanche	1972-73 (WHA)	1 WHA (1977) 2 Cups (1996, 2001)	•Quebec City (1972-95) Denver (1995—)
Columbus Blue Jackets	2000-01 (NHL)	None	•Columbus, OH (2000—)
Dallas Stars	1967-68 (NHL)	1 Cup (1999)	•Bloomington, MN (1967-93) Dallas (1993—)
Detroit Red Wings	1926-27 (NHL)	10 Cups (1936-37,43,50,52,54-55,97,98, 2002)	•Detroit (1926—)
Edmonton Oilers	1972-73 (WHA)	5 Cups (1984-85,87-88,90)	•Edmonton (1972—)
Los Angeles Kings	1967-68 (NHL)	None	•Inglewood, CA (1967-99) Los Angeles (1999—)
Minnesota Wild	2000-01 (NHL)	None	•St. Paul, MN (2000—)
Nashville Predators	1998-99 (NHL)	None	•Nashville, TN (1998—)
Phoenix Coyotes	1972-73 (WHA)	3 WHA (1976, 78-79)	•Winnipeg (1972-96) Phoenix (1996—)
St. Louis Blues	1967-68 (NHL)	None	•St. Louis (1967—)
San Jose Sharks	1991-92 (NHL)	None	•San Francisco (1991-93) San Jose (1993—)
Vancouver Canucks	1970-71 (NHL)	None	•Vancouver (1970—)

Eastern Conference

	First Season	League Titles	Franchise Stops
Atlanta Thrashers	1999-00 (NHL)	None	•Atlanta (1999—)
Boston Bruins	1924-25 (NHL)	5 Cups (1929,39,41,70,72)	•Boston (1924—)
Buffalo Sabres	1970-71 (NHL)	None	•Buffalo (1970—)
Carolina Hurricanes	1972-73 (WHA)	1 WHA (1973)	•Boston (1972-74) W. Springfield, MA (1974-75) Hartford, CT (1975-78) Springfield, MA (1978-80) Hartford (1980-97) Greensboro, NC (1997-99) Raleigh, NC (1999—)
Florida Panthers	1993-94 (NHL)	None	•Miami (1993-98) Sunrise, FL (1998—)
Montreal Canadiens	1909-10 (NHA)	2 NHA (1916-17) 2 NHL (1924-25) 24 Cups (1916,24,30-31,44,46,53,56-60,65-66,68-69,71,73,76-79,86,93)	•Montreal (1909—)
New Jersey Devils	1974-75 (NHL)	3 Cups (1995, 2000,03)	•Kansas City (1974-76) Denver (1976-82) E. Rutherford, NJ (1982—)
New York Islanders	1972-73 (NHL)	4 Cups (1980-83)	•Uniondale, NY (1972—)
New York Rangers	1926-27 (NHL)	4 Cups (1928,33,40,94)	•New York (1926—)
Ottawa Senators	1992-93 (NHL)	None	•Ottawa (1992-1996) Kanata, Ont. (1996—)
Philadelphia Flyers	1967-68 (NHL)	2 Cups (1974-75)	•Philadelphia (1967—)
Pittsburgh Penguins	1967-68 (NHL)	2 Cups (1991-92)	•Pittsburgh (1967—)
Tampa Bay Lightning	1992-93 (NHL)	None	•Tampa, FL (1992-93) St. Petersburg, FL (1993-96) Tampa, FL (1996—)
Toronto Maple Leafs	1916-17 (NHA)	2 NHL (1918,22) 13 Cups (1918,22,32,42,45,47-49,51,62-64,67)	•Toronto (1916—)
Washington Capitals	1974-75 (NHL)	None	•Landover, MD (1974-97) Washington, D.C. (1997—)

Note: The Hartford Civic Center roof collapsed after a snowstorm in January 1978, forcing the Whalers to move their home games to Springfield, Mass., for two years.

The Growth of the NHL

Of the four franchises that comprised the National Hockey League (NHL) at the start of the 1917-18 season, only two remain—the Montreal Canadiens and the Toronto Maple Leafs (originally the Toronto Arenas). From 1919-26, eight new teams joined the league, but only four—the Boston Bruins, Chicago Blackhawks (originally Black Hawks), Detroit Red Wings (originally Cougars) and New York Rangers—survived.

It was 41 years before the NHL expanded again, doubling in size for the 1967-68 season with new teams in Bloomington (Minn.), Los Angeles, Oakland, Philadelphia, Pittsburgh and St. Louis. The league had 16 clubs by the start of the 1972-73 season, but it also had a rival in the **World Hockey Association,** which debuted that year with 12 teams.

The NHL added two more teams in 1974 and merged the struggling Cleveland Barons (originally the Oakland Seals) and Minnesota North Stars in 1978, before absorbing four WHA clubs—the Edmonton Oilers, Hartford Whalers, Quebec Nordiques and Winnipeg Jets—in time for the 1979-80 season. Seven expansion teams joined the league in the 1990s, with two more being added in 2000 to make it an even 30.

Expansion/Merger Timetable
For teams currently in NHL.

1919—Quebec Bulldogs finally take the ice after sitting out NHL's first two seasons; **1924**—Boston Bruins and Montreal Maroons; **1925**—New York Americans and Pittsburgh Pirates; **1926**—Chicago Black Hawks (now Blackhawks), Detroit Cougars (now Red Wings) and New York Rangers; **1932**—Ottawa Senators return after sitting out 1931-32 season.

1967—California-Oakland Seals (later Cleveland Barons), Los Angeles Kings, Minnesota North Stars, Philadelphia Flyers, Pittsburgh Penguins and St. Louis Blues.

1970—Buffalo Sabres and Vancouver Canucks; **1972**—Atlanta Flames (now Calgary) and New York Islanders; **1974**—Kansas City Scouts (now New Jersey Devils) and Washington Capitals; **1978**—Cleveland Barons merge with Minnesota North Stars (now Dallas Stars) and team remains in Minnesota; **1979**—added WHA's Edmonton Oilers, Hartford Whalers (now Carolina Hurricanes), Quebec Nordiques (now Colorado Avalanche) and Winnipeg Jets (now Phoenix Coyotes).

1991—San Jose Sharks; **1992**—Ottawa Senators and Tampa Bay Lightning; **1993**—Mighty Ducks of Anaheim and Florida Panthers; **1998**—Nashville Predators; **1999**—Atlanta Thrashers.

2000—Columbus Blue Jackets and Minnesota Wild.

City and Nickname Changes

1919—Toronto Arenas renamed St. Pats; **1920**—Quebec Bulldogs move to Hamilton and becomes Tigers (will fold in 1925); **1926**—Toronto St. Pats renamed Maple Leafs; **1929**—Detroit Cougars renamed Falcons.

1930—Pittsburgh Pirates move to Philadelphia and become Quakers (will fold in 1931); **1932**—Detroit Falcons renamed Red Wings; **1934**—Ottawa Senators move to St. Louis and become Eagles (will fold in 1935); **1941**—New York Americans renamed Brooklyn Americans (will fold in 1942).

1967—California Seals renamed Oakland Seals three months into first season; **1970**—Oakland Seals renamed California Golden Seals; **1975**—California Golden Seals renamed Seals; **1976**—California Seals move to Cleveland and become Barons, while Kansas City Scouts move to Denver and become Colorado Rockies; **1978**—Cleveland Barons merge with Minnesota North Stars and become Minnesota North Stars.

1980—Atlanta Flames move to Calgary; **1982**—Colorado Rockies move to East Rutherford, N.J., and become New Jersey Devils; **1986**—Chicago Black Hawks renamed Blackhawks; **1993**—Minnesota North Stars move to Dallas and become Stars. **1995**—Quebec Nordiques move to Denver and become Colorado Avalanche; **1996**—Winnipeg Jets move to Phoenix and become Coyotes; **1997**—Hartford Whalers move to Greensboro, N.C. and become Carolina Hurricanes; **1999**—Carolina Hurricanes move to Raleigh, N.C.

Defunct NHL Teams
Teams that once played in the NHL, but no longer exist.

Brooklyn—Americans (1941-42, formerly NY Americans from 1925-41); **Cleveland**—Barons (1976-78, originally California-Oakland Seals from 1967-76); **Hamilton (Ont.)**—Tigers (1920-25, originally Quebec Bulldogs from 1919-20); **Montreal**—Maroons (1924-38) and Wanderers (1917-18); **New York**—Americans (1925-41, later Brooklyn Americans for 1941-42); **Oakland**—Seals (1967-76, also known as California Seals and Golden Seals and later Cleveland Barons from 1976-78); **Ottawa**—Senators (1917-31 and 1932-34, later St. Louis Eagles for 1934-35); **Philadelphia**—Quakers (1930-31, originally Pittsburgh Pirates from 1925-30); **Pittsburgh**—Pirates (1925-30, later Philadelphia Quakers for 1930-31); **Quebec**—Bulldogs (1919-20, later Hamilton Tigers from 1920-25); **St. Louis**—Eagles (1934-35), originally Ottawa Senators (1917-31 and 1932-34).

WHA Teams (1972-79)

Baltimore—Blades (1975); **Birmingham**—Bulls (1976-78); **Calgary**—Cowboys (1975-77); **Chicago**—Cougars (1972-75); **Cincinnati**—Stingers (1975-79); **Cleveland**—Crusaders (1972-76, moved to Minnesota); **Denver**—Spurs (1975-76, moved to Ottawa); **Edmonton**—Oilers (1972-79, originally called Alberta Oilers in 1972-73); **Houston**—Aeros (1972-78); **Indianapolis**—Racers (1974-78).

Los Angeles—Sharks (1972-74, moved to Michigan); **Michigan**—Stags (1974-75, moved to Baltimore); **Minnesota**—Fighting Saints (1972-76) and New Fighting Saints (1976-77); **New England**—Whalers (1972-79, played in Boston from 1972-74, West Springfield, MA from 1974-75, Hartford from 1975-78 and Springfield, MA in 1979); **New Jersey**—Knights (1973-74, moved to San Diego); **New York**—Raiders (1972-73, renamed Golden Blades in 1973, moved to New Jersey).

Ottawa—Nationals (1972-73, moved to Toronto) and Civics (1976); **Philadelphia**—Blazers (1972-73, moved to Vancouver); **Phoenix**—Roadrunners (1974-77); **Quebec**—Nordiques (1972-79); **San Diego**—Mariners (1974-77); **Toronto**—Toros (1973-76, moved to Birmingham, AL); **Vancouver**—Blazers (1973-75, moved to Calgary); **Winnipeg**—Jets (1972-79).

Annual NHL Leaders
Art Ross Trophy (Scoring)

Given to the player who leads the league in points scored and named after the former Boston Bruins general manager-coach. First presented in 1948, names of prior leading scorers have been added retroactively. A tie for the scoring championship is broken three ways: 1. total goals; 2. fewest games played; 3. first goal scored.

Multiple Winners: Wayne Gretzky (10); Gordie Howe and Mario Lemieux (6); Phil Esposito and Jaromir Jagr (5); Stan Mikita (4); Bobby Hull and Guy Lafleur (3); Max Bentley, Charlie Conacher, Bill Cook, Babe Dye, Bernie Geoffrion, Elmer Lach, Newsy Lalonde, Joe Malone, Dickie Moore, Howie Morenz, Bobby Orr and Sweeney Schriner (2).

Year		Gm	G	A	Pts	Year		Gm	G	A	Pts
1918	Joe Malone, Mon	20	44	0	44	1961	Bernie Geoffrion, Mon	64	50	45	95
1919	Newsy Lalonde, Mon	17	23	9	32	1962	Bobby Hull, Chi.	70	50	34	84
1920	Joe Malone, Que	24	39	6	45	1963	Gordie Howe, Det	70	38	48	86
1921	Newsy Lalonde, Mon	24	33	8	41	1964	Stan Mikita, Chi	70	39	50	89
1922	Punch Broadbent, Ott	24	32	14	46	1965	Stan Mikita, Chi	70	28	59	87
1923	Babe Dye, Tor	22	26	11	37	1966	Bobby Hull, Chi	65	54	43	97
1924	Cy Denneny, Ott	21	22	1	23	1967	Stan Mikita, Chi	70	35	62	97
1925	Babe Dye, Tor	29	38	6	44	1968	Stan Mikita, Chi	72	40	47	87
1926	Nels Stewart, Maroons	36	34	8	42	1969	Phil Esposito, Bos	74	49	77	126
1927	Bill Cook, NYR	44	33	4	37	1970	Bobby Orr, Bos	76	33	87	120
1928	Howie Morenz, Mon	43	33	18	51	1971	Phil Esposito, Bos	78	76	76	152
1929	Ace Bailey, Tor	44	22	10	32	1972	Phil Esposito, Bos	76	66	67	133
1930	Cooney Weiland, Bos	44	43	30	73	1973	Phil Esposito, Bos	78	55	75	130
1931	Howie Morenz, Mon	39	28	23	51	1974	Phil Esposito, Bos	78	68	77	145
1932	Busher Jackson, Tor	48	28	25	53	1975	Bobby Orr, Bos	80	46	89	135
1933	Bill Cook, NYR	48	28	22	50	1976	Guy Lafleur, Mon	80	56	69	125
1934	Charlie Conacher, Tor	42	32	20	52	1977	Guy Lafleur, Mon	80	56	80	136
1935	Charlie Conacher, Tor	47	36	21	57	1978	Guy Lafleur, Mon	79	60	72	132
1936	Sweeney Schriner, NYA.	48	19	26	45	1979	Bryan Trottier, NYI	76	47	87	134
1937	Sweeney Schriner, NYA.	48	21	25	46	1980	Marcel Dionne, LA	80	53	84	137
1938	Gordie Drillon, Tor	48	26	26	52	1981	Wayne Gretzky, Edm	80	55	109	164
1939	Toe Blake, Mon	48	24	23	47	1982	Wayne Gretzky, Edm	80	92	120	212
1940	Milt Schmidt, Bos	48	22	30	52	1983	Wayne Gretzky, Edm	80	71	125	196
1941	Bill Cowley, Bos	46	17	45	62	1984	Wayne Gretzky, Edm	74	87	118	205
1942	Bryan Hextall, NYR	48	24	32	56	1985	Wayne Gretzky,Edm	80	73	135	208
1943	Doug Bentley, Chi.	50	33	40	73	1986	Wayne Gretzky, Edm	80	52	163	215
1944	Herbie Cain, Bos	48	36	46	82	1987	Wayne Gretzky, Edm	79	62	121	183
1945	Elmer Lach, Mon.	50	26	54	80	1988	Mario Lemieux, Pit	77	70	98	168
1946	Max Bentley, Chi	47	31	30	61	1989	Mario Lemieux, Pit	76	85	114	199
1947	Max Bentley, Chi	60	29	43	72	1990	Wayne Gretzky, LA.	73	40	102	142
1948	Elmer Lach, Mon.	60	30	31	61	1991	Wayne Gretzky, LA	78	41	122	163
1949	Roy Conacher, Chi	60	26	42	68	1992	Mario Lemieux, Pit.	64	44	87	131
1950	Ted Lindsay, Det	69	23	55	78	1993	Mario Lemieux, Pit.	60	69	91	160
1951	Gordie Howe, Det	70	43	43	86	1994	Wayne Gretzky, LA.	81	38	92	130
1952	Gordie Howe, Det	70	47	39	86	1995	jaromir Jagr, Pit	48	32	38	70
1953	Gordie Howe, Det	70	49	46	95	1996	Mario Lemieux, Pit	70	69	92	161
1954	Gordie Howe, Det	70	33	48	81	1997	Mario Lemieux, Pit	76	50	72	122
1955	Bernie Geoffrion, Mon.	70	38	37	75	1998	Jaromir Jagr, Pit	77	35	67	102
1956	Jean Beliveau, Mon.	70	47	41	88	1999	Jaromir Jagr, Pit	81	44	83	127
1957	Gordie Howe, Det	70	44	45	89	2000	Jaromir Jagr, Pit	63	42	54	96
1958	Dickie Moore, Mon.	70	36	48	84	2001	Jaromir Jagr, Pit	81	52	69	121
1959	Dickie Moore, Mon.	70	41	55	96	2002	Jarome Iginla, Calg.	82	52	44	96
1960	Bobby Hull, Chi	70	39	42	81	2003	Peter Forsberg, Col.	75	29	77	106

Note: The three times players have tied for total points in one season the player with more goals has won the trophy. In 1961-62, Hull outscored Andy Bathgate of NY Rangers, 50 goals to 28. In 1979-80, Dionne outscored Wayne Gretzky of Edmonton, 53-51. In 1995, Jagr outscored Eric Lindros of Philadelphia, 32-29.

Goals

Multiple Winners: Bobby Hull (7); Phil Esposito (6); Charlie Conacher, Wayne Gretzky, Gordie Howe and Maurice Richard (5); Bill Cooke, Babe Dye, Brett Hull, Mario Lemieux, Pavel Bure and Teemu Selanne (3); Jean Beliveau, Doug Bentley, Peter Bondra, Mike Bossy, Bernie Geoffrion, Bryan Hextall, Joe Malone and Nels Stewart (2).

Year		No	Year		No	Year		No
1918	Joe Malone, Mon	44	1927	Bill Cook, NYR	33	1936	Charlie Conacher, Tor	23
1919	Odie Cleghorn, Mon	23	1928	Howie Morenz, Mon	33		& Bill Thoms, Tor	23
	& Newsy Lalonde, Mon	23	1929	Ace Bailey, Tor.	22	1937	Larry Aurie, Det	23
1920	Joe Malone, Que	39	1930	Cooney Weiland, Bos.	43		& Nels Stewart, Bos-NYA	23
1921	Babe Dye, Ham-Tor.	35	1931	Charlie Conacher, Tor.	31	1938	Gordie Drillon, Tor	26
1922	Punch Broadbent, Ott	32	1932	Charlie Conacher, Tor.	34	1939	Roy Conacher, Bos.	26
1923	Babe Dye, Tor	26		& Bill Cook, NYR	34	1940	Bryan Hextall, NYR	24
1924	Cy Denneny, Ott	22	1933	Bill Cook, NYR.	28	1941	Bryan Hextall, NYR	26
1925	Babe Dye, Tor	38	1934	Charlie Conacher, Tor.	32	1942	Lynn Patrick, NYR.	32
1926	Nels Stewart, Maroons	34	1935	Charlie Conacher, Tor.	36	1943	Doug Bentley, Chi.	33

Annual NHL Leaders (Cont.)

Year		No	Year		No	Year		No
1944	Doug Bentley, Chi.	38	1964	Bobby Hull, Chi	43	1984	Wayne Gretzky, Edm	87
1945	Maurice Richard, Mon	50	1965	Norm Ullman, Tor	42	1985	Wayne Gretzky, Edm	73
1946	Gaye Stewart, Tor	37	1966	Bobby Hull, Chi	54	1986	Jari Kurri, Edm	68
1947	Maurice Richard, Mon	45	1967	Bobby Hull, Chi	52	1987	Wayne Gretzky, Edm	62
1948	Ted Lindsay, Det	33	1968	Bobby Hull, Chi	44	1988	Mario Lemieux, Pit	70
1949	Sid Abel, Det	28	1969	Bobby Hull, Chi	58	1989	Mario Lemieux, Pit	85
1950	Maurice Richard, Mon	43	1970	Phil Esposito, Bos	43	1990	Brett Hull, St.L	72
1951	Gordie Howe, Det	43	1971	Phil Esposito, Bos	76	1991	Brett Hull, St.L	86
1952	Gordie Howe, Det	47	1972	Phil Esposito, Bos	66	1992	Brett Hull, St.L	70
1953	Gordie Howe, Det	49	1973	Phil Esposito, Bos	55	1993	Alexander Mogilny, Buf.	76
1954	Maurice Richard, Mon	37	1974	Phil Esposito, Bos	68		& Teemu Selanne, Win	76
1955	Bernie Geoffrion, Mon	38	1975	Phil Esposito, Bos	61	1994	Pavel Bure, Van	60
	& Maurice Richard, Mon.	38	1976	Reggie Leach, Phi.	61	1995	Peter Bondra, Wash	34
1956	Jean Beliveau, Mon	47	1977	Steve Shutt, Mon	60	1996	Mario Lemieux, Pit	69
1957	Gordie Howe, Det	44	1978	Guy Lafleur, Mon	60	1997	Keith Tkachuk, Pho	52
1958	Dickie Moore, Mon	36	1979	Mike Bossy, NYI	69	1998	Teemu Selanne, Ana	52
1959	Jean Beliveau, Mon	45	1980	Danny Gare, Buf	56		& Peter Bondra, Wash	52
1960	Bronco Horvath, Bos	39		Charlie Simmer, LA	56	1999	Teemu Selanne, Ana	47
	& Bobby Hull, Chi	39		& Blaine Stoughton, Hart.	56	2000	Pavel Bure, Fla	58
1961	Bernie Geoffrion, Mon	50	1981	Mike Bossy, NYI	68	2001	Pavel Bure, Fla	59
1962	Bobby Hull, Chi	50	1982	Wayne Gretzky, Edm	92	2002	Jarome Iginla, Calg.	52
1963	Gordie Howe, Det	38	1983	Wayne Gretzky, Edm	71	2003	Milan Hejduk, Col.	50

Assists

Multiple Winners: Wayne Gretzky (16); Bobby Orr (5); Adam Oates, Frank Boucher, Bill Cowley, Phil Esposito, Gordie Howe, Jaromir Jagr, Elmer Lach, Mario Lemieux, Stan Mikita and Joe Primeau (3); Syl Apps, Andy Bathgate, Jean Beliveau, Doug Bentley, Art Chapman, Bobby Clarke, Ron Francis, Ted Lindsay, Bert Olmstead, Henri Richard and Bryan Trottier (2).

Year		No	Year		No	Year		No
1918	No official records kept.		1948	Doug Bentley, Chi.	37	1977	Guy Lafleur, Mon	80
1919	Newsy Lalonde, Mon	9	1949	Doug Bentley, Chi.	43	1978	Bryan Trottier, NYI	77
1920	Corbett Denneny, Tor	12	1950	Ted Lindsay, Det	55	1979	Bryan Trottier, NYI	87
1921	Louis Berlinquette, Mon	9	1951	Gordie Howe, Det	43	1980	Wayne Gretzky, Edm	86
	Harry Cameron, Tor	9		& Teeder Kennedy, Tor	43	1981	Wayne Gretzky, Edm	109
	& Joe Matte, Ham	9	1952	Elmer Lach, Mon	50	1982	Wayne Gretzky, Edm	120
1922	Punch Broadbent, Ott	14	1953	Gordie Howe, Det	46	1983	Wayne Gretzky, Edm	125
	& Leo Reise, Ham	14	1954	Gordie Howe, Det	48	1984	Wayne Gretzky, Edm	118
1923	Ed Bouchard, Ham	12	1955	Bert Olmstead, Mon	48	1985	Wayne Gretzky, Edm	135
1924	King Clancy, Ott	8	1956	Bert Olmstead, Mon	56	1986	Wayne Gretzky, Edm	163
1925	Cy Denneny, Ott	15	1957	Ted Lindsay, Det	55	1987	Wayne Gretzky, Edm	121
1926	Frank Nighbor, Ott	13	1958	Henri Richard, Mon	52	1988	Wayne Gretzky, Edm	109
1927	Dick Irvin, Chi	18	1959	Dickie Moore, Mon	55	1989	Wayne Gretzky, LA	114
1928	Howie Morenz, Mon	18	1960	Don McKenney, Bos	49		& Mario Lemieux, Pit	114
1929	Frank Boucher, NYR	16	1961	Jean Beliveau, Mon	58	1990	Wayne Gretzky, LA	102
1930	Frank Boucher, NYR	36	1962	Andy Bathgate, NYR	56	1991	Wayne Gretzky, LA	122
1931	Joe Primeau, Tor	32	1963	Henri Richard, Mon	50	1992	Wayne Gretzky, LA	90
1932	Joe Primeau, Tor	37	1964	Andy Bathgate, NYR-Tor	58	1993	Adam Oates, Bos.	97
1933	Frank Boucher, NYR	28	1965	Stan Mikita, Chi	59	1994	Wayne Gretzky, LA	92
1934	Joe Primeau, Tor	32	1966	Jean Beliveau, Mon	48	1995	Ron Francis, Pit	48
1935	Art Chapman, NYA	34		Stan Mikita, Chi	48	1996	Ron Francis, Pit	92
1936	Art Chapman, NYA	28		& Bobby Rousseau, Mon	48		& Mario Lemieux, Pit	92
1937	Syl Apps, Tor	29	1967	Stan Mikita, Chi	62	1997	Mario Lemieux, Pit	72
1938	Syl Apps, Tor	29	1968	Phil Esposito, Bos	49		& Wayne Gretzky, NYR	72
1939	Bill Cowley, Bos	34	1969	Phil Esposito, Bos	77	1998	Jaromir Jagr, Pit	67
1940	Milt Schmidt, Bos	30	1970	Bobby Orr, Bos	87		& Wayne Gretzky, NYR	67
1941	Bill Cowley, Bos	45	1971	Bobby Orr, Bos	102	1999	Jaromir Jagr, Pit	83
1942	Phil Watson, NYR	37	1972	Bobby Orr, Bos	80	2000	Mark Recchi, Phi	63
1943	Bill Cowley, Bos	45	1973	Phil Esposito, Bos	75	2001	Jaromir Jagr, Pit	69
1944	Clint Smith, Chi	49	1974	Bobby Orr, Bos	90		& Adam Oates, Wash	69
1945	Elmer Lach, Mon	54	1975	Bobby Clarke, Phi	89	2002	Adam Oates, Wash-Phi.	64
1946	Elmer Lach, Mon	34		& Bobby Orr, Bos.	89	2003	Peter Forsberg, Col.	77
1947	Billy Taylor, Det	46	1976	Bobby Clarke, Phi	89			

Goals Against Average

Average determined by games played through 1942-43 season and by minutes played since then. Minimum of 15 games from 1917-18 season through 1925-26; minimum of 25 games since 1926-27 season. Not to be confused with the Vezina Trophy. Goaltenders who posted the season's lowest goals against average, but did not win the Vezina are in **bold** type.

Multiple Winners: Jacques Plante (9); Clint Benedict and Bill Durnan (6); Johnny Bower, Ken Dryden and Tiny Thompson (4); Patrick Roy and Georges Vezina (3); Ed Belfour, Frankie Brimsek, Turk Broda, George Hainsworth, Dominik Hasek, Harry Lumley, Bernie Parent, Pete Peeters, Terry Sawchuk and Marty Turco (2).

Year	GAA	Year	GAA	Year	GAA
1918 Georges Vezína, Mon	3.82	1947 Bill Durnan, Mon	2.30	1976 Ken Dryden, Mon	2.03
1919 Clint Benedict, Ott	2.94	1948 Turk Broda, Tor	2.38	1977 Bunny Larocque, Mon	2.09
1920 Clint Benedict, Ott	2.67	1949 Bill Durnan, Mon	2.10	1978 Ken Dryden, Mon	2.05
1921 Clint Benedict, Ott	3.13	1950 Bill Durnan, Mon	2.20	1979 Ken Dryden, Mon	2.30
1922 Clint Benedict, Ott	3.50	1951 Al Rollins, Tor	1.77	1980 Bob Sauve, Buf	2.36
1923 Clint Benedict, Ott	2.25	1952 Terry Sawchuk, Det	1.90	1981 Richard Sevigny, Mon	2.40
1924 Georges Vezina, Mon	2.00	1953 Terry Sawchuk, Det	1.90	1982 **Denis Herron,** Mon	2.64
1925 Georges Vezina, Mon	1.87	1954 Harry Lumley, Tor	1.86	1983 Pete Peeters, Bos	2.36
1926 Alex Connell, Ott	1.17	1955 **Harry Lumley,** Tor	1.94	1984 **Pat Riggin,** Wash	2.66
1927 **Clint Benedict,** Mon-M	1.51	1956 Jacques Plante, Mon	1.86	1985 **Tom Barrasso,** Buf	2.66
1928 Geo. Hainsworth, Mon	1.09	1957 Jacques Plante, Mon	2.02	1986 **Bob Froese,** Phi	2.55
1929 Geo. Hainsworth, Mon	0.98	1958 Jacques Plante, Mon	2.11	1987 **Brian Hayward,** Mon	2.81
1930 Tiny Thompson, Bos	2.23	1959 Jacques Plante, Mon	2.16	1988 Pete Peeters, Wash	2.78
1931 Roy Worters, NYA	1.68	1960 Jacques Plante, Mon	2.54	1989 Patrick Roy, Mon	2.47
1932 Chuck Gardiner, Chi	1.92	1961 Johnny Bower, Tor	2.50	1990 **Mike Liut,** Hart-Wash	2.53
1933 Tiny Thompson, Bos	1.83	1962 Jacques Plante, Mon	2.37	1991 Ed Belfour, Chi	2.47
1934 **Wilf Cude,** Det-Mon	1.57	1963 **Jacques Plante,** Mon	2.49	1992 Patrick Roy, Mon	2.36
1935 Lorne Chabot, Chi	1.83	1964 **Johnny Bower,** Tor	2.11	1993 **Felix Potvin,** Tor	2.50
1936 Tiny Thompson, Bos	1.71	1965 Johnny Bower, Tor	2.38	1994 Dominik Hasek, Buf	1.95
1937 Norm Smith, Det	2.13	1966 **Johnny Bower,** Tor	2.25	1995 Dominik Hasek, Buf	2.11
1938 Tiny Thompson, Bos	1.85	1967 Glenn Hall, Chi	2.38	1996 **Ron Hextall,** Phi	2.17
1939 Frankie Brimsek, Bos	1.58	1968 Gump Worsley, Mon	1.98	1997 **Martin Brodeur,** NJ	1.88
1940 Dave Kerr, NYR	1.60	1969 **Jacques Plante,** St.L	1.96	1998 **Ed Belfour,** Dal	1.88
1941 Turk Broda, Tor	2.06	1970 **Ernie Wakely,** St.L	2.11	1999 **Ron Tugnutt,** Ott	1.79
1942 Frankie Brimsek, Bos	2.45	1971 **Jacques Plante,** Tor	1.88	2000 **Brian Boucher,** Phi	1.91
1943 John Mowers, Det	2.47	1972 Tony Esposito, Chi	1.77	2001 **Marty Turco,** Dal	1.90
1944 Bill Durnan, Mon	2.18	1973 Ken Dryden, Mon	2.26	2002 **Patrick Roy,** Col	1.94
1945 Bill Durnan, Mon	2.42	1974 Bernie Parent, Phi	1.89	2003 **Marty Turco,** Dal	1.72
1946 Bill Durnan, Mon	2.60	1975 Bernie Parent, Phi	2.03		

Penalty Minutes

Multiple Winners: Red Horner (8); Gus Mortson and Dave Schultz (4); Bert Corbeau, Lou Fontinato and Tiger Williams (3); Matthew Barnaby, Billy Boucher, Carl Brewer, Red Dutton, Pat Egan, Bill Ezinicki, Joe Hall, Tim Hunter, Keith Magnuson, Chris Nilan, Jimmy Orlando and Rob Ray (2).

Year	Min	Year	Min	Year	Min
1918 Joe Hall, Mon	60	1947 Gus Mortson, Tor	133	1976 Steve Durbano, Pit-KC	370
1919 Joe Hall, Mon	85	1948 Bill Barilko, Tor	147	1977 Tiger Williams, Tor	338
1920 Cully Wilson, Tor	79	1949 Bill Ezinicki, Tor	145	1978 Dave Schultz, LA-Pit	405
1921 Bert Corbeau, Mon	86	1950 Bill Ezinicki, Tor	144	1979 Tiger Williams, Tor	298
1922 Sprague Cleghorn, Mon	63	1951 Gus Mortson, Tor	142	1980 Jimmy Mann, Win	287
1923 Billy Boucher, Mon	52	1952 Gus Kyle, Bos	127	1981 Tiger Williams, Van	343
1924 Bert Corbeau, Tor	55	1953 Maurice Richard, Mon	112	1982 Paul Baxter, Pit	409
1925 Billy Boucher, Mon	92	1954 Gus Mortson, Chi	132	1983 Randy Holt, Wash	275
1926 Bert Corbeau, Tor	121	1955 Fern Flaman, Bos	150	1984 Chris Nilan, Mon	338
1927 Nels Stewart, Mon-M	133	1956 Lou Fontinato, NYR	202	1985 Chris Nilan, Mon	358
1928 Eddie Shore, Bos	165	1957 Gus Mortson, Chi	147	1986 Joey Kocur, Det	377
1929 Red Dutton, Mon-M	139	1958 Lou Fontinato, NYR	152	1987 Tim Hunter, Calg	361
1930 Joe Lamb, Ott	119	1959 Ted Lindsay, Chi	184	1988 Bob Probert, Det	398
1931 Harvey Rockburn, Det	118	1960 Carl Brewer, Tor	150	1989 Tim Hunter, Calg	375
1932 Red Dutton, NYA	107	1961 Pierre Pilote, Chi	165	1990 Basil McRae, Min	351
1933 Red Horner, Tor	144	1962 Lou Fontinato, Mon	167	1991 Rob Ray, Buf	350
1934 Red Horner, Tor	146	1963 Howie Young, Det	273	1992 Mike Peluso, Chi	408
1935 Red Horner, Tor	125	1964 Vic Hadfield, NYR	151	1993 Marty McSorley, LA	399
1936 Red Horner, Tor	167	1965 Carl Brewer, Tor	177	1994 Tie Domi, Win	347
1937 Red Horner, Tor	124	1966 Reg Fleming, Bos-NYR	166	1995 Enrico Ciccone, TB	225
1938 Red Horner, Tor	82	1967 John Ferguson, Mon	177	1996 Matthew Barnaby, Buf.	335
1939 Red Horner, Tor	85	1968 Barclay Plager, St.L	153	1997 Gino Odjick, Van	371
1940 Red Horner, Tor	87	1969 Forbes Kennedy, Phi-Tor	219	1998 Donald Brashear, Van	372
1941 Jimmy Orlando, Det	99	1970 Keith Magnuson, Chi	213	1999 Rob Ray, Buf	261
1942 Pat Egan, NYA	124	1971 Keith Magnuson, Chi	291	2000 Denny Lambert, Atl	219
1943 Jimmy Orlando, Det	99	1972 Bryan Watson, Pit	212	2001 Matthew Barnaby, Pit-TB	265
1944 Mike McMahon, Mon	98	1973 Dave Schultz, Phi	259	2002 Peter Worrell, Fla	354
1945 Pat Egan, Bos	86	1974 Dave Schultz, Phi	348	2003 Jody Shelley, Clb	249
1946 Jack Stewart, Det	73	1975 Dave Schultz, Phi	472		

All-Time NHL Regular Season Leaders

Through 2003 regular season.

CAREER

Players active during 2003 season in **bold** type.

Points

		Yrs	Gm	G	A	Pts
1	Wayne Gretzky	20	1487	894	1963	2857
2	Gordie Howe	26	1767	801	1049	1850
3	**Mark Messier**	24	1680	676	1168	1844
4	Marcel Dionne	18	1348	731	1040	1771
5	**Ron Francis**	22	1651	536	1222	1758
6	**Mario Lemieux**	15	879	682	1010	1692
7	**Steve Yzerman**	20	1378	660	1010	1670
8	Phil Esposito	18	1282	717	873	1590
9	Ray Bourque	22	1612	410	1169	1579
10	Paul Coffey	21	1409	396	1135	1531
11	Stan Mikita	22	1394	541	926	1467
12	Bryan Trottier	18	1279	524	901	1425
13	**Doug Gilmour**	20	1474	450	964	1414
14	Dale Hawerchuk	16	1188	518	891	1409
15	**Adam Oates**	18	1277	339	1063	1402
16	Jari Kurri	17	1251	601	797	1398
17	John Bucyk	23	1540	556	813	1369
18	Guy Lafleur	17	1126	560	793	1353
19	Denis Savard	17	1196	473	865	1338
20	Mike Gartner	19	1432	708	627	1335
21	Gilbert Perreault	17	1191	512	814	1326
22	**Brett Hull**	18	1183	716	606	1322
23	**Luc Robitaille**	17	1286	631	688	1319
24	**Joe Sakic**	15	1074	509	806	1315
25	Alex Delvecchio	24	1549	456	825	1281
	Dave Andreychuk	21	1515	613	668	1281
27	**Al MacInnis**	22	1413	340	932	1272
28	Jean Ratelle	21	1281	491	776	1267
29	Peter Stastny	15	977	450	789	1239
30	**Jaromir Jagr**	13	950	506	729	1235

Goals

		Yrs	Gm	No
1	Wayne Gretzky	20	1487	894
2	Gordie Howe	26	1767	801
3	Marcel Dionne	18	1348	731
4	Phil Esposito	18	1282	717
5	**Brett Hull**	18	1183	716
6	Mike Gartner	19	1432	708
7	**Mario Lemieux**	15	879	682
8	**Mark Messier**	24	1680	676
9	**Steve Yzerman**	20	1378	660
10	**Luc Robitaille**	17	1286	631
11	**Dave Andreychuk**	21	1515	613
12	Bobby Hull	16	1063	610
13	Dino Ciccarelli	19	1232	608
14	Jari Kurri	17	1251	601
15	Mike Bossy	10	752	573
16	Guy Lafleur	17	1126	560
17	John Bucyk	23	1540	556
18	Michel Goulet	15	1089	548
19	Maurice Richard	18	978	544
20	Stan Mikita	22	1394	541
21	**Ron Francis**	22	1651	536
22	Frank Mahovlich	18	1181	533
	Brendan Shanahan	16	1186	533
24	Bryan Trottier	18	1279	524
25	Pat Verbeek	20	1424	522
26	Dale Hawerchuk	16	1188	518
27	Gilbert Perreault	17	1191	512
28	**Joe Nieuwendyk**	17	1113	511
29	**Joe Sakic**	15	1074	509
30	Jean Beliveau	20	1125	507

Assists

		Yrs	Gm	No
1	Wayne Gretzky	20	1487	1963
2	**Ron Francis**	22	1651	1222
3	Ray Bourque	22	1612	1169
4	**Mark Messier**	24	1680	1168
5	Paul Coffey	21	1409	1135
6	**Adam Oates**	18	1277	1063
7	Gordie Howe	26	1767	1049
8	Marcel Dionne	18	1348	1040
9	**Steve Yzerman**	20	1378	1010
	Mario Lemieux	15	879	1010
11	**Doug Gilmour**	20	1474	964
12	**Al MacInnis**	22	1413	932
13	Larry Murphy	21	1615	929
14	Stan Mikita	22	1394	926
15	Bryan Trottier	18	1279	901
16	**Phil Housley**	21	1495	894
17	Dale Hawerchuk	16	1188	891
18	Phil Esposito	18	1281	873
19	Denis Savard	17	1196	865
20	Bobby Clarke	15	1144	852

Penalty Minutes

		Yrs	Gm	Min
1	Tiger Williams	14	962	3966
2	Dale Hunter	19	1407	3565
3	Marty McSorley	17	961	3381
4	Bob Probert	16	935	3300
5	**Tie Domi**	14	863	3198
6	**Rob Ray**	14	894	3193
7	**Craig Berube**	17	1054	3149
8	Tim Hunter	16	815	3146
9	Chris Nilan	13	688	3043
10	Rick Tocchet	18	1144	2972
11	Pat Verbeek	20	1424	2905
12	Dave Manson	16	1103	2792
13	**Scott Stevens**	21	1597	2763
14	**Chris Chelios**	20	1326	2634
15	Willi Plett	12	834	2572

NHL-WHA Top 15

All-time regular season scoring leaders, including games played in World Hockey Association (1972-79). NHL players with WHA experience are listed in CAPITAL letters. Players active during 2003 are in **bold** type.

Points

		Yrs	G	A	Pts
1	WAYNE GRETZKY	21	940	2027	2967
2	GORDIE HOWE	32	975	1383	2358
3	**MARK MESSIER**	25	677	1178	1855
4	BOBBY HULL	23	913	895	1808
5	Marcel Dionne	18	731	1040	1771
6	**Ron Francis**	22	536	1222	1758
7	**Mario Lemieux**	15	682	1010	1692
8	**Steve Yzerman**	20	660	1010	1670
9	Phil Esposito	18	717	873	1590
10	Ray Bourque	22	410	1169	1579
11	Paul Coffey	21	396	1135	1531
12	Stan Mikita	22	541	926	1467
13	Bryan Trottier	18	524	901	1425
14	**Doug Gilmour**	20	450	964	1414
15	Dale Hawerchuk	16	518	891	1409

WHA Totals: GRETZKY (1 yr, 80 gm, 46-64—110); HOWE (6 yrs, 419 gm, 174-334—508); MESSIER (1 yr, 52 gm, 1-10—11); HULL (7 yrs, 411 gm, 303-335—638).

Years Played

		Yrs	Career	Gm
1	Gordie Howe	26	1946-71, 79-80	1767
2	Alex Delvecchio	24	1950-74	1549
	Tim Horton	24	1949-50, 51-74	1446
	Mark Messier	24	1979–	1680
5	John Bucyk	23	1955-78	1540
6	Ray Bourque	22	1979-2001	1612
	Ron Francis	22	1981–	1651
	Al MacInnis	22	1982–	1413
	Stan Mikita	22	1958-80	1394
	Doug Mohns	22	1953-75	1390
	Dean Prentice	22	1952-74	1378
12	Fourteen tied with 21 years each:

Dave Andreychuk, George Armstrong, Paul Coffey, **Phil Housley**, Harry Howell, Larry Murphy, Eric Nesterenko, Marcel Pronovost, Jean Ratelle, Terry Sawchuk, Allan Stanley, **Scott Stevens**, Ron Stewart and Gump Worsley.

Note: Combined NHL-WHA years played: Howe (32); Messier (25); Howell (24); Bobby Hull (23); Norm Ullman, Nesterenko, Frank Mahovlich and Dave Keon (22); Wayne Gretzky (21).

Games Played

		Yrs	Career	Gm
1	Gordie Howe	26	1946–71, 79–80	1767
2	**Mark Messier**	24	1979–	1680
3	**Ron Francis**	22	1981–	1651
4	Larry Murphy	21	1980-2001	1615
5	Ray Bourque	22	1979-2001	1612
6	**Scott Stevens**	21	1982–	1597
7	Alex Delvecchio	24	1950-74	1549
8	John Bucyk	23	1955–78	1540
9	**Dave Andreychuk**	21	1982–	1515
10	**Phil Housley**	21	1982–	1495
11	Wayne Gretzky	20	1979-99	1487
12	**Doug Gilmour**	20	1983–	1474
13	Tim Horton	24	1949–50, 51–74	1446
14	Mike Gartner	19	1979-98	1432
15	Pat Verbeek	20	1982-2002	1424

Note: Combined NHL-WHA games played: Howe (2,186), Messier (1,732), Dave Keon (1,597), Harry Howell (1,581), Gretzky (1,567), Norm Ullman (1,554), Gartner (1,510) and Bobby Hull (1,474).

Goaltending

Wins

		Yrs	Gm	W	L	T	Pct
1	**Patrick Roy**	19	1029	551	315	131	.618
2	Terry Sawchuk	21	971	447	330	172	.562
3	Jacques Plante	18	837	434	247	146	.614
4	Tony Esposito	16	886	423	306	152	.566
5	Glenn Hall	18	906	407	326	163	.545
6	Grant Fuhr	19	868	403	295	114	.567
7	**Ed Belfour**	15	797	401	262	105	.590
8	Mike Vernon	19	781	385	273	92	.575
19	**Curtis Joseph**	14	767	380	279	87	.568
10	John Vanbiesbrouck	20	882	374	346	119	.517
11	Andy Moog	18	713	372	209	88	.622
12	**Tom Barrasso**	19	777	369	277	86	.563
13	**Martin Brodeur**	11	665	365	191	94	.634
14	Rogie Vachon	16	795	355	291	127	.541
15	Gump Worsley	21	861	335	352	150	.490
16	Harry Lumley	16	804	330	329	143	.501
17	Billy Smith	18	680	305	233	105	.556
18	Turk Broda	12	629	302	224	101	.562
19	**Mike Richter**	15	666	301	258	73	.534
20	Ron Hextall	13	608	296	214	69	.571

Losses

		Yrs	Gm	W	L	T	Pct
1	Gump Worsley	21	861	335	352	150	.490
2	Gilles Meloche	18	788	270	351	131	.446
3	John Vanbiesbrouck	20	882	374	346	119	.517
4	Terry Sawchuk	21	971	447	330	172	.562
5	Harry Lumley	16	804	330	329	143	.501

Goals Against Average
Minimum of 300 games played.

Before 1950

		Gm	Min	GA	GAA
1	George Hainsworth	465	29,415	937	1.91
2	Alex Connell	417	26,050	830	1.91
3	Chuck Gardiner	316	19,687	664	2.02
4	Lorne Chabot	411	25,307	860	2.04
5	Tiny Thompson	553	34,175	1183	2.08

Since 1950

		Gm	Min	GA	GAA
1	**Martin Brodeur**	665	38,956	1419	2.19
2	Dominik Hasek	581	33,745	1254	2.23
3	Ken Dryden	397	23,352	870	2.24
4	**Roman Turek**	310	18,064	694	2.31
5	Jacques Plante	837	49,533	1965	2.38

Shutouts

		Yrs	Games	No
1	Terry Sawchuk	21	971	103
2	George Hainsworth	11	465	94
3	Glenn Hall	18	906	84
4	Jacques Plante	18	837	82
5	Alex Connell	12	417	81
	Tiny Thompson	12	553	81
7	Tony Esposito	16	886	76
8	Lorne Chabot	11	411	73
9	Harry Lumley	16	804	71
10	Roy Worters	12	484	66
	Patrick Roy	19	1029	66
12	**Ed Belfour**	15	797	65
13	**Martin Brodeur**	11	665	64
14	Turk Broda	14	629	62
15	Dominik Hasek	12	581	61

NHL-WHA Top 15

All-time regular season wins leaders, including games played in World Hockey Association (1972-79). NHL goaltenders with WHA experience are listed in CAPITAL LETTERS. Players active during 2003 are in bold type.

Wins

		Yrs	W	L	T	Pct
1	**Patrick Roy**	19	551	315	131	.618
2	JACQUES PLANTE	19	449	261	147	.610
3	Terry Sawchuk	21	447	330	172	.562
4	Tony Esposito	16	423	306	152	.566
5	Glenn Hall	18	407	326	163	.545
6	Grant Fuhr	19	403	295	114	.567
7	**Ed Belfour**	15	401	262	105	.590
8	Mike Vernon	19	385	273	92	.575
9	**Curtis Joseph**	14	380	279	87	.568
10	John Vanbiesbrouck	20	374	346	119	.517
11	Andy Moog	18	372	209	88	.622
12	**Tom Barrasso**	19	369	277	86	.563
13	**Martin Brodeur**	11	365	191	94	.634
14	Rogie Vachon	16	355	291	127	.541
15	Gump Worsley	21	335	352	150	.490

WHA Totals: PLANTE (1 yr, 31 gm, 15-14-1).

All-Time NHL Regular Season Leaders (Cont.)
SINGLE SEASON

Scoring
Points

		Season	G	A	Pts
1	Wayne Gretzky, Edm	1985-86	52	163	215
2	Wayne Gretzky, Edm	1981-82	92	120	212
3	Wayne Gretzky, Edm	1984-85	73	135	208
4	Wayne Gretzky, Edm	1983-84	87	118	205
5	Mario Lemieux, Pit	1988-89	85	114	199
6	Wayne Gretzky, Edm	1982-83	71	125	196
7	Wayne Gretzky, Edm	1986-87	62	121	183
8	Mario Lemieux, Pit	1987-88	70	98	168
	Wayne Gretzky, LA	1988-89	54	114	168
10	Wayne Gretzky, Edm	1980-81	55	109	164
11	Wayne Gretzky, LA	1990-91	41	122	163
12	Mario Lemieux, Pit	1995-96	69	92	161
13	Mario Lemieux, Pit	1992-93	69	91	160
14	Steve Yzerman, Det	1988-89	65	90	155
15	Phil Esposito, Bos	1970-71	76	76	152
16	Bernie Nicholls, LA	1988-89	70	80	150
17	Jaromir Jagr, Pit	1995-96	62	87	149
	Wayne Gretzky, Edm	1987-88	40	109	149
19	Pat LaFontaine, Buf	1992-93	53	95	148
20	Mike Bossy, NYI	1981-82	64	83	147

WHA 150 points or more: 154—Marc Tardif, Que. (1977-78).

Goals

		Season	Gm	No
1	Wayne Gretzky, Edm	1981-82	80	92
2	Wayne Gretzky, Edm	1983-84	74	87
3	Brett Hull, St.L	1990-91	78	86
4	Mario Lemieux, Pit	1988-89	76	85
5	Alexander Mogilny, Buf.	1992-93	77	76
	Phil Esposito, Bos	1970-71	78	76
	Teemu Selanne, Win	1992-93	84	76
8	Brett Hull, St.L	1984-85	80	73
9	Brett Hull, St.L	1989-90	80	72
10	Jari Kurri, Edm	1984-85	73	71
	Wayne Gretzky, Edm	1982-83	80	71
12	Brett Hull, St.L	1991-92	73	70
	Mario Lemieux, Pit	1987-88	77	70
	Bernie Nicholls, LA	1988-89	79	70
15	Mario Lemieux, Pit	1992-93	60	69
	Mario Lemieux, Pit	1995-96	70	69
	Mike Bossy, NYI	1978-79	80	69
18	Phil Esposito, Bos	1973-74	78	68
	Jari Kurri, Edm	1985-86	78	68
	Mike Bossy, NYI	1980-81	79	68

WHA 70 goals or more: 77—Bobby Hull, Win. (1974-75); 75—Real Cloutier, Que. (1978-79); 71—Marc Tardif, Que. (1975-76); 70—Anders Hedberg, Win. (1976-77).

Assists

		Season	Gm	No
1	Wayne Gretzky, Edm	1985-86	80	163
2	Wayne Gretzky, Edm	1984-85	80	135
3	Wayne Gretzky, Edm	1982-83	80	125
4	Wayne Gretzky, LA	1990-91	78	122
5	Wayne Gretzky, Edm	1986-87	79	121
6	Wayne Gretzky, Edm	1981-82	80	120
7	Wayne Gretzky, Edm	1983-84	74	118
8	Mario Lemieux, Pit	1988-89	76	114
	Wayne Gretzky, LA	1988-89	78	114
10	Wayne Gretzky, Edm	1987-88	64	109
	Wayne Gretzky, Edm	1980-81	80	109
12	Wayne Gretzky, LA	1989-90	73	102
	Bobby Orr, Bos	1970-71	78	102
14	Mario Lemieux, Pit	1987-88	77	98
15	Adam Oates, Bos	1992-93	84	97

WHA 95 assists or more: 106—Andre Lacroix, San Diego (1974-75).

Goaltending
Wins

		Season	Record
1	Bernie Parent, Phi	1973-74	47-13-12
2	Bernie Parent, Phi	1974-75	44-14-9
	Terry Sawchuk, Det	1950-51	44-13-13
	Terry Sawchuk, Det	1951-52	44-14-12
5	Martin Brodeur, NJ	1999-00	43-20-8
	Martin Brodeur, NJ	1997-98	43-17-8
	Tom Barrasso, Pit	1992-93	43-14-5
	Ed Belfour, Chi	1990-91	43-19-7
9	Jacques Plante, Mon	1955-56	42-12-10
	Jacques Plante, Mon	1961-62	42-14-14
	Ken Dryden, Mon	1975-76	42-10-8
	Mike Richter, NYR	1993-94	42-12-6
	Roman Turek, St.L	1999-00	42-15-9
	Martin Brodeur, NJ	2000-01	42-17-11

Most WHA wins in one season: 44—Richard Brodeur, Que. (1975-76).

Losses

		Season	Record
1	Gary Smith, Cal	1970-71	19-48-4
2	Al Rollins, Chi	1953-54	12-47-7
3	Peter Sidorkiewicz, Ott	1992-93	8-46-3
4	Harry Lumley, Chi	1951-52	17-44-9
5	Three tied with 41 losses each.		

Most WHA losses in one season: 36—Don McLeod, Van. (1974-75) and Andy Brown, Ind. (1974-75).

Shutouts

		Season	Gm	No
1	George Hainsworth, Mon	1928-29	44	22
2	Alex Connell, Ott	1925-26	36	15
	Alex Connell, Ott	1927-28	44	15
	Hal Winkler, Bos	1927-28	44	15
	Tony Esposito, Chi	1969-70	63	15

Most WHA shutouts in one season: 5—Gerry Cheevers, Cle. (1972-73) and Joe Daly, Win. (1975-76).

Goals Against Average
Before 1950

		Season	Gm	GAA
1	George Hainsworth, Mon	1928-29	44	0.98
2	George Hainsworth, Mon	1927-28	44	1.09
3	Alex Connell, Ott	1925-26	36	1.17
4	Tiny Thompson, Bos	1928-29	44	1.18
5	Roy Worters, NY Americans	1928-29	38	1.21

Since 1950

		Season	Gm	GAA
1	**Marty Turco**, Dal	2002-03	55	1.72
2	Tony Esposito, Chi	1971-72	48	1.77
3	Al Rollins, Tor	1950-51	40	1.77
4	Ron Tugnutt, Ott	1998-99	43	1.79
5	**Roman Cechmanek**, Phi.	2002-03	58	1.83

Penalty Minutes

		Season	PM
1	Dave Schultz, Phi	1974-75	472
2	Paul Baxter, Pit	1981-82	409
3	Mike Peluso, Chi	1991-92	408
4	Dave Schultz, LA-Pit	1977-78	405
5	Marty McSorley, LA	1992-93	399
6	Bob Probert, Det	1987-88	398
7	Basil McRae, Min	1987-88	382
8	Joey Kocur, Det	1985-86	377
9	Tim Hunter, Calg	1988-89	375
10	Donald Brashear, Van	1997-98	372

WHA 355 minutes or more: 365—Curt Brackenbury, Min-Que. (1975-76).

SINGLE GAME
Scoring

Points

	Date	G-A—Pts
Darryl Sittler, Tor vs Bos	2/7/76	6-4—10
Maurice Richard, Mon vs Det	12/28/44	5-3— 8
Bert Olmstead, Mon vs Chi.	1/9/54	4-4— 8
Tom Bladon, Phi vs Cle.	12/11/77	4-4— 8
Bryan Trottier, NYI vs NYR	12/23/78	5-3— 8
Peter Stastny, Que at Wash.	2/22/81	4-4— 8
Anton Stastny, Que at Wash	2/22/81	3-5— 8
Wayne Gretzky, Edm vs NJ.	11/19/83	3-5— 8
Wayne Gretzky, Edm vs Min.	1/4/84	4-4— 8
Paul Coffey, Edm vs Det	3/14/86	2-6— 8
Mario Lemieux, Pit vs St.L	10/15/88	2-6— 8
Bernie Nicholls, LA vs Tor	12/1/88	2-6— 8
Mario Lemieux, Pit vs NJ.	12/31/88	5-3— 8

Goals

	Date	No
Joe Malone, Que vs Tor	1/31/20	7
Newsy Lalonde, Mon vs Tor	1/10/20	6
Joe Malone, Que vs Ott	3/10/20	6
Corb Denneny, Tor vs Ham	1/26/21	6
Cy Denneny, Ott vs Ham	3/7/21	6
Syd Howe, Det vs NYR	2/3/44	6
Red Berenson, St.L at Phi	11/7/68	6
Darryl Sittler, Tor vs Bos	2/7/76	6

Assists

	Date	No
Billy Taylor, Det at Chi.	3/16/47	7
Wayne Gretzky, Edm vs Wash	2/15/80	7
Wayne Gretzky, Edm at Chi.	12/11/85	7
Wayne Gretzky, Edm vs Que	2/14/86	7
24 players tied with 6 each.		

Penalty Minutes

	Date	Min
Randy Holt, LA at Phi.	3/11/79	67
Reed Low, St.L at Calg	2/28/02	57
Frank Bathe, Phi vs LA	3/11/79	55
Reed Low, St.L at Det	12/31/02	53
Russ Anderson, Pit vs Edm	1/19/80	51

Penalties

	Date	No
Chris Nilan, Bos vs Har	3/31/91	10*
Nine tied with 9 each.		

* Nilan accumulated six minors, two majors, one 10-minute misconduct and one game misconduct.

All-Time Winningest NHL Coaches

Top 20 NHL career victories through the 2002-03 season. Career, regular season and playoff records are noted along with NHL titles won. Coaches active during 2002-03 season in **bold** type. **Note:** In the following tables, overtime losses are considered losses.

		Yrs	W	Career L	T	Pct	W	Regular Season L	T	Pct	W	Playoffs L	T	Pct	Stanley Cups
1	Scotty Bowman	.30	1467	714	313	.651	1244	584	313	.654	223	130	0	.632	9 (1973, 76-79, 92, 97-98, 2002)
2	Al Arbour	22	904	663	248	.566	781	577	248	.564	123	86	0	.589	4 (1980-83)
3	Dick Irvin	.26	790	609	228	.556	690	521	226	.559	100	88	2	.532	4 (1932,44,46,53)
4	**Mike Keenan**	.17	670	552	145	.543	.579	483	145	.540	91	69	0	.569	1 (1994)
5	**Pat Quinn**	.17	659	521	144	.552	571	439	144	.557	88	82	0	.518	None
6	Billy Reay	.17	599	445	175	.563	542	385	175	.571	57	60	0	.487	None
7	Toe Blake	13	582	292	159	.640	500	255	159	.634	82	37	0	.689	8 (1956-60,65-66,68)
8	**Glen Sather**	12	564	318	114	.623	475	281	114	.611	89	37	0	.706	4 (1984-85,87-88)
9	Bryan Murray	12	547	457	131	.540	513	413	131	.547	34	44	0	.436	None
10	**Pat Burns**	13	535	407	139	.559	458	340	139	.563	77	67	0	.535	1 (2003)
11	Roger Neilson	.17	511	436	159	.534	460	381	159	.540	51	55	0	.481	None
12	Jack Adams	.21	465	442	162	.511	413	390	161	.512	52	52	1	.500	3 (1936-37, 43)
13	Jacques Demers	.14	464	510	130	.479	409	467	130	.471	55	43	0	.561	1 (1993)
14	**Brian Sutter**	14	459	426	129	.516	431	386	129	.524	28	40	0	.412	None
15	Fred Shero	.10	451	272	119	.606	390	225	119	.612	61	47	0	.565	2 (1974-75)
16	Punch Imlach	.15	439	384	148	.528	395	336	148	.534	44	48	0	.478	4 (1962-64,67)
17	Emile Francis	.13	433	326	112	.561	393	273	112	.577	40	53	0	.430	None
18	Sid Abel	.16	414	470	155	.473	382	426	155	.477	32	44	0	.421	None
19	Terry Murray	11	406	331	89	.545	360	288	89	.549	46	43	0	.517	None
20	**Jacques Martin**	.10	399	340	109	.535	364	297	109	.544	35	43	0	.449	None

Where They Coached

Abel—Chicago (1952-54), Detroit (1957-68,69-70), St. Louis (1971-72), Kansas City (1975-76); **Adams**—Toronto (1922-23), Detroit (1927-47); **Arbour**—St. Louis (1970-73), NY Islanders (1973-86,88-94); **Blake**—Montreal (1955-68); **Bowman**—St. Louis (1967-71), Montreal (1971-79), Buffalo (1979-87), Pittsburgh (1991-93), Detroit (1993-2002); **Burns**—Montreal (1988-92), Toronto (1992-96), Boston (1997-2000), New Jersey (2002-). **Demers**—Quebec (1979-80), St. Louis (1983-86), Detroit (1986-90), Montreal (1992-95), Tampa Bay (1997-99); **Francis**—NY Rangers (1965-75), St. Louis (1976-77,81-83); **Imlach**—Toronto (1958-69), Buffalo (1970-72), Toronto (1979-81); **Irvin**—Chicago (1930-31,55-56), Toronto (1931-40), Montreal (1940-55); **Keenan**—Philadelphia (1984-88), Chicago (1988-92), NY Rangers (1993-94), St. Louis (1994-96), Vancouver (1997-99), Boston (2000-01), Florida (2001-); **Martin**—St. Louis (1986-88), Ottawa (1995-); **B. Murray**—Washington (1982-90), Detroit (1990-93), Florida (1997-98), Anaheim (2001-02); **T. Murray**— Washington (1990-94), Philadelphia (1994-97), Florida (1998-2000). **Neilson**—Toronto (1977-79), Buffalo (1979-81), Vancouver (1982-83), Los Angeles (1984), NY Rangers (1989-93), Florida (1993-95), Philadelphia (1998-00), Ottawa (2002); **Quinn**—Philadelphia (1978-82), Los Angeles (1984-87), Vancouver (1990-94, 96), Toronto (1998—); **Reay**—Toronto (1957-59), Chicago (1963-77); **Sather**—Edmonton (1979-89, 93-94), NY Rangers (2003-); **Shero**—Philadelphia (1971-78), NY Rangers (1978-81); **Sutter**—St. Louis (1988-92), Boston (1992-95), Calgary (1997-2000), Chicago (2001-).

Top Winning Percentages

Minimum of 275 victories, including playoffs.

		Yrs	W	L	T	Pct.
1	Scotty Bowman	30	1467	714	313	**.651**
2	Toe Blake	13	582	292	159	**.640**
3	**Glen Sather**	12	564	318	114	**.623**
4	**Ken Hitchcock**	8	375	230	73	**.607**
5	Fred Shero	10	451	272	119	**.606**
6	Don Cherry	6	281	177	77	**.597**
7	Tommy Ivan	9	324	205	111	**.593**
8	**Joel Quenneville**	7	312	218	70	**.578**
9	Al Arbour	22	904	663	248	**.566**
10	Billy Reay	16	599	445	175	**.563**
11	Emile Francis	13	433	326	112	**.561**
12	**Marc Crawford**	9	366	276	93	**.561**
13	**Pat Burns**	13	535	407	139	**.559**
14	Hap Day	10	308	237	81	**.557**
15	Dick Irvin	26	790	609	228	**.556**
16	Lester Patrick	13	312	242	115	**.552**
17	**Pat Quinn**	17	659	521	144	**.552**
18	Art Ross	18	393	310	95	**.552**
19	Bob Johnson	6	275	223	58	**.547**
20	**Jacques Lemaire**	10	397	321	104	**.546**
21	Terry Murray	11	406	331	89	**.545**
22	**Mike Keenan**	17	670	552	145	**.543**
23	Bryan Murray	14	547	457	131	**.540**
24	**Jacques Martin**	10	399	340	109	**.535**
25	Roger Neilson	16	511	436	159	**.534**
26	Punch Imlach	15	439	384	148	**.528**
27	**Darryl Sutter**	9	350	320	94	**.520**
28	Terry Crisp	9	310	286	78	**.518**
29	**Brian Sutter**	12	459	426	129	**.516**
30	Jack Adams	21	465	442	162	**.511**

Active Coaches' Victories

Through 2002-03 season, including playoffs.

		Yrs	W	L	T	Pct.
1	Mike Keenan, Fla.	17	**670**	552	145	.543
2	Pat Quinn, Tor.	17	**659**	521	144	.552
3	Glen Sather, NYR	12	**564**	318	114	.623
4	Pat Burns, NJ	13	**535**	407	139	.559
5	Brian Sutter, Chi.	12	**459**	426	129	.516
6	Jacques Martin, Ott.	10	**399**	340	109	.535
7	Jacques Lemaire, Min.	10	**397**	321	104	.546
8	Ken Hitchcock, Phi.	8	**375**	230	73	.607
9	Marc Crawford, Van.	9	**366**	276	93	.561
10	Darryl Sutter, Calg.	9	**350**	320	94	.520
	Ron Wilson, SJ	10	**350**	367	89	.489
12	Joel Quenneville, St.L	7	**312**	218	70	.578
13	Paul Maurice, Car.	8	**277**	311	91	.475
14	Bob Hartley, Atl.	5	**261**	164	53	.601
15	Lindy Ruff, Buf.	6	**248**	227	71	.519
16	Andy Murray, LA	4	**160**	150	42	.514
17	Bob Francis, Pho.	4	**147**	146	45	.501
18	Barry Trotz, Nash.	5	**145**	216	49	.413
19	Craig MacTavish, Edm.	3	**117**	106	35	.521
20	Doug MacLean, Clb.	4	**111**	108	37	.506
21	John Tortorella, TB	4	**80**	113	29	.426
22	Mike Babcock, Ana.	1	**55**	39	9	.578
23	Dave Tippett, Dal.	1	**52**	27	15	.633
24	Dave Lewis, Det.	1	**48**	28	10	.616
25	Bruce Cassidy, Wash.	1	**41**	39	8	.511
26	Tony Granato, Col.	1	**35**	19	4	.638
27	Claude Julien, Mon.	1	**12**	21	3	.375
28	Ed Olczyk, Pit.	0	**0**	0	0	.000
	Steve Stirling, NYI	0	**0**	0	0	.000
	Mike Sullivan, Bos.	0	**0**	0	0	.000

Annual Awards
Hart Memorial Trophy

Awarded to the player "adjudged to be the most valuable to his team" and named after Cecil Hart, the former manager-coach of the Montreal Canadiens. Winners selected by Pro Hockey Writers Assn. (PHWA). Winners' scoring statistics or goaltender W-L records and goals against average are provided; (*) indicates led or tied for league lead.

Multiple Winners: Wayne Gretzky (9); Gordie Howe (6); Eddie Shore (4); Bobby Clarke, Mario Lemieux, Howie Morenz and Bobby Orr (3); Jean Beliveau, Bill Cowley, Phil Esposito, Dominik Hasek, Bobby Hull, Guy Lafleur, Mark Messier, Stan Mikita and Nels Stewart (2).

Year		G	A	Pts
1924	Frank Nighbor, Ottawa, C	10	3	13
1925	Billy Burch, Hamilton, C	20	4	24
1926	Nels Stewart, Maroons, C	34	8	42*
1927	Herb Gardiner, Mon., D	6	6	12
1928	Howie Morenz, Mon., C	33	18	51
1929	Roy Worters, NYA, G	16-13-9;		1.21
1930	Nels Stewart, Maroons, C	39	16	55
1931	Howie Morenz, Mon., C	28	23	51*
1932	Howie Morenz, Mon., C	24	25	49
1933	Eddie Shore, Bos., D	8	27	35
1934	Aurel Joliat, Mon., LW	22	15	37
1935	Eddie Shore, Bos., D	7	26	33
1936	Eddie Shore, Bos., D	3	16	19
1937	Babe Siebert, Mon., D	8	20	28
1938	Eddie Shore, Bos., D	3	14	17
1939	Toe Blake, Mon., LW	24	23	47*
1940	Ebbie Goodfellow, Det., D	11	17	28
1941	Bill Cowley, Bos., C	17	45	62*
1942	Tommy Anderson, NYA, D	12	29	41
1943	Bill Cowley, Bos., C	27	45	72
1944	Babe Pratt, Tor., D	17	40	57
1945	Elmer Lach, Mon., C	26	54	80*
1946	Max Bentley, Chi., C	31	30	61*
1947	Maurice Richard, Mon., RW	45	26	71
1948	Buddy O'Connor, NYR, C	24	36	60
1949	Sid Abel, Det., C	28	26	54
1950	Chuck Rayner, NYR, G	28-30-11;		2.62

Year		G	A	Pts
1950	Chuck Rayner, NYR, G	28-30-11;		2.62
1951	Milt Schmidt, Bos., C	22	39	61
1952	Gordie Howe, Det., RW	47	39	86*
1953	Gordie Howe, Det., RW	49	46	95*
1954	Al Rollins, Chi., G	12-47-7;		3.23
1955	Ted Kennedy, Tor., C	10	42	52
1956	Jean Beliveau, Mon., C	47	41	88
1957	Gordie Howe, Det., RW	44	45	89*
1958	Gordie Howe, Det., RW	33	44	77
1959	Andy Bathgate, NYR, RW	40	48	88
1960	Gordie Howe, Det., RW	28	45	73
1961	Bernie Geoffrion, Mon., RW	50	45	95*
1962	Jacques Plante, Mon., G	42-14-14;		2.37*
1963	Gordie Howe, Det., RW	38	48	86*
1964	Jean Beliveau, Mon., C	28	50	78
1965	Bobby Hull, Chi., LW	39	32	71
1966	Bobby Hull, Chi., LW	54	43	97*
1967	Stan Mikita, Chi., C	35	62	97*
1968	Stan Mikita, Chi., C	40	47	87*
1969	Phil Esposito, Bos., C	49	77	126*
1970	Bobby Orr, Bos., D	33	87	120*
1971	Bobby Orr, Bos., D	37	102	139
1972	Bobby Orr, Bos., D	37	80	117
1973	Bobby Clarke, Phi., C	37	67	104
1974	Phil Esposito, Bos., C	68	77	145*
1975	Bobby Clarke, Phi., C	27	89	116
1976	Bobby Clarke, Phi., C	30	89	119
1977	Guy Lafleur, Mon., RW	56	80	136*

Year		G	A	Pts	Year		G	A	Pts
1978	Guy Lafleur, Mon., RW	60	72	132*	1991	Brett Hull, St. L., RW	86	45	131
1979	Bryan Trottier, NYI., C	47	87	134*	1992	Mark Messier, NYR, C	35	72	107
1980	Wayne Gretzky, Edm., C	51	86	137*	1993	Mario Lemieux, Pit., C	69	91	160*
1981	Wayne Gretzky, Edm., C	55	109	164*	1994	Sergei Fedorov, Det., C	56	64	120
1982	Wayne Gretzky, Edm., C	92	120	212*	1995	Eric Lindros, Phi., C	29	41	70*
1983	Wayne Gretzky, Edm., C	71	125	196*	1996	Mario Lemieux, Pit., C	69	92	161*
1984	Wayne Gretzky, Edm., C	87	118	205*	1997	Dominik Hasek, Buf., G	37-20-10;		2.27
1985	Wayne Gretzky, Edm., C	73	135	208*	1998	Dominik Hasek, Buf., G	33-23-13;		2.09
1986	Wayne Gretzky, Edm., C	52	163	215*	1999	Jaromir Jagr, Pit., RW	44	83	127*
1987	Wayne Gretzky, Edm., C	62	121	183*	2000	Chris Pronger, St.L, D	14	48	62
1988	Mario Lemieux, Pit., C	70	98	168*	2001	Joe Sakic, Col., C	54	64	118
1989	Wayne Gretzky, LA, C	54	114	168	2002	Jose Theodore, Mon., G	30-24-10;		2.11
1990	Mark Messier, Edm., C	45	84	129	2003	Peter Forsberg, Col., C	29	77	106*

Calder Memorial Trophy

Awarded to the most outstanding rookie of the year and named after Frank Calder, the late NHL president (1917-43). Since the 1990-91 season, all eligible candidates must not have attained their 26th birthday by Sept. 15 of their rookie year. Winners selected by PHWA. Winners' scoring statistics or goaltender W-L record & goals against average are provided.

Year		G	A	Pts	Year		G	A	Pts
1933	Carl Voss, NYR-Det., C	8	15	23	1969	Danny Grant, Min., LW	34	31	65
1934	Russ Blinco, Maroons, C	14	9	23	1970	Tony Esposito, Chi., G	38-17-8;		2.17
1935	Sweeney Schriner, NYA, LW	18	22	40	1971	Gilbert Perreault, Buf., C	38	34	72
1936	Mike Karakas, Chi., G	21-19-8;		1.92	1972	Ken Dryden, Mon., G	39-8-15;		2.24
1937	Syl Apps, Tor., C	16	29	45	1973	Steve Vickers, NYR, LW	30	23	53
1938	Cully Dahlstrom, Chi., C	10	9	19	1974	Denis Potvin, NYI, D	17	37	54
1939	Frankie Brimsek, Bos., G	33-9-1;		1.58	1975	Eric Vail, Atl., LW	39	21	60
1940	Kilby MacDonald, NYR, LW	15	13	28	1976	Bryan Trottier, NYI, C	32	63	95
1941	John Quilty, Mon., C	18	16	34	1977	Willi Plett, Atl., RW	33	23	56
1942	Knobby Warwick, NYR, RW	16	17	33	1978	Mike Bossy, NYI, RW	53	38	91
1943	Gaye Stewart, Tor., LW	24	23	47	1979	Bobby Smith, Min., C	30	44	74
1944	Gus Bodnar, Tor., C	22	40	62	1980	Ray Bourque, Bos., D	17	48	65
1945	Frank McCool, Tor., G	24-22-4;		3.22	1981	Peter Stastny, Que., C	39	70	109
1946	Edgar Laprade, NYR, C	15	19	34	1982	Dale Hawerchuk, Win., C	45	58	103
1947	Howie Meeker, Tor., RW	27	18	45	1983	Steve Larmer, Chi., RW	43	47	90
1948	Jim McFadden, Det., C	24	24	48	1984	Tom Barrasso, Buf., G	26-12-3;		2.84
1949	Penny Lund, NYR, RW	14	16	30	1985	Mario Lemieux, Pit., C	43	57	100
1950	Jack Gelineau, Bos., G	22-30-15;		3.28	1986	Gary Suter, Calg., D	18	50	68
1951	Terry Sawchuk, Det., G	44-13-13;		1.99	1987	Luc Robitaille, LA, LW	45	39	84
1952	Bernie Geoffrion, Mon., RW	30	24	54	1988	Joe Nieuwendyk, Calg., C	51	41	92
1953	Gump Worsley, NYR, G	13-29-8;		3.06	1989	Brian Leetch, NYR, D	23	48	71
1954	Camille Henry, NYR, LW	24	15	39	1990	Sergei Makarov, Calg., RW	24	62	86
1955	Ed Litzenberger, Mon-Chi., RW	23	28	51	1991	Ed Belfour, Chi., G	43-19-7;		2.47
1956	Glenn Hall, Det., G	30-24-16;		2.11	1992	Pavel Bure, Van., RW	34	26	60
1957	Larry Regan, Bos., RW	14	19	33	1993	Teemu Selanne, Win., RW	76	56	132
1958	Frank Mahovlich, Tor., LW	20	16	36	1994	Martin Brodeur, NJ, G	27-11-8;		2.40
1959	Ralph Backstrom, Mon., C	18	22	40	1995	Peter Forsberg, Que., C	15	35	50
1960	Billy Hay, Chi., C	18	37	55	1996	Daniel Alfredsson, Ott., RW	26	35	61
1961	Dave Keon, Tor., C	20	25	45	1997	Bryan Berard, NYI, D	8	40	48
1962	Bobby Rousseau, Mon., RW	21	24	45	1998	Sergei Samsonov, Bos., LW	22	25	47
1963	Kent Douglas, Tor., D	7	15	22	1999	Chris Drury, Col., C	20	24	44
1964	Jacques Laperriere, Mon., D	2	28	30	2000	Scott Gomez, NJ, C	19	51	70
1965	Roger Crozier, Det., G	40-23-7;		2.42	2001	Evgeni Nabokov, SJ, G	32-21-7;		2.19
1966	Brit Selby, Tor., LW	14	13	27	2002	Dany Heatley, Atl., RW	26	41	67
1967	Bobby Orr, Bos., D	13	28	41	2003	Barret Jackman, St.L, D	3	16	19
1968	Derek Sanderson, Bos., C	24	25	49					

Vezina Trophy

From 1927-80, given to the principal goaltender(s) on the team allowing the fewest goals during the regular season. Trophy named after 1920's goalie Georges Vezina of the Montreal Canadiens, who died of tuberculosis in 1926. Since the 1980-81 season, the trophy has been awarded to the most outstanding goaltender of the year as selected by the league's general managers.

Multiple Winners: Jacques Plante (7, one of them shared); Bill Durnan and Dominik Hasek (6); Ken Dryden (5, three shared); Bunny Larocque (4, all shared); Terry Sawchuk (4, one shared); Tiny Thompson (4); Tony Esposito (3, one shared); George Hainsworth (3); Glenn Hall (3, two shared); Patrick Roy (3); Ed Belfour (2); Johnny Bower (2, one shared); Frankie Brimsek (2); Turk Broda (2); Chuck Gardiner (2); Charlie Hodge (2, one shared); Bernie Parent (2, one shared); Gump Worsley (2, both shared).

Year		Record	GAA	Year		Record	GAA
1927	George Hainsworth, Mon	28-14-2	1.52	1932	Chuck Gardiner, Chi	18-19-11	1.92
1928	George Hainsworth, Mon	26-11-7	1.09	1933	Tiny Thompson, Bos	25-15-8	1.83
1929	George Hainsworth, Mon	22-7-15	0.98	1934	Chuck Gardiner, Chi	20-17-11	1.73
1930	Tiny Thompson, Bos	38-5-1	2.23	1935	Lorne Chabot, Chi	26-17-5	1.83
1931	Roy Worters, NYA	18-16-10	1.68	1936	Tiny Thompson, Bos	22-20-6	1.71

Annual Awards (Cont.)

Year		Record	GAA	Year		Record	GAA
1937	Norm Smith, Det	25-14-9	2.13	1972	Tony Esposito, Chi	31-10-6	1.77
1938	Tiny Thompson, Bos	30-11-7	1.85		& Gary Smith, Chi	14-5-6	2.42
1939	Frankie Brimsek, Bos.	33-9-1	1.58	1973	Ken Dryden, Mon	33-7-13	2.26
1940	Dave Kerr, NYR	27-11-10	1.60	1974	(Tie) Bernie Parent, Phi	47-13-12	1.89
1941	Turk Broda, Tor	28-14-6	2.06		Tony Esposito, Chi	34-14-21	2.04
1942	Frankie Brimsek, Bos.	24-17-6	2.45	1975	Bernie Parent, Phi.	44-14-10	2.03
1943	John Mowers, Det	25-14-11	2.47	1976	Ken Dryden, Mon.	42-10-8	2.03
1944	Bill Durnan, Mon	38-5-7	2.18	1977	Ken Dryden, Mon	41-6-8	2.14
1945	Bill Durnan, Mon	38-8-4	2.42		& Bunny Larocque, Mon	19-2-4	2.09
1946	Bill Durnan, Mon	24-11-5	2.60	1978	Ken Dryden, Mon	37-7-7	2.05
1947	Bill Durnan, Mon	34-16-10	2.30		& Bunny Larocque, Mon.	22-3-4	2.67
1948	Turk Broda, Tor	32-15-13	2.38	1979	Ken Dryden, Mon	30-10-7	2.30
1949	Bill Durnan, Mon	28-23-9	2.10		& Bunny Larocque, Mon.	22-7-4	2.84
1950	Bill Durnan, Mon	26-21-17	2.20	1980	Bob Sauve, Buf	20-8-4	2.36
1951	Al Rollins, Tor.	27-5-8	1.77		& Don Edwards, Buf.	27-9-12	2.57
1952	Terry Sawchuk, Det.	44-14-12	1.90	1981	Richard Sevigny, Mon.	20-4-3	2.40
1953	Terry Sawchuk, Det.	32-15-16	1.90		Denis Herron, Mon.	6-9-6	3.50
1954	Harry Lumley, Tor	32-24-13	1.86		& Bunny Larocque, Mon.	16-9-3	3.03
1955	Terry Sawchuk, Det.	40-17-11	1.96	1982	Billy Smith, NYI	32-9-4	2.97
1956	Jacques Plante, Mon.	42-12-10	1.86	1983	Pete Peeters, Bos	40-11-9	2.36
1957	Jacques Plante, Mon.	31-18-12	2.02	1984	Tom Barrasso, Buf.	26-12-3	2.84
1958	Jacques Plante, Mon.	34-14-8	2.11	1985	Pelle Lindbergh, Phi	40-17-7	3.02
1959	Jacques Plante, Mon.	38-16-13	2.16	1986	John Vanbiesbrouck, NYR	31-21-5	3.32
1960	Jacques Plante, Mon.	40-17-12	2.54	1987	Ron Hextall, Phi	37-21-6	3.00
1961	Johnny Bower, Tor	33-15-10	2.50	1988	Grant Fuhr, Edm.	40-24-9	3.43
1962	Jacques Plante, Mon.	42-14-14	2.37	1989	Patrick Roy, Mon	33-5-6	2.47
1963	Glenn Hall, Chi	30-20-16	2.55	1990	Patrick Roy, Mon	31-16-5	2.53
1964	Charlie Hodge, Mon	33-18-11	2.26	1991	Ed Belfour, Chi.	43-19-7	2.47
1965	Johnny Bower, Tor	13-13-8	2.38	1992	Patrick Roy, Mon.	36-22-8	2.36
	& Terry Sawchuk, Tor	17-13-6	2.56	1993	Ed Belfour, Chi.	41-18-11	2.59
1966	Gump Worsley, Mon	29-14-6	2.36	1994	Dominik Hasek, Buf	30-20-6	1.95
	& Charlie Hodge, Mon.	12-7-2	2.58	1995	Dominik Hasek, Buf	19-14-7	2.11
1967	Glenn Hall, Chi	19-5-5	2.38	1996	Jim Carey, Wash	35-24-9	2.26
	& Denis Dejordy, Chi	22-12-7	2.46	1997	Dominik Hasek, Buf	37-20-10	2.27
1968	Gump Worsley, Mon	19-9-8	1.98	1998	Dominik Hasek, Buf	33-23-13	2.09
	& Rogie Vachon, Mon	23-13-2	2.48	1999	Dominik Hasek, Buf	30-18-14	1.87
1969	Jacques Plante, St.L	18-12-6	1.96	2000	Olaf Kolzig, Wash	41-20-11	2.24
	& Glenn Hall, St.L	19-12-8	2.17	2001	Dominik Hasek, Buf	37-24-4	2.11
1970	Tony Esposito, Chi	38-17-8	2.17	2002	Jose Theodore, Mon.	30-24-10	2.11
1971	Ed Giacomin, NYR	27-10-7	2.16	2003	Martin Brodeur, NJ.	41-23-9	2.02
	& Gilles Villemure, NYR	22-8-4	2.30				

Lady Byng Memorial Trophy

Awarded to the player "adjudged to have exhibited the best type of sportsmanship and gentlemanly conduct combined with a high standard of playing ability" and named after Lady Evelyn Byng, the wife of former Canadian Governor General (1921-26) Baron Byng of Vimy. Winners selected by PHWA.

Multiple winners: Frank Boucher (7); Wayne Gretzky (5); Red Kelly (4); Bobby Bauer, Mike Bossy, Alex Delvecchio and Ron Francis (3); Johnny Bucyk, Marcel Dionne, Paul Kariya, Dave Keon, Stan Mikita, Joey Mullen, Frank Nighbor, Jean Ratelle, Clint Smith and Sid Smith (2).

Year		Year		Year	
1925	Frank Nighbor, Ott., C	1943	Max Bentley, Chi., C	1961	Red Kelly, Tor., D
1926	Frank Nighbor, Ott., C	1944	Clint Smith, Chi., C	1962	Dave Keon, Tor., C
1927	Billy Burch, NYA, C	1945	Bill Mosienko, Chi., RW	1963	Dave Keon, Tor., C
1928	Frank Boucher, NYR, C	1946	Toe Blake, Mon., LW	1964	Ken Wharram, Chi., RW
1929	Frank Boucher, NYR, C	1947	Bobby Bauer, Bos., RW	1965	Bobby Hull, Chi., LW
1930	Frank Boucher, NYR, C	1948	Buddy O'Connor, NYR, C	1966	Alex Delvecchio, Det., LW
1931	Frank Boucher, NYR, C	1949	Bill Quackenbush, Det., D	1967	Stan Mikita, Chi., C
1932	Joe Primeau, Tor., C	1950	Edgar Laprade, NYR, C	1968	Stan Mikita, Chi., C
1933	Frank Boucher, NYR, C	1951	Red Kelly, Det., D	1969	Alex Delvecchio, Det., LW
1934	Frank Boucher, NYR, C	1952	Sid Smith, Tor., LW	1970	Phil Goyette, St.L., C
1935	Frank Boucher, NYR, C	1953	Red Kelly, Det., D	1971	Johnny Bucyk, Bos., LW
1936	Doc Romnes, Chi., F	1954	Red Kelly, Det., D	1972	Jean Ratelle, NYR, C
1937	Marty Barry, Det., C	1955	Sid Smith, Tor., LW	1973	Gilbert Perreault, Buf., C
1938	Gordie Drillon, Tor., RW	1956	Earl Reibel, Det., C	1974	Johnny Bucyk, Bos., LW
1939	Clint Smith, NYR, C	1957	Andy Hebenton, NYR, RW	1975	Marcel Dionne, Det., C
1940	Bobby Bauer, Bos., RW	1958	Camille Henry, NYR, LW	1976	Jean Ratelle, NY-Bos., C
1941	Bobby Bauer, Bos., RW	1959	Alex Delvecchio, Det., LW	1977	Marcel Dionne, LA, C
1942	Syl Apps, Tor., C	1960	Don McKenney, Bos., C	1978	Butch Goring, LA, C

Year

1979 Bob MacMillan, Atl., RW
1980 Wayne Gretzky, Edm., C
1981 Rick Kehoe, Pit., RW
1982 Rick Middleton, Bos., RW
1983 Mike Bossy, NYI, RW
1984 Mike Bossy, NYI, RW
1985 Jari Kurri, Edm., RW
1986 Mike Bossy, NYI, RW
1987 Joey Mullen, Calg., RW

Year

1988 Mats Naslund, Mon., LW
1989 Joey Mullen, Calg., RW
1990 Brett Hull, St.L., RW
1991 Wayne Gretzky, LA, C
1992 Wayne Gretzky, LA, C
1993 Pierre Turgeon, NYI, C
1994 Wayne Gretzky, LA, C
1995 Ron Francis, Pit., C
1996 Paul Kariya, Ana., LW

Year

1997 Paul Kariya, Ana., LW
1998 Ron Francis, Pit., C
1999 Wayne Gretzky, NYR, C
2000 Pavol Demitra, St.L, RW
2001 Joe Sakic, Col., C
2002 Ron Francis, Car., C
2003 Alexander Mogilny, Tor., RW

Note: Bill Quackenbush and Red Kelly are the only defensemen to win the Lady Byng.

James Norris Memorial Trophy

Awarded to the most outstanding defenseman of the year and named after James Norris, the late Detroit Red Wings owner-president. Winners selected by PHWA.

Multiple winners: Bobby Orr (8); Doug Harvey (7); Ray Bourque (5); Chris Chelios, Paul Coffey, Nicklas Lidstrom, Pierre Pilote and Denis Potvin (3); Rod Langway, Brian Leetch and Larry Robinson (2).

Year

1954 Red Kelly, Detroit
1955 Doug Harvey, Montreal
1956 Doug Harvey, Montreal
1957 Doug Harvey, Montreal
1958 Doug Harvey, Montreal
1959 Tom Johnson, Montreal
1960 Doug Harvey, Montreal
1961 Doug Harvey, Montreal
1962 Doug Harvey, NY Rangers
1963 Pierre Pilote, Chicago
1964 Pierre Pilote, Chicago
1965 Pierre Pilote, Chicago
1966 Jacques Laperriere, Montreal
1967 Harry Howell, NY Rangers
1968 Bobby Orr, Boston
1969 Bobby Orr, Boston
1970 Bobby Orr, Boston

Year

1971 Bobby Orr, Boston
1972 Bobby Orr, Boston
1973 Bobby Orr, Boston
1974 Bobby Orr, Boston
1975 Bobby Orr, Boston
1976 Denis Potvin, NY Islanders
1977 Larry Robinson, Montreal
1978 Denis Potvin, NY Islanders
1979 Denis Potvin, NY Islanders
1980 Larry Robinson, Montreal
1981 Randy Carlyle, Pittsburgh
1982 Doug Wilson, Chicago
1983 Rod Langway, Washington
1984 Rod Langway, Washington
1985 Paul Coffey, Edmonton
1986 Paul Coffey, Edmonton
1987 Ray Bourque, Boston

Year

1988 Ray Bourque, Boston
1989 Chris Chelios, Montreal
1990 Ray Bourque, Boston
1991 Ray Bourque, Boston
1992 Brian Leetch, NY Rangers
1993 Chris Chelios, Chicago
1994 Ray Bourque, Boston
1995 Paul Coffey, Detroit
1996 Chris Chelios, Chicago
1997 Brian Leetch, NY Rangers
1998 Rob Blake, Los Angeles
1999 Al MacInnis, St. Louis
2000 Chris Pronger, St. Louis
2001 Nicklas Lidstrom, Detroit
2002 Nicklas Lidstrom, Detroit
2003 Nicklas Lidstrom, Detroit

Frank Selke Trophy

Awarded to the outstanding defensive forward of the year and named after the late Montreal Canadiens general manager. Winners selected by the PHWA.

Multiple winners: Bob Gainey (4); Guy Carbonneau and Jere Lehtinen (3); Sergei Fedorov and Michael Peca (2).

Year

1978 Bob Gainey, Mon., LW
1979 Bob Gainey, Mon., LW
1980 Bob Gainey, Mon., LW
1981 Bob Gainey, Mon., LW
1982 Steve Kasper, Bos., C
1983 Bobby Clarke, Phi., C
1984 Doug Jarvis, Wash., C
1985 Craig Ramsay, Buf., LW
1986 Troy Murray, Chi., C

Year

1987 Dave Poulin, Phi., C
1988 Guy Carbonneau, Mon., C
1989 Guy Carbonneau, Mon., C
1990 Rick Meagher, St.L., C
1991 Dirk Graham, Chi., RW
1992 Guy Carbonneau, Mon., C
1993 Doug Gilmour, Tor., C
1994 Sergei Fedorov, Det., C
1995 Ron Francis, Pit., C

Year

1996 Sergei Fedorov, Det., C
1997 Michael Peca, Buf., C
1998 Jere Lehtinen, Dal., RW
1999 Jere Lehtinen, Dal., RW
2000 Steve Yzerman, Det., C
2001 John Madden, NJ, LW
2002 Michael Peca, NYI, C
2003 Jere Lehtinen, Dal., RW

Jack Adams Award

Awarded to the coach "adjudged to have contributed the most to his team's success" and named after the late Detroit Red Wings coach and general manager. Winners selected by NHL Broadcasters' Assn.; (*) indicates division champion.

Multiple winners: Pat Burns (3); Scotty Bowman, Jacques Demers and Pat Quinn (2).

Year		Improvement		Year		Improvement	
1974	Fred Shero, Phi.	37-30-11	to 50-16-12*	1989	Pat Burns, Mon	45-22-13	to 53-18- 9*
1975	Bob Pulford, LA.	41-14-23	to 37-35-8	1990	Bob Murdoch, Win	26-42-12	to 37-32-11
1976	Don Cherry, Bos	40-26-14	to 48-15-17*	1991	Brian Sutter, St.L	37-34-9	to 47-22-11
1977	Scotty Bowman, Mon	58-11-11*	to 60-8-12*	1992	Pat Quinn, Van	28-43-9	to 42-26-12*
1978	Bobby Kromm, Det	6-55-9	to 32-34-14	1993	Pat Burns, Tor	30-43-7	to 44-29-11
1979	Al Arbour, NYI	48-17-15*	to 51-15-14*	1994	Jacques Lemaire, NJ	40-37-7	to 47-25-12
1980	Pat Quinn, Phi	40-25-15	to 48-12-20*	1995	Marc Crawford, Que	34-42-8	to 30-13-5*
1981	Red Berenson, St.L	34-34-12	to 45-18-17*	1996	Scotty Bowman, Det	33-11-4*	to 62-13-7*
1982	Tom Watt, Win	9-57-14	to 33-33-14	1997	Ted Nolan, Buf	33-42-7	to 40-30-12*
1983	Orval Tessier, Chi	30-38-12	to 47-23-10	1998	Pat Burns, Bos	26-47-9	to 39-30-13
1984	Bryan Murray, Wash	39-25-16	to 48-27-5	1999	Jacques Martin, Ott	34-33-15	to 44-23-15*
1985	Mike Keenan, Phi	44-26-10	to 53-20-7*	2000	Joel Quenneville, St.L.	37-32-13	to 51-20-11*
1986	Glen Sather, Edm	49-20-11*	to 56-17-7*	2001	Bill Barber, Phi	45-25-12	to 43-25-11-3
1987	Jacques Demers, Det	17-57-6	to 34-36-10	2002	Bob Francis, Pho	35-27-17-3	to 40-27-9-6
1988	Jacques Demers, Det	34-36-10	to 41-28-11*	2003	Jacques Lemaire, Minn.	26-35-12-9	to 42-29-10-1

Annual Awards (Cont.)
Lester B. Pearson Award

Awarded to the season's most outstanding player and named after the former diplomat, Nobel Peace Prize winner and Canadian prime minister. Winners selected by the NHL Players Assn.

Multiple winners: Wayne Gretzky (5); Mario Lemieux (4); Guy Lafleur (3); Marcel Dionne, Phil Esposito, Dominik Hasek, Jaromir Jagr and Mark Messier (2).

Year		Year		Year	
1971	Phil Esposito, Bos., C	1982	Wayne Gretzky, Edm., C	1993	Mario Lemieux, Pit., C
1972	Jean Ratelle, NYR, C	1983	Wayne Gretzky, Edm., C	1994	Sergei Fedorov, Det., C
1973	Bobby Clarke, Phi., C	1984	Wayne Gretzky, Edm., C	1995	Eric Lindros, Phi., C
1974	Phil Esposito, Bos., C	1985	Wayne Gretzky, Edm., C	1996	Mario Lemieux, Pit., C
1975	Bobby Orr, Bos., D	1986	Mario Lemieux, Pit., C	1997	Dominik Hasek, Buf., G
1976	Guy Lafleur, Mon., RW	1987	Wayne Gretzky, Edm., C	1998	Dominik Hasek, Buf., G
1977	Guy Lafleur, Mon., RW	1988	Mario Lemieux, Pit., C	1999	Jaromir Jagr, Pit., RW
1978	Guy Lafleur, Mon., RW	1989	Steve Yzerman, Det., C	2000	Jaromir Jagr, Pit., RW
1979	Marcel Dionne, LA, C	1990	Mark Messier, Edm., C	2001	Joe Sakic, Col., C
1980	Marcel Dionne, LA, C	1991	Brett Hull, St.L., RW	2002	Jarome Iginla, Calg., RW
1981	Mike Liut, St.L., G	1992	Mark Messier, NYR, C	2003	Markus Naslund, Van., LW

King Clancy Memorial Trophy

Awarded to the player who "best exemplifies leadership on and off the ice and who has made a noteworthy humanitarian contribution to his community" and named after former player, coach, official and executive Frank "King" Clancy. Presented by the NHL's Board of Governors.

Year		Year		Year	
1988	Lanny McDonald, Calg., RW	1994	Adam Graves, NYR, LW	2000	Curtis Joseph, Tor., G
1989	Bryan Trottier, NYI, C	1995	Joe Nieuwendyk, Calg., C	2001	Shjon Podein, Col., LW
1990	Kevin Lowe, Edm., D	1996	Kris King, Win., LW	2002	Ron Francis, Car., C
1991	Dave Taylor, LA, RW	1997	Trevor Linden, Van., C	2003	Brendan Shanahan, Det., LW
1992	Ray Bourque, Bos., D	1998	Kelly Chase, St.L, RW		
1993	Dave Poulin, Bos., C	1999	Rob Ray, Buf., RW		

Bill Masterton Trophy

Awarded to the player who "best exemplifies the qualities of perseverance, sportsmanship and dedication to hockey" and named after the 29-year-old rookie center of the Minnesota North Stars who died of a head injury sustained in a 1968 NHL game. Presented by the PHWA.

Year		Year		Year	
1968	Claude Provost, Mon., RW	1980	Al MacAdam, Min., RW	1992	Mark Fitzpatrick, NYI, G
1969	Ted Hampson, Oak., C	1981	Blake Dunlop, St.L., C	1993	Mario Lemieux, Pit., C
1970	Pit Martin, Chi., C	1982	Chico Resch, Colo., G	1994	Cam Neely, Bos., RW
1971	Jean Ratelle, NYR, C	1983	Lanny McDonald, Calg., RW	1995	Pat LaFontaine, Buf., C
1972	Bobby Clarke, Phi., C	1984	Brad Park, Det., D	1996	Gary Roberts, Calg., LW
1973	Lowell MacDonald, Pit., RW	1985	Anders Hedberg, NYR, RW	1997	Tony Granato, SJ, LW
1974	Henri Richard, Mon., C	1986	Charlie Simmer, Bos., LW	1998	Jamie McLennan, St.L, G
1975	Don Luce, Buf., C	1987	Doug Jarvis, Hart., C	1999	John Cullen, TB, C
1976	Rod Gilbert, NYR, RW	1988	Bob Bourne, LA, C	2000	Ken Daneyko, NJ, D
1977	Ed Westfall, NYI, RW	1989	Tim Kerr, Phi., C	2001	Adam Graves, NYR, LW
1978	Butch Goring, LA, C	1990	Gord Kluzak, Bos., D	2002	Saku Koivu, Mon., C
1979	Serge Savard, Mon., D	1991	Dave Taylor, LA, RW	2003	Steve Yzerman, Det., C

Number One Draft Choices

Overall first choices in the NHL draft since the league staged its first universal amateur draft in 1969. Players are listed with team that selected them; those who became Rookie of the Year are in **bold** type.

Year		Year		Year	
1969	Rejean Houle, Mon., LW	1981	**Dale Hawerchuk,** Win., C	1993	Alexandre Daigle, Ott., C
1970	**Gilbert Perreault,** Buf., C	1982	Gord Kluzak, Bos., D	1994	Ed Jovanovski, Fla., D
1971	Guy Lafleur, Mon., RW	1983	Brian Lawton, Min., C	1995	**Bryan Berard,** Ott., D
1972	Billy Harris, NYI, RW	1984	**Mario Lemieux,** Pit., C	1996	Chris Phillips, Ott., D
1973	**Denis Potvin,** NYI, D	1985	Wendel Clark, Tor., LW/D	1997	Joe Thornton, Bos., C
1974	Greg Joly, Wash., D	1986	Joe Murphy, Det., C	1998	Vincent Lecavalier, TB, C
1975	Mel Bridgman, Phi., C	1987	Pierre Turgeon, Buf., C	1999	Patrik Stefan, Atl., C
1976	Rick Green, Wash., D	1988	Mike Modano, Min., C	2000	Rick DiPietro, NYI, G
1977	Dale McCourt, Det., C	1989	Mats Sundin, Que., RW	2001	Ilya Kovalchuk, Atl., RW
1978	**Bobby Smith,** Min., C	1990	Owen Nolan, Que., RW	2002	Rick Nash, Clb., LW
1979	Rob Ramage, Colo., D	1991	Eric Lindros, Que., C	2003	Marc-Andre Fleury, Pit., G
1980	Doug Wickenheiser, Mon., C	1992	Roman Hamrlik, TB, D		

World Hockey Association
WHA Finals

The World Hockey Association began play in 1972-73 as a 12-team rival of the 56-year-old NHL. The WHA played for the AVCO World Trophy in its seven playoff finals (Avco Financial Services underwrote the playoffs).

Multiple winners: Winnipeg (3); Houston (2).

Year	Winner	Head Coach	Series	Loser	Head Coach
1973	New England Whalers	Jack Kelley	4-1 (WWLWW)	Winnipeg Jets	Bobby Hull
1974	Houston Aeros	Bill Dineen	4-0	Chicago Cougars	Pat Stapleton
1975	Houston Aeros	Bill Dineen	4-0	Quebec Nordiques	Jean-Guy Gendron
1976	Winnipeg Jets	Bobby Kromm	4-0	Houston Aeros	Bill Dineen
1977	Quebec Nordiques	Marc Boileau	4-3 (LWLWWLW)	Winnipeg Jets	Bobby Kromm
1978	Winnipeg Jets	Larry Hillman	4-0	NE Whalers	Harry Neale
1979	Winnipeg Jets	Larry Hillman	4-2 (WWLWLW)	Edmonton Oilers	Glen Sather

Playoff MVPs—1973—No award; **1974**—No award; **1975**—Ron Grahame, Houston, G; **1976**—Ulf Nilsson, Winnipeg, C; **1977**—Serg Bernier, Quebec, C; **1978**—Bobby Guindon, Winnipeg, C; **1979**—Rich Preston, Winnipeg, RW.

Most Valuable Player

(Gordie Howe Trophy, 1976-79)

Year		G	A	Pts
1973	Bobby Hull, Win., LW	51	52	103
1974	Gordie Howe, Hou., RW	31	69	100
1975	Bobby Hull, Win., LW	77	65	142
1976	Marc Tardif, Que., LW	71	77	148
1977	Robbie Ftorek, Pho., C	46	71	117
1978	Marc Tardif, Que., LW	65	89	154
1979	Dave Dryden, Edm., G	41-17-2; 2.89		

Scoring Leaders

Year		Gm	G	A	Pts
1973	Andre Lacroix, Phi	78	50	74	124
1974	Mike Walton, Min	78	57	60	117
1975	Andre Lacroix, S. Diego	78	41	106	147
1976	Marc Tardif, Que	81	71	77	148
1977	Real Cloutier, Que	76	66	75	141
1978	Marc Tardif, Que	78	65	89	154
1979	Real Cloutier, Que	77	75	54	129

Note: In 1979, 18 year-old Rookie of the Year Wayne Gretzky finished third in scoring (46-64—110).

Rookie of the Year

Year		G	A	Pts
1973	Terry Caffery, N. Eng., C	39	61	100
1974	Mark Howe, Hou., LW	38	41	79
1975	Anders Hedberg, Win., RW	53	47	100
1976	Mark Napier, Tor., RW	43	50	93
1977	George Lyle, N. Eng., LW	39	33	72
1978	Kent Nilsson, Win., C	42	65	107
1979	Wayne Gretzky, Ind.-Edm., C	46	64	110

Best Goaltender

Year		Record	GAA
1973	Gerry Cheevers, Cleveland	32-20-0	2.84
1974	Don McLeod, Houston	33-13-3	2.56
1975	Ron Grahame, Houston	33-10-0	3.03
1976	Michel Dion, Indianapolis	14-15-1	2.74
1977	Ron Grahame, Houston	27-10-2	2.74
1978	Al Smith, New England	30-20-3	3.22
1979	Dave Dryden, Edmonton	41-17-2	2.89

Best Defenseman

Year	
1973	J.C. Tremblay, Quebec
1974	Pat Stapleton, Chicago
1975	J.C. Tremblay, Quebec
1976	Paul Shmyr, Cleveland
1977	Ron Plumb, Cincinnati
1978	Lars-Erik Sjoberg, Winnipeg
1979	Rick Ley, New England

Coach of the Year

Year			Improvement
1973	Jack Kelley, N. Eng		46-30-2*
1974	Billy Harris, Tor	35-39-4	to 41-33-4
1975	Sandy Hucul, Pho	Expan.	to 39-31-8
1976	Bobby Kromm, Win	38-35-5	to 52-27-2*
1977	Bill Dineen, Hou	53-27-0 *	to 50-24-6*
1978	Bill Dineen, Hou	50-24-6 *	to 42-34-4
1979	John Brophy, Birm	36-41-3	to 32-42-6

*Won Division.

WHA All-Star Game

The WHA All-Star Game was an Eastern Division vs Western Division contest from 1973-75. In 1976, the league's five Canadian-based teams played the nine teams in the US. Over the final three seasons—East played West in 1977; AVCO Cup champion Quebec played a WHA All-Star team in 1978; and in 1979, a full WHA All-Star team played a three-game series with Moscow Dynamo of the Soviet Union.

Year	Result	Host	Coaches	Most Valuable Player
1973	East 6, West 2	Quebec	Jack Kelley, Bobby Hull	Wayne Carleton, Ottawa
1974	East 8, West 4	St. Paul, MN	Jack Kelley, Bobby Hull	Mike Walton, Minnesota
1975	West 6, East 4	Edmonton	Bill Dineen, Ron Ryan	Rejean Houle, Quebec
1976	Canada 6, USA 1	Cleveland	Jean-Guy Gendron, Bill Dineen	Can—Real Cloutier, Que. USA—Paul Shmyr, Cleve.
1977	East 4, West 2	Hartford	Jacques Demers, Bobby Kromm	East—L. Levasseur, Min. West—W. Lindstrom, Win.
1978	Quebec 5, WHA 4	Quebec	Marc Boileau, Bill Dineen	Quebec—Marc Tardif WHA—Mark Howe, NE
1979	WHA def. Moscow Dynamo 3 games to none (4-2, 4-2, 4-3)	Edmonton	Larry Hillman, P. Iburtovich	No awards

World Championship
Men

The World Hockey Championship tournament has been played regularly since 1930. The International Ice Hockey Federation (IIHF), which governs both the World and Winter Olympic tournaments, considers the Olympic champions from 1920-68 to also be the World champions. However the IIHF has not recognized an Olympic champion as World champion since 1968. The IIHF has sanctioned separate World Championships in Olympic years four times–in 1972, 1976, 1992 and 2002. The world championship is officially vacant for the three Olympic years from 1980-88.

Multiple winners: Soviet Union/Russia (23); Canada (22); Sweden (7); Czechoslovakia (6) Czech Republic (4), USA (2).

Year		Year		Year		Year	
1920	Canada	1951	Canada	1969	Soviet Union	1987	Sweden
1924	Canada	1952	Canada	1970	Soviet Union	1988	Not held
1928	Canada	1953	Sweden	1971	Soviet Union	1989	Soviet Union
1930	Canada	1954	Soviet Union	1972	Czechoslovakia	1990	Soviet Union
1931	Canada	1955	Canada	1973	Soviet Union	1991	Sweden
1932	Canada	1956	Soviet Union	1974	Soviet Union	1992	Sweden
1933	United States	1957	Sweden	1975	Soviet Union	1993	Russia
1934	Canada	1958	Canada	1976	Czechoslovakia	1994	Canada
1935	Canada	1959	Canada	1977	Czechoslovakia	1995	Finland
1936	Great Britain	1960	United States	1978	Soviet Union	1996	Czech Republic
1937	Canada	1961	Canada	1979	Soviet Union	1997	Canada
1938	Canada	1962	Sweden	1980	Not held	1998	Sweden
1939	Canada	1963	Soviet Union	1981	Soviet Union	1999	Czech Republic
1940-46	Not held	1964	Soviet Union	1982	Soviet Union	2000	Czech Republic
1947	Czechoslovakia	1965	Soviet Union	1983	Soviet Union	2001	Czech Republic
1948	Canada	1966	Soviet Union	1984	Not held	2002	Slovakia
1949	Czechoslovakia	1967	Soviet Union	1985	Czechoslovakia	2003	Canada
1950	Canada	1968	Soviet Union	1986	Soviet Union		

Women

The women's World Hockey Championship tournament is governed by the International Ice Hockey Federation (IIHF).
Multiple winners: Canada (7).

Year		Year		Year		Year	
1990	Canada	1994	Canada	1999	Canada	2001	Canada
1992	Canada	1997	Canada	2000	Canada		

Canada vs. USSR Summits

The first competition between the Soviet National Team and the NHL took place Sept. 2-28, 1972. A team of NHL All-Stars emerged as the winner of the heralded 8-game series, but just barely–winning with a record of 4-3-1 after trailing 1-3-1.

Two years later a WHA All-Star team played the Soviet Nationals and could win only one game and tie three others in eight contests. Two other Canada vs USSR series took place during NHL All-Star breaks: the three-game Challenge Cup at New York in 1979, and the two-game Rendez-Vous '87 in Quebec City in 1987.

The NHL All-Stars played the USSR in a three-game Challenge Cup series in 1979.

1972 Team Canada vs. USSR
NHL All-Stars vs Soviet National Team.

Date	City	Result	Goaltenders
9/2	Montreal	USSR, 7-3	Tretiak/Dryden
9/4	Toronto	Canada, 4-1	Esposito/Tretiak
9/6	Winnipeg	Tie, 4-4	Tretiak/Esposito
9/8	Vancouver	USSR, 5-3	Tretiak/Dryden
9/22	Moscow	USSR, 5-4	Tretiak/Esposito
9/24	Moscow	Canada, 3-2	Dryden/Tretiak
9/26	Moscow	Canada, 4-3	Esposito/Tretiak
9/28	Moscow	Canada, 6-5	Dryden/Tretiak

Standings

	W	L	T	Pts	GF	GA
Team Canada (NHL)	4	3	1	9	32	32
Soviet Union	3	4	1	7	32	32

Leading Scorers

1. Phil Esposito, Canada, (7-6—13); **2.** Aleksandr Yakushev, USSR (7-4—11); **3.** Paul Henderson, Canada (7-2—9); **4.** Boris Shadrin, USSR (3-5—8); **5.** Valeri Kharlamov, USSR (3-4—7) and Vladimir Petrov, USSR (3-4—7).

1974 Team Canada vs. USSR
WHA All-Stars vs Soviet National Team.

Date	City	Result	Goaltenders
9/17	Quebec City	Tie, 3-3	Tretiak/Cheevers
9/19	Toronto	Canada, 4-1	Cheevers/Tretiak
9/21	Winnipeg	USSR, 8-5	Tretiak/McLeod
9/23	Vancouver	Tie, 5-5	Tretiak/Cheevers
10/1	Moscow	USSR, 3-2	Tretiak/Cheevers
10/3	Moscow	USSR, 5-2	Tretiak/Cheevers
10/5	Moscow	Tie, 4-4	Cheevers/Tretiak
10/6	Moscow	USSR, 3-2	Sidelinkov/Cheevers

Standings

	W	L	T	Pts	GF	GA
Soviet Union	4	1	3	11	32	27
Team Canada (WHA)	1	4	3	5	27	32

Leading Scorers

1. Bobby Hull, Canada (7-2—9); **2.** Aleksandr Yakushev, USSR (6-2—8), Ralph Backstrom, Canada (4-4—8) and Valeri Kharlamov, USSR (2-6—8); **5.** Gordie Howe, Canada (3-4—7), Andre Lacroix, Canada (1-6—7) and Vladimi Petrov, USSR (1-6—7).

1979 Challenge Cup Series
NHL All-Stars vs Soviet National Team

Date	City	Result	Goaltenders
2/8	New York	NHL, 4-2	K. Dryden/Tretiak
2/10	New York	USSR, 5-4	Tretiak/K. Dryden
2/11	New York	USSR, 6-0	Myshkin/Cheevers

Rendez-Vous '87
NHL All-Stars vs Soviet National Team

Date	City	Result	Goaltenders
2/11	Quebec	NHL, 4-3	Fuhr/Belosheykhin
2/13	Quebec	USSR, 5-3	Belosheykhin/Fuhr

The Canada Cup

After organizing the historic 8-game Team Canada-Soviet Union series of 1972, NHL Players Association executive director Alan Eagleson and the NHL created the Canada Cup in 1976. For the first time, the best players from the world's six major hockey powers—Canada, Czechoslovakia, Finland, Russia, Sweden and the USA—competed together in one tournament.

1976
Round Robin Standings

	W	L	T	Pts	GF	GA
Canada	4	1	0	8	22	6
Czechoslovakia	3	1	1	7	19	9
Soviet Union	2	2	1	5	23	14
Sweden	2	2	1	5	16	18
United States	1	3	1	3	14	21
Finland	1	4	0	2	16	42

Finals (Best of 3)

Date	City	Score
9/13	Toronto	Canada 6, Czechoslovakia 0
9/15	Montreal	Canada 5, Czechoslovakia 4 (OT)

Note: Darryl Sittler scored the winning goal for Canada at 11:33 in overtime to clinch the Cup, 2 games to none.

Leading Scorers

1. Victor Hluktov, USSR (5-4—9), Bobby Orr, Canada (2-7—9) and Denis Potvin, Canada (1-8—9); **4.** Bobby Hull, Canada (5-3—8) and Milan Novy, Czechoslovakia (5-3—8).

Team MVPs

Canada—Rogie Vachon   Sweden—Borje Salming
Czech.—Milan Novy   USA—Robbie Ftorek
USSR—Alexandr Maltsev   Finland—Matti Hagman
Tournament MVP—Bobby Orr, Canada

1981
Round Robin Standings

	W	L	T	Pts	GF	GA
Canada	4	0	1	9	32	13
Soviet Union	3	1	1	7	20	13
Czechoslovakia	2	1	2	6	21	13
United States	2	2	1	5	17	19
Sweden	1	4	0	2	13	20
Finland	0	4	1	1	6	31

Semifinals

Date	City	Score
9/11	Ottawa	USSR 4, Czechoslovakia 1
9/11	Montreal	Canada 4, United States 1

Finals

Date	City	Score
9/13	Montreal	USSR 8, Canada 1

Leading Scorers

1. Wayne Gretzky, Canada (5-7—12); **2.** Mike Bossy, Canada (8-3—11), Bryan Trottier, Canada (3-8—11), Guy Lafleur, Canada (2-9—11), Alexei Kasatonov, USSR (1-10—11).

All-Star Team

Goal—Vladislav Tretiak, USSR; **Defense**—Arnold Kadlec, Czech. and Alexei Kasatonov, USSR; **Forwards**—Mike Bossy, Canada, Gil Perreault, Canada, and Sergei Shepelev, USSR. **Tournament MVP**—Tretiak.

1984
Round Robin Standings

	W	L	T	Pts	GF	GA
Soviet Union	5	0	0	10	22	7
United States	3	1	1	7	21	13
Sweden	3	2	0	6	15	16
Canada	2	2	1	5	23	18
West Germany	0	4	1	1	13	29
Czechoslovakia	0	4	1	1	10	21

Semifinals

Date	City	Score
9/12	Edmonton	Sweden 9, United States 2
9/15	Montreal	Canada 3, USSR 2 (OT)

Note: Mike Bossy scored the winning goal for Canada at 12:29 in overtime.

Finals (Best of 3)

Date	City	Score
9/16	Calgary	Canada 5, Sweden 2
9/18	Edmonton	Canada 6, Sweden 5

Leading Scorers

1. Wayne Gretzky, Canada (5-7—12); **2.** Michel Goulet, Canada (5-6—11), Kent Nilsson, Sweden (3-8—11), Paul Coffey, Canada (3-8—11); **5.** Hakan Loob, Sweden (6-4—10).

All-Star Team

Goal—Vladimir Myshkin, USSR; **Defense**—Paul Coffey, Canada and Rod Langway, USA; **Forwards**—Wayne Gretzky, Canada, John Tonelli, Canada, and Sergei Makarov, USSR. **Tournament MVP**—Tonelli.

1987
Round Robin Standings

	W	L	T	Pts	GF	GA
Canada	3	0	2	8	19	13
Soviet Union	3	1	1	7	22	13
Sweden	3	2	0	6	17	14
Czechoslovakia	2	2	1	5	12	15
United States	2	3	0	4	13	14
Finland	1	0	5	0	9	23

Semifinals

Date	City	Score
9/8	Hamilton	USSR 4, Sweden 2
9/9	Montreal	Canada 5, Czechoslovakia 3

Finals (Best of 3)

Date	City	Score
9/11	Montreal	USSR 6, Canada 5 (OT)
9/13	Hamilton	Canada 6, USSR 5 (2 OT)
9/15	Hamilton	Canada 6, USSR 5

Note: In Game 1, Alexander Semak of USSR scored at 5:33 in overtime. In Game 2, Mario Lemieux of Canada scored at 10:01 in the second overtime period. Lemieux also won Game 3 on a goal with 1:26 left in regulation time.

Leading Scorers

1. Wayne Gretzky, Canada (3-18—21); **2.** Mario Lemieux, Canada (11-7—18); **3.** Sergei Makarov, USSR (7-8—15); **4.** Vladimir Krutov, USSR (7-7—14); **5.** Viacheslav Bykov, USSR (2-7—9); **6.** Ray Bourque, Canada (2-6—8).

All-Star Team

Goal—Grant Fuhr, Canada; **Defense**—Ray Bourque, Canada and Viacheslav Fetisov, USSR; **Forwards**—Wayne Gretzky, Canada, Mario Lemieux, Canada, and Vladimir Krutov, USSR. **Tournament MVP**—Gretzky.

1991

Round Robin Standings

	W	L	T	Pts	GF	GA
Canada	3	0	2	8	21	11
United States	4	1	0	8	19	15
Finland	2	2	1	5	10	13
Sweden	2	3	0	4	13	17
Soviet Union	1	3	1	3	14	14
Czechoslovakia	1	4	0	2	11	18

Semifinals

Date	City	Score
9/11	Hamilton	United States 7, Finland 3
9/12	Toronto	Canada 4, Sweden 0

Finals (Best of 3)

Date	City	Score
9/14	Montreal	Canada 4, United States 1
9/16	Hamilton	Canada 4, United States 2

Leading Scorers

1. Wayne Gretzky, Canada (4-8—12); **2.** Steve Larmer, Canada (6-5—11); **3.** Brett Hull, USA (2-7—9); **4.** Mike Modano, USA (2-7—9); **5.** Mark Messier, Canada (2-6—8).

All-Star Team

Goal—Bill Ranford, Canada; **Defense**—Al MacInnis, Canada and Chris Chelios, USA; **Forwards**—Wayne Gretzky, Canada, Jeremy Roenick, USA and Mats Sundin, Sweden. **Tournament MVP**—Bill Ranford.

The World Cup

Formed jointly by the NHL and the NHL Players Association in cooperation with the International Ice Hockey Federation. The inaugural World Cup held games in nine different cities throughout North America and Europe, the most ever by a single international hockey tournament.

1996

Round Robin Standings

European Pool	W	L	T	Pts	GF	GA
Sweden	3	0	0	6	14	3
Finland	2	1	0	4	17	11
Germany	1	2	0	2	11	15
Czech Republic	0	3	0	0	4	17

North American Pool	W	L	T	Pts	GF	GA
United States	3	0	0	6	19	8
Canada	2	1	0	4	11	10
Russia	1	2	0	2	12	14
Slovakia	0	3	0	0	10	18

Semifinals

Date	City	Score
9/7	Philadelphia	Canada 3, Sweden 2 (OT)
9/8	Ottawa	United States 5, Russia 2

Finals (Best of 3)

Date	City	Score
9/10	Philadelphia	Canada 4, United States 3 (OT)
9/12	Montreal	United States 5, Canada 2
9/14	Montreal	United States 5, Canada 2

Leading Scorers

1. Brett Hull, USA (7-4—11); **2.** John LeClair, USA (6-4—10); **3.** Mats Sundin, Sweden (4-3—7); Wayne Gretzky, Canada (3-4—7); Doug Weight, USA (3-4—7); Paul Coffey, Canada (0-7—7); Brian Leetch, USA (0-7—7).

All-Tournament Team

Goal—Mike Richter, USA; **Defense**—Calle Johansson, Sweden and Chris Chelios, USA; **Forwards**—Brett Hull, USA; John LeClair, USA and Mats Sundin, Sweden. **Tournament MVP**—Mike Richter, USA.

U.S. DIVISION I COLLEGE HOCKEY

NCAA Frozen Four

The NCAA Division I hockey tournament began in 1948 and was played at the Broadmoor Ice Palace in Colorado Springs from 1948-57. Since 1958, the tournament has moved around the country, stopping for consecutive years only at Boston Garden from 1972-74. Consolation games to determine third place were played from 1949-89 and discontinued in 1990.

Multiple winners: Michigan (9); North Dakota (7); Denver, Minnesota and Wisconsin (5); Boston University (4); Lake Superior St. and Michigan Tech (3); Boston College, Colorado College, Cornell, Maine, Michigan St. and RPI (2).

Year	Champion	Head Coach	Score	Runner-up	Third Place		
1948	Michigan	Vic Heyliger	8-4	Dartmouth	Colorado College and Boston College		

Year	Champion	Head Coach	Score	Runner-up	Third Place	Score	Fourth Place
1949	Boston College	Snooks Kelley	4-3	Dartmouth	Michigan	10-4	Colorado Col.
1950	Colorado College	Cheddy Thompson	13-4	Boston Univ.	Michigan	10-6	Boston College
1951	Michigan	Vic Heyliger	7-1	Brown	Boston Univ.	7-4	Colorado College
1952	Michigan	Vic Heyliger	4-1	Colorado Col.	Yale	4-1	St. Lawrence
1953	Michigan	Vic Heyliger	7-3	Minnesota	RPI	6-3	Boston Univ.
1954	RPI	Ned Harkness	5-4 *	Minnesota	Michigan	7-2	Boston College
1955	Michigan	Vic Heyliger	5-3	Colorado Col.	Harvard	6-3	St. Lawrence
1956	Michigan	Vic Heyliger	7-5	Michigan Tech	St. Lawrence	6-2	Boston College
1957	Colorado College	Tom Bedecki	13-6	Michigan	Clarkson	2-1†	Harvard
1958	Denver	Murray Armstrong	6-2	North Dakota	Clarkson	5-1	Harvard
1959	North Dakota	Bob May	4-3 *	Michigan St.	Boston College	7-6†	St. Lawrence
1960	Denver	Murray Armstrong	5-3	Michigan Tech	Boston Univ.	7-6	St. Lawrence
1961	Denver	Murray Armstrong	12-2	St. Lawrence	Minnesota	4-3	RPI
1962	Michigan Tech	John MacInnes	7-1	Clarkson	Michigan	5-1	St. Lawrence
1963	North Dakota	Barry Thorndycraft	6-5	Denver	Clarkson	5-3	Boston College
1964	Michigan	Allen Renfrew	6-3	Denver	RPI	2-1	Providence
1965	Michigan Tech	John MacInnes	8-2	Boston College	North Dakota	9-5	Brown
1966	Michigan St.	Amo Bessone	6-1	Clarkson	Denver	4-3	Boston Univ.

Year	Champion	Head Coach	Score	Runner-up	Third Place	Score	Fourth Place
1967	Cornell	Ned Harkness	4-1	Boston Univ.	Michigan St.	6-1	North Dakota
1968	Denver	Murray Armstrong	4-0	North Dakota	Cornell	6-1	Boston College
1969	Denver	Murray Armstrong	4-3	Cornell	Harvard	6-5†	Michigan Tech
1970	Cornell	Ned Harkness	6-4	Clarkson	Wisconsin	6-5	Michigan Tech
1971	Boston Univ.	Jack Kelley	4-2	Minnesota	Denver	1-0	Harvard
1972	Boston Univ.	Jack Kelley	4-0	Cornell	Wisconsin	5-2	Denver
1973	Wisconsin	Bob Johnson	4-2	Denver	Boston College	3-1	Cornell
1974	Minnesota	Herb Brooks	4-2	Michigan Tech	Boston Univ.	7-5	Harvard
1975	Michigan Tech	John MacInnes	6-1	Minnesota	Boston Univ.	10-5	Harvard
1976	Minnesota	Herb Brooks	6-4	Michigan Tech	Brown	8-7	Boston Univ.
1977	Wisconsin	Bob Johnson	6-5*	Michigan	Boston Univ.	6-5	N. Hampshire
1978	Boston Univ.	Jack Parker	5-3	Boston College	Bowl. Green	4-3	Wisconsin
1979	Minnesota	Herb Brooks	4-3	North Dakota	Dartmouth	7-3	N. Hampshire
1980	North Dakota	Gino Gasparini	5-2	N. Michigan	Dartmouth	8-4	Cornell
1981	Wisconsin	Bob Johnson	6-3	Minnesota	Mich. Tech	5-2	N. Michigan
1982	North Dakota	Gino Gasparini	5-2	Wisconsin	Northeastern	10-4	N. Hampshire
1983	Wisconsin	Jeff Sauer	6-2	Harvard	Providence	4-3	Minnesota
1984	Bowling Green	Jerry York	5-4*	Minn-Duluth	North Dakota	6-5†	Michigan St.
1985	RPI	Mike Addesa	2-1	Providence	Minn-Duluth	7-6†	Boston College
1986	Michigan St.	Ron Mason	6-5	Harvard	Minnesota	6-4	Denver
1987	North Dakota	Gino Gasparini	5-3	Michigan St.	Minnesota	6-3	Harvard
1988	Lake Superior St.	Frank Anzalone	4-3*	St. Lawrence	Maine	5-2	Minnesota
1989	Harvard	Billy Cleary	4-3*	Minnesota	Michigan St.	7-4	Maine

Year	Champion	Head Coach	Score	Runner-up	Third Place
1990	Wisconsin	Jeff Sauer	7-3	Colgate	Boston College and Boston Univ.
1991	Northern Michigan	Rick Comley	8-7*	Boston Univ.	Maine and Clarkson
1992	Lake Superior St.	Jeff Jackson	5-3	Wisconsin	Michigan and Michigan St.
1993	Maine	Shawn Walsh	5-4	Lake Superior St.	Boston Univ. and Michigan
1994	Lake Superior St.	Jeff Jackson	9-1	Boston Univ.	Harvard and Minnesota
1995	Boston Univ.	Jack Parker	6-2	Maine	Michigan and Minnesota
1996	Michigan	Red Berenson	3-2*	Colorado Col.	Vermont and Boston Univ.
1997	North Dakota	Dean Blais	6-4	Boston Univ.	Colorado College and Michigan
1998	Michigan	Red Berenson	3-2*	Boston College	New Hampshire and Ohio St.
1999	Maine	Shawn Walsh	3-2*	New Hampshire	Boston College and Michigan St.
2000	North Dakota	Dean Blais	4-2	Boston College	St. Lawrence and Maine
2001	Boston College	Jerry York	3-2*	North Dakota	Michigan and Michigan St.
2002	Minnesota	Don Lucia	4-3*	Maine	Michigan and New Hampshire
2003	Minnesota	Don Lucia	5-1	New Hampshire	Michigan and Cornell

*Championship game overtime goals: **1954**—1:54; **1959**—4:22; **1977**—0: 23; **1984**—7:11 in 4th OT; **1988**—4:46; **1989**—4:16; **1991**—1:57 in 3rd OT; **1996**—3:35; **1998**—17:51; **1999**—10:50; **2001**—4:43; **2002**—16:58.
†Consolation game overtimes ended in 1st OT except in 1957, '59, and '69, which all ended in 2nd OT.
Note: Runners-up Denver (1973) and Wisconsin (1992) had participation voided by the NCAA for using ineligible players.

Most Outstanding Player

The Most Outstanding Players of each NCAA Div. I tournament since 1948. Winners of the award who did not play for the tournament champion are in **bold** type. In 1960, three players, none on the winning team, shared the award.
   Multiple winners: Lou Angotti and Marc Behrend (2).

Year	Year	Year
1948 **Joe Riley,** Dartmouth, F	1966 Gaye Cooley, Mich. St., G	1986 Mike Donnelly, Mich. St., F
1949 **Dick Desmond,** Dart., G	1967 Walt Stanowski, Cornell, D	1987 Tony Hrkac, N. Dakota, F
1950 **Ralph Bevins,** Boston U., G	1968 Gerry Powers, Denver, G	1988 Bruce Hoffort, Lk. Superior, G
1951 **Ed Whiston,** Brown, G	1969 Keith Magnuson, Denver, D	1989 Ted Donato, Harvard, F
1952 **Ken Kinsley,** Colo. Col., G	1970 Dan Lodboa, Cornell, D	1990 Chris Tancill, Wisconsin, F
1953 John Matchefts, Mich., F	1971 Dan Brady, Boston U., G	1991 Scott Beattie, No. Mich., F
1954 Abbie Moore, RPI, F	1972 Tim Regan, Boston, U., G	1992 Paul Constantin, Lk. Superior, F
1955 **Phil Hilton,** Colo. Col., D	1973 Dean Talafous, Wisc., F	1993 Jim Montgomery, Maine, F
1956 Lorne Howes, Mich., G	1974 Brad Shelstad, Minn., G	1994 Sean Tallaire, Lk. Superior, F
1957 Bob McCusker, Colo. Col., F	1975 Jim Warden, Mich. Tech, G	1995 Chris O'Sullivan, Boston U., F
1958 Murray Massier, Denver, F	1976 Tom Vanelli, Minn., F	1996 Brendan Morrison, Michigan, F
1959 Reg Morelli, N. Dakota, F	1977 Julian Baretta, Wisc., F	1997 Matt Henderson, N. Dakota, F
1960 **Lou Angotti,** Mich. Tech, F;	1978 Jack O'Callahan, Boston U., D	1998 Marty Turco, Michigan, G
Bob Marquis, Boston U., F;	1979 Steve Janaszak, Minn., G	1999 Alfie Michaud, Maine, G
& **Barry Urbanski,** BU, G	1980 Doug Smail, N. Dakota, F	2000 Lee Goren, N. Dakota, F
1961 Bill Masterton, Denver, F	1981 Marc Behrend, Wisc., G	2001 Chuck Kobasew, Boston College, F
1962 Lou Angotti, Mich. Tech, F	1982 Phil Sykes, N. Dakota, F	2002 Grant Potulny, Minnesota, F
1963 Al McLean, N. Dakota, F	1983 Marc Behrend, Wisc., G	2003 Thomas Vanek, Minnesota, F
1964 Bob Gray, Michigan, G	1984 Gary Kruzich, Bowl. Green, G	
1965 Gary Milroy, Mich. Tech, F	1985 **Chris Terreri,** Prov., G	

U.S. Division I College Hockey (Cont.)
Hobey Baker Award

College hockey's Player of the Year award; voted on by a national panel of sportswriters, broadcasters, college coaches and pro scouts (plus a fan vote beginning in 2003). First presented in 1981 by the Decathlon Athletic Club of Bloomington, Minn., in the name of the Princeton collegiate hockey and football star who was killed in a plane crash.

Year	Year	Year
1981 Neal Broten, Minnesota, F	1989 Lane MacDonald, Harvard, F	1997 Brendan Morrison, Michigan, F
1982 George McPhee, Bowl. Green, F	1990 Kip Miller, Michigan St., F	1998 Chris Drury, Boston U., F
1983 Mark Fusco, Harvard, D	1991 Dave Emma, Boston College, F	1999 Jason Krog, UNH, F
1984 Tom Kurvers, Minn-Duluth, D	1992 Scott Pellerin, Maine, F	2000 Mike Mottau, Boston College, D
1985 Bill Watson, Minn-Duluth, F	1993 Paul Kariya, Maine, F	2001 Ryan Miller, Michigan St., G
1986 Scott Fusco, Harvard, F	1994 Chris Marinucci, Minn-Duluth, F	2002 Jordan Leopold, Minnesota, D
1987 Tony Hrkac, North Dakota, F	1995 Brian Holzinger, Bowl. Green, F	2003 Peter Sejna, Colorado Coll., F
1988 Robb Stauber, Minnesota, G	1996 Brian Bonin, Minnesota, F	

Coach of the Year

The Penrose Memorial Trophy, voted on by the American Hockey Coaches Association and first presented in 1951 in the name of Colorado gold and copper magnate Spencer T. Penrose. Penrose built the Broadmoor hotel and athletic complex in Colorado Springs that originally hosted the NCAA hockey championship from 1948-57.

Multiple winners: Len Ceglarski and Charlie Holt (3); Dean Blais, Rick Comley, Eddie Jeremiah, Snooks Kelly, John MacInnes, Joe Marsh, Jack Parker, Jack Riley and Cooney Weiland (2).

Year	Year	Year
1951 Eddie Jeremiah, Dartmouth	1970 John MacInnes, Michigan Tech	1990 Terry Slater, Colgate
1952 Cheddy Thompson, Colo. Col.	1971 Cooney Weiland, Harvard	1991 Rick Comley, No. Michigan
1953 John Mariucci, Minnesota	1972 Snooks Kelly, BC	1992 Ron Mason, Michigan St.
1954 Vic Heyliger, Michigan	1973 Len Ceglarski, BC	1993 George Gwozdecky, Miami-OH
1955 Cooney Weiland, Harvard	1974 Charlie Holt, New Hampshire	1994 Don Lucia, Colorado Col.
1956 Bill Harrison, Clarkson	1975 Jack Parker, BU	1995 Shawn Walsh, Maine
1957 Jack Riley, Army	1976 John MacInnes, Michigan Tech	1996 Bruce Crowder, UMass-Lowell
1958 Harry Cleverly, BU	1977 Jerry York, Clarkson	1997 Dean Blais, N. Dakota
1959 Snooks Kelly, BC	1978 Jack Parker, BU	1998 Tim Taylor, Yale
1960 Jack Riley, Army	1979 Charlie Holt, New Hampshire	1999 Dick Umile, UNH
1961 Murray Armstrong, Denver	1980 Rick Comley, No. Michigan	
1962 Jack Kelley, Colby	1981 Bill O'Flarety, Clarkson	2000 Joe Marsh, St. Lawrence
1963 Tony Frasca, Colorado Col.	1982 Fern Flaman, Northeastern	2001 Dean Blais, N. Dakota
1964 Tom Eccleston, Providence	1983 Bill Cleary, Harvard	2002 Tim Whitehead, Maine
1965 Jim Fulllerton, Brown	1984 Mike Sertich, Minn-Duluth	2003 Bob Daniels, Ferris St.
1966 Amo Bessone, Michigan St.	1985 Len Ceglarski, BU	**Note:** 1960 winner Jack Riley won the
& Len Ceglarski, Clarkson	1986 Ralph Backstrom, Denver	award for coaching the USA to its first
1967 Eddie Jeremiah, Dartmouth	1987 Gino Gasparini, N. Dakota	hockey gold medal in the Winter
1968 Ned Harkness, Cornell	1988 Frank Anzalone, Lk. Superior	Olympics at Squaw Valley.
1969 Charlie Holt, New Hampshire	1989 Joe Marsh, St. Lawrence	

NCAA Women's Frozen Four

Women's college hockey was officially introduced as an NCAA Division I sport in 2000-01.
Multiple winner: Minnesota-Duluth (3).

Year	Champion	Head Coach	Score	Runner-up	Third Place	Score	Fourth Place
2001	Minnesota-Duluth	Shannon Miller	4-2	St. Lawrence	Harvard	3-2	Dartmouth
2002	Minnesota-Duluth	Shannon Miller	3-2	Brown	(tie) Niagara and Minnesota, 2-2		
2003	Minnesota-Duluth	Shannon Miller	4-3*	Harvard	Dartmouth	4-2	Minnesota

*Championship game overtime goal: 2003—4:19 in 2nd OT.

Most Outstanding Player

The Most Outstanding Players of each NCAA Women's Division I tournament since 2001. Winner of the award who did not play for the tournament champion in **bold** type.

Year	Year	Year
2001 Maria Rooth, Minn.-Duluth, F	2002 **Kristy Zamora**, Brown, F	2003 Caroline Ouellette, Minn.-Duluth, F

Patty Kazmaier Award

Awarded annually to the women's Division I player who displays the highest standards of personal and team excellence during the season; voted on by a 13-member panel of national media, college coaches and one USA Hockey member. First presented in 1998, in the name of the Princeton collegiate hockey and lacrosse star who died in 1990 of a rare blood disease.
Multiple winner: Jennifer Botterill (2).

Year	Year	Year
1998 Brandy Fisher, New Hampshire, F	2000 Ali Brewer, Brown, G	2002 Brooke Whitney, Northeastern, F
1999 A.J. Mleczko, Harvard, F	2001 Jennifer Botterill, Harvard, F	2003 Jennifer Botterill, Harvard, F

College Sports

Former Indiana president **Myles Brand** took the office of president of the NCAA in 2003.

Moral Exam

Programs are left to clean up from a wave of embarrassing coaching scandals that rocked the NCAA.

Michael Morrison
is co-editor of the ESPN Sports Almanac.

Article 11.1.1 under the "Coaching" section of the 2003-04 NCAA Manual states,

"Individuals employed by…a member institution to administer, conduct or coach intercollegiate athletics shall act with honesty and sportsmanship at all times so that they and their institutions represent the honor and dignity of fair play and high standards associated with wholesome competitive sports."

It's safe to say that in 2002-03, Article 11.1.1 took a major beating.

In 2001-02 the scandal-du-jour in the NCAA was coaches "exaggerating" on their resumes. This year coaches truly sunk to new depths on the debauchery-meter. The rap sheet read like the description of a "Lifetime" mini-series.

Gambling…drinking…sex…murder cover-up. You name it, they did it.

The first sign of trouble occurred in late December in Nashville. Tennessee State basketball coach Nolan Richardson III,

his team off to a sluggish 2-5 start, became embroiled in a heated argument with assistant Hosea Lewis at a practice on Christmas night. An enraged Richardson reportedly stormed off to his car and returned to the gym a few minutes later looking for Lewis, claiming he "had something for him." It turned out the "something" Richardson had was a handgun.

Whether it was loaded or not is disputed. Richardson claims it wasn't. For athletic director Teresa Phillips, it didn't matter and Richardson was forced to resign two weeks later.

"I'm really ready to move forward and look to bring some positive, new leadership for Tennessee State men's basketball," said Phillips.

Instead, she named Lewis the head coach for the remainder of the season. The team, obviously enthused by the change, went 0-19 the rest of the way, including one game when Phillips herself

AP/Wide World Photos

*Baylor basketball coach **Davis Bliss**, left, and athletic director **Tom Stanton**, right, bow their heads at a memorial service for Patrick Dennehy. Both men would resign the following day.*

assumed coaching duties after Lewis was suspended for his role in a bench-clearing brawl.

In March 2003 Georgia basketball coach Jim Harrick and his son, Jim Harrick Jr., were each sent packing amidst charges of academic fraud and improper payments to athletes. Evidently Harrick Jr. decided to help out former player Tony Cole by paying various bills for him and giving him an "A" in a course ("Coaching Principles and Strategies of Basketball") that Cole later admitted he never even attended. Harrick Jr. was fired. His dad technically resigned, and then retired, putting an end to a success-

ful coaching career on the court, but one riddled with NCAA compliance issues at almost every stop.

Two months later, the ugliness continued and the embarrassment picked up. In early May, Iowa State hoops coach Larry Eustachy resigned after pictures were released on the internet of him partying it up with students in Missouri after a game. The photos showed, among other things, a glassy-eyed Eustachy at a frat house with a can of beer in one hand and a blonde co-ed in the other. That's usually a bad move in the professional world.

Eustachy pled for his job, in the process admitting he was an alcoholic, but in the end the highest-paid state employee in Iowa agreed to resign (with a substantial cash settlement) and get the help he needs.

Also in early May, Alabama fired football coach Mike Price before he even coached a game, when it was reported he had a romp in a Florida hotel room with at least one stripper, who then rung up a $1,000 room service bill to Price's credit card. Illegal? Nope. Immoral? You better believe it, especially for a highly ranked, well paid, not to mention married, school official whose two sons were also on the coaching staff.

In June the coaching scandal "wheel of misfortune" landed on Washington when it was reported that football coach Rick Neuheisel won $12,123 on the past two NCAA Basketball Tournaments. Sure, it may seem to some like a paltry offense, especially compared with the litany of wrongdoings by some of his coaching peers. Literally millions of people sit in their cubicles and paperclip a $5 bill to a bracket each year. But that doesn't mean it's not illegal. For an employee in the athletic department of an NCAA institution, it's even more illegal. Every staff member, from the athletic director to the receptionist to the department intern, is made aware that any form of gambling is a no-no. Surely the head coach of a major Division I program should have known better. Still, Neuheisel pled ignorance,

Brian Bahr/Getty Images

*Iowa State's **Larry Eustachy** was done in by pictures of him partying with students.*

and in the end, he traded his $1.2 million salary for a cool $12,123. Not such a good bet after all.

All of these cases turned out to be just a prelude to what is clearly the worst offense of the year. When news broke about the disappearance, and later, the tragic death of Baylor basketball player Patrick Dennehy, head coach Dave Bliss publicly acted sympathetic. Secretly (or so he thought), he couldn't have been more devious.

To keep investigators from discovering that he paid part of Dennehy's tuition,

continued on page 438 ▶

The Ten Biggest Stories
of the Year in College Sports

10 In order to remain in compliance with Title IX regulations, University of Maryland makes cheerleading a varsity sport. By offering 12 cheerleading scholarships over the next three years (along with eight more in women's water polo), the school will be allowed to dole out 20 additional scholarships to men's teams.

9 Indiana president Myles Brand is elected the new president of the NCAA, replacing Cedric Dempsey, who had held the position since 1994. He is the first university president to hold the NCAA's top post.

8 U. of Michigan sues former player Chris Webber for $695,000 to recoup funds the school says it lost in NCAA tournament earnings, legal fees, and other penalties caused by Webber's actions.

7 Stanford once again proves it is the best overall Division I college athletics program, winning the Directors' Cup for the ninth consecutive year. UC-Davis (Division II), Williams, MA (Division III) and Lindenwood, MO (NAIA) also win their respective divisions.

6 Ohio St. running back Maurice Clarett is suspended for the entire 2003 season for accepting improper payments and lying to the NCAA. In September, he sues the NFL in an attempt to do away with the league's rule prohibiting players from entering the draft unless they have been out of high school for three years.

5 Lewis University, a school with roughly 3,400 students located in Romeoville, Illinois, storms its way into the NCAA men's national collegiate volleyball tournament, then shocks top-seeded Brigham Young in five games to win the title. It is the first Division II school to win the NCAA volleyball championship.

4 In what could be a sign of things to come, Vanderbilt dismantles its athletic department, folding it into the school's Division of Student Life and University Affairs, which is overseen by Chancellor Gordon Gee. According to Gee, the move is meant to "bring some balance back into the nature of intercollegiate athletics."

3 After much speculation, Miami-FL and Virginia Tech are chosen to join the Atlantic Coast Conference, beginning in 2004. The impending exodus sends shockwaves through the Big East, whose leaders immediately begin the search for replacements.

2 In the first week of May, Iowa State hoops coach Larry Eustachy and Alabama football coach Mike Price both lose their jobs after details emerge regarding their behavior.

1 Baylor basketball coach Dave Bliss resigns after a secret tape recording reveals an attempt to cover up numerous NCAA violations in the aftermath of the death of Patrick Dennehy.

Bliss enlisted the help of certain assistant coaches and players to say Dennehy was a drug dealer and used that money to pay his tuition. What he didn't realize was that assistant Abar Rouse was recording the conversations.

"If there's any way that we can even create the perception of the fact that Pat may have been a dealer ... even if we had to kind of make some things look a little better than they are, that can save us," Bliss was heard saying.

While his plan was to impugn the reputation of a dead student-athlete, he ended up damaging his school's, the NCAA's and destroying his own. After his resignation, Bliss applied for volunteer work at a Texas jail, which is probably where he belongs.

For his part, NCAA President Myles Brand is staying optimistic and considering the poor behavior of these coaches as the exception, not the norm.

"Some coaches, a small minority, must feel as though their marketability makes them immune from social norms," said Brand. "That is absurd. And they are being exposed and fired."

There are 327 Division I men's basketball head coaches and 240 football coaches. Many, even most, follow the code set forth in Article 11.1.1. Sadly they're overshadowed by the famous few that didn't.

Winning in Style

Rice's 14-2 victory over Stanford in the College Baseball World Series title game was the largest margin of victory ever in a Series-clinching game.

	Opponent	Diff.
2003 Rice (14-2)	Stanford	12
2001 Miami-FL (12-1)	Stanford	11
1956 Minnesota (12-1)	Arizona	11
1969 Arizona St. (10-1)	Tulsa	9
1967 Arizona St. (11-2)	Houston	9
1994 Oklahoma (13-5)	Ga. Tech	8
1993 LSU (8-0)	Wichita St.	8
1986 Arizona (10-2)	Florida St.	8

Joltin' Damian?

Division III Salve Regina OF Damian Costantino broke the all-divisions consecutive game hitting streak mark held by current major leaguer Robin Ventura. His streak started April 1, 2001 and finally ended on March 11, 2003.

Source: NCAA News

	Gms
Damian Costantino, Salve Regina, 2003	60
Robin Ventura, Oklahoma St., 1987	58
Phil Stephensen, Wichita St., 1981	47
Corey Breyne, Aurora, 1998	46
Roger Schmuck, Arizona St., 1971	45

Note: Year given indicates the end of the streak.

NCAA Schools & Champs

SPORTS ALMANAC

NCAA Division I-A Football Schools
2003 Season
Conferences and coaches as of Sept. 28, 2003.

Joining Conference USA in 2003: SOUTH FLORIDA from Independent.
Joining Sun Belt in 2003: UTAH STATE from Independent.
Move approved to Division I-A in 2004: FLORIDA A&M from I-AA Mid-Eastern.
Joining ACC in 2004: MIAMI-FL and VIRGINIA TECH from Big East.
Joining Big East in 2004: CONNECTICUT from Independent.
Joining Sun Belt in 2004: TROY ST. from Independent.
Leaving Conference USA in 2005: ARMY to Independent.

	Nickname	Conference	Head Coach	Location	Colors
Air Force	Falcons	Mountain West	Fisher DeBerry	Colo. Springs, CO	Blue/Silver
Akron	Zips	Mid-American	Lee Owens	Akron, OH	Blue/Gold
Alabama	Crimson Tide	SEC-West	Mike Shula	Tuscaloosa, AL	Crimson/White
Arizona	Wildcats	Pac-10	Mike Hankwitz	Tucson, AZ	Cardinal/Navy
Arizona St.	Sun Devils	Pac-10	Dirk Koetter	Tempe, AZ	Maroon/Gold
Arkansas	Razorbacks	SEC-West	Houston Nutt	Fayetteville, AR	Cardinal/White
Arkansas St.	Indians	Sun Belt	Steve Roberts	State Univ., AR	Scarlet/Black
Army	Cadets, Black Knights	USA	Todd Berry	West Point, NY	Black/Gold/Gray
Auburn	Tigers	SEC-West	Tommy Tuberville	Auburn, AL	Orange/Blue
Ball St.	Cardinals	Mid-American	Brady Hoke	Muncie, IN	Cardinal/White
Baylor	Bears	Big 12	Guy Morriss	Waco, TX	Green/Gold
Boise St.	Broncos	WAC	Dan Hawkins	Boise, ID	Orange/Blue
Boston College	Eagles	Big East	Tom O'Brien	Chestnut Hill, MA	Maroon/Gold
Bowling Green	Falcons	Mid-American	Gregg Brandon	Bowling Green, OH	Orange/Brown
Brigham Young	Cougars	Mountain West	Gary Crowton	Provo, UT	Royal Blue/White
Buffalo	Bulls	Mid-American	Jim Hofher	Buffalo, NY	Royal Blue/White
California	Golden Bears	Pac-10	Jeff Tedford	Berkeley, CA	Blue/Gold
Central Florida	Golden Knights	Mid-American	Mike Kruczek	Orlando, FL	Black/Gold
Central Michigan	Chippewas	Mid-American	Mike DeBord	Mt. Pleasant, MI	Maroon/Gold
Cincinnati	Bearcats	USA	Rick Minter	Cincinnati, OH	Red/Black
Clemson	Tigers	ACC	Tommy Bowden	Clemson, SC	Purple/Orange
Colorado	Buffaloes	Big 12	Gary Barnett	Boulder, CO	Silver/Gold/Black
Colorado St.	Rams	Mountain West	Sonny Lubick	Ft. Collins, CO	Green/Gold
Connecticut	Huskies	Independent	Randy Edsall	Storrs, CT	Blue/White
Duke	Blue Devils	ACC	Carl Franks	Durham, NC	Royal Blue/White
East Carolina	Pirates	USA	John Thompson	Greenville, NC	Purple/Gold
Eastern Michigan	Eagles	Mid-American	Jeff Woodruff	Ypsilanti, MI	Green/White
Florida	Gators	SEC-East	Ron Zook	Gainesville, FL	Orange/Blue
Florida St.	Seminoles	ACC	Bobby Bowden	Tallahassee, FL	Garnet/Gold
Fresno St.	Bulldogs	WAC	Pat Hill	Fresno, CA	Cardinal/Blue
Georgia	Bulldogs	SEC-East	Mark Richt	Athens, GA	Red/Black
Georgia Tech	Yellow Jackets	ACC	Chan Gailey	Atlanta, GA	Old Gold/White
Hawaii	Warriors	WAC	June Jones	Honolulu, HI	Green/White
Houston	Cougars	USA	Art Briles	Houston, TX	Scarlet/White
Idaho	Vandals	Sun Belt	Tom Cable	Moscow, ID	Silver/Gold
Illinois	Fighting Illini	Big Ten	Ron Turner	Champaign, IL	Orange/Blue
Indiana	Hoosiers	Big Ten	Gerry DiNardo	Bloomington, IN	Cream/Crimson
Iowa	Hawkeyes	Big Ten	Kirk Ferentz	Iowa City, IA	Old Gold/Black
Iowa St.	Cyclones	Big 12	Dan McCarney	Ames, IA	Cardinal/Gold
Kansas	Jayhawks	Big 12	Mark Mangino	Lawrence, KS	Crimson/Blue
Kansas St.	Wildcats	Big 12	Bill Snyder	Manhattan, KS	Purple/White
Kent St.	Golden Flashes	Mid-American	Dean Pees	Kent, OH	Navy Blue/Gold
Kentucky	Wildcats	SEC-East	Rich Brooks	Lexington, KY	Blue/White
LSU	Fighting Tigers	SEC-West	Nick Saban	Baton Rouge, LA	Purple/Gold
LA-Lafayette	Ragin' Cajuns	Sun Belt	Rickey Bustle	Lafayette, LA	Vermilion/White
LA-Monroe	Indians	Sun Belt	Charlie Weatherbie	Monroe, LA	Maroon/Gold
Louisiana Tech	Bulldogs	WAC	Jack Bicknell III	Ruston, LA	Red/Blue
Louisville	Cardinals	USA	Bob Petrino	Louisville, KY	Red/Black/White

	Nickname	Conference	Head Coach	Location	Colors
Marshall	Thundering Herd	Mid-American	Bob Pruett	Huntington, WV	Green/White
Maryland	Terrapins, Terps	ACC	Ralph Friedgen	College Park, MD	Red/White/Black/Gold
Memphis	Tigers	USA	Tommy West	Memphis, TN	Blue/Gray
Miami-FL	Hurricanes	Big East	Larry Coker	Coral Gables, FL	Orange/Grn./Wt.
Miami-OH	RedHawks	Mid-American	Terry Hoeppner	Oxford, OH	Red/White
Michigan	Wolverines	Big Ten	Lloyd Carr	Ann Arbor, MI	Maize/Blue
Michigan St.	Spartans	Big Ten	John L. Smith	E. Lansing, MI	Green/White
Middle Tenn. St.	Blue Raiders	Sun Belt	Andy McCollum	Murfreesboro, TN	Blue/White
Minnesota	Golden Gophers	Big Ten	Glen Mason	Minneapolis, MN	Maroon/Gold
Mississippi	Ole Miss, Rebels	SEC-West	David Cutcliffe	Oxford, MS	Cardinal/Navy Bl.
Mississippi St.	Bulldogs	SEC-West	Jackie Sherrill	Starkville, MS	Maroon/White
Missouri	Tigers	Big 12	Gary Pinkel	Columbia, MO	Old Gold/Black
Navy	Midshipmen	Independent	Paul Johnson	Annapolis, MD	Navy Blue/Gold
Nebraska	Cornhuskers	Big 12	Frank Solich	Lincoln, NE	Scarlet/Cream
Nevada	Wolf Pack	WAC	Chris Tormey	Reno, NV	Silver/Blue
New Mexico	Lobos	Mountain West	Rocky Long	Albuquerque, NM	Cherry/Silver
New Mexico St.	Aggies	Sun Belt	Tony Samuel	Las Cruces, NM	Crimson/White
North Carolina	Tar Heels	ACC	John Bunting	Chapel Hill, NC	Carolina Blue/Wt.
North Carolina St.	Wolfpack	ACC	Chuck Amato	Raleigh, NC	Red/White
North Texas	Mean Green	Sun Belt	Darrell Dickey	Denton, TX	Green/White
Northern Illinois	Huskies	Mid-American	Joe Novak	De Kalb, IL	Cardinal/Black
Northwestern	Wildcats	Big Ten	Randy Walker	Evanston, IL	Purple/White
Notre Dame	Fighting Irish	Independent	Tyrone Willingham	Notre Dame, IN	Gold/Blue
Ohio University	Bobcats	Mid-American	Brian Knorr	Athens, OH	Hunter Green/Wt.
Ohio St.	Buckeyes	Big Ten	Jim Tressel	Columbus, OH	Scarlet/Gray
Oklahoma	Sooners	Big 12	Bob Stoops	Norman, OK	Crimson/Cream
Oklahoma St.	Cowboys	Big 12	Les Miles	Stillwater, OK	Orange/Black
Oregon	Ducks	Pac-10	Mike Bellotti	Eugene, OR	Green/Yellow
Oregon St.	Beavers	Pac-10	Mike Riley	Corvallis, OR	Orange/Black
Penn St.	Nittany Lions	Big Ten	Joe Paterno	University Park, PA	Blue/White
Pittsburgh	Panthers	Big East	Walt Harris	Pittsburgh, PA	Blue/Gold
Purdue	Boilermakers	Big Ten	Joe Tiller	W. Lafayette, IN	Old Gold/Black
Rice	Owls	WAC	Ken Hatfield	Houston, TX	Blue/Gray
Rutgers	Scarlet Knights	Big East	Greg Schiano	New Brunswick, NJ	Scarlet
San Diego St.	Aztecs	Mountain West	Tom Craft	San Diego, CA	Scarlet/Black
San Jose St.	Spartans	WAC	Fitz Hill	San Jose, CA	Gold/White/Blue
South Carolina	Gamecocks	SEC-East	Lou Holtz	Columbia, SC	Garnet/Black
South Florida	Bulls	USA	Jim Leavitt	Tampa, FL	Green/Gold
SMU	Mustangs	WAC	Phil Bennett	Dallas, TX	Red/Blue
Southern Miss.	Golden Eagles	USA	Jeff Bower	Hattiesburg, MS	Black/Gold
Stanford	Cardinal	Pac-10	Buddy Teevens	Stanford, CA	Cardinal/White
Syracuse	Orangemen	Big East	Paul Pasqualoni	Syracuse, NY	Orange
Temple	Owls	Big East	Bobby Wallace	Philadelphia, PA	Cherry/White
Tennessee	Volunteers	SEC-East	Phillip Fulmer	Knoxville, TN	Orange/White
Texas	Longhorns	Big 12	Mack Brown	Austin, TX	Burnt Orange/Wt.
Texas A&M	Aggies	Big 12	Dennis Franchione	College Station, TX	Maroon/White
TCU	Horned Frogs	USA	Gary Patterson	Ft. Worth, TX	Purple/White
Texas Tech	Red Raiders	Big 12	Mike Leach	Lubbock, TX	Scarlet/Black
Toledo	Rockets	Mid-American	Tom Amstutz	Toledo, OH	Blue/Gold
Troy State	Trojans	Independent	Larry Blakeney	Troy, AL	Cardinal/Slvr./Blk.
Tulane	Green Wave	USA	Chris Scelfo	New Orleans, LA	Olive Grn./Sky Bl.
Tulsa	Golden Hurricane	WAC	Steve Kragthorpe	Tulsa, OK	Blue/Gold
UAB	Blazers	USA	Watson Brown	Birmingham, AL	Green/Gold
UCLA	Bruins	Pac-10	Karl Dorrell	Los Angeles, CA	Blue/Gold
UNLV	Rebels	Mountain West	John Robinson	Las Vegas, NV	Scarlet/Gray
USC	Trojans	Pac-10	Pete Carroll	Los Angeles, CA	Cardinal/Gold
Utah	Utes	Mountain West	Urban Meyer	Salt Lake City, UT	Crimson/White
Utah St.	Aggies	Sun Belt	Mick Dennehy	Logan, UT	Navy Blue/White
UTEP	Miners	WAC	Gary Nord	El Paso, TX	Orange/Blue/Wt.
Vanderbilt	Commodores	SEC-East	Bobby Johnson	Nashville, TN	Black/Gold
Virginia	Cavaliers	ACC	Al Groh	Charlottesville, VA	Orange/Blue
Virginia Tech	Hokies, Gobblers	Big East	Frank Beamer	Blacksburg, VA	Orange/Maroon
Wake Forest	Demon Deacons	ACC	Jim Grobe	Winston-Salem, NC	Old Gold/Black
Washington	Huskies	Pac-10	Keith Gilbertson	Seattle, WA	Purple/Gold
Washington St.	Cougars	Pac-10	Bill Doba	Pullman, WA	Crimson/Gray
West Virginia	Mountaineers	Big East	Rich Rodriguez	Morgantown, WV	Old Gold/Blue
Western Michigan	Broncos	Mid-American	Gary Darnell	Kalamazoo, MI	Brown/Gold
Wisconsin	Badgers	Big Ten	Barry Alvarez	Madison, WI	Cardinal/White
Wyoming	Cowboys	Mountain West	Joe Glenn	Laramie, WY	Brown/Yellow

NCAA Division I-AA Football Schools
2003 Season
Conferences and coaches as of Sept. 28, 2003.

Joining Big South in 2003: VIRGINIA MILITARY INSTITUTE from Southern and COASTAL CAROLINA (new program).
Joining Southern in 2003: ELON from Big South.
Joining Ohio Valley in 2003: JACKSONVILLE ST. from Southland and SAMFORD from Independent.
To I-AA Independent in 2003: SOUTHEASTERN LOUISIANA (program reinstated), UC-DAVIS and NORTHERN COLORADO (as transitional members from Division II).
Leaving Metro Atlantic in 2003: CANISIUS and FAIRFIELD (programs discontinued).
Leaving Northeast in 2003: ST. JOHN'S (program discontinued).
Leaving I-AA Independent in 2003: MORRIS BROWN (program suspended).
Joining Atlantic 10 in 2004: TOWSON from Patriot.
Leaving Southern in 2004: EAST TENNESSEE ST. (program discontinued).
To I-AA Independent in 2004: SOUTH DAKOTA ST. from Division II.
Joining Southland in 2005: SOUTHEASTERN LOUISIANA from Independent.

	Nickname	Conference	Head Coach	Location	Colors
Alabama A&M	Bulldogs	SWAC	Anthony Jones	Huntsville, AL	Maroon/White
Alabama St.	Hornets	SWAC	Charles Coe	Montgomery, AL	Black/Gold
Albany	Great Danes	Northeast	Bob Ford	Albany, NY	Purple/Gold
Alcorn St.	Braves	SWAC	Johnny Thomas	Lorman, MS	Purple/Gold
Appalachian St.	Mountaineers	Southern	Jerry Moore	Boone, NC	Black/Gold
Ark.-Pine Bluff	Golden Lions	SWAC	Lee Hardman	Pine Bluff, AR	Black/Gold
Austin Peay St.	Governors	Pioneer	Carroll McCray	Clarksville, TN	Red/White
Bethune-Cookman	Wildcats	Mid-Eastern	Alvin Wyatt	Daytona Beach, FL	Maroon/Gold
Brown	Bears	Ivy	Phil Estes	Providence, RI	Brown/Red/White
Bucknell	Bison	Patriot	Tim Landis	Lewisburg, PA	Orange/Blue
Butler	Bulldogs	Pioneer	Kit Cartwright	Indianapolis, IN	Blue/White
Cal Poly	Mustangs	Independent	Rich Ellerson	San Luis Obispo, CA	Green/Gold
Central Conn. St.	Blue Devils	Northeast	Paul Schudel	New Britain, CT	Blue/White
Charleston So.	Buccaneers	Big South	Jay Mills	Charleston, SC	Blue/Gold
Chattanooga	Mocs	Southern	Rodney Allison	Chattanooga, TN	Navy Blue/Old Gold
The Citadel	Bulldogs	Southern	Ellis Johnson	Charleston, SC	Blue/White
Coastal Carolina	Chanticleers	Big South	David Bennett	Conway, SC	Green/Bronze/Black
Colgate	Raiders	Patriot	Dick Biddle	Hamilton, NY	Maroon/White/Gray
Columbia	Lions	Ivy	Bob Shoop	New York, NY	Lt. Blue/White
Cornell	Big Red	Ivy	Tim Pendergast	Ithaca, NY	Carnelian/White
Dartmouth	Big Green	Ivy	John Lyons	Hanover, NH	Green/White
Davidson	Wildcats	Pioneer	Mike Toop	Davidson, NC	Red/Black
Dayton	Flyers	Pioneer	Mike Kelly	Dayton, OH	Red/Blue
Delaware	Blue Hens	Atlantic 10	K.C. Keeler	Newark, DE	Blue/Gold
Delaware St.	Hornets	Mid-Eastern	Ben Blacknall	Dover, DE	Red/Blue
Drake	Bulldogs	Pioneer	Rob Ash	Des Moines, IA	Blue/White
Duquesne	Dukes	Metro Atlantic	Greg Gattuso	Pittsburgh, PA	Red/Blue
East Tenn. St.	Buccaneers	Southern	Paul Hamilton	Johnson City, TN	Blue/Gold
Eastern Illinois	Panthers	Ohio Valley	Bob Spoo	Charleston, IL	Blue/Gray
Eastern Kentucky	Colonels	Ohio Valley	Danny Hope	Richmond, KY	Maroon/White
Eastern Washington	Eagles	Big Sky	Paul Wulff	Cheney, WA	Red/White
Elon	Phoenix	Southern	Al Seagraves	Elon, NC	Maroon/Gold
Florida A&M	Rattlers	Mid-Eastern	Billy Joe	Tallahassee, FL	Orange/Green
Florida Atlantic	Owls	Independent	H. Schnellenberger	Boca Raton, FL	Blue/Red
Florida Int'l	Golden Panthers	Independent	Don Strock	Miami, FL	Blue/Gold
Fordham	Rams	Patriot	Dave Clawson	Bronx, NY	Maroon/White
Furman	Paladins	Southern	Bobby Lamb	Greenville, SC	Purple/White
Gardner-Webb	Bulldogs	Big South	Steve Patton	Boiling Springs, NC	Scarlet/Black
Georgetown	Hoyas	Patriot	Bob Benson	Washington, DC	Blue/Gray
Georgia Southern	Eagles	Southern	Mike Sewak	Statesboro, GA	Blue/White
Grambling St.	Tigers	SWAC	Doug Williams	Grambling, LA	Black/Gold
Hampton	Pirates	Mid-Eastern	Joe Taylor	Hampton, VA	Royal Blue/White
Harvard	Crimson	Ivy	Tim Murphy	Cambridge, MA	Crimson/Black/White
Hofstra	Pride	Atlantic 10	Joe Gardi	Hempstead, NY	Gold/White/Blue
Holy Cross	Crusaders	Patriot	Dan Allen	Worcester, MA	Royal Purple
Howard	Bison	Mid-Eastern	Rayford T. Petty	Washington, DC	Blue/Wt./Red
Idaho St.	Bengals	Big Sky	Larry Lewis	Pocatello, ID	Orange/Black
Illinois St.	Redbirds	Gateway	Denver Johnson	Normal, IL	Red/White
Indiana St.	Sycamores	Gateway	Tim McGuire	Terre Haute, IN	Royal Blue/White
Iona	Gaels	Metro Atlantic	Fred Mariani	New Rochelle, NY	Maroon/Gold
Jackson St.	Tigers	SWAC	James Bell	Jackson, MS	Blue/White
Jacksonville	Dolphins	Pioneer	Steve Gilbert	Jacksonville, FL	Green/White
Jacksonville St.	Gamecocks	Ohio Valley	Jack Crowe	Jacksonville, AL	Red/White
James Madison	Dukes	Atlantic 10	Mickey Matthews	Harrisonburg, VA	Purple/Gold

	Nickname	Conference	Head Coach	Location	Colors
Lafayette	Leopards	Patriot	Frank Tavani	Easton, PA	Maroon/White
La Salle	Explorers	Metro Atlantic	Archie Stalcup	Philadelphia, PA	Blue/Gold
Lehigh	Engineers	Patriot	Pete Lembo	Bethlehem, PA	Brown/White
Liberty	Flames	Big South	Ken Karcher	Lynchburg, VA	Red/White/Blue
Maine	Black Bears	Atlantic 10	Jack Cosgrove	Orono, ME	Blue/White
Marist	Red Foxes	Metro Atlantic	Jim Parady	Poughkeepsie, NY	Red/White
Massachusetts	Minutemen	Atlantic 10	Mark Whipple	Amherst, MA	Maroon/White
McNeese St.	Cowboys	Southland	Tommy Tate	Lake Charles, LA	Blue/Gold
Miss. Valley St.	Delta Devils	SWAC	Willie Totten	Itta Bena, MS	Green/White
Monmouth	Hawks	Northeast	Kevin Callahan	W. Long Branch, NJ	Royal Blue/White
Montana	Grizzlies	Big Sky	Bobby Hauck	Missoula, MT	Maroon/Gray
Montana St.	Bobcats	Big Sky	Mike Kramer	Bozeman, MT	Blue/Gold
Morehead St.	Eagles	Pioneer	Matt Ballard	Morehead, KY	Blue/Gold
Morgan St.	Bears	Mid-Eastern	Stanley Mitchell	Baltimore, MD	Blue/Orange
Murray St.	Racers	Ohio Valley	Joe Pannunzio	Murray, KY	Blue/Gold
New Hampshire	Wildcats	Atlantic 10	Sean McDonnell	Durham, NH	Blue/White
Nicholls St.	Colonels	Southland	Daryl Daye	Thibodaux, LA	Red/Gray
Norfolk State	Spartans	Mid-Eastern	Willie Gillus	Norfolk, VA	Green/Gold
North Carolina A&T	Aggies	Mid-Eastern	George Small	Greensboro, NC	Blue/Gold
Northeastern	Huskies	Atlantic 10	Don Brown	Boston, MA	Red/Black
Northern Arizona	Lumberjacks	Big Sky	Jerome Souers	Flagstaff, AZ	Blue/Gold
Northern Colorado	Bears	Independent	O. Kay Dalton	Greeley, CO	Blue/Gold
Northern Iowa	Panthers	Gateway	Mark Farley	Cedar Falls, IA	Purple/Old Gold
Northwestern St.	Demons	Southland	Scott Stoker	Natchitoches, LA	Purple/White
Pennsylvania	Quakers	Ivy	Al Bagnoli	Philadelphia, PA	Red/Blue
Portland St.	Vikings	Big Sky	Tim Walsh	Portland, OR	Green/Gray
Prairie View A&M	Panthers	SWAC	C.L. Whittington	Prairie View, TX	Purple/Gold
Princeton	Tigers	Ivy	Roger Hughes	Princeton, NJ	Orange/Black
Rhode Island	Rams	Atlantic 10	Tim Stowers	Kingston, RI	Light Blue/Navy/Wt.
Richmond	Spiders	Atlantic 10	Jim Reid	Richmond, VA	Red/Blue
Robert Morris	Colonials	Northeast	Joe Walton	Moon Township, PA	Blue/White
Sacramento St.	Hornets	Big Sky	Steve Mooshagian	Sacramento, CA	Green/Gold
Sacred Heart	Pioneers	Northeast	Bill Lacey	Fairfield, CT	Scarlet/White
St. Francis-PA	Red Flash	Northeast	Dave Opfar	Loretto, PA	Red/White
Saint Mary's-CA	Gaels	Independent	Vincent White	Moraga, CA	Red/Blue
Saint Peter's	Peacocks	Metro Atlantic	Scott Kochman	Jersey City, NJ	Blue/White
Sam Houston St.	Bearkats	Southland	Ron Randleman	Huntsville, TX	Orange/White
Samford	Bulldogs	Ohio Valley	Bill Gray	Birmingham, AL	Crimson/Blue
San Diego	Toreros	Pioneer	Kevin McGarry	San Diego, CA	Lt. Blue/Navy
Savannah St.	Tigers	Independent	Richard Basil	Savannah, GA	Orange/Blue
Siena	Saints	Metro Atlantic	Jay Bateman	Loudonville, NY	Green/Gold
South Carolina St.	Bulldogs	Mid-Eastern	Oliver Pough	Orangeburg, SC	Garnet/Blue
SE Missouri St.	Indians	Ohio Valley	Tim Billings	Cape Girardeau, MO	Red/Black
SE Louisiana	Lions	Independent	Hal Mumme	Hammond, LA	Green/Gold
Southern-BR	Jaguars	SWAC	Pete Richardson	Baton Rouge, LA	Blue/Gold
Southern Illinois	Salukis	Gateway	Jerry Kill	Cardondale, IL	Maroon/White
Southern Utah	Thunderbirds	Independent	Gary Andersen	Cedar City, UT	Scarlet/White
SW Missouri St.	Bears	Gateway	Randy Ball	Springfield, MO	Maroon/White
S.F. Austin St.	Lumberjacks	Southland	Mike Santiago	Nacogdoches, TX	Purple/White
Stony Brook	Seawolves	Northeast	Sam Kornhauser	Stony Brook, NY	Scarlet/Gray
Tennessee-Martin	Skyhawks	Ohio Valley	Matt Griffin	Martin, TN	Orange/White/Blue
Tennessee St.	Tigers	Ohio Valley	James Reese	Nashville, TN	Blue/White
Tennessee Tech	Golden Eagles	Ohio Valley	Mike Hennigan	Cookeville, TN	Purple/Gold
Texas Southern	Tigers	SWAC	Bill Thomas	Houston, TX	Maroon/Gray
Texas St.-San Marcos	Bobcats	Southland	Manny Matsakis	San Marcos, TX	Maroon/Gold
Towson	Tigers	Patriot	Gordy Combs	Towson, MD	Gold/White
UC-Davis	Aggies	Independent	Bob Biggs	Davis, CA	Yale Blue/Gold
Valparaiso	Crusaders	Pioneer	Tom Horne	Valparaiso, IN	Brown/Gold
Villanova	Wildcats	Atlantic 10	Andy Talley	Villanova, PA	Blue/White
VMI	Keydets	Big South	Cal McCombs	Lexington, VA	Red/White/Yellow
Wagner	Seahawks	Northeast	Walt Hameline	Staten Island, NY	Green/White
Weber St.	Wildcats	Big Sky	Jerry Graybeal	Ogden, UT	Royal Purple/White
Western Carolina	Catamounts	Southern	Kent Briggs	Cullowhee, NC	Purple/Gold
Western Illinois	Leathernecks	Gateway	Don Patterson	Macomb, IL	Purple/Gold
Western Kentucky	Hilltoppers	Gateway	David Elson	Bowling Green, KY	Red/White
William & Mary	Tribe	Atlantic 10	Jimmye Laycock	Williamsburg, VA	Green/Gold/Silver
Wofford	Terriers	Southern	Mike Ayers	Spartanburg, SC	Old Gold/Black
Yale	Bulldogs, Elis	Ivy	Jack Siedlecki	New Haven, CT	Yale Blue/White
Youngstown St.	Penguins	Gateway	Jon Heacock	Youngstown, OH	Red/White

NCAA Division I Basketball Schools
2003-2004 Season
Conferences and coaches as of Sept. 28, 2003.

Joining America East in 2003-2004: MARYLAND-BALTIMORE COUNTY from Northeast.
Joining Atlantic Sun in 2003-2004: LIPSCOMB from Independent.
Joining Big South in 2003-2004: VIRGINIA MILITARY INSTITUTE from Southern.
Joining Mid-Continent in 2003-2004: CENTENARY from Independent.
Joining Ohio Valley in 2003-2004: JACKSONVILLE ST., SAMFORD from Atlantic Sun.
Joining Southern in 2003-2004: ELON from Big South.
To Div. I Independent in 2003-04: LONGWOOD, NORTHERN COLORADO, UC-DAVIS, UTAH VALLEY ST. from Div. II.
Leaving Independent in 2003-04: MORRIS BROWN (program suspended).
Joining ACC in 2004-05: MIAMI-FL and VIRGINIA TECH from Big East.
Joining Big West in 2004-05: UC-DAVIS from Independent.
To Div. I Independent in 2004-05: SOUTH DAKOTA ST. from Div. II.
Joining Sun Belt in 2005-06: IDAHO and UTAH ST. from Big West, TROY ST. from Atlantic Sun.

	Nickname	Conference	Head Coach	Location	Colors
Air Force	Falcons	Mountain West	Joe Scott	Colo. Springs, CO	Blue/Silver
Akron	Zips	Mid-American	Dan Hipsher	Akron, OH	Blue/Gold
Alabama	Crimson Tide	SEC-West	Mark Gottfried	Tuscaloosa, AL	Crimson/White
Alabama A&M	Bulldogs	SWAC	Vann Pettaway	Huntsville, AL	Maroon/White
Alabama St.	Hornets	SWAC	Rob Spivery	Montgomery, AL	Black/Gold
Albany	Great Danes	America East	Will Brown	Albany, NY	Purple/Gold
Alcorn St.	Braves	SWAC	Samuel West	Lorman, MS	Purple/Gold
American	Eagles	Patriot	Jeff Jones	Washington, DC	Red/Blue
Appalachian St.	Mountaineers	Southern	Houston Fancher	Boone, NC	Black/Gold
Arizona	Wildcats	Pac-10	Lute Olson	Tucson, AZ	Cardinal/Navy
Arizona St.	Sun Devils	Pac-10	Rob Evans	Tempe, AZ	Maroon/Gold
Arkansas	Razorbacks	SEC-West	Stan Heath	Fayetteville, AR	Cardinal/White
Ark.-Little Rock	Trojans	Sun Belt	Steve Shields	Little Rock, AR	Maroon/White
Ark.-Pine Bluff	Golden Lions	SWAC	Van Holt	Pine Bluff, AR	Black/Gold
Arkansas St.	Indians	Sun Belt	Dickey Nutt	State Univ., AR	Scarlet/Black
Army	Black Knights	Patriot	Jim Crews	West Point, NY	Black/Gold/Gray
Auburn	Tigers	SEC-West	Cliff Ellis	Auburn, AL	Orange/Blue
Austin Peay St.	Governors	Ohio Valley	Dave Loos	Clarksville, TN	Red/White
Ball St.	Cardinals	Mid-American	Tim Buckley	Muncie, IN	Cardinal/White
Baylor	Bears	Big 12	Scott Drew	Waco, TX	Green/Gold
Belmont	Bruins	Atlantic Sun	Rick Byrd	Nashville, TN	Navy Blue/Red
Bethune-Cookman	Wildcats	Mid-Eastern	Clifford Reed	Daytona Beach, FL	Maroon/Gold
Binghamton	Bearcats	America East	Al Walker	Binghamton, NY	Green/Black/White
Birmingham Southern	Panthers	Big South	Duane Reboul	Birmingham, AL	Black/Gold
Boise St.	Broncos	WAC	Greg Graham	Boise, ID	Orange/Blue
Boston College	Eagles	Big East	Al Skinner	Chestnut Hill, MA	Maroon/Gold
Boston University	Terriers	America East	Dennis Wolff	Boston, MA	Scarlet/White
Bowling Green	Falcons	Mid-American	Dan Dakich	Bowling Green, OH	Orange/Brown
Bradley	Braves	Mo. Valley	Jim Les	Peoria, IL	Red/White
Brigham Young	Cougars	Mountain West	Steve Cleveland	Provo, UT	Royal Blue/White
Brown	Bears	Ivy	Glen Miller	Providence, RI	Brown/Cardinal/White
Bucknell	Bison	Patriot	Pat Flannery	Lewisburg, PA	Orange/Blue
Buffalo	Bulls	Mid-American	R. Witherspoon	Buffalo, NY	Royal Blue/White
Butler	Bulldogs	Horizon	Todd Lickliter	Indianapolis, IN	Blue/White
California	Golden Bears	Pac-10	Ben Braun	Berkeley, CA	Blue/Gold
Cal Poly	Mustangs	Big West	Kevin Bromley	San Luis Obispo, CA	Green/Gold
CS-Fullerton	Titans	Big West	Bob Burton	Fullerton, CA	Blue/Orange/White
CS-Northridge	Matadors	Big West	Bobby Braswell	Northridge, CA	Red/White/Black
Campbell	Fighting Camels	Atlantic Sun	Robbie Laing	Buies Creek, NC	Orange/Black
Canisius	Golden Griffins	Metro Atlantic	Mike MacDonald	Buffalo, NY	Blue/Gold
Centenary	Gents, Gentlemen	Mid-Continent	Kevin Johnson	Shreveport, LA	Maroon/White
Central Conn. St.	Blue Devils	Northeast	Howie Dickenman	New Britain, CT	Blue/White
Central Florida	Golden Knights	Atlantic Sun	Kirk Speraw	Orlando, FL	Black/Gold
Central Michigan	Chippewas	Mid-American	Jay Smith	Mt. Pleasant, MI	Maroon/Gold
Charleston So.	Buccaneers	Big South	Jim Platt	Charleston, SC	Blue/Gold
Charlotte	49ers	USA	Bobby Lutz	Charlotte, NC	Green/White
Chattanooga	Mocs	Southern	Jeff Lebo	Chattanooga, TN	Navy Blue/Old Gold
Chicago St.	Cougars	Mid-Continent	Kevin Jones	Chicago, IL	Green/White
Cincinnati	Bearcats	USA	Bob Huggins	Cincinnati, OH	Red/Black
The Citadel	Bulldogs	Southern	Pat Dennis	Charleston, SC	Blue/White
Clemson	Tigers	ACC	Oliver Purnell	Clemson, SC	Purple/Orange
Cleveland St.	Vikings	Horizon	Mike Garland	Cleveland, OH	Forest Green/White
Coastal Carolina	Chanticleers	Big South	Pete Strickland	Conway, SC	Green/Bronze/Black
Colgate	Raiders	Patriot	Emmett Davis	Hamilton, NY	Maroon/Gray/White

NCAA Division I Basketball Schools (Cont.)

	Nickname	Conference	Head Coach	Location	Colors
College of Charleston	Cougars	Southern	Tom Herrion	Charleston, SC	Maroon/White
Colorado	Buffaloes	Big 12	Ricardo Patton	Boulder, CO	Silver/Gold/Black
Colorado St.	Rams	Mountain West	Dale Layer	Ft. Collins, CO	Green/Gold
Columbia	Lions	Ivy	Joseph Jones	New York, NY	Lt. Blue/White
Connecticut	Huskies	Big East	Jim Calhoun	Storrs, CT	Blue/White
Coppin St.	Eagles	Mid-Eastern	Ron Mitchell	Baltimore, MD	Royal Blue/Gold
Cornell	Big Red	Ivy	Steve Donahue	Ithaca, NY	Carnelian/White
Creighton	Bluejays	Mo. Valley	Dana Altman	Omaha, NE	Blue/White
Dartmouth	Big Green	Ivy	Dave Faucher	Hanover, NH	Green/White
Davidson	Wildcats	Southern	Bob McKillop	Davidson, NC	Red/Black
Dayton	Flyers	Atlantic 10	Brian Gregory	Dayton, OH	Red/Blue
Delaware	Fightin' Blue Hens	Colonial	David Henderson	Newark, DE	Blue/Gold
Delaware St.	Hornets	Mid-Eastern	Greg Jackson	Dover, DE	Red/Columbia Blue
Denver	Pioneers	Sun Belt	Terry Carroll	Denver, CO	Crimson/Gold
DePaul	Blue Demons	USA	Dave Leitao	Chicago, IL	Scarlet/Blue
Detroit Mercy	Titans	Horizon	Perry Watson	Detroit, MI	Red/White/Blue
Drake	Bulldogs	Mo. Valley	Tom Davis	Des Moines, IA	Blue/White
Drexel	Dragons	Colonial	Bruiser Flint	Philadelphia, PA	Navy Blue/Gold
Duke	Blue Devils	ACC	Mike Krzyzewski	Durham, NC	Royal Blue/White
Duquesne	Dukes	Atlantic 10	Danny Nee	Pittsburgh, PA	Red/Blue
East Carolina	Pirates	USA	Bill Herrion	Greenville, NC	Purple/Gold
East Tenn. St.	Buccaneers	Southern	Murry Bartow	Johnson City, TN	Blue/Gold
Eastern Illinois	Panthers	Ohio Valley	Rick Samuels	Charleston, IL	Blue/Gray
Eastern Kentucky	Colonels	Ohio Valley	Travis Ford	Richmond, KY	Maroon/White
Eastern Michigan	Eagles	Mid-American	Jim Boone	Ypsilanti, MI	Green/White
Eastern Washington	Eagles	Big Sky	Ray Giacoletti	Cheney, WA	Red/White
Elon	Phoenix	Southern	Ernie Nestor	Elon, NC	Maroon/Gold
Evansville	Aces	Mo. Valley	Steve Merfeld	Evansville, IN	Purple/White
Fairfield	Stags	Metro Atlantic	Tim O'Toole	Fairfield, CT	Cardinal Red
Fairleigh Dickinson	Knights	Northeast	Tom Green	Teaneck, NJ	Maroon/Blue
Florida	Gators	SEC-East	Billy Donovan	Gainesville, FL	Orange/Blue
Florida A&M	Rattlers	Mid-Eastern	Mike Gillespie	Tallahassee, FL	Orange/Green
Florida Atlantic	Owls	Atlantic Sun	Sidney Green	Boca Raton, FL	Blue/Red
Florida Int'l	Golden Panthers	Sun Belt	Donnie Marsh	Miami, FL	Blue/Gold
Florida St.	Seminoles	ACC	Leonard Hamilton	Tallahassee, FL	Garnet/Gold
Fordham	Rams	Atlantic 10	Dereck Whittenburg	Bronx, NY	Maroon/White
Fresno St.	Bulldogs	WAC	Ray Lopes	Fresno, CA	Cardinal/Blue
Furman	Paladins	Southern	Larry Davis	Greenville, SC	Purple/White
Gardner-Webb	Bulldogs	Atlantic Sun	Rick Scruggs	Boiling Springs, NC	Scarlet/Black
George Mason	Patriots	Colonial	Jim Larranaga	Fairfax, VA	Green/Gold
George Washington	Colonials	Atlantic 10	Karl Hobbs	Washington, DC	Buff/Blue
Georgetown	Hoyas	Big East	Craig Esherick	Washington, DC	Blue/Gray
Georgia	Bulldogs, 'Dawgs	SEC-East	Dennis Felton	Athens, GA	Red/Black
Georgia Southern	Eagles	Southern	Jeff Price	Statesboro, GA	Blue/White
Georgia St.	Panthers	Atlantic Sun	Michael Perry	Atlanta, GA	Roy. Blue/White
Georgia Tech	Yellow Jackets	ACC	Paul Hewitt	Atlanta, GA	Old Gold/White
Gonzaga	Bulldogs, Zags	West Coast	Mark Few	Spokane, WA	Blue/White/Red
Grambling St.	Tigers	SWAC	Larry Wright	Grambling, LA	Black/Gold
Hampton	Pirates	Mid-Eastern	Bobby Collins	Hampton, VA	Royal Blue/White
Hartford	Hawks	America East	Larry Harrison	W. Hartford, CT	Scarlet/White
Harvard	Crimson	Ivy	Frank Sullivan	Cambridge, MA	Crimson/Black/White
Hawaii	Rainbows	WAC	Riley Wallace	Honolulu, HI	Green/White
High Point	Panthers	Big South	Bart Lundy	High Point, NC	Purple/White
Hofstra	Pride	Colonial	Tom Pecora	Hempstead, NY	Blue/Gold/White
Holy Cross	Crusaders	Patriot	Ralph Willard	Worcester, MA	Royal Purple
Houston	Cougars	USA	Ray McCallum	Houston, TX	Scarlet/White
Howard	Bison	Mid-Eastern	Frankie Allen	Washington, DC	Blue/White/Red
Idaho	Vandals	Big West	Leonard Perry	Moscow, ID	Silver/Gold
Idaho St.	Bengals	Big Sky	Doug Oliver	Pocatello, ID	Orange/Black
Illinois	Fighting Illini	Big Ten	Bruce Weber	Champaign, IL	Orange/Blue
Illinois-Chicago	Flames	Horizon	Jim Collins	Chicago, IL	Navy Blue/Red
Illinois St.	Redbirds	Mo. Valley	Porter Moser	Normal, IL	Red/White
Indiana	Hoosiers	Big Ten	Mike Davis	Bloomington, IN	Cream/Crimson
IPFW	Mastodons	Independent	Doug Noll	Fort Wayne, IN	Royal Blue/White
IUPUI	Jaguars	Mid-Continent	Ron Hunter	Indianapolis, IN	Red/Gold
Indiana St.	Sycamores	Mo. Valley	Royce Waltman	Terre Haute, IN	Blue/White
Iona	Gaels	Metro Atlantic	Jeff Ruland	New Rochelle, NY	Maroon/Gold
Iowa	Hawkeyes	Big Ten	Steve Alford	Iowa City, IA	Old Gold/Black

	Nickname	Conference	Head Coach	Location	Colors
Iowa St.	Cyclones	Big 12	Wayne Morgan	Ames, IA	Cardinal/Gold
Jackson St.	Tigers	SWAC	Tevester Anderson	Jackson, MS	Blue/White
Jacksonville	Dolphins	Atlantic Sun	Hugh Durham	Jacksonville, FL	Green/White
Jacksonville St.	Gamecocks	Ohio Valley	Mike LaPlante	Jacksonville, AL	Red/White
James Madison	Dukes	Colonial	Sherman Dillard	Harrisonburg, VA	Purple/Gold
Kansas	Jayhawks	Big 12	Bill Self	Lawrence, KS	Crimson/Blue
Kansas St.	Wildcats	Big 12	Jim Wooldridge	Manhattan, KS	Purple/White
Kent St.	Golden Flashes	Mid-American	Jim Christian	Kent, OH	Navy Blue/Gold
Kentucky	Wildcats	SEC-East	Tubby Smith	Lexington, KY	Blue/White
La Salle	Explorers	Atlantic 10	Bill Hahn	Philadelphia, PA	Blue/Gold
Lafayette	Leopards	Patriot	Fran O'Hanlon	Easton, PA	Maroon/White
Lamar	Cardinals	Southland	Billy Tubbs	Beaumont, TX	Red/White
Lehigh	Mountain Hawks, Engineers	Patriot	Bill Taylor	Bethlehem, PA	Brown/White
Liberty	Flames	Big South	Randy Dunton	Lynchburg, VA	Red/White/Blue
Lipscomb	Bisons	Atlantic Sun	Scott Sanderson	Nashville, TN	Purple/Gold
Long Beach St.	49ers	Big West	Larry Reynolds	Long Beach, CA	Black/Gold
Longwood	Lancers	Independent	Mike Gillian	Farmville, VA	Blue/White
LIU-Brooklyn	Blackbirds	Northeast	Jim Ferry	Brooklyn, NY	Black/Silver/Blue
LSU	Fighting Tigers	SEC-West	John Brady	Baton Rouge, LA	Purple/Gold
LA-Lafayette	Ragin' Cajuns	Sun Belt	Jessie Evans	Lafayette, LA	Vermilion/White
LA-Monroe	Indians	Southland	Mike Vining	Monroe, LA	Maroon/Gold
Louisiana Tech	Bulldogs	WAC	Keith Richard	Ruston, LA	Red/Blue
Louisville	Cardinals	USA	Rick Pitino	Louisville, KY	Red/Black/White
Loyola Marymount	Lions	West Coast	Steve Aggers	Los Angeles, CA	Crimson/Blue
Loyola-IL	Ramblers	Horizon	Larry Farmer	Chicago, IL	Maroon/Gold
Loyola-MD	Greyhounds	Metro Atlantic	Scott Hicks	Baltimore, MD	Green/Gray
Maine	Black Bears	America East	John Giannini	Orono, ME	Blue/White
Manhattan	Jaspers	Metro Atlantic	Bobby Gonzalez	Riverdale, NY	Kelly Green/White
Marist	Red Foxes	Metro Atlantic	Dave Magarity	Poughkeepsie, NY	Red/White
Marquette	Golden Eagles	USA	Tom Crean	Milwaukee, WI	Blue/Gold
Marshall	Thundering Herd	Mid-American	Ron Jirsa	Huntington, WV	Green/White
Maryland	Terrapins, Terps	ACC	Gary Williams	College Park, MD	Red/Wt./Black/Gold
MD-Balt. County	Retrievers	America East	Tom Sullivan	Baltimore, MD	Black/Gold/Red
MD-Eastern Shore	Hawks	Mid-Eastern	Thomas Trotter	Princess Anne, MD	Maroon/Gray
Massachusetts	Minutemen	Atlantic 10	Steve Lappas	Amherst, MA	Maroon/White
McNeese St.	Cowboys	Southland	Tic Price	Lake Charles, LA	Blue/Gold
Memphis	Tigers	USA	John Calipari	Memphis, TN	Blue/Gray
Mercer	Bears	Atlantic Sun	Mark Slonaker	Macon, GA	Orange/Black
Miami-FL	Hurricanes	Big East	Perry Clark	Coral Gables, FL	Orange/Grn./White
Miami-OH	RedHawks	Mid-American	Charlie Coles	Oxford, OH	Red/White
Michigan	Wolverines	Big Ten	Tommy Amaker	Ann Arbor, MI	Maize/Blue
Michigan St.	Spartans	Big Ten	Tom Izzo	East Lansing, MI	Green/White
Middle Tenn. St.	Blue Raiders	Sun Belt	Kermit Davis Jr.	Murfreesboro, TN	Blue/White
Minnesota	Golden Gophers	Big Ten	Dan Monson	Minneapolis, MN	Maroon/Gold
Mississippi	Ole Miss, Rebels	SEC-West	Rod Barnes	Oxford, MS	Red/Blue
Mississippi St.	Bulldogs	SEC-West	Rick Stansbury	Starkville, MS	Maroon/White
Miss. Valley St.	Delta Devils	SWAC	Lafayette Stribling	Itta Bena, MS	Green/White
Missouri	Tigers	Big 12	Quin Snyder	Columbia, MO	Old Gold/Black
Missouri-KC	Kangaroos	Mid-Continent	Rich Zvosec	Kansas City, MO	Blue/Gold
Monmouth	Hawks	Northeast	Dave Calloway	W. Long Branch, NJ	Midnight Blue/White
Montana	Grizzlies	Big Sky	Pat Kennedy	Missoula, MT	Copper/Silver/Gold
Montana St.	Bobcats	Big Sky	Mick Durham	Bozeman, MT	Blue/Gold
Morehead St.	Eagles	Ohio Valley	Kyle Macy	Morehead, KY	Blue/Gold
Morgan St.	Bears	Mid-Eastern	Butch Beard	Baltimore, MD	Blue/Orange
Mt. St. Mary's	Mountaineers	Northeast	Milan Brown	Emmitsburg, MD	Blue/White
Murray St.	Racers	Ohio Valley	Mick Cronin	Murray, KY	Blue/Gold
Navy	Midshipmen	Patriot	Don DeVoe	Annapolis, MD	Navy Blue/Gold
Nebraska	Cornhuskers	Big 12	Barry Collier	Lincoln, NE	Scarlet/Cream
Nevada	Wolf Pack	WAC	Trent Johnson	Reno, NV	Silver/Blue
New Hampshire	Wildcats	America East	Phil Rowe	Durham, NH	Blue/White
New Mexico	Lobos	Mountain West	Ritchie McKay	Albuquerque, NM	Cherry/Silver
New Mexico St.	Aggies	Sun Belt	Lou Henson	Las Cruces, NM	Crimson/White
New Orleans	Privateers	Sun Belt	Monte Towe	New Orleans, LA	Royal Blue/Silver
Niagara	Purple Eagles	Metro Atlantic	Joe Mihalich	Lewiston, NY	Purple/White/Gold
Nicholls St.	Colonels	Southland	Ricky Blanton	Thibodaux, LA	Red/Gray
Norfolk State	Spartans	Mid-Eastern	Dwight Freeman	Norfolk, VA	Green/Gold
North Carolina	Tar Heels	ACC	Roy Williams	Chapel Hill, NC	Carolina Blue/Wht.
North Carolina A&T	Aggies	Mid-Eastern	Jerry Eaves	Greensboro, NC	Blue/Gold
North Carolina St.	Wolfpack	ACC	Herb Sendek	Raleigh, NC	Red/White
NC-Asheville	Bulldogs	Big South	Eddie Biedenbach	Asheville, NC	Royal Blue/White

NCAA Division I Basketball Schools (Cont.)

	Nickname	Conference	Head Coach	Location	Colors
NC-Greensboro	Spartans	Southern	Fran McCaffrey	Greensboro, NC	Gold/White/Navy
NC-Wilmington	Seahawks	Colonial	Brad Brownell	Wilmington, NC	Green/Gold/Navy
North Texas	Mean Green	Sun Belt	Johnny Jones	Denton, TX	Green/White
Northeastern	Huskies	America East	Ron Everhart	Boston, MA	Red/Black
Northern Arizona	Lumberjacks	Big Sky	Mike Adras	Flagstaff, AZ	Blue/Gold
Northern Colorado	Bears	Independent	Craig Rasmuson	Greeley, CO	Blue/Gold
Northern Illinois	Huskies	Mid-American	Rob Judson	De Kalb, IL	Cardinal/Black
Northern Iowa	Panthers	Mo. Valley	Greg McDermott	Cedar Falls, IA	Purple/Old Gold
Northwestern	Wildcats	Big Ten	Bill Carmody	Evanston, IL	Purple/White
Northwestern St.	Demons	Southland	Mike McConathy	Natchitoches, LA	Purple/Orange/Wt.
Notre Dame	Fighting Irish	Big East	Mike Brey	Notre Dame, IN	Gold/Blue
Oakland-MI	Golden Grizzlies	Mid-Continent	Greg Kampe	Rochester, MI	Black/Gold
Ohio University	Bobcats	Mid-American	Tim O'Shea	Athens, OH	Hunter Green/White
Ohio St.	Buckeyes	Big Ten	Jim O'Brien	Columbus, OH	Scarlet/Gray
Oklahoma	Sooners	Big 12	Kelvin Sampson	Norman, OK	Crimson/Cream
Oklahoma St.	Cowboys	Big 12	Eddie Sutton	Stillwater, OK	Orange/Black
Old Dominion	Monarchs	Colonial	Blaine Taylor	Norfolk, VA	Slate Blue/Silver
Oral Roberts	Golden Eagles	Mid-Continent	Scott Sutton	Tulsa, OK	Navy Blue/White
Oregon	Ducks	Pac-10	Ernie Kent	Eugene, OR	Green/Yellow
Oregon St.	Beavers	Pac-10	Jay John	Corvallis, OR	Orange/Black
Pacific	Tigers	Big West	Bob Thomason	Stockton, CA	Orange/Black
Pennsylvania	Quakers	Ivy	Fran Dunphy	Philadelphia, PA	Red/Blue
Penn St.	Nittany Lions	Big Ten	Ed DeChellis	University Park, PA	Blue/White
Pepperdine	Waves	West Coast	Paul Westphal	Malibu, CA	Blue/Orange
Pittsburgh	Panthers	Big East	Jamie Dixon	Pittsburgh, PA	Gold/Blue
Portland	Pilots	West Coast	Mike Holton	Portland, OR	Purple/White
Portland St.	Vikings	Big Sky	Heath Schroyer	Portland, OR	Green/White
Prairie View A&M	Panthers	SWAC	Jerry Francis	Prairie View, TX	Purple/Gold
Princeton	Tigers	Ivy	J. Thompson III	Princeton, NJ	Orange/Black
Providence	Friars	Big East	Tim Welsh	Providence, RI	Black/White
Purdue	Boilermakers	Big Ten	Gene Keady	W. Lafayette, IN	Old Gold/Black
Quinnipiac	Bobcats	Northeast	Joe DeSantis	Hamden, CT	Navy/Gold
Radford	Highlanders	Big South	Byron Samuels	Radford, VA	Blue/Red/Green/Wt.
Rhode Island	Rams	Atlantic 10	Jim Baron	Kingston, RI	Lt. Blue/White/Navy
Rice	Owls	WAC	Willis Wilson	Houston, TX	Blue/Gray
Richmond	Spiders	Atlantic 10	Jerry Wainwright	Richmond, VA	Red/Blue
Rider	Broncs	Metro Atlantic	Don Harnum	Lawrenceville, NJ	Cranberry/White
Robert Morris	Colonials	Northeast	Mark Schmidt	Moon Township, PA	Blue/Red/White
Rutgers	Scarlet Knights	Big East	Gary Waters	New Brunswick, NJ	Scarlet
Sacramento St.	Hornets	Big Sky	Jerome Jenkins	Sacramento, CA	Green/Gold
Sacred Heart	Pioneers	Northeast	Dave Bike	Fairfield, CT	Scarlet/White
St. Bonaventure	Bonnies	Atlantic 10	Anthony Solomon	St. Bonaventure, NY	Brown/White
St. Francis-NY	Terriers	Northeast	Ron Ganulin	Brooklyn, NY	Red/Blue
St. Francis-PA	Red Flash	Northeast	Bobby Jones	Loretto, PA	Red/White
St. John's	Red Storm	Big East	Mike Jarvis	Jamaica, NY	Red/White
Saint Joseph's	Hawks	Atlantic 10	Phil Martelli	Philadelphia, PA	Crimson/Gray
Saint Louis	Billikens	USA	Brad Soderberg	St. Louis, MO	Blue/White
Saint Mary's-CA	Gaels	West Coast	Randy Bennett	Moraga, CA	Red/Blue
Saint Peter's	Peacocks	Metro Atlantic	Bob Leckie	Jersey City, NJ	Blue/White
Sam Houston St.	Bearkats	Southland	Bob Marlin	Huntsville, TX	Orange/White
Samford	Bulldogs	Ohio Valley	Jimmy Tillette	Birmingham, AL	Red/Blue
San Diego	Toreros	West Coast	Brad Holland	San Diego, CA	Lt. Blue/Navy
San Diego St.	Aztecs	Mountain West	Steve Fisher	San Diego, CA	Scarlet/Black
San Francisco	Dons	West Coast	Phil Mathews	San Francisco, CA	Green/Gold
San Jose St.	Spartans	WAC	Phil Johnson	San Jose, CA	Gold/White/Blue
Santa Clara	Broncos	West Coast	Dick Davey	Santa Clara, CA	Bronco Red/White
Savannah St.	Tigers	Independent	Edward Daniels	Savannah, GA	Orange/Blue
Seton Hall	Pirates	Big East	Louis Orr	South Orange, NJ	Blue/White
Siena	Saints	Metro Atlantic	Rob Lanier	Loudonville, NY	Green/Gold
South Alabama	Jaguars	Sun Belt	John Pelphrey	Mobile, AL	Red/White/Blue
South Carolina	Gamecocks	SEC-East	Dave Odom	Columbia, SC	Garnet/Black
South Carolina St.	Bulldogs	Mid-Eastern	Benjamin Betts Jr.	Orangeburg, SC	Garnet/Blue
South Florida	Bulls	USA	Robert McCullum	Tampa, FL	Green/Gold
SE Missouri St.	Indians	Ohio Valley	Gary Garner	Cape Girardeau, MO	Red/Black
SE Louisiana	Lions	Southland	Billy Kennedy	Hammond, LA	Green/Gold
Southern-BR	Jaguars	SWAC	Michael Grant	Baton Rouge, LA	Blue/Gold
Southern Illinois	Salukis	Mo. Valley	Matt Painter	Carbondale, IL	Maroon/White
SMU	Mustangs	WAC	Mike Dement	Dallas, TX	Red/Blue

	Nickname	Conference	Head Coach	Location	Colors
Southern Miss	Golden Eagles	USA	James Green	Hattiesburg, MS	Black/Gold
Southern Utah	Thunderbirds	Mid-Continent	Bill Evans	Cedar City, UT	Scarlet/White
SW Missouri St.	Bears	Mo. Valley	Barry Hinson	Springfield, MO	Maroon/White
Stanford	Cardinal	Pac-10	Mike Montgomery	Stanford, CA	Cardinal/White
S.F. Austin St.	Lumberjacks	Southland	Danny Kaspar	Nacogdoches, TX	Purple/White
Stetson	Hatters	Atlantic Sun	Derek Waugh	DeLand, FL	Green/White
Stony Brook	Seawolves	America East	Nick Macarchuk	Stony Brook, NY	Scarlet/Gray
Syracuse	Orangemen	Big East	Jim Boeheim	Syracuse, NY	Orange
Temple	Owls	Atlantic 10	John Chaney	Philadelphia, PA	Cherry/White
Tennessee	Volunteers	SEC-East	Buzz Peterson	Knoxville, TN	Orange/White
Tenn-Martin	Skyhawks	Ohio Valley	Bret Campbell	Martin, TN	Orange/Wt./Blue
Tennessee St.	Tigers	Ohio Valley	Cy Alexander	Nashville, TN	Blue/White
Tennessee Tech	Golden Eagles	Ohio Valley	Mike Sutton	Cookeville, TN	Purple/Gold
Texas	Longhorns	Big 12	Rick Barnes	Austin, TX	Burnt Orange/White
Texas A&M	Aggies	Big 12	Melvin Watkins	College Station, TX	Maroon/White
TX A&M Corpus-Christi	Islanders	Independent	Ronnie Arrow	Corpus Christi, TX	Blue/Green/Silver
TCU	Horned Frogs	USA	Neil Dougherty	Ft. Worth, TX	Purple/White
Texas Southern	Tigers	SWAC	Ronnie Courtney	Houston, TX	Maroon/Gray
Texas St.-San Marcos	Bobcats	Southland	Dennis Nutt	San Marcos, TX	Maroon/Gold
Texas Tech	Red Raiders	Big 12	Bob Knight	Lubbock, TX	Scarlet/Black
TX-Arlington	Mavericks	Southland	Eddie McCarter	Arlington, TX	Royal Blue/White
TX-Pan American	Broncs	Independent	Bob Hoffman	Edinburg, TX	Green/White
TX-San Antonio	Roadrunners	Southland	Tim Carter	San Antonio, TX	Orange/Navy/White
Toledo	Rockets	Mid-American	Stan Joplin	Toledo, OH	Blue/Gold
Towson	Tigers	Colonial	Michael Hunt	Towson, MD	Gold/White/Black
Troy St.	Trojans	Atlantic Sun	Don Maestri	Troy, AL	Cardinal/Silver/Black
Tulane	Green Wave	USA	Shawn Finney	New Orleans, LA	Olive Grn./Sky Blue
Tulsa	Golden Hurricane	WAC	John Phillips	Tulsa, OK	Blue/Red/Gold
UAB	Blazers	USA	Mike Anderson	Birmingham, AL	Green/Gold
UC-Irvine	Anteaters	Big West	Pat Douglass	Irvine, CA	Blue/Gold
UCLA	Bruins	Pac-10	Ben Howland	Los Angeles, CA	Blue/Gold
UC-Davis	Aggies	Independent	Gary Stewart	Davis, CA	Yale Blue/Gold
UC-Riverside	Highlanders	Big West	John Masi	Riverside, CA	Blue/Gold
UC-Santa Barbara	Gauchos	Big West	Bob Williams	Santa Barbara, CA	Blue/Gold
UNLV	Runnin' Rebels	Mountain West	Charlie Spoonhour	Las Vegas, NV	Scarlet/Gray
USC	Trojans	Pac-10	Henry Bibby	Los Angeles, CA	Cardinal/Gold
Utah	Utes	Mountain West	Rick Majerus	Salt Lake City, UT	Crimson/White
Utah St.	Aggies	Big West	Stew Morrill	Logan, UT	Navy Blue/White
Utah Valley St.	Wolverines	Independent	Dick Hunsaker	Orem, UT	Green/Gold/White
UTEP	Miners	WAC	Jason Rabedeaux	El Paso, TX	Orange/Blue/White
Valparaiso	Crusaders	Mid-Continent	Homer Drew	Valparaiso, IN	Brown/Gold
Vanderbilt	Commodores	SEC-East	Kevin Stallings	Nashville, TN	Black/Gold
Vermont	Catamounts	America East	Tom Brennan	Burlington, VT	Green/Gold
Villanova	Wildcats	Big East	Jay Wright	Villanova, PA	Blue/White
Virginia	Cavaliers	ACC	Pete Gillen	Charlottesville, VA	Orange/Blue
VCU	Rams	Colonial	Jeff Capel III	Richmond, VA	Black/Gold
VMI	Keydets	Big South	Bart Bellairs	Lexington, VA	Red/White/Yellow
Virginia Tech	Hokies, Gobblers	Big East	Seth Greenberg	Blacksburg, VA	Orange/Maroon
Wagner	Seahawks	Northeast	Mike Deane	Staten Island, NY	Green/White
Wake Forest	Demon Deacons	ACC	Skip Prosser	Winston-Salem, NC	Old Gold/Black
Washington	Huskies	Pac-10	Lorenzo Romar	Seattle, WA	Purple/Gold
Washington St.	Cougars	Pac-10	Dick Bennett	Pullman, WA	Crimson/Gray
Weber St.	Wildcats	Big Sky	Joe Cravens	Ogden, UT	Purple/White
West Virginia	Mountaineers	Big East	John Beilein	Morgantown, WV	Old Gold/Blue
Western Carolina	Catamounts	Southern	Steve Shurina	Cullowhee, NC	Purple/Gold
Western Illinois	Leathernecks	Mid-Continent	Derek Thomas	Macomb, IL	Purple/Gold
Western Kentucky	Hilltoppers	Sun Belt	Darrin Horn	Bowling Green, KY	Red/White
Western Michigan	Broncos	Mid-American	Steve Hawkins	Kalamazoo, MI	Brown/Gold
Wichita St.	Shockers	Mo. Valley	Mark Turgeon	Wichita, KS	Yellow/Black
William & Mary	Tribe	Colonial	Tony Shaver	Williamsburg, VA	Green/Gold/Silver
Winthrop	Eagles	Big South	Gregg Marshall	Rock Hill, SC	Garnet/Gold
Wisconsin	Badgers	Big Ten	Bo Ryan	Madison, WI	Cardinal/White
WI-Green Bay	Phoenix	Horizon	Tod Kowalczyk	Green Bay, WI	Green/White/Red
WI-Milwaukee	Panthers	Horizon	Bruce Pearl	Milwaukee, WI	Black/Gold
Wofford	Terriers	Southern	Mike Young	Spartanburg, SC	Old Gold/Black
Wright St.	Raiders	Horizon	Paul Biancardi	Dayton, OH	Green/Gold
Wyoming	Cowboys	Mountain West	Steve McClain	Laramie, WY	Brown/Yellow
Xavier	Musketeers	Atlantic 10	Thad Matta	Cincinnati, OH	Blue/Gray/White
Yale	Bulldogs, Elis	Ivy	James Jones	New Haven, CT	Yale Blue/White
Youngstown St.	Penguins	Horizon	John Robic	Youngstown, OH	Red/White

	Alabama	Utah	North Carolina	UCLA
Mike Shula	**Urban Meyer**	**Roy Williams**	**Ben Howland**
Dolphins to 'Bama	Bowling Green to Utah	Kansas to N. Carolina	Pitt to UCLA

Coaching Changes

New head coaches were named at 18 Division 1-A and 19 Division 1-AA football schools while 46 Division 1 basketball schools changed head coaches after the 2002-03 season. Coaching changes listed below are as of September 1, 2003.

Division I-A Football

	Old Coach	Record	Why Left?	New Coach	Old Job
Alabama	Dennis Franchione	10-3	to Texas A&M*.	Mike Price	Coach, Washington St.
	Mike Price	—	fired†	Mike Shula	QB coach, NFL Miami
Ball State	Bill Lynch	6-6	fired	Brady Hoke	Asst., Michigan
Baylor	Kevin Steele	3-9	fired	Guy Morriss	Coach, Kentucky
Bowling Green . . .	Urban Meyer	9-3	to Utah*	Gregg Brandon	Off. coord., Bowling Green
East Carolina	Steve Logan	4-8	fired	John Thompson	Def. coord., Florida
Houston	Dana Dimel	5-7	fired	Art Briles	Asst., Texas Tech
Kentucky	Guy Morriss	7-5	to Baylor*	Rich Brooks	Fmr def. coord., NFL Atl.
LA-Monroe	Mike Collins	3-9@	resigned	Charlie Weatherbie	Former coach, Navy
Louisville	John L. Smith	7-6	to Michigan St.*	Bob Petrino	Off. coord., Auburn
Michigan St.	Bobby Williams	4-8#	fired	John L. Smith	Coach, Louisville
Oregon St.	Dennis Erickson	8-5	to NFL San Fran*	Mike Riley	Asst., NFL New Orleans
Texas A&M	R.C. Slocum	6-6	fired	Dennis Franchione	Coach, Alabama
Tulsa	Keith Burns	1-11	resigned	Steve Kragthorpe	Asst., NFL Buffalo
UCLA	Bob Toledo	8-5&	fired	Karl Dorrell	WR coach, NFL Denver
Utah	Ron McBride	5-6	fired	Urban Meyer	Coach, Bowling Green
Washington	Rick Neuheisel	7-6	fired	Keith Gilbertson	Off. coord., Washington
Washington St. . . .	Mike Price	1Q-3	to Alabama*	Bill Doba	Def. coord., Washington St.
Wyoming	Vic Koenning	2-10	fired	Joe Glenn	Coach, Montana

* as head coach
† Price was fired after four months as Alabama head coach when various details emerged about his inappropriate behavior.
@ Def. coord. Collins (3-6) took over head coaching duties on Sept. 19, 2002 after head coach Bobby Keasler (0-3) resigned.
# Williams (3-6) was fired on Nov. 4 and replaced on an interim basis by offensive coordinator Morris Watts (1-2).
& Toledo (7-5) was fired on Dec. 9, 2002. Asst. AD of Acad. Services Ed Kezirian (1-0) coached the final game (Las Vegas Bowl).

Division I-AA Football

	Old Coach	Record	Why Left?	New Coach	Old Job
Alabama St.	L.C. Cole	6-6	fired	Charles Coe	Asst., Memphis
Austin Peay	Bill Schmitz	7-5	fired	Carroll McCray	Asst., Mississippi St.
Bucknell	Tom Gadd	2-9	resigned†	Tim Landis	Coach, St. Mary's-CA
Charleston So. . . .	David Dowd	4-8	resigned	Jay Mills	Off. coord., Harvard
Chattanooga	Donnie Kirkpatrick	2-10	fired	Rodney Allison	Asst., Clemson
Columbia	Ray Tellier	1-9	fired	Bob Shoop	Def. coord., Boston Coll.
Eastern Kentucky . .	Roy Kidd	8-4	retired	Danny Hope	Asst., Louisville
Jackson St.	Robert Hughes	7-4	fired	James Bell	Coach, Chavez (TX) HS
Montana	Joe Glenn	11-3	to Wyoming*	Bobby Hauck	Asst., Washington
Norfolk St.	Mo Forte	5-6	resigned	Willie Gillus	Off. coord., Virginia Union
N. Carolina A&T . .	Bill Hayes	4-8	fired	George Small	Def. coord., Hampton
Prairie View A&M .	Larry Dorsey	1-10	resigned	C.L. Whittington	Former asst., NFLE Frankfurt
Sacramento St. . . .	John Volek	5-7	fired	Steve Mooshagian	Asst., NFL Cincinnati
Saint Mary's-CA . .	Tim Landis	6-6	to Bucknell*	Vincent White	Asst., Utah
Saint Peter's	Rob Stern	6-5	fired	Scott Kochman	Asst., St. Peter's
Southern Utah . . .	C. Ray Gregory	1-10	fired	Gary Andersen	Asst., Utah
Tenn.-Martin	Sam McCorkle	2-10@	fired	Matt Griffin	Asst., Maine
Tex. St.-San Marcos	Bob DeBesse	4-7	fired	Manny Matsakis	Asst., Texas Tech
Western Kentucky	Jack Harbaugh	12-3	resigned	David Elson	Def. coord., Western Ky.

* as head coach
† Gadd took the entire 2002 season off while battling cancer. Former def. coord. Dave Kotuslki served as acting head coach.
@ McCorkle (2-6) was fired on Nov. 1, 2002 and replaced on an interim basis by defensive line coach Johnny Jernigan (0-4).

Division I Basketball

	Old Coach	Record	Why Left?	New Coach	Old Job
Alcorn St.	Davey Whitney	14-19	retired	Samuel West	Asst., Alcorn St.
Ark.-Little Rock	Porter Moser	18-12	to Illinois St.*	Steve Shields	Asst., Ark.-Little Rock
Baylor	Dave Bliss	14-14	resigned	Scott Drew	Coach, Valparaiso
CS-Fullerton	Donny Daniels	10-19	to UCLA**	Bob Burton	Asst., Fresno St.
Campbell	Billy Lee	5-22	resigned	Robbie Laing	Asst., Kansas St.
Chicago St.	Bo Ellis	3-27 †	fired	Kevin Jones	Asst., Chicago St.
Clemson	Larry Shyatt	15-13	resigned	Oliver Purnell	Coach, Dayton
Cleveland St.	Rollie Massimino	8-22	resigned	Mike Garland	Asst., Michigan St.
Columbia	Armond Hill	2-25	fired	Joseph Jones	Asst., Villanova
Dayton	Oliver Purnell	24-6	to Clemson*	Brian Gregory	Asst., Michigan St.
Drake	Kurt Kanaskie	10-20	resigned	Tom Davis	Former coach, Iowa
East Tenn. St.	Ed DeChellis	20-11	to Penn St.*	Murry Bartow	Former coach, UAB
Elon	Mark Simons	12-15	resigned	Ernie Nestor	Asst., South Carolina
Fordham	Bob Hill	2-26	resigned	Dereck Whittenburg	Coach, Wagner
Georgia	Jim Harrick	19-8	resigned	Dennis Felton	Coach, Western Ky.
Georgia St.	Lefty Driesell	14-15@	retired	Michael Perry	Asst., Georgia St.
High Point	Jerry Steele	7-20	retired	Bart Lundy	Coach, Queens Univ.
Illinois	Bill Self	25-7	to Kansas*	Bruce Weber	Coach, Southern Illinois
Illinois St.	Tom Richardson	8-21	fired	Porter Moser	Coach, Ark.-Little Rock
Iowa St.	Larry Eustachy	17-14	resigned	Wayne Morgan	Asst., Iowa St.
Jackson St.	Andy Stoglin	10-18	fired	Tevester Anderson	Coach, Murray St.
Kansas	Roy Williams	30-8	to North Carolina*	Bill Self	Coach, Illinois
Lamar	Mike Deane	13-14	to Wagner*#	Billy Tubbs	AD, Lamar
Marshall	Greg White	14-15	to Charleston*	Ron Jirsa	Asst., Clemson
Mt. St. Mary's	Jim Phelan	11-16	retired	Milan Brown	Asst., Mt. St. Mary's
Murray St.	Tevester Anderson	17-12	to Jackson St.*&	Mick Cronin	Asst., Louisville
North Carolina	Matt Doherty	19-16	resigned	Roy Williams	Coach, Kansas
North Carolina A&T	Curtis Hunter	1-26	fired	Jerry Eaves	Asst., NBA Cleveland
Penn St.	Jerry Dunn	7-21	resigned	Ed DeChellis	Coach, East Tenn. St.
Pittsburgh	Ben Howland	28-5	to UCLA*	Jamie Dixon	Asst., Pittsburgh
St. Bonaventure	Jan van Breda Kolff	7-22 $	fired	Anthony Solomon	Asst., Notre Dame
South Carolina St.	Cy Alexander	20-11	to Tennessee St.*	Benjamin Betts Jr.	Asst., VCU
South Florida	Seth Greenberg	15-14	to Virginia Tech*	Robert McCullum	Coach, Western Michigan
Southern-BR	Ben Jobe	9-20	retired	Michael Grant	Coach Central St.
Southern Illinois	Bruce Weber	24-7	to Illinois	Matt Painter	Asst., Southern Illinois
Tennessee St.	Nolan Richardson III	2-25 +	resigned	Cy Alexander	Coach, South Carolina St.
UCLA	Steve Lavin	10-19	fired	Ben Howland	Coach, Pittsburgh
Valparaiso	Scott Drew	20-11	to Baylor*	Homer Drew	Former coach, Valparaiso
Virginia Tech	Ricky Stokes	11-18	fired	Seth Greenberg	Coach, South Florida
Wagner	Dereck Whittenburg	21-11	to Fordham*	Mike Deane	Coach, Lamar
Washington St.	Paul Graham	7-20	fired	Dick Bennett	Former coach, Wisconsin
Western Illinois	Jim Kerwin	7-21	resigned	Derek Thomas	Asst., UNLV
Western Kentucky	Dennis Felton	24-9	to Georgia*	Darrin Horn	Asst., Marquette
Western Michigan	Robert McCullum	20-11	to South Florida*	Steve Hawkins	Asst., Western Michigan
William & Mary	Rick Boyages	12-16	to Ohio St.**	Tony Shaver	Coach, Hampden-Sydney
Wright St.	Ed Schilling	10-18	fired	Paul Biancardi	Asst., Ohio St.

* as head coach
** as assistant coach

† Ellis (3-15) was fired on Jan. 22 and replaced by assistant Jones (0-12) for the remainder of the season. On Apr. 23 Jones was given the job on a permanent basis.

@ Driesell (4-6) retired on Jan. 3 and was replaced by assistant Michael Perry (10-9) for the remainder of the season. On Apr. 3 Perry was given the job on a permanent basis.

Deane was reassigned to another position at Lamar on March 20 when AD Billy Tubbs decided to take over the head coaching duties. He was named coach at Wagner on June 3.

& Anderson announced his retirement from Murray St. on Mar. 23. He accepted the job at Jackson St. on Apr. 8.

$ St. Bonaventure stood at 13-14 on March 4 with two regular season games remaining when the Atlantic 10 Conference announced it was stripping the team of six conference wins and barring it from the postseason conference tournament due to the Bonnies' use of an ineligible player. The team subsequently voted to forfeit its final two games.

+ Richardson (2-5) was suspended on Dec. 27, 2002 and later resigned on Jan. 8 after it was learned he brought a gun into the school's gym during practice. He was replaced by asst. Hosea Lewis (0-19) for the remainder of the season. When Lewis was suspended on Feb. 10 for one game after a bench-clearing brawl, he was replaced by school AD Teresa Phillips (0-1).

2002-03 Directors' Cup

Developed as a joint effort between the National Association of Collegiate Directors of Athletics (NACDA) and USA Today. Introduced in 1993-94 to honor the nation's best overall NCAA Division I athletic department (combining men's and women's sports). Winners in NCAA Division II and III and NAIA were named for the first time following the 1995-96 season.

Standings are computed by NACDA with points awarded for each Div. I school's finish in 20 sports (top 10 scoring sports for both men and women). Div. II schools are awarded points in 14 sports (top 7 scoring sports for both men and women). Div III schools are awarded points in 18 sports (top 9 scoring sports for both men and women). NAIA schools are awarded points in 12 sports (top 6 scoring sports for both men and women). National champions in each sport earn 100 points, while 2nd through 64th-place finishers earn decreasing points depending on the size of the tournament field. Division I-A football points are based on the final ESPN/USA Today Coaches' Top 25 poll. Listed below are team conferences (for Div. I only), combined Final Four finishes (1st through 4th place) for men's and women's programs, overall points in **bold** type, and the previous year's ranking (for Div. I only).

Multiple winners: Stanford (9); Williams, MA (7); UC-Davis (6); Simon Fraser, BC (5); Lindenwood, MO (2).

Division I

		Conf	1-2-3-4	Pts	01-02 Rank			Conf	1-2-3-4	Pts	01-02 Rank
1	Stanford	Pac-10	2-6-2-0	**1420.5**	1	15	Georgia	SEC	0-1-2-0	**784.75**	8
2	Texas	Big 12	0-2-5-0	**1094**	2	16	Arizona	Pac-10	0-0-1-0	**760**	9
3	Ohio St.	Big Ten	1-1-0-2	**1074.8**	14	17	Washington	Pac-10	0-0-1-0	**732**	25
4	Michigan	Big Ten	0-0-1-2	**1034.3**	6	18	South Carolina	SEC	0-1-1-0	**701**	11
5	Penn St.	Big Ten	0-2-2-0	**993**	24	19	Virginia	ACC	1-1-0-0	**690**	27
6	UCLA	Pac-10	4-0-2-0	**943.75**	5	20	Oklahoma	Big 12	1-0-1-0	**643.25**	17
7	Florida	SEC	1-1-1-2	**935.75**	3	21	Duke	ACC	0-0-2-0	**643**	30
8	North Carolina	ACC	0-0-1-0	**933.5**	4	22	Maryland	ACC	0-0-3-0	**620.5**	44
9	California	Pac-10	0-2-1-1	**884.75**	20	23	LSU	SEC	2-0-0-2	**597.25**	10
10	Arizona St.	Pac-10	0-0-0-0	**860.75**	15	24	Nebraska	Big 12	0-0-1-1	**596.5**	22
11	Minnesota	Big Ten	1-0-0-0	**845**	7	25	Wisconsin	Big Ten	0-1-0-0	**579**	33
12	Auburn	SEC	2-2-0-0	**822.75**	19						
13	Notre Dame	Big East	1-0-1-0	**822.5**	13						
	USC	Pac-10	2-0-2-1	**822.5**	15						

Division II

		1-2-3-4	Pts			1-2-3-4	Pts
1	UC-Davis	2-0-0-1	**857**	14	Adams St., CO	0-1-1-0	**437.25**
2	Grand Valley St., MI	1-0-2-1	**797.5**	15	Barry, FL	0-1-1-0	**416**
3	North Florida	1-0-0-0	**628.5**	16	Nebraska-Kearney	0-1-0-0	**410**
4	CS-Bakersfield	0-1-1-1	**597.5**	17	UMass-Lowell	0-0-0-0	**409.75**
5	South Dakota St.	1-0-0-1	**562**	18	Indiana, PA	0-0-0-0	**408**
6	Northern Colorado	0-0-2-0	**555.5**	19	Ashland, OH	0-0-0-0	**398.5**
7	Abilene Christian, TX	2-2-0-1	**539**	20	Drury, MO	1-1-0-0	**394.5**
8	Truman St., MO	1-1-0-0	**492.5**	21	North Dakota St.	0-0-3-1	**393.5**
9	Central Missouri St.	1-0-0-1	**488**	22	Minnesota St.-Mankato	0-0-0-0	**393.25**
10	Nebraska-Omaha	0-1-1-0	**472**	23	Northwest Missouri St.	0-0-0-0	**389.25**
11	Western St., CO	2-1-1-0	**468.5**	24	St. Cloud St., MN	0-0-0-0	**385.5**
12	California-San Diego	0-0-1-1	**467**	25	Rollins, FL	1-1-0-0	**379**
13	Indianapolis	0-0-0-0	**450.5**				

Division III

		1-2-3-4	Pts			1-2-3-4	Pts
1	Williams, MA	2-2-2-0	**1158.25**	14	Johns Hopkins, MD	0-2-0-0	**482**
2	Emory, GA	2-0-2-1	**789**	15	Cortland St., NY	0-0-1-0	**481.5**
3	College of New Jersey	0-0-2-0	**695.75**	16	Messiah, PA	1-2-0-0	**478.5**
4	Trinity, TX	1-1-3-0	**680**		Wisconsin-Stevens Point	0-0-1-0	**478.5**
5	Washington, MO	0-1-1-1	**638.75**	18	Salisbury, MD	1-1-1-0	**468**
6	Gustavus Adolphus, MN	0-1-1-1	**637**	19	Mary Washington, VA	0-0-0-0	**448.5**
7	Wartburg, IA	1-0-1-0	**624.5**	20	Wittenberg, OH	0-0-0-0	**408.25**
8	Wisconsin-Oshkosh	1-1-1-1	**561.5**	21	Wheaton, MA	2-0-0-0	**405.25**
9	Ithaca, NY	0-0-0-0	**550.5**	22	Calvin, MI	0-1-0-0	**403.75**
10	Wisconsin-La Crosse	2-0-1-0	**512.5**	23	Ohio Wesleyan	1-0-1-0	**363.5**
11	Amherst, MA	1-0-0-1	**502.5**	24	Nebraska Wesleyan	0-0-1-2	**355**
12	Middlebury, VT	0-3-1-1	**499.5**	25	Keene St., NH	0-0-0-0	**343.25**
13	Wheaton, IL	0-0-0-0	**494**				

NAIA

		1-2-3-4	Pts			1-2-3-4	Pts
1	Lindenwood, MO	1-2-2-0	746.5	14	Westmont, CA	1-0-0-0	469.5
2	Simon Fraser, BC	3-0-0-1	718	15	Spring Hill, AL	0-0-1-0	459
3	Azusa Pacific, CA	3-2-1-0	643	16	Southern Nazarene, OK	1-0-0-0	444.5
4	Mary, ND	0-0-0-1	580	17	Lewis-Clark, ID	1-0-0-0	441.5
5	Oklahoma City	1-3-0-0	568	18	Olivet Nazarene, IL	0-0-1-0	441
6	Pt. Loma Nazarene, CA	0-0-1-0	566	19	McKendree, IL	0-0-2-0	428.5
7	Oklahoma Christian	1-0-0-1	530.5	20	Indiana Wesleyan	0-0-0-0	417
8	Cumberland, KY	0-0-1-0	517.5	21	Warner Southern, FL	0-0-1-0	414.5
9	Berry, GA	0-1-0-0	507	22	Hastings, NE	1-0-0-0	379.5
10	Embry-Riddle, FL	0-0-1-0	491.5	23	Brescia, KY	0-0-0-1	378.5
11	Dickinson St., ND	0-1-0-0	477	24	Concordia, CA	1-0-0-0	369
12	Concordia, NE	0-1-1-0	476.5	25	Mobile, AL	1-1-0-0	360.75
13	Oklahoma Baptist	0-0-1-1	475.5				

NCAA Division I Schools on Probation

As of Sept. 25, 2003, there were 26 Division I member institutions serving NCAA probations.

School	Sport	Yrs	Penalty To End	School	Sport	Yrs	Penalty To End
South Alabama	M Basketball	2	12/18/03	Jackson St.	M Track and XC	5	5/16/05
Nebraska	M Swimming	2	1/22/04	New Mexico St.	M Basketball	4	6/19/05
	& Wrestling	2	1/22/04	Marshall	Football	4	12/20/05
Rutgers	Ten Sports	2	3/31/04		& M Basketball	4	12/20/05
Northern Arizona	Football	3	4/17/04	California	Football	5	3/7/06
Stetson	M Basketball	2	5/8/04	Arkansas	Football	3	4/15/06
Maryland	Football	1	8/10/04		& M Basketball	3	4/15/06
Colorado	Football	2	10/7/04	Utah	M Basketball	3	7/29/06
Texas	Baseball	2	11/5/04	Jacksonville	M Soccer	5	8/29/06
Howard	Baseball	3	11/26/04		& W Rowing	5	8/29/06
	M & W Swimming	3	11/26/04	Wisconsin	M Basketball	5	9/30/06
	& M & W Basketball	3	11/26/04		& Football	5	9/30/06
UNLV	M Basketball	4	12/11/04	Minnesota	W Basketball	4	10/22/06
Kentucky	Football	3	1/30/05		& M Basketball	6	10/22/06
Washington	M Basketball	2	2/9/05	Fresno St.	M Basketball	4	12/4/06
San Diego St.	Football	2	2/23/05	Alabama	Football	5	1/31/07
Miami-FL	Baseball	2	2/26/05	Michigan	M Basketball	4	5/6/07

Remaining postseason and TV sanctions

2003-2004 postseason ban: Alabama football, Baylor basketball (self-imposed) and Fresno St. basketball (self-imposed).
2002-2003 television ban: None.

NCAA Graduation Rates

The following table compares graduation rates of NCAA Division I student athletes with the entire student body in those schools. Years given denote the year in which students entered college. Rates are based on students who enrolled as freshmen, received an athletics scholarship and graduated in six years or less. All figures are percentages.
Source: NCAA Graduation-Rates Report, 2003.

	1991	1992	1993	1994	1995	1996
All Student Athletes	57	58	58	58	60	62
Entire Student Body	56	56	56	56	58	59
Male Student Athletes	51	52	51	51	54	55
Male Student Body	53	54	54	54	56	56
Female Student Athletes	67	68	68	69	69	70
Female Student Body	58	59	59	59	61	62
Div. I-A Football Players	50	51	48	51	53	54
Male Basketball Players	41	41	42	40	43	44
Female Basketball Players	66	62	63	65	65	66

2002-03 NCAA Team Champions

Fifteen schools won two or more national championships during the 2002-03 academic year, led by Division I UCLA with four.

Multiple winners: Four—UCLA (Div. I men's soccer, National Div. women's gymnastics, Div. I softball, National Div. women's water polo). **Three**—BYU-HAWAII (Div. II women's volleyball, Div. II men's and women's tennis).

Two—ABILENE CHRISTIAN (Div. II men's indoor and outdoor track); ARKANSAS (Div. I men's indoor and outdoor track); AUBURN (Div. I men's and women's swimming & diving); EMORY, GA (Div. III men's and women's tennis); KENYON, OH (Div. III men's and women's swimming & diving); LSU (Div. I women's indoor and outdoor track); STANFORD (Div. I men's cross country, National Div. men's water polo); UC DAVIS (Div. II women's rowing, Div. II softball); USC (Div. I women's volleyball, Div. I women's golf); WESTERN ST., CO (Div. II men's and women's cross country); WHEATON, MA (Div. III women's indoor and outdoor track); WILLIAMS, MA (Div. III women's cross country, Div. III men's basketball); WISC-LA CROSSE (Div. III men's indoor and outdoor track).

Overall titles in parentheses; (*) indicates defending champions.

FALL

Cross Country

Men

Div.	Winner	Runner-Up	Score
I	Stanford (3)	Wisconsin	47-107
II	Western St., CO* (5)	Abilene Christian	35-81
III	Wisc.-Oshkosh (4)	Calvin, MI	66-122

Women

Div.	Winner	Runner-Up	Score
I	Brigham Young* (4)	Stanford	85-113
II	Western St., CO* (3)	Adams St., CO	43-46
III	Williams, MA (1)	Middlebury, VT*	42-145

Field Hockey

Div.	Winner	Runner-Up	Score
I	Wake Forest (1)	Penn St.	2-0
II	Bloomsburg, PA (7)	Bentley, MA*	5-0
III	Rowan, NJ (1)	Messiah, PA	1-0

Football

Div.	Winner	Runner-Up	Score
I-A	Ohio St. (7)	Miami-FL*	31-24 (2OT)
I-AA	Western Kentucky (1)	McNeese St.	34-14
II	Grand Valley St., MI (1)	Valdosta St., GA	31-24
III	Mt. Union, OH* (7)	Trinity, TX	48-7

Note: There is no official Div. I-A playoff. Ohio St. defeated Miami-FL in the BCS Championship Game (Fiesta Bowl).

Soccer

Men

Div.	Winner	Runner-Up	Score
I	UCLA (4)	Stanford	1-0
II	Sonoma St., CA (1)	So. New Hampshire	4-3
III	Messiah, PA (2)	Otterbein, OH	1-0

Women

Div.	Winner	Runner-Up	Score
I	Portland (1)	Santa Clara*	2-1 (OT)
II	Christian Brothers, TN (1)	Nebraska-Omaha	2-1
III	Ohio Wesleyan* (2)	Messiah, PA	1-0

Volleyball

Women

Div.	Winner	Runner-Up	Score
I	USC (2)	Stanford*	3-1
II	BYU-Hawaii (2)	Truman St., MO	3-0
III	Wisc.-Whitewater (1)	Washington, MO	3-0

Water Polo

Men

Div.	Winner	Runner-Up	Score
National	Stanford* (10)	California	7-6

WINTER

Basketball

Men

Div.	Winner	Runner-Up	Score
I	Syracuse (1)	Kansas	81-78
II	Northeastern St., OK (1)	Kentucky Wesleyan†	75-64
III	Williams, MA (1)	Gustavus Adolphus	67-65

† Ky. Wesleyan was later forced to vacate its second-place finish due to the use of an ineligible player.

Women

Div.	Winner	Runner-Up	Score
I	Connecticut* (4)	Tennessee	73-68
II	South Dakota St. (1)	Northern Kentucky	65-50
III	Trinity, TX (1)	Eastern Conn. St.	60-58

Fencing

Div.	Winner	Runner-Up	Score
Combined	Notre Dame (6)	Penn St.*	182-179

Gymnastics

Div.	Winner	Runner-Up	Margin
Men	Oklahoma* (5)	Ohio St.	by 1.900
Women	UCLA (4)	Alabama	by .550

Ice Hockey

Men

Div.	Winner	Runner-Up	Score
I	Minnesota* (5)	New Hampshire	5-1
III	Norwich, VT (2)	Oswego St., NY	2-1

Women

Div.	Winner	Runner-Up	Score
I	Minn.-Duluth* (3)	Harvard	4-3 (2OT)
III	Elmira, NY (2)	Manhattanville, NY	5-1

Rifle

Div.	Winner	Runner-Up	Score
Combined	AK-Fairbanks* (6)	Xavier	6287-6197

Skiing

Div.	Winner	Runner-Up	Score
Combined	Utah (10)	Vermont	682-551

Swimming & Diving

Men

Div.	Winner	Runner-Up	Score
I	Auburn (3)	Texas*	609½-413
II	Drury, MO (2)	CS-Bakersfield*	612-535
III	Kenyon, OH* (24)	Johns Hopkins	756½-384½

Women

Div.	Winner	Runner-Up	Score
I	Auburn* (2)	Georgia	536-373
II	Truman, MO* (3)	Drury, MO	682-412
III	Kenyon, OH* (19)	Williams, MA	560½-350

Indoor Track
Men

Div.	Winner		Runner-Up	Score
I	Arkansas	(17)	Auburn	52-28
II	Abilene Christian*	(10)	Western St., CO	58-54
III	Wisc.-La Crosse*	(10)	Wisc.-Oshkosh	71-34

Women

Div.	Winner		Runner-Up	Score
I	LSU*	(10)	(tie) Florida & South Carolina	62-44
II	St. Augustine's, NC	(4)	Abilene Christian	73-53
III	Wheaton, MA*	(5)	Lehman, NY	54-48

Wrestling
Men

Div.	Winner		Runner-Up	Score
I	Oklahoma St.	(31)	Minnesota*	143-104½
II	Central Oklahoma*	(6)	Neb.-Kearney	87½-73½
III	Wartburg, IA	(3)	Augsburg, MN*	166½-84½

SPRING
Baseball

Div.	Winner		Runner-Up	Score
I	Rice	(1)	Stanford	14-2
II	Central Missouri St.	(2)	Tampa	11-4
III	Chapman, CA	(1)	Chris. Newport, VA	15-7

Golf
Men

Div.	Winner		Runner-Up	Score
I	Clemson	(1)	Oklahoma St.	1191-1193
II	Francis Marion, SC	(1)	Rollins, FL*	1149-1163
III	Averett, VA	(1)	Wesley, DE	1175-1180

Women

Div.	Winner		Runner-Up	Score
I	USC	(1)	Pepperdine	1197-1212
II	Rollins, FL	(1)	Fla. Southern*	1237-1276
III	Methodist, NC*	(7)	Mary Hardin-Baylor	1295-1348

Lacrosse
Men

Div.	Winner		Runner-Up	Score
I	Virginia	(3)	Johns Hopkins	9-7
II	New York Tech	(2)	Limestone, SC*	9-4
III	Salisbury, MD	(4)	Middlebury, VT*	14-13 (OT)

Women

Div.	Winner		Runner-Up	Score
I	Princeton*	(3)	Virginia	8-7 (OT)
II	Stonehill, MA	(1)	Longwood, VA	9-8
III	Amherst, MA	(1)	Middlebury, VT*	11-9

Rowing
Women

Div.	Winner		Runner-Up	Score
I	Harvard	(1)	Brown*	59-57
II	UC Davis*	(2)	Western Wash.	59-57
III	Colby, ME	(1)	Puget Sound, WA	10-12

Note: In 2001-02, women's rowing was inaugurated as an official NCAA sport at the Division II and III levels. Since 1997, all three divisions had been grouped into one "National Collegiate Championship."

Softball

Div.	Winner		Runner-Up	Score
I	UCLA	(9)	California*	1-0 (9 inn.)
II	UC Davis	(1)	Georgia Coll. & St.	7-0
III	Central, IA	(4)	Salisbury, MD	5-3

Tennis

Note that both Div. II tournaments were team-only.

Men

Div.	Winner		Runner-Up	Score
I	Illinois	(1)	Vanderbilt	4-3
II	BYU-Hawaii*	(2)	Hawaii Pacific	5-4
III	Emory, GA	(1)	Williams, MA*	4-0

Women

Div.	Winner		Runner-Up	Score
I	Florida	(4)	Stanford*	4-3
II	BYU-Hawaii*	(4)	Barry, FL	5-3
III	Emory, GA	(2)	Washington & Lee, VA	5-1

Outdoor Track
Men

Div.	Winner		Runner-Up	Score
I	Arkansas	(10)	Auburn	59-50
II	Abilene Christian*	(13)	St. Augustine's, NC	102-69
III	Wisc.-La Crosse*	(8)	Lincoln, MO	88-64

Women

Div.	Winner		Runner-Up	Score
I	LSU	(13)	Texas	64-50
II	Lincoln, MO	(1)	St. Augustine's, NC*	98-67
III	Wheaton, MA*	(3)	Lehman, NY	72-52

Volleyball
Men

Div.	Winner		Runner-Up	Score
National	Lewis, IL	(1)	Brigham Young	3-2

Water Polo
Women

Div.	Winner		Runner-Up	Score
National	UCLA	(2)	Stanford*	4-3

Real Gender Equity

Schools whose men's and women's teams won NCAA championships in the same sport, or its equivalent during the 2002-03 season.

School	Div.	Sports
Auburn	I	Men's Swimming & Diving Women's Swimming & Diving
BYU-Hawaii	II	Men's Tennis Women's Tennis
Emory, GA	III	Men's Tennis Women's Tennis
Kenyon, OH	III	Men's Swimming & Diving Women's Swimming & Diving
Western St., CO	II	Men's Cross Country Women's Cross Country

North Carolina
Shalane Flanagan
Cross Country

Oklahoma
Daniel Furney
Gymnastics

Utah
Katrin Smigun
Skiing

Oklahoma St.
Johnny Thompson
Wrestling

2002-03 Division I Individual Champions
Repeat champions in **bold** type.

FALL
Cross Country

Men (10,000 meters)	Time
1 Jorge Torres, Colorado	29:04.7
2 Alistair Cragg, Arkansas	29:06.0
3 Grant Robison, Stanford	29:36.7

Women (6,000 meters)	Time
1 Shalane Flanagan, North Carolina	19:36.0
2 Kate O'Neill, Yale	19:45.9
3 Alicia Craig, Stanford	19:48.0

WINTER
Fencing
Men

Event		Score
Foil	**Non Panchan**, Penn St.	15-14
Epee	Weston Kelsey, Air Force	8-7
Sabre	Adam Crompton, Ohio St.	15-13

Women

Event		Score
Foil	**Alicja Kryczalo**, Notre Dame	15-13
Epee	Katarzyna Trzopek, Penn St.	15-12
Sabre	Alexis Jemal, Rutgers	15-12

Gymnastics
Men

Event		Points
All-Around	Daniel Furney, Oklahoma	56.100
Floor Exercise	Josh Landis, Oklahoma	9.675
Pommel Horse	Josh Landis, Oklahoma	9.687
Rings	Kevin Tan, Penn St.	9.762
Vault	Andrew DiGiore, Michigan	9.650
Parallel Bars	Daniel Furney, Oklahoma	9.475
Horizontal Bar	Linas Gaveika, Iowa	9.712

Women

Event		Points
All-Around	Richelle Simpson, Nebraska	39.800
Vault	Ashley Miles, Alabama	9.9375
Uneven Bars	Jamie Dantzcher, UCLA & Kate Richardson, UCLA	9.900
Balance Beam	Kate Richardson, UCLA	9.938
Floor Exercise	Richelle Simpson, Nebraska	9.963

Rifle
Combined
Number in parentheses denotes inner tens.
Smallbore

	Points
1 **Matthew Emmons**, AK-Fairbanks	1191 (89)
2 Bradley Wheeldon, Kentucky	1183 (78)
3 Jamie Beyerle, AK-Fairbanks	1182 (83)

Air Rifle

	Points
1 Jamie Beyerle, AK-Fairbanks	395 (32)
2 Per Sandberg, AK-Fairbanks	394 (31)
3 Bradley Wheeldon, Kentucky	393 (26)

Skiing
Men

Event		Time
Slalom	Bradley Wall, Dartmouth	1:40.28
Giant Slalom	Ben Thornhill, Utah	1:59.78
10-k Freestyle	Jimmy Vika, New Mexico	24:03.9
20-k Classic	Chris Cook, Northern Michigan	58:43.4

Women

Event		Time
Slalom	Lina Johansson, Utah	1:35.03
Giant Slalom	Jamie Kingsbury, Vermont	2:06.71
5-k Freestyle	Katrin Smigun, Utah	13:29.7
15-k Classic	Katrin Smigun, Utah	46:30.7

Wrestling

Wgt	Champion	Runner-Up
125	Travis Lee, Cornell	C. Fleeger, Purdue
133	**Johnny Thompson**, Okla. St.	Ryan Lewis, Minnesota
141	Teyon Ware, Oklahoma	D. Long, N. Iowa
149	Eric Larkin, Arizona St.	Jared Lawrence, Minnesota
157	Ryan Bertin, Michigan	A. Tirapelle, Illinois
165	Matt Lackey, Illinois	T. Letters, Lehigh
174	Robbie Waller, Oklahoma	C. Fronhofer, Pitt.
184	Jake Rosholt, Okla. St.	S. Barker, Missouri
197	Damion Hahn, Minnesota	J. Trenge, Lehigh
Hvy	Steve Mocco, Iowa	K. Hoy, Air Force

Arizona St.
Alejandro Canizares
Golf

Arkansas
Alistair Cragg
Track & Field/XC

LSU
Muna Lee
Track & Field

Stanford
Amber Liu
Tennis

Swimming & Diving
(*) indicates meet record.

Men

Event (yards)		Time
50 free	Fred Bousquet, Auburn	19.31
100 free	Duje Draganja, California	42.02
200 free	Simon Burnett, Arizona	1:33.69
500 free	Erik Vendt, USC	4:15.75
1650 free	**Erik Vendt**, USC	14:29.85
100 back	**Peter Marshall**, Stanford	45.57
200 back	Aaron Peirsol, Texas	1:39.16*
100 breast	**Brendan Hansen**, Texas	51.96*
200 breast	**Brendan Hansen**, Texas	1:52.62*
100 butterfly	**Ian Crocker**, Texas	45.67
200 butterfly	**Stefan Gherghel**, Alabama	1:42.35
200 IM	George Bovell, Auburn	1:42.66*
400 IM	Robert Margalis, Georgia	3:39.92
200 free relay	**Stanford**	1:17.03
400 free relay	**California**	2:48.99*
800 free relay	Texas	6:18.62
200 medley relay	Texas	1:24.46*
400 medley relay	Texas	3:04.47*

Diving		Points
1-meter	Joona Puhakka, Arizona St.	395.80
3-meter	Phillip Jones, Tennessee	649.70
Platform	(tie) Caesar Garcia, Auburn & Jason Coben, Michigan	575.80

Women

Event (yards)		Time
50 free	**Maritza Correia**, Georgia	21.83
100 free	**Maritza Correia**, Georgia	47.29*
200 free	(tie) Jessi Perruquet, North Carolina & Heather Kemp, Auburn	1:45.01
500 free	**Flavia Rigamonti**, SMU	4:37.72
1650 free	**Flavia Rigamonti**, SMU	15:43.90
100 back	**Natalie Coughlin**, California	50.92
200 back	**Natalie Coughlin**, California	1:50.86
100 breast	**Tara Kirk**, Stanford	58.62*
200 breast	**Tara Kirk**, Stanford	2:08.79
100 butterfly	**Natalie Coughlin**, California	50.62
200 butterfly	Mary DeScenza, Georgia	1:53.51
200 IM	**Maggie Bowen**, Auburn	1:55.33
400 IM	**Maggie Bowen**, Auburn	4:06.15
200 free relay	**Georgia**	1:28.96
400 free relay	Auburn	3:14.15
800 free relay	Auburn	7:02.72*
200 medley relay	Auburn	1:36.69*
400 medley relay	Auburn	3:31.45*

Diving		Points
1-meter	Yulia Pakhalina, Houston	339.70
3-meter	**Yulia Pakhalina**, Houston	657.30
Platform	Natalia Diea, Ohio St.	476.65

Indoor Track
(*) indicates meet record

Men

Event		Time
60 meters	Pierre Browne, Mississippi St.	6.60
200 meters	Leo Bookman, Kansas	20.53
400 meters	Gary Kikaya, Tennessee	45.71
800 meters	Nate Brannen, Michigan	1:47.79
Mile	Chris Mulvaney, Arkansas	4:05.70
3000 meters	Alistair Cragg, Arkansas	7:55.68
5000 meters	**Alistair Cragg**, Arkansas	13:28.93*
60-m hurdles	Jabari Greer, Tennessee	7.55
4x400-m relay	LSU	3:04.79
Distance medley relay	**Villanova**	9:29.12

Event		Hgt/Dist
High Jump	Adam Shunk, North Carolina	7-2½
Pole Vault	Brad Walker, Washington	19-0¼
Long Jump	Brian Johnson, Southern	27-2
Triple Jump	Allen Simms, USC	56-7½
Shot Put	**Carl Meyerscough**, Nebraska	70-6¼*
35-lb Throw	Thomas Freeman, Manhattan	71-2½

Note: East Carolina's Julien Dunkley and Cal State-Northridge's Jerrick Holmes were originally thought to be winners of the 60-m dash and high jump, respectively, but were later disqualified for undisclosed reasons.

Women

Event		Time
60 meters	Muna Lee, LSU	7.17
200 meters	**Muna Lee**, LSU	22.61*
400 meters	LeShinda Demus, S. Carolina	51.79
800 meters	Lena Nilsson, UCLA	2:05.13
Mile	Johanna Nilsson, N. Arizona	4:32.49
3000 meters	Shalane Flanagan, N. Carolina	9:01.05
5000 meters	Sara Gorton, Colorado	15:39.25*
60-m hurdles	Lolo Jones, LSU	8.00
4x400-m relay	Texas	3:27.66*
Distance medley relay	North Carolina	11:00.20

Event		Hgt/Dist
High Jump	Nevena Lendel, SMU	6-2¼
Pole Vault	Lacy Janson, Florida St.	14-7¼
Long Jump	**Elva Goulbourne**, Auburn	22-4¼*
Triple Jump	Elva Goulbourne, Auburn	45-2½
Shot Put	Laura Gerraughty, North Carolina	59-3
20-lb Throw	Erin Gilreath, Florida	72-3¾

SPRING
Golf
Men

		Total
1	Alejandro Canizares, Arizona St.	77-70-71-69—287
2	Lee Williams, Auburn	69-72-71-77—289
3	Matthew Rosenfeld, Texas	71-76-71-72—290
	Chris Stroud, Lamar	70-77-70-73—290

Golf (cont.)
Women

		Total
1	Mikaela Parmlid, USC	77-73-70-77 —297†
	Andrea Vander Lende, Florida	77-74-69-77 —297
3	Erica Blasberg, Arizona	78-81-70-69 —298
	Irene Cho, USC	74-79-73-72 —298

† Parmlid defeated Vander Lende by two strokes on the first sudden-death playoff hole.

Tennis
Men
Singles— Amer Delic (Illinois) def. Benedikt Dorsch (Baylor), 6-4, 6-3.
Doubles— Rajeev Ram & Brian Wilson (Illinois) def. Oliver Maiberger & Ryan Redondo (San Diego St.), 6-4, 5-7, 6-1.
Women
Singles— Amber Liu (Stanford) def. Vilmarie Castellvi (Tennessee), 7-6(5), 6-2.
Doubles— Christina Fusano & Raquel Kops-Jones (California) def. Sarah Witten & Amy Trefethen (Kentucky), 6-1, 6-2.

Outdoor Track
(*) indicates meet record
Men

Event		Time
100 meters	Mardy Scales, Mid. Tenn. St.	10.25
200 meters	Leo Bookman, Kansas	20.47
400 meters	Adam Steele, Minnesota	44.57
800 meters	Sam Burley, Pennsylvania	1:46.50
1500 meters	Grant Robison, Stanford	3:40.39
5000 meters	Alistair Cragg, Arkansas	13:47.87
10,000 meters	Dan Lincoln, Arkansas	28:20.20
110-m hurdles	Ryan Wilson, USC	13.35
400-m hurdles	Dean Griffiths, Auburn	48.55
3000-m steeple	**Dan Lincoln**, Arkansas	8:26.65
4x100-m relay	**LSU**	38.65
4x400-m relay	LSU	3:02.01

Event		Hgt/Dist
High Jump	David Jaworski, USC	7-5¾
Pole Vault	Eric Eshbach, Nebraska	17-10½
Long Jump	Leevan Sands, Auburn	26-5
Triple Jump	Julien Kapek, USC	56-2
Shot Put	Carl Myerscough, Nebraska	71-11
Discus	Hannes Hopley, SMU	200-11
Javelin	Brian Chaput, Pennsylvania	258-2
Hammer	Lucais MacKay, Georgia	230-3
Decathlon	Stephen Harris, Tennessee	8061 pts

Women

Event		Time
100 meters	Aleen Bailey, South Carolina	11.18
200 meters	Aleen Bailey, South Carolina	22.65
400 meters	Sanya Richards, Texas	50.58
800 meters	**Alice Schmidt**, N. Carolina	2:01.16
1500 meters	Tiffany McWilliams, Miss. St.	4:06.75*
5000 meters	**Lauren Fleshman**, Stanford	15:24.06*
10,000 meters	Alicia Craig, Stanford	32:40.03
100-m hurdles	**Perdita Felicien**, Illinois	12.74
400-m hurdles	Sheena Johnson, UCLA	54.24*
3000-m steeple	Kassi Andersen, BYU	9:44.95*
4x100-m relay	LSU	42.55
4x400-m relay	Texas	3:26.76

Event		Hgt/Dist
High Jump	Whitney Evans, Washington St.	6-1¼
Pole Vault	Becky Holliday, Oregon	14-5½*
Long Jump	**Elva Goulbourne**, Auburn	22-2¼
Triple Jump	Ineta Radevica, Nebraska	45-8½
Shot Put	Becky Breisch, Nebraska	58-3¼
Discus	Deshaya Williams, Penn St.	181-9
Javelin	Irina Kharun, Indiana	202-10*
Hammer	Candice Scott, Florida	229-0*
Heptathlon	Hyleas Fountain, Georgia	5999 pts

Championships Most Outstanding Players
Men

Baseball	John Hudgins, Stanford
Basketball	Carmelo Anthony, Syracuse
Cross Country	Jorge Torres, Colorado*
Golf	Alejandro Canizares, Arizona St.*
Gymnastics	Daniel Furney, Oklahoma*
Ice Hockey	Thomas Vanek, Minnesota
Lacrosse	Tillman Johnson, Virginia
Soccer: Offense	Aaron Lopez, UCLA
Soccer: Defense	Zach Wells, UCLA
Swimming & Diving	Aaron Peirsol, Texas
Tennis	Clayton Moss, Kentucky
Tennis	Amer Delic, Illinois*
Track: Indoor	Alistair Cragg, Arkansas*
Track: Outdoor	Dan Lincoln, Arkansas*
Volleyball	Gustavo Meyer, Lewis, IL
Water Polo	Tony Azevedo, Stanford
Wrestling	Eric Larkin, Arizona St.

Women

Basketball	Diana Taurasi, Connecticut
Cross Country	Shalane Flanagan, North Carolina*
Golf	Mikaela Parmlid, USC*
Gymnastics	Richelle Simpson, Nebraska*
Ice Hockey	Caroline Ouellette, Minnesota-Duluth
Lacrosse	Rachael Becker, Princeton
Soccer: Offense	Christine Sinclair, Portland
Soccer: Defense	Jessica Ballweg, Santa Clara
Softball	Keira Goerl, UCLA
Swimming & Diving	Natalie Coughlin, California
	Yulia Pakhalina, Houston
Tennis	Amber Liu, Stanford*
Track: Indoor	Elva Goulbourne, Auburn*
Track: Outdoor	Aleen Bailey, South Carolina*
Volleyball	Keao Burdine, USC
Water Polo	Robin Beauregard, UCLA

(*) indicates won individual or all-around NCAA championship; There were no official Outstanding Players in fencing, field hockey, I-AA football, riflery, rowing and skiing. Outstanding players in indoor and outdoor track are the individuals earning the most points in the NCAA Championships.

2002-03 NAIA Team Champions
Total NAIA titles in parentheses.

FALL
Cross Country: MEN'S–Minot St., ND (1); WOMEN'S–Northwest, WA (1). **Football:** MEN'S–Carroll, MT (1). **Soccer:** MEN'S–Mobile, AL (1); WOMEN'S– Westmont, CA (4). **Volleyball:** WOMEN'S–National American, SD (1).

WINTER
Basketball: MEN'S–Division I: Concordia, CA (1) and Division II: Northwestern, IA (2); WOMEN'S–Division I: Southern Nazarene, OK (6) and Division II: Hastings, NE (2). **Swimming & Diving:** MEN'S–Simon Fraser, BC (15); WOMEN'S– Simon Fraser, BC (9). **Indoor Track:** MEN'S–Azusa Pacific, CA (3); WOMEN'S–Azusa Pacific, CA (1). **Wrestling:** MEN'S–Missouri Valley (3).

SPRING
Baseball: MEN'S–Lewis-Clark St., ID (13). **Golf:** MEN'S–Oklahoma City (3); WOMEN'S–Northwood, FL (1). **Softball:** WOMEN'S–Simon Fraser, BC (2). **Tennis:** MEN'S–Oklahoma Christian (1); WOMEN'S–Northwood, FL (1). **Outdoor Track:** MEN'S–Lindenwood, MO (1); WOMEN'S–Azusa Pacific, CA (1).

Annual NCAA Division I Team Champions

Men's and women's NCAA Division I team champions from cross country to wrestling. Also see team champions for baseball, basketball, football, golf, ice hockey, soccer and tennis in the appropriate chapters throughout the almanac. See pages 454-456 for list of 2002-03 individual champions.

CROSS COUNTRY

Men

Stanford placed four of its runners in the top 10 and eased to its third overall Division I cross country title. Grant Robison (third), Louis Luchini (fifth), Donald Sage (sixth) and Ian Dobson (eighth) led the Cardinal, who finished with 47 points, well ahead of runner-up Wisconsin (107) and Eastern Michigan (165). Colorado's Jorge Torres, last year's runner-up, took the individual title, completing the 10,000-meter course in 29:04.7. (*Terre Haute, IN; Nov. 25, 2002.*)

Multiple winners: Arkansas (11); Michigan St. (8); UTEP (7); Oregon and Villanova (4); Drake, Indiana, Penn St., Stanford and Wisconsin (3); Iowa St., San Jose St. and Western Michigan (2).

Year	Year	Year	Year	Year
1938 Indiana	1951 Syracuse	1965 Western Mich.	1979 UTEP	1993 Arkansas
1939 Michigan St.	1952 Michigan St.	1966 Villanova	1980 UTEP	1994 Iowa St.
1940 Indiana	1953 Kansas	1967 Villanova	1981 UTEP	1995 Arkansas
1941 Rhode Island	1954 Oklahoma St.	1968 Villanova	1982 Wisconsin	1996 Stanford
1942 Indiana	1955 Michigan St.	1969 UTEP	1983 Vacated	1997 Stanford
& Penn St.	1956 Michigan St.	1970 Villanova	1984 Arkansas	1998 Arkansas
1943 Not held	1957 Notre Dame	1971 Oregon	1985 Wisconsin	1999 Arkansas
1944 Drake	1958 Michigan St.	1972 Tennessee	1986 Arkansas	2000 Arkansas
1945 Drake	1959 Michigan St.	1973 Oregon	1987 Arkansas	2001 Colorado
1946 Drake	1960 Houston	1974 Oregon	1988 Wisconsin	2002 Stanford
1947 Penn St.	1961 Oregon St.	1975 UTEP	1989 Iowa St.	
1948 Michigan St.	1962 San Jose St.	1976 UTEP	1990 Arkansas	
1949 Michigan St.	1963 San Jose St.	1977 Oregon	1991 Arkansas	
1950 Penn St.	1964 Western Mich.	1978 UTEP	1992 Arkansas	

Women

Brigham Young won its second consecutive Division I cross country title and fourth in the past six years, outdistancing Stanford, 85-113. Notre Dame finished in third with 170 points. Michaela Manova was once again BYU's top finisher with a fifth-place showing while freshman teammate Kassie Anderson contributed a sixth-place finish. North Carolina's Shalane Flanagan ran away with the individual title, completing the 6,000-meter course in 19:36.0. (*Terre Haute, IN; Nov. 25, 2002.*)

Multiple winners: Villanova (7); Brigham Young (4); Oregon, Virginia and Wisconsin (2).

Year	Year	Year	Year	Year
1981 Virginia	1986 Texas	1991 Villanova	1996 Stanford	2001 Brigham Young
1982 Virginia	1987 Oregon	1992 Villanova	1997 Brigham Young	2002 Brigham Young
1983 Oregon	1988 Kentucky	1993 Villanova	1998 Villanova	
1984 Wisconsin	1989 Villanova	1994 Villanova	1999 Brigham Young	
1985 Wisconsin	1990 Villanova	1995 Providence	2000 Colorado	

FENCING

Men & Women

After finishing in either second or third for the past eight years, Notre Dame can once again call itself champion as the Fighting Irish captured its second fencing title with a 182-179 nailbiter over perennial champ Penn State. St. John's, winner of the 2001 title, took third with 171 points. Alicja Kryczalo was Notre Dame's only individual winner as she successfully defended her title in the women's foil. (*Colorado Springs, CO; Mar. 20-23, 2003.*)

Multiple winners: Penn St. (9); Columbia/Barnard and Notre Dame (2). **Note:** Prior to 1990, men and women held separate championships. Men's multiple winners included: NYU (12); Columbia (11); Wayne St. (7); Navy, Notre Dame and Penn (3); Illinois (2). Women's multiple winners included: Wayne St. (3); Yale (2).

Year	Year	Year	Year
1990 Penn St.	1994 Notre Dame	1998 Penn St.	2002 Penn St.
1991 Penn St.	1995 Penn St.	1999 Penn St.	2003 Notre Dame
1992 Columbia/Barnard	1996 Penn St.	2000 Penn St.	
1993 Columbia/Barnard	1997 Penn St.	2001 St. John's	

FIELD HOCKEY

Women

Wake Forest shutout Penn State, 2-0, to win its first Division I field hockey championship and the school's first NCAA women's title in any sport. Kelly Doton and senior Heather Aughinbaugh scored first-half goals and the Demon Deacon defense took over from there, limiting Penn State to just four shots for the game. Goaltender Katie Ridd recorded the shutout, her fifth consecutive. Wake Forest closed out the year with a 20-2 record, while Penn State fell to 19-5. (*Louisville, KY; Nov. 24, 2002.*)

Multiple winners: Old Dominion (9); North Carolina (4); Maryland (3); Connecticut (2).

Year	Year	Year	Year	Year
1981 Connecticut	1986 Iowa	1991 Old Dominion	1996 North Carolina	2001 Michigan
1982 Old Dominion	1987 Maryland	1992 Old Dominion	1997 North Carolina	2002 Wake Forest
1983 Old Dominion	1988 Old Dominion	1993 Maryland	1998 Old Dominion	
1984 Old Dominion	1989 North Carolina	1994 J. Madison	1999 Maryland	
1985 Connecticut	1990 Old Dominion	1995 North Carolina	2000 Old Dominion	

Annual NCAA Division I Team Champions (Cont.)

GYMNASTICS

Men

Senior Daniel Furney led Oklahoma to its second consecutive national collegiate gymnastics title and its fifth overall. With its win at the NCAA championships, the Sooners ran their record to 26-0 to become just the second team to record a perfect season. Furney captured the all-around individual title, defeating defending champ Raj Bhavsar of Ohio State. Oklahoma amassed 222.600 points to beat runner-up Ohio State (220.700) and Penn State (219.950). *(Philadelphia, PA; Apr. 11-13, 2003.)*

Multiple winners: Penn St. (10); Illinois (9); Nebraska (8); Oklahoma (5); California and So. Illinois (4); Iowa St., Michigan, Ohio St. and Stanford (3); Florida St and UCLA (2).

Year	Year	Year	Year	Year
1938 Chicago	1956 Illinois	1969 Iowa	1980 Nebraska	1994 Nebraska
1939 Illinois	1957 Penn St.	& Michigan (T)	1981 Nebraska	1995 Stanford
1940 Illinois	1958 Michigan St.	1970 Michigan	1982 Nebraska	1996 Ohio St.
1941 Illinois	& Illinois	& Michigan (T)	1983 Nebraska	1997 California
1942 Illinois	1959 Penn St.	1971 Iowa St.	1984 UCLA	1998 California
1943-47 Not held	1960 Penn St.	1972 So. Illinois	1985 Ohio St.	1999 Michigan
1948 Penn St.	1961 Penn St.	1973 Iowa St.	1986 Arizona St.	2000 Penn St.
1949 Temple	1962 USC	1974 Iowa St.	1987 UCLA	2001 Ohio St.
1950 Illinois	1963 Michigan	1975 California	1988 Nebraska	2002 Oklahoma
1951 Florida St.	1964 So. Illinois	1976 Penn St.	1989 Illinois	2003 Oklahoma
1952 Florida St.	1965 Penn St.	1977 Indiana St.	1990 Nebraska	
1953 Penn St.	1966 So. Illinois	& Oklahoma	1991 Oklahoma	(T) indicates won
1954 Penn St.	1967 So. Illinois	1978 Oklahoma	1992 Stanford	trampoline competi-
1955 Illinois	1968 California	1979 Nebraska	1993 Stanford	tion (1969-70).

Women

UCLA won three of the four team event contests to capture its third NCAA women's gymnastics title in the last four years and its fourth overall. The Bruins took the top team scores in the balance beam, the floor exercise and the bars and finished runner-up to host Nebraska in the vault. UCLA registered 197.825 points overall for the victory, the Crimson Tide of Alabama took second (197.275) while Nebraska finished third (197.150). In front of her home crowd, Husker Richelle Simpson won the individual all-around title, edging UCLA's Jamie Dantzcher by a quarter point. *(Lincoln, NE; Apr. 24-26, 2003.)*

Multiple winners: Utah (9); Georgia (5); Alabama and UCLA (4).

Year	Year	Year	Year	Year
1982 Utah	1987 Georgia	1992 Utah	1997 UCLA	2002 Alabama
1983 Utah	1988 Alabama	1993 Georgia	1998 Georgia	2003 UCLA
1984 Utah	1989 Georgia	1994 Utah	1999 Georgia	
1985 Utah	1990 Utah	1995 Utah	2000 UCLA	
1986 Utah	1991 Alabama	1996 Alabama	2001 UCLA	

LACROSSE

Men

Midfielder A.J. Shannon scored four goals and Chris Rotelli chipped in a goal and four assists to lead Virginia to a 9-7 victory over top-seeded Johns Hopkins in the Division I men's lacrosse championship game. It is the Cavaliers' third win overall and first since 1999. Virginia jumped out to an early 5-0 lead, carried a 6-4 lead into halftime and held on against the fierce Johns Hopkins offense. Virginia goaltender Tillman Johnson stopped 13 shots in the title game and a career-high 18 in the semifinals against Maryland to earn Most Outstanding Player honors for the tournament. *(Baltimore, MD; May 26, 2003.)*

Multiple winners: Johns Hopkins and Syracuse (7); Princeton (6); North Carolina (4); Cornell and Virginia (3); Maryland (2).

Year	Year	Year	Year	Year
1971 Cornell	1978 Johns Hopkins	1985 Johns Hopkins	1992 Princeton	1999 Virginia
1972 Virginia	1979 Johns Hopkins	1986 North Carolina	1993 Syracuse	2000 Syracuse
1973 Maryland	1980 Johns Hopkins	1987 Johns Hopkins	1994 Princeton	2001 Princeton
1974 Johns Hopkins	1981 North Carolina	1988 Syracuse	1995 Syracuse	2002 Syracuse
1975 Maryland	1982 North Carolina	1989 Syracuse	1996 Princeton	2003 Virginia
1976 Cornell	1983 Syracuse	1990 Syracuse*	1997 Princeton	
1977 Cornell	1984 Johns Hopkins	1991 North Carolina	1998 Princeton	

*Title was later vacated due to action by the NCAA Committee on Infractions.

Women

Despite losing seven seniors from its 2002 championship squad, Princeton successfully defended its Division I women's lacrosse title with an 8-7 overtime win vs. Virginia. It is the Tigers' third title in the last ten years. Virginia held a 7-6 lead for the latter part of the second half until Princeton's Whitney Miller finally broke through with 1:39 remaining to send the game into overtime. Then with just 1:29 left in the first OT period, junior Theresa Sherry netted the game winner. Defender Rachael Becker was spectacular for the Tigers and was voted Most Outstanding Player of the tournament. *(Syracuse, NY; May 18, 2003.)*

Multiple winners: Maryland (9); Princeton (3); Penn St., Temple and Virginia (2).

Year	Year	Year	Year	Year
1982 Massachusetts	1987 Penn St.	1992 Maryland	1997 Maryland	2002 Princeton
1983 Delaware	1988 Temple	1993 Virginia	1998 Maryland	2003 Princeton
1984 Temple	1989 Penn St.	1994 Princeton	1999 Maryland	
1985 New Hampshire	1990 Harvard	1995 Maryland	2000 Maryland	
1986 Maryland	1991 Virginia	1996 Maryland	2001 Maryland	

RIFLE
Men & Women

It was business as usual for Alaska-Fairbanks at the 2003 NCAA Rifle Championships as the Nanooks captured their fifth consecutive title and sixth overall. Matt Emmons, Jamie Beyerle and Per Sandberg led the Nanooks to an NCAA record 6287 points, defeating runner-up Xavier (6197) and third-place Murray State (6158). Alaska-Fairbanks swept the air rifle and small-bore disciplines, setting another NCAA mark in the smallbore with 4717 points. (West Point, NY; Mar. 14-15, 2003.)

Multiple winners: West Virginia (13); Alaska-Fairbanks (6); Tennessee Tech (3); Murray St. (2).

Year		Year		Year		Year		Year	
1980	Tenn. Tech	1985	Murray St.	1990	West Virginia	1995	West Virginia	2000	AK-Fairbanks
1981	Tenn. Tech	1986	West Virginia	1991	West Virginia	1996	West Virginia	2001	AK-Fairbanks
1982	Tenn. Tech	1987	Murray St.	1992	West Virginia	1997	West Virginia	2002	AK-Fairbanks
1983	West Virginia	1988	West Virginia	1993	West Virginia	1998	West Virginia	2003	AK-Fairbanks
1984	West Virginia	1989	West Virginia	1994	AK-Fairbanks	1999	AK-Fairbanks		

ROWING
NCAA Championships
Women

After six years of domination by Washington and Brown, there is new blood at the top of the Division I women's rowing world. Harvard/Radcliffe won the closely-contested grand finals of the Varsity Eights event, giving it 59 total points for the weekend, enough to edge defending champ Brown (57 points) and third-place Washington (55) for the title. Harvard's Varsity Eights completed the 2,000-meter course in 6:26.98, taking control in the final 500 meters to prevail over runner-up Michigan (6:28.58) and Stanford (6:29.54). The Brown crew took the Varsity Fours and the Varsity II Eights. (Indianapolis, IN; May 30-June 1, 2003).

Multiple winners: Brown and Washington (3).

Year	Overall winner	Varsity Eights	Year	Overall winner	Varsity Eights
1997	Washington	Washington	2001	Washington	Washington
1998	Washington	Washington	2002	Brown	Washington
1999	Brown	Brown	2003	Harvard	Harvard
2000	Brown	Brown			

Intercollegiate Rowing Association Regatta
VARSITY EIGHTS
Men

Harvard pulled away after the first 1,000 meters and and cruised to its first Varsity Eights title in 5:43.41 at the 101st IRA Championships Regatta. Due to academic and scheduling conflicts, it was just Harvard's fourth appearance at the IRA Championships. Washington's crew came in second in 5:47.23 while California, looking for a record fifth consecutive title, placed third in 5:48.33. (Cooper River, Camden, NJ; May 29-31, 2003.)

The IRA was formed in 1895 by several Northeastern colleges after Harvard and Yale quit the Rowing Association (established in 1871) to stage an annual-race of their own. Since then the IRA Regatta has been contested over courses of varying lengths in Poughkeepsie, N.Y., Marietta, Ohio, Syracuse, N.Y. and Camden, N.J.

Distances: 4 miles (1895-97,1899-1916,1925-41); 3 miles (1898,1921-24,1947-49,1952-63,1965-67); 2 miles (1920,1950-51); 2000 meters (1964, since 1968).

Multiple winners: Cornell (24); California (14); Navy (13); Washington (11); Penn (9); Brown and Wisconsin (7); Syracuse (6); Columbia (4); Princeton (3); Northeastern (2).

Year		Year		Year		Year		Year	
1895	Columbia	1916	Syracuse	1939	California	1964	California	1985	Princeton
1896	Cornell	1917-19	Not held	1940	Washington	1965	Navy	1986	Brown
1897	Cornell					1966	Wisconsin	1987	Brown
1898	Penn	1920	Syracuse	1941	Washington	1967	Penn	1988	Northeastern
1899	Penn	1921	Navy	1942-46	Not held	1968	Penn	1989	Penn
		1922	Navy	1947	Navy	1969	Penn		
1900	Penn	1923	Washington	1948	Washington			1990	Wisconsin
1901	Cornell	1924	Washington	1949	California	1970	Washington	1991	Northeastern
1902	Cornell	1925	Navy			1971	Cornell	1992	Dartmouth,
1903	Cornell	1926	Washington	1950	Washington	1972	Penn		Navy & Penn†
1904	Syracuse	1927	Columbia	1951	Wisconsin	1973	Wisconsin	1993	Brown
1905	Cornell	1928	California	1952	Navy	1974	Wisconsin	1994	Brown
1906	Cornell	1929	Columbia	1953	Navy	1975	Wisconsin	1995	Brown
1907	Cornell			1954	Navy*	1976	California	1996	Princeton
1908	Syracuse	1930	Cornell	1955	Cornell	1977	Cornell	1997	Washington
1909	Cornell	1931	Navy	1956	Cornell	1978	Syracuse	1998	Princeton
		1932	California	1957	Cornell	1979	Brown	1999	California
1910	Cornell	1933	Not held	1958	Cornell				
1911	Cornell	1934	California	1959	Wisconsin	1980	Navy	2000	California
1912	Cornell	1935	California			1981	Cornell	2001	California
1913	Syracuse	1936	Washington	1960	California	1982	Cornell	2002	California
1914	Columbia	1937	Washington	1961	California	1983	Brown	2003	Harvard
1915	Cornell	1938	Navy	1962	Cornell	1984	Cornell		
				1963	Cornell				

*In 1954, Navy was disqualified because of an ineligible coxswain; no trophies were given.
†First dead heat in history of IRA Regatta.

Annual NCAA Division I Team Champions (Cont.)

National Rowing Championship
VARSITY EIGHTS
· Men

National championship raced annually from 1982-96 in Bantam, Ohio over a 2,000-meter course on Lake Harsha. Winner received the Herschede Cup. Regatta discontinued in 1997.
   Multiple winners: Harvard (6); Brown (3); Wisconsin (2).

Year	Champion	Time	Runner-up	Time	Year	Champion	Time	Runner-up	Time
1982	Yale	5:50.8	Cornell	5:54.15	1990	Wisconsin	5:52.5	Harvard	5:56.84
1983	Harvard	5:59.6	Washington	6:00.0	1991	Penn	5:58.21	Northeastern	5:58.48
1984	Washington	5:51.1	Yale	5:55.6	1992	Harvard	5:33.97	Dartmouth	5:34.28
1985	Harvard	5:44.4	Princeton	5:44.87	1993	Brown	5:54.15	Penn	5:56.98
1986	Wisconsin	5:57.8	Brown	5:59.9	1994	Brown	5:24.52	Harvard	5:25.83
1987	Harvard	5:35.17	Brown	5:35.63	1995	Brown	5:23.40	Princeton	5:25.83
1988	Harvard	5:35.98	Northeastern	5:37.07	1996	Princeton	5:57.47	Penn	6:03.28
1989	Harvard	5:36.6	Washington	5:38.93	1997	discontinued			

Women

National championship held over various distances at 10 different venues from 1979-96. Distances— 1000 meters (1979-81); 1500 meters (1982-83); 1000 meters (1984); 1750 meters (1985); 2000 meters (1986-88, 1991-96); 1852 meters (1989-90). Winner received the Ferguson Bowl. Regatta discontinued in 1997.
   Multiple winners: Washington (7); Princeton (4); Boston University (2).

Year	Champion	Time	Runner-up	Time	Year	Champion	Time	Runner-up	Time
1979	Yale	3:06	California	3:08.6	1988	Washington	6:41.0	Yale	6:42.37
1980	California	3:05.4	Oregon St.	3:05.8	1989	Cornell	5:34.9	Wisconsin	5:37.5
1981	Washington	3:20.6	Yale	3:22.9	1991	Boston Univ.	7:03.2	Cornell	7:06.21
1982	Washington	4:56.4	Wisconsin	4:59.83	1992	Boston Univ.	6:28.79	Cornell	6:32.79
1983	Washington	4:57.5	Dartmouth	5:03.02	1993	Princeton	6:40.75	Washington	6:43.86
1984	Washington	3:29.48	Radcliffe	3:31.08	1994	Princeton	6:11.38	Yale	6:14.46
1985	Washington	5:28.4	Wisconsin	5:32.0	1995	Princeton	6:11.98	Washington	6:12.69
1986	Wisconsin	6:53.28	Radcliffe	6:53.34	1996	Brown	6:45.7	Princeton	6:49.3
1987	Washington	6:33.8	Yale	6:37.4	1997	discontinued			

The Harvard-Yale Regatta

To virtually no one's surprise, Harvard made it four in a row and 17 of the last 19 by sweeping Yale at the 138th running of the Harvard/Yale Regatta on June 7, 2003. The win gave the Harvard crew is first undefeated season since 1980. Harvard's Varsity Eights squad finished the four-mile course on the Thames River in New London, Conn. in 18:54.4, the fourth-fastest upstream time in race history. Yale (19:44.2) came in 49.8 seconds later, the largest margin of victory since 1911. The Harvard/Yale Regatta is the nation's oldest intercollegiate sporting event. Harvard holds an 85-53 series edge.

SKIING
Men & Women

Utah won its first NCAA skiing title since 1997 and its tenth overall. The Utes won four of the eight individual events and piled up an amazing 682 points to put themselves way out of reach of runner-up Vermont (551 points) and third-place Colorado (546½). New Mexico followed in fourth while three-time defending champion Denver fell to fifth. The Utes went into the final day 100 points ahead of the rest of the pack, based on a first-place finish by Ben Thornkill in the men's giant slalom and a double win by two-time Olympian Katrin Smigun. Smigun, a native of Estonia, took the women's 5-k freestyle and the 15-k classic to complete a sweep of the women's Nordic events. The Utes extended their lead on the final day thanks to junior Lina Johansson, who won the women's slalom over Colby freshman Jenny Lathrop. (*Hanover, NH; March 5-8, 2003*)
   Multiple winners: Denver (17); Colorado (15); Utah (10); Vermont (5); Dartmouth and Wyoming (2).

Year		Year		Year		Year		Year	
1954	Denver	1965	Denver	1976	Colorado	1986	Utah	1997	Utah
1955	Denver	1966	Denver		& Dartmouth	1987	Utah	1998	Colorado
1956	Denver	1967	Denver	1977	Colorado	1988	Utah	1999	Colorado
1957	Denver	1968	Wyoming	1978	Colorado	1989	Vermont	2000	Denver
1958	Dartmouth	1969	Denver	1979	Colorado	1990	Vermont	2001	Denver
1959	Colorado	1970	Denver	1980	Vermont	1991	Colorado	2002	Denver
1960	Colorado	1971	Denver	1981	Utah	1992	Vermont	2003	Utah
1961	Denver	1972	Colorado	1982	Colorado	1993	Utah		
1962	Denver	1973	Colorado	1983	Utah	1994	Vermont		
1963	Denver	1974	Colorado	1984	Utah	1995	Colorado		
1964	Denver	1975	Colorado	1985	Wyoming	1996	Utah		

SOFTBALL
Women

Keira Goerl picked a perfect time to spin her second no-hitter of the season, leading UCLA to a 1-0, nine-inning win over defending champion California in the 2003 NCAA Div. I softball championship game. The junior whiffed four California batters and traded goose eggs with Bears hurler Kelly Anderson through eight innings. In the top of the ninth, UCLA centerfielder Stephanie Ramos laced a leadoff double off the wall and was moved to third on a bunt by Emily Zaplatosch. Senior designated hitter Toria Auelua singled to left to give the Bruins all the offense they would need as Goerl shut the door on California in the bottom of the ninth. Goerl was named tournament most outstanding player, pitching all 47 innings for UCLA in the tournament. (Oklahoma City, OK; May 22-26, 2003.)

Multiple winners: UCLA (9); Arizona (6); Texas A&M (2).

Year	Year	Year	Year	Year
1982 UCLA	1987 Texas A&M	1992 UCLA	1997 Arizona	2002 California
1983 Texas A&M	1988 UCLA	1993 Arizona	1998 Fresno St.	2003 UCLA
1984 UCLA	1989 UCLA	1994 Arizona	1999 UCLA	
1985 UCLA	1990 UCLA	1995 UCLA*	2000 Oklahoma	
1986 CS-Fullerton	1991 Arizona	1996 Arizona	2001 Arizona	

*Title was later vacated due to action by the NCAA Committee on Infractions.

SWIMMING & DIVING
Men

Auburn became just the second team in Division I championships history to crack the 600-point barrier in winning its third NCAA men's swimming and diving title. Balance was the key for the Tigers who amassed 609½ points despite winning just three of the 21 individual events. Every one of Auburn's 19 team members contributed to the score. Three-time defending champ and meet host Texas finished runner-up with 413 points while Stanford placed third with 374.

Fred Bousquet and George Bovell were individual winners for the Tigers, claiming titles in the 50-yard freestyle and 200-yard individual medley, respectively. Additionally, Caesar Garcia tied for first with Michigan's Jason Coben in the platform dive. Texas' Brendan Hansen set meet records in the 100- and 200-yard breaststrokes, winning each of those events for the third consecutive year. His Longhorn teammate Ian Crocker successfully defended his title in the 100-yard butterfly, but it was Texas freshman Aaron Piersol who was named NCAA Swimmer of the Year, setting an American record in the 200-yard backstroke, just one of three American records he broke during the meet. (Austin, TX; Mar. 27-29, 2003.)

Multiple winners: Michigan and Ohio St. (11); Texas and USC (9); Stanford (8); Indiana (6); Yale (4); Auburn (3); California and Florida (2).

Year	Year	Year	Year	Year
1937 Michigan	1951 Yale	1965 USC	1979 California	1993 Stanford
1938 Michigan	1952 Ohio St.	1966 USC	1980 California	1994 Stanford
1939 Michigan	1953 Yale	1967 Stanford	1981 Texas	1995 Michigan
1940 Michigan	1954 Ohio St.	1968 Indiana	1982 UCLA	1996 Texas
1941 Michigan	1955 Ohio St.	1969 Indiana	1983 Florida	1997 Auburn
1942 Yale	1956 Ohio St.	1970 Indiana	1984 Florida	1998 Stanford
1943 Ohio St.	1957 Michigan	1971 Indiana	1985 Stanford	1999 Auburn
1944 Yale	1958 Michigan	1972 Indiana	1986 Stanford	2000 Texas
1945 Ohio St.	1959 Michigan	1973 Indiana	1987 Stanford	2001 Texas
1946 Ohio St.	1960 USC	1974 USC	1988 Texas	2002 Texas
1947 Ohio St.	1961 Michigan	1975 USC	1989 Texas	2003 Auburn
1948 Michigan	1962 Ohio St.	1976 USC	1990 Texas	
1949 Ohio St.	1963 USC	1977 USC	1991 Texas	
1950 Ohio St.	1964 USC	1978 Tennessee	1992 Stanford	

Women

If there was a theme for the 2003 Division I women's swimming and diving championships, it had to be "repeat champion." Winners from the 2002 championships repeated their title in 13 of the 21 individual events, and perhaps most importantly, Auburn successfully defended its team title in its home pool, collecting 536 points to finish well ahead of runner-up Georgia (373) and third-place USC (284).

Senior Maggie Bowen was the catalyst for the Tigers, once again winning the 200- and 400-yard individual medleys and leading Auburn to wins in four of the meet's five relay races. For the third straight year, Swimmer of the Year Natalie Coughlin of California won the 100-yard butterfly and the 100- and 200-yard backstrokes. Other double winners were Georgia's Maritza Correia (50- and 100-yard freestyle), SMU's Flavia Rigamonti (500- and 1650-yard freestyles), Stanford's Tara Kirk (100- and 200-yard breaststrokes) and Houston's Yulia Pakhalina (1-meter and 3-meter dive). (Auburn, AL; Mar. 20-22, 2003.)

Multiple winners: Stanford (8); Texas (7); Georgia (3); Auburn (2).

Year	Year	Year	Year	Year
1982 Florida	1987 Texas	1992 Stanford	1997 USC	2002 Auburn
1983 Stanford	1988 Texas	1993 Stanford	1998 Stanford	2003 Auburn
1984 Texas	1989 Stanford	1994 Stanford	1999 Georgia	
1985 Texas	1990 Texas	1995 Stanford	2000 Georgia	
1986 Texas	1991 Texas	1996 Stanford	2001 Georgia	

Annual NCAA Division I Team Champions (Cont.)

INDOOR TRACK
Men

After a two-year hiatus, Arkansas returned to the top of the indoor track and field world with its 17th Division I men's indoor championship. After a slow start, the Razorbacks took control thanks to Chris Mulvaney's win in the mile and a double win by Alistair Cragg. The South African set a meet record of 13:28.93 in the 5000-meters to win for the second consecutive year and also added a win in the 3000-meters to his resume. Arkansas amassed 52 points for the title, Auburn finished in second with 28 and Nebraska placed third with 26. Husker Carl Myerscough successfully defended his title in the shot put, setting a meet record of 70-6¼; missing the collegiate record by just a quarter-inch. *(Fayetteville, AR; Mar. 14-15, 2003.)*

Multiple winners: Arkansas (17); UTEP (7); Kansas and Villanova (3); USC (2).

Year	Year	Year	Year	Year
1965 Missouri	1973 Manhattan	1981 UTEP	1989 Arkansas	1997 Arkansas
1966 Kansas	1974 UTEP	1982 UTEP	1990 Arkansas	1998 Arkansas
1967 USC	1975 UTEP	1983 SMU	1991 Arkansas	1999 Arkansas
1968 Villanova	1976 UTEP	1984 Arkansas	1992 Arkansas	2000 Arkansas
1969 Kansas	1977 Washington St.	1985 Arkansas	1993 Arkansas	2001 LSU
1970 Kansas	1978 UTEP	1986 Arkansas	1994 Arkansas	2002 Tennessee
1971 Villanova	1979 Villanova	1987 Arkansas	1995 Arkansas	2003 Arkansas
1972 USC	1980 UTEP	1988 Arkansas	1996 George Mason	

Women

Sprinter Muna Lee's double win led LSU to its second consecutive title at the Division I women's indoor track and field championships and its tenth overall. The Lady Tigers recorded 62 points while Florida and South Carolina tied for second with 44. Lee successfully defended her title in the 200-meters, then had to come from behind to nip Auburn's Elva Goulbourne in the 60-meter race. She won the 200 with a time of 22.61 seconds, but it was her 22.49 in the prelims that broke the collegiate record that had stood for 21 years. In addition to her second-place finish in the 60, Goulbourne won both the long jump and the triple jump, setting a meet record in the long jump with a leap of 22-4¼. Texas' 4x400-meter relay team set a new collegiate record with a scorching time of 3:27.66. *(Fayetteville, AR; Mar. 14-15, 2003.)*

Multiple winners: LSU (10); Texas (5); Nebraska and UCLA (2).

Year	Year	Year	Year	Year
1983 Nebraska	1988 Texas	1993 LSU	1998 Texas	2003 LSU
1984 Nebraska	1989 LSU	1994 LSU	1999 Texas	
1985 Florida St.	1990 Texas	1995 LSU	2000 UCLA	
1986 Texas	1991 LSU	1996 LSU	2001 UCLA	
1987 LSU	1992 Florida	1997 LSU	2002 LSU	

OUTDOOR TRACK
Men

The distance combo of Dan Lincoln and Alistair Cragg racked up 38 points between them to carry Arkansas to its tenth Division I outdoor track and field title and first since its string of eight consecutive from 1992-99. The Razorbacks registered 59 points overall to beat runner-up Auburn (50) and third-place USC (41½). Lincoln captured his second straight steeplechase title and also won the 10,000-meters in 28:20.20. Cragg finished just behind Lincoln in the 10-k, and clinched the title for the Razorbacks with his win in the 5-k. Chris Mulvaney gave Arkansas much-needed points, finishing runner-up to Stanford's Grant Robison in the 1,500. Auburn's Dean Griffiths took the 400-m hurdles title and teammate Leevan Sands was victorious in the long jump to keep the Tigers close. *(Sacramento, CA; June 11-14, 2003.)*

Multiple winners: USC (26); Arkansas (10); UCLA (8); UTEP (6); Illinois and Oregon (5); LSU and Stanford (4); Kansas and Tennessee (3); SMU (2).

Year	Year	Year	Year	Year
1921 Illinois	1938 USC	1955 USC	1971 UCLA	1988 UCLA
1922 California	1939 USC	1956 UCLA	1972 UCLA	1989 LSU
1923 Michigan	1940 USC	1957 Villanova	1973 UCLA	1990 LSU
1924 Not held	1941 USC	1958 USC	1974 Tennessee	1991 Tennessee
1925 Stanford*	1942 USC	1959 Kansas	1975 UTEP	1992 Arkansas
1926 USC*	1943 USC	1960 Kansas	1976 USC	1993 Arkansas
1927 Illinois*	1944 Illinois	1961 USC	1977 Arizona St.	1994 Arkansas
1928 Stanford	1945 Navy	1962 Oregon	1978 UCLA & UTEP	1995 Arkansas
1929 Ohio St.	1946 Illinois	1963 USC	1979 UTEP	1996 Arkansas
1930 USC	1947 Illinois	1964 Oregon	1980 UTEP	1997 Arkansas
1931 USC	1948 Minnesota	1965 Oregon & USC	1981 UTEP	1998 Arkansas
1932 Indiana	1949 USC	1966 UCLA	1982 UTEP	1999 Arkansas
1933 LSU	1950 USC	1967 USC	1983 SMU	
1934 Stanford	1951 USC	1968 USC	1984 Oregon	2000 Stanford
1935 USC	1952 USC	1969 San Jose St.	1985 Arkansas	2001 Tennessee
1936 USC	1953 USC	1970 BYU, Kansas	1986 SMU	2002 LSU
1937 USC	1954 USC	& Oregon	1987 UCLA	2003 Arkansas

(*) indicates unofficial championship.

*Division II **Lewis, IL** stunned two-time champion Brigham Young in five games to win the national collegiate men's volleyball title on May 3.*

Women

Aleen Bailey of South Carolina defeated LSU's Muna Lee in both the 100- and 200-meter sprints, but LSU just had too much firepower, cruising to its 13th Division I women's outdoor title. LSU finished with 64 points (43 on the final day of competition), followed by runner-up Texas with 50, and South Carolina with 47. In each sprint event, Bailey chased down a shocked Lee in the final meters for her double win, but Lee's two second-place finishes and the Lady Tigers' win in the 4x100-m relay carried LSU to the title.

Stanford junior Lauren Fleshman won her third consecutive 5000-meters with a meet record 15:24.06. North Carolina's Alice Schmidt (800-m), Illinois' Perdita Felicien (100-m hurdles) and Auburn's Elva Goulbourne (long jump) also repeated as individual champions. (*Sacramento, CA; June 11-14, 2003.*)

Multiple winners: LSU (13); Texas (3); UCLA (2).

Year	Year	Year	Year	Year
1982 UCLA	1987 LSU	1992 LSU	1997 LSU	2002 South Carolina
1983 UCLA	1988 LSU	1993 LSU	1998 Texas	2003 LSU
1984 Florida St.	1989 LSU	1994 LSU	1999 Texas	
1985 Oregon	1990 LSU	1995 LSU	2000 LSU	
1986 Texas	1991 LSU	1996 LSU	2001 USC	

VOLLEYBALL

Men

Division II Lewis, IL made history, becoming the first non-Division I school to win the national collegiate men's volleyball title, upsetting top seed Brigham Young in five sets. Lewis, seeded third, used a 7-1 run in the final game to defeat Brigham Young, 42-44, 30-27, 30-21, 23-30, 15-12. Tournament most outstanding player Gustavo Meyer blasted 21 kills and blocked four shots for the Flyers and teammate Jose Martins recorded 55 assists. Rafael Paal led BYU with 20 kills and ten digs. Lewis (29-5) defeated Pepperdine to reach the finals while BYU (23-7) took down Penn State. (*Long Beach, CA; May 3, 2003.*)

Multiple winners: UCLA (18); Pepperdine and USC (4); Brigham Young (2).

Year	Year	Year	Year	Year
1970 UCLA	1978 Pepperdine	1986 Pepperdine	1994 Penn St.	2002 Hawaii†
1971 UCLA	1979 UCLA	1987 UCLA	1995 UCLA	2003 Lewis, IL*
1972 UCLA	1980 USC	1988 USC	1996 UCLA	
1973 San Diego St.	1981 UCLA	1989 UCLA	1997 Stanford	*Division II
1974 UCLA	1982 UCLA	1990 USC	1998 UCLA	†Title was later vacat-
1975 UCLA	1983 UCLA	1991 Long Beach St.	1999 Brigham Young	ed due to action by
1976 UCLA	1984 UCLA	1992 Pepperdine	2000 UCLA	the NCAA Committee
1977 USC	1985 Pepperdine	1993 UCLA	2001 Brigham Young	on Infractions.

Annual NCAA Division I Team Champions (Cont.)
Women

Top-seeded USC won its first Division I women's volleyball title since 1981, taking down defending champ Stanford, 30-27, 23-30, 30-24, 30-26. The four-game victory avenged USC's loss to Stanford earlier in the season, its only blemish in an otherwise perfect season. Keao Burdine was selected Most Outstanding Player of the tournament, registering 15 digs against the Cardinal, while teammate Katie Olsovsky slammed 16 kills. Ogonna Nnamani led Stanford with 19 kills and Logan Tom tallied 16 kills and 13 digs in her final collegiate performance. (*New Orleans, LA; Dec. 21, 2002.*)

Multiple winners: Stanford (5); Hawaii, Long Beach St. and UCLA (3); Nebraska, Pacific and USC (2).

Year	Year	Year	Year	Year
1981 USC	1986 Pacific	1991 UCLA	1996 Stanford	2001 Stanford
1982 Hawaii	1987 Hawaii	1992 Stanford	1997 Stanford	2002 USC
1983 Hawaii	1988 Texas	1993 Long Beach St.	1998 Long Beach St.	
1984 UCLA	1989 Long Beach St.	1994 Stanford	1999 Penn St.	
1985 Pacific	1990 UCLA	1995 Nebraska	2000 Nebraska	

WATER POLO
Men

Stanford defeated California, 7-6, to win its second consecutive national water polo championship and tenth overall. Sophomore phenom Tony Azevedo scored four goals for the Cardinal en route to his second straight tournament MVP award. Down 7-4, California staged a ferocious fourth quarter rally, cutting the lead to 7-6 with just over a minute left on Will Quist's third goal of the game, but an Azevedo steal on Cal's final attempt solidified the win for Stanford. (*Los Angeles, CA; Dec. 8, 2002.*)

Multiple winners: California (11); Stanford (10); UCLA (7); UC-Irvine (3).

Year	Year	Year	Year	Year
1969 UCLA	1976 Stanford	1983 California	1990 California	1997 Pepperdine
1970 UC-Irvine	1977 California	1984 California	1991 California	1998 USC
1971 UCLA	1978 Stanford	1985 Stanford	1992 California	1999 UCLA
1972 UCLA	1979 UC-S. Barbara	1986 Stanford	1993 Stanford	2000 UCLA
1973 California	1980 Stanford	1987 California	1994 Stanford	2001 Stanford
1974 California	1981 Stanford	1988 California	1995 UCLA	2002 Stanford
1975 California	1982 UC-Irvine	1989 UC-Irvine	1996 UCLA	

Women

In a thrilling title game, UCLA edged Stanford, 4-3, to become the first two-time NCAA women's water polo champion. The Bruins found themselves down 2-0 at halftime, stymied by the Cardinal defense and goaltender Jackie Frank. But third-period goals by Kelly Rulon and Jessica Lopez knotted the score heading into the fourth. Lauren Heineck gave the Bruins a 3-2 lead, and tournament MVP Robin Beauregard scored to give UCLA some much-needed breathing room. (*La Jolla, CA; May 11, 2003.*)

Multiple winner: UCLA (2).

Year	Year	Year
2001 UCLA	2002 Stanford	2003 UCLA

WRESTLING
Men

Individual titles by Johnny Thompson and Jake Rosholt vaulted Oklahoma State back to its familiar spot as champion of the Division I wrestling world. The Cowboys collected 143 points for its first title since 1994 and 31st overall. Two-time defending champ Minnesota finished in second place with 104½ points and Oklahoma placed third with 78. Thompson faced Minnesota's Ryan Lewis in the title match at 133 pounds in a rematch of the 2002 final match and once again it was Thompson who came out on top. Arizona State's 149 pound champ Eric Larkin was named Outstanding Wrestler of the tournament (*Kansas City, MO; Mar. 20-22, 2003.*)

Multiple winners: Oklahoma St. (31); Iowa (20); Iowa St. (8); Oklahoma (7); Minnesota (2).

Year	Year	Year	Year	Year
1928 Okla. A&M*	1942 Okla. A&M	1959 Okla. St.	1974 Oklahoma	1989 Okla. St.
1929 Okla. A&M	1943-45 Not held	1960 Oklahoma	1975 Iowa	1990 Okla. St.
1930 Okla. A&M	1946 Okla. A&M	1961 Okla. St.	1976 Iowa	1991 Iowa
1931 Okla. A&M*	1947 Cornell Col.	1962 Okla. St.	1977 Iowa St.	1992 Iowa
1932 Indiana*	1948 Okla. A&M	1963 Oklahoma	1978 Iowa	1993 Iowa
1933 Okla. A&M*	1949 Okla. A&M	1964 Okla. St.	1979 Iowa	1994 Okla. St.
& Iowa St.*	1950 Northern Iowa	1965 Iowa St.	1980 Iowa	1995 Iowa
1934 Okla. A&M	1951 Oklahoma	1966 Okla. St.	1981 Iowa	1996 Iowa
1935 Okla. A&M	1952 Oklahoma	1967 Michigan St.	1982 Iowa	1997 Iowa
1936 Oklahoma	1953 Penn St.	1968 Okla. St.	1983 Iowa	1998 Iowa
1937 Okla. A&M	1954 Okla. A&M	1969 Iowa St.	1984 Iowa	1999 Iowa
1938 Okla. A&M	1955 Okla. A&M	1970 Iowa St.	1985 Iowa	2000 Iowa
1939 Okla. A&M	1956 Okla. A&M	1971 Okla. St.	1986 Iowa	2001 Minnesota
1940 Okla. A&M	1957 Oklahoma	1972 Iowa St.	1987 Iowa St.	2002 Minnesota
1941 Okla. A&M	1958 Okla. St.	1973 Iowa St.	1988 Arizona St.	2003 Okla. St.

(*) indicates unofficial champions. **Note:** Oklahoma A&M became Oklahoma St. in 1958.

Halls of Fame & Awards

NFL great **Elvin Bethea** hugs his son at his induction at the Pro Football Hall of Fame in 2003.

AP/Wide World Photos

BASEBALL

National Baseball Hall of Fame & Museum

Established in 1935 by Major League Baseball to celebrate the game's 100th anniversary. **Address:** P.O. Box 590, Cooperstown, NY 13326. **Telephone:** (607) 547-7200.

Eligibility: In August 2001, the Hall of Fame announced changes in the way players are elected via the Veterans Committee. The voting done by Baseball Writers' Association of America remains unchanged. Nominated players must have played at least parts of 10 seasons in the major leagues and be retired for at least five. Certain nominated players not elected by the writers can become eligible via the Veterans Committee. The new Veterans Committee will be comprised of all living Hall of Famers (currently 58 people) as well as all living winners of the Ford Frick (13) and J.G. Taylor Spink (12) Awards and three members of the old 15-member Veterans Committee with unexpired terms. There was no Veterans Committee vote in 2002. Beginning in 2003 the new Veterans Committee votes every two years on former players and every four years on managers, umpires and executives. Previously, the committee voted annually.

Also, the eligibility of all players that had been dropped from the ballots for not receiving five percent of the vote was restored and those players can now be immediately considered by the new Veterans Committee. The players on baseball's ineligible list are still excluded from consideration. Pete Rose is the only living ex-player on that list.

Class of 2003 (2): BBWAA vote—catcher **Gary Carter**, Montreal (1974-84, 92), New York Mets (1985-89), San Francisco (1990) and Los Angeles (1991); **Eddie Murray**, Baltimore (1977-88, 96), Los Angeles (1989-1991, 97), New York Mets (1992-1993), Cleveland (1994-96), Anaheim (1997).

2003 Top 10 vote-getters (496 BBWAA ballots cast, 372 needed to elect): 1. **Eddie Murray** (423), 2. **Gary Carter** (387), 3. **Bruce Sutter** (266), 4. **Jim Rice** (259), 5. **Andre Dawson** (248), 6. **Ryne Sandberg** (244), 7. **Lee Smith** (210), 8. **Rich Gossage** (209), 9. **Bert Blyleven** (145), 10. **Steve Garvey** (138).

Elected first year on ballot (38): Hank Aaron, Ernie Banks, Johnny Bench, George Brett, Lou Brock, Rod Carew, Steve Carlton, Ty Cobb, Bob Feller, Bob Gibson, Reggie Jackson, Al Kaline, Sandy Koufax, Mickey Mantle, Christy Mathewson, Willie Mays, Willie McCovey, Joe Morgan, Eddie Murray, Stan Musial, Jim Palmer, Kirby Puckett, Brooks Robinson, Frank Robinson, Jackie Robinson, Babe Ruth, Nolan Ryan, Mike Schmidt, Tom Seaver, Ozzie Smith, Warren Spahn, Willie Stargell, Honus Wagner, Ted Williams, Dave Winfield, Carl Yastrzemski and Robin Yount.

Members are listed with years of induction; (+) indicates deceased members.

Catchers

Bench, Johnny	1989	+ Cochrane, Mickey	1947	+ Hartnett, Gabby	1955
Berra, Yogi	1972	+ Dickey, Bill	1954	+ Lombardi, Ernie	1986
+ Bresnahan, Roger	1945	+ Ewing, Buck	1939	+ Schalk, Ray	1955
+ Campanella, Roy	1969	+ Ferrell, Rick	1984		
Carter, Gary	2003	Fisk, Carlton	2000		

1st Basemen

+ Anson, Cap	1939	+ Connor, Roger	1976	McCovey, Willie	1986
+ Beckley, Jake	1971	+ Foxx, Jimmie	1951	+ Mize, Johnny	1981
+ Bottomley, Jim	1974	+ Gehrig, Lou	1939	Murray, Eddie	2003
+ Brouthers, Dan	1945	+ Greenberg, Hank	1956	Perez, Tony	2000
Cepeda, Orlando	1999	+ Kelly, George	1973	+ Sisler, George	1939
+ Chance, Frank	1946	Killebrew, Harmon	1984	+ Terry, Bill	1954

2nd Basemen

Carew, Rod	1991	+ Gehringer, Charlie	1949	+ McPhee, Bid	2000
+ Collins, Eddie	1939	+ Herman, Billy	1975	Morgan, Joe	1990
Doerr, Bobby	1986	+ Hornsby, Rogers	1942	+ Robinson, Jackie	1962
+ Evers, Johnny	1946	+ Lajoie, Nap	1937	Schoendienst, Red	1989
+ Fox, Nellie	1997	+ Lazzeri, Tony	1991		
+ Frisch, Frankie	1947	Mazeroski, Bill	2001		

Shortstops

Aparicio, Luis	1984	+ Jackson, Travis	1982	+ Tinker, Joe	1946
+ Appling, Luke	1964	+ Jennings, Hugh	1945	+ Vaughan, Arky	1985
+ Bancroft, Dave	1971	+ Maranville, Rabbit	1954	+ Wagner, Honus	1936
Banks, Ernie	1977	+ Reese, Pee Wee	1984	+ Wallace, Bobby	1953
+ Boudreau, Lou	1970	Rizzuto, Phil	1994	+ Ward, Monte	1964
+ Cronin, Joe	1956	+ Sewell, Joe	1977	Yount, Robin	1999
+ Davis, George	1998	Smith, Ozzie	2002		

3rd Basemen

+ Baker, Frank	1955	Kell, George	1983	Robinson, Brooks	1983
Brett, George	1999	+ Lindstrom, Fred	1976	Schmidt, Mike	1995
+ Collins, Jimmy	1945	+ Mathews, Eddie	1978	+ Traynor, Pie	1948

Center Fielders

+ Ashburn, Richie	1995	+ Doby, Larry	1998	+ Roush, Edd	1962
+ Averill, Earl	1975	+ Duffy, Hugh	1945	Snider, Duke	1980
+ Carey, Max	1961	+ Hamilton, Billy	1961	+ Speaker, Tris	1937
+ Cobb, Ty	1936	+ Mantle, Mickey	1974	+ Waner, Lloyd	1967
+ Combs, Earle	1970	Mays, Willie	1979	+ Wilson, Hack	1979
+ DiMaggio, Joe	1955	Puckett, Kirby	2001		

Left Fielders

Brock, Lou 1985	+ Kelley, Joe 1971	+ Simmons, Al 1953
+ Burkett, Jesse 1946	Kiner, Ralph 1975	+ Stargell, Willie 1988
+ Clarke, Fred 1945	+ Manush, Heinie 1964	+ Wheat, Zack 1959
+ Delahanty, Ed 1945	+ Medwick, Joe 1968	Williams, Billy 1987
+ Goslin, Goose 1968	Musial, Stan 1969	+ Williams, Ted 1966
+ Hafey, Chick 1971	+ O'Rourke, Jim 1945	Yastrzemski, Carl 1989

Right Fielders

Aaron, Hank 1982	Kaline, Al 1980	+ Ruth, Babe 1936
+ Clemente, Roberto 1973	+ Keeler, Willie 1939	+ Slaughter, Enos 1985
+ Crawford, Sam 1957	+ Kelly, King 1945	+ Thompson, Sam 1974
+ Cuyler, Kiki 1968	+ Klein, Chuck 1980	+ Waner, Paul 1952
+ Flick, Elmer 1963	+ McCarthy, Tommy 1946	Winfield, Dave 2001
+ Heilmann, Harry 1952	+ Ott, Mel 1951	+ Youngs, Ross 1972
+ Hooper, Harry 1971	+ Rice, Sam 1963	
Jackson, Reggie 1993	Robinson, Frank 1982	

Pitchers

+ Alexander, Grover 1938	+ Coveleski, Stan 1969	+ Galvin, Pud 1965
+ Bender, Chief 1953	+ Dean, Dizzy 1953	Gibson, Bob 1981
+ Brown, Mordecai 1949	+ Drysdale, Don 1984	+ Gomez, Lefty 1972
Bunning, Jim 1996	+ Faber, Red 1964	+ Grimes, Burleigh 1964
Carlton, Steve 1994	Feller, Bob 1962	+ Grove, Lefty 1947
+ Chesbro, Jack 1946	Fingers, Rollie 1992	+ Haines, Jess 1970
+ Clarkson, John 1963	Ford, Whitey 1974	+ Hoyt, Waite 1969

Major League Baseball's All-Time Team—Then and Now

The Baseball Writers' Association of America originally selected an all-time team as part of major league baseball's 100th anniversary, announcing the outcome of its vote on July 21, 1969. Vote totals were not released. Recently, another vote was released when a panel of 36 BWAA members picked an all-time team for the Classic Sports Network just before the 1997 All-Star Game. This time vote totals were given, the single outfield category was divided into three (left, center and right) and two recently popularized positions—the designated hitter and relief pitcher—were added. In the most recent vote two points were awarded for first-place votes and one point for second place. Point totals follow the names with the number of first-place votes in parentheses. All-time team members are listed in **bold** type

1969 Vote

C   **Mickey Cochrane**, Bill Dickey, Roy Campanella
1B   **Lou Gehrig**, George Sisler, Stan Musial
2B   **Rogers Hornsby**, Charlie Gehringer, Eddie Collins
SS   **Honus Wagner**, Joe Cronin, Ernie Banks
3B   **Pie Traynor**, Brooks Robinson, Jackie Robinson
OF   **Babe Ruth, Ty Cobb, Joe DiMaggio**, Ted Williams, Tris Speaker, Willie Mays

RHP **Walter Johnson**, Christy Mathewson, Cy Young
LHP **Lefty Grove**, Sandy Koufax, Carl Hubbell
Mgr. **John McGraw**, Casey Stengel, Joe McCarthy

1969 Vote All-Time Outstanding Player: **Ruth**, Cobb, Wagner, DiMaggio

1997 Vote

C   **Johnny Bench** (24) 52; Yogi Berra (4) 22; Roy Campanella (4) 17; Mickey Cochrane (1) 5; Bill Dickey (1) 4; Gabby Hartnett (1) 3; Carlton Fisk 2.
1B   **Lou Gehrig** (31) 661/2; Jimmie Foxx (3) 19; George Sisler (4) 8; Willie McCovey 6; Hank Greenberg 21/2; Stan Musial, Eddie Murray, Mark McGwire and Frank Thomas 1.
2B   **Rogers Hornsby** (17) 44; Joe Morgan (6) 23; Jackie Robinson (6) 15; Charley Gehringer (4) and Napolean Lajoie (3) 11; Eddie Collins (1) 3; Rod Carew 2; Ryne Sandberg 1.
SS   **Honus Wagner** (23) 55; Cal Ripken Jr. (6) 24; Ozzie Smith (5) 16; Ernie Banks (1) 8; Lou Boudreau and Luke Appling 1.
3B   **Mike Schmidt** (21) 50; Brooks Robinson (13) 37; Eddie Mathews 5; George Brett (1) 8; Pie Traynor 3; Pete Rose (1) 2; Frank Baker, Al Rosen and Wade Boggs 1.
LF   **Ted Williams** (32) 68; Stan Musial (4) 36; Pete Rose, Ralph Kiner, Rickey Henderson and Barry Bonds 1.
CF   **Willie Mays** (25) 57; Ty Cobb (7) 22; Joe DiMaggio (3) 17; Mickey Mantle (1) 10; Tris Speaker 2.
RF   **Babe Ruth** (31) 67; Hank Aaron (5) 36; Frank Robinson 2; Al Kaline, Roberto Clemente and Tony Gwynn 1.

DH   **Paul Molitor** (22) 48; Harold Baines (3) 12; Don Baylor (1) 10; Edgar Martinez (2) 9; Ty Cobb (2) 6; Hal McRae (1) 5; Mickey Mantle (1) and Dave Parker (1) 3; Joe DiMaggio (1) 2; Lee May, Frank Robinson and Tony Oliva 1.
RHP **Walter Johnson** (9) 30; Cy Young (12) 25; Christy Mathewson (5) 18; Bob Feller (4) 10; Bob Gibson (2) 9; Nolan Ryan (2) 7; Tom Seaver (1) 3; Greg Maddux (1), Grover Cleveland Alexander and Juan Marichal 2.
LHP **Sandy Koufax** (11) 32; Warren Spahn (11) 28; Lefty Grove (8) 25; Steve Carlton (4) 12; Carl Hubbell 6; Whitey Ford (1) 3; Eddie Plank (1) 2.
RP   **Dennis Eckersley** (16) 40; Rollie Fingers (9) 29; Lee Smith (4) 13; Hoyt Wilhelm (3) 10; Rich Gossage (3) 9; Bruce Sutter (1) 6, Dan Quisenberry 1.
Mgr. **Casey Stengel** (6) 22; Joe McCarthy (6) 18; Connie Mack (7) 17; John McGraw (6) 14; Sparky Anderson (3) 11; Leo Durocher (2) 6; Dick Williams (1) 4; Billy Martin (1) 3; Al Lopez (1), Ned Hanlon (1), Whitey Herzog (1), Earl Weaver and Bobby Cox 2; Tony La Russa 1.

Baseball (Cont.)

+ Hubbell, Carl 1947	Niekro, Phil 1997	Seaver, Tom 1992
+ Hunter, Catfish 1987	+ Newhouser, Hal 1992	Spahn, Warren 1973
Jenkins, Ferguson 1991	+ Nichols, Kid 1949	Sutton, Don 1998
+ Johnson, Walter 1936	Palmer, Jim 1990	+ Vance, Dazzy 1955
+ Joss, Addie 1978	+ Pennock, Herb 1948	+ Waddell, Rube 1946
+ Keefe, Tim 1964	Perry, Gaylord 1991	+ Walsh, Ed 1946
Koufax, Sandy 1972	+ Plank, Eddie 1946	+ Welch, Mickey 1973
+ Lemon, Bob 1976	+ Radbourne, Old Hoss 1939	+ Wilhelm, Hoyt 1985
+ Lyons, Ted 1955	+ Rixey, Eppa 1963	+ Willis, Vic 1995
Marichal, Juan 1983	Roberts, Robin 1976	+ Wynn, Early 1972
+ Marquard, Rube 1971	+ Ruffing, Red 1967	+ Young, Cy 1937
+ Mathewson, Christy 1936	+ Rusie, Amos 1977	
+ McGinnity, Joe 1946	Ryan, Nolan 1999	

Managers

+ Alston, Walter 1983	Lasorda, Tommy 1997	+ Robinson, Wilbert 1945
Anderson, Sparky 2000	Lopez, Al 1977	+ Selee, Frank 1999
+ Durocher, Leo 1994	+ Mack, Connie 1937	+ Stengel, Casey 1966
+ Hanlon, Ned 1996	+ McCarthy, Joe 1957	Weaver, Earl 1996
+ Harris, Bucky 1975	+ McGraw, John 1937	
+ Huggins, Miller 1964	+ McKechnie, Bill 1962	

Umpires

+ Barlick, Al 1989	+ Connolly, Tom 1953	+ Klem, Bill 1953
+ Chylak, Nestor 1999	+ Evans, Billy 1973	+ McGowan, Bill 1992
+ Conlan, Jocko 1974	+ Hubbard, Cal 1976	

From Negro Leagues

+ Bell, Cool Papa (OF) 1974	+ Foster, Willie (P) 1996	+ Paige, Satchel (P) 1971
+ Charleston, Oscar (1B-OF) .1976	+ Gibson, Josh (C) 1972	+ Rogan, Wilber (P) 1998
+ Dandridge, Ray (3B) 1987	Irvin, Monte (OF) 1973	+ Smith, Hilton 2001
+ Day, Leon (P-OF-2B) 1995	+ Johnson, Judy (3B) 1975	+ Stearns, Turkey (OF) 2000
+ Dihigo, Martin (P-OF) 1977	+ Leonard, Buck (1B) 1972	+ Wells, Willie (SS) 1997
+ Foster, Rube (P-Mgr) 1981	+ Lloyd, Pop (SS) 1977	+ Williams, Joe (P) 1999

Pioneers and Executives

+ Barrow, Ed 1953	+ Giles, Warren 1979	+ Rickey, Branch 1967
+ Bulkeley, Morgan 1937	+ Griffith, Clark 1946	+ Spalding, Al 1939
+ Cartwright, Alexander 1938	+ Harridge, Will 1972	+ Veeck, Bill 1991
+ Chadwick, Henry 1938	+ Hulbert, William 1995	+ Weiss, George 1971
+ Chandler, Happy 1982	+ Johnson, Ban 1937	+ Wright, George 1937
+ Comiskey, Charles 1939	+ Landis, Kenesaw 1944	+ Wright, Harry 1953
+ Cummings, Candy 1939	+ MacPhail, Larry 1978	+ Yawkey, Tom 1980
+ Frick, Ford 1970	MacPhail, Lee 1998	

Ford Frick Award

First presented in 1978 by the Hall of Fame for meritorious contributions by baseball broadcasters. Named in honor of the late newspaper reporter, broadcaster, National League president and commissioner, the Frick Award does not constitute induction into the Hall of Fame.

Year		Year		Year	
1978	Mel Allen & Red Barber	1987	Jack Buck	1996	Herb Carneal
1979	Bob Elson	1988	Lindsey Nelson	1997	Jimmy Dudley
1980	Russ Hodges	1989	Harry Caray	1998	Jaime Jarrin
1981	Ernie Harwell	1990	Byrum Saam	1999	Arch McDonald
1982	Vin Scully	1991	Joe Garagiola	2000	Marty Brennaman
1983	Jack Brickhouse	1992	Milo Hamilton	2001	Felo Ramirez
1984	Curt Gowdy	1993	Chuck Thompson	2002	Harry Kalas
1985	Buck Canel	1994	Bob Murphy	2003	Bob Uecker
1986	Bob Prince	1995	Bob Wolff		

J.G. Taylor Spink Award

First presented in 1962 by the Baseball Writers' Association of America for meritorious contributions by members of the BBWAA. Named in honor of the late publisher of *The Sporting News*, the Spink Award does not constitute induction into the Hall of Fame. Winners are honored in the year following their selection.

Year		Year		Year	
1962	J.G. Taylor Spink	1972	Dan Daniel, Fred Lieb	1978	Tim Murnane & Dick Young
1963	Ring Lardner		& J. Roy Stockton	1979	Bob Broeg & Tommy Holmes
1964	Hugh Fullerton	1973	Warren Brown, John	1980	Joe Reichler & Milt Richman
1965	Charley Dryden		Drebinger & John F. Kieran	1981	Bob Addie & Allen Lewis
1966	Grantland Rice	1974	John Carmichael	1982	Si Burick
1967	Damon Runyon		& James Isaminger	1983	Ken Smith
1968	H.G. Salsinger	1975	Tom Meany & Shirley Povich	1984	Joe McGuff
1969	Sid Mercer	1976	Harold Kaese & Red Smith	1985	Earl Lawson
1970	Heywood C. Broun	1977	Gordon Cobbledick	1986	Jack Lang
1971	Frank Graham		& Edgar Munzel	1987	Jim Murray

Year		Year		Year	
1988	Bob Hunter & Ray Kelly	1993	John Wendell Smith	1999	Hal Lebovitz
1989	Jerome Holtzman	1994	No award	2000	Ross Newhan
1990	Phil Collier	1995	Joseph Durso	2001	Joe Falls
1991	Ritter Collett	1996	Charley Feeney	2002	Hal McCoy
1992	Leonard Koppett	1997	Sam Lacy		
	& Buzz Saidt	1998	Bob Stevens		

BASKETBALL

Naismith Memorial Basketball Hall of Fame

Established in 1949 by the National Association of Basketball Coaches in memory of the sport's inventor, Dr. James Naismith. Original Hall opened in 1968 and a renovated version of the Hall opened in 1985. A completely new building opened Sept. 28, 2002. **Address:** 1000 West Columbus Avenue, Springfield, MA 01105. **Telephone:** (413) 781-6500.

Eligibility: Nominated players and referees must be retired for five years, coaches must have coached 25 years or be retired for five, and contributors must have already completed their noteworthy service to the game. Voting done by 24-member honors committee made up of media representatives, Hall of Fame members and trustees. Any nominee not elected after five years becomes eligible for consideration by the Veterans' Committee after a five-year wait.

Class of 2003 (7): PLAYERS—center **Robert Parish**, Golden State (1977-80), Boston (1981-1994), Charlotte (1995-96), Chicago (1997), forward **James Worthy**, Los Angeles Lakers (1983-1994), CONTRIBUTOR—Harlem Globetrotter **Meadowlark Lemon**; COACHES—**Leon Barmore**. INTERNATIONAL—**Dino Meneghin**; VETERANS—**Earl Lloyd**; BROADCASTER— **Francis "Chick" Hearn.**

2003 finalists (nominated but not elected): PLAYERS—Maurice Cheeks, Adrian Dantley, Walter Davis, Dennis Johnson, Gus Johnson, Bobby Jones and Chet Walker. COACHES—Forrest Anderson, Lefty Driesell, Guy Lewis, Harley Redin, Cathy Rush, Bill Sharman, Norm Stewart, and Eddie Sutton. CONTRIBUTORS—Vic Bubas, Jerry Colangelo, Junius Kellogg and Tex Winter. REFEREE—Hank Nichols. VETERAN—Grady Lewis. INTERNATIONAL—Drazen Dalipagic and Pedro Ferrandiz.

Note: John Wooden and **Lenny Wilkens**, who was rehonored by the Hall in 1998, are the only members to be inducted as both a player and a coach.

Members are listed with years of induction; (+) indicates deceased members.

Men

Abdul-Jabbar, Kareem	..1995	Greer, Hal	...1981	Mikkelsen, Vern	...1995
Archibald, Nate	...1991	+ Gruenig, Robert	...1963	Monroe, Earl	...1990
Arizin, Paul	...1977	Hagan, Cliff	...1977	Murphy, Calvin	...1993
+ Barlow, Thomas (Babe)	..1980	+ Hanson, Victor	...1960	+ Murphy, Charles (Stretch)	1960
Barry, Rick	...1987	Havlicek, John	...1983	+ Page, Harlan (Pat)	...1962
Baylor, Elgin	...1976	Hawkins, Connie	...1992	Parish, Robert	...2003
+ Beckman, John	...1972	Hayes, Elvin	...1990	+ Petrovic, Drazen	...2002
Bellamy, Walt	...1993	Haynes, Marques	...1998	Pettit, Bob	...1970
Belov, Sergei	...1992	Heinsohn, Tom	...1986	+ Phillip, Andy	...1961
Bing, Dave	...1990	+ Holman, Nat	...1964	+ Pollard, Jim	...1977
Bird, Larry	...1998	Houbregs, Bob	...1987	Ramsey, Frank	...1981
+ Borgmann, Bennie	...1961	Howell, Bailey	...1997	Reed, Willis	...1981
Bradley, Bill	...1982	Hyatt, Chuck	...1959	Risen, Arnie	...1998
+ Brennan, Joe	...1974	Issel, Dan	...1993	Robertson, Oscar	...1979
Cervi, Al	...1984	+ Jeannette, Buddy	...1994	+ Roosma, John	...1961
+ Chamberlain, Wilt	...1978	+ Johnson, Bill (Skinny)	...1976	Russell, Bill	...1974
+ Cooper, Charles (Tarzan)	1976	Johnson, Earvin (Magic)	.2002	+ Russell, John (Honey)	...1964
+ Cosic, Kresimir	...1996	+ Johnston, Neil	...1990	Schayes, Dolph	...1972
Cousy, Bob	...1970	Jones, K. C	...1989	+ Schmidt, Ernest J	...1973
Cowens, Dave	...1991	Jones, Sam	...1983	+ Schommer, John	...1959
Cunningham, Billy	...1986	+ Krause, Edward (Moose)	..1975	+ Sedran, Barney	...1962
+ Davies, Bob	...1969	Kurland, Bob	...1961	Sharman, Bill	...1975
+ DeBernardi, Forrest	...1961	Lanier, Bob	...1992	+ Steinmetz, Christian	...1961
+ DeBusschere, Dave	...1982	+ Lapchick, Joe	...1966	Thomas, Isiah	...2000
+ Dehnert, Dutch	...1968	Lovellette, Clyde	...1988	Thompson, David	...1996
+ Endacott, Paul	...1971	Lucas, Jerry	...1979	+ Thompson, John (Cat)	...1962
English, Alex	...1997	Luisetti, Hank	...1959	Thurmond, Nate	...1984
Erving, Julius (Dr. J)	...1993	Macauley, Ed	...1960	Twyman, Jack	...1982
+ Foster, Bud	...1964	Malone, Moses	...2001	Unseld, Wes	...1988
Frazier, Walt	...1987	+ Maravich, Pete	...1987	+ Vandivier, Robert (Fuzzy)	1974
+ Friedman, Marty	...1971	Martin, Slater	...1981	+ Wachter, Ed	...1961
+ Fulks, Joe	...1977	McAdoo, Bob	...2000	Walton, Bill	...1993
+ Gale, Laddie	...1976	+ McCracken, Branch	...1960	Wanzer, Bobby	...1987
Gallatin, Harry	...1991	+ McCracken, Jack	...1962	West, Jerry	...1979
+ Gates, William (Pop)	...1989	+ McDermott, Bobby	...1988	Wilkens, Lenny	...1989
Gervin, George	...1996	McGuire, Dick	...1993	Wooden, John	...1960
Gola, Tom	...1975	McHale, Kevin	...1999	Worthy, James	...2003
Goodrich, Gail	...1996	Mikan, George	...1959	Yardley, George	...1996

Women

Blazejowski, Carol	...1994	Harris-Stewart, Lucia	...1992	Semenova, Uljana	...1993
Crawford, Joan	...1997	Lieberman, Nancy	...1996	White, Nera	...1992
Curry, Denise	...1997	Meyers, Ann	...1993		
Donovan, Anne	...1995	Miller, Cheryl	...1995		

Basketball (Cont.)

Teams

Buffalo Germans 1961	Harlem Globetrotters 2002	Original Celtics 1959
First Team 1959	New York Renaissance 1963	

Referees

+ Enright, Jim 1978	+ Leith, Lloyd 1982	+ Shirley, J. Dallas 1979
+ Hepbron, George 1960	+ Mihalik, Red 1986	+ Strom, Earl 1995
+ Hoyt, George 1961	+ Nucatola, John 1977	+ Tobey, Dave 1961
+ Kennedy, Pat 1959	+ Quigley, Ernest (Quig) 1961	+ Walsh, David 1961

Coaches

+ Allen, Forrest (Phog) 1959	+ Gill, Amory (Slats) 1967	+ Meanwell, Walter (Doc) 1959
+ Anderson, Harold (Andy) . .1984	Gomelsky, Aleksandr 1995	Meyer, Ray 1978
Auerbach, Red 1968	+ Hannum, Alex 1998	+ Miller, Ralph 1988
Barmore, Leon 2003	Harshman, Marv 1984	Moore, Billie 1999
+ Barry, Sam 1978	Haskins, Don 1997	Newell, Pete 1978
+ Blood, Ernest (Prof) 1960	+ Hickey, Eddie 1978	+ Nikolic, Aleksandar 1998
Brown, Larry 2002	+ Hobson, Howard (Hobby) . . .1965	Olson, Lute 2002
+ Cann, Howard 1967	+ Holzman, Red 1986	Ramsay, Jack 1992
+ Carlson, Henry (Doc) 1959	+ Iba, Hank 1968	Rubini, Cesare 1994
Carnesecca, Lou 1992	+ Julian, Alvin (Doggie) 1967	+ Rupp, Adolph 1968
Carnevale, Ben 1969	+ Keaney, Frank 1960	+ Sachs, Leonard 1961
Carril, Pete 1997	+ Keogan, George 1961	+ Shelton, Everett 1979
+ Case, Everett 1981	Knight, Bob 1991	Smith, Dean 1982
Chaney, John 2001	Krzyzewski, Mike 2001	Summitt, Pat 2000
Conradt, Jody 1998	Kundla, John 1995	+ Taylor, Fred 1986
Crum, Denny 1994	+ Lambert, Ward (Piggy) 1960	Thompson, John 1999
Daly, Chuck 1994	+ Litwack, Harry 1975	+ Wade, Margaret 1984
+ Dean, Everett 1966	+ Loeffler, Ken 1964	Watts, Stan 1985
+ Diaz-Miguel, Antonio 1997	+ Lonborg, Dutch 1972	Wilkens, Lenny 1998
+ Diddle, Ed 1971	+ McCutchan, Arad 1980	Wooden, John 1972
+ Drake, Bruce 1972	+ McGuire, Al 1992	+ Woolpert, Phil 1992
Gaines, Clarence (Bighouse) .1981	+ McGuire, Frank 1976	Wooten, Morgan 2000
+ Gardner, Jack 1983	+ McLendon, John 1978	Yow, Kay 2002

Contributors

+ Abbott, Senda Berenson . . .1984	+ Hickox, Ed 1959	+ Porter, Henry (H.V.) 1960
+ Bee, Clair 1967	+ Hinkle, Tony 1965	+ Reid, William A 1963
+ Biasone, Danny 2000	+ Irish, Ned 1964	+ Ripley, Elmer 1972
+ Brown, Walter A 1965	+ Jones, R. William 1964	+ St. John, Lynn W 1962
+ Bunn, John 1964	+ Kennedy, Walter 1980	+ Saperstein, Abe 1970
+ Douglas, Bob 1971	Lemon, Meadowlark 2003	+ Schabinger, Arthur 1961
+ Duer, Al 1981	+ Liston, Emil (Liz) 1974	+ Stagg, Amos Alonzo 1959
Embry, Wayne 1999	+ Mokray, Bill 1965	Stankovic, Boris 1991
+ Fagan, Clifford B 1983	+ Morgan, Ralph 1959	+ Steitz, Ed 1983
+ Fisher, Harry 1973	+ Morgenweck, Frank (Pop) . .1962	+ Taylor, Chuck 1968
+ Fleisher, Larry 1991	+ Naismith, James 1959	+ Teague, Bertha 1984
+ Gottlieb, Eddie 1971	Newton, Charles M. 2000	+ Tower, Oswald 1959
+ Gulick, Luther 1959	+ O'Brien, John J. (Jack) 1961	+ Trester, Arthur (A.L.) 1961
+ Harrison, Les 1979	+ O'Brien, Larry 1991	+ Wells, Cliff 1971
+ Hearn, Francis (Chick) 2003	+ Olsen, Harold G 1959	+ Wilke, Lou 1982
+ Hepp, Ferenc 1980	+ Podoloff, Maurice 1973	+ Zollner, Fred 1999

Curt Gowdy Award

First presented in 1990 by the Hall of Fame Board of Trustees for meritorious contributions by the media. Named in honor of the former NBC sportscaster, the Gowdy Award does not constitute induction into the Hall of Fame.

Year		Year		Year	
1990	Curt Gowdy & Dick Herbert	1995	Dick Enberg & Bob Hammel	2000	Dave Kindred & Hubie Brown
1991	Dave Dorr & Marty Glickman	1996	Billy Packer & Bob Hentzen	2001	Dick Stockton
1992	Sam Goldaper & Chick Hearn	1997	Marv Albert & Bob Ryan		& Curry Kirkpatrick
1993	Leonard Lewin & Johnny Most	1998	Dick Vitale, Larry Donald	2002	Jim Nantz & Jim O'Connell
1994	Leonard Koppett		& Dick Weiss	2003	Sid Hartman
	& Cawood Ledford	1999	Smith Barrier & Bob Costas		& Hot Rod Hundley

BOWLING

International Bowling Hall of Fame & Museum

The National Bowling Hall is one museum with separate wings for honorees of the American Bowling Congress (ABC), Professional Bowlers' Association (PBA) and Women's International Bowling Congress (WIBC). The museum does not include the Pro Women Bowlers Hall of Fame, which is located in Las Vegas. **Address:** 111 Stadium Plaza, St. Louis, MO 63102. **Telephone:** (314) 231-6340.

Professional Bowlers Association

Established in 1975. **Eligibility:** The criteria was revamped in 2002. Nominees must now be retired from full-time competition on the PBA Tour for a minimum of at least five years, or reached the age of 50, and must have won a minimum of 10 PBA Tour titles or two major titles.

Members are listed with years of induction; (+) indicates deceased members.

Performance

+ Allen, Bill 1983	+ Fazio, Buzz 1976	Roth, Mark 1987
+ Anthony, Earl 1986	Ferraro, Dave 1997	Salvino, Carmen 1975
Aulby, Mike 1996	+ Godman, Jim 1987	Semiz, Teata 1998
Berardi, Joe 1990	Hardwick, Billy 1977	Smith, Harry 1975
Bluth, Ray 1975	Holman, Marshall 1990	Soutar, Dave 1979
Bohn, Parker III 2000	Hudson, Tommy 1989	Stefanich, Jim 1980
Buckley, Roy 1992	Husted, Dave 1996	Voss, Brian 1994
Burton, Nelson Jr 1979	Johnson, Don 1977	Webb, Wayne 1993
Carter, Don 1975	Laub, Larry 1985	Weber, Dick 1975
Colwell, Paul 1991	Monacelli, Amleto 1997	Weber, Pete 1998
Cook, Steve 1993	Ozio, David 1995	+ Welu, Billy 1975
Davis, Dave 1978	Pappas, George 1986	Williams, Mark 1999
Dickinson, Gary 1988	Petraglia, John 1982	Williams, Walter Ray Jr. 1995
Durbin, Mike 1984	Ritger, Dick 1978	Zahn, Wayne 1981

Veterans

Allison, Glenn 1984	+ Joseph, Joe 1985	Schlegel, Ernie 1997
Asher, Barry 1988	Limongello, Mike 1994	+ St. John, Jim 1989
Baker, Tom 1999	Marzich, Andy 1990	Strampe, Bob 1987
Foremsky, Skee 1992	McCune, Don 1991	
Guenther, Johnny 1986	McGrath, Mike 1988	

Meritorious Service

+ Antenora, Joe 1993	+ Fitzgerald, Jim 2000	Nakano, Keijiro 1999
Archibald, John 1989	+ Frantz, Lou 1978	Pezzano, Chuck 1975
Clemens, Chuck 1994	Golden, Harry 1983	Reichert, Jack 1992
+ Elias, Eddie 1976	Hoffman, Ted Jr 1985	+ Richards, Joe 1976
Esposito, Frank 1975	Jowdy, John 1988	Schenkel, Chris 1976
Evans, Dick 1986	Kelley, Joe 1989	Stitzlein, Lorraine 1980
Firestone, Raymond 1987	Lichstein, Larry 1996	Thompson, Al 1991
Fisher, E.A. (Bud) 1984	+ Nagy, Steve 1977	Zeller, Roger 1995

American Bowling Congress

Established in 1941 and open to professional and amateur bowlers. **Eligibility:** Nominated bowlers must have competed in at least 20 years of ABC tournaments. Voting done by 170-member panel made up of ABC officials, Hall of Fame members and media representatives.

Class of 2003 (2): PERFORMANCE—**Lowell Jackson**; MERITORIOUS SERVICE—**Nick Mormando**.

Members are listed with years of induction; (+) indicates deceased members.

Performance

Allison, Glenn 1979	+ Castellano, Graz 1976	Hoover, Dick 1974
+ Anthony, Earl 1986	+ Clause, Frank 1980	Horn, Bud 1992
Asher, Barry 1998	Cohn, Alfred 1985	Howard, George 1986
+ Asplund, Harold 1978	Colwell, Paul 1999	Jackson, Eddie 1988
Aulby, Mike 2001	+ Crimmins, Johnny 1962	+ Jackson, Lowell 2003
Baer, Gordy 1987	Davis, Dave 1990	+ Johnson, Don 1982
Beach, Bill 1991	+ Daw, Charlie 1941	Johnson, Earl 1987
+ Benkovic, Frank 1958	+ Day, Ned 1952	+ Joseph, Joe 1969
Berlin, Mike 1994	Dickinson, Gary 1992	+ Jouglard, Lee 1979
+ Billick, George 1982	Duke, Norm 2002	+ Kartheiser, Frank 1967
+ Blouin, Jimmy 1953	+ Easter, Sarge 1963	+ Kawolics, Ed 1968
Bluth, Ray 1973	Ellis, Don 1981	+ Kissoff, Joe 1976
+ Bodis, Joe 1941	+ Falcaro, Joe 1968	Klares, John 1982
+ Bomar, Buddy 1966	+ Faragalli, Lindy 1968	+ Knox, Billy 1954
Bower, Gary 2001	+ Fazio, Buzz 1963	+ Koster, John 1941
+ Brandt, Allie 1960	Fehr, Steve 1993	+ Krems, Eddie 1973
Brosius, Eddie 1976	+ Gersonde, Russ 1968	Kristof, Joe 1968
+ Bujack, Fred 1967	+ Gibson, Therm 1965	+ Krumske, Paul 1968
Bunetta, Bill 1968	+ Godman, Jim 1987	+ Lange, Herb 1941
Burton, Nelson Jr 1981	Goike, Robert 1996	+ Lauman, Hank 1976
+ Burton, Nelson Sr 1964	+ Golembiewski, Billy 1979	Lillard, Bill 1972
+ Campi, Lou 1968	Griffo, Greg 1995	Lindemann, Tony 1979
+ Carlson, Adolph 1941	Guenther, Johnny 1988	+ Lindsey, Mort 1941
Carter, Don 1970	Hardwick, Billy 1985	+ Lippe, Harry 1989
+ Caruana, Frank 1977	Hart, Bob 1994	
+ Cassio, Marty 1972	+ Hennessey, Tom 1976	

Bowling (Cont.)

Lubanski, Ed 1971	Schlegel, Ernie 1997	Toft, Rod 1991
+ Lucci, Vince Sr 1978	Schroeder, Jim 1990	+ Totsky, Mike ..*......1996
+ Marino, Hank 1941	+ Schwoegler, Connie 1968	Tountas, Pete 1989
+ Martino, John 1969	Scudder, Don 1999	Tucker, Bill 1988
Marzich, Andy 1993	Semiz, Teata 1991	Tuttle, Tommy 1995
McGrath, Mike 1993	+ Sielaff, Lou 1968	+ Varipapa, Andy 1957
+ McMahon, Junie 1967	+ Sinke, Joe 1977	+ Ward, Walter 1959
+ Meisel, Darold 1998	+ Sixty, Billy 1961	Weber, Dick 1970
+ Mercurio, Skang 1967	Smith, Harry 1978	Weber, Pete 2002
Meyers, Norm 1984	+ Smith, Jimmy 1941	+ Welu, Billy 1975
+ Nagy, Steve 1963	Soutar, Dave 1985	Wilcox, John 1999
+ Norris, Joe 1954	+ Sparando, Tony 1968	+ Wilman, Joe 1951
+ O'Donnell, Chuck 1968	Spigner, Bill 2001	+ Wolf, Phil 1961
Pappas, George 1989	+ Spinella, Barney 1968	Wonders, Rich 1990
+ Patterson, Pat 1974	+ Steers, Harry 1941	+ Young, George 1959
+ Powell, John (Junior) ...2000	Stefanich, Jim 1983	Zahn, Wayne 1980
Ritger, Dick 1984	+ Stein, Otto Jr 1971	Zikes, Les 1983
+ Rogoznica, Andy 1993	Stoudt, Bud 1991	+ Zunker, Gil 1941
Salvino, Carmen 1979	Strampe, Bob 1977	
Schissler, Les 1991	+ Thoma, Sykes 1971	

Pioneers

+ Allen, Lafayette Jr. 1994	+ Hall, William Sr. 1994	+ Satow, Masao 1994
+ Briell, Frank 1996	Hirashima, Hirohito 1995	+ Schutte, Louis 1993
+ Carow, Rev. Charles 1995	+ Karpf, Samuel 1993	Shimada, Fuzzy 1997
+ Celestine, Sydney 1993	+ Moore, Henry 1996	+ Stein, Louis 1997
+ Curtis, Thomas 1993	+ Pasdeloup, Frank 1993	+ Thompson, William V. ...1993
+ de Freitas, Eric 1994	+ Rhodman, Bill 1997	+ Timm, Dr. Henry 1993

Meritorious Service

+ Allen, Harold 1966	+ Franklin, Bill 1992	+ Petersen, Louie 1963
Archibald, John 1996	+ Hagerty, Jack 1963	Pezzano, Chuck 1982
+ Baker, Frank 1975	+ Hattstrom, H.A. (Doc) ...1980	Picchietti, Remo 1993
+ Baumgarten, Elmer 1963	+ Hermann, Cornelius 1968	Pluckhahn, Bruce 1989
Bellisimo, Lou 1986	+ Howley, Pete 1941	+ Raymer, Milt 1972
+ Bensinger, Bob 1969	Jensen, Mark 2002	+ Reed, Elmer 1978
Borden, Fred 2002	Jowdy, John 2001	Reichert, Jack 1998
+ Chase, LeRoy 1972	+ Kennedy, Bob 1981	Rudo, Milt 1984
+ Coker, John 1980	+ Langtry, Abe 1963	Schenkel, Chris 1988
+ Collier, Chuck 1963	+ Levine, Sam 1971	Skelton, Max 2002
+ Cruchon, Steve 1983	+ Luby, David 1969	+ Sweeney, Dennis 1974
+ Ditzen, Walt 1973	Luby, Mort Jr. 1988	Tessman, Roger 1994
+ Dobs, Darold 1999	+ Luby, Mort Sr. 1974	+ Thum, Joe 1980
+ Doehrman, Bill 1968	Matzelle, Al 1995	Weinstein, Sam 1970
+ Elias, Eddie 1985	+ McCullough, Howard 1971	+ Whitney, Eli 1975
Esposito, Frank 1997	+ Mormando, Nick 2003	+ Wolf, Fred 1976
Evans, Dick 1992	+ Patterson, Morehead 1985	

Women's International Bowling Congress

Established in 1953. **Eligibility:** Performance nominees must have won at least one WIBC Championship Tournament title, a WIBC Queens tournament title or an international competition title and have bowled in at least 15 national WIBC Championship Tournaments (unless injury or illness cut career short).

Class of 2003 (3): PERFORMANCE—**Linda Kelly**; MERITORIOUS SERVICE—**Bernice Bennie** and **Joyce Deitch**.

Members are listed with years of induction; (+) indicates deceased members.

Performance

Abel, Joy 1984	Dryer, Pat 1978	Havlish, Jean 1987
Adamek, Donna 1996	Duval, Helen 1970	+ Hoffman, Martha 1979
Ann, Patty 1995	+ Fellmeth, Catherine 1970	Holm, Joan 1974
Bolt, Mae 1978	Fothergill, Dotty 1980	+ Humphreys, Birdie 1979
Bouvia, Gloria 1987	+ Fulton, Louise 2001	Ignizio, Millie Martorella ..1975
Boxberger, Loa 1984	Fritz, Deane 1966	Jacobson, D.D 1981
Buckner, Pam 1990	Garms, Shirley 1971	+ Jaeger, Emma 1953
+ Burling, Catherine 1958	Gianulias, Nikki 1997	Johnson, Tish 2002
+ Burns, Nina 1977	+ Gloor, Olga 1976	Kelly, Annese 1985
Cantaline, Anita 1979	Gonzalez, Ashie 1998	Kelly, Linda 2003
Carter, LaVerne 1977	Graham, Linda 1992	+ Knechtges, Doris 1983
Carter, Paula 1994	Graham, Mary Lou 1989	Kuczynski, Betty 1981
Coburn, Doris 1976	Greenwald, Goldie 1953	Ladewig, Marion 1964
Coburn-Carroll, Cindy ...1998	Grinfelds, Vesma 1991	+ Matthews, Merle 1974
Costello, Pat 1986	+ Harman, Janet 1985	+ McCutcheon, Floretta ...1956
Costello, Patty 1989	+ Hartrick, Stella 1972	Merrick, Marge 1980
Daniels, Cheryl 2002	+ Hatch, Grayce 1953	+ Mikiel, Val 1979

Miller-Mackey, Dana 2000	+ Powers, Connie 1973	+ Simon, Violet (Billy) 1960
Miller, Carol 1997	Reichley, Susie 2000	+ Small, Tess 1971
+ Miller, Dorothy 1954	Rickard, Robin 1994	+ Smith, Grace 1968
Mivelaz, Betty 1991	+ Robinson, Leona 1969	Soutar, Judy 1976
Mohacsi, Mary 1994	Romeo, Robin 1995	+ Stockdale, Louise 1953
Morris, Betty 1983	+ Rump, Anita 1962	Toepfer, Elvira 1976
Naccarato, Jeanne 1999	+ Ruschmeyer, Addie 1961	+ Twyford, Sally 1964
Nichols, Lorrie Koch 1989	+ Ryan, Esther 1963	Wagner, Lisa 2000
Norman, Carol 2001	+ Sablatnik, Ethel 1979	+ Warmbier, Marie 1953
Norman, Edie Jo 1993	Sandelin, Lucy 1999	Wene-Martin, Sylvia 1966
Norton, Virginia 1988	+ Schulte, Myrtle 1965	Wilkinson, Dorothy 1990
Notaro, Phyllis 1979	+ Shablis, Helen 1977	+ Winandy, Cecelia 1975
Ortner, Bev 1972	Sill, Aleta 1996	Zimmerman, Donna 1982

Meritorious Service

+ Baetz, Helen 1977	+ Haas, Dorothy 1977	+ Mraz, Jo 1959
+ Baker, Helen 1989	Hagin, Elaine 2000	O'Connor, Billie 1992
+ Banker, Gladys 1994	+ Herold, Mitzi 1998	+ Phaler, Emma 1965
+ Bayley, Clover 1992	+ Higley, Margaret 1969	+ Porter, Cora 1986
Bennie, Bernice 2003	+ Hochstadter, Bee 1967	+ Quin, Zoe 1979
+ Berger, Winifred 1976	+ Kay, Nora 1964	+ Rishling, Gertrude 1972
+ Bohlen, Philena 1955	Keller, Pearl 1999	Robinson, Jeanette 2000
Borschuk, Lo 1988	+ Kelly, Ellen 1979	Simone, Anne 1991
+ Botkin, Freda 1986	Kelone, Theresa 1978	Sloan, Catherine 1985
+ Chapman, Emily 1957	+ Knepprath, Jeannette ...1963	+ Speck, Berdie 1966
Chapman, Nancy 2002	+ Lasher, Iolia 1967	Spitalnick, Mildred 1994
+ Crowe, Alberta 1982	+ Marrs, Mabel 1979	+ Spring, Alma 1979
Deitch, Joyce 2003	+ McBride, Bertha 1968	+ Switzer, Pearl 1973
+ Dornblaser, Gertrude ...1979	McLeary, Hazel 2000	+ Todd, Trudy 1993
Duffy, Agnes 1987	+ Menne, Catherine 1979	+ Veatch, Georgia 1974
Finke, Gertrude 1990	Mitchell, Flora 1996	+ White, Mildred 1975
+ Fisk, Rae 1983	Morton, Clara 2001	+ Wood, Ann 1970

Professional Women Bowlers Hall of Fame

Established in 1995 by the Ladies Pro Bowlers Tour. The LPBT has since been renamed the Professional Women Bowlers Association. **Address:** Sam's Town Hotel, Gambling Hall and Bowling Center, 5111 Boulder Highway, Las Vegas, NV 89122. **Telephone:** (815) 332-5756.

Eligibility: Nominees in performance category must have at least five titles from organizations including All-Star, World Invitational, LPBT, WPBA, PWBA, TPA and LPBA. Voting done by 10-member committee of bowling writers appointed by PWBA president John Falzone.

Class of 2003 (2): PERFORMANCE—**Anne Marie Duggan** and **Virginia Norton**.

Members are listed with year of induction; (+) indicates deceased member.

Performance

Adamek, Donna 1995	Grinfelds, Vesma 1997	Nichols, Lorrie 1996
Coburn-Carroll, Cindy 1997	Johnson, Tish 1998	Norton, Virginia 2003
Costello, Pat 1997	Ladewig, Marion 1995	Romeo, Robin 1996
Costello, Patty 1995	Martorella, Millie 1995	Sill, Aleta 1998
Duggan, Anne Marie 2003	Miller-Mackie, Dana 2002	Wagner, Lisa 1996
Fothergill, Dotty 1995	Morris, Betty 1995	
Gianulias, Nikki 1996	Naccarato, Jeanne 2002	

Pioneers

Able, Joy 1998	Coburn, Doris 1996	Ortner, Bev 1998
Boxberger, Loa 1997	Duval, Helen 1995	Soutar, Judy 1997
Carter, LaVerne 1995	Garms, Shirley 1995	Zimmerman, Donna 1996

Builders

+ Buehler, Janet 1996	Robinson, Jeanette 1996	+ Veatch, Georgia 1995
Keller, Pearl 1997	Sommer Jr., John 1997	

BOXING

International Boxing Hall of Fame

Established in 1984 and opened in 1989. **Address:** 1 Hall of Fame Drive, Canastota, NY 13032. **Tel.:** (315) 697-7095.

Eligibility: All nominees must be retired for five years. Voting done by 142-member panel made up of Boxing Writers' Association members and world-wide boxing historians.

Class of 2003 (16): MODERN ERA—**Fred Apostoli, Curtis Cokes, George Foreman, Nicolino Locche** and **Mike McCallum**. OLD TIMERS—**Battling Battalino, Louis "Kid" Kaplan, Tom Sharkey** and **Jess Willard**. PIONEER—**Caleb Baldwin** and **Joe Goss**. NON-PARTICIPANTS—**Dan Duva, Dewey Fragetta** and **Al Weill**. OBSERVERS—**Jack Fiske** and **Budd Schulberg**

Members are listed with year of induction; (+) indicates deceased member.

Boxing (Cont.)

Modern Era

Ali, Muhammad 1990	+ Galindez, Victor 2002	Olivares, Ruben 1991
+ Angott, Sammy 1998	Gavilan, Kid 1990	+ Olson, Carl (Bobo) 2000
+ Apostoli, Fred 2003	Giardello, Joey 1993	Ortiz, Carlos 1991
Arguello, Alexis 1992	Gomez, Wilfredo 1995	+ Ortiz, Manuel 1996
+ Armstrong, Henry 1990	+ Graham, Billy 1992	Papp, Laszlo 2001
Basilio, Carmen 1990	+ Graziano, Rocky 1991	+ Pastrano, Willie 2001
Benitez, Wilfredo 1996	Griffith, Emile 1990	Patterson, Floyd 1991
Benvenuti, Nino 1992	Hagler, Marvelous Marvin .1993	Pedroza, Eusebio 1999
+ Berg, Jackie (Kid) 1994	Harada, Masahiko (Fighting) 1995	Pep, Willie 1990
Bivins, Jimmy 1999	Jack, Beau 1991	+ Perez, Pascual 1995
+ Brown, Joe 1996	+ Jenkins, Lew 1999	Pryor, Aaron 1996
Buchanan, Ken 2000	Jofre, Eder 1992	Ramos, Ultiminio 2001
+ Burley, Charley 1992	Johansson, Ingemar 2002	+ Robinson, Sugar Ray 1990
Canto, Miguel 1998	Johnson, Harold 1993	+ Rodriguez, Luis 1997
+ Carter, Jimmy 2000	Laguna, Ismael 2001	+ Saddler, Sandy 1990
+ Cerdan, Marcel 1991	LaMotta, Jake 1990	+ Saldivar, Vicente 1999
Cervantes, Antonio 1998	Leonard, Sugar Ray 1997	+ Sanchez, Salvador 1991
Chandler, Jeff 2000	+ Liston, Sonny 1991	Schmeling, Max 1992
+ Charles, Ezzard 1990	Locche, Nicolino 2003	Spinks, Michael 1994
Cokes, Curtis 2003	+ Louis, Joe 1990	+ Tiger, Dick 1991
+ Conn, Billy 1990	+ Marciano, Rocky 1990	Torres, Jose 1997
Cuevas, Pipino 2002	+ Maxim, Joey 1994	+ Turpin, Randy 2001
+ Elorde, Gabriel (Flash) 1993	McCallum, Mike 2003	+ Walcott, Jersey Joe 1990
Fenech, Jeff 2002	+ Montgomery, Bob 1995	+ Williams, Ike 1990
Foreman, George 2003	+ Monzon, Carlos 1990	+ Wright, Chalky 1997
Foster, Bob 1990	+ Moore, Archie 1990	+ Zale, Tony 1991
Frazier, Joe 1990	Muhammad, Matthew Saad 1998	Zarate, Carlos 1994
Fullmer, Gene 1991	Napoles, Jose 1990	+ Zivic, Fritzie 1993
Galaxy, Khaosai 1999	Norton, Ken 1992	

Old-Timers

+ Ambers, Lou 1992	+ Gans, Joe 1990	McLarnin, Jimmy 1991
+ Attell, Abe 1990	+ Genaro, Frankie 1998	+ McVey, Sam 1999
+ Baer, Max 1995	+ Gibbons, Mike 1992	+ Miller, Freddie 1997
+ Barry, Jimmy 2000	+ Gibbons, Tommy 1993	+ Mitchell, Charley 2002
+ Bass, Benny 2002	+ Greb, Harry 1990	+ Moran, Owen 2002
+ Battalino, Battling 2003	+ Griffo, Young 1991	+ Nelson, Battling 1992
+ Berlenbach, Paul 2001	+ Harris, Harry 2002	+ O'Brien, Philadelphia Jack . .1994
+ Braddock, Jim 2001	+ Herman, Pete 1997	+ Papke, Billy 2001
+ Britton, Jack 1990	+ Jackson, Peter 1990	+ Petrolle, Billy 2000
+ Brown, Aaron (Dixie Kid) . .2002	+ Jeanette, Joe 1997	+ Rosenbloom, Maxie 1993
+ Brown, Panama Al 1992	+ Jeffries, James J 1990	+ Ross, Barney 1990
+ Burns, Tommy 1996	+ Johnson, Jack 1990	+ Ryan, Tommy 1991
+ Canzoneri, Tony 1990	+ Kaplan, Louis (Kid) 2003	+ Sharkey, Jack 1994
+ Carpentier, Georges 1991	+ Ketchel, Stanley 1990	+ Sharkey, Tom 2003
+ Chocolate, Kid 1991	+ Kilbane, Johnny 1995	+ Steele, Freddie 1999
+ Choynski, Joe 1998	+ LaBarba, Fidel 1996	+ Stribling, Young 1996
+ Corbett, James J. 1990	+ Langford, Sam 1990	+ Tendler, Lew 1999
+ Coulon, Johnny 1999	+ Lavigne, George (Kid) 1998	+ Tunney, Gene 1990
+ Darcy, Les 1993	+ Leonard, Benny 1990	+ Villa, Pancho 1994
+ Delaney, Jack 1996	+ Levinsky, Battling 2000	+ Walcott, Joe (Barbados) . . .1991
+ Dempsey, Jack 1990	+ Lewis, John Henry 1994	+ Walker, Mickey 1990
+ Dempsey, Jack (Nonpareil) .1992	+ Lewis, Ted (Kid) 1992	+ Welsh, Freddie 1997
+ Dillon, Jack 1995	+ Loughran, Tommy 1991	+ Wilde, Jimmy 1990
+ Dixon, George 1990	+ Lynch, Benny 1998	+ Willard, Jess 2003
+ Driscoll, Jim 1990	+ Mandell, Sammy 1998	+ Williams, Kid 1996
+ Dundee, Johnny 1991	+ McAuliffe, Jack 1995	+ Wills, Harry 1992
+ Escobar, Sixto 2002	+ McCoy, Charles (Kid) 1991	+ Wolgast, Ad 2000
+ Fitzsimmons, Bob 1990	+ McFarland, Packey 1992	+ Wolgast, Midget 2001
+ Flowers, Theodore (Tiger) . .1993	+ McGovern, Terry 1990	

Pioneers

+ Aaron, Barney 2001	+ Goss, Joe 2003	Morrissey, John 1996
+ Baldwin, Caleb 2003	+ Figg, James 1992	+ Pearce, Henry 1993
+ Belcher, Jem 1992	+ Heenan, John C. 2002	+ Richmond, Bill 1999
+ Brain, Ben 1994	+ Jackson, Gentleman John . .1992	+ Sam, Dutch 1997
+ Broughton, Jack 1990	+ Johnson, Tom 1995	+ Sam, Young Dutch 2002
+ Burke, James (Deaf) 1992	+ King, Tom 1992	+ Sayers, Tom 1990
+ Chambers, Arthur 2000	+ Langham, Nat 1992	+ Spring, Tom 1992
+ Cribb, Tom 1991	+ Mace, Jem 1990	+ Sullivan, John L 1990
+ Donovan, Prof. Mike 1998	+ Mendoza, Daniel 1990	+ Thompson, William 1991
+ Duffy, Paddy 1994	+ Molineaux, Tom 1997	+ Ward, Jem 1995

Non-Participants

+ Andrews, Thomas S 1992
+ Arcel, Ray 1991
  Arum, Bob 1999
+ Ballarati, Giuseppe 1999
  Benton, George 2001
+ Blackburn, Jack 1992
+ Brady, William A. 1998
  Brenner, Teddy 1993
+ Chambers, John Graham . .1990
  Chargin, Don 2001
  Clancy, Gil 1993
+ Coffroth, James W. 1991
+ Cohen, Irving 2002
+ D'Amato, Cus. 1995
  Dickson, Jeff 2000
+ Donovan, Arthur 1993
  Duff, Mickey 1999
  Dundee, Angelo 1992
+ Dundee, Chris 1994
+ Dunphy, Don 1993

+ Duva, Dan 2003
  Duva, Lou 1998
+ Eaton, Aileen 2002
+ Egan, Pierce 1991
+ Fleischer, Nat 1990
+ Fox, Richard K. 1997
+ Fragetta, Dewey 2003
+ Futch, Eddie 1994
+ Goldman, Charley 1992
+ Goldstein, Ruby 1994
  Goodman, Murray 1999
+ Humphreys, Joe 1997
+ Ichinose, Sam 2001
+ Jacobs, Jimmy 1993
+ Jacobs, Mike 1990
+ Johnston, Jimmy 1999
+ Kearns, Jack (Doc) 1990
  King, Don 1997
  Lectoure, Tito 2000
+ Liebling, A.J 1992

+ Lonsdale, Lord 1990
+ Markson, Harry 1992
  Mercante, Arthur 1995
+ Morgan, Dan 2000
+ Muldoon, William 1996
  Odd, Gilbert 1995
+ O'Rourke, Tom 1999
+ Parker, Dan 1993
+ Parnassus, George 1991
+ Queensberry, Marquis of . .1990
+ Rickard, Tex 1990
+ Rudd, Irving 1999
+ Siler, George 1995
+ Silverman, Sam 2002
+ Solomons, Jack 1995
  Steward, Emanuel 1996
+ Taub, Sam 1994
+ Taylor, Herman 1998
+ Walker, James J. (Jimmy) . .1992
+ Weill, Al 2003

Observers

+ Bromberg, Lester 2001
+ Cannon, Jimmy 2002
  Citro, Ralph 2001

  Gallo, Bill 2001
  Gutteridge, Reg 2002
  Fiske, Jack 2003

+ Runyon, Damon 2002
  Schulberg, Budd 2003

Old *Ring* Hall Members Not in Int'l. Boxing Hall

Nat Fleischer, the late founder and editor-in-chief of *The Ring*, established his magazine's Boxing Hall of Fame in 1954, but it was abandoned after the 1987 inductions. One hundred and twenty-seven members of the old *Ring* Hall have been elected to the International Hall since 1989. The 27 boxers and one sportswriter who have yet to be elected to the International Hall are listed below with their year of induction into the *Ring* Hall.

Modern Group

+ Garcia, Ceferino 1977

+ Lesnevich, Gus 1973

+ Shirai, Yoshio 1977

Old-Timers

+ Britt, Jimmy 1976
+ Chaney, George (K.O.) . . .1974
+ Corbett, Young II 1965
+ Fields, Jackie 1977

+ Houck, Leo 1969
+ Jeffra, Harry 1982
+ Klaus, Frank 1974
+ Maher, Peter 1978

+ Ritchie, Willie 1962
+ Root, Jack 1961
+ Smith, Jeff 1969
+ Taylor, Bud 1986

Pioneers

+ Chandler, Tom 1972
+ Clark, Nobby 1971
+ Collyer, Sam 1964
+ Donnelly, Dan 1960
+ Gully, John 1959

+ Hyer, Jacob 1968
+ Hyer, Tom 1954
+ Jackling, Thomas 1985
+ Kilrain, Jack 1965
+ Price, Ned 1962

+ Ryan, Paddy 1973

Non-Participant

+ Daniel, Dan (sportswriter) . .1977

FOOTBALL

College Football Hall of Fame

Established in 1955 by the National Football Foundation. **Address:** 111 South St. Joseph St., South Bend, IN 46601. **Telephone:** (574) 235-9999.

Eligibility: Nominated players must be out of college 10 years and a first team All-America pick by a major selector during their careers; coaches must be retired three years. Voting done by 12-member panel of athletic directors, conference and bowl officials and media representatives. The first year representatives from NCAA Div. I-AA, II, and III, and the NAIA were eligible for induction was 1996.

Class of 2003 (13): LARGE COLLEGE—RB **Ricky Bell**, USC (1973-76); DB **Murry Bowden**, Dartmouth (1967-70); G **Tom Brown**, Minnesota (1958-60); OT **Jimbo Covert**, Pittsburgh (1980-83); E **Jerry Levias**, SMU (1965-68); T **Billy Neighbors**, Alabama (1959-61); LB **Ron Pritchard**, Arizona St. (1966-68); QB **John Rauch**, Georgia (1945-48); TB **Barry Sanders**, Oklahoma St. (1986-88); QB **Joe Theismann**, Notre Dame (1968-70); DB **Roger Wehrli**, Missouri (1966-68). COACHES—**Doug Dickey**, Tennessee (1964-69), Florida (1970-78); **Hayden Fry**, SMU (1962-72), North Texas St. (1973-78), Iowa (1979-98).

Note: Bobby Dodd and **Amos Alonzo Stagg** are the only members to be honored as both players and coaches.

Players are listed with final year they played in college and coaches are listed with year of induction; (+) indicates deceased members.

Players

+ Abell, Earl-Colgate 1915
  Agase, Alex-Purdue/Ill 1946
+ Agganis, Harry-Boston U . . .1952
  Albert, Frank-Stanford 1941
+ Aldrich, Ki-TCU 1938

+ Aldrich, Malcolm-Yale 1921
+ Alexander, Joe-Syracuse . . .1920
  Allen, Marcus-USC 1981
  Alworth, Lance-Arkansas . . .1961
+ Ameche, Alan-Wisconsin . . .1954

+ Ames, Knowlton-Princeton . .1889
+ Amling, Warren-Ohio St . . .1946
  Anderson, Dick-Colorado . . .1967
  Anderson, Donny-Tex.Tech . .1966
+ Anderson, Hunk-N.Dame . .1921

College Football Hall of Fame (Cont.)

Arnett, Jon-USC 1956
Atkins, Doug-Tennessee . . . 1952
Babich, Bob-Miami-OH 1968
+ Bacon, Everett-Wesleyan . . .1912
Bagnell, Reds-Penn 1950
+ Baker, Hobey-Princeton 1913
+ Baker, John-USC 1931
+ Baker, Moon-N'western 1926
Baker, Terry-Oregon St 1962
+ Ballin, Harold-Princeton 1914
Banker, Bill-Tulane 1929
Banonis, Vince-Detroit 1941
+ Barnes, Stan-California 1921
Barrett, Charles-Cornell 1915
Baston, Bert-Minnesota 1916
Battles, Cliff-WV Wesleyan .1931
Baugh, Sammy-TCU 1936
Baughan, Maxie-Ga.Tech . .1959
Bausch, James-Kansas 1930
Beagle, Ron-Navy 1955
Beasley, Terry-Auburn 1971
Beban, Gary-UCLA 1967
Bechtol, Hub-Texas 1946
Beck, Ray-Ga. Tech 1951
+ Beckett, John-Oregon 1916
Bednarik, Chuck-Penn 1948
Behm, Forrest-Nebraska . . .1940
Bell, Bobby-Minnesota 1962
Bell, Ricky-USC 1976
Bellino, Joe-Navy 1960
Below, Marty-Wisconsin . . .1923
+ Benbrook, Al-Michigan 1910
+ Berry, Charlie-Lafayette 1924
+ Bertelli, Angelo-N.Dame . . .1943
+ Berwanger, Jay-Chicago . . .1935
+ Bettencourt, L.-St.Mary's . . .1927
Biletnikoff, Fred-Fla.St. 1964
Blanchard, Doc-Army 1946
+ Blozis, Al-Georgetown 1942
Bock, Ed-Iowa St 1938
Bomar, Lynn-Vanderbilt 1924
+ Bomeisler, Bo-Yale 1913
+ Booth, Albie-Yale 1931
+ Borries, Fred-Navy 1934
+ Bosley, Bruce-West Va 1955
Bosseler, Don-Miami,FL . . .1956
Bottari, Vic-California 1938
Bowden, Murry-Dartmouth .1970
+ Boynton, Ben-Williams 1920
+ Brewer, Charles-Harvard . . .1895
+ Bright, Johnny-Drake 1951
Brodie, John-Stanford 1956
+ Brooke, George-Penn 1895
Brosky, Al-Illinois 1952
Brown, Bob-Nebraska 1963
Brown, Geo-Navy/S.Diego St .1947
+ Brown, Gordon-Yale 1900
Brown, Jim-Syracuse 1956
+ Brown, John, Jr.-Navy 1913
+ Brown, Johnny Mack-Ala . . .1925
+ Brown, Tay-USC 1932
Brown, Tom-Minnesota 1960
Browner, Ross-Notre Dame .1977
Buddie, Brad-USC 1979
+ Bunker, Paul-Army 1902
Burford, Chris-Stanford 1959
+ Burris, Kurt-Oklahoma 1954
Burton, Ron-N'western 1959
Butkus, Dick-Illinois 1964
Butler, Kevin-Georgia 1984
+ Butler, Robert-Wisconsin . . .1912
Cafego, George-Tenn 1939
+ Cagle, Red-SWLa/Army 1929
+ Cain, John-Alabama 1932

Cameron, Ed-Wash.& Lee . .1924
+ Campbell, David-Harvard . . .1901
Campbell, Earl-Texas 1977
+ Cannon, Jack-N.Dame 1929
Cappelletti, John-Penn St . . .1973
+ Carideo, Frank-N.Dame 1930
+ Carney, Charles-Illinois 1921
Caroline, J.C.-Illinois 1954
Carpenter, Bill-Army 1959
+ Carpenter, Hunter-Va.Tech . .1905
Carroll, Chas.-Washington . .1928
Carter, Anthony-Michigan . .1982
Casanova, Tommy-LSU 1971
+ Casey, Edward-Harvard 1919
Cassady, Howard-Ohio St . .1955
+ Chamberlin, Guy-Neb. 1915
Chapman, Sam-California . .1938
Chappuis, Bob-Michigan . . .1947
+ Christman, Paul-Missouri . . .1940
+ Clark, Dutch-Colo. Col. 1929
Cleary, Paul-USC 1947
+ Clevenger, Zora-Indiana 1903
Cloud, Jack-Wm. & Mary . .1948
+ Cochran, Gary-Princeton 1897
+ Cody, Josh-Vanderbilt 1919
Coleman, Don-Mich.St 1951
+ Conerly, Charlie-Miss 1947
Connor, George-HC/ND 1947
+ Corbin, William-Yale 1888
Corbus, William-Stanford . .1933
+ Covert, Jimbo-Pittsburgh . . .1983
+ Cowan, Hector-Princeton . . .1889
+ Coy, Edward (Tad)-Yale 1909
+ Crawford, Fred-Duke 1933
Crow, John David-Tex.A&M .1957
+ Crowley, Jim-Notre Dame . . .1924
Csonka, Larry-Syracuse 1967
Cutter, Slade-Navy 1934
+ Czarobski, Ziggie-N.Dame . .1947
Dale, Carroll-Va.Tech 1959
+ Dalrymple, Gerald-Tulane . . .1931
+ Dalton, John-Navy 1911
+ Daly, Chas.-Harvard/Army . .1902
Daniell, Averell-Pitt 1936
+ Daniell, James-Ohio St 1941
+ Davies, Tom-Pittsburgh 1921
Davis, Ernie-Syracuse 1961
Davis, Glenn-Army 1946
Davis, Robert-Ga.Tech 1947
Dawkins, Pete-Army 1958
DeLong, Steve-Tennessee . .1964
+ DeRogatis, Al-Duke 1948
+ DesJardien, Paul-Chicago . . .1914
Devine, Aubrey-Iowa 1921
DeWitt, John-Princeton 1903
Dial, Buddy-Rice 1958
Dicus, Chuck-Arkansas 1970
Dierdorf, Dan-Michigan 1970
Ditka, Mike-Pittsburgh 1960
Dobbs, Glenn-Tulsa 1942
+ Dodd, Bobby-Tennessee 1930
Donan, Holland-Princeton . .1950
+ Donchess, Joseph-Pitt 1929
Dorsett, Tony-Pitt 1976
+ Dougherty, Nathan-Tenn . . .1909
Dove, Bob-Notre Dame 1942
Drahos, Nick-Cornell 1940
+ Driscoll, Paddy-N'western . . .1917
+ Drury, Morley-USC 1927
Duden, Dick-Navy 1945
Dudley, Bill-Virginia 1941
Duncan, Randy-Iowa 1958
Easley, Kenny-UCLA 1980
+ Eckersall, Walter-Chicago . . .1906

+ Edwards, Turk-Wash.St 1931
+ Edwards, Wm.-Princeton . . .1899
+ Eichenlaub, Ray-N.Dame . . .1914
Eisenhauer, Steve-Navy 1953
Elkins, Larry-Baylor 1964
Elliott, Bump-Mich/Purdue .1947
Elliott, Pete-Michigan 1947
Elmendorf, Dave-Tex. A&M .1970
Elway, John-Stanford 1982
+ Evans, Ray-Kansas 1947
+ Exendine, Albert-Carlisle . . .1907
Falaschi, Nello-S.Clara 1936
Fears, Tom-S.Clara/UCLA . .1947
+ Feathers, Beattie-Tenn 1933
Fenimore, Bob-Okla.St 1946
+ Fenton, Doc-LSU 1909
Ferguson, Bob-Ohio St. 1961
+ Ferraro, John-USC 1944
Fesler, Wes-Ohio St. 1930
+ Fincher, Bill-Ga.Tech 1920
Fischer, Bill-Notre Dame . . .1948
+ Fish, Hamilton-Harvard 1909
+ Fisher, Robert-Harvard 1911
+ Flowers, Allen-Ga.Tech 1920
Flowers, Charlie-Ole Miss. . .1959
+ Fortmann Danny-Colgate . . .1935
Fralic, Bill-Pittsburgh 1984
+ Francis, Sam-Nebraska 1936
Franck, George-Minnesota . .1940
Franco, Ed-Fordham 1937
+ Frank, Clint-Yale 1937
Franz, Rodney-California . . .1949
Frederickson, Tucker-Auburn 1964
+ Friedman, Benny-Michigan .1926
Gabriel, Roman-N.C. State .1961
Gain, Bob-Kentucky 1950
+ Galiffa, Arnold-Army 1949
+ Gallarneau, Hugh-Stanford .1940
+ Garbisch, Edgar-W.& J./Army .1924
Garrett, Mike-USC 1965
+ Gelbert, Charles-Penn 1896
Geyer, Forest-Oklahoma . . .1915
Gibbs, Jake-Miss 1960
+ Giel, Paul-Minnesota 1953
Gifford, Frank-USC 1951
Gilbert, Chris-Texas 1968
+ Gilbert, Walter-Auburn 1936
Gilmer, Harry-Alabama 1947
+ Gipp, George-N.Dame 1920
+ Gladchuk, Chet-Boston Col .1940
Glass, Bill-Baylor 1956
Glover, Rich-Nebraska 1972
Goldberg, Marshall-Pitt 1938
Goodreault, Gene-BC 1940
+ Gordon, Walter-Calif 1918
+ Governali, Paul-Columbia . . .1942
Grabowski, Jim-Illinois 1965
Gradishar, Randy-Ohio St. . .1973
Graham, Otto-N'western . . .1943
+ Grange, Red-Illinois 1925
Grayson, Bobby-Stanford . .1935
Green, Hugh-Pitt 1980
+ Green, Jack-Tulane/Army . . .1945
Green, Tim-Syracuse 1985
Greene, Joe-N.Texas St 1968
Griese, Bob-Purdue 1966
Griffin, Archie-Ohio St 1975
Groom, Jerry-Notre Dame . .1950
+ Gulick, Merle-Toledo/Hobart 1929
Guglielmi, Ralph-N.Dame . .1954
+ Guyon, Joe-Ga.Tech 1918
Hadl, John-Kansas 1961
+ Hale, Edwin-Miss.College . .1921
Hall, Parker-Miss 1938

College Football Hall of Fame (Cont.)

Olsen, Merlin-Utah St 1961
Onkotz, Dennis-Penn St. 1969
+ Oosterbaan, Bennie-Mich . .1927
O'Rourke, Charles-BC 1940
+ Orsi, John-Colgate 1931
+ Osgood, Win-Cornell/Penn .1892
Osmanski, Bill-Holy Cross 1938
+ Outland, John-Penn. 1899
+ Owen, George-Harvard 1922
Owens, Jim-Oklahoma 1949
Owens, Steve-Oklahoma 1969
+ Page, Alan-Notre Dame 1966
Palumbo, Joe-Virginia 1951
Pardee, Jack-Texas A&M 1956
Parilli, Babe-Kentucky 1951
Parker, Ace-Duke 1936
Parker, Jackie-Miss.St 1953
Parker, Jim-Ohio St 1956
+ Pazzetti, Vince-Lehigh 1912
+ Peabody, Chub-Harvard 1941
+ Peck, Robert-Pittsburgh 1916
Pellegrini, Bob-Maryland . . .1955
+ Pennock, Stan-Harvard 1914
Pfann, George-Cornell 1923
+ Phillips, H.D.-Sewanee 1904
Phillips, Loyd-Arkansas 1966
Pihos, Pete-Indiana 1946
Pingel, John-Michigan St 1938
+ Pinckert, Erny-USC 1931
Plunkett, Jim-Stanford 1970
+ Poe, Arthur-Princeton 1899
+ Pollard, Fritz-Brown 1916
Poole, B.-Miss/NC/Army . . .1947
Powell, Marvin-USC 1976
Pregulman, Merv-Michigan . .1943
+ Price, Eddie-Tulane 1949
Pritchard, Ron-Arizona St. . . .1968
Pruitt, Greg-Oklahoma 1972
+ Pund, Peter-Georgia Tech . . .1928
Ramsey, D.-Wm&Mary 1942
Rauch, John-Georgia 1948
Redman, Rick-Wash 1964
+ Reeds, Claude-Oklahoma . . .1913
Reid, Mike-Penn St 1969
Reid, Steve-Northwestern . . .1936
+ Reid, William-Harvard 1899
Reifsnyder, Bob-Navy 1958
Renfro, Mel-Oregon 1963
+ Rentner, Pug-N'western 1932
Ressler, Glenn-Penn St. 1964
+ Reynolds, Bob-Stanford 1935
+ Reynolds, Bobby-Nebraska . .1952
Rhino, Randy-Georgia Tech . .1974
Rhome, Jerry-SMU/Tulsa . . .1964
Richter, Les-California 1951
Richter, Pat-Wisconsin 1962
+ Riley, Jack-Northwestern 1931
Rimington, Dave-Nebraska . .1982
+ Rinehart, Chas.-Lafayette . . .1897
Ritcher, Jim-NC St. 1979
Roberts, J. D.-Oklahoma . . .1953
+ Robeson, Paul-Rutgers 1918
Robinson, Dave-Penn St. . . .1962
Robinson, Jerry-UCLA 1978
+ Rodgers, Ira-West Va 1919
Rodgers, Johnny-Nebraska . .2000
+ Rogers, Ed-Carlisle/Minn . . .1903
Rogers, George-S. Carolina .1980
Roland, Johnny-Missouri 1965
Romig, Joe-Colorado 1961
+ Rosenberg, Aaron-USC 1933
+ Rote, Kyle-SMU 1950
+ Routt, Joe-Texas A&M 1937
+ Salmon, Red-Notre Dame . . .1903

Sanders, Barry-Okla. St. 1988
Sarkisian, Alex 1948
+ Sauer, George-Nebraska 1933
Savitsky, George-Penn 1947
Saxton, Jimmy-Texas 1961
Sayers, Gale-Kansas 1964
Scarbath, Jack-Maryland 1952
+ Scarlett, Hunter-Penn 1908
Schloredt, Bob-Wash 1960
Schmidt, Joe-Pittsburgh 1952
+ Schoonover, Wear-Ark. 1929
+ Schreiner, Dave-Wisconsin . .1942
+ Schultz, Germany-Mich 1908
+ Schwab, Dutch-Lafayette . . .1922
+ Schwartz, Marchy-N.Dame . .1931
+ Schwegler, Paul-Wash 1931
Scott, Clyde-Navy/Arkansas .1948
Scott, Richard-Navy 1947
Scott, Tom-Virginia 1953
+ Seibels, Henry-Sewanee 1899
Sellers, Ron-Florida St 1968
Selmon, Lee Roy-Okla 1975
Sewell, Harley-Texas 1952
+ Shakespeare, Bill-N.Dame . . .1935
Shell, Donnie-S.Carolina St. . .1998
+ Shelton, Murray-Cornell 1915
+ Shevlin, Tom-Yale 1905
+ Shively, Bernie-Illinois 1926
+ Simons, Monk-Tulane 1934
Simpson, O.J.-USC 1968
Sims, Billy-Oklahoma 1979
Singletary, Mike-Baylor 1980
Sington, Fred-Alabama 1930
+ Sinkwich, Frank-Georgia 1942
Sisemore, Jerry-Texas 1972
+ Sitko, Emil-Notre Dame 1949
+ Skladany, Joe-Pittsburgh 1933
+ Slater, Duke-Iowa 1921
Smith, Billy Ray-Arkansas . . .1982
+ Smith, Bruce-Minnesota 1941
+ Smith, Bubba-Michigan St . . .1966
+ Smith, Clipper-N.Dame 1927
+ Smith, Ernie-USC 1932
Smith, Harry-USC 1939
Smith, Jim Ray-Baylor 1954
Smith, Riley-Alabama 1935
+ Smith, Vernon-Georgia 1931
+ Snow, Neil-Michigan 1901
Spani, Gary-Kansas St. 1977
Sparlis, Al-UCLA 1945
+ Spears, Clarence-Dart 1915
Spears, W.D.-Vanderbilt 1927
+ Sprackling, Wm.-Brown 1911
+ Sprague, Bud-Army/Texas . .1928
Spurrier, Steve-Florida 1966
Stafford, Harrison-Texas 1932
+ Stagg, Amos Alonzo-Yale . . .1889
Stanfill, Bill-Georgia 1968
Starcevich, Max-Wash 1936
Staubach, Roger-Navy 1964
+ Steffen, Walter-Chicago 1908
Steffy, Joe-Tenn/Army 1947
+ Stein, Herbert-Pitt 1921
Steuber, Bob-Missouri 1943
+ Stevens, Mal-Yale 1923
Stillwagon, Jim-Ohio St. 1970
+ Stinchcomb, Pete-Ohio St. . .1920
+ Stevenson, Vincent-Penn 1905
Strom, Brock-Air Force 1959
+ Strong, Ken-NYU 1928
+ Strupper, Ev-Ga.Tech 1917
+ Stuhldreher, Harry-N.Dame .1924
+ Sturhan, Herb-Yale 1926
+ Stydahar, Joe-West Va 1935

+ Suffridge, Bob-Tennessee . . .1940
+ Suhey, Steve-Penn St 1947
Sullivan, Pat-Auburn ς. 1971
+ Sundstrom, Frank-Cornell . . .1923
Swann, Lynn-USC 1973
+ Swanson, Clarence-Neb 1921
+ Swiacki, Bill-Columbia/HC . .1947
Swink, Jim-TCU 1956
+ Talboom, Eddie-Wyoming . . .1950
Taliaferro, Geo.-Indiana 1948
Tarkenton, Fran-Georgia 1960
+ Tavener, John-Indiana 1944
+ Taylor, Chuck-Stanford 1942
Theismann, Joe-Notre Dame 1970
Thomas, Aurelius-Ohio St . .1957
+ Thompson, Joe-Pittsburgh . . .1907
+ Thorne, Samuel-Yale 1895
+ Thorpe, Jim-Carlisle 1912
+ Ticknor, Ben-Harvard 1930
+ Tigert, John-Vanderbilt 1904
+ Tinsley, Gaynell-LSU 1936
+ Tipton, Eric-Duke 1938
+ Tonnemaker, Clayton-Minn . .1949
+ Torrey, Bob-Pennsylvania . . .1905
+ Travis, Brick-Missouri 1920
Trippi, Charley-Georgia 1946
+ Tryon, Edward-Colgate 1925
Tubbs, Jerry-Oklahoma 1956
Turner, Bulldog-H.Simmons . .1939
Twilley, Howard-Tulsa 1965
+ Utay, Joe-Texas A&M 1907
+ Van Brocklin, Norm-Ore 1948
Van Pelt, Brad-Michigan St. .1972
+ Van Sickel, Dale-Florida 1929
+ Van Surdam, H.-Wesleyan . . .1905
+ Very, Dexter-Penn St 1912
+ Vessels, Billy-Oklahoma 1952
+ Vick, Ernie-Michigan 1921
+ Wagner, Hube-Pittsburgh . . .1913
+ Walker, Doak-SMU 1949
Walker, Herschel-Georgia . . .1982
+ Wallace, Bill-Rice 1935
+ Walsh, Adam-N.Dame 1924
+ Warburton, Cotton, USC . . .1934
Ward, Bob-Maryland 1951
+ Warner, William-Cornell 1904
+ Washington, Kenny-UCLA . .1939
+ Weatherall, Jim-Okla. 1951
Webster, George-Mich. St . .1966
+ Wedemeyer, H.-St. Mary's . .1947
+ Weekes, Harold-Columbia . .1902
Wehrli, Roger-Minnesota . . .1968
Weiner, Art-N. Carolina 1949
+ Weir, Ed-Nebraska 1925
+ Welch, Gus-Carlisle 1914
+ Weller, John-Princeton 1935
+ Wendell, Percy-Harvard 1912
+ West, Belford-Colgate 1919
+ Westfall, Bob-Michigan 1941
+ Weyand, Babe-Army 1915
+ Wharton, Buck-Penn 1896
+ Wheeler, Arthur-Princeton . .1894
+ White, Byron-Colorado 1938
White, Charles-USC 1979
White, Danny-Ariz. St. 1973
White, Ed-Cal.Berkeley 1968
White, Randy-Maryland 1974
White, Reggie-Tennessee . . .1983
Whitmire, Don-Navy/Ala . . .1944
+ Wickhorst, Frank-Navy 1926
+ Widseth, Ed-Minnesota 1936
+ Wildung, Dick-Minnesota . . .1942
Williams, Bob-N. Dame 1950
Williams, Froggie-Rice 1949

Willis, Bill-Ohio St 1944
+ Wilson, Bobby-SMU 1935
+ Wilson, George-Lafayette . .1928
+ Wilson, George-Wash 1925
+ Wilson, Harry-Army/Penn St .1926
Wilson, Marc-BYU 1979
Wilson, Mike-Lafayette 1928
Winslow, Kellen-Missouri . .1978
Wistert, Albert-Michigan . . .1942

Wistert, Alvin-Michigan . . .1949
+ Wistert, Whitey-Michigan . .1933
+ Wojciechowicz, Alex-Fordham 1937
+ Wood, Barry-Harvard 1931
+ Wyant, Andy-Chicago 1894
+ Wyatt, Bowden-Tenn 1938
+ Wyckoff, Clint-Cornell 1895
+ Yarr, Tommy-N.Dame 1931
Yary, Ron-USC 1967

+ Yoder, Lloyd-Carnegie 1926
+ Young, Claude-Illinois 1946
+ Young, Harry-Wash.& Lee . .1916
Young, Steve-Brigham Young .1983
+ Young, Waddy-Okla 1938
Youngblood, Jack-Florida . . .1970
+ Younger, Paul-GRamblin . . .1948
Zarnas, Gustave-Ohio St. . . .1937

Coaches

+ Aillet, Joe 1989
+ Alexander, Bill 1951
+ Anderson, Ed 1971
+ Armstrong, Ike 1957
+ Bachman, Charlie 1978
+ Banks, Earl 1992
+ Baujan, Harry 1990
+ Bell, Matty 1955
+ Bezdek, Hugo 1954
+ Bible, Dana X 1951
+ Bierman, Bernie 1955
Blackman, Bob 1987
+ Blaik, Earl (Red) 1965
Broyles, Frank 1983
Bruce, Earle 2002
+ Bryant, Paul (Bear) 1986
+ Butts, Wally 1997
+ Caldwell, Charlie 1961
+ Camp, Walter 1951
Casanova, Len 1977
+ Cavanaugh, Frank 1954
+ Claiborne, Jerry 1999
+ Colman, Dick 1990
Coryell, Don 1999
Cozza, Carmen 2002
+ Crisler, Fritz 1954
+ Daugherty, Duffy 1984
+ Devaney, Bob 1981
+ Devine, Dan 1985
Dickey, Doug 2003
+ Dobie, Gil 1951
+ Dodd, Bobby 1993
Donahue, Tom 2000
+ Donohue, Michael 1951
Dooley, Vince 1994
+ Dorais, Gus 1954
+ Edwards, Bill 1986
+ Engle, Rip 1973
Evashevski, Forest 2000
Faurot, Don 1961
Fry, Hayden 2003
+ Gaither, Jake 1973
Gillman, Sid 1989
+ Godfrey, Ernest 1972
Graves, Ray 1990
+ Gustafson, Andy 1985

+ Hall, Edward 1951
+ Harding, Jack 1980
+ Harlow, Richard 1954
+ Harman, Harvey 1981
+ Harper, Jesse 1971
+ Haughton, Percy 1951
+ Hayes, Woody 1983
+ Heisman, John W 1954
+ Higgins, Robert 1954
+ Hollingberry, Babe 1979
+ Howard, Frank 1989
+ Ingram, Bill 1973
James, Don 1997
+ Jennings, Morley 1973
+ Jones, Biff 1954
+ Jones, Howard 1951
+ Jones, Tad 1958
+ Jordan, Lloyd 1978
+ Jordan, Ralph (Shug) 1982
+ Kerr, Andy 1951
Kush, Frank 1995
+ Leahy, Frank 1970
+ Little, George 1955
+ Little, Lou 1960
+ Madigan, Slip 1974
Maurer, Dave 1991
+ McClendon, Charley 1986
+ McCracken, Herb 1973
+ McGugin, Dan 1951
+ McKay, John 1988
+ McKeen, Allyn 1991
+ McLaughry, Tuss 1962
+ Merritt, John 1994
+ Meyer, Dutch 1956
+ Mollenkopf, Jack 1988
+ Moore, Bernie 1954
+ Moore, Scrappy 1980
+ Morrison, Ray 1954
+ Munger, George 1976
+ Munn, Clarence (Biggie) . . .1959
+ Murray, Bill 1974
+ Murray, Frank 1983
+ Mylin, Ed (Hooks) 1974
+ Neale, Earle (Greasy) 1967
+ Neely, Jess 1971
+ Nelson, David 1987

+ Neyland, Robert 1956
+ Norton, Homer 1971
+ O'Neill, Frank (Buck) 1951
+ Osborne, Tom 1998
+ Owen, Bennie 1951
Parseghian, Ara 1980
+ Perry, Doyt 1988
+ Phelan, Jimmy 1973
+ Prothro, Tommy 1991
Ralston, John 1992
+ Robinson, E.N. 1955
+ Rockne, Knute 1951
+ Romney, Dick 1954
+ Roper, Bill 1951
Royal,Darrell 1983
+ Sanders, Henry (Red) 1996
+ Sanford, George 1971
Schembechler, Bo 1993
+ Schmidt, Francis 1971
+ Schwartzwalder, Ben 1982
+ Shaughnessy, Clark 1968
+ Shaw, Buck 1972
+ Smith, Andy 1951
+ Snavely, Carl 1965
+ Stagg, Amos Alonzo 1951
+ Sutherland, Jock 1951
Switzer, Barry 2001
+ Tatum, Jim 1984
Teaff, Grant 2001
+ Thomas, Frank 1951
+ Vann, Thad 1987
Vaught, Johnny 1979
+ Wade, Wallace 1955
+ Waldorf, Lynn (Pappy) 1966
+ Warner, Glenn (Pop) 1951
+ Wieman, E.E. (Tad) 1956
+ Wilce, John 1954
+ Wilkinson, Bud 1969
+ Williams, Henry 1951
+ Woodruff, George 1963
+ Woodson, Warren 1989
+ Wyatt, Bowden 1997
Yeoman, Bill 2001
Young, Jim 1999
+ Yost, Fielding (Hurry Up) . . .1951
+ Zuppke, Bob 1951

Pro Football Hall of Fame

Established in 1963 by National Football League to commemorate the sport's professional origins. **Address:** 2121 George Halas Drive NW, Canton, OH 44708. **Telephone:** (330) 456-8207.

Eligibility: Nominated players must be retired five years, coaches must be retired, and contributors can still be active. Voting done by 39-member panel made up of media representatives from all 31 NFL cities (two from New York), one PFWA representative and six selectors-at-large.

Class of 2003 (5): PLAYERS—RB **Marcus Allen**, L.A. Raiders (1982-92), Kansas City (1993-97); WR **James Lofton**, Green Bay (1978-86), L.A. Raiders (1987-88), Buffalo (1989-92), L.A. Rams (1993), Philadelphia (1993); DE **Elvin Bethea**, Houston (1968-83) and G **Joe DeLamielleure**, Buffalo (1973-79, 85), Cleveland (1980-84); COACHES—**Hank Stram**, Dallas Texans (1960-62), Kansas City (1963-74), New Orleans (1976-77).

Quarterbacks

Baugh, Sammy 1963	Griese, Bob 1990	Starr, Bart 1977
Blanda, George (also PK) ..1981	+ Herber, Arnie 1966	Staubach, Roger 1985
Bradshaw, Terry 1989	Jurgensen, Sonny 1983	Tarkenton, Fran 1986
+ Clark, Dutch 1963	Kelly, Jim 2002	Tittle, Y.A 1971
+ Conzelman, Jimmy 1964	+ Layne, Bobby 1967	+ Unitas, Johnny 1979
Dawson, Len 1987	+ Luckman, Sid 1965	+ Van Brocklin, Norm 1971
+ Driscoll, Paddy 1965	Montana, Joe 2000	+ Waterfield, Bob 1965
Fouts, Dan 1993	Namath, Joe 1985	
Graham, Otto 1965	Parker, Clarence (Ace) ...1972	

Running Backs

Allen, Marcus 2003	+ Hinkle, Clarke 1964	+ Payton, Walter 1993
+ Battles, Cliff 1968	Hornung, Paul 1986	Perry, Joe 1969
Brown, Jim 1971	Johnson, John Henry 1987	Riggins, John 1992
Campbell, Earl 1991	Kelly, Leroy 1994	Sayers, Gale 1977
Canadeo, Tony 1974	+ Leemans, Tuffy 1978	Simpson, O.J 1985
Csonka, Larry 1987	Matson, Ollie 1972	+ Strong, Ken 1967
Dickerson, Eric 1999	McAfee, George 1966	Taylor, Jim 1976
Dorsett, Tony 1994	McElhenny, Hugh 1970	+ Thorpe, Jim 1963
Dudley, Bill 1966	+ McNally, Johnny (Blood) ..1963	Trippi, Charley 1968
Gifford, Frank 1977	Moore, Lenny 1975	Van Buren, Steve 1965
+ Grange, Red 1963	+ Motley, Marion 1968	+ Walker, Doak 1986
+ Guyon, Joe 1966	+ Nagurski, Bronko 1963	
Harris, Franco 1990	+ Nevers, Ernie 1963	

Ends & Wide Receivers

Alworth, Lance 1978	+ Hutson, Don 1963	Newsome, Ozzie 1999
+ Badgro, Red 1981	Joiner, Charlie 1996	Pihos, Pete 1970
Berry, Raymond 1973	Largent, Steve 1995	Smith, Jackie 1994
Biletnikoff, Fred 1988	Lavelli, Dante 1975	Stallworth, John 2002
Casper, Dave 2002	Lofton, James 2003	Swann, Lynn 2001
+ Chamberlin, Guy 1965	Mackey, John 1992	Taylor, Charley 1984
Ditka, Mike 1988	Maynard, Don 1987	Warfield, Paul 1983
+ Fears, Tom 1970	McDonald, Tommy 1998	Winslow, Kellen 1995
+ Hewitt, Bill 1971	+ Millner, Wayne 1968	
Hirsch, Elroy (Crazylegs) ..1968	Mitchell, Bobby 1983	

Linemen (pre-World War II)

+ Edwards, Turk (T) 1969	+ Hubbard, Cal (T) 1963	+ Musso, George (T-G) 1982
+ Fortmann, Dan (G) 1985	+ Kiesling, Walt (G) 1966	+ Stydahar, Joe (T) 1967
+ Healey, Ed (T) 1964	+ Kinard, Bruiser (T) 1971	+ Trafton, George (C) 1964
+ Hein, Mel (C) 1963	+ Lyman, Link (T) 1964	+ Turner, Bulldog (C) 1966
+ Henry, Pete (T) 1963	+ Michalske, Mike (G) 1964	+ Wojciechowicz, Alex (C) ..1968

Offensive Linemen

Bednarik, Chuck (C-LB) 1967	Little, Larry (G) 1993	St. Clair, Bob (T) 1990
Brown, Roosevelt (T) 1975	Mack, Tom (G) 1999	Shaw, Billy (G) 1999
DeLamielleure, Joe (G) 2003	McCormack, Mike (T) 1984	Shell, Art (T) 1989
Dierdorf, Dan (T) 1996	Mix, Ron T-G) 1979	Slater, Jackie (T) 2001
Gatski, Frank (C) 1985	Munchak, Mike (G) 2001	Stephenson, Dwight (C) ..1998
Gregg, Forrest (T-G) 1977	Munoz, Anthony (T) 1998	Upshaw, Gene (G) 1987
+ Groza, Lou (T-PK) 1974	+ Musso, George (T-G) 1982	Yary, Ron (T) 2001
Hannah, John (G) 1991	Otto, Jim (C) 1980	+ Webster, Mike (C) 1997
Jones, Stan (T-G-DT) 1991	Parker, Jim (G) 1973	
Langer, Jim (C) 1987	Ringo, Jim (C) 1981	

Defensive Linemen

Atkins, Doug 1982	Hampton, Dan 2002	Page, Alan 1988
Bethea, Elvin 2003	Jones, Deacon 1980	Robustelli, Andy 1971
+ Buchanan, Buck 1990	+ Jordan, Henry 1995	Selmon, Lee Roy 1995
Creekmur, Lou 1996	Lilly, Bob 1980	Stautner, Ernie 1969
Davis, Willie 1981	Long, Howie 2000	+ Weinmeister, Arnie 1984
Donovan, Art 1968	Marchetti, Gino 1972	White, Randy 1994
+ Ford, Len 1976	+ Nomellini, Leo 1969	Willis, Bill 1977
Greene, Joe 1987	Olsen, Merlin 1982	Youngblood, Jack 2001

Linebackers

Bell, Bobby 1983	Ham, Jack 1988	+ Nitschke, Ray 1978
Buoniconti, Nick 2001	Hendricks, Ted 1990	Schmidt, Joe 1973
Butkus, Dick 1979	Huff, Sam 1982	Singletary, Mike 1998
Connor, George (DT-OT) . . .1975	Lambert, Jack 1990	Taylor, Lawrence 1999
+ George, Bill 1974	Lanier, Willie 1986	Wilcox, Dave 2000

Defensive Backs

Adderley, Herb 1980	Houston, Ken 1986	Renfro, Mel 1996
Barney, Lem 1992	Johnson, Jimmy 1994	+ Tunnell, Emlen 1967
Blount, Mel 1989	Krause, Paul 1998	Wilson, Larry 1978
Brown, Willie 1984	+ Lane, Dick (Night Train) . . .1974	Wood, Willie 1989
+ Christiansen, Jack 1970	Lary, Yale 1979	
Haynes, Michael 1997	Lott, Ronnie 2000	

Placekicker

Stenerud, Jan 1991

Coaches

+ Allen, George 2002	Grant, Bud 1994	+ Neale, Earle (Greasy) 1969
+ Brown, Paul 1967	+ Halas, George 1963	Noll, Chuck 1993
+ Ewbank, Weeb 1978	+ Lambeau, Curly 1963	+ Owen, Steve 1966
+ Flaherty, Ray 1976	+ Landry, Tom 1990	Shula, Don 1997
Gibbs, Joe 1996	Levy, Marv 2001	Stram, Hank 2003
Gillman, Sid 1983	+ Lombardi, Vince 1971	Walsh, Bill 1993

Contributors

+ Bell, Bert 1963	Hunt, Lamar 1972	+ Rooney, Art 1964
+ Bidwill, Charles 1967	+ Mara, Tim 1963	Rooney, Dan 2000
+ Carr, Joe 1963	Mara, Wellington 1997	+ Rozelle, Pete 1985
Davis, Al 1992	+ Marshall, George 1963	Schramm, Tex 1991
+ Finks, Jim 1995	+ Ray, Hugh (Shorty) 1966	
+ Halas, George 1963	+ Reeves, Dan 1967	

NFL's All-Time Team

Selected by the Pro Football Hall of Fame voters and released Aug. 1, 2000 as part of the NFL Century celebration.

Offense

Wide Receivers: Don Hutson and Jerry Rice
Tight End: John Mackey
Tackles: Roosevelt Brown and Anthony Munoz
Guards: John Hannah and Jim Parker
Center: Mike Webster
Quarterback: Johnny Unitas
Running Backs: Jim Brown and Walter Payton

Defense

Ends: Deacon Jones and Reggie White
Tackles: Joe Greene and Bob Lilly
Linebackers: Dick Butkus, Jack Ham and Lawrence Taylor
Cornerbacks: Mel Blount and Dick (Night Train) Lane
Safeties: Ronnie Lott and Larry Wilson

Specialists

Placekicker: Jan Stenerud
Punter: Ray Guy
Kick Returner: Gale Sayers

Punt Returner: Deion Sanders
Special Teams: Steve Tasker

GOLF

World Golf Hall of Fame

The World Golf Hall of Fame opened its doors in 1998 at the World Golf Village outside of Jacksonville, Fla. **Address:** 21 World Golf Place, St. Augustine, FL 32092. **Telephone:** (904) 940-4000. **Eligibility:** Professionals have three avenues into the WGHF. A PGA Tour player qualifies for the ballot if he has at least 10 victories in approved tournaments, or at least two victories among The Players Championship, Masters, U.S. Open, British Open and PGA Championship, is at least 40 years old and has been a member of the Tour for 10 years. A senior PGA Tour player qualifies if he has been a Senior Tour member for five years and has 20 wins between the PGA Tour and Senior Tour or five wins among the PGA majors, the Players Championship and the senior majors (U.S. Senior Open, Tradition, PGA Seniors' Championship and Senior Players Championship). Final selections for both Veteran's and Lifetime Achievement Categories are made by the Executive Committee of the World Golf Hall of Fame, which includes leaders from the major golf organizations.

Any player qualifying for the LPGA Hall automatically qualifies for the WGHF. Until 1999, nominees must have had played 10 years on the LPGA tour and won 30 official events, including two major championships; 35 official events and one major; or 40 official events and no majors. The eligibility requirements were loosened somewhat in 1999. The new guidelines are based on a system which awards two points for winning a major and one point for winning other tournaments, the Vare trophy (for lowest scoring average) and the player of the year award. Players must win at least one major, Vare trophy, or player of the year award and accumulate a total of 27 points to be inducted. For players not eligible for either the PGA Tour or the LPGA Hall of Fame, a body of over 300 international golf writers and historians will vote each year.

Members are listed with year of induction; (+) indicates deceased members.

Class of 2003 (3): MEN—**Leo Diegel** and **Nick Price**; WOMEN—**Chako Higuchi**;

Note: Annika Sorenstam (2003) and Karrie Webb (2005) already have enough points for entrance into the Hall but will be inducted after their 10th LPGA season.

Men

+ Anderson, Willie 1975	Faldo, Nick 1997	Nicklaus, Jack 1974
+ Armour, Tommy 1976	Floyd, Ray 1989	Norman, Greg 2001
+ Ball, John, Jr 1977	+ Guldahl, Ralph 1981	+ Ouimet, Francis 1974
Ballesteros, Seve 1999	+ Hagen, Walter 1974	Palmer, Arnold 1974
+ Barnes, Jim 1989	+ Hilton, Harold 1978	Player, Gary 1974
Beman, Deane 2000	+ Hogan, Ben 1974	Price, Nick 2003
Bolt, Tommy 2002	Irwin, Hale 1992	+ Robertson, Allan 2001
Bonallack, Sir Michael 2000	Jacklin, Tony 2002	+ Runyan, Paul 1990
+ Boros, Julius 1982	Jacobs, John 2000	+ Sarazen, Gene 1974
+ Braid, James 1976	+ Jones, Bobby 1974	Smith, Horton 1990
Burke, Jack Jr. 2000	Langer, Bernhard 2002	+ Snead, Sam 1974
Casper, Billy 1978	+ Little, Lawson 1980	+ Stewart, Payne 2001
Coles, Neil 2000	Littler, Gene 1990	+ Taylor, John H 1975
+ Cooper, Lighthorse Harry . .1992	+ Locke, Bobby 1977	Thomson, Peter 1988
+ Cotton, Sir Henry 1980	+ Mangrum, Lloyd 1998	+ Travers, Jerry 1976
Crenshaw, Ben 2002	+ Middlecoff, Cary 1986	+ Travis, Walter 1979
+ Demaret, Jimmy 1983	Miller, Johnny 1996	Trevino, Lee 1981
De Vicenzo, Roberto 1989	+ Morris, Tom Jr 1975	+ Vardon, Harry 1974
+ Diegel, Leo 2003	+ Morris, Tom Sr 1976	Watson, Tom 1988
+ Evans, Chick 1975	Nelson, Byron 1974	

Women

Alcott, Amy 1999	Higuchi, Chako 2003	Rawls, Betsy 1987
Berg, Patty 1974	+ Howe, Dorothy C.H 1978	Sheehan, Patty 1993
Bradley, Pat 1986	Inkster, Julie 2000	Suggs, Louise 1979
Carner, JoAnne 1985	Jameson, Betty 1951	+ Vare, Glenna Collett 1975
Caponi, Donna 2001	King, Betsy 1995	+ Wethered, Joyce 1975
Daniel, Beth 1999	Lopez, Nancy 1989	Whitworth, Kathy 1982
Hagge, Marlene 2002	Mann, Carol 1977	Wright, Mickey 1976
Haynie, Sandra 1977	Rankin, Judy 2000	+ Zaharias, Babe Didrikson . .1974

Contributors

Bell, Judy 2001	+ Harlow, Robert 1988	+ Ross, Donald 1977
Campbell, William 1990	+ Hope, Bob 1983	+ Solheim, Karsten 2001
+ Corcoran, Fred 1975	+ Jones, Robert Trent 1987	+ Shore, Dinah 1994
+ Crosby, Bing 1978	+ Penick, Harvey 2002	+ Tufts, Richard 1992
+ Dey, Joe 1975	+ Roberts, Clifford 1978	
+ Graffis, Herb 1977	Rodriguez, Chi Chi 1992	

Old PGA Hall Members Not in PGA/World Hall

The original PGA Hall of Fame was established in 1940 by the PGA of America, but abandoned after the 1982 inductions in favor of the PGA/World Hall of Fame. Thirty members of the old PGA Hall have been elected to the PGA/World Hall since then. Players yet to make the cut are listed below with year of induction into old PGA Hall.

+ Brady, Mike 1960	+ Ghezzi, Vic 1965	+ Picard, Henry 1961
+ Burke, Billy 1966	+ Harbert, Chick 1968	+ Revolta, Johnny 1963
+ Cruickshank, Bobby 1967	Harper, Chandler 1969	+ Shute, Denny 1957
+ Dudley, Ed 1964	+ Harrison, Dutch 1962	+ Smith, Alex 1940
+ Dutra, Olin 1962	+ Hutchison, Jock Sr 1959	+ Smith, Macdonald 1954
+ Farroll, Johnny 1961	+ McDermott, John 1940	+ Wood, Craig 1956
Ford, Doug 1975	+ McLeod, Fred 1960	

HOCKEY

Hockey Hall of Fame

Established in 1945 by the National Hockey League and opened in 1961. **Address:** BCE Place, 30 Yonge Street, Toronto, Ontario, M5E 1X8. **Telephone:** (416) 360-7735.

Eligibility: Nominated players and referees must be retired three years. However that waiting period has now been waived 10 times. Players that have had the waiting period waived are indicated with an asterisk. Voting done by 18-member panel made up of pro and amateur hockey personalities and media representatives. A 15-member Veterans Committee that selected older players was eliminated in 2000.

Class of 2003 (4): PLAYERS—G **Grant Fuhr**, Edmonton (1981-1991), Toronto (1992-93), Buffalo (1993-95), Los Angeles (1995), St. Louis (1996-99), Calgary (2000); C **Pat LaFontaine**, N.Y. Islanders (1984–91), Buffalo (1992-97), N.Y. Rangers (1998). BUILDER—**Mike Ilitch**, owner, and **Brian Kilrea**, coach.

Members are listed with year of induction; (+) indicates deceased members.

Forwards

+ Abel, Sid 1969	+ Gardner, Jimmy 1962	+ Nighbor, Frank 1947
+ Adams, Jack 1959	Gartner, Mike 2001	+ Noble, Reg 1962
+ Apps, Syl 1961	Geoffrion, Bernie 1972	+ O'Connor, Buddy 1988
Armstrong, George 1975	+ Gerard, Eddie 1945	+ Oliver, Harry 1967
Bailey, Ace 1975	Gilbert, Rod 1982	Olmstead, Bert 1985
+ Bain, Dan 1945	Gillies, Clark 2002	+ Patrick, Lynn 1980
+ Baker, Hobey 1945	+ Gilmour, Billy 1962	Perreault, Gilbert 1990
Barber, Bill 1990	Goulet, Michel 1998	+ Phillips, Tom 1945
+ Barry, Marty 1965	Gretzky, Wayne* 1999	+ Primeau, Joe 1963
Bathgate, Andy 1978	+ Griffis, Si 1950	Pulford, Bob 1991
+ Bauer, Bobby 1996	Hawerchuk, Dale 2001	+ Rankin, Frank 1961
Beliveau, Jean* 1972	+ Hay, George 1958	Ratelle, Jean 1985
+ Bentley, Doug 1964	+ Hextall, Bryan 1969	Richard, Henri 1979
+ Bentley, Max 1966	+ Hooper, Tom 1962	+ Richard, Maurice (Rocket)* 1961
+ Blake, Toe 1966	+ Howe, Gordie* 1972	+ Richardson, George 1950
Bossy, Mike 1991	+ Howe, Syd 1965	+ Roberts, Gordie 1971
+ Boucher, Frank 1958	Hull, Bobby 1983	+ Russel, Blair 1965
+ Bowie, Dubbie 1945	+ Hyland, Harry 1962	+ Russell, Ernie 1965
+ Broadbent, Punch 1962	+ Irvin, Dick 1958	+ Ruttan, Jack 1962
Bucyk, John (Chief) 1981	+ Jackson, Busher 1971	Savard, Denis 2000
+ Burch, Billy 1974	Joliat, Aurel 1947	+ Scanlan, Fred 1965
Clarke, Bobby 1987	+ Keats, Duke 1958	Schmidt, Milt 1961
+ Colville, Neil 1967	Kennedy, Ted (Teeder) 1966	+ Schriner, Sweeney 1962
+ Conacher, Charlie 1961	Keon, Dave 1986	+ Seibert, Oliver 1961
Conacher, Roy 1998	Kurri, Jari 2001	Shutt, Steve 1993
+ Cook, Bill 1952	Lach, Elmer 1966	+ Siebert, Babe 1964
+ Cook, Bun 1995	Lafleur, Guy 1988	Sittler, Darryl 1989
Cournoyer, Yvan 1982	LaFontaine, Pat 2003	+ Smith, Alf 1962
+ Cowley, Bill 1968	+ Lalonde, Newsy 1950	Smith, Clint 1991
+ Crawford, Rusty 1962	Laprade, Edgar 1993	+ Smith, Hooley 1972
+ Darragh, Jack 1962	Lemaire, Jacques 1984	+ Smith, Tommy 1973
+ Davidson, Scotty 1950	Lemieux, Mario* 1997	+ Stanley, Barney 1962
+ Day, Hap 1961	+ Lewis, Herbie 1989	Stastny, Peter 1998
Delvecchio, Alex 1977	Lindsay, Ted* 1966	+ Stewart, Nels 1962
+ Denneny, Cy 1959	+ MacKay, Mickey 1952	+ Stuart, Bruce 1961
Dionne, Marcel 1992	Mahovlich, Frank 1981	+ Taylor, Fred (Cyclone) 1947
Drillon, Gordie 1975	+ Malone, Joe 1950	+ Trihey, Harry 1950
+ Drinkwater, Graham 1950	Marshall, Jack 1965	Trottier, Bryan 1997
Dumart, Woody 1992	+ Maxwell, Fred 1962	Ullman, Norm 1982
+ Dunderdale, Tommy 1974	McDonald, Lanny 1992	+ Walker, Jack 1960
Dye, Babe 1970	+ McGee, Frank 1945	+ Walsh, Marty 1962
Esposito, Phil 1984	+ McGimsie, Billy 1962	Watson, Harry 1994
+ Farrell, Arthur 1965	Mikita, Stan 1983	+ Watson, Harry (Moose) 1962
Federko, Bernie 2002	Moore, Dickie 1974	+ Weiland, Cooney 1971
+ Foyston, Frank 1958	+ Morenz, Howie 1945	+ Westwick, Harry (Rat) 1962
+ Frederickson, Frank 1958	+ Mosienko, Bill 1965	+ Whitcroft, Fred 1962
Gainey, Bob 1992	Mullen, Joe 2000	

Goaltenders

+ Benedict, Clint 1965	Giacomin, Eddie 1987	+ Plante, Jacques 1978
Bower, Johnny 1976	+ Hainsworth, George 1961	Rayner, Chuck 1973
+ Brimsek, Frankie 1966	Hall, Glenn 1975	+ Sawchuk, Terry* 1971
+ Broda, Turk 1967	+ Hern, Riley 1962	Smith, Billy 1993
Cheevers, Gerry 1985	+ Holmes, Hap 1972	+ Thompson, Tiny 1959
+ Connell, Alex 1958	+ Hutton, J.B. (Bouse) 1962	Tretiak, Vladislav 1989
Dryden, Ken 1983	+ Lehman, Hughie 1958	+ Vezina, Georges 1945
+ Durnan, Bill 1964	+ LeSueur, Percy 1961	Worsley, Gump 1980
Esposito, Tony 1988	+ Lumley, Harry 1980	+ Worters, Roy 1969
Fuhr, Grant 2003	+ Moran, Paddy 1958	
+ Gardiner, Chuck 1945	Parent, Bernie 1984	

Defensemen

Boivin, Leo	1986	+ Hall, Joe	1961	+ Pitre, Didier	1962
+ Boon, Dickie	1952	+ Harvey, Doug	1973	Potvin, Denis	1991
Bouchard, Butch	1966	Horner, Red	1965	+ Pratt, Babe	1966
+ Boucher, George	1960	+ Horton, Tim	1977	Pronovost, Marcel	1978
+ Cameron, Harry	1962	Howell, Harry	1979	+ Pulford, Harvey	1945
+ Clancy, King	1958	+ Johnson, Ching	1958	Quackenbush, Bill	1976
+ Clapper, Dit*	1947	+ Johnson, Ernie	1952	Reardon, Kenny	1966
+ Cleghorn, Sprague	1958	Johnson, Tom	1970	Robinson, Larry	1995
+ Conacher, Lionel	1994	Kelly, Red*	1969	+ Ross, Art	1945
Coulter, Art	1974	Langway, Rod	2002	Salming, Borje	1996
+ Dutton, Red	1958	Laperriere, Jacques	1987	Savard, Serge	1986
Fetisov, Viacheslav	2001	Lapointe, Guy	1993	Seibert, Earl	1963
Flaman, Fernie	1990	+ Laviolette, Jack	1962	+ Shore, Eddie	1947
Gadsby, Bill	1970	+ Mantha, Sylvio	1960	+ Simpson, Joe	1962
+ Gardiner, Herb	1958	+ McNamara, George	1958	Stanley, Allan	1981
+ Goheen, F.X. (Moose)	1952	Orr, Bobby*	1979	+ Stewart, Jack	1964
+ Goodfellow, Ebbie	1963	Park, Brad	1988	+ Stuart, Hod	1945
+ Grant, Mike	1950	+ Patrick, Lester	1947	+ Wilson, Gordon (Phat)	1962
+ Green, Wilf (Shorty)	1962	Pilote, Pierre	1975		

Referees & Linesmen

Armstrong, Neil	1991	+ Hayes, George	1988	+ Smeaton, J. Cooper	1961
Ashley, John	1981	+ Hewitson, Bobby	1963	Storey, Red	1967
Chadwick, Bill	1964	+ Ion, Mickey	1961	Udvari, Frank	1973
D'Amico, John	1993	Pavelich, Matt	1987	van Hellemond, Andy	1999
+ Elliott, Chaucer	1961	+ Rodden, Mike	1962		

Builders

+ Adams, Charles	1960	+ Hewitt, W.A	1945	+ Patrick, Frank	1958
+ Adams, Weston W. Sr	1972	+ Hume, Fred	1962	+ Pickard, Allan	1958
+ Ahearn, Frank	1962	+ Ilitch, Mike	2003	+ Pilous, Rudy	1985
+ Ahearne, J.F. (Bunny)	1977	+ Imlach, Punch	1984	Poile, Bud	1990
+ Allan, Sir Montagu	1945	+ Ivan, Tommy	1964	Pollock, Sam	1978
Allen, Keith	1992	+ Jennings, Bill	1975	+ Raymond, Donat	1958
Arbour, Al	1996	+ Johnson, Bob	1992	+ Robertson, John Ross	1945
+ Ballard, Harold	1977	+ Juckes, Gordon	1979	+ Robinson, Claude	1945
+ Bauer, Fr. David	1989	+ Kilpatrick, John	1960	+ Ross, Philip	1976
+ Bickell, J.P.	1978	Kilrea, Brian	2003	Sather, Glen	1997
Bowman, Scotty	1991	+ Knox, Seymour III	1993	Sebetzki, Gunther	1995
+ Brown, George	1961	+ Leader, Al	1969	+ Selke, Frank	1960
+ Brown, Walter	1962	LeBel, Bob	1970	Sinden, Harry	1983
+ Buckland, Frank	1975	+ Lockhart, Tom	1965	+ Smith, Frank	1962
Bush, Walter	2000	+ Loicq, Paul	1961	+ Smythe, Conn	1958
Butterfield, Jack	1980	+ Mariucci, John	1985	Snider, Ed	1988
+ Calder, Frank	1945	Mathers, Frank	1992	+ Stanley, Lord of Preston	1945
+ Campbell, Angus	1964	+ McLaughlin, Frederic	1963	+ Sutherland, James	1945
+ Campbell, Clarence	1966	+ Milford, Jake	1984	+ Tarasov, Anatoli	1974
+ Cattarinich, Joseph	1977	Molson, Hartland	1973	Torrey, Bill	1995
+ Dandurand, Leo	1963	Morrison, Ian (Scotty)	1999	+ Turner, Lloyd	1958
Dilio, Frank	1964	+ Murray, Athol (Pere)	1998	+ Tutt, William Thayer	1978
+ Dudley, George	1958	+ Nelson, Francis	1945	Voss, Carl	1974
+ Dunn, James	1968	Neilson, Roger	2002	+ Waghorne, Fred	1961
Francis, Emile	1982	+ Norris, Bruce	1969	+ Wirtz, Arthur	1971
+ Gibson, Jack	1976	+ Norris, James D	1962	Wirtz, Bill	1976
+ Gorman, Tommy	1963	+ Norris, James Sr	1958	Ziegler, John	1987
+ Griffiths, Frank A.	1993	+ Northey, William	1945		
+ Hanley, Bill	1986	O'Brien, J.A	1962	**Note:** Alan Eagleson was inducted
+ Hay, Charles	1984	O'Neill, Brian	1994	into the Hockey Hall of Fame in 1989
+ Hendy, Jim	1968	Page, Fred	1993	but resigned in 1998 after being found
+ Hewitt, Foster	1965	Patrick, Craig	2001	guilty of fraud.

Foster Hewitt Award

First presented in 1984 by the NHL Broadcasters' Association for meritorious contributions by members of the NHLBA. Named in honor of Canada's legendary "Voice of Hockey," the Hewitt Award does not constitute induction into the Hall of Fame and is not necessarily an annual presentation.

Year		Year		Year		Year	
1984	Fred Cusick, Foster Hewitt, Danny Gallivan & Rene Lecavelier	1986	Wes McKnight & Lloyd Pettit	1992	Jim Robson	1999	Richard Garneau
		1987	Bob Wilson	1993	Al Shaver	2000	Bob Miller
		1988	Dick Irvin	1994	Ted Darling	2001	Mike Lange
		1989	Dan Kelly	1995	Brian McFarlane	2002	Gilles Tremblay
1985	Budd Lynch & Doug Smith	1990	Jiggs McDonald	1996	Bob Cole	2003	Rod Phillips
		1991	Bruce Martyn	1997	Gene Hart		
				1998	Howie Meeker		

Elmer Ferguson Award

First presented in 1984 by the Professional Hockey Writers' Association for meritorious contributions by members of the PHWA. Named in honor of the late Montreal newspaper reporter, the Ferguson Award does not constitute induction into the Hall of Fame and is not necessarily an annual presentation.

Year		Year		Year	
1984	Jacques Beauchamp, Jim Burchard, Red Burnett, Dink Carroll, Jim Coleman, Ted Damata, Marcel Desjardins, Jack Dulmage, Milt Dunnell, Elmer Ferguson, Tom Fitzgerald, Trent Frayne, Al Laney, Joe Nichols, Basil O'Meara, Jim Vipond & Lewis Walter	1986	Dick Johnston, Leo Monahan & Tim Moriarty	1995	Jake Gatecliff
		1987	Bill Brennan, Rex MacLeod, Ben Olan & Fran Rosa	1996	No award
				1997	Ken McKenzie
		1988	Jim Proudfoot & Scott Young	1998	Yvon Pedneault
		1989	Claude Larochelle & Frank Orr	1999	Russ Conway
		1990	Bertrand Raymond	2000	Jim Matheson
		1991	Hugh Delano	2001	Eric Duhatschek
1985	Charlie Barton, Red Fisher, George Gross, Zotique L'Esperance, Charles Mayer & Andy O'Brien	1992	No award	2002	Kevin Paul Dupont
		1993	Al Strachan	2003	Michael Farber
		1994	No award		

U.S. Hockey Hall of Fame

Established in 1968 by the Eveleth (Minn.) Civic Association Project H Committee and opened in 1973. **Address:** 801 Hat Trick Ave., P.O. Box 657, Eveleth, MN 55734. **Telephone:** (218) 744-5167.

Eligibility: Nominated players and referees must be American-born and retired five years; coaches must be American-born and must have coached predominantly American teams. Voting done by 12-member panel made up of Hall of Fame members and U.S. hockey officials.

Class of 2003 (4): COACH—**John Cunniff**; PLAYERS—**Richard Dougherty**, **Mark Howe** and **Pat LaFontaine**.

Members are listed with year of induction; (+) indicates deceased members.

Players

+ Abel, Clarence (Taffy)	1973	Fusco, Mark	2002	McCartan, Jack	1983
+ Baker, Hobey	1973	Fusco, Scott	2002	Moe, Bill	1974
Bartholome, Earl	1977	+ Garrison, John	1974	Morrow, Ken	1995
+ Bessone, Peter	1978	Garrity, Jack	1986	+ Moseley, Fred	1975
Blake, Bob	1985	+ Goheen, Frank (Moose)	1973	Mullen, Joe	1998
Boucha, Henry	1995	Grant, Wally	1994	+ Murray, Hugh (Muzz) Sr	1987
+ Brimsek, Frankie	1973	+ Harding, Austie	1975	+ Nelson, Hub	1978
Broten, Neal	2000	Howe, Mark	2003	+ Nyrop, William D.	1997
Cavanaugh, Joe	1994	Iglehart, Stewart	1975	Olson, Eddie	1977
+ Chaisson, Ray	1974	Ikola, Willard	1990	+ Owen, George	1973
Chase, John	1973	Johnson, Paul	2001	+ Palmer, Winthrop	1973
Christian, Bill	1984	Johnson, Virgil	1974	Paradise, Bob	1989
Christian, Dave	2001	+ Karakas, Mike	1973	+ Purpur, Clifford (Fido)	1974
Christian, Roger	1989	Kirrane, Jack	1987	Ramsey, Mike	2001
Cleary, Bill	1976	LaFontaine, Pat	2003	Riley, Bill	1977
Cleary, Bob	1981	+ Lane, Myles	1973	Riley, Joe	2002
+ Conroy, Tony	1975	Langevin, Dave	1993	+ Romnes, Elwin (Doc)	1973
Curran, Mike	1998	Langway, Rod	1999	+ Rondeau, Dick	1985
+ Dahlstrom, Carl (Cully)	1973	Larson, Reed	1996	Sheehy, Timothy	1997
+ DesJardins, Vic	1974	+ Linder, Joe	1975	Watson, Gordie	1999
+ Desmond, Richard	1988	+ LoPresti, Sam	1973	+ Williams, Tom	1981
+ Dill, Bob	1979	+ Mariucci, John	1973	+ Winters, Frank (Coddy)	1973
Dougherty, Richard	2003	Matchefts, John	1991	+ Yackel, Ken	1986
+ Everett, Doug	1974	+ Mather, Bruce	1998		
Ftorek, Robbie	1991	Mayasich, John	1976		

Coaches

+ Almquist, Oscar	1983	Heyliger, Vic	1974	Pleban, Connie	1990
Bessone, Amo	1992	+ Holt Jr., Charles E.	1997	Ramsay, Mike	2001
+ Brooks, Herb	1990	Ikola, Willard	1990	Riley, Jack	1979
Ceglarski, Len	1992	+ Jeremiah, Eddie	1973	+ Ross, Larry	1988
+ Cunniff, John	2003	Johnson, Bob	1991	+ Thompson, Cliff	1973
+ Fullerton, James	1992	Johnson, Paul	2001	+ Stewart, Bill	1982
Gambucci, Sergio	1996	Kelley, Jack	1993	Watson, Sid	1999
+ Gordon, Malcolm	1973	+ Kelly, John (Snooks)	1974	+ Winsor, Ralph	1973
Harkness, Ned	1994	Nanne, Lou	1998	Woog, Doug	2002

Referee

Chadwick, Bill 1974

Contributor

+ Schulz, Charles M. 1993

Administrators

+ Brown, George	1973	+ Jennings, Bill	1981	Pleau, Larry	2000
+ Brown, Walter	1973	+ Kahler, Nick	1980	Ridder, Bob	1976
Bush, Walter	1980	+ Lockhart, Tom	1973	Trumble, Hal	1970
Clark, Don	1978	Marvin, Cal	1982	+ Tutt, Thayer	1973
Claypool, Jim	1995	Palazzari, Doug	2000	Wirtz, Bill	1967
+ Gibson, J.L. (Doc)	1973	Patrick, Craig	1996	+ Wright, Lyle	1973

HORSE RACING

National Museum of Racing and Hall of Fame

Established in 1950 by the Saratoga Springs Racing Association and opened in 1955. **Address:** National Museum of Racing and Hall of Fame, 191 Union Ave., Saratoga Springs, NY 12866. **Telephone:** (518) 584-0400.

Eligibility: Nominated horses must be retired five years; jockeys must be active at least 15 years; trainers must be active at least 25 years. Voting done by 125-member panel of horse racing media.

Class of 2003 (4): JOCKEY—**Mike Smith**. TRAINER—**Hubert "Sonny" Hine**. HORSES—**Dance Smartly** and **Precisionist**.

Members are listed with year of induction; (+) indicates deceased members.

Jockeys

+ Adams, Frank (Dooley)* 1970	+ Garner, Andrew (Mack) 1969	+ Patrick, Gil 1970
+ Adams, John 1965	+ Garrison, Snapper 1955	Pincay, Laffit Jr. 1975
+ Aitcheson, Joe Jr.* 1978	+ Gomez, Avelino 1982	+ Purdy, Sam 1970
+ Arcaro, Eddie 1958	+ Griffin, Henry 1956	+ Reiff, John 1956
Atkinson, Ted 1957	+ Guerin, Eric 1972	+ Robertson, Alfred 1971
Baeza, Braulio 1976	Hartack, Bill 1959	Rotz, John L. 1983
Bailey, Jerry 1995	Hawley, Sandy 1992	+ Sande, Earl 1955
+ Barbee, George 1996	+ Johnson, Albert 1971	+ Schilling, Carroll 1970
+ Bassett, Carroll* 1972	+ Knapp, Willie 1969	Shoemaker, Bill 1958
Baze, Russell 1999	Krone, Julie 2000	+ Simms, Willie 1977
+ Blum, Walter 1987	+ Kummer, Clarence 1972	+ Sloan, Todhunter 1955
+ Bostwick, George H.* 1968	+ Kurtsinger, Charley 1967	Smith, Mike 2003
+ Boulmetis, Sam 1973	+ Loftus, Johnny 1959	+ Smithwick, A. Patrick* 1973
+ Brooks, Steve 1963	Longden, Johnny 1958	Stevens, Gary 1997
Brumfield, Don 1996	Maher, Danny 1955	+ Stout, James 1968
+ Burns, Tommy 1983	McAtee, Linus 1956	+ Taral, Fred 1955
+ Butwell, Jimmy 1984	McCarron, Chris 1989	+ Tuckman, Bayard Jr.* 1973
+ Byers, J.D. (Dolly) 1967	+ McCreary, Conn 1975	Turcotte, Ron 1979
Cauthen, Steve 1994	+ McKinney, Rigan 1968	+ Turner, Nash 1955
+ Coltiletti, Frank 1970	+ McLaughlin, James 1955	Ussery, Robert 1980
Cordero, Angel Jr. 1988	+ Miller, Walter 1955	Vasquez, Jacinto 1998
+ Crawford, Robert (Specs)* . . .1973	+ Murphy, Isaac 1955	Velasquez, Jorge 1990
Day, Pat 1991	+ Neves, Ralph 1960	+ Westrope, Jack 2002
Delahoussaye, Eddie 1993	+ Notter, Joe 1963	+ Woolfe, George 1955
Ensor, Lavelle (Buddy) 1962	+ O'Connor, Winnie 1956	+ Workman, Raymond 1956
+ Fator, Laverne 1955	+ Odom, George 1955	Ycaza, Manuel 1977
Fires, Earlie 2001	+ O'Neill, Frank 1956	
Fishback, Jerry* 1992	+ Parke, Ivan 1978	*Steeplechase jockey

Harness Racing Museum & Hall of Fame

Established by the U.S. Harness Writers Association (USHWA) in 1958. **Address:** Trotting Horse Museum, 240 Main Street, P.O. Box 590, Goshen, NY 10924; **Telephone:** (845) 294-6330.

Eligibility: Open to all harness racing drivers, trainers and executives. Voting done by USHWA membership. There are 84 members of the Living Hall of Fame, but only the 47 drivers and trainer-drivers are listed below.

Class of 2003 (3): TRAINER/DRIVERS—**James Doherty, Berndt Lindstedt** and **Robert McIntosh.**

Members are listed with years of induction; (+) indicates deceased members.

Trainer-Drivers

Abbatiello, Carmine 1986	Farrington, Bob 1980	Miller, Del 1969
Abbatiello, Tony 1995	Filion, Herve 1976	+ O'Brien, Joe 1971
Ackerman, Doug 1995	+ Garnsey, Glen 1983	O'Donnell, Bill 1991
+ Avery, Earle 1975	Galbraith, Clint 1990	Patterson, John Sr 1994
+ Baldwin, Ralph 1972	Gilmour, Buddy 1990	+ Pownall, Harry 1971
Beissinger, Howard 1975	Harner, Levi 1986	Remmem, Ray 1998
Bostwick, Dunbar 1989	Harvey, Harry M. 2002	Riegle, Gene 1992
+ Cameron, Del 1975	+ Haughton, Billy 1969	+ Russell, Sanders 1971
Campbell, John 1991	+ Hodgins, Clint 1973	+ Shively, Bion 1968
+ Chapman, John 1980	Insko, Del 1981	Sholty, George 1985
Cruise, Jimmy 1987	Kopas, Jack 1996	Simpson, John Sr 1972
Dancer, Stanley 1970	Lachance, Mike 1996	+ Smart, Curly 1970
Dancer, Vernon 2001	Lindstedt, Berndt 2003	Sylvester, Charles 1998
Dennis, Jim 2002	Magee, Dave 2001	Waples, Keith 1987
Doherty, James 2003	Manzi, Catello 2002	Waples, Ron 1994
+ Ervin, Frank 1969	McIntosh, Robert 2003	

Horse Racing (Cont.)
Trainers

+ Barrera, Laz 1979
+ Bedwell, H. Guy 1971
+ Brown, Edward D. 1984
   Burch, Elliot 1980
+ Burch, Preston M. 1963
+ Burch, W.P. 1955
+ Burlew, Fred 1973
+ Childs, Frank E. 1968
+ Clark, Henry 1982
+ Cocks, W. Burling 1985
   Conway, James P. 1996
   Croll, Jimmy 1994
   Delp, Bud 2002
   Drysdale, Neil 2000
+ Duke, William 1956
+ Feustel, Louis 1964
+ Fitzsimmons, J. (Sunny Jim) . 1958
   Frankel, Bobby 1995
+ Gaver, John M. 1966
+ Healey, Thomas 1955
+ Hildreth, Samuel 1955
+ Hine, Hubert (Sonny) 2003
+ Hirsch, Max 1959
+ Hirsch, W.J. (Buddy) 1982
+ Hitchcock, Thomas Sr. 1973
+ Hughes, Hollie 1973

+ Hyland, John 1956
+ Jacobs, Hirsch 1958
   Jerkens, H. Allen 1975
   Johnson, Philip 1997
+ Johnson, William R. 1986
+ Jolley, LeRoy 1987
+ Jones, Ben A. 1958
+ Jones, H.A. (Jimmy) 1959
+ Joyner, Andrew 1955
   Kelly, Tom 1993
+ Laurin, Lucien 1977
+ Lewis, J. Howard 1969
   Lukas, D. Wayne 1999
+ Luro, Horatio 1980
   Mandella, Richard 2001
+ Madden, John 1983
+ Maloney, Jim 1989
   Martin, Frank (Pancho) 1981
   McAnally, Ron 1990
+ McDaniel, Henry 1956
+ Miller, MacKenzie 1987
+ Molter, William, Jr. 1960
   Mott, Bill 1998
+ Mulholland, Winbert 1967
+ Neloy, Eddie 1983
   Nerud, John 1972

+ Parke, Burley . . . . , . . 1986
+ Penna, Angel Sr. 1988
+ Pincus, Jacob 1988
+ Rogers, John 1955
+ Rowe, James Sr. 1955
   Schulhofer, Scotty 1992
   Sheppard, Jonathan 1990
+ Smith, Robert A. 1976
   Smith, Tom 2001
+ Smithwick, Mike 1976
+ Stephens, Woody 1976
   Tenny, Mesh 1991
+ Thompson, H.J. 1969
+ Trotsek, Harry 1984
   Van Berg, Jack 1985
+ Van Berg, Marion 1970
+ Veitch, Sylvester 1977
+ Walden, Robert 1970
   Walsh, Michael 1997
+ Ward, Sherrill 1978
   Whiteley, Frank Jr. 1978
+ Whittingham, Charlie 1974
+ Williamson, Ansel 1998
   Winfrey, W.C. (Bill) 1971

Horses
Year foaled in parentheses.

   A.P. Indy (1989) 2000
+ Ack Ack (1966) 1986
   Affectionately (1960) 1989
+ Affirmed (1975) 1980
   All-Along (1979) 1990
+ Alsab (1939) 1976
+ Alydar (1975) 1989
   Alysheba (1984) 1993
+ American Eclipse (1814) . . . 1970
+ Armed (1941) 1963
+ Artful (1902) 1956
+ Arts and Letters (1966) 1994
+ Assault (1943) 1964
+ Battleship (1927) 1969
+ Bayakoa (1984) 1998
+ Bed O'Roses (1947) 1976
+ Beldame (1901) 1956
+ Ben Brush (1893) 1955
+ Bewitch (1945) 1977
+ Bimelech (1937) 1990
+ Black Gold (1919) 1989
+ Black Helen (1932) 1991
+ Blue Larkspur (1926) 1957
+ Bold 'n Determined (1977) . . 1997
+ Bold Ruler (1954) 1973
+ Bon Nouvel (1960) 1976
+ Boston (1833) 1955
+ Broomstick (1901) 1956
+ Buckpasser (1963) 1970
+ Busher (1942) 1964
+ Bushranger (1930) 1967
+ Cafe Prince (1970) 1985
+ Carry Back (1958) 1975
+ Cavalcade (1931) 1993
+ Challendon (1936) 1977
+ Chris Evert (1971) 1988
+ Cicada (1959) 1967
   Cigar (1990) 2002
+ Citation (1945) 1959
+ Coaltown (1945) 1983
+ Colin (1905) 1956
+ Commando (1898) 1956

+ Count Fleet (1940) 1961
+ Crusader (1923) 1995
+ Dahlia (1971) 1981
+ Damascus (1964) 1974
   Dance Smartly (1989) 2003
+ Dark Mirage (1965) 1974
+ Davona Dale (1976) 1985
+ Desert Vixen (1970) 1979
+ Devil Diver (1939) 1980
+ Discovery (1931) 1969
+ Domino (1891) 1955
+ Dr. Fager (1964) 1971
   Easy Goer (1986) 1997
+ Eight 30 (1936) 1994
+ Elkridge (1938) 1966
+ Emperor of Norfolk (1885) . . 1988
+ Equipoise (1928) 1957
+ Exceller (1973) 1999
+ Exterminator (1915) 1957
+ Fairmount (1921) 1985
+ Fair Play (1905) 1956
+ Firenze (1885) 1981
   Flatterer (1979) 1994
+ Foolish Pleasure (1972) 1995
+ Forego (1971) 1979
+ Fort Marcy (1964) 1998
+ Gallant Bloom (1966) 1977
+ Gallant Fox (1927) 1957
+ Gallant Man (1954) 1987
+ Gallorette (1942) 1962
+ Gamely (1964) 1980
   Genuine Risk (1977) 1986
+ Good and Plenty (1900) . . . 1956
+ Go For Wand (1987) 1996
+ Granville (1933) 1997
+ Grey Lag (1918) 1957
+ Gun Bow (1960) 1999
+ Hamburg (1895) 1986
+ Hanover (1884) 1955
+ Henry of Navarre (1891) . . . 1985
+ Hill Prince (1947) 1991
+ Hindoo (1878) 1955

   Holy Bull (1991) 2001
+ Imp (1894) 1965
+ Jay Trump (1957) 1971
   John Henry (1975) 1990
+ Johnstown (1936) 1992
+ Jolly Roger (1922) 1965
+ Kingston (1884) 1955
+ Kelso (1957) 1967
+ Kentucky (1861) 1983
   Lady's Secret (1982) 1992
+ La Prevoyante (1970) 1995
+ L'Escargot (1963) 1977
+ Lexington (1850) 1955
+ Longfellow (1867) 1971
+ Luke Blackburn (1877) 1956
+ Majestic Prince (1966) 1988
+ Man o' War (1917) 1957
   Maskette (1906) 2001
   Miesque (1984) 1999
+ Miss Woodford (1880) 1967
+ Myrtlewood (1933) 1979
+ Nashua (1952) 1965
+ Native Dancer (1950) 1963
+ Native Diver (1959) 1978
+ Needles (1953) 2000
+ Neji (1950) 1966
+ Noor (1945) 2002
+ Northern Dancer (1961) . . . 1976
+ Oedipus (1941) 1978
+ Old Rosebud (1911) 1968
+ Omaha (1932) 1965
+ Pan Zareta (1910) 1972
+ Parole (1873) 1984
   Personal Ensign (1984) 1993
   Paseana (1987) 2001
+ Peter Pan (1904) 1956
   Precisionist (1983) 2003
   Princess Rooney (1980) 1991
+ Real Delight (1949) 1987
+ Regret (1912) 1957
+ Reigh Count (1925) 1978
   Riva Ridge (1969) 1998

+ Roamer (1911) 1981	+ Silver Spoon (1956) 1978	+ Tom Fool (1949) 1960
+ Roseben (1901) 1956	+ Sir Archy (1805) 1955	+ Top Flight (1929) 1966
+ Round Table (1954) 1972	+ Sir Barton (1916) 1957	+ Tosmah (1961) 1984
+ Ruffian (1972) 1976	Slew o'Gold (1980) 1992	+ Twenty Grand (1928) 1957
+ Ruthless (1864) 1975	+ Sun Beau (1925) 1996	+ Twilight Tear (1941) 1963
+ Salvator (1886) 1955	+ Sunday Silence (1986) 1996	+ War Admiral (1934) 1958
+ Sarazen (1921) 1957	+ Stymie (1941) 1975	+ Whirlaway (1938) 1959
+ Seabiscuit (1933) 1958	+ Susan's Girl (1969) 1976	+ Whisk Broom II (1907) 1979
+ Searching (1952) 1978	+ Swaps (1952) 1966	Winning Colors (1985) . . .2000
+ Seattle Slew (1974) 1981	+ Sword Dancer (1956) 1977	Zaccio (1976) 1990
+ Secretariat (1970) 1974	+ Sysonby (1902) 1956	+ Zev (1920) 1983
Serena's Song (1992) 2002	+ Ta Wee (1966) 1994	
+ Shuvee (1966) 1975	+ Tim Tam (1955) 1985	

Exemplars of Racing

+ Hanes, John W 1982	+ Mellon, Paul 1989	Widener, George D 1971
+ Jeffords, Walter M 1973		

MEDIA

National Sportscasters and Sportswriters Hall of Fame

Established in 1959 by the National Sportscasters and Sportswriters Association. A permanent museum for the NSSA Hall of Fame opened on May 1, 2000. **Address:** 322 East Innes St., Salisbury, NC 28144. **Telephone:** (704) 633-4275.

Eligibility: Nominees must be active for at least 25 years. Voting done by NSSA membership and other media representatives.
Class of 2003 (2): **Will McDonough** and **Bob Wolff**.

Members are listed with year of induction; (+) indicates deceased members.

Sportscasters

+ Allen, Mel 1972	Harwell, Ernie 1989	+ Nelson, Lindsey 1979
+ Barber, Walter (Red) 1973	+ Hearn, Chick 1997	+ Prince, Bob 1986
+ Brickhouse, Jack 1983	+ Hodges, Russ 1975	Schenkel, Chris 1981
+ Buck, Jack 1990	+ Hoyt, Waite 1987	+ Scott, Ray 1982
+ Caray, Harry 1989	+ Husing, Ted 1963	Scully, Vin 1991
+ Cosell, Howard 1993	Jackson, Keith 1995	Simpson, Jim 2000
+ Dean, Dizzy 1976	+ McCarthy, Clem 1970	+ Stern, Bill 1974
+ Dunphy, Don 1986	McKay, Jim 1987	Summerall, Pat 1994
+ Elson, Bob 1995	+ McNamee, Graham 1964	Whitaker, Jack 2001
Enberg, Dick 1996	Michaels, Al 1998	Wolff, Bob 2003
+ Glickman, Marty 1992	Miller, Jon 1999	
Gowdy, Curt 1981	Murphy, Bob 2002	

Sportswriters

Anderson, Dave 1990	+ Graham, Frank Sr. 1995	+ Povich, Shirley 1984
Bisher, Furman 1989	+ Grimsley, Will 1987	+ Rice, Grantland 1962
Broeg, Bob 1997	Heinz, W.C. 2001	+ Runyon, Damon 1964
+ Burick, Si 1985	Izenberg, Jerry 2000	Russell, Fred 1988
+ Cannon, Jimmy 1986	Jenkins, Dan 1996	Sherrod, Blackie 1991
+ Carmichael, John P. 1994	+ Kieran, John 1971	+ Smith, Walter (Red) 1977
Collins, Bud 2002	+ Lardner, Ring 1967	+ Spink, J.G. Taylor 1969
+ Connor, Dick 1992	+ McDonough, Will 2003	+ Stedman, John 1999
+ Considine, Bob 1980	+ Murphy, Jack 1988	Vecsey, George 2001
+ Daley, Arthur 1976	+ Murray, Jim 1978	+ Ward, Arch 1973
Deford, Frank 1998	Olderman, Murray 1993	+ Woodward, Stanley 1974
Durslag, Mel 1995	+ Parker, Dan 1975	
+ Gould, Alan 1990	Pope, Edwin 1994	

MOTORSPORTS

Motorsports Hall of Fame of America

Established in 1989. **Mailing Address:** P.O. Box 194, Novi, MI 48376. **Telephone:** (248) 349-7223.

Eligibility: Nominees must be retired at least three years or engaged in their area of motorsports for at least 20 years. Areas include: open wheel, stock car, dragster, sports car, motorcycle, off road, power boat, air racing, land speed records, historic and at-large.

Class of 2003 (8): DRIVERS—**Tommy Hinnershitz** (sprint cars), **Mel Kenyon** (midget cars), **Gary Nixon** (motorcycles) and **Darrell Waltrip** (stock cars). CONTRIBUTORS—**Bob Bondurant**, **Ed Donovan**, **Ted Jones** and **Bill Simpson**.

Members are listed with year of induction; (+) indicates deceased members.

Drivers

Allison, Bobby 1992	Breedlove, Craig 1993	Chrisman, Art 1997
Andretti, Mario 1990	Bryan, Jimmy 1999	+ Clark, Jim 1990
Arfons, Art 1991	+ Campbell, Sir Malcolm 1994	+ Cook, Betty 1996
+ Baker, Buck 1998	+ Cantrell, Bill 1992	+ Cooper, Earl 2001
+ Baker, Cannonball 1989	+ Chenoweth, Dean 1991	Cunningham, Briggs 1997
+ Bettenhausen, Tony 1997	+ Chevrolet, Gaston 2002	+ Davis, Jim 1997

Motorsports (Cont.)

D'Eath, Tom 2000	Johncock, Gordon 2002	Ongais, Danny 2000
DeCoster, Roger 1994	Johnson, Junior 1991	Parks, Wally 1993
+ DePalma, Ralph 1992	Jones, Parnelli 1992	Pearson, David 1993
+ DePaolo, Peter 1995	Kalitta, Connie 1992	+ Petrali, Joe 1992
+ Donahue, Mark 1990	Kenyon, Mel 2003	+ Petty, Lee 1996
+ Earnhardt, Dale 2002	+ Kurtis, Frank 1999	Petty, Richard 1989
Fittipaldi, Emerson 2001	Lawson, Eddie 2002	Prudhomme, Don 1991
Flock, Tim 1999	Leonard, Joe 1991	Resweber, Carroll 1998
Follmer, George 1999	+ Lockhart, Frank 1999	Redman, Brian 2002
Foyt, A.J. 1989	Lorenzen, Fred 2001	+ Revson, Peter 1996
Garlits, Don 1989	+ McLaren, Bruce 1995	+ Roberts, Fireball 1995
Glidden, Bob 1994	Mann, Dick 1993	Roberts, Kenny 1990
+ Gregg, Peter 2000	Markle, Bart 1999	Rutherford, Johnny 1996
Gurney, Dan 1991	+ Mays, Rex 1995	Seebold, Bill 1999
Hanauer, Chip 1995	McEwen, Tom 2001	+ Shaw, Wilbur 1991
Hannah, Bob 2000	Mears, Rick 1998	Slovak, Mira 2001
+ Hanks, Sam 2000	+ Meyer, Louis 1993	Smith, Malcolm 1996
+ Harroun, Ray 2000	+ Miles, Ken 2001	Spencer, Freddie 2001
Hart, C.J. 1999	+ Milton, Tommy 1998	+ Thompson, Mickey 1990
Hill, Eddie 2002	Muldowney, Shirley 1990	Unser, Al 1991
Hill, Phil 1989	+ Muncy, Bill 1989	Unser, Bobby 1994
+ Hinnershitz, Tommy 2003	+ Murphy, Jimmy 1998	+ Vukovich, Bill Sr 1992
+ Holbert, Al 1993	+ Musson, Ron 1993	Waltrip, Darrell 2003
+ Horn, Ted 1993	Nickelson, Don 1998	Ward, Rodger 1995
+ Hulme, Denis 1998	Nixon, Gary 2003	+ Wood, Gar 1990
·Jarrett, Ned 1997	+ Nordskog, Bob 1997	Yarborough, Cale 1994
Jenkins, Bill (Grumpy) 1996	+ Oldfield, Barney 1989	

Pilots

Cleland, Cook 2000	+ Earhart, Amelia 1992	+ Mantz, Paul 2002
+ Cochran, Jacqueline 1993	+ Falck, Bill 1994	Shelton, Lyle 1999
+ Curtiss, Glenn 1990	Greenmayer, Darryl 1997	+ Turner, Roscoe 1991
+ Doolittle, Jimmy 1989	LeVier, Tony 2001	+ Steve Wittman 2002

Contributors

+ Agajanian, J.C 1992	+ Ford, Henry 1996	Penske, Roger 1995
Bignotti, George 1993	+ France, Bill Sr. 1990	+ Rickenbacker, Eddie 1994
Black, Keith 1995	Granatelli, Andy 2001	+ Rose, Mauri 1996
Bondurant, Bob 2003	Hall, Jim 1994	Shelby, Carroll 1992
+ Brawner, Clint 1998	+ Hulman, Tony 1991	Simpson, Bill 2003
Chapman, Colin 1997	+ Jones, Ted 2003	Watson, A.J. 1996
+ Chevrolet, Louis 1995	+ Kiekhaefer, Carl 1998	Wood, Glen 2000
+ Donovan, Ed 2003	Little, Bernie 1994	Wood, Leonard 2000
Duesenberg, Fred 1997	+ Miller, Harry 1999	+ Yunick, Smokey 2000
Economaki, Chris 1994	+ Offenhauser, Fred 2002	

International Motorsports Hall of Fame

Established in 1990 by the International Motorsports Hall of Fame Commission. **Mailing Address:** P.O. Box 1018, Talladega, AL 35160. **Telephone:** (256) 362-5002.

Eligibility: Nominees must be retired from their specialty in motorsports for five years. Voting done by 150-member panel made up of the world-wide auto racing media.

Class of 2003 (5): DRIVERS—**Emerson Fittipaldi** (Open Wheel) and **Mel Kenyon** (Midget Cars). CONTRIBUTORS—**A.J. Watson**, **Ray Fox** and **Briggs Cunningham**.

Members are listed with year of induction; (+) indicates deceased members.

Drivers

Allison, Bobby 1993	Foyt, A.J. 2000	Lorenzen, Fred 1991
Andretti, Mario 2000	+ Gregg, Peter 1992	+ Lund, Tiny 1994
+ Ascari, Alberto 1992	Gurney, Dan 1990	+ Mays, Rex 1993
+ Ascari, Alberto 1992	Hailwood, Mike 2001	+ McLaren, Bruce 1991
+ Baker, Buck 1990	+ Haley, Donald 1996	+ Meyer, Louis 1992
Bonnett, Neil 2001	+ Hill, Graham 1990	Moss, Stirling 1990
Bettenhausen, Tony 1991	Hill, Phil 1991	+ Nuvolari, Tazio 1998
Brabham, Jack 1990	+ Holbert, Al 1993	+ Oldfield, Barney 1990
Bryan, Jimmy 2001	+ Hulme, Denis 2002	Parsons, Benny 1994
+ Campbell, Sir Malcolm 1990	Ickx, Jacky 2002	Pearson, David 1993
+ Caracciola, Rudolph 1998	+ Isaac, Bobby 1996	+ Petty, Lee 1990
+ Clark, Jim 1990	Jarrett, Ned 1991	Piquet, Nelson 2000
+ DePalma, Ralph 1991	Johncock, Gordon 1999	Prodhomme, Don 2000
+ Donahue, Mark 1990	Johnson, Junior 1990	Prost, Alain 1999
+ Evans, Richie 1996	Jones, Parnelli 1990	+ Richmond, Tim 2002
+ Fangio, Juan Manuel 1990	Kenyon, Mel 2003	+ Roberts, Fireball 1990
Fittipaldi, Emerson 2003	+ Kulwicki, Alan 2002	Roberts, Kenny 1992
Flock, Tim 1991	Lauda, Niki 1993	Rose, Mauri 1994

Rutherford, Johnny 1996	
Scott, Wendell 1999	
+ Senna, Ayrton 2000	
+ Shaw, Wilbur 1991	
Smith, Louise 1999	
Stewart, Jackie 1990	

Surtees, John 1996
+ Thomas, Herb 1994
+ Turner, Curtis 1992
Unser, Al Sr. 1998
Unser, Bobby 1990
+ Vukovich, Bill 1991

Ward Rodger 1992
+ Weatherly, Joe 1994
Wood, Glen 2002
Yarborough, Cale 1993

Contributors

Bignotti, George 1993
Breedlove, Craig 2000
+ Bugatti, Ettore 2002
+ Chapman, Colin 1994
+ Chevrolet, Louis 1992
+ Cunningham, Briggs 2003
+ Ferrari, Enzo 1994
+ Ford, Henry 1993
Fox, Ray 2003

+ France, Bill Sr 1990
Granatelli, Andy 1992
+ Hulman, Tony 1990
Hyde, Harry 1999
Marcum, John 1994
+ Matthews, Banjo 1998
Moody, Ralph 1994
+ Offenhauser, Fred 2001
Parks, Wally 1992

Penske, Roger 1998
+ Porsche, Ferdinand 1996
+ Rickenbacker, Eddie 1992
Shelby, Carroll 1991
+ Thompson, Mickey 1990
Watson, A.J. 2003
+ Yunick, Smokey 1990

OLYMPICS

U.S. Olympic Hall of Fame

Established in 1983 by the United States Olympic Committee. **Mailing Address:** U.S. Olympic Committee, 1750 East Boulder Street, Colorado Springs, CO 80909. Plans for a permanent museum site have been suspended due to lack of funding. **Telephone:** (719) 866-4529.

Eligibility: Nominated athletes must be five years removed from active competition. Voting done by National Sportscasters and Sportswriters Association, Hall of Fame members and the USOC board members of directors.

Voting for membership in the Hall was suspended in 1993.

Members are listed with year of induction; (+) indicates deceased members.

Teams

1956 Basketball Dick Boushka, Carl Cain, Chuck Darling, Bill Evans, Gib Ford, Burdy Haldorson, Bill Hougland, Bob Jeangerard, K.C. Jones, Bill Russell, Ron Tomsic, +Jim Walsh and coach +Gerald Tucker.
1960 Basketball Jay Arnette, Walt Bellamy, Bob Boozer, Terry Dischinger, Burdy Haldorson, Darrall Imhoff, Allen Kelley, +Lester Lane, Jerry Lucas, Oscar Robertson, Adrian Smith, Jerry West and coach Pete Newell.
1964 Basketball Jim Barnes, Bill Bradley, Larry Brown, Joe Caldwell, Mel Counts, Richard Davies, Walt Hazzard, Luke Jackson, John McCaffrey, Jeff Mullins, Jerry Shipp, George Wilson and coach Hank Iba.
1960 Ice Hockey Billy Christian, Roger Christian, Billy Cleary, Bob Cleary, Gene Grazia, Paul Johnson, Jack Kirrane, John Mayasich, Jack McCartan, Bob McKay, Dick Meredith, Weldon Olson, Ed Owen, Rod Paavola, Larry Palmer, Dick Rodenheiser, +Tom Williams and coach Jack Riley.
1980 Ice Hockey Bill Baker, Neal Broten, Dave Christian, Steve Christoff, Jim Craig, Mike Eruzione, John Harrington, Steve Janaszak, Mark Johnson, Ken Morrow, Rob McClanahan, Jack O'Callahan, Mark Pavelich, Mike Ramsey, Buzz Schneider, Dave Silk, Eric Strobel, Bob Suter, Phil Verchota, Mark Wells and coach Herb Brooks.

Alpine Skiing

Mahre, Phil 1992

Bobsled

+ Eagan, Eddie (see Boxing) .1983

Boxing

Clay, Cassius* 1983
+ Eagan, Eddie (see Bobsled) .1983
Foreman, George 1990
Frazier, Joe 1989
Leonard, Sugar Ray 1985
Patterson, Floyd 1987
*Clay changed name to Muhammad Ali in 1964.

Cycling

Carpenter-Phinney, Connie .1992

Diving

King, Miki 1992
Lee, Sammy 1990
Louganis, Greg 1985
McCormick, Pat 1985

Figure Skating

Albright, Tenley 1988
Button, Dick 1983
Fleming, Peggy 1983
Hamill, Dorothy 1991
Hamilton, Scott 1990

Gymnastics

Conner, Bart 1991
Retton, Mary Lou 1985
Vidmar, Peter 1991

Rowing

+ Kelly, Jack Sr. 1990

Speed Skating

Heiden, Eric 1983

Swimming

Babashoff, Shirley 1987
Caulkins, Tracy 1990
+ Daniels, Charles 1988
de Varona, Donna 1987
+ Kahanamoku, Duke 1984
+ Madison, Helene 1992
Meyer, Debbie 1986
Naber, John 1984
Schollander, Don 1983
Spitz, Mark 1983
+ Weissmuller, Johnny 1983

Track & Field

Beamon, Bob 1983
Boston, Ralph 1985
+ Calhoun, Lee 1991
Campbell, Milt 1992
+ Davenport, Willie 1991
Davis, Glenn 1986
+ Didrikson, Babe 1983
Dillard, Harrison 1983
Evans, Lee 1989
+ Ewry, Ray 1983
Fosbury, Dick 1992
Jenner, Bruce 1986
Johnson, Rafer 1983
+ Kraenzlein, Alvin 1985
Lewis, Carl 1985
Mathias, Bob 1983

Mills, Billy 1984
Morrow, Bobby 1989
Moses, Edwin 1985
O'Brien, Parry 1984
Oerter, Al 1983
+ Owens, Jesse 1983
+ Paddock, Charley 1991
Richards, Bob 1983
+ Rudolph, Wilma 1983
+ Sheppard, Mel 1989
Shorter, Frank 1984
+ Thorpe, Jim 1983
Toomey, Bill 1984
Tyus, Wyomia 1985
Whitfield, Mal 1988
+ Wykoff, Frank 1984

Weight Lifting

+ Davis, John 1989
Kono, Tommy 1990

Wrestling

Gable, Dan 1985

Contributors

+ Arledge, Roone 1989
+ Brundage, Avery 1983
+ Bushnell, Asa 1990
Hull, Col. Don 1992
+ Iba, Hank 1985
+ Kane, Robert 1986
+ Kelly, Jack Jr. 1992
McKay, Jim 1988
Miller, Don 1984
+ Simon, William 1991
Walker, LeRoy 1987

SOCCER

International Football Hall of Champions

Established in 1998 by FIFA, soccer's international governing body. Located at Disneyland Paris.

Eligibility: Nominated players and coaches must be retired at least five years. Nominations made by a committee composed of FIFA members, the Hall of Champions management and three ad hoc members then submit a list to a panel of 32 soccer journalists from around the world who also have the chance to add nominees of their own as well as voting for a specific number of candidates in each category.

Note: There have been no inductions since 2001.

Players

+ Andrade, José Leandro (URU) 2001
  Beckenbauer, Franz (W. Ger) 1998
  Best, George (N. Ire) 2000
  Charlton, Sir Bobby (ENG) . .1998
  Cruyff, Johan (NED) 1998
+ Didi (BRA) 2000
  Distefano, Alfredo (ARG/SPA) 1998
  Eusebio (POR) 1998
  Fontaine, Just (FRA) 1999
+ Garrincha (BRA) 1999
+ Matthews, Sir Stanley (ENG) .1998
+ Meazza, Giuseppe (ITA) 2001
+ Moore, Bobby (ENG) 1999
  Müller, Gerd (W. Ger) 1999
  Pele (BRA) 1998
  Plantini, Michel (FRA) 1998
  Puskas, Ferenc (HUN/SPA) . .1998
  Van Basten, Marko (HOL) . . .2000

+ Yashin, Lev (RUS) 1998
  Zico (BRA) 2000
  Zoff, Dino (ITA) 1999

Managers

+ Busby, Sir Matt (SCO) 1998
  Michels, Rinus (NED) 1998
+ Pozzo, Vittorio (ITA) 2001
+ Shankly, Bill (SCO) 1999

Referees

Taylor, Jack (ENG) 1999
Vautrot, Michel (FRA) 1998

Pioneers

Havelange, Joao (BRA) 1999
+ Rimet, Jules (FRA) 1998

Club Teams

Ajax Amsterdam (NED) 1999
FC Barcelona (SPA) 2000
Real Madrid (SPA) 1998

National Teams

Argentina 2001
Brazil 1998
Germany 1999
Italy 2000

Media

Ferran, Jacques (FRA) 1999
Goddett, Jacques (FRA) 1998

For the Good of the Game

+ Dassler, Horst (GER) 1998
+ Sastre, Fernard (FRA) 1999

National Soccer Hall of Fame

Established in 1950 by the Philadelphia Oldtimers Association. First exhibit unveiled in Oneonta, NY in 1982. Moved into new Hall of Fame building in the summer of 1999. **Address:** 18 Stadium Circle, Oneonta, NY 13820. **Telephone:** (607) 432-3351.

Eligibility: Nominated players must have represented the U.S. in international competition and be retired five years; other categories include Meritorious Service and Special Commendation. The Class of 2003 was inducted to honor the North American Soccer League (1967-84).

Nominations made by state organizations and a veterans' committee. Voting done by nine-member committee made up of Hall of Famers, U.S. Soccer officials and members of the national media.

Class of 2003 (16): **Carlos Alberto, Paul Child, Ahmet Ertegun, Nesuhi Ertegun, Karl-Heinz Granitza, Ted Howard, Bob Lenarduzzi, Arnie Mausser, Ace Ntsoelengoe, Elizabeth Robbie, Joe Robbie, Steve Ross, Lee Stern, Clive Toye, Alan Willey** and **Bruce Wilson.**

Members are listed with home state and year of induction; (+) indicates deceased members.

Members

Abronzino, Umberto (CA) . .1971
Aimi, Milton (TX) 1991
Alberto, Carlos (Bra) 2003
+ Alonso, Julie (NY) 1972
+ Andersen, William (NY) . . .1956
  Annis, Robert (MO) 1976
+ Ardizzone, John (CA) 1971
+ Armstrong, James (NY) 1952
+ Auld, Andrew (RI) 1986
  Bachmeier, Adolph (IL) 2002
  Bahr, Walter (PA) 1976
+ Barr, George (NY) 1983
+ Barriskill, Joe (NY) 1953
+ Beardsworth, Fred (MA) . . .1965
  Beckenbauer, Franz (Ger) . .1998
  Berling, Clay (CA) 1995
  Bernabei, Ray (PA) 1978
+ Best, John O. (CA) 1982
  Bogicevic, Vladislav (Yug) . .2002
+ Bookie, Michael (PA) 1986
+ Booth, Joseph (CT) 1952
  Borghi, Frank (MO) 1976
+ Boulos, Frenchy (NY) 1980
+ Boxer, Matt (CA) 1961
  Bradley, Gordon (Eng) 1996
+ Briggs, Lawrence E. (MA) . .1978
+ Brittan, Harold (PA) 1951
+ Brock, John (MA) 1950
+ Brown, Andrew M. (OH) . . .1950
  Brown, David (NJ) 1951
  Brown, George (NJ) 1995

+ Brown, James (NY) 1986
+ Cahill, Thomas W (NY) 1950
+ Carenza, Joe (MO) 1982
+ Caraffi, Ralph (OH) 1959
  Chacurian, Chico (CT) 1992
+ Chesney, Stan (NY) 1966
  Child, Paul (Eng) 2003
  Chinaglia, Giorgio (Italy) . . .2000
+ Chyzowych, Walter (PA) . . .1997
+ Coll, John (NY) 1986
+ Collins, George M. (MA) . . .1951
  Collins, Peter (NY) 1998
+ Colombo, Charlie (MO) 1976
+ Commander, Colin (OH) 1967
  Coombes, Geoff (MI) 1976
+ Cordery, Ted (CA) 1975
+ Craddock, Robert (PA) 1959
  Craddock Jr., Robert (PA) . .1976
+ Craggs, Edmund (WA) 1969
  Craggs, George (WA) 1981
+ Cummings, Wilfred R. (IL) . . .1953
  Danilo, Paul (PA) 1997
  Davis, Rick (CA) 2001
+ Delach, Joseph (PA) 1973
  DeLuca, Enzo (NY) 1979
+ Dick, Walter (CA) 1989
  Diorio, Nick (PA) 1974
+ Donaghy, Edward J. (NY) . . .1951
+ Donelli, Buff (PA) 1954
+ Donnelly, George (NY) 1989
+ Douglas, Jimmy (NJ) 1953

+ Dresmich, John W. (PA) 1968
+ Duff, Duncan (CA) 1972
+ Duggan, Thomas (NJ) 1951
+ Dunn, James (MO) 1974
+ Edwards, Gene (WI) 1985
  Ely, Alexander (PA) 1997
+ Epperlein, Rudy (NJ) 1951
  Ertegun, Ahmet (NY) 2003
  Ertegun, Nesuhi (NY) 2003
+ Fairfield, Harry (PA) 1951
  Feibusch, Ernst (CA) 1984
+ Ferguson, John (PA) 1950
+ Fernley, John A. (MA) 1951
+ Ferro, Charles (NY) 1958
+ Fishwick, George E. (IL) 1974
+ Flamhaft, Jack (NY) 1964
+ Fleming, Harry G. (PA) 1967
+ Florie, Thomas (NJ) 1986
+ Foulds, Pal (MA) 1953
+ Foulds, Sam (MA) 1969
+ Fowler, Dan (NY) 1970
+ Fowler, Peg (NY) 1979
+ Fricker, Werner (PA) 1992
+ Fryer, William J. (NJ) 1951
  Gabarra, Carin (CA) 2000
+ Gaetjens, Joe (NY) 1976
+ Gallagher, James (NY) 1986
+ Garcia, Pete (MO) 1964
  Gard, Gino (IL) 1976
+ Gentle, James (PA) 1986
  Getzinger, Rudy (IL) 1991

+ Giesler, Walter (MO) 1962
+ Glover, Teddy (NY) 1965
+ Gonsalves, Billy (MA) 1950
  Gormley, Bob (PA) 1989
+ Gould, David L. (PA) 1953
+ Govier, Sheldon (IL) 1950
  Granitza, Karl-Heinz (Ger) .2003
+ Greer, Don (CA) 1985
  Gryzik, Joe (IL) 1973
+ Guelker, Bob (MO) 1980
  Guennel, Joe (CO) 1980
  Harker, Al (PA) 1979
+ Healey, George (MI) 1951
  Heilpern, Herb (NY) 1988
  Heinrichs, April (CO) 1998
+ Hemmings, William (IL) . . .1961
  Hermann, Robert (MO) 2001
  Higgins, Shannon (NC) 2002
  Howard, Ted (NY) 2003
+ Hudson, Maurice (CA) 1966
  Hunt, Lamar (TX) 1982
  Hynes, John (NY) 1977
+ Iglehart, Alfredda (MD) 1951
+ Japp, John (PA) 1953
+ Jeffrey, William (PA) 1951
+ Johnston, Jack (IL) 1952
+ Kabanica, Mike (WI) 1987
  Kehoe, Bob (MO) 1990
+ Kelly, Frank (NJ) 1994
+ Kempton, George (WA) 1950
  Keough, Harry (MO) 1976
+ Klein, Paul (NJ) 1953
  Kleinaitis, Al (IN) 1995
+ Kozma, Oscar (CA) 1964
+ Kracher, Frank (IL) 1983
  Kraft, Granny (MD) 1984
+ Kraus, Harry (NY) 1963
  Kropfelder, Nicholas 1996
+ Kunter, Rudy (NY) 1963
+ Lamm, Kurt (NY) 1979
  Lang, Millard (MD) 1950
  Larson, Bert (CT) 1988
  Lenarduzzi, Bob (Can) 2003
+ Lewis, H. Edgar (PA) 1950
  Lombardo, Joe (NY) 1984
  Long, Denny (MO) 1993
+ Looby, Bill (MO) 2001
+ MacEwan, John J. (MI) 1953
+ Maca, Joe (NY) 1976
+ Magnozzi, Enzo (NY) 1977
+ Maher, Jack (IL) 1970

+ Manning, Dr. Randolf (NY) .1950
+ Marre, John (MO) 1953
  Mausser, Arnie (RI) 2003
  McBride, Pat (MO) 1994
+ McClay, Allan (MA) 1971
+ McGhee, Bart (NY) 1986
+ McGrath, Frank (MA) 1978
+ McGuire, Jimmy (NY) 1951
+ McGuire, John (NY) 1951
+ McIlveney, Eddie (PA) 1976
  McLaughlin, Bennie (PA) . . .1977
+ McSkimming, Dent (MO) . . .1951
+ Merovich, Pete (PA) 1971
+ Mieth, Werner (NJ) 1974
+ Millar, Robert (NY) 1950
  Miller, Al (OH) 1995
+ Miller, Milton (NY) 1971
+ Mills, Jimmy (PA) 1954
+ Monsen, Lloyd (NY) 1994
+ Moore, James F. (MO) 1971
  Moore, Johnny (CA) 1997
+ Moorehouse, George (NY) .1986
+ Morrison, Robert (PA) 1951
+ Morrissette, Bill (MA) 1967
  Murphy, Edward (IL) 1998
  Nanoski, Jukey (PA) 1993
+ Netto, Fred (IL) 1958
  Newman, Ron (CA) 1992
+ Niotis, D.J. (IL) 1963
  Ntsoelengoe, Ace (S.Afr.) . .2003
+ O'Brien, Shamus (NY) 1990
  Olaff, Gene (NJ) 1971
+ Oliver, Arnie (MA) 1968
  Oliver, Len (PA) 1996
+ Palmer, William (PA) 1952
  Pariani, Gino (MO) 1976
+ Patenaude, Bert (MA) 1971
+ Pearson, Eddie (GA) 1990
+ Peel, Peter (IL) 1951
  Pel|fe (Brazil) 1993
+ Peters, Wally (NJ) 1967
  Phillipson, Don (CO) 1987
+ Piscopo, Giorgio (NY) 1978
+ Pomeroy, Edgar (CA) 1955
+ Ramsden, Arnold (TX) 1957
+ Ratican, Harry (MO) 1950
+ Reese, Doc (MD) 1957
+ Renzulli, Pete (NY) 1951
  Ringsdorf, Gene (MD) 1979
  Robbie, Elizabeth (FL) 2003
+ Robbie, Joe (FL) 2003

+ Roe, Jimmy (MO) 1997
  Ross, Steve (NY) 2003
  Roth, Werner (NY) 1989
+ Rottenberg, Jack (NJ) 1971
  Roy, Willy (IL) 1989
+ Ryan, Hun (PA) 1958
+ Sager, Tom (PA) 1968
  Saunders, Harry (NY) 1981
  Schaller, Willy (IL) 1995
  Schellscheidt, Mannie (NJ) .1990
+ Schillinger, Emil (PA) 1960
+ Schroeder, Elmer (PA) 1951
+ Scwarcz, Erno (NY) 1951
+ Shields, Fred (PA) 1968
+ Single, Erwin (NY) 1981
  Slone, Philip (NY) 1986
+ Smith, Alfred (PA) 1951
  Smith, Patrick (OH) 1998
+ Souza, Ed (MA) 1976
  Souza, Clarkie (MA) 1976
+ Spalding, Dick (PA) 1951
  Spath, Reinhold (NY) 1997
+ Stark, Archie (NJ) 1950
+ Steelink, Nicolaas (CA) 1971
  Stern, Lee (IL) 2003
+ Steur, August (NY) 1969
+ Stewart, Douglas (PA) 1950
+ Stone, Robert T. (CO) 1971
+ Swords, Thomas (MA) 1951
+ Tintle, Joseph (NJ) 1952
  Toye, Clive (NY) 2003
+ Tracey, Ralph (MO) 1986
+ Triner, Joseph (IL) 1951
+ Vaughn, Frank (MO) 1986
+ Walder, Jimmy (PA) 1971
+ Wallace, Frank (MO) 1976
+ Washauer, Adolph (CA) 1977
+ Webb, Tom (WA) 1987
+ Weir, Alex (NY) 1975
+ Weston, Victor (WA) 1956
  Willey, Alan (Eng) 2003
  Wilson, Bruce (Can) 2003
+ Wilson, Peter (NJ) 1950
  Wolanin, Adam (IL) 1976
+ Wood, Alex (MI) 1986
+ Woods, John W. (IL) 1952
  Woosnam, Phil (GA) 1997
  Yeagley, Jerry (IN) 1989
+ Young, John (CA) 1958
+ Zampini, Dan (PA) 1963
  Zerhusen, Al (CA) 1978

SWIMMING

International Swimming Hall of Fame

Established in 1965 by the U.S. College Coaches' Swim Forum. **Address:** One Hall of Fame Drive, Ft. Lauderdale, FL 33316.
Telephone: (954) 462-6536.

Categories for induction are: swimming, diving, water polo, synchronized swimming, coaching, pioneers and contributors. Coaches and contributors are not included in the following list. Only U.S. men and women listed below.
Class of 2003 (2): U.S. WOMEN—**Laura Val**; U.S. MEN—**Mark Lenzi**.
Members are listed with year of induction; (+) indicates deceased members.

U.S. Men

+ Anderson, Miller 1967
  Barrowman, Mike 1997
  Biondi, Matt 1997
+ Boggs, Phil 1985
  Breen, George 1975
+ Browning, Skippy 1975
  Bruner, Mike 1988
  Burton, Mike 1977
+ Cann, Tedford 1967
  Carey, Rick 1993
  Clark, Earl 1972
  Clark, Steve 1966
+ Cleveland, Dick 1991
  Clotworthy, Robert 1980

+ Crabbe, Buster 1965
+ Daniels, Charlie 1965
  Degener, Dick 1971
  DeMont, Rick 1990
  Dempsey, Frank 1996
+ Desjardins, Pete 1966
  Dysdale, Taylor 1994
  Edgar, David 1996
+ Faricy, John 1990
+ Farrell, Jeff 1968
+ Fick, Peter 1978
+ Flanagan, Ralph 1978
  Ford, Alan 1966
  Furniss, Bruce 1987

  Gaines, Rowdy 1995
  Garton, Tim 1997
+ Glancy, Harrison 1990
  Goodell, Brian 1986
+ Goodwin, Budd 1971
  Graef, Jed 1988
  Haines, George 1977
  Hall Sr., Gary 1981
+ Harlan, Bruce 1973
  Harper, Don 1998
+ Hebner, Harry 1968
  Heidenreich, Jerry 1992
  Hencken, John 1988
  Hickcox, Charles 1976

Higgins, John 1971
+ Holiday, Harry 1991
Hough, Richard 1970
Irwin, Juno Stover 1980
Graham, Johnston 1998
Jager, Tom 2001
Jastremski, Chet 1977
+ Kahanamoku, Duke 1965
+ Kealoha, Warren 1968
Kiefer, Adolph 1965
Kinsella, John 1986
+ Kojac, George 1968
Konno, Ford 1972
+ Kruger, Stubby 1986
+ Kuehn, Louis 1988
+ Langer, Ludy 1988
+ Langner, G. Harold 1995
Larson, Lance 1980
Laufer, Walter 1973
Lee, Dr. Sammy 1968
Lemmon, Kelley 1999
+ LeMoyne, Harry 1988
Lenzi, Mark 2003
Louganis, Greg 1993
Lundquist, Steve 1990
Mann, Thompson 1984
+ Martin, G. Harold 1999
McCormick, Pat 1965
+ McDermott, Turk 1969

+ McGillivray, Perry 1981
McKee, Tim 1998
McKenzie, Don 1989
McKinney, Frank 1975
McLane, Jimmy 1970
+ Medica, Jack 1966
Montgomery, Jim 1986
Morales, Pablo 1998
Mulliken, Bill 1984
Naber, John 1982
Nakama, Keo 1975
+ O'Connor, Wally 1966
Oyakawa, Yoshi 1973
+ Patnik, Al 1969
Prew, William 1998
+ Riley, Mickey 1977
+ Ris, Wally 1966
Robie, Carl 1976
Ross, Clarence 1988
+ Ross, Norman 1967
Roth, Dick 1987
Rouse, Jeff 2001
+ Ruddy Sr., Joe 1986
Russell, Doug 1985
Saari, Roy 1976
+ Schaeffer, E. Carroll 1968
Scholes, Clarke 1980
Schollander, Don 1965
Schroeder, Terry 2002

Shaw, Tim 1989
+ Sheldon, George 1989
Sitzberger, Ken 1994
+ Skelton, Robert 1988
Smith, Bill 1966
+ Smith, Dutch 1979
+ Smith, Jimmy 1992
Spitz, Mark 1977
+ Stack, Allen 1979
Stewart, Melvin 2002
Stickles, Ted 1995
Stock, Tom 1989
+ Swendsen, Clyde 1991
Taft, Ray 1996
Tobian, Gary 1978
Troy, Mike 1971
Vande Weghe, Albert 1990
Vassallo, Jesse 1997
+ Verdeur, Joe 1966
Vogel, Matt 1996
+ Vollmer, Hal 1990
+ Wayne, Marshall 1981
Webster, Bob 1970
+ Weissmuller, Johnny 1965
+ White, Al 1965
Wiggins, Al 1994
Wrightson, Bernie 1984
Yorzyk, Bill 1971

U.S. Women

Andersen, Teresa 1986
Atwood, Sue 1992
Babashoff, Shirley 1982
Babb-Sprague, Kristen 1999
Ball, Catie 1976
+ Bauer, Sybil 1967
Bean, Dawn Pawson 1996
Belote, Melissa 1983
Bleibtrey, Ethelda 1967
+ Boyle, Charlotte 1988
Bruner, Jayne Owen 1998
Burke, Lynn 1978
Bush, Lesley 1986
Callen, Gloria 1984
Caretto, Patty 1987
Carr, Cathy 1988
Caulkins, Tracy 1990
+ Chadwick, Florence 1970
Chandler, Jennifer 1987
Cohen, Tiffany 1996
+ Coleman, Georgia 1966
Cone, Carin 1984
Costie, Candy 1995
Cox, Lynne 2000
Crlenkovich, Helen 1981
Curtis, Ann 1966
Daniel, Ellie 1997
de Varona, Donna 1969
Dean, Penny 1996
+ Dorfner, Olga 1970
Draves, Vickie 1969
Duenkel, Ginny 1985
Dunbar, Barbara 2000
Ederle, Gertrude 1965
Ellis, Kathy 1991
Elsener, Patty 2002
Evans, Janet 2001
Fauntz, Jane 1991
Ferguson, Cathy 1978
Finneran, Sharon 1985

+ Fulton, Patty Robinson 2001
+ Galligan, Claire 1970
+ Garatti-Seville, Eleanor 1992
Gestring, Marjorie 1976
Gossick, Sue 1988
+ Guest, Irene 1990
Gundling, Buelah 1965
Hall, Kaye 1979
Henne, Jan 1979
Hogan, Peg 2002
Hogshead, Nancy 1994
Holm, Eleanor 1966
Hunt-Newman, Virginia 1993
Johnson, Gail 1983
Josephson, Karen 1997
Josephson, Sarah 1997
+ Kaufman, Beth 1967
+ Kight, Lenore 1981
King, Micki 1978
Kolb, Claudia 1975
+ Lackie, Ethel 1969
+ Landon, Alice Lord 1993
Linehan, Kim 1997
+ Madison, Helene 1966
Mann, Shelly 1966
McCormick, Kelly 1999
McGrath, Margo 1989
McKim, Josephine 1991
Meagher, Mary T. 1993
+ Meany, Helen 1971
Merlino, Maxine 1999
Meyer, Debbie 1977
Mitchell, Betsy 1998
Mitchell, Michele 1995
Moe, Karen 1992
Morris, Pam 1965
Mueller, Ardeth 1996
Neilson, Sandra 1986
Neyer, Megan 1997
+ Norelius, Martha 1967

Olsen, Zoe Ann 1989
O'Rourke, Heidi 1980
+ Osipowich, Albina 1986
Pedersen, Susan 1995
Pinkston, Betty Becker 1967
Pope, Paula Jean Meyers . . .1979
Potter, Cynthia 1987
+ Poynton, Dorothy 1968
+ Rawls, Katherine 1965
Redmond, Carol 1989
Riggin, Aileen 1967
Roper, Gail 1997
Ross, Anne 1984
Rothhammer, Keena 1991
Ruiz-Conforto, Tracie 1993
Ruuska, Sylvia 1976
Sanders, Summer 2002
Schuler, Carolyn 1989
Seller, Peg 1988
+ Smith, Caroline 1988
Steinseifer, Carrie 1999
Sterkel, Jill 2002
Stouder, Sharon 1972
+ Toner, Vee 1995
Val, Laura 2003
+ Vilen, Kay 1978
Von Saltza, Chris 1966
+ Wainwright, Helen 1972
Walker, Clara Lamore 1995
+ Watson, Lillian (Pokey) 1984
Wayte, Mary 2000
Wehselau, Mariechen 1989
Welshons, Kim 1988
Wichman, Sharon 1991
Williams, Esther 1966
+ Woodbridge, Margaret 1989
Woodhead, Cynthia 1994
Wyland, Wendy 2001

TENNIS

International Tennis Hall of Fame

Originally the National Tennis Hall of Fame. Established in 1953 by James Van Alen and sanctioned by the U.S. Tennis Association in 1954. Renamed the International Tennis Hall of Fame in 1976. **Address:** 194 Bellevue Ave., Newport, RI 02840. **Telephone:** (401) 849-3990.

Eligibility: Nominated players must be five years removed from being a "significant factor" in competitive tennis. Voting done by members of the international tennis media.

Class of 2003 (4): PLAYERS—**Boris Becker, Françoise "Frankie" Dürr** and **Nancy Richey**. CONTRIBUTOR—**Brian Tobin**.

Members are listed with year of induction; (+) indicates deceased members.

Men

+ Adee, George 1964
+ Alexander, Fred 1961
+ Allison, Wilmer 1963
+ Alonso, Manuel 1977
  Anderson, Malcolm 2000
+ Ashe, Arthur 1985
+ Austin, Bunny 1997
  Becker, Boris 2003
+ Behr, Karl 1969
  Borg, Bjorn 1987
+ Borotra, Jean 1976
+ Bromwich, John 1984
+ Brookes, Norman 1977
+ Brugnon, Jacques 1976
+ Budge, Don 1964
+ Campbell, Oliver 1955
+ Chace, Malcolm 1961
+ Clark, Clarence 1983
+ Clark, Joseph 1955
+ Clothier, William 1956
+ Cochet, Henri 1976
  Connors, Jimmy 1998
  Cooper, Ashley 1991
+ Crawford, Jack 1979
+ David, Herman 1998
+ Doeg, John 1962
+ Doherty, Lawrence 1980
+ Doherty, Reginald 1980
+ Drobny, Jaroslav 1983
+ Dwight, James 1955
  Emerson, Roy 1982
+ Etchebaster, Pierre 1978
  Falkenburg, Bob 1974
  Fraser, Neale 1984
+ Garland, Chuck 1969
+ Gonzalez, Pancho 1968
+ Grant, Bryan (Bitsy) 1972
+ Griffin, Clarence 1970

+ Hackett, Harold 1961
  Hewitt, Bob 1992
+ Hoad, Lew 1980
+ Hovey, Fred 1974
+ Hunt, Joe 1966
+ Hunter, Frank 1961
+ Johnston, Bill 1958
+ Jones, Perry 1970
  Kelleher, Robert 2000
  Kodes, Jan 1990
  Kramer, Jack 1968
+ Lacoste, Rene 1976
+ Larned, William 1956
  Larsen, Art 1969
  Laver, Rod 1981
  Lendl, Ivan 2001
+ Lott, George 1964
  Mako, Gene 1973
  McEnroe, John 1999
  McGregor, Ken 1999
+ McKinley, Chuck 1986
+ McLoughlin, Maurice 1957
  McMillan, Frew 1992
+ McNeill, Don 1965
  Mulloy, Gardnar 1972
+ Murray, Lindley 1958
+ Myrick, Julian 1963
  Nastase, Ilie 1991
  Newcombe, John 1986
+ Nielsen, Arthur 1971
  Olmedo, Alex 1987
+ Osuna, Rafael 1979
+ Parker, Frank 1966
+ Patterson, Gerald 1989
  Patty, Budge 1977
+ Perry, Fred 1975
+ Pettitt, Tom 1982

  Pietrangeli, Nicola 1986
+ Quist, Adrian 1984
  Ralston, Dennis 1987
+ Renshaw, Ernest 1983
+ Renshaw, William 1983
+ Richards, Vincent 1961
+ Riggs, Bobby 1967
  Roche, Tony 1986
  Rose, Mervyn 2001
  Rosewall, Ken 1980
  Santana, Manuel 1984
  Savitt, Dick 1976
  Schroeder, Ted 1966
+ Sears, Richard 1955
  Sedgman, Frank 1979
  Segura, Pancho 1984
  Seixas, Vic 1971
+ Shields, Frank 1964
+ Slocum, Henry 1955
  Smith, Stan 1987
  Stolle, Fred 1985
  Talbert, Bill 1967
+ Tilden, Bill 1959
  Trabert, Tony 1970
+ Van Ryn, John 1963
  Vilas, Guillermo 1991
+ Vines, Ellsworth 1962
+ von Cramm, Gottfried 1977
+ Ward, Holcombe 1956
+ Washburn, Watson 1965
+ Whitman, Malcolm 1955
  Wilander, Mats 2002
+ Wilding, Anthony 1978
+ Williams, Richard 2nd 1957
  Wood, Sidney 1964
+ Wrenn, Robert 1955
+ Wright, Beals 1956

Women

+ Atkinson, Juliette 1974
  Austin, Tracy 1992
+ Barger-Wallach, Maud 1958
  Betz Addie, Pauline 1965
+ Bjurstedt Mallory, Molla . . . 1958
  Bowrey, Lesley Turner 1997
  Brough Clapp, Louise 1967
+ Browne, Mary 1957
  Bueno, Maria 1978
+ Cahill, Mabel 1976
  Casals, Rosie 1996
+ Connolly Brinker, Maureen . . 1968
+ Dod, Charlotte (Lottie) 1983
  Douglass Chambers, Dorothy 1981
  Dürr, Françoise 2003
  Evert, Chris 1995
  Fry Irvin, Shirley 1970

+ Gibson, Althea 1971
  Goolagong Cawley, Evonne 1988
+ Hansell, Ellen 1965
  Hard, Darlene 1973
  Hart, Doris 1969
  Haydon Jones, Ann 1985
  Heldman, Gladys 1979
+ Hotchkiss Wightman, Hazel 1957
+ Jacobs, Helen Hull 1962
  King, Billie Jean 1987
+ Lenglen, Suzanne 1978
  Mandlikova, Hana 1994
+ Marble, Alice 1964
+ McKane Godfree, Kitty 1978
+ Moore, Elisabeth 1971
  Mortimer Barrett, Angela . . 1993

  Navratilova, Martina 2000
+ Nuthall Shoemaker, Betty . 1977
  Osborne duPont, Margaret . 1967
+ Palfrey Danzig, Sarah 1963
  Richey, Nancy 2003
+ Roosevelt, Ellen 1975
+ Round Little, Dorothy 1986
+ Ryan, Elizabeth 1972
+ Sears, Eleanora 1968
  Shriver, Pam 2002
  Smith Court, Margaret 1979
+ Sutton Bundy, May 1956
+ Townsend Toulmin, Bertha . 1974
  Wade, Virginia 1989
+ Wagner, Marie 1969
+ Wills Moody Roark, Helen . 1959

Contributors

+ Hester, W.E. (Slew) 1981
+ Hopman, Harry 1978
  Hunt, Lamar 1993
+ Laney, Al 1979
  Martin, Alastair 1973
+ Martin, William M. 1982
+ Maskell, Dan 1996
+ Outerbridge, Mary 1981

+ Baker, Lawrence Sr 1975
+ Chatrier, Philippe 1992
  Collins, Bud 1994
+ Cullman, Joseph F. 3rd 1990
+ Danzig, Allison 1968
+ Davis, Dwight 1956
+ Gray, David 1985
+ Gustaf, V (King of Sweden) . 1980

+ Pell, Theodore 1966
+ Tingay, Lance 1982
+ Tinling, Ted 1986
  Tobin, John 2003
+ Van Alen, James 1965
+ Wingfield, Walter Clopton . 1997

TRACK & FIELD

National Track & Field Hall of Fame

Established in 1974 by the The Athletics Congress (now USA Track & Field). Originally located in Charleston, WV, the Hall moved to Indianapolis in 1983 and opened at the Hoosier Dome (now RCA Dome) in 1986. The Hall moved to Manhattan and was scheduled to reopen at the 168th Street Armory in early 2004. **Address:** One RCA Dome, Indianapolis, IN 46225. **Telephone:** (317) 261-0500.

Eligibility: Nominated athletes must be retired three years and coaches must have coached at least 20 years if retired or 35 years if still coaching. Voting done by 800-member panel made up of Hall of Fame and USA Track & Field officials, Hall of Fame members, current U.S. champions and members of the Track & Field Writers of America.

Class of 2002 (4): MEN—**Earl Bell** (pole vault), **Steve Scott** (middle distance), **Larry Young** (race walk). WOMEN— **Gwen Torrence** (sprint). Members are listed with year of induction; (+) indicates deceased members.

Men

+ Albritton, Dave 1980	Jenkins, Charlie 1992	+ Ray, Joie 1976
Ashenfelter, Horace 1975	Jenner, Bruce 1980	+ Rice, Greg 1977
Banks, Willie 1999	+ Johnson, Cornelius 1994	Richards, Rev. Bob 1975
+ Bausch, James 1979	Johnson, Rafer 1974	Robinson, Arnie 2000
Beamon, Bob 1977	Jones, Hayes 1976	Rodgers, Bill 1999
Beatty, Jim 1990	Kelley, John 1980	+ Rose, Ralph 1976
Bell, Earl 2002	+ Kiviat, Abel 1985	Ryun, Jim 1980
Bell, Greg 1988	+ Kraenzlein, Alvin 1974	Salazar, Alberto 2001
+ Boeckmann, Dee 1976	Laird, Ron 1986	+ Scholz, Jackson 1977
Boston, Ralph 1974	+ Lash, Don 1995	Schul, Bob 1991
+ Borican, Jonn 2000	+ Laskau, Henry 1997	Scott, Steve 2002
Bragg, Don 1996	Lewis, Carl 2001	Seagren, Bob 1986
+ Calhoun, Lee 1974	Liquori, Marty 1995	+ Sheppard, Mel 1976
Campbell, Milt 1989	Long, Dr. Dallas 1996	+ Sheridan, Martin 1988
Carr, Henry 1997	Marsh, Henry 2001	Shorter, Frank 1989
+ Clark, Ellery 1991	Mathias, Bob 1974	Silvester, Jay 1998
Connolly, Harold 1984	Matson, Randy 1984	Sime, Dave 1981
Courtney, Tom 1978	McCluskey, Joe 1996	+ Simpson, Robert 1974
+ Cunningham, Glenn 1974	+ Meadows, Earle 1996	Smith, Tommie 1978
+ Curtis, William 1979	+ Meredith, Ted 1982	+ Stanfield, Andy 1977
+ Davenport, Willie 1982	Metcalfe, Ralph 1975	Steers, Les 1974
Davis, Glenn 1974	+ Milburn, Rod 1993	Stones, Dwight 1998
Davis, Harold 1974	Mills, Billy 1976	+ Taylor, Frederick Morgan ..2000
Dillard, Harrison 1974	Moore, Charles 1999	+ Tewksbury, Dr. Walter ..1996
Dumas, Charles 1990	Moore, Tom 1988	Thomas, John 1985
Evans, Lee 1983	Morrow, Bobby 1975	+ Thomson, Earl 1977
+ Ewell, Barney 1986	+ Mortensen, Jess 1992	+ Thorpe, Jim 1975
Ewry, Ray 1974	Moses, Edwin 1994	Tolan, Eddie 1982
+ Flanagan, John 1975	+ Myers, Lawrence 1974	Toomey, Bill 1975
Fosbury, Dick 1981	Myricks, Larry 2001	+ Towns, Forrest (Spec) ...1976
Foster, Greg 1998	Nehemiah, Renaldo 1997	Warmerdam, Cornelius 1974
+ Gordien, Fortune 1979	O'Brien, Parry 1974	Whitfield, Mal 1974
Greene, Charles 1992	Oerter, Al 1974	Wilkins, Mac 1993
+ Hahn, Archie 1983	+ Osborn, Harold 1974	+ Williams, Archie 1992
+ Hardin, Glenn 1978	+ Owens, Jesse 1974	Wohlhuter, Rick 1990
Hayes, Bob 1976	+ Paddock, Charlie 1976	Woodruff, John 1978
Held, Bud 1987	Patton, Mel 1985	Wottle, Dave 1982
Hines, Jim 1979	+ Peacock, Eulace 1987	+ Wykoff, Frank 1977
+ Houser, Bud 1979	+ Prefontaine, Steve 1976	Young, George 1981
+ Hubbard, DeHart 1979	Prinstein, Meyer 2000	Young, Larry 2002

Women

Ashford, Evelyn 1997	Heritage, Doris Brown 1990	Schmidt, Kate 1994
Brisco, Valerie 1995	+ Jackson, Nell 1989	Seidler, Maren 2000
Cheeseborough, Chandra ..2000	Larrieu Smith, Francie ...1998	+ Shiley Newhouse, Jean ...1993
Coachman, Alice 1975	Manning-Mims, Madeline ..1984	+ Stephens, Helen 1975
+ Copeland, Lillian 1994	McDaniel, Mildred 1983	Torrance, Gwen 2002
+ Didrikson, Babe 1974	McGuire, Edith 1979	Tyus, Wyomia 1980
+ Faggs, Mae 1976	Ritter, Louise 1995	+ Walsh, Stella 1975
Ferrell, Barbara 1988	+ Robinson, Betty 1977	Watson, Martha 1987
+ Griffith Joyner, Florence ..1995	+ Rudolph, Wilma 1974	White, Willye 1981
+ Hall Adams, Evelyne 1988		

Coaches

+ Abbott, Cleve 1996	+ Easton, Bill 1975	+ Hurt, Edward 1975
+ Baskin, Weems 1982	+ Ellis, Larry 1999	+ Hutsell, Wilbur 1975
+ Beard, Percy 1981	+ Elliott, Jumbo 1981	+ Jones, Thomas 1977
Bell, Sam 1992	+ Giegengack, Bob 1978	Jordan, Payton 1982
+ Botts, Tom 1983	+ Hamilton, Brutus 1974	+ Littlefield, Clyde 1981
+ Bowerman, Bill 1981	+ Haydon, Ted 1975	+ Moakley, Jack 1988
+ Bush, Jim 1987	+ Hayes, Billy 1976	+ Murphy, Michael 1974
+ Cromwell, Dean 1974	+ Haylett, Ward 1979	Rosen, Mel 1995
Dellinger, Bill 2000	+ Higgins, Ralph 1982	+ Snyder, Larry 1978
+ Doherty, Ken 1976	+ Hillman, Harry 1976	Temple, Ed 1989

+ Templeton, Dink 1976
  Walker, LeRoy 1983
+ Wilt, Fred 1981

+ Winter, Bud 1985
+ Wolfe, Vern 1996
  Wright, Stan 1993

+ Yancy, Joseph 1984

Contributors

+ Ferris, Dan 1974
+ Griffith, John 1979
+ Lebow, Fred 1994
+ Nelson, Bert 1991

Nelson, Cordner 1988
+ Sullivan, James 1977

WOMEN

International Women's Sports Hall of Fame

Established in 1980 by the Women's Sports Foundation. **Address:** Women's Sports Foundation, Eisenhower Park, East Meadow, NY 11554. **Telephone:** (516) 542-4700.

Eligibility: Nominees' achievements and commitment to the development of women's sports must be internationally recognized. Athletes are elected in two categories—Pioneer (before 1960) and Contemporary (since 1960). Members are divided below by sport for the sake of easy reference; (*) indicates member inducted in Pioneer category. Coaching nominees must have coached at least 10 years. Members are listed with year of induction; (+) indicates deceased members.

Class of 2003 (4): CONTEMPORARY—**Jackie Joyner-Kersee** (track and field) and **Min Gao** (diving); PIONEER—**Heather McKay** (squash); COACH—**Linda Vollstedt** (golf).

Note: Charlotte Dod is inducted for tennis, as well as archery and golf; **Marie Marvingt** is inducted for aviation, as well as mountaineering; **Eleanora Sears** is inducted for golf, as well as polo and squash.

Alpine Skiing
  Cranz, Christl* 1991
+ Golden Brosnihan, Diana .1997
- Lawrence, Andrea Mead* .1983
  Moser-Proell, Annemarie . .1982

Auto Racing
  Guthrie, Janet 1980

Aviation
+ Coleman, Bessie* 1992
+ Earhart, Amelia* 1980
+ Marvingt, Marie* 1987

Badminton
  Hashman, Judy Devlin* . . .1995

Baseball
  Stone, Toni* 1993

Basketball
  Meyers, Ann 1985
  Miller, Cheryl 1991

Bowling
  Ladewig, Marion* 1984

Cycling
  Carpenter Phinney, Connie .1990

Diving
  Gao, Min 2003
  King, Micki 1983
  McCormick, Pat* 1984
  Riggin, Aileen* 1988

Equestrian
  Hartel, Lis 1994

Fencing
  Schacherer-Elek, Ilona* . . .1989

Figure Skating
  Albright, Tenley* 1983
+ Blanchard, Theresa Weld* .1989
  Fleming, Peggy 1981
  Heiss Jenkins, Carol* 1992
+ Henie, Sonja* 1982
  Protopopov, Ludmila 1992
  Rodnina, Irena 1988
  Scott-King, Barbara Ann* . .1997
  Torvill, Jayne 2002

Golf
  Berg, Patty* 1980
  Carner, JoAnne 1987
  Haynie, Sandra 1999
  Hicks, Betty* 1995
  Jameson, Betty* 1999

  Mann, Carol 1982
  Rawls, Betsy* 1986
+ Sears, Eleanora 1984
  Suggs, Louise* 1987
+ Vare, Glenna Collett* 1981
  Whitworth, Kathy 1984
  Wright, Mickey 1981

Golf/Track & Field
+ Zaharias, Babe Didrikson* .1980

Gymnastics
  Caslavska, Vera 1991
  Comaneci, Nadia 1990
  Korbut, Olga 1982
  Latynina, Larysa* 1985
  Retton, Mary Lou 1993
  Tourischeva, Lyudmila 1987

Orienteering
  Kringstad, Annichen 1995

Shooting
  Murdock, Margaret 1988

Softball
  Joyce, Joan 1989

Speed Skating
+ Klein Outland, Kit* 1993
  Young, Sheila 1981

Squash
  McKay, Heather* 2003

Swimming
  Caulkins, Tracy 1986
+ Chadwick, Florence* 1996
  Curtis Cuneo, Ann* 1985
  de Varona, Donna 1983
  Ederle, Gertrude* 1980
  Fraser, Dawn 1985
  Holm, Eleanor* 1980
  Meagher, Mary T. 1993
  Meyer-Reyes, Debbie 1987
  Ruiz-Confronto, Tracie 2001

Tennis
+ Connolly, Maureen* 1987
+ Dod, Charlotte (Lottie)* 1986
  Evert, Chris 1981
+ Gibson, Althea* 1980
  Goolagong Cawley, Evonne 1989
+ Hotchkiss Wightman, Hazel*1986
  King, Billie Jean 1980

+ Lenglen, Suzanne* 1984
  Navratilova, Martina 1984
  Osbourne du Pont,Margaret*1998
+ Sears, Eleanora* 1984
  Smith Court, Margaret 1986

Track & Field
  Ashford, Evelyn 1997
  Blankers-Koen, Fanny* 1982
  Brisco, Valerie 2002
  Cheng, Chi 1994
  Coachman Davis, Alice* . .1991
  Cuthbert, Betty* 2002
+ Faggs Star, Aeriwentha Mae* 1996
+ Griffith Joyner, Florence . . .1998
  Joyner-Kersee, Jackie 2003
  Manning Mims, Madeline . .1987
  Nelson, Marjorie Jackson* .2001
+ Rudolph, Wilma 1980
  Samuelson, Joan Benoit . . .1999
+ Stephens, Helen* 1983
  Strickland de la Hunty, Shirley*1998
  Szewinska, Irena 1992
  Tyus, Wyomia 1981
  Waitz, Grete 1995
  White, Willye 1988

Volleyball
+ Hyman, Flo 1986

Water Skiing
  McGuire, Willa Worthington* 1990

Coaches
+ Applebee, Constance 1991
  Backus, Sharron 1993
  Carver, Chris 2001
  Conradt, Judy 1995
  Emery, Gail 1997
  Franke, Nikki 2002
  Green, Tina Sloan 1999
  Grossfeld, Muriel 1991
  Holum, Diana 1996
  Jacket, Barbara 1995
+ Jackson, Nell 1990
  Kanakogi, Rusty 1994
  Summitt, Pat Head 1990
  Van Derveer, Tara 1998
  Vollstedt, Linda 2003
+ Wade, Margaret 1992

RETIRED NUMBERS
Major League Baseball

The New York Yankees have retired the most uniform numbers (14) in the major leagues; followed by the Brooklyn/Los Angeles Dodgers (10), the St. Louis Cardinals (9), the Chicago White Sox and the Pittsburgh Pirates (8) and the New York/San Francisco Giants (7). **Jackie Robinson** had his #42 retired by Major League Baseball in 1997. Players who were already wearing the number were allowed to continue to do so. Los Angeles had already retired Robinson's number so he's only listed with the Dodgers below. **Nolan Ryan** has had his number retired by three teams—#34 by Texas and Houston and #30 by California (now Anaheim). Five players and a manager have had their numbers retired by two teams: **Hank Aaron**—#44 by the Boston/Milwaukee/Atlanta Braves and the Milwaukee Brewers; **Rod Carew**—#29 by Minnesota and California (now Anaheim); **Rollie Fingers**—#34 by Milwaukee and Oakland; **Carlton Fisk**—#27 by Boston and #72 by the Chicago White Sox; **Frank Robinson**—#20 by Cincinnati and Baltimore; **Casey Stengel**—#37 by the New York Yankees and New York Mets.

Number retired in 2003 (2): CHICAGO CUBS—#10 worn by Ron Santo (1960-73 with Cubs); NEW YORK YANKEES—#49 worn by **Ron Guidry** (1975-88 with Yankees).

American League

Two AL teams—the Seattle Mariners and the Toronto Blue Jays—have not retired any numbers. The Blue Jays have a "level of excellence" which includes Dave Steib (#11), George Bell (#37), and Cito Gaston (#43). All numbers have been used in recent years, however.

Anaheim Angels
11	Jim Fregosi
26	Gene Autry
29	Rod Carew
30	Nolan Ryan
50	Jimmie Reese

Baltimore Orioles
4	Earl Weaver
5	Brooks Robinson
8	Cal Ripken Jr.
20	Frank Robinson
22	Jim Palmer
33	Eddie Murray

Boston Red Sox
1	Bobby Doerr
4	Joe Cronin
8	Carl Yastrzemski
9	Ted Williams
27	Carlton Fisk

Chicago White Sox
2	Nellie Fox
3	Harold Baines
4	Luke Appling
9	Minnie Minoso
11	Luis Aparicio
16	Ted Lyons
19	Billy Pierce
72	Carlton Fisk

Cleveland Indians
3	Earl Averill
5	Lou Boudreau
14	Larry Doby
18	Mel Harder
19	Bob Feller
21	Bob Lemon
455	Fans (# of consecutive sellouts)

Detroit Tigers
2	Charlie Gehringer
5	Hank Greenberg
6	Al Kaline
16	Hal Newhouser
23	Willie Horton

Kansas City Royals
5	George Brett
10	Dick Howser
20	Frank White

Minnesota Twins
3	Harmon Killebrew
6	Tony Oliva
14	Kent Hrbek
29	Rod Carew
34	Kirby Puckett

Oakland Athletics
27	Catfish Hunter
34	Rollie Fingers

New York Yankees
1	Billy Martin
3	Babe Ruth
4	Lou Gehrig
5	Joe DiMaggio
7	Mickey Mantle
8	Yogi Berra & Bill Dickey
9	Roger Maris
10	Phil Rizzuto
15	Thurman Munson
16	Whitey Ford
23	Don Mattingly
32	Elston Howard
37	Casey Stengel
44	Reggie Jackson
49	Ron Guidry

Tampa Bay Devil Rays
12	Wade Boggs

Texas Rangers
34	Nolan Ryan

National League

Two NL teams—the Arizona Diamondbacks and Colorado Rockies—have not retired any numbers. San Francisco has honored former NY Giants Christy Mathewson and John McGraw even though they played before numbers were worn. As did the Philadelphia Phillies for Grover Cleveland Alexander and Chuck Klein.

Atlanta Braves
3	Dale Murphy
21	Warren Spahn
35	Phil Niekro
41	Eddie Mathews
44	Hank Aaron

Chicago Cubs
10	Ron Santo
14	Ernie Banks
26	Billy Williams

Cincinnati Reds
1	Fred Hutchinson
5	Johnny Bench
8	Joe Morgan
18	Ted Kluszewski
20	Frank Robinson
24	Tony Perez

Florida Marlins
5	Carl Barger

Houston Astros
25	Jose Cruz
32	Jim Umbricht
33	Mike Scott
34	Nolan Ryan
40	Don Wilson
49	Larry Dierker

Los Angeles Dodgers
1	Pee Wee Reese
2	Tommy Lasorda
19	Duke Snider
19	Jim Gilliam
20	Don Sutton
24	Walter Alston
32	Sandy Koufax
39	Roy Campanella
42	Jackie Robinson
53	Don Drysdale

Milwaukee Brewers
4	Paul Molitor
19	Robin Yount
34	Rollie Fingers
44	Hank Aaron

Montreal Expos
8	Gary Carter
10	Rusty Staub & Andre Dawson

New York Mets
14	Gil Hodges
37	Casey Stengel
41	Tom Seaver

Philadelphia Phillies
1	Richie Ashburn
14	Jim Bunning
20	Mike Schmidt
32	Steve Carlton
36	Robin Roberts

Pittsburgh Pirates
1	Billy Meyer
4	Ralph Kiner
8	Willie Stargell
9	Bill Mazeroski
20	Pie Traynor
21	Roberto Clemente
33	Honus Wagner
40	Danny Murtaugh

St. Louis Cardinals
1	Ozzie Smith
2	Red Schoendienst
6	Stan Musial
9	Enos Slaughter
14	Ken Boyer
17	Dizzy Dean
20	Lou Brock
45	Bob Gibson
85	August (Gussie) Busch

San Diego Padres
6	Steve Garvey
31	Dave Winfield
35	Randy Jones

San Francisco Giants
3	Bill Terry
4	Mel Ott
11	Carl Hubbell
24	Willie Mays
27	Juan Marichal
30	Orlando Cepeda
44	Willie McCovey

Retired Numbers (Cont.)
National Basketball Association

Boston has retired the most numbers (21) in the NBA, followed by Portland (9); Syracuse Nats/Philadelphia 76ers and New York Knicks (8); Detroit, Los Angeles Lakers, Milwaukee, Phoenix Suns and the KC/Sacramento Kings have (7); Cleveland, New Jersey, the Rochester/Cincinnati Royals have (6). **Wilt Chamberlain** is the only player to have his number retired by three teams: #13 by the LA Lakers, Golden State and Philadelphia. Seven players have had their numbers retired by two teams: **Kareem Abdul-Jabbar**—#33 by LA Lakers and Milwaukee; **Clyde Drexler**—#22 by Houston and Portland; **Julius Erving**—#6 by Philadelphia and #32 by New Jersey; **Bob Lanier**—#16 by Detroit and Milwaukee; **Pete Maravich**—#7 by Utah and New Orleans; **Oscar Robertson**—#1 by Milwaukee and #14 by Sacramento; **Nate Thurmond**—#42 by Cleveland and Golden State.

Numbers retired in 2002-03 (5): BOSTON—#31 worn by **Cedric Maxwell** (1978-85 with Celtics); HOUSTON—#34 worn by **Hakeem Olajuwon** (1984-2001 with Rockets); NEW ORLEANS—#7 worn by **Pete Maravich** (1975-79 with New Orleans Jazz); NEW YORK—#33 worn by **Patrick Ewing** (1986-2000 with Knicks); SAN ANTONIO—#50 worn by **David Robinson** (1987-2003 with Spurs).

Eastern Conference

Two Eastern teams—the Miami Heat and Toronto Raptors—have not retired any numbers.

Atlanta Hawks
9 Bob Pettit
21 Dominique Wilkins
23 Lou Hudson

Boston Celtics
1 Walter A. Brown
2 Red Auerbach
3 Dennis Johnson
6 Bill Russell
10 Jo Jo White
14 Bob Cousy
15 Tom Heinsohn
16 Tom (Satch) Sanders
17 John Havlicek
18 Dave Cowens
19 Don Nelson
21 Bill Sharman
22 Ed Macauley
23 Frank Ramsey
24 Sam Jones
25 K.C. Jones
31 Cedric Maxwell
32 Kevin McHale
33 Larry Bird
35 Reggie Lewis
00 Robert Parish
Loscy Jim Loscutoff (#18)

Radio mic Johnny Most
Chicago Bulls
4 Jerry Sloan
10 Bob Love
23 Michael Jordan

Cleveland Cavaliers
7 Bingo Smith
22 Larry Nance
25 Mark Price
34 Austin Carr
42 Nate Thurmond
43 Brad Daugherty

Detroit Pistons
2 Chuck Daly
4 Joe Dumars
11 Isiah Thomas
15 Vinnie Johnson
16 Bob Lanier
21 Dave Bing
40 Bill Laimbeer

Indiana Pacers
30 George McGinnis
34 Mel Daniels
35 Roger Brown
529 Bob "Slick" Leonard

Milwaukee Bucks
1 Oscar Robertson
2 Junior Bridgeman
4 Sidney Moncrief
14 Jon McGlocklin
16 Bob Lanier
32 Brian Winters
33 Kareem Abdul-Jabbar

New York Knicks
10 Walt Frazier
12 Dick Barnett
15 Dick McGuire
   & Earl Monroe
19 Willis Reed
22 Dave DeBusschere
24 Bill Bradley
33 Patrick Ewing
613 Red Holzman

New Jersey Nets
3 Drazen Petrovic
4 Wendell Ladner
23 John Williamson
25 Bill Melchionni
32 Julius Erving
52 Buck Williams

New Orleans Hornets
7 Pete Maravich
13 Bobby Phills

Orlando Magic
6 Fans ("Sixth Man")

Philadelphia 76ers
2 Moses Malone
6 Julius Erving
10 Maurice Cheeks
13 Wilt Chamberlain
15 Hal Greer
24 Bobby Jones
32 Billy Cunningham
34 Charles Barkley
P.A. mic Dave Zinkoff

Washington Wizards
11 Elvin Hayes
25 Gus Johnson
41 Wes Unseld

Western Conference

Two Western teams—the Los Angeles Clippers and Memphis Grizzlies—have not retired any numbers.

Dallas Mavericks
15 Brad Davis
22 Rolando Blackman

Denver Nuggets
2 Alex English
33 David Thompson
40 Byron Beck
44 Dan Issel

Golden St. Warriors
13 Wilt Chamberlain
14 Tom Meschery
16 Al Attles
24 Rick Barry
42 Nate Thurmond

Houston Rockets
22 Clyde Drexler
23 Calvin Murphy
24 Moses Malone
34 Hakeem Olajuwon
45 Rudy Tomjanovich

Los Angeles Lakers
13 Wilt Chamberlain
22 Elgin Baylor
25 Gail Goodrich
32 Magic Johnson
33 Kareem Abdul-Jabbar
42 James Worthy
44 Jerry West
Radio mic Chick Hearn

Minnesota Timberwolves
2 Malik Sealy

Phoenix Suns
5 Dick Van Arsdale
6 Walter Davis
7 Kevin Johnson
24 Tom Chambers
33 Alvan Adams
42 Connie Hawkins
44 Paul Westphal

Portland Trail Blazers
1 Larry Weinberg
13 Dave Twardzik
15 Larry Steele
20 Maurice Lucas
22 Clyde Drexler
32 Bill Walton
36 Lloyd Neal
45 Geoff Petrie
77 Jack Ramsay

Sacramento Kings
1 Nate Archibald
6 Fans ("Sixth Man")
11 Bob Davies
12 Maurice Stokes
14 Oscar Robertson
27 Jack Twyman
44 Sam Lacey

San Antonio Spurs
13 James Silas
44 George Gervin
50 David Robinson
00 Johnny Moore

Seattle SuperSonics
10 Nate McMillan
19 Lenny Wilkens
32 Fred Brown
43 Jack Sikma
Radio mic Bob Blackburn

Utah Jazz
1 Frank Layden
7 Pete Maravich
35 Darrell Griffith
53 Mark Eaton

National Football League

The Chicago Bears have retired the most uniform numbers (13) in the NFL; followed by the New York Giants (11); the Dallas Texans/Kansas City Chiefs, Boston-New England Patriots and San Francisco (8); the Baltimore-Indianapolis Colts (7); Detroit and Philadelphia (6); Cleveland (5). No player has ever had his number retired by more than one NFL team. The NFL has recently discouraged (though not eliminated) the practice of retiring numbers. As a result, the Green Bay Packers retired the jersey (but not the #92) of defensive end Reggie White in 1999. Nonetheless, Packers GM Ron Wolf announced that there are no plans to reissue the number.

Number retired in 2003 (1): MINNESOTA—#80 worn by **Cris Carter** (1990-2001 with Vikings).

AFC

Four AFC teams—the Baltimore Ravens, Houston Texans, Jacksonville Jaguars and Oakland Raiders—have not retired any numbers.

Buffalo Bills
12 Jim Kelly

Cincinnati Bengals
54 Bob Johnson

Cleveland Browns
14 Otto Graham
32 Jim Brown
45 Ernie Davis
46 Don Fleming
76 Lou Groza

Denver Broncos
7 John Elway
18 Frank Tripucka
44 Floyd Little

Indianapolis Colts
19 Johnny Unitas
22 Buddy Young
24 Lenny Moore
70 Art Donovan
77 Jim Parker
82 Raymond Berry
89 Gino Marchetti

Kansas City Chiefs
3 Jan Stenerud
16 Len Dawson
28 Abner Haynes
33 Stone Johnson
36 Mack Lee Hill
63 Willie Lanier
78 Bobby Bell
86 Buck Buchanan

Miami Dolphins
12 Bob Griese
13 Dan Marino
39 Larry Csonka

New England Patriots
20 Gino Cappelletti
40 Mike Haynes
56 Andre Tippett
57 Steve Nelson
73 John Hannah
78 Bruce Armstrong
79 Jim Lee Hunt
89 Bob Dee

New York Jets
12 Joe Namath
13 Don Maynard

Pittsburgh Steelers
70 Ernie Stautner

San Diego Chargers
14 Dan Fouts

Tennessee Titans
34 Earl Campbell
43 Jim Norton
63 Mike Munchak
65 Elvin Bethea

NFC

Dallas and the Carolina Panthers are the only NFC teams that haven't officially retired any numbers. The Falcons haven't issued uniform #10 (Steve Bartkowski) and #78 (Mike Kenn) since those players retired. The Cowboys have a "Ring of Honor" at Texas Stadium that includes 10 players, one coach and one president/GM—Tony Dorsett, Bob Hayes, Chuck Howley, Lee Roy Jordan, Tom Landry, Bob Lilly, Don Meredith, Don Perkins, Mel Renfro, Tex Schramm, Roger Staubach and Randy White. The Panthers have a Hall of Honor that includes Mike McCormack and Sam Mills.

Arizona Cardinals
8 Larry Wilson
77 Stan Mauldin
88 J.V. Cain
99 Marshall Goldberg

Atlanta Falcons
31 William Andrews
57 Jeff Van Note
60 Tommy Nobis

Chicago Bears
3 Bronko Nagurski
5 George McAfee
7 George Halas
28 Willie Galimore
34 Walter Payton
40 Gale Sayers
41 Brian Piccolo
42 Sid Luckman
51 Dick Butkus
56 Bill Hewitt
61 Bill George
66 Bulldog Turner
77 Red Grange

Detroit Lions
7 Dutch Clark
22 Bobby Layne
37 Doak Walker
56 Joe Schmidt
85 Chuck Hughes
88 Charlie Sanders

Green Bay Packers
3 Tony Canadeo
14 Don Hutson
15 Bart Starr
66 Ray Nitschke

Minnesota Vikings
10 Fran Tarkenton
53 Mick Tingelhoff
70 Jim Marshall
77 Korey Stringer
80 Cris Carter
88 Alan Page

New Orleans Saints
31 Jim Taylor
81 Doug Atkins

New York Giants
1 Ray Flaherty
4 Tuffy Leemans
7 Mel Hein
11 Phil Simms
14 Y.A. Tittle
16 Frank Gifford
32 Al Blozis
40 Joe Morrison
42 Charlie Conerly
50 Ken Strong
56 Lawrence Taylor

Philadelphia Eagles
15 Steve Van Buren
40 Tom Brookshier
44 Pete Retzlaff
60 Chuck Bednarik
70 Al Wistert
99 Jerome Brown

St. Louis Rams
7 Bob Waterfield
29 Eric Dickerson
74 Merlin Olsen
78 Jackie Slater
85 Jack Youngblood

San Francisco 49ers
12 John Brodie
16 Joe Montana
34 Joe Perry
37 Jimmy Johnson
39 Hugh McElhenny
70 Charlie Krueger
73 Leo Nomellini
79 Bob St. Clair
87 Dwight Clark

Seattle Seahawks
12 Fans ("12th Man")
80 Steve Largent

Tampa Bay Bucs
63 Lee Roy Selmon

Wash. Redskins
33 Sammy Baugh

National Hockey League

The Boston Bruins have retired the most uniform numbers (10) in the NHL; followed by Montreal (7); N.Y. Islanders (6); Chicago and Detroit (5). Following his retirement in 1999, the NHL announced that the league would retire **Wayne Gretzky**'s #99. Three other players have had their numbers retired by two teams: **Gordie Howe**—#9 by Detroit and Hartford; **Bobby Hull**—#9 by Chicago and Winnipeg (now Phoenix); and **Ray Bourque**—#77 by Boston and Colorado.

Numbers retired in 2003-04 (2): BOSTON—#8 worn by **Cam Neely** (1986-96 with Bruins); #35 worn by **Mike Richter** (1990-2002 with Rangers).

Eastern Conference

Five Eastern teams—the Atlanta Thrashers, Carolina Hurricanes, Florida Panthers, New Jersey Devils and Tampa Bay Lightning—have not retired any numbers. The Hartford Whalers had retired three numbers: #2 Rick Ley, #9 Gordie Howe and #19 John McKenzie. Mario Lemieux's retired #66 with Pittsburgh has been temporarily unretired during his recent comeback.

Boston Bruins
2 Eddie Shore
3 Lionel Hitchman
4 Bobby Orr
5 Dit Clapper
7 Phil Esposito
8 Cam Neely
9 John Bucyk
15 Milt Schmidt
24 Terry O'Reilly
77 Ray Bourque

Buffalo Sabres
2 Tim Horton
7 Rick Martin
11 Gilbert Perreault
14 Rene Robert

Montreal Canadiens
1 Jacques Plante
2 Doug Harvey
4 Jean Beliveau
7 Howie Morenz
9 Maurice Richard
10 Guy Lafleur
16 Henri Richard

New York Islanders
5 Denis Potvin
9 Clark Gilles
19 Bryan Trottier
22 Mike Bossy
23 Bob Nystrom
31 Billy Smith

New York Rangers
1 Eddie Giacomin
7 Rod Gilbert
35 Mike Richter

Ottawa Senators
8 Frank Finnigan

Philadelphia Flyers
1 Bernie Parent
4 Barry Ashbee
7 Bill Barber
16 Bobby Clarke

Pittsburgh Penguins
21 Michel Briere
66 Mario Lemieux

Toronto Maple Leafs
5 Bill Barilko
6 Ace Bailey

Washington Capitals
5 Rod Langway
7 Yvon Labre
32 Dale Hunter

Western Conference

Four Western teams—the Columbus Blue Jackets, Mighty Ducks of Anaheim, Nashville Predators and San Jose Sharks—have not retired any numbers. Note, the Quebec Nordiques retired the numbers of J.C. Tremblay (3), Marc Tardif (8) and Michel Goulet (16) but these numbers have been worn since the team moved to Colorado. Detroit has not officially retired the number of Larry Aurie (6) but has kept it "out of circulation."

Calgary Flames
9 Lanny McDonald

Chicago Blackhawks
1 Glenn Hall
9 Bobby Hull
18 Denis Savard
21 Stan Mikita
35 Tony Esposito

Colorado Avalanche
77 Ray Bourque

Dallas Stars
7 Neal Broten
8 Bill Goldsworthy
19 Bill Masterton

Detroit Red Wings
1 Terry Sawchuk
7 Ted Lindsay
9 Gordie Howe
10 Alex Delvecchio
12 Sid Abel

Edmonton Oilers
3 Al Hamilton
17 Jari Kurri
99 Wayne Gretzky

Los Angeles Kings
16 Marcel Dionne
18 Dave Taylor
30 Rogie Vachon
99 Wayne Gretzky

Minnesota Wild
1 Fans

Phoenix Coyotes
9 Bobby Hull
25 Thomas Steen

St. Louis Blues
3 Bob Gassoff
8 Barclay Plager
11 Brian Sutter
24 Bernie Federko

Vancouver Canucks
12 Stan Smyl

AWARDS

Associated Press Athletes of the Year

Selected annually by AP newspaper sports editors since 1931.

Male

Lance Armstrong won his fourth consecutive Tour de France in 2002. The cancer survivor started a little slow, losing a long-distance time trial for the first time during his startling four-year streak, but soon dominated the competition, beat all comers as well as suspicions of performance enhancers. Armstrong, who has never failed a drug test, thanked his U.S. Postal Service teammates for their support and his continued success.

The top 3 vote-getters (first place votes in parentheses): 1. **Lance Armstrong**, cycling (45), 292 pts; 2. **Barry Bonds**, baseball (31), 233 pts; 3. **Tiger Woods**, golf (7), 110 pts.

Multiple winners: Michael Jordan and Tiger Woods (3); Don Budge, Sandy Koufax, Carl Lewis, Joe Montana and Byron Nelson (2).

Year		Year		Year	
1931	**Pepper Martin**, baseball	1941	**Joe DiMaggio**, baseball	1951	**Dick Kazmaier**, col. football
1932	**Gene Sarazen**, golf	1942	**Frank Sinkwich**, col. football	1952	**Bob Mathias**, track
1933	**Carl Hubbell**, baseball	1943	**Gunder Haegg**, track	1953	**Ben Hogan**, golf
1934	**Dizzy Dean**, baseball	1944	**Byron Nelson**, golf	1954	**Willie Mays**, baseball
1935	**Joe Louis**, boxing	1945	**Byron Nelson**, golf	1955	**Hopalong Cassady**, col. football
1936	**Jesse Owens**, track	1946	**Glenn Davis**, college football		
1937	**Don Budge**, tennis	1947	**Johnny Lujack**, col. football	1956	**Mickey Mantle**, baseball
1938	**Don Budge**, tennis	1948	**Lou Boudreau**, baseball	1957	**Ted Williams**, baseball
1939	**Nile Kinnick**, college football	1949	**Leon Hart**, college football	1958	**Herb Elliott**, track
1940	**Tom Harmon**, college football	1950	**Jim Konstanty**, baseball	1959	**Ingemar Johansson**, boxing

Year		Year		Year	
1960	**Rafer Johnson**, track	1976	**Bruce Jenner**, track	1992	**Michael Jordan**, pro basketball
1961	**Roger Maris**, baseball	1977	**Steve Cauthen**, horse racing	1993	**Michael Jordan**, pro basketball
1962	**Maury Wills**, baseball	1978	**Ron Guidry**, baseball	1994	**George Foreman**, boxing
1963	**Sandy Koufax**, baseball	1979	**Willie Stargell**, baseball	1995	**Cal Ripken Jr.**, baseball
1964	**Don Schollander**, swimming	1980	**U.S. Olympic hockey team**	1996	**Michael Johnson**, track
1965	**Sandy Koufax**, baseball	1981	**John McEnroe**, tennis	1997	**Tiger Woods**, golf
1966	**Frank Robinson**, baseball	1982	**Wayne Gretzky**, hockey	1998	**Mark McGwire**, baseball
1967	**Carl Yastrzemski**, baseball	1983	**Carl Lewis**, track	1999	**Tiger Woods**, golf
1968	**Denny McLain**, baseball	1984	**Carl Lewis**, track	2000	**Tiger Woods**, golf
1969	**Tom Seaver**, baseball	1985	**Dwight Gooden**, baseball	2001	**Barry Bonds**, baseball
1970	**George Blanda**, pro football	1986	**Larry Bird**, pro basketball	2002	**Lance Armstrong**, cycling
1971	**Lee Trevino**, golf	1987	**Ben Johnson**, track		
1972	**Mark Spitz**, swimming	1988	**Orel Hershiser**, baseball		
1973	**O.J. Simpson**, pro football	1989	**Joe Montana**, pro football		
1974	**Muhammad Ali**, boxing	1990	**Joe Montana**, pro football		
1975	**Fred Lynn**, baseball	1991	**Michael Jordan**, pro basketball		

Female

Serena Williams won three of the four Grand Slam titles and became the world's top-ranked player in 2002. In 2001, Williams had gone 0-4 against 2001 AP Female Athlete of the Year Jennifer Capriati and big sister Venus, but in 2002 she went 9-0 against them and lost just five matches all year.

The top 3 vote-getters (first place votes in parentheses): 1. **Serena Williams**, tennis (53), 351 pts; 2. **Annika Sorenstam** (27), golf, 193 pts; 3. **Sarah Hughes**, skating (12), 158 pts.

Multiple winners: Babe Didrikson Zaharias (6); Chris Evert (4); Patty Berg and Maureen Connolly (3); Tracy Austin, Althea Gibson, Billie Jean King, Nancy Lopez, Alice Marble, Martina Navratilova, Wilma Rudolph, Monica Seles, Kathy Whitworth and Mickey Wright (2).

Year		Year		Year	
1931	**Helene Madison**, swimming	1955	**Patty Berg**, golf	1979	**Tracy Austin**, tennis
1932	**Babe Didrikson**, track	1956	**Pat McCormick**, diving	1980	**Chris Evert Lloyd**, tennis
1933	**Helen Jacobs**, tennis	1957	**Althea Gibson**, tennis	1981	**Tracy Austin**, tennis
1934	**Virginia Van Wie**, golf	1958	**Althea Gibson**, tennis	1982	**Mary Decker Tabb**, track
1935	**Helen Wills Moody**, tennis	1959	**Maria Bueno**, tennis	1983	**Martina Navratilova**, tennis
1936	**Helen Stephens**, track	1960	**Wilma Rudolph**, track	1984	**Mary Lou Retton**, gymnastics
1937	**Katherine Rawls**, swimming	1961	**Wilma Rudolph**, track	1985	**Nancy Lopez**, golf
1938	**Patty Berg**, golf	1962	**Dawn Fraser**, swimming	1986	**Martina Navratilova**, tennis
1939	**Alice Marble**, tennis	1963	**Mickey Wright**, golf	1987	**Jackie Joyner-Kersee**, track
1940	**Alice Marble**, tennis	1964	**Mickey Wright**, golf	1988	**Florence Griffith Joyner**, track
1941	**Betty Hicks Newell**, golf	1965	**Kathy Whitworth**, golf	1989	**Steffi Graf**, tennis
1942	**Gloria Callen**, swimming	1966	**Kathy Whitworth**, golf	1990	**Beth Daniel**, golf
1943	**Patty Berg**, golf	1967	**Billie Jean King**, tennis	1991	**Monica Seles**, tennis
1944	**Ann Curtis**, swimming	1968	**Peggy Fleming**, skating	1992	**Monica Seles**, tennis
1945	**Babe Didrikson Zaharias**, golf	1969	**Debbie Meyer**, swimming	1993	**Sheryl Swoopes**, basketball
1946	**Babe Didrikson Zaharias**, golf	1970	**Chi Cheng**, track	1994	**Bonnie Blair**, speed skating
1947	**Babe Didrikson Zaharias**, golf	1971	**Evonne Goolagong**, tennis	1995	**Rebecca Lobo**, col. basketball
1948	**Fanny Blankers-Koen**, track	1972	**Olga Korbut**, gymnastics	1996	**Amy Van Dyken**, swimming
1949	**Marlene Bauer**, golf	1973	**Billie Jean King**, tennis	1997	**Martina Hingis**, tennis
1950	**Babe Didrikson Zaharias**, golf	1974	**Chris Evert**, tennis	1998	**Se Ri Pak**, golf
1951	**Maureen Connolly**, tennis	1975	**Chris Evert**, tennis	1999	**U.S. Soccer Team**
1952	**Maureen Connolly**, tennis	1976	**Nadia Comaneci**, gymnastics	2000	**Marion Jones**, track
1953	**Maureen Connolly**, tennis	1977	**Chris Evert**, tennis	2001	**Jennifer Capriati**, tennis
1954	**Babe Didrikson Zaharias**, golf	1978	**Nancy Lopez**, golf	2002	**Serena Williams**, tennis

USOC Sportsman & Sportswoman of the Year

To the outstanding overall male and female athletes from within the U.S. Olympic Committee member organizations. Winners are chosen from nominees of the national governing bodies for Olympic and Pan American Games and affiliated organizations. Voting is done by members of the national media, USOC board of directors and Athletes' Advisory Council.

Sportsman

Multiple winners: Lance Armstrong, Eric Heiden and Michael Johnson (3); Matt Biondi and Greg Louganis (2).

Year		Year		Year	
1974	**Jim Bolding**, track	1984	**Edwin Moses**, track	1994	**Dan Jansen**, speed skating
1975	**Clint Jackson**, boxing	1985	**Willie Banks**, track	1995	**Michael Johnson**, track
1976	**John Naber**, swimming	1986	**Matt Biondi**, swimming	1996	**Michael Johnson**, track
1977	**Eric Heiden**, speed skating	1987	**Greg Louganis**, diving	1997	**Pete Sampras**, tennis
1978	**Bruce Davidson**, equestrian	1988	**Matt Biondi**, swimming	1998	**Jonny Moseley**, skiing
1979	**Eric Heiden**, speed skating	1989	**Roger Kingdom**, track	1999	**Lance Armstrong**, cycling
1980	**Eric Heiden**, speed skating	1990	**John Smith**, wrestling	2000	**Rulon Gardner**, wrestling
1981	**Scott Hamilton**, fig. skating	1991	**Carl Lewis**, track	2001	**Lance Armstrong**, cycling
1982	**Greg Louganis**, diving	1992	**Pablo Morales**, swimming	2002	**Lance Armstrong**, cycling
1983	**Rick McKinney**, archery	1993	**Michael Johnson**, track		

Awards (Cont.)
Sportswoman

Multiple winners: Bonnie Blair, Tracy Caulkins, Jackie Joyner-Kersee, Picabo Street and Sheila Young Ochowicz (2).

Year	Year	Year
1974 **Shirley Babashoff**, swimming	1983 **Tamara McKinney**, skiing	1993 **Gail Devers**, track
1975 **Kathy Heddy**, swimming	1984 **Tracy Caulkins**, swimming	1994 **Bonnie Blair**, speed skating
1976 **Sheila Young**, speedskating	1985 **Mary Decker Slaney**, track	1995 **Picabo Street**, skiing
1977 **Linda Fratianne**, fig. skating	1986 **Jackie Joyner-Kersee**, track	1996 **Amy Van Dyken**, swimming
1978 **Tracy Caulkins**, swimming	1987 **Jackie Joyner-Kersee**, track	1997 **Tara Lipinski**, figure skating
1979 **Sippy Woodhead**, swimming	1988 **Florence Griffith Joyner**, track	1998 **Picabo Street**, skiing
1980 **Beth Heiden**, speed skating	1989 **Janet Evans**, swimming	1999 **Jenny Thompson**, swimming
1981 **Sheila Ochowicz**, speed skating & cycling	1990 **Lynn Jennings**, track	2000 **Marion Jones**, track
	1991 **Kim Zmeskal**, gymnastics	2001 **Jennifer Capriati**, tennis
1982 **Melanie Smith**, equestrian	1992 **Bonnie Blair**, speed skating	2002 **Sarah Hughes**, figure skating

UPI International Athletes of the Year

Selected annually by United Press International's European newspaper sports editors from 1974-95.

Male

Multiple winners: Sebastian Coe, Alberto Juantorena and Carl Lewis (2).

Year	Year	Year
1974 **Muhammad Ali**, boxing	1982 **Daley Thompson**, track	1990 **Stefan Edberg**, tennis
1975 **Joao Oliveira**, track	1983 **Carl Lewis**, track	1991 **Sergei Bubka**, track
1976 **Alberto Juantorena**, track	1984 **Carl Lewis**, track	1992 **Kevin Young**, track
1977 **Alberto Juantorena**, track	1985 **Steve Cram**, track	1993 **Miguel Indurain**, cycling
1978 **Henry Rono**, track	1986 **Diego Maradona**, soccer	1994 **Johan Olav Koss**, speed skating
1979 **Sebastian Coe**, track	1987 **Ben Johnson**, track	
1980 **Eric Heiden**, speed skating	1988 **Matt Biondi**, swimming	1995 **Jonathan Edwards**, track
1981 **Sebastian Coe**, track	1989 **Boris Becker**, tennis	1996 discontinued

Female

Multiple winners: Nadia Comaneci, Steffi Graf, Marita Koch and Monica Seles (2).

Year	Year	Year
1974 **Irena Szewinska**, track	1982 **Marita Koch**, track	1990 **Merlene Ottey**, track
1975 **Nadia Comaneci**, gymnastics	1983 **Jarmila Kratochvilova**, track	1991 **Monica Seles**, tennis
1976 **Nadia Comaneci**, gymnastics	1984 **Martina Navratilova**, tennis	1992 **Monica Seles**, tennis
1977 **Rosie Ackermann**, track	1985 **Mary Decker Slaney**, track	1993 **Wang Junxia**, track
1978 **Tracy Caulkins**, swimming	1986 **Heike Drechsler**, track	1994 **Le Jingyi**, swimming
1979 **Marita Koch**, track	1987 **Steffi Graf**, tennis	1995 **Gwen Torrence**, track
1980 **Hanni Wenzel**, alpine skiing	1988 **Florence Griffith Joyner**, track	1996 discontinued
1981 **Chris Evert Lloyd**, tennis	1989 **Steffi Graf**, tennis	

American-International Athlete Trophy

Formerly known as the Jesse Owens International Trophy, the trophy has been presented annually by the International Amateur Athletic Association since 1981 and selected by a worldwide panel of electors.

Multiple winners: Michael Johnson and Marion Jones (2).

Year	Year	Year
1981 **Eric Heiden**, speed skating	1990 **Roger Kingdom**, track	1997 **Michael Johnson**, track
1982 **Sebastian Coe**, track	1991 **Greg LeMond**, cycling	1998 **Haile Gebrselassie**, track
1983 **Mary Decker**, track	1992 **Mike Powell**, track	1999 **Marion Jones**, track
1984 **Edwin Moses**, track	1993 **Vitaly Scherbo**, gymnastics	2000 **Lance Armstrong**, cycling
1985 **Carl Lewis**, track	1994 **Wang Junxia**, track	2001 **Marion Jones**, track
1986 **Said Aouita**, track	1995 **Johan Olva Koss**, speed skating	2002 **Ian Thorpe**, swimming
1987 **Greg Louganis**, diving		
1988 **Ben Johnson**, track	1996 **Michael Johnson**, track	

Honda-Broderick Cup

To the outstanding collegiate woman athlete of the year in NCAA competition. Winner is chosen from nominees in each of the NCAA's 10 competitive sports. Final voting is done by member athletic directors. Award is named after founder and sportswear manufacturer Thomas Broderick.

Multiple winner: Tracy Caulkins (2).

Year		Year	
1977 **Lucy Harris**, Delta St	basketball	1987 **Mary T. Meagher**, California	swimming
1978 **Ann Meyers**, UCLA	basketball	1988 **Teresa Weatherspoon**, La. Tech	basketball
1979 **Nancy Lieberman**, Old Dominion	basketball	1989 **Vicki Huber**, Villanova	track
1980 **Julie Shea**, N.C. State	track & field	1990 **Suzy Favor**, Wisconsin	track
1981 **Jill Sterkel**, Texas	swimming	1991 **Dawn Staley**, Virginia	basketball
1982 **Tracy Caulkins**, Florida	swimming	1992 **Missy Marlowe**, Utah	gymnastics
1983 **Deitre Collins**, Hawaii	volleyball	1993 **Lisa Fernandez**, UCLA	softball
1984 **Tracy Caulkins**, Florida & **Cheryl Miller**, USC	swimming / basketball	1994 **Mia Hamm**, North Carolina	soccer
1985 **Jackie Joyner**, UCLA	track & field	1995 **Rebecca Lobo**, UConn	basketball
1986 **Kamie Ethridge**, Texas	basketball	1996 **Jennifer Rizzotti**, UConn	basketball
		1997 **Cindy Daws**, Notre Dame	soccer

Year		
1998 **Chamique Holdsclaw**, Tennessee . . .basketball		
1999 **Misty May**, Long Beach St. . . . . .volleyball		
2000 **Cristina Teuscher**, Columbia . . . . . . .swimming		

Year		
2001 **Jackie Stiles**, SW Missouri St. . . . . . .basketball
2002 **Angela Williams**, USC . . . . .track
2003 **Natasha Watley**, UCLA . . . . .softball

Flo Hyman Award

Presented annually since 1987 by the Women's Sports Foundation for "exemplifying dignity, spirit and commitment to excellence" and named in honor of the late captain of the 1984 U.S. Women's Volleyball team. Voting by WSF members.

Year	Year	Year
1987 **Martina Navratilova**, tennis	1993 **Lynette Woodward**, basketball	1999 **Bonnie Blair**, speed skating
1988 **Jackie Joyner-Kersee**, track	1994 **Patty Sheehan**, golf	2000 **Monica Seles**, tennis
1989 **Evelyn Ashford**, track	1995 **Mary Lou Retton**, gymnastics	2001 **Lisa Leslie**, basketball
1990 **Chris Evert**, tennis	1996 **Donna de Varona**, swimming	2002 **Dot Richardson**, softball
1991 **Diana Golden**, skiing	1997 **Billie Jean King**, tennis	2003 **Nawal El Moutawakel**, track
1992 **Nancy Lopez**, golf	1998 **Nadia Comaneci**, gymnastics	

James E. Sullivan Memorial Award

Presented annually by the Amateur Athletic Union since 1930. The Sullivan Award is named after the former AAU president and given to the aihlete who, "by his or her performance, example and influence as an amateur, has done the most during the year to advance the cause of sportsmanship." An athlete cannot win the award more than once.

Olympic figure skater **Sarah Hughes** won the 2002 Sullivan Award. Hughes was the surprise winner of the 2002 olympic women's figure skating gold medal at Salt Lake City. The four additional finalists are listed alphabetically: **Natalie Coughlin**, swimming; **Apolo Anton Ohno**, short track speed skating; **Cael Sanderson**, wrestling; **Chris Waddell**, paralympic skiing. Vote totals were not released.

Year	Year	Year
1930 **Bobby Jones**, golf	1955 **Harrison Dillard**, track	1980 **Eric Heiden**, speed skating
1931 **Barney Berlinger**, track	1956 **Pat McCormick**, diving	1981 **Carl Lewis**, track
1932 **Jim Bausch**, track	1957 **Bobby Morrow**, track	1982 **Mary Decker**, track
1933 **Glenn Cunningham**, track	1958 **Glenn Davis**, track	1983 **Edwin Moses**, track
1934 **Bill Bonthron**, track	1959 **Parry O'Brien**, track	1984 **Greg Louganis**, diving
1935 **Lawson Little**, golf	1960 **Rafer Johnson**, track	1985 **Joan B. Samuelson**, track
1936 **Glenn Morris**, track	1961 **Wilma Rudolph**, track	1986 **Jackie Joyner-Kersee**, track
1937 **Don Budge**, tennis	1962 **Jim Beatty**, track	1987 **Jim Abbott**, baseball
1938 **Don Lash**, track	1963 **John Pennel**, track	1988 **Florence Griffith Joyner**, track
1939 **Joe Burk**, rowing	1964 **Don Schollander**, swimming	1989 **Janet Evans**, swimming
1940 **Greg Rice**, track	1965 **Bill Bradley**, basketball	1990 **John Smith**, wrestling
1941 **Leslie MacMitchell**, track	1966 **Jim Ryun**, track	1991 **Mike Powell**, track
1942 **Cornelius Warmerdam**, track	1967 **Randy Matson**, track	1992 **Bonnie Blair**, speed skating
1943 **Gilbert Dodds**, track	1968 **Debbie Meyer**, swimming	1993 **Charlie Ward**, football
1944 **Ann Curtis**, swimming	1969 **Bill Toomey**, track	1994 **Dan Jansen**, speed skating
1945 **Doc Blanchard**, football	1970 **John Kinsella**, swimming	1995 **Bruce Baumgartner**, wrestling
1946 **Arnold Tucker**, football	1971 **Mark Spitz**, swimming	1996 **Michael Johnson**, track
1947 **John B. Kelly, Jr.**, rowing	1972 **Frank Shorter**, track	1997 **Peyton Manning**, football
1948 **Bob Mathias**, track	1973 **Bill Walton**, basketball	1998 **Chamique Holdsclaw**,
1949 **Dick Button**, skating	1974 **Rich Wohlhuter**, track	basketball
1950 **Fred Wilt**, track	1975 **Tim Shaw**, swimming	1999 **Coco and Kelly Miller**,
1951 **Bob Richards**, track	1976 **Bruce Jenner**, track	basketball
1952 **Horace Ashenfelter**, track	1977 **John Naber**, swimming	2000 **Rulon Gardner**, wrestling
1953 **Sammy Lee**, diving	1978 **Tracy Caulkins**, swimming	2001 **Michelle Kwan**, figure skating
1954 **Mal Whitfield**, track	1979 **Kurt Thomas**, gymnastics	2002 **Sarah Hughes**, figure skating

ESPY Awards

The ESPY Awards, which represent the convergence of the sports and entertainment communities, were created by ESPN in 1993 and are given for Excellence in Sports Performance in more than 30 categories. ESPYs are awarded by a panel of sports executives, journalists and retired athletes whose decisions are based on the performances of the nominees during the year preceding the awards ceremony. Note that not all categories are listed below.

Breakthrough Athlete

1993 Gary Sheffield, San Diego Padres	1999 Randy Moss, Minnesota Vikings
1994 Mike Piazza, Los Angeles Dodgers	2000 Kurt Warner, St. Louis Rams
1995 Jeff Bagwell, Houston Astros	2001 Daunte Culpepper, Minnesota Vikings
1996 Hideo Nomo, Los Angeles Dodgers	2002 Tom Brady, New England Patriots
1997 Tiger Woods, golf	2003 Alfonso Soriano, New York Yankees
1998 Nomar Garciaparra, Boston Red Sox	

504   HALLS OF FAME & AWARDS

ESPY Awards (Cont.)

Best Coach/Manager

1993 Jimmy Johnson, Dallas Cowboys
1994 Jimmy Johnson, Dallas Cowboys
1995 George Siefert, San Francisco 49ers
1996 Gary Barnett, Northwestern
1997 Joe Torre, New York Yankees
1998 Jim Leyland, Florida Marlins
1999 Joe Torre, New York Yankees
2000 Joe Torre, New York Yankees
2001 Joe Torre, New York Yankees
2002 Phil Jackson, Los Angeles Lakers
2003 Jon Gruden, Tampa Bay Buccaneers

Best Comeback Athlete

1993 Dave Winfield, Toronto Blue Jays
1994 Mario Lemieux, Pittsburgh Penguins
1995 Dan Marino, Miami Dolphins
1996 Michael Jordan, Chicago Bulls
1997 Evander Holyfield, boxer
1998 Roger Clemens, Toronto Blue Jays
1999 Eric Davis, Baltimore Orioles
2000 Lance Armstrong, cycling
2001 Andres Galarraga, baseball
2002 Jennifer Capriati, tennis
2003 Tommy Maddox, Pittsburgh Steelers

Best Female Athlete

1993 Monica Seles, tennis
1994 Julie Krone, jockey
1995 Bonnie Blair, speed skater
1996 Rebecca Lobo, basketball
1997 Amy Van Dyken, swimming
1998 Mia Hamm, soccer
1999 Chamique Holdsclaw, college basketball
2000 Mia Hamm, soccer
2001 Marion Jones, track
2002 Venus Williams, tennis
2003 Serena Williams, tennis

Best Male Athlete

1993 Michael Jordan, Chicago Bulls
1994 Barry Bonds, San Francisco Giants
1995 Steve Young, San Francisco 49ers
1996 Cal Ripken, Baltimore Orioles
1997 Michael Johnson, Olympic sprinter
1998 Tiger Woods, golf
1999 Mark McGwire, St. Louis Cardinals
2000 Tiger Woods, golf
2001 Tiger Woods, golf
2002 Tiger Woods, golf
2003 Lance Armstrong, cycling

Outstanding Performance Under Pressure

1993 Christian Laettner, Duke
1994 Joe Carter, Toronto Blue Jays
1995 Mark Messier, New York Rangers
1996 Martin Broduer, New Jersey Devils
1997 Kerri Strug, Olympic gymnast
1998 Terrell Davis, Denver Broncos
1999 Mark O'Meara, golf
2000 discontinued

Best Team

1993 Dallas Cowboys
1994 Toronto Blue Jays
1995 New York Rangers
1996 UConn women's hoops
1997 New York Yankees
1998 Denver Broncos
1999 New York Yankees
2000 U.S. Women's World Cup Soccer Team
2001 New York Yankees
2002 Los Angeles Lakers
2003 Anaheim Angels

Best Baseball Player

1993 Dennis Eckersley, Oakland A's
1994 Barry Bonds, San Francisco Giants
1995 Jeff Bagwell, Houston Astros
1996 Greg Maddux, Atlanta Braves
1997 Ken Caminiti, San Diego Padres
1998 Larry Walker, Colorado Rockies
1999 Mark McGwire, St. Louis Cardinals
2000 Pedro Martinez, Boston Red Sox
2001 Pedro Martinez, Boston Red Sox
2002 Barry Bonds, San Francisco Giants
2003 Barry Bonds, San Francisco Giants

Best NFL Player

1993 Emmitt Smith, Dallas Cowboys
1994 Emmitt Smith, Dallas Cowboys
1995 Barry Sanders, Detroit Lions
1996 Brett Favre, Green Bay Packers
1997 Brett Favre, Green Bay Packers
1998 Barry Sanders, Detroit Lions
1999 Terrell Davis, Denver Broncos
2000 Kurt Warner, St. Louis Rams
2001 Marshall Faulk, St. Louis Rams
2002 Marshall Faulk, St. Louis Rams
2003 Michael Vick, Atlanta Falcons

Best NBA Player

1993 Michael Jordan, Chicago Bulls
1994 Charles Barkley, Phoenix Suns
1995 Hakeem Olajuwon, Houston Rockets
1996 Hakeem Olajuwon, Houston Rockets
1997 Michael Jordan, Chicago Bulls
1998 Michael Jordan, Chicago Bulls
1999 Michael Jordan, Chicago Bulls
2000 Tim Duncan, San Antonio Spurs
2001 Shaquille O'Neal, Los Angeles Lakers
2002 Shaquille O'Neal, Los Angeles Lakers
2003 Tim Duncan, San Antonio Spurs

Best WNBA Player

1998 Cynthia Cooper, Houston Comets
1999 Cynthia Cooper, Houston Comets
2000 Cynthia Cooper, Houston Comets
2001 Sheryl Swoopes, Houston Comets
2002 Lisa Leslie, Los Angeles Sparks
2003 Lisa Leslie, Los Angeles Sparks

Best NHL Player

1993 Mario Lemieux, Pittsburgh Penguins
1994 Mario Lemieux, Pittsburgh Penguins
1995 Mark Messier, New York Rangers
1996 Eric Lindros, Philadelphia Flyers
1997 Joe Sakic, Colorado Avalanche
1998 Mario Lemieux, Pittsburgh Penguins
1999 Dominik Hasek, Buffalo Sabres
2000 Dominik Hasek, Buffalo Sabres
2001 Chris Pronger, St. Louis Blues
2002 Jarome Iginla, Calgary Flames
2003 Jean-Sebastien Giguere, Anaheim Mighty Ducks

Outstanding College Football Performer of the Year

1993 Garrison Hearst, Georgia
1994 Charlie Ward, Florida State
1995 Rashaan Salaam, Colorado
1996 Eddie George, Ohio State
1997 Danny Wuerffel, Florida
1998 Peyton Manning, Tennessee
1999 Ricky Williams, Texas
2000 Michael Vick, Virginia Tech
2001 Chris Weinke, Florida State
2002 discontinued

Outstanding College Basketball Performer of the Year

1993 Christian Laettner, Duke
1994 Bobby Hurley, Duke
1995 Grant Hill, Duke
1996 Ed O'Bannon, UCLA
1997 Tim Duncan, Wake Forest
1998 Keith Van Horn, Utah
1999 Antawn Jamison, North Carolina
2000 Elton Brand, Duke
2001 Kenyon Martin, Cincinnati
2002 discontinued

Outstanding Women's College Hoops Performer of the Year

1993 Dawn Staley, Virginia
1994 Sheryl Swoopes, Texas Tech
1995 Charlotte Smith, North Carolina
1996 Rebecca Lobo, Connecticut
1997 Saudia Roundtree, Georgia
1998 Chamique Holdsclaw, Tennessee
1999 Chamique Holdsclaw, Tennessee
2000 Chamique Holdsclaw, Tennessee
2001 Tamika Catchings, Tennessee
2002 discontinued

Best Men's Tennis Player

1993	Jim Courier	1999	Pete Sampras
1994	Pete Sampras	2000	Andre Agassi
1995	Pete Sampras	2001	Pete Sampras
1996	Pete Sampras	2002	Lleyton Hewitt
1997	Pete Sampras	2003	Andre Agassi
1998	Pete Sampras		

Best Women's Tennis Player

1993	Monica Seles	2000	Lindsay Davenport
1994	Steffi Graf	2001	Venus Williams
1995	A. Sanchez Vicario	2002	Venus Williams
1996	Steffi Graf	2002	Venus Williams
1997	Steffi Graf	2003	Serena Williams
1998	Martina Hingis		
1999	Lindsay Davenport		

Best Men's Golfer

1993	Fred Couples	2000	Tiger Woods
1994	Nick Price	2001	Tiger Woods
1995	Nick Price	2002	Tiger Woods
1996	Corey Pavin	2003	Tiger Woods
1997	Tom Lehman		
1998	Tiger Woods		
1999	Mark O'Meara		

Best Women's Golfer

1993	Dottie Mochrie	1999	Annika Sorenstam
1994	Betsy King	2000	Julie Inkster
1995	Laura Davies	2001	Karrie Webb
1996	Annika Sorenstam	2002	Annika Sorenstam
1997	Karrie Webb	2003	Annika Sorenstam
1998	Annika Sorenstam		

Best Jockey

1994	Mike Smith	1999	Kent Desormeaux
1995	Chris McCarron	2000	Chris Antley
1996	Jerry Bailey	2001	Kent Desormeaux
1997	Jerry Bailey	2002	Victor Espinoza
1998	Gary Stevens	2003	Jose Santos

Best Bowler

1995	Norm Duke	2000	Parker Bohn III
1996	Mike Aulby	2001	Walter Ray Williams Jr.
1997	Bob Learn Jr.	2002	Pete Weber
1998	Walter Ray Williams Jr.	2003	Walter Ray Williams Jr.
1999	Walter Ray Williams Jr.		

Best Driver

1993	Nigel Mansell	1999	Jeff Gordon
1994	Nigel Mansell	2000	Dale Jarrett
1995	Al Unser Jr.	2001	Bobby Labonte
1996	Jeff Gordon	2002	Michael Schumacher
1997	Jimmy Vasser	2003	Tony Stewart
1998	Jeff Gordon		

Best Men's Track Athlete

1993	Kevin Young	1999	Maurice Greene
1994	Michael Johnson	2000	Michael Johnson
1995	Dennis Mitchell	2001	Maurice Greene
1996	Michael Johnson	2002	Maurice Greene
1997	Michael Johnson	2003	Tim Montgomery
1998	Wilson Kipketer		

Best Women's Track Athlete

1993	Evelyn Ashford	1999	Marion Jones
1994	Gail Devers	2000	Marion Jones
1995	Gwen Torrence	2001	Marion Jones
1996	Kim Batten	2002	Marion Jones
1997	Marie-Jose Perec	2003	Gail Devers
1998	Marion Jones		

Game of the Year

1996 AFC championship between Colts and Steelers
1997 Rose Bowl, Ohio State edges Arizona St.
1998 Super Bowl XXXII, Broncos over Packers
1999-
2001 not awarded
2002 World Series Game 7, Diamondbacks-Yankees
2003 Fiesta Bowl, Ohio State beat Miami-FL in OT

Best Boxer

1993	Riddick Bowe	1999	Oscar De La Hoya
1994	Evander Holyfield	2000	Roy Jones Jr.
1995	George Foreman	2001	Felix Trinidad
1996	Roy Jones Jr.	2002	Lennox Lewis
1997	Evander Holyfield	2003	Roy Jones Jr.
1998	Evander Holyfield		

Best Male College Athlete

2002 Cael Sanderson, Iowa St. wrestling
2003 Carmelo Anthony, Syracuse basketball

Best Female College Athlete

2002 Sue Bird, UConn basketball
2003 Diana Taurasi, UConn basketball

Best Male Soccer Player

2002 Landon Donovan
2003 Ronaldo

Best Female Soccer Player

2002 Tiffeny Milbrett
2003 Katia

Best Outdoors Athlete

2002 Kevin VanDam, fishing
2003 Jay Yelas, fishing

Best Action Sports Athlete

2002 Kelly Clark, snowboarding
2003 Shaun White, snowboarding

Presidential Medal of Freedom

Since President John F. Kennedy established the Medal of Freedom as America's highest civilian honor in 1963, only 11 sports figures have won the award. Note that (*) indicates the presentation was made posthumously.

Year		President	Year		President
1963	**Bob Kiphuth**, swimming	Kennedy	1991	**Ted Williams**, baseball	Bush
1976	**Jesse Owens**, track & field	Ford	1992	**Richard Petty**, auto racing	Bush
1977	**Joe DiMaggio**, baseball	Ford	1993	**Arthur Ashe***, tennis	Clinton
1983	**Paul (Bear) Bryant***, football	Reagan	2002	**Hank Aaron**, baseball	Bush
1984	**Jackie Robinson***, baseball	Reagan	2003	**John Wooden**, basketball	Bush
1986	**Earl (Red) Blaik**, football	Reagan			

Arthur Ashe Award for Courage

Presented since 1993 on the annual ESPN "ESPYs" telecast. Given to a member of the sports community who has exemplified the same courage, spirit and determination to help others despite personal hardship that characterized Arthur Ashe, the late tennis champion and humanitarian. Voting done by select 26-member committee of media and sports personalities.

Year		Year		Year	
1993	**Jim Valvano**, basketball	1998	**Dean Smith**, college basketball	2002	**Todd Beamer, Mark Bingham, Tom Burnett** and **Jeremy Glick**, Flight 93
1994	**Steve Palermo**, baseball	1999	**Billie Jean King**, tennis		
1995	**Howard Cosell**, TV & radio	2000	**Dave Sanders**, Columbine H.S. coach	2003	**Pat Tillman**, football & **Kevin Tillman**, baseball
1996	**Loretta Clairborne**, special olympics	2001	**Cathy Freeman**, track		
1997	**Muhammad Ali**, boxing				

The Hickok Belt

Officially known as the S. Rae Hickok Professional Athlete of the Year Award and presented by the Kickik Manufacturing Co. of Arlington, Texas, from 1950-76. The trophy was a large belt of gold, diamonds and other jewels, reportedly worth $30,000 in 1976, the last year it was handed out. Voting was done by 270 newspaper sports editors from around the country.

Multiple winner: Sandy Koufax (2).

Year		Year		Year	
1950	**Phil Rizzuto**, baseball	1960	**Arnold Palmer**, golf	1970	**Brooks Robinson**, baseball
1951	**Allie Reynolds**, baseball	1961	**Roger Maris**, baseball	1971	**Lee Trevino**, golf
1952	**Rocky Marciano**, boxing	1962	**Maury Wills**, baseball	1972	**Steve Carlton**, baseball
1953	**Ben Hogan**, golf	1963	**Sandy Koufax**, baseball	1973	**O.J. Simpson**, football
1954	**Willie Mays**, baseball	1964	**Jim Brown**, football	1974	**Muhammad Ali**, boxing
1955	**Otto Graham**, football	1965	**Sandy Koufax**, baseball	1975	**Pete Rose**, baseball
1956	**Mickey Mantle**, baseball	1966	**Frank Robinson**, baseball	1976	**Ken Stabler**, football
1957	**Carmen Basilio**, boxing	1967	**Carl Yastrzemski**, baseball	1977	Discontinued
1958	**Bob Turley**, baseball	1968	**Joe Namath**, football		
1959	**Ingemar Johansson**, boxing	1969	**Tom Seaver**, baseball		

ABC's "Wide World of Sports" Athlete of the Year

Selected annually by the producers of ABC Sports since 1962.

Multiple winners: Greg LeMond and Tiger Woods (2).

Year		Year		Year	
1962	**Jim Beatty**, track	1975	**Jack Nicklaus**, golf	1989	**Greg LeMond**, cycling
1963	**Valery Brumel**, track	1976	**Nadia Comaneci**, gymnastics	1990	**Greg LeMond**, cycling
1964	**Don Schollander**, swimming	1977	**Steve Cauthen**, horse racing	1991	**Carl Lewis**, track & **Kim Zmeskal**, gymnastics
1965	**Jim Clark**, auto racing	1978	**Ron Guidry**, baseball		
1966	**Jim Ryun**, track	1979	**Willie Stargell**, baseball	1992	**Bonnie Blair**, speed skating
1967	**Peggy Fleming**, figure skating	1980	**U.S. Olympic hockey team**	1993	**Evander Holyfield**, boxing
1968	**Bill Toomey**, track	1981	**Sugar Ray Leonard**, boxing	1994	**Al Unser Jr.**, auto racing
1969	**Mario Andretti**, auto racing	1982	**Wayne Gretzky**, hockey	1995	**Miguel Indurlfain**, cycling
1970	**Willis Reed**, basketball	1983	**Australia II**, yachting	1996	**Michael Johnson**, track
1971	**Lee Trevino**, golf	1984	**Edwin Moses**, track	1997	**Tiger Woods**, golf
1972	**Olga Korbut**, gymnastics	1985	**Pete Rose**, baseball	1998	**Mark McGwire**, baseball
1973	**O.J. Simpson**, football & **Jackie Stewart**, auto racing	1986	**Debi Thomas**, figure skating	1999	**Lance Armstrong**, cycling
		1987	**Dennis Conner**, yachting	2000	**Tiger Woods**, golf
1974	**Muhammad Ali**, boxing	1988	**Greg Louganis**, diving	2001	discontinued

Time Person of the Year

Since Charles Lindbergh was named *Time* magazine's first Man of the Year for 1927, two individuals with significant sports credentials have won the honor.

Year
1984 **Peter Ueberroth**, president of the Los Angeles Olympic Organizing Committee.
1991 **Ted Turner**, owner-president of Turner Broadcasting System, founder of CNN cable news network, owner of the Atlanta Braves (NL) and Atlanta Hawks (NBA), and former winning America's Cup skipper.

TROPHY CASE

From the first organized track meet at Olympia in 776 B.C., to the Athens Summer Olympics over 2,700 years later, championships have been officially recognized with prizes that are symbolically rich and eagerly pursued. Here are 15 of the most coveted trophies in America.

(Illustrations by Lynn Mercer Michaud)

America's Cup

First presented by England's Royal Yacht Squadron to the winner of an invitational race around the Isle of Wight on Aug. 22, 1851 . . . originally called the Hundred Guinea Cup . . . renamed after the U.S. boat America, winner of the first race . . . made of sterling silver and designed by London jewelers R. & G. Garrard . . . measures 2 feet, 3 inches high and weighs 16 lbs . . . originally cost 100 guineas ($500), now valued at $250,000 . . . bell-shaped base added in 1958 . . . challenged for every three to four years . . . trophy held by yacht club sponsoring winning boat . . . Cup was badly damaged when a Maori protester repeatedly smashed it with a sledgehammer on March 14, 1997. It was sent back to the original maker and fully restored.

Vince Lombardi Trophy

First presented at the AFL-NFL World Championship Game (now Super Bowl) on Jan. 15, 1967 . . . originally called the World Championship Game Trophy . . . renamed in 1971 in honor of former Green Bay Packers GM-coach and two-time Super Bowl winner Vince Lombardi, who died in 1970 as coach of Washington . . . made of sterling silver and designed by Tiffany & Co. of New York . . . measures 21 inches high and weighs 7 lbs (football depicted is regulation size) . . . valued at $12,500 . . . competed for annually . . . winning team keeps trophy.

Olympic Gold Medal

First presented by International Olympic Committee in 1908 (until then winners received silver medals) . . . second and third place finishers also got medals of silver and bronze for first time in 1908 . . . each medal must be at least 2.4 inches in diameter and 0.12 inches thick . . . the gold medal is actually made of silver, but must be gilded with at least 6 grams (0.21 ounces) of pure gold . . . the medals for the 1996 Atlanta Games were designed by Malcolm Grear Designers and produced by Reed & Barton of Taunton, Mass . . . 604 gold, 604 silver and 630 bronze medals were made . . . competed for every two years as Winter and Summer Games alternate . . . winners keep medals.

Awards (Cont.)

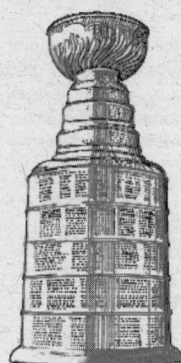

Stanley Cup

Donated by Lord Stanley of Preston, the Governor General of Canada and first presented in 1893 . . . original cup was made of sterling silver by an unknown London silversmith and measured 7 inches high with an 11½-inch diameter . . . in order to accommodate all the rosters of winning teams, the cup now measures 35½ inches high with a base 54 inches around and weighs 32 lbs . . . in order to add new names each year, bands on the trophy are often retired and displayed at the Hall of Fame . . . originally bought for 10 guineas ($48.67), it is now insured for $75,000 . . . actual cup retired to Hall of Fame and replaced in 1970 . . . presented to NHL playoff champion since 1918 . . . trophy loaned to winning team for one year.

World Cup

First presented by the Federation Internationale de Football Association (FIFA) . . . originally called the World Cup Trophy . . . renamed the Jules Rimet Cup (after the then FIFA president) in 1946, but retired by Brazil after that country's third title in 1970 . . . new World Cup trophy created in 1974 . . . designed by Italian sculptor Silvio Gazzaniga and made of solid 18 carat gold with two malachite rings inlaid at the base . . . measures 14.2 inches high and weighs 11 lbs . . . insured for $200,000 (U.S.) . . . competed for every four years . . . winning team gets gold-plated replica.

Commissioner's Trophy

First presented by the Commissioner of baseball to the winner of the 1967 World Series . . . also known as the World Championship Trophy . . . made of brass and gold plate with an ebony base and a baseball in the center made of pewter with a silver finish . . . designed by Balfour & Co. of Attleboro, Mass . . . 30 pennants represent 14 AL and 16 NL teams . . . measures 30 inches high and 36 inches around at the base and weighs 30 lbs . . . valued at $15,000 . . . competed for annually . . . winning team keeps trophy.

Larry O'Brien Trophy

First presented in 1978 to winner of NBA Finals . . . originally called the Walter A. Brown Trophy after the league pioneer and Boston Celtics owner (an earlier NBA championship bowl was also named after Brown) . . . renamed in 1984 in honor of outgoing commissioner O'Brien, who served from 1975-84 . . . made of sterling silver with 24 carat gold overlay and designed by Tiffany & Co. of New York . . . measures 2 feet high and weighs 14½ lbs (basketball depicted is regulation size) . . . valued at $13,500 . . . competed for annually . . . winning team keeps trophy.

Heisman Trophy

First presented in 1935 to the best college football player east of the Mississippi by the Downtown Athletic Club of New York . . . players across the entire country eligible since 1936 . . . originally called the DAC Trophy . . . renamed in 1936 following the death of DAC athletic director and former college coach John W. Heisman . . . made of bronze and designed by New York sculptor Frank Eliscu, it measures 13½ in. high, 6½ in. wide and 14 in. long at the base and weighs 25 lbs . . . valued at $2,000 . . . voting done by national media and former Heisman winners . . . trophy sponsor American Suzuki announced plans for limited fan voting starting in 1999 . . . awarded annually . . . winner keeps trophy.

James E. Sullivan Memorial Award

First presented by the Amateur Athletic Union (AAU) in 1930 as a gold medal and given to the nation's outstanding amateur athlete . . . trophy given since 1933 . . . named after the amateur sports movement pioneer, who was a founder and past president of AAU and the director of the 1904 Olympic Games in St. Louis . . . made of bronze with a marble base, it measures 17½ in. high and 11 in. wide at the base and weighs 13½ lbs . . . valued at $2,500 . . . voting done by AAU and USOC officials, former winners and selected media . . . awarded annually . . . winner keeps trophy.

Ryder Cup

Donated in 1927 by English seed merchant Samuel Ryder, who offered the gold cup for a biennial match between teams of golfing pros from Great Britain and the United States . . . the format changed in 1977 to include the best players on the European PGA Tour . . . made of 14 carat gold on a wood base and designed by Mappin and Webb of London . . . the golfer depicted on the top of the trophy is Ryder's friend and teaching pro Abe Mitchell . . . the cup measures 16 in. high and weighs 4 lbs . . . insured for $50,000 . . . competed for every two years at alternating European and U.S. sites . . . the cup is held by the PGA headquarters of the winning side.

Davis Cup

Donated by American college student and U.S. doubles champion Dwight F. Davis in 1900 and presented by the International Tennis Federation (ITF) to the winner of the annual 16-team men's competition . . . officially called the International Lawn Tennis Challenge Trophy . . . made of sterling silver and designed by Shreve, Crump and Low of Boston, the cup has a matching tray (added in 1921) and a very heavy two-tiered base containing rosters of past winning teams . . . it stands 34½ in. high and 108 in. around at the base and weighs 400 lbs . . . insured for $150,000 . . . competed for annually . . . trophy loaned to winning country for one year.

Borg-Warner Trophy

First presented by the Borg-Warner Automotive Co. of Chicago in 1936 to the winner of the Indianapolis 500 . . . replaced the Wheeler-Schebler Trophy which went to the 400-mile leader from 1911-32 . . . made of sterling silver with bas-relief sculptured heads of each winning driver and a gold bas-relief head of Tony Hulman, the owner of the Indy Speedway from 1945-77 . . . designed by Robert J. Hill and made by Gorham, Inc. of Rhode Island . . . measures 51½ in. high and weighs over 80 lbs . . . new base added in 1988 and the entire trophy restored in 1991 . . . competed for annually . . . insured for $1 million . . . trophy stays at Speedway Hall of Fame . . . winner gets a 14-in. high replica valued at $30,000.

NCAA Championship Trophy

First presented in 1952 by the NCAA to all 1st, 2nd and 3rd place teams in sports with sanctioned tournaments . . . 1st place teams receive gold-plated awards, 2nd place award is silver-plated and 3rd is bronze . . . replaced silver cup given to championship teams from 1939-51 . . . made of walnut, the trophy stands 24¾ in. high, 14⅛ in. wide and 4½ in. deep at the base and weighs 15 lbs . . . designed by Medallic Art Co. of Danbury, Conn. and made by House of Usher of Kansas City since 1990 . . . valued at $500 . . . competed for annually . . . winning teams keep trophies.

World Championship Belt

First presented in 1921 by the World Boxing Association, one of the three organizations (the World Boxing Council and International Boxing Federation are the others) generally accepted as sanctioning legitimate world championship fights . . . belt weighs 8 lbs. and is made of hand tanned leather . . . the outsized buckle measures 10½ in. high and 8 in. wide, is made of pewter with 24 carat gold plate and contains crystal and semi-precious stones . . . side panels of polished brass are for engraving title bout results . . . currently made by Champbelts by Ronn Scala in Pittsburgh . . . champions keep belts even if they lose their title.

World Championship Ring

Rings decorated with gems and engraving date back to ancient Egypt where the wealthy wore heavy gold and silver rings to indicate social status . . . championship rings in sports serve much the same purpose, indicating the wearer is a champion . . . As an example, the Dallas Cowboys' ring for winning Superbowl XXX on Jan. 28, 1996 was designed by Diamond Cutters International of Houston . . . each ring is made of 14 carat yellow gold, weighs 48-51 penny weights and features five trimmed marquis diamonds interlocking in the shape of the Cowboys' star logo as well as five more marquis diamonds (for the team's five Super Bowl wins) on a bed of 51 smaller diamonds . . . rings were appraised at over $30,000 each.

Who's Who

Julius Erving was a star with the New York Nets in
the ABA before joining the NBA's Philadelphia 76ers.

AP/Wide World Photos

Sports Personalities

Nine hundred thirty entries dating back to the 19th century. Entries updated through September 30, 2003.

Hank Aaron (b. Feb. 5, 1934): Baseball OF; led NL in HRs and RBI 4 times each and batting twice with Milwaukee and Atlanta Braves; MVP in 1957; played in 24 All-Star Games, all-time leader in HRs (755), RBI (2,297), total bases (6,856), 3rd in hits (3,771); won 3 Gold Gloves; executive with Braves.

Kareem Abdul-Jabbar (b. Lew Alcindor, Apr. 16, 1947): Basketball C; led UCLA to 3 NCAA titles (1967-69); Final 4 MOP 3 times; Player of Year twice; led Milwaukee (1) and LA Lakers (5) to 6 NBA titles; playoff MVP twice (1971,85), regular season MVP 6 times (1971-72,74,76-77,80); retired in 1989 after 20 seasons as all-time leader in over 20 categories.

Andre Agassi (b. Apr. 29, 1970): Tennis; 58 career tournament wins including the career grand slam; Wimbledon (1992), U.S. Open (1994,99), Australian Open (1995,2000,01,03), French Open (1999); helped U.S. win 2 Davis Cup finals (1990,92), regained the world No. 1 ranking in 1999 for the first time since 1996.

Troy Aikman (b. Nov. 21, 1966): Football QB; consensus All-America at UCLA (1988); 1st overall pick in 1989 NFL Draft (by Dallas); led Cowboys to 3 Super Bowl titles (1992,93,95 seasons); MVP of Super Bowl XXVII.

Marv Albert (b. June 12, 1941): Radio-TV; NBC announcer and radio broadcaster for the New York Knicks, Rangers and Giants who pled guilty to a misdemeanor assault charge amid embarrassing allegations of his sex life. Rehired to MSG and Turner networks in 1998 and NBC in '99.

Tenley Albright (b. July 18, 1935): Figure skater; 2-time world champion (1953,55); won Olympic silver (1952) and gold (1956) medals; became a surgeon.

Amy Alcott (b. Feb. 22, 1956): Golfer; 29 career wins, including five majors; inducted into World Golf Hall of Fame in 1999.

Grover Cleveland (Pete) Alexander (b. Feb. 26, 1887, d. Nov. 4, 1950): Baseball RHP; won 20 or more games 9 times; 373 career wins and 90 shutouts.

Muhammad Ali (b. Cassius Clay, Jan. 17, 1942): Boxer; 1960 Olympic light heavyweight champion; 3-time world heavyweight champion (1964-67, 1974-78,1978-79); defeated Sonny Liston (1964), George Foreman (1974) and Leon Spinks (1978) for title; fought Joe Frazier in 3 memorable bouts (1971-75), winning twice; adopted Black Muslim faith in 1964 and changed name; stripped of title in 1967 after conviction for refusing induction into U.S. Army; verdict reversed by Supreme Court in 1971; career record of 56-5 with 37 KOs and 19 successful title defenses; lit the flaming cauldron to signal the beginning of the 1996 Summer Olympics in Atlanta.

Forrest (Phog) Allen (b. Nov. 18, 1885, d. Sept. 16, 1974): Basketball; college coach 48 years; directed Kansas to NCAA title (1952); 746 wins.

Bobby Allison (b. Dec. 3, 1937): Auto racer; 3-time winner of Daytona 500 (1978,82,88); NASCAR national champ in 1983; father of Davey.

Davey Allison (b. Feb. 25, 1961, d. July 13, 1993): Auto racer; stock car Rookie of Year (1987); winner of 19 NASCAR races, including 1992 Daytona 500; killed at age 32 in helicopter accident at Talladega Superspeedway; son of Bobby.

Roberto Alomar (b. Feb. 5, 1968): Baseball; perennial Gold Glove second baseman and All-Star; MVP of 1992 ALCS; became known well beyond baseball for spitting in the face of umpire John Hirschbeck during final weekend of 1996 season; named MVP of 1998 All-Star Game.

Walter Alston (b. Dec. 1, 1911, d. Oct. 1, 1984): Baseball; managed Brooklyn-LA Dodgers 23 years, won 7 pennants and 4 World Series (1955,59,63,65); retired after 1976 season with 2,063 wins (2,040 regular season and 23 postseason).

Gary Anderson (b. July 16, 1959): Football K; all-time leading scorer in NFL history; had perfect regular season in 1998 (59/59 PAT, 35/35 FG); holds NFL record for consecutive FG made (40); led AFC in scoring 3 times (1983-85 with Steelers) and NFC once (1998 with Vikings).

Sparky Anderson (b. Feb. 22, 1934): Baseball; only manager to win World Series in each league—Cincinnati in NL (1975-76) and Detroit in AL (1984); 3rd-ranked skipper on all-time career list with 2,228 wins (2,194 regular season and 34 postseason); inducted into the Baseball Hall of Fame in 2000.

Mario Andretti (b. Feb. 28, 1940): Auto racer; 4-time USAC-CART national champion (1965-66,69,84); only driver to win Daytona 500 (1967), Indy 500 (1969) and Formula One world title (1978); Indy 500 Rookie of Year (1965); retired after 1994 racing season ranked 1st in poles (67) and starts (407) and 2nd in wins (52) on all-time CART list; father of Michael and Jeff, uncle of John.

Michael Andretti (b. Oct. 5, 1962): Auto racer; 1991 CART national champion with single-season record 8 wins; Indy 500 Rookie of Year (1984); left IndyCar circuit for ill-fated Formula One try in 1993; returned to IndyCar (now CART) in '94; son of Mario.

Earl Anthony (b. Apr. 27, 1938, d. Aug. 14, 2001): Bowler; 6-time PBA Bowler of Year; 41 career titles; first to earn $100,000 in 1 season (1975); first to earn $1 million in career; won 10 Majors (2 Tournamnet of Champions, 6 PBA National Championships and 2 ABC Masters).

Said Aouita (b. Nov. 2, 1959): Moroccan runner; won gold (5000m) and bronze (800m) in 1984 Olympics; won 5000m at 1987 World Championships; formerly held 2 world records recognized by IAAF—2000m and 5000m.

Luis Aparicio (b. Apr. 29, 1934): Baseball SS; retired as all-time leader in most games, assists and double plays by shortstop; led AL in stolen bases 9 times (1956-64); 506 career steals.

Al Arbour (b. Nov. 1, 1932): Hockey; coached NY Islanders to 4 straight Stanley Cup titles (1980-83); retired after 1993-94 season; 2nd on all-time career list with 904 wins (781 regular season and 123 postseason); elected to Hockey Hall of Fame in 1996.

Eddie Arcaro (b. Feb. 19, 1916, d. Nov. 14, 1997): Jockey; 2-time Triple Crown winner (Whirlaway in 1941, Citation in '48); he won Kentucky Derby 5 times, Preakness and Belmont 6 times each.

Roone Arledge (b. July 8, 1931, d. Dec. 5, 2002): Sports TV pioneer; innovator of live events, anthology shows, Olympic coverage, "Monday Night Football" and "Wide World of Sports"; ran ABC Sports from 1968-86; ran ABC News from 1977-98.

Henry Armstrong (b. Dec. 12, 1912, d. Oct. 22, 1988): Boxer; held feather-, light- and welterweight titles simultaneously in 1938; pro record 152-21-8 with 100 KOs.

Lance Armstrong (b. Sept. 18, 1971): Cyclist; This Texan is the fifth 5-time winner of the Tour de France (1999-2003) and just the 2nd man (Miguel Indurain) to win 5 straight; member of the U.S. Postal Service team; returned from treatment for testicular cancer to become the world's top cyclist; only the 2nd American winner (Greg Lemond) in the race's history.

Arthur Ashe (b. July 10, 1943, d. Feb. 6, 1993): Tennis; first black man to win U.S. Championship (1968) and Wimbledon (1975); 1st U.S. player to earn $100,000 in 1 year (1970); won Davis Cup as player (1968-70) and captain (1981-82); wrote black sports history, *Hard Road to Glory*; announced in 1992 that he was infected with AIDS virus from a blood transfusion during 1983 heart surgery; in 1997, the new home for the U.S. Open was named Arthur Ashe Stadium.

Evelyn Ashford (b. Apr. 15, 1957): Track & Field; winner of 4 Olympic gold medals—100m in 1984, and 4x100m in 1984, '88 and '92; also won silver medal in 100m in '88; member of 5 U.S. Olympic teams (1976-92); Inducted into Track and Field and Women's Sports Halls of Fame in 1997.

Red Auerbach (b. Sept. 20, 1917): Basketball; 4th winningest coach (regular season and playoffs) in NBA history; won 1,037 times in 20 years; as coach-GM, led Boston to 9 NBA titles, including 8 in a row (1959-66); also coached defunct Washington Capitols (1946-49); NBA Coach of the Year award named after him; retired as Celtics coach in 1966 and as GM in '84; club president from 1970 to 1997 and then again beginning in 2001.

Tracy Austin (b. Dec. 12, 1962): Tennis; youngest player to win U.S. Open (age 16 in 1979); won 2nd U.S. Open in '81; named AP Female Athlete of Year twice before she was 20; recurring neck and back injuries shortened career after 1983; youngest player ever inducted into Tennis Hall of Fame (age 29 in 1992).

Paul Azinger (b. Jan. 6, 1960): Golf; PGA Player of Year (1987); 12 career wins, including '93 PGA Championship; missed most of '94 season overcoming lymphoma (a form of cancer) in right shoulder blade; member of 4 U.S. Ryder Cup teams (1989,91,93,2002).

Bob Baffert (b. Jan. 13, 1953): Horse racing; 3-time Eclipse Award winner as outstanding trainer (1997-99); trained 3 Kentucky Derby winners (1997,98,02), 4 Preakness winners (1997,98,01,02) and 1 Belmont Stakes winner (2001); 4-time leading annual money leader for trainers (1998-01).

Donovan Bailey (b. Dec. 16, 1967): Track; Jamaican-born Canadian sprinter who set world record in the 100m (9.84) in gold medal-winning performance at 1996 Olympics which stood until '99; set indoor record in 50m (5.56) in 1996; member of Canadian 4x100 relay that won gold in 1996 Olympics.

Oksana Baiul (b. Feb. 26, 1977): Ukrainian figure skater; 1993 world champion at age 15; edged Nancy Kerrigan by a 5-4 judges' vote for 1994 Olympic gold medal.

Hobey Baker (b. Jan. 15, 1892, d. Dec. 21, 1918): Football and hockey star at Princeton (1911-14); member of college football and pro hockey Halls of Fame; college hockey Player of Year award named after him; killed in plane crash.

Seve Ballesteros (b. Apr. 9, 1957): Spanish golfer; has won British Open 3 times (1979,84,88) and Masters twice (1980,83); 3-time European Golfer of Year (1986,88,91); has led Europe to 5 Ryder Cup titles (1985,87,89,95,97).

Ernie Banks (b. Jan. 31, 1931): Baseball SS-1B; led NL in home runs and RBI twice each; 2-time MVP (1958-59) with Chicago Cubs; 512 career HRs.

Roger Bannister (b. Mar. 23, 1929): British runner; first to run mile in less than 4 minutes (3:59.4 on May 6, 1954).

Walter (Red) Barber (b. Feb. 17, 1908, d. Oct. 22, 1992): Radio-TV; renowned baseball play-by-play broadcaster for Cincinnati, Brooklyn and N.Y. Yankees from 1934-66; won Peabody Award for radio commentary in 1991.

Charles Barkley (b. Feb. 20, 1963): Basketball F; 5-time All-NBA 1st team with Philadelphia and Phoenix; U.S. Olympic Dream Team member in '92; NBA regular season MVP in 1993; currently a basketball announcer for TNT.

Leon Barmore (b. June 3, 1944): college basketball coach; respected coach of Louisiana Tech Lady Techsters; retired in Aug. 2002; career win pct. of .869 (576-87, 20 yrs) is best all-time; won national championship with Louisiana Tech in 1988.

Rick Barry (b. Mar. 28, 1944): Basketball F; only player to lead both NBA and ABA in scoring; 5-time All-NBA 1st team; Finals MVP with Golden St. in 1975. Perfected the underhand foul shot.

Sammy Baugh (b. Mar. 17, 1914): Football QB-DB-P; led Washington to NFL titles in 1937 (his rookie year) and '42; led league in passing 6 times, punting 4 times and interceptions once.

Elgin Baylor (b. Sept. 16, 1934): Basketball F; MVP of Final 4 in 1958; led Minneapolis-LA Lakers to 8 NBA Finals; 10-time All-NBA 1st team (1959-65,67-69); LA Clippers' vice president of basketball operations.

Bob Beamon (b. Aug. 29, 1946): Track & Field; won 1968 Olympic gold medal in long jump with world record (29-ft, 2½in.) that shattered old mark by nearly 2 feet; record finally broken by 2 inches in 1991 by Mike Powell.

Franz Beckenbauer (b. Sept. 11, 1945): Soccer; captain of West German World Cup champions in 1974 then coached West Germany to World Cup title in 1990; invented sweeper position; played in U.S. for NY Cosmos (1977-80,83); Member of International Soccer Hall of Champions.

Boris Becker (b. Nov. 22, 1967): German tennis player; 3-time Wimbledon champ (1985-86,89); youngest male (17) to win Wimbledon; led country to 1st Davis Cup win in 1988; has also won U.S. (1989) and Australian (1991,96) Opens.

Chuck Bednarik (b. May 1, 1925): Football C-LB; 2-time All-America at Penn and 7-time All-Pro with NFL Eagles as both center (1950) and linebacker (1951-56); missed only 3 games in 14 seasons; led Eagles to 1960 NFL title as a 35-year-old two-way player.

Clair Bee (b. Mar. 2, 1896, d. May 20, 1983): Basketball coach who led LIU to 2 undefeated seasons (1936,39) and 2 NIT titles (1939,41); his teams won 95 percent of their games between 1931-51, including 43 in a row from 1935-37; coached NBA Baltimore Bullets from 1952-54, but was only 34-116; contributions to game include 1-3-1 zone defense, 3-second rule and NBA 24-second clock.

Jean Beliveau (b. Aug. 31, 1931): Hockey C; led Montreal to 10 Stanley Cups in 17 playoffs; playoff MVP (1965); 2-time regular season MVP (1956,64).

Bert Bell (b. Feb. 25, 1895, d. Oct. 11, 1959): Football; team owner and 2nd NFL commissioner (1946-59); proposed college draft in 1935 and instituted TV blackout rule.

James (Cool Papa) Bell (b. May 17, 1903, d. Mar. 8, 1991): Baseball; member of the Negro Leagues; widely considered the fastest player ever to play baseball; also coached for the Kansas City Monarchs, teaching such players as Jackie Robinson; member of the National Baseball Hall of Fame.

Deane Beman (b. Apr. 22, 1938): Golf; 1st commissioner of PGA Tour (1974-94); introduced "stadium golf" and created The Players Championship; as player, won U.S. Amateur twice and British Amateur once; inducted into the World Golf Hall of Fame in 2000.

Johnny Bench (b. Dec. 7, 1947): Baseball C; led NL in HRs twice and RBI 3 times; 2-time regular season MVP (1970,72) with Cincinnati, World Series MVP in 1976; 389 career HRs.

Patty Berg (b. Feb. 13, 1918): Golfer; 57 career pro wins, including 15 majors; 3-time AP Female Athlete of Year (1938,43,55).

Chris Berman (b. May 10, 1955): Radio-TV; 6-time National Sportscaster of Year known for his nicknames and jovial studio anchoring on ESPN; narrated weekly highlights on "Monday Night Football" 1996-99.

Yogi Berra (b. May 12, 1925): Baseball C; played on 10 World Series winners with NY Yankees; holds WS records for games played (75), at bats (259) and hits (71); 3-time AL MVP (1951,54-55); managed both Yankees (1964) and NY Mets (1973) to pennants.

Jay Berwanger (b. Mar. 19, 1914, d. June 26, 2002): Football HB; Univ. of Chicago star; won 1st Heisman Trophy in 1935; top selection in the 1st-ever NFL Draft (1936).

Gary Bettman (b. June 2, 1952): Hockey; former NBA executive, who was named first commissioner of NHL on Dec. 11, 1992; took office on Feb. 1, 1993.

Abebe Bikila (b. Aug. 7, 1932, d. Oct. 25, 1973): Ethiopian runner; 1st to win consecutive Olympic marathons (1960,64).

Matt Biondi (b. Oct. 8, 1965): Swimmer; won 7 medals in 1988 Olympics, including 5 gold (2 individual, 3 relay); won a total of 11 medals (8 gold, 2 silver and a bronze) in 3 Olympics (1984,88,92).

Larry Bird (b. Dec. 7, 1956): Basketball F; college Player of Year (1979) at Indiana St.; 1980 NBA Rookie of Year; 9-time All-NBA 1st team; 3-time regular season MVP (1984-86); led Boston to 3 NBA titles (1981,84, 86); 2-time Finals MVP (1984,86); U.S. Olympic Dream Team member in '92; inducted into Hall of Fame in 1998; in 1997, named coach of Indiana Pacers and won Coach of the Year honors in first season; led the Pacers to the NBA Finals in 2000 but lost in 6 games to the Lakers and retired; named president of basketball operations of Pacers in 2003.

The Black Sox: Eight Chicago White Sox players who were banned from baseball for life in 1921 for allegedly throwing the 1919 World Series— RHP Eddie Cicotte (1884-1969), OF Happy Felsch (1891-1964), 1B Chick Gandil (1887-1970), OF Shoeless Joe Jackson (1889-1951), INF Fred McMullin (1891-1952), SS Swede Risberg (1894-1975), 3B-SS Buck Weaver (1890-1956), and LHP Lefty Williams (1893-1959).

Earl (Red) Blaik (b. Feb. 15, 1897, d. May 6, 1989): Football; coached Army to consecutive national titles in 1944-45; 166 career wins and 3 Heisman winners (Blanchard, Davis, Dawkins).

Bonnie Blair (b. Mar. 18, 1964): Speed skater; only American woman to win 5 Olympic gold medals in Winter Games; won 500-meters in 1988, then 500m and 1,000m in both 1992 and '94; added 1,000m bronze in 1988; Sullivan Award winner (1992); retired on 31st birthday as reigning world sprint champ.

Hector (Toe) Blake (b. Aug. 21, 1912, d. May 17, 1995): Hockey LW; led Montreal to 2 Stanley Cups as a player and 8 more as coach; regular season MVP in 1939.

Felix (Doc) Blanchard (b. Dec. 11, 1924): Football FB; 3-time All-America; led Army to national titles in 1944-45; Glenn Davis' running mate; won Heisman Trophy and Sullivan Award in 1945.

George Blanda (b. Sept. 17, 1927): Football QB-PK; was pro football's all-time leading scorer (2,002 points) until 2000 when he was finally passed by kicker Gary Anderson; led Houston to 2 AFL titles (1960-61); played 26 pro seasons; retired at age 48.

Fanny Blankers-Koen (b. Apr. 26, 1918): Dutch sprinter; 30-year-old mother of two, who won 4 gold medals (100m, 200m, 800m hurdles and 4x100m relay) at 1948 Olympics.

Drew Bledsoe (b. Feb. 14, 1972): Football QB; 1st overall pick in 1993 NFL draft (by New England); holds NFL season record for most passes attempted (691) and game records for most passes completed (45) and attempted (70); traded to Buffalo before 2002 season.

Wade Boggs (b. June 15, 1958): Baseball 3B; 5 AL batting titles (1983,85-88) with Boston Red Sox; 11-time All-Star; two Gold Gloves; later played with NY Yankees and Tampa Bay; got 3000th career hit with a home run Aug. 7, 1999 against Cleveland.

Barry Bonds (b. July 24, 1964): Baseball OF; set MLB single-season HR in 2001 with 73 also set single-season walks record in 2001 with 177 and then bettered his mark in 2002 with 198 BB; 5-time NL MVP, 2 with Pittsburgh (1990, 92) and 3 with San Francisco (1993,2001-02); one of only 3 players with 40 HRs and 40 SBs in same season (1996); became the 4th player to reach 600 career HRs in Aug., 2002; hit .370 in 2002 at age 38; check baseball chapter for career HR total through 2003; son of Bobby.

Bjorn Borg (b. June 6, 1956): Swedish tennis player; 2-time Player of Year (1979-80); won 6 French Opens and 5 straight Wimbledons (1976-80); led Sweden to 1st Davis Cup win in 1975; retired in 1983 at age 26; attempted unsuccessful comeback in 1991.

Mike Bossy (b. Jan. 22, 1957): Hockey RW; led NY Isles to 4 Stanley Cups; playoff MVP in 1982; 50 goals or more 9 straight years; 573 career goals.

Ralph Boston (b. May 9, 1939): Track & Field; medaled in 3 consecutive Olympic long jumps— gold (1960), silver (1964), bronze (1968).

Ray Bourque (b. Dec. 28, 1960): Hockey D; 12-time All-NHL 1st team; won Norris Trophy 5 times (1987-88,1990-91,94) with Boston; '96 All-Star Game MVP; all-time leader for points and assists by a defenseman; won Stanley Cup in 2001 with Colorado Avalanche; retired in 2001 ranked 8th in scoring (1,579 points) and 3rd in games played (1,612).

Bobby Bowden (b. Nov. 8, 1929): Football; coached Florida St. to 2 national titles (1993,99); entered 2003 season with 332 wins (second only to Joe Paterno) including a 18-7-1 bowl record in 37 years as coach at Samford, West Va. and FSU; father of Clemson head coach Tommy and former Auburn coach Terry.

Riddick Bowe (b. Aug. 10, 1967): Boxer; won world heavyweight title with unanimous dec. over champion Evander Holyfield on Nov. 13, 1992; lost title to Holyfield on maj. dec. Nov. 6, 1993; in 1996, was fined $250k because members of his entourage caused a riot at Madison Square Garden after opponent Andrew Golota was DQ'd for repeated low blows; joined Marines in 1997 but quit after a few days.

Scotty Bowman (b. Sept. 18, 1933): Hockey coach; all-time winningest NHL coach in both regular season (1,244) and playoffs (223) over 30 seasons; coached a record nine Stanley Cup winners with Montreal (1973,76-79), Pittsburgh (1992) and Detroit (1997,98,2002); retired after 2001-02 season.

Jack Brabham (b. Apr. 2, 1926): Australian auto racer; 3-time Formula One champion (1959-60,66); 14 career wins; member of the Hall of Fame.

Bill Bradley (b. July 28, 1943): Basketball F; 2-time All-America at Princeton; Player of the Year and Final 4 MOP in 1965; captain of gold medal-winning 1964 U.S. Olympic team; Sullivan Award winner (1965); led NY Knicks to 2 NBA titles (1970,73); U.S. Senator (D, N.J.) 1979-95; ran for President in 2000.

Pat Bradley (b. Mar. 24, 1951): Golfer; 2-time LPGA Player of Year (1986,91); has won all four majors on LPGA tour, including 3 du Maurier Classics; inducted into the LPGA Hall of Fame on Jan. 18, 1992; among all-time LPGA money leaders and tournament winners (31); captained the 2000 U.S. Solheim Cup team.

Terry Bradshaw (b. Sept. 2, 1948): Football QB; led Pittsburgh to 4 Super Bowl titles (1975-76,79-80); 2-time Super Bowl MVP (1979-80) and regular season MVP in 1978; Fox TV studio analyst.

George Brett (b. May 15, 1953): Baseball 3B-1B; AL batting champion in 3 different decades (1976,80,90); MVP in 1980; led KC to World Series title in 1985; retired after 1993 season with 3,154 hits and .305 average; inducted into Hall of Fame in '99.

Valerie Brisco-Hooks (b. July 6, 1960): Track & Field; won three gold medals at the 1984 Olympics (200 meters, 400 meters and 4x100 relay); first athlete to ever win the 200 and 400 in the same Olympics.

Lou Brock (b. June 18, 1939): Baseball OF; former all-time stolen base leader (938); led NL in steals 8 times; led St. Louis to 2 World Series titles (1964,67); had 3,023 career hits.

Herb Brooks (b. Aug. 5, 1937, d. Aug. 11, 2003): Hockey; former U.S. Olympic coach (1964,68) who coached 1980 "Miracle on Ice" team to gold medal and 2002 U.S. team to silver medal; coached Minnesota to 3 NCAA titles (1974,76,78); also coached NY Rangers, Minnesota, New Jersey and Pittsburgh in NHL.

Jim Brown (b. Feb. 17, 1936): Football FB; All-America at Syracuse (1956) and NFL Rookie of Year (1957); led NFL in rushing 8 times; 8-time All-Pro (1957-61,63-65); 3-time MVP (1958,63,65) with Cleveland; ran for 12,312 yards and scored 126 touchdowns in just 9 seasons; went to jail for 4 mos in 2002 after he was convicted of vandalizing his wife's car and refused court ordered counseling.

Larry Brown (b. Sept. 14, 1940): Basketball; played in ACC, AAU, 1964 Olympics and ABA; 3-time assist leader (1968-70) and 3-time Coach of Year (1973,75-76) in ABA; coached ABA's Carolina and Denver and NBA's Denver, N.J., San Antonio, LA Clippers, Indiana, Philadelphia and Detroit; also coached UCLA to NCAA Final (1980) and Kansas to NCAA title (1988).

Mordecai (Three-Finger) Brown (b. Oct. 18, 1876, d. Feb. 14, 1948): Baseball; nickname derived from injury in a childhood accident that left him with three digits on right hand; injury gave him a particularly nasty curve ball; won the decisive game of the the 1907 World Series as a Chicago Cub; in 1908, first pitcher to record 4 consecutive shutouts and finished at 29-9; career record of 239-130 with lifetime ERA of 2.06; member of Hall of Fame.

Paul Brown (b. Sept. 7, 1908, d. Aug. 5, 1991): Football innovator; coached Ohio St. to national title in 1942; in pros, directed Cleveland Browns to 4 straight AAFC titles (1946-49) and 3 NFL titles (1950,54-55); formed Cincinnati Bengals as head coach and part owner in 1968 (reached playoffs in '70).

Valery Brumel (b. Apr. 14, 1942): Soviet high jumper; dominated event from 1961-64; broke world record 5 times; won silver medal in 1960 Olympics and gold in 1964; highest jump was 7-5¾.

Avery Brundage (b. Sept. 28, 1887, d. May 5, 1975): Amateur sports czar for over 40 years as president of AAU (1928-35), U.S. Olympic Committee (1929-53) and Int'l Olympic Committee (1952-72).

Kobe Bryant (b. Aug. 23, 1978): Basketball; G/F for the LA Lakers; graduated from Lower Merion (Penn.) HS and made the jump directly to the NBA; youngest player (18 yrs., 2 mos., 11 days) ever to appear in an NBA game; became the youngest all-star in NBA history in 1998 and scored a team-high 18 points; won 3 consecutive titles with the Lakers (2000,01,02); accused of rape in 2003 and awaiting trial.

Paul (Bear) Bryant (b. Sept. 11, 1913, d. Jan. 26, 1983): Football; coached at 4 colleges over 38 years; directed Alabama to 6 national titles (1961,64-65,73,78-79); retired as the winningest coach of all-time (323-85-17 record) finally passed by Joe Paterno in 2001; 15 bowl wins, including 8 Sugar Bowls.

Sergey Bubka (b. Dec. 4, 1963): Ukrainian pole vaulter; 1st man to clear 20 feet both indoors and out (1991); holder of indoor (20-2) and outdoor (20-1¾) world records as of Sept. 1, 2002; 6-time world champion (1983,87,91,93,95,97); won Olympic gold medal in 1988, but failed to clear any height in 1992 Games.

Buck Buchanan (b. Sept. 10, 1940, d. July 16, 1992): Football; played both ways in college at Grambling; first player chosen in the first AFL draft by the Dallas Texans who later became the KC Chiefs; missed one game in a 13-year pro career; played in six AFL All-Star games and two Pro Bowls at def. tackle; defensive star of the Chiefs team that won Super Bowl IV; later coached for the New Orleans Saints and Cleveland Browns; member of Pro Football Hall of Fame.

Jack Buck (b. Aug. 21, 1924, d. June 18, 2002): Radio-TV; broadcast baseball games for St. Louis Cardinals from 1954-2001; CBS Radio voice for Monday Night Football (1978-96) and announcer for 1st televised AFL game in 1960; recipient of Baseball Hall of Fame's Ford Frick Award (1987) and Football Hall of Fame's Pete Rozelle Award (1996); received the Purple Heart in WWII; father of sportscaster Joe.

Don Budge (b. June 13, 1915, d. Jan. 26, 2000): Tennis; in 1938 became 1st player to win the Grand Slam— the French, Wimbledon, U.S. and Australian titles in 1 year; led U.S. to 2 Davis Cups (1937-38); turned pro in late '38.

Maria Bueno (b. Oct. 11, 1939): Brazilian tennis player; won 4 U.S. Championships (1959,63-64,66) and 3 Wimbledons (1959-60,64).

Leroy Burrell (b. Feb. 21, 1967): Track & Field; set former world record of 9.85 in 100 meters, July 6, 1994; previously held record (9.90) in 1991; member of 4 world record-breaking 4x100m relay teams.

Susan Butcher (b. Dec. 26, 1956): Sled Dog racer; 4-time winner of Iditarod Trail race (1986-88,90).

Dick Butkus (b. Dec. 9, 1942): Football LB; 2-time All-America at Illinois (1963-64); All-Pro 7 of 9 NFL seasons with Chicago Bears; worked with XFL in 2001.

Dick Button (b. July 18, 1929): Figure skater; 5-time world champion (1948-52); 2-time Olympic champ (1948,52); Sullivan Award winner (1949); won Emmy Award as Best Analyst for 1980-81 TV season.

Walter Byers (b. Mar. 13, 1922): College athletics; 1st exec. director of NCAA, serving from 1951-88.

Frank Calder (b. Nov. 17, 1877, d. Feb. 4, 1943): Hockey; 1st NHL president (1917-43); guided league through its formative years; NHL's Rookie of the Year award named after him.

Lee Calhoun (b. Feb. 23, 1933, d. June 22, 1989): Track & Field; won consecutive Olympic gold medals in the 110m hurdles (1956,60).

Walter Camp (b. Apr. 7, 1859, d. Mar. 14, 1925): Football coach and innovator; established scrimmage line, center snap, downs, 11 players per side; elected 1st All-America team (1889).

Roy Campanella (b. Nov. 19, 1921, d. June 26, 1993): Baseball C; 3-time NL MVP (1951,53,55); led Brooklyn to 5 pennants and 1st World Series title (1955); career cut short when 1958 car accident left him paralyzed.

Clarence Campbell (b. July 9, 1905, d. June 24, 1984): Hockey; 3rd NHL president (1946-77); league tripled in size from 6 to 18 teams during his tenure.

Earl Campbell (b. Mar. 29, 1955): Football RB; won Heisman Trophy in 1977; led NFL in rushing 3 times; 3-time All-Pro; 2-time MVP (1978-79) at Houston.

John Campbell (b. Apr. 8, 1955): Harness racing; 5-time winner of Hambletonian (1987,88,90,95,98); 3-time Driver of Year; first driver to go over $100 million in career winnings.

Milt Campbell (b. Dec. 9, 1933): Track & Field; won silver medal in 1952 Olympic decathlon and gold medal in '56.

Jimmy Cannon (b. 1910, d. Dec. 5, 1973): Tough, opinionated New York sportswriter and essayist who viewed sports as an extension of show business; protégé of Damon Runyon; covered World War II for Stars & Stripes.

Jose Canseco (b. July 2, 1964): Baseball OF/DH; AL Rookie of the Year in 1986 and MVP in 1988 with the Oakland A's; in 1988 he became the 1st player in MLB history with 40 HRs and 40 steals in a season; led AL in HRs in 1988 and tied for lead in 1991; retired in 2003 with 462 career HRs.

Tony Canzoneri (b. Nov. 6, 1908, d. Dec. 9, 1959): Boxer; 2-time world lightweight champion (1930-33,35-36); pro record 141-24-10 with 44 KOs.

Jennifer Capriati (b. Mar. 29, 1976): Tennis; youngest Grand Slam semifinalist ever (age 14 in 1990 French Open); surprise gold medal winner at 1992 Olympics; left tour from 1994 to '96 due to personal problems including an arrest for marijuana possession; surprised many with comeback, winning French Open (2001) and 2 Australian Opens (2001,02).

Harry Caray (b. Mar. 1, 1917, d. Feb. 18, 1998): Radio-TV; baseball play-by-play broadcaster for St. Louis Cardinals, Oakland, Chicago White Sox and Cubs 1945-98; father of sportscaster Skip and grandfather of sportscaster Chip.

Rod Carew (b. Oct. 1, 1945): Baseball 2B-1B; led AL in batting 7 times (1969,72-75,77-78) with Minnesota; MVP in 1977; had 3,053 career hits.

Steve Carlton (b. Dec. 22, 1944): Baseball LHP; won 20 or more games 6 times; 4-time Cy Young winner (1972,77,80,82) with Philadelphia; 329-244 career record; 4,136 career Ks, 2nd all-time (Ryan).

JoAnne Carner (b. Apr. 4, 1939): Golfer; 5-time U.S. Amateur champion; 2-time U.S. Open champ; 3-time LPGA Player of Year (1974,81-82); 7th in career wins (42).

Cris Carter (b. Nov. 25, 1965): Football; WR with Philadelphia (1987-89), Minnesota (1990-2001) and Miami (2002); twice caught 122 passes in a season (1994, '95), the first time establishing an NFL record for catches in a season that was beaten a year later; 2nd player to reach 1000 career catches.

Don Carter (b. July 29, 1926): Bowler; 6-time Bowler of Year (1953-54,57-58,60-61); voted Greatest of All-Time in 1970.

Joe Carter (b. Mar. 7, 1960): Baseball OF; 3-time All-America at Wichita St. (1979-81); won 1993 World Series for Toronto with 3-run HR in bottom of the 9th of Game 6.

Alexander Cartwright (b. Apr. 17, 1820, d. July 12, 1892): Baseball; engineer and draftsman who spread gospel of baseball from New York City to California gold fields; widely regarded as the father of modern game; his guidelines included setting 3 strikes for an out and 3 outs for each half inning.

Billy Casper (b. June 24, 1931): Golfer; 2-time PGA Player of Year (1966,70); has won U.S. Open (1959,66), Masters (1970), U.S. Senior Open (1983); compiled 51 PGA Tour wins and 9 on Senior Tour.

Tracy Caulkins (b. Jan. 11, 1963): Swimmer; won 3 gold medals (2 individual) at 1984 Olympics; set 5 world records and won 48 U.S. national titles from 1978-84; Sullivan Award winner (1978); 2-time Honda Broderick Cup winner (1982,84).

Steve Cauthen (b. May 1, 1960): Jockey; became youngest jockey (18) to win the Triple Crown with Affirmed in 1978; won a record $6.1 million in 1977, winning the Eclipse Award as the nation's top rider and the award for AP male athlete of the year.

Evonne Goolagong Cawley (b. July 31, 1951): Australian tennis player; won Australian Open 4 times, Wimbledon twice (1971,80), French once (1971).

Florence Chadwick (b. Nov. 9, 1917, d. Mar. 15, 1995): Distance swimmer of 1950s; set English Channel records from France to England (1950) and England to France (1951 and '55).

Wilt Chamberlain (b. Aug. 21, 1936, d. Oct. 12, 1999): Basketball C; consensus All-America in 1957 and '58 at Kansas; Final Four MOP in 1957; led NBA in scoring 7 times and rebounding 11 times; 7-time All-NBA first team; 4-time MVP (1960,66-68) in Philadelphia; scored 100 points vs. NY Knicks in Hershey, Pa., Mar. 2, 1962; led 76ers (1967) and LA Lakers (1972) to NBA titles; Finals MVP in 1972.

A.B. (Happy) Chandler (b. July 14, 1898, d. June 15, 1991): Baseball; former Kentucky governor and U.S. Senator who succeeded Judge Landis as commissioner in 1945; backed Branch Rickey's move in 1947 to make Jackie Robinson 1st black player in major leagues; deemed too pro-player and ousted by owners in 1951.

Michael Chang (b. Feb. 22, 1972): Tennis; won the 1989 French Open , becoming the youngest men's champion of a grand slam event (17 years, 3 months.); went 11 consecutive years (1988-98) with at least one title; finished in top 10 in the ATP year-end rankings from 1992-97 (career high no. 2 in 1996).

Julio Cesar Chavez (b. July 12, 1962): Mexican boxer; world jr. welterweight champ (1989-94); also held titles as jr. lightweight (1984-87) and lightweight (1987-89); won over 100 bouts; 90-bout unbeaten streak ended 1/29/94 when Frankie Randall won title on split decision; Chavez won title back 4 months later.

Linford Christie (b. Apr. 2, 1960): British sprinter; won 100-meter gold medals at both 1992 Olympics (9.96) and '93 World Championships (9.87).

Jim Clark (b. Mar. 14, 1936, d. Apr. 7, 1968): Scottish auto racer; 2-time Formula One world champion (1963,65); won Indy 500 in 1965; killed in car crash.

Bobby Clarke (b. Aug. 13, 1949): Hockey C; led Philadelphia Flyers to consecutive Stanley Cups in 1974-75; 3-time regular season MVP (1973,75-76); currently Flyers GM.

Ron Clarke (b. Feb. 21, 1937): Australian runner; from 1963-70 set 17 world records in races from 2 miles to 20,000m; never won Olympic gold medal.

Roger Clemens (b. Aug. 4, 1962): Baseball RHP; twice fanned MLB record 20 batters in 9-inning game (April 29, 1986 and Sept. 18, 1996); won a record 6 Cy Young Awards with Boston (1986-87,91), Toronto (1997,98) and N.Y. Yankees (2001); AL MVP in 1986; won pitching Triple Crown in 1997 and 98; won 2 World Series with Yankees (1999-2000); got 300th win and 4000th strikeout in 2003.

Roberto Clemente (b. Aug. 18, 1934, d. Dec. 31, 1972): Baseball OF; hit over .300 13 times with Pittsburgh; led NL in batting 4 times; World Series MVP in 1971; regular season MVP in 1966; had 3,000 career hits; killed in plane crash; MLB Man of the Year award is named for him.

Alice Coachman (b. Nov. 9, 1923): Track & Field; became the first black woman to win an Olympic gold medal with her win in the high jump in 1948 (London); broke the high school and college high jump records despite not wearing any shoes; member of the National Track & Field Hall of Fame.

Ty Cobb (b. Dec. 18, 1886, d. July 17, 1961): Baseball OF; all-time highest career batting average (.367); hit over .400 3 times; led AL in batting 12 times and stolen bases 6 times with Detroit; MVP in 1911; had 4,191 career hits, 2,245 career runs and 892 steals; played 24 years (22 with Detroit, 2 with Philadelphia); nicknamed "The Georgia Peach"; part of Baseball Hall of Fame's inaugural class.

Mickey Cochrane (b. Apr. 6, 1903, d. June 28, 1962): Baseball C; led Philadelphia A's (1929-30) and Detroit (1935) to 3 World Series titles; 2-time AL MVP (1928,34).

Sebastian Coe (b. Sept. 29, 1956): British runner; won gold medal in 1500m and silver medal in 800m at both 1980 and '84 Olympics; long-time world record holder in 800m and 1000m; elected to Parliament as Conservative in 1992.

Paul Coffey (b. June 1, 1961): Hockey D; 3-time Norris Trophy winner; member of 4 Stanley Cup champions at Edmonton (1984-85,87) and Pittsburgh (1991); ranks 10th on NHL all-time scoring list.

Rocky Colavito (b. August 10, 1933): Baseball OF; six-time all-star who hit 374 HRs over his 14-year career; hugely popular in Cleveland where he played from 1955-59 and then 1965-67; led the league in HRs in 1959 with 42 and RBI in 1965 with 108; hit four consecutive HRs in one game.

Eddie Collins (b. May 2, 1887, d. Mar. 25, 1951): Baseball 2B; led Philadelphia A's (1910-11) and Chicago White Sox (1917) to 3 World Series titles; AL MVP in 1914; had 3,311 career hits and 743 stolen bases.

Nadia Comaneci (b. Nov. 12, 1961): Romanian gymnast; first to record perfect 10 in Olympics; won 3 individual golds at 1976 Olympics and 2 more in '80.

Lionel Conacher (b. May 24, 1901, d. May 26, 1954): Canada's greatest all-around athlete; NHL hockey (2 Stanley Cups), CFL football (1 Grey Cup), minor league baseball, soccer, lacrosse, track, amateur boxing champion; member of Parliament (1949-54).

Tony Conigliaro (b. Jan. 7, 1945, d. Feb. 24, 1990): Baseball OF; youngest (20 years old) to lead the AL in HRs (32 in 1965); hit in the face with a fastball in 1967; came back to hit 36 HRs in 1970 but was never the same.

Gene Conley (b. Nov. 10, 1930): Baseball and Basketball; played for World Series and NBA champions with Milwaukee Braves (1957) and Boston Celtics (1959-61); winning pitcher in 1954 All-Star Game; 91-96 record in 11 seasons.

Billy Conn (b. Oct. 8, 1917, d. May 29, 1993): Boxer; Pittsburgh native and world light heavyweight champion from 1939-41; nearly upset heavyweight champ Joe Louis in 1941 title bout, but was knocked out in 13th round; pro record 63-11-1 with 14 KOs.

Dennis Conner (b. Sept. 16, 1942): Sailing; 3-time America's Cup-winning skipper aboard *Freedom* (1980), *Stars & Stripes* (1987) and the *Stars & Stripes* catamaran (1988); only American skipper to lose Cup, first in 1983 when *Australia II* beat *Liberty* and again in '95 when New Zealand's *Black Magic* swept Conner and his *Stars & Stripes* crew aboard the borrowed *Young America*.

Maureen Connolly (b. Sept. 17, 1934, d. June 21, 1969): Tennis; 1st woman to win Grand Slam (in 1953 at age 18); horse riding accident ended her career in '54 at age 19; won 3 Wimbledons (1952-54), 3 U.S. Opens (1951-53), 2 French Opens (1953-54) and 1 Australian Open (1953); 3-time AP Female Athlete of Year (1951-53).

Jimmy Connors (b. Sept. 2, 1952): Tennis; No.1 player in world 5 times (1974-78); won 5 U.S. Opens, 2 Wimbledons and 1 Australian; rose from No. 936 at the close of 1990 to U.S. Open semifinals in 1991 at age 39; NCAA singles champ (1971); all-time leader in pro singles titles (109) and matches won at U.S. Open (98) and Wimbledon (84).

Jack Kent Cooke (b. Oct. 25, 1912, d. April 6, 1997): Football; sole owner of NFL Washington Redskins from 1985-97; teams won 2 Super Bowls (1988,92); also owned NBA Lakers and NHL Kings in LA; built LA Forum for $12 million in 1967.

Cynthia Cooper (b. April 14, 1963): Women's basketball G; won two NCAA basketball titles at USC (1983-84); won gold medal with U.S. team in 1988; 2-time WNBA MVP and 4-time league champion with Houston Comets; coach of WNBA's Phoenix Mercury 2001-02.

Angel Cordero Jr. (b. Nov. 8, 1942): Jockey; retired third on all-time list with 7,057 wins in 38,646 starts; won Kentucky Derby 3 times (1974,76,85), Preakness twice and Belmont once; 2-time Eclipse Award winner (1982-83).

Howard Cosell (b. Mar. 25, 1920, d. Apr. 23, 1995): Radio-TV; former ABC commentator on *Monday Night Football* and *Wide World of Sports*, who energized TV sports journalism with abrasive "tell it like it is" style.

Bob Costas (b. Mar. 22, 1952): Radio-TV; NBC broadcaster who has been anchor for NBA, NFL and Summer Olympics as well as baseball play-by-play man; 12-time Emmy winner as studio host/play-by-play and 8-time National Sportscaster of Year.

James (Doc) Counsilman (b. Dec. 28, 1920): Swimming; coached Indiana men's swim team to 6 NCAA championships (1968-73); coached the 1964 and '76 U.S. men's Olympic teams that won a combined 21 of 24 gold medals; in 1979 became oldest person (59) to swim English Channel; retired in 1990 with dual meet record of 287-36-1.

Fred Couples (b. Oct. 3, 1959): Golfer; 2-time PGA Tour Player of the Year (1991,92); 15 Tour victories, including 1992 Masters.

Jim Courier (b. Aug. 17, 1970): Tennis; No. 1 player in world in 1992, won 2 Australian Opens (1992-93) and 2 French Opens (1991-92); played on 1992 Davis Cup winner; Nick Bollettieri Academy classmate of Andre Agassi.

Margaret Smith Court (b. July 16, 1942): Australian tennis player; won Grand Slam in both singles (1970) and mixed doubles (1963 with Ken Fletcher); record 24 Grand Slam singles titles—11 Australian, 5 U.S., 5 French and 3 Wimbledon.

Bob Cousy (b. Aug. 9, 1928): Basketball G; led NBA in assists 8 times; 10-time All-NBA 1st team; 1957 MVP; led Boston to 6 NBA titles (1957,59-63); elected to Hall of Fame in 1970, one of NBA's 50 Greatest Players.

Buster Crabbe (b. Feb. 7, 1908, d. Apr. 23, 1983): Swimmer; 2-time Olympic freestyle medalist with bronze in 1928 (1500m) and gold in '32 (400m); became movie star and King of Serials as Flash Gordon and Buck Rogers.

Ben Crenshaw (b. Jan. 11, 1952): Golfer; co-NCAA champion with Tom Kite in 1972; battled Graves' disease in mid-1980s; 19 career Tour victories; won Masters for second time in 1995 and dedicated it to 90-year-old mentor Harvey Penick, who had died a week earlier; captain of 1999 Ryder Cup team.

Joe Cronin (b. Oct. 12, 1906, d. Sept. 7, 1984): Baseball SS; hit over .300 and drove in over 100 runs 8 times each; player-manager in Washington and Boston (1933-47); AL president (1959-73).

Larry Csonka (b. Dec. 25, 1946): Football RB; powerful runner and blocker who gained 8,081 yards in 11 seasons in the AFL and NFL; won two consecutive Super Bowls with the Miami Dolphins (1973-74) and was named MVP in the latter, rushing for 145 yards and two TDs; member of the College and Pro Football Halls of Fame.

Ann Curtis (b. Mar. 6, 1926): Swimming; won 2 gold medals and 1 silver in 1948 Olympics; set 4 world and 18 U.S. records during career; 1st woman and swimmer to win Sullivan Award (1944).

Betty Cuthbert (b. Apr. 20, 1938): Australian runner; won gold medals in 100 and 200 meters and 4x100m relay at 1956 Olympics; also won 400m gold at 1964 Olympics.

Bjorn Dählie (b. June 19, 1967): Norwegian cross-country skier; winner of a record eight gold and 12 overall Winter Olympic medals from 1992-98.

Chuck Daly (b. July 20, 1930): Basketball; coached Detroit to two NBA titles (1989-90) before leaving in 1992 to coach New Jersey; coached NBA "Dream Team" to gold medal in 1992 Olympics; retired in 1994 but returned in 1997 to coach Orlando Magic for two seasons.

John Daly (b. Apr. 28, 1966): Golfer; this big hitter was the surprise winner of 1991 PGA Championship as unknown 25-year old; battled through personal troubles in 1994 to return in '95 and win 2nd major at British Open, beating Italy's Costantino Rocca in 4-hole playoff.

Stanley Dancer (b. July 25, 1927): Harness racing; winner of 4 Hambletonians; trainer-driver of Triple Crown winners in trotting (Nevele Pride in 1968 and Super Bowl in '72) and pacing (Most Happy Fella in 1970).

Beth Daniel (b. Oct. 14, 1956): Golfer; 32 career wins, including 1 major; inducted into World Golf Hall of Fame in 1999.

Alvin Dark (b. Jan. 7, 1922): Baseball OF and MGR; hit .322 to win the NL Rookie of the Year award in 1948 with the Boston Braves; traded to the N.Y. Giants where he led the league in doubles (41) in 1951; won 994 games as a manager and led the Oakland A's to a World Series win in 1974.

Tamas Darnyi (b. June 3, 1967): Hungarian swimmer; 2-time double gold medal winner in 200m and 400m individual medley at 1988 and '92 Olympics; also won both events in 1986 and '91 world championships; set world records in both at '91 worlds; 1st swimmer to break 2 minutes in 200m IM (1:59:36).

Lindsay Davenport (b. June 8, 1976): Tennis player; became first American female to be ranked No. 1 in the world (1998) since Chris Evert in 1985; won U.S. Open (1998), Wimbledon (1999) and Australian Open (2000); Olympic gold medalist at Atlanta in 1996.

Al Davis (b. July 4, 1929): Football; GM-coach of Oakland 1963-66; helped force AFL-NFL merger as AFL commissioner in 1966; returned to Oakland as managing general partner and directed club to 3 Super Bowl wins (1977,81,84); defied fellow NFL owners and moved Raiders to LA in 1982; turned down owners' 1995 offer to build him a new stadium in LA and moved back to Oakland instead.

Dwight Davis (b. July 5, 1879, d. Nov. 28, 1945): Tennis; donor of Davis Cup; played for winning U.S. team in 1st two Cup finals (1900,02); won U.S. and Wimbledon doubles titles in 1901; Secretary of War (1925-29) under President Coolidge.

Ernie Davis (b. Dec. 14, 1939, d. May 18, 1963): Football; star running back at Syracuse University; first black player to win the Heisman Trophy in 1961; drafted by the Washington Redskins and traded to Cleveland but died the following year of leukemia before playing a pro game.

Glenn Davis (b. Dec. 26, 1924): Football HB; 3-time All-America; led Army to national titles in 1944-45; Doc Blanchard's running mate; won Heisman Trophy in 1946.

John Davis (b. Jan. 12, 1921, d. July 13, 1984): Weightlifting; 6-time world champion; 2-time Olympic super-heavyweight champ (1948,52); undefeated from 1938-53.

Terrell Davis (b. Oct. 28, 1972): Football RB; 1998 NFL MVP, rushing for a league-leading 2,008 yards (3rd all-time); played for two Super Bowl winners in Denver (XXXII and XXXIII), earning MVP honors in the former with Super Bowl-record 3 rushing TDs; retired in Aug. 2002 after 3 injury-plagued seasons.

Pat Day (b. Oct. 13, 1953): Jockey; 4-time Eclipse award winner; became all-time leader in earnings in 2002; over 8,000 career victories; won Kentucky Derby (1992), 5 Preaknesses (1985,90,94-96) and 3 Belmonts (1989,94,2000); inducted into Hall of Fame in 1991.

Ron Dayne (b. Mar. 14, 1978): Football RB; NCAA Div. I-A all-time leading rusher, gaining 6,397 yards at Wisconsin (1996-99); 1999 Heisman Trophy winner; selected in 1st round (11th overall) of 2000 NFL draft by NY Giants.

Dizzy Dean (b. Jan. 16 1911, d. July 17, 1974): Baseball RHP; led NL in strikeouts and complete games 4 times; last NL pitcher to win 30 games (30-7 in 1934); MVP in 1934 with St. Louis; 150-83 record.

Dave DeBusschere (b. Oct. 16, 1940, d. May, 14, 2003): Basketball F; youngest coach in NBA history (24 in 1964); player-coach of Detroit Pistons (1964-67); played in 8 All-Star games; won 2 NBA titles as player with NY Knicks; ABA commissioner (1975-76); also pitched 2 seasons for Chicago White Sox (1962-63) with 3-4 record.

Pierre de Coubertin (b. Jan. 1, 1863, d. Sept. 2, 1937): French educator; father of the Modern Olympic Games; IOC president from 1896-1925.

Anita DeFrantz (b. Oct. 4, 1952): Olympics; attorney who became the International Olympic Committee's first female vice president in 1997; first woman to represent U.S. on IOC (elected in 1986); member of USOC Executive Committee; member of bronze medal U.S. women's eight-oared shell at Montreal in 1976.

Oscar De La Hoya (b. Feb. 4, 1973): Boxer; 1992 Olympic gold medallist (lightweight); has held world titles in 4 weight classes (lightweight, super lightweight, welterweight and jr. middleweight); was unbeaten until losing WBC Welterweight belt to Felix Trinidad in a majority decision in 1999; has since moved to jr. middleweight and won WBA and WBC belts.

Cedric Dempsey (b. Apr. 14, 1932): College sports; succeeded Dick Schultz as NCAA executive director (title later changed to president) in 1993 and served until the end of 2002; former athletic director at Pacific (1967-79), San Diego St. (1979), Houston (1979-82) and Arizona (1983-93).

Jack Dempsey (b. June 24, 1895, d. May 31, 1983): Boxer; world heavyweight champion from 1919-26; lost title to Gene Tunney, then lost "Long Count" rematch in 1927 when he floored Tunney in 7th round but failed to retreat to neutral corner; pro record 64-6-9 with 49 KOs.

Bob Devaney (b. April 13, 1915, d. May 9, 1997): Football; head coach at Wyoming from 1957-1961; from 1962 to 1972 built Nebraska into a college football power; won two consecutive national championships in 1970-71; won eight Big Eight Conference titles; later served as Nebraska's athletic director.

Donna de Varona (b. Apr. 26, 1947): Swimming; won gold medals in 400 IM and 400 freestyle relay at 1964 Olympics; set 18 world records during career; co-founder of Women's Sports Foundation in 1974.

Gail Devers (b. Nov. 19, 1966): Track & Field; won Olympic gold medal in 100 meters in 1992 and '96; world champion in 100 meters (1993) and 100-meter hurdles (1993,95,99); overcame thyroid disorder (Graves' disease) that sidelined her in 1989-90 and nearly resulted in having both feet amputated.

Klaus Dibiasi (b. Oct. 6, 1947): Italian diver; won 3 consecutive Olympic gold medals in platform event (1968,72,76).

Eric Dickerson (b. Sept. 2, 1960): Football RB; led NFL in rushing 4 times (1983-84,86,88); ran for single-season record 2,105 yards in 1984; NFC Rookie of Year in 1983; All-Pro 5 times; traded from LA Rams to Indianapolis (Oct. 31, 1987) in 3-team, 10-player deal (including draft picks) that also involved Buffalo; 4th on all-time career rushing list with 13,259 yards in 11 seasons.

Harrison Dillard (b. July 8, 1923): Track & Field; only man to win Olympic gold medals in both sprints (100m in 1948) and hurdles (110m in 1952).

Joe DiMaggio (b. Nov. 25, 1914, d. Mar. 8, 1999): Baseball OF; hit safely in 56 straight games (1941); led AL in batting, HRs and RBI twice each; 3-time MVP (1939,41,47); hit .325 with 361 HRs over 13 seasons; led NY Yankees to 10 World Series titles.

Marcel Dionne (b. Aug. 3, 1951): Hockey C; fourth on NHL's all-time points list (1,771) and third on goals list (731) through 2003; tied Wayne Gretzky for the league lead in points (137) in 1980; scored 50 goals in a season 6 times; won the Lady Byng Award for gentlemanly play in 1975 and 1977; member of the Hockey Hall of Fame.

Mike Ditka (b. Oct. 18, 1939): Football; All-America at Pitt (1960); NFL Rookie of Year (1961); 5-time Pro Bowl tight end for Chicago Bears; returned to Chicago as head coach in 1982 and won Super Bowl XX in 1986; left Bears in 1992 and worked as a broadcaster at NBC for four years; coached the New Orleans Saints from 1997-99; compiled 127-101-0 record in 14 seasons.

Larry Doby (b. Dec. 13, 1924, d. June 18, 2003): Baseball OF; first black player in the AL; joined the Cleveland Indians in July 1947, three months after Jackie Robinson entered the Majors with the NL's Brooklyn Dodgers; an all-star centerfielder from 1949-55; managed the Chicago White Sox in 1978, becoming the second black major league manager; inducted into the Hall of Fame in 1998.

Charlotte (Lottie) Dod (b. Sept. 24, 1871, d. June 27, 1960): British athlete; was 5-time Wimbledon singles champion (1887-88,91-93); youngest player ever to win Wimbledon (15 in 1887); archery silver medalist at 1908 Olympics; member of national field hockey team in 1899; British Amateur golf champ in 1904.

Tony Dorsett (b. Apr. 7, 1954): Football RB; won Heisman Trophy leading Pitt to national title in 1976; 3rd all-time in NCAA Div. I-A rushing with 6,082 yards; led Dallas to Super Bowl title as NFC Rookie of Year (1977); NFC Player of Year (1981); ranks 5th on all-time NFL list with 12,739 yards gained in 12 years.

James (Buster) Douglas (b. Apr. 7, 1960): Boxer; 42-1 shot who knocked out undefeated Mike Tyson in 10th round on Feb. 10, 1990 to win heavyweight title in Tokyo; 8½ months later, lost only title defense to Evander Holyfield by KO in 3rd round.

Vicki Manalo Draves (b. Dec. 31, 1924): Diver; First woman in olympic history to win gold medals in both platform diving and springboard diving; inducted into Int'l Swimming Hall of Fame in 1969.

The Dream Team Head coach Chuck Daly's "Best Ever" 12-man NBA All-Star squad that headlined the 1992 Summer Olympics in Barcelona and easily won the basketball gold medal; co-captained by Larry Bird and Magic Johnson, with veterans Charles Barkley, Clyde Drexler, Patrick Ewing, Michael Jordan, Karl Malone, Chris Mullin, Scottie Pippen, David Robinson, John Stockton and Duke's Christian Laettner.

Heike Drechsler (b. Dec. 16, 1964): German long jumper and sprinter; East German before reunification in 1991; set world long jump record (24-2¼) in 1988; won long jump gold medals at 1992 Olympics and 1983 and '93 World Championships; won silver medal in long jump and bronze medals in both 100- and 200-meter sprints at 1988 Olympics.

Ken Dryden (b. Aug. 8, 1947): Hockey G; led Montreal to 6 Stanley Cup titles; playoff MVP as rookie in 1971; won or shared 5 Vezina trophies; 2.24 career GAA.

Don Drysdale (b. July 23, 1936, d. July 3, 1993): Baseball RHP; led NL in strikeouts 3 times and games started 4 straight years; pitched record 6 shutouts in a row in 1968; won Cy Young (1962); had 209-166 record and hit 29 HRs in 14 years.

Charley Dumas (b. Feb. 12, 1937): U.S. high jumper; first man to clear 7 feet (7-0½) on June 29, 1956; won gold medal at 1956 Olympics.

Tim Duncan (b. Apr. 25, 1976): Basketball C/F; This 7-foot shot-blocker and shot-maker is a 2-time NBA Finals MVP (1999, 2003); 2-time NBA MVP (2002-03); 1997 College Player of the Year at Wake Forest; #1 overall pick by San Antonio (1997); 1998 NBA Rookie of the Year.

Margaret Osborne du Pont (b. Mar. 4, 1918): Tennis; won 5 French, 7 Wimbledon and an unprecedented 25 U.S. national titles in singles, doubles and mixed doubles from 1941-62.

Roberto Duran (b. June 16, 1951): Panamanian boxer; one of only 6 fighters to hold 4 different world titles— lightweight (1972-79), welterweight (1980), junior middleweight (1983) and middleweight (1989-90); lost famous "No Mas" welterweight title bout when he quit in 8th round against Sugar Ray Leonard (1980); finally retired in 2002 at the age of 50 with a record of 104-16 (69 KOs).

Leo Durocher (b. July 27, 1905, d. Oct. 7, 1991): Baseball; managed in NL 24 years; won 2,015 games, including postseason; 3 pennants with Brooklyn (1941) and NY Giants (1951,54); won World Series in 1954.

Eddie Eagan (b. Apr. 26, 1898, d. June 14, 1967): Only athlete to win gold medals in both Summer and Winter Olympics (Boxing—1920, Bobsled—1932).

Alan Eagleson (b. Apr. 24, 1933): Hockey; Toronto lawyer, agent and 1st executive director of NHL Players Assn. (1967-90); midwifed Team Canada vs. Soviet series (1972) and Canada Cup; charged with racketeering and defrauding NHLPA in indictment handed down by U.S. grand jury in 1994; was sentenced to 18 months in jail in Jan. 1998 after pleading guilty but only served 6 months; resigned from Hall of Fame in 1998.

Dale Earnhardt (b. Apr. 29, 1951, d. Feb. 18, 2001): Auto racer; 7-time NASCAR national champion (1980,86-87,90-91,93-94); Rookie of Year in 1979; was all-time NASCAR money leader (now 2nd) with over $34 million won and 6th on career wins list with 76 when he died; finally won Daytona 500 in 1998 on 20th attempt; died in last lap crash at the 2001 Daytona 500.

James Easton (b. July 26, 1935): Olympics; archer and sporting goods manufacturer (Easton softball bats); one of 4 American delegates to the International Olympic Committee; president of International Archery Federation (FITA); member of LA Olympic Organizing Committee in 1984.

Dennis Eckersley (b. Oct. 3, 1954): Baseball P; began his career as a starter in 1975 with Cleveland; no-hit Angels in 1977; won 20 games in 1978 with Boston; moved to the bullpen after 12 seasons as a starter and became one of the best closers of all-time with Oakland; won 1992 AL Cy Young and MVP.

Stefan Edberg (b. Jan. 19, 1966): Swedish tennis player; 2-time No.1 player (1990-91); 2-time winner of Australian Open (1985,87), Wimbledon (1988,90) and U.S. Open (1991-92).

Gertrude Ederle (b. Oct. 23, 1906): Swimmer; 1st woman to swim English Channel, breaking men's record by 2 hours in 1926; won 3 medals in 1924 Olympics.

Krisztina Egerszegi (b. Aug. 16, 1974): Hungarian swimmer; 3-time gold medal winner (100m and 200m backstroke and 400m IM) at 1992 Olympics; also won a gold (200m back) and silver (100m back) at 1988 Games; youngest (14) ever to win swimming gold. Won fifth gold medal (200m back) at '96 Games.

Lee Elder (b. July 14, 1934): Golf; in 1975, became the first black golfer to play in the Masters Tournament; also played in the 1977 Masters; member of the 1979 U.S. Ryder Cup team; played in South Africa's first integrated tournament in 1972.

Todd Eldredge (b. Aug. 28, 1971): Figure Skater; 6-time U.S. champion (1990,91,95,97,98,2002); 1996 World Champion; won U.S. titles at all three levels (novice, junior and senior); most decorated American figure skater without an Olympic medal.

Bill Elliott (b. Oct. 8, 1955): Auto racer; 2-time winner of Daytona 500 (1985,87); NASCAR national champ in 1988; 43 NASCAR wins as of Sept. 2002.

Herb Elliott (b. Feb. 25, 1938): Australian runner; undefeated from 1958-60; ran 17 sub-4:00 miles; 3 world records; won gold medal in 1500 meters at 1960 Olympics; retired at age 22.

Ernie Els (b. Oct. 17, 1969): Golfer; sweet swinging South African; 1994 PGA Tour Rookie of the Year and European Golfer of the Year; 2-time U.S. Open winner (1994,97); won 3rd major in 2002 British Open playoff; #2 ranked player in the world in 2003.

John Elway (b. June 28, 1960): Football QB; All-American at Stanford; #1 overall pick in the famous quarterback draft of 1983; known for his last-minute, game-winning scoring drives; led Broncos to 3 Super Bowl losses before back-to-back wins in Super Bowl XXXII and XXXIII; 1987 NFL MVP; 4-time Pro Bowler; one of only two quarterbacks (Marino) to throw for over 50,000 yards.

Roy Emerson (b. Nov. 3, 1936): Australian tennis player; won 12 majors in singles— 6 Australian, 2 French, 2 Wimbledon and 2 U.S. from 1961-67.

Kornelia Ender (b. Oct. 25, 1958): East German swimmer; 1st woman to win 4 gold medals at one Olympics (1976), all in world-record time.

Julius Erving (b. Feb. 22, 1950): Basketball F; "Dr. J"; in ABA (1971-76)— 3-time MVP, 2-time playoff MVP, led NY Nets to 2 titles (1974,76); in NBA (1976-87)— 5-time All-NBA 1st team, MVP in 1981, led Philadelphia 76ers to title in 1983.

Phil Esposito (b. Feb. 20, 1942): Hockey C; 1st NHL player to score 100 points in a season (126 in 1969); 6-time All-NHL 1st team with Boston (1969-74); 2-time MVP (1969,74); 5-time scoring champ; star of 1972 Canada-Soviet series; former president-GM of Tampa Bay Lightning.

Janet Evans (b. Aug. 28, 1971): Swimmer; won 3 individual gold medals (400m & 800m freestyle, 400m IM) at 1988 Olympics; 1989 Sullivan Award winner; won 1 gold (800m) and 1 silver (400m) at 1992 Olympics.

Lee Evans (b. Feb. 25, 1947): Track & Field; dominant quarter-miler in world from 1966-72; world record in 400m set at 1968 Olympics stood 20 years.

Chris Evert (b. Dec. 21, 1954): Tennis; No. 1 player in world 5 times (1975-77,80-81); won at least 1 Grand Slam singles title every year from 1974-86; 18 majors in all— 7 French, 6 U.S., 3 Wimbledon and 2 Australian; retired after 1989 season with 154 singles titles and $8,896,195 in career earnings.

Weeb Ewbank (b. May 6, 1907, d. Nov. 18, 1998): Football; only coach to win NFL and AFL titles; led Baltimore to 2 NFL titles (1958-59) and NY Jets to Super Bowl III win.

Patrick Ewing (b. Aug. 5, 1962): Basketball C; 3-time All-America; led Georgetown to 3 NCAA Finals and 1984 title; Final 4 MOP in '84; 1986 NBA Rookie of Year with New York; All-NBA (1990); on U.S. Olympic gold medal-winning teams in 1984 and '92; named one of the NBA's 50 Greatest Players; retired after 2001-02 season.

Ray Ewry (b. Oct. 14, 1873, d. Sept. 29, 1937): Track & Field; won 10 gold medals (although 2 are not recognized by IOC) over 4 consecutive Olympics (1900,04,06,08); all events he won (Standing HJ, LJ and TJ) were discontinued in 1912.

Nick Faldo (b. July 18, 1957): British golfer; 3-time winner of British Open (1987,90,92) and Masters (1989, 90, 96); 3-time European Golfer of Year (1989-90,92); PGA Player of Year in 1990.

Juan Manuel Fangio (b. June 24, 1911-, d. July 17, 1995): Argentine auto racer; 5-time Formula One world champion (1951,54-57); 24 career wins, retired in 1958.

Marshall Faulk (b. Feb. 26, 1973): Football RB; 3-time consensus All-America at San Diego St.; 2-time NCAA Div. I-A rushing leader (1991-92); 2nd overall pick (Indianapolis) of the 1994 NFL draft; traded to St.L Rams in 1999; 3-time AP Offensive Player of the Year (1999-2001); NFL MVP in 2000 (AP/PFWA) and 2001 (Bell/PFWA); set NFL record with 26 TDs (18 rush, 8 rec.) in 2000.

Brett Favre (b. Oct. 10, 1969): Football QB; Selected in the second round (33rd overall) by the Atlanta Falcons in the 1991 NFL draft; traded to Green Bay Packers in 1992; league MVP in 1995, '96 and '97; 6-time Pro Bowl QB; 100th TD pass came in his 62nd game, third-fastest in league history; 39 TD passes in 1996 season broke his own NFC record of 38 set in 1995 (since broken by Kurt Warner — 41 in 1999); led Packers to Super Bowl victory in 1997.

Sergei Fedorov (b. Dec. 13, 1969): Hockey C; first Russian to win NHL Hart Trophy as 1993-94 regular season MVP; 5-time All-Star and 3-time Stanley Cup winner (1997,98,2002) with Detroit.

Donald Fehr (b. July 18, 1948): Baseball labor leader; protégé of Marvin Miller; executive director and general counsel of Major League Players Assn. since 1983; led players in 1994 "salary cap" strike that lasted eight months and resulted in first cancellation of World Series since 1904.

Bob Feller (b. Nov. 3, 1918): Baseball RHP; led AL in strikeouts 7 times and wins 6 times with Cleveland; threw 3 no-hitters and 12 one-hitters; 266-162 record.

Tom Ferguson (b. Dec. 20, 1950): Rodeo; 6-time All-Around champion (1974-79); 1st cowboy to win $100,000 in one season (1978); 1st to win $1 million in career (1986).

Herve Filion (b. Feb. 1, 1940): Harness racing; 10-time Driver of Year; all-time leader in races won with 14,783 in 35 years.

Rollie Fingers (b. Aug. 25, 1946): Baseball RHP; relief ace with 341 career saves; won AL MVP and Cy Young awards in 1981 with Milwaukee; World Series MVP in 1974 with Oakland.

Charles O. Finley (b. Feb. 22, 1918, d. Feb. 19, 1997): Baseball owner; moved KC A's to Oakland in 1968; won 3 straight World Series from 1972-74; also owned teams in NHL and ABA.

Bobby Fischer (b. Mar. 9, 1943): Chess; at 15, became youngest international grandmaster in chess history; only American to hold world championship (1972-75); was stripped of title in 1975 after refusing to defend against Anatoly Karpov and became recluse; re-emerged to defeat old foe and former world champion Boris Spassky in 1992.

Carlton Fisk (b. Dec. 26, 1947): Baseball C; holds all-time major league record for games caught (2,229); also all-time HR leader for catchers (376); AL Rookie of Year (1972) and 10-time All-Star; hit epic, 12th-inning Game 6 homer for Boston Red Sox in 1975 World Series; inducted into the Baseball Hall of Fame in 2000.

Emerson Fittipaldi (b. Dec. 12, 1946): Brazilian auto racer; 2-time Formula One world champion (1972,74); 2-time winner of Indy 500 (1989,93); won overall IndyCar title in 1989.

Bob Fitzsimmons (b. May 26, 1863, d. Oct. 22, 1917): British boxer; held three world titles— middleweight (1881-97), heavyweight (1897-99) and light heavyweight (1903-05); pro record 40-11 with 32 KOs.

James (Sunny Jim) Fitzsimmons (b. July 23, 1874, d. Mar. 11, 1966): Horse racing; trained horses that won over 2,275 races, including 2 Triple Crown winners— Gallant Fox in 1930 and Omaha in '35.

Jim Fixx (b. Apr. 23, 1932, d. July 20, 1984): Running; author who popularized the sport of running; his 1977 bestseller The Complete Book of Running, is credited with helping start America's fitness revolution; died of a heart attack while running.

Larry Fleisher (b. Sept. 26, 1930, d. May 4, 1989): Basketball; led NBA players union from 1961-89; increased average yearly salary from $9,400 in 1967 to $600,000 without a strike.

Peggy Fleming (b. July 27, 1948): Figure skating; 3-time world champion (1966-68); won Olympic gold medal in 1968.

Curt Flood (b. Jan. 18, 1938, d. Jan. 20, 1997): Baseball OF; played 15 years (1956-69,71) mainly with St. Louis; hit over .300 6 times with 7 Gold Gloves; refused trade to Phillies in 1969; lost challenge to baseball's reserve clause in Supreme Court in 1972.

Ray Floyd (b. Sept. 14, 1942): Golfer; has 22 PGA victories in 4 decades; joined Senior PGA Tour in 1992 and has 14 Senior wins; has won Masters (1976), U.S. Open (1986), PGA twice (1969,82) and PGA Seniors Championship (1995); first player to win on PGA and Senior tours in same year (1992); member of 8 Ryder Cup teams and captain in 1989.

Doug Flutie (b. Oct. 23, 1962): Football QB; won Heisman Trophy with Boston College (1984); has played in USFL, NFL and CFL; 6-time CFL MVP with B.C. Lions (1991), Calgary (1992-94) and Toronto (1996-97); led Calgary (1992) and Toronto (1996-97) to Grey Cup titles; returned to NFL in 1998 with Buffalo and became part of QB controversy with Rob Johnson; signed by San Diego in 2001.

Whitey Ford (b. Oct. 21, 1928): Baseball LHP; all-time leader in World Series wins (10); led AL in wins 3 times; won Cy Young and World Series MVP in 1961 with NY Yankees; 236-106 record.

George Foreman (b. Jan. 10, 1949): Boxer; Olympic heavyweight champ (1968); world heavyweight champ (1973-74, 94-95); lost title to Muhammad Ali (KO-8th) in '74; recaptured it on Nov. 5, 1994 at age 45 with a 10-round KO of WBA/IBF champ Michael Moorer, becoming the oldest man to win heavyweight crown; named AP Male Athlete of Year 20 years after losing title to Ali; stripped of WBA title in 1995 after declining to fight No. 1 contender; successfully defended title at age 46 against 26-year-old Axel Schulz in controversial maj. decision; gave up IBF title after refusing rematch with Schulz.

Dick Fosbury (b. Mar. 6, 1947): Track & Field; revolutionized high jump with back-first "Fosbury Flop"; won gold medal at 1968 Olympics.

Greg Foster (b. Aug. 4, 1958): Track & Field; 3-time winner of World Championship in 110-m hurdles (1983,87,91); won silver in 1984 Olympics; world indoor champion in 1991.

The Four Horsemen Senior backfield that led Notre Dame to national collegiate football championship in 1924; put together as sophomores by Irish coach Knute Rockne; immortalized by sportswriter Grantland Rice, whose report of the Oct. 19, 1924, Notre Dame-Army game began: "Outlined against a blue, gray October sky the Four Horsemen rode again . . ."; HB Jim Crowley (b. Sept. 10, 1902, d. Jan. 15, 1986), FB Elmer Layden (b. May 4, 1903, d. June 30, 1973), HB Don Miller (b. May 30, 1902, d. July 28, 1979) and QB Harry Stuhldreher (b. Oct. 14, 1901, d. Jan. 26, 1965).

The Four Musketeers French quartet that dominated men's tennis in 1920s and '30s, winning 8 straight French singles titles (1925-32), 6 Wimbledons in a row (1924-29) and 6 consecutive Davis Cups (1927-32) — Jean Borotra (b. Aug. 13, 1898, d. July 17, 1994), Jacques Brugnon (b. May 11, 1895, d. Mar. 20, 1978), Henri Cochet (b. Dec. 14, 1901, d. Apr. 1, 1987), Rene Lacoste (b. July 2, 1905, d. Oct. 13, 1996).

Nellie Fox (b. Dec. 25, 1927, d. Dec. 1, 1975): Baseball 2B; batted .306 in 1959 to win the AL MVP award with the pennant-winning Chicago White Sox; led the league in fielding percentage six times, hits four times and triples once; ended his 19-year career with 2,663 hits, 1,279 runs and .288 average.

Jimmie Foxx (b. Oct. 22, 1907, d. July 21, 1967): Baseball 1B; led AL in HRs 4 times and batting twice; won Triple Crown in 1933; 3-time MVP (1932-33,38) with Philadelphia and Boston; hit 30 HRs or more 12 years in a row; 534 career HRs.

A.J. Foyt (b. Jan. 16, 1935): Auto racer; 7-time USAC-CART national champion (1960-61,63-64,67,75,79); 4-time Indy 500 winner (1961,64,67,77); only driver in history to win Indy 500, Daytona 500 (1972) and 24 Hours of LeMans (1967 with Dan Gurney); retired in 1993 as all-time CART wins leader with 67.

Bill France Sr. (b. Sept. 26, 1909, d. June 7, 1992): Stock car pioneer and promoter; founded NASCAR in 1948; guided race circuit through formative years; built both Daytona (Fla.) Int'l Speedway and Talladega (Ala.) Superspeedway.

Dawn Fraser (b. Sept. 4, 1937): Australian swimmer; won gold medals in 100m freestyle at 3 consecutive Olympics (1956,60,64).

Joe Frazier (b. Jan. 12, 1944): Boxer; 1964 Olympic heavyweight champion; world heavyweight champ (1970-73); fought Muhammad Ali 3 times and won once; pro record 32-4-1 with 27 KOs.

Walt Frazier (b. March 29, 1945): Basketball G; won the NBA championship two times (1970 and 73) with the New York Knicks; 35 points and 19 assists in the 1970 championship game vs. the Lakers; averaged 18.9 PPG and 6.1 APG over his career; four-time all-NBA and a member of the Hall of Fame; nicknamed "Clyde" after well-dressed gangster Clyde Barrow.

Cathy Freeman (b. Feb. 16, 1973): Track & Field; Australian Aborigine who lit the cauldron at the start of the 2000 Olympic Games in Sydney and provided one of the games' most memorable moments by winning gold in the 400-meters on her home soil; 2-time world champion in the 400-meters (1997,99); won silver in the 400 at the 1996 Olympics in Atlanta.

Ford Frick (b. Dec. 19, 1894, d. Apr. 8, 1978): Baseball; sportswriter and radio announcer who served as NL president (1934-51) and commissioner (1951-65); convinced record-keepers to list Roger Maris' and Babe Ruth's season records separately; major leagues moved to West Coast and expanded from 16 to 20 teams during his tenure.

Frankie Frisch (b. Sept. 9, 1898, d. Mar. 12, 1973): Baseball 2B; played on 8 NL pennant winners in 19 years with NY and St. Louis; hit .300 or better 11 years in a row (1921-31); MVP in 1931; player-manager from 1933-37.

Dan Gable (b. Oct. 25, 1948): Wrestling; career wrestling record of 118-1 at Iowa St., where he was a 2-time NCAA champ (1968,69) and tourney MVP in 1969 (137 lbs); won gold medal (149 lbs) at 1972 Olympics; coached U.S. freestyle team in 1988; coached Iowa to 9 straight NCAA titles (1978-86) and 15 overall in 21 years.

Eddie Gaedel (b. June 8, 1925, d. June 18, 1961): Baseball PH; St. Louis Browns' 3-foot-7 player whose career lasted one at bat (he walked) on Aug 19, 1951; hired as a publicity stunt by eccentric owner Bill Veeck.

Clarence (Big House) Gaines (b. May 21, 1924): Basketball; retired as coach of Div. II Winston-Salem after 1992-93 season with 828-447 record in 47 years; ranks 4th on all-time NCAA list behind Dean Smith (879), Adolph Rupp (876) and Jim Phelan (830).

Alonzo (Jake) Gaither (b. Apr. 11, 1903, d. Feb. 18, 1994): Football; head coach at Florida A&M for 25 years; led Rattlers to 6 national black college titles; retired after 1969 season with record of 203-36-4 and a winning percentage of .844; coined phrase, "I like my boys agile, mobile and hostile."

Cito Gaston (b. Mar. 17, 1944): Baseball; managed Toronto to consecutive World Series titles (1992-93); first black manager to win Series; shared *The Sporting News* 1993 Man of Year award with Blue Jays GM Pat Gillick.

Rulon Gardner (b. Aug. 16, 1971): Olympic wrestler; surprise winner of the super heavyweight Greco-Roman wrestling gold medal at the 2000 Sydney Games; beat unbeatable Russian legend Alexandre Kareline, 1-0; won 2000 Sullivan Award and USOC Sportsman of the Year Award.

Lou Gehrig (b. June 19, 1903, d. June 2, 1941): Baseball 1B; played in 2,130 consecutive games from 1925-39 a major league record until Cal Ripken Jr. surpassed it in 1995; led AL in RBI 5 times and HRs 3 times; drove in 100 runs or more 13 years in a row; 2-time MVP (1927,36); hit .340 with 493 HRs over 17 seasons; led NY Yankees to 6 World Series titles; died at age 37 of Amyotrophic Lateral Sclerosis (ALS), a rare and incurable disease of the nervous system now better known as Lou Gehrig's disease.

Bernie Geoffrion (b. Feb. 14, 1931): Hockey RW; credited with popularizing the slap shot, earning his nickname "Boom Boom"; scored 30 goals in 1952 to win the NHL's Calder Trophy (Rookie of the Year Award); won the MVP award (Hart) in 1955; became the second player in history to score 50 goals in one season; led the league in points in 1955 and 61; won 6 Stanley Cups with Montreal; member of the Hockey Hall of Fame.

George Gervin (b. April 27, 1952): Basketball G/F; joined the ABA in 1972 and came to the NBA with San Antonio in 1976; a five-time NBA all-star; led the league in scoring four times; scored 26,595 points with an average of 25.1 per game; known as the "Iceman" because of his cool style; elected to the Hall of Fame in 1996.

A. Bartlett Giamatti (b. Apr. 14, 1938, d. Sept. 1, 1989): Scholar and 7th commissioner of baseball; banned Pete Rose for life for betting on Major League games and associating with known gamblers; also served as president of Yale (1978-86) and National League (1986-89).

Joe Gibbs (b. Nov. 25, 1940): Football; coached Washington to 140 victories and 3 Super Bowl titles in 12 seasons before retiring in 1993; owner of NASCAR racing team that won 1993 Daytona 500 and 2000 Winston Cup title.

Althea Gibson (b. Aug. 25, 1927, d. Sept. 28, 2003): Tennis; won both Wimbledon and U.S. championships in 1957 and '58; 1st black to play in either tourney and 1st to win each title.

Bob Gibson (b. Nov. 9, 1935): Baseball RHP; won 20 or more games 5 times; won 2 NL Cy Youngs (1968,70); MVP in 1968; led St. Louis to 2 World Series titles (1964,67); his ERA of 1.12 in 1968 is the lowest for a starter since 1914; 251-174 record.

Josh Gibson (b. Dec. 21, 1911, d. Jan. 20, 1947): Baseball C; the "Babe Ruth of the Negro Leagues": Satchel Paige's battery mate with Pittsburgh Crawfords. The Negro Leagues did not keep accurate records but Gibson hit 84 home runs in one season and his Baseball Hall of Fame plaque says he hit "almost 800" home runs in his seventeen-year career.

Kirk Gibson (b. May 28, 1957): Baseball OF; All-America flanker at Mich. St. in 1978; chose baseball career and was AL playoff MVP with Detroit in 1984 and NL regular season MVP with Los Angeles in 1988; hit famous pinch-hit home run against Oakland's Dennis Eckersley in Game 1 of the 1988 World Series to vault the Dodgers to the title.

Frank Gifford (b. Aug. 16, 1930): Football HB; 4-time All-Pro (1955-57,59); NFL MVP in 1956; led NY Giants to 3 NFL title games; longtime TV sportscaster, beginning career in 1958 while still a player; scandal struck the married Gifford after he was videotaped in a compromising position with a former stewardess in 1997.

Sid Gillman (b. Oct. 26, 1911): Football innovator; coach elected to both College and Pro Football Halls of Fame; led college teams at Miami-OH and Cincinnati to combined 81-19-2 record from 1944-54; coached LA Rams (1955-59) in NFL, then led LA-San Diego Chargers to 5 Western titles and 1 league championship in first six years of AFL.

George Gipp (b. Feb. 18, 1895, d. Dec. 14, 1920): Football FB; died of throat infection 2 weeks before he made All-America; rushed for 2,341 yards, scored 156 points and averaged 38 yards a punt in 4 years (1917-20).

Marc Girardelli (b. July 18, 1963): Luxembourg Alpine skier; Austrian native who refused to join Austrian Ski Federation because he wanted to be coached by his father; won unprecedented 5th overall World Cup title in 1993; winless at Olympics, although he won 2 silver medals in 1992.

Tom Glavine (b. Mar. 26, 1966): Baseball LHP; led the majors in wins from 1991-95 with 91; NL Cy Young winner in 1991 and '98; seven-time All-Star and was the NL starter twice; World Series MVP with Atlanta in 1995.

Tom Gola (b. Jan. 13, 1933): Basketball F; 4-time All-America and 1955 Player of Year at La Salle; MOP in 1952 NIT and '54 NCAA Final 4, leading Pioneers to both titles; won NBA title as rookie with Philadelphia Warriors in 1956; 4-time NBA All-Star.

Marshall Goldberg (b. Oct. 24, 1917): Football HB; 2-time consensus All-America at Pittsburgh (1937-38); led Pitt to national championship in 1937; played with NFL champion Chicago Cardinals 10 years later.

Lefty Gomez (b. Nov. 26, 1908, d. Feb. 17, 1989): Baseball LHP; 4-time 20-game winner with NY Yankees; holds World Series record for most wins (6) without a defeat; pitched on 5 world championship clubs in 1930s.

Pancho Gonzales (b. May 9, 1928, d. July 3, 1995): Tennis; won consecutive U.S. Championships in 1947-48 before turning pro at 21; dominated pro tour from 1950-61; in 1969 at age 41, played longest Wimbledon match ever (5:12), beating Charlie Pasarell 22-24,1-6,16-14,6-3,11-9.

Bob Goodenow (b. Oct. 29, 1952): Hockey; succeeded Alan Eagleson as executive director of NHL Players Assn. in 1990; led players out on 10-day strike (Apr. 1-10) in 1992 and during 103-day owners' lockout in 1994-95.

Gail Goodrich (b. April 23, 1943): Basketball G; starred at UCLA and won two national championships in 1964 and 1965 under legendary coach John Wooden's tutelage; won the NBA championship with the L.A. Lakers in 1972 and led the team in scoring (25.9 ppg); averaged 18.6 ppg over his 14-year career.

Jeff Gordon (b. Aug. 4, 1971): Auto racer; NASCAR Rookie of Year (1993); 4-time Winston Cup champion (1995,97,98,2001); won inaugural Brickyard 400 in 1994; in 1997, at 25 became youngest winner of the Daytona 500; in 1998 he tied Richard Petty for the modern-era record for wins in a single season with 13; NASCAR's all-time leading money winner and currently 7th on the all-time victory list.

Goose Gossage (b. July 5, 1951): Baseball RHP; Nine-time All Star (1975-78, 80-82, 84-85); intimidating relief pitcher; Fireman of the Year in 1975 with White Sox and 1978 with Yankees; led AL in saves with 26 (1975), 27 (1978); 1,002 career appearances; 310 saves.

Shane Gould (b. Nov. 23, 1956): Australian swimmer; set world records in 5 different women's freestyle events between July 1971 and Jan. 1972; won 3 gold medals, a silver and bronze in 1972 Olympics then retired at age 16.

Alf Goullet (b. Apr. 5, 1891, d. Mar. 11, 1995): Cycling; Australian who gained fame and fortune early in century as premier performer on U.S. 6-day bike race circuit; won 8 annual races at Madison Square Garden with 6 different partners from 1913-23.

Curt Gowdy (b. July 31, 1919): Radio-TV; former radio voice of NY Yankees and then Boston Red Sox from 1949-66; TV play-by-play man for AFL, NFL and major league baseball; has broadcast World Series, All-Star Games, Rose Bowls, Super Bowls, Olympics and NCAA Final Fours for 3 networks; hosted "The American Sportsman."

Steffi Graf (b. June 14, 1969): German tennis player; won Grand Slam and Olympic gold medal in 1988 at age 19; won three of four majors in 1993, '95 and '96; won 22 Grand Slam singles titles— 7 at Wimbledon, 6 French, 5 U.S. and 4 Australian Opens, retired in 1999 as 3rd all-time with 107 career singles titles and as all-time tour leader in career earnings with over $21 million in prize money; married to André Agassi.

Otto Graham (b. Dec. 6, 1921): Football QB and basketball All-America at Northwestern; in pro ball, led Cleveland Browns to 7 league titles in 10 years, winning 4 AAFC championships (1946-49) and 3 NFL (1950,54-55); 5-time All-Pro; 2-time NFL MVP (1953,55).

Cammi Granato (b. Mar. 25, 1971): Hockey; American women's hockey pioneer; captain of U.S. team that won gold at the inaugural olympic women's hockey competition in 1998 at Nagano; sister of NHL veteran Tony.

Red Grange (b. June 13, 1903, d. Jan. 28, 1991): Football HB; 3-time All-America at Illinois who brought 1st huge crowds to pro football when he signed with Chicago Bears in 1925; formed 1st AFL with manager-promoter C.C. Pyle in 1926, but league folded and he returned to Bears.

Bud Grant (b. May 20, 1927): Football and Basketball; only coach to win 100 games in both CFL and NFL and only member of both CFL and U.S. Pro Football Halls of Fame; led Winnipeg to 4 Grey Cup titles (1958-59,61-62) in 6 appearances, but his Minnesota Vikings lost all 4 Super Bowl attempts in 1970s; accumulated 122 CFL wins and 168 NFL wins; also All-Big Ten at Minnesota in both football and basketball in late 1940s; a 3-time CFL All-Star offensive end; also member of 1950 NBA champion Minneapolis Lakers.

Rocky Graziano (b. June 7, 1922, d. May 22, 1990): Boxer; world middleweight champion (1946-47); fought Tony Zale for title 3 times in 21 months, losing twice; pro record 67-10-6 with 52 KOs; movie "Somebody Up There Likes Me" based on his life.

Hank Greenberg (b. Jan. 1, 1911, d. Sept. 4, 1986): Baseball 1B; led AL in HRs and RBI 4 times each; 2-time MVP (1935,40) with Detroit; 331 career HRs, including 58 in 1938.

Joe Greene (b. Sept. 24, 1946): Football DT; 5-time All-Pro (1972-74,77,79); led Pittsburgh to 4 Super Bowl titles in 1970s; nicknamed "Mean Joe."

Maurice Greene (b. July 23, 1974): Track & Field; world 100m champion in 1997, 99 and 2001 and 200m champion in 1999; former world record holder (9.79) in the 100m; injury forced him out of the 1996 Olympics in Atlanta; won the gold medal in the 100m at the 2000 Olympics in Sydney; 100m WR broken by Tim Montgomery in Sept. 2002 (9.78).

Bud Greenspan (b. Sept. 18, 1926): Filmmaker specializing in the Olympic Games; has won Emmy awards for 22-part "The Olympiad" (1976-77) and historical vignettes for ABC-TV's coverage of 1980 Winter Games; won 1994 Emmy award for edited special on Lillehammer Winter Olympics; won The Peabody Award in 1996 for his outstanding service in chronicling the Olympic Games.

Wayne Gretzky (b. Jan. 26, 1961): Hockey C; 10-time NHL scoring champion; 9-time regular season MVP (1979-87,89) and 9-time All-NHL first team; scored 200 points or more in a season 4 times; led Edmonton to 4 Stanley Cups (1984-85,87-88); 2-time playoff MVP (1985,88); traded to LA Kings (Aug. 9, 1988); broke Gordie Howe's all-time NHL goal scoring record of 801 on Mar. 23, 1994; all-time NHL leader in points (2857), goals (894) and assists (1963); also all-time Stanley Cup leader in points, goals and assists; spent the end of the 1996 season with the St. Louis Blues and then signed a free agent contract with the New York Rangers; retired in 1999 at age 38 with 61 NHL scoring records in 20 seasons; became part-owner of NHL's Coyotes in 2000.

Bob Griese (b. Feb. 3, 1945): Football QB; 2-time All-Pro (1971,77); led Miami to undefeated season (17-0) in 1972 and consecutive Super Bowl titles (1973-74); father of Brian.

Ken Griffey Jr. (b. Nov. 21, 1969): Baseball OF; overall 1st pick of 1987 draft by Seattle; 10-time Gold Glove winner; 11-time All-Star; 1997 AL MVP; Mariners all-time leader in home runs and RBIs; MVP of 1992 All-Star game at age 23; hit home runs in 8 consecutive games in 1993; son of Ken Sr. and in 1990 they became the first father-son combination to appear in the same major league lineup; traded to the Cincinnati Reds before the 2000 season but has been plagued with injuries since.

Archie Griffin (b. Aug. 21, 1954): Football RB; only college player to win two Heisman Trophies (1974-75); rushed for 5,177 yards in career at Ohio St. and played in four straight Rose Bowls; drafted by Cincinnati Bengals and played 8 years in NFL.

Emile Griffith (b. Feb. 3, 1938): Boxer; world welterweight champion (1961,62-63,63-65); world middleweight champ (1966-67,67-68); pro record 85-24-2 with 23 KOs.

Dick Groat (b. Nov. 4, 1930): Basketball G and Baseball SS; 2-time basketball All-America at Duke and college Player of Year in 1951; won NL MVP award as shortstop with Pittsburgh in 1960; won World Series with Pirates (1960) and St. Louis (1964).

Lefty Grove (b. Mar. 6, 1900, d. May 23, 1975): Baseball LHP; won 20 or more games 8 times; led AL in ERA 9 times and strikeouts 7 times; 31-4 record and MVP in 1931 with Philadelphia; 300-141 record; real name: Robert Moses Grove

Lou Groza (b. Jan. 25, 1924, d. Nov. 29, 2000): Football T-PK; 6-time All-Pro; played in 13 championship games for Cleveland from 1946-67; kicked winning field goal in 1950 NFL title game; 1,608 career points (1,349 in NFL).

Janet Guthrie (b. Mar. 7, 1938): Auto racer; in 1977, became 1st woman to race in Indianapolis 500; placed 9th at Indy in 1978.

Tony Gwynn (b. May 9, 1960): Baseball OF; 8-time NL batting champion (1984,87-89,94-97) with San Diego, 15-time All-Star; got 3,000th career hit Aug. 6, 1999 at Montreal; played basketball at San Diego St. leaving as school's all-time assist leader; drafted in 10th round of 1981 NBA draft by then San Diego Clippers.

Harvey Haddix (b. Sept. 18, 1925, d. Jan. 9, 1994): Baseball LHP; pitched 12 perfect innings for Pittsburgh, but lost to Milwaukee in the 13th, 1-0 (May 26, 1959); won Game 7 of 1960 World Series.

Walter Hagen (b. Dec. 21, 1892, d. Oct. 5, 1969): Pro golf pioneer; won 2 U.S. Opens (1914,19), 4 British Opens (1922,24,28-29), 5 PGA Championships (1921,24-27) and 5 Western Opens; retired with 40 PGA wins; 6-time U.S. Ryder Cup captain.

Marvin Hagler (b. May 23, 1954): Boxer; world middleweight champion 1980-87; enjoyed his nickname "Marvelous Marvin" so much he had his name legally changed; pro record of 62-3-2 with 52 KOs.

Mika Hakkinen (b. Sept. 28, 1968): Finnish auto racer; won two consecutive Formula One world drivers championships in 1998 and '99; recorded eight wins in '98 and five in '99; 20 career F1 wins.

George Halas (b. Feb. 2, 1895, d. Oct. 31, 1983): Football pioneer; MVP in 1919 Rose Bowl; player-coach-owner of Chicago Bears from 1920-83; signed Red Grange in 1925; coached Bears for 40 seasons and won 8 NFL titles (1921,32-33,40-41,43,46,63); 2nd on all-time career list with 324 wins; elected to NFL Hall of Fame in 1963.

Dorothy Hamill (b. July 26, 1956): Figure skater; won Olympic gold medal and world championship in 1976; Ice Capades headliner from 1977-84; bought the financially-strapped Ice Capades in 1993 and sold it several years later.

Scott Hamilton (b. Aug. 28, 1958): Figure skater; 4-time world champion (1981-84); won gold medal at 1984 Olympics.

Mia Hamm (b. Mar. 17, 1972): Soccer F; became all-time leading scorer in international soccer with her 108th goal on May 22, 1999; member of 1996 and 2000 U.S. Olympic teams, the 1991, 1995, 1999 and 2003 U.S. World Cup teams; made the U.S. National Team at 15; a three-time collegiate All-American; led UNC to 4 national titles (1989,90,92,93).

Tonya Harding (b. Nov. 12, 1970): Figure skater; 1991 U.S. women's champion; involved in bizarre plot hatched by ex-husband Jeff Gillooly to injure rival Nancy Kerrigan on Jan. 6, 1994 and keep her off Olympic team; won '94 U.S. women's title in Kerrigan's absence; denied any role in assault and sued USOC when her berth on Olympic team was threatened; finished 8th at Lillehammer (Kerrigan recovered and won silver medal); pled guilty on Mar. 16 to conspiracy to hinder investigation; stripped of 1994 title by U.S. Figure Skating Association.

Tom Harmon (b. Sept. 28, 1919, d. Mar. 17, 1990): Football HB; 2-time All-America at Michigan; won Heisman Trophy in 1940; played with AFL NY Americans in 1941 and NFL LA Rams (1946-47);World War II fighter pilot who won Silver Star and Purple Heart; became radio-TV commentator.

Franco Harris (b. Mar. 7, 1950): Football RB; ran for over 1,000 yards in a season 8 times; rushed for 12,120 yards in 13 years; led Pittsburgh to 4 Super Bowl titles.

Leon Hart (b. Nov. 2, 1928, d. Sept. 24, 2002): Football E; only player to win 3 national championships in college and 3 more in the NFL; won his titles at Notre Dame (1946-47,49) and with Detroit Lions (1952-53,57); 3-time All-America and last lineman to win Heisman Trophy (1949); All-Pro on both offense and defense in 1951.

Bill Hartack (b. Dec. 9, 1932): Jockey; won Kentucky Derby 5 times (1957,60,62,64,69), Preakness 3 times (1956,64,69), and the Belmont once (1960).

Doug Harvey (b. Dec. 19, 1924, d. Dec. 26, 1989): Hockey D; 10-time All-NHL 1st team; won Norris Trophy 7 times (1955-58,60-62); led Montreal to 6 Stanley Cups.

Dominik Hasek (b. Jan. 29, 1965): Czech hockey G; 2-time NHL MVP (1997,98) with Buffalo; 6-time Vezina Trophy winner (1994,95,97,98,99,2001); led Czech Republic to Olympic gold medal in 1998 at Nagano; won Stanley Cup with Detroit in 2002.

Billy Haughton (b. Nov. 2, 1923, d. July 15, 1986): Harness racing; 4-time winner of Hambletonian; trainer-driver of one Pacing Triple Crown winner (1968); 4,910 career wins.

João Havelange (b. May 8, 1916): Soccer; Brazilian-born president of Federation Internationale de Football Assoc. (FIFA) 1974-98; also member of International Olympic Committee.

John Havlicek (b. Apr. 8, 1940): Basketball F; played in 3 NCAA Finals at Ohio St. (1960-62); led Boston to 8 NBA titles (1963-66,68-69,74,76); Finals MVP in 1974; 4-time All-NBA 1st team.

Bob Hayes (b. Dec. 20, 1942, d. Sept. 18, 2002): Track & Field and Football; won gold medal in 100m at 1964 Olympics; all-pro SE for Dallas in 1966; won Super Bowl with Cowboys in 1972; convicted of drug trafficking in 1979 and served 18 months of a 5-year sentence.

Elvin Hayes (b. Nov. 17, 1945): Basketball C; Known as "the Big E"; Overall number one pick of the 1968 NBA draft; three-time All-NBA first team (1975,77,79); 1978 Finals MVP; 12-time NBA all-star (1969-80); named to NBA's 50 Greatest Players; 6th leading scorer in NBA history with 27,313 points and 4th leading rebounder with 16,279; member of NBA Hall of Fame.

Woody Hayes (b. Feb. 14, 1913, d. Mar. 12, 1987): Football; coached Ohio St. to 6 national titles (1954,57,61,68,70) and 4 Rose Bowl victories; 238 career wins in 28 seasons at Denison, Miami-OH and OSU; his coaching career ended abruptly in 1978 after he attacked an opposing player on the sidelines.

Thomas Hearns (b. Oct. 18, 1958): Boxer; held world titles as welterweight, junior middleweight, middleweight and light heavyweight; four career losses came against Ray Leonard, Marvin Hagler and twice to Iran Barkley; pro record of 59-4-1, 46 KOs.

Eric Heiden (b. June 14, 1958): Speed skater; 3-time overall world champion (1977-79); won all 5 men's gold medals at 1980 Olympics, setting records in each; Sullivan Award winner (1980).

Mel Hein (b. Aug. 22, 1909, d. Jan. 31, 1992): Football C; NFL All-Pro 8 straight years (1933-40); MVP in 1938 with Giants; didn't miss a game in 15 years.

John W. Heisman (b. Oct. 23, 1869, d. Oct. 3, 1936): Football; coached at 9 colleges from 1892-1927; won 185 games; Director of Athletics at Downtown Athletic Club in NYC (1928-36); DAC named Heisman Trophy after him.

Carol Heiss (b. Jan. 20, 1940): Figure skater; 5-time world champion (1956-60); won Olympic silver medal in 1956 and gold in '60; married 1956 men's gold medalist Hayes Jenkins.

Rickey Henderson (b. Dec. 25, 1958): Baseball OF; AL playoff MVP (1989) and AL regular season MVP (1990); set single-season base stealing record of 130 in 1982; has led AL in steals a record 12 times; broke Lou Brock's all-time record of 938 on May 1, 1991; all-time leader in runs, steals, walks and HRs as leadoff batter.

Sonja Henie (b. Apr. 8, 1912, d. Oct. 12, 1969): Norwegian figure skater; 10-time world champion (1927-36); won 3 consecutive Olympic gold medals (1928,32,36); became movie star.

Foster Hewitt (b. Nov. 21, 1902, d. Apr. 21, 1985): Radio-TV; Canada's premier hockey play-by-play broadcaster from 1923-81; coined phrase, "He shoots, he scores!"

Damon Hill (b. Sept. 17, 1960): British auto racer; 1996 Formula One champion; 22 F1 wins places him 10th all-time; retired following 1999 season.

Graham Hill (b. Feb. 15, 1929, d. Nov. 29, 1975): British auto racer; 2-time Formula One world champion (1962,68); won Indy 500 in 1966; killed in plane crash; father of Damon.

Phil Hill (b. Apr. 20, 1927): Auto racer; first U.S. driver to win Formula One championship (1961); 3 career wins (1958-64).

Martina Hingis (b. Sept. 30, 1980): Tennis player; in March 1997 at 16 years, 6 months, she became the youngest No. 1 ranked player since the ranking system began in 1975; has won Wimbledon (1997), U.S. Open (1997) and 3 Australian Opens (1997,98,99); first woman to surpass the $3 million mark in earnings for one season (1997).

Max Hirsch (b. July 30, 1880, d. Apr. 3, 1969): Horse racing; trained 1,933 winners from 1908-68; won Triple Crown with Assault in 1946.

Tommy Hitchcock (b. Feb. 11, 1900, d. Apr. 19, 1944): Polo; world class player at 20; achieved 10-goal rating 18 times from 1922-40.

Lew Hoad (b. Nov. 23, 1934, d. July 3, 1994): Australian tennis player; 2-time Wimbledon winner (1956-57); won Australian, French and Wimbledon titles in 1956, but missed capturing Grand Slam at Forest Hills when beaten by Ken Rosewall in 4-set final.

Gil Hodges (b. Apr. 4, 1924, d. Apr. 2, 1972): Baseball 1B-Manager; tied Major League record with four home runs in one game on Aug 31, 1950; won three Gold Gloves (1957-59); drove in 100 runs in seven consecutive seasons (1949-55); hit 370 home runs and 1,274 RBIs lifetime; won 660 games as a manager (Senators and Mets).

Ben Hogan (b. Aug. 13, 1912, d. July 25, 1997): Golfer; 4-time PGA Player of Year; one of only five players to win all four Grand Slam titles (others are Nicklaus, Player, Sarazen and Woods); won 4 U.S. Opens, 2 Masters, 2 PGAs and 1 British Open between 1946-53; one of only two players (Woods) to win three of the four current majors in one year when he won Masters, U.S. Open and British Open in 1953; nearly killed in Feb. 2, 1949 car accident, but came back to win U.S. Open in '50; third on all-time list with 63 career wins.

Chamique Holdsclaw (b. Aug. 9, 1977): Basketball F; 2-time national player of the year, leading Tennessee to 3 straight national championships (1996,97,98); 1998 Sullivan Award winner; top selection by the Washington Mystics in the 1999 WNBA draft; 1999 Rookie of the Year.

Eleanor Holm (b. Dec. 6, 1913): Swimmer; won gold medal in 100m backstroke at 1932 Olympics; thrown off '36 U.S. team for drinking champagne in public and shooting craps on boat to Germany.

Nat Holman (b. Oct. 18, 1896, d. Feb. 12, 1995): Basketball pioneer; played with Original Celtics (1920-28); coached CCNY to both NCAA and NIT titles in 1950 (a year later, several of his players were caught up in a point-shaving scandal); 423 career wins.

Larry Holmes (b. Nov. 3, 1949): Boxer; heavyweight champion (WBC or IBF) from 1978-85; successfully defended title 20 times before losing to Michael Spinks; returned from first retirement in 1988 and was KO'd in 4th by champ Mike Tyson; launched second comeback in 1991; fought and lost title bids against Evander Holyfield in '92 and Oliver McCall in '95; beat Eric "Butterbean" Esch in a one-fight comeback in 2002; pro record of 69-6 and 44 KOs.

Lou Holtz (b. Jan. 6, 1937): Football; coached Notre Dame to national title in 1988; 2-time Coach of Year (1977,88); coached six schools in all — Wm. & Mary (3 years), N.C. State (4), Arkansas (7), Minnesota (2), ND (11) and S. Carolina (5+); also coached NFL N.Y. Jets for 13 games (3-10) in 1976.

Evander Holyfield (b. Oct. 19, 1962): Boxer; KO'd Buster Douglas in 3rd round to become work hvywt. champion in 1990; lost title to Riddick Bowe in 1992; beat Bowe to reclaim title in 1993; lost title again to Michael Moorer in 1994; defeated Mike Tyson in 1996 to win WBA belt; in 1997 rematch, Tyson was DQ'd for twice biting Holyfield's ear; escaped with controversial draw in 1999 unification bout with Lennox Lewis, then lost the rematch later that year; defeated John Ruiz in Aug. 2000 for vacant WBA belt then lost rematch and belt in March, 2001; the pair fought again in Dec. 2001, this time to a draw.

Red Holzman (b. Aug. 10, 1920, d. Nov. 13, 1998): Basketball; played for NBL and NBA champions at Rochester (1946,51); coached NY Knicks to 2 NBA titles (1970,73); Coach of Year (1970); 754 career NBA wins.

Rogers Hornsby (b. Apr. 27, 1896, d. Jan. 5, 1963): Baseball 2B; hit .400 3 times, including .424 in 1924; led NL in batting 7 times; 2-time MVP (1925,29); career BA of .358 over 23 years is highest in NL.

Paul Hornung (b. Dec. 23, 1935): Football HB-PK; only Heisman Trophy winner to play for losing team (2-8 Notre Dame in 1956); 3-time NFL scoring leader (1959-61) at Green Bay; 176 points in 1960, an all-time record; MVP in 1961; suspended by NFL for 1963 season for betting on his own team.

Gordie Howe (b. Mar. 31, 1928): Hockey RW; played 32 seasons in NHL and WHA from 1946-80; led NHL in scoring 6 times; All-NHL 1st team 12 times; MVP 6 times in NHL (1952-53,57-58,60,63) with Detroit and once in WHA (1974) with Houston; ranks 2nd on all-time NHL list in goals (801) and points (1,850) to Wayne Gretzky; played with sons Mark and Marty at Houston (1973-77) and New England-Hartford (1977-80).

Cal Hubbard (b. Oct. 31, 1900, d. Oct. 17, 1977): Member of college football, pro football and baseball halls of fame; 9 years in NFL; 4-time All-Pro at end and tackle; AL umpire (1936-51).

William DeHart Hubbard (b. Nov. 25, 1903, d. June 23, 1976): Track & Field; won the long jump at the 1924 Olympics, becoming the first black athlete to win an Olympic gold medal in an individual event; set the long jump world record in 1925 (25-10¾) and tied the 100-yard dash record (9.6) in 1926.

Carl Hubbell (b. June 22, 1903, d. Nov. 21, 1988): Baseball LHP; led NL in wins and ERA 3 times each; 2-time MVP (1933,36) with NY Giants; fanned Ruth, Gehrig, Foxx, Simmons and Cronin in succession in 1934 All-Star Game; 253-154 career record.

Sam Huff (b. Oct. 4, 1934): Football LB; glamorized NFL's middle linebacker position with NY Giants from 1956-63; subject of "The Violent World of Sam Huff" TV special in 1961; helped club win 6 division titles and a world championship (1956).

Miller Huggins (b. Mar. 27, 1878, d. Sept. 25, 1929): Baseball; managed NY Yankees from 1918 until his death late in '29 season; led Yanks to 6 pennants and 3 World Series titles from 1921-28.

Bobby Hull (b. Jan. 3, 1939): Hockey LW; led NHL in scoring 3 times; 2-time MVP (1965-66) with Chicago; All-NHL first team 10 times; jumped to WHA in 1972, 2-time MVP there (1973,75) with Winnipeg; scored 913 goals in both leagues; father of Brett.

Brett Hull (b. Aug. 9, 1964): Hockey RW; NHL MVP in 1991 with St. Louis; holds single season RW scoring record with 86 goals; he and father Bobby have both won Hart (MVP), Lady Byng (sportsmanship) and All-Star Game MVP trophies; won Stanley Cup with Dallas in 1999 and Detroit in 2002.

Lamar Hunt (b. Aug. 2, 1932): Football/Soccer; Founder of the Kansas City Chiefs (formerly Dallas Texans); instrumental in forming the AFL in 1959 and merging the league with the NFL in 1966; elected to the Pro Football Hall of Fame in 1972; AFC Championship trophy is named for him; investor/operator of 3 Major League Soccer teams (Columbus, Dallas and Kansas City).

Jim (Catfish) Hunter (b. Apr. 8, 1946, d. Sept. 9, 1999): Baseball RHP; won 20 games or more 5 times (1971-75); played on 5 World Series winners with Oakland and NY Yankees; threw perfect game in 1968; won AL Cy Young Award in 1974; 224-166 career record.

Ibrahim Hussein (b. June 3, 1958): Kenyan distance runner; 3-time winner of Boston Marathon (1988,91-92) and 1st African runner to win in Boston; won New York Marathon in 1987.

Don Hutson (b. Jan. 31, 1913, d. June 24, 1997): Football E-PK; led NFL in receptions 8 times and interceptions once; 9-time All-Pro (1936,38-45) for Green Bay; 99 career TD catches.

Flo Hyman (b. July 31, 1954, d. Jan. 24, 1986): Volleyball; 3-time All-America spiker at Houston and captain of 1984 U.S. Women's Olympic team; died of heart attack caused by Marfan Syndrome during a match in Japan in 1986; namesake of award given out annually by the Women's Sports Foundation.

Hank Iba (b. Aug. 6, 1904, d. Jan. 15, 1993): Basketball; coached Oklahoma A&M to 2 straight NCAA titles (1945-46); 767 career wins in 41 years; coached U.S. Olympic team to 2 gold medals (1964,68), but lost to Soviets in controversial '72 final.

Punch Imlach (b. Mar. 15, 1918, d. Dec. 1, 1987): Hockey; directed Toronto to 4 Stanley Cups (1962-64,67) in 11 seasons as GM-coach.

Miguel Induráin (b. July 16, 1964): Spanish cyclist; won 5 straight Tour de Frances (1991-95), one of only 5 5-time winners; won gold in time trial at '96 Olympics; retired in 1997.

Juli Inkster (b. June 24, 1960): Golfer; 30 career LPGA victories; winner of 7 major LPGA tournaments and 3 consecutive U.S. Women's Amateur tournaments (1980-82); inducted into the World Golf Hall of Fame in 2000; LPGA Rookie of the Year in 1984.

Hale Irwin (b. June 3, 1945): Golfer; oldest player ever to win U.S. Open (45 in 1990); NCAA champion in 1967; 20 PGA victories, including 3 U.S. Opens (1974,79,90); 5-time Ryder Cup team member; joined senior PGA tour in 1995 and has already won 37 titles.

Allen Iverson (b. June 7, 1975): Basketball G; former Georgetown Hoya chosen first overall by the Philadelphia 76ers in the 1996 NBA Draft; NBA Rookie of the Year (1997); 2-time NBA scoring leader (2001-02) and steals leader (2001-02); voted regular season MVP in 2001 and led 76ers to NBA Finals.

Bo Jackson (b. Nov. 30, 1962): Baseball OF and Football RB; won Heisman Trophy in 1985 and MVP of baseball All-Star Game in 1989; starter for both baseball's KC Royals and NFL's LA Raiders in 1988 and '89; severely injured left hip Jan. 13, 1991, in NFL playoffs; waived by Royals but signed by Chicago White Sox in 1991; missed entire 1992 season recovering from hip surgery; played for White Sox in 1993 and California in '94 before retiring.

Joe Jackson (b. July 16, 1889, d. Dec. 5, 1951): Baseball OF; hit .300 or better 11 times; nicknamed "Shoeless Joe"; career average of .356, third highest all-time; was placed on MLB's ineligible list in 1921 following the Black Sox scandal in which he and 7 teammates were accussed of fixing 1919 World Series.

Phil Jackson (b. Sept. 17, 1945): Basketball; NBA champion as reserve forward with New York in 1973 (injured when Knicks won in '70); coached Chicago to six NBA titles in eight years (1991-93, 96-98); coach of the year in 1996 and 97; returned to coach the LA Lakers in 1999 and has won 3 more titles (2000,01,02); all-time leader in winning pct. for NBA coaches with 350 or more wins; all-time NBA leader in playoff wins (162).

Reggie Jackson (b. May 18, 1946): Baseball OF; led AL in HRs 4 times; MVP in 1973; played on 5 World Series winners with Oakland and NY Yankees; 1977 Series MVP with 5 HRs; 563 career HRs; all-time strikeout leader (2,597); member of the Hall of Fame.

Dr. Robert Jackson (b. Aug. 6, 1932): Surgeon; revolutionized sports medicine by popularizing the use of arthroscopic surgery to treat injuries; learned technique from Japanese physician that allowed athletes to return quickly from potentially career-ending injuries.

Helen Jacobs (b. Aug. 6, 1908, d. June 2, 1997): Tennis; 4-time winner of U.S. Championship (1932-35); Wimbledon winner in 1936; lost 4 Wimbledon finals to arch-rival Helen Wills Moody.

Jaromir Jagr (b. Feb. 15, 1972): Czech Hockey RW; fifth overall pick by Pittsburgh (1990); NHL All-Rookie team (1991); NHL MVP (1999); Won Art Ross Trophy (1995,98,99,00,01); 7-time All-NHL First Team; NHL single season record for most points by a right wing (149); NHL single season record for most assists by a RW (87); traded to Washington in 2001.

LeBron James (b. Dec. 30, 1984): Basketball; highly touted top pick in 2003 NBA Draft (Cleveland) out of an Ohio high school; has signed several megamillion dollar endorsement deals since.

Dan Jansen (b. June 17, 1965): Speed skater; fell in 500m and 1,000m in 1988 Olympics just after sister Jane's death; placed 4th in 500m and didn't attempt 1,000m in 1992; fell in 500m at '94 Games, but finally won an Olympic medal with world record (1:12.43) effort in 1,000m, then took victory lap with baby daughter Jane in his arms; won 1994 Sullivan Award.

Dale Jarrett (b. Nov. 26, 1956): Auto racer; 1999 Winston Cup champion; 3-time Daytona 500 champion (1993,96,2000); son of driver Ned Jarrett.

James J. Jeffries (b. Apr. 15, 1875, d. Mar. 3, 1953): Boxer; world heavyweight champion (1899-1905); retired undefeated but came back to fight Jack Johnson in 1910 and lost (KO, 15th).

David Jenkins (b. June 29, 1936): Figure skater; brother of Hayes; 3-time world champion (1957-59); won gold medal at 1960 Olympics.

Hayes Jenkins (b. Mar. 23, 1933): Figure skater; 4-time world champion (1953-56); won gold medal at 1956 Olympics; married 1960 women's gold medalist Carol Heiss.

Bruce Jenner (b. Oct. 28, 1949): Track & Field; won gold medal in 1976 Olympic decathlon.

Jackie Jensen (b. Mar. 9, 1927, d. July 14, 1982): Football RB and Baseball OF; All-America at Cal in 1948; AL MVP with Boston Red Sox in 1958.

Ben Johnson (b. Dec. 30, 1961): Canadian sprinter; set 100m world record (9.83) at 1987 World Championships; won 100m at 1988 Olympics, but flunked drug test and forfeited gold medal; 1987 world record revoked in '89 for admitted steroid use; returned drug-free in 1991, but performed poorly; banned for life by IAAF in 1993 for testing positive again.

Bob Johnson (b. Mar. 4, 1931, d. Nov. 26, 1991): Hockey; coached Pittsburgh Penguins to 1st Stanley Cup title in 1991; led Wisconsin to 3 NCAA titles (1973,77,81); also coached 1976 U.S. Olympic team and NHL Calgary Flames (1982-87).

Earvin (Magic) Johnson (b. Aug. 14, 1959): Basketball G; led Michigan St. to NCAA title in 1979 and was Final 4 MOP; All-NBA 1st team 9 times; 3-time MVP (1987,89-90); led LA Lakers to 5 NBA titles; 3-time Finals MVP (1980, 82, 87); 3rd all-time in NBA assists with 10,141; retired on Nov. 7, 1991 after announcing he was HIV-positive; returned to score 25 points in 1992 NBA* All-Star Game; U.S. Olympic Dream Team co-captain; announced NBA comeback then retired again before start of 1992-93 season; named head coach of Lakers on Mar. 23, 1994, but finished season at 5-11 and quit; later became minority owner of team; came back a final time and played 32 games during 1995-96 season.

Jack Johnson (b. Mar. 31, 1878, d. June 10, 1946): Boxer; controversial heavyweight champion (1908-15) and 1st black to hold title; defeated Tommy Burns for crown at age 30; fled to Europe in 1913 after Mann Act conviction; lost title to Jess Willard in Havana, but claimed to have taken a dive; pro record 78-8-12 with 45 KOs.

Jimmy Johnson (b. July 16, 1943): Football; All-SWC defensive lineman on Arkansas' 1964 national championship team; coached Miami-FL to national title in 1987; college record of 81-34-3 in 10 years; hired by old friend and new Dallas owner Jerry Jones to succeed Tom Landry in 1989; went 1-15 in '89, then led Cowboys to consecutive Super Bowl victories in 1992 and '93 seasons; quit in 1994 after feuding with Jones; became TV analyst; replaced Don Shula as Miami Dolphins head coach from 1996-99.

Judy Johnson (b. Oct. 26, 1899, d. June 13, 1989): Baseball IF; one of the great stars of the Negro Leagues; a terrific fielding third baseman who regularly batted over .300; when baseball integrated Johnson's playing days were over but he coached and scouted for the Philadelphia Athletics, Boston Braves and Philadelphia Phillies; member of Hall of Fame.

Junior Johnson (b. June 28, 1931): Auto Racing; won Daytona 500 in 1960; also won 13 NASCAR races in 1965, including the Rebel 300 at Darlington; retired from racing to become a highly successful car owner; his first driver was Bobby Allison.

Michael Johnson (b. Sep 13, 1967): Track & Field; Shattered world record in 200m (19.32) and set Olympic record in 400m (43.49) to become first man to win the gold in both races in the same Olympic Games at Atlanta in 1996; two-time world champion in 200 (1991,95) and four-time world champ in 400 (1993,95,97,99); set world record in 400m (43.18) at '99 world championships in Seville; won the 400 in Sydney in 2000 to become the only man to win the event in two consecutive Olympics; retired in 2001.

Rafer Johnson (b. Aug. 18, 1935): Track & Field; won silver medal in 1956 Olympic decathlon and gold medal in 1960.

Randy Johnson (b. Sept. 10, 1963): Baseball LHP; 6'10" flamethrower; threw no-hitter June 2, 1990 for Seattle; struck out over 300 batters 6 times (1993,98,99,00,01,02); led AL in Ks 4 times (1992-95) and NL 4 times (1999-2002); struck out 20 batters in a game (5/8/01); 5-time Cy Young Award winner (AL-1995, NL-1999,00,01,02); traded to Houston in 1998 and signed as a free agent with Arizona in 1999; won 3 games in 2001 World Series to earn first ring and co-MVP honors (Curt Schilling).

Walter Johnson (b. Nov. 6, 1887, d. Dec. 10, 1946): Baseball RHP; won 20 games or more 10 straight years; led AL in ERA 5 times, wins 6 times and strikeouts 12 times; twice MVP (1913, 24) with Washington; all-time leader in shutouts (110) and 2nd in wins (417); nicknamed "Big Train."

Ben A. Jones (b. Dec. 31, 1882, d. June 13, 1961): Horse racing; Calumet Farm trainer (1939-47); saddled 6 Kentucky Derby champions, including 2 Triple Crown winners—Whirlaway in 1941 and Citation in '48.

Bobby Jones (b. Mar. 17, 1902, d. Dec. 18, 1971): Won U.S. and British Opens plus U.S. and British Amateurs in 1930 to become golf's only Grand Slam winner ever; from 1922-30, won 4 U.S. Opens, 5 U.S. Amateurs, 3 British Opens, and played in 6 Walker Cups; founded Masters tournament in 1934.

Deacon Jones (b. Dec. 9, 1938): Football DE; 5-time All-Pro (1965-69) with LA Rams; unofficially 3rd all-time in NFL sacks with 173½ in 14 years; inducted into Pro Football Hall of Fame in 1980.

Jerry Jones (b. Oct. 13, 1942): Football; owner-GM of Dallas Cowboys; maverick who bought declining team (3-13) and Texas Stadium for $140 million in 1989; hired pal Jimmy Johnson to replace legendary Tom Landry as coach; their partnership led to 2 Super Bowl titles (1993-94); when feud developed in 1994, he fired Johnson and hired Barry Switzer and won Super Bowl in 1996; defied NFL by signing separate sponsorship deals with Pepsi and Nike in 1995, causing NFL to file a $300 million lawsuit against him; Jones countersued and both sides eventually settled; hired proven winner Bill Parcells as head coach in 2003 following 3 losing seasons.

Marion Jones (b. Oct. 12, 1975): Track & Field; American sprinter who won 3 golds (100, 200, 4x100) at Sydney Games in 2000; 5-time world champion: 100m (1997,99), 200m (2001), 4x100m (1997,01); former college basketball star at North Carolina; voted Women's Athlete of the Year by *Track & Field News* in 1997,98 and 2000; 1999 Jesse Owens Award winner; 2000 AP and USOC Female Athlete of the Year.

Roy Jones Jr. (b. Jan. 16, 1969): Boxing; robbed of gold medal at 1988 Olympics due to a scoring error; still voted Outstanding Boxer of the Games; won IBF middleweight crown, beating Bernard Hopkins in 1993; moved up to super middleweight and won IBF title from James Toney in 1994; moved up to light heavyweight, winning WBC (1997), WBA (1998) and IBF titles (1999); suffered only pro loss in a DQ to Montel Griffin which he avenged with a 1st rd. KO 5 months later; made move to heavyweight in 2003, beating John Ruiz in a unanimous decision for WBA belt.

Michael Jordan (b. Feb. 17, 1963): Basketball G; College Player of Year with North Carolina in 1984; NBA Rookie of the Year (1985); led NBA in scoring 7 years in a row (1987-93) and also 1996-98; 10-time All-NBA 1st team; 5-time regular season MVP (1988,91-92,96,98) and 6-time MVP of NBA Finals (1991-93,96-98); 3-time AP Male Athlete of Year; led U.S. Olympic team to gold in 1984 and '92; stunned sports world when he retired at age 30 on Oct. 6, 1993; signed as OF with Chi. White Sox and spent summer of '94 in AA with Birmingham; struggled with .204 average; made one of the most anticipated comebacks in sports history when he returned to the Bulls lineup on Mar. 19, 1995 but Bulls were eliminated by Orlando in 2nd round of playoffs later that season; led Bulls to NBA titles the next 3 years for 6 titles in all (1991-93,96-98); retired in 1999; became pres. of Wash. Wizards before unretiring again in 2001 and returning to play with Wizards for 2 seasons.

Florence Griffith Joyner (b. Dec. 21, 1959, d. Sept. 21, 1998): Track & Field; set world records in 100 and 200 meters in 1988; won 3 gold medals at '88 Olympics (100m, 200m, 4x100m relay); Sullivan Award winner (1988); retired in 1989; named as co-chairperson of President's Council on Physical Fitness and Sports in 1993; sister-in-law of Jackie Joyner-Kersee; died of suffocation during an epileptic seizure in 1998.

Jackie Joyner-Kersee (b. Mar. 3, 1962): Track & Field; 2-time world champion in both long jump (1987,91) and heptathlon (1987,93); won heptathlon gold medals at 1988 and '92 Olympics and LJ gold at '88 Games; also won Olympic silver (1984) in heptathlon and bronze (1992,96) in LJ; Sullivan Award winner (1986); only woman to receive *The Sporting News* Man of Year award.

Alberto Juantorena (b. Nov. 21, 1950): Cuban runner; won both 400m and 800m gold medals at 1976 Olympics.

Sonny Jurgensen (b. Aug. 23, 1934): Football QB; played 18 seasons with Philadelphia and Washington; led NFL in passing twice (1967,69); All-Pro in 1961; 255 career TD passes.

Duke Kahanamoku (b. Aug. 24, 1890, d. Jan. 22, 1968): Swimmer; won 3 gold medals and 2 silver over 3 Olympics (1912,20,24); also surfing pioneer.

Al Kaline (b. Dec. 19, 1934): Baseball; youngest player (at age 20) to win batting title (led AL with .340 in 1955); had 3,007 hits, 399 HRs in 22 years with Detroit.

Paul Kariya (b. Oct. 16, 1974): Hockey LW; first-ever selection of Anaheim (4th overall in 1993); led Maine to a NCAA Div. I national title in 1993; won Hobey Baker Award in 1993 as a freshman.

Anatoly Karpov (b. May 23, 1951): Chess; Soviet world champion from 1975-85; regained International Chess Federation (FIDE) version of championship in 1993 when countryman Garry Kasparov was stripped of title after forming new Professional Chess Association; held FIDE title until 1999.

Garry Kasparov (b. Apr. 13, 1963): Chess; Azerbaijani who became youngest player (22 years, 210 days) ever to win world championship as Soviet in 1985; defeated countryman Anatoly Karpov for title; split with International Chess Federation (FIDE) to form Professional Chess Association (PCA) in 1993; stripped of FIDE title in '93 but successfully defended PCA title against Briton Nigel Short; beat IBM supercomputer "Deep Blue" 4 games to 2 in 1996 much-publicized match in New York; lost rematch to computer in 1997; finally lost world title to Vladimir Kramnik in 2000.

Mike Keenan (b. Oct. 21, 1949): Hockey; coach who finally led NY Rangers to Stanley Cup title in 1994 after 53 unsuccessful years; ranked 4th all-time on NHL coaching wins list.

Kipchoge (Kip) Keino (b. Jan. 17, 1940): Kenyan runner; policeman who· beat USA's Jim Ryun to win 1,500m gold medal at 1968 Olympics; won again in steeplechase at 1972 Summer Games; his success spawned long line of distance champions from Kenya.

Johnny Kelley (b. Sept. 6, 1907): Distance runner; ran in his 61st and final Boston Marathon at age 84 in 1992, finishing in 5:58:36; won Boston twice (1935,45) and was 2nd seven times.

Jim Kelly (b. Feb. 14, 1960): Football QB; led Buffalo to four straight Super Bowls, and is only QB to lose four times; named to AFC Pro Bowl team 5 times; inducted into Pro Football Hall of Fame in 2002.

Leroy Kelly (b. May 20, 1942): Football; replaced Jim Brown in the Cleveland Browns backfield; in 1967, he led the NFL in rushing yards (1,205), rushing average (5.1 per carry) and rushing touchdowns (11).

Walter Kennedy (b. June 8, 1912, d. June 26, 1977): Basketball; 2nd NBA commissioner (1963-75), league doubled in size to 18 teams during his tenure.

Nancy Kerrigan (b. Oct. 13, 1969): Figure skating; 1993 U.S. women's champion and Olympic medalist in 1992 (bronze) and '94 (silver); victim of Jan. 6, 1994 assault at U.S. nationals in Detroit when Shane Stant clubbed her in right knee with metal baton after a practice session; conspiracy hatched by Jeff Gillooly, ex-husband of rival Tonya Harding; although unable to compete in nationals, she recovered and was granted berth on Olympic team; finished 2nd in Lillehammer to Oksana Baiul of Ukraine by a 5-4 judges' vote.

Billy Kidd (b. Apr. 13, 1943): Skiing; the first great Amercian male Alpine skier; first American male to win an Olympic medal when he won a silver in the slalom and a bronze in the Alpine combined in 1964; competed respectably with the great Jean-Claude Killy; won the world Alpine combined event in 1970, which was the first world championship for an American male.

Harmon Killebrew (b. June 29, 1936): Baseball 3B-1B; led AL in HRs 6 times and RBI 3 times; MVP in 1969 with Minnesota; 573 career HRs ranks 7th.

Jean-Claude Killy (b. Aug. 30, 1943): French alpine skier; 2-time World Cup champion (1967-68); won 3 gold medals at 1968 Olympics in Grenoble; co-president of 1992 Winter Games in Albertville; president of coordination commission for 2006 Turin Games.

Ralph Kiner (b. Oct. 27, 1922): Baseball OF; led NL in home runs 7 straight years (1946-52) with Pittsburgh; 369 career HRs and 1,015 RBI in 10 seasons; long-time NY Mets announcer.

Betsy King (b. Aug. 13, 1955): Golfer; 2-time LPGA Player of Year (1984,89); 3-time winner of Dinah Shore (1987,90,97) and 2-time winner of U.S. Open (1989,90); 34 overall Tour wins; 1st player in LPGA history to break $5 million mark in career earnings; member of LPGA Hall of Fame.

Billie Jean King (b. Nov. 22, 1943): Tennis; women's rights pioneer; Wimbledon singles champ 6 times; U.S. champ 4 times; first woman athlete to earn $100,000 in one year (1971); beat 55-year-old Bobby Riggs 6-4,6-3,6-3, in "Battle of the Sexes" to win $100,000 at Astrodome in 1973; founded the Women's Sports Foundation in 1974; captained the U.S. Olympic team in 1996 and 2000.

Don King (b. Aug. 20, 1931): Boxing promoter; first major black promoter who has controlled heavyweight title off and on since 1978; first big promotion was Muhammad Ali's fight against George Foreman in 1974; former numbers operator who served 4 years for manslaughter (1967-70); acquitted of tax evasion and fraud in 1985; also promoted Larry Holmes, Mike Tyson, Evander Holyfield, Roberto Duran and Julio Cesar Chavez among others; has been accused of bilking his fighters out of money; famous for his gravity-defying hairstyle and his catchphrase "Only in America".

Karch Kiraly (b. Nov. 3, 1960): Volleyball; USA's preeminent volleyball player; led UCLA to three NCAA championships (1979,81,82); played on US national teams that won Olympic gold medals in 1984 and '88, world championships in '82 and '86; won the inaugural gold medal for Olympic beach volleyball with Kent Steffes in 1996.

Tom Kite (b. Dec. 9, 1949): Golfer; co-NCAA champion with Ben Crenshaw (1972); PGA Rookie of Year (1973); PGA Player of Year (1989); finally won 1st major with victory in 1992 U.S. Open at Pebble Beach; captain of 1997 US Ryder Cup team; 19 career PGA wins, played on the Senior tour since 2000.

Gene Klein (b. Jan. 29, 1921, d. Mar. 12, 1990): Horseman; won 3 Eclipse awards as top owner (1985-87); his filly Winning Colors won 1988 Kentucky Derby; also owned San Diego Chargers football team (1966-84).

Bob Knight (b. Oct. 25, 1940): Basketball; coached Indiana to 3 NCAA titles (1976,81,87); 3-time Coach of Year (1975-76,89); coached 1984 U.S. Olympic team to gold medal; his volatile temper finally cost him when he was fired from Indiana in Sept. 2000 after a string of unacceptable incidents that included choking one of his players; returned to coaching with Texas Tech in 2001; 4th on all-time NCAA list with 808 wins in 37 years.

Phil Knight (b. Feb. 24, 1938): Founder and chairman of Nike, Inc., the multi-billion dollar shoe and fitness company founded in 1972 and based in Beaverton, Ore.; named "The Most Powerful Man in Sports" by *The Sporting News* in 1992.

Bill Koch (b. June 7, 1955): Cross country skiing; first highly accomplished American male in his sport; first American male to win a cross country Olympic medal when he took home a silver in the 30-kilometer race in 1976; In 1982, he was the first American male to win the Nordic World Cup.

Tommy Kono (b. June 27, 1930): weight lifter; won 2 olympic gold medals for U.S. (1952,56) and 1 silver (1960); all 3 medals were in different weight classes; set world records in four different classes; inducted into U.S. Olympic Hall of Fame in 1990.

Olga Korbut (b. May 16, 1955): Soviet gymnast; became the media darling of the 1972 Olympics in Munich by winning 3 gold medals (balance beam, floor exercise and team all-around); came back in the 1976 Olympics in Montreal and was a part of the USSR's gold medal winning all-around team; first to perform back somersault on balance beam; was inducted into the International Women's Sports Hall of Fame in 1982, the first gymnast to be inducted.

Johann Olav Koss (b. Oct. 29, 1968): Norwegian speed skater; won three gold medals at 1994 Olympics in Lillehammer with world records in the 1,500m, 5,000m and 10,000m; also won 1,500m gold and 10,000m silver in 1992 Games; retired shortly after '94 Olympics.

Sandy Koufax (b. Dec. 30, 1935): Baseball LHP; led NL in strikeouts 4 times and ERA 5 straight years; won 3 Cy Young Awards (1963,65,66) with LA Dodgers; MVP in 1963; 2-time World Series MVP (1963, 65); threw perfect game against Chicago Cubs (1-0, Sept. 9, 1965) and had 3 other no-hitters, 40 shutouts and 137 complete games in a career that ended prematurely due to an arm injury.

Alvin Kraenzlein (b. Dec. 12, 1876, d. Jan. 6, 1928): Track & Field; won 4 individual gold medals in 1900 Olympics (60m, long jump and the 110m and 200m hurdles).

Jack Kramer (b. Aug. 1, 1921): Tennis; Wimbledon singles champ 1947; U.S. champ 1946-47; promoter and Open pioneer.

Lenny Krayzelburg (b. Sept. 28, 1975): Swimming; born in Ukraine but became an American citizen in 1995; won gold for U.S. in the 100m backstroke and 200m backstroke at the Sydney Games in 2000; was also part of U.S. team that set a world record in the 4x100m medley relay in Sydney; world record holder in the 50 and 100 meter backstrokes.

Ingrid Kristiansen (b. Mar. 21, 1956): Norwegian runner; 2-time Boston Marathon winner (1986,89); won New York City Marathon in 1989; former world record holder in the marathon.

Julie Krone (b. July 24, 1963): Jockey; only woman to ride winning horse in a Triple Crown race when she captured Belmont Stakes aboard Colonial Affair in 1993; retired in 1999 as all-time winningest female jockey with over 3,000 wins; in 2000 became the first female jockey elected to thoroughbred racing's hall of fame; unretired in 2002.

Mike Krzyzewski (b. Feb. 13, 1947): Basketball; has coached Duke to 9 Final Four appearances and 3 NCAA titles (1991-92,2001); has coached at Army (1976-80) and Duke (1981–); inducted into Hall of Fame in 2001.

Bowie Kuhn (b. Oct. 28, 1926): Baseball Commissioner; Elected commissioner on Feb. 4, 1969 and served until Sept. 30, 1984; kept Willie Mays and Mickey Mantle out of baseball for their employment with casinos; handed down one-year suspensions of several players for drug involvement; nixed Charlie Finley's sale of three players for $3.5 million; baseball enjoyed unprecedented attendance and television contracts during his reign.

Alan Kulwicki (b. Dec. 14, 1954, d. Apr. 1, 1993): Auto racer; 1992 NASCAR national champion; 1st college grad and Northerner to win title; NASCAR Rookie of Year in 1986; famous for driving car backwards on victory lap; killed at age 38 in plane crash near Bristol, Tenn.

Michelle Kwan (b. July 7, 1980): Figure Skater; 1998 Olympic silver medalist at Nagano and 2002 bronze medalist at Salt Lake City; 7-time U.S. Champion (1996,98-03) and 5-time World Champ (1996,98,00,01,03); holds U.S. record with 8 career overall medals at the World Championships (5 gold, 3 silver); was U.S. alternate to the Olympics in 1994 as a 13-year-old.

Marion Ladewig (b. Oct. 30, 1914): Bowler; named Woman Bowler of the Year 9 times (1950-54,57-59,63).

Guy Lafleur (b. Sept. 20, 1951): Hockey RW; led NHL in scoring 3 times (1976-78); 2-time MVP (1977-78), played for 5 Stanley Cup winners in Montreal; playoff MVP in 1977; returned to NHL as player in 1988 after election to Hall of Fame; retired again in 1991 with 560 goals and 1,353 points.

Napoleon (Nap) Lajoie (b. Sept. 5, 1874, d. Feb. 7, 1959): Baseball 2B; led AL in batting 3 times (1901,03-04); batted .422 in 1901; hit .339 for career with 3,251 hits.

Jack Lambert (b. July 8, 1952): Football LB; 6-time All-Pro (1975-76,79-82); led Pittsburgh to 4 Super Bowl titles.

Kenesaw Mountain Landis (b. Nov. 20, 1866, d. Nov. 25, 1944): U.S. District Court judge who became first baseball commissioner (1920-44); banned eight Chicago Black Sox from baseball for life.

Tom Landry (b. Sept. 11, 1924, d. Feb. 12, 2000): Football; All-Pro DB for NY Giants (1954); coached Dallas for 29 years (1960-88); won 2 Super Bowls (1972,78); 3rd on NFL all-time list with 270 wins.

Steve Largent (b. Sept. 28, 1954): Football WR; retired in 1989 after 14 years in Seattle with then NFL records in passes caught (819) and TD passes caught (100); elected to U.S. House of Representatives (R, Okla.) in 1994 and Pro Football Hall of Fame in '95; ran for governor of Oklahoma in 2002 but suffered a narrow defeat.

Don Larsen (b. Aug. 7, 1929): Baseball RHP; NY Yankees hurler who pitched the only perfect game in World Series history— a 2-0 victory over Brooklyn in Game 5 of the 1956 Series (Oct. 8); Series MVP that year; had career record of 81-91 in 14 seasons with 6 clubs.

Tommy Lasorda (b. Sept. 22, 1927): Baseball; managed LA Dodgers to 2 World Series titles (1981,88) in 4 appearances; retired as manager during 1996 season with 1,599 regular-season wins in 21 years; named interim GM of Dodgers in 1998; member of Baseball Hall of Fame; managed gold-medal winning U.S. Olympic team in 2000 at Sydney.

Larissa Latynina (b. Dec. 27, 1934): Soviet gymnast; won total of 18 medals, (9 gold) in 3 Olympics (1956,60,64).

Nikki Lauda (b. Feb. 22, 1949): Austrian auto racer; 3-time world Formula One champion (1975,77,84); 25 career wins from 1971-85.

Rod Laver (b. Aug. 9, 1938): Australian tennis player; only player to win Grand Slam twice (1962,69); Wimbledon champion 4 times; 1st to earn $1 million in prize money, won 11 Grand Slam singles titles.

Andrea Mead Lawrence (b. Apr. 19, 1932): Alpine skier; won 2 gold medals at 1952 Olympics.

Bobby Layne (b. Dec. 19, 1926, d. Dec. 1, 1986): Football QB; college star at Texas; master of 2-minute offense; led Detroit to 4 divisional titles and 3 NFL championships in 1950s.

Frank Leahy (b. Aug. 27, 1908, d. June 21, 1973): Football; coached Notre Dame to four national titles (1943,46-47,49); career record of 107-13-9 for a winning pct. of .864.

Jeanette Lee (b. July 9, 1971): Billiards; known as "The Black Widow"; won the 1994 Women's Professional Billiards Assoc. (WPBA) National Championship and vaulted to the No. 1 women's player in the world; voted 1994 WPBA Player of the Year and 1998 WPBA Sportsperson of the Year.

Sammy Lee (b. Aug. 1, 1920): Diving; won Olympic gold medals for U.S. in the platform diving event in 1948 and 1952, the first male diver in history to win 2 golds in that event; Sullivan Award winner (1953); former doctor in U.S. Army; trained Greg Louganis.

Brian Leetch (b. Mar. 3, 1968): Hockey D; NHL Rookie of Year in 1989; won Norris Trophy as top defenseman in 1992; Conn Smythe Trophy winner as playoffs' MVP in 1994 when he helped lead NY Rangers to 1st Stanley Cup title in 54 years.

Jacques Lemaire (b. Sept. 7, 1945): Hockey C; member of 8 Stanley Cup champions in Montreal; scored 366 goals in 12 seasons; coached Canadiens (1983-85) and NJ Devils (1993-98), won 1995 Stanley Cup with New Jersey; returned to coaching with the expansion Minnesota Wild in 2000.

Mario Lemieux (b. Oct. 5, 1965): Hockey C; 6-time NHL scoring leader (1988-89,92-93,96,97); Rookie of Year (1985); 4-time All-NHL 1st team (1988-89,93,96); 3-time regular season MVP (1988,93,96); 3-time All-Star Game MVP; led Pittsburgh to consecutive Stanley Cup titles (1991 and '92) and was play-off MVP both years; won 1993 scoring title despite missing 24 games to undergo radiation treatments for Hodgkin's disease; missed 62 games during 1993-94 season and entire 94-95 season due to back injuries and fatigue; returned in 1995-96 to lead NHL in scoring and win the MVP trophy; retired after 1996-97 season and inducted into the Hall of Fame; headed group of investors that bought bankrupt Penguins in 1999; made surprising return to the ice in 2001.

Greg LeMond (b. June 26, 1961): Cyclist; 3-time Tour de France winner (1986,89-90); only non-European to win the event until Lance Armstrong in 1999; retired in Dec. 1994 after being diagnosed with a rare muscular disease known as mitochondrial myopathy.

Ivan Lendl (b. Mar. 7, 1960): Czech tennis player; No. 1 player in world 4 times (1985-87,89); won both French and U.S. Opens 3 times and Australian twice; owns 94 career tournament wins.

Suzanne Lenglen (b. May 24, 1899, d. July 4, 1938): French tennis player; dominated women's tennis from 1919-26; won both Wimbledon and French singles titles 6 times.

Sugar Ray Leonard (b. May 17, 1956): Boxer; light welterweight Olympic champ (1976); won world welterweight title 1979 and four more times; retired after losing to Terry Norris on Feb. 9, 1991, with record of 36-2-1 and 25 KOs; misguided comeback in 1997 resulted in resounding defeat by Hector Camacho.

Walter (Buck) Leonard (b. Sept. 8, 1907, d. Nov. 27, 1997): Baseball 1B; won Negro League championship nine years in a row with the Homestead Grays; hit .391 in 1948 to lead the league; usually batted cleanup behind Josh Gibson; retired at the age of 48; member of the National Baseball Hall of Fame.

Lisa Leslie (b. July 7, 1972): Basketball C; 2-time WNBA Finals MVP (2001-02) with the champion Los Angeles Sparks; 2001 regular season MVP; 3-time WNBA All-Star Game MVP (1999,2001-02); 2-time Olympic gold medalist (1996,2000); consensus National Player of the Year at USC (1994).

Marv Levy (b. Aug. 3, 1928): Football; coached Buffalo to four consecutive Super Bowls, but is one of two coaches who are 0-4 (Bud Grant is the other); won 50 games and two CFL Grey Cups with Montreal (1974,77).

Bill Lewis (b. Nov. 30, 1868, d. Jan. 1, 1949): Football; college star at Amherst College and then Harvard; first black player to be selected as an All-American (1892-93); also the first black admitted to the American Bar Association (1911); was U.S. Assistant Attorney General.

Carl Lewis (b. July 1, 1961): Track & Field; won 9 Olympic gold medals; 4 in 1984 (100m, 200m, 4x100m, LJ), 2 in '88 (100m, LJ), 2 in '92 (4x100m, LJ) and 1 in '96 (LJ); has record 8 World Championship titles and 9 medals in all; Sullivan Award winner (1981); two-time AP Athlete of the Year (1983-84).

Lennox Lewis (b. Sept. 2, 1965): British boxer; won 1988 Olympic super heavyweight gold medal for Canada; was awarded WBC heavyweight belt when Riddick Bowe tossed it in a London trash can in 1993; lost title in a 2nd round TKO loss to Oliver McCall; won rematch 3 years later when McCall suffered emotional breakdown in the ring; unified titles in his rematch with Evander Holyfield in Nov. 1999; lost belts in upset loss to Hasim Rahman in South Africa in April 2001 but regained them 7 months later; recorded 8th-round KO of Mike Tyson in June 2002.

Nancy Lieberman (b. July 1, 1958): Basketball; 3-time All-America and 2-time Player of Year (1979-80); led Old Dominion to consecutive AIAW titles in 1979 and '80; played in defunct WPBL and WABA and became 1st woman to play in men's pro league (USBL) in 1986; played in the inaugural season of the WNBA for the Phoenix Mercury and served as coach/GM of Detroit Shock (1998-2000).

Eric Lindros (b. Feb. 28, 1973): Hockey C; No. 1 pick in 1991 NHL draft by the Nordiques; sat out 1991-92 season rather than play in Quebec; traded to Philadelphia in 1992 for 6 players, 2 No. 1 picks and $15 million; elected Flyers captain at age 22; won Hart Trophy as league MVP in 1995; suffered series of concussions in 1999-00 but was traded to NY Rangers and inked big money deal with team in 2001.

Tara Lipinski (b. June 10, 1982): Figure Skater; won the 1998 women's figure skating gold medal at the Olympics in Nagano, becoming the youngest in history (15 yrs., 7 mos.) to do so; she and Michelle Kwan gave the U.S. its first 1-2 finish in that event since 1956; 1997 U.S. and World champion; turned pro in April 1998.

Sonny Liston (b. May 8, 1932, d. Dec. 30, 1970): Boxer; heavyweight champion (1962-64), who knocked out Floyd Patterson twice in the first round, then lost title to Muhammad Ali (then Cassius Clay) in 1964; pro record of 50-4 with 39 KOs.

Vince Lombardi (b. June 11, 1913, d. Sept. 3, 1970): Football; coached Green Bay to 5 NFL titles; won first 2 Super Bowls (1967-68); died as NFL's all-time winningest coach with percentage of .740 (105-35-6); Super Bowl trophy named in his honor.

Johnny Longden (b. Feb. 14, 1907): Jockey; first to win 6,000 races; rode Count Fleet to Triple Crown in 1943.

Jeannie Longo (b. Oct. 31, 1958): French cyclist; 12-time world cycling champion and 1996 olympic road race gold medallist.

Nancy Lopez (b. Jan. 6, 1957): Golfer; 4-time LPGA Player of the Year (1978-79,85,88); Rookie of Year (1977); 3-time winner of LPGA Championship; reached Hall of Fame by age 30 with 35 victories; 48 career wins.

Donna Lopiano (b. Sept. 11, 1946): Former basketball and softball star who was women's AD at Texas for 18 years before leaving to become executive director of Women's Sports Foundation in 1992.

Greg Louganis (b. Jan. 29, 1960): U.S. diver; widely considered the greatest diver in history; won platform and springboard gold medals at both 1984 and '88 Olympics; also won a silver medal at the 1976 Olympics at the age of 16; won five world championships and 47 U.S. National Diving titles; revealed on Feb. 22, 1995 that he has AIDS.

Joe Louis (b. May 13, 1914, d. Apr. 12, 1981): Boxer; world heavyweight champion from June 22, 1937 to Mar. 1, 1949; his reign of 11 years, 8 months longest in division history; successfully defended title 25 times; retired in 1949, but returned to lose title shot against successor Ezzard Charles in 1950 and then to Rocky Marciano in '51; pro record of 63-3 with 49 KOs.

Sid Luckman (b. Nov. 21, 1916, d. July 5, 1998): Football QB; 6-time All-Pro; led Chicago Bears to 4 NFL titles (1940,41,43,46); MVP in 1943.

Hank Luisetti (b. June 16, 1916): Basketball F; 3-time All-America at Stanford (1935-38); revolutionized game with one-handed shot.

Johnny Lujack (b. Jan. 4, 1925): Football QB; led Notre Dame to three national titles (1943,46-47); won Heisman Trophy in 1947.

Darrell Wayne Lukas (b. Sept. 2, 1935): Horse racing; 4-time Eclipse-winning trainer who saddled Horses of Year Lady's Secret in 1988 and Criminal Type in 1990; first trainer to earn over $100 million in purses; led nation in earnings 14 times since 1983; Grindstone's Kentucky Derby win in 1996 gave him six Triple Crown wins in a row; has won Preakness 5 times, Kentucky Derby 4 times and Belmont 4 times; his most recent Triple Crown victory came in the 2000 Belmont with Commendable; leads all Breeders' Cup trainers with 16 victories.

Gen. Douglas MacArthur (b. Jan. 26, 1880, d. Apr. 5, 1964): Controversial U.S. general of World War II and Korea; president of U.S. Olympic Committee (1927-28); college football devotee, National Football Foundation MacArthur Bowl named after him.

Connie Mack (b. Dec. 22, 1862, d. Feb. 8, 1956): Baseball owner; managed Philadelphia A's until he was 87 (1901-50); all-time major league wins leader with 3,755, including World Series; won 9 AL pennants and 5 World Series (1910-11,13,29-30); also finished last 17 times.

Andy MacPhail (b. Apr. 5, 1953): Baseball; Chicago Cubs president/CEO who was GM of 2 World Series champions in Minnesota (1987,91); won first title at age 34; son of Lee, grandson of Larry.

Larry MacPhail (b. Feb. 3, 1890, d. Oct. 1, 1975): Baseball executive and innovator; introduced major leagues to night games at Cincinnati (May 24, 1935); won pennant in Brooklyn (1941) and World Series with NY Yankees (1947); father of Lee.

Lee MacPhail (b. Oct. 25, 1917): Baseball; AL president (1974-83); president of owners' Player Relations Committee (1984-85); also GM of Baltimore (1959-65) and NY Yankees (1967-74); son of Larry and father of Andy.

Wendy Macpherson (b. Jan. 28, 1968): Bowling; voted Bowler of the Decade for the 1990s; Major titles include the 1986 BPAA U.S. Open, 1988, 2000 and 2003 WIBC Queens and 1999 Sam's Town Invitational; annual PWBA money winner 4 times (1996,97,99,2000).

John Madden (b. Apr. 10, 1936): Football and Radio-TV; won 112 games and a Super Bowl (1976 season) as coach of Oakland Raiders; has won 13 Emmy Awards since 1982 as NFL analyst; signed 4-year, $32 million deal with Fox in 1994— a richer contract than any NFL player at the time; joined Al Michaels in ABC's Monday Night Football booth in 2002 after 21 seasons alongside Pat Summerall.

Greg Maddux (b. Apr. 14, 1966): Baseball RHP; won unprecedented 4 straight NL Cy Young Awards with Cubs (1992) and Atlanta (1993-95); has led NL in ERA four times (1993-95,98); won 13th straight gold glove in 2002; first to win at least 15 games in 16 straight seasons (1988-2003).

Larry Mahan (b. Nov. 21, 1943): Rodeo; 6-time All-Around world champion cowboy (1966-70,73).

Phil Mahre (b. May 10, 1957): Alpine skier; 3-time World Cup overall champ (1981-83); finished 1-2 with twin brother Steve in 1984 Olympic slalom.

Karl Malone (b. July 24, 1963): Basketball F; 11-time All-NBA 1st team (1989-99) with Utah; member of the 1992 and '96 Olympic gold medal teams; 2-time NBA MVP (1997,99); all-time NBA leader in free throws made (9,619), 2nd in career points (36,374) and 2nd in field goals made (13,335); named one of the NBA's 50 greatest players; signed as a free agent with L.A. Lakers in 2003.

Moses Malone (b. Mar. 23, 1955): Basketball C; signed with Utah of ABA out of high school at age 19; led NBA in rebounding 6 times; 4-time All-NBA 1st team; 3-time NBA MVP (1979,82-83); Finals MVP with Philadelphia in 1983; played in 21st pro season in 1994-95.

Nigel Mansell (b. Aug. 8, 1953): British auto racer; won 1992 Formula One driving championship with record 9 victories and 14 poles; quit Grand Prix circuit to race Indy cars in 1993; 1st rookie to win IndyCar title; 3rd driver to win IndyCar and F1 titles; returned to F1 after 1994 IndyCar season and won '94 Australian Grand Prix; left F1 again on May 23, 1995 with 31 wins and 32 poles in 15 years.

Mickey Mantle (b. Oct. 20, 1931, d. Aug. 13, 1995): Baseball CF; led AL in home runs 4 times; won Triple Crown in 1956; hit 52 HRs in 1956 and 54 in '61; 3-time MVP (1956-57,62); hit 536 career HRs; played in 12 World Series with NY Yankees and won 7 times; all-time World Series leader in HRs (18), RBI (40), runs (42) and strikeouts (54); inducted into Baseball Hall of Fame in 1974.

Diego Maradona (b. Oct. 30, 1960): Soccer F; captain and MVP of 1986 World Cup champion Argentina; also led national team to 1990 World Cup final; consensus Player of Decade in 1980s; led Napoli to 2 Italian League titles (1987,90) and UEFA Cup (1989); tested positive for cocaine and suspended 15 months by FIFA in 1991; returned to World Cup as Argentine captain in 1994, but was kicked out of tournament after two games when doping test found 5 banned substances in his urine.

Pete Maravich (b. June 27, 1947, d. Jan. 5, 1988): Basketball; NCAA scoring leader 3 times at LSU (1968-70); averaged NCAA-record 44.2 points a game over career; Player of Year in 1970; NBA scoring champ in '77 with New Orleans.

Alice Marble (b. Sept. 28, 1913, d. Dec. 13, 1990): Tennis; 4-time U.S. champion (1936,38-40); won Wimbledon in 1939; swept U.S. singles, doubles and mixed doubles from 1938-40.

Gino Marchetti (b. Jan. 2, 1927): Football DE; 8-time NFL All-Pro (1957-64) with Baltimore Colts.

Rocky Marciano (b. Sept. 1, 1923, d. Aug. 31, 1969): Boxer; heavyweight champion (1952-56); retired undefeated; pro record of 49-0 with 43 KOs; killed in plane crash in Iowa.

Juan Marichal (b. Oct. 20, 1938): Baseball RHP; won 21 or more games 6 times for S.F. Giants from 1963-69; ended 16-year career at 243-142.

Dan Marino (b. Sept. 15, 1961): Football QB; 4-time leading passer in AFC (1983-84,86,89); set NFL single-season records for TD passes (48) and passing yards (5,084) in 1984; all-time leader in career TD passes, passing yards, attempts and completions.

Roger Maris (b. Sept. 10, 1934, d. Dec. 14, 1985): Baseball OF; broke Babe Ruth's season HR record with 61 in 1961 and held record until 1998 (passed by M. McGwire and S. Sosa); 2-time AL MVP (1960-61) with NY Yankees; 275 HRs in 12 years.

Jim Marshall (b. Dec. 30, 1937): Football; long-time Vikings DE and NFL ironman; played in an NFL-record 282 consecutive games (1960-1979); also famous for picking up a fumble and running 66 yards the wrong way into the opponent's (49ers) endzone.

Billy Martin (b. May 16, 1928, d. Dec. 25, 1989): Baseball; 5-time manager of NY Yankees; won 2 pennants and 1 World Series (1977); also managed Minnesota, Detroit, Texas and Oakland; played on 5 Yankee world champions in 1950s.

Casey Martin (b. June 2, 1972): Golfer; suffers from a birth defect in his right leg known as Klippel-Trenauney-Webber Syndrome; won lawsuit against the PGA Tour for the right to use a golf cart during competition under the Americans with Disabilities Act.

Pedro Martinez (b. Oct. 25, 1971): Baseball RHP; one of baseball's premier pitchers; won 1997 NL Cy Young award with Montreal; traded to Boston Red Sox in Nov. 1997; 2-time AL Cy Young Award winner with Boston (1999,2000).

Eddie Mathews (b. Oct. 13, 1931, d. Feb. 18, 2001): Baseball 3B; led NL in HRs twice (1953,59); hit 30 or more home runs 9 straight years; 512 career HRs.

Christy Mathewson (b. Aug. 12, 1880, d. Oct. 7, 1925): Baseball RHP; won 22 or more games 12 straight years (1903-14); 373 career wins; pitched 3 shutouts in 1905 World Series.

Bob Mathias (b. Nov. 17, 1930): Track & Field; youngest winner of decathlon with gold medal in 1948 Olympics at age 17; first to repeat as decathlon champ in 1952; Sullivan Award winner (1948); 4-term member of U.S. Congress (R, Calif.) from 1967-74.

Ollie Matson (b. May 1, 1930): Football HB; All-America at San Francisco (1951); bronze medal winner in 400m at 1952 Olympics; 4-time All-Pro for NFL Chicago Cardinals (1954-57); traded to LA Rams for 9 players in 1959; accounted for 12,884 all-purpose yards and scored 73 TDs in 14 seasons.

Don Mattingly (b. Apr. 20, 1961): Baseball 1B; American League MVP (1985); won AL batting title in 1984 (.343); led majors with 145 RBI in 1985; led AL with 238 hits (Yankee record) and 53 doubles in 1986; won 9 Gold Glove Awards at 1B (1985-89, 91-94); back injury shortened career.

Willie Mays (b. May 6, 1931): Baseball OF; nicknamed the "Say Hey Kid"; led NL in HRs and stolen bases 4 times each; 2-time MVP (1954,65) with NY-SF Giants; Hall of Famer who played in 24 All-Star Games, earning MVP honors twice (1963,68); 12-time Gold Glove winner; 660 HRs and 3,283 hits in career.

Bill Mazeroski (b. Sept. 5, 1936): Baseball 2B; career .260 hitter who won the 1960 World Series for Pittsburgh with a lead-off HR in the bottom of the 9th inning of Game 7; the pitcher was Ralph Terry of the NY Yankees, the count was 1-0 and the score was tied 9-9; also a sure-fielder, Maz won 8 Gold Gloves in 17 seasons.

Bob McAdoo (b. Sept. 25, 1951): Basketball F/C; 1972 *Sporting News* First Team All-American; NBA Rookie of the Year (1973); NBA MVP (1975); All-NBA First Team (1975); Led NBA in scoring three consecutive years (1974-76); 5-time All-Star (1974-78); two championships with LA Lakers (1982,85).

Joe McCarthy (b. Apr. 21, 1887, d. Jan. 13, 1978): Baseball; first manager to win pennants in both leagues (Chicago Cubs in 1929 and NY Yankees in 1932); greatest success came with Yankees when he won seven pennants and six World Series championships from 1936 to 1943; first manager to win four World Series in a row (1936-39); finished his career with the Boston Red Sox (1948-'50); lifetime record of 2125-1333; member of Baseball Hall of Fame.

Pat McCormick (b. May 12, 1930): U.S. diver; won women's platform and springboard gold medals in both 1952 and '56 Olympics.

Willie McCovey (b. Jan. 10, 1938): Baseball 1B; led NL in HRs 3 times and RBI twice; MVP in 1969 with SF; 521 career HRs; indicted for tax evasion in July 1995, pled guilty; "McCovey Cove," the bay outside the rightfield fence at San Francisco's Pacific Bell Park is named for him.

John McEnroe (b. Feb. 16, 1959): Tennis; No.1 player in the world 4 times (1981-84); 4-time U.S. Open champ (1979-81,84); 3-time Wimbledon champ (1981,83-84); played on 5 Davis Cup winners (1978,79,81,82,92); won NCAA singles title (1978); finished career with 77 singles championships, 77 more in men's doubles (including 9 Grand Slam titles), and U.S. Davis Cup records for years played (13) and singles matches won (41).

John McGraw (b. Apr. 7, 1873, d. Feb. 25, 1934): Baseball; managed NY Giants to 9 NL pennants between 1905-24; won 3 World Series (1905,21-22); 2nd on all-time career list with 2,866 wins in 33 seasons (2,840 regular season and 26 World Series).

Frank McGuire (b. Nov. 8, 1916, d. Oct. 11, 1994): Basketball; winner of 731 games as high school, college and pro coach; won at least 100 games at 3 colleges— St. John's (103), North Carolina (164) and South Carolina (283); won 550 games in 30 college seasons; 1957 UNC team went 32-0 and beat Kansas 54-53 in triple OT to win NCAA title; coached NBA Philadelphia Warriors to 49-31 record in 1961-62 season, but refused to move with team to San Francisco.

Mark McGwire (b. Oct. 1, 1963): Baseball 1B; *Sporting News* college player of the year (1984); Member of 1984 U.S. Olympic baseball team; won AL Rookie of the Year and hit rookie-record 49 HRs in 1987; shattered Roger Maris' season home run record (61) in 1998 with St. Louis (70); followed that magical season with 65 HRs and 147 RBI in 1999.

Jim McKay (b. Sept. 24, 1921): Radio-TV; host and commentator of ABC's Olympic coverage and "Wide World of Sports" show since 1961; 12-time Emmy winner; also given Peabody Award in 1988 and Life Achievement Emmy in 1990; became part owner of Baltimore Orioles in 1993.

Tamara McKinney (b. Oct. 16, 1962): Skiing; first American woman to win overall Alpine World Cup championship (1983); won World Cup slalom (1984) and giant slalom titles twice (1981,83).

Denny McLain (b. Mar. 29, 1944): Baseball RHP; last pitcher to win 30 games (1968); 2-time Cy Young winner (1968-69) with Detroit; convicted of racketeering, extortion and drug possession in 1985, served 29 months of 25-year jail term, sentence overturned when court ruled he had not received a fair trial; he has faced subsequent legal troubles.

Rick Mears (b. Dec. 3, 1951): Auto racer; 3-time CART national champ (1979,81-82); 4-time winner of Indy 500 (1979,84,88,91) and only driver to win 6 Indy 500 poles; Indy 500 Rookie of Year (1978); retired in 1992 with 29 CART wins and 40 poles.

Mark Messier (b. Jan. 18, 1961): Hockey C; 2-time NHL MVP with Edmonton (1990) and NY Rangers (1992); captain of 1994 Rangers team that won 1st Stanley Cup since 1940; ranks 2nd in all-time playoff points, goals and assists; signed free agent contract with Vancouver Canucks in 1997 but returned to the Rangers in 2000; 3rd on all-time regular season points list (1,844).

Anne Meyers (b. Mar. 26, 1955): Basketball G; In 1974, became first high schooler to play for U.S. national team; 4-time All-American at UCLA (1976-79); member of 1976 U.S. Olympic team; Broderick Award and Cup winner (1978); Signed $50,000 no cut contract with NBA's Indiana Pacers (1980); married Dodger great Don Drysdale.

Debbie Meyer (b. Aug. 14, 1952): Swimmer; 1st swimmer to win 3 individual gold medals at one Olympics (1968).

George Mikan (b. June 18, 1924): Basketball C; 3-time All-America (1944-46); led DePaul to NIT title (1945); led Minneapolis Lakers to 5 NBA titles in 6 years (1949-54); first commissioner of ABA (1967-69).

Stan Mikita (b. May 20, 1940): Hockey C; led NHL in scoring 4 times; won both MVP and Lady Byng awards in 1967 and '68 with Chicago.

Bode Miller (b. Oct. 12, 1977): Alpine Skier; won 2 silver medals at 2002 Winter Games; 2 golds, 1 silver at 2003 World Championships; 2nd overall in 2003 World Cup standings.

Cheryl Miller (b. Jan. 3, 1964): Basketball; 3-time College Player of Year (1984-86); led USC to NCAA title and U.S. to Olympic gold medal in 1984; coached USC to 44-14 record in 2 years; coached WNBA's Phoenix Mercury for 4 years; sister of NBA's Reggie.

Del Miller (b. July 5, 1913, d. Aug. 19, 1996): Harness racing; driver, trainer, owner, breeder, seller and track owner; drove to 2,441 wins from 1929-90.

Marvin Miller (b. Apr. 14, 1917): Baseball labor leader; executive director of Players' Assn. from 1966-82; increased average salary from $19,000 to over $240,000; led 13-day strike in 1972 and 50-day walkout in '81.

Shannon Miller (b. Mar. 10, 1977): Gymnast; won 5 medals in 1992 Olympics and 2 golds in '96 Games; All-Around women's world champion in 1993 and '94.

Billy Mills (b. June 30, 1938): Track & Field; Native American who was upset winner of 10,000m gold medal at 1964 Olympics.

Bora Milutinovic (b. Sept. 7, 1944): Soccer; Serbian who coached United States national team from 1991-95; led Mexico (1986), Costa Rica ('90), USA ('94) and Nigeria ('98) into the 2nd round of the World Cup; coached China to its 1st World Cup in 2002 but went 0-3 in the 1st round.

Tommy Moe (b. Feb. 17, 1970): Alpine skier; won Downhill gold and Super-G silver at 1994 Winter Olympics; 1st U.S. man to win 2 Olympic alpine medals in one year.

Paul Molitor (b. Aug. 22, 1956): Baseball DH-1B; All-America SS at Minnesota in 1976; spent 15 years with Milwaukee, then 3 each with Toronto and Minnesota; led Blue Jays to 2nd straight World Series title as MVP (1993); hit .418 in 2 Series appearances (1982,93); holds World Series record with five hits in one game.

Joe Montana (b. June 11, 1956): Football QB; led Notre Dame to national title in 1977; led San Francisco to 4 Super Bowl titles in 1980s; only 3-time Super Bowl MVP; 2-time NFL MVP (1989-90); led NFL in passing 5 times; traded to K.C. in 1993; ranks 3rd all-time in passing efficiency (92.3), 7th in TD passes (273) and 7th in yards passing (40,551); inducted into Pro Football Hall of Fame in 2000.

Helen Wills Moody (b. Oct. 6, 1905, d. Jan. 1, 1998): Tennis; won 8 Wimbledon singles titles, 7 U.S. and 4 French from 1923-38.

Warren Moon (b. Nov. 18, 1956): Football QB; MVP of 1978 Rose Bowl with Washington; MVP of CFL with Edmonton in 1983; led Eskimos to 5 consecutive Grey Cup titles (1978-82) and was playoff MVP twice (1980,82); entered NFL in 1984 and played for four different teams; picked for 9 Pro Bowls including a QB-record 8 straight (1988-95).

Archie Moore (b. Dec. 13, 1913, d. Dec. 9, 1998): Boxer; world light-heavyweight champion (1952-60); pro record 199-26-8 with a record 145 KOs.

Noureddine Morceli (b. Feb. 28, 1970): Algerian runner; 3-time world champion at 1,500 meters (1991,93,95) and 1996 Olympic gold medal winner; former holder of world records in several middle distance events.

Howie Morenz (b. June 21, 1902, d. Mar. 8, 1937): Hockey C; 3-time NHL MVP (1928,31,32); led Montreal Canadiens to 3 Stanley Cups; voted Outstanding Player of the Half-Century in 1950.

Joe Morgan (b. Sept. 19, 1943): Baseball 2B; led NL in walks 4 times; regular-season MVP both years he led Cincinnati to World Series titles (1975-76); 5th behind Rickey Henderson, Babe Ruth, Ted Williams and Barry Bonds in career walks with 1,865.

Bobby Morrow (b. Oct. 15, 1935): Track & Field; won 3 gold medals at 1956 Olympics (100m, 200m and 4x400m relay).

Willie Mosconi (b. June 27, 1913, d. Sept. 12, 1993): Pocket Billiards; 14-time world champion from 1941-57.

Annemarie Moser-Pröll (b. Mar. 27, 1953): Austrian alpine skier; won World Cup overall title 6 times (1971-75,79); all-time women's World Cup leader in career wins with 61; won Downhill in 1980 Olympics.

Edwin Moses (b. Aug. 31, 1955): Track & Field; won 400m hurdles at 1976 and '84 Olympics, bronze medal in '88; also winner of 122 consecutive races from 1977-87.

Stirling Moss (b. Sept. 17, 1929): Auto racer; won 194 of 466 career races and 16 Formula One events, but was never world champion.

Marion Motley (b. June 5, 1920, d. June 27, 1999): Football FB; all-time leading AAFC rusher; rushed for over 4,700 yards and 31 TDs for Cleveland Browns (1946-53).

Shirley Muldowney (b. June 19, 1940): Drag Racer; "Cha Cha"; women's racing pioneer; 3-time Winston drag racing Top Fuel champion (1977,80,82); recorded 18 career NHRA National Event Victories.

Anthony Munoz (b. Aug. 19, 1958): Football OT; drafted 3rd overall in 1980 out of USC; 11-time All Pro with Cincinnati; member of NFL 75th Anniv. All-Time Team; elected to Hall of Fame in 1998.

Calvin Murphy (b. May 9, 1948): Basketball G; NBA All-Rookie team (1971); holds NBA single season free throw percentage (.958); third all-time career free throw pct. (.892); elected to Basketball Hall of Fame in 1992; though only 5'9" and 165 pounds, he is regarded as one of the best guards ever.

Dale Murphy (b. Mar. 12, 1956): Baseball OF; led NL in RBI 3 times and HRs twice; 2-time MVP (1982-83) with Atlanta; also played with Philadelphia and Colorado; retired in 1993 with 398 HRs.

Jack Murphy (b. Feb. 5, 1923, d. Sept. 24, 1980): Sports editor and columnist of *The San Diego Union* from 1951-80; instrumental in bringing AFL Chargers south from LA in 1961, landing Padres as NL expansion team in '69; and lobbying for 54,000-seat San Diego stadium that would later bear his name.

Eddie Murray (b. Feb. 24, 1956): Baseball 1B-DH; AL Rookie of Year in 1977; became 20th player in history, but only 2nd switch hitter (after Pete Rose) to get 3,000 hits; one of only 3 men (Aaron and Mays) with 500 HRs and 3,000 hits.

Jim Murray (b. Dec. 29, 1919, d. Aug. 16, 1998): Sports columnist for *LA Times* 1961-98; 14-time Sportswriter of the Year; won Pulitzer Prize for commentary in 1990.

Ty Murray (b. Oct. 11, 1969): Rodeo cowboy; 7-time All-Around world champion (1989-94,98); Rookie of Year in 1988; youngest (age 20) to win All-Around title; set single season earnings mark with $297,896 in 1993; career hampered by injury.

Stan Musial (b. Nov. 21, 1920): Baseball OF-1B; led NL in batting 7 times and RBI 2 times; 3-time MVP (1943,46,48) with St. Louis; played in 24 All-Star Games; had 3,630 career hits (4th all-time) and .331 average.

John Naber (b. Jan. 20, 1956): Swimmer; won 4 gold medals and a silver in 1976 Olympics.

Bronko Nagurski (b. Nov. 3, 1908, d. Jan. 7, 1990): Football FB-T; All-America at Minnesota (1929); All-Pro with Chicago Bears (1932-34); charter member of college and pro Halls of Fame.

James Naismith (b. Nov. 6, 1861, d. Nov. 28, 1939): Canadian physical education instructor who invented basketball in 1891 at the YMCA Training School (now Springfield College) in Springfield, Mass.

Joe Namath (b. May 31, 1943): Football QB; signed for unheard-of $400,000 as rookie with AFL's NY Jets in 1965; 2-time All-AFL (1968-69) and All-NFL (1972); led Jets to Super Bowl upset as MVP in '69 after making brash prediction of victory.

Ilie Nastase (b. July 19, 1946): Romanian tennis player; No.1 in the world twice (1972-73); won U.S. (1972) and French (1973) Opens; has since entered Romanian politics.

Martina Navratilova (b. Oct. 18, 1956): Tennis player; No.1 player in the world 7 times (1978-79,82-86); won her record 9th Wimbledon singles title in 1990; also won 4 U.S. Opens, 3 Australian and 2 French; in all, won 18 Grand Slam singles titles and 37 Grand Slam doubles titles; all-time leader among men and women in singles titles (167); 2nd all-time behind Graf on women's career money list ($20.9 million); still active in very limited competition; inducted into International Tennis Hall of Fame in 2000.

Cosmas Ndeti (b. Nov. 24, 1971): Kenyan distance runner; winner of three consecutive Boston Marathons (1993-95); set what is still the course record of 2:07:15 in 1994.

Earle (Greasy) Neale (b. Nov. 5, 1891, d. Nov. 2, 1973): Baseball and Football; hit .357 for Cincinnati in 1919 World Series; also played with pre-NFL Canton Bulldogs; later coached Philadelphia Eagles to 2 NFL titles (1948-49).

Primo Nebiolo (b. July 14, 1923, d. Nov. 7, 1999): Italian president of International Amateur Athletic Federation (IAAF) since 1981; also an at-large member of International Olympic Committee; regarded as dictatorial, but credited with elevating track & field to world class financial status.

Byron Nelson (b. Feb. 4, 1912): Golfer; 2-time winner of both Masters (1937,42) and PGA (1940,45); also U.S. Open champion in 1939; won 19 tournaments in 1945, including 11 in a row; also set all-time PGA stroke average with 68.33 strokes per round over 120 rounds in '45.

Lindsey Nelson (b. May 25, 1919, d. June 10, 1995): Radio-TV; all-purpose play-by-play broadcaster for CBS, NBC and others; 4-time Sportscaster of the Year (1959-62); voice of Cotton Bowl for 25 years and NY Mets from 1962-78; given Life Achievement Emmy Award in 1991.

Ernie Nevers (b. June 11, 1903, d. May 3, 1976): Football FB; earned 11 letters in four sports at Stanford; played pro football, baseball and basketball; scored 40 points for Chicago Cardinals in one NFL game (1929).

Paula Newby-Fraser (b. June 2, 1962): Zimbabwean triathlete; 8-time winner of Ironman Triathlon in Hawaii; established women's record of 8:55:28 in 1992.

John Newcombe (b. May 23, 1944): Australian tennis player; No.1 player in world 3 times (1967,70-71); won Wimbledon 3 times and U.S. and Australian championships twice each.

Pete Newell (b. Aug. 31, 1915): Basketball; coached at Univ. of San Francisco, Michigan St. and the Univ. of California; first coach to win NIT (San Francisco-1949), NCAA (California-1959) and Olympic gold medal (1960); later served as the general manager of the San Diego Rockets and LA Lakers in the NBA; member of Basketball Hall of Fame.

Jack Nicklaus (b. Jan. 21, 1940): Golfer; all-time leader in major tournament wins with 18— 6 Masters, 5 PGAs, 4 U.S. Opens and 3 British Opens; oldest player to win Masters (46 in 1986); PGA Player of Year 5 times (1967,72-73,75-76); named Golfer of the Century by PGA in 1988; 6-time Ryder Cup player and 2-time captain (1983,87); won NCAA title (1961) and 2 U.S. Amateurs (1959,61); 70 PGA Tour wins (2nd to Sam Snead's 81); fourth win in Tradition in 1996 gave him 8 majors on Senior PGA Tour; nicknamed "the Golden Bear."

Chuck Noll (b. Jan. 5, 1932): Football; coached Pittsburgh to 4 Super Bowl titles (1975-76,79-80); retired after 1991 season ranked 5th on all-time list with 209 wins (including playoffs) in 23 years.

Greg Norman (b. Feb. 10, 1955): Australian golfer; 73 tournament wins worldwide including 18 PGA Tour victories; 2-time British Open winner (1986,93); lost Masters by a stroke in both 1986 (to Jack Nicklaus) and '87 (to Larry Mize in sudden death); 1995 PGA Tour Player of the Year.

James D. Norris (b. Nov. 6, 1906, d. Feb. 25, 1966): Boxing promoter and NHL owner; president of International Boxing Club from 1949 until U.S. Supreme Court ordered its break-up (for anti-trust violations) in 1958; only NHL owner to win Stanley Cups in two cities: Detroit (1936-37,43) and Chicago (1961).

Paavo Nurmi (b. June 13, 1897, d. Oct. 2, 1973): Finnish runner; won 9 gold medals (6 individual) in 1920, '24 and '28 Olympics; from 1921-31 broke 23 world outdoor records in events ranging from 1,500 to 20,000 meters.

Dan O'Brien (b. July 18, 1966): Track & Field; Olympic decathlon gold medalist (1996); set former world record in decathlon (8,891 pts) in 1992, after shockingly failing to qualify for event at U.S. Olympic Trials; three-time gold medalist at World Championships (1991,93,95).

Larry O'Brien (b. July 7, 1917, d. Sept. 27, 1990): Basketball; former U.S. Postmaster General and 3rd NBA commissioner (1975-84); league absorbed 4 ABA teams and created salary cap during his term in office.

Parry O'Brien (b. Jan. 28, 1932): Track & Field; in 4 consecutive Olympics, won two gold medals, a silver and placed 4th in the shot put (1952-64).

Al Oerter (b. Sept. 19, 1936): Track & Field; his 4 discus gold medals in consecutive Olympics from 1956-68 is an unmatched Olympic record.

Sadaharu Oh (b. May 20, 1940): Baseball 1B; led Japan League in HRs 15 times; 9-time MVP for Tokyo Giants; hit 868 HRs in 22 years.

Hakeem Olajuwon (b. Jan. 21, 1963): Basketball C; Nigerian native who was All-America in 1984 and Final Four MOP in 1983 for Houston; overall 1st pick by Houston Rockets in 1984 NBA draft; led Rockets to back-to-back NBA titles (1994-95); regular season MVP (1994) and 2-time Finals MVP ('94-95); 6-time All-NBA 1st team (1987-89,93-95); all-time NBA blocks leader.

Jose Maria Olazabal (b. Feb. 5, 1966): Spanish golfer; has 28 worldwide victories including 2 Masters (1994,99); played on 6 European Ryder Cup teams.

Barney Oldfield (b. Jan. 29, 1878, d. Oct. 4, 1946): Auto racing pioneer; drove cars built by Henry Ford; first man to drive car a mile per minute (1903).

Walter O'Malley (b. Oct. 9, 1903, d. Aug. 9, 1979): Baseball owner; moved Brooklyn Dodgers to Los Angeles after 1957 season; won 4 World Series (1955,59,63,65).

Shaquille O'Neal (b. Mar. 6, 1972): Basketball C; 2-time All-America at LSU (1991-92); overall 1st pick (as a junior) by Orlando in 1992 NBA draft; Rookie of Year in 1993; 2-time NBA scoring leader (1995,2000); regular season MVP (2000) and 3-time NBA Finals MVP (2000,01,02); named one of the NBA's 50 Greatest Players.

Bobby Orr (b. Mar. 20, 1948): Hockey D; league's only 8-time Norris Trophy winner as best defenseman (1968-75); credited with revolutionizing the position; 3-time Hart Trophy winner as NHL regular season MVP (1970-72); led NHL in scoring twice and assists 5 times; All-NHL 1st team 8 times; playoff MVP twice (1970,72) with Boston.

Tom Osborne (b. Feb. 23, 1937): Football; Nebraska head coach from 1973-97; career record of 255-49-3; his win pct. of .836 is fifth all-time; won national championships in 1994 and '95 and shared national title with Michigan in '97; elected to U.S. Congress (R., Neb.) in 2000.

Mel Ott (b. Mar. 2, 1909, d. Nov. 21, 1958): Baseball OF; joined NY Giants at age 16; led NL in HRs 6 times; had 511 HRs and 1,860 RBI in 22 years.

Kristin Otto (b. Feb. 7, 1966): East German swimmer; 1st woman to win 6 gold medals (4 individual) at one Olympics (1988).

Francis Ouimet (b. May 8, 1893, d. Sept. 3, 1967): Golfer; won 1913 U.S. Open as 20-year-old amateur playing on Brookline, Mass. course where he used to caddie; won U.S. Amateur twice; 8-time Walker Cup player.

Steve Owen (b. Apr. 21, 1898, d. May 17, 1964): Football; All-Pro guard (1927); coached NY Giants for 23 years (1931-53); won 153 career games and 2 NFL titles (1934,38).

Jesse Owens (b. Sept. 12, 1913, d. Mar. 31, 1980): Track & Field; set 4 world records in one afternoon competing for Ohio State at the Big Ten Championships (May 25, 1935); a year later, he soundly debunked Adolph Hitler's "master race" claims, winning 4 gold medals (100m, 200m, 4x100m relay and long jump) at 1936 Summer Olympics in Berlin.

Alan Page (b. Aug. 7, 1945): Football DE; All-America at Notre Dame in 1966 and member of two national championship teams; 6-time NFL All-Pro and 1971 Player of Year with Minnesota Vikings; later a lawyer who was elected to Minnesota Supreme Court in 1992.

Satchel Paige (b. July 7, 1906, d. June 6, 1982): Baseball RHP; pitched 55 career no-hitters over 20 seasons in Negro Leagues; entered major leagues with Cleveland in 1948 at age 42; had 28-31 record in 5 years; returned to AL at age 59 to start 1 game for Kansas City in 1965 (went 3 innings, gave up a hit and got a strikeout); elected to Baseball Hall of Fame in 1971.

Se Ri Pak (b. Sept. 28, 1977): Golfer; won two Majors as an LPGA rookie in 1998 (LPGA Championship and U.S. Open); youngest player to win the U.S. Open (20); won British Open in 2001 and added her 2nd LPGA Championship in 2002.

Arnold Palmer (b. Sept. 10, 1929): Golfer; winner of 4 Masters, 2 British Opens and a U.S. Open; 2-time PGA Player of Year (1960,62); 1st player to earn over $1 million in career (1968); annual PGA Tour money leader award named after him; 60 wins on PGA Tour and 10 more on Senior Tour; made 48 consecutive Masters starts.

Jim Palmer (b. Oct. 15, 1945): Baseball RHP; 3-time Cy Young Award winner (1973,75-76); won 20 or more games 8 times with Baltimore; elected to the Baseball Hall of Fame in 1990; 1991 comeback attempt at age 45 scrubbed in spring training.

Bill Parcells (b. Aug. 22, 1941): Football; coached NY Giants to 2 Super Bowl titles (1987,91); retired after 1990 season then returned in 1993 as coach of New England; took hapless Pats from 2-14 in 1992 to Super Bowl (loss to Green Bay) in 1997; left Patriots after Super Bowl to coach the New York Jets; coached 3 seasons with the Jets (1997-99), turning them from 1-15 doormat to AFC East champ in 2 years; retired again in 2000 but returned to the sidelines in 2003 as head coach of the Dallas Cowboys.

Jack Pardee (b. Apr. 19, 1936): Football; All-America linebacker at Texas A&M; 2-time All-Pro with LA Rams (1963) and Washington (1971); 2-time NFL Coach of Year (1976,79) and winner of 87 games in 11 seasons; only man hired as head coach in NFL, WFL, USFL and CFL; also coached at University of Houston.

Bernie Parent (b. Apr. 3, 1945): Hockey G; led Philadelphia Flyers to 2 Stanley Cups as playoff MVP (1974,75); 2-time Vezina Trophy winner; posted 55 career shutouts and 2.55 GAA in 13 seasons.

Joe Paterno (b. Dec. 21, 1926): Football; became all-time wins leader in college football in 2001, passing Bear Bryant; coached Penn St. to 336-101-3 record, 20-10-1 bowl record and 2 national titles (1982,86) in 37 years; also had three unbeaten teams that didn't finish No. 1; 4-time Coach of Year (1968,78,82,86).

Craig Patrick (b. May 20, 1946): Hockey; 3rd generation Patrick to have name inscribed on Stanley Cup; GM of 2-time Cup champion Pittsburgh Penguins (1991-92); also captain of 1969 NCAA champion at Denver; assistant coach-GM of 1980 gold medal-winning U.S. Olympic team; grandson of Lester.

Lester Patrick (b. Dec. 30, 1883, d. June 1, 1960): Hockey; pro hockey pioneer as player, coach and general manager for 43 years; led NY Rangers to Stanley Cups as coach (1928,33) and GM (1940); grandfather of Craig.

Floyd Patterson (b. Jan. 4, 1935): Boxer; Olympic middleweight champ in 1952; world heavyweight champion (1956-59,60-62); 1st to regain heavyweight crown; fought Ingemar Johansson 3 times in 22 months from 1959-61 and won last two; pro record 55-8-1 with 40 KOs.

Walter Payton (b. July 25, 1954, d. Nov. 1, 1999): Football RB; formerly NFL's alltime leading rusher with 16,726 yards (1984-2002, passed by Emmitt Smith); scored 125 career TDs; All-Pro 7 times with Chicago; led NFC in rushing 5 times (1976-80); league MVP in 1977 (AP & PFWA) and 1985 (Bell); won ring with Bears in Super Bowl XX; known as superb runner, receiver and blocker; nicknamed "Sweetness."

Calvin Peete (b. July 18, 1943): Golf; began playing golf at the age of 23; earned over $2 million in career earnings; selected to the U.S. Ryder Cup teams in 1983 and 1985.

Pelé (b. Oct. 23, 1940): Brazilian soccer F; given name— Edson Arantes do Nascimento; led Brazil to 3 World Cup titles (1958,62,70); came to U.S. in 1975 to play for NY Cosmos in NASL; scored 1,281 goals in 22 years including 12 goals in the World Cup; served as Brazil's minister of sport (1990-98); named IOC Athlete of the Century and FIFA's co-Player of the Century (along with Diego Maradona).

Roger Penske (b. Feb. 20, 1937): Auto racing; national sports car driving champion (1964); established racing team in 1961; co-founder of Championship Auto Racing Teams (CART); Penske Racing has won 13 Indianapolis 500s and 11 CART points titles; announced surprising move to IRL for 2002 season.

Willie Pep (b. Sept. 19, 1922): Boxer; 2-time world featherweight champion (1942-48,49-50); pro record 230-11-1 with 65 KOs.

Marie-Jose Perec (b. 1968): Track & Field; French sprinter who became 2nd woman to win the 200m and 400m events in the same Olympics (1996); her time in the 400 (48.25) set an Olympic record; also won the 400 in 1992 Games.

Fred Perry (b. May 18, 1909, d. Feb. 2, 1995): British tennis player; 3-time Wimbledon champ (1934-36); first player to win all four Grand Slam singles titles, though not in same year; last native to win All-England men's title.

Gaylord Perry (b. Sept. 15, 1938): Baseball RHP; was only pitcher to win a Cy Young Award in both leagues until 1999 when Randy Johnson and Pedro Martinez joined him; retired in 1983 with 314-265 record and 3,534 strikeouts over 22 years and with 8 teams; brother Jim won 215 games for family total of 529.

Bob Pettit (b. Dec. 12, 1932): Basketball F; All-NBA 1st team 10 times (1955-64); 2-time MVP (1956,59) with St. Louis Hawks; first player to score 20,000 points.

Richard Petty (b. July 2, 1937): Auto racer; 7-time winner of Daytona 500; 7-time NASCAR national champ (1964,67,71-72,74-75,79); first stock car driver to win $1 million in career; all-time NASCAR leader in races won (200), poles (127) and wins in a single season (27 in 1967); retired after 1992 season; son of Lee (55 career wins), father of Kyle (8 career wins), grandfather of Adam; nicknamed "The King."

Laffit Pincay Jr. (b. Dec. 29, 1946): Jockey; 5-time Eclipse Award winner (1971,73-74,79,85); winner of 3 Belmonts and 1 Kentucky Derby (aboard Swale in 1984); with his 8834th win in Dec., 1999 he passed Bill Shoemaker to become thoroughbred racing's all-time winningest jockey.

Scottie Pippen (b. Sept. 25, 1965): Basketball F; started on six NBA champions with Chicago (1991-93, 96-98); 3-time All-NBA first team (1994-96). Voted one of NBA's 50 Greatest Players.

Uta Pippig (b. Sept. 7, 1965): German marathoner; won three-straight Boston Marathons (1994,95,96); set a course record in '94 (since broken in 2002).

Nelson Piquet (b. Aug. 17, 1952): Brazilian auto racer; 3-time Formula One world champion (1981,83, 87); left circuit in 1991 with 23 career wins.

Rick Pitino (b. Sept. 18, 1952): Basketball; won 1996 NCAA title in his 7th year at Kentucky; previously coached the New York Knicks in the NBA (96-81 overall), Providence College (42-23) and Boston University (46-24); in 1997, became coach and president of Boston Celtics; resigned from Celtics in 2001 and returned to college coaching with Louisville.

Jacques Plante (b. Jan. 17, 1929, d. Feb. 27, 1986): Hockey G; led Montreal to 6 Stanley Cups (1953,56-60); won 7 Vezina Trophies; MVP in 1962; first goalie to regularly wear a mask; posted 82 shutouts with 2.38 GAA.

Gary Player (b. Nov. 1, 1936): South African golfer; 3-time winner of Masters and British Open; only player in 20th century to win British Open in three different decades (1959,68,74); one of only five players to win all four Grand Slam titles (others are Hogan, Nicklaus, Sarazen and Woods); has also won 2 PGAs, a U.S. Open and 2 U.S. Senior Opens; owner of 21 wins on PGA Tour and 19 more on Senior Tour.

Jim Plunkett (b. Dec. 5, 1947): Football QB; Heisman Trophy winner (Stanford) in 1970; AFL Rookie of the Year in 1971; led Oakland-LA Raiders to Super Bowl wins in 1981 and '84; MVP in '81.

Maurice Podoloff (b. Aug. 18, 1890, d. Nov. 24, 1985): Basketball; engineered merger of Basketball Assn. of America and National Basketball League into NBA in 1949; NBA commissioner (1949-63); league MVP trophy named after him.

Fritz Pollard (b. Jan. 27, 1894, d. May 11, 1986): Football; 1st black All-America RB (1916 at Brown); 1st black to play in Rose Bowl; 7-year NFL pro (1920-26); 1st black NFL coach, at Milwaukee and Hammond, Ind.

Sam Pollock (b. Dec. 15, 1925): Hockey GM; managed NHL Montreal Canadiens to 9 Stanley Cups in 14 years (1965-78).

Denis Potvin (b. Oct. 29, 1953): Hockey D; won Norris Trophy 3 times (1976,78-79); 5-time All-NHL 1st-team; led NY Islanders to 4 Stanley Cups.

Mike Powell (b. Nov. 10, 1963): Track & Field; broke Bob Beamon's 23-year-old long jump world record by 2 inches with leap of 29-ft., 4½ in. at the 1991 World Championships; Sullivan Award winner (1991); won long jump silver medals in 1988 and '92 Olympics; repeated as world champion in 1993.

Steve Prefontaine (b. Jan. 25, 1951, d. May 30, 1975): Track & Field; All-America distance runner at Oregon; first athlete to win same event at NCAA championships 4 straight years (5,000 meters from 1970-73); finished 4th in 5,000 at 1972 Munich Olympics; first athlete to endorse Nike running shoes; killed in a one-car accident.

Nick Price (b. Jan. 28, 1957): Zimbabwean golfer; PGA Tour Player of Year in 1993 and '94; became 1st since Nick Faldo in 1990 to win 2 Grand Slam titles in same year when he took British Open and PGA Championship in 1994; also won PGA in '92.

Alain Prost (b. Feb. 24, 1955): French auto racer; 4-time Formula One world champion (1985-86,89,93); sat out 1992 then returned to win title in 1993; retired after '93 season as all-time F1 wins leader with 51 (passed by Michael Schumacher in 2001).

Kirby Puckett (b. Mar. 14, 1961): Baseball OF; led Minnesota Twins to World Series titles in 1987 and '91; retired in 1996 due to an eye ailment with a batting title (1989), 2,304 hits and a .318 career average in 12 seasons; elected to Hall of Fame in 2001; charged with sexual assault in 2003 but acquitted at trial.

C.C. Pyle (b. 1882, d. Feb. 3, 1939): Promoter; known as "Cash and Carry"; hyped Red Grange's pro football debut by arranging 1925 barnstorming tour with Chicago Bears; had Grange bolt NFL for new AFL in 1926 (AFL folded in '27); also staged 2 Transcontinental Races (1928-29), known as "Bunion Derbies."

Bobby Rahal (b. Jan. 10, 1953): Auto racer; 3-time PPG Cup champ (1986,87,92); 24 career Indy-Car wins, including 1986 Indy 500; current CART team owner; acted as interim president-CEO of CART in 2000 but resigned to assume position with Jaguar Formula One team.

Jack Ramsay (b. Feb. 21, 1925): Basketball; coach who won 239 college games with St. Joseph's-PA in 11 seasons and 906 NBA games (including playoffs) with 4 teams over 21 years; placed 3rd in 1961 Final Four; led Portland to NBA title in 1977.

Bill Rassmussen (b. Oct. 15, 1932): Radio-TV; unemployed radio broadcaster who founded ESPN, the nation's first 24-hour all-sports cable-TV network, in 1978; bought out by Getty Oil in 1981.

Willis Reed (b. June 25, 1942): Basketball C; led NY Knicks to NBA titles in 1970 and '73, Finals MVP both years; regular season MVP 1970. Voted one of NBA's 50 Greatest Players.

Pee Wee Reese (b. July 23, 1918, d. Aug. 14, 1999): Baseball SS; member of Brooklyn/Los Angeles Dodgers from 1940-58; led NL in runs scored (132) in 1949 and stolen bases (30) in 1952; hit over .300 in a season once (.309 in 1954); led the NL in putouts four times; real name was Harold H. Reese.

Mary Lou Retton (b. Jan. 24, 1968): Gymnast; won gold medal in women's All-Around at the 1984 Olympics; also won 2 silvers and 2 bronzes.

Manon Rheaume (b. Feb. 24, 1972): Hockey; 2-time gold medallist (1992,94) at the Women's World Hockey Championships as goaltender for Canada; first woman to sign a professional hockey contract; started in goal in an exhibition game for the Tampa Bay Lightning on Sept. 23, 1992 to become the only woman to play in an NHL game.

Grantland Rice (b. Nov. 1, 1880, d. July 13, 1954): First celebrated American sportswriter; chronicled the Golden Age of Sport in 1920s; immortalized Notre Dame's "Four Horsemen."

Jerry Rice (b. Oct. 13, 1962): Football WR; 2-time Div. I-AA All-America at Mississippi Valley St. (1983-84); won 3 Super Bowls with San Francisco (1989,90,95); 10-time All-Pro; regular season MVP in 1987 and Super Bowl MVP in 1989; NFL all-time regular season and Super Bowl leader in touchdowns, receptions and receiving yards.

Henri Richard (b. Feb. 29, 1936): Hockey C; leap year baby who played on more Stanley Cup championship teams (11) than anybody else; at 5-foot-7, known as the "Pocket Rocket"; brother of Maurice.

Maurice Richard (b. Aug. 4, 1921, d. May 27, 2000): Hockey RW; the "Rocket"; 8-time NHL 1st team All-Star; MVP in 1947; 1st to score 50 goals in one season (1944-45); 544 career goals; played on 8 Stanley Cup winners in Montreal.

Bob Richards (b. Feb. 2, 1926): Track & Field; pole vaulter, ordained minister and original *Wheaties* pitchman, remains only 2-time Olympic pole vault champ (1952,56).

Nolan Richardson (b. Dec. 27, 1941): Basketball; coached Arkansas to consecutive NCAA finals, beating Duke in 1994 and losing to UCLA in '95; school bought out his contract in 2002, ending his 17-year reign.

Tex Rickard (b. Jan. 2, 1870, d. Jan. 6, 1929): Promoter who handled boxing's first $1 million gate (Dempsey vs. Carpentier in 1921); built Madison Square Garden in 1925; founded NY Rangers as Garden tenant in 1926 and named NHL team after himself (Tex's Rangers); also built Boston Garden in 1928.

Eddie Rickenbacker (b. Oct. 8, 1890, d. July 23, 1973): Mechanic and auto racer; became America's top flying ace (22 kills) in World War I; owned Indianapolis Speedway (1927-45) and ran Eastern Air Lines (1938-59).

Branch Rickey (b. Dec. 20, 1881, d. Dec. 9, 1965): Baseball innovator; revolutionized game with creation of modern farm system while GM of St. Louis Cardinals (1917-42); integrated major leagues in 1947 as president-GM of Brooklyn Dodgers when he brought up Jackie Robinson (whom he had signed on Oct. 23, 1945); later GM of Pittsburgh Pirates.

Leni Riefenstahl (b. Aug. 22, 1902, d. Sept. 8, 2003): German filmmaker of 1930s; directed classic sports documentary "Olympia" on 1936 Berlin Summer Olympics; infamous, however, for also making 1934 Hitler propaganda film "Triumph of the Will."

Roy Riegels (b. Apr. 4, 1908, d. Mar. 26, 1993): Football; California center who picked up fumble in 2nd quarter of 1929 Rose Bowl and raced 70 yards in the wrong direction to set up a 2-point safety in 8-7 loss to Georgia Tech.

Bobby Riggs (b. Feb. 25, 1918, d. Oct. 25, 1995): Tennis; won Wimbledon once (1939) and U.S. title twice (1939,41); legendary hustler who made his biggest score in 1973 as 55-year-old male chauvinist challenging the best women players; beat No. 1 Margaret Smith Court 6-2,6-1, but was thrashed by No. 2 Billie Jean King, 6-4,6-3,6-3 in nationally televised "Battle of the Sexes" on Sept. 20, before 30,492 at the Astrodome.

Pat Riley (b. Mar. 20, 1945): Basketball; coached LA Lakers to 4 of their 5 NBA titles in 1980s (1982,85,87-88); coached New York Knicks from 1991-95, then signed with Miami Heat as coach, team president and part-owner; 3-time Coach of Year (1990,93,97); 2nd on list of all-time coaching victories behind Lenny Wilkens.

Cal Ripken Jr. (b. Aug. 24, 1960): Baseball SS; broke Lou Gehrig's major league Iron Man record of 2,130 consecutive games played on Sept. 6, 1995; record streak began on May 30, 1982 and ended Sept. 19, 1998 after 2,632 games; 2-time AL MVP (1983,91) for Baltimore; AL Rookie of Year (1982); AL starter in All-Star Game from 1984-2001; 2-time All-Star Game MVP (1991,2001); holds record for career home runs by a shortstop.

Phil Rizzuto (b. Sept. 25, 1918): Baseball SS; nicknamed "the Scooter"; AL MVP with the Yankees in 1950; 5-time All-Star; retired in 1956 and became Yankees radio and television announcer; elected to the Hall of Fame in 1994.

Oscar Robertson (b. Nov. 24, 1938): Basketball G; 3-time College Player of Year (1958-60) at Cincinnati; led 1960 U.S. Olympic team to gold medal; NBA Rookie of Year (1961); 9-time All-NBA 1st team; MVP in 1964 with Cincinnati Royals; NBA champion in 1971 with Milwaukee Bucks; 6-time annual NBA assist leader; 4th in career assists with 9,887; 8th in career points with 26,710.

Paul Robeson (b. Apr. 8, 1898, d. Jan. 23, 1976): Black 4-sport star and 2-time football All-America (1917-18) at Rutgers; 3-year NFL pro; also scholar, lawyer, singer, actor and political activist; long-tainted by Communist sympathies, he was finally inducted into College Football Hall of Fame in 1995.

Brooks Robinson (b. May 18, 1937): Baseball 3B; led AL in fielding 12 times from 1960-72 with Baltimore; AL MVP in 1964; World Series MVP in 1970; 16 Gold Gloves; entered Hall of Fame in 1983.

David Robinson (b. Aug. 6, 1965): Basketball C; 1987 College Player of Year at Navy; overall 1st pick by San Antonio in 1987 NBA draft; served in military (1987-89); NBA Rookie of Year (1990) and MVP (1995); 2-time All-NBA 1st team (1991,92); led NBA in scoring in 1994; member of 1988, '92 and '96 U.S. Olympic teams; won 2 NBA titles (1999, 2003).

Eddie Robinson (b. Feb. 13, 1919): Football; head coach at Div. I-AA Grambling from 1941-97; winningest coach in college history (408-165-15); led Tigers to 8 national black college titles.

Frank Robinson (b. Aug. 31, 1935): Baseball OF; won MVP in NL (1961) and AL (1966); Triple Crown winner and World Series MVP in 1966 with Baltimore; 5th on all-time home run list with 586; 1st black manager in major leagues with Cleveland in 1975; also managed in SF, Baltimore and Montreal; served as the league's VP of on-field operations (2000-01) before managing Monteal Expos in 2002.

Jackie Robinson (b. Jan. 31, 1919, d. Oct. 24, 1972): Baseball 1B-2B-3B; 4-sport athlete at UCLA (baseball, basketball, football and track); hit .387 with Kansas City Monarchs of Negro Leagues in 1945; signed by Brooklyn Dodgers' Branch Rickey on Oct. 23, 1945. Played in minors (Montreal) in 1946 and broke Major League Baseball's color line in 1947; Rookie of Year in 1947 and NL's MVP in 1949; hit .311 over 10 seasons. His #42 was retired by Major League Baseball in 1997.

Sugar Ray Robinson (b. May 3, 1921, d. Apr. 12, 1989): Boxer; arguably the greatest pound-for-pound prizefighter of all-time; world welterweight champion (1946-51); 5-time middleweight champ; retired at age 45 after 25 years in the ring; pro record 174-19-6 with 109 KOs.

Knute Rockne (b. Mar. 4, 1888, d. Mar. 31, 1931): Football; coached Notre Dame to 3 consensus national titles (1924,29,30), highest winning percentage in college history (.881) with record of 105-12-5 over 13 seasons; killed in plane crash.

Bill Rodgers (b. Dec. 23, 1947): Distance runner; won Boston and New York City marathons 4 times each from 1975-80.

Dennis Rodman (b. May 13, 1961): Basketball F; superb rebounder and defender; also known for dyeing his hair various colors and for getting suspended regularly; in 1997, he was suspended for 11 games for kicking a courtside cameraman; led NBA in rebounding 7 years in a row (1992-98); member of 5 NBA champion teams with Detroit (1989,90) and Chicago (1996-98); 2-time defensive player of the year (1990-91).

Irina Rodnina (b. Sept. 12, 1949): Soviet figure skater; won 10 world championships and 3 Olympic gold medals in pairs competition from 1971-80.

Alex Rodriguez (b. July 27, 1975): Baseball SS; one of baseball's best all-around players; debuted with Seattle and led AL in hitting (.358) his first full season in the majors (1996); in 1998 became third player ever with 40 HRs and 40 steals in one season; signed a 10-year, $252m deal (the biggest in U.S. sports history) with Texas in 2000; has hit at least 40 homers the last six years (1998-2003).

Juan (Chi Chi) Rodriguez (b. Oct. 23, 1935): Golfer; popular player with 8 PGA Tour victories and 22 Senior Tour wins; 1973 U.S. Ryder Cup Team.

Ronaldo (b. Sept. 22, 1976): Soccer; Brazilian forward who has been compared to the great Pele; signed with a first division club in Brazil, Cruzeiro Belo Horizonte, before he was 18 and scored 58 goals in 60 games; named to the Brazilian National Team when he was 17; named FIFA Player of the Year in 1996 and '97; European Player of the Year in '97; named 1998 World Cup MVP; led Brazil to World Cup victory in 2002, scoring 8 times in the tournament including both of Brazil's goals in its 2-0 win over Germany in the final.

Art Rooney (b. Jan. 27, 1901, d. Aug. 25, 1988): Race track legend and pro football pioneer; bought Pittsburgh Steelers franchise in 1933 for $2,500; finally won NFL title with 1st of 4 Super Bowls in 1974 season.

Theodore Roosevelt (b. Oct. 27, 1858, d. Jan. 6, 1919): 26th President of the U.S.; physical fitness buff who boxed as undergraduate at Harvard; credited with presidential pigskin in forming of Intercollegiate Athletic Assn. (now NCAA) in 1905-06.

Mauri Rose (b. May 26, 1906, d. Jan. 1, 1981): Auto racer; 3-time winner of Indy 500 (1941,47-48).

Murray Rose (b. Jan. 6, 1939): Australian swimmer; won 3 gold medals at 1956 Olympics; added a gold, silver and bronze in 1960.

Pete Rose (b. Apr. 14, 1941): Baseball OF-IF; all-time hits leader with 4,256 and games leader with 3562; led NL in batting 3 times; regular-season MVP in 1973; World Series MVP in 1975; had 44-game hitting streak in '78; managed Cincinnati (1984-89); banned for life in 1989 for conduct detrimental to baseball; convicted of tax evasion in 1990 and sentenced to 5 months in prison; released Jan. 7, 1991.

Ken Rosewall (b. Nov. 2, 1934): Tennis; won French and Australian singles titles at age 18; U.S. champ twice, but never won Wimbledon.

Mark Roth (b. Apr. 10, 1951): Bowler; 4-time PBA Player of Year (1977-79,84); has 34 tournament wins and over $1.5 million in career earnings; U.S. Open champ in 1984.

Alan Rothenberg (b. Apr. 10, 1939): Soccer; president of U.S. Soccer 1990-98; surprised European skeptics by directing hugely successful 1994 World Cup tournament; successfully got oft-delayed outdoor Major League Soccer off ground in 1996.

Chad Rowan (Akebono) (b. May 8, 1969): Sumo Wrestling; 6-foot-9, 510-pound naturalized Japanese citizen born in Hawaii; first foreign grand champion in sumo wrestling's 2,000-year history; retired in 2001.

Patrick Roy (b. Oct. 5, 1965): Hockey G; led Montreal to 2 Stanley Cup titles (1986,93) and won 3rd and 4th Cups with Colorado (1996,2001); 3-time playoff MVP (as rookie in 1986,93,2001); won Vezina Trophy 3 times (1989-90,92); led NHL in goals against average 3 times (1989,92,2002); all-time leader in career regular season wins (551) and playoff wins (151).

Pete Rozelle (b. Mar. 1, 1926, d. December 6, 1996): Football; NFL Commissioner from 1960-89; presided over growth of league from 12 to 28 teams, merger with AFL, creation of Super Bowl and advent of huge TV rights fees.

Wilma Rudolph (b. June 23, 1940, d. Nov. 12, 1994): Track & Field; won 3 gold medals (100m, 200m and 4x100m relay) at 1960 Olympics; also won relay silver in '56 Games at age 16; 2-time AP Athlete of Year (1960-61) and Sullivan Award winner in 1961; suffered from polio and wore leg braces until she was 9.

John Ruiz (b. Jan. 4, 1972): Boxer; defeated Evander Holyfield by decision in 2001 for the WBA heavyweight title; the first-ever Hispanic heavyweight champ; lost belt to Roy Jones Jr. on unanimous dec. in 2003.

Damon Runyon (b. Oct. 4, 1884, d. Dec. 10, 1946): Kansas native who gained fame as New York journalist, sports columnist and short-story writer; best known for 1932 story collection, "Guys and Dolls."

Adolph Rupp (b. Sept. 2, 1901, d. Dec. 10, 1977): Basketball; 2nd in all-time college coaching wins with 876; led Kentucky to 4 NCAA championships (1948-49,51,58) and 1 NIT title (1946).

Bill Russell (b. Feb. 12, 1934): Basketball C; won titles in college (with San Francisco in 1955,56), Olympics (1956) and pros; 5-time NBA MVP (1958,61,62, 63,65); led Boston to 11 titles from 1957-69; 4-time NBA rebound leader (1958-59,64-65); 2nd on all-time rebound list with 21,620; became first black NBA (and major pro sports) head coach in 1966.

Babe Ruth (b. Feb. 6, 1895, d. Aug. 16, 1948): Baseball LHP-OF; two-time 20-game winner with Boston Red Sox (1916-17); had a 94-46 record with a 2.28 ERA, while he was 3-0 in the World Series with an ERA of 0.87; sold to New York Yankees for $100,000 in 1920; AL MVP in 1923; led AL in slugging average 13 times, HRs 12 times, RBI 6 times and batting once (.378 in 1924); hit 60 HRs in 1927 and at least 54 3 other times; ended career with Boston Braves in 1935 with 714 HRs, 2,211 RBI, 2,062 walks and a batting average of .342; remains all-time leader in slugging percentage (.690); member of the Hall of Fame's inaugural class of 1936.

Johnny Rutherford (b. Mar. 12, 1938): Auto racer; 3-time winner of Indy 500 (1974,76,80); CART national champion in 1980.

Nolan Ryan (b. Jan. 31, 1947): Baseball RHP; recorded 7 no-hitters against Kansas City and Detroit (1973), Minnesota (1974), Baltimore (1975), LA Dodgers (1981), Oakland A's (1990) and Toronto (1991 at age 44); 2-time 20-game winner (1973-74); 2-time NL leader in ERA (1981,87); led AL in strikeouts 9 times and NL twice in 27 years; retired after 1993 season with 324 wins, 292 losses and all-time records for strikeouts (5,714) and walks (2,795); never won Cy Young Award; had his number retired by three teams (California, Houston, Texas).

Samuel Ryder (b. Mar. 24, 1858, d. Jan. 2, 1936): Golf; English seed merchant who donated the Ryder Cup in 1927 for competition between pro golfers from Great Britain and the U.S.; made his fortune by coming up with idea of selling seeds in small packages.

Toni Sailer (b. Nov. 17, 1935): Austrian skier; 1st to win 3 alpine gold medals in Winter Olympics—taking downhill, slalom and giant slalom events in 1956.

Alberto Salazar (b. Aug. 7, 1958): Track and Field; set one world and six U.S. records during his career; broke 12-year-old record at New York Marathon in 1981 and broke Boston Marathon record in 1982; won three straight NY Marathons (1980-82); qualified for the 1980 and 1984 U.S. Olympic teams.

Juan Antonio Samaranch (b. July 17, 1920): president of International Olympic Committee (1980-2001); the native of Barcelona was re-elected in 1996 after IOC's move in '95 to bump membership age limit to 80; replaced by Belgian Jacques Rogge.

Pete Sampras (b. Aug. 12, 1971): Tennis; No.1 in world (1993-98); youngest ever U.S. Open men's champ (19 years, 28 days) in 1990; his win at 2002 U.S. Open was record 14th grand slam singles title; won 2 Australian Opens (1994,97), 7 Wimbledons (1993-95, 1997-2000) and 5 U.S. Opens (1990,93, 95-96,2002); career money leader on ATP Tour.

Joan Benoit Samuelson (b. May 16, 1957): Distance runner; won Boston Marathon twice (1979,83); won first women's Olympic marathon in 1984 Games; Sullivan Award recipient in 1985.

Arantxa Sanchez Vicario (b. Dec. 18, 1971): Spanish tennis player; won 29 tour singles titles including 3 French Opens (1989,94,98) and 1 U.S. Open (1994); 6 doubles and 4 mixed doubles grand slam titles; finalist in three of four Grand Slam finals in '95; teamed with Conchita Martinez to win 5 Federation Cups from 1991-98.

Earl Sande (b. Nov. 13, 1898, d. Aug. 19, 1968): Jockey; rode Gallant Fox to Triple Crown in 1930; won 5 Belmonts and 3 Kentucky Derbies.

Barry Sanders (b. July 16, 1968): Football RB; won 1988 Heisman Trophy as junior at Oklahoma St.; all-time NCAA single season leader in rushing (2,628 yards), scoring (234 points) and TDs (39); 4-time NFL rushing leader with Detroit Lions (1990,94,96,97); NFC Rookie of Year (1988); 2-time NFL Player of Year (1991,97); NFC MVP (1994); rushed for 2,053 yards in 1997, second-best season total ever; No. 3 all-time rusher (15,269 yds); abruptly retired just prior to 1999 season.

Deion Sanders (b. Aug. 9, 1967): Baseball OF and Football DB-KR-WR; 2-time All-America at Florida St. in football (1987-88); 7-time NFL All-Pro CB with Atlanta, San Fran. and Dallas (1991-94,96-98); led majors in triples (14) with Braves in 1992 and hit .533 in World Series that year; played on 2 Super Bowl winners (SF in XXIX, and Dallas in XXX); first 2-way starter in NFL since 1962 (Chuck Bednarik); only athlete to play in both World Series and Super Bowl.

Cael Sanderson (b. June 20, 1979): Wrestling; first 4-time undefeated NCAA college wrestling champion (1999-2002); went 159-0 during 4-year career at Iowa State; 4-time NCAA Most Outstanding Wrestler.

Abe Saperstein (b. July 4, 1901, d. Mar. 15, 1966): Basketball; founded all-black, Harlem Globetrotters barnstorming team in 1927; coached sharp-shooting comedians to 1940 world pro title in Chicago and established troupe as game's foremost goodwill ambassadors; also served as 1st commissioner of American Basketball League (1961-62).

Gene Sarazen (b. Feb. 27, 1902, d. May 13, 1999): Golfer; one of only five players to win all four Grand Slam titles (others are Hogan, Nicklaus, Player and Woods); won Masters, British Open, 2 U.S. Opens and 3 PGA titles between 1922-35; invented sand wedge in 1930.

Glen Sather (b. Sept. 2, 1943): Hockey; GM-coach of 4 Stanley Cup winners in Edmonton (1984-85,87-88) and GM-only for another in 1990; ranks 8th on all-time NHL coaching list with 553 wins (including playoffs); entered Hockey Hall of Fame in 1997; named Pres-GM of NY Rangers in 2000.

Terry Sawchuk (b. Dec. 28, 1929, d. May 31, 1970): Hockey G; recorded 103 shutouts in 21 NHL seasons; 4-time Vezina Trophy winner; played on 4 Stanley Cup winners at Detroit and Toronto; posted career 2.52 GAA.

Gale Sayers (b. May 30, 1943): Football HB; 2-time All-America at Kansas; NFL Rookie of Year (1965) and 5-time All-Pro with Chicago; scored then-record 22 TDs in rookie year; led league in rushing twice (1966,69).

Chris Schenkel (b. Aug. 21, 1923): Radio-TV; 4-time Sportscaster of Year; easy-going baritone who covered basketball, bowling, football, golf and the Olympics for ABC and CBS; host of ABC's Pro Bowlers Tour for 33 years; received lifetime achievement Emmy Award in 1992.

Vitaly Scherbo (b. Jan. 13, 1972): Russian gymnast; winner of unprecedented 6 gold medals in gymnastics, including men's All-Around, for Unified Team in 1992 Olympics; also won 3 bronze in '96 Games.

Curt Schilling (b. Nov. 14, 1966): Baseball RHP; led majors in strikeouts twice (1997-98) with Philadelphia Phillies; Traded to Arizona in 2000; 2-time 20-game winner (2001-02); shared 2001 World Series MVP award with Diamondbacks teammate Randy Johnson.

Mike Schmidt (b. Sept. 27, 1949): Baseball 3B; led NL in HRs 8 times; 3-time MVP (1980,81,86) with Philadelphia; 548 career HRs and 10 Gold Gloves; inducted into Hall of Fame in 1995.

Don Schollander (b. Apr. 30, 1946): Swimming; won 4 gold medals at 1964 Olympics, plus one gold and one silver in 1968; won Sullivan Award in 1964.

Dick Schultz (b. Sept. 5, 1929): Reform-minded executive director of NCAA from 1988-93; announced resignation on May 11, 1993 in wake of special investigator's report citing Univ. of Virginia with improper student-athlete loan program during Schultz's tenure as athletic director (1981-87); executive director of the USOC 1995-2000.

Michael Schumacher (b. Jan. 3, 1969): German auto racer; Formula One's all-time win leader with 70 grand prix victories; 5-time world champion (1994,95,00,01,02); broke the all-time F1 single-season record with 10 wins in 2002.

Bob Seagren (b. Oct. 17, 1946): Track & Field; won gold medal in pole vault at 1968 Olympics; broke world outdoor record 5 times.

Tom Seaver (b. Nov. 17, 1944): Baseball RHP; won 3 Cy Young Awards (1969,73,75); led NL in K 5 times (1970,71,73,75,76); pitched no-hitter in 1978 for Cin.; had 311 wins, 3,640 strikeouts and 2.86 ERA over 20 years.

Peter Seitz (b. May 17, 1905, d. Oct. 17, 1983): Baseball arbitrator; ruled on Dec. 23, 1975 that players who perform for one season without a signed contract can become free agents; decision ushered in big money era for players.

Monica Seles (b. Dec. 2, 1973): Tennis; No. 1 in the world in 1991 and '92 after winning Australian, French and U.S. Opens both years; won 4 Australian, 3 French and 2 US Opens; winner of 30 singles titles in just 5 years before she was stabbed in the back by Steffi Graf fan Gunter Parche on Apr. 30, 1993 during match in Hamburg, Germany; spent remainder of 1993, all of '94 and most of '95 recovering; returned to tennis with win at the 1995 Canadian Open; won 1996 Australian Open; winner of 53 WTA tournaments.

Bud Selig (b. July 30, 1934): Baseball; Milwaukee car dealer who bought AL Seattle Pilots for $10.8 million in 1970 and moved team to Midwest; as de facto commissioner, he presided over 232-day players' strike that resulted in cancellation of World Series for first time since 1904; officially named baseball's ninth commissioner on July 2, 1998; made the controversial decision to end the 2002 All-Star Game after 11 inns., tied 7-7.

Frank Selke (b. May 7, 1893, d. July 3, 1985): Hockey; GM of 6 Stanley Cup champions in Montreal (1953,56-60); the annual NHL trophy for best defensive forward bears his name.

Ayrton Senna (b. Mar. 21, 1960, d. May 1, 1994): Brazilian auto racer; 3-time Formula One champion (1988,90-91); died as all-time F1 leader in poles (65) and 2nd in wins (41, currently in 3rd place); killed in crash at Imola, Italy during '94 San Marino Grand Prix.

Wilbur Shaw (b. Oct. 13, 1902, d. Oct. 30, 1954): Auto racer; 3-time winner and 3-time runner-up of Indy 500 from 1933-1940.

Patty Sheehan (b. Oct. 27, 1956): Golfer; LPGA Player of Year in 1983; clinched entry into LPGA Hall of Fame with her 30th career win in 1993; her 6 major titles include 3 LPGA Champ. (1983-84,93), 2 U.S. Opens (1992,94) 1 Dinah Shore (1996).

Bill Shoemaker (b. Aug. 19, 1931): Jockey; ranks second all-time in career wins with 8,833 (passed by Laffit Pincay Jr. in Dec. 1999); 3-time Eclipse Award winner as jockey (1981) and special award recipient (1976,81); won Belmont 5 times, Kentucky Derby 4 times and Preakness twice; oldest jockey to win Kentucky Derby (age 54, aboard Ferdinand in 1986); retired in 1990 to become trainer; paralyzed in 1991 auto accident but continued to train horses.

Eddie Shore (b. Nov. 25, 1902, d. Mar. 16, 1985): Hockey D; only NHL defenseman to win Hart Trophy as MVP 4 times (1933,35-36,38); led Boston Bruins to Stanley Cup titles in 1929 and '39; had 105 goals and 1,047 penalty minutes in 14 seasons.

Frank Shorter (b. Oct. 31, 1947): Track & Field; won gold medal in marathon at 1972 Olympics, 1st American to win in 64 years.

Don Shula (b. Jan. 4, 1930): Football; retired after 1995 season with an NFL-record 347 career wins (including playoffs) and a winning percentage of .665; took six teams to Super Bowl and won twice with Miami (VII, VIII); 4-time Coach of Year, twice with Baltimore (1964,68) and twice with Miami (1970-71); coached 1972 Dolphins to 17-0 record, the only undefeated team in NFL history.

Charlie Sifford (b. June 2, 1922): Golf; won the Hartford Open in 1967 with a final-round 64, becoming the first black player to win a PGA event; won the PGA Seniors Championship in 1975; amassed over $1 million in career earnings; published his autobiography "Just Let Me Play" in 1992.

Al Simmons (b. May 22, 1902, d. May 26, 1956): Baseball OF; led AL in batting twice (1930-31) with Philadelphia A's and knocked in 100 runs or more 11 straight years (1924-34).

O.J. Simpson (b. July 9, 1947): Football RB; won Heisman Trophy in 1968 at USC; ran for 2,003 yards in NFL in 1973; All-Pro 5 times; MVP in 1973; rushed for 11,236 career yards; TV analyst and actor after career ended; arrested June 17, 1994 as suspect in double murder of ex-wife Nicole Brown Simpson and her friend Ronald Goldman; acquitted on Oct. 3, 1995 by a Los Angeles jury in criminal trial but forced to make financial reparations after losing wrongful death suit.

George Sisler (b. Mar. 24, 1893, d. Mar. 26, 1973): Baseball 1B; hit over .400 twice (1920,22) and batted over .300 in 13 of his 15 seasons; his 257 hits in 1920 is still a major league record; played most of his career with the St. Louis Browns; inducted into Baseball Hall of Fame in 1939.

Mary Decker Slaney (b. Aug. 4, 1958): U.S. middle distance runner; has held 7 separate American track & field records from the 800 to 10,000 meters; won both 1,500 and 3,000 meters at 1983 World Championships in Helsinki, but no Olympic medals.

Raisa Smetanina (b. Feb. 29, 1952): Russian Nordic skier; all-time leading female Winter Olympics medalist with 10 cross country medals (4 gold, 5 silver and a bronze) in 5 appearances (1976,80,84,88,92) for USSR and Unified Team.

Billy Smith (b. Dec. 12, 1950): Hockey G; led NY Islanders to 4 consecutive Stanley Cups (1980-83); won Vezina Trophy in 1982; Stanley Cup MVP in 1983.

Dean Smith (b. Feb. 28, 1931): Basketball; No. 1 on all-time NCAA coaches victory list (879); led North Carolina to 25 NCAA tournaments in 34 years, reaching Final Four 10 times and winning championship twice (1982,93); coached U.S. Olympic team to gold medal in 1976.

Emmitt Smith (b. May 15, 1969): Football RB; passed Walter Payton in 2002 to become the NFL's all-time leading rusher; also holds all-time record for rushing TDs (153); 4-time NFL rushing leader (1991-93,95); 11 straight 1,000-yard seasons (1991-2001); regular season and Super Bowl MVP in 1993; played on three Super Bowl champions (1993,94,96); consensus All-America (1989) at Florida.

John Smith (b. Aug. 9, 1965): Wrestler; 2-time NCAA champion for Oklahoma St. at 134 lbs (1987-88) and Most Outstanding Wrestler of '88 championships; 3-time world champion; gold medal winner at 1988 and '92 Olympics at 137 lbs; won Sullivan Award (1990); coached Oklahoma St. to 1994 NCAA title and brother Pat was Most Outstanding Wrestler.

Lee Smith (b. Dec. 4, 1957): Baseball RHP; 3-time NL saves leader (1983,91-92); retired as all-time saves leader with 478 and a ERA of 3.03; 10 seasons with 30+ saves and 3 times saved over 40.

Michelle Smith deBruin (b. Apr. 7, 1969): Irish swimmer; won three gold medals at the 1996 Olympics; accused of using performance-enhancing drugs but passed all tests until she was suspended for 4 years by FINA in 1998 for tampering with a urine sample.

Ozzie Smith (b. Dec. 26, 1954): Baseball SS; won 13 straight Gold Gloves (1980-92); played in 12 straight All-Star Games (1981-92); MVP of 1985 NL playoffs; all-time MLB assist leader (8,375); inducted into Baseball Hall of Fame in 2002.

Walter (Red) Smith (b. Sept. 25, 1905, d. Jan. 15, 1982): Sportswriter for newspapers in Philadelphia and New York from 1936-82; won Pulitzer Prize for commentary in 1976.

Conn Smythe (b. Feb. 1, 1895, d. Nov. 18, 1980): Hockey pioneer; built Maple Leaf Gardens in 1931; managed Toronto to 7 Stanley Cups.

Sam Snead (b. May 27, 1912, d. May 23, 2002): Golfer; won both Masters and PGA 3 times and British Open once; runner-up in U.S. Open 4 times; PGA Player of Year in 1949; oldest player (52 years, 10 months) to win PGA event with Greater Greensboro Open title in 1965; all-time PGA Tour career victory leader with 81.

Peter Snell (b. Dec. 17, 1938): Track & Field; New Zealander who won gold medal in 800m at 1960 Olympics, then won both the 800m and 1,500m at 1964 Games.

Duke Snider (b. Sept. 19, 1926): Baseball OF; hit 40 or more home runs five straight seasons (1953-57); led the league in runs scored 1953-55; played in six World Series with the Dodgers and batted .286 with 11 home runs; nicknamed "Duke of Flatbush"; in 18 seasons hit 407 home runs, scored 1,259 runs and had 1,333 RBI.

Annika Sorenstam (b. Oct. 9, 1970): Swedish golfer; won 2 U.S. Opens (1995-96) and 2 Nabisco Championship titles (2001-02); 5-time Rolex Player of the Year (1995,97-98, 2001-02); shot an LPGA-record 59 in round 2 of the 2001 Standard Register Ping; LPGA all-time leading money winner; in 2003 she became first woman in 58 years to play on men's PGA Tour (via a sponsor's exemption); shot 71-74 but missed the cut at the Colonial by 4 strokes.

Sammy Sosa (b. Nov. 12, 1968): Baseball OF; slugging Chicago Cub who surpassed Roger Maris' season home run record (61), just after Mark McGwire did, in 1998 and finished the year with 66; followed that up with seasons of 63, 50 and 64 HR; NL MVP (1998); 6-time NL all-star (1995,98-2002).

Javier Sotomayor (b. Oct. 13, 1967): Cuban high jumper; first man to clear 8 feet (8-0) on July 29, 1989; won gold medal at 1992 Olympics with jump of only 7-ft, 8-in.; broke world record with leap of 8-0½ in 1993; had a controversial drug suspension reduced, which allowed him to participate in 2000 Olympics; won the silver medal in Sydney with a leap of 7-7¼.

Warren Spahn (b. Apr. 23, 1921): Baseball LHP; led NL in wins 8 times; won 20 or more games 13 times; Cy Young winner in 1957; most career wins (363) by a lefthander.

Tris Speaker (b. Apr. 4, 1888, d. Dec. 8, 1958): Baseball; all-time leader in outfield assists (449) and doubles (792); had .344 career BA and 3,515 hits.

J.G. Taylor Spink (b. Nov. 6, 1888, d. Dec. 7, 1962): Publisher of The Sporting News from 1914-62; BWAA annual meritorious service award named after him.

Leon Spinks (b. July 11, 1953): Boxing; won heavyweight crown in split decision over Muhammad Ali in Feb. 1978; Ali regained title seven months later; won gold medal in light heavyweight division at 1976 Olympics; brother Michael won the heavyweight title in 1983; were the only brothers to hold world titles; known more for frequent traffic violations and lavish lifestyle than bouts late in career; filed for bankruptcy in 1986.

Mark Spitz (b. Feb. 10, 1950): Swimmer; set 23 world and 35 U.S. records; won all-time record 7 gold medals (4 individual, 3 relay) in 1972 Olympics; also won 4 medals (2 gold, a silver and a bronze) in 1968 Games for a total of 11; comeback attempt at age 41 foundered in 1991.

Latrell Sprewell (b. Sept. 8, 1970): Basketball G; became an NBA All-Star in just his second pro season out of Alabama; made headlines in 1997 after being suspended by the NBA for attacking Golden State Warriors head coach P.J. Carlesimo during a practice.

Lyn St. James (b. Mar. 13, 1947): Auto racer; one of just 3 women to qualify for the Indianapolis 500; best finish in the race came in 1992 when she came in 11th and won Indianapolis 500 Rookie of the Year.

Amos Alonzo Stagg (b. Aug. 16, 1862, d. Mar. 17, 1965): Football innovator; coached at U. of Chicago for 41 seasons and College of the Pacific for 14 more; 314-199-35 record; elected to both college football and basketball Halls of Fame.

Willie Stargell (b. Mar. 6, 1940, d. Apr. 9, 2001): Baseball OF-1B; "Pops"; led NL in home runs twice (1971,73); 475 career HRs; NL co-MVP and World Series MVP in 1979.

Bart Starr (b. Jan. 9, 1934): Football QB; led Green Bay to 5 NFL titles and 2 Super Bowl wins from 1961-67; regular season MVP in 1966; MVP of Super Bowls I and II.

Roger Staubach (b. Feb. 5, 1942): Football QB; Heisman Trophy winner as Navy junior in 1963; led Dallas to 2 Super Bowl titles (1972,78) and was Super Bowl MVP in 1972; 5-time leading passer in NFC (1971,73,77-79).

George Steinbrenner (b. July 4, 1930): Baseball; principal owner of NY Yankees since 1973; teams have won 9 pennants and 6 World Series (1977-78,96,98,99,00); has changed managers 21 times and GMs 11 times in 30 years; ordered by baseball commish Fay Vincent in 1990 to surrender control of club for dealings with small-time gambler; reinstated in 1993.

Casey Stengel (b. July 30, 1890, d. Sept. 29, 1975): Baseball; player for 14 years and manager for 25; outfielder and lifetime .284 hitter with 5 clubs (1912-25); guided NY Yankees to 10 AL pennants and 7 World Series titles from 1949-60; 1st NY Mets skipper from 1962-65.

Ingemar Stenmark (b. Mar. 18, 1956): Swedish alpine skier; 3-time World Cup overall champ (1976-78); posted 86 World Cup wins in 16 years; won 2 gold medals at 1980 Olympics.

Helen Stephens (b. Feb. 3, 1918, d. Jan. 17, 1994): Track & Field; set 3 world records in 100-yard dash and 4 more in 100 meters in 1935-36; won gold medals in 100 meters and 4x100-meter relay in 1936 Olympics; retired in 1937.

Woody Stephens (b. Sept. 1, 1913, d. Aug. 22, 1998): Horse racing; trainer who saddled an unprecedented 5 straight winners in Belmont Stakes (1982-86); also had two Kentucky Derby winners (1974,84) and one Preakness winner (1952); trained 1982 Horse of Year Conquistador Cielo; won Eclipse award as nation's top trainer in 1983.

David Stern (b. Sept. 22, 1942): Basketball; marketing expert and NBA commissioner since 1984; took office the year Michael Jordan turned pro; has presided over stunning artistic and financial success of NBA both nationally and internationally; league has grown from 23 teams to 29 during his watch and opened offices worldwide; oversaw launch of WNBA in 1997.

Teófilo Stevenson (b. Mar. 29, 1952): Cuban boxer; won 3 consecutive gold medals as Olympic heavyweight (1972,76,80); did not turn pro.

Jackie Stewart (b. June 11, 1939): Auto racer; won 27 Formula One races and 3 world driving titles from 1965-73.

John Stockton (b. Mar 26, 1962): Basketball G; all-time NBA leader in every major assist category, including most in a season (1,164), highest average in a season (14.5 per game) and most overall (15,806); also the NBA's all-time leader in steals (3,265); All-NBA team in '94 and '95; member of 1992 and '96 US Olympic basketball Dream Teams; 10-time All-Star; played 19 seasons with Utah Jazz—18 of them with Karl Malone—perfecting the pick and roll; retired in 2003.

Curtis Strange (b. Jan. 30, 1955): Golfer; won consecutive U.S. Open titles (1988-89); 3-time leading money winner on PGA Tour (1985,87-88); first PGA player to win $1 million in one year (1988); captain of the 2002 U.S. Ryder Cup team.

Picabo Street (b. Apr. 3, 1971): Skiing; 2-time Olympic medalist, gold (Super G in 1998) and silver (downhill in 1994); her 1995 World Cup downhill series title first-ever by U.S. woman, she repeated the feat in 1996.

Kerri Strug (b. Nov. 19, 1977): Gymnastics; delivered the most dramatic moment of the 1996 Summer Olympics when she completed a vault (9.712) after spraining her ankle; the second vault assured the first all-around gold medal for a US Women's gymnastics team; a poor performance by the Russian team on the beam had clinched the gold medal for the US but Strug was unaware when she made the second vault.

Louise Suggs (b. Sept. 7, 1923): Golfer; won 11 majors and 50 LPGA events overall from 1949-62.

James E. Sullivan (b. Nov. 18, 1862, d. Sept. 16, 1914): Track & Field; pioneer who founded Amateur Athletic Union (AAU) in 1888; director of St. Louis Olympic Games in 1904; AAU's annual Sullivan Award for performance and sportsmanship named after him.

John L. Sullivan (b. Oct. 15, 1858, d. Feb. 2, 1918): Boxer; world heavyweight champion (1882-92); last of bare-knuckle champions.

Pat Summitt (b. June 14, 1952): Basketball; women's basketball coach at Tennessee (1974—); entered 2003-04 season as all-time leader in career victories with 821; coached 1984 US women's basketball team to its first Olympic gold medal; has coached Lady Vols to 6 national championships (1987,89,91,96,97,98).

Don Sutton (b. April 2, 1945): Baseball RHP; won 324 games and tossed 58 shutouts in his 23-year career; recorded NL record five career 1-hitters; played with Dodgers, Astros, Brewers, Athletics, Angels and was a 4-time All-Star; elected to Hall of Fame in 1998.

Ichiro Suzuki (b. Oct. 22, 1973): Baseball OF; speedy Seattle Mariners RF who in 2001 became the 2nd player (Fred Lynn) to win AL Rookie of the Year and MVP in same year; 1st Japanese-born position player to play in the majors; won 7 consecutive Japanese batting titles (1994-2000).

Lynn Swann (b. Mar. 7, 1952): Football WR; played nine seasons with Pittsburgh (1974-82); appeared in four Super Bowls and had 16 catches for 364 yards and three TDs; named MVP of Super Bowl X for 4 catch, 161 yard, 1 TD performance.

Barry Switzer (b. Oct. 5, 1937): Football; coached Oklahoma to 3 national titles (1974-75,85); 4th on all-time winning pct list at .837 (157-29-4); resigned in 1989 after OU was slapped with 3-year NCAA probation; hired as Dallas Cowboys head coach in 1994 and led team to victory in Super Bowl XXX in 1996.

Sheryl Swoopes (b. Mar. 25, 1971): Basketball; forward for WNBA's Houston Comets; 3-time WNBA regular season MVP (2000,02,03); Defensive Player of the Year in 2000, 2-time olympic gold medalist (1996,2000); led Texas Tech to Div. I NCAA championship in 1993; consensus National Player of the Year in 1993.

Paul Tagliabue (b. Nov. 24, 1940): Football; NFL attorney who was elected league's 4th commissioner in 1989; ushered in salary cap in 1994; the league has expanded from 28 teams to 32 in his tenure.

Anatoli Tarasov (b. 1918, d. June 23, 1995): Hockey; coached Soviet Union to 9 straight world championships and 3 Olympic gold medals (1964,68,72).

Jerry Tarkanian (b. Aug. 30, 1930): Basketball; amassed 778 wins in 31 years at Long Beach St., UNLV and Fresno St.; led UNLV to 4 Final Fours and 1 national title (1990); fought battle with NCAA over purity of UNLV program; quit as coach after going 26-2 in 1991-92; fired after 20 games (9-11) as coach of NBA San Antonio Spurs in 1992; unretired in 1995 to coach his alma mater, Fresno St.; retired again in 2002.

Fran Tarkenton (b. Feb. 3, 1940): Football QB; 2-time NFL All-Pro (1973,75); Player of Year (1975); threw for 47,003 yards and 342 TDs (both former NFL records) in 18 seasons with Vikings and Giants.

Chuck Taylor (b. June 24, 1901, d. June 23, 1969): Converse traveling salesman whose name came to grace the classic, high-top canvas basketball sneakers known as "Chucks"; over 500 million pairs have been sold since 1917; he also ran clinics worldwide and edited Converse Basketball Yearbook (1922-68).

Lawrence Taylor (b. Feb. 4, 1959): Football LB; All-America at North Carolina (1980); only defensive player in NFL history to be consensus Player of Year (1986); led NY Giants to Super Bowl titles in 1986 and '90 seasons; played in 10 Pro Bowls (1981-90); retired after 1993 season with 132½ sacks and has had several drug-related arrests since; inducted into Hall of Fame in 1999.

Marshall (Major) Taylor (b. Nov. 26, 1878, d. June 21, 1932): Cyclist; Considered one of the first African-American sports heroes; held seven world cycling records at the turn of the century, racing mostly in Europe, Australia and New Zealand after being barred from many events in the U.S. due to racial prejudices; won the world 1-mile championship in 1899.

Gustavo Thoeni (b. Feb. 28, 1951): Italian alpine skier; 4-time World Cup overall champion (1971-73,75); won giant slalom at 1972 Olympics.

Isiah Thomas (b. Apr. 30, 1961): Basketball; led Indiana to NCAA title as sophomore and Final 4 MOP in 1981; consensus All-America guard in '81; led Detroit to 2 NBA titles (1989, 1990); NBA Finals MVP in 1990; 3-time All-NBA 1st team (1984-86); retired in 1994 at age 33 after tearing right Achilles tendon; following a failed tenure as owner of the CBA, he coached NBA's Indiana Pacers from 2000-03; elected to Hall of Fame in 2000.

Thurman Thomas (b. May 16, 1966): Football RB; 3-time AFC rushing leader (1990-91,93); 2-time All-Pro (1990-91); NFL Player of Year (1991); led Buffalo to 4 straight Super Bowls (1991-94).

Daley Thompson (b. July 30, 1958): British Track & Field; won consecutive gold medals in decathlon at 1980 and '84 Olympics.

Jenny Thompson (b. Feb. 26, 1973): Swimmer; 8-time Olympic gold medalist (all in relays) and winner of 10 Olympic medals overall, more than any other American woman; won 3 gold (4x100 free, 4x200 free, 4x100 medley) and 1 bronze (100m freestyle) for the U.S. at the 2000 Olympics in Sydney.

John Thompson (b. Sept. 2, 1941): Basketball; coached centers Patrick Ewing, Alonzo Mourning and Dikembe Mutombo at Georgetown; reached NCAA tourney final 3 out of 4 years with Ewing, winning title in 1984; also led Hoyas to 6 Big East tourney titles; coached 1988 U.S. Olympic team to bronze medal; retired abruptly during 1999 season with 27-year mark of 596-239.

Bobby Thomson (b. Oct. 25, 1923): Baseball OF; career .270 hitter who won the 1951 NL pennant for the NY Giants with a 1-out, 3-run HR in the bottom of the 9th inning of Game 3 of a best-of-3 playoff with Brooklyn; the pitcher was Ralph Branca, the count was 0-1 and the Dodgers were ahead 4-2; the Giants had trailed Brooklyn by 13½ games on Aug. 11.

Ian Thorpe (b. Oct. 13, 1982): Swimming; Australian who won gold at Sydney Olympics in the 400m free (breaking his own world record) and silver in the 200m freestyle; was also part of relay team that won gold and broke the world record in the 4x100m and 4x200 freestyle relays; broke world records in the 200, 400 and 800m free at the 2001 world championships; won 3 golds at 2003 world championships; 2002 Jesse Owens Award winner.

Jim Thorpe (b. May 28, 1888, d. May 28, 1953): 2-time All-America in football; won both pentathlon and decathlon at 1912 Olympics; stripped of medals a month later for playing semi-pro baseball prior to Games; medals restored in 1982; played major league baseball (1913-19) and pro football (1920-26,28); chosen "Athlete of the Half Century" by AP in 1950.

Bill Tilden (b. Feb. 10, 1893, d. June 5, 1953): Tennis; won 7 U.S. and 3 Wimbledon titles in 1920s; led U.S. to 7 straight Davis Cup victories (1920-26).

Tinker to Evers to Chance Chicago Cubs double play combination from 1903-10; immortalized in poem by New York sportswriter Franklin P. Adams—SS Joe Tinker (1880-1948), 2B Johnny Evers (1883-1947) and 1B Frank Chance (1877-1924); all 3 managed the Cubs and made the Hall of Fame.

Y.A. Tittle (b. Oct. 24, 1926): Football QB; Yelberton Abraham Tittle played 17 years in AAFC and NFL; All-Pro 4 times; league MVP with San Francisco (1957) and NY Giants (1962); passed for 28,339 career yards.

Alberto Tomba (b. Dec. 19, 1966): Italian alpine skier; winner of 5 Olympic medals (3 gold, 2 silver); became 1st alpine skier to win gold medals in 2 consecutive Winter Games when he won the slalom and giant slalom in 1988 then repeated in the GS in '92; also won silvers in slalom in 1992 and '94.

Dara Torres (b. April 15, 1967): Swimmer; her 9 career Olympic medals (4G, 1S, 4B) are the 2nd-most for an American woman; took a 7-year hiatus before returning to the pool to win 5 medals in Sydney in 2000; participated in 4 olympic games overall (1984,88,92,2000).

Vladislav Tretiak (b. Apr. 25, 1952): Hockey G; led USSR to Olympic gold medals in 1972 and '76; starred for Soviets against Team Canada in 1972, and again in 2 Canada Cups (1976,81).

Lee Trevino (b. Dec. 1, 1939): Golfer; 2-time winner of 3 majors—U.S. Open (1968, 71), British Open (1971-72) and PGA (1974,84); Player of Year once on PGA Tour (1971) and 3 times with Seniors (1990,92,94); 27 PGA Tour and 30 Senior Tour wins.

Felix Trinidad (b. Jan. 10, 1973): Puerto Rican boxer; former WBC/IBF welterweight champion; won WBC belt with a majority decision over Oscar De La Hoya in Sept., 1999; stepped up to junior middleweight and won the WBA title from David Reid in March, 2000; moved to middleweight and lost in a 12th-round TKO to Bernard Hopkins in Sept. 2001; announced retirement in 2002 with a record of 41-1 and 34 KOs.

Bryan Trottier (b. July 17, 1956): Hockey C; led NY Islanders to 4 straight Stanley Cups (1980-83); Rookie of Year (1976); scoring champion (134 points) and regular season MVP in 1979; playoff MVP (1980); added 5th and 6th Cups with Pittsburgh in 1991 and '92; entered Hockey Hall of Fame in 1997; head coach of NY Rangers in 2002, fired in 2003.

Gene Tunney (b. May 25, 1897, d. Nov. 7, 1978): Boxer; world heavyweight champion from 1926-28; beat 31-year-old champ Jack Dempsey in unanimous 10 round decision in 1926; beat him again in famous "long count" rematch in '27; quit while still champion in 1928 with 65-1-1 record and 47 KOs.

Ted Turner (b. Nov. 19, 1938): Sportsman and TV mogul; skippered Courageous to America's Cup win in 1977; one-time owner of MLB Atlanta Braves, NBA Hawks and NHL Thrashers; founder of CNN, TNT and TBS; founder of Goodwill Games; 1991 Time Man of Year.

Mike Tyson (b. June 30, 1966): Boxer; youngest (age 19) to win heavyweight title (WBC in 1986); undisputed champ from 1987 until upset loss to 42-1 shot Buster Douglas on Feb. 10, 1990, in Tokyo; found guilty on Feb. 10, 1992, of raping 18-year-old Miss Black America contestant Desiree Washington in Indianapolis on July 19, 1991; sentenced to 6-year prison term; released May 9, 1995 after serving 3 years; reclaimed WBC and WBA belts with wins over Frank Bruno and Bruce Seldon in 1996; lost WBA title to Evander Holyfield in 1996; he bit Holyfield's ear twice during their 1997 WBA title rematch; was KO'd in 8th round by Lennox Lewis in 2002; despite earning $300m in his career, he filed for bankruptcy in 2003.

Wyomia Tyus (b. Aug. 29, 1945): Track & Field; 1st woman to win consecutive Olympic gold medals in 100m (1964-68).

Peter Ueberroth (b. Sept. 2, 1937): Organizer of 1984 Summer Olympics in LA; 1984 *Time* Man of Year; baseball commissioner from 1984-89; headed Rebuild Los Angeles for one year after 1992 riots.

Johnny Unitas (b. May 7, 1933, d. Sept. 11, 2002): Football QB; led Baltimore Colts to 2 NFL titles (1958-59) and a Super Bowl win (1971); All-Pro 5 times; 3-time MVP (1959,64,67); passed for 40,239 career yards and 290 TDs.

Al Unser Jr. (b. Apr. 19, 1962): Auto racer; 2-time CART-IndyCar national champion (1990,94); captured Indy 500 for 2nd time in 3 years in '94, giving Unser family 9 overall titles at the Brickyard; 31 CART wins in 18 years; left CART for Indy Racing League at the start of the 2000 season; son of Al and nephew of Bobby.

Al Unser Sr. (b. May 29, 1939): Auto racer; 3-time USAC-CART national champion (1970,83,85); 4-time winner of Indy 500 (1970-71,78,87); retired in 1994 ranked 3rd (now 4th) on all-time CART list with 39 wins; younger brother of Bobby and father of Al Jr.

Bobby Unser (b. Feb. 20, 1934): Auto racer; 2-time USAC-CART national champion (1968,74); 3-time winner of Indy 500 (1968,75,81); retired after 1981 season; ranks 5th on all-time CART list with 35 career wins.

Gene Upshaw (b. Aug. 15, 1945): Football G; 2-time All-AFL and 3-time All-NFL selection with Oakland; helped lead Raiders to 2 Super Bowl titles in 1976 and '80 seasons; executive director of NFL Players Assn. since 1987; agreed to application of salary cap in 1994.

Jim Valvano (b. Mar. 10, 1946, d. Apr. 28, 1993): Basketball; coach at N.C. State whose team upset Houston to win national title in 1983; in 19 seasons as a coach appeared in 8 NCAA tournaments; twice voted ACC Coach of the Year; career record 346-212; AD at N.C. State (1986-89) when a recruiting and admissions scandal forced him out of the job; worked as a broadcaster for ESPN and ABC; died after a year-long battle with cancer; The V Foundation for cancer research is named for him.

Norm Van Brocklin (b. Mar. 15, 1926, d. May 2, 1983): Football QB-P; led NFL in passing 3 times and punting twice; led LA Rams (1951) and Philadelphia (1960) to NFL titles; MVP in 1960.

Amy Van Dyken (b. Feb. 17, 1973): Swimming; first American woman to win four gold medals in one Olympics (1996); won the individual 50m freestyle, 100m butterfly, and was on the US team for the 4x100 freestyle and 4x50 medley; won gold at Sydney in 2000 as part of the US 4x100 freestyle relay.

Johnny Vander Meer (b. Nov. 2, 1914, d. Oct. 6, 1997): Baseball LHP; only major leaguer to pitch consecutive no-hitters (June 11 & 15, 1938).

Harold S. Vanderbilt (b. July 6, 1884, d. July 4, 1970): Sportsman; successfully defended America's Cup 3 times (1930, 34,37); also invented contract bridge in 1926.

Glenna Collett Vare (b. June 20, 1903, d. Feb. 10, 1989): Golfer; won record 6 U.S. Women's Amateur titles from 1922-35; "the female Bobby Jones."

Andy Varipapa (b. Mar. 31, 1891, d. Aug. 25, 1984): Bowler; trick-shot artist; won consecutive All-Star match game titles (1947-48) at age 55 and 56.

Bill Veeck (b. Feb. 9, 1914, d. Jan. 2, 1986): Maverick baseball executive; owned AL teams in Cleveland, St. Louis and Chicago from 1946-80; introduced ballpark giveaways, exploding scoreboards, Wrigley Field's ivy-covered walls and midget Eddie Gaedel; won World Series with Indians (1948) and pennant with White Sox (1959).

Jacques Villeneuve (b. Apr. 9, 1971): Canadian auto racer; Indianapolis 500 runner-up and Indy-Car Rookie of Year in 1994; won 500 and IndyCar driving championship in 1995; jumped to Formula One racing in 1996 and won the F1 title in 1997.

Fay Vincent (b. May 29, 1938): Baseball; became 8th commissioner after death of A. Bartlett Giamatti in 1989; presided over World Series earthquake, owners' lockout and banishment of NY Yankees owner George Steinbrenner in his first year on the job; contentious relationship with owners resulted in his resignation on Sept. 7, 1992, four days after 18-9 "no confidence" vote.

Lasse Viren (b. July 22, 1949): Finnish runner; won gold medals at 5,000 and 10,000 meters in 1972 Munich Olympics; repeated 5,000/10,000 double in 1976 Games and added a fifth place finish in the marathon.

Dick Vitale (b. June 9, 1939): Broadcaster; Radio and television commentator for ESPN and ABC Sports known for his enthusiastic, almost spastic style; had successful college and pro basketball coaching career with the University of Detroit (1973-77) and the Detroit Pistons (1978-79).

Lanny Wadkins (b. Dec. 5, 1949): Golfer; member of 8 U.S. Ryder Cup teams and captain of 1995 team; 21 PGA Tour wins.

Honus Wagner (b. Feb. 24, 1874, d. Dec. 6, 1955): Baseball SS; hit .300 for 17 consecutive seasons (1897-1913) with Louisville and Pittsburgh; led NL in batting 8 times; ended career with 3,430 career hits, a .329 average and 722 stolen bases.

Lisa Wagner (b. May 19, 1961): Bowler; 4-time LPBT Player of Year (1983,86,88,93); 1980's Bowler of Decade; first woman to earn $100,000 in a season; winner of 32 pro titles.

Grete Waitz (b. Oct. 1, 1953): Norwegian runner; 9-time winner of New York City Marathon from 1978-88; won silver medal at 1984 Olympics.

Jersey Joe Walcott (b. Jan. 31, 1914, d. Feb. 27, 1994): Boxer; oldest heavyweight (37) to win the championship (until George Foreman beat his record in 1994); lost four championship bouts before knocking out Ezzard Charles in the seventh round in 1951; lost the title the following year to Rocky Marciano; won 50 bouts, 30 by knockout, lost 17 and fought one draw as a professional; later became sheriff of Camden County, NJ.

Doak Walker (b. Jan. 1, 1927, d. Sept. 27, 1998): Football HB; won Heisman Trophy as SMU junior in 1948; led Detroit to 2 NFL titles (1952-53); All-Pro 4 times in 6 years.

Herschel Walker (b. Mar. 3, 1962): Football RB; led Georgia to national title as freshman in 1980; won Heisman in 1982 then jumped to upstart USFL in '83; signed by Dallas Cowboys after USFL folded; led NFL in rushing in 1988; traded to Minnesota in 1989 for 5 players and 6 draft picks.

Rusty Wallace (b. Aug. 14, 1956): Auto racing; NASCAR Winston Cup champion in 1989 and runner-up in 1980, 1988 and 1993; recorded 54 victories and has won over $30 million in earnings in 24 years of racing.

Bill Walsh (b. Nov. 30, 1931): Football; Hall of Fame coach and GM of 3 Super Bowl winners with San Francisco (1982,85,89); retired after 1989 Super Bowl; returned to college coaching in 1992 for his second stint at Stanford; retired again after 1994 season; returned as 49er GM from 1999-2001.

Bill Walton (b. Nov. 5, 1952): Basketball C; 3-time College Player of Year (1972-74); led UCLA to 2 national titles (1972-73); led Portland to NBA title as MVP in 1977; regular season MVP in 1978; successful basketball analyst.

Darrell Waltrip (b. Feb. 5, 1947): Auto racing; 3-time NASCAR Winston Cup champion (1981,82,85); 84 career Winston Cup wins and 59 poles.

Arch Ward (b. Dec. 27, 1896, d. July 9, 1955): Promoter and sports editor of *Chicago Tribune* from 1930-55; founder of baseball All-Star Game (1933), Chicago College All-Star Football Game (1934) and the All-America Football Conference (1946-49).

Charlie Ward (b. Oct. 12, 1970): Football QB and Basketball G; first Heisman winner to play for national champs (Florida St. in 1993) since Tony Dorsett in 1976; won Sullivan Award (1993); 3-year starter for FSU basketball team; not taken in NFL draft (because he made public his intentions to pursue basketball); 1st round pick of NY Knicks in 1994 NBA draft.

Glenn (Pop) Warner (b. Apr. 5, 1871, d. Sept. 7, 1954): Football innovator; coached at 7 colleges over 49 years; 319 career wins, fourth all-time; produced 47 All-Americas, including Jim Thorpe and Ernie Nevers.

Kurt Warner (b. June 22, 1971): Football QB; former Arena leaguer who led the St. Louis Rams to 2000 Super Bowl title over Tennessee; threw for a record 414 yards and was voted Super Bowl MVP; brought Rams back to the Super Bowl in 2002 and lost to the Patriots; 2-time NFL MVP (1999,2001).

Tom Watson (b. Sept. 4, 1949): Golfer; 6-time PGA Player of the Year (1977-80,82,84); has won 5 British Opens, 2 Masters and a U.S. Open; 4-time Ryder Cup member and captain of 1993 team; 34 PGA tour wins.

Earl Weaver (b. Aug. 14, 1930): Baseball; managed the Baltimore Orioles to 6 Eastern Division titles, four AL pennants and a World Series victory in 1970; was ejected 91 times and suspended four times for outbursts against umpires; record of 1,480-1,060 from 1968-82 and 1985-86.

Alan Webb (b. Jan. 13, 1983): Track; on May 27, 2001 at the Prefontaine Classic, he ran a mile in 3:53.43 to break Jim Ryun's 36-year-old national high school record; collegiate track star at Michigan.

Karrie Webb (b. Dec. 21, 1974): Golfer; youngest woman to win career Grand Slam; her win in the 2002 British Open made her the first player to win the "Super Grand Slam" (5 different majors) and gave her 6 major titles; 2-time Rolex Player of the Year (1999-2000)

Dick Weber (b. Dec. 23, 1929): Bowler; 3-time PBA Bowler of the Year (1961,63,65); won 30 PBA titles in 4 decades; father of Pete.

Pete Weber (b. Aug. 21, 1962): Bowler; 2nd on all-time PBA money list; 1990 PBA Rookie of the Year; inducted into PBA Hall of Fame (1998); has 29 PBA titles; son of Dick.

Johnny Weissmuller (b. June 2, 1904, d. Jan. 20 1984): Swimmer; won 3 gold medals at 1924 Olympics and 2 more at 1928 Games; became Hollywood's most famous Tarzan.

Jerry West (b. May 28, 1938): Basketball G; 2-time All-America and NCAA Final 4 MOP (1959) at West Virginia; led 1960 U.S. Olympic team to gold medal; 10-time All-NBA 1st-team; NBA finals MVP (1969); led LA Lakers to NBA title once as player (1972) and then 6 more times (1980,82,85,87,88,00) as an executive in various positions with the club; hired as President of Basketball Ops. by Memphis Grizzlies in 2002; his silhouette serves as the NBA's logo.

Pernell Whitaker (b. Jan. 2, 1964): Boxer; won Olympic gold medal as lightweight in 1984; won 4 world championships as lightweight, jr. welterweight, welterweight and jr. middleweight; outfought but failed to beat Julio Cesar Chavez when 1993 welterweight title defense ended in controversial draw; pro record of 41-3-1 (17 KOs); nicknamed "Sweet Pea".

Bill White (b. Jan. 28, 1934): Baseball; former NL president and highest ranking black executive in sports from 1989-94; as 1st baseman, won 7 Gold Gloves and hit .286 with 202 HRs in 13 seasons.

Byron (Whizzer) White (b. June 8, 1917, d. Apr. 15, 2002): Football; All-America HB at Colorado (1937); signed with Pittsburgh in 1938 for the then largest contract in pro history ($15,800); took Rhodes Scholarship in 1939; returned to NFL in 1940 to lead league in rushing and retired in 1941; named to U.S. Supreme Court by President Kennedy in 1962 and stepped down in 1993.

Reggie White (b. Dec. 19, 1961): Football DE; consensus All-America in 1983 at Tennessee; 7-time All-NFL (1986-92) with Philadelphia; signed as free agent with Green Bay in 1993 for $17 million over 4 years; played key role in Packers 1997 Super Bowl victory; made headlines in 1998 after making controversial public comments about gays and minorities; retired in 1999 but returned with the Carolina Panthers in 2000; NFL leader in sacks (198).

Kathy Whitworth (b. Sept. 27, 1939): Golf; 7-time LPGA Player of the Year (1966-69,71-73); won 6 majors; 88 tour wins, most on LPGA or PGA tour.

Hoyt Wilhelm (b. July 26, 1923, d. Aug. 23, 2002): Baseball RHP; Knuckleballer who is 3rd all-time in games pitched (1,070) and 1st in games finished (651) and games won in relief (123); career ERA of 2.52 and 227 saves; 1st reliever inducted into Hall of Fame (1985); threw no-hitter vs. NY Yankees (1958); also hit lone HR of career in first major league at bat (1952); won Purple Heart at the Battle of the Bulge.

Lenny Wilkens (b. Oct. 28, 1937): Basketball; NBA's all-time winningest coach; MVP of 1960 NIT as Providence guard; played 15 years in NBA, including 4 as player-coach; MVP of 1971 All-Star Game; coached Seattle to NBA title in 1979; Coach of Year in 1994 with Atlanta; one of only two men (John Wooden) to be honored by the Hall of Fame as player and coach; career record of 1372-1208 including playoffs with 5 NBA teams.

Dominique Wilkins (b. Jan. 12, 1960): Basketball F; last player to lead NBA in scoring (1986) before Michael Jordan's 7-year reign; All-NBA 1st team in 1986; elder statesman of Dream Team II.

Bud Wilkinson (b. Apr. 23, 1916, d. Feb. 9, 1994): Football; played on 1936 national championship team at Minnesota; coached Oklahoma to 3 national titles (1950, 55, 56); won 4 Orange and 2 Sugar Bowls; teams had winning streaks of 47 (1953-57) and 31 (1948-50); retired after 1963 season with 145-29-4 record in 17 years; also coached St. Louis of NFL to 9-20 record from 1978-79.

Ricky Williams (b. May 21, 1977): Football RB; became all-time NCAA Div. I-A leader in rushing yards (6,279) and touchdowns (75) at Texas but has since been passed in both categories; 1998 Heisman Trophy winner; Mike Ditka and New Orleans Saints traded their entire draft to take him fifth overall in 1999 NFL draft; traded to Miami Dolphins in 2002.

Serena Williams (b. Sept. 26, 1981): Tennis; beat Martina Hingis for 1999 U.S. Open championship to become the first African-American woman to win a Grand Slam title since Althea Gibson in 1958; won Wimbledon, the French Open and U.S. Open in 2002 and Australian and Wimbledon in 2003, defeating sister Venus in the final of each; has won career doubles grand slam with Venus.

Ted Williams (b. Aug. 30, 1918, d. July 5, 2002): Baseball OF; led AL in batting 6 times, and HRs and RBI 4 times each; won Triple Crown twice (1942,47); 2-time MVP (1946,49); last player to bat .400 when he hit .406 in 1941; Marine Corps combat pilot who missed 3 full seasons during WWII (1943-45) and most of two others (1952-53) during Korean War; hit .344 lifetime with 521 HRs in 19 years with Boston Red Sox; also known as avid fisherman; furor erupted following his death when plans to keep his body frozen at a cryogenic lab were made public.

Venus Williams (b. June 17, 1980): Tennis; won career doubles grand slam with sister Serena; recorded fastest serve in WTA history with 127 mph blast; winner of 2 Wimbledon (2000,01) and 2 U.S. Open (2000,01) singles titles; 2000 Olympic singles and doubles (w/Serena) gold medalist.

Walter Ray Williams Jr. (b. Oct. 6, 1959): Bowling and Horseshoes; 6-time PBA Bowler of Year (1986,93,96,97,98,2003); all-time leading money winner on the PBA Tour; has 37 PBA titles; won 6 World Horseshoe Pitching titles.

Hack Wilson (b. Apr. 26, 1900, d. Nov. 23, 1948): Baseball; as a Chicago Cub, he produced one of baseball's most outstanding seasons in 1930 with 56 home runs, .356 batting average, 105 walks and, most amazingly, a major league record 191 RBIs that still stands; finished career with 1,461 hits, 244 homers, 1,062 RBIs; member of Baseball Hall of Fame.

Dave Winfield (b. Oct. 3, 1951): Baseball OF-DH; selected in 4 major sports league drafts in 1973— NFL, NBA, ABA, and MLB; chose baseball and played in 12 All-Star Games over 22-year career; at age 41, helped lead Toronto to World Series title in 1992; 3,110 hits and 465 HRs.

Katarina Witt (b. Dec. 3, 1965): East German figure skater; 4-time world champion (1984-85,87-88); won consecutive Olympic gold medals (1984,88).

John Wooden (b. Oct. 14, 1910): Basketball; College Player of Year at Purdue in 1932; coached UCLA to 10 national titles (1964-65,67-73,75); one of only two men (Lenny Wilkens) to be honored by the Hall of Fame as player and coach.

Tiger Woods (b. Dec. 30, 1975): Golfer; youngest (18) and first minority to win U.S. Amateur in 1994, won it again in '95 and '96; in first full year on the PGA tour, he won 6 of 25 events and broke the single season money record; won 1997 Masters by a record 18 under par and 13 stroke margin of victory; won second major at 1999 PGA Championship; in 2000 won the U.S. Open at Pebble Beach by a record 15 strokes, the British Open by 8 strokes and the PGA Championship in a playoff; one of only five players to win all four Grand Slam titles (others are Hogan, Nicklaus, Player and Sarazen); held all four Major titles simultaneously after his win at 2001 Masters; won 2 more majors in 2002 (Masters and U.S. Open); the all-time career money leader on the PGA Tour.

Mickey Wright (b. Feb. 14, 1935): Golfer; won 3 of 4 majors (LPGA, U.S. Open, Titleholders) in 1961; 4-time winner of both U.S. Open and LPGA titles; 82 career wins including 13 majors.

Early Wynn (b. Jan. 6, 1920, d. Mar. 4, 1999): Baseball RHP; won 20 games 5 times; Cy Young winner in 1959; 300-244 record in 23 years.

Kristi Yamaguchi (b. July 12, 1971): Figure Skating; finished second in the 1991 American nationals but won the world title that year; dominated the sport in 1992 by winning the national, world and Olympic titles and then turned professional.

Cale Yarborough (b. Mar. 27, 1940): Auto racer; 3-time NASCAR national champion (1976-78); 4-time winner of Daytona 500 (1968,77,83-84); ranks 5th on NASCAR all-time win list with 83 wins.

Carl Yastrzemski (b. Aug. 22, 1939): Baseball OF; led AL in batting 3 times; won Triple Crown and MVP in 1967; had 3,419 hits and 452 HRs in 23 years with Boston Red Sox; member of Hall of Fame.

Cy Young (b. Mar. 29, 1867, d. Nov. 4, 1955): Baseball RHP; all-time leader in wins (511), losses (313), complete games (751) and innings pitched (7,356); had career 2.63 ERA in 22 years (1890-1911); 30-game winner 5 times and 20-game winner 11 other times; threw three no-hitters and a perfect game (1904); annual AL and NL pitching awards named after him.

Dick Young (b. Oct. 17, 1917, d. Aug. 31, 1987): Confrontational sportswriter for 44 years with NY tabloids; as baseball beat writer and columnist, he lead change from flowery prose to hard-nosed reporting.

Sheila Young (b. Oct. 14, 1950): Speed skater and cyclist; 1st U.S. athlete to win 3 medals at Winter Olympics (1976); won speed skating overall and sprint cycling world titles in 1976.

Steve Young (b. Oct. 11, 1961): Football QB; All-America at BYU (1983); NFL Player of Year (1992) with SF 49ers; only QB to lead NFL in passer rating 4 straight years (1991-94); rating of 112.8 in 1994 was highest ever; threw record 6 TD passes in MVP performance in Super Bowl XXIX; retired with NFL records for highest passer rating (96.8) and completion percentage (64.4); 232 career TD passes and 33,124 yards.

Robin Yount (b. Sept. 16, 1955): Baseball SS-OF; AL MVP at 2 positions— as SS in 1982 and OF in '89; retired after 1993 season with 3,142 hits, 251 HRs and a major-league-record 123 sacrifice flies after 20 seasons with Milwaukee Brewers; inducted into Hall of Fame in 1999.

Steve Yzerman (b. May 9, 1965): Hockey C; Captained the Detroit Red Wings to Stanley Cup wins in 1997, 98 and 2002; won the Conn Smythe Trophy as the playoff MVP in 1998; one of only 14 NHL players to score 600 goals; 7th in career scoring (1,670 points).

Mario Zagalo (b. Aug. 9, 1931): Soccer; Brazilian forward who is one of only two men (Franz Beckenbauer is the other) to serve as both captain (1962) and coach (1970,94) of World Cup champion.

Babe Didrikson Zaharias (b. June 26, 1911, d. Sept. 27, 1956): All-around athlete who was chosen AP Female Athlete of Year 6 times from 1932-54; won 2 gold medals (javelin and 80-meter hurdles) and a silver (high jump) at 1932 Olympics; played baseball and acquired the nickname "Babe" for her tape measure home runs; real first name was Mildred; took up golf in 1935 and went on to win 55 pro and amateur events; won 10 majors, including 3 U.S. Opens (1948,50,54); helped found LPGA in 1949; chosen female "Athlete of the Half Century" by AP in 1950; when asked if there was anything she didn't play, she replied, "Yeah, dolls."

Tony Zale (b. May 29, 1913, d. March 20, 1997): Boxer; 2-time world middleweight champion (1941-47,48); fought Rocky Graziano for title 3 times in 21 months in 1947-48, winning twice; pro record 67-18-2 with 44 KOs.

Frank Zamboni (b. Jan. 16, 1901, d. July 27, 1988): Mechanic, ice salesman and skating rink owner in Paramount, Calif.; invented ice-resurfacing machine in 1949; now there are few skating rinks without one as thousands have been sold in over 35 countries.

Emil Zatopek (b. Sept. 19, 1922, d. Nov. 22, 2000): Czech distance runner; winner of 1948 Olympic gold medal at 10,000 meters; 4 years later, won unprecedented Olympic triple crown (5,000 meters, 10,000 meters and marathon) at 1952 Games in Helsinki.

Zinedine Zidane (b. June 23, 1972): Frech soccer player; 2-time FIFA World Player of the Year (1998, 2000); led host nation France to 1998 World Cup title, scoring twice in final against Brazil; a record $64M transfer fee sent the midfielder from Juventus to Real Madrid in 2001.

John Ziegler (b. Feb. 9, 1934): Hockey; NHL president from 1977-92; negotiated settlement with rival WHA in 1979 that led to inviting four WHA teams (Edmonton, Hartford, Quebec and Winnipeg) to join NHL; stepped down June 12, 1992, 2 months after settling 10-day players' strike.

Kim Zmeskal (b. Feb. 6, 1976): Gymnastics; Won 3 U.S. national championships (1990-92); first American gymnast to win the all-around title at the world championship (1991).

Pirmin Zurbriggen (b. Feb. 4, 1963): Swiss alpine skier; 4-time World Cup overall champ (1984,87-88,90) and 3-time runner-up; 40 World Cup wins in 10 years; won gold and bronze medals at 1988 Olympics.

Ballparks & Arenas

Chicago's **Soldier Field**, the home of the Bears, underwent a total renovation and reopened in 2003.

AP/Wide World Photos

Coming Attractions

SPORTS ALMANAC

2003

BASEBALL

Cincinnati (NL): The Great American Ballpark (Great American Insurance is the title sponsor) opened for business Mar. 28, 2003 with an exhibition game between the Reds and cross-state rivals Cleveland Indians. Cleveland beat Cincinnati 6-1 in front of 40,888 fans. The stadium site overlaps the current site of Cinergy Field (formerly known as Riverfront Stadium). The grass-field, baseball-only park cost $290 million to build and seats 42,059. Home plate of the new park is set 580 feet from the Ohio River, probably a little too far·for splashdown homers that have been made famous at San Francisco's Pacific Bell Park. Interesting ballpark elements include smokestacks that emit vapor and fireworks following Reds home runs, outstanding plays and victories.

NBA BASKETBALL

Houston (West): Grand opening of the Toyota Center (Toyota Motor Sales is the title sponsor) for the Rockets and WNBA Comets was scheduled for September 2003. The multi-purpose complex will seat 18,300 for basketball and 17,800 for hockey, including 92 luxury suites and 2,900 club seats; estimated cost: $175 million; The arena is located in downtown Houston on a four-block site bounded by LaBranch, Jackson, Bell and Polk streets.

NFL FOOTBALL

Chicago (NFC): Grand re-opening of Soldier Field following a total renovation (originally built in 1924) took place Sept. 29, 2003. Part of a larger lakefront improvement project; estimated cost of entire project including the stadium, underground parking structure and additional infrastructure: $606 million. The improved stadium seats an estimated 63,000 including 133 luxury suites and 8,600 club seats. Bears played their home games of the 2002 season and the 2003 preseason at the University of Illinois' Memorial Stadium and returned to Soldier Field on Sept. 29, 2003 for the team's 2003 regular season home opener against the Green Bay Packers. The Bears lost XX-XX in front of a crowd of XXX.

Green Bay (NFC): A $295 million renovation of 43-year-old Lambeau Field was set to be completed by the fall of 2003. Unlike most stadium renovations, lack of luxury suites was not the issue here. The newly renovated stadium will actually have 32 fewer suites. Approximately 10,000 seats (including about 4,300 additional club seats) will be added bringing the total seating capacity to 72,515, including 167 luxury suites. Plans also called for the team and the city of Green Bay to seek naming rights before the 2003 season. A minimum bid of $120 million would have to be considered; the team and city would split the proceeds. As of yet corporate interest in renaming the storied stadium has been cool. One of the major features of the renovated stadium will be the atrium which is built to include a new Packer Hall of Fame and pro shop.

Philadelphia (NFC): Lincoln Financial Field (Lincoln Financial Group is the title sponsor) opened for business on Aug. 3, 2003 with a soccer match between European professional teams, Manchester United and FC Barcelona. Man. U. won the match, 3-1. The stadium, located at 11th Street and Pattison Avenue in South Philadelphia, cost $512 million to build and seats 68,532, including 10,828 club seats and 172 luxury suites. The city was responsible for site acquisition and preparation while the Eagles covered construction and overrun costs.

NHL HOCKEY

Phoenix (West): Construction of Glendale Arena, the new home to the Phoenix Coyotes, was scheduled to be completed in late 2003. The multi-purpose arena located at 101 Freeway and Glendale Avenue in Glendale, Ariz. (15 miles west of Phoenix), is the anchor and first building to be completed in the new 223-acre Westgate mixed-use project which features entertainment, retail, restaurants, office, hotel and residential venues. The stadium seats 17,500 and includes 87 luxury suites. The Coyotes will open the 2003-04 regular season at America West Arena before their move to the new digs, which is scheduled for Dec. 27, 2003. The cost of the stadium is approximately $206 million. The city owns the arena, but the team will get all of the revenue from the building for 30 years.

2004

BASEBALL

Philadelphia (NL): Construction on Citizens Bank Park (Citizens Bank is the title sponsor) is well underway. The baseball-only, grass-field park is located adjacent to Veterans Stadium in South Philadelphia on the north side of Pattison Avenue, between 11th and Darien Streets and offer scenic views of the Philadelphia skyline. The ballpark will seat 43,000, including 4,700 club seats and 71 luxury suites. Estimated cost of project is $346 million. One of the more impressive design features of the new park will be a 50-foot high neon Liberty Bell that will light up and ring following Phillies home runs. The Phillies home opener is set for April 2004.

San Diego (NL): Construction of PETCO Park (PETCO Animal Supplies, Inc. is the title sponsor) is nearing completion. The open-air, grass-field park is located on a one-square-block downtown lot and be part of a larger redevelopment project that will include a new hotel, office space and retail space. The park will seat approximately 46,000, including 6,000 club seats and 58 luxury suites, and cost an estimated $294.1 million. The adjacent historic Western Metal Supply Company building will be incorporated as a portion of the left field wall and foul pole. The Padres' home opener is set for April 2004.

NBA BASKETBALL

Memphis (East): Construction on the FedExForum (FedEx Corp. is the title sponsor) is well underway. The new $250 million home of the Grizzlies, located between Third and Fourth Streets and Lt. George W. Lee and Linden Avenues, will seat 18,400 for basketball (including 64 luxury suites) and 12,500 for hockey. The grand opening is set for September 2004.

AP/Wide World Photos

The Cincinnati Reds opened their new home in 2003. **The Great American Ballpark** saw baseball action for the first time on Mar. 28, 2003 in an exhibition game against the Cleveland Indians.

2005

BASEBALL

St. Louis (NL): New ballpark for the Cardinals is in the planning stages. The proposed site is south of the existing Busch Stadium on the south stadium parking lot. The proposed open-air, baseball-only ballpark would offer a spectacular view of the Gateway Arch. Since the new site partially overlaps the current stadium site, for the first year the park would offer about 40,000 permanent and temporary seats, but by year two the stadium would be complete and the seating capacity would grow to 47,900. Estimated cost (including a new Cardinals Hall of Fame and Museum) is $370 million. Earliest opening would be April 2005.

Florida (NL): The team is currently in discussions with the city of Miami involving financing for a new domed or retractable-roofed ballpark for the Marlins. Preliminary plans call for a $325 million ballpark to be built in downtown Miami. No realistic timetable has been set forth but the earliest home opener would likely be no earlier than April 2005.

NBA BASKETBALL

Charlotte (expansion): Construction on the new Uptown Arena (title sponsor pending) for the NBA expansion Charlotte Bobcats and the WNBA Charlotte Sting began with a ceremonial "groundblasting" on July 29, 2003. The arena, which will seat 18,500 for basketball (including 60 luxury suites) and 14,100 for hockey, is being built by the City of Charlotte and will cost an estimated $200 million. The building will be located in Center City Charlotte bounded by East Trade, Fifth and North Caldwell streets and the South Corridor Light Rail Line. The Bobcats will begin play in the NBA in 2004 and will play their first season at the Charlotte Coliseum before moving to the new Uptown Arena in November 2005 for the start of their second season.

New Jersey (East): New arena for the Nets is stalled in the planning stages. Funding from a new lease on Newark Airport would help pay for the project. Arena would be located in downtown Newark near Penn Station and would house the Nets and NHL's New Jersey Devils; estimated cost: $355 million. Earliest opening would be fall 2005. As part of a larger redevelopment plan for the site, New Jersey state officials and Meadowlands officials are investigating the possibility of renovating Continental Airlines Arena to meet the needs of the Nets and Devils.

NHL HOCKEY

New Jersey (East): New arena for the Devils is stalled in the planning stages. Funding from a new lease on Newark Airport would help pay for the project. Arena would be located in downtown Newark near Penn Station and would house the Devils and NBA's New Jersey Nets; estimated cost: $355 million. Earliest opening would be fall 2005. As part of a larger redevelopment plan for the site, New Jersey state officials and Meadowlands officials are investigating the possibility of renovating Continental Airlines Arena to meet the needs of the Devils and Nets.

2006

NFL FOOTBALL

Arizona (NFC): Excavation on a new home to the Arizona Cardinals and Fiesta Bowl began July 30, 2003. The 63,000-seat (expandable to 73,000) stadium will be located in Glendale, Ariz. (15 miles west of Phoenix) on a site on the Loop 101 (Agua Fria Freeway) south of Glendale Avenue and adjacent to the new home of the NHL's Coyotes. The stadium will feature a bold design, with a partially retractable roof and wall and feature a natural grass field that can be rolled out into the adjoining parking lot in order to help it grow. The stadium would include 88 luxury suites and 7,000 club seats; estimated cost: $365 million. Earliest Cardinals' home opener will be fall 2006.

Other Ballparks & Stadia in the Works

Plans for a new *Fenway Park* in Boston have been put on hold by the new Red Sox ownership...Proposals in Minnesota for new homes for both the Twins and Vikings to replace the *HHH Metrodome* have run into some trouble over financing issues...The San Francisco 49ers have explored replacing *Candlestick Park* with a new stadium as part of a larger retail and entertainment complex to be located at Candlestick Point...Groups in Washington, D.C. and Portland, Ore. have also floated plans for new ballparks in order to attract the fiscally troubled Montreal Expos...The A's are trying to get a new ballpark built in Oakland so they can leave *Network Associates Coliseum* to the Raiders...Stay tuned.

Home, Sweet Home

The home fields, home courts and home ice of the AL, NL, NBA, NFL, NHL, NCAA Division I-A college football and Division I basketball. Also included are MLS stadiums, Formula One, CART, Indy Racing League and NASCAR auto racing tracks.

Attendance figures for the 2002 NFL regular season and the 2002-03 NBA and NHL regular seasons are provided. See Baseball chapter for 2003 AL and NL attendance figures.

MAJOR LEAGUE BASEBALL

American League

| | | | | | Outfield Fences | | | |
	Built	Capacity	LF	LCF	CF	RCF	RF	Field
Anaheim Angels . . . .**Edison International Field of Anaheim**	1966	45,030	365	387	400	370	365	Grass
Baltimore Orioles . . . . .**Oriole Park at Camden Yards**	1992	48,190	337	376	406	391	320	Grass
Boston Red Sox . . . .**Fenway Park**	1912	34,892	310	379	390*	380	302	Grass
Chicago White Sox . . . .**U.S. Cellular Field**	1991	46,943	330	377	400	372	335	Grass
Cleveland Indians . . . .**Jacobs Field**	1994	43,068	325	370	405	375	325	Grass
Detroit Tigers . . . .**Comerica Park**	2000	40,120	345	395	420	365	330	Grass
Kansas City Royals . . . .**Kauffman Stadium**	1973	40,793	330	375	400	375	330	Grass
Minnesota Twins . . .**Hubert H. Humphrey Metrodome**	1982	48,678	343	385	408	367	327	Turf
New York Yankees . . . .**Yankee Stadium**	1923	57,478	318	399	408	385	314	Grass
Oakland Athletics . . . .**Network Associates Coliseum**	1966	43,662	330	367	400	367	330	Grass
Seattle Mariners . . . .**SAFECO Field**	1999	47,116	331	390	405	387	327	Grass
Tampa Bay Devil Rays . . . .**Tropicana Field**	1990	43,761	315	370	404	370	322	Turf
Texas Rangers . . . .**The Ballpark in Arlington**	1994	49,115	332	390	400	381	325	Grass
Toronto Blue Jays . . . .**SkyDome**	1989	50,516	328	375	400	375	328	Turf

*The straightaway center-field fence at Fenway Park is 390 feet from home plate but the deepest part of center-field, a.k.a. "the Triangle," is 420 feet away. The left-field fence, known as "the Green Monster," is 37 feet tall. Two hundred and seventy seats were added to the top of the wall in 2003 replacing the 23-foot screen that previously topped the Monster.

National League

| | | | | | Outfield Fences | | | |
	Built	Capacity	LF	LCF	CF	RCF	RF	Field
Arizona Diamondbacks . . . .**Bank One Ballpark**	1998	49,033	330	376	407	376	334	Grass
Atlanta Braves . . . .**Turner Field**	1996	50,091	335	380	401	390	330	Grass
Chicago Cubs . . . .**Wrigley Field**	1914	39,111	355	368	400	368	353	Grass
Cincinnati Reds . . . .**Great American Ballpark**	2003	42,059	328	379	404	370	325	Grass
Colorado Rockies . . . .**Coors Field**	1995	50,449	347	390	415	375	350	Grass
Florida Marlins . . . .**Pro Player Stadium**	1987	36,331	330	385	434	385	345	Grass
Houston Astros . . . .**Minute Maid Park**	2000	40,950	315	362	436	373	326	Grass
Los Angeles Dodgers . . . .**Dodger Stadium**	1962	56,000	330	385	395	385	330	Grass
Milwaukee Brewers . . . .**Miller Park**	2001	42,400	340	374	400	378	345	Grass
Montreal Expos . . . .**Olympic Stadium**	1976	46,500	325	375	404	375	325	Turf
& Hiram Bithorn Stadium*	1962	18,000	315	360	399	360	313	Turf
New York Mets . . . .**Shea Stadium**	1964	56,749	338	378	410	378	338	Grass
Philadelphia Phillies . . . .**Citizens Bank Park**	2004	43,000	329	369	401*	369	330	Grass
Pittsburgh Pirates . . . .**PNC Park**	2001	37,898	326	368	399*	375	324	Grass
St. Louis Cardinals . . . .**Busch Stadium**	1966	49,814	330	372	402	372	330	Grass
San Diego Padres . . . .**PETCO Park**	2004	46,000	334	367	396*	387	322	Grass
San Francisco Giants . . . .**Pacific Bell Park**	2000	41,467	339	364	399	421	309	Grass

*In 2003, the Montreal Expos played 22 games in San Juan, Puerto Rico at Hiram Bithorn Stadium and likely will return there for part of their 2004 schedule. Also, the deepest part of PNC Park is 410 feet between straightaway center and left-center. The deepest part of Citizens Bank Park is 409 feet in part of left-center. The deepest part of PETCO Park is 411 feet in part of right-center.

Rank by Capacity

AL		NL	
New York	57,478	New York	56,749
Toronto	50,516	Los Angeles	56,000
Texas	49,115	Colorado	50,449
Minnesota	48,678	Atlanta	50,091
Baltimore	48,190	St. Louis	49,814
Seattle	47,116	Arizona	49,033
Chicago	46,943	Montreal	46,500
Anaheim	45,030	San Diego	46,000
Tampa Bay	43,761	Philadelphia	43,000
Oakland	43,662	Milwaukee	42,400
Cleveland	43,068	Cincinnati	42,059
Kansas City	40,793	San Francisco	41,467
Detroit	40,120	Houston	40,950
Boston	34,892	Chicago	39,111
		Pittsburgh	37,898
		Florida	36,331

Rank by Age

AL		NL	
Boston	1912	Chicago	1914
New York	1923	Los Angeles	1962
Anaheim	1966	New York	1964
Oakland	1966	St. Louis	1966
Kansas City	1973	Montreal	1976
Minnesota	1982	Florida	1987
Toronto	1989	Atlanta	1993
Tampa Bay	1990	Colorado	1995
Chicago	1991	Arizona	1998
Baltimore	1992	Houston	2000
Cleveland	1994	San Francisco	2000
Texas	1994	Milwaukee	2001
Seattle*	1999	Pittsburgh	2001
Detroit	2000	Cincinnati	2003
		Philadelphia	2004
		San Diego	2004

Note: New York's Yankee Stadium (AL) was rebuilt in 1976.

Home Fields

Listed below are the principal home fields used through the years by current American and National League teams. The NL became a major league in 1876, the AL in 1901.

The capacity figures in the right-hand column indicate the largest seating capacity of the ballpark while the club played there. Capacity figures before 1915 (and the introduction of concrete grandstands) are sketchy at best and have been left blank.

American League

Anaheim Angels

1961	Wrigley Field (Los Angeles)	.20,457
1962-65	Dodger Stadium	.56,000
1966–	Edison International Field of Anaheim	45,030
	(1966 capacity—43,250)	

Baltimore Orioles

1901	Lloyd Street Grounds (Milwaukee) . . .	—
1902-53	Sportsman's Park II (St. Louis)	.30,500
1954-91	Memorial Stadium (Baltimore)	.53,371
1992–	Oriole Park at Camden Yards	48,190

Boston Red Sox

1901-11	Huntington Ave. Grounds	—
1912–	Fenway Park	.34,892
	(1934 capacity—27,000)	

Chicago White Sox

1901-10	Southside Park	—
1910-90	Comiskey Park I	.43,931
1991–	U.S. Cellular Field	.46,943

Cleveland Indians

1901-09	League Park I	—
1910-46	League Park II	.21,414
1932-93	Cleveland Stadium	.74,483
1994–	Jacobs Field	.43,068

Detroit Tigers

1901-11	Bennett Park	—
1912-99	Tiger Stadium	.46,945
2000–	Comerica Park	.40,120
	(1912 capacity—23,000)	

Kansas City Royals

1969-72	Municipal Stadium	.35,020
1973–	Kauffman Stadium	.40,793
	(1973 capacity—40,762)	

Minnesota Twins

1901-02	American League Park (Washington, DC)	—
1903-60	Griffith Stadium	.27,410
1960-81	Metropolitan Stadium	
	(Bloomington, MN)	.45,919
1982–	HHH Metrodome (Minneapolis)	.48,678
	(1982 capacity—54,000)	

New York Yankees

1901-02	Oriole Park (Baltimore)	—
1903-12	Hilltop Park (New York)	—
1913-22	Polo Grounds II	.38,000
1923-73	Yankee Stadium I	.67,224
1974-75	Shea Stadium	.55,101
1976–	Yankee Stadium II	.57,478
	(1976 capacity—57,145)	

Oakland Athletics

1901-08	Columbia Park (Philadelphia)	—
1909-54	Shibe Park	.33,608
1955-67	Municipal Stadium (Kansas City) . . .	.35,020
1968–	Network Associates Coliseum	.43,662
	(1968 capacity—48,621)	

Seattle Mariners

1977-99	The Kingdome	.59,166
1999–	SAFECO Field	.47,116

Tampa Bay Devil Rays

1990–	Tropicana Field	.43,761

Texas Rangers

1961	Griffith Stadium (Washington, DC) . . .	.27,410
1962-71	RFK Stadium	.45,016
1972-93	Arlington Stadium (Texas)	.43,521
1994–	The Ballpark in Arlington	.49,115

Toronto Blue Jays

1977-89	Exhibition Stadium	.43,737
1989–	SkyDome	.50,516
	(1989 capacity—49,500)	

Ballpark Name Changes: ANAHEIM—**Edison International Field of Anaheim** originally Anaheim Stadium (1966-98); CHICAGO—**Comiskey Park I** originally White Sox Park (1910-12), then Comiskey Park in 1913, then White Sox Park again in 1962, then Comiskey Park again in 1976; **U.S. Cellular Field** originally Comiskey Park (1991-2002); CLEVELAND—**League Park** renamed Dunn Field in 1920, then League Park again in 1928; **Cleveland Stadium** originally Municipal Stadium (1932-74); DETROIT—**Tiger Stadium** originally Navin Field (1912-37), then Briggs Stadium (1938-60); KANSAS CITY—**Kauffman Stadium** originally Royals Stadium (1973-93); LOS ANGELES—**Dodger Stadium** referred to as Chavez Revine by AL while Angels played there (1962-65); OAKLAND—**Network Associates Coliseum** originally Oakland Alameda Coliseum (1968-98); PHILADELPHIA—**Shibe Park** renamed Connie Mack Stadium in 1953; ST. LOUIS—**Sportsman's Park** renamed Busch Stadium in 1953; WASHINGTON—**Griffith Stadium** originally National Park (1892-1920), **RFK Stadium** originally D.C. Stadium (1961-68).

National League

Arizona Diamondbacks

1998–	Bank One Ballpark	.49,033

Atlanta Braves

1876-94	South End Grounds I (Boston)	—
1894-1914	South End Grounds II	—
1915-52	Braves Field	.40,000
1953-65	County Stadium (Milwaukee)	.43,394
1966-96	Atlanta-Fulton County Stadium	.52,769
	(1966 capacity—50,000)	
1997–	Turner Field	.50,091

Chicago Cubs

1876-77	State Street Grounds	—
1878-84	Lakefront Park	—
1885-91	West Side Park	—
1891-93	Brotherhood Park	—
1893-1915	West Side Grounds	—
1916–	Wrigley Field	.39,111
	(1916 capacity—16,000)	

Cincinnati Reds

1876-79	Avenue Grounds	—
1880	Bank Street Grounds	—
1890-1901	Redland Field I	—
1902-11	Palace of the Fans	—
1912-70	Crosley Field	.29,603
1970-2002	Cinergy Field	.40,007
	(1970 capacity—52,000)	
2003–	Great American Ballpark	.42,059

Major League Baseball (Cont.)

Colorado Rockies

1993–94	Mile High Stadium (Denver)	.76,100
1995–	Coors Field	.50,449

Florida Marlins

1993–	Pro Player Stadium (Miami)	.36,331
	(1993 capacity—47,662)	

Houston Astros

1962–64	Colt Stadium	.32,601
1965–99	The Astrodome	.54,370
	(1965 capacity—45,011)	
2000–	Minute Maid Park	.40,950

Los Angeles Dodgers

1890	Washington Park I (Brooklyn)	—
1891–97	Eastern Park	—
1898–1912	Washington Park II	—
1913–56	Ebbets Field	.31,497
1957	Ebbets Field	.31,497
	& Roosevelt Stadium (Jersey City)	.24,167
1958–61	Memorial Coliseum (Los Angeles)	.93,600
1962–	Dodger Stadium	.56,000

Milwaukee Brewers

1969	Sick's Stadium (Seattle)	.59,166
1970–	County Stadium (Milwaukee)	.53,192
2000	(1970 capacity—46,620)	
2001–	Miller Park	.42,400

Montreal Expos

1969–76	Jarry Park	.28,000
1977–2002	Olympic Stadium	.46,500
2003–	Olympic Stadium	.46,500
	& Hiram Bithon Stadium (San Juan)	.18,000

New York Mets

1962–63	Polo Grounds	.55,987
1964–	Shea Stadium	.56,749
	(1964 capacity—55,101)	

Philadelphia Phillies

1883–86	Recreation Park	—
1887–94	Huntingdon Ave. Grounds	—
1895–1938	Baker Bowl	.18,800
1938–70	Shibe Park	.33,608
1971–2003	Veterans Stadium	.62,418
2004–	Citizens Bank Park	.43,000

Pittsburgh Pirates

1887–90	Recreation Park	—
1891–1909	Exposition Park	—
1909–70	Forbes Field	.35,000
1970–2000	Three Rivers Stadium	.47,687
	(1970 capacity—50,235)	
2001–	PNC Park	.37,898

St. Louis Cardinals

1876–77	Sportsman's Park I	—
1885–86	Vandeventer Lot	—
1892–1920	Robison Field	.18,000
1920–66	Sportsman's Park II	.30,500
1966–	Busch Stadium	.49,814
	(1966 capacity—50,126)	

San Diego Padres

1969–2003	Qualcomm Stadium	.66,083
2004–	PETCO Park	.46,000

San Francisco Giants

1876	Union Grounds (Brooklyn)	—
1883–88	Polo Grounds I (New York)	—
1889–90	Manhattan Field	—
1891–1957	Polo Grounds II	.55,987
1958–59	Seals Stadium (San Francisco)	.22,900
1960–99	3Com Park	.63,000
	(1960 capacity—42,553)	
2000–	Pacific Bell Park	.41,467

Ballpark Name Changes: ATLANTA—**Atlanta-Fulton County Stadium** originally Atlanta Stadium (1966-74), **Turner Field** originally Centennial Olympic Stadium (1996); CHICAGO—**Wrigley Field** originally Weeghman Park (1914-17), then Cubs Park (1918-25); CINCINNATI—**Redland Field** originally League Park (1890-93), **Crosley Field** originally Redland Field II (1912-33) and **Cinergy Field** originally Riverfront Stadium (1970-96); FLORIDA—**Pro Player Stadium** originally Joe Robbie Stadium (1987-96); HOUSTON—**Astrodome** originally Harris County Domed Stadium before it opened in 1965; **Enron Field** renamed Astros Field briefly and then Minute Maid Park in 2002; PHILADELPHIA—**Shibe Park** renamed Connie Mack Stadium in 1953; ST. LOUIS—**Robison Field** originally Vandeventer Lot, then League Park, then Cardinal Park all before becoming Robison Field in 1901, **Sportsman's Park** renamed Busch Stadium in 1953, and **Busch Stadium** originally Busch Memorial Stadium (1966-82); SAN DIEGO—**Qualcomm Stadium** originally San Diego Stadium (1967-81) and San Diego/Jack Murphy Stadium (1982-96); SAN FRANCISCO—**3Com Park** originally Candlestick Park (1960-95).

NATIONAL BASKETBALL ASSOCIATION

Western Conference

		Location	Built	Capacity
Dallas Mavericks	**American Airlines Center**	Dallas, Texas	2001	**19,200**
Denver Nuggets	**Pepsi Center**	Denver, Colo.	1999	**19,099**
Golden State Warriors	**The Arena in Oakland**	Oakland, Calif.	1997	**19,596**
Houston Rockets	**Toyota Center**	Houston, Texas	2003	**18,300**
Los Angeles Clippers	**Staples Center**	Los Angeles, Calif.	1999	**18,694**
Los Angeles Lakers	**Staples Center**	Los Angeles, Calif.	1999	**18,997**
Memphis Grizzlies	**The Pyramid**	Memphis, Tenn.	1990	**19,342**
Minnesota Timberwolves	**Target Center**	Minneapolis, Minn.	1990	**19,006**
Phoenix Suns	**America West Arena**	Phoenix, Ariz.	1992	**19,023**
Portland Trail Blazers	**Rose Garden**	Portland, Ore.	1995	**19,980**
Sacramento Kings	**ARCO Arena**	Sacramento, Calif.	1988	**17,317**
San Antonio Spurs	**SBC Center**	San Antonio, Texas	2002	**18,500**
Seattle SuperSonics	**KeyArena at Seattle Center**	Seattle, Wash.	1962	**17,072**
Utah Jazz	**Delta Center**	Salt Lake City, Utah	1991	**19,911**

Notes: Seattle's KeyArena was originally the Seattle Center Coliseum before being rebuilt in 1995; The Staples Center has different listed capacities for Clippers games and Lakers games because of different floor seating arrangements.

Eastern Conference

		Location	Built	Capacity
Atlanta Hawks	**Philips Arena**	Atlanta, Ga.	1999	**19,445**
Boston Celtics	**FleetCenter**	Boston, Mass.	1995	**18,624**
Chicago Bulls	**United Center**	Chicago, Ill.	1994	**21,711**
Cleveland Cavaliers	**Gund Arena**	Cleveland, Ohio	1994	**20,562**
Detroit Pistons	**The Palace of Auburn Hills**	Auburn Hills, Mich.	1988	**22,076**
Indiana Pacers	**Conseco Fieldhouse**	Indianapolis, Ind.	1999	**18,345**
Miami Heat	**AmericanAirlines Arena**	Miami, Fla.	1999	**16,500**
Milwaukee Bucks	**Bradley Center**	Milwaukee, Wisc.	1988	**18,717**
New Jersey Nets	**Continental Airlines Arena**	E. Rutherford, N.J.	1981	**20,049**
New Orleans Hornets	**New Orleans Arena**	New Orleans, La.	1999	**18,500**
New York Knicks	**Madison Square Garden**	New York, N.Y.	1968	**19,763**
Orlando Magic	**TD Waterhouse Centre**	Orlando, Fla.	1989	**17,248**
Philadelphia 76ers	**Wachovia Center**	Philadelphia, Penn.	1996	**20,444**
Toronto Raptors	**Air Canada Centre**	Toronto, Ont.	1999	**19,800**
Washington Wizards	**MCI Center**	Washington, D.C.	1997	**20,674**

Rank by Capacity

Western		Eastern	
Portland	19,980	Detroit	22,076
Utah	19,911	Chicago	21,711
Golden State	19,596	Washington	20,674
Memphis	19,342	Cleveland	20,562
Dallas	19,200	Philadelphia	20,444
Denver	19,099	New Jersey	20,049
Phoenix	19,023	Toronto	19,800
Minnesota	19,006	New York	19,763
LA Lakers	18,997	Atlanta	19,445
LA Clippers	18,694	Milwaukee	18,717
San Antonio	18,500	Boston	18,624
Houston	18,300	New Orleans	18,500
Sacramento	17,317	Indiana	18,345
Seattle	17,072	Orlando	17,248
		Miami	16,500

Rank by Age

Western		Eastern	
Seattle	1962	New York	1968
Sacramento	1988	New Jersey	1981
Memphis	1990	Detroit	1988
Minnesota	1990	Milwaukee	1988
Utah	1991	Orlando	1989
Phoenix	1992	Chicago	1994
Portland	1995	Cleveland	1994
Golden St.	1997	Boston	1995
Denver	1999	Philadelphia	1996
LA Clippers	1999	Washington	1997
LA Lakers	1999	Toronto	1999
Dallas	2001	New Orleans	1999
San Antonio	2002	Atlanta	1999
Houston	2003	Indiana	1999
		Miami	1999

Note: The Seattle Center Coliseum was rebuilt and renamed KeyArena in 1995.

2002-03 NBA Attendance

Official overall attendance in the NBA for the 2002-03 season was 20,074,388 for an average per game crowd of 16,883 over 1,189 games. Teams in each conference are ranked by attendance over 41 home games based on total tickets distributed. Rank column refers to rank in entire league. Numbers in parentheses indicate conference rank in 2001-02.

Western Conference

		Attendance	Rank	Average
1	Dallas (2)	816,429	3	19,912
2	Portland (3)	796,258	6	19,420
3	Utah (5)	786,034	7	19,171
4	LA Lakers (4)	777,888	9	18,972
5	San Antonio (1)	735,970	11	17,950
6	Sacramento (8)	709,997	12	17,317
7	LA Clippers (6)	706,471	14	17,231
8	Phoenix (9)	666,559	16	16,257
9	Minnesota (7)	643,684	18	15,699
10	Seattle (11)	637,194	20	15,541
11	Golden St. (12)	634,935	21	15,486
12	Memphis (13)	611,322	24	14,910
13	Denver (10)	607,813	25	14,824
14	Houston (14)	565,166	27	13,784
	TOTAL	9,695,720	—	16,891

Eastern Conference

		Attendance	Rank	Average
1	Detroit (6)	839,278	1	20,470
2	Washington (2)	827,093	2	20,173
3	Philadelphia (1)	807,097	4	19,685
4	Chicago (5)	804,309	5	19,617
5	New York (3)	779,479	8	19,011
6	Toronto (4)	777,507	10	18,963
7	Boston (9)	709,049	13	17,293
8	Indiana (8)	670,461	15	16,352
9	Milwaukee (7)	665,966	17	16,243
10	New Orleans (15)	641,683	19	15,650
11	Miami (10)	628,242	22	15,322
12	New Jersey (13)	622,574	23	15,184
13	Orlando (11)	605,901	26	14,778
14	Atlanta (14)	528,655	28	12,894
15	Cleveland (12)	471,374	29	11,496
	TOTAL	10,378,668	—	16,876

Note: The Charlotte Hornets moved to New Orleans following the 2001-02 season.

National Basketball Association (Cont.)
Home Courts

Listed below are the principal home courts used through the years by current NBA teams. The largest capacity of each arena is noted in the right-hand column. ABA arenas (1967-76) are included for Denver, Indiana, New Jersey and San Antonio.

Western Conference

Dallas Mavericks

1980–2000	Reunion Arena	.18,187
2001–	American Airlines Center	.19,200

Denver Nuggets

1967–75	Auditorium Arena	.6,841
1975–99	McNichols Sports Arena	.17,171
	(1975 capacity—16,700)	
1999–	Pepsi Center	.19,099

Golden State Warriors

1946–52	Philadelphia Arena	.7,777
1952–62	Convention Hall (Philadelphia)	.9,200
	& Philadelphia Arena	.7,777
1962–64	Cow Palace (San Francisco)	.13,862
1964–66	Civic Auditorium	.7,500
	& (USF Memorial Gym)	.6,000
1966–67	Cow Palace, Civic Auditorium	
	& Oakland Coliseum Arena	.15,000
1967–71	Cow Palace	.14,500
1971–96	Oakland Coliseum Arena	.15,025
	(1971 capacity—12,905)	
1996–97	San Jose Arena	.18,500
1997–	The Arena in Oakland	.19,596

Houston Rockets

1967–71	San Diego Sports Arena	.14,000
1971–72	Hofheinz Pavilion (Houston)	.10,218
1972–73	Hofheinz Pavilion	.10,218
	& HemisFair Arena (San Antonio)	.10,446
1973–75	Hofheinz Pavilion	.10,218
1975–2002	Compaq Center	.16,285
2003–	Toyota Center	.18,300

Los Angeles Clippers

1970–78	Memorial Auditorium (Buffalo)	.17,300
1978–84	San Diego Sports Arena	.12,167
1985–94	Los Angeles Sports Arena	.16,005
1994–99	Los Angeles Sports Arena	.16,021
	& Arrowhead Pond	.18,211
1999–	Staples Center	.18,694

Los Angeles Lakers

1948–60	Minneapolis Auditorium	.10,000
1960–67	Los Angeles Sports Arena	.14,781
1967–99	Great Western Forum (Inglewood, CA)	.17,505
	(1967 capacity—17,086)	
1999–	Staples Center	.18,997

Memphis Grizzlies

1995–2001	General Motors Place (Vancouver)	.19,193
2001–	The Pyramid (Memphis, TN)	.19,342

Minnesota Timberwolves

1989–90	Hubert H. Humphrey Metrodome	.23,000
1990–	Target Center	.19,006

Phoenix Suns

1968–92	Arizona Veterans' Memorial Coliseum	14,487
1992–	America West Arena	.19,023

Portland Trail Blazers

1970–95	Memorial Coliseum	.12,888
1995–	Rose Garden	.19,980
	(1995 capacity—21,538)	

Sacramento Kings

1948–55	Edgarton Park Arena (Rochester, NY)	.5,000
1955–58	Rochester War Memorial	.10,000
1958–72	Cincinnati Gardens	.11,438
1972–74	Municipal Auditorium (Kansas City)	.9,929
	& Omaha (NE) Civic Auditorium	.9,136
1974–78	Kemper Arena (Kansas City)	.16,785
	& Omaha Civic Auditorium	.9,136
1978–85	Kemper Arena	.16,785
1985–88	ARCO Arena I	.10,333
1988–	ARCO Arena II	.17,317
	(1988 capacity—16,517)	

San Antonio Spurs

1967–70	Memorial Auditorium (Dallas)	.8,088
	& Moody Coliseum (Dallas)	.8,500
1970–71	Moody Coliseum	.8,500
	Tarrant Convention Center (Ft. Worth)	.13,500
	& Municipal Coliseum (Lubbock)	.10,400
1971–73	Moody Coliseum	.9,500
	& Memorial Auditorium	.8,088
1973–93	HemisFair Arena (San Antonio)	.16,057
1993–2002	The Alamodome	.20,557
2002–	SBC Center	.18,500

Seattle SuperSonics

1967–78	Seattle Center Coliseum	.14,098
1978–85	Kingdome	.40,192
1985–94	Seattle Center Coliseum	.14,252
1994–95	Tacoma Dome	.19,000
1995–	KeyArena at Seattle Center	.17,072

Utah Jazz

1974–75	Municipal Auditorium (New Orleans)	.7,853
	& Louisiana Superdome	.47,284
1975–79	Superdome	.47,284
1979–83	Salt Palace (Salt Lake City)	.12,519
1983–84	Salt Palace	.12,519
	& Thomas & Mack Center (Las Vegas)	.18,500
1984–91	Salt Palace	.12,616
1991–	Delta Center	.19,911

Eastern Conference

Atlanta Hawks

1949–51	Wharton Field House (Moline, IL)	.6,000
1951–55	Milwaukee Arena	.11,000
1955–68	Kiel Auditorium (St. Louis)	.10,000
1968–72	Alexander Mem. Coliseum (Atlanta)	.7,166
1972–96	The Omni	.16,378
1997–99	Georgia Dome	.21,570
	& Alexander Mem. Coliseum	.9,300
1999–	Philips Arena	.19,445

Boston Celtics

1946–95	Boston Garden	.14,890
1995–	FleetCenter	.18,624

Note: From 1975-95 the Celtics played some regular season games at the Hartford Civic Center (15,418).

Chicago Bulls

1966–67	Chicago Amphitheater	.11,002
1967–94	Chicago Stadium	.18,676
1994–	United Center	.21,711

Cleveland Cavaliers

1970–74	Cleveland Arena	.11,000
1974–94	The Coliseum (Richfield, OH)	.20,273
1994–	Gund Arena	.20,562

Detroit Pistons

1948–52	North Side H.S. Gym (Ft. Wayne, IN)	3,800
1952–57	Memorial Coliseum (Ft. Wayne)	9,306
1957–61	Olympia Stadium (Detroit)	.14,000
1961–78	Cobo Arena	.11,147
1978–88	Silverdome (Pontiac, MI)	.22,366
1988–	The Palace of Auburn Hills	.22,076

Indiana Pacers

1967–74	State Fairgrounds (Indianapolis)	9,479
1974–99	Market Square Arena	.16,530
	(1974 capacity—17,287)	
1999–	Conseco Fieldhouse	.18,345

Miami Heat

1988–99	Miami Arena	.15,200
2000–	AmericanAirlines Arena	.16,500

Milwaukee Bucks

1968–88	Milwaukee Arena (The Mecca)	.11,052
1988–	Bradley Center	.18,717

New Jersey Nets

1967–68	Teaneck (NJ) Armory	3,500
1968–69	Long Island Arena (Commack, NY)	6,500
1969–71	Island Garden (W. Hempstead, NY)	5,200
1971–77	Nassau Coliseum (Uniondale, NY)	.15,500
1977–81	Rutgers Ath. Center (Piscataway, NJ)	9,050
1981–	Continental Airlines Arena (E. Ruth., NJ)	.20,049

New Orleans Hornets

1988-	Charlotte Coliseum	.19,925
2002	(1988 capacity—23,500)	
2002-	New Orleans Arena	.18,500

New York Knicks

1946–68	Madison Sq. Garden III (50th St.)	.18,496
1968-	Madison Sq. Garden IV (33rd St.)	.19,763
	(1968 capacity—19,694)	

Orlando Magic

1989–	TD Waterhouse Centre	.17,248

Philadelphia 76ers

1949–51	State Fair Coliseum (Syracuse, NY)	.7,500
1951–63	Onondaga County (NY) War Memorial	.8,000
1963–67	Convention Hall (Philadelphia)	.12,000
	& Philadelphia Arena	.7,777
1967–96	CoreStates Spectrum	.18,136
1996–	Wachovia Center	.20,444

Toronto Raptors

1995–99	SkyDome	.20,125
1999–	Air Canada Centre	.19,800

Washington Wizards

1961–62	Chicago Amphitheater	.11,000
1962–63	Chicago Coliseum	.7,100
1963–73	Baltimore Civic Center	.12,289
1973–97	USAir Arena (Landover, MD)	.18,756
1997–	MCI Center	.20,674

Note: From 1988-96 the Wizards (then Bullets) played four regular season games at Baltimore Arena (12,756).

Building Name Changes: HOUSTON—**Compaq Center** originally The Summit (1975-97); NEW JERSEY—**Continental Airlines Arena** originally Byrne Meadowlands Arena (1981-96); ORLANDO—**TD Waterhouse Centre** originally Orlando Arena (1989-99); PHILADELPHIA—**Wachovia Center** originally the CoreStates Center (1996-98), then the First Union Center (1998-2003) and **CoreStates Spectrum** originally The Spectrum (1967-94); WASHINGTON—**USAir Arena** originally Capital Centre (1973-93).

NATIONAL FOOTBALL LEAGUE

American Football Conference

		Location	Built	Capacity	Field
Baltimore Ravens	**Ravens Stadium**	Baltimore, Md.	1998	**69,084**	Grass
Buffalo Bills	**Ralph Wilson Stadium**	Orchard Park, N.Y.	1973	**73,967**	Turf
Cincinnati Bengals	**Paul Brown Stadium**	Cincinnati, Ohio	2000	**65,352**	Grass
Cleveland Browns	**Cleveland Browns Stadium**	Cleveland, Ohio	1999	**73,200**	Grass
Denver Broncos	**INVESCO Field at Mile High**	Denver, Colo.	2001	**76,125**	Grass
Houston Texans	**Reliant Stadium**	Houston, Tex.	2002	**69,500**	Grass
Indianapolis Colts	**RCA Dome**	Indianapolis, Ind.	1984	**56,127**	Turf
Jacksonville Jaguars	**ALLTEL Stadium**	Jacksonville, Fla.	1995	**73,000**	Grass
Kansas City Chiefs	**Arrowhead Stadium**	Kansas City, Mo.	1972	**79,451**	Grass
Miami Dolphins	**Pro Player Stadium**	Miami, Fla.	1987	**75,540**	Grass
New England Patriots	**Gillette Stadium**	Foxboro, Mass.	2002	**68,000**	Grass
New York Jets	**Giants Stadium**	E. Rutherford, N.J.	1976	**80,062**	Grass
Oakland Raiders	**Network Associates Coliseum**	Oakland, Calif.	1966	**63,132**	Grass
Pittsburgh Steelers	**Heinz Field**	Pittsburgh, Pa.	2001	**64,450**	Grass
San Diego Chargers	**Qualcomm Stadium**	San Diego, Calif.	1967	**71,000**	Grass
Tennessee Titans	**The Coliseum**	Nashville, Tenn.	1999	**68,798**	Grass

National Football Conference

		Location	Built	Capacity	Field
Arizona Cardinals	**Sun Devil Stadium**	Tempe, Ariz.	1958	**73,273**	Grass
Atlanta Falcons	**Georgia Dome**	Atlanta, Ga.	1992	**71,228**	Turf
Carolina Panthers	**Ericsson Stadium**	Charlotte, N.C.	1996	**73,500**	Grass
Chicago Bears	**Soldier Field**	Chicago, Ill.	1924	**63,000**	Grass
Dallas Cowboys	**Texas Stadium**	Irving, Texas	1971	**65,639**	Turf
Detroit Lions	**Ford Field**	Detroit, Mich.	2002	**65,000**	Turf
Green Bay Packers	**Lambeau Field**	Green Bay, Wis.	1957	**72,515**	Grass
Minnesota Vikings	**Hubert H. Humphrey Metrodome**	Minneapolis, Minn.	1982	**64,121**	Turf
New Orleans Saints	**Louisiana Superdome**	New Orleans, La.	1975	**68,395**	Turf
New York Giants	**Giants Stadium**	E. Rutherford, N.J.	1976	**80,062**	Grass
Philadelphia Eagles	**Lincoln Financial Field**	Philadelphia, Pa.	2003	**68,532**	Grass
St. Louis Rams	**Edward Jones Dome**	St. Louis, Mo.	1995	**66,000**	Turf
San Francisco 49ers	**Candlestick Park**	San Francisco, Calif.	1960	**69,400**	Grass
Seattle Seahawks	**Seahawks Stadium**	Seattle, Wash.	2002	**67,000**	Grass
Tampa Bay Buccaneers	**Raymond James Stadium**	Tampa, Fla.	1998	**65,657**	Grass
Washington Redskins	**FedEx Field**	Raljon, Md.	1997	**86,484**	Grass

National Football League (Cont.)

Rank by Capacity

AFC		NFC	
NY Jets	80,062	Washington	86,484
Kansas City	79,451	NY Giants	80,062
Denver	76,125	Arizona	73,273
Miami	75,540	Carolina	73,500
Buffalo	73,967	Green Bay	72,515
Cleveland	73,200	Atlanta	71,228
Jacksonville	73,000	San Francisco	69,400
San Diego	71,000	Philadelphia	68,532
Houston	69,500	New Orleans	68,395
Baltimore	69,084	Seattle	67,000
Tennessee	68,798	St. Louis	66,000
New England	68,000	Tampa Bay	65,657
Cincinnati	65,352	Dallas	65,639
Pittsburgh	64,450	Detroit	65,000
Oakland	63,132	Minnesota	64,121
Indianapolis	56,127	Chicago	63,000

Rank by Age

AFC		NFC	
Oakland	1966	Chicago	1924
San Diego	1967	Green Bay	1957
Kansas City	1972	Arizona	1958
Buffalo	1973	San Francisco	1960
NY Jets	1976	Dallas	1971
Indianapolis	1984	New Orleans	1975
Miami	1987	NY Giants	1976
Jacksonville	1995	Minnesota	1982
Baltimore	1998	Atlanta	1992
Cleveland	1999	St. Louis	1995
Tennessee	1999	Carolina	1996
Cincinnati	2000	Washington	1997
Denver	2001	Tampa Bay	1998
Pittsburgh	2001	Seattle	2002
New England	2002	Detroit	2002
Houston	2002	Philadelphia	2003

Notes: Chicago's Soldier Field was rebuilt and Green Bay's Lambeau Field was renovated in 2003.

2002 NFL Attendance

Official overall paid attendance in the NFL for the 2002 season was 16,979,369 for an average per game crowd of 66,326 over 256 games. Teams in each conference are ranked by attendance over eight home games. Rank column indicates rank in entire league. Numbers in parentheses indicate conference rank in 2001. Note that Houston was an expansion team in 2002.

AFC

		Attendance	Rank	Average
1	N.Y. Jets (1)	628,812	3	78,601
2	Kansas City (2)	625,503	4	78,187
3	Denver (3)	604,904	5	75,613
4	Cleveland (5)	586,294	6	73,286
5	Miami (4)	585,523	7	73,190
6	Houston	559,322	9	69,915
7	Baltimore (6)	554,724	10	69,340
8	Tennessee (7)	550,437	12	68,804
9	Buffalo (8)	547,702	13	68,462
10	New England (12)	547,488	14	68,436
11	San Diego (13)	494,973	24	61,871
12	Pittsburgh (9)	490,274	25	61,284
13	Oakland (14)	485,092	28	60,636
14	Indianapolis (16)	453,357	29	56,669
15	Jacksonville (10)	450,216	30	56,277
16	Cincinnati (15)	422,235	31	52,779
	TOTAL	8,586,856	—	67,085

NFC

		Attendance	Rank	Average
1	Washington (2)	643,950	1	80,493
2	NY Giants (1)	629,211	2	78,651
3	Carolina (4)	572,015	8	71,501
4	Atlanta (14)	550,974	11	66,871
5	New Orleans (5)	542,796	15	67,849
6	San Francisco (6)	541,593	16	67,699
7	St. Louis (8)	528,498	17	66,062
8	Tampa Bay (10)	525,029	18	65,628
9	Philadelphia (9)	523,535	19	65,441
10	Minnesota (11)	512,517	20	64,064
11	Green Bay (13)	508,788	21	63,598
12	Dallas (12)	504,717	22	63,089
13	Seattle (11)	504,621	23	63,077
14	Detroit (3)	489,742	26	61,217
15	Chicago (7)	487,255	27	60,906
16	Arizona (15)	327,272	32	40,909
	TOTAL	8,392,513	—	65,567

Home Fields

Listed below are the principal home fields used through the years by current NFL teams. The largest capacity of each stadium is noted in the right-hand column. All-America Football Conference stadiums (1946-49) are included for Cleveland and San Francisco.

AFC

Baltimore Ravens

1996–97	Memorial Stadium	65,000
1998–	Ravens Stadium	69,084

Buffalo Bills

1960–72	War Memorial Stadium	45,748
1973–	Ralph Wilson Stadium (Orchard Park, NY)	73,967
	(1973 capacity—80,020)	

Cincinnati Bengals

1968–69	Nippert Stadium (Univ. of Cincinnati)	26,500
1970–99	Cinergy Field	60,389
	(1970 capacity—56,200)	
2000–	Paul Brown Stadium	65,352

Cleveland Browns

1946–95	Cleveland Stadium	78,512
	(1946 capacity—85,703)	
1999–	Cleveland Browns Stadium	73,200

Denver Broncos

1960–	Mile High Stadium	76,123
2000	(1960 capacity—34,000)	
2001–	INVESCO Field at Mile High	76,125

Houston Texans

2002–	Reliant Stadium	69,500

Indianapolis Colts

1953–83	Memorial Stadium (Baltimore)	60,020
1984–	RCA Dome (Indianapolis)	56,127
	(1984 capacity—60,127)	

Jacksonville Jaguars

1995–	ALLTEL Stadium	.73,000

Kansas City Chiefs

1960–62	Cotton Bowl (Dallas)	.72,000
1963–71	Municipal Stadium (Kansas City)	.47,000
1972–	Arrowhead Stadium	.79,451
	(1972 capacity—78,097)	

Miami Dolphins

1966–86	Orange Bowl	.75,206
1987–	Pro Player Stadium	.75,540

New England Patriots

1960–62	Nickerson Field (Boston Univ.)	.17,369
1963–68	Fenway Park	.33,379
1969	Alumni Stadium (Boston College)	.26,000
1970	Harvard Stadium	.37,300
1971-2001	Foxboro Stadium	.60,292
	(1971 capacity—61,114)	
2002–	Gillette Stadium	.68,000

New York Jets

1960–63	Polo Grounds	.55,987
1964–83	Shea Stadium	.60,372
1984–	Giants Stadium (E. Rutherford, NJ)	.80,062

Oakland Raiders

1960	Kesar Stadium (San Francisco)	.59,636
1961	Candlestick Park	.42,500
1962–65	Frank Youell Field (Oakland)	.20,000
1966–81	Oakland-Alameda County Coliseum	.54,587
1982–94	Memorial Coliseum (Los Angeles)	.67,800
1995–	Network Associates Coliseum	.63,132

Pittsburgh Steelers

1933–57	Forbes Field	.35,000
1958–63	Forbes Field	.35,000
	& Pitt Stadium	.54,500
1964–69	Pitt Stadium	.54,500
1970– 2000	Three Rivers Stadium	.59,600
	(1970 capacity—49,000)	
2001–	Heinz Field	.64,450

San Diego Chargers

1960	Memorial Coliseum (Los Angeles)	.92,604
1961–66	Balboa Stadium (San Diego)	.34,000
1967–	Qualcomm Stadium	.71,000
	(1967 capacity—54,000)	

Tennessee Titans

1960–64	Jeppesen Stadium (Houston)	.23,500
1965–67	Rice Stadium (Rice Univ.)	.70,000
1968–96	Astrodome	.59,969
1997	Liberty Bowl (Memphis)	.62,380
1998	Vanderbilt Stadium (Nashville)	.41,600
1999–	The Coliseum (Nashville)	.68,798

Ballpark Name Changes: BALTIMORE—PSInet Stadium originally named Ravens Stadium (1998-99) and renamed **Ravens Stadium** in 2002; BUFFALO—**Ralph Wilson Stadium** originally Rich Stadium (1973-99); CINCINNATI—**Cinergy Field** originally Riverfront Stadium (1970-96); CLEVELAND—**Cleveland Stadium** originally Municipal Stadium (1932-74); DENVER—**Mile High Stadium** originally Bears Stadium (1948-66); INDIANAPOLIS—**RCA Dome** originally Hoosier Dome (1984-94); JACKSONVILLE—**ALLTEL Stadium** originally Jacksonville Municipal Stadium (1995-97); MIAMI—**Pro Player Stadium** originally Joe Robbie Stadium (1987-96); NEW ENGLAND—**Foxboro Stadium** originally Schaefer Stadium (1971-82), then Sullivan Stadium (1983-89); **Gillette Stadium** originally CMGI Field; OAKLAND—**Network Associates Coliseum** originally Oakland Alameda Coliseum (1995-99); SAN DIEGO—**Qualcomm Stadium** originally San Diego Stadium (1967-81) then San Diego/Jack Murphy Stadium (1981-96); TENNESSEE—**The Coliseum** originally Adelphia Coliseum (1999-2001).

NFC

Arizona Cardinals

1920–21	Normal Field (Chicago)	.7,500
1922–25	Comiskey Park	.28,000
1926–28	Normal Field	.7,500
1929–59	Comiskey Park	.52,000
1960–65	Busch Stadium (St. Louis)	.34,000
1966–87	Busch Memorial Stadium	.54,392
1988–	Sun Devil Stadium (Tempe, AZ)	.73,273

Atlanta Falcons

1966-91	Atlanta-Fulton County Stadium	.59,643
1992–	Georgia Dome	.71,228

Carolina Panthers

1995	Memorial Stadium (Clemson, SC)	.81,473
1996–	Ericsson Stadium	.73,500

Chicago Bears

1920	Staley Field (Decatur, IL)	—
1921–70	Wrigley Field (Chicago)	.37,741
1971–2001	Soldier Field	.66,944
	(1971 capacity—55,049)	
2002	Memorial Stadium (Champaign, IL)	.69,249
2003–	Soldier Field	.63,000

Dallas Cowboys

1960–70	Cotton Bowl	.72,132
1971–	Texas Stadium (Irving, TX)	.65,639
	(1971 capacity—65,101)	

Detroit Lions

1930–33	Spartan Stadium (Portsmouth, OH)	.8,200
1934–37	Univ. of Detroit Stadium	.25,000
1938–74	Tiger Stadium	.54,468
1975-2001	Pontiac Silverdome	.80,311
	(1975 capacity—80,638)	
2002–	Ford Field	.65,000

Green Bay Packers

1921–22	Hagemeister Brewery Park	—
1923–24	Bellevue Park	—
1925–56	City Stadium I	.24,800
1957–	Lambeau Field	.72,515
	(1957 capacity—32,150)	
	(2002 capacity—62,500)	

Note: The Packers played games in Milwaukee from 1933-94: at Borchert Field, State Fair Park and Marquette Stadium (1933-52), and County Stadium (1953-94).

Minnesota Vikings

1961–81	Metropolitan Stadium (Bloomington)	.48,446
1982–	HHH Metrodome (Minneapolis)	.64,121
	(1982 capacity—62,220)	

New Orleans Saints

1967–74	Tulane Stadium	.80,997
1975–	Louisiana Superdome	.68,395
	(1975 capacity—74,472)	

New York Giants

1925–55	Polo Grounds II	.55,200
1956–73	Yankee Stadium I	.63,800
1973–74	Yale Bowl (New Haven, CT)	.70,896
1975	Shea Stadium	.60,372
1976–	Giants Stadium (E. Rutherford, NJ)	.80,062
	(1976 capacity—76,800)	

National Football League (Cont.)

Philadelphia Eagles

1933–35	Baker Bowl	.18,800
1936–39	Municipal Stadium	.73,702
1940	Shibe Park	.33,608
1941	Municipal Stadium	.73,702
1942	Shibe Park	.33,608
1943	Forbes Field (Pittsburgh)	.34,528
1944–57	Shibe Park	.33,608
1958–70	Franklin Field (Univ. of Penn.)	.60,546
1971–2002	Veterans Stadium	.65,352
2003–	Lincoln Financial Field	.68,532

St. Louis Rams

1937–42	Municipal Stadium (Cleveland)	.85,703
1937	League Park (Cleveland)	—
1938	Shaw Stadium (Cleveland)	—
1937	League Park	—
1943	Suspended operations for one year.	
1944–45	Municipal Stadium	.85,703
1946–79	Memorial Coliseum (Los Angeles)	.92,604
1980–94	Anaheim Stadium	.69,008
1995	Busch Stadium	.60,000
1995–	Edward Jones Dome	.66,000

San Francisco 49ers

1946–70	Kezar Stadium	.59,636
1971–	Candlestick Park	.69,400
	(1971 capacity—61,246)	

Seattle Seahawks

1976–94	Kingdome	.66,000
1994	Kingdome	.66,400
	&–Husky Stadium	.72,500
1995–99	Kingdome	.66,400
2000-01	Husky Stadium	.72,500
2002–	Seahawks Stadium	.67,000

Tampa Bay Buccaneers

1976–97	Houlihan's Stadium	.74,300
1998–	Raymond James Stadium	.65,657

Washington Redskins

1932	Braves Field (Boston)	.40,000
1933–36	Fenway Park	.27,000
1937–60	Griffith Stadium (Washington, DC)	.35,000
1961–97	RFK Stadium	.56,454
1997–	FedEx Field (Raljon, MD)	.86,484

Ballpark Name Changes: ATLANTA—**Atlanta-Fulton County Stadium** originally Atlanta Stadium (1966-74); CHICAGO—**Wrigley Field** originally Cubs Park (1916-25); DETROIT—**Tiger Stadium** originally Navin Field (1912-37), then Briggs Stadium (1938-60), also, **Pontiac Silverdome** originally Pontiac Metropolitan Stadium (1975); GREEN BAY—**Lambeau Field** originally City Stadium II (1957-64); PHILADELPHIA—**Shibe Park** renamed Connie Mack Stadium in 1953; ST. LOUIS—**Busch Memorial Stadium** renamed Busch Stadium in 1983, **Edward Jones Dome** originally Trans World Dome (1995-99), then The Dome at America's Center (2000-01); SAN FRANCISCO—**Candlestick Park** originally Candlestick Park (1960-94), then 3Com Park (1995-2001); TAMPA BAY—**Raymond James Stadium** originally Tampa Stadium (1976-96), then **Houlihan's Stadium** (1996-98); WASHINGTON—**RFK Stadium** originally D.C. Stadium (1961-68), also, **FedEx Field** originally Jack Kent Cooke Stadium (1997-99).

NATIONAL HOCKEY LEAGUE

Western Conference

		Location	Built	Capacity
Anaheim, Mighty Ducks of	**Arrowhead Pond**	Anaheim, Calif.	1993	**17,174**
Calgary Flames	**Pengrowth Saddledome**	Calgary, Alb.	1983	**17,135**
Chicago Blackhawks	**United Center**	Chicago, Ill.	1994	**20,500**
Colorado Avalanche	**Pepsi Center**	Denver, Colo.	1999	**18,007**
Columbus Blue Jackets	**Nationwide Arena**	Columbus, Ohio	2000	**18,136**
Dallas Stars	**American Airlines Center**	Dallas, Texas	2001	**18,532**
Detroit Red Wings	**Joe Louis Arena**	Detroit, Mich.	1979	**20,058**
Edmonton Oilers	**Skyreach Centre**	Edmonton, Alb.	1974	**16,839**
Los Angeles Kings	**Staples Center**	Los Angeles, Calif.	1999	**18,118**
Minnesota Wild	**Xcel Energy Center**	St. Paul, Minn.	2000	**18,064**
Nashville Predators	**Gaylord Entertainment Center**	Nashville, Tenn.	1994	**17,113**
Phoenix Coyotes	**Glendale Arena**	Glendale, Ariz.	2003	**17,500**
St. Louis Blues	**Savvis Center**	St. Louis, Mo.	1994	**19,022**
San Jose Sharks	**Compaq Center at San Jose**	San Jose, Calif.	1993	**17,496**
Vancouver Canucks	**General Motors Place**	Vancouver, B.C.	1995	**18,422**

Eastern Conference

		Location	Built	Capacity
Atlanta Thrashers	**Philips Arena**	Atlanta, Ga.	1999	**18,545**
Boston Bruins	**FleetCenter**	Boston, Mass.	1995	**17,565**
Buffalo Sabres	**HSBC Arena**	Buffalo, N.Y.	1996	**18,690**
Carolina Hurricanes	**RBC Center**	Raleigh, N.C.	1999	**18,730**
Florida Panthers	**Office Depot Center**	Sunrise, Fla.	1998	**19,250**
Montreal Canadiens	**Bell Centre**	Montreal, Que.	1996	**21,273**
New Jersey Devils	**Continental Airlines Arena**	E. Rutherford, N.J.	1981	**19,040**
New York Islanders	**Nassau Veterans' Mem. Coliseum**	Uniondale, N.Y.	1972	**16,234**
New York Rangers	**Madison Square Garden**	New York, N.Y.	1968	**18,200**
Ottawa Senators	**Corel Centre**	Kanata, Ont.	1996	**18,500**
Philadelphia Flyers	**Wachovia Center**	Philadelphia, Penn.	1996	**18,523**
Pittsburgh Penguins	**Mellon Arena**	Pittsburgh, Penn.	1961	**16,958**
Tampa Bay Lightning	**St. Pete Times Forum**	Tampa Bay, Fla.	1996	**19,758**
Toronto Maple Leafs	**Air Canada Centre**	Toronto, Ont.	1999	**18,819**
Washington Capitals	**MCI Center**	Washington, D.C.	1997	**18,672**

Rank by Capacity

Western		Eastern	
Chicago	.20,500	Montreal	.21,273
Detroit	.20,058	Tampa Bay	.19,758
St. Louis	.19,022	Florida	.19,250
Dallas	.18,532	New Jersey	.19,040
Vancouver	.18,422	Toronto	.18,819
Columbus	.18,136	Carolina	.18,730
Los Angeles	.18,118	Buffalo	.18,690
Minnesota	.18,064	Washington	.18,672
Colorado	.18,007	Atlanta	.18,545
Phoenix	.17,500	Philadelphia	.18,523
San Jose	.17,496	Ottawa	.18,500
Anaheim	.17,174	NY Rangers	.18,200
Calgary	.17,135	Boston	.17,565
Nashville	.17,113	Pittsburgh	.16,958
Edmonton	.16,839	NY Islanders	.16,234

Rank by Age

Western		Eastern	
Edmonton	.1974	Pittsburgh	.1961
Detroit	.1979	NY Rangers	.1968
Calgary	.1983	NY Islanders	.1972
Anaheim	.1993	New Jersey	.1981
San Jose	.1993	Boston	.1995
Chicago	.1994	Montreal	.1996
St. Louis	.1994	Ottawa	.1996
Nashville	.1994	Buffalo	.1996
Vancouver	.1995	Philadelphia	.1996
Colorado	.1999	Tampa Bay	.1996
Los Angeles	.1999	Washington	.1997
Columbus	.2000	Florida	.1998
Minnesota	.2000	Toronto	.1999
Dallas	.2001	Carolina	.1999
Phoenix	.2003	Atlanta	.1999

2002-03 NHL Attendance

Official overall paid attendance for the 2002-03 season according to the NHL accounting office was 20,390,908 (paid tickets) for an average per game crowd of 16,578 over 1,230 games. Teams in each conference are ranked by attendance over 41 home games. Rank column refers to rank in entire league. Numbers in parentheses indicate conference rank in 2001-02.

Western Conference

		Attendance	Rank	Average
1	Detroit (1)	.822,378	2	20,058
2	St. Louis (2)	.761,388	5	18,570
3	Dallas (3)	.759,812	6	18,532
4	Minnesota (4)	.758,536	7	18,500
5	Vancouver (7)	.754,247	8	18,396
6	Colorado (6)	.738,287	10	18,007
7	Columbus (5)	.727,522	11	17,744
8	Los Angeles (9)	.720,366	12	17,569
9	San Jose (8)	.711,386	13	17,350
10	Edmonton (10)	.682,960	15	16,657
11	Calgary (11)	.665,808	17	16,239
12	Chicago (12)	.606,580	24	14,794
13	Anaheim (15)	.573,524	26	13,988
14	Phoenix (14)	.542,404	29	13,229
15	Nashville (13)	.542,367	30	13,228
	TOTAL	.10,367,565	—	16,858

Eastern Conference

		Attendance	Rank	Average
1	Montreal (1)	.847,586	1	20,672
2	Philadelphia (2)	.792,333	3	19,325
3	Toronto (3)	.788,847	4	19,240
4	NY Rangers (4)	.744,068	9	18,148
5	Ottawa (9)	.705,124	14	17,198
6	Tampa Bay (12)	.678,354	16	16,545
7	Washington (9)	.647,272	18	15,787
8	Carolina (14)	.642,973	19	15,682
9	Florida (13)	.632,552	20	15,428
10	Boston (10)	.616,197	21	15,029
11	NY Islanders (15)	.612,154	22	14,930
12	New Jersey (8)	.609,218	23	14,858
13	Pittsburgh (7)	.604,728	25	14,749
14	Atlanta (11)	.552,535	27	13,476
15	Buffalo (5)	.549,402	28	13,735
	TOTAL	.10,023,343	—	16,298

Home Ice

Listed below are the principal home buildings used through the years by current NHL teams. The largest capacity of each arena is noted in the right hand column. World Hockey Association arenas (1972-79) are included for Edmonton, Hartford (now Carolina), Quebec (now Colorado) and Winnipeg (now Phoenix).

Western Conference

Anaheim, Mighty Ducks of

1993–	Arrowhead Pond	.17,174

Calgary Flames

1972–80	The Omni (Atlanta)	.15,278
1980–83	Calgary Corral	.7,424
1983–	Pengrowth Saddledome	.17,135
	(1983 capacity—16,674)	

Chicago Blackhawks

1926–29	Chicago Coliseum	.5,000
1929–94	Chicago Stadium	.17,317
1994–	United Center	.20,500

Colorado Avalanche

1972–95	Le Colisee de Quebec	.15,399
1995–99	McNichols Arena (Denver)	.16,061
1999–	Pepsi Center	.18,007

Columbus Blue Jackets

2000–	Nationwide Arena	.18,136

Dallas Stars

1967–93	Met Center (Bloomington, MN)	.15,174
1993–2000	Reunion Arena (Dallas)	.17,001
2001–	American Airlines Center	.18,532

Detroit Red Wings

1926–27	Border Cities Arena (Windsor, Ont.)	.3,200
1927–79	Olympia Stadium (Detroit)	.16,700
1979–	Joe Louis Arena	.20,058

Edmonton Oilers

1972–74	Edmonton Gardens	.7,200
1974–	Skyreach Centre	.16,839
	(1974 capacity—15,513)	

Los Angeles Kings

1967–99	Great Western Forum (Inglewood)	.16,005
	(1967 capacity—15,651)	
1999–	Staples Center	.18,118

Note: The Kings played 17 games at Long Beach Sports Arena and LA Sports Arena at the start of the 1967-68 season.

National Hockey League (Cont.)

Minnesota Wild
2000–	Xcel Energy Center (St. Paul)	18,064

Nashville Predators
1998–	Gaylord Entertainment Center	17,113

Phoenix Coyotes
1972–96	Winnipeg Arena	15,393
	(1972 capacity—10,177)	
1996–2002	America West (Phoenix)	16,210
2003–	Glendale Arena (Glendale, Ariz.)	17,500

St. Louis Blues
1967–94	St. Louis Arena	17,188
1994–	Savvis Center	19,022

San Jose Sharks
1991–93	Cow Palace (Daly City, CA)	11,100
1993–	Compaq Center at San Jose	17,496

Vancouver Canucks
1970–95	Pacific Coliseum	16,150
1995–	General Motors Place	18,422

Building Name Changes: CALGARY—**Pengrowth Saddledome** formerly named Canadian Airlines Saddledome (1996-2000) which was originally Olympic Saddledome (1983-95); DALLAS—**Met Center** in Minneapolis originally Metropolitan Sports Center (1967-82); EDMONTON—**Skyreach Centre** formerly named Edmonton Coliseum (1995-99) which was originally Northlands Coliseum (1974-94); LOS ANGELES—**Great Western Forum** originally The Forum (1967-88); NASHVILLE—**Gaylord Entertainment Center** originally Nashville Arena (1994-99); ST. LOUIS—**Savvis Center** originally Kiel Center (1994-2000), **St. Louis Arena** renamed The Checkerdome in 1977, then St. Louis Arena again in 1982; SAN JOSE—**Compaq Center at San Jose** originally San Jose Arena (1993-2000).

Eastern Conference

Atlanta Thrashers
1999–	Philips Arena	18,545

Boston Bruins
1924–28	Boston Arena	6,200
1928–95	Boston Garden	14,448
1995–	FleetCenter	17,565

Buffalo Sabres
1970–96	Memorial Auditorium (The Aud)	16,284
	(1970 capacity—10,429)	
1996–	HSBC Arena	18,690

Carolina Hurricanes
1972–73	Boston Garden	14,442
1973–74	Boston Garden (regular season)	14,442
	West Springfield (MA) Big E (playoffs)	5,513
1974–75	West Springfield Big E	5,513
	& Hartford (CT) Civic Center	10,507
1975–77	Hartford Civic Center	10,507
1977–78	Hartford Civic Center	10,507
	& Springfield (MA) Civic Center	7,725
1978–79	Springfield Civic Center	7,725
1979–80	Springfield Civic Center	7,725
	& Hartford Civic Center II	14,250
1980–97	Hartford Civic Center II	15,635
1997–99	Greensboro Coliseum	21,500
1999–	RBC Center	18,730

Note: The Hartford Civic Center roof caved in January 1978, forcing the Whalers to move their home games to Springfield, MA for two years.

Florida Panthers
1993–98	Miami Arena	14,703
1998–	Office Depot Center	19,250

Montreal Canadiens
1910–21	Jubilee Arena	3,200
1913–18	Montreal Arena (Westmount)	6,000
1918–26	Mount Royal Arena	6,750
1926–68	Montreal Forum I	15,500
1968–96	Montreal Forum II	17,959
1996–	Bell Centre	21,273

New Jersey Devils
1974–76	Kemper Arena (Kansas City)	16,300
1976–82	McNichols Arena (Denver)	15,900
1982–	Continental Airlines Arena	19,040
	(1982 capacity—19,023)	

New York Islanders
1972–	Nassau Veterans' Mem. Coliseum	16,234
	(1972 capacity—14,500)	

New York Rangers
1925–68	Madison Square Garden III	15,925
1968–	Madison Square Garden IV	18,200
	(1968 capacity—17,250)	

Ottawa Senators
1992–96	Ottawa Civic Center	10,755
1996–	Corel Centre (Kanata)	18,500

Philadelphia Flyers
1967–96	CoreStates Spectrum	17,380
	(1967 capacity—14,558)	
1996–	Wachovia Center	18,523

Pittsburgh Penguins
1967–	Mellon Arena	16,958
	(1967 capacity—12,508)	

Tampa Bay Lightning
1992–93	Expo Hall (Tampa)	10,500
1993–96	ThunderDome (St. Petersburg)	26,000
1996–	St. Pete Times Forum	19,758

Toronto Maple Leafs
1917–31	Mutual Street Arena	8,000
1931–99	Maple Leaf Gardens	15,746
	(1931 capacity—13,542)	
1999–	Air Canada Centre	18,819

Washington Capitals
1974–97	USAir Arena (Landover, MD)	18,130
1997–	MCI Center	18,672

Building Name Changes: BUFFALO—**HSBC Arena** originally Marine Midland Arena (1996-99); CALGARY—**Pengrowth Saddledome** originally Canadian Airlines Arena (1983-2000); CAROLINA—**RBC Center** originally Raleigh Entertainment and Sports Arena (1999-2002); DALLAS—**American Airlines Center** originally Reunion Arena (1993-2000); FLORIDA—**Office Depot Center** originally National Car Rental Center (1998-2002); MONTREAL—**Bell Centre** originally Molson Centre (1996-2002); NEW JERSEY—**Continental Airlines Arena** originally Meadowlands Arena (1982-96); PHILADELPHIA—**Wachovia Center** originally the CoreStates Center (1996-98), then First Union Center (1998-2003) and **CoreStates Spectrum** originally The Spectrum (1967-94); PITTSBURGH—**Mellon Arena** originally Civic Arena (1967-2000); TAMPA BAY—**St. Pete Times Forum** originally Ice Palace (1996-2002); WASHINGTON—**USAir Arena** originally Capital Centre (1974-93).

AUTO RACING

Formula One, NASCAR Winston Cup, CART and Indy Racing League (IRL) racing circuits. Qualifying records accurate as of Sept. 30, 2003. Capacity figures for NASCAR, CART and IRL tracks are approximate and pertain to grandstand seating only. Standing room and hillside terrain seating featured at most road courses are not included.

CART

	Location	Miles	Qual.mph record	Set by	Seats
Burke Lakefront Airport	Cleveland, Ohio	2.106**	134.385	Jimmy Vasser (1998)	36,000
California Speedway	Fontana, Calif.	2.029	241.428†	Gil de Ferran (2000)	122,000
Concord Pacific Place	Vancouver, B.C.	1.781**	106.260	Cristiano da Matta (2002)	65,000
EuroSpeedway	Lausitz, Germany	2.023	153.553	Kenny Brack (2001)	120,000
Exhibition Place	Toronto, Ont.	1.755**	110.565	Gil de Ferran (1999)	60,000
Fundidora Park	Monterrey, Mexico	2.104*	101.076	Sebastien Bourdais (2003)	61,871
Circuit Gilles Villeneuve	Montreal, Que.	2.709*	123.512	Christiano da Matta (2002)	
Grand Prix of the Americas	Miami, Fla.	1.387**	81.503	Tony Kanaan (2002)	
Grand Prix of Denver	Denver, Colo.	1.647**	96.093	Bruno Junqueira (2002)	
Mazda Raceway at Laguna Seca	Monterey, Calif.	2.238*	118.969	Helio Castroneves (2000)	8,000
Long Beach	Long Beach, Calif.	1.968**	104.969	Gil de Ferran (2000)	63,000
Mexico Gran Premio	Mexico City, Mexico	2.75*	116.703	Bruno Junqueira (2002)	
Mid-Ohio Sports Car Course	Lexington, Ohio	2.258*	124.394	Dario Franchitti (1999) & Gil de Ferran (2000)	6,000
The Milwaukee Mile	West Allis, Wisc.	1.032	185.500	Patrick Carpentier (1998)	36,800
Portland International Raceway	Portland, Ore.	1.969*	122.768	Helio Castroneves (2000)	50,000
Road America	Elkhart Lake, Wisc.	4.048*	145.924	Dario Franchitti (2000)	10,000
Rockingham Motor Speedway	Corby, England	1.5	210.859	Patrick Carpentier (2001)	27,500
Surfers Paradise	Queensland, Australia	2.795**	111.547	Cristiano da Matta (2002)	55,000

*Road courses (not ovals). **Temporary street circuits. †Indicates world closed-course record for auto racing.

Indy Racing League

Founded by Indianapolis Motor Speedway president Tony George, the Indy Racing League competes with CART and fielded 16 races, anchored by the Indianapolis 500, in 2003. Note that the track records listed are for normally-aspirated IRL cars unless otherwise noted by an asterisk.

	Location	Miles	Qual.mph Record	Set by	Seats
California Speedway	Fontana, Calif.	2.0	221.422	Eddie Cheever Jr. (2002)	92,109
Chicagoland Speedway	Joliet, Ill.	1.5	222.137	Robbie Buhl (2001)	75,000
Gateway International Raceway	Madison, Ill.	1.25	175.965	Helio Castroneves (2003)	60,000
Homestead-Miami Speedway	Homestead, Fla.	1.5	203.560	Tony Kanaan (2003)	65,000
Indianapolis Motor Speedway	Indianapolis, Ind.	2.5	237.498	Arie Luyendyk (1996)*	250,000+
Kansas Speedway	Kansas City, Kan.	1.5	218.085	Scott Dixon (2003)	75,000
Kentucky Speedway	Sparta, Ky.	1.5	219.191	Scott Goodyear (2000)	70,000
Michigan Intl. Speedway	Brooklyn, Mich.	2.0	222.458	Tomas Scheckter (2003)	136,373
Nashville Superspeedway	Nashville, Tenn.	1.33	206.211	Scott Dixon (2003)	50,000
Nazareth Speedway	Nazareth, Penn.	1.0	172.778	Gil de Ferran (2002)	44,044
Phoenix International Raceway	Phoenix, Ariz.	1.0	183.599	Arie Luyendyk (1996)*	78,450
Pikes Peak Int'l. Raceway	Fountain, Colo.	1.0	179.874	Greg Ray (2000)	42,787
Richmond International Raceway	Richmond, Va.	0.75	168.138	Scott Dixon (2003)	95,920
Texas Motor Speedway	Fort Worth, Texas	1.5	225.979	Billy Boat (1998)	154,861
Twin Ring Motegi	Motegi, Japan	1.549	206.996	Scott Dixon (2003)	50,000

NASCAR

	Location	Miles	Qual.mph Record	Set by	Seats
Atlanta Motor Speedway	Hampton, Ga.	1.54	197.478	Geoff Bodine (1997)	124,000
Bristol Motor Speedway	Bristol, Tenn.	0.533	128.709	Ryan Newman (2003)	147,000
California Speedway	Fontana, Calif.	2.0	187.432	Ryan Newman (2002)	92,000
Chicagoland Speedway	Joliet, Ill.	1.5	184.786	Tony Stewart (2003)	75,000
Darlington International Raceway	Darlington, S.C.	1.366	173.797	Ward Burton (1996)	65,000
Daytona International Speedway	Daytona Beach, Fla.	2.5	210.364	Bill Elliott (1987)	168,000
Dover International Speedway	Dover, Del.	1.0	159.964	Rusty Wallace (1999)	140,000
Homestead-Miami Speedway	Homestead, Fla.	1.5	156.440	Steve Park (2000)	72,000
Indianapolis Motor Speedway	Indianapolis, Ind.	2.5	184.343	Kevin Harvick (2003)	250,000+
Infineon Raceway	Sonoma, Calif.	1.949*	99.309	Rusty Wallace (2000)	42,500
Kansas Speedway	Kansas City, Kan.	1.5	177.924	Dale Earnhardt Jr. (2002)	75,000
Las Vegas Motor Speedway	Las Vegas, Nev.	1.5	173.016	Bobby Labonte (2003)	126,000
Lowe's Motor Speedway	Concord, N.C.	1.5	186.464	Jimmie Johnson (2002)	167,000
Martinsville Speedway	Martinsville, Va.	0.526	95.371	Tony Stewart (2000)	91,000
Michigan Speedway	Brooklyn, Mich.	2.0	191.149	Dale Earnhardt Jr. (2000)	136,384
New Hampshire Int'l Speedway	Loudon, N.H.	1.058	132.240	Ryan Newman (2002)	91,000
North Carolina Speedway	Rockingham, N.C.	1.017	158.035	Rusty Wallace (2000)	60,113
Phoenix International Raceway	Phoenix, Ariz.	1.0	134.178	Rusty Wallace (2000)	76,812
Pocono Raceway	Long Pond, Penn.	2.5	172.391	Tony Stewart (2000)	77,000

Auto Racing (Cont.)

	Location	Miles	Qual.mph Record	Set by	Seats
Richmond International Raceway	Richmond, Va.	0.75	127.389	Ward Burton (2002)	100,000+
Talladega Superspeedway	Talladega, Ala.	2.66	212.809	Bill Elliott (1987)	143,000
Texas Motor Speedway	Ft. Worth, Texas	1.5	194.224	Bill Elliott (2002)	154,861
Watkins Glen International	Watkins Glen, N.Y.	2.45*	124.580	Jeff Gordon (2003)	40,000

*Road courses (not ovals).

Note: Richmond sells reserved seats only (no infield) for Winston Cup races.

Formula One

Race track capacity figures unavailable.

Grand Prix		Miles	Qual.mph Record	Set by
Australian	**Albert Park** (Melbourne)	3.295	137.883	Rubens Barrichello (2002)
Austrian	**A1-Ring** (Zeltwig, Austria)	2.684	141.595	Rubens Barrichello (2002)
Belgian	**Spa-Francorchamps**	4.333	143.418	Mika Hakkinen (1998)
Brazilian	**Interlagos** (Sao Paulo)	2.684	193.747	Rubens Barrichello (2003)
British	**Silverstone** (Towcester)	3.194	148.043	Nigel Mansell (1992)
Canadian	**Circuit Gilles Villeneuve** (Montreal)	2.747	133.941	Juan Montoya (2002)
European	**Nürburgring** (Nürburg, Germany)	2.822	135.959	Michael Schumacher (2001)
French	**Magny Cours** (Nevers)	2.641	159.757	Juan Montoya (2002)
German	**Hockenheim** (Germany)	2.796	204.450	Michael Schumacher (2002)
Hungarian	**Hungaroring** (Budapest)	2.468	120.984	Rubens Barrichello (2002)
Italian	**Autodromo Nazionale di Monza** (Milan)	3.585	159.951	Ayrton Senna (1991)
Japanese	**Suzuka** (Nagoya)	3.644	138.515	Gerhard Berger (1991)
Malaysian	**Sepang** (Kuala Lumpur)	3.444	130.218	Michael Schumacher (2001)
Monaco	**Monte Carlo** (Monaco)	2.082	141.595	Rubens Barrichello (2002)
San Marino	**Autodromo Enzo e Dino Ferrari** (Imola, Italy)	3.063	138.265	Ayrton Senna (1994)
Spanish	**Catalunya** (Barcelona)	2.937	138.250	Michael Schumacher (2002)
United States	**Indianapolis Motor Speedway**	2.606	126.355	Michael Schumacher (2000)

SOCCER

World's Premier Soccer Stadiums

(Listed alphabetically by city)

Stadium	Location	Seats	Stadium	Location	Seats
Spiros Louis	Athens, Greece	74,443	Estadio Azteca	Mexico City, Mexico	106,000
Eden Park	Auckland, New Zealand	50,000	Meazza (San Siro)	Milan, Italy	85,700
Nou Camp	Barcelona, Spain	98,000	Centenario	Montevideo, Uruguay	73,609
Workers'	Beijing, China	72,000	Luzhniki Stadion	Moscow, Russia	80,840
Olympiastadion	Berlin, Germany	76,243	Olympiastadion	Munich, Germany	63,000
Népstadion	Budapest, Hungary	65,000	San Paolo	Naples, Italy	78,210
Antonio Liberti	Buenos Aires, Argentina	76,689	Stade de France	Paris, France	80,000
National	Cairo, Egypt	90,000	Rungnado (May Day)	Pyongyang, N. Korea	150,000
Salt Lake	Calcutta, India	120,000	Maracana	Rio de Janeiro, Brazil	122,268
Millennium	Cardiff, Wales	72,500	King Fahd II	Riyadh, Saudi Arabia	79,000
Westfalenstadion	Dortmund, Germany	68,600	Olimpico	Rome, Italy	82,307
Lansdowne Road	Dublin, Ireland	48,000	Nacional	Santiago, Chile	77,000
Celtic Park	Glasgow, Scotland	60,506	Morumbi	Sao Paulo, Brazil	80,000
Hampden Park	Glasgow, Scotland	52,670	Chasmil	Seoul, S. Korea	100,000
FNB Stadium	Johannesburg, S. Africa	90,000	Stadium Australia	Sydney, Australia	80,000
Olympic Stadium	Kiev, Ukraine	83,160	Azadi	Tehran, Iran	100,000
new Estadio da Luz	Lisbon, Portugal	65,000	Delle Alpi	Turin, Italy	69,041
Santiago Bernabeu	Madrid, Spain	87,000	Ernst Happel	Vienna, Austria	47,500
Old Trafford	Manchester, England	67,650	International	Yokohama, Japan	77,000

Major League Soccer

The 10-team MLS is the only U.S. Division I professional outdoor league sanctioned by FIFA and U.S. Soccer. Note that all capacity figures are approximate given the adjustments of football stadium seating to soccer.

Western Conference

	Stadium	Built	Seats	Field
Colorado Rapids	INVESCO Field	2001	17,500	Grass
Dallas Burn	Cotton Bowl	1935	22,528	Grass
Kansas City Wizards	Arrowhead	1972	20,571	Grass
L.A. Galaxy	Home Depot Center	2003	27,000	Grass
San Jose Earthquakes	Spartan	1933	26,000	Grass

Eastern Conference

	Stadium	Built	Seats	Field
Chicago Fire	Soldier Field*	1924	25,000	Grass
Columbus Crew	Columbus Crew	1999	22,555	Grass
D.C. United	RFK	1961	26,169	Grass
Metro Stars (N.Y./N.J.)	Giants	1976	25,576	Grass
N.E. Revolution	Gillette	2002	21,000	Grass

*Chicago played temporarily at North Central College's Cardinal Stadium in Naperville, Ill. and will return to Soldier Field in 2004 following the current renovations.

Horse Racing
Triple Crown race tracks

Race	Racetrack	Seats	Infield
Kentucky Derby . . . . .Churchill Downs		48,500	65,000
Preakness Stakes .Pimlico Race Course		13,047	60,000
Belmont Stakes . . . . . . .Belmont Park		32,941	N/A

Record crowds: Kentucky Derby—163,628 (1974); Preakness—104,454 (2001); Belmont—103,222 (2002).

Note: Belmont Park does not open infield for Belmont Stakes.

Tennis
Grand Slam center courts

Event	Main Stadium	Seats
Australian Open . . . . .Melbourne Park		15,021
French Open . . . . .Stade Roland Garros		16,300
Wimbledon . . . . .Centre Court		13,813
U.S. Open . . . . .Arthur Ashe Stadium		22,547

COLLEGE BASKETBALL
The 50 Largest Arenas

The 50 largest arenas in Division I for the 2003-04 NCAA regular season. Note that (*) indicates part-time home court.

	Seats	Home Team		Seats	Home Team
1 Carrier Dome	**33,000**	Syracuse	26 Herb Kohl Center	**17,142**	Wisconsin
2 Thompson-Boling Arena .	**24,535**	Tennessee	27 Assembly Hall	**16,450**	Illinois
3 Rupp Arena	**23,500**	Kentucky	28 Frank Erwin Center	**16,331**	Texas
4 Marriott Center	**22,700**	BYU	29 Allen Fieldhouse	**16,300**	Kansas
5 Dean Smith Center	**21,750**	N. Carolina	30 Hartford Civic Center . . .	**16,294**	UConn*
6 MCI Center	**20,674**	Georgetown*	31 L.A. Sports Arena	**16,161**	USC
7 The Pyramid	**20,142**	Memphis	32 Carver-Hawkeye Arena . .	**15,500**	Iowa
8 Continental Airlines Arena	**20,049**	Seton Hall	Pepsi Arena	**15,500**	Siena
9 Savvis Center	**20,000**	Saint Louis	34 Bryce Jordan Center	**15,261**	Penn St.
10 The Rose Garden	**19,980**	Portland St.*	35 United Spirit Arena	**15,050**	Texas Tech
11 RBC Center	**19,722**	N.C. State	36 Coleman Coliseum	**15,043**	Alabama
12 Value City Arena	**19,500**	Ohio St.	37 Arena-Auditorium	**15,028**	Wyoming
13 Bud Walton Arena	**19,200**	Arkansas	38 Huntsman Center	**15,000**	Utah
14 Wachovia Center	**19,010**	Villanova*	39 Breslin Events Center . . .	**14,992**	Michigan St.
15 Freedom Hall	**18,865**	Louisville	40 LJVM Coliseum	**14,665**	Wake Forest
16 Bradley Center	**18,717**	Marquette	41 Williams Arena	**14,625**	Minnesota
17 Thomas & Mack Center .	**18,500**	UNLV	42 McKale Center	**14,545**	Arizona
18 Madison Square Garden .	**18,470**	St. John's*	43 Maravich Assembly Ctr .	**14,236**	LSU
19 University Arena (The Pit)	**18,018**	New Mexico	44 Wells Fargo Arena	**14,198**	Arizona St.
20 Alltel Arena	**18,000**	Arkansas-Little Rock	45 Memorial Gym	**14,168**	Vanderbilt
21 Comcast Center	**17,950**	Maryland	46 Mackey Arena	**14,123**	Purdue
22 New Orleans Arena	**17,832**	Tulane*	47 James H. Hilton Coliseum .	**14,092**	Iowa St.
23 Carolina Center	**17,600**	South Carolina	48 WVU Coliseum	**14,000**	West Virginia
24 Allstate Arena	**17,500**	DePaul	49 Crisler Arena	**13,751**	Michigan
25 Assembly Hall	**17,257**	Indiana	50 CSU Convocation Center .	**13,610**	Cleveland St.

Division I Conference Home Courts

NCAA Division I conferences for the 2003-04 season. Teams with home games in more than one arena are noted.

America East

	Home Floor	Seats
Albany . . . . .Rec & Convocation Ctr.		5,000
Binghamton . . . . .West Gym		2,275
Boston University . . . . .Case Gym		1,800
Hartford . . . . .Chase Family Arena		4,475
Maine . . . . .Alfond Arena		5,712
MD-Balt. County . . . . . . .Retriever Activity Center		4,024
New Hampshire . . . . .Lundholm Gym		3,500
Northeastern . . . . .Solomon Court		1,500
Stony Brook . . . . .USB Sports Complex		4,103
Vermont . . . . .Patrick Gym		3,228

Atlantic Coast

	Home Floor	Seats
Clemson . . . . .Littlejohn Coliseum		11,020
Duke . . . . .Cameron Indoor Stadium		9,314
Florida St. . . . .Tallahassee-Leon Cty Civic Center		12,200
Georgia Tech . . . . .Alexander Memorial Stadium		10,000
Maryland . . . . .Comcast Center		17,950
North Carolina . . . . .Dean Smith Center		21,750
N.C. State .RBC Center		19,722
Virginia .University Hall		8,864
Wake Forest . . . . .LJVM Coliseum		14,665

Atlantic Sun

	Home Floor	Seats
Belmont . . . . .Municipal Auditorium		5,000
Campbell .Carter Gym		1,050
Central Fla. . . . . .UCF Arena		5,100
Fla. Atlantic .FAU Gym		5,000
Gardner-Webb . . . . .Paul Porter Arena		5,000
Georgia St. . . . . .GSU Sports Arena		5,500
Jacksonville . . . . .Swisher Gym		1,500
Lipscomb . . . . .Lipscomb U. Arena		5,028
Mercer. . . . . .Porter Gym		1,000
Stetson . . . . .Edmunds Center		5,000
Troy St. .Trojan Arena		3,000

Atlantic 10

	Home Floor	Seats
Dayton . . . . .U. of Dayton Arena		13,266
Duquesne . . . . .Palumbo Center		6,200
Fordham . . . . .Rose Hill Gym		3,470
George Washington . . . . .Smith Center		5,000
La Salle . . . . .Tom Gola Arena		4,000
Massachusetts . . . . .Mullins Center		9,493
Rhode Island . . . . .Ryan Center		7,800
Richmond . . . . .Robins Center		9,171
St. Bonaventure . . . . .Reilly Center		6,000
St. Joseph's-PA . . . . .Alumni Mem. Fieldhouse		3,200
Temple . . . . .Liacouras Center		10,206
Xavier-OH . . . . .Cintas Center		10,200

College Basketball (Cont.)

Big East

	Home Floor	Seats
Boston College	Conte Forum	8,606
Connecticut	Gampel Pavilion	10,027
	& Hartford Civic Center	16,294
Georgetown	MCI Center	20,674
	& McDonough Arena	2,500
Miami-FL	Convocation Center	7,000
Notre Dame	Joyce Center	11,418
Pittsburgh	Petersen Event Center	12,500
Providence	Dunkin Donuts Center	12,993
Rutgers	Louis Brown Athletic Center	9,000
St. John's	Alumni Hall	6,008
	& Madison Square Garden	18,470
Seton Hall	Continental Airlines Arena	20,049
Syracuse	Carrier Dome	33,000
Villanova	The Pavilion	6,500
	& Wachovia Center	19,010
Virginia Tech	Cassell Coliseum	10,052
West Virginia	WVU Coliseum	14,000

Big Sky

	Home Floor	Seats
Eastern Wash	Reese Court	6,000
Idaho St.	Reed Gym	3,600
Montana	Adams Center	7,500
Montana St.	Worthington Arena	7,250
Northern Arizona	Walkup Skydome	7,000
Portland St.	Rose Garden	19,980
	& Stott Center	1,775
Sacramento St.	Hornet Gym	1,500
Weber St.	Dee Events Center	12,000

Big South

	Home Floor	Seats
Birmingham-Southern	Bill Battle Coliseum	2,000
Charleston Southern	CSU Fieldhouse	1,500
Coastal Carolina	Kimbel Gymnasium	1,037
High Point	Millis Center	3,000
Liberty	Vines Center	9,000
NC-Asheville	Justice Center	1,100
	& Asheville Civic Center	6,000
Radford	Dedmon Center	5,000
VMI	Cameron Hall	5,029
Winthrop	Winthrop Coliseum	6,100

Big Ten

	Home Floor	Seats
Illinois	Assembly Hall	16,450
Indiana	Assembly Hall	17,257
Iowa	Carver-Hawkeye Arena	15,500
Michigan	Crisler Arena	13,751
Michigan St.	Breslin Events Center	14,759
Minnesota	Williams Arena	14,625
Northwestern	Welsh-Ryan Arena	8,117
Ohio St.	Value City Arena	19,200
Penn St.	Bryce Jordan Center	15,261
Purdue	Mackey Arena	14,123
Wisconsin	Kohl Center	17,142

Big 12

	Home Floor	Seats
Colorado	Coors Events Conference Ctr.	11,076
Iowa St.	Hilton Coliseum	14,092
Kansas	Allen Fieldhouse	16,300
Kansas St.	Bramlage Coliseum	13,500
Missouri	Hearnes Center	13,545
Nebraska	Devaney Sports Center	13,500
Baylor	Ferrell Center	10,284
Oklahoma	Lloyd Noble Center	11,100
Oklahoma St.	Gallagher-Iba Arena	13,611
Texas	Erwin Center	16,175
Texas A&M	Reed Arena	12,700
Texas Tech	United Spirit Arena	15,050

Big West

	Home Floor	Seats
Cal Poly	Mott Gym	3,032
CS-Fullerton	Titan Gym	3,500
CS-Northridge	The Matadome	1,600
Idaho	Cowan Spectrum	7,000
Long Beach St.	The Pyramid	5,000
Pacific	Spanos Center	6,150
UC-Irvine	Bren Events Center	5,000
UC-Riverside	Student Rec. Center	3,168
UC-Santa Barbara	The Thunderdome	6,000
Utah St.	The Smith Spectrum	10,270

Colonial

	Home Floor	Seats
Delaware	Bob Carpenter Center	5,000
Drexel	Daskalis Athletic Center	2,300
George Mason	Patriot Center	10,000
Hofstra	Hofstra Arena	5,124
James Madison	JMU Convocation Center	7,156
NC-Wilmington	Trask Coliseum	6,100
Old Dominion	Ted Constant Convocation Ctr.	8,650
Towson	Towson Center	5,000
VCU	Siegel Center	7,500
Wm. & Mary	William &Mary Hall	8,600

Conference USA

	Home Floor	Seats
UAB	Bartow Arena	8,500
Charlotte	Halton Arena	9,105
Cincinnati	Shoemaker Center	13,176
DePaul	Allstate Arena	17,500
East Carolina	Minges Coliseum	8,000
Houston	Hofheinz Pavilion	8,479
Louisville	Freedom Hall	18,865
Marquette	Bradley Center	18,717
Memphis	The Pyramid	20,142
Saint Louis	Savvis Center	20,000
South Florida	Sun Dome	10,411
Southern Miss	Green Coliseum	8,095
TCU	Daniel-Meyer Coliseum	7,166
Tulane	New Orleans Arena	17,832
	& Fogelman Arena	3,600

Horizon League

	Home Floor	Seats
Butler	Hinkle Fieldhouse	11,043
Cleveland St.	CSU Convocation Center	13,610
Detroit Mercy	Calihan Hall	8,837
IL-Chicago	UIC Pavilion	8,000
Loyola-IL	Gentile Center	5,200
WI-Green Bay	Rush Center	10,400
WI-Milwaukee	Klotsche Center	5,000
Wright St.	Nutter Center	10,632
Youngstown St.	Beeghly Center	8,000

Ivy League

	Home Floor	Seats
Brown	Pizzitola Sports Center	2,800
Columbia	Levien Gymnasium	3,408
Cornell	Newman Arena	4,473
Dartmouth	Leede Arena	2,200
Harvard	Lavietes Pavilion	2,195
Penn	The Palestra	8,700
Princeton	Jadwin Gymnasium	6,854
Yale	Payne Whitney Gym	3,100

Metro Atlantic

	Home Floor	Seats
Canisius	Koessler Athletic Center	2,176
Fairfield	Bridgeport Arena	9,500
Iona	Mulcahy Center	3,200
Loyola-MD	Reitz Arena	3,000
Manhattan	Draddy Gymnasium	3,000
Marist	McCann Center	3,944
Niagara	Gallagher Center	2,400
Rider	Alumni Gymnasium	1,650
St. Peter's	Yanitelli Center	3,200
Siena	Pepsi Arena	15,500

Mid-American

	Home Floor	Seats
Akron	JAR Arena	5,942
Ball St.	John E. Wortham Arena	11,500
Bowling Green	Anderson Arena	5,000
Buffalo	Alumni Arena	8,500
Central Mich.	Rose Arena	5,200
Eastern Mich.	Convocation Center	8,824
Kent St.	MAC Center	6,327
Marshall	Cam Henderson Center	9,043
Miami-OH	Millett Hall	9,200
Northern Illinois	Convocation Center	9,100
Ohio Univ.	Convocation Center	13,000
Toledo	Savage Hall	9,000
Western Mich.	University Arena	5,800

Mid-Continent

	Home Floor	Seats
Centenary	Gold Dome	3,000
Chicago St.	Dickens Athletic Center	2,500
IUPUI	IUPUI Gym	2,000
Missouri-KC	Municipal Auditorium	9,287
Oakland	Oakland Arena	3,000
Oral Roberts	Mabee Center	10,575
Southern Utah	Centrum	5,300
Valparaiso	Athletics-Recreation Center	4,500
Western Ill.	Western Hall	5,139

Mid-Eastern Athletic

	Home Floor	Seats
Bethune-Cookman	Moore Gym	3,000
Coppin St.	Coppin Center	3,000
Delaware St.	Memorial Hall	3,000
Florida A&M	Gaither Gym	3,365
Hampton	Hampton Convocation Center	7,500
Howard	Burr Gym	2,200
MD-East.Shore	W.P. Hytche Center	5,500
Morgan St.	Hill Fieldhouse	4,500
Norfolk St.	Echols Hall	7,600
N. Carolina A&T	Corbett Sports Center	6,700
South Carolina St.	SHM Center	3,200

Missouri Valley

	Home Floor	Seats
Bradley	Carver Arena	11,300
Creighton	Omaha Civic Auditorium	9,377
Drake	Knapp Center	7,002
Evansville	Roberts Stadium	12,144
Illinois St.	Redbird Arena	10,200
Indiana St.	Hulman Center	10,200
Northern Iowa	UNI-Dome	10,000
Southern Ill.	SIU Arena	10,000
SW Missouri St.	Hammons Student Center	8,846
Wichita St.	Levitt Arena	10,556

Mountain West

	Home Floor	Seats
Air Force	Clune Arena	6,002
BYU	Marriott Center	22,700
Colorado St.	Moby Arena	8,745
San Diego St.	Cox Arena at the Aztec Bowl	12,414
UNLV	Thomas & Mack Center	18,500
New Mexico	The Pit	18,018
Utah	Huntsman Center	15,000
Wyoming	Arena-Auditorium	15,028

Northeast

	Home Floor	Seats
Central Conn. St.	Detrick Gym	3,200
Farleigh Dickinson	Rothman Center	5,000
LIU-Brooklyn	Schwartz Athletic Center	1,200
Monmouth	Boylan Gym	2,500
Mt. St. Mary's	Knott Arena	3,196
Quinnipiac	Burt Kahn Court	1,500
Robert Morris	Sewall Center	3,056
Sacred Heart	Pitt Center	2,100
St. Francis-NY	Pope Center	1,200
St. Francis-PA	DeGol Arena	3,500
Wagner	Spiro Sports Center	2,100

Ohio Valley

	Home Floor	Seats
Austin Peay	Dunn Center	9,000
Eastern Illinois	Lantz Gym	5,300
Eastern Ky.	McBrayer Arena	6,500
Jacksonville St.	Mathews Coliseum	5,500
Morehead St.	Johnson Arena	6,500
Murray St.	Regional Special Events Ctr.	8,600
Samford	Seibert Hall	4,000
SE Missouri St.	Show Me Center	7,000
Tennessee-Martin	Skyhawk Arena	6,700
Tennessee St.	Gentry Complex	10,500
Tennessee Tech	Eblen Center	10,152

Pacific-10

	Home Floor	Seats
Arizona	McKale Center	14,545
Arizona St.	Wells Fargo Arena	14,198
California	Haas Pavilion	12,172
Oregon	McArthur Court	9,087
Oregon St.	Gill Coliseum	10,400
Stanford	Maples Pavilion	7,500
UCLA	Pauley Pavilion	12,819
USC	LA Sports Arena	16,161
Washington	Bank of America Arena	10,000
Washington. St.	Friel Court	12,058

Patriot League

	Home Floor	Seats
American	Bender Arena	5,000
Army	Christl Arena	5,043
Bucknell	The Rack Pavilion	4,000
Colgate	Cotterell Court	3,000
Holy Cross	Hart Recreation Center	3,600
Lafayette	Kirby Field House	3,500
Lehigh	Stabler Arena	5,600
Navy	Alumni Hall	5,710

College Basketball (Cont.)

Southeastern

Eastern	Home Floor	Seats
Florida	O'Connell Center	12,000
Georgia	Stegeman Coliseum	10,523
Kentucky	Rupp Arena	23,500
South Carolina	Carolina Center	17,600
Tennessee	Thompson-Boling Arena	24,535
Vanderbilt	Memorial Gymnasium	14,168

Western	Home Floor	Seats
Alabama	Coleman Coliseum	15,316
Arkansas	Bud Walton Arena	19,200
Auburn	Eaves-Memorial Coliseum	10,500
LSU	Maravich Assembly Center	14,164
Mississippi	Tad Smith Coliseum	8,135
Mississippi St.	Humphrey Coliseum	10,500

Southern

	Home Floor	Seats
Appalachian St.	Seby Jones Arena	8,300
The Citadel	McAlister Field House	6,200
Coll. of Charleston	John Kresse Arena	3,500
Davidson	Belk Arena	5,700
E. Tenn. St.	Memorial Center	12,000
Elon	Koury Center	2,000
Furman	Timmons Arena	5,000
Ga. Southern	Hanner Fieldhouse	5,500
NC-Greensboro	Fleming Gymnasium	2,320
Chattanooga	McKenzie Arena	11,218
W. Carolina	Ramsey Center	7,286
Wofford	Johnson Arena	3,500

Southland

	Home Floor	Seats
Lamar	Montagne Center	10,080
Louisiana-Monroe	Fant-Ewing Coliseum	8,000
McNeese St.	Burton Coliseum	8,000
Nicholls St.	Stopher Gym	3,800
Northwestern St.	Prather Coliseum	4,300
Sam Houston St.	Johnson Coliseum	6,172
SE Louisiana	University Center	7,500
S.F. Austin St.	W.R. Johnson Coliseum	7,200
TX-Arlington	Texas Hall	4,200
TX-San Antonio	Convocation Center	5,100
Texas St.-San Marcos	Strahan Coliseum	7,200

Southwestern Athletic

	Home Floor	Seats
Alabama A&M	Elmore Healh/Science Building	6,000
Alabama St.	Joe Reed Acadome	8,000
Alcorn St.	Whitney Complex	7,000
Arkansas-Pine Bluff	HPER Complex	4,500
Grambling St.	Tiger Memorial Gym	4,500
Jackson St.	Williams Center	8,000
Miss.Valley St.	Harrison HPER Athletic Complex	6,000
Prairie View A&M	The Baby Dome	6,600
Southern-BR	Clark Activity Center	7,500
TX Southern	Health & P.E. Building	8,100

Sun Belt

	Home Floor	Seats
Arkansas-Little Rock	Alltel Arena	18,000
Arkansas St	Convocation Center	10,563
Denver	Magness Arena	7,200
Florida International	Golden Panther Arena	5,000
LA-Lafayette	The Cajundome	12,800
Middle Tenn. St.	Murphy Center	11,520
New Mexico St.	Pan American Center	13,071
New Orleans	Lakefront Arena	10,000
North Texas	The Super Pit	10,000
South Alabama	Mitchell Center	10,000
Western Ky.	E.A. Diddle Arena	11,300

West Coast

	Home Floor	Seats
Gonzaga	Martin Centre	4,000
Loyola Marymount	Gersten Pavilion	4,156
Pepperdine	Firestone Fieldhouse	3,104
Portland	Chiles Center	5,000
St. Mary's-CA	McKeon Pavilion	3,500
San Diego	Jenny Craig Pavilion	5,100
San Francisco	War Memorial Gym	5,300
Santa Clara	Leavy Center	5,000

Western Athletic

	Home Floor	Seats
Boise St.	BSU Pavilion	12,380
Fresno St.	Selland Arena	10,220
Hawaii	Stan Sherif Center	10,300
Louisiana Tech	Thomas Assembly Center	8,000
Nevada	Lawlor Events Center	11,200
Rice	Autry Court	5,000
San Jose St.	The Events Center	5,000
SMU	Moody Coliseum	8,998
Tulsa	Reynolds Center	8,355
UTEP	Haskins Center	12,000

Independents

	Home Floor	Seats
IPFW	Hilliard Gates Sports Center	2,700
Morris Brown	John H. Lewis Gym	2,000
Savannah St.	Wiley Gym	2,100
Texas A&M-Corpus Christi	Memorial Coliseum	4,000
Texas-Pan Am	Health/PE Fieldhouse	3,500

Future NCAA Final Four Sites

Men

Year	Arena	Seats	Location
2004	Alamodome	20,557*	San Antonio
2005	Edward Jones Dome	66,000	St. Louis
2006	RCA Dome	47,100	Indianapolis
2007	Georgia Dome	40,000	Atlanta
2008	Alamodome	20,557*	San Antonio
2009	Ford Field	TBA	Detroit
2010	RCA Dome	47,100	Indianapolis
2011	Reliant Stadium	TBA	Houston

Women

Year	Arena	Seats	Location
2004	New Orleans Arena	17,832	New Orleans
2005	RCA Dome	56,127	Indianapolis
2006	FleetCenter	18,624	Boston
2007	Gund Arena	20,562	Cleveland
2008	St. Pete Times Forum	TBA	Tampa
2009	Edward Jones Dome	TBA	St. Louis
2010	Alamodome	20,557*	San Antonio

*This was the listed capacity for Spurs games at the Alamodome before the moved to the SBC Center. It is likely that the seating will be reconfigured to fit more spectators for the Final Four.

The 40 Largest I-A Stadiums

The 40 largest stadiums in NCAA Division I-A college football heading into the 2003 season. Note that (*) indicates stadium not on campus.

		Location	Seats	Home Team	Conference	Built	Field
1	Michigan Stadium	Ann Arbor, Mich.	107,501	Michigan	Big Ten	1927	Turf
2	Beaver Stadium	University Park, Penn.	107,282	Penn St.	Big Ten	1960	Grass
3	Neyland Stadium	Knoxville, Tenn.	104,079	Tennessee	SEC-East	1921	Grass
4	Ohio Stadium	Columbus, Ohio	101,568	Ohio St.	Big Ten	1922	Grass
5	Rose Bowl*	Pasadena, Calif.	98,636	UCLA	Pac-10	1922	Grass
6	Sanford Stadium	Athens, Ga.	92,020	Georgia	SEC-East	1929	Grass
7	LA Memorial Coliseum*	Los Angeles, Calif.	92,000	USC	Pac-10	1923	Grass
8	Tiger Stadium	Baton Rouge, La.	91,600	LSU	SEC-West	1924	Grass
9	Ben Hill Griffin Stadium at Florida Field	Gainesville, Fla.	88,548	Florida	SEC-East	1929	Grass
10	Jordan-Hare Stadium	Auburn, Ala.	86,063	Auburn	SEC-West	1939	Grass
11	Stanford Stadium	Stanford, Calif.	85,500	Stanford	Pac-10	1921	Grass
12	Bryant-Denny Stadium	Tuscaloosa, Ala.	83,818	Alabama	SEC-West	1929	Grass
13	Legion Field*	Birmingham, Ala.	83,091	Alabama/UAB	SEC-West/USA	1927	Grass
14	Memorial Stadium	Clemson, S.C.	81,474	Clemson	ACC	1942	Grass
15	Notre Dame Stadium	Notre Dame, Ind.	80,795	Notre Dame	Independent	1930	Grass
16	Kyle Field	College Station, Texas	80,650	Texas A&M	Big 12-South	1925	Grass
17	Williams-Brice Stadium	Columbia, S.C.	80,250	South Carolina	SEC-East	1934	Grass
18	Darrell K. Royal-Texas Memorial Stadium	Austin, Texas	80,082	Texas	Big 12-South	1924	Grass
19	Doak Campbell Stadium	Tallahasse, Fla.	80,000	Florida St.	ACC	1950	Grass
20	Camp Randall Stadium	Madison, Wis.	76,634	Wisconsin	Big Ten	1917	Turf
21	Memorial Stadium	Berkeley, Calif.	75,028	California	Pac-10	1923	Grass
22	Memorial Stadium	Lincoln, Neb.	73,918	Nebraska	Big 12-North	1923	Turf
23	Sun Devil Stadium	Tempe, Ariz.	73,379	Arizona St.	Pac-10	1959	Grass
24	Gaylord Family-Oklahoma Memorial Stadium	Norman, Okla.	72,765	Oklahoma	Big 12-South	1924	Grass
25	Husky Stadium	Seattle, Wash.	72,500	Washington	Pac-10	1920	Turf
26	Orange Bowl*	Miami, Fla.	72,319	Miami-FL	Big East	1935	Grass
27	Spartan Stadium	East Lansing, Mich.	72,027	Michigan St.	Big Ten	1957	Turf
28	Donald W. Reynolds Razorback Stadium	Fayetteville, Ark.	72,000	Arkansas	SEC-West	1938	Grass
29	Kinnick Stadium	Iowa City, Iowa	70,397	Iowa	Big Ten	1929	Grass
30	Citrus Bowl*	Orlando, Fla.	70,188	Central Florida	Mid-American	1936	Grass
31	Rice Stadium	Houston, Texas	70,000	Rice	WAC	1950	Turf
32	Superdome*	New Orleans, La.	69,767	Tulane	USA	1975	Turf
33	Memorial Stadium	Champaign, Ill.	69,249	Illinois	Big Ten	1923	Turf
34	Lincoln Financial Field*	Philadelphia, Penn.	68,532	Temple	Big East	2003	Grass
35	Commonwealth	Lexington, Ky.	67,530	Kentucky	SEC-East	1973	Grass
36	Ross-Ade Stadium	W. Lafayette, Ind.	66,295	Purdue	Big Ten	1924	Grass
37	Lane Stadium	Blacksburg, Va.	65,115	Va. Tech	Big East	1965	Grass
38	LaVell Edwards Stadium	Provo, Utah	65,000	BYU	Mountain West	1964	Grass
39	Heinz Field*	Pittsburgh, Penn.	64,450	Pittsburgh	Big East	2001	Grass
40	HHH Metrodome*	Minneapolis, Minn.	64,172	Minnesota	Big Ten	1982	Turf

Note: The capacities for several stadiums including the Rose Bowl, Louisiana Superdome and Sun Devil Stadium are often listed differently for other events, such as bowl games, which they host.

2003 Conference Home Fields

NCAA Division I-A conference by conference listing includes member teams heading into the 2003 season. Note that (*) indicates stadium is not on campus.

Atlantic Coast

	Stadium	Built	Seats	Field
Clemson	Memorial	1942	81,474	Grass
Duke	Wallace Wade	1929	33,941	Grass
Florida St.	Doak Campbell	1950	80,000	Grass
Ga. Tech	Bobby Dodd Stadium at Historic Grant Field	1913	55,000	Grass
Maryland	Byrd	1950	48,055	Grass
N. Carolina	Kenan Memorial	1927	60,000	Grass
N.C. State	Carter-Finley	1966	51,500	Grass
Virginia	Scott	1931	61,500	Grass
Wake Forest	Groves	1968	31,500	Grass

Big East

	Stadium	Built	Seats	Field
Boston Col.	Alumni	1957	44,500	Turf
Miami-FL	Orange Bowl*	1935	72,319	Grass
Pittsburgh	Heinz Field*	2001	64,450	Grass
Rutgers	Rutgers	1994	41,500	Grass
Syracuse	Carrier Dome	1980	49,550	Turf
Temple	Lincoln Financial Field*	2003	68,532	Grass
Va. Tech	Lane	1965	65,115	Grass
West Va.	Mountaineer	1980	63,500	Turf

Note: Miami and Virginia Tech will move to the ACC and Connecticut will join the Big East in 2004.

College Football (Cont.)

Big Ten

	Stadium	Built	Seats	Field
Illinois	Memorial	1923	69,249	Turf
Indiana	Memorial	1960	52,354	Turf
Iowa	Kinnick	1929	70,397	Grass
Michigan	Michigan	1927	107,501	Turf
Michigan St.	Spartan	1957	72,027	Turf
Minnesota	HHH Metrodome*	1982	64,172	Turf
Northwestern	Ryan Field	1926	47,130	Grass
Ohio St.	Ohio	1922	101,568	Grass
Penn St.	Beaver	1960	107,282	Grass
Purdue	Ross-Ade	1924	66,295	Grass
Wisconsin	Camp Randall	1917	76,634	Turf

Big 12

NORTH	Stadium	Built	Seats	Field
Colorado	Folsom Field	1924	53,750	Turf
Iowa St.	Jack Trice Field	1975	45,814	Grass
Kansas	Memorial	1921	50,250	Turf
Kansas St.	Wagner Field	1968	50,000	Turf
Missouri	Faurot Field	1926	62,000	Turf
Nebraska	Memorial	1923	73,918	Turf
SOUTH	**Stadium**	**Built**	**Seats**	**Field**
Baylor	Floyd Casey	1950	50,000	Grass
Oklahoma	Gaylord Family-Oklahoma Memorial	1924	81,000	Grass
Oklahoma St.	Lewis Field	1920	48,000	Turf
Texas	Royal-Memorial	1924	80,082	Grass
Texas A&M	Kyle Field	1925	82,600	Grass
Texas Tech	Jones SBC	1947	53,702	Turf

Note: The annual Oklahoma-Texas game has been played at the Cotton Bowl (capacity 68,252) in Dallas since 1937.

Conference USA

	Stadium	Built	Seats	Field
UAB	Legion Field	1927	83,091	Grass
Army	Michie	1924	39,929	Turf
Cincinnati	Nippert	1924	35,000	Turf
E. Carolina	Dowdy-Ficklen	1963	43,000	Grass
Houston	Robertson	1942	32,000	Grass
Louisville	Papa John's Cardinal	1998	42,000	Turf
Memphis	Liberty Bowl*	1965	62,380	Grass
S. Florida	Raymond James*	1988	41,444	Grass
Southern Miss	M.M. Roberts	1976	33,000	Grass
TCU	Amon G. Carter	1929	44,008	Grass
Tulane	Superdome*	1975	69,767	Turf

Mid-American

	Stadium	Built	Seats	Field
Akron	Rubber Bowl*	1940	35,202	Turf
Ball St.	Ball State	1967	21,581	Grass
Bowling Green	Doyt Perry	1966	30,599	Grass
Buffalo	UB	1993	31,000	Grass
C. Florida	Citrus Bowl	1936	70,188	Grass
Central Mich.	Kelly/Shorts	1972	30,199	Turf
Eastern Mich.	Rynearson	1969	30,200	Turf
Kent	Dix	1969	30,520	Turf
Marshall	Marshall	1991	38,019	Turf
Miami-OH	Fred Yager	1983	30,012	Grass
Northern Ill.	Huskie	1965	31,000	Turf
Ohio Univ.	Peden	1929	24,000	Grass
Toledo	Glass Bowl	1937	26,248	Turf
Western Mich.	Waldo	1939	30,200	Grass

Mountain West

	Stadium	Built	Seats	Field
Air Force	Falcon	1962	52,480	Grass
BYU	LaVell Edwards	1964	65,000	Grass
Colorado St.	Hughes	1968	30,000	Grass
New Mexico	University	1960	37,370	Grass
San Diego St.	Qualcomm*	1967	54,000	Grass
UNLV	Sam Boyd*	1971	36,800	Grass
Utah	Rice-Eccles	1927	45,634	Grass
Wyoming	War Memorial	1950	33,500	Grass

Pacific-10

	Stadium	Built	Seats	Field
Arizona	Arizona	1928	56,002	Grass
Arizona St.	Sun Devil	1958	73,379	Grass
California	Memorial	1923	75,028	Grass
Oregon	Autzen	1967	53,800	Turf
Oregon St.	Reser	1953	35,362	Turf
Stanford	Stanford	1921	85,500	Grass
UCLA	Rose Bowl*	1922	98,636	Grass
USC	LA Memorial Coliseum*	1923	92,000	Grass
Washington	Husky	1920	72,500	Turf
Washington St.	Martin	1972	37,600	Turf

Southeastern

EAST	Stadium	Built	Seats	Field
Florida	Florida Field	1929	90,000	Grass
Georgia	Sanford	1929	92,020	Grass
Kentucky	Commonwealth	1973	67,530	Grass
S. Carolina	Williams-Brice	1934	80,250	Grass
Tennessee	Neyland	1921	104,079	Grass
Vanderbilt	Vanderbilt	1981	41,600	Grass
WEST	**Stadium**	**Built**	**Seats**	**Field**
Alabama	Bryant-Denny	1929	83,818	Grass
	& Legion Field	1927	83,091	Grass
Arkansas	Donald W. Reynolds Razorback	1938	72,000	Grass
	& War Memorial*	1948	53,727	Grass
Auburn	Jordan-Hare	1939	86,063	Grass
LSU	Tiger	1924	91,600	Grass
Mississippi	Vaught-Hemingway	1915	60,580	Grass
Miss. St.	Davis-Wade	1915	52,884	Grass

Note: EAST–Vanderbilt Stadium was rebuilt in 1981.

Sun Belt

	Stadium	Built	Seats	Field
Arkansas St.	Indian	1974	33,410	Grass
Idaho	Kibbie Dome	1975	16,000	Turf
UL-Lafayette	Cajun Field	1971	31,000	Grass
UL-Monroe	Malone	1978	30,427	Grass
Middle Tennessee St.	Johnny Red Floyd	1933	30,788	Turf
New Mexico St.	Aggie Memorial	1978	30,343	Grass
North Texas	Fouts Field	1952	30,500	Turf
Utah St.	Romney	1968	30,257	Grass

Western Athletic

	Stadium	Built	Seats	Field
Boise St.	Bronco	1970	30,000	Turf
Fresno St.	Bulldog	1980	41,031	Grass
Hawaii	Aloha*	1975	50,000	Grass
Louisiana Tech	Joe Aillet	1968	30,600	Grass
Nevada	Mackay	1967	31,545	Grass
Rice	Rice	1950	70,000	Grass
San Jose St.	Spartan	1933	30,456	Grass
SMU	Gerald J. Ford Stadium	2000	32,000	Grass
Tulsa	Skelly	1930	40,385	Turf
UTEP	Sun Bowl*	1963	51,500	Turf

I-A Independents

	Stadium	Built	Seats	Field
Connecticut	Rentschler Field*	2003	40,000	Grass
Navy	Navy-Marine Corps Memorial	1959	30,000	Grass
Notre Dame	Notre Dame	1930	80,795	Grass
Troy State	Movie Gallery Veterans	1950	30,000	Turf

Business

Billionaire **Arturo "Arte" Moreno** sports an
Angels sombrero after purchasing the team in May.

2002-03 Top Rated TV Sports Events

Final 2002-03 network television ratings for the top nationally telecast sports events, according to Nielsen Media Research. Covers period from Sept. 1, 2002 through Aug. 31, 2003. Events are listed with ratings points and audience share; each ratings point represents 1,067,000 households and shares indicate percentage of TV sets in use.

Multiple entries: SPORTS—NFL Football (55); Major League Baseball (6); NCAA Football bowl games (2). NETWORKS—FOX (26); ABC (20); CBS (1).

	Date	Net	Rtg/Sh
1 **Super Bowl XXXVII**			
(Buccaneers vs Raiders) ..1/26/03		ABC	40.7/61
2 **AFC Championship Game**			
(Titans at Raiders) 1/19/03		CBS	24.6/38
3 **NFC Championship Game**			
(Buccaneers at Eagles) ..1/19/03		FOX	23.8/45
4 **AFC Div. Playoff Game**			
(Jets at Raiders) 1/12/03		CBS	22.1/38
5 **NFC Div. Playoff Game**			
(49ers at Buccaneers) ...1/12/03		FOX	18.3/39
6 **NFC Wild Card Game**			
(Giants at 49ers) 1/5/03		FOX	18.2/32
7 **AFC Wild Card Game**			
(Browns at Steelers) 1/5/03		CBS	18.1/40
AFC Div. Playoff Game			
(Steelers at Titans) 1/11/03		CBS	18.1/35
9 **MLB World Series—Game 7**			
(Giants at Angels) 10/27/02		FOX	17.9/28
10 **Fiesta Bowl**			
(Miami-FL vs Ohio St.) 1/3/03		ABC	17.2/29
11 **NFC Playoff Game**			
(Falcons at Packers) 1/4/03		ABC	16.0/27
12 **NFL Regular Season Late Game**			
(Various teams) 12/29/02		FOX	15.6/30
13 **NFC Div. Playoff Game**			
(Falcons at Eagles) 1/11/03		FOX	14.8/25
14 **NFL Regular Season Late Game**			
(Various teams) 12/15/02		FOX	14.3/27
15 **NFL Regular Season Late Game**			
(Various teams) 11/24/02		FOX	14.0/26
16 **NFL Regular Season Late Game**			
(Various teams) 12/1/02		FOX	13.7/24
17 **NFL Regular Season Late Game**			
(Various teams) 10/20/02		FOX	13.5/26
NFL Regular Season Late Game			
(Various teams) 11/3/02		FOX	13.5/26
19 **NFL Regular Season Late Game**			
(Various teams) 9/8/02		FOX	13.2/27
20 **AFC Playoff Game**			
(Colts at Jets) 1/4/03		ABC	13.0/27
21 **NFL Regular Season Late Game**			
(Various teams) 12/22/02		CBS	12.9/27
22 **NFL Monday Night Football**			
(Steelers at Patriots) 9/9/02		ABC	12.8/23
NFL Monday Night Football			
(Dolphins at Packers) 11/4/02		ABC	12.8/21
NFL Regular Season Early Game			
(Various teams) 12/8/02		FOX	12.8/29
25 **NFL Regular Season Early Game**			
(Various teams) 11/17/02		FOX	12.6/27
NCAA Men's Basketball Championship Game			
(Syracuse vs Kansas) 4/7/03		CBS	12.6/19
27 **NFL Monday Night Football**			
(Rams at Buccaneers) 9/23/02		ABC	12.5/21
28 **NFL Regular Season Late Game**			
(Various teams) 9/22/02		FOX	12.4/26
NFL Monday Night Football			
(Raiders at Broncos) ...11/11/02		ABC	12.4/21
30 **NFL Monday Night Football**			
(Jets at Raiders) 12/2/02		ABC	12.2/21
31 **NFL Regular Season Late Game**			
(Various teams) 9/15/02		CBS	12.0/23
NFL Regular Season Late Game			
(Various teams) 12/8/02		CBS	12.0/23
33 **MLB World Series—Game 2**			
(Giants at Angels) 10/20/02		FOX	11.9/20

	Date	Net	Rtg/Sh
34 **NFL Monday Night Football**			
(Eagles at Redskins) 9/6/02		ABC	11.8/21
MLB World Series—Game 4			
(Angels at Giants) 10/23/02		FOX	11.8/19
MLB World Series—Game 6			
(Giants at Angels) 10/26/02		FOX	11.8/21
NFL Regular Season Late Game			
(Various teams) 10/27/02		CBS	11.8/23
NFL Regular Season Late Game			
(Various teams) 11/10/02		CBS	11.8/23
NFL Thanksgiving Day Late Game			
(Redskins at Cowboys) ..11/28/02		FOX	11.8/31
40 **NFL Monday Night Football**			
(Bears at Rams) 11/18/02		ABC	11.7/20
41 **NFL Monday Night Football**			
(Steelers at Buccaneers) .12/23/02		ABC	11.6/20
42 **NFL Regular Season Late Game**			
(Various teams) 9/29/02		CBS	11.5/24
NFL Monday Night Football			
(Broncos at Ravens) 9/30/02		ABC	11.5/20
44 **NFL Monday Night Football**			
(Eagles at 49ers) 11/25/02		ABC	11.4/19
NFL Thanksgiving Day Early Game			
(Patriots at Lions) 11/28/02		CBS	11.4/30
46 **Rose Bowl**			
(Oklahoma vs Wash. St.) ..1/1/03		ABC	11.3/20
47 **NFL Regular Season Early Game**			
(Various teams) 10/27/02		FOX	11.2/25
NFL Monday Night Football			
(Patriots at Titans) 12/16/02		ABC	11.2/19
49 **NFL Regular Season Late Game**			
(Various teams) 10/13/02		CBS	11.1/22
NFL Regular Season Late Game			
(Various teams) 11/17/02		CBS	11.1/21
51 **NFL Regular Season Early Game**			
(Various teams) 10/13/02		FOX	10.9/25
NFL Monday Night Football			
(Giants at Eagles) 10/28/02		ABC	10.9/19
53 **MLB World Series—Game 3**			
(Angels at Giants) 10/22/02		FOX	10.8/18
54 **NFL Monday Night Football**			
(Bears at Dolphins) 12/9/02		ABC	10.7/18
NFL Regular Season Early Game			
(Various teams) 12/15/02		CBS	10.7/25
Belmont Stakes			
(Funny Cide denied) 6/7/03		NBC	10.7/25
57 **NFL Regular Season Late Game**			
(Various teams) 10/6/02		FOX	10.6/22
NFL Monday Night Football			
(Packers at Bears) 10/7/02		ABC	10.6/18
NFL Monday Night Football			
(Colts at Steelers) 10/21/02		ABC	10.6/18
60 **NFL Regular Season Early Game**			
(Various teams) 9/15/02		FOX	10.3/23
NFL Regular Season Early Game			
(Eagles at Giants) 12/28/02		FOX	10.3/27
62 **NFL Regular Season Early Game**			
(Various teams) 10/6/02		CBS	10.2/24
63 **NFL Regular Season Early Game**			
(Various teams) 12/1/02		CBS	10.1/22
64 **NFL Regular Season Early Game**			
(Various teams) 9/15/02		CBS	10.0/23
MLB World Series—Game 5			
(Angels at Giants) 10/24/02		FOX	10.0/17

All-Time Top-Rated TV Programs

NFL Football dominates television's All-Time Top-Rated 50 Programs with 22 Super Bowls and the 1981 NFC Championship Game making the list. Rankings based on surveys taken from January 1961 through August 31, 2003; include only sponsored programs seen on individual networks; and programs under 30 minutes scheduled duration are excluded. Programs are listed with ratings points, audience share and number of households watching, according to Nielsen Media Research.

Multiple entries: The Super Bowl (22); "Roots" (7); "The Beverly Hillbillies" and "The Thorn Birds" (3); "The Bob Hope Christmas Show," "The Ed Sullivan Show," "Gone With The Wind" and 1994 Winter Olympics (2).

	Program	Episode/Game	Net	Date	Rating	Share	Households
1	M*A*S*H (series)	Final episode	CBS	2/28/83	60.2	77	50,150,000
2	Dallas (series)	"Who Shot J.R.?"	CBS	11/21/80	53.3	76	41,470,000
3	Roots (mini-series)	Part 8	ABC	1/30/77	51.1	71	36,380,000
4	**Super Bowl XVI**	49ers 26, Bengals 21	CBS	1/24/82	49.1	73	40,020,000
5	**Super Bowl XVII**	Redskins 27, Dolphins 17	NBC	1/30/83	48.6	69	40,480,000
6	**XVII Winter Olympics**	Women's Figure Skating	CBS	2/23/94	48.5	64	45,690,000
7	**Super Bowl XX**	Bears 46, Patriots 10	NBC	1/26/86	48.3	70	41,490,000
8	Gone With The Wind (movie)	Part 1	NBC	11/7/76	47.7	65	33,960,000
9	Gone With The Wind (movie)	Part 2	NBC	11/8/76	47.4	64	33,750,000
10	**Super Bowl XII**	Cowboys 27, Broncos 10	CBS	1/15/78	47.2	67	34,410,000
11	**Super Bowl XIII**	Steelers 35, Cowboys 31	NBC	1/21/79	47.1	74	35,090,000
12	Bob Hope Special	Christmas Show	NBC	1/15/70	46.6	64	27,260,000
13	**Super Bowl XVIII**	Raiders 38, Redskins 9	CBS	1/22/84	46.4	71	38,800,000
	Super Bowl XIX	49ers 38, Dolphins 16	ABC	1/20/85	46.4	63	39,390,000
15	**Super Bowl XIV**	Steelers 31, Rams 19	CBS	1/20/80	46.3	67	35,330,000
16	**Super Bowl XXX**	Cowboys 27, Steelers 17	NBC	1/28/96	46.0	68	44,114,400
	ABC Theater (special)	"The Day After"	ABC	11/20/83	46.0	62	38,550,000
18	Roots (mini-series)	Part 6	ABC	1/28/77	45.9	66	32,680,000
	The Fugitive (series)	Final episode	ABC	8/29/67	45.9	72	25,700,000
20	**Super Bowl XXI**	Giants 39, Broncos 20	CBS	1/25/87	45.8	66	40,030,000
21	Roots (mini-series)	Part 5	ABC	1/27/77	45.7	71	32,540,000
22	**Super Bowl XXVIII**	Cowboys 30, Bills 13	NBC	1/30/94	45.5	66	42,860,000
	Cheers (series)	Final episode	NBC	5/20/93	45.5	64	42,360,500
24	The Ed Sullivan Show	Beatles' 1st appearance	CBS	2/9/64	45.3	60	23,240,000
25	**Super Bowl XXVII**	Cowboys 52, Bills 17	NBC	1/31/93	45.1	66	41,988,100
26	Bob Hope Special	Christmas Show	NBC	1/14/71	45.0	61	27,050,000
27	Roots (mini-series)	Part 3	ABC	1/25/77	44.8	68	31,900,000
28	**Super Bowl XXXII**	Broncos 31, Packers 24	NBC	1/25/98	44.5	67	43,630,000
29	**Super Bowl XI**	Raiders 32, Vikings 14	NBC	1/9/77	44.4	73	31,610,000
	Super Bowl XV	Raiders 27, Eagles 10	NBC	1/25/81	44.4	63	34,540,000
31	**Super Bowl VI**	Cowboys 24, Dolphins 3	CBS	1/16/72	44.2	74	27,450,000
32	XVII Winter Olympics	Women's Figure Skating	CBS	2/25/94	44.1	64	41,540,000
	Roots (mini-series)	Part 2	ABC	1/24/77	44.1	62	31,400,000
34	The Beverly Hillbillies (series)	Regular episode	CBS	1/8/64	44.0	65	22,570,000
35	Roots (mini-series)	Part 4	ABC	1/26/77	43.8	66	31,190,000
	The Ed Sullivan Show	Beatles' 2nd appearance	CBS	2/16/64	43.8	60	22,445,000
37	**Super Bowl XXIII**	49ers 20, Bengals 16	NBC	1/22/89	43.5	68	39,320,000
38	The Academy Awards	John Wayne wins Oscar	ABC	4/7/70	43.4	78	25,390,000
39	**Super Bowl XXXI**	Packers 35, Patriots 21	FOX	1/26/97	43.3	65	42,000,000
	Super Bowl XXXIV	Rams 23, Titans 16	ABC	1/30/00	43.3	63	43,618,000
41	The Thorn Birds (mini-series)	Part 3	ABC	3/29/83	43.2	62	35,990,000
42	The Thorn Birds (mini-series)	Part 4	ABC	3/30/83	43.1	62	35,900,000
43	**NFC Championship Game**	49ers 28, Cowboys 27	CBS	1/10/82	42.9	62	34,940,000
44	The Beverly Hillbillies (series)	Regular episode	CBS	1/15/64	42.8	62	21,960,000
45	**Super Bowl VII**	Dolphins 14, Redskins 7	NBC	1/14/73	42.7	72	27,670,000
46	The Thorn Birds (mini-series)	Part 2	ABC	3/28/83	42.5	59	35,400,000
47	**Super Bowl IX**	Steelers 16, Vikings 6	NBC	1/12/75	42.4	72	29,040,000
	The Beverly Hillbillies (series)	Regular episode	CBS	2/26/64	42.4	60	21,750,000
49	**Super Bowl X**	Steelers 21, Cowboys 17	CBS	1/18/76	42.3	78	29,440,000
	ABC Sunday Night Movie	"Airport"	ABC	11/11/73	42.3	63	28,000,000
	ABC Sunday Night Movie	"Love Story"	ABC	10/1/72	42.3	62	27,410,000
	Cinderella	Musical special	CBS	2/22/65	42.3	59	22,250,000
	Roots (mini-series)	Part 7	ABC	1/29/77	42.3	65	30,120,000

All-Time Top-Rated Cable TV Sports Events

All-time cable television for sports events, according to ESPN, Turner Sports research and *The Sports Business Daily*. Covers period from Sept. 1, 1980 through Aug. 31, 2003.

NFL Telecasts

		Date	Net	Rtg
1	Chicago at Minnesota	12/6/87	ESPN	17.6
2	Detroit at Miami	12/25/94	ESPN	15.1
3	Chicago at Minnesota	12/3/89	ESPN	14.7
4	Cleveland at San Fran	11/29/87	ESPN	14.2
5	Pittsburgh at Houston	12/30/90	ESPN	13.8

Non-NFL Telecasts

		Date	Net	Rtg
1	MLB: Chicago (NL)-St. Louis	9/7/98	ESPN	9.5
2	NBA: Detroit-Boston	6/1/88	TBS	8.8
3	NBA: Chicago-Detroit	5/31/89	TBS	8.2
4	NBA: Detroit-Boston	5/26/88	TBS	8.1
	MLB: Giants-Chicago (NL)	9/28/98	ESPN	8.0

Teams Bought in 2003

Five major league clubs acquired new majority owners from Sept. 21, 2002 through Sept. 25, 2003.

Major League Baseball

Anaheim Angels: On May 15, 2003 MLB owners approved the sale of the world champion Angels from The Walt Disney Co. to 56-year-old billboard magnate Arturo "Arte" Moreno. The deal was worth a reported $184 million and made Moreno the first Hispanic majority owner of a major league franchise. Moreno, worth an estimated $940 million, made his wealth from the sale of his outdoor advertising business, Outdoor Systems. He is just the third owner in the Angels' 42-year history.

NBA Basketball

Boston Celtics: On Dec. 31, 2002 NBA owners approved the $360 million sale of the storied franchise to a new ownership group headed by three longtime Celtics fans. The deal included a 52 percent stake in the team held by the Gaston family and the remaining 48 percent, which was owned by a publicly-traded limited partnership. The group is headed by venture capitalist Wyc Grousbeck of Highland Capital Partners. The sale smashed the previous NBA record of $280 million, paid by Mark Cuban for the Dallas Mavericks in 2000.

Charlotte Bobcats: On Jan. 10, 2003 the NBA Board of Governors approved Black Entertainment Television (BET) founder and CEO Robert Johnson to own and operate the Charlotte, N.C. expansion team, later named the Bobcats, and the WNBA's Charlotte Sting. Johnson paid $300 million as an expansion fee and is the first African-American majority owner of a professional sports franchise. The Bobcats begin play in 2004-05.

NHL Hockey

Buffalo Sabres: On April 10, 2003 U.S. Bankruptcy Court judge Michael Kaplan approved the sale of the Sabres to 61-year-old Paychex founder and chairman B. Thomas Golisano for $92 million. The team had been owned by Adelphia Communications chairman John Rigas until June 2002 when the NHL assumed control after Adelphia's bankruptcy and Rigas' ensuing legal troubles. Also included in the sale were the HSBC Arena and the Buffalo Bandits of the National Lacrosse League.

Ottawa Senators: On Aug. 26, 2003 the sale of the Senators and the Corel Centre was finalized to Canadian billionaire Eugene Melnyk, owner of Capital Sports & Entertainment Inc. and Capital Sports Properties Inc. and founder/CEO of pharmaceutical company Biovail. Financial details of the transaction were not disclosed but the deal was reportedly between $130 and $150 million (U.S.). The team was approximately $160 million in debt and had declared bankruptcy on Jan. 9.

Also of note:

1) Maple Leaf Sports & Entertainment Ltd., owner of the NHL's Toronto Maple Leafs, NBA's Toronto Raptors and Air Canada Centre, still owns those entities but the ownership structure in the company has changed. Chairman Steve Stavro sold all of his interest in the company, and Kilmer Sports, Inc. owner Larry Tanenbaum was named the new chairman of MLSEL.

2) On Sept. 15, 2003, the NBA's Atlanta Hawks, NHL's Atlanta Thrashers and the rights to Philips Arena were sold from AOL Time Warner to Atlanta Spirit LLC. At press time, however, the deal still needed approval from each league's Board of Governors and from AOL Time Warner's Board of Directors.

Top 10 Salaries In Each Sport

The top 10 highest paid athletes over the 2002-03 season for the NBA and NHL, 2003 for Major League Baseball and the 2002 season for the NFL. Figures are in millions of dollars.

Sources: *USA Today, Street & Smith's SportsBusiness Journal,* NHLPA and AP.

NFL

		Position	Team	Salary
1	Michael Strahan	Def. Lineman	NY Giants	$20.600
2	Donovan McNabb	Quarterback	Philadelphia	14.736
3	Curtis Martin	Running Back	NY Jets	13.504
4	Larry Allen	Off. Lineman	Dallas	13.003
5	David Carr	Quarterback	Houston	11.960
6	Rod Smith	Receiver	Denver	11.664
7	Jeff Garcia	Quarterback	San Fran.	11.600
8	Marshall Faulk	Running Back	St. Louis	11.595
9	Aaron Glenn	Def. Back	Houston	11.343
10	Tarik Glenn	Off. Lineman	Indianapolis	11.300
	League Avg			1.250

MLB

		Position	Team	Salary
1	Alex Rodriguez	Shortstop	Texas	$22.000
2	Manny Ramirez	Left Field	Boston	20.000
3	Carlos Delgado	First Base	Toronto	18.700
4	Mo Vaughn	First Base	NY Mets	17.167
5	Sammy Sosa	Right Field	Chicago-NL	16.000
6	Kevin Brown	Pitcher	Los Angeles	15.714
7	Shawn Green	Right Field	Los Angeles	15.667
8	Derek Jeter	Shortstop	NY Yankees	15.600
9	Mike Piazza	Catcher	NY Mets	15.571
10	Barry Bonds	Left Field	San Fran.	15.500
	Pedro Martinez	Pitcher	Boston	15.500
	League Avg			2.555

NBA

		Position	Team	Salary
1	Kevin Garnett	Forward	Minnesota	$25.200
2	Shaquille O'Neal	Center	LA Lakers	23.571
3	Alonzo Mourning	Center	Miami	20.633
4	Juwan Howard	Forward	Denver	20.152
5	Scottie Pippen	Forward	Portland	19.728
6	Karl Malone	Forward	Utah	19.250
7	Dikembe Mutombo	Center	New Jersey	16.105
8	Shawn Kemp	Forward	Orlando	15.019
9	Rasheed Wallace	Forward	Portland	14.926
10	Allan Houston	Guard	New York	14.344
	Chris Webber	Forward	Sacramento	14.344
	League Avg			4.920

NHL

		Position	Team	Salary
1	Jaromir Jagr	Right Wing	Washington	$11.483
2	Keith Tkachuk	Left Wing	St. Louis	11.000
3	Nicklas Lidstrom	Defense	Detroit	10.500
4	Pavel Bure	Right Wing	NY Rangers	10.000
	Paul Kariya	Left Wing	Anaheim	10.000
6	Joe Sakic	Center	Colorado	9.856
7	Brian Leetch	Defense	NY Rangers	9.680
8	Bobby Holik	Center	NY Rangers	9.600
9	Chris Pronger	Defense	St. Louis	9.500
	Peter Forsberg	Center	Colorado	9.500
	League Avg			1.790

2002-03 Team Payrolls

Team payrolls for active players during the 2002-03 season for the NBA and NHL, the 2002 season for the NFL and the 2003 season (as of July 16) for Major League Baseball. Figures are in millions of dollars. **Note:** The NFL and NBA use a salary cap to set payroll. In 2002, the NFL's cap was $71.1 million. In 2002-03 the NBA's cap was $40.27 million. Teams can circumvent the cap, however, via bonuses and other exceptions. **Sources**: *USA Today*, NHLPA, NFLPA and AP.

	NBA		MLB		NHL		NFL
1	Portland $104.3	1	NY Yankees $180.3	1	NY Rangers $69.2	1	Pittsburgh $85.3
2	New York 93.0	2	NY Mets 116.3	2	Detroit 68.0	2	Atlanta 85.1
3	Dallas 79.8	3	Los Angeles 109.2	3	St. Louis 61.8	3	NY Jets 84.7
4	Sacramento 70.4	4	Texas 106.3	4	Dallas 61.8	4	Oakland 83.9
5	Philadelphia 65.3	5	Boston 104.9	5	Colorado 60.8	5	Houston 83.8
6	LA Lakers 62.6	6	Atlanta 103.9	6	Philadelphia 55.7	6	Philadelphia 81.9
7	Memphis 60.5	7	St. Louis 101.8	7	Toronto 54.9	7	NY Giants 77.8
8	New Jersey 60.4	8	San Francisco . . .100.1	8	New Jersey 51.2	8	San Francisco 75.1
9	Milwaukee 60.0	9	Philadelphia 95.3	9	Washington 50.4	9	Dallas 74.1
10	Minnesota 59.5	10	Arizona 92.7	10	Montreal 48.6	10	Cleveland 72.2
11	Miami 57.6	11	Seattle 92.3	11	San Jose 45.1	11	Chicago 71.9
12	Atlanta 56.4	12	Chicago-NL 86.6	12	Chicago 44.4	12	Kansas City 71.5
13	Toronto 55.4	13	Anaheim 83.2	13	Phoenix 43.9	13	St. Louis 70.7
14	Phoenix 55.2	14	Houston 79.9	14	Los Angeles 41.8	14	Arizona 67.0
15	Boston 53.8	15	Colorado 78.7	15	NY Islanders 41.5	15	Indianapolis 65.7
16	Indiana 53.5	16	Baltimore 75.5	16	Anaheim 38.8	16	Tampa Bay 64.5
17	San Antonio 52.8	17	Chicago-AL 71.3	17	Carolina 38.4	17	Detroit 64.3
18	Orlando 51.9	18	Minnesota 65.3	18	Boston 36.9	18	Miami 63.4
19	Seattle 51.8	19	Cincinnati 65.1	19	Vancouver 35.3	19	Denver 62.6
20	Utah 50.5	20	Florida 63.3	20	Calgary 33.6	20	Washington 61.1
21	Houston 50.2	21	Pittsburgh 62.3	21	Buffalo 31.5	21	San Diego 60.7
22	Detroit 47.8	22	Toronto 61.2	22	Edmonton 31.5	22	Buffalo 59.6
23	Cleveland 47.6	23	Detroit 59.0	23	Florida 31.2	23	Seattle 58.3
24	Golden St. 47.4	24	Cleveland 58.1	24	Pittsburgh 31.2	24	Cincinnati 57.9
25	Washington 46.6	25	San Diego 57.9	25	Tampa Bay 28.9	25	Baltimore 55.7
26	New Orleans 45.2	26	Oakland 56.6	26	Ottawa 28.5	26	Tennessee 54.3
27	Chicago 44.5	27	Kansas City 48.5	27	Columbus 27.4	27	New Orleans 54.3
28	LA Clippers 42.8	28	Milwaukee 47.3	28	Atlanta 27.0	28	Carolina 54.2
29	Denver 41.0	29	Montreal 45.9	29	Nashville 23.3	29	Green Bay 50.0
		30	Tampa Bay 31.7	30	Minnesota 21.1	30	Jacksonville 49.6
						31	New England 46.2
						32	Minnesota 43.5

Highest and Lowest Ticket Prices

The most expensive and least expensive average ticket prices for NFL franchises over the 2002 season, MLB franchises over the 2003 season and NBA and NHL franchises for the 2002-03 season. Note that average ticket prices for each league are as follows: **NFL** $50.02, **MLB** $18.69, **NBA** $43.65 and **NHL** $41.56. **Source**: *Team Marketing Report*

NFL

	Highest	**Venue**	**Avg. Price**
1	New England . . . . . .Gillette Stadium	$76.19
2	Washington . . . . .FedEx Field	68.06
3	Jacksonville . . . . .ALLTEL Stadium	62.85
4	Oakland . . . . . . .Network Assoc. Col.	58.89
5	San Francisco . . . . . . .Candlestick Park	58.00

	Lowest	**Venue**	**Avg. Price**
1	Atlanta . . . . .Georgia Dome	$29.78
2	Arizona . . . . .Sun Devil Stadium	33.68
3	Buffalo . . . . .Ralph Wilson Stadium	37.61
4	Tennessee . . . . .The Coliseum	40.66
5	Carolina . . . . .Ericsson Stadium	42.27

MLB

	Highest	**Venue**	**Avg. Price**
1	Boston . . . . .Fenway Park	$42.34
2	NY Yankees . . . . .Yankee Stadium	24.86
3	Chicago Cubs . . . . .Wrigley Field	24.21
4	Seattle . . . . .SAFECO Field	23.92
5	NY Mets . . . . .Shea Stadium	22.53

	Lowest	**Venue**	**Avg. Price**
1	Montreal . . . . .Olympic Stadium	$9.00
2	Kansas City . . . . . .Kauffman Stadium	12.13
3	Florida . . . . .Pro Player Stadium	12.78
4	Minnesota . . . . .HHH Metrodome	14.40
5	Tampa Bay . . . . .Tropicana Field	14.49

NBA

	Highest	**Venue**	**Avg. Price**
1	LA Lakers . . . . .Staples Center	$71.06
2	New York . . . . . .Madison Sq. Garden	64.10
3	Sacramento . . . . .ARCO Arena	58.83
4	New Jersey . .Continental Airlines Arena	54.36
5	Houston . . . . .Compaq Center	54.21

	Lowest	**Venue**	**Avg. Price**
1	Golden St. . . . . .The Arena in Oakland	$26.38
2	Detroit . . . . .The Palace	30.60
3	Toronto . . . . .Air Canada Centre	31.01
4	Denver . . . . .Pepsi Center	32.77
5	Seattle . . . . .KeyArena	34.01

NHL

	Highest	**Venue**	**Avg. Price**
1	Philadelphia . . . . . .First Union Center	$57.06
2	Detroit . . . . .Joe Louis Arena	56.72
3	New Jersey . .Continental Airlines Arena	54.67
4	Boston . . . . .FleetCenter	51.37
5	Toronto . . . . .Air Canada Centre	48.48

	Lowest	**Venue**	**Avg. Price**
1	Edmonton . . . . .Skyreach Centre	$29.36
2	Tampa Bay . . . . . .St. Pete Times Forum	29.93
3	Calgary . . . . . .Pengrowth Saddledome	30.68
4	Phoenix . . . . .America West Arena	31.32
5	Carolina . . . . .RBC Center	31.77

The Peabody Award

Presented annually since 1940 for outstanding achievement in radio and television broadcasting. Named after Georgia banker and philanthropist George Foster Peabody, the awards are administered by the Henry W. Grady College of Journalism and Mass Communication at the University of Georgia.

Television

Year
1960 **CBS** for coverage of 1960 Winter and Summer Olympic Games
1966 ABC's **"Wide World of Sports"** (for Outstanding Achievement in Promotion of International Understanding).
1968 **ABC Sports** coverage of both the 1968 Winter and Summer Olympic Games.
1972 **ABC Sports** coverage of the 1972 Summer Olympics in Munich.
1973 **Joe Garagiola** of NBC Sports (for "The Baseball World of Joe Garagiola").
1976 **ABC Sports** coverage of both the 1976 Winter and Summer Olympic Games.
1984 **Roone Arledge**, president of ABC News & Sports (for significant contributions to news and sports programming).
1986 **WFAA-TV**, Dallas for its investigation of the Southern Methodist University football program.
1988 **Jim McKay** of ABC Sports (for pioneering efforts and career accomplishments in the world of TV sports).
1991 **CBS Sports** coverage of the 1991 Masters golf tournament
    & **HBO Sports** and **Black Canyon Productions** for the baseball special "When It Was A Game."
1995 **Kartemquin Educational Films** and **KTCA-TV** in St. Paul, MN, presented on PBS for "Hoop Dreams"
    & **Turner Original Productions** for the baseball special "Hank Aaron: Chasing the Dream."
1996 **HBO Sports** for its documentary "The Journey of the African-American Athlete"
    & **Bud Greenspan**, a personal award for excellence in chronicling the Olympic Games.
1997 **HBO Pictures** and **The Thomas Carter Company** for the original movie "Don King: Only in America."
1998 **KTVX-TV**, Salt Lake City for its investigation into the policies and practices of the IOC during the Olympic bribery scandal & **HBO Sports** for its ongoing series of sports documentaries.
1999 **WCPO-TV**, Cincinnati for its investigation of fraud and misrepresentation in the construction of new sports stadiums, **HBO Sports** for its documentary "Dare to Compete: The Struggle of Women in Sports," and its documentary "Fists of Freedom: The Story of the '68 Summer Games" & **ESPN** for its "SportsCentury" series.
2000 **HBO Sports** for its documentary "Ali-Frazier 1: One Nation...Divisible."
2001 **The Ciesla Foundation** and **Cinemax** for the documentary "The Life and Times of Hank Greenberg."
2002 **ESPN** for "The Complete Angler," its documentary celebrating nature, art and fly-fishing.

Radio

Year
1974 **WSB** radio in Atlanta for "Henry Aaron: A Man with a Mission."
1991 **Red Barber** of National Public Radio (for his six decades as a broadcaster and his 10 years as a commentator on NPR's "Morning Edition").

National Emmy Awards
Sports Programming

Presented by the Academy of Television Arts and Sciences since 1948. Eligibility period covered the calendar year from 1948-57 and since 1988.
   Multiple major award winners: ABC "Wide World of Sports" (20), NFL Films Football coverage (13); ABC Olympics coverage (9); ABC "Monday Night Football" (8); FOX MLB coverage (7); CBS NFL Football coverage, NBC Olympics coverage (9); ESPN "Outside the Lines" series (8); HBO "Real Sports with Bryant Gumbel" (7); "ESPN "SportsCenter" (6); CBS NCAA Basketball coverage and CBS "NFL Today" (5); ESPN "GameDay/Sunday NFL Countdown (4); ABC "The American Sportsman," ABC Indianapolis 500 coverage, ESPN "SportsCentury" series and FOX "NFL Sunday" (3); ABC Kentucky Derby coverage, ABC "Sportsbeat," Bud Greenspan Olympic specials, CBS Olympics coverage, CBS Golf coverage, ESPN "Speedworld," MTV Sports series, The NBA on NBC and NBC World Series coverage (2).

1949
Coverage—"Wrestling" (KTLA, Los Angeles)

1950
Program—"Rams Football" (KNBH-TV, Los Angeles)

1954
Program—"Gillette Cavalcade of Sports" (NBC)

1965-66
Programs—"Wide World of Sports" (ABC), "Shell's Wonderful World of Golf" (NBC) and "CBS Golf Classic" (CBS)

1966-67
Program—"Wide World of Sports" (ABC)

1967-68
Program—"Wide World of Sports" (ABC)

1968-69
Program—"1968 Summer Olympics" (ABC)

1969-70
Programs—"NFL Football" (CBS) and "Wide World of Sports" (ABC)

1970-71
Program—"Wide World of Sports" (ABC)

1971-72
Program—"Wide World of Sports" (ABC)

1972-73
News Special—"Coverage of Munich Olympic Tragedy" (ABC)
Sports Programs—"1972 Summer Olympics" (ABC) and "Wide World of Sports" (ABC)

1973-74
Program—"Wide World of Sports" (ABC)

1974-75

Non-Edited Program— "Jimmy Connors vs. Rod Laver Tennis Challenge" (CBS)
Edited Program— "Wide World of Sports" (ABC)

1975-76

Live Special— "1975 World Series: Cincinnati vs. Boston" (NBC)
Live Series— "NFL Monday Night Football" (ABC)
Edited Specials— "1976 Winter Olympics" (ABC) and "Triumph and Tragedy: The Olympic Experience" (ABC)
Edited Series— "Wide World of Sports" (ABC)

1976-77

Live Special— "1976 Summer Olympics" (ABC)
Live Series— "The NFL Today/NFL Football" (CBS)
Edited Special— "1976 Summer Olympics Preview" (ABC)
Edited Series— "The Olympiad" (PBS)

1977-78

Live Special— "Muhammad Ali vs. Leon Spinks Heavyweight Championship Fight" (CBS)
Live Series— "The NFL Today/NFL Football" (CBS)
Edited Special— "The Impossible Dream: Ballooning Across the Atlantic" (CBS)
Edited Series— "The Way It Was" (PBS)

1978-79

Live Special— "Super Bowl XIII: Pittsburgh vs Dallas" (NBC)
Live Series— "NFL Monday Night Football" (ABC)
Edited Special— "Spirit of '78: The Flight of Double Eagle II" (ABC)
Edited Series— "The American Sportsman" (ABC)

1979-80

Live Special— "1980 Winter Olympics" (ABC)
Live Series— "NCAA College Football" (ABC)
Edited Special— "Gossamer Albatross: Flight of Imagination" (CBS)
Edited Series— "NFL Game of the Week" (NFL Films)

1980-81

Live Special— "1981 Kentucky Derby" (ABC)
Live Series— "PGA Golf Tour" (CBS)
Edited Special— "Wide World of Sports 20th Anniversary Show" (ABC)
Edited Series— "The American Sportsman" (ABC)

1981-82

Live Special— "1982 NCAA Basketball Final: North Carolina vs Georgetown" (CBS)
Live Series— "NFL Football" (CBS)
Edited Special— "1982 Indianapolis 500" (ABC)
Edited Series— "Wide World of Sports" (ABC)

1982-83

Live Special— "1982 World Series: St. Louis vs Milwaukee" (NBC)
Live Series— "NFL Football" (CBS)
Edited Special— "Wimbledon '83" (NBC)
Edited Series— "Wide World of Sports" (ABC)
Journalism— "ABC Sportsbeat" (ABC)

1983-84

No awards given

1984-85

Live Special— "1984 Summer Olympics" (ABC)
Live Series— No award given
Edited Special— "Road to the Super Bowl '85" (NFL Films)
Edited Series— "The American Sportsman" (ABC)
Journalism— "ABC Sportsbeat" (ABC), "CBS Sports Sunday" (CBS), Dick Schaap features (ABC) and 1984 Summer Olympic features (ABC)

1985-86

No awards given

1986-87

Live Special— "1987 Daytona 500" (CBS)
Live Series— "NFL Football" (CBS)
Edited Special— "Wide World of Sports 25th Anniversary Special" (ABC)
Edited Series— "Wide World of Sports" (ABC)

1987-88

Live Special— "1987 Kentucky Derby" (ABC)
Live Series— "NFL Monday Night Football" (ABC)
Edited Special— "Paris-Roubaix Bike Race" (CBS)
Edited Series— "Wide World of Sports" (ABC)

1988

Live Special— "1988 Summer Olympics" (NBC)
Live Series— "1988 NCAA Basketball" (CBS)
Edited Special— "Road to the Super Bowl '88" (NFL Films)
Edited Series— "Wide World of Sports" (ABC)
Studio Show— "NFL GameDay" (ESPN)
Journalism— 1988 Summer Olympic reporting (NBC)

1989

Live Special— "1989 Indianapolis 500" (ABC)
Live Series— "NFL Monday Night Football" (ABC)
Edited Special— "Trans-Antarctica! The International Expedition" (ABC)
Edited Series— "This is the NFL" (NFL Films)
Studio Show— "NFL Today" (CBS)
Journalism— 1989 World Series Game 3 earthquake coverage (ABC)

1990

Live Special— "1990 Indianapolis 500" (ABC)
Live Series— "1990 NCAA Basketball Tournament" (CBS)
Edited Special— "Road to Super Bowl XXIV" (NFL Films)
Edited Series— "Wide World of Sports" (ABC)
Studio Show— "SportsCenter" (ESPN)
Journalism— "Outside the Lines: The Autograph Game" (ESPN)

1991

Live Special— "1991 NBA Finals: Chicago vs LA Lakers" (NBC)
Live Series— "1991 NCAA Basketball Tournament" (CBS)
Edited Special— "Wide World of Sports 30th Anniversary Special" (ABC)
Edited Series— "This is the NFL" (NFL Films)
Studio Show— "NFL GameDay" (ESPN) and "NFL Live" (NBC)
Journalism— "Outside the Lines: Steroids–Whatever It Takes" (ESPN)

1992

Live Special— "1992 Breeders' Cup" (NBC)
Live Series— "1992 NCAA Basketball Tournament" (CBS)
Edited Special— "1992 Summer Olympics" (NBC)
Edited Series— "MTV Sports" (MTV)
Studio Show— "The NFL Today" (CBS)
Journalism— "Outside the Lines: Portraits in Black and White" (ESPN)

1993

Live Special— "1993 World Series" (CBS)
Live Series— "Monday Night Football" (ABC)
Edited Special— "Road to the Super Bowl" (NFL Films)
Edited Series— "This is the NFL" (NFL Films)
Studio Show— "The NFL Today" (CBS)
Journalism (TIE)— "Outside the Lines: Mitch Ivey Feature" (ESPN) and "SportsCenter: University of Houston Football" (ESPN).
Feature— "Arthur Ashe: His Life, His Legacy" (NBC).

National Emmy Awards (Cont.)

1994

Live Special—"NHL Stanley Cup Finals" (ESPN)
Live Series—"Monday Night Football" (ABC)
Edited Special—"Lillehammer '94: 16 Days of Glory" (Disney/Cappy Productions)
Edited Series—"MTV Sports" (MTV)
Studio Show—"NFL GameDay" (ESPN)
Journalism—"1994 Winter Olympic Games: Mossad feature" (CBS)
Feature (TIE)—"Heroes of Telemark" on Winter Olympic Games (CBS); and "SportsCenter: Vanderbilt running back Brad Gaines" (ESPN).

"Baseball" Wins Prime Time Emmy

Ken Burns's miniseries "Baseball" won the 1994 Emmy Award for Outstanding Informational Series. The nine-part documentary aired from Sept. 18-28, 1994 and ran more than 18 hours, drawing the largest audience in PBS history.

1995

Live Special—"Cal Ripken 2131" (ESPN)
Live Series—"ESPN Speedworld" (ESPN)
Edited Special (quick turn-around)—"Outside the Lines: Playball–Opening Day in America" (ESPN)
Edited Special (long turn-around)—"Lillehammer, an Olympic Diary" (CBS)
Edited Series—"NFL Films Presents" (NFL Films)
Studio Show (TIE)—"NFL GameDay" (ESPN) and "FOX NFL Sunday"(FOX)
Journalism—"Real Sports with Bryant Gumbel: Broken Promises" (HBO)
Feature (TIE)—"SportsCenter: Jerry Quarry" (ESPN) and "Real Sports with Bryant Gumbel: Coach" (HBO).

1996

Live Special—"1996 World Series" (FOX)
Live Series—"ESPN Speedworld" (ESPN)
Edited Special—"Football America" (TNT/NFL Films)
Edited Series—"NFL Films Presents" (NFL Films)
Live Event Turnaround—"The Centennial Olympic Games" (NBC)
Studio Show—"SportsCenter" (ESPN)
Journalism—"Outside the Lines: AIDS in Sports" (ESPN)
Feature—"Real Sports with Bryant Gumbel: 1966 Texas Western NCAA Champs" (HBO).

1997

Live Special—"The NBA Finals" (NBC)
Live Series—"NFL Monday Night Football" (ABC)
Edited Special—"Ironman Triathlon World Championship" (NBC/World Triathlon Corporation)
Edited Series—"NFL Films Presents" (NFL Films)
Live Event Turnaround—"Outside The Lines: Inside The Kentucky Derby" (ESPN)
Studio Show—"FOX NFL Sunday" (FOX)
Journalism—"Real Sports with Bryant Gumbel: Pros and Cons" (HBO)
Feature—"NFL Films Presents: Eddie George" (NFL Films).

1998

Live Special—"McGwire's 62nd Home Run Game" (FOX)
Live Series—"NBC Golf Tour" (NBC)
Edited Special—"A Cinderella Season: The Lady Vols Fight Back" (HBO)
Edited Series—"Real Sports with Bryant Gumbel" (HBO)
Live Event Turnaround—"Wimbledon '98" (NBC)
Studio Show—"FOX NFL Sunday" (FOX)
Journalism (TIE)—"Real Sports with Bryant Gumbel: Winning At All Costs" (HBO) and "Real Sports with Bryant Gumbel: Diamond Bucks" (HBO)
Feature—"NFL Films Presents: Steve Mariucci" (ESPN2 and NFL Films).

1999

Live Special—"2000 MLB All-Star Game" (FOX)
Live Series—"MLB Regular Season" (FOX)
Edited Special—"Ironman Triathlon World Championship" (NBC)
Edited Series—"SportsCentury: 50 Greatest Athletes" (ESPN)
Live Event Turnaround—"The World Track & Field Championships" (NBC)
Studio Show—"MLB Pre-Game Show" (FOX)
Journalism—"Real Sports with Bryant Gumbel: Fake Golf Clubs" (HBO)
Feature—"NFL Films Presents: Lt. Kalsu" (ESPN2)

2000

Live Special—"2000 World Series" (FOX)
Live Series—"NFL Sunday Night Football" (ESPN)
Edited Special—"Hoops and Hoosiers: The Story of the Final Four 2000" (CBS)
Edited Series—"SportsCentury: The Top 50 & Beyond" (ESPN)
Live Event Turnaround—"The Games of the XXVII Olympiad" (NBC)
Studio Show—"FOX NFL Sunday" (FOX)
Journalism—"Real Sports with Bryant Gumbel: Dominican Free-For-All" (HBO)
Feature—"The Games of the XXVII Olympiad" (NBC)

2001

Live Special—"2001 World Series" (FOX)
Live Series—"NASCAR on FOX" (FOX)
Edited Special—"ABC's Wide World of Sports 40th Anniversary Special" (ABC)
Edited Series—"SportsCentury" (ESPN Classic)
Live Event Turnaround—"Tour de France" (CBS)
Studio Show—Weekly—"Sunday NFL Countdown" (ESPN)
Studio Show—Daily—"Inside the NBA" (TNT/TBS)
Journalism—"Real Sports with Bryant Gumbel: Amare Stoudemire" (HBO)
Feature—"NFL Films Presents: Gerry Faust—The Golden Dream" (ESPN2)
Documentary—"Do You Believe in Miracles? The Story of the 1980 U.S. Hockey Team" (HBO)

2002

Live Special—"XIX Olympic Winter Games" (NBC)
Live Series—"The NBA on NBC" (NBC)
Edited Special—"America's Heroes: The Bravest vs. The Finest" (NBC)
Edited Series—"Real Sports with Bryant Gumbel" (HBO)
Live Event Turnaround—"Tour de France" (CBS)
Studio Show—Weekly—"Inside the NFL" (HBO & NFL Films)
Studio Show—Daily—"Baseball Tonight" (ESPN)
Journalism—"Outside the Lines, Weekly: Eligibility for Sale" (ESPN) and "Outside the Lines, Weekly: Iraqi Atletes, Tales of Torture" (ESPN)
Long Feature—"SportsCenter: Flight 93" (ESPN)
Short Feature—"SportsCenter: Chris Paul" (ESPN), "XIX Olympic Winter Games: Bill Johnson" (NBC) and "XIX Olympic Winter Games: The Sheas" (NBC)
Documentary—"Our Greatest Hopes, Our Worst Fears: The Tragedy of the Munich Games" (ABC)

Sportscasters of the Year
National Emmy Awards

An Emmy Award for Sportscasters was first introduced in 1968 and given for Outstanding Host/Commentator for the 1967-68 TV season. Two awards, one for Outstanding Host or Play-by-Play and the other for Outstanding Analyst, were first presented in 1981 for the 1980-81 season. Three awards, for Outstanding Studio Host, Play-by-Play and Studio Analyst, have been given since the 1993 season, and one more, Sports Event Analyst, was added in 1997.

Multiple winners: John Madden (13); Bob Costas (12); Jim McKay (9); Dick Enberg and Al Michaels (4); Joe Buck, Cris Collinsworth, Keith Jackson and Tim McCarver (3); Terry Bradshaw and James Brown (2). Note that Jim McKay has won a total of 12 Emmy awards: eight for Host/Commentator, one for Host/Play-by-Play, two for Sports Writing, and one for News Commentary.

Season	Host/Commentator	Season	Host/Play-by-Play	Season	Analyst
1967-68	Jim McKay, ABC	1980-81	Dick Enberg, NBC	1980-81	Dick Button, ABC
1968-69	No award	1981-82	Jim McKay, ABC	1981-82	John Madden, CBS
1969-70	No award	1982-83	Dick Enberg, NBC	1982-83	John Madden, CBS
1970-71	Jim McKay, ABC	1983-84	No award	1983-84	No award
	& Don Meredith, ABC	1984-85	George Michael, NBC	1984-85	No award
1971-72	No award	1985-86	No award	1985-86	No award
1972-73	Jim McKay, ABC	1986-87	Al Michaels, ABC	1986-87	John Madden, CBS
1973-74	Jim McKay, ABC	1987-88	Bob Costas, NBC	1987-88	John Madden, CBS
1974-75	Jim McKay, ABC	1988	Bob Costas, NBC	1988	John Madden, CBS
1975-76	Jim McKay, ABC	1989	Al Michaels, ABC	1989	John Madden, CBS
1976-77	Frank Gifford, ABC	1990	Dick Enberg, NBC	1990	John Madden, CBS
1977-78	Jack Whitaker, CBS	1991	Bob Costas, NBC	1991	John Madden, CBS
1978-79	Jim McKay, ABC	1992	Bob Costas, NBC	1992	John Madden, CBS
1979-80	Jim McKay, ABC				

Studio Host

Year		Year		Year	
1993	Bob Costas, NBC	1997	Dan Patrick, ESPN	2001	Bob Costas, HBO &
1994	Bob Costas, NBC	1998	James Brown, FOX		Ernie Johnson, TNT/TBS
1995	Bob Costas, NBC	1999	James Brown, FOX	2002	Bob Costas, HBO/NBC
1996	Bob Costas, NBC	2000	Bob Costas, NBC		

Play-by-Play

Year		Year		Year	
1993	Dick Enberg, NBC	1997	Bob Costas, NBC	2001	Joe Buck, FOX
1994	Keith Jackson, ABC	1998	Keith Jackson, ABC	2002	Joe Buck, FOX
1995	Al Michaels, ABC	1999	Joe Buck, FOX		
1996	Keith Jackson, ABC	2000	Al Michaels, ABC		

Studio Analyst

Year		Year		Year	
1993	Billy Packer, CBS	1997	Cris Collinsworth, HBO/NBC	2001	Terry Bradshaw, FOX
1994	John Madden, FOX	1998	Cris Collinsworth, HBO/FOX	2002	Cris Collinsworth, HBO
1995	John Madden, FOX	1999	Terry Bradshaw, FOX		
1996	Howie Long, FOX	2000	Steve Lyons, FOX		

Sports Events Analyst

Year		Year		Year	
1997	Joe Morgan, ESPN	1999	John Madden, FOX	2001	Tim McCarver, FOX
1998	John Madden, FOX	2000	Tim McCarver, FOX	2002	Tim McCarver, FOX

Lifetime Achievement Emmy Award

Year		Year		Year		Year	
1989	Jim McKay	1993	Pat Summerall	1997	Jim Simpson	2001	Herb Granath
1990	Lindsey Nelson	1994	Howard Cosell	1998	Keith Jackson	2002	Roone Arledge*
1991	Curt Gowdy	1995	Vin Scully	1999	Jack Buck		
1992	Chris Schenkel	1996	Frank Gifford	2000	Dick Enberg		

*Arledge is the only recipient of two Lifetime Achievement Emmy Awards. In addition to sports, he won the lifetime award for "News and Documentary" in 2002.

National Sportscasters and Sportswriters Assn. Award

Sportscaster of the Year presented annually since 1959 by the National Sportscasters and Sportswriters Association, based in Salisbury, N.C. Voting is done by NSSA members and selected national media.

Multiple winners: Bob Costas (8); Chris Berman (6) Keith Jackson (5); Lindsey Nelson and Chris Schenkel (4); Dick Enberg, Al Michaels and Vin Scully (3); Curt Gowdy and Ray Scott (2).

Year		Year		Year		Year	
1959	Lindsey Nelson	1971	Ray Scott	1982	Vin Scully	1994	Chris Berman
1960	Lindsey Nelson	1972	Keith Jackson	1983	Al Michaels	1995	Bob Costas
1961	Lindsey Nelson	1973	Keith Jackson	1984	John Madden	1996	Chris Berman
1962	Lindsey Nelson	1974	Keith Jackson	1985	Bob Costas	1997	Bob Costas
1963	Chris Schenkel	1975	Keith Jackson	1986	Al Michaels	1998	Jim Nantz
1964	Chris Schenkel	1976	Keith Jackson	1987	Bob Costas	1999	Dan Patrick
1965	Vin Scully	1977	Pat Summerall	1988	Bob Costas	2000	Bob Costas
1966	Curt Gowdy	1978	Vin Scully	1989	Chris Berman	2001	Chris Berman
1967	Chris Schenkel	1979	Dick Enberg	1990	Chris Berman	2002	Joe Buck
1968	Ray Scott	1980	Dick Enberg	1991	Bob Costas		
1969	Curt Gowdy		& Al Michaels	1992	Bob Costas		
1970	Chris Schenkel	1981	Dick Enberg	1993	Chris Berman		

The Pulitzer Prize

The Pulitzer Prizes for journalism, letters, drama and music have been presented annually since 1917 in the name of Joseph Pulitzer (1847-1911), the publisher of the *New York World.* Prizes are awarded by the president of Columbia University on the recommendation of a board of review. Sixteen Pulitzers have been awarded for newspaper sports reporting, sports commentary and sports photography.

News Coverage

1935 **Bill Taylor,** NY *Herald Tribune,* for his reporting on the 1934 America's Cup yacht races.

Special Citation

1952 **Max Kase,** NY *Journal-American,* for his reporting on the 1951 college basketball point-shaving scandal.

Meritorious Public Service

1954 **Newsday** (Garden City, N.Y.) for its expose of New York State's race track scandals and labor racketeering.

General Reporting

1956 **Arthur Daley,** NY *Times,* for his 1955 columns.

Investigative Reporting

1981 **Clark Hallas** & **Robert Lowe,** (Tucson) *Arizona Daily Star,* for their 1980 investigation of the University of Arizona athletic department.

1986 **Jeffrey Marx** & **Michael York,** Lexington (Ky.) *Herald-Leader,* for their 1985 investigation of the basketball program at the University of Kentucky and other major colleges.

Photography

1949 **Nat Fein,** NY *Herald Tribune,* for his photo, "Babe Ruth Bows Out."

1952 **John Robinson** & **Don Ultang,** Des Moines (Iowa) *Register and Tribune,* for their sequence of six pictures of the 1951 Drake-Oklahoma A&M football game, in which Drake's Johnny Bright had his jaw broken.

Specialized Reporting

1985 **Randall Savage** & **Jackie Crosby,** Macon (Ga.) *Telegraph and News,* for their 1984 investigation of athletics and academics at the University of Georgia and Georgia Tech.

Beat Reporting

2000 **George Dohrmann,** St. Paul (Min.) *Pioneer Press,* for his investigation that revealed academic fraud in the men's basketball program at the University of Minnesota.

Feature Writing

1997 **Lisa Pollak,** Baltimore Sun, for her story about baseball umpire John Hirschbeck dealing with the death of one son and the illness of another from the same disease.

Commentary

1976 **Red Smith,** NY *Times,* for his 1975 columns.

1981 **Dave Anderson,** NY *Times,* for his 1980 columns.

1990 **Jim Murray,** LA *Times,* for his 1989 columns.

1985 **The Photography Staff** of the *Orange County* (Calif.) *Register,* for their coverage of the 1984 Summer Olympics in Los Angeles.

1993 **William Snyder** & **Ken Geiger,** The *Dallas Morning News,* for their coverage of the 1992 Summer Olympics in Barcelona, Spain.

Red Smith Award

Presented annually by the Associated Press Sports Editors (APSE) to a person who has made "major contributions to sports journalism."

Year		Year		Year	
1981	Red Smith, NY Times	1990	Dave Smith, Dallas Morning News	1998	Sam Lacy, Baltimore Afro-American
1982	Jim Murray, LA Times	1991	Dave Kindred, National Sports Daily	1999	Bud Collins, Boston Globe
1983	Shirley Povich, Washington Post	1992	Ed Storin, Miami Herald	2000	Jerry Izenberg, Newark Star Ledger
1984	Fred Russell, Nashville Banner	1993	Tom McEwen, Tampa Tribune	2001	John Steadman, Baltimore Sun
1985	Blackie Sherrod, Dallas Morning News	1994	Dave Anderson, NY Times	2002	Dick Schaap, ESPN "The Sports Reporters"
1986	Si Burick, Dayton Daily News	1995	Richard Sandler, Newsday	2003	George Solomon, Washington Post
1987	Will Grimsley, AP	1996	Bill Dwyre, LA Times		
1988	Furman Bisher, Atlanta Journal	1997	Jerome Holtzman, Chicago Tribune		
1989	Edwin Pope, Miami Herald				

BUSINESS

577

Sportswriter of the Year
NSSA Award

Presented annually since 1959 by the National Sportscasters and Sportswriters Association, based in Salisbury, N.C. Voting is done by NSSA members and selected national media.

Multiple winners: Jim Murray (14); Rick Reilly (8); Frank Deford (6); Red Smith (5); Will Grimsley (4); Peter Gammons (3).

Year		Year		Year	
1959	Red Smith, *NY Herald-Tribune*	1976	Jim Murray, *LA Times*	1993	Peter Gammons, *Boston Globe*
1960	Red Smith, *NY Herald-Tribune*	1977	Jim Murray, *LA Times*	1994	Rick Reilly, *Sports Ill.*
1961	Red Smith, *NY Herald-Tribune*	1978	Will Grimsley, AP	1995	Rick Reilly, *Sports Ill.*
1962	Red Smith, *NY Herald-Tribune*	1979	Jim Murray, *LA Times*	1996	Rick Reilly, *Sports Ill.*
1963	Arthur Daley, *NY Times*	1980	Will Grimsley, AP	1997	Dave Kindred, *The Sporting*
1964	Jim Murray, *LA Times*	1981	Will Grimsley, AP		*News*
1965	Red Smith, *NY Herald-Tribune*	1982	Frank Deford, *Sports Ill.*	1998	Mitch Albom, *Detroit Free Press*
1966	Jim Murray, *LA Times*	1983	Will Grimsley, AP	1999	Rick Reilly, *Sports Ill.*
1967	Jim Murray, *LA Times*	1984	Frank Deford, *Sports Ill.*	2000	Bob Ryan, *Boston Globe*
1968	Jim Murray, *LA Times*	1985	Frank Deford, *Sports Ill.*	2001	Rick Reilly, *Sports Ill.*
1969	Jim Murray, *LA Times*	1986	Frank Deford, *Sports Ill.*	2002	Rick Reilly, *Sports Ill.*
1970	Jim Murray, *LA Times*	1987	Frank Deford, *Sports Ill.*		
1971	Jim Murray, *LA Times*	1988	Frank Deford, *Sports Ill.*		
1972	Jim Murray, *LA Times*	1989	Peter Gammons, *Sports Ill.*		
1973	Jim Murray, *LA Times*	1990	Peter Gammons, *Boston Globe*		
1974	Jim Murray, *LA Times*	1991	Rick Reilly, *Sports Ill.*		
1975	Jim Murray, *LA Times*	1992	Rick Reilly, *Sports Ill.*		

Best Newspaper Sports Sections of 2002

Winners of the annual Associated Press Sports Editors contest for best daily and Sunday sports sections. Awards are divided into different categories, based on circulation figures. Selections are made by a committee of APSE members.

Circulation Over 250,000

Top 10 Daily

Boston Globe · *Minneapolis Star Tribune* · *Dallas Morning News* · *Star-Ledger (Newark, NJ)* · *Detroit Free Press* · *New York Times* · *Fort Worth Star-Telegram* · *USA Today* · *Los Angeles Times* · *Washington Post*

Top 10 Sunday

Atlanta Journal-Constitution · *Los Angeles Times* · *Boston Globe* · *Minneapolis Star Tribune* · *Dallas Morning News* · *Daily News (NY)* · *Fort Worth Star-Telegram* · *Newsday (NY)* · *Kansas City Star* · *Orlando Sentinel*

Circulation 100,000-250,000

Top 10 Daily

Calgary Herald · *Palm Beach Post* · *Contra Costa Times (Walnut Creek, CA)* · *Pittsburgh Post-Gazette* · *Seattle Post-Intelligencer* · *Hartford Courant* · *Seattle Times* · *The Commercial Appeal (Memphis)* · *St. Paul Pioneer Press* · *Tampa Tribune*

Top 10 Sunday

Charlotte Observer · *Raleigh News & Observer* · *Contra Costa Times (Walnut Creek, CA)* · *St. Paul Pioneer Press* · *San Antonio Express-News* · *Des Moines Register* · *Seattle Times* · *Hartford Courant* · *The State (Columbia, SC)* · *Palm Beach Post*

Best Sportswriting of 2002

Winners of the annual Associated Press Sports Editors Contest for best sportswriting in 2002. Eventual winners were chosen from five finalists in each writing division. Selections are made by a committee of APSE members. Note the investigative writing division included all circulation categories.

Circulation over 250,000

Column: Joe Posnanski, *Kansas City Star*
Game story: Rick Morrissey, *Chicago Tribune*
News story: Twenty-one writers, *USA Today*
Feature: Linda Robertson, *Miami Herald*

Enterprise: Tony Barnhart, Mark Schlabach, David Markiewicz, Al Levine, Michael Carvell, Mark Bradley and Carroll Rogers, *Atlanta Journal-Constitution*

Circulation 100,000-250,000

Column: Adrian Wojnarowski, *The Record (Hackensack, NJ)*
Game story: Bob Klapisch, *The Record (Hackensack, NJ)*

News story: Brian Ettkin, *Herald-Tribune (Sarasota, FL)*
Feature: John Erardi, *Cincinnati Enquirer*
Enterprise: Lori Shontz, *Pittsburgh Post-Gazette*

All Categories

Investigative: Scott M. Reid, Marla Jo Fisher and Natalya Shulyakovskaya, *Orange County Register*

Directory of Organizations

Listing of the major sports organizations, teams and media addresses and officials as of Sept. 30, 2003.

AUTO RACING

CART
(Championship Auto Racing Teams, Inc.)
5350 Lakeview Pkwy South Drive, Indianapolis, IN 46268
(317) 715-4100   www.cart.com
President-CEO .Christopher Pook
V.P. of Communications . . . . .Adam Saal

IRL
(Indy Racing League)
4565 West 16th St., Indianapolis, IN 46222
(317) 484-6526   www.indyracing.com
President-CEO . . . . .Tony George
Sr. Dir. of Racing Operations . . . . .John Lewis
Director of Public Relations . . . . .Tom Savage

FIA—Formula One
(Federation Internationale de L'Automobile)
8 Place de la Concorde, Paris 75008 France
TEL: 011-33-1-43-12-58-15   www.fia.com
President . . . . .Max Mosley
Deputy President (Sport) . . . . .Marco Piccinini

NASCAR
(National Assn. for Stock Car Auto Racing)
P.O. Box 2875, Daytona Beach, FL 32120
(386) 253-0611   www.nascar.com
Chairman-CEO . . . . .Brian France
President . . . . .Michael Helton
V.P. of Corporate Communications . . . . .Jim Hunter

NHRA
(National Hot Rod Association)
2035 Financial Way, Glendora, CA 91741
(626) 914-4761   www.nhra.com
President . . . . .Tom Compton
Sr. V.P. of Racing Operations . . . . .Graham Light
V.P. of Communications . . . . .Jerry Archambeault

MAJOR LEAGUE BASEBALL

Office of the Commissioner
245 Park Ave., 31st Floor, New York, NY 10167
(212) 931-7800   www.mlb.com
Commissioner . . . . .Bud Selig
President-COO . . . . .Robert DuPuy
Exec. V.P. of Baseball Ops. . . . . .Sandy Alderson
General Counsel . . . . .Thomas Ostertag
Senior Vice President . . . . .Richard Levin
Sr. V.P. of Corporate Communications . . . . .Jim Gallagher

Player Relations Committee
245 Park Ave.
New York, NY 10160
(212) 931-7800
Executive V.P. for Labor Relations . . . . .Rob Manfred
Chief Labor Negotiator . . . . .Frank Coonelly

Major League Baseball Players Association
12 East 49th St., 24th Floor
New York, NY 10017
(212) 826-0808
Exec. Director & General Counsel . . . . .Donald Fehr
Associate General Counsel . . . . .Gene Orza

AL

American League Office
245 Park Ave., 31st Floor, New York, NY 10167
(212) 931-7800

Anaheim Angels
2000 Gene Autry Way, Anaheim, CA 92806
(888) 796-4256   www.angelsbaseball.com
Owner . . . . .Arturo Moreno
Senior V.P. of Business Ops. . . . . .Kevin Uhlich
V.P. & General Manager . . . . .Bill Stoneman
V.P. of Communications . . . . .Tim Mead

Baltimore Orioles
333 West Camden St., Baltimore, MD 21201
(410) 685-9800   www.theorioles.com
CEO . . . . .Peter Angelos
Vice Chairman & COO . . . . .Joseph Foss
V.P. of Baseball Operations . . . . .Jim Beattie
V.P. of Baseball Operations . . . . .Mike Flanagan
Director of Public Relations . . . . .Bill Stetka

Boston Red Sox
Fenway Park, 4 Yawkey Way, Boston, MA 02215
(617) 267-9440   www.redsox.com
Principal Owner .John Henry
President-CEO . . . . .Larry Lucchino
Senior V.P./General Manager . . . . .Theo Epstein
Director of Media Relations . . . . .Kevin Shea

Chicago White Sox
U.S. Cellular Field, 333 W. 35th St., Chicago, IL 60616
(312) 674-1000   www.whitesox.com
Chairman . . . . .Jerry Reinsdorf
Vice Chairman . . . . .Eddie Einhorn
Senior V.P./General Manager . . . . .Ken Williams
Director of Public Relations . . . . .Scott Reifert

Cleveland Indians
Jacobs Field, 2401 Ontario St., Cleveland, OH 44115
(216) 420-4200   www.indians.com
Owner-Chairman-CEO . . . . .Lawrence Dolan
Exec. V.P./General Manager . . . . .Mark Shapiro
V.P., Public Relations . . . . .Bob DiBiasio

Detroit Tigers
Comerica Park, 2100 Woodward Ave., Detroit, MI 48201
(313) 962-4000   www.detroittigers.com
Owner and Director . . . . .Mike Ilitch
President/CEO/GM . . . . .Dave Dombrowski
Sr. Dir. of Communications . . . . .Cliff Russell

Kansas City Royals
One Royal Way, Kansas City, MO 64129
(816) 921-8000   www.kcroyals.com
Owner/CEO . . . . .David Glass
Executive V.P./COO . . . . .Herk Robinson
Senior V.P./General Manager . . . . .Allard Baird
V.P. of Broadcasting and Public Relations . . . .David Witty

Minnesota Twins
Hubert H. Humphrey Metrodome
34 Kirby Puckett Place, Minneapolis, MN 55415
(612) 375-1366   www.mntwins.com
Owner . . . . .Carl Pohlad
President . . . . .Dave St. Peter
V.P./General Manager . . . . .Terry Ryan
Director of Communications . . . . .Brad Ruiter
Manager of Media Relations . . . . .Sean Harlin

New York Yankees

Yankee Stadium, 161st St. and River Ave., Bronx, NY 10451
(718) 293-4300   www.yankees.com
Principal Owner . . . . George Steinbrenner
President . . . . .Randy Levine
Sr. V.P./General Manager . . . . .Brian Cashman
Dir. of Media Relations/Publicity . . . . Rick Cerrone

Oakland Athletics

7000 Coliseum Way
Oakland, CA 94621
(510) 638-4900   www.oaklandathletics.com
Co-Owners . . . . .Steve Schott and Ken Hofmann
President . . . . .Mike Crowley
V.P./General Manager . . . . .Billy Beane
Baseball Information Manager . . . . .Mike Selleck

Seattle Mariners

Safeco Field, P.O. Box 4100 , Seattle, WA 98104
(206) 346-4000   www.mariners.org
Chairman-CEO . . . . :.Howard Lincoln
President-COO . . . . .Chuck Armstrong
Executive V.P./General Manager . . . . .TBA
Director of Baseball Information . . . . .Tim Hevly

Tampa Bay Devil Rays

Tropicana Field, One Tropicana Dr.
St. Petersburg, FL 33705
(727) 825-3137   www.devilrays.com
Managing General Partner/CEO . . . . .Vincent J. Naimoli
Senior V.P., Baseball Ops./GM . . . . .Chuck LaMar
V.P. of Public Relations . . . . .Rick Vaughn

Texas Rangers

1000 Ballpark Way #400, Arlington, TX 76011
(817) 273-5222   www.texasrangers.com
Owner . . . . .Thomas Hicks
Executive V.P., General Manager . . . . .John Hart
Senior V.P. of Communications . . . . .John Blake

Toronto Blue Jays

SkyDome, One Blue Jays Way, Suite 3200
Toronto, Ontario M5V 1J1
(416) 341-1000   www.bluejays.com
Majority Owner . . . . .Rogers Communications
President & CEO . . . . .Paul Godfrey
Sr. V.P. of Baseball Ops./GM . . . . .J.P. Ricciardi
Director of Communications . . . . .Jay Stenhouse

NL

National League Office

245 Park Ave., 31st Floor, New York, NY 10167
(212) 931-7800

Arizona Diamondbacks

P.O. Box 2095, Phoenix, AZ 85001
(602) 462-6500   www.azdiamondbacks.com
Chairman/CEO . . . . Jerry Colangelo
President . . . . .Richard H. Dozer
V.P./General Manager . . . . .Joe Garagiola Jr.
Director of Public Relations . . . . .Mike Swanson

Atlanta Braves

P.O. Box 4064, Atlanta, GA 30302
(404) 522-7630   www.atlantabraves.com
President . . . . .Stan Kasten
Exec. V.P./General Manager . . . . .John Schuerholz
Director of Public Relations . . . . Jim Schultz

Chicago Cubs

1060 West Addison St., Chicago, IL 60613
(773) 404-2827   www.cubs.com
Owner .The Tribune Company
President/CEO . . . . .Andy MacPhail
General Manager .Jim Hendry
Director of Media Relations . . . . .Sharon Pannozzo

Cincinnati Reds

Great American Ballpark, 100 Main St., Cincinnati, OH 45202
(513) 421-4510   www.cincinnatireds.com
Majority Owner-CEO . . . . .Carl Lindner
General Manager . . . . .TBA
Director of Media Relations . . . . .Rob Butcher

Colorado Rockies

Coors Field, 2001 Blake St., Denver, CO 80205
(303) 292-0200   www.coloradorockies.com
Chairman/CEO . . . . .Charles Monfort
President . . . . .Keli McGregor
Executive V.P./General Manager . . . . .Dan O'Dowd
Sr. Director Comm./PR . . . . .Jay Alves

Florida Marlins

2267 Dan Marino Blvd., Miami, FL 33056
(305) 626-7400   www.flamarlins.com
Owner/Chairman/CEO . . . . .Jeffrey Loria
President . . . . .David Samson
Senior V.P./General Manager . . . . .Larry Beinfest
Director of Media Relations . . . . .Steve Copses

Houston Astros

Minute Maid Park, P.O. Box 288, Houston, TX 77001
(713) 259-8000   www.astros.com
Chairman-CEO . . . . .Drayton McLane Jr.
President of Baseball Ops. . . . . .Tal Smith
General Manager . . . . .Gerry Hunsicker
Senior V.P., Communications . . . . .Jay Lucas

Los Angeles Dodgers

1000 Elysian Park Ave., Los Angeles, CA 90012
(323) 224-1500   www.dodgers.com
Owner . . . . .Bob Daly & News Corp
President/COO . . . . .Bob Graziano
Executive V.P./General Manager . . . . .Dan Evans
Director of Public Relations . . . . .John Olguin

Milwaukee Brewers

Miller Park, One Brewers Way, Milwaukee, WI 53214
(414) 902-4400   www.milwaukeebrewers.com
President/CEO .Ulice Payne
Senior V.P./General Manager . . . . .Doug Melvin
Director of Media Relations . . . . .Jon Greenberg

Montreal Expos

P.O. Box 500, Station M, Montreal, Quebec H1V 3P2
(514) 253-3434   www.montrealexpos.com
President . . . . .Tony Tavares
V.P./General Manager . . . . .Omar Minaya
Director of Media Services . . . . .Monique Giroux

New York Mets

123-01 Roosevelt Ave., Flushing, NY 11368
(718) 507-6387   www.mets.com
Chairman/CEO . . . . .Fred Wilpon
President . . . . .Saul Katz
Interim General Manager . . . . .Jim Duquette
V.P. of Media Relations . . . . .Jay Horwitz

Philadelphia Phillies

3501 South Broad St., Philadelphia, PA 19148
(215) 463-6000   www.phillies.com
General Partner/Pres./CEO . . . . .David Montgomery
Partner/Chairman . . . . .Bill Giles
General Manager & V.P. . . . . .Ed Wade
V.P. of Public Relations . . . . .Larry Shenk

Pittsburgh Pirates

115 Federal St., Pittsburgh, PA 15212
(412) 323-5000   www.pirateball.com
CEO/Managing General Partner . . . . . .Kevin McClatchy
Senior V.P. & General Manager . . . . .Dave Littlefield
Director of Media Relations . . . . .Jim Trdinich

St. Louis Cardinals
250 Stadium Plaza, St. Louis, MO 63102
(314) 421-3060 · www.stlcardinals.com
Chairman/General Partner ....William O. DeWitt Jr.
Chairman ....Frederick O. Hanser
V.P./General Manager ....Walt Jocketty
Director of Media Relations ....Brian Bartow

San Diego Padres
P.O. Box 122000, San Diego, CA 92112
(619) 881-6500 www.padres.com
Chairman ....John Moores
President-COO ....Dick Freeman
Executive V.P./General Manager ⌐........Kevin Towers
Director of Media Relations ....Luis Garcia

San Francisco Giants
Pacific Bell Park, 24 Willie Mays Plaza
San Francisco, CA 94107
(415) 972-2000 www.sfgiants.com
President ....Peter Magowan
Executive V.P./COO ....Laurence Baer
Senior V.P./General Manager ....Brian Sabean
Manager of Media Relations ....Jim Moorehead

PRO BASKETBALL

NBA

League Office
Olympic Tower, 645 Fifth Ave., New York, NY 10022
(212) 407-8000 www.nba.com
Commissioner ....David Stern
Senior V.P. of Basketball Ops. ....Stuart Jackson
Deputy Commissioner ....Russell Granik
Sr. V.P. Sports Media Relations ....Brian McIntyre
Executive V.P. Global Media ....Heidi Ueberroth

NBA Players Association
Two Penn Plaza, Suite 2430, New York, NY 10121
(212) 655-0880 www.nbapa.com
Executive Director ....William Hunter
General Counsel ....Ron Klempner
President ....Michael Curry

Atlanta Hawks
One CNN Center
Atlanta, GA 30303
(404) 827-3800 www.hawks.com
Owner ....AOL-Time Warner
President ....Stan Kasten
General Manager ....Billy Knight
V.P. of Communications ....Arthur Triche

Boston Celtics
151 Merrimac St., 4th Floor, Boston, MA 02114
(617) 854-8000 www.celtics.com
CEO/Managing Partner ....Wyc Grousbeck
President ....Red Auerbach
Exec. Director of Basketball Ops. ....Danny Ainge
V.P. of Media Relations ....Jeff Twiss

Charlotte Bobcats
(Team begins play in 2004-05)
129 West Trade St., Suite 700, Charlotte, NC 28202
(704) 424-4120 www.bobcatsbasketball.com
Chairman/President ....Robert L. Johnson
Exec. V.P./COO ....Ed Tapscott
Exec. V.P. of Corporate Affairs ....Chris Weiller

Chicago Bulls
United Center, 1901 West Madison St., Chicago, IL 60612
(312) 455-4000 www.bulls.com
Chairman ....Jerry Reinsdorf
General Manager ....John Paxson
Sr. Director of Media Services ....Tim Hallam

Cleveland Cavaliers
Gund Arena, One Center Court, Cleveland, OH 44115
(216) 420-2000 www.cavs.com
Owner-Chairman ....Gordon Gund
Owner-Vice Chairman ....George Gund III
President ....Len Komoroski
President & General Manager ....Jim Paxson
V.P., Communications ....Tad Carper

Dallas Mavericks
2909 Taylor St., Dallas, TX 75226
(214) 747-6287 www.dallasmavericks.com
Owner ....Mark Cuban
President/CEO ....Terdema Ussery
GM & Head Coach ....Don Nelson
Sr. V.P., Marketing and Communications ...Matt Fitzgerald

Denver Nuggets
1000 Chopper Cir., Denver, CO 80204
(303) 405-1100 www.nuggets.com
Owner ....Stan Kroenke
General Manager ....Kiki Vandeweghe
Manager of Media Relations ....Eric Sebastian

Detroit Pistons
The Palace of Auburn Hills
Two Championship Dr., Auburn Hills, MI 48326
(248) 377-0100 www.pistons.com
Managing Partner ....William Davidson
President ....Tom Wilson
President of Basketball Operations ....Joe Dumars
V.P. of Public Relations ....Matt Dobek

Golden State Warriors
1011 Broadway, Oakland, CA 94607
(510) 986-2200 www.warriors.com
Owner-CEO ....Chris Cohan
General Manager ....Garry St. Jean
Director of Public Relations ....Raymond Ridder

Houston Rockets
2 Greenway Plaza, Suite 400, Houston, TX 77046
(713) 627-3865 www.rockets.com
Owner ....Leslie L. Alexander
President-CEO ....George Postolos
General Manager ....Carroll Dawson
Director of Media Relations ....Nelson Luis

Indiana Pacers
125 S. Pennsylvania Street, Indianapolis, IN 46204
(317) 917-2500 www.pacers.com
Owners ....Melvin Simon & Herb Simon
CEO ....Donnie Walsh
President of Basketball Ops. ....Larry Bird
Director of Media Relations ....David Benner

Los Angeles Clippers
Staples Center
1111 S. Figueroa St., Suite 1100
Los Angeles, CA 90015
(213) 742-7500 www.clippers.com
Owner-Chairman ....Donald T. Sterling
Executive V.P. ....Andy Roeser
V.P., Basketball Operations ....Elgin Baylor
V.P. of Communications ....Joe Safety

Los Angeles Lakers
555 N. Nash St., El Segundo, CA 90245
(310) 426-6000 www.lakers.com
Owner ....Jerry Buss
General Manager ....Mitch Kupchak
Director of Public Relations ....John Black

Memphis Grizzlies
175 Toyota Plaza, Suite 150
Memphis, TN 38103
(901) 205-1234   www.grizzlies.com
Owner ....Michael Heisley
President of Basketball Ops. ....Jerry West
General Manager ....Dick Versace
Media Relations Director ....Kirk Clayborn

Miami Heat
AmericanAirlines Arena, 601 Biscayne Blvd.
Miami, FL 33132
(786) 777-4328   www.heat.com
Managing General Partner ....Micky Arison
President & Head Coach ....Pat Riley
General Manager & President Basketball Ops. .Randy Pfund
V.P. of Sports Media Relations ....Tim Donovan

Milwaukee Bucks
Bradley Center, 1001 N. Fourth St., Milwaukee, WI 53203
(414) 227-0500   www.bucks.com
President ....Sen. Herb Kohl (D., Wisc.)
General Manager ....Larry Harris
Director of Public Relations ....Cheri Hanson

Minnesota Timberwolves
Target Center
600 First Ave. North, Minneapolis, MN 55403
(612) 673-1600   www.timberwolves.com
Owner ....Glen Taylor
President ....Rob Moor
V.P., Basketball Operations/GM ....Kevin McHale
Dir. of Communications ....Ted Johnson

New Jersey Nets
390 Murray Hill Pkwy., East Rutherford, NJ 07073
(201) 935-8888   www.njnets.com
Co-Chair/Owner ....Lewis Katz
Co-Chairman/CEO ....Lou Lamoriello
President/GM ....Rod Thorn
Director of Public Relations ....Gary Sussman

New Orleans Hornets
1501 Girod St., New Orleans, LA 70113
(504) 301-4000   www.hornets.com
Owners ....George Shinn and Ray Wooldridge
Executive V.P./COO ....Jack Capella
Executive V.P., Basketball Ops./GM ....Bob Bass
V.P. of Public Relations ....Harold Kaufman

New York Knickerbockers
Madison Square Garden
2 Penn Plaza, 14th Floor, New York, NY 10121
(212) 465-6471   www.knicks.com
Owner ....Cablevision Systems Inc.
President (Cablevision) ....James Dolan
President/General Manager ....Scott Layden
V.P. of Communications ....Joe Favorito

Orlando Magic
2 Magic Place
8701 Maitland Summit Blvd., Orlando, FL 32810
(407) 916-2400   www.orlandomagic.com
Owner ....Rich DeVos
COO ....John Weisbrod
V.P., Basketball Ops. & GM ....John Gabriel
Director of Media Relations ....Joel Glass

Philadelphia 76ers
Wachovia Center
3601 S. Broad St., Philadelphia, PA 19148
(215) 339-7600   www.76ers.com
Owner ....Comcast-Spectacor
Chairman ....Ed Snider
President/General Manager ....Billy King
V.P. of Communications ....Karen Frascona

Phoenix Suns
201 E Jefferson St., Phoenix, AZ 85004
(602) 379-7900   www.suns.com
Chairman-CEO/Managing Gen. Partner .Jerry Colangelo
President/General Manager ....Bryan Colangelo
Sr. V.P. of Player Personnel ....Dick Van Arsdale
V.P. of Basketball Communications ....Julie Fie

Portland Trail Blazers
One Center Court, Suite 200, Portland, OR 97227
(503) 234-9291   www.blazers.com
Owner-Chairman ....Paul Allen
President ....Steve Patterson
General Manager ....John Nash
Executive Dir. of Communications ....Mike Hanson

Sacramento Kings
One Sports Parkway, Sacramento, CA 95834
(916) 928-0000   www.kings.com
Controlling Partners ....Joe and Gavin Maloof
President, Basketball Operations ....Geoff Petrie
V.P., Basketball Operations ....Wayne Cooper
Director of Media Relations ....Troy Hanson

San Antonio Spurs
One SBC Center
San Antonio, TX 78219
(210) 554-7700   www.spurs.com
Chairman ....Peter Holt
General Manager ...................R.C. Buford
V.P., Director of Player Personnel ....Sam Schuler
Director of Media Services ....Tom James

Seattle SuperSonics
351 Elliott Ave. West, Suite 500
Seattle, WA 98119
(206) 281-5800   www.supersonics.com
Chairman ....Howard Schultz
President & CEO ....Wally Walker
General Manager ....Rick Sund
Executive Vice President ....Billy McKinney
Director of Public Relations ....Marc Moquin

Toronto Raptors
40 Bay St., Suite 400
Toronto, Ontario M5J 2X2
(416) 815-5600   www.raptors.com
Chairman ....Larry Tanenbaum
President/CEO ....Richard Peddie
Sr. V.P./General Manager ....Glen Grunwald
Director of Media Relations ....Jim LaBumbard

Utah Jazz
Delta Center, 301 West South Temple
Salt Lake City, UT 84101
(801) 325-2500   www.utahjazz.com
Owner ....Larry Miller
President ....Dennis Haslam
Sr. V.P. of Basketball Operations ....Kevin O'Connor
Director of Media Relations ....Kim Turner

Washington Wizards
MCI Center, 601 F Street NW
Washington, D.C., 20004
(202) 661-5000   www.washingtonwizards.com
Chairman ....Abe Pollin
President ....Susan O'Malley
President of Basketball Ops. ....Ernie Grunfeld
Director of Player Personnel ....Milt Newton
Director of Public Relations ....Nicole Hawkins

Other Men's Pro Leagues

Continental Basketball Association
1412 W. Idaho St., Ste. 235
Boise, ID 83702
(208) 429-0101   www.cbahoopsonline.com
Commissioner . . . . .Gary Hunter
Dir. of Public/Media Relations . . . . .Todd Anderson
 Member teams (7): Dakota Wizards, Gary Steel-heads, Great Lakes Storm, Idaho Stampede, Rockford Light-ning, Sioux Falls Skyforce and Yakima Sun Kings.

United States Basketball League
46 Quirk Road, Milford, CT 06460
(203) 877-9508   www.usbl.com
Commissioner . . . . .Daniel T. Meisenheimer III
Dir. of Public Relations . . . . .Dennis Truax
 Member teams (10): Adirondack (NY) Wildcats, Brevard (FL) Blue Ducks, Brooklyn Kings, Cedar Rapids River Raiders, Dodge City Legend, Kansas Cagerz, Oklahoma Storm, Pennsylvania ValleyDawgs, Texas Rim Rockers and Westchester (NY) Wildfire.

National Basketball Development League
24 Vardry Street, Suite 201, Greenville, SC 29601
(864) 248-1100   www.nbdl.com
President . . . . .Philip Evans
Director of Communications . . . . .Kent Partridge
 Member teams (6): Asheville (NC) Altitude; Columbus (GA) Riverdragons; Fayetteville (NC) Patriots; Huntsville (AL) Flight; North Charleston (SC) Lowgators; Roanoke (VA) Dazzle.

WNBA

League Office
645 5th Ave., New York, NY 10022
(212) 688-9622   www.wnba.com
President . . . . .Val Ackerman
V.P. of Player Personnel . . . . .Renee Brown
Dir. of Basketball Communications . . . . . . .John Maxwell

Charlotte Sting
100 Hive Drive, Charlotte, NC 28217
(704) 357-0252   www.charlottesting.com
Owner/President . . . . .Robert L. Johnson
General Manager . . . . .Bernie Bickerstaff
Director of Public Relations . . . . .Karen Kase

Cleveland Rockers
Gund Arena, One Center Court
Cleveland, OH 44115
(216) 420-2000   www.clevelandrockers.com
President . . . . .Len Komoroski
V.P., Communications . . . . .Tad Carper
(Team has ceased operations as of Sept. 19, 2003)

Connecticut Sun
One Mohegan Sun Blvd., Uncasville, CT 06382
(860) 862-4000   www.wnba.com/sun
President . . . . .Paul Munick
General Manager . . . . .Christopher Sienko
Director of Public Relations . . . . .Saverio Mancini

Detroit Shock
The Palace of Auburn Hills
Two Championship Dr., Auburn Hills, MI 48326
(248) 377-0100   www.detroitshock.com
President . . . . .Thomas S. Wilson
Head Coach/Dir. of Player Personnel . . . . .Bill Laimbeer
Dir. of Public Relations & Business Ops. . . .Dennis Sampier

Houston Comets
Two Greenway Plaza, Suite 400
Houston, TX 77046-3865
(713) 627-9622   www.houstoncomets.com
Owner/President . . . . .Leslie L. Alexander
GM/Head Coach . . . . .Van Chancellor
Director of Media Relations . . . . .Nelson Luis

Indiana Fever
125 S. Pennsylvania St., Indianapolis, IN 46204
(317) 917-2500   www.wnba.com/fever
CEO . . . . .Donnie Walsh
Sr. VP/COO . . . . .Kelly Krauskopf
Director of Media Relations . . . . .Kevin Messenger

Los Angeles Sparks
555 N. Nash St., El Segundo, CA 90245
(310) 330-2434   www.lasparks.com
Chairman . . . . .Jerry Buss
General Manager . . . . .Penny Toler
Director of Media Relations . . . . .Kristal Shipp

Minnesota Lynx
Target Center
600 First Ave. N., Minneapolis, MN 55403
(612) 673-1600   www.wnba.com/lynx
Owner . . . . .Glen Taylor
Head Coach . . . . .Suzie McConnell Serio
Manager of Media Relations . . . . .Mike Cristaldi

New York Liberty
Madison Square Garden
Two Penn Plaza, New York, NY 10121
(212) 564-9622   www.nyliberty.com
Owner .Cablevision Systems Inc.
Senior V.P/General Manager . . . . . . .Carol Blazejowski
Manager of Communications . . . . .Larry Torres

Phoenix Mercury
America West Arena, 201 E. Jefferson St.
Phoenix, AZ 85004
(602) 514-8333   www.phoenixmercury.com
President . . . . .Bryan Colangelo
V.P., General Manager . . . . .Seth Sulka
Director of Communications . . . . .Tami Nealy

Sacramento Monarchs
ARCO Arena, One Sports Pkwy.
Sacramento, CA 95834
(916) 928-0000 www.sacramentomonarchs.com
President, Basketball Ops. . . . . .John Thomas
General Manager . . . . .John Whisenant
Manager of Media Relations . . . . .Kimberly Williams

San Antonio Silver Stars
One SBC Center
San Antonio, TX 78219
(210) 444-5000   www.wnba.com/silverstars
Chairman/CEO . . . . .Peter Holt
COO . . . . .Clarissa Davis-Wrightsil
Manager, Media Services . . . . .Kris Davis

Seattle Storm
351 Elliott Ave. W., Suite 500
Seattle, WA 98119
(206) 281-5800   www.wnba.com/storm
President & CEO . . . . .Wally Walker
General Manager/Exec. V.P. . . . . .Billy McKinney
Sr. Director of Media Relations . . . . .Valerie O'Neil

Washington Mystics
MCI Center, 601 F St. NW
Washington D.C. 20004
(202) 661-5000   www.wnba.com/mystics
President . . . . .Susan O'Malley
Sr. V.P. Business & Basketball Ops. . . . .Judy Holland-Burton
Dir. of Public Relations . . . . .Dyani Gordon

BOWLING

ABC
(American Bowling Congress)
5301 South 76th St., Greendale, WI 53129
(800) 514-2695   www.bowl.com/bowl/abc
Executive Director . . . . .Roger Dalkin
President . . . . .Alton Forbes

BPAA
(Bowling Proprietors' Assn. of America)
P.O. Box 5802
Arlington, TX 76011
(817) 649-5105 www.bpaa.com
Executive Director . . . . .John F. Berglund
President . . . . .Jack Moran
Director of Public Relations . . . . .Cary Richmond

PWBA
(Professional Women's Bowling Association)
7171 Cherryvale Blvd.
Rockford, IL 61112
(815) 332-5756 www.pwba.com
Owner . . . . .Pinacle Events
President . . . . .John Falzone
Media Director . . . . .Gary Kohn

PBA
(Professional Bowlers Association)
719 Second Ave., Suite 701
Seattle, WA 98104
(206) 332-9688 www.pba.com
Chairman . . . . .Chris Peters
President/CEO . . . . .Steve Miller
Dir. of Corporate Communications . . . . . . .Beth Marshall

WIBC
(Women's International Bowling Congress, Inc.)
5301 South 76th St., Greendale, WI 53129
(414) 421-9000 www.bowl.com/bowl/wibc
President . . . . .Sylvia Broyles
Executive Director . . . . .Roseann Kuhn

BOXING

IBF
(International Boxing Federation)
134 Evergreen Place, 9th Floor, East Orange, NJ 07018
(973) 414-0300 www.ibf-usba-boxing.com
President . . . . .Marian Muhammad
Treasurer-Ratings Chairman . . . . .Daryl Peoples

WBA
(World Boxing Association)
P.O. Box 377, Maracay 2101-A, Estado Aragua
Venezuela
TEL: 011-58-244-663-1584 www.wbaonline.com
President . . . . .Gilberto Mendoza
General Counsel/U.S. Spokesman . . . . .Jimmy Binns
300 Walnut St., Philadelphia, PA 19106
(215) 922-4000
Ratings Chairman . . . . Jose Oliver Gomez
TEL: (507) 638-0527

WBC
(World Boxing Council)
Genova 33-503, Col. Juarez,
MEXICO, 06600, D.F., Mexico
TEL: 011-525-525-3787 www.wbcboxing.com
President . . . . .Jose Sulaiman
Ratings Chairman . . . . .Frank Quill
Press Information/U.S. Spokesman . . . . .John Brister
(831) 423-4824

WBO
(World Boxing Organization)
1st Federal Bldg.
1056 Ave Munoz Rivera, Suite 711
San Juan, P.R. 00927
(787) 765-4444 www.wbo-int.com
President . . . . .Francisco "Paco" Valcarcel
Past Pres./Chairman Champ. Committee . . .Luis Batista Salas
Ratings Chairman .Luis Perez

Don King Productions, Inc.
501 Fairway Dr.
Deerfield Beach, FL 33441
(954) 418-5800 www.donking.com
President . . . . .Don King
V.P. of Boxing Ops. . . . . .Dana Jamison
V.P., Boxing Ops./Public Relations . . . . . . .Bob Goodman

Top Rank
3980 Howard Hughes Pkwy. Ste. 580
Las Vegas, NV 89109
(702) 732-2717 www.toprank.com
Chairman . . . . .Bob Arum
Director of Public Relations . . . . .Lee Samuels

COLLEGE SPORTS

NAIA
(National Assn. of Intercollegiate Athletics)
23500 W. 105th Street, Olathe, KS 66051
(913) 791-0044 www.naia.org
President-CEO . . . . .Steve Baker
Director of Sports Information . . . . .Dawn Harmon

NCAA
(National Collegiate Athletic Association)
P.O. Box 6222, Indianapolis, IN 46206
(317) 917-6222 www.ncaa.com
President . . . . .Myles Brand
Senior Vice President . . . . .TBA
V.P. of Enforcement . . . . .David Price
Director of Public Relations . . . . .Jeff Howard

WSF
(Women's Sports Foundation)
Eisenhower Park, East Meadow, NY 11554
(516) 542-4700 www.womenssportsfoundation.org
Founder . . . . .Billie Jean King
Executive Director . . . . .Donna Lopiano
President . . . . .Dawn Riley
Sr. Comm. Coordinator . . . . .Ellie Seifert

Major NCAA Conferences

See pages 439-447 for football coaches, basketball
coaches, nicknames and colors of all Division I-A and I-AA
football schools and Division I basketball schools.

ATLANTIC COAST CONFERENCE
P.O. Drawer ACC
Greensboro, NC 27417-6724
(336) 854-8787 www.theacc.com
854-8788
Founded: 1953
Commissioner . . . . John Swofford
Asst. Commis. of Media Relations . . . . . .Brian Morrison
2003-04 members: BASKETBALL & FOOTBALL (9)—
Clemson, Duke, Florida St., Georgia Tech, Maryland, North
Carolina, N.C. State, Virginia and Wake Forest.

Clemson University
Clemson, SC 29633
SID: (864) 656-2114 www.clemsontigers.com
Founded: 1889 . . . . .Enrollment: 16,403
President . . . . .James F. Barker
Athletic Director . . . . .Terry Don Phillips
Asst. AD, Sports Information . . . . .Tim Bourret

Duke University
Durham, NC 27708
SID: (919) 684-2633 www.goduke.com
Founded: 1838 Enrollment: 6,347
President . . . . .Nannerl Keohane
Athletic Director .Joe Alleva
Sports Information Director . . . . .Jon Jackson

Florida State University
Tallahassee, FL 32306
SID: (850) 644-1403   www.seminoles.com
Founded: 1851   Enrollment: 36,683
President . . . . .Dr. T.K. Wetherell
Athletic Director . . . . .Dave Hart Jr.
Sports Information Director . . . . .Rob Wilson

Georgia Tech
Atlanta, GA 30332
SID: (404) 894-5445   www.ramblinwreck.com
Founded: 1885   Enrollment: 15,000
President . . . . .Wayne Clough
Athletic Director .Dave Braine
Sports Information Director . . . . .Allison George

University of Maryland
College Park, MD 20741
SID: (301) 314-7064   www.umterps.com
Founded: 1807   Enrollment: 34,801
President .Dr. Clayton D. Mote Jr.
Athletic Director .Deborah Yow
Assoc. AD, Media Relations . . . . .Doug Dull

University of North Carolina
Chapel Hill, NC 27514
SID: (919) 962-2123   www.tarheelblue.com
Founded: 1789   Enrollment: 25,972
Chancellor . . . . .James Moeser
Athletic Director . . . . .Dick Baddour
Sports Information Director . . . . .Steve Kirschner

North Carolina State University
Raleigh, NC 27695
SID: (919) 515-2102   www.gopack.com
Founded: 1887   Enrollment: 29,286
Chancellor . . . . .Marye Anne Fox
Athletic Director .Lee Fowler
Asst. AD for Media Relations . . . . . . .Annabelle Vaughan

University of Virginia
Charlottesville, VA 22903
SID: (434) 982-5500   www.virginiasports.com
Founded: 1819   Enrollment: 19,197
President .John T. Casteen III
Athletic Director . . . . .Craig Littlepage
Sports Information Director . . . . .Rich Murray

Wake Forest University
Winston-Salem, NC 27109
SID: (336) 758-5640   www.wakeforestsports.com
Founded: 1834   Enrollment: 6,264
President .Thomas K. Hearn Jr.
Athletic Director . . . . .Ron Wellman
Asst. Athletic Director/Media Relations . . . . .Dean Buchan

*   *   *

BIG EAST CONFERENCE
222 Richmond Street, Suite 110
Providence, RI 02903
(401) 272-9108   www.bigeast.org
Founded: 1979
Commissioner . . . . .Mike Tranghese
Assoc. Commissioner/Communications . . . John Paquette
  2003-04 members: BASKETBALL (14)—Boston
College, Connecticut, Georgetown, Miami-FL, Notre Dame,
Pittsburgh, Providence, Rutgers, St. John's, Seton Hall,
Syracuse, Villanova, Virginia Tech and West Virginia; FOOT-
BALL (8)—Boston College, Miami-FL, Pittsburgh, Rutgers,
Syracuse, Temple, Virginia Tech and West Virginia.

Boston College
Chestnut Hill, MA 02467
SID: (617) 552-3004   www.bceagles.com
Founded: 1863   Enrollment: 14,830
President . . . . .Rev. William P. Leahy, S.J.
Athletic Director . . . . .Gene DeFilippo
Sports Information Director . . . . .Chris Cameron

University of Connecticut
Storrs, CT 06269
SID: (860) 486-3531   www.uconnhuskies.com
Founded:1881   Enrollment: 17,652
President . . . . .Philip Austin
Athletic Director . . . . .Jeffrey Hathaway
Sports Information Director . . . . .Michael Enright

Georgetown University
Washington, DC 20057
SID: (202) 687-2492   www.guhoyas.com
Founded: 1789   Enrollment: 6,374
President . . . . .John J. DeGioia, Ph. D.
Athletic Director . . . . .Joseph C. Lang
Sr. Sports Communication Director . . . . . . .Bill Shapland

University of Miami
Coral Gables, FL 33146
SID: (305) 284-3244   www.hurricanesports.com
Founded: 1926   Enrollment: 13,842
President . . . . .Dr. Donna E. Shalala
Athletic Director . . . . .Paul Dee
Asst. Athletic Director/Communications . . . . . .Mark Pray

University of Notre Dame
Notre Dame, IN 46556
SID: (574) 631-7516   www.und.com
Founded: 1842   Enrollment: 10,126
President . . . . .Rev. Edward (Monk) Malloy
Athletic Director . . . . .Kevin White
Sports Information Director . . . . .John Heisler

University of Pittsburgh
Pittsburgh, PA 15260
SID: (412) 648-8240   www.pittsburghpanthers.com
Founded: 1787   Enrollment: 33,544
Chancellor . . . . .Mark A. Nordenberg
Athletic Director . . . . .Jeff Long
Sports Information Director . . . . .E.J. Borghetti

Providence College
Providence, RI 02918
SID: (401) 865-2272   www.friars.com
Founded: 1917   Enrollment: 3,596
President . . . . .Philip A. Smith, O.P.
Athletic Director . . . . .Robert Driscoll
Sports Information Director . . . . .Arthur Parks

Rutgers University
New Brunswick, NJ 08903
SID: (732) 445-4200   www.scarletknights.com
Founded: 1766   Enrollment: 33,500
President . . . . .Richard L. McCormick
Athletic Director . . . . .Robert E. Mulcahy III
Sports Information Director . . . . .John Wooding

St. John's University
Jamaica, NY 11439
SID: (718) 990-1520   www.redstormsports.com
Founded: 1870   Enrollment: 18,300
President . . . . .Rev. Donald J. Harrington, CM
Athletic Director . . . . .David Wegrzyn
Sports Information Director . . . . .Dominic Scianna

Seton Hall University
South Orange, NJ 07079
SID: (973) 761-9493   www.shupirates.com
Founded: 1856   Enrollment: 9,604
President   Monsignor Robert Sheeran
Athletic Director . . . . .Jeff Fogelson
Sports Information Director . . . . .Marie Wozniak

Syracuse University
Syracuse, NY 13244
SID: (315) 443-2608 — www.suathletics.com
Founded: 1870 — Enrollment: 10,000
Chancellor ....Kenneth Shaw
Athletic Director ....Jake Crouthamel
Sports Information Director ....Sue Edson

Temple University
Philadelphia, PA 19122
SID: (215) 204-7445 — www.owlsports.com
Founded: 1884 — Enrollment: 30,000
President ....Dr. David Adamany
Athletic Director ....Bill Bradshaw
Sports Information Director ....Kevin Lorincz

Villanova University
Villanova, PA 19085
SID: (610) 519-4120 — www.villanova.com
Founded: 1842 — Enrollment: 6,295
President ....Rev. Edmund J. Dobbin, OSA
Athletic Director ....Vince Nicastro
Sports Information Director ....Dean Kenefick

Virginia Tech
Blacksburg, VA 24061
SID: (540) 231-6726 — www.hokiesports.com
Founded: 1872 — Enrollment: 24,812
President ....Charles Steger
Athletic Director ....Jim Weaver
Sports Information Director ....Dave Smith

West Virginia University
Morgantown, WV 26507
SID: (304) 293-2821 — www.wvu.edu/~sports
Founded: 1867 — Enrollment: 21,500
President ....David Hardesty
Athletic Director ....Ed Pastilong
Sports Information Director ....Shelly Poe

*   *   *

BIG 12 CONFERENCE
2201 Stemmons Fwy., 28th Floor
Dallas, TX 75207
(214) 742-1212 — www.big12sports.com
Founded: 1996
Commissioner ....Kevin Weiberg
Assoc. Commis./Media Relations ....Bo Carter
2003-04 members: BASKETBALL & FOOTBALL (12)—
Baylor, Colorado, Iowa St., Kansas, Kansas St., Missouri,
Nebraska, Oklahoma, Oklahoma St., Texas, Texas A&M
and Texas Tech.

Baylor University
Waco, TX 76711
SID: (254) 710-2743 — www.baylorbears.com
Founded: 1845 — Enrollment: 14,159
President ....Robert B. Sloan
Athletic Director ....Ian McCaw
Director of Media Relations ....Heath Nielsen

University of Colorado
Boulder, CO 80309
SID: (303) 492-5626 — www.cubuffs.com
Founded: 1876 — Enrollment: 27,954
President ....Dr. Elizabeth Hoffman
Athletic Director ....Dick Tharp
Sports Information Director ....Dave Plati

Iowa State University
Ames, IA 50011
SID: (515) 294-3372 — www.cyclones.com
Founded: 1858 — Enrollment: 27,898
President ....Gregory Geoffroy
Athletic Director ....Bruce Van De Velde
Sports Information Director ....Tom Kroeschell

University of Kansas
Lawrence, KS 66045
SID: (785) 864-3417 — www.kuathletics.com
Founded: 1866 — Enrollment: 27,463
Chancellor ....Robert Hemenway
Athletic Director ....Lew Perkins
Director of Media Relations ....Mitch Germann

Kansas State University
Manhattan, KS 66502
SID: (785) 532-6735 — www.kstatesports.com
Founded: 1863 — Enrollment: 22,762
President ....Jon Wefald
Athletic Director ....Tim Weiser
Sports Information Director ....Garry Bowman

University of Missouri
Columbia, MO 65205
SID: (573) 882-0712 — www.mutigers.com
Founded: 1839 — Enrollment: 23,666
President ....Dr. Elson Floyd
Athletic Director ....Michael Alden
Media Relations Director ....Chad Moller

University of Nebraska
Lincoln, NE 68588
SID: (402) 472-2263 — www.huskers.com
Founded: 1869 — Enrollment: 25,000
Chancellor ....Harvey Perlman
Athletic Director ....Steve Pederson
Sports Information Director ....Chris Anderson

University of Oklahoma
Norman, OK 73019
SID: (405) 325-8231 — www.soonersports.com
Founded: 1890 — Enrollment: 28,954
President ....David Boren
Athletic Director ....Joe Castiglione
Dir. of Athletic Media Relations ....Kenny Mossman

Oklahoma State University
Stillwater, OK 74078
SID: (405) 744-7714 — www.okstate.com
Founded: 1890 — Enrollment: 21,000
President ....Dr. David J. Schimdly
Athletic Director ....Harry Birdwell
Assoc. AD, Media Relations ....Steve Buzzard

University of Texas
Austin, TX 78713
SID: (512) 471-7437 — www.texassports.com
Founded: 1883 — Enrollment: 49,411
President ....Dr. Larry Faulkner
Athletic Director ....DeLoss Dodds
Asst. AD for Media Relations ....John Bianco

Texas A&M University
College Station, TX 77843
SID: (979) 845-5725 — www.aggieathletics.com
Founded: 1876 — Enrollment: 45,083
President ....Dr. Robert Gates
Athletic Director ....Bill Byrne
Asst. AD for Media Relations ....Alan Cannon

Texas Tech University
Lubbock, TX 79409
SID: (806) 742-2770 — www.texastech.com
Founded: 1923 — Enrollment: 27,000
Chancellor ....David R. Smith
Athletic Director ....Gerald Myers
Asst. AD for Media Relations ....Chris Cook

*   *   *

BIG TEN CONFERENCE
1500 West Higgins Road
Park Ridge, IL 60068-6300
(847) 696-1010   www.bigten.org
Founded: 1896
Commissioner . . . . .James E. Delany
Assoc. Commissioner of Media Relations . . . . .Sue Lister
   2003-04 members: BASKETBALL & FOOTBALL (11)—
Illinois, Indiana, Iowa, Michigan, Michigan St., Minnesota,
Northwestern, Ohio St., Penn St., Purdue and Wisconsin.

University of Illinois
Champaign, IL 61820
SID: (217) 244-6533
Founded: 1867   Enrollment: 36,738
President .James J. Stukel
Athletic Director . . . . .Ron Guenther
Dir. of Communications . . . . .Kent Brown
www.fightingillini.com

Indiana University
Bloomington, IN 47408
SID: (812) 855-9399   www.iuhoosiers.com
Founded: 1820   Enrollment: 36,000
President . . . . .Dr. Adam W. Herbert
Athletic Director . . . . .Terry Clapacs
Asst. AD, Media Relations . . . . .Jeff Fanter

University of Iowa
Iowa City, IA 52242
SID: (319) 335-9411   www.hawkeyesports.com
Founded: 1847   Enrollment: 28,705
President . . . . .David Skorton
Athletic Director . . . . .Bob Bowlsby
Sports Information Director . . . . .Phil Haddy

University of Michigan
Ann Arbor, MI 48109
SID: (734) 763-4423   www.mgoblue.com
Founded: 1817   Enrollment: 37,197
President . . . . .Mary Sue Coleman
Athletic Director . . . . .William Martin
Sports Information Director . . . . .Bruce Madej

Michigan State University
East Lansing, MI 48824
SID: (517) 355-2271   www.msuspartans.com
Founded: 1855   Enrollment: 43,159
President . . . . .Peter McPherson
Athletic Director . . . . .Ron Mason
Asst. AD for Media Relations . . . . . . .John Lewandowski

University of Minnesota
Minneapolis, MN 55455
SID: (612) 625-4090   www.gophersports.com
Founded: 1851   Enrollment: 45,361
President . . . . .Robert Bruininks
Athletic Director . . . . .Joel Maturi
Director of Media Relations . . . . .Nick Joos

Northwestern University
Evanston, IL 60208
SID: (847) 491-7503   www.nusports.com
Founded: 1851   Enrollment: 7,400
President . . . . .Henry S. Bienen
Athletic Director . . . . .Mark Murphy
Asst. Athletic Director/Media Services . . . . . .Mike Wolf

Ohio State University
Columbus, OH 43210
SID: (614) 292-6861   www.ohiostatebuckeyes.com
Founded: 1870   Enrollment: 54,989
President . . . . .Karen A. Holbrook
Athletic Director . . . . .Andy Geiger
Asst. AD, Athletic Communications . . . . . . .Steve Snapp

Penn State University
University Park, PA 16802
SID: (814) 865-1757   www.gopsusports.com
Founded: 1855   Enrollment: 40,571
President . . . . .Graham Spanier
Athletic Director . . . . .Tim Curley
Assoc. AD, Communications . . . . .Jeff Nelson

Purdue University
West Lafayette, IN 47907
SID: (765) 494-3201   www.purduesports.com
Founded: 1869   Enrollment: 37,871
President . . . . .Martin C. Jischke
Athletic Director . . . . .Morgan Burke
Sports Information Director . . . . .Tom Schott

University of Wisconsin
Madison, WI 53711
SID: (608) 262-1811   www.uwbadgers.com
Founded: 1848   Enrollment: 41,522
Chancellor . . . . .John Wiley
Athletic Director . . . . .Pat Richter
Sports Information Director . . . . .Justin Doherty

      *****   *****   *****

CONFERENCE USA
35 East Wacker Drive, Suite 650, Chicago, IL 60601
(312) 553-0483   www.conferenceusa.com
Founded: 1995
Commissioner . . . . .Britton Banowsky
Asst. Comm. for Media Relations . . . . . .Russell Anderson
   2003-04 members: BASKETBALL (14)—UAB, Char-
lotte, Cincinnati, DePaul, East Carolina, Houston, Louisville,
Marquette, Memphis, Saint Louis, South Florida, Southern
Miss, TCU and Tulane; FOOTBALL (11)—UAB, Army, Cincin-
nati, East Carolina, Houston, Louisville, Memphis, South
Florida, Southern Miss, TCU and Tulane.

University of Alabama at Birmingham
Birmingham, AL 35294
SID: (205) 934-0723   www.uabsports.com
Founded: 1969   Enrollment: 15,850
President . . . . .Carol Z. Garrison
Athletic Director . . . . .Watson Brown
Asst. AD for Media Relations . . . . .Norm Reilly

Army—U.S. Military Academy
West Point, NY 10996
SID: (845) 938-3303   www.goarmysports.com
Founded: 1802   Enrollment: 4,000
Superintendent . . . . .Lt. Gen. William J. Lennox, Jr.
Athletic Director . . . . .Rick Greenspan
Asst. AD for Media Relations . . . . .Bob Beretta

University of Cincinnati
Cincinnati, OH 45221
SID: (513) 556-5191   www.ucbearcats.com
Founded: 1819   Enrollment: 34,000
President . . . . .Dr. Nancy L. Zimpher
Athletic Director . . . . .Bob Goin
Asst. AD for Media Relations . . . . .Tom Hathaway

DePaul University
Chicago, IL 60614
SID: (773) 325-7525   www.depaulbluedemons.com
Founded: 1898   Enrollment: 18,565
President . . . . .Rev. John P. Minogue
Athletic Director . . . . .Jean Lenti Ponsetto
Sports Information Director . . . . .Scott Reed

East Carolina University
Greenville, NC 27858
SID: (252) 328-4522   www.ecupirates.com
Founded: 1907   Enrollment: 20,615
Chancellor . . . . .Dr. William V. Muse
Interim Athletic Director . . . . .Nick Floyd
Sports Information Director . . . . .Craig Wells

University of Houston
Houston, TX 77204
SID: (713) 743-9404   www.uhcougars.com
Founded: 1927   Enrollment: 30,757
President . . . . .Dr. Jay Gogue
Athletic Director .Dave Maggard
Sports Information Director . . . . .Chris Burkhalter

University of Louisville
Louisville, KY 40292
SID: (502) 852-6581   www.uoflsports.com
Founded: 1798   Enrollment: 22,000
President . . . . .James Ramsey
Athletic Director . . . . .Tom Jurich
Sports Information Director . . . . .Kenny Klein

Marquette University
Milwaukee, WI 53233
SID: (414) 288-7447   www.gomarquette.com
Founded: 1881   Enrollment: 11,000
President . . . . .Rev. Robert A. Wild S.J.
Athletic Director . . . . .Bill Cords
Sports Information Director . . . . .John Farina

University of Memphis
Memphis, TN 38152
SID: (901) 678-2337   www.gotigersgo.com
Founded: 1912   Enrollment: 20,332
President . . . . .Dr. Shirley Raines
Athletic Director .R.C. Johnson
Asst. AD, Media Relations . . . . .Bob Winn

University of North Carolina at Charlotte
Charlotte, NC 28223
SID: (704) 687-6312   www.charlotte49ers.com
Founded: 1946   Enrollment: 16,395
Chancellor . . . . .James Woodward
Athletic Director . . . . .Judy Rose
Asst. AD, Media Relations . . . . .Tom Whitestone

Saint Louis University
St. Louis, MO 63103
SID: (314) 977-3462   www.slubillikens.com
Founded: 1818   Enrollment: 11,274
President . . . . .Rev. Lawrence Biondi, S.J.
Athletic Director .Doug Woolard
Sport Information Director . . . . .Doug McIlhagga

University of South Florida
Tampa, FL 33620
SID: (813) 974-4086   www.gousfbulls.com
Founded: 1956   Enrollment: 37,000
President . . . . .Judy Genshaft
Athletic Director . . . . .Lee Roy Selmon
Sports Information Director . . . . .John Gerdes

University of Southern Mississippi
Hattiesburg, MS 39406
SID: (601) 266-4507   www.southernmiss.com
Founded: 1910   Enrollment: 15,259
President . . . . .Dr. Shelby Thames
Athletic Director . . . . .Rich Giannini
Asst. AD for Media Relations . . . . .Mike Montoro

TCU—Texas Christian University
Fort Worth, TX 76129
SID: (817) 257-7969   www.gofrogs.com
Founded: 1873   Enrollment: 8,066
Chancellor . . . . .Dr. Victor Boschini
Athletic Director .Eric Hyman
Director of Media Relations . . . . .Steve Fink

Tulane University
New Orleans, LA 70118
SID: (504) 865-5506   www.tulanegreenwave.com
Founded: 1834   Enrollment: 12,381
President . . . . .Dr. Scott S. Cowen
Athletic Director .Rick Dickson
Asst. AD for Media Relations . . . . .Donna Turner

*   *   *

MID-AMERICAN CONFERENCE
24 Public Square, 15th Floor, Cleveland, OH 44113
(216) 566-4622   www.mac-sports.com
Founded: 1946
Commissioner . . . . .Rick Chryst
Director of Communications . . . . .Gary Richter
   2003-04 members: FOOTBALL (14)—Akron, Ball St.,
Bowling Green, Buffalo, Central Florida, Central Michigan,
Eastern Michigan, Kent St., Marshall, Miami-OH, Northern
Illinois, Ohio University, Toledo and Western Michigan;
BASKETBALL (13)—all except Central Florida.

University of Akron
Akron, OH 44325
SID: (330) 972-7468   www.gozips.com
Founded: 1870   Enrollment: 24,358
President . . . . .Luis Proenza
Athletic Director . . . . .Michael J. Thomas
Director of Media Relations . . . . .Shawn Nestor

Ball State University
Muncie, IN 47306
SID: (765) 285-8242   www.ballstatesports.com
Founded: 1918   Enrollment: 18,528
President . . . . .Dr. Blaine Brownell
Athletic Director . . . . .Lawrence "Bubba" Cunningham
Assoc. AD for External Affairs . . . . .Joe Hernandez

Bowling Green State University
Bowling Green, OH 43403
SID: (419) 372-7075   www.bgsufalcons.com
Founded: 1910   Enrollment: 20,650
President . . . . .Sidney Ribeau
Athletic Director . . . . .Paul Krebs
Director of Athletic Communications . . . . . .J.D. Campbell

University of Buffalo
Buffalo, NY 14260
SID: (716) 645-6311   www.ubathletics.buffalo.edu
Founded: 1846   Enrollment: 25,838
President . . . . .TBA
Interim Athletic Director . . . . .William Maher
Sports Information Director . . . . .Paul Vecchio

University of Central Florida
Orlando, FL 32816
SID: (407) 823-2729   www.ucfathletics.com
Founded: 1963   Enrollment: 40,000
President . . . . .Dr. John C. Hitt
Athletic Director .Steve Orsini
Asst. AD for Media Relations . . . . .John Marini

Central Michigan University
Mt. Pleasant, MI 48859
SID: (989) 774-3277   www.cmuchippewas.com
Founded: 1892   Enrollment: 28,015
President . . . . .Michael Rao
Athletic Director . . . . .Herb Deromedi
Sports Information Director . . . . .Fred Stabley Jr.

Eastern Michigan University
Ypsilanti, MI 48197
SID: (734) 487-0317   www.emich.edu/goeagles
Founded: 1849   Enrollment: 24,000
President .Dr. Samuel Kirkpatrick
Athletic Director . . . . .Dr. David Diles
Sports Information Director . . . . .Jim Streeter

Kent State University
Kent, OH 44242
SID: (330) 672-2110   www.kent.edu/athletics
Founded: 1910   Enrollment: 33,000
President . . . . .Carol Cartwright
Athletic Director . . . . .Laing Kennedy
Sports Information Director . . . . .Will Roleson

Marshall University
Huntington, WV 25715
SID: (304) 696-4660   www.herdzone.com
Founded: 1837   Enrollment: 16,038
President . . . . .Dan Angel
Athletic Director . . . . .Bob Marcum
Assoc. Sports Information Director . . . . . . .Randy Burnside

Miami University
Oxford, OH 45056
SID: (513) 529-4327   www.muredhawks.com
Founded: 1809   Enrollment: 16,300
President . . . . .James C. Garland
Athletic Director . . . . .Brad Bates
Asst. AD for External Affairs . . . . .Mike Harris

Northern Illinois University
DeKalb, IL 60115
SID: (815) 753-1706   www.niuhuskies.com
Founded: 1895   Enrollment: 24,948
President . . . . .John G. Peters
Athletic Director . . . . .Cary Groth
Sports Information Director . . . . .Michael Korcek

Ohio University
Athens, OH 45701
SID: (740) 593-1298   www.ohiobobcats.com
Founded: 1804   Enrollment: 28,197
President . . . . .Robert Glidden
Athletic Director .Tom Boeh
Dir. of Broadcasting and Media Relations . . . .Derek Scott

University of Toledo
Toledo, OH 43606
SID: (419) 530-4920   www.utrockets.com
Founded: 1872   Enrollment: 20,014
President . . . . .Dr. Daniel Johnson
Athletic Director . . . . .Mike O'Brien
Assoc. AD, Media Relations . . . . .Paul Helgren

Western Michigan University
Kalamazoo, MI 49008
SID: (616) 387-4138   www.wmubroncos.com
Founded: 1903   Enrollment: 29,732
President . . . . .Dr. Judith I. Bailey
Athletic Director . . . . .Kathy Beauregard
Sports Information Director . . . . .Dan Jankowski

*   *   *

MOUNTAIN WEST CONFERENCE
15455 Gleneagle Drive, Suite 200
Colorado Springs, CO 80921
(719) 488-4040   www.themwc.com
Founded: 1999
Commissioner . . . . .Craig Thompson
Associate Comm./Communications . . . . .Bob Burda
   2003-04 members: BASKETBALL & FOOTBALL (8)—
Air Force, BYU, Colorado St., UNLV, New Mexico, San
Diego St., Utah and Wyoming.

U.S. Air Force Academy
US Academy, CO 80840
SID: (719) 333-9263   www.airforcesports.com
Founded: 1959   Enrollment: 4,000
Superintendent . . . . .Lt. Gen. John W. Rosa Jr.
Athletic Director . . . . .Col. Randall W. Spetman
Asst. AD for Media Relations . . . . .Troy Garnhart

Brigham Young University
Provo, UT 84602
SID: (801) 422-4910   www.byucougars.com
Founded: 1875   Enrollment: 30,069
President . . . . .Cecil O. Samuelson
Athletic Director . . . . .Val Hale
Assoc. Director, External Relations . . . . .Duff Tittle

Colorado State University
Fort Collins, CO 80523
SID: (970) 491-5067   www.csurams.com
Founded: 1870   Enrollment: 23,934
President . . . . .Dr. Larry Penley
Athletic Director . . . . .Mark Driscoll
Asst. AD, Media Relations Director . . . . . . .Gary Ozzello

University of New Mexico
Albuquerque, NM 87131
SID: (505) 925-5520   www.golobos.com
Founded: 1889   Enrollment: 24,250
President . . . . .Louis Caldera
Athletic Director . . . . .Rudy Davalos
Assoc. AD, Media Relations . . . . .Greg Remington

San Diego State University
San Diego, CA 92182
SID: (619) 594-5547   www.goaztecs.com
Founded: 1897   Enrollment: 34,171
President . . . . .Dr. Stephen L. Weber
Interim Athletic Director . . . . .Gene Bartow
Assoc. AD, Media Relations . . . . .Kevin Klintworth

UNLV—University of Nevada, Las Vegas
Las Vegas, NV 89154
SID: (702) 895-3207   www.unlvrebels.com
Founded: 1957   Enrollment: 24,000
President . . . . .Dr. Carol Harter
Athletic Director . . . . .Mike Hamrick
Sports Information Director . . . . .Andy Grossman

University of Utah
Salt Lake City, UT 84112
SID: (801) 581-3510   www.utahutes.com
Founded: 1850   Enrollment: 25,391
President . . . . .Dr. Bernard Machen
Athletic Director . . . . .Dr. Chris Hill
Asst. AD, Sports Information . . . . .Liz Abel

University of Wyoming
Laramie, WY 82071
SID: (307) 766-2256   www.wyomingathletics.com
Founded: 1886   Enrollment: 12,402
President . . . . .Philip L. Dubois
Athletic Director . . . . .Gary Barta
Sports Information Director . . . . .Kevin McKinney

*   *   *

PACIFIC-10 CONFERENCE
800 South Broadway, Suite 400
Walnut Creek, CA 94596
(925) 932-4411   www.pac-10.org
Founded: 1915
Commissioner . . . . .Thomas Hansen
Asst. Commissioner, Public Relations . . . . . .Jim Muldoon
   2003-04 members: BASKETBALL & FOOTBALL (10)—
Arizona, Arizona St., California, Oregon, Oregon St.,
Stanford, UCLA, USC, Washington and Washington St.

University of Arizona
Tucson, AZ 85721
SID: (520) 621-4163   www.arizonaathletics.com
Founded: 1885   Enrollment: 35,400
President . . . . .Peter Likins
Athletic Director . . . . .Jim Livengood
Sports Information Director . . . . .Tom Duddleston

Arizona State University
Tempe, AZ 85287
SID: (480) 965-5799   www.thesundevils.com
Founded: 1885   Enrollment: 43,372
President . . . . .Michael Crow
Athletic Director .Gene Smith
Sports Information Director . . . . .Mark Brand

University of California
Berkeley, CA 94720
SID: (510) 642-5363   www.calbears.com
Founded: 1868   Enrollment: 33,000
Chancellor . . . . .Robert Berdahl
Athletic Director . . . . .Steve Gladstone
Exec. Assoc. AD for Communications . . . . .Bob Rose

University of Oregon
Eugene, OR 97401
SID: (541) 346-5488   www.goducks.com
Founded: 1876   Enrollment: 20,044
President . . . . .Dave Frohnmayer
Athletic Director . . . . .Bill Moos
Sports Information Director . . . . .Dave Williford

Oregon State University
Corvallis, OR 97331
SID: (541) 737-3720   www.osubeavers.com
Founded: 1868   Enrollment: 19,000
President . . . . .Dr. Edward Ray
Athletic Director . . . . .Bob De Carolis
Sports Information Director . . . . .Hal Cowan

Stanford University
Stanford, CA 94305
SID: (650) 723-4418   www.gostanford.com
Founded: 1891   Enrollment: 13,075
President . . . . .John L. Hennessy
Athletic Director .Ted Leland
Sports Information Director . . . . .Gary Migdol

UCLA—Univ. of California, Los Angeles
Los Angeles, CA 90024
SID: (310) 206-6831   www.uclabruins.com
Founded: 1919   Enrollment: 36,890
Chancellor .Albert Carnesale
Athletic Director . . . . .Dan Guerrero
Sports Information Director . . . . .Marc Dellins

USC—Univ. of Southern California
Los Angeles, CA 90089
SID: (213) 740-8480   www.usctrojans.com
Founded: 1880   Enrollment: 28,600
President . . . . .Steven Sample
Athletic Director . . . . .Mike Garrett
Sports Information Director . . . . .Tim Tessalone

University of Washington
Seattle, WA 98195
SID: (206) 543-2230   www.gohuskies.com
Founded: 1861   Enrollment: 26,800
Acting President . . . . .Lee Huntsman
Athletic Director . . . . .Barbara Hedges
Asst. AD for Media Relations . . . . .Jim Daves

Washington State University
Pullman, WA 99164
SID: (509) 335-2684   www.wsucougars.com
Founded: 1890   Enrollment: 22,000
President . . . . .V. Lane Rawlins
Athletic Director . . . . .Jim Sterk
Sports Information Director . . . . .Rod Commons

        *   *   *

SOUTHEASTERN CONFERENCE
2201 Richard Arrington Blvd. North
Birmingham, AL 35203
(205) 458-3000   www.secsports.com
Founded: 1933
Commissioner . . . . .Mike Slive
Assoc. Commis. of Media Relations . . . . .Charles Bloom
   2003-04 members: BASKETBALL & FOOTBALL (12)—
Alabama, Arkansas, Auburn, Florida, Georgia, Kentucky,
LSU, Mississippi St., Ole Miss, South Carolina, Tennessee
and Vanderbilt.

University of Alabama
Tuscaloosa, AL 35487
SID: (205) 348-6084   www.rolltide.com
Founded: 1831   Enrollment: 19,400
President . . . . .Dr. Robert Witt
Athletic Director . . . . .Mal Moore
Assoc. AD for Media Relations . . . . .Larry White

University of Arkansas
Fayetteville, AR 72701   www.hogwired.com
SID: (479) 575-2751   www.ladybacks.com
Founded: 1871   Enrollment: 16,035
Chancellor . . . . .John White
Athletic Director . . . . .Frank Broyles
Women's Athletic Director . . . . .Bev Lewis
Asst. AD, Sports Information . . . . .Kevin Trainor

Auburn University
Auburn, AL 36831
SID: (334) 844-9800   www.auburntigers.com
Founded: 1856   Enrollment: 21,775
President .William F. Walker
Athletic Director . . . . .David Housel
Asst. AD, Media Relations . . . . .Meredith Jenkins

University of Florida
Gainesville, FL 32604
SID: (352) 375-4683 ext. 6100   www.gatorzone.com
Founded: 1853   Enrollment: 47,373
President .Charles E. Young
Athletic Director . . . . .Jeremy Foley
Asst. AD for Sports Information . . . . .Steve McClain

University of Georgia
Athens, GA 30603
SID: (706) 542-1621   www.georgiadogs.com
Founded: 1785   Enrollment: 32,317
President .Michael F. Adams
Athletic Director . . . . .Vince Dooley
Sports Information Director . . . . .Claude Felton

University of Kentucky
Lexington, KY 40506
SID: (859) 257-3838   www.ukathletics.com
Founded: 1865   Enrollment: 34,182
President . . . . .Dr. Lee Todd
Athletic Director . . . . .Mitch Barnhart
Asst. AD/Media Relations . . . . .Scott Stricklin

LSU—Louisiana State University
Baton Rouge, LA 70894
SID: (225) 578-8226   www.lsusports.net
Founded: 1860   Enrollment: 29,022
Chancellor . . . . .Dr. Mark A. Emmert
Athletic Director . . . . .Skip Bertman
Sports Information Director . . . . .Michael Bonnette

Mississippi State University
Starkville, MS 39762
SID: (662) 325-2703   www.mstateathletics.com
Founded: 1878   Enrollment: 16,610
President . . . . .Dr. J. Charles Lee
Athletic Director . . . . .Larry Templeton
Assoc. AD, Media & Public Relations . . . . . .Mike Nemeth

Ole Miss—University of Mississippi
University, MS 38677
SID: (662) 915-7522   www.olemisssports.com
Founded: 1848   Enrollment: 14,960
Chancellor . . . . .Dr. Robert C. Khayat
Athletic Director . . . . .Pete Boone
Assoc. AD for Media Relations . . . . . . .Langston Rogers

University of South Carolina
Columbia, SC 29208
SID: (803) 777-5204   www.uscsports.com
Founded: 1801   Enrollment: 23,728
President . . . . .Dr. Andrew Sorensen
Athletic Director .Mike McGee
Sports Information Director . . . . .Kerry Tharp

University of Tennessee
Knoxville, TN 37996   www.utsports.com
SID: (865) 974-1212   www.utladyvols.com
Founded: 1794   Enrollment: 25,793
Interim President . . . . .Dr. Joseph E. Johnson
Athletic Director .Mike Hamilton
Women's Athletic Director . . . . .Joan Cronan
Sports Information Director . . . . .Bud Ford

Vanderbilt University
Nashville, TN 37212
SID: (615) 322-4121   www.vucommodores.com
Founded: 1873   Enrollment: 6,037
Chancellor . . . . .Gordon Gee
Asst. Vice Chancellor . . . . .Brock Williams
Assoc. AD, Communications . . . . .Rod Williamson

         *   *   *

SUN BELT CONFERENCE
601 Poydras Street, Suite 2355
New Orleans, LA 70130
(504) 299-9066   www.sunbeltsports.org
Founded: 1976
Commissioner .Wright Waters
Assoc. Commissioner/Media Relations . . . . . Judy Wilson
   2003-04 members: BASKETBALL (11)—Arkansas-Little Rock, Arkansas St., Denver, Florida International, LA-Lafayette, Middle Tenn. St., New Mexico St., New Orleans, North Texas, South Alabama and Western Kentucky; FOOTBALL (8)—Arkansas St., Idaho, LA-Lafayette, LA-Monroe, Middle Tenn. State, New Mexico St., North Texas and Utah St.

Arkansas-Little Rock
Little Rock, AR 72204
SID: (501) 569-3449   www.ualr.edu/~athletics
Founded: 1927   Enrollment: 12,000
Chancellor . . . . .Joel E. Anderson
Athletic Director .Chris Peterson
Sports Information Director . . . . .Kevin Tankersley

Arkansas State
Jonesboro, AR 72467
SID: (870) 972-2541   www.asuindians.com
Founded: 1909   Enrollment: 16,303
President .Dr. J. Leslie Wyatt
Athletic Director .Dr. Dean Lee
Asst. AD/Media Relations . . . . .Gina Bowman

University of Denver
Denver, CO 80208
SID: (303) 871-4990   www.denverpioneers.com
Founded: 1864   Enrollment: 9,271
Chancellor . . . . .Daniel L. Ritchie
Athletic Director . . . . .Dr. M. Dianne Murphy
Director of Sports Media Relations . . . . .Marla Rodriguez

Florida International University
Miami, FL 33199
SID: (305) 348-3164   www.fiusports.com
Founded: 1889   Enrollment: 34,000
President . . . . .Modesto A. Maidique
Athletic Director . . . . .Rick Mello
Asst. AD/Media Relations . . . . .Rich Kelch

University of Idaho
Moscow, ID 83844
SID: (208) 885-0245   www.uiathletics.com
Founded: 1889   Enrollment: 11,430
Acting President .Gary Michael
Athletic Director . . . . .Mike Bohn
Asst. AD/Media Relations . . . . .Becky Paull

University of Louisiana at Lafayette
Lafayette, LA 70506
SID: (337) 851-2255   www.ragincajuns.com
Founded: 1898   Enrollment: 15,150
President . . . . .Ray Authement
Athletic Director . . . . .Nelson Schexnayder
Sports Information Director . . . . .Daryl Cetnar

University of Louisiana at Monroe
Monroe, LA 71209
SID: (318) 342-5442   www.ulmathletics.com
Founded: 1931   Enrollment: 9,400
President .Dr. James E. Cofer
Athletic Director .Bruce Hanks
Sports Information Director . . . . .Hank Largin

Middle Tennessee State
Murfreesboro, TN 37132
SID: (615) 898-2450   www.goblueraiders.com
Founded: 1911   Enrollment: 21,663
President . . . . .Dr. Sidney A. McPhee
Athletic Director . . . . .Boots Donnelly
Sports Information Director . . . . .Mark Owens

New Mexico State
Las Cruces, NM 88003
SID: (505) 646-3929   www.nmstatesports.com
Founded: 1888   Enrollment: 15,243
Interim President . . . . .William V. Flores
Athletic Director .Brian Faison
Asst. AD/Media Relations . . . . .Sean Johnson

University of New Orleans
New Orleans, LA 70148
SID: (504) 280-6284   www.unoprivateers.com
Founded: 1958   Enrollment: 16,138
Chancellor . . . . .Dr. Gregory O'Brien
Athletic Director . . . . .Jim Miller
Sports Information Director . . . . .Bob Boyle

University of North Texas
Denton, TX 76203
SID: (940) 565-2476   www.unt.edu/meangreen
Founded: 1890   Enrollment: 30,000
President . . . . .Dr. Norval F. Pohl
Athletic Director .Rick Villarreal
Asst. AD/Media Relations . . . . .Eric Capper

University of South Alabama
Mobile, AL 36688
SID: (251) 460-7035   www.usajaguars.com
Founded: 1963   Enrollment: 12,500
President . . . . .V. Gordon Moulton
Athletic Director .Joe Gottfried
Director of Athletic Media Relations . . . . .Matt Smith

Utah State University
Logan, UT 84322
SID: (435) 797-1361   www.utahstateaggies.com
Founded: 1888   Enrollment: 21,490
President . . . . .Dr. Kermit L. Hall
Athletic Director . . . . .Rance Pugmire
Asst. AD for Media Relations . . . . .Mike Strauss

Western Kentucky University
Bowling Green, KY 42101
SID: (270) 745-4298   www.wkusports.com
Founded: 1906   Enrollment: 17,770
President . . . . .Dr. Gary Ransdell
Athletic Director . . . . .Dr. Camden Wood Selig
Dir. of Athletic Media Relations . . . . .Brian Fremund

*   *   *

WESTERN ATHLETIC CONFERENCE
9250 East Costilla Ave., Suite 300
Englewood, CO 80112
(303) 799-9221   www.wacsports.com
Founded: 1962
Commissioner . . . . .Karl Benson
Asst. Commiss./Media Relations . . . . .Dave Chaffin
  2003-04 members: BASKETBALL & FOOTBALL (10)—
Boise St., Fresno St., Hawaii, Louisiana Tech, Nevada,
Rice, San Jose St., SMU, Tulsa and UTEP.

Boise State
Boise, ID 83725
SID: (208) 426-1515   www.broncosports.com
Founded: 1932   Enrollment: 17,745
President . . . . .Dr. Robert Kustra
Athletic Director . . . . .Gene Bleymaier
Asst. AD/Media Relations . . . . .Max Corbet

Fresno State University
Fresno, CA 93740
SID: (559) 278-2509   www.gobulldogs.com
Founded: 1911   Enrollment: 21,389
President . . . . .Dr. John D. Welty
Athletic Director . . . . .Scott Johnson
Asst. AD/Communications . . . . .Steve Weakland

University of Hawaii
Honolulu, HI 96822
SID: (808) 956-7523   www.uhathletics.hawaii.edu
Founded: 1907   Enrollment: 18,706
President . . . . .Dr. Evan Dobelle
Athletic Director . . . . .Herman Frazier
Media Relations Director . . . . .Lois Manin

Louisiana Tech University
Ruston, LA 71272
SID: (318) 257-3144   www.latechsports.com
Founded: 1894   Enrollment: 11,280
President. . . . . .Dan Reneau
Athletic Director . . . . .Jim Oakes
Sports Information Director . . . . .Malcolm Butler

University of Nevada
Reno, NV 89557
SID: (775) 784-6900   www.nevadawolfpack.com
Founded: 1874   Enrollment: 15,700
President . . . . .Dr. John Lilley
Athletic Director . . . . .Chris Ault
Media Services Director . . . . .Jamie Klund

Rice University
Houston, TX 77005
SID: (713) 348-5775   www.riceowls.com
Founded: 1912   Enrollment: 4,785
President . . . . .Dr. Malcolm Gillis
Athletic Director .Bobby May
Asst. AD/Sports Information Director . . . . .Bill Cousins

San Jose State University
San Jose, CA 95192
SID: (408) 924-1217   www.sjsuspartans.com
Founded: 1857   Enrollment: 30,067
Interim President . . . . .Dr. Joseph N. Crowley
Athletic Director . . . . .Chuck Bell
Sports Information Director . . . . .Lawrence Fan

SMU—Southern Methodist University
Dallas, TX 75275
SID: (214) 768-2883   www.smumustangs.com
Founded: 1911   Enrollment: 10,038
President .Dr. R. Gerald Turner
Athletic Director . . . . .Jim Copeland
Asst. AD/Media Relations . . . . .Brad Sutton

University of Tulsa
Tulsa, OK 74104
SID: (918) 631-2395   www.tulsahurricane.com
Founded: 1894   Enrollment: 4,100
President . . . . .Dr. Bob Lawless
Athletic Director . . . . .Judy MacLeod
Asst. AD/Media Relations . . . . .Don Tomkalski

UTEP—University of Texas at El Paso
El Paso, TX 79902
SID: (915) 747-6653   www.utepathletics.com
Founded: 1914   Enrollment: 17,232
President .Dr. Diana Natalicio
Athletic Director .Bob Stull
Assoc. AD/Media Relations . . . . .Jeff Darby

*   *   *

Major Independents
Division I-A football independents in 2003.

University of Connecticut
Storrs, CT 06269
SID: (860) 486-3531   www.uconnhuskies.com
Founded:1881   Enrollment: 17,652
President . . . . .Philip Austin
Athletic Director . . . . .Jeffrey Hathaway
Sports Information Director . . . . .Michael Enright

Navy—U.S. Naval Academy
Annapolis, MD 21402
SID: (410) 293-2700   www.navysports.com
Founded: 1845   Enrollment: 4,123
Superintendent . . . . .Vice Adm. Rodney P. Rempt
Athletic Director . . . . .Chet Gladchuk
Asst. AD/Sports Information Director . . . .Scott Strasemeier

University of Notre Dame
Notre Dame, IN 46556
SID: (574) 631-7516   www.und.com
Founded: 1842   Enrollment: 10,301
President . . . . .Rev. Edward (Monk) Malloy
Athletic Director . . . . .Kevin White
Assoc. AD/Media Relations . . . . .John Heisler
Sports Information Director . . . . .Bernadette Cafarelli

Troy State University
Troy, AL 36082
SID: (334) 670-3229   www.troystate.com
Founded: 1887   Enrollment: 18,222
Chancellor . . . . .Dr. Jack Hawkins Jr.
Athletic Director . . . . .Johnny Williams
Athletics Media Relations Dir. . . . . .Tom Strother

*   *   *

Other Major Division I Conferences

Conferences that play either Division I basketball or Division I-AA football, or both.

America East
10 High St., Suite 860, Boston, MA 02110
(617) 695-6369   www.americaeast.com
Founded: 1979
Commissioner ....Chris Monasch
Dir. of Communications ....Matt Bourque
   2003-04 members: BASKETBALL (10)—Albany, Binghamton, Boston University, Hartford, Maine, Maryland-Baltimore County, New Hampshire, Northeastern, Stony Brook and Vermont.

Atlantic Sun Conference
3370 Vineyville Ave., Suite 108-B
Macon, GA 31204
(478) 474-3394   www.atlanticsun.org
Founded: 1978
Commissioner ....Bill Bibb
Asst. Commissioner ....Devlin Pierce
   2003-04 members: BASKETBALL (11)—Belmont, Campbell, Central Florida, Florida Atlantic, Gardner-Webb, Georgia St., Jacksonville, Lipscomb, Mercer, Stetson and Troy St.

Atlantic 10 Conference
230 S. Broad St., Suite 1700
Philadelphia, PA 19102
(215) 545-6678   www.atlantic10.org
Founded: 1976   A-10 Football founded: 1997
Commissioner ....Linda Bruno
Asst. Commissioner/P.R. ....Ray Cella
   2003-04 members: BASKETBALL (12)—Dayton, Duquesne, Fordham, George Washington, La Salle, Massachusetts, Rhode Island, Richmond, St. Bonaventure, St. Joseph's-PA, Temple and Xavier-OH. FOOTBALL (11)—Delaware, Hofstra, James Madison, Maine, Massachusetts, New Hampshire, Northeastern, Rhode Island, Richmond, Villanova and William & Mary.

Big Sky Conference
2491 Washington Blvd. Suite 201
Ogden, UT 84401
(801) 392-1978   www.bigskyconf.com
Founded: 1963
Commissioner ....Douglas Fullerton
Asst. Commissioner, Media Relations .....Dusty Clements
   2003-04 members: BASKETBALL & FOOTBALL (8)—Eastern Washington, Idaho St., Montana, Montana St., Northern Arizona, Portland St., Sacramento St., and Weber St.

Big South Conference
6428 Bannington Dr., Ste A
Charlotte, NC 28226
(704) 341-7990   www.bigsouthsports.com
Founded: 1983
Commissioner ....Kyle Kallander
Asst. Commissioner ....Drew Dickerson
   2003-04 members: BASKETBALL (9)—Birmingham Southern, Charleston Southern, Coastal Carolina, High Point, Liberty, NC-Asheville, Radford, VMI and Winthrop. FOOTBALL (5)—Charleston Southern, Coastal Carolina, Gardner-Webb, Liberty and VMI.

Big West Conference
Two Corporate Park, Suite 206
Irvine, CA 92606
(949) 261-2525   www.bigwest.org
Founded: 1969
Commissioner ....Dennis Farrell
Information Director ....Mike Villamor
   2003-04 members: BASKETBALL (10)—CS-Fullerton, CS-Northridge, Cal Poly, Idaho, Long Beach St., Pacific, UC-Irvine, UC-Riverside, UC-Santa Barbara and Utah St.

Colonial Athletic Association
8625 Patterson Ave.,
Richmond, VA 23229
(804) 754-1616   www.caasports.com
Founded: 1985
Commissioner ....Thomas E. Yeager
Asst. Commissioner/Commun. ....Rob Washburn
   2003-04 members: BASKETBALL (10)—Delaware, Drexel, George Mason, Hofstra, James Madison, NC-Wilmington, Old Dominion, Towson, Virginia Commonwealth and William & Mary.

Gateway Football Conference
1818 Chouteau Ave.
St. Louis, MO 63103
(314) 421-2268   www.gatewayfootball.org
Founded: 1985
Commissioner ....Patty Viverito
Asst. Commissioner ....Mike Kern
   2003 members: FOOTBALL (8)—Illinois St., Indiana St., Northern Iowa, Southern Illinois, SW Missouri St., Western Illinois, Western Kentucky and Youngstown St.

Horizon League
201 South Capitol Ave., Suite 500
Indianapolis, IN 46225
(317) 237-5622   www.horizonleague.org
Founded: 1979
Commissioner ....Jon LeCrone
Associate Commissioner ....Terry Powers
   2003-04 members: BASKETBALL (9)—Butler, Cleveland St., Detroit Mercy, Illinois-Chicago, Loyola-IL, Wisconsin-Green Bay, Wisconsin-Milwaukee, Wright St. and Youngstown St.

Ivy League
228 Alexander Street
Princeton, NJ 08544
(609) 258-6426   www.ivyleaguesports.com
Founded: 1954
Executive Director ....Jeffrey Orleans
Assistant Director ....Brett Hoover
   2003-04 members: BASKETBALL & FOOTBALL (8)—Brown, Columbia, Cornell, Dartmouth, Harvard, Pennsylvania, Princeton and Yale.

Metro Atlantic Athletic Conference
712 Amboy Avenue
Edison, NJ 08837
(732) 738-5455   www.maacsports.com
Founded: 1980
Commissioner ....Richard Ensor
Director of Media Relations ....Jill Skotarczak
   2003-04 members: BASKETBALL (10)—Canisius, Fairfield, Iona, Loyola-MD, Manhattan, Marist, Niagara, Rider, St. Peter's and Siena. FOOTBALL (6)—Duquesne, Iona, La Salle, Marist, St. Peter's and Siena.

Mid-Continent Conference
340 West Butterfield Rd., Ste 3D
Elmhurst, IL 60126
(630) 516-0661   www.mid-con.com
Founded: 1982
Commissioner ....Ron Bertovich
Director of Media Relations ....Tony Hamilton
   2003-04 members: BASKETBALL (9)—Centenary, Chicago St., IUPUI, UMKC, Oakland, Oral Roberts, Southern Utah, Valparaiso and Western Illinois.

Mid-Eastern Athletic Conference
102 North Elm St.
SE Building, Suite 401
Greensboro, NC 27401
(336) 275-9961   www.meacsports.com
Founded: 1970
Commissioner .... Dr. Dennis Thomas
Director of Media Relations .... Michelle Jinks
   2003-04 members: BASKETBALL (11)—Bethune-Cookman, Coppin St., Delaware St., Florida A&M, Hampton, Howard, MD-Eastern Shore, Morgan St., Norfolk St., North Carolina A&T and South Carolina St.; FOOTBALL (9)—all but Coppin St. and MD-Eastern Shore.

Missouri Valley Conference
1818 Chouteau Ave.
St. Louis, MO 63103
(314) 421-0339   www.mvc-sports.com
Founded: 1907
Commissioner .... Doug Elgin
Assoc. Commissioner, Communications .... Mike Kern
   2003-04 members: BASKETBALL (10)—Bradley, Creighton, Drake, Evansville, Illinois St., Indiana St., Northern Iowa, Southern Illinois, SW Missouri St. and Wichita St.

Northeast Conference
200 Cottontail Lane, Vantage Court North
Somerset, NJ 08823
(732) 469-0440   www.northeastconference.org
Founded: 1981
Commissioner .... John Iamarino
Associate Commissioner .... Ron Ratner
   2003-04 members: BASKETBALL (11)—Cent. Conn. St., Fairleigh Dickinson, LIU-Brooklyn, Monmouth, Mount St. Mary's, Quinnipiac, Robert Morris, Sacred Heart, St. Francis-NY, St. Francis-PA and Wagner. FOOTBALL (8)—Albany, Cent. Conn. St., Monmouth, Robert Morris, Sacred Heart, St. Francis-PA, Stony Brook and Wagner.

Ohio Valley Conference
278 Franklin Road, Suite103
Brentwood, TN 37027
(615) 371-1698   www.ovcsports.com
Founded: 1948
Commissioner .... Dr. Jon A. Steinbrecher
Asst. Commissioner for Media Relations ..... Kim Melcher
   2003-04 members: BASKETBALL (11)—Austin Peay St., Eastern Illinois, Eastern Kentucky, Jacksonville St., Morehead St., Murray St., Samford, SE Missouri St., Tennessee-Martin, Tennessee St. and Tennessee Tech; FOOTBALL (9)—all but Austin Peay St. and Morehead St.

Patriot League
3773 Corporate Pkwy, Suite 190
Center Valley, PA 18034
(610) 289-1950   www.patriotleague.com
Founded: 1984
Executive Director .... Carolyn Schlie Femovich
Asst. Exec. Dir. for Media Relations .... Tom Byrnes
   2003-04 members: BASKETBALL (8)—American, Army, Bucknell, Colgate, Holy Cross, Lafayette, Lehigh and Navy; FOOTBALL (8)—Bucknell, Colgate, Fordham, Georgetown, Holy Cross, Lafayette, Lehigh and Towson.

Pioneer Football League
1818 Chouteau Ave.
St. Louis, MO 63103
(314) 421-2268   www.pioneer-football.org
Founded: 1993
Commissioner .... Patty Viverito
Sports Information Director .... Cody Bush
   2003 members: FOOTBALL (9): Austin Peay St., Butler, Davidson, Dayton, Drake, Jacksonville, Morehead St., San Diego and Valparaiso.

Southern Conference
905 East Main St.
Spartanburg, SC 29302
(864) 591-5100   www.soconsports.com
Founded: 1921
Commissioner .... Dr. Daniel B. Morrison Jr.
Assoc. Commissioner for Public Affairs ...... Steve Shutt
   2003-04 members: BASKETBALL (12)—Appalachian St., Chattanooga, The Citadel, College of Charleston, Davidson, East Tennessee St., Elon, Furman, Georgia Southern, NC-Greensboro, Western Carolina and Wofford; FOOTBALL (9)—all except College of Charleston, Davidson and NC-Greensboro.

Southland Conference
1700 Alma Drive, Suite 550
Plano, TX 75075
(972) 422-9500   www.southland.org
Founded: 1963
Commissioner .... Tom Burnett
Asst. Commissioner for Media Relations .... Bruce Ludlow
   2003-04 members: BASKETBALL (11)—Lamar, LA-Monroe, McNeese St., Nicholls St., Northwestern St., Sam Houston St., SE Louisiana, Stephen F. Austin St., Texas-Arlington, Texas-San Antonio and Texas St.-San Marcos; FOOTBALL (6)—McNeese St., Nicholls St., Northwestern St., Sam Houston St., Stephen F. Austin St. and Texas St.-San Marcos.

Southwestern Athletic Conference
1527 Fifth Ave. North
Birmingham, AL 35204
(205) 251-7573   www.swac.org
Founded: 1920
Commissioner .... Robert C. Vowels Jr.
Asst. Comm. for Media Relations ..... Wallace Dooley Jr.
   2003-04 members: BASKETBALL & FOOTBALL (10)—Alabama A&M, Alabama St., Alcorn St., Arkansas-Pine Bluff, Grambling St., Jackson St., Mississippi Valley St., Prairie View A&M, Southern-Baton Rouge and Texas Southern.

West Coast Conference
1200 Bayhill Dr., Suite 302
San Bruno, CA 94066
(650) 873-8622   www.wccsports.com
Founded: 1952
Commissioner .... Michael Gilleran
Asst. Comm. for Media Relations .... Brad Walker
   2003-04 members: BASKETBALL (8)—Gonzaga, Loyola Marymount, Pepperdine, Portland, Saint Mary's-CA, San Diego, San Francisco and Santa Clara.

PRO FOOTBALL

National Football League

League Office
280 Park Ave.
New York, NY 10017
(212) 450-2000   www.nfl.com
Commissioner .... Paul Tagliabue
Exec. Vice President/League Counsel .... Jeff Pash
Exec. V.P., Communications, Public Affairs ... Joe Browne
AFC Info. Coordinator .... Steve Alic
NFC Info. Coordinator .... Mike Signora

NFL Management Council
280 Park Ave.
New York, NY 10017
(212) 450-2000
Chairman .... Harold Henderson
Sr. V.P. of Broadcast/Network TV .... Dennis Lewin

NFL Players Association
2021 L Street NW, Suite 600
Washington, DC 20036
(202) 463-2200   www.nflpa.org
Executive Director . . . . .Gene Upshaw
Asst. Exec. Director . . . . .Doug Allen
General Counsel . . . . .Richard Berthelsen
Director of Communications . . . . .Carl Francis

AFC

Baltimore Ravens
11001 Owings Mills Blvd.
Owings Mills, MD 21117
(410) 654-6200   www.baltimoreravens.com
Owner/CEO . . . . .Arthur B. Modell
President/COO . . . . .David Modell
V.P. of Public & Community Relations . . . . . .Kevin Byrne

Buffalo Bills
One Bills Drive, Orchard Park, NY 14127
(716) 648-1800   www.buffalobills.com
Chairman & Owner . . . . .Ralph C. Wilson Jr.
President & GM . . . . .Tom Donahue
V.P. of Communications . . . . .Scott Berchtold

Cincinnati Bengals
One Paul Brown Stadium, Cincinnati, OH 45202
(513) 621-3550   www.bengals.com
President . . . . .Mike Brown
Sr. Vice President . . . . .Pete Brown
Public Relations Director . . . . .Jack Brennan

Cleveland Browns
76 Lou Groza Blvd., Berea, OH 44017
(440) 891-5000   www.clevelandbrowns.com
Owner/Chairman . . . . .Randolph Lerner
President/CEO . . . . .Carmen Policy
Exec. Dir. of Commun./Media Relations . . . .Todd Stewart

Denver Broncos
13655 Broncos Parkway, Englewood, CO 80112
(303) 649-9000   www.denverbroncos.com
Owner-President-CEO . . . . .Pat Bowlen
General Manager . . . . .Ted Sundquist
V.P. of Public Relations . . . . .Jim Saccomano

Houston Texans
Two Reliant Park
Houston, TX 77054
(832) 667-2000   www.houstontexans.com
Chairman & CEO . . . . .Robert C. McNair
Sr. V.P. & GM of Football Ops. . . . . . . .Charley Casserly
V.P. of Communications . . . . .Tony Wyllie

Indianapolis Colts
7001 W 56th St., Indianapolis, IN 46254
(317) 297-2658   www.colts.com
Owner-CEO . . . . .Jim Irsay
President . . . . .Bill Polian
Dir. of Football Operations . . . . .Dom Anile
V.P. of Public Relations . . . . .Craig Kelley

Jacksonville Jaguars
One ALLTEL Stadium Place
Jacksonville, FL 32202
(904) 633-6000   www.jaguars.com
Chairman & CEO . . . . .Wayne Weaver
Sr. V.P., Football Operations . . . . .Paul Vance
Exec. Dir. of Comm. & Broadcasting . . . . .Dan Edwards

Kansas City Chiefs
One Arrowhead Drive, Kansas City, MO 64129
(816) 920-9300   www.kcchiefs.com
Owner-Founder . . . . .Lamar Hunt
Chairman . . . . .Jack Steadman
President-CEO-General Manager . . . . .Carl Peterson
Director of Public Relations . . . . .Bob Moore

Miami Dolphins
7500 SW 30th St., Davie, FL 33314
(954) 452-7000   www.miamidolphins.com
Owner-Chairman . . . . .H. Wayne Huizenga
President . . . . .Eddie Jones
Sr. V.P. Football Ops & Player Personnel . . .Rick Spielman
Sr. V.P. of Media Relations . . . . .Harvey Greene

New England Patriots
One Patriot Place, Foxboro, MA 02035
(508) 543-8200   www.patriots.com
Owner & Chairman . . . . .Bob Kraft
Dir. of Player Personnel . . . . .Scott Pioli
Director of Media Relations . . . . .Stacey James

New York Jets
1000 Fulton Ave., Hempstead, NY 11550
(516) 560-8100   www.newyorkjets.com
Owner & Chairman . . . . .Robert Wood Johnson IV
President . . . . .Jay Cross
General Manager . . . . .Terry Bradway
V.P. of Public Relations . . . . .Ron Colangelo

Oakland Raiders
1220 Harbor Bay Parkway, Alameda, CA 94502
(510) 864-5000   www.raiders.com
Owner —Manager of General Partners . . . . .Al Davis
Executive Assistant . . . . .Al LoCasale
Director of Public Relations . . . . .Mike Taylor

Pittsburgh Steelers
3400 South Water Street, Pittsburgh, PA 15203
(412) 432-7800   www.steelers.com
Chairman . . . . .Dan Rooney
President . . . . .Art Rooney II
Vice Presidents . . . . .John McGinley & Art Rooney Jr.
Communications Coordinator . . . . .Ron Wahl

San Diego Chargers
4020 Murphy Canyon Rd.
San Diego, CA 92123
(858) 874-4500   www.chargers.com
Owner-Chairman . . . . .Alex Spanos
President-CEO . . . . .Dean Spanos
Exec. V.P./General Manager . . . . .A.J. Smith
Director of Public Relations . . . . .Bill Johnston

Tennessee Titans
460 Great Circle Road, Nashville, TN 37228
(615) 565-4000   www.titansonline.com
Owner/Chairman/CEO . . . . .K.S. (Bud) Adams Jr.
President/COO . . . . .Jeff Diamond
Exec. V.P./General Manager . . . . .Floyd Reese
Director of Media Services . . . . .Robbie Bohren

NFC

Arizona Cardinals
8701 S. Hardy Drive, Tempe, AZ 85284
(602) 379-0101   www.azcardinals.com
Owner-President . . . . .Bill Bidwill Sr.
Vice President . . . . .Bill Bidwill Jr.
V.P. of Football Operations . . . . .Rod Graves
Public Relations Director . . . . .Paul Jensen

Atlanta Falcons
4400 Falcon Pkwy
Flowery Branch, GA 30542
(770) 965-3115   www.atlantafalcons.com
Owner-CEO . . . . .Arthur Blank
V.P. of Football Operations . . . . .Ron Hill
Director of Football Communications . . . . . . .Aaron Salkin

Carolina Panthers
800 South Mint St.
Charlotte, NC 28202-1502
(704) 358-7000   www.panthers.com
Founder-Owner . . . . .Jerry Richardson
President . . . . .Mark Richardson
General Manager . . . . .Marty Hurney
Director of Communications . . . . .Charlie Dayton

Chicago Bears
1000 Football Drive, Lake Forest, IL 60045
(847) 295-6600   www.chicagobears.com
Chairman . . . . .Michael McCaskey
President-CEO . . . . .Ted Phillips
General Manager . . . . .Jerry Angelo
Director of Public Relations . . . . .Scott Hagel

Dallas Cowboys
Cowboys Center
One Cowboys Parkway
Irving, TX 75063
(972) 556-9900   www.dallascowboys.com
Owner-President-GM . . . . Jerry Jones
Exec. V.P./Dir. of Player Personnel/COO . . .Stephen Jones
Public Relations Director . . . . .Rich Dalrymple

Detroit Lions
222 Republic Drive, Allen Park, MI 48101
(313) 216-4000   www.detroitlions.com
Owner . . . . .William Clay Ford
President & CEO . . . . .Matt Millen
Dir. of Pro Personnel . . . . .Sheldon White
Director of Media Relations . . . . .Matt Barnhart

Green Bay Packers
1265 Lombardi Ave.
Green Bay, WI 54304
(920) 496-5700   www.packers.com
President & CEO . . . . .Bob Harlan
Exec. V.P./GM & Head Coach . . . . .Mike Sherman
Exec. Dir. of Public Relations . . . . .Lee Remmel

Minnesota Vikings
9520 Viking Drive, Eden Prairie, MN 55344
(952) 828-6500   www.vikings.com
Owner . . . . .Red McCombs
President . . . . .Gary Woods
Executive Vice President . . . . .Michael Kelly
Director of Public Relations . . . . .Bob Hagan

New Orleans Saints
5800 Airline Drive, Metairie, LA 70003
(504) 731-1799   www.neworleanssaints.com
Owner . . . . .Tom Benson
Exec. V.P./GM of Football Ops. . . . . .Mickey Loomis
Dir. of Player Personnel . . . . .Rick Mueller
Director of Media/Public Relations . . . . .Greg Bensel

New York Giants
Giants Stadium
East Rutherford, NJ 07073
(201) 935-8111   www.giants.com
President/co-CEO . . . . .Wellington Mara
Chairman/co-CEO . . . . .Preston Robert Tisch
Senior V.P. & General Manager . . . . .Ernie Accorsi
V.P. of Communications . . . . .Pat Hanlon

Philadelphia Eagles
NovaCare Complex
One NovaCare Way
Philadelphia, PA 19145
(215) 463-2500   www.philadelphiaeagles.com
Owner-Chairman-CEO . . . . .Jeffrey Lurie
President/COO .Joe Banner
Head Coach/Exec. V.P. of Football Ops. . . . . .Andy Reid
Dir. of Football Media Services . . . . .Derek Boyko

St. Louis Rams
One Rams Way, St. Louis, MO 63045
(314) 982-7267   www.stlouisrams.com
Owner-Chairman . . . . .Georgia Frontiere
Owner-Vice Chairman . . . . .Stan Kroenke
President . . . . .John Shaw
Pres. of Football Operations . . . . .Jay Zygmunt
Director of Football Media . . . . .Duane Lewis

San Francisco 49ers
4949 Centennial Blvd.
Santa Clara, CA 95054
(408) 562-4949   www.sf49ers.com
Owner . . . . .Denise DeBartolo-York
President/CEO .Peter Harris
General Manager . . . . .Terry Donahue
Director of Public Relations . . . . .Kirk Reynolds

Seattle Seahawks
11220 NE 53rd Street, Kirkland, WA 98033
(425) 827-9777   www.seahawks.com
Owner . . . . .Paul Allen
President . . . . .Bob Whitsitt
General Manager . . . . .Bob Ferguson
Public Relations Director . . . . .Dave Pearson

Tampa Bay Buccaneers
One Buccaneer Place, Tampa, FL 33607
(813) 870-2700   www.buccaneers.com
Owner-President . . . . .Malcolm Glazer
General Manager . . . . .Rich McKay
Communications Manager . . . . .Jeff Kamis

Washington Redskins
21300 Redskins Park
Ashburn, VA 20147
(703) 726-7000   www.redskins.com
Owner .Daniel M. Snyder
V.P. of Football Operations . . . . .Vinny Cerrato
Director of Public Relations . . . . .Michelle Tessier

Canadian Football League

League Office
50 Wellington St. East, 3rd Floor
Toronto, Ontario M5E 1C8
(416) 322-9650   www.cfl.ca
Commissioner . . . . .Tom Wright
V.P. of Football Operations . . . . .Ed Chalupka
Director, Football Media . . . . .Shawn Lackie
   Member teams (9): West Division—British Columbia Lions, Calgary Stampeders, Edmonton Eskimos, Saskatchewan Roughriders and Winnipeg Blue Bombers. East Division—Hamilton Tiger-Cats, Montreal Alouettes, Ottawa Renegades and Toronto Argonauts.

CFL Players Association
603 Argus Rd., Suite 207
Oakville, Ontario L6J 6G6
(905) 844-7852   www.cflpa.com
President . . . . .Stu Laird
Legal Counsel .Ed Molstad

NFL Europe

New York Office
280 Park Avenue
New York, NY 10017
(212) 450-2000   www.nfleurope.com
Vice President of Football Ops. . . . . .John Beake
Managing Director . . . . .Jim Connelly
Director of Public Relations . . . . .David Tossell
Public Relations Assistant . . . . .Neil Reynolds
   Member teams (6): Amsterdam Admirals, Barcelona Dragons, Berlin Thunder, Frankfurt Galaxy, Rhein Fire (Dusseldorf), Scottish Claymores (Edinburgh).

Arena Football League

20 North Wacker Dr., Suite 1231
Chicago, IL 60606
(312) 621-7000   www.arenafootball.com
(212) 252-8100 (N.Y. office)
Commissioner : . . . . .C. David Baker
V.P. of Football Operations . . . . Jerry Trice
V.P. of Communications . . . . .Chris McCloskey
   Member teams (18): American Conference—Arizona
Rattlers, Chicago Rush, Colorado Crush, Dallas Desperados,
Grand Rapids Rampage, Indiana Firebirds, Los Angeles
Avengers and San Jose SaberCats. National Conference—
Carolina Cobras, Columbus Destroyers, Detroit Fury, Geor-
gia Force, Las Vegas Gladiators, New York Dragons, Orlan-
do Predators and Tampa Bay Storm.
   Joining the league in 2004: New Orleans Voodoo,
Philadelphia Soul.

GOLF

LPGA Tour
(Ladies' Professional Golf Association)
100 International Golf Drive
Daytona Beach, FL 32124
(386) 274-6200   www.lpga.com
Commissioner . . . . .Ty Votaw
Director of Media Relations . . . . .Connie Wilson

PGA of America
100 Avenue of the Champions
Palm Beach Gardens, FL 33410
(561) 624-8400   www.pga.com
President . . . . .M.G. Orender
CEO . . . . Jim Awtrey
Director of Public Relations . . . . Julius Mason

PGA European Tour
Wentworth Drive, Virginia Water
Surrey, England GU25 4LX
TEL: 011-44-1344-840400   www.europeantour.com
Executive Director . . . . .Ken Schofield
Director of P.R./Corporate Affairs . . . . .Mitchell Platts
Director of Communications . . . . .Gordon Simpson

PGA Tour
112 PGA Tour Blvd.
Ponte Vedra, FL 32082
(904) 285-3700   www.pgatour.com
Commissioner . . . . .Tim Finchem
Senior V.P./Chief of Operations . . . . .Henry Hughes
Senior V.P. of Communications . . . . .Bob Combs

USGA
(United States Golf Association)
P.O. Box 708, Liberty Corner Road
Far Hills, NJ 07931
(908) 234-2300   www.usga.org
President . . . . .Reed McKenzie
Executive Director .David Fay
Sr. Director of Communications . . . . .Marty Parkes

PRO HOCKEY

NHL
National Hockey League

Commissioner .Gary Bettman
Pres., NHL Enterprises . . . . .Ed Horne
Exec. V.P., Dir. of Hockey Ops. . . . . .Colin Campbell
V.P. of Media Relations . . . . .Frank Brown

League Offices

Montreal
1800 McGill College Ave., Suite 2600
Montreal, Quebec H3A 3J6
(514) 841-9220

New York
1251 Avenue of the Americas, 47th Floor, New York, NY 10020
(212) 789-2000

Toronto
50 Bay St., 11th Floor
Toronto, Ontario M5J 2X8
(416) 981-2777   www.nhl.com

NHL Players' Association
777 Bay St., Suite 2400
P.O. Box 121
Toronto, Ontario M5G 2C8
(416) 408-4040   www.nhlpa.com
Executive Director . . . . .Bob Goodenow
Senior Director . . . . .Ted Saskin
Media Relations . . . . .Jonathan Weatherdon

Anaheim, Mighty Ducks of
Arrowhead Pond of Anaheim
2695 Katella Ave.
Anaheim, CA 92806
(714) 940-2900   www.mightyducks.com
Owner . . . . .Walt Disney Co.
Governor . . . . .Jay Rasulo
Senior V.P./General Manager . . . . .Bryan Murray
Mngr., Communications and Team Services . .Alex Gilchrist

Atlanta Thrashers
1 CNN Center
12th Floor, South Tower
Atlanta, GA 30303
(404) 584-7825   www.atlantathrashers.com
Owner . . . . .AOL-Time Warner
President/Governor . . . . .Stan Kasten
V.P./General Manager . . . . .Don Waddell
Director of Media Relations . . . . .Tom Hughes

Boston Bruins
1 FleetCenter, Suite 250
Boston, MA 02114
(617) 624-1900   www.bostonbruins.com
Owner . . . . .Jeremy Jacobs
President . . . . .Harry Sinden
V.P & General Manager . . . . .Mike O'Connell
Director of Media Relations . . . . .Heidi Holland

Buffalo Sabres
HSBC Arena
One Seymour H. Knox III Plaza
Buffalo, NY 14203-3096
(716) 855-4100   www.sabres.com
Owner . . . . .B. Thomas Golisano
General Manager . . . . .Darcy Regier
V.P. of Communications . . . . .Michael Gilbert

Calgary Flames
Pengrowth Saddledome, P.O. Box 1540
Station M Calgary, Alberta T2P 3B9
(403) 777-2177   www.calgaryflames.com
Owners . . . . .Harley Hotchkiss, Murray Edwards,
   Alvin G. Libin, Allan P. Markin, J.R. McCaig,
   Clay Riddell, Byron and Daryl Seamen
President & CEO . . . . .Ken King
General Manager/Head Coach . . . . .Darryl Sutter
Director of Communications . . . . .Peter Hanlon

Carolina Hurricanes
RBC Center
1400 Edwards Mill Rd., Raleigh, NC 27607
(919) 467-7825   www.caneshockey.com
Owner . . . . .Peter Karmanos Jr.
President & General Manager . . . . .Jim Rutherford
Dir., Media Relations . . . . .Mike Sundheim

Chicago Blackhawks
United Center, 1901 West Madison St.
Chicago, IL 60612
(312) 455-7000   www.chicagoblackhawks.com
Owner-President . . . . .William Wirtz
General Manager . . . . .Mike Smith
Executive Director of Communications . . . . .Jim DeMaria

Colorado Avalanche
1000 Chopper Cir., Denver, CO 80204
(303) 405-1100   www.coloradoavalanche.com
Owner . . . . .Stan Kroenke
President/GM/Alt. Governor . . . . .Pierre Lacroix
V.P. of Comm. & Team Services . . . . . . .Jean Martineau

Columbus Blue Jackets
200 W. Nationwide Blvd., Suite Level
Columbus, OH 43215
(614) 246-4625   www.bluejackets.com
Owner . . . . .John H. McConnell
President/GM/Head Coach . . . . .Doug MacLean
Director of Communications . . . . .Todd Sharrock

Dallas Stars
211 Cowboys Parkway, Irving, TX 75063
(972) 831-2453   www.dallasstars.com
Owner . . . . .Thomas O. Hicks
President . . . . .Jim Lites
General Manager . . . . .Doug Armstrong
Sr. Director of Hockey Comm. . . . . .Rob Scichili

Detroit Red Wings
Joe Louis Arena, 600 Civic Center Drive
Detroit, MI 48226
(313) 396-7544   www.detroitredwings.com
Owner/President .Mike Ilitch
Owner/Secretary-Treasurer . . . . .Marian Ilitch
General Manager . . . . .Ken Holland
Sr. Director of Communications . . . . .John Hahn

Edmonton Oilers
11230 110th St., Edmonton, Alberta, T5G 3H7
(780) 414-4000   www.edmontonoilers.com
Owners . . . . .Edmonton Investors Group, Ltd.
President & CEO . . . . .Patrick LaForge
Exec. V.P./General Manager . . . . .Kevin Lowe
V.P./Public Relations . . . . .Bill Tuele

Florida Panthers
Office Depot Center
One Panther Parkway, Sunrise, FL 33323
(954) 835-7000   www.flpanthers.com
Chairman/CEO .Alan Cohen
President .Jordan Zimmerman
General Manager . . . . .Rick Dudley
Dir. of Media Relations . . . . .Randy Sieminski

Los Angeles Kings
Staples Center
1111 S. Figueroa, Los Angeles, CA 90015
(310) 535-4543   www.lakings.com
Majority Owners . . . . .Philip Anschutz and Ed Roski
President/Governor . . . . .Tim Leiweke
Sr. V.P. & General Manager . . . . .Dave Taylor
Director of Media Relations . . . . .Mike Altieri

Minnesota Wild
317 Washington Street
St. Paul, MN 55102
(651) 602-6000   www.wild.com
Owner . . . . .Bob Naegele Jr.
CEO . . . . .Jac Sperling
President/General Manager . . . . .Doug Risebrough
V.P. of Comm. & Broadcast . . . . .Bill Robertson

Montreal Canadiens
Bell Centre, 1260 Gauchetiere St. West
Montreal, Quebec H3B 5E8
(514) 989-2829   www.canadiens.com
Owner . . . . .George N. Gillett Jr.
President . . . . .Pierre Boivin
Exec. V.P./General Manager . . . . .Bob Gainey
V.P. of Communications . . . . .Donald Beauchamp

Nashville Predators
501 Broadway, Nashville, TN 37203
(615) 770-2300   www.nashvillepredators.com
Chairman and Maj. Owner . . . . .Craig Leipold
President/COO . . . . .Jack Diller
Exec. V.P. & General Manager . . . . .David Poile
V.P. of Communications . . . . .Gerry Helper

New Jersey Devils
Continental Airlines Arena, P.O. Box 504
East Rutherford, NJ 07073
(201) 935-6050   www.newjerseydevils.com
Owner . . . . .YankeeNets
President-GM-CEO . . . . .Lou Lamoriello
Director of Public Relations . . . . .Jeff Altstadter

New York Islanders
1535 Old Country Road, Plainview, NY 11083
(516) 501-6700   www.newyorkislanders.com
Owner . . . . .Charles Wang & Sanjay Kumar
General Manager . . . . .Mike Milbury
V.P. of Communications . . . . .Chris Botta

New York Rangers
2 Penn Plaza, 14th Floor
New York, NY 10121
(212) 465-6486   www.newyorkrangers.com
Owner . . . . .Cablevision Systems Inc.
President (MSG) . . . . .James Dolan
President/GM/Head Coach . . . . .Glen Sather
V.P. of Public Relations . . . . .John Rosasco

Ottawa Senators
1000 Palladium Dr., Kanata, Ontario, K2V 1A5
(613) 599-0250   www.ottawasenators.com
Owner/Chairman/Governor . . . . .Eugene Melnyk
President & CEO . . . . .Roy Mlakar
General Manager . . . . .John Muckler
Director of Communications . . . . .Steve Keogh

Philadelphia Flyers
3601 S. Broad St., Philadelphia, PA 19148
(215) 465-4500   www.philadelphiaflyers.com
Chairman . . . . .Ed Snider
President . . . . .Ron Ryan
General Manager . . . . .Bob Clarke
Sr. Director of Communications . . . . .Zack Hill

Phoenix Coyotes
Alltel Ice Den, 9375 E. Bell Rd., Scottsdale, AZ 85260
(480) 473-5600   www.phoenixcoyotes.com
Chairman/CEO . . . . .Steve Ellman
President/COO . . . . .Douglas Moss
Exec. V.P. & General Manager . . . . .Michael Barnett
V.P. of Communications . . . . .Richard Nairn

Pittsburgh Penguins
Mellon Arena, 66 Mario Lemieux Place
Pittsburgh, PA 15219
(412) 642-1800   www.pittsburghpenguins.com
Owner/Chairman/CEO . . . . .Mario Lemieux
President/CEO . . . . .Ken Sawyer
Exec. V.P. & General Manager . . . . .Craig Patrick
V.P. of Communications . . . . .Tom McMillan

St. Louis Blues
Savvis Center, 1401 Clark Ave.
St. Louis, MO 63103
(314) 622-2500   www.stlouisblues.com
Owners .Bill and Nancy Laurie
President/CEO . . . . .Mark Sauer
Senior V.P./General Manager . . . . .Larry Pleau
Director of Communications . . . . .Frank Buonomo

San Jose Sharks
525 West Santa Clara St., San Jose, CA 95113
(408) 287-7070   www.sjsharks.com
Owner . . . .San Jose Sports and Entertainment Enterprises
President-CEO . . . . .Greg Jamison
Exec. V.P. & General Manager . . . . .Doug Wilson
Sr. Dir. of Media Relations/Publishing . . . . . .Ken Arnold

Tampa Bay Lightning
401 Channelside Drive, Tampa, FL 33602
(813) 301-6500   www.tampabaylightning.com
Owner . . . . .Palace Sports & Ent.
CEO & Governor .Tom Wilson
Exec. V.P. & General Manager . . . . .Jay Feaster
Director of Public Relations . . . . Jay Preble

Toronto Maple Leafs
Air Canada Centre
40 Bay Street, Ste. 400, Toronto, Ontario M5J 2X2
(416) 815-5500   www.mapleleafs.com
Owner . . . . .Maple Leaf Sports & Entertainment, Ltd
President/CEO .Richard Peddie
Vice Chairman . . . . .Ken Dryden
General Manager . . . . .John Ferguson
Director of Media Relations . . . . .Pat Park

Vancouver Canucks
General Motors Place, 800 Griffiths Way
Vancouver, B.C. V6B 6G1
(604) 899-4600   www.canucks.com
Owners . . . . .John McCaw
COO . . . . .David Cobb
President & General Manager . . . . .Brian Burke
Manager of Media Relations . . . . .Chris Brumwell

Washington Capitals
MCI Center, 401 Ninth St., Suite 750
Washington, D.C. 20004
(202) 266-2200   www.washingtoncaps.com
Majority Owner/Chairman . . . . .Ted Leonsis
President . . . . .Dick Patrick
V.P./General Manager . . . . .George McPhee
Manager of Media Relations . . . . .Brian Potter

IIHF

International Ice Hockey Federation
Brandschenkestrasse 50, Postfach
CH-8039 Zurich, Switzerland
TEL: 011-411-562-2200   www.iihf.com
President . . . . .Rene Fasel
General Secretary . . . . .Jan-Ake Edvinsson
Director of P.R./Marketing . . . . .Kimmo Leinonen

AHL

American Hockey League
One Monarch Place, Springfield, MA 01144
(413) 781-2030   www.theahl.com
President/CEO .David Andrews
V.P. of Hockey Ops. .Jim Mill
Dir. of Communications/Media Services . . . . .Bret Stothart
Member teams (28): Eastern Conference—Albany
River Rats, Binghamton Senators, Bridgeport Sound Tigers,
Hartford Wolf Pack, Hershey Bears, Lowell Lock Monsters,
Manchester Monarchs, Norfolk Admirals, Philadelphia Phan-
toms, Portland Pirates, Providence Bruins, Springfield Falcons,
Wilkes-Barre/Scranton Penguins and Worcester IceCats.
   Western Conference—Chicago Wolves, Cincinnati
Mighty Ducks, Cleveland Barons, Grand Rapids Griffins,
Hamilton Bulldogs, Houston Aeros, Manitoba Moose, Mil-
waukee Admirals, Rochester Americans, St. John's Maple
Leafs, San Antonio Rampage, Syracuse Crunch, Toronto
Roadrunners and Utah Grizzlies.

HORSE RACING

Breeders' Cup Limited
PO Box 4230, Lexington, KY 40544-4230
(859) 223-5444   www.breederscup.com
President/NTRA Vice Chairman . . . . . .D.G. Van Clief, Jr.
V.P./Breeders' Cup & Event Mktg. . . . . . .Damon Thayer

NTRA
(National Thoroughbred Racing Association)
444 Madison Ave., Suite 503
New York, NY 10022
(212) 907-9280   www.ntra.com
CEO-Commissioner . . . . .Tim Smith
Deputy Commissioner & COO . . . . .Greg Avioli
Sr. Director of Media Relations . . . . .Eric Wing

TRA
(Thoroughbred Racing Associations of N. America, Inc.)
420 Fair Hill Drive, Suite 1, Elkton, MD 21921
(410) 392-9200   www.tra-online.com
President . . . . .Joe Harper
Executive V.P. . . . . .Christopher N. Scherf

USTA
(United States Trotting Association)
750 Michigan Ave., Columbus, OH 43215
(614) 224-2291   www.ustrotting.com
President .F. Phillip Langley
Executive V.P. . . . . .Fred Noe
Director of Public Relations . . . . .John Pawlak

MEDIA

PERIODICALS

ESPN, The Magazine
19 E 34th St., 7th Floor, New York, NY 10016
(212) 515-1000   www.espnmag.com
Editor in Chief .Gary Hoenig
Executive Editors . .Gary Belsky, Neil Fine and Steve Wulf
Sr. Vice President/GM . . . . .Geoff Reiss
Sr. Vice President/Editorial Dir. . . . . .John Papanek

Sports Illustrated
135 West 50th St., New York, NY 10020
(212) 522-9797   www.cnnsi.com
President/CEO . . . . .E. Bruce Hallett
Managing Editor . . . . .Terry McDonell
Executive Editors . . . . .Michael Bevans, Rob Fleder
                                     and Charlie Leerhsen

The Sporting News
10176 Corporate Square Dr., Suite 200
St. Louis, MO 63132
(314) 997-7111   www.sportingnews.com
Senior V.P./Editorial Director . . . . John D. Rawlings
President/CEO . . . . .C. Richard Allen

The Sports Business Daily
120 West Morehead St., Ste. 220
Charlotte, NC 28202
(704) 973-1500   www.sportsbizdaily.com
Executive Editor . . . . .Abe Madkour
Editor-at-Large . . . . .Terry Lefton
Media Relations Manager . . . . .Bill Magrath

USA Today
7950 Jones Branch Drive., McLean, VA 22108
(703) 854-3400   www.usatoday.com
Owner . . . . .Gannett Co.
President-Publisher . . . . .Tom Curley
Managing Editor/Sports . . . . .Monte Lorell

WIRE SERVICES

Associated Press
50 Rockefeller Plaza 5th Floor, New York, NY 10020
(212) 621-1630   www.ap.org
Sports Editor . . . . .Terry Taylor
Deputy Sports Editor . . . . .Aaron Watson

United Press International
1510 H Street NW, Washington, DC 20005
(202) 898-8000   www.upi.com
Managing Editor, Sports . . . . .Ron Colbert

The Sports Network
2200 Byberry Rd., Suite 200
Hatboro, PA 19040
(215) 441-8444   www.sportsnetwork.com
CEO/President .Mickey Charles
Director of Operations . . . . .Phil Sokol

Sportsticker
800 Plaza Two, Harborside Financial Ctr., Jersey City, NJ 07311
(201) 309-1200   www.sportsticker.com
Dir., Customer Marketing & Communication . . .Lou Monaco
                                                (201) 938-4537

TV NETWORKS

ABC Sports
47 West 66th St., 13th Floor
New York, NY 10023
(212) 456-4867   www.abcsports.com
President .George Bodenheimer
Senior V.P., Exec. Producer . . . . .Mike Pearl
V.P. of Media Relations . . . . .Mark Mandel

CBC Sports
250 Front St. West, P.O. Box 500, Station A
Toronto, Ontario M5W 1E6
(416) 205-6523   www.cbc.ca/sports
Executive Director-Sports . . . . .Nancy Lee
Sr. Executive Producer . . . . .Mike Brannagan

CBS Sports
51 West 52nd St., 25th Floor
New York, NY 10019
(212) 975-5230   www.cbs.sportsline.com
President . . . . .Sean McManus
Executive Producer . . . . .Tony Petitti
Sr. V.P., Programming . . . . .Rob Correa and Mike Aresco
V.P., Communications . . . . .Leslie Anne Wade

ESPN
ESPN Plaza, Bristol, CT 06010
(860) 766-2000   www.espn.go.com
President . . . . .George Bodenheimer
Sr. V.P. & Executive Editor . . . . .John Walsh
Executive V.P. of Programming . . . . .Mark Shapiro
Sr. V.P. of Programming . . . . .John Wildhack
Vice President/Director of News . . . . .Vince Doria
Director of Communications . . . . .Mike Soltys

FOX Sports
10201 W. Pico Blvd., Los Angeles, CA 90035
(310) 369-1000   www.foxsports.com
Chairman-CEO . . . . :. . . .David Hill
President . . . . .Ed Goren
Sr. V.P. of Media Relations (NYC) . . . . .Lou D'Ermilio

The Golf Channel
7580 Commerce Center Drive
Orlando, FL 32819
(407) 363-4653   www.thegolfchannel.com
Co-founder & Chairman . . . . .Arnold Palmer
President-CEO . . . . .David Manougian
V.P./Executive Producer . . . . .Tony Tortorici
Director of Public Relations . . . . .Dan Higgins

HBO Sports
1100 Ave. of the Americas
New York, NY 10036
(212) 512-1987   www.hbo.com/sports
President-CEO . . . . .Ross Greenburg
Sr. V.P./Exec. Producer . . . . .Rick Bernstein
Sr. V.P., Programming . . . . .Kery Davis
Director of Publicity . . . . .Ray Stallone

NBC Sports
30 Rockefeller Plaza, New York, NY 10112
(212) 664-2160   www.nbcsports.com
Chairman . . . . .Dick Ebersol
President . . . . .Ken Schanzer
Executive Producer . . . . .Tommy Roy
V.P. of Communications . . . . .Kevin Sullivan

NFL Network
280 Park Ave.
New York, NY 10017
(212) 450-2000   www.nfl.com/nflnetwork
President/CEO . . . . .Steve Bornstein
V.P. of Programming . . . . .Charles Coplin
Director of Media Services . . . . .Seth Palansky

TSN—The Sports Network
Nine Channel Nine Court
Scarborough, Ontario, M1S 4B5
(416) 332-7660   www.tsn.ca
President . . . . .Keith Pelley
Communications Manager . . . . .Andrea Goldstein

Turner Sports
One CNN Center
13th Floor, Atlanta, GA 30303
(404) 827-1735   www.cnnsi.com/turnersports
President . . . . .David R. Levy
Senior V.P./Coordinating Producer . . . . .Jeff Behnke
Senior V.P. of Public Relations . . . . .Greg Hughes

USA Network
1230 Ave. of the Americas, New York, NY 10020
(212) 413-5000   www.usanetwork.com/sports
Sr. V.P., Exec. Producer . . . . .Gordon Beck
V.P., Sports Programming . . . . .Kevin Landy
Sports Publicity . . . . .Tom Caraccioli

OLYMPICS

IOC
(International Olympic Committee)
Chateau de Vidy
CH-1007 Lausanne, Switzerland
TEL: 011-41-21-621-6111
President ....Jacques Rogge
Director General ....Francois Carrard
Director of Communications ....Giselle Davies

COC
(Canadian Olympic Committee)
2070 Peel St., Suite 300
Montreal, Quebec H3A 1W6
(514) 861-3371   www.olympic.ca
CEO ....Chris Rudge
President ....Michael Chambers
IOC members ....Charmaine Crooks, Paul Henderson,
          Richard Pound, James Worrall (Honourary)
Director of Communications ....Jackie DeSouza

USOC
(United States Olympic Committee)
One Olympic Plaza
Colorado Springs, CO 80909
(719) 632-5551   www.usoc.org
Acting President ....William C. Martin
CEO ....TBA
IOC members ..Anita DeFrantz, James Easton & Bob Ctvrlik
Chief Communications Officer ....Darryl Seibel

2004 SUMMER GAMES

Athens Olympic Organizing Committee
Iolkou 8 & Filikis Etaireias, 142 34 Nea Ionia, Athens, Greece
TEL: 011-30-12004-000   www.athens.olympic.org
     Time difference: 7 hours ahead of New York (EDT)
Chairman ....Gianna Angelopoulos-Daskalaki
Managing Director ....Ioannis Spanudakis
Chairman of Coord. Commission ....Denis Oswald
     (XXVIIIth Olympic Summer Games, Aug. 13-29)

2006 WINTER GAMES

Turin Olympic Organizing Committee
Via Nizza 262/58
10126 Turin, Italy
TEL: 011-39-011-631-0511   www.torino2006.org
President ....Valentino Castellani
Deputy President ....Evelina Christillin
Chairman of Coord. Commission .....Jean Claude-Killy
Media Relations Manager ....Giuseppe Gattino
     (XXth Olympic Winter Games, Feb. 10-26)

2008 SUMMER GAMES

Beijing Olympic Organizing Committee
24 Dongsi Shitiao St.
Beijing, China 100007
TEL: 86-10-65-28-20-09   www.beijing-2008.org
President ....Liu Qi
Executive President ....Yuan Weimin
Executive President ....Wang Qishan
Secretary General ....Wang Wei
     (XXIXth Olympic Summer Games, July 25-Aug. 10)

2010 WINTER GAMES

Vancouver 2010 Bid Corporation
TEL: 604-806-1019   www.winter2010.com
Chairman and CEO ....Jack Poole
Media Relations ....Sam Corea
     (XXIth Olympic Winter Games, Feb. 12-28)

U.S. OLYMPICS TRAINING CENTERS

Colorado Springs Training Center
One Olympic Plaza, Colorado Springs, CO 80909
(719) 866-4500
Director ....Lloyd Ward

Lake Placid Training Center
421 Old Military Road, Lake Placid, NY 12946
(518) 523-2600
Director ....Jack Favro

Arco Olympic Training Center
2800 Olympic Parkway, Chula Vista, CA 91915
(619) 656-1500
Director ....Patrice Milkovich

U.S. OLYMPIC ORGANIZATIONS

National Archery Association
One Olympic Plaza, Colorado Springs, CO 80909
(719) 866-4576   www.usarchery.org
President ....Mark Miller
Executive Director ....Brad Camp
Comm./Media Relations Mgr. ....Mary Beth Vorwerk

U.S. Badminton Association
One Olympic Plaza, Colorado Springs, CO 80909
(719) 866-4808   www.usabadminton.org
President ....Don Chew
Executive Director ....Dan Cloppas
Programs & Financial Services ....Peggy Savosik

USA Baseball
PO Box 1131, Durham, NC 27702
(919) 474-8721   www.usabaseball.com
President ....Mike Gaski
Executive Director & CEO ....Paul Seiler
Dir. of Communications ....David Fannucchi

USA Basketball
5465 Mark Dabling Blvd.
Colorado Springs, CO 80918
(719) 590-4800   www.usabasketball.com
President ....Tom Jernstedt
Executive Director ....James Tooley
Asst. Exec. Director/Communications ......Craig Miller

U.S. Biathlon Association
29 Ethan Allen Ave.
Colchester, VT 05446
(802) 654-7833   www.usbiathlon.org
President ....Lyle Nelson
Exec. Director ....Stephen Sands
Director of Winter Biathlon ....Max Cobb
Director of Summer Biathlon ....Marc Sheppard
Public Relations Contact ....Jerry Kokesh

U.S. Bobsled and Skeleton Federation
421 Old Military Road
Lake Placid, NY 12946
(518) 523-1842   www.usbsf.com
President ....Jim Morris
Executive Director ....Matt Roy
Media/P.R. Manager ....Tom LaDue

USA Boxing
One Olympic Plaza, Colorado Springs, CO 80909
(719) 866-4506   www.usaboxing.org
President ....Dr. Robert Voy
Executive Director ....Eric Parthen
Director of Media/Public Relations .....Julie Goldsticker

U.S. Canoe and Kayak Team
230 South Tyron St., Suite 220
Charlotte, NC 28202
(704) 348-4330 www.usack.org
President . . . . Anne Blanchard
Executive Director . . . . David Yarborough

USA Curling
1100 CenterPoint Drive, PO Box 866
Stevens Point, WI 54481
(715) 344-1199 www.usacurl.org
President . . . . Robert Fenson
Executive Director . . . . David Garber
Communications Director . . . . Rick Patzke

USA Cycling
One Olympic Plaza
Colorado Springs, CO 80909
(719) 866-4581 www.usacycling.org
President . . . . Jim Ochowicz
Exec. Director/CEO . . . . Gerard Bisceglia
Communications Mgrs. . . . . Andy Lee/Kelly Walker

United States Diving, Inc.
201 South Capitol Avenue, Suite 430
Indianapolis, IN 46205
(317) 237-5252 www.usdiving.org
President . . . . Dave Burgering
Executive Director . . . . Todd Smith
Director of Communications . . . . Kelli Servizzi

U.S. Equestrian Team
Pottersville Road, PO Box 355, Gladstone, NJ 07934
(908) 234-1251 www.uset.com
President . . . . Armand Leone, Jr.
Executive Director . . . . Bonnie B. Jenkins
Director of Communications . . . . Marty Bauman
(508) 698-6810

U.S. Fencing Association
One Olympic Plaza, Colorado Springs, CO 80909
(719) 866-4511 www.usfencing.org
President . . . . Stacey Johnson
Executive Director . . . . Michael Massik
Media Relations Contact . . . . Cindy Bent

U.S. Field Hockey Association
One Olympic Plaza, Colorado Springs, CO 80909
(719) 866-4567 www.usfieldhockey.com
President . . . . Sharon Taylor
Executive Director . . . . Sheila Walker
Director of Sport/Public Info. . . . . Howard Thomas

U.S. Figure Skating Association
20 First Street, Colorado Springs, CO 80906
(719) 635-5200 www.usfsa.org
President . . . . Chuck Foster
Executive Director . . . . John LeFevre
Director of Events . . . . Greg Johnston
Director of Communications . . . . Bob Dunlop

USA Gymnastics (Artistic & Rhythmic)
Pan American Plaza, Suite 300
201 South Capitol Avenue, Indianapolis, IN 46225
(317) 237-5050 www.usa-gymnastics.org
President-Exec. Director . . . . Robert V. Colarossi
Communications Manager . . . . Brian Eaton

USA Hockey, Inc.
1775 Bob Johnson Dr., Colorado Springs, CO 80906
(719) 576-8724 www.usahockey.com
President . . . . Ron DeGregorio
Executive Director . . . . Doug Palazzari
Dir. of Public and Media Relations . . . . Chuck Menke

United States Judo, Inc.
One Olympic Plaza, Suite 202
Colorado Springs, CO 80909
(719) 866-4730 www.usjudo.org
President . . . . Dr. Ron Tripp
Exec. Director . . . . William Rosenberg
Director of Operations . . . . John Miller

U.S. Luge Association
35 Church Street, Lake Placid, NY 12946
(518) 523-2071 www.usaluge.org
President . . . . Doug Bateman
Executive Director . . . . Ron Rossi
Public/Media Relations Manager . . . . Jon Lundin

U.S. Modern Pentathlon
5415 Bandera Rd., Suite 512, San Antonio, TX 78238
(210) 229-2004 usmpa.home.texas.net
President . . . . Ralph Bender
Executive Director . . . . Robert Marbut
Media Coordinator . . . . Elaine Cheris

U.S. Rowing
201 South Capitol Avenue, Suite 400
Indianapolis, IN 46225
(317) 237-5656 www.usrowing.org
President . . . . Monk Terry
Executive Director . . . . John Dane
Director of Communications . . . . Brett Johnson

U.S. Sailing Association
P.O. Box 1260, 15 Maritime Drive, Portsmouth, RI 02871
(401) 683-0800 www.ussailing.org
President . . . . David Rosekrans
Executive Director . . . . Nick Craw
Communications Manager . . . . . Marlieke de Lange Eaton

U.S. Shooting Team
One Olympic Plaza, Colorado Springs, CO 80909
(719) 866-4670 www.usashooting.com
President . . . . Michael English
Executive Director . . . . Robert Mitchell
Media Director . . . . Sara Greenlee

U.S. Ski & Snowboard Association
P.O. Box 100, 1500 Kearns Blvd.
Park City, UT 84060
(435) 649-9090 www.ussa.org
CEO/President . . . . Bill Marolt
V.P. of Public Relations/Member Svcs. . . . . Tom Kelly
Public Relations Director . . . . Juliann Fritz

U.S. Soccer Federation
U.S. Soccer House
1801-1811 South Prairie Ave.
Chicago, IL 60616
(312) 808-1300 www.ussoccer.com
President . . . . Dr. S. Robert Contiguglia
Secretary General . . . . Dan Flynn
Director of Communications . . . . Jim Moorhouse

Amateur Softball Association
2801 N.E. 50th Street
Oklahoma City, OK 73111
(405) 424-5266 www.softball.org
President . . . . H. Franklin Taylor III
Executive Director . . . . Ron Radigonda
Director of Communications . . . . Brian McCall

U.S. Speed Skating
P.O. Box 450639, Westlake, OH 44145
(440) 899-0128 www.usspeedskating.org
President . . . . Andy Gabel
Executive Director . . . . Katie Marquard
Public Relations Director . . . . Bill Kellick

USA Swimming
One Olympic Plaza, Colorado Springs, CO 80909
(719) 866-4578   www.usswim.com
President ....Ron Van Pool
Executive Director ....,....Chuck Wielgus
Communications Director ....Mary Wagner

U.S. Synchronized Swimming, Inc.
201 South Capitol Avenue, Suite 901
Indianapolis, IN 46225
(317) 237-5700   www.usasynchro.org
President ....Betty Hazle
Executive Director ....Terry Harper
Media Relations Director ....Amy McClintock

USA Table Tennis
One Olympic Plaza, Colorado Springs, CO 80909
(719) 866-4583   www.usatt.org
President ....Sherri Soderberg Pittman
Executive Director ....Doru Gheorghe
Program and Marketing Coord. ....Tommy Perkins

U.S. Taekwondo Union
One Olympic Plaza, Suite 104-C
Colorado Springs, CO 80909
(719) 866-4632   www.ustu.org
President ....Sang Chul Lee
Executive Director ....Bruce Harris

USA Team Handball
One Olympic Plaza
Colorado Springs, CO 80909
(719) 866-4036   www.usateamhandball.org
President ....Bob Djokovich
Executive Director ....Mike Cavanaugh
Program Directors ....Lindalisa Severo, Kim Miller

U.S. Tennis Association
70 West Red Oak Lane
White Plains, NY 10604
(914) 696-7000   www.usta.com
Chairman/President ....Alan Schwartz
Executive Director ....D. Lee Hamilton
Director of Communications/Marketing ...David Newman

USA Track and Field
One RCA Dome, Suite 140
Indianapolis, IN 46225
(317) 261-0500   www.usatf.org
President ....Bill Roe
CEO ....Craig Masback
Director of Communications ....Jill Geer

USA Triathlon
616 W. Monument St., Colorado Springs, CO 80905
(719) 597-9090   www.usatriathlon.org
President ....Valerie Ellsworth-Gattis
Executive Director ....Steven M. Locke
Communications Director ........B.J. Hoeptner-Evans

USA Volleyball
715 S. Circle Dr., 2nd Floor
Colorado Springs, CO 80910
(719) 228-6800   www.usavolleyball.org
President ....Albert Monaco
CEO ....Rebecca Howard .
Manager P.R./Publications ....Paul Soriano

United States Water Polo
1685 W. Uintah St., Colorado Springs, CO 80904
(719) 634-0699   www.usawaterpolo.org
President ....Rich Foster
Executive Director ....Tom Seitz
Dir. of Media/Marketing ....Eric Velazquez

USA Weightlifting
One Olympic Plaza, Colorado Springs, CO 80909
(719) 866-4508   www.usaweightlifting.org
President ....Dennis Snethen
Exec. Director ....Wes Barnett
Communications Coordinator ....Beth Connolly

USA Wrestling
6155 Lehman Drive, Colorado Springs, CO 80918
(719) 598-8181   www.usawrestling.org
President ....Stan Dziedzic
Executive Director ....Rich Bender
Dir. of Comm./Special Projects ....Gary Abbott

SOCCER

FIFA

(Federation Internationale de Football Assn.)
P.O. Box 85, 8030 Zurich, Switzerland
TEL: 011-41-1-384-9595   www.fifa.com
President ....Joseph Blatter
General Secretary ....Dr. Urs Linsi
Director of Communications ....Markus Siegler

MLS

Major League Soccer
110 E. 42nd Street, 10th Floor
New York, NY 10017
(212) 450-1200   www.mlsnet.com
Founder ....Alan I. Rothenberg
Commissioner ....Don Garber
Senior Dir. of Communications ....Trey Fitz-Gerald

Chicago Fire
980 N. Michigan Ave., Suite 1998
Chicago, IL 60611
(312) 705-7200   www.chicago-fire.com
Investor/Operator ....Philip F. Anschutz (AEG)
General Manager ....Peter Wilt
Director of Communications ....Diana Lopez

Colorado Rapids
555 17th Street, Suite 3350, Denver, CO 80202
(303) 299-1570   www.coloradorapids.com
Investor/Operator ....Kroenke Sports Enterprises
General Manager ....Dan Counce
Director of Media Relations ....Jurgen Mainka

Columbus Crew
Columbus Crew Stadium
One Black & Gold Blvd., Columbus, OH 43211
(614) 447-2739   www.thecrew.com
Investor/Operator ....Hunt Sports Group
President/GM ....Jim Smith
Director of Public Relations ....Jeff Wuerth

Dallas Burn
14800 Quorum Drive, Suite 300
Dallas, TX 75254
(214) 979-0303   www.dallasburn.com
Investor/Operator ....Hunt Sports Group
President/GM ....Greg Elliott
Sr. Director of Media Services ....Chris Ward

D.C. United
14120 Newbrook Drive, Suite 170
Chantilly, VA 20151
(703) 478-6600   www.dcunited.com
Investor/Operator ....Philip F. Anschutz (AEG)
Senior V.P./Managing Dir. of AEG Soccer ...Kevin Payne
V.P., Communications ....Doug Hicks

Kansas City Wizards
2 Arrowhead Drive
Kansas City, MO 64129
(816) 920-9300   www.kcwizards.com
Investor/Operator . . . . .Hunt Sports Group
General Manager .Curt Johnson
Assoc. Manager of Public Relations . Justin Gorman, Staci
       Schottman

Los Angeles Galaxy
18400 Avalon Blvd., Ste. 200, Carson, CA 90746
(626) 432-1540   www.lagalaxy.com
Investor/Operator . . . . .Philip F. Anschutz (AEG)
V.P./General Manager . . . . .Doug Hamilton
Manager of Communications . . . . .Patrick Donnelly

MetroStars
One Harmon Plaza, 3rd Floor
Secaucus, NJ 07094
(201) 583-7000   www.metrostars.com
Investor/Operator . . . . .Philip F. Anschutz (AEG)
President/GM .Nick Sakiewicz
Manager of Communications . . . . .Matthew Chmura

New England Revolution
Gillette Stadium, One Patriot Place
Foxboro, MA 02035
(508) 543-5001   www.revolutionsoccer.net
Investor/Operator . . . . .Robert Kraft/Jonathan Kraft
Vice President/COO . . . . .Lou Imbriano
Managing Director . . . . .Sunil Gulati

San Jose Earthquakes
3550 Stevens Creek Blvd., Suite 200
San Jose, CA 95117
(408) 241-9922   www.sjearthquakes.com
Investor/Operator . . . . .San Jose Sports and Entertainment
       Enterprises & AEG
General Manager . . . . .Johnny Moore
Director of Media Relations . . . . .Jed Mettee

Other Soccer

CONCACAF
(Confederation of North, Central American & Caribbean Association Football)
725 Fifth Ave., 17th Floor, New York, NY 10022
(212) 308-0044   www.concacaf.com
President .Jack Austin Warner
General Secretary . . . . .Chuck Blazer
Senior Consultant .Clive Toye
Press Officer . . . . .Steven Torres

U.S. Soccer
(United States Soccer Federation)
U.S. Soccer House, 1801-1811 South Prairie Ave.
Chicago, IL 60616
(312) 808-1300   www.ussoccer.com
President . . . . .Dr. S. Robert Contiguglia
Secretary General .Dan Flynn
Director of Communications . . . . .Jim Moorhouse

MISL
(Major Indoor Soccer League)
1175 Post Road East
Westport, CT 06880
(203) 222-4900   www.misl.net
Commissioner . . . . .Steve Ryan
Director, Soccer Operations . . . . .David Grimaldi
Director of Communications . . . . .Lou Corletto
    Member teams (9): Baltimore Blast, Cleveland Force, Dallas Sidekicks, Kansas City Comets, Milwaukee Wave, Monterrey (Mex.) Fury, Philadelphia Kixx, St. Louis Steamers and San Diego Sockers.

WUSA
(Women's United Soccer Association)
6205 Peachtree Dunwoody Rd., 15th Floor
Atlanta, GA 30328
(678) 645-0800   www.wusa.com
President/CEO .Lynn Morgan
Commissioner .Tony DiCicco
V.P. of Communications/Bus. Dev. . . . . . .Dan Courtemanche
    Member teams (8): Atlanta Beat, Boston Breakers, Carolina Courage, New York Power, Philadelphia Charge, San Diego Spirit, San Jose CyberRays and Washington Freedom. (League has suspended operations as of Sept. 15, 2003)

SWIMMING

FINA
(Federation Internationale de Natation Amateur)
4 ave de l'Avante Poste
1005 Lausanne, Switzerland
TEL: 011-4121-310-4710   www.fina.org
President .Mustapha Larfaoui
Executive Director . . . . .Cornel Marculescu
Honorary Secretary . . . . .Bartolo Consolo

USA Swimming
One Olympic Plaza, Colorado Springs, CO 80909
(719) 866-4578   www.usswim.org
President . . . . .Ron Van Pool
Executive Director . . . . .Chuck Wielgus
Communications Director . . . . .Mary Wagner

TENNIS

ATP Tour
(Association of Tennis Professionals)
201 ATP Boulevard
Ponte Vedra Beach, FL 32082
(904) 285-8000   www.atptennis.com
Chief Executive Officer . . . . .Mark Miles
V.P. of Corporate Comm. . . . . .David Higdon
Dir. of Public Relations . . . . .J.J. Carter

ITF
(International Tennis Federation)
Bank Lane, Roehampton
London, England SW15 5XZ
TEL: 011-44-208-878-6464   www.itftennis.com
President . . . . .Francesco Ricci Bitti
Executive V.P. . . . . .Juan Margets
Head of Communications . . . . .Barbara Travers

World TeamTennis
250 Park Ave. South, 9th Floor
New York, NY 10003
(212) 979-0202   www.worldteamtennis.com
Director/Co-Founder . . . . .Billie Jean King
Commissioner & CEO . . . . .Ilana Kloss
Public Relations . . . . .Katie Fassbinder—GEM Group
       (303-237-0616)
    Member teams (10): Delaware Smash, Hartford FoxForce, Kansas City Explorers, New York Buzz, New York Sportimes, Newport Beach Breakers, Philadelphia Freedoms, Sacramento Capitals, Springfield (Mo.) Lasers and St. Louis Aces.

U.S. Tennis Association
70 West Red Oak Lane
White Plains, NY 10604
(914) 696-7000   www.usta.com
Chairman/President . . . . .Alan Schwartz
Executive Director . . . . .D. Lee Hamilton
Director of Communications/Marketing . . .David Newman

WTA Tour
(Women's Tennis Association)
133 First Street N.E., St. Petersburg, FL 33701
(727) 895-5000 www.wtatour.com
Chairman/CEO ....Larry Scott
Senior V.P., Tour Operations ....Peachy Kellmeyer
Dir. of Corporate Communications ....Darrell Fry
Sr. Manager, Communications ....John Dolan

TRACK & FIELD

IAAF
(International Association of Athletics Federations)
17 rue Princesse Florestine, BP 359
MC 98007 Monaco
TEL: 011-377-93-10-8888 www.iaaf.org
President ....Lamine Diack
Senior V.P. ....Dr. Arne Ljungquist
General Secretary ....Istvan Gyulai

USA Track & Field
One RCA Dome, Suite 140
Indianapolis, IN 46225
(317) 261-0500 www.usatf.org
President ....Bill Roe
CEO ....Craig Masback
Director of Communications ....Jill Geer

MISCELLANEOUS

AAU
(Amateur Athletic Union)
P.O. Box 22409
Lake Buena Vista, FL 32830
(407) 934-7200 www.aausports.org
President/CEO ....Bobby Dodd
Media/Public Relations Director ....Melissa Wilson

All-American Soap Box Derby
P.O. Box 7225, Akron, OH 44306
(330) 733-8723 www.aasbd.org
Executive Director ....Tony DeLuca
General Manager ....Jeff Iula
Public Relations Director ....Bob Troyer

American Power Boat Association
17640 Nine Mile Road
Eastpointe, MI 48021
(586) 773-9700 www.apba.org
Chairman ....Don Allen
Executive Administrator ....Gloria Urbin

Association of Surfing Professionals
P.O. Box 1095, Coolangatta
Queensland, Australia 4225
011-61-7-5599-1550 www.aspworldtour.com
President/CEO ....Wayne "Rabbit" Bartholomew
Media Director ....Jesse Faen

BASS, Inc.
(Bass Anglers Sportsmen Society)
5845 Carmichael Road
Montgomery, AL 36141
(334) 272-9530 www.bassmaster.com
Owner ....ESPN
V.P., General Manager ....Dean Kessel
Tournament Director ....Trip Weldon
Director of Communications ....George McNeilly

Iditarod Trail Committee
P.O. Box 870800
Wasilla, AK 99687
(907) 376-5155 www.iditarod.com
Executive Director ....Stan Hooley
Race Director ....Joanne Potts

Little League Baseball, Incorporated
P.O. Box 3485, Williamsport, PA 17701
(570) 326-1921 www.littleleague.org
CEO-President ....Stephen Keener
Director of Comm. & Media Relations ...Lance Van Auken

Major League Lacrosse
One Harmon Plaza, 3rd Floor, Secaucus, NJ 07094
(201) 325-0800 www.majorleaguelacrosse.com
Executive Director ....Matthew Pace
Dir. of Communications ....Jaye Cavallo
 Member teams (6): Baltimore Bayhawks, Boston Cannons, Bridgeport Barrage, Long Island Lizards, New Jersey Pride and Rochester Rattlers.

National Lacrosse League
1212 Avenue of the Americas, 5th Floor
New York, NY 10036
(917) 510-9200 www.nll.com
Commissioner ....Jim Jennings
Dir. of Public Relations ....Doug Fritts
 Member teams (10): Anaheim Storm, Arizona (TBA), Buffalo Bandits, Calgary Roughnecks, Colorado Mammoth, Philadelphia Wings, Rochester Knighthawks, San Jose Stealth, Toronto Rock and Vancouver Ravens.

Professional Rodeo Cowboys Association
101 Pro Rodeo Drive
Colorado Springs, CO 80919
(719) 593-8840 www.prorodeo.com
Commissioner ....Steven J. Hatchell
Director of Communications ....Leslie King

Special Olympics
1325 G St. NW Suite 500
Washington, DC 20005
(202) 628-3630 www.specialolympics.org
Founder/Honorary Chairman ....Eunice Kennedy Shriver
Chairman Emeritus ....Sargent Shriver
Chairman ....Timothy 'P. Shriver
Media Relations Coordinator ....Jo-Ann Enwezor

U.S. Association of Blind Athletes
33 N. Institute St.
Colorado Springs, CO 80903
(719) 630-0422 www.usaba.org
Executive Director ....Mark Lucas
Communications Director ....Nicole Jomantas

U.S. Polo Association
771 Corporate Dr., Suite 505
Lexington, KY 40503
(859) 219-1000 www.us-polo:org
Chairman ....Orrin H. Ingram
Executive Director ....David Cummings

USA Rugby
1033 Walnut St., Suite 200
Boulder, CO 80302
(719) 637-1022 www.usarugby.org
CEO ....Doug Arnot
Communications Manager ....Deborah Engen

Wheelchair Sports, USA
3595 East Fountain Blvd., Suite L-1
Colorado Springs, CO 80910
(719) 574-1150 www.wsusa.org
Chairman ....Paul DePace
Executive Director ....Patricia Shepherd

Women's Professional Billiard Association
6407 South Blvd.
Charlotte, NC 28217
(704) 556-1128 www.wpba.com
President ....Ewa Mataya Laurance
Director of Operations ....Peg Ledman

International Sports

Michael Phelps, shows how many world records
he set at the 2003 Swimming World Championships.

Down, But Not Out

Gerry Brown is co-editor of the ESPN Sports Almanac.

Lance Armstrong picked himself up off the asphalt to bag his fifth consecutive Tour de France in 2003.

Lance Armstrong had to know winning his fifth straight Tour de France wouldn't be a piece of pastry. All he would have to do was review history, the Tour de France has 100 years of it.

And the only men to win five Tours, Jacques Anquetil, Eddy Merckx, Bernard Hinault and Miguel Indurain, all had a difficult time in their fifth and final victory. History notwithstanding, he may not have suspected it would be quite this hard or that he would have this many obstacles.

Then again the adage says, "nothing worth having comes without a fight." And unlike previous years, Armstrong had to fight for the yellow jersey in 2003. It's not that the other riders weren't trying in the past, it's just that they were irrelevant.

Armstrong's apparent mortality was in some ways a complete surprise to his competitors. His apparent weakness gave them a hope that they had forgotten about for several years and weakness was the last thing Armstrong wanted to show.

But this year was different because Armstrong was. A virus punched him in the gut early on in the race and he didn't seem to have the pedal power like in years past.

And a proven champion, Jan Ullrich, was lurking. Ullrich was suspended for the 2002 race for taking a recreational drug. For the big German it was starting to look like he had a chance to go from Ecstasy to ecstasy in one year.

For Armstrong, the agony continued as the race rolled on. After escaping serious injury in a mass crash at the end of Stage 1—the same crash that gave fellow American Tyler Hamilton a broken collarbone—he very nearly avoided complete disaster on a long steep descent in Stage 9 when he was able

AP/Wide World Photos

Lance Armstrong hit the deck hard and took out Spanish rider Iban Mayo when his handlebars hooked a spectator's handbag. Main rival Jan Ullrich (right, on bike) passed Armstrong but waited for him to catch up instead of taking advantage.

to swerve at the last instant to avoid fallen foe Joseba Beloki. The evasive maneuver sent him rolling down a grassy hill. He had to hop off the bike and jump over a trench before rejoining the race. It could easily have been a lot worse. If there were rocks or a cliff, instead of grass, it could have been a race, career or even life-ending event.

Armstrong fought not only his body, the terrain and the other riders but the crowd as well. In the race's most compelling moment, Armstrong was standing up on his pedals, during Stage 15's Luz-Ardiden climb in the French Pyrenees. He was riding alongside the crowds of cheering spectators when his right handle bar caught the strap of fan's musette bag and his bike was pulled out from under him. Suddenly, the invincible Armstrong was down and Ullrich, the 1997 champion and four-time runner up, was going by, leaving him behind.

But Armstrong got up, got back in the saddle and got angry. With his adrenaline feeding his legs, Armstrong chewed up the hill and soon left Ullrich (who repaid an old debt by not taking advantage of Armstrong's misfortune) and every other rider, for that matter, behind.

AP/Wide World Photos

American **Kelli White** swept the 100 and 200 meter dashes at the Track and Field World Championships but raised suspicions when she tested positive for a stimulant.

It was Armstrong's first stage win of the race and it was just what he needed to remind everyone why they had lost all hope in the first place.

But with just a 65-second lead over Ullrich in the race's final days and a 30-mile time trial in the Tour's penultimate stage looming, things looked like they could go either way. Armstrong had never lost the final time trial at the Tour de France since his streak began in 1999 but it was in a time trial stage earlier in the race that Ullrich nearly destroyed a dehydrated Armstrong, beating him by one minute, 36 seconds.

But when the day arrived it was rainy. And when a desperate Ullrich pushed his luck and his bike slipped away on the wet pavement, so did any hope of catching Armstrong.

During the ceremonial parade into Paris on the race's final day, despite the fact that the margin of victory would be the narrowest of his five Tour wins, the smile on his face was definitely the widest.

So, in the end, Armstrong proved beatable but unbeaten. And with a promise to come back in 2004 for a shot at an historic sixth Tour de France victory, the only hope he left the peloton with was that if he does win again and makes history, *he'll* be history by retiring someday, giving somebody else a shot.

The Ten Biggest Stories
of the Year in International Sports

10   American sprinter Jon Drummond gets disqualified for a false start in a preliminary heat of the 100 meters at the Track and Field World Championships and throws a tirade, arguing with officials and laying down on the track, ultimately disrupting the meet for nearly an hour.

9   The United States wins one gold and six silver medals, including one by former undefeated collegian Cael Sanderson, at the Freestyle Wrestling World Championships at New York City's Madison Square Garden. The American men's team finishes second to former Soviet Republic Georgia in the standings and the American women tie Japan but take second on the tiebreaker.

8   Regina Jacobs breaks four minutes and a 13-year-old world record in the women's indoor 1,500 meters in Boston.

7   The men's and women's marathon world records fall. Britain's Paula Radcliffe destroys her world mark with a win at the London Marathon and Kenya's Paul Tergat bests Khalid Khannouchi's world record by 43 seconds with a time of 2:04:55 at the Berlin Marathon.

6   Michelle Kwan joins Carol Heiss and Dick Button as the only Americans to win five World Championship gold medals. Kwan also wins her seventh U.S. Championship in 2003.

5   American skier Bode Miller has a super season on the slopes. Miller wins two golds (giant slalom and combined) and a silver (Super G) at the World Championship at St. Moritz. On the World Cup circuit, Miller finishes first in the combined event and second to Austrian Stephan Eberharter in the overall standings for the best finish by an American since Phil Mahre in 1983.

4   American sprinter Kelli White sweeps the 100 and 200 meter dashes, winning two gold medals at the Track and Field World Championships in Paris. Controversy swirls however, when White tests positive for the stimulant modafinil, which she purportedly took to treat narcolepsy. White avoids suspension but waits to hear whether she will keep the medals.

3   The United States women's team, depleted by injury and illness, wins America's first team gold (men or women) at the World Gymnastics Championships. Russia's Svetlana Khorkina becomes the first three-time all-around women's champion. On the men's side, China wins the team gold but Paul Hamm becomes the first American to win the individual all-around gold medal.

2 American teenager Michael Phelps breaks five world records, including two in separate events on the same afternoon, at the World Swimming Championships in Barcelona. Phelps, nicknamed the Baltimore Bullet, gives the world a preview of what could be dominance at the 2004 Athens Games and a run at Mark Spitz's record of seven gold medals.

1 Super cyclist Lance Armstrong struggles, a bit, but eventually returns to greatness as he extends his incredible streak with a fifth straight victory in his sport's biggest event, the Tour de France. The cancer survivor and wiry Texan will attempt to eclipse cycling's all-time greats with an unprecedented sixth consecutive Tour de France victory in 2004.

Kwan Do

American figure skating star Michelle Kwan continued to add to her huge numbers in two of ice skating's most important competitions in 2003 but still has yet to win a gold medal on the world's biggest stage, the Olympic Games.

	Championships
U.S. Championships	7
World Championships	5
Olympics	0

Note: Kwan's totals in the U.S. Championships and World Championships are second all-time.

Back-to-Back-to-Back-to-Back-to-Back

Lance Armstrong has dominated his sport like no one else in recent years. Here's how he compares to the turnover of champions in the four major professional sports since Armstrong's streak began in 1999.

	Different Winners
Super Bowl	5
Stanley Cup	4
World Series	3
NBA Championship	2
Tour de France	1

2002-2003
Season in Review

SPORTS ALMANAC

TRACK & FIELD

2003 IAAF World Championships

The 9th IAAF World Championships in Athletics held in Paris, France, Aug. 23-31, 2003. Note that (WR) indicates world record, (CR) indicates championship meet record and (TR) indicates meet record was tied.

Final Medal Leaders

		G	S	B	Total			G	S	B	Total
1	United States	10	8	2	20	6	Sweden	2	1	2	5
2	Russia	6	8	5	19		Jamaica	0	3	2	5
3	Ethiopia	3	2	2	7		Spain	0	3	2	5
	Belarus	3	1	3	7	9	Seven countries tied with 4 medals each.				
	France	2	3	2	7						

MEN

Event		Time	
100 meters	Kim Collins, SKN	10.07	
200 meters	John Capel, USA	20.30	
400 meters	Jerome Young, USA	44.50	
800 meters	Djabir Said-Guerni, ALG	1:44.81	
1500 meters	Hicham El Guerrouj, MOR	3:31.77	
5000 meters	Eliud Kipchoge, KEN	12:52.79	CR
10,000 meters	Kenenisa Bekele, ETH	26:49.57	CR
Marathon	Jaouad Gharib, MOR	2:08:31	CR
4x100m relay	USA (Capel, Williams, Patton, Johnson)	38.06	
4x400m relay	USA (Harrison, Washington, Brew, Young)	2:58.88	
110m hurdles	Allen Johnson, USA	13.12	
400m hurdles	Felix Sanchez, DOM	47.25	
3000m steeple	Saif Saaeed Shaheen, QAT	8:04.39	
20k walk	Jefferson Perez, ECU	1:17:21	WR
50k walk	Robert Korzeniowski, POL	3:36:03	WR

Event		Hgt/Dist
High Jump	Jacques Freitag, RSA	7-8½
Pole Vault	Giuseppe Gibilisco, ITA	19-4¼
Long Jump	Dwight Phillips, USA	27-3¾
Triple Jump	Christian Olsson, SWE	58-1¾
Shot Put	Andrei Mikhnevich, BLR	71-2
Discus	Virgilijus Alekna, LTU	228-7
Hammer	Ivan Tikhon, BLR	272-5
Javelin	Sergey Makarov, RUS	280-3
Decathlon	Tom Pappas, USA	8750 pts

WOMEN

Event		Time	
100 meters	Kelli White, USA	10.85	
200 meters	Kelli White, USA	22.05	
400 meters	Ana Guevara, MEX	48.89	
800 meters	Maria de Lourdes Mutola, MOZ	1:59.89	
1500 meters	Tatyana Tomashova, RUS	3:58.52	CR
5000 meters	Tirunesh Dibaba, ETH	14:51.72	
10,000 meters	Berhane Adere, ETH	30:04.18	CR
Marathon	Catherine Ndereba, KEN	2:23:55	CR
4x100m relay	France (Girard, Hurtis, Felix, Arron)	41.78	
4x400m relay	USA (Barber, Washington, Miles Clark, Richards)	3:22.63	
100m hurdles	Perdita Felicien, CAN	12.53	
400m hurdles	Jana Pittman, AUS	53.22	
20k walk	Yelena Nikolayeva, RUS	1:26:52	CR

Event		Hgt/Dist	
High Jump	Hestrie Cloete, RSA	6-9	
Pole Vault	Svetlana Feofanova, RUS	15-7	TR
Long Jump	Eunice Barber, FRA	22-11¼	
Triple Jump	Tatyana Lebedeva, RUS	49-9¾	
Shot Put	Svetlana Krivelyova, RUS	67-8¼	
Discus	Irina Yatchenko, BLR	220-10	
Hammer	Yipsi Moreno, CUB	240-7	
Javelin	Mirela Manjani, GRE	218-3	
Heptathlon	Carolina Kluft, SWE	7001 pts	

World Outdoor Records Set in 2003

World outdoor records set or equaled between Oct. 1, 2002 and Sept. 28, 2003; (p) indicates record is pending ratification by the IAAF; (†) indicates the IAAF does not officially recognize world records in that event.

MEN

Event	Name	Record	Old Mark	Former Holder
Marathon†	**Paul Tergat**, KEN	2:04:55	2:05:38	Khalid Khannouchi, USA (2002)
20k walk†	**Jefferson Perez**, ECU	1:17:21	1:17:22	Francisco Fernandez, ESP (2002)
50k walk†	**Robert Korzeniowski**, POL	3:36:03	3:36:39	Robert Korzeniowski, POL (2002)

WOMEN

Event	Name	Record	Old Mark	Former Holder
Marathon†	**Paula Radcliffe**, GBR	2:15:25	2:17:18	Paula Radcliffe, GBR (2002)
400m hurdles	**Yuliya Pechonkina**, RUS	52.34	52.61	Kim Batten, USA (1995)
3000m steeplechase	**Gulnara Samitova**, RUS	9:08.33p	9:16.51	Alesya Turova, BLR (2002)
Pole Vault	**Yelena Isinbayeva**, RUS	15-9¾p	15-9¼	Stacy Dragila, USA (2001)

World, Olympic and American Records
As of Sept. 28, 2003
World outdoor records officially recognized by the International Amateur Athletics Federation (IAAF); (p) indicates record is pending ratification.

MEN
Running

Event		Time		Date Set	Location
100 meters:	**World**	9.78	**Tim Montgomery**, USA	Sept. 14, 2002	Paris
	Olympic	9.84	Donovan Bailey, Canada	July 27, 1996	Atlanta
	American	9.78	Montgomery (same as World)	—	—
200 meters:	**World**	19.32	**Michael Johnson**, USA	Aug. 1, 1996	Atlanta
	Olympic	19.32	Johnson (same as World)	—	—
	American	19.32	Johnson (same as World)	—	—
400 meters:	**World**	43.18	**Michael Johnson**, USA	Aug. 26, 1999	Seville
	Olympic	43.49	Michael Johnson, USA	July 29, 1996	Atlanta
	American	43.18	Johnson (same as World)	—	—
800 meters:	**World**	1:41.11	**Wilson Kipketer**, Denmark	Aug. 24, 1997	Cologne
	Olympic	1:42.58	Vebjoern Rodal, Norway	July 31, 1996	Atlanta
	American	1:42.60	Johnny Gray	Aug. 28, 1985	Koblenz, W. Ger.
1000 meters:	**World**	2:11.96	**Noah Ngeny**, Kenya	Sept. 5, 1999	Rieti, ITA
	Olympic		Not an event	—	—
	American	2:13.9	Rick Wohlhuter	July 30, 1974	Oslo
1500 meters:	**World**	3:26.00	**Hicham El Guerrouj**, Morocco	July 14, 1998	Rome
	Olympic	3:32.07	Noah Ngeny, Kenya	Sept. 29, 2000	Sydney
	American	3:29.77	Sydney Maree	Aug. 25, 1985	Cologne
Mile:	**World**	3:43.13	**Hicham El Guerrouj**, Morocco	July 7, 1999	Rome
	Olympic		Not an event	—	—
	American	3:47.69	Steve Scott	July 7, 1982	Oslo
2000 meters:	**World**	4:44.79	**Hicham El Guerrouj**, Morocco	Sept. 7, 1999	Berlin
	Olympic		Not an event	—	—
	American	4:52.44	Jim Spivey	Sept. 15, 1987	Lausanne, SWI
3000 meters:	**World**	7:20.67	**Daniel Komen**, Kenya	Sept. 1, 1996	Rieti, ITA
	Olympic		Not an event	—	—
	American	7:30.84	Bob Kennedy	Aug. 8, 1998	Monte Carlo
5000 meters:	**World**	12:39.36	**Haile Gebrselassie**, Ethiopia	June 13, 1998	Helsinki
	Olympic	13:05.59	Said Aouita, Morocco	Aug. 11, 1984	Los Angeles
	American	12:58.21	Bob Kennedy	Aug. 14, 1996	Zurich
10,000 meters:	**World**	26:22.75	**Haile Gebrselassie**, Ethiopia	June 1, 1998	Hengelo, NED
	Olympic	27:07.34	Haile Gebrselassie, Ethiopia	July 29, 1996	Atlanta
	American	27:13.98	Meb Keflezighi	May 4, 2001	Stanford, Calif.
20,000 meters:	**World**	56:55.6	**Arturo Barrios**, Mexico	Mar. 30, 1991	La Fleche, FRA
	Olympic		Not an event	—	—
	American	58:15.0	Bill Rodgers	Aug. 9, 1977	Boston
Marathon:	**World**	2:04:55†	**Paul Tergat**, KEN	Sept. 28, 2003	Berlin
	Olympic	2:09:21	Carlos Lopes, Portugal	Aug. 12, 1984	Los Angeles
	American	2:05:38	Khalid Khannouchi	Apr. 14, 2002	London

Note: The Mile run is 1,609.344 meters and the Marathon is 42,194.988 meters (26 miles, 385 yards).
†Marathon records are not officially recognized by the IAAF.

Relays

Event		Time		Date Set	Location
4 x 100m:	**World**	37.40	**USA** (Marsh, Burrell, Mitchell, C. Lewis)	Aug. 8, 1992	Barcelona
		37.40	**USA** (Drummond, Cason, Mitchell, Burrell)	Aug. 21, 1993	Stuttgart
	Olympic	37.40	USA (same as World)	—	—
	American	37.40	USA (same as World)	—	—
4 x 200m:	**World**	1:18.68	**USA** (Marsh, Burrell, Heard, C. Lewis)	Apr. 17, 1994	Walnut, Calif.
	Olympic		Not an event	—	—
	American	1:18.68	USA (same as World)	—	—
4 x 400m:	**World**	2:54.20	**USA** (Young, Pettigrew, Washington, Johnson)	July 22,1998	Uniondale, N.Y.
	Olympic	2:55.74	USA (Valmon, Watts, Johnson, S. Lewis)	Aug. 8, 1992	Barcelona
	American	2:54.20	USA (same as World)	—	—
4 x 800m:	**World**	7:03.89	**Great Britain** (Elliott, Cook, Cram, Coe)	Aug. 30, 1982	London
	Olympic		Not an event	—	—
	American	7:06.5	Santa Monica TC (J. Robinson, Mack, E. Jones, Gray)	Apr. 26, 1986	Walnut, Calif.
4 x 1500m:	**World**	14:38.8	**West Germany** (Wessinghage, Hudak, Lederer, Fleschen)	Aug.17, 1977	Cologne
	Olympic		Not an event	—	—
	American	14:46.3	USA (Aldredge, Clifford, Harbour, Duits)	June 24, 1979	Bourges, FRA

Hurdles

Event		Time		Date Set	Location
110 meters:	**World**	12.91	**Colin Jackson**, Great Britain	Aug. 20, 1993	Stuttgart
	Olympic	12.95	Allen Johnson, USA	July 29, 1996	Atlanta
	American	12.92	Roger Kingdom	Aug. 16, 1989	Zurich
		12.92	Allen Johnson	June 23, 1996	Atlanta
400 meters:	**World**	46.78	**Kevin Young**, USA	Aug. 6, 1992	Barcelona
	Olympic	46.78	Young (same as World)	—	—
	American	46.78	Young (same as World)	—	—

Note: The 10 hurdles at 110 meters are 3 feet, 6 inches high and those at 400 meters are 3 feet.

Walking

Event		Time		Date Set	Location
20 km:	**World**	1:17:21p	**Jefferson Perez**, Ecuador	Aug. 23, 2003	Paris
	Olympic	1:18:59	Robert Korzeniowski, Poland	Sept. 22, 2000	Sydney
	American	1:22:17	Tim Lewis	Sept. 24, 1989	Dearborn, Mich.
50 km:	**World**	3:36:03	**Robert Korzeniowski**, Poland	Aug. 27, 2003	Paris
	Olympic	3:38:29	Vyacheslav Ivanenko, USSR	Sept. 30, 1988	Seoul
	American	3:48:04	Curt Clausen	May. 2, 1999	Deauville, FRA

Steeplechase

Event		Time		Date Set	Location
3000 meters:	**World**	7:53.17 p	**Brahim Boulami**, Morocco	Aug. 16, 2002	Zurich
	Olympic	8:05.51	Julius Kariuki, Kenya	Sept. 30, 1988	Seoul
	American	8:09.17	Henry Marsh	Aug. 28, 1985	Koblenz, W. Ger

Note: A men's steeplechase course consists of 28 hurdles (3 feet high) and seven water jumps (12 feet long).

Field Events

Event		Mark		Date Set	Location
High Jump:	**World**	8-0½	Javier Sotomayor, Cuba	July 27, 1993	Salamanca, SPA
	Olympic	7-10	Charles Austin, USA	July 28, 1996	Atlanta
	American	7-10½	Charles Austin	Aug. 7, 1991	Zurich
Pole Vault:	**World**	20-1¾	**Sergey Bubka**, Ukraine	July 31, 1994	Sestriere, ITA
	Olympic	19-5¼	Jean Galfione, France	Aug. 2, 1996	Atlanta
		19-5¼	Igor Trandenkov, Russia	Aug. 2, 1996	Atlanta
		19-5¼	Andrei Tiwontschik, Germany	Aug. 2, 1996	Atlanta
	American	19-9¼	Jeff Hartwig	June 14, 2000	Jonesboro, Ark.
Long Jump:	**World**	29-4¾*	**Ivan Pedroso**, Cuba	July 29, 1995	Sestriere, ITA
		29-4½	**Mike Powell**, USA	Aug. 30, 1991	Tokyo
	Olympic	29-2½	Bob Beamon, USA	Oct. 18, 1968	Mexico City
	American	29-4½	Powell (same as World)	—	—
Triple Jump:	**World**	60-0¼	**Jonathan Edwards**, GBR	Aug. 7, 1995	Göteborg, SWE
	Olympic	59-4¼	Kenny Harrison, USA	July 27, 1996	Atlanta
	American	59-4¼	Kenny Harrison (same as Olympic)	—	—
Shot Put:	**World**	75-10¼	**Randy Barnes**, USA	May 20, 1990	Los Angeles
	Olympic	73-8¾	Ulf Timmermann, East Germany	Sept. 23, 1988	Seoul
	American	75-10¼	Barnes (same as World)	—	—
Discus:	**World**	243-0	**Jurgen Schult**, East Germany	June 6, 1986	Neubrandenburg
	Olympic	227-8	Lars Riedel, Germany	July 31, 1996	Atlanta
	American	237-4	Ben Plucknett	July 7, 1981	Stockholm
Javelin:	**World**	323-1	**Jan Zelezny**, Czech Republic	May 25, 1996	Jena, GER
	Olympic	295-10	Jan Zelezny, Czech Republic	Sept. 23, 2000	Sydney
	American	285-10	Tom Pukstys	May 25, 1997	Jena, GER
Hammer:	**World**	284-7	**Yuriy Sedykh**, USSR	Aug. 30, 1986	Stuttgart
	Olympic	278-2	Sergey Litvinov, USSR	Sept. 26, 1988	Seoul
	American	270-9	Lance Deal	Sept. 7, 1996	Milan

Note: The international weights for men—**Shot** (16 lbs); **Discus** (4 lbs/6.55 oz); **Javelin** (minimum 1 lb/12¼ oz.); **Hammer** (16 lbs).
*Apparent world record disallowed because of interference with wind gauge at altitude.

Decathlon

Event		Points		Date Set	Location
Ten Events:	**World**	9026	**Roman Sebrle**, Czech Republic	May 26-27, 2001	Gotzis, AUT
	Olympic	8847	Daley Thompson, Great Britain	Aug. 8-9, 1984	Los Angeles
	American	8891	Dan O'Brien	Sept. 4-5, 1992	Talence, FRA

Note: Sebrle's WR times and distances, in order over two days—**100m** (10.64); **LJ** (26-7¼); **Shot** (50-3½); **HJ** (6-11½); **400m** (47.79); **110m H** (13.92); **Discus** (157-3); **PV** (15-9); **Jav** (230-2); **1500m** (4:21.98).

WOMEN
Running

Event		Time		Date Set	Location
100 meters:	**World**	10.49	**Florence Griffith Joyner**, USA	July 16, 1988	Indianapolis
	Olympic	10.62	Florence Griffith Joyner, USA	Sept. 24, 1988	Seoul
	American	10.49	Griffith Joyner (same as World)	—	—
200 meters:	**World**	21.34	**Florence Griffith Joyner**, USA	Sept. 29, 1988	Seoul
	Olympic	21.34	Griffith Joyner (same as World)	—	—
	American	21.34	Griffith Joyner (same as World)	—	—

Track & Field (Cont.)

Event		Time		Date Set	Location
400 meters:	World	47.60	**Marita Koch**, East Germany	Oct. 6, 1985	Canberra, AUS
	Olympic	48.25	Marie-Jose Perec, France	July 29, 1996	Atlanta
	American	48.83	Valerie Brisco	Aug. 6, 1984	Los Angeles
800 meters:	World	1:53.28	**Jarmila Kratochvilova**, Czech.	July 26, 1983	Munich
	Olympic	1:53.42	Nadezhda Olizarenko, USSR	July 27, 1980	Moscow
	American	1:56.40	Jearl Miles-Clark	Aug. 11, 1999	Zurich
1000 meters:	World	2:28.98	**Svetlana Masterkova**, Russia	Aug. 23, 1996	Brussels
	Olympic		Not an event	—	—
	American	2:31.80	Regina Jacobs	July 3, 1999	Brunswick, Me.
1500 meters:	World	3:50.46	**Qu Yunxia**, China	Sept. 11, 1993	Beijing
	Olympic	3:53.96	Paula Ivan, Romania	Oct. 1, 1988	Seoul
	American	3:57.12	Mary Slaney	July 26, 1983	Stockholm
Mile:	World	4:12.56	**Svetlana Masterkova**, Russia	Aug. 14, 1996	Zurich
	Olympic		Not an event	—	—
	American	4:16.71	Mary Slaney	Aug. 21, 1985	Zurich
2000 meters:	World	5:25.36	**Sonia O'Sullivan**, Ireland	July 8, 1994	Edinburgh
	Olympic		Not an event	—	—
	American	5:32.7	Mary Slaney	Aug. 3, 1984	Eugene, Ore.
3000 meters:	World	8:06.11	**Wang Junxia**, China	Sept. 13, 1993	Beijing
	Olympic	8:26.53	Tatyana Samolenko, USSR	Sept. 25, 1988	Seoul
	American	8:25.83	Mary Slaney	Sept. 7, 1985	Rome
5000 meters:	World	14:28.09	**Jiang Bo**, China	Oct. 23, 1997	Shanghai
	Olympic	14:40.79	Gabriela Szabo, Romania	Sept. 25, 2000	Sydney
	American	14:45.35	Regina Jacobs	July 27, 2000	Sacramento
10,000 meters:	World	29:31.78	**Wang Junxia**, China	Sept. 8, 1993	Beijing
	Olympic	30:17.49	Derartu Tulu, Ethiopia	Sept. 30, 2000	Sydney
	American	30:50:32p	Deena Drossin	May 3, 2002	Stanford, Calif.
Marathon:	World	2:15:25†	**Paula Radcliffe**, Great Britain	Apr. 13, 2003	London
	Olympic	2:23:14	Naoko Takahashi, Japan	Sept. 24, 2000	Sydney
	American	2:21:16	Deena Drossin	Apr. 13, 2003	London

Note: The Mile run is 1,609.344 meters and the Marathon is 42,194.988 meters (26 miles, 385 yards).
†Marathon records are not officially recognized by the IAAF.

Relays

Event		Time		Date Set	Location
4 x 100m:	World	41.37	**East Germany** (Gladisch, Rieger, Auerswald, Gohr)	Oct. 6, 1985	Canberra, AUS
	Olympic	41.60	East Germany (Muller, Wockel, Auerswald, Gohr)	Aug. 1, 1980	Moscow
	American	41.47	USA (Gaines, Jones, Miller, Devers)	Aug. 9, 1997	Athens
4 x 200m:	World	1:27.46	**USA** (Jenkins, Colander-Richardson, Perry, Jones)	Apr. 29, 2000	Philadelphia
	Olympic		Not an event	—	—
	American	1:27.46	USA (same as World)	—	—
4 x 400m:	World	3:15.17	**USSR** (Ledovskaya, Nazarova, Pinigina, Bryzgina)	Oct. 1, 1988	Seoul
	Olympic	3:15.17	USSR (same as World)	—	—
	American	3:15.51	USA (Howard, Dixon, Brisco, Griffith Joyner)	Oct. 1, 1988	Seoul
4 x 800m:	World	7:50.17	**USSR** (Olizarenko, Gurina, Borisova, Podyalovskaya)	Aug. 5, 1984	Moscow
	Olympic		Not an event	—	—
	American	8:17.09	Athletics West (Addison, Arbogast, Decker Slaney, Mullen)	Apr. 24, 1983	Walnut, Calif.

Hurdles

Event		Time		Date Set	Location
100 meters:	World	12.21	**Yordanka Donkova**, Bulgaria	Aug. 20, 1988	Stara Zagora, BUL
	Olympic	12.38	Yordanka Donkova, Bulgaria	Sept. 30, 1988	Seoul
	American	12.33	Gail Devers	July 23, 2000	Sacramento
400 meters:	World	52.34	**Yuliya Pechonkina**, RUS	Aug. 8, 2003	Tula, RUS
	Olympic	52.82	Deon Hemmings, Jamaica	July 31, 1996	Atlanta
	American	52.61	Kim Batten	Aug. 11, 1995	Göteborg, SWE

Note: The 10 hurdles at 110 meters are 3 feet, 6 inches high and those at 400 meters are 3 feet.

Walking

Event		Time		Date Set	Location
20 km:	World	1:24:50	**Olimpiada Ivanova**, Russia	Mar. 4, 2001	Adler, RUS
	Olympic	1:29:05	Wang Liping, China	Sept. 28, 2000	Sydney
	American	1:31:51	Michelle Rohl	May 13, 2000	Kenosha, Wis.

Steeplechase

Event	Time		Date Set	Location
3000 meters:	**World** 9:08.33p	**Gulnara Samitova**, Russia	Aug. 10, 2003	Tula, RUS
	Olympic	Not an event	—	—
	American . . 9:41.94	Elizabeth Jackson	Sept. 4, 2001	Brisbane

Note: A women's steeplechase course consists of 28 hurdles (30 inches high) and seven water jumps (10 feet long).

Field Events

Event	Mark		Date Set	Location
High Jump:	**World** 6-10¼	**Stefka Kostadinova,** Bulgaria	Aug. 30, 1987	Rome
	Olympic . . . 6-8¾	Stefka Kostadinova, Bulgaria	Aug. 3, 1996	Atlanta
	American. 6-8	Louise Ritter	July 8, 1988	Austin, Texas
Pole Vault:	**World** 15-9¾p	**Yelena Isinbayeva**, RUS	July 13, 2003	Gateshead, ENG
	Olympic 15-1	Stacy Dragila, USA	Sept. 25, 2000	Sydney
	American. . . . 15-9¼	Stacy Dragila	June 9, 2001	Palo Alto, Calif
Long Jump:	**World** 24-8¼	**Galina Chistyakova**, USSR	June 11, 1988	Leningrad
	Olympic . . . 24-3¼	Jackie Joyner-Kersee, USA	Sept. 29, 1988	Seoul
	American. . . . 24-7	Jackie Joyner-Kersee	May 22, 1994	New York
Triple Jump:	**World** 50-10¼	**Inessa Kravets**, Ukraine	Aug. 8, 1995	Göteborg, SWE
	Olympic . . . 50-3½	Inessa Kravets, Ukraine	July 31, 1996	Atlanta
	American. . . . 47-3½	Sheila Hudson	July 8, 1996	Stockholm
Shot Put:	**World** 74-3	**Natalya Lisovskaya**, USSR	June 7, 1987	Moscow
	Olympic . . . 73-6¼	Ilona Slupianek, E. Germany	July 24, 1980	Moscow
	American. . . . 66-2½	Ramona Pagel	June 25, 1988	San Diego
Discus:	**World** 252-0	**Gabriele Reinsch**, E. Germany	July 9, 1988	Neubrandenburg
	Olympic . . 237-2½	Martina Hellmann, E. Germany	Sept. 29, 1988	Seoul
	American. . 227-10	Suzy Powell	Apr. 27, 2002	La Jolla, Calif.
Javelin:	**World** . . . 234-8	**Osleidys Menendez**, Cuba	July 1, 2001	Rethymno, GRE
	Olympic . . 226-1	Trine Hattestad, Norway	Sept. 30, 2000	Sydney
	American. . . 199-8 p	Kim Kreiner	Aug. 7, 2003	Santo Domingo
Hammer:	**World** . . . 249-7	**Mihaela Melinte**, Romania	Aug. 29, 1999	Rudlingen, SWI
	Olympic . . 233-5¾	Kamila Skolimowska, Poland	Sept. 29, 2000	Sydney
	American. . . 236-3	Anna Norgren-Mahon	July 28, 2002	Walnut, Calif.

Note: The international weights for women—**Shot** (8 lbs/13 oz); **Discus** (2 lbs/3.27 oz); **Javelin** (minimum 1 lb/5.16 oz); **Hammer** (8 lbs/13 oz).

Heptathlon

Event	Points		Date Set	Location
Seven Events:	**World** 7291	**Jackie Joyner-Kersee**, USA	Sept. 23-24, 1988	Seoul
	Olympic 7291	Joyner-Kersee (same as World)	—	—
	American . . . 7291	Joyner-Kersee (same as World)	—	—

Note: Joyner-Kersee's WR times and distances, in order over two days—**100m H** (12.69); **HJ** (61¼); **Shot** (51-10); **200m** (22.56); **LJ** (2310¼); **Jav** (149-10); **800m** (2:08.51).

2003 IAAF World Indoor Championships

The 9th IAAF World Indoor Championships in Athletics held in Birmingham, England, Mar. 14-16, 2003. Note that (WR) indicates world record and (CR) indicates championships meet record.

Final Medal Leaders

	G	S	B	Total			G	S	B	Total
1 United States 10		3	4	17	5 Sweden 4		0	0		4
2 Russia 5		4	3	12	Germany 1		1	2		4
3 Great Britain & N.I. .2		2	3	7	7 Five tied with 3 medals each.					
4 Spain 1		4	1	6						

MEN

Event	Time
60 meters . . . . .Justin Gatlin, USA	6.46
200 meters . . . .Marlon Devonish, GBR	20.62
400 meters . . .Tyree Washington, USA	45.34
800 meters . David Krummenacker, USA	1:45.69
1500 meters . . . .Driss Maazouzi, FRA	3:42.59
3000 meters . .Haile Gebrselassie, ETH	7:40.97
60m hurdles . . . .Allen Johnson, USA	7.47
4x400m relay . . . .USA (James, Young,	3:04.09
Campbell, Washington)	

Event	Hgt/Dist
High Jump . . . . .Stefan Holm, SWE	7-8½
Pole Vault . . . . .Tim Lobinger, GER	19-0¼
Long Jump . . . .Dwight Phillips, USA	27-2½
Triple Jump . . . .Christian Olsson, SWE	58-1
Shot Put . . . . . .Manuel Martinez, ESP	69-8¼
Heptathlon . . . . .Tom Pappas, USA	6361 pts

WOMEN

Event	Time
60 meters . . . . . . .Zhanna Block, UKR	7.04
200 meters . . . .Michelle Collins, USA	22.18
400 meters . . . .Natalya Nazarova, RUS	50.83
800 meters . M. de Lourdes Mutola, MOZ	1:58.94
1500 meters . . . .Regina Jacobs, USA	4:01.67 CR
3000 meters . . . . .Berhane Adere, ETH	8:40.25
60m hurdles . . . . . .Gail Devers, USA	7.81
4x400m relay . . . . . .Russia (Antyukh,	3:28.45
Pechonkina, Zykina, Nazarova)	

Event	Hgt/Dist
High Jump . . . .Kajsa Bergqvist, SWE	6-7¼
Pole Vault . . .Svetlana Feofanova, RUS	15-9 **WR**
Long Jump . . . .Tatyana Kotova, RUS	22-5¼
Triple Jump . . . . .Ashia Hansen, GBR	49-3
Shot Put . . . .Irina Korzhanenko, RUS	67-5¼ CR
Pentathlon . . . . .Carolina Kluft, SWE	4933 pts CR

World and American Indoor Records
As of Sept. 28, 2003

World indoor records officially recognized by the International Amateur Athletics Federation (IAAF); (p) indicates record is pending ratification by the IAAF; (a) indicates record was set at an altitude over 1000 meters.

MEN
Running

Event		Time		Date Set	Location
50 meters:	**World**	.5.56a	**Donovan Bailey**, Canada	Feb. 9, 1996	Reno, Nev.
		5.56	**Maurice Greene**, USA	Feb. 13, 1999	Los Angeles
	American	.5.56	Greene (same as World)	Feb. 13, 1999	Los Angeles
60 meters:	**World**	.6.39	**Maurice Greene**, USA	Feb. 3, 1998	Madrid
		6.39	**Maurice Greene**, USA	March 3, 2001	Atlanta
	American	.6.39	Greene (same as World)	—	—
200 meters:	**World**	.19.92	**Frankie Fredericks**, Namibia	Feb. 18, 1996	Lievin, FRA
	American	.20.26	John Capel	Mar. 11, 2000	Fayetteville, Ark.
		20.26	Shawn Crawford	Mar. 11, 2000	Fayetteville, Ark.
400 meters:	**World**	.44.63	**Michael Johnson**, USA	Mar. 4, 1995	Atlanta
	American	.44.63	Johnson (same as World)	—	—
800 meters:	**World**	.1:42.67	**Wilson Kipketer**, Denmark	Mar. 9, 1997	Paris
	American	.1:45.00	Johnny Gray	Mar. 8, 1992	Sindelfingen, GER
1000 meters:	**World**	.2:14.96	**Wilson Kipketer**, Denmark	Feb. 20, 2000	Birmingham, ENG
	American	.2:17.86	David Krummenacker	Jan. 27, 2002	Boston
1500 meters:	**World**	.3:31.18	**Hicham El Guerrouj**, Morocco	Feb. 2, 1997	Stuttgart
	American	.3:38.12	Jeff Atkinson	Mar. 5, 1989	Budapest
Mile:	**World**	.3:48.45	**Hicham El Guerrouj**, Morocco	Feb. 12, 1997	Ghent, BEL
	American	.3:51.8	Steve Scott	Feb. 20, 1981	San Diego
3000 meters:	**World**	.7:24.90	**Daniel Komen**, Kenya	Feb. 6, 1998	Budapest
	American	.7:39.23	Tim Broe	Jan. 27, 2002	Boston
5000 meters:	**World**	.12:50.38	**Haile Gebrselassie**, Ethiopia	Feb. 14, 1999	Birmingham, ENG
	American	.13:20.55	Doug Padilla	Feb. 12, 1982	New York

Note: The Mile run is 1,609.344 meters.

Hurdles

Event		Time		Date Set	Location
50 meters:	**World**	6.25	**Mark McKoy**, Canada	Mar. 5, 1986	Kobe, JPN
	American	6.35	Greg Foster	Jan. 27, 1985	Rosemont, Ill.
		6.35	Greg Foster	Jan. 31, 1987	Ottawa
60 meters:	**World**	7.30	**Colin Jackson**, Great Britain	Mar. 6, 1994	Sindelfingen, GER
	American	7.36	Greg Foster	Jan. 16, 1987	Los Angeles

Note: The hurdles for both distances are 3 feet, 6 inches high. There are four hurdles in the 50 meters and five in the 60.

Walking

Event		Time		Date Set	Location
5000 meters:	**World**	18:07.08	**Mikhail Shchennikov**, Russia	Feb. 14, 1995	Moscow
	American	19:18.40	Tim Lewis	Mar. 7, 1987	Indianapolis

Relays

Event		Time		Date Set	Location
4 x 200 meters:	**World**	1:22.11	**Great Britain**	Mar. 3, 1991	Glasgow
	American	1:22.71	National Team	Mar. 3, 1991	Glasgow
4 x 400 meters:	**World**	3:02.83	**United States**	Mar. 7, 1999	Maebashi, JPN
	American	3:02.83	National Team (same as World)	Mar. 7, 1999	Maebashi, JPN
4 x 800 meters:	**World**	7:13.94	**United States**	Feb. 6, 2000	Boston
	American	7:13.94	Global Athletics (same as World)	Feb. 6, 2000	Boston

Field Events

Event		Mark		Date Set	Location
High Jump:	**World**	7-11½	**Javier Sotomayor**, Cuba	Mar. 4, 1989	Budapest
	American	7-10½	Hollis Conway	Mar. 10, 1991	Seville
Pole Vault:	**World**	20-2	**Sergey Bubka**, Ukraine	Feb. 21, 1993	Donyetsk, UKR
	American	19-9	Jeff Hartwig	Mar. 10, 2002	Sindelfingen, GER
Long Jump:	**World**	28-10¼	**Carl Lewis**, USA	Jan. 27, 1984	New York
	American	28-10¼	Lewis (same as World)	—	—
Triple Jump:	**World**	58-6	**Aliecer Urrutia**, Cuba	Mar. 1, 1997	Sindelfingen, GER
	American	58-3¼	Mike Conley	Feb. 27, 1987	New York

World Indoor Records Set in 2003
World indoor records set or equaled between Oct. 1, 2002 and Sept. 28, 2003.
WOMEN

Event	Name	Record	Old Mark	Former Holder
1500 meters	**Regina Jacobs**, USA	3:59.98p	4:00.27	Doina Melinte, ROM (1990)
3000m walk	**Gillian O'Sullivan**, IRL	11:35.34p	11:40.33	Claudia Stef, ROM (1999)
Pole Vault	**Svetlana Feofanova**, RUS	15-9p	15-8¼	Stacy Dragila, USA (2003)

Note: Feofanova broke her own women's pole vault record on Feb. 2 (15-7¼) and again on Feb. 21 (15-7¾). Dragila then broke Feofanova's record on Mar. 2 (15-8¼). Feofanova set the current mark (15-9) on Mar. 16.

Event	Mark		Date Set	Location
Shot Put:	**World** 74-4¼	**Randy Barnes**, USA	Jan. 20, 1989	Los Angeles
	American . . . 74-4¼	Barnes (same as World)	—	—

Note: The international shot put weight for men is 16 lbs.

Heptathlon

Event	Points		Date Set	Location
Seven Events:	**World** 6476	**Dan O'Brien**, USA	Mar. 13-14, 1993	Toronto
	American 6476	O'Brien (same as World)	—	—

Note: O'Brien's WR times and distances, in order over two days—**60m** (6.67); **LJ** (25-8¾); **SP** (52-6¾); **HJ** (6-11¾); **60m H** (7.85); **PV** (17-0¾); **1000m** (2:57.96).

WOMEN
Running

Event	Time		Date Set	Location
50 meters:	**World** 5.96	**Irina Privalova**, Russia	Feb. 9, 1995	Madrid
	American 6.02	Gail Devers	Feb. 21, 1999	Lievin, FRA
60 meters:	**World** 6.92	**Irina Privalova**, Russia	Feb. 11, 1993	Madrid
	. . . . .6.92	**Irina Privalova**, Russia	Feb. 9, 1995	Madrid
	American 6.95	Gail Devers	Mar. 12, 1993	Toronto
	. . . . .6.95	Marion Jones	Mar. 7, 1998	Maebashi, JPN
200 meters:	**World** 21.87	**Merlene Ottey**, Jamaica	Feb. 13, 1993	Lievin, FRA
	American 22.18	Michelle Collins	Mar. 15, 2003	Birmingham, ENG
400 meters:	**World** 49.59	**Jarmila Kratochvilova**, Czech.	Mar. 7, 1982	Milan
	American 50.64	Diane Dixon	Mar. 10, 1991	Seville
800 meters:	**World** 1:55.82	**Jolanda Ceplak**, Slovenia	Mar. 3, 2002	Vienna
	American . . .1:58.71	Nicole Teter	Mar. 2, 2002	New York
1000 meters:	**World** 2:30.94	**Maria Mutola**, Mozambique	Feb. 25, 1999	Stockholm
	American . . .2:35.29	Regina Jacobs	Feb. 6, 2000	Boston
1500 meters:	**World** 3:59.98p	**Regina Jacobs**, USA	Feb. 1, 2003	Boston
	American . . .3:59.98p	Jacobs (same as World)	—	—
Mile:	**World** 4:17.14	**Doina Melinte**, Romania	Feb. 9, 1990	E. Rutherford, N.J.
	American 4:20.5	Mary Slaney	Feb. 19, 1982	San Diego
3000 meters:	**World** 8:29.15	**Berhane Adere**, Ethiopia	Feb. 3, 2002	Stuttgart
	American . . .8:39.14	Regina Jacobs	Mar. 7, 1999	Maebashi, JPN
5000 meters:	**World** . . .14:47.35	**Gabriela Szabo**, Romania	Feb. 13, 1999	Dortmund, GER
	American . .15:07.33	Marla Runyan	Feb. 18, 2001	New York City

Note: The Mile run is 1,609.344 meters.

Hurdles

Event	Time		Date Set	Location
50 meters:	**World** 6.58	**Cornelia Oschkenat**, E. Ger.	Feb. 20, 1988	East Berlin
	American 6.67a	Jackie Joyner-Kersee	Feb. 10, 1995	Reno, Nev.
60 meters:	**World** 7.69	**Ludmila Engquist**, USSR	Feb. 4, 1990	Chelyabinsk, USSR
	American 7.74	Gail Devers	Mar. 1, 2003	Boston

Note: The hurdles for both distances are 2 feet, 9 inches high. There are four hurdles in the 50 meters and five in the 60.

Walking

Event	Time		Date Set	Location
3000 meters:	**World** . . .11:35.34p	**Gillian O'Sullivan**, IRL	Feb. 15, 2003	Belfast
	American . .12:20.79	Debbi Lawrence	Mar. 12, 1993	Toronto

Relays

Event	Time		Date Set	Location
4 x 200 meters:	**World** 1:32.55	**West Germany**	Feb. 20, 1988	Dortmund, W. Ger.
	1:32.55	Germany	Feb.21, 1999	Karlsruhe, GER
	American 1:33.24	National Team	Feb. 12, 1994	Glasgow
4 x 400 meters:	**World** . . 3:24.25	**Russia**	Mar. 7, 1999	Maebashi, JPN
	American . . 3:27.59	National Team	Mar. 7, 1999	Maebashi, JPN
4 x 800 meters:	**World** . . . 8:18.71	**Russia**	Feb. 4, 1994	Moscow
	American . 8:25.5	Villanova	Feb. 7, 1987	Gainesville, Fla.

Field Events

Event	Mark		Date Set	Location
High Jump:	**World** 6-9½	Heike Henkel, Germany	Feb. 9, 1992	Karlsruhe, GER
	American 6-7	Tisha Waller	Feb. 28, 1998	Atlanta
Pole Vault:	**World** 15-9p	**Svetlana Feofanova**, RUS	Mar. 16, 2003	Birmingham, ENG
	American . . 15-8¼	Stacy Dragila	Mar. 2, 2003	Boston
Long Jump:	**World** 24-2¼	**Heike Drechsler**, E. Germany	Feb. 13, 1988	Vienna
	American . . 23-4¾a	Jackie Joyner-Kersee	Mar. 5, 1994	Atlanta
Triple Jump:	**World** 49-9	**Ashia Hansen**, Great Britain	Feb. 28, 1998	Valencia, SPA
	American . . 46-8¼	Sheila Hudson	Mar. 4, 1995	Atlanta
Shot Put:	**World** 73-10	**Helena Fibingerova**, Czech.	Feb. 19, 1977	Jablonec, CZE
	American . . 65-0¾	Ramona Pagel	Feb. 20, 1987	Inglewood, Calif.

Note: The international shotput weight for women is 8 lbs. and 13 oz.

Pentathlon

Event	Points		Date Set	Location
Five Events:	**World** 4991	**Irina Byelova**, Russia	Feb. 14-15, 1992	Berlin
	American 4753	DeDee Nathan	Mar. 4-5, 1999	Maebashi, JPN

Note: Byelova's WR times and distances, in order over two days—**60m H** (8.22); **HJ** (6-4); **SP** (43-5¾); **LJ** (21-1¾); **800m** (2:10.26).

SWIMMING

2003 FINA World Championships

The 10th FINA World Championships in swimming, diving, synchronized swimming and water polo held in Barcelona, Spain, July 12-27, 2003. Note that (WR) indicates world record and (CR) indicates championship meet record.

Final Medal Leaders—Swimming Top 10

		G	S	B	Total			G	S	B	Total
1	United States	11	12	5	28	7	Ukraine	2	2	2	6
2	Australia	6	10	6	22		Japan	2	1	3	6
3	Germany	5	1	2	8	9	Netherlands	2	2	1	5
	Great Britain	2	3	3	8		Hungary	0	4	1	5
5	Russia	3	2	2	7						
	China	3	0	4	7						

MEN

Event		Time	
50m free	Aleksandr Popov, RUS	21.92	CR
100m free	Aleksandr Popov, RUS	48.42	
200m free	Ian Thorpe, AUS	1:45.14	
400m free	Ian Thorpe, AUS	3:42.58	
800m free	Grant Hackett, AUS	7:43.82	
1500m free	Grant Hackett, AUS	14:43.14	
50m back	Thomas Rupprath, GER	24.80	WR
100m back	Aaron Peirsol, USA	53.61	CR
200m back	Aaron Peirsol, USA	1:55.92	
50m breast	James Gibson, GBR	27.56	
100m breast	Kosuke Kitajima, JPN	59.78	WR
200m breast	Kosuke Kitajima, JPN	2:09.42	WR
50m fly	Matthew Welsh, AUS	23.43	WR
100m fly	Ian Crocker, USA	50.98	WR
200m fly	Michael Phelps, USA	1:54.35	
200m I.M.	Michael Phelps, USA	1:56.04	WR
400m I.M.	Michael Phelps, USA	4:09.09	WR

WOMEN

Event		Time	
50m free	Inge de Bruijn, NED	24.47	
100m free	Hanna-Maria Seppala, FIN	54.37	
200m free	Alena Popchenko, BLR	1:58.32	
400m free	Hannah Stockbauer, GER	4:06.75	
800m free	Hannah Stockbauer, GER	8:23.66	CR
1500m free	Hannah Stockbauer, GER	16:00.18	CR
50m back	Nina Zhivanevskaya, ESP	28.48	CR
100m back	Antje Buschschulte, GER	1:00.50	
200m back	Katy Sexton, GBR	2:08.74	
50m breast	Luo Xuejuan, CHN	30.67	
100m breast	Luo Xuejuan, CHN	1:06.80	
200m breast	Amanda Beard, USA	2:22.99	WR
50m fly	Inge de Bruijn, NED	25.84	CR
100m fly	Jenny Thompson, USA	57.96	
200m fly	Otylia Jedrzejczak, POL	2:07.56	
200m I.M.	Yana Klochkova, UKR	2:10.75	
400m I.M.	Yana Klochkova, UKR	4:36.74	

Men's Relays

Event		Time	
4x100m free	Russia (Kapralov, Usov, Pimankov, Popov)	3:14.06	CR
4x200m free	Australia (Hackett, Stevens, Sprenger, Thorpe)	7:08.58	
4x100m medley	USA (Peirsol, Hansen, Crocker, Lezak)	3:31.54	WR

Women's Relays

Event		Time	
4x100m free	USA (Coughlin, Benko, Jeffrey, Thompson)	3:38.09	
4x200m free	USA (Benko, Komisarz, Jeffrey, Munz)	7:55.70	CR
4x100m medley	China (Zhan, Luo, Zhou, Yang)	3:59.89	CR

Diving

Men

Event		Points
1m springboard	Xu Xiang, CHN	431.94
3m springboard	Alexander Dobroskok, RUS	788.37
10m platform	Alexandre Despatie, CAN	716.91
3m springboard (synchronized)	Alexander Dobroskok & Dmitri Sautin, RUS	369.18
10m platform (synchronized)	Mathew Helm & Robert Newbery, AUS	384.60

Women

Event		Points
1m springboard	Irina Lashko, AUS	299.97
3m springboard	Guo Jingjing, CHN	617.94
10m platform	Emilie Heymans, CAN	597.45
3m springboard (synchronized)	Wu Mingxia & Guo Jingjing, CHN	357.30
10m platform (synchronized)	Lao Lishi & Li Ting, CHN	344.58

Synchronized Swimming

Event		Points
Solo	Virginie Dedieu, FRA	99.251
Duet	Anastasia Davydova & Anastasia Ermakova, RUS	99.084
Team	Russia	99.500
Free	Japan	98.500

Water Polo

Men's Final

Hungary	2	2	2	2	1	2	—	11
Italy	1	3	1	3	0	1	—	9

Women's Final

Italy	2	1	1	2	—	6
United States	1	2	3	2	—	8

World, Olympic and American Records

As of September 28, 2003

World long course records officially recognized by the Federation Internationale de Natation Amateur (FINA). Note that (p) indicates preliminary heat; (r) relay lead-off split; and (s) indicates split time. Note that (*) denotes that a record is awaiting ratification.

MEN

Freestyle

Distance		Time		Date Set	Location
50 meters:	World	21.64	Aleksandr Popov, Russia	June 16, 2000	Moscow
	Olympic	21.91	Aleksandr Popov, Unified Team	July 30, 1992	Barcelona
	American	21.76	Gary Hall Jr.	Aug. 15, 2000	Indianapolis
100 meters:	World	47.84p	P. van den Hoogenband, Netherlands	Sept. 19, 2000	Sydney
	Olympic	47.84	P. van den Hoogenband, NED (same as World)	—	—
	American	48.33	Anthony Ervin	July 27, 2001	Fukuoka, JPN
200 meters:	World	1:44.06	Ian Thorpe, Australia	July 25, 2001	Fukuoka, JPN
	Olympic	1:45.35p	P. van den Hoogenband, NED	Sept. 18, 2000	Sydney
	American	1:46.73	Josh Davis	Sept. 18, 2000	Sydney
400 meters:	World	3:40.08	Ian Thorpe, Australia	July 30, 2002	Manchester, GBR
	Olympic	3:40.59	Ian Thorpe, Australia	Sept. 16, 2000	Sydney
	American	3:47.00	Klete Keller	Sept. 16, 2000	Sydney
800 meters:	World	7:39.16	Ian Thorpe, Australia	July 24, 2001	Fukuoka, JPN
	Olympic		Not an event		
	American	7:48.09	Larsen Jensen	July 25, 2003	Barcelona
1500 meters:	World	14:34.56	Grant Hackett, Australia	July 29, 2001	Fukuoka, JPN
	Olympic	14:43.48	Kieren Perkins, Australia	July 31, 1992	Barcelona
	American	14:56.81	Chris Thompson	Sept. 23, 2000	Sydney

Backstroke

Distance		Time		Date Set	Location
50 meters:	World	24.80	Thomas Rupprath, Germany	July 27, 2003	Barcelona
	Olympic		Not an event	—	—
	American	24.99	Lenny Krayzelburg	Aug. 28, 1999	Sydney
100 meters:	World	53.60	Lenny Krayzelburg, USA	Aug. 24, 1999	Sydney
	Olympic	53.72	Lenny Krayzelburg, USA	Sept. 18, 2000	Sydney
	American	53.60	Krayzelburg (same as World)	—	—
200 meters:	World	1:55.15	Aaron Peirsol, USA	Mar. 20, 2002	Minneapolis
	Olympic	1:56.76	Lenny Krayzelburg, USA	Sept. 21, 2000	Sydney
	American	1:55.15	Peirsol (same as World)	—	—

Breaststroke

Distance		Time		Date Set	Location
50 meters:	World	27.18	Oleg Lisogor, Ukraine	Aug. 1, 2002	Berlin
	Olympic		Not an event	—	—
	American	27.39	Ed Moses	Mar. 31, 2001	Austin, Texas
100 meters:	World	59.78	Kosuke Kitajima, Japan	July 21, 2003	Barcelona
	Olympic	1:00.46	Domenico Fioravanti, Italy	Sept. 17, 2000	Sydney
	American	1:00.21	Brendan Hansen	July 21, 2003	Barcelona
200 meters:	World	2:09.42	Kosuke Kitajima, Japan	July 24, 2003	Barcelona
	Olympic	2:10.16	Mike Barrowman	July 29, 1992	Barcelona
	American	2:10.16	Barrowman (same as Olympic)	—	—

Butterfly

Distance		Time		Date Set	Location
50 meters:	World	23.43	Matthew Welsh, Australia	July 21, 2003	Barcelona
	Olympic		Not an event	—	—
	American	23.47	Ian Crocker	July 20, 2003	Barcelona
100 meters:	World	50.98	Ian Crocker, USA	July 26, 2003	Barcelona
	Olympic	51.96p	Geoff Huegill, Australia	Sept. 21, 2000	Sydney
	American	50.98	Crocker (same as World)	—	—
200 meters:	World	1:53.93p	Michael Phelps, USA	July 22, 2003	Barcelona
	Olympic	1:55.35	Tom Malchow, USA	Sept. 19, 2000	Sydney
	American	1:53.93p	Phelps (same as World)	—	—

Individual Medley

Distance		Time		Date Set	Location
200 meters:	World	1:56.04	Michael Phelps, USA	July 25, 2003	Barcelona
	Olympic	1:58.98	Massimiliano Rosolino, ITA	Sept. 21, 2000	Sydney
	American	1:56.04	Phelps (same as World)	—	—
400 meters:	World	4:09.09	Michael Phelps, USA	July 27, 2003	Barcelona
	Olympic	4:11.76	Tom Dolan, USA	Sept. 17, 2000	Sydney
	American	4:09.09	Phelps (same as World)	—	—

Swimming (Cont.)

Relays

Distance		Time		Date Set	Location
4x100m free:	World	3:13.67	**Australia** (Klim, Fydler, Callus, Thorpe)	Sept. 16, 2000	Sydney
	Olympic	3:13.67	Australia (same as world)	—	—
	American	3:13.86	USA (Ervin, Walker, Lezak, Hall Jr.)	Sept. 16, 2000	Sydney
4x200m free:	World	7:04.66	**Australia** (Hackett, Klim, Kirby, Thorpe)	July 27, 2001	Fukuoka, JPN
	Olympic	7:07.05	**Australia** (Thorpe, Klim, Pearson, Kirby)	Sept. 19, 2000	Sydney
	American	7:10.26	USA (Phelps, Dusing, Peirsol, Keller)	July 23, 2003	Barcelona
4x100m medley:	World	3:31.54	**USA** (Peirsol, Hansen, Crocker, Lezak)	July 27, 2003	Barcelona
	Olympic	3:33.73	USA (Krayzelburg, Moses, Crocker, Hall Jr.)	Sept. 23, 2000	Sydney
	American	3:31.54	USA (same as World)	—	—

WOMEN

Freestyle

Distance		Time		Date Set	Location
50 meters:	World	24.13p	**Inge de Bruijn**, Netherlands	Sept. 22, 2000	Sydney
	Olympic	24.13	de Bruijn (same as World)	—	—
	American	24.63	Dara Torres	Sept. 23, 2000	Sydney
100 meters:	World	53.77p	**Inge de Bruijn**, Netherlands	Sept. 20, 2000	Sydney
	Olympic	53.77	de Bruijn (same as World)	—	—
	American	53.99	Natalie Coughlin	Aug. 29, 2002	Yokohama, JPN
200 meters:	World	1:56.64	**Franziska van Almsick**, Ger.	Aug. 3, 2002	Berlin
	Olympic	1:57.65	Heike Friedrich, E. Germany	Sept. 21, 1988	Seoul
	American	1:57.41r	Lindsay Benko	July 24, 2003	Barcelona
400 meters:	World	4:03.85	**Janet Evans**, USA	Sept. 22, 1988	Seoul
	Olympic	4:03.85	Evans (same as World)	—	—
	American	4:03.85	Evans (same as World)	—	—
800 meters:	World	8:16.22	**Janet Evans**, USA	Aug. 20, 1989	Tokyo
	Olympic	8:19.67	Brooke Bennett, USA	Sept. 22, 2000	Sydney
	American	8:16.22	Evans (same as World)	—	—
1500 meters:	World	15:52.10	**Janet Evans**, USA	Mar. 26, 1988	Orlando
	Olympic		Not an event	—	—
	American	15:52.10	Evans (same as World)	—	—

Backstroke

Distance		Time		Date Set	Location
50 meters:	World	28.25	**Sandra Volker**, Germany	June 17, 2000	Berlin
	Olympic		Not an event	—	—
	American	28.49p	Natalie Coughlin	July 23, 2001	Fukuoka, JPN
100 meters:	World	59.58	**Natalie Coughlin**, USA	Aug. 13, 2002	Ft. Lauderdale, Fla.
	Olympic	1:00.21	Diana Mocanu, Romania	Sept. 18, 2000	Sydney
	American	59.58	Coughlin (same as World)	—	—
200 meters:	World	2:06.62	**Krisztina Egerszegi**, Hungary	Aug. 25, 1991	Athens
	Olympic	2:07.06	Krisztina Egerszegi, Hungary	July 31, 1992	Barcelona
	American	2:08.53	Natalie Coughlin	Aug. 16, 2002	Ft. Lauderdale, Fla.

Breaststroke

Distance		Time		Date Set	Location
50 meters:	World	30.57	**Zoe Baker**, Great Britain	July 30, 2002	Manchester, GBR
	Olympic		Not an event	—	—
	American	31.34p	Megan Quann	Aug. 11, 2000	Indianapolis
100 meters:	World	1:06.37p	**Leisel Jones**, Australia	July 21, 2003	Barcelona
	Olympic	1:07.02	Penny Heyns, South Africa	July 21, 1996	Atlanta
	American	1:07.05	Megan Quann	Sept. 18, 2000	Sydney
200 meters:	World	2:22.99	**Hui Qi**, China	Apr. 13, 2001	Hangzhou, China
		2:22.99	**Amanda Beard**, USA	July 25, 2003	Barcelona
	Olympic	2:24.35	Agnes Kovacs, Hungary	Sept. 21, 2000	Sydney
	American	2:22.99	Beard (same as World)	—	—

World Swimming Records Set in 2003

World long course records set or equaled between Oct. 1, 2002 and Sept. 28, 2003; (*) indicates record is awaiting ratification.

MEN

Event	Name	Record	Old Mark	Former Holder
50m backstroke	**Thomas Rupprath,** GER	24.80	24.99	Lenny Krayzelburg, USA (1999)
100m breaststroke	**Kosuke Kitajima,** JPN	59.78	59.94	Roman Sloudnov, RUS (2001)
200m breaststroke	**Kosuke Kitajima,** JPN	2:09.42	2:09.52	Dmitri Komornikov, RUS (2003)
50m butterfly	**Matthew Welsh,** AUS	23.43	23.44	Geoff Huegill, AUS (2001)
100m butterfly	**Ian Crocker,** USA	50.98	51.47	Michael Phelps, USA (2003)
200m butterfly	**Michael Phelps,** USA	1:53.93	1:54.58	Michael Phelps, USA (2001)
200m IM	**Michael Phelps,** USA	1:56.04	1:57.52	Michael Phelps, USA (2003)
400m IM	**Michael Phelps,** USA	4:09.09	4:10.73	Michael Phelps, USA (2003)
4x100m . . . . medley	**USA**—Peirsol, Hansen, Crocker, Lezak	3:31.54	3:33.48	USA—Peirsol, Hansen Phelps, Lezak (2002)

WOMEN

Event	Name	Record	Old Mark	Former Holder
100m breaststroke	**Leisel Jones,** AUS	1:06.37	1:06.52	Penny Heyns, RSA (1999)
200m breaststroke	**Amanda Beard,** USA	2:22.99	—	Hui Qi, CHN (2001)

Note: Beard equaled the mark set by Hui in 2001.

Butterfly

Distance		Time		Date Set	Location
50 meters:	**World**	25.57	**Anna-Karin Kammerling**, SWE	July 30, 2002	Berlin
	Olympic		Not an event	—	—
	American	26.00	Jenny Thompson	July 26, 2003	Barcelona
100 meters:	**World**	56.61	**Inge de Bruijn**, Netherlands	Sept. 17, 2000	Sydney
	Olympic	56.61	de Bruijn (same as World)	—	—
	American	57.58p	Dara Torres	Aug. 9, 2000	Indianapolis
200 meters:	**World**	2:05.78	**Otylia Jedrejczak**, Poland	Aug. 4, 2002	Berlin
	Olympic . .	2:05.88	Misty Hyman, USA	Sept. 20, 2000	Sydney
	American . .	2:05.88	Misty Hyman	Sept. 20, 2000	Sydney

Individual Medley

Distance		Time		Date Set	Location
200 meters:	**World**	2:09.72	**Wu Yanyan**, China	Oct. 17, 1997	Shanghai
	Olympic . . .	2:10.68	Yana Klochkova, Ukraine	Sept. 19, 2000	Sydney
	American . .	2:11.91	Summer Sanders	July 30, 1992	Barcelona
400 meters:	**World**	4:33.59	**Yana Klochkova**, Ukraine	Sept. 16, 2000	Sydney
	Olympic . . .	4:33.59	Klochkova, UKR (same as World)	—	—
	American . .	4:37.58	Summer Sanders	July 26, 1992	Barcelona

Relays

Distance		Time		Date Set	Location
4x100m free:	**World**	3:36.00	**Germany** (Meissner, Dallmann, Volker, van Almsick)	July 29, 2002	Berlin
	Olympic . . .	3:36.61	USA (Van Dyken, Torres, Shealy, Thompson)	Sept. 16, 2000	Sydney
	American . .	3:36.61	USA (same as Olympic)	—	—
4x200m free:	**World**	7:55.47	**E. Germany** (Stellmach, Strauss, Mohring, Friedrich)	Aug. 18, 1987	Strasbourg, FRA
	Olympic . . .	7:57.80	USA (Arsenault, Munz, Benko, Thompson)	Sept. 20, 2000	Sydney
	American . .	7:55.70	USA (Benko, Komisarz, Jeffrey Munz)	July 24, 2003	Barcelona
4x100m medley:	**World**	3:58.30	**USA** (Bedford, Quann, Thompson, Torres)	Sept. 23, 2000	Sydney
	Olympic . . .	3:58.30	USA (same as World)	—	—
	American . .	3:58.30	USA (same as World)	—	—

WINTER SPORTS

Alpine Skiing
World Cup Champions
Top Five Standings
MEN

Overall 1. Stephan Eberharter, AUT (1333 pts); 2. Bode Miller, USA (1100); 3. Kjetil Andre Aamodt, NOR (940); 4. Kalle Palander, FIN (718); 5. Didier Cuche, SWI (709).

Downhill 1. Stephan Eberharter, AUT (790 pts); 2. Daron Rahlves, USA (593); 3. Michael Walchhofer, AUT (430); 4. Bruno Kernen, SWI (351); 5. Hannes Trinkl, AUT (341).

Slalom 1. Kalle Palander, FIN (658 pts); 2. Ivica Kostelic, CRO (580); 3. Rainer Schoenfelder, AUT (473); 4. Giorgio Rocca, ITA (438); 5. Manfred Pranger, AUT (385). *Best USA*—Bode Miller (17th, 144 pts).

Giant Slalom 1. Michael Von Gruenigen, SWI (542 pts); 2. Bode Miller, USA (425); 3. Hans Knauss, AUT (365); 4. Frederic Covili, FRA (296); 5. Heinz Schilchegger, AUT & Massimiliano Blardone, ITA (449).

Super G 1. Stephan Eberharter, AUT (356 pts); 2. Marco Buechel, LIE (280); 3. Didier Cuche, SWI (270); 4. Kjetil Andre Aamodt, NOR (251); 5. Hannes Reichelt, AUT (214). *Best USA*—Bode Miller (t-12th, 138 pts).

Combined 1. Bode Miller, USA (125 pts); 2. Kjetil Andre Aamodt, NOR & Michael Walchhofer, AUT (100); 4. Aksel Lund Svindal, NOR (80); 5. Bruno Kernen, SWI & Ambrosi Hoffmann, SWI (72).

Nation's Cup Champion: Austria

WOMEN

Overall 1. Janica Kostelic, CRO (1570 pts); 2. Karen Putzer, ITA (1100); 3. Anja Paerson, SWE (1042); 4. Michaela Dorfmeister, AUT (972); 5. Martina Ertl, GER (922). *Best USA*—Kirsten Clark (9th, 661 pts).

Downhill 1. Michaela Dorfmeister, AUT (372 pts); 2. Renate Goetschl, AUT (368); 3. Karen Putzer, ITA (316); 4. Carole Montillet, FRA (313); 5. Corinne Rey Bellet, SWI (230).

Slalom 1. Janica Kostelic, CRO (710 pts); 2. Anja Paerson, SWE (498); 3. Tanja Poutiainen, FIN (367); 4. Christel Pascal, FRA (359); 5. Marlies Schild, AUT (342). *Best USA*—Kristina Koznick (11th, 212 pts).

Giant Slalom 1. Anja Paerson, SWE (514 pts); 2. Karen Putzer, ITA (513); 3. Janica Kostelic, CRO (343); 4. Nicole Hosp, AUT (332); 5. Sonja Nef, SWI (329). *Best USA*—Sarah Schleper (21st, 140 pts).

Super G 1. Carole Montillet, FRA (493 pts); 2. Renate Goetschl, AUT (458); 3. Karen Putzer, ITA (394); 4. Alexandra Meissnitzer, AUT (350); 5. Michaela Dorfmeister, AUT (298). *Best USA*—Kirsten Clark (10th, 252 pts).

Combined 1. Janica Kostelic, CRO (100 pts); 2. Martine Ertl, GER (80); 3. Maria Riesch, GER (60); 4. Karen Putzer, ITA (50); 5. Julia Mancuso, USA (45).

Nation's Cup Champion: Austria

2003 World Championships
at St. Moritz, Switzerland (Feb. 1-16)

MEN

Downhill	Michael Walchhofer, Austria
Slalom	Ivica Kostelic, Croatia
Giant Slalom	Bode Miller, United States
Super G	Stephan Eberharter, Austria
Combined	Bode Miller, United States

WOMEN

Downhill	Melanie Turgeon, Canada
Slalom	Janica Kostelic, Croatia
Giant Slalom	Anja Paerson, Sweden
Super G	Michaela Dorfmeister, Austria
Combined	Janica Kostelic, Croatia

Freestyle Skiing
World Cup Champions
MEN

Overall	Dmitri Arkhipov, Russia
Aerials	Dmitri Arkhipov, Russia
Moguls	Travis Cabral, United States
Dual Moguls	Janne Lahtela, Finland
Ski Cross	Hiroomi Takizawa, Japan

WOMEN

Overall	Kari Traa, Norway
Aerials	Alisa Camplin, Australia
Moguls	Shannon Bahrke, United States
Dual Moguls	Margarita Marbler, Austria
Ski Cross	Valentine Scuotto, France

2003 World Championships
at Deer Valley, Utah (Jan. 29-Feb. 1)

MEN

Aerials	Dmitri Arkhipov, Russia
Moguls	Mikko Ronkainen, Finland
Dual Moguls	Jeremy Bloom, United States

WOMEN

Aerials	Alisa Camplin, Australia
Moguls	Kari Traa, Norway
Dual Moguls	Kari Traa, Norway

Nordic Skiing
World Cup Champions
MEN

Cross Country - Overall	Mathias Fredriksson, Sweden
Cross Country - Sprint	Thobias Fredriksson, Sweden
Ski Jumping - Overall	Adam Malysz, Poland
Ski Jumping - Four Hills	Janne Ahonen, Finland
Nordic Combined - Overall	Ronny Ackermann, Germany
Nordic Combined - Sprint	Ronny Ackermann, Germany

WOMEN

Cross Country - Overall	Bente Skari, Norway
Cross Country - Sprint	Marit Bjoergen, Norway

2003 World Championships
at Val di Fiemme, Italy (Feb. 18-Mar. 1)

MEN

Sprint	Thobias Fredriksson, Sweden
15-k Classic	Axel Teichmann, Germany
30-k Classic	Thomas Alsgaard, Norway
50-k Freestyle	Martin Koukal, Czech Republic
20-k Skiathlon	Per Elofsson, Sweden
4x10-k Relay	Norway
Nordic Combined (Ind.)	Ronny Ackermann, Germany
Nordic Combined (Sprint)	Johnny Spillane, United States
Nordic Combined (Team)	Austria
Ski Jumping (K95m)	Adam Malysz, Poland
Ski Jumping (K120m)	Adam Malysz, Poland
Ski Jumping (K120m Team)	Finland

WOMEN

Sprint	Marit Bjoergen, Norway
10-k Classic	Bente Skari, Norway
15-k Classic	Bente Skari, Norway
30-k Freestyle	Olga Savialova, Russia
10-k Skiathlon	Kristina Smigun, Estonia
4x5-k Relay	Germany

Bobsled
2003 World Championships
MEN
at Lake Placid, N.Y. (Feb. 15-23)

Two-Man . . . . .Germany II (Lange, Kuske)
  Best USA—Hays, Jones (5th).
Four-Man . . . . .Germany I
  (Lange, Hoppe, Kuske, Embach)
  Best USA—Hays, Schuffenhauer, Jones, Hines (2nd).

WOMEN
at Winterberg, Germany (Feb. 1-2)

Two-Woman . . . . . . .Germany II (Erdmann, Dietrich)
  Best USA—Racine, Flowers (6th).

Snowboarding
World Cup Champions
MEN
Overall . . . . .Jasey Jay Anderson, Canada
Halfpipe . . . . .Xavier Hoffmann, Germany
Parallel Slalom . . . . .Mathieu Bozzetto, France
Snowboardcross . . . . .Xavier Delerue, France
Big Air . . . . Jukka Eratuli, Finland

WOMEN
Overall . . . . .Karine Ruby, France
Halfpipe . . . . .Manuela Laura Pesko, Switzerland
Parallel Slalom . . . . .Ursula Bruhin, Switzerland
Snowboardcross . . . . .Karine Ruby, France

2003 World Championships
at Kreischberg, Austria (Jan. 11-19)
MEN
Halfpipe . . . . .Markus Keller, Switzerland
Parallel Slalom . . . . .Sigi Grabner, Austria
Parallel Giant Slalom . . . . .Dejan Kosir, Slovenia
Snowboardcross . . . . .Xavier Delerue, France
Big Air . . . . .Risto Mattila, Finland

WOMEN
Halfpipe . . . . .Doriane Vidal, France
Parallel Slalom . . . . .Isabelle Blanc, France
Parallel Giant Slalom . . . . .Ursula Bruhin, Switzerland
Snowboardcross . . . . .Karine Ruby, France

Speed Skating
World Cup Champions
MEN
500 meters . . . . Jeremy Wotherspoon, Canada
1000 meters . . . . .Erben Wennemars, Netherlands
1500 meters . . . . .Yevgeny Lalenkov, Russia
5000/10,000 meters . . . . . .Carl Verheijen, Netherlands

WOMEN
500 meters . . . . . . .Monique Garbrecht-Enfeldt, Germany
1000 meters . . . . . .Monique Garbrecht-Enfeldt, Germany
1500 meters . . . . .Cindy Klassen, Canada
3000/5000 meters . . . . . . .Claudia Pechstein, Germany

2003 World Championships
at Göteborg, Sweden (Feb. 8-9)
MEN
500 meters . . . . .Ids Postma, Netherlands
1500 meters . . . . .Yevgeny Lalenkov, Russia
5000 meters . . . . .Gianni Romme, Netherlands
10,000 meters . . . . .Gianni Romme, Netherlands
All-Around . . . . .Gianni Romme, Netherlands

WOMEN
500 meters . . . . .Jennifer Rodriguez, United States
1500 meters . . . . .Maki Tabata, Japan
3000 meters . . . . .Claudia Pechstein, Germany
5000 meters . . . . .Clara Hughes, Canada
All-Around . . . . .Cindy Klassen, Canada

2003 World Short Track Championships
at Warsaw, Poland (March 21-23)
MEN
500 meters .Li Jiajun, China
1000 meters . . . . .Li Jiajun, China
1500 meters . . . . .Ahn Hyun-Soo, South Korea
3000 meters . . . . .Ahn Hyun-Soo, South Korea
5000 meter relay . . . . .South Korea
All-Around . . . . .Ahn Hyun-Soo, South Korea

WOMEN
500 meters . . . . .Yang Yang (A), China
1000 meters . . . . .Evgenia Radanova, Bulgaria
1500 meters . . . . .Choi Eun-Kyung, South Korea
3000 meters . . . . .Kim Min-Jee, South Korea
3000 meter relay . . . . .China
All-Around . . . . .Choi Eun-Kyung, South Korea

Figure Skating

World Championships
at Washington, D.C. (March 24-30)

Men's —1. Evgeni Plushenko, Russia; 2. Tim Goebel, USA; 3. Honda Takeshi, Japan; 4. Li Chengjiang, China; 5. Michael Weiss, USA.

Women's —1. Michelle Kwan, USA; 2. Elena Sokolova, Russia; 3. Fumie Suguri, Japan; 4. Sasha Cohen, USA; 5. Viktoria Volchkova, Russia.

Pairs —1. Xue Shen & Hongbo Zhao, China; 2. Tatiana Totmianina & Maxim Marinin, Russia; 3. Maria Petrova & Alexei Tikhonov, Russia; 4. Qing Pang & Jian Tong, China; 5. Anabelle Langlois & Patrice Archetto, Canada.

Ice Dance —1. Shae-Lynn Bourne & Victor Kraatz, Canada; 2. Irina Lobacheva & Ilia Averbukh, Russia; 3. Albena Denkova & Maxim Staviyski, Bulgaria; 4. Tatiana Navka & Roman Kostomarov, Russia; 5. Elena Grushina & Ruslan Goncharov, Ukraine.

U.S. Championships
at Dallas, Tex. (Jan. 12-19)

Men's . . . . .Michael Weiss
Women's . . . . .Michelle Kwan
Pairs . . . . .Tiffany Scott
                       & Philip Dulebohn
Ice Dance . . . . .Naomi Lang
                     & Peter Tchernyshev

European Championships
at Malmö, Sweden (Jan. 20-26)

Men's . . . . .Evgeni Plushenko, Russia
Women's . . . . .Irina Slutskaya, Russia
Pairs . . . . .Tatiana Totmianina
                   & Maxim Marinin, Russia
Ice Dance . . . . .Irina Lobacheva
                   & Ilia Averbukh, Russia

SUMMER SPORTS

Cross Country
IAAF World Championships
The 31st IAAF World Cross Country Championships held in Lausanne, Switzerland (March 29-30).

MEN		WOMEN	
12.355 km . . . . .1. Kenenisa Bekele, Ethiopia 35:56		8 km . . . . .1. Werknesh Kidane, Ethiopia 25:53	
(7.68 mi)	2. Patrick Ivuti, Kenya 36:09	(4.97 mi)	2. Deena Drossin, USA 26:02
	3. Gebre-egziabher Gebremariam, Ethioia 36:17		3. Merima Denboba, Ethiopia 26:28
	Best USA—Mebrahtom Keflezighi, 11th 37:16		

Cycling
Tour de France
The 90th Tour de France (July 5-27) ran 20 stages plus a prologue, covering 2,130 miles starting in Paris, winding through the French countryside, passing through the Alps and Pyrenees and finishing back in Paris on the Avenue des Champs-Elysees.

U.S. Postal Service rider Lance Armstrong survived a nasty spill, stomach flu and an unexpected trip across a French field to win his fifth straight Tour. He completed the grueling event in 83 hours, 41 minutes and 12 seconds, defeating his closest rival, Jan Ullrich of Germany, by just over a minute. It was the most closely contested of his five wins. He is one of only five men in history to win five Tours, and one of only two men (Miguel Indurain) to win five consecutive.

	Team	Behind		Team	Behind
1 Lance Armstrong, USA	U.S. Postal	—	6 Iban Mayo, ESP	Euskaltel-Euskadi	7:06
2 Jan Ullrich, GER	Bianchi	1:01	7 Ivan Basso, ITA	Fassa Bortolo	10:12
3 Alexandre Vinokourov, KAZ	Telekom	4:14	8 Christophe Moreau, FRA	Credit Agricole	12:28
4 Tyler Hamilton, USA	CSC	6:17	9 Carlos Sastre, ESP	CSC	18:49
5 Haimar Zubeldia, ESP	Euskaltel-Euskadi	6:51	10 Francisco Mancebo, ESP	iBanesto.com	19:15

Other Worldwide Champions
2003 Major UCI (Union Cycliste Internationale) Road results through Sept. 15. Note that in some instances, the date shown below is the final day of that particular race.

MEN

Race	Winner	Race	Winner
Jan. 26: Tour Down Under (AUS)	Mikel Astarloza, ESP	Mar. 30: Criterium Int'l (FRA)	Laurent Brochard, FRA
Feb. 6: Challenge Illes Balears (ESP)	Alejandro Valverde, ESP	Apr. 6: Tour de Flanders (BEL)	Peter Van Petegem, BEL
Feb. 9: Tour de Langwaki (MAS)	Tom Danielson, USA	Apr. 9: Ghent-Wevelgem (BEL)	Andreas Klier, GER
Feb. 16: Mediterranean Tour (FRA)	Paolo Bettini, ITA	Apr. 13: Paris-Roubaix (FRA)	Peter Van Petegem, BEL
Feb. 20: Ruta del Sol (ESP)	Javier Pascual Llorente, ESP	Apr. 23: Fleche Wallonne (BEL)	Igor Astarloa, ESP
Mar. 1: Tour de Valencia (ESP)	Dario Frigo, ITA	May 4: Tour de Romandie (SWI)	Tyler Hamilton, USA
Mar. 1: Omloop Het Volk (BEL)	Johan Museeuw, BEL	May 11: Four Days of Dunkirk (FRA)	Christophe Moreau, Fra
Mar. 16: Paris-Nice (FRA)	Alexandre Vinokourov, KAZ	June 1: Giro d'Italia (ITA)	Gilberto Simoni, ITA
Mar. 19: Tirreno-Adriatico (ITA)	Filippo Pozzato, ITA	June 15: Dauphine Libere (FRA)	Lance Armstrong, USA
Mar. 22: Milan-San Remo (ITA)	Paolo Bettini, ITA	June 25: Tour of Switzerland (SWI)	A. Vinokourov, KAZ
Mar. 28: Setmana Catalana (ESP)	Dario Frigo, ITA	Aug. 23: Tour of the Netherlands (NED)	V. Ekimov, RUS

WOMEN

Race	Winner	Race	Winner
Mar. 6: Geelong World Cup (AUS)	Sara Carrigan, AUS	June 8: Liberty Classic (USA)	Lyne Bessette, CAN
Mar. 22: Primavera Rosa (ITA)	Zoulfia Zabirova, RUS	July 13: Giro d'Italia Femminile (ITA)	Nicole Braendli, SWI
Apr. 23: Fleche Wallonne (BEL)	Nicole Cooke, GBR	Aug. 17: Grande Boucle Feminine (FRA)	Joane
May 25: Tour de L'Aude (FRA)	Judith Arndt, GER		Somarriba Arrola, ESP
May 31: Montreal World Cup (CAN)	G. Jeanson, CAN	Sept. 7: Rotterdam Tour (NED)	Chantal Beltman, NED

Gymnastics
2003 World Championships
at Anaheim, Calif. (Aug. 16-24)

MEN		WOMEN	
All-Around	Paul Hamm, United States	All-Around	Svetlana Khorkina, Russia
Horizontal Bar	Takehiro Kashima, Japan	Vault	Oksana Chusovitina, Uzbekistan
Parallel Bars	Li Xiao-Peng, China	Uneven Bars	Hollie Vise, United States
Vault	Li Xiao-Peng, China	Balance Beam	Fan Ye, China
Pommel Horse	Teng Haibin, China	Floor Exercise	Daiane Dos Santos, Brazil
Rings	Jordan Jovtchev, Bulgaria	Team	United States
Floor Exercise	Paul Hamm, United States		
Team	China		

Marathons
2003 Boston Marathon

The 107th edition of the Boston Marathon was held Monday, April 21, 2003 and run, as always, from Hopkinton through Ashland, Framingham, Natick, Wellesley, Newton and Brookline to Boston, Mass. Kenyan dominance continued in the men's race as 24-year-old Robert Kipoech Cheruiyot won won the coveted laurel wreath (and the $80,000 that comes with it) with a time of 2:10:11. It was the 12th time in the last 13 years that a Kenyan has won the world's oldest annual marathon.

In the women's division, 32-year-old Svetlana Zakharova became the first Russian winner in 10 years, breaking the tape in 2:25:20 and snapping a three-year winning streak by the Kenyans. **Distance:** 26.2 miles.

MEN

		Time
1	Robert Kipoech Cheruiyot, Kenya	2:10:11
2	Benjamin Kosgei Kimutai, Kenya	2:10:34
3	Martin Lel, Kenya	2:11:11
4	Timothy Cherigat, Kenya	2:11:28
5	Christopher Cheboiboch, Kenya	2:12:45

Best USA: 10th—Eddy Hellebuyck, New Mexico, 2:17:18

WOMEN

		Time
1	Svetlana Zakharova, Russia	2:25:20
2	Lyubov Denisova, Russia	2:26:51
3	Joyce Chepchumba, Kenya	2:27:20
4	Margaret Okayo, Kenya	2:27:39
5	Marla Runyan, Oregon (USA)	2:30:28

Other 2003 Winners

Tokyo
Feb. 9	Men	Zebedayo Bayo, TAN	2:09:07
	(No women's division)		

Los Angeles
Mar. 2	Men	Mark Yatich, KEN	2:09:52
	Women	Tatyana Pozdnyakova, UKR	2:29:40

Paris
Apr. 6	Men	Michael Rotich, KEN	2:06:33
	Women	Beatrice Omwanza, KEN	2:27:44

London
Apr. 13	Men	Gezahegne Abera, ETH	2:07:56
	Women	Paula Radcliffe, GBR	2:15:25*

* world record

Turin
Apr. 13	Men	Daniele Caimmi, ITA	2:10:08
	Women	Stine Larsen, NOR	2:27:12

Rotterdam
Apr. 13	Men	William Kiplagat, KEN	2:07:42
	Women	Olivera Jevtic, SER	2:25:23

Late 2002

Chicago
Oct. 13	Men	Khalid Khannouchi, USA	2:05:56
	Women	Paula Radcliffe, GBR	2:17:18*

* world record (later broken on Apr. 13, 2003)

New York City
Nov. 3	Men	Rodgers Rop, KEN	2:08:07
	Women	Joyce Chepchumba, KEN	2:25:56

Tokyo Women's
Nov. 17	Women	Banuelia Mrashani, TAN	2:24:59

Fukuoka
Dec. 1	Men	Gezahegne Abera, ETH	2:09:13
	(No women's division)		

Rowing
2003 World Championships
at Milan, Italy (Aug. 24-31)

MEN

Eights	Canada, 6:00.44
Coxed Pairs	United States, 7:10.11
Coxed Fours	United States, 6:04.68
Coxless Pairs	Australia, 6:19.31
Coxless Fours	Canada, 5:52.91
Single Sculls	Olaf Tufte, Norway, 6:46.15
Double Sculls	France, 6:13.93
Quad Sculls	Germany, 6:12.26

WOMEN

Eights	Germany, 6:41.23
Coxless Pairs	Great Britain, 7:04.88
Coxless Fours	United States, 6:53.08
Single Sculls	Roumiana Neykova, Bulgaria, 7:18.12
Double Sculls	New Zealand, 6:45.79
Quad Sculls	Australia, 6:46.52

Freestyle Wrestling
2003 World Championships
at New York, N.Y. (Sept. 12-15)

MEN

55kg (121 pounds)	Dilshod Mansurov, Uzbekistan
60kg (132)	Abdullaev Yadulla, Azerbaijan
66kg (145¼)	Irbek Farniev, Russia
74kg (163)	Bouvaisa Saytiev, Russia
84kg (185)	Sajid Sajidov, Russia
96kg (211¼)	Eldar Kurtanidze, Georgia
120kg (264)	Artur Taymazov, Uzbekistan
Team	Georgia

WOMEN

48kg (105½ pounds)	Irini Merleni, Ukraine
51kg (112¼)	Chiharu Icho, Japan
55kg (121)	Saori Yoshida, Japan
59kg (130)	Seiko Yamamoto, Japan
63kg (138½)	Kaori Icho, Japan
67kg (147½)	Kristie Marano, United States
72kg (158½)	Kyoko Hamaguchi, Japan
Team	Japan

1882-2003
Through the Years

TRACK & FIELD

IAAF World Championships

While the Summer Olympics have served as the unofficial world outdoor championships for track and field throughout the centuries, a separate World Championship meet was started in 1983 by the International Amateur Athletic Federation (IAAF). The meet was held every four years from 1983-91, but began an every-other-year cycle in 1993. World Championship sites include Helsinki (1983), Rome (1987), Tokyo (1991), Stuttgart (1993), Göteborg, Sweden (1995), Athens (1997), Seville, Spain (1999), Edmonton (2001) and Paris (2003). Looking forward, the Championships will be held in Helsinki (2005) and Osaka, Japan (2007). Note that (WR) indicates world record and (CR) indicates championship meet record.

MEN

Multiple gold medals (including relays): Michael Johnson (9); Carl Lewis (8); Sergey Bubka (6); Maurice Greene and Lars Riedel (5); Hicham El Guerrouj, Haile Gebrselassie, Allen Johnson, Ivan Pedroso, Antonio Pettigrew and Calvin Smith (4); Donovan Bailey, Tomas Dvorak, Greg Foster, John Godina, Werner Gunthor, Wilson Kipketer, Moses Kiptanui, Robert Korzeniowski, Dennis Mitchell, Noureddine Morceli, Dan O'Brien, Butch Reynolds, Jerome Young and Jan Zelezny (3); Andrey Abduvaliyev, Abel Anton, Derrick Brew, Leroy Burrell, John Capel, Andre Cason, Maurizio Damilano, Jon Drummond, Jonathan Edwards, Colin Jackson, Ismael Kirui, Billy Konchellah, Sergey Litvinov, Tim Montgomery, Edwin Moses, Mike Powell, Felix Sanchez, Javier Sotomayor, Angelo Taylor and Bernard Williams (2).

100 Meters

Year		Time	
1983	Carl Lewis, USA	10.07	
1987	Carl Lewis, USA	9.93	
1991	Carl Lewis, USA	9.86	WR
1993	Linford Christie, GBR	9.87	
1995	Donovan Bailey, CAN	9.97	
1997	Maurice Greene, USA	9.86	
1999	Maurice Greene, USA	9.80	CR
2001	Maurice Greene, USA	9.82	
2003	Kim Collins, SKN	10.07	

Note: Ben Johnson was the original winner in 1987, but was stripped of his title and world record time (9.83) following his 1989 admission of drug taking.

200 Meters

Year		Time	
1983	Calvin Smith, USA	20.14	
1987	Calvin Smith, USA	20.16	
1991	Michael Johnson, USA	20.01	
1993	Frank Fredericks, NAM	19.85	
1995	Michael Johnson, USA	19.79	CR
1997	Ato Boldon, USA	20.04	
1999	Maurice Greene, USA	19.90	
2001	Konstantinos Kenteris, GRE	20.04	
2003	John Capel, USA	20.30	

400 Meters

Year		Time	
1983	Bert Cameron, JAM	45.05	
1987	Thomas Schonlebe, E. Ger	44.33	
1991	Antonio Pettigrew, USA	44.57	
1993	Michael Johnson, USA	43.65	
1995	Michael Johnson, USA	43.39	
1997	Michael Johnson, USA	44.12	
1999	Michael Johnson, USA	43.18	WR
2001	Avard Moncur, BAH	44.64	
2003	Jerome Young, USA	44.50	

800 Meters

Year		Time	
1983	Willi Wülbeck, W. Ger	1:43.65	
1987	Billy Konchellah, KEN	1:43.06	CR
1991	Billy Konchellah, KEN	1:43.99	
1993	Paul Ruto, KEN	1:44.71	
1995	Wilson Kipketer, DEN	1:45.08	
1997	Wilson Kipketer, DEN	1:43.38	
1999	Wilson Kipketer, DEN	1:43.30	
2001	Andre Bucher, SWI	1:43.70	
2003	Djabir Said-Guerni, ALG	1:44.81	

1500 Meters

Year		Time	
1983	Steve Cram, GBR	3:41.59	
1987	Abdi Bile, SOM	3:36.80	
1991	Noureddine Morceli, ALG	3:32.84	
1993	Noureddine Morceli, ALG	3:34.24	
1995	Noureddine Morceli, ALG	3:33.73	
1997	Hicham El Guerrouj, MOR	3:35.83	
1999	Hicham El Guerrouj, MOR	3:27.65	CR
2001	Hicham El Guerrouj, MOR	3:30.68	
2003	Hicham El Guerrouj, MOR	3:31.77	

5000 Meters

Year		Time	
1983	Eammon Coghlan, IRL	13:28.53	
1987	Said Aouita, MOR	13:26.44	
1991	Yobes Ondieki, KEN	13:14.45	
1993	Ismael Kirui, KEN	13:02.75	
1995	Ismael Kirui, KEN	13:16.77	
1997	Daniel Komen, KEN	13:07.38	
1999	Salah Hissou, MOR	12:58.13	
2001	Richard Limo, KEN	13:00.77	
2003	Eliud Kipchoge, KEN	12:52.79	CR

10,000 Meters

Year		Time		Year		Time	
1983	Alberto Cova, ITA	28:01.04		1997	Haile Gebrselassie, ETH	27:24.58	
1987	Paul Kipkoech, KEN	27:38.63		1999	Haile Gebrselassie, ETH	27:57.27	
1991	Moses Tanui, KEN	27:38.74		2001	Charles Kamathi, KEN	27:53.25	
1993	Haile Gebrselassie, ETH	27:46.02		2003	Kenenisa Bekele, ETH	26:49.57	CR
1995	Haile Gebrselassie, ETH	27:12.95					

Marathon

Year		Time
1983	Rob de Castella, AUS	2:10:03
1987	Douglas Wakiihuri, KEN	2:11:48
1991	Hiromi Taniguchi, JPN	2:14:57
1993	Mark Plaatjes, USA	2:13:57
1995	Martin Fíz, SPA	2:11:41
1997	Abel Anton, SPA	2:13:16
1999	Abel Anton, SPA	2:13:36
2001	Gezahegne Abera, ETH	2:12:42
2003	Jaouad Gharib, MOR	2:08:31 CR

110-Meter Hurdles

Year		Time
1983	Greg Foster, USA	13.42
1987	Greg Foster, USA	13.21
1991	Greg Foster, USA	13.06
1993	Colin Jackson, GBR	12.91 WR
1995	Allen Johnson, USA	13.00
1997	Allen Johnson, USA	12.93
1999	Colin Jackson, GBR	13.04
2001	Allen Johnson, USA	13.04
2003	Allen Johnson, USA	13.12

400-Meter Hurdles

Year		Time
1983	Edwin Moses, USA	47.50
1987	Edwin Moses, USA	47.46
1991	Samuel Matete, ZAM	47.64
1993	Kevin Young, USA	47.18 CR
1995	Derrick Adkins, USA	47.98
1997	Stephane Diagana, FRA	47.70
1999	Fabrizio Mori, ITA	47.72
2001	Felix Sanchez, DOM	47.49
2003	Felix Sanchez, DOM	47.25

3000-Meter Steeplechase

Year		Time
1983	Patriz Ilg, W. Ger	8:15.06
1987	Francesco Panetta, ITA	8:08.57
1991	Moses Kiptanui, KEN	8:12.59
1993	Moses Kiptanui, KEN	8:06.36
1995	Moses Kiptanui, KEN	8:04.16 CR
1997	Wilson B. Kipketer, KEN	8:05.84
1999	Christopher Koskei, KEN	8:11.76
2001	Reuben Kosgei, KEN	8:15.16
2003	Saif Saaeed Shaheen, QAT	8:04.39

4 x 100-Meter Relay

Year		Time
1983	United States	37.86 WR
1987	United States	37.90
1991	United States	37.50 WR
1993	United States	37.48 CR
1995	Canada	38.31
1997	Canada	37.86
1999	United States	37.59
2001	United States	37.96
2003	United States	38.06

4 x 400-Meter Relay

Year		Time
1983	Soviet Union	3:00.79
1987	United States	2:57.29
1991	Great Britain	2:57.53
1993	United States	2:54.29 WR
1995	United States	2:57.32
1997	United States	2:56.47
1999	United States	2:56.45
2001	United States	2:57.54
2003	United States	2:58.88

20-Kilometer Walk

Year		Time
1983	Ernesto Canto, MEX	1:20.49
1987	Maurizio Damilano, ITA	1:20.45
1991	Maurizio Damilano, ITA	1:19.37
1993	Valentin Massana, SPA	1:22.31
1995	Michele Didoni, ITA	1:19.59
1997	Daniel Garcia, MEX	1:21.43
1999	Ilya Markov, RUS	1:23:34
2001	Roman Rasskazov, RUS	1:20:31
2003	Jefferson Perez, ECU	1:17:21 WR

50-Kilometer Walk

Year		Time
1983	Ronald Weigel, E. Ger	3:43:08
1987	Hartwig Gauder, E. Ger	3:40:53
1991	Aleksandr Potashov, USSR	3:53:09
1993	Jesus Angel Garcia, SPA	3:41:41
1995	Valentin Kononen, FIN	3:43.42
1997	Robert Korzeniowski, POL	3:44:46
1999	German Skurygin, RUS	3:44:23
2001	Robert Korzeniowski, POL	3:42:08
2003	Robert Korzeniowski, POL	3:36:03 WR

High Jump

Year		Height
1983	Gennedy Avdeyenko, USSR	7- 7¼
1987	Patrik Sjoberg, SWE	7- 9¾
1991	Charles Austin, USA	7- 9¾
1993	Javier Sotomayor, CUB	7-10½ CR
1995	Troy Kemp, BAH	7- 9¼
1997	Javier Sotomayor, CUB	7- 9¼
1999	Vyacheslav Voronin, RUS	7- 9¼
2001	Martin Buss, GER	7- 8¾
2003	Jacques Freitag, RSA	7- 8½

Pole Vault

Year		Height
1983	Sergey Bubka, USSR	18- 8¼
1987	Sergey Bubka, USSR	19- 2¼
1991	Sergey Bubka, USSR	19- 6¼
1993	Sergey Bubka, UKR	19- 8¼
1995	Sergey Bubka, UKR	19- 5
1997	Sergey Bubka, UKR	19- 8½
1999	Maksim Tarasov, RUS	19- 9
2001	Dmitri Markov, AUS	19-10¼ CR
2003	Giuseppe Gibilisco, ITA	19- 4¼

Long Jump

Year		Distance
1983	Carl Lewis, USA	28- 0¾
1987	Carl Lewis, USA	28- 0¼
1991	Mike Powell, USA	29- 4½ WR
1993	Mike Powell, USA	28- 2¼
1995	Ivan Pedroso, CUB	28- 6½
1997	Ivan Pedroso, CUB	27- 7½
1999	Ivan Pedroso, CUB	28- 1
2001	Ivan Pedroso, CUB	27- 6¾
2003	Dwight Phillips, USA	27- 3¾

Triple Jump

Year		Distance
1983	Zdzislaw Hoffmann, POL	57- 2
1987	Khristo Markov, BUL	58- 9
1991	Kenny Harrison, USA	58- 4
1993	Mike Conley, USA	58- 7¼
1995	Jonathan Edwards, GBR	60- 0¼ WR
1997	Yoelvis Quesada, CUB	58- 6¾
1999	Charles Michael Friedek, GER	57- 8½
2001	Jonathan Edwards, GBR	58- 9½
2003	Christian Olsson, SWE	58- 1¾

Track & Field (Cont.)

Shot Put

Year		Distance	
1983	Edward Sarul, POL	70- 2¼	
1987	Werner Günthör SWI	72-11¼	CR
1991	Werner Günthör, SWI	71- 1¼	
1993	Werner Günthör, SWI	72- 1	
1995	John Godina, USA	70- 5¼	
1997	John Godina, USA	70- 4¼	
1999	C.J. Hunter, USA	71- 6	
2001	John Godina, USA	71- 9	
2003	Andrei Mikhnevich, BLR	71- 2	

Discus

Year		Distance	
1983	Imrich Bugar, CZE	222- 2	
1987	Jurgen Schult, E. Ger	225- 6	
1991	Lars Riedel, GER	217- 2	
1993	Lars Riedel, GER	222- 2	
1995	Lars Riedel, GER	225- 7	
1997	Lars Riedel, GER	224-10	
1999	Anthony Washington, USA	226- 7	
2001	Lars Riedel, GER	228- 9	
2003	Virgilijus Alekena, LTA	228- 7	CR

Hammer Throw

Year		Distance	
1983	Sergey Litvinov, USSR	271- 3	
1987	Sergey Litvinov, USSR	272- 6	
1991	Yuri Sedykh, USSR	268- 0	
1993	Andrey Abduvaliyev, TAJ	267-10	
1995	Andrey Abduvaliyev, TAJ	267- 7	
1997	Heinz Weis, GER	268- 4	
1999	Karsten Kobs, GER	263- 3	
2001	Szymon Ziolkowski, POL	273- 7	CR
2003	Ivan Tikhon, BLR	272- 5	

Javelin

Year		Distance	
1983	Detlef Michel, E. Ger	293-7	
1987	Seppo Raty, FIN	274-1	
1991	Kimmo Kinnunen, FIN	297-11	
1993	Jan Zelezny, CZR	282-1	
1995	Jan Zelezny, CZR	293-11	
1997	Marius Corbett, S. Afr.	290-0	
1999	Aki Parviainen, FIN	293-8	
2001	Jan Zelezny, CZR	304- 5	CR
2003	Sergey Makarov, RUS	280- 3	

Decathlon

Year		Points	
1983	Daley Thompson, GBR	8714	
1987	Torsten Voss, E. Ger	8680	
1991	Dan O'Brien, USA	8812	
1993	Dan O'Brien, USA	8817	
1995	Dan O'Brien, USA	8695	

Year		Points	
1997	Tomas Dvorak, CZR	8837	
1999	Tomas Dvorak, CZR	8744	
2001	Tomas Dvorak, CZR	8902	CR
2003	Tom Pappas, USA	8750	

WOMEN

Multiple gold medals (including relays): Gail Devers and Marion Jones (5), Jearl Miles Clark and Jackie Joyner-Kersee (4); Tatyana Samolenko Dorovskikh, Chryste Gaines, Silke Gladisch, Marita Koch, Astrid Kumbernuss, Inger Miller, Maria Mutola, Merlene Ottey, Gabriela Szabo, Gwen Torrence and Kelli White (3); Hassiba Boulmerka, Sabine Braun, Olga Bryzgina, Hestrie Cloete, Mary Decker, Stacy Dragila, Heike Daute Drechsler, Lyudmila Narozhilenko Enquist, Cathy Freeman, Trine Hattestad, Martina Optiz Hellmann, Stefka Kostadinova, Katrin Krabbe, Jarmila Kratochvilova, Tatyana Lebedeva, Mirela Manjani, Fiona May, Yipsi Moreno, Marie-José Pérec, Zhanna Pintusevich-Block, Ana Quirot and Huang Zhihong (2).

100 Meters

Year		Time	
1983	Marlies Gohr, E. Ger	10.97	
1987	Silke Gladisch, E. Ger	10.90	
1991	Katrin Krabbe, GER	10.99	
1993	Gail Devers, USA	10.81	CR
1995	Gwen Torrence, USA	10.85	
1997	Marion Jones, USA	10.83	
1999	Marion Jones, USA	10.70	CR
2001	Zhanna Pintusevich-Block, UKR	10.82	
2003	Kelli White, USA	10.85	

200 Meters

Year		Time	
1983	Marita Koch, E. Ger	22.13	
1987	Silke Gladisch, E. Ger	21.74	CR
1991	Katrin Krabbe, GER	22.09	
1993	Merlene Ottey, JAM	21.98	
1995	Merlene Ottey, JAM	22.12	
1997	Zhanna Pintusevich, UKR	22.32	
1999	Inger Miller, USA	21.77	
2001	Marion Jones, USA	22.39	
2003	Kelli White, USA	22.05	

400 Meters

Year		Time	
1983	Jarmila Kratochvilova, CZE	47.99	WR
1987	Olga Bryzgina, USSR	49.38	
1991	Marie-José Pérec, FRA	49.13	
1993	Jearl Miles, USA	49.82	
1995	Marie-José Pérec, FRA	49.28	
1997	Cathy Freeman, AUS	49.77	
1999	Cathy Freeman, AUS	49.67	
2001	Amy Mbacke Thiam , SEN	49.86	
2003	Ana Guevara, MEX	48.89	

800 Meters

Year		Time	
1983	Jarmila Kratochvilova, CZE	1:54.68	CR
1987	Sigrun Wodars, E. Ger	1:55.26	
1991	Lilia Nurutdinova, USSR	1:57.50	
1993	Maria Mutola, MOZ	1:55.43	
1995	Ana Quirot, CUB	1:56.11	
1997	Ana Quirot, CUB	1:57.14	
1999	Ludmila Formanova, CZR	1:56.68	
2001	Maria Mutola, MOZ	1:57.17	
2003	Maria Mutola, MOZ	1:59.89	

1500 Meters

Year		Time	
1983	Mary Decker, USA	4:00.90	
1987	Tatiana Samolenko, USSR	3:58.56	
1991	Hassiba Boulmerka, ALG	4:02.21	
1993	Liu Dong, CHN	4:00.50	
1995	Hassiba Boulmerka, ALG	4:02.42	
1997	Carla Sacramento, POR	4:04.24	
1999	Svetlana Masterkova, RUS	3:59.53	
2001	Gabriela Szabo, ROM	4:00.57	
2003	Tatyana Tomashova, RUS	3:58.52	CR

5000 Meters

Held as 3000-meter race from 1983-93

Year		Time	
1983	Mary Decker, USA	8:34.62	
1987	Tatyana Samolenko, USSR	8:38.73	
1991	T. Samolenko Dorovskikh, USSR	8:35.82	
1993	Qu Yunxia, CHN	8:28.71	
1995	Sonia O'Sullivan, IRL	14:46.47	
1997	Gabriela Szabo, ROM	14:57.68	
1999	Gabriela Szabo, ROM	14:41.82	CR
2001	Olga Yegorova, RUS	15:03.39	
2003	Tirunesh Dibaba, ETH	14:51.72	

10,000 Meters

Year		Time
1983	Not held	
1987	Ingrid Kristiansen, NOR	31:05.85
1991	Liz McColgan, GBR	31:14.31
1993	Wang Junxia, CHN	30:49.30
1995	Fernanda Ribeiro, POR	31:04.99
1997	Sally Barsosio, KEN	31:32.92
1999	Gete Wami, ETH	30:24.56
2001	Derartu Tulu, ETH	31:48.81
2003	Berhane Adere, ETH	30:04.18 CR

Marathon

Year		Time
1983	Grete Waitz, NOR	2:28:09
1987	Rose Mota, POR	2:25:17
1991	Wanda Panfil, POL	2:29:53
1993	Junko Asari, JPN	2:30:03
1995	Manuela Machado, POR	2:25:39
1997	Hiromi Suzuki, JPN	2:29:48
1999	Jong Song-Ok, N. Kor	2:26:59
2001	Lidia Simon, ROM	2:26:01
2003	Catherine Ndereba, KEN	2:23:55 CR

100-Meter Hurdles

Year		Time
1983	Bettine Jahn, E. Ger	12.35w
1987	Ginka Zagorcheva, BUL	12.34 CR
1991	Lyudmila Narozhilenko, USSR	12.59
1993	Gail Devers, USA	12.46
1995	Gail Devers, USA	12.68
1997	Ludmila Enquist, SWE	12.50
1999	Gail Devers, USA	12.37
2001	Anjanette Kirkland, USA	12.42
2003	Perdita Felicien, CAN	12.53

w indicates wind-aided.

400-Meter Hurdles

Year		Time
1983	Yekaterina Fesenko, USSR	54.14
1987	Sabine Busch, E. Ger	53.62
1991	Tatiana Ledovskaya, USSR	53.11
1993	Sally Gunnell, GBR	52.74 WR
1995	Kim Batten, USA	52.61 WR
1997	Nezha Bidouane, MOR	52.97
1999	Daima Pernia, CUB	52.89
2001	Nezha Bidouane, MOR	53.34
2003	Jana Pittman, AUS	53.22

4 x 100-Meter Relay

Year		Time
1983	East Germany	41.76
1987	United States	41.58
1991	Jamaica	41.94
1993	Russia	41.49
1995	United States	42.12
1997	United States	41.47 CR
1999	Bahamas	41.92
2001	United States	41.71
2003	France	41.78

4 x 400-Meter Relay

Year		Time
1983	East Germany	3:19.73
1987	East Germany	3:18.63
1991	Soviet Union	3:18.43
1993	United States	3:16.71 CR
1995	United States	3:22.39
1997	Germany	3:20.92
1999	Russia	3:21.98
2001	Jamaica	3:20.65
2003	United States	3:22.63

20-Kilometer Walk

Held as 10-Kilometer race from 1987-97

Year		Time
1983	Not held	
1987	Irina Strakhova, USSR	44:12
1991	Alina Ivanova, USSR	42:57
1993	Sari Essayah, FIN	42:59
1995	Irina Stankina, RUS	42:13
1997	Anna Sidoti, ITA	42:55
1999	Hongyu Liu, CHN	1:30:50
2001	Olimpiada Ivanova, RUS	1:27:48
2003	Yelena Nikolayeva, RUS	1:26:52 CR

High Jump

Year		Height
1983	Tamara Bykova, USSR	6-7
1987	Stefka Kostadinova, BUL	6-10¼ WR
1991	Heike Henkel, GER	6-8¾
1993	Ioamnet Quintero, CUB	6-6¼
1995	Stefka Kostadinova, BUL	6-7
1997	Hanne Haugland, NOR	6-6¼
1999	Inga Babakova, UKR	6-6¼
2001	Hestrie Cloete, RSA	6-6¾
2003	Hestrie Cloete, RSA	6-9

Pole Vault

Year		Height
1999	Stacy Dragila, USA	15-1
2001	Stacy Dragila, USA	15-7 CR
2003	Svetlana Feofanova, RUS	15-7 CR

Long Jump

Year		Distance
1983	Heike Daute, E. Ger	23-10¼w
1987	Jackie Joyner-Kersee, USA	24-1¾ CR
1991	Jackie Joyner-Kersee, USA	24-0¼
1993	Heike Drechsler, GER	23-4
1995	Fiona May, ITA	22-10¾w
1997	Lyudmila Galkina, RUS	23-1¾
1999	Niurka Montalvo, SPA	23-2
2001	Fiona May, ITA	23-0½
2003	Eunice Barber, FRA	22-11¼

w indicates wind-aided.

Triple Jump

Year		Distance
1993	Ana Biryukova, RUS	46-6¼ WR
1995	Inessa Kravets, UKR	50-10¾ WR
1997	Sarka Kasparkova, CZR	49-10½
1999	Paraskevi Tsiamita, GRE	48-10
2001	Tatyana Lebedeva, RUS	50-0½
2003	Tatyana Lebedeva, RUS	49-9¾

Shot Put

Year		Distance
1983	Helena Fibingerova, CZE	69-0
1987	Natalia Lisovskaya, USSR	69-8 CR
1991	Huang Zhihong, CHN	68-4
1993	Huang Zhihong, CHN	67-6
1995	Astrid Kumbernuss, GER	69-7½
1997	Astrid Kumbernuss, GER	67-11½
1999	Astrid Kumbernuss, GER	65-1½
2001	Yanina Korolchik, BLR	67-7½
2003	Svetlana Krivelyova, RUS	67-8¼

Discus

Year		Distance
1983	Martina Opitz, E. Ger	226-2
1987	Martina Opitz Hellmann, E. Ger	235-0 CR
1991	Tsvetanka Khristova, BUL	233-0
1993	Olga Burova, RUS	221-1
1995	Ellina Zvereva, BLR	225-2
1997	Beatrice Faumuina, NZE	219-3
1999	Franka Dietzsch, GER	223-6
2001	Natalya Sadova, RUS	224-11
2003	Irina Yatchenko, BLR	220-10

Track & Field (Cont.)

Hammer Throw

Year		Distance	
1999	Mihaela Melinte, ROM	246-8¾	CR
2001	Yipsi Moreno, CUB	231-9	
2003	Yipsi Moreno, CUB	240-7	

Javelin

Year		Distance	
1983	Tiina Lillak, FIN	232-4	
1987	Fatima Whitbread, GBR	251-5	CR
1991	Xu Demei, CHN	225-8	
1993	Trine Hattestad, NOR	227-0	
1995	Natalya Shikolenko, BLR	221-8	
1997	Trine Hattestad, NOR	225-8	
1999	Mirela Manjani-Tzelili, GRE	220-1	
2001	Osleidys Menendez, CUB	228-1	CR
2003	Mirela Manjani, GRE	218-3	

Heptathlon

Year		Points	
1983	Ramona Neubert, E. Ger	6770	
1987	Jackie Joyner-Kersee, USA	7128	CR
1991	Sabine Braun, GER	6672	
1993	Jackie Joyner-Kersee, USA	6837	
1995	Ghada Shouaa, SYR	6651	
1997	Sabine Braun, GER	6739	
1999	Eunice Barber, FRA	6861	
2001	Yelena Prokhorova, RUS	6694	
2003	Carolina Kluft, SWE	7001	

World Cross Country Championships

MEN

Multiple winners: John Ngugi and Paul Tergat (5); Carlos Lopes (3); Kenenisa Bekele, Mohammed Mourhit, Khalid Skah, William Sigei, John Treacy and Craig Virgin (2).

Year		Year		Year	
1973	Pekka Paivarinta, Finland	1984	Carlos Lopes, Portugal	1995	Paul Tergat, Kenya
1974	Eric DeBeck, Belgium	1985	Carlos Lopes, Portugal	1996	Paul Tergat, Kenya
1975	Ian Stewart, Scotland	1986	John Ngugi, Kenya	1997	Paul Tergat, Kenya
1976	Carlos Lopes, Portugal	1987	John Ngugi, Kenya	1998	Paul Tergat, Kenya
1977	Leon Schots, Belgium	1988	John Ngugi, Kenya	1999	Paul Tergat, Kenya
1978	John Treacy, Ireland	1989	John Ngugi, Kenya	2000	Mohammed Mourhit, Belgium
1979	John Treacy, Ireland	1990	Khalid Skah, Morocco	2001	Mohammed Mourhit, Belgium
1980	Craig Virgin, USA	1991	Khalid Skah, Morocco	2002	Kenenisa Bekele, Ethiopia
1981	Craig Virgin, USA	1992	John Ngugi, Kenya	2003	Kenenisa Bekele, Ethiopia
1982	Mohammed Kedir, Ethiopia	1993	William Sigei, Kenya		
1983	Bekele Debele, Ethiopia	1994	William Sigei, Kenya		

WOMEN

Multiple winners: Grete Waitz (5); Lynn Jennings and Derartu Tulu (3); Zola Budd, Paola Cacchi, Maricica Puica, Paula Radcliffe, Annette Sergent, Carmen Valero and Gete Wami (2).

Year		Year		Year	
1973	Paola Cacchi, Italy	1984	Maricica Puica, Romania	1995	Derartu Tulu, Ethiopia
1974	Paola Cacchi, Italy	1985	Zola Budd, England	1996	Gete Wami, Ethiopia
1975	Julie Brown, USA	1986	Zola Budd, England	1997	Derartu Tulu, Ethiopia
1976	Carmen Valero, Spain	1987	Annette Sergent, France	1998	Sonia O'Sullivan, Ireland
1977	Carmen Valero, Spain	1988	Ingrid Kristiansen, Norway	1999	Gete Wami, Ethiopia
1978	Grete Waitz, Norway	1989	Annette Sergent, France	2000	Derartu Tulu, Ethiopia
1979	Grete Waitz, Norway	1990	Lynn Jennings, USA	2001	Paula Radcliffe, Gr. Britain
1980	Grete Waitz, Norway	1991	Lynn Jennings, USA	2002	Paula Radcliffe, Gr. Britain
1981	Grete Waitz, Norway	1992	Lynn Jennings, USA	2003	Werknesh Kidane, Ethiopia
1982	Maricica Puica, Romania	1993	Albertina Dias, Portugal		
1983	Grete Waitz, Norway	1994	Helen Chepngeno, Kenya		

Marathons

Boston

America's oldest regularly contested foot race, the Boston Marathon is held on Patriots' Day every April. It has been run at four different distances: 24 miles, 1232 yards (1897-1923); 26 miles, 209 yards (1924-26); 26 miles, 385 yards (1927-52, since 1957); 25 miles, 958 yards (1953-56).

MEN

Multiple winners: Clarence DeMar (7); Gerard Cote and Bill Rodgers (4); Ibrahim Hussein, Cosmas Ndeti, Eino Oksanen and Leslie Pawson (3); Tarzan Brown, Jim Caffrey, John A. Kelley, John Miles, Toshihiko Seko, Geoff Smith, Moses Tanui and Aurele Vandendriessche (2).

Year		Time	Year		Time
1897	John McDermott, New York	2:55:10	1903	J.C. Lorden, Massachusetts	2:41:29
1898	Ronald McDonald, Massachusetts	2:42:00	1904	Mike Spring, New York	2:38:04
1899	Lawrence Brignolia, Massachusetts	2:54:38	1905	Fred Lorz, New York	2:38:25
			1906	Tim Ford, Massachusetts	2:45:45
1900	Jim Caffrey, Canada	2:39:44	1907	Tom Longboat, Canada	2:24:24
1901	Jim Caffrey, Canada	2:29:23	1908	Tom Morrissey, New York	2:25:43
1902	Sam Mellor, New York	2:43:12	1909	Henri Renaud, New Hampshire	2:53:36

Year		Time
1910	Fred Cameron, Nova Scotia	2:28:52
1911	Clarence DeMar, Massachusetts	2:21:39
1912	Mike Ryan, Illinois	2:21:18
1913	Fritz Carlson, Minnesota	2:25:14
1914	James Duffy, Canada	2:25:01
1915	Edouard Fabre, Canada	2:31:41
1916	Arthur Roth, Massachusetts	2:27:16
1917	Bill Kennedy, New York	2:28:37
1918	World War relay race	
1919	Carl Linder, Massachusetts	2:29:13
1920	Peter Trivoulidas, New York	2:29:31
1921	Frank Zuna, New Jersey	2:18:57
1922	Clarence DeMar, Massachusetts	2:18:10
1923	Clarence DeMar, Massachusetts	2:23:37
1924	Clarence DeMar, Massachusetts	2:29:40
1925	Charles Mellor, Illinois	2:33:00
1926	John Miles, Nova Scotia	2:25:40
1927	Clarence DeMar, Massachusetts	2:40:22
1928	Clarence DeMar, Massachusetts	2:37:07
1929	John Miles, Nova Scotia	2:33:08
1930	Clarence DeMar, Massachusetts	2:34:48
1931	James Henigan, Massachusetts	2:46:45
1932	Paul deBruyn, Germany	2:33:36
1933	Leslie Pawson, Rhode Island	2:31:01
1934	Dave Komonen, Canada	2:32:53
1935	John A. Kelley, Massachusetts	2:32:07
1936	Ellison (Tarzan) Brown, Rhode Island	2:33:40
1937	Walter Young, Canada	2:33:20
1938	Leslie Pawson, Rhode Island	2:35:34
1939	Ellison (Tarzan) Brown, Rhode Island	2:28:51
1940	Gerard Cote, Canada	2:28:28
1941	Leslie Pawson, Rhode Island	2:30:38
1942	Joe Smith, Massachusetts	2:26:51
1943	Gerard Cote, Canada	2:28:25
1944	Gerard Cote, Canada	2:31:50
1945	John A. Kelley, Massachusetts	2:30:40
1946	Stylianos Kyriakides, Greece	2:29:27
1947	Yun Bok Suh, Korea	2:25:39
1948	Gerard Cote, Canada	2:31:02
1949	Karle Leandersson, Sweden	2:31:50
1950	Kee Yonh Ham, Korea	2:32:39
1951	Shigeki Tanaka, Japan	2:27:45
1952	Doroteo Flores, Guatemala	2:31:53
1953	Keizo Yamada, Japan	2:18:51
1954	Veiko Karvonen, Finland	2:20:39
1955	Hideo Hamamura, Japan	2:18:22
1956	Antti Viskari, Finland	2:14:14
1957	John J. Kelley, Connecticut	2:20:05

Year		Time
1958	Franjo Mihalic, Yugoslavia	2:25:54
1959	Eino Oksanen, Finland	2:22:42
1960	Paavo Kotila, Finland	2:20:54
1961	Eino Oksanen, Finland	2:23:39
1962	Eino Oksanen, Finland	2:23:48
1963	Aurele Vandendriessche, Belgium	2:18:58
1964	Aurele Vandendriessche, Belgium	2:19:59
1965	Morio Shigematsu, Japan	2:16:33
1966	Kenji Kimihara, Japan	2:17:11
1967	David McKenzie, New Zealand	2:15:45
1968	Amby Burfoot, Connecticut	2:22:17
1969	Yoshiaki Unetani, Japan	2:13:49
1970	Ron Hill, England	2:10:30
1971	Alvaro Mejia, Colombia	2:18:45
1972	Olavi Suomalainen, Finland	2:15:39
1973	Jon Anderson, Oregon	2:16:03
1974	Neil Cusack, Ireland	2:13:39
1975	Bill Rodgers, Massachusetts	2:09:55
1976	Jack Fultz, Pennsylvania	2:20:19
1977	Jerome Drayton, Canada	2:14:46
1978	Bill Rodgers, Massachusetts	2:10:13
1979	Bill Rodgers, Massachusetts	2:09:27
1980	Bill Rodgers, Massachusetts	2:12:11
1981	Toshihiko Seko, Japan	2:09:26
1982	Alberto Salazar, Oregon	2:08:52
1983	Greg Meyer, New Jersey	2:09:00
1984	Geoff Smith, England	2:10:34
1985	Geoff Smith, England	2:14:05
1986	Rob de Castella, Australia	2:07:51
1987	Toshihiko Seko, Japan	2:11:50
1988	Ibrahim Hussein, Kenya	2:08:43
1989	Abebe Mekonnen, Ethiopia	2:09:06
1990	Gelindo Bordin, Italy	2:08:19
1991	Ibrahim Hussein, Kenya	2:11:06
1992	Ibrahim Hussein, Kenya	2:08:14
1993	Cosmas Ndeti, Kenya	2:09:33
1994	Cosmas Ndeti, Kenya	2:07:15*
1995	Cosmas Ndeti, Kenya	2:09:22
1996	Moses Tanui, Kenya	2:09:16
1997	Lameck Aguta, Kenya	2:10:34
1998	Moses Tanui, Kenya	2:07:34
1999	Joseph Chebet, Kenya	2:09:52
2000	Elijah Lagat, Kenya	2:09:47
2001	Lee Bong-Ju, South Korea	2:09:43
2002	Rodgers Rop, Kenya	2:09:02
2003	Robert Kipoech Cheruiyot, Kenya	2:10:11

*Course record.

WOMEN

Multiple winners: Rosa Mota, Uta Pippig and Fatuma Roba (3); Joan Benoit, Miki Gorman, Ingrid Kristiansen, Olga Markova and Catherine Ndereba (2).

Year		Time
1972	Nina Kuscsik, New York	3:08:58
1973	Jacqueline Hansen, California	3:05:59
1974	Miki Gorman, California	2:47:11
1975	Liane Winter, West Germany	2:42:24
1976	Kim Merritt, Wisconsin	2:47:10
1977	Miki Gorman, California	2:48:33
1978	Gayle Barron, Georgia	2:44:52
1979	Joan Benoit, Maine	2:35:15
1980	Jacqueline Gareau, Canada	2:34:28
1981	Allison Roe, New Zealand	2:26:46
1982	Charlotte Teske, West Germany	2:29:33
1983	Joan Benoit, Maine	2:22:43
1984	Lorraine Moller, New Zealand	2:29:28
1985	Lisa Larsen Weidenbach, Mass	2:34:06
1986	Ingrid Kristiansen, Norway	2:24:55
1987	Rosa Mota, Portugal	2:25:21
1988	Rosa Mota, Portugal	2:24:30

Year		Time
1989	Ingrid Kristiansen, Norway	2:24:33
1990	Rosa Mota, Portugal	2:25:23
1991	Wanda Panfil, Poland	2:24:18
1992	Olga Markova, CIS	2:23:43
1993	Olga Markova, Russia	2:25:27
1994	Uta Pippig, Germany	2:21:45
1995	Uta Pippig, Germany	2:25:11
1996	Uta Pippig, Germany	2:27:12
1997	Fatuma Roba, Ethiopia	2:26:23
1998	Fatuma Roba, Ethiopia	2:23:21
1999	Fatuma Roba, Ethiopia	2:23:25
2000	Catherine Ndereba, Kenya	2:26:11
2001	Catherine Ndereba, Kenya	2:23:53
2002	Margaret Okayo, Kenya	2:20:43*
2003	Svetlana Zakharova, Russia	2:25:20

*Course record.

Track & Field (Cont.)
New York City

Started in 1970, the New York City Marathon is run in the fall, usually on the first Sunday in November. The route winds through all of the city's five boroughs and finishes in Central Park.

MEN

Multiple winners: Bill Rodgers (4); Alberto Salazar (3); Tom Fleming, John Kagwe, Orlando Pizzolato and German Silva (2).

Year		Time	Year		Time	Year		Time
1970	Gary Muhrcke, USA	2:31:38	1982	Alberto Salazar, USA	2:09:29	1994	German Silva, MEX	2:11:21
1971	Norman Higgins, USA	2:22:54	1983	Rod Dixon, NZE	2:08:59	1995	German Silva, MEX	2:11:00
1972	Sheldon Karlin, USA	2:27:52	1984	Orlando Pizzolato, ITA	2:14:53	1996	Giacomo Leone, ITA	2:09:54
1973	Tom Fleming, USA	2:21:54	1985	Orlando Pizzolato, ITA	2:11:34	1997	John Kagwe, KEN	2:08:12
1974	Norbert Sander, USA	2:26:30	1986	Gianni Poli, ITA	2:11:06	1998	John Kagwe, KEN	2:08:45
1975	Tom Fleming, USA	2:19:27	1987	Ibrahim Hussein, KEN	2:11:01	1999	Joseph Chebet, KEN	2:09:14
1976	Bill Rodgers, USA	2:10:09	1988	Steve Jones, WAL	2:08:20	2000	Abdelkhader El Mouaziz,	
1977	Bill Rodgers, USA	2:11:28	1989	Juma Ikangaa, TAN	2:08:01		MOR	2:10:08
1978	Bill Rodgers, USA	2:12:12	1990	Douglas Wakiihuri, KEN	2:12:39	2001	Tesfaye Jifar, ETH	2:07:43*
1979	Bill Rodgers, USA	2:11:42	1991	Salvador Garcia, MEX	2:09:28	2002	Rodgers Rop, KEN	2:08:07
1980	Alberto Salazar, USA	2:09:41	1992	Willie Mtolo, S. Afr.	2:09:29	*Course record.		
1981	Alberto Salazar, USA	2:08:13	1993	Andres Espinosa, MEX	2:10:04			

WOMEN

Multiple winners: Grete Waitz (9); Miki Gorman, Nina Kuscsik and Tegla Loroupe (2).

Year		Time	Year		Time	Year		Time
1970	No Finisher		1982	Grete Waitz, NOR	2:27:14	1994	Tegla Loroupe, KEN	2:27:37
1971	Beth Bonner, USA	2:55:22	1983	Grete Waitz, NOR	2:27:00	1995	Tegla Loroupe, KEN	2:28:06
1972	Nina Kuscsik, USA	3:08:41	1984	Grete Waitz, NOR	2:29:30	1996	Anuta Catuna, ROM	2:28:18
1973	Nina Kuscsik, USA	2:57:07	1985	Grete Waitz, NOR	2:28:34	1997	F. Rochat-Moser, SWI	2:28:43
1974	Katherine Switzer, USA	3:07:29	1986	Grete Waitz, NOR	2:28:06	1998	Franca Fiacconi, ITA	2:25:17
1975	Kim Merritt, USA	2:46:14	1987	Priscilla Welch, GBR	2:30:17	1999	Adriana Fernandez, MEX	2:25:06
1976	Miki Gorman, USA	2:39:11	1988	Grete Waitz, NOR	2:28:07	2000	Ludmila Petrova, RUS	2:25:45
1977	Miki Gorman, USA	2:43:10	1989	Ingrid Kristiansen, NOR	2:25:30	2001	Margaret Okayo, KEN	2:24:21*
1978	Grete Waitz, NOR	2:32:30	1990	Wanda Panfil, POL	2:30:45	2002	Joyce Chepchumba, KEN	2:25:56
1979	Grete Waitz, NOR	2:27:33	1991	Liz McColgan, GBR	2:27:23	*Course record.		
1980	Grete Waitz, NOR	2:25:41	1992	Lisa Ondieki, AUS	2:24:40			
1981	Allison Roe, NZE	2:25:29	1993	Uta Pippig, GER	2:26:24			

Annual Awards
Track & Field News Athletes of the Year

Voted on by an international panel of track and field experts and presented since 1959 for men and 1974 for women.

MEN

Multiple winners: Hicham El Guerrouj and Carl Lewis (3); Sergey Bubka, Sebastian Coe, Haile Gebrselassie, Michael Johnson, Alberto Juantorena, Noureddine Morceli, Jim Ryun and Peter Snell (2).

Year		Event	Year		Event
1959	Martin Lauer, W. Germany	110H/Decathlon	1981	Sebastian Coe, Great Britain	800/1500
1960	Rafer Johnson, USA	Decathlon	1982	Carl Lewis, USA	100/200/Long Jump
1961	Ralph Boston, USA	Long Jump/110 Hurdles	1983	Carl Lewis, USA	100/200/Long Jump
1962	Peter Snell, New Zealand	800/1500	1984	Carl Lewis, USA	100/200/Long Jump
1963	C.K. Yang, Taiwan	Decathlon/Pole Vault	1985	Said Aouita, Morocco	1500/5000
1964	Peter Snell, New Zealand	800/1500	1986	Yuri Sedykh, USSR	Hammer Throw
1965	Ron Clarke, Australia	5000/10,000	1987	Ben Johnson, Canada	100
1966	Jim Ryun, USA	800/1500	1988	Sergey Bubka, USSR	Pole Vault
1967	Jim Ryun, USA	1500	1989	Roger Kingdom, USA	110 Hurdles
1968	Bob Beamon, USA	Long Jump	1990	Michael Johnson, USA	200/400
1969	Bill Toomey, USA	Decathlon	1991	Sergey Bubka, USSR	Pole Vault
1970	Randy Matson, USA	Shot Put	1992	Kevin Young, USA	400 Hurdles
1971	Rod Milburn, USA	110 Hurdles	1993	Noureddine Morceli, Algeria	Mile/1500/3000
1972	Lasse Viren, Finland	5000/10,000	1994	Noureddine Morceli, Algeria	Mile/1500/3000
1973	Ben Jipcho, Kenya	1500/5000/Steeplechase	1995	Haile Gebrselassie, Ethiopia	5000/10,000
1974	Rick Wohlhuter, USA	800/1500	1996	Michael Johnson, USA	200/400
1975	John Walker, New Zealand	800/1500	1997	Wilson Kipketer, Denmark	800
1976	Alberto Juantorena, Cuba	400/800	1998	Haile Gebrselassie, Ethiopia	3000/5000/10,000
1977	Alberto Juantorena, Cuba	400/800	1999	Hicham El Guerrouj, Morocco	Mile/1500
1978	Henry Rono, Kenya	5000/10,000/Steeplechase	2000	Virgilijus Alekna , Lithuania	Discus
1979	Sebastian Coe, Great Britain	800/1500	2001	Hicham El Guerrouj, Morocco	Mile/1500
1980	Edwin Moses, USA	400 Hurdles	2002	Hicham El Guerrouj, Morocco	Mile/1500

WOMEN

Multiple winners: Marita Koch (4); Marion Jones and Jackie Joyner-Kersee (3); Evelyn Ashford (2).

Year		Event
1974	Irena Szewinska, Poland	100/200/400
1975	Faina Melnik, USSR	Shot Put/Discus
1976	Tatiana Kazankina, USSR	800/1500
1977	Rosemarie Ackermann, E. Germany	High Jump
1978	Marita Koch, E. Germany	100/200/400
1979	Marita Koch, E. Germany	100/200/400
1980	Ilona Briesenick, E. Germany	Shot Put
1981	Evelyn Ashford, USA	100/200
1982	Marita Koch, E. Germany	100/200/400
1983	Jarmila Kratochvilova, Czech	200/400/800
1984	Evelyn Ashford, USA	100
1985	Marita Koch, E. Germany	100/200/400
1986	Jackie Joyner-Kersee, USA	Heptathlon/Long Jump
1987	Jackie Joyner-Kersee, USA	100H/Heptathlon/LJ
1988	Florence Griffith Joyner, USA	100/200

Year		Event
1989	Ana Quirot, Cuba	400/800
1990	Merlene Ottey, Jamaica	100/200
1991	Heike Henkel, Germany	High Jump
1992	Heike Drechsler, Germany	Long Jump
1993	Wang Junxia, China	1500/3000/10,000
1994	Jackie Joyner-Kersee, USA	100H/Heptathlon/LJ
1995	Sonia O'Sullivan, Ireland	1500/3000/5000
1996	Svetlana Masterkova, Russia	800/1500
1997	Marion Jones, USA	100/200
1998	Marion Jones, USA	100/200/LJ
1999	Gabriela Szabo, Romania	3000/5000
2000	Marion Jones, USA	100/200/LJ
2001	Stacy Dragila, USA	Pole Vault
2002	Paula Radcliffe, Gr. Britain	3000/5000/10k/Mar

SWIMMING & DIVING

FINA World Championships

While the Summer Olympics have served as the unofficial world championships for swimming and diving throughout the centuries, a separate World Championship meet was started in 1973 by the Federation Internationale de Natation Amateur (FINA). The meet has varied between being held every two years, every three years or every four years. Currently it is held every two years. Sites have been Belgrade (1973); Cali, COL (1975); West Berlin (1978); Guayaquil, ECU (1982); Madrid (1986); Perth (1991 & 98), Rome (1994), Fukuoka, JPN (2001) and Barcelona (2003). Looking forward, the Championships will be held in Montreal (2005) and Melbourne (2007).

MEN

Most gold medals (including relays): Ian Thorpe (11); Grant Hackett and Jim Montgomery (7); Matt Biondi, Michael Klim and Aleksandr Popov (6); Rowdy Gaines (5); Joe Bottom, Tamas Darnyi, Michael Gross, Tom Jager, David McCagg, Aaron Peirsol, Michael Phelps, Vladimir Salnikov, Tim Shaw and Matt Welsh (4); Billy Forrester, Andras Hargitay, Roland Matthes, John Murphy, Jeff Rouse, Norbert Rozsa and David Wilkie (3).

50-Meter Freestyle

Year		Time	
1973-82 Not held			
1986	Tom Jager, USA	22.49	
1991	Tom Jager, USA	22.16	
1994	Aleksandr Popov, RUS	22.17	
1998	Bill Pilczuk, USA	22.29	
2001	Anthony Ervin, USA	22.09	
2003	Aleksandr Popov, RUS	21.92	CR

100-Meter Freestyle

Year		Time	
1973	Jim Montgomery, USA	51.70	
1975	Tim Shaw, USA	51.25	
1978	David McCagg, USA	50.24	
1982	Jorg Woithe, E. Ger	50.18	
1986	Matt Biondi, USA	48.94	
1991	Matt Biondi, USA	49.18	
1994	Aleksandr Popov, RUS	49.12	
1998	Aleksandr Popov, RUS	48.93	
2001	Anthony Ervin, USA	48.33	CR
2003	Aleksandr Popov, RUS	48.42	

200-Meter Freestyle

Year		Time	
1973	Jim Montgomery, USA	1:53.02	
1975	Tim Shaw, USA	1:52.04	
1978	Billy Forrester, USA	1:51.02	
1982	Michael Gross, W. Ger	1:49.84	
1986	Michael Gross, W. Ger	1:47.92	
1991	Giorgio Lamberti, ITA	1:47.27	
1994	Antti Kasvio, FIN	1:47.32	
1998	Michael Klim, AUS	1:47.41	
2001	Ian Thorpe, AUS	1:44.06	WR
2003	Ian Thorpe, AUS	1:45.14	

400-Meter Freestyle

Year		Time	
1973	Rick DeMont, USA	3:58.18	
1975	Tim Shaw, USA	3:54.88	
1978	Vladimir Salnikov, USSR	3:51.94	
1982	Vladimir Salnikov, USSR	3:51.30	
1986	Rainer Henkel, W. Ger	3:50.05	
1991	Jorg Hoffman, GER	3:48.04	
1994	Kieren Perkins, AUS	3:43.80	WR
1998	Ian Thorpe, AUS	3:46.29	
2001	Ian Thorpe, AUS	3:40.17	WR
2003	Ian Thorpe, AUS	3:42.58	

800-Meter Freestyle

Year		Time	
1973-98 Not held			
2001	Ian Thorpe, AUS	7:39.16	WR
2003	Grant Hackett, AUS	7:43.82	

1500-Meter Freestyle

Year		Time	
1973	Stephen Holland, AUS	15:31.85	
1975	Tim Shaw, USA	15:28.92	
1978	Vladimir Salnikov, USSR	15:03.99	
1982	Vladimir Salnikov, USSR	15:01.77	
1986	Rainer Henkel, W. Ger	15:05.31	
1991	Jorg Hoffman, GER	14:50.36	WR
1994	Kieren Perkins, AUS	14:50.52	
1998	Grant Hackett, AUS	14:51.70	
2001	Grant Hackett, AUS	14:34.56	WR
2003	Grant Hackett, AUS	14:43.14	

50-Meter Backstroke

Year		Time	
1973-98 Not held			
2001	Randall Bal, USA	25.34	
2003	Thomas Rupprath, GER	24.80	WR

Swimming & Diving (Cont.)

100-Meter Backstroke

Year		Time
1973	Roland Matthes, E. Ger	.57.47
1975	Roland Matthes, E. Ger	.58.15
1978	Bob Jackson, USA	.56.36
1982	Dirk Richter, E. Ger	.55.95
1986	Igor Polianski, USSR	.55.58
1991	Jeff Rouse, USA	.55.23
1994	Martin Lopez-Zubero, SPA	.55.17
1998	Lenny Krayzelburg, USA	.55.00
2001	Matt Welsh, AUS	.54.31
2003	Aaron Peirsol, USA	.53.61 CR

200-Meter Backstroke

Year		Time
1973	Roland Matthes, E. Ger	2:01.87
1975	Zoltan Varraszto, HUN	2:05.05
1978	Jesse Vassallo, USA	2:02.16
1982	Rick Carey, USA	2:00.82
1986	Igor Polianski, USSR	1:58.78
1991	Martin Zubero, SPA	1:59.52
1994	Vladimir Selkov, RUS	1:57.42
1998	Lenny Krayzelburg, USA	1:58.84
2001	Aaron Peirsol, USA	1:57.13
2003	Aaron Peirsol, USA	1:55.92

50-Meter Breaststroke

Year		Time
1973-98 Not held		
2001	Oleg Lisogor, UKR	.27.52
2003	James Gibson, GBR	.27.56

100-Meter Breaststroke

Year		Time
1973	John Hencken, USA	1:04.02
1975	David Wilkie, GBR	1:04.26
1978	Walter Kusch, W. Ger	1:03.56
1982	Steve Lundquist, USA	1:02.75
1986	Victor Davis, CAN	1:02.71
1991	Norbert Rozsa, HUN	1:01.45
1994	Norbert Rozsa, HUN	1:01.24
1998	Frederik deBurghgraeve, BEL	1:01.34
2001	Roman Sloudnov, RUS	1:00.16
2003	Kosuke Kitajima, JPN	.59.78 WR

200-Meter Breaststroke

Year		Time
1973	David Wilkie, GBR	2:19.28
1975	David Wilkie, GBR	2:18.23
1978	Nick Nevid, USA	2:18.37
1982	Victor Davis, CAN	2:14.77 WR
1986	Jozsef Szabo, HUN	2:14.27
1991	Mike Barrowman, USA	2:11.23 WR
1994	Norbert Rozsa, HUN	2:12.81
1998	Kurt Grote, USA	2:13.40
2001	Brendan Hansen, USA	2:10.69
2003	Kosuke Kitajima, JPN	2:09.42 WR

50-Meter Butterfly

Year		Time
1973-98 Not held		
2001	Geoff Huegill, AUS	.23.50
2003	Matt Welsh, AUS	.23.43 WR

100-Meter Butterfly

Year		Time
1973	Bruce Robertson, CAN	.55.69
1975	Greg Jagenburg, USA	.55.63
1978	Joe Bottom, USA	.54.30
1982	Matt Gribble, USA	.53.88
1986	Pablo Morales, USA	.53.54
1991	Anthony Nesty, SUR	.53.29
1994	Rafal Szukala, POL	.53.51
1998	Michael Klim, AUS	.52.25
2001	Lars Frolander, SWE	.52.10
2003	Ian Crocker, USA	.50.98 WR

200-Meter Butterfly

Year		Time
1973	Robin Backhaus, USA	2:03.32
1975	Billy Forrester, USA	2:01.95
1978	Mike Bruner, USA	1:59.38
1982	Michael Gross, W. Ger	1:58.85
1986	Michael Gross, W. Ger	1:56.53
1991	Melvin Stewart, USA	1:55.69 WR
1994	Denis Pankratov, RUS	1:56.54
1998	Denys Sylantyev, UKR	1:56.61
2001	Michael Phelps, USA	1:54.58 WR
2003	Michael Phelps, USA	1:54.35

200-Meter Individual Medley

Year		Time
1973	Gunnar Larsson, SWE	2:08.36
1975	Andras Hargitay, HUN	2:07.72
1978	Graham Smith, CAN	2:03.65 WR
1982	Alexander Sidorenko, USSR	2:03.30
1986	Tamás Darnyi, HUN	2:01.57
1991	Tamás Darnyi, HUN	1:59.36 WR
1994	Janis Sievinen, FIN	1:58.16 WR
1998	Marcel Wouda, NET	2:01.18
2001	Massimiliano Rosolino, ITA	1:59.71
2003	Michael Phelps, USA	1:56.04 WR

400-Meter Individual Medley

Year		Time
1973	Andras Hargitay, HUN	4:31.11
1975	Andras Hargitay, HUN	4:32.57
1978	Jesse Vassallo, USA	4:20.05 WR
1982	Ricardo Prado, BRA	4:19.78 WR
1986	Tamás Darnyi, HUN	4:18.98
1991	Tamás Darnyi, HUN	4:12.36 WR
1994	Tom Dolan, USA	4:12.30 WR
1998	Tom Dolan, USA	4:14.95
2001	Alessio Boggiatto, ITA	4:13.15
2003	Michael Phelps, USA	4:09.09 WR

4 x 100-Meter Freestyle Relay

Year		Time
1973	United States	3:27.18
1975	United States	3:24.85
1978	United States	3:19.74
1982	United States	3:19.26 WR
1986	United States	3:19.98
1991	United States	3:17.15
1994	United States	3:16.90
1998	United States	3:16.69
2001	Australia	3:14.10
2003	Russia	3:14.06 WR

4 x 200-Meter Freestyle Relay

Year		Time
1973	United States	7:33.22 WR
1975	West Germany	7:39.44
1978	United States	7:20.82
1982	United States	7:21.09
1986	East Germany	7:15.91
1991	Germany	7:13.50 CR
1994	Sweden	7:17.34
1998	Australia	7:12.48
2001	Australia	7:04.66 WR
2003	Australia	7:08.58

4 x 100-Meter Medley Relay

Year		Time
1973	United States	3:49.49
1975	United States	3:49.00
1978	United States	3:44.63
1982	United States	3:40.84 WR
1986	United States	3:41.25
1991	United States	3:39.66
1994	United States	3:37.74
1998	Australia	3:37.98
2001	Australia	3:35.35
2003	United States	3:31.54 WR

WOMEN

Most gold medals (including relays): Kornelia Ender (8); Kristin Otto (7); Jenny Thompson (6); Inge De Bruijn, Hannah Stockbauer and Luo Xuejuan (5); Tracy Caulkins, Heike Friedrich, Le Jingyi, Jana Klochkova, Rosemarie Kother and Ulrike Richter (4); Hannalore Anke, Lu Bin, He Cihong, Janet Evans, Nicole Haislett, Lui Limin, Birgit Meineke, Joan Pennington, Manuela Stellmach, Petria Thomas, Amy Van Dyken, Renate Vogel and Cynthia Woodhead (3).

50-Meter Freestyle

Year		Time	
1973-82 Not held			
1986	Tamara Costache, ROM	.25.28	WR
1991	Zhuang Yong, CHN	.25.47	
1994	Le Jingyi, CHN	.24.51	WR
1998	Amy Van Dyken, USA	.25.15	
2001	Inge de Bruijn, NED	.24.47	
2003	Inge de Bruijn, NED	.24.47	

100-Meter Freestyle

Year		Time	
1973	Kornelia Ender, E. Ger	.57.54	
1975	Kornelia Ender, E. Ger	.56.50	
1978	Barbara Krause, E. Ger	.55.68	
1982	Birgit Meineke, E. Ger	.55.79	
1986	Kristin Otto, E. Ger	.55.05	
1991	Nicole Haislett, USA	.55.17	
1994	Le Jingyi, CHN	.54.01	WR
1998	Jenny Thompson, USA	.54.95	
2001	Inge de Bruijn, NED	.54.18	
2003	Hanna-Maria Seppala, FIN	.54.37	

200-Meter Freestyle

Year		Time	
1973	Keena Rothhammer, USA	.2:04.99	
1975	Shirley Babashoff, USA	.2:02.50	
1978	Cynthia Woodhead, USA	.1:58.53	WR
1982	Annemarie Verstappen, NED	.1:59.53	
1986	Heike Friedrich, E. Ger	.1:58.26	
1991	Hayley Lewis, AUS	.2:00.48	
1994	Franziska Van Almsick, GER	.1:56.78	WR
1998	Claudia Poll, CRC	.1:58.90	
2001	Giaan Rooney, AUS	.1:58.57	
2003	Alena Popchenko, BLR	.1:58.32	

400-Meter Freestyle

Year		Time	
1973	Heather Greenwood, USA	.4:20.28	
1975	Shirley Babashoff, USA	.4:22.70	
1978	Tracey Wickham, AUS	.4:06.28	WR
1982	Carmela Schmidt. E. Ger	.4:08.98	
1986	Heike Friedrich, E. Ger	.4:07.45	
1991	Janet Evans, USA	.4:08.63	
1994	Yang Aihua, CHN	.4:09.64	
1998	Yan Chen, CHN	.4:06.72	
2001	Yana Klochkova, UKR	.4:07.30	
2003	Hannah Stockbauer, GER	.4:06.75	

800-Meter Freestyle

Year		Time	
1973	Novella Calligaris, ITA	.8:52.97	
1975	Jenny Turrall, AUS	.8:44.75	
1978	Tracey Wickham, AUS	.8:25.94	
1982	Kim Linehan, USA	.8:27.48	
1986	Astrid Strauss, E. Ger	.8:28.24	
1991	Janet Evans, USA	.8:24.05	
1994	Janet Evans, USA	.8:29.85	
1998	Brooke Bennett, USA	.8:28.71	
2001	Hannah Stockbauer, GER	.8:24.66	
2003	Hannah Stockbauer, GER	.8:23.66	CR

1500-Meter Freestyle

Year		Time	
1973-98 Not held			
2001	Hannah Stockbauer, GER	.16:01.02	
2003	Hannah Stockbauer, GER	.16:00.18	CR

50-Meter Backstroke

Year		Time	
1973-98 Not held			
2001	Haley Cope, USA	.28.51	
2003	Nina Zhivanevskaya, ESP	.28.48	CR

100-Meter Backstroke

Year		Time	
1973	Ulrike Richter, E. Ger	.1:05.42	
1975	Ulrike Richter, E. Ger	.1:03.30	
1978	Linda Jezek, USA	.1:02.55	
1982	Kristin Otto, E. Ger	.1:01.30	
1986	Betsy Mitchell, USA	.1:01.74	
1991	Krisztina Egerszegi, HUN	.1:01.78	
1994	He Cihong, CHN	.1:00.57	WR
1998	Lea Maurer, USA	.1:01.16	
2001	Natalie Coughlin, USA	.1:00.37	
2003	Antje Buschschulte, GER	.1:00.50	

200-Meter Backstroke

Year		Time	
1973	Melissa Belote, USA	.2:20.52	
1975	Birgit Treiber, E. Ger	.2:15.46	WR
1978	Linda Jezek, USA	.2:11.93	WR
1982	Cornelia Sirch, E. Ger	.2:09.91	WR
1986	Cornelia Sirch, E. Ger	.2:11.37	
1991	Krisztina Egerszegi, HUN	.2:09.15	
1994	He Cihong, CHN	.2:07.40	
1998	Roxanna Maracineanu, FRA	.2:11.26	
2001	Diana Iuliana Mocanu, ROM	.2:09.94	
2003	Katy Sexton, GBR	.2:08.74	

50-Meter Breaststroke

Year		Time	
1973-82 Not held			
2001	Luo Xuejuan, CHN	.30.84	
2003	Luo Xuejuan, CHN	.30.67	

100-Meter Breaststroke

Year		Time	
1973	Renate Vogel, E. Ger	.1:13.74	
1975	Hannalore Anke, E. Ger	.1:12.72	
1978	Julia Bogdanova, USSR	.1:10.31	WR
1982	Ute Geweniger, E. Ger	.1:09.14	
1986	Sylvia Gerasch, E. Ger	.1:08.11	WR
1991	Linley Frame, AUS	.1:08.81	
1994	Samantha Riley, AUS	.1:07.69	WR
1998	Kristy Kowal, USA	.1:08.42	
2001	Luo Xuejuan, CHN	.1:07.18	CR
2003	Luo Xuejuan, CHN	.1:06.80	

200-Meter Breaststroke

Year		Time	
1973	Renate Vogel, E. Ger	.2:40.01	
1975	Hannalore Anke, E. Ger	.2:37.25	
1978	Lina Kachushite, USSR	.2:31.42	WR
1982	Svetlana Varganova, USSR	.2:28.82	
1986	Silke Hoerner, E. Ger	.2:27.40	WR
1991	Elena Volkova, USSR	.2:29.53	
1994	Samantha Riley, AUS	.2:26.87	
1998	Agnes Kovacs, HUN	.2:25.45	
2001	Agnes Kovacs, HUN	.2:24.90	
2003	Amanda Beard, USA	.2:22.99	WR

50-Meter Butterfly

Year		Time	
1973-98 Not held			
2001	Inge de Bruijn, NED	.25.90	
2003	Inge de Bruijn, NED	.25.84	CR

Swimming & Diving (Cont.)

100-Meter Butterfly

Year		Time	
1973	Kornelia Ender, E. Ger	1:02.53	
1975	Kornelia Ender, E. Ger	1:01.24	**WR**
1978	Joan Pennington, USA	1:00.20	
1982	Mary T. Meagher, USA	.59.41	
1986	Kornelia Gressler, E. Ger	.59.51	
1991	Qian Hong, CHN	.59.68	
1994	Liu Limin, CHN	.58.98	
1998	Jenny Thompson, USA	.58.46	
2001	Petria Thomas, AUS	.58.27	
2003	Jenny Thompson, USA	.57.96	

200-Meter Butterfly

Year		Time	
1973	Rosemarie Kother, E. Ger	2:13.76	
1975	Rosemarie Kother, E. Ger	2:15.92	
1978	Tracy Caulkins, USA	2:09.78	**WR**
1982	Ines Geissler, E. Ger	2:08.66	
1986	Mary T. Meagher, USA	2:08.41	
1991	Summer Sanders, USA	2:09.24	
1994	Liu Limin, CHN	2:07.25	**CR**
1998	Susie O'Neill, AUS	2:07.93	
2001	Petria Thomas, AUS	2:06.73	**CR**
2003	Otylia Jedrzejczak, POL	2:07.56	

200-Meter Individual Medley

Year		Time	
1973	Andre Huebner, E. Ger	2:20.51	
1975	Kathy Heddy, USA	2:19.80	
1978	Tracy Caulkins, USA	2:19.80	**WR**
1982	Petra Schneider, E. Ger	2:11.79	
1986	Kristin Otto, E. Ger	2:15.56	
1991	Lin Li, CHN	2:13.40	
1994	Lu Bin, CHN	2:12.34	
1998	Yanyan Wu, CHN	2:10.88	
2001	Maggie Bowen, USA	2:11.93	
2003	Yana Klochkova, UKR	2:10.75	

400-Meter Individual Medley

Year		Time	
1973	Gudrun Wegner, E. Ger	4:57.71	
1975	Ulrike Tauber, E. Ger	4:52.76	
1978	Tracy Caulkins, USA	4:40.83	**WR**
1982	Petra Schneider, E. Ger	4:36.10	**WR**
1986	Kathleen Nord, E. Ger	4:43.75	
1991	Lin Li, CHN	4:41.45	
1994	Dai Guohong, CHN	4:39.14	
1998	Yan Chen, CHN	4:36.66	
2001	Yana Klochkova, UKR	4:36.98	
2003	Yana Klochkova, UKR	4:36.74	

4 x 100-Meter Freestyle Relay

Year		Time	
1973	East Germany	3:52.45	
1975	East Germany	3:49.37	
1978	United States	3:43.43	**WR**
1982	East Germany	3:43.97	
1986	East Germany	3:40.57	
1991	United States	3:43.26	
1994	China	3:37.91	**WR**
1998	United States	3:42.11	
2001	Germany	3:39.58	
2003	United States	3:38.09	

4 x 200-Meter Freestyle Relay

Year		Time	
1973-82	Not held		
1986	East Germany	7:59.33	**WR**
1991	Germany	8:02.56	
1994	China	7:57.96	
1998	Germany	8:01.46	
2001	Great Britain	7:58.69	
2003	United States	7:55.70	**CR**

4 x 100-Meter Medley Relay

Year		Time		Year		Time	
1973	East Germany	4:16.84		1991	United States	4:06.51	
1975	East Germany	4:14.74		1994	China	4:01.67	**CR**
1978	United States	4:08.21		1998	United States	4:01.93	
1982	East Germany	4:05.80	**WR**	2001	Australia	4:01.50	**CR**
1986	East Germany	4:04.82		2003	China	3:59.89	**CR**

Diving

Multiple Gold Medals: MEN—Greg Louganis and Dmitri Sautin (5); Phil Boggs (3); Klaus Dibiasi, Tian Liang and Yu Zhuocheng (2). WOMEN—Guo Jingjing (4); Irina Kalinina and Gao Min (3); Irina Lashko, Fu Mingxia and Wu Mingxia (2).

MEN

1-Meter Springboard

Year		Pts
1973-86	Not Held	
1991	Edwin Jongejans, NED	588.51
1994	Evan Stewart, ZIM	382.14
1998	Yu Zhuocheng, CHN	417.54
2001	Wang Feng, CHN	444.03
2003	Xu Xiang, CHN	431.94

3-Meter Springboard

Year		Pts
1973	Phil Boggs, USA	618.57
1975	Phil Boggs, USA	597.12
1978	Phil Boggs, USA	913.95
1982	Greg Louganis, USA	752.67
1986	Greg Louganis, USA	750.06
1991	Kent Ferguson, USA	650.25
1994	Yu Zhuocheng, CHN	655.44

Year		Pts
1998	Dmitri Sautin, RUS	746.79
2001	Dmitri Sautin, RUS	725.82
2003	Alexander Dobroskok, RUS	788.37

Platform

Year		Pts
1973	Klaus Dibiasi, ITA	559.53
1975	Klaus Dibiasi, ITA	547.98
1978	Greg Louganis, USA	844.11
1982	Greg Louganis, USA	634.26
1986	Greg Louganis, USA	668.58
1991	Sun Shuwei, CHN	626.79
1994	Dmitri Sautin, RUS	634.71
1998	Dmitri Sautin, RUS	750.99
2001	Tian Liang, CHN	688.77
2003	Alexandre Despatie, CAN	716.91

3-Meter Synchronized

Year		Pts
1973-98	Not held	
2001	Peng Bo & Wang Kenan, CHN	342.63
2003	Alexander Dobroskok & Dmitri Sautin, RUS	369.18

10-Meter Synchronized

Year		Pts
1973-98	Not held	
2001	Tian Liang & Hu Jia, CHN	361.41
2003	Mathew Helm & Robert Newbery, AUS	384.60

WOMEN

1-Meter Springboard

Year		Pts
1973-86	Not held	
1991	Gao Min, CHN	478.26
1994	Chen Lixia, CHN	279.30
1998	Irina Lashko, RUS	296.07
2001	Blythe Hartley, CAN	300.81
2003	Irina Lashko, AUS	299.97

3-Meter Springboard

Year		Pts
1973	Christa Koehler, E. Ger	442.17
1975	Irina Kalinina, USSR	489.81
1978	Irina Kalinina, USSR	691.43
1982	Megan Neyer, USA	501.03
1986	Gao Min, CHN	582.90
1991	Gao Min, CHN	539.01
1994	Tan Shuping, CHN	548.49
1998	Yulia Pakhalina, RUS	544.52
2001	Guo Jingjing, CHN	596.67
2003	Guo Jingjing, CHN	617.94

Platform

Year		Pts
1973	Ulrike Knape, SWE	406.77
1975	Janet Ely, USA	403.89

Year		Pts
1978	Irina Kalinina, USSR	412.71
1982	Wendy Wyland, USA	438.79
1986	Chen Lin, CHN	449.67
1991	Fu Mingxia, CHN	426.51
1994	Fu Mingxia, CHN	434.04
1998	Olena Zhupyna	550.41
2001	Xu Mian, CHN	532.65
2003	Emilie Heymans, CAN	597.45

3-Meter Synchronized

Year		Pts
1973-98	Not held	
2001	Wu Minxia & Guo Jingjing, CHN	347.31
2003	Wu Minxia & Guo Jingjing, CHN	357.30

10-Meter Synchronized

Year		Pts
1973-98	Not held	
2001	Duan Qing & Sang Xue, CHN	329.94
2003	Lao Lishi & Li Ting, CHN	344.58

ALPINE SKIING

World Cup Overall Champions

World Cup Overall Champions (downhill and slalom events combined) since the tour was organized in 1967.

MEN

Multiple winners: Marc Girardelli (5), Gustavo Thoeni and Pirmin Zurbriggen (4); Phil Mahre, Hermann Maier and Ingemar Stenmark (3); Stephan Eberharter, Jean-Claude Killy, Lasse Kjus and Karl Schranz (2).

Year		Year		Year	
1967	Jean-Claude Killy, France	1980	Andreas Wenzel, Liechtenstein	1993	Marc Girardelli, Luxembourg
1968	Jean-Claude Killy, France	1981	Phil Mahre, USA	1994	Kjetil Andre Aamodt, Norway
1969	Karl Schranz, Austria	1982	Phil Mahre, USA	1995	Alberto Tomba, Italy
		1983	Phil Mahre, USA	1996	Lasse Kjus, Norway
1970	Karl Schranz, Austria	1984	Pirmin Zurbriggen, Switzerland	1997	Luc Alphand, France
1971	Gustavo Thoeni, Italy	1985	Marc Girardelli, Luxembourg	1998	Hermann Maier, Austria
1972	Gustavo Thoeni, Italy	1986	Marc Girardelli, Luxembourg	1999	Lasse Kjus, Norway
1973	Gustavo Thoeni, Italy	1987	Pirmin Zurbriggen, Switzerland		
1974	Piero Gros, Italy	1988	Pirmin Zurbriggen, Switzerland	2000	Hermann Maier, Austria
1975	Gustavo Thoeni, Italy	1989	Marc Girardelli, Luxembourg	2001	Hermann Maier, Austria
1976	Ingemar Stenmark, Sweden			2002	Stephan Eberharter, Austria
1977	Ingemar Stenmark, Sweden	1990	Pirmin Zurbriggen, Switzerland	2003	Stephan Eberharter, Austria
1978	Ingemar Stenmark, Sweden	1991	Marc Girardelli, Luxembourg		
1979	Peter Luescher, Switzerland	1992	Paul Accola, Switzerland		

WOMEN

Multiple winners: Annemarie Moser-Proell (6); Petra Kronberger and Vreni Schneider (3); Janica Kostelic, Michela Figini, Nancy Greene, Erika Hess, Katja Seizinger, Maria Walliser and Hanni Wenzel (2).

Year		Year		Year	
1967	Nancy Greene, Canada	1975	Annemarie Moser-Pröll, Austria	1982	Erika Hess, Switzerland
1968	Nancy Greene, Canada	1976	Rosi Mittermaier, W. Germany	1983	Tamara McKinney, USA
1969	Gertrud Gabi, Austria	1977	Lise-Marie Morerod, Switzerland	1984	Erika Hess, Switzerland
1970	Michele Jacot, France	1978	Hanni Wenzel, Liechtenstein	1985	Michela Figini, Switzerland
1971	Annemarie Pröll, Austria	1979	Annemarie Moser-Pröll, Austria	1986	Maria Walliser, Switzerland
1972	Annemarie Pröll, Austria	1980	Hanni Wenzel, Liechtenstein	1987	Maria Walliser, Switzerland
1973	Annemarie Pröll, Austria	1981	Marie-Therese Nadig, Switzerland	1988	Michela Figini, Switzerland
1974	Annemarie Pröll, Austria			1989	Vreni Schneider, Switzerland

Alpine Skiing (Cont.)

Year		Year		Year	
1990	Petra Kronberger, Austria	1995	Vreni Schneider, Switzerland	2000	Renate Goetschl, Austria
1991	Petra Kronberger, Austria	1996	Katja Seizinger, Germany	2001	Janica Kostelic, Croatia
1992	Petra Kronberger, Austria	1997	Pernilla Wiberg, Sweden	2002	Michaela Dorfmeister, Austria
1993	Anita Wachter, Austria	1998	Katja Seizinger, Germany	2003	Janica Kostelic, Croatia
1994	Vreni Schneider, Switzerland	1999	Alexandra Meissnitzer, Austria		

World Cup Event Champions

World Cup Champions in each individual event since the tour was organized in 1967.

MEN

Downhill

Multiple winners: Franz Klammer (5); Luc Alphand, Franz Heinzer and Peter Muller (3); Roland Collumbin, Stephan Eberharter, Marc Girardelli, Helmut Hoflehner, Hermann Maier, Bernard Russi, Karl Schranz and Pirmin Zurbriggen (2).

Year		Year		Year	
1967	Jean-Claude Killy, France	1979	Peter Muller, Switzerland	1991	Franz Heinzer, Switzerland
1968	Gerhard Nenning, Austria	1980	Peter Muller, Switzerland	1992	Franz Heinzer, Switzerland
1969	Karl Schranz, Austria	1981	Harti Weirather, Austria	1993	Franz Heinzer, Switzerland
1970	Karl Schranz, Austria	1982	Steve Podborski, Canada	1994	Marc Girardelli, Luxembourg
	Karl Cordin, Austria		Peter Muller, Switzerland	1995	Luc Alphand, France
1971	Bernard Russi, Switzerland	1983	Franz Klammer, Austria	1996	Luc Alphand, France
1972	Bernard Russi, Switzerland	1984	Urs Raber, Switzerland	1997	Luc Alphand, France
1973	Roland Collumbin, Switzerland	1985	Helmut Hoflehner, Austria	1998	Andreas Schifferer, Austria
1974	Roland Collumbin, Switzerland	1986	Peter Wirnsberger, Austria	1999	Lasse Kjus, Norway
1975	Franz Klammer, Austria	1987	Pirmin Zurbriggen, Switzerland	2000	Hermann Maier, Austria
1976	Franz Klammer, Austria	1988	Pirmin Zurbriggen, Switzerland	2001	Hermann Maier, Austria
1977	Franz Klammer, Austria	1989	Marc Girardelli, Luxembourg	2002	Stephan Eberharter, Austria
1978	Franz Klammer, Austria	1990	Helmut Hoflehner, Austria	2003	Stephan Eberharter, Austria

Slalom

Multiple winners: Ingemar Stenmark (8); Alberto Tomba (4); Jean-Noel Augert and Marc Girardelli (3); Armin Bittner, Thomas Sykora and Gustavo Thoeni (2).

Year		Year		Year	
1967	Jean-Claude Killy, France	1979	Ingemar Stenmark, Sweden	1992	Alberto Tomba, Italy
1968	Domeng Giovanoli, Switzerland	1980	Ingemar Stenmark, Sweden	1993	Tomas Fogdof, Sweden
1969	Jean-Noel Augert, France	1981	Ingemar Stenmark, Sweden	1994	Alberto Tomba, Italy
1970	Patrick Russel, France	1982	Phil Mahre, USA	1995	Alberto Tomba, Italy
	Alain Penz, France	1983	Ingemar Stenmark, Sweden	1996	Sebastien Amiez, France
1971	Jean-Noel Augert, France	1984	Marc Girardelli, Luxembourg	1997	Thomas Sykora, Austria
1972	Jean-Noel Augert, France	1985	Marc Girardelli, Luxembourg	1998	Thomas Sykora, Austria
1973	Gustavo Thoeni, Italy	1986	Rok Petrovic, Yugoslavia	1999	Thomas Stangassinger, Austria
1974	Gustavo Thoeni, Italy	1987	Bojan Krizaj, Yugoslavia	2000	Kjetil Andre Aamodt, Norway
1975	Ingemar Stenmark, Sweden	1988	Alberto Tomba, Italy	2001	Benjamin Raich, Austria
1976	Ingemar Stenmark, Sweden	1989	Armin Bittner, West Germany	2002	Ivica Kostelic, Croatia
1977	Ingemar Stenmark, Sweden	1990	Armin Bittner, West Germany	2003	Kalle Palander, Finland
1978	Ingemar Stenmark, Sweden	1991	Marc Girardelli, Luxembourg		

Giant Slalom

Multiple winners: Ingemar Stenmark (8); Michael von Gruenigen and Alberto Tomba (4); Hermann Maier and Pirmin Zurbriggen (3); Joel Gaspoz, Jean-Claude Killy, Phil Mahre and Gustavo Thoeni (2).

Year		Year		Year	
1967	Jean-Claude Killy, France	1981	Ingemar Stenmark, Sweden	1993	Kjetil Andre Aamodt, Norway
1968	Jean-Claude Killy, France	1982	Phil Mahre, USA	1994	Christian Mayer, Austria
1969	Karl Schranz, Austria	1983	Phil Mahre, USA	1995	Alberto Tomba, Italy
1970	Gustavo Thoeni, Italy	1984	Ingemar Stenmark, Sweden	1996	Michael von Gruenigen, Switzerland
1971	Patrick Russel, France		Pirmin Zurbriggen, Switzerland		
1972	Gustavo Thoeni, Italy	1985	Marc Girardelli, Luxembourg	1997	Michael von Gruenigen, Switzerland
1973	Hans Hinterseer, Austria	1986	Joel Gaspoz, Switzerland		
1974	Piero Gros, Italy	1987	Joel Gaspoz, Switzerland	1998	Hermann Maier, Austria
1975	Ingemar Stenmark, Sweden		Pirmin Zurbriggen, Switzerland	1999	Michael von Gruenigen, Switzerland
1976	Ingemar Stenmark, Sweden	1988	Alberto Tomba, Italy		
1977	Heini Hemmi, Switzerland	1989	Pirmin Zurbriggen, Switzerland	2000	Hermann Maier, Austria
	Ingemar Stenmark, Sweden	1990	Ole-Cristian Furuseth, Norway	2001	Hermann Maier, Austria
1978	Ingemar Stenmark, Sweden		Gunther Mader, Austria	2002	Frederic Covili, France
1979	Ingemar Stenmark, Sweden	1991	Alberto Tomba, Italy	2003	Michael von Gruenigen, Switzerland
1980	Ingemar Stenmark, Sweden	1992	Alberto Tomba, Italy		

Super G

Multiple winners: Hermann Maier and Pirmin Zurbriggen (4); Stephan Eberharter (2).

Year		Year		Year	
1986	Markus Wasmeier, W. Ger.	1992	Paul Accola, Switzerland	1998	Hermann Maier, Austria
1987	Pirmin Zurbriggen, Switzerland	1993	Kjetil Andre Aamodt, Norway	1999	Hermann Maier, Austria
1988	Pirmin Zurbriggen, Switzerland	1994	Jan Einar Thorsen, Norway	2000	Hermann Maier, Austria
1989	Pirmin Zurbriggen, Switzerland	1995	Peter Runggaldier, Italy	2001	Hermann Maier, Austria
1990	Pirmin Zurbriggen, Switzerland	1996	Atle Skaardal, Norway	2002	Stephan Eberharter, Austria
1991	Franz Heinzer, Switzerland	1997	Luc Alphand, France	2003	Stephan Eberharter, Austria

Combined

Multiple winners: Marc Girardelli and Andreas Wenzel (4); Kjetil Andre Aamodt and Phil Mahre (3); Pirmin Zurbriggen (2).

Year		Year		Year	
1979	Andreas Wenzel, Liechtenstein	1987	Pirmin Zurbriggen, Switzerland	1995	Marc Girardelli, Luxembourg
1980	Andreas Wenzel, Liechtenstein	1988	Hubert Strolz, Austria	1996	Gunther Mader, Austria
1981	Phil Mahre, USA	1989	Marc Girardelli, Luxembourg	1997-99	Not awarded
1982	Phil Mahre, USA	1990	Pirmin Zurbriggen, Switzerland	2000	Kjetil Andre Aamodt, Norway
1983	Phil Mahre, USA	1991	Marc Girardelli, Luxembourg	2001	Lasse Kjus, Norway
1984	Andreas Wenzel, Liechtenstein	1992	Paul Accola, Switzerland	2002	Kjetil Andre Aamodt, Norway
1985	Andreas Wenzel, Liechtenstein	1993	Marc Girardelli, Luxembourg	2003	Bode Miller, United States
1986	Markus Wasmeier, W. Ger	1994	Kjetil Andre Aamodt, Norway		

WOMEN
Downhill

Multiple winners: Annemarie Moser-Pröll (7); Michela Figini and Katja Seizinger (4); Renate Goetschl, Isolde Kostner, Isabelle Mir, Marie-Therese Nadig, Picabo Street, Bridgitte Totschnig-Habersatter and Maria Walliser (2).

Year		Year		Year	
1967	Marielle Goitschel, France	1978	Annemarie Moser-Pröll, Austria	1991	Chantal Bournissen, SWI
1968	Isabelle Mir, France	1979	Annemarie Moser-Pröll, Austria	1992	Katja Seizinger, Germany
	Olga Pall, Austria	1980	Marie-Therese Nadig, SWI	1993	Katja Seizinger, Germany
1969	Wiltrud Drexel, Austria	1981	Marie-Therese Nadig, SWI	1994	Katja Seizinger, Germany
1970	Isabelle Mir, France	1982	Marie-Cecile Gros-Gaudenier,	1995	Picabo Street, USA
1971	Annemarie Pröll, Austria		France	1996	Picabo Street, USA
1972	Annemarie Pröll, Austria	1983	Doris De Agostini, Switzerland	1997	Renate Goetschl, Austria
1973	Annemarie Pröll, Austria	1984	Maria Walliser, Switzerland	1998	Katja Seizinger, Germany
1974	Annemarie Pröll, Austria	1985	Michela Figini, Switzerland	1999	Renate Goetschl, Austria
1975	Annemarie Moser-Pröll, Austria	1986	Maria Walliser, Switzerland	2000	Regina Haeusl, Germany
1976	Bridgitte Totschnig-Habersatter,	1987	Michela Figini, Switzerland	2001	Isolde Kostner, Italy
	Austria	1988	Michela Figini, Switzerland	2002	Isolde Kostner, Italy
1977	Bridgitte Totschnig-Habersatter,	1989	Michela Figini, Switzerland	2003	Michaela Dorfmeister, Austria
	Austria	1990	Katrin Gutensohn-Knopf, GER		

Slalom

Multiple winners: Vreni Schneider (6); Erika Hess (5); Janica Kostelic, Marielle Goitschel, Britt Lafforgue, Lisa-Marie Morerod and Roswitha Steiner (2).

Year		Year		Year	
1967	Marielle Goitschel, France	1978	Hanni Wenzel, Liechtenstein	1991	Petra Kronberger, Austria
1968	Marielle Goitschel, France	1979	Regina Sackl, Austria	1992	Vreni Schneider, Switzerland
1969	Gertrud Gabl, Austria	1980	Perrine Pelene, France	1993	Vreni Schneider, Switzerland
1970	Ingrid Lafforgue, France	1981	Erika Hess, Switzerland	1994	Vreni Schneider, Switzerland
1971	Britt Lafforgue, France	1982	Erika Hess, Switzerland	1995	Vreni Schneider, Switzerland
1972	Britt Lafforgue, France	1983	Erika Hess, Switzerland	1996	Elfi Eder, Austria
1973	Patricia Emonet, France	1984	Tamara McKinney, USA	1997	Pernilla Wiberg, Sweden
1974	Christa Zechmeister,	1985	Erika Hess, Switzerland	1998	Ylva Nowen, Sweden
	West Germany	1986	Roswitha Steiner, Austria	1999	Sabine Egger, Austria
1975	Lisa-Marie Morerod,		Erika Hess, Switzerland	2000	Spela Pretnar, Slovenia
	Switzerland	1987	Corrine Schmidhauser,	2001	Janica Kostelic, Croatia
1976	Rosi Mittermaier,		Switzerland	2002	Laure Pequegnot, France
	West Germany	1988	Roswitha Steiner, Austria	2003	Janica Kostelic, Croatia
1977	Lisa-Marie Morerod,	1989	Vreni Schneider, Switzerland		
	Switzerland	1990	Vreni Schneider, Switzerland		

Giant Slalom

Multiple winners: Vreni Schneider (5); Lisa-Marie Morerod and Annemarie Moser-Pröll (3); Martina Ertl, Nancy Greene, Carole Merle, Sonja Nef, Anita Wachter and Hanni Wenzel (2).

Year		Year		Year	
1967	Nancy Greene, Canada	1971	Annemarie Pröll, Austria	1976	Lisa-Marie Morerod, SWI
1968	Nancy Greene, Canada	1972	Annemarie Pröll, Austria	1977	Lisa-Marie Morerod, SWI
1969	Marilyn Cochran, USA	1973	Monika Kaserer, Austria	1978	Lisa-Marie Morerod, SWI
1970	Michele Jacot, France	1974	Hanni Wenzel, Liechtenstein	1979	Christa Kinshofer, W. Ger.
	Francoise Macchi, France	1975	Annemarie Moser-Pröll, Austria	1980	Hanni Wenzel, Liechtenstein

Alpine Skiing (Cont.)

Year		Year		Year	
1981	Marie-Therese Nadig, SWI	1988	Mateja Svet, Yugoslavia	1997	Deborah Compagnoni, Italy
1982	Irene Epple, West Germany	1989	Vreni Schneider, Switzerland	1998	Martina Ertl, Germany
1983	Tamara McKinney, USA	1990	Anita Wachter, Austria	1999	Alexandra Meissnitzer, Austria
1984	Erika Hess, Switzerland	1991	Vreni Schneider, Switzerland	2000	Michaela Dorfmeister, Austria
1985	Maria Keihl, West Germany	1992	Carole Merle, France	2001	Sonja Nef, Switzerland
	Michela Figini, Switzerland	1993	Carole Merle, France	2002	Sonja Nef, Switzerland
1986	Vreni Schneider, Switzerland	1994	Anita Wachter, Austria	2003	Anja Paerson, Sweden
1987	Vreni Schneider, Switzerland	1995	Vreni Schneider, Switzerland		
	Maria Walliser, Switzerland	1996	Martina Ertl, Germany		

Super G

Multiple winners: Katja Seizinger (5); Carole Merle (4); Hilde Gerg (2).

Year		Year		Year	
1986	Maria Kiehl, West Germany	1992	Carole Merle, France	1998	Katja Seizinger, Germany
1987	Maria Walliser, Switzerland	1993	Katja Seizinger, Germany	1999	Alexandra Meissnitzer, Austria
1988	Michela Figini, Switzerland	1994	Katja Seizinger, Germany	2000	Renate Goetschl, Austria
1989	Carole Merle, France	1995	Katja Seizinger, Germany	2001	Regine Cavagnoud, France
1990	Carole Merle, France	1996	Katja Seizinger, Germany	2002	Hilde Gerg, Germany
1991	Carole Merle, France	1997	Hilde Gerg, Germany	2003	Carole Montillet, France

Combined

Multiple winners: Brigitte Oertli (5); Anita Wachter and Hanni Wenzel (3); Sabine Ginther, Renate Goetschl, Janica Kostelic and Pernilla Wiberg (2).

Year		Year		Year	
1979	Annemarie Moser-Pröll, Austria	1986	Maria Walliser, Switzerland	1994	Pernilla Wiberg, Sweden
	Hanni Wenzel, Liechtenstein	1987	Brigitte Oertli, Switzerland	1995	Pernilla Wiberg, Sweden
1980	Hanni Wenzel, Liechtenstein	1988	Brigitte Oertli, Switzerland	1996	Anita Wachter, Austria
1981	Maria-Therese Nadig,	1989	Brigitte Oertli, Switzerland	1997–99	Not Awarded
	Switzerland	1989	Brigitte Oertli, Switzerland	2000	Renate Goetschl, Austria
1982	Irene Epple, West Germany	1990	Anita Wachter, Austria	2001	Janica Kostelic, Croatia
1983	Hanni Wenzel, Liechtenstein	1991	Sabine Ginther, Austria	2002	Renate Goetschl, Austria
1984	Erika Hess, Switzerland	1992	Sabine Ginther, Austria	2003	Janica Kostelic, Croatia
1985	Brigitte Oertli, Switzerland	1993	Anita Wachter, Austria		

TOUR DE FRANCE

The world's premier cycling event, the Tour de France is staged throughout the country (sometimes passing through neighboring countries) over four weeks. The 1946 Tour, however, the first after World War II, was only a five-day race.

Multiple winners: Jacques Anquetil, Lance Armstrong, Bernard Hinault, Miguel Induráin and Eddy Merckx (5); Louison Bobet, Greg LeMond and Philippe Thys (3); Gino Bartali Ottavio Bottecchia, Fausto Coppi, Laurent Fignon, Nicholas Frantz, Firmin Lambot, André Leducq, Sylvere Maes, Antonin Magne, Lucien Petit-Breton and Bernard Thevenet (2).

Year		Year		Year	
1903	Maurice Garin, France	1937	Roger Lapebie, France	1973	Luis Ocana, Spain
1904	Henri Cornet, France	1938	Gino Bartali, Italy	1974	Eddy Merckx, Belgium
1905	Louis Trousselier, France	1939	Sylvere Maes, Belgium	1975	Bernard Thevenet, France
1906	René Pottier, France	1940-45	Not held	1976	Lucien van Impe, Belgium
1907	Lucien Petit-Breton, France	1946	Jean Lazarides, France	1977	Bernard Thevenet, France
1908	Lucien Petit-Breton, France	1947	Jean Robic, France	1978	Bernard Hinault, France
1909	Francois Faber, Luxembourg	1948	Gino Bartali, Italy	1979	Bernard Hinault, France
1910	Octave Lapize, France	1949	Fausto Coppi, Italy	1980	Joop Zoetemelk, Netherlands
1911	Gustave Garrigou, France	1950	Ferdinand Kubler, Switzerland	1981	Bernard Hinault, France
1912	Odile Defraye, Belgium	1951	Hugo Koblet, Switzerland	1982	Bernard Hinault, France
1913	Philippe Thys, Belgium	1952	Fausto Coppi, Italy	1983	Laurent Fignon, France
1914	Philippe Thys, Belgium	1953	Louison Bobet, France	1984	Laurent Fignon, France
1915-18	Not held	1954	Louison Bobet, France	1985	Bernard Hinault, France
1919	Firmin Lambot, Belgium	1955	Louison Bobet, France	1986	Greg LeMond, USA
1920	Philippe Thys, Belgium	1956	Roger Walkowiak, France	1987	Stephen Roche, Ireland
1921	Léon Scieur, Belgium	1957	Jacques Anquetil, France	1988	Pedro Delgado, Spain
1922	Firmin Lambot, Belgium	1958	Charly Gaul, Luxembourg	1989	Greg LeMond, USA
1923	Henri Pelissier, France	1959	Federico Bahamontes, Spain	1990	Greg LeMond, USA
1924	Ottavio Bottecchia, Italy	1960	Gastone Nencini, Italy	1991	Miguel Induráin, Spain
1925	Ottavio Bottecchia, Italy	1961	Jacques Anquetil, France	1992	Miguel Induráin, Spain
1926	Lucien Buysse, Belgium	1962	Jacques Anquetil, France	1993	Miguel Induráin, Spain
1927	Nicholas Frantz, Luxembourg	1963	Jacques Anquetil, France	1994	Miguel Induráin, Spain
1928	Nicholas Frantz, Luxembourg	1964	Jacques Anquetil, France	1995	Miguel Induráin, Spain
1929	Maurice Dewaele, Belgium	1965	Felice Gimondi, Italy	1996	Bjarne Riis, Denmark
1930	André Leducq, France	1966	Lucien Aimar, France	1997	Jan Ullrich, Germany
1931	Antonin Magne, France	1967	Roger Pingeon, France	1998	Marco Pantani, Italy
1932	André Leducq, France	1968	Jan Janssen, Netherlands	1999	Lance Armstrong, USA
1933	Georges Speicher, France	1969	Eddy Merckx, Belgium	2000	Lance Armstrong, USA
1934	Antonin Magne, France	1970	Eddy Merckx, Belgium	2001	Lance Armstrong, USA
1935	Romain Maes, Belgium	1971	Eddy Merckx, Belgium	2002	Lance Armstrong, USA
1936	Sylvere Maes, Belgium	1972	Eddy Merckx, Belgium	2003	Lance Armstrong, USA

FIGURE SKATING
World Champions
Skaters who won World and Olympic championships in the same year are listed in **bold** type.

MEN

Multiple winners: Ulrich Salchow (10); Karl Schafer (7); Dick Button (5); Willy Bockl, Kurt Browning, Scott Hamilton and Hayes Jenkins and Alexei Yagudin (4); Emmerich Danzer, Gillis Grafstrom, Gustav Hugel, David Jenkins, Fritz Kachler, Ondrej Nepela and Elvis Stojko (3); Brian Boitano, Gilbert Fuchs, Jan Hoffmann, Felix Kaspar, Vladimir Kovalev, Evgeni Plushenko, and Tim Wood (2).

Year		Year		Year	
1896	Gilbert Fuchs, Germany	1935	Karl Schafer, Austria	1973	Ondrej Nepela, Czechoslovakia
1897	Gustav Hugel, Austria	1936	**Karl Schafer**, Austria	1974	Jan Hoffmann, E. Germany
1898	Henning Grenander, Sweden	1937	Felix Kaspar, Austria	1975	Sergie Volkov, USSR
1899	Gustav Hugel, Austria	1938	Felix Kaspar, Austria	1976	**John Curry**, Britain
1900	Gustav Hugel, Austria	1939	Graham Sharp, Britain	1977	Vladimir Kovalev, USSR
1901	Ulrich Salchow, Sweden	1940-46	Not held	1978	Charles Tickner, USA
1902	Ulrich Salchow, Sweden	1947	Hans Gerschwiler, Switzerland	1979	Vladimir Kovalev, USSR
1903	Ulrich Salchow, Sweden	1948	**Dick Button**, USA	1980	Jan Hoffmann, E. Germany
1904	Ulrich Salchow, Sweden	1949	Dick Button, USA	1981	Scott Hamilton, USA
1905	Ulrich Salchow, Sweden	1950	Dick Button, USA	1982	Scott Hamilton, USA
1906	Gilbert Fuchs, Germany	1951	Dick Button, USA	1983	Scott Hamilton, USA
1907	Ulrich Salchow, Sweden	1952	**Dick Button**, USA	1984	**Scott Hamilton**, USA
1908	**Ulrich Salchow**, Sweden	1953	Hayes Jenkins, USA	1985	Alexander Fadeev, USSR
1909	Ulrich Salchow, Sweden	1954	Hayes Jenkins, USA	1986	Brian Boitano, USA
1910	Ulrich Salchow, Sweden	1955	Hayes Jenkins, USA	1987	Brian Orser, Canada
1911	Ulrich Salchow, Sweden	1956	**Hayes Jenkins**, USA	1988	**Brian Boitano**, USA
1912	Fritz Kachler, Austria	1957	David Jenkins, USA	1989	Kurt Browning, Canada
1913	Fritz Kachler, Austria	1958	David Jenkins, USA	1990	Kurt Browning, Canada
1914	Gosta Sandhal, Sweden	1959	David Jenkins, USA	1991	Kurt Browning, Canada
1915-21	Not held	1960	Alan Giletti, France	1992	**Viktor Petrenko**, CIS
1922	Gillis Grafstrom, Sweden	1961	Not held	1993	Kurt Browning, Canada
1923	Fritz Kachler, Austria	1962	Donald Jackson, Canada	1994	Elvis Stojko, Canada
1924	**Gillis Grafstrom,** Sweden	1963	Donald McPherson, Canada	1995	Elvis Stojko, Canada
1925	Willy Bockl, Austria	1964	**Manfred Schnelldorfer,** W. Ger	1996	Todd Eldredge, USA
1926	Willy Bockl, Austria			1997	Elvis Stojko, Canada
1927	Willy Bockl, Austria	1965	Alain Calmat, France	1998	Alexei Yagudin, Russia
1928	Willy Bockl, Austria	1966	Emmerich Danzer, Austria	1999	Alexei Yagudin, Russia
1929	Gillis Grafstrom, Sweden	1967	Emmerich Danzer, Austria	2000	Alexei Yagudin, Russia
1930	Karl Schafer, Austria	1968	Emmerich Danzer, Austria	2001	Evgeni Plushenko, Russia
1931	Karl Schafer, Austria	1969	Tim Wood, USA	2002	**Alexei Yagudin**, Russia
1932	**Karl Schafer**, Austria	1970	Tim Wood, USA	2003	Evgeni Plushenko, Russia
1933	Karl Schafer, Austria	1971	Ondrej Nepela, Czechoslovakia		
1934	Karl Schafer, Austria	1972	**Ondrej Nepela**, Czechoslovakia		

WOMEN

Multiple winners: Sonja Henie (10); Carol Heiss, Michelle Kwan and Herma Planck Szabo (5); Lily Kronberger and Katarina Witt (4); Sjoukje Dijkstra, Peggy Fleming and Meray Horvath (3); Tenley Albright, Linda Fratianne, Anett Poetzsch, Beatrix Schuba, Barbara Ann Scott, Gabriele Seyfert, Megan Taylor, Alena Vrzanova and Kristi Yamaguchi (2).

Year		Year		Year	
1906	Madge Syers, Britain	1932	**Sonja Henie**, Norway	1958	Carol Heiss, USA
1907	Madge Syers, Britain	1933	Sonja Henie, Norway	1959	Carol Heiss, USA
1908	Lily Kronberger, Hungary	1934	Sonja Henie, Norway	1960	**Carol Heiss**, USA
1909	Lily Kronberger, Hungary	1935	Sonja Henie, Norway	1961	Not held
1910	Lily Kronberger, Hungary	1936	**Sonja Henie**, Norway	1962	Sjoukje Dijkstra, Netherlands
1911	Lily Kronberger, Hungary	1937	Cecilia Colledge, Britain	1963	Sjoukje Dijkstra, Netherlands
1912	Meray Horvath, Hungary	1938	Megan Taylor, Britain	1964	**Sjoukje Dijkstra**, Netherlands
1913	Meray Horvath, Hungary	1939	Megan Taylor, Britain	1965	Petra Burka, Canada
1914	Meray Horvath, Hungary	1940-46	Not held	1966	Peggy Fleming, USA
1915-21	Not held	1947	Barbara Ann Scott, Canada	1967	Peggy Fleming, USA
1922	Herma Planck-Szabo, Austria	1948	**Barbara Ann Scott**, Canada	1968	**Peggy Fleming**, USA
1923	Herma Planck-Szabo, Austria	1949	Alena Vrzanova, Czechoslovakia	1969	Gabriele Seyfert, E. Germany
1924	**Herma Planck-Szabo**, Austria	1950	Alena Vrzanova, Czechoslovakia	1970	Gabriele Seyfert, E. Germany
1925	Herma Planck-Szabo, Austria	1951	Jeannette Altwegg, Britain	1971	Beatrix Schuba, Austria
1926	Herma Planck-Szabo, Austria	1952	Jacqueline Du Bief, France	1972	**Beatrix Schuba**, Austria
1927	Sonja Henie, Norway	1953	Tenley Albright, USA	1973	Karen Magnussen, Canada
1928	**Sonja Henie**, Norway	1954	Gundi Busch, W. Germany	1974	Christine Errath, E. Germany
1929	Sonja Henie, Norway	1955	Tenley Albright, USA	1975	Dianne DeLeeuw, Netherlands
1930	Sonja Henie, Norway	1956	Carol Heiss, USA	1976	**Dorothy Hamill**, USA
1931	Sonja Henie, Norway	1957	Carol Heiss, USA	1977	Linda Fratianne, USA
				1978	Anett Poetzsch, E. Germany

Figure Skating (Cont.)

Year		Year		Year	
1979	Linda Fratianne, USA	1988	**Katarina Witt**, E. Germany	1997	Tara Lipinski, USA
1980	**Anett Poetzsch**, E. Germany	1989	Midori Ito, Japan	1998	Michelle Kwan, USA
1981	Denise Biellmann, Switzerland	1990	Jill Trenary, USA	1999	Maria Butyrskaya, Russia
1982	Elaine Zayak, USA	1991	Kristi Yamaguchi, USA	2000	Michelle Kwan, USA
1983	Rosalyn Sumners, USA	1992	**Kristi Yamaguchi**, USA	2001	Michelle Kwan, USA
1984	**Katarina Witt**, E. Germany	1993	Oksana Baiul, Ukraine	2002	Irina Slutskaya, Russia
1985	Katarina Witt, E. Germany	1994	Yuka Sato, Japan	2003	Michelle Kwan, USA
1986	Debi Thomas, USA	1995	Lu Chen, China		
1987	Katarina Witt, E. Germany	1996	Michelle Kwan, USA		

PAIRS

Year		Year		Year	
1908	**Anna Hubler & Heinrich Burger**, GER	1949	Andrea Kekessy & Ede Kiraly, HUN	1977	Irina Rodnina & Aleksandr Zaitsev, USSR
1909	Phyllis Johnson & James H. Johnson, GBR	1950	Karol Kennedy & Peter Kennedy, USA	1978	Irina Rodnina & Aleksandr Zaitsev, USSR
1910	Anna Hubler & Heinrich Burger, GER	1951	Ria Baran & Paul Falk, W. Ger	1979	Tai Babilonia & Randy Gardner, USA
1911	Ludowika Eilers, GER & Walter Jakobsson, FIN	1952	**Ria Falk-Baran & Paul Falk**, W. Ger	1980	Maria Cherkasova & Sergei Shakhrai, USSR
1912	Phyllis Johnson & James H. Johnson, GBR	1953	Jennifer Nicks & John Nicks, GBR	1981	Irina Vorobieva & Igor Lisovsky, USSR
1913	Helene Engelmann & Karl Majstrik, GER	1954	Frances Dafoe & Norris Bowden, CAN	1982	Sabine Baess & Tassilio Thierbach, E. Ger
1914	Ludowika Jakobsson-Eilers & Walter Jakobsson-Eilers, FIN	1955	Frances Dafoe & Norris Bowden, CAN	1983	Elena Valova & Oleg Vasiliev, USSR
1915-21	Not held	1956	**Elisabeth Schwarz & Kurt Oppelt**, AUT	1984	Barbara Underhill & Paul Martini, CAN
1922	**Helene Engelmann & Alfred Berger**, AUT	1957	Barbara Wagner & Robert Paul, CAN	1985	Elena Valova & Oleg Vasiliev, USSR
1923	Ludowika Jakobsson-Eilers & Walter Jakobsson-Eilers, FIN	1958	Barbara Wagner & Robert Paul, CAN	1986	Ekaterina Gordeeva & Sergei Grinkov, USSR
1924	Helene Engelmann & Alfred Berger, GER	1959	Barbara Wagner & Robert Paul, CAN	1987	Ekaterina Gordeeva & Sergei Grinkov, USSR
1925	Herma Jaross-Szabo & Ludwig Wrede, AUT	1960	**Barbara Wagner & Robert Paul**, CAN	1988	Elena Valova & Oleg Vasiliev, USSR
1926	Andree Joly & Pierre Brunet, FRA	1961	Not held	1989	Ekaterina Gordeeva & Sergei Grinkov, USSR
1927	Herma Jaross-Szabo & Ludwig Wrede, AUT	1962	Maria Jelinek & Otto Jelinek, CAN	1990	Ekaterina Gordeeva & Sergei Grinkov, USSR
1928	**Andree Joly & Pierre Brunet**, FRA	1963	Marika Kilius & H.J. Baumler, W. Ger	1991	Natalya Mishkutienok & Arhtur Dmitriev, USSR
1929	Lilly Scholz & Otto Kaiser, AUT	1964	Marika Kilius & H.J. Baumler, W. Ger	1992	**Natalya Mishkutienok & Arthur Dmitriev**, USSR
1930	Andree Brunet-Joly & Pierre Brunet-Joly, FRA	1965	Ludmila Protopopov & Oleg Protopopov, USSR	1993	Isabelle Brasseur & Lloyd Eisler, CAN
1931	Emilie Rotter & Laszlo Szollas, HUN	1966	Ludmila Protopopov & Oleg Protopopov, USSR	1994	Evgenia Shishkova & Vadim Naumov, RUS
1932	**Andree Brunet-Joly & Pierre Brunet-Joly**, FRA	1967	Ludmila Protopopov & Oleg Protopopov, USSR	1995	Radka Kovarikova & Rene Novotny, CZR
1933	Emilie Rotter & Laszlo Szollas, HUN	1968	**Ludmila Protopopov & Oleg Protopopov**, USSR	1996	Marina Eltsova & Andrey Buskhov, RUS
1934	Emilie Rotter & Laszlo Szollas, HUN	1969	Irina Rodnina & Alexsei Ulanov, USSR	1997	Mandy Wotzel & Ingo Steuer, GER
1935	Emilie Rotter & Laszlo Szollas, HUN	1970	Irina Rodnina & Aleksei Ulanov, USSR	1998	Jenni Meno & Todd Sand, USA
1936	**Maxi Herber & Ernst Baier**, GER	1971	Irina Rodnina & Aleksei Ulanov, USSR	1999	Elena Berezhnaya & Anton Sikharulidze, RUS
1937	Maxi Herber & Ernst Baier, GER	1972	**Irina Rodnina & Aleksei Ulanov**, USSR	2000	Maria Petrova & Alexei Tikhonov, RUS
1938	Maxi Herber & Ernst Baier, GER	1973	Irina Rodnina & Aleksandr Zaitsev, USSR	2001	Jamie Sale & David Pelletier, CAN
1939	Maxi Herber & Ernst Baier, GER	1974	Irina Rodnina & Aleksandr Zaitsev, USSR	2002	Xue Shen & Hongbo Zhao, CHN
1940-46	Not held	1975	Irina Rodnina & Aleksandr Zaitsev, USSR	2003	Xue Shen & Hongbo Zhao, CHN
1947	Micheline Lannoy & Pierre Baugniet, BEL	1976	**Irina Rodnina & Aleksandr Zaitsev**, USSR		
1948	**Micheline Lannoy & Pierre Baugniet**, BEL				

AP/Wide World Photos

*Five-time world champ **Carol Heiss**, top, shakes hands with Austrian runners-up Ingrid Wendl, left, and Hanna Walter after retaining her world title on Feb. 15, 1958.*

DANCE

Year
1950 Lois Waring
& Michael McGean, USA
1951 Jean Westwood
& Lawrence Demmy, GBR
1952 Jean Westwood
& Lawrence Demmy, GBR
1953 Jean Westwood
& Lawrence Demmy, GBR
1954 Jean Westwood
& Lawrence Demmy, GBR
1955 Jean Westwood
& Lawrence Demmy, GBR
1956 Pamela Wieght
& Paul Thomas, GBR
1957 June Markham
& Courtney Jones, GBR
1958 June Markham
& Courtney Jones, GBR
1959 Doreen D. Denny
& Courtney Jones, GBR

1960 Doreen D. Denny
& Courtney Jones, GBR
1961 Not held
1962 Eva Romanova
& Pavel Roman, CZE
1963 Eva Romanova
& Pavel Roman, CZE
1964 Eva Romanova
& Pavel Roman, CZE
1965 Eva Romanova
& Pavel Roman, CZE
1966 Diane Towler
& Bernard Ford, GBR
1967 Diane Towler
& Bernard Ford, GBR
1968 Diane Towler
& Bernard Ford, GBR

Year
1969 Diane Towler
& Bernard Ford, GBR
1970 Lyudmila Pakhomova
& Aleksandr Gorshkov, USSR
1971 Lyudmila Pakhomova
& Aleksandr Gorshkov, USSR
1972 Lyudmila Pakhomova
& Aleksandr Gorshkov, USSR
1973 Lyudmila Pakhomova
& Aleksandr Gorshkov, USSR
1974 Lyudmila Pakhomova
& Aleksandr Gorshkov, USSR
1975 Irina Moiseeva
& Andreij Minenkov, USSR
1976 **Lyudmila Pakhomova**
& Aleksandr Gorshkov,
USSR
1977 Irina Moiseeva
& Andreij Minenkov, USSR
1978 Natalia Linichuk
& Gennadi Karponosov, USSR
1979 Natalia Linichuk
& Gennadi Karponosov, USSR

1980 Krisztina Regoeczy
& Andras Sallai, HUN
1981 Jayne Torvill
& Christopher Dean, GBR
1982 Jayne Torvill
& Christopher Dean, GBR
1983 Jayne Torvill
& Christopher Dean, GBR
1984 **Jayne Torvill**
& Christopher Dean, GBR
1985 Natalia Bestemianova
& Andrei Bukin, USSR
1986 Natalia Bestemianova
& Andrei Bukin, USSR

Year
1987 Natalia Bestemianova
& Andrei Bukin, USSR
1988 **Natalia Bestemianova**
& Andrei Bukin, USSR
1989 Marina Klimova
& Sergei Ponomarenko, USSR
1990 Marina Klimova
& Sergei Ponomarenko, USSR
1991 Isabelle Duchesnay
& Paul Duchesnay, FRA
1992 **Marina Klimova**
& Sergei Ponomarenko,
USSR
1993 Renee Roca
& Gorsha Sur, USA
1994 **Oksana Grishuk**
& Evgeny Platov, RUS
1995 Oksana Grishuk
& Evgeny Platov, RUS
1996 Oksana Grishuk
& Evgeny Platov, RUS
1997 Oksana Grishuk
& Evgeny Platov, RUS
1998 Anjelika Krylova
& Oleg Ovsyannikov, RUS
1999 Anjelika Krylova
& Oleg Ovsyannikov, RUS
2000 Marina Anissina
& Gwendal Peizerat, FRA
2001 Barbara Fusar Poli
& Maurizio Margaglio, ITA
2002 Irina Lobacheva
& Ilia Averbukh, RUS
2003 Shae-Lynn Bourne
& Victor Kraatz, CAN

U.S. Champions
Skaters who won U.S., World and Olympic championships in same year are in **bold** type.

MEN

Multiple winners: Dick Button and Roger Turner (7); Todd Eldredge (6); Sherwin Badger and Robin Lee (5); Brian Boitano, Scott Hamilton, David Jenkins, Hayes Jenkins and Charles Tickner (4); Gordon McKellen, Nathaniel Niles, Michael Weiss and Tim Wood (3); Scott Allen, Christopher Bowman, Scott Davis, Eugene Turner and Gary Visconti (2).

Year		Year		Year		Year	
1914	Norman Scott	1938	Robin Lee	1961	Bradley Lord	1983	Scott Hamilton
1915-17	Not held	1939	Robin Lee	1962	Monty Hoyt	1984	**Scott Hamilton**
1918	Nathaniel Niles	1940	Eugene Turner	1963	Thomas Litz	1985	Brian Boitano
1919	Not held	1941	Eugene Turner	1964	Scott Allen	1986	Brian Boitano
1920	Sherwin Badger	1942	Robert Specht	1965	Gary Visconti	1987	Brian Boitano
1921	Sherwin Badger	1943	Arthur Vaughn	1966	Scott Allen	1988	**Brian Boitano**
1922	Sherwin Badger	1944-45	Not held	1967	Gary Visconti	1989	Christopher Bowman
1923	Sherwin Badger	1946	Dick Button	1968	Tim Wood	1990	Todd Eldredge
1924	Sherwin Badger	1947	Dick Button	1969	Tim Wood	1991	Todd Eldredge
1925	Nathaniel Niles	1948	**Dick Button**	1970	Tim Wood	1992	Christopher Bowman
1926	Chris Christenson	1949	Dick Button	1971	John (Misha) Petkevich	1993	Scott Davis
1927	Nathaniel Niles	1950	Dick Button	1972	Ken Shelley	1994	Scott Davis
1928	Roger Turner	1951	Dick Button	1973	Gordon McKellen	1995	Todd Eldredge
1929	Roger Turner	1952	**Dick Button**	1974	Gordon McKellen	1996	Rudy Galindo
1930	Roger Turner	1953	Hayes Jenkins	1975	Gordon McKellen	1997	Todd Eldredge
1931	Roger Turner	1954	Hayes Jenkins	1976	Terry Kubicka	1998	Todd Eldredge
1932	Roger Turner	1955	Hayes Jenkins	1977	Charles Tickner	1999	Michael Weiss
1933	Roger Turner	1956	**Hayes Jenkins**	1978	Charles Tickner	2000	Michael Weiss
1934	Roger Turner	1957	David Jenkins	1979	Charles Tickner	2001	Tim Goebel
1935	Robin Lee	1958	David Jenkins	1980	Charles Tickner	2002	Todd Eldredge
1936	Robin Lee	1959	David Jenkins	1981	Scott Hamilton	2003	Michael Weiss
1937	Robin Lee	1960	David Jenkins	1982	Scott Hamilton		

WOMEN

Multiple winners: Maribel Vinson (9); Michelle Kwan (7); Theresa Weld Blanchard and Gretchen Merrill (6); Tenley Albright, Peggy Fleming and Janet Lynn (5); Linda Fratianne and Carol Heiss (4); Dorothy Hamill, Beatrix Loughran, Rosalyn Summers, Joan Tozzer and Jill Trenary (3); Yvonne Sherman and Debi Thomas (2).

Year		Year		Year		Year	
1914	Theresa Weld	1938	Joan Tozzer	1960	**Carol Heiss**	1982	Rosalyn Sumners
1915-17	Not held	1939	Joan Tozzer	1961	Laurence Owen	1983	Rosalyn Sumners
1918	Rosemary Beresford	1940	Joan Tozzer	1962	Barbara Pursley	1984	Rosalyn Sumners
1919	Not held	1941	Jane Vaughn	1963	Lorraine Hanlon	1985	Tiffany Chin
1920	Theresa Weld	1942	Jane Sullivan	1964	Peggy Fleming	1986	Debi Thomas
1921	Theresa Blanchard	1943	Gretchen Merrill	1965	Peggy Fleming	1987	Jill Trenary
1922	Theresa Blanchard	1944	Gretchen Merrill	1966	Peggy Fleming	1988	Debi Thomas
1923	Theresa Blanchard	1945	Gretchen Merrill	1967	Peggy Fleming	1989	Jill Trenary
1924	Theresa Blanchard	1946	Gretchen Merrill	1968	**Peggy Fleming**	1990	Jill Trenary
1925	Beatrix Loughran	1947	Gretchen Merrill	1969	Janet Lynn	1991	Tonya Harding
1926	Beatrix Loughran	1948	Gretchen Merrill	1970	Janet Lynn	1992	**Kristi Yamaguchi**
1927	Beatrix Loughran	1949	Yvonne Sherman	1971	Janet Lynn	1993	Nancy Kerrigan
1928	Maribel Vinson	1950	Yvonne Sherman	1972	Janet Lynn	1994	vacated*
1929	Maribel Vinson	1951	Sonya Klopfer	1973	Janet Lynn	1995	Nicole Bobek
1930	Maribel Vinson	1952	Tenley Albright	1974	Dorothy Hamill	1996	Michelle Kwan
1931	Maribel Vinson	1953	Tenley Albright	1975	Dorothy Hamill	1997	Tara Lipinski
1932	Maribel Vinson	1954	Tenley Albright	1976	**Dorothy Hamill**	1998	Michelle Kwan
1933	Maribel Vinson	1955	Tenley Albright	1977	Linda Fratianne	1999	Michelle Kwan
1934	Suzanne Davis	1956	Tenley Albright	1978	Linda Fratianne	2000	Michelle Kwan
1935	Maribel Vinson	1957	Carol Heiss	1979	Linda Fratianne	2001	Michelle Kwan
1936	Maribel Vinson	1958	Carol Heiss	1980	Linda Fratianne	2002	Michelle Kwan
1937	Maribel Vinson	1959	Carol Heiss	1981	Elaine Zayak	2003	Michelle Kwan

* Tonya Harding was stripped of the 1994 women's title and banned from membership in the U.S. Figure Skating Assn. for life on June 30, 1994 for violating the USFSA Code of Ethics after she pleaded guilty to a charge of conspiracy to hinder the prosecution related to the Jan. 6, 1994 attack on Nancy Kerrigan.

RUGBY

World Cup

The inaugural Rugby World Cup was held in 1987. Like soccer's World Cup, it is held every four years. Sixteen national teams were assembled for the first three tournaments but beginning in 1999, 20 teams played for the William Webb Ellis Cup, named for the game's inventor. The Rugby World Cup is now billed as the world's third largest athletic event, behind the Olympics and the soccer World Cup. The 2003 competition was scheduled for Oct. 10-Nov. 22 in Australia.

Year	Winner	Score	Runner up	Host Country
1987	New Zealand	29-9	France	Australia & New Zealand
1991	Australia	12-6	England	United Kingdom & France
1995	South Africa	15-12	New Zealand	South Africa
1999	Australia	35-12	France	Wales

Olympics

Greek Olympic Committee President **Gianna Angelopoulos-Daskalaki** displays images of the Athens 2004 Summer Olympic medals.

1896-2000
Through the Years

SPORTS ALMANAC

Modern Olympic Games

The original Olympic Games were celebrated as a religious festival from 776 B.C. until 393 A.D., when Roman emperor Theodosius I banned all pagan festivals (the Olympics celebrated the Greek god Zeus). On June 23, 1894, French educator Baron Pierre de Coubertin, speaking at the Sorbonne in Paris to a gathering of international sports leaders, proposed that the ancient games be revived on an international scale. The idea was enthusiastically received and the Modern Olympics were born. The first Olympics were held two years later in Athens, where 245 athletes from 14 nations competed in the ancient Panathenaic stadium to large and ardent crowds. Americans captured nine out of 12 track and field events, but Greece won the most medals with 47.

The Summer Olympics

Year	No	Location	Dates	Nations	Most medals	USA medals	
1896	I	Athens, GRE	Apr. 6-15	14	Greece (10-19-18—47)	11- 6- 2— 19	(2nd)
1900	II	Paris, FRA	May 20-Oct. 28	26	France (26-37-32—95)	18-14-15— 47	(2nd)
1904	III	St. Louis, USA. . . .	July 1-Nov. 23	13	USA (78-84-82—244)	78-84-82—244	(1st)
1906-a	—	Athens, GRE	Apr. 22-May 2	20	France (15-9-16—40)	12-6- 6— 24	(3rd)
1908	IV	London, GBR	Apr. 27-Oct. 31	22	Britain (54-46-38—138)	23-12-12— 47	(2nd)
1912	V	Stockholm, SWE .	May 5-July 22	28	Sweden (23-24-17—64)	25-18-20— 63	(2nd)
1916	VI	Berlin, GER	Cancelled (WWI)				
1920	VII	Antwerp, BEL	Apr. 20-Sept. 12	29	USA (41-27-27—95)	41-27-27— 95	(1st)
1924	VIII	Paris, FRA	May 4-July 27	44	USA (45-27-27—99)	45-27-27— 99	(1st)
1928	IX	Amsterdam, NED . .	May 17-Aug. 12	46	USA (22-18-16—56)	22-18-16— 56	(1st)
1932	X	Los Angeles, USA. .	July 30-Aug. 14	37	USA (41-32-30—103)	41-32-30—103	(1st)
1936	XI	Berlin, GER	Aug. 1-16	49	Germany (33-26-30—89)	24-20-12— 56	(2nd)
1940-b	XII	Tokyo, JPN	Cancelled (WWII)				
1944	XIII	London, GBR	Cancelled (WWII)				
1948	XIV	London, GBR	July 29-Aug. 14	59	USA (38-27-19—84)	38-27-19— 84	(1st)
1952-cd	XV	Helsinki, FIN	July 19-Aug. 3	69	USA (40-19-17—76)	40-19-17— 76	(1st)
1956-e	XVI	Melbourne, AUS . .	Nov. 22-Dec. 8	72	USSR (37-29-32—98)	32-25-17— 74	(2nd)
1960	XVII	Rome, ITA	Aug. 25-Sept. 11	83	USSR (43-29-31—103)	34-21-16— 71	(2nd)
1964	XVIII	Tokyo, JPN	Oct. 10-24	93	USSR (30-31-35—96)	36-26-28— 90	(2nd)
1968-f	XIX	Mexico City, MEX	Oct. 12-27	112	USA (45-28-34—107)	45-28-34—107	(1st)
1972	XX	Munich, W. GER .	Aug. 26-Sept. 10	121	USSR (50-27-22—99)	33-31-30— 94	(2nd)
1976-g	XXI	Montreal, CAN . . .	July 17-Aug. 1	92	USSR (49-41-35—125)	34-35-25— 94	(3rd)
1980-h	XXII	Moscow, USSR . .	July 19-Aug. 3	80	USSR (80-69-46—195)	Boycotted games	
1984-i	XXIII	Los Angeles, USA. .	July 28-Aug. 12	140	USA (83-61-30—174)	83-61-30—174	(1st)
1988	XXIV	Seoul, S. KOR . . .	Sept. 17-Oct. 2	159	USSR (55-31-46—132)	36-31-27— 94	(3rd)
1992-j	XXV	Barcelona, SPA . . .	July 25-Aug. 9	169	UT (45-38-29—112)	37-34-37—108	(2nd)
1996	XXVI	Atlanta, USA	July 20-Aug. 4	197	USA (44-32-25—101)	44-32-25—101	(1st)
2000	XXVII	Sydney, AUS	Sept. 15-Oct. 1	199	USA (40-24-33—97)	40-24-33— 97	(1st)
2004	XXVIII	Athens, GRE	Aug. 13-29				
2008	XXIX	Beijing, CHN	July 25-Aug. 10				

a—The 1906 Intercalated Games in Athens are considered unofficial by the IOC because they did not take place in the four-year cycle established in 1896. However, most record books include these interim games with the others.

b—The 1940 Summer Games are originally scheduled for Tokyo, but Japan resigns as host after the outbreak of the Sino-Japanese War in 1937. Helsinki is the next choice, but the IOC cancels the Games after Soviet troops invade Finland in 1939.

c—Germany and Japan are allowed to rejoin the Olympic community for the first Summer Games since 1936. Though a divided country, the Germans send a joint East-West team until 1964.

d—The Soviet Union (USSR) participates in its first Olympics, Winter or Summer, since the Russian revolution in 1917 and takes home the second most medals (22-30-19—71).

e—Due to Australian quarantine laws, the equestrian events for the 1956 Games are held in Stockholm, June 10-17.

f—East Germany and West Germany send separate teams for the first time and will continue to do so through 1988.

g—The 1976 Games are boycotted by 32 nations, most of them from black Africa, because the IOC will not ban New Zealand. Earlier that year, a rugby team from New Zealand had toured racially segregated South Africa.

h—The 1980 Games are boycotted by 64 nations, led by the USA, to protest the Soviet invasion of Afghanistan on Dec. 27, 1979.

i—The 1984 Games are boycotted by 14 Eastern Bloc nations, led by the USSR, to protest America's overcommercialization of the Games, inadequate security and an anti-Soviet attitude by the U.S. government. Most believe, however, the communist walkout is simply revenge for 1980.

j—Germany sends a single team after East and West German reunification in 1990 and the USSR competes as the Unified Team after the breakup of the Soviet Union in 1991.

1896

Athens

The ruins of ancient Olympia were excavated by the German archaeologist Ernst Curtius from 1875-81.

Among the remains uncovered was the ancient stadium where the original Olympic Games were celebrated from 776 B.C. to 393 A.D., when Roman emperor Theodosius I banned all pagan festivals.

Athletics played an important role in the religious festivals of the ancient Greeks, who believed competitive sports pleased the spirits of the dead. The festivals honoring gods like Zeus were undertaken by many Greek tribes and cities and usually held every four years.

During the first 13 Olympiads (an Olympiad is an interval of four years between celebrations of the Olympic Games), the only contested event was a foot race of 200 yards. Longer races were gradually introduced and by 708 B.C., field events like the discus, javelin throw and the long jump were part of the program. Wrestling and boxing followed and in 640 B.C., four-horse chariot races became a fixture at the Games.

During the so-called Golden Age of Greece, which most historians maintain lasted from 477 to 431 B.C., Olympia was considered holy ground. Victorious athletes gave public thanks to the gods and were revered as heroes. Three-time winners had statues erected in their likeness and received various gifts and honors, including exemption from taxation.

Eventually, however, winning and the rewards that went with victory corrupted the original purpose of the Ancient Games. Idealistic amateurs gave way to skilled foreign athletes who were granted the citizenship needed to compete and were paid handsomely by rich Greek gamblers.

There is evidence to suggest that the Games continued until the temples of Olympia were physically demolished in 426 A.D. by a Roman army sent by Theodosius II. Over the next 15 centuries, earthquakes and floods buried the site, until its discovery in 1875.

On June 23, 1894, French educator Baron Pierre de Coubertin, speaking at the Sorbonne in Paris to a gathering of international sports leaders from nine nations— including the United States and Russia— proposed that the ancient Games be revived on an international scale. The idea was enthusiastically received and the Modern Olympics, as we know them, were born.

The first Olympiad was celebrated two years later in Athens, where an estimated 245 athletes (all men) from 14 nations competed in the ancient Panathenaic stadium before large and ardent crowds.

Americans won nine of the 12 track and field events, but Greece won the most medals with 47. The highlight was the victory by native peasant Spiridon Louis in the first marathon race, which was run over the same course covered by the Greek hero Pheidippides after the battle of Marathon in 490 B.C.

Top 10 Standings

National medal standings are not recognized by the IOC. The unofficial point totals are based on 3 points for a gold medal, 2 for a silver and 1 for a bronze.

		Gold	Silver	Bronze	Total	Pts
1	Greece	10	19	18	47	86
2	USA	11	6	2	19	47
3	Germany	7	5	3	15	34
4	France	5	4	2	11	25
5	Great Britain	3	3	1	7	16
6	Denmark	1	2	4	7	11
	Hungary	2	1	3	6	11
8	Austria	2	0	3	5	9
9	Switzerland	1	2	0	3	7
10	Australia	2	0	0	2	6

Leading Medal Winners

Number of individual medals won on the left; gold, silver and bronze breakdown to the right.

No		Sport	G-S-B
6	Hermann Weingärtner, GER	Gymnastics	3-2-1
4	Karl Schuman, GER	Gymnastics & Wrestling	4-0-0
4	Alfred Flatow, GER	Gymnastics	3-1-0
4	Bob Garrett, USA	Track/Field	2-1-1
4	Viggo Jensen, DEN	Shooting & Weightlifting	1-2-1
3	Paul Masson, FRA	Cycling	3-0-0
3	Teddy Flack, AUS	Track/Field & Tennis	2-0-1
3	Jules Zutter, SWI	Gymnastics	1-2-0
3	James Connolly, USA	Track/Field	1-1-1
3	Leon Flameng, FRA	Cycling	1-1-1
3	Adolf Schmal, AUT	Cycling	1-0-2
3	Efstathios Chorophas, GRE	Swimming	0-1-2
3	Holger Nielsen, DEN	Shooting	0-1-2

Track & Field

Event		Time
100m	Tom Burke, USA	12.0
400m	Tom Burke, USA	54.2
800m	Teddy Flack, AUS	2:11.0
1500m	Teddy Flack, AUS	4:33.2
Marathon	Spiridon Louis, GRE	2:58:50
110m H	Tom Curtis, USA	17.6

Event		Mark
High Jump	Ellery Clark, USA	5-11¼
Pole Vault	William Hoyt, USA	10-10
Long Jump	Ellery Clark, USA	20-10
Triple Jump	James Connolly, USA	44-11¾
Shot Put	Bob Garrett, USA	36-9¾
Discus	Bob Garrett, USA	95-7½

Swimming

Event		Time
100m Free	Alfréd Hajós, HUN	1:22.2
500m Free	Paul Neumann, AUT	8:12.6
1200m Free	Alfréd Hajós, HUN	18:22.2

Other		Time
Sailors'		
100m Free	Ioannis Malokinis, GRE	2:20.4

Team Sports

None

Also Contested

Cycling, Fencing, Gymnastics, Shooting, Tennis, Weightlifting and Greco-Roman Wrestling.

1900

Paris

The success of the revived Olympics moved Greece to declare itself the rightful host of all future Games, but de Coubertin and the International Olympic Committee were determined to move the athletic feast around. In France, however, the Games were overshadowed by the brand new Eiffel Tower and all but ignored by the organizers of the 1900 Paris Exposition.

Despite their sideshow status, the Games attracted 1,225 athletes from 26 nations and enjoyed more publicity, if not bigger crowds, than in Athens.

University of Pennsylvania roommates Alvin Kraenzlein, Irving Baxter and John Tewksbury and Purdue grad Ray Ewry dominated the 23 track and field events, winning 11 and taking five seconds and a third. Kraenzlein remains the only track and fielder to win four individual titles in one year. Women were invited to compete for the first time and Britain's Charlotte Cooper won the singles and mixed doubles in tennis.

No gold medals were given out in Paris. Winners received silver medals with bronze for second place.

Top 10 Standings

National team medal standings are not recognized by the IOC. The unofficial point totals are based on 3 points for a gold medal, 2 for a silver and 1 for a bronze.

		Gold	Silver	Bronze	Total	Pts
1	France	26	37	32	95	184
2	USA	18	14	15	47	97
3	Great Britain	16	6	8	30	68
4	Belgium	6	5	5	16	33
5	Switzerland	6	1	1	8	21
6	Germany	3	2	2	7	15
7	Denmark	1	3	2	6	11
	Hungary	1	3	2	6	11
9	Australia	2	0	4	6	10
	Holland	1	2	3	6	10

Leading Medal Winners

Number of individual medals won on the left; gold, silver and bronze breakdown to the right.

MEN

No		Sport	G-S-B
5	Irving Baxter, USA	Track/Field	2-3-0
5	John W. Tewksbury, USA	Track/Field	2-2-1
4	Alvin Kraenzlein, USA	Track/Field	4-0-0
4	Konrad Stäheli, SWI	Shooting	3-0-1
4	Achille Paroche, FRA	Shooting	1-2-1
4	Stan Rowley, AUS	Track/Field	1-0-3
4	Ole Ostmo, NOR	Shooting	0-2-2
3	Ray Ewry, USA	Track/Field	3-0-0
3	Charles Bennett, GBR	Track/Field	2-1-0
3	Emil Kellenberger, SWI	Shooting	2-1-0
3	Laurie Doherty, GBR	Tennis	2-0-1
3	Reggie Doherty, GBR	Tennis	2-0-1
3	E. Michelet, FRA	Yachting	1-0-2
3	F. Michelet, FRA	Yachting	1-0-2

No		Sport	G-S-B
3	Anders Nielsen, DEN	Shooting	0-3-0
3	Zoltán Halmay, HUN	Swimming	0-2-1
3	Léon Moreaux, FRA	Shooting	0-2-1

WOMEN

No		Sport	G-S-B
2	Charlotte Cooper, GBR	Tennis	2-0-0
2	Marion Jones, USA	Tennis	0-0-2

Track & Field

Event		Time	
60m	Alvin Kraenzlein, USA	7.0	WR
100m	Frank Jarvis, USA	11.0	OR
200m	John W. Tewksbury, USA	22.2	
400m	Maxey Long, USA	49.4	OR
800m	Alfred Tysoe, GBR	2:01.2	
1500m	Charles Bennett, GBR	4:06.2	WR
Marathon	Michel Théato, FRA	2:59:45	
110m H	Alvin Kraenzlein, USA	15.4	OR
200m H	Alvin Kraenzlein, USA	25.4	
400m H	John W. Tewksbury, USA	57.6	
3000m Steeple	George Orton, CAN	7:34.4	
4000m Steeple	John Rimmer, GBR	12:58.4	
5000m Team	GBR (Charles Bennett, John Rimmer, Sidney Robinson, Alfred Tysoe, Stanley Rowley)	26 pts	

Event		Mark	
High Jump	Irving Baxter, USA	6-2¾	OR
Pole Vault	Irving Baxter, USA	10-10	OR
Long Jump	Alvin Kraenzlein, USA	23-6¾	OR
Triple Jump	Meyer Prinstein, USA	47-5¾	OR
Shot Put	Richard Sheldon, USA	46-3	OR
Discus	Rudolf Bauer, HUN	118-3	OR
Hammer	John Flanagan, USA	163-1	

Standing		Mark	
High Jump	Ray Ewry, USA	5-5	WR
Long Jump	Ray Ewry, USA	10-6¼	
Triple Jump	Ray Ewry, USA	34-8½	

Swimming

Event		Time
220yd Free	Frederick Lane, AUS	2:25.2
1000m Free	John Jarvis, GBR	13:40.2
4000m Free	John Jarvis, GBR	58:24.0
200m Back	Ernst Hoppenberg, GER	2:47.0
200m Team	GER (Ernst Hoppenberg, Max Hainle, Max Schone, Julius Frey, Herbert von Petersdorff)	32 pts

Team Sports

Sport	Champion
Cricket	Great Britain
Polo	Great Britain/USA
Rugby	France
Soccer	Great Britain
Tug-of-War	Sweden/Norway
Water Polo	Great Britain

Note: In Polo, Foxhunters Hurlingham defeated Club Rugby in a contest of teams made up of British and American players. A combined 6-man team of Swedes and Norwegians won the Tug-of-War.

Also Contested

Archery, Croquet, Cycling, Equestrian, Fencing, Golf, Gymnastics, Rowing, Shooting, Tennis and Yachting.

1904

St. Louis

Originally scheduled for Chicago, the Games were moved to St. Louis and held in conjunction with the centennial celebration of the Louisiana Purchase.

The program included more sports than in Paris, but with only 13 nations sending athletes, the first Olympics to be staged in the United States had a decidedly All-American flavor—over 500 of the 687 competitors were Americans. Little wonder the home team won 80 percent of the medals.

The rout was nearly total in track and field where the U.S.–led by triple-winners Ray Ewry, Archie Hahn, Jim Lightbody and Harry Hillman–took 23 of 25 gold medals and swept 20 events.

The marathon, which was run over dusty roads in brutally hot weather, was the most bizarre event of the Games. Thomas Hicks of the U.S. won, but only after his handlers fed him painkillers during the race. And an impostor nearly stole the victory when Fred Lorz, who dropped out after nine miles, was seen trotting back to the finish line to retrieve his clothes. Amused that officials thought he had won the race, Lorz played along until he was found out shortly after the medal ceremony. Banned for life by the AAU, Lorz was reinstated a year later and won the 1905 Boston Marathon.

Top 10 Standings

National medal standings are not recognized by the IOC. The unofficial point totals are based on 3 points for a gold medal, 2 for a silver and 1 for a bronze.

		Gold	Silver	Bronze	Total	Pts
1	USA	78	84	82	244	484
2	Germany	4	4	4	12	24
3	Canada	4	1	1	6	15
4	Hungary	2	1	1	4	9
	Cuba	3	0	0	3	9
6	Austria	1	1	1	3	6
	Britain/Ireland	1	1	1	3	6
8	Greece	1	0	1	2	4
	Switzerland	1	0	1	2	4
10	Cuba/USA	1	0	0	1	3

Leading Medal Winners

Number of individual medals won on the left; gold, silver and bronze breakdown to the right.

MEN

No		Sport	G-S-B
6	Anton Heida, USA	Gymnastics	5-1-0
6	George Eyser, USA	Gymnastics	3-2-1
6	Burton Downing, USA	Cycling	2-3-1
5	Marcus Hurley, USA	Cycling	4-0-1
5	Charles Daniels, USA	Swimming	3-1-1

No		Sport	G-S-B
5	Albertson Van Zo Post, USA	Fencing	2-1-2
5	William Merz, USA	Gymnastics	0-1-4
4	Jim Lightbody, USA	Track/Field	3-1-0
4	Francis Gailey, USA	Swimming	0-3-1
4	Teddy Billington, USA	Cycling	0-1-3
4	Frank Kungler, USA	Weightlifting, Wrestling & Tug of War	0-1-3
3	Ray Ewry, USA	Track/Field	3-0-0
3	Ramón Fonst, CUB	Fencing	3-0-0
3	Archie Hahn, USA	Track/Field	3-0-0
3	Harry Hillman, USA	Track/Field	3-0-0
3	Julius Lenhart, AUT	Gymnastics	2-1-0
3	George Bryant, USA	Archery	2-0-1
3	Emil Rausch, GER	Swimming	2-0-1
3	Robert Williams, USA	Archery	1-2-0
3	Ralph Rose, USA	Track/Field	1-1-1
3	William Thompson, USA	Archery	1-0-2
3	Charles Tatham, USA	Fencing	0-2-1
3	William Hogenson, USA	Track/Field	0-1-2
3	Emil Voigt, USA	Gymnastics	0-1-2

WOMEN

No		Sport	G-S-B
2	Lida Howell, USA	Archery	2-0-0
2	Emma Cooke, USA	Archery	0-2-0
2	Jessie Pollack, USA	Archery	0-0-2

Track & Field

Event		Time	
60m	Archie Hahn, USA	.7.0	=WR
100m	Archie Hahn, USA	11.0	
200m	Archie Hahn, USA	21.6	OR
400m	Harry Hillman, USA	49.2	OR
800m	Jim Lightbody, USA	1:56.0	OR
1500m	Jim Lightbody, USA	4:05.4	WR
Marathon	Thomas Hicks, USA	3:28:53	
110m H	Frederick Schule, USA	16.0	
200m H	Harry Hillman, USA	24.6	
400m H	Harry Hillman, USA	53.0	OR
3000m Steeple	Jim Lightbody, USA	7:39.6	
4-mile Team	New York AC (Arthur Newton, George Underwood, Paul Pilgrim, Howard Valentine, David Munson)	27 pts	

Event		Mark	
High Jump	Sam Jones, USA	.5-11	
Pole Vault	Charles Dvorak, USA	11-5¾	
Long Jump	Meyer Prinstein, USA	.24-1	OR
Triple Jump	Meyer Prinstein, USA	.47-1	
Shot Put	Ralph Rose, USA	.48-7	WR
56-lb Throw	Étienne Desmarteau, CAN	.34-4	
Discus	Martin Sheridan, USA	128-10	OR
Hammer	John Flanagan, USA	168-1	OR
Triathlon	Max Emmerich, USA	.35.7 pts	
Decathlon	Tom Kiely, IRL	.6036 pts	

Note: Sheridan won Discus throw-off after tying with Rose for 1st.

Standing		Mark	
High Jump	Ray Ewry, USA	.5-3	
Long Jump	Ray Ewry, USA	11-4⅞	WR
Triple Jump	Ray Ewry, USA	34-7¼	

Swimming

Event		Time
50yd Free	Zoltán Halmay, HUN	.28.0
100yd Free	Zoltán Halmay, HUN	1:02.8
220yd Free	Charles Daniels, USA	2:44.2
440yd Free	Charles Daniels, USA	6:16.2
880yd Free	Emil Rausch, GER	13:11.4
Mile Free	Emil Rausch, GER	27:18.2
100yd Back	Walter Brack, GER	1:16.8
400yd Brst	Georg Zacharias, GER	7:23.6
4x50yd Free	USA (Joe Ruddy, Leo Goodwin, Louis Handle, Charles Daniels)	2:04.6

Note: Halmay won 50-Free in swim-off with Scott Leary of USA.

Diving		Points
Platform	George Sheldon, USA	12.66

Plunge		Mark
for Distance	William Dickey, USA	62-6

Team Sports

Sport	Champion
Lacrosse	Canada (Shamrock-Winnipeg)
Soccer	Canada (Galt Football Club)
Tug-of-War	USA (Milwaukee AC)
Water Polo	USA (New York AC)

Also Contested

Archery, Boxing, Cycling, Fencing, Golf, Gymnastics, Roque (Croquet), Rowing, Tennis, Weightlifting and Freestyle Wrestling.

1906
Athens

After disappointing receptions in Paris and St. Louis, the Olympic movement returned to Athens for the Intercalated Games of 1906.

The mutual desire of Greece and Baron de Coubertin to recapture the spirit of the 1896 Games led to an understanding that the Greeks would host an interim games every four years between Olympics.

Nearly 900 athletes from 20 countries came to Athens, including, for the first time, an official American team picked by the USOC.

As usual, the U.S. dominated track and field, taking 11 of 21 events, including double wins by Martin Sheridan (shot put and freestyle discus), Ray Ewry (standing high and long jumps) and Paul Pilgrim (400 and 800 meters). The previously unknown Pilgrim had been an 11th-hour addition to the team.

Verner Järvinen, the first Finn to compete in the Olympics, won the Greek-style discus throw and placed second in the freestyle discus. He returned home a national hero and inspired Finland to become a future Olympic power.

The Intercalated Games were cancelled due to political unrest in 1910 and never reappeared. Medals won are considered unofficial by the IOC.

Top 10 Standings

National medal standings are not recognized by the IOC. The unofficial point totals are based on 3 points for a gold medal, 2 for a silver and 1 for a bronze.

		Gold	Silver	Bronze	Total	Pts
1	France	15	9	16	40	79
2	Greece	8	13	12	33	62
3	USA	12	6	6	24	54
4	Great Britain	8	11	5	24	51
5	Italy	7	6	3	16	36
6	Switzerland	5	6	4	15	31
7	Germany	4	6	5	15	29
8	Sweden	2	5	7	14	23
9	Hungary	2	5	3	10	19
10	Austria	3	3	2	8	17
	Norway	4	2	1	7	17

Leading Medal Winners

Number of individual medals won on the left; gold, silver and bronze breakdown to the right.

MEN

No		Sport	G-S-B
6	Louis Richardet, SWI	Shooting	4-2-0
5	Martin Sheridan, USA	Track/Field	2-3-0
5	Konrad Stäheli, SWI	Shooting	2-2-1
5	Léon Moreaux, FRA	Shooting	2-1-2
5	Jean Reich, SWI	Shooting	1-1-3
4	Gudbrand Skatteboe, NOR	Shooting	3-1-0
4	Gustav Casmir, GER	Fencing	2-2-0
4	Eric Lemming, SWE	Track/Field & Tug of War	1-0-3
3	Francesco Verri, ITA	Cycling	3-0-0
3	Enrico Bruna, ITA	Rowing	3-0-0
3	Georgio Cesana, ITA	Rowing	3-0-0
3	Max Decugis, FRA	Tennis	3-0-0
3	Emilio Fontanella, ITA	Rowing	3-0-0
3	Georges Dillon-Cavanaugh, FRA	Fencing	2-1-0
3	Henry Taylor, GBR	Swimming	1-1-1
3	Fernand Vast, FRA	Cycling	1-0-2
3	Raoul de Boigne, FRA	Shooting	0-1-2
3	John Jarvis, GBR	Swimming	0-1-2

WOMEN

No		Sport	G-S-B
2	Sophia Marinou, GRE	Tennis	0-2-0

Track & Field

Event		Time
100m	Archie Hahn, USA	11.2
400m	Paul Pilgrim, USA	53.2
800m	Paul Pilgrim, USA	2:01.5
1500m	Jim Lightbody, USA	4:12.0
5 Miles	Henry Hawtrey, GBR	26:11.8
Marathon	Billy Sherring, CAN	2:51:23.6
110m H	Robert Leavitt, USA	16.2
500m Walk	George Bonhag, USA	7:12.6
3000m Walk	György Sztantics, HUN	15:13.2

Event		Mark
High Jump	Con Leahy, GBR/IRL	5-10
Pole Vault	Fernand Gonder, FRA	11-5¾
Long Jump	Meyer Prinstein, USA	23-7½
Triple Jump	Peter O'Connor, GBR/IRL	46-2¼
Shot Put	Martin Sheridan, USA	40-5¼
Stone Throw	Nicolaos Georgantas, GRE	65-4½
Discus	Martin Sheridan, USA	136-0
Greek Discus	Verner Järvinen, FIN	115-4½
Freestyle		
Javelin	Eric Lemming, SWE	176-10 **WR**
Pentathlon	Hjalmar Mellander, SWE	24 pts

Notes: Weight in Stone Throw was 14.08 lbs; spinning not allowed in Greek-style Discus.

Standing		Mark
High Jump	Ray Ewry, USA	5-1¼
Long Jump	Ray Ewry, USA	10-10

Swimming

Event		Time
100m Free	Charles Daniels, USA	1:13.4
400m Free	Otto Scheff, AUT	6:23.8
Mile Free	Henry Taylor, GBR	28:28.0
4x250m Free	HUN (József Ónody, Henrik Hajós, Geza Kiss, Zoltán Halmay)	16:52.4

Diving		Points
Platform	Gottlob Walz, GER	156.0

Team Sports

Sport	Champion
Soccer	Denmark
Tug-of-War	Germany

Also Contested

Canoeing, Cycling, Fencing, Gymnastics, Rowing, Shooting, Tennis, Weightlifting and Greco-Roman Wrestling.

1908

London

The fourth Olympic Games were certainly the wettest and probably the most contentious in history.

Held at a new 68,000-seat stadium in the Shepherds Bush section of London, the 1908 Games were played out under continually rainy skies and suffered from endless arguments between British officials and many of the other countries involved—especially the United States.

"The Battle of Shepherds Bush" began almost immediately, when the U.S. delegation noticed that there was no American flag among the national flags decorating the stadium for the opening ceremonies. U.S. flag bearer and discus champion Martin Sheridan responded by refusing to dip the Stars and Stripes when he passed King Edward VII's box in the parade of athletes. "This flag dips to no earthly king," Sheridan said. And it hasn't since.

The Americans, at least, got to march with their flag. Finland, then ruled by Russia, could not. Informed they would have to use a Russian flag, the furious Finns elected to march with no flag at all.

Once again the marathon proved to be the Games' most memorable event. Laid out over a 26-mile, 365-yard course that stretched from Windsor Castle to the royal box at Shepherds Bush, the race ended in controversy when leader Dorando Pietri of Italy staggered into the packed stadium, took a wrong turn, collapsed, was helped up by doctors, wobbled and fell three more times before

being half-carried across the finish line by race officials. Caught up in the drama of Pietri's agony, the cheering crowd hardly noticed that he was declared the winner just as second place runner, Johnny Hayes of the U.S., entered the stadium.

Pietri was later disqualified in favor of Hayes, but only after British and U.S. officials argued for an hour and fights had broken out in the stands.

Top 10 Standings

National medal standings are not recognized by the IOC. The unofficial point totals are based on 3 points for a gold medal, 2 for a silver and 1 for a bronze

		Gold	Silver	Bronze	Total	Pts
1	Great Britain	54	46	38	138	292
2	USA	23	12	12	47	105
3	Sweden	8	6	11	25	47
4	France	5	5	9	19	34
5	Canada	3	3	10	16	25
6	Germany	3	5	5	13	24
7	Hungary	3	4	2	9	19
8	Norway	2	3	3	8	15
	Belgium	1	5	2	8	15
10	Italy	2	2	0	4	10

Leading Medal Winners

Number of individual medals won on the left; gold, silver and bronze breakdown to the right.

MEN

No		Sport	G-S-B
3	Mel Sheppard, USA	Track/Field	3-0-0
3	Henry Taylor, GBR	Swimming	3-0-0
3	Benjamin Jones, GBR	Cycling	2-1-0
3	Martin Sheridan, USA	Track/Field	2-0-1
3	Oscar Swahn, SWE	Shooting	2-0-1
3	Josiah Ritchie, GBR	Tennis	1-1-1
3	Ted Ranken, GBR	Shooting	0-3-0

WOMEN

No		Sport	G-S-B
2	Madge Syers, GBR	Figure Skating	1-0-1

Note: Figure Skating was part of the Summer Olympics in 1908 and '20.

Track & Field

Event		Time	
100m	Reggie Walker, S. Afr.	10.8	=OR
200m	Bobby Kerr, CAN	22.6	
400m	Wyndham Halswelle, GBR	50.0	
800m	Mel Sheppard, USA	1:52.8	WR
1500m	Mel Sheppard, USA	4:03.4	OR
5 Miles	Emil Voigt, GBR	25:11.2	
Marathon	Johnny Hayes, USA	2:55:18.4	OR
110m H	Forrest Smithson, USA	15.0	WR
400m H	Charley Bacon, USA	55.0	WR
3200m Steeple	Arthur Russell, GBR	10:47.8	
3500m Walk	George Larner, GBR	14:55.0	
10-mi Walk	George Larner, GBR	1:15:57.4	
Medley Relay	USA (William Hamilton, Nathaniel Cartmell, John Taylor, Mel Sheppard)	3:29.4	
3-mile Relay	GBR (Joseph Deakin, Archie Robertson, Wilfred Coales)	.6 pts	

Note: Medley Relay made up of two 200m runs, a 400m and an 800m.

Event		Mark	
High Jump	Harry Porter, USA	6- 3	OR
Pole Vault	Edward Cooke, USA	12- 2	OR
Long Jump	Frank Irons, USA	24- 6½	OR
Triple Jump	Timothy Ahearne, GBR/IRL	48-11½	OR
Shot Put	Ralph Rose, USA	46- 7½	
Discus	Martin Sheridan, USA	134- 2	OR
Greek Discus	Martin Sheridan, USA	128- 4	OR
Hammer	John Flanagan, USA	170- 4	OR
Javelin	Eric Lemming, SWE	179-10	WR
Freestyle Javelin	Eric Lemming, SWE	178- 7½	

Note: Spinning not allowed in Greek-style Discus.

Standing		Mark
High Jump	Ray Ewry, USA	5- 2
Long Jump	Ray Ewry, USA	10-11¼

Swimming
MEN

Event		Time	
100m Free	Charles Daniels, USA	1:05.6	WR
400m Free	Henry Taylor, GBR	5:36.8	
1500m Free	Henry Taylor, GBR	22:48.4	WR
100m Back	Arno Bieberstein, GER	1:24.6	WR
200m Brst	Frederick Holman, GBR	3:09.2	WR
4x200m Free	GBR (John Derbyshire, Paul Radmilovic, William Foster, Henry Taylor)	10:55.6	WR

Diving		Points
Platform	Hjalmar Johansson, SWE	83.75
Spring	Albert Zürner, GER	85.5

Team Sports

Sport	Champion
Field Hockey	Great Britain (England)
Lacrosse	Canada
Polo	Great Britain (Roehampton)
Rugby	Australia
Soccer	Great Britain
Tug-of-War	Great Britain (City Police)
Water Polo	Great Britain

Also Contested
Archery, Boxing, Cycling, Fencing, Figure Skating, Gymnastics, Jeu de Paume (court tennis), Racquets, Rowing, Shooting, Tennis, Freestyle Wrestling, Greco-Roman Wrestling and Yachting.

1912
Stockholm

The belligerence of 1908 was replaced with benevolence four years later, as Sweden provided a well-organized and pleasant haven for the troubled Games.

And then there were Jim Thorpe and Hannes Kolehmainen.

Thorpe, a 24-year-old American Indian who was a two-time consensus All-America football player at Carlisle (Pa.) Institute, won the two most demanding events in track and field—the pentathlon and decath-

lon. And he did it with ease. "You sir," said the Swedes' King Gustav V at the medal ceremony, "are the greatest athlete in the world." To which Thorpe is said to have replied, "Thanks, King."

Kolehmainen, a 22-year-old Finnish vegetarian, ran away with three distance events being run for the first time—the 5,000 and 10,000-meter races and the 12,000-meter cross-country run. He also picked up a silver medal in the 12,000-meter team race.

Ralph Craig of the U.S. was the only other winner of two individual track gold medals, taking both the 100 and 200-meter runs. The 100 final had seven false starts, one with Craig sprinting the entire distance before being called back.

Although Thorpe returned to the U.S. a hero, a year later it was learned that he had played semi-pro baseball for $25 a week in 1909 and 1910. The IOC, with the full support of the American Olympic Committee, stripped him of his medals and erased his records.

The medals and records were restored in 1982—29 years after Thorpe's death.

Top 10 Standings
National medal standings are not recognized by the IOC. The unofficial point totals are based on 3 points for a gold medal, 2 for a silver and 1 for a bronze.

		Gold	Silver	Bronze	Total	Pts
1	Sweden	23	24	17	64	134
2	USA	25	18	20	63	131
3	Great Britain	10	15	16	41	76
4	Finland	9	8	9	26	52
5	Germany	5	13	7	25	48
6	France	7	4	3	14	32
7	Denmark	1	6	5	12	20
8	Norway	3	2	5	10	18
9	Canada	3	2	3	8	16
	Hungary	3	2	3	8	16
	South Africa	4	2	0	6	16

Leading Medal Winners
Number of individual medals won on the left; gold, silver and bronze breakdown to the right.

MEN

No		Sport	G-S-B
6	Louis Richardet, SWI	Shooting	4-2-0
5	Wilhelm Carlberg, SWE	Shooting	3-2-0
4	Hannes Kolehmainen, FIN	Track/Field	3-1-0
4	Eric Carlberg, SWE	Shooting	2-2-0
4	Johan von Holst, SWE	Shooting	2-1-1
4	Carl Osburn, USA	Shooting	1-2-1
3	Alfred Lane, USA	Shooting	3-0-0
3	Åke Lundeberg, SWE	Shooting	2-1-0
3	Frederick Hird, USA	Shooting	2-0-1
3	Jean Cariou, FRA	Equestrian	1-1-1
3	Charles Dixon, GBR	Tennis	1-1-1
3	Harold Hardwick, AUS	Swimming	1-0-2
3	Jack Hatfield, GBR	Swimming	0-2-1
3	Charles Stewart, GBR	Shooting	0-0-3

WOMEN

No		Sport	G-S-B
2	Edith Hannam, GBR	Tennis	2-0-0
2	Jennie Fletcher, GBR	Swimming	1-0-1
2	Sigrid Fick, SWE	Tennis	0-1-1

Track & Field

Event		Time	
100m	Ralph Craig, USA	.10.8	=OR
200m	Ralph Craig, USA	.21.7	
400m	Charlie Reidpath, USA	.48.2	OR
800m	Ted Meredith, USA	1:51.9	WR
1500m	Arnold Jackson, GBR	3:56.8	OR
5000m	Hannes Kolehmainen, FIN	14:36.6	WR
10,000m	Hannes Kolehmainen, FIN	.31:20.8	
X-country (12,000m)	Hannes Kolehmainen, FIN	.45:11.6	
Marathon	Kenneth McArthur, S. Afr	2:36:54.8	
110m H	Frederick Kelly, USA	.15.1	
10k Walk	George Goulding, CAN	.46:28.4	
4x100m	GBR (David Jacobs, Harold Macintosh, Victor d'Arcy, William Applegarth)	.42.4	OR
4x400m	USA (Mel Sheppard, Edward Lindberg, Ted Meredith, Charlie Reidpath)	3:16.6	WR
3000m Team	USA (Tel Berna, Norman Taber, George Bonhag)	.9 pts	
X-country (12,000m)	SWE (Hjalmar Andersson, John Eke, Josef Ternström)	.10 pts	

Event		Mark	
High Jump	Alma Richards, USA	.6- 4	OR
Pole Vault	Harry Babcock, USA	.12-11½	OR
Long Jump	Albert Gutterson, USA	.24-11¼	OR
Triple Jump	Gustaf Lindblom, SWE	.48-5¼	
Shot Put	Babe McDonald, USA	.50- 4	OR
Discus	Armas Taipale, FIN	.148- 3	OR
Hammer	Matt McGrath, USA	.179- 7	OR
Javelin	Eric Lemming, SWE	.198-11	WR
Pentathlon	Jim Thorpe, USA	.7 pts	
Decathlon	Jim Thorpe, USA	.8412 pts	WR

Event		Mark
High Jump	Platt Adams, USA	.5-4¼
Long Jump	Constantin Tsiklitiras, GRE	.11-0¾

Both Hands		Mark
Shot Put	Ralph Rose, USA	.90-10½
Discus	Armas Taipale, FIN	.271-10
Javelin	Juho Saaristo, FIN	.359- 0

Swimming
MEN

Event		Time	
100m Free	Duke Kahanamoku, USA	1:03.4	
400m Free	George Hodgson, CAN	5:24.4	
1500m Free	George Hodgson, CAN	.22:00.0	WR
100m Back	Harry Hebner, USA	1:21.2	
200m Brst	Walter Bathe, GER	3:01.8	OR
400m Brst	Walter Bathe, GER	6:29.6	OR
4x200m Free	AUS (Cecil Healy, Malcolm Champion, Leslie Boardman, Harold Hardwick)	.10:11.6	WR

Diving		Points
Spring	Paul Günther, GER	.79.23
Platform	Erik Adlerz, SWE	.73.94
Plain High	Erik Adlerz, SWE	.40.0

WOMEN

Event		Time	
100m Free	Fanny Durack, AUS	1:22.2	
4x100m Free	GBR (Bella Moore, Jennie Fletcher, Annie Speirs, Irene Steer)	5:52.8	WR

Diving		Points
Platform	Greta Johansson, SWE	.39.9

Team Sports

Sports		Champion
Soccer		.Great Britain
Tug-of-War		.Sweden
Water Polo		.Great Britain

Also Contested

Cycling, Equestrian, Fencing, Gymnastics, Modern Pentathlon, Rowing, Shooting, Tennis, Greco-Roman Wrestling and Yachting.

1920
Antwerp

The Olympic quadrennial, scheduled for Berlin in 1916, was interrupted by World War I—the so-called "War to End All Wars," which had involved 28 countries and killed nearly 10 million troops in four years.

The four-year cycle of Olympiads—Berlin would have been the sixth—is still counted, however, even though the Games were not played.

Less than two years after the armistice, the Olympics resumed in Belgium, a symbolic and austere choice considering it had been occupied for four years by enemy forces. Still, 29 countries (one more than participated in the war) sent a record 2,600 athletes to the Games. Germany and Austria, the defeated enemies of Belgium and the Allies, were not invited.

The United States turned in the best overall team performance, winning 41 gold medals, but the talk of the Games was 23-year-old distance runner Paavo Nurmi of Finland. Nurmi won the 10,000-meter run and 8,000-meter cross-country, took a third gold in the team cross-country and silver in the 5,000-meter run. In all, Finland won nine track and field gold medals to break the U.S. dominance in the sport.

Elsewhere, Albert Hill of Britain made his Olympic debut at age 36 and won both the 800 and 1,500-meter runs. World record holder Charley Paddock of the U.S. won the 100 meters, but was upset in the 200 by teammate Allen Woodring, who was a last-minute addition to the team. And in swimming, the U.S. won 11 of 15 events, led by triple gold medalists Norman Ross and Ethelda Bleibtrey, defending men's 100-meter freestyle champion Duke Kahanamoku and 14-year-old springboard diving champion Aileen Riggin.

The Antwerp Games were also noteworthy for the introduction of the Olympic oath—uttered for the first time by Belgium fencer Victor Bion—and the Olympic flag, with its five multicolored, intersecting rings.

Top 10 Standings

National medal standings are not recognized by the IOC. The unofficial point totals are based on 3 points for a gold medal, 2 for a silver and 1 for a bronze.

		Gold	Silver	Bronze	Total	Pts
1	USA	41	27	27	95	204
2	Sweden	19	20	25	64	122
3	Great Britain	14	15	13	42	85
4	France	9	19	13	41	78
5	Finland	15	10	9	34	74
	Belgium	13	11	11	35	72
7	Norway	13	9	9	31	66
8	Italy	13	5	5	23	54
9	Denmark	3	9	1	13	28
10	Holland	4	2	5	11	21

Leading Medal Winners

Number of individual medals won on the left; gold, silver and bronze breakdown to the right.

MEN

No		Sport	G-S-B
7	Willis Lee, USA	Shooting	5-1-1
7	Lloyd Spooner, USA	Shooting	4-1-2
6	Hubert van Innis, BEL	Archery	4-2-0
6	Carl Osburn, USA	Shooting	4-1-1
5	Nedo Nadi, ITA	Fencing	5-0-0
5	Otto Olsen, NOR	Shooting	3-2-0
5	Larry Nuesslein, USA	Shooting	2-1-2
5	Julien Brulé, FRA	Archery	1-3-1
4	Dennis Fenton, USA	Shooting	3-0-1
4	Aldo Nadi, ITA	Fencing	3-1-0
4	Paavo Nurmi, FIN	Track/Field	3-1-0
4	Harold Natvig, NOR	Shooting	2-1-1
4	Östen Östensen, NOR	Shooting	0-2-2
4	Erik Backman, SWE	Track/Field	0-1-3
4	Fritz Kuchen, SWI	Shooting	0-0-4
3	Norman Ross, USA	Swimming	3-0-0
3	Albert Hill, GBR	Track/Field	2-1-0
3	Morris Kirksey, USA	Track/Field & Rugby	2-1-0
3	Charley Paddock, USA	Track/Field	2-1-0
3	Bevil Rudd, S. Afr.	Track/Field	1-0-2
3	Ettore Caffaratti, ITA	Equestrian	0-1-2

Fourteen shooters tied with 3 each.

WOMEN

No		Sport	G-S-B
3	Ethelda Bleibtrey, USA	Swimming	3-0-0
3	Suzanne Lenglen, FRA	Tennis	2-0-1
3	Kitty McKane, GBR	Tennis	1-1-1
3	Frances Schroth, USA	Swimming	1-0-2
2	Irene Guest, USA	Swimming	1-1-0
2	Margaret Woodbridge, USA	Swimming	1-1-0
2	Dorothy Holman, GBR	Tennis	0-2-0

Track & Field

Event		Time
100m	Charley Paddock, USA	10.8
200m	Allen Woodring, USA	22.0
400m	Bevil Rudd, S. Afr.	49.6
800m	Albert Hill, GBR	1:53.4
1500m	Albert Hill, GBR	4:01.8
5000m	Joseph Guillemot, FRA	14:55.6
10,000m	Paavo Nurmi, FIN	31:45.8
X-country (8000m)	Paavo Nurmi, FIN	27:15.0
Marathon	Hannes Kolehmainen, FIN	2:32:35.8	WB
110m H	Earl Thomson, CAN	14.8	WR
400m H	Frank Loomis, USA	54.0	WR
3000m Steeple	Percy Hodge, GBR	10:00.4	OR
3k Walk	Ugo Frigerio, ITA	13:14.2	OR

Event		Time	
10k Walk	Ugo Frigerio, ITA	48:06.2	
4x100m	USA (Charley Paddock, Jackson Scholz, Loren Murchison, Morris Kirksey)	42.2	WR
4x100m	GBR (Cecil Griffiths, Robert Lindsay, John Ainsworth-Davis, Guy Butler)	3:22.2	
3000m Team	USA (Horace Brown, Arlie Schardt, Ivan Dresser)	10 pts	
X-country (8000m)	FIN (Paavo Nurmi, Heikki Liimatainen, Teodor Koskenniemi)	10 pts	

Event		Mark	
High Jump	Richmond Landon, USA	6-4	=OR
Pole Vault	Frank Foss, USA	13-5	WR
Long Jump	William Petersson, SWE	23-5½	
Triple Jump	Vilho Tuulos, FIN	47-7	
Shot Put	Ville Pörhölä, FIN	48-7¼	
56-lb Throw	Babe McDonald, USA	36-11½	OR
Discus	Elmer Niklander, FIN	146-7	
Hammer	Pat Ryan, USA	173-5	
Javelin	Jonni Myyrä, FIN	215-10	OR
Pentathlon	Eero Lehtonen, FIN	14 pts	
Decathlon	Helge Lövland, NOR	6803 pts	

Swimming

MEN

Event		Time	
100m Free	Duke Kahanamoku, USA	1:01.4	
400m Free	Norman Ross, USA	5:26.8	
1500m Free	Norman Ross, USA	22:23.2	
100m Back	Warren Kealoha, USA	1:15.2	
200m Brst	Håkan Malmroth, SWE	3:04.4	
400m Brst	Håkan Malmroth, SWE	6:31.8	
4x200m Free	USA (Perry McGillivray, Pua Kealoha, Norman Ross, Duke Kahanamoku)	10:04.4	WR

Diving		Points
Plain High	Arvid Wallman, SWE	183.5
Platform	Clarence Pinkston, USA	100.67
Spring	Louis Kuehn, USA	675.4

WOMEN

Event		Time	
100m Free	Ethelda Bleibtrey, USA	1:13.6	WR
300m Free	Ethelda Bleibtrey, USA	4:34.0	WR
4x100m Free	USA (Margaret Woodbridge, Frances Schroth, Irene Guest, Ethelda Bleibtrey)	5:11.6	WR

Diving		Points
Platform	Stefani Fryland-Clausen, DEN	34.6
Spring	Aileen Riggin, USA	539.9

Team Sports

Sport	Champion
Field Hockey	Great Britain
Ice Hockey	Canada
Polo	Great Britain
Soccer	Belgium
Rugby	United States
Tug-of-War	Great Britain
Water Polo	Great Britain/Ireland

Also Contested

Archery, Boxing, Cycling, Equestrian, Fencing, Figure Skating, Gymnastics, Modern Pentathlon, Rowing, Shooting, Tennis, Weightlifting, Freestyle Wrestling, Greco-Roman Wrestling and Yachting.

1924

Paris

Paavo Nurmi may have been the talk of Antwerp in 1920, but he was the sensation of Paris four years later.

It wasn't just that the "Flying Finn" won five gold medals, it was the way he did it. Running with a stopwatch on his wrist, Peerless Paavo captured the 1,500 and 5,000-meter finals within an hour of each other and set Olympic records in both. Two days later, he blew away the field in the 10,000-meter cross-country run where the heat and an unusually difficult course combined to knock out 23 of 38 starters (Finland also won the team gold in the event). And finally, the next day he led the Finns to victory in the 3,000-meter team race. His performance overshadowed the four gold medals of teammate Ville Ritola.

The gold medals won by British runners Harold Abrahams in the 100 meters and Eric Liddell in the 400 were chronicled in the 1981 Academy Award-winning film "Chariots of Fire." The movie, however, was not based on fact. Liddell, a devout Christian, knew months in advance that the preliminary for the 100 (his best event) was on a Sunday, so he had plenty of time to change plans and train for the 400. Also, he and Abrahams never competed against each other in real life.

Speaking of the movies, Johnny Weissmuller of the U.S. won three swimming gold medals in the 100 and 400-meter freestyles and the 4x200 freestyle relay. He would later become Hollywood's most famous Tarzan.

Top 10 Standings

National medal standings are not recognized by the IOC. The unofficial point totals are based on 3 points for a gold medal, 2 for a silver and 1 for a bronze.

		Gold	Silver	Bronze	Total	Pts
1	USA	45	27	27	99	216
2	France	13	15	10	38	79
3	Finland	14	13	10	37	78
4	Great Britain	9	13	12	34	65
5	Sweden	4	13	12	29	50
6	Switzerland	7	8	10	25	47
7	Italy	8	3	5	16	35
8	Belgium	3	7	3	13	26
9	Norway	5	2	3	10	22
10	Holland	4	1	5	10	19

Leading Medal Winners

Number of individual medals won on the left; gold, silver and bronze breakdown to the right.

MEN

No		Sport	G-S-B
6	Ville Ritola, FIN	Track/Field	4-2-0
5	Paavo Nurmi, FIN	Track/Field	5-0-0
5	Roger Ducret, FRA	Fencing	3-2-0
4	Johnny Weissmuller, USA	Swimming & Water Polo	3-0-1

No		Sport	G-S-B
3	Ole Lilloe-Olsen, NOR	Shooting	2-1-0
3	Vincent Richards, USA	Tennis	2-1-0
3	Albert Séquin, FRA	Gymnastics	1-2-0
3	Boy Charlton, AUS	Swimming	1-1-1
3	August Güttinger, SWI	Gymnastics	1-0-2
3	Robert Prazák, CZE	Gymnastics	0-3-0
3	Arne Borg, SWE	Swimming	0-2-1
3	Jean Gutweniger, SWI	Gymnastics	0-2-1
3	Henri Hoevenaers, BEL	Cycling	0-2-1

WOMEN

No		Sport	G-S-B
3	Gertrude Ederle, USA	Swimming	1-0-2
2	Ethel Lackie, USA	Swimming	2-0-0
2	Hazel Wightman, USA	Tennis	2-0-0
2	Helen Wills, USA	Tennis	2-0-0
2	Betty Becker, USA	Diving	1-1-0
2	Mariechen Wehselau, USA	Swimming	1-1-0
2	Kitty McKane, GBR	Tennis	0-1-1
2	Aileen Riggin, USA	Swimming & Diving	0-1-1

Track & Field

Event		Time	
100m	Harold Abrahams, GBR	10.6	=OR
200m	Jackson Scholz, USA	21.6	
400m	Eric Liddell, GBR	47.6	OR
800m	Douglas Lowe, GBR	1:52.4	
1500m	Paavo Nurmi, FIN	3:53.6	OR
5000m	Paavo Nurmi, FIN	14:31.2	OR
10,000m	Ville Ritola, FIN	30:23.2	WR
X-country (10,000m)	Paavo Nurmi, FIN	32:54.8	
Marathon	Albin Stenroos, FIN	2:41:22.6	
110m H	Daniel Kinsey, USA	15.0	
400m H	Morgan Taylor, USA	52.6	
3000m Steeple	Ville Ritola, FIN	9:33.6	OR
10k Walk	Ugo Frigerio, ITA	47:49.0	
4x100m	USA (Francis Hussey, Louis Clarke, Loren Murchison, Alfred Leconey)	41.0	=WR
4x400M	USA (C.S. Cochrane, Alan Helffrich, J.O. MacDonald, William Stevenson)	3:16.0	WR
3000m Team	FIN (Paavo Nurmi, Ville Ritola, Elias Katz)	8 pts	
X-country (10,000m)	FIN (Paavo Nurmi, Ville Ritola, Hekki Liimatainen)	11 pts	

Event		Mark	
High Jump	Harold Osborn, USA	6- 6	OR
Pole Vault	Lee Barnes, USA	12-11	
Long Jump	De Hart Hubbard, USA	24-5	
Triple Jump	Nick Winter, AUS	50-11¼	WR
Shot Put	Bud Houser, USA	49-2¼	
Discus	Bud Houser, USA	151- 4	OR
Hammer	Fred Tootell, USA	174-10	
Javelin	Jonni Myyrä, FIN	206- 7	
Pentathlon	Eero Lehtonen, FIN	14 pts	
Decathlon	Harold Osborn, USA	7711 pts	WR

Swimming

MEN

Event		Time	
100m Free	Johnny Weissmuller, USA	59.0	OR
400m Free	Johnny Weissmuller, USA	5:04.2	OR
1500m Free	Boy Charlton, AUS	20:06.6	WR
100m Back	Warren Kealoha, USA	1:13.2	
200m Brst	Robert Skelton, USA	2:56.6	

Event		Time	
4x200m Free	USA (Wallace O'Connor, Harry Glancy, Ralph Breyer, Johnny Weissmuller)	9:53.4	**WR**

Diving		Points
Plain High	Richmond Eve, AUS	160.0
Platform	Albert White, USA	97.46
Spring	Albert White, USA	696.4

WOMEN

Event		Time	
100m Free	Ethel Lackie, USA	1:12.4	
400m Free	Martha Norelius, USA	6:02.2	**OR**
100m Back	Sybil Bauer, USA	1:23.2	**OR**
200m Brst	Lucy Morton, GBR	3:33.2	**OR**
4x100m Free	USA (Gertrude Ederle, Euphrasia Donnelly, Ethel Lackie, Mariechen Wehselau)	4:58.8	**WR**

Diving		Points
Platform	Caroline Smith, USA	33.2
Spring	Elizabeth Becker, USA	474.5

Team Sports

Sport	Champion
Polo	Argentina
Rugby	United States
Soccer	Uruguay
Water Polo	France

Also Contested

Boxing, Cycling, Equestrian, Fencing, Gymnastics, Modern Pentathlon, Rowing, Shooting, Tennis, Weightlifting, Freestyle Wrestling, Greco-Roman Wrestling and Yachting.

1928

Amsterdam

"We are here to represent the greatest country on earth. We did not come here to lose gracefully. We came here to win—and win decisively."

So ordered American Olympic Committee president Gen. Douglas MacArthur before the start of the 1928 Games. His athletes could deliver, easily winning the unofficial national standings for the third Olympiad in a row.

The U.S. men won eight gold medals in track and field, but were victorious in only one individual running race (Ray Barbuti in the 400 meters). In the sprints, Canada's Percy Williams became the first non-American to win both the 100 and 200. Finland claimed four running titles, including Paavo Nurmi's victory in the 10,000 meters—his ninth overall gold medal in three Olympic Games. Teammate and arch-rival Ville Ritola placed second in the 10,000 and outran Nurmi in the 5,000.

These Games marked Germany's return to the Olympic fold after serving a 10-year probation for its "aggressiveness" in World War I. It was also the first Olympics that women were allowed to partici-

pate in track and field (despite objections from Pope Pius IX). And in swimming, the U.S. got double gold performances from Martha Norelius, Albina Osipowich and Johnny Weissmuller, as well as diver Pete Desjardins.

Top 10 Standings

National medal standings are not recognized by the IOC. The unofficial point totals are based on 3 points for a gold medal, 2 for a silver and 1 for a bronze.

		Gold	Silver	Bronze	Total	Pts
1	USA	22	18	16	56	118
2	Germany	10	7	14	31	58
3	Finland	8	8	9	25	49
4	Sweden	7	6	12	25	45
5	France	6	10	5	21	43
6	Holland	6	9	4	19	40
7	Italy	7	5	7	19	38
8	Great Britain	3	10	7	20	36
9	Switzerland	7	4	4	15	33
10	Canada	4	4	7	15	27

Leading Medal Winners

Number of individual medals won on the left; gold, silver and bronze breakdown to the right.

MEN

No		Sport	G-S-B
4	Georges Miez, SWI	Gymnastics	3-1-0
4	Hermann Hänggi, SWI	Gymnastics	2-1-1
3	Lucien Gaudin, FRA	Fencing	2-1-0
3	Eugen Mack, SWI	Gymnastics	2-0-1
3	Paavo Nurmi, FIN	Track/Field	1-2-0
3	Ladislav Vácha, CZE	Gymnastics	1-2-0
3	Leon Stukelj, YUG	Gymnastics	1-0-2
3	Emanuel Löffler, CZE	Gymnastics	0-2-1

WOMEN

No		Sport	G-S-B
3	Joyce Cooper, GBR	Swimming	0-1-2
2	Martha Norelius, USA	Swimming	2-0-0
2	Albina Osipowich, USA	Swimming	2-0-0
2	Maria Braun, NED	Swimming	1-1-0
2	Eleanor Garatti, USA	Swimming	1-1-0
2	Betty Robinson, USA	Track/Field	1-1-0
2	Fanny Rosenfeld, CAN	Track/Field	1-1-0
2	Ethel Smith, CAN	Track/Field	1-0-1
2	Ellen King, GBR	Swimming	0-2-0
2	Georgia Coleman, USA	Diving	0-1-1

Track & Field

MEN

Event		Time	
100m	Percy Williams, CAN	10.8	
200m	Percy Williams, CAN	21.8	
400m	Ray Barbuti, USA	47.8	
800m	Douglas Lowe, GBR	1:51.8	**OR**
1500m	Harri Larva, FIN	3:53.2	**OR**
5000m	Ville Ritola, FIN	14:38.0	
10,000m	Paavo Nurmi, FIN	30:18.8	**OR**
Marathon	Mohamed El Ouafi, FRA	2:32:57.0	
110m H	Syd Atkinson, S. Afr.	14.8	
400m H	David Burghley, GBR	53.4	**OR**
3000m Steeple	Toivo Loukola, FIN	9:21.8	**WR**
4x100m	USA (Frank Wykoff, Jimmy Quinn, Charley Borah, Hank Russell)	41.0	**WR**
4x100m	USA (George Baird, Bud Spencer, Fred Alderman, Ray Barbuti)	3:14.2	**WR**

Event		Mark	
High Jump	Bob King, USA	.6-4½	
Pole Vault	Sabin Carr, USA	.13-9¼	OR
Long Jump	Ed Hamm, USA	.25- 4½	OR
Triple Jump	Mikio Oda, JPN	.49-11	
Shot Put	Johnny Kuck, USA	.52-0¾	WR
Discus	Bud Houser, USA	.155- 3	OR
Hammer	Pat O'Callaghan, IRL	.168- 7	
Javelin	Erik Lundkvist, SWE	.218- 6	OR
Decathlon	Paavo Yrjölä, FIN	.8053 pts	WR

WOMEN

Event		Time	
100m	Betty Robinson, USA	.12.2	=WR
800m	Lina Radke, GER	.2:16.8	WR
4x100m	CAN (Fanny Rosenfeld, Ethel Smith, Florence Bell, Myrtle Cook)	.48.4	WR

Event		Mark	
High Jump	Ethel Catherwood, CAN	.5- 2½	
Discus	Halina Konopacka, POL	.129-11¾	WR

Swimming

MEN

Event		Time	
100m Free	Johnny Weissmuller, USA	.58.6	OR
400m Free	Alberto Zorrilla, ARG	.5:01.6	OR
1500m Free	Arne Borg, SWE	.19:51.8	OR
100m Back	George Kojac, USA	.1:08.2	WR
200m Brst	Yoshiyuki Tsuruta, JPN	.2:48.8	OR

Event		Time	
4x200m Free	USA (Austin Clapp, Walter Laufer, Gorge Kojac, Johnny Weissmuller)	.9:36.2	WR

Diving		Points
Platform	Pete Desjardins, USA	.98.74
Spring	Pete Desjardins, USA	.185.04

WOMEN

Event		Time	
100m Free	Albina Osipowich, USA	.1:11.0	OR
400m Free	Martha Norelius, USA	.5:42.8	WR
100m Back	Maria Braun, NED	.1:22.0	
200m Brst	Hilde Schrader, GER	.3:12.6	
4x100m Free	USA (Adelaide Lambert, Eleanor Garatti, Albina Osipowich, Martha Norelius)	.4:47.6	WR

Diving		Points
Platform	Elizabeth Becker Pinkston, USA	.31.6
Spring	Helen Meany, USA	.78.62

Team Sports

Sport	Champion
Field Hockey	India
Soccer	Uruguay
Water Polo	Germany

Also Contested

Boxing, Cycling, Equestrian, Fencing, Gymnastics, Modern Pentathlon, Rowing, Weightlifting, Freestyle Wrestling, Greco-Roman Wrestling and Yachting.

1932

Los Angeles

Despite a world-wide economic depression and predictions that the 1932 Summer Olympics were doomed to failure, 37 countries sent over 1,300 athletes to southern California and the Games were a huge success.

Energized by perfect weather and the buoyant atmosphere of the first Olympic Village, the competition was fierce. Sixteen world and Olympic records fell in men's track and field alone.

In women's track, 21-year-old Babe Didrikson, who had set world records in the 80-meter hurdles, javelin and high jump at the AAU Olympic Trials three weeks before, came to L.A. and announced, "I am out to beat everybody in sight." She almost did toowinning the hurdles and javelin, but taking second in the high jump (despite tying teammate Jean Shiley for first) when her jumping style was ruled illegal.

Didrikson's heroics, along with American Eddie Tolan's double in the 100 and 200 meters and Italian Luigi Beccali's upset victory in the 1,500, were among the Games' highlights, but they didn't quite make up for the absence of Finland's famed distance runner Paavo Nurmi.

Just before the Games, the IOC said that Nurmi would not be allowed to participate in his fourth Olympics because he had received excessive expense money on a trip to Germany in 1929. The ruling came as no surprise in the track world where it was said, "Nurmi has the lowest heartbeat and the highest asking price of any athlete in the world."

The Japanese men and American women dominated in swimming, each winning five of six events. Helene Madison of the U.S. won two races and anchored the winning relay team.

Top 10 Standings

National medal standings are not recognized by the IOC. The unofficial point totals are based on 3 points for a gold medal, 2 for a silver and 1 for a bronze.

		Gold	Silver	Bronze	Total	Pts
1	USA	41	32	30	103	217
2	Italy	12	12	12	36	72
3	Sweden	9	5	9	23	46
4	France	10	5	4	19	44
5	Finland	5	8	12	25	43
6	Germany	3	12	5	20	38
7	Japan	7	7	4	18	39
8	Great Britain	4	7	5	16	31
	Hungary	6	4	5	15	31
10	Canada	2	5	8	15	24

Leading Medal Winners

Number of individual medals won on the left; gold, silver and bronze breakdown to the right.

MEN

No		Sport	G-S-B
4	István Pelle, HUN	Gymnastics	2-2-0
4	Giulio Gaudini, ITA	Fencing	0-3-1
4	Heikki Savolainen, FIN	Gymnastics	0-1-3
3	Romeo Neri, ITA	Gymnastics	3-0-0
3	Alex Wilson, CAN	Track/Field	0-1-2
3	Philip Edwards, CAN	Track/Field	0-0-3

WOMEN

No		Sport	G-S-B
3	Helene Madison, USA . . . . .Swimming		3-0-0
3	Babe Didrikson, USA . . . . .Track/Field		2-1-0
2	Georgia Coleman, USA . . . . .Diving		1-1-0
2	Eleanor Garatti, USA . . . . .Swimming		1-0-1
2	Willy den Ouden, HOL . . . . . .Swimming		0-2-0
2	Valerie Davies, GBR . . . . .Swimming		0-0-2

Track & Field

MEN

Event		Time	
100m	Eddie Tolan, USA 10.3		OR
200m	Eddie Tolan, USA 21.2		OR
400m	Bill Carr, USA 46.2		WR
800m	Tommy Hampson, GBR 1:49.7		WR
1500m	Luigi Beccali, ITA 3:51.2		OR
5000m	Lauri Lehtinen, FIN 14:30.0		OR
10,000m	Janusz Kusocinski, POL 30:11.4		OR
Marathon	Juan Carlos Zabala, ARG .2:31:36.0		OR
110m H	George Saling, USA 14.6		
400m H	Bob Tisdall, IRL 51.7		
3000m Steeple	Volmari Iso-Hollo, FIN 10:33.4		
50k Walk	Thomas Green, GBR 4:50:10		
4x100m	USA (Bob Kiesel, Emmett Toppino, Hector Dyer, Frank Wykoff) 40.0		WR
4x100m	USA (Ivan Fuqua, Edgar Ablowich, Karl Warner, Bill Carr) 3:08.2		WR

Note: Due to a lap count error, the 3000-meter steeplechase actually went 3460 meters, or one lap too many.

Event		Mark	
High Jump	Duncan McNaughton, CAN . .6- 5½		
Pole Vault	Bill Miller, USA 14- 1¾		OR
Long Jump	Edward Gordon, USA 25- 0¾		
Triple Jump	Chuhei Nambu, JPN 51- 7		WR
Shot Put	Leo Sexton, USA 52- 6		OR
Discus	John Anderson, USA 162- 4		OR
Hammer	Pat O'Callaghan, IRL 176-11		
Javelin	Matti Järvinen, FIN 238- 6		OR
Decathlon	Jim Bausch, USA . . . . . . .8462 pts		WR

WOMEN

Event		Time	
100m	Stella Walsh, POL* 11.9		=WR
80m H	Babe Didrikson, USA 11.7		WR
4x100m	USA (Mary Carew, Evelyn Furtsch, Annette Rogers, Wilhelmina Von Bremen) 46.9		WR

*An autopsy performed after Walsh's death in 1980 revealed that she was a man.

Event		Mark	
High Jump	Jean Shiley, USA 5-5		WR
Discus	Lillian Copeland, USA 133-2		OR
Javelin	Babe Didrikson, USA 143-4		OR

Swimming

MEN

Event		Time	
100m Free	Yasuji Miyazaki, JPN 58.2		
400m Free	Buster Crabbe, USA 4:48.4		OR
1500m Free	Kusuo Kitamura, JPN 19:12.4		OR
100m Back	Masaji Kiyokawa, JPN 1:08.6		
200m Brst	Yoshiyuki Tsuruta, JPN 2:45.4		
4x200m Free	JPN (Yasuji Miyazaki, Masonori Yusa, Takashi Yokoyama, Hisakichi Toyoda) 8:58.4		WR

Diving		Points
Platform	Harold Smith, USA 124.80	
Spring	Michael Galitzen, USA 161.38	

WOMEN

Event		Time	
100m Free	Helene Madison, USA . . .1:06.8		OR
400m Free	Helene Madison, USA . . .5:28.5		WR
100m Back	Eleanor Holm, USA 1:19.4		
200m Brst	Clare Dennis, AUS 3:06.3		OR
4x100m Free	USA (Josephine McKim, Helen Johns, Eleanor Saville-Garatti, Helene Madison) 4:38.0		WR

Diving		Points
Platform	Dorothy Poynton, USA 40.26	
Spring	Georgia Coleman, USA 87.52	

Team Sports

Sport		Champion
Field Hockey . . . . .India		
Water Polo . . . . .Hungary		

Also Contested

Boxing, Cycling, Equestrian, Fencing, Gymnastics, Modern Pentathlon, Rowing, Shooting, Weightlifting, Freestyle Wrestling, Greco-Roman Wrestling and Yachting.

1936

Berlin

At the Big Ten Track and Field Championships of 1935, Ohio State's Jesse Owens equaled or set world records in four events: the 100 and 220-yard dashes, 200-yard low hurdles and the long jump. He was also credited with world marks in the 200-meter run and 200-meter hurdles. That's six world records in one afternoon, and he did it all in 45 minutes!

The following year, he swept the 100 and 200 meters and long jump at the Olympic Trials and headed for Germany favored to win all three.

In Berlin, dictator Adolf Hitler and his Nazi followers felt sure that the Olympics would be the ideal venue to demonstrate Germany's oft-stated racial superiority. He directed that $25 million be spent on the finest facilities, the cleanest streets and the temporary withdrawal of all outward signs of the state-run anti-Jewish campaign. By the time over 4,000 athletes from 49 countries arrived for the Games, the stage was set.

Then Owens, a black sharecropper's son from Alabama, stole the show—winning his three individual events and adding a fourth gold medal in the 4x100-meter relay. The fact that four other American blacks also won did little to please Herr Hitler, but the applause from the German crowds, especially for Owens, was thunderous. As it was for New Zealander Jack Lovelock's thrilling win over Glenn Cunningham and defending champ Luigi Beccali in the 1,500 meters.

Germany won only five combined gold medals

in men's and women's track and field, but saved face for the "master race" in the overall medal count with an 89-56 margin over the United States.

The top female performers in Berlin were 17-year-old Dutch swimmer Rie Mastenbroek, who won three gold medals, and 18-year-old American runner Helen Stephens, who captured the 100 meters and anchored the winning 4x100-meter relay team.

Basketball also made its debut as a medal sport and was played outdoors. The U.S. men easily won the first gold medal championship game with a 19-8 victory over Canada in the rain.

Top 10 Standings

National medal standings are not recognized by the IOC. The unofficial point totals are based on 3 points for a gold medal, 2 for a silver and 1 for a bronze.

		Gold	Silver	Bronze	Total	Pts
1	Germany	33	26	30	89	181
2	USA	24	20	12	56	124
3	Italy	8	9	5	22	47
4	Finland	7	6	6	19	39
	France	7	6	6	19	39
6	Sweden	6	5	9	20	37
	Hungary	10	1	5	16	37
8	Japan	6	4	8	18	34
9	Holland	6	4	7	17	33
10	Great Britain	4	7	3	14	29

Leading Medal Winners

Number of individual medals won on the left; gold, silver and bronze breakdown to the right.

MEN

No		Sport	G-S-B
6	Konrad Frey, GER	Gymnastics	3-1-2
5	Alfred Schwarzmann, GER	Gymnastics	3-0-2
5	Eugen Mack, SWI	Gymnastics	0-4-1
4	Jesse Owens, USA	Track/Field	4-0-0
3	Robert Charpentier, FRA	Cycling	3-0-0
3	Guy Lapébie, FRA	Cycling	2-1-0
3	Jack Medica, USA	Swimming	1-2-0
3	Matthias Volz, GER	Gymnastics	1-0-2

WOMEN

No		Sport	G-S-B
4	Rie Mastenbroek, NED	Swimming	3-1-0
2	Helen Stephens, USA	Track/Field	2-0-0
2	Dorothy Poynton Hill, USA	Diving	1-0-1
2	Gisela Arendt, GER	Swimming	0-1-1

Track & Field

MEN

Event		Time	
100m	Jesse Owens, USA	10.3	
200m	Jesse Owens, USA	20.7	OR
400m	Archie Williams, USA	46.5	
800m	John Woodruff, USA	1:52.9	
1500m	Jack Lovelock, NZE	3:47.8	WR
5000m	Gunnar Höckert, FIN	14:22.2	OR
10,000m	Ilmari Salminen, FIN	30:15.4	
Marathon	Sohn Kee-chung, JPN	2:29:19.2	OR
110m H	Forrest Towns, USA	14.2	
400m H	Glenn Hardin, USA	52.4	
3000m Steeple	Volmari Iso-Hollo, FIN	9:03.8	WR
50k walk	Harold Whitlock, GBR	4:30:41.4	OR

Note: Marathon winner Sohn was a Korean, but was forced to run for Japan, which occupied his country.

Event		Time	
4x100m	USA (Jesse Owens, Ralph Metcalfe, Foy Draper, Frank Wykoff)	39.8	WR
4x400m	GBR (Frederick Wolff, Godfrey Rampling, William Roberts, A.G. Brown)	3:09.0	

Event		Mark	
High Jump	Cornelius Johnson, USA	6-8	OR
Pole Vault	Earle Meadows, USA	14-3¼	OR
Long Jump	Jesse Owens, USA	26-5½	OR
Triple Jump	Naoto Tajima, JPN	52-6	WR
Shot Put	Hans Woellke, GER	53-1¾	OR
Discus	Ken Carpenter, USA	165-7	OR
Hammer	Karl Hein, GER	185-4	OR
Javelin	Gerhard Stöck, GER	235-8	
Decathlon	Glenn Morris, USA	7900 pts	WR

WOMEN

Event		Time	
100m	Helen Stephens, USA	11.5^W	
80m H	Trebisonda Valla, ITA	11.7	
4x100m	USA (Harriet Bland, Annette Rogers, Betty Robinson, Helen Stephens)	46.9	

^{W} indicates wind-aided.

Event		Mark	
High Jump	Ibolya Csák, HUN	5-3	
Discus	Gisela Mauermayer, GER	156-3	OR
Javelin	Tilly Fleischer, GER	148-3	OR

Swimming

MEN

Event		Time	
100m Free	Ferenc Csík, HUN	57.6	
400m Free	Jack Medica, USA	4:44.5	OR
1500m Free	Noboru Terada, JPN	19:13.7	
100m Back	Adolf Kiefer, USA	1:05.9	OR
200m Brst	Tetsuo Hamuro, JPN	2:41.5	OR
4x200m Free	JPN (Masanori Yusa, Shigeo Sugiura, Masaharu Taguchi, Shigeo Arai)	8:51.5	WR

Diving		Points
Platform	Marshall Wayne, USA	113.58
Spring	Richard Degener, USA	163.57

WOMEN

Event		Time	
100m Free	Rie Mastenbroek, NED	1:05.9	OR
400m Free	Rie Mastenbroek, NED	5:26.4	OR
100m Back	Nida Senff, NED	1:18.9	
200m Brst	Hideko Maehata, JPN	3:03.6	
4x100m Free	NED (Johanna Selbach, Catherina Wagner, Willemijntje den Ouden, Rie Mastenbroek)	4:36.0	OR

Diving		Points
Platform	Dorothy Poynton Hill, USA	33.93
Spring	Marjorie Gestring, USA	89.27

Team Sports

Sport	Champion
Basketball	United States
Field Hockey	India
Handball	Germany
Polo	Argentina
Soccer	Italy
Water Polo	Hungary

Note: In Water Polo, both Hungary and Germany finished with records of 8-0-1. The Hungarians were awarded the gold medal on total goals (57-56).

Also Contested

Boxing, Canoeing, Cycling, Equestrian, Fencing, Gymnastics, Modern Pentathlon, Rowing, Shooting, Weightlifting, Freestyle Wrestling, Greco-Roman Wrestling and Yachting.

OLYMPIC GAMES

29 JULY 1948 14 AUGUST
L O N D O N

1948

London

The Summer Olympics were scheduled for Tokyo in 1940, but by mid-1938, Japan was at war with China and withdrew as host. The IOC immediately transferred the Games to Helsinki and the Finns eagerly began preparations only to be invaded by the Soviet Union in 1939.

By then, of course, Germany had marched into Poland and World War II was on. The Japanese attacked Pearl Harbor two years later, and the bombs didn't stop falling until 1945. Against this backdrop of global conflict, the Olympic Games were cancelled again in 1940 and '44. Many of the participants in the 1936 Games died in the war.

Eager to come back after two dormant Olympiads, the IOC offered the 1948 Games to London. Much of the British capital had been reduced to rubble in the blitz, but the offer was accepted and the Games went on—successfully, without frills, and without invitations extended to Germany and Japan. The Soviet Union was invited, but chose not to show.

The United States reclaimed its place at the top of the overall medal standings, but the primary individual stars were a 30-year-old Dutch mother of two and a 17-year-old kid from California.

Fanny Blankers-Koen duplicated Jesse Owens' track and field grand slam of 12 years before by winning the 100-meter and 200-meter runs, the 80-meter hurdles, and anchoring the women's 4x100-meter relay.

And Bob Mathias, just two months after graduating from Tulare High School, won the gold medal in the decathlon, an event he had taken up for the first time earlier in the year.

Top 10 Standings

National medal standings are not recognized by the IOC. The unofficial point totals are based on 3 points for a gold medal, 2 for a silver and 1 for a bronze.

		Gold	Silver	Bronze	Total	Pts
1	USA	38	27	19	84	187
2	Sweden	16	11	17	44	87
3	Italy	8	12	9	29	57
4	France	10	6	13	29	55
5	Hungary	10	5	12	27	52
6	Great Britain	3	14	6	23	43
	Finland	8	7	5	20	43
8	Switzerland	5	10	5	20	40
9	Denmark	5	7	8	20	37
10	Holland	5	2	9	16	28
	Turkey	6	4	2	12	28

Leading Medal Winners

Number of individual medals won on the left; gold, silver and bronze breakdown to the right.

MEN

No		Sport	G-S-B
5	Veikko Huhtanen, FIN	Gymnastics	3-1-1
4	Paavo Aaltonen, FIN	Gymnastics	3-0-1
3	Jimmy McLane, USA	Swimming	2-1-0
3	Humberto Mariles, MEX	Equestrian	2-0-1
3	Mal Whitfield, USA	Track/Field	2-0-1
3	Barney Ewell, USA	Track/Field	1-2-0
3	Michael Reusch, SWI	Gymnastics	1-2-0
3	Josef Stalder, SWI	Gymnastics	1-1-1
3	Ferenc Pataki, HUN	Gymnastics	1-0-2
3	Walter Lehmann, SWI	Gymnastics	0-3-0
3	Edoardo Mangiarotti, ITA	Fencing	0-2-1
3	János Mogyorósi, HUN	Gymnastics	0-1-2

WOMEN

No		Sport	G-S-B
4	Fanny Blankers-Koen, NED	Track/Field	4-0-0
3	Ann Curtis, USA	Swimming	2-1-0
3	Micheline Ostermeyer, FRA	Track/Field	2-0-1
3	Karen-Margrete Harup, DEN	Swimming	1-2-0
3	Shirley Strickland, AUS	Track/Field	0-1-2

Track & Field

MEN

Event		Time	
100m	Harrison Dillard, USA	10.3	=OR
200m	Mel Patton, USA	21.1	
400m	Arthur Wint, JAM	46.2	
800m	Mal Whitfield, USA	1:49.2	OR
1500m	Henri Eriksson, SWE	3:49.8	
5000m	Gaston Reiff, BEL	14:17.6	OR
10,000m	Emil Zátopek, CZE	29:59.6	OR
Marathon	Delfo Cabrera, ARG	2:34:51.6	
110m H	Bill Porter, USA	13.9	OR
400m H	Roy Cochran, USA	51.1	OR
3000m Steeple	Thore Sjöstrand, SWE	9:04.6	
10k Walk	John Mikaelsson, SWE	45:13.2	
50k Walk	John Ljunggren, SWE	4:41:52	
4x100m	USA (Barney Ewell, Lorenzo Wright, Harrison Dillard, Mel Patton)	40.6	
4x100m	USA (Art Harnden, Cliff Bourland, Roy Cochran, Mal Whitfield)	3:10.4	

Event		Mark	
High Jump	John Winter, AUS	6-6	
Pole Vault	Guinn Smith, USA	14-1¼	
Long Jump	Willie Steele, USA	25-8	
Triple Jump	Arne Åhman, SWE	50-6¼	
Shot Put	Wilbur Thompson, USA	56-2	OR
Discus	Adolfo Consolini, ITA	173-2	OR
Hammer	Imre Németh, HUN	183-11	
Javelin	Tapio Rautavaara, FIN	228-10	
Decathlon	Bob Mathias, USA	7139 pts	

WOMEN

Event		Time	
100m	Fanny Blankers-Koen, NED	11.9	
200m	Fanny Blankers-Koen, NED	24.4	
80m H	Fanny Blankers-Koen, NED	11.2	OR
4x100m	NED (Xenia Stad-de Jong, Jeanette Witziers-Timmer, Gerda van der Kade-Koudijs, Fanny Blankers-Koen)	47.5	

Event		Mark	
High Jump	Alice Coachman, USA	.5- 6	OR
Long Jump	Olga Gyarmati, HUN	18- 8¼	
Shot Put	Micheline Ostermeyer, FRA	.45- 1½	
Discus	Micheline Ostermeyer, FRA	.137- 6	
Javelin	Herma Bauma, AUT	149- 6	

Note: Coachman and Dorothy Odam of Britain tied for 1st place, but Coachman was awarded gold medal for making height on first try.

Swimming

MEN

Event		Time	
100m Free	Wally Ris, USA	.57.3	OR
400m Free	Bill Smith, USA	.4:41.0	OR
1500m Free	Jimmy McLane, USA	19:18.5	
100m Back	Allen Stack, USA	1:06.4	
200m Brst	Joe Verdeur, USA	2:39.3	OR
4x200m Free	USA (Wally Ris, Jimmy McLane, Wally Wolf, Bill Smith)	8:46.0	WR

Diving		Points
Platform	Sammy Lee, USA	130.05
Spring	Bruce Harlan, USA	163.64

WOMEN

Event		Time	
100m Free	Greta Andersen, DEN	1:06.3	
400m Free	Ann Curtis, USA	5:17.8	OR
100m Back	Karen M. Harup, DEN	1:14.4	OR
200m Brst	Nel van Vliet, NED	2:57.2	
4x100m Free	USA (Marie Corridon, Thelma Kalama, Brenda Helser, Ann Curtis)	4:29.2	OR

Diving		Points
Platform	Vicki Draves, USA	.68.87
Spring	Vicki Draves, USA	108.74

Team Sports

Sport	Champion
Basketball	United States
Field Hockey	India
Soccer	Sweden
Water Polo	Italy

Also Contested

Boxing, Canoeing, Cycling, Equestrian, Fencing, Gymnastics, Modern Pentathlon, Rowing, Shooting, Weightlifting, Freestyle Wrestling, Greco-Roman Wrestling and Yachting.

1952

Helsinki

The Soviet Union returned to the Olympic fold in 1952 after a 40-year absence, a period of time that included a revolution and two world wars. Ironically, the Soviets chose to make their comeback in Finland, a country they had invaded twice during World War II.

This time it was the United States that was surprised by the Soviets, and the USA had to scramble on the last day of competition to hold off the USSR's assault on first place in the overall standings. It was the beginning of an all-consuming 36-year Cold War rivalry.

Despite the Soviets' impressive debut, it was a Communist from another Iron Curtain country who turned in the most memorable individual performance of the Games. Emil Zátopek of Czechoslovakia, the 10,000-meter champion in London, not only repeated at 10,000 meters, but also won at 5,000 and in the marathon—an event he had never run before. He also set Olympic records in each race and topped it off by watching his wife Dana Zátopková win the women's javelin.

Zátopek's unique triple was wildly applauded by the distance-minded Finns, but their greatest outburst came in the opening ceremonies when legendary countryman Paavo Nurmi, now 56, ran into the stadium with the Olympic torch and handed it off to another native legend Hannes Kolehmainen, now 62, who lit the flame to start the Games.

Also, Harrison Dillard of the U.S. won the 110-meter hurdles. In 1948, Dillard, the world's best hurdler, failed to qualify for the hurdles and won the 100-meter dash instead.

Top 10 Standings

National medal standings are not recognized by the IOC. The unofficial point totals are based on 3 points for a gold medal, 2 for a silver and 1 for a bronze.

		Gold	Silver	Bronze	Total	Pts
1	USA	40	19	17	76	175
2	USSR	21	30	18	69	141
3	Hungary	16	10	16	42	84
4	Sweden	12	13	10	35	72
5	Italy	8	9	4	21	46
6	Finland	6	3	13	22	37
7	France	6	6	6	18	36
8	Germany	0	7	17	24	31
9	Czechoslovakia	7	3	3	13	30
10	Australia	6	2	3	11	25

Leading Medal Winners

Number of individual medals won on the left; gold, silver and bronze breakdown to the right.

MEN

No		Sport	G-S-B
6	Viktor Chukarin, USSR	Gymnastics	4-2-0
4	Edoardo Mangiarotti, ITA	Fencing	2-2-0
4	Grant Shaginyan, USSR	Gymnastics	2-2-0
4	Josef Stalder, SWI	Gymnastics	0-2-2
3	Emil Zátopek, CZE	Track/Field	3-0-0
3	Ford Konno, USA	Swimming	2-1-0
3	Herb McKenley, JAM	Track/Field	1-2-0
3	Hans Eugster, SWI	Gymnastics	1-1-1

WOMEN

No		Sport	G-S-B
7	Maria Gorokhovskaya, USSR	Gymnastics	2-5-0
6	Margit Korondi, HUN	Gymnastics	1-1-4
4	Nina Bocharova, USSR	Gymnastics	2-2-0
4	Ágnes Keleti, HUN	Gymnastics	1-1-2
3	Yekaterina Kalinchuk, USSR	Gymnastics	2-1-0
3	Éva Novák, HUN	Swimming	1-2-0
3	Galina Minaicheva, USSR	Gymnastics	1-1-1
3	Aleksandra Chudina, USSR	Track/Field	0-2-1

Track & Field
MEN

Event		Time	
100m	Lindy Remigino, USA	.10.4	
200m	Andy Stanfield, USA	.20.7	
400m	George Rhoden, JAM	.45.9	OR
800m	Mal Whitfield, USA	1:49.2	=OR
1500m	Josy Barthel, LUX	3:45.1	OR
5000m	Emil Zátopek, CZE	14:06.6	OR
10,000m	Emil Zátopek, CZE	.29:17.0	OR
Marathon	Emil Zátopek, CZE	2:23:03.2	OR
110m H	Harrison Dillard, USA	.13.7	OR
400m H	Charley Moore, USA	.50.8	OR
3000m Steeple	Horace Ashenfelter, USA	.8:45.4	WR
10k Walk	John Mikaelsson, SWE	.45:02.8	OR
50k Walk	Giuseppe Dordoni, ITA	.4:28:07.8	OR
4x100m	USA (Dean Smith, Harrison Dillard, Lindy Remigino,Andy Stanfield)	.40.1	
4x100m	JAM (Arthur Wint, Leslie Laing, Herb McKenley, George Rhoden)	3:03.9	WR

Event		Mark	
High Jump	Walt Davis, USA	.6-8½	OR
Pole Vault	Bob Richards, USA	.14-11	OR
Long Jump	Jerome Biffle, USA	.24-10	
Triple Jump	Adhemar da Silva, BRA	.53-2¾	WR
Shot Put	Parry O'Brien, USA	.57-1½	OR
Discus	Sim Iness, USA	.180-6	OR
Hammer	József Csermák, HUN	.197-11	WR
Javelin	Cy Young, USA	.242-1	OR
Decathlon	Bob Mathias, USA	.7887 pts	WR

WOMEN

Event		Time	
100m	Marjorie Jackson, AUS	.11.5	WR
200m	Marjorie Jackson, AUS	.23.7	
80m H	Shirley Strickland, AUS	.10.9	WR
4x100m	USA (Mae Faggs, Barbara Jones, Janet Moreau, Catherine Hardy)	.45.9	WR

Event		Mark	
High Jump	Esther Brand, S.Afr.	.5-5¾	
Long Jump	Yvette Williams, NZE	.20-5¾	OR
Shot Put	Galina Zybina, USSR	.50-1¾	WR
Discus	Nina Romaschkova, USSR	.168-8	OR
Javelin	Dana Zátopková, CZE	.165-7	

Swimming
MEN

Event			Time	
100m Free	Clarke Scholes, USA		.57.4	
400m Free	Jean Boiteux, FRA		4:30.7	OR
1500m Free	Ford Konno, USA		18:30.3	OR
100m Back	Yoshi Oyakawa, USA		1:05.4	OR
200m Brst	John Davies, AUS		2:34.4	OR
4x200m Free	USA (Wayne Moore, Bill Woolsey, Ford Konno, Jimmy McLane)		.8:31.1	OR

Diving		Points	
Platform	Sammy Lee, USA	.156.28	
Spring	Skippy Browning, USA	.205.29	

WOMEN

Event			Time	
100m Free	Katalin Szöke, HUN		1:06.8	
400m Free	Valéria Gyenge, HUN		5:12.1	OR
100m Back	Joan Harrison, S. Afr.		1:14.3	
200m Brst	Éva Szekely, HUN		2:51.7	OR
4x100m Free	HUN (Ilona Novák, Judit Temes, Eva Novák, Katalin Szöke)		4:24.4	WR

Diving		Points
Platform	Pat McCormick, USA	.79.37
Spring	Pat McCormick, USA	.147.30

Team Sports

Sport	Champion
Basketball	United States
Field Hockey	India
Soccer	Hungary
Water Polo	Hungary

Also Contested

Boxing, Canoeing, Cycling, Equestrian, Fencing, Gymnastics, Modern Pentathlon, Rowing, Shooting, Weightlifting, Freestyle Wrestling, Greco-Roman Wrestling and Yachting.

1956
Melbourne

Armed conflicts in Egypt and Hungary threatened to disrupt the 1956 Games, which were scheduled to begin on Nov. 22 (during the summer Down Under).

In July, Egypt seized the Suez Canal from British and French control. In October, Britain and France invaded Egypt in an attempt to retake the canal. Then in November, Soviet tanks rolled into Hungary to crush an anti-Communist revolt.

The only direct bearing these events had in Melbourne came when the Soviet water polo team met the Hungarians in the semifinals. Hungary won 4-0, but the match turned ugly after a Hungarian player was pulled bleeding from the pool with a deep gash over his eye from a Soviet head butt. A brawl quickly ensued involving both players and spectators and the police had to step in to prevent a riot.

Otherwise, the Soviets outmedaled the U.S. for the first time, cleaning up in gymnastics and winning their first track and field titles when Vladimir Kuts ran off with the 5,000 and 10,000 meters.

The American men won 15 track and field titles, including three golds for sprinter Bobby Morrow and Al Oerter's first victory in the discus.

Harold Connolly of the U.S. won the hammer throw and the heart of the women's discus champion, Olga Fikotová of Czechoslovakia. Their romance captured the imagination of the world and three months after the Games they were married.

Emil Zátopek, the Czech hero of Helsinki, returned to defend his marathon title but came in sixth. Winner Alain Mimoun of France had finished second to Zátopek three times in previous Olympic races.

Top 10 Standings

National medal standings are not recognized by the IOC. The unofficial point totals are based on 3 points for a gold medal, 2 for a silver and 1 for a bronze.

		Gold	Silver	Bronze	Total	Pts
1	USSR	37	29	32	98	201
2	USA	32	25	17	74	163
3	Australia	13	8	14	35	69
4	Hungary	9	10	7	26	54
5	Germany	6	13	7	26	51
6	Italy	8	8	9	25	49
7	Great Britain	6	7	11	24	43
8	Sweden	8	5	6	19	40
9	Japan	4	10	5	19	37
10	Romania	5	3	5	13	26
	France	4	4	6	14	26

Leading Medal Winners

Number of individual medals won on the left; gold, silver and bronze breakdown to the right.

MEN

No		Sport	G-S-B
5	Viktor Chukarin, USSR	Gymnastics	3-1-1
5	Takashi Ono, JPN	Gymnastics	1-3-1
4	Valentin Muratov, USSR	Gymnastics	3-1-0
4	Yuriy Titov, USSR	Gymnastics	1-1-2
4	Masao Takemoto, JPN	Gymnastics	0-1-3
3	Bobby Morrow, USA	Track/Field	3-0-0
3	Murray Rose, AUS	Swimming	3-0-0
3	Edoardo Mangiarotti, ITA	Fencing	2-0-1
3	Thane Baker, USA	Track/Field	1-1-1
3	Masami Kubota, JPN	Gymnastics	0-2-1
3	George Breen, USA	Swimming	0-1-2

WOMEN

No		Sport	G-S-B
6	Agnes Keleti, HUN	Gymnastics	4-2-0
6	Larissa Latynina, USSR	Gymnastics	4-1-1
4	Tamara Manina, USSR	Gymnastics	1-2-1
4	Sofiya Muratova, USSR	Gymnastics	1-0-3
3	Betty Cuthbert, AUS	Track/Field	3-0-0
3	Lorraine Crapp, AUS	Swimming	2-1-0
3	Dawn Fraser, AUS	Swimming	2-1-0
3	Olga Tass, HUN	Gymnastics	1-1-1

Track & Field

MEN

Event		Time	
100m	Bobby Morrow, USA	10.5	
200m	Bobby Morrow, USA	20.6	OR
400m	Charley Jenkins, USA	46.7	
800m	Tom Courtney, USA	1:47.7	OR
1500m	Ron Delany, IRL	3:41.2	OR
5000m	Vladimir Kuts, USSR	13:39.6	OR
10,000m	Vladimir Kuts, USSR	28:45.6	OR
Marathon	Alain Mimoun, FRA	2:25:00.0	
110m H	Lee Calhoun, USA	13.5	OR
400m H	Glenn Davis, USA	50.1	=OR
3000m Steeple	Chris Brasher, GBR	8:41.2	OR
20k Walk	Leonid Spirin, USSR	1:31:27.4	
50k Walk	Norman Read, NZE	4:30:42.8	
4x100m	USA (Ira Murchison, Leamon King, Thane Baker, Bobby Morrow)	39.5	WR
4x400m	USA (Lou Jones, Jesse Mashburn, Charlie Jenkins, Tom Courtney)	3:04.8	

Event		Mark	
High Jump	Charley Dumas, USA	6-11½	OR
Pole Vault	Bob Richards, USA	14-11½	OR
Long Jump	Greg Bell, USA	25-8¼	
Triple Jump	Adhemar da Silva, BRA	53-7¾	OR
Shot Put	Parry O'Brien, USA	60-11½	OR
Discus	Al Oerter, USA	184-11	OR
Hammer	Harold Connolly, USA	207-3	OR
Javelin	Egil Danielson, NOR	281-2	WR
Decathlon	Milt Campbell, USA	7937 pts	OR

WOMEN

Event		Time	
100m	Betty Cuthbert, AUS	11.5	
200m	Betty Cuthbert, AUS	23.4	=OR
80m H	Shirley Strickland, AUS	10.7	OR
4x100m	AUS (Shirley Strickland, Norma Croker, Fleur Mellor, Betty Cuthbert)	44.5	WR

Event		Mark	
High Jump	Mildred McDaniel, USA	5-9¼	WR
Long Jump	Elzbieta Krzesinska, POL	20-10	=WR
Shot Put	Tamara Tyshkevich, USSR	54-5	OR
Discus	Olga Fikotová, CZE	176-1	OR
Javelin	Inese Jaunzeme, USSR	176-8	

Swimming

MEN

Event		Time	
100m Free	Jon Henricks, AUS	55.4	OR
400m Free	Murray Rose, AUS	4:27.3	OR
1500m Free	Murray Rose, AUS	17:58.9	
100m Back	David Theile, AUS	1:02.2	OR
200m Brst	Masaru Furukawa, JPN	2:34.7	OR
200m Fly	Bill Yorzyk, USA	2:19.3	OR
4x200m Free	AUS (Kevin O'Halloran, John Devitt, Murray Rose, Jon Henricks)	8:23.6	WR

Diving		Points
Platform	Joaquin Capilla, MEX	152.44
Spring	Bob Clotworthy, USA	159.56

WOMEN

Event		Time	
100m Free	Dawn Fraser, AUS	1:02.0	WR
400m Free	Lorraine Crapp, AUS	4:54.6	OR
100m Back	Judy Grinham, GBR	1:12.9	OR
200m Brst	Ursula Happe, GER	2:53.1	OR
100m Fly	Shelly Mann, USA	1:11.0	OR
4x100m Free	AUS (Dawn Fraser, Faith Leech, Sandra Morgan, Lorraine Crapp)	4:17.1	WR

Diving		Points
Platform	Pat McCormick, USA	84.85
Spring	Pat McCormick, USA	142.36

Team Sports

Sport	Champion
Basketball	United States
Field Hockey	India
Soccer	Soviet Union
Water Polo	Hungary

Also Contested

Boxing, Canoeing, Cycling, Equestrian, Fencing, Gymnastics, Modern Pentathlon, Rowing, Shooting, Weightlifting, Freestyle Wrestling, Greco-Roman Wrestling and Yachting.

Note: Equestrian events were held in Stockholm, Sweden, June 10-17, due to Australian quarantine laws.

JEUX DE LA XVII OLYMPIADE
ROMA 25.VIII-11.IX

1960

Rome

Free of political entanglements, save the ruling that Nationalist China had to compete as Formosa, the 1960 Games attracted a record 5,348 athletes from 83 countries. More importantly, it was the first Summer Games covered by U.S. television. CBS bought the rights for $394,000.

Rome was a coming-out party for 18-year-old Louisville boxer Cassius Clay. The brash but engaging Clay, who would later change his name to Muhammad Ali and hold the world heavyweight title three times, won the Olympic light heavyweight crown, pummeling Polish opponent Zbigniew Pietry-skowsky in the final. Clay was so proud of his gold medal that he didn't take it off for two days.

Sprinter Wilma Rudolph and swimmer Chris von Saltza each won three gold medals for the U.S. Rudolph, who was one of her father's 22 children and who couldn't walk without braces until she was nine, struck gold at 100 and 200 meters and anchored the winning 400-meter relay team. Von Saltza won the 400-meter freestyle, placed second in the 100-free and anchored the winning 4x100-free and medley relays.

The U.S. men won nine track and field titles, including repeat gold medals for Lee Calhoun, Glenn Davis and Al Oerter. Rafer Johnson and C.K. Yang of Formosa, college teammates at UCLA, finished 1-2 in the decathlon.

Among the other stars in Rome were barefoot Ethiopian marathoner Abebe Bikila, Australia's Herb Elliott in the 1,500 meters, Soviet gymnasts Boris Shakhlin and Larissa Latynina.

Finally, the greatest amateur basketball team ever assembled represented the U.S. and won easily. The 12-man roster included Oscar Robertson, Jerry West, Jerry Lucas, Walt Bellamy and Terry Dischinger—four of whom would become NBA Rookies of the Year from 1961-64.

Top 10 Standings

National medal standings are not recognized by the IOC. The unofficial point totals are based on 3 points for a gold medal, 2 for a silver and 1 for a bronze.

		Gold	Silver	Bronze	Total	Pts
1	USSR	43	29	31	103	218
2	USA	34	21	16	71	160
3	Germany	12	19	11	42	85
4	Italy	13	10	13	36	72
5	Australia	8	8	6	22	46
6	Hungary	6	8	7	21	41
7	Poland	4	6	11	21	35
8	Japan	4	7	7	18	33
9	Great Britain	2	6	12	20	30
10	Turkey	7	2	0	9	25

Leading Medal Winners

Number of individual medals won on the left; gold, silver and bronze breakdown to the right.

MEN

No		Sport	G-S-B
7	Boris Shakhlin, USSR	Gymnastics	4-2-1
6	Takashi Ono, JPN	Gymnastics	3-1-2
3	Murray Rose, AUS	Swimming	1-1-1
3	John Konraads, AUS	Swimming	1-0-2
3	Yuri Titov, USSR	Gymnastics	0-2-1

WOMEN

No		Sport	G-S-B
6	Larissa Latynina, USSR	Gymnastics	3-2-1
4	Chris von Saltza, USA	Swimming	3-1-0
4	Polina Astakhova, USSR	Gymnastics	2-1-1
4	Sofia Muratova, USSR	Gymnastics	1-2-1
3	Wilma Rudolph, USA	Track/Field	3-0-0
3	Dawn Fraser, AUS	Swimming	1-2-0
3	Tamara Lyukhina, USSR	Gymnastics	1-0-2

Track & Field

MEN

Event		Time	
100m	Armin Hary, GER	10.2	OR
200m	Livio Berruti, ITA	20.5	=WR
400m	Otis Davis, USA	44.9	WR
800m	Peter Snell, NZE	1:46.3	OR
1500m	Herb Elliott, AUS	3:35.6	WR
5000m	Murray Halberg, NZE	13:43.4	
10,000m	Pyotr Bolotnikov, USSR	28:32.2	OR
Marathon	Abebe Bikila, ETH	2:15:16.2	WB
110m H	Lee Calhoun, USA	13.8	
400m H	Glenn Davis, USA	49.3	=OR
3000m Steeple	Zdzislaw Krzyszkowiak, POL	8:34.2	
20k Walk	Vladimir Golubnichiy, USSR	1:34:07.2	
50k Walk	Don Thompson, GBR	4:25:30.0	OR
4x100m	GER (Bernd Cullmann, Armin Hary, Walter Mahlendorf, Martin Lauer)	39.5	=WR
4x400m	USA (Jack Yerman, Earl Young, Glenn Davis, Otis Davis)	3:02.2	WR

Event		Mark	
High Jump	Robert Shavlakadze, USSR	7-1	OR
Pole Vault	Don Bragg, USA	15-5	OR
Long Jump	Ralph Boston, USA	26-7¾	OR
Triple Jump	József Schmidt, POL	55-2	
Shot Put	Bill Nieder, USA	64-6¾	OR
Discus	Al Oerter, USA	194-2	OR
Hammer	Vasily Rudenkov, USSR	220-2	OR
Javelin	Viktor Tsibulenko, USSR	277-8	
Decathlon	Rafer Johnson, USA	8392 pts	OR

WOMEN

Event		Time	
100m	Wilma Rudolph, USA	11.0ᵂ	
200m	Wilma Rudolph, USA	24.0	
800m	Lyudmila Shevtsova, USSR	2:04.3	=WR
80m H	Irina Press, USSR	10.8	
4x100m	USA (Martha Hudson, Lucinda Williams, Barbara Jones, Wilma Rudolph)	44.5	

ᵂ indicates wind-aided.

Event		Mark	
High Jump	Iolanda Balas, ROM	6-0¾	OR
Long Jump	Vyera Krepkina, USSR	20-10¾	OR
Shot Put	Tamara Press, USSR	56-10	OR
Discus	Nina R. Ponomaryeva, USSR	180-9	OR
Javelin	Elvira Ozolina, USSR	183-8	OR

Boxing

Weight Class	Champion
Flyweight (112 lbs)	Gyula Török, HUN
Bantamweight (119)	Oleg Grigoryev, USSR
Featherweight (125)	Francesco Musso, ITA
Lightweight (132)	Kazimierz Pazdzior, POL
Lt. Welterweight (139)	Bohumil Nemecek, CZE
Welterweight (148)	Nino Benvenuti, ITA
Lt. Middleweight (156)	Skeeter McClure, USA
Middleweight (165)	Eddie Crook, USA
Lt. Heavyweight (178)	Cassius Clay, USA
Heavyweight (178+)	Franco De Piccoli, ITA

Gymnastics

MEN

Individual		Points
All-Around	Boris Shakhlin, USSR	115.95
Floor	Nobuyuki Aihara, JPN	19.45
Horiz.Bar	Takashi Ono, JPN	19.60
Paral.Bars	Boris Shakhlin, USSR	19.40
Rings	Albert Azaryan, USSR	19.725
Side Horse	Boris Shakhlin, USSR Eugen Ekman, FIN	19.375
Vault	Boris Shakhlin, USSR Takashi Ono, JPN	19.35

Team		Points
All-Around	JPN (Ono, Tsurumi, Aihara, Endo, Takemoto, Mitsukuri)	575.20

WOMEN

Individual		Points
All-Around	Larissa Latynina, USSR	77.031
Bal.Beam	Eva Bosáková, CZE	19.283
Floor	Larissa Latynina, USSR	19.583
Uneven Bars	Polina Astakhova, USSR	19.616
Vault	Margarita Nikolayeva, USSR	19.316

Team		Points
All-Around	USSR (Latynina, Muratova, Astakhova, Nikolayeva, Ivanova, Lyukhina)	382.320

Swimming

MEN

Event		Time	
100m Free	John Devitt, AUS	55.2	OR
400m Free	Murray Rose, AUS	4:18.3	OR
1500m Free	John Konrads, AUS	17:19.6	OR
100m Back	David Theile, AUS	1:09.9	OR
200m Brst	Bill Mulliken, USA	2:37.4	
200m Fly	Mike Troy, USA	2:12.8	WR
4x200m Free	USA (George Harrison, Dick Blick, Mike Troy, Jeff Farrell)	8:10.2	WR
4x100m Mdly	USA (Frank McKinney, Paul Hait, Lance Larson, Jeff Farrell)	4:05.4	WR

Diving		Points
Platform	Bob Webster, USA	165.56
Spring	Gary Tobian, USA	170.00

WOMEN

Event		Time	
100m Free	Dawn Fraser, AUS	1:01.2	OR
400m Free	Chris von Saltza, USA	4:50.6	OR
100m Back	Lynn Burke, USA	1:09.3	OR
200m Brst	Anita Lonsbrough, GBR	2:49.5	WR
100m Fly	Carolyn Schuler, USA	1:09.5	OR
4x100m Free	USA (Joan Spillane, Shirley Stobs, Carolyn Wood, Chris von Saltza)	4:08.9	WR
4x100m Mdly	USA (Lynn Burke, Patty Kempner, Carolyn Schuler, Chris von Saltza)	4:41.1	WR

Diving

Platform	Ingrid Krämer, GER	Points 91.28
Spring	Ingrid Krämer, GER	155.81

Team Sports

Men	Champion
Basketball	United States
Field Hockey	Pakistan
Soccer	Yugoslavia
Water Polo	Italy

Also Contested

Canoeing, Cycling, Equestrian, Fencing, Modern Pentathlon, Rowing, Shooting, Weightlifting, Freestyle Wrestling, Greco-Roman Wrestling and Yachting.

1964

Tokyo

Twenty-six years after Japan's wartime government forced the Japanese Olympic Committee to resign as hosts of the 1940 Summer Games, Tokyo welcomed the world to the first Asian Olympics. The new Japan spared no expense—a staggering $3 billion was spent to rebuild the city—and was rewarded with a record-breaking fortnight.

Twelve world and six Olympic records fell in swimming alone, with Americans accounting for 13. Eighteen-year-old Don Schollander led the way, winning two individual and two relay gold medals to become the first swimmer to win four events in one Games. Sharon Stouder collected three golds and a silver for the U.S. women, but the most remarkable performance of all belonged to Australian Dawn Fraser, who won the 100-meter freestyle for the third straight Olympics.

In track and field, Al Oerter of the U.S. won the discus for the third straight time. His record toss was one of 25 world and Olympic marks broken. Another fell when Billy Mills of the U.S. electrified the Games by coming from behind for an upset win in the 10,000 meters. New Zealander Peter Snell, the defending 800-meter champion, won both the 800 and 1,500 (last done in 1920).

Sprinter Bob Hayes of the U.S. equaled the world record of 10 seconds flat in the 100 meters, but stunned the crowd with a sub-nine second, come-from-behind anchor leg to lead the U.S. to set a world record in the 4x100 meters.

Abebe Bikila of Ethiopia became the first runner to win consecutive marathons. The remarkable Betty Cuthbert of Australia, who won three sprint gold medals in Melbourne, came back eight years later at age 26 to win the 400. And Soviet gymnast Larissa Latynina won six medals for the second Olympics in a row.

Top 10 Standings

National medal standings are not recognized by the IOC. The unofficial point totals are based on 3 points for a gold medal, 2 for a silver and 1 for a bronze.

		Gold	Silver	Bronze	Total	Pts
1	USA	36	26	28	90	188
2	USSR	30	31	35	96	187
3	Germany	10	22	18	50	92
4	Japan	16	5	8	29	66
5	Italy	10	10	7	27	57
6	Hungary	10	7	5	22	49
7	Poland	7	6	10	23	43
8	Great Britain	4	12	2	18	38
9	Australia	6	2	10	18	32
10	Czechoslovakia	5	6	3	14	30

Leading Medal Winners

Number of individual medals won on the left; gold, silver and bronze breakdown to the right.

MEN

No		Sport	G-S-B
4	Don Schollander, USA	Swimming	4-0-0
4	Yukio Endo, JPN	Gymnastics	3-1-0
4	Shuji Tsurumi, JPN	Gymnastics	1-3-0
4	Boris Shakhlin, USSR	Gymnastics	1-2-1
4	Viktor Lisitsky, USSR	Gymnastics	0-4-0
4	Hans-Joachim Klein, GER	Swimming	0-3-1
3	Steve Clark, USA	Swimming	3-0-0
3	Franco Menichelli, ITA	Gymnastics	1-1-1
3	Frank Wiegard, GER	Swimming	0-3-0

WOMEN

No		Sport	G-S-B
6	Larissa Latynina, USSR	Gymnastics	2-2-2
4	Vera Cáslavská, CZE	Gymnastics	3-1-0
4	Polina Astakhova, USSR	Gymnastics	2-1-1
4	Sharon Stouder, USA	Swimming	3-1-0
4	Kathy Ellis, USA	Swimming	2-0-2
3	Irena Kirszenstein, POL	Track/Field	1-2-0
3	Ada Kok, NED	Swimming	1-2-0
3	Edith Maguire, USA	Track/Field	1-2-0
3	Mary Rand, GBR	Track/Field	1-1-1

Track & Field

MEN

Event		Time	
100m	Bob Hayes, USA	10.0	=WR
200m	Henry Carr, USA	20.3	OR
400m	Mike Larrabee, USA	45.1	
800m	Peter Snell, NZE	1:45.1	OR
1500m	Peter Snell, NZE	3:38.1	
5000m	Bob Schul, USA	13:48.8	
10,000m	Billy Mills, USA	28:24.4	OR
Marathon	Abebe Bikila, ETH	2:12:11.2	WB
110m H	Hayes Jones, USA	13.6	
400m H	Rex Cawley, USA	49.6	
3000m Steeple	Gaston Roelants, BEL	8:30.8	OR
20k Walk	Ken Matthews, GBR	1:29:34.0	OR
50k Walk	Abdon Pamich, ITA	4:11:12.4	OR
4x100m	USA (Paul Drayton, Gerald Ashworth, Richard Stebbins, Bob Hayes)	39.0	WR
4x400m	USA (Ollan Cassell, Mike Larrabee, Ulis Williams, Henry Carr)	3:00.7	WR

WB indicates world best.

Event		Mark	
High Jump	Valery Brumel, USSR	7- 1¾	OR
Pole Vault	Fred Hansen, USA	16- 8¾	OR
Long Jump	Lynn Davies, GBR	26- 5¾	
Triple Jump	Józef Schmidt, POL	55- 3½	OR
Shot Put	Dallas Long, USA	66- 8½	OR
Discus	Al Oerter, USA	200- 1	OR
Hammer	Romuald Klim, USSR	228-10	OR
Javelin	Pauli Nevala, FIN	271- 2	
Decathlon	Willi Holdorf, GER	7887 pts	

WOMEN

Event		Time	
100m	Wyomia Tyus, USA	11.4	
200m	Edith McGuire, USA	23.0	OR
400m	Betty Cuthbert, AUS	52.0	OR
800m	Ann Packer, GBR	2:01.1	OR
80m H	Karin Balzer, GER	10.5W	
4x100m	POL (Teresa Ciepla, Irena Kirszenstein, Halina Górecka, Ewa Klobukowska)	43.6	

W indicates wind-aided.

Event		Mark	
High Jump	Iolanda Balas, ROM	6-2¾	OR
Long Jump	Mary Rand GBR	22-2¼	WR
Shot Put	Tamara Press, USSR	59-6¼	OR
Discus	Tamara Press, USSR	187-10	OR
Javelin	Mihaela Penes, ROM	198-7	
Pentathlon	Irina Press, USSR	5246 pts	WR

Boxing

Weight Class	Champion
Flyweight (112 lbs)	Fernando Atzori, ITA
Bantamweight (119)	Takao Sakurai, JPN
Featherweight (125)	Stanislav Stepashkin, USSR
Lightweight (132)	Józef Grudzien, POL
Lt. Welterweight (139)	Jerzy Kulej, POL
Welterweight (148)	Marian Kasprzyk, POL
Lt. Middleweight (156)	Boris Lagutin, USSR
Middleweight (165)	Valery Popenchenko, USSR
Lt. Heavyweight (178)	Cosimo Pinto, ITA
Heavyweight (178+)	Joe Frazier, USA

Gymnastics

MEN

Individual		Points
All-Around	Yukio Endo, JPN	115.95
Floor	Franco Menichelli, ITA	19.45
Horiz.Bar	Boris Shakhlin, USSR	19.625
Paral.Bars	Yukio Endo, JPN	19.675
Rings	Takuji Haytta, JPN	19.475
Side Horse	Miroslav Cerar, YUG	19.525
Vault	Haruhiro Yamashita, JPN	19.60

Team		Points
All-Around	JPN (Endo, Tsurumi, Yamashita, Hayata, Mitsukuri, Ono)	577.95

WOMEN

Individual		Points
All-Around	Vera Cáslavská, CZE	77.564
Bal.Beam	Vera Cáslavská, CZE	19.449
Floor	Larissa Latynina, USSR	19.599
Uneven Bars	Polina Astakhova, USSR	19.332
Vault	Vera Cáslavská, CZE	19.483

Team		Points
All-Around	USSR (Latynina, Astakhova, Volchetskaya, Zamotailova, Manina, Gromova)	280.890

Swimming
MEN

Event		Time	
100m Free	Don Schollander, USA	.53.4	**OR**
400m Free	Don Schollander, USA	.4:12.2	**WR**
1500m Free	Robert Windle, AUS	17:01.7	**WR**
200m Back	Jed Graef, USA	2:10.3	**WR**
200m Brst	Ian O'Brien, AUS	2:27.8	**WR**
200m Fly	Kevin Berry, AUS	2:06.6	**WR**
400m I.M.	Dick Roth, USA	4:45.4	**WR**
4x100m Free	USA (Steve Clark, Mike Austin, Gary Ilman, Don Schollander)	3:32.3	**WR**
4x200m Free	USA (Steve Clark, Roy Saari, Gary Ilman, Don Schollander)	7:52.1	**WR**
4x100m Mdly	USA (Thompson Mann, Bill Craig, Fred Schmidt, Steve Clark)	3:58.4	**WR**

Diving		Points
Platform	Bob Webster, USA	.148.58
Spring	Ken Sitzberger, USA	159.90

WOMEN

Event		Time	
100m Free	Dawn Fraser, AUS	.59.5	**OR**
400m Free	Ginny Duenkel, USA	4:43.3	**OR**
100m Back	Cathy Ferguson, USA	1:07.7	**WR**
200m Brst	G. Prozumenshikova, USSR	2:46.4	**OR**
100m Fly	Sharon Stouder, USA	1:04.7	**WR**

Event		Time	
400m Mdly	Donna de Varona, USA	5:18.7	**OR**
4x100m Free	USA (Sharon Stouder, Donna de Varona, Pokey Watson, Kathy Ellis)	4:03.8	**WR**
4x100m Mdly	USA (Cathy Ferguson, Cynthia Goyette, Sharon Stouder, Kathy Ellis)	4:33.9	**WR**

Diving		Points
Platform	Lesley Bush, USA	.99.80
Spring	Ingrid Engel-Krämer, GER	.145.00

Team Sports

Men	Champion
Basketball	United States
Field Hockey	India
Soccer	Hungary
Volleyball	Soviet Union
Water Polo	Hungary

Women	Champion
Volleyball	Japan

Also Contested

Canoeing, Cycling, Equestrian, Fencing, Judo, Modern Pentathlon, Rowing, Shooting, Weightlifting, Freestyle Wrestling, Greco-Roman Wrestling and Yachting.

1968
Mexico City

The Games of the Nineteenth Olympiad were the highest and most controversial ever held.

Staged at 7,349 feet above sea level where the thin air was a major concern to many competing countries, the Mexico City Olympics were another chapter in a year buffeted by the Vietnam War, the assassinations of Martin Luther King and Robert Kennedy, the Democratic Convention in Chicago, and the Soviet invasion of Czechoslovakia.

Ten days before the Olympics were scheduled to open on Oct. 12, over 30 Mexico City university students were killed by army troops when a campus protest turned into a riot. Still, the Games began on time and were free of discord until black Americans Tommie Smith and John Carlos, who finished 1-3 in the 200-meter run, bowed their heads and gave the Black Power salute during the national anthem as a protest against racism in the U.S.

They were immediately thrown off the team by the USOC.

The thin air helped shatter records in every men's and women's race up to 1,500 meters and may have played a role in U.S. long jumper Bob Beamon's incredible gold medal leap of 29 feet, 2½ inches –beating the existing world mark by nearly two feet.

Other outstanding American performances included Al Oerter's record fourth consecutive discus title, Debbie Meyer's three individual swimming gold medals, the innovative Dick Fosbury winning the high jump with his backwards "flop" and Wyomia Tyus becoming the first woman to win back-to-back golds in the 100 meters.

Top 10 Standings

National medal standings are not recognized by the IOC. The unofficial point totals are based on 3 points for a gold medal, 2 for a silver and 1 for a bronze.

		Gold	Silver	Bronze	Total	Pts
1	USA	45	28	34	107	225
2	USSR	29	32	30	91	181
3	Hungary	10	10	12	32	62
4	Japan	11	7	7	25	54
5	E. Germany	9	9	7	25	52
6	W. Germany	5	10	10	25	45
7	Australia	5	7	5	17	34
8	France	7	3	5	15	32
9	Poland	5	2	11	18	30
10	Czechoslovakia	7	2	4	13	29
	Romania	4	6	5	15	29

Leading Medal Winners

Number of individual medals won on the left; gold, silver and bronze breakdown to the right.

MEN

No		Sport	G-S-B
7	Mikhail Voronin, USSR	Gymnastics	2-4-1
6	Akinori Nakayama, JPN	Gymnastics	4-1-1
4	Charles Hickcox, USA	Swimming	3-1-0
4	Sawao Kato, JPN	Gymnastics	3-0-1
4	Mark Spitz, USA	Swimming	2-1-1
4	Mike Wenden, AUS	Swimming	2-1-1
3	Roland Matthes, E. Ger	Swimming	2-1-0
3	Ken Walsh, USA	Swimming	2-1-0
3	Pierre Trentin, FRA	Cycling	2-0-1
3	Vladimir Kosinski, USSR	Swimming	0-2-1
3	Leonid Ilyichev, USSR	Swimming	0-1-2

WOMEN

No		Sport	G-S-B
6	Vera Cáslavská, CZE . . . . .Gymnastics		4-2-0
4	Sue Pedersen, USA . . . . .Swimming		2-2-0
4	Natalya Kuchinskaya, USSR . . .Gymnastics		2-0-2
4	Jan Henne, USA . . . . .Swimming		2-1-1
4	Zinaida Voronina, USSR . . . . . .Gymnastics		1-1-2
3	Debbie Meyer, USA . . . . .Swimming		3-0-0
3	Kaye Hall, USA . . . . .Swimming		2-0-1
3	Larissa Petrik, USSR . . . . .Gymnastics		2-0-1
3	Ellie Daniel, USA . . . . .Swimming		1-1-1
3	Linda Gustavson, USA . . . . .Swimming		1-1-1
3	Elaine Tanner, CAN . . . . .Swimming		0-2-1

Track & Field
MEN

Event		Time	
100m	Jim Hines, USA 9.95		**WR**
200m	Tommie Smith, USA 19.83		**WR**
400m	Lee Evans, USA 43.86		**WR**
800m	Ralph Doubell, AUS 1:44.3		**=WR**
1500m	Kip Keino, KEN 3:34.9		**OR**
5000m	Mohamed Gammoudi, TUN .14:05.0		
10,000m	Naftali Temu, KEN 29:27.4		
Marathon	Mamo Wolde, ETH 2:20:26.4		
110m H	Willie Davenport, USA 13.3		**OR**
400m H	David Hemery, GBR 48.12		**WR**
3000m			
Steeple	Amos Biwott, KEN 8:51.0		
20k Walk	Vladimir Golubnichiy, USSR .1:33:58.4		
50k Walk	Christoph Höhne, E. Ger . .4:20:13.6		
4x100m	USA (Charlie Greene, Mel Pender,		
	Ronnie Ray Smith, Jim Hines) . . .38.2		**WR**
4x400m	USA (Vince Matthews, Ron Freeman,		
	Larry James, Lee Evans) 2:56.16		**WR**

Event		Mark	
High Jump	Dick Fosbury, USA 7-4¼		**OR**
Pole Vault	Bob Seagren, USA 17-8½		**OR**
Long Jump	Bob Beamon, USA 29-2½		**WR**
Triple Jump	Viktor Saneyev, USSR 57-0¾		**WR**
Shot Put	Randy Matson, USA 67-4¾		
Discus	Al Oerter, USA 212-6		**OR**
Hammer	Gyula Zsivóyzky, HUN 240-8		**OR**
Javelin	Janis Lusis, USSR 295-7		**OR**
Decathlon	Bill Toomey, USA . . . . .8193 pts		**OR**

WOMEN

Event		Time	
100m	Wyomia Tyus, USA 11.0		**WR**
200m	Irena K. Szewinska, POL 22.5		**WR**
400m	Colette Besson, FRA 52.0		**=OR**
800m	Madeline Manning, USA . .2:00.9		**OR**
80m H	Maureen Caird, AUS 10.3		**OR**
4x100m	USA (Barbara Ferrell, Margaret Bailes,		
	Mildrette Netter, Wyomia Tyus) .42.8		**WR**

Event		Mark	
High Jump	Miloslava Rezková, CZE 5-11½		
Long Jump	Viorica Viscopoleanu, ROM . .22-4½		**WR**
Shot Put	Margitta Gummel, E. Ger 64-4		**WR**
Discus	Lia Manoliu, ROM 191-2		**OR**
Javelin	Angéla Németh, HUN 198-0		
Pentathlon	Ingrid Becker, GER . . . . . . .5098 pts		

Boxing

Weight Class	Champion
Lt. Flyweight (106 lbs) . . . . . . .Francisco Rodriquez, VEN	
Flyweight (112) . . . . .Ricardo Delgado, MEX	
Bantamweight (119) . . . . .Valery Sokolov, USSR	
Featherweight (125) . . . . .Antonio Roldan, MEX	
Lightweight (132) . . . . .Ron Harris, USA	
Lt. Welterweight (139) . . . . .Jerzy Kulej, POL	

Weight Class	Champion
Welterweight (148) . . . . .Manfred Wolke, E. Ger	
Lt. Middleweight (156) . . . . .Boris Lagutin, USSR	
Middleweight (165) . . . . .Chris Finnegan, GBR	
Lt. Heavyweight (178) . . . . .Dan Poznjak, USSR	
Heavyweight (178+) . . . . .George Foreman, USA	

Gymnastics
MEN

Individual		Points
All-Around	Sawao Kato, JPN 115.9	
Floor	Sawao Kato, JPN 19.475	
Horiz.Bar	Akinori Nakayama, JPN	
	Mikhail Voronin, USSR 19.55	
Paral.Bars	Akinori Nakayama, JPN 19.475	
Rings	Akinori Nakayama, JPN 19.45	
Side Horse	Miroslav Cerar, YUG 19.325	
Vault	Mikhail Voronin, USSR 19.00	

Team		Points
All-Around	JPN (Kato, Nakayama, Kenmotsu,	
	Kato, Endo, Tsukahara) 575.90	

WOMEN

Individual		Points
All-Around	Vera Cáslavská, CZE 78.25	
Bal.Beam	Natayla Kuchinskaya, USSR 19.65	
Floor	Vera Cáslavská, CZE	
	Larissa Petrik, USSR 19.675	
Uneven Bars	Vera Cáslavská, CZE 19.65	
Vault	Vera Cáslavská, CZE 19.775	

Team		Points
All-Around	USSR (Voronina, Kuchinskaya, Petrik,	
	Karasseva, Tourischeva, Burda) 382.85	

Swimming
MEN

Event		Time	
100m Free	Mike Wenden, AUS 52.2		**WR**
200m Free	Mike Wenden, AUS 1:55.2		**OR**
400m Free	Mike Burton, USA 4:09.0		**OR**
1500m Free	Mike Burton, USA 16:38.9		**OR**
100m Back	Roland Matthes, E. Ger 58.7		**OR**
200m Back	Roland Matthes, E. Ger 2:09.6		**OR**
100m Brst	Don McKenzie, USA 1:07.7		**OR**
200m Brst	Felipe Muñoz, MEX 2:28.7		
100m Fly	Doug Russell, USA 55.9		**OR**
200m Fly	Carl Robie, USA 2:08.7		
200m I.M.	Charles Hickcox, USA 2:12.0		**OR**
400m I.M.	Charles Hickcox, USA 4:48.4		
4x100m Free	USA (Zack Zorn, Steve Rerych,		
	Mark Spitz, Ken Walsh) . . .3:31.7		**WR**
4x200m Free	USA (John Nelson, SteveRerych,		
	Mark Spitz, Don Schollander) 7:52.33		
4x100m Mdly	USA (Charles Hickcox, Don		
	McKenzie, Doug Russell,		
	Ken Walsh) 3:54.9		**WR**

Diving		Points
Platform	Klaus Dibiasi, ITA 164.18	
Spring	Bernie Wrightson, USA 170.15	

WOMEN

Event		Time	
100m Free	Jan Henne, USA 1:00.0		
200m Free	Debbie Meyer, USA 2:10.5		**OR**
400m Free	Debbie Meyer, USA 4:31.8		**OR**
800m Free	Debbie Meyer, USA 9:24.0		**OR**
100m Back	Kaye Hall, USA 1:06.2		**WR**
200m Back	Pokey Watson, USA 2:24.8		**OR**
100m Brst	Djurdjica Bjedov, YUG 1:15.8		**OR**
200m Brst	Sharon Wichman, USA 2:44.4		**OR**

Event		Time	
100m Fly	Lyn McClements, AUS	1:05.5	
200m Fly	Ada Kok, NED	2:24.7	**OR**
200m I.M.	Claudia Kolb, USA	2:24.7	**OR**
400m I.M.	Claudia Kolb, USA	5:08.5	**OR**
4x100m Free	USA (Jane Barkman, Linda Gustavson, Sue Pedersen, Jan Henne)	4:02.5	**OR**
4x100m Mdly	USA (Kaye Hall, Catie Ball, Ellie Daniel, Sue Pedersen)	4:28.3	**OR**

Diving		Points
Platform	Milena Duchková, CZE	109.59
Spring	Sue Gossick, USA	150.77

Team Sports

Men	Champion
Basketball	United States
Field Hockey	Pakistan
Soccer	Hungary
Volleyball	Soviet Union
Water Polo	Yugoslavia

Women	Champion
Volleyball	Soviet Union

Also Contested

Canoeing, Cycling, Equestrian, Fencing, Modern Pentathlon, Rowing, Shooting, Weightlifting, Freestyle Wrestling, Greco-Roman Wrestling and Yachting.

1972
Munich

On Sept. 5, with six days left in the Games, eight Arab commandos slipped into the Olympic Village, killed two Israeli team members and seized nine others as hostages. Early the next morning, all nine were killed in a shootout between the terrorists and West German police at a military airport.

The tragedy stunned the world and stopped the XXth Olympiad in its tracks. But after suspending competition for 24 hours and holding a memorial service attended by 80,000 at the main stadium, 84-year-old outgoing IOC president Avery Brundage and his committee ordered "the Games must go on."

They went on without 22-year-old swimmer Mark Spitz, who had set an Olympic gold medal record by winning four individual and three relay events, all in world record times. Spitz, an American Jew, was an inviting target for further terrorism and agreed with West German officials when they advised him to leave the country.

The pall that fell over Munich quieted an otherwise boisterous Games in which American swimmer Rick DeMont was stripped of a gold medal for taking asthma medication and track medalists Vince Matthews and Wayne Collett of the U.S. were banned for life for fooling around on the victory stand during the American national anthem.

The United States also lost an Olympic basketball game for the first time ever (they were 62-0) when the Soviets were given three chances to convert a last-second inbound pass and finally won, 51-50. The U.S. refused the silver medal.

Munich was also where 17-year-old Soviet gymnast Olga Korbut and 16-year-old swimmer Shane Gould of Australia won three gold medals each and Britain's 33-year-old Mary Peters won the pentathlon.

Top 10 Standings

National medal standings are not recognized by the IOC. The unofficial point totals are based on 3 points for a gold medal, 2 for a silver and 1 for a bronze.

		Gold	Silver	Bronze	Total	Pts
1	USSR	50	27	22	99	226
2	USA	33	31	30	94	191
3	E. Germany	20	23	23	66	129
4	W. Germany	13	11	16	40	77
5	Japan	13	8	8	29	63
6	Hungary	6	13	16	35	60
7	Bulgaria	6	10	5	21	43
8	Australia	8	7	2	17	40
	Poland	7	5	9	21	40
10	Italy	5	3	10	18	31
	Great Britain	4	5	9	18	31

Leading Medal Winners

Number of individual medals won on the left; gold, silver and bronze breakdown to the right.

MEN

No		Sport	G-S-B
7	Mark Spitz, USA	Swimming	7-0-0
5	Sawao Kato, JPN	Gymnastics	3-2-0
4	Jerry Heidenreich, USA	Swimming	2-1-1
4	Roland Matthes, E. Ger	Swimming	2-1-1
4	Akinori Nakayama, JPN	Gymnastics	2-1-1
4	Shigeru Kasamatsu, JPN	Gymnastics	1-1-2
4	Eizo Kenmotsu, JPN	Gymnastics	1-1-2
3	Valery Borsov, USSR	Track/Field	2-1-0
3	Mitsuo Tsukahara, JPN	Gymnastics	2-0-1
3	Steve Genter, USA	Swimming	1-2-0
3	Viktor Klimenko, USSR	Gymnastics	1-2-0
3	Mike Stamm, USA	Swimming	1-2-0
3	Vladimir Bure, USSR	Swimming	0-1-2

WOMEN

No		Sport	G-S-B
5	Shane Gould, AUS	Swimming	3-1-1
5	Karin Janz, E. Ger	Gymnastics	2-2-1
4	Olga Korbut, USSR	Gymnastics	3-1-0
4	Lyudmila Tourischeva, USSR	Gymnastics	2-1-1
4	Tamara Lazakovitch, USSR	Gymnastics	1-1-2

Track & Field
MEN

Event		Time	
100m	Valery Borzov, USSR	10.14	
200m	Valery Borzov, USSR	20.00	
400m	Vince Matthews, USA	44.66	
800m	Dave Wottle, USA	1:45.9	
1500m	Pekka Vasala, FIN	3:36.3	
5000m	Lasse Viren, FIN	13:26.4	**OR**
10,000m	Lasse Viren, FIN	27:38.4	**WR**
Marathon	Frank Shorter, USA	2:12:19.8	
110m H	Rod Milburn, USA	13.24	**=WR**
400m H	John Akii-Bua, UGA	47.82	**WR**
3000m Steeple	Kip Keino, KEN	8:23.6	**OR**
20k Walk	Peter Frenkel, E. Ger	1:26:42.4	**OR**
50k Walk	Bernd Kannenberg, W. Ger	3:56:11.6	**OR**

Event		Time
4x100m	USA (Larry Black, Robert Taylor, Gerald Tinker, Eddie Hart)	.38.19 =WR
4x400m	KEN (Charles Asati, Hezaklah Nyamau, Robert Ouko, Julius Sang)	.2:59.8

Event		Mark	
High Jump	Yuri Tarmak, USSR	.7-3¾	
Pole Vault	Wolfgang Nordwig, E. Ger	.18-0½	OR
Long Jump	Randy Williams, USA	.27-0½	
Triple Jump	Viktor Saneyev, USSR	.56-11¼	
Shot Put	Wladyslaw Komar, POL	.69-6	OR
Discus	Ludvik Danek, CZE	.211-3	
Hammer	Anatoly Bondarchuk, USSR	.247-8	OR
Javelin	Klaus Wolfermann, W. Ger	.296-10	OR
Decathlon	Nikolai Avilov, USSR	.8454 pts	WR

WOMEN

Event		Time	
100m	Renate Stecher, E. Ger	.11.07	
200m	Renate Stecher, E. Ger	.22.40	=WR
400m	Monika Zehrt, E. Ger	.51.08	OR
800m	Hildegard Falck, W. Ger	.1:58.55	OR
1500m	Lyudmila Bragina, USSR	.4:01.4	WR
100m H	Annelie Ehrhardt, E. Ger	.12.59	WR
4x100m	W. Ger. (Christiane Krause, Ingrid Mickler, Annegret Richter, Heidemarie Rosendahl)	.42.81	=WR
4x400m	E. Ger. (Dägmar Käsling, Rita Kühne, Helga Seidler, Monika Zehrt)	.3:23.0	WR

Event		Mark	
High Jump	Ulrike Meyfarth, W. Ger	.6-3½	=WR
Long Jump	Heidemarie Rosendahl, W. Ger	.22-3	
Shot Put	Nadezhda Chizhova, USSR	.69-0	WR
Discus	Faina Melnik, USSR	.218-7	OR
Javelin	Ruth Fuchs, E. Ger	.209-7	OR
Pentathlon	Mary Peters, GBR	.4801 pts	WR

Boxing

Weight Class		Champion
Lt. Flyweight (106 lbs)		György Gedó, HUN
Flyweight (112)		Georgi Kostadinov, BUL
Bantamweight (119)		Orlando Martinez, CUB
Featherweight (125)		Boris Kousnetsov, USSR
Lightweight (132)		Jan Szczepanski, POL
Lt. Welterweight (139)		Ray Seales, USA
Welterweight (148)		Emilio Correa, CUB
Lt. Middleweight (156)		Dieter Kottysch, W. Ger
Middleweight (165)		Vyacheslav Lemechev, USSR
Lt. Heavyweight (178)		Mate Parlov, YUG
Heavyweight (178+)		Teófilo Stevenson, CUB

Gymnastics
MEN

Individual		Points
All-Around	Sawao Kato, JPN	.114.650
Floor	Nikolai Andrianov, USSR	.19.175
Horiz.Bar	Mitsuo Tsukahara, JPN	.19.725
Paral.Bars	Sawao Kato, JPN	.19.475
Rings	Akinori Nakayama, JPN	.19.35
Side Horse	Viktor Klimenko, USSR	.19.125
Vault	Klaus Köste, E. Ger	.18.85

Team		Points
All-Around	JPN (Kato, Kenmotsu, Kasamatsu, Nakayama, Tsukahara, Okamura)	.571.25

WOMEN

Individual		Points
All-Around	Lyudmila Tourischeva, USSR	.77.025
Bal.Beam	Olga Korbut, USSR	.19.40
Floor	Olga Korbut, USSR	.19.575
Uneven Bars	Karin Janz, E. Ger	.19.675
Vault	Karin Janz, E. Ger	.19.525

Team		Points
All-Around	USSR (Tourischeva, Korbut, Lazakovitch, Burda, Saadi, Koshel)	.380.50

Swimming
MEN

Event		Time	
100m Free	Mark Spitz, USA	.51.22	WR
200m Free	Mark Spitz, USA	.1:52.78	WR
400m Free	Brad Cooper, USA	.4:00.27	OR
1500m Free	Mike Burton, USA	.15:52.58	WR
100m Back	Roland Matthes, E. Ger	.56.58	OR
200m Back	Roland Matthes, E. Ger	.2:02.82	=WR
100m Brst	Nobutaka Taguchi, JPN	.1:04.94	WR
200m Brst	John Hencken, USA	.2:21.55	WR
100m Fly	Mark Spitz, USA	.54.27	WR
200m Fly	Mark Spitz, USA	.2:00.70	WR
200m I.M.	Gunnar Larsson, SWE	.2:07.17	WR
400m I.M.	Gunnar Larsson, SWE	.4:31.98	OR
4x100m Free	USA (Dave Edgar, John Murphy, Jerry Heidenreich, Mark Spitz)	.3:26.42	WR
4x200m Free	USA (John Kinsella, Fred Tyler, Steve Genter, Mark Spitz)	.7:35.78	WR
4x100m Mdly	USA (Mike Stamm, Tom Bruce, Mark Spitz, Jerry Heidenreich)	.3:48.16	WR

Diving		Points
Platform	Klaus Dibiasi, ITA	.504.12
Spring	Vladimir Vasin, USSR	.594.09

WOMEN

Event		Time	
100m Free	Sandra Neilson, USA	.58.59	OR
200m Free	Shane Gould, AUS	.2:03.56	WR
400m Free	Shane Gould, AUS	.4:19.44	WR
800m Free	Keena Rothhammer, USA	.8:53.68	WR
100m Back	Melissa Belote, USA	.1:05.78	OR
200m Back	Melissa Belote, USA	.2:19.19	WR
100m Brst	Cathy Carr, USA	.1:13.58	WR
200m Brst	Beverly Whitfield, AUS	.2:41.71	OR
100m Fly	Mayumi Aoki, JPN	.1:03.34	WR
200m Fly	Karen Moe, USA	.2:15.57	WR
200m I.M.	Shane Gould, AUS	.2:23.07	WR
400m I.M.	Gail Neall, AUS	.5:02.97	WR
4x100m Free	USA (Sandra Neilson, Jennifer Kemp, Jane Barkman, Shirley Babashoff)	.3:55.19	WR
4x100m Mdly	USA (Melissa Belote, Cathy Carr, Deena Deardurff, Sandra Neilson)	.4:20.75	WR

Diving		Points
Platform	Ulrika Knape, SWE	.390.00
Spring	Micki King, USA	.450.03

Team Sports

Men	Champion
Basketball	Soviet Union
Field Hockey	West Germany
Handball	Yugoslavia
Soccer	Poland
Volleyball	Japan
Water Polo	Soviet Union

Women	Champion
Volleyball	Soviet Union

Also Contested

Archery, Canoeing, Cycling, Equestrian, Fencing, Judo, Modern Pentathlon, Rowing, Shooting, Weightlifting, Freestyle Wrestling, Greco-Roman Wrestling and Yachting.

CANADA
1976

1976
Montreal

In 1970, when Montreal was named to host the Summer Olympics '76, organizers estimated it would cost $310 million to stage the Games. However, due to political corruption, mismanagement, labor disputes, inflation and a $100 million outlay for security to prevent another Munich, the final bill came to more than $1.5 billion.

Then, right before the Games were scheduled to open in July, 32 nations, most of them from black Africa, walked out when the IOC refused to ban New Zealand because its national rugby team was touring racially segregated South Africa. Taiwan also withdrew when Communist China pressured trading partner Canada to deny the Taiwanese the right to compete as the Republic of China.

When the Games finally got started they were quickly stolen by 14-year-old Romanian gymnast Nadia Comaneci, who scored seven perfect 10s on her way to three gold medals.

East Germany's Kornelia Ender did Comaneci one better, winning four times as the GDR captured 11 of 13 events in women's swimming. John Naber (4 gold) and the U.S. men did the East German women one better when they won 12 of 13 gold medals in swimming.

In track and field, Cuba's Alberto Juantorena won the 400 and 800-meter runs, and Finland's Lasse Viren took the 5,000 and 10,000. Viren missed a third gold when he placed fifth in the marathon.

Four Americans who became household names during the Games were decathlon winner Bruce Jenner and three future world boxing champions—Ray Leonard and the Spinks brothers, Michael and Leon.

Top 10 Standings

National medal standings are not recognized by the IOC. The unofficial point totals are based on 3 points for a gold medal, 2 for a silver and 1 for a bronze.

		Gold	Silver	Bronze	Total	Pts
1	USSR	49	41	35	125	264
2	USA	34	35	25	94	197
3	E. Germany	40	25	25	90	195
4	W. Germany	10	12	17	39	71
5	Japan	9	6	10	25	49
6	Poland	7	6	13	26	46
7	Romania	4	9	14	27	44
8	Bulgaria	6	9	7	22	43
9	Cuba	6	4	3	13	29
10	Hungary	4	5	13	22	35

Leading Medal Winners

Number of individual medals won on the left; gold, silver and bronze breakdown to the right.

MEN

No		Sport	G-S-B
7	Nikolai Andrianov, USSR	Gymnastics	4-2-1
5	John Naber, USA	Swimming	4-1-0
5	Mitsuo Tsukahara, JPN	Gymnastics	2-1-2
4	Jim Montgomery, USA	Swimming	3-0-1
3	John Hencken, USA	Swimming	2-1-0
3	Sawao Kato, JPN	Gymnastics	2-1-0
3	Eizo Kenmotsu, JPN	Gymnastics	1-2-0
3	Rüdiger Helm, E. Ger	Canoeing	1-0-2

WOMEN

No		Sport	G-S-B
5	Kornelia Ender, E. Ger	Swimming	4-1-0
5	Nadia Comaneci, ROM	Gymnastics	3-1-1
5	Shirley Babashoff, USA	Swimming	1-4-0
4	Nelli Kim, USSR	Gymnastics	3-1-0
4	Andrea Pollack, E. Ger	Swimming	2-2-0
4	Lyudmila Tourischeva, USSR	Gymnastics	1-2-1
3	Ulrike Richter, E. Ger	Swimming	3-0-0
3	Annagret Richter, W. Ger	Track/Field	1-2-0
3	Renate Stecher, E. Ger	Track/Field	1-1-1
3	Teodora Ungureanu, ROM	Gymnastics	0-2-1

Track & Field
MEN

Event		Time	
100m	Hasely Crawford, TRI	10.06	
200m	Donald Quarrie, JAM	20.23	
400m	Alberto Juantorena, CUB	44.26	
800m	Alberto Juantorena, CUB	1:43.50	WR
1500m	John Walker, NZE	3:39.17	
5000m	Lasse Viren, FIN	13:24.76	
10,000m	Lasse Viren, FIN	27:40.38	
Marathon	Waldemar Cierpinski, E. Ger	2:09:55	OR
110m H	Guy Drut, FRA	13.30	
400m H	Edwin Moses, USA	47.64	WR
3000m Steeple	Anders Gärdeud, SWE	8:08.2	WR
20k Walk	Daniel Bautista, MEX	1:24:40.6	OR
4x100m	USA (Harvey Glance, Johnny Jones, Millard Hampton, Steve Riddick)	38.33	
4x400m	USA (Herman Frazier, Benjamin Brown, Fred Newhouse, Maxie Parks)	2:58.65	

Event		Mark	
High Jump	Jacek Wszola, POL	7-4½	OR
Pole Vault	Tadeusz Slusarski, POL	18-0½	=OR
Long Jump	Arnie Robinson, USA	27-4¾	
Triple Jump	Viktor Saneyev, USSR	56-8¾	
Shot Put	Udo Beyer, E. Ger	69-0¾	
Discus	Mac Wilkins, USA	221-5	
Hammer	Yuri Sedykh, USSR	254-4	OR
Javelin	Miklos Nèmeth, HUN	310-4	WR
Decathlon	Bruce Jenner, USA	8617 pts	WR

WOMEN

Event		Time	
100m	Annegret Richter, W. Ger	11.08	
200m	Bärbel Eckert, E. Ger	22.37	OR
400m	Irena K. Szewinska, POL	49.29	WR
800m	Tatyana Kazankina, USSR	1:54.94	WR
1500m	Tatyana Kazankina, USSR	4:05.48	
100m H	Johanna Schaller, E. Ger	12.77	

Event		Time
4x100m	E. Ger. (Marlies Oelsner, Renate Stecher, Carla Bodendorf, Barbel Eckert)	.42.55 **OR**
4x400m	E. Ger. (Doris Maletzki, Brigitte Rohde, Ellen Streidt, Christina Brehmer)	.3:19.23 **WR**

Event		Mark
High Jump	Rosemarie Ackermann, E. Ger	..6-4 **OR**
Long Jump	Angela Voigt, E. Ger	.22-0¾
Shot Put	Ivanka Hristova, BUL	.69-5¼
OR Discus	Evelin Schlaak, E. Ger	.226-4 **OR**
Javelin	Ruth Fuchs, E. Ger	.216-4 **OR**
Pentathlon	Siegrun Siegl, E. Ger	.4745 pts

Boxing

Weight Class	Champion
Lt. Flyweight (106 lbs)	Jorge Hernandez, CUB
Flyweight (112)	Leo Randolph, USA
Bantamweight (119)	Gu Yong-Ju, N. Kor
Featherweight (125)	Angel Herrera, CUB
Lightweight (132)	Howard Davis, USA
Lt. Welterweight (139)	Ray Leonard, USA
Welterweight (148)	Jochen Bachfeld, E. Ger
Lt. Middleweight (156)	Jerzy Rybicki, POL
Middleweight (165)	Michael Spinks, USA
Lt. Heavyweight (178)	Leon Spinks, USA
Heavyweight (178+)	Teófilo Stevenson, CUB

Gymnastics
MEN

Individual		Points
All-Around	Nikolai Andrianov, USSR	.116.65
Floor	Nikolai Andrianov, USSR	.19.45
Horiz.Bar	Mitsuo Tsukahara, JPN	.19.675
Paral.Bars	Sawao Kato, JPN	.19.675
Rings	Nikolai Andrianov, USSR	.19.65
Side Horse	Zoltan Magyar, HUN	.19.70
Vault	Nikolai Andrianov, USSR	.19.45

Team		Points
All-Around	JPN (Kato, Tsukahara, Kajiyama, Kenmotsu, Igarashi, Fujimoto)	.576.85

WOMEN

Individual		Points
All-Around	Nadia Comaneci, ROM	.79.275
Bal.Beam	Nadia Comaneci, ROM	.19.95
Floor	Nelli Kim, USSR	.19.85
Uneven Bars	Nadia Comaneci, ROM	.20.00
Vault	Nelli Kim, USSR	.19.80

Team		Points
All-Around	USSR (Kim, Touriacheva, Korbut, Saadi, Filatova, Grozdova)	.466.00

Swimming
MEN

Event		Time	
100m Free	Jim Montgomery, USA	.49.99	**WR**
200m Free	Bruce Furniss, USA	.1:50.29	**WR**
400m Free	Brian Goodell, USA	.3:51.93	**WR**
1500m Free	Brian Goodell, USA	.15:02.40	**WR**
100m Back	John Naber, USA	.55.49	**WR**
200m Back	John Naber, USA	.1:59.19	**WR**
100m Brst	John Hencken, USA	.1:03.11	**WR**
200m Brst	David Wilkie, GBR	.2:15.11	**WR**
100m Fly	Matt Vogel, USA	.54.35	
200m Fly	Mike Bruner, USA	.1:59.23	**WR**
400m I.M.	Rod Strachan, USA	.4:23.68	**WR**
4x200m Free	USA (Mike Bruner, Bruce Furniss, John Naber, Jim Montgomery)	.7:23.22	**WR**

Event		Time	
4x100m Mdly	USA (John Naber, John Hencken, Matt Vogel, Jim Montgomery)	.3:42.22	**WR**

Diving		Points
Platform	Klaus Dibiasi, ITA	.600.51
Spring	Phil Boggs, USA	.619.05

WOMEN

Event		Time	
100m Free	Kornelia Ender, E. Ger	.55.65	**WR**
200m Free	Kornelia Ender, E. Ger	.1:59.26	**WR**
400m Free	Petra Thümer, E. Ger	.4:09.89	**WR**
800m Free	Petra Thümer, E. Ger	.8:37.14	**WR**
100m Back	Ulrike Richter, E. Ger	.1:01.83	**OR**
200m Back	Ulrike Richter, E. Ger	.2:13.43	**OR**
100m Brst	Hannelore Anke, E. Ger	.1:11.16	
200m Brst	Marina Koshevaia, USSR	.2:33.35	**WR**
100m Fly	Kornelia Ender, E. Ger	.1:00.13	**WR**
200m Fly	Andrea Pollack, E. Ger	.2:11.41	**OR**
400m I.M.	Ulrike Tauber, E. Ger	.4:42.77	**WR**
4x100m Free	USA (Kim Peyton, Wendy Boglioli, Jill Sterkel, Shirley Babashoff)	.3:44.82	**WR**
4x100m Mdly	E. Ger. (Ulrike Richter, Hannelore Anke, Andrea Pollack, Kornelia Ender)	.4:07.95	**WR**

Diving		Points
Platform	Elena Vaytsekhovskaya, USSR	.406.59
Spring	Jennifer Chandler, USA	.506.19

Team Sports

Men	Champion
Basketball	United States
Field Hockey	New Zealand
Handball	Soviet Union
Soccer	East Germany
Volleyball	Poland
Water Polo	Hungary

Women	Champion
Basketball	Soviet Union
Handball	Soviet Union
Volleyball	Japan

Also Contested

Archery, Canoeing, Cycling, Equestrian, Fencing, Judo, Modern Pentathlon, Rowing, Shooting, Weightlifting, Freestyle Wrestling, Greco-Roman Wrestling and Yachting.

1980
Moscow

Four years after 32 nations walked out of the Montreal Games, twice that many chose to stay away from Moscow—many in support of an American-led boycott to protest the December 1979, Soviet invasion of Afghanistan.

Unable to persuade the IOC to cancel or move the Summer Games, U.S. President Jimmy Carter pressured the USOC to officially withdraw in April. Many western governments, like West Germany and Japan, followed suit and withheld their athletes. But others, like Britain and France, while supporting the boycott, allowed their Olympic committees to participate if they wished.

The first Games to be held in a Communist country opened in July with 8 nations competing and were dominated by the USSR and East Germany. They were also plagued by charges of rigged judging and poor sportsmanship by Moscow fans who, without the Americans around, booed the Poles and East Germans unmercifully.

While Soviet gymnast Aleksandr Dityatin became the first athlete to win eight medals in one year, the belle of Montreal, Nadia Comaneci of Romania, returned to win two more gold medals and Cuban heavyweight Teofilo Stevenson became the first boxer to win three golds in the same weight division.

In track and field, Miruts Yifter of Ethiopia won at 5,000 and 10,000 meters, but the most thrilling moment of the Games came in the last lap of the 1,500 meters where Sebastian Coe of Great Britain outran countryman Steve Ovett and Jurgen Straub of East Germany for the gold.

Top 10 Standings

National medal standings are not recognized by the IOC. The unofficial point totals are based on 3 points for a gold medal, 2 for a silver and 1 for a bronze.

		Gold	Silver	Bronze	Total	Pts
1	USSR	80	69	46	195	424
2	E. Germany	47	37	42	126	257
3	Bulgaria	8	16	17	41	73
4	Hungary	7	10	15	32	56
5	Poland	3	14	15	32	52
6	Cuba	8	7	5	20	43
	Romania	6	6	13	25	43
8	Great Britain	5	7	9	21	38
9	Italy	8	3	4	15	34
10	France	6	5	3	14	31

Leading Medal Winners

Number of individual medals won on the left; gold, silver and bronze breakdown to the right.

MEN

No		Sport	G-S-B
8	Aleksandr Dityatin, USSR	Gymnastics	3-4-1
5	Nikolai Andrianov, USSR	Gymnastics	2-2-1
4	Roland Brückner, E. Ger	Gymnastics	1-1-2
3	Vladimir Parfenovich, USSR	Canoeing	3-0-0
3	Vladimir Salnikov, USSR	Swimming	3-0-0
3	Sergei Kopliakov, USSR	Swimming	2-1-0
3	Aleksandr Tkachyov, USSR	Gymnastics	2-1-0
3	Andrei Krylov, USSR	Swimming	1-2-0
3	Arsen Miskarov, USSR	Swimming	0-2-1

WOMEN

No		Sport	G-S-B
5	Ines Diers, E. Ger	Swimming	2-2-1
4	Caren Metschuck, E. Ger	Swimming	3-1-0
4	Nadia Comaneci, ROM	Gymnastics	2-2-0
4	Natalya Shaposhnikova, USSR	Gymnastics	2-0-2
4	Maxi Gnauck, E. Ger	Gymnastics	1-1-2
3	Barbara Krause, E. Ger	Swimming	3-0-0
3	Rica Reinisch, E. Ger	Swimming	3-0-0
3	Yelena Davydova, USSR	Gymnastics	2-1-0
3	Steffi Kraker, E. Ger	Gymnastics	0-1-2
3	Melita Ruhn, ROM	Gymnastics	0-1-2

Track & Field

MEN

Event		Time	
100m	Allan Wells, GBR	10.25	
200m	Pietro Mennea, ITA	20.19	
400m	Viktor Markin, USSR	44.60	
800m	Steve Ovett, GBR	1:45.4	
1500m	Sebastian Coe, GBR	3:38.4	
5000m	Miruts Yifter, ETH	13:21.0	
10,000m	Miruts Yifter, ETH	27:42.7	
Marathon	Waldemar Cierpinski, E. Ger	2:11:03	
110m H	Thomas Munkelt, E. Ger	13.39	
400m H	Volker Beck, E. Ger	48.70	
3000m Steeple	Bronislaw Malinowski, POL	8:09.7	
20k Walk	Maurizio Damilano, ITA	1:23:35.5	OR
50k Walk	Hartwig Gauder, E. Ger	3:49:24.0	
4x100m	USSR (Vladimir Muravyov, Nikolai Sidorov, Aleksandr Aksinin, Andrei Prokofiev)	38.26	
4x400m	USSR (Remigius Valiulis, Mikhail Linge, Nikolai Chernetsky, Viktor Markin)	3:01.1	

Event		Mark	
High Jump	Gerd Wessig, E. Ger	7-8	WR
Pole Vault	Wladyslaw Kozakiewicz, POL	18-11½	WR
Long Jump	Lutz Dombrowski, E. Ger	28-0¼	
Triple Jump	Jaak Uudmäe, USSR	56-11¼	
Shot Put	Vladimir Kiselyov, USSR	70-0½	OR
Discus	Viktor Rashchupkin, USSR	218-8	
Hammer	Yuri Sedykh, USSR	268-4	WR
Javelin	Dainis Kula, USSR	299-2	
Decathlon	Daley Thompson, GBR	8495 pts	

WOMEN

Event		Time	
100m	Lyudmila Kondratyeva, USSR	11.06	
200m	Bärbel E. Wöckel, E. Ger	22.03	OR
400m	Marita Koch, E. Ger	48.88	OR
800m	Nadezhda Olizarenko, USSR	1:53.42	OR
1500m	Tatyana Kazankina, USSR	3:56.6	OR
100m H	Vera Komisova, USSR	12.56	OR
4x100m	E. Ger. (Romy Müller, Bärbel E. Wöckel, Ingrid Auerswald, Marlies O. Göhr)	41.60	WR
4x400m	USSR (Tatyana Prorochenko, Tatyana Goistchik, Nina Zyuskova, Irina Nazarova)	3:20.2	

Event		Mark	
High Jump	Sara Simeoni, ITA	6-5½	OR
Long Jump	Tatiana Kolpakova, USSR	23-2	OR
Shot Put	Ilona Slupianke, E. Ger	73-6¼	OR
Discus	Evelin S. Jahl, E. Ger	229-6	OR
Javelin	Maria Colon, CUB	224-5	OR
Pentathlon	Nadezhda Tkachenko, USSR	5083 pts	WR

Boxing

Weight Class	Champion
Lt. Flyweight (106 lbs)	Shamil Sabyrov, USSR
Flyweight (112)	Peter Lessov, BUL
Bantamweight (119)	Juan Hernandez, CUB
Featherweight (125)	Rudi Fink, E. Ger
Lightweight (132)	Angel Herrera, CUB
Lt. Welterweight (139)	Patrizio Oliva, ITA
Welterweight (148)	Andres Aldama, CUB
Lt. Middleweight (156)	Armando Martinez, CUB
Middleweight (165)	Jose Gomez, CUB
Lt. Heavyweight (178)	Slobodan Kacar, YUG
Heavyweight (178+)	Teofilo Stevenson, CUB

Gymnastics
MEN

Individual		Points
All-Around	Aleksandr Dityatin, USSR	118.65
Floor	Roland Brückner, E. Ger	19.75
Horiz.Bar	Stoyan Deltchev, BUL	19.825
Paral.Bars	Aleksandr Tkachyov, USSR	19.775
Rings	Aleksandr Dityatin, USSR	19.875
Side Horse	Zoltán Magyar, HUN	19.925
Vault	Nikolai Andrianov, USSR	19.825

Team		Points
All-Around	USSR (Dityatin, Andrianov, Azaryan, Tkachyov, Makuts, Markelov)	598.60

WOMEN

Individual		Points
All-Around	Yelena Davydova, USSR	79.15
Bal.Beam	Nadia Comaneci, ROM	19.80
Floor	Nadia Comaneci, ROM & Nelli Kim, USSR	19.875
Uneven Bars	Maxi Gnauk, E. Ger	19.875
Vault	Natalya Shaposhnikova, USSR	19.725

Team		Points
All-Around	USSR (Shaposhnikova, Davydova, Kim, Filatova, Zakharova, Naimuschina)	394.90

Swimming
MEN

Event		Time	
100m Free	Jörg Woithe, E. Ger	50.40	
200m Free	Sergei Kopliakov, USSR	1:49.91	OR
400m Free	Vladimir Salnikov, USSR	3:51.31	OR
1500m Free	Vladimir Salnikov, USSR	14:58.27	WR
100m Back	Bengt Baron, SWE	56.33	
200m Back	Sándor Wladár, HUN	2:01.93	
100m Brst	Duncan Goodhew, GBR	1:03.44	
200m Brst	Robertas Zhulpa, USSR	2:15.85	
100m Fly	Pär Arvidsson, SWE	54.92	
200m Fly	Sergei Fesenko, USSR	1:59.76	
400m I.M.	Aleksandr Sidorenko, USSR	4:22.89	OR
4x200m Free	USSR (Sergei Kopliakov, Vladimir, Salnikov, Ivar Stukolkin, Andrei Krylov)	7:23.50	
4x100m Mdly	AUS (Mark Kerry, Peter Evans, Mark Tonelli, Neil Brooks)	3:45.70	

Diving		Points
Platform	Falk Hoffmann, E. Ger	835.650
Spring	Aleksandr Portnov, USSR	905.025

WOMEN

Event		Time	
100m Free	Barbara Krause, E. Ger	54.79	WR
200m Free	Barbara Krause, E. Ger	1:58.33	OR
400m Free	Ines Diers, E. Ger	4:08.76	OR
800m Free	Michelle Ford, AUS	8:28.90	
100m Back	Rica Reinisch, E. Ger	1:00.86	WR
200m Back	Rica Reinisch, E. Ger	2:11.77	WR
100m Brst	Ute Geweniger, E. Ger	1:10.22	
200m Brst	Lina Kaciusyté, USSR	2:29.54	OR
100m Fly	Caren Metschuck, E. Ger	1:00.42	
200m Fly	Ines Geissler, E. Ger	2:10.44	OR
400m I.M.	Petra Schneider, E. Ger	4:36.29	WR
4x100m Free	E. Ger. (Barbara Krause, Caren Metschuck, Ines Diers, Sarina Hülsenbeck)	3:42.71	WR
4x100m Mdly	E. Ger. (Rica Reinisch, Ute Geweniger, Andrea Pollack, Caren Metschuck)	4:06.67	WR

Diving		Points
Platform	Martina Jäschke, E. Ger	596.25
Spring	Irina Kalinina, USSR	725.91

Team Sports

Men	Champion
Basketball	Yugoslavia
Field Hockey	India
Handball	East Germany
Soccer	Czechoslovakia
Volleyball	Soviet Union
Water Polo	Soviet Union

Women	Champion
Basketball	Soviet Union
Field Hockey	Zimbabwe
Handball	Soviet Union
Volleyball	Soviet Union

Also Contested

Archery, Canoeing, Cycling, Equestrian, Fencing, Judo, Modern Pentathlon, Rowing, Shooting, Weightlifting, Freestyle Wrestling, Greco-Roman Wrestling and Yachting.

1984
Los Angeles

For the third consecutive Olympiad, a boycott prevented all member nations from attending the Summer Games. This time, the Soviet Union and 13 Communist allies stayed home in an obvious payback for the West's snub of Moscow in 1980. Romania was the only Warsaw Pact country to come to L.A.

While a record 140 nations did show up, the level of competition was hardly what it might have been had the Soviets and East Germans made the trip. As a result, the United States won a record 83 gold medals in the most lopsided Summer Games since St. Louis 80 years before.

The American gold rush was led by 23-year-old Carl Lewis, who duplicated Jesse Owens' 1936 track and field grand slam by winning the 100 and 200 meters and the long jump, and anchoring the 4x100 meter relay. Teammate Valerie Brisco-Hooks won three times, taking the 200, 400 and 4x100 relay.

Sebastian Coe of Britain became the first repeat winner of the 1,500 meters since Jim Lightbody of the U.S. in 1906. Other repeaters were Briton Daley Thompson in the decathlon and U.S. hurdler Edwin Moses, who won in 1976 but was not allowed to defend his title in '80.

Romanian gymnast Ecaterina Szabó matched Lewis' four gold medals and added a silver, but the darling of the Games was little (4-foot-8¾), 16-year-old Mary Lou Retton, who won the women's All-Around with a pair of 10s in her last two events.

The L.A. Olympics were the first privately financed Games ever and made an unheard of profit of $215 million. Time magazine was so impressed it named organizing president Peter Ueberroth its Man of the Year.

Top 10 Standings

National medal standings are not recognized by the IOC. The unofficial point totals are based on 3 points for a gold medal, 2 for a silver and 1 for a bronze.

		Gold	Silver	Bronze	Total	Pts
1	USA	83	61	30	174	401
2	W. Germany	17	19	23	59	112
3	Romania	20	16	17	53	109
4	Canada	10	18	16	44	82
5	China	15	8	9	32	70
6	Italy	14	6	12	32	66
7	Japan	10	8	14	32	60
8	Great Britain	5	11	21	37	58
9	France	5	7	16	28	45
10	Australia	4	8	12	24	40

Leading Medal Winners

Number of individual medals won on the left; gold, silver and bronze breakdown to the right.

MEN

No		Sport	G-S-B
6	Li Ning, CHN	Gymnastics	3-2-1
5	Koji Gushiken, JPN	Gymnastics	2-1-2
4	Carl Lewis, USA	Track/Field	4-0-0
4	Mike Heath, USA	Swimming	3-1-0
4	Michael Gross, W. Ger	Swimming	2-2-0
4	Mitch Gaylord, USA	Gymnastics	1-1-2
3	Rick Carey, USA	Swimming	3-0-0
3	Ian Ferguson, NZE	Canoeing	3-0-0
3	Rowdy Gaines, USA	Swimming	3-0-0
3	Peter Vidmar, USA	Gymnastics	2-1-0
3	Victor Davis, CAN	Swimming	1-2-0
3	Pablo Morales, USA	Swimming	1-2-0
3	Lou Yun, CHN	Gymnastics	1-2-0
3	Shinji Morisue, JPN	Gymnastics	1-1-1
3	Lars-Erik Moberg, SWE	Canoeing	0-3-0
3	Mark Stockwell, AUS	Swimming	0-2-1

WOMEN

No		Sport	G-S-B
5	Ecaterina Szabó, ROM	Gymnastics	4-1-0
5	Mary Lou Retton, USA	Gymnastics	1-2-2
4	Nancy Hogshead, USA	Swimming	3-1-0
3	Valerie Brisco-Hooks, USA	Track/Field	3-0-0
3	Tracy Caulkins, USA	Swimming	3-0-0
3	Mary T. Meagher, USA	Swimming	3-0-0
3	Agneta Andersson, SWE	Canoeing	2-1-0
3	Chandra Cheeseborough, USA	Track/Field	2-1-0
3	Simona Pauca, ROM	Gymnastics	2-0-1
3	Julie McNamara, USA	Gymnastics	1-2-0
3	Anne Ottenbrite, CAN	Swimming	1-1-1
3	Karin Seick, W. Ger	Swimming	0-1-2
3	Annemarie Verstappen, NED	Swimming	0-1-2

Track & Field

MEN

Event		Time	
100m	Carl Lewis, USA	9.99	
200m	Carl Lewis, USA	19.80	OR
400m	Alonzo Babers, USA	44.27	
800m	Joaquim Cruz, BRA	1:43.00	OR
1500m	Sebastian Coe, GBR	3:32.53	OR
5000m	Said Aouita, MOR	13:05.59	OR
10,000m	Alberto Cova, ITA	27:47.54	
Marathon	Carlos Lopes, POR	2:09:21	OR
110m H	Roger Kingdom, USA	13.20	OR
400m H	Edwin Moses, USA	47.75	
3000m Steeple	Julius Korir, KEN	8:11.80	
20k Walk	Ernesto Canto, MEX	1:23:13.0	OR
50k Walk	Raúl González, MEX	3:47:26.0	OR
4x100m	USA (Sam Graddy, Ron Brown, Calvin Smith, Carl Lewis)	37.83	WR

Event		Time	
4x400m	USA (Sunder Nix, Ray Armstead, Alonzo Babers, Antonio McKay)	2:57.91	

Event		Mark	
High Jump	Dietmar Mögenburg, W. Ger	7-8½	
Pole Vault	Pierre Quinon, FRA	18-10¼	
Long Jump	Carl Lewis, USA	28-0¼	
Triple Jump	Al Joyner, USA	56-7½	
Shot Put	Alessandro Andrei, ITA	69-9	
Discus	Rolf Danneberg, W. Ger	218-6	
Hammer	Juha Tiainen, FIN	256-2	
Javelin	Arto Härkönen, FIN	284-8	
Decathlon	Daley Thompson, GBR	8798 pts	=WR

WOMEN

Event		Time	
100m	Evelyn Ashford, USA	10.97	OR
200m	Valerie Brisco-Hooks, USA	21.81	OR
400m	Valerie Brisco-Hooks, USA	48.83	OR
800m	Doina Melinte, ROM	1:57.60	
1500m	Gabriella Dorio, ITA	4:03.25	
3000m	Maricica Puica, ROM	8:35.96	OR
Marathon	Joan Benoit, USA	2:24.52	
100m H	Benita Fitzgerald-Brown, USA	12.84	
400m H	Nawal El Moutawakel, MOR	54.61	OR
4x100m	USA (Alice Brown, Jeanette Bolden, Chandra Cheeseborough, Evelyn Ashford)	41.65	
4x400m	USA (Lillie Leatherwood, Sherri Howard, Valerie Brisco-Hooks, Chandra Cheeseborough)	3:18.29	OR

Event		Mark	
High Jump	Ulrike Meyfarth, W. Ger	6-7½	OR
Long Jump	Anisoara Stanciu, ROM	22-10	
Shot Put	Claudia Losch, W. Ger	67-2¼	
Discus	Ria Stalman, NED	214-5	
Javelin	Tessa Sanderson, GBR	228-2	OR
Heptathlon	Glynis Nunn, AUS	6390 pts	OR

Boxing

Weight Class	Champion
Lt. Flyweight (106 lbs)	Paul Gonzales, USA
Flyweight (112)	Steve McCrory, USA
Bantamweight (119)	Maurizio Stecca, ITA
Featherweight (125)	Meldrick Taylor, USA
Lightweight (132)	Pernell Whitaker, USA
Lt. Welterweight (139)	Jerry Page, USA
Welterweight (148)	Mark Breland, USA
Lt. Middleweight (156)	Frank Tate, USA
Middleweight (165)	Shin Joon-Sup, S. Kor
Lt. Heavyweight (178)	Anton Josipovic, YUG
Heavyweight (200)	Henry Tillman, USA
Super Heavyweight (200+)	Tyrell Biggs, USA

Gymnastics

MEN

Individual		Points
All-Around	Koji Gushiken, JPN	118.7
Floor	Li Ning, CHN	19.925
Horiz.Bar	Shinji Morisue, JPN	20.00
Paral.Bars	Bart Conner, USA	19.95
Rings	Koji Gushiken, JPN	
	Li Ning, CHN	19.85
Side Horse	Li Ning, CHN	
	Peter Vidmar, USA	19.95
Vault	Lou Yun, CHN	19.95

Team		Points
All-Around	USA (Peter Vidmar, Bart Conner, Mitch Gaylord, Tim Daggett, James Hartung, Scott Johnson)	591.40

WOMEN

Individual		Points
All-Around	Mary Lou Retton, USA	79.175
Bal.Beam	Simona Pauco, ROM	
	Ecaterina Szabó, ROM	19.80
Floor	Ecaterina Szabó, ROM	19.975
Uneven Bars	Julie McNamara, USA	
	Ma Yanhong, CHN	19.95
Vault	Ecaterina Szabó, ROM	19.875

Team		Points
All-Around	ROM (Szabó, Cutina, Pauca, Grigoras, Stanulet, Agache)	392.02

Rhythmic		Points
All-Around	Lori Fung, CAN	57.950

Swimming
MEN

Event		Time	
100m Free	Rowdy Gaines, USA	49.80	OR
200m Free	Michael Gross, W. Ger	1:47.44	WR
400m Free	George DiCarlo, USA	3:51.23	OR
1500m Free	Mike O'Brien, USA	15:05.20	
100m Back	Rick Carey, USA	55.79	
200m Back	Rick Carey, USA	2:00.23	
100m Brst	Steve Lundquist, USA	1:01.65	WR
200m Brst	Victor Davis, CAN	2:13.34	WR
100m Fly	Michael Gross, W. Ger	53.08	WR
200m Fly	Jon Sieben, AUS	1:57.04	WR
200m I.M.	Alex Baumann, CAN	2:01.42	WR
400m I.M.	Alex Baumann, CAN	4:17.41	WR
4x100m Free	USA (Chris Cavanaugh, Mike Heath, Matt Biondi, Rowdy Gaines)	3:19.03	WR
4x200m Free	USA (Mike Heath, David Larson, Jeff Float, Bruce Hayes)	7:15.69	WR
4x100m Mdly	USA (Rick Carey, Steve Lundquist, Pablo Morales, Rowdy Gaines)	3:39.30	WR

Diving		Points
Platform	Greg Louganis, USA	710.91
Spring	Greg Louganis, USA	754.41

WOMEN

Event		Time	
100m Free	Nancy Hogshead, USA	55.92	
200m Free	Mary Wayte, USA	1:59.23	
400m Free	Tiffany Cohen, USA	4:07.10	OR
800m Free	Tiffany Cohen, USA	8:24.95	OR
100m Back	Theresa Andrews, USA	1:02.55	
200m Back	Jolanda de Rover, NED	2:12.38	
100m Brst	Petra van Staveren, NED	1:09.88	OR
200m Brst	Anne Ottenbrite, CAN	2:30.38	
100m Fly	Mary T. Meagher, USA	59.26	
200m Fly	Mary T. Meagher, USA	2:06.90	OR
200m I.M.	Tracy Caulkins, USA	2:12.64	OR
400m I.M.	Tracy Caulkins, USA	4:39.24	
4x100m Free	USA (Jenna Johnson, Carrie Steinseifer, Dara Torres, Nancy Hogshead)	3:43.43	
4x100m Mdly	USA (Theresa Andrews, Tracy Caulkins, Mary T. Meagher, Nancy Hogshead)	4:08.34	

Diving		Points
Platform	Zhou Jihong, CHN	435.51
Spring	Sylvie Bernier, CAN	530.70

Team Sports

Men		Champion
Basketball		United States

Men		Champion
Field Hockey		Pakistan
Handball		Yugoslavia
Soccer		France
Volleyball		United States
Water Polo		Yugoslavia

Women		Champion
Basketball		United States
Field Hockey		Holland
Handball		Yugoslavia
Volleyball		China

Also Contested

Archery, Canoeing, Cycling, Equestrian, Fencing, Judo, Modern Pentathlon, Rowing, Shooting, Synchronized Swimming, Weightlifting, Freestyle Wrestling, Greco-Roman Wrestling and Yachting.

SÉOUL 1988

1988
Seoul

For the first time since Munich in 1972, there was no organized boycott of the Summer Olympics. Cuba and Ethiopia stayed away in support of North Korea (the IOC turned down the North Koreans' demand to co-host the Games, so they refused to participate), but that was about it.

More countries (159) sent more athletes (9,465) to South Korea than to any previous Olympics. There were also more security personnel (100,000) than ever before given Seoul's proximity (30 miles) to the North and the possibility of student demonstrations for reunification.

Ten days into the Games, Canadian Ben Johnson beat defending champion Carl Lewis in the 100-meter dash with a world record time of 9.79. Two days later, however, Johnson was stripped of his gold medal and sent packing by the IOC when his post-race drug test indicated steroid use.

Lewis, who finished second in the 100, was named the winner. He also repeated in the long jump, but was second in the 200 and did not run the 4x100-relay. Teammate Florence Griffith Joyner claimed four medals—gold in the 100, 200 and 4x100-meter relay, and silver in the 4x400 relay. Her sister-in-law, Jackie Joyner-Kersee, won the long jump and heptathlon.

The most gold medals were won by swimmers—Kristin Otto of East Germany (6) and American Matt Biondi (5). Otherwise, Steffi Graf added an Olympic gold medal to her Grand Slam sweep in tennis, Greg Louganis won both men's diving events for the second straight time, and the U.S. men's basketball team had to settle for third place after losing to the gold medal-winning Soviets, 82-76, in the semifinals.

Top 10 Standings

National medal standings are not recognized by the IOC. The unofficial point totals are based on 3 points for a gold medal, 2 for a silver and 1 for a bronze.

		Gold	Silver	Bronze	Total	Pts
1	USSR	55	31	46	132	273
2	E. Germany	37	35	30	102	211
3	USA	36	31	27	94	197
4	W. Germany	11	14	15	40	76
5	Bulgaria	10	12	13	35	67
	South Korea	12	10	11	33	67
7	Hungary	11	6	6	23	51
8	China	5	11	12	28	49
	Romania	7	11	6	24	49
10	Great Britain	5	10	9	24	44

Leading Medal Winners

Number of individual medals won on the left; gold, silver and bronze breakdown to the right.

MEN

No		Sport	G-S-B
7	Matt Biondi, USA	Swimming	5-1-1
5	Vladimir Artemov, USSR	Gymnastics	4-1-0
4	Dmitri Bilozerchev, USSR	Gymnastics	3-0-1
4	Valeri Lyukin, USSR	Gymnastics	2-2-0
3	Chris Jacobs, USA	Swimming	2-1-0
3	Carl Lewis, USA	Track/Field	2-1-0
3	Holger Behrendt, E. Ger	Gymnastics	1-1-1
3	Uwe Dassler, E. Ger	Swimming	1-1-1
3	Paul McDonald, NZE	Canoeing	1-1-1
3	Igor Polianski, USSR	Swimming	1-0-2
3	Gennadi Prigoda, USSR	Swimming	0-1-2
3	Sven Tippelt, E. Ger	Gymnastics	0-1-2

WOMEN

No		Sport	G-S-B
6	Kristin Otto, E. Ger	Swimming	6-0-0
6	Daniela Silivas, ROM	Gymnastics	3-2-1
4	Florence Griffith Joyner, USA	Track/Field	3-1-0
4	Svetlana Boguinskaya, USSR	Gymnastics	2-1-1
4	Elena Shushunova, USSR	Gymnastics	2-1-1
3	Janet Evans, USA	Swimming	3-0-0
3	Silke Hörner, E. Ger	Swimming	2-0-1
3	Daniela Hunger, E. Ger	Swimming	2-0-1
3	Katrin Meissner, E. Ger	Swimming	2-0-1
3	Birgit Schmidt, E. Ger	Canoeing	2-1-0
3	Birte Weigang, E. Ger	Swimming	1-2-0
3	Vania Guecheva, BUL	Canoeing	1-1-1
3	Gabriela Potorac, ROM	Gymnastics	0-2-1
3	Heike Drechsler, E. Ger	Track/Field	0-1-2

Track & Field
MEN

Event		Time	
100m	Carl Lewis, USA	9.92	OR
200m	Joe DeLoach, USA	19.75	OR
400m	Steve Lewis, USA	43.87	
800m	Paul Ereng, KEN	1:43.45	
1500m	Peter Rono, KEN	3:35.96	
5000m	John Ngugi, KEN	13:11.70	
10,000m	Brahim Boutaib, MOR	27:21.46	OR
Marathon	Gelindo Bordin, ITA	2:10:32	
110m H	Roger Kingdom, USA	12.98	OR
400m H	Andre Phillips, USA	47.19	OR
3000m			
Steeple	Julius Kariuki, KEN	8:05.51	OR
20k Walk	Jozef Pribilinec, CZE	1:19:57	OR
50k Walk	Viacheslav Ivanenko, USSR	3:38:29	OR
4x100m	USSR (Victor Bryzgine, Vladimir Krylov, Vladimir Mouraviev, Vitaly Savine)	38.19	

Event		Time	
4x400m	USA (Danny Everett, Steve Lewis, Kevin Robinzine, Butch Reynolds)	2:56.16	=WR

Event		Mark	
High Jump	Guennadi Avdeenko, USSR	7-9¾	OR
Pole Vault	Sergey Bubka, USSR	19-4¼	OR
Long Jump	Carl Lewis, USA	28-7¼	
Triple Jump	Hristo Markov, BUL	57-9¼	OR
Shot Put	Ulf Timmermann, E. Ger	73-8¾	OR
Discus	Jürgen Schult, E. Ger	225-9	OR
Hammer	Sergey Litvinov, USSR	278-2	OR
Javelin	Tapio Korjus, FIN	276-6	
Decathlon	Christian Schenk, E. Ger	8488 pts	

WOMEN

Event		Time	
100m	Florence Griffith Joyner, USA	10.54	OR
200m	Florence Griffith Joyner, USA	21.34	WR
400m	Olga Bryzgina, USSR	48.65	OR
800m	Sigrun Wodars, E. Ger	1:56.10	
1500m	Paula Ivan, ROM	3:53.96	OR
3000m	Tatiana Samolenko, USSR	8:26.53	OR
10,000m	Olga Bondarenko, USSR	31:05.21	OR
Marathon	Rosa Mota, POR	2:25:40	
100m H	Yordanka Donkova, BUL	12.38	OR
400m H	Debra Flintoff-King, AUS	53.17	OR
4x100m	USA (Alice Brown, Sheila Echols, Florence Griffith Joyner, Evelyn Ashford)	41.98	
4x400m	USSR (Tatyana Ledovskaia, Olga Nazarova, Maria Piniguina, Olga Bryzgina)	3:15.18	WR

Event		Mark	
High Jump	Louise Ritter, USA	6-8	OR
Long Jump	Jackie Joyner-Kersee, USA	24-3¼	OR
Shot Put	Natalya Lisovskaya, USSR	72-11¼	
Discus	Martina Hellmann, E. Ger	237-2½	OR
Javelin	Petra Felke, E. Ger	245-0	OR
Heptathlon	Jackie Joyner-Kersee, USA	7291 pts	WR

Boxing

Weight Class	Champion
Lt. Flyweight (106 lbs)	Ivailo Hristov, BUL
Flyweight (112)	Kim Kwang-Sun, S. Kor
Bantamweight (119)	Kennedy McKinney, USA
Featherweight (125)	Giovanni Parisi, ITA
Lightweight (132)	Andreas Zuelow, E. Ger
Lt. Welterweight (139)	Vyacheslav Yanovsky, USSR
Welterweight (148)	Robert Wangila, KEN
Lt. Middleweight (156)	Park Si-Hun, S. Kor
Middleweight (165)	Henry Maske, E. Ger
Lt. Heavyweight (178)	Andrew Maynard, USA
Heavyweight (200)	Ray Mercer, USA
Super Heavyweight (200+)	Lennox Lewis, CAN

Gymnastics
MEN

Individual		Points
All-Around	Vladimir Artemov, USSR	119.125
Floor	Sergey Kharkov, USSR	19.925
Horiz.Bar	Vladimir Artemov, USSR	
	Valeri Lyukin, USSR	19.900
Paral.Bars	Vladimir Artemov, USSR	19.925
Rings	Dmitri Bilozerchev, USSR	
	Holger Behrendt, E. Ger	19.925
Side Horse	Dmitri Bilozerchev, USSR,	
	Lyubomir Geraskov, BUL,	
	Zsolt Borkai, HUN	19.950
Vault	Lou Yun, CHN	19.875

Team		Points
All-Around	USSR (Artemov, Bilozerchev, Kharkov, Lyukin, Gogoladze, Nouvikov)	593.350

WOMEN

Individual		Points
All-Around	Yelena Shushunova, USSR	79.662
Bal.Beam	Daniela Silivas, ROM	19.924
Floor	Daniela Silivas, ROM	19.937
Uneven Bars	Daniela Silivas, ROM	20.000
Vault	Svetlana Boguinskaya, USSR	19.905

Team		Points
All-Around	USSR (Shushunova, Boguinskaya, Baitova, Chevtchenko, Strajeva, Lachtchenova)	395.475

Rhythmic		Points
All-Around	Marina Lobatch, USSR	60.0

Swimming

MEN

Event		Time	
50m Free	Matt Biondi, USA	22.14	WR
100m Free	Matt Biondi, USA	48.63	OR
200m Free	Duncan Armstrong, AUS	1:47.25	WR
400m Free	Uwe Dassler, E. Ger	3:46.95	WR
1500m Free	Vladimir Salnikov, USSR	15:00.04	
100m Back	Daichi Suzuki, JPN	55.05	
200m Back	Igor Polianski, USSR	1:59.37	
100m Brst	Adrian Moorhouse, GBR	1:02.04	
200m Brst	József Szabó, HUN	2:13.52	
100m Fly	Anthony Nesty, SUR	53.00	OR
200m Fly	Michael Gross, W. Ger	1:56.94	OR
200m I.M.	Tamás Darnyi, HUN	2:00.17	WR
400m I.M.	Tamás Darnyi, HUN	4:14.75	WR
4x100mFree	USA (Chris Jacobs, Troy Dalbey, Tom Jager, Matt Biondi)	3:16.53	WR
4x200m Free	USA (Troy Dalbey, Matt Cetlinski, Doug Gjertsen, Matt Biondi)	7:12.51	WR

Event		Time	
4x100m Med	USA (David Berkoff, Rich Schroeder, Matt Biondi, Chris Jacobs)	3:36.93	WR

Diving		Points
Platform	Greg Louganis, USA	638.61
Spring	Greg Louganis, USA	730.80

WOMEN

Event		Time	
50m Free	Kristin Otto, E. Ger	25.49	OR
100m Free	Kristin Otto, E. Ger	54.93	
200m Free	Heike Freidrich, E. Ger	1:57.65	OR
400m Free	Janet Evans, USA	4:03.85	WR
800m Free	Janet Evans, USA	8:20.20	
100m Back	Kristin Otto, E. Ger	1:00.89	
200m Back	Krisztina Egerszegi, HUN	2:09.29	OR
100m Brst	Tania Dangalakova, BUL	1:07.95	OR
200m Brst	Silke Hörner, E. Ger	2:26.71	WR
100m Fly	Kristin Otto, E. Ger	59.00	OR
200m Fly	Kathleen Nord, E. Ger	2:09.51	
200m I.M.	Daniela Hunger, E. Ger	2:12.59	OR
400m I.M.	Janet Evans, USA	4:37.76	
4x100m Free	E. Ger. (Kristin Otto, Katrin Meissner, Daniela Hunger, Manuela Stellmach)	3:40.63	OR
4x100m Med	E. Ger. (Kristin Otto, Silke Horner, Birte Weigang, Katrin Meissner)	4:03.74	OR

Diving		Points
Platform	Xu Yanmei, CHN	445.20
Spring	Gao Min, CHN	580.23

Tennis

MEN

Singles: Miloslav Mecir, CZE, def. Tim Mayotte, USA, 3-6, 6-2, 6-4, 6-2

Doubles: Ken Flach & Robert Seguso, USA, def. Emilio Sanchez & Sergio Casal, SPA, 6-3, 6-4, 6-7, 6-7, 9-7

WOMEN

Singles: Steffi Graf, W. Ger, def. Gabriela Sabatini, ARG, 6-3,6-3

Doubles: Pam Shriver and Zina Garrison, USA, def. Jana Novotna and Helena Sukova, CZE, 4-6, 6-2,10-8

Team Sports

Men	Champion
Basketball	Soviet Union
Field Hockey	Great Britain
Handball	Soviet Union
Soccer	Soviet Union
Volleyball	United States
Water Polo	Yugoslavia

Women	Champion
Basketball	United States
Field Hockey	Australia
Handball	South Korea
Volleyball	Soviet Union

Also Contested

Archery, Canoeing, Cycling, Equestrian, Fencing, Judo, Modern Pentathlon, Shooting, Synchronized Swimming, Table Tennis, Weightlifting, Freestyle Wrestling, Greco-Roman Wrestling and Yachting.

1992

Barcelona

The year IOC president Juan Antonio Samaranch brought the Olympics to his native Spain marked the first renewal of the Summer Games since the fall of communism in Eastern Europe and the reunification of Germany in 1990.

A record 10,563 athletes from 172 nations gathered without a single country boycotting the Games. Both Cuba and North Korea returned after 12 years and South Africa was welcomed back after 32, following the national government's denunciation of apartheid racial policies.

While Germany competed under one flag for the first time since 1964, 12 nations from the former Soviet Union joined forces one last time as the Unified Team.

This was also the year the IOC threw open the gates to professional athletes after 96 years of high-minded opposition. Basketball was the chief beneficiary as America's popular "Dream Team" of NBA All-Stars easily won the gold.

Carl Lewis earned his seventh and eighth career gold medals with a third consecutive Olympic win in the long jump, and an anchor-leg performance on the American 4x100-meter relay team that helped establish a world record. Gail Devers of the U.S., whose feet had nearly been amputated by doctors in 1990 as a result of radiation treatment for Graves' disease, won the women's 100 meters.

Other track and field athletes stumbled, however. After Olympic favorite and world champion Dan O'Brien failed to even make the U.S. team, Dave Johnson, the new favorite, settled for the bronze. Ukrainian pole vaulter Sergey Bubka, who had dominated the sport for the past decade, was the heavy favorite, but he failed to clear any height.

China's Fu Mingxia, 13, won the women's platform diving gold, becoming the second-youngest person to win an individual gold medal. In gymnastics, Vitaly Scherbo of Belarus, competing for the Unified Team, won six golds. Cuba made its Olympic return rewarding, capturing seven boxing golds as well as the gold in baseball.

Top 10 Standings

National medal standings are not recognized by the IOC. The unofficial point totals are based on 3 points for a gold medal, 2 for a silver and 1 for a bronze.

		Gold	Silver	Bronze	Total	Pts
1	Unified Team	45	38	29	112	240
2	United States	37	34	37	108	216
3	Germany	33	21	28	82	169
4	China	16	22	16	54	108
5	Cuba	14	6	11	31	65
6	Hungary	11	12	7	30	64
7	South Korea	12	5	12	29	58
8	Spain	13	7	2	22	55
9	France	8	5	16	29	50
	Australia	7	9	11	27	50

Leading Medal Winners

Number of individual medals won on the left; gold, silver and bronze breakdown to the right.

MEN

No		Sport	G-S-B
6	Vitaly Scherbo, UT	Gymnastics	6-0-0
5	Grigory Misiutin, UT	Gymnastics	1-4-0
4	Aleksandr Popov, UT	Gymnastics	2-2-0
3	Yevgeny Sadovyi, UT	Swimming	3-0-0
3	Matt Biondi, USA	Swimming	2-1-0
3	Jon Olsen, USA	Swimming	2-0-1
3	Mel Stewart, USA	Swimming	2-0-1
3	Vladimir Pychnenko, UT	Swimming	1-2-0
3	Li Xiaosahuang, CHN	Gymnastics	1-1-1
3	Li Jing, CHN	Gymnastics	0-3-0
3	Anders Holmertz, SWE	Swimming	0-2-1
3	Andreas Wecker, GER	Gymnastics	0-1-2

WOMEN

No		Sports	G-S-B
5	Shannon Miller, USA	Gymnastics	0-2-3
4	Tatiana Gutsu, UT	Gymnastics	2-1-1
4	Lavinia Milosovici, ROM	Gymnastics	2-1-1
4	Summer Sanders, USA	Swimming	2-1-1
4	Franziska van Almsick, GER	Swimming	0-2-2
3	Krisztina Egerszegi, HUN	Swimming	3-0-0
3	Nicole Haislett, USA	Swimming	3-0-0
3	Crissy Ahmann-Leighton, USA	Swimming	2-1-0
3	Jenny Thompson, USA	Swimming	2-1-0
3	Gwen Torrence, USA	Track/Field	2-1-0
3	Tatyana Lysenko, UT	Gymnastics	2-0-1
3	Lin Li, CHN	Swimming	1-2-0
3	Dagmar Hase, GER	Swimming	1-2-0
3	Zhuang Yong, CHN	Swimming	1-2-0
3	Rita Koban, HUN	Kayaking	1-1-1
3	Anita Hall, USA	Swimming	1-1-1
3	Daniela Hunger, GER	Swimming	0-1-2

Track & Field

MEN

Event		Time	
100m	Linford Christie, GBR	9.96	
200m	Mike Marsh, USA	20.01	
400m	Quincy Watts, USA	43.50	OR
800m	William Tanui, KEN	1:43.66	
1500m	Fermin Cacho, SPA	3:40.12	
5000m	Dieter Baumann, GER	13:12.52	
10,000m	Khalid Skah, MOR	27:46.70	
Marathon	Hwang Young-Cho, S. Kor	2:13.23	
110m H	Mark McKoy, CAN	13.12	
400m H	Kevin Young, USA	46.78	WR
3000m			
Steeple	Matthew Birir, KEN	8:08.84	
20k Walk	Daniel Plaza Montero, SPA	1:21:45	
50k Walk	Andrei Perlov, UT	3:50:13	
4x100m	USA (Mike Marsh, Leroy Burrell, Dennis Mitchell, Carl Lewis)	37.40	WR
4x400m	USA (Andrew Valmon, Quincy Watts, Michael Johnson, Steve Lewis)	2:55.74	WR

Event		Mark	
High Jump	Javier Sotomayor, CUB	7-8	
Pole Vault	Maksim Tarasov, UT	19-0¼	
Long Jump	Carl Lewis, USA	28-5½	
Triple Jump	Mike Conley, USA	59-7½W	
Shot Put	Michael Stulce, USA	71-2½	
Discus	Romas Ubartas, LIT	213-8	
Hammer	Andrei Abduvaliyev, UT	270-9	
Javelin	Jan Zelezny, CZE	294-2	OR
Decathlon	Robert Zmelik, CZE	8611 pts	

W indicates wind-aided.

WOMEN

Event		Time
100m	Gail Devers, USA	10.82
200m	Gwen Torrence, USA	21.81
400m	Marie-Jose Perec, FRA	48.83
800m	Ellen van Langen, NED	1:55.54
1500m	Hassiba Boulmerka, ALG	3:55.30
3000m	Elena Romanova, UT	8:46.04
10,000m	Derartu Tulu, ETH	31:06.02
Marathon	Valentina Yegorova, UT	2:32:41
100m H	Paraskevi Patoulidou, GRE	12.64
400m H	Sally Gunnell, GBR	53.23
10K Walk	Chen Yueling, CHN	44.32
4x100m	USA (Evelyn Ashford, Esther Jones, Carlette Guidry-White, Gwen Torrence)	42.11
4x400m	UT (Yelena Ruzina, Lyudmila Dzhigalova, Olga Nazarova, Olga Bryzgina)	3:20.20

Event		Mark
High Jump	Heike Henkel, GER	6-7½
Long Jump	Heike Drechsler, GER	23-5¼
Shot Put	Svetlana Krivaleva, UT	69-1¼
Discus	Maritza Marten, CUB	229-10
Javelin	Silke Renk, GER	224-2
Heptathlon	Jackie Joyner-Kersee, USA	7044 pts

Boxing

Weight Class	Champion
Lt. Flyweight (106 lbs)	Rogelio Marcelo, CUB
Flyweight (112)	Su Choi-Chol, N. Kor
Bantamweight (119)	Joel Casamayor, CUB
Featherweight (125)	Andreas Tews, GER
Lightweight (132)	Oscar De La Hoya, USA
Lt. Welterweight (139)	Hector Vinent, CUB
Welterweight (147)	Michael Carruth, IRE
Lt. Middleweight (156)	Juan Lemus, CUB

Weight Class	Champion
Middleweight (165)	Ariel Hernandez, CUB
Lt. Heavyweight (178)	Torsten May, GER
Heavyweight (201)	Felix Savon, CUB
Super Heavyweight (200+)	Roberto Balado, CUB

Gymnastics
MEN

Individual		Points
All-Around	Vitaly Scherbo, UT	59.025
Floor	Li Xiaosahuang, CHN	9.925
Horiz.Bar	Trent Dimas, USA	9.875
Paral.Bars	Vitaly Scherbo, UT	9.900
Rings	Vitaly Scherbo, UT	9.937
Side Horse	Vitaly Scherbo, UT	
	Pae Gil-Su, N. Kor	9.925
Vault	Vitaly Scherbo, UT	9.856

Team		Points
All Around	UT (Scherbo, Belenki, Misiutin, Korobchinski, Voropayev, Sharipov)	585.450

WOMEN

Individual		Points
All-Around	Tatiana Gutsu, UT	39.737
Bal.Beam	Tatiana Lyssenko, UT	9.975
Floor	Lavinia Milosovici, ROM	10.000
Uneven Bars	Lu Li, CHN	10.000
Vault	Henrietta Onodi, HUN	
	& Lavinia Milosovici, ROM	9.925

Team		Points
All Around	UT (Boginskaya, Lyssenko, Galiyeva, Gautsou, Grudneva, Chusovitina)	395.666

Rythmic		Points
All Around	Aleksandra Timoshenko, UT	59.037

Swimming
MEN

Event		Time	
50m Free	Aleksandr Popov, UT	21.91	OR
100m Free	Aleksandr Popov, UT	49.02	
200m Free	Yevgeny Sadovyi, UT	1:46.70	OR
400m Free	Yevgeny Sadovyi, UT	3:45.00	WR
1500m Free	Kieren Perkins, AUS	14:43.48	WR
100m Back	Mark Tewksbury, CAN	53.98	OR
200m Back	Martin Lopez-Zubero, SPA	1:58.47	OR
100m Brst	Nelson Diebel, USA	1:01.50	OR
200m Brst	Mike Barrowman, USA	2:10.16	WR
100m Fly	Pablo Morales, USA	53.32	
200m Fly	Mel Stewart, USA	1:56.26	OR
200m I.M.	Tamas Darnyi, HUN	2:00.76	
400m I.M.	Tamas Darnyi, HUN	4:14.23	
4x100m Free	USA (Joe Hudepohl, Matt Biondi, Tom Jager, Jon Olsen)	3:16.74	
4x200m Free	UT (Dmitri Lepikov, Vladimir Pyshnenko, Veniamin Tayanovich, Yevgeny Sadovyi)	7:11.95	WR

Diving		Points
Platform	Sun Shuwei, CHN	677.31
Spring	Mark Lenzi, USA	676.53

WOMEN

Event		Time	
50m Free	Yang Wenyi, CHN	24.79	WR
100m Free	Zhuang Yong, CHN	54.64	OR
200m Free	Nicole Haislett, USA	1:57.90	
400m Free	Dagmar Hase, GER	4:07.18	
800m Free	Janet Evans, USA	8:25.52	
100m Back	Krisztina Egerszegi, HUN	1:00.68	OR
200m Back	Krisztina Egerszegi, HUN	2:07.06	OR
100m Brst	Yelena Rudkovskaya, UT	1:08.00	
200m Brst	Kyoko Iwasaki, JPN	2:26.65	OR
100m Fly	Qian Hong, CHN	58.62	OR

Event		Time	
200m Fly	Summer Sanders, USA	2:08.67	
200m I.M.	Lin Li, CHN	2:11.65	WR
400m I.M.	Krisztina Egerszegi, HUN	4:36.54	
4x100m Free	USA (Nicole Haislett, Dara Torres, Angel Martino, Jenny Thompson)	3:39.46	WR
4x100m Med	USA (Lea Loveless, Anita Nall, Crissy Ahmann-Leighton, Jenny Thompson)	4:02.54	WR

Diving		Points
Platform	Fu Mingxia, CHN	461.43
Spring	Gao Min, CHN	572.40

Tennis
MEN

Singles:	Marc Rosset, SWI, def. Jordi Arrese, SPA, 7-6, 6-4, 3-6, 4-6, 8-6.
Doubles:	Boris Becker and Michael Stich, GER, def. Wayne Ferreira and Piet Norval, RSA, 7-6, 4-6, 7-6, 6-3.

WOMEN

Singles:	Jennifer Capriati, USA, def. Steffi Graf, GER, 3-6, 6-3, 6-4.
Doubles:	Gigi Fernandez and Mary Joe Fernandez, USA, def. Conchita Martinez and Arantxa Sanchez Vicario, SPA, 7-5, 2-6, 6-2.

Team Sports

Men	Champion
Baseball	Cuba
Basketball	United States
Field Hockey	Germany
Handball	Unified Team
Soccer	Spain
Volleyball	Brazil
Water Polo	Italy

Women	Champion
Basketball	Unified Team
Field Hockey	Spain
Handball	South Korea
Volleyball	Cuba

Also Contested

Archery, Badminton, Canoeing, Cycling, Equestrian, Fencing, Judo, Modern Pentathlon, Shooting, Table Tennis, Weightlifting, Freestyle Wrestling, Greco-Roman Wrestling and Yachting.

1996
Atlanta

The Atlanta Games were certainly the largest (a record 197 nations competed), most logistically complicated Olympics to date and perhaps the most hyped and overcommercialized as well. Despite all the troubles that organizers faced, from computer scoring snafus and transportation problems to a horrific terrorist attack, these Olympics had some of the best stories ever.

The Games began so joyously with Muhammad Ali, the world's best-known sports figure now stricken by illness, igniting the Olympic cauldron.

Sadly, just eight days later horror was the prevailing mood after a terrorist's bomb ripped apart a peaceful Friday evening in Centennial Olympic Park. In the explosion, one women was killed, 111 were injured and the entire world was reminded of the terror and tragedy of Munich in 1972.

As they did in '72, the Games would go on. In track and field, Michael Johnson delivered on his much-anticipated, yet still startling, double in the 200 and 400 meters. One thing that many didn't foresee is that he would be matched by France's Marie-Jose Perec, who converted her own 200-400 double, albeit with much less attention. Carl Lewis pulled out one last bit of magic to win the long jump for the ninth gold medal of his amazing Olympic career. Donovan Bailey set a world record in the 100 and led Canada to a win over a faltering U.S. team in the 4x100 relay.

The U.S. women's gymnastics squad took the team gold after Kerri Strug hobbled up and completed her final gutsy vault in the Games' most compelling moment. Swimmer Amy Van Dyken became the first American woman to win four golds in a single Games. Ireland's Michelle Smith won three golds (and a bronze) of her own, but her victories were somewhat tainted by controversy surrounding unproven charges of drug use.

The USA faired well in team sports also. The men's basketball "Dream Team" was back and, predictably, stomped the competition on its way back to the winners' podium. Also the U.S. women won gold at the Olympic debut of two sports—softball and soccer.

Top 10 Standings

National medal standings are not recognized by the IOC. The unofficial point totals are based on 3 points for a gold medal, 2 for a silver and 1 for a bronze.

		Gold	Silver	Bronze	Total	Pts
1	United States	44	32	25	101	221
2	Russia	26	21	16	63	136
3	Germany	20	18	27	65	123
4	China	16	22	12	50	104
5	France	15	7	15	37	74
6	Italy	13	10	12	35	71
7	Australia	9	9	23	41	68
8	South Korea	7	15	5	27	56
9	Cuba	9	8	8	25	51
10	Ukraine	9	2	12	23	43

Leading Medal Winners

Number of individual medals won on the left; gold, silver and bronze breakdown to the right.

MEN

No		Sport	G-S-B
6	Alexei Nemov, RUS	Gymnastics	2-1-3
4	Gary Hall Jr., USA	Swimming	2-2-0
4	Aleksandr Popov, RUS	Swimming	2-2-0
4	Josh Davis, USA	Swimming	3-0-0
3	Denis Pankratov, RUS	Swimming	2-1-0
3	Daniel Kowalski, AUS	Swimming	0-1-2
3	Vitaly Scherbo, BEL	Gymnastics	0-0-3

WOMEN

No		Sport	G-S-B
4	Amy Van Dyken, USA	Swimming	4-0-0
4	Michelle Smith, IRL	Swimming	3-0-1
4	Angel Martino, USA	Swimming	2-0-2
4	Simona Amanar, ROM	Gymnastics	1-1-2
4	Dagmar Hase, GER	Swimming	0-3-1
4	Gina Gogean, ROM	Gymnastics	0-1-3
3	Jenny Thompson, USA	Swimming	3-0-0
3	Lilia Podkopayeva, UKR	Gymnastics	2-1-0
3	Amanda Beard, USA	Swimming	1-2-0
3	Le Jingyi, CHN	Swimming	1-2-0
3	Wendy Hedgepeth, USA	Swimming	1-2-0
3	Susan O'Neill, AUS	Swimming	1-1-1
3	Merlene Ottey, JAM	Track & Field	0-2-1
3	Franziska van Almsick, GER	Swimming	0-2-1
3	Sandra Volker, GER	Swimming	0-1-2

Track & Field

MEN

Event		Time	
100m	Donovan Bailey, CAN	9.84	WR
200m	Michael Johnson, USA	19.32	WR
400m	Michael Johnson, USA	43.49	OR
800m	Vebjoern Rodal, NOR	1:42.58	OR
1500m	Noureddine Morceli, ALG	3:35.78	
5000m	Venuste Niyongabo, BUR	13:07.96	
10,000m	Haile Gebrselassie, ETH	27:07.34	OR
Marathon	Josia Thugwane, RSA	2:12:36	
110m H	Allen Johnson, USA	12.95	OR
400m H	Derrick Adkins, USA	47.54	
3000m Steeple	Joseph Keter, KEN	8:07.12	
20k Walk	Jefferson Perez, ECU	1:20:07	
50k Walk	Robert Korzeniowski, POL	3:43:30	
4x100m	Canada (Donovan Bailey, Robert Esmie, Glenroy Gilbert, Bruny Surin, Carlton Chambers)	37.69	
4x400m	USA (Anthuan Maybank, Derek Mills, LaMont Smith, Alvin Harrison, Jason Rouser)	2:55.99	

Event		Mark	
High Jump	Charles Austin, USA	7-10	OR
Pole Vault	Jean Galfione, FRA	19-5¼	OR
Long Jump	Carl Lewis, USA	27-10¾	
Triple Jump	Kenny Harrison, USA	59-4¼	OR
Shot Put	Randy Barnes, USA	70-11¼	
Discus	Lars Riedel, GER	227-8	
Hammer	Balazs Kiss, HUN	266-6	
Javelin	Jan Zelezny, CZE	289-3	
Decathlon	Dan O'Brien, USA	8824 pts	

WOMEN

Event		Time	
100m	Gail Devers, USA	10.94	
200m	Marie-Jose Perec, FRA	22.12	
400m	Marie-Jose Perec, FRA	48.25	OR
800m	Svetlana Masterkova, RUS	1:57.73	
1500m	Svetlana Masterkova, RUS	4:00.83	
5000m	Wang Junxia, CHN	14:59.88	
10,000m	Fernanda Ribeiro, POR	31:01.63	OR
Marathon	Fatuma Roba, ETH	2:26:05	
100m H	Ludmila Engquist, SWE	12.58	
400m H	Deon Hemmings, JAM	52.82	OR
10K Walk	Yelena Nikolayeva, RUS	41:49	
4x100m	USA (Chryste Gaines, Gail Devers, Inger Miller, Gwen Torrence)	41.95	
4x400m	USA (Rochelle Stevens, Maicel Malone, Kim Graham, Jearl Miles, Linetta Wilson)	3:20.91	

Event		Mark	
High Jump	Stefka Kostadinova, BUL	6-8¾	
Long Jump	Chioma Ajunwa, NGR	23-4½	
Triple Jump	Inessa Kravets, UKR	50-3½	

Shot Put	Astrid Kumbernuss, GER	.67-5½
Discus	Ilke Wyludda, GER	.228-6
Javelin	Heli Rantanen, FIN	.222-11
Heptathlon	Ghada Shouaa, SYR	.6780 pts

Boxing

Weight Class	Champion
Lt. Flyweight (106 lbs)	Daniel Petrov Bojilov, BUL
Flyweight (112)	Maikro Romero, CUB
Bantamweight (119)	Istvan Kovacs, HUN
Featherweight (125)	Somluck Kamsing, THA
Lightweight (132)	Hocine Soltani, ALG
Lt. Welterweight (139)	Hector Vinent, CUB
Welterweight (147)	Oleg Saitov, RUS
Lt. Middleweight (156)	David Reid, USA
Middleweight (165)	Ariel Hernandez, CUB
Lt. Heavyweight (178)	Vasilii Jirov, KAZ
Heavyweight (201)	Felix Savon, CUB
Super Heavyweight (200+)	Vladimir Klichko, UKR

Gymnastics
MEN

Individual		Points
All-Around	Li Xiaosahuang, CHN	.58.423
Floor	Ioannis Melissanidis, GRE	.9.850
Horiz.Bar	Andreas Wecker, GER	.9.850
Paral.Bars	Rustam Sharipov, UKR	.9.837
Rings	Yuri Chechi, ITA	.9.887
Side Horse	Li Donghua, SWI	.9.875
Vault	Alexei Nemov, RUS	.9.787

Team		Points
All-Around	Russia	.576.778

WOMEN

Individual		Points
All-Around	Lilia Podkopayeva, UKR	.39.255
Bal.Beam	Shannon Miller, USA	.9.862
Floor	Lilia Podkopayeva, UKR	.9.887
Uneven Bars	Svetlana Chorkina, RUS	.9.850
Vault	Simona Amanar, ROM	.9.775

Team		Points
All-Around	USA (Borden, Chow, Dawes, Miller, Moceanu, Phelps and Strug)	.389.225

Rythmic		Points
All-Around	Ekaterina Serebryanskaya, UKR	.39.683
Team	Spain	.38.933

Swimming
MEN

Event		Time
50m Free	Aleksandr Popov, RUS	.22.13
100m Free	Aleksandr Popov, RUS	.48.74
200m Free	Danyon Loader, NZE	.1:47.63
400m Free	Danyon Loader, NZE	.3:47.97
1500m Free	Kieren Perkins, AUS	.14:56.40
100m Back	Jeff Rouse, USA	.54.10
200m Back	Brad Bridgewater, USA	.1:58.54
100m Brst	Fred Deburghgraeve, BEL	.1:00.60
200m Brst	Norbert, Rozsa, HUN	.2:12.57
100m Fly	Denis Pankratov, RUS	.52.27
200m Fly	Denis Pankratov, RUS	.1:56.51
200m I.M.	Attila Czene, HUN	.1:59.51
400m I.M.	Tom Dolan, USA	.4:14.90
4x100m Free	USA (Jon Olsen, Josh Davis, Bradley Schumacher, Gary Hall Jr.)	.3:15.41
4x200m Free	USA (Josh Davis, Joe Hudepohl, Ryan Berube, Bradley Schumacher)	7:14.84
4x100m Med.	USA (Jeff Rouse, Mark Henderson, Gary Hall Jr., Jeremy Linn)	.3:34.84

Diving		Points
Platform	Dmitri Saoutine, RUS	.692.34
Spring	Xiong Ni, CHN	.701.46

WOMEN

Event		Time
50m Free	Amy Van Dyken, USA	.24.87
100m Free	Le Jingyi, CHN	.54.50
200m Free	Claudia Poll, CRC	.1:58.16
400m Free	Michelle Smith, IRL	.4:07.25
800m Free	Brooke Bennett, USA	.8:27.89
100m Back	Beth Botsford, USA	.1:01.19
200m Back	Krisztina Egerszegi, HUN	.2:07.83
100m Brst	Penny Heyns, RSA	.1:07.73
200m Brst	Penny Heyns, RSA	.2:25.41
100m Fly	Amy Van Dyken, USA	.59.13
200m Fly	Susan O'Neill, AUS	.2:07.76
200m I.M.	Michelle Smith, IRL	.2:13.93
400m I.M.	Michelle Smith, IRL	.4:39.18
4x100m Free	USA (Angel Martino, Amy Van Dyken, Catherine Fox, Jenny Thompson)	.3:39.29
4x200m Free	USA (Jenny Thompson, Sheila Taorima, Trina Jackson, Christina Teuscher)	.7:59.87
4x100m Med	USA (Angel Martino, Amy Van Dyken, Amanda Beard, Beth Botsford)	.4:02.88

Diving		Points
Platform	Fu Mingxia, CHN	.521.58
Spring	Fu Mingxia, CHN	.547.68

Tennis
MEN

Singles:	Andre Agassi, USA, def. Sergi Bruguera, SPA, 6-2, 6-3, 6-1.
Doubles:	Todd Woodbridge and Mark Woodforde, AUS, def. Neil Broad and Tim Henman, GBR, 6-4, 6-4, 6-2.

WOMEN

Singles:	Lindsay Davenport, USA, def. Arantxa Sanchez Vicario, SPA, 7-6 (8-6), 6-2.
Doubles:	Gigi Fernandez and Mary Joe Fernandez, USA, def. Jana Novotna and Helena Sukova, CZE, 7-6 (8-6), 6-4.

Team Sports

Men	Champion
Baseball	Cuba
Basketball	United States
Field Hockey	Netherlands
Handball	Croatia
Soccer	Nigeria
Volleyball	Netherlands
Water Polo	Spain

Women	Champion
Basketball	United States
Field Hockey	Australia
Handball	Denmark
Soccer	United States
Softball	United States
Volleyball	Cuba

Also Contested

Archery, Badminton, Beach Volleyball, Canoeing, Cycling, Equestrian, Fencing, Judo, Modern Pentathlon, Mountain Biking, Rowing, Sailing, Shooting, Table Tennis, Weightlifting, Freestyle Wrestling, Greco-Roman Wrestling and Yachting.

2000
Sydney

Billed as the Games of the New Millennium, the Sydney Summer Olympics were the largest in history—with 10,651 athletes competing—but were praised for their superb organization.

Aussie sprinter Cathy Freeman lit the Olympic torch then warmed the hearts of a nation and a people with her performance in the 400 meters, becoming the first Australian aborigine to win Olympic gold.

Local boy Ian Thorpe also wowed the home crowds with an eye-popping performance in the pool, winning three golds and two silvers. The 17-year-old "Thorpedo" broke his own world record in the 400-meter freestyle and just an hour later, in front of 17,500 screaming fans, he anchored the Aussie 4x100 meter freestyle relay team. Thorpe came from behind to edge American anchor Gary Hall Jr. in a thrilling finish.

Germany's Birgit Fischer earned two gold medals in Kayak, becoming the first woman in any sport to win medals 20 years apart. Ryoko Tamura lost in the final in both Barcelona and Atlanta, but came back to win the gold medal for Japan in the extra light-weight division of women's judo. Great Britain's Steve Redgrave became the first rower to win gold medals at five consecutive Olympics.

American sprinter Marion Jones made a highly publicized play to become the first track and field athlete to win five gold medals at a single games. Jones was golden in the 100 meters, 200 meters and 4x400 meter relay, but "fell short" of complete success, taking bronze in the long jump and 4x100 meter relay. Jones was still the first female to win five track and field medals at a single games.

Another American came out of obscurity to win a gold medal. In one of the biggest upsets in Olympic history, Greco-Roman wrestler Rulon Gardner shocked the world by beating the previously unbeatable Alexandre Kareline of Russia in the super heavyweight gold medal match.

The United States also took gold with a surprising run in baseball and a bounce-back victory in softball after losing three straight games before the medal round.

Top 10 Standings

National medal standings are not recognized by the IOC. The unofficial point totals are based on 3 points for a gold medal, 2 for a silver and 1 for a bronze.

		Gold	Silver	Bronze	Total	Pts
1	United States	40	24	33	97	201
2	Russia	32	28	28	88	180
3	China	28	16	15	59	131
4	Australia	16	25	17	58	115
5	Germany	13	17	26	56	99
6	France	13	14	11	38	78
7	Italy	13	8	13	34	68
8	Cuba	11	11	7	29	62
9	Great Britain	11	10	7	28	60
10	Netherlands	12	9	4	25	58

Leading Medal Winners

Number of individual medals won on the left; gold, silver and bronze breakdown to the right.

MEN

No		Sport	G-S-B
6	Alexei Nemov, RUS	Gymnastics	2-1-3
5	Ian Thorpe, Aus	Swimming	3-2-0
4	Michael Klim, Aus	Swimming	2-2-0
4	Gary Hall Jr., USA	Swimming	2-1-1
4	P. van den Hoogenband, NED	Swimming	2-0-2
4	Dmitri Sautin, RUS	Diving	1-1-2
3	Lenny Krayzelburg, USA	Swimming	3-0-0
3	Florian Rousseau, FRA	Cycling	2-1-0
3	Massimiliano Rosolino, ITA	Swimming	1-1-1
3	Matthew Welsh, AUS	Swimming	0-2-1

WOMEN

No		Sport	G-S-B
5	Marion Jones, USA	Track & Field	3-0-2
5	Dara Torres, USA	Swimming	2-0-3
4	Inge de Bruijn, NED	Swimming	3-1-0
4	Leontien Zijlaard, NED	Cycling	3-1-0
4	Jenny Thompson, USA	Swimming	3-0-1
4	Susie O'Neill, AUS	Swimming	1-3-0
3	Yana Klochkova, UKR	Swimming	2-1-0
3	Elena Zamolodtchikova, RUS	Gymnastics	2-1-0
3	Simona Amanar, ROM	Gymnastics	2-0-1
3	Svetlana Khorkina, RUS	Gymnastics	1-2-0
3	Liu Xuan, CHN	Gymnastics	1-0-2
3	Therese Alshammer, SWE	Swimming	0-2-1
3	Ekaterina Lobazniouk, RUS	Gymnastics	0-2-1
3	Petria Thomas, AUS	Swimming	0-2-1

Track & Field
MEN

Event		Time
100m	Maurice Greene, USA	9.87
200m	Konstantinos Kenteris, GRE	20.09
400m	Michael Johnson, USA	43.84
800m	Nils Schumann, GER	1:45.08
1500m	Noah Ngeny, KEN	3:32.07 **OR**
5000m	Millon Wolde, ETH	13:35.49
10,000m	Haile Gebrselassie, ETH	27:18.20
Marathon	Gezahenge Abera, ETH	2:10:11
110m H	Anier Garcia, CUB	13.00
400m H	Angelo Taylor, USA	47.50
3000m Steeple	Reuben Kosgei, KEN	8:21.43
20k Walk	Robert Korzeniowski, POL	1:18:59 **OR**
50k Walk	Robert Korzeniowski, POL	3:42:22
4x100m	USA (Jonathan Drummond, Bernard Williams III, Brian Lewis, Maurice Greene)	37.61
4x400m	USA (Alvin Harrison, Antonio Pettigrew, Calvin Harrison, Michael Johnson)	2:56.35

Event		Mark
High Jump	Sergey Kliugin, RUS	.7–8½
Pole Vault	Nick Hysong, USA	.19-4¼
Long Jump	Ivan Pedroso, CUB	.28-0¾
Triple Jump	Jonathan Edwards, GBR	.58-1¼
Shot Put	Arsi Harju, FIN	.69-10¼
Discus	Virgilijus Alekna, LIT	.227-4
Hammer	Szymon Ziolkowski, POL	.262-6
Javelin	Jan Zelezny, CZE	.295-10 OR
Decathlon	Erki Nool, EST	.8641 pts

WOMEN

Event		Time
100m	Marion Jones, USA	.10.75
200m	Marion Jones, USA	.21.84
400m	Cathy Freeman, AUS	.49.11
800m	Maria Mutola, MOZ	.1:56.15
1500m	Nouria Merah-Benida, ALG	.4:05.10
5000m	Gabriela Szabo, ROM	.14:40.79 OR
10,000m	Derartu Tulu, ETH	.30:17.49 OR
Marathon	Naoko Takahashi, JPN	.2:23:14
100m H	Olga Shishigina, KAZ	.12.65
400m H	Irina Privilova, RUS	.53.02
20K Walk	Wang Liping, CHN	.1:29:05 OR
4x100m	BAH (Sevatheda Fynes, Chandra Sturrup, Pauline Davis-Thompson, Debbie Ferguson)	.41.95
4x400m	USA (Jearl Miles-Clark, Monique Hennagan, Marion Jones, LaTasha Colander-Richardson)	.3:22.62

Event		Mark
High Jump	Yelena Yelesina, RUS	.6-7
Long Jump	Heike Drechsler, GER	.22-11¼
Triple Jump	Tereza Marinova, BUL	.49-10½
Pole Vault	Stacy Dragila, USA	.15-1 OR
Shot Put	Yanina Korolchik, BLR	.67-5½
Discus	Ellina Zvereva, BLR	.224-5
Hammer	Kamila Skolimowska, POL	.233-5¾ OR
Javelin	Trine Hattestad, NOR	.226-1
Heptathlon	Denise Lewis, GBR	.6584 pts

Boxing

Weight Class	Champion
Lt. Flyweight (106 lbs)	Brahim Asloum, FRA
Flyweight (112)	Winjan Ponlid, THA
Bantamweight (119)	Guillermo Rigondeaux, CUB
Featherweight (125)	Bekzat Sattarkhanova, KAZ
Lightweight (132)	Mario Kindelan, CUB
Lt. Welterweight (139)	Mahamadkadyz Abdullaev, UZB
Welterweight (147)	Oleg Saitov, RUS
Lt. Middleweight (156)	Yermakhan Ibraimov, KAZ
Middleweight (165)	Jorge Guitierrez, CUB
Lt. Heavyweight (178)	Alexander Lebziak, RUS
Heavyweight (201)	Felix Savon, CUB
Super Heavyweight (200+)	Audley Harrison, GBR

Gymnastics
MEN

Individual		Points
All-Around	Alexei Nemov, RUS	.58.474
Floor	Igors Vihrovs, LAT	.9.812
Horiz.Bar	Alexei Nemov, RUS	.9.878
Paral.Bars	Li Xiaopeng, CHN	.9.825
Rings	Szilveszter Csollany, HUN	.9.850
Side Horse	Marius Urzica, ROM	.9.862
Vault	Gervasio Deferr, SPA	.9.712

Team		Points
All-Around	China	.231.919

WOMEN

Individual		Points
All-Around	Simona Amanar, ROM*	.38.642
Bal. Beam	Liu Xuan, CHN	.9.825
Floor	Elena Zamolodtchikova, RUS	.9.850
Uneven Bars	Svetlana Khorkina, RUS	.9.862
Vault	Elena Zamolodtchikova, RUS	.9.731

*Romania's Andreea Raducan was stripped of her all-around gold medal after testing positive for a banned substance. She was, however, allowed to keep her team gold and the silver she won in the vault.

Team		Points
All-Around	Romania	.154.608

Rythmic		Points
All-Around	Yulia Barsukova, RUS	.39.632
Team	Russia*	.39.500

*Russia and Belarus both finished with 39.500 points but Russia won the gold on a tie-breaker by posting a higher score in qualifying.

Swimming
MEN

Event		Time	
50m Free	Anthony Ervin, USA	.21.98	
	Gary Hall Jr., USA	.21.98	

Note: Ervin and Hall finished in a dead heat and were each awarded the gold medal.

100m Free	P. van den Hoogenband, NED	.48.30	
200m Free	P. van den Hoogenband, NED	.1:45.35	WR
400m Free	Ian Thorpe, AUS	.3:40.59	WR
1500m Free	Grant Hackett, AUS	.14:48.33	
100m Back	Lenny Krayzelburg, USA	.53.72	OR
200m Back	Lenny Krayzelburg, USA	.1:56.76	OR
100m Brst	Domenico Fioravanti, ITA	.1:00.46	OR
200m Brst	Domenico Fioravanti, ITA	.2:10.87	
100m Fly	Lars Frolander, SWE	.52.00	
200m Fly	Tom Malchow, USA	.1:55.35	
200m I.M.	Massimiliano Rodolino, ITA	.1:58.98	OR
400m I.M.	Tom Dolan, USA	.4:11.76	WR
4x100m Free	AUS (Michael Klim, Chris Fydler, Ashley Callus, Ian Thorpe)	.3:13.67	WR
4x200m Free	AUS (Ian Thorpe, Michael Klim, Todd Pearson, William Kirby)	.7:07.05	WR
4x100m Med.	USA (Lenny Krayzelburg, Ed Moses, Ian Crocker, Gary Hall Jr.)	.3:33.73	WR

Diving		Points
10m Platform	Tian Liang, CHN	.724.53
3m Spring	Xiong Ni, CHN	.708.72
Synch.Spring	Xiao Hailiang & Xiong Ni, CHN	.365.58
Synch.Platform	Igor Loukachine & Dmitri Sautin, RUS	.365.04

WOMEN

Event		Time	
50m Free	Inge de Bruijn, NED	.24.32	
100m Free	Inge de Bruijn, NED	.53.83	
200m Free	Susie O'Neill, AUS	.1:58.24	
400m Free	Brooke Bennett, USA	.4:05.80	
800m Free	Brooke Bennett, USA	.8:19.67	OR
100m Back	Diana Mocanu, ROM	.1:00.21	OR
200m Back	Diana Mocanu, ROM	.2:08.16	
100m Brst	Megan Quann, USA	.1:07.05	
200m Brst	Agnes Kovacs, HUN	.2:24.35	
100m Fly	Inge de Bruijn, NED	.56.61	OR
200m Fly	Misty Hyman, USA	.2:05.88	OR
200m I.M.	Yana Klochkova, UKR	.2:10.68	OR
400m I.M.	Yana Klochkova, UKR	.4:33.59	WR
4x100m Free	USA (Amy Van Dyken, Dara Torres, Courtney Shealy, Jenny Thompson)	.3:36.61	

4x200m Free USA (Samantha Arsenault, Diana Munz, Lindsay Benko, Jenny Thompson) ....7:57.80 **OR**
4x100m Med USA (B.J. Bedford, Megan Quann, Jenny Thompson, Dara Torres) ....3:58.30 **WR**

Diving		Points
10m Platform	Laura Wilkinson, USA	.543.75
3m Spring	Fu Mingxia, CHN	.609.42
Synch.Spring	Vera Ilyina & Yulia Pakhalina, RUS	.332.64
Synch.Platform	Li Na & Sang Zue, CHN	.345.12

Tennis
MEN
Singles: Yevgeny Kafelnikov, RUS, def. Tommy Haas, GER, 7-6 (7-4), 3-6, 6-2, 4-6, 6-3.

Doubles: Sebastien Lareau & Daniel Nestor, CAN, def. Todd Woodbridge & Mark Woodforde, AUS, 4-7, 6-3, 6-4, 7-6 (7-2).

WOMEN
Singles: Venus Williams, USA, def. Elena Dementieva, RUS, 6-2, 6-4.

Doubles: Serena Williams & Venus Williams, USA, def. Kristie Boogert & Miriam Oremans, NED, 6-1, 6-1.

Triathlon
1.5k swim, 40k bike ride and 10k run.
MEN
Simon Whitfield, CAN 1:48:24.02
WOMEN
Brigitte McMahon, SWI 2:00:40.52

Team Sports

Men	Champion
Baseball	United States
Basketball	United States
Field Hockey	Netherlands
Handball	Russia
Soccer	Cameroon
Volleyball	Yugoslavia
Water Polo	Hungary

Women	Champion
Basketball	United States
Field Hockey	Australia
Handball	Denmark
Soccer	Norway
Softball	United States
Volleyball	Cuba
Water Polo	Australia

Also Contested
Archery, Badminton, Beach Volleyball, Canoeing, Cycling, Equestrian, Fencing, Judo, Modern Pentathlon, Mountain Biking, Rowing, Sailing, Shooting, Table Tennis, Taekwondo, Weightlifting, Freestyle Wrestling, Greco-Roman Wrestling and Yachting.

ATHENS 2004
Will They Be Ready?
Not long after Athens was awarded the 2004 Summer Olympics, questions started surfacing whether the organizers would be ready to host the world's biggest sporting event in time, no small feat when you consider that Athens has less green space than any other European capital.

The ultimate answers to those questions will be revealed Aug. 13, 2004 when the Games of XXVIII Olympiad begin in and around the Ancient City.

Test events held in August 2003, one year before the show must go on, revealed that while problems remained International Olympic Committee inspectors gave an over-all positive report. Construction delays on several venues, including the sports complex at the old airport of Hellenikon, caused the biggest worries. The complex is set to house a number of sports including baseball, softball and preliminary basketball games.

One of the infrastructure projects that ran into trouble is in the Athens suburb of Paleo Faliron, where residents have battled the construction of a coastal tram line that is designed to alleviate traffic to seaside venues during the games.

The main Olympic Stadium, site of the track and field events as well as the opening and closing ceremonies, will have a magnificent steel-and-glass roof designed by renowned Spanish architect Santiago Calatrava. That is if they can finish the complex job in time.

One stadium was finished awhile back. It is Kallimarmaro, the all-marble stadium that was used for the first modern Olympiad in 1896. That stadium was actually built on the ancient Stadium dating from 329 B.C. The "new" stadium, being refurbished for the 2004 Games, will host the archery competitions and the finish of the marathon.

IOC President Jacques Rogge officially invited a record number of nations to compete, 201 to be exact. Afghanistan was recently reinstated by the IOC following the fall of the ruling Taliban. Two nations were invited for the first time: East Timor and the pacific island nation of Kiribati.

If all the countries that have been invited accept, it would set a record, and with the multitudes of spectators and media members set to invade (not to mention an estimated 10,500 athletes) it will be readily apparent if time ran out.

Event-by-Event

Gold medal winners from 1896-2000 in the following events: Baseball, Basketball, Boxing, Diving, Field Hockey, Gymnastics, Soccer, Softball, Swimming, Tennis and Track & Field.

BASEBALL

Multiple gold medals: Cuba (2).

Year		Year	
1992	**Cuba**, Taiwan, Japan	2000	**United States**, Cuba, South Korea
1996	**Cuba**, Japan, United States		

U.S. Medal-Winning Baseball Teams

1996 (bronze medal): P–Kris Benson, R.A. Dickey, Seth Greisinger, Billy Koch, Braden Looper, Jim Parque and Jeff Weaver; C–A.J. Hinch, Matt LeCroy and Brian Lloyd; INF–Troy Glaus, Kip Harkrider, Travis Lee, Warren Morris, Augie Ojeda and Jason Williams; OF–Chad Allen, Chad Green, Jacque Jones and Mark Kotsay; Manager–Skip Bertman. Final: Cuba over Japan, 13-9

2000 (gold medal): P–Kurt Ainsworth, Ryan Franklin, Chris George, Shane Heams, Rick Krivda, Roy Oswalt, Jon Rauch, Bobby Seay, Ben Sheets, Todd Williams and Tim Young; C–Pat Borders, Marcus Jensen and Mike Kinkade; INF–Brent Abernathy, Sean Burroughs, John Cotton, Gookie Dawkins, Adam Everett and Doug Mientkiewicz; OF–Mike Neill, Anthony Sanders, Brad Wilkerson and Ernie Young; Manager–Tommy Lasorda. Final: USA over Cuba, 4-0.

BASKETBALL

MEN

Multiple gold medals: USA (12), USSR (2).

Year		Year	
1936	**United States**, Canada, Mexico	1976	**United States**, Yugoslavia, Soviet Union
1948	**United States**, France, Brazil	1980	**Yugoslavia**, Italy, Soviet Union
1952	**United States**, Soviet Union, Uruguay	1984	**United States**, Spain, Yugoslavia
1956	**United States**, Soviet Union, Uruguay	1988	**Soviet Union**, Yugoslavia, United States
1960	**United States**, Soviet Union, Brazil	1992	**United States**, Croatia, Lithuania
1964	**United States**, Soviet Union, Brazil	1996	**United States**, Yugoslavia, Lithuania
1968	**United States**, Yugoslavia, Soviet Union	2000	**United States**, France, Lithuania
1972	**Soviet Union**, United States, Cuba		

U.S. Medal-Winning Men's Basketball Teams

1936 (gold medal): Sam Balter, Ralph Bishop, Joe Fortenberry, Tex Gibbons, Francis Johnson, Carl Knowles, Frank Lubin, Art Mollner, Don Piper, Jack Ragland, Carl Shy, Willard Schmidt, Duane Swanson and William Wheatley. Coach–Jim Needles; Assistant–Gene Johnson. Final: USA over Canada, 19-8.

1948 (gold medal): Cliff Barker, Don Barksdale, Ralph Beard, Louis Beck, Vince Boryla, Gordon Carpenter, Alex Groza, Wallace Jones, Bob Kurland, Ray Lumpp, R.C. Pitts, Jesse Renick, Robert (Jackie) Robinson and Ken Rollins. Coach–Omar Browning; Assistant–Adolph Rupp. Final: USA over France, 65-21.

1952 (gold medal): Ron Bontemps, Mark Freiberger, Wayne Glasgow, Charlie Hoag, Bill Hougland, John Keller, Dean Kelley, Bob Kenney, Bob Kurland, Bill Lienhard, Clyde Lovellette, Frank McCabe, Dan Pippin and Howie Williams. Coach–Warren Womble; Assistant–Forrest (Phog) Allen. Final: USA over USSR, 36-25.

1956 (gold medal): Dick Boushka, Carl Cain, Chuck Darling, Bill Evans, Gib Ford, Burdy Haldorson, Bill Hougland, Bob Jeangerard, K.C. Jones, Bill Russell, Ron Tomsic and Jim Walsh. Coach–Gerald Tucker; Assistant–Bruce Drake. Final: USA over USSR, 89-55.

1960 (gold medal): Jay Arnette, Walt Bellamy, Bob Boozer, Terry Dischinger, Jerry Lucas, Oscar Robertson, Adrian Smith, Burdy Haldorson, Darrall Imhoff, Allen Kelley, Lester Lane and Jerry West. Coach–Pete Newell; Assistant–Warren Womble. Final round: USA defeated USSR (81-57), Italy (112-81) and Brazil (90-63) in round robin.

1964 (gold medal): Jim (Bad News) Barnes, Bill Bradley, Larry Brown, Joe Caldwell, Mel Counts, Dick Davies, Walt Hazzard, Lucious Jackson, Pete McCaffrey, Jeff Mullins, Jerry Shipp and George Wilson. Coach–Hank Iba; Assistant–Henry Vaughn. Final: USA over USSR, 73-59.

1968 (gold medal): Mike Barrett, John Clawson, Don Dee, Cal Fowler, Spencer Haywood, Bill Hosket, Jim King, Glynn Saulters, Charlie Scott, Mike Silliman, Ken Spain, and Jo Jo White. Coach–Hank Iba; Assistant–Henry Vaughn. Final: USA over Yugoslavia, 65-50.

1972 (silver medal refused): Mike Bantom, Jim Brewer, Tom Burleson, Doug Collins, Kenny Davis, Jim Forbes, Tom Henderson, Bobby Jones, Dwight Jones, Kevin Joyce, Tom McMillen and Ed Ratleff. Coach–Hank Iba; Assistants– John Bach and Don Haskins. Final: USSR over USA, 51-50.

1976 (gold medal): Tate Armstrong, Quinn Buckner, Kenny Carr, Adrian Dantley, Walter Davis, Phil Ford, Ernie Grunfeld, Phil Hubbard, Mitch Kupchak, Tommy LaGarde, Scott May and Steve Sheppard. Coach–Dean Smith; Assistants–Bill Guthridge and John Thompson. Final: USA over Yugoslavia, 95-74.

1980 (no medal): USA boycotted Moscow Games. Final: Yugoslavia over Italy, 86-77.

1984 (gold medal): Steve Alford, Patrick Ewing, Vern Fleming, Michael Jordan, Joe Kleine, Jon Koncak, Chris Mullin, Sam Perkins, Alvin Robertson, Wayman Tisdale, Jeff Turner and Leon Wood. Coach–Bobby Knight; Assistants– Don Donoher and George Raveling. Final: USA over Spain, 96-65.

1988 (bronze medal): Stacey Augmon, Willie Anderson, Bimbo Coles, Jeff Grayer, Hersey Hawkins, Dan Majerle, Danny Manning, Mitch Richmond, J.R. Reid, David Robinson, Charles D. Smith and Charles E. Smith. Coach–John Thompson; Assistants–George Raveling and Mary Fenlon. Final: USSR over Yugoslavia, 76-63.

1992 (gold medal): Charles Barkley, Larry Bird, Clyde Drexler, Patrick Ewing, Magic Johnson, Michael Jordan, Christian Laettner, Karl Malone, Chris Mullin, Scottie Pippen, David Robinson and John Stockton. Coach–Chuck Daly; Assistants–Lenny Wilkens, Mike Krzyzewski and P.J. Carlesimo. Final: USA over Croatia, 117-85.

1996 (gold medal): Charles Barkley, Anfernee Hardaway, Grant Hill, Karl Malone, Reggie Miller, Hakeem Olajuwon, Shaquille O'Neal, Gary Payton, Scottie Pippen, David Robinson and John Stockton. Coach–Lenny Wilkens; Assistants–Bobby Cremins, Clem Haskins and Jerry Sloan. Final: USA over Yugoslavia, 95-69.

2000 (gold medal): Shareef Abdur-Rahim, Ray Allen, Vin Baker, Vince Carter, Kevin Garnett, Tim Hardaway, Allan Houston, Jason Kidd, Antonio McDyess, Alonzo Mourning, Gary Payton and Steve Smith. Coach–Rudy Tomjanovich; Assistants–Larry Brown, Gene Keady and Tubby Smith. Final: USA over France, 85-75.

WOMEN

Multiple gold medals: USA (4), USSR/UT (3).

Year		Year	
1976	**Soviet Union**, United States, Bulgaria	1992	**Unified Team**, China, United States
1980	**Soviet Union**, Bulgaria, Yugoslavia	1996	**United States**, Brazil, Australia
1984	**United States**, South Korea, China	2000	**United States**, Australia, Brazil
1988	**United States**, Yugoslavia, Soviet Union		

U.S. Gold Medal-Winning Women's Basketball Teams

1984 (gold medal): Cathy Boswell, Denise Curry, Anne Donovan, Teresa Edwards, Lea Henry, Janice Lawrence, Pamela McGee, Carol Menken-Schaudt, Cheryl Miller, Kim Mulkey, Cindy Noble and Lynette Woodard. Coach–Pat Summitt; Assistant–Kay Yow. Final: USA over South Korea, 85-55.

1988 (gold medal): Cindy Brown, Vicky Bullett, Cynthia Cooper, Anne Donovan, Teresa Edwards, Kamie Ethridge, Jennifer Gillom, Bridgette Gordon, Andrea Lloyd, Katrina McClain, Suzie McConnell and Teresa Weatherspoon. Coach–Kay Yow; Assistants–Sylvia Hatchell and Susan Yow. Final: USA over Yugoslavia, 77-70.

1996 (gold medal): Jennifer Azzi, Ruthie Bolton, Teresa Edwards, Venus Lacy, Lisa Leslie, Rebecca Lobo, Katrina McClain, Nikki McCray, Carla McGee, Dawn Staley, Katy Steding and Sheryl Swoopes. Coach—Tara VanDerveer; Assistants–Ceal Barry, Nancy Darsch and Marian Washington. Final: USA over Brazil, 111-87.

2000 (gold medal): Ruthie Bolton-Holyfield, Teresa Edwards, Yolanda Griffith, Chamique Holdsclaw, Lisa Leslie, Nikki McCray, Delisha Milton, Katie Smith, Dawn Staley, Sheryl Swoopes, Natalie Williams and Kara Wolters. Coach—Nell Fortner; Assistants--Geno Auriemma and Peggie Gillom. Final: USA over Australia, 76-54.

BOXING

Multiple gold medals: László Papp, Felix Savon and Teófilo Stevenson (3); Ariel Hernandez, Angel Herrera, Oliver Kirk, Jerzy Kulej, Boris Lagutin, Harry Mallin, Oleg Saitov and Hector Vinent (2). All fighters won titles in consecutive Olympics, except Kirk, who won both the bantamweight and featherweight titles in 1904 (he only had to fight once in each division).

Light Flyweight (106 lbs)

Year		Final Match	Year		Final Match
1968	Francisco Rodriguez, VEN	Decision, 3-2	1988	Ivailo Hristov, BUL	Decision, 5-0
1972	György Gedó, HUN	Decision, 5-0	1992	Rogelio Marcelo, CUB	Decision, 24-10
1976	Jorge Hernandez, CUB	Decision, 4-1	1996	Daniel Petrov Bojilov, BUL	Decision, 19-6
1980	Shamil Sabyrov, USSR	Decision, 3-2	2000	Brahim Asloum, FRA	Decision, 23-10
1984	Paul Gonzales, USA	Default			

Flyweight (112 lbs)

Year		Final Match	Year		Final Match
1904	George Finnegan, USA	Stopped, 1st	1964	Fernando Atzori, ITA	Decision, 4-1
1920	Frank Di Gennara, USA	Decision	1968	Ricardo Delgado, MEX	Decision, 5-0
1924	Fidel LaBarba, USA	Decision	1972	Georgi Kostadinov, BUL	Decision, 5-0
1928	Antal Kocsis, HUN	Decision	1976	Leo Randolph, USA	Decision, 3-2
1932	István Énekes, HUN	Decision	1980	Peter Lessov, BUL	Stopped, 2nd
1936	Willi Kaiser, GER	Decision	1984	Steve McCrory, USA	Decision, 4-1
1948	Pascual Perez, ARG	Decision	1988	Kim Kwang-Sun, S. Kor	Decision, 4-1
1952	Nate Brooks, USA	Decision, 3-0	1992	Su Choi-Chol, N. Kor	Decision, 12-2
1956	Terence Spinks, GBR	Decision	1996	Maikro Romero, CUB	Decision, 12-11
1960	Gyula Török, HUN	Decision, 3-2	2000	Wijan Ponlid, THA	Decision, 19-12

Bantamweight (119 lbs)

Year		Final Match	Year		Final Match
1904	Oliver Kirk, USA	Stopped, 3rd	1964	Takao Sakurai, JPN	Stopped, 2nd
1908	Henry Thomas, GBR	Decision	1968	Valery Sokolov, USSR	Stopped, 2nd
1920	Clarence Walker, RSA	Decision	1972	Orlando Martinez, CUB	Decision, 5-0
1924	William Smith, RSA	Decision	1976	Gu Yong-Ju, N. Kor	Decision, 5-0
1928	Vittorio Tamagnini, ITA	Decision	1980	Juan Hernandez, CUB	Decision, 5-0
1932	Horace Gwynne, CAN	Decision	1984	Maurizio Stecca, ITA	Decision, 4-1
1936	Ulderico Sergo, ITA	Decision	1988	Kennedy McKinney, USA	Decision, 5-0
1948	Tibor Csik, HUN	Decision	1992	Joel Casamayor, CUB	Decision, 14-8
1952	Pentti Hämäläinen, FIN	Decision, 2-1	1996	Istvan Kovacs, HUN	Decision, 14-7
1956	Wolfgang Behrendt, GER	Decision	2000	Guillermo Rigondeaux, CUB	Decision, 18-12
1960	Oleg Grigoryev, USSR	Decision			

Featherweight (125 lbs)

Year		Final Match	Year		Final Match
1904	Oliver Kirk, USA	Decision	1964	Stanislav Stepashkin, USSR	Decision, 3-2
1908	Richard Gunn, GBR	Decision	1968	Antonio Roldan, MEX	Won on Disq.
1920	Paul Fritsch, FRA	Decision	1972	Boris Kousnetsov, USSR	Decision, 3-2
1924	John Fields, USA	Decision	1976	Angel Herrera, CUB	KO, 2nd
1928	Lambertus van Klaveren, NED	Decision	1980	Rudi Fink, E. Ger	Decision, 4-1
1932	Carmelo Robledo, ARG	Decision	1984	Meldrick Taylor, USA	Decision, 5-0
1936	Oscar Casanovas, ARG	Decision	1988	Giovanni Parisi, ITA	Stopped, 1st
1948	Ernesto Formenti, ITA	Decision	1992	Andreas Tews, GER	Decision, 16-7
1952	Jan Zachara, CZE	Decision, 2-1	1996	Somluck Kamsing, THA	Decision, 8-5
1956	Vladimir Safronov, USSR	Decision	2000	Bekzat Sattarkhanov, KAZ	Decision, 22-14
1960	Francesco Musso, ITA	Decision, 4-1			

Boxing (Cont.)
Lightweight (132 lbs)

Year		Final Match	Year		Final Match
1904	Harry Spanger, USA	Decision	1964	Józef Grudzien, POL	Decision
1908	Frederick Grace, GBR	Decision	1968	Ronnie Harris, USA	Decision, 5-0
1920	Samuel Mosberg, USA	Decision	1972	Jan Szczepanski, POL	Decision, 5-0
1924	Hans Nielsen, DEN	Decision	1976	Howard Davis, USA	Decision, 5-0
1928	Carlo Orlandi, ITA	Decision	1980	Angel Herrera, CUB	Stopped, 3rd
1932	Lawrence Stevens, S. Afr	Decision	1984	Pernell Whitaker, USA	Foe quit, 2nd
1936	Imre Harangi, HUN	Decision	1988	Andreas Zuelow, E. Ger	Decision, 5-0
1948	Gerald Dreyer, S. Afr	Decision	1992	Oscar De La Hoya, USA	Decision, 7-2
1952	Aureliano Bolognesi, ITA	Decision, 2-1	1996	Hocine Soltani, ALG	Tiebreak, 3-3
1956	Richard McTaggart, GBR	Decision	2000	Mario Kindelan, CUB	Decision, 14-4
1960	Kazimierz Pazdzior, POL	Decision, 4-1			

Light Welterweight (139 lbs)

Year		Final Match	Year		Final Match
1952	Charles Adkins, USA	Decision, 2-1	1980	Patrizio Oliva, ITA	Decision, 4-1
1956	Vladimir Yengibaryan, USSR	Decision	1984	Jerry Page, USA	Decision, 5-0
1960	Bohumil Nemecek, CZE	Decision, 5-0	1988	Vyacheslav Yanovsky, USSR	Decision, 5-0
1964	Jerzy Kulej, POL	Decision, 5-0	1992	Hector Vinent, CUB	Decision, 11-1
1968	Jerzy Kulej, POL	Decision, 3-2	1996	Hector Vinent, CUB	Decision, 20-13
1972	Ray Seales, USA	Decision, 3-2	2000	Mahamadkadyz Abdullaev, UZB	Decision, 27-20
1976	Ray Leonard, USA	Decision, 5-0			

Welterweight (147 lbs)

Year		Final Match	Year		Final Match
1904	Albert Young, USA	Decision	1964	Marian Kasprzyk, POL	Decision, 4-1
1920	Bert Schneider, CAN	Decision	1968	Manfred Wolke, E. Ger	Decision, 4-1
1924	Jean Delarge, BEL	Decision	1972	Emilio Correa, CUB	Decision, 5-0
1928	Edward Morgan, NZE	Decision	1976	Jochen Bachfeld, E. Ger	Decision, 3-2
1932	Edward Flynn, USA	Decision	1980	Andrés Aldama, CUB	Decision, 4-1
1936	Sten Suvio, FIN	Decision	1984	Mark Breland, USA	Decision, 5-0
1948	Julius Torma, CZE	Decision	1988	Robert Wangila, KEN	KO, 2nd
1952	Zygmunt Chychla, POL	Decision, 3-0	1992	Michael Carruth, IRE	Decision, 13-10
1956	Nicolae Linca, ROM	Decision, 3-2	1996	Oleg Saitov, RUS	Decision, 14-9
1960	Nino Benvenuti, ITA	Decision, 4-1	2000	Oleg Saitov, RUS	Decision, 24-16

Light Middleweight (156 lbs)

Year		Final Match	Year		Final Match
1952	László Papp, HUN	Decision, 3-0	1980	Armando Martinez, CUB	Decision, 4-1
1956	László Papp, HUN	Decision	1984	Frank Tate, USA	Decision, 5-0
1960	Skeeter McClure, USA	Decision, 4-1	1988	Park Si-Hun, S. Kor	Decision, 3-2
1964	Boris Lagutin, USSR	Decision, 4-1	1992	Juan Lemus, CUB	Decision, 6-1
1968	Boris Lagutin, USSR	Decision, 5-0	1996	David Reid, USA	KO, 3rd
1972	Dieter Kottysch, W. Ger	Decision, 3-2	2000	Yermakhan Ibraimov, KAZ	Decision, 25-23
1976	Jerzy Rybicki, POL	Decision, 5-0			

Middleweight (165 lbs)

Year		Final Match	Year		Final Match
1904	Charles Mayer, USA	Stopped, 3rd	1964	Valery Popenchenko, USSR	Stopped, 1st
1908	John Douglas, GBR	Decision	1968	Christopher Finnegan, GBR	Decision, 3-2
1920	Harry Mallin, GBR	Decision	1972	Vyacheslav Lemechev, USSR	KO, 1st
1924	Harry Mallin, GBR	Decision	1976	Michael Spinks, USA	Stopped, 3rd
1928	Piero Toscani, ITA	Decision	1980	José Gomez, CUB	Decision, 4-1
1932	Carmen Barth, USA	Decision	1984	Shin Joon-Sup, S. Kor	Decision, 3-2
1936	Jean Despeaux, FRA	Decision	1988	Henry Maske, E. Ger	Decision, 5-0
1948	László Papp, HUN	Decision	1992	Ariel Hernandez, CUB	Decision, 12-7
1952	Floyd Patterson, USA	KO, 1st	1996	Ariel Hernandez, CUB	Decision, 11-3
1956	Gennady Schatkov, USSR	KO, 1st	2000	Jorge Gutierrez, CUB	Decision, 17-15
1960	Eddie Crook, USA	Decision, 3-2			

Light Heavyweight (178 lbs)

Year		Final Match	Year		Final Match
1920	Eddie Eagan, USA	Decision	1968	Dan Poznjak, USSR	Default
1924	Harry Mitchell, GBR	Decision	1972	Mate Parlov, YUG	Stopped, 2nd
1928	Victor Avenda|fno, ARG	Decision	1976	Leon Spinks, USA	Stopped, 3rd
1932	David Carstens, S. Afr	Decision	1980	Slobodan Kacar, YUG	Decision, 4-1
1936	Roger Michelot, FRA	Decision	1984	Anton Josipovic, YUG	Default
1948	George Hunter, S. Afr	Decision	1988	Andrew Maynard, USA	Decision, 5-0
1952	Norvel Lee, USA	Decision, 3-0	1992	Torsten May, GER	Decision, 8-3
1956	Jim Boyd, USA	Decision	1996	Vasilii Jirov, KAZ	Decision, 17-4
1960	Cassius Clay, USA	Decision, 5-0	2000	Alexander Lebziak, RUS	Decision, 20-6
1964	Cosimo Pinto, ITA	Decision, 3-2			

Note: Cassius Clay changed his name to Muhammad Ali after winning the world heavyweight championship in 1964.

Heavyweight (201 lbs)

Year		Final Match	Year		Final Match
1984	Henry Tillman, USA	Decision, 5-0	1996	Felix Savon, CUB	Decision, 20-2
1988	Ray Mercer, USA	KO, 1st	2000	Felix Savon, CUB	Decision, 21-13
1992	Felix Savon, CUB	Decision, 14-1			

Super Heavyweight (Unlimited)

Year		Final Match	Year		Final Match
1904	Samuel Berger, USA	Decision	1964	Joe Frazier, USA	Decision, 3-2
1908	Albert Oldham, GBR	KO, 1st	1968	George Foreman, USA	Stopped, 2nd
1920	Ronald Rawson, GBR	Decision	1972	Teófilo Stevenson, CUB	Default
1924	Otto von Porat, NOR	Decision	1976	Teófilo Stevenson, CUB	KO, 3rd
1928	Arturo Rodriguez Jurado, ARG	Stopped, 1st	1980	Teófilo Stevenson, CUB	Decision, 4-1
1932	Santiago Lovell, ARG	Decision	1984	Tyrell Biggs, USA	Decision, 4-1
1936	Herbert Runge, GER	Decision	1988	Lennox Lewis, CAN	Stopped, 2nd
1948	Rafael Iglesias, ARG	KO, 2nd	1992	Roberto Balado, CUB	Decision, 13-2
1952	Ed Sanders, USA	Won on Disq.*	1996	Vladimir Klichko, UKR	Decision, 7-3
1956	Pete Rademacher, USA	Stopped, 1st	2000	Audley Harrison, GBR	Decision, 30-16
1960	Franco De Piccoli, ITA	KO, 1st			

* Sanders' opponent, Ingemar Johansson, was disqualified in 2nd round for not trying.
Note: Called heavyweight through 1980.

DIVING

MEN

Multiple gold medals: Greg Louganis (4); Klaus Dibiasi (3); Pete Desjardins, Sammy Lee, Xiong Ni, Bob Webster and Albert White (2).

Springboard

Year		Points	Year		Points
1908	Albert Z)rner, GER	85.5	1964	Ken Sitzberger, USA	159.90
1912	Paul Günther, GER	79.23	1968	Bernie Wrightson, USA	170.15
1920	Louis Kuehn, USA	675.4	1972	Vladimir Vasin, USSR	594.09
1924	Albert White, USA	696.4	1976	Phil Boggs, USA	619.05
1928	Pete Desjardins, USA	185.04	1980	Aleksandr Portnov, USSR	905.03
1932	Michael Galitzen, USA	161.38	1984	Greg Louganis, USA	754.41
1936	Richard Degener, USA	163.57	1988	Greg Louganis, USA	730.80
1948	Bruce Harlan, USA	163.64	1992	Mark Lenzi, USA	676.53
1952	David Browning, USA	205.29	1996	Xiong Ni, CHN	701.46
1956	Bob Clotworthy, USA	159.56	2000	Xiong Ni, CHN	708.72
1960	Gary Tobian, USA	170.00			

Platform

Year		Points	Year		Points
1904	George Sheldon, USA	12.66	1960	Bob Webster, USA	165.56
1906	Gottlob Walz, GER	156.0	1964	Bob Webster, USA	148.58
1908	Hjalmar Johansson, SWE	83.75	1968	Klaus Dibiasi, ITA	164.18
1912	Erik Adlerz, SWE	73.94	1972	Klaus Dibiasi, ITA	504.12
1920	Clarence Pinkston, USA	100.67	1976	Klaus Dibiasi, ITA	600.51
1924	Albert White, USA	97.46	1980	Falk Hoffmann, E. Ger	835.65
1928	Pete Desjardins, USA	98.74	1984	Greg Louganis, USA	710.91
1932	Harold Smith, USA	124.80	1988	Greg Louganis, USA	638.61
1936	Marshall Wayne, USA	113.58	1992	Sun Shuwei, CHN	677.31
1948	Sammy Lee, USA	130.05	1996	Dmitri Sautin, RUS	692.34
1952	Sammy Lee, USA	156.28	2000	Tian Liang, CHN	724.53
1956	Joaquin Capilla, MEX	152.44			

WOMEN

Multiple gold medals: Pat McCormick and Fu Mingxia (4); Ingrid Engel-Krämer (3); Vicki Draves, Dorothy Poynton Hill and Gao Min (2).

Springboard

Year		Points	Year		Points
1920	Aileen Riggin, USA	539.9	1968	Sue Gossick, USA	150.77
1924	Elizabeth Becker, USA	474.5	1972	Micki King, USA	450.03
1928	Helen Meany, USA	78.62	1976	Jennifer Chandler, USA	506.19
1932	Georgia Coleman, USA	87.52	1980	Irina Kalinina, USSR	725.91
1936	Marjorie Gestring, USA	89.27	1984	Sylvie Bernier, CAN	530.70
1948	Vicki Draves, USA	108.74	1988	Gao Min, CHN	580.23
1952	Pat McCormick, USA	147.30	1992	Gao Min, CHN	572.40
1956	Pat McCormick, USA	142.36	1996	Fu Mingxia, CHN	547.68
1960	Ingrid Krämer, GER	155.81	2000	Fu Mingxia, CHN	609.42
1964	Ingrid Engel-Kräamer, GER	145.00			

DIVING (Cont.)
Platform

Year		Points	Year		Points
1912	Greta Johansson, SWE	39.9	1964	Lesley Bush, USA	99.80
1920	Stefani Fryland-Clausen, DEN	34.6	1968	Milena Duchková, CZE	109.59
1924	Caroline Smith, USA	33.2	1972	Ulrika Knape, SWE	390.00
1928	Elizabeth Becker Pinkston, USA	31.6	1976	Elena Vaytsekhovskaya, USSR	406.59
1932	Dorothy Poynton, USA	40.26	1980	Martina Jäschke, E. Ger	596.25
1936	Dorothy Poynton-Hill, USA	33.93	1984	Zhou Jihong, CHN	435.51
1948	Vicki Draves, USA	68.87	1988	Xu Yanmei, CHN	445.20
1952	Pat McCormick, USA	79.37	1992	Fu Mingxia, CHN	461.43
1956	Pat McCormick, USA	84.85	1996	Fu Mingxia, CHN	521.58
1960	Ingrid Krämer, GER	91.28	2000	Laura Wilkinson, USA	543.75

FIELD HOCKEY
MEN

Multiple gold medals: India (8); Great Britain and Pakistan (3); West Germany/Germany and Netherlands (2).

Year		Year	
1908	**Great Britain**, Ireland, Scotland	1968	**Pakistan**, Australia, India
1920	**Great Britain**, Denmark, Belgium	1972	**West Germany**, Pakistan, India
1928	**India**, Netherlands, Germany	1976	**New Zealand**, Australia, Pakistan
1932	**India**, Japan, United States	1980	**India**, Spain, Soviet Union
1936	**India**, Germany, Netherlands	1984	**Pakistan**, West Germany, Great Britain
1948	**India**, Great Britain, Netherlands	1988	**Great Britain**, West Germany, Netherlands
1952	**India**, Netherlands, Great Britain	1992	**Germany**, Australia, Pakistan
1956	**India**, Pakistan, Germany	1996	**Netherlands**, Spain, Australia
1960	**Pakistan**, India, Spain	2000	**Netherlands**, South Korea, Australia
1964	**India**, Pakistan, Australia		

WOMEN

Multiple gold medals: Australia (3).

Year		Year	
1980	**Zimbabwe**, Czechoslovakia, Soviet Union	1992	**Spain**, Germany, Great Britain
1984	**Netherlands**, West Germany, United States	1996	**Australia**, South Korea, Netherlands
1988	**Australia**, South Korea, Netherlands	2000	**Australia**, Argentina, Netherlands

GYMNASTICS
MEN

At least 4 gold medals (including team events): Sawao Kato (8); Nikolai Andrianov, Viktor Chukarin and Boris Shakhlin (7); Akinori Nakayama and Vitaly Scherbo (6); Yukio Endo, Anton Heida, Mitsuo Tsukahara and Takashi Ono (5); Vladimir Artemov, Georges Miez, Valentin Muratov and Alexei Nemov (4).

All-Around

Year		Points	Year		Points
1900	Gustave Sandras, FRA	302	1956	Viktor Chukarin, USSR	114.25
1904	Julius Lenhart, AUT	69.80	1960	Boris Shakhlin, USSR	115.95
1906	Pierre Payssé, FRA	97.0	1964	Yukio Endo, JPN	115.95
1908	Alberto Braglia, ITA	317.0	1968	Sawao Kato, JPN	115.9
1912	Alberto Braglia, ITA	135.0	1972	Sawao Kato, JPN	114.650
1920	Giorgio Zampori, ITA	88.35	1976	Nikolai Andrianov, USSR	116.65
1924	Leon Stukelj, YUG	110.340	1980	Aleksandr Dityatin, USSR	118.65
1928	Georges Miez, SWI	247.500	1984	Koji Gushiken, JPN	118.7
1932	Romeo Neri, ITA	140.625	1988	Vladimir Artemov, USSR	119.125
1936	Alfred Schwarzmann, GER	113.100	1992	Vitaly Scherbo, UT	59.025
1948	Veikko Huhtanen, FIN	229.7	1996	Li Xiaoshuang, CHN	58.423
1952	Viktor Chukarin, USSR	115.7	2000	Alexei Nemov, RUS	58.474

Horizontal Bar

Year		Points	Year		Points
1896	Hermann Weing|f3rtner, GER	–	1968	(TIE) Akinori Nakayama, JPN	19.55
1904	(TIE) Anton Heida, USA	40		& Mikhail Voronin, USSR	19.55
	& Edward Hennig, USA	40	1972	Mitsuo Tsukahara, JPN	19.725
1924	Leon Stukelj, YUG	19.73	1976	Mitsuo Tsukahara, JPN	19.675
1928	Georges Miez, SWI	19.17	1980	Stoyan Deltchev, BUL	19.825
1932	Dallas Bixler, USA	18.33	1984	Shinji Morisue, JPN	20.00
1936	Aleksanteri Saarvala, FIN	19.367	1988	(TIE) Vladimir Artemov, USSR	19.900
1948	Josef Stalder, SWI	19.85		& Valeri Lyukin, USSR	19.900
1952	Jack G)nthard, SWI	19.55	1992	Trent Dimas, USA	9.875
1956	Takashi Ono, JPN	19.60	1996	Andreas Wecker, GER	9.850
1960	Takashi Ono, JPN	19.60	2000	Alexei Nemov, RUS	9.787
1964	Boris Shakhlin, USSR	19.625			

Parallel Bars

Year		Points	Year		Points
1896	Alfred Flatow, GER	.–	1964	Yukio Endo, JPN	19.675
1904	George Eyser, USA	.44	1968	Akinori Nakayama, JPN	19.475
1924	August G)ttinger, SWI	21.63	1972	Sawao Kato, JPN	19.475
1928	Ladislav Vácha, CZE	18.83	1976	Sawao Kato, JPN	19.675
1932	Romeo Neri, ITA	18.97	1980	Aleksandr Tkachyov, USSR	19.775
1936	Konrad Frey, GER	19.067	1984	Bart Conner, USA	19.95
1948	Michael Reusch, SWI	19.75	1988	Vladimir Artemov, USSR	19.925
1952	Hans Eugster, SWI	19.65	1992	Vitaly Scherbo, UT	9.900
1956	Viktor Chukarin, USSR	19.20	1996	Rustam Sharipov, UKR	9.837
1960	Boris Shakhlin, USSR	19.40	2000	Li Xiaopeng, CHN	9.825

Vault

Year		Points	Year		Points
1896	Karl Schumann, GER	.–	1964	Haruhiro Yamashita, JPN	19.60
1904	(TIE) George Eyser, USA	.36	1968	Mikhail Voronin, USSR	19.00
	& Anton Heida, USA	.36	1972	Klaus Köste, E. Ger	18.85
1924	Frank Kriz, USA	9.98	1976	Nikolai Andrianov, USSR	19.45
1928	Eugen Mack, SWI	9.58	1980	Nikolai Andrianov, USSR	19.825
1932	Savino Guglielmetti, ITA	18.03	1984	Lou Yun, CHN	19.95
1936	Alfred Schwarzmann, GER	19.20	1988	Lou Yun, CHN	19.875
1948	Paavo Aaltonen, FIN	19.55	1992	Vitaly Scherbo, UT	9.856
1952	Viktor Chukarin, USSR	19.20	1996	Alexei Nemov, RUS	9.787
1956	(TIE) Helmut Bantz, GER	18.85	2000	Gervasio Deferr, SPA	9.712
	& Valentin Muratov, USSR	18.85			
1960	(TIE) Takashi Ono, JPN	19.35			
	& Boris Shakhlin, USSR	19.35			

Pommel Horse

Year		Points	Year		Points
1896	Louis Zutter, SWI	.–	1968	Miroslav Cerar, YUG	19.325
1904	Anton Heida, USA	.42	1972	Viktor Klimenko, SOV	19.125
1924	Josef Wilhelm, SWI	21.23	1976	Zoltán Magyar, HUN	19.70
1928	Hermann H|f3nggi, SWI	19.75	1980	Zoltán Magyar, HUN	19.925
1932	Istv|f3n Pelle, HUN	19.07	1984	(TIE) Li Ning, CHN	19.95
1936	Konrad Frey, GER	19.333		& Peter Vidmar, USA	19.95
1948	(TIE) Paavo Aaltonen, FIN	19.35	1988	(TIE) Dmitri Bilozerchev, USSR,	19.95
	Veikko Huhtanen, FIN	19.35		Zsolt Borkai, HUN	19.95
	& Heikki Savolainen, FIN	19.35		& Lyubomir Geraskov, BUL	19.95
1952	Viktor Chukarin, USSR	19.50	1992	(TIE) Pae Gil-Su, N. Kor	9.925
1956	Boris Shakhlin, USSR	19.25		& Vitaly Scherbo, UT	9.925
1960	(TIE) Eugen Ekman, FIN	19.375	1996	Li Donghua, SWI	9.875
	& Boris Shakhlin, USSR	19.375	2000	Marius Urzica, ROM	9.862
1964	Miroslav Cerar, YUG	19.525			

Rings

Year		Points	Year		Points
1896	Ioannis Mitropoulos, GRE	.–	1968	Akinori Nakayama, JPN	19.45
1904	Hermann Glass, USA	.45	1972	Akinori Nakayama, JPN	19.35
1924	Francesco Martino, ITA	21.553	1976	Nikolai Andrianov, USSR	19.65
1928	Leon Stukelj, YUG	19.25	1980	Aleksandr Dityatin, USSR	19.875
1932	George Gulack, USA	18.97	1984	(TIE) Koji Gushiken, JPN	19.85
1936	Alois Hudec, CZE	19.433		& Li Ning, CHN	19.85
1948	Karl Frei, SWI	19.80	1988	(TIE) Holger Behrendt, E. Ger	19.925
1952	Grant Shaginyan, USSR	19.75		& Dmitri Bilozerchev, USSR	19.925
1956	Albert Azaryan, USSR	19.35	1992	VitalyScherbo, UT	9.937
1960	Albert Azaryan, USSR	19.725	1996	Yuri Chechi, ITA	9.887
1964	Takuji Haytta, JPN	19.475	2000	Szilveszter Csollany, HUN	9.850

Floor Exercise

Year		Points	Year		Points
1932	Istvan Pelle, HUN	9.60	1972	Nikolai Andrianov, USSR	19.175
1936	Georges Miez, SWI	18.666	1976	Nikolai Andrianov, USSR	19.45
1948	Ferenc Pataki, HUN	19.35	1980	Roland Br)ckner, E. Ger	19.75
1952	William Thoresson, SWE	19.25	1984	Li Ning, CHN	19.925
1956	Valentin Muratov, USSR	19.20	1988	Sergei Kharkov, USSR	19.925
1960	Nobuyuki Aihara, JPN	19.45	1992	Li Xiaosahuang, CHN	9.925
1964	Franco Menichelli, ITA	19.45	1996	Ioannis Melissanidis, GRE	9.850
1968	Sawao Kato, JPN	19.475	2000	Igors Vihrovs, LAT	9.812

Gymnastics (Cont.)
Team Combined Exercises

Year		Points	Year		Points
1904	United States	374.43	1960	Japan	575.20
1906	Norway	19.00	1964	Japan	577.95
1908	Sweden	.438	1968	Japan	575.90
1912	Italy	265.75	1972	Japan	571.25
1920	Italy	359.855	1976	Japan	576.85
1924	Italy	839.058	1980	Soviet Union	598.60
1928	Switzerland	1718.625	1984	United States	591.40
1932	Italy	541.850	1988	Soviet Union	593.35
1936	Germany	657.430	1992	Unified Team	585.45
1948	Finland	1358.30	1996	Russia	576.778
1952	Soviet Union	574.40	2000	China	231.919
1956	Soviet Union	568.25			

WOMEN

At least 4 gold medals (including team events): Larissa Latynina (9); Vera Cáslavská (7); Polina Astakhova, Nadia Comaneci, Agnes Keleti and Nelli Kim (5); Olga Korbut, Ecaterina Szabó and Lyudmila Tourischeva (4).

All-Around

Year		Points	Year		Points
1952	Maria Gorokhovskaya, USSR	76.78	1980	Yelena Davydova, USSR	79.15
1956	Larissa Latynina, USSR	74.933	1984	Mary Lou Retton, USA	79.175
1960	Larissa Latynina, USSR	77.031	1988	Yelena Shushunova, USSR	79.662
1964	Vera Cáslavská, CZE	77.564	1992	Tatiana Gutsu, UT	39.737
1968	Vera Cáslavská, CZE	78.25	1996	Lilia Podkopayeva, UKR	39.255
1972	Lyudmila Tourischeva, USSR	77.025	2000	Simona Amanar, ROM*	38.642
1976	Nadia Comaneci, ROM	79.275			

*Amanar finished second to Andreea Raducan, Romania, who was disqualified for testing positive for pseudo-ephedrine, a drug banned by the IOC and found in Nurofen—an over-the-counter medicine she purportedly took to treat a cold.

Vault

Year		Points	Year		Points
1952	Yekaterina Kalinchuk, USSR	19.20	1980	Natalia Shaposhnikova, USSR	19.725
1956	Larissa Latynina, USSR	18.833	1984	Ecaterina Szabó, ROM	19.875
1960	Margarita Nikolayeva, USSR	19.316	1988	Svetlana Boginskaya, USSR	19.905
1964	Vera Cáslavská, CZE	19.483	1992	(TIE) Henrietta Onodi, HUN	9.925
1968	Vera Cáslavská, CZE	19.775		& Lavinia Milosovici, ROM	9.925
1972	Karin Janz, E. Ger	19.525	1996	Simona Amanar, ROM	9.775
1976	Nelli Kim, USSR	19.80	2000	Elena Zamolodtchikova, RUS	9.731

Uneven Bars

Year		Points	Year		Points
1952	Margit Korondi, HUN	19.40	1980	Maxi Gnauck, E. Ger	19.875
1956	Agnes Keleti, HUN	18.966	1984	(TIE) Julianne McNamora, USA	19.95
1960	Polina Astakhova, USSR	19.616		& Ma Yanhong, CHN	19.95
1964	Polina Astakhova, USSR	19.332	1988	Daniela Silivas, ROM	20.00
1968	Vera Cáslavská, CZE	19.65	1992	Lu Li, CHN	10.00
1972	Karin Janz, E. Ger	19.675	1996	Svetlana Khorkina, RUS	9.850
1976	Nadia Comaneci, ROM	20.00	2000	Svetlana Khorkina, RUS	9.862

Balance Beam

Year		Points	Year		Points
1952	Nina Bocharova, USSR	19.22	1980	Nadia Comaneci, ROM	19.80
1956	Agnes Keleti, HUN	18.80	1984	(TIE) Simona Pauca, ROM	19.80
1960	Eva Bosakova, CZE	19.283		& Ecaterina Szabó, ROM	19.80
1964	Vera Cáslavská, CZE	19.449	1988	Daniela Silivas, ROM	19.924
1968	Natalya Kuchinskaya, USSR	19.65	1992	Tatiana Lyssenko, UT	9.975
1972	Olga Korbut, USSR	19.40	1996	Shannon Miller, USA	9.862
1976	Nadia Comaneci, ROM	19.95	2000	Liu Xuan, CHN	9.825

Floor Exercise

Year		Points	Year		Points
1952	Agnes Keleti, HUN	19.36	1976	Nelli Kim, USSR	19.85
1956	(TIE) Agnes Keleti, HUN	18.733	1980	(TIE) Nadia Comaneci, ROM	19.875
	& Larissa Latynina, USSR	18.733		& Nelli Kim, USSR	19.875
1960	Larissa Latynina, USSR	19.583	1984	Ecaterina Szabó, ROM	19.975
1964	Larissa Latynina, USSR	19.599	1988	Daniela Silivas, ROM	19.937
1968	(TIE) Vera Cáslavská, CZE	19.675	1992	Lavinia Milosovici, ROM	10.000
	& Larissa Petrik, USSR	19.675	1996	Lilia Podkopayeva, UKR	9.887
1972	Olga Korbut, USSR	19.575	2000	Elena Zamolodtchikova, RUS	9.850

Team Combined Exercises

Year		Points	Year		Points
1928	Netherlands	316.75	1972	Soviet Union	380.50
1936	Germany	506.50	1976	Soviet Union	466.00
1948	Czechoslovakia	445.45	1980	Soviet Union	394.90
1952	Soviet Union	527.03	1984	Romania	392.02
1956	Soviet Union	444.800	1988	Soviet Union	395.475
1960	Soviet Union	382.320	1992	Unified Team	395.666
1964	Soviet Union	280.890	1996	United States	389.225
1968	Soviet Union	382.85	2000	Romania	154.608

SOCCER

MEN

Multiple gold medals: Great Britain and Hungary (3); Uruguay and USSR (2).

Year		Year	
1900	**Great Britain**, France, Belgium	1960	**Yugoslavia**, Denmark, Hungary
1904	**Canada**, USA I, USA II	1964	**Hungary**, Czechoslovakia, Germany
1906	**Denmark**, Smyrna (Int'l entry), Greece	1968	**Hungary**, Bulgaria, Japan
1908	**Great Britain**, Denmark, Netherlands	1972	**Poland**, Hungary, East Germany & Soviet Union
1912	**Great Britain**, Denmark, Netherlands	1976	**East Germany**, Poland, Soviet Union
1920	**Belgium**, Spain, Netherlands	1980	**Czechoslovakia**, East Germany, Soviet Union
1924	**Uruguay**, Switzerland, Sweden	1984	**France**, Brazil, Yugoslavia
1928	**Uruguay**, Argentina, Italy	1988	**Soviet Union**, Brazil, West Germany
1936	**Italy**, Austria, Norway	1992	**Spain**, Poland, Ghana
1948	**Sweden**, Yugoslavia, Denmark	1996	**Nigeria**, Argentina, Brazil
1952	**Hungary**, Yugoslavia, Sweden	2000	**Cameroon**, Spain, Chile
1956	**Soviet Union**, Yugoslavia, Bulgaria		

WOMEN

Year		Year	
1996	**United States**, China, Norway	2000	**Norway**, United States, Germany

SOFTBALL

Multiple gold medals: United States (2).

Year		Year	
1996	**United States**, China, Australia	2000	**United States**, Japan, Australia

U.S. Medal-Winning Softball Teams

1996 (gold medal): P–Lisa Fernandez, Michele Granger, Lori Harrigan and Michele Smith; C–Gillian Boxx and Shelly Stokes; INF–Sheila Cornell, Kim Maher, Leah O'Brien, Dot Richardson, Julie Smith and Dani Tyler; OF–Laura Berg, Dionna Harris; Manager–Ralph Raymond. Final: USA over China, 3-1.

2000 (gold medal): P–Lisa Fernandez, Lori Harrigan, Danielle Henderson, Michele Smith and Christa Williams; C–Stacey Nuveman and Michelle Venturella; INF–Jennifer Brundage, Crystl Bustos, Sheila Douty, Jennifer McFalls and Dot Richardson; OF–Christie Ambrosi, Laura Berg, Leah O'Brien-Amico; Manager–Ralph Raymond. Final: USA over Japan, 2-1.

SWIMMING

World and Olympic records below that appear to be broken or equaled by winning times in subsequent years, but are not so indicated, were all broken in preliminary heats leading up to the finals. Some events were not held at every Olympics.

MEN

At least 4 gold medals (including relays): Mark Spitz (9); Matt Biondi (8); Charles Daniels, Tom Jager, Don Schollander, and Johnny Weissmuller (5); Tamás Darnyi, Gary Hall Jr., Roland Matthes, John Naber, Aleksandr Popov, Murray Rose, Vladimir Salnikov and Henry Taylor (4).

50-meter Freestyle

Year		Time		Year		Time	
1904	Zoltán Halmay, HUN (50 yds)	28.0		1996	Aleksandr Popov, RUS	22.13	
1906-84	Not held			2000	(TIE) Anthony Ervin, USA	21.98	
1988	Matt Biondi, USA	22.14	**WR**		& Gary Hall Jr., USA	21.98	
1992	Aleksandr Popov, UT	21.91	**OR**				

100-meter Freestyle

Year		Time		Year		Time	
1896	Alfréd Hajós, HUN	1:22.2	**OR**	1936	Ferenc Csik, HUN	57.6	
1904	Zoltán Halmay, HUN (100 yds)	1:02.8		1948	Wally Ris, USA	57.3	**OR**
1906	Charles Daniels, USA	1:13.4		1952	Clarke Scholes, USA	57.4	
1908	Charles Daniels, USA	1:05.6	**WR**	1956	Jon Henricks, AUS	55.4	**OR**
1912	Duke Kahanamoku, USA	1:03.4		1960	John Devitt, AUS	55.2	**OR**
1920	Duke Kahanamoku, USA	1:00.4	**WR**	1964	Don Schollander, USA	53.4	**OR**
1924	Johnny Weissmuller, USA	59.0	**OR**	1968	Michael Wenden, AUS	52.2	**WR**
1928	Johnny Weissmuller, USA	58.6	**OR**	1972	Mark Spitz, USA	51.22	**WR**
1932	Yasuji Miyazaki, JPN	58.2		1976	Jim Montgomery, USA	49.99	**WR**

Swimming (Cont.)

Year		Time		Year		Time	
1980	Jorg Woithe, E. Ger	.50.40		1992	Aleksandr Popov, UT	.49.02	
1984	Rowdy Gaines, USA	.49.80	**OR**	1996	Aleksandr Popov, RUS	.48.74	
1988	Matt Biondi, USA	.48.63	**OR**	2000	Pieter van den Hoogenband, NED	.48.30	

200-meter Freestyle

Year		Time		Year		Time	
1900	Frederick Lane, AUS (220 yds)	.2:25.2	**OR**	1984	Michael Gross, W. Ger	.1:47.44	**WR**
1904	Charles Daniels, USA (220 yds)	.2:44.2		1988	Duncan Armstrong, AUS	.1:47.25	**WR**
1968	Michael Wenden, AUS	.1:55.2	**OR**	1992	Yevgeny Sadovyi, UT	.1:46.70	**OR**
1972	Mark Spitz, USA	.1:52.78	**WR**	1996	Danyon Loader, NZE	.1:47.63	
1976	Bruce Furniss, USA	.1:50.29	**WR**	2000	Pieter van den Hoogenband, NED	.1:45.35	**WR**
1980	Sergei Kopliakov, USSR	.1:49.81	**OR**				

400-meter Freestyle

Year		Time		Year		Time	
1896	Paul Neumann, AUT (550m)	.8:12.6		1956	Murray Rose, AUS	.4:27.3	**OR**
1904	Charles Daniels, USA (440 yds)	.6:16.2		1960	Murray Rose, AUS	.4:18.3	**OR**
1906	Otto Scheff, AUT	.6:23.8		1964	Don Schollander, USA	.4:12.2	**WR**
1908	Henry Taylor, GBR	.5:36.8		1968	Mike Burton, USA	.4:09.0	**OR**
1912	George Hodgson, CAN	.5:24.4		1972	Bradford Cooper, AUS*	.4:00.27	**OR**
1920	Norman Ross, USA	.5:26.8		1976	Brian Goodell, USA	.3:51.93	**WR**
1924	Johnny Weissmuller, USA	.5:04.2	**OR**	1980	Vladimir Salnikov, USSR	.3:51.31	**OR**
1928	Alberto Zorilla, ARG	.5:01.6	**OR**	1984	George DiCarlo, USA	.3:51.23	**OR**
1932	Buster Crabbe, USA	.4:48.4	**OR**	1988	Uwe Dassler, E. Ger	.3:46.95	**WR**
1936	Jack Medica, USA	.4:44.5	**OR**	1992	Yevgeny Sadovyi, UT	.3:45.00	**WR**
1948	Bill Smith, USA	.4:41.0	**OR**	1996	Danyon Loader, NZE	.3:47.97	
1952	Jean Boiteux, FRA	.4:30.7	**OR**	2000	Ian Thorpe, AUS	.3:40.59	**WR**

*Cooper finished second to Rick DeMont of the U.S., who was disqualified when he flunked the post-race drug test (his asthma medication was on the IOC's banned list).

1500-meter Freestyle

Year		Time		Year		Time	
1896	Alfréd Hajós, HUN (1200m)	.18:22.2	**OR**	1956	Murray Rose, AUS	.17:58.9	
1900	John Arthur Jarvis, GBR (1000m)	.13:40.2		1960	Jon Konrads, AUS	.17:19.6	**OR**
1904	Emil Rausch, GER (1 mile)	.27:18.2		1964	Robert Windle, AUS	.17:01.7	**OR**
1906	Henry Taylor, GBR (1 mile)	.28:28.0		1968	Mike Burton, USA	.16:38.9	**OR**
1908	Henry Taylor, GBR	.22:48.4	**WR**	1972	Mike Burton, USA	.15:52.58	**WR**
1912	George Hodgson, CAN	.22:00.0	**WR**	1976	Brian Goodell, USA	.15:02.40	**WR**
1920	Norman Ross, USA	.22:23.2		1980	Vladimir Salnikov, USSR	.14:58.27	**WR**
1924	Andrew (Boy) Charlton, AUS	.20:06.6	**WR**	1984	Mike O'Brien, USA	.15:05.20	
1928	Arne Borge, SWE	.19:51.8	**OR**	1988	Vladimir Salnikov, USSR	.15:00.40	
1932	Kusuo Kitamura, JPN	.19:12.4	**OR**	1992	Kieren Perkins, AUS	.14:43.48	**WR**
1936	Noboru Terada, JPN	.19:13.7		1996	Kieren Perkins, AUS	.14:56.40	
1948	James McLane, USA	.19:18.5		2000	Grant Hackett, AUS	.14:48.33	
1952	Ford Konno, USA	.18:30.3	**OR**				

100-meter Backstroke

Year		Time		Year		Time	
1904	Walter Brack, GER (100 yds)	.1:16.8		1960	David Theile, AUS	.1:01.9	**OR**
1908	Arno Bieberstein, GER	.1:24.6	**WR**	1968	Roland Matthes, E. Ger	.58.7	**OR**
1912	Harry Hebner, USA	.1:21.2		1972	Roland Matthes, E. Ger	.56.58	**OR**
1920	Warren Kealoha, USA	.1:15.2		1976	John Naber, USA	.55.49	**WR**
1924	Warren Kealoha, USA	.1:13.2	**OR**	1980	Bengt Baron, SWE	.56.33	
1928	George Kojac, USA	.1:08.2	**WR**	1984	Rick Carey, USA	.55.79	
1932	Masaji Kiyokawa, JPN	.1:08.6		1988	Daichi Suzuki, JPN	.55.05	
1936	Adolf Kiefer, USA	.1:05.9	**OR**	1992	Mark Tewksbury, CAN	.53.98	**OR**
1948	Allen Stack, USA	.1:06.4		1996	Jeff Rouse, USA	.54.10	
1952	Yoshinobu Oyakawa, USA	.1:05.4	**OR**	2000	Lenny Krayzelburg, USA	.53.72	**OR**
1956	David Theile, AUS	.1:02.2	**OR**				

200-meter Backstroke

Year		Time		Year		Time	
1900	Ernst Hoppenberg, GER	.2:47.0		1984	Rick Carey, USA	.2:00.23	
1964	Jed Graef, USA	.2:10.3	**WR**	1988	Igor Poliansky, USSR	.1:59.37	
1968	Roland Matthes, E. Ger	.2:09.6	**OR**	1992	Martin Lopez-Zubero, SPA	.1:58.47	**OR**
1972	Roland Matthes, E. Ger	.2:02.82	**=WR**	1996	Brad Bridgewater, USA	.1:58.54	
1976	John Naber, USA	.1:59.19	**WR**	2000	Lenny Krayzelburg, USA	.1:56.76	**OR**
1980	Sándor Wládár, HUN	.2:01.93					

100-meter Breaststroke

Year		Time		Year		Time	
1968	Don McKenzie, USA	1:07.7	**OR**	1988	Adrian Moorhouse, GBR	1:02.04	
1972	Nobutaka Taguchi, JPN	1:04.94	**WR**	1992	Nelson Diebel, USA	1:01.50	**OR**
1976	John Hencken, USA	1:03.11	**WR**	1996	Fred deBurghgraeve, BEL	1:00.60	
1980	Duncan Goodhew, GBR	1:03.44		2000	Domenico Fioravanti, ITA	1:00.46	**OR**
1984	Steve Lundquist, USA	1:01.65	**WR**				

200-meter Breaststroke

Year		Time		Year		Time	
1908	Frederick Holman, GBR	3:09.2	**WR**	1964	Ian O'Brien, AUS	2:27.8	**WR**
1912	Walter Bathe, GER	3:01.8	**OR**	1968	Felipe Muñoz, MEX	2:28.7	
1920	Hakan Malmroth, SWE	3:04.4		1972	John Hencken, USA	2:21.55	**WR**
1924	Robert Skelton, USA	2:56.6		1976	David Wilkie, GBR	2:15.11	**WR**
1928	Yoshiyuki Tsuruta, JPN	2:48.8	**OR**	1980	Robertas Zhulpa, USSR	2:15.85	
1932	Yoshiyuki Tsuruta, JPN	2:45.4		1984	Victor Davis, CAN	2:13.34	**WR**
1936	Tetsuo Hamuro, JPN	2:41.5	**OR**	1988	József Szabó, HUN	2:13.52	
1948	Joseph Verdeur, USA	2:39.3	**OR**	1992	Mike Barrowman, USA	2:10.16	**WR**
1952	John Davies, AUS	2:34.4	**OR**	1996	Norbert Rozsa, HUN	2:12.57	
1956	Masaru Furukawa, JPN	2:34.7*	**OR**	2000	Domenico Fioravanti, ITA	2:10.87	
1960	Bill Mulliken, USA	2:37.4					

*In 1956, the butterfly stroke and breaststroke were separated into two different events.

100-meter Butterfly

Year		Time		Year		Time	
1968	Doug Russell, USA	55.9	**OR**	1988	Anthony Nesty, SUR	53.0	**OR**
1972	Mark Spitz, USA	54.27	**WR**	1992	Pablo Morales, USA	53.32	
1976	Matt Vogel, USA	54.35		1996	Dennis Pankratov, RUS	52.27	
1980	Pär Arvidsson, SWE	54.92		2000	Lars Frolander, SWE	52.00	
1984	Michael Gross, W. Ger	53.08	**WR**				

200-meter Butterfly

Year		Time		Year		Time	
1956	Bill Yorzyk, USA	2:19.3	**OR**	1980	Sergei Fesenko, USSR	1:59.76	
1960	Mike Troy, USA	2:12.8	**WR**	1984	Jon Sieben, AUS	1:57.04	**WR**
1964	Kevin Berry, AUS	2:06.6	**WR**	1988	Michael Gross, W. Ger	1:56.94	**OR**
1968	Carl Robie, USA	2:08.7		1992	Melvin Stewart, USA	1:56.26	**OR**
1972	Mark Spitz, USA	2:00.70	**WR**	1996	Dennis Pankratov, RUS	1:56.51	
1976	Mike Bruner, USA	1:59.23	**WR**	2000	Tom Malchow, USA	1:55.35	**OR**

200-meter Individual Medley

Year		Time		Year		Time	
1968	Charles Hickcox, USA	2:12.0	**OR**	1992	Tamás Darnyi, HUN	2:00.76	
1972	Gunnar Larsson, SWE	2:07.17	**WR**	1996	Attila Czene, HUN	1:59.91	
1984	Alex Baumann, CAN	2:01.42	**WR**	2000	Massimiliano Rosolino, ITA	1:58.98	**OR**
1988	Tamás Darnyi, HUN	2:00.17	**WR**				

400-meter Individual Medley

Year		Time		Year		Time	
1964	Richard Roth, USA	4:45.4	**WR**	1984	Alex Baumann, CAN	4:17.41	**WR**
1968	Charles Hickcox, USA	4:48.4		1988	Tamás Darnyi, HUN	4:14.75	**WR**
1972	Gunnar Larsson, SWE	4:31.98	**OR**	1992	Tamás Darnyi, HUN	4:14.23	**WR**
1976	Rod Strachan, USA	4:23.68	**WR**	1996	Tom Dolan, USA	4:14.90	
1980	Aleksandr Sidorenko, USSR	4:22.89	**OR**	2000	Tom Dolan, USA	4:11.76	**WR**

4x100-meter Freestyle Relay

Year		Time		Year		Time	
1964	United States	3:32.2	**WR**	1988	United States	3:16.53	**WR**
1968	United States	3:31.7	**WR**	1992	United States	3:16.74	
1972	United States	3:26.42	**WR**	1996	United States	3:15.41	
1976-80	Not held			2000	Australia	3:13.67	**WR**
1984	United States	3:19.03	**WR**				

4x200-meter Freestyle Relay

Year		Time		Year		Time	
1906	Hungary (x250m)	16:52.4		1948	United States	8:46.0	**WR**
1908	Great Britain	10:55.6	**WR**	1952	United States	8:31.1	**OR**
1912	Australia/New Zealand	10:11.6	**WR**	1956	Australia	8:23.6	**WR**
1920	United States	10:04.4	**WR**	1960	United States	8:10.2	**WR**
1924	United States	9:53.4	**WR**	1964	United States	7:52.1	**WR**
1928	United States	9:36.2	**WR**	1968	United States	7:52.33	
1932	Japan	8:58.4	**WR**	1972	United States	7:35.78	**WR**
1936	Japan	8:51.5	**WR**	1976	United States	7:23.22	**WR**

Swimming (Cont.)

Year	Time		Year	Time	
1980 Soviet Union	7:23.50		1992 Unified Team	7:11.95	**WR**
1984 United States	7:15.69	**WR**	1996 United States	7:14.84	
1988 United States	7:12.51	**WR**	2000 Australia	7:07.05	**WR**

4x100-meter Medley Relay

Year	Time		Year	Time	
1960 United States	4:05.4	**WR**	1984 United States	3:39.30	**WR**
1964 United States	3:58.4	**WR**	1988 United States	3:36.93	**WR**
1968 United States	3:54.9	**WR**	1992 United States	3:36.93	**=WR**
1972 United States	3:48.16	**WR**	1996 United States	3:34.84	
1976 United States	3:42.22	**WR**	2000 United States	3:33.73	**WR**
1980 Australia	3:45.70				

WOMEN

At least 4 gold medals (including relays): Jenny Thompson (8); Kristin Otto and Amy Van Dyken (6); Krisztina Egerszegi (5), Kornelia Ender, Janet Evans, Dawn Fraser and Dara Torres (4).

50-meter Freestyle

Year	Time		Year	Time	
1988 Kristin Otto, E. Ger	25.49	**OR**	1996 Amy Van Dyken, USA	24.87	
1992 Yang Wenyi, CHN	24.79	**WR**	2000 Inge de Bruijn, NED	24.32	

100-meter Freestyle

Year	Time		Year	Time	
1912 Fanny Durack, AUS	1:22.2		1968 Jan Henne, USA	1:00.0	
1920 Ethelda Bleibtrey, USA	1:13.6	**WR**	1972 Sandra Neilson, USA	58.59	**OR**
1924 Ethel Lackie, USA	1:12.4		1976 Kornelia Ender, E. Ger	55.65	**WR**
1928 Albina Osipowich, USA	1:11.0	**OR**	1980 Barbara Krause, E. Ger	54.79	**WR**
1932 Helene Madison, USA	1:06.8	**OR**	1984 (TIE) Nancy Hogshead, USA	55.92	
1936 Rie Mastenbroek, NED	1:05.9	**OR**	& Carrie Steinseifer, USA	55.92	
1948 Greta Andersen, DEN	1:06.3		1988 Kristin Otto, E. Ger	54.93	
1952 Katalin Sz|f·ke, HUN	1:06.8		1992 Zhuang Yong, CHN	54.65	**OR**
1956 Dawn Fraser, AUS	1:02.0	**WR**	1996 Le Jingyi, CHN	54.50	
1960 Dawn Fraser, AUS	1:01.2	**OR**	2000 Inge de Bruijn, NED	53.83	
1964 Dawn Fraser, AUS	59.5	**OR**			

200-meter Freestyle

Year	Time		Year	Time	
1968 Debbie Meyer, USA	2:10.5	**OR**	1988 Heike Friedrich, E. Ger	1:57.65	**OR**
1972 Shane Gould, AUS	2:03.56	**WR**	1992 Nicole Haislett, USA	1:57.90	
1976 Kornelia Ender, E. Ger	1:59.26	**WR**	1996 Claudia Poll, CRC	1:58.16	
1980 Barbara Krause, E. Ger	1:58.33	**OR**	2000 Susie O'Neill, AUS	1:58.24	
1984 Mary Wayte, USA	1:59.23				

400-meter Freestyle

Year	Time		Year	Time	
1920 Ethelda Bleibtrey, USA (300m)	4:34.0	**WR**	1968 Debbie Meyer, USA	4:31.8	**OR**
1924 Martha Norelius, USA	6:02.2	**OR**	1972 Shane Gould, AUS	4:19.44	**WR**
1928 Martha Norelius, USA	5:42.8	**WR**	1976 Petra Th)mer, E. Ger	4:09.89	**WR**
1932 Helene Madison, USA	5:28.5	**WR**	1980 Ines Diers, E. Ger	4:08.76	**OR**
1936 Rie Mastenbroek, NED	5:26.4	**OR**	1984 Tiffany Cohen, USA	4:07.10	**OR**
1948 Ann Curtis, USA	5:17.8	**OR**	1988 Janet Evans, USA	4:03.85	**WR**
1952 Valéria Gyenge, HUN	5:12.1	**OR**	1992 Dagmar Hase, GER	4:07.18	
1956 Lorraine Crapp, AUS	4:54.6	**OR**	1996 Michelle Smith, IRE	4:07.25	
1960 Chris von Saltza, USA	4:50.6	**OR**	2000 Brooke Bennett, USA	4:05.80	
1964 Ginny Duenkel, USA	4:43.3	**OR**			

800-meter Freestyle

Year	Time		Year	Time	
1968 Debbie Meyer, USA	9:24.0	**OR**	1988 Janet Evans, USA	8:20.20	**OR**
1972 Keena Rothhammer, USA	8:53.68	**WR**	1992 Janet Evans, USA	8:25.52	
1976 Petra Th)mer, E. Ger	8:37.14	**WR**	1996 Brooke Bennett, USA	8:27.89	
1980 Michelle Ford, AUS	8:28.90	**OR**	2000 Brooke Bennett, USA	8:19.67	**OR**
1984 Tiffany Cohen, USA	8:24.95	**OR**			

100-meter Backstroke

Year	Time		Year	Time	
1924 Sybil Bauer, USA	1:23.2	**OR**	1968 Kaye Hall, USA	1:06.2	**OR**
1928 Maria Braun, NED	1:22.0		1972 Melissa Belote, USA	1:05.78	**OR**
1932 Eleanor Holm, USA	1:19.4		1976 Ulrike Richter, E. Ger	1:01.83	**OR**
1936 Dina Senff, NED	1:18.9		1980 Rica Reinisch, E. Ger	1:00.86	**WR**
1948 Karen-Margrete Harup, DEN	1:14.4	**OR**	1984 Theresa Andrews, USA	1:02.55	
1952 Joan Harrison, S. Afr.	1:14.3		1988 Kristin Otto, E. Ger	1:00.89	
1956 Judy Grinham, GBR	1:12.9	**OR**	1992 Krisztina Egerszegi, HUN	1:00.68	**OR**
1960 Lynn Burke, USA	1:09.3	**OR**	1996 Beth Botsford, USA	1:01.19	
1964 Cathy Ferguson, USA	1:07.7	**WR**	2000 Diana Mocanu, ROM	1:00.21	**OR**

200-meter Backstroke

Year		Time		Year		Time	
1968	Pokey Watson, USA	2:24.8	OR	1988	Krisztina Egerszegi, HUN	2:09.29	OR
1972	Melissa Belote, USA	2:19.19	WR	1992	Krisztina Egerszegi, HUN	2:07.06	OR
1976	Ulrike Richter, E. Ger	2:13.43	OR	1996	Krisztina Egerszegi, HUN	2:07.83	
1980	Rica Reinisch, E. Ger	2:11.77	WR	2000	Diana Mocanu, ROM	2:08.16	
1984	Jolanda de Rover, NED	2:12.38					

100-meter Breaststroke

Year		Time		Year		Time	
1968	Djurdjica Bjedov, YUG	1:15.8	OR	1988	Tania Dangalakova, BUL	1:07.95	OR
1972	Cathy Carr, USA	1:13.58	WR	1992	Yelena Rudkovskaya, UT	1:08.00	
1976	Hannelore Anke, E. Ger	1:11.16		1996	Penny Heyns, RSA.	1:07.73	
1980	Ute Geweniger, E. Ger	1:10.22		2000	Megan Quann, USA	1:07.05	
1984	Petra van Staveren, NED	1:09.88	OR				

200-meter Breaststroke

Year		Time		Year		Time	
1924	Lucy Morton, GBR	3:33.2	OR	1968	Sharon Wichman, USA	2:44.4	OR
1928	Hilde Schrader, GER	3:12.6		1972	Beverley Whitfield, AUS	2:41.71	OR
1932	Clare Dennis, AUS	3:06.3	OR	1976	Marina Koshevaya, USSR	2:33.35	WR
1936	Hideko Maehata, JPN	3:03.6		1980	Lina Kaciusyte, USSR	2:29.54	OR
1948	Petronella van Vliet, NED	2:57.2		1984	Anne Ottenbrite, CAN	2:30.38	
1952	éva Székely, HUN	2:51.7	OR	1988	Silke Hörner, E. Ger	2:26.71	WR
1956	Ursula Happe, GER	2:53.1	OR	1992	Kyoko Iwasaki, JPN	2:26.65	OR
1960	Anita Lonsbrough, GBR	2:49.5	WR	1996	Penny Heyns, RSA	2:25.41	
1964	Galina Prozumenshikova, USSR	2:46.4	OR	2000	Agnes Kovacs, HUN	2:24.35	

100-meter Butterfly

Year		Time		Year		Time	
1956	Shelly Mann, USA	1:11.0	OR	1980	Caren Metschuck, E. Ger	1:00.42	
1960	Carolyn Schuler, USA	1:09.5	OR	1984	Mary T. Meagher, USA	.59.26	
1964	Sharon Stouder, USA	1:04.7	WR	1988	Kristin Otto, E. Ger	.59.00	OR
1968	Lynn McClements, AUS	1:05.5		1992	Qian Hong, CHN	.58.62	OR
1972	Mayumi Aoki, JPN	1:03.34	WR	1996	Amy Van Dyken, USA	.59.13	
1976	Kornelia Ender, E. Ger	1:00.13	=WR	2000	Inge de Bruijn, NED	.56.61	WR

200-meter Butterfly

Year		Time		Year		Time	
1968	Ada Kok, NED	2:24.7	OR	1988	Kathleen Nord, E. Ger	2:09.51	
1972	Karen Moe, USA	2:15.57	OR	1992	Summer Sanders, USA	2:08.67	
1976	Andrea Pollack, E. Ger	2:11.41	OR	1996	Susie O'Neill, AUS	2:07.76	
1980	Ines Geissler, E. Ger	2:10.44	OR	2000	Misty Hyman, USA	2:05.88	OR
1984	Mary T. Meagher, USA	2:06.90	OR				

200-meter Individual Medley

Year		Time		Year		Time	
1968	Claudia Kolb, USA	2:24.7	OR	1992	Lin Li, CHN	2:11.65	WR
1972	Shane Gould, AUS	2:23.07	WR	1996	Michelle Smith, IRE	2:13.93	
1984	Tracy Caulkins, USA	2:12.64	OR	2000	Yana Klochkova, UKR	2:10.68	OR
1988	Daniela Hunger, E. Ger	2:12.59	OR				

400-meter Individual Medley

Year		Time		Year		Time	
1964	Donna de Varona, USA	5:18.7	OR	1984	Tracy Caulkins, USA	4:39.24	
1968	Claudia Kolb, USA	5:08.5	OR	1988	Janet Evans, USA	4:37.76	
1972	Gail Neall, AUS	5:02.97	WR	1992	Krisztina Egerszegi, HUN	4:36.54	
1976	Ulrike Tauber, E. Ger	4:42.77	WR	1996	Michelle Smith, IRE	4:39.18	
1980	Petra Schneider, E. Ger	4:36.29	WR	2000	Yana Klochkova, UKR	4:33.59	WR

4x100-meter Freestyle Relay

Year		Time		Year		Time	
1912	Great Britain	5:52.8	WR	1964	United States	4:03.8	WR
1920	United States	5:11.6	WR	1968	United States	4:02.5	OR
1924	United States	4:58.8	WR	1972	United States	3:55.19	WR
1928	United States	4:47.6	WR	1976	United States	3:44.82	WR
1932	United States	4:38.0	WR	1980	East Germany	3:42.71	WR
1936	Netherlands	4:36.0	OR	1984	United States	3:43.43	
1948	United States	4:29.2	OR	1988	East Germany	3:40.63	OR
1952	Hungary	4:24.4	WR	1992	United States	3:39.46	WR
1956	Australia	4:17.1	WR	1996	United States	3:39.29	
1960	United States	4:08.9	WR	2000	United States	3:36.61	WR

4x200-meter Freestyle Relay

Year		Time		Year		Time	
1996	United States	7:59.87		2000	United States	7:57.80	OR

Swimming (Cont.)
4x100-meter Medley Relay

Year		Time		Year		Time	
1960	United States	4:41.1	**WR**	1984	United States	4:08.34	
1964	United States	4:33.9	**WR**	1988	East Germany	4:03.74	**OR**
1968	United States	4:28.3	**OR**	1992	United States	4:02.54	**WR**
1972	United States	4:20.75	**WR**	1996	United States	4:02.88	
1976	East Germany	4:07.95	**WR**	2000	United States	3:58.30	**WR**
1980	East Germany	4:06.67	**WR**				

TENNIS

MEN

Multiple gold medals (including men's doubles): John Boland, Max Decugis, Laurie Doherty, Reggie Doherty, Arthur Gore, Andre Grobert, Vincent Richards, Charles Winslow and Beals Wright (2).

Singles

Year			Year		
1896	John Boland	Great Britain/Ireland	1920	Louis Raymond	South Africa
1900	Laurie Doherty,	Great Britain	1924	Vincent Richards	United States
1904	Beals Wright	United States	1928-84	Not held	
1906	Max Decugis	France	1988	Miloslav Mecir	Czechoslovakia
1908	Josiah Ritchie	Great Britain	1992	Marc Rosset	Switzerland
	(Indoor) Arthur Gore	Great Britain	1996	Andre Agassi	United States
1912	Charles Winslow	South Africa	2000	Yevgeny Kafelnikov	Russia
	(Indoor) André Gobert	France			

Doubles

Year		Year	
1896	John Boland, IRE & Fritz Traun, GER	1920	Noel Turnbull & Max Woosnam, GBR
1900	Laurie and Reggie Doherty, GBR	1924	Vincent Richards & Frank Hunter, USA
1904	Edgar Leonard & Beals Wright, USA	1928-84	Not held
1906	Max Decugis & Maurice Germot, FRA	1988	Ken Flach & Robert Seguso, USA
1908	George Hillyard & Reggie Doherty, GBR	1992	Boris Becker & Michael Stich, GER
	(Indoor) Arthur Gore & Herbert Barrett, GBR	1996	Todd Woodbridge & Mark Woodforde, AUS
1912	Charles Winslow & Harold Kitson, S. Afr.	2000	Sebastien Lareau & Daniel Nestor, CAN
	(Indoor) Andre Gobert & Maurice Germot, FRA		

WOMEN

Multiple gold medals (including women's doubles): Helen Wills, Gigi Fernandez, Mary Joe Fernandez and Venus Williams (2).

Singles

Year			Year		
1900	Charlotte Cooper	Great Britain	1924	Helen Wills	United States
1906	Esmee Simiriotou	Greece	1928-84	Not held	
1908	Dorothea Chambers	Great Britain	1988	Steffi Graf	West Germany
	(Indoor) Gwen Eastlake-Smith	Great Britain	1992	Jennifer Capriati	United States
1912	Marguerite Broquedis	France	1996	Lindsay Davenport	United States
	(Indoor) Edith Hannam	Great Britain	2000	Venus Williams	United States
1920	Suzanne Lenglen	France			

Doubles

Year		Year	
1920	Winifred McNair & Kitty McKane, GBR	1992	Gigi Fernandez & Mary Joe Fernandez, USA
1924	Hazel Wightman & Helen Wills, USA	1996	Gigi Fernandez & Mary Joe Fernandez, USA
1928-84	Not held	2000	Serena Williams & Venus Williams, USA
1988	Pam Shriver & Zina Garrison, USA		

TRACK & FIELD

World and Olympic records below that appear to be broken or equaled by winning times, heights and distances in subsequent years, but are not so indicated, were all broken in preliminary races and field events leading up to the finals.

MEN

At least 4 gold medals (including relays and discontinued events): Ray Ewry (10); Carl Lewis and Paavo Nurmi (9); Ville Ritola and Martin Sheridan (5); Harrison Dillard, Archie Hahn, Michael Johnson, Hannes Kolehmainen, Alvin Kraenzlein, Eric Lemming, Jim Lightbody, Al Oerter, Jesse Owens, Meyer Prinstein, Mel Sheppard, Lasse Viren and Emil Zátopek (4). Note that all of Ewry's gold medals came before 1912, in the Standing High Jump, Standing Long Jump and Standing Triple Jump.

100 meters

Year		Time		Year		Time	
1896	Tom Burke, USA	12.0		1920	Charley Paddock, USA	10.8	
1900	Frank Jarvis, USA	11.0		1924	Harold Abrahams, GBR	10.6	**=OR**
1904	Archie Hahn, USA	11.0		1928	Percy Williams, CAN	10.8	
1906	Archie Hahn, USA	11.2		1932	Eddie Tolan, USA	10.3	**OR**
1908	Reggie Walker, S. Afr.	10.8	**=OR**	1936	Jesse Owens, USA	10.3ᵂ	
1912	Ralph Craig, USA	10.8		1948	Harrison Dillard, USA	10.3	**=OR**

Year		Time	Year		Time
1952	Lindy Remigino, USA	10.4	1980	Allan Wells, GBR	10.25
1956	Bobby Morrow, USA	10.5	1984	Carl Lewis, USA	9.99
1960	Armin Hary, GER	10.2 OR	1988	Carl Lewis, USA*	9.92 WR
1964	Bob Hayes, USA	10.0 =WR	1992	Linford Christie, GBR	9.96
1968	Jim Hines, USA	9.95 WR	1996	Donovan Bailey, CAN	9.84 WR
1972	Valery Borzov, USSR	10.14	2000	Maurice Greene, USA	9.87
1976	Hasely Crawford, TRI	10.06			

Windicates wind-aided.

*Lewis finished second to Ben Johnson of Canada, who set a world record of 9.79 seconds. Two days later, Johnson was stripped of his gold medal and his record when he tested positive for steroid use in a post-race drug test.

200 meters

Year		Time	Year		Time
1900	Walter Tewksbury, USA	22.2	1960	Livio Berruti, ITA	20.5 =WR
1904	Archie Hahn, USA	21.6 OR	1964	Henry Carr, USA	20.3 OR
1908	Bobby Kerr, CAN	22.6	1968	Tommie Smith, USA	19.83 WR
1912	Ralph Craig, USA	21.7	1972	Valery Borzov, USSR	20.00
1920	Allen Woodring, USA	22.0	1976	Donald Quarrie, JAM	20.23
1924	Jackson Scholz, USA	21.6	1980	Pietro Mennea, ITA	20.19
1928	Percy Williams, CAN	21.8	1984	Carl Lewis, USA	19.80 OR
1932	Eddie Tolan, USA	21.2 OR	1988	Joe DeLoach, USA	19.75 OR
1936	Jesse Owens, USA	20.7 OR	1992	Mike Marsh, USA	20.01
1948	Mel Patton, USA	21.1	1996	Michael Johnson,USA	19.32 WR
1952	Andy Stanfield, USA	20.7	2000	Konstantinos Kenteris,GRE	20.09
1956	Bobby Morrow, USA	20.6 OR			

400 meters

Year		Time	Year		Time
1896	Tom Burke, USA	54.2	1956	Charley Jenkins, USA	46.7
1900	Maxey Long, USA	49.4 OR	1960	Otis Davis, USA	44.9 WR
1904	Harry Hillman, USA	49.2 OR	1964	Mike Larrabee, USA	45.1
1906	Paul Pilgrim, USA	53.2	1968	Lee Evans, USA	43.86 WR
1908	Wyndham Halswelle, GBR	50.0	1972	Vince Matthews, USA	44.66
1912	Charlie Reidpath, USA	48.2 OR	1976	Alberto Juantorena, CUB	44.26
1920	Bevil Rudd, S. Afr.	49.6	1980	Viktor Markin, USSR	44.60
1924	Eric Liddell, GBR	47.6 OR	1984	Alonzo Babers, USA	44.27
1928	Ray Barbuti, USA	47.8	1988	Steve Lewis, USA	43.87
1932	Bill Carr, USA	46.2 WR	1992	Quincy Watts, USA	43.50 OR
1936	Archie Williams, USA	46.5	1996	Michael Johnson, USA	43.49 OR
1948	Arthur Wint, JAM	46.2	2000	Michael Johnson, USA	43.84
1952	George Rhoden, JAM	45.9 OR			

800 meters

Year		Time	Year		Time
1896	Teddy Flack, AUS	2:11.0	1956	Tom Courtney, USA	1:47.7 OR
1900	Alfred Tysoe, GBR	2:01.2	1960	Peter Snell, NZE	1:46.3 OR
1904	Jim Lightbody, USA	1:56.0 OR	1964	Peter Snell, NZE	1:45.1 OR
1906	Paul Pilgrim, USA	2:01.5	1968	Ralph Doubell, AUS	1:44.3 =WR
1908	Mel Sheppard, USA	1:52.8 WR	1972	Dave Wottle, USA	1:45.9
1912	Ted Meredith, USA	1:51.9 WR	1976	Alberto Juantorena, CUB	1:43.50 WR
1920	Albert Hill, GBR	1:53.4	1980	Steve Ovett, GBR	1:45.4
1924	Douglas Lowe, GBR	1:52.4	1984	Joaquim Cruz, BRA	1:43.00 OR
1928	Douglas Lowe, GBR	1:51.8 OR	1988	Paul Ereng, KEN	1:43.45
1932	Tommy Hampson, GBR	1:49.7 WR	1992	William Tanui, KEN	1:43.66
1936	John Woodruff, USA	1:52.9	1996	Vebjoern Rodal, NOR	1:42.58 OR
1948	Mal Whitfield, USA	1:49.2 OR	2000	Nils Schumann, GER	1:45.08
1952	Mal Whitfield, USA	1:49.2 =OR			

1500 meters

Year		Time	Year		Time
1896	Teddy Flack, AUS	4:33.2	1956	Ron Delany,IRE	3:41.2 OR
1900	Charles Bennett, GBR	4:06.2 WR	1960	Herb Elliott, AUS	3:35.6 WR
1904	Jim Lightbody, USA	4:05.4 WR	1964	Peter Snell, NZE	3:38.1
1906	Jim Lightbody, USA	4:12.0	1968	Kip Keino, KEN	3:34.9 OR
1908	Mel Sheppard, USA	4:03.4 OR	1972	Pekka Vasala, FIN	3:36.3
1912	Arnold Jackson, GBR	3:56.8 OR	1976	John Walker, NZE	3:39.17
1920	Albert Hill, GBR	4:01.8	1980	Sebastian Coe, GBR	3:38.4
1924	Paavo Nurmi, FIN	3:53.6 OR	1984	Sebastian Coe, GBR	3:32.53 OR
1928	Harry Larva, FIN	3:53.2 OR	1988	Peter Rono, KEN	3:35.96
1932	Luigi Beccali, ITA	3:51.2 OR	1992	Fermin Cacho, SPA	3:40.12
1936	John Lovelock, NZE	3:47.8 WR	1996	Noureddine Morceli, ALG	3:35.78
1948	Henry Eriksson, SWE	3:49.8	2000	Noah Ngeny, KEN	3:32.07 OR
1952	Josy Barthel, LUX	3:45.1 OR			

Track & Field (Cont.)

5000 meters

Year		Time		Year		Time	
1912	Hannes Kolehmainen, FIN	14:36.6	WR	1964	Bob Schul, USA	13:48.8	
1920	Joseph Guillemot, FRA	14:55.6		1968	Mohamed Gammoudi, TUN	14:05.0	
1924	Paavo Nurmi, FIN	14:31.2	OR	1972	Lasse Viren, FIN	13:26.4	OR
1928	Ville Ritola, FIN	14:38.0		1976	Lasse Viren, FIN	13:24.76	
1932	Lauri Lehtinen, FIN	14:30.0	OR	1980	Miruts Yifter, ETH	13:21.0	
1936	Gunnar Höckert, FIN	14:22.2	OR	1984	Said Aouita, MOR	13:05.59	OR
1948	Gaston Reiff, BEL	14:17.6	OR	1988	John Ngugi, KEN	13:11.70	
1952	Emil Zátopek, CZE	14:06.6	OR	1992	Dieter Baumann, GER	13:12.52	
1956	Vladimir Kuts, USSR	13:39.6	OR	1996	Venuste Niyongabo, BUR	13:07.96	
1960	Murray Halberg, NZE	13:43.4		2000	Millon Wolde, ETH	13:35.49	

10,000 meters

Year		Time		Year		Time	
1912	Hannes Kolehmainen, FIN	31:20.8		1964	Billy Mills, USA	28:24.4	OR
1920	Paavo Nurmi, FIN	31:45.8		1968	Naftali Temu, KEN	29:27.4	
1924	Ville Ritola, FIN	30:23.2	WR	1972	Lasse Viren, FIN	27:38.4	WR
1928	Paavo Nurmi, FIN	30:18.8	OR	1976	Lasse Viren, FIN	27:40.38	
1932	Janusz Kusocinski, POL	30:11.4	OR	1980	Miruts Yifter, ETH	27:42.7	
1936	Ilmari Salminen, FIN	30:15.4		1984	Alberto Cova, ITA	27:47.54	
1948	Emil Zátopek, CZE	29:59.6	OR	1988	Brahim Boutaib, MOR	27:21.46	OR
1952	Emil Zátopek, CZE	29:17.0	OR	1992	Khalid Skah, MOR	27:46.70	
1956	Vladimir Kuts, USSR	28:45.6	OR	1996	Haile Gebrselassie, ETH	27:07.34	OR
1960	Pyotr Bolotnikov, USSR	28:32.2	OR	2000	Haile Gebrselassie, ETH	27:18.20	

Marathon

Year		Time		Year		Time	
1896	Spiridon Louis, GRE	2:58:50		1956	Alain Mimoun, FRA	2:25:00.0	
1900	Michel Théato, FRA	2:59:45		1960	Abebe Bikila, ETH	2:15:16.2	WB
1904	Thomas Hicks, USA	3:28:53		1964	Abebe Bikila, ETH	2:12:11.2	WB
1906	Billy Sherring, CAN	2:51:23.6		1968	Mamo Wolde, ETH	2:20:26.4	
1908	Johnny Hayes, USA*	2:55:18.4	OR	1972	Frank Shorter, USA	2:12:19.8	
1912	Kenneth McArthur, S. Afr.	2:36:54.8		1976	Waldemar Cierpinski, E. Ger	2:09:55.0	OR
1920	Hannes Kolehmainen, FIN	2:32:35.8	WB	1980	Waldemar Cierpinski, E. Ger	2:11:03.0	
1924	Albin Stenroos, FIN	2:41:22.6		1984	Carlos Lopes, POR	2:09:21.0	OR
1928	Bough|f4ra El Ouafi, FRA	2:32:57.0		1988	Gelindo Bordin, ITA	2:10:32	
1932	Juan Carlos Zabala, ARG	2:31:36.0	OR	1992	Hwang Young-Cho, S. Kor	2:13:23	
1936	Sohn Kee-Chung, JPN†	2:29:19.2	OR	1996	Josia Thugwane, RSA	2:12:36	
1948	Delfo Cabrera, ARG	2:34:51.6		2000	Gezahenge Abera, ETH	2:10.11	
1952	Emil Zátopek, CZE	2:23:03.2	OR				

*Dorando Pietri of Italy placed first, but was disqualified for being helped across the finish line.

†Sohn was a Korean, but he was forced to compete under the name Kitei Son by Japan, which occupied Korea at the time.

Note: Marathon distances—40,000 meters (1896,1904); 40,260 meters (1900); 41,860 meters (1906); 42,195 meters (1908 and since 1924); 40,200 meters (1912); 42,750 meters (1920). Current distance of 42,195 meters measures 26 miles, 385 yards.

110-meter Hurdles

Year		Time		Year		Time	
1896	Tom Curtis, USA	17.6		1956	Lee Calhoun, USA	13.5	OR
1900	Alvin Kraenzlein, USA	15.4	OR	1960	Lee Calhoun, USA	13.8	
1904	Frederick Schule, USA	16.0		1964	Hayes Jones, USA	13.6	
1906	Robert Leavitt, USA	16.2		1968	Willie Davenport, USA	13.3	OR
1908	Forrest Smithson, USA	15.0	WR	1972	Rod Milburn, USA	13.24	=WR
1912	Frederick Kelly, USA	15.1		1976	Guy Drut, FRA	13.30	
1920	Earl Thomson, CAN	14.8	WR	1980	Thomas Munkelt, E. Ger	13.39	
1924	Daniel Kinsey, USA	15.0		1984	Roger Kingdom, USA	13.20	OR
1928	Syd Atkinson, S. Afr.	14.8		1988	Roger Kingdom, USA	12.98	OR
1932	George Saling, USA	14.6		1992	Mark McKoy, CAN	13.12	
1936	Forrest (Spec) Towns, USA	14.2		1996	Allen Johnson, USA	12.95	OR
1948	William Porter, USA	13.9	OR	2000	Anier Garcia, CUB	13.00	
1952	Harrison Dillard, USA	13.7	OR				

400-meter Hurdles

Year		Time		Year		Time	
1900	Walter Tewksbury, USA	57.6		1960	Glenn Davis, USA	49.3	OR
1904	Harry Hillman, USA	53.0		1964	Rex Cawley, USA	49.6	
1908	Charley Bacon, USA	55.0	WR	1968	David Hemery, GBR	48.12	WR
1920	Frank Loomis, USA	54.0	WR	1972	John Akii-Bua, UGA	47.82	WR
1924	Morgan Taylor, USA	52.6		1976	Edwin Moses, USA	47.64	WR
1928	David Burghley, GBR	53.4	OR	1980	Volker Beck, E. Ger	48.70	
1932	Bob Tisdall, IRE	51.7		1984	Edwin Moses, USA	47.75	
1936	Glenn Hardin, USA	52.4		1988	Andre Phillips, USA	47.19	OR
1948	Roy Cochran, USA	51.1	OR	1992	Kevin Young, USA	46.78	WR
1952	Charley Moore, USA	50.8	OR	1996	Derrick Adkins, USA	47.54	
1956	Glenn Davis, USA	50.1	=OR	2000	Angelo Taylor, USA	47.50	

3000-meter Steeplechase

Year		Time		Year		Time	
1900	George Orton, CAN	7:34.4		1960	Zdzislaw Krzyszkowiak, POL	8:34.2	OR
1904	Jim Lightbody, USA	7:39.6		1964	Gaston Roelants, BEL	8:30.8	OR
1908	Arthur Russell, GBR	10:47.8		1968	Amos Biwott, KEN	8:51.0	
1920	Percy Hodge, GBR	10:00.4	OR	1972	Kip Keino, KEN	8:23.6	OR
1924	Ville Ritola, FIN	9:33.6	OR	1976	Anders G|f3rderud, SWE	8:08.2	WR
1928	Toivo Loukola, FIN	9:21.8	WR	1980	Bronislaw Malinowski, POL	8:09.7	
1932	Volmari Iso-Hollo, FIN	10:33.4*		1984	Julius Korir, KEN	8:11.80	
1936	Volmari Iso-Hollo, FIN	9:03.8	WR	1988	Julius Kariuki, KEN	8:05.51	OR
1948	Thore Sjöstrand, SWE	9:04.6		1992	Matthew Birir, KEN	8:08.84	
1952	Horace Ashenfelter, USA	8:45.4	WR	1996	Joseph Keter, KEN	8:07.12	
1956	Chris Brasher, GBR	8:41.2	OR	2000	Reuben Kosgei, KEN	8:21.43	

*Iso-Hollo ran one extra lap due to lap counter's mistake.

Note: Other steeplechase distances– 2500 meters (1900); 2590 meters (1904); 3200 meters (1908) and 3460 meters (1932).

4x100-meter Relay

Year		Time		Year		Time	
1912	Great Britain	42.4		1964	United States	39.0	WR
1920	United States	42.2	WR	1968	United States	38.23	WR
1924	United States	41.0	=WR	1972	United States	38.19	WR
1928	United States	41.0	=WR	1976	United States	38.33	
1932	United States	40.0	WR	1980	Soviet Union	38.26	
1936	United States	39.8	WR	1984	United States	37.83	WR
1948	United States	40.6		1988	Soviet Union	38.19	
1952	United States	40.1		1992	United States	37.40	WR
1956	United States	39.5	WR	1996	Canada	37.69	
1960	Germany	39.5	=WR	2000	United States	37.61	

4x400-meter Relay

Year		Time		Year		Time	
1908	United States	3:29.4		1964	United States	3:00.7	WR
1912	United States	3:16.6	WR	1968	United States	2:56.16	WR
1920	Great Britain	3:22.2		1972	Kenya	2:59.8	
1924	United States	3:16.0	WR	1976	United States	2:58.65	
1928	United States	3:14.2	WR	1980	Soviet Union	3:01.1	
1932	United States	3:08.2	WR	1984	United States	2:57.91	
1936	Great Britain	3:09.0		1988	United States	2:56.16	=WR
1948	United States	3:10.4		1992	United States	2:55.74	WR
1952	Jamaica	3:03.9	WR	1996	United States	2:55.99	
1956	United States	3:04.8		2000	United States	2:56.35	
1960	United States	3:02.2	WR				

20-kilometer Walk

Year		Time		Year		Time	
1956	Leonid Spirin, USSR	1:31:27.4		1980	Maurizio Damilano, ITA	1:23:35.5	OR
1960	Vladimir Golubnichiy, USSR	1:34:07.2		1984	Ernesto Canto, MEX	1:23:13	OR
1964	Ken Matthews, GBR	1:29:34.0	OR	1988	Jozef Pribilinec, CZE	1:19:57	OR
1968	Vladimir Golubnichiy, USSR	1:33:58.4		1992	Daniel Plaza Montero, SPA	1:21:45	
1972	Peter Frenkel, E. Ger	1:26:42.4	OR	1996	Jefferson Perez, ECU	1:20:07	
1976	Daniel Bautista, MEX	1:24:40.6	OR	2000	Robert Korzeniowski, POL	1:18.59	OR

50-kilometer Walk

Year		Time		Year		Time	
1932	Thomas Green, GBR	4:50:10		1972	Bernd Kannenberg, W. Ger	3:56:11.6	OR
1936	Harold Whitlock, GBR	4:30:41.4	OR	1976	Not held		
1948	John Ljunggren, SWE	4:41:52		1980	Hartwig Gauder, E. Ger	3:49:24.0	OR
1952	Giuseppe Dordoni, ITA	4:28:07.8	OR	1984	Raul Gonzalez, MEX	3:47:26	OR
1956	Norman Read, NZE	4:30:42.8		1988	Vyacheslav Ivanenko, USSR	3:38:29	OR
1960	Don Thompson, GBR	4:25:30.0	OR	1992	Andrei Perlov, UT	3:50:13	
1964	Abdon Pamich, ITA	4:11:12.4	OR	1996	Robert Korzeniowski, POL	3:43:30	
1968	Christoph Höhne, E. Ger	4:20:13.6		2000	Robert Korzeniowski, POL	3:42.22	

High Jump

Year		Height		Year		Height	
1896	Ellery Clark, USA	5-11¼		1956	Charley Dumas, USA	6-11½	OR
1900	Irving Baxter, USA	6- 2¾	OR	1960	Robert Shavlakadze, USSR	7- 1	OR
1904	Sam Jones, USA	5-11		1964	Valery Brumel, USSR	7- 1¾	OR
1906	Cornelius Leahy, GBR/IRE	5-10		1968	Dick Fosbury, USA	7- 4¼	OR
1908	Harry Porter, USA	6- 3	OR	1972	Yuri Tarmak, USSR	7- 3¾	
1912	Alma Richards, USA	6- 4	OR	1976	Jacek Wszola, POL	7- 4½	OR
1920	Richmond Landon, USA	6- 4	=OR	1980	Gerd Wessig, E. Ger	7- 8¾	WR
1924	Harold Osborn, USA	6- 6	OR	1984	Dietmar Mögenburg, W. Ger	7- 8½	
1928	Bob King, USA	6- 4½		1988	Gennady Avdeyenko, USSR	7- 9¾	OR
1932	Duncan McNaughton, CAN	6- 5½		1992	Javier Sotomayor, CUB	7- 8	
1936	Cornelius Johnson, USA	6- 8	OR	1996	Charles Austin, USA	7-10	OR
1948	John Winter, AUS	6- 6		2000	Sergey Klugin, RUS	7- 8½	
1952	Walt Davis, USA	6- 8½	OR				

Track & Field (Cont.)

Pole Vault

Year		Height	
1896	William Hoyt, USA	10-10	
1900	Irving Baxter, USA	10-10	
1904	Charles Dvorak, USA	11- 5¾	
1906	Fernand Gonder, FRA	11- 5¾	
1908	(TIE) Edward Cooke, USA	12- 2	
	& Alfred Gilbert, USA	12- 2	OR
1912	Harry Babcock, USA	12-11½	OR
1920	Frank Foss, USA	13- 5	WR
1924	Lee Barnes, USA	12-11½	
1928	Sabin Carr, USA	13- 9¼	OR
1932	Bill Miller, USA	14-1¾	OR
1936	Earle Meadows, USA	14- 3¼	OR
1948	Guinn Smith, USA	14-1¼	

Year		Height	
1952	Bob Richards, USA	14-11	OR
1956	Bob Richards, USA	14-11½	OR
1960	Don Bragg, USA	15- 5	OR
1964	Fred Hansen, USA	16- 8¾	OR
1968	Bob Seagren, USA	17-8½	OR
1972	Wolfgang Nordwig, E. Ger	18- 0½	OR
1976	Tadeusz Slusarski, POL	18- 0½	=OR
1980	Wladyslaw Kozakiewicz, POL	18-11½	WR
1984	Pierre Quinon, FRA	18-10¼	
1988	Sergey Bubka, USSR	19- 4¼	OR
1992	Maksim Tarasov, UT	19-0¼	
1996	Jean Galfione, FRA	19- 5¼	OR
2000	Nick Hysong, USA	19-4¼	

Long Jump

Year		Distance	
1896	Ellery Clark, USA	20-10	
1900	Alvin Kraenzlein, USA	23- 6¾	OR
1904	Meyer Prinstein, USA	24- 1	OR
1906	Meyer Prinstein, USA	23- 7½	OR
1908	Frank Irons, USA	24- 6½	OR
1912	Albert Gutterson, USA	24-11¼	OR
1920	William Petersson, SWE	23-5½	
1924	De Hart Hubbard, USA	24- 5	
1928	Ed Hamm, USA	25- 4½	OR
1932	Ed Gordon, USA	25- 0¾	
1936	Jesse Owens, USA	26-5½	OR
1948	Willie Steele, USA	25- 8	
1952	Jerome Biffle, USA	24-10	

Year		Distance	
1956	Greg Bell, USA	25- 8¼	
1960	Ralph Boston, USA	26-7¾	OR
1964	Lynn Davies, GBR	26- 5¾	
1968	Bob Beamon, USA	29- 2½	WR
1972	Randy Williams, USA	27-0½	
1976	Arnie Robinson, USA	27- 4¾	
1980	Lutz Dombrowski, E. Ger	28- 0¼	
1984	Carl Lewis, USA	28-0¼	
1988	Carl Lewis, USA	28- 7¼	
1992	Carl Lewis, USA	28- 5½	
1996	Carl Lewis, USA	27-10¾	
2000	Ivan Pedroso, CUB	28- 0¾	

Triple Jump

Year		Distance	
1896	James Connolly, USA	44-11¾	
1900	Meyer Prinstein, USA	47- 5¾	OR
1904	Meyer Prinstein, USA	47- 1	
1906	Peter O'Connor, GBR/IRE	46-2¼	
1908	Timothy Ahearne, GBR/IRE	48-11¼	OR
1912	Gustaf Lindblom, SWE	48-5¼	
1920	Vilho Tuulos, FIN	47- 7	
1924	Nick Winter, AUS	50-11¼	WR
1928	Mikio Oda, JPN	49-11	
1932	Chuhei Nambu, JPN	51- 7	WR
1936	Naoto Tajima, JPN	52- 6	WR
1948	Arne Ahman, SWE	50- 6¼	
1952	Adhemar da Silva, BRA	53-2¾	WR

Year		Distance	
1956	Adhemar da Silva, BRA	53- 7¾	OR
1960	Józef Schmidt, POL	55- 2	
1964	Józef Schmidt, POL	55-3½	OR
1968	Viktor Saneyev, USSR	57- 0¾	WR
1972	Viktor Saneyev, USSR	56-11¼	
1976	Viktor Saneyev, USSR	56- 8¾	
1980	Jaak Uudmäf3e, USSR	56-11¼	
1984	Al Joyner, USA	56-7½	
1988	Khristo Markov, BUL	57- 9¼	OR
1992	Mike Conley, USA	59-7½W	OR
1996	Kenny Harrison, USA	59-4¼	OR
2000	Jonathan Edwards, GBR	58-1¼	

Windicates wind-aided.

Shot Put

Year		Distance	
1896	Bob Garrett, USA	36- 9¾	
1900	Richard Sheldon, USA	46- 3¼	OR
1904	Ralph Rose, USA	48- 7	WR
1906	Martin Sheridan, USA	40- 5¼	
1908	Ralph Rose, USA	46- 7½	
1912	Patrick McDonald, USA	50- 4	OR
1920	Ville Pörhöl f3, FIN	48-7¼	
1924	Bud Houser, USA	49- 2¼	
1928	John Kuck, USA	52- 0¾	WR
1932	Leo Sexton, USA	52- 6	OR
1936	Hans Woellke, GER	53- 1¾	OR
1948	Wilbur Thompson, USA	56- 2	OR
1952	Parry O'Brien, USA	57- 1½	OR

Year		Distance	
1956	Parry O'Brien, USA	60-11¼	OR
1960	Bill Nieder, USA	64-6¾	OR
1964	Dallas Long, USA	66- 8½	OR
1968	Randy Matson, USA	67-4¾	
1972	Wladyslaw Komar, POL	69- 6	OR
1976	Udo Beyer, E. Ger	69- 0¾	
1980	Vladimir Kiselyov, USSR	70- 0½	OR
1984	Alessandro Andrei, ITA	69- 9	
1988	Ulf Timmermann, E. Ger	73- 8¾	OR
1992	Mike Stulce, USA	71-2½	
1996	Randy Barnes, USA	70-11¼	
2000	Arsi Harju, FIN	69-10¼	

Discus Throw

Year		Distance		Year		Distance	
1896	Bob Garrett, USA	95- 7½		1956	Al Oerter, USA	184-11	OR
1900	Rudolf Bauer, HUN	118- 3	OR	1960	Al Oerter, USA	194- 2	OR
1904	Martin Sheridan, USA	128-10½	OR	1964	Al Oerter, USA	200- 1	OR
1906	Martin Sheridan, USA	136- 0		1968	Al Oerter, USA	212- 6	OR
1908	Martin Sheridan, USA	134- 2	OR	1972	Ludvik Danek, CZE	211- 3	
1912	Armas Taipale, FIN	148- 3	OR	1976	Mac Wilkins, USA	221- 5	
1920	Elmer Niklander, FIN	146- 7		1980	Viktor Rashchupkin, USSR	218- 8	
1924	Bud Houser, USA	151- 4	OR	1984	Rolf Danneberg, W. Ger	218- 6	
1928	Bud Houser, USA	155- 3	OR	1988	J]rgen Schult, E. Ger	225- 9	OR
1932	John Anderson, USA	162- 4	OR	1992	Romas Ubartas, LIT	213- 8	
1936	Ken Carpenter, USA	165- 7	OR	1996	Lars Riedel, GER	227-8	
1948	Adolfo Consolini, ITA	173- 2	OR	2000	Virgilijus Alekna, LIT	227-4	
1952	Sim Iness, USA	180- 6	OR				

Hammer Throw

Year		Distance		Year		Distance	
1900	John Flanagan, USA	163- 1		1960	Vasily Rudenkov, USSR	220- 2	OR
1904	John Flanagan, USA	168- 1	OR	1964	Romuald Klim, USSR	228-10	OR
1908	John Flanagan, USA	170- 4	OR	1968	Gyula Zsivótzky, HUN	240- 8	OR
1912	Matt McGrath, USA	179- 7	OR	1972	Anatoly Bondarchuk, USSR	247- 8	OR
1920	Pat Ryan, USA	173- 5		1976	Yuri Sedykh, USSR	254- 4	OR
1924	Fred Tootell, USA	174-10		1980	Yuri Sedykh, USSR	268- 4	WR
1928	Pat O'Callaghan, IRE	168- 7		1984	Juha Tiainen, FIN	256- 2	
1932	Pat O'Callaghan, IRE	176-11		1988	Sergey Litvinov, USSR	278- 2	OR
1936	Karl Hein, GER	185- 4	OR	1992	Andrei Abduvaliyev, UT	270- 9	
1948	Imre Németh, HUN	183-11		1996	Balazs Kiss, HUN	266-6	
1952	József Csérmák, HUN	197-11	WR	2000	Szymon Ziolkowski, POL	262-6	
1956	Harold Connolly, USA	207- 3	OR				

Javelin Throw

Year		Distance		Year		Distance	
1908	Eric Lemming, SWE	179-10	WR	1964	Pauli Nevala, FIN	271- 2	
1912	Eric Lemming, SWE	198-11	WR	1968	Jänis L]sis, USSR	295- 7	OR
1920	Jonni Myyrä, FIN	215-10	OR	1972	Klaus Wolfermann, W. Ger	296-10	OR
1924	Jonni Myyrä, FIN	206- 7		1976	Miklos Németh, HUN	310- 4	WR
1928	Erik Lundkvist, SWE	218- 6	OR	1980	Dainis Kula, USSR	299- 2	
1932	Matti Järvinen, FIN	238- 6	OR	1984	Arto Härkönen, FIN	284-8	
1936	Gerhard Stöck, GER	235- 8		1988	Tapio Korjus, FIN	276- 6	
1948	Kai Tapio Rautavaara, FIN	228-10		1992	Jan Zelezny, CZE	294- 2*	OR
1952	Cy Young, USA	242- 1	OR	1996	Jan Zelezny, CZE	289- 3	
1956	Egil Danielson, NOR	281- 2	WR	2000	Jan Zelezny, CZR	295- 10	OR
1960	Viktor Tsibulenko, USSR	277- 8					

*In 1986 the balance point of the javelin was modified and new records have been kept since.

Decathlon

Year		Points		Year		Points	
1904	Thomas Kiely, IRE	6036		1960	Rafer Johnson, USA	8392	OR
1906-08	Not held			1964	Willi Holdorf, GER	7887	
1912	Jim Thorpe, USA	8412	WR	1968	Bill Toomey, USA	8193	OR
1920	Helge Lövland, NOR	6803		1972	Nikolai Avilov, USSR	8454	WR
1924	Harold Osborn, USA	7711	WR	1976	Bruce Jenner, USA	8617	WR
1928	Paavo Yrjölä, FIN	8053	WR	1980	Daley Thompson, GBR	8495	
1932	Jim Bausch, USA	8462	WR	1984	Daley Thompson, GBR	8798	=WR
1936	Glenn Morris, USA	7900	WR	1988	Christian Schenk, E. Ger	8488	
1948	Bob Mathias, USA	7139		1992	Robert Zmelik, CZE	8611	
1952	Bob Mathias, USA	7887	WR	1996	Dan O'Brien, USA	8824	
1956	Milt Campbell, USA	7937	OR	2000	Erki Nool, EST	8641	

WOMEN

At least 4 gold medals (including relays): Evelyn Ashford, Fanny Blankers-Koen, Betty Cuthbert and Bärbel Eckert Wöckel (4).

100 meters

Year		Time		Year		Time	
1928	Betty Robinson, USA	12.2	=WR	1972	Renate Stecher, E. Ger	11.07	
1932	Stella Walsh, POL*	11.9	=WR	1976	Annegret Richter, W. Ger	11.08	
1936	Helen Stephens, USA	11.5W		1980	Lyudmila Kondratyeva, USSR	11.06	
1948	Fanny Blankers-Koen, NED	11.9		1984	Evelyn Ashford, USA	10.97	OR
1952	Marjorie Jackson, AUS	11.5	=WR	1988	Florence Griffith Joyner, USA	10.54W	
1956	Betty Cuthbert, AUS	11.5		1992	Gail Devers, USA	10.82	
1960	Wilma Rudolph, USA	11.0W		1996	Gail Devers, USA	10.94	
1964	Wyomia Tyus, USA	11.4		2000	Marion Jones, USA	10.75	
1968	Wyomia Tyus, USA	11.08	WR				

*An autopsy performed after Walsh's death in 1980 revealed that she was a man.
Windicates wind-aided.

Track & Field (Cont.)

200 meters

Year		Time		Year		Time	
1948	Fanny Blankers-Koen, NED	.24.4		1976	Bärbel Eckert, E. Ger	.22.37	OR
1952	Marjorie Jackson, AUS	.23.7	OR	1980	Bärbel Eckert Wockel, E. Ger	.22.03	OR
1956	Betty Cuthbert, AUS	.23.4	=OR	1984	Valerie Brisco-Hooks, USA	.21.81	OR
1960	Wilma Rudolph, USA	.24.0		1988	Florence Griffith Joyner, USA	.21.34	WR
1964	Edith McGuire, USA	.23.0	OR	1992	Gwen Torrence, USA	.21.81	
1968	Irena Szewinska, POL	.22.5	WR	1996	Marie-Jose Perec, FRA	.22.12	
1972	Renate Stecher, E. Ger	.22.40	=WR	2000	Marion Jones, USA	.21.84	

400 meters

Year		Time		Year		Time	
1964	Betty Cuthbert, AUS	.52.0		1984	Valerie Brisco-Hooks, USA	.48.83	OR
1968	Colette Besson, FRA	.52.03	=OR	1988	Olga Bryzgina, USSR	.48.65	OR
1972	Monika Zehrt, E. Ger	.51.08	OR	1992	Marie-Jose Perec, FRA	.48.83	
1976	Irena Szewinska, POL	.49.29	WR	1996	Marie-Jose Perec, FRA	.48.25	OR
1980	Marita Koch, E. Ger	.48.88	OR	2000	Cathy Freeman, AUS	.49.11	

800 meters

Year		Time		Year		Time	
1928	Lina Radke, GER	.2:16.8	WR	1980	Nadezhda Olizarenko, USSR	.1:53.42	WR
1932-56	Not held			1984	Doina Melinte, ROM	.1:57.60	
1960	Lyudmila Shevtsova, USSR	.2:04.3	=WR	1988	Sigrun Wodars, E. Ger	.1:56.10	
1964	Ann Packer, GBR	.2:01.1	OR	1992	Ellen van Langen, NED	.1:55.54	
1968	Madeline Manning, USA	.2:00.9	OR	1996	Svetlana Masterkova, RUS	.1:57.73	
1972	Hildegard Falck, W. Ger	.1:58.55	OR	2000	Maria Mutola, MOZ	.1:56.15	
1976	Tatyana Kazankina, USSR	.1:54.94	WR				

1500 meters

Year		Time		Year		Time	
1972	Lyudmila Bragina, USSR	.4:01.4	WR	1988	Paula Ivan, ROM	.3:53.96	OR
1976	Tatyana Kazankina, USSR	.4:05.48		1992	Hassiba Boulmerka, ALG	.3:55.30	
1980	Tatyana Kazankina, USSR	.3:56.6	OR	1996	Svetlana Masterkova, RUS	.4:00.83	
1984	Gabriella Dorio, ITA	.4:03.25		2000	Nouria Merah-Benida, ALG	.4:05.10	

5000 meters

Year		Time		Year		Time	
1984	Maricica Puica, ROM	.8:35.96		1996	Wang Junxia, CHN	.14:59.88	
1988	Tatyana Samolenko, USSR	.8:26.53	OR	2000	Gabriela Szabo, ROM	.14:40.79	OR
1992	Elena Romanova, UT	.8:46.04		**Note:** Event held over 3000 meters from 1984-92.			

10,000 meters

Year		Time		Year		Time	
1988	Olga Bondarenko, USSR	.31:05.21	OR	1996	Fernanda Ribeiro, POR	.31:01.63	OR
1992	Derartu Tulu, ETH	.31:06.02		2000	Derartu Tulu, ETH	.30:17.49	OR

Marathon

Year		Time	Year		Time
1984	Joan Benoit, USA	.2:24:52	1996	Fatuma Roba, ETH	.2:26:05
1988	Rosa Mota, POR	.2:25:40	2000	Naoko Takahashi, JPN	.2:23:14
1992	Valentina Yegorova, UT	.2:32:41			

100-meter Hurdles

Year		Time		Year		Time	
1932	Babe Didrikson, USA	.11.7	WR	1976	Johanna Schaller, E. Ger	.12.77	
1936	Trebisonda Valla, ITA	.11.7		1980	Vera Komisova, USSR	.12.56	OR
1948	Fanny Blankers-Koen, NED	.11.2	OR	1984	Benita Fitzgerald-Brown, USA	.12.84	
1952	Shirley Strickland, AUS	.10.9	WR	1988	Yordanka Donkova, BUL	.12.38	OR
1956	Shirley Strickland, AUS	.10.7	OR	1992	Paraskevi Patoulidou, GRE	.12.64	
1960	Irina Press, USSR	.10.8		1996	Ludmila Enquist, SWE	.12.58	
1964	Karin Balzer, GER	.10.5^w		2000	Olga Shishigina, KAZ	.12.65	
1968	Maureen Caird, AUS	.10.3	OR	^{w}indicates wind-aided.			
1972	Annelie Ehrhardt, E. Ger	.12.59	WR	**Note:** Event held over 80 meters from 1932-68.			

400-meter Hurdles

Year		Time		Year		Time	
1984	Nawal El Moutawakel, MOR	.54.61	OR	1996	Deon Hemmings, JAM	.52.82	OR
1988	Debra Flintoff-King, AUS	.53.17	OR	2000	Irina Privalova, RUS	.53.02	
1992	Sally Gunnell, GBR	.53.23					

4x100-meter Relay

Year		Time		Year		Time	
1928	Canada	48.4	WR	1972	West Germany	42.81	WR
1932	United States	46.9	WR	1976	East Germany	42.55	OR
1936	United States	46.9		1980	East Germany	41.60	WR
1948	Holland	47.5		1984	United States	41.65	
1952	United States	45.9	WR	1988	United States	41.98	
1956	Australia	44.5	WR	1992	United States	42.11	
1960	United States	44.5		1996	United States	41.95	
1964	Poland	43.6		2000	Bahamas	42.20	
1968	United States	42.87	WR				

4x400-meter Relay

Year		Time		Year		Time	
1972	East Germany	3:23.0	WR	1988	Soviet Union	3:15.18	WR
1976	East Germany	3:19.23	WR	1992	Unified Team	3:20.20	
1980	Soviet Union	3:20.2		1996	United States	3:20.91	
1984	United States	3:18.29	OR	2000	United States	3:22.62	

20-kilometer Walk

Year		Time	Year		Time
1992	Chen Yueling, CHN	44:32	2000	Wang Liping, CHN	1:29.05
1996	Yelena Ninikolayeva, RUS	41:49			

Note: Event was held over 10 kilometers from 1992-96.

High Jump

Year		Height		Year		Height	
1928	Ethel Catherwood, CAN	5- 2½		1972	Ulrike Meyfarth, W. Ger	6- 3½	=WR
1932	Jean Shiley, USA	5- 5¼	WR	1976	Rosemarie Ackermann, E. Ger	6-4	OR
1936	Ibolya Csák, HUN	5- 3		1980	Sara Simeoni, ITA	6- 5½	OR
1948	Alice Coachman, USA	5- 6	OR	1984	Ulrike Meyfarth, W. Ger	6-7½	OR
1952	Esther Brand, RSA	5- 5¾		1988	Louise Ritter, USA	6- 8	OR
1956	Mildred McDaniel, USA	5- 9¼	WR	1992	Heike Henkel, GER	6-7½	
1960	Iolanda Balas, ROM	6-0¾	OR	1996	Stefka Kostadinova, BUL	6- 8¾	
1964	Iolanda Balas, ROM	6- 2¾	OR	2000	Yelena Yelesina, RUS	6- 7	
1968	Miloslava Rezkova, CZE	5-11½					

Pole Vault

Year		Height	
2000	Stacy Dragila, USA	15- 1	OR

Long Jump

Year		Distance		Year		Distance	
1948	Olga Gyarmati, HUN	18- 8¼		1976	Angela Voigt, E. Ger	22- 0¾	
1952	Yvette Williams, NZE	20- 5¾	OR	1980	Tatyana Kolpakova, USSR	23- 2	OR
1956	Elzbieta Krzesinska, POL	20-10	=WR	1984	Anisoara Cusmir-Stanciu, ROM	22- 10	
1960	Vyera Krepkina, USSR	20-10¾	OR	1988	Jackie Joyner-Kersee, USA	24- 3¼	OR
1964	Mary Rand, GBR	22- 2¼	WR	1992	Heike Drechsler, GER	23-5¼	
1968	Viorica Viscopoleanu, ROM	22- 4½	WR	1996	Chioma Ajunwa, NGR	23- 4½	
1972	Heidemarie Rosendahl, W. Ger	22- 3		2000	Heike Drechsler, GER	22- 11¼	

Triple Jump

Year		Distance	Year		Distance
1996	Inessa Kravets, UKR	50-3½	2000	Tereza Marinova, BUL	49- 10½

Shot Put

Year		Distance		Year		Distance	
1948	Micheline Ostermeyer, FRA	45- 1½		1976	Ivanka Hristova, BUL	69-5¼	OR
1952	Galina Zybina, USSR	50- 1¾	WR	1980	Ilona Slupianek, E. Ger	73- 6¼	OR
1956	Tamara Tyshkevich, USSR	54- 5	OR	1984	Claudia Losch, W. Ger	67-2¼	
1960	Tamara Press, USSR	56- 10	OR	1988	Natalia Lisovskaya, USSR	72- 11¾	
1964	Tamara Press, USSR	59- 6¼	OR	1992	Svetlana Krivaleva, UT	69- 1¼	
1968	Margitta Gummel, E. Ger	64- 4	WR	1996	Astrid Kumbernuss, GER	67-5½	
1972	Nadezhda Chizhova, USSR	69- 0	WR	2000	Yanina Korolchik, BLR	67- 5½	

Track & Field (Cont.)
Discus Throw

Year		Distance		Year		Distance	
1928	Halina Konopacka, POL	129-11¾	WR	1972	Faina Melnik, USSR	218-7	OR
1932	Lillian Copeland, USA	133-2	OR	1976	Evelin Schlaak, E. Ger	226-4	OR
1936	Gisela Mauermeyer, GER	156-3	OR	1980	Evelin Schlaak Jahl, E. Ger	229-6	OR
1948	Micheline Ostermeyer, FRA	137-6		1984	Ria Stalman, NED	214-5	
1952	Nina Romaschkova, USSR	168-8	OR	1988	Martina Hellmann, E. Ger	237-2½	OR
1956	Olga Fikotová, CZE	176-1	OR	1992	Maritza Marten, CUB	229-10	
1960	Nina Ponomaryeva, USSR	180-9	OR	1996	Ilke Wyludda, GER	228-6	
1964	Tamara Press, USSR	187-10	OR	2000	Ellina Zvereva, BLR	224-5	
1968	Lia Manoliu, ROM	191-2	OR				

Hammer Throw

Year		Distance	
2000	Kamila Skolimowska, POL	233-5¾	OR

Javelin Throw

Year		Distance		Year		Distance	
1932	Babe Didrikson, USA	143-4		1972	Ruth Fuchs, E. Ger	209-7	OR
1936	Tilly Fleischer, GER	148-3	OR	1976	Ruth Fuchs, E. Ger	216-4	OR
1948	Herma Bauma, AUT	149-6	OR	1980	Maria Colon Rueñes, CUB	224-5	OR
1952	Dana Zátopková, CZE	165-7	OR	1984	Tessa Sanderson, GBR	228-2	OR
1956	Ineze Jaunzeme, USSR	176-8	OR	1988	Petra Felke, E. Ger	245-0	OR
1960	Elvira Ozolina, USSR	183-8	OR	1992	Silke Renk, GER	224-2	
1964	Mihaela Penes, ROM	198-7	OR	1996	Heli Rantanen, FIN	222-11	
1968	Angéla Németh, HUN	198-0		2000	Trine Hattestad, NOR	226-1	OR

Heptathlon

Year		Points		Year		Points	
1964	Irina Press, USSR	5246	WR	1984	Glynis Nunn, AUS	6390	OR
1968	Ingrid Becker, W. Ger	5098		1988	Jackie Joyner-Kersee, USA	7291	WR
1972	Mary Peters, GBR	4801	WR	1992	Jackie Joyner-Kersee, USA	7044	
1976	Siegrun Siegl, E. Ger	4745		1996	Ghada Shouaa, SYR	6780	
1980	Nadezhda Tkachenko, USSR	5083	WR	2000	Denise Lewis, GBR	6584	

Note: Seven-event Heptathlon replaced five-event Pentathlon in 1984.

All-Time Leading Medal Winners – Single Games

Athletes who have won the most medals in a single Summer Olympics. Totals include individual, relay and team medals. U.S. athletes are in **bold** type.

MEN

No		Sport	G-S-B	No		Sport	G-S-B
8	Aleksandr Dityatin, USSR (1980)	Gym	3-4-1	6	Viktor Chukarin, USSR (1956)	Gym	4-2-0
7	**Mark Spitz**, USA (1972)	Swim	7-0-0	6	Konrad Frey, GER (1936)	Gym	3-1-2
7	**Willis Lee**, USA (1920)	Shoot	5-1-1	6	Ville Ritola, FIN (1924)	Track	4-2-0
7	**Matt Biondi**, USA (1988)	Swim	5-1-1	6	Hubert Van Innis, BEL (1920)	Arch	4-2-0
7	Boris Shakhlin, USSR (1960)	Gym	4-2-1	6	**Carl Osburn**, USA (1920)	Shoot	4-1-1
6	**Lloyd Spooner**, USA (1920)	Shoot	4-1-2	6	Louis Richardet, SWI (1906)	Shoot	3-3-0
7	Mikhail Voronin, USSR (1968)	Gym	2-4-1	6	**Anton Heida**, USA (1904)	Gym	5-1-0
7	Nikolai Andrianov, USSR (1976)	Gym	2-4-1	6	**George Eyser**, USA (1904)	Gym	3-2-1
6	Vitaly Scherbo, UT (1992)	Gym	6-0-0	6	**Burton Downing**, USA (1904)	Cycle	2-3-1
6	Li Ning, CHN (1984)	Gym	3-2-1	6	Alexei Nemov, RUS (1996)	Gym	2-1-3
6	Akinori Nakayama, JPN (1968)	Gym	4-1-1	6	Alexei Nemov, RUS (2000)	Gym	2-1-3
6	Takashi Ono, JPN (1960)	Gym	3-1-2				

WOMEN

No		Sport	G-S-B	No		Sport	G-S-B
7	Maria Gorokhovskaya, USSR (1952)	Gym	2-5-0	5	Ecaterina Szabó, ROM (1984)	Gym	4-1-0
6	Kristin Otto, E. Ger (1988)	Swim	6-0-0	5	Shane Gould, AUS (1972)	Swim	3-1-1
6	Agnes Keleti, HUN (1956)	Gym	4-2-0	5	Nadia Comaneci, ROM (1976)	Gym	3-1-1
6	Vera Cáslavská, CZE (1968)	Gym	4-2-0	5	Karin Janz, E. Ger (1972)	Gym	2-2-1
6	Larisa Latynina, USSR (1956)	Gym	4-1-1	5	Ines Diers, E. Ger (1980)	Swim	2-2-1
6	Larisa Latynina, USSR (1960)	Gym	3-2-1	5	**Shirley Babashoff**, USA (1976)	Swim	1-4-0
6	Daniela Silivas, ROM (1988)	Gym	3-2-1	5	**Mary Lou Retton**, USA (1984)	Gym	1-2-2
6	Larisa Latynina, USSR (1964)	Gym	2-2-2	5	**Shannon Miller**, USA (1992)	Gym	0-2-3
6	Margit Korondi, HUN, (1956)	Gym	1-1-4	5	**Marion Jones**, USA (2000)	Track	3-0-2
5	Kornelia Ender, E. Ger (1976)	Swim	4-1-0	5	**Dara Torres**, USA (2000)	Swim	2-0-3

All-Time Leading Medal Winners – Career

MEN

No		Sport	G-S-B	No		Sport	G-S-B
15	Nikolai Andrianov, USSR	Gymnastics	7-5-3	10	Carl Lewis, USA	Track/Field	9-1-0
13	Boris Shakhlin, USSR	Gymnastics	7-4-2	10	Aladár Gerevich, HUN	Fencing	7-1-2
13	Edoardo Mangiarotti, ITA	Fencing	6-5-2	10	Akinori Nakayama, JPN	Gymnastics	6-2-2
13	Takashi Ono, JPN	Gymnastics	5-4-4	10	Aleksandr Dityatin, USSR	Gymnastics	3-6-1
12	Paavo Nurmi, FIN	Track/Field	9-3-0	10	Vitaly Scherbo, BLR	Gymnastics	6-0-3
12	Sawao Kato, JPN	Gymnastics	8-3-1	9*	**Martin Sheridan**, USA	Track/Field	5-3-1
12	Alexei Nemov, RUS	Gymnastics	4-2-6	9*	Zoltán Halmay, HUN	Swimming	3-5-1
11	**Mark Spitz**, USA	Swimming	9-1-1	9	Giulio Gaudini, ITA	Fencing	3-4-2
11†	**Matt Biondi**, USA	Swimming	8-2-1	9	Mikhail Voronin, USSR	Gymnastics	2-6-1
11	Viktor Chukarin, USSR	Gymnastics	7-3-1	9	Heikki Savolainen, FIN	Gymnastics	2-1-6
11	**Carl Osburn**, USA	Shooting	5-4-2	9	Yuri Titov, USSR	Gymnastics	1-5-3
10*	**Ray Ewry**, USA	Track/Field	10-0-0				

†Includes gold medal as preliminary member of 1st-place relay team.

*Medals won by Ewry (2-0-0), Sheridan (2-3-0) and Halmay (1-1-0) at the 1906 Intercalated games are not officially recognized by the IOC.

Games Participated In

Andrianov (1972,76,80); **Biondi** (1984,88,92); **Chukarin** (1952,56); **Dityatin** (1976,80); **Ewry** (1900,04,06,08); **Gerevich** (1932,36,48,52,56,60); **Gaudini** (1928,32,36); **Halmay** (1900,04,06,08); **Kato** (1968,72,76); **Lewis** (1984,88,92,96); **Mangiarotti** (1936,48,52,56,60); **Nakayama** (1968,72); **Nemov** (1996,2000) **Nurmi** (1920,24,28); **Ono** (1952,56,60,64); **Osburn** (1912,20, 24); **Savolainen** (1928,32,36,48,52); **Scherbo** (1992,96); **Shakhlin** (1956,60,64); **Sheridan** (1904,06,08); **Spitz** (1968,72); **Titov** (1956,60,64); **Voronin** (1968,72).

WOMEN

No		Sport	G-S-B
18	Larissa Latynina, USSR	Gymnastics	9-5-4
11	Vera Cáslavská, CZE	Gymnastics	7-4-0
10	Birgit Fischer, GER	Canoe/Kayak	7-3-0
10	Jenny Thompson, USA	Swimming	8-1-1
10	Agnes Keleti, HUN	Gymnastics	5-3-2
10	Polina Astakhova, USSR	Gymnastics	5-2-3
9	Nadia Comaneci, ROM	Gymnastics	5-3-1
9	Lyudmila Tourischeva, USSR	Gymnastics	4-3-2
9	**Dara Torres**, USA	Swimming	4-1-4
8	Kornelia Ender, E. Ger.	Swimming	4-4-0
8	Dawn Fraser, AUS	Swimming	4-4-0
8	**Shirley Babashoff**, USA	Swimming	2-6-0
8	Sofia Muratova, USSR	Gymnastics	2-2-4
7	Krisztina Egerszegi, HUN	Swimming	5-1-1
7	Irena Kirszenstein Szewinska, POL	Track/Field	3-2-2
7	Shirley Strickland, AUS	Track/Field	3-1-3
7	Maria Gorokhovskaya, USSR	Gymnastics	2-5-0
7	Ildiko Sagine-Ujlaki-Rejto, HUN	Fencing	2-3-2
7	**Shannon Miller**, USA	Gymnastics	2-2-3
7	Susie O'Neill, AUS	Swimming	2-4-1
7	Merlene Ottey, JAM	Track/Field	0-2-5

Games Participated In

Astakhova (1956,60,64); **Babashoff** (1972,76); **Cáslavská** (1960,64,68); **Comaneci** (1976,80); **Egerszegi** (1988,92,96); **Ender** (1972,76); **Fischer** (1980,92,96,2000); **Fraser** (1956,60,64); **Gorokhovskaya** (1952); **Keleti** (1952,56); **Latynina** (1956,60,64); **Miller** (1992,96); **Muratova** (1956,60); **O'Neill** (1996,2000) **Ottey** (1980,84,88,92,96) **Sagine-Ujlaki-Rejto** (1960,64, 68,72,76); **Strickland** (1948,52,56); **Szewinska** (1964,68,72,76,80); **Thompson** (1992,96,2000); **Torres** (1984,88,92,2000) **Tourischeva** (1968, 72,76).

Most Gold Medals

MEN

No		Sport	G-S-B	No		Sport	G-S-B
10*	**Ray Ewry**, USA	Track/Field	10-0-0	7	Boris Shakhlin, USSR	Gymnastics	7-4-2
9	Paavo Nurmi, FIN	Track/Field	9-3-0	7	Viktor Chukarin, USSR	Gymnastics	7-3-1
9	**Mark Spitz**, USA	Swimming	9-1-1	7	Aladar Gerevich, HUN	Fencing	7-1-2
9	**Carl Lewis**, USA	Track/Field	9-1-0				
8	Sawao Kato, JPN	Gymnastics	8-3-1	*Medals won by Ewry (2-0-0) at the 1906 Intercalated games are not officially recognized by the IOC.			
8†	**Matt Biondi**, USA	Swimming	8-2-1				
7	Nikolai Andrianov, USSR	Gymnastics	7-5-3	†Includes gold medal as preliminary member of 1st-place relay team.			

WOMEN

No		Sport	G-S-B	No		Sport	G-S-B
9	Larissa Latynina, USSR	Gymnastics	9-5-4	4	Lyudmila Tourischeva, USSR	Gymnastics	4-3-2
8	**Jenny Thompson**, USA	Swimming	8-1-1	4	**Dara Torres**, USA	Swimming	4-1-4
7	Vera Cáslavská, CZE	Gymnastics	7-4-0	4	**Evelyn Ashford**, USA	Track/Field	4-1-0
7	Birgit Fischer, GER	Canoe/Kayak	7-3-0	4	**Janet Evans**, USA	Swimming	4-1-0
6†	Kristin Otto, E. Ger.	Swimming	6-0-0	4	Fu Mingxia, CHN	Diving	4-1-0
6†	**Amy Van Dyken**, USA	Swimming	6-0-0	4	Fanny Blankers-Koen, NED	Track/Field	4-0-0
5	Agnes Keleti, HUN	Gymnastics	5-3-2	4	Betty Cuthbert, AUS	Track/Field	4-0-0
5	Nadia Comaneci, ROM	Gymnastics	5-3-1	4	**Pat McCormick**, USA	Diving	4-0-0
5	Polina Astakhova, USSR	Gymnastics	5-2-3	4	Bärbel Eckert Wäckel, E. Ger.	Track/Field	4-0-0
5	Krisztina Egerszegi, HUN	Swimming	5-1-1	†Includes gold medal as preliminary member of 1st-place relay team.			
4	Kornelia Ender, E. Ger.	Swimming	4-4-0				
4	Dawn Fraser, AUS	Swimming	4-4-0				

All-Time Leading Medal Winners – Career (Cont.)
Most Silver Medals

No	MEN	Sport	G-S-B	No	WOMEN	Sport	G-S-B
6	Alexandr Dityatin, USSR	Gymnastics	3-6-1	6	**Shirley Babashoff**, USA	Swimming	2-6-0
6	Mikhail Voronin, USSR	Gymnastics	2-6-1	5	Larissa Latynina, USSR	Gymnastics	9-5-4
5	Nikolai Andrianov, USSR	Gymnastics	7-5-3	5	Maria Gorokhovskaya, USSR	Gymnastics	2-5-0
5	Edoardo Mangiarotti, ITA	Fencing	6-5-2	4	Vera Cáslavská, CZE	Gymnastics	7-4-0
5	Zoltán Halmay, HUN	Swimming	3-5-1	4	Kornelia Ender, E. Ger	Swimming	4-4-0
5	Gustavo Marzi, ITA	Fencing	2-5-0	4	Dawn Fraser, AUS	Swimming	4-4-0
5	Yuri Titov, USSR	Gymnastics	1-5-3	4	Erica Zuchold, E. Ger	Gymnastics	0-4-1
5	Viktor Lisitsky, USSR	Gymnastics	0-5-0				

Most Bronze Medals

No	MEN	Sport	G-S-B	No	WOMEN	Sport	G-S-B
6	Alexei Nemov, RUS	Gymnastics	4-2-6	5	Merlene Ottey, JAM	Track/Field	0-2-5
6	Heikki Savolainen, FIN	Gymnastics	2-1-6	4	Larissa Latynina, USSR	Gymnastics	9-5-4
5	Daniel Revenu, FRA	Fencing	1-0-5	4	**Dara Torres**, USA	Swimming	4-1-4
5	Philip Edwards, CAN	Track/Field	0-0-5	4	Sofia Muratova, USSR	Gymnastics	2-2-4
5	Adrianus Jong, NED	Fencing	0-0-5				

All-Time Leading USA Medal Winners
Most Overall Medals
MEN

No		Sport	G-S-B	No		Sport	G-S-B
11	Mark Spitz	Swimming	9-1-1	6	Anton Heida	Gymnastics	5-1-0
11†	Matt Biondi	Swimming	8-2-1	6	Don Schollander	Swimming	5-1-0
11	Carl Osburn	Shooting	5-4-2	6	Johnny Weissmuller	Swim/Water Polo	5-0-1
10*	Ray Ewry	Track/Field	10-0-0	6	Alfred Lane	Shooting	5-0-1
10	Carl Lewis	Track/Field	9-1-0	6	Jim Lightbody	Track/Field	4-2-0
9*	Martin Sheridan	Track/Field	5-3-1	6	George Eyser	Gymnastics	3-2-1
8	Charles Daniels	Swimming	5-1-2	6	Ralph Rose	Track/Field	3-2-1
8	Gary Hall Jr.	Swimming	4-3-1	6	Michael Plumb	Equestrian	2-4-0
7‡	Tom Jager	Swimming	5-1-1	6	Burton Downing	Cycling	2-3-1
7	Willis Lee	Shooting	5-1-1	6	Bob Garrett	Track/Field	2-2-2
7	Lloyd Spooner	Shooting	4-1-2				

†Includes gold medal as prelim. member of 1st-place relay team.
*Medals won by Ewry (2-0-0) and Sheridan (2-3-0) at the 1906 Intercalated games are not officially recognized by the IOC.
‡Includes 3 gold medals as prelim. member of 1st-place relay teams.

Games Participated In
Biondi (1984,88,92); **Daniels** (1904,06,08); **Downing** (1904); **Ewry** (1900,04,06,08); **Eyser** (1904); **Garrett** (1896,1900); **Hall** (1996,2000) **Heida** (1904); **Jager** (1984,88,92); **Lane** (1912,20); **Lee** (1920); **Lewis** (1984,88,92,96); **Lightbody** (1904,06); **Osburn** (1912,20,24); **Plumb** (1960, 64,68,72,76,84); **Rose** (1904,08,12); **Schollander** (1964, 68); **Sheridan** (1904,06,08); **Spitz** (1968,72); **Spooner** (1920); **Weissmuller** (1924,28).

WOMEN

No		Sport	G-S-B	No		Sport	G-S-B
10	Jenny Thompson	Swimming	8-1-1	4	Nancy Hogshead	Swimming	3-1-0
9	Dara Torres	Swimming	4-1-4	4	Sharon Stouder	Swimming	3-1-0
8	Shirley Babashoff	Swimming	2-6-0	4	Wyomia Tyus	Track/Field	3-1-0
7	Shannon Miller	Gymnastics	2-2-3	4	Wilma Rudolph	Track/Field	3-0-1
6†	Amy Van Dyken	Swimming	6-0-0	4	Chris von Saltza	Swimming	3-1-0
6	Jackie Joyner-Kersee	Track/Field	3-1-2	4	Sue Pedersen	Swimming	2-2-0
6	Angel Martino	Swimming	3-0-3	4	Eleanor Garatti Saville	Swimming	2-1-1
5	Evelyn Ashford	Track/Field	4-1-0	4	Jan Henne	Swimming	2-1-1
5	Janet Evans	Swimming	4-1-0	4	Mary Wayte	Swimming	2-1-1
5	Florence Griffith Joyner	Track/Field	3-2-0	4	Dorothy Poynton Hill	Diving	2-1-1
5†	Mary T. Meagher	Swimming	3-1-1	4‡	Summer Sanders	Swimming	2-1-1
5	Gwen Torrence	Track/Field	3-2-0	4	Kathy Ellis	Swimming	2-0-2
5	Marion Jones	Track/Field	3-0-2	4	Jill Sterkel	Swimming	2-0-2
5	Mary Lou Retton	Gymnastics	1-2-2	4	Amanda Beard	Swimming	1-2-1
4	Pat McCormick	Diving	4-0-0	4	Georgia Coleman	Diving	1-2-1
4	Valerie Brisco-Hooks	Track/Field	3-1-0	4	Ellie Daniel	Swimming	1-1-2

†Includes gold medal as prelim. member of 1st-place relay team.

Games Participated In
Ashford (1976,84,88,92); **Babashoff** (1972,76); **Beard** (1996,2000); **Brisco-Hooks** (1984,88); **Coleman** (1928,32); **Daniel** (1968,72); **Ellis** (1964); **Evans** (1988,92,96); **Garatti Saville** (1928,32); **Griffith Joyner** (1984,88); **Henne** (1968); **Hogshead** (1984); **Jones** (2000); **Joyner-Kersee** (1984,88,92,96); **Martino** (1992,96); **McCormick** (1952,56); **Meagher** (1984,88); **Miller** (1992, 96); **Pedersen** (1968); **Poynton Hill** (1928,32,36); **Retton** (1984); **Rudolph** (1956,60); **Sanders** (1992); **Sterkel** (1976,84,88); **Stouder** (1964); **Thompson** (1988,92,96,2000); **Torrence** (1988,92,96); **Torres** (1984,88,92,2000); **Tyus** (1964,68); **Van Dyken** (1996,2000); **von Saltza** (1960); **Wayte** (1984,88).

Most Gold Medals

MEN

No		Sport	G-S-B
10*	Raymond Ewry	Track/Field	10-0-0
9	Mark Spitz	Swimming	9-1-1
9	Carl Lewis	Track/Field	9-1-0
8†	Matt Biondi	Swimming	8-2-1
5	Carl Osburn	Shooting	5-4-2
5*	Martin Sheridan	Track/Field	5-3-1
5	Charles Daniels	Swimming	5-1-2
5‡	Tom Jager	Swimming	5-1-1
5	Willis Lee	Shooting	5-1-1
5	Anton Heida	Gymnastics	5-1-0
5	Don Schollander	Swimming	5-1-0
5	Johnny Weissmuller	Swim/Water Polo	5-0-1
5	Alfred Lane	Shooting	5-0-1
5	Morris Fisher	Shooting	5-0-0
4	Gary Hall Jr.	Swimming	4-3-1
4	Jim Lightbody	Track/Field	4-2-0
4	Lloyd Spooner	Shooting	4-1-2
4	Greg Louganis	Diving	4-1-0
4	John Naber	Swimming	4-1-0
4	Meyer Prinstein	Track/Field	4-1-0
4	Mel Sheppard	Track/Field	4-1-0
4	Marcus Hurley	Cycling	4-0-1
4	Marcus Hurley	Cycling	4-0-1
4†	Jon Olsen	Swimming	4-0-1
4	Archie Hahn	Track/Field	4-0-0
4	Alvin Kraenzlein	Track/Field	4-0-0
4	Al Oerter	Track/Field	4-0-0
4	Jesse Owens	Track/Field	4-0-0

*Medals won by Ewry (2-0-0) and Sheridan (2-3-0) at the 1906 Intercalated games are not officially recognized by the IOC.
†Includes gold medal as prelim. member of 1st-place relay team.
‡Includes 3 gold medals as prelim. member of 1st-place relay teams.

WOMEN

No		Sport	G-S-B
8	Jenny Thompson	Swimming	8-1-1
6†	Amy Van Dyken	Swimming	6-0-0
4	Dara Torres	Swimming	4-1-4
4	Evelyn Ashford	Track/Field	4-1-0
4	Janet Evans	Swimming	4-1-0
4	Pat McCormick	Diving	4-0-0
3	Florence Griffith Joyner	Track/Field	3-2-0
3	Jackie Joyner-Kersee	Track/Field	3-1-2
3†	Mary T. Meagher	Swimming	3-1-1
3	Gwen Torrence	Track/Field	3-1-1
3	Valerie Brisco-Hooks	Track/Field	3-1-0
3	Nancy Hogshead	Swimming	3-1-0
3	Sharon Stouder	Swimming	3-1-0
3	Wyomia Tyus	Track/Field	3-1-0
3	Chris von Saltza	Swimming	3-1-0
3	Wilma Rudolph	Track/Field	3-0-1
3	Melissa Belote	Swimming	3-0-0
3	Ethelda Bleibtrey	Swimming	3-0-0
3	Tracy Caulkins	Swimming	3-0-0
3†	Nicole Haislett	Swimming	3-0-0
3	Helen Madison	Swimming	3-0-0
3	Debbie Meyer	Swimming	3-0-0
3	Sandra Neilson	Swimming	3-0-0
3	Martha Norelius	Swimming	3-0-0
3†	Carrie Steinseifer	Swimming	3-0-0
3‡	Ashley Tappin	Swimming	3-0-0

†Includes gold medal as prelim. member of 1st-place relay team.
‡Includes 3 gold medals as prelim. member of 1st-place relay teams.

Most Silver Medals

MEN

No		Sport	G-S-B
4	Carl Osburn	Shooting	5-4-2
4	Michael Plumb	Equestrian	2-4-0
3	Martin Sheridan	Track/Field	5-3-1
3	Burton Downing	Cycling	2-3-1
3	Irving Baxter	Track/Field	2-3-0

No		Sport	G-S-B
3	Earl Thomson	Equestrian	2-3-0
3	Alexander McKee	Swimming	0-3-0

WOMEN

No		Sport	G-S-B
6	Shirley Babashoff	Swimming	2-6-0

All-Time Medal Standings, 1896-2000

All-time Summer Games medal standings, based on *The Golden Book of the Olympic Games*. Medal counts include the 1906 Intercalated Games, which are not recognized by the IOC.

		G	S	B	Total
1	United States	872	658	586	2116
2	USSR (1952-88)	395	319	296	1010
3	Great Britain	180	233	225	638
4	France	188	193	217	598
5	Italy	179	143	157	479
6	Sweden	136	156	177	469
7	East Germany (1968-88)	159	150	136	445
8	Hungary	150	135	158	443
9	Germany (1896-64,92–)	137	138	160	435
10	Australia	102	110	138	350
11	West Germany (1968-88)	77	104	120	301
12	Finland	101	81	114	296
	Japan	97	97	102	296
14	Romania	74	83	108	265
15	Poland	56	72	113	241
16	Canada	51	81	98	230
17	China	80	79	64	223
18	Netherlands	61	67	85	213
19	Bulgaria	48	82	65	195
20	Switzerland	47	75	61	183
21	Denmark	40	63	58	161
22	Russia (1896-1912, 96–)	58	52	46	156
23	South Korea	46	52	56	154
24	Czechoslovakia (1924-92)	49	49	44	142
25	Belgium	37	51	52	140
26	Cuba	55	44	38	137
27	Norway	49	44	41	134
28	Greece	32	48	46	126
29	Unified Team (1992)	45	38	29	112
30	Yugoslavia (1924-88, 96–)	28	32	33	93
31	Austria	20	32	34	86
32	Spain	25	28	22	75
33	New Zealand	30	12	32	74
34	Brazil	12	19	35	66
35	Turkey	33	16	15	64
36	Rep. of S. Africa (1904-60, 92–)	19	20	24	63

All-Time Medal Standings, 1896-2000 (Cont.)

		G	S	B	Total
37	Argentina	13	23	18	54
	Kenya	16	20	18	54
39	Mexico	10	15	22	47
40	Iran	8	13	19	40
41	Jamaica	5	20	12	37
42	North Korea	8	7	15	30
43	Estonia	8	6	12	26
44	Ethiopia	12	2	10	24
45	Ukraine	3	10	10	23
46	Great Britain/Ireland	6	11	3	20
	Ireland	8	6	6	20
48	Czech Republic	6	6	7	19
49	Portugal	3	4	10	17
	Belarus	3	3	11	17
	Nigeria	2	8	7	17
52	India	8	3	5	16
	Egypt	6	5	5	16
	Indonesia	4	7	5	16
	Morocco	4	3	9	16
56	Mongolia	0	5	9	14
57	Algeria	4	1	7	12
58	Trinidad & Tobago	1	3	7	11
59	Pakistan	3	3	4	10
	Uruguay	2	2	6	10
	Latvia	1	6	3	10
	Chinese Taipei	0	4	6	10
63	Lithuania	3	0	6	9
	Thailand	2	1	6	9
	Chile	0	6	3	9
	Philippines	0	2	7	9
67	Slovakia	2	4	2	8
	Venezuela	1	2	5	8
	Georgia	0	0	8	8
70	Kazakhstan	3	4	0	7
	Croatia	2	2	3	7
	Colombia	1	2	4	7
73	Bahamas	2	2	2	6
	Slovenia	2	2	2	6
	Uganda	1	3	2	6
	Tunisia	1	2	3	6
	Uzbekistan	1	2	3	6
	Bohemia	0	1	5	6
	Puerto Rico	0	1	5	6
80	Azerbaijan	2	1	1	4
	Peru	1	3	0	4
	Costa Rica	1	1	2	4
	Namibia	0	4	0	4
	Lebanon	0	2	2	4
	Moldova	0	2	2	4
	Ghana	0	1	3	4
	Israel	0	1	3	4
88	Luxembourg	2	1	0	3
	Armenia	1	1	1	3
	Cameroon	1	1	1	3
	Iceland	0	1	2	3
	Malaysia	0	1	2	3

		G	S	B	Total
93	Syria	1	1	0	2
	Japan/Korea	1	0	1	2
	Mozambique	1	0	1	2
	Surinam	1	0	1	2
	Tanzania	0	2	0	2
	Great Britain/USA	0	1	1	2
	Haiti	0	1	1	2
	Russia/Estonia	0	1	1	2
	Saudi Arabia	0	1	1	2
	United Arab Republic	0	1	1	2
	Zambia	0	1	1	2
	The Antilles	0	0	2	2
	Panama	0	0	2	2
	Qatar	0	0	2	2
107	Australia/New Zealand	1	0	0	1
	Burkina Faso	1	0	0	1
	Cuba/USA	1	0	0	1
	Denmark/Sweden	1	0	0	1
	Ecuador	1	0	0	1
	Gr. Britain/Ireland/Germany	1	0	0	1
	Gr. Britain/Ireland/USA	1	0	0	1
	Hong Kong	1	0	0	1
	Ireland/USA	1	0	0	1
	Zimbabwe	1	0	0	1
	Belgium/Greece	0	1	0	1
	Ceylon	0	1	0	1
	France/USA	0	1	0	1
	France/Gr. Britain/Ireland	0	1	0	1
	Ivory Coast	0	1	0	1
	Netherlands Antilles	0	1	0	1
	Senegal	0	1	0	1
	Singapore	0	1	0	1
	Smyrna	0	1	0	1
	Tonga	0	1	0	1
	Vietnam	0	1	0	1
	Virgin Islands	0	1	0	1
	Australia/Great Britain	0	0	1	1
	Barbados	0	0	1	1
	Bermuda	0	0	1	1
	Bohemia/Great Britain	0	0	1	1
	Djibouti	0	0	1	1
	Dominican Republic	0	0	1	1
	France/Great Britain	0	0	1	1
	Guyana	0	0	1	1
	Iraq	0	0	1	1
	Kuwait	0	0	1	1
	Kyrgyzstan	0	0	1	1
	Macedonia	0	0	1	1
	Mexico/Spain	0	0	1	1
	Niger	0	0	1	1
	Scotland	0	0	1	1
	Sri Lanka	0	0	1	1
	Thessalonika	0	0	1	1
	Wales	0	0	1	1

Combined totals:	G	S	B	Total
USSR/UT/Russia	498	409	371	1278
Germany/E. Ger/W. Ger	374	392	416	1182

Notes: Athletes from the USSR participated in the Summer Games from 1952-88, returned as the Unified Team in 1992 after the breakup of the Soviet Union (in 1991) and have competed as independent republics since the 1994 Winter Games. Germany was barred from the Olympics in 1924 and 1948 following World Wars I and II. Divided into East and West Germany after WWII, both countries competed together from 1952-64, then separately from 1968-88. Germany was reunified in 1990. Czechoslovakia split into Slovakia and the Czech Republic in 1993. Croatia and Bosnia-Herzegovina gained independence from Yugoslavia in 1991. Yugoslavia was not invited to the 1992 games (though Serbian and Montenegrin athletes were allowed to compete as independent athletes) but returned in 1996. South Africa was banned from 1964-88 for using the apartheid policy in the selection of its teams. It returned in 1992 as the Republic of South Africa (RSA).

1924-2002
Through the Years

SPORTS ALMANAC

The Winter Olympics

The move toward a winter version of the Olympics began in 1908 when figure skating made an appearance at the Summer Games in London. Ten-time world champion Ulrich Salchow of Sweden, who originated the backwards, one revolution jump that bears his name, and Madge Syers of Britain were the first singles champions. Germans Anna Hubler and Heinrich Berger won the pairs competition.

Organizers of the 1916 Summer Games in Berlin planned to introduce a "Skiing Olympia," featuring nordic events in the Black Forest, but the Games were cancelled after the outbreak of World War I in 1914.

The Games resumed in 1920 at Antwerp, Belgium, where figure skating returned and ice hockey was added as a medal event. Sweden's Gillis Grafstrom and Magda Julin took individual honors, while Ludovika and Walter Jakobsson were the top pair. In hockey, Canada won the gold medal with the United States second and Czechoslovakia third.

Despite the objections of Modern Olympics' founder Baron Pierre de Coubertin and the resistance of the Scandinavian countries, which had staged their own Nordic championships every four or five years from 1901-26 in Sweden, the International Olympic Committee sanctioned an "International Winter Sports Week" at Chamonix, France, in 1924. The 11-day event, which included nordic skiing, speed skating, figure skating, ice hockey and bobsledding, was a huge success and was retroactively called the first Olympic Winter Games.

Seventy years after those first cold weather Games, the 17th edition of the Winter Olympics took place in Lillehammer, Norway, in 1994. The event ended the four-year Olympic cycle of staging both Winter and Summer Games in the same year and began a new schedule that calls for the two Games to alternate every two years.

Year	No	Location	Dates	Nations	Most medals	USA medals
1924	I	Chamonix, FRA	Jan. 25-Feb. 4	16	Norway (4-7-6–17)	1-2-1–4 (3rd)
1928	II	St. Moritz, SWI	Feb. 11-19	25	Norway (6-4-5–15)	2-2-2– 6 (2nd)
1932	III	Lake Placid, USA	Feb. 4-15	17	USA (6-4-2–12)	6-4-2–12 (1st)
1936	IV	Garmisch-Partenkirchen, GER	Feb. 6-16	28	Norway (7-5-3–15)	1-0-3– 4 (T-5th)
1940-a	–	Sapporo, JPN	Cancelled (WWII)			
1944	–	Cortina d'Ampezzo, ITA	Cancelled (WWII)			
1948	V	St. Moritz, SWI	Jan. 30-Feb. 8	28	Norway (4-3-3–10), Sweden (4-3-3–10) & Switzerland (3-4-3–10)	3-4-2– 9 (4th)
1952-b	VI	Oslo, NOR	Feb. 14-25	30	Norway (7-3-6–16)	4-6-1–11 (2nd)
1956-c	VII	Cortina d'Ampezzo, ITA	Jan. 26-Feb. 5	32	USSR (7-3-6–16)	2-3-2– 7 (T-4th)
1960	VIII	Squaw Valley, USA	Feb. 18-28	30	USSR (7-5-9–21)	3-4-3–10 (2nd)
1964	IX	Innsbruck, AUT	Jan. 29-Feb. 9	36	USSR (11-8-6–25)	1-2-3– 6 (7th)
1968-d	X	Grenoble, FRA	Feb. 6-18	37	Norway (6-6-2–14)	1-5-1– 7 (T-7th)
1972	XI	Sapporo, JPN	Feb. 3-13	35	USSR (8-5-3–16)	3-2-3– 8 (6th)
1976-e	XII	Innsbruck, AUT	Feb. 4-15	37	USSR (13-6-8–27)	3-3-4–10 (T-3rd)
1980	XIII	Lake Placid, USA	Feb. 14-23	37	E. Germany (9-7-7–23)	6-4-2–12 (3rd)
1984	XIV	Sarajevo, YUG	Feb. 7-19	49	USSR (6-10-9–25)	4-4-0– 8 (T-5th)
1988	XV	Calgary, CAN	Feb. 13-28	57	USSR (11-9-9–29)	2-1-3– 6 (T-8th)
1992-f	XVI	Albertville, FRA	Feb. 8-23	63	Germany (10-10-6–26)	5-4-2–11 (6th)
1994-g	XVII	Lillehammer, NOR	Feb. 12-27	67	Norway (10-11-5–26)	6-5-2–13 (5th)
1998	XVIII	Nagano, JPN	Feb. 7-22	72	Germany (12-9-8–29)	6-3-4–13 (5th)
2002	XIX	Salt Lake City, USA	Feb. 8-24	78	Germany (12-16-7–35)	10-13-11–34 (2nd)
2006	XX	Turin, ITA	Feb. 10-26			
2010	XXI	Vancouver, CAN	TBA			

a–The 1940 Winter Games are originally scheduled for Sapporo, but Japan resigns as host in 1937 when the Sino-Japanese war breaks out. St. Moritz is the next choice, but the Swiss feel that ski instructors should not be considered professionals and the IOC withdraws its offer. Finally, Garmisch-Partenkirchen is asked to serve again as host, but the Germans invade Poland in 1939 and the Games are eventually cancelled.

b–Germany and Japan are allowed to rejoin the Olympic community for the first time since World War II. Though a divided country, the Germans send a joint East-West team through 1964.

c–The Soviet Union (USSR) participates in its first Winter Olympics and takes home the most medals, including the gold medal in ice hockey.

d–East Germany and West Germany officially send separate teams for the first time and will continue to do so through 1988.

e–The IOC grants the 1976 Winter Games to Denver in May 1970, but in 1972 Colorado voters reject a $5 million bond issue to finance the undertaking. Denver immediately withdraws as host and the IOC selects Innsbruck, the site of the 1964 Games, to take over.

f–Germany sends a single team after East and West German reunification in 1990 and the USSR competes as the Unified Team after the breakup of the Soviet Union in 1991.

g–The IOC moves the Winter Games' four-year cycle ahead two years in order to separate them from the Summer Games and alternate Olympics every two years.

Event-by-Event

Gold medal winners from 1924-2002 in the following events: Alpine Skiing, Biathlon, Bobsled, Cross Country Skiing, Curling, Figure Skating, Freestyle Skiing, Ice Hockey, Luge, Nordic Combined, Skeleton, Ski Jumping, Snowboarding and Speed Skating.

ALPINE SKIING

MEN

Multiple gold medals: Kjetil Andre Aamodt, Jean-Claude Killy, Toni Sailer and Alberto Tomba (3); Hermann Maier, Henri Oreiller, Ingemar Stenmark and Markus Wasmeier (2).

Downhill

Year		Time	Year		Time
1948	Henri Oreiller, FRA	2:55.0	1980	Leonhard Stock, AUS	1:45.50
1952	Zeno Colò, ITA	2:30.8	1984	Bill Johnson, USA	1:45.59
1956	Toni Sailer, AUT	2:52.2	1988	Pirmin Zurbriggen, SWI	1:59.63
1960	Jean Vuarnet, FRA	2:06.0	1992	Patrick Ortlieb, AUT	1:50.37
1964	Egon Zimmermann, AUT	2:18.16	1994	Tommy Moe, USA	1:45.75
1968	Jean-Claude Killy, FRA	1:59.85	1998	Jean-Luc Cretier, FRA	1:50.11
1972	Bernhard Russi, SWI	1:51.43	2002	Fritz Strobl, AUT	1:39.13
1976	Franz Klammer AUT	1:45.73			

Slalom

Year		Time	Year		Time
1948	Edi Reinalter, SWI	2:10.3	1980	Ingemar Stenmark, SWE	1:44.26
1952	Othmar Schneider, AUT	2:00.0	1984	Phil Mahre, USA	1:39.41
1956	Toni Sailer, AUT	3:14.7	1988	Alberto Tomba, ITA	1:39.47
1960	Ernst Hinterseer, AUT	2:08.9	1992	Finn Christian Jagge, NOR	1:44.39
1964	Pepi Stiegler, AUT	2:11.13	1994	Thomas Stangassinger, AUT	2:02.02
1968	Jean-Claude Killy, FRA	1:39.73	1998	Hans-Petter Buraas, NOR	1:49.31
1972	Francisco Ochoa, SPA	1:49.27	2002	Jean-Pierre Vidal, FRA	1:41.06
1976	Piero Gros, ITA	2:03.29			

Giant Slalom

Year		Time	Year		Time
1952	Stein Eriksen, NOR	2:25.0	1980	Ingemar Stenmark, SWE	2:40.74
1956	Toni Sailer, AUT	3:00.1	1984	Max Julen, SWI	2:41.18
1960	Roger Staub, SWI	1:48.3	1988	Alberto Tomba, ITA	2:06.37
1964	Francois Bonlieu, FRA	1:46.71	1992	Alberto Tomba, ITA	2:06.98
1968	Jean-Claude Killy, FRA	3:29.28	1994	Markus Wasmeier, GER	2:52.46
1972	Gustav Thöni, ITA	3:09.62	1998	Hermann Maier, AUT	2:38.51
1976	Heini Hemmi, SWI	3:26.97	2002	Stephan Eberharter, AUT	2:23.28

Super G

Year		Time	Year		Time
1988	Frank Piccard, FRA	1:39.66	1998	Hermann Maier, AUT	1:34.82
1992	Kjetil Andre Aamodt, NOR	1:13.04	2002	Kjetil Andre Aamodt, NOR	1:21.58
1994	Markus Wasmeier, GER	1:32.53			

Alpine Combined

Year		Points	Year		Time
1936	Franz Pfnür, GER	99.25	1994	Lasse Kjus, NOR	3:17.53
1948	Henri Oreiller, FRA	3.27	1998	Mario Reiter, AUT	3:08.06
1952-84	Not held		2002	Kjetil Andre Aamodt, NOR	3:17.56
1988	Hubert Strolz, AUT	36.55			
1992	Josef Polig, ITA	14.58			

WOMEN

Multiple gold medals: Deborah Compagnoni, Janica Kostelic, Vreni Schneider and Katja Seizinger (3); Marielle Goitschel, Trude Jochum-Beiser, Petra Kronberger, Andrea Mead Lawrence, Rosi Mittermaier, Marie-Theres Nadig, Hanni Wenzel and Pernilla Wiberg (2).

Downhill

Year		Time	Year		Time
1948	Hedy Schlunegger, SWI	2:28.3	1980	Annemarie Moser-Pröll, AUT	1:37.52
1952	Trude Jochum-Beiser, AUT	1:47.1	1984	Michela Figini, SWI	1:13.36
1956	Madeleine Berthod, SWI	1:40.7	1988	Marina Kiehl, W. Ger	1:25.86
1960	Heidi Biebl, GER	1:37.6	1992	Kerrin Lee-Gartner, CAN	1:52.55
1964	Christl Haas, AUT	1:55.39	1994	Katja Seizinger, GER	1:35.93
1968	Olga Pall, AUT	1:40.87	1998	Katja Seizinger, GER	1:28.89
1972	Marie-Theres Nadig, SWI	1:36.68	2002	Carole Montillet, FRA	1:39.56
1976	Rosi Mittermaier, W. Ger	1:46.16			

Slalom

Year		Time	Year		Time
1948	Gretchen Fraser, USA	1:57.2	1980	Hanni Wenzel, LIE	1:25.09
1952	Andrea Mead Lawrence, USA	2:10.6	1984	Paoletta Magoni, ITA	1:36.47
1956	Renée Colliard, SWI	1:52.3	1988	Vreni Schneider, SWI	1:36.69
1960	Anne Heggtveit, CAN	1:49.6	1992	Petra Kronberger, AUT	1:32.68
1964	Christine Goitschel, FRA	1:29.86	1994	Vreni Schneider, SWI	1:56.01
1968	Marielle Goitschel, FRA	1:25.86	1998	Hilde Gerg, GER	1:32.40
1972	Barbara Cochran, USA	1:31.24	2002	Janica Kostelic, CRO	1:46.10
1976	Rosi Mittermaier, W. Ger	1:30.54			

Giant Slalom

Year		Time	Year		Time
1952	Andrea Mead Lawrence, USA	2:06.8	1980	Hanni Wenzel, LIE	2:41.66
1956	Ossi Reichert, GER	1:56.5	1984	Debbie Armstrong, USA	2:20.98
1960	Yvonne Rügg, SWI	1:39.9	1988	Vreni Schneider, SWI	2:06.49
1964	Marielle Goitschel, FRA	1:52.24	1992	Pernilla Wiberg, SWE	2:12.74
1968	Nancy Greene, CAN	1:51.97	1994	Deborah Compagnoni, ITA	2:30.97
1972	Marie-Theres Nadig, SWI	1:29.90	1998	Deborah Compagnoni, ITA	2:50.59
1976	Kathy Kreiner, CAN	1:29.13	2002	Janica Kostelic, CRO	2:30.01

Super G

Year		Time	Year		Time
1988	Sigrid Wolf, AUT	1:19.03	1998	Picabo Street, USA	1:18.02
1992	Deborah Compagnoni, ITA	1:21.22	2002	Daniela Ceccarelli, ITA	1:13.59
1994	Diann Roffe-Steinrotter, USA	1:22.15			

Alpine Combined

Year		Points	Year		Time
1936	Christl Cranz, GER	97.06	1994	Pernilla Wiberg, SWE	3:05.16
1948	Trude Beiser, AUT	6.58	1998	Katja Seizinger, GER	2:40.74
1952-84	Not held		2002	Janica Kostelic, CRO	2:43.28
1988	Anita Wachter, AUT	29.25			
1992	Petra Kronberger, AUT	2.55			

BIATHLON

MEN

Multiple gold medals (including relays): Ole Einar Bjoerndalen (5); Aleksandr Tikhonov (4); Mark Kirchner and Ricco Gross (3); Anatoly Alyabyev, Ivan Biakov, Sergei Chepikov, Sven Fischer, Halvard Hanevold, Frank Luck, Viktor Mamatov, Frank-Peter Roetsch, Magnar Solberg and Dmitri Vasilyev (2).

10 kilometers

Year		Time	Year		Time
1980	Frank Ulrich, E. Ger	32:10.69	1994	Sergei Chepikov, RUS	28:07.0
1984	Erik Kvalfoss, NOR	30:53.8	1998	Ole Einar Bjoerndalen, NOR	27:16.2
1988	Frank-Peter Roetsch, E. Ger	25:08.1	2002	Ole Einar Bjoerndalen, NOR	24:51.3
1992	Mark Kirchner, GER	26:02.3			

12.5 kilometers

Year		Time
2002	Ole Einar Bjoerndalen, NOR	32:34.6

20 kilometers

Year		Time	Year		Time
1960	Klas Lestander, SWE	1:33:21.6	1984	Peter Angerer, W. Ger	1:11:52.7
1964	Vladimir Melanin, USSR	1:20:26.8	1988	Frank-Peter Roetsch, E. Ger	56:33.3
1968	Magnar Solberg, NOR	1:13:45.9	1992	Yevgeny Redkine, UT	57:34.4
1972	Magnar Solberg, NOR	1:15:55.50	1994	Sergei Tarasov, RUS	57:25.3
1976	Nikolai Kruglov, USSR	1:14:12.26	1998	Halvard Hanevold, NOR	56:16.4
1980	Anatoly Alyabyev, USSR	1:08:16.31	2002	Ole Einar Bjoerndalen, NOR	51:03.3

4x7.5-kilometer Relay

Year		Time	Year		Time	Year		Time
1968	Soviet Union	2:13:02.4	1984	Soviet Union	1:38:51.7	1998	Germany	1:21:36.2
1972	Soviet Union	1:51:44.92	1988	Soviet Union	1:22:30.0	2002	Norway	1:23:42.3
1976	Soviet Union	1:57:55.64	1992	Germany	1:24:43.5			
1980	Soviet Union	1:34:03.27	1994	Germany	1:30:22.1			

BIATHLON (Cont.)
WOMEN

Multiple gold medals (including relays): Myriam Bedard, Andrea Henkel, Anfisa Reztsova and Kati Wilhelm (2). Note that Reztsova won a third gold medal in 1988 in the cross country 4x5-kilometer relay.

7.5 kilometers

Year		Time	Year		Time
1992	Anfisa Reztsova, UT	24:29.2	1998	Galina Koukleva, RUS	23:08.0
1994	Myriam Bedard, CAN	26:08.8	2002	Kati Wilhelm, GER	20:41.4

10 kilometers

Year		Time
2002	Olga Pyleva, RUS	31:07.7

15 kilometers

Year		Time	Year		Time
1992	Antje Misersky, GER	51:47.2	1998	Ekaterina Dafovska, BUL	54:52.0
1994	Myriam Bedard, CAN	52:06.6	2002	Andrea Henkel, GER	47:29.1

4x7.5-kilometer Relay

Year		Time	Year		Time
1992	France	1:15:55.6	1998	Germany	1:40:13.6
1994	Russia	1:47:19.5	2002	Germany	1:27:55.0

Note: Event featured three skiers per team in 1992.

BOBSLED

A two-woman bobsled event was added in 2002. Only drivers are listed in parentheses.

Multiple gold medals: DRIVERS–Meinhard Nehmer (3); Billy Fiske, Wolfgang Hoppe, Christoph Langen, Eugenio Monti, Andreas Ostler and Gustav Weder (2). CREW–Bernard Germeshausen (3); Donat Acklin, Luciano De Paolis, Cliff Gray, Lorenz Nieberl and Dietmar Schauerhammer (2).

Two-Man

Year		Time	Year		Time
1932	United States (Hubert Stevens)	8:14.74	1976	East Germany (Meinhard Nehmer)	3:44.42
1936	United States (Ivan Brown)	5:29.29	1980	Switzerland (Erich Schärer)	4:09.36
1948	Switzerland (Felix Endrich)	5:29.2	1984	East Germany (Wolfgang Hoppe)	3:25.56
1952	Germany (Andreas Ostler)	5:24.54	1988	Soviet Union (Janis Kipurs)	3:54.19
1956	Italy (Lamberto Dalla Costa)	5:30.14	1992	Switzerland I (Gustav Weder)	4:03.26
1960	Not held		1994	Switzerland I (Gustav Weder)	3:30.81
1964	Great Britain (Anthony Nash)	4:21.90	1998	(TIE) Italy I (Guenther Huber)	3:37.24
1968	Italy (Eugenio Monti)	4:41.54		& Canada I (Pierre Lueders)	3:37.24
1972	West Germany (Wolfgang Zimmerer)	4:57.07	2002	Germany I (Christoph Langen)	3:10.11

Two-Woman

Year		Time
2002	United States II (Jill Bakken)	1:37.76

Four-Man

Year		Time	Year		Time
1924	Switzerland (Eduard Scherrer)	5:45.54	1972	Switzerland (Jean Wicki)	4:43.07
1928	United States (Billy Fiske)	3:20.5	1976	East Germany (Meinhard Nehmer)	3:40.43
1932	United States (Billy Fiske)	7:53.68	1980	East Germany (Meinhard Nehmer)	3:59.92
1936	Switzerland (Pierre Musy)	5:19.85	1984	East Germany (Wolfgang Hoppe)	3:20.22
1948	United States (Francis Tyler)	5:20.1	1988	Switzerland (Ekkehard Fasser)	3:47.51
1952	Germany (Andreas Ostler)	5:07.84	1992	Austria I (Ingo Appelt)	3:53.90
1956	Switzerland (Franz Kapus)	5:10.44	1994	Germany II (Harald Czudaj)	3:27.78
1960	Not held		1998	Germany II (Christoph Langen)	2:39.41
1964	Canada (Vic Emery)	4:14.46	2002	Germany II (Andre Lange)	3:07.51
1968	Italy (Eugenio Monti)	2:17.39			

Note: Five-man sleds were used in 1928.

CROSS COUNTRY SKIING

Starting with the 1988 Winter Games in Calgary, the classical and freestyle (i.e., skating) techniques were designated for specific events. The Pursuit race was introduced in 1992 and revamped after the 1998 Nagano Games. The Sprint was added in 2002.

MEN

Multiple gold medals (including relays): Bjorn Dählie (8); Thomas Alsgaard, Sixten Jernberg, Gunde Svan, Thomas Wassberg and Nikolai Zimyatov (4); Veikko Hakulinen, Eero Mäntyranta and Vegard Ulvang (3); Hallgeir Brenden, Harald Grönningen, Thorleif Haug, Johann Muehlegg, Jan Ottoson, Kristen Skjeldal, Pål Tyldum and Vyacheslav Vedenine (2).

Multiple gold medals (including Nordic Combined): Johan Gröttumsbråten and Thorleif Haug (3).

1.5-kilometer Sprint

New event in 2002.

Year		Time
2002	Tor Arne Hetland, NOR	2:56.9

10 kilometers

Held as a classical event..

Year		Time	Year		Time
1992	Vegard Ulvang, NOR	27:36.0	1998	Bjorn Dählie, NOR	27:24.5
1994	Bjorn Dählie, NOR	24:20.1	2002	Not held	

Combined Pursuit (10km)

From 1992-98 the pursuit included a 10-km classical race and a 15-km freestyle race contested on separate days. Beginning in 2002, the pursuit was shortened to two 5-kilometer races held on the same day.

Year		Time	Year		Time
1992	Bjorn Dählie, NOR	1:05:37.9	1998	Thomas Alsgaard, NOR	1:07:01.7
1994	Bjorn Dählie, NOR	1:00:08.8	2002	Johann Muehllegg, SPA	49:20.4

15 kilometers

Held over 18 kilometers from 1924-52. Held as a classical event from 1956-88, and since 2002. Replaced by the 15-km combined pursuit (1992-98).

Year		Time	Year		Time
1924	Thorleif Haug, NOR	1:14:31.0	1968	Harald Grönningen, NOR	47:54.2
1928	Johan Gröttumsbr äten, NOR	1:37:01.0	1972	Sven-Ake Lundback, SWE	45:28.24
1932	Sven Utterström, SWE	1:23:07.0	1976	Nikolai Bazhukov, USSR	43:58.47
1936	Erik-August Larsson, SWE	1:14:38.0	1980	Thomas Wassberg, SWE	41:57.63
1948	Martin Lundström, SWE	1:13:50.0	1984	Gunde Svan, SWE	41:25.6
1952	Hallgeir Brenden, NOR	1:01:34.0	1988	Mikhail Devyatyarov, USSR	41:18.9
1956	Hallgeir Brenden, NOR	49:39.0	1992-98	Not held	
1960	Hakon Brusveen, NOR	51:55.5	2002	Andrus Veerpalu, EST	37:07.4
1964	Eero Mäntyranta, FIN	50:54.1			

30 kilometers

Held as a freestyle event from 1956-94, and since 2002. Held as a classical event in 1998.

Year		Time	Year		Time
1956	Veikko Hakulinen, FIN	1:44:06.0	1984	Nikolai Zimyatov, USSR	1:28:56.3
1960	Sixten Jernberg, SWE	1:51:03.9	1988	Alexei Prokurorov, USSR	1:24:26.3
1964	Eero Mäntyranta, FIN	1:30:50.7	1992	Vegard Ulvang, NOR	1:22:27.8
1968	Franco Nones, ITA	1:35:39.2	1994	Thomas Alsgaard, NOR	1:12:26.4
1972	Vyacheslav Vedenine, USSR	1:36:31.15	1998	Mika Myllylae, FIN	1:33:55.8
1976	Sergei Saveliev, USSR	1:30:29.38	2002	Johann Muehllegg, SPA	1:09:28.9
1980	Nikolai Zimyatov, USSR	1:27:02.80			

50 kilometers

Held as a classical event from 1924-94, and since 2002. Held as a freestyle event in 1998.

Year		Time	Year		Time
1924	Thorleif Haug, NOR	3:44:32.0	1972	Päl Tyldum, NOR	2:43:14.75
1928	Per Erik Hedlund, SWE	4:52:03.0	1976	Ivar Formo, NOR	2:37:30.05
1932	Veli Saarinen, FIN	4:28:00.0	1980	Nikolai Zimyatov, USSR	2:27:24.60
1936	Elis Wiklund, SWE	3:30:11.0	1984	Thomas Wassberg, SWE	2:15:55.8
1948	Nils Karlsson, SWE	3:47:48.0	1988	Gunde Svan, SWE	2:04:30.9
1952	Veikko Hakulinen, FIN	3:33:33.0	1992	Bjorn Dählie, NOR	2:03:41.5
1956	Sixten Jernberg, SWE	2:50:27.0	1994	Vladimir Smirnov, KAZ	2:07:20.3
1960	Kalevi Hämäläinen, FIN	2:59:06.3	1998	Bjorn Dählie, NOR	2:05:08.2
1964	Sixten Jernberg, SWE	2:43:52.6	2002	Mikhail Ivanov, RUS*	2:06:20.8
1968	Ole Ellefsaeter, NOR	2:28:45.8			

*Ivanov finished second to Johann Muehllegg of Spain, who was disqualified for failing a drug test.

4x10-kilometer Mixed Relay

Two classical and two freestyle legs.

Year		Time	Year		Time	Year		Time
1936	Finland	2:41:33.0	1968	Norway	2:08:33.5	1992	Norway	1:39:26.0
1948	Sweden	2:32:08.0	1972	Soviet Union	2:04:47.94	1994	Italy	1:41:15.0
1952	Finland	2:20:16.0	1976	Finland	2:07:59.72	1998	Norway	1:40:55.7
1956	Soviet Union	2:15:30.0	1980	Soviet Union	1:57:03.46	2002	Norway	1:32:45.5
1960	Finland	2:18:45.6	1984	Sweden	1:55:06.3			
1964	Sweden	2:18:34.6	1988	Sweden	1:43:58.6			

CROSS COUNTRY SKIING (Cont.)
WOMEN

Multiple gold medals (including relays): Lyubov Egorova (6); Larissa Lazutina (5); Galina Kulakova and Raisa Smetanina (4); Claudia Boyarskikh, Olga Danilova and Marja-Liisa Hämäläinen and Elena Valbe (3); Stefania Belmondo, Manuela Di Centa, Nina Gavriluk, Toini Gustafsson, Barbara Petzold and Julija Tchepalova (2).

Multiple gold medals (including relays and Biathlon): Anfisa Reztsova (2).

1.5-kilometer Sprint
New event in 2002.

Year		Time
2002	Julija Tchepalova, RUS	3:10.6

5 kilometers
Held as a classical event from 1964-98. From 1992-98 it was half of the combined pursuit event. Discontinued after 1998.

Year		Time	Year		Time
1964	Claudia Boyarskikh, USSR	17:50.5	1984	Marja-Liisa Hämäläinen, FIN	17:04.0
1968	Toini Gustafsson, SWE	16:45.2	1988	Marjo Matikainen, FIN	15:04.0
1972	Galina Kulakova, USSR	17:00.50	1992	Marjut Lukkarinen, FIN	14:13.8
1976	Helena Takalo, FIN	15:48.69	1994	Lyubov Egorova, RUS	14:08.8
1980	Raisa Smetanina, USSR	15:06.92	1998	Larissa Lazutina, RUS	17:37.9

Combined Pursuit (10km)
From 1992-98 the pursuit consisted of a 10-km freestyle race in which the starting order was determined by order of finish in the 5-km classical race contested on separate days. Beginning in 2002, the pursuit was shortened to a 5-km classical race followed by a 5-km freestyle race contested on the same day. The 5-km classical is no longer a separate medal event.

Year		Time	Year		Time
1992	Lyubov Egorova, UT	40:07.7	1998	Larissa Lazutina, RUS	46:06.9
1994	Lyubov Egorova, RUS	41:38.1	2002	Olga Danilova, RUS	24:52.1

10 kilometers
Held as a classical event from 1952-88, and since 2002. Replaced by 10-km combined pursuit from 1992-98.

Year		Time	Year		Time
1952	Lydia Wideman, FIN	41:40.0	1976	Raisa Smetanina, USSR	30:13.41
1956	Lyubov Kosyreva, USSR	38:11.0	1980	Barbara Petzold, E. Ger	30:31.54
1960	Maria Gusakova, USSR	39:46.6	1984	Marja-Liisa Hämäläinen, FIN	31:44.2
1964	Claudia Boyarskikh, USSR	40:24.3	1988	Vida Venciene, USSR	30:08.3
1968	Toini Gustafsson, SWE	36:46.5	1992-98 Not held		
1972	Galina Kulakova, USSR	34:17.82	2002	Bente Skari, NOR	28:05.6

15 kilometers
Held as a freestyle event from 1992-94, and since 2002. Held as a classical event in 1998.

Year		Time	Year		Time
1992	Lyubov Egorova, UT	42:20.8	1998	Olga Danilova, RUS	46:55.4
1994	Manuela Di Centa, ITA	39:44.5	2002	Stefania Belmondo, ITA	39:54.4

20 kilometers
Held as a classical event from 1984-88. Discontinued in 1992 and replaced by the 30-kilometer freestyle.

Year		Time	Year		Time
1984	Marja-Liisa Hämäläinen, FIN	1:01:45.0	1988	Tamara Tikhonova, USSR	55:53.6

30 kilometers
Replaced 20-km classical event in 1992. Held as a freestyle event 1992-98. Held as a classical event since 2002.

Year		Time	Year		Time
1992	Stefania Belmondo, ITA	1:22:30.1	1998	Julija Tchepalova, RUS	1:22:01.5
1994	Manuela Di Centa, ITA	1:25:41.6	2002	Gabriella Paruzzi, ITA*	1:30:57.1

*Paruzzi finished second to Larissa Lazutina of Russia, who was disqualified after failing a drug test.

4x5-kilometer Relay
Two classical and two freestyle legs since 1992. Event featured three skiers per team from 1956-72.

Year	Time	Year	Time	Year	Time
1956 Finland	1:09:01.0	1976 Soviet Union	1:07:49.75	1994 Russia	57:12.5
1960 Sweden	1:04:21.4	1980 East Germany	1:02:11.10	1998 Russia	55:13.5
1964 Soviet Union	59:20.2	1984 Norway	1:06:49.7	2002 Germany	49:30.6
1968 Norway	57:30.0	1988 Soviet Union	59:51.1		
1972 Soviet Union	48:46.15	1992 Unified Team	59:34.8		

CURLING

MEN		WOMEN	
Year		**Year**	
1998	**Switzerland**, Canada, Norway	1998	**Canada**, Denmark, Sweden
2002	**Norway**, Canada, Switzerland	2002	**Great Britain**, Switzerland, Canada

FIGURE SKATING

MEN

Multiple gold medals: Gillis Grafström (3); Dick Button and Karl Schäfer (2).

Year			Year			Year		
1908	Ulrich Salchow	SWE	1952	Dick Button	USA	1984	Scott Hamilton	USA
1912	Not held		1956	Hayes Alan Jenkins	USA	1988	Brian Boitano	USA
1920	Gillis Grafström	SWE	1960	David Jenkins	USA	1992	Victor Petrenko	UT
1924	Gillis Grafström	SWE	1964	Manfred Schnelldorfer	GER	1994	Alexei Urmanov	RUS
1928	Gillis Grafström	SWE	1968	Wolfgang Schwarz	AUT	1998	Ilia Kulik	RUS
1932	Karl Schäfer	AUT	1972	Ondrej Nepela	CZE	2002	Alexei Yagudin	RUS
1936	Karl Schäfer	AUT	1976	John Curry	GBR			
1948	Dick Button	USA	1980	Robin Cousins	GBR			

WOMEN

Multiple gold medals: Sonja Henie (3); Katarina Witt (2).

Year			Year			Year		
1908	Madge Syers	GBR	1952	Jeanette Altwegg	GBR	1984	Katarina Witt	E. Ger
1912	Not held		1956	Tenley Albright	USA	1988	Katarina Witt	E. Ger
1920	Magda Julin-Mauroy	SWE	1960	Carol Heiss	USA	1992	Kristi Yamaguchi	USA
1924	Herma Planck-Szabö	AUT	1964	Sjoukje Dijkstra	NED	1994	Oksana Baiul	UKR
1928	Sonja Henie	NOR	1968	Peggy Fleming	USA	1998	Tara Lipinski	USA
1932	Sonja Henie	NOR	1972	Beatrix Schuba	AUT	2002	Sarah Hughes	USA
1936	Sonja Henie	NOR	1976	Dorothy Hamill	USA			
1948	Barbara Ann Scott	CAN	1980	Anett Pötzsch	E. Ger			

Pairs

Multiple gold medals: MEN–Pierre Brunet, Artur Dmitriev, Sergei Grinkov, Oleg Protopopov and Aleksandr Zaitsev (2). WOMEN–Irina Rodnina (3); Ludmila Belousova, Ekaterina Gordeeva and Andree Joly Brunet (2).

Year			Year		
1908	Anna Hübler & Heinrich Burger	Germany	1968	Ludmila Belousova & Oleg Protopopov	USSR
1912	Not held		1972	Irina Rodnina & Aleksei Ulanov	USSR
1920	Ludovika & Walter Jakobsson	Finland	1976	Irina Rodnina & Aleksandr Zaitsev	USSR
1924	Helene Engelmann & Alfred Berger	Austria	1980	Irina Rodnina & Aleksandr Zaitsev	USSR
1928	Andrée Joly & Pierre Brunet	France	1984	Elena Valova & Oleg Vasiliev	USSR
1932	Andrée & Pierre Brunet	France	1988	Ekaterina Gordeeva & Sergei Grinkov	USSR
1936	Maxi Herber & Ernst Baier	Germany	1992	Natalia Mishkutienok & Arthur Dmitriev	UT
1948	Micheline Lannoy & Pierre Baugniet	Belgium	1994	Ekaterina Gordeeva & Sergei Grinkov	RUS
1952	Ria & Paul Falk	Germany	1998	Oksana Kazakova & Artur Dmitriev	RUS
1956	Elisabeth Schwartz & Kurt Oppelt	Austria	2002	Elena Berezhnaya & Anton Sikharulidze	RUS
1960	Barbara Wagner & Robert Paul	Canada		Jamie Sale & David Pelletier*	CAN
1964	Ludmila Belousova & Oleg Protopopov	USSR			

*Originally awarded silver medals, Sale & Pelletier later had them upgraded to gold after an investigation by the International Olympic Committee and the International Skating Union concluded that a judge was guilty of misconduct.

Ice Dancing

Multiple gold medals: Oksana Grishuk & Yevgeny Platov (2).

Year			Year		
1976	Lyudmila Pakhomova & Aleksandr Gorshkov	USSR	1992	Marina Klimova & Sergei Ponomarenko	UT
1980	Natalia Linichuk & Gennady Karponosov	USSR	1994	Oksana Grishuk & Yevgeny Platov	RUS
1984	Jayne Torvill & Christopher Dean	Great Britain	1998	Oksana Grishuk & Yevgeny Platov	RUS
1988	Natalia Bestemianova & Andrei Bukin		2002	Marina Anissina & Gwendal Peizerat	FRA

FREESTYLE SKIING

MEN			WOMEN		
Aerials			**Aerials**		
Year		Points	Year		Points
1994	Andreas Schoebaechler, SWI	234.67	1994	Lina Cherjazova, UZB	166.84
1998	Eric Bergoust, USA	255.64	1998	Nikki Stone, USA	193.00
2002	Ales Valenta, CZR	257.02	2002	Alisa Camplin, AUS	193.47
Moguls			**Moguls**		
Year		Points	Year		Points
1994	Jean-Luc Brassard, CAN	27.24	1994	Stine Lise Hattestad, NOR	25.97
1998	Jonny Moseley, USA	26.93	1998	Tae Satoya, JPN	25.06
2002	Janne Lahtela, FIN	27.97	2002	Kari Traa, NOR	25.94

ICE HOCKEY
MEN

Multiple gold medals: Soviet Union/Unified Team (8); Canada (7); United States (2).

Year		Year	
1920	**Canada**, United States Czechoslovakia	1980	**United States**, Soviet Union, Sweden
1924	**Canada**, United States, Great Britain	1984	**Soviet Union**, Czechoslovakia, Sweden
1928	**Canada**, Sweden, Switzerland	1988	**Soviet Union**, Finland, Sweden
1932	**Canada**, United States, Germany	1992	**Unified Team**, Canada, Czechoslovakia
1936	**Great Britain**, Canada, United States	1994	**Sweden**, Canada, Finland
1948	**Canada**, Czechoslovakia, Switzerland	1998	**Czech Republic**, Russia, Finland
1952	**Canada**, United States, Sweden	2002	**Canada**, United States, Russia
1956	**Soviet Union**, United States, Canada		
1960	**United States**, Canada, Soviet Union		**WOMEN**
1964	**Soviet Union**, Sweden, Czechoslovakia	Year	
1968	**Soviet Union**, Czechoslovakia, Canada	1998	**United States**, Canada, Finland
1972	**Soviet Union**, United States, Czechoslovakia	2002	**Canada**, United States, Sweden
1976	**Soviet Union**, Czechoslovakia, West Germany		

U.S. Gold Medal Hockey Teams
1960

Forwards: Billy Christian, Roger Christian, Billy Cleary, Gene Grazia, Paul Johnson, Bob McVey, Dick Meredith, Weldy Olson, Dick Rodenheiser and Tom Williams. **Defensemen:** Bob Cleary, Jack Kirrane (captain), John Mayasich, Bob Owen and Rod Paavola. **Goaltenders:** Jack McCartan and Larry Palmer. **Coach:** Jack Riley.

1980

Forwards: Neal Broten, Steve Christoff, Mike Eruzione (captain), John Harrington, Mark Johnson, Rob McClanahan, Mark Pavelich, Buzz Schneider, Dave Silk, Eric Strobel, Phil Verchota and Mark Wells. **Defensemen:** Bill Baker, Dave Christian, Ken Morrow, Jack O'Callahan, Mike Ramsey and Bob Suter. **Goaltenders:** Jim Craig and Steve Janaszak. **Coach:** Herb Brooks.

1998

Forwards: Laurie Baker, Alana Blahoski, Lisa Brown-Miller, Karen Bye, Tricia Dunn, Cammi Granato, Katie King, Shelley Looney, A.J. Mleczko, Jenny Schmidgall, Gretchen Ulion, Sandra Whyte. **Defensemen:** Chris Bailey, Colleen Coyne, Sue Mertz, Tara Mounsey, Vicki Movessian, Angela Ruggiero. **Goaltenders:** Sarah DeCosta and Sarah Tueting. **Coach:** Ben Smith.

LUGE
MEN

Multiple gold medals: (including doubles): Georg Hackl (3); Jan Behrendt, Norbert Hahn, Paul Hildgartner, Thomas Köhler, Stefan Krausse and Hans Rinn (2).

Singles

Year		Time	Year		Time
1964	Thomas Köhler, GER	3:26.77	1988	Jens Müller, E. Ger	3:05.548
1968	Manfred Schmid, AUT	2:52.48	1992	Georg Hackl, GER	3:02.363
1972	Wolfgang Scheidel, E. Ger	3:27.58	1994	Georg Hackl, GER	3:21.571
1976	Dettlef Günther, E. Ger	3:27.688	1998	Georg Hackl, GER	3:18.436
1980	Bernhard Glass, E. Ger	2:54.796	2002	Armin Zoeggeler, ITA	2:57.941
1984	Paul Hildgartner, ITA	3:04.258			

Doubles

Year		Time	Year		Time
1964	Josef Feistmantl & Manfred Stengl, AUT	1:41.62	1988	Joerg Hoffmann & Jochen Pietzsch, E. Ger.	1:31.940
1968	Klaus Bonsack & Thomas Köhler, E. Ger.	1:35.85	1992	Jan Behrendt & Stefan Krausse, GER	1:32.053
1972	(TIE) Paul Hildgartner/Walter Plaikner, ITA	1:28.35	1994	Kurt Brugger & Wilfred Huber, ITA	1:36.720
	& Richard Bredow/Horst Hornlein, E. Ger.	1:28.35	1998	Jan Behrendt & Stefan Krausse, GER	1:41.105
1976	Norbert Hahn & Hans Rinn, E. Ger.	1:25.604	2002	Patric-Fritz Leitner & Alexander Resch, GER	1:26.082
1980	Norbert Hahn & Hans Rinn, E. Ger.	1:19.331			
1984	Hans Stangassinger & Franz Wembacher, W. Ger.	1:23.620			

WOMEN

Multiple gold medals: Steffi Martin Walter (2).

Singles

Year		Time	Year		Time
1964	Ortrun Enderlein, GER	3:24.67	1988	Steffi Martin Walter, E. Ger	3:03.973
1968	Erica Lechner, ITA	2:28.66	1992	Doris Neuner, AUT	3:06.696
1972	Anna-Maria Müller, E. Ger	2:59.18	1994	Gerda Weissensteiner, ITA	3:15.517
1976	Margit Schumann, E. Ger	2:50.621	1998	Silke Kraushaar, GER	3:23.779
1980	Vera Zozulya, USSR	2:36.537	2002	Sylke Otto, GER	2:52.464
1984	Steffi Martin, E. Ger	2:46.570			

Ski jumping followed by a cross country race. Judges stopped converting cross country times into points after the 1994 Games. The times listed are final cross country times adjusted to include the competitors' staggered start time. The staggered start is determined by the Gundersen Method, which is a table that converts final ski jumping point differentials into time intervals.

Multiple gold medals: Samppa Lajunen and Ulrich Wehling (3); Bjarte Engen Vik, Johan Gröttumsbråten, Fred Boerre Lundberg, Takanori Kono and Kenji Ogiwara (2).

Individual

Year		Points	Year		Points
1924	Thorleif Haug, NOR	18.906	1972	Ulrich Wehling, E. Ger	413.340
1928	Johan Gröttumsbråten, NOR	17.833	1976	Ulrich Wehling, E. Ger	423.39
1932	Johan Gröttumsbråten, NOR	446.00	1980	Ulrich Wehling, E. Ger	432.200
1936	Oddbjörn Hagen, NOR	430.3	1984	Tom Sandberg, NOR	422.595
1948	Heikki Hasu, FIN	448.80	1988	Hippolyt Kempf, SWI	432.230
1952	Simon Slattvik, NOR	451.621	1992	Fabrice Guy, FRA	426.470
1956	Sverre Stenersen, NOR	455.000	1994	Fred Borre Lundberg, NOR	457.970
1960	Georg Thoma, GER	457.952			**Time**
1964	Tormod Knutsen, NOR	469.28	1998	Bjarte Engen Vik, NOR	41:21.1
1968	Franz Keller, W. Ger	449.04	2002	Samppa Lajunen, FIN	39:11.7

Sprint
New event in 2002.

Year		Time
2002	Samppa Lajunen, FIN	16:40.1

Team

Year		Points			Time
1988	West Germany	792.08	1998	Norway	54:11.5
1992	Japan	1247.180	2002	Finland	48:42.2
1994	Japan	1368.860			

MEN Singles			**WOMEN** Singles		
Year		Time	Year		Time
1928	Jennison Heaton, USA	3:01.8	2002	Tristan Gale, USA	1:45.11
1932-36	Not held				
1948	Nino Bibbia, ITA	5:23.2			
1952-98	Not held				
2002	Jim Shea, USA	1:41.96			

Note: This event was called Cresta when it was held in 1928 and 1948.

Multiple gold medals (including team jumping): Matti Nykänen (4); Jens Weissflog (3); Simon Ammann, Birger Ruud and Toni Nieminen (2).

Normal Hill–90 Meters

Year		Points	Year		Points
1924-60	Not held		1984	Jens Weissflog, E. Ger	215.2
1964	Veikko Kankkonen, FIN	229.9	1988	Matti Nykänen, FIN	229.1
1968	Jiri Raska, CZE	216.5	1992	Ernst Vettori, AUT	222.8
1972	Yukio Kasaya, JPN	244.2	1994	Espen Bredesen, NOR	282.0
1976	Hans-Georg Aschenbach, E. Ger	252.0	1998	Jani Soininen, FIN	234.5
1980	Anton Innauer, AUT	266.3	2002	Simon Ammann, SWI	269.0

Note: Jump held at 70 meters from 1964-92.

Large Hill–120 Meters

Year		Points	Year		Points
1924	Jacob Tullin Thams, NOR	18.960	1972	Wojciech Fortuna, POL	219.9
1928	Alf Andersen, NOR	19.208	1976	Karl Schäabl, AUT	234.8
1932	Birger Ruud, NOR	228.1	1980	Jouko Törmänen, FIN	271.0
1936	Birger Ruud, NOR	232.0	1984	Matti Nykänen, FIN	231.2
1948	Petter Hugsted, NOR	228.1	1988	Matti Nykänen, FIN	224.0
1952	Arnfinn Bergmann, NOR	226.0	1992	Toni Nieminen, FIN	239.5
1956	Antti Hyvärinen, FIN	227.0	1994	Jens Weissflog, GER	274.5
1960	Helmut Recknagel, GER	227.2	1998	Kazuyoshi Funaki, JPN	272.3
1964	Toralf Engan, NOR	230.7	2002	Simon Ammann, SWI	281.4
1968	Vladimir Beloussov, USSR	231.3			

Note: Jump held at various lengths from 1924-56; at 80 meters from 1960-64; and at 90 meters from 1968-88.

SKI JUMPING (Cont.)
Team Large Hill

Year		Points	Year		Points
1988	Finland	.634.4	1998	Japan	.933.0
1992	Finland	.644.4	2002	Germany	.974.1
1994	Germany	.970.1			

SNOWBOARDING

MEN
Halfpipe

Year		Points
1998	Gian Simmen, SWI	.85.2
2002	Ross Powers, USA	.46.1

Giant Slalom (Discont.)
Discontinued after 1998, replaced by Parallel Giant Slalom.

Year		Time
1998	Ross Rebagliati, CAN	.2:03.96

Parallel Giant Slalom

Year		
2002	Philipp Schoch	.SWI

WOMEN
Halfpipe

Year		Points
1998	Nicola Thost, GER	.74.6
2002	Kelly Clark, USA	.47.9

Giant Slalom (Discont.)
Discontinued after 1998, replaced by Parallel Giant Slalom.

Year		Time
1998	Karine Ruby, FRA	.2:17.34

Parallel Giant Slalom

Year		
2002	Isabelle Blanc	.FRA

SPEED SKATING

MEN

Multiple gold medals: Eric Heiden and Clas Thunberg (5); Ivar Ballangrud, Yevgeny Grishin and Johann Olav Koss (4); Hjalmar Andersen, Tomas Gustafson, Irving Jaffee and Ard Schenk (3); Gaétan Boucher, Knut Johannesen, Erhard Keller, Uwe-Jens Mey, Gianni Romme, Jack Shea and Jochem Uytdehaage (2). Note that Thunberg's total includes the All-Around, which was contested for the only time in 1924.

500 meters

Year		Time		Year		Time	
1924	Charles Jewtraw, USA	.44.0		1968	Erhard Keller, W. Ger	.40.3	
1928	(TIE) Bernt Evensen, NOR	.43.4	OR	1972	Erhard Keller, W. Ger	.39.44	OR
	& Clas Thunberg, FIN	.43.4	OR	1976	Yevgeny Kulikov, USSR	.39.17	OR
1932	Jack Shea, USA	.43.4	=OR	1980	Eric Heiden, USA	.38.03	OR
1936	Ivar Ballangrud, NOR	.43.4	=OR	1984	Sergei Fokichev, USSR	.38.19	
1948	Finn Helgesen, NOR	.43.1	OR	1988	Uwe-Jens Mey, E. Ger	.36.45	WR
1952	Ken Henry, USA	.43.2		1992	Uwe-Jens Mey, GER	.37.14	
1956	Yevgeny Grishin, USSR	.40.2	=WR	1994	Aleksandr Golubev, RUS	.36.33	OR
1960	Yevgeny Grishin, USSR	.40.2	=WR	1998	Hiroyashu Shimizu, JPN	.71.35*	OR
1964	Terry McDermott, USA	.40.1	OR	2002	Casey FitzRandolph, USA	.69.23	OR

*The two-race final was introduced; skater with the lowest combined time wins gold.

1000 meters

Year		Time		Year		Time	
1924-72	Not held			1992	Olaf Zinke, GER	.1:14.85	
1976	Peter Mueller, USA	.1:19.32		1994	Dan Jansen, USA	.1:12.43	WR
1980	Eric Heiden, USA	.1:15.18	OR	1998	Ids Postma, NED	.1:10.64	OR
1984	Gaétan Boucher, CAN	.1:15.80		2002	Gerard van Velde, NED	.1:07.18	WR
1988	Nikolai Gulyaev, USSR	.1:13.03	OR				

1500 meters

Year		Time		Year		Time	
1924	Clas Thunberg, FIN	.2:20.8		1968	Kees Verkerk, NED	.2:03.4	OR
1928	Clas Thunberg, FIN	.2:21.1		1972	Ard Schenk, NED	.2:02.96	OR
1932	Jack Shea, USA	.2:57.5		1976	Jan Egil Storholt, NOR	.1:59.38	OR
1936	Charles Mathisen, NOR	.2:19.2	OR	1980	Eric Heiden, USA	.1:55.44	OR
1948	Sverre Farstad, NOR	.2:17.6	OR	1984	Gaétan Boucher, CAN	.1:58.36	
1952	Hjalmar Andersen, NOR	.2:20.4		1988	Andre Hoffman, E. Ger	.1:52.06	WR
1956	(TIE) Yevgeny Grishin, USSR	.2:08.6	WR	1992	Johann Olav Koss, NOR	.1:54.81	
	& Yuri Mikhailov, USSR	.2:08.6	WR	1994	Johann Olav Koss, NOR	.1:51.29	WR
1960	(TIE) Roald Aas, NOR	.2:10.4		1998	Aadne Sondral, NOR	.1:47.87	WR
	& Yevgeny Grishin, USSR	.2:10.4		2002	Derek Parra, USA	.1:43.95	WR
1964	Ants Antson, USSR	.2:10.3					

5000 meters

Year		Time		Year		Time	
1924	Clas Thunberg, FIN	.8:39.0		1932	Irving Jaffee, USA	.9:40.8	
1928	Ivar Ballangrud, NOR	.8:50.5		1936	Ivar Ballangrud, NOR	.8:19.6	OR

Year		Time		Year		Time	
1948	Reidar Liaklev, NOR	8:29.4		1980	Eric Heiden, USA	7:02.29	OR
1952	Hjalmar Andersen, NOR	8:10.6	OR	1984	Tomas Gustafson, SWE	7:12.28	
1956	Boris Shilkov, USSR	7:48.7	OR	1988	Tomas Gustafson, SWE	6:44.63	WR
1960	Viktor Kosichkin, USSR	7:51.3		1992	Geir Karlstad, NOR	6:59.97	
1964	Knut Johannesen, NOR	7:38.4	OR	1994	Johann Olav Koss, NOR	6:34.96	WR
1968	Fred Anton Maier, NOR	7:22.4	WR	1998	Gianni Romme, NED	6:22.20	WR
1972	Ard Schenk, NED	7:23.61		2002	Jochem Uytdehaage, NED	6:14.66	WR
1976	Sten Stensen, NOR	7:24.48					

10,000 meters

Year		Time		Year		Time	
1924	Julius Skutnabb, FIN	18:04.8		1972	Ard Schenk, NED	15:01.35	OR
1928	Irving Jaffee, USA*	18:36.5		1976	Piet Kleine, NED	14:50.59	OR
1932	Irving Jaffee, USA	19:13.6		1980	Eric Heiden, USA	14:28.13	WR
1936	Ivar Ballangrud, NOR	17:24.3	OR	1984	Igor Malkov, USSR	14:39.90	
1948	Ake Seyffarth, SWE	17:26.3		1988	Tomas Gustafson, SWE	13:48.20	WR
1952	Hjalmar Andersen, NOR	16:45.8	OR	1992	Bart Veldkamp, NED	14:12.12	
1956	Sigvard Ericsson, SWE	16:35.9	OR	1994	Johann Olav Koss, NOR	13:30.55	WR
1960	Knut Johannesen, NOR	15:46.6	WR	1998	Gianni Romme, NED	13:15.33	WR
1964	Jonny Nilsson, SWE	15:50.1		2002	Jochem Uytdehaage, NED	12:58.92	WR
1968	Johnny Höglin, SWE	15:23.6	OR				

*Unofficial, according to the IOC. Jaffee recorded the fastest time, but the event was called off in progress due to thawing ice.

WOMEN

Multiple gold medals: Lydia Skoblikova (6); Bonnie Blair (5); Claudia Pechstein (4); Karin Enke, Gunda Niemann-Stirnemann and Yvonne van Gennip (3); Tatiana Averina, Catriona Lemay-Doan, Christa Rothenburger and Marianne Timmer (2).

500 meters

Year		Time		Year		Time	
1960	Helga Haase, GER	45.9		1984	Christa Rothenburger, E. Ger	41.02	OR
1964	Lydia Skoblikova, USSR	45.0	OR	1988	Bonnie Blair, USA	39.10	WR
1968	Lyudmila Titova, USSR	46.1		1992	Bonnie Blair, USA	40.33	
1972	Anne Henning, USA	43.33	OR	1994	Bonnie Blair, USA	39.25	
1976	Sheila Young, USA	42.76	OR	1998	Catriona Lemay-Doan, CAN	76.60*	OR
1980	Karin Enke, E. Ger	41.78	OR	2002	Catriona Lemay-Doan, CAN	74.75	OR

*The two-race final was introduced; skater with the lowest combined time wins gold.

1000 meters

Year		Time		Year		Time	
1960	Klara Guseva, USSR	1:34.1		1984	Karin Enke, E. Ger	1:21.61	OR
1964	Lydia Skoblikova, USSR	1:33.2	OR	1988	Christa Rothenburger, E. Ger	1:17.65	WR
1968	Carolina Geijssen, NED	1:32.6	OR	1992	Bonnie Blair, USA	1:21.90	
1972	Monika Pflug, W. Ger	1:31.40	OR	1994	Bonnie Blair, USA	1:18.74	
1976	Tatiana Averina, USSR	1:28.43	OR	1998	Marianne Timmer, NED	1:16.51	OR
1980	Natalia Petruseva, USSR	1:24.10	OR	2002	Chris Witty, USA	1:13.83	WR

1500 meters

Year		Time		Year		Time	
1960	Lydia Skoblikova, USSR	2:25.2	WR	1984	Karin Enke, E. Ger	2:03.42	OR
1964	Lydia Skoblikova, USSR	2:22.6	OR	1988	Yvonne van Gennip, NED	2:00.68	OR
1968	Kaija Mustonen, FIN	2:22.4	OR	1992	Jacqueline Börner, GER	2:05.87	
1972	Dianne Holum, USA	2:20.85	OR	1994	Emese Hunyady, AUT	2:02.19	
1976	Galina Stepanskaya, USSR	2:16.58	OR	1998	Marianne Timmer, NED	1:57.58	WR
1980	Annie Borckink, NED	2:10.95	OR	2002	Anni Friesinger, GER	1:54.02	WR

3000 meters

Year		Time		Year		Time	
1960	Lydia Skoblikova, USSR	5:14.3		1984	Andrea Schöne, E. Ger	4:24.79	OR
1964	Lydia Skoblikova, USSR	5:14.9		1988	Yvonne van Gennip, NED	4:11.94	WR
1968	Johanna Schut, NED	4:56.2	OR	1992	Gunda Niemann, GER	4:19.90	
1972	Christina Baas-Kaiser, NED	4:52.14	OR	1994	Svetlana Bazhanova, RUS	4:17.43	
1976	Tatiana Averina, USSR	4:45.19	OR	1998	Gunda Niemann-Stirnemann, GER	4:07.29	OR
1980	Bjorg Eva Jensen, NOR	4:32.13	OR	2002	Claudia Pechstein, GER	3:57.70	WR

5000 meters

Year		Time		Year		Time	
1960-84 Not held				1994	Claudia Pechstein, GER	7:14.37	
1988	Yvonne van Gennip, NED	7:14.13	WR	1998	Claudia Pechstein, GER	6:59.61	WR
1992	Gunda Niemann, GER	7:31.57		2002	Claudia Pechstein, GER	6:46.91	WR

SHORT TRACK SPEED SKATING

MEN

Multiple gold medals (including relays): Marc Gagnon and Kim Ki-Hoon (3).

500 meters

Year		Time	
1994	Chae Ji-Hoon, S. Kor.	.43.45	
1998	Takafumi Nishitani, JPN	.42.862	
2002	Marc Gagnon, CAN	.41.802	**OR**

1000 meters

Year		Time	
1992	Kim Ki-Hoon, S. Kor.	1:30.76	**WR**
1994	Kim Ki-Hoon, S. Kor.	1:34.57	
1998	Kim Dong-Sung, S. Kor.	1:32.375	
2002	Steven Bradbury, AUS	1:29.109	

1500 meters

Year		Time
2002	Apolo Anton Ohno, USA*	2:18.541

*Ohno finished second to South Korea's Kim Dong-Sung, who was disqualifed for cross-tracking.

5000-m Relay

Year		Time	
1992	South Korea	.7:14.02	**WR**
1994	Italy	.7:11.74	**OR**
1998	Canada	.7:06.075	
2002	Canada	.6:51.579	

WOMEN

Multiple gold medals (including relays): Chun Lee-Kyung (4); Kim Yun-Mi, Annie Perrault, Cathy Turner, Won Hye-Kyung and Yang Yang (A) (2)

500 meters

Year		Time	
1992	Cathy Turner, USA	.47.04	
1994	Cathy Turner, USA	.45.98	**OR**
1998	Annie Perrault, CAN	.46.568	
2002	Yang Yang (A), CHN	.44.187	

1000 meters

Year		Time
1994	Chun Lee-Kyung, S. Kor.	1:36.87
1998	Chun Lee-Kyung, S. Kor.	1:42.776
2002	Yang Yang (A), CHN	1:36.391

1500 meters

Year		Time
2002	Ko Gi-Hyun, S. Kor.	2:31.581

3000-m Relay

Year		Time	
1992	Canada	.4:36.62	
1994	South Korea	.4:26.64	**WR**
1998	South Korea	.4:16.260	**WR**
2002	South Korea	.4:12.793	**WR**

Athletes with Winter and Summer Medals

Only three athletes have won medals in both the Winter and Summer Olympics:
Eddie Eagan, USA–Light Heavyweight Boxing gold (1920) and Four-man Bobsled gold (1932).
Jacob Tullin Thams, Norway–Ski Jumping gold (1924) and 8-meter Yachting silver (1936).
Christa Luding-Rothenburger, East Germany–Speed Skating gold at 500 meters (1984) and 1,000m (1988), silver at 500m (1988) and bronze at 500m (1992) and Match Sprint Cycling silver (1988). Luding-Rothenburger is the only athlete to ever win medals in both Winter and Summer Games in the same year.

All-Time Leading Medal Winners
MEN

No		Sport	G-S-B
12	Bjorn Dählie, NOR	Cross Country	8-4-0
9	Sixten Jernberg, SWE	Cross Country	4-3-2
7	Clas Thunberg, FIN	Speed Skating	5-1-1
7	Ivar Ballangrud, NOR	Speed Skating	4-2-1
7	Ricco Gross, GER	Biathlon	3-3-1
7	Veikko Hakulinen, FIN	Cross Country	3-3-1
7	Kjetil Andre Aamodt, NOR	Alpine	3-2-2
7	Eero Mäntyranta, FIN	Cross Country	3-2-2
7	Bogdan Musiol, E. Ger/GER	Bobsled	1-5-1
6	Ole Einar Bjoerndalen, NOR	Biathlon	5-1-0
6	Thomas Alsgaard, NOR	Cross Country	4-2-0
6	Gunde Svan, SWE	Cross Country	4-1-1
6	Vegard Ulvang, NOR	Cross Country	3-2-1
6	Johan Gröttumsbråten, NOR	Nordic	3-1-2
6	Wolfgang Hoppe, E. Ger/GER	Bobsled	2-3-1
6	Eugenio Monti, ITA	Bobsled	2-2-2
6	Vladimir Smirnov, USSR/UT/KAZ	X-country	1-4-1
6	Mika Myllylae, FIN	Cross Country	1-1-4
6	Roald Larsen, NOR	Speed Skating	0-2-4
6	Harri Kirvesniemi, FIN	Cross Country	0-0-6
5	**Eric Heiden, USA**	Speed Skating	5-0-0
5	Yevgeny Grishin, USSR	Speed Skating	4-1-0
5	Johann Olav Koss, NOR	Speed Skating	4-1-0
5	Matti Nykänen, FIN	Ski Jumping	4-1-0
5	Aleksandr Tikhonov, USSR	Biathlon	4-1-0
5	Nikolai Zimyatov, USSR	Cross Country	4-1-0
5	Georg Hackl, GER	Luge	3-2-0
5	Samppa Lajunen, FIN	Cross Country	3-2-0
5	Alberto Tomba, ITA	Alpine	3-2-0
5	Marc Gagnon, CAN	ST Sp. Skating	3-0-2
5	Harald Grönningen, NOR	Cross Country	2-3-0
5	Frank Luck, GER	Biathlon	2-3-0
5	Pål Tyldum, NOR	Cross Country	2-3-0
5	Sven Fischer, GER	Biathlon	2-2-1
5	Knut Johannesen, NOR	Speed Skating	2-2-1
5	Lasse Kjus, NOR	Alpine	1-3-1
5	Peter Angerer, W. Ger/GER	Biathlon	1-2-2
5	Juha Mieto, FIN	Cross Country	1-2-2
5	Fritz Feierabend, SWI	Bobsled	0-3-2
5	Rintje Ritsma, NED	Speed Skating	0-2-3

WOMEN

No		Sport	G-S-B
10	Raisa Smetanina, USSR/UT	Cross Country	4-5-1
9	Lyubov Egorova, UT/RUS	Cross Country	6-3-0
9	Larissa Lazutina, UT/RUS	Cross Country	5-3-1
9	Stefania Belmondo, ITA	Cross Country	2-3-4
8	Galina Kulakova, USSR	Cross Country	4-2-2
8	Karin (Enke) Kania, E. Ger	Speed Skating	3-4-1
8	Gunda Neimann-Stirnemann, GER	Speed Skating	3-4-1
8	Ursula Disl, GER	Biathlon	2-4-2
7	Claudia Pechstein, GER	Speed Skating	4-1-2
7	Marja-Liisa (Hämäläinen) Kirvesniemi, FIN	Cross Country	3-0-4

No		Sport	G-S-B	No		Sport	G-S-B
7	Elena Valbe, UT/RUS	Cross Country	3-0-4	5	Anfisa Reztsova, USSR/UT	CC/Biathlon	3-1-1
7	Andrea (Mitscherlich,			5	Vreni Schneider, SWI	Alpine	3-1-1
	Schöne) Ehrig, E. Ger	Speed Skating	1-5-1	5	Katja Seizinger, GER	Alpine	3-0-2
6	Lydia Skoblikova, USSR	Speed Skating	6-0-0	5	Helena Takalo, FIN	Cross Country	1-3-1
6	**Bonnie Blair, USA**	Speed Skating	5-0-1	5	Bente (Martinsen) Skari, NOR	Cross Country	1-2-2
6	Manuela Di Centa, ITA	Cross Country	2-2-2	5	Alevtina Kolchina, USSR	Cross Country	1-1-3
5	Lee-Kyung Chun, S. Kor	ST Sp. Skating	4-0-1	5	Yang Yang (S), CHN	ST Sp. Skating	0-4-1
5	Olga Danilova, RUS	Cross Country	3-2-0	5	Anita Moen, NOR	Cross Country	0-3-2

Games Medaled In

MEN–**Aamodt** (1992,94,2002); **Alsgaard** (1994,98,2002); **Angerer** (1980,84,88); **Ballangrud** (1928,32,36); **Bjoerndalen** (1998,2002); **Dählie** (1992,94,98); **Feierabend** (1936,48,52); **Fischer** (1994,98,2002); **Gagnon** (1994,98,2002); **Grishin** (1956,60,64); **Gross** (1992,94,98,2002); **Gröttumsbråten** (1924,28,32); **Grönningen** (1960,64,68); **Hackl** (1988,92,94,98,2002) **Hakulinen** (1952,56,60); **Heiden** (1980); **Hoppe** (1984,88,92,94); **Jernberg** (1956,60,64); **Johannesen** (1956,60,64); **Kirvesniemi** (1980,84,92,94,98); **Kjus** (1994,98,2002); **Koss** (1992,94); **Lajunen** (1998,2002);**Larsen** (1924,28); **Luck** (1994,98,2002); **Mäntyranta** (1960,64,68); **Mieto** (1976,80,84); **Monti** (1956,60,64,68); **Musiol** (1980,84,88,92); **Myllylae** (1994,98); **Nykänen** (1984,88); **Ritsma** (1994,98); **Smirnov** (1988,92,94,98); **Svan** (1984,88); **Thunberg** (1924,28); **Tikhonov** (1968,72,76,80); **Tomba** (1988,92,94); **Tyldum** (1968,72,76); **Ulvang** (1988,92,94); **Zimyatov** (1980,84).

WOMEN–**Belmondo** (1992,94,98,2002); **Blair** (1988,92,94); **Chun** (1994,98); **Danilova** (1998,2002); **Di Centa** (1992,94); **Disl** (1992,94,98,2002); **Egorova** (1992,94); **Ehrig** (1976,80,84,88); **Kania** (1980,84,88); **Kirvesniemi** (1984,88,94); **Kolchina** (1956,64,68); **Kulakova** (1968,72,76,80); **Lazutina** (1992,94,98,2002); **Moen** (1994,98,2002); **Niemann-Stirnemann** (1992,94,98); **Pechstein** (1992,94,98,2002); **Reztsova** (1988,92,94); **Schneider** (1988,92,94); **Seizinger** (1992,94,98); **Skari** (1998,2002); **Skoblikova** (1960,64); **Smetanina** (1976,80,84,88,92); **Takalo** (1972,76,80); **Valbe** (1992,94,98); **Yang** (1998,2002).

Most Gold Medals

MEN

No		Sport	G-S-B	No		Sport	G-S-B
8	Bjorn Dählie, NOR	Cross Country	8-4-0	4	Thomas Wassberg, SWE	Cross Country	4-0-0
5	Clas Thunberg, FIN	Speed Skating	5-1-1				
5	Ole Einar Bjoerndalen, NOR	Biathlon	5-1-0			**WOMEN**	
5	**Eric Heiden, USA**	Speed Skating	5-0-0	No		Sport	G-S-B
4	Sixten Jernberg, SWE	Cross Country	4-3-2	6	Lyubov Egorova, UT/RUS	Cross Country	6-3-0
4	Ivar Ballangrud, NOR	Speed Skating	4-2-1	6	Lydia Skoblikova, USSR	Speed Skating	6-0-0
4	Thomas Alsgaard, NOR	Cross Country	4-2-0	5	Larissa Lanina, USSR/UT	Cross Country	4-5-1
4	Gunde Svan, SWE	Cross Country	4-1-1	4	Galina Kulakova, USSR	Cross Country	4-2-2
4	Yevgeny Grishin, USSR	Speed Skating	4-1-0	4	Claudia Pechstein, GER	ST Sp. Skating	4-1-2
4	Johann Olav Koss, NOR	Speed Skating	4-1-0	4	Lee-Kyung Chun, S. Kor.	ST Sp. Skating	4-0-1
4	Matti Nykänen, FIN	Ski Jumping	4-1-0				
4	Aleksandr Tikhonov, USSR	Biathlon	4-1-0				
4	Nikolai Zimyatov, USSR	Cross Country	4-1-0				

All-Time Leading USA Medalists
MEN

No		Sport	G-S-B	No		Sport	G-S-B
5	Eric Heiden	Speed Skating	5-0-0	2	Terry McDermott	Speed Skating	1-1-0
3*	Irving Jaffee	Speed Skating	3-0-0	2	Dick Meredith	Ice Hockey	1-1-0
3	Pat Martin	Bobsled	1-2-0	2	Tommy Moe	Alpine	1-1-0
3	John Heaton	Bobsled/Skeleton	0-2-1	2	Weldy Olson	Ice Hockey	1-1-0
2	Dick Button	Figure Skating	2-0-0	2	Derek Parra	Speed Skating	1-1-0
2†	Eddie Eagan	Boxing/Bobsled	2-0-0	2	Dick Rodenheiser	Ice Hockey	1-1-0
2	Billy Fiske	Bobsled	2-0-0	2	Ross Powers	Snowboarding	1-0-1
2	Cliff Gray	Bobsled	2-0-0	2	Stan Benham	Bobsled	0-2-0
2	Jack Shea	Speed Skating	2-0-0	2	Herb Drury	Ice Hockey	0-2-0
2	Apolo Anton Ohno	ST Sp. Skating	1-1-0	2	Eric Flaim	Sp. Skate/ST Sp. Skate	0-2-0
2	Billy Cleary	Ice Hockey	1-1-0	2	Bode Miller	Alpine	0-2-0
2	Jennison Heaton	Bobsled/Skeleton	1-1-0	2	Frank Synott	Ice Hockey	0-2-0
2	David Jenkins	Figure Skating	1-1-0	2	John Garrison	Ice Hockey	0-1-1
2	John Mayasich	Ice Hockey	1-1-0				

*Jaffee is generally given credit for a third gold medal in the 10,000-meter Speed Skating race of 1928. He had the fastest time before the race was cancelled due to thawing ice. The IOC considers the race unofficial.

†Eagan won the light heavyweight boxing title at the 1920 Summer Games in Antwerp and the four-man Bobsled at the 1932 Winter Games in Lake Placid. He is the only athlete ever to win gold medals in both the Winter and Summer Olympics.

WOMEN

No		Sport	G-S-B	No		Sport	G-S-B
6	Bonnie Blair	Speed Skating	5-0-1	2	Carol Heiss	Figure Skating	1-1-0
4	Cathy Turner	ST Sp. Skating	2-1-1	2	Katie King	Ice Hockey	1-1-0
4	Dianne Holum	Speed Skating	1-2-1	2	Shelley Looney	Ice Hockey	1-1-0
3	Chris Witty	Speed Skating	1-1-1	2	Sue Merz	Ice Hockey	1-1-0
3	Sheila Young	Speed Skating	1-1-1	2	A.J. Mleczko	Ice Hockey	1-1-0
3	Leah Poulos Mueller	Speed Skating	0-3-0	2	Tara Mounsey	Ice Hockey	1-1-0
3	Beatrix Loughran	Figure Skating	0-2-1	2	Diann Roffe-Steinrotter	Alpine	1-1-0
3	Amy Peterson	ST Sp. Skating	0-2-1	2	Angela Ruggiero	Ice Hockey	1-1-0
2	Andrea Mead Lawrence	Alpine	2-0-0	2	Picabo Street	Alpine	1-1-0
2	Tenley Albright	Figure Skating	1-1-0	2	Sarah Teuting	Ice Hockey	1-1-0
2	Chris Bailey	Ice Hockey	1-1-0	2	Anne Henning	Speed Skating	1-0-1
2	Laurie Baker	Ice Hockey	1-1-0	2	Penny Pitou	Alpine	0-2-0
2	Karyn Bye	Ice Hockey	1-1-0	2	Nancy Kerrigan	Figure Skating	0-1-1
2	Sara DeCosta	Ice Hockey	1-1-0	2	Michelle Kwan	Figure Skating	0-1-1
2	Tricia Dunn	Ice Hockey	1-1-0	2	Jean Saubert	Alpine	0-1-1
2	Gretchen Fraser	Alpine	1-1-0	2	Nikki Ziegelmeyer	ST Sp. Skating	0-1-1
2	Cammi Granato	Ice Hockey	1-1-0	2	Jennifer Rodriguez	Speed Skating	0-0-2

Note: The term ST Sp. Skating refers to Short Track (or pack) Speed Skating.

All-Time Medal Standings, 1924-2002

All-time Winter Games medal standings, according to *The Golden Book of the Olympic Games*. Medal counts include figure skating medals (1908 and '20) and hockey medals (1920) awarded at the Summer Games. National medal standings for the Winter and Summer Games are not recognized by the IOC.

		G	S	B	Total			G	S	B	Total
1	Norway	94	94	75	263	25	Czech Republic (1998–)	2	1	2	5
2	Soviet Union (1956-88)	78	57	59	194		Kazakhstan (1994–)	1	2	2	5
3	**United States**	69	72	52	193		Belgium	1	1	3	5
4	Austria	41	57	64	162		Bulgaria	1	1	3	5
5	Finland	42	51	49	142		Belarus (1994–)	0	2	3	5
6	Germany (1928-36, 52-64, 92–)	47	46	32	125	30	Croatia	3	1	0	4
7	East Germany (1968-88)	43	39	36	118		Spain	3	0	1	4
8	Sweden	39	30	39	108		Australia	2	0	2	4
9	Switzerland	32	33	38	103		Yugoslavia (1924-88)	0	3	1	4
10	Canada	31	28	37	96		Slovenia	0	0	4	4
11	Italy	31	31	27	89	35	Estonia	1	1	1	3
12	France	22	22	28	72		Ukraine (1994–)	1	1	1	3
13	Netherlands	22	28	19	69		Slovakia (1992–)	0	0	3	3
14	Russia (1994–)	27	20	11	58	38	Luxembourg	0	2	0	2
15	West Germany (1968-88)	18	20	19	57		North Korea	0	1	1	2
16	Japan	8	10	13	31	40	Uzbekistan (1994–)	1	0	0	1
17	Great Britain	8	4	14	26		Denmark	0	1	0	1
	Czechoslovakia (1924-92)	2	8	16	26		New Zealand	0	1	0	1
19	Unified Team (1992)	9	6	8	23		Romania	0	0	1	1
20	China	2	12	8	22						
21	South Korea	11	5	4	20	**Combined totals**		**G**	**S**	**B**	**Total**
22	Liechtenstein	2	2	5	9	Germany/E. Ger/W. Ger		108	105	87	300
23	Poland	1	2	3	6	USSR/UT/Russia		114	83	78	275
	Hungary	0	2	4	6						

Notes: Athletes from the USSR participated in the Winter Games from 1956-88, returned as the Unified Team in 1992 after the breakup of the Soviet Union (in 1991) and then competed for the independent republics of Belarus, Kazakhstan, Russia, Ukraine, Uzbekistan and three others in 1994. Yugoslavia divided into Croatia and Bosnia-Herzegovina in 1992, while Czechoslovakia split into Slovakia and the Czech Republic in 1993.

Germany was barred from the Olympics in 1924 and 1948 as an aggressor nation in both World Wars I and II. Divided into East and West Germany after WWII, both countries competed under one flag from 1952-64, then as separate teams from 1968-88. Germany was reunified in 1990.

Soccer

David Beckham joined Ronaldo and Zinedine Zidane on a star-studded roster when Manchester United sold him to Real Madrid for $41 million.

AP/Wide World Photos

Tough Losses

The WUSA folds and Team USA loses in the semis, ending the World Cup careers of a key group of veterans.

Gerry Brown
is co-editor of the ESPN Sports Almanac

Winter came early for women's soccer in the United States in 2003.

The spring had sprung with such optimism. The Women's United Soccer Association, a growing women's professional league with teams comprised of some of the world's best players, began its third season in April and by May word came that the Women's World Cup would be returning to the States for the second straight quadrennial due to the SARS scare in Asia.

The U.S. women's national team, the defending World Cup champions, were expecting big things in 2003 as it was and now, with a home-field advantage, a repeat championship seemed to be a good bet.

The WUSA season culminated on a flawless, sunny summer day in San Diego with a dramatic win by Mia Hamm's Washington Freedom in the league's championship game, the Founders' Cup III.

Hamm is the league's marquee player but in the Freedom's 2-1 overtime win over Atlanta in the Founders' Cup, the Freedom got both goals from rising national team superstar Abby Wambach.

Just a few days after the thrilling women's soccer showcase, Clive Charles, a fixture for years in U.S. national team soccer as well as the men's and women's college game, died following an extended fight with prostate cancer.

Charles, the U.S. Olympic team coach, was also the longtime coach of both the men's and women's programs at the University of Portland and after eight trips to the Final Four, had just led Portland's Lady Pilots to the school's first national title at the NCAA Division I championship in December 2002.

For the dozens of WUSA players from around the world planning to represent their countries in the upcoming World Cup, the end of the season

AP/Wide World Photos

*Reigning World Player of the Year **Mia Hamm** was looking for answers in the aftermath of the U.S. team's 3-0 loss to Germany in the semifinal round of the 2003 Women's World Cup.*

gave them time to prepare for the fast growing international event.

Then just five days before the start of the fourth Women's World Cup, the WUSA's board of governors abruptly announced that they planned to suspend operations immediately because of a $20 million shortfall from a crippling lack of corporate sponsorship.

The recent downward trend in the league's attendance figures and rock-bottom television ratings didn't help. Average league attendance fell from more than 8,000 the first season to about 6,700 a game in 2003.

Reeling from the bad news the U.S. national team, whose entire roster played in the WUSA and was now effectively laid off, began the defense of its World Cup championship.

Things started fine. The U.S. opened group play with a 3-1 win over scrappy Sweden. That was followed by shutout wins over Nigeria and North Korea, propelling Team USA into the quarterfinals without a loss or tie and having allowed just one goal in three games.

The 1-0 quarterfinal win against Norway was a symbolic passing of the torch from Hamm to players like Wambach who dominated the first half, scoring the only goal of the game.

AP/Wide World Photos

*Fourteen-year-old American soccer phenom **Freddy Adu** starred for the Under-17 U.S. national team at the 2003 FIFA Under-17 World Championship.*

Everything appeared on track for another World Cup title entering the team's first real test in their semifinal match with high-scoring Germany. It was a test the team failed, 3-0, but not by as much as the final grade indicated.

Germany got a first-half goal off a corner kick and the US was trailing for the first time in the tournament.

The team responded and went on the attack but was unable to score. As time grew shorter the desperation grew and Germany counter attacked well, scoring two goals late in the match.

On the field after the loss, the team, with at least five players who won't be back in 2007 for the next World Cup (including Hamm), was stunned and plenty of tears mixed with all the sweat they left on the field.

But as is often the case, out of disappointment comes hope and with a win over continental rival Canada in the Cup's third-place game and the Summer Olympics less than a year away comes a real chance at redemption for Team USA on the international stage.

Also, talk of reviving the WUSA has already begun and before long the winter will end and the flawless, sunny days will return, signaling another spring.

The Ten Biggest
Stories of the Year in Soccer

10 European soccer powers and Serie A rivals, AC Milan and Juventus, meet in an all-Italian final at the 2003 UEFA Champions League at Old Trafford. Depending on how one looks at it, the result was either a brilliant defensive battle or a complete snoozer. No goals were scored in 90 minutes of regulation or in the 30 minutes of overtime. The game was finally decided on penalty kicks as AC Milan prevailed on Andriy Shevchenko's clutch kick.

9 UCLA beats cross-state and Pac-10 conference rival Stanford, 1-0, for the third time in 2002, winning the 2002 NCAA Men's College Cup on a goal by Bruin defender Aaron Lopez in the game's 89th minute.

8 Cameroon midfielder Marc-Vivien Foe, 28, collapses in the heat and dies in a semifinal match against Colombia in the FIFA Confederations Cup. Cameroon won the game but went on to lose to host-team France, 1-0, in the final.

7 Portland beats West Coast Conference rival and defending national champions Santa Clara, 2-1, behind two scores, including a golden goal from leading scorer Christine Sinclair, in two overtimes at the 2002 NCAA Women's College Cup. The Lady Pilots overcame the loss of senior starting goalkeeper Lauren Arase, who was kneed in the head four minutes into the first overtime.

6 The Women's World Cup, originally set to be played in China in 2003, is moved to the United States in the aftermath of the SARS (Severe Acute Respiratory Syndrome) outbreak in Asia. The 2007 Women's World Cup will go to China instead.

5 England's marquee team Manchester United sells star midfielder, England national team captain and international heart throb David Beckham to Spanish club Real Madrid for a $41 million transfer fee. Beckham joins all-world players Ronaldo, Roberto Carlos, Luis Figo and Zinedine Zidane in Madrid.

4 American soccer prodigy Freddy Adu has a big year. He earns his U.S. citizenship in February, signs a $1 million endorsement deal with Nike in May, turns 14 years old in June, and makes his debut with the U.S. Under-20 national team in October.

3 Faced with a bleak financial outlook, organizers of the eight-team Women's United Soccer Association (WUSA), the world's top women's professional soccer league, decide to cease operations following the 2003 season and on the eve of the Women's World Cup.

2   Germany eliminates the defending champion United States, 3-0, in the semifinals and then goes on to win its first Women's World Cup with a 2-1 win over Sweden in overtime. Germany is led by forward Birgit Prinz who wins the Golden Ball Award as tournament MVP, with seven goals and five assists, 2003 WUSA MVP midfielder Maren Meinert who tallies four goals and seven assists and goalkeeper Silke Rottenberg.

1   The United States women's national team, looking to repeat as World Cup champion, falls short losing to Germany in the semifinals. The team bounces back to beat Canada, 3-1, in the third-place game but it is a disappointing finish, especially for team veterans like Brandi Chastain, Joy Fawcett, Julie Foudy, Mia Hamm and Kristine Lilly who plan to retire from soccer before the next World Cup is held in 2007.

The "United" States Tour

England's Manchester United finished a 2003 four-game U.S. tour with a perfect record of 4-0. Manchester's game with Celtic established a record crowd at the year-old Seahawks Stadium in Seattle. A sellout record crowd of over 79,000, the largest ever at a soccer game at Giants Stadium, witnessed the match with Juventus.

Date	Result	Attendance
July 21	def. Juventus, 4-1	79,005
July 22	def. Celtic, 4-0	66,722
July 27	def. Club America, 3-1	57,365
Aug. 3	def. FC Barcelona, 3-1	68,396
Average attendance: 67,872		

Top of the World

The 2003 Women's World Cup saw some high scoring games including 25 goals from Cup winners Germany, with seven coming from Golden Ball winner Birgit Prinz alone. Here's a look at the all-time list of Women's World Cup goal scoring leaders through 2003.

Player	Years Played	Goals
Michelle Akers, USA	91,95,99	12
Sun Wen, CHN	91,95,99,03	11
Ann Kristin Aarones, NOR	95,99	10
Heidi Mohr, GER	91,95	10
B. Wiegmann, GER	91,95,99,03	10
Birgit Prinz, GER	1995,99,03	9
Mia Hamm USA	91,95,99,03	8
Tiffeny Milbrett, USA	91, 95, 99, 03	8

2002-2003
Season in Review

ESPN
SPORTS ALMANAC

2003 Women's World Cup Tournament

The FIFA Women's World Cup is held every four years to determine the best women's national team in the world. In 2003 it was moved from planned host nation China to the United States due to the SARS outbreak in Asia. Contested Sept. 20-Oct. 12, 2003 for the fourth time since its inception in 1991.

First Round

Round robin; each team played the other three teams in its group once. Note that three points were awarded for a win and one point for a tie. (*) indicates team advanced to second round.

Group A	W	L	T	Pts	GF	GA
USA	3	0	0	9	11	1
Sweden	2	1	0	6	5	3
North Korea	1	2	0	3	3	4
Nigeria	0	3	0	0	0	11

Results

Date	Site (attendance)	Result
Sept. 20	Philadelphia (24,347)	North Korea 3, Nigeria 0
Sept. 21	Wash., D.C. (35,000)	USA 3, Sweden 1
Sept. 25	Philadelphia (31,553)	Sweden 1, North Korea 0
Sept. 25	Philadelphia (31,553)	USA 5, Nigeria 0
Sept. 28	Columbus (22,828)	Sweden 3, Nigeria 0
Sept. 28	Columbus (22,828)	USA 3, North Korea 0

Group B	W	L	T	Pts	GF	GA
Brazil	2	0	1	7	8	2
Norway	2	1	0	6	10	5
France	1	1	1	4	2	3
South Korea	0	3	0	0	1	11

Results

Date	Site (attendance)	Result
Sept. 20	Philadelphia (13,486)	Norway 2, France 0
Sept. 21	Wash., D.C. (34,144)	Brazil 3, South Korea 0
Sept. 24	Wash., D.C. (15,490)	Brazil 4, Norway 1
Sept. 24	Wash., D.C. (16,316)	France 1, South Korea 0
Sept. 27	Foxboro (14,356)	Norway 7, South Korea 1
Sept. 27	Wash., D.C. (17,618)	Brazil 1, France 1

Group C	W	L	T	Pts	GF	GA
Germany	3	0	0	9	13	2
Canada	2	1	0	6	7	5
Japan	1	2	0	3	7	6
Argentina	0	3	0	0	1	15

Results

Date	Site (attendance)	Result
Sept. 20	Columbus (16,340)	Germany 4, Canada 1
Sept. 20	Columbus (16,404)	Japan 6, Argentina 0
Sept. 24	Columbus (15,490)	Germany 3, Japan 0
Sept. 24	Columbus (15,529)	Canada 3, Argentina 0
Sept. 27	Foxboro (14,356)	Canada 3, Japan 1
Sept. 27	Wash., D.C. (17,618)	Germany 6, Argentina 1

Group D	W	L	T	Pts	GF	GA
China	2	0	1	7	3	1
Russia	2	1	0	6	5	2
Ghana	1	2	0	3	2	5
Australia	0	2	1	1	3	5

Results

Date	Site (attendance)	Result
Sept. 21	Carson (8,500)	Russia 2, Australia 1
Sept. 21	Carson (10,027)	China 1, Ghana 0
Sept. 25	Carson (13,929)	Russia 3, Ghana 0
Sept. 25	Carson (13,329)	China 1, Australia 1
Sept. 28	Portland (19,132)	Ghana 2, Australia 1
Sept. 28	Portland (19,132)	China 1, Russia 0

Quarterfinals

Date	Site (attendance)	Result
Oct. 1	Foxboro (25,103)	USA 1, Norway 0
Oct. 1	Foxboro (25,103)	Sweden 2, Brazil 1
Oct. 2	Portland (20,021)	Germany 7, Russia 1
Oct. 2	Portland (20,021)	Canada 1, China 0

Semifinals

Date	Site (attendance)	Result
Oct. 5	Portland (27,623)	Germany 3, USA 0
Oct. 5	Portland (27,623)	Sweden 2, Canada 1

Third Place

Date	Site (attendance)	Result
Oct. 11	Carson (25,253)	USA 3, Canada 1

Final

Date	Site (attendance)	Result
Oct. 12	Carson (26,137)	Germany 2, Sweden 1 OT

Goals: Hanna Ljungberg, SWE (41st minute); Maren Meinert, GER (46th); Nia Kuenzer, GER (98th).

Top Scorers
Goals Scored

	Goals
Birgit Prinz, Germany	7
Kerstin Garefrekes, Germany	4
Katia, Brazil	4
Maren Meinert, Germany	4
Nine players tied at	3

Assists

	Assists
Maren Meinert, Germany	7
Mia Hamm, USA	5
Birgit Prinz, Germany	5
Victoria Svensson, Sweden	4
Ten players tied at	2

Most Valuable Player

Officially, the Golden Ball Award. Second and third place finishers win the Silver and Bronze Ball Awards, respectively.

1   Birgit Prinz, Germany
2   Victoria Svensson, Sweden
3   Maren Meinert, Germany

FIFA Top 50 World Rankings

FIFA announced a new monthly world ranking system on Aug. 13, 1993 designed to "provide a constant international comparison of national team performances." The rankings are based on a mathematical formula that weighs strength of schedule, importance of matches and goals scored for and against. Games considered include World Cup qualifying and final rounds, Continental championship qualifying and final rounds, and friendly matches.

The formula was altered slightly in January 1999. Now the rankings annually take into account a team's seven best matches of the last eight years, thereby favoring some teams that have been consistent over a long period of time but that may have stumbled just recently. At the end of the year, FIFA designates a Team of the Year. Teams of the Year so far have been Germany (1993), Brazil (1994-2000, 2002) and France (2001). The USA reached their highest-ever ranking (8th) in Sept. 2002. Serbia & Montenegro was formerly listed as Yugoslavia.

2002

		Points	2001 Rank			Points	2001 Rank			Points	2001 Rank
1	Brazil	.856	3	18	Paraguay	.679	13	35	Morocco	.621	36
2	France	.787	1	19	Serbia & Montenegro	.677	11	36	Slovenia	.620	25
3	Spain	.779	7	20	South Korea	.669	42	37	Colombia	.617	5
4	Germany	.761	12	21	Costa Rica	.652	30	38	Saudi Arabia	.608	31
5	Argentina	.751	2	22	Japan	.650	34	39	Egypt	.592	41
6	Netherlands	.746	8		Russia	.650	21	40	Honduras	.591	25
7	England	.734	10	24	Romania	.649	15	41	Tunisia	.586	28
8	Mexico	.732	9		Sweden	.649	16	42	Bulgaria	.582	51
9	Turkey	.729	23	26	Norway	.648	25	43	Finland	.580	46
10	**USA**	.723	24	27	Senegal	.646	65	44	Switzerland	.576	45
11	Portugal	.710	4	28	Uruguay	.643	22	45	Ukraine	.575	45
12	Denmark	.707	17	29	Nigeria	.642	39	46	Israel	.568	49
13	Italy	.705	6	30	South Africa	.636	34	47	Trinidad and Tobago	.567	32
14	Ireland	.697	17	31	Ecuador	.634	37	48	Greece	.563	57
15	Czech Republic	.687	14	32	Croatia	.629	19	49	New Zealand	.561	83
16	Cameroon	.685	38	33	Iran	.628	29	50	Australia	.557	48
17	Belgium	.682	20		Poland	.628	33				

2003 (as of Oct. 22)

		Points	2002 Rank			Points	2002 Rank			Points	2002 Rank
1	Brazil	.854	1	18	Sweden	.681	24	35	Ecuador	.624	31
2	France	.827	2	19	Costa Rica	.680	21	36	Colombia	.622	37
3	Spain	.777	3	20	Croatia	.664	32	37	Norway	.620	26
4	Argentina	.747	5	21	Romania	.657	24	38	Morocco	.617	35
5	Netherlands	.746	6	22	South Korea	.654	28	39	Bulgaria	.615	42
6	England	.745	7		Uruguay	.654	28	40	Egypt	.614	39
7	Germany	.744	4	24	Paraguay	.647	18	41	Finland	.610	43
8	Italy	.742	13	25	Japan	.645	22	42	Iran	.599	33
	Turkey	.742	9	26	Greece	.640	48	43	Switzerland	.592	44
	Mexico	.742	8		Poland	.640	33	44	Honduras	.586	40
11	Czech Republic	.739	15	28	Russia	.637	22	45	Tunisia	.576	41
12	**USA**	.731	10	29	Slovenia	.636	36	46	Jamaica	.573	51
13	Cameroon	.711	16	30	Saudi Arabia	.634	38	47	Israel	.566	46
14	Denmark	.707	12	31	South Africa	.630	30	48	Zimbabwe	.562	56
15	Ireland	.705	14	32	Nigeria	.627	29	49	Slovakia	.560	55
16	Belgium	.696	17		Serbia & Montenegro	.627	19	50	Kuwait	.556	83
17	Portugal	.686	11	34	Senegal	.625	27				

FIFA Women's World Rankings

As part of its growing recognition of women's soccer FIFA began ranking the women's national teams in 2002 following the inaugural FIFA Women's U19 World Championship in Canada. The rankings are currently released four times a year and are calculated in a similar manner to the men's rankings. The first women's international was held on April 17, 1971 (France vs. the Netherlands). The Top 30 teams are listed below.

2003 (as of Oct. 24)

		Points	2002 Rank			Points	2002 Rank			Points	2002 Rank
1	Germany	2201	3	11	Canada	1911	14	21	New Zealand	1760	21
2	**USA**	2166	1	12	Russia	1897	11	22	Chinese Taipei	1746	19
3	Norway	2131	2	13	England	1861	12	23	Czech Republic	1741	24
4	Sweden	2095	13	14	Japan	1841	13	24	Nigeria	1738	23
5	China	2064	4	15	Netherlands	1815	15	25	South Korea	1721	28
6	Brazil	2042	6	16	Australia	1810	15	26	Hungary	1717	25
7	North Korea	1994	7	17	Iceland	1796	18	27	Belgium	1715	26
8	Denmark	1981	8	18	Ukraine	1778	17	28	Switzerland	1697	29
9	France	1967	9	19	Finland	1773	20	29	Serbia & Montenegro	1693	27
10	Italy	1947	10	20	Spain	1767	22	30	Scotland	1679	32

U.S. Women's National Team
2003 Schedule and Results

Through Oct. 11, 2003. Games in **bold type** are World Cup matches.

Date		Result	USA Goals	Site
Jan. 12	Japan	T, 0-0	—	San Diego
Jan. 23	Norway	W, 3-1	Bryan, Milbrett, O'Reilly	Yiwu, China
Jan. 26	China	L, 0-2	—	Wuhan , China
Jan. 29	Germany	W, 1-0	Hawkins	Shanghai, China
Feb. 16	Iceland	W, 1-0	Hamm	Charleston, S.C.
Mar. 14	Canada	T, 1-1	Wagner	Olhao, Portugal
Mar. 16	Norway	W, 1-0	MacMillan	Ferreiras, Portugal
Mar. 18	Sweden	T, 1-1	Wagner	Real San Antonio, Portugal
Mar. 20	China	W, 2-0	MacMillan, Hamm	Loule, Portugal
Apr. 26	Canada	W, 6-1	MacMillan (4), Foudy, Lilly	Washington, D.C.
May 17	England	W, 6-0	Parlow (4), Hamm, Milbrett	Birmingham, Ala.
June 14	Ireland	W, 5-0	O'Reilly, Foudy, Wambach (2), Hamm	Salt Lake City, Utah
July 13	Brazil	W, 1-0	Milbrett	New Orleans
Sept. 1	Costa Rica	W, 5-0	Parlow, Wagner, Hamm, Boxx, Wambach	Carson, Calif.
Sept. 7	Mexico	W, 5-0	Boxx, Wambach, Chastain, Hamm, Wagner	San Jose, Calif.
Sept. 21	**Sweden**	W, 3-1	Lilly, Parlow, Boxx	Washington
Sept. 25	**Nigeria**	W, 5-0	Hamm (2), Parlow, Wambach, Foudy	Philadelphia
Sept. 28	**North Korea**	W, 3-0	Wambach, Reddick (2)	Columbus, Ohio
Oct. 1	**Norway**	W, 1-0	Wambach	Foxboro, Mass.
Oct. 5	**Germany**	L, 0-3	—	Portland, Ore.
Oct. 11	**Canada**	W, 3-1	Lilly, Boxx, Milbrett	Carson, Calif.

Overall record: 16-2-3.
Team Scoring: Goals for–53; Goals against–11.

2003 U.S. Women's National Team Statistics

Individual records through Oct. 11, 2003. Note that the column labeled "Career C/G" refers to career caps and goals.

Forwards	GP	GS	Mins	G	A	Pts	Career C/G
Mia Hamm	16	14	1263	8	7	23	245/144
Shannon MacMillan	12	6	539	6	3	15	164/58
Tiffeny Milbrett	16	6	701	4	1	9	198/99
Heather O'Reilly	10	1	285	2	0	4	18/3
Cindy Parlow	18	6	1064	7	1	15	134/64
Abby Wambach	12	8	778	7	0	14	20/12

Defenders	GP	GS	Mins	G	A	Pts	Career C/G
Jenny Benson	5	3	270	0	0	0	8/0
Kylie Bivens	7	4	399	0	0	0	7/0
Thori Bryan	4	3	278	1	0	2	63/1
Brandi Chastain	14	13	1080	1	1	3	179/30
Joy Fawcett	19	18	1575	0	1	1	223/26
Heather Mitts	1	0	45	0	0	0	4/0
Christie Pearce	15	13	1125	0	1	1	98/4
Catherine Reddick	17	12	1239	2	1	5	42/3
Danielle Slaton	6	1	207	0	0	0	37/1
Kate Sobrero	20	19	1530	0	0	0	93/0

Midfielders	GP	GS	Mins	G	A	Pts	Career C/G
Shannon Boxx	7	7	582	4	0	8	7/4
Lorrie Fair	7	6	436	0	0	0	113/7
Julie Foudy	17	16	1237	3	7	13	237/42
Devvyn Hawkins	2	1	92	0	0	0	9/1
Angela Hucles	15	6	698	0	0	0	20/1
Jena Kluegel	4	1	172	0	0	0	24/1
Kristine Lilly	17	16	1304	3	3	9	261/93
Tiffany Roberts	13	7	669	0	2	2	82/6
Lindsay Tarpley	7	2	325	0	0	0	6/0
Aly Wagner	19	13	1140	4	7	15	53/12

Goalkeepers	GP	GS	Mins	W-L-T	SO	GAA	Career Caps
LaKeysia Beene	5	3	270	2-1-0	0	0.67	17
Siri Mullinix	7	3	380	1-0-3	1	0.24	38
Briana Scurry	15	15	1240	13-1-0	7	0.58	127

Yellow Cards: Parlow 2, Benson, Fair, Hawkins, Lilly, Milbrett, Roberts, Scurry, Wagner, Wambach.
Red Cards: none.
Head coach: April Heinrichs
General Manager: Nils Krumins

U.S. Men's National Team
2003 Schedule and Results

Through Oct. 30, 2003. Games in **bold** type are Gold Cup matches. (*) denotes FIFA Confederations Cup match.

Date		Result	USA Goals	Site
Jan. 18	Canada	W, 4-0	Bocanegra, Mathis, Klein and Ralston	Ft. Lauderdale, Fla.
Feb. 8	Argentina	L, 0-1	—	Miami, Fla.
Feb. 12	Jamaica	W, 2-1	Bocanegra, Klein	Kingston, Jamaica
Mar. 29	Venezuela	W, 2-0	Kirovski, Donovan	Seattle, Wash.
May 8	Mexico	T, 0-0	—	Houston, Texas
May 26	Wales	W, 2-0	Donovan, Lewis	San Jose, Calif.
June 8	New Zealand	W, 2-1	Klein, Kirovski	Richmond, Va.
June 19	Turkey*	L, 1-2	Beasley	St. Etienne, France
June 21	Brazil*	L, 0-1	—	Lyon, France
June 23	Cameroon*	T, 0-0	—	Lyon, France
July 6	Paraguay	W, 2-0	Donovan, Stewart	Columbus, Ohio
July 12	**El Salvador**	W, 2-0	Lewis, McBride	Foxboro, Mass.
July 14	**Martinique**	W, 2-0	McBride (2)	Foxboro, Mass.
July 19	**Cuba**	W, 5-0	Donovan (4), Ralston	Foxboro, Mass.
July 23	**Brazil**	L, -1-2 (OT)	Bocanegra	Miami, Fla.
July 26	**Costa Rica**	W, 3-2	Bocanegra, Stewart, Convey	Miami, Fla.

Overall record: 10-4-2. **Team scoring:** Goals For–28; Goals Against–10.

FIFA Under-17 Men's World Championships

Contested for the 10th time since its inception in 1985. Held Aug. 13-30, 2003 in Finland.

First Round

Round robin; each team played the other three teams in its group once. Note that three points were awarded for a win and one point for a tie. (*) indicates team advanced to second round.

Group A	W	L	T	Pts	GF	GA
*Colombia	2	0	1	7	11	2
*Mexico	1	0	2	5	5	3
Finland	1	2	0	3	3	12
China	0	2	1	1	5	7

Group B	W	L	T	Pts	GF	GA
*Argentina	3	0	0	9	5	0
*Costa Rica	1	1	1	4	3	3
Nigeria	1	1	1	4	3	3
Australia	0	3	0	0	1	6

Group C	W	L	T	Pts	GF	GA
*Brazil	2	0	1	7	9	1
*Portugal	1	1	1	4	9	13
Cameroon	0	0	3	3	7	7
Yemen	0	2	1	1	4	8

Group D	W	L	T	Pts	GF	GA
*Spain	2	0	1	7	8	5
*USA	2	1	0	6	8	4
South Korea	1	2	0	3	6	11
Sierra Leone	0	2	1	1	6	8

Quarterfinals

Date	Site	Result
Aug. 23	Helsinki	Colombia 2, Costa Rica 0
Aug. 23	Lahti	Argentina 2, Mexico 0
Aug. 24	Turku	Brazil 3, USA 0
Aug. 24	Tampere	Spain 5, Portugal 2

Semifinals

Date	Site	Result
Aug. 27	Tampere	Brazil 2, Colombia 0
Aug. 27	Helsinki	Spain 3, Argentina 2 OT

Third Place

Date	Site	Result
Aug. 30	Helsinki	Argentina 1, Colombia 1

Final

Date	Site (attendance)	Result
Aug. 30	Helsinki (10,452)	Brazil 1, Spain 0

Leading Goal Scorers

	Goals
Cesc, Spain	5
Carlos Hidalgo, Colombia	5
Curto Manuel, Portugal	5
Abuda, Brazil	4
Freddy Adu, USA	4
Evandro, Brazil	4

Club Team Competition
2002 European/South American Cup

Also known as the Toyota Cup and the Intercontinental Cup; a year-end match for the Club World Championship between the UEFA Champions League (formerly the European Cup) and Copa Libertadores winners. Its winner is generally recognized as the Club World Champion but with the recent advent of FIFA's Club World Championship that could change. However that may be some time off considering the recent starts and stops that FIFA's new club tournament has endured. The next FIFA World Club Championship is scheduled for 2005. The 2003 edition of the European/South American Cup was set to be played between Boca Juniors (Argentina) and AC Milan (Italy).

Final

Dec. 3 at International Stadium, Yokohama, Japan. **Attendance:** 66,070

Real Madrid (Spain) 2 . . . . Olimpia (Paraguay) 0

Scoring: Real Madrid–Ronaldo (14th), Jose Maria Guiterres (84th).

Referee: Carlos Eugenio Simon, Brazil

SOUTH AMERICA

2003 Libertadores Cup

Contested by the league champions of South America's football union. Two-leg Semifinals and two-leg Final; home teams listed first. Winner Boca Juniors of Argentina was to play UEFA Champions League winner AC Milan of Italy in the 2003 Europe/South America Cup in Yokohama, Japan in December.

Final Four: America de Cali (Colombia), Boca Juniors (Argentina), Independiente Medellin (Colombia) and Santos (Brazil).

Semifinals

America de Cali vs. Boca Juniors

Boca Juniors 2 . . . . .America de Cali 0
Boca Juniors 4 . . . . .America de Cali 0
Boca Juniors won 6-0 on aggregate

Independiente Medellin vs. Santos

Santos 1 . . . . .Independiente Medellin 0
Santos 3 . . . . .Independiente Medellin 2
Santos won 4-2 on aggregate

Final

Matches played June 25 in Buenos Aires, Argentina and July 2 in Sao Paulo, Brazil.

Boca Juniors 2 . . . . .Santos 0
Boca Juniors 3 . . . . .Santos 1
Boca Juniors won 5-1 on aggregate

EUROPE

There are two major European club competitions sanctioned by the Union of European Football Associations (UEFA). The constantly evolving **Champions League** is currently a 74-team tournament made up from UEFA member countries. The teams are ranked 1-74 depending on how they finish in their own domestic leagues. UEFA ranks the quality of the 52 European national football associations (from number one Spain to number 52 Kazakhstan) and assigns each association a number weighted by their respective ranking (UEFA calls this number a coefficient). Each team's domestic league finish is then multiplied by the coefficient and the teams are finally ranked (countries can enter a maximum of four teams).

The defending champions Real Madrid and the other 15 highest-ranked teams form Group 1 and are given a direct entry into the League but the remaining 16 teams are determined by dividing teams 17-74 into three groups—Group 2 (teams 17-34), Group 3 (35-50) and Group 4 (51-74). The 24 teams in the lowest Group (Group 4) play two-leg, total goal elimination series. The 12 survivors advance to the Second Qualifying Phase and join the 16 teams from Group 3 to play 14 two-leg, total goal elimination series. The 14 clubs that survive this phase join the 18 teams from Group 2 to play in the Third Qualifying Phase. The winning clubs from the 16 two-leg, total goal elimination series advance to the Champions League for the right to play against the top-ranked 16 teams in Europe.

The 32 teams are separated into eight groups of four and play a round-robin series of home-and-home matches. Starting for the 2003-04 Champions League, the eight group winners and eight group runners-up advance to the next round where they are paired and play two home-and-home matches. Formerly, including the 2002-03 League recapped below, there was a second four-group, four-team group stage where the group winners and runners-up advanced. The eight winners then advance to the quarterfinals where home-and-home series are played through the semi-finals until ultimately a single championship match for the European club championship is held. Winner AC Milan plays Liberatadores Cup champion Boca Juniors of Argentina in the 2003 European/South American Cup in Japan.

The updated **UEFA Cup**, which is basically a combination of the what was known as the Cup Winners' Cup (played between national cup champions) and the old UEFA Cup (sort of a "best of the rest" tournament), is single-elimination throughout and features 121 additional teams plus 24 teams that have been already eliminated from the Champions League.

2002-03 Champions League

Following the first three qualifying phases, the first group phase starts with six-game double round-robin format in eight four-team groups (Sept. 13-Nov. 13); top two teams in each group advance to second group phase (Nov. 26-Mar. 19) where four, four-team groups compete in the same format. Group winners and runners-up advance to the quarterfinals. While the third-place team from each of the eight groups moves to the third round of the UEFA Cup tournament. (*) indicates team advanced to the next round (of the Champions League). Note that in results listing under each table the home team is listed first.

First Group Phase

Group A	W	L	T	GF	GA	Pts
*Arsenal (England)	3	2	1	9	4	10
*Borussia Dortmund (Germany)	3	2	1	8	7	10
Auxerre	2	3	1	4	7	7
PSV	1	2	3	5	8	6

RESULTS: **Sept. 17**–Arsenal 2, Borussia Dortmund 0; Auxerre 0, PSV 0; **Sept. 25**–Borussia Dortmund 2, Auxerre 1; PSV 0, Arsenal 4; **Oct. 2**–Auxerre 0, Arsenal 1; PSV 1, Borussia Dortmund 3; **Oct. 22**–Arsenal 1, Auxerre 2; Borussia Dortmund 1, PSV 1; **Oct. 30**–Borussia Dortmund 2, Arsenal 1; PSV 3, Auxerre 0; **Nov. 12**–Arsenal 0, PSV 0; Auxerre 1, Borussia Dortmund 0.

Group B	W	L	T	GF	GA	Pts
*Valencia	5	0	1	17	4	16
*Basel	2	1	3	12	12	9
Liverpool (England)	2	2	2	12	8	8
Spartak Moscow (Russia)	0	6	0	1	18	0

RESULTS: **Sept. 17**–Basle 2, Spartak Moscow 0; Valencia 2, Liverpool 0; **Sept. 25**–Liverpool 1, Basle 1; Spartak Moscow 0, Valencia 3; **Oct. 2**–Liverpool 5, Spartak Moscow 0; Valencia 6, Basle 2; **Oct. 22**–Basle 2, Valencia 2; Spartak Moscow 1, Liverpool 3; **Oct. 30**–Liverpool 0, Valencia 1; **Nov. 5**–Spartak Moscow 0, Basle 2; **Nov. 12**–Basle 3, Liverpool 1; Valencia 3, Spartak Moscow 0.

EUROPE (Cont.)

Group C	W	L	T	GF	GA	Pts
*Real Madrid (Spain)	2	1	3	15	7	9
*Roma (Italy)	2	1	3	4	9	9
AEK Athens (Greece)	0	0	6	7	7	6
Genk (Belgium)	0	2	4	2	9	4

RESULTS: **Sept. 17**–Genk 0, AEK Athens 0; Roma 0, Real Madrid 1; **Sept. 25**–AEK Athens 0, Roma 0; Real Madrid 6, Genk 0; **Oct. 2**–AEK Athens 3, Real Madrid 3; Genk 0, Roma 1; **Oct. 22**–Real Madrid 2, AEK Athens 2; Roma 0, Genk 0; **Oct. 30**–AEK Athens 1, Genk 1; Real Madrid 0, Roma 1; **Nov. 12**–Genk 1, Real Madrid 1; Roma 1, AEK Athens 1.

Group D	W	L	T	GF	GA	Pts
*Inter Milan (Italy)	3	1	2	12	8	11
*Ajax (Netherlands)	2	2	2	6	5	8
Lyon (France)	2	2	2	12	9	8
Rosenborg	0	2	4	4	12	4

RESULTS: **Sept. 17**–Ajax 2, Lyon 1; Rosenborg 2, Inter Milan 2 ; **Sept. 25**–Inter Milan 1, Ajax 0; Lyon 5, Rosenborg 0; **Oct. 2**–Inter Milan 1, Lyon 2; Rosenborg 0, Ajax 0; **Oct. 22**–Ajax 1, Rosenborg 0; Lyon 3, Inter Milan 3; **Oct. 30**–Inter Milan 3, Rosenborg 0; Lyon 0, Ajax 2; **Nov. 12**–Ajax 1, Inter Milan 0; Rosenborg 2, Lyon 1.

Group E	W	L	T	GF	GA	Pts
*Juventus (Italy)	4	1	1	12	3	13
*Newcastle United (England)	3	3	0	6	8	9
Dynamo Kiev (Ukraine)	2	3	1	6	9	7
Feyenoord	1	3	2	4	8	5

RESULTS: **Sept. 18**–Dynamo Kiev 2, Newcastle United 0; Feyenoord 1, Juventus 1; **Sept. 24**–Juventus 5, Dynamo Kiev 0; Newcastle United 0, Feyenoord 1; **Oct. 1**–Feyenoord 0, Dynamo Kiev 0; Juventus 2, Newcastle United 0; **Oct. 23**–Dynamo Kiev 2, Feyenoord 0; Newcastle United 1, Juventus 0; **Oct. 29**–Juventus 1, Feyenoord 0; Newcastle United 2, Dynamo Kiev 1; **Nov. 13**–Dynamo Kiev 1, Juventus 2; Feyenoord 2, Newcastle United 3.

Group F	W	L	T	GF	GA	Pts
*Manchester United (England)	5	1	0	16	8	15
*Bayer Leverkusen (Germany)	3	3	0	9	11	9
Maccabi Haifa	2	3	1	12	12	7
Olympiakos (Greece)	1	4	1	11	17	4

RESULTS: **Sept. 18**–Manchester United 5, Maccabi Haifa 2; Olympiakos 6, Bayer Leverkusen 2; **Sept. 24**–Bayer Leverkusen 1, Manchester United 2; Maccabi Haifa 3, Olympiakos 0; **Oct. 1**–Maccabi Haifa 0, Bayer Leverkusen 2; Manchester United 4, Olympiakos 0; **Oct. 23**–Bayer Leverkusen 2, Maccabi Haifa 1; Olympiakos 2, Manchester United 3; **Oct. 29**–Bayer Leverkusen 2, Olympiakos 0; Maccabi Haifa 3, Manchester United 0; **Nov. 13**–Manchester United 2, Bayer Leverkusen 0; Olympiakos 3, Maccabi Haifa 3.

Group G	W	L	T	GF	GA	Pts
*AC Milan (Italy)	4	2	0	12	7	12
*Deportivo La Coruna	4	2	0	11	12	12
Lens	2	2	2	11	11	8
Bayern Munich (Germany)	0	4	2	9	13	2

RESULTS: **Sept. 18**–AC Milan 2, Lens 1; Bayern Munich 2, Deportivo La Coruna 0; **Sept. 24**–Deportivo La Coruna 0, AC Milan 4; Lens 1, Bayern Munich 1; **Oct. 1**–Bayern Munich 1, AC Milan 2; Deportivo La Coruna 3, Lens 1; **Oct. 23**–AC Milan 2, Bayern Munich 1; Lens 3, Deportivo La Coruna 1; **Oct. 29**–Deportivo La Coruna 2, Bayern Munich 1; Lens 2, AC Milan 1; **Nov. 13**–AC Milan 1, Deportivo La Coruna 2; Bayern Munich 3, Lens 3.

Group H	W	L	T	GF	GA	Pts
*Barcelona (Spain)	6	0	0	13	4	18
*Lokomotiv Moscow (Russia)	2	3	1	5	7	7
Club Brugge	1	3	2	5	7	5
Galatasaray (Turkey)	1	4	1	5	10	4

RESULTS: **Sept. 18**–Barcelona 3, Club Brugge 1; Lokomotiv Moscow 1, Galatasaray 0; **Sept. 24**–Club Brugge 0, Lokomotiv Moscow 0; Galatasaray 0, Barcelona 2; **Oct. 1**–Galatasaray 0, Club Brugge 0; Lokomotiv Moscow 1, Barcelona 3; **Oct. 23**–Barcelona 1, Lokomotiv Moscow 0; Club Brugge 3, Galatasaray 1; **Oct. 29**–Club Brugge 0, Barcelona 1; Galatasaray 1, Lokomotiv Moscow 2; **Nov. 13**–Barcelona 3, Galatasaray 1; Lokomotiv Moscow 2, Club Brugge 0.

Second Group Phase

Group A	W	L	T	GF	GA	Pts
*Barcelona	5	0	1	12	2	16
*Inter Milan	3	1	2	11	8	11
Newcastle	2	3	1	10	13	7
Leverkusen	0	6	0	5	15	0

RESULTS: **Nov. 27**–Bayer Leverkusen 1, Barcelona 2; Newcastle United 1, Inter Milan 4; **Dec. 10**–Inter Milan 3, Bayer Leverkusen 2; **Dec. 11**–Barcelona 3, Newcastle United 1; **Feb. 18**–Barcelona 3, Inter Milan 3; Bayer Leverkusen 1, Newcastle United 3; **Feb. 26**–Inter Milan 0, Barcelona 0; Newcastle United 3, Bayer Leverkusen 1; **Mar. 11**–Barcelona 2, Bayer Leverkusen 0; Inter Milan 2, Newcastle 0; **Mar. 19**–Bayer Leverkusen 0, Inter Milan 2; Newcastle 0, Barcelona 2.

Group B	W	L	T	GF	GA	Pts
*Valencia	2	1	3	5	6	9
*Ajax	1	0	5	6	5	8
Arsenal	1	1	4	6	5	7
Roma	1	3	2	7	8	5

RESULTS: **Nov. 27**–Roma 1, Arsenal 3; Valencia 1, Ajax 1; **Dec. 10**–Ajax 0, Roma 1; Arsenal 0, Valencia 0; **Feb. 18**–Arsenal 1, Ajax 1; Roma 0, Valencia 1; **Feb. 26**–Ajax 0, Arsenal 0; Valencia 0, Roma 3; **Mar. 11**–Ajax 1, Valencia 1; Arsenal 1, Roma 1; **Mar. 19**–Roma 1, Ajax 1; Valencia 2, Arsenal 1.

Group C	W	L	T	GF	GA	Pts
*AC Milan	4	2	0	5	4	12
*Real Madrid	3	1	2	9	6	11
Borussia Dortmund	3	2	1	8	5	10
Lokomotiv Moscow	0	5	1	3	10	1

RESULTS: **Nov. 26**–AC Milan 1, Real Madrid 0; Lokomotiv Moscow 1, Borussia Dortmund 2; **Dec. 11**–Borussia Dortmund 0, AC Milan 1; Real Madrid 2, Lokomotiv Moscow 2; **Feb. 19**–AC Milan 1, Lokomotiv Moscow 0; Real Madrid 2, Borussia Dortmund 1; **Feb. 25**–Borussia Dortmund 1, Real Madrid 1; Lokomotiv Moscow 0, AC Milan; **Mar. 12**–Borussia Dortmund 3, Lokomotiv Moscow 0; Real Madrid 3, AC Milan 1; **Mar. 18**–AC Milan 0, Borussia Dortmund 1; Lokomotiv Moscow 0, Real Madrid 1.

Group D	W	L	T	GF	GA	Pts
*Manchester United	4	1	1	11	5	13
*Juventus	2	3	1	11	11	7
Basel	2	3	1	5	10	7
Deportivo	2	3	1	3	7	7

RESULTS: **Nov. 26**–Basle 1, Manchester United 3; Deportivo La Coruna 2, Juventus 2; **Dec. 11**–Juventus 4, Basle 0; Manchester United 2, Deportivo La Coruna 0; **Dec. 4**–Basle 3, Juventus 1; Bayer Leverkusen 3, Deportivo La Coruna 0; **Feb. 19**–Basle 1, Deportivo La Coruna 0; Manchester United 2, Juventus 1; **Feb. 25**–Deportivo La Coruna 1, Basle 0; Juventus 0, Manchester United 3; **Mar. 12**–Juventus 3, Deportivo La Coruna 2; Manchester United 1, Basle 1; **Mar. 18**–Basle 2, Juventus 1; Deportivo La Coruna 2, Manchester United 0.

Quarterfinals

Two legs, total goals; home team listed first.

Ajax vs. AC Milan

Apr. 8   Ajax 0 . . . . .AC Milan 0
Apr. 23 AC Milan 3 . . . . .Ajax 2
AC Milan wins 3-2 on aggregate

Inter Milan vs. Valencia

Apr. 3   Inter Milan 1 . . . . .Valencia 0
Apr. 22 Valencia 2 . . . . .Inter Milan 1
Aggregate tied 2-2. Inter Milan wins on away goal

Real Madrid vs. Manchester United

Apr. 8   Real Madrid 3 . . . . .Manchester United 1
Apr. 23 Manchester United 4 . . . . .Real Madrid 3
Real Madrid wins 6-5 on aggregate

Juventus vs. Barcelona

Apr. 3   Juventus 1 . . . . .Barcelona 1
Apr. 22 Barcelona 1 . . . . .Juventus 2
Juventus wins 3-2 on aggregate

Semifinals

Two legs, total goals; home team listed first.

Real Madrid vs. Juventus

May 6   Real Madrid 2 . . . . .Juventus 1
May 14 Juventus 3 . . . . .Real Madrid 1
Juventus wins 4-3 on aggregate

AC Milan vs. Inter Milan

May 7   AC Milan 0 . . . . .Inter Milan 0
May 13 Inter Milan 1 . . . . .AC Milan 1
AC Milan wins on away goals

Final

May 28 at Old Trafford, Manchester, England. **Attendance:** 63,215

AC Milan 0 . . . . Juventus 0

AC Milan won 3-2 on penalty kick shootout

Shootout: JUVENTUS–saved (David Trezeguet), goal (Alessandro Birindelli), saved (Marcelo Zalayeta), saved (Paolo Montero), goal (Alessandro Del Piero); AC MILAN–goal (Serginho), saved (Clarence Seedorf), saved (Kakka Kaladze), goal (Alessandro Nesta), goal (Andriy Shevchenko).

2003 UEFA Cup

Two-leg Quarterfinals and Semifinals, one-game Final; home team listed first.

Final Eight: FC Porto (Portugal), Panathinaikos (Greece), Malaga (Spain), Boavista (Portugal), Celtic (Scotland), Liverpool (England), Lazio (Italy), Besiktas (Turkey).

Quarterfinals

FC Porto vs. Panathinaikos

Mar. 13 FC Porto 0 . . . . .Panathinaikos 1
Mar. 20 Panathinaikos 0 . . . . .FC Porto 2
FC Porto wins 2-1 on aggregate

Celtic vs. Liverpool

Mar. 12 Celtic 1 .Liverpool 1
Mar. 20 Liverpool 0 .Celtic 2
Celtic wins 3-1 on aggregate

Malaga vs. Boavista

Mar. 13 Malaga 1 . . . . .Boavista 0
Mar. 20 Boavista 0 . . . . .Malaga 0
Aggregate tied 1-1. Boavista wins 4-1 on penalty kicks

Lazio vs. Besiktas

Mar. 13 Lazio 1 . . . . .Besiktas 0
Mar. 20 Besiktas 1 .Lazio 2
Lazio wins 3-1 on aggregate

Semifinals

FC Porto vs. Lazio

Apr. 10 FC Porto 4 . . . . .Lazio 1
Apr. 24 Lazio 0 .FC Porto 0
FC Porto wins 4-1 on aggregate

Celtic vs. Boavista

Apr. 10 Celtic 1 .Boavista 1
Apr. 24 Boavista 0 .Celtic 1
Celtic wins 2-1 on aggregate

Final

May 21 in Seville, Spain. **Attendance:** 52,972

FC Porto 3 . . . . .OT . . . . .Celtic 2

Scoring: FC Porto–Derlei (46th) and (115th) and Dmitry Alenitchev (54th); Celtic–Henrik Larsson (48th) and (56th).

2003 U.S. Open Cup

Dating back to 1914, the U.S. Open Cup is the oldest soccer competition in the United States and is among the oldest in the world. The U.S. Open Cup is a single-elimination tournament open to all amateur and professional teams in the United States. Thirty-four teams competed for the 90-year-old Dewar Cup trophy in the 2003 U.S. Open Cup.

Quarterfinals

L.A. Galaxy (MLS) def. Seattle Sounders (A-League), 5-1
D.C. United (MLS) def. Wilmington Hammerheads (Pro Select), 1-0
Chicago Fire (MLS) def. Colorado Rapids (MLS), 2-1
MetroStars (MLS) def. New England Revolution (MLS), 2-1 (OT)

Semifinals

MetroStars def. D.C. United, 3-2
Chicago Fire def. Los Angeles Galaxy, 3-2

Final

Oct. 15, 2003
Chicago Fire def. MetroStars, 1-0

Major League Soccer
2003 Final Regular Season Standings

Conference champions (*) and playoff qualifiers (†) are noted. Teams receive three points for a win and one for a tie. The GF and GA columns refer to Goals For and Goals Against in regulation play. Number of seasons listed after each head coach refers to current tenure with club through the 2003 season.

Eastern Conference

Team	W	L	T	Pts	GF	GA
*Chicago Fire	15	7	8	53	53	43
†N.E. Revolution	12	9	9	45	55	47
†MetroStars	11	10	9	42	40	40
†D.C. United	10	11	9	39	38	36
Columbus Crew	10	12	8	38	44	44

Head Coaches: Chi—Dave Sarachan (1st season); **NE**—Steve Nicol (2nd); **Met**—Bob Bradley (1st); **DC**—Ray Hudson (2nd); **Clb**—Greg Andrulis (3rd).

Western Conference

Team	W	L	T	Pts	GF	GA
*San Jose Earthquakes	14	7	9	51	45	35
†Kansas City Wizards	11	10	9	42	48	44
†Colorado Rapids	11	12	7	40	40	45
†Los Angeles Galaxy	9	12	9	36	35	35
Dallas Burn	6	19	5	23	35	64

Head Coaches: SJ—Frank Yallop (3rd season); **KC**—Bob Gansler (5th); **Colo**—Tim Hankinson (3rd); **LA**—Sigi Schmid (5th); **Dal**—Mike Jeffries (3rd).

Leading Scorers

Points

	Gm	G	A	Pts
Preki, KC	30	12	17	41
Carlos Ruiz, LA	26	15	5	35
Ante Razov, Chi	26	14	6	34
Taylor Twellman, NE	22	15	4	34
John Spencer, Col	27	14	5	33
Landon Donovan, SJ	22	12	6	30
Mark Chung, Col	29	11	6	28
Damani Ralph, Chi	25	11	6	28
Brian McBride, Clb	24	12	3	27
Pat Noonan, NE	28	10	7	27
Edson Buddle, Clb	21	10	4	24

Goals

	Gm	No
Carlos Ruiz, LA	26	15
Taylor Twellman, NE	22	15
Ante Razov, Chi	26	14
John Spencer, Col	27	14
Landon Donovan, SJ	22	12
Brian McBride, Clb	24	12
Preki, KC	30	12
Mark Chung, Col	29	11
Damani Ralph, Chi	21	10
Pat Noona, NE	28	10

Assists

	Gm	No
Preki, KC	30	17
Mark Lisi, Met	24	11
Amado Guevara, Met	25	10
Brian Mullan, SJ	30	9
Chris Carrieri, Col	30	8
Cobi Jones, LA	28	8

11 players tied with 7 each.

Shots

	Gm	No
Ante Razov, Chi	26	119
Preki, KC	30	92
Damani Ralph, Chi	25	91
Taylor Twellman, NE	22	90
Clint Mathis, Met	22	84
Carlos Ruiz, LA	26	84
John Spencer, Col	27	81
Mamadou Diallo, Met	24	81
Mark Chung, Col	29	78
Amado Guevara, Met	25	72
Brian McBride, Clb	24	68

Shots on Goal

	Gm	No
Taylor Twellman, NE	28	58
Ante Razov, Chi	25	56
Carlos Ruiz, LA	26	56
Mamadou Diallo, Met	24	51
Rodrigo Faria, Met	28	49
Preki, KC	25	44
Ariel Graziani, SJ	28	39
Jason Kreis, Dal	27	38
Jeff Cunningham, Clb	27	37
Mark Chung, Col	27	33

Game-Winning Goals

	Gm	GWG
Preki, KC	30	5
Chris Carrieri, Col	30	4
Amado Guevara, Met	25	4
Kyle Beckerman, Col	28	3
Mark Chung, Col	29	3
Mark Lisi, Met	24	3
Richard Mulrooney, SJ	25	3
Damani Ralph, Chi	25	3
Ante Razov, Chi	26	3

Fourteen tied with 2 each.

MLS All-Star Game
MLS All-Stars 3, Chivas 1

Played Saturday, August 2, 2003 at the Home Depot Center in Carlsbad, Calif. between an MLS All-Star team and the CD Guadalajara Chivas, a Mexican first division club. **Attendance:** 27,000; **Coaches:** Bob Bradley, MLS All-Stars and Eduardo de la Torre, CD Guadalajara; **MVP:** Carlos Ruiz, MLS All-Stars.

	1	2	Final
Guadalajara Chivas	0	1	—1
MLS	0	3	—3

Scoring

2nd Half: MLS—Ante Razov (Landon Donovan, Mauricio Cienfuegos) 57th; CDJ—Jair Garcia (Manuel Sol) 66th; MLS—Carlos Ruiz (Carlos Bocanegra) 68th; MLS—DaMarcus Beasley (unassisted) 83rd.

Goaltenders

Saves: MLS—Kevin Hartman 9; CDJ—Oswaldo Sanchez 1.

Fouls Committed

	Gm	No
Carlos Ruiz, LA	26	76
Dema Kovalenko, DC	26	67
Shalrie Joseph, NE	28	62
Oscar Pareja, Dal	24	58
Chad Deering, Dal	27	57
Brian Mullan, SJ	30	57
Evan Whitfield, Chi	27	57
Chris Albright, LA	27	56
Chris Maisonneuve, Clb	23	55

Fouls Suffered

	Gm	No
DaMarcus Beasley, Chi	22	96
Carlos Ruiz, LA	26	87
Ben Olsen, DC	26	80
Kyle Martino, Clb	22	79
Brian McBride, Clb	24	78
Dema Kovalenko, DC	26	68
Cobi Jones, LA	28	65
Jose Cancela, NE	13	64
Amado Guevara, Met	25	64

Offsides

	Gm	Offs
Carlos Ruiz, LA	26	46
Ante Razov, Chi	26	37
Chris Carrieri, Col	30	27
Jeff Cunningham, Clb	21	26
John Spencer, Col	27	24
Chris Henderson, Col	26	23
Taylor Twellman, NE	22	23
Damani Ralph, Chi	25	22
Edson Buddle, Clb	21	21

Cautions

	Gm	No
Carlos Llamosa, NE	24	9
Oscar Pareja, Dal	24	9
Mike Petke, DC	25	9
Carlos Bocanegra, Chi	19	8
Eight tied with seven each.		

Corner Kicks

	Gm	CKs
Cobi Jones, LA	28	129
Marco Etcheverry, DC	25	97
Amando Guevara, Met	25	96
Ross Paule, Clb	25	86
Preki, KC	30	84
Ante Razov, Chi	26	71
Richard Mulrooney, SJ	25	64
Brad Davis, Dal	26	59
Mark Chung, Col	29	57
Jose Cancela, NE	13	54

Minutes Played

	Mins
Tony Meola, KC	2797
Kevin Hartman, LA	2796
Todd Dunivant, SJ	2778
Jimmy Conrad, KC	2777
Jim Curtin, Chi	2733
Zach Thornton, Chi	2728
Brian Mullan, SJ	2723
Nick Garcia, KC	2689
Preki, KC	2678
Mike Clark, Clb	2673

2003 MLS Attendance

Number in parentheses indicates last year's rank.

	Gm	Total	Avg
Los Angeles (2)	15	329,752	21,983
Colorado (1)	15	251,578	16,772
Columbus (4)	15	243,756	16,250
MetroStars (3)	15	237,326	15,822
Kansas City (9)	15	233,594	15,573
D.C. United (6)	15	233,476	15,565
New England (5)	15	219,611	14,641
Chicago (8)	15	210,080	14,005
San Jose (10)	15	156,989	10,466
Dallas (7)	15	118,585	7,906
TOTAL	150	2,234,747	14,898

Leading Goaltenders
Goals Against Average

	Gm	Min	Shts	Svs	GAA	W-L-T
Jonny Walker, Met	14	1325	69	55	0.95	4-5-5
Pat Onstad, SJ	27	2510	132	103	1.04	14-5-8
Nick Rimando, DC	25	2318	129	100	1.13	10-9-6
Kevin Hartman, LA	30	2796	184	149	1.13	9-12-9
Zach Thornton, Chi	30	2728	160	123	1.22	15-6-8
Tim Howard, Met	13	1222	92	74	1.33	6-3-4
Adin Brown, NE	25	2347	132	95	1.42	11-6-8
Tony Meola, KC	30	2789	165	121	1.42	11-10-9
Jon Busch, Clb	24	2194	139	104	1.44	9-8-6
Scott Garlick, Col	26	2346	121	83	1.46	11-10-5

Saves

	Gm	No
Kevin Hartman, LA	30	149
Zach Thornton, Chi	30	123
Tony Meola, KC	30	121
D.J. Countess, Dal	24	115
Jon Busch, Clb	24	104

Shutouts

	Gm	No
Scott Garlick, Col	26	9
Pat Onstad, SJ	27	9
Zach Thornton, Chi	30	8
Nick Rimando, DC	25	7
Four players wited with 4 each.		

Save Percentage

	Svs	SOG	SV Pct
Jonny Walkers, Met	55	70	78.6
Kevin Hartman, LA	149	190	78.4
Tim Howard, Met	74	96	77.1
Nick Rimando, DC	100	131	76.3
Pat Onstad, SJ	103	138	74.6
Zach Thornton, Chi	123	165	74.5

Catches & Punches

	Gm	C/P
Pat Onstad, SJ	27	117
Adin Brown, NE	25	115
Scott Garlick, Col	26	97
Jon Busch, Clb	27	88
D.J. Countess, Dal	24	88
Tony Meola, KC	30	82
Zach Thornton, Chi	30	82

Major League Soccer (Cont.)
Team-by-Team Statistics
Players who played with more than one club during the season are listed with final team.

Eastern Conference
Chicago Fire

	Pos	Gm	Min	G	A	Pts
Ante Razov	F	26	2270	14	6	34
Damani Ralph	F	22	1985	11	6	28
DaMarcus Beasley	M	22	1969	7	5	19
Andy Williams	M	14	1360	2	7	11
Jesse Marsch	M	19	1465	5	0	10
Chris Armas	M	25	2267	2	4	8
Nate Jaqua	F	20	712	2	2	6
Kelly Gray	D/M	28	1910	2	1	5
Carlos Bocanegra	D	19	1784	1	2	4
Orlando Perez	D	21	1635	2	0	4
Dipsy Selolwane	F	5	165	1	1	3

	Pos	Gm	Min	G	A	Pts
Evan Whitfield	M/D	27	2329	1	1	3
Jonathan Bolanos	M	2	92	0	1	1
C.J. Brown	D	21	1728	0	1	1
Jim Curtin	D	30	2733	0	1	1
Ryan Futagaki	M	6	218	0	1	1
Craig Capano	F	5	122	0	0	0
Logan Pause	M	23	1354	0	0	0

Goalkeepers	Gm	Min	W-L-T	Shts	Svs	GAA
Henry Ring	1	11	0-0-0	1	1	0.00
Zach Thornton	30	2728	15-6-8	165	123	1.22

Columbus Crew

	Pos	Gm	Min	G	A	Pts
Brian McBride	F	24	2183	12	3	27
Edson Buddle	F	21	1509	10	4	24
Jeff Cunningham	F	21	1405	5	7	17
Ross Paule	M	25	2212	4	7	15
Brian West	M/F	24	1543	4	4	12
Freddy Garcia	M	22	1278	1	6	8
Kyle Martino	M	22	1765	2	4	8
Eric Denton	M/D	26	2336	2	1	5
Frankie Hejduk	D/M	23	2128	0	4	4
Brian Maisonneuve	M	23	1730	1	0	2
Jeff Matteo	M	6	286	1	0	2
Alex Pineda Chacon	M	14	703	0	2	2
Jake Traeger	D	1	12	0	2	2
Diego Walsh	M	14	612	1	0	2
Mike Clark	D	29	2673	0	1	1
Nelson Akwari	D	11	488	0	0	0
Chad McCarty	D	19	1226	0	0	0
Duncan Oughton	M/F	23	1717	0	0	0
Michael Ritch	F	3	21	0	0	0
Daniel Torres	D	8	562	0	0	0
Mark Williams	D	5	391	0	0	0

Goalkeepers	Gm	Min	W-L-T	Shts	Svs	GAA
Tom Presthus	7	613	1-4-2	30	21	1.32
Jon Busch	24	2194	9-8-6	144	104	1.44

D.C. United

	Pos	Gm	Min	G	A	Pts
Marco Etcheverry	M	25	2006	6	7	19
Ben Olsen	M	26	2239	4	7	15
Hristo Stoitchkov	F	21	901	5	5	15
Dema Kovalenko	M	26	2401	6	0	12
Ronald Cerritos	F	25	1767	4	2	10
Eliseo Quintanilla	M/F	18	1179	3	3	9
Alecko Eskandarian	F	23	728	3	2	8
Mike Petke	D	25	2343	3	0	6
Bobby Convey	M	19	1576	2	1	5
Santino Quaranta	F	12	738	1	3	5
Earnie Stewart	F	21	1923	1	2	4
Galin Ivanov	D	24	2011	1	1	3
Ryan Nelsen	D/M	25	2314	1	0	2
Jose Alegria	M	17	1093	0	1	1
Bryan Namoff	D	22	1665	0	1	1
Davin Barclay	F/M	3	113	0	0	0
Thiago Martins	F	5	359	0	0	0
Brandon Prideaux	D	28	2586	0	0	0
Trevor Perea	M	2	38	0	0	0

Goalkeepers	Gm	Min	W-L-T	Shts	Svs	GAA
Clint Baumstark	1	100	0-0-1	1	0	0.90
Nick Rimando	25	2318	10-9-6	131	100	1.13
Doug Warren	5	404	0-2-2	404	33	1.34

MetroStars

	Pos	Gm	Min	G	A	Pts
Clint Mathis	M/F	22	2019	9	1	19
Amado Guevara	M	25	2264	3	10	16
Mike Magee	M	29	1709	7	2	16
Mark Lisi	M	24	1829	1	11	13
John Wolyniec	F	25	1385	5	2	12
Steve Jolley	D	24	2194	4	0	8
Ricardo Clark	M	28	2590	3	1	7
Jacob LeBlanc	D	7	225	2	0	4
Jaime Moreno	F	11	517	2	0	4
Craig Ziadie	D	22	1913	1	2	4
Eddie Gaven	M	12	691	1	1	3
Andrzej Juskowiak	F	5	160	1	0	2
Eddie Pope	D	20	1724	0	2	2
Richie Williams	M	26	2337	0	2	2
Joseph Addo	D	8	700	0	0	0
Kenny Arena	D	10	458	0	0	0
Edgar Bartolomeu	D	13	1000	0	0	0
Joey DiGiamarino	D/M	18	1446	0	0	0
Juan Forchetti	M	10	775	0	0	0
Jose Galvan	M	9	266	0	0	0
Chris Leitch	D	15	993	0	0	0
Mike Nugent	F	1	90	0	0	0
Tim Regan	D/M	15	747	0	0	0

Goalkeepers	Gm	Min	W-L-T	Shts	Svs	GAA
Jonny Walker	14	1325	4-5-5	70	55	0.95
Tim Howard	13	1222	6-3-4	96	74	1.33
Paul Grafer	3	270	1-2-0	24	14	2.67

New England Revolution

	Pos	Gm	Min	G	A	Pts
Taylor Twellman	F	22	1893	15	4	34
Pat Noonan	F	28	1646	10	7	27
Brian Kamler	M	28	2322	6	5	17
Joe-Max Moore	F	16	1187	4	7	15
Steve Ralston	M	26	2348	4	7	15
Chris Brown	M/F	21	1327	5	2	12
Jose Cancela	M	13	1142	1	7	9
Jay Heaps	D/M	28	2579	3	1	7
Joe Franchino	D	25	2355	1	4	6
Shalrie Joseph	M	28	2466	2	2	6
Dario Fabbro	F	16	690	2	0	4
Leo Cullen	M	26	1564	0	2	2
Daniel Hernandez	M	9	520	0	2	2
Chris Bagley	F	3	59	0	0	0
Daouda Kante	D	16	1319	0	0	0
Ibrahim Kante	F	2	65	0	0	0
Marshall Leonard	D	10	550	0	0	0
Carlos Llamosa	D	24	2001	0	0	0
Jason Moore	M	13	328	0	0	0
Rusty Pierce	D	21	1878	0	0	0

Goalkeepers	Gm	Min	W-L-T	Shts	Svs	GAA
Adin Brown	25	2347	11-6-8	136	95	1.42
Matt Reis	5	458	1-3-1	23	12	1.97

Western Conference

Colorado Rapids

	Pos	Gm	Min	G	A	Pts
John Spencer	F	27	2265	14	5	33
Mark Chung	M	29	2639	11	6	28
Chris Carrieri	F	30	2458	3	8	14
Chris Henderson	M	26	2180	4	6	14
Zizi Roberts	F	12	729	5	0	10
Kyle Beckerman	M	28	2124	0	5	5
Ritchie Kotschau	D	26	2333	1	1	3
Seth Trembly	M	16	1112	1	1	3
Matt Crawford	D	16	750	1	0	2
Wes Hart	D/M	29	2623	0	2	2
Zach Kingsley	M	12	480	0	2	2
Pablo Mastroeni	M/D	18	1655	0	2	2
Casey Schmidt	F	13	363	0	2	2
Alex Blake	F	3	24	0	0	0
Nat Borchers	D	23	2101	0	0	0
Robin Fraser	D	26	2335	0	0	0
Steven Herdsman	D	3	198	0	0	0
Darryl Powell	M	5	335	0	0	0
Alberto Rizo	D	6	297	0	0	0
Jeff Stewart	D	8	608	0	0	0

Goalkeepers	Gm	Min	W-L-T	Shts	Svs	GAA
Joe Cannon	1	45	0-0-0	0	0	0.00
Scott Garlick	26	2346	11-10-5	123	83	1.46
Scott Vallow	4	380	0-2-2	22	14	1.66

Dallas Burn

	Pos	Gm	Min	G	A	Pts
Brad Davis	M	26	1910	6	5	17
Jason Kreis	F	18	1543	7	2	16
Ali Curtis	F	25	1509	2	6	10
Toni Nhleko	F	11	792	2	4	8
Joselito Vaca	M	27	1871	2	4	8
Chad Deering	M	27	2187	1	5	7
Brian Dunseth	D	28	2395	2	3	7
Edward Johnson	F	22	1265	3	0	6
Oscar Pareja	M	24	1982	1	4	6
Bobby Rhine	F	25	1034	2	1	5
Chris Gbandi	D	22	1573	1	2	4
Ezra Hendrickson	M/D	28	2305	1	1	3
Gavin Glinton	F	19	672	1	1	3
Ronnie O'Brien	M	6	317	1	0	2
Shavar Thomas	D	15	1252	1	0	2
Matt Behncke	D	13	827	0	0	0
Tenywa Bonseu	D	20	1789	0	0	0
Steve Morrow	D	17	1484	0	0	0
Philip Salyer	M	8	491	0	0	0
Jordan Stone	M	16	1057	0	0	0
Mandi Urbas	M	3	40	0	0	0

Goalkeepers	Gm	Min	W-L-T	Shts	Svs	GAA
D.J. Countess	24	2193	5-15-4	173	115	1.97
Jeff Cassar	7	562	1-4-1	40	23	2.56

Kansas City Wizards

	Pos	Gm	Min	G	A	Pts
Preki	M	30	2678	12	17	41
Igor Simutenkov	F	21	1435	7	3	17
Chris Klein	M	27	2527	6	4	16
Eric Quill	M/F	27	2261	3	7	13
Jimmy Conrad	D	30	2777	4	1	9
Francisco Gomez	M	26	1644	3	3	9
Davy Arnaud	F	18	818	3	0	6
Wolde Harris	F	27	1416	2	2	6
Josh Wolff	F	13	872	2	1	5
Stephen Armstrong	M	23	1102	2	0	4
Kerry Zavagnin	M	29	2487	1	2	4
Chris Brunt	F	4	166	1	0	2
Alex Zotinca	M/D	20	1239	1	0	2
Carey Talley	D	20	1344	0	1	1
Jorge Vazquez	M	4	497	0	1	1
Jose Burciaga Jr.	D	4	347	0	0	0
Nick Garcia	D	29	2689	0	0	0
Taylor Graham	D	2	10	0	0	0
Diego Gutierrez	D/M	20	1559	0	0	0
Jack Jewsbury	M/F	2	61	0	0	0

Goalkeepers	Gm	Min	W-L-T	Shts	Svs	GAA
Bo Oshoniyi	1	8	0-0-0	0	0	0.00
Tony Meola	30	2789	11-10-9	172	121	1.42

Los Angeles Galaxy

	Pos	Gm	Min	G	A	Pts
Carlos Ruiz	F	26	2331	15	5	35
Alejandro Moreno	F	24	1117	6	2	14
Cobi Jones	M	28	2574	2	8	12
Chris Albright	M/F	27	1966	3	4	10
Diego Serna	F	10	660	3	2	8
Sasha Victorine	M	20	1797	2	1	5
Simon Elliottt	M	24	2141	1	2	4
Alexi Lalas	D	22	1760	1	1	3
Antonio Martinez	M	14	776	1	1	3
Danny Califf	D	23	2162	0	2	2
Mauricio Cienfuegos	M	20	1344	0	2	2
Ryan Suarez	D	15	1357	1	0	2
Hong Myung-Bo	D	25	2296	0	2	2
Kevin Hartman	GK	30	2796	0	1	1
Isaias Bardales Jr.	F	1	21	0	0	0
Paul Broome	D	11	749	0	1	1
Hercules Gomez	F	1	5	0	0	0
Guillermo Gonzalez	M	6	129	0	0	0
Ricky Lewis	D	13	798	0	0	0
Tyrone Marshall	D	25	1882	0	0	0
Jesus Ochoa	M	10	571	0	0	0
Jose Retiz	M	5	111	0	0	0
Arturo Torres	F	9	335	0	0	0
Peter Vagenas	M	20	1724	0	0	0

Goalkeepers	Gm	Min	W-L-T	Shts	Svs	GAA
Dan Popik	1	16	0-0-0	0	0	0.00
Kevin Hartman	30	2796	9-12-9	190	149	1.13

San Jose Earthquakes

	Pos	Gm	Min	G	A	Pts
Landon Donovan	F	22	1182	12	6	30
Brian Mullan	M/F	30	2723	6	9	21
Brian Ching	F	15	1235	6	2	14
Dwayne De Rosario	F	11	686	4	3	11
Manny Lagos	F/M	27	1545	3	5	11
Todd Dunivant	D	30	2778	1	6	8
Jamil Walkers	M/F	19	365	4	0	8
Richard Mulrooney	M	25	2330	0	7	7
Jeff Agoos	D	28	2593	2	2	6
Chris Roner	D	23	1939	2	2	6
Ronnie Ekelund	M	22	1457	1	3	5
Ian Russell	M	18	1339	0	5	5
Ramiro Corrales	M/D	25	2080	1	2	4
Arturo Alvarez	M/F	15	655	1	1	3
Eddie Robinson	D	13	1121	1	1	3
Craig Waibel	D	24	1991	0	2	2
Rodrigo Faria	F	9	579	0	1	1
Troy Dayak	D	9	785	0	0	0
Roger Levesque	F	3	43	0	0	0

Goalkeepers	Gm	Min	W-L-T	Shts	Svs	GAA
Pat Onstad	27	2510	14-5-8	138	103	1.04
Jon Conway	3	280	0-2-1	18	11	1.93

Women's United Soccer Association

2003 WUSA Final Standings

Three points awarded for a win, one point for a tie; (*) indicates team advanced to semifinals.

	W	L	T	Pts	GF	GA
*Boston	10	4	7	37	33	29
*Atlanta	9	4	8	35	34	19
*San Diego	8	6	7	31	27	26
*Washington	9	8	4	31	40	31
*New York	7	9	5	26	33	43
San Jose	7	10	4	25	23	30
Carolina	7	10	4	25	31	33
Philadelphia	5	11	5	20	30	40

Annual Awards

Most Valuable Player . . . . . . .Maren Meinert, Boston
Defender of the Year . . . . . . .Joy Fawcett, San Diego
Executive of the Year . . . . . . .Joe Cummings, Boston

All-WUSA First Team

F	Maren Meinert, Bos	**M**	Homare Sawa, Atl
F	Dagny Mellgren, Bos	**D**	Jennifer Grubb, Wash
F	Abby Wambach, Wash	**D**	Sharolta Nonen, At
M	Kristine Lilly, Bos	**D**	Joy Fawcett, SD
M	Mia Hamm, Wash	**GK**	Briana Scurry, Atl
M	Shannon Boxx, NY		

League Leaders

Points

	G	A	Pts
Mia Hamm, Washington	11	11	33
Abby Wambach, Washington	13	7	33
Marinette Pichon, Philadelphia	14	3	31
Dagny Mellgren, Boston	14	2	30
Charmaine Hooper, Atlanta	11	7	29

Goals

	Goals
Marinette Pichon, Philadelphia	14
Dagny Mellgren, Boston	14
Abby Wambach, Washington	13
Mia Hamm, Washington	11
Charmaine Hooper, Atlanta	11
Julie Fleeting, San Diego	11
Birgit Prinz, Carolina	11

Assists

	Assists
Mia Hamm, Washington	11
Maren Meinert, Boston	10
Shannon Boxx, New York	8
Abby Wambach, Washington	7
Charmaine Hooper, Atlanta	7

Goal Against Average

	GAA
Melanie Wilson, Atlanta	0.50
Briana Scurry, Atlanta	0.95
Jaime Pagliarulo, San Diego	1.21
Hope Solo, Philadelphia	1.25
Siri Mullinix, Washington	1.27

Playoffs

Semifinals

Games played Aug. 16-17, 2003.

Washington 0 . . . . .OT . . . . .at Boston 0
Washington wins on penalty kicks, 3-1

at Atlanta 2 . . . . .OT . . . . .San Diego 1

Final

Founders Cup III was held Aug. 24, 2003 at Torero Stadium, San Diego, Calif.; **Attendance:** 7,106

Washington 2 . . . . .OT . . . .:Atlanta 1

Scoring

1st Half: WASH—Abby Wambach (Sandra Minnert, Carrie Moore) 7th minute.; ATL—Charmaine Hooper (penalty kick), 46th minute. **2nd Half:** WASH—Wambach (Jennifer Meier, Jacqui Little) 96th.

MVP: Abby Wambach, Washington

Team-by-Team Statistics

Atlanta Beat

	Pos	Gm	Min	G	A	Pts
Charmaine Hooper	F	21	1834	11	7	29
Maribel Dominguez	F	18	1196	7	4	18
Conny Pohlers	F	17	1121	4	5	13
Cindy Parlow	F	18	1441	3	5	11
Homare Sawa	M	15	1323	3	4	10
Abby Crumpton	F	18	657	3	2	8
Kylie Bivens	D	18	1547	1	3	5
Nikki Serlenga	M	20	1670	0	3	3
Ifeoma Dieke	D	13	756	1	0	2
Leslie Gaston	D	18	1415	0	1	1
Sharolta Nonen	D	21	1825	0	1	1
Katie Antongiovanni	M	1	9	0	0	0
Julie Augustyniak	D	13	669	0	0	0
Nancy Augustyniak	F	20	1775	0	0	0
Emily Burt	F	3	13	0	0	0
Marci Miller	M	15	854	0	0	0
Tara Minnax	F/M	1	1	0	0	0
Kristen Warren	M	12	516	0	0	0
Callie Withers	M	12	224	0	0	0

Goalkeepers	Gm	Min	W-L-T	Shts	Svs	GAA
Melanie Wilson	2	180	1-0-1	12	9	0.50
Briana Scurry	19	1710	8-4-7	88	70	0.95

Boston Breakers

	Pos	Gm	Min	G	A	Pts
Dagny Mellgren	F	20	1751	14	2	30
Maren Meinert	F/M	21	1870	9	10	28
Kristine Lilly	M	19	1678	3	4	10
Angela Hucles	M	17	1424	1	4	6
Mary-Franes Monroe	M	12	1068	1	2	4
Monica Gonzalez	D	14	1068	1	2	4
Devvyn Hawkins	M	15	823	1	2	4
Jena Kluegel	D	19	1677	0	4	4
Heather Aldama	D	19	1521	1	1	3
Ragnhild Gulbrandsen	F	7	174	1	1	3
Kate Sobrero	D	19	1710	0	3	3
Stephanie Mugneret-Beghe	M	17	1273	0	2	2
Sarah Popper	M	14	889	0	2	2
Rebekah McDowell	M	10	488	0	1	1
Christine McCann	D	18	1347	0	0	0
Erin O'Grady	F	9	319	0	0	0
Rebekah Splaine	F/M	1	9	0	0	0
Marcia Wallis	F	3	97	0	0	0

Goalkeepers	Gm	Min	W-L-T	Shts	Svs	GAA
Karina LeBlanc	21	1890	10-4-7	123	91	1.38

Carolina Courage

	Pos	Gm	Min	G	A	Pts
Birgit Prinz	F	20	1790	11	3	25
Danielle Fotopoulos	F	12	1029	7	6	20
Venus James	M	20	1301	5	1	11
Nel Fettig	D	21	1890	2	2	6
Unni Lehn	M	20	1670	0	6	6
Erin Baxter	D/M	20	1719	2	1	5
Danielle Slaton	D	18	1154	2	1	5
Danielle Borgman	D	17	403	2	0	4
Staci Burt	D/M	21	1800	0	4	4
Brooke O'Hanley	M	21	1484	0	4	4
Breanna Boyd	D	16	1180	0	2	2
Carla Overbeck	D/M	15	839	0	2	2
Tiffany Roberts	M	18	1620	0	2	2
Robin McCullough	F	12	371	0	1	1
Kim Montgomery	M	7	168	0	1	1
Hege Riise	M	2	125	0	1	1
Marcia Walls	F	8	204	0	0	0

Goalkeepers	Gm	Min	W-L-T	Shts	Svs	GAA
Kristin Luckenbill	18	1575	7-7-4	98	68	1.43
Maite Zabala	3	225	0-2-0	19	13	2.40

New York Power

	Pos	Gm	Min	G	A	Pts
Tiffeny Milbrett	F	17	1462	5	6	16
Christie Welsh	F	12	921	6	0	12
Margaret Tietjen	D	21	1871	2	6	10
Shannon Boxx	M	21	1868	1	8	10
Emily Janss	M	21	1243	4	1	9
Krista Davey	M	17	531	3	2	8
Anita Rapp	M	19	1389	2	4	8
Cheryl Salisbury	D	13	1098	3	1	7
Joanne Peters	M	17	1397	2	2	6
Justi Baumgardt	M	19	808	1	4	6
Jaclyn Raveia	D	20	1761	2	1	5
Tammy Pearman	F/D	15	679	1	2	4
Heather Beem	F	12	735	1	0	2
Lindsey Jones	D	9	408	0	2	2
Lauren Orlandos	D	18	820	0	1	1
Christie Pearce	D	18	1620	0	1	1
Keri Sarver	F	1	1	0	0	0
Kristy Whelchel	D/M	5	231	0	0	0

Goalkeepers	Gm	Min	W-L-T	Shts	Svs	GAA
Saskia Webber	13	1126	4-4-4	72	50	1.52
Carly Smolak	9	764	3-5-1	54	30	2.83

Philadelphia Charge

	Pos	Gm	Min	G	A	Pts
Marinette Pichon	F	18	1583	14	3	31
Melanie Hoffmann	F/M	20	1640	5	5	15
Stacey Tullock	D/M	21	1862	3	5	11
Emily Burt	F	15	998	2	2	6
Pavlina Scasna	M	7	319	1	2	4
Jennifer Tietjen-Prozzo	D	21	1890	1	2	4
Delliah Arrington	F	5	313	1	1	3
Kelly Smith	F	6	242	1	1	3
Lorrie Fair	M	18	1501	0	3	3
Rachel Kruze	M	15	1054	0	2	2
Trina Maso de Moya	F	9	253	0	2	2
Erin Misaki	M	14	1023	0	2	2
Heather Mitts	D	14	1176	0	2	2
Jenny Benson	D	20	1777	0	1	1
Mary McVeigh	D	18	1477	0	1	1
Alexa Borisjuk	M	2	18	0	0	0
Karyn Hall	D	6	75	0	0	0
Anne Makinen	M	17	1429	0	0	0
Mary-Frances Monroe	M	1	81	0	0	0

Goalkeepers	Gm	Min	W-L-T	Shts	Svs	GAA
Hope Solo	8	720	3-4-1	35	22	1.25
Melissa Moore	13	1170	2-7-4	81	50	2.31

San Diego Spirit

	Pos	Gm	Min	G	A	Pts
Julie Fleeting	F	18	1538	11	4	26
Christine Latham	F	19	1551	6	3	15
Julie Foudy	M	20	1742	3	2	8
Aly Wagner	M	20	1778	2	4	8
Zhang Ouying	F	20	1196	1	4	6
Shannon MacMillan	F	6	461	1	3	5
Allie Sullivan	F/M	17	830	1	3	5
Daniela	M	17	1075	0	3	3
Kerry Connors	D/M	21	1830	0	2	2
Susan Bush	M	12	525	0	1	1
Joy Fawcett	D	18	1535	0	1	1
Lisa Krzykowski	D	21	1826	0	1	1
Jennifer Nielsen	M	16	623	0	1	1
Andrea Alfiler	M	2	68	0	0	0
Ronnie Fair	F	15	339	0	0	0
Kim Pickup	D	21	1826	0	0	0
Shauna Rohbock	F	4	21	0	0	0
Rhiannon Tanaka	D	1	51	0	0	0

Goalkeepers	Gm	Min	W-L-T	Shts	Svs	GAA
Jaime Pagliarulo	12	1044	4-4-4	69	52	1.21
Jenni Branam	11	846	4-2-3	47	36	1.28

San Jose CyberRays

	Pos	Gm	Min	G	A	Pts
Pretinha	F	13	1111	5	5	15
Katia	F	18	1291	5	2	12
Sissi	M	20	1404	3	5	11
Tisha Venturini-Hoch	M	20	1161	3	2	8
Keri Sanchez	D	21	1676	1	5	7
Brandi Chastain	D	15	1269	1	4	6
Katie Barnes	M	18	882	2	1	5
Michelle French	D	21	1806	0	4	4
Katie Antongiovanni	M	11	584	1	1	3
Dianne Alagich	D	11	764	1	0	2
Betsy Barr	D	20	1703	1	0	2
Mandy Clemens	F	16	671	0	2	2
Christina Bell	F	10	285	0	1	1
Ann Cook	M	11	308	0	1	1
Amanda Cromwell	D	18	1452	0	1	1
Thori Bryan	D	20	1779	0	0	0
Melinda Carr	D	1	1	0	0	0
Kelly Lindsey	D	10	704	0	0	0
Kim Patrick	F	1	4	0	0	0

Goalkeepers	Gm	Min	W-L-T	Shts	Svs	GAA
LaKeysia Beene	19	1710	7-8-4	113	83	1.37
Dawn Greathouse	2	180	0-2-0	11	7	2.00

Washington Freedom

	Pos	Gm	Min	G	A	Pts
Abby Wambach	F	18	1620	13	7	33
Mia Hamm	F/M	19	1527	11	11	33
Jacqui Little	F/M	20	1545	2	6	10
Lindsay Stoecker	D	21	1636	4	1	9
Steffi Jones	D	21	1831	2	4	8
Kelly Golebiowski	M	17	1057	2	3	7
Jennifer Grubb	D	21	1890	2	1	5
Lori Lindsey	M	19	991	2	1	5
Sandra Minnert	D	12	1003	1	2	4
Casey Zimny	M	14	410	1	1	3
Skylar Little	D	20	1741	0	2	2
Emmy Barr	D	11	889	0	1	1
Jennifer Meier	F	4	69	0	1	1
Carrie Moore	D	21	1890	0	1	1
Sarah Kate Noftsinger	M	6	56	0	1	1
Laura Schott	F	7	163	0	1	1
Meredith Beard	F	14	487	0	0	0

Goalkeepers	Gm	Min	W-L-T	Shts	Svs	GAA
Siri Mullinix	19	1699	9-6-4	100	74	1.27
Nicci Wright	2	101	0-1-0	7	4	1.78
Erin Regan	1	90	0-1-0	8	3	5.00

Colleges
MEN
2002 Final Soccer America Top 25

Final 2002 regular season poll including games through Nov. 18. Conducted by the national weekly *Soccer America* and released in the Dec. 2 issue. Listing includes records through conference playoffs as well as NCAA tournament record and team lost to. Teams in **bold** type went on to reach NCAA Final Four. All tournament games decided by penalty kicks are considered ties.

	Nov. 18 Record	NCAA Recap		Nov. 18 Record	NCAA Recap
1 **Maryland**	17-4-0	3-1 (UCLA)	14 Clemson	12-4-3	1-1-1 (Stanford)
2 Wake Forest	14-1-4	1-1 (Clemson)	15 **Creighton**	15-3-2	3-1 (Stanford)
3 St. John's	12-2-5	1-1 (Creighton)	16 Portland	12-5-1	1-1 (Stanford)
4 Indiana	14-3-2	1-1 (Connecticut)	17 Saint Louis	14-3-2	1-1 (Maryland)
5 Boston College	16-4-0	1-1 (Creighton)	18 Loyola Marymount	14-3-2	1-1 (UCLA)
6 **UCLA**	13-3-3	5-0	19 North Carolina	13-6-1	1-1 (Penn St.)
7 SMU	15-2-3	1-1 (Boston College)	20 Notre Dame	11-5-3	1-1 (Indiana)
8 Furman	17-2-1	1-1-1 (Stanford)	21 San Diego	14-5-0	1-1 (UC Santa Barb)
9 Connecticut	15-5-0	2-1 (Maryland)	22 VCU	15-4-1	0-1 (Furman)
10 **Stanford**	14-4-2	3-1-1 (UCLA)	23 UC Santa Barbara	17-2-1	1-1 (California)
11 Virginia	15-6-0	0-0-1 (Wm.& Mary)	24 Penn State	14-7-0	2-1 (UCLA)
12 California	13-5-2	1-1 (UCLA)	25 Pennsylvania	11-3-1	1-1 (Connecticut)
13 Wisc-Milwaukee	18-1-1	1-1 (Creighton)			

NCAA Division I Tournament

First Round (Nov. 22 or 23)

at Old Dominion 3 . . . . .Richmond 0
Coastal Carolina . . . . . . .2 OT . . .at South Carolina 1
at Portland 2 . . . . .Oregon St. 0
at Furman 2 . . . . .Loyola (MD) 0
Northeastern 1 .Lehigh 1
Northeastern advanced on PKs
at Florida International 2 . . . . .Central Florida 1
at Wisc-Milwaukee 2 . . . . .Oakland 1
at Fairleigh Dickinson 1 . . . . .Holy Cross 1
Fairleigh Dickinson advanced on PKs
at Loyola Marymount 1 . . . . .CS Northridge 0
at UC Santa Barbara 2 . . . . .San Diego 1
at North Carolina 6 . . . . .Winthrop 0
William & Mary 2 . . . . .at Duke 1
at Pennsylvania 1 . . . . .OT . . . . . . .Seton Hall 0
at Notre Dame 3 . . . . .Akron 1
New Mexico 2 . . . . .at Bradley 1
at American 1 . . . . .George Washington 0

Second Round (Nov. 27)

at Wake Forest 1 . . . . .Old Dominion 0
at Clemson 1 . . . . .Coastal Carolina 1
Clemson advanced on PKs
at Stanford 0 . . . . .Portland 0
Stanford advanced on PKs
Furman 0 . . . . .at Virginia Commonwealth 0
Furman advanced on PKs
Boston College 2 . . . . .at Northeastern 1
at Southern Methodist 3 . . . . .Florida International 1
at Creighton 3 . . . . .Wisc-Milwaukee 2
at St. John's 2 . . . . .2 OT . .Fairleigh Dickinson 1
at UCLA 4 . . . . .Loyola Marymount 2
at California 2 . . . . .UC Santa Barbara 1
at Penn St. 1 . . . . .2 OT . . . .North Carolina 0
William & Mary 1 . . . . .at Virginia 1
William & Mary advanced on PKs
at Connecticut 4 . . . . .Pennsylvania 0
at Indiana 1 . . . . .Notre Dame 0
at Saint Louis 1 . . . . .New Mexico 0
at Maryland 1 . . . . .American 0

Third Round (Nov. 30 or Dec. 1)

Clemson 2 . . . . .OT . . . . . . .Wake Forest 1
at Stanford 2 . . . . .2 OT . . . . .Furman 1
Boston College 4 . . . . .Southern Methodist 4
Boston College advanced on PKs
Creighton 1 . . . . .OT . . . . . . .at St. John's 0
at UCLA 3 . . . . .California 2
at Penn St. 1 . . . . .OT . . . .William & Mary 0
at Connecticut 1 . . . . .Indiana 0
at Maryland 1 . . . . .OT . . . . . . .Saint Louis 0

Quarterfinals (Dec. 7 or 8)

at Stanford 2 . . . . .Clemson 0
Creighton 6 . . . . .at Boston College 2
at UCLA 7 . . . . .Penn State 1
at Maryland 3 . . . . .Connecticut 0

2002 College Cup
at Dallas, Tex. (Dec. 13 & 15)

Semifinals

Stanford 1 . . . . .2 OT . . . . .Creighton 0
UCLA 1 . . . . .Maryland 0

Championship

UCLA 1 . . . . .Stanford 0

Scoring:
Second Half: UCLA—Aaron Lopez (Ryan Futagaki), 88:58
Attendance: 8,498
Final records: UCLA (18-3-3); Stanford (18-5-2).
Offensive MVP: Aaron Lopez, UCLA, D
Defensive MVP: Zach Wells, UCLA, GK.

All-Tournament Team: Lopez, Wells, Adolfo Gregorio, Matt Taylor and Scot Thompson from UCLA, Joe Wieland and Mike Tranchilla from Creighton, Sumed Ibrahim from Maryland, Chad Marshall, Roger Levesque, and Todd Dunivant from Stanford.

WOMEN
2002 Final *Soccer America* Top 25

Final 2002 regular season poll including games through Nov. 11. Conducted by the national weekly *Soccer America* and released in the Dec. 2 issue. Listing includes records through conference playoffs as well as NCAA tournament record and team lost to. Teams in **bold** type went on to reach NCAA Final Four. All tournament games decided by penalty kicks are considered ties.

		Nov.11 Record	NCAA Recap			Nov.11 Record	NCAA Recap
1	Stanford	18-1-0	3-1 (Portland)	13	**Penn St.**	15-3-1	4-1 (Portland)
2	**North Carolina**	17-1-4	4-1 (Santa Clara)	14	Clemson	14-7-0	0-1 (Richmond)
3	UCLA	16-3-0	2-1 (Texas A&M)	15	Denver	17-1-2	0-1 (California)
4	**Santa Clara**	15-4-1	5-1 (Portland)	16	Washington St.	11-6-2	0-1 (Arizona St.)
5	Pepperdine	16-1-2	2-1 (Michigan)	17	Brigham Young	16-5-0	0-1 (Utah)
6	Connecticut	18-2-1	3-1 (Penn St.)	18	California	11-7-1	1-1 (Stanford)
7	**Portland**	14-4-2	5-0-1	19	Maryland	12-7-2	1-1 (Penn St.)
8	West Virginia	17-2-1	1-1 (Virginia)	20	Villanova	14-2-4	0-1 (Yale)
9	Texas A&M	15-3-1	2-1-1 (N. Carolina)	21	Duke	9-9-2	did not play
10	Nebraska	14-5-3	2-1 (Santa Clara)	22	Cincinnati	16-3-3	1-1 (Tennessee)
11	Texas	15-4-1	0-1 (SMU)	23	Charlotte	16-1-2	0-1 (J. Madison)
12	Tennessee	16-5-1	2-1 (N. Carolina)	24	Virginia	11-6-2	2-1 (Penn St.)
				25	Arizona St.	11-6-2	1-1 (Santa Clara)

NCAA Division I Tournament

First Round (Nov. 15)

at Stanford 4	Cal Poly 0
California 2	Denver 1
at Notre Dame 3	Ohio St. 1
Purdue 1	Eastern Illinois 1
Purdue advanced on PKs	
James Madison 1	at Charlotte 0
Richmond 1	Clemson 0
Utah 3 OT	BYU 2
Portland 3	Idaho St. 0
at West Virginia 3	Loyola (Md.) 1
Virginia 3	Dayton 2
Penn St. 2	Princeton 0
at Maryland 1	American 0
Auburn 2	Central Florida 1
at Florida St. 2	Mississippi 1
Rhode Island 2 2 OT	Dartmouth 1
at Connecticut 2	Central Conn. St. 0
Pepperdine 2	Wisc-Milwaukee 2
Wisconsin 3	at Marquette 2
Miami-OH 2	Michigan St. 1
at Michigan 1	Oakland 0
Yale 0	at Villanova 0
Yale advanced on PKs	
Nebraska 2	Hartford 0
Arizona St. 2	Washington 1
at Santa Clara 5	Creighton 0
at UCLA 4	Loyola Marymount 0
USC 1	San Diego 0
Southern Methodist 2	Texas 1
at Texas A&M 8	Northwestern St. 0
at Tennessee 5	Furman 0
Cincinnati 1	Kentucky 0
Wake Forest 2	at William & Mary 0
at North Carolina 6	Radford 1

Second Round (Nov. 17)

Pepperdine 2	Wisconsin 1
at Michigan 4	Miami-OH 0
Nebraska 1	Yale 0
at Santa Clara 5	Arizona St. 1
at UCLA 1 2 OT	USC 0
Texas A&M 1	SMU 1
Texas A&M advanced on PKs	
Tennessee 2	Cincinnati 1
at North Carolina 3	Wake Forest 1
at Stanford 1 OT	California 0
Notre Dame 3	Purdue 1

at Portland 3	Utah 0
Virginia 1	West Virginia 0
at Penn St. 2	Maryland 1
Florida St. 2	Auburn 1
at Connecticut 2 OT	Rhode Island 1

Third Round (Nov. 22-24)

at Stanford 1	Notre Dame 0
at Portland 4	Richmond 0
at Penn St. 3	Virginia 0
at Connecticut 1	Florida St. 0
at Michigan 2	Pepperdine 0
at Santa Clara 3	Nebraska 2
Texas A&M 0	at UCLA 0
Texas A&M advanced on PKs	
at North Carolina 3	Tennessee 1

Quarterfinals (Nov. 29-Dec. 1)

at Santa Clara 3	Michigan 1
at North Carolina 3	Texas A&M 0
Portland 0	at Stanford 0
Portland advanced on PKs	
Penn St. 2	at Connecticut 1

2002 College Cup
at Austin, Texas (Dec. 6 & 8)
Semifinals

Portland 2	Penn St. 1
Santa Clara 2	North Carolina 1

Championship

Portland 2 2 OT	Santa Clara 1

Scoring:
2nd Half: SC— Devyn Hawkins (Chardonnay Poole), 52:08. PORT— Christine Sinclair (unassisted), 60:18.
2nd Overtime: PORT— Sinclair (unassisted), 103:27
Attendance: 10,027
Final records: Portland (20-4-2); Santa Clara (20-5-1).
Offensive MVP: Christine Sinclair, Portland, F
Defensive MVP: Jessica Ballweg, Santa Clara, D.
All Tournament Team: Sinclair, Lauren Orlandos, Lauren Arase and Erin Misaki from Portland; Aly Wagner, Devvyn Hawkins, Veronica Zepeda and Ballweg from Santa Clara; Joanna Lohman from Penn St.; Catherine Reddick and Lindsay Tarpley from North Carolina.

Colleges (Cont.)
2002 Annual Awards

Men's Players of the Year

MAC/Hermann Trophy . . .Alecko Eskandarian, Virginia, M
Soccer America . . . . .Alecko Eskandarian, Virginia, M
NCAA Div. II . . . . . .Mounir Tajiou, So. New Hampshire, M
NCAA Div. III . . . . .Hayden Woodworth, Messiah, M
JuCo Div. I . . . . .Jordan McKee, Yavapai, D
JuCo Div. III . . . . .Eric Zegle, Dutchess CC, F

Women's Players of the Year

MAC/Hermann Trophy . . . . .Aly Wagner, Santa Clara, M
Soccer America . . . . .Christine Sinclair, Portland, F
NCAA Div. II . . . . . . .Missy Gregg, Christian Brothers, F
NCAA Div. III . . . . . . .Leah Cornwell, William Smith, GK
JuCo . . . . .Kim Jents, Long Beach CC, F

NSCAA Coaches of the Year

Women's Div. I . . . . .Clive Charles, Portland
Men's Div. I . . . . .Tom Fitzgerald, UCLA
Women's Div. II . . . . . .Don Klosterman, Nebraska-Omaha
Men's Div. II . . . . .Marcus Ziemer, Sonoma St.
Women's Div. III . . . . .Bob Barnes, Ohio Wesleyan
Men's Div. III . . . . .Dave Brandt, Messiah
Women's NAIA . . . . .Mike Giuliano, Wesmont
Men's NAIA . . . . .Peter Fuller, Mobile
Men's Juco Div. I . . . . .Mike Pantalione, Yavapai
Men's JuCo Div. III . . . . .Sean Worley, Richland
Women's JuCo . . . . .Dennis Grassini, CC of Rhode Island

Division I All-America Teams

MEN

The 2002 first team All-America selections of the National Soccer Coaches Association of America (NSCAA). Holdovers from the 2001 NSCAA All-America team are in **bold** type.

GOALKEEPER—Doug Warren, Clemson.

DEFENDERS—Todd Dunivant, Stanford; John Swann, Indiana; Chris Wingert, St. John's.

MIDFIELDERS—Ricardo Clark, Furman; Sumed Ibrahim, Maryland; Andres Murriagui, Loyola Marymount; **Diego Walsh**, SMU.

FORWARDS—Alecko Eskandarian, Virginia; **Pat Noonan**, Indiana; Tim Pierce, UCLA; Mike Tranchilla, Creighton.

WOMEN

The 2002 first team All-America selections of the National Soccer Coaches Association of America (NSCAA). Holdovers from the 2001 NSCAA All-America team are in **bold** type.

GOALKEEPER—Nicole Barnhardt, Stanford.

DEFENDERS—Lauren Orlandos, Portland; Catherine Reddick, North Carolina; Nandi Pryce, UCLA.

MIDFIELDERS—Callie Withers, Stanford; **Joanna Lohman**, Penn St.; Sarah Popper, Connecticut; **Aly Wagner**, Santa Clara.

FORWARDS—Chrissie Abbott, West Virginia; Marcia Wallis, Stanford; Courtney Crandell, UNC-Charlotte; **Christine Sinclair**, Portland.

Small College Final Fours

MEN
NCAA Division II
at Virginia Beach, Va. (Dec. 6-8)

Semifinals: Sonoma St. def. Central Arkansas, 2-1 (2 OT); So. New Hampshire def. Mercyhurst, 2-1.
Championship: Sonoma St. def. So. New Hampshire, 4-3. Final records: Sonoma St. (20-3-1), So. New Hampshire (20-3-2).

NCAA Division III
at Canton, N.Y. (Nov. 29-30)

Semifinals: Otterbein def. Trinity (Texas), 3-2; Messiah 3, St. Lawrence 0.
Championship: Messiah def. Otterbein, 1-0; Final records: Messiah (23-2-1), Otterbein (22-3-2).

NAIA
at Bowling Green, Ky. (Nov. 25-26)

Semifinals: Mobile def. Auburn Montgomery, 2-1; Park def. Lindsey Wilson, 2-2 (4-3 on PKs).
Championship: Mobile def. Park, 2-1; Final records: Mobile (18-4-1), Park (21-3-2).

WOMEN
NCAA Division II
at Virginia Beach, Va. (Dec. 6-8)

Semifinals: Nebraska-Omaha def. Franklin Pierce, 3-1; Christian Brothers def. Metropolitan St., 1-0 (OT).
Championship: Christian Brothers def. Nebraska-Omaha, 2-1. Final records: Christian Brothers (24-1-0), Nebraska-Omaha (22-1-0).

NCAA Division III
at Geneva, N.Y. (Nov. 29-30)

Semifinals: Ohio Wesleyan def. William Smith, 3-0; Messiah def. Trinity (Texas), 0-0 (3-1 on PKs).
Championship: Ohio Wesleyan def. Messiah, 1-0. Final records: Ohio Wesleyan (24-0-0), Messiah (22-1-1).

NAIA
at St. Charles, Mo. (Nov. 25-26)

Semifinals: Azusa Pacific (Calif.) def. Lindenwood (Mo.), 1-0 (OT); Westmont (Calif.) def. Union (Ky.), 4-0.
Championship: Westmont def. Azusa Pacific 2-1; Final records: Westmont (20-1-3), Azusa Pacific (16-4-0).

1900-2003
Through the Years

SPORTS ALMANAC

The World Cup

The Federation Internationale de Football Association (FIFA) began the World Cup championship tournament in 1930 with a 13-team field in Uruguay. Sixty-four years later, 138 countries competed in qualifying rounds to fill 24 berths in the 1994 World Cup finals. FIFA increased the World Cup '98 tournament field from 24 to 32 teams, and it remained at 32 in 2002 including automatic berths for defending champion France and co-hosts Japan and South Korea. The other 29 slots were allotted by region: Europe (13), Africa (5), South America (4), CONCACAF (3), Asia (2), the two remaining positions were determined via two home-and-away playoff series. One was between the #14 European team (Ireland) and the #3 Asian team (Iran) and the other was between the #5 South American team (Uruguay) and the champion of Oceania (Australia).

Tournaments have been played once in Asia (Japan/South Korea), three times in North America (Mexico 2 and U.S.), four times in South America (Argentina, Chile, Brazil and Uruguay) and nine times in Europe (France 2, Italy 2, England, Spain, Sweden, Switzerland and West Germany). Following an outcry when Germany was awarded the 2006 World Cup over South Africa, FIFA announced that, starting in 2010, the World Cup will be rotated among six continents.

Brazil retired the first World Cup (called the Jules Rimet Trophy after FIFA's first president) in 1970 after winning it for the third time. The new trophy, first presented in 1974, is known as simply the World Cup.

Multiple winners: Brazil (5); Italy and West Germany (3); Argentina and Uruguay (2).

Year	Champion	Manager	Score	Runner-up	Host Country	Third Place
1930	Uruguay	Alberto Suppici	4-2	Argentina	Uruguay	No game
1934	Italy	Vittório Pozzo	2-1*	Czechoslovakia	Italy	Germany 3, Austria 2
1938	Italy	Vittório Pozzo	4-2	Hungary	France	Brazil 4, Sweden 2
1942-46 Not held						
1950	Uruguay	Juan Lopez	2-1	Brazil	Brazil	No game
1954	West Germany	Sepp Herberger	3-2	Hungary	Switzerland	Austria 3, Uruguay 1
1958	Brazil	Vicente Feola	5-2	Sweden	Sweden	France 6, W. Ger. 3
1962	Brazil	Aimoré Moreira	3-1	Czechoslovakia	Chile	Chile 1, Yugoslavia 0
1966	England	Alf Ramsey	4-2*	W. Germany	England	Portugal 2, USSR 1
1970	Brazil	Mario Zagalo	4-1	Italy	Mexico	W. Ger. 1, Uruguay 0
1974	West Germany	Helmut Schoen	2-1	Netherlands	W. Germany	Poland 1, Brazil 0
1978	Argentina	Cesar Menotti	3-1*	Netherlands	Argentina	Brazil 2, Italy 1
1982	Italy	Enzo Bearzot	3-1	W. Germany	Spain	Poland 3, France 2
1986	Argentina	Carlos Bilardo	3-2	W. Germany	Mexico	France 4, Belgium 2*
1990	West Germany	Franz Beckenbauer	1-0	Argentina	Italy	Italy 2, England 1
1994	Brazil	Carlos Parreira	0-0†	Italy	USA	Sweden 4, Bulgaria 0
1998	France	Aimé Jacquet	3-0	Brazil	France	Croatia 2, Netherlands 1
2002	Brazil	Luiz Felipe Scolari	2-0	Germany	Japan/S. Korea	Turkey 3, S. Korea 2
2006	at Germany (June 9-July 9)					

*Winning goals scored in overtime (no sudden death); †Brazil defeated Italy in shootout (3-2) after scoreless overtime period.

All-Time World Cup Leaders

Career Goals

World Cup scoring leaders through 2002. Years listed are years played in World Cup.

	No
Gerd Müller, West Germany (1970, 74)	14
Just Fontaine, France (1958)	13
Pelé, Brazil (1958, 62, 66, 70)	12
Ronaldo, Brazil (1994, 98, 2002)	12
Sandor Kocsis, Hungary (1954)	11
Juergen Klinsmann, Germany (1990, 94, 98)	11
Helmut Rahn, West Germany (1954, 58)	10
Teofilo Cubillas, Peru (1970, 78)	10
Gregorz Lato, Poland (1974, 78, 82)	10
Gary Lineker, England (1986, 90)	10

Most Valuable Player

Officially, the Golden Ball Award, the Most Valuable Player of the World Cup tournament has been selected since 1982 by a panel of international soccer journalists.

Year		Year	
1982	Paolo Rossi, Italy	1994	Romario, Brazil
1986	Diego Maradona, Arg.	1998	Ronaldo, Brazil
1990	Toto Schillaci, Italy	2002	Oliver Kahn, Germany

Single Tournament Goals

World Cup tournament scoring leaders through 2002.

Year		Gm	No
1930	Guillermo Stabile, Argentina	4	8
1934	Angelo Schiavio, Italy	3	4
	Oldrich Nejedly, Czechoslovakia	4	4
	Edmund Conen, Germany	4	4
1938	Leônidas, Brazil	3	8
1950	Ademir, Brazil	6	7
1954	Sandor Kocsis, Hungary	5	11
1958	Just Fontaine, France	6	13
1962	Drazen Jerkovic, Yugoslavia	6	5
1966	Eusébio, Portugal	6	9
1970	Gerd Müller, West Germany	6	10
1974	Grzegorz Lato, Poland	7	7
1978	Mario Kempes, Argentina	7	6
1982	Paolo Rossi, Italy	7	6
1986	Gary Lineker, England	5	6
1990	Toto Schillaci, Italy	7	6
1994	Oleg Salenko, Russia	3	6
	Hristo Stoitchkov, Bulgaria	6	6
1998	Davor Suker, Croatia	7	6
2002	Ronaldo, Brazil	7	8

All-Time World Cup Ranking Table

Since the first World Cup in 1930, Brazil is the only country to play in all 17 final tournaments. The FIFA all-time table below ranks all nations that have ever qualified for a World Cup final tournament by points earned through 2002. Victories, which earned two points from 1930-90, were awarded three points starting in 1994. Note that Germany's appearances include 10 made by West Germany from 1954-90. Participants in the 2002 World Cup final are in **bold** type.

		App	Gm	W	L	T	Pts	GF	GA			App	Gm	W	L	T	Pts	GF	GA
1	**Brazil**	17	87	60	13	14	141	191	82	36	Morocco	4	13	2	7	4	8	12	18
2	**Germany**	15	85	50	17	18	123	176	106		Colombia	4	13	3	8	2	8	14	23
3	**Italy**	15	70	39	14	17	96	110	67		**Costa Rica**	2	7	3	3	1	8	9	12
4	**Argentina**	13	60	30	19	11	72	102	71		**Senegal**	1	5	2	1	2	8	7	6
5	**England**	11	50	26	13	15	61	68	45	40	Norway	2	8	2	3	3	7	7	8
6	**Spain**	11	45	20	15	10	54	71	53		**Japan**	2	7	2	4	1	7	6	7
7	**France**	11	44	21	16	7	49	86	61	42	East Germany	1	6	2	2	2	6	5	5
8	**Sweden**	10	42	15	16	10	42	71	65		**South Africa**	2	6	1	2	3	6	8	11
9	**Russia**	9	37	17	14	6	41	64	44	44	**Saudi Arabia**	3	10	2	7	1	5	7	25
10	Yugoslavia	9	37	16	13	8	40	60	46		Algeria	2	6	2	3	1	5	6	10
	Uruguay	10	40	15	10	15	40	65	57		Wales	1	5	1	1	3	5	4	4
12	Netherlands	7	31	14	9	9	37	56	36		**Tunisia**	3	9	1	5	3	5	5	11
13	**Poland**	6	28	14	9	5	34	42	36	48	Iran	2	6	1	4	1	3	4	12
14	Hungary	9	32	15	14	3	33	87	57		North Korea	1	4	1	2	1	3	5	9
	Mexico	12	41	10	20	11	33	43	80		Cuba	1	3	1	1	1	3	5	12
16	**Belgium**	11	36	10	17	9	30	46	63		Jamaica	1	3	1	2	0	3	3	9
	Austria	7	29	12	13	4	28	43	47	52	**Ecuador**	1	3	1	2	0	2	2	4
18	Czech Republic	8	30	11	14	5	27	44	45		Egypt	2	4	0	2	2	2	3	6
19	Romania	7	21	8	8	5	21	30	32		Honduras	1	3	0	1	2	2	2	3
20	Chile	7	25	7	12	6	20	31	40		Israel	1	3	0	1	2	2	1	3
21	**Paraguay**	6	19	5	8	6	18	25	34	56	Bolivia	3	6	0	5	1	1	1	20
	Denmark	3	13	7	4	2	18	24	18		Australia	1	3	0	2	1	1	0	5
23	**South Korea**	6	21	4	12	5	17	19	49		Kuwait	1	3	0	2	1	1	2	6
24	**Cameroon**	5	17	4	6	7	16	15	29	59	El Salvador	2	6	0	6	0	0	1	22
	USA	7	22	6	14	2	16	25	45		Canada	1	3	0	3	0	0	0	5
26	Portugal	3	12	7	5	0	15	25	16		East Indies	1	1	0	1	0	0	0	6
	Scotland	8	23	4	12	7	15	25	41		Greece	1	3	0	3	0	0	0	10
	Switzerland	7	22	6	13	3	15	33	51		Haiti	1	3	0	3	0	0	2	14
	Turkey	2	10	4	4	1	15	20	17		Iraq	1	3	0	3	0	0	1	4
30	Bulgaria	7	26	3	15	8	14	22	53		**Slovenia**	1	3	0	2	1	0	2	7
31	**Croatia**	2	10	6	4	0	13	13	8		New Zealand	1	3	0	2	1	0	2	12
32	**Ireland**	3	13	2	4	7	12	10	10		UAE	1	3	0	3	0	0	2	11
33	Peru	4	15	4	8	3	11	19	31		**China**	1	3	0	3	0	0	0	9
	No. Ireland	3	13	3	5	5	11	13	23		Zaire	1	3	0	3	0	0	0	14
35	**Nigeria**	3	11	4	6	1	9	14	16										

The United States in the World Cup

While the United States has fielded a national team every year of the World Cup, only seven of those teams have been able to make it past the preliminary competition and qualify for the final World Cup tournament. The 1994 national team automatically qualified because the U.S. served as host of the event for the first time. The U.S. played in three of the first four World Cups (1930, '34 and '50) and each of the last four (1990, '94, '98 and 2002). The Americans have a record of 6-14-2 in 22 World Cup matches.

1930

1st Round Matches

United States 3 . . . . Belgium 0
United States 3 . . . . Paraguay 0

Semifinals

Argentina 6 . . . . United States 1

U.S. Scoring—Bert Patenaude (3), Bart McGhee (2), James Brown and Thomas Florie.

1934

1st Round Match

Italy 7 . . . . United States 1

U.S. Scoring—Buff Donelli (who later became a noted college and NFL football coach).

1950

1st Round Matches

Spain 3 . . . . United States 1
United States 1 . . . . England 0
Chile 5 . . . . United States 2

U.S. Scoring—Joe Gaetjens, Joe Maca, John Souza and Frank Wallace.

1990

1st Round Matches

Czechoslovakia 5 . . . . United States 1
Italy 1 . . . . United States 0
Austria 2 . . . . United States 1

U.S. Scoring—Paul Caligiuri and Bruce Murray.

1994

1st Round Matches

United States 1 . . . . Switzerland 1
United States 2 . . . . Colombia 1
Romania 1 . . . . United States 0

Round of 16

Brazil 1 . . . . United States 0

U.S. Scoring—Eric Wynalda, Earnie Stewart and own goal (Colombia defender Andres Escobar).

1998
1st Round Matches

Germany 2 . . . . .United States 0
Iran 2 . . . . .United States 1
Yugoslavia 1 . . . . .United States 0

U.S. Scoring–Brian McBride.

2002
1st Round Matches

United States 3 . . . . .Portugal 2
United States 1 . . . . .So. Korea 1
Poland 3 . . . . .United States 1

Round of 16

United States 2 . . . . .Mexico 0

Round of 8

Germany 1 . . . . .United States 0

U.S. Scoring– Landon Donovan (2), Brian McBride (2), John O'Brien, own goal (Portugal defender Jorge Costa) and Clint Mathis.

World Cup Finals

Brazil and Germany (formerly West Germany) have played in the most Cup finals with seven but faced each other for the first time in a final in 2002. Note that a four-team round robin determined the 1950 championship–the deciding game turned out to be the last one of the tournament between Uruguay and Brazil.

1930
Uruguay 4, Argentina 2
(at Montevideo, Uruguay)

		1	2–T
July 30	Uruguay (4-0) 1		3–4
	Argentina (4-1) 2		0–2

Goals: Uruguay–Pablo Dorado (12th minute), Pedro Cea (54th), Santos Iriarte (68th), Castro (89th); Argentina–Carlos Peucelle (20th), Guillermo Stabile (37th).
Uruguay–Ballesteros, Nasazzi, Mascheroni, Andrade, Fernandez, Gestido, Dorado, Scarone, Castro, Cea, Iriarte.
Argentina–Botasso, Della Torre, Paternoster, J. Evaristo, Monti, Suarez, Peucelle, Varallo, Stabile, Ferreira, M. Evaristo.
Attendance: 90,000. **Referee:** Langenus (Belgium).

1934
Italy 2, Czechoslovakia 1 (OT)
(at Rome)

		1	2	OT–T
June 10	Italy (4-0-1) 0		1	1–2
	Czechoslovakia (3-1) 0		1	0–1

Goals: Italy–Raimondo Orsi (80th minute), Angelo Schiavio (95th); Czechoslovakia–Puc (70th).
Italy–Combi, Monzeglio, Allemandi, Ferraris IV, Monti, Bertolini, Guaita, Meazza, Schiavio, Ferrari, Orsi.
Czechoslovakia–Planicka, Zenisek, Ctyroky, Kostalek, Cambal, Krcil, Junek, Svoboda, Sobotka, Nejedly, Puc.
Attendance: 55,000. **Referee:** Eklind (Sweden).

1938
Italy 4, Hungary 2
(at Paris)

		1	2–T
June 19	Italy (4-0) 3		1–4
	Hungary (3-1) 1		1–2

Goals: Italy–Gino Colaussi (5th minute), Silvio Piola (16th), Colaussi (35th), Piola (82nd); Hungary–Titkos (7th), Georges Sarosi (70th).
Italy–Olivieri, Foni, Rava, Serantoni, Andreolo, Locatelli, Biavati, Meazza, Piola, Ferrari, Colaussi.
Hungary–Szabo, Polgar, Biro, Szalay, Szucs, Lazar, Sas, Vincze, G. Sarosi, Szengeller, Titkos.
Attendance: 65,000. **Referee:** Capdeville (France).

1950
Uruguay 2, Brazil 1
(at Rio de Janeiro)

		1	2–T
July 16	Uruguay (3-0-1) 0		2–2
	Brazil (4-1-1) 0		1–1

Goals: Uruguay–Juan Schiaffino (66th minute), Chico Ghiggia (79th); Brazil–Friaca (47th).
Uruguay–Maspoli, M. Gonzales, Tejera, Gambetta, Varela, Andrade, Ghiggia, Perez, Miguez, Schiaffino, Moran.
Brazil–Barbosa, Augusto, Juvenal, Bauer, Danilo, Bigode, Friaça, Zizinho, Ademir, Jair, Chico.
Attendance: 199,854. **Referee:** Reader (England).

1954
West Germany 3, Hungary 2
(at Berne, Switzerland)

		1	2–T
July 4	West Germany (4-1) 2		1–3
	Hungary (4-1) 2		0–2

Goals: West Germany–Max Morlock (10th minute), Helmut Rahn (18th), Rahn (84th); Hungary–Ferenc Puskas (4th), Zoltan Czibor (9th).
West Germany–Turek, Posipal, Liebrich, Kohlmeyer, Eckel, Mai, Rahn, Morlock, O. Walter, F. Walter, Schaefer.
Hungary–Grosics, Buzansky, Lorant, Lantos, Bozsik, Zakarias, Czibor, Kocsis, Hidegkuti, Puskas, J. Toth.
Attendance: 60,000. **Referee:** Ling (England).

1958
Brazil 5, Sweden 2
(at Stockholm)

		1	2–T
June 29	Brazil (5-0-1) 2		3–5
	Sweden (4-1-1) 1		1–2

Goals: Brazil–Vava (9th minute), Vava (32nd), Pelé (55th), Mario Zagalo (68th), Pelé (90th); Sweden–Nils Liedholm (3rd), Agne Simonsson (80th).
Brazil–Gilmar, D. Santos, N. Santos, Zito, Bellini, Orlando, Garrincha, Didi, Vava, Pelé, Zagalo.
Sweden–Svensson, Bergmark, Axbom, Boerjesson, Gustavsson, Parling, Hamrin, Gren, Simonsson, Liedholm, Skoglund.
Attendance: 49,737. **Referee:** Guigue (France).

World Cup Finals (Cont.)

1962
Brazil 3, Czechoslovakia 1
(at Santiago, Chile)

		1	2–T
June 17	Brazil (5-0-1) 1		2–3
	Czechoslovakia (3-2-1) 1		0–1

Goals: Brazil–Amarildo (17th minute), Zito (68th), Vava (77th); Czechoslovakia–Josef Masopust (15th).

Brazil–Gilmar, D. Santos, N. Santos, Zito, Mauro, Zozimo, Garrincha, Didi, Vava, Amarildo, Zagalo.

Czechoslovakia–Schroiff, Tichy, Novak, Pluskal, Popluhar, Masopust, Pospichal, Scherer, Kvasniak, Kadraba, Jelinek.

Attendance: 68,679. **Referee:** Latishev (USSR).

1966
England 4, West Germany 2 (OT)
(at London)

		1	2	OT–T
July 30	England (5-0-1) 1		1	2–4
	West Germany (4-1-1) 1		1	0–2

Goals: England–Geoff Hurst (18th minute), Martin Peters (78th), Hurst (101st), Hurst (120th); West Germany–Helmut Haller (12th), Wolfgang Weber (90th).

England–Banks, Cohen, Wilson, Stiles, J. Charlton, Moore, Ball, Hurst, B. Charlton, Hunt, Peters.

West Germany–Tilkowski, Hottges, Schnellinger, Beckenbauer, Schulz, Weber, Haller, Seeler, Held, Overath, Emmerich.

Attendance: 93,802. **Referee:** Dienst (Switzerland).

1970
Brazil 4, Italy 1
(at Mexico City)

		1	2–T
June 21	Brazil (6-0) 1		3–4
	Italy (3-1-2) 1		0–1

Goals: Brazil–Pelé (18th minute), Gerson (65th), Jairzinho (70th), Carlos Alberto (86th); Italy–Roberto Boninsegna (37th).

Brazil–Felix, C. Alberto, Everaldo, Clodoaldo, Brito, Piazza, Jairzinho, Gerson, Tostão, Pelé, Rivelino.

Italy–Albertosi, Burgnich, Facchetti, Bertini (Juliano, 73rd), Rosato, Cera, Domenghini, Mazzola, Boninsegna (Rivera, 84th), De Sisti, Riva.

Attendance: 107,412. **Referee:** Glockner (E. Germany).

1974
West Germany 2, Netherlands 1
(at Munich)

		1	2–T
July 7	West Germany (6-1) 2		0–2
	Netherlands (5-1-1) 1		0–1

Goals: West Germany–Paul Breitner (25th minute, penalty kick), Gerd Müller (43rd); Netherlands–Johan Neeskens (1st, penalty kick).

West Germany–Maier, Beckenbauer, Vogts, Breitner, Schwarzenbeck, Overath, Bonhof, Hoeness, Grabowski, Muller, Holzenbein.

Netherlands–Jongbloed, Suurbier, Rijsbergen (De Jong, 58th), Krol, Haan, Jansen, Van Hanegem, Neeskens, Rep, Cruyff, Rensenbrink (R. Van de Kerkhof, 46th).

Attendance: 77,833. **Referee:** Taylor (England).

1978
Argentina 3, Netherlands 1 (OT)
(at Buenos Aires)

		1	2	OT–T
June 25	Argentina (5-1-1) 1		0	2–3
	Netherlands (3-2-2) 0		1	0–1

Goals: Argentina–Mario Kempes (37th minute), Kempes (104th), Daniel Bertoni (114th); Netherlands–Dirk Nanninga (81st).

Argentina–Fillol, Olguin, L. Galvan, Passarella, Tarantini, Ardiles (Larrosa, 65th), Gallego, Kempes, Luque, Bertoni, Ortiz (Houseman, 77th).

Netherlands–Jongbloed, Jansen (Suurbier, 72nd), Brandts, Krol, Poortvliet, Haan, Neeskens, W. Van de Kerkhof, R. Van de Kerkhof, Rep (Nanninga, 58th), Rensenbrink.

Attendance: 77,260. **Referee:** Gonella (Italy).

1982
Italy 3, West Germany 1
(at Madrid)

		1	2–T
July 11	Italy (4-0-3) 0		3–3
	West Germany (4-2-1) 0		1–1

Goals: Italy–Paolo Rossi (57th minute), Marco Tardelli (68th), Alessandro Altobelli (81st); West Germany–Paul Breitner (83rd).

Italy–Zoff, Scirea, Gentile, Cabrini, Collovati, Bergomi, Tardelli, Oriali, Conti, Rossi, Graziani (Altobelli, 8th, and Causio, 89th).

West Germany–Schumacher, Stielike, Kaltz, Briegel, K.H. Forster, B. Forster, Breitner, Dremmler (Hrubesch, 61st), Littbarski, Fischer, Rummenigge (Muller, 69th).

Attendance: 90,080. **Referee:** Coelho (Brazil).

1986
Argentina 3, West Germany 2
(at Mexico City)

		1	2–T
June 29	Argentina (6-0-1) 1		2–3
	West Germany (4-2-1) 0		2–2

Goals: Argentina–Jose Brown (22nd minute), Jorge Valdano (55th), Jorge Burruchaga (83rd); West Germany–Karl-Heinz Rummenigge (73rd), Rudi Voller (81st).

Argentina–Pumpido, Cuciuffo, Olarticoechea, Ruggeri, Brown, Batista, Burruchaga (Trobbiani, 89th), Giusti, Enrique, Maradona, Valdano.

West Germany–Schumacher, Jakobs, B. Forster, Berthold, Briegel, Eder, Brehme, Matthaus, Rummenigge, Magath (Hoeness, 61st), Allofs (Voller, 46th).

Attendance: 114,590. **Referee:** Filho (Brazil).

1990
West Germany 1, Argentina 0
(at Rome)

		1	2–T
July 8	West Germany (6-0-1) 0		1–1
	Argentina (4-2-1) 0		0–0

Goals: West Germany–Andreas Brehme (85th minute, penalty kick).

West Germany–Illgner, Berthold (Reuter, 73rd), Kohler, Augenthaler, Buchwald, Brehme, Haessler, Matthaus, Littbarski, Klinsmann, Voller.

Argentina: Goycochea, Ruggeri (Monzon, 46th), Simon, Serrizuela, Lorenzo, Basualdo, Troglio, Burruchaga (Calderon, 53rd), Sensini, Dezotti, Maradona.

Attendance: 73,603. **Referee:** Codesal (Mexico).

1994
Brazil 0, Italy 0 (Shootout)

(at Pasadena, Calif.)

		1	2	OT–	T
July 17	Brazil (6-0-1)	0	0	0–	0*
	Italy (4-2-1)	0	0	0–	0

*Brazil wins shootout, 3-2.

Shootout (five shots each, alternating): ITA–Baresi (miss, 0-0); BRA–Santos (blocked, 0-0); ITA– Albertini (goal, 1-0); BRA–Romario (goal, 1-1); ITA–Evani (goal, 2-1); BRA–Branco (goal, 2-2); ITA–Massaro (blocked, 2-2); BRA–Dunga (goal, 2-3); ITA–R. Baggio (miss, 2-3).

Brazil–Taffarel, Jorginho (Cafu, 21st minute), Branco, Aldair, Santos, Mazinho, Silva, Dunga, Zinho (Viola, 106th), Bebeto, Romario.

Italy–Pagliuca, Mussi (Apolloni, 35th minute), Baresi, Benarrivo, Maldini, Albertini, D. Baggio (Evani, 95th), Berti, Donadoni, R. Baggio, Massaro.

Attendance: 94,194. **Referee:** Puhl (Hungary).

1998
France 3, Brazil 0

(at Paris)

		1	2–	T
July 12	Brazil (6-1)	0	0–	0
	France (7-0)	2	1–	3

Goals: France–Zinedine Zidane (27th and 46th minutes), Petit (92).

Brazil–Taffarel, Cafu, Aldair, Baiano, Carlos, Sampaio (Edmundo, 74th minute), Dunga, Rivaldo, Leonardo (Denilson, 46th minute), Bebeto, Ronaldo.

France–Barthez, Lizarazu, Desailly, Thuram, Leboeuf, Djorkaeff (Viera, 75th minute), Deschamps, Zidane, Petit, Karembeu (Boghossian, 57th minute), Guivarc'h, Dugarry.

Attendance: 75,000. **Referee:** Belqola (Morocco).

2002
Brazil 2, Germany 0

(at Yokohama, Japan)

		1	2–	T
June 30	Germany (5-2)	0	0–	0
	Brazil (7-0)	0	2–	2

Goals: Brazil–Ronaldo (67th and 79th minutes).

Germany–Kahn, Linke, Ramelow, Neuville, Hamann, Klose (Bierhoff, 74th minute), Jeremies (Asamoah, 77th minute), Bode (Ziege, 84th minute), Schneider, Metzelder, Frings.

Brazil–Marcos, Cafu, Lucio, Junior, Edmilson, Carlos, Silva, Ronaldo (Denilson, 90th minute), Rivaldo, Ronaldinho (Paulista, 85th minute), Kleberson.

Attendance: 69,029. **Referee:** Collina (Italy).

Year-by-Year Comparisons

How the 17 World Cup tournaments have compared in nations qualifying, matches played, players participating, goals scored, average goals per game, overall attendance and attendance per game.

Year	Host	Continent	Nations	Matches	Players	Goals Scored	Goals Per Game	Attendance Overall	Attendance Per Game
1930	Uruguay	So. America	13	18	189	70	3.8	589,300	32,739
1934	Italy	Europe	16	17	208	70	4.1	361,000	21,235
1938	France	Europe	15	18	210	84	4.7	376,000	20,889
1942-46	Not held								
1950	Brazil	So. America	13	22	192	88	4.0	1,044,763	47,489
1954	Switzerland	Europe	16	26	233	140	5.3	872,000	33,538
1958	Sweden	Europe	16	35	241	126	3.6	819,402	23,411
1962	Chile	So. America	16	32	252	89	2.8	892,812	27,900
1966	England	Europe	16	32	254	89	2.8	1,464,944	45,780
1970	Mexico	No. America	16	32	270	95	3.0	1,690,890	52,840
1974	West Germany	Europe	16	38	264	97	2.6	1,809,953	47,630
1978	Argentina	So. America	16	38	277	102	2.7	1,685,602	44,358
1982	Spain	Europe	24	52	396	146	2.8	2,108,723	40,552
1986	Mexico	No. America	24	52	414	132	2.5	2,393,031	46,020
1990	Italy	Europe	24	52	413	115	2.2	2,516,354	48,391
1994	United States	No. America	24	52	437	140	2.7	3,587,088	68,982
1998	France	Europe	32	64	704	171	2.7	2,775,400	43,366
2002	Japan/So. Korea	Asia	32	64	736	161	2.5	2,705,197	42,269

World Cup Shootouts
Introduced in 1982; winning sides in **bold** type.

Year	Round		Final	SO	Year	Round		Final	SO
1982	Semi	**W. Germany** vs. France	3-3	(5-4)	1994	Second	**Bulgaria** vs. Mexico	1-1	(3-1)
1986	Quarter	**Belgium** vs. Spain	1-1	(5-4)		Quarter	**Sweden** vs. Romania	2-2	(5-4)
	Quarter	**France** vs. Brazil	1-1	(4-3)		Final	**Brazil** vs. Italy	0-0	(3-2)
	Quarter	**W. Germany** vs. Mexico	0-0	(4-1)	1998	Second	**Argentina** vs. England	2-2	(4-3)
1990	Second	**Ireland** vs. Romania	0-0	(5-4)		Quarter	**France** vs. Italy	0-0	(4-3)
	Quarter	**Argentina** vs. Yugoslavia	0-0	(3-2)	2002	Second	**Spain** vs. Ireland	1-1	(3-2)
	Semi	**Argentina** vs. Italy	1-1	(4-3)		Quarter	**So. Korea** vs. Spain	0-0	(5-3)
	Semi	**W. Germany** vs. England	1-1	(4-3)					

World Team of the 20th Century

The team, comprised of the century's best players, was voted on by a panel that included 250 international soccer journalists and released on June 10, 1998 in conjunction with the opening of the 1998 World Cup. The panel first selected the European and South American Teams of the Century and then chose the World Team from those two lists.

World Team

Pos		Pos	
GK	Lev Yashin, Soviet Union	MF	Alfredo Di Stefano, Argentina
D	Carlos Alberto, Brazil	MF	Michel Platini, France
D	Franz Beckenbauer, West Germany	F	Pele, Brazil
D	Bobby Moore, England	F	Garrincha, Brazil
D	Nilton Santos, Brazil	F	Diego Maradona, Argentina
MF	Johan Cruyff, Netherlands		

European Team

Pos	
GK	Lev Yashin, Soviet Union
D	Paolo Maldini, Italy
D	Franz Beckenbauer, West Germany
D	Bobby Moore, England
D	Franco Baresi, Italy
MF	Johan Cruyff, Netherlands
MF	Eusebio, Portugal
MF	Michel Platini, France
F	Ferenc Puskas, Hungary
F	Bobby Charlton, England
F	Marco Van Basten, Netherlands

South American Team

Pos	
GK	Ubaldo Fillol, Argentina
D	Carlos Alberto, Brazil
D	Elias Figueroa, Chile
D	Daniel Passarella, Argentina
D	Nilton Santos, Brazil
MF	Didi, Brazil
MF	Alfredo Di Stefano, Argentina
MF	Rivelino, Brazil
F	Pele, Brazil
F	Garrincha, Brazil
F	Diego Maradona, Argentina

OTHER WORLDWIDE COMPETITION

The Olympic Games

Held every four years since 1896, except during World War I (1916) and World War II (1940-44). Soccer was not a medal sport in 1896 at Athens or in 1932 at Los Angeles. By agreement between FIFA and the IOC, Olympic soccer competition is currently limited to players 23 years old and under with a few exceptions.

Multiple winners: England and Hungary (3); Soviet Union and Uruguay (2).

MEN

Year		Year	
1900	**England**, France, Belgium	1960	**Yugoslavia**, Denmark, Hungary
1904	**Canada**, USA I, USA II	1964	**Hungary**, Czechoslovakia, Germany
1906	**Denmark**, Smyrna (Int'l entry), Greece	1968	**Hungary**, Bulgaria, Japan
1908	**England**, Denmark, Netherlands	1972	**Poland**, Hungary, East Germany & Soviet Union
1912	**England**, Denmark, Netherlands	1976	**East Germany**, Poland, Soviet Union
1920	**Belgium**, Spain, Netherlands	1980	**Czechoslovakia**, East Germany, Soviet Union
1924	**Uruguay**, Switzerland, Sweden	1984	**France**, Brazil, Yugoslavia
1928	**Uruguay**, Argentina, Italy	1988	**Soviet Union**, Brazil, West Germany
1936	**Italy**, Austria, Norway	1992	**Spain**, Poland, Ghana
1948	**Sweden**, Yugoslavia, Denmark	1996	**Nigeria**, Argentina, Brazil
1952	**Hungary**, Yugoslavia, Sweden	2000	**Cameroon**, Spain, Chile
1956	**Soviet Union**, Yugoslavia, Bulgaria	2004	(at Athens, Greece)

WOMEN

Year		Year	
1996	**USA**, China, Norway	2004	(at Athens, Greece)
2000	**Norway**, USA, Germany		

The Under-20 World Cup

Held every two years since 1977. Officially, the FIFA World Youth Championship.

Multiple winners: Argentina (4); Brazil (3); Portugal (2).

Year		Year	
1977	Soviet Union	1991	Portugal
1979	Argentina	1993	Brazil
1981	West Germany	1995	Argentina
1983	Brazil	1997	Argentina
1985	Brazil	1999	Spain
1987	Yugoslavia	2001	Argentina
1989	Portugal	2003	(at UAE)

The Under-17 World Cup

Held every two years since 1985. Officially, the FIFA U-17 World Championship.

Multiple winners: Brazil (3); Ghana and Nigeria (2).

Year		Year	
1985	Nigeria	1995	Ghana
1987	Soviet Union	1997	Brazil
1989	Saudi Arabia	1999	Brazil
1991	Ghana	2001	France
1993	Nigeria	2003	Brazil

Indoor World Championship

First held in 1989. Officially, the FIFA Futsal World Championship. **Multiple winner:** Brazil (3).

Year		Year	
1989	Brazil	1996	Brazil
1992	Brazil	2000	Spain

Women's World Cup

First held in 1991. Officially, the FIFA Women's World Championship.

Multiple winner: United States (2).

Year		Year	
1991	United States	1999	United States
1995	Norway	2003	Germany

Confederations Cup

First held in 1992. Contested by the Continental champions of Africa, Asia, Europe, North America and South America and originally called the Intercontinental Championship for the King Fahd Cup until it was redubbed the FIFA/Confederations Cup for the King Fahd Trophy in 1997.

Year		Year	
1992	Argentina	1999	Mexico
1995	Denmark	2001	France
1997	Brazil	2003	France

CONTINENTAL COMPETITION

European Championship

Held every four years since 1960. Officially, the European Football Championship. Winners receive the Henri Delaunay trophy, named for the Frenchman who first proposed the idea of a European Soccer Championship in 1927. The first one would not be played until five years after his death in 1955.

Multiple winners: Germany/West Germany (3); France (2).

Year		Year		Year		Year	
1960	Soviet Union	1972	West Germany	1984	France	1996	Germany
1964	Spain	1976	Czechoslovakia	1988	Netherlands	2000	France
1968	Italy	1980	West Germany	1992	Denmark	2004	(at Portugal)

Copa America

Held irregularly since 1916. Unofficially, the Championship of South America.

Multiple winners: Argentina and Uruguay (14); Brazil (6); Paraguay and Peru (2).

Year		Year		Year		Year		Year	
1916	Uruguay	1925	Argentina	1942	Uruguay	1957	Argentina	1987	Uruguay
1917	Uruguay	1926	Uruguay	1945	Argentina	1958	Argentina	1989	Brazil
1919	Brazil	1927	Argentina	1946	Argentina	1959	Uruguay	1991	Argentina
1920	Uruguay	1929	Argentina	1947	Argentina	1963	Bolivia	1993	Argentina
1921	Argentina	1935	Uruguay	1949	Brazil	1967	Uruguay	1995	Uruguay
1922	Brazil	1937	Argentina	1953	Paraguay	1975	Peru	1997	Brazil
1923	Uruguay	1939	Peru	1955	Argentina	1979	Paraguay	1999	Brazil
1924	Uruguay	1941	Argentina	1956	Uruguay	1983	Uruguay	2001	Colombia
								2004	(at Peru)

African Nations Cup

Contested since 1957 and held every two years since 1968.

Multiple winners: Cameroon, Egypt and Ghana (4); Congo/Zaire (3); Nigeria (2).

Year		Year		Year		Year		Year	
1957	Egypt	1968	Zaire	1978	Ghana	1988	Cameroon	1998	Egypt
1959	Egypt	1970	Sudan	1980	Nigeria	1990	Algeria	2000	Cameroon
1962	Ethiopia	1972	Congo	1982	Ghana	1992	Ivory Coast	2002	Cameroon
1963	Ghana	1974	Zaire	1984	Cameroon	1994	Nigeria	2004	(at Tunisia)
1965	Ghana	1976	Morocco	1986	Egypt	1996	South Africa		

CONCACAF Gold Cup

The Confederation of North, Central American and Caribbean Football Championship. Contested irregularly from 1963-81 and revived as CONCACAF Gold Cup in 1991.

Multiple winners: Mexico (6); Costa Rica (2).

Year		Year		Year		Year		Year	
1963	Costa Rica	1969	Costa Rica	1977	Mexico	1993	Mexico	2000	Canada
1965	Mexico	1971	Mexico	1981	Honduras	1996	Mexico	2004	(at USA)
1967	Guatemala	1973	Haiti	1991	United States	1998	Mexico		

CLUB COMPETITION
European/South American Cup

Also known as the Toyota Cup and Intercontinental Cup. Contested annually in December between the winners of the European Champions League (formerly European Cup) and South America's Copa Libertadores for the unofficial World Club Championship. Four European Cup winners refused to participate in the championship match in the 1970s and were replaced each time by the European Cup runner-up: Panathinaikos (Greece) for Ajax Amsterdam (Netherlands) in 1971; Juventus (Italy) for Ajax in 1973; Atlético Madrid (Spain) for Bayern Munich (West Germany) in 1974; and Malmo (Sweden) for Nottingham Forest (England) in 1979. Another European Cup winner, Marseille of France, was prohibited by the Union of European Football Associations (UEFA) from playing for the 1993 Toyota Cup because of its involvement in a match-rigging scandal.

Best-of-three game format from 1960-68, then a two-game/total goals format from 1969-79. Toyota became Cup sponsor in 1980, changed the format to a one-game championship and moved it to Toyko.

Multiple winners: AC Milan, Nacional, Penarol and Real Madrid (3); Ajax Amsterdam, Bayern Munich, Boca Juniors, Independiente, Inter Milan, Juventus, Santos and Sao Paulo (2).

Year		Year		Year	
1960	Real Madrid (Spain)	1975	Not held	1990	AC Milan (Italy)
1961	Penarol (Uruguay)	1976	Bayern Munich (W. Germany)	1991	Red Star (Yugoslavia)
1962	Santos (Brazil)	1977	Boca Juniors (Argentina)	1992	Sao Paulo (Brazil)
1963	Santos (Brazil)	1978	Not held	1993	Sao Paulo (Brazil)
1964	Inter Milan (Italy)	1979	Olimpia (Paraguay)	1994	Velez Sarsfield (Argentina)
1965	Inter Milan (Italy)	1980	Nacional (Uruguay)	1995	Ajax Amsterdam (Netherlands)
1966	Penarol (Uruguay)	1981	Flamengo (Brazil)	1996	Juventus (Italy)
1967	Racing Club (Argentina)	1982	Penarol (Uruguay)	1997	Borussia Dortmund (Germany)
1968	Estudiantes (Argentina)	1983	Gremio (Brazil)	1998	Real Madrid (Spain)
1969	AC Milan (Italy)	1984	Independiente (Argentina)	1999	Manchester United (England)
1970	Feyenoord (Netherlands)	1985	Juventus (Italy)	2000	Boca Juniors (Argentina)
1971	Nacional (Uruguay)	1986	River Plate (Argentina)	2001	Bayern Munich (Germany)
1972	Ajax Amsterdam (Netherlands)	1987	FC Porto (Portugal)	2002	Real Madrid (Spain)
1973	Independiente (Argentina)	1988	Nacional (Uruguay)		
1974	Atlético Madrid (Spain)	1989	AC Milan (Italy)		

European Cup/UEFA Champions League

Contested annually since the 1955-56 season by the league champions of the member countries of the Union of European Football Associations (UEFA). In 1999, UEFA announced the formation of a new competition called the UEFA Champions League to take the place of the Cup competition.

Multiple winners: Real Madrid (9); AC Milan (6); Ajax Amsterdam, Bayern Munich and Liverpool (4); Benfica, Inter-Milan, Juventus and Nottingham Forest (2).

Year		Year		Year	
1956	Real Madrid (Spain)	1973	Ajax Amsterdam (Netherlands)	1990	AC Milan (Italy)
1957	Real Madrid (Spain)	1974	Bayern Munich (W. Germany)	1991	Red Star Belgrade (Yugo.)
1958	Real Madrid (Spain)	1975	Bayern Munich (W. Germany)	1992	Barcelona (Spain)
1959	Real Madrid (Spain)	1976	Bayern Munich (W. Germany)	1993	Marseille (France)*
1960	Real Madrid (Spain)	1977	Liverpool (England)	1994	AC Milan (Italy)
1961	Benfica (Portugal)	1978	Liverpool (England)	1995	Ajax Amsterdam (Netherlands)
1962	Benfica (Portugal)	1979	Nottingham Forest (England)	1996	Juventus (Italy)
1963	AC Milan (Italy)	1980	Nottingham Forest (England)	1997	Borussia Dortmund (Germany)
1964	Inter Milan (Italy)	1981	Liverpool (England)	1998	Real Madrid (Spain)
1965	Inter Milan (Italy)	1982	Aston Villa (England)	1999	Manchester United (England)
1966	Real Madrid (Spain)	1983	SV Hamburg (W. Germany)	2000	Real Madrid (Spain)
1967	Glasgow Celtic (Scotland)	1984	Liverpool (England)	2001	Bayern Munich (Germany)
1968	Manchester United (England)	1985	Juventus (Italy)	2002	Real Madrid (Spain)
1969	AC Milan (Italy)	1986	Steaua Bucharest (Romania)	2003	AC Milan (Italy)
1970	Feyenoord (Netherlands)	1987	FC Porto (Portugal)	*title vacated	
1971	Ajax Amsterdam (Netherlands)	1988	PSV Eindhoven (Netherlands)		
1972	Ajax Amsterdam (Netherlands)	1989	AC Milan (Italy)		

European Cup Winner's Cup

Contested annually from the 1960-61 season through the 1999-2000 season by the cup winners of the member countries of the Union of European Football Associations (UEFA). The Cup Winner's Cup was absorbed by the UEFA Cup in 2000.

Multiple winners: Barcelona (4); AC Milan, RSC Anderlecht, Chelsea and Dinamo Kiev (2).

Year		Year		Year	
1961	Fiorentina (Italy)	1972	Glasgow Rangers (Scotland)	1983	Aberdeen (Scotland)
1962	Atletico Madrid (Spain)	1973	AC Milan (Italy)	1984	Juventus (Italy)
1963	Tottenham Hotspur (England)	1974	FC Magdeburg (E. Germany)	1985	Everton (England)
1964	Sporting Lisbon (Portugal)	1975	Dinamo Kiev (USSR)	1986	Dinamo Kiev (USSR)
1965	West Ham United (England)	1976	RSC Anderlecht (Belgium)	1987	Ajax Amsterdam (Netherlands)
1966	Borussia Dortmund (W.Germany)	1977	SV Hamburg (W. Germany)	1988	Mechelen (Belgium)
1967	Bayern Munich (W. Germany)	1978	RSC Anderlecht (Belgium)	1989	Barcelona (Spain)
1968	AC Milan (Italy)	1979	Barcelona (Spain)	1990	Sampdoria (Italy)
1969	Slovan Bratislava (Czech.)	1980	Valencia (Spain)	1991	Manchester United (England)
1970	Manchester City (England)	1981	Dinamo Tbilisi (USSR)	1992	Werder Bremen (Germany)
1971	Chelsea (England)	1982	Barcelona (Spain)	1993	Parma (Italy)

Year		Year		Year	
1994	Arsenal (England)	1997	Barcelona (Spain)	1999	Lazio (Italy)
1995	Real Zaragoza (Spain)	1998	Chelsea (England)	2000	discontinued
1996	Paris St. Germain (France)				

UEFA Cup

Contested annually since the 1957-58 season by teams other than league champions and cup winners of the Union of European Football Associations (UEFA). Teams selected by UEFA based on each country's previous performance in the tournament. Teams from England were banned from UEFA Cup play from 1985-90 for the criminal behavior of their supporters. In 1999, with the formation of the new Champions League, UEFA announced that the UEFA Cup would be expanded and include any teams that would have normally played in the Cup Winner's Cup.

Multiple winners: Barcelona, Inter Milan, Juventus and Liverpool (3); Borussia Mönchengladbach, Feyenoord, IFK Göteborg, Leeds United, Parma, Real Madrid, Tottenham Hotspur and Valencia (2).

Year		Year		Year	
1958	Barcelona (Spain)	1974	Feyenoord (Netherlands)	1988	Bayer Leverkusen (W. Germany)
1959	Not held	1975	Borussia Mönchengladbach (W. Germany)	1989	Napoli (Italy)
1960	Barcelona (Spain)	1976	Liverpool (England)	1990	Juventus (Italy)
1961	AS Roma (Italy)	1977	Juventus (Italy)	1991	Inter Milan (Italy)
1962	Valencia (Spain)	1978	PSV Eindhoven (Netherlands)	1992	Ajax Amsterdam (Netherlands)
1963	Valencia (Spain)	1979	Borussia Mönchengladbach (W. Germany)	1993	Juventus (Italy)
1964	Real Zaragoza (Spain)			1994	Inter Milan (Italy)
1965	Ferencvaros (Hungary)			1995	Parma (Italy)
1966	Barcelona (Spain)	1980	Eintracht Frankfurt (W. Germany)	1996	Bayern Munich (Germany)
1967	Dinamo Zagreb (Yugoslavia)	1981	Ipswich Town (England)	1997	Schalke 04 (Germany)
1968	Leeds United (England)	1982	IFK Göteborg (Sweden)	1998	Inter Milan (Italy)
1969	Newcastle United (England)	1983	RSC Anderlecht (Belgium)	1999	Parma (Italy)
		1984	Tottenham Hotspur (England)		
1970	Arsenal (England)	1985	Real Madrid (Spain)	2000	Galatasaray (Turkey)
1971	Leeds United (England)	1986	Real Madrid (Spain)	2001	Liverpool (England)
1972	Tottenham Hotspur (England)	1987	IFK Göteborg (Sweden)	2002	Feyenoord (Netherlands)
1973	Liverpool (England)			2003	FC Porto (Portugal)

Copa Libertadores

Contested annually since the 1955-56 season by the league champions of South America's football union.

Multiple winners: Independiente (7); Boca Juniors and Peñarol (5); Estudiantes, Nacional-Uruguay and Olimpia (3); Cruzeiro, Gremio, River Plate, Santos and São Paulo (2).

Year		Year		Year	
1960	Peñarol (Uruguay)	1975	Independiente (Argentina)	1990	Olimpia (Paraguay)
1961	Peñarol (Uruguay)	1976	Cruzeiro (Brazil)	1991	Colo Colo (Chile)
1962	Santos (Brazil)	1977	Boca Juniors (Argentina)	1992	São Paulo (Brazil)
1963	Santos (Brazil)	1978	Boca Juniors (Argentina)	1993	São Paulo (Brazil)
1964	Independiente (Argentina)	1979	Olimpia (Paraguay)	1994	Velez Sarsfield (Argentina)
1965	Independiente (Argentina)			1995	Gremio (Brazil)
1966	Peñarol (Uruguay)	1980	Nacional (Uruguay)	1996	River Plate (Argentina)
1967	Racing Club (Argentina)	1981	Flamengo (Brazil)	1997	Cruzeiro (Brazil)
1968	Estudiantes de la Plata (Argentina)	1982	Peñarol (Uruguay)	1998	Vasco da Gama (Brazil)
1969	Estudiantes de la Plata (Argentina)	1983	Gremio (Brazil)	1999	Palmeiras (Brazil)
		1984	Independiente (Argentina)		
1970	Estudiantes de la Plata (Argentina)	1985	Argentinos Jrs. (Argentina)	2000	Boca Juniors (Argentina)
1971	Nacional (Uruguay)	1986	River Plate (Argentina)	2001	Boca Juniors (Argentina)
1972	Independiente (Argentina)	1987	Peñarol (Uruguay)	2002	Olimpia (Paraguay)
1973	Independiente (Argentina)	1988	Nacional (Uruguay)	2003	Boca Juniors (Argentina)
1974	Independiente (Argentina)	1989	Nacional Medellin (Colombia)		

Annual Awards
World Player of the Year

Presented by FIFA, the European Sports Magazine Association (ESM) and Adidas, the sports equipment manufacturer, since 1991. Winners are selected by national team coaches from around the world.

Multiple winners: Ronaldo (3); Zinedine Zidane (2).

Year		Nat'l Team	Year		Nat'l Team
1991	Lothar Matthäus, Inter Milan	Germany	1997	Ronaldo, Inter Milan	Brazil
1992	Marco Van Basten, AC Milan	Netherlands	1998	Zinedine Zidane, Juventus	France
1993	Roberto Baggio, Juventus	Italy	1999	Rivaldo, Barcelona	Brazil
1994	Romario, Barcelona	Brazil	2000	Zinedine Zidane, Juventus	France
1995	George Weah, AC Milan	Liberia	2001	Luis Figo, Real Madrid	Portugal
1996	Ronaldo, Barcelona	Brazil	2002	Ronaldo, Real Madrid	Brazil

Women's World Player of the Year

Presented by FIFA since 2001. Winners are selected by national team coaches from around the world.

Multiple winner: Mia Hamm (2).

Year		Nat'l Team	Year		Nat'l Team
2001	Mia Hamm, Washington Freedom	USA	2002	Mia Hamm, Washington Freedom	USA

European Player of the Year

Officially, the "Ballon d'Or," or "Golden Ball," and presented by *France Football* magazine since 1956. Candidates are limited to European players in European leagues and winners are selected by a poll of European soccer journalists.

Multiple winners: Johan Cruyff, Michel Platini and Marco Van Basten (3); Franz Beckenbauer, Alfredo di Stéfano, Kevin Keegan, Ronaldo and Karl-Heinz Rummenigge (2).

Year		Nat'l Team	Year		Nat'l Team
1956	Stanley Matthews, Blackpool	England	1980	K.H. Rummenigge, Bayern Munich	W. Ger.
1957	Alfredo di Stéfano, Real Madrid	Arg./Spain	1981	K.H. Rummenigge, Bayern Munich	W. Ger.
1958	Raymond Kopa, Real Madrid	France	1982	Paolo Rossi, Juventus	Italy
1959	Alfredo di Stéfano, Real Madrid	Arg./Spain	1983	Michel Platini, Juventus	France
1960	Luis Suarez, Barcelona	Spain	1984	Michel Platini, Juventus	France
1961	Enrique Sivori, Juventus	Arg./Italy	1985	Michel Platini, Juventus	France
1962	Josef Masopust, Dukla Prague	Czech.	1986	Igor Belanov, Dinamo Kiev	Soviet Union
1963	Lev Yashin, Dinamo Moscow	Soviet Union	1987	Ruud Gullit, AC Milan	Netherlands
1964	Denis Law, Manchester United	Scotland	1988	Marco Van Basten, AC Milan	Netherlands
1965	Eusébio, Benfica	Portugal	1989	Marco Van Basten, AC Milan	Netherlands
1966	Bobby Charlton, Manchester United	England	1990	Lothar Matthäus, Inter Milan	W. Ger.
1967	Florian Albert, Ferencvaros	Hungary	1991	Jean-Pierre Papin, Marseille	France
1968	George Best, Manchester United	No. Ireland	1992	Marco Van Basten, AC Milan	Netherlands
1969	Gianni Rivera, AC Milan	Italy	1993	Roberto Baggio, Juventus	Italy
1970	Gerd Müller, Bayern Munich	W. Ger.	1994	Hristo Stoitchkov, Barcelona	Bulgaria
1971	Johan Cruyff, Ajax Amsterdam	Netherlands	1995	George Weah, AC Milan	Liberia
1972	Franz Beckenbauer, Bayern Munich	W. Ger.	1996	Matthias Sammer, Bor. Dortmund	Germany
1973	Johan Cruyff, Barcelona	Netherlands	1997	Ronaldo, Inter Milan	Brazil
1974	Johan Cruyff, Barcelona	Netherlands	1998	Zinedine Zidane, Juventus	France
1975	Oleg Blokhin, Dinamo Kiev	Soviet Union	1999	Rivaldo, Barcelona	Brazil
1976	Franz Beckenbauer, Bayern Munich	W. Ger.	2000	Luis Figo, Real Madrid	Portugal
1977	Allan Simonsen, B. Mönchengladbach	Denmark	2001	Michael Owen, Liverpool	England
1978	Kevin Keegan, SV Hamburg	England	2002	Ronaldo, Real Madrid	Brazil
1979	Kevin Keegan, SV Hamburg	England			

South American Player of the Year

Presented by *El Mundo* of Venezuela from 1971-1985 and *El Pais* of Uruguay since 1986. Candidates are limited to South American players in South American leagues and winners are selected by a poll of South American sports editors.

Multiple winners: Elias Figueroa and Zico (3); Enzo Francescoli, Diego Maradona and Carlos Valderrama (2).

Year		Nat'l Team	Year		Nat'l Team
1971	Tostao, Cruzeiro	Brazil	1987	Carlos Valderrama, Deportivo Cali	Colombia
1972	Teofilo Cubillas, Alianza Lima	Peru	1988	Ruben Paz, Racing Buenos Aires	Uruguay
1973	Pelé, Santos	Brazil	1989	Bebeto, Vasco da Gama	Brazil
1974	Elias Figueroa, Internacional	Chile	1990	Raul Amarilla, Olimpia	Paraguay
1975	Elias Figueroa, Internacional	Chile	1991	Oscar Ruggeri, Velez Sarsfield	Argentina
1976	Elias Figueroa, Internacional	Chile	1992	Rai, Sao Paulo	Brazil
1977	Zico, Flamengo	Brazil	1993	Carlos Valderrama, Atl. Junior	Colombia
1978	Mario Kempes, Valencia	Argentina	1994	Cafu, Sao Paulo	Brazil
1979	Diego Maradona, Argentinos Juniors	Argentina	1995	Enzo Francescoli, River Plate	Uruguay
1980	Diego Maradona, Boca Juniors	Argentina	1996	Jose Luis Chilavert, Velez Sarsfield	Paraguay
1981	Zico, Flamengo	Brazil	1997	Marcelo Salas, River Plate	Chile
1982	Zico, Flamengo	Brazil	1998	Martin Palermo, Boca Juniors	Argentina
1983	Socrates, Corinthians	Brazil	1999	Javier Saviola, River Plate	Argentina
1984	Enzo Francescoli, River Plate	Uruguay	2000	Romario, Vasco da Gama	Brazil
1985	Julio Cesar Romero, Fluminense	Paraguay	2001	Juan Roman Riquelme, Boca Juniors	Argentina
1986	Antonio Alzamendi, River Plate	Uruguay	2002	Jose Cardozo, Toluca	Paraguay

African Player of the Year

Officially, the African "Ballon d'Or" and presented by *France Football* magazine from 1970-96. The Arican Player of the Year award has been presented by the CAF (African Football Confederation) since 1997. All African players are eligible for the award.

Multiple winners: George Weah and Abedi Pelé (3); El Hadji Diouf, Nwankwo Kanu, Roger Milla and Thomas N'Kono (2).

Year		Year		Year	
1970	Salif Keita, Mali	1981	Lakhdar Belloumi, Algeria	1992	Abedi Pelé, Ghana
1971	Ibrahim Sunday, Ghana	1982	Thomas N'Kono, Cameroon	1993	Abedi Pelé, Ghana
1972	Cherif Souleymane, Guinea	1983	Mahmoud Al-Khatib, Egypt	1994	George Weah, Liberia
1973	Tshimimu Bwanga, Zaire	1984	Theophile Abega, Cameroon	1995	George Weah, Liberia
1974	Paul Moukila, Congo	1985	Mohamed Timoumi, Morocco	1996	Nwankwo Kanu, Nigeria
1975	Ahmed Faras, Morocco	1986	Badou Zaki, Morocco	1997	Victor Ikpeba, Nigeria
1976	Roger Milla, Cameroon	1987	Rabah Madjer, Algeria	1998	Mustapha Hadji, Morocco
1977	Dhiab Tarak, Tunisia	1988	Kalusha Bwalya, Zambia	1999	Nwankwo Kanu, Nigeria
1978	Abdul Razak, Ghana	1989	George Weah, Liberia	2000	Patrick Mboma, Cameroon
1979	Thomas N'Kono, Cameroon	1990	Roger Milla, Cameroon	2001	El Hadji Diouf, Senegal
1980	Jean Manga Onguene, Cameroon	1991	Abedi Pelé, Ghana	2002	El Hadji Diouf, Senegal

U.S. Player of the Year

Presented by Honda and the Spanish-speaking radio show "Futbol de Primera" since 1991. Candidates are limited to American players who have played with the U.S. National Team and winners are selected by a panel of U.S. soccer journalists.

Multiple winners: Landon Donovan and Eric Wynalda (2).

Year		Year		Year		Year	
1991	Hugo Perez	1995	Alexi Lalas	1999	Kasey Keller	2003	Landon Donovan
1992	Eric Wynalda	1996	Eric Wynalda	2000	Claudio Reyna		
1993	Thomas Dooley	1997	Eddie Pope	2001	Earnie Stewart		
1994	Marcelo Balboa	1998	Cobi Jones	2002	Landon Donovan		

U.S. PRO LEAGUES

OUTDOOR
Major League Soccer

Sanctioned by U.S. Soccer and FIFA, the international soccer federation. MLS was founded on the heels of the successful 1994 World Cup tournament hosted by the United States and it remains the only FIFA-sanctioned division I outdoor league in the United States. The annual MLS title game is known as the MLS Cup.

Multiple winner: D.C. United (3).

MLS Cup

Year	Winner	Head Coach	Score	Loser	Head Coach	Site
1996	D.C. United	Bruce Arena	3-2 OT	Los Angeles Galaxy	Lothar Osiander	Foxboro, Mass.
1997	D.C. United	Bruce Arena	2-1	Colorado Rapids	Glen Myernick	Washington, D.C.
1998	Chicago Fire	Bob Bradley	2-0	D.C. United	Bruce Arena	Pasadena, Calif.
1999	D.C. United	Thomas Rongen	2-0	Los Angeles Galaxy	Sigi Schmid	Foxboro, Mass.
2000	K.C. Wizards	Bob Gansler	1-0	Chicago Fire	Bob Bradley	Washington, D.C.
2001	San Jose Earthquakes	Frank Yallop	2-1 OT	Los Angeles Galaxy	Sigi Schmid	Columbus, Ohio
2002	Los Angeles Galaxy	Sigi Schmid	1-0 2OT	N.E. Revolution	Steve Nicol	Foxboro, Mass.

MLS Cup '96
D.C. United, 3-2 (OT)
Oct. 20 at Foxboro Stadium, Foxboro, Mass.
Attendance: 34,643

	1	2	OT	
Los Angeles Galaxy	1	1	0	—2
D.C. United	0	2	1	—3

First Half: LA–Eduardo Hurtado (Mauricio Cienfuegos), 5th minute.

Second Half: LA–Chris Armas (unassisted), 56th; DC–Tony Sanneh (Marco Etcheverry), 73rd; DC–Shawn Medved (unassisted), 82nd.

Overtime: DC–Eddie Pope (Etcheverry), 94th.

MVP: Marco Etcheverry, D.C. United, Midfielder

MLS Cup '97
D.C. United, 2-1
Oct. 26 at RFK Stadium, Washington, D.C.
Attendance: 57,431

	1	2	
Colorado Rapids	0	1	—1
D.C. United	1	1	—2

First Half: DC–Jaime Moreno (Tony Sanneh, David Vaudreuil), 37th minute.

Second Half: DC–Sanneh (John Harkes, Richie Williams), 68th; COL–Adrian Paz (David Patino, Matt Kmosko), 75th.

MVP: Jaime Moreno, D.C. United, Forward

MLS Cup '98
Chicago Fire, 2-0
Oct. 25 at the Rose Bowl, Pasadena, Calif.
Attendance: 51,350

	1	2	
D.C. United	0	0	—0
Chicago	2	0	—2

First Half: CHI–Jerzy Podbrozny (Peter Nowak, Ante Razov), 29th minute; CHI–Diego Gutierrez (Nowak), 45th.

MVP: Nowak, Chicago, Midfielder

MLS Cup '99
D.C. United, 2-0
Nov. 21 at Foxboro Stadium, Foxboro, Mass.
Attendance: 44,910

	1	2	
D.C. United	2	0	—2
Los Angeles	0	0	—0

First Half: DC–Jaime Moreno (Roy Lassiter), 19th minute; DC–Ben Olsen (unassisted), 48th

MVP: Olsen, D.C. United, Midfielder

MLS Cup 2000
Kansas City Wizards, 1-0
Oct. 15 at RFK Stadium, Washington, D.C.
Attendance: 39,159

	1	2	
Chicago	0	0	—0
Kansas City	1	0	—1

First Half: DC– Miklos Molnar (Chris Klein), 11th minute.

MVP: Tony Meola, Kansas City, Goalkeeper

MLS Cup 2001
San Jose Earthquakes, 2-1 (OT)
Oct. 21 at Crew Stadium, Columbus, Ohio
Attendance: 21,626

	1	2	OT	
San Jose	1	0	1	—2
Los Angeles	1	0	0	—1

First Half: LA–Luis Hernandez (Greg Vanney, Kevin Hartman), 21st minute; SJ–Landon Donovan (Ian Russell, Richard Mulrooney), 43rd.

Overtime: SJ–Dwayne DeRosario (Ronnie Ekelund, Zak Ibsen), 96th.

MVP: Dwayne DeRosario, San Jose, Forward

U.S. Pro Leagues (Cont.)

MLS Cup 2002
Los Angeles, 1-0 (2 OT)
Oct. 20 at Gillette Stadium, Foxboro, Mass.
Attendance: 61,316

	1	2	1OT	2OT	F
Los Angeles	0	0	0	1	—1
New England	0	0	0	0	—0

2nd OT: LA–Carlos Ruiz, (Tyrone Marshall, Chris Albright), 113th minute.
MVP: Carlos Ruiz, Los Angeles, F

Regular Season

MLS Most Valuable Player
1996 Carlos Valderrama, Tampa Bay
1997 Preki, Kansas City
1998 Marco Etcheverry, D.C.
1999 Jason Kreis, Dallas
2000 Tony Meola, Kansas City
2001 Alex Pineda Chacón, Miami
2002 Carlos Ruiz, LA

MLS Leading Scorer		G	A	Pts
1996 Roy Lassiter, Tampa Bay		27	4	58
1997 Preki, Kansas City		12	17	41
1998 Stern John, Columbus		26	5	57
1999 Jason Kreis, Dallas		18	15	51
2000 Mamadou Diallo, Tampa Bay		26	4	56
2001 Alex Pineda Chacón		19	9	47
2002 Taylor Twellman, New England		23	6	52

Women's United Soccer Association

The eight-team WUSA was formed in 2000 as the top women's outdoor professional league and play began in 2001. The league championship game is known as the Founders Cup.

Founders Cup

Year	Winner	Score	Loser
2001	Bay Area CyberRays	3-3*	Atlanta Beat
2002	Carolina Courage	3-2	Washington Freedom
2003	Washington Freedom	2-1 OT	Atlanta Beat

*Bay Area won shoot-out, 4-2.

National Professional Soccer League (1967)

Not sanctioned by FIFA, the international soccer federation. The NPSL recruited individual players to fill the rosters of its 10 teams. The league lasted only one season.

Playoff Final

Year	Winner	Scores	Loser
1967	Oakland Clippers	0-1, 4-1	Baltimore Bays

Regular Season

Leading Scorer		G	A	Pts
Yanko Daucik, Toronto		20	8	48

United Soccer Association (1967)

Sanctioned by FIFA. Originally called the North American Soccer League, it became the USA to avoid being confused with the National Professional Soccer League (see above). Instead of recruiting individual players, the USA imported 12 entire teams from Europe to represent its 12 franchises. It, too, only lasted a season. The league champion Los Angeles Wolves were actually Wolverhampton of England and the runner-up Washington Whips were Aberdeen of Scotland.

Playoff Final

Year	Winner	Score	Loser
1967	Los Angeles Wolves	6-5 (OT)	Washington Whips

Regular Season

Leading Scorer		G	A	Pts
Roberto Boninsegna, Chicago		10	1	21

North American Soccer League (1968-84)

The NPSL and USA merged to form the NASL in 1968 and the new league lasted through 1984. The NASL championship was known as the Soccer Bowl from 1975-84. One game decided the NASL title every year but five. There were no playoffs in 1969; a two-game/aggregate goals format was used in 1968 and '70; and a best-of-three games format was used in 1971 and '84; (*) indicates overtime and (†) indicates game decided by shootout.

Multiple winners: NY Cosmos (5); Chicago (2).

Playoff Final

Regular Season

Year	Winner	Score(s)	Loser	Leading Scorer		G	A	Pts
1968	Atlanta Chiefs	0-0, 3-0	San Diego Toros	John Kowalik, Chicago		30	9	69
1969	Kansas City Spurs	No game	Atlanta Chiefs	Kaiser Motaung, Atlanta		16	4	36
1970	Rochester Lancers	3-0, 1-3	Washington Darts	Kirk Apostolidis, Dallas		16	3	35
1971	Dallas Tornado	1-2*, 4-1, 2-0	Atlanta Chiefs	Carlos Metidieri, Rochester		19	8	46
1972	New York Cosmos	2-1	St. Louis Stars	Randy Horton, New York		9	4	22
1973	Philadelphia Atoms	2-0	Dallas Tornado	Kyle Rote Jr., Dallas		10	10	30
1974	Los Angeles Aztecs	3-3†	Miami Toros	Paul Child, San Jose		15	6	36
1975	Tampa Bay Rowdies	2-0	Portland Timbers	Steve David, Miami		23	6	52
1976	Toronto Metros	3-0	Minnesota Kicks	Giorgio Chinaglia, New York		19	11	49
1977	New York Cosmos	2-1	Seattle Sounders	Steve David, Los Angeles		26	6	58
1978	New York Cosmos	3-1	Tampa Bay Rowdies	Giorgio Chinaglia, New York		34	11	79
1979	Vancouver Whitecaps	2-1	Tampa Bay Rowdies	Oscar Fabbiani, Tampa Bay		25	8	58
1980	New York Cosmos	3-0	Ft. Laud. Strikers	Giorgio Chinaglia, New York		32	13	77
1981	Chicago Sting	0-0†	New York Cosmos	Giorgio Chinaglia, New York		29	16	74
1982	New York Cosmos	1-0	Seattle Sounders	Giorgio Chinaglia, New York		20	15	55
1983	Tulsa Roughnecks	2-0	Toronto Blizzard	Roberto Cabanas, New York		25	16	66
1984	Chicago Sting	2-1, 3-2	Toronto Blizzard	Steve Zungul, Golden Bay		20	10	50

Note: In 1969, Kansas City won the NASL regular season championship with 110 points to 109 for Atlanta. There were no playoffs.

Regular Season MVP

Regular season Most Valuable Player as designated by the NASL.

Multiple winner: Carlos Metidieri (2).

Year	Year	Year
1967 Rueben Navarro, Phila (NPSL)	1973 Warren Archibald, Miami	1979 Johan Cruyff, Los Angeles
1968 John Kowalik, Chicago	1974 Peter Silvester, Baltimore	1980 Roger Davies, Seattle
1969 Cirilio Fernandez, KC	1975 Steve David, Miami	1981 Giorgio Chinaglia, New York
1970 Carlos Metidieri, Rochester	1976 Pelé, New York	1982 Peter Ward, Seattle
1971 Carlos Metidieri, Rochester	1977 Franz Beckenbauer, New York	1983 Roberto Cabanas, New York
1972 Randy Horton, New York	1978 Mike Flanagan, New England	1984 Steve Zungul, Golden Bay

A-League (American Professional Soccer League)

The American Professional Soccer League was formed in 1990 with the merger of the Western Soccer League and the New American Soccer League. The APSL was officially sanctioned as an outdoor pro league in 1992 and changed its name to the A-League in 1995.

Multiple winners: Rochester (3); Colorado, Milwaukee and Seattle (2).

Year	Year	Year
1990 Maryland Bays	1995 Seattle Sounders	2000 Rochester Rhinos
1991 SF Bay Blackhawks	1996 Seattle Sounders	2001 Rochester Rhinos
1992 Colorado Foxes	1997 Milwaukee Rampage	2002 Milwaukee Rampage
1993 Colorado Foxes	1998 Rochester Rhinos	2003 Charleston Battery
1994 Montreal Impact	1999 Minnesota Thunder	

INDOOR

Major Soccer League (1978-92)

Originally the Major Indoor Soccer League from 1978-79 season through 1989-90. The MISL championship was decided by one game in 1980 and 1981; a best-of-three games series in 1979, best-of-five games in 1982 and 1983; and best-of-seven games since 1984. The MSL folded after the 1991-92 season.

Multiple winners: San Diego (8); New York (4).

Playoff Final

Year	Winner	Series	Loser
1979	New York Arrows	2-0	Philadelphia
1980	New York Arrows	7-4 (1 game)	Houston
1981	New York Arrows	6-5 (1 game)	St. Louis
1982	New York Arrows	3-2 (LWWLW)	St. Louis
1983	San Diego Sockers	3-2 (WWLLW)	Baltimore
1984	Baltimore Blast	4-1 (LWWWW)	St. Louis
1985	San Diego Sockers	4-1 (WWLWW)	Baltimore
1986	San Diego Sockers	4-3 (WLLLWWW)	Minnesota
1987	Dallas Sidekicks	4-3 (LLWWLWW)	Tacoma
1988	San Diego Sockers	4-0	Cleveland
1989	San Diego Sockers	4-3 (LWWWLLW)	Baltimore
1990	San Diego Sockers	4-2 (LWWWLW)	Baltimore
1991	San Diego Sockers	4-2 (WLWLWW)	Cleveland
1992	San Diego Sockers	4-2 (WWWLLW)	Dallas

Regular Season

Leading Scorer	G	A	Pts
Fred Grgurev, Philadelphia	46	28	74
Steve Zungul, New York	90	46	136
Steve Zungul, New York	108	44	152
Steve Zungul, New York	103	60	163
Steve Zungul, NY/Golden Bay	75	47	122
Stan Stamenkovic, Baltimore	34	63	97
Steve Zungul, San Diego	68	68	136
Steve Zungul, Tacoma	55	60	115
Tatu, Dallas	73	38	111
Eric Rasmussen, Wichita	55	57	112
Preki, Tacoma	51	53	104
Tatu, Dallas	64	49	113
Tatu, Dallas	78	66	144
Zoran Karic, Cleveland	39	63	102

Playoff MVPs

MSL playoff Most Valuable Players, selected by a panel of soccer media covering the playoffs.

Multiple winners: Steve Zungul (4); Brian Quinn (2).

Year	Year
1979 Shep Messing, NY	1986 Brian Quinn, SD
1980 Steve Zungul, NY	1987 Tatu, Dallas
1981 Steve Zungul, NY	1988 Hugo Perez, SD
1982 Steve Zungul, NY	1989 Victor Nogueira, SD
1983 Juli Veee, SD	1990 Brian Quinn, SD
1984 Scott Manning, Bal.	1991 Ben Collins, SD
1985 Steve Zungul, SD	1992 Thompson Usiyan, SD

Regular Season MVPs

MSL regular season Most Valuable Players, selected by a panel of soccer media from every city in the league.

Multiple winners: Steve Zungul (6); Victor Nogueira and Tatu (2).

Year	Year
1979 Steve Zungul, NY	1986 Steve Zungul, SD/Tac.
1980 Steve Zungul, NY	1987 Tatu, Dallas
1981 Steve Zungul, NY	1988 Erik Rasmussen, Wich.
1982 Steve Zungul, NY & Stan Terlecki, Pit.	1989 Preki, Tacoma
1983 Alan Mayer, SD	1990 Tatu, Dallas
1984 Stan Stamenkovic, Bal.	1991 Victor Nogueira, SD
1985 Steve Zungul, SD	1992 Victor Nogueira, SD

NASL Indoor Champions (1980-84)

The North American Soccer League started an indoor league in the fall of 1979. The indoor NASL, which featured many of the same teams and players who played in the outdoor NASL, crowned champions from 1980-82 before suspending play. It was revived for the 1983-84 indoor season but folded for good in 1984. The NASL held indoor tournaments in 1975 (San Jose Earthquakes won) and 1976 (Tampa Bay Rowdies won) before the indoor league was started.

Multiple winner: San Diego (2).

Year	Year	Year	Year
1980 Tampa Bay Rowdies	1982 San Diego Sockers	1983 Play suspended	1984 San Diego Sockers
1981 Edmonton Drillers			

U.S. Pro Leagues (Cont.)
Major Indoor Soccer League

The winter indoor MISL began as the American Indoor Soccer Association in 1984-85, then changed its name to the National Professional Soccer League in 1989-90 and was known as the NPSL until 2001 when the name was changed again and the league was relaunched as the MISL.

Multiple winners: Canton (5); Cleveland and Milwaukee (3); Kansas City (2).

Year		Year		Year		Year	
1985	Canton (OH) Invaders	1990	Canton Invaders	1995	St. Louis Ambush	2000	Milwaukee Wave
1986	Canton Invaders	1991	Chicago Power	1996	Cleveland Crunch	2001	Milwaukee Wave
1987	Louisville Thunder	1992	Detroit Rockers	1997	Kansas City Attack	2002	Philadelphia Kixx
1988	Canton Invaders	1993	Kansas City Attack	1998	Milwaukee Wave	2003	Baltimore Blast
1989	Canton Invaders	1994	Cleveland Crunch	1999	Cleveland Crunch		

Continental Indoor Soccer League (1993-97)

The summer indoor CISL played its first season in 1993 and folded following the 1997 season.

Multiple winner: Monterrey (2).

Year		Year		Year	
1993	Dallas Sidekicks	1995	Monterrey La Raza	1997	Seattle Seadogs
1994	Las Vegas Dustdevils	1996	Monterrey La Raza		

U.S. COLLEGES

NCAA Men's Division I Champions

NCAA Division I champions since the first title was contested in 1959. The championship has been shared three times—in 1967, 1968 and 1989. There was a playoff for third place from 1974-81.

Multiple winners: Saint Louis (10); Indiana, San Francisco and Virginia (5); UCLA (4); Clemson, Connecticut, Howard and Michigan St. (2).

Year	Winner	Head Coach	Score	Runner-up	Host/Site	Semifinalists
1959	Saint Louis	Bob Guelker	5-2	Bridgeport	Connecticut	West Chester, CCNY
1960	Saint Louis	Bob Guelker	3-2	Maryland	Brooklyn	West Chester, Connecticut
1961	West Chester	Mel Lorback	2-0	Saint Louis	Saint Louis	Bridgeport, Rutgers
1962	Saint Louis	Bob Guelker	4-3	Maryland	Saint Louis	Mich. St., Springfield
1963	Saint Louis	Bob Guelker	3-0	Navy	Rutgers	Army, Maryland
1964	Navy	F.H. Warner	1-0	Michigan St.	Brown	Army, Saint Louis
1965	Saint Louis	Bob Guelker	1-0	Michigan St.	Saint Louis	Army, Navy
1966	San Francisco	Steve Negoesco	5-2	LIU-Brooklyn	California	Army, Mich. St.
1967-a	Michigan St. & Saint Louis	Gene Kenney Harry Keough	0-0	–	Saint Louis	LIU-Bklyn, Navy
1968-b	Michigan St. & Maryland	Gene Kenney Doyle Royal	2-2 (2 OT)	–	Ga. Tech	Brown, San Jose St.
1969	Saint Louis	Harry Keough	4-0	San Francisco	San Jose St.	Harvard, Maryland
1970	Saint Louis	Harry Keough	1-0	UCLA	SIU-Ed'sville	Hartwick, Howard
1971-c	Howard	Lincoln Phillips	3-2	Saint Louis	Miami	Harvard, San Fran.
1972	Saint Louis	Harry Keough	4-2	UCLA	Miami	Cornell, Howard
1973	Saint Louis	Harry Keough	2-1 (OT)	UCLA	Miami	Brown, Clemson

Year	Winner	Head Coach	Score	Runner-up	Host/Site	Third Place
1974	Howard	Lincoln Phillips	2-1 (4OT)	Saint Louis	Saint Louis	Hartwick 3, UCLA 1
1975	San Francisco	Steve Negoesco	4-0	SIU-Ed'sville	SIU-Ed'sville	Brown 2, Howard 0
1976	San Francisco	Steve Negoesco	1-0	Indiana	Penn	Hartwick 4, Clemson 3
1977	Hartwick	Jim Lennox	2-1	San Francisco	California	SIU-Ed'sville 3, Brown 2
1978-d	San Francisco	Steve Negoesco	4-3 (OT)	Indiana	Tampa	Clemson 6, Phi. Textile 2
1979	SIU-Ed'sville	Bob Guelker	3-2	Clemson	Tampa	Penn St. 2, Columbia 1
1980	San Francisco	Steve Negoesco	4-3 (OT)	Indiana	Tampa	Ala. A&M 2, Hartwick 0
1981	Connecticut	Joe Morrone	2-1 (OT)	Alabama A&M	Stanford	East. Ill. 4, Phi. Textile 2

Year	Winner	Head Coach	Score	Runner-up	Host/Site	Semifinalists
1982	Indiana	Jerry Yeagley	2-1 (8 OT)	Duke	Ft. Lauderdale	Connecticut, SIU-Ed'sville
1983	Indiana	Jerry Yeagley	1-0 (2 OT)	Columbia	Ft. Lauderdale	Connecticut, Virginia
1984	Clemson	I.M. Ibrahim	2-1	Indiana	Seattle	Hartwick, UCLA
1985	UCLA	Sigi Schmid	1-0 (8 OT)	American	Seattle	Evansville, Hartwick
1986	Duke	John Rennie	1-0	Akron	Tacoma	Fresno St., Harvard
1987	Clemson	I.M. Ibrahim	2-0	San Diego St.	Clemson	Harvard, N. Carolina
1988	Indiana	Jerry Yeagley	1-0	Howard	Indiana	Portland, S. Carolina
1989-e	Santa Clara & Virginia	Steve Sampson Bruce Arena	1-1 (2 OT)	– –	Rutgers	Indiana, Rutgers
1990-f	UCLA	Sigi Schmid	0-0 (PKs)	Rutgers	South Fla.	Evansville, N.C. State
1991-g	Virginia	Bruce Arena	0-0 (PKs)	Santa Clara	Tampa	Indiana, Saint Louis

Year	Winner	Head Coach	Score	Runner-up	Host/Site	Semifinalists
1992	Virginia	Bruce Arena	2-0	San Diego	Davidson	Davidson, Duke
1993	Virginia	Bruce Arena	2-0	South Carolina	Davidson	CS-Fullerton, Princeton
1994	Virginia	Bruce Arena	1-0	Indiana	Davidson	Rutgers, UCLA
1995	Wisconsin	Jim Launder	2-0	Duke	Richmond	Portland, Virginia
1996	St. John's	Dave Masur	4-1	Fla. International	Richmond	Creighton, NC-Charlotte
1997	UCLA	Sigi Schmid	2-0	Virginia	Richmond	Indiana, Saint Louis
1998	Indiana	Jerry Yeagley	3-1	Stanford	Richmond	Maryland, Santa Clara
1999	Indiana	Jerry Yeagley	1-0	Santa Clara	Charlotte	Connecticut, UCLA
2000	Connecticut	Ray Reid	2-0	Creighton	Charlotte	Indiana, Southern Methodist
2001	North Carolina	Elmar Bolowich	2-0	Indiana	Columbus	St. John's, Stanford
2002	UCLA	Tom Fitzgerald	1-0	Stanford	Dallas	Creighton, Maryland

a–game declared a draw due to inclement weather after regulation time; **b**–game declared a draw after two overtimes; **c**–Howard vacated title for using ineligible player; **d**–San Francisco vacated title for using ineligible player; **e**–game declared a draw due to inclement weather after two overtimes. **f**–UCLA wins on penalty kicks (4-3) after four overtimes; **g**–Virginia wins on penalty kicks (3-1) after four overtimes.

Women's NCAA Division I Champions

NCAA Division I women's champions since the first tournament was contested in 1982.

Multiple winner: North Carolina (16).

Year	Winner	Coach	Score	Runner-up	Host/Site
1982	North Carolina	Anson Dorrance	2-0	Central Florida	Central Florida
1983	North Carolina	Anson Dorrance	4-0	George Mason	Central Florida
1984	North Carolina	Anson Dorrance	2-0	Connecticut	North Carolina
1985	George Mason	Hank Leung	2-0	North Carolina	George Mason
1986	North Carolina	Anson Dorrance	2-0	Colorado College	George Mason
1987	North Carolina	Anson Dorrance	1-0	Massachusetts	Massachusetts
1988	North Carolina	Anson Dorrance	4-1	N.C. State	North Carolina
1989	North Carolina	Anson Dorrance	2-0	Colorado College	N.C. State
1990	North Carolina	Anson Dorrance	6-0	Connecticut	North Carolina
1991	North Carolina	Anson Dorrance	3-1	Wisconsin	North Carolina
1992	North Carolina	Anson Dorrance	9-1	Duke	North Carolina
1993	North Carolina	Anson Dorrance	6-0	George Mason	North Carolina
1994	North Carolina	Anson Dorrance	5-0	Notre Dame	Portland
1995	Notre Dame	Chris Petrucelli	1-0 (3OT)	Portland	North Carolina
1996	North Carolina	Anson Dorrance	1-0 (2OT)	Notre Dame	Santa Clara
1997	North Carolina	Anson Dorrance	2-0	Connecticut	NC-Greensboro
1998	Florida	Becky Burleigh	1-0	North Carolina	NC-Greensboro
1999	North Carolina	Anson Dorrance	2-0	Notre Dame	San Jose, Calif.
2000	North Carolina	Anson Dorrance	2-1	UCLA	San Jose, Calif.
2001	Santa Clara	Jerry Smith	1-0	North Carolina	Dallas
2002	Portland	Clive Charles	2-1 (2OT)	Santa Clara	Austin

Annual Awards
MEN
Hermann Trophy

College Player of the Year. Voted on by Division I college coaches and selected sportswriters and first presented in 1967 in the name of Robert Hermann, one of the founders of the North American Soccer League.

Multiple winners: Mike Fisher, Mike Seerey, Ken Snow and Al Trost (2).

Year		Year		Year	
1967	Dov Markus, LIU	1979	Jim Stamatis, Penn St.	1991	Alexi Lalas, Rutgers
1968	Manuel Hernandez, San Jose St.	1980	Joe Morrone, Jr. Connecticut	1992	Brad Friedel, UCLA
1969	Al Trost, Saint Louis	1981	Armando Betancourt, Indiana	1993	Claudio Reyna, Virginia
1970	Al Trost, Saint Louis	1982	Joe Ulrich, Duke	1994	Brian Maisonneuve, Indiana
1971	Mike Seerey, Saint Louis	1983	Mike Jeffries, Duke	1995	Mike Fisher, Virginia
1972	Mike Seerey, Saint Louis	1984	Amr Aly, Columbia	1996	Mike Fisher, Virginia
1973	Dan Counce, Saint Louis	1985	Tom Kain, Duke	1997	Johnny Torres, Creighton
1974	Farrukh Quraishi, Oneonta St.	1986	John Kerr, Duke	1998	Wojtek Krakowiak, Clemson
1975	Steve Ralbovsky, Brown	1987	Bruce Murray, Clemson	1999	Ali Curtis, Duke
1976	Glenn Myernick, Hartwick	1988	Ken Snow, Indiana	2000	Chris Gbandi, Connecticut
1977	Billy Gazonas, Hartwick	1989	Tony Meola, Virginia	2001	Luchi Gonzalez, SMU
1978	Angelo DiBernardo, Indiana	1990	Ken Snow, Indiana	2002	Alecko Eskandarian, Virginia

U.S. Colleges (Cont.)
Missouri Athletic Club Award

College Player of the Year. Voted on by men's team coaches around the country from Division I to junior college level and first presented in 1986 by the Missouri Athletic Club of St. Louis.

Multiple winners: Claudio Reyna and Ken Snow (2).

Year	Year	Year
1986 John Kerr, Duke	1992 Claudio Reyna, Virginia	1998 Jay Heaps, Duke
1987 John Harkes, Virginia	1993 Claudio Reyna, Virginia	1999 Sasha Victorine, UCLA
1988 Ken Snow, Indiana	1994 Todd Yeagley, Indiana	2000 Ali Curtis, Duke
1989 Tony Meola, Virginia	1995 Matt McKeon, St. Louis	2001 Luchi Gonzalez, SMU
1990 Ken Snow, Indiana	1996 Mike Fisher, Virginia	2002 merged with Hermann Trophy.
1991 Alexi Lalas, Rutgers	1997 Johnny Torres, Creighton	

Coach of the Year

Men's Coach of the Year. Voted on by the National Soccer Coaches Association of America. From 1973-81 all Senior College coaches were eligible. In 1982, the award was split into several divisions. The Division I Coach of the Year is listed since 1982.

Multiple winner: Jerry Yeagley (5).

Year	Year	Year
1973 Robert Guelker, SIU-Edwardsville	1983 Dieter Ficken, Columbia	1993 Bob Bradley, Princeton
1974 Jack MacKenzie, Quincy College	1984 James Lennox, Hartwick	1994 Jerry Yeagley, Indiana
1975 Paul Reinhardt, Vermont	1985 Peter Mehleft, American	1995 Jim Launder, Wisconsin
1976 Jerry Yeagley, Indiana	1986 Steve Parker, Akron	1996 Dave Masur, St. John's
1977 Klass Deboer, Cleveland St.	1987 Anson Dorrance, N. Carolina	1997 Sigi Schmid, UCLA
1978 Cliff McCrath, Seattle Pacific	1988 Keith Tucker, Howard	1998 Jerry Yeagley, Indiana
1979 Walter Bahr, Penn St.	1989 Steve Sampson, Santa Clara	1999 Jerry Yeagley, Indiana
1980 Jerry Yeagley, Indiana	1990 Bob Reasso, Rutgers	2000 Ray Reid, Connecticut
1981 Schellas Hyndman, E. Illinois	1991 Mitch Murray, Santa Clara	2001 Elmar Bolowich, North Carolina
1982 John Rennie, Duke	1992 Charles Slagle, Davidson	2002 Tom Fitzgerald, UCLA

WOMEN
Hermann Trophy

Women's College Player of the year. Voted on by Division I college coaches and selected sportswriters and first presented in 1988 in the name of Robert Hermann, one of the founders of the North American Soccer League.

Multiple winners: Mia Hamm and Cindy Parlow (2).

Year	Year	Year
1988 Michelle Akers, Central Fla.	1993 Mia Hamm, N. Carolina	1998 Cindy Parlow, N. Carolina
1989 Shannon Higgins, N. Carolina	1994 Tisha Venturini, N. Carolina	1999 Mandy Clemens, Santa Clara
1990 April Kater, Massachusetts	1995 Shannon McMillan, Portland	2000 Anne Makinen, Notre Dame
1991 Kristine Lilly, N. Carolina	1996 Cindy Daws, Notre Dame	2001 Christie Welsh, Penn St.
1992 Mia Hamm, N. Carolina	1997 Cindy Parlow, N. Carolina	2002 Aly Wagner, Santa Clara

Missouri Athletic Club Award

Women's College Player of the Year. Voted on by women's team coaches around the country from Division I to junior college level and first presented in 1991 by the Missouri Athletic Club of St. Louis.

Multiple winners: Mia Hamm and Cindy Parlow (2).

Year	Year	Year
1991 Kristine Lilly, N. Carolina	1995 Shannon McMillan, Portland	1999 Mandy Clemens, Santa Clara
1992 Mia Hamm, N. Carolina	1996 Cindy Daws, Notre Dame	2000 Anne Makinen, Notre Dame
1993 Mia Hamm, N. Carolina	1997 Cindy Parlow, N. Carolina	2001 Christie Welsh, Penn St.
1994 Tisha Venturini, N. Carolina	1998 Cindy Parlow, N. Carolina	2002 merged with Hermann Trophy.

Coach of the Year

Women's Coach of the Year. Voted on by the National Soccer Coaches Association of America. From 1982-87 all Senior College coaches were eligible. In 1988, the award was split into several divisions. The Division I Coach of the Year is listed since 1988.

Multiple winners: Kalenkeni M. Banda, Anson Dorrance and Chris Petrucelli (2).

Year	Year	Year
1982 Anson Dorrance, N. Carolina	1989 Austin Daniels, Hartford	1996 John Walker, Nebraska
1983 David Lombardo, Keene St.	1990 Lauren Gregg, Virginia	1997 Len Tsantiris, Connecticut
1984 Phillip Picince, Brown	1991 Greg Ryan, Wisc-Madison	1998 Becky Burleigh, Florida
1985 Kalenkeni M. Banda, UMass	1992 Bell Hempen, Duke	1999 Patrick Farmer, Penn St.
1986 Anson Dorrance, N. Carolina	1993 Jac Cicala, George Mason	2000 Jillian Ellis, UCLA
1987 Kalenkeni M. Banda, UMass	1994 Chris Petrucelli, Norte Dame	2001 Jerry Smith, Santa Clara
1988 Larry Gross, N.C. State	1995 Chris Petrucelli, Norte Dame	2002 Clive Charles, Portland

Bowling

Bowling's "bad boy" **Pete Weber** won his second straight Tar Heel Open in February.

PBA Tour

Dead-Eye's Double

Walter Ray Williams Jr. adds to his resume by capturing two more major titles in a record-breaking season.

Michael Morrison
is co-editor of the ESPN Sports Almanac.

Think, for a second, about what it might take to become the best in the world at something. Regardless of what it is, what would it take? Talent? Hard work? Dedication? Sure, but even if you had all of those attributes, odds on becoming the best in the entire world are pretty long.

Now consider this. Walter Ray Williams Jr. has been the best in the world...at two different things.

He's the greatest bowler on the Professional Bowlers Association Tour. He's also a six-time world horseshoe pitching champion. He's a member of both the PBA Hall of Fame and the National Horseshoe Pitching Association Hall of Fame. When most people think of two-sport stars, Bo Jackson and Deion Sanders are usually the first names brought up. But Walter Ray may have them both beat! Oh yeah, he's also a three-handicap in golf.

Nicknamed "Dead-Eye" (for what should be obvious reasons), the 43-year-old from Ocala, Fla. ruled the lanes in 2002-03, winning three tournaments, placing second in three and third in three more. He smashed the PBA single-season earnings record with $419,700 (the previous high was $298,237 set in 1989) and became the first bowler to top $3 million in career earnings. Williams joined the late Earl Anthony as the only two bowlers to win six PBA Player of the Year awards.

As usual, Williams saved his best for the biggest tournaments. His first win came in November, 2002 at the Greater Detroit Open, and it gave Williams his 35th career victory, pushing him past Mark Roth and into second place on the all-time list (Anthony heads the list with 41). It was only fitting, as former Detroit Red Wings star Gordie Howe, second on

AP/Wide World Photos

Walter Ray Williams Jr. *reacts after winning his 36th PBA Tour title in February at the 60th U.S. Open in Fountain Valley, Calif.*

the all-time National Hockey League points list behind Wayne Gretzky, rolled out the ceremonial first ball. Williams began the finals of the championship round with four strikes and never looked back, defeating Mark Roth, 215-193, for the title.

His other two victories came in what many consider to be the two biggest PBA tournaments of the year—the U.S. Open and the PBA World Championship. Those two tournaments along with the Tournament of Champions and the American Bowling Congress Masters constitute the four majors in men's bowling.

At the 60th U.S. Open in February, Williams defeated Michael Haugen Jr. in the finals, 236-198, for his fourth major victory. Haugen, who had bowled a 300 earlier in the tournament, left the 4-6-7 pins in frame 6, and that's all Williams needed.

"I threw one bad shot today and I paid the price for it," said Haugen.

PBA Tour

Jason Couch, left, and *Bryon Smith* claimed victories in the two men's majors not won by Walter Ray Williams Jr. Smith won the ABC Masters while Couch made it three straight TOCs.

"When you're bowling someone like Walter Ray, you can't afford to make mistakes."

Six weeks later at the season-ending PBA World Championship, Williams was at it again. As if he hadn't already clinched Player of the Year honors, he threw in one more major title for good measure. After automatically qualifying for the Super 16 Round (for being one of the top eight performers in the season point standings), Williams advanced to the Round of Eight in style. He lost the first game of the best-of-five round to Dale Traber, then roared back to take the next three, rolling a 279, 246...and a 300.

After defeating Ryan Shafer, 3-1, and then the ever enthusiastic Pete Weber in the semifinals, Williams grabbed the title with a 226-205 victory over Brian Kretzer. He took home $120,000 for the win in what was his tenth ESPN finals appearance of the 2002-03 season. So what's his encore?

"A goal of mine has always been to win the PBA Player of the Year and be the World Champion in horseshoes in the same year," he said in a PBA.com interview. "So I am going to try for that."

If his 2002-03 season is any indication, don't bet against him.

The Ten Biggest Stories of the Year in Bowling

10 Floridian Lesley Boczar, who had bowled a perfect 300 in 1997 with her right hand, bowls another 300 on July 22, this time with her left hand. The 39-year-old originally switched hands six years ago after suffering a damaged nerve in a finger on her right hand. She becomes the first player in Women's International Bowling Congress history to bowl a pefect game with each hand.

9 Norm Duke defeats Billy Traber at the Cambridge Credit Classic in December, 2002 in the closest final match in PBA Tour history. The two tied, 245-245. The PBA uses a sudden-death, one-ball roll-off to break ties. On the first sudden-death roll, each bowler threw a nine. On the second, each threw a strike. On the third, Traber rolled a nine while Duke came through with a strike for the victory.

8 Wendy Macpherson wins her 20th career title and her sixth major with a 218-193 finals victory over Kendra Gaines at the 43rd WIBC Queen's Tournament on April 11. Trailing by six pins going into the eighth frame, she rattles off five consecutive strikes to take control of the match.

7 At the ABC Masters in January, Bryon Smith defeats Walter Ray Williams Jr., 236-220 in the finals for the victory. Not only is it his first major win, it is the first title of his career in his 194th tournament.

6 New Jersey native Kelly Kulick makes her first career PWBA Tour win a major one with her victory at the 2003 U.S. Open. She takes the hard road to the title, beating 2002 Player of the Year Michelle Feldman in the semis, then 2001 Player of the Year Carolyn Dorin-Ballard in the finals.

5 While Tiffany Stanbrough captures two consecutive titles in June in Terre Haute, Ind. and Rockford, Ill., it is Carolyn Dorin-Ballard once again who leads all women in earnings and average through the spring/summer tour.

4 Jason Couch beats Ryan Shafer, 266-224, in the finals of the PBA Tournament of Champions in December, 2002 to become the first bowler in history to win the prestigious event three straight times. The only other player to have three TOC wins is hall of famer Mike Durbin.

3 PBA ownership and new Commissioner Fred Schreyer continue to tinker with the PBA Tour with the hopes of elevating the sport to the next level. In 2004-05, the 16 non-major tournaments will be limited to 64 bowlers, 60 of whom will be exempt for the entire season. PBA Tour Trials (similar to the PGA's Q-school) will be introduced in 2004 and the top ten finishers will earn full exemption.

continued on page 768 ▶

2 Despite increased television ratings, the PWBA cancels its fall tour and shuts down operations in August due to a lack of operating funds. The following month, founder and owner John Sommer announces that he has relinquished ownership of the league to Pinacle Events, saying, "this is the best option I had to insure a good long-term future for the tour." As of October, Pinacle president Steve Sanders was hopeful for a 2004 season.

1 Walter Ray Williams Jr. wins three tournaments in 2002-03 and earns $419,700, shattering the PBA single-season money record and pushing him over the $3 million mark in career earnings. His titles include wins at the U.S. Open in February and PBA World Championship in March, the fourth and fifth majors of his 37 career victories. He matches Earl Anthony with his sixth PBA Player of the Year award.

Model of Consistency

Walter Ray Williams Jr. won three titles in 2002-03, but it was his first one at the Greater Detroit Open that gave him 10 consecutive seasons with at least one PBA Tour win. Listed are the longest streaks in history.

		Seasons
Earl Anthony	1970-83	14
Don Johnson	1966-77	12
Brian Voss	1987-98	12
Pete Weber	1984-93	10
W.R. Williams Jr.	1993—	10

Source: Professional Bowlers Association

Tube Tops

Wendy Macpherson is the PWBA Tour's all-time leader in television appearances (final rounds are generally shown on TV). Below are the top-five through the 2003 spring/summer tour.

	App.
Wendy Macpherson	106
Leanne Barrette	99
Tish Johnson	99
Lisa Wagner	89
Aleta Sill	88

Source: Professional Women's Bowling Association

Perfectionists

Norm Duke and Billy Traber's 245-245 match in Dec., 2002 was the tightest in PBA history because it went to three sudden-death roll-offs. But Duke has also been involved in two of the PBA's four 300-300 matches.

300-300 Games	Year
Tom Baker vs Pete Weber	1981
Purvis Granger vs Norm Duke	1987
Davis Ozio vs Mike Edwards	1993
Doug Wallace vs Norm Duke	1995

Source: Professional Bowlers Association

2002-2003
Season in Review

SPORTS ALMANAC

Tournament Results

Winners of stepladder finals in all PBA, Seniors and PWBA tournaments from Sept. 2, 2002 through Aug. 27, 2003; major tournaments in **bold** type. Note (a) indicates amateur.

PBA
2002-03 Season

Final	Event	Winner	Earnings	Score	Runner-up
Sept. 2	Dream Bowl 2002 (Yokohama)	Hugh Miller	$44,000	431-428	Yukio Yamazaki
Sept. 8	Japan Cup	Robert Smith	50,000	224-222	Chris Barnes
Oct. 13	Wichita Open	Dave D'Entremont	40,000	202-179	Chris Barnes
Oct. 20	Greater Kansas City Classic	Patrick Healey Jr.	40,000	243-227	Michael Gaither
Oct. 27	Memphis Open	Brian Voss	40,000	253-247	Danny Wiseman
Nov. 3	Miller High Life Open	Danny Wiseman	40,000	277-237	Walter Ray Williams Jr.
Nov. 10	Greater Detroit Open	Walter Ray Williams Jr.	40,000	215-193	Brian Voss
Nov. 17	Banquet Classic	Eugene McCune	40,000	224-186	Walter Ray Williams Jr.
Nov. 24	Pepsi Open	Randy Pederson	40,000	216-210	Chris Barnes
Dec. 1	Cambridge Credit Classic	Norm Duke	40,000	245-245*	David Traber
Dec. 8	Empire State Open	Doug Kent	40,000	257-204	Chris Barnes
Dec. 15	**Tournament of Champions**	Jason Couch	100,000	266-224	Ryan Shafer
	at Mohegan Sun				
Jan. 6	Geico Earl Anthony Classic	Mike DeVaney	40,000	279-248	Norm Duke
Jan. 12	Medford Open	Bryan Goebel	40,000	257-212	Danny Wiseman
Jan. 19	**ABC Masters**	Bryon Smith	100,000	236-220	Walter Ray Williams Jr.
Jan. 23	Storm Las Vegas Classic	Lonnie Waliczek	40,000	260-246	Patrick Allen
	presented by The Castaways				
Feb. 2	**U.S. Open**	Walter Ray Williams Jr.	100,000	236-198	Michael Haugen Jr.
	presented by Jackson Hewitt Tax Service				
Feb. 9	Days Inn Open	Chris Barnes	40,000	244-194	Parker Bohn III
Feb. 16	VIA Bowling Open	Chris Hayden	40,000	236-227	Jason Couch
Feb. 23	Tar Heel Open	Pete Weber	40,000	245-182	Brian Voss
Mar. 2	Odor-Eaters Open	Lonnie Waliczek	40,000	218-194	Tommy Jones
Mar. 17	**PBA World Championship**	Walter Ray Williams Jr.	120,000	226-205	Brian Kretzer

*The PBA uses a sudden-death, one-ball roll-off to decide ties. On the first roll each bowler knocked down nine pins, forcing a second roll-off. On the second roll each bowler threw a strike. Finally on the third roll Traber scored a nine, while Duke threw a strike for the victory.
Note: The ABC Masters is not an official PBA Tour event.

2003-04 PBA Tour Schedule

Major tournaments are in **bold** type. See Updates chapter for results through mid-October.

September—Dream Bowl 2003*, Yokohama, JPN (Sept. 12-15); Japan Cup*, Tokyo, JPN (Sept. 18-21).

October—Banquet Open, Council Bluffs, Iowa (Oct. 8-12); Greater Kansas City Classic, Blue Springs, Mo. (Oct. 15-19); Miller High Life Open, Vernon Hills, Ill. (Oct. 22-26).

November—Pepsi Open, Grand Rapids, Mich. (Oct. 29-Nov. 2); Toledo Open, Toledo, Ohio (Nov. 5-9); Greater Philadelphia Open, Springfield, Penn. (Nov. 12-16); Empire State Open, Latham, N.Y. (Nov. 19-23); Geico Open, West Babylon, N.Y. (Nov. 26-30).

December—Cambridge Credit Classic, Windsor Locks, Conn. (Dec. 3-7); **Dexter Tournament of Champions**, Uncasville, Conn. (Dec. 11-14).

January 2004—Earl Anthony Classic, Tacoma, Wash. (Jan. 7-11); Medford Open, Medford, Ore. (Jan. 14-18); **ABC Masters**, Reno, Nev. (Jan. 20-25); Reno Open, Reno, Nev. (Jan. 25-29).

February—**U.S. Open** presented by Jackson Hewitt Tax Service, Fountain Valley, Calif. (Feb. 2-8); Odor-Eaters Open, Tucson, Ariz. (Feb. 11-15); Days Inn Open, Dallas, Texas (Feb. 18-22); Greater St. Louis Open, O'Fallon, Ill. (Feb. 25-29).

March—Indianapolis Open, Indianapolis, Ind. (Mar. 3-7); **PBA World Championship**, Taylor, Mich. (Mar. 15-21).

*Tournament doesn't count towards PBA season points total.

Tournament Results (Cont.)

Senior PBA

2003 Spring/Summer Tour

Final	Event	Winner	Earnings	Score	Runner-up
May 6	Chillicothe Open	Steve Neff	$8,000	246-187, 266-170	Mark Roth
May 13	Greater Detroit Open	John Bennett	8,000	216-203, 246-203	Dale Eagle
May 30	**ABC Senior Masters**	Dale Eagle	20,000	718-550, 707-654	Bob Glass
June 6	**Senior Storm U.S. Open**	Dave Soutar	20,000	204-164	Gary Dickinson
	presented by The Castaways				
June 11	Northern California Classic	Ernie Schlegel	8,000	221-203, 214-179	Norb Wetzel
June 18	Epicenter Classic	Lee Snow	8,000	228-202, 234-224	Henry Gonzalez
June 25	Northwest Classic	Bob Handley	8,000	221-179, 279-223	John Bennett
Aug. 5	Manassas Open	Don Sylvia	8,000	216-203, 246-203	Gary Hiday
Aug. 12	Clarksville Open	Ron Winger	8,000	208-237, 224-175 222-183	Gene Stus
	presented by Georgia Boot				
Aug. 20	Lake County Horseshoe Casino Open	Vince Mazzanti Jr.	8,000	222-215, 287-254	Charlie Tapp
Aug. 27	Days Inn Open	Bob Chamberlain	9,000	269-234, 279-165	Sal Bongiorno

Note: In 2003, all tournaments on the Senior PBA Tour followed a best-of-three match-play final-round format with the exception of the Senior Storm U.S. Open, which used a traditional step-ladder single-match final round. The ABC Senior Masters used a best-of-three match format, however each match was comprised of three games.

PWBA

2002 Fall Tour

Final	Event	Winner	Earnings	Score	Runner-up
Sept. 19	Three Rivers Open	Leanne Barrette	$9,000	225-166	Marianne DiRupo
Sept. 26	Burlington Open	Carolyn Dorin-Ballard	9,000	255-184	Kendra Gaines
Oct. 3	Lady Ebonite Classic	Liz Johnson	12,000	205-198	Leanne Barrette
Oct. 10	Greater Pasadena Open	Tish Johnson	9,000	246-187	Liz Johnson
Oct. 18	Rollers and Pro Bowlers	Tom Hein, John Handegard & Kim Terrell	15,000	668-617	Ziggy Traczenko, Hobo Boothe & Wendy Macpherson
Oct. 24	Wheelchair Awareness Classic	Tiffany Stanbrough	9,000	194-188	Kelly Kulick
Nov. 1	Greater San Diego Open	Michelle Feldman	9,000	236-204	Wendy Macpherson
Nov. 8	Storm Las Vegas PWBA Challenge	Tiffany Stanbrough	12,000	236-189	Kendra Gaines
Nov. 8	Storm Las Vegas Shootout	Liz Johnson	8,000	—*	Kendra Gaines

* In the Storm Las Vegas Shootout, the top eight PWBA season point leaders participate in a competition similar to golf's Skins Game. Players must strike to win or split a frame.

2003 Spring/Summer Tour

Final	Event	Winner	Earnings	Score	Runner-up
April 11	**WIBC Queens**	Wendy Macpherson	$14,000	218-193	Kendra Gaines
June 1	**U.S. Open**	Kelly Kulick	30,000	261-195	Carolyn Dorin-Ballard
June 8	Greater Terre Haute Open	Tiffany Stanbrough	15,000	205-186	Lisa Bishop
June 15	Pepsi Rockford Classic	Tiffany Stanbrough	15,000	266-241	Michelle Feldman
June 15	Pepsi Women's Collegiate Shootout	Jennifer Petrick (Stark St. Comm. Coll.)	4,000*	243-150	Shannon Pluhowsky (Nebraska)
June 22	Greater Cincinnati Open	Carolyn Dorin-Ballard	15,000	243-200	Liz Johnson
June 29	Greater Harrisburg Open	Dede Davidson	15,000	185-184	Cara Honeychurch
July 6	Greater Memphis Open	Tennelle Milligan	15,000	205-203	Cara Honeychurch
July 13	Dallas Open	Michelle Feldman	15,000	250-170	Kendra Gaines

*Petrick won $4,000 in scholarship funds.
Note: The Women's International Bowling Congress Queens tournament is not an official PWBA Tour event.

2003 PWBA Fall Tour Cancelled

The PWBA's four-week fall tour, scheduled for Sept. 14-Oct. 10, was cancelled due to a lack of operating funds. The tour is scheduled to resume in 2004 under new league ownership.

Tour Leaders

Official standings for 2002-03. Note that (TB) indicates Tournaments Bowled; (CR) Championship Rounds as Stepladder or Match-play Finalist; and (1st) Titles Won.

PBA
2002-03

Top 10 Money Winners

		TB	CR	1st	Earnings
1	Walter Ray Williams Jr.	21	10	3	$419,700
2	Chris Barnes	22	5	1	183,930
3	Jason Couch	21	3	1	150,470
4	Norm Duke	22	5	1	145,000
5	Bryon Smith	21	2	1	136,700
6	Pete Weber	20	5	1	134,350
7	Lonnie Waliczek	20	4	2	125,720
8	Danny Wiseman	21	3	1	120,150
9	Brian Voss	22	3	1	115,675
10	Ryan Shafer	22	4	0	100,740

Note: Earnings include ABC Masters and U.S. Open.

Top 10 Averages

		TB	Games	Avg
1	Walter Ray Williams Jr.	21	569	224.94
2	Chris Barnes	22	564	222.91
3	Norm Duke	22	517	221.78
4	Pete Weber	20	437	220.73
5	Ryan Shafer	22	461	220.29
6	Brian Voss	22	495	220.16
7	Danny Wiseman	21	484	219.53
8	Tommy Delutz Jr.	22	512	219.43
9	Parker Bohn III	21	446	218.95
10	Tommy Jones	20	503	218.10

Senior PBA
2003

Top 10 Money Winners

		TB	CR	1st	Earnings
1	Dale Eagle	11	3	1	$34,000
2	Dave Soutar	11	2	1	31,310
3	Bob Handley	5	3	1	25,200
4	Bob Chamberlain	11	3	1	24,400
5	Robert Glass	11	2	0	23,700
6	George Pappas	7	5	0	22,450
7	Steve Neff	10	3	1	22,250
8	Henry Gonzalez	10	1	0	19,000
9	Ron Winger	11	1	1	18,050
	Ernie Schlegel	9	1	1	18,050

Note: Earnings include ABC Senior Masters.

Top 10 Averages

		TB	Games	Avg
1	George Pappas	7	247	216.98
2	Gary Dickinson	5	157	216.07
3	Henry Gonzalez	10	297	216.00
4	Dale Eagle	11	283	215.92
5	Bob Chamberlain	11	321	215.32
6	Robert Glass	11	275	214.99
7	Mark Roth	5	102	214.59
8	Steve Neff	10	271	213.91
9	Bob Handley	5	163	213.64
10	Ray Johnson	5	104	213.54

PWBA
2002

Top 10 Money Winners

		TB	CR	1st	Earnings
1	Michelle Feldman	19	9	3	$80,905
2	Leanne Barrette	19	9	3	72,960
3	Kim Terrell	19	8	1	69,488
4	Kendra Gaines	19	8	1	67,800
5	Carolyn Dorin-Ballard	19	9	2	65,673
6	Kim Adler	19	4	1	59,770
7	Liz Johnson	19	5	1	53,498
8	Wendy Macpherson	19	8	0	52,400
9	Tiffany Stanbrough	19	5	2	51,930
10	Marianne DiRupo	19	4	1	44,275

Note: Earnings include WIBC Queens.

Top 10 Averages

		TB	Games	Avg
1	Leanne Barrette	19	717	216.45
2	Carolyn Dorin-Ballard	19	738	215.46
3	Wendy Macpherson	19	741	214.39
4	Michelle Feldman	19	745	213.93
5	Kendra Gaines	19	743	213.57
6	Liz Johnson	19	633	213.00
7	Cara Honeychurch	14	481	212.48
8	Kim Terrell	19	747	211.32
9	Marianne DiRupo	19	689	210.97
10	Kelly Kulick	18	618	210.86

2003

Top 10 Money Winners

		TB	CR	1st	Earnings
1	Carolyn Dorin-Ballard	8	4	1	$53,750
2	Michelle Feldman	8	3	1	45,900
3	Kelly Kulick	8	2	1	44,350
4	Wendy Macpherson	8	4	1	43,225
5	Tiffany Stanbrough	8	3	2	40,410
6	Dede Davidson	8	4	1	35,875
7	Kendra Gaines	8	2	0	35,350
8	Liz Johnson	8	2	0	31,870
9	Tish Johnson	8	3	0	31,600
10	Cara Honeychurch	8	2	0	31,250

Note: Earnings include WIBC Queens and U.S. Open.

Top 10 Averages

		TB	Games	Avg
1	Carolyn Dorin-Ballard	8	305	215.22
2	Cara Honeychurch	8	276	214.00
3	Wendy Macpherson	8	301	212.74
4	Tiffany Stanbrough	8	253	212.40
5	Tish Johnson	8	269	212.09
6	Marianne DiRupo	8	302	212.00
7	Jackie Mitskavich	5	128	211.49
8	Rachel Perez	8	275	211.32
9	Michelle Feldman	8	304	211.21
10	Kendra Gaines	8	298	210.50

1942-2003
Through the Years

ESPN
SPORTS ALMANAC

Major Championships
MEN
U.S. Open

Started in 1941 by the Bowling Proprietors' Association of America, 18 years before the founding of the Professional Bowlers Association. Originally the BPAA All-Star Tournament, it became the U.S. Open in 1971.

Multiple winners: Don Carter and Dick Weber (4); Dave Husted (3); Del Ballard Jr., Marshall Holman, Junie McMahon, Connie Schwoegler, Andy Varipapa, Pete Weber and Walter Ray Williams Jr. (2).

Year		Year		Year		Year	
1942	John Crimmins	1958	Don Carter	1974	Larry Laub	1990	Ron Palombi Jr.
1943	Connie Schwoegler	1959	Billy Welu	1975	Steve Neff	1991	Pete Weber
1944	Ned Day	1960	Harry Smith	1976	Paul Moser	1992	Robert Lawrence
1945	Buddy Bomar	1961	Bill Tucker	1977	Johnny Petraglia	1993	Del Ballard Jr.
1946	Joe Wilman	1962	Dick Weber	1978	Nelson Burton Jr.	1994	Justin Hromek
1947	Andy Varipapa	1963	Dick Weber	1979	Joe Berardi	1995	Dave Husted
1948	Andy Varipapa	1964	Bob Strampe	1980	Steve Martin	1996	Dave Husted
1949	Connie Schwoegler	1965	Dick Weber	1981	Marshall Holman	1997	Not held
1950	Junie McMahon	1966	Dick Weber	1982	Dave Husted	1998	Walter Ray Williams Jr.
1951	Dick Hoover	1967	Les Schissler	1983	Gary Dickinson	1999	Bob Learn Jr.
1952	Junie McMahon	1968	Jim Stefanich	1984	Mark Roth	2000	Robert Smith
1953	Don Carter	1969	Billy Hardwick	1985	Marshall Holman	2001	Miko Koivuniemi
1954	Don Carter	1970	Bobby Cooper	1986	Steve Cook	2003	Walter Ray Williams Jr.
1955	Steve Nagy	1971	Mike Limongello	1987	Del Ballard Jr.		
1956	Bill Lillard	1972	Don Johnson	1988	Pete Weber		
1957	Don Carter	1973	Mike McGrath	1989	Mike Aulby		

PBA World Championship

The Professional Bowlers Association was formed in 1958 and its first national championship tournament was held in Memphis in 1960. Formerly known as the PBA National Championship, the name was changed in 2002. The tournament was held in various locations (1960-80), Toledo, Ohio (1981-2002) and Taylor, Mich. (2003-).

Multiple winners: Earl Anthony (6); Mike Aulby, Dave Davis, Mike McGrath, Pete Weber, Walter Ray Williams Jr. and Wayne Zahn (2).

Year		Year		Year		Year	
1960	Don Carter	1971	Mike Limongello	1982	Earl Anthony	1993	Ron Palombi Jr.
1961	Dave Soutar	1972	Johnny Guenther	1983	Earl Anthony	1994	David Traber
1962	Carmen Salvino	1973	Earl Anthony	1984	Bob Chamberlain	1995	Scott Alexander
1963	Billy Hardwick	1974	Earl Anthony	1985	Mike Aulby	1996	Butch Soper
1964	Bob Strampe	1975	Earl Anthony	1986	Tom Crites	1997	Rick Steelsmith
1965	Dave Davis	1976	Paul Colwell	1987	Randy Pedersen	1998	Pete Weber
1966	Wayne Zahn	1977	Tommy Hudson	1988	Brian Voss	1999	Tim Criss
1967	Dave Davis	1978	Warren Nelson	1989	Pete Weber	2000	Norm Duke
1968	Wayne Zahn	1979	Mike Aulby	1990	Jim Pencak	2001	Walter Ray Williams Jr.
1969	Mike McGrath	1980	Johnny Petraglia	1991	Mike Miller	2002	Doug Kent
1970	Mike McGrath	1981	Earl Anthony	1992	Eric Forkel	2003	Walter Ray Williams Jr.

Tournament of Champions

Originally the Firestone Tournament of Champions (1965-93), the tournament has also been sponsored by General Tire (1994), Brunswick Corp. (1995-2000) and Dexter (2002-). Held in Akron, Ohio in 1965, then Fairlawn, Ohio (1966-94), Lake Zurich, Ill. (1995-96, 2000), Reno, N.V. (1997), Overland Park, Kan. (1998-99) and Uncasville, Conn. (2002-).

Multiple winners: Jason Couch and Mike Durbin (3); Earl Anthony, Dave Davis, Jim Godman, Marshall Holman and Mark Williams (2).

Year		Year		Year		Year	
1965	Billy Hardwick	1975	Dave Davis	1985	Mark Williams	1995	Mike Aulby
1966	Wayne Zahn	1976	Marshall Holman	1986	Marshall Holman	1996	Dave D'Entremont
1967	Jim Stefanich	1977	Mike Berlin	1987	Pete Weber	1997	John Gant
1968	Dave Davis	1978	Earl Anthony	1988	Mark Williams	1998	Bryan Goebel
1969	Jim Godman	1979	George Pappas	1989	Del Ballard Jr.	1999	Jason Couch
1970	Don Johnson	1980	Wayne Webb	1990	Dave Ferraro	2000	Jason Couch
1971	Johnny Petraglia	1981	Steve Cook	1991	David Ozio	2001	Not held
1972	Mike Durbin	1982	Mike Durbin	1992	Marc McDowell	2002	Jason Couch
1973	Jim Godman	1983	Joe Berardi	1993	George Branham III		
1974	Earl Anthony	1984	Mike Durbin	1994	Norm Duke		

ABC Masters Tournament

Sponsored by the American Bowling Congress, the Masters is not a PBA event, but is considered one of the four major tournaments on the men's tour and is open to qualified pros and amateurs.

Multiple winners: Mike Aulby (3); Earl Anthony, Billy Golembiewski, Dick Hoover and Billy Welu (2).

Year		Year		Year		Year	
1951	Lee Jouglard	1965	Billy Welu	1979	Doug Myers	1993	Norm Duke
1952	Willard Taylor	1966	Bob Strampe	1980	Neil Burton	1994	Steve Fehr
1953	Rudy Habetler	1967	Lou Scalia	1981	Randy Lightfoot	1995	Mike Aulby
1954	Red Elkins	1968	Pete Tountas	1982	Joe Berardi	1996	Ernie Schlegel
1955	Buzz Fazio	1969	Jim Chestney	1983	Mike Lastowski	1997	Jason Queen
1956	Dick Hoover	1970	Don Glover	1984	Earl Anthony	1998	Mike Aulby
1957	Dick Hoover	1971	Jim Godman	1985	Steve Wunderlich	1999	Brian Boghosian
1958	Tom Hennessey	1972	Bill Beach	1986	Mark Fahy	2000	Mika Koivuniemi
1959	Ray Bluth	1973	Dave Soutar	1987	Rick Steelsmith	2001	Parker Bohn III
1960	Billy Golembiewski	1974	Paul Colwell	1988	Del Ballard Jr.	2002	Brett Wolfe
1961	Don Carter	1975	Eddie Ressler Jr.	1989	Mike Aulby	2003	Bryon Smith
1962	Billy Golembiewski	1976	Nelson Burton Jr.	1990	Chris Warren		
1963	Harry Smith	1977	Earl Anthony	1991	Doug Kent		
1964	Billy Welu	1978	Frank Ellenburg	1992	Ken Johnson		

WOMEN
U.S. Open

Started by the Bowling Proprietors' Association of America in 1949. Originally the BPAA Women's All-Star Tournament (1949-70); and U.S. Open since 1971. There were two BPAA All-Star tournaments in 1955, in January and December.

Multiple winners: Marion Ladewig (8); Donna Adamek, Paula Sperber Carter, Pat Costello, Dotty Fothergill, Dana Miller-Mackie, Aleta Sill and Sylvia Wene (2).

Year		Year		Year		Year	
1949	Marion Ladewig	1962	Shirley Garms	1976	Patty Costello	1990	Dana Miller-Mackie
1950	Marion Ladewig	1963	Marion Ladewig	1977	Betty Morris	1991	Anne Marie Duggan
1951	Marion Ladewig	1964	LaVerne Carter	1978	Donna Adamek	1992	Tish Johnson
1952	Marion Ladewig	1965	Ann Slattery	1979	Diana Silva	1993	Dede Davidson
1953	Not held	1966	Joy Abel	1980	Patty Costello	1994	Aleta Sill
1954	Marion Ladewig	1967	Gloria Simon	1981	Donna Adamek	1995	Cheryl Daniels
1955	Sylvia Wene	1968	Dotty Fothergill	1982	Shinobu Saitoh	1996	Liz Johnson
1955	Anita Cantaline	1969	Dotty Fothergill	1983	Dana Miller	1997	Not held
1956	Marion Ladewig	1970	Mary Baker	1984	Karen Ellingsworth	1998	Aleta Sill
1957	Not held	1971	Paula Sperber	1985	Pat Mercatanti	1999	Kim Adler
1958	Merle Matthews	1972	Lorrie Koch	1986	Wendy Macpherson	2000	Tennelle Grijalva
1959	Marion Ladewig	1973	Millie Martorella	1987	Carol Norman	2001	Kim Terrell
1960	Sylvia Wene	1974	Patty Costello	1988	Lisa Wagner	2002	Not held
1961	Phyllis Notaro	1975	Paula Sperber Carter	1989	Robin Romeo	2003	Kelly Kulick

WIBC Queens

Sponsored by the Women's International Bowling Congress, the Queens is not a PWBA event, but is open to qualified pros and amateurs.

Multiple winners: Wendy Macpherson and Millie Martorella (3); Donna Adamek, Dotty Fothergill, Aleta Sill and Katsuko Sugimoto (2).

Year		Year		Year		Year	
1961	Janet Harman	1972	Dotty Fothergill	1983	Aleta Sill	1994	Anne Marie Duggan
1962	Dorothy Wilkinson	1973	Dotty Fothergill	1984	Kazue Inahashi	1995	Sandra Postma
1963	Irene Monterosso	1974	Judy Soutar	1985	Aleta Sill	1996	Lisa Wagner
1964	D.D. Jacobson	1975	Cindy Powell	1986	Cora Fiebig	1997	Sandra Jo Odom
1965	Betty Kuczynski	1976	Pam Rutherford	1987	Cathy Almeida	1998	Lynda Norry
1966	Judy Lee	1977	Dana Stewart	1988	Wendy Macpherson	1999	Leanne Barrette
1967	Millie Martorella	1978	Loa Boxberger	1989	Carol Gianotti	2000	Wendy Macpherson
1968	Phyllis Massey	1979	Donna Adamek	1990	Patty Ann	2001	Carolyn Dorin-Ballard
1969	Ann Feigel	1980	Donna Adamek	1991	Dede Davidson	2002	Kim Terrell
1970	Millie Martorella	1981	Katsuko Sugimoto	1992	Cindy Coburn-Carroll	2003	Wendy Macpherson
1971	Millie Martorella	1982	Katsuko Sugimoto	1993	Jan Schmidt		

WPBA National Championship (1960-1980)

The Women's Professional Bowling Association National Championship tournament was discontinued when the WPBA broke up in 1981. The WPBA changed its name from the Professional Women Bowlers Association (PWBA) in 1978.

Multiple winners: Patty Costello (3); Dotty Fothergill (2).

Year		Year		Year		Year	
1960	Marion Ladewig	1966	Judy Lee	1972	Patty Costello	1978	Toni Gillard
1961	Shirley Garms	1967	Betty Mivelaz	1973	Betty Morris	1979	Cindy Coburn
1962	Stephanie Balogh	1968	Dotty Fothergill	1974	Pat Costello	1980	Donna Adamek
1963	Janet Harman	1969	Dotty Fothergill	1975	Pam Buckner		
1964	Betty Kuczynski	1970	Bobbe North	1976	Patty Costello		
1965	Helen Duval	1971	Patty Costello	1977	Vesma Grinfelds		

Annual Leaders
Average
PBA Tour

The George Young Memorial Award, named after the late ABC Hall of Fame bowler. Based on at least 16 national PBA tournaments from 1959-78, and at least 400 games of tour competition since 1979.

Multiple winners: Mark Roth (6); Earl Anthony and Walter Ray Williams Jr. (5); Marshall Holman (3); Parker Bohn III, Norm Duke, Billy Hardwick, Don Johnson and Wayne Zahn (2).

Year	Avg	Year	Avg	Year	Avg
1962 Don Carter	212.84	1976 Mark Roth	215.97	1990 Amleto Monacelli	218.16
1963 Billy Hardwick	210.35	1977 Mark Roth	218.17	1991 Norm Duke	218.21
1964 Ray Bluth	210.51	1978 Mark Roth	219.83	1992 Dave Ferraro	219.70
1965 Dick Weber	211.90	1979 Mark Roth	221.66	1993 Walter Ray Williams Jr.	222.98
1966 Wayne Zahn	208.63	1980 Earl Anthony	218.54	1994 Norm Duke	222.83
1967 Wayne Zahn	212.14	1981 Mark Roth	216.70	1995 Mike Aulby	225.49
1968 Jim Stefanich	211.90	1982 Marshall Holman	216.15	1996 Walter Ray Williams Jr.	225.37
1969 Billy Hardwick	212.96	1983 Earl Anthony	216.65	1997 Walter Ray Williams Jr.	222.00
1970 Nelson Burton Jr.	214.91	1984 Marshall Holman	213.91	1998 Walter Ray Williams Jr.	226.13
1971 Don Johnson	213.98	1985 Mark Baker	213.72	1999 Parker Bohn III	228.04
1972 Don Johnson	215.29	1986 John Gant	214.38	2000 Chris Barnes	220.93
1973 Earl Anthony	215.80	1987 Marshall Holman	216.80	2002 Parker Bohn III	221.54
1974 Earl Anthony	219.34	1988 Mark Roth	218.04	2003 Walter Ray Williams Jr.	224.94
1975 Earl Anthony	219.06	1989 Pete Weber	215.43		

Note: After its first nine events of 2001, the PBA instituted a new September-to-March schedule with the statistics for those first nine tournaments rolled over into players' final 2001-02 statistics.

PWBA Tour

The Professional Women's Bowling Association (PWBA) went by the name Ladies Professional Bowling Tour (LPBT) from 1981-97 and the Women's Professional Bowling Association prior to that. This table is based on at least 282 games of tour competition, with the expection of 2003 when the minimum was 122 games. In 2003 the fall season was unexpectedly cancelled, shortening the year to eight tournaments.

Multiple winners: Leanne Barrette (4); Nikki Gianulias, Wendy Macpherson and Lisa Rathgeber Wagner (3); Carolyn Dorin-Ballard, Anne Marie Duggan and Aleta Sill (2).

Year	Avg	Year	Avg	Year	Avg
1981 Nikki Gianulias	213.71	1989 Lisa Wagner	211.87	1997 Wendy Macpherson	214.68
1982 Nikki Gianulias	210.63	1990 Leanne Barrette	211.53	1998 Dede Davidson	217.25
1983 Lisa Rathgeber	208.50	1991 Leanne Barrette	211.48	1999 Wendy Macpherson	218.85
1984 Aleta Sill	210.68	1992 Leanne Barrette	211.36	2000 Cara Honeychurch	215.18
1985 Aleta Sill	211.10	1993 Tish Johnson	215.39	2001 Carolyn Dorin-Ballard	214.73
1986 Nikki Gianulias	213.89	1994 Anne Marie Duggan	213.47	2002 Leanne Barrette	216.45
1987 Wendy Macpherson	211.11	1995 Anne Marie Duggan	215.79	2003 Carolyn Dorin-Ballard	215.22
1988 Lisa Wagner	213.02	1996 Tammy Turner	215.23		

Money Won
PBA Tour

Since 1998 annual totals have included two non-PBA Tour events: BPAA U.S. Open and ABC Masters.

Multiple winners: Earl Anthony and Walter Ray Williams Jr. (6); Mark Roth and Dick Weber (4); Mike Aulby (3); Parker Bohn III, Don Carter and Norm Duke (2).

Year	Earnings	Year	Earnings	Year	Earnings
1959 Dick Weber	$7,672	1974 Earl Anthony	$99,585	1989 Mike Aulby	$298,237
1960 Don Carter	22,525	1975 Earl Anthony	107,585	1990 Amleto Monacelli	204,775
1961 Dick Weber	26,280	1976 Earl Anthony	110,833	1991 David Ozio	225,585
1962 Don Carter	49,972	1977 Mark Roth	105,583	1992 Marc McDowell	176,215
1963 Dick Weber	46,333	1978 Mark Roth	134,500	1993 Walter Ray Williams Jr.	296,370
1964 Bob Strampe	33,592	1979 Mark Roth	124,517	1994 Norm Duke	273,752
1965 Dick Weber	47,675	1980 Wayne Webb	116,700	1995 Mike Aulby	219,792
1966 Wayne Zahn	54,720	1981 Earl Anthony	164,735	1996 Walter Ray Williams Jr.	244,630
1967 Dave Davis	54,165	1982 Earl Anthony	134,760	1997 Walter Ray Williams Jr.	240,544
1968 Jim Stefanich	67,375	1983 Earl Anthony	135,605	1998 Walter Ray Williams Jr.	238,225
1969 Billy Hardwick	64,160	1984 Mark Roth	158,712	1999 Parker Bohn III	232,595
1970 Mike McGrath	52,049	1985 Mike Aulby	201,200	2000 Norm Duke	136,900
1971 Johnny Petraglia	85,065	1986 Walter Ray Williams Jr.	145,550	2002 Parker Bohn III	245,200
1972 Don Johnson	56,648	1987 Pete Weber	179,516	2003 Walter Ray Williams Jr.	419,700
1973 Don McCune	69,000	1988 Brian Voss	225,485		

Note: After its first nine events of 2001, the PBA instituted a new September-to-March schedule with the statistics for those first nine tournaments rolled over into players' final 2001-02 statistics.

WPBA and PWBA Tours

WPBA leaders through 1980; PWBA leaders since 1981. Totals include the WIBC Queens, but do not include TV incentives.
Multiple winners: Aleta Sill (6); Donna Adamek and Wendy Macpherson (4); Patty Costello, Tish Johnson and Betty Morris (3); Carolyn Dorin-Ballard and Dotty Fothergill (2).

Year	Earnings	Year	Earnings	Year	Earnings
1965 Betty Kuczynski	$ 3,792	1978 Donna Adamek	$31,000	1991 Leanne Barrette	$87,618
1966 Joy Abel	5,795	1979 Donna Adamek	26,280	1992 Tish Johnson	96,872
1967 Shirley Garms	4,920	1980 Donna Adamek	31,907	1993 Aleta Sill	57,995
1968 Dotty Fothergill	16,170	1981 Donna Adamek	41,270	1994 Aleta Sill	126,325
1969 Dotty Fothergill	9,220	1982 Nikki Gianulias	45,875	1995 Tish Johnson	123,440
1970 Patty Costello	9,317	1983 Aleta Sill	42,525	1996 Wendy Macpherson	107,230
1971 Vesma Grinfelds	4,925	1984 Aleta Sill	81,452	1997 Wendy Macpherson	165,425
1972 Patty Costello	11,350	1985 Aleta Sill	52,655	1998 Carol Gianotti-Block	150,350
1973 Judy Cook	11,200	1986 Aleta Sill	36,212	1999 Wendy Macpherson	86,265
1974 Betty Morris	30,037	1987 Betty Morris	55,095	2000 Wendy Macpherson	108,525
1975 Judy Soutar	20,395	1988 Lisa Wagner	105,500	2001 Carolyn Dorin-Ballard	135,045
1976 Patty Costello	39,585	1989 Robin Romeo	113,750	2002 Michelle Feldman	80,905
1977 Betty Morris	23,802	1990 Tish Johnson	94,420	2003 Carolyn Dorin-Ballard	53,750

All-Time Leaders

All-time leading money winners on the PBA and PWBA tours, through Sept., 2003. PBA figures date back to 1959, while PWBA figures include Women's Pro Bowlers Association (WPBA) earnings through 1980. National tour titles are also listed.

Money Won

PBA Top 20

		Titles	Earnings
1	Walter Ray Williams Jr.	37	$3,131,901
2	Pete Weber	29	2,539,737
3	Parker Bohn III	29	2,286,810
4	Mike Aulby	27	2,080,210
5	Brian Voss	22	1,998,148
6	Amleto Monacelli	18	1,872,884
7	Norm Duke	20	1,851,879
8	Marshall Holman	22	1,699,390
9	Dave Husted	14	1,612,723
10	Mark Roth	34	1,611,886
11	Earl Anthony	41	1,441,061
12	Wayne Webb	20	1,399,341
13	David Ozio	11	1,369,516
14	Gary Dickinson	8	1,284,806
15	Tom Baker	9	1,225,020
16	Bob Learn Jr.	5	1,202,518
17	Jason Couch	10	1,184,220
18	Del Ballard Jr.	12	1,170,232
19	Mark Williams	7	1,169,527
20	Dave Soutar	17	1,114,537

WPBA-PWBA Top 10

		Titles	Earnings
1	Wendy Macpherson	20	$1,238,960
2	Tish Johnson	25	1,098,563
3	Aleta Sill	31	1,071,194
4	Leanne Barrette	26	1,028,994
5	Anne Marie Duggan	15	955,809
6	Carol Gianotti-Block	16	918,777
7	Carolyn Dorin-Ballard	20	916,477
8	Lisa (Rathgeber) Wagner	32	853,796
9	Kim Adler	15	827,493
10	Cheryl Daniels	10	754,545

Senior PBA Top 5

		Titles	Earnings
1	Dave Soutar	7	$455,715
2	Gene Stus	11	451,130
3	John Handegard	14	444,593
4	Gary Dickinson	10	420,046
5	Teata Semiz	8	388,778

Annual Awards
MEN
BWAA Bowler of the Year
Winners selected by Bowling Writers Association of America.
Multiple winners: Earl Anthony, Don Carter and Walter Ray Williams Jr. (6); Mark Roth (4); Mike Aulby and Dick Weber (3); Parker Bohn III, Buddy Bomar, Ned Day, Norm Duke, Billy Hardwick, Don Johnson and Steve Nagy (2).

Year	Year	Year	Year
1942 John Crimmins	1958 Don Carter	1974 Earl Anthony	1990 Amleto Monacelli
1943 Ned Day	1959 Ed Lubanski	1975 Earl Anthony	1991 David Ozio
1944 Ned Day	1960 Don Carter	1976 Earl Anthony	1992 Marc McDowell
1945 Buddy Bomar	1961 Dick Weber	1977 Mark Roth	1993 Walter Ray Williams Jr.
1946 Joe Wilman	1962 Don Carter	1978 Mark Roth	1994 Norm Duke
1947 Buddy Bomar	1963 Dick Weber	1979 Mark Roth	1995 Mike Aulby
1948 Andy Varipapa	1964 Billy Hardwick	1980 Wayne Webb	1996 Walter Ray Williams Jr.
1949 Connie Schwoegler	1965 Dick Weber	1981 Earl Anthony	1997 Walter Ray Williams Jr.
1950 Junie McMahon	1966 Wayne Zahn	1982 Earl Anthony	1998 Walter Ray Williams Jr.
1951 Lee Jouglard	1967 Dave Davis	1983 Earl Anthony	1999 Parker Bohn III
1952 Steve Nagy	1968 Jim Stefanich	1984 Mark Roth	2000 Norm Duke
1953 Don Carter	1969 Billy Hardwick	1985 Mike Aulby	2001 Parker Bohn III
1954 Don Carter	1970 Nelson Burton Jr.	1986 Walter Ray Williams Jr.	2002 Walter Ray Williams Jr.
1955 Steve Nagy	1971 Don Johnson	1987 Marshall Holman	
1956 Bill Lillard	1972 Don Johnson	1988 Brian Voss	
1957 Don Carter	1973 Don McCune	1989 Mike Aulby	

Annual Awards (Cont.)
PBA Player of the Year

Named after longtime broadcaster Chris Schenkel, winners are selected by members of Professional Bowlers Association. The PBA Player of the Year has differed from the BWAA Bowler of the Year four times–in 1963, '64, '89 and '92.

Multiple winners: Earl Anthony and Walter Ray Williams Jr. (6); Mark Roth (4); Mike Aulby, Parker Bohn III, Norm Duke, Billy Hardwick, Don Johnson and Amleto Monacelli (2).

Year		Year		Year		Year	
1963	Billy Hardwick	1973	Don McCune	1983	Earl Anthony	1993	Walter Ray Williams Jr.
1964	Bob Strampe	1974	Earl Anthony	1984	Mark Roth	1994	Norm Duke
1965	Dick Weber	1975	Earl Anthony	1985	Mike Aulby	1995	Mike Aulby
1966	Wayne Zahn	1976	Earl Anthony	1986	Walter Ray Williams Jr.	1996	Walter Ray Williams Jr.
1967	Dave Davis	1977	Mark Roth	1987	Marshall Holman	1997	Walter Ray Williams Jr.
1968	Jim Stefanich	1978	Mark Roth	1988	Brian Voss	1998	Walter Ray Williams Jr.
1969	Billy Hardwick	1979	Mark Roth	1989	Amleto Monacelli	1999	Parker Bohn III
1970	Nelson Burton Jr.	1980	Wayne Webb	1990	Amleto Monacelli	2000	Norm Duke
1971	Don Johnson	1981	Earl Anthony	1991	David Ozio	2002	Parker Bohn III
1972	Don Johnson	1982	Earl Anthony	1992	Dave Ferraro	2003	Walter Ray Williams Jr.

Note: After its first nine events of 2001, the PBA instituted a new September-to-March schedule with the statistics for those first nine tournaments rolled over into players' final 2001-02 statistics. Individual awards were handed out in 2002.

PBA Rookie of the Year

Named after PBA Hall of Famer Harry Golden, who was the PBA's national tournament director for 30 years. Winners selected by members of Professional Bowlers Association.

Year		Year		Year		Year	
1964	Jerry McCoy	1974	Cliff McNealy	1984	John Gant	1994	Tony Ament
1965	Jim Godman	1975	Guy Rowbury	1985	Tom Crites	1995	Billy Myers Jr.
1966	Bobby Cooper	1976	Mike Berlin	1986	Marc McDowell	1996	C.K. Moore
1967	Mike Durbin	1977	Steve Martin	1987	Ryan Shafer	1997	Anthony Lombardo
1968	Bob McGregor	1978	Joseph Groskind	1988	Rick Steelsmith	1998	Chris Barnes
1969	Larry Lichstein	1979	Mike Aulby	1989	Steve Hoskins	1999	Paul Fleming
1970	Denny Krick	1980	Pete Weber	1990	Brad Kiszewski	2000	Joe Ciccone
1971	Tye Critchlow	1981	Mark Fahy	1991	Ricky Ward	2002	Tommy Jones
1972	Tommy Hudson	1982	Mike Steinbach	1992	Jason Couch	2003	Brad Angelo
1973	Steve Neff	1983	Toby Contreras	1993	Mark Scroggins		

Note: After its first nine events of 2001, the PBA instituted a new September-to-March schedule with the statistics for those first nine tournaments rolled over into players' final 2001-02 statistics. Individual awards were handed out in 2002.

WOMEN
BWAA Bowler of the Year

Winners selected by Bowling Writers Association of America.

Multiple winners: Marion Ladewig (9); Donna Adamek, Lisa Rathgeber Wagner and Wendy Macpherson (4); Tish Johnson and Betty Morris (3); Leanne Barrette, Patty Costello, Dotty Fothergill, Shirley Garms, Val Mikiel, Aleta Sill, Judy Soutar and Sylvia Wene (2).

Year		Year		Year		Year	
1948	Val Mikiel	1962	Shirley Garms	1976	Patty Costello	1990	Tish Johnson
1949	Val Mikiel	1963	Marion Ladewig	1977	Betty Morris	1991	Leanne Barrette
1950	Marion Ladewig	1964	LaVerne Carter	1978	Donna Adamek	1992	Tish Johnson
1951	Marion Ladewig	1965	Betty Kuczynski	1979	Donna Adamek	1993	Lisa Wagner
1952	Marion Ladewig	1966	Joy Abel	1980	Donna Adamek	1994	Anne Marie Duggan
1953	Marion Ladewig	1967	Millie Martorella	1981	Donna Adamek	1995	Tish Johnson
1954	Marion Ladewig	1968	Dotty Fothergill	1982	Nikki Gianulias	1996	Wendy Macpherson
1955	Sylvia Wene	1969	Dotty Fothergill	1983	Lisa Rathgeber	1997	Wendy Macpherson
1956	Anita Cantaline	1970	Mary Baker	1984	Aleta Sill	1998	Carol Gianotti-Block
1957	Marion Ladewig	1971	Paula Sperber	1985	Aleta Sill	1999	Wendy Macpherson
1958	Marion Ladewig	1972	Patty Costello	1986	Lisa Wagner	2000	Wendy Macpherson
1959	Marion Ladewig	1973	Judy Soutar	1987	Betty Morris	2001	Carolyn Dorin-Ballard
1960	Sylvia Wene	1974	Betty Morris	1988	Lisa Wagner	2002	Leanne Barrette
1961	Shirley Garms	1975	Judy Soutar	1989	Robin Romeo		

PWBA Player of the Year

Winners selected by members of Professional Women's Bowling Association. The PWBA Player of the Year has differed from the BWAA Bowler of the Year four times–in 1985, '86, '90 and 2002. This award was known as the LPBT Player of the Year Award from 1983-97.

Multiple winners: Wendy Macpherson (4); Lisa Rathgeber Wagner (3); Leanne Barrette and Tish Johnson (2).

Year		Year		Year		Year	
1983	Lisa Rathgeber	1988	Lisa Wagner	1993	Lisa Wagner	1998	Carol Gianotti-Block
1984	Aleta Sill	1989	Robin Romeo	1994	Anne Marie Duggan	1999	Wendy Macpherson
1985	Patty Costello	1990	Leanne Barrette	1995	Tish Johnson	2000	Wendy Macpherson
1986	Jeanne Maiden	1991	Leanne Barrette	1996	Wendy Macpherson	2001	Carolyn Dorin-Ballard
1987	Betty Morris	1992	Tish Johnson	1997	Wendy Macpherson	2002	Michelle Feldman

Horse Racing

Jockey **Jose Santos** celebrates Funny Cide's stirring win in the 2003 Preakness.

Cide Out

Funny Cide wins the Kentucky Derby and the Preakness but comes up short in his Triple Crown bid.

Michael Morrison
is co-editor of the ESPN Sports Almanac.

So close, yet so far. For a second consecutive year and fifth in the last seventh, a horse won the first two legs of the Triple Crown and was thwarted at the Belmont. No horse has won thoroughbred racing's Triple Crown since Affirmed accomplished the feat in 1978.

This year, most experts expected a horse to step up and make a strong bid. Well they were right. They just had the wrong horse.

Empire Maker was bred to be a champion, sired by former Kentucky Derby winner Unbridled, owned and bred by renowned Juddmonte Farms, trained by hall of famer Bobby Frankel and ridden by another hall of famer Jerry Bailey. Between them, they boast five Triple Crown wins, 16 Breeders' Cup wins and 14 Eclipse Awards.

Funny Cide, on the other hand, is a New York-bred gelding sired by relatively unknown Distorted Humor and purchased for a mere $75,000 by Sackatoga Stable. While Juddmonte Farms owns approximately 300 horses, Sackatoga Stable has

owned just nine thoroughbreds since the partnership was formed in 1995.

Funny Cide was trained by journeyman Barclay Tagg (whose most accomplished horse prior to Funny Cide may be Miss Josh) and ridden by Jose Santos. Between them, they have won one Eclipse Award and one Triple Crown race winner (Santos rode Lemon Drop Kid to victory in the Belmont Stakes).

So with *Seabiscuit* on the best-seller list and the highly anticipated movie by the same name to be released two months later, there was another horse racing drama about to be played out in real life.

In Triple Crown preliminary events, Empire Maker did nothing to dispel his lofty reputation. He cruised to victory at the Florida Derby in March by $9^3/4$ lengths. At the Wood Memorial at Aqueduct in April, just three weeks before the Kentucky Derby, he won again, this time edging Funny Cide by a half a length.

Funny Cide came into the Derby with no victories in 2003. But second-place finishes to Frankel's other Triple Crown hope-

AP/Wide World Photos

It wasn't quite Secretariat's 31-length win in the 1973 Belmont Stakes, but Funny Cide had an easy time in the 2003 Preakness, cruising to a 9 ³/₄ length victory.

ful, Peace Rules, in the Louisiana Derby in March, and then his performance at the Wood made him a worthy candidate for the Run for the Roses.

"If he hadn't run as well as he did, it would have taken pressure off of going to the Kentucky Derby," said Tagg. "Now we have to go. At a mile and a quarter, he just might beat that other horse."

At 5-to-2 Empire Maker was the pre-race Derby favorite, and a foot bruise suffered at the Wood kept the odds higher than they might have been.

Odds on Funny Cide were set at 12-to-1. Starting from the five-spot, he bumped with Offlee Wild at the start before moving to third place at the first turn. Meanwhile Empire Maker ran comfortably in eighth.

At the three-quarter mark, they made their move. Down the stretch it was Funny Cide, Peace Rules and Empire Maker. And then Funny Cide broke free, squeezing between Frankel's two horses for a 1³/₄ length win.

A shocked crowd of 148,530 saw Funny Cide become the first gelding to win the Derby since Clyde Van Dusen in 1929.

When asked about the Preakness, Tagg in his usual unassuming fashion, said, "I guess I'll have to bring him now."

In the weeks before the Preakness, photos from the Derby win prompted allegations that Santos carried an electrical buzzer. He was Eventually cleared when "the buzzer" turned out to be shadows. So his focus returned to racing.

Juddmonte Farms' **John Chandler** *(2nd from left), trainer* **Bobby Frankel** *(center) and jockey* **Jerry Bailey** *(2nd from right) enjoy Empire Maker's win with N.Y. governor* **George Pataki***.*

Ten horses were entered in the Preakness, but no Empire Maker. Funny Cide was dealt the ninth post position. Early on, he sat back and watched Scrimshaw and Peace Rules battle for the lead. And then at the far turn, Funny Cide put on a burst of speed that made the other horses look like they were standing still.

As he crossed the finished line an amazing 9¾ lengths ahead of runner-up Midway Road, Santos stood up, smiled and showed the crowd of 100,268 his palm. Nothing but skin and sweat. It was sweet vindication for Santos and it was the largest margin of victory at the Preakness since the very first edition in 1873.

"The only machine I had was the horse that was carrying me," said Santos.

Tagg worried that Santos may have worked him a little too hard. "It looks impressive to win by nine," he said. "But you'd rather they win by one and be able to win by nine. It takes a little less out of your horse."

The fairytale story was all set. Like War Emblem in 2002 and Silver Charm, Real Quiet and Charismatic in the late '90s, Funny Cide won the first two legs of the Triple Crown. And now he was heading to his home track to win the Triple Crown.

A jubilant crowd of 101,864 jammed into Belmont Park on June 7, while over 11 million watched at home. Only five other horses stood in the way of history, but one of them was a well-rested Empire Maker.

continued on page 782 ▶

The Ten Biggest Stories of the Year in Horse Racing

10 Five-year-old Azeri, the 2002 Breeders' Cup Distaff winner and reigning Horse of the Year, sees her 11-race winning streak come to an end in the Lady's Secret Handicap at Santa Anita. Owner Michael Paulson blames jockey Mike Smith for dropping back in the pack early in the race.

9 Harness horse No Pan Intended wins the first two legs of the pacing Triple Crown—the Cane Pace and the Little Brown Jug—and needed a win in the Messenger Stakes to become the tenth horse in history to win all three.

8 With seven wins and two seconds in nine starts, including late-season wins in the Woodward and Jockey Club Gold Cup, Will Farish's Mineshaft stakes its claim as Horse of the Year. He is then retired in October with an ankle injury before the Breeders' Cup Classic.

7 Jockey Gary Stevens is thrown from his horse, Storming Home, after crossing the finish line at the Arlington Million in August. He suffers a punctured lung and other assorted injuries, but is back racing just three weeks later.

6 Candy Ride, undefeated in six career starts, defeats Medaglia d'Oro at the million-dollar Pacific Classic. Usual jockey Gary Stevens is forced to skip the race after his spill and is replaced by Julie Krone. Candy Ride's handlers later choose to skip the Breeders' Cup Classic.

5 Legendary horse Spectacular Bid dies of a heart attack in June at age 27. The winner of the 1979 Kentucky Derby and Preakness won 26 of 30 career starts.

4 *Seabiscuit*, based on Laura Hillenbrand's best-selling book about the rags-to-riches story of the famed 1938 Horse of the Year, becomes one of the hottest movies of the summer.

3 Bill Shoemaker, thoroughbred racing's second-winningest jockey of all-time, dies in his sleep on Oct. 12 at the age of 72. Just four-foot-11,"The Shoe" won 8,833 races (including four Kentucky Derbys, two Preaknesses and five Belmonts) over his 42-year career.

2 Juddmonte Farms' Empire Maker, the early favorite to win the Triple Crown, overcomes a disappointing second-place finish in the Kentucky Derby to edge Ten Most Wanted by ¾ of a length in the Belmont Stakes. The win gives trainer Bobby Frankel his first victory in a Triple Crown race. A hoof injury then forces Empire Maker to retire in the fall.

1 Funny Cide, a relatively unknown gelding based out of New York, shocks Empire Maker in the Kentucky Derby, then romps to a 9¾ length win in the Preakness. He becomes the fifth horse in the last seven years to win the first two jewels in the Triple Crown, only to be denied in the Belmont.

Early morning downpours created a sloppy track. Funny Cide left from the four-spot, grabbed an early lead at the first turn and held onto it as he passed the mile mark. This time, however, it was Empire Maker doing the stalking and he passed Funny Cide shortly thereafter. Down the stretch it was Empire Maker in first, Ten Most Wanted trailing and Funny Cide in third falling further and further back. He made a valiant run, but in the end, Empire Maker was the better horse on this day.

At a mile and a half, the Belmont Stakes is the longest of the three races, making Empire Maker's rest and Funny Cide's strenuous performance in the Preakness even more of a factor. In addition, many believed Funny Cide's workout on the Tuesday before the race was too taxing.

Tagg disputed the claims.

"I don't know if it was the extra quarter-mile," said Tagg. "He looks all right, but I can't talk to him."

Bailey guided Empire Maker to the winner's circle amidst a smattering of boos. As accomplished a trainer as Frankel is, this was his first victory in a Triple Crown race.

"I don't feel bad that Funny Cide didn't win the Triple Crown," he said. "I'm sure the sport would have liked to have seen him win after 25 years without a Triple Crown winner. But I'm very happy."

While everyone anticipated a rematch between the two three-year-olds, first at the Travers and later at the Breeders' Cup, it never materialized. Ultimately Empire Maker's recurring foot problem forced him to retire to stud after just eight starts.

Box Office Smash

Seabiscuit, released in the summer of 2003, became the fifth-highest grossing sports movie of all time in the U.S.

Note: Figures are as of Oct. 7, 2003.

	Gross (millions)	Year
The Waterboy	$161.456	1998
Jerry Maguire	153.620	1996
Rocky IV	127.874	1985
Rocky III	122.823	1982
Seabiscuit	118,252	2003
Rocky	117,235	1976
Remember the Titans	115,849	2000
A League of Their Own	107,439	1992

Sources: *Exhibitor Relations* and *AP.*

Golden Geldings

Since 1908, 106 geldings have competed in the Kentucky Derby (records were sketchy before that), but Funny Cide is the first in 74 years to win it. Listed below are the winners.

2003	Funny Cide
1929	Clyde Van Dusen
1920	Paul Jones
1918	Extermintaor
1914	Old Rosebud
1888	MacBeth II
1882	Apollo
1876	Vagrant

Source: *The Thoroughbred Times Racing Almanac.*

2002-2003
Season in Review

SPORTS ALMANAC

Thoroughbred Racing
Major Stakes Races
Winners of major stakes races from Nov. 24, 2002 through Sept. 23, 2003; (T) indicates turf race course; F indicates furlongs.

Late 2002

Date	Race	Track	Miles	Winner	Jockey	Purse
Nov. 24	Japan Cup*	Nakayama	1½ (T)	Falbrav	Frankie Dettori	$3,869,919
Dec. 1	Matriarch Stakes	Hollywood	1⅛ (T)	Dress to Thrill	Patrick Smullen	500,000
Dec. 1	Hollywood Derby	Hollywood	1⅛ (T)	Johar	Alex Solis	500,000
Dec. 15	Hong Kong Cup*	Sha Tin	1¼ (T)	Precision	Mick Kinane	2,325,203
Dec. 21	Hollywood Futurity	Hollywood	1¹⁄₁₆	Toccet	Jorge Chavez	409,500

2003 (through Sept. 23)

Date	Race	Track	Miles	Winner	Jockey	Purse
Feb. 1	Charles H. Strub Stakes	Santa Anita	1⅛	Medaglia d'Oro	Jerry Bailey	$400,000
Feb. 1	San Vicente Stakes	Santa Anita	7 F	Kafwain	Victor Espinoza	150,000
Feb. 15	Hutcheson Stakes	Gulfstream	7 F	Lion Tamer	John Velazquez	150,000
Feb. 15	Fountain of Youth Stakes	Gulfstream	1¹⁄₁₆	Trust N Luck	Cornelio Velazquez	200,000
Feb. 22	Donn Handicap	Gulfstream	1⅛	Harlan's Holiday	John Velazquez	500,000
Mar. 1	San Rafael Stakes	Santa Anita	1	Rojo Toro	Jerry Bailey	200,000
Mar. 1	Santa Anita Handicap	Santa Anita	1¼	Milwaukee Brew	Edgar Prado	1,000,000
Mar. 8	El Camino Real Derby	Golden Gate	1¹⁄₁₆	Ocean Terrace	Mike Smith	200,000
Mar. 8	Santa Anita Oaks	Santa Anita	1¹⁄₁₆	Composure	Jerry Bailey	300,000
Mar. 9	Louisiana Derby	Fair Grounds	1¹⁄₁₆	Peace Rules	Edgar Prado	750,000
Mar. 15	Florida Derby	Gulfstream	1⅛	Empire Maker	Jerry Bailey	1,000,000
Mar. 15	Swale Stakes	Gulfstream	7 F	Midas Eyes	Jerry Bailey	150,000
Mar. 16	San Felipe Stakes	Santa Anita	1¹⁄₁₆	Buddy Gil	Gary Stevens	250,000
Mar. 16	Gotham Stakes	Aqueduct	1	Alysweep	Richard Migliore	200,000
Mar. 16	Tampa Bay Derby	Tampa Bay	1¹⁄₁₆	Region Of Merit	Eibar Coa	250,000
Mar. 22	Lane's End Stakes	Turfway	1⅛	New York Hero	Norberto Arroyo Jr.	500,000
Mar. 29	UAE Derby	Nad al-Sheba	1¼	Victory Moon	Wayne Smith	2,000,000
Mar. 29	Dubai World Cup	Nad al-Sheba	1¼	Moon Ballad	Frankie Dettori	6,000,000
Mar. 30	WinStar Derby	Sunland	1¹⁄₁₆	Excessivepleasure	Pat Day	500,000
Apr. 5	Santa Anita Derby	Santa Anita	1⅛	Buddy Gil	Gary Stevens	750,000
Apr. 5	Ashland Stakes	Keeneland	1¹⁄₁₆	Elloluv	Robby Albarado	500,000
Apr. 5	The Oaklawn Handicap	Oaklawn	1⅛	Medaglia d'Oro	Jerry Bailey	500,000
Apr. 5	Apple Blossom Handicap	Oaklawn	1¹⁄₁₆	Azeri	Mike Smith	500,000
Apr. 5	Illinois Derby	Hawthorne	1⅛	Ten Most Wanted	Pat Day	500,000
Apr. 12	Wood Memorial	Aqueduct	1⅛	Empire Maker	Jerry Bailey	750,000
Apr. 12	Blue Grass Stakes	Keeneland	1⅛	Peace Rules	Edgar Prado	750,000
Apr. 12	Arkansas Derby	Oaklawn	1⅛	Sir Cherokee	Terry Thompson	500,000
Apr. 19	Lexington Stakes	Keeneland	1¹⁄₁₆	Scrimshaw	Edgar Prado	363,675
Apr. 20	San Juan Capistrano H.	Santa Anita	1¾	Passinetti	Brice Blanc	400,000
Apr. 27	Queen Elizabeth II Cup*	Sha Tin	1¼ (T)	Eishin Preston	Yuichi Fukunaga	1,808,492
May 2	Kentucky Oaks	Churchill Downs	1⅛	Bird Town	Edgar Prado	573,800
May 2	Louisville Breeders' Cup H	Churchill Downs	1¹⁄₁₆	You	Jerry Bailey	325,500
May 3	**Kentucky Derby**	Churchill Downs	1¼	Funny Cide	Jose Santos	1,100,200
May 10	Lone Star Derby	Lone Star	1⅛	Dynever	Edgar Prado	500,000
May 16	Black-Eyed Susan Stakes	Pimlico	1⅛	Roar Emotion	John Velazquez	200,000
May 16	Pimlico Special	Pimlico	1³⁄₁₆	Mineshaft	Robby Albarado	600,000
May 17	**Preakness Stakes**	Pimlico	1³⁄₁₆	Funny Cide	Jose Santos	1,000,000
May 24	Peter Pan Stakes	Belmont	1⅛	Go Rockin' Robin	Shaun Bridgmohan	200,000
May 26	Gamely BC Handicap	Hollywood	1⅛ (T)	Tates Creek	Pat Valenzuela	439,600
May 26	Shoemaker BC Mile	Hollywood	1 (T)	Redattore	Alex Solis	475,000
May 26	Metropolitan Mile	Belmont	1	Aldebaran	Jerry Bailey	750,000
June 6	Acorn Stakes	Belmont	1	Bird Town	Edgar Prado	250,000
June 8	Riva Ridge BC Stakes	Belmont	7 F	Posse	Corey Lanerie	200,000
June 8	**Belmont Stakes**	Belmont	1½	Empire Maker	Jerry Bailey	1,000,000
June 8	Manhattan Handicap	Belmont	1¼ (T)	Denon	Jerry Bailey	400,000
June 8	Vodafone English Derby	Epsom Downs	1½ (T)	Kris Kin	Kieren Fallon	1,400,000
June 14	Charles Whittingham H	Hollywood Park	1¼ (T)	Storming Home	Gary Stevens	350,000

Major Stakes Races (Cont.)

Date	Race	Track	Miles	Winner	Jockey	Purse
June 14	The Californian	Hollywood Park	1⅛	Kudos	Alex Solis	$400,000
June 14	Hollywood Oaks	Hollywood Park	1¹⁄₁₆	Santa Catarina	Gary Stevens	250,000
June 14	Stephen Foster Handicap	Churchill Downs	1⅛	Perfect Drift	Pat Day	856,500
June 21	Ogden Phipps Handicap	Belmont	1¹⁄₁₆	Sightseek	Jerry Bailey	300,000
June 21	Vanity Handicap	Hollywood Park	1⅛	Azeri	Mike Smith	250,000
June 21	Ohio Derby	Thistledown	1⅛	Wild and Wicked	Shane Sellers	300,000
June 22	Queen's Plate	Woodbine	1¼	Wando	Patrick Husbands	1,000,000
June 28	Mother Goose Stakes	Belmont	1⅛	Spoken Fur	Jerry Bailey	300,000
June 29	Irish Derby	Curragh	1½ (T)	Alamshar	Johnny Murtagh	1,485,640
July 5	Suburban Handicap	Belmont	1¼	Mineshaft	Robby Albarado	500,000
July 5	American Oaks	Hollywood Park	1¼ (T)	Dimitrova	David Flores	750,000
July 13	Hollywood Gold Cup	Hollywood Park	1¼	Congaree	Jerry Bailey	750,000
July 13	Swaps Stakes	Hollywood Park	1⅛	During	Jerry Bailey	400,000
July 19	Washington Park H.	Arlington	1³⁄₁₆	Perfect Drift	Pat Day	400,000
July 19	Coaching Club Am. Oaks	Belmont	1½	Spoken Fur	Jerry Bailey	500,000
July 20	Delaware Handicap	Delaware	1¼	Wild Spirit	Jerry Bailey	750,000
July 26	Test Stakes	Saratoga	7 F	Lady Tak	Jerry Bailey	250,000
July 26	Diana Handicap	Saratoga	1⅛	Voodoo Dancer	Corey Nakatani	500,000
July 26	K. George VI and Q. Elizabeth Diamond Stakes*	Ascot	1½ (T)	Alamshar	Johnny Murtagh	1,242,000
July 27	Eddie Read Handicap	Del Mar	1⅛ (T)	Special Ring	David Flores	400,000
July 27	Go for Wand Handicap	Saratoga	1⅛	Sightseek	Jerry Bailey	250,000
Aug. 2	Whitney Handicap	Saratoga	1⅛	Medaglia d'Oro	Jerry Bailey	750,000
Aug. 2	Jim Dandy Stakes	Saratoga	1⅛	Strong Hope	John Velazquez	500,000
Aug. 3	Haskell Invitational	Monmouth	1⅛	Peace Rules	Edgar Prado	1,000,000
Aug. 9	Sword Dancer Invitational*	Saratoga	1½	Whitmore's Conn	Jean-Luc Samyn	500,000
Aug. 16	Arlington Million*	Arlington	1¼ (T)	Sulamani	David Flores	1,000,000
Aug. 16	Bevery D. Stakes	Arlington	1³⁄₁₆ (T)	Heat Haze	Jose Valdivia	700,000
Aug. 16	Alabama Stakes	Saratoga	1¼	Island Fashion	John Velazquez	750,000
Aug. 16	Saratoga BC Handicap	Saratoga	1¼	Puzzlement	Jorge Chavez	300,000
Aug. 22	Personal Ensign Handicap	Saratoga	1¼	Passing Shot	Jose Santos	400,000
Aug. 23	Travers Stakes	Saratoga	1¼	Ten Most Wanted	Pat Day	1,000,000
Aug. 23	King's Bishop Stakes	Saratoga	7 F	Valid Video	Joe Bravo	200,000
Aug. 24	Pacific Classic	Del Mar	1¼	Candy Ride	Julie Krone	1,000,000
Sept. 6	Gazelle Handicap	Belmont	1⅛	Buy the Sport	Pat Day	250,000
Sept. 6	Man o' War Stakes	Belmont	1³⁄₈ (T)	Lunar Sovereign	Richard Migliore	500,000
Sept. 6	The Woodward Stakes	Belmont	1⅛	Mineshaft	Robby Albarado	500,000
Sept. 6	Irish Champion Stakes*	Leopardstown	1¼ (T)	High Chaparral	Mick Kinane	1,148,776
Sept. 7	Grosser Bugatti Preis*	Baden-Baden	1½ (T)	Mamool	Frankie Dettori	999,435
Sept. 13	Kentucky Cup Classic	Turfway	1⅛	Perfect Drift	Pat Day	350,000
Sept. 13	Ruffian Handicap	Belmont	1¹⁄₁₆	Wild Spirit	Jerry Bailey	300,000
Sept. 14	Atto Mile	Woodbine	1 (T)	Touch of the Blues	Kent Desormeaux	1,000,000
Sept. 14	Matron Stakes	Belmont	1	Marylebone	Edgar Prado	200,000
Sept. 14	Futurity Stakes	Belmont	1	Cuvee	Jerry Bailey	200,000
Sept. 20	Super Derby XXIV	Louisiana Downs	1⅛	Ten Most Wanted	Pat Day	500,000
Sept. 20	Kentucky Cup Turf	Kentucky Downs	1½ (T)	Rochester	Eddie Martin Jr.	200,000

*World Series Racing Championship series race (see standings on page 786).

NTRA National Thoroughbred Poll

The NTRA Thoroughbred Poll conducted by National Thoroughbred Racing Association, covering races through Sept. 23, 2003. Rankings are based on the votes of horse racing media representatives on a 10-9-8-7-6-5-4-3-2-1 basis. First place votes are in parentheses.

		Pts	Age	Sex	'03 Record Sts—1-2-3	Owner	Trainer
1	Mineshaft (13)	193	4	Colt	8—6-2-0	William Farish, James Elkins Jr. & Temple Webber Jr.	Neil Howard
2	Azeri (7)	180	5	Mare	4—4-0-0	Allen Paulson Living Trust	Laura de Seroux
3	Candy Ride	121	4	Colt	3,—3-0-0	Sidney H. & Jenny Craig	Ronal McAnally
4	Perfect Drift	91	4	Gelding	6—4-0-0	Dr. William Reed/Stonecrest Farm	Murray Johnson
5	Medaglia D'Oro	89	4	Colt	4—3-1-0	Edmund Gann	Bobby Frankel
6	Empire Maker	85	3	Colt	6—3-3-0	Juddmonte Farms, Inc.	Bobby Frankel
7	Aldebaran	66	5	Horse	7—5-1-1	Flaxman Holdings	Bobby Frankel
8	Ten Most Wanted	62	3	Colt	9—4-2-1	James Chisholm, Michael Jarvis, J. Paul Reddam & Horizon Stable	Wallace Dollase
9	Funny Cide	59	3	Gelding	7—2-3-1	Sackatoga Stable	Barclay Tagg
10	Congaree	44	5	Horse	7—4-2-0	Stonerside Stable	Bob Baffert

Others receiving votes: 11. Sightseek (36 points); **12.** Storming Home (24); **13.** Heat Haze (13); **14.** Wild Spirit & Peace Rules (10); **16.** High Chaparral (8); **17.** Cuvee (3); **18.** Silver Wagon & Take Charge Lady (2); **20.** Tenpins & Halfbridled (1).

The 2003 Triple Crown

129TH KENTUCKY DERBY

Grade I for three-year-olds; 10th race at Churchill Downs in Louisville. **Date**—May 3, 2003; **Distance**—1¼ miles; **Stakes Purse**—$1,100,200 ($800,200 to winner; $170,000 for 2nd; $85,000 for 3rd; $45,000 for 4th); **Track**—Fast; **Off**—6:08 p.m. EDT; **Favorite**—Empire Maker (5-2 odds). **Winner**—Funny Cide; **Field**—16 horses; **Time**—2:01.19; **Start**—Good for all; **Won**—Driving; **Sire**—Distorted Humor; **Dam**—Belle's Good Cide; **Record** (going into race)—6 starts, 3 wins, 2 second, 0 third; **Last start**—2nd in Wood Memorial (Apr. 12); **Breeder**—Win Star Farm (N.Y.).

Order of Finish	Jockey	PP	1/4	1/2	3/4	Mile	Stretch	Finish	To $1
Funny Cide	Jose Santos	5	4-½	3-½	3-1½	2-1	1-hd	1-1¾	12.80
Empire Maker	Jerry Bailey	11	8-½	8-2½	8-1½	3-1½	3-1½	2-hd	2.50
Peace Rules	Edgar Prado	4	2-1½	2-1½	2-1½	1-½	2-½	3-hd	6.30
Atswhatimtalknbout	David Flores	3	10-1½	12-2	11-2	10-½	5-½	4-2¾	8.90
Eye of the Tiger	Eibar Coa	12	3-hd	4-1½	4-½	4-1	4-1½	5-1	41.50
Buddy Gil	Gary Stevens	7	13-hd	13-2½	13-4	11-1	6-½	6-¾	7.20
Outta Here	Kent Desormeaux	14	15-1½	14-hd	16	15-3	14-1½	7-1	39.70
Ten Cents a Shine	Calvin Borel	13	16	16	15-½	14-3½	11-1	8-nk	37.20
Ten Most Wanted	Pat Day	15	12-1½	10-½	10-1½	9-½	10-½	9-1¾	6.60
Domestic Dispute	Alex Solis	10	7-½	7-1	5-hd	7-hd	7-½	10-1	44.00
Scrimshaw	Cornelio Velasquez	16	5-½	6-½	7-hd	8-hd	8-½	11-1	16.50
Offlee Wild	Robby Albarado	6	11-1½	11-1½	9-1½	6-½	9-1	12-5½	29.90
Supah Blitz	Rosemary Homeister Jr.	1	9-2½	9-½	12-2½	13-hd	12-1	13-1¾	43.10
Indian Express	Tyler Baze	8	6-½	5-hd	6-hd	12-hd	15-2½	14-1¼	10.80
Lone Star Sky	Shane Sellers	9	14-1½	15-1	14-½	16	16	15-1	52.10
Brancusi	Tony Farina	2	1-½	1-½	1-hd	5-hd	13-1½	16	29.30

Times—22.78; 46.23; 1:10.48; 1:35.75; 2:01.19.

$2 Mutual Prices—#6 Funny Cide ($27.60, $12.40, $8.20); #12 Empire Maker ($5.80, $4.40); #5 Peace Rules ($6.00). **Exacta**—(6-12) for $97.00; **Trifecta**—(6-12-5) for $664.80; **Superfecta**—(6-12-5-4) for $2,795.80; **Pick Six**—(2/6-3-4-2-9-6) for $453,285.40; **Scratched**—Sir Cherokee; **Overweights**—none; **Attendance**—148,530; **TV Rating**—7.6/20 share (NBC).

Trainers & Owners (by finish): **1**—Barclay Tagg & Sackatoga Stable; **2**—Bobby Frankel & Juddmonte Farms, Inc.; **3**—Bobby Frankel & Edmund Gann; **4**—Ronald Ellis & B. Wayne Hughes/Biscuit Stables; **5**—Jerry Hollendorfer & John D. Gunther; **6**—Jeff Mullens & Desperado Stables; **7**—Bill Currin & Bill Currin/Al Eisman; **8**—D. Wayne Lukas & Kenneth/Sarah Ramsey; **9**—Wallace Dollase & James Chisholm/Michael Jarvis/J. Paul Reddam/Horizon Stable; **10**—Patrick Gallagher & Chuck Winner/David Bienstock; **11**—D. Wayne Lukas & Bob/Beverly Lewis; **12**—Thomas V. Smith & Azalea Stables; **13**—Emanuel Tortora & Bee Bee Stables/Jacqueline Tortora; **14**—Bob Baffert & Phil Chess; **15**—Thomas Amoss & Walter New; **16**—Patrick Biancone & Michael Tabor.

128TH PREAKNESS STAKES

Grade I for three-year-olds; 12th race at Pimlico in Baltimore. **Date**—May 17, 2003; **Distance**—1$\frac{3}{16}$ miles; **Stakes Purse**—$1,000,000 ($650,000 to winner; $200,000 for 2nd; $100,000 for 3rd; $50,000 for 4th); **Track**—Good; **Off**—6:14 p.m. EDT; **Favorite**—Funny Cide (9-5 odds). **Winner**—Funny Cide; **Field**—10 horses; **Time**—1:55.61; **Start**—Good for all; **Won**—Driving; **Sire**—Distorted Humor; **Dam**—Belle's Good Cide; **Record** (going into race)—7 starts, 4 wins, 2 second, 0 third; **Last start**—1st in Kentucky Derby (May 3); **Breeder**—Win Star Farm (N.Y.).

Order of Finish	Jockey	PP	1/4	1/2	3/4	Stretch	Finish	To $1
Funny Cide	Jose Santos	9	3-1	2-1	2-1½	1-5	1-9¾	1.90
Midway Road	Robby Albarado	6	7-2	5-1½	3-½	4-3	2-¾	20.00
Scrimshaw	Gary Stevens	2	1-hd	3-1½	4-1	2-hd	3-no	4.90*
Peace Rules	Edgar Prado	7	2-2	1-1	1-½	3-1	4-2	2.40
Senor Swinger	Pat Day	10	10	10	10	6-hd	5-hd	4.90*
New York Hero	Jorge Chavez	8	5-hd	6-1½	6-1	5-3½	6-3¼	19.60
Foufa's Warrior	Ramon Dominguez	3	9-4½	8-hd	7-3	7-hd	7-1¼	22.40
Cherokee's Boy	Ryan Fogelsonger	1	4-1½	4-½	5-2	8-3	8-5¾	9.70
Ten Cents a Shine	Jerry Bailey	5	8-hd	9-4½	8-2½	9-3½	9-1	8.50
Kissin Saint	Richard Migliore	4	6-1½	7-2½	9-hd	10	10	10.20

*coupled

Times—23.37; 47.14; 1:11.62; 1:36.42; 1:55.61.

$2 Mutual Prices—#9 Funny Cide ($5.80, $4.60, $3.40); #6 Midway Road ($15.40, $9.00); #1 Scrimshaw ($4.00).

Exacta—(9-6) for $120.60; **Trifecta**—(9-6-1) for $684.20; **Superfecta**—(9-6-1-7) for $792.20; **Pick Three**—(10-8-9) for $652.40; **Scratched**—none; **Overweights**—none; **Attendance**—100,268; **TV Rating**—5.6/15 share (NBC).

Trainers & Owners (by finish): **1**—Barclay Tagg & Sackatoga Stable; **2**—Neil Howard & William S. Farish; **3**—D. Wayne Lukas & Robert/Beverly Lewis; **4**—Bobby Frankel & Edmund Gann; **5**—Bob Baffert & Robert/Beverly Lewis; **6**—Jennifer Pederson & Paraneck Stable; **7**—Lawrence E. Murray & Sondra D. Bender; **8**—Gary Capuano & ZWP Stable; **9**—D. Wayne Lukas & Kenneth/Sarah Ramsey; **10**—Lisa L. Lewis & Peter F. Karches/Michael Rankowitz.

The 2003 Triple Crown (Cont.)

135TH BELMONT STAKES

Grade I for three-year-olds; 11th race at Belmont Park in Elmont, N.Y. **Date**—June 7, 2003; **Distance**—1½ miles; **Stakes Purse**—$1,000,000 ($600,000 to winner; $200,000 for 2nd; $110,000 for 3rd; $60,000 for 4th; $30,000 for 5th); **Track**—Sloppy; **Off**—6:40 p.m. EDT; **Favorite**—Funny Cide (even odds). **Winner**—Empire Maker; **Field**—6 horses; **Time**—2:28.26; **Start**—Good for all; **Won**—Driving; **Sire**—Unbridled; **Dam**—Toussaud; **Record** (going into race)—6 starts, 3 wins, 2 second, 1 third; **Last Start**—2nd in Kentucky Derby (May 3); **Breeder**—Juddmonte Farms, Inc. (Ky.).

Order of Finish	Jockey	PP	1/4	1/2	Mile	1-1/4	Stretch	Finish	To $1
Empire Maker	Jerry Bailey	1	3-2	2-1	2-1½	1-1	1-1½	1-¾	2.00
Ten Most Wanted	Pat Day	6	4-½	5-5	4-hd	3-4	2-1½	2-4¼	9.70
Funny Cide	Jose Santos	4	1-1	1-1	1-hd	2-1	3-5	3-5¼	1.00
Dynever	Edgar Prado	5	5-4	4-hd	5-7	4-3	4-10	4-15¼	8.50
Supervisor	John Velazquez	2	6	6	6	6	5-1	5-4½	14.80
Scrimshaw	Gary Stevens	3	2-1½	3-1	3-hd	5-4	6	6	11.00

Times—23.85; 48.70; 1:13.51; 1:38.05; 2:02.62; 2:28.26.
$2 Mutual Prices—#1 Empire Maker ($6.00, $3.70, $2.80); #6 Ten Most Wanted ($5.80, $3.20); #4 Funny Cide ($2.70).
Exacta—(1-6) for $44.00; **Trifecta**—(1-6-4) for $67.50; **Pick Six**—(5-6-2-5-10-1) for $900.00; **Scratched**—none; **Overweights**—none; **Attendance**—101,864; **TV Rating**—10.7/25 share (NBC).

Trainers & Owners (by finish): **1**—Bobby Frankel & Juddmonte Farms, Inc.; **2**—Wallace Dollase & James Chisholm/Michael Jarvis/J. Paul Reddam/Horizon Stable; **3**—Barclay Tagg & Sackatoga Stable; **4**—Christophe Clement & Peter F. Karches/Catherine Wills; **5**—Linda Rice & Rodney G. Lundock; **6**—D. Wayne Lukas & Robert/Beverly Lewis.

2002-03 Money Leaders

Official Top 10 standings for 2002 and unofficial Top 10 standings for 2003, through Sept. 23, 2003.

FINAL 2002

HORSES	Age	Sts	1-2-3	Earnings
Street Cry (IRE)	4	3	2-1-0	$4,266,615
War Emblem	3	10	5-0-0	3,455,000
Volponi	4	8	3-3-1	2,389,200
Medaglia d'Oro	3	9	4-3-0	2,260,600
Azeri	4	9	8-1-0	2,181,540
Falbrav (IRE)	4	2	1-0-0	2,063,794
Sarafan	5	12	2-4-2	2,039,765
Grandera (IRE)	4	6	2-0-1	1,851,519
Came Home	3	8	6-0-0	1,624,500
Harlan's Holiday	3	10	3-2-1	1,606,000

JOCKEYS	Mts	1st	Earnings
Jerry Bailey	833	214	$22,871,814
Edgar Prado	1527	289	18,024,429
John Velazquez	1394	289	16,361,445
Pat Day	1155	258	15,904,396
Jorge Chavez	1196	223	13,721,254
Victor Espinoza	1143	188	12,590,646
Patrick Valenzuela	1298	221	12,544,098
Alex Solis	1123	217	12,027,315
Jose Santos	1161	176	11,917,955
Kent Desormeaux	977	160	11,676,407

TRAINERS	Sts	1st	Earnings
Bobby Frankel	480	117	$17,748,340
Bob Baffert	686	133	12,029,115
Saeed bin Suroor	77	18	10,837,975
Steve Asmussen	1810	407	10,248,260
Todd Pletcher	699	147	8,702,228
Scott Lake	1790	400	8,307,347
Bill Mott	710	149	7,521,998
Ken McPeek	469	81	6,647,289
D. Wayne Lukas	474	82	5,996,362
Jerry Hollendorfer	1119	265	5,909,710

2003 (Through Sept. 23)

HORSES	Age	Sts	1-2-3	Earnings
Moon Ballad (IRE)	4	2	1-0-0	$3,633,318
Wando	3	7	5-1-0	1,972,025
Funny Cide	3	7	2-2-2	1,963,200
Empire Maker	3	6	3-3-0	1,936,200
Peace Rules	3	6	3-1-1	1,850,000
Harlan's Holiday	4	6	2-2-0	1,685,100
Mineshaft	4	8	6-2-0	1,609,686
Ten Most Wanted	3	9	4-2-1	1,544,860
Medaglia d'Oro	4	4	3-1-0	1,190,000
Congaree	5	7	4-2-0	1,170,000

JOCKEYS	Mts	1st	Earnings
Jerry Bailey	653	175	$17,319,303
Edgar Prado	1177	213	14,223,544
John Velazquez	1029	249	12,738,992
Patrick Valenzuela	1125	225	11,148,787
Pat Day	764	150	10,084,511
Jose Santos	959	145	9,773,708
Alex Solis	843	147	9,279,336
Robby Albarado	919	146	8,608,786
Todd Kabel	551	111	8,461,096
David Flores	814	127	8,384,936

TRAINERS	Sts	1st	Earnings
Bobby Frankel	291	89	$15,107,191
Todd Pletcher	621	149	10,411,956
Steve Asmussen	1359	319	8,711,295
Bob Baffert	498	99	7,519,562
Scott Lake	1504	349	6,987,730
Saeed bin Suroor	18	3	5,420,247
Bill Mott	559	109	5,379,245
Cole Norman	880	243	4,574,056
Jerry Hollendorfer	891	201	4,507,974
Doug O'Neill	540	92	4,459,782

2003 World Series Racing Championship

The 2003 World Series Racing Championship includes 12 prestigious thoroughbred races in nine countries on four continents. Points are awarded to the top six finishers in each race. Through Sept. 23, 2003 and five series races.

Horses

	Horses	Pts
1	Sulamani (IRE)	18
2	Alamshar (IRE)	15
3	Mamool (IRE)	12
	High Chaparral (IRE)	12
	Eishin Preston (USA)	12

Jockeys

	Jockeys	Pts
1	Frankie Dettori	20
2	Mick Kinane	18
3	Johnny Murtagh	15
4	Yuichi Fukunaga	12
	David Flores	12

Trainers

	Trainers	Pts
1	Saeed bin Suroor	32
2	Aidan O'Brien	19
3	John Oxx	15
4	Shuji Kitahashi	12
5	Andreas Wohler	10

Harness Racing
2002-03 Major Stakes Races

Winners of major stakes races from Oct. 19, 2002 through Sept. 23, 2003; all paces and trots cover one mile; (BC) indicates year-end Breeders' Crown series.

Late 2002

Date	Race	Raceway	Winner	Time	Driver	Purse
Oct. 19	BC 3-Yr-Old Colt Pace	Woodbine	Art Major	1:51	John Campbell	$500,000
Oct. 19	BC 3-Yr-Old Filly Pace	Woodbine	Allamerican Nadia	1:53	Chris Christoforou	500,000
Oct. 19	BC 3-Yr-Old Colt Trot	Woodbine	Kadabra	1:54⅕	David Miller	542,500
Oct. 19	BC 3-Yr-Old Filly Trot	Woodbine	Cameron Hall	1:55⅘	Trevor Ritchie	542,500
Oct. 19	BC 2-Yr-Old Colt Pace	Woodbine	Totally Western	1:52⅗	Mario Baillargeon	594,600
Oct. 19	BC 2-Yr-Old Filly Pace	Woodbine	Ambro Amoretto	1:53	Luc Ouellette	522,300
Oct. 19	BC 2-Yr-Old Colt Trot	Woodbine	Broadway Hall	1:57⅖	John Campbell	475,500
Oct. 19	BC 2-Yr-Old Filly Trot	Woodbine	Pick Me Up	1:57⅗	Luc Ouellette	484,600
Oc. 26	**Messenger Stakes**	The Meadows	Allamerican Ingot	1:50⅗	David Miller	400,000
Dec. 7	Goldsmith Maid	Meadowlands	Pizza Dolce	1:58⅕	David Miller	370,000
Dec. 7	Three Diamonds Pace	Meadowlands	Dream of Mimi	1:55⅕	Jack Moiseyev	370,000
Dec. 7	Valley Victory	Meadowlands	Garden Spot	1:57⅖	Stephen Smith	410,000
Dec. 7	Governor's Cup	Meadowlands	Allamerican Native	1:53⅕	John Campbell	520,000

2003 (through Sept. 23)

Date	Race	Raceway	Winner	Time	Driver	Purse
May 30	Hoosier Cup	Hoosier Park	Jr. Mint	1:53⅕	Paul MacDonell	$450,000
May 31	New Jersey Classic	Meadowlands	Artesian	1:50⅘	Mike Lachance	500,000
June 21	North America Cup	Woodbine	Yankee Cruiser	1:49⅗	Dean Magee	1,542,500
July 11	Del Miller Memorial	Meadowlands	Luby	1:54⅘	Jim Doherty	410,000
July 11	Stanley Dancer Trot	Meadowlands	Power to Charm	1:53⅗	John Campbell	412,000
July 12	Meadowlands Pace	Meadowlands	Allamerican Theory	1:49⅗	Mike Lachance	1,000,000
July 31	Peter Haughton Memorial	Meadowlands	Tom Ridge	1:56⅕	Ron Pierce	440,000
July 31	Merrie Annabelle Final	Meadowlands	Ladylind	1:57⅗	Cat Manzi	350,000
Aug. 1	Sweetheart Pace	Meadowlands	So Artsi	1:53⅖	John Campbell	430,000
Aug. 1	Woodrow Wilson Pace	Meadowlands	Modern Art	1:51⅗	David Miller	640,000
Aug. 2	**Hambletonian**	Meadowlands	Amigo Hall	1:54	Mike Lachance	1,000,000
Aug. 2	Hambletonian Oaks	Meadowlands	Southwind Allaire	1:53⅘	Ron Pierce	500,000
Aug. 2	Mistletoe Shalee	Meadowlands	Armbro Amoretto	1:50⅕	Luc Ouellette	400,000
Aug. 2	Nat Ray	Meadowlands	Rotation	1:52⅗	Trevor Ritchie	450,000
Aug. 16	Canadian Pacing Derby	Woodbine	Art Major	1:49⅕	John Campbell	609,760
Aug. 17	Confederation Cup XXVII	Flamboro	Stonebridge Premio	1:54⅗	Mike Lachance	558,000
Aug. 23	**Yonkers Trot**	Yonkers	Sugar Trader	1:58⅗	Cat Manzi	337,229
Aug. 30	BC Open Pace	Woodbine	Art Major	1:49⅘	John Campbell	540,000
Aug. 30	BC Open Trot	Woodbine	Fool's Goal	1:52⅘	Jack Moiseyev	800,000
Aug. 30	BC Open Mare Pace	Woodbine	Eternal Camnation	1:51⅕	Eric Ledford	300,000
Aug. 30	Metro Pace	Woodbine	Camelot Hall	1:51	George Brennan	1,100,000
Sept. 1	**Cane Pace**	Freehold	No Pan Intended	1:53⅗	David Miller	331,000
Sept. 13	Maple Leaf Trot	Mohawk	Rotation	1:53⅖	Trevor Ritchie	851,500
Sept. 18	**Little Brown Jug**	Delaware	No Pan Intended	1:53	David Miller	605,050

2002-03 Money Leaders

Official Top 10 standings for 2002 and unofficial Top 10 standings for 2003 through Sept. 23, 2003.

FINAL 2002

HORSES	Age	Sts	1-2-3	Earnings
Art Major	3ph	31	20-3-2	$1,562,779
McArdle	3ph	27	14-8-1	1,382,949
Fool's Goal	7tg	15	7-3-1	1,277,640
Mach Three	3ph	18	11-2-2	1,215,547
Kadabra	3th	14	11-2-0	1,215,496
Like A Prayer	3th	18	7-7-2	1,088,504
Cameron Hall	3tm	15	11-3-0	1,075,006
Real Desire	4ph	13	10-1-1	1,059,790
Allamerican Native	2ph	14	8-1-1	948,017
Worldly Beauty	3pm	15	12-3-0	905,742

DRIVERS	Mts	1st	Earnings
John Campbell	1709	323	$11,943,027
David Miller	2508	393	10,578,711
Luc Ouellette	2240	373	9,440,669
Mike Lachance	1965	225	8,549,281
Ron Pierce	1752	248	6,892,780
Chris Christoforou	2976	517	6,816,393
Randall Waples	2178	430	5,189,526
Mario Baillargeon	2288	276	5,120,629
Tony Morgan	3521	700	5,112,006
George Brennan	1918	226	4,940,181

2003 (through Sept. 23)

HORSES	Age	Sts	1-2-3	Earnings
Art Major	4ph	11	8-3-0	$1,082,930
McArdle	4ph	17	7-3-5	849,222
Mr. Muscleman	3tg	13	6-3-2	836,415
Allamerican Theory	3ph	17	9-2-1	794,247
Yankee Cruiser	3ph	15	5-4-1	724,549
No Pan Intended	3ph	14	11-2-0	715,363
Rotation	4th	9	3-3-0	661,690
Fool's Goal	8tg	11	3-1-5	639,363
Camelot Hall	2ph	6	2-1-3	635,595
Amigo Hall	3th	11	4-4-2	634,941

DRIVERS	Mts	1st	Earnings
David Miller	1913	325	$7,937,212
Ron Pierce	1621	229	6,826,412
Mike Lachance	1604	175	6,438,113
Chris Christoforou	2430	433	6,234,488
Luc Ouellette	1688	248	5,727,164
John Campbell	681	103	4,920,321
Randall Waples	2153	416	4,823,022
George Brennan	2026	289	4,406,246
James Morrill Jr.	1697	278	4,300,513
Cat Manzi	2042	285	4,264,777

1867-2003
Through the Years

SPORTS ALMANAC

Thoroughbred Racing

The Triple Crown

The term "Triple Crown" was coined by sportswriter Charles Hatton while covering the 1930 victories of Gallant Fox in the Kentucky Derby, Preakness Stakes and Belmont Stakes. Before then, only Sir Barton (1919) had won all three races in the same year. Since then, nine horses have won the Triple Crown. Two trainers, James (Sunny Jim) Fitzsimmons and Ben A. Jones, have saddled two Triple Crown champions, while Eddie Arcaro is the only jockey to ride two champions.

Year		Jockey	Trainer	Owner	Sire/Dam
1919	**Sir Barton**	Johnny Loftus	H. Guy Bedwell	J.K.L. Ross	Star Shoot/Lady Sterling
1930	**Gallant Fox**	Earl Sande	J.E. Fitzsimmons	Belair Stud	Sir Gallahad III/Marguerite
1935	**Omaha**	Willie Saunders	J.E. Fitzsimmons	Belair Stud	Gallant Fox/Flambino
1937	**War Admiral**	Charley Kurtsinger	George Conway	Samuel Riddle	Man o' War/Brushup
1941	**Whirlaway**	Eddie Arcaro	Ben A. Jones	Calumet Farm	Blenheim II/Dustwhirl
1943	**Count Fleet**	Johnny Longden	Don Cameron	Mrs. J.D. Hertz	Reigh Count/Quickly
1946	**Assault**	Warren Mehrtens	Max Hirsch	King Ranch	Bold Venture/Igual
1948	**Citation**	Eddie Arcaro	Ben A. Jones	Calumet Farm	Bull Lea/Hydroplane II
1973	**Secretariat**	Ron Turcotte	Lucien Laurin	Meadow Stable	Bold Ruler/Somethingroyal
1977	**Seattle Slew**	Jean Cruguet	Billy Turner	Karen Taylor	Bold Reasoning/My Charmer
1978	**Affirmed**	Steve Cauthen	Laz Barrera	Harbor View Farm	Exclusive Native/Won't Tell You

Note: Gallant Fox (1930) is the only Triple Crown winner to sire another Triple Crown winner, Omaha (1935). Wm. Woodward Sr., owner of Belair Stud, was breeder-owner of both horses and both were trained by Sunny Jim Fitzsimmons.

Triple Crown Near Misses

Forty-seven horses have won two legs of the Triple Crown. Of those, seventeen won the Kentucky Derby (KD) and Preakness Stakes (PS) only to be beaten in the Belmont Stakes (BS). Two others, Burgoo King (1932) and Bold Venture (1936), won the Derby and Preakness, but were forced out of the Belmont with the same injury—a bowed tendon—that effectively ended their racing careers. In 1978, Alydar finished second to Affirmed in all three races, the only time that has happened. Note that the Preakness preceded the Kentucky Derby in 1922, '23 and '31; (*) indicates won on disqualification.

Year		KD	PS	BS
1877	**Cloverbrook**	DNS	won	won
1878	**Duke of Magenta**	DNS	won	won
1880	**Grenada**	DNS	won	won
1881	**Saunterer**	DNS	won	won
1895	**Belmar**	DNS	won	won
1920	**Man o' War**	DNS	won	won
1922	**Pillory**	DNS	won	won
1923	**Zev**	won	12th	won
1931	**Twenty Grand**	won	2nd	won
1932	**Burgoo King**	won	won	DNS
1936	**Bold Venture**	won	won	DNS
1939	**Johnstown**	won	5th	won
1940	**Bimelech**	2nd	won	won
1942	**Shut Out**	won	5th	won
1944	**Pensive**	won	won	2nd
1949	**Capot**	2nd	won	won
1950	**Middleground**	won	2nd	won
1953	**Native Dancer**	2nd	won	won
1955	**Nashua**	2nd	won	won
1956	**Needles**	won	2nd	won
1958	**Tim Tam**	won	won	2nd
1961	**Carry Back**	won	won	7th
1963	**Chateaugay**	won	2nd	won
1964	**Northern Dancer**	won	won	3rd

Year		KD	PS	BS
1966	**Kauai King**	won	won	4th
1967	**Damascus**	3rd	won	won
1968	**Forward Pass**	won*	won	2nd
1969	**Majestic Prince**	won	won	2nd
1971	**Canonero II**	won	won	4th
1972	**Riva Ridge**	won	4th	won
1974	**Little Current**	5th	won	won
1976	**Bold Forbes**	won	3rd	won
1979	**Spectacular Bid**	won	won	3rd
1981	**Pleasant Colony**	won	won	3rd
1984	**Swale**	won	7th	won
1987	**Alysheba**	won	won	4th
1988	**Risen Star**	3rd	won	won
1989	**Sunday Silence**	won	won	2nd
1991	**Hansel**	10th	won	won
1994	**Tabasco Cat**	6th	won	won
1995	**Thunder Gulch**	won	3rd	won
1997	**Silver Charm**	won	won	2nd
1998	**Real Quiet**	won	won	2nd
1999	**Charismatic**	won	won	3rd
2001	**Point Given**	5th	won	won
2002	**War Emblem**	won	won	8th
2003	**Funny Cide**	won	won	3rd

The Triple Crown Challenge (1987-93)

Seeking to make the Triple Crown more than just a media event and to insure that owners would not be attracted to more lucrative races, officials at Churchill Downs, the Maryland Jockey Club and the New York Racing Association created Triple Crown Productions in 1985 and announced that a $1 million bonus would be given to the horse that performs best in the Kentucky Derby, Preakness Stakes and Belmont Stakes. Furthermore, a bonus of $5 million would be presented to any horse winning all three races.

Revised in 1991, the rules stated that the winning horse must: 1. finish all three races; 2. earn points by finishing first, second, third or fourth in at least one of the three races; and 3. earn the highest number of points based on the following system—10 points to win, five to place, three to show and one to finish fourth. In the event of a tie, the $1 million is distributed equally among the top point-getters. From 1987-90, the system was five points to win, three to place and one to show. The Triple Crown Challenge was discontinued in 1994.

Year		KD	PS	BS	Pts
1987	1 **Bet Twice**	2nd	2nd	1st—	11
	2 Alysheba	1st	1st	4th—	10
	3 Cryptoclearance	4th	3rd	2nd—	4
1988	1 **Risen Star**	3rd	1st	1st—	11
	2 Winning Colors	1st	3rd	6th—	6
	3 Brian's Time	6th	2nd	3rd—	4
1989	1 **Sunday Silence**	1st	1st	2nd—	13
	2 Easy Goer	2nd	2nd	1st—	11
	3 Hawkster	5th	5th	5th—	0
1990	1 **Unbridled**	1st	2nd	4th—	8
	2 Summer Squall	2nd	1st	DNR—	8
	3 Go and Go	DNR	DNR	1st—	5
	(Unbridled was only horse to run all three races.)				

Year		KD	PS	BS	Pts
1991	1 **Hansel**	10th	1st	1st—	20
	2 Strike the Gold	1st	6th	2nd—	15
	3 Mane Minister	3rd	3rd	3rd—	9
1992	1 **Pine Bluff**	5th	1st	3rd—	13
	2 Casual Lies	2nd	3rd	5th—	8
	(No other horses ran all three races.)				
1993	1 **Sea Hero**	1st	5th	7th—	10
	2 Wild Gale	3rd	8th	3rd—	6
	(No other horses ran all three races.)				

Kentucky Derby

For three-year-olds. Held the first Saturday in May at Churchill Downs in Louisville, Ky. Inaugurated in 1875. Originally run at 1½ miles (1875-95), shortened to present 1¼ miles in 1896.

Trainers with most wins: Ben Jones (6); D. Wayne Lukas and Dick Thompson (4); Bob Baffert, Sunny Jim Fitzsimmons and Max Hirsch (3).

Jockeys with most wins: Eddie Arcaro and Bill Hartack (5); Bill Shoemaker (4); Angel Cordero Jr., Issac Murphy, Earl Sande and Gary Stevens (3).

Winning fillies: Regret (1915), Genuine Risk (1980) and Winning Colors (1988).

Year	Winner (Margin)	Time	Jockey	Trainer	2nd place	3rd place
1875	**Aristides** (1)	2:37¾	Oliver Lewis	Ansel Anderson	Volcano	Verdigris
1876	**Vagrant** (2)	2:38¼	Bobby Swim	James Williams	Creedmore	Harry Hill
1877	**Baden-Baden** (2)	2:38	Billy Walker	Ed Brown	Leonard	King William
1878	**Day Star** (2)	2:37¼	Jimmy Carter	Lee Paul	Himyar	Leveler
1879	**Lord Murphy** (1)	2:37	Charlie Shauer	George Rice	Falsetto	Strathmore
1880	**Fonso** (1)	2:37½	George Lewis	Tice Hutsell	Kimball	Bancroft
1881	**Hindoo** (4)	2:40	Jim McLaughlin	James Rowe Sr.	Lelex	Alfambra
1882	**Apollo** (½)	2:40¼	Babe Hurd	Green Morris	Runnymede	Bengal
1883	**Leonatus** (3)	2:43	Billy Donohue	John McGinty	Drake Carter	Lord Raglan
1884	**Buchanan** (2)	2:40¼	Isaac Murphy	William Bird	Loftin	Audrain
1885	**Joe Cotton** (nk)	2:37¼	Babe Henderson	Alex Perry	Bersan	Ten Booker
1886	**Ben Ali** (½)	2:36½	Paul Duffy	Jim Murphy	Blue Wing	Free Knight
1887	**Montrose** (2)	2:39¼	Isaac Lewis	John McGinty	Jim Gore	Jacobin
1888	**MacBeth II** (1)	2:38¼	George Covington	John Campbell	Gallifet	White
1889	**Spokane** (ns)	2:34½	Thomas Kiley	John Rodegap	Proctor Knott	Once Again
1890	**Riley** (2)	2:45	Isaac Murphy	Edward Corrigan	Bill Letcher	Robespierre
1891	**Kingman** (1)	2:52¼	Isaac Murphy	Dud Allen	Balgowan	High Tariff
1892	**Azra** (ns)	2:41½	Lonnie Clayton	John Morris	Huron	Phil Dwyer
1893	**Lookout** (5)	2:39¼	Eddie Kunze	Wm. McDaniel	Plutus	Boundless
1894	**Chant** (2)	2:41	Frank Goodale	Eugene Leigh	Pearl Song	Sigurd
1895	**Halma** (3)	2:37½	Soup Perkins	Byron McClelland	Basso	Laureate
1896	**Ben Brush** (ns)	2:07¾	Willie Simms	Hardy Campbell	Ben Eder	Semper Ego
1897	**Typhoon II** (hd)	2:12½	Buttons Garner	J.C. Cahn	Ornament	Dr. Catlett
1898	**Plaudit** (nk)	2:09	Willie Simms	John E. Madden	Lieber Karl	Isabey
1899	**Manuel** (2)	2:12	Fred Taral	Robert Walden	Corsini	Mazo
1900	**Lieut. Gibson** (4)	2:06¼	Jimmy Boland	Charles Hughes	Florizar	Thrive
1901	**His Eminence** (2)	2:07¾	Jimmy Winkfield	F.B. Van Meter	Sannazarro	Driscoll
1902	**Alan-a-Dale** (ns)	2:08¾	Jimmy Winkfield	T.C. McDowell	Inventor	The Rival
1903	**Judge Himes** (¾)	2:09	Hal Booker	J.P. Mayberry	Early	Bourbon
1904	**Elwood** (½)	2:08½	Shorty Prior	C.E. Durnell	Ed Tierney	Brancas
1905	**Agile** (2)	2:10¾	Jack Martin	Robert Tucker	Ram's Horn	Layson
1906	**Sir Huon** (2)	2:08⅘	Roscoe Troxler	Pete Coyne	Lady Navarre	James Reddick
1907	**Pink Star** (2)	2:12⅗	Andy Minder	W.H. Fizer	Zal	Ovelando
1908	**Stone Street** (1)	2:15⅕	Arthur Pickens	J.W. Hall	Sir Cleges	Dunvegan
1909	**Wintergreen** (4)	2:08⅕	Vincent Powers	Charles Mack	Miami	Dr. Barkley

Kentucky Derby (Cont.)

Year	Winner (Margin)	Time	Jockey	Trainer	2nd place	3rd place
1910	**Donau** (½)	2:06⅖	Fred Herbert	George Ham	Joe Morris	Fighting Bob
1911	**Meridian** (¾)	2:05	George Archibald	Albert Ewing	Governor Gray	Colston
1912	**Worth** (nk)	2:09⅖	C.H. Shilling	Frank Taylor	Duval	Flamma
1913	**Donerail** (½)	2:04⅘	Roscoe Goose	Thomas Hayes	Ten Point	Gowell
1914	**Old Rosebud** (8)	2:03⅖	John McCabe	F.D. Weir	Hodge	Bronzewing
1915	**Regret** (2)	2:05⅖	Joe Notter	James Rowe Sr.	Pebbles	Sharpshooter
1916	**George Smith** (nk)	2:04	Johnny Loftus	Hollie Hughes	Star Hawk	Franklin
1917	**Omar Khayyam** (2)	2:04⅗	Charles Borel	C.T. Patterson	Ticket	Midway
1918	**Exterminator** (1)	2:10⅘	William Knapp	Henry McDaniel	Escoba	Viva America
1919	**SIR BARTON** (5)	2:09⅘	Johnny Loftus	H. Guy Bedwell	Billy Kelly	Under Fire
1920	**Paul Jones** (hd)	2:09	Ted Rice	Billy Garth	Upset	On Watch
1921	**Behave Yourself** (hd)	2:04⅕	Charles Thompson	Dick Thompson	Black Servant	Prudery
1922	**Morvich** (1½)	2:04⅗	Albert Johnson	Fred Burlew	Bet Mosie	John Finn
1923	**Zev** (1½)	2:05⅖	Earl Sande	David Leary	Martingale	Vigil
1924	**Black Gold** (½)	2:05⅕	John Mooney	Hanly Webb	Chilhowee	Beau Butler
1925	**Flying Ebony** (1½)	2:07⅗	Earl Sande	William Duke	Captain Hal	Son of John
1926	**Bubbling Over** (5)	2:03⅘	Albert Johnson	Dick Thompson	Bagenbaggage	Rock Man
1927	**Whiskery** (hd)	2:06	Linus McAtee	Fred Hopkins	Osmand	Jock
1928	**Reigh Count** (3)	2:10⅖	Chick Lang	Bert Michell	Misstep	Toro
1929	**Clyde Van Dusen** (2)	2:10⅘	Linus McAtee	Clyde Van Dusen	Naishapur	Panchio
1930	**GALLANT FOX** (2)	2:07⅗	Earl Sande	Jim Fitzsimmons	Gallant Knight	Ned O.
1931	**Twenty Grand** (4)	2:01⅘	Charley Kurtsinger	James Rowe Jr.	Sweep All	Mate
1932	**Burgoo King** (5)	2:05⅕	Eugene James	Dick Thompson	Economic	Stepenfetchit
1933	**Brokers Tip** (ns)	2:06⅘	Don Meade	Dick Thompson	Head Play	Charley O.
1934	**Cavalcade** (2½)	2:04	Mack Garner	Bob Smith	Discovery	Agrarian
1935	**OMAHA** (1½)	2:05	Willie Saunders	Jim Fitzsimmons	Roman Soldier	Whiskolo
1936	**Bold Venture** (hd)	2:03⅗	Ira Hanford	Max Hirsch	Brevity	Indian Broom
1937	**WAR ADMIRAL** (1¾)	2:03⅕	Charley Kurtsinger	George Conway	Pompoon	Reaping Reward
1938	**Lawrin** (1)	2:04⅘	Eddie Arcaro	Ben Jones	Dauber	Can't Wait
1939	**Johnstown** (8)	2:03⅖	James Stout	Jim Fitzsimmons	Challedon	Heather Broom
1940	**Gallahadion** (1½)	2:05	Carroll Bierman	Roy Waldron	Bimelech	Dit
1941	**WHIRLAWAY** (8)	2:01⅖	Eddie Arcaro	Ben Jones	Staretor	Market Wise
1942	**Shut Out** (2½)	2:04⅖	Wayne Wright	John Gaver	Alsab	Valdina Orphan
1943	**COUNT FLEET** (3)	2:04	Johnny Longden	Don Cameron	Blue Swords	Slide Rule
1944	**Pensive** (4½)	2:04⅕	Conn McCreary	Ben Jones	Broadcloth	Stir Up
1945	**Hoop Jr** (6)	2:07	Eddie Arcaro	Ivan Parke	Pot O'Luck	Darby Dieppe
1946	**ASSAULT** (8)	2:06⅗	Warren Mehrtens	Max Hirsch	Spy Song	Hampden
1947	**Jet Pilot** (hd)	2:06⅘	Eric Guerin	Tom Smith	Phalanx	Faultless
1948	**CITATION** (3½)	2:05⅖	Eddie Arcaro	Ben Jones	Coaltown	My Request
1949	**Ponder** (3)	2:04⅕	Steve Brooks	Ben Jones	Capot	Palestinian
1950	**Middleground** (1¼)	2:01⅗	William Boland	Max Hirsch	Hill Prince	Mr. Trouble
1951	**Count Turf** (4)	2:02⅗	Conn McCreary	Sol Rutchick	Royal Mustang	Ruhe
1952	**Hill Gail** (2)	2:01⅗	Eddie Arcaro	Ben Jones	Sub Fleet	Blue Man
1953	**Dark Star** (hd)	2:02	Hank Moreno	Eddie Hayward	Native Dancer	Invigorator
1954	**Determine** (1½)	2:03	Raymond York	Willie Molter	Hasty Road	Hasseyampa
1955	**Swaps** (1½)	2:01⅘	Bill Shoemaker	Mesh Tenney	Nashua	Summer Tan
1956	**Needles** (¾)	2:03⅖	David Erb	Hugh Fontaine	Fabius	Come On Red
1957	**Iron Liege** (ns)	2:02⅕	Bill Hartack	Jimmy Jones	Gallant Man	Round Table
1958	**Tim Tam** (½)	2:05	Ismael Valenzuela	Jimmy Jones	Lincoln Road	Noureddin
1959	**Tomy Lee** (ns)	2:02⅕	Bill Shoemaker	Frank Childs	Sword Dancer	First Landing
1960	**Venetian Way** (3½)	2:02⅖	Bill Hartack	Victor Sovinski	Bally Ache	Victoria Park
1961	**Carry Back** (¾)	2:04	John Sellers	Jack Price	Crozier	Bass Clef
1962	**Decidedly** (2¼)	2:00⅖	Bill Hartack	Horatio Luro	Roman Line	Ridan
1963	**Chateaugay** (1¼)	2:01⅘	Braulio Baeza	James Conway	Never Bend	Candy Spots
1964	**Northern Dancer** (nk)	2:00	Bill Hartack	Horatio Luro	Hill Rise	The Scoundrel
1965	**Lucky Debonair** (nk)	2:01⅕	Bill Shoemaker	Frank Catrone	Dapper Dan	Tom Rolfe
1966	**Kauai King** (½)	2:02	Don Brumfield	Henry Forrest	Advocator	Blue Skyer
1967	**Proud Clarion** (1)	2:00⅗	Bobby Ussery	Loyd Gentry	Barbs Delight	Damascus
1968	**Forward Pass*** (nk)	—	Ismael Valenzuela	Henry Forrest	Francie's Hat	T.V. Commercial
1969	**Majestic Prince** (nk)	2:01⅘	Bill Hartack	Johnny Longden	Arts and Letters	Dike
1970	**Dust Commander** (5)	2:03⅖	Mike Manganello	Don Combs	My Dad George	High Echelon
1971	**Canonero II** (3¼)	2:03⅕	Gustavo Avila	Juan Arias	Jim French	Bold Reason
1972	**Riva Ridge** (3¼)	2:01⅘	Ron Turcotte	Lucien Laurin	No Le Hace	Hold Your Peace
1973	**SECRETARIAT** (2½)	1:59⅖	Ron Turcotte	Lucien Laurin	Sham	Our Native
1974	**Cannonade** (2¼)	2:04	Angel Cordero Jr.	Woody Stephens	Hudson County	Agitate
1975	**Foolish Pleasure** (1¾)	2:02	Jacinto Vasquez	LeRoy Jolley	Avatar	Diabolo
1976	**Bold Forbes** (1)	2:01⅗	Angel Cordero Jr.	Laz Barrera	Honest Pleasure	Elocutionist
1977	**SEATTLE SLEW** (1¾)	2:02⅕	Jean Cruguet	Billy Turner	Run Dusty Run	Sanhedrin
1978	**AFFIRMED** (1½)	2:01⅕	Steve Cauthen	Laz Barrera	Alydar	Believe It

Year	Winner (Margin)	Time	Jockey	Trainer	2nd place	3rd place
1979	**Spectacular Bid** (2¾)	2:02⅖	Ron Franklin	Bud Delp	General Assembly	Golden Act
1980	**Genuine Risk** (1)	2:02	Jacinto Vasquez	LeRoy Jolley	Rumbo	Jaklin Klugman
1981	**Pleasant Colony** (¾)	2:02	Jorge Velasquez	John Campo	Woodchopper	Partez
1982	**Gato Del Sol** (2½)	2:02⅖	E. Delahoussaye	Eddie Gregson	Laser Light	Reinvested
1983	**Sunny's Halo** (2)	2:02⅕	E. Delahoussaye	David Cross Jr.	Desert Wine	Caveat
1984	**Swale** (3¼)	2:02⅖	Laffit Pincay Jr.	Woody Stephens	Coax Me Chad	At The Threshold
1985	**Spend A Buck** (5¼)	2:00⅕	Angel Cordero Jr.	Cam Gambolati	Stephan's Odyssey	Chief's Crown
1986	**Ferdinand** (2¼)	2:02⅘	Bill Shoemaker	Chas. Whittingham	Bold Arrangement	Broad Brush
1987	**Alysheba** (¾)	2:03⅖	Chris McCarron	Jack Van Berg	Bet Twice	Avies Copy
1988	**Winning Colors** (nk)	2:02⅕	Gary Stevens	D. Wayne Lukas	Forty Niner	Risen Star
1989	**Sunday Silence** (2½)	2:05	Pat Valenzuela	Chas. Whittingham	Easy Goer	Awe Inspiring
1990	**Unbridled** (3½)	2:02	Craig Perret	Carl Nafzger	Summer Squall	Pleasant Tap
1991	**Strike the Gold** (1¾)	2:03	Chris Antley	Nick Zito	Best Pal	Mane Minister
1992	**Lil E. Tee** (1)	2:03	Pat Day	Lynn Whiting	Casual Lies	Dance Floor
1993	**Sea Hero** (2½)	2:02⅖	Jerry Bailey	Mack Miller	Prairie Bayou	Wild Gale
1994	**Go For Gin** (2)	2:03⅗	Chris McCarron	Nick Zito	Strodes Creek	Blumin Affair
1995	**Thunder Gulch** (2¼)	2:01⅕	Gary Stevens	D. Wayne Lukas	Tejano Run	Timber Country
1996	**Grindstone** (ns)	2:01	Jerry Bailey	D. Wayne Lukas	Cavonnier	Prince of Thieves
1997	**Silver Charm** (hd)	2:02⅖	Gary Stevens	Bob Baffert	Captain Bodgit	Free House
1998	**Real Quiet** (½)	2:02⅕	Kent Desormeaux	Bob Baffert	Victory Gallop	Indian Charlie
1999	**Charismatic** (nk)	2:03⅕	Chris Antley	D. Wayne Lukas	Menifee	Cat Thief
2000	**Fusaichi Pegasus** (1½)	2:01⅕	Kent Desormeaux	Neil Drysdale	Aptitude	Impeachment
2001	**Monarchos** (4¾)	1:59⅘	Jorge Chavez	John Ward Jr.	Invisible Ink	Congaree
2002	**War Emblem** (4)	2:01	Victor Espinoza	Bob Baffert	Proud Citizen	Perfect Drift
2003	**Funny Cide** (1¾)	2:01	Jose Santos	Barclay Tagg	Empire Maker	Peace Rules

*Dancer's Image finished first (in 2:02½), but was disqualified after traces of prohibited medication were found in his system.

Preakness Stakes

For three-year-olds. Held two weeks after the Kentucky Derby at Pimlico Race Course in Baltimore. Inaugurated 1873. Note that the 1918 race was held over two divisions. Originally run at 1½ miles (1873-88), then at 1¼ miles (1889), 1½ miles (1890), 1$\frac{1}{16}$ miles (1894-1900), 1 mile & 70 yards (1901-07), 1$\frac{1}{16}$ miles (1908), 1 mile (1909-1910), 1⅛ miles (1911-24), and the present 1$\frac{3}{16}$ miles since 1925.

Trainers with most wins: Robert W. Walden (7); T.J. Healey and D. Wayne Lukas (5); Bob Baffert, Sunny Jim Fitzsimmons and Jimmy Jones (4); J. Whalen (3).

Jockeys with most wins: Eddie Arcaro (6); Pat Day (5); G. Barbee, Bill Hartack and Lloyd Hughes (3).

Winning fillies: Flocarline (1903), Whimsical (1906), Rhine Maiden (1915) and Nellie Morse (1924).

Year	Winner (Margin)	Time	Jockey	Trainer	2nd place	3rd place
1873	**Survivor** (10)	2:43	G. Barbee	A.D. Pryor	John Boulger	Artist
1874	**Culpepper** (¾)	2:56½	W. Donohue	H. Gaffney	King Amadeus	Scratch
1875	**Tom Ochiltree** (2)	2:43½	L. Hughes	R.W. Walden	Viator	Bay Final
1876	**Shirley** (4)	2:44¾	G. Barbee	W. Brown	Rappahannock	Compliment
1877	**Cloverbrook** (2)	2:45½	C. Holloway	J. Walden	Bombast	Lucifer
1878	**Duke of Magenta** (2)	2:41¾	C. Holloway	R.W. Walden	Bayard	Albert
1879	**Harold** (1)	2:40½	L. Hughes	R.W. Walden	Jericho	Rochester
1880	**Grenada** (¾)	2:40½	L. Hughes	R.W. Walden	Oden	Emily F.
1881	**Saunterer** (½)	2:40½	T. Costello	R.W. Walden	Compensation	Baltic
1882	**Vanguard** (nk)	2:44½	T. Costello	R.W. Walden	Heck	Col. Watson
1883	**Jacobus** (4)	2:42½	G. Barbee	R. Dwyer	Parnell	(2-horse race)
1884	**Knight of Ellerslie** (2)	2:39½	S. Fisher	T.B. Doswell	Welcher	(2-horse race)
1885	**Tecumseh** (2)	2:49	Jim McLaughlin	C. Littlefield	Wickham	John C.
1886	**The Bard** (3)	2:45	S. Fisher	J. Huggins	Eurus	Elkwood
1887	**Dunboyne** (1)	2:39½	W. Donohue	W. Jennings	Mahoney	Raymond
1888	**Refund** (3)	2:49	F. Littlefield	R.W. Walden	Bertha B.*	Glendale
1889	**Buddhist** (8)	2:17½	W. Anderson	J. Rogers	Japhet	(2-horse race)
1890	**Montague** (3)	2:36¾	W. Martin	E. Feakes	Philosophy	Barrister
1891-93	Not held					
1894	**Assignee** (3)	1:49¼	F. Taral	W. Lakeland	Potentate	Ed Kearney
1895	**Belmar** (1)	1:50½	F. Taral	E. Feakes	April Fool	Sue Kittie
1896	**Margrave** (1)	1:51	H. Griffin	Byron McClelland	Hamilton II	Intermission
1897	**Paul Kauvar** (1½)	1:51¼	T. Thorpe	T.P. Hayes	Elkins	On Deck
1898	**Sly Fox** (2)	1:49¾	W. Simms	H. Campbell	The Huguenot	Nuto
1899	**Half Time** (1)	1:47	R. Clawson	F. McCabe	Filigrane	Lackland
1900	**Hindus** (hd)	1:48⅖	H. Spencer	J.H. Morris	Sarmatian	Ten Candles
1901	**The Parader** (2)	1:47⅕	F. Landry	T.J. Healey	Sadie S.	Dr. Barlow
1902	**Old England** (ns)	1:45⅘	L. Jackson	G.B. Morris	Maj. Daingerfield	Namtor
1903	**Flocarline** (½)	1:44⅘	W. Gannon	H.C. Riddle	Mackey Dwyer	Rightful
1904	**Bryn Mawr** (1)	1:44⅕	E. Hildebrand	W.F. Presgrave	Wotan	Dolly Spanker
1905	**Cairngorm** (hd)	1:45⅘	W. Davis	A.J. Joyner	Kiamesha	Coy Maid
1906	**Whimsical** (4)	1:45	Walter Miller	T.J. Gaynor	Content	Larabie
1907	**Don Enrique** (1)	1:45⅖	G. Mountain	J. Whalen	Ethon	Zambesi

Preakness Stakes (Cont.)

Year	Winner (Margin)	Time	Jockey	Trainer	2nd place	3rd place
1908	**Royal Tourist** (4)	1:46⅖	Eddie Dugan	A.J. Joyner	Live Wire	Robert Cooper
1909	**Effendi** (1)	1:39⅘	Willie Doyle	F.C. Frisbie	Fashion Plate	Hill Top
1910	**Layminster** (½)	1:40⅗	R. Estep	J.S. Healy	Dalhousie	Sager
1911	**Watervale** (1)	1:51	Eddie Dugan	J. Whalen	Zeus	The Nigger
1912	**Colonel Holloway** (5)	1:56⅗	C. Turner	D. Woodford	Bwana Tumbo	Tipsand
1913	**Buskin** (nk)	1:53⅖	James Butwell	J. Whalen	Kleburne	Barnegat
1914	**Holiday** (¾)	1:53⅘	A. Schuttinger	J.S. Healy	Brave Cunarder	Defendum
1915	**Rhine Maiden** (1½)	1:58	Douglas Hoffman	F. Devers	Half Rock	Runes
1916	**Damrosch** (1½)	1:54⅘	Linus McAtee	A.G. Weston	Greenwood	Achievement
1917	**Kalitan** (2)	1:54⅖	E. Haynes	Bill Hurley	Al M. Dick	Kentucky Boy
1918	**War Cloud** (¾)	1:53⅗	Johnny Loftus	W.B. Jennings	Sunny Slope	Lanius
1918	**Jack Hare Jr** (2)	1:53⅖	Charles Peak	F.D. Weir	The Porter	Kate Bright
1919	**SIR BARTON** (4)	1:53	Johnny Loftus	H. Guy Bedwell	Eternal	Sweep On
1920	**Man o' War** (1½)	1:51⅗	Clarence Kummer	L. Feustel	Upset	Wildair
1921	**Broomspun** (¾)	1:54⅕	F. Coltiletti	James Rowe Sr.	Polly Ann	Jeg
1922	**Pillory** (hd)	1:51⅗	L. Morris	Thomas Healey	Hea	June Grass
1923	**Vigil** (1¼)	1:53⅗	B. Marinelli	Thomas Healey	General Thatcher	Rialto
1924	**Nellie Morse** (1½)	1:57⅕	John Merimee	A.B. Gordon	Transmute	Mad Play
1925	**Coventry** (4)	1:59	Clarence Kummer	William Duke	Backbone	Almadel
1926	**Display** (hd)	1:59⅘	John Maiben	Thomas Healey	Blondin	Mars
1927	**Bostonian** (½)	2:01⅗	Whitey Abel	Fred Hopkins	Sir Harry	Whiskery
1928	**Victorian** (ns)	2:00⅕	Sonny Workman	James Rowe Jr.	Toro	Solace
1929	**Dr. Freeland** (1)	2:01⅗	Louis Schaefer	Thomas Healey	Minotaur	African
1930	**GALLANT FOX** (¾)	2:00⅗	Earl Sande	Jim Fitzsimmons	Crack Brigade	Snowflake
1931	**Mate** (1½)	1:59	George Ellis	J.W. Healy	Twenty Grand	Ladder
1932	**Burgoo King** (hd)	1:59⅘	Eugene James	Dick Thompson	Tick On	Boatswain
1933	**Head Play** (4)	2:02	Charley Kurtsinger	Thomas Hayes	Ladysman	Utopian
1934	**High Quest** (ns)	1:58⅕	Robert Jones	Bob Smith	Cavalcade	Discovery
1935	**OMAHA** (6)	1:58⅖	Willie Saunders	Jim Fitzsimmons	Firethorn	Psychic Bid
1936	**Bold Venture** (ns)	1:59	George Woolf	Max Hirsch	Granville	Jean Bart
1937	**WAR ADMIRAL** (hd)	1:58⅖	Charley Kurtsinger	George Conway	Pompoon	Flying Scot
1938	**Dauber** (7)	1:59⅘	Maurice Peters	Dick Handlen	Cravat	Menow
1939	**Challedon** (1¼)	1:59⅘	George Seabo	Louis Schaefer	Gilded Knight	Volitant
1940	**Bimelech** (3)	1:58⅗	F.A. Smith	Bill Hurley	Mioland	Gallahadion
1941	**WHIRLAWAY** (5½)	1:58⅘	Eddie Arcaro	Ben Jones	King Cole	Our Boots
1942	**Alsab** (1)	1:57	Basil James	Sarge Swenke	Requested & Sun Again (dead heat)	
1943	**COUNT FLEET** (8)	1:57⅖	Johnny Longden	Don Cameron	Blue Swords	Vincentive
1944	**Pensive** (¾)	1:59⅕	Conn McCreary	Ben Jones	Platter	Stir Up
1945	**Polynesian** (2½)	1:58⅘	W.D. Wright	Morris Dixon	Hoop Jr.	Darby Dieppe
1946	**ASSAULT** (nk)	2:01⅖	Warren Mehrtens	Max Hirsch	Lord Boswell	Hampden
1947	**Faultless** (1¼)	1:59	Doug Dodson	Jimmy Jones	On Trust	Phalanx
1948	**CITATION** (5½)	2:02⅖	Eddie Arcaro	Jimmy Jones	Vulcan's Forge	Bovard
1949	**Capot** (hd)	1:56	Ted Atkinson	J.M. Gaver	Palestinian	Noble Impulse
1950	**Hill Prince** (5)	1:59⅕	Eddie Arcaro	Casey Hayes	Middleground	Dooly
1951	**Bold** (7)	1:56⅖	Eddie Arcaro	Preston Burch	Counterpoint	Alerted
1952	**Blue Man** (3½)	1:57⅖	Conn McCreary	Woody Stephens	Jampol	One Count
1953	**Native Dancer** (nk)	1:57⅘	Eric Guerin	Bill Winfrey	Jamie K.	Royal Bay Gem
1954	**Hasty Road** (nk)	1:57⅖	Johnny Adams	Harry Trotsek	Correlation	Hasseyampa
1955	**Nashua** (1)	1:54⅗	Eddie Arcaro	Jim Fitzsimmons	Saratoga	Traffic Judge
1956	**Fabius** (¾)	1:58⅖	Bill Hartack	Jimmy Jones	Needles	No Regrets
1957	**Bold Ruler** (2)	1:56⅕	Eddie Arcaro	Jim Fitzsimmons	Iron Liege	Inside Tract
1958	**Tim Tam** (1½)	1:57⅕	Ismael Valenzuela	Jimmy Jones	Lincoln Road	Gone Fishin'
1959	**Royal Orbit** (4)	1:57	William Harmatz	R. Cornell	Sword Dancer	Dunce
1960	**Bally Ache** (4)	1:57⅗	Bobby Ussery	Jimmy Pitt	Victoria Park	Celtic Ash
1961	**Carry Back** (¾)	1:57⅗	Johnny Sellers	Jack Price	Globemaster	Crozier
1962	**Greek Money** (ns)	1:56⅕	John Rotz	V.W. Raines	Ridan	Roman Line
1963	**Candy Spots** (3½)	1:56⅕	Bill Shoemaker	Mesh Tenney	Chateaugay	Never Bend
1964	**Northern Dancer** (2¼)	1:56⅘	Bill Hartack	Horatio Luro	The Scoundrel	Hill Rise
1965	**Tom Rolfe** (nk)	1:56⅕	Ron Turcotte	Frank Whiteley	Dapper Dan	Hail To All
1966	**Kauai King** (1¾)	1:55⅖	Don Brumfield	Henry Forrest	Stupendous	Amberoid
1967	**Damascus** (2¼)	1:55⅕	Bill Shoemaker	Frank Whiteley	In Reality	Proud Clarion
1968	**Forward Pass** (6)	1:56⅘	Ismael Valenzuela	Henry Forrest	Out Of the Way	Nodouble
1969	**Majestic Prince** (hd)	1:55⅗	Bill Hartack	Johnny Longden	Arts and Letters	Jay Ray
1970	**Personality** (nk)	1:56⅕	Eddie Belmonte	John Jacobs	My Dad George	Silent Screen
1971	**Canonero II** (1½)	1:54	Gustavo Avila	Juan Arias	Eastern Fleet	Jim French
1972	**Bee Bee Bee** (1¼)	1:55⅗	Eldon Nelson	Red Carroll	No Le Hace	Key To The Mint
1973	**SECRETARIAT** (2½)	1:54⅖	Ron Turcotte	Lucien Laurin	Sham	Our Native
1974	**Little Current** (7)	1:54⅗	Miguel Rivera	Lou Rondinello	Neapolitan Way	Cannonade
1975	**Master Derby** (1)	1:56⅖	Darrel McHargue	Smiley Adams	Foolish Pleasure	Diabolo

Year	Winner (Margin)	Time	Jockey	Trainer	2nd place	3rd place
1976	**Elocutionist** (3½)	1:55	John Lively	Paul Adwell	Play The Red	Bold Forbes
1977	**SEATTLE SLEW** (1½)	1:54⅖	Jean Cruguet	Billy Turner	Iron Constitution	Run Dusty Run
1978	**AFFIRMED** (nk)	1:54⅖	Steve Cauthen	Laz Barrera	Alydar	Believe It
1979	**Spectacular Bid** (3½)	1:54⅕	Ron Franklin	Bud Delp	Golden Act	Screen King
1980	**Codex** (4¾)	1:54⅕	Angel Cordero Jr.	D. Wayne Lukas	Genuine Risk	Colonel Moran
1981	**Pleasant Colony** (1)	1:54⅗	Jorge Velasquez	John Campo	Bold Ego	Paristo
1982	**Aloma's Ruler** (½)	1:55⅖	Jack Kaenel	John Lenzini Jr.	Linkage	Cut Away
1983	**Deputed Testamony** (2¾)	1:55⅖	Donald Miller Jr.	Bill Boniface	Desert Wine	High Honors
1984	**Gate Dancer** (1½)	1:53⅗	Angel Cordero Jr.	Jack Van Berg	Play On	Fight Over
1985	**Tank's Prospect** (hd)	1:53⅖	Pat Day	D. Wayne Lukas	Chief's Crown	Eternal Prince
1986	**Snow Chief** (4)	1:54⅘	Alex Solis	Melvin Stute	Ferdinand	Broad Brush
1987	**Alysheba** (½)	1:55⅘	Chris McCarron	Jack Van Berg	Bet Twice	Cryptoclearance
1988	**Risen Star** (1¼)	1:56⅕	E. Delahoussaye	Louie Roussel III	Brian's Time	Winning Colors
1989	**Sunday Silence** (ns)	1:53⅘	Pat Valenzuela	Chas. Whittingham	Easy Goer	Rock Point
1990	**Summer Squall** (2¼)	1:53⅗	Pat Day	Neil Howard	Unbridled	Mister Frisky
1991	**Hansel** (7)	1:54	Jerry Bailey	Frank Brothers	Corporate Report	Mane Minister
1992	**Pine Bluff** (¾)	1:55⅗	Chris McCarron	Tom Bohannan	Alydeed	Casual Lies
1993	**Prairie Bayou** (½)	1:56⅗	Mike Smith	Tom Bohannan	Cherokee Run	El Bakan
1994	**Tabasco Cat** (¾)	1:56⅖	Pat Day	D. Wayne Lukas	Go For Gin	Concern
1995	**Timber Country** (½)	1:54⅖	Pat Day	D. Wayne Lukas	Oliver's Twist	Thunder Gulch
1996	**Louis Quatorze** (3¼)	1:53⅖	Pat Day	Nick Zito	Skip Away	Editor's Note
1997	**Silver Charm** (hd)	1:54⅖	Gary Stevens	Bob Baffert	Free House	Captain Bodgit
1998	**Real Quiet** (2¼)	1:54⅘	Kent Desormeaux	Bob Baffert	Victory Gallop	Classic Cat
1999	**Charismatic** (1½)	1:55⅕	Chris Antley	D. Wayne Lukas	Menifee	Badge
2000	**Red Bullet** (3¾)	1:56	Jerry Bailey	Joe Orseno	Fusaichi Pegasus	Impeachment
2001	**Point Given** (2¼)	1:55⅖	Gary Stevens	Bob Baffert	A P Valentine	Congaree
2002	**War Emblem** (¾)	1:56⅕	Victor Espinoza	Bob Baffert	Magic Weisner	Proud Citizen
2003	**Funny Cide** (9¾)	1:55⅗	Jose Santos	Barclay Tagg	Midway Road	Scrimshaw

* Later named Judge Murray.

Belmont Stakes

For three-year-olds. Held three weeks after Preakness Stakes at Belmont Park in Elmont, N.Y. Inaugurated in 1867 at Jerome Park, moved to Morris Park in 1890 and then to Belmont Park in 1905.

Originally run at 1 mile and 5 furlongs (1867-89), then 1¼ miles (1890-1905), 1⅜ miles (1906-25), and the present 1½ miles since 1926.

Trainers with most wins: James Rowe Sr. (8); Sam Hildreth (7); Sunny Jim Fitzsimmons (6); Woody Stephens (5); Max Hirsch, D. Wayne Lukas and Robert W. Walden (4); Elliott Burch, Lucien Laurin, F. McCabe and D. McDaniel (3).

Jockeys with most wins: Eddie Arcaro and Jim McLaughlin (6); Earl Sande and Bill Shoemaker (5); Braulio Baeza, Pat Day, Laffit Pincay Jr., Gary Stevens and James Stout (3).

Winning fillies: Ruthless (1867) and Tanya (1905).

Year	Winner (Margin)	Time	Jockey	Trainer	2nd place	3rd place
1867	**Ruthless** (½)	3:05	J. Gilpatrick	A.J. Minor	DeCourcey	Rivoli
1868	**General Duke** (2)	3:02	Bobby Swim	A. Thompson	Northumberland	Fanny Ludlow
1869	**Fenian** (6)	3:04¼	C. Miller	J. Pincus	Glenelg	Invercauld
1870	**Kingfisher** (nk)	2:59½	W. Dick	R. Colston	Foster	Midday
1871	**Harry Bassett** (3)	2:56	W. Miller	D. McDaniel	Stockwood	By the Sea
1872	**Joe Daniels** (¾)	2:58¼	James Roe	D. McDaniel	Meteor	Shylock
1873	**Springbok** (¾)	3:01¾	James Roe	D. McDaniel	Count d'Orsay	Strachino
1874	**Saxon** (nk)	2:39½	G. Barbee	W. Prior	Grinstead	Aaron Pennington
1875	**Calvin** (2)	2:42¼	Bobby Swim	A. Williams	Aristides	Milner
1876	**Algerine** (½)	2:40½	Billy Donohue	Major Doswell	Fiddlesticks	Barricade
1877	**Cloverbrook** (1)	2:46	C. Holloway	J. Walden	Loiterer	Baden-Baden
1878	**Duke of Magenta** (2)	2:43½	L. Hughes	R.W. Walden	Bramble	Sparta
1879	**Spendthrift** (6)	2:42¾	George Evans	T. Puryear	Monitor	Jericho
1880	**Grenada** (nk)	2:47	L. Hughes	R.W. Walden	Ferncliffe	Turenne
1881	**Saunterer** (nk)	2:47	T. Costello	R.W. Walden	Eole	Baltic
1882	**Forester** (5)	2:43	Jim McLaughlin	L. Stuart	Babcock	Wyoming
1883	**George Kinney** (3)	2:42½	Jim McLaughlin	James Rowe Sr.	Trombone	Renegade
1884	**Panique** (nk)	2:42	Jim McLaughlin	James Rowe Sr.	Knight of Ellerslie	Himalaya
1885	**Tyrant** (3)	2:43	Paul Duffy	W. Claypool	St. Augustine	Tecumseh
1886	**Inspector B** (1)	2:41	Jim McLaughlin	F. McCabe	The Bard	Linden
1887	**Hanover** (15)	2:43½	Jim McLaughlin	F. McCabe	Oneko	(2-horse race)
1888	**Sir Dixon** (15)	2:40¼	Jim McLaughlin	F. McCabe	Prince Royal	(2-horse race)
1889	**Eric** (½)	2:47¼	W. Hayward	J. Huggins	Diablo	Zephyrus
1890	**Burlington** (2)	2:07¾	Pike Barnes	A. Cooper	Devotee	Padishah
1891	**Foxford** (nk)	2:08¾	Ed Garrison	M. Donavan	Montana	Laurestan
1892	**Patron** (6)	2:12	W. Hayward	L. Stuart	Shellbark	(2-horse race)
1893	**Commanche** (hd)	1:53¼	Willie Simms	G. Hannon	Dr. Rice	Rainbow
1894	**Henry of Navarre** (1½)	1:56½	Willie Simms	B. McClelland	Prig	Assignee

Belmont Stakes (Cont.)

Year	Winner (Margin)	Time	Jockey	Trainer	2nd place	3rd place
1895	**Belmar** (hd)	2:11½	Fred Taral	E. Feakes	Counter Tenor	Nanki Poo
1896	**Hastings** (hd)	2:24½	H. Griffin	J.J. Hyland	Handspring	Hamilton II
1897	**Scottish Chieftain** (1)	2:23¼	J. Scherrer	M. Byrnes	On Deck	Octagon
1898	**Bowling Brook** (6)	2:32	F. Littlefield	R.W. Walden	Previous	Hamburg
1899	**Jean Beraud** (hd)	2:23	R. Clawson	Sam Hildreth	Half Time	Glengar
1900	**Ildrim** (ns)	2:21¼	Nash Turner	H.E. Leigh	Petruchio	Missionary
1901	**Commando** (2)	2:21	H. Spencer	James Rowe Sr.	The Parader	All Green
1902	**Masterman** (2)	2:22⅗	John Bullman	J.J. Hyland	Renald	King Hanover
1903	**Africander** (2)	2:21¾	John Bullman	R. Miller	Whorler	Red Knight
1904	**Delhi** (4)	2:06⅗	George Odom	James Rowe Sr.	Graziallo	Rapid Water
1905	**Tanya** (½)	2:08	E. Hildebrand	J.W. Rogers	Blandy	Hot Shot
1906	**Burgomaster** (4)	2:20	Lucien Lyne	J.W. Rogers	The Quail	Accountant
1907	**Peter Pan** (1)	N/A	G. Mountain	James Rowe Sr.	Superman	Frank Gill
1908	**Colin** (hd)	N/A	Joe Notter	James Rowe Sr.	Fair Play	King James
1909	**Joe Madden** (8)	2:21⅗	E. Dugan	Sam Hildreth	Wise Mason	Donald MacDonald
1910	**Sweep** (6)	2:22	James Butwell	James Rowe Sr.	Duke of Ormonde	(2-horse race)
1911-12	Not held					
1913	**Prince Eugene** (½)	2:18	Roscoe Troxler	James Rowe Sr.	Rock View	Flying Fairy
1914	**Luke McLuke** (8)	2:20	Merritt Buxton	J.F. Schorr	Gainer	Charlestonian
1915	**The Finn** (4)	2:18⅖	George Byrne	E.W. Heffner	Half Rock	Pebbles
1916	**Friar Rock** (3)	2:22	E. Haynes	Sam Hildreth	Spur	Churchill
1917	**Hourless** (10)	2:17⅘	James Butwell	Sam Hildreth	Skeptic	Wonderful
1918	**Johren** (2)	2:20⅖	Frank Robinson	A. Simons	War Cloud	Cum Sah
1919	**SIR BARTON** (5)	2:17⅖	John Loftus	H. Guy Bedwell	Sweep On	Natural Bridge
1920	**Man o' War** (20)	2:14⅕	Clarence Kummer	L. Feustel	Donnacona	(2-horse race)
1921	**Grey Lag** (3)	2:16⅘	Earl Sande	Sam Hildreth	Sporting Blood	Leonardo II
1922	**Pillory** (2)	2:18⅘	C.H. Miller	T.J. Healey	Snob II	Hea
1923	**Zev** (1½)	2:19	Earl Sande	Sam Hildreth	Chickvale	Rialto
1924	**Mad Play** (2)	2:18⅘	Earl Sande	Sam Hildreth	Mr. Mutt	Modest
1925	**American Flag** (8)	2:16⅘	Albert Johnson	G.R. Tompkins	Dangerous	Swope
1926	**Crusader** (1)	2:32⅕	Albert Johnson	George Conway	Espino	Haste
1927	**Chance Shot** (1½)	2:32⅖	Earl Sande	Pete Coyne	Bois de Rose	Flambino
1928	**Vito** (3)	2:33⅕	Clarence Kummer	Max Hirsch	Genie	Diavolo
1929	**Blue Larkspur** (¾)	2:32⅘	Mack Garner	C. Hastings	African	Jack High
1930	**GALLANT FOX** (3)	2:31⅗	Earl Sande	Jim Fitzsimmons	Whichone	Questionnaire
1931	**Twenty Grand** (10)	2:29⅗	Charley Kurtsinger	James Rowe Jr.	Sun Meadow	Jamestown
1932	**Faireno** (1½)	2:32⅘	Tom Malley	Jim Fitzsimmons	Osculator	Flag Pole
1933	**Hurryoff** (1½)	2:32⅗	Mack Garner	H. McDaniel	Nimbus	Union
1934	**Peace Chance** (6)	2:29⅕	W.D. Wright	Pete Coyne	High Quest	Good Goods
1935	**OMAHA** (1½)	2:30⅗	Willie Saunders	Jim Fitzsimmons	Firethorn	Rosemont
1936	**Granville** (ns)	2:30	James Stout	Jim Fitzsimmons	Mr. Bones	Hollyrood
1937	**WAR ADMIRAL** (3)	2:28⅗	Charley Kurtsinger	George Conway	Sceneshifter	Vamoose
1938	**Pasteurized** (nk)	2:29⅖	James Stout	George Odom	Dauber	Cravat
1939	**Johnstown** (5)	2:29⅗	James Stout	Jim Fitzsimmons	Belay	Gilded Knight
1940	**Bimelech** (¾)	2:29⅗	Fred Smith	Bill Hurley	Your Chance	Andy K.
1941	**WHIRLAWAY** (2½)	2:31	Eddie Arcaro	Ben Jones	Robert Morris	Yankee Chance
1942	**Shut Out** (2)	2:29⅕	Eddie Arcaro	John Gaver	Alsab	Lochinvar
1943	**COUNT FLEET** (25)	2:28⅕	Johnny Longden	Don Cameron	Fairy Manhurst	Deseronto
1944	**Bounding Home** (½)	2:32⅕	G.L. Smith	Matt Brady	Pensive	Bull Dandy
1945	**Pavot** (5)	2:30⅕	Eddie Arcaro	Oscar White	Wildlife	Jeep
1946	**ASSAULT** (3)	2:30⅘	Warren Mehrtens	Max Hirsch	Natchez	Cable
1947	**Phalanx** (5)	2:29⅖	R. Donoso	Syl Veitch	Tide Rips	Tailspin
1948	**CITATION** (8)	2:28⅕	Eddie Arcaro	Jimmy Jones	Better Self	Escadru
1949	**Capot** (½)	2:30⅕	Ted Atkinson	John Gaver	Ponder	Palestinian
1950	**Middleground** (1)	2:28⅗	William Boland	Max Hirsch	Lights Up	Mr. Trouble
1951	**Counterpoint** (4)	2:29	David Gorman	Syl Veitch	Battlefield	Battle Morn
1952	**One Count** (2½)	2:30⅕	Eddie Arcaro	Oscar White	Blue Man	Armageddon
1953	**Native Dancer** (nk)	2:28⅗	Eric Guerin	Bill Winfrey	Jamie K.	Royal Bay Gem
1954	**High Gun** (nk)	2:30⅘	Eric Guerin	Max Hirsch	Fisherman	Limelight
1955	**Nashua** (9)	2:29	Eddie Arcaro	Jim Fitzsimmons	Blazing Count	Portersville
1956	**Needles** (nk)	2:29⅘	David Erb	Hugh Fontaine	Career Boy	Fabius
1957	**Gallant Man** (8)	2:26⅗	Bill Shoemaker	John Nerud	Inside Tract	Bold Ruler
1958	**Cavan** (6)	2:30⅕	Pete Anderson	Tom Barry	Tim Tam	Flamingo
1959	**Sword Dancer** (¾)	2:28⅖	Bill Shoemaker	Elliott Burch	Bagdad	Royal Orbit
1960	**Celtic Ash** (5½)	2:29⅕	Bill Hartack	Tom Barry	Venetian Way	Disperse
1961	**Sherluck** (2¼)	2:29⅕	Braulio Baeza	Harold Young	Globemaster	Guadalcanal
1962	**Jaipur** (ns)	2:28⅘	Bill Shoemaker	B. Mulholland	Admiral's Voyage	Crimson Satan
1963	**Chateaugay** (2½)	2:30⅕	Braulio Baeza	James Conway	Candy Spots	Choker
1964	**Quadrangle** (2)	2:28⅖	Manuel Ycaza	Elliott Burch	Roman Brother	Northern Dancer

Year	Winner (Margin)	Time	Jockey	Trainer	2nd place	3rd place
1965	**Hail to All** (nk)	2:28⅖	John Sellers	Eddie Yowell	Tom Rolfe	First Family
1966	**Amberoid** (2½)	2:29⅗	William Boland	Lucien Laurin	Buffle	Advocator
1967	**Damascus** (2½)	2:28⅘	Bill Shoemaker	F.Y. Whiteley Jr.	Cool Reception	Gentleman James
1968	**Stage Door Johnny** (1¼)	2:27⅕	Gus Gustines	John Gaver	Forward Pass	Call Me Prince
1969	**Arts and Letters** (5½)	2:28⅘	Braulio Baeza	Elliott Burch	Majestic Prince	Dike
1970	**High Echelon** (¾)	2:34	John Rotz	John Jacobs	Needles N Pens	Naskra
1971	**Pass Catcher** (¾)	2:30⅖	Walter Blum	Eddie Yowell	Jim French	Bold Reason
1972	**Riva Ridge** (7)	2:28	Ron Turcotte	Lucien Laurin	Ruritania	Cloudy Dawn
1973	**SECRETARIAT** (31)	2:24	Ron Turcotte	Lucien Laurin	Twice A Prince	My Gallant
1974	**Little Current** (7)	2:29⅕	Miguel Rivera	Lou Rondinello	Jolly Johu	Cannonade
1975	**Avatar** (nk)	2:28⅕	Bill Shoemaker	Tommy Doyle	Foolish Pleasure	Master Derby
1976	**Bold Forbes** (nk)	2:29	Angel Cordero Jr.	Laz Barrera	McKenzie Bridge	Great Contractor
1977	**SEATTLE SLEW** (4)	2:29⅗	Jean Cruguet	Billy Turner	Run Dusty Run	Sanhedrin
1978	**AFFIRMED** (hd)	2:26⅘	Steve Cauthen	Laz Barrera	Alydar	Darby Creek Road
1979	**Coastal** (3¼)	2:28⅗	Ruben Hernandez	David Whiteley	Golden Act	Spectacular Bid
1980	**Temperence Hill** (2)	2:29⅘	Eddie Maple	Joseph Cantey	Genuine Risk	Rockhill Native
1981	**Summing** (nk)	2:29	George Martens	Luis Barerra	Highland Blade	Pleasant Colony
1982	**Conquistador Cielo** (14)	2:28⅕	Laffit Pincay Jr.	Woody Stephens	Gato Del Sol	Illuminate
1983	**Caveat** (3½)	2:27⅘	Laffit Pincay Jr.	Woody Stephens	Slew o' Gold	Barberstown
1984	**Swale** (4)	2:27⅕	Laffit Pincay Jr.	Woody Stephens	Pine Circle	Morning Bob
1985	**Creme Fraiche** (½)	2:27	Eddie Maple	Woody Stephens	Stephan's Odyssey	Chief's Crown
1986	**Danzig Connection** (1¼)	2:29⅘	Chris McCarron	Woody Stephens	Johns Treasure	Ferdinand
1987	**Bet Twice** (14)	2:28⅕	Craig Perret	Jimmy Croll	Cryptoclearance	Gulch
1988	**Risen Star** (14¾)	2:26⅖	E. Delahoussaye	Louie Roussel III	Kingpost	Brian's Time
1989	**Easy Goer** (8)	2:26	Pat Day	Shug McGaughey	Sunday Silence	Le Voyageur
1990	**Go And Go** (8¼)	2:27⅕	Michael Kinane	Dermot Weld	Thirty Six Red	Baron de Vaux
1991	**Hansel** (hd)	2:28	Jerry Bailey	Frank Brothers	Strike the Gold	Mane Minister
1992	**A.P. Indy** (¾)	2:26	E. Delahoussaye	Neil Drysdale	My Memoirs	Pine Bluff
1993	**Colonial Affair** (2)	2:29⅘	Julie Krone	Scotty Schulhofer	Kissin Kris	Wild Gale
1994	**Tabasco Cat** (2)	2:26⅘	Pat Day	D. Wayne Lukas	Go For Gin	Strodes Creek
1995	**Thunder Gulch** (2)	2:32	Gary Stevens	D. Wayne Lukas	Star Standard	Citadeed
1996	**Editor's Note** (1)	2:28⅘	Rene Douglas	D. Wayne Lukas	Skip Away	My Flag
1997	**Touch Gold** (¾)	2:28⅘	Chris McCarron	David Hofmans	Silver Charm	Free House
1998	**Victory Gallop** (ns)	2:29	Gary Stevens	Elliott Walden	Real Quiet	Thomas Jo
1999	**Lemon Drop Kid** (hd)	2:27⅘	Jose Santos	Scotty Schulhofer	Vision and Verse	Charismatic
2000	**Commendable** (1½)	2:31⅕	Pat Day	D. Wayne Lukas	Aptitude	Unshaded
2001	**Point Given** (12¼)	2:26⅖	Gary Stevens	Bob Baffert	A P Valentine	Monarchos
2002	**Sarava** (½)	2:29⅗	Edgar Prado	Ken McPeek	Medaglia d'Oro	Sunday Break
2003	**Empire Maker** (¾)	2:28⅕	Jerry Bailey	Bobby Frankel	Ten Most Wanted	Funny Cide

Breeders' Cup Championship

Inaugurated on Nov. 10, 1984, the Breeders' Cup World Thoroughbred Championships consists of eight races on one track on one day late in the year to determine thoroughbred racing's principle champions.

The Breeders' Cup has been (will be) held at the following tracks (in alphabetical order): Aqueduct Racetrack (N.Y.) in 1985; Arlington Park (Ill.) in 2002; Belmont Park (N.Y.) in 1990, '95 and 2001; Churchill Downs (Ky.) in 1988, '91, '94, '98 and 2000; Gulfstream Park (Fla.) in 1989, '92 and '99; Hollywood Park (Calif.) in 1984, '87 and '97; Lone Star Park (Texas) in 2004; Santa Anita Park (Calif.) in 1986, '93 and 2003 and Woodbine (Toronto) in 1996.

Horses with most wins: Bayakoa, Da Hoss, Lure, Miesque and Tiznow (2).

Trainers with most wins: D. Wayne Lukas (17); Shug McGaughey (8); Neil Drysdale (6); Bill Mott (5); Ron McAnally (4); Bob Baffert, Francois Boutin, Patrick Byrne and Andre Fabre (3).

Jockeys with most wins: Jerry Bailey (13); Pat Day (12); Mike Smith (10); Chris McCarron (9); Gary Stevens (8); Eddie Delahoussaye, Laffit Pincay Jr. and Jose Santos (7); Pat Valenzuela (6); Corey Nakatani (5); Angel Cordero Jr., Craig Perret and John Velazquez (4); Frankie Dettori and Randy Romero (3).

Juvenile

Distances: one mile (1984-85, 87); 1 1/16 miles (1986, 1988-2001), 1⅛ miles (2002).

Year	Winner (Margin)	Time	Jockey	Trainer	2nd place	3rd place
1984	**Chief's Crown** (¾)	1:36⅕	Don MacBeth	Roger Laurin	Tank's Prospect	Spend A Buck
1985	**Tasso** (ns)	1:36⅕	Laffit Pincay Jr.	Neil Drysdale	Storm Cat	Scat Dancer
1986	**Capote** (1¼)	1:43⅘	Laffit Pincay Jr.	D. Wayne Lukas	Qualify	Alysheba
1987	**Success Express** (1¾)	1:35⅕	Jose Santos	D. Wayne Lukas	Regal Classic	Tejano
1988	**Is It True** (1¼)	1:46⅗	Laffit Pincay Jr.	D. Wayne Lukas	Easy Goer	Tagel
1989	**Rhythm** (2)	1:43⅗	Craig Perret	Shug McGaughey	Grand Canyon	Slavic
1990	**Fly So Free** (3)	1:43⅖	Jose Santos	Scotty Schulhofer	Take Me Out	Lost Mountain
1991	**Arazi** (4¾)	1:44⅗	Pat Valenzuela	Francois Boutin	Bertrando	Snappy Landing
1992	**Gilded Time** (¾)	1:43⅖	Chris McCarron	Darrell Vienna	It'sali'lknownfact	River Special
1993	**Brocco** (5)	1:42⅘	Gary Stevens	Randy Winick	Blumin Affair	Tabasco Cat
1994	**Timber Country** (½)	1:44⅖	Pat Day	D. Wayne Lukas	Eltish	Tejano Run
1995	**Unbridled's Song** (nk)	1:41⅗	Mike Smith	James Ryerson	Hennessy	Editor's Note
1996	**Boston Harbor** (nk)	1:43⅖	Jerry Bailey	D. Wayne Lukas	Acceptable	Ordway
1997	**Favorite Trick** (5½)	1:41⅖	Pat Day	Patrick Byrne	Dawson's Legacy	Nationalore

Breeders' Cup Championship (Cont.)

Year	Winner (Margin)	Time	Jockey	Trainer	2nd place	3rd place
1998	**Answer Lively** (hd)	1:44	Jerry Bailey	Bobby Barnett	Aly's Alley	Cat Thief
1999	**Anees** (2½)	1:42⅕	Gary Stevens	Alex Hassinger Jr.	Chief Seattle	High Yield
2000	**Macho Uno** (ns)	1:42	Jerry Bailey	Joe Orseno	Point Given	Street Cry
2001	**Johannesburg** (2¼)	1:42⅕	Michael Kinane	Aidan O'Brien	Repent	Siphonic
2002	**Vindication** (2¾)	1:49⅗	Mike Smith	Bob Baffert	Kafwain	Hold That Tiger

Juvenile Fillies

Distances: one mile (1984-85, 87); 1 1/16 miles (1986, 1988-2001); 1⅛ miles (2002).

Year	Winner (Margin)	Time	Jockey	Trainer	2nd place	3rd place
1984	**Outstandingly***	1:37⅘	Walter Guerra	Pancho Martin	Dusty Heart	Fine Spirit
1985	**Twilight Ridge** (1)	1:35⅘	Jorge Velasquez	D. Wayne Lukas	Family Style	Steal A Kiss
1986	**Brave Raj** (5½)	1:43⅕	Pat Valenzuela	Melvin Stute	Tappiano	Saros Brig
1987	**Epitome** (ns)	1:36⅖	Pat Day	Phil Hauswald	Jeanne Jones	Dream Team
1988	**Open Mind** (1¾)	1:46⅗	Angel Cordero Jr.	D. Wayne Lukas	Darby Shuffle	Lea Lucinda
1989	**Go for Wand** (2¾)	1:44⅕	Randy Romero	Wm. Badgett Jr.	Sweet Roberta	Stella Madrid
1990	**Meadow Star** (5)	1:44	Jose Santos	LeRoy Jolley	Private Treasure	Dance Smartly
1991	**Pleasant Stage** (nk)	1:46⅖	Eddie Delahoussaye	Chris Speckert	La Spia	Cadillac Women
1992	**Eliza** (nk)	1:42⅘	Pat Valenzuela	Alex Hassinger	Educated Risk	Boots 'n Jackie
1993	**Phone Chatter** (hd)	1:43	Laffit Pincay Jr.	Richard Mandella	Sardula	Heavenly Prize
1994	**Flanders** (hd)	1:45⅕	Pat Day	D. Wayne Lukas	Serena's Song	Stormy Blues
1995	**My Flag** (½)	1:42⅖	Jerry Bailey	Shug McGaughey	Cara Rafaela	Golden Attraction
1996	**Storm Song** (4½)	1:43⅗	Craig Perret	Nick Zito	Love That Jazz	Critical Factor
1997	**Countess Diana** (8½)	1:42⅕	Shane Sellers	Patrick Byrne	Career Collection	Primaly
1998	**Silverbulletday** (½)	1:43⅗	Gary Stevens	Bob Baffert	Excellent Meeting	Three Ring
1999	**Cash Run** (1¼)	1:43⅕	Jerry Bailey	D. Wayne Lukas	Chilukki	Surfside
2000	**Caressing** (½)	1:42⅗	John Velazquez	David Vance	Platinum Tiara	She's a Devil Due
2001	**Tempera** (1½)	1:41⅖	David Flores	Eoin Harty	Imperial Gesture	Bella Bellucci
2002	**Storm Flag Flying** (½)	1:49⅗	John Velazquez	Shug McGaughey	Composure	Santa Catarina

*In 1984, winner Fran's Valentine was disqualified for interference in the stretch and placed 10th.

Sprint

Distance: six furlongs (since 1984).

Year	Winner (Margin)	Time	Jockey	Trainer	2nd place	3rd place
1984	**Eillo** (ns)	1:10⅕	Craig Perret	Budd Lepman	Commemorate	Fighting Fit
1985	**Precisionist** (¾)	1:08⅖	Chris McCarron	L.R. Fenstermaker	Smile	Mt. Livermore
1986	**Smile** (1¼)	1:08⅖	Jacinto Vasquez	Scotty Schulhofer	Pine Tree Lane	Bedside Promise
1987	**Very Subtle** (4)	1:08⅘	Pat Valenzuela	Melvin Stute	Groovy	Exclusive Enough
1988	**Gulch** (¾)	1:10⅖	Angel Cordero Jr.	D. Wayne Lukas	Play The King	Afleet
1989	**Dancing Spree** (nk)	1:09	Angel Cordero Jr.	Shug McGaughey	Safely Kept	Dispersal
1990	**Safely Kept** (nk)	1:09⅗	Craig Perret	Alan Goldberg	Dayjur	Black Tie Affair
1991	**Sheikh Albadou** (nk)	1:09⅕	Pat Eddery	Alexander Scott	Pleasant Tap	Robyn Dancer
1992	**Thirty Slews** (nk)	1:08⅕	Eddie Delahoussaye	Bob Baffert	Meafara	Rubiano
1993	**Cardmania** (nk)	1:08⅗	Eddie Delahoussaye	Derek Meredith	Meafara	Gilded Time
1994	**Cherokee Run** (nk)	1:09⅖	Mike Smith	Frank Alexander	Soviet Problem	Cardmania
1995	**Desert Stormer** (nk)	1:09	Kent Desormeaux	Frank Lyons	Mr. Greeley	Lit de Justice
1996	**Lit de Justice** 1¼)	1:08⅗	Corey Nakatani	Jenine Sahadi	Paying Dues	Honour and Glory
1997	**Elmhurst** ½)	1:08⅕	Corey Nakatani	Jenine Sahadi	Hesabull	Bet On Sunshine
1998	**Reraise** (2)	1:09	Corey Nakatani	Craig Dollase	Grand Slam	Kona Gold
1999	**Artax** (½)	1:07⅘	Jorge Chavez	Louis Albertrani	Kona Gold	Big Jag
2000	**Kona Gold** (½)	1:07⅗	Alex Solis	Bruce Headley	Honest Lady	Bet On Sunshine
2001	**Squirtle Squirt** (½)	1:08⅖	Jerry Bailey	Bobby Frankel	Xtra Heat	Caller One
2002	**Orientate** (½)	1:08⅘	Jerry Bailey	D. Wayne Lukas	Thunderello	Crafty C.T.

Mile

Year	Winner (Margin)	Time	Jockey	Trainer	2nd place	3rd place
1984	**Royal Heroine** (1½)	1:32⅗	Fernando Toro	John Gosden	Star Choice	Cozzene
1985	**Cozzene** (2¼)	1:35	Walter Guerra	Jan Nerud	Al Mamoon*	Shadeed
1986	**Last Tycoon** (hd)	1:35⅕	Yves St.-Martin	Robert Collet	Palace Music	Fred Astaire
1987	**Miesque** (3½)	1:32⅘	Freddie Head	Francois Boutin	Show Dancer	Sonic Lady
1988	**Miesque** (4)	1:38⅗	Freddie Head	Francois Boutin	Steinlen	Simply Majestic
1989	**Steinlen** (¾)	1:37⅕	Jose Santos	D. Wayne Lukas	Sabona	Most Welcome
1990	**Royal Academy** (nk)	1:35⅕	Lester Piggott	M.V. O'Brien	Itsallgreektome	Priolo
1991	**Opening Verse** (2¼)	1:37⅖	Pat Valenzuela	Dick Lundy	Val des Bois	Star of Cozzene
1992	**Lure** (3)	1:32⅘	Mike Smith	Shug McGaughey	Paradise Creek	Brief Truce
1993	**Lure** (2¼)	1:33⅖	Mike Smith	Shug McGaughey	Ski Paradise	Fourstars Allstar
1994	**Barathea** (hd)	1:34⅖	Frankie Dettori	Luca Cumani	Johann Quatz	Unfinished Symph
1995	**Ridgewood Pearl** (2)	1:43⅗	John Murtagh	John Oxx	Fastness	Sayyedati
1996	**Da Hoss** (1½)	1:35⅘	Gary Stevens	Michael Dickinson	Spinning World	Same Old Wish
1997	**Spinning World** (2)	1:32⅗	Cash Asmussen	Jonathan Pease	Geri	Decorated Hero
1998	**Da Hoss** (hd)	1:35⅕	John Velazquez	Michael Dickinson	Hawksley Hill	Labeeb
1999	**Silic** (nk)	1:34⅕	Corey Nakatani	Julio Canani	Tuzla	Docksider
2000	**War Chant** (nk)	1:34⅗	Gary Stevens	Neil Drysdale	North East Bound	Dansili
2001	**Val Royal** (1¾)	1:32	Jose Valdivia	Julio Canani	Forbidden Apple	Bach
2002	**Domedriver** (¾)	1:36⅘	Thierry Thulliez	Pascal Bary	Rock of Gibraltar	Good Journey

*In 1985, 2nd place finisher Palace Music was disqualified for interference and placed 9th.

Distaff

Distances: 1¼ miles (1984-87); 1⅛ miles (since 1988).

Year	Winner (Margin)	Time	Jockey	Trainer	2nd place	3rd place
1984	**Princess Rooney** (7)	2:02⅖	Eddie Delahoussaye	Neil Drysdale	Life's Magic	Adored
1985	**Life's Magic** (6¼)	2:02	Angel Cordero Jr.	D. Wayne Lukas	Lady's Secret	DontstopThemusic
1986	**Lady's Secret** (2½)	2:01⅕	Pat Day	D. Wayne Lukas	Fran's Valentine	Outstandingly
1987	**Sacahuista** (2¼)	2:02⅘	Randy Romero	D. Wayne Lukas	Clabber Girl	Oueee Bebe
1988	**Personal Ensign** (ns)	1:52	Randy Romero	Shug McGaughey	Winning Colors	Goodbye Halo
1989	**Bayakoa** (1½)	1:47⅖	Laffit Pincay Jr.	Ron McAnally	Gorgeous	Open Mind
1990	**Bayakoa** (6¾)	1:49⅕	Laffit Pincay Jr.	Ron McAnally	Colonial Waters	Valay Maid
1991	**Dance Smartly** (½)	1:50⅘	Pat Day	Jim Day	Versailles Treaty	Brought to Mind
1992	**Paseana** (4)	1:48	Chris McCarron	Ron McAnally	Versailles Treaty	Magical Maiden
1993	**Hollywood Wildcat** (ns)	1:48⅕	Eddie Delahoussaye	Neil Drysdale	Paseana	Re Toss
1994	**One Dreamer** (nk)	1:50⅗	Gary Stevens	Thomas Proctor	Heavenly Prize	Miss Dominique
1995	**Inside Information** (13½)	1:46	Mike Smith	Shug McGaughey	Heavenly Prize	Lakeway
1996	**Jewel Princess** (1½)	1:48⅕	Corey Nakatani	Wallace Dollase	Serena's Song	Different
1997	**Ajina** (2)	1:47⅕	Mike Smith	Bill Mott	Sharp Cat	Escena
1998	**Escena** (ns)	1:49⅘	Gary Stevens	Bill Mott	Banshee Breeze	Keeper Hill
1999	**Beautiful Pleasure** (¾)	1:47⅖	Jorge Chavez	John Ward Jr.	Banshee Breeze	Heritage of Gold
2000	**Spain** (1½)	1:47⅗	Victor Espinoza	D. Wayne Lukas	Surfside	Heritage of Gold
2001	**Unbridled Elaine** (hd)	1:49⅕	Pat Day	Dallas Stewart	Spain	Two Item Limit
2002	**Azeri** (5)	1:48⅗	Mike Smith	Laura de Seroux	Farda Amiga	Imperial Gesture

Turf

Distance: 1½ miles (since 1984).

Year	Winner (Margin)	Time	Jockey	Trainer	2nd place	3rd place
1984	**Lashkari** (nk)	2:25⅕	Yves St.-Martin	de Royer-Dupre	All Along	Raami
1985	**Pebbles** (nk)	2:27	Pat Eddery	Clive Brittain	StrawberryRoad II	Mourjane
1986	**Manila** (nk)	2:25⅖	Jose Santos	Leroy Jolley	Theatrical	Estrapade
1987	**Theatrical** (½)	2:24⅖	Pat Day	Bill Mott	Trempolino	Village Star II
1988	**Gt. Communicator** (½)	2:35⅕	Ray Sibille	Thad Ackel	Sunshine Forever	Indian Skimmer
1989	**Prized** (hd)	2:28	Eddie Delahoussaye	Neil Drysdale	Sierra Roberta	Star Lift
1990	**In The Wings** (½)	2:29⅗	Gary Stevens	Andre Fabre	With Approval	El Senor
1991	**Miss Alleged** (2)	2:30⅘	Eric Legrix	Pascal Bary	Itsallgreektome	Quest for Fame
1992	**Fraise** (ns)	2:24	Pat Valenzuela	Bill Mott	Sky Classic	Quest for Fame
1993	**Kotashaan** (½)	2:25	Kent Desormeaux	Richard Mandella	Bien Bien	Luazur
1994	**Tikkanen** (1½)	2:26⅖	Mike Smith	Jonathan Pease	Hatoof	Paradise Creek
1995	**Northern Spur** (nk)	2:42	Chris McCarron	Ron McAnally	Freedom Cry	Carnegie
1996	**Pilsudski** (1¼)	2:30⅕	Walter Swinburn	Michael Stoute	Singspiel	Swain
1997	**Chief Bearhart** (¾)	2:24	Jose Santos	Mark Frostad	Borgia	Flag Down
1998	**Buck's Boy** (1¼)	2:28⅗	Shane Sellers	Noel Hickey	Yagli	Dushyantor
1999	**Daylami** (2½)	2:24⅗	Frankie Dettori	Saeed bin Suroor	Royal Anthem	Buck's Boy
2000	**Kalanisi** (½)	2:26⅘	John Murtagh	Sir Michael Stoute	Quiet Resolve	John's Call
2001	**Fantastic Light** (¾)	2:24⅕	Frankie Dettori	Saeed bin Suroor	Milan	Timboroa
2002	**High Chaparral** (1¼)	2:30⅕	Michael Kinane	Aidan O'Brien	With Anticipation	Falcon Flight

Filly & Mare Turf

Distance: 1⅜ miles (1999-2000); 1¼ miles (since 2001).

Year	Winner (Margin)	Time	Jockey	Trainer	2nd place	3rd place
1999	**Soaring Softly** (¾)	2:13⅘	Jerry Bailey	James J. Toner	Coretta	Zomarradah
2000	**Perfect Sting** (¾)	2:13	Jerry Bailey	Joe Orseno	Tout Charmant	Catella
2001	**Banks Hill** (5½)	2:00⅕	Olivier Peslier	Andre Fabre	Spook Express	Spring Oak
2002	**Starine** (1½)	2:03⅗	John Velazquez	Bobby Frankel	Banks Hill	Islington

Classic

Distance: 1¼ miles (since 1984).

Year	Winner (Margin)	Time	Jockey	Trainer	2nd place	3rd place
1984	**Wild Again** (hd)	2:03⅖	Pat Day	Vincent Timphony	Slew o' Gold	Gate Dancer*
1985	**Proud Truth** (hd)	2:00⅘	Jorge Velasquez	John Veitch	Gate Dancer	Turkoman
1986	**Skywalker** (1¼)	2:00⅖	Laffit Pincay Jr.	M. Whittingham	Turkoman	Precisionist
1987	**Ferdinand** (ns)	2:01⅖	Bill Shoemaker	C. Whittingham	Alysheba	Judge Angelucci
1988	**Alysheba** (ns)	2:04⅘	Chris McCarron	Jack Van Berg	Seeking the Gold	Waquoit
1989	**Sunday Silence** (½)	2:00⅕	Chris McCarron	C. Whittingham	Easy Goer	Blushing John
1990	**Unbridled** (1)	2:02⅕	Pat Day	Carl Nafzger	Ibn Bey	Thirty Six Red
1991	**Black Tie Affair** (1¼)	2:02⅘	Jerry Bailey	Ernie Poulos	Twilight Agenda	Unbridled
1992	**A.P. Indy** (2)	2:00⅕	Eddie Delahoussaye	Neil Drysdale	Pleasant Tap	Jolypha
1993	**Arcangues** (2)	2:00⅘	Jerry Bailey	Andre Fabre	Bertrando	Kissin Kris
1994	**Concern** (nk)	2:02⅖	Jerry Bailey	Richard Small	Tabasco Cat	Dramatic Gold
1995	**Cigar** (2½)	1:59⅖	Jerry Bailey	Bill Mott	L'Carriere	Unaccounted For
1996	**Alphabet Soup** (ns)	2:01	Chris McCarron	David Hofmans	Louis Quatorze	Cigar
1997	**Skip Away** (6)	1:59⅕	Mike Smith	Hubert Hine	Deputy Commander	Dowty
1998	**Awesome Again** (¾)	2:02	Pat Day	Patrick Byrne	Silver Charm	Swain
1999	**Cat Thief** (1¼)	1:59⅖	Pat Day	D. Wayne Lukas	Budroyale	Golden Missile
2000	**Tiznow** (nk)	2:00⅗	Chris McCarron	Jay Robbins	Giant's Causeway	Captain Steve
2001	**Tiznow** (ns)	2:00⅗	Chris McCarron	Jay Robbins	Sakhee	Albert the Great
2002	**Volponi** (6½)	2:01⅖	Jose Santos	Philip Johnson	Medaglia d'Oro	Milwaukee Brew

*In 1984, 2nd place finisher Gate Dancer was disqualified for interference and placed 3rd.

Breeders' Cup Leaders

The all-time money-winning horses and jockeys in the history of the Breeders' Cup through 2002.

Top 10 Horses

		Sts	1-2-3	Earnings
1	Tiznow	2	2-0-0	$4,560,400
2	Awesome Again	1	1-0-0	2,662,400
3	Skip Away	2	1-0-0	2,288,000
4	Cat Thief	3	1-0-1	2,200,000
5	Alysheba	2	1-1-1	2,133,000
6	Alphabet Soup	1	1-0-0	2,080,000
	Volponi	1	1-0-0	2,080,000
8	Cigar	2	1-0-1	2,040,000
9	Spain	3	1-1-0	1,755,200
10	Unbridled	2	1-0-1	1,710,000

Top 10 Jockeys

		Sts	1-2-3	Earnings
1	Pat Day	107	12-17-11	$22,730,600
2	Chris McCarron	101	9-12-7	17,669,600
3	Jerry Bailey	82	13-7-9	15,768,120
4	Gary Stevens	88	8-15-10	13,441,160
5	Mike Smith	48	10-4-4	10,148,920
6	Jose Santos	55	7-2-4	7,948,200
7	Eddie Delahoussaye	68	7-3-6	7,775,000
8	Laffit Pincay Jr.	61	7-4-9	6,811,000
9	Corey Nakatani	45	5-6-6	6,500,280
10	Angel Cordero Jr.	48	4-7-7	6,020,000

Annual Money Leaders

Horses

Annual money-leading horses since 1910, according to *The American Racing Manual*.

Multiple leaders: Round Table, Buckpasser, Alysheba and Cigar (2).

Year		Age	Sts	1-2-3	Earnings	Year		Age	Sts	1-2-3	Earnings
1910	Novelty	2	16	11—	$72,630	1957	Round Table	3	22	15-1-3	$600,383
1911	Worth	2	13	10—	16,645	1958	Round Table	4	20	14-4-0	662,780
1912	Star Charter	4	17	6—	14,655	1959	Sword Dancer	3	13	8-4-0	537,004
1913	Old Rosebud	2	14	12—	19,057	1960	Bally Ache	3	15	10-3-1	445,045
1914	Roamer	3	16	12—	29,105	1961	Carry Back	3	16	9-1-3	565,349
1915	Borrow	7	9	4—	20,195	1962	Never Bend	2	10	7-1-2	402,969
1916	Campfire	2	9	6—	49,735	1963	Candy Spots	3	12	7-2-1	604,481
1917	Sun Briar	2	9	5—	59,505	1964	Gun Bow	4	16	8-4-2	580,100
1918	Eternal	2	8	6—	56,173	1965	Buckpasser	2	11	9-1-0	568,096
1919	Sir Barton	3	13	8-3-2	88,250	1966	Buckpasser	3	14	13-1-0	669,078
1920	Man o' War	3	11	11-0-0	166,140	1967	Damascus	3	16	12-3-1	817,941
1921	Morvich	2	11	11-0-0	115,234	1968	Forward Pass	3	13	7-2-0	546,674
1922	Pillory	3	7	4-1-1	95,654	1969	Arts and Letters	3	14	8-5-1	555,604
1923	Zev	3	14	12-1-0	272,008	1970	Personality	3	18	8-2-1	444,049
1924	Sarzen	3	12	8-1-1	95,640	1971	Riva Ridge	2	9	7-0-0	503,263
1925	Pompey	2	10	7-2-0	121,630	1972	Droll Role	4	19	7-3-4	471,633
1926	Crusader	3	15	9-4-0	166,033	1973	Secretariat	3	12	9-2-1	860,404
1927	Anita Peabody	2	7	6-0-1	111,905	1974	Chris Evert	3	8	5-1-2	551,063
1928	High Strung	2	6	5-0-0	153,590	1975	Foolish Pleasure	3	11	5-4-1	716,278
1929	Blue Larkspur	3	6	4-1-0	153,450	1976	Forego	6	8	6-1-1	401,701
1930	Gallant Fox	3	10	9-1-0	308,275	1977	Seattle Slew	3	7	6-1-1	641,370
1931	Gallant Flight	2	7	7-0-0	219,000	1978	Affirmed	3	11	8-2-0	901,541
1932	Gusto	3	16	4-3-2	145,940	1979	Spectacular Bid	3	12	10-1-1	1,279,334
1933	Singing Wood	2	9	3-2-2	88,050	1980	Temperence Hill	3	17	8-3-1	1,130,452
1934	Cavalcade	3	7	6-1-0	111,235	1981	John Henry	6	10	8-0-0	1,798,030
1935	Omaha	3	9	6-1-2	142,255	1982	Perrault (GBR)	5	8	4-1-2	1,197,400
1936	Granville	3	11	7-3-0	110,295	1983	All Along (FRA)	4	7	4-1-1	2,138,963
1937	Seabiscuit	4	15	11-2-2	168,580	1984	Slew o' Gold	4	6	5-1-0	2,627,944
1938	Stagehand	3	15	8-2-3	189,710	1985	Spend A Buck	3	7	5-1-1	3,552,704
1939	Challedon	3	15	9-2-3	184,535	1986	Snow Chief	3	9	6-1-1	1,875,200
1940	Bimelech	3	7	4-2-1	110,005	1987	Alysheba	3	10	3-3-1	2,511,156
1941	Whirlaway	3	20	13-5-2	272,386	1988	Alysheba	4	9	7-1-0	3,808,600
1942	Shut Out	3	12	8-2-0	238,872	1989	Sunday Silence	3	9	7-2-0	4,578,454
1943	Count Fleet	3	6	6-0-0	174,055	1990	Unbridled	3	11	4-3-2	3,718,149
1944	Pavot	2	8	8-0-0	179,040	1991	Dance Smartly	3	8	8-0-0	2,876,821
1945	Busher	3	13	10-2-1	273,735	1992	A.P. Indy	3	7	5-0-1	2,622,560
1946	Assault	3	15	8-2-3	424,195	1993	Kotashaan (FRA)	5	10	6-3-0	2,619,014
1947	Armed	6	17	11-4-1	376,325	1994	Paradise Creek	5	11	8-2-1	2,610,187
1948	Citation	3	20	19-1-0	709,470	1995	Cigar	5	10	10-0-0	4,819,800
1949	Ponder	3	21	9-5-2	321,825	1996	Cigar	6	8	5-2-1	4,910,000
1950	Noor	5	12	7-4-1	346,940	1997	Skip Away	4	11	4-5-2	4,089,000
1951	Counterpoint	3	15	7-2-1	250,525	1998	Silver Charm	4	9	6-2-0	4,696,506
1952	Crafty Admiral	4	16	9-4-1	277,225	1999	Almutawakel	4	4	1-1-1	3,290,000
1953	Native Dancer	3	10	9-1-0	513,425	2000	Dubai Millennium (GBR)	4	1	1-0-0	3,600,000
1954	Determine	3	16	10-3-2	328,700	2001	Captain Steve	4	6	2-1-1	4,201,200
1955	Nashua	3	12	10-1-1	752,550	2002	Street Cry (IRE)	4	3	2-1-0	4,266,615
1956	Needles	3	8	4-2-0	440,850						

Jockeys

Annual money-leading jockeys since 1910, according to *The American Racing Manual.*

Multiple leaders: Bill Shoemaker (10); Laffit Pincay Jr. (7); Eddie Arcaro (6); Braulio Baeza and Jerry Bailey (5); Chris McCarron and Jose Santos (4); Angel Cordero Jr. and Earl Sande (3); Ted Atkinson, Pat Day, Laverne Fator, Mack Garner, Bill Hartack, Charley Kurtsinger, Johnny Longden, Mike Smith, Gary Stevens, Sonny Workman and Wayne Wright (2).

Year		Mts	Wins	Earnings	Year		Mts	Wins	Earnings
1910	Carroll Shilling	.506	172	$176,030	1957	Bill Hartack	1238	341	$3,060,501
1911	Ted Koerner	.813	162	88,308	1958	Bill Shoemaker	1133	300	2,961,693
1912	Jimmy Butwell	.684	144	79,843	1959	Bill Shoemaker	1285	347	2,843,133
1913	Merritt Buxton	.887	146	82,552	1960	Bill Shoemaker	1227	274	2,123,961
1914	J. McCahey	.824	155	121,845	1961	Bill Shoemaker	1256	304	2,690,819
1915	Mack Garner	.775	151	96,628	1962	Bill Shoemaker	1126	311	2,916,844
1916	John McTaggart	.832	150	155,055	1963	Bill Shoemaker	1203	271	2,526,925
1917	Frank Robinson	.731	147	148,057	1964	Bill Shoemaker	1056	246	2,649,553
1918	Lucien Luke	.756	178	201,864	1965	Braulio Baeza	1245	270	2,582,702
1919	John Loftus	.177	65	252,707	1966	Braulio Baeza	1341	298	2,951,022
1920	Clarence Kummer	.353	87	292,376	1967	Braulio Baeza	1064	256	3,088,888
1921	Earl Sande	.340	112	263,043	1968	Braulio Baeza	1089	201	2,835,108
1922	Albert Johnson	.297	43	345,054	1969	Jorge Velasquez	1442	258	2,542,315
1923	Earl Sande	.430	122	569,394	1970	Laffit Pincay Jr.	1328	269	2,626,526
1924	Ivan Parke	.844	205	290,395	1971	Laffit Pincay Jr.	1627	380	3,784,377
1925	Laverne Fator	.315	81	305,775	1972	Laffit Pincay Jr.	1388	289	3,225,827
1926	Laverne Fator	.511	143	361,435	1973	Laffit Pincay Jr.	1444	350	4,093,492
1927	Earl Sande	.179	49	277,877	1974	Laffit Pincay Jr.	1278	341	4,251,060
1928	Linus McAtee	.235	55	301,295	1975	Braulio Baeza	1190	196	3,674,398
1929	Mack Garner	.274	57	314,975	1976	Angel Cordero Jr.	1534	274	4,709,500
1930	Sonny Workman	.571	152	420,438	1977	Steve Cauthen	2075	487	6,151,750
1931	Charley Kurtsinger	.519	93	392,095	1978	Darrel McHargue	1762	375	6,188,353
1932	Sonny Workman	.378	87	385,070	1979	Laffit Pincay Jr.	1708	420	8,183,535
1933	Robert Jones	.471	63	226,285	1980	Chris McCarron	1964	405	7,666,100
1934	Wayne Wright	.919	174	287,185	1981	Chris McCarron	1494	326	8,397,604
1935	Silvio Coucci	.749	141	319,760	1982	Angel Cordero Jr.	1838	397	9,702,520
1936	Wayne Wright	.670	100	264,000	1983	Angel Cordero Jr.	1792	362	10,116,807
1937	Charley Kurtsinger	.765	120	384,202	1984	Chris McCarron	1565	356	12,038,213
1938	Nick Wall	.658	97	385,161	1985	Laffit Pincay Jr.	1409	289	13,415,049
1939	Basil James	.904	191	353,333	1986	Jose Santos	1636	329	11,329,297
1940	Eddie Arcaro	.783	132	343,661	1987	Jose Santos	1639	305	12,407,355
1941	Don Meade	1164	210	398,627	1988	Jose Santos	1867	370	14,877,298
1942	Eddie Arcaro	.687	123	481,949	1989	Jose Santos	1459	285	13,847,003
1943	Johnny Longden	.871	173	573,276	1990	Gary Stevens	1504	283	13,881,198
1944	Ted Atkinson	1539	287	899,101	1991	Chris McCarron	1440	265	14,456,073
1945	Johnny Longden	.778	180	981,977	1992	Kent Desormeaux	1568	361	14,193,006
1946	Ted Atkinson	1377	233	1,036,825	1993	Mike Smith	1510	343	14,024,815
1947	Douglas Dodson	.646	141	1,429,949	1994	Mike Smith	1484	317	15,979,820
1948	Eddie Arcaro	.726	188	1,686,230	1995	Jerry Bailey	1367	287	16,311,876
1949	Steve Brooks	.906	209	1,316,817	1996	Jerry Bailey	1187	298	19,465,376
1950	Eddie Arcaro	.888	195	1,410,160	1997	Jerry Bailey	1136	269	18,206,013
1951	Bill Shoemaker	1161	257	1,329,890	1998	Gary Stevens	.869	178	19,358,840
1952	Eddie Arcaro	.807	188	1,859,591	1999	Pat Day	1265	254	18,092,845
1953	Bill Shoemaker	1683	485	1,784,187	2000	Pat Day	1219	267	17,479,838
1954	Bill Shoemaker	1251	380	1,876,760	2001	Jerry Bailey	.912	227	22,597,720
1955	Eddie Arcaro	.820	158	1,864,796	2002	Jerry Bailey	.833	214	22,871,814
1956	Bill Hartack	1387	347	2,343,955					

Trainers

Annual money-leading trainers since 1908, according to *The American Racing Manual.*

Multiple Leaders: D. Wayne Lukas (14); Sam Hildreth (9); Charlie Whittingham (7); Sunny Jim Fitzsimmons and Jimmy Jones (5); Bob Baffert, Laz Barrera, Ben Jones and Willie Molter (4); Hirsch Jacobs, Eddie Neloy and James Rowe Sr. (3); H. Guy Bedwell, Jack Gaver, John Schorr, Humming Bob Smith, Silent Tom Smith and Mesh Tenney (2).

Year		Wins	Earnings	Year		Wins	Earnings
1908	James Rowe Sr.	.50	$284,335	1917	Sam Hildreth	.23	$61,698
1909	Sam Hildreth	.73	123,942	1918	H. Guy Bedwell	.53	80,296
1910	Sam Hildreth	.84	148,010	1919	H. Guy Bedwell	.63	208,728
1911	Sam Hildreth	.67	49,418	1920	Louis Feustel	.22	186,087
1912	John Schorr	.63	58,110	1921	Sam Hildreth	.85	262,768
1913	James Rowe Sr.	.18	45,936	1922	Sam Hildreth	.74	247,014
1914	R.C. Benson	.45	59,315	1923	Sam Hildreth	.75	392,124
1915	James Rowe Sr.	.19	75,596	1924	Sam Hildreth	.77	255,608
1916	Sam Hildreth	.39	70,950	1925	G.R. Tompkins	.30	199,245

Annual Money Leaders (Cont.)

Year		Wins	Earnings	Year		Sts	Wins	Earnings
1926	Scott Harlan	.21	$205,681	1965	Hirsch Jacobs	.610	91	$1,331,628
1927	W.H. Bringloe	.63	216,563	1966	Eddie Neloy	.282	93	2,456,250
1928	John Schorr	.65	258,425	1967	Eddie Neloy	.262	72	1,776,089
1929	James Rowe Jr.	.25	314,881	1968	Eddie Neloy	.212	52	1,233,101
1930	Sunny Jim Fitzsimmons	.47	397,355	1969	Elliott Burch	.156	26	1,067,936
1931	Big Jim Healy	.33	297,300	1970	Charlie Whittingham	.551	82	1,302,354
1932	Sunny Jim Fitzsimmons	.68	266,650	1971	Charlie Whittingham	.393	77	1,737,115
1933	Humming Bob Smith	.53	135,720	1972	Charlie Whittingham	.429	79	1,734,020
1934	Humming Bob Smith	.43	249,938	1973	Charlie Whittingham	.423	85	1,865,385
1935	Bud Stotler	.87	303,005	1974	Pancho Martin	.846	166	2,408,419
1936	Sunny Jim Fitzsimmons	.42	193,415	1975	Charlie Whittingham	.487	3	2,437,244
1937	Robert McGarvey	.46	209,925	1976	Jack Van Berg	.2362	496	2,976,196
1938	Earl Sande	.15	226,495	1977	Laz Barrera	.781	127	2,715,848
1939	Sunny Jim Fitzsimmons	.45	266,205	1978	Laz Barrera	.592	100	3,307,164
1940	Silent Tom Smith	.14	269,200	1979	Laz Barrera	.492	98	3,608,517
1941	Ben Jones	.70	475,318	1980	Laz Barrera	.559	99	2,969,151
1942	Jack Gaver	.48	406,547	1981	Charlie Whittingham	.376	74	3,993,302
1943	Ben Jones	.73	267,915	1982	Charlie Whittingham	.410	63	4,587,457
1944	Ben Jones	.60	601,660	1983	D. Wayne Lukas	.595	78	4,267,261
1945	Silent Tom Smith	.52	510,655	1984	D. Wayne Lukas	.805	131	5,835,921
1946	Hirsch Jacobs	.99	560,077	1985	D. Wayne Lukas	.1140	218	11,155,188
1947	Jimmy Jones	.85	1,334,805	1986	D. Wayne Lukas	.1510	259	12,345,180
1948	Jimmy Jones	.81	1,118,670	1987	D. Wayne Lukas	.1735	343	17,502,110
1949	Jimmy Jones	.76	978,587	1988	D. Wayne Lukas	.1500	318	17,842,358
1950	Preston Burch	.96	637,754	1989	D. Wayne Lukas	.1398	305	16,103,998
1951	Jack Gaver	.42	616,392	1990	D. Wayne Lukas	.1396	267	14,508,871
1952	Ben Jones	.29	662,137	1991	D. Wayne Lukas	.1497	289	15,942,223
1953	Harry Trotsek	.54	1,028,873	1992	D. Wayne Lukas	.1349	230	9,806,436
1954	Willie Molter	.136	1,107,860	1993	Bobby Frankel	.345	79	8,933,252
1955	Sunny Jim Fitzsimmons	.66	1,270,055	1994	D. Wayne Lukas	.693	147	9,247,457
1956	Willie Molter	.142	1,227,402	1995	D. Wayne Lukas	.837	194	12,834,483
1957	Jimmy Jones	.70	1,150,910	1996	D. Wayne Lukas	.1006	192	15,966,344
1958	Willie Molter	.69	1,116,544	1997	D. Wayne Lukas	.824	169	9,993,569
1959	Willie Molter	.71	847,290	1998	Bob Baffert	.538	139	15,000,870
1960	Hirsch Jacobs	.97	748,349	1999	Bob Baffert	.735	169	16,934,607
1961	Jimmy Jones	.62	759,856	2000	Bob Baffert	.678	146	11,831,605
1962	Mesh Tenney	.58	1,099,474	2001	Bob Baffert	.660	138	16,354,996
				2002	Bobby Frankel	.480	117	17,748,340

Year		Sts	Wins	Earnings
1963	Mesh Tenney	.192	40	$860,703
1964	Bill Winfrey	.287	61	1,350,534

All-Time Leaders

The all-time money-winning horses and race-winning jockeys of North America, according to the *The American Racing Manual* and *The Thoroughbred Times Racing Almanac*. Records include all available information on races in foreign countries.

Top 30 Horses—Money Won

Note that horses who raced in 2002 are in **bold** type. Records are through May 19, 2003.

		Sts	1st	2nd	3rd	Earnings			Sts	1st	2nd	3rd	Earnings
1	Cigar	.33	19	4	5	$9,999,815	16	Daylami	.21	11	3	4	$4,614,762
2	Skip Away	.38	18	10	6	9,616,360	17	Behrens	.27	9	8	3	4,563,500
3	Fantastic Light	.25	12	5	3	8,486,957	18	Unbridled	.24	8	6	6	4,489,475
4	Silver Charm	.24	12	7	2	6,944,369	19	**Silver Charm**	.24	12	7	2	4,444,369
5	Captain Steve	.25	9	3	7	6,828,356	20	Awesome Again	.12	9	0	2	4,374,590
6	Alysheba	.26	11	8	2	6,679,242	21	Spend A Buck	.15	10	3	2	4,220,689
7	John Henry	.83	39	15	9	6,591,860	22	Pilsudski	.22	10	6	2	4,080,297
8	Tiznow	.15	8	4	2	6,427,830	23	Broad Appeal	.34	12	5	5	4,032,632
9	Singspiel	.20	9	8	0	5,952,825	24	Creme Fraiche	.64	17	12	13	4,024,727
10	Best Pal	.47	18	11	4	5,668,245	25	Seeking the Pearl	.21	8	2	3	4,021,716
11	Taiki Blizzard	.23	6	8	2	5,523,549	26	Point Given	.13	9	3	0	3,968,500
12	**Street Cry**	.12	5	6	1	5,150,837	27	Cat Thief	.30	4	9	8	3,951,012
13	**Jim and Tonic**	.39	13	13	4	4,975,807	28	Devil His Due	.41	11	12	3	3,920,405
14	Sunday Silence	.14	9	5	0	4,968,554	29	Sandpit	.40	14	11	6	3,812,597
15	Easy Goer	.20	14	5	1	4,873,770	30	Swain	.22	10	4	6	3,797,566

Top 30 Jockeys—Races Won

Note that jockeys active in 2002 are in **bold** type. Records are through April 8, 2003.

		Yrs	Wins	Earnings			Yrs	Wins	Earnings
1	**Laffit Pincay Jr.**	.37	9530	$237,157,192	16	Jacinto Vasquez	.37	5231	$80,764,853
2	Bill Shoemaker	.42	8833	123,375,524	17	**Ron Ardoin**	.31	5225	58,908,059
3	**Pat Day**	.31	8437	276,005,646	18	**Mario Pino**	.26	5118	78,874,454
4	**Russell Baze**	.30	8193	120,353,063	19	Rudy Baez	.25	4875	30,474,225
5	David Gall	.43	7396	24,972,821	20	**Rick Wilson**	.31	4810	74,437,043
6	**Chris McCarron**	.29	7139	264,380,651	21	**Edgar Prado**	.20	4794	116,298,075
7	Angel Cordero Jr.	.35	7057	164,561,227	22	Eddie Arcaro	.31	4779	30,039,543
8	Jorge Velasquez	.33	6795	125,544,379	23	**Gary Stevens**	.25	4771	216,149,422
9	Sandy Hawley	.31	6449	88,681,292	24	Don Brumfield	.37	4573	43,567,861
10	Larry Snyder	.35	6388	47,207,289	25	**Anthony Black**	.33	4532	49,021,891
11	**E. Delahoussaye**	.36	6384	195,801,624	26	**Mark Guidry**	.30	4485	74,434,462
12	Carl Gambardella	.39	6349	29,389,041	27	Steve Brooks	.34	4451	18,239,817
13	**Earlie Fires**	.39	6210	79,367,510	28	Eddie Maple	.34	4398	105,338,573
14	John Longden	.41	6032	24,665,800	29	Walter Blum	.22	4382	26,497,189
15	**Jerry Bailey**	.29	5430	258,357,133	30	**Craig Perret**	.37	4357	110,124,037

Eclipse Awards

The Eclipse Awards, honoring the Horse of the Year and other champions of the sport, are sponsored by the National Thoroughbred Racing Association (NTRA), *Daily Racing Form* and the National Turf Writers Assn. In 1998, the NTRA replaced the Thoroughbred Racing Associations of North America as co-sponsor.

The awards are named after the 18th century racehorse and sire, Eclipse, who began racing at age five and was unbeaten in 18 starts (eight wins were walkovers). As a stallion, Eclipse sired winners of 344 races, including three Epsom Derby champions.

Horses listed in CAPITAL letters won the Triple Crown that year. Age of horse in parentheses where necessary.

Multiple winners: (horses): Forego (8); John Henry (7); Affirmed, Lonesome Glory and Secretariat (5); Cigar, Flatterer, Seattle Slew, Skip Away and Spectacular Bid (4); Ack Ack, Susan's Girl, Tiznow and Zaccio (3); All Along, Alysheba, Azeri, Bayakoa, Black Tie Affair, Cafe Prince, Charismatic, Conquistador Cielo, Desert Vixen, Favorite Trick, Ferdinand, Flawlessly, Flat Top, Go for Wand, Holy Bull, Housebuster, Kotashaan, Lady's Secret, Life's Magic, Miesque, Morley Street, Open Mind, Paseana, Point Given, Riva Ridge, Silverbulletday, Slew o' Gold and Spend A Buck (2).

Multiple winners: (people): Jerry Bailey and Laffit Pincay Jr. (6); Laz Barrera, Pat Day, Bobby Frankel, John Franks, Juddmonte Farms, D. Wayne Lukas, Allen Paulson, Ogden Phipps and Frank Stronach (4); Bob Baffert, Steve Cauthen, Harbor View Farm, Fred W. Hooper, Nelson Bunker Hunt, Mr. & Mrs. Gene Klein, Dan Lasater, John & Betty Mabee, Paul Mellon, Bill Shoemaker, Edward Taylor and Charlie Whittingham (3); Braulio Baeza, C.T. Chenery, Claiborne Farm, Angel Cordero Jr., Kent Desormeaux, Richard Englander, William S. Farish, John W. Galbreath, Chris McCarron, Bill Mott and Mike Smith (2).

Horse of the Year

Year		Year		Year		Year	
1971	Ack Ack (5)	1979	Affirmed (4)	1987	Ferdinand (4)	1995	Cigar (5)
1972	Secretariat (2)	1980	Spectacular Bid (4)	1988	Alysheba (4)	1996	Cigar (6)
1973	SECRETARIAT (3)	1981	John Henry (6)	1989	Sunday Silence (3)	1997	Favorite Trick (2)
1974	Forego (4)	1982	Conquistador Cielo (3)	1990	Criminal Type (5)	1998	Skip Away (5)
1975	Forego (5)	1983	All Along (4)	1991	Black Tie Affair (5)	1999	Charismatic (3)
1976	Forego (6)	1984	John Henry (9)	1992	A.P. Indy (3)	2000	Tiznow (3)
1977	SEATTLE SLEW (3)	1985	Spend A Buck (4)	1993	Kotashaan (5)	2001	Point Given (3)
1978	AFFIRMED (3)	1986	Lady's Secret (4)	1994	Holy Bull (3)	2002	Azeri (4)

Horse of the Year (1936-70)

In 1971, the *Daily Racing Form*, the Thoroughbred Racing Associations, and the National Turf Writers Assn. joined forces to create the Eclipse Awards. Before then, however, the *Racing Form* (1936-70) and the TRA (1950-70) issued separate selections for Horse of the Year. Their picks differed only four times from 1950-70 and are so noted. Horses listed in CAPITAL letters are Triple Crown winners; (f) indicates female.

Multiple winners: Kelso (5); Challedon, Native Dancer and Whirlaway (2).

Year		Year		Year		Year	
1936	Granville	1946	ASSAULT	1955	Nashua	1964	Kelso
1937	WAR ADMIRAL	1947	Armed	1956	Swaps	1965	Roman Brother (DRF)
1938	Seabiscuit	1948	CITATION	1957	Bold Ruler (DRF)		Moccasin (TRA)
1939	Challedon	1949	Capot		Dedicate (TRA)	1966	Buckpasser
1940	Challedon	1950	Hill Prince	1958	Round Table	1967	Damascus
1941	WHIRLAWAY	1951	Counterpoint	1959	Sword Dancer	1968	Dr. Fager
1942	Whirlaway	1952	One Count (DRF)	1960	Kelso	1969	Arts and Letters
1943	COUNT FLEET		Native Dancer (TRA)	1961	Kelso	1970	Fort Marcy (DRF)
1944	Twilight Tear (f)	1953	Tom Fool	1962	Kelso		Personality (TRA)
1945	Busher (f)	1954	Native Dancer	1963	Kelso		

Eclipse Awards (Cont.)

Older Male

Year		Year		Year		Year	
1971	Ack Ack (5)	1979	Affirmed (4)	1987	Ferdinand (4)	1995	Cigar (5)
1972	Autobiography (4)	1980	Spectacular Bid (4)	1988	Alysheba (4)	1996	Cigar (6)
1973	Riva Ridge (4)	1981	John Henry (6)	1989	Blushing John (4)	1997	Skip Away (4)
1974	Forego (4)	1982	Lemhi Gold (4)	1990	Criminal Type (5)	1998	Skip Away (5)
1975	Forego (5)	1983	Bates Motel (4)	1991	Black Tie Affair (5)	1999	Victory Gallop (4)
1976	Forego (6)	1984	Slew o' Gold (4)	1992	Pleasant Tap (5)	2000	Lemon Drop Kid (4)
1977	Forego (7)	1985	Vanlandingham (4)	1993	Bertrando (4)	2001	Tiznow (4)
1978	Seattle Slew (4)	1986	Turkoman (4)	1994	The Wicked North (4)	2002	Left Bank (5)

Older Female

Year		Year		Year		Year	
1971	Shuvee (5)	1979	Waya (5)	1987	North Sider (5)	1995	Inside Information (4)
1972	Typecast (6)	1980	Glorious Song (4)	1988	Personal Ensign (4)	1996	Jewel Princess (4)
1973	Susan's Girl (4)	1981	Relaxing (5)	1989	Bayakoa (5)	1997	Hidden Lake (4)
1974	Desert Vixen (4)	1982	Track Robbery (6)	1990	Bayakoa (6)	1998	Escena (5)
1975	Susan's Girl (6)	1983	Amb. of Luck (4)	1991	Queena (5)	1999	Beautiful Pleasure (4)
1976	Proud Delta (4)	1984	Princess Rooney (4)	1992	Paseana (5)	2000	Riboletta (5)
1977	Cascapedia (4)	1985	Life's Magic (4)	1993	Paseana (6)	2001	Gourmet Girl (6)
1978	Late Bloomer (4)	1986	Lady's Secret (4)	1994	Sky Beauty (4)	2002	Azeri (4)

3-Year-Old Male

Year		Year		Year		Year	
1971	Canonero II	1979	Spectacular Bid	1987	Alysheba	1995	Thunder Gulch
1972	Key to the Mint	1980	Temperence Hill	1988	Risen Star	1996	Skip Away
1973	SECRETARIAT	1981	Pleasant Colony	1989	Sunday Silence	1997	Silver Charm
1974	Little Current	1982	Conquistador Cielo	1990	Unbridled	1998	Real Quiet
1975	Wajima	1983	Slew o' Gold	1991	Hansel	1999	Charismatic
1976	Bold Forbes	1984	Swale	1992	A.P. Indy	2000	Tiznow
1977	SEATTLE SLEW	1985	Spend A Buck	1993	Prairie Bayou	2001	Point Given
1978	AFFIRMED	1986	Snow Chief	1994	Holy Bull	2002	War Emblem

3-Year-Old Filly

Year		Year		Year		Year	
1971	Turkish Trousers	1979	Davona Dale	1987	Sacahuista	1995	Serena's Song
1972	Susan's Girl	1980	Genuine Risk	1988	Winning Colors	1996	Yanks Music
1973	Desert Vixen	1981	Wayward Lass	1989	Open Mind	1997	Ajina
1974	Chris Evert	1982	Christmas Past	1990	Go for Wand	1998	Banshee Breeze
1975	Ruffian	1983	Heartlight No. One	1991	Dance Smartly	1999	Silverbulletday
1976	Revidere	1984	Life's Magic	1992	Saratoga Dew	2000	Surfside
1977	Our Mims	1985	Mom's Command	1993	Hollywood Wildcat	2001	Xtra Heat
1978	Tempest Queen	1986	Tiffany Lass	1994	Heavenly Prize	2002	Farda Amiga

2-Year-Old Male

Year		Year		Year		Year	
1971	Riva Ridge	1979	Rockhill Native	1987	Forty Niner	1995	Maria's Mon
1972	Secretariat	1980	Lord Avie	1988	Easy Goer	1996	Boston Harbor
1973	Protagonist	1981	Deputy Minister	1989	Rhythm	1997	Favorite Trick
1974	Foolish Pleasure	1982	Roving Boy	1990	Fly So Free	1998	Answer Lively
1975	Honest Pleasure	1983	Devil's Bag	1991	Arazi	1999	Anees
1976	Seattle Slew	1984	Chief's Crown	1992	Gilded Time	2000	Macho Uno
1977	Affirmed	1985	Tasso	1993	Dehere	2001	Johannesburg
1978	Spectacular Bid	1986	Capote	1994	Timber Country	2002	Vindication

2-Year-Old Filly

Year		Year		Year		Year	
1971	Numbered Account	1979	Smart Angle	1988	Open Mind	1997	Countess Diana
1972	La Prevoyante	1980	Heavenly Cause	1989	Go for Wand	1998	Silverbulletday
1973	Talking Picture	1981	Before Dawn	1990	Meadow Star	1999	Chilukki
1974	Ruffian	1982	Landaluce	1991	Pleasant Stage	2000	Caressing
1975	Dearly Precious	1983	Althea	1992	Eliza	2001	Tempera
1976	Sensational	1984	Outstandingly	1993	Phone Chatter	2002	Storm Flag Flying
1977	Lakeville Miss	1985	Family Style	1994	Flanders		
1978	(TIE) Candy Eclair	1986	Brave Raj	1995	Golden Attraction		
	& It's in the Air	1987	Epitome	1996	Storm Song		

Champion Turf Horse

Year		Year		Year		Year	
1971	Run the Gantlet (3)	1973	SECRETARIAT (3)	1975	Snow Knight (4)	1977	Johnny D (3)
1972	Cougar II (6)	1974	Dahlia (4)	1976	Youth (3)	1978	Mac Diarmida (3)

Champion Male Turf Horse

Year		Year		Year		Year	
1979	Bowl Game (5)	1985	Cozzene (4)	1991	Tight Spot (4)	1997	Chief Bearhart (4)
1980	John Henry (5)	1986	Manila (3)	1992	Sky Classic (5)	1998	Buck's Boy (5)
1981	John Henry (6)	1987	Theatrical (5)	1993	Kotashaan (5)	1999	Daylami (5)
1982	Perrault (5)	1988	Sunshine Forever (3)	1994	Paradise Creek (5)	2000	Kalanisi (4)
1983	John Henry (8)	1989	Steinlen (6)	1995	Northern Spur (4)	2001	Fantastic Light (5)
1984	John Henry (9)	1990	Itsallgreektome (3)	1996	Singspiel (4)	2002	High Chaparral (3)

Champion Female Turf Horse

Year		Year		Year		Year	
1979	Trillion (5)	1985	Pebbles (4)	1991	Miss Alleged (4)	1997	Ryafan (3)
1980	Just A Game II (4)	1986	Estrapade (6)	1992	Flawlessly (4)	1998	Fiji (4)
1981	De La Rose (3)	1987	Miesque (3)	1993	Flawlessly (5)	1999	Soaring Softly (4)
1982	April Run (4)	1988	Miesque (4)	1994	Hatoof (5)	2000	Perfect Sting (4)
1983	All Along (4)	1989	Brown Bess (7)	1995	Possibly Perfect (5)	2001	Banks Hill (3)
1984	Royal Heroine (4)	1990	Laugh and Be Merry (5)	1996	Wandesta (5)	2002	Golden Apples (4)

Sprinter

Year		Year		Year		Year	
1971	Ack Ack (5)	1979	Star de Naskra (4)	1988	Gulch (4)	1997	Smoke Glacken (3)
1972	Chou Croute (4)	1980	Plugged Nickle (3)	1989	Safely Kept (3)	1998	Reraise (3)
1973	Shecky Greene (3)	1981	Guilty Conscience (5)	1990	Housebuster (3)	1999	Artax (4)
1974	Forego (4)	1982	Gold Beauty (3)	1991	Housebuster (4)	2000	Kona Gold (6)
1975	Gallant Bob (3)	1983	Chinook Pass (4)	1992	Rubiano (5)	2001	Squirtle Squirt (3)
1976	My Juliet (4)	1984	Eillo (4)	1993	Cardmania (7)	2002	Orientate (4)
1977	What a Summer (4)	1985	Precisionist (4)	1994	Cherokee Run (4)		
1978	(TIE) Dr. Patches (4)	1986	Smile (4)	1995	Not Surprising (4)		
	& J.O. Tobin (4)	1987	Groovy (4)	1996	Lit de Justice (6)		

Steeplechase or Hurdle Horse

Year		Year		Year		Year	
1971	Shadow Brook (7)	1979	Martie's Anger (4)	1987	Inlander (6)	1995	Lonesome Glory (7)
1972	Soothsayer (5)	1980	Zaccio (4)	1988	Jimmy Lorenzo (6)	1996	Correggio (5)
1973	Athenian Idol (5)	1981	Zaccio (5)	1989	Highland Bud (4)	1997	Lonesome Glory (9)
1974	Gran Kan (8)	1982	Zaccio (6)	1990	Morley Street (6)	1998	Flat Top (5)
1975	Life's Illusion (4)	1983	Flatterer (4)	1991	Morley Street (7)	1999	Lonesome Glory (11)
1976	Straight and True (6)	1984	Flatterer (5)	1992	Lonesome Glory (4)	2000	All Gong (6)
1977	Cafe Prince (7)	1985	Flatterer (6)	1993	Lonesome Glory (5)	2001	Pompeyo (8)
1978	Cafe Prince (8)	1986	Flatterer (7)	1994	Warm Spell (6)	2002	Flat Top (9)

Outstanding Jockey

Year		Year		Year		Year	
1971	Laffit Pincay Jr.	1979	Laffit Pincay Jr.	1987	Pat Day	1995	Jerry Bailey
1972	Braulio Baeza	1980	Chris McCarron	1988	Jose Santos	1996	Jerry Bailey
1973	Laffit Pincay Jr.	1981	Bill Shoemaker	1989	Kent Desormeaux	1997	Jerry Bailey
1974	Laffit Pincay Jr.	1982	Angel Cordero Jr.	1990	Craig Perret	1998	Gary Stevens
1975	Braulio Baeza	1983	Angel Cordero Jr.	1991	Pat Day	1999	Jorge Chavez
1976	Sandy Hawley	1984	Pat Day	1992	Kent Desormeaux	2000	Jerry Bailey
1977	Steve Cauthen	1985	Laffit Pincay Jr.	1993	Mike Smith	2001	Jerry Bailey
1978	Darrel McHargue	1986	Pat Day	1994	Mike Smith	2002	Jerry Bailey

Outstanding Apprentice Jockey

Year		Year		Year		Year	
1971	Gene St. Leon	1980	Frank Lovato Jr.	1988	Steve Capanas	1996	Neil Poznansky
1972	Thomas Wallis	1981	Richard Migliore	1989	Michael Luzzi	1997	Roberto Rosado
1973	Steve Valdez	1982	Alberto Delgado	1990	Mark Johnston		& Philip Teator
1974	Chris McCarron	1983	Declan Murphy	1991	Mickey Walls	1998	Shaun Bridgmohan
1975	Jimmy Edwards	1984	Wesley Ward	1992	Rosemary Homeister	1999	Ariel Smith
1976	George Martens	1985	Art Madrid Jr.	1993	Juan Umana	2000	Tyler Baze
1977	Steve Cauthen	1986	Allen Stacy	1994	Dale Beckner	2001	Jeremy Rose
1978	Ron Franklin	1987	Kent Desormeaux	1995	Ramon B. Perez	2002	Ryan Fogelsonger
1979	Cash Asmussen						

Outstanding Trainer

Year		Year		Year		Year	
1971	Charlie Whittingham	1979	Laz Barrera	1987	D. Wayne Lukas	1995	Bill Mott
1972	Lucien Laurin	1980	Bud Delp	1988	Shug McGaughey	1996	Bill Mott
1973	H. Allen Jerkens	1981	Ron McAnally	1989	Charlie Whittingham	1997	Bob Baffert
1974	Sherill Ward	1982	Charlie Whittingham	1990	Carl Nafzger	1998	Bob Baffert
1975	Steve DiMauro	1983	Woody Stephens	1991	Ron McAnally	1999	Bob Baffert
1976	Laz Barrera	1984	Jack Van Berg	1992	Ron McAnally	2000	Bobby Frankel
1977	Laz Barrera	1985	D. Wayne Lukas	1993	Bobby Frankel	2001	Bobby Frankel
1978	Laz Barrera	1986	D. Wayne Lukas	1994	D. Wayne Lukas	2002	Bobby Frankel

Eclipse Awards (Cont.)
Outstanding Owner

Year		Year		Year		Year	
1971	Mr. & Mrs. E.E. Fogleson	1980	Mr. & Mrs. Bertram Firestone	1988	Ogden Phipps	1997	Carolyn Hine
1972-73	No award	1981	Dotsam Stable	1989	Ogden Phipps	1998	Frank Stronach
1974	Dan Lasater	1982	Viola Sommer	1990	Frances Genter	1999	Frank Stronach
1975	Dan Lasater	1983	John Franks	1991	Sam-Son Farms	2000	Frank Stronach
1976	Dan Lasater	1984	John Franks	1992	Juddmonte Farms	2001	Richard Englander
1977	Maxwell Gluck	1985	Mr. & Mrs. Gene Klein	1993	John Franks	2002	Richard Englander
1978	Harbor View Farm	1986	Mr. & Mrs. Gene Klein	1994	John Franks		
1979	Harbor View Farm	1987	Mr. & Mrs. Gene Klein	1995	Allen Paulson		
				1996	Allen Paulson		

Outstanding Breeder

Year		Year		Year		Year	
1971	Paul Mellon	1979	Claiborne Farm	1987	Nelson Bunker Hunt	1995	Juddmonte Farms
1972	C.T. Chenery	1980	Mrs. Henry Paxson	1988	Ogden Phipps	1996	Farnsworth Farms
1973	C.T. Chenery	1981	Golden Chance Farm	1989	North Ridge Farm	1997	John & Betty Mabee
1974	John W. Galbreath	1982	Fred W. Hooper	1990	Calumet Farm	1998	John & Betty Mabee
1975	Fred W. Hooper	1983	Edward P. Taylor	1991	John & Betty Mabee	1999	William S. Farish
1976	Nelson Bunker Hunt	1984	Claiborne Farm	1992	William S. Farish	2000	Frank Stronach
1977	Edward P. Taylor	1985	Nelson Bunker Hunt	1993	Allan Paulson	2001	Juddmonte Farms
1978	Harbor View Farm	1986	Paul Mellon	1994	William T. Young	2002	Juddmonte Farms

Award of Merit

Year		Year		Year		Year	
1976	Jack J. Dreyfus	1985	Keene Daingerfield	1992	Joe Hirsch & Robert P. Strub	1998	D.G. Van Clief Jr.
1977	Steve Cauthen	1986	Herman Cohen	1993	Paul Mellon	2000	Jim McKay
1978	Dinny Phipps	1987	J.B. Faulconer	1994	Alfred G. Vanderbilt	2001	Pete Pederson & Harry T. Mangurian
1979	Jimmy Kilroe	1988	John Forsythe	1995	Ted Bassett III		
1980	John D. Shapiro	1989	Michael Sandler	1996	Allen Paulson	2002	Ogden Phipps & Howard Battle
1981	Bill Shoemaker	1990	Warner L. Jones	1997	Bob & Beverly Lewis		
1984	John Gaines	1991	Fred W. Hooper				

Special Award

Year		Year		Year		Year	
1971	Robert J. Kleberg	1985	Arlington Park	1995	Russell Baze	2001	Sheikh Mohammed al-Maktoum
1974	Charles Hatton	1987	Anheuser-Busch	1998	Oak Tree Racing Assoc.		
1976	Bill Shoemaker	1988	Edward J. DeBartolo Sr.	1999	Laffit Pincay Jr.	2002	Keeneland Library
1980	John T. Landry & Pierre E. Bellocq	1989	Richard Duchossois	2000	John Hettinger		
1984	C.V. Whitney	1994	Eddie Arcaro & John Longden				

HARNESS RACING

Triple Crown Winners
PACERS

Nine three-year-olds have won the Cane Pace, Little Brown Jug and Messenger Stakes in the same year since the Pacing Triple Crown was established in 1956. No trainer or driver has won it more than once. **Note:** As of the closing time for the Horse Racing chaper, No Pan Intended had won the Cane Pace and Little Brown Jug. See Updates for results from Messenger Stakes.

Year		Driver	Trainer	Owner
1959	**Adios Butler**	Clint Hodgins	Paige West	Paige West & Angelo Pellillo
1965	**Bret Hanover**	Frank Ervin	Frank Ervin	Richard Downing
1966	**Romeo Hanover**	Bill Myer & George Sholty*	Jerry Silverman	Lucky Star Stables & Morton Finder
1968	**Rum Customer**	Billy Haughton	Billy Haughton	Kennilworth Farms & L.C. Mancuso
1970	**Most Happy Fella**	Stanley Dancer	Stanley Dancer	Egyptian Acres Stable
1980	**Niatross**	Clint Galbraith	Clint Galbraith	Niagara Acres, Niatross Stables & Clint Galbraith
1983	**Ralph Hanover**	Ron Waples	Stew Firlotte	Waples Stable, Pointsetta Stable, Grant's Direct Stable & P.J. Baugh
1997	**Western Dreamer**	Mike Lachance	Bill Robinson Stable	Matthew, Daniel and Patrick Daly
1999	**Blissful Hall**	Ron Pierce	Benn Wallace	Daniel Plouffe

*Myer drove Romeo Hanover in the Cane, Sholty in the other two races.

TROTTERS

Six three-year-olds have won the Yonkers Trot, Hambletonian and Kentucky Futurity in the same year since the Trotting Triple Crown was established in 1955. Stanley Dancer is the only driver/trainer to win it twice.

Year		Driver/Trainer	Owner
1955	**Scott Frost**	Joe O'Brien	S.A. Camp Farms
1963	**Speedy Scot**	Ralph Baldwin	Castleton Farms
1964	**Ayres**	John Simpson Sr.	Charlotte Sheppard
1968	**Nevele Pride**	Stanley Dancer	Nevele Acres & Lou Resnick
1969	**Lindy's Pride**	Howard Beissinger	Lindy Farms
1972	**Super Bowl**	Stanley Dancer	Rachel Dancer & Rose Hild Breeding Farm

Triple Crown Near Misses

PACERS

Nine horses have won the first two legs of the Triple Crown, but not the third. The Cane Pace (CP), Little Brown Jug (LBJ), and Messenger Stakes (MS) have not always been run in the same order so numbers after races won indicate sequence for that year.

Year		CP	LBJ	MS
1957	Torpid	won, 1	won, 2	DNF*
1960	Countess Adios	won, 2	NE	won, 1
1971	Albatross	won, 2	2nd*	won, 1
1976	Keystone Ore	won, 1	won, 2	2nd*
1986	Barberry Spur	won, 1	won, 2	2nd*
1990	Jake and Elwood	won, 1	NE	won, 2
1992	Western Hanover	won, 1	2nd*	won, 2
1993	Rijadh	won, 1	2nd*	won, 2
1998	Shady Character	won, 1	won, 2	6th*

*Winning horses: Meadow Lands (1957), Nansemond (1971), Windshield Wiper (1976), Amity Chef (1986), Fake Left (1992), Life Sign (1993), Fit for Life (1998).

Note: Torpid (1957) scratched before the final heat; Countess Adios (1960) and Jake and Elwood (1990) not eligible for Little Brown Jug.

TROTTERS

Eight horses have won the first two legs of the Triple Crown–the Yonkers Trot (YT) and the Hambletonian (Ham)–but not the third. The winner of the Ky. Futurity (KF) is listed.

Year		YT	Ham	KF
1962	A.C.'s Viking	won	won	Safe Mission
1976	Steve Lobell	won	won	Quick Pay
1977	Green Speed	won	won	Texas
1978	Speedy Somolli	won	won	Doublemint
1987	Mack Lobell	won	won	Napoletano
1993	American Winner	won	won	Pine Chip
1996	Continentalvictory	won	won	Running Sea
1998	Muscles Yankee	won	won	Trade Balance

Note: Green Speed (1977) not eligible for Ky. Futurity; Continentalvictory (1996) was withdrawn from the Ky. Futurity due to a leg injury.

The Hambletonian

For three-year-old trotters. Inaugurated in 1926 and has been held in Syracuse, N.Y.; Lexington, Ky.; Goshen, N.Y.; Yonkers, N.Y.; Du Quoin, Ill.; and since 1981 at The Meadowlands in East Rutherford, N.J.

Run at one mile since 1947. Winning horse must win two heats.

Drivers with most wins: John Campbell (5); Stanley Dancer, Billy Haughton, Mike Lachance and Ben White (4); Howard Beissinger, Del Cameron and Henry Thomas (3).

Year		Driver	Fastest Heat	Year		Driver	Fastest Heat
1926	Guy McKinney	Nat Ray	2:04¾	1966	Kerry Way	Frank Ervin	1:58⅘
1927	Iosola's Worthy	Marvin Childs	2:03¾	1967	Speedy Streak	Del Cameron	2:00
1928	Spencer	W.H. Lessee	2:02½	1968	Nevele Pride	Stanley Dancer	1:59⅖
1929	Walter Dear	Walter Cox	2:02¾	1969	Lindy's Pride	Howard Beissinger	1:57⅗
1930	Hanover's Bertha	Tom Berry	2:03	1970	Timothy T	John Simpson Jr.	1:58⅖
1931	Calumet Butler	R.D. McMahon	2:03¼	1971	Speedy Crown	Howard Beissinger	1:57⅖
1932	The Marchioness	Will Caton	2:01¼	1972	Super Bowl	Stanley Dancer	1:56⅖
1933	Mary Reynolds	Ben White	2:03¾	1973	Flirth	Ralph Baldwin	1:57⅕
1934	Lord Jim	Doc Parshall	2:02¾	1974	Christopher T	Billy Haughton	1:58⅗
1935	Greyhound	Sep Palin	2:02¼	1975	Bonefish	Stanley Dancer	1:59
1936	Rosalind	Ben White	2:01¾	1976	Steve Lobell	Billy Haughton	1:56⅖
1937	Shirley Hanover	Henry Thomas	2:01½	1977	Green Speed	Billy Haughton	1:55⅗
1938	McLin Hanover	Henry Tomas	2:02¼	1978	Speedy Somolli	Howard Beissinger	1:55
1939	Peter Astra	Doc Parshall	2:04¼	1979	Legend Hanover	George Sholty	1:56⅕
1940	Spencer Scott	Fred Egan	2:02	1980	Burgomeister	Billy Haughton	1:56⅗
1941	Bill Gallon	Lee Smith	2:05	1981	Shiaway St. Pat	Ray Remmen	2:01⅕
1942	The Ambassador	Ben White	2:04	1982	Speed Bowl	Tommy Haughton	1:56⅘
1943	Volo Song	Ben White	2:02½	1983	Duenna	Stanley Dancer	1:57⅖
1944	Yankee Maid	Henry Thomas	2:04	1984	Historic Freight	Ben Webster	1:56⅖
1945	Titan Hanover	Harry Pownall Sr.	2:04	1985	Prakas	Bill O'Donnell	1:54⅗
1946	Chestertown	Thomas Berry	2:02½	1986	Nuclear Kosmos	Ulf Thoresen	1:55⅖
1947	Hoot Mon	Sep Palin	2:00	1987	Mack Lobell	John Campbell	1:53⅗
1948	Demon Hanover	Harrison Hoyt	2:02	1988	Armbro Goal	John Campbell	1:54⅗
1949	Miss Tilly	Fred Egan	2:01⅖	1989	Park Avenue Joe & Probe *	Ron Waples Bill Fahy	1:54⅗
1950	Lusty Song	Del Miller	2:02	1990	Harmonious	John Campbell	1:54⅕
1951	Mainliner	Guy Crippen	2:02⅗	1991	Giant Victory	Jack Moiseyev	1:54⅗
1952	Sharp Note	Bion Shively	2:02⅖	1992	Alf Palema	Mickey McNichol	1:56⅖
1953	Helicopter	Harry Harvey	2:01⅗	1993	American Winner	Ron Pierce	1:53⅕
1954	Newport Dream	Del Cameron	2:02⅘	1994	Victory Dream	Mike Lachance	1:54⅕
1955	Scott Frost	Joe O'Brien	2:00⅗	1995	Tagliabue	John Campbell	1:54⅗
1956	The Intruder	Ned Bower	2:01⅖	1996	Continentalvictory	Mike Lachance	1:52⅖
1957	Hickory Smoke	John Simpson Sr.	2:00⅕	1997	Malabar Man	Mal Burroughs	1:55
1958	Emily's Pride	Flave Nipe	1:59⅘	1998	Muscles Yankee	John Campbell	1:52⅖
1959	Diller Hanover	Frank Ervin	2:01⅕	1999	Self Possessed	Mike Lachance	1:51⅗
1960	Blaze Hanover	Joe O'Brien	1:59⅗	2000	Yankee Paco	Trevor Ritchie	1:53⅖
1961	Harlan Dean	James Arthur	1:58⅖	2001	Scarlet Knight	Stefan Melander	1:53⅘
1962	A.C.'s Viking	Sanders Russell	1:59⅗	2002	Chip Chip Hooray	Eric Ledford	1:53⅗
1963	Speedy Scot	Ralph Baldwin	1:57⅗	2003	Amigo Hall	Mike Lachance	1:54
1964	Ayres	John Simpson Sr.	1:56⅘				
1965	Egyptian Candor	Del Cameron	2:03⅘				

*In 1989, Park Avenue Joe and Probe finished in a dead heat in the race-off. They were later declared co-winners, but Park Avenue Joe was awarded 1st place money because his three-race summary (2-1-1) was better than Probe's (1-9-1).

Harness Racing (Cont.)
All-Time Leaders

The all-time winning trotters, pacers and drivers through 2002, according to *The Trotting and Pacing Guide*. Purses for horses include races in foreign countries. Earnings and wins for drivers include only races held in North America.

Top 10 Horses—Money Won

		T/P	Yrs	Earnings
1	Varenne	T	1998-2002	$5,636,255
2	Moni Maker	T	1995-2000	5,589,256
3	Peace Corps	T	1988-93	4,137,737
4	Ourasi	T	1988-90	4,010,105
5	Gallo Blue Chip	P	1999—	3,944,512
6	Mack Lobell	T	1986-91	3,917,594
7	Reve d'Udon	T	1985-92	3,611,351
8	Zoogin	T	1992-99	3,513,324
9	Victory Tilly	T	1997—	3,386,387
10	General du Pommeau	T	1996—	3,247,727
11	Nihilator	P	1984-85	3,225,653
12	Real Desire	P	2000—	3,159,814
13	Sea Cove	T	1989-95	3,138,986
14	Magician	T	1997—	3,133,025
15	Artsplace	P	1990-92	3,085,083

Top 10 Drivers—Races Won

		Yrs	1st	Earnings
1	Herve Filion	36	14,857	$85,574,660
2	Walter Case Jr.	25	10,826	43,006,418
3	Cat Manzi	35	9,652	88,643,353
4	Mike Lachance	35	9,267	147,936,357
5	Dave Magee	30	9,228	72,421,402
6	John Campbell	31	9,145	213,776,639
7	Dave Palone	21	8,852	36,973,349
8	Jack Moiseyev	27	8,314	88,886,711
9	Eddie Davis	39	8,141	45,554,423
10	Bill (Zeke) Parker Jr.	32	8,069	19,857,432
11	Tony Morgan	29	8,017	50,837,977
12	Doug Brown	30	7,774	80,452,423
13	Carmine Abbatiello	46	7,170	50,323,736
14	Leigh Fitch	41	7,084	7,720,029
15	Ron Waples	32	6,764	71,810,527

Annual Awards
Harness Horse of the Year

Selected since 1947 by U.S. Trotting Association and the U.S. Harness Writers Association; age of winning horse is noted; (t) indicates trotter and (p) indicates pacer.

Multiple winners: Bret Hanover and Nevele Pride (3); Adios Butler, Albatross, Cam Fella, Good Time, Mack Lobell, Moni Maker, Niatross and Scott Frost (2).

Year		Year		Year		Year	
1947	Victory Song (4t)	1963	Speedy Scot (3t)	1979	Niatross (2p)	1995	CR Kay Suzie (3t)
1948	Rodney (4t)	1964	Bret Hanover (2p)	1980	Niatross (3p)	1996	Continentalvictory (3t)
1949	Good Time (3p)	1965	Bret Hanover (3p)	1981	Fan Hanover (3p)	1997	Malabar Man (3t)
1950	Proximity (8t)	1966	Bret Hanover (4p)	1982	Cam Fella (3p)	1998	Moni Maker (5t)
1951	Pronto Don (6t)	1967	Nevele Pride (2t)	1983	Cam Fella (4p)	1999	Moni Maker (6t)
1952	Good Time (6p)	1968	Nevele Pride (3t)	1984	Fancy Crown (3t)	2000	Gallo Blue Chip (3p)
1953	Hi Lo's Forbes (5p)	1969	Nevele Pride (4t)	1985	Nihilator (3p)	2001	Bunny Lake (3p)
1954	Stenographer (3t)	1970	Fresh Yankee (7t)	1986	Forrest Skipper (4p)	2002	Real Desire (4p)
1955	Scott Frost (3t)	1971	Albatross (3p)	1987	Mack Lobell (3t)		
1956	Scott Frost (4t)	1972	Albatross (4p)	1988	Mack Lobell (4t)		
1957	Torpid (3p)	1973	Sir Dalrae (4p)	1989	Matt's Scooter (4p)		
1958	Emily's Pride (3t)	1974	Delmonica Hanover (5t)	1990	Beach Towel (3p)		
1959	Bye Bye Byrd (4t)	1975	Savoir (7t)	1991	Precious Bunny (3p)		
1960	Adios Butler (4p)	1976	Keystone Ore (3p)	1992	Artsplace (4p)		
1961	Adios Butler (5p)	1977	Green Speed (3t)	1993	Staying Together (4p)		
1962	Su Mac Lad (8t)	1978	Abercrombie (3p)	1994	Cam's Card Shark (3p)		

Driver of the Year

Determined by Universal Driving Rating System (UDR) and presented by the Harness Tracks of America since 1968. Eligible drivers must have at least 1,000 starts for the season.

Multiple winners: Herve Filion (10); John Campbell, Walter Case Jr. and Mike Lachance (3); Tony Morgan, Bill O'Donnell, Luc Ouellette, Dave Palone and Ron Waples (2).

Year		Year		Year		Year	
1968	Stanley Dancer	1978	Carmine Abbatiello & Herve Filion	1987	Mike Lachance	1996	Tony Morgan & Luc Ouellette
1969	Herve Filion			1988	John Campbell		
1970	Herve Filion	1979	Ron Waples	1989	Herve Filion	1997	Tony Morgan
1971	Herve Filion	1980	Ron Waples	1990	John Campbell	1998	Walter Case Jr.
1972	Herve Filion	1981	Herve Filion	1991	Walter Case Jr.	1999	Dave Palone
1973	Herve Filion	1982	Bill O'Donnell	1992	Walter Case Jr.		
1974	Herve Filion	1983	John Campbell	1993	Jack Moiseyev	2000	Dave Palone
1975	Joe O'Brien	1984	Bill O'Donnell	1994	Dave Magee	2001	Stephane Bouchard
1976	Herve Filion	1985	Mike Lachance	1995	Luc Ouellette	2002	Tony Morgan
1977	Donald Dancer	1986	Mike Lachance				

Tennis

Andy Roddick can't believe his big win in the 2003 U.S. Open for his first Grand Slam title.

AP/Wide World Photos

Passing the Torch

No sooner had Pete Sampras hung it up at the U.S. Open than Andy Roddick won his first Grand Slam.

Gerry Brown
is co-editor of the ESPN Sports Almanac.

Pete Sampras has a problem. He has a picture perfect family, enough trophies to fill a dozen mantles, millions of dollars in the bank and nothing left to prove to himself.

It's no wonder Sampras decided to call it a career in 2003, walking away from the sport he dominated for the last decade. The only question remaining is why hadn't he done it sooner. Surely he'd proven everything he'd had to prove long ago.

Whenever a great player retires, talk turns to where they fit on the list of all-time greats. Although he was never as popular a player as Jimmy Connors, John McEnroe or Andre Agassi, Sampras was better than all of them. And while Australian legend Rod Laver won the Grand Slam twice and Sampras could never win the French Open, there's never been a champion like Sampras. His 14 Grand Slam titles are the best ever and he finished the year ranked first in the world six times, a number that has never been, and may

never be, surpassed.

The "problem" with Sampras was always was that he is dull. But compared to some of his contemporaries, most people would come off as dull. Connors was captivating, McEnroe was anything but dull and Agassi is certainly more fun. It seemed like Agassi was his only competition on the court and even that's a rivalry that was won decisively by Sampras, finishing his career with a 20-14 record in their head-to-head meetings, including 6-3 in Grand Slam matches.

But does Sampras think he's the greatest ever?

"I will never sit here and say I'm the greatest ever. I've done what I've done in the game. I've won a number of majors—I think that's kind of the answer to everything," Sampras said at a news conference at the U.S. Open.

"I don't know if there's one best player of all time. I feel my game will match up to just about anybody. I played perfect tennis at times, in my mind."

AP/Wide World Photos

*Tennis legend **Pete Sampras** waved goodbye from center court one final time in 2003, leaving the game with nothing left to prove to himself.*

The Sampras goodbye party was held at the National Tennis Center during the 2003 U.S. Open, especially appropriate for the best American tennis player in history. Although he won more Grand Slam titles in England, it was at the U.S. Open that Sampras won his first and last majors, each time over Agassi.

In 1990, a teenage Sampras became the youngest champion in tournament history and in 2002, at age 31, he became the oldest to win it since Ken Rosewall in 1970.

Speaking of the 2002 U.S. Open, it was a special way to end a special career, winning a major in his final match.

Fellow U.S. standard-bearer Agassi is not rushing to follow Sampras into retirement. In fact, he won his eighth Grand Slam title at the 2003 Australian Open. However it's not Agassi that is expected to carry the flag for American men's tennis in the coming years.

Andy Roddick won what should be just the first in a pile of Grand Slam titles with his breakthrough win at the 2003 U.S. Open, a dominating 6-3, 7-6, 6-3 victory over top-ranked Juan Carlo Ferrero.

But while the 21-year-old Roddick has attributes that Sampras never had, he can still only aspire to and may never achieve what Sampras did.

While Sampras retired because he

AP/Wide World Photos

*With the Williams sisters out of action for part of the year it was a Belgian invasion atop the WTA Tour in 2003 as **Justine Henin-Hardenne** beat **Kim Clijsters** at the French Open. Despite the loss, Clijsters earned the world number one ranking in August.*

had nothing left to prove, Roddick is only beginning to prove that he deserves to be mentioned with the likes of a champion like Sampras.

Appropriately, Roddick used a Sampras-like game—bombing big serves and scoring lots of winners—to overpower Ferrero in the Open final. Perhaps it was a tennis lesson learned firsthand from the master himself one year before.

At the 2002 U.S. Open an aging but still dangerous Sampras was still jealously guarding any torches. And, seeded 17th in the tournament, he surprised many when, in the quarterfinals, he completely stomped the young gun Roddick in straight sets on his way to that 14th and final Grand Slam singles title.

A year later it was Roddick giving the lessons and lifting the trophy.

Sampras could strike a tennis ball like few others who ever played. His consistently dominating serve was one of the biggest weapons in the history of tennis and he won 65 ATP Tour singles titles with it.

He never struck a chord with the public the same way he struck the tennis ball. Maybe that's our problem. Not his.

The Ten Biggest Stories of the Year in Tennis

10 Russia wins its first Davis Cup ever in December 2002 when young Mikhail Youzhny, a late substitute in the deciding singles match, manages an amazing comeback to beat Paul-Henri Mathieu 3-6, 2-6, 6-3, 7-5, 6-4. Youzhny is the first player to come from two sets down in the final singles to win the Davis Cup and he gets a bear hug from former president and self-proclaimed Russian team mascot Boris Yeltsin for his efforts.

9 Tennis trailblazer Althea Gibson dies at age 72. Gibson broke down barriers becoming the first African-American to win Wimbledon and the U.S. championship (the predecessor of the U.S. Open).

8 Belgian Kim Clijsters, who has never won a Grand Slam title, takes over the world number one ranking from an injured Serena Williams on Aug. 11.

7 Serena Williams wins the "Serena Slam" with her win at the Australian Open. She becomes the first player since Steffi Graf in 1994 to win four straight Grand Slam titles.

6 Thirty-two-year-old Andre Agassi wins his eighth career Grand Slam title with his lopsided victory at the Australian Open, becoming the oldest man to win a Grand Slam singles title since Ken Rosewall won the 1972 Australian Open title at age 37.

5 Belgium's Justine Henin-Hardenne ends Serena's grand slam run with her 6-0, 6-4, win over countrywoman Kim Clijsters at the French Open. It is the first Grand Slam title of her career and the first in Belgium's history. Henin-Hardenne gets her second Grand Slam win at the U.S. Open as both Williams sisters are sidelined with injuries.

4 Martina Navratilova wins her 20th Wimbledon title—this one in mixed doubles with partner Leander Paes. The victory ties Billie Jean King's Wimbledon record. King earned her 20th Wimbledon title playing doubles with Navratilova in 1979. The 46-year-old Navratilova becomes the oldest Wimbledon champion ever.

3 The seemingly ever-spry Martina Navratilova is chosen by captain Billie Jean King to lead the U.S. Fed Cup team against Belgium in November. Navratilova, undefeated in Fed Cup play with a record of 37-0, was to be 47 years old at the time of the competition and would be the oldest player ever to compete in the event. She was expected to play doubles.

2　　Young American Andy Roddick steps to the fore and wins his first Grand Slam title, beating the world's top-ranked player Juan Carlos Ferrero, 6-3, 7-6 (2), 6-3 at a rain-soaked U.S. Open. The 21-year-old Roddick overpowers Ferrero, by blasting 23 aces and never getting his serve broken.

1　　Pete Sampras officially announces his retirement from tennis at the U.S. Open in an emotional on-court ceremony after a dominating professional career in which he won 64 singles titles and a record 14 grand slam tournaments, including the 2002 U.S. Open in his final match.

Smashing Baby!

Andy Roddick tied Greg Rusedski's record for the fastest serve when he blasted a 149 m.p.h. rocket at Andre Agassi at the Stella Artois Championships. He also launched one 147 m.p.h. earlier in the tournament. Below are the fastest recorded serves each year since 1999.

Year		MPH
2003	Andy Roddick	149
2002	Andy Roddick	144
2001	Taylor Dent	144
2000	Taylor Dent	140
1999	Greg Rusedski	143

Source: ATP Tour Communications.

30-Somethings

With four more wins (through Oct. 12) in 2003, Andre Agassi is steadily moving up the list of all-time ATP wins by players over 30 years old.

	Titles
Rod Laver	44
Ken Rosewall	29
Arthur Ashe	20
Jimmy Connors	15
Andre Agassi	13

Streaking

With no wins in 2003 (through Oct. 12), Monica Seles was in danger of having her streak of consecutive years with a WTA singles title stopped at eight. Listed are the longest streaks in the open era.

	Years
Martina Navratilova, 1974-94	21
Chris Evert, 1971-88	18
Steffi Graf, 1986-99	14
E. Goolagong-Cawley, 1970-80	11
Virginia Wade, 1968-78	11

Source: WTA Tour Communications.

Tennis Anyone?

New Jersey leads all states with 13.1 percent of its population playing tennis at least once over the last twelve months. The state with the lowest percentage is N. Dakota (4.1 percent).

	Pct. of Population
New Jersey	13.1
Maryland	12.9
Minnesota	12.5
Washington D.C.	11.8
Wisconsin	11.2

Sources: USA Today, USTA and Tennis Industry Assoc.

2002-2003
Season in Review

SPORTS ALMANAC

Tournament Results

Winners of men's and women's pro singles championships from Nov. 3, 2002 through Sept. 28, 2003.

Men's ATP Tour

Late 2002

Finals	Tournament	Winner	Earnings	Runner-Up	Score
Nov. 3	TMS—Paris	Marat Safin	$448,000	L. Hewitt	76 60 64
Nov. 17	Tennis Masters Cup (Shanghai)	Lleyton Hewitt	700,000	J.C. Ferrero	75 75 26 26 64
Dec. 1	Davis Cup Final (Paris)	Russia	—	France	3-2

2003

Finals	Tournament	Winner	Earnings	Runner-Up	Score
Jan. 5	AAPT Championships (Adelaide)	Nikolay Davydenko	$48,600	K. Vliegen	62 76
Jan. 5	Qatar Open (Doha)	Stafen Koubek	142,000	J-M Gambill	64 64
Jan. 6	Tata Open (Chennai)	Paradorn Srichaphan	52,000	K. Kucera	63 61
Jan. 11	adidas International (Sydney)	Hyung-Taik Lee	48,600	J.C. Ferrero	46 76 76
Jan. 11	Heineken Open (Auckland)	Gustavo Kuerten	48,600	D. Hrbaty	63 75
Jan. 26	**Australian Open** (Melbourne)	Andre Agassi	654,000	R. Schuettler	62 62 61
Feb. 2	Milan Indoors	Martin Verkerk	55,960	Y. Kafelnikov	64 57 75
Feb. 16	Marseille Open	Roger Federer	66,700	J. Bjorkman	62 76
Feb. 16	Siebel Open (San Jose)	Andre Agassi	52,000	D. Sanguinetti	62 76
Feb. 16	BellSouth Open (Vina Del Mar)	David Sanchez	47,000	M. Rios	16 63 63
Feb. 23	Kroger St. Jude (Memphis)	Taylor Dent	128,000	A. Roddick	61 64
Feb. 23	ABN/AMRO World Tennis Tournament (Rotterdam)	Max Mirnyi	154,000	R. Sluiter	76 64
Feb. 23	Copa AT&T Cup (Buenos Aires)	Carlos Moya	52,000	G. Coria	63 46 64
Mar. 1	Mexican Open (Acapulco)	Agustin Calleri	128,000	M. Zabaleta	75 36 63
Mar. 2	Dubai Open	Roger Federer	187,500	J. Novak	61 76
Mar. 2	Copenhagen Open	Karol Kucera	52,000	O. Rochus	76 64
Mar. 9	International Tennis Champs. (Delray Beach)	Jan-Michael Gambill	52,000	M. Fish	60 76
Mar. 9	Franklin Templeton Classic (Scottsdale)	Lleyton Hewitt	52,000	M. Philippoussis	64 64
Mar. 16	TMS—Indian Wells	Lleyton Hewitt	400,000	G. Kuerten	61 61
Mar. 31	TMS—Miami	Andre Agassi	500,000	C. Moya	63 63
Apr. 13	Estoril Open	Nikolay Davydenko	78,640	A. Calleri	64 63
Apr. 13	Grand Prix Hassan II (Casablanca)	Julien Boutter	59,147	Y. El Aynaoui	62 26 61
Apr. 20	TMS—Monte Carlo	Juan Carlos Ferrero	434,268	G. Coria	62 62
Apr. 27	Open Seat Godo (Barcelona)	Carlos Moya	168,288	M. Safin	57 62 62
Apr. 27	U.S. Claycourt Championships (Houston)	Andre Agassi	52,000	A. Roddick	36 63 64
May 4	BMW Open (Munich)	Roger Federer	58,615	J. Nieminen	61 64
May 4	Valencia Open	Juan Carlos Ferrero	58,615	C. Rochus	62 64
May 11	TMS—Rome	Felix Mantilla	462,303	R. Federer	75 62 76
May 18	TMS—Hamburg	Guillermo Coria	461,725	A. Calleri	63 64 64
May 24	ATP World Team Championship (Dusseldorf)	Chile	515,490	Czech Republic	2-1
May 24	Int'l Raiffeisen Grand Prix (St. Poelten)	Andy Roddick	61,700	N. Davydenko	63 62
June 8	**French Open** (Paris)	Juan Carlos Ferrero	983,000	M. Verkerk	61 63 62
June 15	Gerry Weber Open (Halle)	Roger Federer	112,224	N. Kiefer	61 63
June 15	Stella Artois Championships (London)	Andy Roddick	112,224	S. Grosjean	63 63
June 21	Samsung Open (Nottingham)	Greg Rusedski	60,060	M. Fish	63 62
June 21	Ordina Open (s'Hertogenbosch)	Sjeng Schalken	60,060	A. Clement	63 64
July 6	**Wimbledon** (London)	Roger Federer	960,250	M. Philippoussis	76 62 76
July 13	Swedish Open (Bastad)	Mariano Zabaleta	58,667	N. Lapentti	63 64
July 13	Swiss Open (Gstaad)	Jiri Novak	86,308	R. Federer	57 63 63 16 63
July 13	Hall of Fame Championships (Newport)	Robby Ginepri	52,000	J. Melzer	64 67 61
July 20	Mercedes Cup (Stuttgart)	Guillermo Coria	132,739	T. Robredo	62 62 61
July 20	Dutch Open (Amersfoort)	Nicolas Massu	58,588	R. Sluiter	64 76 62
July 27	Croatia Open (Umag)	Carlos Moya	63,250	F. Volandri	64 36 75
July 27	Generali Open (Kitzbuhel)	Guillermo Coria	183,547	N. Massu	61 64 62
July 27	RCA Championships (Indianapolis)	Andy Roddick	74,250	P. Srichaphan	76 64

Tournament Results (Cont.)

Finals	Tournament	Winner	Earnings	Runner-Up	Score
Aug. 3	Idea Prokom Open (Sopot)	Guillermo Coria	$61,900	D. Ferrer	75 61
Aug. 3	Legg Mason Classic (Washington D.C.)	Tim Henman	74,250	F. Gonzalez	63 64
Aug. 3	Mercedes-Benz Cup (Los Angeles)	Wayne Ferreira	52,000	L. Hewitt	63 46 75
Aug. 10	TMS—Montreal	Andy Roddick	400,000	D. Nalbandian	61 63
Aug. 17	TMS—Cincinnati	Andy Roddick	400,000	M. Fish	46 76 76
Aug. 24	TD Waterhouse Cup (Commack)	Paradorn Srichaphan	52,000	J. Blake	62 64
Sept. 7	**U.S. Open** (Flushing)	Andy Roddick	1,000,000	J.C. Ferrero	63 76 63
Sept. 14	Romanian Open (Bucharest)	David Sanchez	58,785	N. Massu	62 62
Sept. 14	Brazil Open (Costa do Sauipe)	Sjeng Schalken	52,000	R. Scheuttler	62 64
Sept. 28	Thailand Open (Bangkok)	Taylor Dent	76,500	J.C. Ferrero	63 76
Sept. 28	Heineken Open (Shanghai)	Mark Philippoussis	52,000	J. Novak	62 61
Sept. 28	International Championship of Sicily (Palermo)	Nicolas Massu	60,230	P-H Mathieu	16 62 76

Note: TMS indicates tournament is part of the Tennis Masters Series.

Women's WTA Tour

Late 2002

Finals	Tournament	Winner	Earnings	Runner-Up	Score
Nov. 3	Fed Cup Final	Slovakia	—	Spain	3-1
Nov. 10	Volvo Open (Pattaya City)	Angelique Widjaja	$16,000	Y. J. Cho	62 64
Nov. 11	WTA Championships (Los Angeles)	Kim Clijsters	765,000	S. Williams	75 63

2003

Finals	Tournament	Winner	Earnings	Runner-Up	Score
Jan. 4	Uncle Toby's Hardcourts (Gold Coast)	Nathalie Dechy	$27,000	M-G Mikaelian	63 36 63
Jan. 4	ASB Bank Classic (Auckland)	Eleni Daniilidou	22,000	Y. J. Cho	64 46 76
Jan. 10	Moorilla International (Hobart)	Alicia Molik	16,000	A. Frazier	62 46 64
Jan. 11	Canberra International	Meghann Shaughnessy	16,000	F. Schiavone	61 61
Jan. 11	adidas International (Sydney)	Kim Clijsters	93,000	L. Davenport	64 63
Jan. 25	**Australian Open** (Melbourne)	Serena Williams	654,000	V. Williams	76 36 64
Feb. 2	Pan Pacific Open (Tokyo)	Lindsay Davenport	189,000	M. Seles	67 61 62
Feb. 9	Open Gaz de France (Paris)	Serena Williams	93,000	A. Mauresmo	63 62
Feb. 9	Indian Open (Hyderabad)	Tamarine Tanasugarn	22,000	I. Tulyaganova	64 64
Feb. 16	Proximus Diamond Games (Antwerp)	Venus Williams	93,000	K. Clijsters	62 64
Feb. 16	Qatar Open (Doha)	Anastasia Myskina	27,000	E. Likhovtseva	63 61
Feb. 22	Dubai Open	Justine Henin-Hardenne	93,000	M. Seles	46 76 75
Feb. 22	Kroger St. Jude (Memphis)	Lisa Raymond	27,000	A. Coetzer	63 62
Feb. 22	Copa Colsanitas (Bogota)	Fabiola Zuluaga	27,000	A. Medina Garrigues	63 62
Mar. 2	State Farm Tennis Classic (Scottsdale)	Ai Sugiyama	93,000	K. Clijsters	36 75 64
Mar. 2	Mexican Open (Acapulco)	Amanda Coetzer	27,000	M. Diaz-Oliva	75 63
Mar. 16	Pacific Life Open (Indian Wells)	Kim Clijsters	332,000	L. Davenport	64 75
Mar. 29	Nasdaq 100 Open (Miami)	Serena Williams	393,000	J. Capriati	46 64 61
Apr. 5	Grand Prix De S.A.R. (Casablanca)	Rita Grande	16,000	A. Serra Zanetti	62 46 61
Apr. 6	Sarasota Open	Anastasia Myskina	22,000	A. Molik	64 61
Apr. 13	Estoril Open	Magui Serna	22,000	J. Schruff	64 61
Apr. 13	Family Circle Cup (Charleston)	Justine Henin-Hardenne	189,000	S. Williams	63 64
Apr. 20	Bausch & Lomb Championships (Amelia Island)	Elena Dementieva	93,000	L. Davenport	46 75 63
Apr. 20	Budapest Grand Prix	Magui Serna	16,000	A. Molik	36 75 64
May 4	J&S Cup (Warsaw)	Amelie Mauresmo	103,500	V. Williams	67 60 30 (ret.)
May 4	Croatian Bol Open	Vera Zvonareva	27,000	C. Martinez Granados	61 63
May 11	German Open (Berlin)	Justine Henin-Hardenne	182,000	K. Clijsters	64 46 75
May 18	Italian Masters (Rome)	Kim Clijsters	189,000	A. Mauresmo	36 76 60
May 24	Strasbourg International	Silvia Farina Elia	27,000	K. Sprem	63 46 64
May 24	Madrid Open	Chanda Rubin	27,000	M.A. Sanchez Lorenzo	64 57 64
June 7	**French Open** (Paris)	Justine Henin-Hardenne	958,000	K. Clijsters	60 64
June 14	Wien Energie Grand Prix (Vienna)	Paola Suarez	27,000	K. Sprem	76 26 64
June 15	DFS Classic (Birmingham)	Magdalena Maleeva	27,000	S. Asagoe	61 64
June 21	Ordina Open ('s-Hertogenbosch)	Kim Clijsters	27,000	J. Henin-Hardenne	67 30 (ret.)
June 21	Hastings Direct Int'l Champs (Eastbourne)	Chanda Rubin	93,000	C. Martinez	64 36 64
July 7	**Wimbledon** (London)	Serena Williams	954,000	V. Williams	46 64 62
July 14	Palermo International	Dinara Safina	16,000	K. Srebotnik	63 64
July 27	Bank of the West Classic (Stanford)	Kim Clijsters	97,000	J. Capriati	46 64 62
Aug. 3	Acura Classic (San Diego)	Justine Henin-Hardenne	165,500	K. Clijsters	36 62 63
Aug. 3	Idea Prokom Polish Open (Sopot)	Anna Pistolesi	50,000	K. Koukalova	62 60

Finals	Tournament	Winner	Earnings	Runner-Up	Score
Aug. 10	JP Morgan Chase Open (Los Angeles)	Kim Clijsters	$97,000	L. Davenport	61 36 61
Aug. 10	Nordea Nordic Light Open (Helsinki)	Anna Pistolesi	22,000	J. Kostanic	46 64 60
Aug. 17	Rogers AT&T Cup (Toronto)	Justine Henin-Hardenne	192,000	L. Krasnoroutskaya	61 60
Aug. 23	Pilot Pen Tennis (New Haven)	Jennifer Capriati	96,000	L. Davenport	62 40 (ret.)
Sept. 6	**U.S. Open** (Flushing)	J. Henin-Hardenne	1,000,000	K. Clijsters	75 61
Sept. 14	Wismilak International (Bali)	Elena Dementieva	32,000	C. Rubin	62 61
Sept. 21	Polo Open (Shanghai)	Elena Dementieva	93,000	C. Rubin	63 76
Sept. 28	Sparkassen Cup (Leipzig)	Anastasia Myskina	93,000	J. Henin-Hardenne	36 63 63

2003 Grand Slam Tournaments

Australian Open

MEN'S SINGLES

FINAL EIGHT—#2 Andre Agassi; #4 Juan Carlos Ferrero; #9 Andy Roddick; #10 David Nalbandian; #12 Sebastien Grosjean; #18 Younes El Aynaoui; #31 Rainer Schuettler; plus unseeded Wayne Ferreira.

Quarterfinals

Roddick def. El Aynaoui		46 76(5) 46 64 21-19
Schuettler def. Nalbandian		63 57 61 60
Ferreira def. Ferrero		76(4) 76(5) 61
Agassi def. Grosjean		63 62 62

Semifinals

Schuettler def. Roddick		75 26 63 63
Agassi def. Ferreira		62 62 63

Final

Agassi def. Schuettler		62 62 61

WOMEN'S SINGLES

FINAL EIGHT—#1 Serena Williams; #2 Venus Williams; #4 Kim Clijsters; #5 Justine Henin-Hardenne; #7 Daniela Hantuchova; #8 Anastasia Myskina; #25 Meghann Shaughnessy; plus unseeded Virginia Ruano Pascual.

Quarterfinals

S. Williams def. Shaughnessy	62 62
Clijsters def. Myskina	62 64
Henin-Hardenne def. Ruano Pascual	62 62
V. Williams def. Hantuchova	64 63

Semifinals

S. Williams def. Clijsters	46 63 75
V. Williams def. Henin-Hardenne	63 63

Final

S. Williams def. V. Williams	76(4) 36 64

DOUBLES FINALS

Men—#8 Michael Llodra & Fabrice Santoro def. #1 Mark Knowles & Daniel Nestor, 6-4, 3-6, 6-3.

Women—#1 Venus Williams & Serena Williams def. #2 Virginia Ruano Pascual & Paola Suarez, 4-6, 6-4, 6-3.

Mixed—Leander Paes & Martina Navratilova def. Todd Woodbridge & Eleni Daniilidou, 6-4, 7-5.

French Open

MEN'S SINGLES

FINAL EIGHT—#2 Andre Agassi; #3 Juan Carlos Ferrero; #4 Carlos Moya; #7 Guillermo Coria; #9 Albert Costa; #19 Fernando Gonzalez; #28 Tommy Robredo; plus unseeded Martin Verkerk.

Quarterfinals

Ferrero def. Gonzalez	61 36 61 57 64
Costa def. Robredo	26 36 64 75 62
Coria def. Agassi	46 63 62 64
Verkerk def. Moya	63 64 57 46 86

Semifinals

Ferrero def. Costa	63 76(5) 64
Verkerk def. Coria	76(4) 64 76(0)

Final

Ferrero def. Verkerk	61 63 62

WOMEN'S SINGLES

FINAL EIGHT—#1 Serena Williams; #2 Kim Clijsters; #4 Justine Henin-Hardenne; #5 Amelie Mauresmo; #8 Chanda Rubin; #22 Vera Zvonareva; #24 Conchita Martinez; plus unseeded Nadia Petrova.

Quarterfinals

Williams def. Mauresmo	61 62
Clijsters def. Martinez	62 61
Henin-Hardenne def. Rubin	63 62
Petrova def. Zvonareva	61 46 63

Semifinals

Henin-Hardenne def. Williams	62 46 75
Clijsters def. Petrova	75 61

Final

Henin-Hardenne def. Clijsters	60 64

DOUBLES FINALS

Men—#3 Bob Bryan & Mike Bryan def. #11 Paul Haarhuis & Yevgeny Kafelnikov, 7-6 (7-3), 6-3.

Women—#2 Kim Clijsters & Ai Sugiyama def. #1 Virginia Ruano Pascual & Paola Suarez, 6-7(5-7), 6-2, 9-7.

Mixed—#2 Lisa Raymond & Mike Bryan def. #3 Elena Likhovtseva & Mahesh Bhupathi, 6-3, 6-4.

Wimbledon

MEN'S SINGLES

FINAL EIGHT—#4 Roger Federer; #5 Andy Roddick; #8 Sjeng Schalken; #10 Tim Henman; #13 Sebastien Grosjean; plus unseeded Jonas Bjorkman, Mark Philippoussis and Alexander Popp.

Quarterfinals

Roddick def. Bjorkman 64 62 64
Federer def. Schalken 63 64 64
Grosjean def. Henman . . . . .76(8) 36 63 64
Philippoussis def. Popp 46 46 63 63 86

Semifinals

Federer def. Roddick . . . . .76(6) 63 63
Philippoussis def. Grosjean . . . . .76(3) 63 63

Final

Federer def. Philippoussis . . . . .76(5) 62 76(3)

WOMEN'S SINGLES

FINAL EIGHT—#1 Serena Williams; #2 Kim Clijsters; #3 Justine Henin-Hardenne; #4 Venus Williams; #5 Lindsay Davenport; #8 Jennifer Capriati; #27 Silvia Farina Elia; #33 Svetlana Kuznetsova.

Quarterfinals

S. Williams def. Capriati 26 62 63
Henin-Hardenne def. Kutnetsova 62 62
V. Williams def. Davenport 62 26 61
Clijsters def. Farina Elia 57 60 61

Semifinals

S. Williams def. Henin-Hardenne 63 62
V. Williams def. Clijsters 46 63 61

Final

S. Williams def. V. Williams 46 64 62

DOUBLES FINALS

Men—#4 Jonas Bjorkman & Todd Woodbridge def. #1 Mahesh Bhupathi & Max Mirnyi, 3-6, 6-3, 7-6 (7-4), 6-3.

Women—#2 Kim Clijsters & Ai Sugiyama def. #1 Virginia Ruano Pascual & Paola Suarez, 6-4, 6-4.

Mixed—#5 Martina Navratilova & Leander Paes def. Anastassia Rodionova & Andy Ram, 6-3, 6-3.

U.S. Open

MEN'S SINGLES

FINAL EIGHT—#1 Andre Agassi; #3 Juan Carlos Ferrero; #4 Andy Roddick; #5 Guillermo Coria; #6 Lleyton Hewitt; #12 Sjeng Schalken; #13 David Nalbandian; and #22 Younes El Aynaoui.

Quarterfinals

Agassi def. Coria 64 63 75
Ferrero def. Hewitt . . . . .46 63 76(5) 61
Roddick def. Schalken 64 62 63
Nalbandian def. El Aynaoui . . . . .76(2) 62 36 75

Semifinals

Ferrero def. Agassi 64 63 36 64
Roddick def. Nalbandian . . . . . .67(4) 36 76(7) 61 63

Final

Roddick def. Ferrero . . . . .63 76(2) 63

WOMEN'S SINGLES

FINAL EIGHT—#1 Kim Clijsters; #2 Justine Henin-Hardenne; #3 Lindsay Davenport; #5 Amelie Mauresmo; #6 Jennifer Capriati; #7 Anastasia Myskina; #24 Paola Suarez; and #29 Francesca Schiavone.

Quarterfinals

Clijsters def. Mauresmo 61 64
Davenport def. Suarez 64 60
Capriati def. Schiavone 61 63
Henin-Hardenne def. Myskina 62 63

Semifinals

Clijsters def. Davenport 62 63
Henin-Hardenne def. Capriati . . . . .46 75 76(4)

Final

Henin-Hardenne def. Clijsters 75 61

DOUBLES FINALS

Men—#4 Jonas Bjorkman & Todd Woodbridge def. #2 Bob Bryan & Mike Bryan 5-7, 6-0, 7-5.

Women—#2 Virginia Ruano Pascual & Paola Suarez def. #4 Svetlana Kuznetsova & Martina Navratilova 6-2, 6-3.

Mixed—#8 Katarina Srebotnik & Bob Bryan def. #5 Lina Krasnoroutskaya & Daniel Nestor 5-7, 7-5, 7-6 (10-5).

Fed Cup

Originally the Federation Cup and started in 1963 by the International Tennis Federation as the Davis Cup of women's tennis.

2002 FINAL
Slovakia 3, Spain 1

at Maspalomas, Gran Canaria, Spain (Nov. 2-3)

Singles—Conchita Martinez (ESP) def. Janette Husarova (SVK) 6-4, 7-6 (8-6); Daniela Hantuchova (SVK) def. Magui Serna (ESP) 6-2, 6-1; Hantuchova (SVK) def. Martinez (ESP) 6-7 (8-10), 7-5, 6-4; Husarova (SVK) def. Arantxa Sanchez-Vicario (ESP) 6-0, 6-2.

Doubles—canceled.

2003 Early Rounds
First Round
(April 27-28)

Winner	Loser
at United States 5 . . . . .Czech Republic 0	
Slovenia 3 . . . . .at Argentina 2	
Italy 3 . . . . .at Sweden 2	
at Belgium 5 . . . . .Austria 0	
Slovakia 3 . . . . .at Germany 2	
at Russia 4 . . . . .Croatia 1	

Winner	Loser
at Spain 3 . . . . .Australia 2	
at France 5 . . . . .Colombia 0	

Quarterfinals
(July 19-20)

Winner	Loser
at United States 5 .Italy 0	
at Belgium 5 . . . . .Slovakia 0	
Russia 5 .at Slovenia 0	
France 4 . . . . .at Spain 1	

SEMIFINALS & FINAL

The 2003 Fed Cup semifinals and final was to be held on the carpet at the Olympic Stadium in Moscow, Russia from Nov. 19-23. Belgium was to play the United States, while host Russia was to take on France in the semifinals. These four countries have won five of the past seven Fed Cups, the U.S. leading the way with three of those wins and 17 overall.

Singles Leaders

Official Top 20 rankings and money leaders of men's and women's tours for 2002 and unofficial rankings for 2003 (through Sept. 29), as compiled by the ATP Tour (Association of Tennis Professionals) and WTA (Women's Tennis Association). Note that money lists include doubles earnings.

Final 2002 Rankings and Money Won

Listed are events won and times a finalist and semifinalist (Finish, 1-2-SF), match record (W-L), and earnings for the year.

MEN

		Finish 1-2-SF	W-L	Earnings
1	Lleyton Hewitt	5-2-3	61-15	$4,619,386
2	Andre Agassi	5-2-2	53-12	2,186,006
3	Marat Safin	1-2-2	56-26	1,719,408
4	Juan Carlos Ferrero	2-3-2	48-25	2,761,498
5	Carlos Moya	4-2-5	59-21	1,772,314
6	Roger Federer	3-2-3	58-22	1,995,027
7	Jiri Novak	0-2-6	53-26	1,454,130
8	Tim Henman	1-3-2	50-19	1,194,899
9	Albert Costa	1-2-0	35-22	1,434,439
10	Andy Roddick	2-2-4	56-22	1,060,878
11	Tommy Haas	0-1-4	45-21	1,163,569
12	David Nalbandian	2-1-0	36-24	914,882
13	Pete Sampras	1-1-1	27-17	1,222,999
14	Thomas Johansson	1-0-1	29-24	1,028,691
15	Guillermo Canas	2-2-2	45-23	1,276,617
16	Sebastien Grosjean	1-0-3	43-22	1,331,157
17	Fernando Gonzalez	2-1-1	40-22	735,682
18	Paradorn Srichaphan	2-2-3	49-25	651,089
19	Alex Corretja	2-0-2	39-19	780,986
20	Sjeng Schalken	1-1-2	37-29	888,581

WOMEN

		Finish 1-2-SF	W-L	Earnings
1	Serena Williams	8-2-1	56-5	$3,514,731
2	Venus Williams	7-4-3	62-9	2,123,316
3	Jennifer Capriati	1-3-5	48-16	1,617,409
4	Kim Clijsters	4-2-4	51-17	1,538,779
5	Justine Henin-Hardenne	2-4-4	52-21	1,056,843
6	Amelie Mauresmo	2-0-6	48-15	986,293
7	Monica Seles	2-1-6	47-14	949,613
8	Daniela Hantuchova	1-1-4	56-25	943,486
9	Jelena Dokic	2-3-6	53-26	743,407
10	Martina Hingis	2-2-2	34-10	908,506
11	Anastasia Myskina	1-3-1	50-29	533,214
12	Lindsay Davenport	0-4-3	24-9	637,208
13	Chanda Rubin	2-1-1	30-13	444,167
14	Magdalena Maleeva	1-1-1	35-24	540,341
15	Patty Schnyder	1-1-1	35-25	534,525
16	Anna Pistolesi	4-0-1	46-25	392,911
17	Silvia Farina Elia	1-0-2	44-28	475,647
18	Alexandra Stevenson	0-2-1	46-25	301,717
19	Elena Dementieva	0-1-2	37-27	420,682
20	Nathalie Dechy	0-0-2	34-26	276,056

2003 Tour Rankings (through Sept. 29)

Listed are tournaments won and times a finalist and semifinalist (Finish, 1-2-SF), match record (W-L), and points earned (Pts). The **ATP Champions Race** replaced the men's pro tennis tour's 27-year-old computer ranking system in 2000. Under the new system players start from zero on Jan. 1 and accumulate points during the calendar year with the player accumulating the most points becoming the World No. 1. Points are awarded in 18 tournaments: nine Tennis Masters Series events, four Grand Slams and five other International Series events.

MEN

Final ATP Tour singles rankings will be based on points earned from 18 tournaments played in 2003. Tournaments, titles and match won-lost records are for 2003 only.

Rank 03	(02)		Finish 1-2-SF	W-L	Pts
1	10	Andy Roddick	6-2-3	63-14	807
2	4	Juan Carlos Ferrero	3-3-2	57-14	726
3	6	Roger Federer	5-2-2	62-14	629
4	9	Andre Agassi	4-0-3	44-8	605
5	57	Guillermo Coria	4-2-1	54-14	589
6	33	Rainer Schuettler	0-2-4	54-25	493
7	5	Carlos Moya	3-1-2	49-17	398
8	12	David Nalbandian	0-1-2	37-18	358
9	72	Mark Philippoussis	1-2-1	30-16	310
10	1	Lleyton Hewitt	2-1-0	36-10	290
11	20	Sjeng Schalken	2-0-1	40-19	283
12	16	Sebastien Grosjean	0-1-2	28-16	255
	18	Paradorn Srichaphan	2-1-1	39-22	255
14	123	Martin Verkerk	1-2-1	23-21	252
15	22	Younes El Aynaoui	0-1-2	37-21	250
16	36	Gustavo Kuerten	1-1-3	33-18	243
	30	Tommy Robredo	0-1-3	34-21	243
18	7	Jiri Novak	1-3-0	36-21	242
19	51	Felix Mantilla	1-0-2	25-17	237
20	47	Agustin Calleri	1-2-1	31-19	231

WOMEN

WTA Tour singles ranking system based on total Round and Quality Points for each tournament played during the last 12 months (capped at 17 tournaments). Tournaments, titles and match won-lost records, however, are for 2003 only.

Rank 03	(02)		Finish 1-2-SF	W-L	Pts
1	4	Kim Clijsters	6-6-3	75-11	6579
2	5	Justine Henin-Hardenne	7-2-5	66-8	6291
3	1	Serena Williams	4-1-2	38-3	4400
4	12	Lindsay Davenport	1-5-3	46-14	3577
5	3	Jennifer Capriati	1-2-6	40-14	2809
6	2	Venus Williams	1-3-0	26-5	2508
7	6	Amelie Mauresmo	1-2-3	38-10	2341
8	19	Elena Dementieva	3-0-3	44-20	2299
9	13	Chanda Rubin	2-2-2	39-14	2150
10	11	Anastasia Myskina	3-0-0	35-16	1905
11	14	Magdalena Maleeva	1-0-0	25-19	1685
12	24	Ai Sugiyama	1-0-3	34-19	1680
13	111	Nadia Petrova	0-0-2	36-18	1604
14	8	Daniela Hantuchova	0-0-1	27-20	1598
15	45	Vera Zvonareva	1-0-2	40-17	1563
16	34	Conchita Martinez	0-1-1	29-19	1498
17	27	Paola Suarez	1-0-2	34-20	1414
18	21	Amada Coetzer	1-1-0	27-16	1410
19	30	Meghann Shaughnessy	1-0-1	32-18	1373
20	15	Patty Schnyder	0-0-2	20-19	1333

2003 Money Winners
Amounts include singles and doubles earnings through Sept. 29, 2003.

MEN

		Earnings			Earnings			Earnings
1	Andy Roddick	.$2,705,662	11	Jonas Bjorkman	....$854,567	21	Yeveny Kafelnikov	..$623,979
2	Juan Carlos Ferrero	.2,458,330	12	Mark Philippoussis	.834,838	22	Tommy Robredo	612,745
3	Roger Federer	2,147,580	13	Martin Verkerk	804,486	23	Sebastien Grosjean	..605,722
4	Andre Agassi	1,830,929	14	Jiri Novak	736,591	24	Albert Costa	588,077
5	Guillermo Coria	1,588,982	15	Felix Mantilla	703,238	25	Gustavo Kuerten	583,017
6	Rainer Schuettler	1,167,002	16	Sjeng Schalken	680,529	26	Radek Stepanek	542,885
7	Carlos Moya	1,015,255	17	Fernando Gonzalez	..676,520	27	Nicolas Massu	535,151
8	Max Mirnyi	1,008,247	18	Younes El Aynaoui	..652,699	28	Fabrice Santoro	532,763
9	David Nalbandian	...986,783	19	Paradorn Srichaphan	.630,272	29	Mardy Fish	523,613
10	Lleyton Hewitt	873,598	20	Agustin Calleri	629,520	30	Bob Bryan	516,879

WOMEN

		Earnings			Earnings			Earnings
1	J. Henin-Hardenne	..$3,035,264	11	Virginia Ruano Pascual	$645,866	21	Elena Likhovtseva	...$414,174
2	Kim Clijsters	2,811,764	12	Elena Dementieva	643,557	22	Magdalena Maleeva	..401,867
3	Serena Williams	2,249,038	13	Anastasia Myskina	...515,919	23	Vera Zvonareva	385,275
4	Lindsay Davenport	..1,278,593	14	Lisa Raymond	507,820	24	Lina Krasnoroutskaya	.355,200
5	Venus Williams	998,222	15	Nadia Petrova	504,319	25	Francesca Schiavone	.354,471
6	Jennifer Capriati	987,481	16	Svetlana Kuznetsova	..502,359	26	Silvia Farina Elia	354,069
7	Ai Sugiyama	888,974	17	Conchita Martinez	472,509	27	Martina Navratilova	..352,469
8	Paola Suarez	876,936	18	Daniela Hantuchova	..465,702	28	Cara Black	337,607
9	Chanda Rubin	693,538	19	Meghann Shaughnessy	.419,563	29	Katarina Srebotnik	...329,560
10	Amelie Mauresmo	...662,494	20	Jelena Dokic	415,550	30	Nathalie Dechy	323,181

Davis Cup

Russia won its first Davis Cup title in 2002 with a shocking 3-2, come-from-behind victory over host France. While Marat Safin provided two singles victories for Russia, it was 20-year-old former ballboy Mikhail Youzhny, a late substitute, who brought home the title with a five-set thriller over Paul-Henri Mathieu.

2002 FINAL
Russia 3, France 2
at Paris, France (Nov. 29–Dec. 1)

Day One—Marat Safin (RUS) def. Paul-Henri Mathieu (FRA) 6-4, 3-6, 6-1, 6-4; Sebastien Grosjean (FRA) def. Yevgeny Kafelnikov (RUS) 7-6 (7-3), 6-3, 6-0.

Day Two—Nicolas Escude & Fabrice Santoro (FRA) def. Kafelnikov & Safin (RUS) 6-3, 3-6, 5-7, 6-3, 6-4.

Day Three—Safin (RUS) def. Grosjean (FRA) 6-3, 6-2, 7-6 (13-11); Mikhail Youzhny (RUS) def. Mathieu (FRA) 3-6, 2-6, 6-3, 7-5, 6-4.

2003 Early Rounds
FIRST ROUND
(Feb. 7-9)

Winner	Loser
at Croatia 4	.United States 1
France 4	.at Romania 1
at Australia 4	.Great Britain 1
at Argentina 5	.Germany 0
Switzerland 3	.at Netherlands 2
at Sweden 3	.Brazil 1
at Spain 5	.Belgium 0
Russia 3	.at Czech Republic 2

QUARTERFINALS
(Apr. 4-6)

Winner	Loser
Switzerland 3	.at France 2
Australia 5	.at Sweden 0
at Spain 5	.Croatia 0
at Argentina 5	.Russia 0

SEMIFINALS
Australia 3, Switzerland 2
at Melbourne, Australia (Sept. 19-21)

Day One—Lleyton Hewitt (AUS) def. Michel Kratochvil (SWI) 6-4, 6-4, 6-1; Roger Federer (SWI) def. Mark Philippoussis (AUS) 6-3, 6-4, 7-6 (7-3).

Day Two—Wayne Arthurs & Todd Woodbridge (AUS) def. Federer & Marc Rosset (SWI) 4-6, 7-6 (7-5), 5-7, 6-4, 6-4.

Day Three—Hewitt (AUS) def. Federer (SWI) 5-7, 2-6, 7-6 (7-4), 7-5, 6-1; Kratochvil (SWI) def. Woodbridge (AUS) 6-4, retired.

Spain 3, Argentina 2
at Malaga, Spain (Sept. 19-21)

Day One—Juan Carlos Ferrero (ESP) def. Gaston Gaudio (ARG) 6-4, 6-0, 6-0; Carlos Moya (ESP) def. Mariano Zabaleta (ARG) 5-7, 2-6, 6-2, 6-0, 6-1.

Day Two—Lucas Arnold & Agustin Calleri (ARG) def. Alex Corretja & Albert Costa (ESP) 6-3, 1-6, 6-4, 6-2.

Day Three—Calleri (ARG) def. Ferrero (ESP) 6-4, 7-5, 6-1; Moya (ESP) def. Gaudio (ARG) 6-1, 6-4, 6-2.

2003 FINAL

The 2003 Davis Cup final between Australia and Spain was to be held from Nov. 28-30 on the grass courts of Rod Laver Arena in Melbourne, Australia. Host Australia is 3-1 lifetime against Spain, but the two countries most recently battled in the 2000 Final in Barcelona, with Spain coming away with the 3-1 victory.

1877-2003
Through the Years

SPORTS ALMANAC

Grand Slam Championships
Australian Open
MEN

Became an Open Championship in 1969. Two tournaments were held in 1977; the first in January, the second in December. Tournament moved back to January in 1987, so no championship was decided in 1986. **Surface:** Synpave Rebound Ace (hardcourt surface composed of polyurethane and synthetic rubber).

Multiple winners: Roy Emerson (6); Andre Agassi, Jack Crawford and Ken Rosewall (4); James Anderson, Rod Laver, Adrian Quist, Mats Wilander and Pat Wood (3); Boris Becker, Jack Bromwich, Ashley Cooper, Jim Courier, Stefan Edberg, Rodney Heath, Johan Kriek, Ivan Lendl, John Newcombe, Pete Sampras, Frank Sedgman, Guillermo Vilas and Tony Wilding (2).

Year	Winner	Loser	Score
1905	Rodney Heath	A. Curtis	46 63 64 64
1906	Tony Wilding	H. Parker	60 64 64
1907	Horace Rice	H. Parker	63 64 64
1908	Fred Alexander	A. Dunlop	36 36 60 62 63
1909	Tony Wilding	E. Parker	61 75 62
1910	Rodney Heath	H. Rice	64 63 62
1911	Norman Brookes	H. Rice	61 62 63
1912	J. Cecil Parke	A. Beamish	36 63 16 61 75
1913	Ernie Parker	H. Parker	26 61 62 63
1914	Pat Wood	G. Patterson	64 63 57 61
1915	Francis Lowe	H. Rice	46 61 61 64
1916-18	Not held World War I		
1919	A.R.F. Kingscote	E. Pockley	64 60 63
1920	Pat Wood	R. Thomas	63 46 68 61 63
1921	Rhys Gemmell	A. Hedeman	75 61 64
1922	James Anderson	G. Patterson	60 36 36 63 62
1923	Pat Wood	C.B. St. John	61 61 63
1924	James Anderson	R. Schlesinger	63 64 36 57 63
1925	James Anderson	G. Patterson	11-9 26 62 63
1926	John Hawkes	J. Willard	63 63 62
1927	Gerald Patterson	J. Hawkes	36 64 36 18-16 63
1928	Jean Borotra	R.O. Cummings	64 61 46 57 63
1929	John Gregory	R. Schlesinger	62 62 57 75
1930	Gar Moon	H. Hopman	63 61 63
1931	Jack Crawford	H. Hopman	64 62 26 61
1932	Jack Crawford	H. Hopman	46 63 36 63 61
1933	Jack Crawford	K. Gledhill	26 75 63 62
1934	Fred Perry	J. Crawford	63 75 61
1935	Jack Crawford	F. Perry	26 64 64 64
1936	Adrian Quist	J. Crawford	62 63 46 36 97
1937	Viv McGrath	J. Bromwich	63 16 60 26 61
1938	Don Budge	J. Bromwich	64 62 61
1939	Jack Bromwich	A. Quist	64 61 63
1940	Adrian Quist	J. Crawford	63 61 62
1941-45	Not held World War II		
1946	Jack Bromwich	D. Pails	57 63 75 36 62
1947	Dinny Pails	J. Bromwich	46 64 36 75 86
1948	Adrian Quist	J. Bromwich	64 36 63 26 63
1949	Frank Sedgman	J. Bromwich	63 63 62
1950	Frank Sedgman	K. McGregor	63 64 46 61
1951	Dick Savitt	K. McGregor	63 26 63 61
1952	Ken McGregor	F. Sedgman	75 12-10 26 62
1953	Ken Rosewall	M. Rose	60 63 64
1954	Mervyn Rose	R. Hartwig	62 06 64 62
1955	Ken Rosewall	L. Hoad	97 64 64
1956	Lew Hoad	K. Rosewall	64 36 64 75
1957	Ashley Cooper	N. Fraser	63 9-11 64 62

Year	Winner	Loser	Score
1958	Ashley Cooper	M. Anderson	75 63 64
1959	Alex Olmedo	N. Fraser	61 62 36 63
1960	Rod Laver	N. Fraser	57 36 63 86 86
1961	Roy Emerson	R. Laver	16 63 75 64
1962	Rod Laver	R. Emerson	86 06 64 64
1963	Roy Emerson	K. Fletcher	63 63 61
1964	Roy Emerson	F. Stolle	63 64 62
1965	Roy Emerson	F. Stolle	79 26 64 75 61
1966	Roy Emerson	A. Ashe	64 68 62 63
1967	Roy Emerson	A. Ashe	64 61 61
1968	Bill Bowrey	J. Gisbert	75 26 97 64
1969	Rod Laver	A. Gimeno	63 64 75
1970	Arthur Ashe	D. Crealy	64 97 62
1971	Ken Rosewall	A. Ashe	61 75 63
1972	Ken Rosewall	M. Anderson	76 63 75
1973	John Newcombe	O. Parun	63 67 75 61
1974	Jimmy Connors	P. Dent	76 64 46 63
1975	John Newcombe	J. Connors	75 36 64 75
1976	Mark Edmondson	J. Newcombe	67 63 76 61
1977	Roscoe Tanner	G. Vilas	63 63 63
	Vitas Gerulaitis	J. Lloyd	63 76 57 36 62
1978	Guillermo Vilas	J. Marks	64 64 36 63
1979	Guillermo Vilas	J. Sadri	76 63 62
1980	Brian Teacher	K. Warwick	75 76 63
1981	Johan Kriek	S. Denton	62 76 67 64
1982	Johan Kriek	S. Denton	63 63 62
1983	Mats Wilander	I. Lendl	61 64 64
1984	Mats Wilander	K. Curren	67 64 76 62
1985	Stefan Edberg	M. Wilander	64 63 63
1986	Not held		
1987	Stefan Edberg	P. Cash	63 64 36 57 63
1988	Mats Wilander	P. Cash	63 67 36 61 86
1989	Ivan Lendl	M. Mecir	62 62 62
1990	Ivan Lendl	S. Edberg	46 76 52 (ret.)
1991	Boris Becker	I. Lendl	16 64 64 64
1992	Jim Courier	S. Edberg	63 36 64 62
1993	Jim Courier	S. Edberg	62 61 26 75
1994	Pete Sampras	T. Martin	76 64 64
1995	Andre Agassi	P. Sampras	46 61 76 64
1996	Boris Becker	M. Chang	62 64 26 62
1997	Pete Sampras	C. Moya	62 63 63
1998	Petr Korda	M. Rios	62 62 62
1999	Yevgeny Kafelnikov	T. Enqvist	46 60 63 76
2000	Andre Agassi	Y. Kafelnikov	36 63 62 64
2001	Andre Agassi	A. Clement	64 62 62
2002	Thomas Johansson	M. Safin	36 64 64 76
2003	Andre Agassi	R. Schuettler	62 62 61

WOMEN

Became an Open Championship in 1969. Two tournaments were held in 1977, the first in January, the second in December. Tournament moved back to January in 1987, so no championship was decided in 1986.

Multiple winners: Margaret Smith Court (11); Nancye Wynne Bolton (6); Daphne Akhurst (5); Evonne Goolagong Cawley, Steffi Graf and Monica Seles (4); Joan Hartigan, Martina Hingis and Martina Navratilova (3); Coral Buttsworth, Jennifer Capriati, Chris Evert Lloyd, Thelma Long, Hana Mandlikova, Mall Molesworth and Mary Carter Reitano (2).

Year	Winner	Loser	Score
1922	Mall Molesworth	E. Boyd	63 10-8
1923	Mall Molesworth	E. Boyd	61 75
1924	Sylvia Lance	E. Boyd	63 36 64
1925	Daphne Akhurst	E. Boyd	16 86 64
1926	Daphne Akhurst	E. Boyd	61 63
1927	Esna Boyd	S. Harper	57 61 62
1928	Daphne Akhurst	E. Boyd	75 62
1929	Daphne Akhurst	L. Bickerton	61 57 62
1930	Daphne Akhurst	S. Harper	10-8 26 75
1931	Coral Buttsworth	M. Crawford	16 63 64
1932	Coral Buttsworth	K. Le Messurier	97 64
1933	Joan Hartigan	C. Buttsworth	64 63
1934	Joan Hartigan	M. Molesworth	61 64
1935	Dorothy Round	N. Lyle	16 61 63
1936	Joan Hartigan	N. Bolton	64 64
1937	Nancye Wynne	E. Westacott	63 57 64
1938	Dorothy Bundy	D. Stevenson	63 62
1939	Emily Westacott	N. Hopman	61 62
1940	Nancye Wynne	T. Coyne	57 64 60
1941-45	Not held World War II		
1946	Nancye Bolton	J. Fitch	64 64
1947	Nancye Bolton	N. Hopman	63 62
1948	Nancye Bolton	M. Toomey	63 61
1949	Doris Hart	N. Bolton	63 64
1950	Louise Brough	D. Hart	64 36 64
1951	Nancye Bolton	T. Long	61 75
1952	Thelma Long	H. Angwin	62 63
1953	Maureen Connolly	J. Sampson	63 62
1954	Thelma Long	J. Staley	63 64
1955	Beryl Penrose	T. Long	64 63
1956	Mary Carter	T. Long	36 62 97
1957	Shirley Fry	A. Gibson	63 64
1958	Angela Mortimer	L. Coghlan	63 64
1959	Mary Reitano	T. Schuurman	62 63
1960	Margaret Smith	J. Lehane	75 62
1961	Margaret Smith	J. Lehane	61 64
1962	Margaret Smith	J. Lehane	60 62
1963	Margaret Smith	J. Lehane	62 62
1964	Margaret Smith	L. Turner	63 62
1965	Margaret Smith	M. Bueno	57 64 52 (ret)

Year	Winner	Loser	Score
1966	Margaret Smith	N. Richey	walkover
1967	Nancy Richey	L. Turner	61 64
1968	Billie Jean King	M. Smith	61 62
1969	Margaret Court	B.J. King	64 61
1970	Margaret Court	K. Melville	61 63
1971	Margaret Court	E. Goolagong	26 76 75
1972	Virginia Wade	E. Goolagong	64 64
1973	Margaret Court	E. Goolagong	64 75
1974	Evonne Goolagong	C. Evert	76 46 60
1975	Evonne Goolagong	M. Navratilova	63 62
1976	Evonne Cawley	R. Tomanova	62 62
1977	Kerry Reid	D. Balestrat	75 62
	Evonne Cawley	H. Gourlay	63 60
1978	Chris O'Neil	B. Nagelsen	63 76
1979	Barbara Jordan	S. Walsh	63 63
1980	Hana Mandlikova	W. Turnbull	60 75
1981	Martina Navratilova	C. Evert Lloyd	67 64 75
1982	Chris Evert Lloyd	M. Navratilova	63 26 63
1983	Martina Navratilova	K. Jordan	62 76
1984	Chris Evert Lloyd	H. Sukova	67 61 63
1985	Martina Navratilova	C. Evert Lloyd	62 46 62
1986	Not held		
1987	Hana Mandlikova	M. Navratilova	75 76
1988	Steffi Graf	C. Evert	61 76
1989	Steffi Graf	H. Sukova	64 64
1990	Steffi Graf	M.J. Fernandez	63 64
1991	Monica Seles	J. Novotna	57 63 61
1992	Monica Seles	M.J. Fernandez	62 63
1993	Monica Seles	S. Graf	46 63 62
1994	Steffi Graf	A.S. Vicario	60 62
1995	Mary Pierce	A.S. Vicario	63 62
1996	Monica Seles	A. Huber	64 61
1997	Martina Hingis	M. Pierce	62 62
1998	Martina Hingis	C. Martinez	63 63
1999	Martina Hingis	A. Mauresmo	62 63
2000	Lindsay Davenport	M. Hingis	61 75
2001	Jennifer Capriati	M. Hingis	64 63
2002	Jennifer Capriati	M. Hingis	46 76 62
2003	Serena Williams	V. Williams	76 36 64

French Open
MEN

From 1891 to 1925, entry was restricted to members of French clubs. Became an Open Championship in 1968, but closed to contract pros in 1972. Note that Max Decugis won eight tournaments before 1925 (1903-04, 1907-09, 1912-14) to lead all men. **Surface:** Red clay.

Multiple winners (since 1925): Bjorn Borg (6); Henri Cochet (4); Gustavo Kuerten, Rene Lacoste, Ivan Lendl and Mats Wilander (3); Sergi Bruguera, Jim Courier, Jaroslav Drobny, Roy Emerson, Jan Kodes, Rod Laver, Frank Parker, Nicola Pietrangeli, Ken Rosewall, Manuel Santana, Tony Trabert and Gottfried von Cramm (2).

Year	Winner	Loser	Score
1925	Rene Lacoste	J. Borotra	75 61 64
1926	Henri Cochet	R. Lacoste	62 64 63
1927	Rene Lacoste	B. Tilden	64 46 57 63 11-9
1928	Henri Cochet	R. Lacoste	57 63 61 63
1929	Rene Lacoste	J. Borotra	63 26 60 26 86
1930	Henri Cochet	B. Tilden	36 86 63 61
1931	Jean Borotra	C. Boussus	26 64 75 64
1932	Henri Cochet	G. de Stefani	60 64 46 63
1933	Jack Crawford	H. Cochet	86 61 63
1934	Gottfried von Cramm	J. Crawford	64 79 36 75 63
1935	Fred Perry	G. von Cramm	63 36 61 63
1936	Gottfried von Cramm	F. Perry	60 26 62 26 60
1937	Henner Henkel	H. Austin	61 64 63

Year	Winner	Loser	Score
1938	Don Budge	R. Menzel	63 62 64
1939	Don McNeill	B. Riggs	75 60 63
1941-45	Not held World War II		
1946	Marcel Bernard	J. Drobny	36 26 61 64 63
1947	Joseph Asboth	E. Sturgess	86 75 64
1948	Frank Parker	J. Drobny	64 75 57 86
1949	Frank Parker	B. Patty	63 16 61 64
1950	Budge Patty	J. Drobny	61 62 36 57 75
1951	Jaroslav Drobny	E. Sturgess	63 63 63
1952	Jaroslav Drobny	F. Sedgman	62 60 36 64
1953	Ken Rosewall	V. Seixas	63 64 16 62
1954	Tony Trabert	A. Larsen	64 75 61
1955	Tony Trabert	S. Davidson	26 61 64 63

Year	Winner	Loser	Score	Year	Winner	Loser	Score
1956	Lew Hoad	S. Davidson	64 86 63	1980	Bjorn Borg	V. Gerulaitis	64 61 62
1957	Sven Davidson	H. Flam	63 64 64	1981	Bjorn Borg	I. Lendl	61 46 62 36 61
1958	Mervyn Rose	L. Ayala	63 64 64	1982	Mats Wilander	G. Vilas	16 76 60 64
1959	Nicola Pietrangeli	I. Vermaak	36 63 64 61	1983	Yannick Noah	M. Wilander	62 75 76
				1984	Ivan Lendl	J. McEnroe	36 26 64 75 75
1960	Nicola Pietrangeli	L. Ayala	36 63 64 46 63	1985	Mats Wilander	I. Lendl	36 64 62 62
1961	Manuel Santana	N. Pietrangeli	46 61 36 60 62	1986	Ivan Lendl	M. Pernfors	63 62 64
1962	Rod Laver	R. Emerson	36 26 63 97 62	1987	Ivan Lendl	M. Wilander	75 62 36 76
1963	Roy Emerson	P. Darmon	36 61 64 64	1988	Mats Wilander	H. Leconte	75 62 61
1964	Manuel Santana	N. Pietrangeli	63 61 46 75	1989	Michael Chang	S. Edberg	61 36 46 64 62
1965	Fred Stolle	T. Roche	36 60 62 63				
1966	Tony Roche	I. Gulyas	61 64 75	1990	Andres Gomez	A. Agassi	63 26 64 64
1967	Roy Emerson	T. Roche	61 64 26 62	1991	Jim Courier	A. Agassi	36 64 26 61 64
1968	Ken Rosewall	R. Laver	63 61 26 62	1992	Jim Courier	P. Korda	75 62 61
1969	Rod Laver	K. Rosewall	64 63 64	1993	Sergi Bruguera	J. Courier	64 26 62 36 63
				1994	Sergi Bruguera	A. Berasategui	63 75 26 61
1970	Jan Kodes	Z. Franulovic	62 64 60	1995	Thomas Muster	M. Chang	75 62 64
1971	Jan Kodes	I. Nastase	86 62 26 75	1996	Yevgeny Kafelnikov	M. Stich	76 75 76
1972	Andres Gimeno	P. Proisy	46 63 61 61	1997	Gustavo Kuerten	S. Bruguera	63 64 62
1973	Ilie Nastase	N. Pilic	63 63 60	1998	Carlos Moya	A. Corretja	63 75 63
1974	Bjorn Borg	M. Orantes	26 67 60 61 61	1999	Andre Agassi	A. Medvedev	16 26 64 63 64
1975	Bjorn Borg	G. Vilas	62 63 64				
1976	Adriano Panatta	H. Solomon	61 64 46 76	2000	Gustavo Kuerten	M. Norman	62 63 26 76
1977	Guillermo Vilas	B. Gottfried	60 63 60	2001	Gustavo Kuerten	A. Corretja	67 75 62 60
1978	Bjorn Borg	G. Vilas	61 61 63	2002	Albert Costa	J. C. Ferrero	61 60 46 63
1979	Bjorn Borg	V. Pecci	63 61 67 64	2003	Juan Carlos Ferrero	M. Verkerk	61 63 62

WOMEN

From 1897 to 1925, entry was restricted to members of French clubs. Became an Open Championship in 1968, but closed to contract pros in 1972. Note that Suzanne Lenglen won two titles prior to 1925, giving her six total.

Multiple winners (since 1925): Chris Evert Lloyd (7); Steffi Graf (6); Margaret Smith Court (5); Helen Wills Moody (4); Arantxa Sanchez Vicario, Monica Seles and Hilde Sperling (3); Maureen Connolly, Margaret Osborne duPont, Doris Hart, Ann Haydon Jones, Suzanne Lenglen, Simone Mathieu, Margaret Scriven, Martina Navratilova and Lesley Turner (2).

Year	Winner	Loser	Score	Year	Winner	Loser	Score
1925	Suzanne Lenglen	K. McKane	61 62	1967	Francoise Durr	L. Turner	46 63 64
1926	Suzanne Lenglen	M. Browne	61 60	1968	Nancy Richey	A. Jones	57 64 61
1927	Kea Bouman	I. Peacock	62 64	1969	Margaret Court	A. Jones	61 46 63
1928	Helen Wills	E. Bennett	61 62				
1929	Helen Wills	S. Mathieu	63 64	1970	Margaret Court	H. Niessen	62 64
				1971	Evonne Goolagong	H. Gourlay	63 75
1930	Helen Moody	H. Jacobs	62 61	1972	Billie Jean King	E. Goolagong	63 63
1931	Cilly Aussem	B. Nuthall	86 61	1973	Margaret Court	C. Evert	67 76 64
1932	Helen Moody	S. Mathieu	75 61	1974	Chris Evert	O. Morozova	61 62
1933	Margaret Scriven	S. Mathieu	62 46 64	1975	Chris Evert	M. Navratilova	26 62 61
1934	Margaret Scriven	H. Jacobs	75 46 61	1976	Sue Barker	R. Tomanova	62 06 62
1935	Hilde Sperling	S. Mathieu	62 61	1977	Mima Jausovec	F. Mihai	62 67 61
1936	Hilde Sperling	S. Mathieu	63 64	1978	Virginia Ruzici	M. Jausovec	62 62
1937	Hilde Sperling	S. Mathieu	62 64	1979	Chris Evert Lloyd	W. Turnbull	62 60
1938	Simone Mathieu	N. Landry	60 63				
1939	Simone Mathieu	J. Jedrzejowska	63 86	1980	Chris Evert Lloyd	V. Ruzici	60 63
				1981	Hana Mandlikova	S. Hanika	62 64
1940-45 Not held World War II				1982	Martina Navratilova	A. Jaeger	76 61
1946	Margaret Osborne	P. Betz	16 86 75	1983	Chris Evert Lloyd	M. Jausovec	61 62
1947	Patricia Todd	D. Hart	63 36 64	1984	Martina Navratilova	C. Evert Lloyd	63 61
1948	Nelly Landry	S. Fry	62 06 60	1985	Chris Evert Lloyd	M. Navratilova	63 67 75
1949	Margaret duPont	N. Adamson	75 62	1986	Chris Evert Lloyd	M. Navratilova	26 63 63
				1987	Steffi Graf	M. Navratilova	64 46 86
1950	Doris Hart	P. Todd	64 46 62	1988	Steffi Graf	N. Zvereva	60 60
1951	Shirley Fry	D. Hart	63 36 63	1989	A. Sanchez Vicario	S. Graf	76 36 75
1952	Doris Hart	S. Fry	64 64				
1953	Maureen Connolly	D. Hart	62 64	1990	Monica Seles	S. Graf	76 64
1954	Maureen Connolly	G. Bucaille	64 61	1991	Monica Seles	A.S. Vicario	63 64
1955	Angela Mortimer	D. Knode	26 75 10-8	1992	Monica Seles	S. Graf	62 36 10-8
1956	Althea Gibson	A. Mortimer	60 12-10	1993	Steffi Graf	M.J. Fernandez	46 62 64
1957	Shirley Bloomer	D. Knode	61 63	1994	A. Sanchez Vicario	M. Pierce	64 64
1958	Susi Kormoczi	S. Bloomer	64 16 62	1995	Steffi Graf	A.S. Vicario	76 46 60
1959	Christine Truman	S. Kormoczi	64 75	1996	Steffi Graf	A.S. Vicario	63 61
				1997	Iva Majoli	M. Hingis	64 62
1960	Darlene Hard	Y. Ramirez	63 64	1998	A. Sanchez Vicario	M. Seles	76 06 62
1961	Ann Haydon	Y. Ramirez	62 61	1999	Steffi Graf	M. Hingis	46 75 62
1962	Margaret Smith	L. Turner	63 36 75				
1963	Lesley Turner	A. Jones	26 63 75	2000	Mary Pierce	C. Martinez	62 75
1964	Margaret Smith	M. Bueno	57 61 62	2001	Jennifer Capriati	K. Clijsters	16 64 1210
1965	Lesley Turner	M. Smith	63 64	2002	Serena Williams	V. Williams	75 63
1966	Ann Jones	N. Richey	63 61	2003	J. Henin-Hardenne	K. Clijsters	60 64

Wimbledon
MEN

Officially called "The Lawn Tennis Championships" at the All England Club, Wimbledon. Challenge round system (defending champion qualified for following year's final) used from 1877-1921. Became an Open Championship in 1968, but closed to contract pros in 1972. **Surface:** Grass.

Multiple winners: Willie Renshaw and Pete Sampras (7); Bjorn Borg and Laurie Doherty (5); Reggie Doherty, Rod Laver and Tony Wilding (4); Wilfred Baddeley, Boris Becker, Arthur Gore, John McEnroe, John Newcombe, Fred Perry and Bill Tilden (3); Jean Borotra, Norman Brookes, Don Budge, Henri Cochet, Jimmy Connors, Stefan Edberg, Roy Emerson, John Hartley, Lew Hoad, Rene Lacoste, Gerald Patterson and Joshua Pim (2).

Year	Winner	Loser	Score
1877	Spencer Gore	W. Marshall	61 62 64
1878	Frank Hadow	S. Gore	75 61 97
1879	John Hartley	V. St. L. Gould	62 64 62
1880	John Hartley	H. Lawford	60 62 26 63
1881	Willie Renshaw	J. Hartley	60 62 61
1882	Willie Renshaw	E. Renshaw	61 26 46 62 62
1883	Willie Renshaw	E. Renshaw	26 63 63 46 63
1884	Willie Renshaw	H. Lawford	60 64 97
1885	Willie Renshaw	H. Lawford	75 62 46 75
1886	Willie Renshaw	H. Lawford	60 57 63 64
1887	Herbert Lawford	E. Renshaw	16 63 36 64 64
1888	Ernest Renshaw	H. Lawford	63 75 60
1889	Willie Renshaw	E. Renshaw	64 61 36 60
1890	William Hamilton	W. Renshaw	68 62 36 61 61
1891	Wilfred Baddeley	J. Pim	64 16 75 60
1892	Wilfred Baddeley	J. Pim	46 63 63 62
1893	Joshua Pim	W. Baddeley	36 61 63 62
1894	Joshua Pim	W. Baddeley	10-8 62 86
1895	Wilfred Baddeley	W. Eaves	46 26 86 62 63
1896	Harold Mahony	W. Baddeley	62 68 57 86 63
1897	Reggie Doherty	H. Mahony	64 64 63
1898	Reggie Doherty	L. Doherty	63 63 26 57 61
1899	Reggie Doherty	A. Gore	16 46 62 63 63
1900	Reggie Doherty	S. Smith	68 63 61 62
1901	Arthur Gore	R. Doherty	46 75 64 64
1902	Laurie Doherty	A. Gore	64 63 36 60
1903	Laurie Doherty	F. Riseley	75 63 60
1904	Laurie Doherty	F. Riseley	61 75 86
1905	Laurie Doherty	N. Brookes	86 62 64
1906	Laurie Doherty	F. Riseley	64 46 62 63
1907	Norman Brookes	A. Gore	64 62 62
1908	Arthur Gore	R. Barrett	63 62 46 36 64
1909	Arthur Gore	M. Ritchie	68 16 62 62 62
1910	Tony Wilding	A. Gore	64 75 46 62
1911	Tony Wilding	R. Barrett	64 46 26 62 (ret)
1912	Tony Wilding	A. Gore	64 64 46 64
1913	Tony Wilding	M. McLoughlin	86 63 10-8
1914	Norman Brookes	T. Wilding	64 64 75
1915-18	Not held World War I		
1919	Gerald Patterson	N. Brookes	63 75 62
1920	Bill Tilden	G. Patterson	26 63 62 64
1921	Bill Tilden	B. Norton	46 26 61 60 75
1922	Gerald Patterson	R. Lycett	63 64 62
1923	Bill Johnston	F. Hunter	60 63 61
1924	Jean Borotra	R. Lacoste	61 36 61 36 64
1925	Rene Lacoste	J. Borotra	63 63 46 86
1926	Jean Borotra	H. Kinsey	86 61 63
1927	Henri Cochet	J. Borotra	46 46 63 64 75
1928	Rene Lacoste	H. Cochet	61 46 64 62
1929	Henri Cochet	J. Borotra	64 63 64
1930	Bill Tilden	W. Allison	63 97 64
1931	Sidney Wood	F. Shields	walkover
1932	Ellsworth Vines	H. Austin	64 62 60
1933	Jack Crawford	E. Vines	46 11-9 62 26 64
1934	Fred Perry	J. Crawford	63 60 75
1935	Fred Perry	G. von Cramm	62 64 64
1936	Fred Perry	G. von Cramm	61 61 60
1937	Don Budge	G. von Cramm	63 64 62
1938	Don Budge	H. Austin	61 60 63
1939	Bobby Riggs	E. Cooke	26 86 36 63 62

Year	Winner	Loser	Score
1940-45	Not held World War II		
1946	Yvon Petra	G. Brown	62 64 79 57 64
1947	Jack Kramer	T. Brown	61 63 62
1948	Bob Falkenburg	J. Bromwich	75 06 62 36 75
1949	Ted Schroeder	J. Drobny	36 60 63 46 64
1950	Budge Patty	F. Sedgman	61 8-10 62 63
1951	Dick Savitt	K. McGregor	64 64 64
1952	Frank Sedgman	J. Drobny	46 62 63 62
1953	Vic Seixas	K. Nielsen	97 63 64
1954	Jaroslav Drobny	K. Rosewall	13-11 46 62 97
1955	Tony Trabert	K. Nielsen	63 75 61
1956	Lew Hoad	K. Rosewall	62 46 75 64
1957	Lew Hoad	A. Cooper	62 61 62
1958	Ashley Cooper	N. Fraser	36 63 64 13-11
1959	Alex Olmedo	R. Laver	64 63 64
1960	Neale Fraser	R. Laver	64 36 97 75
1961	Rod Laver	C. McKinley	63 61 64
1962	Rod Laver	M. Mulligan	62 62 61
1963	Chuck McKinley	F. Stolle	96 61 64
1964	Roy Emerson	F. Stolle	64 12-10 46 63
1965	Roy Emerson	F. Stolle	62 64 64
1966	Manuel Santana	D. Ralston	64 11-9 64
1967	John Newcombe	W. Bungert	63 61 61
1968	Rod Laver	T. Roche	63 64 62
1969	Rod Laver	J. Newcombe	64 57 64 64
1970	John Newcombe	K. Rosewall	57 63 62 36 61
1971	John Newcombe	S. Smith	63 57 26 64 64
1972	Stan Smith	I. Nastase	46 63 63 46 75
1973	Jan Kodes	A. Metreveli	61 98 63
1974	Jimmy Connors	K. Rosewall	61 61 64
1975	Arthur Ashe	J. Connors	61 61 57 64
1976	Bjorn Borg	I. Nastase	64 62 97
1977	Bjorn Borg	J. Connors	36 62 61 57 64
1978	Bjorn Borg	J. Connors	62 62 63
1979	Bjorn Borg	R. Tanner	67 61 36 63 64
1980	Bjorn Borg	J. McEnroe	16 75 63 67 86
1981	John McEnroe	B. Borg	46 76 76 64
1982	Jimmy Connors	J. McEnroe	36 63 67 76 64
1983	John McEnroe	C. Lewis	62 62 62
1984	John McEnroe	J. Connors	61 61 62
1985	Boris Becker	K. Curren	63 67 76 64
1986	Boris Becker	I. Lendl	64 63 75
1987	Pat Cash	I. Lendl	76 62 75
1988	Stefan Edberg	B. Becker	46 76 64 62
1989	Boris Becker	S. Edberg	60 76 64
1990	Stefan Edberg	B. Becker	62 62 36 36 64
1991	Michael Stich	B. Becker	64 76 64
1992	Andre Agassi	G. Ivanisevic	67 64 64 16 64
1993	Pete Sampras	J. Courier	76 76 36 63
1994	Pete Sampras	G. Ivanisevic	76 76 60
1995	Pete Sampras	B. Becker	67 62 64 62
1996	Richard Krajicek	M. Washington	63 64 63
1997	Pete Sampras	C. Pioline	64 62 64
1998	Pete Sampras	G. Ivanisevic	67 76 64 36 62
1999	Pete Sampras	A. Agassi	63 64 75
2000	Pete Sampras	P. Rafter	67 76 64 62
2001	Goran Ivanisevic	P. Rafter	63 36 63 26 97
2002	Lleyton Hewitt	D. Nalbandian	61 63 62
2003	Roger Federer	M. Philippoussis	76 62 76

WOMEN

Officially called "The Lawn Tennis Championships" at the All England Club, Wimbledon. Challenge round system (defending champion qualified for following year's final) used from 1877-1921. Became an Open Championship in 1968, but closed to contract pros in 1972.

Multiple winners: Martina Navratilova (9); Helen Wills Moody (8); Dorothea Douglass Chambers and Steffi Graf (7); Blanche Bingley Hillyard, Billie Jean King and Suzanne Lenglen (6); Lottie Dod and Charlotte Cooper Sterry (5); Louise Brough (4); Maria Bueno, Maureen Connolly, Margaret Smith Court and Chris Evert Lloyd (3); Evonne Goolagong Cawley, Althea Gibson, Kathleen McKane Godfrey, Dorothy Round, May Sutton, Maud Watson, Serena Williams and Venus Williams (2).

Year	Winner	Loser	Score
1884	Maud Watson	L. Watson	68 63 63
1885	Maud Watson	B. Bingley	61 75
1886	Blanche Bingley	M. Watson	63 63
1887	Lottie Dod	B. Bingley	62 60
1888	Lottie Dod	B. Hillyard	63 63
1889	Blanche Hillyard	L. Rice	46 86 64
1890	Lena Rice	M. Jacks	64 61
1891	Lottie Dod	B. Hillyard	62 61
1892	Lottie Dod	B. Hillyard	61 61
1893	Lottie Dod	B. Hillyard	68 61 64
1894	Blanche Hillyard	E. Austin	61 61
1895	Charlotte Cooper	H. Jackson	75 86
1896	Charlotte Cooper	W. Pickering	62 63
1897	Blanche Hillyard	C. Cooper	57 75 62
1898	Charlotte Cooper	L. Martin	64 64
1899	Blanche Hillyard	C. Cooper	62 63
1900	Blanche Hillyard	C. Cooper	46 64 64
1901	Charlotte Sterry	B. Hillyard	62 62
1902	Muriel Robb	C. Sterry	75 61
1903	Dorothea Douglass	E. Thomson	46 64 62
1904	Dorothea Douglass	C. Sterry	60 63
1905	May Sutton	D. Douglass	63 64
1906	Dorothea Douglass	M. Sutton	63 97
1907	May Sutton	D. Chambers	61 64
1908	Charlotte Sterry	A. Morton	64 64
1909	Dora Boothby	A. Morton	64 46 86
1910	Dorothea Chambers	D. Boothby	62 62
1911	Dorothea Chambers	D. Boothby	60 60
1912	Ethel Larcombe	C. Sterry	63 61
1913	Dorothea Chambers	R. McNair	60 64
1914	Dorothea Chambers	E. Larcombe	75 64
1915-18	Not held World War I		
1919	Suzanne Lenglen	D. Chambers	10-8 46 97
1920	Suzanne Lenglen	D. Chambers	63 60
1921	Suzanne Lenglen	E. Ryan	62 60
1922	Suzanne Lenglen	M. Mallory	62 60
1923	Suzanne Lenglen	K. McKane	62 62
1924	Kathleen McKane	H. Wills	46 64 64
1925	Suzanne Lenglen	J. Fry	62 60
1926	Kathleen Godfrey	L. de Alvarez	62 46 63
1927	Helen Wills	L. de Alvarez	62 64
1928	Helen Wills	L. de Alvarez	62 63
1929	Helen Wills	H. Jacobs	61 62
1930	Helen Moody	E. Ryan	62 62
1931	Cilly Aussem	H. Kranwinkel	62 75
1932	Helen Moody	H. Jacobs	63 61
1933	Helen Moody	D. Round	64 68 63
1934	Dorothy Round	H. Jacobs	62 57 63
1935	Helen Moody	H. Jacobs	63 36 75
1936	Helen Jacobs	H.K. Sperling	62 46 75
1937	Dorothy Round	J. Jedrzejowska	62 26 75
1938	Helen Moody	H. Jacobs	64 60
1939	Alice Marble	K. Stammers	62 60
1940-45	Not held World War II		
1946	Pauline Betz	L. Brough	62 64
1947	Margaret Osborne	D. Hart	62 64
1948	Louise Brough	D. Hart	63 86
1949	Louise Brough	M. duPont	10-8 16 10-8
1950	Louise Brough	M. duPont	61 36 61
1951	Doris Hart	S. Fry	61 60
1952	Maureen Connolly	L. Brough	75 63
1953	Maureen Connolly	D. Hart	86 75
1954	Maureen Connolly	L. Brough	62 75
1955	Louise Brough	B. Fleitz	75 86
1956	Shirley Fry	A. Buxton	63 61
1957	Althea Gibson	D. Hard	63 62
1958	Althea Gibson	A. Mortimer	86 62
1959	Maria Bueno	D. Hard	64 63
1960	Maria Bueno	S. Reynolds	86 60
1961	Angela Mortimer	C. Truman	46 64 75
1962	Karen Susman	V. Sukova	64 64
1963	Margaret Smith	B.J. Moffitt	63 64
1964	Maria Bueno	M. Smith	64 79 63
1965	Margaret Smith	M. Bueno	64 75
1966	Billie Jean King	M. Bueno	63 36 61
1967	Billie Jean King	A. Jones	63 64
1968	Billie Jean King	J. Tegart	97 75
1969	Ann Jones	B.J. King	36 63 62
1970	Margaret Court	B.J. King	14-12 11-9
1971	Evonne Goolagong	M. Court	64 61
1972	Billie Jean King	E. Goolagong	63 63
1973	Billie Jean King	C. Evert	60 75
1974	Chris Evert	O. Morozova	60 64
1975	Billie Jean King	E. Cawley	60 61
1976	Chris Evert	E. Cawley	63 46 86
1977	Virginia Wade	B. Stove	46 63 61
1978	Martina Navratilova	C. Evert	26 64 75
1979	Martina Navratilova	C. Evert Lloyd	64 64
1980	Evonne Cawley	C. Evert Lloyd	61 76
1981	Chris Evert Lloyd	H. Mandlikova	62 62
1982	Martina Navratilova	C. Evert Lloyd	61 36 62
1983	Martina Navratilova	A. Jaeger	60 63
1984	Martina Navratilova	C. Evert Lloyd	76 62
1985	Martina Navratilova	C. Evert Lloyd	46 63 62
1986	Martina Navratilova	H. Mandlikova	76 63
1987	Martina Navratilova	S. Graf	75 63
1988	Steffi Graf	M. Navratilova	57 62 61
1989	Steffi Graf	M. Navratilova	62 67 61
1990	Martina Navratilova	Z. Garrison	64 61
1991	Steffi Graf	G. Sabatini	64 36 86
1992	Steffi Graf	M. Seles	62 61
1993	Steffi Graf	J. Novotna	76 16 64
1994	Conchita Martinez	M. Navratilova	64 36 63
1995	Steffi Graf	A.S. Vicario	46 61 75
1996	Steffi Graf	A.S. Vicario	63 75
1997	Martina Hingis	J. Novotna	26 63 63
1998	Jana Novotna	N. Tauziat	64 76
1999	Lindsay Davenport	S. Graf	64 75
2000	Venus Williams	L. Davenport	63 76
2001	Venus Williams	J. Henin	61 36 60
2002	Serena Williams	V. Williams	76 63
2003	Serena Williams	V. Williams	46 64 62

U.S. Open
MEN

Challenge round system (defending champion qualified for following year's final) used from 1884 to 1911. Known as the Patriotic Tournament in 1917 during World War I. Amateur and Open Championships held in 1968 and '69. Became an exclusively Open Championship in 1970. **Surface:** Decoturf II (acrylic cement).

Multiple winners: Bill Larned, Richard Sears and Bill Tilden (7); Jimmy Connors and Pete Sampras (5); John McEnroe and Robert Wrenn (4); Oliver Campbell, Ivan Lendl, Fred Perry and Malcolm Whitman (3); Andre Agassi, Don Budge, Stefan Edberg, Roy Emerson, Neale Fraser, Pancho Gonzales, Bill Johnston, Jack Kramer, Rene Lacoste, Rod Laver, Maurice McLoughlin, Lindley Murray, John Newcombe, Frank Parker, Patrick Rafter, Bobby Riggs, Ken Rosewall, Frank Sedgman, Henry Slocum Jr., Tony Trabert, Ellsworth Vines and Dick Williams (2).

Year	Winner	Loser	Score	Year	Winner	Loser	Score
1881	Richard Sears	W. Glyn	60 63 62	1944	Frank Parker	B. Talbert	64 36 63 63
1882	Richard Sears	C. Clark	61 64 60	1945	Frank Parker	B. Talbert	14-12 61 62
1883	Richard Sears	J. Dwight	62 60 97	1946	Jack Kramer	T. Brown, Jr.	97 63 60
1884	Richard Sears	H. Taylor	60 16 60 62	1947	Jack Kramer	F. Parker	46 26 61 60 63
1885	Richard Sears	G. Brinley	63 46 60 63	1948	Pancho Gonzales	E. Sturgess	62 63 14-12
1886	Richard Sears	R. Beeckman	46 61 63 64	1949	Pancho Gonzales	F. Schroeder	16-18 26 61 62 64
1887	Richard Sears	H. Slocum Jr.	61 63 62	1950	Arthur Larsen	H. Flam	63 46 57 64 63
1888	Henry Slocum Jr.	H. Taylor	64 61 60	1951	Frank Sedgman	V. Seixas	64 61 61
1889	Henry Slocum Jr.	Q. Shaw	63 61 46 62	1952	Frank Sedgman	G. Mulloy	61 62 63
1890	Oliver Campbell	H. Slocum Jr.	62 46 63 61	1953	Tony Trabert	V. Seixas	63 62 63
1891	Oliver Campbell	C. Hobart	26 75 79 61 62	1954	Vic Seixas	R. Hartwig	36 62 64 64
1892	Oliver Campbell	F. Hovey	75 36 63 75	1955	Tony Trabert	K. Rosewall	97 63 63
1893	Robert Wrenn	F. Hovey	64 36 64 64	1956	Ken Rosewall	L. Hoad	46 62 63 63
1894	Robert Wrenn	M. Goodbody	68 61 64 64	1957	Mal Anderson	A. Cooper	10-8 75 64
1895	Fred Hovey	R. Wrenn	63 62 64	1958	Ashley Cooper	M. Anderson	62 36 46 10-8 86
1896	Robert Wrenn	F. Hovey	75 36 60 16 61	1959	Neale Fraser	A. Olmedo	63 57 62 64
1897	Robert Wrenn	W. Eaves	46 86 63 26 62	1960	Neale Fraser	R. Laver	64 64 97
1898	Malcolm Whitman	D. Davis	36 62 62 61	1961	Roy Emerson	R. Laver	75 63 62
1899	Malcolm Whitman	P. Paret	61 62 36 75	1962	Rod Laver	R. Emerson	62 64 57 64
1900	Malcolm Whitman	B. Larned	64 16 62 62	1963	Rafael Osuna	F. Froehling	75 64 62
1901	Bill Larned	B. Wright	62 68 64 64	1964	Roy Emerson	F. Stolle	64 62 64
1902	Bill Larned	R. Doherty	46 62 64 86	1965	Manuel Santana	C. Drysdale	62 79 75 61
1903	Laurie Doherty	B. Larned	60 63 10-8	1966	Fred Stolle	J. Newcombe	46 12-10 63 64
1904	Holcombe Ward	B. Clothier	10-8 64 97	1967	John Newcombe	C. Graebner	64 64 86
1905	Beals Wright	H. Ward	62 61 11-9	1968	Am-Arthur Ashe	B. Lutz	46 63 8-10 60 64
1906	Bill Clothier	B. Wright	63 60 64		Op-Arthur Ashe	T. Okker	14-12 57 63 36 63
1907	Bill Larned	R. LeRoy	62 62 64	1969	Am-Stan Smith	B. Lutz	97 63 61
1908	Bill Larned	B. Wright	61 62 86		Op-Rod Laver	T. Roche	79 61 63 62
1909	Bill Larned	B. Clothier	61 62 57 16 61	1970	Ken Rosewall	T. Roche	26 64 76 63
1910	Bill Larned	T. Bundy	61 57 60 68 61	1971	Stan Smith	J. Kodes	36 63 62 76
1911	Bill Larned	M. McLoughlin	64 64 62	1972	Ilie Nastase	A. Ashe	36 63 67 64 63
1912	Maurice McLoughlin	W.F. Johnson	36 26 62 64 62	1973	John Newcombe	J. Kodes	64 16 46 62 63
1913	Maurice McLoughlin	R. Williams	64 57 63 61	1974	Jimmy Connors	K. Rosewall	61 60 61
1914	Dick Williams	M. McLoughlin	63 86 10-8	1975	Manuel Orantes	J. Connors	64 63 63
1915	Bill Johnston	M. McLoughlin	16 60 75 10-8	1976	Jimmy Connors	B. Borg	64 36 76 64
1916	Dick Williams	B. Johnston	46 64 06 62 64	1977	Guillermo Vilas	J. Connors	26 63 76 60
1917	Lindley Murray	N. Niles	57 86 63 63	1978	Jimmy Connors	B. Borg	64 62 62
1918	Lindley Murray	B. Tilden	63 61 75	1979	John McEnroe	V. Gerulaitis	75 63 63
1919	Bill Johnston	B. Tilden	64 64 63	1980	John McEnroe	B. Borg	76 61 67 57 64
1920	Bill Tilden	B. Johnston	61 16 75 57 63	1981	John McEnroe	B. Borg	46 62 64 63
1921	Bill Tilden	W. Johnson	61 63 61	1982	Jimmy Connors	I. Lendl	63 62 46 64
1922	Bill Tilden	B. Johnston	46 36 62 63 64	1983	Jimmy Connors	I. Lendl	63 67 75 60
1923	Bill Tilden	B. Johnston	64 61 64	1984	John McEnroe	I. Lendl	63 64 61
1924	Bill Tilden	B. Johnston	61 97 62	1985	Ivan Lendl	J. McEnroe	76 63 64
1925	Bill Tilden	B. Johnston	46 11-9 63 46 63	1986	Ivan Lendl	M. Mecir	64 62 60
1926	Rene Lacoste	J. Borotra	64 60 64	1987	Ivan Lendl	M. Wilander	67 60 76 64
1927	Rene Lacoste	B. Tilden	11-9 63 11-9	1988	Mats Wilander	I. Lendl	64 46 63 57 64
1928	Henri Cochet	F. Hunter	46 64 36 75 63	1989	Boris Becker	I. Lendl	76 16 63 76
1929	Bill Tilden	F. Hunter	36 63 46 62 64	1990	Pete Sampras	A. Agassi	64 63 62
1930	John Doeg	F. Shields	10-8 16 64 16-14	1991	Stefan Edberg	J. Courier	62 64 60
1931	Ellsworth Vines	G. Lott Jr.	79 63 97 75	1992	Stefan Edberg	P. Sampras	36 64 76 62
1932	Ellsworth Vines	H. Cochet	64 64 64	1993	Pete Sampras	C. Pioline	64 64 63
1933	Fred Perry	J. Crawford	63 11-13 46 60 61	1994	Andre Agassi	M. Stich	61 76 75
1934	Fred Perry	W. Allison	64 63 16 86	1995	Pete Sampras	A. Agassi	63 64 75
1935	Wilmer Allison	S. Wood	62 62 63	1996	Pete Sampras	M. Chang	61 64 76
1936	Fred Perry	D. Budge	26 62 86 16 10-8	1997	Patrick Rafter	G. Rusedski	63 62 46 75
1937	Don Budge	G. von Cramm	61 79 61 36 61	1998	Patrick Rafter	M. Philippoussis	63 36 62 60
1938	Don Budge	G. Mako	63 68 62 61	1999	Andre Agassi	T. Martin	64 67 67 63 62
1939	Bobby Riggs	S.W. van Horn	64 62 64	2000	Marat Safin	P. Sampras	64 63 63
1940	Don McNeill	B. Riggs	46 68 63 63 75	2001	Lleyton Hewitt	P. Sampras	76 61 61
1941	Bobby Riggs	F. Kovacs	57 61 63 63	2002	Pete Sampras	A. Agassi	63 64 57 64
1942	Fred Schroeder	F. Parker	86 75 36 46 62	2003	Andy Roddick	J.C. Ferrero	63 76 63
1943	Joe Hunt	J. Kramer	63 68 10-8 60				

WOMEN

Challenge round system used from 1887-1918. Five set final played from 1887 to 1901. Amateur and Open Championships held in 1968 and '69. Became an exclusively Open Championship in 1970.

Multiple winners: Molla Bjurstedt Mallory (8); Helen Wills Moody (7); Chris Evert Lloyd (6); Margaret Smith Court and Steffi Graf (5); Pauline Betz, Maria Bueno, Helen Jacobs, Billie Jean King, Alice Marble, Elizabeth Moore, Martina Navratilova and Hazel Hotchkiss Wightman (4); Juliette Atkinson, Mary Browne, Maureen Connolly and Margaret Osborne duPont (3); Tracy Austin, Mabel Cahill, Sarah Palfrey Cooke, Althea Gibson, Darlene Hard, Doris Hart, Marion Jones, Monica Seles, Bertha Townsend, Serena Williams and Venus Williams (2).

Year	Winner	Loser	Score
1887	Ellen Hansell	L. Knight	61 60
1888	Bertha Townsend	E. Hansell	63 65
1889	Bertha Townsend	L. Voorhes	75 62
1890	Ellen Roosevelt	B. Townsend	62 62
1891	Mabel Cahill	E. Roosevelt	64 61 46 63
1892	Mabel Cahill	E. Moore	57 63 64 46 62
1893	Aline Terry	A. Schultz	61 63
1894	Helen Hellwig	A. Terry	75 36 60 36 63
1895	Juliette Atkinson	H. Hellwig	64 62 61
1896	Elisabeth Moore	J. Atkinson	64 46 62 62
1897	Juliette Atkinson	E. Moore	63 63 46 36 63
1898	Juliette Atkinson	M. Jones	63 57 64 26 75
1899	Marion Jones	M. Banks	61 61 75
1900	Myrtle McAteer	E. Parker	62 62 60
1901	Elizabeth Moore	M. McAteer	64 36 75 26 62
1902	Marion Jones	E. Moore	61 10(ret)
1903	Elizabeth Moore	M. Jones	75 86
1904	May Sutton	E. Moore	61 62
1905	Elizabeth Moore	H. Homans	64 57 61
1906	Helen Homans	M. Barger-Wallach	64 63
1907	Evelyn Sears	C. Neely	63 62
1908	Maud B. Wallach	Ev. Sears	63 16 63
1909	Hazel Hotchkiss	M. Wallach	60 61
1910	Hazel Hotchkiss	L. Hammond	64 62
1911	Hazel Hotchkiss	F. Sutton	8-10 61 97
1912	Mary Browne	E. Sears	64 62
1913	Mary Browne	D. Green	62 75
1914	Mary Browne	M. Wagner	62 16 61
1915	Molla Bjurstedt	H. Wightman	46 62 60
1916	Molla Bjurstedt	L. Raymond	60 61
1917	Molla Bjurstedt	M. Vanderhoef	46 60 62
1918	Molla Bjurstedt	E. Goss	64 63
1919	Hazel Wightman	M. Zinderstein	61 62
1920	Molla Mallory	M. Zinderstein	63 61
1921	Molla Mallory	M. Browne	46 64 62
1922	Molla Mallory	H. Wills	63 61
1923	Helen Wills	M. Mallory	62 61
1924	Helen Wills	M. Mallory	61 63
1925	Helen Wills	K. McKane	36 60 62
1926	Molla Mallory	M. Ryan	46 64 97
1927	Helen Wills	B. Nuthall	61 64
1928	Helen Wills	H. Jacobs	62 61
1929	Helen Wills	P. Watson	64 62
1930	Betty Nuthall	A. Harper	61 64
1931	Helen Moody	E. Whitingstall	64 61
1932	Helen Jacobs	C. Babcock	62 62
1933	Helen Jacobs	H. Moody	86 36 30(ret)
1934	Helen Jacobs	S. Palfrey	61 64
1935	Helen Jacobs	S. Fabyan	62 64
1936	Alice Marble	H. Jacobs	46 63 62
1937	Anita Lizana	J. Jedrzejowska	64 62
1938	Alice Marble	N. Wynne	64 63
1939	Alice Marble	H. Jacobs	60 8-10 64
1940	Alice Marble	H. Jacobs	62 63
1941	Sarah Cooke	P. Betz	75 62
1942	Pauline Betz	L. Brough	46 61 64
1943	Pauline Betz	L. Brough	63 57 63
1944	Pauline Betz	M. Osborne	63 86
1945	Sarah Cooke	P. Betz	36 86 64
1946	Pauline Betz	P. Canning	11-9 63

Year	Winner	Loser	Score
1947	Louise Brough	M. Osborne	86 46 61
1948	Margaret duPont	L. Brough	46 64 15-13
1949	Margaret duPont	D. Hart	64 61
1950	Margaret duPont	D. Hart	64 63
1951	Maureen Connolly	S. Fry	63 16 64
1952	Maureen Connolly	D. Hart	63 75
1953	Maureen Connolly	D. Hart	62 64
1954	Doris Hart	L. Brough	68 61 86
1955	Doris Hart	P. Ward	64 62
1956	Shirley Fry	A. Gibson	63 64
1957	Althea Gibson	L. Brough	63 62
1958	Althea Gibson	D. Hard	36 61 62
1959	Maria Bueno	C. Truman	61 64
1960	Darlene Hard	M. Bueno	64 10-12 64
1961	Darlene Hard	A. Haydon	63 64
1962	Margaret Smith	D. Hard	97 64
1963	Maria Bueno	M. Smith	75 64
1964	Maria Bueno	C. Graebner	61 60
1965	Margaret Smith	B.J. Moffitt	86 75
1966	Maria Bueno	N. Richey	63 61
1967	Billie Jean King	A. Jones	11-9 64
1968	Am-Margaret Court	M. Bueno	62 62
	Op-Virginia Wade	B.J. King	64 62
1969	Am-Margaret Court	V. Wade	46 63 60
	Op-Margaret Court	N. Richey	62 62
1970	Margaret Court	R. Casals	62 26 61
1971	Billie Jean King	R. Casals	64 76
1972	Billie Jean King	K. Melville	63 75
1973	Margaret Court	E. Goolagong	76 57 62
1974	Billie Jean King	E. Goolagong	36 63 75
1975	Chris Evert	E. Cawley	57 64 62
1976	Chris Evert	E. Cawley	63 60
1977	Chris Evert	W. Turnbull	76 62
1978	Chris Evert	P. Shriver	75 64
1979	Tracy Austin	C. Evert Lloyd	64 63
1980	Chris Evert Lloyd	H. Mandlikova	57 61 61
1981	Tracy Austin	M. Navratilova	16 76 76
1982	Chris Evert Lloyd	H. Mandlikova	63 61
1983	Martina Navratilova	C. Evert Lloyd	61 63
1984	Martina Navratilova	C. Evert Lloyd	46 64 64
1985	Hana Mandlikova	M. Navratilova	76 16 76
1986	Martina Navratilova	H. Sukova	63 62
1987	Martina Navratilova	S. Graf	76 61
1988	Steffi Graf	G. Sabatini	63 36 61
1989	Steffi Graf	M. Navratilova	36 75 61
1990	Gabriela Sabatini	S. Graf	62 76
1991	Monica Seles	M. Navratilova	76 61
1992	Monica Seles	A.S. Vicario	63 63
1993	Steffi Graf	H. Sukova	63 63
1994	A. Sanchez Vicario	S. Graf	16 76 64
1995	Steffi Graf	M. Seles	76 06 63
1996	Steffi Graf	M. Seles	75 64
1997	Martina Hingis	V. Williams	60 64
1998	Lindsay Davenport	M. Hingis	63 75
1999	Serena Williams	M. Hingis	63 76
2000	Venus Williams	L. Davenport	64 75
2001	Venus Williams	S. Williams	62 64
2002	Serena Williams	V. Williams	64 63
2003	J. Henin-Hardenne	K. Clijsters	75 61

Grand Slam Summary

Singles winners of the four Grand Slam tournaments–Australian, French, Wimbledon and United States–since the French was opened to all comers in 1925. Note that there were two Australian Opens in 1977 and none in 1986.

MEN

Three wins in one year: Jack Crawford (1933); Fred Perry (1934); Tony Trabert (1955); Lew Hoad (1956); Ashley Cooper (1958); Roy Emerson (1964); Jimmy Connors (1974); Mats Wilander (1988).

Two wins in one year: Roy Emerson and Pete Sampras (4 times); Bjorn Borg (3 times); Rene Lacoste, Ivan Lendl, John Newcombe and Fred Perry (twice); Andre Agassi, Boris Becker, Don Budge, Henri Cochet, Jimmy Connors, Jim Courier, Neale Fraser, Jack Kramer, John McEnroe, Alex Olmedo, Budge Patty, Bobby Riggs, Ken Rosewall, Dick Savitt, Frank Sedgman and Guillermo Vilas (once).

Year	Australian	French	Wimbledon	U.S.
1925	Anderson	Lacoste	Lacoste	Tilden
1926	Hawkes	Cochet	Borotra	Lacoste
1927	Patterson	Lacoste	Cochet	Lacoste
1928	Borotra	Cochet	Lacoste	Cochet
1929	Gregory	Lacoste	Cochet	Tilden
1930	Moon	Cochet	Tilden	Doeg
1931	Crawford	Borotra	Wood	Vines
1932	Crawford	Cochet	Vines	Vines
1933	Crawford	Crawford	Crawford	Perry
1934	Perry	von Cramm	Perry	Perry
1935	Crawford	Perry	Perry	Allison
1936	Quist	von Cramm	Perry	Perry
1937	McGrath	Henkel	Budge	Budge
1938	**Budge**	**Budge**	**Budge**	**Budge**
1939	Bromwich	McNeill	Riggs	Riggs
1940	Quist	—	—	McNeill
1941	—	—	—	Riggs
1942	—	—	—	Schroeder
1943	—	—	—	Hunt
1944	—	—	—	Parker
1945	—	—	—	Parker
1946	Bromwich	Bernard	Petra	Kramer
1947	Pails	Asboth	Kramer	Kramer
1948	Quist	Parker	Falkenburg	Gonzales
1949	Sedgman	Parker	Schroeder	Gonzales
1950	Sedgman	Patty	Patty	Larsen
1951	Savitt	Drobny	Savitt	Sedgman
1952	McGregor	Drobny	Sedgman	Sedgman
1953	Rosewall	Rosewall	Seixas	Trabert
1954	Rose	Trabert	Drobny	Seixas
1955	Rosewall	Trabert	Trabert	Trabert
1956	Hoad	Hoad	Hoad	Rosewall
1957	Cooper	Davidson	Hoad	Anderson
1958	Cooper	Rose	Cooper	Cooper
1959	Olmedo	Pietrangeli	Olmedo	Fraser
1960	Laver	Pietrangeli	Fraser	Fraser
1961	Emerson	Santana	Laver	Emerson
1962	**Laver**	**Laver**	**Laver**	**Laver**
1963	Emerson	Emerson	McKinley	Osuna
1964	Emerson	Santana	Emerson	Emerson

Year	Australian	French	Wimbledon	U.S.
1965	Emerson	Stolle	Emerson	Santana
1966	Emerson	Roche	Santana	Stolle
1967	Emerson	Emerson	Newcombe	Newcombe
1968	Bowrey	Rosewall	Laver	Ashe
1969	**Laver**	**Laver**	**Laver**	**Laver**
1970	Ashe	Kodes	Newcombe	Rosewall
1971	Rosewall	Kodes	Newcombe	Smith
1972	Rosewall	Gimeno	Smith	Nastase
1973	Newcombe	Nastase	Kodes	Newcombe
1974	Connors	Borg	Connors	Connors
1975	Newcombe	Borg	Ashe	Orantes
1976	Edmondson	Panatta	Borg	Connors
1977	Tanner & Gerulaitis	Vilas	Borg	Vilas
1978	Vilas	Borg	Borg	Connors
1979	Vilas	Borg	Borg	McEnroe
1980	Teacher	Borg	Borg	McEnroe
1981	Kriek	Borg	McEnroe	McEnroe
1982	Kriek	Wilander	Connors	Connors
1983	Wilander	Noah	McEnroe	Connors
1984	Wilander	Lendl	McEnroe	McEnroe
1985	Edberg	Wilander	Becker	Lendl
1986	—	Lendl	Becker	Lendl
1987	Edberg	Lendl	Cash	Lendl
1988	Wilander	Wilander	Edberg	Wilander
1989	Chang	Chang	Becker	Becker
1990	Lendl	Gomez	Edberg	Sampras
1991	Becker	Courier	Stich	Edberg
1992	Courier	Courier	Agassi	Edberg
1993	Courier	Bruguera	Sampras	Sampras
1994	Sampras	Bruguera	Sampras	Agassi
1995	Agassi	Muster	Sampras	Sampras
1996	Becker	Kafelnikov	Krajicek	Sampras
1997	Sampras	Kuerten	Sampras	Rafter
1998	Korda	Moya	Sampras	Rafter
1999	Kafelnikov	Agassi	Sampras	Agassi
2000	Agassi	Kuerten	Sampras	Safin
2001	Agassi	Kuerten	Ivanisevic	Hewitt
2002	Johansson	Costa	Hewitt	Sampras
2003	Agassi	Ferrero	Federer	Roddick

Men's, Women's & Mixed Doubles Grand Slam

The tennis Grand Slam has only been accomplished in doubles competition six times in the same calendar year. Here are the doubles teams to accomplish the feat. The two men and three women to win the singles Grand Slam are noted in the Grand Slam Summary tables.

Men's Doubles

1951 . . . . .Frank Sedgman, Australia
& Ken McGregor, Australia

Mixed Doubles

1963 .Ken Fletcher, Australia
& Margaret Smith, Australia
1967 . . . . .Owen Davidson and two partners*

*Davidson's partners: AUS–Lesley Turner; FR/WIM, U.S.–Billie Jean King.

Women's Doubles

1960 . . . . .Maria Bueno, Brazil & two partners†
1984 . . . . .Martina Navratilova, USA
& Pam Shriver, USA
1998 . . . . Martina Hingis, Switzerland & two partners#

†Bueno's partners: AUS–Christine Truman; FR, WIM, U.S.–Darlene Hard.

#Hingis' partners: AUS–Mirjana Lucic; FR, WIM, U.S.–Jana Novotna.

WOMEN

Three in one year: Helen Wills Moody (1928 and '29); Margaret Smith Court (1962, '65, '69 and '73); Billie Jean King (1972); Martina Navratilova (1983 and '84); Steffi Graf (1989, '93, '95 and '96); Monica Seles (1991 and '92); Martina Hingis (1997) and Serena Williams (2002).

Two in one year: Chris Evert Lloyd (5 times); Helen Wills Moody and Martina Navratilova (3 times); Maria Bueno, Maureen Connolly, Margaret Smith Court, Althea Gibson, Billie Jean King and Venus Williams (twice); Cilly Aussem, Pauleen Betz, Louise Brough, Jennifer Capriati, Evonne Goolagong Cawley, Margaret Osborne duPont, Shirley Fry, Darlene Hard, Justine Henin-Hardenne, Suzanne Lenglen, Alice Marble, Arantxa Sanchez Vicario and Serena Williams (once).

Year	Australian	French	Wimbledon	U.S.	Year	Australian	French	Wimbledon	U.S.
1925	Akhurst	Lenglen	Lenglen	Wills	1966	Smith	Jones	King	Bueno
1926	Akhurst	Lenglen	Godfree	Mallory	1967	Richey	Durr	King	King
1927	Boyd	Bouman	Wills	Wills	1968	King	Richey	King	Wade
1928	Akhurst	Wills	Wills	Wills	1969	Court	Court	Jones	Court
1929	Akhurst	Wills	Wills	Wills					
1930	Akhurst	Moody	Moody	Nuthall	**1970**	**Court**	**Court**	**Court**	**Court**
1931	Buttsworth	Aussem	Aussem	Moody	1971	Court	Goolagong	Goolagong	King
1932	Buttsworth	Moody	Moody	Jacobs	1972	Wade	King	King	King
1933	Hartigan	Scriven	Moody	Jacobs	1973	Court	Court	King	Court
1934	Hartigan	Scriven	Round	Jacobs	1974	Goolagong	Evert	Evert	King
1935	Round	Sperling	Moody	Jacobs	1975	Goolagong	Evert	King	Evert
1936	Hartigan	Sperling	Jacobs	Marble	1976	Cawley	Barker	Evert	Evert
1937	Bolton	Sperling	Round	Lizana	1977	Reid	Jausovec	Wade	Evert
1938	Bundy	Mathieu	Moody	Marble		& Cawley			
1939	Westacott	Mathieu	Marble	Marble	1978	O'Neil	Ruzici	Navratilova	Evert
1940	Bolton	—	—	Marble	1979	Jordan	Evert Lloyd	Navratilova	Austin
1941	—	—	—	Cooke	1980	Mandlikova	Evert Lloyd	Cawley	Evert Lloyd
1942	—	—	—	Betz	1981	Navratilova	Mandlikova	Evert Lloyd	Austin
1943	—	—	—	Betz	1982	Evert Lloyd	Navratilova	Navratilova	Evert Lloyd
1944	—	—	—	Betz	1983	Evert Lloyd	Evert Lloyd	Navratilova	Navratilova
1945	—	—	—	Cooke	1984	Evert Lloyd	Navratilova	Navratilova	Navratilova
1946	Bolton	Osborne	Betz	Betz	1985	Navratilova	Evert Lloyd	Navratilova	Mandlikova
1947	Bolton	Todd	Osborne	Brough	1986	–	Evert Lloyd	Navratilova	Navratilova
1948	Bolton	Landry	Brough	du Pont	1987	Mandlikova	Graf	Navratilova	Navratilova
1949	Hart	du Pont	Brough	du Pont	**1988**	**Graf**	**Graf**	**Graf**	**Graf**
1950	Brough	Hart	Brough	du Pont	1989	Graf	Vicario	Graf	Graf
1951	Bolton	Fry	Hart	Connolly	1990	Graf	Seles	Navratilova	Sabatini
1952	Long	Hart	Connolly	Connolly	1991	Seles	Seles	Graf	Seles
1953	**Connolly**	**Connolly**	**Connolly**	**Connolly**	1992	Seles	Seles	Graf	Seles
1954	Long	Connolly	Connolly	Hart	1993	Seles	Graf	Graf	Graf
1955	Penrose	Mortimer	Brough	Hart	1994	Graf	Vicario	Martinez	Vicario
1956	Carter	Gibson	Fry	Fry	1995	Pierce	Graf	Graf	Graf
1957	Fry	Bloomer	Gibson	Gibson	1996	Seles	Graf	Graf	Graf
1958	Mortimer	Kormoczi	Gibson	Gibson	1997	Hingis	Majoli	Hingis	Hingis
1959	Reitano	Truman	Bueno	Bueno	1998	Hingis	Vicario	Novotna	Davenport
1960	Smith	Hard	Bueno	Hard	1999	Hingis	Graf	Davenport	S. Williams
1961	Smith	Haydon	Mortimer	Hard	2000	Davenport	Pierce	V. Williams	V. Williams
1962	Smith	Smith	Susman	Smith	2001	Capriati	Capriati	V. Williams	V. Williams
1963	Smith	Turner	Smith	Bueno	2002	Capriati	S. Williams	S. Williams	S. Williams
1964	Smith	Smith	Bueno	Bueno	2003	S. Williams	Henin-Hardenne	S. Williams	Henin-Hardenne
1965	Smith	Turner	Smith	Smith					

Overall Leaders

All-Time Grand Slam titleists including all singles and doubles championships at the four major tournaments. Titles listed under each heading are singles, doubles and mixed doubles. Players active in 2003 are in **bold** type.

		Career	MEN Australian	French	Wimbledon	U.S.	S-D-M	Total Titles
1	Roy Emerson	1959-71	6-3-0	2-6-0	2-3-0	2-4-0	12-16-0	28
2	John Newcombe	1965-76	2-5-0	0-3-0	3-6-0	2-3-1	7-17-1	25
3	Frank Sedgman	1949-52	2-2-2	0-2-2	1-3-2	2-2-2	5-9-8	22
4	Bill Tilden	1913-30	*	0-0-1	3-1-0	7-5-4	10-6-5	21
	Todd Woodbridge	1988—	0-3-1	0-1-1	0-8-1	0-3-3	0-15-6	21
6	Rod Laver	1959-71	3-4-0	2-1-1	4-1-2	2-0-0	11-6-3	20
7	Jack Bromwich	1938-50	2-8-1	0-0-0	0-2-2	0-3-1	2-13-4	19
	Neale Fraser	1957-62	0-3-1	0-3-0	1-2-1	2-3-3	3-11-5	19
9	Ken Rosewall	1953-72	4-3-0	2-2-0	0-2-0	2-2-1	8-9-1	18
	Jean Borotra	1925-36	1-1-1	1-5-2	2-3-1	0-0-1	4-9-5	18
	Fred Stolle	1962-69	0-3-1	1-2-0	0-2-3	1-3-2	2-10-6	18
12	John McEnroe	1977-93	0-0-0	0-0-1	3-5-0	4-4-0	7-9-1	17
	Jack Crawford	1929-35	4-4-3	1-1-1	1-1-1	0-0-0	6-6-5	17
	Mark Woodforde	1985-2000	0-2-2	0-1-1	0-6-1	0-3-1	0-12-5	17
	Adrian Quist	1936-50	3-10-0	0-1-0	0-2-0	0-1-0	3-14-0	17

WOMEN

		Career	Australian	French	Wimbledon	U.S.	S-D-M	Total Titles
1	Margaret Smith Court	1960-75	11-8-2	5-4-4	3-2-5	5-5-8	24-19-19	62
2	**Martina Navratilova**	1974-95, 2000—	3-8-1	2-7-2	9-7-4	4-9-2	18-31-9	58
3	Billie Jean King	1961-81	1-0-1	1-1-2	6-10-4	4-5-4	12-16-11	39
4	Margaret du Pont	1941-60	*	2-3-0	1-5-1	3-13-9	6-21-10	37
5	Louise Brough	1942-57	1-1-0	0-3-0	4-5-4	1-12-4	6-21-8	35
	Doris Hart	1948-55	1-1-2	2-5-3	1-4-5	2-4-5	6-14-15	35
7	Helen Wills Moody	1923-38	*	4-2-0	8-3-1	7-4-2	19-9-3	31
8	Elizabeth Ryan	1914-34	*	0-4-0	0-12-7	0-1-2	0-17-9	26
9	Suzanne Lenglen	1919-26	*	6-2-2	6-6-3	0-0-0	12-8-5	25
10	Steffi Graf	1982-99	4-0-0	6-0-0	7-1-0	5-0-0	22-1-0	23
11	Pam Shriver	1981-97	0-7-0	0-4-1	0-5-0	0-5-0	0-21-1	22
12	Chris Evert	1974-89	2-0-0	7-2-0	3-1-0	6-0-0	18-3-0	21
	Darlene Hard	1958-69	*	1-3-2	0-4-3	2-6-0	3-13-5	21
14	**Natasha Zvereva**	1989—	0-3-2	0-6-0	0-5-0	0-4-0	0-18-2	20
	Nancye Wynne Bolton	1935-52	6-10-4	0-0-0	0-0-0	0-0-0	6-10-4	20
	Maria Bueno	1958-68	0-1-0	0-1-1	3-5-0	4-5-0	7-12-1	20

All-Time Grand Slam Singles Titles

Men and women with the most singles championships in the Australian, French, Wimbledon and U.S. championships, through 2003. Note that (*) indicates player never played in that particular Grand Slam event; and players active in singles play in 2003 are in **bold** type.

Top 10 Men

		Aus	Fre	Wim	US	Total
1	Pete Sampras	2	0	7	5	14
2	Roy Emerson	6	2	2	2	12
3	Bjorn Borg	0	6	5	0	11
	Rod Laver	3	2	4	2	11
5	Bill Tilden	*	0	3	7	10
6	**Andre Agassi**	4	1	1	2	8
	Jimmy Connors	1	0	2	5	8
	Ivan Lendl	2	3	0	3	8
	Fred Perry	1	1	3	3	8
	Ken Rosewall	4	2	0	2	8

Top 10 Women

		Aus	Fre	Wim	US	Total
1	Margaret Smith Court	11	5	3	5	24
2	Steffi Graf	4	6	7	5	22
3	Helen Wills Moody	*	4	8	7	19
4	Chris Evert	2	7	3	6	18
	Martina Navratilova	3	2	9	4	18
6	Billie Jean King	1	1	6	4	12
	Suzanne Lenglen	*	6	6	0	12
8	Maureen Connolly	1	2	3	3	9
	Monica Seles	4	3	0	2	9
10	Molla Bjurstedt Mallory	*	*	0	8	8

Annual Number One Players

Unofficial world rankings for men and women determined by the *London Daily Telegraph* from 1914-72. Since then, official world rankings computed by men's and women's tours. Rankings included only amateur players from 1914 until the arrival of open (professional) tennis in 1968. No rankings were released during World Wars I and II.

MEN

Multiple winners: Pete Sampras and Bill Tilden (6); Jimmy Connors (5); Henri Cochet, Rod Laver, Ivan Lendl and John McEnroe (4); John Newcombe and Fred Perry (3); Bjorn Borg, Don Budge, Ashley Cooper, Stefan Edberg, Roy Emerson, Neale Fraser, Lleyton Hewitt, Jack Kramer, Rene Lacoste, Ilie Nastase, Frank Sedgman and Tony Trabert (2).

Year		Year		Year		Year	
1914	Maurice McLoughlin	1938	Don Budge	1964	Roy Emerson	1985	Ivan Lendl
1915-18	No rankings	1939	Bobby Riggs	1965	Roy Emerson	1986	Ivan Lendl
1919	Gerald Patterson	1940-45	No rankings	1966	Manuel Santana	1987	Ivan Lendl
1920	Bill Tilden	1946	Jack Kramer	1967	John Newcombe	1988	Mats Wilander
1921	Bill Tilden	1947	Jack Kramer	1968	Rod Laver	1989	Ivan Lendl
1922	Bill Tilden	1948	Frank Parker	1969	Rod Laver	1990	Stefan Edberg
1923	Bill Tilden	1949	Pancho Gonzales	1970	John Newcombe	1991	Stefan Edberg
1924	Bill Tilden	1950	Budge Patty	1971	John Newcombe	1992	Jim Courier
1925	Bill Tilden	1951	Frank Sedgman	1972	Ilie Nastase	1993	Pete Sampras
1926	Rene Lacoste	1952	Frank Sedgman	1973	Ilie Nastase	1994	Pete Sampras
1927	Rene Lacoste	1953	Tony Trabert	1974	Jimmy Connors	1995	Pete Sampras
1928	Henri Cochet	1954	Jaroslav Drobny	1975	Jimmy Connors	1996	Pete Sampras
1929	Henri Cochet	1955	Tony Trabert	1976	Jimmy Connors	1997	Pete Sampras
1930	Henri Cochet	1956	Lew Hoad	1977	Jimmy Connors	1998	Pete Sampras
1931	Henri Cochet	1957	Ashley Cooper	1978	Jimmy Connors	1999	Andre Agassi
1932	Ellsworth Vines	1958	Ashley Cooper	1979	Bjorn Borg	2000	Gustavo Kuerten
1933	Jack Crawford	1959	Neale Fraser	1980	Bjorn Borg	2001	Lleyton Hewitt
1934	Fred Perry	1960	Neale Fraser	1981	John McEnroe	2002	Lleyton Hewitt
1935	Fred Perry	1961	Rod Laver	1982	John McEnroe		
1936	Fred Perry	1962	Rod Laver	1983	John McEnroe		
1937	Don Budge	1963	Rafael Osuna	1984	John McEnroe		

WOMEN

Multiple winners: Helen Wills Moody (9); Steffi Graf (8); Margaret Smith Court and Martina Navratilova (7); Chris Evert Lloyd and Billie Jean King (5); Margaret Osborne duPont (4); Maureen Connolly, Martina Hingis and Monica Seles (3); Maria Bueno, Lindsay Davenport, Althea Gibson and Suzanne Lenglen (2).

Year		Year		Year		Year	
1925	Suzanne Lenglen	1949	Margaret duPont	1968	Billie Jean King	1987	Steffi Graf
1926	Suzanne Lenglen	1950	Margaret duPont	1969	Margaret Court	1988	Steffi Graf
1927	Helen Wills	1951	Doris Hart			1989	Steffi Graf
1928	Helen Wills	1952	Maureen Connolly	1970	Margaret Court		
1929	Helen Wills Moody	1953	Maureen Connolly	1971	Evonne Goolagong	1990	Steffi Graf
		1954	Maureen Connolly	1972	Billie Jean King	1991	Monica Seles
1930	Helen Wills Moody	1955	Louise Brough	1973	Margaret Court	1992	Monica Seles
1931	Helen Wills Moody	1956	Shirley Fry	1974	Billie Jean King	1993	Steffi Graf
1932	Helen Wills Moody	1957	Althea Gibson	1975	Chris Evert	1994	Steffi Graf
1933	Helen Wills Moody	1958	Althea Gibson	1976	Chris Evert	1995	Steffi Graf
1934	Dorothy Round	1959	Maria Bueno	1977	Chris Evert		& Monica Seles*
1935	Helen Wills Moody			1978	Martina Navratilova	1996	Steffi Graf
1936	Helen Jacobs	1960	Maria Bueno	1979	Martina Navratilova	1997	Martina Hingis
1937	Anita Lizana	1961	Angela Mortimer			1998	Lindsay Davenport
1938	Helen Wills Moody	1962	Margaret Smith	1980	Chris Evert Lloyd	1999	Martina Hingis
1939	Alice Marble	1963	Margaret Smith	1981	Chris Evert Lloyd		
		1964	Margaret Smith	1982	Martina Navratilova	2000	Martina Hingis
1940-45	No rankings	1965	Margaret Smith	1983	Martina Navratilova	2001	Lindsay Davenport
1946	Pauline Betz	1966	Billie Jean King	1984	Martina Navratilova	2002	Serena Williams
1947	Margaret Osborne	1967	Billie Jean King	1985	Martina Navratilova		
1948	Margaret duPont			1986	Martina Navratilova		

*Upon her return to the WTA Tour on Aug. 15, 1995, Seles retained her #1 ranking and was co-ranked at #1 through her first six tournaments (August '95–May '96). Seles was on leave since April 1993 when she was stabbed by a fan during a match.

Annual Top 10 World Rankings (since 1968)

Year by year Top 10 world computer rankings for men (ATP Tour) and women (WTA Tour) since the arrival of open tennis in 1968. Rankings from 1968-72 made by Lance Tingay of the *London Daily Telegraph*. Since 1973 the WTA Tour and ATP tour had compiled its own computer rankings. Since 2000, the men's rankings reflect the final standings of the ATP Champions Race.

MEN

1968
1 Rod Laver
2 Arthur Ashe
3 Ken Rosewall
4 Tom Okker
5 Tony Roche
6 John Newcombe
7 Clark Graebner
8 Dennis Ralston
9 Cliff Drysdale
10 Pancho Gonzales

1969
1 Rod Laver
2 Tony Roche
3 John Newcombe
4 Tom Okker
5 Ken Rosewall
6 Arthur Ashe
7 Cliff Drysdale
8 Pancho Gonzales
9 Andres Gimeno
10 Fred Stolle

1970
1 John Newcombe
2 Ken Rosewall
3 Tony Roche
4 Rod Laver
5 Arthur Ashe
6 Ilie Nastase
7 Tom Okker
8 Roger Taylor
9 Jan Kodes
10 Cliff Richey

1971
1 John Newcombe
2 Stan Smith
3 Rod Laver
4 Ken Rosewall
5 Jan Kodes
6 Arthur Ashe
7 Tom Okker
8 Marty Riessen
9 Cliff Drysdale
10 Ilie Nastase

1972
1 Stan Smith
2 Ken Rosewall
3 Ilie Nastase
4 Rod Laver
5 Arthur Ashe
6 John Newcombe
7 Bob Lutz
8 Tom Okker
9 Marty Riessen
10 Andres Gimeno

1973
1 Ilie Nastase
2 John Newcombe
3 Jimmy Connors
4 Tom Okker
5 Stan Smith
6 Ken Rosewall
7 Manuel Orantes
8 Rod Laver
9 Jan Kodes
10 Arthur Ashe

1974
1 Jimmy Connors
2 John Newcombe
3 Bjorn Borg
4 Rod Laver
5 Guillermo Vilas
6 Tom Okker
7 Arthur Ashe
8 Ken Rosewall
9 Stan Smith
10 Ilie Nastase

1975
1 Jimmy Connors
2 Guillermo Vilas
3 Bjorn Borg
4 Arthur Ashe
5 Manuel Orantes
6 Ken Rosewall
7 Ilie Nastase
8 John Alexander
9 Roscoe Tanner
10 Rod Laver

1976
1 Jimmy Connors
2 Bjorn Borg
3 Ilie Nastase
4 Manuel Orantes
5 Raul Ramirez
6 Guillermo Vilas
7 Adriano Panatta
8 Harold Solomon
9 Eddie Dibbs
10 Brian Gottfried

1977
1 Jimmy Connors
2 Guillermo Vilas
3 Bjorn Borg
4 Vitas Gerulaitis
5 Brian Gottfried
6 Eddie Dibbs
7 Manuel Orantes
8 Raul Ramirez
9 Ilie Nastase
10 Dick Stockton

1978
1 Jimmy Connors
2 Bjorn Borg
3 Guillermo Vilas
4 John McEnroe
5 Vitas Gerulaitis
6 Eddie Dibbs
7 Brian Gottfried
8 Raul Ramirez
9 Harold Solomon
10 Corrado Barazzutti

1979
1 Bjorn Borg
2 Jimmy Connors
3 John McEnroe
4 Vitas Gerulaitis
5 Roscoe Tanner
6 Guillermo Vilas
7 Arthur Ashe
8 Harold Solomon
9 Jose Higueras
10 Eddie Dibbs

1980
1 Bjorn Borg
2 John McEnroe
3 Jimmy Connors
4 Gene Mayer
5 Guillermo Vilas
6 Ivan Lendl
7 Harold Solomon
8 Jose-Luis Clerc
9 Vitas Gerulaitis
10 Eliot Teltscher

1981
1 John McEnroe
2 Ivan Lendl
3 Jimmy Connors
4 Bjorn Borg
5 Jose-Luis Clerc
6 Guillermo Vilas
7 Gene Mayer
8 Eliot Teltscher
9 Vitas Gerulaitis
10 Peter McNamara

1982
1 John McEnroe
2 Jimmy Connors
3 Ivan Lendl
4 Guillermo Vilas
5 Vitas Gerulaitis
6 Jose-Luis Clerc
7 Mats Wilander
8 Gene Mayer
9 Yannick Noah
10 Peter McNamara

Annual Top 10 World Rankings (since 1968) (Cont.)

MEN

1983	1987	1991	1995	1999
1 John McEnroe	1 Ivan Lendl	1 Stefan Edberg	1 Pete Sampras	1 Andre Agassi
2 Ivan Lendl	2 Stefan Edberg	2 Jim Courier	2 Andre Agassi	2 Yevgeny Kafelnikov
3 Jimmy Connors	3 Mats Wilander	3 Boris Becker	3 Thomas Muster	3 Pete Sampras
4 Mats Wilander	4 Jimmy Connors	4 Michael Stich	4 Boris Becker	4 Thomas Enqvist
5 Yannick Noah	5 Boris Becker	5 Ivan Lendl	5 Michael Chang	5 Gustavo Kuerten
6 Jimmy Arias	6 Miloslav Mecir	6 Pete Sampras	6 Yevgeny Kafelnikov	6 Nicolas Kiefer
7 Jose Higueras	7 Pat Cash	7 Guy Forget	7 Thomas Enqvist	7 Todd Martin
8 Jose-Luis Clerc	8 Yannick Noah	8 Karel Novacek	8 Jim Courier	8 Nicolas Lapentti
9 Kevin Curren	9 Tim Mayotte	9 Petr Korda	9 Wayne Ferreira	9 Marcelo Rios
10 Gene Mayer	10 John McEnroe	10 Andre Agassi	10 Goran Ivanisevic	10 Richard Krajicek

1984	1988	1992	1996	2000
1 John McEnroe	1 Mats Wilander	1 Jim Courier	1 Pete Sampras	1 Gustavo Kuerten
2 Jimmy Connors	2 Ivan Lendl	2 Stefan Edberg	2 Michael Chang	2 Marat Safin
3 Ivan Lendl	3 Andre Agassi	3 Pete Sampras	3 Yevgeny Kafelnikov	3 Pete Sampras
4 Mats Wilander	4 Boris Becker	4 Goran Ivanisevic	4 Goran Ivanisevic	4 Magnus Norman
5 Andres Gomez	5 Stefan Edberg	5 Boris Becker	5 Thomas Muster	5 Yevgeny Kafelnikov
6 Anders Jarryd	6 Kent Carlsson	6 Michael Chang	6 Boris Becker	6 Andre Agassi
7 Henrik Sundstrom	7 Jimmy Connors	7 Petr Korda	7 Richard Krajicek	7 Lleyton Hewitt
8 Pat Cash	8 Jakob Hlasek	8 Ivan Lendl	8 Andre Agassi	8 Alex Corretja
9 Eliot Teltscher	9 Henri Leconte	9 Andre Agassi	9 Thomas Enqvist	9 Thomas Enqvist
10 Yannick Noah	10 Tim Mayotte	10 Richard Krajicek	10 Wayne Ferreira	10 Tim Henman

1985	1989	1993	1997	2001
1 Ivan Lendl	1 Ivan Lendl	1 Pete Sampras	1 Pete Sampras	1 Lleyton Hewitt
2 John McEnroe	2 Boris Becker	2 Michael Stich	2 Patrick Rafter	2 Gustavo Kuerten
3 Mats Wilander	3 Stefan Edberg	3 Jim Courier	3 Michael Chang	3 Andre Agassi
4 Jimmy Connors	4 John McEnroe	4 Sergi Bruguera	4 Jonas Bjorkman	4 Yevgeny Kafelnikov
5 Stefan Edberg	5 Michael Chang	5 Stefan Edberg	5 Yevgeny Kafelnikov	5 Juan Carlos Ferrero
6 Boris Becker	6 Brad Gilbert	6 Andrei Medvedev	6 Greg Rusedski	6 Sebastien Grosjean
7 Yannick Noah	7 Andre Agassi	7 Goran Ivanisevic	7 Carlos Moya	7 Patrick Rafter
8 Anders Jarryd	8 Aaron Krickstein	8 Michael Chang	8 Sergi Bruguera	8 Tommy Haas
9 Miloslav Mecir	9 Alberto Mancini	9 Thomas Muster	9 Thomas Muster	9 Tim Henman
10 Kevin Curren	10 Jay Berger	10 Cedric Pioline	10 Marcelo Rios	10 Pete Sampras

1986	1990	1994	1998	2002
1 Ivan Lendl	1 Stefan Edberg	1 Pete Sampras	1 Pete Sampras	1 Lleyton Hewitt
2 Boris Becker	2 Boris Becker	2 Andre Agassi	2 Marcelo Rios	2 Andre Agassi
3 Mats Wilander	3 Ivan Lendl	3 Boris Becker	3 Alex Corretja	3 Marat Safin
4 Yannick Noah	4 Andre Agassi	4 Sergi Bruguera	4 Patrick Rafter	4 Juan Carlos Ferrero
5 Stefan Edberg	5 Pete Sampras	5 Goran Ivanisevic	5 Carlos Moya	5 Carlos Moya
6 Henri Leconte	6 Andres Gomez	6 Michael Chang	6 Andre Agassi	6 Roger Federer
7 Joakim Nystrom	7 Thomas Muster	7 Stefan Edberg	7 Tim Henman	7 Jiri Novak
8 Jimmy Connors	8 Emilio Sanchez	8 Alberto Berasategui	8 Karol Kucera	8 Tim Henman
9 Miloslav Mecir	9 Goran Ivanisevic	9 Michael Stich	9 Greg Rusedski	9 Albert Costa
10 Andres Gomez	10 Brad Gilbert	10 Todd Martin	10 Richard Krajicek	10 Andy Roddick

---

Maiden and Married Names of Women's Champions

Maiden Name	Married Name	Maiden Name	Married Name
Blanche Bingley	Blanche Hillyard	Hazel Hotchkiss	Hazel Wightman
Molla Bjurstedt	Molla Mallory	Hilde Krahwinkel	Hilde Sperling
Patricia Canning	Patricia Todd	Kerry Melville	Kerry Reid
Mary Carter	Mary Raitano	Kathleen McKane	Kathleen Godfrey
Charlotte Cooper	Charlotte Sterry	Billie Jean Moffitt	Billie Jean King
Thelma Coyne	Thelma Long	Margaret Osborne	Margaret duPont
Dorothea Douglass	Dorothea Lambert Chambers	Sarah Palfrey	Sarah Fabyan Cooke
Chris Evert	Chris Evert Lloyd*	Margaret Smith	Margaret Smith Court
Evonne Goolagong	Evonne Cawley	Helen Wills	Helen Wills Moody
Louise Hammond	Louise Raymond	Nancye Wynne	Nancye Bolton
Ann Haydon	Ann Haydon Jones		

*Chris Evert Lloyd divorced husband John Lloyd in 1987, and has since gone by the name Chris Evert.

WOMEN

1968
1 Billie Jean King
2 Virginia Wade
3 Nancy Richey
4 Maria Bueno
5 Margaret Court
6 Ann Jones
7 Judy Tegart
8 Annette du Plooy
9 Leslie Bowrey
10 Rosie Casals

1969
1 Margaret Court
2 Ann Jones
3 Billie Jean King
4 Nancy Richey
5 Julie Heldman
6 Rosie Casals
7 Kerry Melville
8 Peaches Bartkowicz
9 Virginia Wade
10 Leslie Bowrey

1970
1 Margaret Court
2 Billie Jean King
3 Rosie Casals
4 Virginia Wade
5 Helga Niessen
6 Kerry Melville
7 Julie Heldman
8 Karen Krantzcke
9 Francoise Durr
10 Nancy R. Gunter

1971
1 Evonne Goolagong
2 Billie Jean King
3 Margaret Court
4 Rosie Casals
5 Kerry Melville
6 Virginia Wade
7 Judy Tegart
8 Francoise Durr
9 Helga N. Masthoff
10 Chris Evert

1972
1 Billie Jean King
2 Evonne Goolagong
3 Chris Evert
4 Margaret Court
5 Kerry Melville
6 Virginia Wade
7 Rosie Casals
8 Nancy R. Gunter
9 Francoise Durr
10 Linda Tuero

1973
1 Margaret S. Court
2 Billie Jean King
3 Evonne G. Cawley
4 Chris Evert
5 Rosie Casals
6 Virginia Wade
7 Kerry Reid
8 Nancy Richey
9 Julie Heldman
10 Helga Masthoff

1974
1 Billie Jean King
2 Evonne G. Cawley
3 Chris Evert
4 Virginia Wade
5 Julie Heldman
6 Rosie Casals
7 Kerry Reid
8 Olga Morozova
9 Lesley Hunt
10 Francoise Durr

1975
1 Chris Evert
2 Billie Jean King
3 Evonne G. Cawley
4 Martina Navratilova
5 Virginia Wade
6 Margaret S. Court
7 Olga Morozova
8 Nancy Richey
9 Francoise Durr
10 Rosie Casals

1976
1 Chris Evert
2 Evonne G. Cawley
3 Virginia Wade
4 Martina Navratilova
5 Sue Barker
6 Betty Stove
7 Dianne Balestrat
8 Mima Jausovec
9 Rosie Casals
10 Francoise Durr

1977
1 Chris Evert
2 Billie Jean King
3 Martina Navratilova
4 Virginia Wade
5 Sue Barker
6 Rosie Casals
7 Betty Stove
8 Dianne Balestrat
9 Wendy Turnbull
10 Kerry Reid

1978
1 Martina Navratilova
2 Chris Evert Lloyd
3 Evonne G. Cawley
4 Virginia Wade
5 Billie Jean King
6 Tracy Austin
7 Wendy Turnbull
8 Kerry Reid
9 Betty Stove
10 Dianne Balestrat

1979
1 Martina Navratilova
2 Chris Evert Lloyd
3 Tracy Austin
4 Evonne G. Cawley
5 Billie Jean King
6 Dianne Balestrat
7 Wendy Turnbull
8 Virginia Wade
9 Kerry Reid
10 Sue Barker

1980
1 Chris Evert Lloyd
2 Tracy Austin
3 Martina Navratilova
4 Hana Mandlikova
5 Evonne G. Cawley
6 Billie Jean King
7 Andrea Jaeger
8 Wendy Turnbull
9 Pam Shriver
10 Greer Stevens

1981
1 Chris Evert Lloyd
2 Tracy Austin
3 Martina Navratilova
4 Andrea Jaeger
5 Hana Mandlikova
6 Sylvia Hanika
7 Pam Shriver
8 Wendy Turnbull
9 Bettina Bunge
10 Barbara Potter

1982
1 Martina Navratilova
2 Chris Evert Lloyd
3 Andrea Jaeger
4 Tracy Austin
5 Wendy Turnbull
6 Pam Shriver
7 Hana Mandlikova
8 Barbara Potter
9 Bettina Bunge
10 Sylvia Hanika

1983
1 Martina Navratilova
2 Chris Evert Lloyd
3 Andrea Jaeger
4 Pam Shriver
5 Sylvia Hanika
6 Jo Durie
7 Bettina Bunge
8 Wendy Turnbull
9 Tracy Austin
10 Zina Garrison

1984
1 Martina Navratilova
2 Chris Evert Lloyd
3 Hana Mandlikova
4 Pam Shriver
5 Wendy Turnbull
6 Manuela Maleeva
7 Helena Sukova
8 Claudia Kohde-Kilsch
9 Zina Garrison
10 Kathy Jordan

1985
1 Martina Navratilova
2 Chris Evert Lloyd
3 Hana Mandlikova
4 Pam Shriver
5 Claudia Kohde-Kilsch
6 Steffi Graf
7 Manuela Maleeva
8 Zina Garrison
9 Helena Sukova
10 Bonnie Gadusek

1986
1 Martina Navratilova
2 Chris Evert Lloyd
3 Steffi Graf
4 Hana Mandlikova
5 Helena Sukova
6 Pam Shriver
7 Claudia Kohde-Kilsch
8 M. Maleeva-Fragniere
9 Zina Garrison
10 Gabriela Sabatini

1987
1 Steffi Graf
2 Martina Navratilova
3 Chris Evert
4 Pam Shriver
5 Hana Mandlikova
6 Gabriela Sabatini
7 Helena Sukova
8 M. Maleeva-Fragniere
9 Zina Garrison
10 Claudia Kohde-Kilsch

1988
1 Steffi Graf
2 Martina Navratilova
3 Chris Evert
4 Gabriela Sabatini
5 Pam Shriver
6 M. Maleeva-Fragniere
7 Natalia Zvereva
8 Helena Sukova
9 Zina Garrison
10 Barbara Potter

1989
1 Steffi Graf
2 Martina Navratilova
3 Gabriela Sabatini
4 Z. Garrison-Jackson
5 A. Sanchez Vicario
6 Monica Seles
7 Conchita Martinez
8 Helena Sukova
9 M. Maleeva-Fragniere
10 Chris Evert

1990
1 Steffi Graf
2 Monica Seles
3 Martina Navratilova
4 Mary Joe Fernandez
5 Gabriela Sabatini
6 Katerina Maleeva
7 A. Sanchez Vicario
8 Jennifer Capriati
9 M. Maleeva-Fragniere
10 Z. Garrison-Jackson

1991
1 Monica Seles
2 Steffi Graf
3 Gabriela Sabatini
4 Martina Navratilova
5 A. Sanchez Vicario
6 Jennifer Capriati
7 Jana Novotna
8 Mary Joe Fernandez
9 Conchita Martinez
10 M. Maleeva-Fragniere

1992
1 Monica Seles
2 Steffi Graf
3 Gabriela Sabatini
4 A. Sanchez Vicario
5 Martina Navratilova
6 Mary Joe Fernandez
7 Jennifer Capriati
8 Conchita Martinez
9 M. Maleeva-Fragniere
10 Jana Novotna

1993
1 Steffi Graf
2 A. Sanchez Vicario
3 Martina Navratilova
4 Conchita Martinez
5 Gabriela Sabatini
6 Jana Novotna
7 Mary Joe Fernandez
8 Monica Seles
9 Jennifer Capriati
10 Anke Huber

1994
1 Steffi Graf
2 A. Sanchez Vicario
3 Conchita Martinez
4 Jana Novotna
5 Mary Pierce
6 Lindsay Davenport
7 Gabriela Sabatini
8 Martina Navratilova
9 Kimiko Date
10 Natasha Zvereva

1995
1 Steffi Graf
  Monica Seles*
2 Conchita Martinez
3 A. Sanchez Vicario
4 Kimiko Date
5 Mary Pierce
6 Magdalena
  Maleeva
7 Gabriela
  Sabatini
8 Mary Joe Fernandez
9 Iva Majoli
10 Anke Huber

1996
1 Steffi Graf
2 Monica Seles†
  A. Sanchez Vicario
3 Jana Novotna
4 Martina Hingis
5 Conchita Martinez
6 Anke Huber
7 Iva Majoli
8 Kimiko Date
9 Lindsay Davenport
10 Barbara Paulus

Annual Top 10 World Rankings (since 1968) (Cont.)
WOMEN

1997
1. Martina Hingis
2. Jana Novotna
3. Lindsay Davenport
4. Amanda Coetzer
5. Monica Seles
6. Iva Majoli
7. Mary Pierce
8. Irina Spirlea
9. A. Sanchez Vicario
10. Mary Joe Fernandez

1998
1. Lindsay Davenport
2. Martina Hingis
3. Jana Novotna
4. A. Sanchez Vicario
5. Venus Williams
6. Monica Seles
7. Mary Pierce
8. Conchita Martinez
9. Steffi Graf
10. Nathalie Tauziat

1999
1. Martina Hingis
2. Lindsay Davenport
3. Venus Williams
4. Serena Williams
5. Mary Pierce
6. Monica Seles
7. Nathalie Tauziat
8. Barbara Schett
9. Julie Halard-Decugis
10. Amelie Mauresmo

2000
1. Martina Hingis
2. Lindsay Davenport
3. Venus Williams
4. Monica Seles
5. Conchita Martinez
6. Serena Williams
7. Mary Pierce
8. Anna Kournikova
9. A. Sanchez Vicario
10. Nathalie Tauziat

2001
1. Lindsay Davenport
2. Jennifer Capriati
3. Venus Williams
4. Martina Hingis
5. Kim Clijsters
6. Serena Williams
7. Justine Henin
8. Jelena Dokic
9. Amelie Mauresmo
10. Monica Seles

2002
1. Serena Williams
2. Venus Williams
3. Jennifer Capriati
4. Kim Clijsters
5. Justine Henin-Hardenne
6. Amelie Mauresmo
7. Monica Seles
8. Daniela Hantuchova
9. Jelena Dokic
10. Martina Hingis

*Returning to the WTA Tour on Aug. 15, 1995, Seles was co-ranked #1 for her first six tournaments. Seles had been absent from the Tour since April 1993 when she was stabbed by a fan during a match. She was ranked #1 at the time of the stabbing.

†Seles' ranking was revised in May 1996. The revision stipulated that her new modified ranking would be calculated using a divisor of the actual number of tournaments she had played (13), and she would be co-ranked with the player whose average is immediately below her average (Sanchez Vicario).

All-Time Leaders
Tournaments Won (singles)

All-time tournament wins from the arrival of open tennis in 1968 through 2002. Men's totals include ATP Tour, Grand Prix and WCT tournaments. Players active in singles play in 2003 are in **bold** type.

MEN

		Total			Total			Total
1	Jimmy Connors	109	11	Thomas Muster	44	21	Vitas Gerulaitis	27
2	Ivan Lendl	94	12	Stefan Edberg	41	22	**Yevgeny Kafelnikov**	26
3	John McEnroe	77	13	Stan Smith	39	23	Jose-Luis Clerc	25
4	Pete Sampras	64	14	**Michael Chang**	34		Brian Gottfried	25
5	Bjorn Borg	62	15	Arthur Ashe	33	25	Jim Courier	23
	Guillermo Vilas	62		Mats Wilander	33		Yannick Noah	23
7	Ilie Nastase	57	17	John Newcombe	32	27	Eddie Dibbs	22
8	**Andre Agassi**	54		Manuel Orantes	32		**Goran Ivanisevic**	22
9	Boris Becker	49		Ken Rosewall	32		Harold Solomon	22
10	Rod Laver	47	20	Tom Okker	31	30	Andres Gomez	21

WOMEN

		Total			Total			Total
1	Martina Navratilova	167	11	**Conchita Martinez**	32	21	Pam Shriver	21
2	Chris Evert	154	12	Olga Morozova	31	22	Julie Heldman	20
3	Steffi Graf	107	13	Tracy Austin	30	23	M. Maleeva-Fragniere	19
4	Margaret Smith Court	92	14	**A. Sanchez Vicario**	29		**Serena Williams**	19
5	E. Goolagong Cawley	68	15	**Venus Williams**	28	25	Virginia Ruzici	17
6	Billie Jean King	67	16	Hana Mandlikova	27		Regina Marsikova	17
7	Virginia Wade	55		Gabriela Sabatini	27	27	Ann Jones	16
8	**Monica Seles**	53	18	Nancy Richey	25	28	Sue Barker	15
9	**Martina Hingis**	40	19	Jana Novotna	24		**Mary Pierce**	15
10	**Lindsay Davenport**	37	20	Kerry Melville Reid	22		Dianne Fromholtz-Balestrat	15

Money Won

All-time money winners from the arrival of open tennis in 1968 through 2002. Totals include doubles earnings.

MEN

		Earnings				Earnings				Earnings
1	Pete Sampras	$43,280,489	11	Michael Stich	$12,590,152	21	Marcelo Rios	$9,404,181
2	Andre Agassi	25,658,496	12	John McEnroe	12,539,622	22	Wayne Ferreira	9,227,992
3	Boris Becker	25,080,956	13	Thomas Muster	12,224,410	23	Jonas Bjorkman	9,114,985
4	Yevgeny Kafelnikov	23,202,345	14	Sergi Bruguera	11,632,199	24	Todd Woodbridge	8,688,899
5	Ivan Lendl	21,262,417	15	Patrick Rafter	11,103,311	25	Jimmy Connors	8,641,040
6	Stefan Edberg	20,630,941	16	Lleyton Hewitt	10,862,801	26	Marat Safin	8,402,773
7	Goran Ivanisevic	19,748,638	17	Petr Korda	10,448,450	27	Carlos Moya	8,376,152
8	Michael Chang	19,070,332	18	Richard Krajicek	9,977,484	28	Mark Woodforde	8,324,401
9	Jim Courier	14,033,132	19	Alex Corretja	9,828,939	29	Tim Henman	8,183,078
10	Gustavo Kuerten	13,456,299	20	Thomas Enqvist	9,784,703	30	Mats Wilander	7,976,256

WOMEN

		Earnings				Earnings				Earnings
1	Steffi Graf	$21,895,277	11	Chris Evert	$8,896,195	21	Anke Huber	$4,768,292
2	Mart. Navratilova	20,527,874	12	Gabriela Sabatini	8,785,850	22	Gigi Fernandez	4,681,906
3	Martina Hingis	18,344,660	13	Natasha Zvereva	7,792,503	23	Z. Garrison Jackson	4,590,816
4	A. Sanchez Vicario	16,917,312	14	Jennifer Capriati	6,974,563	24	Lisa Raymond	4,485,498
5	Lindsay Davenport	14,842,061	15	Nathalie Tauziat	6,645,660	25	Iva Majoli	4,258,381
6	Monica Seles	14,615,549	16	Mary Pierce	6,451,861	26	Larisa Neiland	4,083,936
7	Venus Williams	11,902,908	17	Helena Sukova	6,391,245	27	Sandrine Testud	3,687,384
8	Jana Novotna	11,249,134	18	Pam Shriver	5,460,566	28	Kim Clijsters	3,649,280
9	Conchita Martinez	10,117,481	19	Mary Joe Fernandez	5,258,471	29	Anna Kournikova	3,517,390
10	Serena Williams	10,041,992	20	Amanda Coetzer	5,231,834	30	Lori McNeil	3,441,604

Year-end Tournaments

MEN

Tennis Masters Cup

The year-end championship featuring the top eight players in the Tennis Masters Series rankings. Two groups of four players square off in a round-robin tournament followed by a single-elimination semifinals and finals. Originally called the Masters in 1970, the tournament followed a round-robin format, but was revised in 1972 to include a round-robin to decide the four semifinalists then a single elimination format after that. Replaced by ATP Tour World Championship in 1990 through 1999.

Multiple Winners: Ivan Lendl and Pete Sampras (5); Ilie Nastase (4); Boris Becker and John McEnroe (3); Bjorn Borg and Lleyton Hewitt (2).

Year	Winner		Runner-Up		Year	Winner	Loser	Score
1970	Stan Smith (4-1) *		Rod Laver (4-1)		1986	Ivan Lendl	B. Becker	64 64 64
1971	Ilie Nastase (6-0)		Stan Smith (4-2)		1987	Ivan Lendl	M. Wilander	62 62 63
					1988	Boris Becker	I. Lendl	57 76 36 62 76
Year	**Winner**	**Loser**		**Score**	1989	Stefan Edberg	B. Becker	46 76 63 61
1972	Ilie Nastase	S. Smith		63 62 36 26 63	1990	Andre Agassi	S. Edberg	57 76 75 62
1973	Ilie Nastase	T. Okker		63 75 46 63	1991	Pete Sampras	J. Courier	36 76 63 64
1974	Guillermo Vilas	I. Nastase		76 62 36 36 64	1992	Boris Becker	J. Courier	64 63 75
1975	Ilie Nastase	B. Borg		62 62 61	1993	Michael Stich	P. Sampras	76 26 76 62
1976	Manuel Orantes	W. Fibak		57 62 06 76 61	1994	Pete Sampras	B. Becker	46 63 75 64
1978	Jimmy Connors	B. Borg		64 16 64	1995	Boris Becker	M. Chang	76 60 76
1979	John McEnroe	A. Ashe		67 63 75	1996	Pete Sampras	B. Becker	36 76 76 67 64
1980	Bjorn Borg	V. Gerulaitis		62 62	1997	Pete Sampras	Y. Kafelnikov	63 62 62
1981	Bjorn Borg	I. Lendl		64 62 62	1998	Alex Corretja	C. Moya	36 36 75 63 75
1982	Ivan Lendl	V. Gerulaitis		67 26 76 62 64	1999	Pete Sampras	A. Agassi	61 75 64
1983	Ivan Lendl	J. McEnroe		64 64 62	2000	Gustavo Kuerten	A. Agassi	64 64 64
1984	John McEnroe	I. Lendl		63 64 64	2001	Lleyton Hewitt	S. Grosjean	63 63 64
1985	John McEnroe	I. Lendl		75 60 64	2002	Lleyton Hewitt	J.C. Ferrero	75 75 26 26 64
1986	Ivan Lendl	B. Becker		62 76 63				

*Smith was declared the winner because he beat Laver in their round-robin match (4-6, 6-3, 6-4).
Note: The tournament switched from December to January in 1977-78, then back to December in 1986.

Playing Sites

1970—Tokyo; **1971**—Paris; **1972**—Barcelona; **1973**—Boston; **1974**—Melbourne; **1975**—Stockholm; **1976** & **2003**—Houston; **1977-89**—New York City; **1990-95**—Frankfurt, GER; **1996-99**—Hannover, GER; **2000**—Lisbon, POR; **2001**—Sydney, AUS; **2002**—Shanghai, CHN.

WCT Championship (1971-89)

World Championship Tennis was established in 1967 to promote professional tennis and led the way into the open era. Its major singles and doubles championships were held every May among the top eight regular season finishers on the circuit from 1971 until the WCT folded in 1989.

Multiple winners: John McEnroe (5), Jimmy Connors, Ivan Lendl and Ken Rosewall (2).

Year	Winner	Loser	Score	Year	Winner	Loser	Score
1971	Ken Rosewall	R. Laver	64 16 76 76	1973	Stan Smith	A. Ashe	63 63 46 64
1972	Ken Rosewall	R. Laver	46 60 63 67 76	1974	John Newcombe	B. Borg	46 63 63 62

Year-end Tournaments (Cont.)

Year	Winner	Loser	Score	Year	Winner	Loser	Score
1975	Arthur Ashe	B. Borg	36 64 64 60	1983	John McEnroe	I. Lendl	62 46 63 67 76
1976	Bjorn Borg	G. Vilas	16 61 75 61	1984	John McEnroe	J. Connors	61 62 63
1977	Jimmy Connors	D. Stockton	67 61 64 63	1985	Ivan Lendl	T. Mayotte	76 64 61
1978	Vitas Gerulaitis	E. Dibbs	63 62 61	1986	Anders Jarryd	B. Becker	67 61 61 64
1979	John McEnroe	B. Borg	75 46 62 76	1987	Miloslav Mecir	J. McEnroe	60 36 62 62
1980	Jimmy Connors	J. McEnroe	26 76 61 62	1988	Boris Becker	S. Edberg	64 16 75 62
1981	John McEnroe	J. Kriek	61 62 64	1989	John McEnroe	B. Gilbert	63 63 76
1982	Ivan Lendl	J. McEnroe	62 36 63 63				

WOMEN

WTA Championships

The WTA Tour's year-end tournament took place in March from 1972 until 1986 when the WTA decided to adopt a January-to-November playing season. Given the changeover, two championships were held in 1986. Held in Boca Raton (1972-73), Los Angeles (1974-76, 2002-), New York (1977, 1979-2000), Oakland (1978), Munich (2001).

Multiple winners: Martina Navratilova (8); Steffi Graf (5); Chris Evert (4); Monica Seles (3); Evonne Goolagong, Martina Hingis and Gabriela Sabatini (2).

Year	Winner	Loser	Score	Year	Winner	Loser	Score
1972	Chris Evert	K. Reid	75 64	1988	Gabriela Sabatini	P. Shriver	75 62 62
1973	Chris Evert	N. Richey	63 63	1989	Steffi Graf	M. Navratilova	64 75 26 62
1974	Evonne Goolagong	C. Evert	63 64	1990	Monica Seles	G. Sabatini	64 57 36 64 62
1975	Chris Evert	M. Navratilova	64 62	1991	Monica Seles	M. Navratilova	64 36 75 60
1976	Evonne Goolagong	C. Evert	63 57 63	1992	Monica Seles	M. Navratilova	75 63 61
1977	Chris Evert	S. Barker	26 61 61	1993	Steffi Graf	A. S. Vicario	61 64 36 61
1978	M. Navratilova	E. Goolagong	76 64	1994	Gabriela Sabatini	L. Davenport	63 62 64
1979	M. Navratilova	T. Austin	63 36 62	1995	Steffi Graf	A. Huber	61 26 61 46 63
1980	Tracy Austin	M. Navratilova	62 26 62	1996	Steffi Graf	M. Hingis	63 46 60 46 60
1981	M. Navratilova	A. Jaeger	63 76	1997	Jana Novotna	M. Pierce	76 62 63
1982	Sylvia Hanika	M. Navratilova	16 63 64	1998	Martina Hingis	L. Davenport	75 64 46 62
1983	M. Navratilova	C. Evert	62 60	1999	Lindsay Davenport	M. Hingis	64 62
1984	M. Navratilova	C. Evert	63 75 61	2000	Martina Hingis	M. Seles	67 64 64
1985	M. Navratilova	H. Sukova	63 75 64	2001	Serena Williams	L. Davenport	walkover
1986	M. Navratilova	H. Mandlikova	62 60 36 61	2002	Kim Clijsters	S. Williams	75 63
1986	M. Navratilova	S. Graf	76 63 62				
1987	Steffi Graf	G. Sabatini	46 64 60 64				

Note: The final was best-of-five sets from 1984-98 and best-of-three sets from 1972-83 and since 1999.

Davis Cup

Established in 1900 as an annual international tournament by American player Dwight Davis. Originally called the International Lawn Tennis Challenge Trophy. Challenge round system until 1972. Since 1981, the top 16 nations in the world have played a straight knockout tournament over the course of a year. The format is a best-of-five match of two singles, one doubles and two singles over three days. Note that from 1900-24 Australia and New Zealand competed together as Australasia.

Multiple winners: USA (31); Australia (21); France (9); Sweden (7); Australasia (6); British Isles (5); Britain (4); Germany (3).

Challenge Rounds

Year	Winner	Loser	Score	Site	Year	Winner	Loser	Score	Site
1900	USA	British Isles	3-0	Boston	1927	France	USA	3-2	Philadelphia
1901	Not held				1928	France	USA	4-1	Paris
1902	USA	British Isles	3-2	New York	1929	France	USA	3-2	Paris
1903	British Isles	USA	4-1	Boston	1930	France	USA	4-1	Paris
1904	British Isles	Belgium	5-0	Wimbledon	1931	France	Britain	3-2	Paris
1905	British Isles	USA	5-0	Wimbledon	1932	France	USA	3-2	Paris
1906	British Isles	USA	5-0	Wimbledon	1933	Britain	France	3-2	Paris
1907	Australasia	British Isles	3-2	Wimbledon	1934	Britain	USA	4-1	Wimbledon
1908	Australasia	USA	3-2	Melbourne	1935	Britain	USA	5-0	Wimbledon
1909	Australasia	USA	5-0	Sydney	1936	Britain	Australia	3-2	Wimbledon
1910	Not held				1937	USA	Britain	4-1	Wimbledon
1911	Australasia	USA	5-0	Christchurch, NZ	1938	USA	Australia	3-2	Philadelphia
1912	British Isles	Australasia	3-2	Melbourne	1939	Australia	USA	3-2	Philadelphia
1913	USA	British Isles	3-2	Wimbledon	1940-45	Not held World War II			
1914	Australasia	USA	3-2	New York	1946	USA	Australia	5-0	Melbourne
1915-18	Not held World War I				1947	USA	Australia	4-1	New York
1919	Australasia	British Isles	4-1	Sydney	1948	USA	Australia	5-0	New York
1920	USA	Australasia	5-0	Auckland, NZ	1949	USA	Australia	4-1	New York
1921	USA	Japan	5-0	New York	1950	Australia	USA	4-1	New York
1922	USA	Australasia	4-1	New York	1951	Australia	USA	3-2	Sydney
1923	USA	Australasia	4-1	New York	1952	Australia	USA	4-1	Adelaide
1924	USA	Australia	5-0	Philadelphia	1953	Australia	USA	3-2	Melbourne
1925	USA	France	5-0	Philadelphia	1954	USA	Australia	3-2	Sydney
1926	USA	France	4-1	Philadelphia	1955	Australia	USA	5-0	New York

Year	Winner	Loser	Score	Site	Year	Winner	Loser	Score	Site
1956	Australia	USA	5-0	Adelaide	1962	Australia	Mexico	5-0	Brisbane
1957	Australia	USA	3-2	Melbourne	1963	USA	Australia	3-2	Adelaide
1958	USA	Australia	3-2	Brisbane	1964	Australia	USA	3-2	Cleveland
1959	Australia	USA	3-2	New York	1965	Australia	Spain	4-1	Sydney
1960	Australia	Italy	4-1	Sydney	1966	Australia	India	4-1	Melbourne
1961	Australia	Italy	5-0	Melbourne	1967	Australia	Spain	4-1	Brisbane

Final Rounds

Year	Winner	Loser	Score	Site	Year	Winner	Loser	Score	Site
1968	USA	Australia	4-1	Adelaide	1986	Australia	Sweden	3-2	Melbourne
1969	USA	Romania	5-0	Cleveland	1987	Sweden	India	5-0	Göteborg
1970	USA	W. Germany	5-0	Cleveland	1988	W. Germany	Sweden	4-1	Göteborg
1971	USA	Romania	3-2	Charlotte	1989	W. Germany	Sweden	3-2	Stuttgart
1972	USA	Romania	3-2	Bucharest	1990	USA	Australia	3-2	St. Petersburg
1973	Australia	USA	5-0	Cleveland	1991	France	USA	3-1	Lyon
1974	So. Africa	India	walkover	Not held	1992	USA	Switzerland	3-1	Ft. Worth
1975	Sweden	Czech.	3-2	Stockholm	1993	Germany	Australia	4-1	Dusseldorf
1976	Italy	Chile	4-1	Santiago	1994	Sweden	Russia	4-1	Moscow
1977	Australia	Italy	3-1	Sydney	1995	USA	Russia	3-2	Moscow
1978	USA	Britain	4-1	Palm Springs	1996	France	Sweden	3-2	Malmo
1979	USA	Italy	5-0	San Francisco	1997	Sweden	USA	5-0	Göteborg
1980	Czech.	Italy	4-1	Prague	1998	Sweden	Italy	4-1	Milan
1981	USA	Argentina	3-1	Cincinnati	1999	Australia	France	3-2	Nice
1982	USA	France	4-1	Grenoble	2000	Spain	Australia	3-1	Barcelona
1983	Australia	Sweden	3-2	Melbourne	2001	France	Australia	3-2	Melbourne
1984	Sweden	USA	4-1	Göteborg	2002	Russia	France	3-2	Paris
1985	Sweden	W. Germany	3-2	Munich					

Note: In 1974, India refused to play the final as a protest against the South African government's policies of apartheid.

Fed Cup

Originally the Federation Cup started by the International Tennis Federation as the Davis Cup of women's tennis. Played by 32 teams over one week at one site from 1963-94. Tournament changed to Davis Cup-style format of four rounds and home site in 1995. Currently 16 teams compete in a home-and-away knockout format, with the top four teams advancing to "finals week" at a single location.

Multiple winners: USA (17); Australia (7); Czechoslovakia and Spain (5); Germany (2).

Year	Winner	Loser	Score	Site	Year	Winner	Loser	Score	Site
1963	USA	Australia	2-1	London	1983	Czech.	W. Germany	2-1	Zurich
1964	Australia	USA	2-1	Philadelphia	1984	Czech.	Australia	2-1	Brazil
1965	Australia	USA	2-1	Melbourne	1985	Czech.	USA	2-1	Japan
1966	USA	W. Germany	3-0	Italy	1986	USA	Czech.	3-0	Prague
1967	USA	Britain	2-0	W. Germany	1987	W. Germany	USA	2-1	Vancouver
1968	Australia	Holland	3-0	Paris	1988	Czech.	USSR	2-1	Melbourne
1969	USA	Australia	2-1	Athens	1989	USA	Spain	3-0	Tokyo
1970	Australia	Britain	3-0	W. Germany	1990	USA	USSR	2-1	Atlanta
1971	Australia	Britain	3-0	Perth	1991	Spain	USA	2-1	Nottingham
1972	So. Africa	Britain	2-1	Africa	1992	Germany	Spain	2-1	Frankfurt
1973	Australia	So. Africa	3-0	W. Germany	1993	Spain	Australia	3-0	Frankfurt
1974	Australia	USA	2-1	Italy	1994	Spain	USA	3-0	Frankfurt
1975	Czech.	Australia	3-0	France	1995	Spain	USA	3-2	Valencia
1976	USA	Australia	2-1	Philadelphia	1996	USA	Spain	5-0	Atlantic City
1977	USA	Australia	2-1	Eastbourne	1997	France	Netherlands	4-1	Nice, France
1978	USA	Australia	2-1	Melbourne	1998	Spain	Switzerland	3-2	Geneva
1979	USA	Australia	3-0	Spain	1999	USA	Russia	4-1	Palo Alto
1980	USA	Australia	3-0	W. Germany	2000	USA	Spain	5-0	Las Vegas
1981	USA	Britain	3-0	Tokyo	2001	Belgium	Russia	2-1	Madrid
1982	USA	W. Germany	3-0	Santa Clara	2002	Slovakia	Spain	3-1	Spain

COLLEGES

NCAA team titles were not sanctioned until 1946. NCAA women's individual and team championships started in 1982.

Men's NCAA Individual Champions (1883-1945)

Multiple winners: Malcolm Chace and Pancho Segura (3); Edward Chandler, George Church, E.B. Dewhurst, Fred Hovey, Frank Guernsey, W.P. Knapp, Robert LeRoy, P.S. Sears, Cliff Sutter, Ernest Sutter and Richard Williams (2).

Year		Year		Year	
1883	J. Clark, Harvard (spring)	1886	G.M. Brinley, Trinity, CT	1890	Fred Hovey, Harvard
	H. Taylor, Harvard (fall)	1887	P.S. Sears, Harvard	1891	Fred Hovey, Harvard
1884	W.P. Knapp, Yale	1888	P.S. Sears, Harvard	1891	Fred Hovey, Harvard
1885	W.P. Knapp, Yale	1889	R.P. Huntington Jr., Yale	1892	William Larned, Cornell

Colleges (Cont.)

Year		Year		Year	
1893	Malcolm Chace, Brown	1910	R.A. Holden Jr., Yale	1929	Berkeley Bell, Texas
1894	Malcolm Chace, Yale	1911	E.H. Whitney, Harvard	1930	Cliff Sutter, Tulane
1895	Malcolm Chace, Yale	1912	George Church, Princeton	1931	Keith Gledhill, Stanford
1896	Malcolm Whitman, Harvard	1913	Richard Williams, Harv.	1932	Cliff Sutter, Tulane
1897	S.G. Thompson, Princeton	1914	George Church, Princeton	1933	Jack Tidball, UCLA
1898	Leo Ware, Harvard	1915	Richard Williams, Harv.	1934	Gene Mako, USC
1899	Dwight Davis, Harvard	1916	G.C. Caner, Harvard	1935	Wilbur Hess, Rice
		1917-1918	Not held	1936	Ernest Sutter, Tulane
1900	Ray Little, Princeton	1919	Charles Garland, Yale	1937	Ernest Sutter, Tulane
1901	Fred Alexander, Princeton			1938	Frank Guernsey, Rice
1902	William Clothier, Harvard	1920	Lascelles Banks, Yale	1939	Frank Guernsey, Rice
1903	E.B. Dewhurst, Penn	1921	Philip Neer, Stanford		
1904	Robert LeRoy, Columbia	1922	Lucien Williams, Yale	1940	Don McNeill, Kenyon
1905	E.B. Dewhurst, Penn	1923	Carl Fischer, Phi. Osteo.	1941	Joseph Hunt, Navy
1906	Robert LeRoy, Columbia	1924	Wallace Scott, Wash.	1942	Fred Schroeder, Stanford
1907	G.P. Gardner Jr., Harvard	1925	Edward Chandler, Calif.	1943	Pancho Segura, Miami-FL
1908	Nat Niles, Harvard	1926	Edward Chandler, Calif.	1944	Pancho Segura, Miami-FL
1909	Wallace Johnson, Penn	1927	Wilmer Allison, Texas	1945	Pancho Segura, Miami-FL
		1928	Julius Seligson, Lehigh		

NCAA Men's Division I Champions

Multiple winners (Teams): Stanford (17); USC (16); UCLA (15); Georgia (4); William & Mary (2). (Players): Matias Boeker, Alex Olmedo, Mikael Pernfors, Dennis Ralston and Ham Richardson (2).

Year	Team winner	Individual Champion	Year	Team winner	Individual Champion
1946	USC	Bob Falkenburg, USC	1975	UCLA	Bill Martin, UCLA
1947	Wm. & Mary	Garner Larned, Wm.& Mary	1976	USC & UCLA	Bill Scanlon, Trinity-TX
1948	Wm. & Mary	Harry Likas, San Francisco	1977	Stanford	Matt Mitchell, Stanford
1949	San Francisco	Jack Tuero, Tulane	1978	Stanford	John McEnroe, Stanford
			1979	UCLA	Kevin Curren, Texas
1950	UCLA	Herbert Flam, UCLA			
1951	USC	Tony Trabert, Cincinnati	1980	Stanford	Robert Van't Hof, USC
1952	UCLA	Hugh Stewart, USC	1981	Stanford	Tim Mayotte, Stanford
1953	UCLA	Ham Richardson, Tulane	1982	UCLA	Mike Leach, Michigan
1954	UCLA	Ham Richardson, Tulane	1983	Stanford	Greg Holmes, Utah
1955	USC	Jose Aguero, Tulane	1984	UCLA	Mikael Pernfors, Georgia
1956	UCLA	Alex Olmedo, USC	1985	Georgia	Mikael Pernfors, Georgia
1957	Michigan	Barry MacKay, Michigan	1986	Stanford	Dan Goldie, Stanford
1958	USC	Alex Olmedo, USC	1987	Georgia	Andrew Burrow, Miami-FL
1959	Tulane & Notre Dame	Whitney Reed, San Jose St.	1988	Stanford	Robby Weiss, Pepperdine
			1989	Stanford	Donni Leaycraft, LSU
1960	UCLA	Larry Nagler, UCLA			
1961	UCLA	Allen Fox, UCLA	1990	Stanford	Steve Bryan, Texas
1962	USC	Rafael Osuna, USC	1991	USC	Jared Palmer, Stanford
1963	USC	Dennis Ralston, USC	1992	Stanford	Alex O'Brien Stanford
1964	USC	Dennis Ralston, USC	1993	USC	Chris Woodruff, Tennessee
1965	UCLA	Arthur Ashe, UCLA	1994	USC	Mark Merklein, Florida
1966	USC	Charlie Pasarell, UCLA	1995	Stanford	Sargis Sargisian, Ariz. St.
1967	USC	Bob Lutz, USC	1996	Stanford	Cecil Mamiit, USC
1968	USC	Stan Smith, USC	1997	Stanford	Luke Smith, UNLV
1969	USC	Joaquin Loyo-Mayo, USC	1998	Stanford	Bob Bryan, Stanford
			1999	Georgia	Jeff Morrison, Florida
1970	UCLA	Jeff Borowiak, UCLA			
1971	UCLA	Jimmy Connors, UCLA	2000	Stanford	Alex Kim, Stanford
1972	Trinity-TX	Dick Stockton, Trinity-TX	2001	Georgia	Matias Boeker, Georgia
1973	Stanford	Alex Mayer, Stanford	2002	USC	Matias Boeker, Georgia
1974	Stanford	John Whitlinger, Stanford	2003	Illinois	Amer Delic, Illinois

NCAA Women's Division I Champions

Multiple winners (Teams): Stanford (12); Florida (4); Georgia, Texas and USC (2). (Players): Sandra Birch, Patty Fendick, Laura Granville and Lisa Raymond (2).

Year	Team winner	Individual Champion	Year	Team winner	Individual Champion
1982	Stanford	Alycia Moulton, Stanford	1993	Texas	Lisa Raymond, Florida
1983	USC	Beth Herr, USC	1994	Georgia	Angela Lettiere, Georgia
1984	Stanford	Lisa Spain, Georgia	1995	Texas	Keri Phoebus, UCLA
1985	USC	Linda Gates, Stanford	1996	Florida	Jill Craybas, Florida
1986	Stanford	Patty Fendick, Stanford	1997	Stanford	Lilia Osterloh, Stanford
1987	Stanford	Patty Fendick, Stanford	1998	Florida	Vanessa Webb, Duke
1988	Stanford	Shaun Stafford, Florida	1999	Stanford	Zuzana Lesenarova, S. Diego
1989	Stanford	Sandra Birch, Stanford			
			2000	Georgia	Laura Granville, Stanford
1990	Stanford	Debbie Graham, Stanford	2001	Stanford	Laura Granville, Stanford
1991	Stanford	Sandra Birch, Stanford	2002	Stanford	Bea Bielik, Wake Forest
1992	Florida	Lisa Raymond, Florida	2003	Florida	Amber Liu, Stanford

Golf

Annika Sorenstam became the first woman in 58 years to play in a PGA Tour event.

Making Waves

Four first-timers grab wins at the 2003 PGA majors, and Annika shows us all what the game is about.

Karl Ravech
is an analyst for ESPN's golf coverage.

With all due respect to Tiger Woods, 2003 was one of the most bizarre years on the PGA Tour in quite a while. But a great trivia question for your local sports know-it-all could be, "Who won men's golf's four majors in 2003?"

Very few people would answer, "Mike Weir, Jim Furyk, Ben Curtis and Shaun Micheel."

That foursome in fact won the Masters, US Open, British Open and PGA Championship, respectively. But aside from their friends and family and the guys who finished second in those events—Len Mattiace, Stephen Leaney, Thomas Bjorn and Vijay Singh (finished tied for second at the British Open) and Chad Campbell, (told you it wasn't the most memorable year on tour)—nobody knew who was cashing the first-place checks.

Weir became the first of the four first-time major winners in 2003. We all knew a lefty would win at Augusta some day, we just had the wrong lefty in mind. While Phil Mickelson finished in third, two strokes off the lead, it was Weir wearing the green jacket after winning a one-hole sudden death playoff with Mattiace.

At the U.S. Open, there was no playoff necessary. Furyk held the lead after two rounds and didn't let go, his 272 matching the 72-hole record in the 103-year history of the Open.

Then things really got crazy. Despite not having won a major before this year, Furyk and Weir had at least become recognizable names on tournament leaderboards. But Micheel? Curtis? So while Tiger and Vijay battled for the tour money lead, it was Curtis, the 396th-ranked player, and Micheel, at 169, that showed us anything was possible on the PGA Tour.

AP/Wide World Photos

Ben Curtis, *ranked 396th in the world, holds the Claret Jug and reflects on his shocking win at the 2003 British Open at England's Royal St. George's Golf Club.*

But ask golf fans what the most memorable event of the 2003 PGA season was and they'll tell you, albeit quietly, that it was, in fact, performed by a woman. Yes, a woman.

LPGA star Annika Sorenstam made waves and headlines by teeing it up with the big boys at the PGA Tour's Bank of America Colonial event in late May. She accepted an invitation from the sponsor to play and soon thereafter began an exercise regimen that would make most men in the 101st airborne proud.

As her appeal broadened so did her shoulders. She was the topic of conversation at every sports bar in the world, and how she would do in the tournament became hot stuff at every sports book in Las Vegas. Odds were stacked against her making the cut and once again the oddsmakers were correct. But they did sweat it out for a while.

Following an opening round of 71 despite missing putts all day, she shot a four-over-par 74 on Friday and left before the weekend. But she checked out having left a lasting impression on the men who run the PGA Tour and the guys who play on it.

That week, Sorenstam was bigger

AP/Wide World Photos

Annika Sorenstam experienced quite a range of emotions at the Bank of America Colonial in May. She became the first woman since 1945 to compete in a PGA tour event.

than anything the Tour could put out there. For the first time since Babe Zaharias 58 years earlier, Sorenstam was the shining star on an otherwise cloudy event. Media members, numbering 300 from all over the world, descended on Fort Worth, Texas, to watch her play and chronicle her every move. By the end of the 36 holes we all knew what she wore, how she worked out, when she woke up and how defiantly and delicately she walked away. She taught everyone a lesson in humility. Sorenstam humanized a game which had become robotic.

"I just feel very fortunate to do what I do," she said post-tournament, during yet another grilling from the media.

"I got so much support from my tour. The people who cheered me on. It's been so wonderful and I hope they had a good time as well. I think they all made this week so special."

We watch sports to see how other individuals handle adversity. We attempt to place ourselves in the shoes of the athletes and for the first time in a long time, not too many in the audience jumped up to say, "I can do that."

The Ten Biggest Stories of the Year in Golf

10 Despite suffering from a nasty bout of food poisoning, Tiger Woods wins the Bay Hill Invitational in March for the fourth consecutive year. He plays bogey-free golf for the final 44 holes to win by 11 strokes, the fourth double-digit win of his career. He is the first player since Gene Sarazen won the Miami Open from 1926-30 to win the same tournament in four straight years.

9 Long-hitting 13-year-old Michelle Wie makes her first appearance at an LPGA major tournament, the Kraft Nabisco Championship, and ties for ninth with a score of 288 (par). She puts herself in contention for the win with a third-round 66 (tied for the lowest score in any LPGA event), but struggles on the final day.

8 Tom Watson wins the Senior British Open and the JELD-WEN Tradition, two of the five majors on the Champions Tour. The 53-year-old also cards an opening-round 65 at the U.S. Open at Olympia Fields, where he is accompanied by his long-time caddie Bruce Edwards, who was diagnosed with ALS.

7 Unorthodox swing and all, Jim Furyk wins the U.S. Open, his first major title, by three strokes over Australian Stephen Leaney. Furyk's eight-under 272 ties the record for the lowest 72-hole score in the Open's 103-year history.

6 Hilary Lunke, who had never finished higher than 15th in any LPGA tournament, wins the U.S. Women's Open in a thrilling three-way 18-hole playoff with Angela Stanford and Kelly Robbins. Just after Stanford rolls in a 30-foot putt from just off the green on the 18th playoff hole, Lunke calmly sinks her 15-footer for birdie to win by a stroke.

5 Shaun Micheel, playing in only his third major tournament, wins the PGA Championship in Rochester, N.Y. with a two-stroke victory over Chad Campbell. Up by one stroke on his final hole and in the rough about 175 yards away, Micheel grabs his seven-iron and sticks his shot two inches from the cup, all but clinching the win.

4 After a record-setting 2002 in which she registered 11 wins, Annika Sorenstam continues her torrid pace in 2003, winning five tournaments (through Oct. 5) including her fifth and sixth career majors. In October she is inducted into the LPGA Tour and World Golf Halls of Fame.

3 To the surprise of pretty much everyone, PGA Tour rookie Ben Curtis wins his first major (and his first professional title) at the British Open, defeating veterans Vijay Singh and Thomas Bjorn by a stroke. He is the first player since Francis Ouimet in 1913 to win the first major tournament he enters.

2   Mike Weir dons the coveted green jacket after he defeats Len Mattiace on the first sudden death play-off hole at the Masters. He is the first lefty to win at Augusta and the first Canadian to win any PGA major. Mattiace, five shots off the lead heading into the final day, shoots a final-round 65 to force the playoff. He then suffers through his worst hole of the tournament on the first hole of sudden-death, allowing Weir to grab the title with a bogey.

1   Annika Sorenstam highlights a list of women to play in men's tournaments in 2003. While Michelle Wie plays in two men's tournaments and golf pro Suzy Whaley actually qualifies for the Greater Hartford Open, it is Sorenstam who grabs most of the headlines with her performance at the Bank of America Colonial in May. Sorenstam fails to make the cut, but her accuracy, grace under pressure and cheery demeanor go a long way in silencing many of her critics.

Major Leagues

Tiger who? Ernie who? In 2003 four first-time major winners swept the men's Grand Slam for just the third time in history and first since 1969. As the table below shows, some very prominent players have been a part of these historical feats.

Year		
2003	Weir (Masters)	Curtis (British)
	Furyk (U.S.)	Micheel (PGA)
1969	Archer (Masters)	Jacklin (British)
	Moody (U.S.)	Floyd (PGA)
1959	Wall Jr. (Masters)	Player (British)
	Casper (U.S.)	Rosburg (PGA)

Ladies Night

Not since Babe Zaharias in 1945 (at the Los Angeles Open) has a woman played a PGA Tour event, but that all changed in May when Annika Sorenstam teed off at the Bank of America Colonial. In 2003, five women played in tournaments on various men's tours.

	Tournament (Tour)	Players Beaten
A. Sorenstam	Colonial (PGA)	11
S. Whaley	GHO (PGA)	3
M. Wie	Bay Mills (Canadian)	35
M. Wie	Boise Open (Nationwide)	1
J. Stephenson	Turtle Bay (Champions)	0
L. Davies	Korean Open (Asian)	37

2002-2003
Season In Review

SPORTS ALMANAC

Tournament Results

Schedules and results of PGA, European PGA, Champions and LPGA tournaments from Nov. 3, 2002 through Oct. 5, 2003.

PGA Tour
Late 2002

Last Rd	Tournament	Winner	Earnings	Runner-Up
Nov. 3	Southern Farm Bureau Classic	Luke Donald (201)#	$468,000	D. Pappas (202)
Nov. 3	The Tour Championship	Vijay Singh (268)	900,000	C. Howell III (270)
Nov. 5@	Wendy's Three-Tour Challenge	PGA Tour (5-under par)	450,000	Champions (3-under), LPGA (2-over)
Nov. 17@	Hyundai Team Matches	Rich Beem/	100,000	F. Couples/
		Peter Lonard (2&1)	(each)	M. Calcavecchia
Nov. 24	Franklin Templeton Shootout	Rocco Mediate/	250,000	M. Kuchar/D. Gossett
		Lee Janzen (185)	(each)	& J. Huston/J. Maggert (186)
Nov. 27@	Grand Slam of Golf	Tiger Woods (127)	400,000	J. Leonard & D. Love III (141)
Dec. 1@	Skins Game	Mark O'Meara (8 skins)	405,000	T. Woods (4 skins)
Dec. 8@	Target World Challenge	Padraig Harrington (268)	1,000,000	T. Woods (270)
Dec. 15@	WGC: EMC World Cup	Japan (252)	1,000,000	United States (254)

@ Unofficial PGA Tour money event.
# Weather-shortened.

2003

Last Rd	Tournament	Winner	Earnings	Runner-Up
Jan. 12	Mercedes Championships	Ernie Els (261)	$1,000,000	R. Mediate & K.J. Choi (269)
Jan. 19	Sony Open	Ernie Els (264)*	810,000	A. Baddeley (264)
Jan. 26	Phoenix Open	Vijay Singh (261)	720,000	J. Huston (264)
Feb. 2	Bob Hope Chrysler Classic	Mike Weir (330)+	810,000	J. Haas (332)
Feb. 9	AT&T Pebble Beach Pro-Am	Davis Love III (274)	900,000	T. Lehman (275)
Feb. 16	Buick Invitational	Tiger Woods (272)	810,000	C. Pettersson (276)
Feb. 23	Nissan Open	Mike Weir (275)*	810,000	C. Howell III (275)
Mar. 2	WGC: Accenture Match Play Championship	Tiger Woods (2&1)	1,050,000	D. Toms
Mar. 2	Chrysler Classic of Tucson	Frank LickLiter (269)	540,000	C. Campbell (271)
Mar. 9	Ford Championship	Scott Hoch (271)*	900,000	J. Furyk (271)
Mar. 16	Honda Classic	Justin Leonard (264)	900,000	C. Campbell & D. Love III (265)
Mar. 23	Bay Hill Invitational	Tiger Woods (269)	810,000	4-way tie (280)
Mar. 30	The Players Championship	Davis Love III (271)	1,170,000	J. Haas & P. Harrington (277)
Apr. 6	BellSouth Classic	Ben Crane (272)	720,000	B. Tway (276)
Apr. 13	**The Masters** (Augusta, Ga.)	Mike Weir (281)*	1,080,000	L. Mattiace (281)
Apr. 20	MCI Heritage	Davis Love III (271)*	810,000	W. Austin (271)
Apr. 27	Shell Houston Open	Fred Couples (267)	810,000	3-way tie (271)
May 4	HP Classic of New Orleans	Steve Flesch (267)*	900,000	B. Estes (267)
May 11	Wachovia Championship	David Toms (278)	1,008,000	3-way tie (280)
May 18	EDS Byron Nelson Classic	Vijay Singh (265)	1,008,000	N. Price (267)
May 25	Bank of America Colonial	Kenny Perry (261)	900,000	J. Leonard (267)
June 1	Memorial Tournament	Kenny Perry (275)	900,000	L. Janzen (277)
June 9	FBR Capital Open	Rory Sabbatini (270)	810,000	3-way tie (274)
June 15	**U.S. Open** (Olympia Fields, Ill.)	Jim Furyk (272)	1,080,000	S. Leaney (275)
June 22	Buick Classic	Jonathan Kaye (271)*	900,000	J. Rollins (271)
June 29	FedEx St. Jude Classic	David Toms (264)	810,000	N. Price (267)
July 6	Western Open	Tiger Woods (267)	810,000	R. Beem (272)
July 13	Greater Milwaukee Open	Kenny Perry (268)	630,000	S. Allan & H. Slocum (269)
July 20	**British Open** (Sandwich, Eng.)	Ben Curtis (283)	1,112,720	V. Singh & T. Bjorn (284)
July 20	B.C. Open	Craig Stadler (267)	540,000	A. Cejka & S. Lowery (268)
July 27	Greater Hartford Open	Peter Jacobsen (266)	720,000	C. Riley (268)
Aug. 3	Buick Open	Jim Furyk (274)	720,000	4-way tie (269)
Aug. 10	The International†	Davis Love III (46)	900,000	R. Goosen & V. Singh (34)
Aug. 17	**PGA Championship** (Rochester, N.Y.)	Shaun Micheel (276)	1,080,000	C. Campbell (278)
Aug. 24	WGC: NEC Invitational	Darren Clarke (268)	1,050,000	J. Kaye (272)
Aug. 24	Reno-Tahoe Open	Kirk Triplett (271)	540,000	T. Herron (274)

Tournament Results (Cont.)

Last Rd	Tournament	Winner	Earnings	Runner-Up
Sept. 1	Deutsche Bank U.S. Championship	Adam Scott (264)	$900,000	R. Mediate (268)
Sept. 7	Bell Canadian Open	Bob Tway (272)*	756,000	B. Faxon (272)
Sept. 14	John Deere Classic	Vijay Singh (268)	630,000	3-way tie (272)
Sept. 21	84 Lumber Classic of Pennsylvania	J.L. Lewis (266)	720,000	3-way tie (268)
Sept. 28	Valero Texas Open	Tommy Armour III (254)	630,000	L. Roberts & B. Tway (261)
Oct. 5	WGC: American Express Championship	Tiger Woods (274)	1,050,000	3-way tie (276)
Oct. 5	Southern Farm Bureau Classic	John Huston (268)	540,000	B. Pappas (269)

+This is a five-round, 90-hole event played over five days.

†The scoring for The International is based on a modified Stableford system (8 points for a double eagle, 5 for an eagle, 2 for a birdie, 0 for a par, −1 for a bogey, −3 for double bogey or worse).

*Playoffs: Sony—Els won on 2nd hole; **Nissan**—Weir won on 2nd hole; **Ford**—Hoch won on 3rd hole; **Masters**—Weir won on 1st hole; **MCI Heritage**—Love III won on 4th hole; **HP Classic**—Flesch won on 1st hole; **Buick Classic**—Kaye won on 1st hole; **Bell Canadian**—Tway won on 3rd hole.

Second place ties (3 players or more): 4-WAY—**Bay Hill** (K. Triplett, K. Perry, B. Faxon, S. Cink); **Buick Open** (T. Woods, G. Ogilvy, B. Baird, C. DiMarco). 3-WAY—**Houston** (H. Kuehne, S. Appleby, M. Calcavecchia); **Wachovia** (V. Singh, B. Geiberger, R. Gamez); **FBR Capital** (J. Durant, F. Funk, D. Waldorf); **John Deere** (C. Riley, J.L. Lewis, J. Byrd); **84 Lumber Classic** (F. Lickliter, S. Appleby, T. Petrovic); **American Express** (V. Singh, T. Herron, S. Appleby).

PGA Majors

The Masters

Edition: 67th **Dates:** April 10-13
Site: Augusta National GC, Augusta, Ga.
Par: 36-36—72 (7290 yards) **Purse:** $6,000,000

	1 2 3 4	Tot	Earnings
1 Mike Weir*	70-68-75-68	281	$1,080,000
2 Len Mattiace	73-74-69-65	281	648,000
3 Phil Mickelson	73-70-72-68	283	408,000
4 Jim Furyk	73-72-71-68	284	288,000
5 Jeff Maggert	72-73-66-75	286	240,000
6 Ernie Els	79-66-72-70	287	208,500
Vijay Singh	73-71-70-73	287	208,500
8 Mark O'Meara	76-71-70-71	288	162,000
David Toms	71-73-70-74	288	162,000
Scott Verplank	76-73-70-69	288	162,000
Jose Maria Olazabal	73-71-71-73	288	162,000
Jonathan Byrd	74-71-71-72	288	162,000

*Weir defeated Mattiace on the first hole of sudden death.

Early round leaders: 1st—Darren Clarke (66); 2nd—Weir (138); 3rd—Maggert (211).
Top amateur: Ricky Barnes (291).

U.S. Open

Edition: 103rd **Dates:** June 12-15
Site: Olympia Fields Country Club, Olympia Fields, Ill.
Par: 35-35—70 (7190 yards) **Purse:** $6,000,000

	1 2 3 4	Tot	Earnings
1 Jim Furyk	67-66-67-72	272	$1,080,000
2 Stephen Leaney	67-68-68-72	275	650,000
3 Kenny Perry	72-71-69-67	279	341,367
Mike Weir	73-67-68-71	279	341,367
5 Nick Price	71-65-69-75	280	185,934
David Toms	72-67-70-71	280	185,934
Ernie Els	69-70-69-72	280	185,934
Fredrik Jacobson	69-67-73-71	280	185,934
Justin Rose	70-71-69-70	280	185,934
10 Billy Mayfair	69-71-67-74	281	124,936
Scott Verplank	76-67-68-70	281	124,936
Cliff Kresge	69-70-72-70	281	124,936
Jonathan Kaye	70-70-72-69	281	124,936
Padraig Harrington	69-72-72-68	281	124,936

Early round leaders: 1st—Tom Watson & Brett Quigley (65); 2nd—Furyk & Vijay Singh (133); 3rd—Furyk (200).
Top amateur: Trip Kuehne (290).

British Open

Edition: 132nd **Dates:** July 17-20
Site: Royal St. George's Golf Club, Sandwich, England
Par: 36-35—71 (7106 yards) **Purse:** $6,240,000

	1 2 3 4	Tot	Earnings
1 Ben Curtis	72-72-70-69	283	$1,112,720
2 Vijay Singh	75-70-69-70	284	548,412
Thomas Bjorn	73-70-69-72	284	548,412
4 Tiger Woods	73-72-69-71	285	294,076
Davis Love III	69-72-72-72	285	294,076
6 Brian Davis	77-73-68-68	286	213,801
Fredrik Jacobson	70-76-70-70	286	213,801
8 Nick Faldo	76-74-67-70	287	155,383
Kenny Perry	74-70-70-73	287	155,383
10 Hennie Otto	68-76-75-69	288	108,093
Retief Goosen	73-75-71-69	288	108,093
Gary Evans	71-75-70-72	288	108,093
Phillip Price	74-72-69-73	288	108,093
Sergio Garcia	73-71-70-74	288	108,093

Early round leaders: 1st—Otto (68); 2nd—Love III (141); 3rd—Bjorn (212).
Top amateur: none.

PGA Championship

Edition: 85th **Dates:** Aug. 14-17
Site: Oak Hill Country Club, Rochester, N.Y.
Par: 35-35—70 (7134 yards) **Purse:** $6,000,000

	1 2 3 4	Tot	Earnings
1 Shaun Micheel	69-68-69-70	276	$1,080,000
2 Chad Campbell	69-72-65-72	278	648,000
3 Tim Clark	72-70-68-69	279	408,000
4 Alex Cejka	74-69-68-69	280	288,000
5 Ernie Els	71-70-70-71	282	214,000
Jay Haas	70-74-69-69	282	214,000
7 Fred Funk	69-73-70-72	284	175,667
Loren Roberts	70-73-70-71	284	175,667
Mike Weir	68-71-70-75	284	175,667
10 Charles Howell III	70-72-70-73	285	135,500
Kenny Perry	75-72-70-68	285	135,500
Billy Andrade	67-72-72-74	285	135,500
Niclas Fasth	76-70-71-68	285	135,500

Early round leaders: 1st—Phil Mickelson & Rod Pampling (66); 2nd—Micheel (137); 3rd—Micheel & Campbell (206).
Top amateur: none.

The Official World Golf Ranking

Begun in 1986, the Official World Golf Ranking (formerly the Sony World Ranking) combines the best golfers on the world's leading professional tours—Asian, PGA Tour of Australia, European, European Challenge, Japan Golf Tour, Southern African and U.S. (PGA Tour, Buy.com). Rankings are based on a rolling two-year period and weighted in favor of more recent results. Points are awarded after each worldwide tournament according to finish. Final points-per-tournament averages are determined by dividing a player's total points by the number of tournaments played over that two-year period (through Oct. 5, 2003).

		Avg			Avg			Avg
1	Tiger Woods, USA	17.07	6	Mike Weir, CAN	7.61	11	Phil Mickelson, USA	5.10
2	Ernie Els, RSA	9.89	7	David Toms, USA	6.01	12	Nick Price, ZIM	5.06
3	Vijay Singh, FIJ	9.27	8	Kenny Perry, USA	5.76	13	Darren Clarke, N. IRE	4.87
4	Davis Love III, USA	8.24	9	Retief Goosen, RSA	5.45	14	Justin Leonard, USA	3.88
5	Jim Furyk, USA	7.77	10	Padraig Harrington, IRE	5.41	15	K.J. Choi, KOR	3.83

European PGA Tour

Official money won on the European Tour is presented in euros (E).

Late 2002

Last Rd	Tournament	Winner	Earnings	Runner-Up
Nov. 3	Italian Open	Ian Poulter (197)#	E183,330	P. Lawrie (199)
Nov. 10	Volvo Masters	Bernhard Langher &	435,648	—
		Colin Montgomerie (281)*	435,648	
Nov. 24	BMW Asian Open	Padraig Harrington (273)	247,967	J. Randhawa (274)
Dec. 1	Omega Hong Kong Open	Fredrik Jacobson (260)	113,385	J. Berendt & H. Nystrom (262)
Dec. 15	WGC: EMC World Cup	Japan (252)	991,964	United States (254)

#Weather-shortened

*Playoffs: Volvo Masters—Darkness halted play after two playoff holes. Langher and Montgomerie decided to call it a tie.

2003

Last Rd	Tournament	Winner	Earnings	Runner-Up
Jan. 12	South African Airways Open	Trevor Immelman (274)*	E121,669	T. Clark (274)
Jan. 19	Dunhill Championship	Mark Foster (273)*	120,573	5-way tie (273)
Jan. 26	Caltex Masters	Zhang Lian-Wei (278)	140,713	E. Els (279)
Feb. 2	Heineken Classic	Ernie Els (273)	207,309	N. Faldo & P. Lonard (274)
Feb. 9	ANZ Championship†	Paul Casey (45)	180,934	S. Appleby & N. O'Hern (41)
Feb. 16	Johnnie Walker Classic	Ernie Els (259)	251,263	S. Leaney & A. Stolz (264)
Feb. 23	Malaysian Open	Arjun Atwal (260)	169,765	R. Goosen & B. Kennedy (264)
Mar. 2	WGC: Accenture Match Play Championship	Tiger Woods (2&1)	973,394	D. Toms
Mar. 9	Dubai Desert Classic	Robert-Jan Derksen (271)	291,994	E. Els (272)
Mar. 16	Qatar Masters	Darren Fichardt (275)*	226,983	J. Kingston (275)
Mar. 23	Madeira Island Open	Bradley Dredge (272)	100,000	3-way tie (280)
Apr. 13	The Masters Tournament	Mike Weir (281)*	1,008,312	L. Mattiace (281)
Apr. 20	Portugal Open	Fredrik Jacobsen (283)	208,330	3-way tie (284)
Apr. 27	Canarias Open	Kenneth Ferrie (266)*	291,660	P. Lawrie & P. Hedblom (266)
May 4	Italian Open	Mathias Gronberg (271)	183,330	3-way tie (273)
May 11	Benson & Hedges International	Paul Casey (277)	262,227	P. Harrington (281)
May 18	Deutsche Bank-SAP Open	Padraig Harrington (269)*	450,000	T. Bjorn (269)
May 25	Volvo PGA Championship	Ignacio Garrido (270)*	583,330	T. Immelman (270)
June 1	Celtic Manor Resort Wales Open	Ian Poulter (270)	347,360	3-way tie (273)
June 8	British Masters	Greg Owen (274)	348,312	I. Poulter & C. Cevaer (277)
June 15	U.S. Open	Jim Furyk (272)	923,470	S. Leaney (275)
June 15	Aa St Omer Open	Brett Rumford (269)	66,660	B. Mason (274)
June 22	Diageo Championship	Soren Kjeldsen (279)	281,928	A. Forsyth (281)
June 29	French Open	Philip Golding (273)	416,660	D. Howell (274)
July 6	Smurfit European Open	Phillip Price (272)	481,245	M. McNulty & A. Forsyth (273)
July 13	The Barclay's Scottish Open	Ernie Els (267)	532,888	P. Price & D. Clarke (272)
July 20	British Open	Ben Curtis (283)	1,010,800	T. Bjorn & V. Singh (284)
July 27	Nissan Irish Open	Michael Campbell (277)*	300,000	P. Hedblom & T. Bjorn (277)
Aug. 3	Scandinavian Masters	Adam Scott (277)	316,660	N. Dougherty (279)
Aug. 10	Nordic Open	Ian Poulter (266)	266,660	C. Montgomerie (267)
Aug. 17	PGA Championship	Shaun Micheel (276)	953,979	C. Campbell (278)
Aug. 17	BMW Russian Open	Marcus Fraser (269)*	66,660	M. Wiegele (269)
Aug. 24	WGC: NEC Invitational	Darren Clarke (268)	932,919	J. Kaye (272)
Aug. 31	BMW International Open	Lee Westwood (269)	300,000	A. Cejka (272)
Sept. 7	European Masters	Ernie Els (267)	266,660	M. Campbell (273)
Sept. 14	Trophee Lancome	Retief Goosen (266)	300,000	P. McGinley (270)

Tournament Results (Cont.)

Last Rd	Tournament	Winner	Earnings	Runner-Up
Sept. 21	German Masters	K.J. Choi (262)	500,000	M.A. Jimenez (264)
Sept. 28	Dunhill Links Championship	Lee Westwood (267)	705,093	E. Els (268)
Oct. 5	WGC: American Express			
	Championship	Tiger Woods (274)	914,474	3-way tie (276)

†The scoring for the ANZ Championship is based on a modified Stableford system (8 points for a double eagle, 5 for an eagle, 2 for a birdie, 0 for a par, –1 for a bogey, –3 for double bogey or worse).

*Playoffs: South African—Immelman won on 1st hole; **Dunhill Championship**—Foster won 6-man playoff on 2nd hole; **Qatar**—Fichardt won on 1st hole; **The Masters**—Weir won on 1st hole; **Canarias**—Ferrie won on 2nd hole; **Deutche bank**—Harrington won on 1st hole; **Volvo PGA**—Garrido won on 1st hole; **Irish**—Campbell won on 1st hole; **Russian**—Fraser won on 2nd hole.

Second place ties (3 players or more): 5-WAY—**Dunhill Championship** (P. Lawrie, T. Immelman, D. McGuigan, A. Hansen, B. Vaughan). 3-WAY—**Madeira Island** (B. Davis, A. Marshall, F. Andersson); **Portugal** (B. Davis, B. Dredge, J. Donaldson); **Italian** (J.M. Lara, C. Montgomerie, R. Gonzalez); **Wales** (D. Fichardt, J. Moseley, J. Lomas); **American Express** (T. Herron, S. Appleby, V. Singh).

Champions Tour
(formerly Senior PGA Tour)

Late 2002

Last Rd	Tournament	Winner	Earnings	Runner-Up
Nov. 5@	Wendy's Three-Tour Challenge	PGA Tour (5-under par)	$450,000	Champions (3-under), LPGA (2-over)
Nov. 10@	Senior Slam	Fuzzy Zoeller (138)	300,000	D. Pooley (139)
Nov. 17@	Hyundai Team Matches	Allen Doyle/	100,000	B. Fleisher/
		Dana Quigley (4&3)	(each)	D. Graham
Dec. 15@	Office Depot Father/Son Challenge . .	Craig/Kevin Stadler	100,000	Hale/Steve Irwin
		(120)*	(each)	(120)

*Playoffs: Father/Son—The Stadlers won on 1st hole.

2003

Last Rd	Tournament	Winner	Earnings	Runner-Up
Jan. 26@	Senior Skins Game	Lee Trevino (6 skins)	$240,000	H. Irwin (5)
Feb. 2	MasterCard Championship	Dana Quigley (198)	250,000	L. Nelson (200)
Feb. 9	Royal Caribbean Classic	Dave Barr (207)	217,500	B. Wadkins & G. Morgan (208)
Feb. 16	Ace Group Classic	Vicente Fernandez (202)	240,000	T. Watson & D. Smyth (205)
Feb. 23	Verizon Classic	Bruce Fleisher (205)	240,000	H. Irwin (206)
Mar. 9	MasterCard Classic	David Eger (204)	300,000	4-way tie (205)
Mar. 16	SBC Classic	Tom Purtzer (135)#	225,000	G. Morgan (136)
Mar. 23	Toshiba Classic	Roger Davis (197)	232,500	L. Nelson (201)
Apr. 20	Emerald Coast Classic	Bob Gilder (193)	217,500	3-way tie (197)
Apr. 27@	Liberty Mutual Legends of Golf	Bruce Lietzke (206)	354,000	D. Eger & D. Quigley (207)
May 4	Bruno's Memorial Classic	Tom Jenkins (200)	210,000	B. Fleisher (203)
May 11	Kinko's Classic of Austin	Hale Irwin (208)*	240,000	T. Watson (208)
May 18	Bayer Advantage Invitational	Jay Sigel (205)	240,000	M. McCullough (206)
May 25	Columbus Southern Open	Morris Hatalsky (198)	225,000	A. Doyle (199)
June 1	Music City Championship	Jim Ahern (196)	210,000	J.M. Canizares (200)
June 8	**Senior PGA Championship**			
	(Newtown Square, Penn.)	John Jacobs (276)	360,000	B. Wadkins (278)
June 22	Farmers Charity Classic	Doug Tewell (201)*	225,000	E. Darcy (201)
June 29	**U.S. Senior Open**			
	(Toledo, Ohio)	Bruce Lietzke (277)	470,000	T. Watson (279)
July 13	**Ford Senior Players Championship**			
	(Dearborn, Mich.)	Craig Stadler (271)	375,000	3-way tie (275)
July 27	**Senior British Open**			
	(Turnberry, Scotland)	Tom Watson (263)*	255,731	C. Mason (263)
Aug. 3	FleetBoston Classic	Allen Doyle (198)	225,000	B. Fleisher & B. Gilder (201)
Aug. 10	3M Championship	Wayne Levi (205)	262,500	M. Hatalsky & G. Morgan (206)
Aug. 17	Long Island Classic	Jim Thorpe (195)	225,000	B. Gilder (196)
Aug. 24	Allianz Championship	Don Pooley (200)	225,000	3-way tie (203)
Aug. 31	**JELD-WEN Tradition**			
	(Portland, Ore.)	Tom Watson (273)	330,000	3-way tie (274)
Sept. 7	Kroger Classic	Gil Morgan (200)	225,000	D. Tewell (202)
Sept. 14	Constellation Energy Classic	Larry Nelson (207)	225,000	J. Dent & D. Tewell (209)
Sept. 21	SAS Championship	D.A. Weibring (203)	270,000	T. Kite & B. Wadkins (204)
Sept. 28	Greater Hickory Classic	Craig Stadler (201)	225,000	L. Nelson (203)

#Weather-shortened.
@Unofficial Champions Tour money event.

*Playoffs: Kinko's Classic—Irwin won on 2nd hole; **Farmers Charity**—Tewell won on 3rd hole; **British Open**—Watson won on 2nd hole.

Second place ties (3 players or more): 4-WAY—**MasterCard Classic** (H. Irwin, T. Jenkins, B. Lietzke, E. Darcy). 3-WAY—**Emerald Coast** (L. Nelson, L. Thompson, V. Fernandez); **Players Championship** (T. Kite, J. Thorpe, T. Watson); **Allianz** (B. Fleisher, B. Lietzke, J. Thorpe); **Tradition** (T. Kite, G. Morgan, J. Ahern).

Champions Tour Majors

Senior PGA Championship

Edition: 66th   **Dates:** June 5-8
Site: Aronimink Golf Club, Newtown Square, Penn.
Par: 35-35—70 (6928 yards)   **Purse:** $2,000,000

		1	2	3	4	Tot	Earnings
1	John Jacobs	68	69	71	68	276	$360,000
2	Bobby Wadkins	68	72	68	70	278	216,000
3	Bruce Lietzke	75	67	70	67	279	116,000
	Fuzzy Zoeller	69	70	70	70	279	116,000
5	Doug Tewell	69	73	69	69	280	71,000
	Des Smyth	71	70	65	74	280	71,000
7	Gil Morgan	70	66	73	72	281	58,000
	Allen Doyle	69	67	73	72	281	58,000
	Vicente Fernandez	69	71	72	69	281	58,000
10	Bruce Fleisher	71	71	74	66	282	42,600
	Bob Gilder	77	67	70	68	282	42,600
	Tom Kite	70	68	74	70	282	42,600
	Mark McCumber	71	71	72	68	282	42,600
	Larry Nelson	69	74	69	70	282	42,600

Early round leaders: 1st—Jacobs, Wadkins & Mike San Filippo (68); 2nd—Morgan & Doyle (136); 3rd—Smyth (206).

Top amateur: none.

Ford Sr. Players Championship

Edition: 21st   **Dates:** July 10-13
Site: TPC of Michigan, Dearborn, Mich.
Par: 36-36—72 (7057 yards)   **Purse:** $2,500,000

		1	2	3	4	Tot	Earnings
1	Craig Stadler	67	73	65	66	271	$375,000
2	Tom Kite	66	72	73	63	274	183,000
	Jim Thorpe	68	72	69	65	274	183,000
	Tom Watson	70	64	71	69	274	183,000
5	Tom Jenkins	70	70	69	69	278	97,500
	Mike McCullough	66	71	68	73	278	97,500
	Gil Morgan	64	73	72	69	278	97,500
	Tom Purtzer	67	74	72	65	278	97,500
9	Ed Dougherty	71	71	67	71	280	67,500
	Dave Stockton	69	71	69	71	280	67,500

Early round leaders: 1st—Morgan (64); 2nd—Watson (134); 3rd—Stadler, Watson & McCullough (205).

Top amateur: none.

U.S. Senior Open

Edition: 24th   **Dates:** June 26-29
Site: Inverness Club, Toledo, Ohio
Par: 35-36—71 (6983 yards)   **Purse:** $2,600,000

		1	2	3	4	Tot	Earnings
1	Bruce Lietzke	69	71	64	73	277	$470,000
2	Tom Watson	66	72	70	71	279	280,000
3	Vicente Fernandez	73	64	71	72	280	176,651
4	Fuzzy Zoeller	71	71	74	69	285	111,387
	Allen Doyle	72	69	71	73	285	111,387
6	Wayne Levi	73	73	71	70	287	83,877
	Mike McCullough	70	73	72	72	287	83,877
8	Andy North	77	70	70	71	288	70,360
	Lanny Wadkins	75	73	71	69	288	70,360
10	Tom Jenkins	74	71	75	69	289	60,117
	Craig Stadler	78	69	70	72	289	60,117

Early round leaders: 1st—Watson (66); 2nd—Fernandez (137); 3rd—Lietzke (204).

Top amateur: none.

Senior British Open

Edition: 17th (1st as major)   **Dates:** July 24-27
Site: Westin Turnberry Resort, Turnberry, Scotland
Par: 35-35—70 (6715 yards)   **Purse:** $1,620,000

		1	2	3	4	Tot	Earnings
1	Tom Watson*	66	67	66	64	263	$255,731
2	Carl Mason	67	64	65	67	263	170,568
3	Bruce Summerhays	68	65	66	65	264	96,021
4	Tom Kite	66	67	66	67	266	76,735
5	D.A. Weibring	69	63	65	73	270	65,018
6	Brian Jones	69	69	65	68	271	49,866
	Mark McCumber	67	69	65	70	271	49,866
8	David Eger	71	68	66	67	272	36,358
	Denis Durnian	67	68	69	68	272	36,358
10	Jim Colbert	72	62	66	73	273	28,393
	Graham Marsh	71	68	66	68	273	28,393
	Dana Quigley	71	65	70	67	273	28,393

*Watson defeated Mason on the 2nd hole of sudden death.
Early round leaders: 1st—Watson & Kite (66); 2nd—Mason (131); 3rd—Mason (196).

Top amateur: Arthur Pierse (286).

JELD-WEN Tradition

Edition: 15th   **Dates:** Aug. 28-31
Site: The Reserve Vineyards & Golf Club, Portland, Ore.
Par: 36-36—72 (6994 yards)   **Purse:** $2,200,000

		1	2	3	4	Tot	Earnings
1	Tom Watson	68	62	73	70	273	$330,000
2	Tom Kite	68	68	67	71	274	161,333
	Gil Morgan	69	70	67	68	274	161,333
	Jim Ahern	66	68	68	72	274	161,333
5	Morris Hatalsky	68	68	67	72	275	96,800
	Bruce Summerhays	73	68	68	66	275	96,800
7	Dana Quigley	74	71	64	67	276	70,400
	Jim Thorpe	69	68	68	71	276	70,400
	Hugh Baiocchi	72	69	69	66	276	70,400
10	Hale Irwin	67	67	70	73	277	$50,600
	Jack Nicklaus	72	67	68	70	277	50,600
	Craig Stadler	71	70	69	67	277	50,600
	D.A. Weibring	70	68	70	69	277	50,600

Early round leaders: 1st—Ahern & Fuzzy Zoeller (66); 2nd—Watson (130); 3rd—Ahern (202).

Top amateur: none.

LPGA Tour
Late 2002

Last Rd	Tournament	Winner	Earnings	Runner-Up
Nov. 3	Cisco World Match Play Champ's.	Grace Park (1-up)	$153,000	M. Yoneyama
Nov. 5	Wendy's Three-Tour Challenge	PGA Tour (5-under par)	450,000	Champions (3-under), LPGA (2-over)
Nov. 10	Mizuno Classic	Annika Sorenstam (201)	169,500	G. Park (203)
Nov. 17	Hyundai Team Matches	Lorie Kane/	100,000	D. Pepper/
		Janice Moodie (3&2)	(each)	J. Inkster
Nov. 24	ADT Tour Championship	Annika Sorenstam (275)	215,000	R. Teske (278)

2003

Last Rd	Tournament	Winner	Earnings	Runner-Up
Jan. 26	ConAgra Foods Skins Game	Karrie Webb (12 skins)	$470,000	A. Sorenstam (3)
Mar. 16	Welch's/Fry's Championship	Wendy Doolan (259)	120,000	B. King & L. Kane (262)
Mar. 23	Safeway Ping	Se Ri Pak (265)	150,000	G. Park (266)
Mar. 30	**Kraft Nabisco Championship**			
	(Rancho Mirage, Calif.)	Patricia Meunier-Lebouc (281)	240,000	A. Sorenstam (282)
Apr. 6	Office Depot Championship	Annika Sorenstam (211)	225,000	3-way tie (215)
Apr. 19	Takefuji Classic	Candie Kung (204)	165,000	3-way tie (206)
Apr. 27	Chick-fil-A Charity Championship	Se Ri Pak (200)*	202,500	S. Waugh (200)
May 4	Michelob Light Open	Grace Park (275)	240,000	3-way tie (276)
May 11	Asahi Ryokuken International	Rosie Jones (273)	195,000	W. Ward (276)
May 25	Corning Classic	Juli Inkster (264)	150,000	L. Kane (268)
June 1	Kellogg-Keebler Classic	Annika Sorenstam (199)	180,000	M. McKay (202)
June 8	**McDonald's LPGA Championship**			
	(Wilmington, Del.)	Annika Sorenstam (278)*	240,000	G. Park (278)
June 15	Giant Eagle Classic	Rachel Teske (204)*	150,000	3-way tie (204)
June 22	Wegmen's Rochester	Rachel Teske (277)	180,000	L. Ochoa (281)
June 29	ShopRite Classic	Angela Stanford (197)	195,000	B. Morgan (200)
July 7	**U.S. Women's Open**			
	(North Plains, Ore.)	Hilary Lunke (283)*	560,000	K. Robbins & A. Stanford (283)
July 13	Canadian Women's Open	Beth Daniel (275)	195,000	J. Inkster (276)
July 20	Sybase Big Apple Classic	Hee-Won Han (273)	142,500	M. Mallon (275)
July 26	Evian Masters	Juli Inkster (267)	315,000	H-W Han (273)
Aug. 3	**Weetabix Women's British Open**			
	(Lytham, England)	Annika Sorenstam (278)	254,880	S. R. Pak (279)
Aug. 10	Wendy's Championship for Children	Hee-Won Han (199)*	165,000	W. Ward (199)
Aug. 17	Jamie Farr Kroger Classic	Se Ri Pak (271)	150,000	M. Baena & H-W Han (273)
Aug. 24	Wachovia Classic	Candie Kung (274)	180,000	S.R. Pak & M. Mallon (276)
Aug. 31	State Farm Classic	Candie Kung (202)#	180,000	L. Davies (203)
Sept. 7	John Q. Hammons Hotel Classic	Karrie Webb (200)	150,000	4-way tie (209)
Sept. 14	Solheim Cup	Europe (17½)	—	United States (10½)
Sept. 28	Safeway Classic	Annika Sorenstam (201)	180,000	B. Daniel (202)
Oct. 5	Longs Drugs Challenge	Helen Alfredsson (275)	150,000	5-way tie (276)

Weather-shortened.

*Playoffs: Chick-fil-A—Pak won on 4th hole; **LPGA Championship**—Sorenstam won on 1st hole; **Giant Eagle**—Teske won on 3rd hole; **U.S. Women's Open**—Lunke won 18-hole playoff (see p. 849); **Wendy's**—Han won on 3rd hole.

Second place ties (3 players or more): 5-WAY—**Longs Drugs** (G. Park, J. Y. Lee, P. Hurst, R. Teske, S. R. Pak). 4-WAY—**Hammons** (D. Delasin, C. Kung, J. Hullett, T. Green). 3-WAY—**Office Depot** (S.R. Pak, P. Hurst, H. Bowie); **Takefuji** (S-Y Kang, C. Kerr, A. Sorenstam); **Michelob Light** (K. Webb, L. Ochoa, C. Kerr); **Giant Eagle** (L. Kane, J. Rosales, A. Sorenstam).

LPGA Majors

Nabisco Championship

Edition: 32nd   **Dates:** March 27-30
Site: Mission Hills CC, Rancho Mirage, Calif.
Par: 36-36—72 (6520 yards)   **Purse:** $1,600,000

	1 2 3 4 Tot	Earnings
1 P. Meunier-Lebouc	70-68-70-73—281	$240,000
2 Annika Sorenstam	68-72-71-71—282	146,120
3 Lorena Ochoa	71-70-74-68—283	106,000
4 Laura Davies	70-75-69-70—284	82,000
5 Beth Daniel	75-74-68-70—287	51,200
Catriona Matthew	71-74-72-70—287	51,200
Maria Hjorth	72-72-73-70—287	51,200
Laura Diaz	76-71-69-71—287	51,200
9 Jennifer Rosales	74-70-72-72—288	35,600
a–Michelle Wie	72-74-66-76—288	

Early round leaders: 1st—Sorenstam (68); 2nd—Meunier-Lebouc (138); 3rd—Meunier-Lebouc (208).

LPGA Championship

Edition: 49th   **Dates:** June 5-8
Site: DuPont CC, Wilmington, Del.
Par: 35-36—71 (6408 yards)   **Purse:** $1,600,000

	1 2 3 4 Tot	Earnings
1 Annika Sorenstam*	71-64-72-72—278	$240,000
2 Grace Park	69-72-70-67—278	147,934
3 Rosie Jones	73-68-72-71—284	85,718
Rachel Teske	69-70-74-71—284	85,718
Beth Daniel	71-71-70-72—284	85,718
6 Young-A Yang	73-74-69-69—285	41,873
Joanne Mills	68-73-75-69—285	41,873
Young Kim	70-73-72-70—285	41,873
Becky Morgan	73-70-70-72—285	41,873
Kate Golden	72-70-68-75—285	41,873

*Sorenstam won on the first playoff hole.
Early round leaders: 1st—Hee-Won Han (67); 2nd—Sorenstam (134); 3rd—Sorenstam (206).
Top amateur: none.

U.S. Women's Open

Edition: 58th   **Dates:** July 3-7
Site: Pumpkin Ridge Golf Club, North Plains, Ore.
Par: 36-35–71 (6509 yds Thu. & Fri;
6550 yds Sat., Sun. & Mon.)   **Purse:** $3,100,000

	1	2	3	4	Tot	Earnings
1 Hilary Lunke*	71	69	68	75	283	$560,000
2 Angela Stanford	70	70	69	74	283	275,839
Kelly Robbins	74	69	71	69	283	275,839
4 Annika Sorenstam	72	72	67	73	284	150,994
a–Aree Song	70	73	68	74	285	—
6 Jeong Jang	73	69	69	75	286	115,333
Mhairi McKay	66	70	75	75	286	115,333
8 Juli Inkster	69	71	74	73	287	97,363
9 Rosie Jones	70	72	73	73	288	90,241
10 Grace Park	72	76	73	68	289	79,243
Suzann Pettersen	76	69	69	75	289	79,243

*Lunke (70) defeated Stanford (71) and Robbins (73) in an 18-hole playoff match.
Early round leaders: 1st—McKay (66); 2nd—McKay (136); 3rd—Lunke (208).

Women's British Open

Edition: 10th   **Dates:** July 31-Aug. 3
Site: Royal Lytham & St. Annes GC, Lytham, England
Par: 35-37—72 (6308 yards)   **Purse:** $1,600,000

	1	2	3	4	Tot	Earnings
1 Annika Sorenstam	68	72	68	70	278	$254,880
2 Se Ri Pak	69	69	69	72	279	159,300
3 Grace Park	74	65	71	70	280	99,563
Karrie Webb	67	72	70	71	280	99,563
5 P. Meunier-Lebouc	70	69	67	76	282	71,685
6 V. Goetze-Ackerman	73	71	68	71	283	58,941
Wendy Ward	67	71	69	76	283	58,941
8 Sophie Gustafson	73	69	71	71	284	50,976
9 Young Kim	73	70	72	70	285	46,197
10 Gloria Park	70	75	69	72	286	39,825
Candie Kung	73	71	69	73	286	39,825

Early round leaders: 1st—Webb & Ward (67); 2nd—Heather Bowie (136); 3rd—Meunier-Lebouc (206).
Top amateur: Elisa Serramia (294).

2003 Solheim Cup

The 8th Solheim Cup tournament, Sept. 12-14, at Barseback Golf & Country Club, Malmo, Sweden.

Rosters

The 2003 U.S. Team players were chosen on the basis of points awarded for wins and top-10 finishes at official LPGA events over a two-year qualifying period. The top 10 finishers on the points list automatically qualified for the 12-member team, and U.S. Captain Patty Sheehan selected the final two players.

The 2003 European Team players were chosen on the basis of points awarded weekly to the top 10 finishers at official Ladies European Tour (LET) events. The top seven players in the LET points standings automatically qualify for the 12-member team, and team captain Catrin Nilsmark selected the final five players.

United States: Qualifiers—Beth Daniel, Laura Diaz, Juli Inkster, Rosie Jones, Cristie Kerr, Meg Mallon, Michele Redman, Kelly Robbins, Angela Stanford and Wendy Ward; Captain's selections—Heather Bowie and Kelli Kuehne.

Europe: Qualifiers—Laura Davies (England), Elisabeth Esterl (Germany), Sophie Gustafson (Sweden), Mhairi McKay (Scotland), Ana-Belen Sanchez (Spain), Annika Sorenstam (Sweden) and Iben Tinning (Denmark); Captain's selections—Carin Koch (Sweden), Catriona Matthew (Scotland), Patricia Meunier-Lebouc (France), Janice Moodie (Scotland) and Suzann Pettersen (Norway).

First Day

Foursome Match Results

Winner	Score	Loser
Daniel/Robbins	halved	Koch/Davies
Moodie/Matthew	5&3	Inkster/Ward
Sorenstam/Pettersen	4&3	Diaz/Bowie
Gustafson/Esterl	3&2	Mallon/Jones

Europe wins morning, 3½-½

Four-Ball Match Results

Winner	Score	Loser
Kuehne/Kerr	2&1	Davies/Matthew
Inkster/Daniel	1-up	Sorenstam/Koch
Pettersen/Meunier-Lebouc	3&2	Stanford/Mallon
Redman/Jones	2-up	Tinning/Gustafson

USA wins afternoon, 3-1; (Europe leads, 4½-3½)

Second Day

Foursome Match Results

Winner	Score	Loser
Gustafson/Pettersen	3&1	Kuehne/Kerr
Stanford/Redman	halved	Esterl/Tinning
Sorenstam/Koch	3&2	Ward/Bowie
Mallon/Robbins	halved	Moodie/Matthew

Europe wins morning, 3-1; (Europe leads, 7½-4½)

Four-Ball Match Results

Winner	Score	Loser
Daniel/Inkster	5&4	Sanchez/McKay
Kerr/Kuehne	2&1	Gustafson/Davies
Matthew/Moodie	4&3	Ward/Jones
Sorenstam/Pettersen	1-up	Robbins/Diaz

Teams tie afternoon, 2-2; (Europe leads, 9½-6½)

Third Day
Singles Match Results

Winner	Score	Loser
Moodie	3&2	Kuehne
Inkster	5&4	Koch
Gustafson	5&4	Bowie
Tinning	2&1	Ward
Redman	3&1	Sanchez
Matthew	3&1	Jones

Winner	Score	Loser
Sorenstam	3&2	Stanford
Kerr	*	Pettersen
Davies	*	Mallon
Diaz	5&4	Esterl
McKay	*	Daniel
Meunier-Lebouc	*	Robbins

*Pettersen conceded the match after 15 holes. Mallon and Daniel conceded after 14 holes. Robbins conceded after 11 holes.
Europe wins day, 8-4
Europe wins Solheim Cup, 17½-10½

Money Leaders

Official money leaders of PGA, European PGA, Champions and LPGA tours for 2002 and unofficial money leaders for 2003, as compiled by the PGA, European PGA and LPGA. All European amounts are in euros (*E*).

PGA

Arnold Palmer Award standings: listed are tournaments played (TP); cuts made (CM); 1st, 2nd and 3rd place finishes; and earnings for the year.

	FINAL 2002	TP	CM	Finish 1-2-3	Earnings		2003 (through Oct. 5)	TP	CM	Finish 1-2-3	Earnings
1	Tiger Woods	18	18	5-2-2	$6,912,625	1	Tiger Woods	16	16	5-1-0	$6,278,746
2	Phil Mickelson	26	23	2-1-5	4,311,971	2	Vijay Singh	24	23	3-4-0	6,107,507
3	Vijay Singh	28	24	2-0-2	3,756,563	3	Davis Love III	19	17	4-1-1	5,541,096
4	David Toms	27	25	0-3-1	3,459,740	4	Jim Furyk	23	21	2-1-1	4,815,355
5	Ernie Els	18	17	2-0-0	3,291,895	5	Mike Weir	19	18	3-0-4	4,716,410
6	Jerry Kelly	29	21	2-0-0	2,946,889	6	Kenny Perry	23	21	3-1-1	4,164,976
7	Rich Beem	30	19	2-1-0	2,938,365	7	David Toms	24	17	2-1-0	3,589,255
8	Justin Leonard	26	23	1-1-0	2,738,235	8	Ernie Els	15	15	2-0-0	3,226,997
9	Charles Howell III	32	27	1-1-1	2,702,747	9	Chad Campbell	24	22	0-3-0	2,612,464
10	Retief Goosen	15	14	1-2-0	2,617,004	10	Bob Tway	23	15	1-2-1	2,361,750

European PGA

Volvo Order of Merit standings: listed are tournaments played (TP); cuts made (CM); 1st, 2nd and 3rd place finishes; and earnings for the year.

	FINAL 2002	TP	CM	Finish 1-2-3	Earnings		2003 (through Oct. 5)	TP	CM	Finish 1-2-3	Earnings
1	Retief Goosen	22	21	1-4-0	E2,360,128	1	Ernie Els	16	16	4-3-0	E2,975,374
2	Padraig Harrington	22	21	1-1-2	2,334,655	2	Darren Clarke	17	15	1-1-0	2,159,126
3	Ernie Els	16	16	3-0-0	2,251,708	3	Padraig Harrington	18	15	2-1-0	1,417,336
4	Colin Montgomerie	23	21	1-2-2	1,980,720	4	Ian Poulter	28	19	2-1-2	1,412,075
5	Eduardo Romero	21	20	1-2-0	1,811,330	5	Lee Westwood	22	14	2-0-0	1,307,763
6	Sergio Garcia	11	11	1-0-1	1,488,728	6	Thomas Bjorn	21	16	0-3-0	1,289,873
7	Adam Scott	24	19	2-1-1	1,361,776	7	Paul Casey	22	18	2-0-1	1,216,393
8	Michael Campbell	21	19	1-0-1	1,325,404	8	Phillip Price	19	14	1-1-0	1,196,743
9	Justin Rose	25	18	2-0-1	1,323,529	9	Retief Goosen	16	13	1-1-1	1,115,886
10	Paul Lawrie	25	22	1-3-0	1,151,434	10	Adam Scott	17	10	1-0-1	1,058,333

Champions Tour

	FINAL 2002	TP	CM	Finish 1-2-3	Earnings		2003 (through Oct. 5)	TP	CM	Finish 1-2-3	Earnings
1	Hale Irwin	27	27	4-6-4	$3,028,304	1	Bruce Lietzke	20	19	2-2-1	$1,571,486
2	Bob Gilder	34	34	4-2-3	2,367,637	2	Tom Watson	12	12	2-4-0	1,534,608
3	Bruce Fleisher	31	30	1-4-2	1,860,534	3	Gil Morgan	23	23	1-4-0	1,454,023
4	Tom Kite	23	23	3-0-1	1,631,930	4	Jim Thorpe	27	27	1-2-2	1,340,281
5	Doug Tewell	27	22	2-2-1	1,579,988	5	Tom Jenkins	27	27	1-1-0	1,252,420
6	Dana Quigley	35	35	2-2-0	1,569,972	6	Larry Nelson	22	22	1-4-2	1,224,973
7	Bruce Lietzke	22	22	3-1-1	1,527,676	7	Dana Quigley	28	28	1-1-1	1,217,142
8	Tom Watson	14	14	1-5-0	1,522,437	8	Bruce Fleisher	27	27	1-3-1	1,197,013
9	Jim Thorpe	32	32	1-1-2	1,511,591	9	Doug Tewell	25	25	1-2-1	1,188,591
10	Morris Hatalsky	24	24	1-3-1	1,391,044	10	Allen Doyle	27	27	1-1-0	1,187,772

LPGA

	FINAL 2002	TP	CM	Finish 1-2-3	Earnings		2003 (through Oct. 5)	TP	CM	Finish 1-2-3	Earnings
1	Annika Sorenstam	23	22	11-3-3	$2,863,904	1	Annika Sorenstam	14	14	5-3-1	$1,695,006
2	Se Ri Pak	24	24	5-1-2	1,722,281	2	Se Ri Pak	21	20	3-4-0	1,346,248
3	Juli Inkster	20	18	2-2-0	1,154,349	3	Grace Park	21	19	1-3-4	1,157,572
4	Mi Hyun Kim	28	28	2-3-1	1,049,993	4	Hee-Won Han	22	21	2-2-2	993,575
5	Karrie Webb	21	20	2-0-3	1,009,760	5	Juli Inkster	18	15	2-1-1	967,145
6	Grace Park	28	25	1-1-3	861,943	6	Candie Kung	25	20	3-1-0	874,108
7	Laura Diaz	25	20	2-0-3	843,790	7	Lorena Ochoa	20	19	0-2-3	756,174
8	Carin Koch	25	24	1-0-1	785,817	8	Rosie Jones	16	16	1-0-2	737,255
9	Rachel Teske	27	23	2-1-0	779,329	9	Beth Daniel	19	17	1-1-1	736,349
10	Rosie Jones	24	22	0-1-3	722,412	10	Karrie Webb	19	17	1-1-1	703,766

1860-2003
Through the Years

SPORTS ALMANAC

Major Golf Championships
MEN
The Masters

The Masters has been played every year (except during World War II) since 1934 at the Augusta National Golf Club in Augusta, Ga. Both the course and the tournament were created by Bobby Jones; (*) indicates playoff winner.

Multiple winners: Jack Nicklaus (6); Arnold Palmer (4); Jimmy Demaret, Nick Faldo, Gary Player, Sam Snead and Tiger Woods (3); Seve Ballesteros, Ben Crenshaw, Ben Hogan, Bernhard Langer, Byron Nelson, Jose Maria Olazabal, Horton Smith and Tom Watson (2).

Year	Winner	Score	Runner-up
1934	Horton Smith	284	Craig Wood (285)
1935	Gene Sarazen*	282	Craig Wood (282)
1936	Horton Smith	285	Harry Cooper (286)
1937	Byron Nelson	283	Ralph Guldahl (285)
1938	Henry Picard	285	Ralph Guldahl & Harry Cooper (287)
1939	Ralph Guldahl	279	Sam Snead (280)
1940	Jimmy Demaret	280	Lloyd Mangrum (284)
1941	Craig Wood	280	Byron Nelson (283)
1942	Byron Nelson*	280	Ben Hogan (280)
1943-45	Not held		World War II
1946	Herman Keiser	282	Ben Hogan (283)
1947	Jimmy Demaret	281	Frank Stranahan & Byron Nelson (283)
1948	Claude Harmon	279	Cary Middlecoff (284)
1949	Sam Snead	282	Lloyd Mangrum & John Bulla (285)
1950	Jimmy Demaret	283	Jim Ferrier (285)
1951	Ben Hogan	280	Skee Riegel (282)
1952	Sam Snead	286	Jack Burke Jr. (290)
1953	Ben Hogan	274	Porky Oliver (279)
1954	Sam Snead*	289	Ben Hogan (289)
1955	Cary Middlecoff	279	Ben Hogan (286)
1956	Jack Burke Jr.	289	Ken Venturi (290)
1957	Doug Ford	283	Sam Snead (286)
1958	Arnold Palmer	284	Doug Ford & Fred Hawkins (285)
1959	Art Wall Jr.	284	Cary Middlecoff (285)
1960	Arnold Palmer	282	Ken Venturi (283)
1961	Gary Player	280	Arnold Palmer & Charles R. Coe (281)
1962	Arnold Palmer*	280	Dow Finsterwald & Gary Player (280)
1963	Jack Nicklaus	286	Tony Lema (287)
1964	Arnold Palmer	276	Jack Nicklaus & Dave Marr (282)
1965	Jack Nicklaus	271	Arnold Palmer & Gary Player (280)
1966	Jack Nicklaus*	288	Gay Brewer & Tommy Jacobs (288)
1967	Gay Brewer Jr.	280	Bobby Nichols (281)
1968	Bob Goalby	277	Roberto DeVicenzo (278)
1969	George Archer	281	Billy Casper, George Knudson & Tom Weiskopf (282)
1970	Billy Casper*	279	Gene Littler (279)
1971	Charles Coody	279	Jack Nicklaus & Johnny Miller (281)
1972	Jack Nicklaus	286	Bruce Crampton, Bobby Mitchell & Tom Weiskopf (289)
1973	Tommy Aaron	283	J.C. Snead (284)
1974	Gary Player	278	Tom Weiskopf, & Dave Stockton (280)
1975	Jack Nicklaus	276	Johnny Miller & Tom Weiskopf (277)
1976	Ray Floyd	271	Ben Crenshaw (279)
1977	Tom Watson	276	Jack Nicklaus (278)
1978	Gary Player	277	Hubert Green, Rod Funseth & Tom Watson (278)
1979	Fuzzy Zoeller*	280	Ed Sneed & Tom Watson (280)
1980	Seve Ballesteros	275	Gibby Gilbert & Jack Newton (279)
1981	Tom Watson	280	Jack Nicklaus & Johnny Miller (282)
1982	Craig Stadler*	284	Dan Pohl (284)
1983	Seve Ballesteros	280	Ben Crenshaw & Tom Kite (284)
1984	Ben Crenshaw	277	Tom Watson (279)
1985	Bernhard Langer	282	Curtis Strange, Seve Ballesteros & Ray Floyd (284)
1986	Jack Nicklaus	279	Greg Norman & Tom Kite (280)
1987	Larry Mize*	285	Seve Ballesteros & Greg Norman (285)
1988	Sandy Lyle	281	Mark Calcavecchia (282)
1989	Nick Faldo*	283	Scott Hoch (283)
1990	Nick Faldo*	278	Ray Floyd (278)
1991	Ian Woosnam	277	J.M. Olazabal (278)
1992	Fred Couples	275	Ray Floyd (277)
1993	Bernhard Langer	277	Chip Beck (281)
1994	J.M. Olazabal	279	Tom Lehman (281)
1995	Ben Crenshaw	274	Davis Love III (275)
1996	Nick Faldo	276	Greg Norman (281)
1997	Tiger Woods	270	Tom Kite (282)
1998	Mark O'Meara	279	Fred Couples & David Duval (280)
1999	J.M. Olazabal	280	Davis Love III (282)
2000	Vijay Singh	278	Ernie Els (281)
2001	Tiger Woods	272	David Duval (274)
2002	Tiger Woods	276	Retief Goosen (279)
2003	Mike Weir*	281	Len Mattiace (281)

The Masters (Cont.)

*PLAYOFFS:

1935: Gene Sarazen (144) def. Craig Wood (149) in 36 holes. **1942:** Byron Nelson (69) def. Ben Hogan (70) in 18 holes.
1954: Sam Snead (70) def. Ben Hogan (71) in 18 holes. **1962:** Arnold Palmer (68) def. Gary Player (71) and Dow Fin-
sterwald (77) in 18 holes. **1966:** Jack Nicklaus (70) def. Tommy Jacobs (72) and Gay Brewer Jr. (78) in 18 holes. **1970:**
Billy Casper (69) def. Gene Littler (74) in 18 holes. **1979:** Fuzzy Zoeller (4-3) def. Ed Sneed (4-4) and Tom Watson (4-4) on
2nd hole of sudden death. **1982:** Craig Stadler (4) def. Dan Pohl (5) on 1st hole of sudden death. **1987:** Larry Mize (4-3)
def. Greg Norman (4-4) and Seve Ballesteros (5) on 2nd hole of sudden death. **1989:** Nick Faldo (5-3) def. Scott Hoch (5-
4) on 2nd hole of sudden death. **1990:** Nick Faldo (4-4) def. Raymond Floyd (4) on 2nd hole of sudden death. **2003:** Mike
Weir (5) def. Len Mattiace (6) on 1st hole of sudden death.

U.S. Open

Played at a different course each year, the U.S. Open was launched by the new U.S. Golf Association in 1895. The Open
was a 36-hole event from 1895-97 and has been 72 holes since then. It switched from a 3-day, 36-hole Saturday finish to 4
days of play in 1965. Note that (*) indicates playoff winner and (a) indicates amateur.

Multiple winners: Willie Anderson, Ben Hogan, Bobby Jones and Jack Nicklaus (4); Hale Irwin (3); Julius Boros, Billy
Casper, Ernie Els, Ralph Guldahl, Walter Hagen, Lee Janzen, John McDermott, Cary Middlecoff, Andy North, Gene Sarazen,
Alex Smith, Payne Stewart, Curtis Strange, Lee Trevino and Tiger Woods (2).

Year	Winner	Score	Runner-up	Course	Location
1895	Horace Rawlins 173		Willie Dunn (175)	Newport GC	Newport, R.I.
1896	James Foulis 152		Horace Rawlins (155)	Shinnecock Hills GC	Southampton, N.Y.
1897	Joe Lloyd 162		Willie Anderson (163)	Chicago GC	Wheaton, Ill.
1898	Fred Herd 328		Alex Smith (335)	Myopia Hunt Club	Hamilton, Mass.
1899	Willie Smith 315		George Low, W.H. Way & Val Fitzjohn (326)	Baltimore CC	Baltimore
1900	Harry Vardon 313		J.H. Taylor (315)	Chicago GC	Wheaton, Ill.
1901	Willie Anderson* 331		Alex Smith (331)	Myopia Hunt Club	Hamilton, Mass.
1902	Laurie Auchterlonie....307		Stewart Gardner (313)	Garden City GC	Garden City, N.Y.
1903	Willie Anderson* 307		David Brown (307)	Baltusrol GC	Springfield, N.J.
1904	Willie Anderson 303		Gil Nicholls (308)	Glen View Club	Golf, Ill.
1905	Willie Anderson 314		Alex Smith (316)	Myopia Hunt Club	Hamilton, Mass.
1906	Alex Smith 295		Willie Smith (302)	Onwentsia Club	Lake Forest, Ill.
1907	Alec Ross 302		Gil Nicholls (304)	Phila. Cricket Club	Chestnut Hill, Pa.
1908	Fred McLeod* 322		Willie Smith (322)	Myopia Hunt Club	Hamilton, Mass.
1909	George Sargent 290		Tom McNamara (294)	Englewood GC	Englewood, N.J.
1910	Alex Smith* 298		Macdonald Smith & John McDermott (298)	Phila. Cricket Club	Chestnut Hill, Pa.
1911	John McDermott* 307		George Simpson & Mike Brady (307)	Chicago GC	Wheaton, Ill.
1912	John McDermott 294		Tom McNamara (296)	CC of Buffalo	Buffalo
1913	a-Francis Ouimet* 304		Harry Vardon & Ted Ray (304)	The Country Club	Brookline, Mass.
1914	Walter Hagen 290		a-Chick Evans (291)	Midlothian CC	Blue Island, Ill.
1915	a-John Travers 297		Tom McNamara (298)	Baltusrol GC	Springfield, N.J.
1916	a-Chick Evans 286		Jock Hutchinson (288)	Minikahda Club	Minneapolis
1917-18 Not held			World War I		
1919	Walter Hagen* 301		Mike Brady (301)	Brae Burn CC	West Newton, Mass.
1920	Ted Ray 295		Jock Hutchinson, Jock Burke, Leo Diegel & Harry Vardon (296)	Inverness Club	Toledo, Ohio
1921	Jim Barnes 289		Walter Hagen & Fred McLeod (298)	Columbia CC	Chevy Chase, Md.
1922	Gene Sarazen 288		a-Bobby Jones & John Black (289)	Skokie CC	Glencoe, Ill.
1923	a-Bobby Jones* 296		Bobby Cruickshank (296)	Inwood CC	Inwood, N.Y.
1924	Cyril Walker 297		a-Bobby Jones (300)	Oakland Hills CC	Birmingham, Mich.
1925	Willie Macfarlane* 291		a-Bobby Jones (291)	Worcester CC	Worcester, Mass.
1926	a-Bobby Jones 293		Joe Turnesa (294)	Scioto CC	Columbus, Ohio
1927	Tommy Armour* 301		Harry Cooper (301)	Oakmont CC	Oakmont, Pa.
1928	Johnny Farrell* 294		a-Bobby Jones (294)	Olympia Fields CC	Matteson, Ill.
1929	a-Bobby Jones* 294		Al Espinosa (294)	Winged Foot CC	Mamaroneck, N.Y.
1930	a-Bobby Jones 287		Macdonald Smith (289)	Interlachen CC	Hopkins, Minn.
1931	Billy Burke* 292		George Von Elm (292)	Inverness Club	Toledo, Ohio
1932	Gene Sarazen 286		Bobby Cruickshank & Phil Perkins (289)	Fresh Meadow CC	Flushing, N.Y.
1933	a-Johnny Goodman 287		Ralph Guldahl (288)	North Shore GC	Glenview, Ill.
1934	Olin Dutra 293		Gene Sarazen (294)	Merion Cricket Club	Ardmore, Pa.
1935	Sam Parks Jr. 299		Jimmy Thomson (301)	Oakmont CC	Oakmont, Pa.
1936	Tony Manero 282		Harry E. Cooper (284)	Baltusrol GC	Springfield, N.J.
1937	Ralph Guldahl 281		Sam Snead (283)	Oakland Hills CC	Birmingham, Mich.
1938	Ralph Guldahl 284		Dick Metz (290)	Cherry Hills CC	Denver
1939	Byron Nelson* 284		Craig Wood & Denny Shute (284)	Philadelphia CC	Philadelphia

Year	Winner	Score	Runner-up	Course	Location
1940	Lawson Little*	287	Gene Sarazen (287)	Canterbury GC	Cleveland
1941	Craig Wood	284	Denny Shute (287)	Colonial Club	Ft. Worth
1942-45	Not held		World War II		
1946	Lloyd Mangrum*	284	Byron Nelson & Vic Ghezzi (284)	Canterbury GC	Cleveland
1947	Lew Worsham*	282	Sam Snead (282)	St. Louis CC	Clayton, Mo.
1948	Ben Hogan	276	Jimmy Demaret (278)	Riviera CC	Los Angeles
1949	Cary Middlecoff	286	Clayton Heafner & Sam Snead (287)	Medinah CC	Medinah, Ill.
1950	Ben Hogan*	287	Lloyd Mangrum & George Fazio (287)	Merion Golf Club	Ardmore, Pa.
1951	Ben Hogan	287	Clayton Heafner (289)	Oakland Hills CC	Birmingham, Mich.
1952	Julius Boros	281	Porky Oliver (285)	Northwood Club	Dallas
1953	Ben Hogan	283	Sam Snead (289)	Oakmont CC	Oakmont, Pa.
1954	Ed Furgol	284	Gene Littler (285)	Baltusrol GC	Springfield, N.J.
1955	Jack Fleck*	287	Ben Hogan (287)	Olympic CC	San Francisco
1956	Cary Middlecoff	281	Ben Hogan & Julius Boros (282)	Oak Hill CC	Rochester, N.Y.
1957	Dick Mayer*	282	Cary Middlecoff (282)	Inverness Club	Toledo, Ohio
1958	Tommy Bolt	283	Gary Player (287)	Southern Hills CC	Tulsa
1959	Billy Casper	282	Bob Rosburg (283)	Winged Foot GC	Mamaroneck, N.Y.
1960	Arnold Palmer	280	Jack Nicklaus (282)	Cherry Hills CC	Denver
1961	Gene Littler	281	Doug Sanders & Bob Goalby (282)	Oakland Hills CC	Birmingham, Mich.
1962	Jack Nicklaus*	283	Arnold Palmer (283)	Oakmont CC	Oakmont, Pa.
1963	Julius Boros*	293	Arnold Palmer & Jacky Cupit (293)	The Country Club	Brookline, Mass.
1964	Ken Venturi	278	Tommy Jacobs (282)	Congressional CC	Bethesda, Md.
1965	Gary Player*	282	Kel Nagle (282)	Bellerive CC	St. Louis
1966	Billy Casper*	278	Arnold Palmer (278)	Olympic CC	San Francisco
1967	Jack Nicklaus	275	Arnold Palmer (279)	Baltusrol GC	Springfield, N.J.
1968	Lee Trevino	275	Jack Nicklaus (279)	Oak Hill CC	Rochester, N.Y.
1969	Orville Moody	281	Al Geiberger, Deane Beman & Bob Rosburg (282)	Champions GC	Houston
1970	Tony Jacklin	281	Dave Hill (288)	Hazeltine National GC	Chaska, Minn.
1971	Lee Trevino*	280	Jack Nicklaus (280)	Merion GC	Ardmore, Pa.
1972	Jack Nicklaus	290	Bruce Crampton (293)	Pebble Beach GL	Pebble Beach, Calif.
1973	Johnny Miller	279	John Schlee (280)	Oakmont CC	Oakmont, Pa.
1974	Hale Irwin	287	Forest Fezler (289)	Winged Foot CC	Mamaroneck, N.Y.
1975	Lou Graham*	287	John Mahaffey (287)	Medinah CC	Medinah, Ill.
1976	Jerry Pate	277	Al Geiberger & Tom Weiskopf (279)	Atlanta AC	Duluth, Ga.
1977	Hubert Green	278	Lou Graham (279)	Southern Hills CC	Tulsa
1978	Andy North	285	Dave Stockton & J.C. Snead (286)	Cherry Hills CC	Denver
1979	Hale Irwin	284	Gary Player & Jerry Pate (286)	Inverness Club	Toledo, Ohio
1980	Jack Nicklaus	272	Isao Aoki (274)	Baltusrol GC	Springfield, N.J.
1981	David Graham	273	George Burns & Bill Rogers (276)	Merion GC	Ardmore, Pa.
1982	Tom Watson	282	Jack Nicklaus (284)	Pebble Beach GL	Pebble Beach, Calif.
1983	Larry Nelson	280	Tom Watson (281)	Oakmont CC	Oakmont, Pa.
1984	Fuzzy Zoeller*	276	Greg Norman (276)	Winged Foot GC	Mamaroneck, N.Y.
1985	Andy North	279	Dave Barr, T.C. Chen & Denis Watson (280)	Oakland Hills CC	Birmingham, Mich.
1986	Ray Floyd	279	Lanny Wadkins & Chip Beck (281)	Shinnecock Hills GC	Southampton, N.Y.
1987	Scott Simpson	277	Tom Watson (278)	Olympic Club	San Francisco
1988	Curtis Strange*	278	Nick Faldo (278)	The Country Club	Brookline, Mass.
1989	Curtis Strange	278	Chip Beck, Ian Woosnam & Mark McCumber (279)	Oak Hill CC	Rochester, N.Y.
1990	Hale Irwin*	280	Mike Donald (280)	Medinah CC	Medinah, Ill.
1991	Payne Stewart*	282	Scott Simpson (282)	Hazeltine National GC	Chaska, Minn.
1992	Tom Kite	285	Jeff Sluman (287)	Pebble Beach GL	Pebble Beach, Calif.
1993	Lee Janzen	272	Payne Stewart (274)	Baltusrol GC	Springfield, N.J.
1994	Ernie Els*	279	Colin Montgomerie (279) & Loren Roberts (279)	Oakmont CC	Oakmont, Pa.
1995	Corey Pavin	280	Greg Norman (282)	Shinnecock Hills GC	Southampton, N.Y.
1996	Steve Jones	278	Davis Love III & Tom Lehman (279)	Oakland Hills CC	Bloomfield Hills, Mich.
1997	Ernie Els	276	Colin Montgomerie (277)	Congressional CC	Bethesda, Md.

U.S. Open (Cont.)

Year	Winner	Score	Runner-up	Course	Location
1998	Lee Janzen	280	Payne Stewart (281)	Olympic Club	San Francisco
1999	Payne Stewart	279	Phil Mickelson (280)	Pinehurst CC	Pinehurst, N.C.
2000	Tiger Woods	272	Miguel Angel Jimenez & Ernie Els (287)	Pebble Beach GL	Pebble Beach, Calif.
2001	Retief Goosen*	276	Mark Brooks (276)	Southern Hills CC	Tulsa
2002	Tiger Woods	277	Phil Mickelson (280)	Bethpage State Park (Black Course)	Farmingdale, N.Y.
2003	Jim Furyk	272	Stephen Leaney (275)	Olympia Fields CC	Olympia Fields, Ill.

*PLAYOFFS:

1901: Willie Anderson (85) def. Alex Smith (86) in 18 holes. **1903:** Willie Anderson (82) def. David Brown (84) in 18 holes. **1908:** Fred McLeod (77) def. Willie Smith (83) in 18 holes. **1910:** Alex Smith (71) def. John McDermott (75) & Macdonald Smith (77) in 18 holes. **1911:** John McDermott (80) def. Mike Brady (82) & George Simpson (85) in 18 holes. **1913:** Francis Ouimet (72) def. Harry Vardon (77) & Edward Ray (78) in 18 holes. **1919:** Walter Hagen (77) def. Mike Brady (78) in 18 holes. **1923:** Bobby Jones (76) def. Bobby Cruickshank (78) in 18 holes. **1925:** Willie Macfarlane (75-72—147) def. Bobby Jones (75-73—148) in 36 holes. **1927:** Tommy Armour (76) def. Harry Cooper (79) in 18 holes. **1928:** Johnny Farrell (70-73—143) def. Bobby Jones (73-71—144) in 36 holes. **1929:** Bobby Jones (141) def. Al Espinosa (164) in 36 holes. **1931:** Billy Burke (149-148) def. George Von Elm (149-149) in 72 holes. **1939:** Byron Nelson (68-70) def. Craig Wood (68-73) and Denny Shute (76) in 36 holes. **1940:** Lawson Little (70) def. Gene Sarazen (73) in 18 holes. **1946:** Lloyd Mangrum (72-72—144) def. Byron Nelson (72-73—145) and Vic Ghezzi (72-73—145) in 36 holes. **1947:** Lew Worsham (69) def. Sam Snead (70) in 18 holes. **1950:** Ben Hogan (69) def. Lloyd Mangrum (73) & George Fazio (75) in 18 holes. **1955:** Jack Fleck (69) def. Ben Hogan (72) in 18 holes. **1957:** Dick Mayer (72) def. Cary Middlecoff (79) in 18 holes. **1962:** Jack Nicklaus (71) def. Arnold Palmer (74) in 18 holes. **1963:** Julius Boros (70) def. Jacky Cupit (73) & Arnold Palmer (76) in 18 holes. **1965:** Gary Player (71) def. Kel Nagle (74) in 18 holes. **1966:** Billy Casper (69) def. Arnold Palmer (73) in 18 holes. **1971:** Lee Trevino (68) def. Jack Nicklaus (71) in 18 holes. **1975:** Lou Graham (71) def. John Mahaffey (73) in 18 holes. **1984:** Fuzzy Zoeller (67) def. Greg Norman (75) in 18 holes. **1988:** Curtis Strange (71) def. Nick Faldo (75) in 18 holes. **1990:** Hale Irwin (74-3) def. Mike Donald (74-4) on 1st hole of sudden death after 18 holes. **1991:** Payne Stewart (75) def. Scott Simpson (77) in 18 holes. **1994:** Ernie Els (74-4-4) def. Loren Roberts (74-4-5) and Colin Montgomerie (78) on 2nd hole of sudden death after 18 holes; **2001:** Goosen (70) def. Brooks (72) in 18 holes.

British Open

The oldest of the Majors, the Open began in 1860 to determine "the champion golfer of the world." While only professional golfers participated in the first year of the tournament, amateurs have been invited ever since. Competition was extended from 36 to 72 holes in 1892. Conducted by the Royal and Ancient Golf Club of St. Andrews, the Open is rotated among select golf courses in England and Scotland. Note that (*) indicates playoff winner and (a) indicates amateur winner.

Multiple winners: Harry Vardon (6); James Braid, J.H. Taylor, Peter Thomson and Tom Watson (5); Walter Hagen, Bobby Locke, Tom Morris Sr., Tom Morris Jr. and Willie Park (4); Jamie Anderson, Seve Ballesteros, Henry Cotton, Nick Faldo, Bob Ferguson, Bobby Jones, Jack Nicklaus and Gary Player (3); Harold Hilton, Bob Martin, Greg Norman, Arnold Palmer, Willie Park Jr. and Lee Trevino (2).

Year	Winner	Score	Runner-up	Course	Location
1860	Willie Park	174	Tom Morris Sr. (176)	Prestwick Club	Ayrshire, Scotland
1861	Tom Morris Sr.	163	Willie Park (167)	Prestwick Club	Ayrshire, Scotland
1862	Tom Morris Sr.	163	Willie Park (176)	Prestwick Club	Ayrshire, Scotland
1863	Willie Park	168	Tom Morris Sr. (170)	Prestwick Club	Ayrshire, Scotland
1864	Tom Morris Sr.	167	Andrew Strath (169)	Prestwick Club	Ayrshire, Scotland
1865	Andrew Strath	162	Willie Park (164)	Prestwick Club	Ayrshire, Scotland
1866	Willie Park	169	David Park (171)	Prestwick Club	Ayrshire, Scotland
1867	Tom Morris Sr.	170	Willie Park (172)	Prestwick Club	Ayrshire, Scotland
1868	Tom Morris Jr.	157	Robert Andrew (159)	Prestwick Club	Ayrshire, Scotland
1869	Tom Morris Jr.	154	Tom Morris Sr. (157)	Prestwick Club	Ayrshire, Scotland
1870	Tom Morris Jr.	149	Bob Kirk (161)	Prestwick Club	Ayrshire, Scotland
1871	Not held				
1872	Tom Morris Jr.	166	David Strath (169)	Prestwick Club	Ayrshire, Scotland
1873	Tom Kidd	179	Jamie Anderson (180)	St. Andrews	St. Andrews, Scotland
1874	Mungo Park	159	Tom Morris Jr. (161)	Musselburgh	Musselburgh, Scotland
1875	Willie Park	166	Bob Martin (168)	Prestwick Club	Ayrshire, Scotland
1876	Bob Martin*	176	David Strath (176)	St. Andrews	St. Andrews, Scotland
1877	Jamie Anderson	160	Bob Pringle (162)	Musselburgh	Musselburgh, Scotland
1878	Jamie Anderson	157	Bob Kirk (159)	Prestwick Club	Ayrshire, Scotland
1879	Jamie Anderson	169	Andrew Kirkaldy & James Allan (172)	St. Andrews	St. Andrews, Scotland
1880	Bob Ferguson	162	Peter Paxton (167)	Musselburgh	Musselburgh, Scotland
1881	Bob Ferguson	170	Jamie Anderson (173)	Prestwick Club	Ayrshire, Scotland
1882	Bob Ferguson	171	Willie Fernie (174)	St. Andrews	St. Andrews, Scotland
1883	Willie Fernie*	159	Bob Ferguson (159)	Musselburgh	Musselburgh, Scotland
1884	Jack Simpson	160	Douglas Rolland & Willie Fernie (164)	Prestwick Club	Ayrshire, Scotland
1885	Bob Martin	171	Archie Simpson (172)	St. Andrews	St. Andrews, Scotland
1886	David Brown	157	Willie Campbell (159)	Musselburgh	Musselburgh, Scotland
1887	Willie Park Jr.	161	Bob Martin (162)	Prestwick Club	Ayrshire, Scotland
1888	Jack Burns	171	David Anderson & Ben Sayers (172)	St. Andrews	St. Andrews, Scotland
1889	Willie Park Jr.*	155	Andrew Kirkaldy (155)	Musselburgh	Musselburgh, Scotland

Year	Winner	Score	Runner-up	Course	Location
1890	a-John Ball	164	Willie Fernie (167) & A. Simpson (167)	Prestwick Club	Ayrshire, Scotland
1891	Hugh Kirkaldy	166	Andrew Kirkaldy & Willie Fernie (168)	St. Andrews	St. Andrews, Scotland
1892	a-Harold Hilton	305	John Ball, Sandy Herd & Hugh Kirkaldy (308)	Muirfield	Gullane, Scotland
1893	Willie Auchterlonie	322	Johnny Laidley (324)	Prestwick Club	Ayrshire, Scotland
1894	J.H. Taylor	326	Douglas Rolland (331)	Royal St. George's	Sandwich, England
1895	J.H. Taylor	322	Sandy Herd (326)	St. Andrews	St. Andrews, Scotland
1896	Harry Vardon*	316	J.H. Taylor (316)	Muirfield	Gullane, Scotland
1897	a-Harold Hilton	314	James Braid (315)	Hoylake	Hoylake, England
1898	Harry Vardon	307	Willie Park Jr. (308)	Prestwick Club	Ayrshire, Scotland
1899	Harry Vardon	310	Jack White (315)	Royal St. George's	Sandwich, England
1900	J.H. Taylor	309	Harry Vardon (317)	St. Andrews	St. Andrews, Scotland
1901	James Braid	309	Harry Vardon (312)	Muirfield	Gullane, Scotland
1902	Sandy Herd	307	Harry Vardon (308)	Hoylake	Hoylake, England
1903	Harry Vardon	300	Tom Vardon (306)	Prestwick Club	Ayrshire, Scotland
1904	Jack White	296	James Braid (297)	Royal St. George's	Sandwich, England
1905	James Braid	318	J.H. Taylor (323) & Rowland Jones (323)	St. Andrews	St. Andrews, Scotland
1906	James Braid	300	J.H. Taylor (304)	Muirfield	Gullane, Scotland
1907	Arnaud Massy	312	J.H. Taylor (314)	Hoylake	Hoylake, England
1908	James Braid	291	Tom Ball (299)	Prestwick Club	Ayrshire, Scotland
1909	J.H. Taylor	295	James Braid (299)	Deal	Deal, England
1910	James Braid	299	Sandy Herd (303)	St. Andrews	St. Andrews, Scotland
1911	Harry Vardon*	303	Arnaud Massy (303)	Royal St. George's	Sandwich, England
1912	Ted Ray	295	Harry Vardon (299)	Muirfield	Gullane, Scotland
1913	J.H. Taylor	304	Ted Ray (312)	Hoylake	Hoylake, England
1914	Harry Vardon	306	J.H. Taylor (309)	Prestwick Club	Ayrshire, Scotland
1915-19	Not held		World War I		
1920	George Duncan	303	Sandy Herd (305)	Deal	Deal, England
1921	Jock Hutchison*	296	Roger Wethered (296)	St. Andrews	St. Andrews, Scotland
1922	Walter Hagen	300	George Duncan & Jim Barnes (301)	Royal St. George's	Sandwich, England
1923	Arthur Havers	295	Walter Hagen (296)	Royal Troon	Troon, Scotland
1924	Walter Hagen	301	Ernest Whitcombe (302)	Hoylake	Hoylake, England
1925	Jim Barnes	300	Archie Compston & Ted Ray (301)	Prestwick Club	Ayrshire, Scotland
1926	a-Bobby Jones	291	Al Watrous (293)	Royal Lytham	Lytham, England
1927	a-Bobby Jones	285	Aubrey Boomer (291)	St. Andrews	St. Andrews, Scotland
1928	Walter Hagen	292	Gene Sarazen (294)	Royal St. George's	Sandwich, England
1929	Walter Hagen	292	Johnny Farrell (298)	Muirfield	Gullane, Scotland
1930	a-Bobby Jones	291	Macdonald Smith & Leo Diegel (293)	Hoylake	Hoylake, England
1931	Tommy Armour	296	Jose Jurado (297)	Carnoustie	Carnoustie, Scotland
1932	Gene Sarazen	283	Macdonald Smith (288)	Prince's	Prince's, England
1933	Denny Shute*	292	Craig Wood (292)	St. Andrews	St. Andrews, Scotland
1934	Henry Cotton	283	Sid Brews (288)	Royal St. George's	Sandwich, England
1935	Alf Perry	283	Alf Padgham (287)	Muirfield	Gullane, Scotland
1936	Alf Padgham	287	Jimmy Adams (288)	Hoylake	Hoylake, England
1937	Henry Cotton	290	Reg Whitcombe (292)	Carnoustie	Carnoustie, Scotland
1938	Reg Whitcombe	295	Jimmy Adams (297)	Royal St. George's	Sandwich, England
1939	Dick Burton	290	Johnny Bulla (292)	St. Andrews	St. Andrews, Scotland
1940-45	Not held		World War II		
1946	Sam Snead	290	Bobby Locke (294) & Johnny Bulla (294)	St. Andrews	St. Andrews, Scotland
1947	Fred Daly	293	Frank Stranahan & Reg Horne (294)	Hoylake	Hoylake, England
1948	Henry Cotton	284	Fred Daly (289)	Muirfield	Gullane, Scotland
1949	Bobby Locke*	283	Harry Bradshaw (283)	Royal St. George's	Sandwich, England
1950	Bobby Locke	279	Roberto de Vicenzo (281)	Royal Troon	Troon, Scotland
1951	Max Faulkner	285	Tony Cerda (287)	Royal Portrush	Portrush, Ireland
1952	Bobby Locke	287	Peter Thomson (288)	Royal Lytham	Lytham, England
1953	Ben Hogan	282	Frank Stranahan, Dai Rees, Tony Cerda & Peter Thomson (286)	Carnoustie	Carnoustie, Scotland
1954	Peter Thomson	283	Sid Scott, Dai Rees & Bobby Locke (284)	Royal Birkdale	Southport, England
1955	Peter Thomson	281	Johny Fallon (283)	St. Andrews	St. Andrews, Scotland
1956	Peter Thomson	286	Flory Van Donck (289)	Hoylake	Hoylake, England
1957	Bobby Locke	279	Peter Thomson (282)	St. Andrews	St. Andrews, Scotland
1958	Peter Thomson*	278	Dave Thomas (278)	Royal Lytham	Lytham, England

British Open (Cont.)

Year	Winner	Score	Runner-up	Course	Location
1959	Gary Player	284	Flory Van Donck & Fred Bullock (286)	Muirfield	Gullane, Scotland
1960	Kel Nagle	278	Arnold Palmer (279)	St. Andrews	St. Andrews, Scotland
1961	Arnold Palmer	284	Dai Rees (285)	Royal Birkdale	Southport, England
1962	Arnold Palmer	276	Kel Nagle (282)	Royal Troon	Troon, Scotland
1963	Bob Charles*	277	Phil Rodgers (277)	Royal Lytham	Lytham, England
1964	Tony Lema	279	Jack Nicklaus (284)	St. Andrews	St. Andrews, Scotland
1965	Peter Thomson	285	Christy O'Connor & Brian Huggett (287)	Royal Birkdale	Southport, England
1966	Jack Nicklaus	282	Doug Sanders & Dave Thomas (283)	Muirfield	Gullane, Scotland
1967	Roberto de Vicenzo	278	Jack Nicklaus (280)	Hoylake	Hoylake, England
1968	Gary Player	289	Jack Nicklaus & Bob Charles (291)	Carnoustie	Carnoustie, Scotland
1969	Tony Jacklin	280	Bob Charles (282)	Royal Lytham	Lytham, England
1970	Jack Nicklaus*	283	Doug Sanders (283)	St. Andrews	St. Andrews, Scotland
1971	Lee Trevino	278	Lu Liang Huan (279)	Royal Birkdale	Southport, England
1972	Lee Trevino	278	Jack Nicklaus (279)	Muirfield	Gullane, Scotland
1973	Tom Weiskopf	276	Johnny Miller & Neil Coles (279)	Royal Troon	Troon, Scotland
1974	Gary Player	282	Peter Oosterhuis (286)	Royal Lytham	Lytham, England
1975	Tom Watson*	279	Jack Newton (279)	Carnoustie	Carnoustie, Scotland
1976	Johnny Miller	279	Seve Ballesteros & Jack Nicklaus (285)	Royal Birkdale	Southport, England
1977	Tom Watson	268	Jack Nicklaus (269)	Turnberry	Turnberry, Scotland
1978	Jack Nicklaus	281	Tom Kite, Ray Floyd, Ben Crenshaw & Simon Owen (283)	St. Andrews	St. Andrews, Scotland
1979	Seve Ballesteros	283	Jack Nicklaus & Ben Crenshaw (286)	Royal Lytham	Lytham, England
1980	Tom Watson	271	Lee Trevino (275)	Muirfield	Gullane, Scotland
1981	Bill Rogers	276	Bernhard Langer (280)	Royal St. George's	Sandwich, England
1982	Tom Watson	284	Peter Oosterhuis & Nick Price (285)	Royal Troon	Troon, Scotland
1983	Tom Watson	275	Hale Irwin & Andy Bean (276)	Royal Birkdale	Southport, England
1984	Seve Ballesteros	276	Bernhard Langer & Tom Watson (278)	St. Andrews	St. Andrews, Scotland
1985	Sandy Lyle	282	Payne Stewart (283)	Royal St. George's	Sandwich, England
1986	Greg Norman	280	Gordon J. Brand (285)	Turnberry	Turnberry, Scotland
1987	Nick Faldo	279	Paul Azinger & Rodger Davis (280)	Muirfield	Gullane, Scotland
1988	Seve Ballesteros	273	Nick Price (275)	Royal Lytham	Lytham, England
1989	Mark Calcavecchia*	275	Greg Norman & Wayne Grady (275)	Royal Troon	Troon, Scotland
1990	Nick Faldo	270	Payne Stewart & Mark McNulty (275)	St. Andrews	St. Andrews, Scotland
1991	Ian Baker-Finch	272	Mike Harwood (274)	Royal Birkdale	Southport, England
1992	Nick Faldo	272	John Cook (273)	Muirfield	Gullane, Scotland
1993	Greg Norman	267	Nick Faldo (269)	Royal St. George's	Sandwich, England
1994	Nick Price	268	Jesper Parnevik (269)	Turnberry	Turnberry, Scotland
1995	John Daly*	282	Costantino Rocca (282)	St. Andrews	St. Andrews, Scotland
1996	Tom Lehman	271	Mark McCumber & Ernie Els (273)	Royal Lytham	Lytham, England
1997	Justin Leonard	272	Jesper Parnevik & Darren Clarke (275)	Royal Troon	Troon, Scotland
1998	Mark O'Meara*	280	Brian Watts (280)	Royal Birkdale	Southport, England
1999	Paul Lawrie*	290	Justin Leonard & Jean Van de Velde (290)	Carnoustie	Carnoustie, Scotland
2000	Tiger Woods	269	Thomas Bjorn & Ernie Els (277)	St. Andrews	St. Andrews, Scotland
2001	David Duval	274	Niclas Fasth (277)	Royal Lytham	Lytham, England
2002	Ernie Els*	278	Thomas Levet, Stuart Appleby & Steve Elkington (278)	Muirfield	Gullane, Scotland
2003	Ben Curtis	283	Vijay Singh & Thomas Bjorn (284)	Royal St. George's	Sandwich, England

*PLAYOFFS:

1876: Bob Martin awarded title when David Strath refused playoff. **1883:** Willie Fernie (158) def. Robert Ferguson (159) in 36 holes. **1889:** Willie Park Jr. (158) def. Andrew Kirkaldy (163) in 36 holes. **1896:** Harry Vardon (157) def. John H. Taylor (161) in 36 holes. **1911:** Harry Vardon won when Arnaud Massy conceded at 35th hole. **1921:** Jock Hutchison (150) def. Roger Wethered (159) in 36 holes. **1933:** Denny Shute (149) def. Craig Wood (154) in 36 holes. **1949:** Bobby Locke (135) def. Harry Bradshaw (147) in 36 holes. **1958:** Peter Thomson (139) def. Dave Thomas (143) in 36 holes. **1963:** Bob Charles (140) def. Phil Rogers (148) in 36 holes. **1970:** Jack Nicklaus (72) def. Doug Sanders (73) in 18 holes. **1975:** Tom Watson (71) def. Jack Newton (72) in 18 holes. **1989:** Mark Calcavecchia (4-3-3-3—13) def. Wayne Grady (4-4-4-4—16) and Greg Norman (3-3-4) in 4 holes. **1995:** John Daly (3-4-4-4—15) def. Costantino Rocca (4-5-7-3—19) in 4 holes. **1998:** Mark O'Meara (4-4-5-4—17) def. Brian Watts (5-4-5-5—19) in 4 holes. **1999:** Paul Lawrie (5-4-3-3—15) def. Justin Leonard (5-4-4-5—18) and Jean Van de Velde (6-4-3-5—18) in 4 holes. **2002:** Els (4-3-5-4—16) and Levet (4-2-5-5—16) remained tied after a four-hole playoff that also included Appleby (4-4-4-5—17) and Elkington (5-3-4-5—17). The pair moved on to sudden death, where Els (4) def. Levet (5) on the 1st hole.

PGA Championship

The PGA Championship began in 1916 as a professional golfers match play tournament, but switched to stroke play in 1958. Conducted by the PGA of America, the tournament is played on a different course each year.

Multiple winners: Walter Hagen and Jack Nicklaus (5); Gene Sarazen and Sam Snead (3); Jim Barnes, Leo Diegel, Ray Floyd, Ben Hogan, Byron Nelson, Larry Nelson, Gary Player, Nick Price, Paul Runyan, Denny Shute, Dave Stockton, Lee Trevino and Tiger Woods (2).

Year	Winner	Score	Runner-up	Course	Location
1916	Jim Barnes	1-up	Jock Hutchison	Siwanoy CC	Bronxville, N.Y.
1917-18 Not held			World War I		
1919	Jim Barnes	6 & 5	Fred McLeod	Engineers CC	Roslyn, N.Y.
1920	Jock Hutchison	1-up	J. Douglas Edgar	Flossmoor CC	Flossmoor, Ill.
1921	Walter Hagen	3 & 2	Jim Barnes	Inwood CC	Inwood, N.Y.
1922	Gene Sarazen	4 & 3	Emmet French	Oakmont CC	Oakmont, Pa.
1923	Gene Sarazen*	1-up/38	Walter Hagen	Pelham CC	Pelham, N.Y.
1924	Walter Hagen	2-up	Jim Barnes	French Lick CC	French Lick, Ind.
1925	Walter Hagen	6 & 5	Bill Mehlhorn	Olympia Fields CC	Matteson, Ill.
1926	Walter Hagen	5 & 3	Leo Diegel	Salisbury GC	Westbury, N.Y.
1927	Walter Hagen	1-up	Joe Turnesa	Cedar Crest CC	Dallas
1928	Leo Diegel	6 & 5	Al Espinosa	Five Farms CC	Baltimore
1929	Leo Diegel	6 & 4	John Farrell	Hillcrest CC	Los Angeles
1930	Tommy Armour	1-up	Gene Sarazen	Fresh Meadow CC	Flushing, N.Y.
1931	Tom Creavy	2 & 1	Denny Shute	Wannamoisett CC	Rumford, R.I.
1932	Olin Dutra	4 & 3	Frank Walsh	Keller GC	St. Paul, Minn.
1933	Gene Sarazen	5 & 4	Willie Goggin	Blue Mound CC	Milwaukee
1934	Paul Runyan*	1-up/38	Craig Wood	Park CC	Williamsville, N.Y.
1935	Johnny Revolta	5 & 4	Tommy Armour	Twin Hills CC	Oklahoma City
1936	Denny Shute	3 & 2	Jimmy Thomson	Pinehurst CC	Pinehurst, N.C.
1937	Denny Shute*	1-up/37	Harold McSpaden	Pittsburgh FC	Aspinwall, Pa.
1938	Paul Runyan	8 & 7	Sam Snead	Shawnee CC	Shawnee-on-Del., Pa.
1939	Henry Picard*	1-up/37	Byron Nelson	Pomonok CC	Flushing, N.Y.
1940	Byron Nelson	1-up	Sam Snead	Hershey CC	Hershey, Pa.
1941	Vic Ghezzi*	1-up/38	Byron Nelson	Cherry Hills CC	Denver
1942	Sam Snead	2 & 1	Jim Turnesa	Seaview CC	Atlantic City, N.J.
1943	Not held		World War II		
1944	Bob Hamilton	1-up	Byron Nelson	Manito G & CC	Spokane, Wash.
1945	Byron Nelson	4 & 3	Sam Byrd	Morraine CC	Dayton, Ohio
1946	Ben Hogan	6 & 4	Porky Oliver	Portland GC	Portland, Ore.
1947	Jim Ferrier	2 & 1	Chick Harbert	Plum Hollow CC	Detroit
1948	Ben Hogan	7 & 6	Mike Turnesa	Norwood Hills CC	St. Louis
1949	Sam Snead	3 & 2	John Palmer	Hermitage CC	Richmond, Va.
1950	Chandler Harper	4 & 3	Henry Williams Jr.	Scioto CC	Columbus, Ohio
1951	Sam Snead	7 & 6	Walter Burkemo	Oakmont CC	Oakmont, Pa.
1952	Jim Turnesa	1-up	Chick Harbert	Big Spring CC	Louisville

Major Championship Leaders

Through 2003; active PGA players in **bold** type.

	US Open	British Open	PGA	Masters	US Am	British Am	Total
Jack Nicklaus	4	3	5	6	2	0	**20**
Bobby Jones	4	3	0	0	5	1	**13**
Walter Hagen	2	4	5	0	0	0	**11**
Tiger Woods	2	1	2	3	3	0	**11**
Ben Hogan	4	1	2	2	0	0	**9**
Gary Player	1	3	2	3	0	0	**9**
John Ball	0	1	0	0	0	8	**9**
Arnold Palmer	1	2	0	4	1	0	**8**
Tom Watson	1	5	0	2	0	0	**8**
Harold Hilton	0	2	0	0	1	4	**7**
Gene Sarazen	2	1	3	1	0	0	**7**
Sam Snead	0	1	3	3	0	0	**7**
Harry Vardon	1	6	0	0	0	0	**7**

Tournaments: U.S. Open, British Open, PGA Championship, Masters, U.S. Amateur and British Amateur.

PGA Championship (Cont.)

Year	Winner	Score	Runner-up	Course	Location
1953	Walter Burkemo	2 & 1	Felice Torza	Birmingham CC	Birmingham, Mich.
1954	Chick Harbert	4 & 3	Walter Burkemo	Keller GC	St. Paul, Minn.
1955	Doug Ford	4 & 3	Cary Middlecoff	Meadowbrook CC	Detroit
1956	Jack Burke	3 & 2	Ted Kroll	Blue Hill CC	Boston
1957	Lionel Hebert	2 & 1	Dow Finsterwald	Miami Valley GC	Dayton, Ohio
1958	Dow Finsterwald	276	Billy Casper (278)	Llanerch CC	Havertown, Pa.
1959	Bob Rosburg	277	Jerry Barber & Doug Sanders (278)	Minneapolis GC	St. Louis Park, Minn.
1960	Jay Hebert	281	Jim Ferrier (282)	Firestone CC	Akron, Ohio
1961	Jerry Barber**	277	Don January (277)	Olympia Fields CC	Matteson, Ill.
1962	Gary Player	278	Bob Goalby (279)	Aronimink GC	Newtown Square, Pa.
1963	Jack Nicklaus	279	Dave Ragan (281)	Dallas AC	Dallas
1964	Bobby Nichols	271	Jack Nicklaus & Arnold Palmer (274)	Columbus CC	Columbus, Ohio
1965	Dave Marr	280	Jack Nicklaus & Billy Casper (282)	Laurel Valley GC	Ligonier, Pa.
1966	Al Geiberger	280	Dudley Wysong (284)	Firestone CC	Akron, Ohio
1967	Don January**	281	Don Massengale (281)	Columbine CC	Littleton, Colo.
1968	Julius Boros	281	Arnold Palmer & Bob Charles (282)	Pecan Valley CC	San Antonio
1969	Ray Floyd	276	Gary Player (277)	NCR GC	Dayton, Ohio
1970	Dave Stockton	279	Arnold Palmer & Bob Murphy (281)	Southern Hills CC	Tulsa
1971	Jack Nicklaus	281	Billy Casper (283)	PGA National GC	Palm Beach Gardens, Fla.
1972	Gary Player	281	Jim Jamieson & Tommy Aaron (283)	Oakland Hills GC	Birmingham, Mich.
1973	Jack Nicklaus	277	Bruce Crampton (281)	Canterbury GC	Cleveland
1974	Lee Trevino	276	Jack Nicklaus (277)	Tanglewood GC	Winston-Salem, N.C.
1975	Jack Nicklaus	276	Bruce Crampton (278)	Firestone CC	Akron, Ohio
1976	Dave Stockton	281	Don January & Ray Floyd (282)	Congressional CC	Bethesda, Md.
1977	Lanny Wadkins**	282	Gene Littler (282)	Pebble Beach GL	Pebble Beach, Calif.
1978	John Mahaffey**	276	Jerry Pate & Tom Watson (276)	Oakmont CC	Oakmont, Pa.
1979	David Graham**	272	Ben Crenshaw (272)	Oakland Hills CC	Birmingham, Mich.
1980	Jack Nicklaus	274	Andy Bean (281)	Oak Hill CC	Rochester, N.Y.
1981	Larry Nelson	273	Fuzzy Zoeller (277)	Atlanta AC	Duluth, Ga.
1982	Ray Floyd	272	Lanny Wadkins (275)	Southern Hills CC	Tulsa
1983	Hal Sutton	274	Jack Nicklaus (275)	Riviera CC	Los Angeles
1984	Lee Trevino	273	Lanny Wadkins & Gary Player (277)	Shoal Creek	Birmingham, Ala.
1985	Hubert Green	278	Lee Trevino (280)	Cherry Hills CC	Denver
1986	Bob Tway	276	Greg Norman (278)	Inverness Club	Toledo, Ohio
1987	Larry Nelson**	287	Lanny Wadkins (287)	PGA National	Palm Beach Gardens, Fla.
1988	Jeff Sluman	272	Paul Azinger 275)	Oak Tree GC	Edmond, Okla.
1989	Payne Stewart	276	Andy Bean, Mike Reid & Curtis Strange (277)	Kemper Lakes GC	Hawthorn Woods, Ill.
1990	Wayne Grady	282	Fred Couples (285)	Shoal Creek	Birmingham, Ala.
1991	John Daly	276	Bruce Lietzke (278)	Crooked Stick GC	Carmel, Ind.
1992	Nick Price	278	Nick Faldo, John Cook, Jim Gallagher & Gene Sauers (281)	Bellerive CC	St. Louis
1993	Paul Azinger**	272	Greg Norman (272)	Inverness Club	Toledo, Ohio
1994	Nick Price	269	Corey Pavin (275)	Southern Hills CC	Tulsa
1995	Steve Elkington**	267	Colin Montgomerie (267)	Riviera CC	Pacific Palisades, Calif.
1996	Mark Brooks**	277	Kenny Perry (277)	Valhalla GC	Louisville, Ky.
1997	Davis Love III	269	Justin Leonard (274)	Winged Foot GC	Mamaroneck, N.Y.
1998	Vijay Singh	271	Steve Stricker (273)	Sahalee CC	Redmond, Wash.
1999	Tiger Woods	277	Sergio Garcia (278)	Medinah CC	Medinah, Ill.
2000	Tiger Woods**	270	Bob May (270)	Valhalla GC	Louisville, Ky.
2001	David Toms	265	Phil Mickelson (266)	Atlanta AC	Duluth, Ga.
2002	Rich Beem	278	Tiger Woods (279)	Hazeltine National GC	Chaska, Minn.
2003	Shaun Micheel	276	Chad Campbell (278)	Oak Hill CC	Rochester, N.Y.

*While the PGA Championship was a match play tournament from 1916-57, the two finalists played 36 holes for the title. In the five years that a playoff was necessary, the match was decided on the 37th or 38th hole.

PLAYOFFS:

1961: Jerry Barber (67) def. Don January (68) in 18 holes. **1967:** Don January (69) def. Don Massengale (71) in 18 holes. **1977:** Lanny Wadkins (4-4-4) def. Gene Littler (4-4-5) on 3rd hole of sudden death. **1978:** John Mahaffey (4-3) def. Jerry Pate (4-4) and Tom Watson (4-5) on 2nd hole of sudden death. **1979:** David Graham (4-4-2) def. Ben Crenshaw (4-4-4) on 3rd hole of sudden death. **1987:** Larry Nelson (4) def. Lanny Wadkins (5) on 1st hole of sudden death. **1993:** Paul Azinger

(4-4) def. Greg Norman (4-5) on 2nd hole of sudden death. **1995:** Steve Elkington (3) def. Colin Montgomerie (4) on 1st hole of sudden death. **1996:** Mark Brooks (4) def. Kenny Perry (5) on 1st hole of sudden death. **2000:** Tiger Woods (3-4-5–12) won a three-hole playoff over Bob May (4-4-5–13).

Grand Slam Summary

The only golfer ever to win a recognized Grand Slam—four major championships in a single season—was Bobby Jones in 1930. That year, Jones won the U.S. and British Opens as well as the U.S. and British Amateurs.

The men's professional Grand Slam—the Masters, U.S. Open, British Open and PGA Championship—did not gain acceptance until 30 years later when Arnold Palmer won the 1960 Masters and U.S. Open. The media wrote that the popular Palmer was chasing the "new" Grand Slam and would have to win the British Open and the PGA to claim it. He did not, but then nobody has before or since.

Three wins in one year (2): Ben Hogan (1953) and Tiger Woods (2000). **Two wins in one year** (20): Jack Nicklaus (5 times); Ben Hogan, Arnold Palmer, Tom Watson and Tiger Woods (twice); Nick Faldo, Mark O'Meara, Gary Player, Nick Price, Sam Snead, Lee Trevino and Craig Wood (once).

Year	Masters	US Open	Brit. Open	PGA	Year	Masters	US Open	Brit. Open	PGA
1934	H. Smith	Dutra	Cotton	Runyan	1964	Palmer	Venturi	Lema	Nichols
1935	Sarazen	Parks	Perry	Revolta	1965	Nicklaus	Player	Thomson	Marr
1936	H. Smith	Manero	Padgham	Shute	1966	Nicklaus	Casper	Nicklaus	Geiberger
1937	B. Nelson	Guldahl	Cotton	Shute	1967	Brewer Jr.	Nicklaus	De Vicenzo	January
1938	Picard	Guldahl	Whitcombe	Runyan	1968	Goalby	Trevino	Player	Boros
1939	Guldahl	B. Nelson	Burton	Picard	1969	Archer	Moody	Jacklin	Floyd
1940	Demaret	Little	—	B. Nelson	1970	Casper	Jacklin	Nicklaus	Stockton
1941	Wood	Wood	—	Ghezzi	1971	Coody	Trevino	Trevino	Nicklaus
1942	B. Nelson	—	—	Snead	1972	Nicklaus	Nicklaus	Trevino	Player
1943	—	—	—	—	1973	Aaron	J. Miller	Weiskopf	Nicklaus
1944	—	—	—	Hamilton	1974	Player	Irwin	Player	Trevino
1945	—	—	—	B. Nelson	1975	Nicklaus	L. Graham	T. Watson	Nicklaus
1946	Keiser	Mangrum	Snead	Hogan	1976	Floyd	J. Pate	Miller	Stockton
1947	Demaret	Worsham	F. Daly	Ferrier	1977	T. Watson	H. Green	T. Watson	L. Wadkins
1948	Harmon	Hogan	Cotton	Hogan	1978	Player	North	Nicklaus	Mahaffey
1949	Snead	Middlecoff	Locke	Snead	1979	Zoeller	Irwin	Ballesteros	D. Graham
1950	Demaret	Hogan	Locke	Harper	1980	Ballesteros	Nicklaus	T. Watson	Nicklaus
1951	Hogan	Hogan	Faulkner	Snead	1981	T. Watson	D. Graham	Rogers	L. Nelson
1952	Snead	Boros	Locke	Turnesa	1982	Stadler	T. Watson	T. Watson	Floyd
1953	Hogan	Hogan	Hogan	Burkemo	1983	Ballesteros	L. Nelson	T. Watson	Sutton
1954	Snead	Furgol	Thomson	Harbert	1984	Crenshaw	Zoeller	Ballesteros	Trevino
1955	Middlecoff	Fleck	Thomson	Ford	1985	Langer	North	Lyle	H. Green
1956	Burke	Middlecoff	Thomson	Burke	1986	Nicklaus	Floyd	Norman	Tway
1957	Ford	Mayer	Locke	L. Hebert	1987	Mize	S. Simpson	Faldo	L. Nelson
1958	Palmer	Bolt	Thomson	Finsterwald	1988	Lyle	Strange	Ballesteros	Sluman
1959	Wall	Casper	Player	Rosburg	1989	Faldo	Strange	Calcavecchia	Stewart
1960	Palmer	Palmer	Nagle	J. Hebert	1990	Faldo	Irwin	Faldo	Grady
1961	Player	Littler	Palmer	J. Barber	1991	Woosnam	Stewart	Baker-Finch	J. Daly
1962	Palmer	Nicklaus	Palmer	Player	1992	Couples	Kite	Faldo	Price
1963	Nicklaus	Boros	Charles	Nicklaus	1993	Langer	Janzen	Norman	Azinger

Vardon Trophy

Awarded since 1937 by the PGA of America to the PGA Tour regular with the lowest adjusted scoring average. The award is named after Harry Vardon, the six-time British Open champion who also won the U.S. Open in 1900. A point system was used from 1937-41.

Multiple winners: Billy Casper and Lee Trevino (5); Arnold Palmer, Sam Snead and Tiger Woods (4); Ben Hogan, Greg Norman and Tom Watson (3); Fred Couples, Bruce Crampton, Tom Kite, Lloyd Mangrum and Nick Price (2).

Year		Pts	Year		Avg	Year		Avg
1937	Harry Cooper	.500	1961	Arnold Palmer	.69.85	1982	Tom Kite	.70.21
1938	Sam Snead	.520	1962	Arnold Palmer	.70.27	1983	Ray Floyd	.70.61
1939	Byron Nelson	.473	1963	Billy Casper	.70.58	1984	Calvin Peete	.70.56
1940	Ben Hogan	.423	1964	Arnold Palmer	.70.01	1985	Don Pooley	.70.36
1941	Ben Hogan	.494	1965	Billy Casper	.70.85	1986	Scott Hoch	.70.08
1942-46	No award		1966	Billy Casper	.70.27	1987	Dan Pohl	.70.25
Year		**Avg**	1967	Arnold Palmer	.70.18	1988	Chip Beck	.69.46
1947	Jimmy Demaret	.69.90	1968	Billy Casper	.69.82	1989	Greg Norman	.69.49
1948	Ben Hogan	.69.30	1969	Dave Hill	.70.34	1990	Greg Norman	.69.10
1949	Sam Snead	.69.37	1970	Lee Trevino	.70.64	1991	Fred Couples	.69.59
1950	Sam Snead	.69.23	1971	Lee Trevino	.70.27	1992	Fred Couples	.69.38
1951	Lloyd Mangrum	.70.05	1972	Lee Trevino	.70.89	1993	Nick Price	.69.11
1952	Jack Burke	.70.54	1973	Bruce Crampton	.70.57	1994	Greg Norman	.68.81
1953	Lloyd Mangrum	.70.22	1974	Lee Trevino	.70.53	1995	Steve Elkington	.69.62
1954	E.J. Harrison	.70.41	1975	Bruce Crampton	.70.51	1996	Tom Lehman	.69.32
1955	Sam Snead	.69.86	1976	Don January	.70.56	1997	Nick Price	.68.98
1956	Cary Middlecoff	.70.35	1977	Tom Watson	.70.32	1998	David Duval	.69.13
1957	Dow Finsterwald	.70.30	1978	Tom Watson	.70.16	1999	Tiger Woods	.68.43
1958	Bob Rosburg	.70.11	1979	Tom Watson	.70.27	2000	Tiger Woods	.67.79
1959	Art Wall	.70.35	1980	Lee Trevino	.69.73	2001	Tiger Woods	.68.81
1960	Billy Casper	.69.95	1981	Tom Kite	.69.80	2002	Tiger Woods	.68.56

Grand Slam Summary (Cont.)

Year	Masters	US Open	Brit. Open	PGA	Year	Masters	US Open	Brit. Open	PGA
1994	Olazabal	Els	Price	Price	1999	Olazabal	Stewart	Lawrie	Woods
1995	Crenshaw	Pavin	Daly	Elkington	2000	Singh	Woods	Woods	Woods
1996	Faldo	S. Jones	Lehman	Brooks	2001	Woods	Goosen	Duval	Toms
1997	Woods	Els	Leonard	Love	2002	Woods	Woods	Els	Beem
1998	O'Meara	Janzen	O'Meara	Singh	2003	Weir	Furyk	Curtis	Micheel

U.S. Amateur

Match play from 1895-64, stroke play from 1965-72, match play 1973-79, 36-hole stroke-play qualifying before match play since 1979.

Multiple winners: Bobby Jones (5); Jerry Travers (4); Walter Travis and Tiger Woods (3); Deane Beman, Charles Coe, Gary Cowan, H. Chandler Egan, Chick Evans, Lawson Little, Jack Nicklaus, Francis Ouimet, Jay Sigel, William Turnesa, Bud Ward, Harvie Ward, and H.J. Whigham (2).

Year		Year		Year		Year	
1895	Charles Macdonald	1922	Jess Sweetser	1951	Billy Maxwell	1978	John Cook
1896	H.J. Whigham	1923	Max Marston	1952	Jack Westland	1979	Mark O'Meara
1897	H.J. Whigham	1924	Bobby Jones	1953	Gene Littler	1980	Hal Sutton
1898	Findlay Douglas	1925	Bobby Jones	1954	Arnold Palmer	1981	Nathaniel Crosby
1899	H.M. Harriman	1926	George Von Elm	1955	Harvie Ward	1982	Jay Sigel
1900	Walter Travis	1927	Bobby Jones	1956	Harvie Ward	1983	Jay Sigel
1901	Walter Travis	1928	Bobby Jones	1957	Hillman Robbins	1984	Scott Verplank
1902	Louis James	1929	Harrison Johnston	1958	Charles Coe	1985	Sam Randolph
1903	Walter Travis	1930	Bobby Jones	1959	Jack Nicklaus	1986	Buddy Alexander
1904	H. Chandler Egan	1931	Francis Ouimet	1960	Deane Beman	1987	Billy Mayfair
1905	H. Chandler Egan	1932	Ross Somerville	1961	Jack Nicklaus	1988	Eric Meeks
1906	Eben Byers	1933	George Dunlap	1962	Labron Harris	1989	Chris Patton
1907	Jerry Travers	1934	Lawson Little	1963	Deane Beman	1990	Phil Mickelson
1908	Jerry Travers	1935	Lawson Little	1964	Bill Campbell	1991	Mitch Voges
1909	Robert Gardner	1936	John Fischer	1965	Bob Murphy	1992	Justin Leonard
1910	W.C. Fownes Jr.	1937	John Goodman	1966	Gary Cowan	1993	John Harris
1911	Harold Hilton	1938	William Turnesa	1967	Bob Dickson	1994	Tiger Woods
1912	Jerry Travers	1939	Bud Ward	1968	Bruce Fleisher	1995	Tiger Woods
1913	Jerry Travers	1940	Richard Chapman	1969	Steve Melnyk	1996	Tiger Woods
1914	Francis Ouimet	1941	Bud Ward	1970	Lanny Wadkins	1997	Matt Kuchar
1915	Robert Gardner	1942-45	Not held	1971	Gary Cowan	1998	Hank Kuehne
1916	Chick Evans	1946	Ted Bishop	1972	Vinny Giles	1999	David Gossett
1917-18	Not held	1947	Skee Riegel	1973	Craig Stadler	2000	Jeff Quinney
1919	Davidson Herron	1948	William Turnesa	1974	Jerry Pate	2001	Bubba Dickerson
1920	Chick Evans	1949	Charles Coe	1975	Fred Ridley	2002	Ricky Barnes
1921	Jesse Guilford	1950	Sam Urzetta	1976	Bill Sander	2003	Nick Flanagan
				1977	John Fought		

British Amateur

Match play since 1885.

Multiple winners: John Ball (8); Michael Bonallack (5); Harold Hilton (4); Joe Carr (3); Horace Hutchinson, Ernest Holderness, Trevor Homer, Johnny Laidley, Lawson Little, Peter McEvoy, Dick Siderowf, Frank Stranahan, Freddie Tait, Cyril Tolley and Gary Wolstenholme (2).

Year		Year		Year		Year	
1885	Allen MacFie	1908	E.A. Lassen	1935	Lawson Little	1963	Michael Lunt
1886	Horace Hutchinson	1909	Robert Maxwell	1936	Hector Thomson	1964	Gordon Clark
1887	Horace Hutchinson	1910	John Ball	1937	Robert Sweeny Jr.	1965	Michael Bonallack
1888	John Ball	1911	Harold Hilton	1938	Charles Yates	1966	Bobby Cole
1889	Johnny Laidley	1912	John Ball	1939	Alexander Kyle	1967	Bob Dickson
1890	John Ball	1913	Harold Hilton	1940-45	Not held	1968	Michael Bonallack
1891	Johnny Laidley	1914	J.L.C. Jenkins	1946	James Bruen	1969	Michael Bonallack
1892	John Ball	1915-19	Not held	1947	William Turnesa	1970	Michael Bonallack
1893	Peter Anderson	1920	Cyril Tolley	1948	Frank Stranahan	1971	Steve Melnyk
1894	John Ball	1921	William Hunter	1949	Samuel McCready	1972	Trevor Homer
1895	Leslie Balfour-Melville	1922	Ernest Holderness	1950	Frank Stranahan	1973	Dick Siderowf
1896	Freddie Tait	1923	Roger Wethered	1951	Richard Chapman	1974	Trevor Homer
1897	Jack Allan	1924	Ernest Holderness	1952	Harvie Ward	1975	Vinny Giles
1898	Freddie Tait	1925	Robert Harris	1953	Joe Carr	1976	Dick Siderowf
1899	John Ball	1926	Jess Sweetser	1954	Douglas Bachli	1977	Peter McEvoy
1900	Harold Hilton	1927	William Tweddell	1955	Joe Conrad	1978	Peter McEvoy
1901	Harold Hilton	1928	Thomas Perkins	1956	John Beharrell	1979	Jay Sigel
1902	Charles Hutchings	1929	Cyril Tolley	1957	Reid Jack	1980	Duncan Evans
1903	Robert Maxwell	1930	Bobby Jones	1958	Joe Carr	1981	Phillipe Ploujoux
1904	Walter Travis	1931	Eric Smith	1959	Deane Beman	1982	Martin Thompson
1905	Arthur Barry	1932	John deForest	1960	Joe Carr	1983	Philip Parkin
1906	James Robb	1933	Michael Scott	1961	Michael Bonallack	1984	Jose-Maria Olazabal
1907	John Ball	1934	Lawson Little	1962	Richard Davies	1985	Garth McGimpsey

Year		Year		Year		Year	
1986	David Curry	1991	Gary Wolstenholme	1996	Warren Bledon	2001	Michael Hoey
1987	Paul Mayo	1992	Stephen Dundas	1997	Craig Watson	2002	Alejandro Larrazabal
1988	Christian Hardin	1993	Ian Pyman	1998	Sergio Garcia	2003	Gary Wolstenholme
1989	Stephen Dodd	1994	Lee James	1999	Graeme Storm		
1990	Rolf Muntz	1995	Gordon Sherry	2000	Mikko Ilonen		

WOMEN
Nabisco Championship

Formerly known as the Colgate Dinah Shore (1972-81) and the Nabisco Dinah Shore (1982-99), the tournament became the LPGA's fourth designated major championship in 1983. Shore's name, which was dropped from the tournament in 2000, is preserved with the Nabisco Dinah Shore Trophy, which is awarded to the winner. The tourney has been played at Mission Hills CC in Rancho Mirage, Calif., since it began; (*) indicates playoff winner.

Multiple winners: (as a major): Amy Alcott and Betsy King (3); Juli Inkster, Dottie Pepper and Annika Sorenstam (2).

Year	Winner	Score	Runner-up	Year	Winner	Score	Runner-up
1972	Jane Blalock	213	Carol Mann & Judy Rankin (216)	1990	Betsy King	283	Kathy Postlewait & Shirley Furlong (285)
1973	Mickey Wright	284	Joyce Kazmierski (286)	1991	Amy Alcott	273	Dottie Pepper (281)
1974	Jo Anne Prentice*	289	Jane Blalock & Sandra Haynie (289)	1992	Dottie Pepper*	279	Juli Inkster (279)
1975	Sandra Palmer	283	Kathy McMullen (284)	1993	Helen Alfredsson	284	Amy Benz & Tina Barrett (286)
1976	Judy Rankin	285	Betty Burfeindt (288)	1994	Donna Andrews	276	Laura Davies (277)
1977	Kathy Whitworth	289	JoAnne Carner & Sally Little (290)	1995	Nanci Bowen	285	Susie Redman (286)
1978	Sandra Post*	283	Penny Pulz (283)	1996	Patty Sheehan	281	Kelly Robbins, Meg Mallon & Annika Sorenstam (276)
1979	Sandra Post	276	Nancy Lopez (277)				
1980	Donna Caponi	275	Amy Alcott (277)				
1981	Nancy Lopez	277	Carolyn Hill (279)	1997	Betsy King	276	Kris Tschetter (278)
1982	Sally Little	278	Hollis Stacy & Sandra Haynie (281)	1998	Pat Hurst	281	Helen Dobson (282)
				1999	Dottie Pepper	269	Meg Mallon (275)
1983	Amy Alcott	282	Beth Daniel & Kathy Whitworth (284)	2000	Karrie Webb	274	Dottie Pepper (284)
1984	Juli Inkster*	280	Pat Bradley (280)	2001	Annika Sorenstam	281	Akiko Fukushima, Janice Moodie, Dottie Pepper, Rachel Teske & Karrie Webb (284)
1985	Alice Miller	275	Jan Stephenson (278)				
1986	Pat Bradley	280	Val Skinner (282)				
1987	Betsy King*	283	Patty Sheehan (283)	2002	Annika Sorenstam	280	Liselotte Neumann (281)
1988	Amy Alcott	274	Colleen Walker (276)	2003	P. Meunier-Lebouc	281	Annika Sorenstam (282)
1989	Juli Inkster	279	Tammie Green & JoAnne Carner (284)				

*PLAYOFFS:

1974: Jo Ann Prentice def. Jane Blalock in sudden death. **1978:** Sandra Post def. Penny Pulz in sudden death. **1984:** Juli Inkster def. Pat Bradley in sudden death. **1987:** Betsy King def. Patty Sheehan in sudden death. **1992:** Dottie Pepper def. Juli Inkster in sudden death.

U.S. Women's Open

The U.S. Women's Open began under the direction of the defunct Women's Professional Golfers Assn. in 1946, passed to the LPGA in 1949 and to the USGA in 1953. The tournament used a match play format its first year then switched to stroke play; (*) indicates playoff winner and (a) indicates amateur.

Multiple winners: Betsy Rawls and Mickey Wright (4); Susie Maxwell Berning, Hollis Stacy and Babe Zaharias (3); JoAnne Carner, Donna Caponi, Juli Inkster, Betsy King, Patty Sheehan, Annika Sorenstam, Louise Suggs and Karrie Webb (2).

Year	Winner	Score	Runner-up	Course	Location
1946	Patty Berg	5&4	Betty Jameson	Spokane CC	Spokane, Wash.
1947	Betty Jameson	295	a-Sally Sessions & a-Polly Riley (301)	Starmount Forest CC	Greensboro, N.C.
1948	Babe Zaharias	300	Betty Hicks (308)	Atlantic City CC	Northfield, N.J.
1949	Louise Suggs	291	Babe Zaharias (305)	Prince Georges CC	Landover, Md.
1950	Babe Zaharias	291	a-Betsy Rawls (300)	Rolling Hills CC	Wichita, Kan.
1951	Betsy Rawls	293	Louise Suggs (298)	Druid Hills CC	Atlanta, Ga.
1952	Louise Suggs	284	Marlene Hagge (291)	Bala GC	Philadelphia, Penn.
1953	Betsy Rawls*	302	Jackie Pung (302)	CC of Rochester	Rochester, N.Y.
1954	Babe Zaharias	291	Betty Hicks (303)	Salem CC	Peabody, Mass.
1955	Fay Crocker	299	Mary Lena Faulk (303)	Wichita CC	Wichita, Kan.
1956	Kathy Cornelius*	302	Barbara McIntire (302)	Northland CC	Duluth, Minn.
1957	Betsy Rawls	299	Patty Berg (305)	Winged Foot GC	Mamaroneck, N.Y.
1958	Mickey Wright	290	Louise Suggs (295)	Forest Lake CC	Detroit, Mich.
1959	Mickey Wright	287	Louise Suggs (289)	Churchill Valley CC	Pittsburgh, Penn.
1960	Betsy Rawls	292	Joyce Ziske (293)	Worcester CC	Worcester, Mass.
1961	Mickey Wright	293	Betsy Rawls (299)	Baltusrol GC	Springfield, N.J.
1962	Murle Breer	301	Jo Anne Prentice & Ruth Jessen (303)	Dunes GC	Myrtle Beach, S.C.

U.S. Women's Open (Cont.)

Year	Winner	Score	Runner-up	Course	Location
1963	Mary Mills	.289	Sandra Haynie & Louise Suggs (292)	Kenwood CC	Cincinnati, Ohio
1964	Mickey Wright*	.290	Ruth Jessen (290)	San Diego CC	Chula Vista, Calif.
1965	Carol Mann	.290	Kathy Cornelius (292)	Atlantic City CC	Northfield, N.J.
1966	Sandra Spuzich	.297	Carol Mann (298)	Hazeltine National GC	Chaska, Minn.
1967	a-Catherine LaCoste	.294	Susie Berning & Beth Stone (296)	Hot Springs GC	Hot Springs, Va.
1968	Susie Berning	.289	Mickey Wright (292)	Moselem Springs GC	Fleetwood, Penn.
1969	Donna Caponi	.294	Peggy Wilson (295)	Scenic Hills CC	Pensacola, Fla.
1970	Donna Caponi	.287	Sandra Haynie (288)	Muskogee CC	Muskogee, Okla.
1971	JoAnne Carner	.288	Kathy Whitworth (295)	Kahkwa CC	Erie, Penn.
1972	Susie Berning	.299	Kathy Ahern, Pam Barnett & Judy Rankin (300)	Winged Foot GC	Mamaroneck, N.Y.
1973	Susie Berning	.290	Gloria Ehret (295)	CC of Rochester	Rochester, N.Y.
1974	Sandra Haynie	.295	Carol Mann & Beth Stone (296)	La Grange CC	La Grange, Ill.
1975	Sandra Palmer	.295	JoAnne Carner, a-Nancy Lopez & Sandra Post (299)	Atlantic City CC	Northfield, N.J.
1976	JoAnne Carner*	.292	Sandra Palmer (292)	Rolling Green CC	Springfield, Penn.
1977	Hollis Stacy	.292	Nancy Lopez (294)	Hazeltine National GC	Chaska, Minn.
1978	Hollis Stacy	.289	JoAnne Carner & Sally Little (290)	CC of Indianapolis	Indianapolis, Ind.
1979	Jerilyn Britz	.284	Debbie Massey & Sandra Palmer (286)	Brooklawn CC	Fairfield, Conn.
1980	Amy Alcott	.280	Hollis Stacy (289)	Richland CC	Nashville, Tenn.
1981	Pat Bradley	.279	Beth Daniel (280)	La Grange CC	La Grange, Ill.
1982	Janet Anderson	.283	Beth Daniel, Sandra Haynie & Donna White (289)	Del Paso CC	Sacramento, Calif.
1983	Jan Stephenson	.290	JoAnne Carner (291)	Cedar Ridge CC	Tulsa, Okla.
1984	Hollis Stacy	.290	Rosie Jones (291)	Salem CC	Peabody, Mass.
1985	Kathy Baker	.280	Judy Dickenson (283)	Baltusrol GC	Springfield, N.J.
1986	Jane Geddes*	.287	Sally Little (287)	NCR GC	Dayton, Ohio
1987	Laura Davies*	.285	Ayako Okamoto & JoAnne Carner (285)	Plainfield CC	Plainfield, N.J.
1988	Liselotte Neumann	.277	Patty Sheehan (280)	Baltimore CC	Baltimore, Md.
1989	Betsy King	.278	Nancy Lopez (282)	Indianwood GC	Lake Orion, Mich.
1990	Betsy King	.284	Patty Sheehan (285)	Atlanta Athletic Club	Duluth, Ga.
1991	Meg Mallon	.283	Pat Bradley (285)	Colonial CC	Ft. Worth, Texas
1992	Patty Sheehan*	.280	Juli Inkster (280)	Oakmont CC	Oakmont, Penn.
1993	Lauri Merten	.280	Donna Andrews & Helen Alfredsson (281)	Crooked Stick GC	Carmel, Ind.
1994	Patty Sheehan	.277	Tammie Green (278)	Indianwood CC	Lake Orion, Mich.
1995	Annika Sorenstam	.278	Meg Mallon (279)	The Broadmoor	Colorado Springs, Colo.
1996	Annika Sorenstam	.272	Kris Tschetter (278)	Pine Needles Lodge & GC	Southern Pines, N.C.
1997	Alison Nicholas	.274	Nancy Lopez (275)	Pumpkin Ridge GC	Cornelius, Ore.
1998	Se Ri Pak*	.290	a-Jenny Chuasiriporn (290)	Blackwolf Run GC	Kohler, Wis.
1999	Juli Inkster	.272	Sherri Turner (277)	Old Waverly GC	West Point, Miss.
2000	Karrie Webb	.282	Cristie Kerr & Meg Mallon (287)	Merit CC	Libertyville, Ill.
2001	Karrie Webb	.273	Se Ri Pak (281)	Pine Needles Lodge & GC	Southern Pines, N.C.
2002	Juli Inkster	.276	Annika Sorenstam (278)	Prairie Dunes CC	Hutchinson, Kan.
2003	Hilary Lunke*	.283	Anglea Stanford & Kelly Robbins (283)	Pumpkin Ridge GC	North Plains, Ore.

*PLAYOFFS:
1953: Betsy Rawls (70) def. Jackie Pung (77) in 18 holes. **1956:** Kathy Cornelius (75) def. Barbara McIntire (82) in 18 holes. **1964:** Mickey Wright (70) def. Ruth Jessen (72) in 18 holes. **1976:** JoAnne Carner (76) def. Sandra Palmer (78) in 18 holes. **1986:** Jane Geddes (71) def. Sally Little (73) in 18 holes. **1987:** Laura Davies (71) def. Ayako Okamoto (73) and JoAnne Carner (74) in 18 holes. **1992:** Patty Sheehan (72) def. Juli Inkster (74) in 18 holes. **1998:** Se Ri Pak def. Jenny Chuasiriporn on the second sudden death hole after both players were tied after an 18-hole playoff. **2003:** Hilary Lunke (70) def. Angela Stanford (71) and Kelly Robbins (73) in 18 holes.

LPGA Championship

Officially the McDonald's LPGA Championship since 1994 (Mazda was the title sponsor from 1987-93), the tournament began in 1955 and has had extended stays at the Stardust CC in Las Vegas (1961-66), Pleasant Valley CC in Sutton, Mass. (1967-68, 70-74), the Jack Nicklaus Sports Center at Kings Island, Ohio (1978-89), Bethesda CC in Maryland (1990-93) and DuPont CC in Wilmington, Del. (since 1994); (*) indicates playoff winner and (#) weather-shortened.

Multiple winners: Mickey Wright (4); Nancy Lopez, Patty Sheehan and Kathy Whitworth (3); Donna Caponi, Laura Davies, Sandra Haynie, Juli Inkster, Mary Mills, Se Ri Pak and Betsy Rawls (2).

Year	Winner	Score	Runner-up
1955	Beverly Hanson	220	Louise Suggs (223)
1956	Marlene Hagge*	...251	Patty Berg (291)
1957	Louise Suggs	.285	Wiffi Smith (288)
1958	Mickey Wright	288	Fay Crocker (294)
1959	Betsy Rawls	288	Patty Berg (289)
1960	Mickey Wright	292	Louise Suggs (295)
1961	Mickey Wright	287	Louise Suggs (296)
1962	Judy Kimball	282	Shirley Spork (286)
1963	Mickey Wright	294	Mary Lena Faulk
			& Mary Mills (296)
1964	Mary Mills	278	Mickey Wright (280)
1965	Sandra Haynie	279	Clifford A. Creed (280)
1966	Gloria Ehret	282	Mickey Wright (285)
1967	Kathy Whitworth	284	Shirley Englehorn (285)
1968	Sandra Post	294	Kathy Whitworth (294)
1969	Betsy Rawls	293	Susie Berning
			& Carol Mann (297)
1970	Shirley Englehorn	285	Kathy Whitworth (285)
1971	Kathy Whitworth	288	Kathy Ahern (292)
1972	Kathy Ahern	293	Jane Blalock (299)
1973	Mary Mills	288	Betty Burfeindt (289)
1974	Sandra Haynie	288	JoAnne Carner (290)
1975	Kathy Whitworth	288	Sandra Haynie (289)
1976	Betty Burfeindt	287	Judy Rankin (288)
1977	Chako Higuchi	279	Pat Bradley, Sandra Post
			& Judy Rankin (282)
1978	Nancy Lopez	275	Amy Alcott (281)
1979	Donna Caponi	279	Jerilyn Britz (282)
1980	Sally Little	285	Jane Blalock (288)

Year	Winner	Score	Runner-up
1981	Donna Caponi	280	Jerilyn Britz
			& Pat Meyers (281)
1982	Jan Stephenson	279	JoAnne Carner (281)
1983	Patty Sheehan	279	Sandra Haynie (281)
1984	Patty Sheehan	272	Beth Daniel
			& Pat Bradley (282)
1985	Nancy Lopez	273	Alice Miller (281)
1986	Pat Bradley	277	Patty Sheehan (278)
1987	Jane Geddes	275	Betsy King (275)
1988	Sherri Turner	281	Amy Alcott (282)
1989	Nancy Lopez	274	Ayako Okamoto (277)
1990	Beth Daniel	280	Rosie Jones (281)
1991	Meg Mallon	274	Pat Bradley
			& Ayako Okamoto (275)
1992	Betsy King	267	JoAnne Carner,
			Karen Noble
			& Liselotte Neumann (278)
1993	Patty Sheehan	275	Lauri Merten (276)
1994	Laura Davies	279	Alice Ritzman (280)
1995	Kelly Robbins	274	Laura Davies (275)
1996	Laura Davies#	213	Julie Piers (214)
1997	Chris Johnson*	281	Leta Lindley (281)
1998	Se Ri Pak	273	Donna Andrews
			& Lisa Hackney (276)
1999	Juli Inkster	268	Liselotte Neumann (272)
2000	Juli Inkster*	281	Stefania Croce (281)
2001	Karrie Webb	270	Laura Diaz (272)
2002	Se Ri Pak	279	Beth Daniel (282)
2003	Annika Sorenstam*	.278	Grace Park (278)

*PLAYOFFS:

1956: Marlene Hagge def. Patti Berg in sudden death. **1968:** Sandra Post (68) def. Kathy Whitworth (75) in 18 holes.
1970: Shirley Englehorn def. Kathy Whitworth in sudden death. **1997:** Chris Johnson def. Leta Lindley in sudden death.
2000: Juli Inkster def. Stefania Croce in sudden death. **2003:** Annika Sorenstam def. Grace Park in sudden death.

Women's British Open

Sponsored by Weetabix, this has been an official stop on the LPGA Tour since 1994, and it became the fourth designated major championship in 2001 when it replaced the du Maurier Classic.
   Multiple winners Karrie Webb (3); and Sherri Steinhauer (2); (as a major): none.

Year	Winner	Score	Runner-up	Course	Location
1994	Liselotte Neumann	280	Dottie Mochrie & Annika Sorenstam (283)	Woburn G&CC	Milton Keynes, England
1995	Karrie Webb	278	Annika Sorenstam & Jill McGill (284)	Woburn G&CC	Milton Keynes, England
1996	Emilee Klein	277	Penny Hammel & Amy Alcott (284)	Woburn G&CC	Milton Keynes, England
1997	Karrie Webb	269	Rosie Jones (277)	Sunningdale GC	Berkshire, England
1998	Sherri Steinhauer	292	Sophie Gustafson & Brandie Burton (293)	Royal Lytham	Lytham, England
1999	Sherri Steinhauer	283	Annika Sorenstam (284)	Woburn G&CC	Milton Keynes, England
2000	Sophie Gustafson	282	Kirsty Taylor, Liselotte Neumann, Becky Iverson & Meg Mallon (284)	Royal Birkdale	Southport, England
2001	Se Ri Pak	277	Mi Hyun Kim (279)	Sunningdale GC	Berkshire, England
2002	Karrie Webb	273	Michelle Ellis & Paula Marti (275)	Turnberry GC	Turnberry, Scotland
2003	Annika Sorenstam	278	Se Ri Pak (279)	Royal Lytham	Lytham, England

du Maurier Classic (1979-2000)

The du Maurier Classic was considered a major title on the women's tour from 1979-2000; (*) indicates playoff winner.
   Multiple winners (as a major): Pat Bradley (3); Brandie Burton (2).

Year		Year		Year		Year	
1973	Jocelyne Bourassa	1980	Pat Bradley	1987	Jody Rosenthal	1994	Martha Nause
1974	Carole Jo Skala	1981	Jan Stephenson	1988	Sally Little	1995	Jenny Lidback
1975	JoAnne Carner	1982	Sandra Haynie	1989	Tammie Green	1996	Laura Davies
1976	Donna Caponi	1983	Hollis Stacy	1990	Cathy Johnston	1997	Colleen Walker
1977	Judy Rankin	1984	Juli Inkster	1991	Nancy Scranton	1998	Brandie Burton
1978	JoAnne Carner	1985	Pat Bradley	1992	Sherri Steinhauer	1999	Karrie Webb
1979	Amy Alcott	1986	Pat Bradley*	1993	Brandie Burton*	2000	Meg Mallon

Titleholders Championship (1937-72)

The Titleholders was considered a major title on the women's tour until it was discontinued after the 1972 tournament.

Multiple winners: Patty Berg (7); Louise Suggs (4); Babe Zaharias (3); Dorothy Kirby, Marilynn Smith, Kathy Whitworth and Mickey Wright (2).

Year		Year		Year		Year	
1937	Patty Berg	1947	Babe Zaharias	1955	Patty Berg	1963	Marilynn Smith
1938	Patty Berg	1948	Patty Berg	1956	Louise Suggs	1964	Marilynn Smith
1939	Patty Berg	1949	Peggy Kirk	1957	Patty Berg	1965	Kathy Whitworth
1940	Betty Hicks	1950	Babe Zaharias	1958	Beverly Hanson	1966	Kathy Whitworth
1941	Dorothy Kirby	1951	Pat O'Sullivan	1959	Louise Suggs	1967-71	Not held
1942	Dorothy Kirby	1952	Babe Zaharias	1960	Fay Crocker	1972	Sandra Palmer
1943-45	Not held	1953	Patty Berg	1961	Mickey Wright		
1946	Louise Suggs	1954	Louise Suggs	1962	Mickey Wright		

Western Open (1930-67)

The Western Open was considered a major title on the women's tour until it was discontinued after the 1967 tournament.

Multiple winners: Patty Berg (7); Louise Suggs and Babe Zaharias (4); Mickey Wright (3); June Beebe, Opal Hill, Betty Jameson and Betsy Rawls (2).

Year		Year		Year		Year	
1930	Mrs. Lee Mida	1940	Babe Zaharias	1950	Babe Zaharias	1960	Joyce Ziske
1931	June Beebe	1941	Patty Berg	1951	Patty Berg	1961	Mary Lena Faulk
1932	Jane Weiller	1942	Betty Jameson	1952	Betsy Rawls	1962	Mickey Wright
1933	June Beebe	1943	Patty Berg	1953	Louise Suggs	1963	Mickey Wright
1934	Marian McDougall	1944	Babe Zaharias	1954	Betty Jameson	1964	Carol Mann
1935	Opal Hill	1945	Babe Zaharias	1955	Patty Berg	1965	Susie Maxwell
1936	Opal Hill	1946	Louise Suggs	1956	Beverly Hanson	1966	Mickey Wright
1937	Betty Hicks	1947	Louise Suggs	1957	Patty Berg	1967	Kathy Whitworth
1938	Bea Barrett	1948	Patty Berg	1958	Patty Berg		
1939	Helen Dettweiler	1949	Louise Suggs	1959	Betsy Rawls		

Grand Slam Summary

From 1955-66, the U.S. Open, LPGA Championship, Western Open and Titleholders tournaments served as the Women's Grand Slam. From 1983-2000, however, the U.S. Open, LPGA, du Maurier Classic and Nabisco Championship were the major events. In 2001, the Weetabix Women's British Open replaced the du Maurier Classic as the tour's fourth major. No one has won a four-event Grand Slam on the women's tour.

Three wins in one year (3): Babe Zaharias (1950), Mickey Wright (1961) and Pat Bradley (1986).

Two wins in one year (19): Patty Berg and Mickey Wright (3 times); Juli Inkster, Louise Suggs and Karrie Webb (twice); Laura Davies, Sandra Haynie, Betsy King, Meg Mallon, Se Ri Pak, Betsy Rawls, Annika Sorenstam and Kathy Whitworth (once).

Year	LPGA	US Open	T'holders	Western	Year	LPGA	US Open	T'holders	Western
1937	—	—	Berg	Hicks	1947	—	Jameson	Zaharias	Suggs
1938	—	—	Berg	Barrett	1948	—	Zaharias	Berg	Berg
1939	—	—	Berg	Dettweiler	1949	—	Suggs	Kirk	Suggs
1940	—	—	Hicks	Zaharias	1950	—	Zaharias	Zaharias	Zaharias
1941	—	—	Kirby	Berg	1951	—	Rawls	O'Sullivan	Berg
1942	—	—	Kirby	Jameson	1952	—	Suggs	Zaharias	Rawls
1943	—	—	—	Berg	1953	—	Rawls	Berg	Suggs
1944	—	—	—	Zaharias	1954	—	Zaharias	Suggs	Jameson
1945	—	—	—	Zaharias	1955	Hanson	Crocker	Berg	Berg
1946	—	Berg	Suggs	Suggs	1956	Hagge	Cornelius	Suggs	Hanson

Major Championship Leaders

Through 2003; active LPGA players in **bold** type.

	US Open	LPGA	Nabisco	British Open	duM	Title	Western	US Am	Brit Am	Total
Patty Berg	1	0	0	0	0	7	7	1	0	**16**
Mickey Wright	4	4	0	0	0	2	3	0	0	**13**
Louise Suggs	2	1	0	0	0	4	4	1	1	**13**
Babe Didrikson Zaharias	3	0	0	0	0	3	4	1	1	**12**
Juli Inkster	2	2	2	0	1	0	0	3	0	**10**
Betsy Rawls	4	2	0	0	0	0	2	0	0	**8**
JoAnne Carner	2	0	0	0	0	0	0	5	0	**7**
Kathy Whitworth	0	3	0	0	0	2	1	0	0	**6**
Pat Bradley	1	1	1	0	3	0	0	0	0	**6**
Betsy King	2	1	3	0	0	0	0	0	0	**6**
Patty Sheehan	2	3	1	0	0	0	0	0	0	**6**
Glenna C. Vare	0	0	0	0	0	0	0	6	0	**6**
Karrie Webb	2	1	1	1	1	0	0	0	0	**6**
Annika Sorenstam	2	1	2	1	0	0	0	0	0	**6**

Tournaments: U.S. Open, LPGA Championship, Nabisco Championship, British Open, du Maurier Classic (1979-2000), Titleholders (1930-72), Western Open (1937-67), U.S. Amateur and British Amateur.

Year	LPGA	US Open	T'holders	Western
1957	Suggs	Rawls	Berg	Berg
1958	Wright	Wright	Hanson	Berg
1959	Rawls	Wright	Suggs	Rawls
1960	Wright	Rawls	Crocker	Ziske
1961	Wright	Wright	Wright	Faulk
1962	Kimball	Lindstrom	Wright	Wright
1963	Wright	Mills	M. Smith	Wright
1964	Mills	Wright	M. Smith	Mann
1965	Haynie	Mann	Whitworth	Maxwell
1966	Ehret	Spuzich	Whitworth	Wright
1967	Whitworth	a-LaCoste	—	Whitworth
1968	Post	Berning	—	—
1969	Rawls	Caponi	—	—
1970	Englehorn	Caponi	—	—
1971	Whitworth	Carner	—	—
1972	Ahern	Berning	Palmer	—
1973	Mills	Berning	—	—
1974	Haynie	Haynie	—	—
1975	Whitworth	Palmer	—	—
1976	Burfeindt	Carner	—	—
1977	Higuchi	Stacy	—	—
1978	Lopez	Stacy	—	—

Year	LPGA	US Open	duMaurier	Nabisco
1979	Caponi	Britz	Alcott	—
1980	Little	Alcott	Bradley	—

Year	LPGA	US Open	duMaurier	Nabisco
1981	Caponi	Bradley	Stephenson	—
1982	Stephenson	Anderson	Haynie	—
1983	Sheehan	Stephenson	Stacy	Alcott
1984	Sheehan	Stacy	Inkster	Inkster
1985	Lopez	Baker	Bradley	Miller
1986	Bradley	Geddes	Bradley	Bradley
1987	Geddes	Davies	Rosenthal	King
1988	Turner	Neumann	Little	Alcott
1989	Lopez	King	Green	Inkster
1990	Daniel	King	Johnston	King
1991	Mallon	Mallon	Scranton	Alcott
1992	King	Sheehan	Steinhauer	Pepper
1993	Sheehan	Merten	Burton	Alfredsson
1994	Davies	Sheehan	Nause	Andrews
1995	Robbins	Sorenstam	Lidback	Bowen
1996	Davies	Sorenstam	Davies	Sheehan
1997	Johnson	Nicholas	Walker	King
1998	Pak	Pak	Burton	Hurst
1999	Inkster	Inkster	Webb	Pepper
2000	Inkster	Webb	Mallon	Webb

Year	LPGA	US Open	Brit. Open	Nabisco
2001	Webb	Webb	Pak	Sorenstam
2002	Pak	Inkster	Webb	Sorenstam
2003	Sorenstam	Lunke	Sorenstam	Meunier-Lebouc

U.S. Women's Amateur

Stroke play in 1895, match play since 1896.

Multiple winners: Glenna Collett Vare (6); JoAnne Gunderson Carner (5); Margaret Curtis, Beatrix Hoyt, Dorothy Campbell Hurd, Juli Inkster, Alexa Stirling, Virginia Van Wie, Anne Quast Decker Welts (3); Kay Cockerill, Beth Daniel, Vicki Goetze, Katherine Harley, Genevieve Hecker, Betty Jameson, Kelli Kuehne and Barbara McIntire (2).

Year		Year		Year		Year	
1895	Mrs. C.S. Brown	1905	Pauline Mackay	1915	Florence Vanderbeck	1926	Helen Stetson
1896	Beatrix Hoyt	1906	Harriot Curtis	1916	Alexa Stirling	1927	Miriam Burns Horn
1897	Beatrix Hoyt	1907	Margaret Curtis	1917-18	Not held	1928	Glenna Collett
1898	Beatrix Hoyt	1908	Katherine Harley	1919	Alexa Stirling	1929	Glenna Collett
1899	Ruth Underhill	1909	Dorothy Campbell	1920	Alexa Stirling	1930	Glenna Collett
1900	Frances Griscom	1910	Dorothy Campbell	1921	Marion Hollins	1931	Helen Hicks
1901	Genevieve Hecker	1911	Margaret Curtis	1922	Glenna Collett	1932	Virginia Van Wie
1902	Genevieve Hecker	1912	Margaret Curtis	1923	Edith Cummings	1933	Virginia Van Wie
1903	Bessie Anthony	1913	Gladys Ravenscroft	1924	Dorothy C. Hurd	1934	Virginia Van Wie
1904	Georgianna Bishop	1914	Katherine Harley	1925	Glenna Collett	1935	Glenna Collett Vare

Vare Trophy

The Vare Trophy for best scoring average by a player on the LPGA Tour has been awarded since 1937 by the LPGA. The award is named after Glenna Collett Vare, winner of six U.S. women's amateur titles from 1922-35.

Multiple winners: Kathy Whitworth (7); JoAnne Carner, Annika Sorenstam and Mickey Wright (5); Patty Berg, Beth Daniel, Nancy Lopez, Judy Rankin and Karrie Webb (3); Pat Bradley and Betsy King (2).

Year		Avg	Year		Avg	Year		Avg
1953	Patty Berg	75.00	1970	Kathy Whitworth	72.26	1987	Betsy King	71.14
1954	Babe Zaharias	75.48	1971	Kathy Whitworth	72.88	1988	Colleen Walker	71.26
1955	Patty Berg	74.47	1972	Kathy Whitworth	72.38	1989	Beth Daniel	70.38
1956	Patty Berg	74.57	1973	Judy Rankin	73.08	1990	Beth Daniel	70.54
1957	Louise Suggs	74.64	1974	JoAnne Carner	72.87	1991	Pat Bradley	70.66
1958	Beverly Hanson	74.92	1975	JoAnne Carner	72.40	1992	Dottie Pepper	70.80
1959	Betsy Rawls	74.03	1976	Judy Rankin	72.25	1993	Betsy King	70.85
1960	Mickey Wright	73.25	1977	Judy Rankin	72.16	1994	Beth Daniel	70.90
1961	Mickey Wright	73.55	1978	Nancy Lopez	71.76	1995	Annika Sorenstam	71.00
1962	Mickey Wright	73.67	1979	Nancy Lopez	71.20	1996	Annika Sorenstam	70.47
1963	Mickey Wright	72.81	1980	Amy Alcott	71.51	1997	Karrie Webb	70.00
1964	Mickey Wright	72.46	1981	JoAnne Carner	71.75	1998	Annika Sorenstam	69.99
1965	Kathy Whitworth	72.61	1982	JoAnne Carner	71.49	1999	Karrie Webb	69.43
1966	Kathy Whitworth	72.60	1983	JoAnne Carner	71.41	2000	Karrie Webb	70.05
1967	Kathy Whitworth	72.74	1984	Patty Sheehan	71.40	2001	Annika Sorenstam	69.42
1968	Carol Mann	72.04	1985	Nancy Lopez	70.73	2002	Annika Sorenstam	68.70
1969	Kathy Whitworth	72.38	1986	Pat Bradley	71.10			

U.S. Women's Amateur (Cont.)

Year		Year		Year		Year	
1936	Pamela Barton	1955	Patricia Lesser	1971	Laura Baugh	1988	Pearl Sinn
1937	Estelle Lawson	1956	Marlene Stewart	1972	Mary Budke	1989	Vicki Goetze
1938	Patty Berg	1957	JoAnne Gunderson	1973	Carol Semple		
1939	Betty Jameson	1958	Anne Quast	1974	Cynthia Hill	1990	Pat Hurst
		1959	Barbara McIntire	1975	Beth Daniel	1991	Amy Fruhwirth
1940	Betty Jameson			1976	Donna Horton	1992	Vicki Goetze
1941	Elizabeth Hicks	1960	JoAnne Gunderson	1977	Beth Daniel	1993	Jill McGill
1942-45	Not held	1961	Anne Quast Decker	1978	Cathy Sherk	1994	Wendy Ward
1946	Babe D. Zaharias	1962	JoAnne Gunderson	1979	Carolyn Hill	1995	Kelli Kuehne
1947	Louise Suggs	1963	Anne Quast Welts			1996	Kelli Kuehne
1948	Grace Lenczyk	1964	Barbara McIntire	1980	Juli Inkster	1997	Silvia Cavalleri
1949	Dorothy Porter	1965	Jean Ashley	1981	Juli Inkster	1998	Grace Park
		1966	JoAnne G. Carner	1982	Juli Inkster	1999	Dorothy Delasin
1950	Beverly Hanson	1967	Mary Lou Dill	1983	Joanne Pacillo		
1951	Dorothy Kirby	1968	JoAnne G. Carner	1984	Deb Richard	2000	Marcy Newton
1952	Jacqueline Pung	1969	Catherine Lacoste	1985	Michiko Hattori	2001	Meredith Duncan
1953	Mary Lena Faulk			1986	Kay Cockerill	2002	Becky Lucidi
1954	Barbara Romack	1970	Martha Wilkinson	1987	Kay Cockerill	2003	V. Nirapathpongporn

British Women's Amateur

Match play since 1893.

Multiple winners: Cecil Leitch and Joyce Wethered (4); May Hezlet, Lady Margaret Scott, Jessie Anderson Valentine, Brigitte Varangot and Enid Wilson (3); Rhona Adair, Pam Barton, Dorothy Campbell, Elizabeth Chadwick, Helen Holm, Rebecca Hudson, Marley Spearman, Frances Stephens and Michelle Walker (2).

Year		Year		Year		Year	
1893	Lady Margaret Scott	1923	Doris Chambers	1954	Frances Stephens	1980	Anne Quast Sander
1894	Lady Margaret Scott	1924	Joyce Wethered	1955	Jessie Valentine	1981	Belle Robertson
1895	Lady Margaret Scott	1925	Joyce Wethered	1956	Wiffi Smith	1982	Kitrina Douglas
1896	Amy Pascoe	1926	Cecil Leitch	1957	Philomena Garvey	1983	Jill Thornhill
1897	Edith Orr	1927	Simone de la Chaume	1958	Jessie Valentine	1984	Jody Rosenthal
1898	Lena Thomson	1928	Nanette le Blan	1959	Elizabeth Price	1985	Lillian Behan
1899	May Hezlet	1929	Joyce Wethered			1986	Marnie McGuire
1900	Rhona Adair	1930	Diana Fishwick	1960	Barbara McIntire	1987	Janet Collingham
1901	Mary Graham	1931	Enid Wilson	1961	Marley Spearman	1988	Joanne Furby
1902	May Hezlet	1932	Enid Wilson	1962	Marley Spearman	1989	Helen Dobson
1903	Rhona Adair	1933	Enid Wilson	1963	Brigitte Varangot		
1904	Lottie Dod	1934	Helen Holm	1964	Carol Sorenson	1990	Julie Wade Hall
1905	Bertha Thompson	1935	Wanda Morgan	1965	Brigitte Varangot	1991	Valerie Michaud
1906	Mrs. W. Kennion	1936	Pam Barton	1966	Elizabeth Chadwick	1992	Bernille Pedersen
1907	May Hezlet	1937	Jessie Anderson	1967	Elizabeth Chadwick	1993	Catriona Lambert
1908	Maud Titterton	1938	Helen Holm	1968	Brigitte Varangot	1994	Emma Duggleby
1909	Dorothy Campbell	1939	Pam Barton	1969	Catherine Lacoste	1995	Julie Wade Hall
1910	Elsie Grant-Suttie	1940-45	Not held	1970	Dinah Oxley	1996	Kelli Kuehne
1911	Dorothy Campbell	1946	Jean Hetherington	1971	Michelle Walker	1997	Alison Rose
1912	Gladys Ravenscroft	1947	Babe Zaharias	1972	Michelle Walker	1998	Kim Rostron
1913	Muriel Dodd	1948	Louise Suggs	1973	Ann Irvin	1999	Marine Monnet
1914	Cecil Leitch	1949	Frances Stephens	1974	Carol Semple		
1915-19	Not held			1975	Nancy Roth Syms	2000	Rebecca Hudson
		1950	Lally de St. Sauveur	1976	Cathy Panton	2001	Marta Prieto
1920	Cecil Leitch	1951	Catherine MacCann	1977	Angela Uzielli	2002	Rebecca Hudson
1921	Cecil Leitch	1952	Moira Paterson	1978	Edwina Kennedy	2003	Elisa Serramia
1922	Joyce Wethered	1953	Marlene Stewart	1979	Maureen Madill		

Champions Tour
(formerly Senior PGA Tour)

The Tradition

Sponsored by window and door manufacturer JELD-WEN since 2003, it was formerly called The Tradition at Desert Mountain (1989-91), The Tradition (1992-99) and The Countrywide Tradition (2000-02). Held at GC at Desert Mountain in Scottsdale, Ariz. (1989-2001), Superstition Mountain (Ariz.) G & CC (2002) and The Reserve Vineyards & GC in Portland, Ore. (2003).

Multiple winners: Jack Nicklaus (4); Gil Morgan (2).

Year		Year		Year		Year	
1989	Don Bies	1993	Tom Shaw	1997	Gil Morgan	2001	Doug Tewell
1990	Jack Nicklaus	1994	Ray Floyd*	1998	Gil Morgan	2002	Jim Thorpe*
1991	Jack Nicklaus	1995	Jack Nicklaus*	1999	Graham Marsh	2003	Tom Watson
1992	Lee Trevino	1996	Jack Nicklaus	2000	Tom Kite		

*PLAYOFFS:

1994: Ray Floyd def. Dale Douglas on 1st extra hole. **1995:** Jack Nicklaus def. Isao Aoki on 3rd extra hole; **2002:** Jim Thorpe def. John Jacobs on 1st extra hole.

Senior PGA Championship

First played in 1937. Two championships played in 1979 and 1984.
Multiple winners: Sam Snead (6); Hale Irwin, Gary Player, Al Watrous and Eddie Williams (3); Julius Boros, Jock Hutchison, Don January, Arnold Palmer, Paul Runyan, Gene Sarazen and Lee Trevino (2).

Year		Year		Year		Year	
1937	Jock Hutchison	1955	Mortie Dutra	1972	Sam Snead	1987	Chi Chi Rodriguez
1938	Fred McLeod*	1956	Pete Burke	1973	Sam Snead	1988	Gary Player
1939	Not held	1957	Al Watrous	1974	Roberto De Vicenzo	1989	Larry Mowry
1940	Otto Hackbarth*	1958	Gene Sarazen	1975	Charlie Sifford*	1990	Gary Player
1941	Jack Burke	1959	Willie Goggin	1976	Pete Cooper	1991	Jack Nicklaus
1942	Eddie Williams	1960	Dick Metz	1977	Julius Boros	1992	Lee Trevino
1943-44	Not held	1961	Paul Runyan	1978	Joe Jiminez*	1993	Tom Wargo*
1945	Eddie Williams	1962	Paul Runyan	1979	Jack Fleck*	1994	Lee Trevino
1946	Eddie Williams*	1963	Herman Barron	1979	Don January	1995	Ray Floyd
1947	Jock Hutchison	1964	Sam Snead	1980	Arnold Palmer*	1996	Hale Irwin
1948	Charles McKenna	1965	Sam Snead	1981	Miller Barber	1997	Hale Irwin
1949	Marshall Crichton	1966	Fred Haas	1982	Don January	1998	Hale Irwin
1950	Al Watrous	1967	Sam Snead	1983	Not held	1999	Allen Doyle
1951	Al Watrous*	1968	Chandler Harper	1984	Arnold Palmer	2000	Doug Tewell
1952	Ernest Newnham	1969	Tommy Bolt	1984	Peter Thomson	2001	Tom Watson
1953	Harry Schwab	1970	Sam Snead	1985	Not held	2002	Fuzzy Zoeller
1954	Gene Sarazen	1971	Julius Boros	1986	Gary Player	2003	John Jacobs

*PLAYOFFS:

1938: Fred McLeod def. Otto Hackbarth in 18 holes. **1940:** Otto Hackbarth def. Jock Hutchison in 36 holes. **1946:** Eddie Williams def. Jock Hutchison in 18 holes. **1951:** Al Watrous def. Jock Hutchison in 18 holes. **1975:** Charlie Sifford def. Fred Wampler on 1st extra hole. **1978:** Joe Jiminez def. Paul Harney on 1st extra hole. **1979:** Jack Fleck def. Bill Johnston on 1st extra hole. **1980:** Arnold Palmer def. Paul Harney on 1st extra hole. **1993:** Tom Wargo def. Bruce Crampton on 2nd extra hole.

U.S. Senior Open

Established in 1980 for senior players 55 years old and over, the minimum age was dropped to 50 (the Champions Tour entry age) in 1981. Arnold Palmer, Billy Casper, Hale Irwin, Orville Moody, Jack Nicklaus and Lee Trevino are the only golfers who have won both the U.S. Open and U.S. Senior Open.
Multiple winners: Miller Barber (3); Hale Irwin, Jack Nicklaus and Gary Player (2).

Year		Year		Year		Year	
1980	Roberto De Vicenzo	1986	Dale Douglass	1992	Larry Laoretti	1998	Hale Irwin
1981	Arnold Palmer*	1987	Gary Player	1993	Jack Nicklaus	1999	Dave Eichelberger
1982	Miller Barber	1988	Gary Player*	1994	Simon Hobday	2000	Hale Irwin
1983	Bill Casper*	1989	Orville Moody	1995	Tom Weiskopf	2001	Bruce Fleisher
1984	Miller Barber	1990	Lee Trevino	1996	Dave Stockton	2002	Don Pooley*
1985	Miller Barber	1991	Jack Nicklaus*	1997	Graham Marsh	2003	Bruce Lietzke

*PLAYOFFS:

1981: Arnold Palmer (70) def. Bob Stone (74) and Billy Casper (77) in 18 holes. **1983:** Tied at 75 after 18-hole playoff, Casper def. Rod Funseth with a birdie on the 1st extra hole. **1988:** Gary Player (68) def. Bob Charles (70) in 18 holes. **1991:** Jack Nicklaus (65) def. Chi Chi Rodriguez (69) in 18 holes. **2002:** Don Pooley and Tom Watson remained tied after a three hole playoff and Pooley won on the second hole of sudden death.

Senior Players Championship

First played in 1983 and contested in Cleveland (1983-86), Ponte Vedra, Fla. (1987-89) and Dearborn, Mich. (since 1990).
Multiple winners: Ray Floyd, Arnold Palmer and Dave Stockton (2).

Year		Year		Year		Year	
1983	Miller Barber	1989	Orville Moody	1995	J.C. Snead*	2001	Allen Doyle*
1984	Arnold Palmer	1990	Jack Nicklaus	1996	Ray Floyd	2002	Stewart Ginn
1985	Arnold Palmer	1991	Jim Albus	1997	Larry Gilbert	2003	Craig Stadler
1986	Chi Chi Rodriguez	1992	Dave Stockton	1998	Gil Morgan		
1987	Gary Player	1993	Jim Colbert	1999	Hale Irwin		
1988	Billy Casper	1994	Dave Stockton	2000	Ray Floyd		

*PLAYOFFS:

1995: J.C. Snead def. Jack Nicklaus on 1st extra hole. **2001:** Allen Doyle def. Doug Tewell on 1st extra hole.

Senior British Open

First played in 1987 and contested in Turnberry, Scotland (1987-90, 2003), Lytham, England (1991-94), Portrush, Ireland (1995-99) and Newcastle, Ireland (2000-02). In 2003 it became the fifth designated major championship on the Champions Tour.
Multiple winners: Gary Player (3); Brian Barnes, Bob Charles and Christy O'Connor Jr. (2). (as a major): none.

Year		Year		Year		Year	
1987	Neil Coles	1992	John Fourie	1997	Gary Player	2002	Noboru Sugai
1988	Gary Player	1993	Bob Charles	1998	Brian Huggett	2003	Tom Watson*
1989	Bob Charles	1994	Tom Wargo	1999	Christy O'Connor Jr.		
1990	Gary Player	1995	Brian Barnes	2000	Christy O'Connor Jr.		
1991	Bobby Verwey	1996	Brian Barnes	2001	Ian Stanley		

*PLAYOFF (as a Major)— **2003:** Tom Watson def. Carl Mason on 2nd extra hole.

Major Senior Championship Leaders

Through 2003. All players are still active. **Note:** The Senior British Open became the Champions Tour's fifth major in 2003.

	Senior PGA	US Open	Senior Players	Trad	Total		Senior PGA	US Open	Senior Players	Trad	Total
1 Jack Nicklaus	1	2	1	4	**8**	4 Ray Floyd	1	0	2	1	**4**
2 Hale Irwin	3	2	1	0	**6**	Lee Trevino	2	1	0	1	**4**
Gary Player	3	2	1	0	**6**						

Grand Slam Summary

The Senior Grand Slam had officially consisted of The Tradition, the Senior PGA Championship, the Senior Players Championship and the U.S. Senior Open from 1990-2002. In 2003, the Senior British Open was added. Jack Nicklaus won three of the four events in 1991, but no one has won all four (or now five) in one season.

Three wins in one year: Jack Nicklaus (1991). **Two wins in one year** (8): Gary Player (twice); Hale Irwin, Gil Morgan, Orville Moody, Jack Nicklaus, Arnold Palmer, Lee Trevino and Tom Watson (once).

Year	Tradition	Sr. PGA	Players	US Open	Year	Tradition	Sr. PGA	Players	US Open
1983	—	—	M. Barber	Casper	1993	Shaw	Wargo	Colbert	Nicklaus
1984	—	Palmer	Palmer	M. Barber	1994	Floyd	Trevino	Stockton	Hobday
1985	—	Thomson	Palmer	M. Barber	1995	Nicklaus	Floyd	Snead	Weiskopf
1986	—	Player	Rodriguez	Douglass	1996	Nicklaus	Irwin	Floyd	Stockton
1987	—	Rodriguez	Player	Player	1997	Morgan	Irwin	Gilbert	Marsh
1988	—	Player	Casper	Player	1998	Morgan	Irwin	Morgan	Irwin
1989	Bies	Mowry	Moody	Moody	1999	Marsh	Doyle	Irwin	Eichelberger
1990	Nicklaus	Player	Nicklaus	Trevino	2000	Kite	Tewell	Floyd	Irwin
1991	Nicklaus	Nicklaus	Albus	Nicklaus	2001	Tewell	Watson	Doyle	Fleisher
1992	Trevino	Trevino	Stockton	Laoretti	2002	Thorpe	Zoeller	Ginn	Pooley

Year	Tradition	Sr. PGA	Players	US Open	Sr. Brit. Open
2003	Watson	Jacobs	Stadler	Lietzke	Watson

Annual Money Leaders

Official annual money leaders on the PGA, European PGA, Champions and LPGA tours.

PGA

Multiple leaders: Jack Nicklaus (8); Ben Hogan, Tom Watson and Tiger Woods (5); Arnold Palmer (4); Greg Norman, Sam Snead and Curtis Strange (3); Julius Boros, Billy Casper, Tom Kite, Byron Nelson and Nick Price (2).

Year		Earnings	Year		Earnings	Year		Earnings
1934	Paul Runyan	$6,767	1957	Dick Mayer	$65,835	1980	Tom Watson	$530,808
1935	Johnny Revolta	9,543	1958	Arnold Palmer	42,608	1981	Tom Kite	375,699
1936	Horton Smith	7,682	1959	Art Wall	53,168	1982	Craig Stadler	446,462
1937	Harry Cooper	14,139	1960	Arnold Palmer	75,263	1983	Hal Sutton	426,668
1938	Sam Snead	19,534	1961	Gary Player	64,540	1984	Tom Watson	476,260
1939	Henry Picard	10,303	1962	Arnold Palmer	81,448	1985	Curtis Strange	542,321
1940	Ben Hogan	10,655	1963	Arnold Palmer	128,230	1986	Greg Norman	653,296
1941	Ben Hogan	18,358	1964	Jack Nicklaus	113,285	1987	Curtis Strange	925,941
1942	Ben Hogan	13,143	1965	Jack Nicklaus	140,752	1988	Curtis Strange	1,147,644
1943	No records kept		1966	Billy Casper	121,945	1989	Tom Kite	1,395,278
1944	Byron Nelson	37,968	1967	Jack Nicklaus	188,998	1990	Greg Norman	1,165,477
1945	Byron Nelson	63,336	1968	Billy Casper	205,169	1991	Corey Pavin	979,430
1946	Ben Hogan	42,556	1969	Frank Beard	164,707	1992	Fred Couples	1,344,188
1947	Jimmy Demaret	27,937	1970	Lee Trevino	157,037	1993	Nick Price	1,478,557
1948	Ben Hogan	32,112	1971	Jack Nicklaus	244,491	1994	Nick Price	1,499,927
1949	Sam Snead	31,594	1972	Jack Nicklaus	320,542	1995	Greg Norman	1,654,959
1950	Sam Snead	35,759	1973	Jack Nicklaus	308,362	1996	Tom Lehman	1,780,159
1951	Lloyd Mangrum	26,089	1974	Johnny Miller	353,022	1997	Tiger Woods	2,066,833
1952	Julius Boros	37,033	1975	Jack Nicklaus	298,149	1998	David Duval	2,591,031
1953	Lew Worsham	34,002	1976	Jack Nicklaus	266,439	1999	Tiger Woods	6,616,585
1954	Bob Toski	65,820	1977	Tom Watson	310,653	2000	Tiger Woods	9,188,321
1955	Julius Boros	63,122	1978	Tom Watson	362,429	2001	Tiger Woods	5,687,777
1956	Ted Kroll	72,836	1979	Tom Watson	462,636	2002	Tiger Woods	6,912,625

Note: In 1944-45, Nelson's winnings were in War Bonds.

Champions Tour

Multiple leaders: Hale Irwin and Don January (3); Miller Barber, Bob Charles, Jim Colbert, Dave Stockton and Lee Trevino (2).

Year		Earnings	Year		Earnings	Year		Earnings
1980	Don January	$44,100	1988	Bob Charles	$533,929	1996	Jim Colbert	$1,627,890
1981	Miller Barber	83,136	1989	Bob Charles	725,887	1997	Hale Irwin	2,343,364
1982	Miller Barber	106,890	1990	Lee Trevino	1,190,518	1998	Hale Irwin	2,861,945
1983	Don January	237,571	1991	Mike Hill	1,065,657	1999	Bruce Fleisher	2,515,705
1984	Don January	328,597	1992	Lee Trevino	1,027,002	2000	Larry Nelson	2,708,005
1985	Peter Thomson	386,724	1993	Dave Stockton	1,175,944	2001	Allen Doyle	2,553,582
1986	Bruce Crampton	454,299	1994	Dave Stockton	1,402,519	2002	Hale Irwin	3,028,304
1987	Chi Chi Rodriguez	509,145	1995	Jim Colbert	1,444,386			

European PGA

Official money in the Volvo Order of Merit was awarded in British pounds from 1961-98 and euros (E) since 1999.

Multiple leaders: Colin Montgomerie (7); Seve Ballesteros (6); Sandy Lyle (3); Gay Brewer Jr., Nick Faldo, Retief Goosen, Bernard Hunt, Bernhard Langer, Peter Thomson and Ian Woosnam (2).

Year		Earnings	Year		Earnings	Year		Earnings
1961	Bernard Hunt	£4,492	1975	Dale Hayes	£20,507	1989	Ronan Rafferty	£465,981
1962	Peter Thomson	5,764	1976	Seve Ballesteros	39,504	1990	Ian Woosnam	737,977
1963	Bernard Hunt	7,209	1977	Seve Ballesteros	46,436	1991	Seve Ballesteros	790,811
1964	Neil Coles	7,890	1978	Seve Ballesteros	54,348	1992	Nick Faldo	1,220,540
1965	Peter Thomson	7,011	1979	Sandy Lyle	49,233	1993	Colin Montgomerie	798,145
1966	Bruce Devlin	13,205	1980	Greg Norman	74,829	1994	Colin Montgomerie	920,647
1967	Gay Brewer Jr.	20,235	1981	Bernhard Langer	95,991	1995	Colin Montgomerie	1,038,718
1968	Gay Brewer Jr.	23,107	1982	Sandy Lyle	86,141	1996	Colin Montgomerie	1,034,752
1969	Billy Casper	23,483	1983	Nick Faldo	140,761	1997	Colin Montgomerie	1,583,904
1970	Christy O'Connor	31,532	1984	Bernhard Langer	160,883	1998	Colin Montgomerie	1,082,833
1971	Gary Player	11,281	1985	Sandy Lyle	254,711	1999	C. Montgomerie	E2,066,885
1972	Bob Charles	18,538	1986	Seve Ballesteros	259,275	2000	Lee Westwood	3,125,147
1973	Tony Jacklin	24,839	1987	Ian Woosnam	439,075	2001	Retief Goosen	2,862,806
1974	Peter Oosterhuis	32,127	1988	Seve Ballesteros	502,000	2002	Retief Goosen	2,360,128

LPGA

Multiple leaders: Kathy Whitworth (8); Annika Sorenstam (5); Mickey Wright (4); Patty Berg, JoAnne Carner, Beth Daniel, Betsy King, Nancy Lopez and Karrie Webb (3); Pat Bradley, Judy Rankin, Betsy Rawls, Louise Suggs and Babe Zaharias (2).

Year		Earnings	Year		Earnings	Year		Earnings
1950	Babe Zaharias	$14,800	1968	Kathy Whitworth	$48,379	1986	Pat Bradley	$492,021
1951	Babe Zaharias	15,087	1969	Carol Mann	49,152	1987	Ayako Okamoto	466,034
1952	Betsy Rawls	14,505	1970	Kathy Whitworth	30,235	1988	Sherri Turner	350,851
1953	Louise Suggs	19,816	1971	Kathy Whitworth	41,181	1989	Betsy King	654,132
1954	Patty Berg	16,011	1972	Kathy Whitworth	65,063	1990	Beth Daniel	863,578
1955	Patty Berg	16,492	1973	Kathy Whitworth	82,864	1991	Pat Bradley	763,118
1956	Marlene Hagge	20,235	1974	JoAnne Carner	87,094	1992	Dottie Pepper	693,335
1957	Patty Berg	16,272	1975	Sandra Palmer	76,374	1993	Betsy King	595,992
1958	Beverly Hanson	12,639	1976	Judy Rankin	150,734	1994	Laura Davies	687,201
1959	Betsy Rawls	26,774	1977	Judy Rankin	122,890	1995	Annika Sorenstam	666,533
1960	Louise Suggs	16,892	1978	Nancy Lopez	189,814	1996	Karrie Webb	1,002,000
1961	Mickey Wright	22,236	1979	Nancy Lopez	197,489	1997	Annika Sorenstam	1,236,789
1962	Mickey Wright	21,641	1980	Beth Daniel	231,000	1998	Annika Sorenstam	1,092,748
1963	Mickey Wright	31,269	1981	Beth Daniel	206,998	1999	Karrie Webb	1,591,959
1964	Mickey Wright	29,800	1982	JoAnne Carner	310,400	2000	Karrie Webb	1,876,853
1965	Kathy Whitworth	28,658	1983	JoAnne Carner	291,404	2001	Annika Sorenstam	2,105,868
1966	Kathy Whitworth	33,517	1984	Betsy King	266,771	2002	Annika Sorenstam	2,863,904
1967	Kathy Whitworth	32,937	1985	Nancy Lopez	416,472			

All-Time Leaders

PGA, Champions Tour and LPGA leaders through 2002. **Note:** In Sept. 2002, the PGA Tour board approved the retroactive awarding of an official victory to British Open winners prior to 1995. The list below reflects the new totals.

Tournaments Won

	PGA	No		Champions	No		LPGA	No
1	Sam Snead	82	1	Hale Irwin	36	1	Kathy Whitworth	88
2	Jack Nicklaus	73	2	Lee Trevino	29	2	Mickey Wright	82
3	Ben Hogan	64	3	Miller Barber	24	3	Patty Berg	60
4	Arnold Palmer	62	4	Bob Charles	23	4	Louise Suggs	58
5	Byron Nelson	52	5	Don January	22	5	Betsy Rawls	55
6	Billy Casper	51		Chi Chi Rodriguez	22	6	Nancy Lopez	48
7	Walter Hagen	44	7	Gil Morgan	21	7	JoAnne Carner	43
8	Cary Middlecoff	40	8	Bruce Crampton	20	8	Sandra Haynie	42
9	Gene Sarazen	39		Jim Colbert	20		Annika Sorenstam	42
	Tom Watson	39	10	George Archer	19	10	Babe Zaharias	41
11	Lloyd Mangrum	36		Gary Player	19	11	Carol Mann	38
12	Tiger Woods	34	12	Mike Hill	18	12	Patty Sheehan	35
13	Horton Smith	32	13	Larry Nelson	16	13	Betsy King	34
14	Harry Cooper	31	14	Bruce Fleisher	15	14	Beth Daniel	32
	Jimmy Demaret	31	15	Dave Stockton	14	15	Pat Bradley	31
16	Leo Diegel	30		Raymond Floyd	14	16	Amy Alcott	29
17	Gene Littler	29	17	Jim Dent	12	17	Juli Inkster	28
	Paul Runyan	29	18	Dale Douglass	11		Karrie Webb	28
	Lee Trevino	29		Orville Moody	11	19	Jane Blalock	27
20	Henry Picard	26		Bob Murphy	11	20	Judy Rankin	26
				Peter Thomson	11		Marlene Hagge	26

All-Time Leaders (Cont.)
Money Won
All-time earnings through 2002.

PGA

		Earnings				Earnings				Earnings
1	Tiger Woods	$33,103,852	10	Hal Sutton	$14,205,947	19	Paul Azinger	$12,457,891
2	Phil Mickelson	22,149,969	11	Jim Furyk	13,856,843	20	Loren Roberts	11,785,232
3	Davis Love III	20,050,850	12	Greg Norman	13,812,130	21	Payne Stewart	11,737,008
4	Vijay Singh	18,281,015	13	Justin Leonard	13,658,234	22	Brad Faxon	11,592,350
5	Nick Price	16,648,337	14	Fred Couples	13,327,971	23	John Cook	11,005,774
6	David Duval	16,150,598	15	Tom Lehman	12,957,027	24	Tom Kite	10,920,309
7	Scott Hoch	16,018,375	16	Jeff Sluman	12,884,759	25	Fred Funk	10,770,922
8	Ernie Els	15,308,529	17	David Toms	12,872,425			
9	Mark Calcavecchia	14,571,858	18	Mark O'Meara	12,755,331			

European PGA

		Earnings				Earnings				Earnings
1	C. Montgomerie	E19,039,963	10	Padraig Harrington	E9,199,440	19	Mark McNulty	E5,786,556
2	Tiger Woods	17,153,559	11	Lee Westwood	9,149,725	20	Paul Lawrie	5,531,524
3	Bernhard Langer	12,918,736	12	Vijay Singh	7,843,853	21	Barry Lane	5,468,651
4	Ernie Els	12,702,620	13	M. A. Jimenez	7,605,868	22	Paul McGinley	5,295,862
5	Ian Woosnam	11,297,761	14	Thomas Bjorn	7,221,500	23	Angel Cabrera	5,079,050
6	Darren Clarke	10,884,369	15	Sam Torrance	7,002,816	24	Costantino Rocca	4,999,613
7	Retief Goosen	10,351,630	16	Eduardo Romero	6,916,811	25	Mark James	4,946,171
8	Nick Faldo	9,528,058	17	Seve Ballesteros	6,860,480			
9	Jose Maria Olazabal	9,479,402	18	Michael Campbell	5,902,490			

Champions Tour

		Earnings				Earnings				Earnings
1	Hale Irwin	$16,950,178	10	George Archer	$8,277,578	19	J.C. Snead	$6,731,859
2	Gil Morgan	11,092,593	11	Jim Dent	8,215,643	20	Bob Murphy	6,635,762
3	Jim Colbert	10,840,374	12	Isao Aoki	8,211,784	21	Chi Chi Rodriguez	6,626,211
4	Dave Stockton	9,735,814	13	Dana Quigley	7,769,279	22	Bruce Summerhays	6,543,445
5	Lee Trevino	9,616,404	14	Mike Hill	7,731,080	23	Tom Wargo	6,456,090
6	Larry Nelson	9,229,621	15	Allen Doyle	7,457,664	24	John Jacobs	6,215,526
7	Bruce Fleisher	9,161,759	16	Jay Sigel	7,266,387	25	Jim Albus	5,868,892
8	Bob Charles	8,763,536	17	Graham Marsh	6,782,754			
9	Ray Floyd	8,435,222	18	Dale Douglass	6,757,725			

LPGA

		Earnings				Earnings				Earnings
1	Annika Sorenstam	$11,170,368	10	Pat Bradley	$5,743,605	19	Tammie Green	$3,711,455
2	Karrie Webb	8,708,059	11	Se Ri Pak	5,724,762	20	Brandie Burton	3,594,946
3	Juli Inkster	7,666,836	12	Patty Sheehan	5,507,155	21	Chris Johnson	3,476,055
4	Betsy King	7,357,253	13	Nancy Lopez	5,320,877	22	Amy Alcott	3,408,074
5	Beth Daniel	6,913,620	14	Kelly Robbins	4,980,460	23	Da. Ammaccapane	3,253,700
6	Dottie Pepper	6,658,613	15	Liselotte Neumann	4,503,573	24	Donna Andrews	3,237,344
7	Meg Mallon	6,418,304	16	Lorie Kane	4,282,840	25	Mi Hyun Kim	3,222,322
8	Rosie Jones	6,406,347	17	Sherri Steinhauer	3,933,900			
9	Laura Davies	6,039,757	18	Jane Geddes	3,787,058			

Official World Ranking

Begun in 1986, the Official World Golf Ranking (formerly the Sony World Ranking) combines the best golfers on the six pro men's tours which make up the International Federation of PGA Tours. Rankings are based on a rolling two-year period and weighed in favor of more recent results. While annual winners are not announced, certain players reaching No. 1 have dominated each year.

Multiple winners (at year's end): Greg Norman and Tiger Woods (6); Nick Faldo (3); Seve Ballesteros (2).

Year		Year		Year		Year	
1986	Seve Ballesteros	1990	Nick Faldo	1993	Nick Faldo	1998	Tiger Woods
1987	Greg Norman		& Greg Norman	1994	Nick Price	1999	Tiger Woods
1988	Greg Norman	1991	Ian Woosnam	1995	Greg Norman	2000	Tiger Woods
1989	Seve Ballesteros	1992	Fred Couples	1996	Greg Norman	2001	Tiger Woods
	& Greg Norman		& Nick Faldo	1997	Tiger Woods	2002	Tiger Woods

Annual Awards

PGA of America Player of the Year

Awarded by the PGA of America; based on points scale that weighs performance in major tournaments, regular events, money earned and scoring average.

Multiple winners: Tom Watson (6); Jack Nicklaus and Tiger Woods (5); Ben Hogan (4); Julius Boros, Billy Casper, Arnold Palmer and Nick Price.

Year		Year		Year		Year	
1948	Ben Hogan	1962	Arnold Palmer	1976	Jack Nicklaus	1990	Nick Faldo
1949	Sam Snead	1963	Julius Boros	1977	Tom Watson	1991	Corey Pavin
1950	Ben Hogan	1964	Ken Venturi	1978	Tom Watson	1992	Fred Couples
1951	Ben Hogan	1965	Dave Marr	1979	Tom Watson	1993	Nick Price
1952	Julius Boros	1966	Billy Casper	1980	Tom Watson	1994	Nick Price
1953	Ben Hogan	1967	Jack Nicklaus	1981	Bill Rogers	1995	Greg Norman
1954	Ed Furgol	1968	No award	1982	Tom Watson	1996	Tom Lehman
1955	Doug Ford	1969	Orville Moody	1983	Hal Sutton	1997	Tiger Woods
1956	Jack Burke	1970	Billy Casper	1984	Tom Watson	1998	Mark O'Meara
1957	Dick Mayer	1971	Lee Trevino	1985	Lanny Wadkins	1999	Tiger Woods
1958	Dow Finsterwald	1972	Jack Nicklaus	1986	Bob Tway	2000	Tiger Woods
1959	Art Wall Jr.	1973	Jack Nicklaus	1987	Paul Azinger	2001	Tiger Woods
1960	Arnold Palmer	1974	Johnny Miller	1988	Curtis Strange	2002	Tiger Woods
1961	Jerry Barber	1975	Jack Nicklaus	1989	Tom Kite		

PGA Tour Player of the Year

Award by the PGA Tour starting in 1990. Winner voted on by tour members from list of nominees. Winner receives the Jack Nicklaus Trophy, which originated in 1997.

Multiple winners: Tiger Woods (5); Fred Couples and Nick Price (2).

Year		Year		Year		Year	
1990	Wayne Levi	1994	Nick Price	1998	Mark O'Meara	2002	Tiger Woods
1991	Fred Couples	1995	Greg Norman	1999	Tiger Woods		
1992	Fred Couples	1996	Tom Lehman	2000	Tiger Woods		
1993	Nick Price	1997	Tiger Woods	2001	Tiger Woods		

PGA Tour Rookie of the Year

Awarded by the PGA Tour in 1990. Winner voted on by tour members from list of first-year nominees.

Year		Year		Year		Year	
1990	Robert Gamez	1994	Ernie Els	1998	Steve Flesch	2002	Jonathan Byrd
1991	John Daly	1995	Woody Austin	1999	Carlos Franco		
1992	Mark Carnevale	1996	Tiger Woods	2000	Michael Clark II		
1993	Vijay Singh	1997	Stewart Cink	2001	Charles Howell III		

Champions Tour Player of the Year

Awarded by the Champions Tour starting in 1990. Winner voted on by tour members from list of nominees.

Multiple winner: Hale Irwin and Lee Trevino (3); Jim Colbert (2).

Year		Year		Year		Year	
1990	Lee Trevino	1993	Dave Stockton	1997	Hale Irwin	2001	Allen Doyle
1991	George Archer	1994	Lee Trevino	1998	Hale Irwin	2002	Hale Irwin
	& Mike Hill	1995	Jim Colbert	1999	Bruce Fleisher		
1992	Lee Trevino	1996	Jim Colbert	2000	Larry Nelson		

European Golfer of the Year

Officially, the Ritz Club Trophy (1985-92), Johnnie Walker Trophy (1993-97) and Asprey Golfer of the Year (1998-present); voting done by panel of European golf writers and tour members.

Multiple winners: Colin Montgomerie (4); Seve Ballesteros and Nick Faldo (3); Ernie Els, Bernhard Langer and Lee Westwood (2).

Year		Year		Year		Year	
1985	Bernhard Langer	1990	Nick Faldo	1995	Colin Montgomerie	2000	Lee Westwood
1986	Seve Ballesteros	1991	Seve Ballesteros	1996	Colin Montgomerie	2001	Retief Goosen
1987	Ian Woosnam	1992	Nick Faldo	1997	Colin Montgomerie	2002	Ernie Els
1988	Seve Ballesteros	1993	Bernhard Langer	1998	Lee Westwood		
1989	Nick Faldo	1994	Ernie Els	1999	Colin Montgomerie		

Annual Awards (Cont.)
LPGA Player of the Year

Sponsored by Rolex and awarded by the LPGA; based on performance points accumulated during the year.

Multiple winners: Kathy Whitworth (7); Annika Sorenstam (5); Nancy Lopez (4); JoAnne Carner, Beth Daniel and Betsy King (3); Pat Bradley, Judy Rankin and Karrie Webb (2).

Year		Year		Year		Year	
1966	Kathy Whitworth	1976	Judy Rankin	1986	Pat Bradley	1996	Laura Davies
1967	Kathy Whitworth	1977	Judy Rankin	1987	Ayako Okamoto	1997	Annika Sorenstam
1968	Kathy Whitworth	1978	Nancy Lopez	1988	Nancy Lopez	1998	Annika Sorenstam
1969	Kathy Whitworth	1979	Nancy Lopez	1989	Betsy King	1999	Karrie Webb
1970	Sandra Haynie	1980	Beth Daniel	1990	Beth Daniel	2000	Karrie Webb
1971	Kathy Whitworth	1981	JoAnne Carner	1991	Pat Bradley	2001	Annika Sorenstam
1972	Kathy Whitworth	1982	JoAnne Carner	1992	Dottie Mochrie	2002	Annika Sorenstam
1973	Kathy Whitworth	1983	Patty Sheehan	1993	Betsy King		
1974	JoAnne Carner	1984	Betsy King	1994	Beth Daniel		
1975	Sandra Palmer	1985	Nancy Lopez	1995	Annika Sorenstam		

LPGA Rookie of the Year

Sponsored by Rolex and awarded by the LPGA; based on performance points accumulated during the year. Winner receives Louise Suggs Trophy, which originated in 2000.

Year		Year		Year		Year	
1962	Mary Mills	1973	Laura Baugh	1984	Juli Inkster	1995	Pat Hurst
1963	Clifford Ann Creed	1974	Jan Stephenson	1985	Penny Hammel	1996	Karrie Webb
1964	Susie Berning	1975	Amy Alcott	1986	Jody Rosenthal	1997	Lisa Hackney
1965	Margie Masters	1976	Bonnie Lauer	1987	Tammie Green	1998	Se Ri Pak
1966	Jan Ferraris	1977	Debbie Massey	1988	Liselotte Neumann	1999	Mi Hyun Kim
1967	Sharron Moran	1978	Nancy Lopez	1989	Pamela Wright	2000	Dorothy Delasin
1968	Sandra Post	1979	Beth Daniel	1990	Hiromi Kobayashi	2001	Hee-Won Han
1969	Jane Blalock	1980	Myra Van Hoose	1991	Brandie Burton	2002	Beth Bauer
1970	JoAnne Carner	1981	Patty Sheehan	1992	Helen Alfredsson	2003	Lorena Ochoa
1971	Sally Little	1982	Patti Rizzo	1993	Suzanne Strudwick		
1972	Jocelyne Bourassa	1983	Stephanie Farwig	1994	Annika Sorenstam		

National Team Competition
MEN
Ryder Cup

The Ryder Cup was presented by British seed merchant and businessman Samuel Ryder in 1927 for competition between professional golfers from Great Britain and the United States. The British team was expanded to include Irish players in 1973 and the rest of Europe in 1979. The 2001 event was postponed due to the attacks on America, causing the event to switch from an odd- to even-year schedule. The United States leads the series 24-8-2 after 34 matches.

Year		Year		Year		Year	
1927	USA, 9½-2½	1951	USA, 9½-2½	1969	Draw, 16-16	1987	Europe, 15-13
1929	Britain-Ireland, 7-5	1953	USA, 6½-5½	1971	USA, 18½-13½	1989	Draw, 14-14
1931	USA, 9-3	1955	USA, 8-4	1973	USA, 19-13	1991	USA, 14½-13½
1933	Great Britain, 6½-5½	1957	Britain-Ireland, 7½-4½	1975	USA, 21-11	1993	USA, 15-13
1935	USA, 9-3	1959	USA, 8½-3½	1977	USA, 12½-13½	1995	Europe, 14½-13½
1937	USA, 8-4	1961	USA, 14½-9½	1979	USA, 17-11	1997	Europe, 14½-13½
1939-45	Not held	1963	USA, 23-9	1981	USA, 18½-9½	1999	USA, 14½-13½
1947	USA, 11-1	1965	USA, 19½-12½	1983	USA, 14½-13½	2002	Europe, 15½-12½
1949	USA, 7-5	1967	USA, 23½-8½	1985	Europe, 16½-11½		

Playing Sites

1927—Worcester CC (Mass.); **1929**—Moortown, England; **1931**—Scioto CC (Ohio); **1933**—Southport & Ainsdale, England; **1935**—Ridgewood CC (N.J.); **1937**—Southport & Ainsdale, England; **1939-45**—Not held. **1947**—Portland CC (Ore.); **1949**—Ganton GC, England; **1951**—Pinehurst CC (N.C.); **1953**—Wentworth, England; **1955**—Thunderbird Ranch & CC (Calif.); **1957**—Lindrick GC, England; **1959**—Eldorado GC (Calif.); **1961**—Royal Lytham & St. Annes, England; **1963**—East Lake CC (Ga.); **1965**—Royal Birkdale, England; **1967**—Champions GC (Tex.); **1969**—Royal Birkdale, England; **1971**—Old Warson CC (Mo.); **1973**—Muirfield, Scotland; **1975**—Laurel Valley GC (Pa.); **1977**—Royal Lytham & St. Annes, England; **1979**—The Greenbrier (W.Va.); **1981**—Walton Heath GC, England; **1983**—PGA National GC (Fla.); **1985**—The Belfry, England; **1987**—Muirfield Village GC (Ohio); **1989**—The Belfry, England; **1991**—Ocean Course (S.C.); **1993**—The Belfry, England; **1995**—Oak Hill CC (N.Y.); **1997**—Valderrama, Costa del Sol, Spain; **1999**—The Country Club (Mass.); **2002**—The Belfry, England; **2004**—Oakland Hills CC (Mich.); **2006**—Kildare Hotel & CC, Ireland; **2008**—Valhalla GC (Ky.); **2010**—Celtic Manor, Wales; **2012**—Medinah CC (Ill.); **2014**—Gleneagles, Scotland.

Walker Cup

The Walker Cup was presented by American businessman George Herbert Walker in 1922 for competition between amateur golfers from Great Britain, Ireland and the United States. The U.S. leads the series against the combined Great Britain-Ireland team, 31-7-1, after 39 matches.

Year		Year		Year		Year	
1922	USA, 8-4	1924	USA, 9-3	1928	USA, 11-1	1932	USA, 9½-2½
1923	USA, 6½-5½	1926	USA, 6½-5½	1930	USA, 10-2	1934	USA, 9½-2½

Year		Year		Year		Year	
1936	USA, 10½-1½	1959	USA, 9-3	1977	USA, 16-8	1993	USA, 19-5
1938	Britain-Ireland, 7½-4½	1961	USA, 11-1	1979	USA, 15½-8½	1995	Britain-Ireland, 14-10
1940-46	Not held	1963	USA, 14-10	1981	USA, 15-9	1997	USA, 18-6
1947	USA, 8-4	1965	Draw, 12-12	1983	USA, 13½-10½	1999	Britain-Ireland, 15-9
1949	USA, 10-2	1967	USA, 15-9	1985	USA, 13-11	2001	Britain-Ireland, 15-9
1951	USA, 7½-4½	1969	USA, 13-11	1987	USA, 16½-7½	2003	Britain-Ireland,
1953	USA, 9-3	1971	Britain-Ireland, 13-11	1989	Britain-Ireland,		12½-11½
1955	USA, 10-2	1973	USA, 14-10		12½-11½		
1957	USA, 8½-3½	1975	USA, 15½-8½	1991	USA, 14-10		

Presidents Cup

The Presidents Cup is a biennial event played in non-Ryder Cup years in which the world's best non-European players compete against players from the United States. The U.S. leads the series, 3-1.

Year		Year		Year	
1994	USA, 20-12	1998	International, 20½-11½	2003	Nov. 18-23
1996	USA, 16½-15½	2000	USA, 21½-10½		

WOMEN

Solheim Cup

The Solheim Cup was presented by the Karsten Manufacturing Co. in 1990 for competition between women professional golfers from Europe and the United States. The event was switched from even- to odd-numbered years after 2002 so it would not conflict with the men's Ryder Cup event. The U.S. leads the series, 5-3.

Year		Year		Year	
1990	USA, 11½-4½	1996	USA, 17-11	2002	USA, 15½-12½
1992	Europe, 11½-6½	1998	USA, 16-12	2003	Europe, 17½-10½
1994	USA, 13-7	2000	Europe, 14½-11½		

Playing Sites

1990—Lake Nona CC (Fla.); **1992**—Dalmahoy CC, Scotland; **1994**—The Greenbrier (W. Va.); **1996**—Marriott St. Pierre Hotel G&CC, Wales; **1998**—Muirfield Village GC (Ohio); **2000**—Loch Lomond GC, Scotland; **2002**—Interlachen CC (Minn.); **2003**—Barseback G&CC, Sweden; **2005**—Crooked Stick GC (Ind.).

Curtis Cup

Named after British golfing sisters Harriot and Margaret Curtis, the Curtis Cup was first contested in 1932 between teams of women amateurs from the United States and the British Isles.

Competed for every other year since 1932 (except during WWII). The U.S. leads the series, 23-6-3, after 32 matches.

Year		Year		Year		Year	
1932	USA, 5½-3½	1956	British Isles, 5-4	1974	USA, 13-5	1992	British Isles, 10-8
1934	USA, 6½-2½	1958	Draw, 4½-4½	1976	USA, 11½-6½	1994	Draw, 9-9
1936	Draw, 4½-4½	1960	USA, 6½-2½	1978	USA, 12-6	1996	British Isles, 11½-6½
1938	USA, 5½-3½	1962	USA, 8-1	1980	USA, 13-5	1998	USA, 10-8
1940-46	Not held	1964	USA, 10½-7½	1982	USA, 14½-3½	2000	USA, 10-8
1948	USA, 6½-2½	1966	USA, 13-5	1984	USA, 9½-8½	2002	USA, 11-7
1950	USA, 7½-1½	1968	USA, 10½-7½	1986	British Isles, 13-5		
1952	British Isles, 5-4	1970	USA, 11½-6½	1988	British Isles, 11-7		
1954	USA, 6-3	1972	USA, 10-8	1990	USA, 14-4		

COLLEGES

Men's NCAA Division I Champions

College championships decided by match play from 1897-1964 and stroke play since 1965.

Multiple winners (Teams): Yale (21); Houston (16); Oklahoma St. (9); Stanford (7); Harvard (6); Florida, LSU and North Texas (4); Wake Forest (3); Arizona St., Michigan, Ohio St. and Texas (2).

Multiple winners (Individuals): Ben Crenshaw and Phil Mickelson (3); Dick Crawford, Dexter Cummings, G.T. Dunlop, Fred Lamprecht and Scott Simpson (2).

Year	Team winner	Individual champion	Year	Team winner	Individual champion
1897	Yale	Louis Bayard, Princeton	1905	Yale	Robert Abbott, Yale
1898	Harvard (spring)	John Reid, Yale	1906	Yale	W.E. Clow Jr., Yale
1898	Yale (fall)	James Curtis, Harvard	1907	Yale	Ellis Knowles, Yale
1899	Harvard	Percy Pyne, Princeton	1908	Yale	H.H. Wilder, Harvard
1900	Not held		1909	Yale	Albert Seckel, Princeton
1901	Harvard	H. Lindsley, Harvard	1910	Yale	Robert Hunter, Yale
1902	Yale (spring)	Chas. Hitchcock Jr., Yale	1911	Yale	George Stanley, Yale
1902	Harvard (fall)	Chandler Egan, Harvard	1912	Yale	F.C. Davison, Harvard
1903	Harvard	F.O. Reinhart, Princeton	1913	Yale	Nathaniel Wheeler, Yale
1904	Harvard	A.L. White, Harvard	1914	Princeton	Edward Allis, Harvard

Colleges (Cont.)

Year	Team winner	Individual champion
1915	Yale	Francis Blossom, Yale
1916	Princeton	J.W. Hubbell, Harvard
1917-18	Not held	
1919	Princeton	A.L. Walker Jr., Columbia
1920	Princeton	Jess Sweetser, Yale
1921	Dartmouth	Simpson Dean, Princeton
1922	Princeton	Pollack Boyd, Dartmouth
1923	Princeton	Dexter Cummings, Yale
1924	Yale	Dexter Cummings, Yale
1925	Yale	Fred Lamprecht, Tulane
1926	Yale	Fred Lamprecht, Tulane
1927	Princeton	Watts Gunn, Georgia Tech
1928	Princeton	Maurice McCarthy, G'town
1929	Princeton	Tom Aycock, Yale
1930	Princeton	G.T. Dunlap Jr., Princeton
1931	Yale	G.T. Dunlap Jr., Princeton
1932	Yale	J.W. Fischer, Michigan
1933	Yale	Walter Emery, Oklahoma
1934	Michigan	Charles Yates, Ga.Tech
1935	Michigan	Ed White, Texas
1936	Yale	Charles Kocsis, Michigan
1937	Princeton	Fred Haas Jr., LSU
1938	Stanford	John Burke, Georgetown
1939	Stanford	Vincent D'Antoni, Tulane
1940	Princeton & LSU	Dixon Brooke, Virginia
1941	Stanford	Earl Stewart, LSU
1942	LSU & Stanford	Frank Tatum Jr., Stanford
1943	Yale	Wallace Ulrich, Carleton
1944	Notre Dame	Louis Lick, Minnesota
1945	Ohio State	John Lorms, Ohio St.
1946	Stanford	George Hamer, Georgia
1947	LSU	Dave Barclay, Michigan
1948	San Jose St.	Bob Harris, San Jose St.
1949	North Texas	Harvie Ward, N.Carolina
1950	North Texas	Fred Wampler, Purdue
1951	North Texas	Tom Nieporte, Ohio St.
1952	North Texas	Jim Vickers, Oklahoma
1953	Stanford	Earl Moeller, Oklahoma St.
1954	SMU	Hillman Robbins, Memphis St.
1955	LSU	Joe Campbell, Purdue
1956	Houston	Rick Jones, Ohio St.
1957	Houston	Rex Baxter Jr., Houston
1958	Houston	Phil Rodgers, Houston
1959	Houston	Dick Crawford, Houston
1960	Houston	Dick Crawford, Houston

Year	Team winner	Individual champion
1961	Purdue	Jack Nicklaus, Ohio St.
1962	Houston	Kermit Zarley, Houston
1963	Oklahoma St.	R.H. Sikes, Arkansas
1964	Houston	Terry Small, San Jose St.
1965	Houston	Marty Fleckman, Houston
1966	Houston	Bob Murphy, Florida
1967	Houston	Hale Irwin, Colorado
1968	Florida	Grier Jones, Oklahoma St.
1969	Houston	Bob Clark, Cal St.-LA
1970	Houston	John Mahaffey, Houston
1971	Texas	Ben Crenshaw, Texas
1972	Texas	Ben Crenshaw, Texas
		& Tom Kite, Texas
1973	Florida	Ben Crenshaw, Texas
1974	Wake Forest	Curtis Strange, W.Forest
1975	Wake Forest	Jay Haas, Wake Forest
1976	Oklahoma St.	Scott Simpson, USC
1977	Houston	Scott Simpson, USC
1978	Oklahoma St.	David Edwards, Okla. St.
1979	Ohio St.	Gary Hallberg, Wake Forest
1980	Oklahoma St.	Jay Don Blake, Utah St.
1981	Brigham Young	Ron Commans, USC
1982	Houston	Billy Ray Brown, Houston
1983	Oklahoma St.	Jim Carter, Arizona St.
1984	Houston	John Inman, N.Carolina
1985	Houston	Clark Burroughs, Ohio St.
1986	Wake Forest	Scott Verplank, Okla. St.
1987	Oklahoma St.	Brian Watts, Oklahoma St.
1988	UCLA	E.J. Pfister, Oklahoma St.
1989	Oklahoma	Phil Mickelson, Ariz. St.
1990	Arizona St.	Phil Mickelson, Ariz. St.
1991	Oklahoma St.	Warren Schuette, UNLV
1992	Arizona	Phil Mickelson, Ariz. St.
1993	Florida	Todd Demsey, Ariz. St.
1994	Stanford	Justin Leonard, Texas
1995	Oklahoma St.	Chip Spratlin, Auburn
1996	Arizona St.	Tiger Woods, Stanford
1997	Pepperdine	Charles Warren, Clemson
1998	UNLV	James McLean, Minnesota
1999	Georgia	Luke Donald, Northwestern
2000	Oklahoma St.	Charles Howell, Oklahoma St.
2001	Florida	Nick Gilliam, Florida
2002	Minnesota	Troy Matteson, Georgia Tech
2003	Clemson	Alejandro Canizares, Ariz. St.

Women's NCAA Division I Champions

College championships decided by stroke play since 1982.

Multiple winners (teams): Arizona St. (6); Arizona, Duke, Florida, San Jose St. and Tulsa (2).

Year	Team winner	Individual champion
1982	Tulsa	Kathy Baker, Tulsa
1983	TCU	Penny Hammel, Miami
1984	Miami-FL	Cindy Schreyer, Georgia
1985	Florida	Danielle Ammaccapane, Ariz.St.
1986	Florida	Page Dunlap, Florida
1987	San Jose St.	Caroline Keggi, New Mexico
1988	Tulsa	Melissa McNamara, Tulsa
1989	San Jose St.	Pat Hurst, San Jose St.
1990	Arizona St.	Susan Slaughter, Arizona
1991	UCLA	Annika Sorenstam, Arizona
1992	San Jose St.	Vicki Goetze, Georgia
1993	Arizona St.	Charlotta Sorenstam, Ariz. St.

Year	Team winner	Individual champion
1994	Arizona St.	Emilee Klein, Ariz. St.
1995	Arizona St.	K. Mourgue d'Algue, Ariz. St.
1996	Arizona	Marisa Baena, Arizona
1997	Arizona St.	Heather Bowie, Texas
1998	Arizona St.	Jennifer Rosales, USC
1999	Duke	Grace Park, Arizona St.
2000	Arizona	Jenna Daniels, Arizona
2001	Georgia	Candy Hannemann, Duke
2002	Duke	Virada Nirapathpongporn, Duke
2003	USC	Mikaela Parmlid, USC

Auto Racing

Gil de Ferran, left, steals the Spider-Man pose from teammate **Helio Castroneves** after the Indy 500.

Fast and Steady

Despite winning just one race through October, Matt Kenseth was primed for the Winston Cup points title.

Michael Morrison
is co-editor of the ESPN Sports Almanac.

In 2002 Matt Kenseth won five races for Roush Racing and finished in eighth place in the Winston Cup points race.

In 2003, with only one win through October in the third race of the year at Las Vegas Motor Speedway, Kenseth had put himself so far ahead in the points race that he was virtually assured of the title with several races remaining.

The NASCAR points system, originally adopted in 1975, rewards consistency as opposed to excellence. So while Kenseth only had one win, he also finished in the top ten 23 times over 33 races, which was more important.

On the flip side of the coin was Ryan Newman, the second-year driver in the No. 12 Dodge, who won eight races through the end of October, six of them coming in an incredible 13-week stretch between July 13 and Aug. 5 when he jumped 20 places in the points race. If not for some tough luck and a flurry of crashes in the beginning of the year,

Newman might have run away with the championship instead of Kenseth.

Newman's ability to balance fuel and power was so remarkable that fellow drivers not-so-quietly wondered whether he and his Penske Racing South Team were cheating. For his part, Newman scoffs at the accusations.

"It's hard to have a smart answer to a dumb question," he said. "They can think what they want, and they can say what they want. Everybody on this team does an awesome job, and the engine company does an awesome job."

Four-time Winston Cup Series champion Jeff Gordon had another solid season for Hendrick Motorsports, but as far as grabbing his fifth title in 2003, it was a case of too little, too late. Gordon won once through mid-October (at the Virginia 500 in Martinsville), then caught fire with late-season wins in Martinsville again (at the Subway 500) and then the Bass Pro Shops MBNA in

Jonathan Ferrey/Getty Images

Matt Kenseth may not have been spectacular in 2003, but his consistency and relentlessness left him sitting pretty for his first NASCAR Winston Cup points title.

Atlanta. With the points title already out of reach, he could only use his double-win as a momentum-builder for 2004.

If Gordon does win the 2004 title, it will be the first since 1971 that won't be known as the Winston Cup Championship. In June NASCAR announced the end of their deal with the R.J. Reynolds tobacco company and a new deal beginning in 2004 with wireless communications company, Nextel.

CART

With continued defections to NASCAR and the Indy Racing League and growing financial difficulties, it was a difficult year off the track for Championship Auto Racing Teams, Inc. In the summer the publicly traded company detailed its worsening situation and claimed losses of an estimated $43.5 million in the first half of 2003 alone. CART executives projected it would need additional cash to successfully make it through the 2004 season. In September the board agreed to sell the company to a group headed by team owner Gerald Forsythe. By the end of October the sale was not completed. The hope is that the sale will ultimately save the series, but there's no doubt that CART is in a precarious situation.

Michael Schumacher is subdued after winning at the Grand Prix of San Marino on April 20 just hours after the death of his mother. The victory was one of six for the six-time world champ.

On the track, the Champ Car World Series belonged to veteran driver Paul Tracy. The Canadian won the first three events of the year en route to seven titles overall. When rival Bruno Junqueira crashed with ten laps to go in the final race of the season, Tracy clinched his first points title.

Indy Racing League

New Zealander Scott Dixon, who made the move to IRL from CART with Target Chip Ganassi in February, acclimated himself to his new racing series quite nicely with a win in Miami in the first event of the year. It was the first of three wins for Dixon on the year, which coupled with five second place finishes, was enough for him to win the IndyCar points title in his first year. Driving a Toyota engine with a G-Force chassis, Dixon fought off valiant challenges from Penske teammates Gil de Ferran and Helio Castroneves.

The most surprising news from the IndyCar Series came out of the Chevy camp in mid-July. Lagging the Toyotas and Hondas by several m.p.h., they had no choice but to team up with Cosworth

continued on page 880 ▶

The Ten Biggest Stories
of the Year in Auto Racing

10 Gil de Ferran beats two-time defending champion and fellow Team Penske driver Helio Castroneves in the third-closest finish ever at the Indianapolis 500 on May 25. England's Scott Wheldon is involved in a spectacular crash that sends him airborne with 14 laps remaining.

9 Tom Kristensen, Rinaldo Capello and Guy Smith give Bentley its first 24 Hours at Le Mans victory since 1930. It is the fourth consecutive Le mans win for Kristensen and fifth overall. The trio complete just shy of 3,200 miles in their Bentley Speed 8.

8 Kurt Busch and Jimmy Spencer are at it again. This time, Spencer is fined and suspended for punching Busch in the face while he sat in his car in the garage area at the GFS Marketplace 400 at the Michigan International Speedway in June.

7 Former CART champion Alex Zanardi returns to competitive racing two years after a gruesome crash took his legs. He places seventh in the season-ending FIA European Touring Car Championship event in Monza, Italy

6 A new NASCAR rule change makes it illegal for drivers to race back to the yellow flag after an accident. The rule is praised for making things safer on the track but criticized for allowing some cars to gain free laps.

5 Michael Waltrip wins a rain-shortened Daytona 500, his second victory in the last three years in stock car racing's most prestigious event. Waltrip passes Jimmie Johnson on a restart on lap 106. The race is then called after lap 109.

4 Indy Racing League driver Tony Renna is killed at the age of 26 when his car spins out of control and crashes during a practice run at the Indianapolis Motor Speedway. He is the 67th person killed at the track and first since Scott Brayton in 1996.

3 Scott Dixon wins the IndyCar points championship for Chip Ganassi, but perhaps the bigger story from the Indy Racing League is Chevy's switch to a Cosworth engine in June, after being outclassed by Honda and Toyota. The engine pays immediate dividends for Sam Hornish Jr., who wins three of the next seven races.

2 NASCAR signs a ten-year title sponsorship agreement with wireless communications company Nextel to begin in 2004. The deal officially ends NASCAR's 33-year partnership with cigarette maker R.J. Reynolds.

1 German Ferrari driver Michael Schumacher wins six Grand Prix races to capture his sixth overall World Driving Championship, more than any driver in Formula One history.

Engineering, which is a wholly-owned subsidiary of Ford. With the new Cosworth engine, 2002 IRL points champion Sam Hornish Jr. won three of the next seven races, after recording no wins before the switch.

Formula One

After the third race of the season, the Brazilian Grand Prix, Ferrari's Michael Schumacher was in trouble. After winning a season-record 11 Grand Prix races in 2002, Schumacher won an unthinkable zero over the first three. All that changed on April 20 at the San Marino Grand Prix. Racing just hours after his mother died, Schumacher won his first race of the year. He stood in silence and fought back the tears on the podium, a spot that is usually meant for celebrating and spraying champagne. After that race, Schumacher won another five to edge Finland's Kimi Raikkonen, 93-91, for his all-time Formula One-record sixth World Driving Championship.

Photo Finishes

Gil de Ferran's 2003 win over Helio Castroneves in the Indy 500 was the races's third closest of all time. Listed are the top-10 closest margins of victory.

Year	Drivers	Margin (Seconds)
1992	Unser Jr. def. Goodyear	0.043
1982	Johncock def. Mears	0.160
2003	de Ferran def. Castroneves	0.299
1997	Luyendyk def. Goodyear	0.570
1996	Lazier def. Jones	0.695
1986	Rahal def. Cogan	1.440
1937	Shaw def. Hepburn	2.160
1985	Sullivan def. Ma. Andretti	2.477
1995	Villeneuve def. C. Fittipaldi	2.481
1993	E. Fittipaldi def. Luyendyk	2.862

Targeting the Title

After four CART titles by three different drivers, Chip Ganassi moved his Target team to the Indy Racing League in Feb., 2003. In his first full season of fielding two cars, Ganassi claimed its first IRL title.

Year	Driver	Series
1996	Jimmy Vasser	CART
1997	Alex Zanardi	CART
1998	Alex Zanardi	CART
1999	Juan Pablo Montoya	CART
2003	Scott Dixon	IRL IndyCar

2002-2003
Season in Review

SPORTS ALMANAC

NASCAR RESULTS
Winston Cup Series

Winners of NASCAR Winston Cup races from Nov. 3, 2002 through Oct. 11, 2003. Note that earnings include bonus money. See Updates chapter for later results.

Late 2002

Date	Event	Location	Winner (Pos.)	Avg.mph	Earnings	Pole	Qual.mph
Nov. 3	Pop Secret 400	Rockingham	Johnny Benson (26)	128.526	$162,965	R. Newman	155.836
Nov. 10	Checker Auto Parts 500	Phoenix	Matt Kenseth (28)	113.857	211,895	R. Newman	132.655
Nov. 17	Ford 400	Homestead	Kurt Busch (1)	116.462	297,100	K. Busch	154.365

Winning cars (2002 season): FORD (14)—Kenseth (5), Busch (4), Jarrett (2), Martin, Newman and Rudd; CHEVROLET (10)—J. Gordon and Johnson (3), Earnhardt Jr. (2), Harvick and Waltrip. DODGE (7)—W. Burton, Elliott and Marlin (2), McMurray; PONTIAC (3)—Stewart (3), Benson and B. Labonte.

2003 Season

Date	Event	Location	Winner (Pos.)	Avg.mph	Earnings	Pole	Qual.mph
Feb. 16	**Daytona 500**†	Daytona	Michael Waltrip (4)	133.870	$1,419,406	J. Green	186.606
Feb. 23	Subway 400	Rockingham	Dale Jarrett (9)	117.852	177,828	D. Blaney	154.683
Mar. 2	UAW-DaimlerChrysler 400	Las Vegas	Matt Kenseth (17)	132.934	365,875	B. Labonte	173.016
Mar. 9	Bass Pro Shops MBNA 500	Atlanta	Bobby Labonte (4)	146.048	209,233	R. Newman	191.417
Mar. 16	Dodge Dealers 400	Darlington	Ricky Craven (31)	126.214	172,150	E. Sadler	170.147
Mar. 23	Food City 500	Bristol	Kurt Busch (9)	76.185	162,790	R. Newman	128.709
Mar. 30	Samsung/Radio Shack 500	Ft. Worth	Ryan Newman (3)	134.517	406,500	B. Labonte	193.514
Apr. 6	Aaron's 499	Talladega	Dale Earnhardt Jr. (13)	144.625	204,367	J. Mayfield	186.489
Apr. 13	Virginia 500	Martinsville	Jeff Gordon (1)	75.557	219,143	J. Gordon	94.308
Apr. 27	Auto Club 500	Fontana	Kurt Busch (16)	140.111	213,150	S. Park	186.838
May 3	Pontiac Excitement 400	Richmond	Joe Nemechek (2)	86.783	159,375	T. Labonte	126.511
May 17@	The Winston	Charlotte	Jimmie Johnson (16)	133.297	1,017,604	B. Elliott	123.192
May 25	**Coca-Cola 600**†	Charlotte	Jimmie Johnson (37)	126.198	271,900	R. Newman	185.312
June 1	MBNA Armed Forces Family 400	Dover	Ryan Newman (1)	106.896	199,325	R. Newman	158.716
June 8	Pocono 500	Long Pond	Tony Stewart (4)	134.892	214,253	J. Johnson	170.645
June 15	Sirius 400	Brooklyn	Kurt Busch (4)	131.219	172,650	B. Labonte	190.365
June 22	Dodge/Save Mart 350	Sonoma	Robby Gordon (2)	73.821	204,512	B. Said	93.620
July 5	Pepsi 400	Daytona	Greg Biffle (30)	166.109	187,975	S. Park	184.752
July 13	Tropicana 400	Joliet	Ryan Newman (14)	134.059	191,000	T. Stewart	184.786
July 20	New England 300	Loudon	Jimmie Johnson (6)	96.924	200,225	M. Kenseth	—**
July 27	Pennsylvania 500	Long Pond	Ryan Newman (1)	127.705	180,575	R. Newman	170.358
Aug. 3	**Brickyard 400**	Indianapolis	Kevin Harvick (1)	134.554	418,253	K. Harvick	184.343
Aug. 10	Sirius at The Glen	Watkins Glen	Robby Gordon (14)	90.441	156,272	J. Gordon	124.580
Aug. 17	GFS Marketplace 400	Brooklyn	Ryan Newman (2)	127.310	155,505	B. Labonte	190.240
Aug. 23	Sharpie 500	Bristol	Kurt Busch (5)	77.421	237,565	J. Gordon	127.597
Aug. 31	**Southern 500**	Darlington	Terry Labonte (3)	120.744	204,736	R. Newman	169.048
Sept. 6	Chevy Rock & Roll 400	Richmond	Ryan Newman (4)	94.945	160,970	M. Skinner	125.792
Sept. 14	Sylvania 300	Loudon	Jimmie Johnson (8)	106.580	200,225	R. Newman	133.357
Sept. 21	MBNA America 400	Dover	Ryan Newman (5)	108.802	160,460	M. Kenseth	—**
Sept. 28	**EA Sports 500**	Talladega	Michael Waltrip (18)	156.045	157,090	E. Sadler	189.943
Oct. 5	Banquet 400	Kansas City	Ryan Newman (11)	121.630	191,000	J. Johnson*	180.373
Oct. 11	UAW-GM Quality 500	Charlotte	Tony Stewart (6)	142.871	312,478	R. Newman	186.657

@ Non-points exhibition event.

†Due to inclement weather the Daytona 500 was shortened from 200 laps to 109, and the Coca-Cola 600 was shortened from 400 laps to 276.

**Qualifying was cancelled due to inclement weather and the pole was awarded to the current Winston Cup points leader.

*Polesitter Johnson crashed in a pre-race practice lap and was forced to use a backup car for the race. He was moved to the back of the field and Mike Skinner, with the second-fastest qualifying lap (179.647), was moved to the pole.

Winning Cars: CHEVROLET (15)—Johnson (3), R. Gordon, Stewart and Waltrip (2), Earnhardt Jr., J. Gordon, Harvick, B. Labonte, T. Labonte and Nemechek; DODGE (8)—Newman (8); FORD (7)—Busch (4), Biffle, Jarrett, Kenseth; PONTIAC (1)—Craven.

2003 NASCAR Winston Cup Race Locations

February—DAYTONA 500 at Daytona International Speedway in Daytona Beach, Fla.; SUBWAY 400 at North Carolina Motor Speedway in Rockingham, N.C.

March—UAW-DAIMLERCHRYSLER 400 at Las Vegas (Nev.) Motor Speedway; BASS PRO SHOPS MBNA 500 at Atlanta (Ga.) Motor Speedway; CAROLINA DODGE DEALERS 400 at Darlington (S.C.) International Raceway; FOOD CITY 500 at Bristol (Tenn.) Motor Speedway; SAMSUNG/RADIO SHACK 500 at Texas Motor Speedway in Ft. Worth, Texas.

April—AARON'S 499 at Talladega (Ala.) Superspeedway; VIRGINIA 500 at Martinsville (Va.) Speedway; AUTO CLUB 500 at California Speedway in Fontana, Calif.

May—PONTIAC EXCITEMENT 400 at Richmond (Va.) International Speedway; THE WINSTON at Lowe's Motor Speedway in Charlotte, N.C.; COCA-COLA 600 at Lowe's.

June—MBNA ARMED FORCES FAMILY 400 at Dover (Del.) Downs International Speedway; POCONO 500 at Pocono International Raceway in Long Pond, Penn.; SIRIUS 400 at Michigan International Speedway in Brooklyn, Mich.; DODGE/SAVE MART 350 at Infineon Raceway in Sonoma, Calif.

July—PEPSI 400 at Daytona; TROPICANA 400 at Chicagoland Speedway in Joliet, Ill.; NEW ENGLAND 300 at New Hampshire International Speedway in Loudon, N.H.; PENNSYLVANIA 500 at Pocono.

August—BRICKYARD 400 at Indianapolis (Ind.) Motor Speedway; SIRIUS AT THE GLEN at Watkins Glen (N.Y.) International; GFS MARKETPLACE 400 at Michigan; SHARPIE 500 at Bristol; MOUNTAIN DEW SOUTHERN 500 at Darlington.

September—CHEVY ROCK & ROLL 400 at Richmond; SYLVANIA 300 at New Hampshire; MBNA AMERICA 400 at Dover Downs; EA SPORTS 500 at Talladega.

October—BANQUET 400 at Kansas Speedway in Kansas City, Mo.; UAW-GM QUALITY 500 at Lowe's; SUBWAY 500 at Martinsville; BASS PRO SHOPS MBNA 500 at Atlanta.

November—CHECKER AUTO PARTS 500 at Phoenix (Ariz.) International Raceway; POP SECRET MICROWAVE POP-CORN 400 at North Carolina; FORD 400 at Miami-Dade Homestead Motorsports Complex in Homestead, Fla.

2003 Daytona 500

Date—Sunday, Feb. 16, 2003, at Daytona International Speedway. **Distance**—272.5 miles (weather shortened from the usual 500); **Course**—2.5 miles; **Field**—43 cars; **Average speed**—133.870 mph; **Margin of victory**—under caution; **Time of race**—2 hours, 2 minutes, 8 seconds; **Caution flags**—5 for 23 laps; **Lead changes**—11 among 8 drivers; **Lap leaders**—Waltrip (68), Earnhardt Jr. (22), Johnson (8), Stewart (6), Kenseth (2), Bodine, Craven and Mears (1). **Pole sitter**—Jeff Green at 186.606 mph; **Attendance**—150,000 (estimated). **Rating**—9.8/21 share (FOX). (r) indicates rookie driver.

	Driver (start pos.)	Sponsor	Car	Laps	Ended	Earnings
1	Michael Waltrip (4)	NAPA Auto Parts	Chevrolet	109	Running	$1,419,406
2	Kurt Busch (36)	Rubbermaid	Ford	109	Running	1,027,101
3	Jimmie Johnson (10)	Lowe's	Chevrolet	109	Running	707,526
4	Kevin Harvick (31)	GM Goodwrench Service	Chevrolet	109	Running	569,630
5	Mark Martin (26)	Viagra	Ford	109	Running	444,609
6	Robby Gordon (3)	Cingular Wireless	Chevrolet	109	Running	362,807
7	Tony Stewart (8)	Home Depot	Chevrolet	109	Running	315,454
8	Jeremy Mayfield (20)	Dodge Dealers	Dodge	109	Running	245,026
9	Mike Wallace (18)	Miccosukee Indian Gaming	Dodge	109	Running	220,051
10	Dale Jarrett (11)	UPS	Ford	109	Running	256,008
11	Jeff Burton (9)	CITGO	Ford	109	Running	233,937
12	Jeff Gordon (13)	DuPont	Chevrolet	109	Running	238,648
13	Kyle Petty (30)	Georgia Pacific	Dodge	109	Running	198,176
14	r-Jack Sprague (24)	NetZero	Pontiac	109	Running	184,901
15	Ricky Rudd (5)	Motorcraft Quality Parts	Ford	109	Running	222,556
16	Kenny Wallace (21)	Stacker 2	Dodge	109	Running	199,420
17	Sterling Marlin (7)	Coors Light	Dodge	109	Running	229,745
18	Todd Bodine (6)	Army National Guard	Ford	109	Running	208,051
19	Johnny Benson (40)	Valvoline	Pontiac	109	Running	208,620
20	Matt Kenseth (35)	DeWalt Power Tools	Ford	109	Running	200,345
21	r-Greg Biffle (27)	Grainger	Ford	109	Running	177,495
22	Joe Nemechek (15)	UAW/Delphi	Chevrolet	109	Running	180,595
23	Elliott Sadler (16)	M&M's	Ford	109	Running	215,901
24	Dave Blaney (39)	Jasper Engines & Transmissions	Ford	109	Running	198,176
25	Rusty Wallace (38)	Miller Lite	Dodge	109	Running	190,692
26	Ricky Craven (25)	Tide	Pontiac	109	Running	194,259
27	r-Casey Mears (29)	Target	Dodge	109	Running	184,420
28	Jerry Nadeau (42)	U.S. Army	Pontiac	109	Running	176,526
29	Steve Park (32)	Pennzoil	Chevrolet	109	Running	191,957
30	Terry Labonte (41)	Kellogg's	Chevrolet	109	Running	200,576
31	r-Jamie McMurray (37)	Havoline	Dodge	109	Running	171,195
32	Bill Elliott (14)	Dodge Dealers	Dodge	109	Running	211,484
33	r-Tony Raines (33)	Staff America	Chevrolet	109	Running	171,851
34	John Andretti (12)	Cheerios	Dodge	108	Running	208,509
35	Christian Fittipaldi (34)	Monaco Coaches	Chevrolet	108	Running	177,856
36	Dale Earnhardt Jr. (2)	Budweiser	Chevrolet	108	Running	243,543
37	Mike Skinner (43)	Kodak	Pontiac	108	Running	167,870
38	Ward Burton (17)	Caterpillar	Dodge	105	Accident	203,751
39	Jeff Green (1)	America Online	Chevrolet	94	Accident	202,720
40	Jimmy Spencer (23)	Sirius Satellite Radio	Dodge	94	Accident	166,620
41	Bobby Labonte (22)	Interstate Batteries	Chevrolet	81	Running	202,134
42	Ken Schrader (28)	1-800-CALLATT	Dodge	57	Accident	166,476
43	Ryan Newman (37)	ALLTEL	Dodge	56	Accident	195,663

Top 5 Finishing Order + Pole
2003 SEASON

No.	Event	Winner	2nd	3rd	4th	5th	Pole
1	Daytona 500	M. Waltrip	K. Busch	J. Johnson	K. Harvick	M. Martin	J. Green
2	Subway 400	D. Jarrett	K. Busch	M. Kenseth	R. Craven	J. McMurray	D. Blaney
3	UAW-DaimlerChrysler 400	M. Kenseth	D. Earnhardt Jr.	M. Waltrip	B. Labonte	T. Stewart	B. Labonte
4	MBNA America 500	B. Labonte	J. Gordon	D. Earnhardt Jr.	M. Kenseth	T. Stewart	R. Newman
5	Dodge Dealers 400	R. Craven	K. Busch	D. Blaney	M. Martin	M. Waltrip	E. Sadler
6	Food City 500	K. Busch	M. Kenseth	B. Labonte	R. Rudd	G. Biffle	R. Newman
7	Samsung/Radio Shack 500	R. Newman	D. Earnhardt Jr.	J. Gordon	J. Nadeau	M. Martin	B. Labonte
8	Aaron's 499	D. Earnhardt Jr.	K. Harvick	E. Sadler	R. Craven	T. Labonte	J. Mayfield
9	Virginia 500	J. Gordon	B. Labonte	D. Earhardt Jr.	J. Burton	E. Sadler	J. Gordon
10	Auto Club 500	K. Busch	B. Labonte	R. Wallace	B. Elliott	J. McMurray	S. Park
11	Pontiac Excitement 400	J. Nemechek	B. Labonte	D. Earhardt Jr.	R. Gordon	M. Martin	T. Labonte
12	Coca-Cola 600	J. Johnson	M. Kenseth	B. Labonte	J. Spencer	R. Newman	R. Newman
13	MBNA Armed Forces Family 400	R. Newman	J. Gordon	B. Labonte	T. Stewart	J. Benson	R. Newman
14	Pocono 500	T. Stewart	M. Martin	M. Kenseth	D. Earnhardt Jr.	R. Newman	J. Johnson
15	Sirius 400	K. Busch	B. Labonte	J. Gordon	M. Kenseth	M. Waltrip	B. Labonte
16	Dodge/Save Mart 350	R. Gordon	J. Gordon	K. Harvick	B. Elliott	J. Gordon	B. Said
17	Pepsi 400	G. Biffle	J. Burton	R. Rudd	T. Labonte	B. Labonte	S. Park
18	Tropicana 400	R. Newman	T. Stewart	J. Johnson	J. Gordon	M. Waltrip	T. Stewart
19	New England 300	J. Johnson	K. Harvick	M. Kenseth	R. Newman	R. Gordon	M. Kenseth
20	Pennsylvania 500	R. Newman	K. Busch	D. Earnhardt Jr.	M. Waltrip	T. Labonte	R. Newman
21	Brickyard 400	K. Harvick	M. Kenseth	J. McMurray	J. Gordon	B. Elliott	K. Harvick
22	Sirius at The Glen	R. Gordon	S. Pruett	D. Earnhardt Jr.	J. Johnson	K. Harvick	J. Gordon
23	GFS Marketplace 400	R. Newman	K. Harvick	T. Stewart	G. Biffle	S. Park	B. Labonte
24	Sharpie 500	K. Busch	K. Harvick	J. McMurray	M. Kenseth	J. Johnson	J. Gordon
25	Southern 500	T. Labonte	K. Harvick	J. Johnson	J. McMurray	B. Elliott	R. Newman
26	Chevy Rock & Roll 400	R. Newman	J. Mayfield	R. Rudd	J. Burton	R. Wallace	M. Skinner
27	Sylvania 300	J. Johnson	R. Rudd	J. Nemechek	B. Elliott	D. Earnhardt Jr.	R. Newman
28	MBNA America 400	R. Newman	J. Mayfield	T. Stewart	K. Harvick	J. Gordon	M. Kenseth
29	EA Sports 500	M. Waltrip	D. Earnhardt Jr.	T. Stewart	R. Newman	J. Gordon	E. Sadler
30	Banquet 400	R. Newman	B. Elliott	J. Mayfield	T. Stewart	J. Gordon	J. Johnson
31	UAW-GM Quality 500	T. Stewart	R. Newman	J. Johnson	D. Elliott	J. Gordon	R. Newman

Winston Cup Point Standings

Official Top 10 NASCAR Winston Cup point leaders and top-10 money leaders for 2002 and unofficial leaders for 2003. Points awarded for all qualifying drivers (winner receives 175) and lap leaders. Earnings include in-season bonuses. Listed are starts (Sts), top-5 finishes (1-2-3-4-5), poles won (PW) and points (Pts).

FINAL 2002

		Finishes			
		Sts	1-2-3-4-5	PW	Pts
1	Tony Stewart	36	3-3-4-2-3	2*	4800
2	Mark Martin	36	1-3-2-3-3	0	4762
3	Kurt Busch	36	4-3-2-3-0	1	4641
4	Jeff Gordon	36	3-2-1-2-5	3	4607
5	Jimmie Johnson	36	3-0-2-1-0	4*	4600
6	Ryan Newman	36	1-5-1-3-4	6	4593
7	Rusty Wallace	36	0-4-1-1-1	1	4574
8	Matt Kenseth	36	5-2-1-2-1	1	4432
9	Dale Jarrett	36	2-1-3-2-2	1	4415
10	Ricky Rudd	36	1-0-4-2-1	1	4323

*Does not include poles awarded for being points leader when qualification was cancelled.

Other wins (13): Ward Burton, Dale Earnhardt Jr., Bill Elliott, Sterling Marlin (2 each); Johnny Benson, Kevin Harvick, Bobby Labonte, Jamie McMurray and Michael Waltrip.

2003 (through Oct. 11)

		Finishes			
		Sts	1-2-3-4-5	PW	Pts
1	Matt Kenseth	31	1-3-3-3-0	0*	4424
2	Kevin Harvick	31	1-5-1-2-1	1	4157
3	Dale Earnhardt Jr.	31	1-3-3-0-1	0	4100
4	Ryan Newman	31	8-1-0-2-3	8	4093
5	Jimmie Johnson	31	3-0-4-1-1	2	4072
6	Jeff Gordon	31	1-3-2-2-4	3	4017
7	Tony Stewart	31	2-1-3-2-2	1	3801
8	Bobby Labonte	31	1-4-3-1-1	4	3800
9	Terry Labonte	31	1-0-0-1-2	1	3620
10	Kurt Busch	31	4-4-0-0-0	0	3615

*Does not include poles awarded for being points leader when qualification was cancelled.

Other wins (8): Robby Gordon, Michael Waltrip (2 each); Greg Biffle, Ricky Craven, Dale Jarrett and Joe Nemechek.

Money Leaders

FINAL 2002

		Earnings
1	Tony Stewart	$9,163,761
2	Mark Martin	7,004,893
3	Jeff Gordon	6,154,475
4	Ryan Newman	5,346,651
5	Kurt Busch	5,105,394
6	Dale Earnhardt Jr.	4,970,034
7	Ward Burton	4,899,884
8	Rusty Wallace	4,785,134
9	Matt Kenseth	4,514,203
10	Ricky Rudd	4,444,614

2003 (through Oct. 11)

		Earnings
1	Jimmie Johnson	$4,828,730
2	Tony Stewart	4,564,610
3	Kurt Busch	4,557,670
4	Kevin Harvick	4,366,680
5	Jeff Gordon	4,319,160
6	Ryan Newman	4,304,420
7	Dale Earnhardt Jr.	4,303,690
8	Michael Waltrip	4,095,760
9	Bobby Labonte	4,002,350
10	Bill Elliott	3,642,950

CART RESULTS

Schedule and results of CART races from Nov. 3, 2002 through Oct. 12, 2003. Officially the "FedEx Championship Series" from 1998-2002 and changed to "Bridgestone Presents The Champ Car World Series Powered By Ford" for the 2003 season. Note that CART does not release per-race winnings. See Updates chapter for later results.

Champ Car World Series

Late 2002

Date	Event	Location	Winner (Pos.)	Time	Avg.mph	Pole	Qual.mph
Nov. 3	The 500 presented by Toyota ....Fontana		Jimmy Vasser (6)	2:33:42.977	197.995	T. Kanaan	232.011
Nov. 17	Gran Premio Telmex/Gigante	Mexico City	Kenny Brack (6)	1:56:48.475	104.468	B. Junqueira	116.703

Winning cars (entire 2002 season): LOLA/TOYOTA (10)—da Matta (7), Junqueira (2), Brack; LOLA/HONDA (4)—Franchitti (3), Tracy; REYNARD/FORD-COSWORTH (2)—Carpentier (2); REYNARD/HONDA (1)—Andretti; LOLA/FORD-COSWORTH (2)—Dominguez and Vasser.

2003 Season

Date	Event	Location	Winner (Pos.)	Time	Avg.mph	Pole	Qual.mph
Feb. 23	GP of St. Petersburg	.St. Petersburg	Paul Tracy (2)	2:04:28.904	91.401	S. Bourdais	106.710
Mar. 23	Monterrey GP ......Monterrey		Paul Tracy (2)	2:03:04.677	87.184	S. Bourdais	101.076
Apr. 13	Toyota GP ....Long Beach		Paul Tracy (2)	1:56:01.792	91.590	M. Jourdain	103.918
May 5	London Champ Car Trophy ....Brands Hatch		Sebastien Bourdais (2)	1:51:56.987	105.412	P. Tracy	115.960
May 11	German 500 ....Lausitz		Sebastien Bourdais (1)	1:49:22.498	170.903	S. Bourdais	196.832
May 31	Milwaukee Mile 250 .Milwaukee		Michel Jourdain (2)	2:16:45.692	113.190	A. Tagliani	—*
June 15	GP of Monterey .....Monterey		Patrick Carpentier (1)	1:48:11.023	107.986	P. Carpentier	115.800
June 22	GP of Portland featuring the G.I. Joe's 200 .....Portland		Adrian Fernandez (3)	1:56:16.626	101.602	P. Tracy	120.565
July 5	Cleveland GP ....Cleveland		Sebastien Bourdais (1)	2:03:51.974	117.315	S. Bourdais	130.686
July 13	Molson Indy ....Toronto		Paul Tracy (1)	2:02:36.488	96.189	P. Tracy	107.378
July 27	Molson Indy ....Vancouver		Paul Tracy (1)	1:57:54.322	90.632	P. Tracy	105.236
Aug. 3	Mario Andretti GP ..Elkhart Lake		Bruno Junqueira (1)	1:35:28.491	86.493	B. Junqueira	140.524
Aug. 10	GP of Mid-Ohio .....Lexington		Paul Tracy (1)	1:56:45.737	106.251	P. Tracy	121.220
Aug. 24	Molson Indy ....Montreal		Michel Jourdain (4)	1:54:23.210	106.573	A. Tagliani	122.418
Aug. 31	GP of Denver ....Denver		Bruno Junqueira (1)	2:03:10.259	85.044	B. Junqueira	96.507
Sept. 28	GP of the Americas .....Miami		Mario Dominguez (8)	2:03:19.401	75.533	A. Fernandez	93.553
Oct. 12	Gran Premio Telmex/Gigante ....Mexico City		Paul Tracy (1)	1:56:51.396	100.133	P. Tracy	112.893

*Qualifying was cancelled due to inclement weather and the pole was awarded based on practice times.

Winning cars (Engine/Chassis): FORD-COSWORTH/LOLA (17)—Tracy (7), Bourdais (3), Jourdain and Junqueira (2), Carpentier, Dominguez and Fernandez.

2003 Race Locations

February—GRAND PRIX OF ST. PETERSBURG in St. Petersburg, Fla.

March—TECATE TELMEX MONTERREY GRAND PRIX at Fundidora Park in Monterrey, Mexico.

April—TOYOTA GRAND PRIX OF LONG BEACH in Long Beach, Calif.

May—LONDON CHAMP CAR TROPHY in Brands Hatch, England; GERMAN 500 at EuroSpeedway, Lausitz, Germany; MILWAUKEE MILE CENTENNIAL 250 Presented by Miller Lite at the Milwaukee Mile in West Allis, Wis.

June—GRAND PRIX OF MONTEREY at Mazda Raceway Laguna Seca in Monterey, Calif.; GRAND PRIX OF PORTLAND FEATURING THE GI JOE'S 200 at Portland (Ore.) International Raceway.

July—THE CLEVELAND GRAND PRIX Presented by U.S. Bank at Burke Lakefront Airport in Cleveland, Ohio; MOLSON INDY TORONTO at Exhibition Place in Toronto, Ontario, Canada; MOLSON INDY VANCOUVER at Concord Pacific Place in Vancouver, B.C., Canada.

August—MARIO ANDRETTI GRAND PRIX Presented by Briggs & Stratton at Road America in Elkhart Lake, Wis.; CHAMP CAR GRAND PRIX OF MID-OHIO at Mid-Ohio Sports Car Course in Lexington, Ohio; MOLSON INDY MONTREAL at Circuit Gilles Villeneuve in Montreal, Quebec, Canada; CENTRIX FINANCIAL GRAND PRIX OF DENVER in Denver, Colo.

September—GRAND PRIX AMERICAS Presented by Sportsbook.com at Bayfront Park, Miami, Fla.

October—MEXICO GRAN PREMIO TELMEX/GIGANTE Presented by Banamex/Visa at Autodromo Hermanos Rodriguez in Mexico City, Mexico; LEXMARK INDY 300 at Surfer's Paradise, Queensland, Australia.

November—CHAMP CAR 500 at California Speedway in Fontana, Calif.

Top 5 Finishing Order + Pole
2003 SEASON

No.	Event	Winner	2nd	3rd	4th	5th	Pole
1	GP of St. Petersburg	P. Tracy	M. Jourdain	B. Junqueira	M. Haberfeld	R. Moreno	S. Bourdais
2	Monterrey GP	P. Tracy	M. Jourdain	A. Tagliani	A. Fernandez	B. Junqueira	S. Bourdais
3	GP of Long Beach	P. Tracy	A. Fernandez	B. Junqueira	J. Vasser	M. Dominguez	M. Jourdain
4	London Champ Car	S. Bourdais	B. Junqueira	M. Dominguez	O. Servia	P. Carpentier	P. Tracy
5	German 500	S. Bourdais	M. Dominguez	M. Jourdain	B. Junqueira	O. Servia	S. Bourdais
6	Milwaukee Mile 250	M. Jourdain	O. Servia	P. Carpentier	D. Manning	A. Tagliani	A. Tagliani
7	GP of Monterey	P. Carpentier	B. Junqueira	P. Tracy	M. Jourdain	M. Haberfeld	P. Carpentier
8	G.I. Joe's 200	A. Fernandez	P. Tracy	A. Tagliani	B. Junqueira	O. Servia	P. Tracy
9	Cleveland GP	S. Bourdais	P. Tracy	B. Junqueira	P. Carpentier	M. Dominguez	S. Bourdais
10	Molson Indy Toronto	P. Tracy	M. Jourdain	B. Junqueira	S. Bourdais	O. Servia	P. Tracy
11	Molson Indy Vancouver	P. Tracy	B. Junqueira	S. Bourdais	M. Jourdain	D. Manning	P. Tracy
12	Mario Andretti GP	B. Junqueira	S. Bourdais	A. Tagliani	M. Papis	P. Carpentier	B. Junqueira
13	GP of Mid-Ohio	P. Tracy	P. Carpentier	R. Hunter-Reay	M. Jourdain	S. Bourdais	P. Tracy
14	Molson Indy Montreal	M. Jourdain	O. Servia	P. Carpentier	A. Tagliani	M. Dominguez	A. Tagliani
15	GP of Denver	B. Junqueira	S. Bourdais	O. Servia	P. Tracy	A. Fernandez	B. Junqueira
16	GP of the Americas	M. Dominguez	R. Moreno	M. Salo	J. Vasser	M. Haberfeld	A. Fernandez
17	Gran Premio	P. Tracy	S. Bourdais	M. Dominguez	M. Jourdain	M. Salo	P. Tracy

CART Point Standings & Money Leaders (through Oct. 12)

Unofficial top-10 Champ Car World Series point leaders and money leaders for 2003. Points awarded for places 1 to 12, pole winner at oval events, fastest driver on each day of qualifying at road/street events and overall lap leader. Listed are starts (Sts), top-5 finishes, poles won (PW) and points (Pts). (r) indicates rookie driver.

Points

		Sts	Finishes 1-2-3-4-5	PW	Pts
1	Paul Tracy	17	7-2-1-1-0	6	226
2	Bruno Junqueira	17	2-3-4-2-1	2	197
3	Michel Jourdain	17	2-3-1-4-0	1	183
4	r-Sebastien Bourdais	17	3-3-1-1-1	4	158
5	Patrick Carpentier	17	1-1-2-1-2	1	136
6	Mario Dominguez	17	1-1-2-0-3	0	115
7	Oriol Servia	17	0-2-1-1-3	0	108
8	Adrian Fernandez	17	1-1-0-1-1	1	104
9	Alex Tagliani	17	0-0-3-1-1	2	91
10	r-Darren Manning	17	0-0-0-1-1	0	87

Earnings

		Earnings
1	Paul Tracy	$893,750
2	Bruno Junqueira	735,500
3	Michel Jourdain	668,000
4	r-Sebastien Bourdais	637,500
5	Patrick Carpentier	526,500
6	Mario Dominguez	456,250
7	Adrian Fernandez	434,500
8	Oriol Servia	430,000
9	Alex Tagliani	386,000
10	r-Darren Manning	331,750

INDY RACING LEAGUE RESULTS

IndyCar Series

Schedule and results of IndyCar Series events during the 2003 season.

2003 Season

Date	Event	Location	Winner (Pos.)	Time	Avg.mph	Pole	Qual.mph
Mar. 2	Toyota 300	Miami	Scott Dixon (12)	1:57:06.2062	153.710	T. Kanaan	203.560
Mar. 23	Purex Dial 200	Phoenix	Tony Kanaan (1)	1:59:54.7395	100.073	T. Kanaan	178.512
Apr. 13	Japan 300	Motegi	Scott Sharp (7)	2:21:17.8256	129.090	S. Dixon	—*
May 25	**Indianapolis 500**	Indianapolis	Gil de Ferran (10)	3:11:56.9891	156.291	H. Castroneves	231.725
June 7	Bombardier 500	Ft. Worth	Al Unser Jr. (7)	1:43:47.8051	168.213	T. Scheckter	219.300
June 15	Honda 125	Pikes Peak	Scott Dixon (6)	1:32:19.9594	146.210	T. Kanaan	—*
June 28	SunTrust Challenge	Richmond	Scott Dixon (5)	1:26:47.9459	106.798	S. Dixon	168.138
July 6	Kansas 300	Kansas City	Bryan Herta (11)	1:48:50.9861	167.570	S. Dixon	218.085
July 19	Firestone 200	Nashville	Gil de Ferran (4)	1:53:18.4386	137.679	S. Dixon	216.211
July 27	Firestone 400	Brooklyn	Alex Barron (6)	2:12:39.4413	180.917	T. Scheckter	222.458
Aug. 10	Emerson 250	St. Louis	Helio Castroneves (1)	1:50:52.5587	135.286	H. Castroneves	175.965
Aug. 17	Belterra Casino 300	Sparta	Sam Hornish Jr. (1)	1:29:44.6120	197.897	S. Hornish Jr.	219.614
Aug 24	Firestone 225	Nazareth	Helio Castroneves (2)	1:42:07.1375	123.606	S. Dixon	171.182
Sept. 7	Delphi 300	Joliet	Sam Hornish Jr. (8)	1:38:58.3310	184.294	R. Hearn	223.159
Sept. 21	Toyota 400	Fontana	Sam Hornish Jr. (10)	1:55:51.4395	207.151	H. Castroneves	226.757
Oct. 12	Chevy 500	Ft. Worth	Gil de Ferran (1)	1:48:56.2674	156.268	G. de Ferran	222.864

*Qualifying was cancelled due to inclement weather and the pole was awarded based on practice times.

Winning cars (Chassis/Engine): DALLARA/TOYOTA (6)—Castroneves and de Ferran (2), Sharp and Unser Jr.; G FORCE/TOYOTA (5)—Dixon (3), Barron and de Ferran; DALLARA/CHEVROLET (3)—Hornish Jr. (3); DALLARA/HONDA (2)—Herta and Kanaan.

Indy Racing League Results (Cont.)
IndyCar Race Locations

March—TOYOTA INDY 300 at Homestead-Miami (Fla.) Speedway; PUREX DIAL INDY 200 at Phoenix (Ari.) International Raceway. **April**—INDY JAPAN 300 at Twin Ring Motegi, Japan. **May**—INDIANAPOLIS 500 at Indianapolis (Ind.) Motor Speedway. **June**—BOMBARDIER 500 at Texas Motor Speedway in Fort Worth, Texas; HONDA INDY 225 at Pikes Peak International Raceway in Colorado Springs, Colo.; SUNTRUST INDY CHALLENGE at Richmond (Va.) International Raceway. **July**—KANSAS INDY 300 at Kansas Speedway in Kansas City, Mo.; FIRESTONE INDY 200 at Nashville (Tenn.) Superspeedway; FIRESTONE INDY 400 at Michigan International Speedway in Brooklyn, Mich. **August**—EMERSON INDY 250 at Gateway International Speedway in St. Louis, Mo; BELTERRA CASINO INDY 300 at Kentucky Speedway in Sparta, Ky.; FIRESTONE INDY 225 at Nazareth (Pa.) Speedway. **September**—DELPHI INDY 300 at Chicagoland Speedway in Joliet, Ill.; TOYOTA INDY 400 at California Speedway in Fontana, Calif.; CHEVY 500 at Texas Motor Speedway.

87th Indianapolis 500

Date—Sunday, May 25, 2003, at Indianapolis Motor Speedway. **Distance**—500 miles; **Course**—2.5 mile oval; **Field**—33 cars; **Winner's average speed**—156.291 mph; **Margin of victory**—0.299 seconds; **Time of race**—3 hours, 11 minutes, 56.9891 seconds; **Caution flags**—9 for 49 laps; **Lead changes**—14 by 8 drivers; **Lap leaders**—Scheckter (63), Castroneves (58), de Ferran (31), Andretti (28), Dixon (15), Kanaan (2), Takagi (2), Vasser (1); **Pole Sitter**—Helio Castroneves at 231.725; **Attendance**—400,000 (est.); **TV Rating**—4.6/14 share (ABC). Note that (r) indicates rookie driver.

	Driver (start pos.)	Country	Car	Laps	Ended	Earnings
1	Gil de Ferran (10)	Brazil	G/T/F	200	Running	$1,353,265
2	Helio Castroneves (1)	Brazil	D/T/F	200	Running	739,065
3	Tony Kanaan (2)	Brazil	D/H/F	200	Running	486,465
4	Tomas Scheckter (12)	South Africa	G/T/F	200	Running	448,415
5	r-Tora Takagi (7)	Japan	G/T/F	200	Running	363,515
6	Alex Barron (25)	United States	G/T/F	200	Running	297,265
7	r-Tony Renna (8)	United States	D/T/F	200	Running	206,315
8	Greg Ray (14)	United States	G/H/F	200	Running	299,065
9	Al Unser Jr. (17)	United States	D/T/F	200	Running	296,565
10	r-Roger Yasukawa (11)	United States	D/H/F	199	Running	288,815
11	r-Buddy Rice (19)	United States	D/C/F	199	Running	323,315
12	r-Vitor Meira (26)	Brazil	D/C/F	199	Running	192,315
13	Jimmy Kite (32)	United States	D/C/F	197	Running	273,565
14	r-Shinji Nakano (15)	Japan	D/H/F	196	Running	269,315
15	Sam Hornish Jr. (18)	United States	D/C/F	195	Engine	271,065
16	Kenny Brack (6)	Sweden	D/H/F	195	Running	271,065
17	r-Scott Dixon (4)	New Zealand	G/T/F	191	Accident	304,315
18	r-A.J. Foyt IV (23)	United States	D/T/F	189	Running	264,315
19	r-Dan Wheldon (5)	England	D/H/F	186	Accident	161,815
20	Scott Sharp (9)	United States	D/T/F	181	Accident	257,815
21	Buddy Lazier (21)	United States	D/C/F	171	Engine	276,065
22	Robby Gordon (3)	United States	D/H/F	169	Gearbox	256,250
23	Robbie Buhl (22)	United States	D/C/F	147	Engine	252,065
24	Airton Dare (33)	Brazil	G/T/F	125	Accident	166,065
25	Robby McGehee (31)	United States	D/C/F	125	Steering	151,565
26	Jimmy Vasser (27)	United States	D/H/F	102	Gearbox	161,265
27	Michael Andretti (13)	United States	D/H/F	94	Throttle	259,415
28	Richie Hearn (28)	United States	G/T/F	61	Accident	142,565
29	Jaques Lazier (20)	United States	D/C/F	61	Accident	240,315
30	Shigeaki Hattori (30)	Japan	D/T/F	19	Fuel System	240,065
31	Sarah Fisher (24)	United States	D/T/F	14	Engine	244,065
32	Billy Boat (29)	United States	D/C/F	7	Engine	139,065
33	Felipe Giaffone (16)	Brazil	G/T/F	6	Electrical	242,815

Car Legend: Chassis/Engine/Tires. D—Dallara, G—Panoz G Force (chassis); C—Chevrolet, H—Honda, T—Toyota (engine); F—Firestone (tires).

"The Double"

Three different drivers in five years have completed "The Double," an auto racing double-header that involves racing in the Indianapolis 500 and NASCAR Winston Cup Series' Coca-Cola 600 on the same day. In addition to the 1,100 miles of racing (600 possible laps) and nearly seven hours of drive time, the feat requires the driver to travel from Indianapolis to Charlotte, N.C. (430 miles) between races. Here is a look at their results. Laps refers to laps completed.

		Indy 500		Coca-Cola 600	
Date	Driver	Finish	Laps	Finish	Laps
5/29/1994	John Andretti	10th	196	36th*	220
5/30/1999	Tony Stewart	9th	196	4th	400
5/27/2001	Tony Stewart	6th	200	3rd	400
5/26/2002	Robby Gordon	8th	200	16th	399
5/25/2003	Robby Gordon	22nd*	169	17th	275

* Did not finish the race.

Note: Robby Gordon attempted "The Double" in 1997 but rain postponed the Indianapolis 500 until the following Monday. He tried again in 2000 but a three hour rain delay at Indianapolis caused him to miss the start of the Coca-Cola 600.

Top 5 Finishing Order + Pole
2003 Season

No. Event	Winner	2nd	3rd	4th	5th	Pole
1 Toyota 300	S. Dixon	G. de Ferran	H. Castroneves	T. Kanaan	S. Sharp	T. Kanaan
2 Purex Dial 200	T. Kanaan	H. Castroneves	F. Giaffone	A. Unser Jr.	K. Brack	T. Kanaan
3 Japan 300	S. Sharp	K. Brack	F. Giaffone	M. Andretti	A. Unser Jr.	S. Dixon
4 Indy 500	G. de Ferran	H. Castroneves	T. Kanaan	T. Scheckter	T. Takagi	H. Castroneves
5 Bombardier 500	A. Unser Jr.	T. Kanaan	T. Takagi	K. Brack	B. Herta	T. Scheckter
6 Honda 225	S. Dixon	T. Kanaan	G. de Ferran	D. Franchitti	S. Hornish Jr.	T. Kanaan
7 SunTrust Challenge	S. Dixon	H. Castroneves	G. de Ferran	S. Hornish Jr.	T. Kanaan	S. Dixon
8 Kansas 300	B. Herta	H. Castroneves	G. de Ferran	T. Kanaan	K. Brack	S. Dixon
9 Firestone 200	G. de Ferran	S. Dixon	H. Castroneves	D. Wheldon	A. Barron	S. Dixon
10 Firestone 400	A. Barron	S. Hornish Jr.	T. Scheckter	S. Sharp	S. Dixon	T. Scheckter
11 Emerson 250	H. Castroneves	T. Kanaan	G. de Ferran	T. Scheckter	D. Wheldon	H. Castroneves
12 Belterra Casino 300	S. Hornish Jr.	S. Dixon	B. Herta	A. Unser Jr.	H. Castroneves	S. Hornish Jr.
13 Firestone 225	H. Castroneves	S. Hornish Jr.	B. Herta	G. de Ferran	K. Brack	S. Dixon
14 Delphi 300	S. Hornish Jr.	S. Dixon	B. Herta	D. Wheldon	T. Scheckter	R. Hearn
15 Toyota 400	S. Hornish Jr.	S. Dixon	T. Kanaan	D. Wheldon	T. Scheckter	H. Castroneves
16 Chevy 500	G. de Ferran	S. Dixon	D. Wheldon	V. Meira	B. Herta	G. de Ferran

Indy Racing League Point Standings & Money Leaders

Official top-10 Indy Racing League driver points leaders and money leaders for 2003. Points awarded for places 1 to 33 (winner receives 50) and overall lap leader. Listed are starts (Sts), top-5 finishes, poles won (PW) and points (Pts).

Points

		Sts	Finishes 1-2-3-4-5	PW	Pts
1	Scott Dixon	16	3-5-0-0-1	5	507
2	Gil de Ferran	15	3-1-4-1-0	1	489
3	Helio Castroneves	16	2-4-2-0-1	3	484
4	Tony Kanaan	16	1-3-2-2-1	3	476
5	Sam Hornish Jr.	16	3-2-0-1-1	1	461
6	Al Unser Jr.	16	1-0-0-2-1	0	374
7	Tomas Scheckter	16	0-0-1-2-2	2	356
8	Scott Sharp	16	1-0-0-1-1	0	351
9	Kenny Brack	16	0-1-0-1-3	0	342
10	Tora Takagi	16	0-0-1-0-1	0	317

Earnings

		Earnings
1	Gil de Ferran	$2,316,815
2	Helio Castroneves	1,764,415
3	Tony Kanaan	1,600,765
4	Scott Dixon	1,481,265
5	Sam Hornish Jr.	1,330,865
6	Tomas Scheckter	1,206,465
7	Al Unser Jr.	1,053,365
8	Tora Takagi	1,027,565
9	Kenny Brack	1,025,015
10	Scott Sharp	1,011,715

Other wins (2): Alex Barron and Bryan Herta.
Other poles (1): Richie Hearn.

FORMULA ONE RESULTS

Results of Formula One Grand Prix races in 2003.

2003 Season

Date	Grand Prix	Location	Winner (Pos.)	Time	Avg.mph	Pole	Qual.mph
Mar. 9	Australian	Melbourne	David Coulthard (11)	1:34:42.124	120.623	M. Schumacher	135.779
Mar. 23	Malaysian	Kuala Lumpur	Kimi Raikkonen (7)	1:32:22.195	125.235	F. Alonso	127.488
Apr. 6	Brazilian	Sao Paulo	Giancarlo Fisichella (8)	1:31:17.748	189.357	R. Barrichello	193.747
Apr. 20	San Marino	Imola	Michael Schumacher (1)	1:28:12.058	128.686	M. Schumacher	134.036
May 4	Spanish	Barcelona	Michael Schumacher (1)	1:33:46.933	121.905	M. Schumacher	130.061
May 18	Austrian	Spielberg	Michael Schumacher (1)	1:24:04.888	127.018	M. Schumacher	139.939
June 1	Monaco	Monaco	Juan Pablo Montoya (3)	1:42:19.010	94.719	R. Schumacher	99.056
June 15	Canadian	Montreal	Michael Schumacher (3)	1:31:13.591	124.280	R. Schumacher	129.121
June 29	European	Nurburgring	Ralf Schumacher (3)	1:34:43.622	121.508	K. Raikkonen	125.546
July 6	French	Magny-Cours	Ralf Schumacher (1)	1:30:49.213	126.676	R. Schumacher	131.471
July 20	British	Silverstone	Rubens Barrichello (1)	1:28:37.554	129.716	R. Barrichello	141.549
Aug. 3	German	Hockenheim	Juan Pablo Montoya (1)	1:28:48.769	128.590	J. Montoya	136.060
Aug. 24	Hungarian	Budapest	Fernando Alonso (1)	1:39:01.460	115.486	F. Alonso	119.998
Sept. 14	Italian	Monza	Michael Schumacher (1)	1:14:19.838	153.775	M. Schumacher	159.985
Sept. 28	U.S.	Indianapolis	Michael Schumacher (7)	1:33:35.997	121.891	K. Raikkonen	130.850
Oct. 12	Japan	Suzuka	Rubens Barrichello (1)	1:25:11.743	134.596	R. Barrichello	141.624

Winning Constructors: FERRARI (8)—M. Schumacher (6), Barrichello (2); WILLIAMS/BMW (4)—Montoya and R. Schumacher (2); MCLAREN/MERCEDES (2)—Coulthard, Raikkonen; JORDAN/FORD (1)—Fisichella; RENAULT (1)—Alonso.

Formula One Results (Cont.)

Top 5 + Pole Finishing Order

No.	Event	Winner	2nd	3rd	4th	5th	Pole
1	Australian	D. Coulthard	J. Montoya	K. Raikkonen	M. Schumacher	J. Trulli	M. Schumacher
2	Malaysian	K. Raikkonen	R. Barrichello	F. Alonso	R. Schumacher	J. Trulli	F. Alonso
3	Brazilian	G. Fisichella	K. Raikkonen	F. Alonso	D. Coulthard	H-H Frentzen	R. Barrichello
4	San Marino	M. Schumacher	K. Raikkonen	R. Barrichello	R. Schumacher	D. Coulthard	M. Schumacher
5	Spanish	M. Schumacher	F. Alonso	R. Barrichello	J. Montoya	R. Schumacher	M. Schumacher
6	Austrian	M. Schumacher	K. Raikkonen	R. Barrichello	J. Button	D. Coulthard	M. Schumacher
7	Monaco	J. Montoya	K. Raikkonen	M. Schumacher	R. Schumacher	F. Alonso	R. Schumacher
8	Canadian	M. Schumacher	R. Schumacher	J. Montoya	F. Alonso	R. Barrichello	R. Schumacher
9	European	R. Schumacher	J. Montoya	R. Barrichello	F. Alonso	M. Schumacher	K. Raikkonen
10	French	R. Schumacher	J. Montoya	M. Schumacher	K. Raikkonen	D. Coulthard	R. Schumacher
11	British	R. Barrichello	J. Montoya	K. Raikkonen	M. Schumacher	D. Coulthard	R. Barrichello
12	German	J. Montoya	D. Coulthard	J. Trulli	F. Alonso	O. Panis	J. Montoya
13	Hungarian	F. Alonso	K. Raikkonen	J. Montoya	R. Schumacher	D. Coulthard	F. Alonso
14	Italian	M. Schumacher	J. Montoya	R. Barrichello	K. Raikkonen	M. Gene	M. Schumacher
15	U.S.	M. Schumacher	K. Raikkonen	H-H Frentzen	J. Trulli	N. Heidfeld	K. Raikkonen
16	Japan	R. Barrichello	K. Raikkonen	D. Coulthard	J. Button	J. Trulli	R. Barrichello

Formula One Point Standings

Official top-10 Formula One World Drivers and Constructors Championship point leaders for 2003. Points awarded for places 1 through 8 only (i.e., 10-8-6-5-4-3-2-1). Listed are starts (Sts), top-8 finishes, poles won (PW) and points (Pts). **Note:** Formula One does not keep money leader standings.

Final 2003 (Drivers)

		Sts	Finishes 1-2-3-4-5-6-7-8	PW	Pts
1	Michael Schumacher	16	6-0-2-2-1-1-1-2	5	93
2	Kimi Raikkonen	16	1-7-2-2-0-1-0-0	2	91
3	Juan Pablo Montoya	16	2-5-2-1-0-1-1-0	1	82
4	Rubens Barrichello	16	2-1-5-0-1-0-1-1	3	65
5	Ralf Schumacher	15	2-1-0-4-1-1-1-1	3	58
6	Fernando Alonso	16	1-1-2-3-1-1-1-1	2	55
7	David Coulthard	16	1-1-1-1-5-0-1-0	0	51
8	Jarno Trulli	16	0-0-1-1-3-2-1-2	0	33
9	Jenson Button	15	0-0-0-2-0-0-2-3	0	17
	Mark Webber	16	0-0-0-0-0-3-4-0	0	17

Other wins (1): Giancarlo Fisichella.

Final 2003 (Constructors)

		Pts
1	Ferrari	158
2	Williams-BMW	144
3	McLaren-Mercedes	142
4	Renault	88
5	BAR-Honda	26
6	Sauber-Petronas	19
7	Jaguar-Cosworth	18
8	Toyota	16
9	Jordan-Ford	13
10	Minardi-Cosworth	0

Major 2003 Endurance Races

24 Hours of Daytona

Feb. 1-2, at Daytona Beach, Fla.

Officially the Rolex 24 at Daytona and first held in 1962 (as a 3-hour race). An IMSA Camel GT race for exotic prototype sports cars and contested over a 3.56-mile road course at Daytona International Speedway. Listed are qualifying position, drivers, chassis, class and laps completed.

1 (16) Kevin Buckler, Michael Schrom, Timo Bernhard and Jorg Bergmeister; PORSCHE GT3 RS; 695 laps (2,474.20 miles) at 103.012 mph; margin of victory nine laps.
2 (17) Ralf Kelleners, Anthony Lazzaro and Johnny Mowlem; FERRARI 360GT; 686 laps.
3 (37) Johannes Van Overbeck, Richard Steranka, Dave Standridge and David Murry; PORSCHE GT3 RS; 684 laps.
4 (1) Scott Maxwell, David Brabham and David Empringham; FORD MULTIMATIC (DP); 679 laps.
5 (3) Hurley Haywood, J.C. France, Scott Goodyear and Scott Sharp; PORSCHE FABCAR (DP); 661 laps.
Top qualifier: Scott Maxwell, FORD MULTIMATIC, 115.969 mph (1:50.512).
Weather: Clear. **Attendance:** 40,000 (est.).

24 Hours of Le Mans

June 14-15, at Le Mans, France

Officially the Le Mans Grand Prix d'Endurance and first held in 1923. Contested over the 8.48-mile Circuit de la Sarthe in Le Mans, France. Listed are qualifying position, drivers, car, and laps completed.

1 (1) Tom Kristensen, Rinaldo Capello and Guy Smith; BENTLEY SPEED 8; 377 laps (3,196 miles).
2 (2) David Brabham, Johnny Herbert and Mark Blundell; BENTLEY SPEED 8; 375 laps.
3 (6) Emanuele Pirro, Stefan Johansson and J.J. Lehto; AUDI R8; 372 laps.
4 (5) Seiji Ara, Jan Magnusen and Marco Werner; AUDI R8; 370 laps.
5 (10) Olivier Beretta, Gunnar Jeannette and Max Papis; PANOZ LMP01; 360 laps.
Top qualifier: Tom Kristensen, BENTLEY SPEED 8, 143.430 (3:32.843).
Weather: Clear. **Attendance:** 250,000 (est.).

NHRA RESULTS

Winners of National Hot Rod Association's POWERade Drag Racing events in the Top Fuel, Funny Car and Pro Stock divisions through Oct. 12, 2003. All times are based on two cars racing head-to-head from a standing start over a straight line, quarter-mile course. Differences in reaction time account for apparently faster losing times.

2003 Season

Date	Event	Event	Winner	Time	MPH	2nd Place	Time	MPH
Feb. 9	K&N Filters Winternationals	Top Fuel	Larry Dixon	4.541	322.04	C. McClenahan	4.597	309.42
		Funny Car	Tony Pedregon	4.765	324.44	J. Gray	4.912	313.66
		Pro Stock	Warren Johnson	6.788	204.01	A. Johnson	6.802	204.73
Feb. 23	Kragen Nationals	Top Fuel	Brandon Bernstein	4.574	322.58	L. Dixon	4.539	321.73
		Funny Car	Ron Caps	4.868	310.13	G. Densham	4.810	318.99
		Pro Stock	Greg Anderson	6.865	201.61	T. Coughlin	6.907	200.83
Mar. 16	Mac Tools Gatornationals	Top Fuel	Brandon Bernstein	4.594	320.05	J. Smith	4.718	315.90
		Funny Car	Gary Densham	4.876	320.85	D. Worsham	4.906	315.67
		Pro Stock	Kurt Johnson	6.825	202.65	J. Coughlin	6.840	201.29
Apr. 6	SummitRacing.com Nationals	Top Fuel	Larry Dixon	4.608	312.57	D. Kalitta	4.695	314.39
		Funny Car	Tony Pedregon	4.916	283.07	W. Bazemore	5.766	172.85
		Pro Stock	Greg Anderson	6.907	200.95	K. Johnson	6.896	201.10
Apr. 13	O'Reilly Spring Nationals	Top Fuel	Doug Kalitta	4.580	323.43	C. McClenahan	6.832	123.27
		Funny Car	Tony Pedregon	4.963	313.07	D. Worsham	4.969	302.96
		Pro Stock	Kurt Johnson	6.780	204.79	S. Geoffrion	6.795	204.14
Apr. 27	Thunder Valley Nationals	Top Fuel	Brandon Bernstein	4.625	324.07	G. Herbert	4.880	282.72
		Funny Car	Del Worsham	4.924	310.41	W. Bazemore	6.500	194.35
		Pro Stock	Kurt Johnson	6.899	200.92	M. Edwards	6.925	199.37
May 4	Southern Nationals	Top Fuel	Larry Dixon	4.569	323.89	D. Russell	9.884	107.52
		Funny Car	Tony Pedregon	4.874	318.77	J. Gray	5.009	304.60
		Pro Stock	Warren Johnson	6.853	201.46	G. Anderson	6.839	202.94
May 18	K&N Filters SuperNationals	Top Fuel	Doug Kalitta	4.494	328.54	L. Dixon	4.554	326.40
		Funny Car	Whit Bazemore	4.869	306.81	R. Capps	8.300	100.52
		Pro Stock	Greg Anderson	6.724	205.98	D. Alderman	6.747	205.38
May 25	O'Reilly Summer Nationals	Top Fuel	Larry Dixon	4.534	322.87	D. Kalitta	4.575	324.20
		Funny Car	Tony Pedregon	4.848	320.66	W. Bazemore	5.126	252.38
		Pro Stock	Greg Anderson	6.808	202.94	K. Johnson	6.845	202.88
June 1	Lucas Oil Route 66 Nationals	Top Fuel	Tony Schumacher	4.530	321.50	L. Dixon	4.615	321.42
		Funny Car	Whit Bazemore	4.872	319.67	T. Johnson Jr.	4.839	316.97
		Pro Stock	Kurt Johnson	6.791	203.40	J. Coughlin	6.833	201.91
June 15	Pontiac Excitement Nationals	Top Fuel	Larry Dixon	4.655	313.58	D. Russell	11.250	91.96
		Funny Car	Tony Pedregon	8.449	134.81	J. Force	—	—*
		Pro Stock	Greg Anderson	6.883	199.88	S. Geoffrion	6.911	198.70
June 29	Sears Craftsman Nationals	Top Fuel	Doug Kalitta	4.602	312.35	S. Weis	4.805	298.27
		Funny Car	Del Worsham	4.884	313.00	J. Force	4.936	314.09
		Pro Stock	Ron Krisher	6.843	201.64	A. Johnson	6.840	201.73
July 20	Mopar Mile-High Nationals	Top Fuel	Larry Dixon	4.737	313.15	D. Kalitta	5.135	228.69
		Funny Car	John Force	5.044	289.45	C. Pedregon	5.060	302.55
		Pro Stock	Warren Johnson	7.225	191.05	J. Coughlin	7.250	190.75
July 27	Carquest Auto Parts Nationals	Top Fuel	Larry Dixon	4.672	316.82	D. Kalitta	4.739	306.95
		Funny Car	John Force	5.036	300.80	W. Bazemore	5.215	272.28
		Pro Stock	Greg Anderson	6.858	202.09	L. Morgan	6.910	200.14
Aug. 3	Fram-Autolite Nationals	Top Fuel	Larry Dixon	4.640	319.67	D. Baca	4.805	298.47
		Funny Car	Gary Scelzi	4.958	312.21	D. Skuza	4.966	306.74
		Pro Stock	Jeg Coughlin	6.839	201.07	G. Anderson	6.798	203.37
Aug. 17	Lucas Oil Nationals	Top Fuel	Doug Kalitta	4.698	311.20	T. Schumacher	4.698	304.19
		Funny Car	Gary Densham	5.009	298.01	T. Wilkerson	5.042	297.29
		Pro Stock	Greg Anderson	6.917	200.05	K. Johnson	6.930	198.82
Sept. 1	Mac Tools U.S. Nationals	Top Fuel	Tony Schumacher	4.498	328.54	D. Russell	4.613	290.19
		Funny Car	Tim Wilkerson	4.841	321.19	J. Gray	4.903	314.24
		Pro Stock	Greg Anderson	6.803	203.40	K. Johnson	6.808	202.39
Sept. 14	Lucas Oil Nationals	Top Fuel	Tony Schumacher	4.584	315.56	J. Head	4.603	322.65
		Funny Car	Tim Wilkerson	4.869	317.94	C. Pedregon	11.909	81.05
		Pro Stock	Warren Johnson	6.755	204.76	T. Coughlin	6.754	199.29
Sept. 21	O'Reilly Mid-South Nationals	Top Fuel	Tony Schumacher	4.581	317.79	L. Dixon	4.651	316.52
		Funny Car	Whit Bazemore	4.894	309.42	D. Skuza	5.225	227.50
		Pro Stock	Greg Anderson	6.814	202.67	J. Coughlin	6.825	200.95
Sept. 28	Carquest Auto Parts Nationals	Top Fuel	Kenny Bernstein	4.503	328.46	L. Dixon	4.638	321.35
		Funny Car	Tony Pedregon	4.769	316.52	P. Burkart	—	—#
		Pro Stock	Jeg Coughlin	6.749	203.22	G. Anderson	6.728	204.93
Oct. 12	O'Reilly Fall Nationals	Top Fuel	Kenny Bernstein	4.514	327.86	S. Kalitta	8.685	84.90
		Funny Car	John Force	4.889	317.68	D. Skuza	5.013	274.30
		Pro Stock	Greg Anderson	6.807	203.66	J. Coughlin	6.833	202.02

*Force was disqualified for crossing over the centerline 800 feet into the race.
Burkart's car began leaking fluid before the final round and could not compete.

1909-2003
Through the Years

SPORTS ALMANAC

NASCAR CIRCUIT
The Crown Jewels

The five biggest races on the NASCAR (National Association for Stock Car Auto Racing) circuit are the Daytona 500, the EA Sports 500, the Coca-Cola 600, the Mountain Dew Southern 500, and the Brickyard 400. They are the Winston Cup Series' biggest (Daytona), fastest (EA Sports), longest (Coca-Cola), oldest (Southern) and richest (Brickyard) races. The only drivers to win three of the races in a year are Lee Roy Yarbrough (1969), David Pearson (1976), Bill Elliott (1985) Dale Jarrett (1996) and Jeff Gordon (1997-98).

Daytona 500

Held over 200 laps on 2.5-mile oval at Daytona International Speedway in Daytona Beach, Fla. First race in 1959, although stock car racing at Daytona dates back to 1936. Winners who started from pole position are in **bold** type.

Multiple winners: Richard Petty (7); Cale Yarborough (4); Bobby Allison and Dale Jarrett (3); Bill Elliott, Jeff Gordon, Sterling Marlin and Michael Waltrip (2). **Multiple poles:** Buddy Baker and Cale Yarborough (4); Bill Elliott, Dale Jarrett, Fireball Roberts and Ken Schrader (3); Donnie Allison (2).

Year	Winner	Car	Owner	MPH	Pole Sitter	MPH
1959	Lee Petty	Oldsmobile	Petty Enterprises	135.521	Bob Welborn	140.121
1960	Junior Johnson	Chevrolet	Ray Fox	124.740	Cotton Owens	149.892
1961	Marvin Panch	Pontiac	Smokey Yunick	149.601	Fireball Roberts	155.709
1962	**Fireball Roberts**	Pontiac	Smokey Yunick	152.529	Fireball Roberts	156.999
1963	Tiny Lund	Ford	Wood Brothers	151.566	Fireball Roberts	160.943
1964	Richard Petty	Plymouth	Petty Enterprises	154.334	Paul Goldsmith	174.910
1965-a	Fred Lorenzen	Ford	Holman-Moody	141.539	Darel Dieringer	171.151
1966-b	**Richard Petty**	Plymouth	Petty Enterprises	160.627	Richard Petty	175.165
1967	Mario Andretti	Ford	Holman-Moody	149.926	Curtis Turner	180.831
1968	**Cale Yarborough**	Mercury	Wood Brothers	143.251	Cale Yarborough	189.222
1969	Lee Roy Yarbrough	Ford	Junior Johnson	157.950	Buddy Baker	188.901
1970	Pete Hamilton	Plymouth	Petty Enterprises	149.601	Cale Yarborough	194.015
1971	Richard Petty	Plymouth	Petty Enterprises	144.462	A.J. Foyt	182.744
1972	A.J. Foyt	Mercury	Wood Brothers	161.550	Bobby Isaac	186.632
1973	Richard Petty	Dodge	Petty Enterprises	157.205	Buddy Baker	185.662
1974-c	Richard Petty	Dodge	Petty Enterprises	140.894	David Pearson	185.017
1975	Benny Parsons	Chevrolet	L.G. DeWitt	153.649	Donnie Allison	185.827
1976	David Pearson	Mercury	Wood Brothers	152.181	Ramo Stott	183.456
1977	Cale Yarborough	Chevrolet	Junior Johnson	153.218	Donnie Allison	188.048
1978	Bobby Allison	Ford	Bud Moore	159.730	Cale Yarborough	187.536
1979	Richard Petty	Oldsmobile	Petty Enterprises	143.977	Buddy Baker	196.049
1980	**Buddy Baker**	Oldsmobile	Ranier Racing	177.602*	Buddy Baker	194.099
1981	Richard Petty	Buick	Petty Enterprises	169.651	Bobby Allison	194.624
1982	Bobby Allison	Buick	DiGard Racing	153.991	Benny Parsons	196.317
1983	Cale Yarborough	Pontiac	Ranier Racing	155.979	Ricky Rudd	198.864
1984	**Cale Yarborough**	Chevrolet	Ranier Racing	150.994	Cale Yarborough	201.848
1985	**Bill Elliott**	Ford	Melling Racing	172.265	Bill Elliott	205.114
1986	Geoff Bodine	Chevrolet	Hendrick Motorsports	148.124	Bill Elliott	205.039
1987	**Bill Elliott**	Ford	Melling Racing	176.263	Bill Elliott	210.364†
1988	Bobby Allison	Buick	Stavola Brothers	137.531	Ken Schrader	198.823
1989	Darrell Waltrip	Chevrolet	Hendrick Motorsports	148.466	Ken Schrader	196.996
1990	Derrike Cope	Chevrolet	Bob Whitcomb	165.761	Ken Schrader	196.515
1991	Ernie Irvan	Chevrolet	Morgan-McClure	148.148	Davey Allison	195.955
1992	Davey Allison	Ford	Robert Yates	160.256	Sterling Marlin	192.213
1993	Dale Jarrett	Chevrolet	Joe Gibbs Racing	154.972	Kyle Petty	189.426
1994	Sterling Marlin	Chevrolet	Morgan-McClure	156.931	Loy Allen	190.158
1995	Sterling Marlin	Chevrolet	Morgan-McClure	141.710	Dale Jarrett	193.498
1996	Dale Jarrett	Ford	Robert Yates	154.308	Dale Earnhardt	189.510
1997	Jeff Gordon	Chevrolet	Rick Hendrick	148.295	Mike Skinner	189.813
1998	Dale Earnhardt	Chevrolet	Richard Childress	172.712	Bobby Labonte	192.415
1999	**Jeff Gordon**	Chevrolet	Rick Hendrick	161.551	Jeff Gordon	195.067
2000	**Dale Jarrett**	Ford	Robert Yates	155.669	Dale Jarrett	191.091
2001	Michael Waltrip	Chevrolet	Dale Earnhardt, Inc.	161.783	Bill Elliott	183.565
2002	Ward Burton	Dodge	Bill Davis	142.971	Jimmie Johnson	185.831
2003-d	Michael Waltrip	Chevrolet	Dale Earnhardt, Inc.	133.870	Jeff Green	186.606

*Track and race record for winning speed. †Track and race record for qualifying speed.
Notes: a—rain shortened 1965 race to 332.5 miles; b—rain shortened 1966 race to 495 miles; c—in 1974, race shortened 50 miles due to energy crisis; d—rain shortened 2003 race to 272.5 miles. **Also:** Pole sitters determined by pole qualifying race (1959-65); by two-lap average (1966-68); by fastest single lap (since 1969).

EA Sports 500

Held over 188 laps on 2.66-mile tri-oval at Talladega Superspeedway in Talladega, Ala.

Previously known as Winston 500 (1970-93, 1997-2000) and Winston Select 500 (1994-96). It's been EA Sports 500 since 2001. Winners who started from pole position are in **bold** type.

Multiple winners: Dale Earnhardt (4); Bobby Allison, Davey Allison, Buddy Baker and David Pearson (3); Dale Earnhardt Jr., Mark Martin, Darrell Waltrip and Cale Yarborough (2).

Year		Year		Year		Year	
1970	Pete Hamilton	1980	Buddy Baker	1990	**Dale Earnhardt**	2000	Dale Earnhardt
1971	**Donnie Allison**	1981	**Bobby Allison**	1991	Harry Gant	2001	Dale Earnhardt Jr.
1972	David Pearson	1982	Darrell Waltrip	1992	Davey Allison	2002	Dale Earnhardt Jr.
1973	David Pearson	1983	Richard Petty	1993	Ernie Irvan	2003	Michael Waltrip
1974	**David Pearson**	1984	**Cale Yarborough**	1994	Dale Earnhardt		
1975	**Buddy Baker**	1985	Bill Elliott	1995	**Mark Martin**		
1976	Buddy Baker	1986	Bobby Allison	1996	Sterling Marlin		
1977	Darrell Waltrip	1987	Davey Allison	1997	Mark Martin		
1978	**Cale Yarborough**	1988	Phil Parsons	1998	Dale Jarrett		
1979	Bobby Allison	1989	Davey Allison	1999	Dale Earnhardt		

Coca-Cola 600

Held over 400 laps on 1.5-mile oval at Lowe's Motor Speedway in Concord, N.C.

Previously known as World 600 (1960-85). It has been Coca-Cola 600 since 1986 (in 2002, sponsors announced a one-time-only name change to The Coca-Cola Racing Family 600). Winners who started from pole position are in **bold** type.

Multiple winners: Darrell Waltrip (5); Bobby Allison, Buddy Baker, Dale Earnhardt, Jeff Gordon and David Pearson (3); Neil Bonnett, Jeff Burton, Fred Lorenzen, Jim Paschal and Richard Petty (2).

Year		Year		Year		Year	
1960	Joe Lee Johnson	1971	Bobby Allison	1982	Neil Bonnett	1993	Dale Earnhardt
1961	David Pearson	1972	Buddy Baker	1983	Neil Bonnett	1994	**Jeff Gordon**
1962	Nelson Stacy	1973	**Buddy Baker**	1984	Bobby Allison	1995	Bobby Labonte
1963	Fred Lorenzen	1974	**David Pearson**	1985	Darrell Waltrip	1996	Dale Jarrett
1964	Jim Paschal	1975	Richard Petty	1986	Dale Earnhardt	1997	**Jeff Gordon***
1965	**Fred Lorenzen**	1976	**David Pearson**	1987	Kyle Petty	1998	**Jeff Gordon**
1966	Marvin Panch	1977	Richard Petty	1988	Darrell Waltrip	1999	Jeff Burton
1967	Jim Paschal	1978	Darrell Waltrip	1989	Darrell Waltrip	2000	Matt Kenseth
1968	Buddy Baker*	1979	Darrell Waltrip	1990	Rusty Wallace	2001	Jeff Burton
1969	Lee Roy Yarbrough	1980	Benny Parsons	1991	Davey Allison	2002	Mark Martin
1970	Donnie Allison	1981	Bobby Allison	1992	Dale Earnhardt	2003	Jimmie Johnson*

* rain-shortened.

Mountain Dew Southern 500

Held over 367 laps on 1.366-mile oval at Darlington International Raceway in Darlington, S.C.

Previously known as Southern 500 (1950-88); Heinz 500 (1989-91); and Pepsi Southern 500 (1998-2000). It was the Mountain Dew Southern 500 from 1992-97, and since 2001. Winners who started from pole position are in **bold** type.

Multiple winners: Jeff Gordon and Cale Yarborough (5); Bobby Allison (4); Buck Baker, Dale Earnhardt, Bill Elliott, David Pearson and Herb Thomas (3); Harry Gant and Fireball Roberts (2).

Year		Year		Year		Year	
1950	Johnny Mantz	1964	Buck Baker	1978	Cale Yarborough	1991	Harry Gant
1951	Herb Thomas	1965	Ned Jarrett	1979	David Pearson	1992	Darrell Waltrip*
1952	**Fonty Flock**	1966	Darel Dieringer	1980	Terry Labonte	1993	Mark Martin*
1953	Buck Baker	1967	**Richard Petty**	1981	Neil Bonnett	1994	Bill Elliott
1954	Herb Thomas	1968	Cale Yarborough	1982	Cale Yarborough	1995	Jeff Gordon
1955	Herb Thomas	1969	Lee Roy Yarbrough*	1983	Bobby Allison	1996	Jeff Gordon
1956	Curtis Turner	1970	Buddy Baker	1984	**Harry Gant**	1997	Jeff Gordon*
1957	Speedy Thompson	1971	**Bobby Allison**	1985	**Bill Elliott**	1998	Jeff Gordon
1958	Fireball Roberts	1972	**Bobby Allison**	1986	**Tim Richmond**	1999	Jeff Burton*
1959	Jim Reed	1973	Cale Yarborough	1987	Dale Earnhardt*	2000	Bobby Labonte*
1960	Buck Baker	1974	Cale Yarborough	1988	**Bill Elliott**	2001	Ward Burton
1961	Nelson Stacy	1975	Bobby Allison	1989	Dale Earnhardt	2002	Jeff Gordon
1962	Larry Frank	1976	**David Pearson**	1990	**Dale Earnhardt**	2003	Terry Labonte
1963	Fireball Roberts	1977	David Pearson				

* rain-shortened.

Brickyard 400

Held over 160 laps at 2.5-mile Indianapolis Motor Speedway in Indianapolis, Ind.

Winners who started from pole position are in **bold** type.

Multiple winners: Jeff Gordon (3); Dale Jarrett (2).

Year		Year		Year		Year		Year	
1994	Jeff Gordon	1996	Dale Jarrett	1998	Jeff Gordon	2000	Bobby Labonte	2002	Bill Elliott
1995	Dale Earnhardt	1997	Ricky Rudd	1999	Dale Jarrett	2001	Jeff Gordon	2003	**Kevin Harvick**

NASCAR Circuit (Cont.)

Winston Cup Series Champions

Originally the Grand National Championship, 1949-70, and based on official NASCAR records. Note that earnings totals include bonus awards.

Multiple winners: (drivers) Dale Earnhardt and Richard Petty (7); Jeff Gordon (4); David Pearson, Lee Petty, Darrell Waltrip and Cale Yarborough (3); Buck Baker, Tim Flock, Ned Jarrett, Terry Labonte, Herb Thomas and Joe Weatherly (2).

Multiple winners: (cars) Chevrolet (22); Ford (6); Plymouth (5); Dodge, Oldsmobile and Pontiac (4); Buick and Hudson (3); and Chrysler (2).

Year	Car #	Driver	Car	Owner	Sts	Wins	Poles	Earnings
1949	22	**Red Byron**	Oldsmobile	Raymond Parks	5	2	1	$5,800
1950	60	**Bill Rexford**	Oldsmobile	Julian Buesink	17	1	0	6,175
1951	92	**Herb Thomas**	Hudson	Herb Thomas	34	7	4	18,200
1952	91	**Tim Flock**	Hudson	Ted Chester	33	8	4	20,210
1953	92	**Herb Thomas**	Hudson	Herb Thomas	37	11	10	27,300
1954	42	**Lee Petty**	Chrysler	Herb Thomas	34	7	3	26,706
1955	300	**Tim Flock**	Chrysler	Carl Kiekhaefer	38	18	19	33,750
1956	300B	**Buck Baker**	Chevrolet	Carl Kiekhaefer	48	14	12	29,790
1957	87	**Buck Baker**	Chevrolet	Buck Baker	40	10	5	24,712
1958	42	**Lee Petty**	Oldsmobile	Petty Enterprises	49	7	4	20,600
1959	42	**Lee Petty**	Plymouth	Petty Enterprises	42	10	2	45,570
1960	4	**Rex White**	Chevrolet	White-Clements	40	6	3	45,260
1961	11	**Ned Jarrett**	Chevrolet	W.G. Holloway Jr.	46	1	4	27,285
1962	8	**Joe Weatherly**	Pontiac	Bud Moore	52	9	6	56,110
1963	8	**Joe Weatherly**	Mercury	Wood Brothers	53	3	6	58,110
1964	43	**Richard Petty**	Plymouth	Petty Enterprises	61	9	8	98,810
1965	11	**Ned Jarrett**	Ford	Bondy Long	54	13	9	77,960
1966	6	**David Pearson**	Dodge	Cotton Owens	42	14	7	59,205
1967	43	**Richard Petty**	Plymouth	Petty Enterprises	48	27	18	130,275
1968	17	**David Pearson**	Ford	Holman-Moody	48	16	12	118,842
1969	17	**David Pearson**	Ford	Holman-Moody	51	11	14	183,700
1970	71	**Bobby Isaac**	Dodge	Nord Krauskopf	47	11	13	121,470
1971	43	**Richard Petty**	Plymouth	Petty Enterprises	46	21	9	309,225
1972	43	**Richard Petty**	Plymouth	Petty Enterprises	31	8	3	227,015
1973	72	**Benny Parsons**	Chevrolet	L.G. DeWitt	28	1	0	114,345
1974	43	**Richard Petty**	Dodge	Petty Enterprises	30	10	7	299,175
1975	43	**Richard Petty**	Dodge	Petty Enterprises	30	13	3	378,865
1976	11	**Cale Yarborough**	Chevrolet	Junior Johnson	30	9	2	387,173
1977	11	**Cale Yarborough**	Chevrolet	Junior Johnson	30	9	3	477,499
1978	11	**Cale Yarborough**	Oldsmobile	Junior Johnson	30	10	8	530,751
1979	43	**Richard Petty**	Chevrolet	Petty Enterprises	31	5	1	531,292
1980	2	**Dale Earnhardt**	Chevrolet	Rod Osterlund	31	5	0	588,926
1981	11	**Darrell Waltrip**	Buick	Junior Johnson	31	12	11	693,342
1982	11	**Darrell Waltrip**	Buick	Junior Johnson	30	12	7	873,118
1983	22	**Bobby Allison**	Buick	Bill Gardner	30	6	0	828,355
1984	44	**Terry Labonte**	Chevrolet	Billy Hagan	30	2	2	713,010
1985	11	**Darrell Waltrip**	Chevrolet	Junior Johnson	28	3	4	1,318,735
1986	3	**Dale Earnhardt**	Chevrolet	Richard Childress	29	5	1	1,783,880
1987	3	**Dale Earnhardt**	Chevrolet	Richard Childress	29	11	1	2,099,243
1988	9	**Bill Elliott**	Ford	Harry Melling	29	6	6	1,574,639
1989	27	**Rusty Wallace**	Pontiac	Raymond Beadle	29	6	4	2,247,950
1990	3	**Dale Earnhardt**	Chevrolet	Richard Childress	29	9	4	3,083,056
1991	3	**Dale Earnhardt**	Chevrolet	Richard Childress	29	4	0	2,396,685
1992	7	**Alan Kulwicki**	Ford	Alan Kulwicki	29	2	6	2,322,561
1993	3	**Dale Earnhardt**	Chevrolet	Richard Childress	30	6	2	3,353,789
1994	3	**Dale Earnhardt**	Chevrolet	Richard Childress	31	4	2	3,400,733
1995	24	**Jeff Gordon**	Chevrolet	Rick Hendrick	31	7	8	4,347,343
1996	5	**Terry Labonte**	Chevrolet	Rick Hendrick	31	2	4	4,030,648
1997	24	**Jeff Gordon**	Chevrolet	Rick Hendrick	32	10	1	6,375,658
1998	24	**Jeff Gordon**	Chevrolet	Rick Hendrick	33	13	7	9,306,584
1999	88	**Dale Jarrett**	Ford	Robert Yates	34	4	0	6,649,596
2000	18	**Bobby Labonte**	Pontiac	Joe Gibbs	34	4	2	7,361,387
2001	24	**Jeff Gordon**	Chevrolet	Rick Hendrick	36	6	6	10,879,757
2002	20	**Tony Stewart**	Pontiac	Joe Gibbs	36	3	2	9,163,761

NASCAR Rookie of the Year

Sponsored by Raybestos, the official brake of NASCAR, and presented to rookie driver who accumulates the most Winston Cup Series Raybestos Rookie of the Year points based on their best 17 finishes.

Year		Year		Year		Year	
1958	Shorty Rollins	1960	David Pearson	1962	Tom Cox	1964	Doug Cooper
1959	Richard Petty	1961	Woodie Wilson	1963	Billy Wade	1965	Sam McQuagg

Year		Year		Year		Year	
1966	James Hylton	1976	Skip Manning	1986	Alan Kulwicki	1996	Johnny Benson
1967	Donnie Allison	1977	Ricky Rudd	1987	Davey Allison	1997	Mike Skinner
1968	Pete Hamilton	1978	Ronnie Thomas	1988	Ken Bouchard	1998	Kenny Irwin
1969	Dick Brooks	1979	Dale Earnhardt	1989	Dick Trickle	1999	Tony Stewart
1970	Bill Dennis	1980	Jody Ridley	1990	Rob Moroso	2000	Matt Kenseth
1971	Walter Ballard	1981	Ron Bouchard	1991	Bobby Hamilton	2001	Kevin Harvick
1972	Larry Smith	1982	Geoff Bodine	1992	Jimmy Hensley	2002	Ryan Newman
1973	Lennie Pond	1983	Sterling Marlin	1993	Jeff Gordon		
1974	Earl Ross	1984	Rusty Wallace	1994	Jeff Burton		
1975	Bruce Hill	1985	Ken Schrader	1995	Ricky Craven		

All-Time Leaders

NASCAR's all-time Top 20 drivers in victories, pole positions and earnings based on records through 2002. Drivers active in 2003 are in **bold** type.

Victories

1	Richard Petty	200	7	**Jeff Gordon**	61	13	Buck Baker	46	19	**Dale Jarrett**	30
2	David Pearson	105	8	Lee Petty	55	14	**Bill Elliott**	43	20	Fred Lorenzen	26
3	Bobby Allison	84	9	**Rusty Wallace**	54	15	Tim Flock	40		Rex White	26
	Darrell Waltrip	84	10	Ned Jarrett	50	16	Bobby Isaac	37			
5	Cale Yarborough	83		Junior Johnson	50	17	Mark Martin	33			
6	Dale Earnhardt	76	12	Herb Thomas	48	18	Fireball Roberts	32			

Pole Positions

1	Richard Petty	126	6	**Bill Elliott**	55	11	**Mark Martin**	41	16	**Rusty Wallace**	36
2	David Pearson	113	7	Bobby Isaac	51	12	Buddy Baker	40	17	Ned Jarrett	35
3	Cale Yarborough	70	8	Junior Johnson	47	13	Tim Flock	39		Fireball Roberts	35
4	Darrell Waltrip	59	9	Buck Baker	44		Herb Thomas	39		Rex White	35
5	Bobby Allison	57	10	**Jeff Gordon**	42	15	**Geoff Bodine**	37	20	Fonty Flock	34

Earnings

1	**Jeff Gordon**	$51,903,055	8	**Terry Labonte**	$29,780,932	15	**Michael Waltrip**	$18,015,845
2	Dale Earnhardt	41,742,384	9	**Ricky Rudd**	28,974,837	16	**Ward Burton**	17,923,194
3	**Dale Jarrett**	37,696,783	10	**Jeff Burton**	27,203,355	17	**Geoff Bodine**	16,054,770
4	**Mark Martin**	36,170,215	11	**Sterling Marlin**	24,128,428	18	**Kyle Petty**	15,529,641
5	**Rusty Wallace**	34,442,853	12	**Tony Stewart**	20,937,721	19	**Bobby Hamilton**	15,187,015
6	**Bill Elliott**	31,418,873	13	**Ken Schrader**	20,560,421	20	**Jimmy Spencer**	14,884,174
7	**Bobby Labonte**	30,136,739	14	Darrell Waltrip	19,416,618			

CART CIRCUIT

Champ Car Series Champions

Officially the "Bridgestone Presents The Champ Car World Series Powered by Ford" since 2003. It was the FedEx Championship Series from 1998-2002. Formerly, AAA (American Automobile Assn., 1909-55), USAC (U.S. Auto Club, 1956-78), CART (Championship Auto Racing Teams, 1979-91). CART was renamed IndyCar in 1992 and then lost use of the name in 1997.

Multiple titles: A.J. Foyt (7); Mario Andretti (4); Jimmy Bryan, Earl Cooper, Ted Horn, Rick Mears, Louie Meyer, Bobby Rahal, Al Unser (3); Tony Bettenhausen, Gil de Ferran, Ralph DePalma, Peter DePaolo, Joe Leonard, Rex Mays, Tommy Milton, Ralph Mulford, Jimmy Murphy, Wilbur Shaw, Al Unser Jr., Bobby Unser, Rodger Ward and Alex Zanardi (2).

AAA

Year		Year		Year		Year	
1909	George Robertson	1920	Tommy Milton	1931	Louis Schneider	1942-45	No racing
1910	Ray Harroun	1921	Tommy Milton	1932	Bob Carey	1946	Ted Horn
1911	Ralph Mulford	1922	Jimmy Murphy	1933	Louie Meyer	1947	Ted Horn
1912	Ralph DePalma	1923	Eddie Hearne	1934	Bill Cummings	1948	Ted Horn
1913	Earl Cooper	1924	Jimmy Murphy	1935	Kelly Petillo	1949	Johnnie Parsons
1914	Ralph DePalma	1925	Peter DePaolo	1936	Mauri Rose	1950	Henry Banks
1915	Earl Cooper	1926	Harry Hartz	1937	Wilbur Shaw	1951	Tony Bettenhausen
1916	Dario Resta	1927	Peter DePaolo	1938	Floyd Roberts	1952	Chuck Stevenson
1917	Earl Cooper	1928	Louie Meyer	1939	Wilbur Shaw	1953	Sam Hanks
1918	Ralph Mulford	1929	Louie Meyer	1940	Rex Mays	1954	Jimmy Bryan
1919	Howard Wilcox	1930	Billy Arnold	1941	Rex Mays	1955	Bob Sweikert

USAC

Year		Year		Year		Year	
1956	Jimmy Bryan	1962	Rodger Ward	1968	Bobby Unser	1974	Bobby Unser
1957	Jimmy Bryan	1963	A.J. Foyt	1969	Mario Andretti	1975	A.J. Foyt
1958	Tony Bettenhausen	1964	A.J. Foyt	1970	Al Unser	1976	Gordon Johncock
1959	Rodger Ward	1965	Mario Andretti	1971	Joe Leonard	1977	Tom Sneva
1960	A.J. Foyt	1966	Mario Andretti	1972	Joe Leonard	1978	A.J. Foyt
1961	A.J. Foyt	1967	A.J. Foyt	1973	Roger McCluskey		

CART Circuit (Cont.)
CART

Year	Driver	Car	Team	Sts	Wins	Poles	Earnings
1979	**Rick Mears**	Penske Ford	Penske	14	3	2	$408,078
1980	**Johnny Rutherford**	Chaparral Ford	Chaparral	12	5	3	503,595
1981	**Rick Mears**	Penske Ford	Penske	11	6	2	323,670
1982	**Rick Mears**	Penske Ford	Penske	11	4	8	306,454
1983	**Al Unser**	Penske Ford	Penske	13	1	0	500,109
1984	**Mario Andretti**	Lola Ford	Newman/Haas	16	6	8	931,929
1985	**Al Unser**	March Ford	Penske	14	1	1	843,885
1986	**Bobby Rahal**	March Ford	TrueSports	17	6	2	1,488,049
1987	**Bobby Rahal**	Lola Ford	TrueSports	15	3	1	1,261,098
1988	**Danny Sullivan**	Penske Chevrolet	Penske	15	4	9	1,222,791
1989	**Emerson Fittipaldi**	Penske Chevrolet	Patrick	15	5	4	2,166,078
1990	**Al Unser Jr.**	Lola Chevrolet	Galles-Kraco	16	6	1	1,946,833
1991	**Michael Andretti**	Lola Chevrolet	Newman/Haas	17	8	8	2,461,734
1992	**Bobby Rahal**	Lola Chevrolet	Rahal-Hogan	16	4	3	2,235,298
1993	**Nigel Mansell**	Lola Ford	Newman/Haas	15	5	7	2,526,953
1994	**Al Unser Jr.**	Penske Ilmor	Marlboro Team Penske	16	8	4	3,535,813
1995	**Jacques Villeneuve**	Reynard Ford	Team Green	17	4	6	2,996,269
1996	**Jimmy Vasser**	Reynard Honda	Target Chip Ganassi	16	4	4	3,071,500
1997	**Alex Zanardi**	Reynard Honda	Target Chip Ganassi	16	5	4	2,096,250
1998	**Alex Zanardi**	Reynard Honda	Target Chip Ganassi	19	7	0	2,229,250
1999	**Juan Montoya**	Reynard Honda	Target Chip Ganassi	20	7	7	1,973,000
2000	**Gil de Ferran**	Reynard Honda	Marlboro Team Penske	20	2	5	1,677,000
2001	**Gil de Ferran**	Reynard Honda	Marlboro Team Penske	20	2	5	1,761,500
2002	**Cristiano da Matta**	Lola Toyota	Newman/Haas	19	7	7	2,053,000

CART Rookie of the Year

Officially, Jim Trueman Rookie of the Year Award. Named after the late founder of the two-time champion TrueSports Racing Team, it's presented to the rookie who accumulates the most Champ Car Series points among first year drivers.

Year		Year		Year		Year	
1979	Bill Alsup	1985	Arie Luyendyk	1991	Jeff Andretti	1997	Patrick Carpentier
1980	Dennis Firestone	1986	Dominic Dobson	1992	Stefan Johansson	1998	Tony Kanaan
1981	Bob Lazier	1987	Fabrizio Barbazza	1993	Nigel Mansell	1999	Juan Montoya
1982	Bobby Rahal	1988	John Jones	1994	Jacques Villeneuve	2000	Kenny Brack
1983	Teo Fabi	1989	Bernard Jourdain	1995	Gil de Ferran	2001	Scott Dixon
1984	Roberto Guerrero	1990	Eddie Cheever	1996	Alex Zanardi	2002	Mario Dominguez

All-Time CART Leaders

CART's all-time Top 20 drivers in victories, pole positions and earnings, based on records through 2002. Drivers active in 2003 are in **bold** type. Totals include victories, poles and earnings before CART was established in 1979. Earnings totals include year-end performance awards. (*) Denotes driver is active, but in Indy Racing League not CART; (†) denotes driver is active, but in Formula One not CART; (**) denotes driver is active, but in NASCAR not CART.

Victories

1	A.J. Foyt 67	8	Johnny Rutherford 27		Emerson Fittipaldi 22
2	Mario Andretti 52	9	Roger Ward 26	16	Earl Cooper 20
3	Michael Andretti* 42	10	Gordon Johncock 25	17	Jimmy Bryan 19
4	Al Unser 39	11	Ralph DePalma 24		Jimmy Murphy 19
5	Bobby Unser 35		Bobby Rahal 24		**Paul Tracy** 19
6	Al Unser Jr.* 31	13	Tommy Milton 23	20	Ralph Mulford 17
7	Rick Mears 29	14	Tony Bettenhausen 22		Danny Sullivan 17

Pole Positions

1	Mario Andretti 67	9	Rex Mays 19		Juan Montoya† 14
2	A.J. Foyt 53		Danny Sullivan 19	18	**Paul Tracy** 13
3	Bobby Unser 49	11	Bobby Rahal 18	19	Parnelli Jones 12
4	Rick Mears 40	12	Emerson Fittipaldi 17	20	Danny Ongais 11
5	Michael Andretti* 32	13	Gil de Ferran* 16		Rodger Ward 11
6	Al Unser 27	14	Tony Bettenhausen 14		Dario Franchitti* 11
7	Johnny Rutherford 23		Don Branson 14		
8	Gordon Johncock 20		Tom Sneva 14		

Earnings

1	Al Unser Jr.* $18,828,406	8	Danny Sullivan ...$8,884,126	15	Alex Zanardi $5,893,750
2	Michael Andretti* ..18,228,119	9	**Paul Tracy** 8,825,270	19	Christian Fittipaldi** .5,526,166
3	Bobby Rahal 16,344,008	10	Arie Luyendyk 7,732,188	16	Scott Pruett** 5,440,144
4	Emerson Fittipaldi ..14,293,625	11	Gil de Ferran* 7,390,703	17	A.J. Foyt 5,357,589
5	Mario Andretti 11,552,154	12	Raul Boesel 6,971,887	18	Teo Fabi 5,045,881
6	Rick Mears 11,050,807	13	Al Unser 6,740,843	20	Dario Franchitti* ...4,935,000
7	**Jimmy Vasser** ...10,627,749	14	**Adrian Fernandez** .6,614,265		

INDY RACING LEAGUE CIRCUIT

Indianapolis 500

Held every Memorial Day weekend; 200 laps around a 2.5-mile oval at Indianapolis Motor Speedway. First race was held in 1911. The Indy Racing League began in 1996 and made the Indianapolis 500 its cornerstone event. Winning drivers are listed with starting positions. Winners who started from pole position are in **bold** type.

Multiple wins: A.J. Foyt, Rick Mears and Al Unser (4); Louis Meyer, Mauri Rose, Johnny Rutherford, Wilbur Shaw and Bobby Unser (3); Helio Castroneves, Emerson Fittipaldi, Gordon Johncock, Arie Luyendyk, Tommy Milton, Al Unser Jr., Bill Vukovich and Rodger Ward (2).

Multiple poles: Rick Mears (6); A.J. Foyt and Rex Mays (4); Mario Andretti, Arie Luyendyk, Johnny Rutherford and Tom Sneva (3); Scott Brayton, Bill Cummings, Ralph DePalma, Leon Duray, Parnelli Jones, Jimmy Murphy, Duke Nalon, Eddie Sachs and Bobby Unser (2).

Year	Winner (Pos.)	Car	MPH	Pole Sitter	MPH
1911	Ray Harroun (28)	Marmon Wasp	74.602	Lewis Strang	–
1912	Joe Dawson (7)	National	78.719	Gil Anderson	–
1913	Jules Goux (7)	Peugeot	75.933	Caleb Bragg	–
1914	Rene Thomas (15)	Delage	82.474	Jean Chassagne	–
1915	Ralph DePalma (2)	Mercedes	89.840	Howard Wilcox	98.90
1916-a	Dario Resta (4)	Peugeot	84.001	John Aitken	96.69
1917-18	Not held	World War I			
1919	Howdy Wilcox (2)	Peugeot	88.050	Rene Thomas	104.78
1920	Gaston Chevrolet (6)	Monroe	88.618	Ralph DePalma	99.15
1921	Tommy Milton (20)	Frontenac	89.621	Ralph DePalma	100.75
1922	**Jimmy Murphy** (1)	Murphy Special	94.484	Jimmy Murphy	100.50
1923	**Tommy Milton** (1)	H.C.S. Special	90.954	Tommy Milton	108.17
1924	L.L. Corum & Joe Boyer (21)	Duesenberg Special	98.234	Jimmy Murphy	108.037
1925	Peter DePaolo (2)	Duesenberg Special	101.127	Leon Duray	113.196
1926-b	Frank Lockhart (20)	Miller Special	95.904	Earl Cooper	111.735
1927	George Souders (22)	Duesenberg	97.545	Frank Lockhart	120.100
1928	Louie Meyer (13)	Miller Special	99.482	Leon Duray	122.391
1929	Ray Keech (6)	Simplex Piston Ring Special	97.585	Cliff Woodbury	120.599
1930	**Billy Arnold** (1)	Miller-Hartz Special	100.448	Billy Arnold	113.268
1931	Louis Schneider (13)	Bowes Seal Fast Special	96.629	Russ Snowberger	112.796
1932	Fred Frame (27)	Miller-Hartz Special	104.144	Lou Moore	117.363
1933	Louie Meyer (6)	Tydol Special	104.162	Bill Cummings	118.530
1934	Bill Cummings (10)	Boyle Products Special	104.863	Kelly Petillo	119.329
1935	Kelly Petillo (22)	Gilmore Speedway Special	106.240	Rex Mays	120.736
1936	Louie Meyer (28)	Ring Free Special	109.069	Rex Mays	119.644
1937	Wilbur Shaw (2)	Shaw-Gilmore Special	113.580	Bill Cummings	123.343
1938	**Floyd Roberts** (1)	Burd Piston Ring Special	117.200	Floyd Roberts	125.681
1939	Wilbur Shaw (3)	Boyle Special	115.035	Jimmy Snyder	130.138
1940	Wilbur Shaw (2)	Boyle Special	114.277	Rex Mays	127.850
1941	Floyd Davis & Mauri Rose (17)	Noc-Out Hose Clamp Special	115.117	Mauri Rose	128.691
1942-45	Not held	World War II			
1946	George Robson (15)	Thorne Engineering Special	114.820	Cliff Bergere	126.471
1947	Mauri Rose (3)	Blue Crown Spark Plug Special	116.338	Ted Horn	126.564
1948	Mauri Rose (3)	Blue Crown Spark Plug Special	119.814	Rex Mays	130.577
1949	Bill Holland (4)	Blue Crown Spark Plug Special	121.327	Duke Nalon	132.939
1950-c	Johnnie Parsons (5)	Wynn's Friction Proofing	124.002	Walt Faulkner	134.343
1951	Lee Wallard (2)	Belanger Special	126.244	Duke Nalon	136.498
1952	Troy Ruttman (7)	Agajanian Special	128.922	Fred Agabashian	138.010
1953	**Bill Vukovich** (1)	Fuel Injection Special	128.740	Bill Vukovich	138.392
1954	Bill Vukovich (19)	Fuel Injection Special	130.840	Jack McGrath	141.033
1955	Bob Sweikert (14)	John Zink Special	128.213	Jerry Hoyt	140.045
1956	**Pat Flaherty** (1)	John Zink Special	128.490	Pat Flaherty	145.596
1957	Sam Hanks (13)	Belond Exhaust Special	135.601	Pat O'Connor	143.948
1958	Jimmy Bryan (7)	Belond AP Parts Special	133.791	Dick Rathmann	145.974
1959	Rodger Ward (6)	Leader Card 500 Roadster	135.857	Johnny Thomson	145.908
1960	Jim Rathmann (2)	Ken-Paul Special	138.767	Eddie Sachs	146.592
1961	A.J. Foyt (7)	Bowes Seal Fast Special	139.130	Eddie Sachs	147.481
1962	Rodger Ward (2)	Leader Card 500 Roadster	140.293	Parnelli Jones	150.370
1963	**Parnelli Jones** (1)	Agajanian-Willard Special	143.137	Parnelli Jones	151.153
1964	A.J. Foyt (5)	Sheraton-Thompson Special	147.350	Jim Clark	158.828
1965	Jim Clark (2)	Lotus Ford	150.686	A.J. Foyt	161.233
1966	Graham Hill (15)	American Red Ball Special	144.317	Mario Andretti	165.899
1967-d	A.J. Foyt (4)	Sheraton-Thompson Special	151.207	Mario Andretti	168.982
1968	Bobby Unser (3)	Rislone Special	152.882	Joe Leonard	171.559
1969	Mario Andretti (2)	STP Oil Treatment Special	156.867	A.J. Foyt	170.568
1970	**Al Unser** (1)	Johnny Lightning Special	155.749	Al Unser	170.221

Indy Racing League Circuit (Cont.)

Year	Winner (Pos.)	Car	MPH	Pole Sitter	MPH
1971	Al Unser (5)	Johnny Lightning Special	157.735	Peter Revson	178.696
1972	Mark Donohue (3)	Sunoco McLaren	162.962	Bobby Unser	195.940
1973-e	Gordon Johncock (11)	STP Double Oil Filters	159.036	Johnny Rutherford	198.413
1974	Johnny Rutherford (25)	McLaren	158.589	A.J. Foyt	191.632
1975-f	Bobby Unser (3)	Jorgensen Eagle	149.213	A.J. Foyt	193.976
1976-g	**Johnny Rutherford** (1)	Hy-Gain McLaren/Goodyear	148.725	Johnny Rutherford	188.957
1977	A.J. Foyt (4)	Gilmore Racing Team	161.331	Tom Sneva	198.884
1978	Al Unser (5)	FNCTC Chaparral Lola	161.363	Tom Sneva	202.156
1979	**Rick Mears** (1)	The Gould Charge	158.899	Rick Mears	193.736
1980	**Johnny Rutherford** (1)	Pennzoil Chaparral	142.862	Johnny Rutherford	192.256
1981-h	**Bobby Unser** (1)	Norton Spirit Penske PC-9B	139.084	Bobby Unser	200.546
1982	Gordon Johncock (5)	STP Oil Treatment	162.029	Rick Mears	207.004
1983	Tom Sneva (4)	Texaco Star	162.117	Teo Fabi	207.395
1984	Rick Mears (3)	Pennzoil Z-7	163.612	Tom Sneva	210.029
1985	Danny Sullivan (8)	Miller American Special	152.982	Pancho Carter	212.583
1986	Bobby Rahal (4)	Budweiser/Truesports/March	170.722	Rick Mears	216.828
1987	Al Unser (20)	Cummins Holset Turbo	162.175	Mario Andretti	215.390
1988	**Rick Mears** (1)	Pennzoil Z-7/Penske Chevy V-8	144.809	Rick Mears	219.198
1989	Emerson Fittipaldi (3)	Marlboro/Penske Chevy V-8	167.581	Rick Mears	223.885
1990	Arie Luyendyk (3)	Domino's Pizza Chevrolet	185.981*	Emerson Fittipaldi	225.301
1991	**Rick Mears** (1)	Marlboro Penske Chevy	176.457	Rick Mears	224.113
1992	Al Unser Jr. (12)	Valvoline Galmer '92	134.477	Roberto Guerrero	232.482
1993	Emerson Fittipaldi (9)	Marlboro Penske Chevy	157.207	Arie Luyendyk	223.967
1994	**Al Unser Jr.** (1)	Marlboro Penske Mercedes	160.872	Al Unser Jr.	228.011
1995	Jacques Villeneuve (5)	Player's Ltd. Reynard Ford	153.616	Scott Brayton	231.604
1996	Buddy Lazier (5)	Reynard Ford	147.956	Tony Stewart	233.100&
1997	**Arie Luyendyk** (1)	G-Force Olds Aurora	145.827	Arie Luyendyk	218.263
1998	Eddie Cheever Jr. (17)	Dallara Olds Aurora	145.155	Billy Boat	223.503
1999	Kenny Brack (8)	Dallara Olds Aurora	153.176	Arie Luyendyk	225.179
2000	Juan Montoya (2)	G-Force Olds Aurora	167.607	Greg Ray	223.471
2001	Helio Castroneves (11)	Dallara Olds Aurora	153.601	Scott Sharp	226.037
2002-i	Helio Castroneves (13)	Dallara Chevrolet	166.499	Bruno Junqueira	231.342
2003	Gil de Ferran (10)	G-Force Toyota	156.291	Helio Castroneves	231.725

*Track record for winning time.

& Scott Brayton won the pole position with an avg. mph of 233.718 but was killed in a practice run. Stewart was given pole position with the next fastest speed.

Notes: a—1916 race scheduled for 300 miles; **b**—rain shortened 1926 race to 400 miles; **c**—rain shortened 1950 race to 345 miles; **d**—1967 race postponed due to rain after 18 laps (May 30), resumed next day (May 31); **e**—rain shortened 1973 race to 332.5 miles; **f**—rain shortened 1975 race to 435 miles; **g**—rain shortened 1976 race to 255 miles; **h**—in 1981, runner-up Mario Andretti was awarded 1st place when winner Bobby Unser was penalized a lap after the race was completed for passing cars illegally under the caution flag. Unser and car-owner Roger Penske appealed the race stewards' decision to the U.S. Auto Club. Four months later, USAC overturned the ruling, saying that the penalty was too harsh and Unser should be fined $40,000 rather than stripped of his championship; **i**—Team Green, runner-up Paul Tracy's team, appealed Castroneves' victory, citing video evidence and driver testimonials that proved Tracy passed Castroneves moments before the caution flag on lap 199. The IRL denied the appeal the following day.

Indy 500 Rookie of the Year

Voted on by a panel of auto racing media. Award does not necessarily go to highest-finishing first-year driver. Graham Hill won the race on his first try in 1966, but the rookie award went to Jackie Stewart, who led with 10 laps to go only to lose oil pressure and finish 6th.

Father and son winners: Mario and Michael Andretti (1965 and 1984); Bill and Billy Vukovich III (1968 and 1988).

Year		Year		Year		Year	
1952	Art Cross	1966	Jackie Stewart	1980	Tim Richmond	1993	Nigel Mansell
1953	Jimmy Daywalt	1967	Denis Hulme	1981	Josele Garza	1994	Jacques Villeneuve
1954	Larry Crockett	1968	Bill Vukovich	1982	Jim Hickman	1995	Christian Fittipaldi
1955	Al Herman	1969	Mark Donohue	1983	Teo Fabi	1996	Tony Stewart
1956	Bob Veith	1970	Donnie Allison	1984	Michael Andretti	1997	Jeff Ward
1957	Don Edmunds	1971	Denny Zimmerman		& Roberto Guerrero	1998	Steve Knapp
1958	George Amick	1972	Mike Hiss	1985	Arie Luyendyk	1999	Robby McGehee
1959	Bobby Grim	1973	Graham McRae	1986	Randy Lanier	2000	Juan Montoya
1960	Jim Hurtubise	1974	Pancho Carter	1987	Fabrizio Barbazza	2001	Helio Castroneves
1961	Parnelli Jones	1975	Bill Puterbaugh	1988	Billy Vukovich III	2002	Alex Barron
	& Bobby Marshman	1976	Vern Schuppan	1989	Bernard Jourdain		& Tomas Scheckter
1962	Jimmy McElreath	1977	Jerry Sneva		& Scott Pruett	2003	Tora Takagi
1963	Jim Clark	1978	Rick Mears	1990	Eddie Cheever		
1964	Johnny White		& Larry Rice	1991	Jeff Andretti		
1965	Mario Andretti	1979	Howdy Holmes	1992	Lyn St. James		

IRL Champions

The Indy Racing Leauge (IRL) announced its split from the open-wheel CART series in 1994. Led by Indianapolis Motor Speedway President Tony George, the league's inaugural three-race series began in January 1996 and ended with the league's keystone event—the Indianapolis 500. Past series' sponsors include Pep Boys (1998-99) and Northern Light Technology, Inc., an Internet search engine (2000-01).

Multiple winner: Sam Hornish Jr. (2).

Year	Driver	Car	Team	Sts	Wins	Poles	Earnings
1996	**Buzz Calkins**	Reynard Ford	A.J. Foyt Enterprises	3	1	0	$345,553
	Scott Sharp	Lola Ford	A.J. Foyt Enterprises	3	0	0	330,303
1997	**Tony Stewart**	Dallara Oldsmobile	Team Menard	10	1	4	1,142,450
1998	**Kenny Brack**	Dallara Oldsmobile	A.J. Foyt Enterprises	11	3	0	2,106,700
1999	**Greg Ray**	Dallara Oldsmobile	Team Menard	10	3	4	2,061,800
2000	**Buddy Lazier**	Dallara Oldsmobile	Hemelgarn Racing	9	2	1	2,176,200
2001	**Sam Hornish Jr.**	Dallara Oldsmobile	Panther Racing	13	3	0	2,477,025
2002	**Sam Hornish Jr.**	Dallara Oldsmobile	Panther Racing	15	5	2	2,470,615
2003	**Scott Dixon**	G-Force Toyota	Target Chip Ganassi	16	3	5	1,481,265

Note: In 1996, Calkins and Sharp were named co-champions after finishing the series tied in drivers' points (246).

IRL Rookie of the Year

Officially the Bombardier Rookie of the Year Award, presented to rookie driver who accumulates the most points in the IRL standings.

Year		Year		Year		Year	
1996	None	1998	Robby Unser	2000	Airton Dare	2002	Laurent Redon
1997	Jim Guthrie	1999	Scott Harrington	2001	Felipe Giaffone	2003	Dan Wheldon

All-Time IRL Leaders

IRL's all-time Top 10 drivers in victories and earnings, and Top 5 in pole positions, based on records through 2002. Earnings totals include season-ending contingency awards. Drivers active in 2003 are in **bold** type. (*) Denotes driver is active, but in NASCAR Winston Cup Series not IRL; (†) Denotes driver is active, but in CART not IRL.

Victories

1	**Buddy Lazier**	8
	Sam Hornish Jr.	8
3	**Scott Ray**	7
4	Eddie Cheever Jr.	5
	Greg Ray	5
5	**Kenny Brack**	4
	Arie Luyendyk	4
8	Scott Goodyear	3
	Tony Stewart*	3
	Helio Castroneves	3

Pole Positions

1	Greg Ray	13
2	Billy Boat	9
3	Tony Stewart*	7
4	Scott Sharp	5
5	Gil de Ferran	4
	Mark Dismore	4
	Arie Luyendyk	4

Earnings

1	**Buddy Lazier**	$8,173,694
2	Eddie Cheever Jr.	6,265,893
3	**Sam Hornish Jr.**	5,469,590
4	Scott Sharp	5,139,143
5	Greg Ray	4,961,040
6	Billy Boat	4,810,440
7	Kenny Brack	4,682,755
8	Jeff Ward	4,586,140
9	Arie Luyendyk	4,161,193
10	**Robbie Buhl**	4,114,393

FORMULA ONE CIRCUIT

United States Grand Prix

Federation Internationale Sportive Automobile (FISA) sanctioned two annual U.S. Grand Prix—USA/East and USA/West—from 1976-80 and 1983-84. Phoenix was the site of the U.S. Grand Prix from 1989-91. Indianapolis Motor Speedway has hosted the U.S. Grand Prix since 2000.

Indianapolis 500

Officially sanctioned as Grand Prix race from 1950-60 only.

U.S. Grand Prix—East

Held from 1959-80 and 1981-88 at the following locations: Sebring, Fla. (1959); Riverside, Calif. (1960); Watkins Glen, N.Y. (1961-80); and Detroit (1982-88). There was no race in 1981. Race discontinued in 1989.

Multiple winners: Jim Clark, Graham Hill and Ayrton Senna (3); James Hunt, Carlos Reutemann and Jackie Stewart (2).

Year		Car	Year		Car
1959	Bruce McLaren, NZE	Cooper Climax	1974	Carlos Reutemann, ARG	Brabham Ford
1960	Stirling Moss, GBR	Lotus Climax	1975	Niki Lauda, AUT	Ferrari
1961	Innes Ireland, GBR	Lotus Climax	1976	James Hunt, GBR	McLaren Ford
1962	Jim Clark, GBR	Lotus Climax	1977	James Hunt, GBR	McLaren Ford
1963	Graham Hill, GBR	BRM	1978	Carlos Reutemann, ARG	Ferrari
1964	Graham Hill, GBR	BRM	1979	Gilles Villeneuve, CAN	Ferrari
1965	Graham Hill, GBR	BRM	1980	Alan Jones, AUS	Williams Ford
1966	Jim Clark, GBR	Lotus BRM	1981	Not held	
1967	Jim Clark, GBR	Lotus Ford	1982	John Watson, GBR	McLaren Ford
1968	Jackie Stewart, GBR	Matra Ford	1983	Michele Alboreto, ITA	Tyrrell Ford
1969	Jochen Rindt, AUT	Lotus Ford	1984	Nelson Piquet, BRA	Brabham BMW Turbo
1970	Emerson Fittipaldi, BRA	Lotus Ford	1985	Keke Rosberg, FIN	Williams Honda Turbo
1971	Francois Cevert, FRA	Tyrrell Ford	1986	Ayrton Senna, BRA	Lotus Renault Turbo
1972	Jackie Stewart, GBR	Tyrrell Ford	1987	Ayrton Senna, BRA	Lotus Honda Turbo
1973	Ronnie Peterson, SWE	Lotus Ford	1988	Ayrton Senna, BRA	McLaren Honda Turbo

Formula One Circuit (Cont.)
U.S. Grand Prix—West

Held from 1976-83 at Long Beach, Calif. Races also held in Las Vegas (1981-82), Dallas (1984) and Phoenix (1989-91). Race discontinued in 1992.

Multiple winners: Alan Jones and Ayrton Senna (2).

Year		Car	Year		Car
1976	Clay Regazzoni, SWI	Ferrari	1983	John Watson, GBR	McLaren Ford
1977	Mario Andretti, USA	Lotus Ford	1984	Keke Rosberg, FIN	Williams Honda Turbo
1978	Carlos Reutemann, ARG	Ferrari	1985-88	Not held	
1979	Gilles Villeneuve, CAN	Ferrari	1989	Alain Prost, FRA	McLaren Honda
1980	Nelson Piquet, BRA	Brabham Ford	1990	Ayrton Senna, BRA	McLaren Honda
1981	Alan Jones, AUS	Williams Ford	1991	Ayrton Senna, BRA	McLaren Honda
1982	Niki Lauda, AUT	McLaren Ford			

U.S. Grand Prix
Held since 2000 at Indianapolis Motor Speedway.

Year		Car	Year		Car
2000	Michael Schumacher, GER	Ferrari	2002	Rubens Barrichello, BRA	Ferrari
2001	Mika Hakkinen, FIN	McLaren Mercedes	2003	Michael Schumacher, GER	Ferrari

World Champions

Officially called the World Championship of Drivers and based on Formula One (Grand Prix) records through the 2003 season.

Multiple winners: Michael Schumacher (6); Juan-Manuel Fangio (5); Alain Prost (4); Jack Brabham, Niki Lauda, Nelson Piquet, Ayrton Senna and Jackie Stewart (3); Alberto Ascari, Jim Clark, Emerson Fittipaldi, Mika Hakkinen and Graham Hill (2).

Year	Driver	Country	Car	Sts	Wins	Poles	Runner(s)-up
1950	Guiseppe Farina	Italy	Alfa Romeo	7	3	2	J.M. Fangio, ARG
1951	Juan-Manuel Fangio	Argentina	Alfa Romeo	8	3	4	A. Ascari, ITA
1952	Alberto Ascari	Italy	Ferrari	8	6	5	G. Farina, ITA
1953	Alberto Ascari	Italy	Ferrari	9	5	6	J.M. Fangio, ARG
1954	Juan-Manuel Fangio	Argentina	Maserati/Mercedes	9	6	5	F. Gonzalez, ARG
1955	Juan-Manuel Fangio	Argentina	Mercedes	7	4	3	S. Moss, GBR
1956	Juan-Manuel Fangio	Argentina	Lancia/Ferrari	8	3	5	S. Moss, GBR
1957	Juan-Manuel Fangio	Argentina	Maserati	8	4	4	S. Moss, GBR
1958	Mike Hawthorn	Great Britain	Ferrari	11	1	4	S. Moss, GBR
1959	Jack Brabham	Australia	Cooper Climax	9	2	1	T. Brooks, GBR
1960	Jack Brabham	Australia	Cooper Climax	10	5	3	B. McLaren, NZE
1961	Phil Hill	United States	Ferrari	8	2	5	W. von Trips, GER
1962	Graham Hill	Great Britain	BRM	9	4	1	J. Clark, GBR
1963	Jim Clark	Great Britain	Lotus Climax	10	7	7	G. Hill, GBR & R. Ginther, USA
1964	John Surtees	Great Britain	Ferrari	10	2	2	G. Hill, GBR
1965	Jim Clark	Great Britain	Lotus Climax	10	6	6	G. Hill, GBR
1966	Jack Brabham	Australia	Brabham Repco	9	4	3	J. Surtees, GBR
1967	Denis Hulme	New Zealand	Brabham Repco	11	2	0	J. Brabham, AUS
1968	Graham Hill	Great Britain	Lotus Ford	12	3	2	J. Stewart, GBR
1969	Jackie Stewart	Great Britain	Matra Ford	11	6	2	J. Ickx, BEL
1970	Jochen Rindt	Austria	Lotus Ford	13	5	3	J. Ickx, BEL
1971	Jackie Stewart	Great Britain	Tyrrell Ford	11	6	6	R. Peterson, SWE
1972	Emerson Fittipaldi	Brazil	Lotus Ford	12	5	3	J. Stewart, GBR
1973	Jackie Stewart	Great Britain	Tyrrell Ford	15	5	3	E. Fittipaldi, BRA
1974	Emerson Fittipaldi	Brazil	McLaren Ford	15	3	2	C. Regazzoni, SWI
1975	Niki Lauda	Austria	Ferrari	14	5	9	E. Fittipaldi, BRA
1976	James Hunt	Great Britain	McLaren Ford	16	6	8	N. Lauda, AUT
1977	Niki Lauda	Austria	Ferrari	17	3	2	J. Scheckter, RSA
1978	Mario Andretti	United States	Lotus Ford	16	6	8	R. Peterson, SWE
1979	Jody Scheckter	South Africa	Ferrari	15	3	1	G. Villeneuve, CAN
1980	Alan Jones	Australia	Williams Ford	14	5	3	N. Piquet, BRA
1981	Nelson Piquet	Brazil	Brabham Ford	15	3	4	C. Reutemann, ARG
1982	Keke Rosberg	Finland	Williams Ford	16	1	1	D. Pironi, FRA & J. Watson, GBR
1983	Nelson Piquet	Brazil	Brabham BMW Turbo	15	3	1	A. Prost, FRA
1984	Niki Lauda	Austria	McL. TAG Turbo	16	5	0	A. Prost, FRA
1985	Alain Prost	France	McL. TAG Turbo	16	5	2	M. Alboreto, ITA
1986	Alain Prost	France	McL. TAG Turbo	16	4	1	N. Mansell, GBR
1987	Nelson Piquet	Brazil	Williams Honda Turbo	16	3	4	N. Mansell, GBR
1988	Ayrton Senna	Brazil	McLaren Honda Turbo	16	8	13	A. Prost, FRA
1989	Alain Prost	France	McLaren Honda	16	4	2	A. Senna, BRA
1990	Ayrton Senna	Brazil	McLaren Honda	16	6	10	A. Prost, FRA
1991	Ayrton Senna	Brazil	McLaren Honda	16	7	8	N. Mansell, GBR
1992	Nigel Mansell	Great Britain	Williams Renault	16	9	14	R. Patrese, ITA
1993	Alain Prost	France	Williams Renault	16	7	13	A. Senna, BRA

Year	Driver	Country	Car	Sts	Wins	Poles	Runner(s)-up
1994	**Michael Schumacher**	Germany	Benetton Ford	14	8	6	D. Hill, GBR
1995	**Michael Schumacher**	Germany	Benetton Renault	17	9	4	D. Hill, GBR
1996	**Damon Hill**	Great Britain	Williams Renault	16	8	9	J. Villeneuve, CAN
1997	**Jacques Villeneuve**	Canada	Williams Renault	17	7	10	H.H. Frentzen, GER
1998	**Mika Hakkinen**	Finland	McLaren Mercedes	16	8	9	M. Schumacher, GER
1999	**Mika Hakkinen**	Finland	McLaren Mercedes	16	5	11	E. Irvine, GBR
2000	**Michael Schumacher**	Germany	Ferrari	17	9	9	M. Hakkinen, FIN
2001	**Michael Schumacher**	Germany	Ferrari	17	9	11	D. Coulthard, GBR
2002	**Michael Schumacher**	Germany	Ferrari	17	11	7	R. Barrichello, BRA
2003	**Michael Schumacher**	Germany	Ferrari	16	6	5	K. Raikkonen, FIN

All-Time Leaders

The all-time Top 15 Grand Prix winning drivers, based on records through 2002. Listed are starts (Sts), poles won (Pole), wins (1st), second place finishes (2nd), and third (3rd). Drivers active in 2003 and career victories in **bold** type.

		Sts	Pole	1st	2nd	3rd			Sts	Pole	1st	2nd	3rd
1	**M. Schumacher**	178	50	**64**	30	17	9	Nelson Piquet	207	24	**23**	20	17
2	Alain Prost	199	33	**51**	35	20	10	Damon Hill	99	20	**22**	15	5
3	Ayrton Senna	161	65	**41**	23	16	11	Mika Hakkinen	163	27	**20**	14	17
4	Nigel Mansell	187	32	**31**	17	11	12	Stirling Moss	66	16	**16**	5	3
5	Jackie Stewart	99	17	**27**	11	5	13	Jack Brabham	126	13	**14**	10	7
6	Jim Clark	72	33	**25**	1	6		Emerson Fittipaldi	144	6	**14**	13	8
	Niki Lauda	171	24	**25**	20	9		Graham Hill	176	13	**14**	15	7
8	Juan-Manuel Fangio	51	28	**24**	10	1							

ENDURANCE RACES

The 24 Hours of Le Mans

Officially, the Le Mans Grand Prix. First run May 22-23, 1923. All subsequent races have been held in June, except in 1956 (July) and 1968 (September). Originally contested on a 10.73-mile track, the circuit was shortened to 8.383 miles in 1932 and has fluxuated around 8.5 miles ever since. The original start of Le Mans, where drivers raced across the track to their unstarted cars, was discontinued in 1970.

Multiple winners: Jacky Ickx (6); Derek Bell and Tom Kristensen (5); Yannick Dalmas, Oliver Gendebien and Henri Pescarolo (4); Woolf Barnato, Frank Biela, Luigi Chinetti, Hurley Haywood, Phil Hill, Al Holbert, Klaus Ludwig and Emanuele Pirro (3); Sir Henry Birkin, Ivoe Bueb, Ron Flockhart, Jean-Pierre Jaussaud, Gerard Larrousse, Andre Rossignol, Raymond Sommer, Hans Stuck, Gijs van Lennep and Jean-Pierre Wimille (2).

Year	Drivers	Car	MPH	Year	Drivers	Car	MPH
1923	Andre Lagache & Rene Leonard	Chenard & Walcker	57.21	1949	Luigi Chinetti & Lord Selsdon	Ferrari	82.28
1924	John Duff & Francis Clement	Bentley	53.78	1950	Louis Rosier & Jean-Louis Rosier	Talbot-Lago	89.71
1925	Gerard de Courcelles & Andre Rossignol	La Lorraine	57.84	1951	Peter Walker & Peter Whitehead	Jaguar C	93.50
1926	Robert Bloch & Andre Rossignol	La Lorraine	66.08	1952	Hermann Lang & Fritz Reiss	Mercedes-Benz	96.67
1927	J.D. Benjafield & Sammy Davis	Bentley	61.35	1953	Tony Rolt & Duncan Hamilton	Jaguar C	98.65
1928	Woolf Barnato & Bernard Rubin	Bentley	69.11	1954	Froilan Gonzalez & Maurice Trintignant	Ferrari 375	105.13
1929	Woolf Barnato & Sir Henry Birkin	Bentley Speed 6	73.63	1955	Mike Hawthorn & Ivor Bueb	Jaguar D	107.05
1930	Woolf Barnato & Glen Kidston	Bentley Speed 6	75.88	1956	Ron Flockhart & Ninian Sanderson	Jaguar D	104.47
1931	Earl Howe & Sir Henry Birkin	Alfa Romeo	78.13	1957	Ron Flockhart & Ivor Bueb	Jaguar D	113.83
1932	Raymond Sommer & Luigi Chinetti	Alfa Romeo	76.48	1958	Oliver Gendebien & Phil Hill	Ferrari 250	106.18
1933	Raymond Sommer & Tazio Nuvolari	Alfa Romeo	81.40	1959	Roy Salvadori & Carroll Shelby	Aston Martin	112.55
1934	Luigi Chinetti & Philippe Etancelin	Alfa Romeo	74.74	1960	Oliver Gendebien & Paul Fräre	Ferrari 250	109.17
1935	John Hindmarsh & Louis Fontes	Lagonda	77.85	1961	Oliver Gendebien & Phil Hill	Ferrari 250	115.88
1936	Not held			1962	Oliver Gendebien & Phil Hill	Ferrari 250	115.22
1937	Jean-Pierre Wimille & Robert Benoist	Bugatti 57G	85.13	1963	Lodovico Scarfiotti & Lorenzo Bandini	Ferrari 250	118.08
1938	Eugene Chaboud & Jean Tremoulet	Delahaye	82.36	1964	Jean Guichet & Nino Vaccarella	Ferrari 275	121.54
1939	Jean-Pierre Wimille & Pierre Veyron	Bugatti 57G	86.86	1965	Masten Gregory & Jochen Rindt	Ferrari 250	121.07
1940-48	Not held						

ENDURANCE RACES (Cont.)

Year	Drivers	Car	MPH
1966	Bruce McLaren & Chris Amon	Ford Mk. II	125.37
1967	A.J. Foyt & Dan Gurney	Ford Mk. IV	135.46
1968	Pedro Rodriguez & Lucien Bianchi	Ford GT40	115.27
1969	Jacky Ickx & Jackie Oliver	Ford GT40	129.38
1970	Hans Herrmann & Richard Attwood	Porsche 917	119.28
1971	Gijs van Lennep & Helmut Marko	Porsche 917	138.13
1972	Graham Hill & Henri Pescarolo	Matra-Simca	121.45
1973	Henri Pescarolo & Gerard Larrousse	Matra-Simca	125.67
1974	Henri Pescarolo & Gerard Larrousse	Matra-Simca	119.27
1975	Derek Bell & Jacky Ickx	Mirage-Ford	118.98
1976	Jacky Ickx & Gijs van Lennep	Porsche 936	123.49
1977	Jacky Ickx, Jurgen Barth & Hurley Haywood	Porsche 936	120.95
1978	Jean-Pierre Jaussaud & Didier Pironi	Renault-Alpine	130.60
1979	Klaus Ludwig, Bill Wittington & Don Whittington	Porsche 935	108.10
1980	Jean-Pierre Jaussaud & Jean Rondeau	Rondeau-Cosworth	119.23
1981	Jacky Ickx & Derek Bell	Porsche 936	124.94
1982	Jacky Ickx & Derek Bell	Porsche 956	126.85
1983	Vern Schuppan, Hurley Haywood & Al Holbert	Porsche 956	130.70
1984	Klaus Ludwig & Henri Pescarolo	Porsche 956	126.88

Year	Drivers	Car	MPH
1985	Klaus Ludwig, Paolo Barilla & John Winter	Porsche 956	131.75
1986	Derek Bell, Hans Stuck & Al Holbert	Porsche 962	128.75
1987	Derek Bell, Hans Stuck & Al Holbert	Porsche 962	124.06
1988	Jan Lammers, Johnny Dumfries & Andy Wallace	Jaguar XJR	137.75
1989	Jochen Mass, Manuel Reuter & Stanley Dickens	Sauber-Mercedes	136.39
1990	John Nielsen, Price Cobb & Martin Brundle	Jaguar XJR-12	126.71
1991	Volker Weider, Johnny Herbert & Bertrand Gachof	Mazda 787B	127.31
1992	Derek Warwick, Yannick Dalmas & Mark Blundell	Peugeot 905B	123.89
1993	Geoff Brabham, Christophe Bouchut & Eric Helary	Peugeot 905	132.58
1994	Yannick Dalmas, Hurley Haywood & Mauro Baldi	Porsche 962LM	129.82
1995	Yannick Dalmas, J.J. Lehto & Masanori Sekiya	McLaren BMW	105.00
1996	Davy Jones, Manuel Reuter & Alexander Wurz	TWR Porsche	124.65
1997	Michele Alberto, Stefan Johansson & Tom Kristensen	TWR Porsche	126.88
1998	Laurent Aiello, Allan McNish & Stephane Ortelli	Porsche 911 GT1	123.86
1999	Yannick Dalmas, Joachim Winkelhock & Pierluigi Martini	BMW V-12 LMR	129.38
2000	Frank Biela, Tom Kristensen & Emanuele Pirro	Audi R8	128.34
2001	Frank Biela, Tom Kristensen & Emanuele Pirro	Audi R8	129.66
2002	Frank Biela, Tom Kristensen & Emanuele Pirro	Audi R8	131.89
2003	Tom Kristensen, Rinaldo Capello & Guy Smith	Bentley Speed 8	143.43

AP/Wide World Photos

*In 2003 drivers **Tom Kristensen**, **Rinaldo Capello** and **Guy Smith** gave Bentley its first 24 Hours of Le Mans title in 73 years. It was Kristensen's fourth consecutive win.*

The 24 Hours of Daytona

Officially, the Rolex 24 at Daytona. First run in 1962 as a three-hour race and won by Dan Gurney in a Lotus 19 Ford. Contested over a 3.56-mile course at Daytona (Fla.) International Speedway. There have been several distance changes since 1962: the event was a three-hour race (1962-63); a 2,000-kilometer race (1964-65); a 24-hour race (1966-71); a six-hour race (1972) and a 24-hour race again since 1973. The race was canceled in 1974 due to a national energy crisis.

Multiple winners: Hurley Haywood (5); Peter Gregg, Pedro Rodriguez and Bob Wollek (4); Derek Bell, Butch Leitzinger, Rolf Stommelen and Andy Wallace (3); Mauro Baldi, A.J. Foyt, Al Holbert, Ken Miles, John Paul Jr., Brian Redman, Elliott Forbes-Robinson, Lloyd Ruby, Didier Theys and Al Unser Jr. (2).

Year	Drivers	Car	MPH
1962	Dan Gurney	Lotus 19 Ford	104.101
1963	Pedro Rodriguez	Ferrari GTO	102.074
1964	Pedro Rodriguez & Phil Hill	Ferrari GTO	98.230
1965	Ken Miles & Lloyd Ruby	Ford GT	99.944
1966	Ken Miles & Lloyd Ruby	Ford Mk. II	108.020
1967	Lorenzo Bandini & Chris Amon	Ferrari 330	105.688
1968	Vic Elford & Jochen Neerpasch	Porsche 907	106.697
1969	Mark Donohue & Chuck Parsons	Lola Chevrolet	99.268
1970	Pedro Rodriguez & Leo Kinnunen	Porsche 917	114.866
1971	Pedro Rodriguez & Jackie Oliver	Porsche 917K	109.203
1972	Mario Andretti & Jacky Ickx	Ferrari 312P	122.573
1973	Peter Gregg & Hurley Haywood	Porsche Carrera	106.225
1974	Not held		
1975	Peter Gregg & Hurley Haywood	Porsche Carrera	108.531
1976	Peter Gregg, Brian Redman & John Fitzpatrick	BMW CSL	104.040
1977	Hurley Haywood, John Graves & Dave Helmick	Porsche Carrera	108.801
1978	Peter Gregg, Rolf Stommelen & Antoine Hezemans	Porsche Turbo	108.743
1979	Hurley Haywood, Ted Field & Danny Ongais	Porsche Turbo	109.249
1980	Rolf Stommelen, Volkert Merl & Reinhold Joest	Porsche Turbo	114.303
1981	Bobby Rahal, Brian Redman & Bob Garretson	Porsche Turbo	113.153
1982	John Paul Sr., John Paul Jr. & Rolf Stommelen	Porsche Turbo	114.794
1983	A.J. Foyt, Preston Henn, Bob Wollek & Claude Ballot-Lena	Porsche Turbo	98.781
1984	Sarel van der Merwe, Tony Martin & Graham Duxbury	March Porsche	103.119
1985	A.J. Foyt, Bob Wollek, Al Unser Sr. & Thierry Boutsen	Porsche 962	104.162
1986	Al Holbert, Derek Bell & Al Unser Jr	Porsche 962	105.484
1987	Al Holbert, Derek Bell, Chip Robinson & Al Unser Jr	Porsche 962	111.599
1988	Raul Boesel, Martin Brundle & John Nielsen	Jaguar XJR-9	107.943
1989	John Andretti, Derek Bell & Bob Wollek	Porsche 962	92.009
1990	Davy Jones, Jan Lammers & Andy Wallace	Jaguar XJR-12	112.857
1991	Hurley Haywood, John Winter, Frank Jelinski, Henri Pescarolo & Bob Wollek	Porsche 962-C	106.633
1992	Masahiro Hasemi, Kazuyoshi Hoshino & Toshio Suzuki	Nissan R-91	112.897
1993	P.J. Jones, Mark Dismore & Rocky Moran	Toyota Eagle	103.537
1994	Paul Gentilozzi, Scott Pruett, Butch Leitzinger & Steve Millen	Nissan 300 ZXT	104.80
1995	Jurgen Lassig, Christophe Bouchut, Giovanni Lavaggi & Marco Werner	Porsche Spyder	102.280
1996	Wayne Taylor, Scott Sharp & Jim Pace	Oldsmobile Arness MK-III	103.32
1997	Rob Dyson, James Weaver, Butch Leitzinger, Andy Wallace, John Paul Jr., Eliot Forbes-Robinson & John Schneider	Ford R&S MK-III	102.29
1998	Mauro Baldi, Arie Luyendyk, Gianpiero Moretti & Didier Theys	Ferrari 333	105.40
1999	Elliot Forbes-Robinson, Butch Leitzinger & Andy Wallace	Riley & Scott Ford	104.957
2000	Olivier Beretta, Dominique Dupuy & Karl Wendlinger	Dodge Viper	107.207
2001	Ron Fellows, Franck Freon, Chris Kneifel & Johnny O'Connell	Chevy Corvette	97.293
2002	Mauro Baldi, Fredy Lienhard, Max Papis & Didier Theys	Dallara LMP900	106.143
2003	Kevin Buckler, Michael Schrom, Timo Bernhard & Jorg Bergmeister	Porsche GT3 RS	115.969

NHRA DRAG RACING

NHRA Champions

Based on points earned during the NHRA POWERade Drag Racing series. The series, originally sponsored by the R.J. Reynolds Tobacco Company's Winston brand, began for Top Fuel, Funny Car and Pro Stock in 1975. The Coca-Cola Company's POWERade brand soft drink began a five-year sponsorship deal with the series in 2002.

Top Fuel

Multiple winners: Joe Amato (5); Don Garlits, Shirley Muldowney and Gary Scelzi (3); Kenny Bernstein and Scott Kalitta (2).

Year		Year		Year		Year	
1975	Don Garlits	1982	Shirley Muldowney	1989	Gary Ormsby	1996	Kenny Bernstein
1976	Richard Tharp	1983	Gary Beck	1990	Joe Amato	1997	Gary Scelzi
1977	Shirley Muldowney	1984	Joe Amato	1991	Joe Amato	1998	Gary Scelzi
1978	Kelly Brown	1985	Don Garlits	1992	Joe Amato	1999	Tony Schumacher
1979	Rob Bruins	1986	Don Garlits	1993	Eddie Hill	2000	Gary Scelzi
1980	Shirley Muldowney	1987	Dick LaHaie	1994	Scott Kalitta	2001	Kenny Bernstein
1981	Jeb Allen	1988	Joe Amato	1995	Scott Kalitta	2002	Larry Dixon

Funny Car

Multiple winners: John Force (12); Don Prudhomme, Kenny Bernstein (4); Raymond Beadle (3); Frank Hawley (2).

Year		Year		Year		Year	
1975	Don Prudhomme	1982	Frank Hawley	1989	Bruce Larson	1996	John Force
1976	Don Prudhomme	1983	Frank Hawley	1990	John Force	1997	John Force
1977	Don Prudhomme	1984	Mark Oswald	1991	John Force	1998	John Force
1978	Don Prudhomme	1985	Kenny Bernstein	1992	Cruz Pedregon	1999	John Force
1979	Raymond Beadle	1986	Kenny Bernstein	1993	John Force	2000	John Force
1980	Raymond Beadle	1987	Kenny Bernstein	1994	John Force	2001	John Force
1981	Raymond Beadle	1988	Kenny Bernstein	1995	John Force	2002	John Force

Pro Stock

Multiple winners: Bob Glidden (9); Warren Johnson (6); Lee Shepherd (4); Darrell Alderman, Jeg Coughlin Jr. and Jim Yates (2).

Year		Year		Year		Year	
1975	Bob Glidden	1982	Lee Shepherd	1989	Bob Glidden	1996	Jim Yates
1976	Larry Lombardo	1983	Lee Shepherd	1990	John Myers	1997	Jim Yates
1977	Don Nicholson	1984	Lee Shepherd	1991	Darrell Alderman	1998	Warren Johnson
1978	Bob Glidden	1985	Bob Glidden	1992	Warren Johnson	1999	Warren Johnson
1979	Bob Glidden	1986	Bob Glidden	1993	Warren Johnson	2000	Jeg Coughlin Jr.
1980	Bob Glidden	1987	Bob Glidden	1994	Darrell Alderman	2001	Warren Johnson
1981	Lee Shepherd	1988	Bob Glidden	1995	Warren Johnson	2002	Jeg Coughlin Jr.

All-Time Leaders
Career Victories

All-time leaders through 2002. Drivers active in 2003 are in **bold**.

	Top Fuel			**Funny Car**			**Pro Stock**	
1	Joe Amato	52	1	John Force	106	1	**Warren Johnson**	88
2	Don Garlits	35	2	Don Prudhomme	35	2	Bob Glidden	85
	Kenny Bernstein	35	3	Kenny Bernstein	30	3	**Jeg Coughlin**	31
4	**Cory McClenathan**	27	4	**Cruz Pedregon**	22	4	**Darrell Alderman**	28
5	**Gary Scelzi**	25	5	**Tony Pedregon**	19	5	Lee Shepherd	26
	Larry Dixon	25						

National-Event Victories (pro categories)

1	**John Force**	106	9	John Myers	33
2	**Warren Johnson**	88	10	**Jeg Coughlin**	31
3	Bob Glidden	85	11	**Matt Hines**	30
4	Kenny Bernstein	65	12	**Darrell Alderman**	28
5	Joe Amato	52		**Angelle Savoie**	28
6	Don Prudhomme	49	14	**Cory McClenathan**	27
7	Dave Schultz	45	15	Lee Shepherd	26
8	Don Garlits	35	16	**Gary Scelzi**	25
				Larry Dixon	25
			18	Terry Vance	24
				Jim Yates	24
			20	**Kurt Johnson**	23
			21	Ed McCulloch	22
				Cruz Pedregon	22
				Mike Dunn	22
			24	Mark Oswald	20

Fastest Mile-Per-Hour Speeds

Fastest performances in NHRA major event history through 2002.

Top Fuel	**Funny Car**	**Pro Stock**
MPH	**MPH**	**MPH**
333.08 Tony Schumacher, 10/6/2001	326.87 . . Gary Densham, 2/9/2002	204.35 . . Mark Osborne, 10/7/2001
332.18 . Kenny Bernstein, 10/6/2001	325.69 . . Whit Bazemore, 9/1/2001	204.03 . . Kurt Johnson, 10/13/2002
331.61 . . . . . Mike Dunn, 3/23/2001	325.69 . . Tony Pedregon, 5/4/2002	203.94 . . Kurt Johnson, 10/13/2002
331.53 . . . . . Mike Dunn, 5/25/2001	325.45 . Whit Bazemore, 9/30/2001	203.83 . . Troy Coughlin, 10/7/2001
330.88 . . Kenny Bernstein, 6/2/2001	325.37 . . W. Bazemore, 10/19/2001	203.77 . Warren Johnson, 5/19/2002

Boxing

Shane Mosley and his father/trainer **Jack** were back on top following an upset win over Oscar De La Hoya in Sept. 2003.

Jones no Junior Heavyweight

Roy Jones Jr. makes a bold statement with his move up to heavyweight and big win over WBA champ John Ruiz.

Gerry Brown
is co-editor of the ESPN Sports Almanac.

Roy Jones Jr. is the reluctant heavyweight.

Jones, who has been the best man in the ring everytime he's fought, has been criticized over the years for not taking enough chances. Not going out of his way to line up marquee fights and for being a pragmatist in choosing his opponents on a strict risk-reward basis.

Then in a effort to end all that talk he inked a preliminary agreement to sign a fight contract with WBA champ John Ruiz that he likely thought Ruiz would never sign because it offered him no guaranteed payday. But Ruiz jumped at the chance and quickly signed the deal, boxing Jones in before he had time for any second thoughts.

Jones had no choice but to go through with the fight, in the process earning the biggest payday of his life and winning the bout with relative ease. Even when this guy takes a risk, the reward is so enormous that in hindsight it doesn't look like much of a risk at all.

And while Ruiz is not going to get confused with Joe Frazier he is a much, bigger guy than Jones has ever fought and history has not been kind to men, including fighters the caliber of Archie Moore and Bob Foster, moving up to the heavyweight ranks to challenge the big boys.

In fact, until Jones managed the feat in 2003, the only former light heavyweight champion to successfully move up and win a heavyweight title was six-foot-three Michael Spinks, who won a controversial 15-round decision over Larry Holmes in 1985. But Holmes only out-weighed Spinks by 18 pounds. Ruiz weighed in at 226 pounds, 33 pounds more than Jones at 193 pounds although by fight-time Ruiz's weight advantage was only 25 pounds.

Before Spinks's gamble, only 12 light heavyweight champions had ever tried to move up and win a heavyweight title, 11 lost and one managed a draw.

Jones, an Olympian at junior middleweight, moved up to middleweight and then super middleweight as a pro even before becoming the undisputed light heavyweight champion.

AP/Wide World Photos

Roy Jones Jr. *(right) was quicker and more accurate than heavyweight opponent John Ruiz and earned the unanimous decision in their historic March meeting.*

Despite having history against him Jones was the 9-5 favorite going into the fight and proved the oddsmakers were right on the money, consistently beating Ruiz to the punch and avoiding any big bombs from the much larger Ruiz.

After an exciting first round, the pace slowed considerably and Jones used his jab and his superior hand speed to earn a unanimous decision.

With his historic win Jones also became only the second former middleweight champion to win the heavyweight title.

The first to do it was 167-pound Bob Fitzsimmons, who scored a famous 14th-round KO of 183-pound heavyweight champion Jim Corbett in 1897.

Jones had announced plans to return to the light heavyweight division following the fight whether he won or lost, rather than challenge the likes of the "real" heavyweight champion Lennox Lewis who outweighs Jones by more than 60 pounds.

The other big fights of the year included the long anticipated Oscar De La Hoya-Shane Mosley rematch. For De La Hoya it was a chance at redemption. Mosley is one of just two men to beat "The Golden Boy" and De La Hoya's grand plan was to beat Mosley and then coax Felix Trinidad, the man responsible for the first loss on his ring record, out of retirement.

But Mosley's master plan obviously disagreed. "Sugar" Shane was being

*Throwback pugilists **Arturo Gatti** (right) and **Micky Ward** fought two more career-defining wars in 2003. Gatti won both brutal bouts by unanimous decision.*

called the pound-for-pound world champion following his thrilling split-decision win over De La Hoya for the welterweight title in 2000.

After three successful title defenses against non-descript opposition, he lost two straight unanimous decisions to Vernon Forrest in 2002 and his career seemed on the ropes. But in his rematch with De La Hoya, this time at 154 pounds, Mosley won, 115-113, on all three judges' scorecards in the close fight, winning the final four rounds.

De La Hoya, who had threatened to retire if he lost the fight, was so stunned following the decision that he promised to launch a full-scale investigation into the decision. Exactly what he meant by that was unclear and he backed off the statement and his immediate plans to retire in the days following the fight.

Another fighter whose career turned around in 2003 is the man who Roy Jones made his name against, James "Lights Out" Toney.

The 34-year-old former middleweight and super middleweight champion had been out of the spotlight since his 1994 defeat at the hands of Jones but came back with a flash, dominating IBF cruiserweight champion Vassiliy Jirov and then sending four-time world champion Evander Holyfield into possible retirement with a ninth-round TKO.

Holyfield, who has had a hall of fame fight career, seemed to age appreciably while in the ring against Toney and was said to be finally contemplating retirement.

The Ten Biggest Stories of the Year in Boxing

10 Former heavyweight champion Mike Tyson files for chapter 11 bankruptcy protection. Tyson, who earned an estimated $400 million in the ring over the years, more money than any fighter in history, is unable to pay his bills.

9 Marco Antonio Barrera, one of the best pound-for-pound fighters in the world doesn't take the easy way out and continues to eschew the championship belts from boxing's sanctioning organizations in order to avoid ho-hum mandatory defenses and arrange bigger, better fights.

8 Undisputed middleweight champion Bernard "The Executioner" Hopkins has all the belts but no fights. The 38-year-old Hopkins, a hard-headed negotiator, can't seem to execute a contract and chooses to defend his title sparingly in 2003, missing out on millions of dollars in potential earnings.

7 Heavyweight champion Lennox Lewis, 37, continues his career denouement, getting beat up, but getting past substitute opponent Vitali Klitschko. Their fight is stopped in the sixth round due to deep gashes over Klitschko's left eye and with Lewis trailing 58-56 on all three judge's cards. Klitschko filled in for an injured Kirk Johnson, Lewis's originally planned opponent.

6 WBC welterweight champion Vernon Forrest, the 2002 Fighter of the Year, meets his match, losing twice to big-swinging WBA titleholder Ricardo Mayorga in 2003. After smoking Forrest in three rounds in their first meeting, Mayorga smoked a cigarette in the ring to celebrate the victory.

5 Forty-year-old heavyweight living legend Evander Holyfield, despite his failing skills and advancing age, stubbornly refuses to hang up the gloves, pledging to fight on in a quest to win a fifth heavyweight title in the aftermath of his loss to ring vet, but heavyweight rookie, James Toney. But word that Holyfield was considering retirement soon got out.

4 Veteran fighter James "Lights Out" Toney revives his career with a big win over IBF cruiserweight champ Vassiliy Jirov and then he moves up to heavyweight, beating the wilting warrior Evander Holyfield with a body-shot knockdown in the ninth round of their pay-per-view bout.

3 After their 2002 Fight of the Year, old school sluggers Arturo Gatti and Micky Ward battle twice more in 2003. In Gatti-Ward III, Gatti shows astounding toughness, overcoming a broken hand to win a hard fought unanimous decision over Ward. Ward retires after the fight.

2 Following back-to-back upset losses to Vernon Forrest in 2002, former pound-for-pound champion "Sugar" Shane Mosley works his way back into the spotlight, getting a controversial decision victory in his highly anticipated rematch with fan favorite Oscar De La Hoya in Las Vegas. Following the defeat, De La Hoya threatens to start an investigation into the decision but later backs off the statement.

1 Undisputed light heavyweight and pound-for-pound champion Roy Jones Jr., criticized for not taking enough risks with his career, takes a sizeable one by moving up two divisions to face a much larger man in heavyweight champion John Ruiz. Jones soundly defeats Ruiz, earning a 12-round unanimous decision and the WBA heavyweight belt, before moving back down to light heavyweight in late 2003.

Financial KO

Former heavyweight champion Mike Tyson filed for bankruptcy in 2003. Tyson, despite earning a reported $400 million over the last two decades, managed to squander the vast majority of it. Here's a look at the creditors holding the largest unsecured financial claims against him.

Creditor	Amount Sought
I.R.S.	$13,368,233
British taxes	$4,000,000
Law firm	$382,028
Insurance agency	$257,555
Las Vegas jeweler	$173,706

Another Black Eye for Boxing

Professional boxing finishes fourth in a poll of 1,020 people conducted by the Sports Marketing Group in Atlanta on the most hated or "disliked a lot" spectator sports in America.

Sport	Pct. Disliked
Dogfighting	81%
Professional Wrestling	56%
Bullfighting	46%
Professional Boxing	31%
PGA Tour	30%
PGA Senior Tour	30%
LPGA Tour	29%
NASCAR	28%
Major League Soccer	28%

2002-2003
Season in Review

SPORTS ALMANAC

Current Champions
WBA, WBC and IBF Titleholders (through Oct. 31, 2003)

The champions of professional boxing's 17 principal weight divisions, as recognized by the Word Boxing Association (WBA), World Boxing Council (WBC) and International Boxing Federation (IBF). Where applicable, records listed below fighters' names indicate wins-losses-draws-no contest.

	Weight Limit	WBA Champion	WBC Champion	IBF Champion
Heavyweight	—	Roy Jones Jr. 48-1-0, 38 KOs	Lennox Lewis 41-2-1, 32 KOs	Chris Byrd 37-2-0, 20 KOs
Cruiserweight	190 lbs	Jean-Marc Mormeck 29-2-0, 21 KOs	Wayne Braithwaite 19-0-0, 16 KOs	James Toney 67-4-2, 43 KOs
Light Heavyweight	175 lbs	Silvio Branco 41-6-2, 21 KOs	Antonio Tarver 22-1-0, 17 KOs	Antonio Tarver 22-1-0, 17 KOs
Super Middleweight	168 lbs	Sven Ottke 31-0-0, 6 KOs	Markus Beyer 27-1-0, 11 KOs	Sven Ottke 31-0-0, 6 KOs
Middleweight	160 lbs	Bernard Hopkins* 42-2-1-1, 31 KOs	Bernard Hopkins 42-2-1-1, 31 KOs	Bernard Hopkins 42-2-1-1, 31 KOs
Jr. Middleweight	154 lbs	Shane Mosley* 38-2-0-1, 35 KOs	Shane Mosley* 38-2-0-1, 35 KOs	Ronald Wright 45-3-0, 25 KOs
Welterweight	147 lbs	Richard Mayorga* 26-3-1-1, 22 KOs	Richard Mayorga 26-3-1-1, 22 KOs	Cory Spinks 31-2-0, 10 KOs
Jr. Welterweight	140 lbs	Kostya Tszyu* 30-1-1, 24 KOs	Kostya Tszyu* 30-1-1, 24 KOs	Kostya Tszyu 30-1-1, 24 KOs
Lightweight	135 lbs	vacant	Floyd Mayweather Jr. 30-0-0, 20 KOs	vacant
Jr. Lightweight	130 lbs	Acelino Freitas* 34-0-0, 31 KOs	Jesus Chavez 40-2-0, 28 KOs	Carlos Hernandez 40-3-1, 24 KOs
Featherweight	126 lbs	Derrick Gainer* 39-5-1, 24 KOs	vacant	Juan Manuel Marquez 41-2-0, 33 KOs
Jr. Featherweight	122 lbs	Mahyar Moshipour 23-2-2, 14 KOs	Oscar Larios 50-3-1, 35 KOs	Manny Pacquiao 37-2-1, 29 KOs
Bantamweight	118 lbs	Johnny Bredahl 53-2-0, 26 KOs	Veerapol Saphrom 41-2-1, 28 KOs	Rafael Marquez 30-3-0, 27 KOs
Jr. Bantamweight	115 lbs	Alexander Munoz 23-0-1, 23 KOs	Masamori Tokuyama 29-2-1, 8 KOs	Luis Perez 21-2-1, 14 KOs
Flyweight	112 lbs	Eric Morel 33-0-0, 18 KOs	Pongsaklek Wonjongkam 47-2-0, 26 KOs	Irene Pacheco 30-0-0, 23 KOs
Jr. Flyweight	108 lbs	Rosendo Alvarez 32-2-1, 20 KOs	Jorge Arce 33-3-1, 24 KOs	Victor Burgos 36-13-2, 21 KOs
Minimumweight	105 lbs	Noel Arambulent 20-2-1-1, 10 KOs	Jose Antonio Aguirre 30-1-1, 19 KOs	Daniel Reyes 33-1-1, 28 KOs

Note: The following weight divisions are also known by these names—**Cruiserweight** as Jr. Heavyweight; **Jr. Middleweight** as Super Welterweight; **Jr. Welterweight** as Super Lightweight; **Jr. Lightweight** as Super Featherweight; **Jr. Featherweight** as Super Bantamweight; **Jr. Bantamweight** as Super Flyweight; **Jr. Flyweight** as Light Flyweight; and **Minimumweight** as Strawweight or Mini-Flyweights.

*Roy Jones Jr. is the WBA light heavyweight "super world champion;" Bernard Hopkins is the WBA middleweight "super world champion;" Shane Mosley is the WBA junior middleweight "super world champion;" Francisco Javier Castillejo (55-5, 36 KOs) is the interim WBC junior middleweight champion; Ricardo Mayorga is the WBA welterweight "super world champion;" Kostya Tszyu is the WBA super lightweight "super world champion" and WBC "champion emeritus;" Acelino Freitas is the WBA super featherweight "super world champion;" Chris John (33-0, 19 KOs) is currently the interim WBA featherweight champion; Oscar Larios (45-3-1, 32 KOs) is currently the interim WBC junior featherweight champion.

Major Bouts, 2002-03

Division by division, from Nov. 1, 2002 through Oct. 31, 2003.

WBA, WBC and IBF champions are listed in **bold** type. Note the following Result columm abbreviations (in alphabetical order): **Disq.** (won by disqualification); **KO** (knockout); **MDraw** (majority draw); **NC** (no contest); **SDraw** (split draw); **TDraw** (technical draw); **TKO** (technical knockout); **TWm** (won by technical majority decision); **TWs** (won by technical split decision); **TWu** (won by technical unanimous decision); **Wm** (won by majority decision); **Ws** (won by split decision) and **Wu** (won by unanimous decision).

Heavyweights

Date	Winner	Loser	Result	Title	Site
Nov. 7	Michael Grant	James Watson	TKO 4	—	Washington, D.C.
Nov. 9	Corrie Sanders	Otis Tisdale	TKO 2	—	Oklahoma City, OK
Nov. 24	Audley Harrison	Shawn Robinson	TKO 1	—	Atlantic City
Nov. 30	David Tua	Russell Chasteen	TKO 2	—	Atlantic City
Dec. 7	Vladimir Klitschko	Jameel McCline	TKO 10	—	Las Vegas
Dec. 7	Kirk Johnson	Jeremy Bates	TKO 2	—	Las Vegas
Dec. 14	Fres Oquendo	George Arias	TKO 11	—	Atlantic City
Dec. 14	Chris Byrd	Evander Holyfield	Wu 12	IBF*	Atlantic City
Jan. 30	Jeremy Williams	Al Cole	MDraw 10	—	Portland, Oregon
Feb. 8	Audley Harrison	Rob Calloway	TKO 5	—	London, England
Feb. 22	Mike Tyson	Clifford Etienne	KO 1	—	Memphis, Tenn.
Mar. 1	Roy Jones Jr.	**John Ruiz**	Wu 12	**WBA**	Las Vegas
Mar. 1	Fres Oquendo	Maurice Harris	KO 10	—	Las Vegas
Mar. 8	Corrie Sanders	Vladimir Klitschko	KO 2	—	Hannover, Germany
Mar. 15	Kirk Johnson	Lou Savarese	TKO 4	—	Dallas, Tex.
Mar. 29	Hasim Rahman	David Tua	SDraw 12	—	Philadelphia
Mar. 29	Audley Harrison	Ratko Draskovic	Wu 8	—	London, England
Apr. 19	Michael Grant	Gilbert Martinez	TKO 8	—	Leemore, Calif.
May 31	Audley Harrison	Matthew Ellis	TKO 2	—	London, England
June 7	Dominick Guinn	Michael Grant	TKO 7	—	Atlantic City
June 21	**Lennox Lewis**	Vitali Klitschko	TKO 6	**WBC**	Los Angeles
Aug. 8	Vassilliy Jirov	Ernest Mateen	TKO 7	—	Temecula, Calif.
Aug. 23	Michael Moorer	Rogerio Lobi	KO 1	—	Coconut Creek, Fla.
Aug. 30	Vladimir Klitschko	Fabio Moli	KO 1	—	Munich, Germany
Sept. 2	Tye Fields	Sherman Williams	Wu 12	—	Chester, W. Va.
Sept. 9	Audley Harrison	Quinn Navarro	KO 3	—	Miami, Fla.
Sept. 20	**Chris Byrd**	Fres Oquendo	Wu 12	**IBF**	Uncasville, Conn.
Sept. 28	Juan Carlos Gomez	Samil Sam	Wu 10	—	Buffalo, NY
Sept. 28	Dominick Guinn	Duncan Dokiwari	Wu 10	—	Buffalo, NY
Sept. 28	Joe Mesi	DaVarryl Williamson	KO 1	—	Buffalo, NY
Oct. 4	James Toney	Evander Holyfield	TKO 9	—	Las Vegas

*Chris Byrd won the IBF that was left vacant by Lennox Lewis when he refused to fight Byrd, the IBF mandatory challenger, in 2002.

Cruiserweights (190 lbs)

(Jr. Heavyweights)

Date	Winner	Loser	Result	Title	Site
Nov. 17	Virgil Hill	Joey DeGrandis	Wu 12	—	Grand Forks, ND
Nov. 23	Johnny Nelson	Guillermo Jones	SDraw 12*	—	Derby, England
Feb. 21	**Wayne Braithwaite**	Ravea Springs	TKO 4	**WBC**	Miami, Fla.
Mar. 1	**Jean-Marc Mormeck**	Alexander Gurov	TKO 8	**WBA**	Las Vegas
Apr. 26	James Toney	**Vassiliy Jirov**	Wu 12	**IBF**	Mashantucket, Conn.
June 13	Rydell Booker	Arthur Williams	Wu 10	—	Detroit, Mich..
July 5	Virgil Hill	Donny Lalonde	Wu 10	—	Winnipeg, Canada

*The Nelson-Jones fight was controversially ruled a split draw. Also, it was reported that Jones tested positive for the banned diuretic frusemide in a post-fight drug test.

Light Heavyweights (175 lbs)

Date	Winner	Loser	Result	Title	Site
Nov. 3	Montell Griffin	George Khalid Jones	Wu 12	—	Friany, Calif.
Nov. 29	Mehdi Sahnoune	Geoffrey Gordian	TKO 7	—	Les Pennes-Mirabeau, France
Mar. 8	Mehdi Sahnoune	**Bruno Girard**	TKO 7	WBA*	Marseille, France
Mar. 29	Dariusz Michalczewski	Derrick Harmon	KO 8	—	Hamburg, Germany
Apr. 26	Antonio Tarver	Montell Griffin	Wu 12	**WBC/IBF**†	Mashantucket, Conn.
Oct. 10	Silvio Branco	**Mehdi Sahnoune**	TKO 11	WBA‡	Marseille, France
Oct. 18	Julio Gonzalez	Dariusz Michalzewski	Ws 12	—	Hamburg, Germany

*Sahnoune captured the WBA belt but note that Roy Jones Jr. was the WBA light heavyweight "super world champion."
†Tarver won the WBC/IBF titles that were vacated by Roy Jones Jr. when he moved up to heavyweight.
‡Sahnoune became the WBA light heavyweight champion when Roy Jones gave up his title of "super world champion" to move up to heavyweight.

Super Middleweights (168 lbs)

Date	Winner	Loser	Result	Title	Site
Nov. 9	Jeff Lacy	Ross Thompson	Wu 12	—	Oklahoma City, OK
Nov. 16	**Sven Ottke**	Rudy Markussen	Wu 12	**IBF**	Nuremberg, Germany
Dec. 14	Joe Calzaghe	Tocker Pudwill	TKO 2	—	Newcastle, England
Feb. 22	Jeff Lacy	Jimmy Crawford	TKO 2	—	Memphis, Tenn.
Mar. 15	**Sven Ottke**	**Byron Mitchell**	Ws 12	**IBF/WBA**	Berlin, Germany
Apr. 4	Markus Beyer	**Eric Lucas**	Ws 12	**WBC**	Leipzig, Germany
June 14	**Sven Ottke**	David Starie	Wu 12	**IBF/WBA**	Magdeburg, Germany
June 28	Joe Calzaghe	Byron Mitchell	TKO 2	—	Cardiff, Wales
Aug. 18	**Markus Beyer**	Danny Green	Disq. 5*	**WBC**	Nurnberg, Germany
Sept. 3	Anthony Mundine	Antwun Echols	Wu 12	WBA†	Sydney, Australia
Sept. 6	**Sven Ottke**	Mads Larsen	Wm 12	**IBF/WBA**	Erfurt, Germany

*Danny Green was controversially disqualified by the referee for intentional head butting following the fifth round. Green was ahead on all three scorecards at the time.
†Mundine won the vacant WBA super middleweight title but note that Sven Ottke is the WBA supper middleweight "super world champion."

Middleweights (160 lbs)

Date	Winner	Loser	Result	Title	Site
Dec. 21	Howard Eastman	Hussain Osman	TKO 4	—	Dagenham, England
Jan. 29	Howard Eastman	Christophe Tendil	TKO 5	—	Nottingham, England
Mar. 5	Howard Eastman	Gary Beardsley	TKO 2	—	London, England
Mar. 29	**Bernard Hopkins**	Morrade Hakkar	TKO 9	**WBA/WBC/IBF**	Philadelphia
Apr. 16	Howard Eastman	Scott Dann	TKO 3	—	Nottingham, England
July 26	Howard Eastman	Hassine Cherifi	TKO 8	—	Norwich, England
Aug. 29	Kingsley Ikeke	Kenny Ellis	KO 6	—	Tacoma, Wash.

Junior Middleweights (154 lbs)
(Super Welterweights)

Date	Winner	Loser	Result	Title	Site
Feb. 8	Shane Mosley	Raul Marquez	NC 3*	—	Las Vegas
Mar. 1	Alex Garcia	Santiago Samaniego	TKO 3	WBA†	Las Vegas
Mar. 1	**Ronald Wright**	J.C. Candelo	Wu 12	**IBF**	Las Vegas
May 3	**Oscar De La Hoya**	Yory Boy Campas	TKO 7	**WBA/WBC**	Las Vegas
May 9	Francisco Javier Castillejo	Diego Gastillo	TKO 1	WBC‡	Madrid, Spain
June 28	Daniel Santos	Fulgencio Zuniga	Wu 12	—	Bayamon, Puerto Rico
July 26	Fernando Vargas	Fitz Vanderpool	TKO 6	—	Los Angeles
Sept. 13	Shane Mosley	**Oscar De La Hoya**	Wu 12	**WBA/WBC**	Las Vegas
Sept. 20	Alex Garcia	Rhoshii Wells	TKO 10	WBA	Uncasville, Conn.

*The Shane Mosley-Raul Marquez bout was ruled a no contest following two accidental head butts left Marquez with deep cuts over both eyes.
†Garcia won the WBA belt but Oscar De La Hoya was the WBA super welterweight "super world champion."
‡Castillejo won the interim WBC belt. Note that Oscar de la Hoya was the WBC super welterweight champion

Welterweights (147 lbs)

Date	Winner	Loser	Result	Title	Site
Jan. 18	Muhammad Abdullaev	Philip Holiday	KO 3	—	Melbourne, Australia
Jan. 25	**Ricardo Mayorga**	**Vernon Forrest**	TKO 3	**WBA/WBC**	Temecula, Calif.
Feb. 8	Antonio Margarito	Andrew Lewis	KO 2	—	Las Vegas
Feb. 15	Juan Valenzuela	Ricardo Williams Jr.	Wu 10	—	Las Vegas
Mar. 22	Cory Spinks	**Michele Piccirillo**	Wu 12	**IBF**	Campione d'Italia, Italy
May 11	Muhammad Abdullaev	Juan Rivera	KO 3	—	Biloxi, Miss.
July 12	**Ricardo Mayorga**	Vernon Forrest	Wm 12	**WBA/WBC**	Las Vegas
Aug. 6	Hector Camacho Jr.	Byron Mackie	Wu 10	—	Washington, D.C.
Sept. 13	Jose Rivera	Michael Trabant	Wu 12	WBA*	Berlin, Germany

*Rivera won the vacant WBA belt but Ricardo Mayorga is the WBA welterweight "super world champion."

Junior Welterweights (140 lbs)
(Super Lightweights)

Date	Winner	Loser	Result	Title	Site
Nov. 2	Ricardo Williams Jr.	Terron Millet	Wu 10	—	Las Vegas
Nov. 9	Sharmba Mitchell	Vince Phillips	Wm 10	—	Oklahoma City, OK
Nov. 12	Arturo Gatti	Micky Ward	Wu 10	—	Atlantic City
Jan. 4	DeMarcus Corley	Randall Bailey	Wu 12	—	Las Vegas
Jan. 18	**Kostya Tszyu**	James Leija	TKO 6	**WBA/WBC/IBF**	Melbourne, Australia
Jan. 25	Sharmba Mitchell	Carlos Vilches	TKO 4	—	Atlantic City
Apr. 5	Ricky Hatton	Vince Phillips	Wu 12	—	Manchester, England
May 17	Sharmba Mitchell	Ben Tackie	Wu 12	—	Reno, Nev.
June 7	Arturo Gatti	Micky Ward	Wu 10	—	Atlantic City
July 12	Vivian Harris	Souleymane M'Baye	Wu 12	WBA*	Las Vegas
July 12	Zab Judah	DeMarcus Corley	Wu 12	—	Las Vegas

*Harris won the WBA belt but note that Kostya Tszyu is the WBA junior welterweight "super world champion."

Major Bouts, 2002-03 (Cont.)
Lightweights (135 lbs)

Date	Winner	Loser	Result	Title	Site
Nov. 9	**Paul Spadafora**	Dennis Holbaek	Wu 12	IBF	Chester, W. Va.
Nov. 22	Juan Diaz	Arthur Cruz	TKO 4	—	Atlantic City
Dec. 7	**Floyd Mayweather Jr.**	Jose Luis Castillo	Wu 12	WBC	Las Vegas
Jan. 18	Artur Grigorian	Matt Zegan	Wu 12	—	Essen, Germany
Jan. 25	Diego Corrales	Michael David	TKO 5	—	Atlantic City
Feb. 1	Juan Diaz	John Bailey	TKO 7	—	Uncasville, Conn.
Feb. 13	Juan Lazcano	Danny Rios	TWu 9*	—	El Paso, Texas
Apr. 19	**Floyd Mayweather Jr.**	Victoriano Sosa	Wu 12	WBC	Fresno, Calif.
May 17	**Paul Spadafora**	**Leonard Dorin**	Draw 12†	IBF/WBA	Pittsburgh
June 20	Diego Corrales	Damian Fuller	KO 3	—	Carson, Calif.

*Lazcano won a technical unanimous decision when the fight went to the scorecards late in the ninth round following an accidental head butt in the eighth round.
†Spadafora (IBF title-holder) and Dorin (WBA title-holder) fought to a draw and each retained their titles.

Junior Lightweights (130 lbs)
(Super Featherweights)

Date	Winner	Loser	Result	Title	Site
Dec. 5	Yodsanan Nanthachai	Lamont Pearson	KO 9	WBA*	Bangkok, Thailand
Dec. 20	Joel Casamayor	Yoni Vargas	TKO 5	—	Miami
Jan. 13	**Sirimonkol Singmanassuk**	Yong-Soo Choi	Wu 12	WBC	Tokyo, Japan
Jan. 25	Joel Casamayor	Nate Campbell	Wu 10	—	Temecula, Calif.
Feb. 1	Carlos Hernandez	David Santos	TKO 8	IBF†	Las Vegas
Feb. 22	Diego Corrales	Roque Cassiani	TKO 1	—	Memphis, Tenn.
Mar. 15	**Acelino Freitas**	Juan Carlos Ramirez	TKO 4	WBA	Chicago
Apr. 24	Diego Corrales	Felix St. Kitts	TKO 3	—	Gulfport, Miss.
Aug. 9	**Acelino Freitas**	Jorge Rodrigo Barrios	TKO 12	WBA	Miami
Aug. 15	Jesus Chavez	**Sirmonkol Singmanassuk**	Wu 12	WBC	Austin, Texas
Oct. 4	Erik Morales	Guty Espadas	KO 3	—	Los Angeles
Oct. 4	**Carlos Hernandez**	Steve Forbes	TWu 10‡	IBF	Los Angeles

*Nanthachai retained with WBA belt but note that Acelino Freitas in the WBA Junior Lightweight "super world champion."
†Hernandez won the vacant IBF title when Santos was unable to continue due to an accidental headbutt in the eighth round.
‡The fight, scheduled for 12 rounds, went to the scorecards in the 10th after an accidental clash of heads left Hernandez with a deep laceration over his right eye.

Featherweights (126 lbs)

Date	Winner	Loser	Result	Title	Site
Nov. 2	Marco Antonio Barrera	Johnny Tapia	Wu 12	—	Las Vegas
Nov. 16	Erik Morales	Paulie Ayala	Wu 12	WBC*	Las Vegas
Nov. 16	Guty Espadas	Clarence Adams	Ws 12	—	Las Vegas
Feb. 1	Juan Manuel Marquez	Manuel Medina	TKO 7	IBF†	Las Vegas
Feb. 1	Ricardo Juarez	Jason Pires	TKO 9	—	Uncasville, Conn.
Feb. 22	**Erik Morales**	Eddie Croft	TKO 3	WBC	Mexico City
Mar. 22	Scott Harrison	Wayne McCullough	Wu 12	—	Glasgow, Scotland
Apr. 12	**Derrick Gainer**	Oscar Leon	Ws 12	WBA	Las Vegas
Apr. 12	Marco Antonio Barrera	Kevin Kelley	TKO 4	—	Las Vegas
May 3	**Erik Morales**	Bobby Boy Velardez	TKO 5	WBC	Las Vegas
July 12	Manuel Medina	Scott Harrison	Ws 12	—	Glasgow, Scotland
July 29	Ricardo Juarez	Antonio Diaz	KO 10	—	Houston, Tex.
Aug. 16	**Juan Manuel Marquez**	Marcos Licona	TKO 9	—	Uncasville, Conn.
Sept. 26	Johnny Tapia	Carlos Contreras	Wu 10	—	Albuquerque, N.M.
Sept. 26	Chris John	Oscar Leon	Ws 12	WBA‡	Bali, Indonesia
Oct. 18	Michael Brodie	Injin Chi	MDraw 12	WBC**	Manchester, England

*Erik Morales regained his WBC featherweight belt that was left vacant when Marco Antonio Barrera declined to accept the title earning a unanimous decision over Morales on June 22, 2002.
†Marquez won the vacant title that was stripped from Johnny Tapia for taking a bigger money fight with Marco Antonio Barrera rather than fight the IBF mandatory challenger. Tapia originally won the title from Medina Apr. 27, 2002.
‡John won the vacant interim WBA belt.
**The fight, which was for the interim WBC belt in the wake of champion Erik Morales' announced plans to move up in weight, was initially ruled a majority decision for Injin Chi, but after a lengthy discussion between ringside judges and WBC president Jose Sulaiman it was discovered that a scoring error was made when two points (instead of one) were deducted from Michael Brodies on one of the scorecards for an accidental first-round clash of heads. The fight was ruled a majority draw, leaving the belt vacant.
Note: Juan Manuel Marquez's IBF title was not at risk in his Aug. 16 bout with Marcos Licona. The fight was originally scheduled as a unification bout with WBA titlist Derrick Gainer but Gainer was forced to bow out with an injured pectoral muscle. Licona filled in for Gainer.

Junior Featherweights (122 lbs)
(Super Bantamweights)

Date	Winner	Loser	Result	Title	Site
Nov. 1	Oscar Larios	**Willie Jorin**	TKO 1	**WBC***	Sacramento, Calif.
Apr. 4	**Salim Medjkoune**	Vincenzo Gigliotti	Wu 12	**WBA**	Clermont-Ferrand, France
July 4	Mahyar Monshipour	**Salim Medjkoune**	KO 12	**WBA**	Poitiers, France
July 26	**Manny Pacquiao**	Emanuel Lucero	TKO 3	**IBF**	Los Angeles
Sept. 7	**Oscar Larios**	Kozo Ishii	TKO 2	**WBC**	Nagoya, Japan

*Oscar Larios was the interim WBC champion and won the belt in a unification bout with reigning but formerly injured champion Willie Jorin.

Bantamweights (118 lbs)

Date	Winner	Loser	Result	Title	Site
Nov. 8	**Johnny Bredahl**	Leo Gamez	Wu 12	**WBA**	Copenhagen, Denmark
Feb. 15	Rafael Marquez	**Tim Austin**	TKO 8	**IBF**	Las Vegas
May 1	**Veerapol Saphrom**	Hugo Dianzo	Wu 12	**WBC**	Bangkok, Thailand
Oct. 4	**Rafael Marquez**	Mauricio Pastrana	Wu 12	**IBF**	Los Angeles

*Veerapol Saphrom's WBC bantamweight title was not at risk for his Mar. 30 bout against Joel Sungahed, his Aug. 24 bout against Daven Bermudez or his Oct. 25 bout against Alex Escaner.

Junior Bantamweights (115 lbs)
(Super Flyweights)

Date	Winner	Loser	Result	Title	Site
Dec. 20	**Masamori Tokuyama**	Gerry Penalosa	Ws 12	**WBC**	Osaka, Japan
Jan. 4	Luis Perez	**Felix Machado**	Ws 12	**IBF**	Washington, D.C.
Jan. 17	Fernando Montiel	Roy Doliguez	TKO 3	—	Los Mochis, Mexico
June 23	**Masamori Tokuyama**	Katsushige Kawashima	Wu 12	**WBC**	Yokohama, Japan
Aug. 16	Mark Johnson	Fernando Montiel	Wm 12	—	Uncasville, Conn.

Flyweights (112 lbs)

Date	Winner	Loser	Result	Title	Site
Nov. 26	**P. Wonjongkam**	Hidenobu Honda	Wu 12	**WBC**	Osaka, Japan
Nov. 29	**Irene Pacheco**	Alejandro Montiel	Wu 12	**IBF**	El Paso, Texas
Dec. 14	Omar Narvaez	Andrea Sarritzu	Ws 12	—	Cagliari, Italy
June 7	Omar Narvaez	Everardo Morales	TKO 5	—	Buenos Aires, Argentina
June 8	**P. Wonjongkam**	Randy Mangybat	Wu 12	**WBC**	Bangkok, Thailand
June 28	**Eric Morel**	Isidro Garcia	Wu 12	**WBA**	Bayamon, Puerto Rico
Aug. 9	Omar Narvaez	Andrea Sarritzu	Draw 12	—	Villasimius, Italy
Sept. 28	**Irene Pacheco**	Damaen Kelly	TKO 6	**IBF**	Barranquilla, Colombia

Junior Flyweights (108 lbs)
(Light Flyweights)

Date	Winner	Loser	Result	Title	Site
Nov. 16	**Jorge Arce**	Augustin Luna	TKO 3	**WBC**	Las Vegas
Feb. 15	Victor Burgos	Alex "Nene" Sanchez	TKO 12	**IBF***	Las Vegas
Feb. 22	**Jorge Arce**	Ernesto Castro	KO 1	**WBC**	Mexico City
Mar. 31	**Rosendo Alvarez**	Beibis Mendoza	Wm 12	**WBA**	Little Rock, Ark.
May 3	**Jorge Arce**	Melchor Cob Castro	TWu 6†	**WBC**	Las Vegas

*Burgos won the IBF title that was left vacant when champion Ricardo Lopez retired.
†Arce won the technical unanimous decision when the fight went to the scorecards after he suffered a deep gash over his right eye following an accidental head butt in the fifth round.

Minimumweights (105 lbs)
(Strawweights or Mini-Flyweights)

Date	Winner	Loser	Result	Title	Site
Nov. 22	Jorge Mata	Jairo Arango	Wu 12	—	Leon, Spain
Dec. 20	**Noel Arambulent**	Keitaro Hoshino	Wm 12	**WBA**	Osaka, Japan
Feb. 22	**Jose Antonio Aguirre** . .	Juan Alfonso Keb	TKO 7	**WBC**	Mexico City
Mar. 22	**Miguel Barrera**	Roberto Leyva	KO 3	**IBF**	Las Vegas
Mar. 28	Eduardo Marquez	Jorge Mata	KO 11	—	Madrid, Spain
May 3	Ivan Calderon	Eduardo Marquez	TWu 9*	—	Las Vegas
May 31	Edgar Cardenas	**Miguel Barrera**	KO 6	**IBF**	Tijuana, Mexico
June 23	**Jose Antonio Aguirre** . .	Keitaro Hoshino	TKO 12	**WBC**	Yokohama, Japan
July 12	**Noel Arambulent**	Yutaka Niida	WS 12	**WBA**	Yokohama, Japan
Sept. 8	Roberto Leyva	Marino Montiel	TKO 5	—	Tijuana, Mexico
Oct. 4	Daniel Reyes	**Edgar Cardenas**	TKO 6	**IBF**	Los Angeles

*Eduardo Ray Marquez was unable to continue due to a cut over his left eye.

1892-2003
Through the Years

ESPN SPORTS ALMANAC

World Heavyweight Championship Fights

Widely accepted world champions in **bold** type. Note following result abbreviations: KO (knockout), TKO (technical knockout), Wu (unanimous decision), Wm (majority decision), Ws (split decision), Ref (referee's decision), ND (no decision), Disq. (won on disqualification).

Year Date	Winner	Age	Wgt	Loser	Wgt	Result	Location
1892 Sept. 7	James J. Corbett	26	178	John L. Sullivan	212	KO 21	New Orleans
1894 Jan. 25	**James J. Corbett**	27	184	Charley Mitchell	158	KO 3	Jacksonville, Fla.
1897 Mar. 17	Bob Fitzsimmons	34	167	**James J. Corbett**	183	KO 14	Carson City, Nev.
1899 June 9	James J. Jeffries	24	206	**Bob Fitzsimmons**	167	KO 11	Coney Island, N.Y.
1899 Nov. 3	**James J. Jeffries**	24	215	Tom Sharkey	183	Ref 25	Coney Island, N.Y.
1900 Apr. 6	**James J. Jeffries**	24	NA	Jack Finnegan	NA	KO 1	Detroit
1900 May 11	**James J. Jeffries**	25	218	James J. Corbett	188	KO 23	Coney Island, N.Y.
1901 Nov. 15	**James J. Jeffries**	26	211	Gus Ruhlin	194	TKO 6	San Francisco
1902 July 25	**James J. Jeffries**	27	219	Bob Fitzsimmons	172	KO 8	San Francisco
1903 Aug. 14	**James J. Jeffries**	28	220	James J. Corbett	190	KO 10	San Francisco
1904 Aug. 25	**James J. Jeffries***	29	219	Jack Munroe	186	TKO 2	San Francisco
1905 July 3	Marvin Hart	28	190	Jack Root	171	KO 12	Reno, Nev.
1906 Feb. 23	Tommy Burns	24	180	**Marvin Hart**	188	Ref 20	Los Angeles
1906 Oct. 2	**Tommy Burns**	25	NA	Jim Flynn	NA	KO 15	Los Angeles
1906 Nov. 28	**Tommy Burns**	25	172	Phila. Jack O'Brien	163½	Draw 20	Los Angeles
1907 May 8	**Tommy Burns**	25	180	Phila. Jack O'Brien	167	Ref 20	Los Angeles
1907 July 4	**Tommy Burns**	26	181	Bill Squires	180	KO 1	Colma, Calif.
1907 Dec. 2	**Tommy Burns**	26	177	Gunner Moir	204	KO 10	London
1908 Feb. 10	**Tommy Burns**	26	NA	Jack Palmer	NA	KO 4	London
1908 Mar. 17	**Tommy Burns**	26	NA	Jem Roche	NA	KO 1	Dublin
1908 Apr. 18	**Tommy Burns**	26	NA	Jewey Smith	NA	KO 5	Paris
1908 June 13	**Tommy Burns**	26	184	Bill Squires	183	KO 8	Paris
1908 Aug. 24	**Tommy Burns**	27	181	Bill Squires	184	KO 13	Sydney
1908 Sept. 2	**Tommy Burns**	27	183	Bill Lang	187	KO 6	Melbourne
1908 Dec. 26	Jack Johnson	30	192	**Tommy Burns**	168	TKO 14	Sydney
1909 Mar. 10	**Jack Johnson**	30	NA	Victor McLaglen	NA	ND 6	Vancouver
1909 May 19	**Jack Johnson**	31	205	Phila. Jack O'Brien	161	ND 6	Philadelphia
1909 June 30	**Jack Johnson**	31	207	Tony Ross	214	ND 6	Pittsburgh
1909 Sept. 9	**Jack Johnson**	31	209	Al Kaufman	191	ND 10	San Francisco
1909 Oct. 16	**Jack Johnson**	31	205½	Stanley Ketchel	170¼	KO 12	Colma, Calif.
1910 July 4	**Jack Johnson**	32	208	James J. Jeffries	227	KO 15	Reno, Nev.
1912 July 4	**Jack Johnson**	34	195½	Jim Flynn	175	TKO 9	Las Vegas, Nev.
1913 Dec. 19	**Jack Johnson**	35	NA	Jim Johnson	NA	Draw 10	Paris
1914 June 27	**Jack Johnson**	36	221	Frank Moran	203	Ref 20	Paris
1915 Apr. 5	Jess Willard	33	230	**Jack Johnson**	205½	KO 26	Havana
1916 Mar. 25	**Jess Willard**	34	225	Frank Moran	203	ND 10	NYC (Mad. Sq. Garden)
1919 July 4	Jack Dempsey	24	187	**Jess Willard**	245	TKO 4	Toledo, Ohio
1920 Sept. 6	**Jack Dempsey**	25	185	Billy Miske	187	KO 3	Benton Harbor, Mich.
1920 Dec. 14	**Jack Dempsey**	25	188¼	Bill Brennan	197	KO 12	NYC (Mad. Sq. Garden)
1921 July 2	**Jack Dempsey**	26	188	Georges Carpentier	172	KO 4	Jersey City, N.J.
1923 July 4	**Jack Dempsey**	28	188	Tommy Gibbons	175½	Ref 15	Shelby, Mont.
1923 Sept. 14	**Jack Dempsey**	28	192½	Luis Firpo	216½	KO 2	NYC (Polo Grounds)
1926 Sept. 23	Gene Tunney	29	189½	**Jack Dempsey**	190	Wu 10	Philadelphia
1927 Sept. 22	**Gene Tunney**	30	189½	Jack Dempsey	192½	Wu 10	Chicago
1928 July 26	**Gene Tunney****	31	192	Tom Heeney	203	TKO 11	NYC (Yankee Stadium)

*James J. Jeffries retired as champion on May 13, 1905, then came out of retirement to fight Jack Johnson for the title in 1910.
**Gene Tunney retired as champion in 1928.

Year	Date	Winner	Age	Wgt	Loser	Wgt	Result	Location
1930	June 12	Max Schmeling	24	188	Jack Sharkey	197	Disq. 4	NYC (Yankee Stadium)
1931	July 3	**Max Schmeling**	25	189	Young Stribling	186½	TKO 15	Cleveland
1932	June 21	Jack Sharkey	29	205	**Max Schmeling**	188	Ws 15	Long Island City, N.Y.
1933	June 29	Primo Carnera	26	260½	**Jack Sharkey**	201	KO 6	Long Island City, N.Y.
1933	Oct. 22	**Primo Carnera**	26	259½	Paulino Uzcudun	229¼	Wu 15	Rome
1934	Mar. 1	**Primo Carnera**	27	270	Tommy Loughran	184	Wu 15	Miami
1934	June 14	Max Baer	25	209½	**Primo Carnera**	263¼	TKO 11	Long Island City, N.Y.
1935	June 13	James J. Braddock	29	193¾	**Max Baer**	209	Wu 15	Long Island City, N.Y.
1937	June 22	Joe Louis	23	197¼	**James J. Braddock**	197	KO 8	Chicago
1937	Aug. 30	**Joe Louis**	23	197	Tommy Farr	204¼	Wu 15	NYC (Yankee Stadium)
1938	Feb. 23	**Joe Louis**	23	200	Nathan Mann	193½	KO 3	NYC (Mad. Sq. Garden)
1938	Apr. 1	**Joe Louis**	23	202½	Harry Thomas	196	KO 5	Chicago
1938	June 22	**Joe Louis**	24	198¾	Max Schmeling	193	KO 1	NYC (Yankee Stadium)
1939	Jan. 25	**Joe Louis**	24	200¼	John Henry Lewis	180¾	KO 1	NYC (Mad. Sq. Garden)
1939	Apr. 17	**Joe Louis**	24	201¼	Jack Roper	204¾	KO 1	Los Angeles
1939	June 28	**Joe Louis**	25	200¾	Tony Galento	233¾	TKO 4	NYC (Yankee Stadium)
1939	Sept. 20	**Joe Louis**	25	200	Bob Pastor	183	KO 11	Detroit
1940	Feb. 9	**Joe Louis**	25	203	Arturo Godoy	202	Ws 15	NYC (Mad. Sq. Garden)
1940	Mar. 29	**Joe Louis**	25	201½	Johnny Paychek	187½	KO 2	NYC (Mad. Sq. Garden)
1940	June 20	**Joe Louis**	26	199	Arturo Godoy	201¼	TKO 8	NYC (Yankee Stadium)
1940	Dec. 16	**Joe Louis**	26	202¼	Al McCoy	180¾	TKO 6	Boston
1941	Jan. 31	**Joe Louis**	26	202½	Red Burman	188	KO 5	NYC (Mad. Sq. Garden)
1941	Feb. 17	**Joe Louis**	26	203½	Gus Dorazio	193½	KO 2	Philadelphia
1941	Mar. 21	**Joe Louis**	26	202	Abe Simon	254½	TKO 13	Detroit
1941	Apr. 8	**Joe Louis**	26	203½	Tony Musto	199½	TKO 9	St. Louis
1941	May 23	**Joe Louis**	27	201½	Buddy Baer	237½	Disq. 7	Washington, D.C.
1941	June 18	**Joe Louis**	27	199½	Billy Conn	174	KO 13	NYC (Polo Grounds)
1941	Sept. 29	**Joe Louis**	27	202¼	Lou Nova	202½	TKO 6	NYC (Polo Grounds)
1942	Jan. 9	**Joe Louis**	27	206¾	Buddy Baer	250	KO 1	NYC (Mad. Sq. Garden)
1942	Mar. 27	**Joe Louis**	27	207½	Abe Simon	255½	KO 6	NYC (Mad. Sq. Garden)
1942-45	World War II							
1946	June 9	**Joe Louis**	32	207	Billy Conn	187	KO 8	NYC (Yankee Stadium)
1946	Sept. 18	**Joe Louis**	32	211	Tami Mauriello	198½	KO 1	NYC (Yankee Stadium)
1947	Dec. 5	**Joe Louis**	33	211½	Jersey Joe Walcott	194½	Ws 15	NYC (Mad. Sq. Garden)
1948	June 25	**Joe Louis***	34	213½	Jersey Joe Walcott	194¾	KO 11	NYC (Yankee Stadium)
1949	June 22	**Ezzard Charles**	27	181¾	Jersey Joe Walcott	195½	Wu 15	Chicago
1949	Aug. 10	**Ezzard Charles**	28	180	Gus Lesnevich	182	TKO 8	NYC (Yankee Stadium)
1949	Oct. 14	**Ezzard Charles**	28	182	Pat Valentino	188½	KO 8	San Francisco
1950	Aug. 15	**Ezzard Charles**	29	183¼	Freddie Beshore	184½	TKO 14	Buffalo
1950	Sept. 27	**Ezzard Charles**	29	184½	Joe Louis	218	Wu 15	NYC (Yankee Stadium)
1950	Dec. 5	**Ezzard Charles**	29	185	Nick Barone	178½	KO 11	Cincinnati
1951	Jan. 12	**Ezzard Charles**	29	185	Lee Oma	193	TKO 10	NYC (Mad. Sq. Garden)
1951	Mar. 7	**Ezzard Charles**	29	186	Jersey Joe Walcott	193	Ws 15	Detroit
1951	May 30	**Ezzard Charles**	29	182	Joey Maxim	181½	Wu 15	Chicago
1951	July 18	Jersey Joe Walcott	37	194	**Ezzard Charles**	182	KO 7	Pittsburgh
1952	June 5	**Jersey Joe Walcott**	38	196	Ezzard Charles	191½	Wu 15	Philadelphia
1952	Sept. 23	Rocky Marciano	29	184	**Jersey Joe Walcott**	196	KO 13	Philadelphia
1953	May 15	**Rocky Marciano**	29	184½	Jersey Joe Walcott	197¾	KO 1	Chicago
1953	Sept. 24	**Rocky Marciano**	30	185	Roland LaStarza	184¾	TKO 11	NYC (Polo Grounds)
1954	June 17	**Rocky Marciano**	30	187½	Ezzard Charles	185½	Wu 15	NYC (Yankee Stadium)
1954	Sept. 17	**Rocky Marciano**	31	187	Ezzard Charles	192½	KO 8	NYC (Yankee Stadium)
1955	May 16	**Rocky Marciano**	31	189	Don Cockell	205	TKO 9	San Francisco
1955	Sept. 21	**Rocky Marciano****	32	188¼	Archie Moore	188	KO 9	NYC (Yankee Stadium)
1956	Nov. 30	Floyd Patterson	21	182¼	Archie Moore	187¾	KO 5	Chicago
1957	July 29	**Floyd Patterson**	22	184	Tommy Jackson	192½	TKO 10	NYC (Polo Grounds)
1957	Aug. 22	**Floyd Patterson**	22	187¼	Pete Rademacher	202	KO 6	Seattle
1958	Aug. 18	**Floyd Patterson**	23	184½	Roy Harris	194	TKO 13	Los Angeles
1959	May 1	**Floyd Patterson**	24	182½	Brian London	206	KO 11	Indianapolis
1959	June 26	Ingemar Johansson	26	196	**Floyd Patterson**	182	TKO 3	NYC (Yankee Stadium)
1960	June 20	Floyd Patterson	25	190	**Ingemar Johansson**	194¾	KO 5	NYC (Polo Grounds)

*Joe Louis retired as champion on Mar. 1, 1949, then came out of retirement to fight Ezzard Charles for the title in 1950.
**Rocky Marciano retired as undefeated champion on Apr. 27, 1956.

World Heavyweight Championship Fights (Cont.)

Year	Date	Winner	Age	Wgt	Loser	Wgt	Result	Location
1961	Mar. 13	**Floyd Patterson**	26	194¾	Ingemar Johansson	206½	KO 6	Miami Beach
1961	Dec. 4	**Floyd Patterson**	26	188½	Tom McNeeley	197	KO 4	Toronto
1962	Sept. 25	Sonny Liston	30	214	**Floyd Patterson**	189	KO 1	Chicago
1963	July 22	**Sonny Liston**	31	215	Floyd Patterson	194½	KO 1	Las Vegas
1964	Feb. 25	Cassius Clay**	22	210½	**Sonny Liston**	218	TKO 7	Miami Beach
1965	Mar. 5	Ernie Terrell WBA	25	199	Eddie Machen	192	Wu 15	Chicago
1965	May 25	**Muhammad Ali**	23	206	Sonny Liston	215¼	KO 1	Lewiston, Maine
1965	Nov. 1	Ernie Terrell WBA	26	206	George Chuvalo	209	Wu 15	Toronto
1965	Nov. 22	**Muhammad Ali**	23	210	Floyd Patterson	196¾	TKO 12	Las Vegas
1966	Mar. 29	**Muhammad Ali**	24	214½	George Chuvalo	216	Wu 15	Toronto
1966	May 21	**Muhammad Ali**	24	201½	Henry Cooper	188	TKO 6	London
1966	June 28	Ernie Terrell WBA	27	209½	Doug Jones	187½	Wu 15	Houston
1966	Aug. 6	**Muhammad Ali**	24	209½	Brian London	201½	KO 3	London
1966	Sept. 10	**Muhammad Ali**	24	203½	Karl Mildenberger	194¼	TKO 12	Frankfurt, W. Ger.
1966	Nov. 14	**Muhammad Ali**	24	212¾	Cleveland Williams	210½	TKO 3	Houston
1967	Feb. 6	**Muhammad Ali**	25	212¼	Ernie Terrell WBA	212¼	Wu 15	Houston
1967	Mar. 22	**Muhammad Ali**	25	211½	Zora Folley	202½	KO 7	NYC (Mad. Sq. Garden)
1968	Mar. 4	Joe Frazier	24	204½	Buster Mathis	243½	TKO 11	NYC (Mad. Sq. Garden)
1968	Apr. 27	Jimmy Ellis	28	197	Jerry Quarry	195	Wm 15	Oakland
1968	June 24	Joe Frazier NY	24	203½	Manuel Ramos	208	TKO 2	NYC (Mad. Sq. Garden)
1968	Aug. 14	Jimmy Ellis WBA	28	198	Floyd Patterson	188	Ref 15	Stockholm
1968	Dec. 10	Joe Frazier NY	24	203	Oscar Bonavena	207	Wu 15	Philadelphia
1969	Apr. 22	Joe Frazier NY	25	204½	Dave Zyglewicz	190½	KO 1	Houston
1969	June 23	Joe Frazier NY	25	203½	Jerry Quarry	198½	TKO 8	NYC (Mad. Sq. Garden)
1970	Feb. 16	Joe Frazier NY	26	205	Jimmy Ellis WBA	201	TKO 5	NYC (Mad. Sq. Garden)
1970	Nov. 18	**Joe Frazier**	26	209	Bob Foster	188	KO 2	Detroit
1971	Mar. 8	**Joe Frazier**	27	205½	Muhammad Ali	215	Wu 15	NYC (Mad. Sq. Garden)
1972	Jan. 15	**Joe Frazier**	28	215½	Terry Daniels	195	TKO 4	New Orleans
1972	May 26	**Joe Frazier**	28	217½	Ron Stander	218	TKO 5	Omaha, Neb.
1973	Jan. 22	George Foreman	24	217½	**Joe Frazier**	214	TKO 2	Kingston, Jamaica
1973	Sept. 1	**George Foreman**	24	219½	Jose (King) Roman	196½	KO 1	Tokyo
1974	Mar. 26	**George Foreman**	25	224¾	Ken Norton	212¾	TKO 2	Caracas, Venezuela
1974	Oct. 30	Muhammad Ali	32	216½	**George Foreman**	220	KO 8	Kinshasa, Zaire
1975	Mar. 24	**Muhammad Ali**	33	223½	Chuck Wepner	225	TKO 15	Cleveland
1975	May 16	**Muhammad Ali**	33	224½	Ron Lyle	219	TKO 11	Las Vegas
1975	June 30	**Muhammad Ali**	33	224½	Joe Bugner	230	Wu 15	Kuala Lumpur, Malaysia
1975	Oct. 1	**Muhammad Ali**	33	224½	Joe Frazier	215	TKO 14	Manila, Philippines
1976	Feb. 20	**Muhammad Ali**	34	226	Jean Pierre Coopman	206	KO 5	San Juan, P.R.
1976	Apr. 30	**Muhammad Ali**	34	230	Jimmy Young	209	Wu 15	Landover, Md.
1976	May 24	**Muhammad Ali**	34	220	Richard Dunn	206½	TKO 5	Munich, W. Ger.
1976	Sept. 28	**Muhammad Ali**	34	221	Ken Norton	217½	Wu 15	NYC (Yankee Stadium)
1977	May 16	**Muhammad Ali**	35	221¼	Alfredo Evangelista	209¼	Wu 15	Landover, Md.
1977	Sept. 29	**Muhammad Ali**	35	225	Earnie Shavers	211¼	Wu 15	NYC (Mad. Sq. Garden)
1978	Feb. 15	Leon Spinks	24	197¼	**Muhammad Ali**	224¼	Ws 15	Las Vegas
1978	June 9	Larry Holmes	28	209	Ken Norton WBC††	220	Ws 15	Las Vegas
1978	Sept. 15	Muhammad Ali†	36	221	**Leon Spinks**	201	Wu 15	New Orleans
1978	Nov. 10	Larry Holmes WBC	29	214	Alfredo Evangelista	208¼	KO 7	Las Vegas
1979	Mar. 23	Larry Holmes WBC	29	214	Osvaldo Ocasio	207	TKO 7	Las Vegas
1979	June 22	Larry Holmes WBC	29	215	Mike Weaver	202	TKO 12	NYC (Mad. Sq. Garden)
1979	Sept. 28	Larry Holmes WBC	29	210	Earnie Shavers	211	TKO 11	Las Vegas
1979	Oct. 20	John Tate	24	240	Gerrie Coetzee	222	Wu 15	Pretoria, S. Africa
1980	Feb. 3	Larry Holmes WBC	30	213½	Lorenzo Zanon	215	KO 6	Las Vegas
1980	Mar. 31	Mike Weaver	27	232	John Tate WBA	232	KO 15	Knoxville, Tenn.
1980	Mar. 31	Larry Holmes WBC	30	211	Leroy Jones	254½	TKO 8	Las Vegas
1980	July 7	Larry Holmes WBC	30	214¼	Scott LeDoux	226	TKO 7	Minneapolis
1980	Oct. 2	Larry Holmes WBC	30	211½	Muhammad Ali	217½	TKO 11	Las Vegas
1980	Oct. 25	Mike Weaver WBA	28	210	Gerrie Coetzee	226½	KO 13	Sun City, S. Africa
1981	Apr. 11	**Larry Holmes**	31	215	Trevor Berbick	215½	Wu 15	Las Vegas
1981	June 12	**Larry Holmes**	31	212½	Leon Spinks	200¼	TKO 3	Detroit
1981	Oct. 3	Mike Weaver WBA	29	215	James (Quick) Tillis	209	Wu 15	Rosemont, Ill.

**After defeating Liston, Cassius Clay announced that he had changed his name to Muhammad Ali. He was later stripped of his title by the WBA and most state boxing commissions after refusing induction into the U.S. Army on Apr. 28, 1967.

† Muhammad Ali retired as champion on June 27, 1979, then came out of retirement to fight Larry Holmes for the title in 1980.

†† WBC recognized Ken Norton as world champion when Leon Spinks refused to meet Norton before Spinks' rematch with Muhammad Ali. Norton had scored a 15-round split decision over Jimmy Young on Nov. 5, 1977 in Las Vegas.

Year	Date	Winner	Age	Wgt	Loser	Wgt	Result	Location
1981	Nov. 6	**Larry Holmes**	32	213¼	Renaldo Snipes	215¾	TKO 11	Pittsburgh
1982	June 11	**Larry Holmes**	32	212½	Gerry Cooney	225½	TKO 13	Las Vegas
1982	Nov. 26	**Larry Holmes**	33	217½	Randall (Tex) Cobb	234¼	Wu 15	Houston
1982	Dec. 10	Michael Dokes	24	216	Mike Weaver WBA	209¾	TKO 1	Las Vegas
1983	Mar. 27	**Larry Holmes**	33	221	Lucien Rodriguez	209	Wu 12	Scranton, Pa.
1983	May 20	Michael Dokes WBA	24	223	Mike Weaver	218½	Draw 15	Las Vegas
1983	May 20	**Larry Holmes**	33	213	Tim Witherspoon	219½	Ws 12	Las Vegas
1983	Sept. 10	**Larry Holmes**	33	223	Scott Frank	211¼	TKO 5	Atlantic City
1983	Sept. 23	Gerrie Coetzee	28	215	Michael Dokes WBA	217	KO 10	Richfield, Ohio
1983	Nov. 25	**Larry Holmes**	34	219	Marvis Frazier	200	TKO 1	Las Vegas
1984	Mar. 9	Tim Witherspoon*	26	220¼	Greg Page	239½	Wm 12	Las Vegas
1984	Aug. 31	Pinklon Thomas	26	216	Tim Witherspoon	217	Wm 12	Las Vegas
1984	Nov. 9	**Larry Holmes** IBF	35	221½	Bonecrusher Smith	227	TKO 12	Las Vegas
1984	Dec. 1	Greg Page	26	236½	Gerrie Coetzee WBA	218	KO 8	Sun City, S. Africa
1985	Mar. 15	**Larry Holmes** IBF	35	223½	David Bey	233¼	TKO 10	Las Vegas
1985	Apr. 29	Tony Tubbs	26	229	Greg Page WBA	239½	Wu 15	Buffalo
1985	May 20	**Larry Holmes** IBF	35	224¼	Carl Williams	215	Wu 15	Las Vegas
1985	June 15	Pinklon Thomas WBC	27	220¼	Mike Weaver	221¼	KO 8	Las Vegas
1985	Sept. 21	Michael Spinks	29	200	**Larry Holmes** IBF	221½	Wu 15	Las Vegas
1986	Jan. 17	Tim Witherspoon	28	227	Tony Tubbs WBA	229	Wm 15	Atlanta
1986	Mar. 22	Trevor Berbick	33	218½	Pinklon Thomas WBC	222¾	Wu 15	Las Vegas
1986	Apr. 19	**Michael Spinks** IBF	29	205	Larry Holmes	223	Ws 15	Las Vegas
1986	July 19	Tim Witherspoon WBA	28	234¾	Frank Bruno	228	TKO 11	Wembley, England
1986	Sept. 6	**Michael Spinks** IBF	30	201	Steffen Tangstad	214¾	TKO 4	Las Vegas
1986	Nov. 22	Mike Tyson	20	221¼	Trevor Berbick WBC	218½	TKO 2	Las Vegas
1986	Dec. 12	Bonecrusher Smith	33	228½	Tim Witherspoon WBA	233½	TKO 1	NYC (Mad. Sq. Garden)
1987	Mar. 7	Mike Tyson WBC	20	219	Bonecrusher Smith WBA	233	Wu 12	Las Vegas
1987	May 30	Mike Tyson	20	218¾	Pinklon Thomas	217¾	TKO 6	Las Vegas
1987	May 30	Tony Tucker**	28	222¼	Buster Douglas	227¼	TKO 10	Las Vegas
1987	June 15	**Michael Spinks**†	30	208¾	Gerry Cooney	238	TKO 5	Atlantic City
1987	Aug. 1	Mike Tyson	21	221	Tony Tucker IBF	221	Wu 12	Las Vegas
1987	Oct. 16	Mike Tyson	21	216	Tyrell Biggs	228¾	TKO 7	Atlantic City
1988	Jan. 22	Mike Tyson	21	215¾	Larry Holmes	225¾	TKO 4	Atlantic City
1988	Mar. 20	Mike Tyson	21	216¼	Tony Tubbs	238¼	KO 2	Tokyo
1988	June 27	Mike Tyson	21	218¼	**Michael Spinks**	212¼	KO 1	Atlantic City
1989	Feb. 25	**Mike Tyson**	22	218	Frank Bruno	228	TKO 5	Las Vegas
1989	July 21	**Mike Tyson**	23	219¼	Carl Williams	218	TKO 1	Atlantic City
1990	Feb. 10	Buster Douglas	29	231½	**Mike Tyson**	220½	KO 10	Tokyo
1990	Oct. 25	Evander Holyfield	28	208	**Buster Douglas**	246	KO 3	Las Vegas
1991	Apr. 19	**Evander Holyfield**	28	208	George Foreman	257	Wu 12	Atlantic City
1991	Nov. 23	**Evander Holyfield**	29	210	Bert Cooper	215	TKO 7	Atlanta
1992	June 19	**Evander Holyfield**	29	210	Larry Holmes	233	Wu 12	Las Vegas
1992	Nov. 13	Riddick Bowe	25	235	**Evander Holyfield**	205	Wu 12	Las Vegas
1993	Feb. 6	**Riddick Bowe**	25	243	Michael Dokes	244	TKO 1	NYC (Mad. Sq. Garden)
1993	May 8	Lennox Lewis WBC‡	27	235	Tony Tucker	235	Wu 12	Las Vegas
1993	May 22	**Riddick Bowe**	25	244	Jesse Ferguson	224	TKO 2	Washington, D.C.
1993	Oct. 1	Lennox Lewis WBC	28	233	Frank Bruno	238	TKO 7	Cardiff, Wales
1993	Nov. 6	Evander Holyfield	31	217	**Riddick Bowe** WBA/IBF	246	Wm 12	Las Vegas
1994	Apr. 22	Michael Moorer	26	214	**Evander Holyfield**	214	Wm 12	Las Vegas
1994	May 6	Lennox Lewis WBC	28	235	Phil Jackson	218	TKO 8	Atlantic City
1994	Sept. 25	Oliver McCall	29	231¼	**Lennox Lewis** WBC	238	TKO 2	London
1994	Nov. 5	George Foreman!	45	250	**Michael Moorer**	222	KO 10	Las Vegas
1995	Apr. 8	Oliver McCall WBC	29	231	Larry Holmes	236	Wu 12	Las Vegas
1995	Apr. 8	Bruce Seldon!	28	236	Tony Tucker	240	TKO 7	Las Vegas
1995	Apr. 22	**George Foreman!**	46	256	Axel Schulz	221	Ws 12	Las Vegas

*WBC recognized winner of Mar. 9, 1984 fight between Tim Witherspoon and Greg Page as world champion after Larry Holmes relinquished title in dispute. IBF then recognized Holmes.

**IBF recognized winner of May 30, 1987 fight between Tony Tucker and James (Buster) Douglas as world champion after Michael Spinks relinquished title in dispute.

†The July 15, 1987 Spinks-Cooney fight was not an official championship bout because it was not sanctioned by any boxing associations, councils or federations.

‡WBC recognized Lennox Lewis as world champion when Riddick Bowe gave up that portion of his title on Dec. 14, 1992, rather than fight Lewis, the WBC's mandatory challenger.

!George Foreman won WBA and IBF championships when he beat Michael Moorer on Nov. 5, 1994. He was stripped of WBA title on Mar. 4, 1995, when he refused to fight No. 1 contender Tony Tucker, and he relinquished IBF title on June 29, 1995, rather than give Axel Schulz a rematch. Tucker lost to Bruce Seldon in their April 8, 2001 fight for vacant WBA title.

World Heavyweight Championship Fights (Cont.)

Year	Date	Winner	Age	Wgt	Loser	Wgt	Result	Location
1995	Aug. 19	Bruce Seldon WBA	28	234	Joe Hipp	223	TKO 10	Las Vegas
1995	Sept. 2	Frank Bruno	33	248	Oliver McCall WBC	235	Wu 12	London
1995	Dec. 9	Frans Botha*	27	237	Axel Schulz	222	Wu 12	Stuttgart, GER
1996	Mar. 16	Mike Tyson	29	220	Frank Bruno WBC	247	TKO 3	Las Vegas
1996	June 22	Michael Moorer*	28	222	Axel Schulz	223	Ws 12	Dortmund, GER
1996	Sept. 7	Mike Tyson WBC†	30	219	Bruce Seldon WBA	229	TKO 1	Las Vegas
1996	Nov. 9	Evander Holyfield	34	215	**Mike Tyson** WBA	222	TKO 11	Las Vegas
1997	Feb. 7	Lennox Lewis†	31	251	Oliver McCall	237	TKO 5	Las Vegas
1997	Mar. 29	Michael Moorer IBF	29	212	Vaughn Bean	212	Wm 12	Las Vegas
1997	June 28	**Evander Holyfield** WBA‡	34	218	Mike Tyson	218	Disq. 3	Las Vegas
1997	July 12	Lennox Lewis WBC	31	242	Henry Akinwande	237½	Disq. 5	Stateline, Nev.
1997	Oct. 4	Lennox Lewis WBC	32	244	Andrew Golota	244	TKO 1	Atlantic City
1997	Nov. 8	Evander Holyfield WBA	35	214	Michael Moorer IBF	223	TKO 8	Las Vegas
1998	Mar. 28	Lennox Lewis WBC	32	243	Shannon Briggs	228	TKO 5	Atlantic City
1998	Sept. 19	**Evander Holyfield** WBA/IBF	35	217	Vaughn Bean	231	Wu 12	Atlanta
1998	Sept. 26	Lennox Lewis WBC	33	250	Zeljko Mavrovic	220	Wu 12	Uncasville, Conn.
1999	Mar. 13	Lennox Lewis WBC	33	246	**Evander Holyfield** WBA/IBF	215	Draw 12	NYC (Mad. Sq. Garden)
1999	Nov. 13	Lennox Lewis WBC	34	240	**Evander Holyfield** WBA/IBF	218	Wu 12	Las Vegas
2000	Apr. 29	**Lennox Lewis** WBC/IBF!	34	247	Michael Grant	250	KO 2	NYC (Mad. Sq. Garden)
2000	July 15	**Lennox Lewis** WBC/IBF	34	250	Frans Botha	237	TKO 2	London
2000	Aug. 12	Evander Holyfield	37	221	John Ruiz	224	Wu 12	Las Vegas
2000	Nov. 11	**Lennox Lewis** WBC/IBF	35	249	David Tua	245	Wu 12	Las Vegas
2001	Mar. 3	John Ruiz	29	227	Evander Holyfield	217	Wu 12	Las Vegas
2001	Apr. 22	Hasim Rahman	28	237	**Lennox Lewis** WBC/IBF	253	KO 5	Johannesburg, S. Africa
2001	Nov. 17	Lennox Lewis	36	247	**Hasim Rahman** WBC/IBF	236	KO 4	Las Vegas
2001	Dec. 15	**John Ruiz** WBA	29	232	Evander Holyfield	219	Draw 12	Mashantucket, Conn.
2002	June 8	**Lennox Lewis** WBC/IBF@	36	249	Mike Tyson	235	KO 8	Memphis, Tenn.
2002	July 27	**John Ruiz** WBA	30	233	Kirk Johnson	238	Disq. 10	Las Vegas
2002	Dec. 14	Chris Byrd	32	214	Evander Holyfield	220	Wu 12	Atlantic City
2003	Mar. 1	Roy Jones Jr.	34	193	**John Ruiz** WBA	226	Wu 12	Las Vegas
2003	June 21	**Lennox Lewis** WBC	37	257	Vitali Klitschko	248	TKO 6	Los Angeles
2003	Sept. 20	**Chris Byrd** IBF	33	212	Fres Oquendo	224	Wu 12	Uncasville, Conn.

*Frans Botha won the vacant IBF title with a controversial 12-round decision over Axel Schulz on Dec. 9, 1995, but after legal sparring, was eventually stripped of the IBF belt for using anabolic steroids. Moorer then claimed the revacated title with his June 22, 1996 win over Schulz.

†Mike Tyson won the WBC belt from Frank Bruno on Mar. 16, 1996 and still held it at the time of his Sept. 7, 1996 win over Bruce Seldon (although it was not at risk for that fight) but was forced to relinquish the title after the bout for not fighting mandatory challenge Lennox Lewis. Tyson also paid Lewis $4 million to step aside and allow the Tyson-Seldon bout to take place. Lewis then fought Oliver McCall for the vacant WBC belt. The fight was stopped 55 seconds into round 5 because, inexplicably, McCall was visibly distraught and stopped throwing punches.

‡Holyfield won the bout by disqualification and retained the WBA belt after Tyson spit out his mouthpiece and bit off a piece of Holyfield's ear. Tyson had received a two-point deduction from referee Mills Lane and after a stern warning and a short delay the fight was allowed to continue. Later in round 3, he bit Holyfield's other ear and Tyson was disqualified.

!Lewis was stripped of the WBA title for choosing to fight Michael Grant instead of John Ruiz, the WBA's #1 challenger. The WBA sanctioned the Evander Holyfield-John Ruiz August 12 bout for its vacant heavyweight belt.

@Lewis effectively sold his IBF title to promoter Don King for $1 million and a Range Rover in September 2002. Lewis stepped aside (in exchange for the car and substantial fee), relinquishing his IBF belt by declining to fight Chris Byrd the mandatory challenger. The IBF sanctioned the Dec. 14, 2002 fight between Byrd and Holyfield for its vacant heavyweight belt.

Muhammad Ali's Career Pro Record

Born Cassius Marcellus Clay, Jr. on Jan. 17, 1942, in Louisville; Amateur record of 100-5; won light-heavyweight gold medal at 1960 Olympic Games; Pro record of 56-5 with 37 KOs in 61 fights.

1960

Date	Opponent (location)	Result
Oct. 29	Tunney Hunsaker, Louisville	Wu 6
Dec. 27	Herb Siler, Miami Beach	TKO 4

1961

Date	Opponent (location)	Result
Jan. 17	Tony Esperti, Miami Beach	TKO 3
Feb. 7	Jim Robinson, Miami Beach	TKO 1
Feb. 21	Donnie Fleeman, Miami Beach	TKO 7
Apr. 19	Lamar Clark, Louisville	KO 2
June 26	Duke Sabedong, Las Vegas	Wu 10
July 22	Alonzo Johnson, Louisville	Wu 10
Oct. 7	Alex Miteff, Louisville	TKO 6
Nov. 29	Willi Besmanoff, Louisville	TKO 7

1962

Date	Opponent (location)	Result
Feb. 10	Sonny Banks, New York	TKO 4
Feb. 28	Don Warner, Miami Beach	TKO 4
Apr. 23	George Logan, Los Angeles	TKO 4
May 19	Billy Daniels, Los Angeles	TKO 7
July 20	Alejandro Lavorante, Los Angeles	KO 5
Nov. 15	Archie Moore, Los Angeles	KO 4

1963

Date	Opponent (location)	Result
Jan. 24	Charlie Powell, Pittsburgh	KO 3
Mar. 13	Doug Jones, New York	Wu 10
June 18	Henry Cooper, London	TKO 5

1964

Date	Opponent (location)	Result
Feb. 25	Sonny Liston, Miami Beach	TKO 7

(won World Heavyweight title)

After the fight, Clay announces he is a member of the Black Muslim religious sect and has changed his name to Muhammad Ali.

1965

Date	Opponent (location)	Result
May 25	Sonny Liston, Lewiston, Me	KO 1
Nov. 22	Floyd Patterson, Las Vegas	TKO 12

1966

Date	Opponent (location)	Result
Mar. 29	George Chuvalo, Toronto	Wu 15
May 21	Henry Cooper, London	TKO 6
Aug. 6	Brian London, London	KO 3
Sept.10	Karl Mildenberger, Frankfurt	TKO 12
Nov. 14	Cleveland Williams, Houston	TKO 3

1967

Date	Opponent (location)	Result
Feb. 6	Ernie Terrell, Houston	Wu 15
Mar. 22	Zora Folley, New York	KO 7
Apr. 28	Refuses induction into U.S. Army and is stripped of world title by WBA and most state commissions the next day.	
June 20	Found guilty of draft evasion in Houston; fined $10,000 and sentenced to 5 years; remains free pending appeals, but is barred from the ring.	

1968-69 (Inactive)

1970

Date	Opponent (location)	Result
Feb. 3	Announces retirement.	
Oct. 26	Jerry Quarry, Atlanta	TKO 3
Dec. 7	Oscar Bonavena, New York	TKO 15

1971

Date	Opponent (location)	Result
Mar. 8	Joe Frazier, New York	Lu 15

(for World Heavyweight title)

June 28	U.S. Supreme Court reverses Ali's 1967 conviction saying he had been drafted improperly.	
July 26	Jimmy Ellis, Houston	TKO 12

(won vacant NABF Heavyweight title)

Nov. 17	Buster Mathis, Houston	Wu 12
Dec. 26	Jurgen Blin, Zurich	KO 7

1972

Date	Opponent (location)	Result
Apr. 1	Mac Foster, Tokyo	Wu 15
May 1	George Chuvalo, Vancouver	Wu 12
June 27	Jerry Quarry, Las Vegas	TKO 7
July 19	Al (Blue) Lewis, Dublin, Ire	TKO 11
Sept.20	Floyd Patterson, New York	TKO 7
Nov. 21	Bob Foster, Stateline, Nev	TKO 8

1973

Date	Opponent (location)	Result
Feb. 14	Joe Bugner, Las Vegas	Wu 12
Mar. 31	Ken Norton, San Diego	Ls 12

(lost NABF Heavyweight title)

Sept.10	Ken Norton, Inglewood, Calif	Ws 12

(regained NABF Heavyweight title)

Oct. 20	Rudi Lubbers, Jakarta, Indonesia	Wu 12

1974

Date	Opponent (location)	Result
Jan. 28	Joe Frazier, New York	Wu 12
Oct. 30	George Foreman, Kinshasa, Zaire	KO 8

(regained World Heavyweight title)

1975

Date	Opponent (location)	Result
Mar. 24	Chuck Wepner, Cleveland	TKO 15
May 16	Ron Lyle, Las Vegas	TKO 11
June 30	Joe Bugner, Kuala Lumpur, Malaysia	Wu 15
Oct. 1	Joe Frazier, Manila, Philippines	TKO 14

1976

Date	Opponent (location)	Result
Feb. 20	Jean Pierre Coopman, San Juan	KO 5
Apr. 30	Jimmy Young, Landover, Md	Wu 15
May 24	Richard Dunn, Munich	TKO 5
Sept.28	Ken Norton, New York	Wu 15

1977

Date	Opponent (location)	Result
May 16	Alfredo Evangelista, Landover	Wu 15
Sept.29	Earnie Shavers, New York	Wu 15

1978

Date	Opponent (location)	Result
Feb. 15	Leon Spinks, Las Vegas	Ls 15

(lost World Heavyweight title)

Sept.15	Leon Spinks, New Orleans	Wu 15

(regained World Heavyweight title)

1979

Date		
June 27	Announces retirement.	

1980

Date	Opponent (location)	Result
Oct. 2	Larry Holmes, Las Vegas	TKO by 11

1981

Date	Opponent (location)	Result
Dec. 11	Trevor Berbick, Nassau	Lu 10

(retires after fight)

Major Titleholders

Note the following sanctioning body abbreviations: NBA (National Boxing Association), WBA (World Boxing Association), WBC (World Boxing Council), GBR (Great Britain), IBF (International Boxing Federation), plus other national and state commissions. Fighters who retired as champion are indicated by (*) and champions who abandoned or relinquished their titles are indicated by (†).

Heavyweights

Widely accepted champions in CAPITAL letters. Current champions in **bold** type (as of Oct. 23, 2001).

Note: Muhammad Ali was stripped of his world title in 1967 after refusing induction into the Army (see Muhammad Ali's Career Pro Record). George Foreman was stripped of his WBA and IBF titles in 1995, but remained active as linear champion.

Champion	Held Title	Champion	Held Title
JOHN L. SULLIVAN	1885–92	Michael Dokes (WBA)	1982–83
JAMES J. CORBETT	1892–97	Gerrie Coetzee (WBA)	1983–84
BOB FITZSIMMONS	1897–99	Tim Witherspoon (WBC)	1984
JAMES J. JEFFRIES	1899–1905*	Pinklon Thomas (WBC)	1984–86
MARVIN HART	1905–06	Greg Page (WBA)	1984–85
TOMMY BURNS	1906–08	MICHAEL SPINKS	1985–87
JACK JOHNSON	1908–15	Tim Witherspoon (WBA)	1986
JESS WILLARD	1915–19	Trevor Berbick (WBC)	1986
JACK DEMPSEY	1919–26	Mike Tyson (WBC)	1986–87
GENE TUNNEY	1926–28*	James (Bonecrusher) Smith (WBA)	1986–87
MAX SCHMELING	1930–32	Tony Tucker (IBF)	1987
JACK SHARKEY	1932–33	MIKE TYSON (WBC, WBA, IBF)	1987–90
PRIMO CARNERA	1933–34	BUSTER DOUGLAS (WBC, WBA, IBF)	1990
MAX BAER	1934–35	EVANDER HOLYFIELD (WBC, WBA, IBF)	1990–92
JAMES J. BRADDOCK	1935–37	RIDDICK BOWE (WBA, IBF)	1992–93
JOE LOUIS	1937–49*	Lennox Lewis (WBC)	1992–94
EZZARD CHARLES	1949–51	EVANDER HOLYFIELD (WBA, IBF)	1993–94
JERSEY JOE WALCOTT	1951–52	MICHAEL MOORER (WBA, IBF)	1994
ROCKY MARCIANO	1952–56*	Oliver McCall (WBC)	1994–95
FLOYD PATTERSON	1956–59	GEORGE FOREMAN (WBA, IBF)	1994–95
INGEMAR JOHANSSON	1959–60	Bruce Seldon (WBA)	1995–96
FLOYD PATTERSON	1960–62	GEORGE FOREMAN	1995–96
SONNY LISTON	1962–64	Frank Bruno (WBC)	1995–96
CASSIUS CLAY (MUHAMMAD ALI)	1964–67	Mike Tyson (WBC)	1996†
Ernie Terrell (WBA)	1965–67	Mike Tyson (WBA)	1996
Joe Frazier (NY)	1968–70	Michael Moorer (IBF)	1996–1997
Jimmy Ellis (WBA)	1968–70	Evander Holyfield (WBA, IBF)	1996–2000
JOE FRAZIER	1970–73	Lennox Lewis (WBC)	1997–2000
GEORGE FOREMAN	1973–74	LENNOX LEWIS (WBA, WBC, IBF)	2000
MUHAMMAD ALI	1974–78	Evander Holyfield (WBA)	2000–01
LEON SPINKS	1978	LENNOX LEWIS (WBC, IBF)	2000–01
Ken Norton (WBC)	1978	John Ruiz (WBA)	2001-03
Larry Holmes (WBC)	1978–80	Hasim Rahman (WBC, IBF)	2001
MUHAMMAD ALI	1978–79*	LENNOX LEWIS (WBC, IBF)	2001–02†
John Tate (WBA)	1979–80	**LENNOX LEWIS** (WBC)	2001–
Mike Weaver (WBA)	1980–82	**Roy Jones Jr.** (WBA)	2003–
LARRY HOLMES	1980–85	**Chris Byrd** (IBF)	2003–

Note: John L. Sullivan held the Bare Knuckle championship from 1882-85.

Cruiserweights

Current champions in **bold** type.

Champion	Held Title	Champion	Held Title
Marvin Camel (WBC)	1980	Massimiliano Duran (WBC)	1990–91
Carlos De Leon (WBC)	1980–82	Bobby Czyz (WBA)	1991–92†
Ossie Ocasio (WBA)	1982–84	Anaclet Wamba (WBC)	1991–95
S.T. Gordon (WBC)	1982–83	James Pritchard (IBF)	1991
Carlos De Leon (WBC)	1983–85	James Warring (IBF)	1991–92
Marvin Camel (IBF)	1983–84	Alfred Cole (IBF)	1992–96
Lee Roy Murphy (IBF)	1984–86	Orlin Norris (WBA)	1993–95
Piet Crous (WBA)	1984–85	Nate Miller (WBA)	1995–97
Alfonso Ratliff (WBC)	1985	Marcelo Dominguez (WBC)	1996–98
Dwight Braxton (WBA)	1985–86	Adolpho Washington (IBF)	1996–97
Bernard Benton (WBC)	1985–86	Uriah Grant (IBF)	1997
Carlos De Leon (WBC)	1986–88	Imamu Mayfield (IBF)	1997–98
Evander Holyfield (WBA)	1986–88	Arthur Williams (IBF)	1998–99
Ricky Parkey (IBF)	1986–87	Fabrice Tiozzo (WBA)	1997–2000
Evander Holyfield (WBA/IBF)	1987–88	Juan Carlos Gomez (WBC)	1998–2002†
Evander Holyfield	1988†	Vassiliy Jirov (IBF)	1999–2003
Toufik Belbouli (WBA)	1989	Virgil Hill (WBA)	2000–02
Robert Daniels (WBA)	1989–91	**Jean-Marc Mormeck** (WBA)	2002–
Carlos De Leon (WBC)	1989–90	**Wayne Braithwaite** (WBC)	2002–
Glenn McCrory (IBF)	1989–90	**James Toney** (IBF)	2003–
Jeff Lampkin (IBF)	1990		

Light Heavyweights

Widely accepted champions in CAPITAL letters. Current champions in **bold** type.

Champion	Held Title
JACK ROOT	1903
GEORGE GARDNER	1903
BOB FITZSIMMONS	1903–05
PHILADELPHIA JACK O'BRIEN	1905–12*
JACK DILLON	1914–16
BATTLING LEVINSKY	1916–20
GEORGES CARPENTIER	1920–22
BATTLING SIKI	1922–23
MIKE McTIGUE	1923–25
PAUL BERLENBACH	1925–26
JACK DELANEY	1926–27†
Jimmy Slattery (NBA)	1927
TOMMY LOUGHRAN	1927-29
JIMMY SLATTERY	1930
MAXIE ROSENBLOOM	1930–34
George Nichols (NBA)	1932
Bob Godwin (NBA)	1933
BOB OLIN	1934–35
JOHN HENRY LEWIS	1935–38
MELIO BETTINA (NY)	1939
Len Harvey (GBR)	1939–42
BILLY CONN	1939–40†
ANTON CHRISTOFORIDIS (NBA)	1941
GUS LESNEVICH	1941–48
Freddie Mills (GBR)	1942–46
FREDDIE MILLS	1948–50
JOEY MAXIM	1950–52
ARCHIE MOORE	1952–62
Harold Johnson (NBA)	1961
HAROLD JOHNSON	1962–63
WILLIE PASTRANO	1963–65
Eddie Cotton (Mich.)	1963–64
JOSE TORRES	1965–66
DICK TIGER	1966–68
BOB FOSTER	1968–74*
Vicente Rondon (WBA)	1971–72
John Conteh (WBC)	1974–77
Victor Galindez (WBA)	1974–78
Miguel A. Cuello (WBC)	1977–78
Mate Parlov (WBC)	1978
Mike Rossman (WBA)	1978–79

Champion	Held Title
Marvin Johnson (WBC)	1978–79
Matthew (Franklin) Saad Muhammad (WBC)	1979–81
Marvin Johnson (WBA)	1979–80
Eddie (Gregory) Mustapha Muhammad (WBA)	1980–81
Michael Spinks (WBA)	1981–83
Dwight (Braxton) Muhammad Qawi (WBC)	1981–83
MICHAEL SPINKS	1983–85†
J.B. Williamson (WBC)	1985–86
Slobodan Kacar (IBF)	1985–86
Marvin Johnson (WBA)	1986–87
Dennis Andries (WBC)	1986–87
Bobby Czyz (IBF)	1986–87
Leslie Stewart (WBA)	1987
Virgil Hill (WBA)	1987–91
Prince Charles Williams (IBF)	1987–93
Thomas Hearns (WBC)	1987
Donny Lalonde (WBC)	1987–88
Sugar Ray Leonard (WBC)	1988
Dennis Andries (WBC)	1989
Jeff Harding (WBC)	1989–90
Dennis Andries (WBC)	1990–91
Jeff Harding (WBC)	1991–94
Thomas Hearns (WBA)	1991–92
Iran Barkley (WBA)	1992†
Virgil Hill (WBA)	1992–97
Henry Maske (IBF)	1993–96
Virgil Hill (WBA/IBF)	1996–97
Mike McCallum (WBC)	1994–95
Fabrice Tiozzo (WBC)	1995–96
Roy Jones Jr. (WBC)	1996
Montell Griffin (WBC)	1996
D. Michaelczewski (WBA/IBF)	1997†
William Guthrie (IBF)	1997–98
Lou Del Valle (WBA)	1997–98
ROY JONES JR. (WBA/WBC)	1997–2003†
Reggie Johnson (IBF)	1998–99
ROY JONES JR. (WBA/WBC/IBF)	1999–2003†
Antonio Tarver (WBC/IBF)	2003–
Mehdi Sahnoune (WBA)	2003
Silvio Branco (WBA)	2003–

Super Middleweights

Current champions in **bold** type.

Champion	Held Title
Murray Sutherland (IBF)	1984
Chong-Pal Park (IBF)	1984–87
Chong-Pal Park (WBA)	1987–88
Graziano Rocchigiani (IBF)	1988–89
Fugencio Obelmejias (WBA)	1988–89
Ray Leonard (WBC)	1988–90†
In-Chut Baek (WBA)	1989–90
Lindell Holmes (IBF)	1990–91
Christophe Tiozzo (WBA)	1990–91
Mauro Galvano (WBC)	1990–92
Victor Cordova (WBA)	1991
Darrin Van Horn (IBF)	1991–92
Iran Barkley (WBA)	1992
Nigel Benn (WBC)	1992–96
James Toney (IBF)	1992–94
Michael Nunn (WBA)	1992–94
Steve Little (WBA)	1994
Frank Liles (WBA)	1994–99

Champion	Held Title
Roy Jones (IBF)	1994–96
Thulane Malinga (WBC)	1996
Vincenzo Nardiello (WBC)	1996
Robin Reid (WBC)	1996–97
Charles Brewer (IBF)	1997–98
Sven Ottke (IBF)	1998–
Thulane Malinga (WBC)	1997–98
Richie Woodhall (WBC)	1998–99
Byron Mitchell (WBA)	1999–2000
Markus Beyer (WBC)	1999–2000
Glenn Gatley (WBC)	2000
Dingaan Thobela (WBC)	2000
Bruno Girard (WBA)	2000–01†
Dave Hilton (WBC)	2000†
Byron Mitchell (WBA)	2001–03
Eric Lucas (WBC)	2001–03
Sven Ottke (IBF/WBA)	2003–
Markus Beyer (WBC)	2003–

Major Titleholders (Cont.)
Middleweights

Widely accepted champions in CAPITAL letters. Current champions in **bold** type.

Champion	Held Title	Champion	Held Title
JACK (NONPAREIL) DEMPSEY	1884–91	SUGAR RAY ROBINSON	1957
BOB FITZSIMMONS	1891–97	CARMEN BASILIO	1957–58
CHARLES (KID) McCOY	1897–98	SUGAR RAY ROBINSON	1958–60
TOMMY RYAN	1898–1907	Gene Fullmer (NBA)	1959–62
STANLEY KETCHEL	1908	PAUL PENDER	1960–61
BILLY PAPKE	1908	TERRY DOWNES	1961–62
STANLEY KETCHEL	1908–10	PAUL PENDER	1962–63
FRANK KLAUS	1913	Dick Tiger (WBA)	1962–63
GEORGE CHIP	1913–14	DICK TIGER	1963
AL McCOY	1914–17	JOEY GIARDELLO	1963–65
Jeff Smith (AUS)	1914	DICK TIGER	1965–66
Mick King (AUS)	1914	EMILE GRIFFITH	1966–67
Jeff Smith (AUS)	1914–15	NINO BENVENUTI	1967
Lee Darcy (AUS)	1915–17	EMILE GRIFFITH	1967–68
MIKE O'DOWD	1917–20	NINO BENVENUTI	1968–70
JOHNNY WILSON	1920–23	CARLOS MONZON	1970–77*
Wm. Bryan Downey (Ohio)	1921–22	Rodrigo Valdez (WBC)	1974–76
Dave Rosenberg (NY)	1922	RODRIGO VALDEZ	1977–78
Jock Malone (Ohio)	1922–23	HUGO CORRO	1978–79
Mike O'Dowd (NY)	1922	VITO ANTUOFERMO	1979–80
Lou Bogash (NY)	1923	ALAN MINTER	1980
HARRY GREB	1923–26	MARVELOUS MARVIN HAGLER	1980–87
TIGER FLOWERS	1926	SUGAR RAY LEONARD	1987
MICKEY WALKER	1926–31†	Frank Tate (IBF)	1987–88
GORILLA JONES	1931–32	Sumbu Kalambay (WBA)	1987–89
MARCEL THIL	1932–37	Thomas Hearns (WBC)	1987–88
Ben Jeby (NY)	1932–33	Iran Barkley (WBC)	1988–89
Lou Brouillard (NBA, NY)	1933	Michael Nunn (IBF)	1988–91
Vince Dundee (NBA, NY)	1933–34	Roberto Duran (WBC)	1989–90*
Teddy Yarosz (NBA, NY)	1934–35	Mike McCallum (WBA)	1989–91
Babe Risko (NBA, NY)	1935–36	Julian Jackson (WBC)	1990–93
Freddie Steele (NBA, NY)	1936–38	James Toney (IBF)	1991–93†
FRED APOSTOLI	1937–39	Reggie Johnson (WBA)	1992–93
Al Hostak (NBA)	1938	Roy Jones Jr. (IBF)	1993–94†
Solly Krieger (NBA)	1938–39	Gerald McClellan (WBC)	1993–95†
Al Hostak (NBA)	1939–40	John David Jackson (WBA)	1993–94
CEFERINO GARCIA	1939–40	Jorge Castro (WBA)	1994–97
KEN OVERLIN	1940–41	Julian Jackson (WBC)	1995
Tony Zale (NBA)	1940–41	**Bernard Hopkins** (IBF)	1995–
BILLY SOOSE	1941	Quincy Taylor (WBC)	1995–96
TONY ZALE	1941–47	Shinji Takehara (WBA)	1995–96
ROCKY GRAZIANO	1947–48	William Joppy (WBA)	1996–97
TONY ZALE	1948	Keith Holmes (WBC)	1996–98
MARCEL CERDAN	1948–49	Julio Cesar Green (WBA)	1997–98
JAKE La MOTTA	1949–51	William Joppy (WBA)	1998–2001
SUGAR RAY ROBINSON	1951	Hassine Cherifi (WBC)	1998–99
RANDY TURPIN	1951	Keith Holmes (WBC)	1999–2001
SUGAR RAY ROBINSON	1951–52*	**Bernard Hopkins** (IBF/WBC)	2001–
CARL (BOBO) OLSON	1953–55	Felix Trinidad (WBA)	2001
SUGAR RAY ROBINSON	1955–57	**BERNARD HOPKINS** (IBF/WBA/WBC)	2001–
GENE FULLMER	1957		

Junior Middleweights

Widely accepted champions in CAPITAL letters. Current champions in **bold** type.

Champion	Held Title	Champion	Held Title
ERNILE GRIFFITH (EBU)	1962–63	Elisha Obed (WBC)	1975–76
DENNIS MOYER	1962–63	KOICHI WAJIMA	1976
RALPH DUPAS	1963	JOSE DURAN	1976
SANDRO MAZZINGHI	1963–65	Eckhard Dagge (WBC)	1976–77
NINO BENVENUTI	1965–66	MIGUEL ANGEL CASTELLINI	1976–77
KI-SOO KIM	1966–68	EDDIE GAZO	1977–78
SANDRO MAZZINGHI	1968	Rocky Mattioli (WBC)	1977–79
FREDDLIE LITTLE	1969–70	MASASHI KUDO	1978–79
CARMELO BOSSI	1970–71	Maurice Hope (WBC)	1979–81
KOICHI WAJIMA	1971–74	AYUB KALULE	1979–81
OSCAR ALBARADO	1974–75	Wilfred Benitez (WBC)	1981–82
KOICHI WAJIMA	1975	SUGAR RAY LEONARD	1981–82
Miguel de Oliveira (WBC)	1975–76	Tadashi Mihara (WBA)	1981–82
JAE-DO YUH	1975–76	Davey Moore (WBA)	1982–83

Champion	Held Title	Champion	Held Title
Thomas Hearns (WBC)	1982–84	Julio Cesar Vasquez (WBA)	1992–95
Roberto Duran (WBA)	1983–84	Simon Brown (WBC)	1994
Mark Medal (IBF)	1984	Terry Norris (WBC)	1994–
THOMAS HEARNS	1984–86	Vincent Pettway (IBF)	1994–95
Mike McCallum (WBA)	1984–87	Paul Vaden (IBF)	1995
Carlos Santos (IBF)	1984–86	Carl Daniels (WBA)	1995
Buster Drayton (IBF)	1986–87	Terry Norris (WBC)	1995–97
Duane Thomas (WBC)	1986–87	Terry Norris (IBF)	1995–96
Matthew Hilton (IBF)	1987–88	Laurent Boudouani (WBA)	1996–99
Lupe Aquino (WBC)	1987	Raul Marquez (IBF)	1997
Gianfranco Rosi (WBC)	1987–88	Keith Mullings (WBC)	1997–99
Julian Jackson (WBA)	1987–90	Yori Boy Campas (IBF)	1997–98
Donald Curry (WBC)	1988–89	Fernando Vargas (IBF)	1998–2000
Robert Hines (IBF)	1988–89	Javier Castillejo (WBC)	1999–2001
Darrin Van Horn (IBF)	1989	David Reid (WBA)	1999–00
Rene Jacquote (WBC)	1989	Felix Trinidad (WBA/IBF)	2000–01†
John Mugabi (WBC)	1989–90	Oscar De La Hoya (WBC)	2001–03
Gianfranco Rosi (IBF)	1989–94	Fernando Vargas (WBA)	2001–02
Terry Norris (WBC)	1990–94	**Ronald Wright** (IBF)	2001–
Gilbert Dele (WBA)	1991	Oscar De La Hoya (WBA/WBC)	2002-03
Vinny Pazienza (WBA)	1991–92	**Shane Mosley** (WBA/WBC)	2003–

Welterweights

Widely accepted champions in CAPITAL letters. Current champions in **bold** type.

Champion	Held Title	Champion	Held Title
PADDY DUFFY	1888–90	TONY DeMARCO	1955
MYSTERIOUS BILLY SMITH	1892–94	CARMEN BASILIO	1955–56
TOMMY RYAN	1894–98	JOHNNY SAXTON	1956
MYSTERIOUS BILLY SMITH	1898–1900	CARMEN BASILIO	1956–57†
MATTY MATTHEWS	1900	VIRGIL AKINS	1958
EDDIE CONNOLLY	1900	DON JORDAN	1958–60
JAMES (RUBE) FERNS	1900	BENNY (KID) PARET	1960–61
MATTY MATHEWS	1900–01	EMILE GRIFFITH	1961
JAMES (RUBE) FERNS	1901	BENNY (KID) PARET	1961–62
JOE WALCOTT	1901–04	EMILE GRIFFITH	1962–63
THE DIXIE KID	1904–05	LUIS RODRIGUEZ	1963
HONEY MELLODY	1906–07	EMILE GRIFFITH	1963–66†
Mike (Twin) Sullivan	1907–08†	Charlie Shipes (Calif.)	1966–67
Harry Lewis	1908–11	CURTIS COKES	1966–69
Jimmy Gardner	1908	JOSE NAPOLES	1969–70
Jimmy Clabby	1910–11	BILLY BACKUS	1970–71
WALDEMAR HOLBERG	1914	JOSE NAPOLES	1971–75
TOM McCORMICK	1914	Hedgemon Lewis (NY)	1972–73
MATT WELLS	1914–15	Angel Espada (WBA)	1975–76
MIKE GLOVER	1915	JOHN H. STRACEY	1975–76
JACK BRITTON	1915	CARLOS PALOMINO	1976–79
TED (KID) LEWIS	1915–16	Pipino Cuevas (WBA)	1976–80
JACK BRITTON	1916–17	WILFREDO BENITEZ	1979
TED (KID) LEWIS	1917–19	SUGAR RAY LEONARD	1979–80
JACK BRITTON	1919–22	ROBERTO DURAN	1980
MICKEY WALKER	1922–26	Thomas Hearns (WBA)	1980–81
PETE LATZO	1926–27	SUGAR RAY LEONARD	1980–82
JOE DUNDEE	1927–29	Donald Curry (WBA)	1983–85
JACKIE FIELDS	1929–30	Milton McCrory (WBC)	1983–85
YOUNG JACK THOMPSON	1930	DONALD CURRY	1985–86
TOMMY FREEMAN	1930–31	LLOYD HONEYGHAN	1986–87
YOUNG JACK THOMPSON	1931	JORGE VACA (WBC)	1987–88
LOU BROUILLARD	1931–32	LLOYD HONEYGHAN (WBC)	1988–89
JACKIE FIELDS	1932–33	Mark Breland (WBA)	1987
YOUNG CORBETT III	1933	Marlon Starling (WBA)	1987–88
JIMMY McLARNIN	1933–34	Tomas Molinares (WBA)	1988–89
BARNEY ROSS	1934	Simon Brown (IBF)	1988–91
JIMMY McLARNIN	1934–35	Mark Breland (WBA)	1989–90
BARNEY ROSS	1935–38	MARLON STARLING (WBC)	1989–90
HENRY ARMSTRONG	1938–40	Aaron Davis (WBA)	1990–91
FRITZIE ZIVIC	1940–41	Maurice Blocker (WBC)	1990–91
Izzy Jannazzo (Md.)	1940–41	Meldrick Taylor (WBA)	1991–92
Freddie (Red) Cochrane	1941–46	Simon Brown (WBC)	1991
MARTY SERVO	1946*	Maurice Blocker (IBF)	1991–93
SUGAR RAY ROBINSON	1946–51†	Buddy McGirt (WBC)	1991–93
Johnny Bratton	1951	Crisanto Espana (WBA)	1992–94
KID GAVILAN	1951–54	Pernell Whitaker (WBC)	1993–97
JOHNNY SAXTON	1954–55	Felix Trinidad (IBF)	1993–99

Major Titleholders (Cont.)
Welterweights (Cont.)

Champion	Held Title	Champion	Held Title
Ike Quartey (WBA)	1994–98†	Vernon Forrest (IBF)	2001–02†
James Page (WBA)	1998–2000†	Vernon Forrest (WBC)	2002–03
Oscar De La Hoya (WBC)	1997–99	**Richard Mayorga** (WBA)	2002–
Felix Trinidad (WBC/IBF)	1999–2000†	Michele Piccirillo (IBF)	2002–03
Oscar De La Hoya (WBC)	2000	**Richard Mayorga** (WBA/WBC)	2003–
Shane Mosley (WBC)	2000–00	**Cory Spinks** (IBF)	2003–
Andrew Lewis (WBA)	2001–02		

Junior Welterweights
Widely accepted champions in CAPITAL letters. Current champions in **bold** type.

Champion	Held Title	Champion	Held Title
PINKEY MITCHELL	1922–25	Ubaldo Sacco (WBA)	1985–86
RED HERRING	1925	Lonnie Smith (WBC)	1985–86
MUSHY CALLAHAN	1926–30	Patrizio Oliva (WBA)	1986–87
JACK (KID) BERG	1930–31	Gary Hinton (IBF)	1986
TONY CANZONERI	1931–32	Rene Arredondo (WBC)	1986
JOHNNY JADICK	1932–33	Tsuyoshi Hamada (WBC)	1986–87
Sammy Fuller	1932–33	Joe Louis Manley (IBF)	1986–87
BATTLING SHAW	1933	Terry Marsh (IBF)	1987
TONY CANZONERI	1933	Juan Coggi (WBA)	1987–90
BARNEY ROSS	1933–35	Rene Arredondo (WBC)	1987
TIPPY LARKIN	1946	Roger Mayweather (WBC)	1987–89
CARLOS ORTIZ	1959–60	James McGirt (IBF)	1988
DUILIO LOI	1960–62	Meldrick Taylor (IBF)	1988–90
EDDIE PERKINS	1962	Julio Cesar Chavez (WBC)	1989–94
DUILIO LOI	1962–63	Julio Cesar Chavez (IBF)	1990–91
Roberto Cruz	1963	Loreto Garza (WBA)	1990–91
EDDIE PERKINS	1963–65	Juan Coggi (WBA)	1991
CARLOS HERNANDEZ	1965–66	Edwin Rosario (WBA)	1991–92
SANDRO LOPOPOLO	1966–67	Rafael Pineda (IBF)	1991–92
PAUL FUJII	1967–68	Akinobu Hiranaka (WBA)	1992
NICOLINO LOCHE	1968–72	Pernell Whitaker (IBF)	1992–93†
Pedro Adigue (WBC)	1968–70	Charles Murray (IBF)	1993–94
Bruno Arcari (WBC)	1970–74	Jake Rodriguez (IBF)	1994–95
ALFONSO FRAZER	1972	Juan Coggi (WBA)	1993–94
ANTONIO CERVANTES	1972–76	Frankie Randall (WBC)	1994
Perico Fernandez (WBC)	1974–75	Frankie Randall (WBA)	1994–96
Saensak Muangsurin (WBC)	1975–76	Juan Coggi (WBA)	1996
WILFRED BENITEZ	1976–79	Julio Cesar Chavez (WBC)	1994–96
Miguel Velasquez (WBC)	1976	Kostya Tszyu (IBF)	1995–97
Saensak Muangsurin (WBC)	1976–78	Frankie Randall (WBA)	1996–97
Antonio Cervantes (WBA)	1977–80	Oscar De La Hoya (WBC)	1996–97†
Sang-Hyun Kim (WBC)	1978–80	Khalid Rahilou (WBA)	1997–98
Saoul Mamby (WBC)	1980–82	Sharmba Mitchell (WBA)	1998–2001
Aaron Pryor (WBA)	1980–83	Vincent Phillips (IBF)	1997–99
Leroy Haley (WBC)	1982–83	Terronn Millet (IBF)	1999–00†
Aaron Pryor (IBF)	1983–85	**Kostya Tszyu** (WBC)	1999–
Bruce Curry (WBC)	1983–84	Zab Judah (IBF)	2000–01
Johnny Bumphus (WBA)	1984	**Kostya Tszyu** (WBA/WBC)	2001–
Bill Costello (WBC)	1984–85	**KOSTYA TSZYU** (IBF/WBA/WBC)	2001–
Gene Hatcher (WBA)	1984–85		

Lightweights
Widely accepted champions in CAPITAL letters. Current champions in **bold** type.

Champion	Held Title	Champion	Held Title
JACK McAULIFFE	1886–94	ROCKY KANSAS	1925–26
GEORGE (KID) LAVIGNE	1896–99	SAMMY MANDELL	1926–30
FRANK ERNE	1899–02	AL SINGER	1930
JOE GANS	1902–04	TONY CANZONERI	1930–33
JIMMY BRITT	1904–05	BARNEY ROSS	1933–35†
BATTLING NELSON	1905–06	TONY CANZONERI	1935–36
JOE GANS	1906–08	LOU AMBERS	1936–38
BATTLING NELSON	1908–10	HENRY ARMSTRONG	1938–39
AD WOLGAST	1910–12	LOU AMBERS	1939–40
WILLIE RITCHIE	1912–14	Sammy Angott (NBA)	1940–41
FREDDIE WELSH	1915–17	LEW JENKINS	1940–41
BENNY LEONARD	1917–25*	SAMMY ANGOTT	1941–42
JIMMY GOODRICH	1925	Beau Jack (NY)	1942–43

Champion	Held Title
Slugger White (Md.)	1943
Bob Montgomery (NY)	1943
Sammy Angott (NBA)	1943–44
Beau Jack (NY)	1943–44
Bob Montgomery (NY)	1944–47
Juan Zurita (NBA)	1944–45
IKE WILLIAMS	1947–51
JAMES CARTER	1951–52
LAURO SALAS	1952
JAMES CARTER	1952–54
PADDY DeMARCO	1954
JAMES CARTER	1954–55
WALLACE (BUD) SMITH	1955–56
JOE BROWN	1956–62
CARLOS ORTIZ	1962–65
Kenny Lane (Mich.)	1963–64
ISMAEL LAGUNA	1965
CARLOS ORTIZ	1965–68
CARLOS TEO CRUZ	1968–69
MANDO RAMOS	1969–70
ISMAEL LAGUNA	1970
KEN BUCHANAN	1970–72
Pedro Carrasco (WBC)	1971–72
Mando Ramos (WBC)	1972
ROBERTO DURAN	1972–79†
Chango Carmona (WBC)	1972
Rodolfo Gonzalez (WBC)	1972–74
Ishimatsu Suzuki (WBC)	1974–76
Esteban De Jesus (WBC)	1976–78
Jim Watt (WBC)	1979–81
Ernesto Espana (WBA)	1979–80
Hilmer Kenty (WBA)	1980–81
Sean O'Grady (WBA,WAA)	1981
Alexis Arguello (WBC)	1981–82
Claude Noel (WBA)	1981
Andrew Ganigan (WAA)	1981–82
Arturo Frias (WBA)	1981–82
Ray Mancini (WBA)	1982–84
ALEXIS ARGUELLO	1982–83
Edwin Rosario (WBC)	1983–84
Choo Choo Brown (IBF)	1984
Livingstone Bramble (WBA)	1984–86
Harry Arroyo (IBF)	1984–85
Jose Luis Ramirez (WBC)	1984–85
Jimmy Paul (IBF)	1985–86
Hector Camacho (WBC)	1985–86
Edwin Rosario (WBA)	1986–87
Greg Haugen (IBF)	1986–87
Julio Cesar Chavez (WBA)	1987–88
Jose Luis Ramirez (WBC)	1987–88
JULIO CESAR CHAVEZ (WBC,WBA)	1988–89
Vinny Pazienza (IBF)	1987–88
Greg Haugen (IBF)	1988–89
Pernell Whitaker (IBF,WBC)	1989–90
Edwin Rosario (WBA)	1989–90
Juan Nazario (WBA)	1990
PERNELL WHITAKER (IBF, WBC, WBA)	1990–92†
Joey Gamache (WBA)	1992
Miguel A. Gonzalez (WBC)	1992–96
Tony Lopez (WBA)	1992–93
Dingaan Thobela (WBA)	1993
Fred Pendleton (IBF)	1993–94
Orzubek Nazarov (WBA)	1993–98
Rafael Ruelas (IBF)	1994–95
Oscar De La Hoya (IBF)	1995†
Phillip Holiday (IBF)	1995–97
Jean-Baptiste Mendy (WBC)	1996–97
Stevie Johnston (WBC)	1997–98
Shane Mosley (IBF)	1997–99†
Cesar Bazan (WBC)	1998–99
Jean-Baptiste Mendy (WBA)	1998–99
Julien Lorcy (WBA)	1999
Stevie Johnston (WBC)	1999–00
Stefano Zoff (WBA)	1999
Israel Cardona (IBF)	1999
Paul Spadafora (IBF)	1999–
Gilberto Serrano (WBA)	1999–00
Takanori Hatakeyama (WBA)	2000–01
Jose Luis Castillo (WBC)	2000–02
Julien Lorcy (WBA)	2001
Raul Balbi (WBA)	2001–02
Leonard Dorin (WBA)	2002–
Floyd Mayweather (WBC)	2002–

Junior Lightweights

Widely accepted champions in CAPITAL letters. Current champions in **bold** type.

Champion	Held Title
JOHNNY DUNDEE	1921–23
JACK BERNSTEIN	1923
JOHNNY DUNDEE	1923–24
STEVE (KID) SULLIVAN	1924–25
MIKE BALLERINO	1925
TOD MORGAN	1925–29
BENNY BASS	1929–31
KID CHOCOLATE	1931–33
FRANKIE KLICK	1933–34
SANDY SADDLER	1949–50
HAROLD GOMES	1959–60
GABRIEL (FLASH) ELORDE	1960–67
YOSHIAKI NUMATA	1967
HIROSHI KOBAYASHI	1967–71
Rene Barrientos (WBC)	1969–70
Yoshiaki Numata (WBC)	1970–71
ALFREDO MARCANO	1971–72
Ricardo Arredondo (WBC)	1971–74
BEN VILLAFLOR	1972–73
KUNIAKI SHIBATA	1973
BEN VILLAFLOR	1973–76
Kuniaki Shibata (WBC)	1974–75
Alfredo Escalera (WBC)	1975–78
SAMUEL SERRANO	1976–80
Alexis Arguello (WBC)	1978–80
YASUTSUNE UEHARA	1980–81
Rafael Limon (WBC)	1980–81
Cornelius Boza-Edwards (WBC)	1981
SAMUEL SERRANO	1981–83
Rolando Navarrete (WBC)	1981–82
Rafael Limon (WBC)	1982
Bobby Chacon (WBC)	1982–83
ROGER MAYWEATHER	1983–84
Hector Camacho (WBC)	1983–84
ROCKY LOCKRIDGE	1984–85
Hwan-Kil Yuh (IBF)	1984–85
Julio Cesar Chavez (WBC)	1984–87
Lester Ellis (IBF)	1985
WILFREDO GOMEZ	1985–86
Barry Michael (IBF)	1985–87
ALFREDO LAYNE	1986
BRIAN MITCHELL	1986–91
Rocky Lockridge (IBF)	1987–88
Azumah Nelson (WBC)	1988–94
Tony Lopez (IBF)	1988–89
Juan Molina (IBF)	1989–90
Tony Lopez (IBF)	1990–91
Joey Gamache (WBA)	1991
Brian Mitchell (IBF)	1991
Genaro Hernandez (WBA)	1991–95
James Leija (WBC)	1994
Juan Molina (IBF)	1991–95
Gabriel Ruelas (WBC)	1994–95
Eddie Hopson (IBF)	1995

Major Titleholders (Cont.)
Junior Lightweights (Cont.)

Champion	Held Title
Tracy Patterson (IBF)	1995
Azumah Nelson (WBC)	1995–97
Choi Yong-Soo (WBA)	1995–98
Arturo Gatti (IBF)	1995–98†
Genaro Hernandez (WBC)	1997–98
Floyd Mayweather Jr. (WBC)	1998–2002†
Takanori Hatakeyama (WBA)	1998–99
Roberto Garcia (IBF)	1998–99
Lavka Sim (WBA)	1999

Champion	Held Title
Diego Corrales (IBF)	1999–2001
Baek Jong-Kwon (WBA)	1999–2000
Joel Casamayor (WBA)	2000–02
Steve Forbes (IBF)	2001-02†
Acelino Freitas (WBA)	2002–
Sirimongkol Singmanassak (WBC)	2002–03
Jesus Chavez (WBC)	2003–
Carlos Hernandez (IBF)	2003–

Featherweights

Widely accepted champions in CAPITAL letters. Current champions in **bold** type.

Champion	Held Title
TORPEDO BILLY MURPHY	1890
YOUNG GRIFFO	1890–92
GEORGE DIXON	1892–97
SOLLY SMITH	1897–98
Ben Jordan (GBR)	1898–99
Eddie Santry (GBR)	1899–1900
DAVE SULLIVAN	1898
GEORGE DIXON	1898–1900
TERRY McGOVERN	1900–01
YOUNG CORBETT II	1901–04
JIMMY BRITT	1904
ABE ATTELL	1904
BROOKLYN TOMMY SULLIVAN	1904–05
ABE ATTELL	1906–12
JOHNNY KILBANE	1912–23
Jem Driscoll (GBR)	1912–13
EUGENE CRIQUI	1923
JOHNNY DUNDEE	1923–24†
LOUIS (KID) KAPLAN	1925–26†
Dick Finnegan (Mass.)	1926–27
BENNY BASS	1927–28
TONY CANZONERI	1928
ANDRE ROUTIS	1928–29
BATTLING BATTALINO	1929–32†
Tommy Paul (NBA)	1932–33
Kid Chocolate (NY)	1932–33
Freddie Miller (NBA)	1933–36
Baby Arizmendi (MEX)	1935–36
Mike Belloise (NY)	1936–37
Petey Sarron (NBA)	1936–37
HENRY ARMSTRONG	1937–38†
Joey Archibald (NY)	1938–39
Leo Rodak (NBA)	1938–39
JOEY ARCHIBALD	1939–40
Petey Scalzo (NBA)	1940–41
Jimmy Perrin (La.)	1940–41
HARRY JEFFRA	1940–41
JOEY ARCHIBALD	1941
Richie Lemos (NBA)	1941
CHALKY WRIGHT	1941–42
Jackie Wilson (NBA)	1941–43
WILLIE PEP	1942–48
Jackie Callura (NBA)	1943
Phil Terranova (NBA)	1943–44
Sal Bartolo (NBA)	1944–46
SANDY SADDLER	1948–49
WILLIE PEP	1949–50
SANDY SADDLER	1950–57*
HOGAN (KID) BASSEY	1957–59
DAVEY MOORE	1959–63
ULTIMINIO (SUGAR) RAMOS	1963–64
VICENTE SALDIVAR	1964–67*
Howard Winstone (GBR)	1968
Raul Rojas (WBA)	1968
Jose Legra (WBC)	1968–69
Shozo Saijyo (WBA)	1968–71
JOHNNY FAMECHON (WBC)	1969–70
VICENTE SALDIVAR (WBC)	1970

Champion	Held Title
KUNIAKI SHIBATA (WBC)	1970–72
Antonio Gomez (WBA)	1971–72
CLEMENTE SANCHEZ (WBC)	1972
Ernesto Marcel (WBA)	1972–74
JOSE LEGRA (WBC)	1972–73
EDER JOFRE (WBC)	1973–74
Ruben Olivares (WBA)	1974
Bobby Chacon (WBC)	1974–75
ALEXIS ARGUELLO (WBA)	1974–76†
Ruben Olivares (WBC)	1975
David (Poison) Kotey (WBC)	1975–76
DANNY (LITTLE RED) LOPEZ (WBC)	1976–80
Rafael Ortega (WBA)	1977
Cecilio Lastra (WBA)	1977–78
Eusebio Pedroza (WBA)	1978–85
SALVADOR SANCHEZ (WBC)	1980–82
Juan LaPorte (WBC)	1982–84
Wilfredo Gomez (WBC)	1984
Min-Keun Oh (IBF)	1984–85
Azumah Nelson (WBC)	1984–88
Barry McGuigan (WBA)	1985–86
Ki-Young Chung (IBF)	1985–86
Steve Cruz (WBA)	1986–87
Antonio Rivera (IBF)	1986–88
Antonio Esparragoza (WBA)	1987–91
Calvin Grove (IBF)	1988
Jorge Paez (IBF)	1988–91†
Jeff Fenech (WBC)	1988–90†
Marcos Villasana (WBC)	1990–91
Yung-Kyun Park (WBA)	1991–93
Troy Dorsey (IBF)	1991
Manuel Medina (IBF)	1991–93
Paul Hodkinson (WBC)	1991–93
Tom Johnson (IBF)	1993–97
Goyo Vargas (WBC)	1993
Kevin Kelley (WBC)	1993–95
Eloy Rojas (WBA)	1993–96
Alejandro Gonzalez (WBC)	1995
Manuel Medina (WBA)	1995–96
Wilfredo Vasquez (WBA)	1996–98†
Luisito Espinosa (WBC)	1995–99
Naseem Hamed (IBF)	1997†
Hector Lizarraga (IBF)	1997–98
Freddie Norwood (WBA)	1998
Manuel Medina (IBF)	1998–99
Antonio Cermeno (WBA)	1998–99
Cesar Soto (WBC)	1999–00
Paul Ingle (IBF)	1999–2000
Mbuelo Botile (IBF)	2000–01
Guty Espadas (WBC)	2000–01
Freddie Norwood (WBA)	1999–00
Derrick Gainer (WBA)	2000–
Erik Morales (WBC)	2001–02
Frankie Toledo (IBF)	2001
Manuel Medina (IBF)	2001–02
Johnny Tapia (IBF)	2002†
Erik Morales (WBC)	2002–03†
Juan Manuel Marquez (IBF)	2003–

Junior Featherweights

Current champions in **bold** type.

Champion	Held Title
Jack (Kid) Wolfe	1922–23
Carl Duane	1923–24
Rigoberto Riasco (WBC)	1976
Royal Kobayashi (WBC)	1976
Dong-Kyun Yum (WBC)	1976–77
Wilfredo Gomez (WBC)	1977–83
Soo-Hwan Hong (WBA)	1977–78
Ricardo Cardona (WBA)	1978–80
Leo Randolph (WBA)	1980
Sergio Palma (WBA)	1980–82
Leonardo Cruz (WBA)	1982–84
Jaime Garza (WBC)	1983
Bobby Berna (IBF)	1983–84
Loris Stecca (WBA)	1984
Seung-Il Suh (IBF)	1984–85
Victor Callejas (WBA)	1984–85
Juan (Kid) Meza (WBC)	1984–85
Ji-Woo Kim (IBF)	1985–86
Lupe Pintor (WBC)	1985–86
Samart Payakaroon (WBC)	1986–87
Seung-Hoon Lee (IBF)	1987–88
Louie Espinoza (WBA)	1987
Jeff French (WBC)	1987
Julio Gervacio (WBA)	1987–88
Daniel Zaragoza (WBC)	1988–90
Jose Sanabria (IBF)	1988–90
Bernardo Pinango (WBA)	1988
Juan Jose Estrada (WBA)	1988–89
Fabrice Benichou (IBF)	1989–90
Jesus Salud (WBA)	1989–90
Welcome Ncita (IBF)	1990–92
Paul Banke (WBC)	1990
Luis Mendoza (WBA)	1990–91
Raul Perez (WBA)	1992
Pedro Decima (WBC)	1990–91
Kiyoshi Hatanaka (WBC)	1991
Daniel Zaragoza (WBC)	1991–92
Tracy Patterson (WBC)	1992–94
Kennedy McKinney (IBF)	1993–94
Wilfredo Vasquez (WBA)	1992–95
Vuyani Bungu (IBF)	1994–99†
Hector Acero Sanchez (WBC)	1994–95
Antonio Cermeno (WBA)	1995–98†
Daniel Zaragoza (WBC)	1995–97
Erik Morales (WBC)	1997–00†
Enrique Sanchez (WBA)	1998
Nestor Garza (WBA)	1998–00
Lehlohonolo Ledwaba (IBF)	1999–2001
Clarence Adams (WBA)	2000–01†
Willie Jorrin (WBC)	2000–02
Manny Pacquiao (IBF)	2001–00
Yorber Ortega (WBA)	2001–02
Yoddamrong Sithyodthong (WBA)	2002
Osamu Sato (WBA)	2002
Salim Medjkoune (WBA)	2002–03
Oscar Larios (WBC)	2002–
Mahyar Monshipour (WBA)	2003–

Bantamweights

Widely accepted champions in CAPITAL letters. Current champions in **bold** type.

Champion	Held Title
TOMMY (SPIDER) KELLY	1887
HUGHEY BOYLE	1887–88
TOMMY (SPIDER) KELLY	1889
CHAPPIE MORAN	1889–90
Tommy (Spider) Kelly	1890–92
GEORGE DIXON	1890–91
Billy Plummer	1892–95
JIMMY BARRY	1894–99
Pedlar Palmer	1895–99
TERRY McGOVERN	1899–1900
HARRY HARRIS	1901–02
DANNY DOUGHERTY	1900–01
HARRY FORBES	1901–03
FRANKIE NEIL	1903–04
JOE BOWKER	1904–05
JIMMY WALSH	1905–06†
OWEN MORAN	1907–08
MONTE ATTELL	1909–10
FRANKIE CONLEY	1910–11
JOHNNY COULON	1911–14
Digger Stanley (GBR)	1910–12
Charles Ledoux (GBR)	1912–13
Eddie Campi (GBR)	1913–14
KID WILLIAMS	1914–17
Johnny Ertle	1915–18
PETE HERMAN	1917–20
Memphis Pal Moore	1918–19
JOE LYNCH	1920–21
PETE HERMAN	1921
JOHNNY BUFF	1921–22
JOE LYNCH	1922–24
ABE GOLDSTEIN	1924
CANNONBALL EDDIE MARTIN	1924–25
PHIL ROSENBERG	1925–27
Teddy Baldock (GBR)	1927
BUD TAYLOR (NBA)	1927–28†
Willie Smith (GBR)	1927–28
Bushy Graham (NY)	1928–29
PANAMA AL BROWN	1929–35
Sixto Escobar (NBA)	1934–35
BALTAZAR SANGCHILLI	1935–36
Lou Salica (NBA)	1935
Sixto Escobar (NBA)	1935–36
TONY MARINO	1936
SIXTO ESCOBAR	1936–37
HARRY JEFFRA	1937–38
SIXTO ESCOBAR	1938–39*
Georgie Pace (NBA)	1939–40
LOU SALICA	1940–42
MANUEL ORTIZ	1942–47
HAROLD DADE	1947
MANUEL ORTIZ	1947–50
VIC TOWEEL	1950–52
JIMMY CARRUTHERS	1952–54*
ROBERT COHEN	1954–56
Raul Macias (NBA)	1955–57
MARIO D'AGATA	1956–57
ALPHONSE HALIMI	1957–59
JOE BECERRA	1959–60*
Johnny Caldwell (EBU)	1961–62
EDER JOFRE	1961–65
MASAHIKO FIGHTING HARADA	1965–68
LIONEL ROSE	1968–69
RUBEN OLIVARES	1969–70
CHUCHO CASTILLO	1970–71
RUBEN OLIVARES	1971–72
RAFAEL HERRERA	1972
ENRIQUE PINDER	1972–73
ROMEO ANAYA	1973
Rafael Herrera (WBC)	1973–74
ARNOLD TAYLOR	1973–74
SOO-HWAN HONG	1974–75
Rodolfo Martinez (WBC)	1974–76
ALFONSO ZAMORA	1975–77
Carlos Zarate (WBC)	1976–79
JORGE LUJAN	1977–80

Major Titleholders (Cont.)
Bantamweights (Cont.)

Champion	Held Title
Lupe Pintor (WBC)	1979–83
JULIAN SOLIS	1980
JEFF CHANDLER	1980–84
Albert Davila (WBC)	1983–85
RICHARD SANDOVAL	1984–86
Satoshi Shingaki (IBF)	1984–85
Jeff Fenech (IBF)	1985
Daniel Zaragoza (WBC)	1985
Miguel (Happy) Lora (WBC)	1985–88
GABY CANIZALES	1986
BERNARDO PINANGO	1986–87
Wilfredo Vasquez (WBA)	1987–88
Kevin Seabrooks (IBF)	1987–88
Kaokor Galaxy (WBA)	1988
Moon Sung-Kil (WBA)	1988–89
Kaokor Galaxy (WBA)	1989
Raul Perez (WBC)	1988–91
Orlando Canizales (IBF)	1988–94†
Luisito Espinosa (WBA)	1989–91
Greg Richardson	1991
Joichiro Tatsuyoshi (WBC)	1991–92
Israel Contreras (WBA)	1991–92
Eddie Cook (WBA)	1992
Victor Rabanales (WBC)	1992–93
Jorge Julio (WBA)	1992–93
Jung-Il Byun (WBC)	1993
Junior Jones (WBA)	1993–94
Yasuei Yakushiji (WBC)	1993–95
John M. Johnson (WBA)	1994
Daorung Chuvatana (WBA)	1994–95
Harold Mestre (IBF)	1995
Mbuelo Botile (IBF)	1995–97
Wayne McCullough (WBC)	1995–96
Veerapol Sahaprom (WBA)	1995–96
Nana Yaw Konadu (WBA)	1996
Daorung Chuvatana (WBA)	1996–97
Nana Yaw Konadu (WBA)	1997–98
Sirimongkol Singmanassak (WBC)	1996–97
Tim Austin (IBF)	1997–2003
Joichiro Tatsuyoshi (WBC)	1997–98
Johnny Tapia (WBA)	1998–99
Veerapol Sahaprom (WBC)	1998–
Paulie Ayala (WBA)	1999–2001
Eidy Moya (WBA)	2001–02
Johnny Bredahl (WBA)	2002–
Rafael Marquez (IBF)	2003–

Junior Bantamweights

Widely accepted champions in CAPITAL letters. Current champions in **bold** type.

Champion	Held Title
Rafael Orono (WBC)	1980–81
Chul-Ho Kim (WBC)	1981–82
Gustavo Ballas (WBA)	1981
Rafael Pedroza (WBA)	1981–82
Jiro Watanabe (WBA)	1982–84
Rafael Orono (WBC)	1982–83
Payao Poontarat (WBC)	1983–84
Joo-Do Chun (IBF)	1983–85
JIRO WATANABE	1984–86
Kaosai Galaxy (WBA)	1984
Ellyas Pical (IBF)	1985–86
Cesar Polanco (IBF)	1986
GILBERTO ROMAN	1986–87
Ellyas Pical (IBF)	1986
Santos Laciar (WBC)	1987
Tae-Il Chang (IBF)	1987
Sugar Rojas (WBC)	1987–88
Ellyas Pical (IBF)	1987–89
Gilberto Roman (WBC)	1988–89
Juan Polo Perez (IBF)	1989–90
Nana Konadu (WBC)	1989–90
Sung-Kil Moon (WBC)	1990–93
Robert Quiroga (IBF)	1990–93
Julio Borboa (IBF)	1993–94
Katsuya Onizuka (WBA)	1993–94
Lee Hyung-Chul (WBA)	1994–95
Jose Luis Bueno (WBC)	1993–94
Hiroshi Kawashima (WBC)	1994–97
Harold Grey (IBF)	1994–95
Alimi Goitia (WBA)	1995–96
Yokthai Sith-Oar (WBA)	1996–97
Carlos Salazar (IBF)	1995–96
Harold Grey (IBF)	1996
Danny Romero (IBF)	1996–97
Gerry Penalosa (WBC)	1997–98
Johnny Tapia (IBF)	1997–98†
Satoshi Iida (WBA)	1997–98
Cho In-Joo (WBC)	1998–00
Jesus Rojas (WBA)	1998–99
Mark Johnson (IBF)	1999–00†
Hideki Todaka (WBA)	1999–2000
Masanori Tokuyama (WBC)	2000–
Felix Machado (IBF)	2000–03
Leo Gamez (WBA)	2000–01
Celes Kobayashi (WBA)	2001–02
Alexander Munoz (WBA)	2002–
Luis Perez (IBF)	2003–

Flyweights

Widely accepted champions in CAPITAL letters. Current champions in **bold** type.

Champion	Held Title
Sid Smith (GBR)	1913
Bill Ladbury (GBR)	1913–14
Percy Jones (GBR)	1914
Joe Symonds (GBR)	1914–16
JIMMY WILDE	1916–23
PANCHO VILLA	1923–25
FIDEL LaBARBA	1925–27*
FRENCHY BELANGER (NBA,IBU)	1927–28
Izzy Schwartz (NY)	1927–29
Johnny McCoy (Calif.)	1927–28
Newsboy Brown (Calif.)	1928
FRANKIE GENARO (NBA,IBU)	1928–29
Johnny Hill (GBR)	1928–29
SPIDER PLADNER (NBA,IBU)	1929
FRANKIE GENARO (NBA,IBU)	1929–31
Willie LaMorte (NY)	1929–30
Midget Wolgast (NY)	1930–35
YOUNG PEREZ (NBA,IBU)	1931–32
JACKIE BROWN (NBA,IBU)	1932–35
BENNY LYNCH	1935–38†
Small Montana (NY,Calif.)	1935–37
PETER KANE	1938–43
Little Dado (NBA,Calif.)	1938–40
JACKIE PATERSON	1943–48

Champion	Held Title
RINTY MONAGHAN	1948–50*
TERRY ALLEN	1950
SALVADOR (DADO) MARINO	1950–52
YOSHIO SHIRAI	1953–54
PASCUAL PEREZ	1954–60
PONE KINGPETCH	1960–62
MASAHIKO (FIGHTING) HARADA	1962–63
PONE KINGPETCH	1963
HIROYUKI EBIHARA	1963–64
PONE KINGPETCH	1964–65
SALVATORE BURRINI	1965–66
Horacio Accavallo (WBA)	1966–68
WALTER McGOWAN	1966
CHARTCHAI CHIONOI	1966–69
EFREN TORRES	1969–70
Hiroyuki Ebihara (WBA)	1969
Bernabe Villacampo (WBA)	1969–70
CHARTCHAI CHIONOI	1970
Berkrerk Chartvanchai (WBA)	1970
Masao Ohba (WBA)	1970–73
ERBITO SALAVARRIA	1970–73
Betulio Gonzalez (WBC)	1972
Venice Borkorsor (WBC)	1972–73
VENICE BORKORSOR	1973
Chartchai Chionoi (WBA)	1973–74
Betulio Gonzalez (WBA)	1973–74
Shoji Oguma (WBC)	1974–75
Susumu Hanagata (WBA)	1974–75
Miguel Canto (WBC)	1975–79
Erbito Salavarria (WBA)	1975–76
Alfonso Lopez (WBA)	1976
Guty Espadas (WBA)	1976–78
Betulio Gonzalez (WBA)	1978–79
Chan-Hee Park (WBC)	1979–80
Luis Ibarra (WBA)	1979–80
Tae-Shik Kim (WBA)	1980
Shoji Oguma (WBC)	1980–81
Peter Mathebula (WBA)	1980–81
Santos Laciar (WBA)	1981
Antonio Avelar (WBC)	1981–82
Luis Ibarra (WBA)	1981
Juan Herrera (WBA)	1981–82
Prudencio Cardona (WBC)	1982
Santos Laciar (WBA)	1982–85
Freddie Castillo (WBC)	1982

Champion	Held Title
Eleoncio Mercedes (WBC)	1982–83
Charlie Magri (WBC)	1983
Frank Cedeno (WBC)	1983–84
Soon-Chun Kwon (IBF)	1983–85
Koji Kobayashi (WBC)	1984
Gabriel Bernal (WBC)	1984
Sot Chitalada (WBC)	1984–88
Hilario Zapate (WBA)	1985–87
Chong-Kwan Chung (IBF)	1985–86
Bi-Won Chung (IBF)	1986
Hi-Sup Shin (IBF)	1986–87
Dodie Penalosa (IBF)	1987
Fidel Bassa (WBA)	1987–89
Choi Chang-Ho (IBF)	1987–88
Rolando Bohol (IBF)	1988
Yong-Kang Kim (WBC)	1988–89
Duke McKenzie (IBF)	1988–89
Dave McAuley (IBF)	1989–92
Sot Chitalada (WBC)	1989–91
Jesus Rojas (WBA)	1989–90
Yul-Woo Lee (WBA)	1990
Leopard Tamakuma (WBA)	1990–91
Muangchai Kittikasem (WBC)	1991–92
Yong-Kang Kim (WBA)	1991–92
Rodolfo Blanco (IBF)	1992
Yuri Arbachakov (WBC)	1992–97
Aquiles Guzman (WBA)	1992
Phichit Sithbangprachan (IBF)	1992–94†
David Griman (WBA)	1992–94
Saen Sor Ploenchit (WBA)	1994–96
Francisco Tejedor (IBF)	1995
Danny Romero (IBF)	1995–96
Mark Johnson (IBF)	1996–99†
Jose Bonilla (WBA)	1996–97
Chatchai Sasakul (WBC)	1997–98
Hugo Soto (WBA)	1998–99
Manny Pacquiao (WBC)	1998–99
Irene Pacheco (IBF)	1999–
Leo Gamez (WBA)	1999
Medgoen Lukchaopormasak (WBC)	1999–00
Sornpichai Kratindaenggym (WBA)	1999–00
Eric Morel (WBA)	2000–
Malcolm Tunacao (WBC)	2000–01
Pongsaklek Wonjongkam (WBC)	2001–

Junior Flyweights
Current champions in **bold** type.

Champion	Held Title
Franco Udella (WBC)	1975
Jaime Rios (WBA)	1975–76
Luis Estaba (WBC)	1975–78
Juan Guzman (WBA)	1976
Yoko Gushiken (WBA)	1976–81
Freddy Castillo (WBC)	1978
Netrnoi Vorasingh (WBC)	1978
Sung-Jun Kim (WBC)	1978–80
Shigeo Nakajima (WBC)	1980
Hilario Zapata (WBC)	1980–82
Pedro Flores (WBA)	1981
Hwan-Jin Kim (WBA)	1981
Katsuo Tokashiki (WBA)	1981–83
Amado Urzua (WBC)	1982
Tadashi Tomori (WBC)	1982
Hilario Zapata (WBC)	1982–83
Jung-Koo Chang (WBC)	1983–88
Lupe Madera (WBA)	1983–84
Dodie Penalosa (IBF)	1983–86
Francisco Quiroz (WBA)	1984–85
Joey Olivo (WBA)	1985
Myung-Woo Yuh (WBA)	1985–91
Jum-Hwan Choi (IBF)	1986–88
Tacy Macalos (IBF)	1988–89
German Torres (WBC)	1988–89
Yul-Woo Lee (WBC)	1989

Champion	Held Title
Muangchai Kittikasem (IBF)	1989–90
Humberto Gonzalez (WBC)	1989–90
Michael Carbajal (IBF)	1990–94
Rolando Pascua (WBC)	1990
Melchor Cob Castro (WBC)	1991
Humberto Gonzalez (WBC)	1991–93
Hirokia Ioka (WBA)	1991–92
Michael Carbajal (WBC)	1993–94
Myung-Woo Yuh (WBA)	1993
Leo Gamez (WBA)	1993–95
Humberto Gonzalez (WBC/IBF)	1994–95
Choi Hi-Yong (WBA)	1995–96
Saman Sor Jaturong (WBC/IBF)	1995–96
Carlos Murillo (WBA)	1996
Keiji Yamaguchi (WBA)	1996
Michael Carbajal (IBF)	1996–97
Saman Sor Jaturong (WBC)	1995–99
Phichit Chor Siriwat (WBA)	1996–00†
Mauricio Pastrana (IBF)	1997–98†
Will Grigsby (IBF)	1999
Choi Yo-Sam (WBA)	1999–2002
Ricardo Lopez (IBF)	1999–
Beibis Mendoza (WBA)	2000–01
Rosendo Alvarez (WBA)	2001–
Jorge Arce (WBC)	2002–

Major Titleholders (Cont.)
Strawweights
Current champions in **bold** type.

Champion	Held Title	Champion	Held Title
Franco Udella (WBC)	1975	Yul-Woo Lee (WBC)	1989
Jaime Rios (WBA)	1975–76	Muangchai Kittikasem (IBF)	1989–90
Luis Estraba (WBC)	1975–78	Humberto Gonzalez (WBC)	1989–90
Juan Guzman (WBA)	1976	Michael Carbajal (IBF)	1990
Yoko Gushiken (WBA)	1976–81	Rolando Pascua (WBC)	1990
Freddy Castillo (WBC)	1978	Melchor Cob Castro (WBC)	1991
Netrnoi Vorasingh (WBC)	1978	Ricardo Lopez (WBC)	1990–98
Sung-Jun Kim (WBC)	1978–80	Ratanapol Voraphin (IBF)	1992–97
Shigeo Nakajima (WBC)	1980	Chana Porpaoin (WBA)	1993–95
Hilario Zapata (WBC)	1980–82	Rosendo Alvarez (WBA)	1995–98
Pedro Flores (WBA)†	1981	Ricardo Lopez (WBA/WBC)	1998–99†
Hwan-Jin Kim (WBA)	1981	Zolani Petelo (IBF)	1997–2001†
Katsuo Tokashiki (WBA)	1981–83	Wandee Chor Chareon (WBC)	1999–00
Amado Urzua (WBC)	1982	Noel Arambulet (WBA)	1999–00†
Tadashi Tomori (WBC)	1982	Joma Gamboa (WBA)	2000
Hilario Zapata (WBC)	1982–83	Keitaro Hoshino (WBA)	2000–01
Jung-Koo Chang (WBC)	1983–88	**Jose Antonio Aguirre** (WBC)	2000–
Lupe Madera (WBA)	1983–84	Chana Porpaoin (WBA)	2001
Dodie Penalosa (IBF)	1983–86	Robert Leyva (IBF)	2001–02
Francisco Quiroz (WBA)	1984–85	Yutaka Niida (WBA)	2001*
Joey Olivo (WBA)	1985	Keitaro Hoshino (WBA)	2002
Myung-Woo Yuh (WBA)	1985–93	**Noel Arambulent** (WBA)	2002–
Jum-Hwan Choi (IBF)	1986–88	Miguel Barrera (IBF)	2002–03
Tacy Macalos (IBF)	1988–89	Edgar Cardenas (IBF)	2003
German Torres (WBC)	1988–89	**Daniel Reyes** (IBF)	2003–

Annual Awards
Ring Magazine Fight of the Year
First presented in 1945 by Nat Fleischer, who started *The Ring* magazine in 1922.

Multiple matchups: Muhammad Ali vs. Joe Frazier, Carmen Basilio vs. Sugar Ray Robinson and Rocky Graziano vs. Tony Zale (2).

Multiple fights: Muhammad Ali (6); Carmen Basilio (5); George Foreman and Joe Frazier (4); Arturo Gatti, Rocky Graziano, Rocky Marciano and Tony Zale (3); Nino Benvenuti, Bobby Chacon, Ezzard Charles, Marvin Hagler, Thomas Hearns, Evander Holyfield, Sugar Ray Leonard, Floyd Patterson, Sugar Ray Robinson, Jersey Joe Walcott and Micky Ward (2).

Year	Winner	Loser	Result	Year	Winner	Loser	Result
1945	Rocky Graziano	Red Cochrane	KO 10	1974	Muhammad Ali	George Foreman	KO 8
1946	Tony Zale	Rocky Graziano	KO 6	1975	Muhammad Ali	Joe Frazier	KO 14
1947	Rocky Graziano	Tony Zale	KO 6	1976	George Foreman	Ron Lyle	KO 4
1948	Marcel Cerdan	Tony Zale	KO 12	1977	Jimmy Young	George Foreman	W 12
1949	Willie Pep	Sandy Saddler	W 15	1978	Leon Spinks	Muhammad Ali	W 15
1950	Jake LaMotta	Laurent Dauthuille	KO 15	1979	Danny Lopez	Mike Ayala	KO 15
1951	Jersey Joe Walcott	Ezzard Charles	KO 7	1980	Saad Muhammad	Yaqui Lopez	KO 14
1952	Rocky Marciano	Jersey Joe Walcott	KO 13	1981	Sugar Ray Leonard	Thomas Hearns	KO 14
1953	Rocky Marciano	Roland LaStarza	KO 11	1982	Bobby Chacon	Rafael Limon	W 15
1954	Rocky Marciano	Ezzard Charles	KO 8	1983	Bobby Chacon	C. Boza-Edwards	W 12
1955	Carmen Basilio	Tony DeMarco	KO 12	1984	Jose Luis Ramirez	Edwin Rosario	KO 4
1956	Carmen Basilio	Johnny Saxton	KO 9	1985	Marvin Hagler	Thomas Hearns	KO 3
1957	Carmen Basilio	Sugar Ray Robinson	W 15	1986	Stevie Cruz	Barry McGuigan	W 15
1958	Sugar Ray Robinson	Carmen Basilio	W 15	1987	Sugar Ray Leonard	Marvin Hagler	W 12
1959	Gene Fullmer	Carmen Basilio	KO 14	1988	Tony Lopez	Rocky Lockridge	W 12
1960	Floyd Patterson	Ingemar Johansson	KO 5	1989	Roberto Duran	Iran Barkley	W 12
1961	Joe Brown	Dave Charnley	W 15	1990	Julio Cesar Chavez	Meldrick Taylor	KO 12
1962	Joey Giardello	Henry Hank	W 10	1991	Robert Quiroga	Akeem Anifowoshe	W 12
1963	Cassius Clay	Doug Jones	W 10	1992	Riddick Bowe	Evander Holyfield	W 12
1964	Cassius Clay	Sonny Liston	KO 7	1993	Michael Carbajal	Humberto Gonzalez	KO 7
1965	Floyd Patterson	George Chuvalo	W 12	1994	Jorge Castro	John David Jackson	TKO 9
1966	Jose Torres	Eddie Cotton	W 15	1995	Saman Sorjaturong	Chiquita Gonzalez	KO 7
1967	Nino Benvenuti	Emile Griffith	W 15	1996	Evander Holyfield	Mike Tyson	TKO 11
1968	Dick Tiger	Frank DePaula	W 10	1997	Arturo Gatti	Gabriel Ruelas	KO 5
1969	Joe Frazier	Jerry Quarry	KO 7	1998	Ivan Robinson	Arturo Gatti	W 10
1970	Carlos Monzon	Nino Benvenuti	KO 12	1999	Paulie Ayala	Johnny Tapia	W 12
1971	Joe Frazier	Muhammad Ali	W 15	2000	Erik Morales	Marco Antonio Barrera	W 12
1972	Bob Foster	Chris Finnegan	KO 14	2001	Micky Ward	Emanuel Burton	W 10
1973	George Foreman	Joe Frazier	KO 2	2002	Micky Ward	Arturo Gatti	W 10

Ring Magazine Fighter of the Year

First presented in 1928 by Nat Fleischer, who started *The Ring* magazine in 1922.

Multiple winners: Muhammad Ali (5); Joe Louis (4); Joe Frazier, Evander Holyfield and Rocky Marciano (3); Ezzard Charles, George Foreman, Marvin Hagler, Thomas Hearns, Ingemar Johansson, Sugar Ray Leonard, Tommy Loughran, Floyd Patterson, Sugar Ray Robinson, Barney Ross, Dick Tiger and Mike Tyson (2).

Year		Year		Year	
1928	Gene Tunney	1953	Carl (Bobo) Olson	1979	Sugar Ray Leonard
1929	Tommy Loughran	1954	Rocky Marciano	1980	Thomas Hearns
1930	Max Schmeling	1955	Rocky Marciano	1981	Sugar Ray Leonard
1931	Tommy Loughran	1956	Floyd Patterson		& Salvador Sanchez
1932	Jack Sharkey	1957	Carmen Basilio	1982	Larry Holmes
1933	No award	1958	Ingemar Johansson	1983	Marvin Hagler
1934	Tony Canzoneri	1959	Ingemar Johansson	1984	Thomas Hearns
	& Barney Ross	1960	Floyd Patterson	1985	Donald Curry
1935	Barney Ross	1961	Joe Brown		& Marvin Hagler
1936	Joe Louis	1962	Dick Tiger	1986	Mike Tyson
1937	Henry Armstrong	1963	Cassius Clay	1987	Evander Holyfield
1938	Joe Louis	1964	Emile Griffith	1988	Mike Tyson
1939	Joe Louis	1965	Dick Tiger	1989	Pernell Whitaker
		1966	No award		
1940	Billy Conn	1967	Joe Frazier	1990	Julio Cesar Chavez
1941	Joe Louis	1968	Nino Benvenuti	1991	James Toney
1942	Sugar Ray Robinson	1969	Jose Napoles	1992	Riddick Bowe
1943	Fred Apostoli			1993	Michael Carbajal
1944	Beau Jack	1970	Joe Frazier	1994	Roy Jones Jr.
1945	Willie Pep	1971	Joe Frazier	1995	Oscar De La Hoya
1946	Tony Zale	1972	Muhammad Ali	1996	Evander Holyfield
1947	Gus Lesnevich		& Carlos Monzon	1997	Evander Holyfield
1948	Ike Williams	1973	George Foreman	1998	Floyd Mayweather Jr.
1949	Ezzard Charles	1974	Muhammad Ali	1999	Paulie Ayala
		1975	Muhammad Ali		
1950	Ezzard Charles	1976	George Foreman	2000	Felix Trinidad
1951	Sugar Ray Robinson	1977	Carlos Zarate	2001	Bernard Hopkins
1952	Rocky Marciano	1978	Muhammad Ali	2002	Vernon Forrest

Note: Cassius Clay changed his name to Muhammad Ali after winning the heavyweight title in 1964.

All-Time Leaders

As compiled by *The Ring Record Book and Encyclopedia*.

Knockouts

	Division		Career	No
1	Archie Moore	Lt. Heavy	1936–63	130
2	Young Stribling	Heavy	1921–33	126
3	Billy Bird	Welter	1920–48	125
4	George Odwel	Welter	1930–45	114
5	Sugar Ray Robinson	Middle	1940–65	110
6	Sandy Saddler	Feather	1944–56	103
7	Sam Langford	Middle	1902–26	102
8	Henry Armstrong	Welter	1931–45	100
9	Jimmy Wilde	Fly	1911–23	98
10	Len Wickwar	Lt. Heavy	1928–47	93

Total Bouts

	Division		Career	No
1	Len Wickwar	Lt. Heavy	1928–47	463
2	Jack Britton	Welter	1905–30	350
3	Johnny Dundee	Feather	1910–32	333
4	Billy Bird	Welter	1920–48	318
5	George Marsden	n/a	1928–46	311
6	Maxie Rosenbloom	Lt. Heavy	1923–39	299
7	Harry Greb	Middle	1913–26	298
8	Young Stribling	Lt. Heavy	1921–33	286
9	Battling Levinsky	Lt. Heavy	1910–29	282
10	Ted (Kid) Lewis	Welter	1909–29	279

Triple Champions

Fighters who have won widely-accepted world titles in more than two divisions. Henry Armstrong is the only fighter listed to hold three titles simultaneously. Note that (*) indicates title claimant.

Sugar Ray Leonard (5) WBC Welterweight (1979-80,80-82); WBA Jr. Middleweight (1981); WBC Middleweight (1987); WBC Super Middleweight (1988-90); WBC Light Heavyweight (1988).

Roy Jones Jr. (4) IBF Middleweight (1993-94); IBF Super Middleweight (1994-96); WBC Light Heavyweight (1996, 1997-2003); WBA Light Heavyweight (1998–); IBF Light Heavyweight (1999-2003); WBA Heavyweight (2003–).

Oscar De La Hoya (4) IBF Lightweight (1995-96); WBC Super Lightweight (1996-97); WBC Welterweight (1997-99); WBC Jr. Middleweight (2001–); WBA Jr. Middleweight (2002–).

Roberto Duran (4) Lightweight (1972-79); WBC Welterweight (1980); WBA Jr. Middleweight (1983-84); WBC Middleweight (1989-90).

Leo Gamez (4) WBA Strawweight (1988-90); WBA Jr. Flyweight (1993-95); WBA Flyweight (1999); WBA Junior Bantamweight (2000-01).

Thomas Hearns (4) WBA Welterweight (1980-81); WBC Jr. Middleweight (1982-84); WBC Light Heavyweight (1987); WBC Middleweight (1987-88); WBA Light Heavyweight (1991).

Pernell Whitaker (4) IBF/WBC/WBA Lightweight (1989-92); IBF Jr. Welterweight (1992-93); WBC Welterweight (1993-97); WBC Jr. Middleweight (1995).

Alexis Arguello (3) WBA Featherweight (1974-77); WBC Jr. Lightweight (1978-80); WBC Lightweight (1981-83).

Henry Armstrong (3) Featherweight (1937-38); Welterweight (1938-40); Lightweight (1938-39).

Iran Barkley (3) WBC Middleweight (1988-89); IBF Super Middleweight (1992-93); WBA Light Heavyweight (1992).

Wilfredo Benitez (3) Jr. Welterweight (1976-79); Welterweight (1979); WBC Jr. Middleweight (1981-82).

Tony Canzoneri (3) Featherweight (1928); Lightweight (1930-33); Jr. Welterweight (1931-32,33).

Julio Cesar Chavez (3) WBC Jr. Lightweight (1984-87); WBA/WBC Lightweight (1987-89); WBC/IBF Jr. Welterweight (1989-91); WBC Jr. Welterweight (1991-94, 1994).

Jeff Fenech (3) IBF Bantamweight (1985); WBC Jr. Featherweight (1986-88); WBC Featherweight (1988-90).

Bob Fitzsimmons (3) Middleweight (1891-97); Light Heavyweight (1903-05); Heavyweight (1897-99).

Wilfredo Gomez (3) WBC Super Bantamweight (1977-83); WBC Featherweight (1984); WBA Jr. Lightweight (1985-86).

Emile Griffith (3) Welterweight (1961,62-63,63-66); Jr. Middleweight (1962-63); Middleweight (1966-67,67-68).

Mike McCallum (3) WBA Jr. Middleweight (1984-88); WBA Middleweight (1989-91); WBC Light Heavyweight (1994-95).

Terry McGovern (3) Bantamweight (1889-1900); Featherweight (1900-01); Lightweight* (1900-01).

Barney Ross (3) Lightweight (1933-35); Jr. Welterweight (1933-35); Welterweight (1934, 35-38).

Johnny Tapia (3) IBF Jr. Bantamweight (1997-98); WBA Bantamweight (1998-99); IBF Featherweight (2002).

James Toney (3) IBF Middleweight (1991-93); IBF Super Middleweight (1992-94); IBF Cruiserweight (2003–).

Felix Trinidad (3) IBF/WBC Welterweight (1993-2000); WBA/IBF Jr. Middleweight (2000-01); WBA Middleweight (2001).

Wilfredo Vazquez (3) WBA Bantamweight (1987-88); WBA Jr. Featherweight (1992-95); WBA Featherweight (1996-98).

All-Time Heavyweight Upsets

Buster Douglas was a 42-1 underdog when he defeated previously-unbeaten heavyweight champion Mike Tyson on Feb. 10, 1990. That 10th-round knockout ranks as the biggest upset in boxing history. By comparison, 45-year-old George Foreman was only a 3-1 underdog before he unexpectedly won the title from Michael Moorer on Nov. 5, 1994.

Here are the best-known upsets in the annals of the heavyweight division. All fights were for the world championship except the Max Schmeling-Joe Louis bout.

Date	Winner	Loser	Result	KO Time	Location
9/7/1892	James J. Corbett	John L. Sullivan	KO 21	1:30	Olympic Club, New Orleans
4/5/1915	Jess Willard	Jack Johnson	KO 26	1:26	Mariano Race Track, Havana
9/23/26	Gene Tunney	Jack Dempsey	Wu 10	–	Sesquicentennial Stadium, Phila.
6/13/35	James J. Braddock	Max Baer	Wu 15	–	Mad. Sq.Garden Bowl, L.I. City
6/19/36	Max Schmeling	Joe Louis	KO 12	2:29	Yankee Stadium, New York
7/18/51	Jersey Joe Walcott	Ezzard Charles	KO 7	0:55	Forbes Field, Pittsburgh
6/26/59	Ingemar Johansson	Floyd Patterson	TKO 3	2:03	Yankee Stadium, New York
2/25/64	Cassius Clay	Sonny Liston	TKO 7	*	Convention Hall, Miami Beach
10/30/74	Muhammad Ali	George Foreman	KO 8	2:58	20th of May Stadium, Zaire
2/15/78	Leon Spinks	Muhammad Ali	Ws 15	–	Hilton Pavilion, Las Vegas
9/21/85	Michael Spinks	Larry Holmes	Wu 15	–	Riviera Hotel, Las Vegas
2/10/90	Buster Douglas	Mike Tyson	KO 10	1:23	Tokyo Dome, Tokyo
11/5/94	George Foreman	Michael Moorer	KO 10	2:03	MGM Grand, Las Vegas
11/9/96	Evander Holyfield	Mike Tyson	TKO 11	0:37	MGM Grand, Las Vegas
4/22/01	Hasim Rahman	Lennox Lewis	KO 5	2:32	Johannesburg, South Africa

*Liston failed to answer bell for Round 7.

Miscellaneous Sports

*Swiss **Team Alinghi** left a broken and beaten Team New Zealand in their wake in 2003, taking the America's Cup in five straight races.*

CHESS

World Champions

Garry Kasparov became the youngest man to win the world chess championship when he beat fellow Russian Anatoly Karpov in 1985 at age 22. In 1993, Kasparov and then-#1 challenger Nigel Short of England broke away from the established International Chess Federation (FIDE) to form the Professional Chess Association (the PCA was disbanded in 1998). FIDE retaliated by stripping Kasparov of the world title and arranging a playoff that was won by Karpov, the former title-holder. Karpov successfully defended the FIDE title several times before failing to show up for the 1999 FIDE World Championship Tournament that was won by Alexander Khalifman. Indian Viswanathan Anand won the 2000 FIDE World Championship. Ruslan Ponomariov won the 2001 FIDE World Championship in Moscow and is the current FIDE World Champion.

In his first title defense in five years, Kasparov faced world #2 Vladimir Kramnik for 16 matches in the unofficial (though more widely recognized) world championship from Oct. 8-Nov. 4, 2000 in London. The 25-year-old Kramnik defeated the longtime world champion 8½-6½ in a stunning result. Kasparov failed to win a single game, but despite the loss is still the top-ranked player in the world.

A plan to unify the world chess championship has been hatched. FIDE will host a knockout tournament in December 2003, the winner of which will play World No. 1 Kasparov. The winner of that match will play the winner of the match between Kramnik, who took Kasparov's title, and Peter Leko of Hungary, winner of the 2002 World Championship Candidates' tournament held in Dortmund, Germany.

Years		Years		Years	
1866-94	Wilhelm Steinitz, Austria	1957-58	Vassily Smyslov, USSR	1975-85	Anatoly Karpov, USSR
1894-1921	Emanuel Lasker, Germany	1958-59	Mikhail Botvinnik, USSR	1985-2000	Garry Kasparov, RUS
1921-27	Jose Capablanca, Cuba	1960-61	Mikhail Tal, USSR	2000–	Vladimir Kramnik, RUS
1927-35	Alexander Alekhine, France	1961-63	Mikhail Botvinnik, USSR	*Fischer defaulted the championship
1935-37	Max Euwe, Holland	1963-69	Tigran Petrosian, USSR	in 1975.	
1937-46	Alexander Alekhine, France	1969-72	Boris Spassky, USSR		
1948-57	Mkhail Botvinnik, USSR	1972-75	Bobby Fischer, USA*		

U.S. Champions

Years		Years		Years	
1857-71	Paul Morphy	1957-61	Bobby Fischer	1988	Michael Wilder
1871-76	George Mackenzie	1961-62	Larry Evans	1989	Roman Dzindzichashvili,
1876-80	James Mason	1962-68	Bobby Fischer		Stuart Rachels
1880-89	George Mackenzie	1968-69	Larry Evans		& Yasser Seirawan
1889-90	Samuel Lipschutz	1969-72	Samuel Reshevsky	1990	Lev Alburt
1890	Jackson Showalter	1972-73	Robert Byrne	1991	Gata Kamsky
1890-91	Max Judd	1973-74	Lubomir Kavalek	1992	Patrick Wolff
1891-92	Jackson Showalter		& John Grefe	1993	Alexander Shabalov
1892-94	Samuel Lipschutz	1974-77	Walter Browne		& Alex Yermolinsky
1894	Jackson Showalter	1978-80	Lubomir Kabalek	1994	Boris Gulko
1894-95	Albert Hodges	1980-81	Larry Evans,	1995	Alexander Ivanov
1895-97	Jackson Showalter		Larry Christiansen	1996	Alexander Yermolinsky
1897-1906	Harry Pillsbury		& Walter Browne	1997	Joel Benjamin
1906-09	Vacant	1981-83	Walter Browne	1998	Nick de Firmian
1909-36	Frank Marshall		& Yasser Seirawan	1999	Boris Gulko
1936-44	Samuel Reshevsky	1983	Roman Dzindzichashvili,	2000	Joel Benjamin, Yasser Seirawan & Alex Shabalov
1944-46	Arnold Denker		Larry Christiansen		
1946-48	Samuel Reshevsky		& Walter Browne	2001	Not held
1948-51	Herman Steiner	1984-85	Lev Alburt	2002	Larry Christiansen
1951-54	Larry Evans	1986	Yasser Seirawan	2003	Alexander Shabalov
1954-57	Arthur Bisguier	1987	Joel Benjamin & Nick DeFirmian		

DOGS

Iditarod Trail Sled Dog Race

In 2003, Robert Sorlie became just the second non-Alaskan to win the Iditarod. The 45-year-old Norwegian firefighter, is an experienced musher but it was only his second Iditarod race (he finished 9th in 2002, setting a rookie record). Sorlie finished the Anchorage-to-Nome race in 9 days, 15 hours and 47 minutes and won $68, 571 and a new pickup truck.

A lack of snow and warm winter weather forced race officials to change the route of this year's race. Instead of canceling the entire event, the race's restart was moved north to Fairbanks. The new route was set to be 70 miles longer than the normal route and covered unfamiliar terrain. In the end, race officials cancelled the route's final leg between Anvik and Shageluk due to icy conditions on the trail, cutting about 50 miles from the race. Sixty-four teams began the race on March 1, 44 would finish. Ramy Brooks finished second for the second straight year. It could be Brooks's year in 2004 however, Sorlie announced he will not be back next year to defend his title.

In even-numbered years the trail follows the 1,151-mile Northern Route, while in odd-numbered years, it takes a slightly different 1,161-mile Southern Route.

Multiple winners: Rick Swenson (5); Martin Buser, Susan Butcher and Doug Swingley (4); Jeff King (3).

Year		Elapsed Time	Year		Elapsed Time
1973	Dick Wilmarth	20 days, 00:49:41	1978	Dick Mackey	14 days, 18:52:24
1974	Carl Huntington	20 days, 15:02:07	1979	Rick Swenson	15 days, 10:37:47
1975	Emmitt Peters	14 days, 14:43:45	1980	Joe May	14 days, 07:11:51
1976	Gerald Riley	18 days, 22:58:17	1981	Rick Swenson	12 days, 08:45:02
1977	Rick Swenson	16 days, 16:27:13	1982	Rick Swenson	16 days, 04:40:10

Year		Elapsed Time	Year		Elapsed Time
1983	Rick Mackey	12 days, 14:10:44	1994	Martin Buser	10 days, 13:02:39
1984	Dean Osmar	12 days, 15:07:33	1995	Doug Swingley	9 days, 02:42:19
1985	Libby Riddles	18 days, 00:20:17	1996	Jeff King	9 days, 05:43:13
1986	Susan Butcher	11 days, 15:06:00	1997	Martin Buser	9 days, 08:31:45
1987	Susan Butcher	11 days, 02:05:13	1998	Jeff King	9 days, 05:52:26
1988	Susan Butcher	11 days, 11:41:40	1999	Doug Swingley	9 days, 14:31:07
1989	Joe Runyan	11 days, 05:24:34	2000	Doug Swingley	9 days, 00:58:06
1990	Susan Butcher	11 days, 01:53:23	2001	Doug Swingley	9 days, 19:55:50
1991	Rick Swenson	12 days, 16:34:39	2002	Martin Buser	8 days, 22:46:02*
1992	Martin Buser	10 days, 19:17:00	2003	Robert Sorlie	9 days, 15:47:36
1993	Jeff King	10 days, 15:38:15	*Race record.		

Westminster Kennel Club

Best in Show

Best in Show at the 127th annual All-Breed Dog Show of the Westminster Kennel Club held February 10-11, 2003, was the Kerry Blue Terrier Ch Torums Scarf Michael. The 6-year-old dog answers to the name "Mick" and is owned by Marilu Hansen. Mick, who was selected among 2,603 dogs in 159 breeds and varieties, has won 113 best in show titles including the Triple Crown of dog shows (Crufts, American Kennel Club Invitational and Westminster). A year ago, Mick was favored to win but got a little jumpy and was beaten out for best in show by a minature poodle.

The Westminster show is the most prestigious dog show in the country, and one of America's oldest annual sporting events.

Multiple winners: Ch. Warren Remedy (3); Ch. Chinoe's Adamant James, Ch. Comejo Wycollar Boy, Ch. Flornell Spicy Piece of Halleston; Ch. Matford Vic, Ch. My Own Brucie, Ch. Pendley Calling of Blarney, Ch. Rancho Dobe's Storm (2).

Year		Breed	Year		Breed
1907	Warren Remedy	Fox Terrier	1956	Wilber White Swan	Toy Poodle
1908	Warren Remedy	Fox Terrier	1957	Shirkhan of Grandeur	Afghan Hound
1909	Warren Remedy	Fox Terrier	1958	Puttencove Promise	Standard Poodle
1910	Sabine Rarebit	Fox Terrier	1959	Fontclair Festoon	Miniature Poodle
1911	Tickle Em Jock	Scottish Terrier	1960	Chick T'Sun of Caversham	Pekingese
1912	Kenmore Sorceress	Airedale	1961	Cappoquin Little Sister	Toy Poodle
1913	Strathway Prince Albert	Bulldog	1962	Elfinbrook Simon	W. Highland Terrier
1914	Brentwood Hero	Old English Sheepdog	1963	Wakefield's Black Knight	English Springer Spaniel
1915	Matford Vic	Old English Sheepdog	1964	Courtenay Fleetfoot of Pennyworth	Whippet
1916	Matford Vic	Old English Sheepdog	1965	Carmichaels Fanfare	Scottish Terrier
1917	Comejo Wycollar Boy	Fox Terrier	1966	Zeloy Mooremaides Magic	Fox Terrier
1918	Haymarket Faultless	Bull Terrier	1967	Bardene Bingo	Scottish Terrier
1919	Briergate Bright Beauty	Airedale	1968	Stingray of Derryabah	Lakeland Terrier
1920	Comejo Wycollar Boy	Fox Terrier	1969	Glamoor Good News	Skye Terrier
1921	Midkiff Seductive	Cocker Spaniel	1970	Arriba's Prima Donna	Boxer
1922	Boxwood Barkentine	Airedale	1971	Chinoe's Adamant James	E.S. Spaniel
1923	No best-in-show award		1972	Chinoe's Adamant James	E.S. Spaniel
1924	Barberryhill Bootlegger	Sealyham	1973	Acadia Command Performance	Standard Poodle
1925	Governor Moscow	Pointer	1974	Gretchenhof Columbia River	German SH Pointer
1926	Signal Circuit	Fox Terrier	1975	Sir Lancelot of Barvan	Old Eng. Sheepdog
1927	Pinegrade Perfection	Sealyham	1976	Jo Ni's Red Baron of Crofton	Lakeland Terrier
1928	Talavera Margaret	Fox Terrier	1977	Dersade Bobby's Girl	Sealyham
1929	Land Loyalty of Bellhaven	Collie	1978	Cede Higgens	Yorkshire Terrier
1930	Pendley Calling of Blarney	Fox Terrier	1979	Oak Tree's Irishtocrat	Irish Water Spaniel
1931	Pendley Calling of Blarney	Fox Terrier	1980	Sierra Cinnar	Siberian Husky
1932	Nancolleth Markable	Pointer	1981	Dhandy Favorite Woodchuck	Pug
1933	Warland Protector of Shelterock	Airedale	1982	St. Aubrey Dragonora of Elsdon	Pekingese
1934	Flornell Spicy Bit of Halleston	Fox Terrier	1983	Kabik's The Challenger	Afghan Hound
1935	Nunsoe Duc de la Terrace of Blakeen	Stan. Poodle	1984	Seaward's Blackbeard	Newfoundland
1936	St. Margaret Magnificent of Clairedale	Sealyham	1985	Braeburn's Close Encounter	Scottish Terrier
1937	Flornell Spicy Bit of Halleston	Fox Terrier	1986	Marjetta National Acclaim	Pointer
1938	Daro of Maridor	English Setter	1987	Covy Tucker Hill's Manhattan	German Shepherd
1939	Ferry v.Rauhfelsen of Giralda	Doberman	1988	Great Elms Prince Charming II	Pomeranian
1940	My Own Brucie	Cocker Spaniel	1989	Royal Tudor's Wild As The Wind	Doberman
1941	My Own Brucie	Cocker Spaniel	1990	Wendessa Crown Prince	Pekingese
1942	Wolvey Pattern of Edgerstoune	W. Highland Terrier	1991	Whisperwind on a Carousel	Stan. Poodle
1943	Pitter Patter of Piperscroft	Miniature Poodle	1992	Lonesome Dove	Fox Terrier
1944	Flornell Rarebit of Twin Ponds	Welsh Terrier	1993	Salilyn's Condor	E.S. Spaniel
1945	Shieling's Signature	Scottish Terrier	1994	Chidley Willum	Norwich Terrier
1946	Hetherington Model Rhythm	Fox Terrier	1995	Gaelforce Post Script	Scottish Terrier
1947	Warlord of Mazelaine	Boxer	1996	Clussex Country Sunrise	Clumber Spaniel
1948	Rock Ridge Night Rocket	Bedling. Terrier	1997	Parsifal di Casa Netzer	Standard Schnauzer
1949	Mazelaine's Zazarac Brandy	Boxer	1998	Fairewood Frolic	Norwich Terrier
1950	Walsing Winning Trick of Edgerstoune	Scot. Terrier	1999	Loteki's Supernatural Being	Papillon
1951	Bang Away of Sirrah Crest	Boxer	2000	Salilyn 'N Erin's Shameless	E.S. Spaniel
1952	Rancho Dobe's Storm	Doberman	2001	Special Times Just Right	Bichon Frise
1953	Rancho Dobe's Storm	Doberman	2002	Surrey Spice Girl	Miniature Poodle
1954	Carmor's Rise and Shine	Cocker Spaniel	2003	Torums Scarf Michael	Kerry Blue Terrier
1955	Kippax Fearnought	Bulldog			

FISHING

IGFA All-Tackle World Records

All-tackle records are maintained for the heaviest fish of any species caught on any line up to 130-lb (60 kg) class and certified by the International Game Fish Association. Records logged through Dec. 31, 2002. **Address:** 300 Gulf Stream Way, Dania Beach, Fla. 33004. **Telephone:** (954) 927-2628.

FRESHWATER FISH

Species	Lbs-Oz	Where Caught	Date	Angler
Barramundi	83-7	N. Queensland, Australia	Sept. 23, 1999	David Powell
Bass, Guadalupe	3-11	Lake Travis, TX	Sept. 25, 1983	Allen Christenson Jr.
Bass, largemouth	22-4	Montgomery Lake, GA	June 2, 1932	George W. Perry
Bass, Roanoke	1-5	Nottoway River, VA	Nov. 11, 1991	Tom Elkins
Bass, rock	3-0	York River, Ontario	Aug. 1, 1974	Peter Gulgin
	3-0	Lake Erie, PA	June 18, 1998	Herbert G. Ratner Jr.
Bass, shoal	8-12	Apalachicola River, FL	Jan. 28, 1995	Carl W. Davis
Bass, smallmouth	10-14	Dale Hollow, TN	Apr. 24, 1969	John T. Gorman
Bass, spotted	10-4	Pine Flat Lake, CA	Apr. 21, 2001	Bryan Shishido
Bass, striped (landlocked)	67-8	O'Neill Forebay, San Luis, CA	May 7, 1992	Hank Ferguson
Bass, Suwannee	3-14	Suwannee River, FL	Mar. 2, 1985	Ronnie Everett
Bass, white	6-13	Lake Orange, VA	July 31, 1989	Ronald L. Sprouse
Bass, whiterock	27-5	Greers Ferry Lake, AR	Apr. 24, 1997	Jerald C. Shaum
Bass, yellow	2-9	Duck River, TN	Feb. 27, 1998	John T. Chappell
Bass, yellow (hybrid)	3-5	Big Cypress Bayou, TX	Mar. 27, 1991	Patrick Collin Myers
Bluegill	4-12	Ketona Lake, AL	Apr. 9, 1950	T.S. Hudson
Bowfin	21-8	Florence, SC	Jan. 29, 1980	Robert L. Harmon
Buffalo, bigmouth	70-5	Bussey Brake, Bastrop, LA	Apr. 21, 1980	Delbert Sisk
Buffalo, black	63-6	Mississippi River, IA	Aug. 14, 1999	Jim Winters
Buffalo, smallmouth	82-3	Athens Lake, AL	June 6, 1993	Randy Collins
Bullhead, black	7-7	Mill Pond, NY	Aug. 25, 1993	Kevin Kelly
Bullhead, brown	6-1	Waterford, NY	Apr. 26, 1998	Bobby Triplett
Bullhead, yellow	4-4	Mormon Lake, AZ	May 11, 1984	Emily Williams
Burbot	18-11	Angenmanelren, Sweden	Oct. 22, 1996	Margit Agren
Carp, bighead	61-15	Old Hickory Lake, TN	Mar. 27, 2002	Rick Richard
Carp, black	40-12	Chiba, Japan	Apr. 1, 2000	Kenichi Hosoi
Carp, common	75-11	St. Cassien, France	May 21, 1987	Leo van der Gugten
Carp, crucian	5-1	Kalterersee, Italy	July 16, 1997	Jorg Marquand
Catfish, blue	116-12	Mississippi River, AR	Aug. 3, 2001	Charles Ashley Jr.
Catfish, channel	58-0	Santee-Cooper Res., SC	July 7, 1964	W.B. Whaley
Catfish, flathead	123-0	Elk City Reservoir, KS	Mar. 14, 1998	Ken Paulie
Catfish, flatwhiskered	16-15	Xingu River, Brazil	Aug. 7, 2001	Ian-Arthur de Sulocki
Catfish, gilded	85-8	Amazon River, Brazil	Nov. 15, 1986	Gilberto Fernandes
Catfish, redtail	97-7	Amazon River, Brazil	July 16, 1988	Gilberto Fernandes
Catfish, sharptoothed	79-5	Orange River, South Africa	Dec. 5, 1992	Hennie Moller
Catfish, white	21-8	East Lyme, CT	Apr. 22, 2001	Thomas Urquahart
Char, Arctic	32-9	Tree River, Canada	July 30, 1981	Jeffery Ward
Crappie, black	4-8	Kerr Lake, VA	Mar. 1, 1981	L. Carl Herring Jr.
Crappie, white	5-3	Enid Dam, MS	July 31, 1957	Fred L. Bright
Dolly Varden	20-14	Wulik River, AK	July 7, 2001	Raz Reid
Dorado	51-5	Corrientes, Argentina	Sept. 27, 1984	Armando Giudice
Drum, freshwater	54-8	Nickajack Lake, TN	Apr. 20, 1972	Benny E. Hull
Gar, alligator	279-0	Rio Grande, TX	Dec. 2, 1951	Bill Valverde
Gar, Florida	10-0	The Everglades, FL	Jan. 28, 2002	Herbert G. Ratner Jr.
Gar, longnose	50-5	Trinity River, TX	July 30, 1954	Townsend Miller
Gar, shortnose	5-12	Rend Lake, IL	July 16, 1995	Donna K. Willmart
Gar, spotted	9-12	Lake Mexia, TX	Apr. 7, 1994	Rick Rivard
Goldfish	6-10	Lake Hodges, CA	Apr. 17, 1996	Florentino M. Abena
Grayling, Arctic	5-15	Katseyedie River, N.W.T.	Aug. 16, 1967	Jeanne P. Branson
Inconnu	53-0	Pah River, AK	Aug. 20, 1986	Lawrence E. Hudnall
Kokanee	9-6	Okanagan Lake, Brit. Columbia	June 18, 1988	Norm Kuhn
Muskellunge	67-8	Hayward, WI	July 24, 1949	Cal Johnson
Muskellunge, tiger	51-3	Lac Vieux-Desert, WI-MI	July 16, 1919	John A. Knobla
Peacock, butterfly	12-9	Chiguao River, Venezuela	Jan. 6, 2000	Antonio Campa G.
Peacock, speckled	27-0	Rio Negro, Brazil	Dec. 4, 1994	Gerald (Doc) Lawson
Perch, Nile	230-0	Lake Nasser, Egypt	Dec. 20, 2000	William Toth
Perch, white	3-1	Forest Hill Park, NJ	May 6, 1989	Edward Tango
Perch, yellow	4-3	Bordentown, NJ	May, 1865	Dr. C.C. Abbot
Pickerel, chain	9-6	Homerville, GA	Feb. 17, 1961	Baxley McQuaig Jr.
Pickerel, grass	1-0	Dewart Lake, IN	June 9, 1990	Mike Berg
Pickerel, redfin	2-4	Gall Berry Swamp, NC	June 27, 1997	Edward C. Davis
Pike, northern	55-1	Lake of Grefeern, Germany	Oct. 16, 1986	Lothar Louis
Redhorse, greater	9-3	Salmon River, Pulaski, NY	May 11, 1985	Jason Wilson

Species	Lbs-Oz	Where Caught	Date	Angler
Redhorse, silver	.11-7	Plum Creek, WI	May 29, 1985	Neal D.G. Long
Salmon, Atlantic	.79-2	Tana River, Norway	1928	Henrik Henriksen
Salmon, chinook	.97-4	Kenai River, AK	May 17, 1985	Les Anderson
Salmon, chum	.35-0	Edye Pass, Brit. Columbia	July 11, 1995	Todd Johansson
Salmon, coho	.33-4	Salmon River, Pulaski, NY	Sept. 27, 1989	Jerry Lifton
Salmon, pink	.14-13	Monroe, WA	Sept. 30, 2001	Alexander Minerich
Salmon, sockeye	.15-3	Kenai River, AK	Aug. 9, 1987	Stan Roach
Sauger	.8-12	Lake Sakakawea, ND	Oct. 6, 1971	Mike Fischer
Shad, American	.11-4	Conn. River, S. Hadley, MA	May 19, 1986	Bob Thibodo
Shad, gizzard	.4-6	Lake Michigan, IN	Mar. 2, 1996	Mike Berg
Sturgeon, lake	.168-0	Georgian Bay, Canada	May 29, 1982	Edward Paszkowski
Sturgeon, white	.468-0	Benicia, CA	July 9, 1983	Joey Pallotta 3rd
Tigerfish, giant	.97-0	Zaire River, Kinshasa, Zaire	July 9, 1988	Raymond Houtmans
Tilapia, spotted	.3-0	Pembroke Pines, FL	Mar. 20, 1999	Jay Wright Jr.
Trout, Apache	.5-3	White Mountain, AZ	May 29, 1991	John Baldwin
Trout, brook	.14-8	Nipigon River, Ontario	July, 1916	Dr. W.J. Cook
Trout, brown	.40-4	Little Red River, AR	May 9, 1992	Rip Collins
Trout, bull	.32-0	Lake Pend Orielle, ID	Oct. 27, 1949	N.L. Higgins
Trout, cutthroat	.41-0	Pyramid Lake, NV	Dec., 1925	John Skimmerhorn
Trout, golden	.11-0	Cooks Lake, WY	Aug. 5, 1948	Charles S. Reed
Trout, lake	.72-0	Great Bear Lake, N.W.T.	Aug. 19, 1995	Lloyd E. Bull
Trout, rainbow	.42-2	Bell Island, AK	June 22, 1970	David Robert White
Trout, tiger	.20-13	Lake Michigan, WI	Aug. 12, 1978	Peter M. Friedland
Walleye	.25-0	Old Hickory Lake, TN	Aug. 2, 1960	Mabry Harper
Warmouth	.2-7	Guess Lake, Holt, FL	Oct. 19, 1985	Tony D. Dempsey
Whitefish, lake	.14-6	Meaford, Ontario	May 21, 1984	Dennis M. Laycock
Whitefish, mountain	.5-8	Elbow River, Manitoba	Aug. 1, 1995	Randy G. Woo
Whitefish, round	.6-0	Putahow River, Manitoba	June 14, 1984	Allan J. Ristori
Zander	.25-2	Trosa, Sweden	June 12, 1986	Harry Lee Tennison

SALTWATER FISH

Species	Lbs-Oz	Where Caught	Date	Angler
Albacore	.88-2	Gran Canaria, Canary Islands	Nov. 19, 1977	Siegfried Dickemann
Amberjack, greater	.155-12	Challenger Bank, Bermuda	Aug. 16, 1992	Larry Trott
Angelfish, gray	.4-0	S.Beach Jetty, Miami, FL	July 12, 1999	Rene G. de Dios
Barracuda, great	.85-0	Christmas Is., Rep. of Kiribati	Apr. 11, 1992	John W. Helfrich
Barracuda, Mexican	.21-0	Phantom Island, Costa Rica	Mar. 27, 1987	E. Greg Kent
Barracuda, pickhandle	.25-5	Scottburgh, South Africa	July 3, 1996	Demetrios Stamatis
Bass, barred sand	.13-3	Huntington Beach, CA	Aug. 29, 198?	Robert Halal
Bass, black sea	.10-4	Virginia Beach, VA	Jan. 1, 2000	Allan P. Paschall
Bass, European	.20-14	Cap d'Agde, France	Sept. 8, 19??	Robert Mari
Bass, giant sea	.563-8	Anacapa Island, CA	Aug. 20, 1?68	J.D. McAdam Jr.
Bass, striped	.78-8	Atlantic City, NJ	Sept. 21, 1982	Albert R. McReynolds
Bluefish	.31-12	Hatteras, NC	Jan. 30, 1972	James M. Hussey
Bonefish	.19-0	Zululand, South Africa	May 26, 1962	Brian W. Batchelor
Bonito, Atlantic	.18-4	Faial Island, Azores	July 8, 1953	D. Gama Higgs
Bonito, Pacific	.21-3	Malibu, CA	July 30, 1978	Gino M. Picciolo
Cabezon	.23-0	Juan de Fuca Strait, WA	Aug. 4, 1990	Wesley Hunter
Cobia	.135-9	Shark Bay, W. Australia	July 9, 1985	Peter W. Goulding
Cod, Atlantic	.98-12	Isle of Shoals, NH	June 8, 1969	Alphonse Bielevich
Cod, Pacific	.35-0	Unalaska Bay, AK	June 16, 1999	Jim Johnson
Conger	.133-4	South Devon, England	June 5, 1995	Vic Evans
Dolphinfish	.88-0	Highbourne Cay, Bahamas	May 5, 1998	Richard D. Evans
Drum, black	.113-1	Lewes, DE	Sept. 15, 1975	Gerald M. Townsend
Drum, red	.94-2	Avon, NC	Nov. 7, 1984	David G. Deuel
Eel, American	.9-4	Cape May, NJ	Nov. 9, 1995	Jeff Pennick
Eel, marbled	.36-1	Durban, South Africa	June 10, 1984	Ferdie van Nooten
Flounder, southern	.20-9	Nassau Sound, FL	Dec. 23, 1983	Larenza Mungin
Flounder, summer	.22-7	Montauk, NY	Sept. 15, 1975	Charles Nappi
Grouper, goliath	.680-0	Fernandina Beach, FL	May 20, 1961	Lynn Joyner
Grouper, Warsaw	.436-12	Gulf of Mexico, Destin, FL	Dec. 22, 1985	Steve Haeusler
Haddock	.14-15	Saltraumen, Germany	Aug. 15, 1997	Heike Neblinger
Halibut, Atlantic	.355-6	Valevag, Norway	Oct. 20, 1997	Odd Arve Gunderstad
Halibut, California	.58-9	Santa Rosa Island, CA	June 26, 1999	Roger W. Borrell
Halibut, Pacific	.459-0	Dutch Harbor, AK	June 11, 1996	Jack Tragis
Jack, almaco (Pacific)	.132-0	La Paz, Baja Calif., Mexico	July 21, 1964	Howard H. Hahn
Jack, crevalle	.58-6	Barra do Kwanza, Angola	Dec. 10, 2000	Nuno A.P. da Silva
Jack, horse-eye	.29-8	Ascencion Island, South Atlantic	May 28, 1993	Mike Hanson
Kawakawa	.29-0	Clarion Island, Mexico	Dec. 17, 1986	Ronald Nakamura
Lingcod	.76-9	Gulf of Alaska	Aug. 11, 2001	Antwan D. Tinsley
Mackerel, cero	.17-2	Islamorada, FL	Apr. 5, 1986	G. Michael Mills

FISHING (Cont.)

Species	Lbs-Oz	Where Caught	Date	Angler
Mackerel, king	93-0	San Juan, Puerto Rico	Apr. 18, 1999	Steve Perez Graulau
Mackerel, Spanish	13-0	Ocracoke Inlet, NC	Nov. 4, 1987	Robert Cranton
Marlin, Atlantic blue	1402-2	Vitoria, Brazil	Feb. 29, 1992	Paulo R.A. Amorim
Marlin, black	1560-0	Cabo Blanco, Peru	Aug. 4, 1953	A.C. Glassell Jr.
Marlin, Pacific blue	1376-0	Kaaiwi Point, Kona, HI	May 31, 1982	Jay W. deBeaubien
Marlin, striped	494-0	Tutakaka, New Zealand	Jan. 16, 1986	Bill Boniface
Marlin, white	181-14	Vitoria, Brazil	Dec. 8, 1979	Evandro Luiz Coser
Permit	56-2	Ft. Lauderdale, FL	June 30, 1997	Thomas Sebestyen
Pollack, European	27-6	Salcombe, Devon, England	Jan. 16, 1986	Robert S. Milkins
Pollock	50-0	Salstraumen, Norway	Nov. 30, 1996	Thor-Magnus Lekang
Pompano, African	50-8	Daytona Beach, FL	Apr. 21, 1990	Tom Sargent
Roosterfish	114-0	La Paz, Baja Calif., Mexico	June 1, 1960	Abe Sackheim
Runner, blue	11-2	Dauphin Island, AL	June 28, 1997	Stacey M. Moiren
Runner, rainbow	37-9	Clarion Island, Mexico	Nov. 21, 1991	Tom Pfleger
Sailfish, Atlantic	141-1	Luanda, Angola	Feb. 19, 1994	Alfredo de Sousa Neves
Sailfish, Pacific	221-0	Santa Cruz Is., Ecuador	Feb. 12, 1947	C.W. Stewart
Seabass, white	83-12	San Felipe, Mexico	Mar. 31, 1953	L.C. Baumgardner
Seatrout, spotted	17-7	Ft. Pierce, FL	May 11, 1995	Craig F. Carson
Shark, blue	528-0	Montauk Point, NY	Aug. 9, 2001	Joe Seidel
Shark, great white	2664-0	Ceduna, S. Australia	Apr. 21, 1959	Alfred Dean
Shark, Greenland	1708-9	Trondheimsfjord, Norway	Oct. 18, 1987	Terje Nordtvedt
Shark, hammerhead	991-0	Sarasota, FL	May 30, 1982	Allen Ogle
Shark, shortfin mako	1221-0	Chatham, MA	July 21, 2001	Luke Sweeney
Shark, porbeagle	507-0	Pentland Firth, Scotland	Mar. 9, 1993	Christopher Bennet
Shark, bigeye thresher	802-0	Tutukaka, New Zealand	Feb. 8, 1981	Dianne North
Shark, tiger	1780-0	Cherry Grove, SC	June 14, 1964	Walter Maxwell
Snapper, cubera	121-8	Cameron, LA	July 5, 1982	Mike Hebert
Snapper, red	50-4	Gulf of Mexico, LA	June 23, 1996	Capt. Doc Kennedy
Snook, Pacific black	57-12	Rio Naranjo, Quepos, Costa Rica	Aug. 23, 1991	George Beck
Spearfish, Mediterranean	90-13	Madeira Island, Portugal	June 2, 1980	Joseph Larkin
Swordfish	1182-0	Iquique, Chile	May 7, 1953	Louis Marron
Tarpon	283-4	Sherbro Is., Sierra Leone	Apr. 16, 1991	Yvon Victor Sebag
Tautog	25-0	Ocean City, NJ	Jan. 20, 1998	Anthony R. Monica
Tuna, Atlantic bigeye	392-6	Gran Canaria, Puerto Rico	July 25, 1996	Dieter Vogel
Tuna, blackfin	45-8	Key West, FL	May 4, 1996	Sam J. Burnett
Tuna, bluefin	1496-0	Aulds Cove, Nova Scotia	Oct. 26, 1979	Ken Fraser
Tuna, longtail	79-2	Montague Is., NSW, Australia	Apr. 12, 1982	Tim Simpson
Tuna, Pacific bigeye	435-0	Cabo Blanco, Peru	Apr. 17, 1957	Dr. Russell Lee
Tuna, skipjack	45-4	Flathead Bank, Mexico	Nov. 16, 1996	Brian Evans
Tuna, southern bluefin	348-5	Whakatane, New Zealand	Jan. 16, 1981	Rex Wood
Tuna, yellowfin	388-12	San Benedicto Island, Mexico	Apr. 1, 1977	Curt Wiesenhutter
Tunny, little	35-2	Cap de Garde, Algeria	Dec. 14, 1988	Jean Yves Chatard
Wahoo	158-8	Loreto, Baja Calif., Mexico	June 10, 1996	Keith Winter
Weakfish	19-2	Jones Beach, Long Island, NY	Oct. 11, 1984	Dennis R. Rooney
	19-2	Delaware Bay, DE	May 20, 1989	William E. Thomas

BASSMASTERS Classic

Michael Iaconelli of Woodbury Heights, N.J., became the 33rd annual CITGO BASSMASTERS Classic champion on the waters of the Louisiana Delta outside New Orleans. Competing in just his fourth Classic, Iaconelli won the 2003 title, with his five fish limit weighing in at 37 pounds, 14 ounces (including a 3-pound catch in the competition's closing minutes) to post a 1-pound-12 ounce margin of victory over Texas veteran angler Gary Klein. Iaconelli earned $200,000 for the victory. Harold Allen, the third-place finisher, had success before getting run off his fishing spot by an irate airboater, who claimed that Allen was trespassing on private, but apparently unposted, property.

The CITGO BASSMASTERS Classic, hosted by B.A.S.S. (Bass Anglers Sportsman Society), is professional bass fishing's world championship. Qualifiers for the three-day event include the 40 top pros on the CITGO BASSMASTER Tour and the five top-ranked anglers from each of three CITGO BASSMASTER Open circuits. Anglers may weigh only five bass per day and each bass must be at least 12 inches long. Only artificial lures are permitted. The first Classic, held at Lake Mead, Nev. in 1971, was a $10,000 winner-take-all event.

Multiple winners: Rick Clunn (4); George Cochran, Bobby Murray and Hank Parker (2).

Year		Weight	Year		Weight
1971	Bobby Murray, Hot Springs, Ark	43-11	1979	Hank Parker, Clover, S.C	31-0
1972	Don Butler, Tulsa, Okla	38-11	1980	Bo Dowden, Natchitoches, La	54-10
1973	Rayo Breckenridge, Paragould, Ark	52-8	1981	Stanley Mitchell, Fitzgerald, Ga	35-2
1974	Tommy Martin, Hemphill, Tex	33-7	1982	Paul Elias, Laurel, Miss	32-8
1975	Jack Hains, Rayne, La	45-4	1983	Larry Nixon, Hemphill, Tex	18-1
1976	Rick Clunn, Montgomery, Tex	59-15	1984	Rick Clunn, Montgomery, Tex	75-9
1977	Rick Clunn, Montgomery, Tex	27-7	1985	Jack Chancellor, Phenix City, Ala	45-0
1978	Bobby Murray, Nashville, Tenn	37-9	1986	Charlie Reed, Broken Bow, Okla	23-9

Year		Weight	Year		Weight
1987	George Cochran, N. Little Rock, Ark	.15-5	1996	George Cochran, Hot Springs, Ark.	.31-14
1988	Guido Hibdon, Gravois Mills, Mo	.28-8	1997	Dion Hibdon, Stover, Mo.	.34-13
1989	Hank Parker, Denver, N.C.	.31-6	1998	Denny Brauer, Camdenton, Mo.	.46-3
1990	Rick Clunn, Montgomery, Tex	.34-5	1999	Davy Hite, Prosperity, S.C.	.55-10
1991	Ken Cook, Meers, Okla	.33-2	2000	Woo Daves, Spring Grove, Va.	.27-13
1992	Robert Hamilton Jr., Brandon, Miss	.59-6	2001	Kevin Van Dam, Kalamazoo, Mich.	.32-5
1993	David Fritts, Lexington, N.C.	.48-6	2002	Jay Yelas, Tyler, Texas	.45-13
1994	Bryan Kerchal, Newtown, Conn	.36-7	2003	Michael Iaconelli, Woodbury Heights, N.J.	.37-14
1995	Mark Davis, Mount Ida, Ark.	.47-14			

LITTLE LEAGUE BASEBALL

World Series

Yuutaro Tanaka struck out 14 batters over six innings as Tokyo, Japan won the Little League World Series for the second time in three years. The eighth time wasn't the charm for Florida as the Sunshine state has placed eight teams in the Little League World Series title game but has never won. Tokyo broke open what was developing as a pitchers' duel in the fourth inning with eight runs punctuated by Hokuto Nakahara's grand slam. With the score 10-0 in the fifth, the kids from Florida barely avoided suffering the "mercy rule" loss when they scored a run in the bottom of the fifth on Michael DeJesus's RBI single.

In the third-place game, Willemstad, Curacao, Netherlands Antilles beat Saugus, Mass., 6-1.

Played annually in late August in Williamsport, Penn. at Original Field in Williamsport, Penn. from 1947-1958 and at Howard J. Lamade Stadium since 1959 and also at newly constructed Volunteer Stadium starting in 2001.

In order to be invited to the World Series, teams must first win their regional tournaments. There are eight regions from the U.S. (Great Lakes, Midwest, Mid-Atlantic, New England, Northwest, Southeast, Southwest and West) and eight outside of the U.S. (Asia, Canada, Caribbean, European, Latin America, Mexico, Pacific and Trans-Atlantic). The eight U.S. regions then play each other and the the eight international regions play each other and the two winners from each meet in the championship game. This insures that a team from the U.S. will always participate in the final game.

Multiple winners: Taiwan (16); Japan (6); California (5); Connecticut, New Jersey and Pennsylvania (4); Mexico (3); New York, South Korea, Texas and Venezuela (2).

Year	Winner	Score	Loser	Year	Winner	Score	Loser
1947	Williamsport, PA	16-7	Lock Haven, PA	1976	Tokyo, Japan	10-3	Campbell, CA
1948	Lock Haven, PA	6-5	St. Petersburg, FL	1977	Li-Teh, Taiwan	7-2	El Cajon, CA
1949	Hammonton, NJ	5-0	Pensacola, FL	1978	Pin-Tung, Taiwan	11-1	Danville, CA
				1979	Hsien, Taiwan	2-1	Campbell, CA
1950	Houston, TX	2-1	Bridgeport, CT				
1951	Stamford, CT	3-0	Austin, TX	1980	Hua Lian, Taiwan	4-3	Tampa, FL
1952	Norwalk, CT	4-3	Monongahela, PA	1981	Tai-Chung, Taiwan	4-2	Tampa, FL
1953	Birmingham, AL	1-0	Schenectady, NY	1982	Kirkland, WA	6-0	Hsien, Taiwan
1954	Schenectady, NY	7-5	Colton, CA	1983	Marietta, GA	3-1	Barahona, D. Rep.
1955	Morrisville, PA	4-3	Merchantville, NJ	1984	Seoul, S. Korea	6-2	Altamonte, FL
1956	Roswell, NM	3-1	Merchantville, NJ	1985	Seoul, S. Korea	7-1	Mexicali, Mex.
1957	Monterrey, Mexico	4-0	La Mesa, CA	1986	Tainan Park, Taiwan	12-0	Tucson, AZ
1958	Monterrey, Mexico	10-1	Kankakee, IL	1987	Hua Lian, Taiwan	21-1	Irvine, CA
1959	Hamtramck, MI	12-0	Auburn, CA	1988	Tai Ping, Taiwan	10-0	Pearl City, HI
				1989	Trumbull, CT	5-2	Kaohsiung, Taiwan
1960	Levittown, PA	5-0	Ft. Worth, TX				
1961	El Cajon, CA	4-2	El Campo, TX	1990	Taipei, Taiwan	9-0	Shippensburg, PA
1962	San Jose, CA	3-0	Kankakee, IL	1991	Taichung, Taiwan	11-0	Danville, CA
1963	Granada Hills, CA	2-1	Stratford, CT	1992	Long Beach, CA	6-0	Zamboanga, Phil.
1964	Staten Island, NY	4-0	Monterrey, Mex.	1993	Long Beach, CA	3-2	Panama
1965	Windsor Locks, CT	3-1	Stoney Creek, Can.	1994	Maracaibo, Venezuela	4-3	Northridge, CA
1966	Houston, TX	8-2	W. New York, NJ	1995	Tainan, Taiwan	17-3	Spring, TX
1967	West Tokyo, Japan	4-1	Chicago, IL	1996	Taipei, Taiwan	13-3	Cranston, RI
1968	Osaka, Japan	1-0	Richmond, VA				(called after 5th inn.)
1969	Taipei, Taiwan	5-0	Santa Clara,CA	1997	Guadalupe, Mexico	5-4	Mission Viejo, CA
				1998	Toms River, NJ	12-9	Kashima, Japan
1970	Wayne, NJ	2-0	Campbell, CA	1999	Osaka, Japan	5-0	Phenix City, AL
1971	Tainan, Taiwan	12-3	Gary, IN				
1972	Taipei, Taiwan	6-0	Hammond, IN	2000	Maracaibo, Venezuela	3-2	Bellaire, TX
1973	Tainan City, Taiwan	12-0	Tucson, AZ	2001	Tokyo, Japan	2-1	Apopka, FL
1974	Kao Hsiung, Taiwan	12-1	Red Bluff, CA	2002	Louisville, KY	1-0	Sendai, Japan
1975	Lakewood, NJ	4-3*	Tampa, FL	2003	Tokyo, Japan	10-1	Boynton Beach, FL

* Foreign teams were banned from the tournament in 1975, but allowed back in the following year.

Note: In 1992, Zamboanga City of the Philippines beat Long Beach, 15-4, but was stripped of the title a month later when it was discovered that the team had used several players from outside the city limits. Long Beach was then awarded the title by forfeit, 6-0 (one run for each inning of the game).

AP/Wide World Photos

*The aptly named **Chris Moneymaker**, who won a spot in the 2003 World Series of Poker through an internet tournament, parlayed his $40 internet entry fee into a cash prize of $2.5 million for beating out the world's best poker players in no-limit Texas hold'em at Binion's Horseshoe Casino in Las Vegas.*

POKER
World Series of Poker

Created by Benny Binion in 1970, the World Series of Poker is held each year at Binion's Horseshoe Casino in Las Vegas, Nev. and brings together the world's greatest poker players. The marquee event is the no-limit Texas hold-'em tournament. The first World Series was a seven-player tournament in which the champion Johnny Moss was chosen by a vote of his peers. The 2003 World Champion, Chris Moneymaker, beat out hundreds of players over four days and won a first prize of $2.5 million—a larger payday than the winner of the Kentucky Derby, Wimbledon, Indianapolis 500 or the Masters receives. Anyone that's over 21 years old and can pay the $10,000 entry fee can compete.
Multiple winners: Johnny Moss and Stu Ungar (3); Doyle Brunson and Johnny Chan (2).

Champions

Year	Champion	Prize Money	Year	Champion	Prize Money
1970	Johnny Moss	n/a	1987	Johnny Chan	$ 625,000
1971	Johnny Moss	$ 30,000	1988	Johnny Chan	700,000
1972	"Amarillo Slim" Preston	80,000	1989	Phil Hellmuth Jr.	755,000
1973	Puggy Pearson	130,000	1990	Mansour Matloubi	895,000
1974	Johnny Moss	160,000	1991	Brad Daugherty	1,000,000
1975	Sailor Roberts	210,000	1992	Hamid Datsmalchi	1,000,000
1976	Doyle Brunson	220,000	1993	Jim Bechtel	1,000,000
1977	Doyle Brunson	340,000	1994	Russ Hamilton	1,000,000
1978	Bobby Baldwin	210,000	1995	Dan Harrington	1,000,000
1979	Hal Fowler	270,000	1996	Huck Seed	1,000,000
1980	Stu Ungar	385,000	1997	Stu Ungar	1,000,000
1981	Stu Ungar	375,000	1998	Scotty Nguyen	1,000,000
1982	Jack Strauss	520,000	1999	Noel Furlong	1,000,000
1983	Tom McEvoy	580,000	2000	Chris Ferguson	1,500,000
1984	Jack Keller	660,000	2001	Carlos Mortensen	1,500,000
1985	Bill Smith	700,000	2002	Robert Varkyoni	2,000,000
1986	Berry Johnston	570,000	2003	Chris Moneymaker	2,500,000

POWER BOAT RACING

APBA Gold Cup

In the race's 100th year, Mitch Evans won the APBA Gold Cup, piloting the piston-powered *Miss Fox Hills Chrysler Jeep-Sun Coatings* to victory Aug. 24, 2003 on the Detroit River. The victory was the first for a non-turbine boat at the Gold Cup in 20 years. Chip Hanauer was the last to do it when drove the Atlas Van Lines boat to a win in 1983 Gold Cup in Evansville, Ind. Evans, in the only piston-powered boat in the unlimited hydroplane fleet, took the lead early on passing the defending champion Dave Villwock and 2001 champion Mike Hanson·in the first turn of lap one. The race itself was in doubt and was postponed from its schedule date in June due to budget troubles. Suppliers and contractors were reportedly owed about $400,000. Three-time Gold Cup champion Tom D'Eath worked with Detroit area Chrysler Jeep Superstores to get the event back on.

The American Power Boat Association Challenge Cup for unlimited hydroplane racing is the oldest active motorsports trophy in North America. The first Gold Cup was competed for on the Hudson River in New York in June and September 1904. Since then several cities have hosted the race, led by Detroit (34 times) and Seattle (14). Note that (*) indicates driver was also owner of the winning boat.

Drivers with multiple wins: Chip Hanauer (11); Bill Muncey (8); Dave Villwock and Gar Wood (5); Dean Chenoweth (4); Caleb Bragg, Tom D'Eath, Lou Fageol, Ron Musson, George Reis and J.M. Wainwright (3); Danny Foster, George Henley, Vic Kliesrath, E.J. Schroeder, Bill Schumacher, Zalmon G. Simmons Jr., Joe Taggart, Mark Tate and George Townsend (2).

Year	Boat	Driver	Avg. MPH	Year	Boat	Driver	Avg. MPH
1904	Standard (June)	Carl Riotte*	23.160	1954	Slo-Mo-Shun V	Lou Fageol	92.613
1904	Vingt-Et-Un II (Sept.)	W. Sharpe Kilmer*	24.900	1955	Gale V	Lee Schoenith	99.552
				1956	Miss Thriftway	Bill Muncey	96.552
1905	Chip I	J.M. Wainwright*	15.000	1957	Miss Thriftway	Bill Muncey	101.787
1906	Chip II	J.M. Wainwright*	25.000	1958	Hawaii Kai III	Jack Regas	103.000
1907	Chip III	J.M. Wainwright*	23.903	1959	Maverick	Bill Stead	104.481
1908	Dixie II	E.J. Schroeder*	29.938	1960	Not held		
1909	Dixie II	E.J. Schroeder*	29.590	1961	Miss Century 21	Bill Muncey	99.678
1910	Dixie III	F.K. Burnham*	32.473	1962	Miss Century 21	Bill Muncey	100.710
1911	MIT II	J.H. Hayden*	37.000	1963	Miss Bardahl	Ron Musson	105.124
1912	P.D.Q. II	A.G. Miles*	39.462	1964	Miss Bardahl	Ron Musson	103.433
1913	Ankle Deep	C.S. Mankowski*	42.779	1965	Miss Bardahl	Ron Musson	103.132
1914	Baby Speed Demon II	Jim Blackton & Bob Edgren	48.458	1966	Tahoe Miss	Mira Slovak	93.019
				1967	Miss Bardahl	Bill Shumacher	101.484
1915	Miss Detroit	Johnny Milot & Jack Beebe	37.656	1968	Miss Bardahl	Bill Shumacher	108.173
				1969	Miss Budweiser	Bill Sterett	98.504
1916	Miss Minneapolis	Bernard Smith	48.860	1970	Miss Budweiser	Dean Chenoweth	99.562
1917	Miss Detroit II	Gar Wood*	54.410	1971	Miss Madison	Jim McCormick	98.043
1918	Miss Detroit II	Gar Wood	51.619	1972	Atlas Van Lines	Bill Muncey	104.277
1919	Miss Detroit III	Gar Wood*	42.748	1973	Miss Budweiser	Dean Chenoweth	99.043
1920	Miss America I	Gar Wood*	62.022	1974	Pay 'n Pak	George Henley	104.428
1921	Miss America I	Gar Wood*	52.825	1975	Pay 'n Pak	George Henley	108.921
1922	Packard Chriscraft	J.G. Vincent*	40.253	1976	Miss U.S.	Tom D'Eath	100.412
1923	Packard Chriscraft	Caleb Bragg	43.867	1977	Atlas Van Lines	Bill Muncey*	111.822
1924	Baby Bootlegger	Caleb Bragg*	45.302	1978	Atlas Van Lines	Bill Muncey*	100.412
1925	Baby Bootlegger	Caleb Bragg*	47.240	1979	Atlas Van Lines	Bill Muncey*	100.765
1926	Greenwich Folly	George Townsend*	47.984	1980	Miss Budweiser	Dean Chenoweth	106.932
				1981	Miss Budweiser	Dean Chenoweth	116.387
1927	Greenwich Folly	George Townsend*	47.662	1982	Atlas Van Lines	Chip Hanauer	120.050
				1983	Atlas Van Lines	Chip Hanauer	118.507
1928	Not held			1984	Atlas Van Lines	Chip Hanauer	130.175
1929	Imp	Richard Hoyt*	48.662	1985	Miller American	Chip Hanauer	120.643
1930	Hotsy Totsy	Vic Kliesrath*	52.673	1986	Miller American	Chip Hanauer	116.523
1931	Hotsy Totsy	Vic Kliesrath*	53.602	1987	Miller American	Chip Hanauer	127.620
1932	Delphine IV	Bill Horn	57.775	1988	Miss Circus Circus	Chip Hanauer & Jim Prevost	123.756
1933	El Lagarto	George Reis*	56.260				
1934	El Lagarto	George Reis*	55.000	1989	Miss Budweiser	Tom D'Eath	131.209
1935	El Lagarto	George Reis*	55.056	1990	Miss Budweiser	Tom D'Eath	143.176
1936	Impshi	Kaye Don	45.735	1991	Winston Eagle	Mark Tate	137.771
1937	Notre Dame	Clell Perry	63.675	1992	Miss Budweiser	Chip Hanauer	136.282
1938	Alagi	Theo Rossi*	64.340	1993	Miss Budweiser	Chip Hanauer	141.296
1939	My Sin	Z.G. Simmons Jr.*	66.133	1994	Smokin' Joe's	Mark Tate	145.532
1940	Hotsy Totsy III	Sidney Allen*	48.295	1995	Miss Budweiser	Chip Hanauer	149.160
1941	My Sin	Z.G. Simmons Jr.*	52.509	1996	Pico/American Dream	Dave Villwock	149.328
1942-45 Not held				1997	Miss Budweiser	Dave Villwock	129.366
1946	Tempo VI	Guy Lombardo*	68.132	1998	Miss Budweiser	Dave Villwock	140.704
1947	Miss Peps V	Danny Foster	57.000	1999	Miss Pico	Chip Hanauer	152.591
1948	Miss Great Lakes	Danny Foster	46.845	2000	Miss Budweiser	Dave Villwock	139.416
1949	My Sweetie	Bill Cantrell	73.612	2001	Tubby's Subs	Mike Hanson	140.519
1950	Slo-Mo-Shun IV	Ted Jones	78.216	2002	Miss Budweiser	Dave Villwock	143.093
1951	Slo-Mo-Shun V	Lou Fageol	90.871	2003	Miss Fox Hills Chrysler Jeep-Sun Coatings	Mitch Evans	144.152
1952	Slo-Mo-Shun IV	Stan Dollar	79.923				
1953	Slo-Mo-Shun IV	Joe Taggart & Lou Fageol	99.108				

PRO RODEO

All-Around Champion Cowboy

Twenty-six-year-old Trevor Brazile of Anson, Texas, won the coveted title of all-around champion cowboy at the 2002 National Finals Rodeo, finishing with a earnings total of $273,998. Brazile is one of just 12 cowboys to qualify for the NFR in three events (calf roping, team roping and steer roping). At the 2002 NFR, Brazile battled with Jesse Bail, of Camp Crook, S.D., for the All-Around Cowboy belt buckle. Bail looked to have the edge as the 2002 NFR's only two-event cowboy but Brazile eventually won out, clinching the title in the 10th and final round in front of a sold-out crowd of 17,681 at the Thomas & Mack Center in Las Vegas.

The Professional Rodeo Cowboys Association (PRCA) title of all-around world champion cowboy goes to the rodeo athlete who wins the most prize money in a single year in two or more events, earning a minimum of $3,000 in each event. Only prize money earned in sanctioned PRCA rodeos is counted. From 1929-44, all-around champions were named by the Rodeo Association of America (earnings for those years are not available).

Multiple winners: Ty Murray (7); Tom Ferguson and Larry Mahan (6); Jim Shoulders (5); Joe Beaver, Lewis Feild and Dean Oliver (3); Everett Bowman, Louis Brooks, Clay Carr, Bill Linderman, Phil Lyne, Gerald Roberts, Casey Tibbs and Harry Tompkins (2).

Year		Year		Year		Year	
1929	Earl Thode	1933	Clay Carr	1937	Everett Bowman	1941	Homer Pettigrew
1930	Clay Carr	1934	Leonard Ward	1938	Burel Mulkey	1942	Gerald Roberts
1931	John Schneider	1935	Everett Bowman	1939	Paul Carney	1943	Louis Brooks
1932	Donald Nesbit	1936	John Bowman	1940	Fritz Truan	1944	Louis Brooks
						1945-46	No award

Year		Earnings	Year		Earnings	Year		Earnings
1947	Todd Whatley	$18,642	1966	Larry Mahan	$40,358	1985	Lewis Feild	$130,347
1948	Gerald Roberts	21,766	1967	Larry Mahan	51,996	1986	Lewis Feild	166,042
1949	Jim Shoulders	21,495	1968	Larry Mahan	49,129	1987	Lewis Feild	144,335
			1969	Larry Mahan	57,726	1988	Dave Appleton	121,546
1950	Bill Linderman	30,715				1989	Ty Murray	134,806
1951	Casey Tibbs	29,104	1970	Larry Mahan	41,493			
1952	Harry Tompkins	30,934	1971	Phil Lyne	49,245	1990	Ty Murray	213,772
1953	Bill Linderman	33,674	1972	Phil Lyne	60,852	1991	Ty Murray	244,231
1954	Buck Rutherford	40,404	1973	Larry Mahan	64,447	1992	Ty Murray	225,992
1955	Casey Tibbs	42,065	1974	Tom Ferguson	66,929	1993	Ty Murray	297,896
1956	Jim Shoulders	43,381	1975	Tom Ferguson	50,300	1994	Ty Murray	246,170
1957	Jim Shoulders	33,299	1976	Tom Ferguson	87,908	1995	Joe Beaver	141,753
1958	Jim Shoulders	32,212	1977	Tom Ferguson	65,981	1996	Joe Beaver	166,103
1959	Jim Shoulders	32,905	1978	Tom Ferguson	83,734	1997	Dan Mortensen	184,559
			1979	Tom Ferguson	96,272	1998	Ty Murray	264,623
1960	Harry Tompkins	32,522				1999	Fred Whitfield	217,819
1961	Benny Reynolds	31,309	1980	Paul Tierney	105,568			
1962	Tom Nesmith	32,611	1981	Jimmie Cooper	105,861	2000	Joe Beaver	225,396
1963	Dean Oliver	31,329	1982	Chris Lybbert	123,709	2001	Cody Ohl	296,419
1964	Dean Oliver	31,150	1983	Roy Cooper	153,391	2002	Trevor Brazile	273,998
1965	Dean Oliver	33,163	1984	Dee Pickett	122,618			

SOAP BOX DERBY

All-American Soap Box Derby

At the 66th annual Soap Box Derby, 14-year-old Anthony Marulli of Rochester, N.Y., rolled to the Masters title in 28.63 seconds in his tiger-striped car. Chicago native Corey Harkins, gave Illinois its first derby world championship when he raced to a win in the Super Stock division and rookie racer Nicholas Sibeto won with a time of 28.99 in the Stock division.

The All-American Soap Box Derby is a coasting race for small gravity-powered cars built by their drivers and assembled within strict guidelines on size, weight and cost. The Derby was started by Dayton, Ohio newsman Myron Scott after he witnessed several boys racing handmade carts down a hill while on a photographic assignment in 1933. Scott decided to start an organized race for kids and the first All-American Soap Box Derby was held in Dayton in 1934. The race got its name because early on most cars were built from wooden soap boxes. The following year, the race was moved to Akron because of its central location and hilly terrain. In 1936, town leaders saw the need for a permanent site for the growing event and with the help of the Works Progress Administration, Derby Downs was constructed.

Held every summer at Derby Downs in Akron, Ohio, the Soap Box Derby is open to all boys and girls from 8 to 17 years old who qualify. There are three competitive divisions: 1. Stock (ages 8-17)— made up of generic, prefab racers that come from Derby-approved kits, can be assembled in four hours and don't exceed 200 pounds when driver, car and wheels are weighed together; 2. Super Stock (ages 10-17)— the same as Stock only with a weight limit of 220 pounds; 3. Masters (ages 11-17)— made up of racers designed by the drivers, but constructed with Derby-approved hardware. The racing ramp at Derby Downs is 989 feet, four inches with an 11 percent grade.

One champion reigned at the All-American Soap Box Derby each year from 1934-75; Junior and Senior division champions from 1976-87; Kit and Masters champions from 1988-91; Stock, Kit and Masters champions from 1992-94; Stock, Super Stock and Masters champions starting in 1995.

Year		Hometown	Age	Year		Hometown	Age
1934	Robert Turner	Muncie, IN	11	1938	Robert Berger	Omaha, NE	14
1935	Maurice Bale Jr.	Anderson, IN	13	1939	Clifton Hardesty	White Plains, NY	11
1936	Herbert Muench Jr.	St. Louis	14	1940	Thomas Fisher	Detroit	12
1937	Robert Ballard	White Plains, NY	12	1941	Claude Smith	Akron, OH	14

Year	Hometown	Age	Year	Hometown	Age
1942-45 Not held			1985 JR: Michael Gallo	Danbury, CT	12
1946 Gilbert Klecan	San Diego	14	SR: Matt Sheffer	York, PA	14
1947 Kenneth Holmboe	Charleston, WV	14	1986 JR: Marc Behan	Dover, NH	9
1948 Donald Strub	Akron, OH	13	SR: Tami Jo Sullivan	Lancaster, OH	13
1949 Fred Derks	Akron, OH	15	1987 JR: Matt Margules	Danbury, CT	11
1950 Harold Williamson	Charleston, WV	14	SR: Brian Drinkwater	Bristol, CT	14
1951 Darwin Cooper	Williamsport, PA	15	1988 KIT: Jason Lamb	Des Moines, IA	10
1952 Joe Lunn	Columbus, GA	11	MAS: David Duffield	Kansas City	13
1953 Fred Mohler	Muncie, IN	14	1989 KIT: David Schiller	Dayton, OH	12
1954 Richard Kemp	Los Angeles	14	MAS: Faith Chavarria	Ventura, CA	12
1955 Richard Rohrer	Rochester, NY	14	1990 MAS: Sami Jones	Salem, OR	13
1956 Norman Westfall	Rochester, NY	14	KIT: Mark Mihal	Valparaiso, IN	12
1957 Terry Townsend	Anderson, IN	14	1991 MAS: Danny Garland	San Diego, CA	14
1958 James Miley	Muncie, IN	15	KIT: Paul Greenwald	Saginaw, MI	13
1959 Barney Townsend	Anderson, IN	13	1992 MAS: Bonnie Thornton	Redding, CA	14
1960 Fredric Lake	South Bend, IN	11	KIT: Carolyn Fox	Sublimity, OR	11
1961 Dick Dawson	Wichita, KS	13	STK: Loren Hurst	Hudson, OH	10
1962 David Mann	Gary, IN	14	1993 MAS: Dean Lutton	Delta, OH	14
1963 Harold Conrad	Duluth, MN	12	KIT: D.M. Del Ferraro	Stow, OH	12
1964 Gregory Schumacher	Tacoma, WA	14	STK: Owen Yuda	Boiling Springs, PA	10
1965 Robert Logan	Santa Ana, CA	12	1994 MAS: D.M. Del Ferraro	Akron, OH	13
1966 David Krussow	Tacoma, WA	12	KIT: Joel Endres	Akron, OH	14
1967 Kenneth Cline	Lincoln, NE	13	STK: Kristina Damond	Jamestown, NY	13
1968 Branch Lew	Muncie, IN	11	1995 MAS: J. Fensterbush	Kingman, AZ	11
1969 Steve Souter	Midland, TX	12	SS: Darcie Davisson	Kingman, AZ	11
1970 Samuel Gupton	Durham, NC	13	STK: Karen Thomas	Jamestown, NY	11
1971 Larry Blair	Oroville, CA	13	1996 MAS: Tim Scrofano	Conneaut, OH	12
1972 Robert Lange Jr.	Boulder, CO	14	SS: Jeremy Phillips	Charlestown, WV	14
1973 Bret Yarborough	Elk Grove, CA	11	STK: Matt Perez	No. Canton, OH	12
1974 Curt Yarborough	Elk Grove, CA	11	1997 MAS: Wade Wallace	Elk Hart, IN	11
1975 Karren Stead	Lower Bucks, PA	11	SS: Dolline Vance	Salem, OR	13
1976 JR: Phil Raber	Sugarcreek, OH	11	STK: Mark Stephens	Waynesboro, VA	13
SR: Joan Ferdinand	Canton, OH	14	1998 MAS: James Marsh	Cleveland, OH	12
1977 JR: Mark Ferdinand	Canton, OH	10	SS: Stacy Sharp	Kingman, AZ	14
SR: Steve Washburn	Bristol, CT	15	STK: Hailey Simpson	Salem, OR	10
1978 JR: Darren Hart	Salem, OR	11	1999 MAS: Allan Endres	Barberton, OH	14
SR: Greg Cardinal	Flint, MI	13	SS: Alisha Ebner	Salem, OR	15
1979 JR: Russell Yurk	Flint, MI	10	STK: Justin Pillow	Deland, FL	12
SR: Craig Kitchen	Akron, OH	14	2000 MAS: Cody Butler	Anderson, IN	12
1980 JR: Chris Fulton	Indianapolis	11	SS: Derek Etherington	Anderson, IN	11
SR: Dan Porul	Sherman Oaks, CA	12	STK: Rachel Curran	Medina, OH	12
1981 JR: Howie Fraley	Portsmouth, OH	11	2001 MAS: Michael Flynn	Harrison Township, MI	12
SR: Tonia Schlegel	Hamilton, OH	13	SS: James Rogers	Hilton, NY	15
1982 JR: Carol A. Sullivan	Rochester, NH	10	STK: Chad Eyerly	Altaloma, CA	11
SR: Matt Wolfgang	Lehigh Val., PA	12	2002 MAS: Evan Griffin	Winter Park, FL	15
1983 JR: Tony Carlini	Del Mar, CA	10	SS: Roger Youmans Jr.	Spencerport, NY	13
SR: Mike Burdgick	Flint, MI	14	STK: C. Vannatta	Anderson, IN	12
1984 JR: Chris Hess	Hamilton, OH	11	2003 MAS: Anthony Marulli	Rochester, NY	14
SR: Anita Jackson	St. Louis	15	SS: Corey Harkins	Chicago	14
			STK: Nicholas Sibeto	New Castle, PA	12

SOFTBALL

Men's and women's national champions since 1933 in Major Fast Pitch, Major Slow Pitch and Super Slow Pitch (men only). Sanctioned by the Amateur Softball Association of America.

MEN
Major Fast Pitch

Multiple winners: Clearwater Bombers (10); Raybestos Cardinals (5); Sealmasters (4); Briggs Beautyware, Decatur Pride, Pay'n Pak and Zollner Pistons (3); Billard Barbell, Frontier Players Casino, Hammer Air Field, Kodak Park, Meierhoffer, National Health Care, Penn Corp and Peterbilt Western (2).

Year	Year	Year
1933 J.L. Gill Boosters, Chicago	1943 Hammer Air Field, Fresno, CA	1953 Briggs Beautyware
1934 Ke-Nash-A, Kenosha, WI	1944 Hammer Air Field	1954 Clearwater Bombers
1935 Crimson Coaches, Toledo, OH	1945 Zollner Pistons, Ft. Wayne, IN	1955 Raybestos Cardinals,
1936 Kodak Park, Rochester, NY	1946 Zollner Pistons	1956 Clearwater Bombers
1937 Briggs Body Team, Detroit	1947 Zollner Pistons	1957 Clearwater Bombers
1938 The Pohlers, Cincinnati	1948 Briggs Beautyware, Detroit	1958 Raybestos Cardinals
1939 Carr's Boosters, Covington, KY	1949 Tip Top Tailors, Toronto	1959 Sealmasters, Aurora, IL
1940 Kodak Park	1950 Clearwater (FL) Bombers	1960 Clearwater Bombers
1941 Bendix Brakes, South Bend, IN	1951 Dow Chemical, Midland, MI	1961 Sealmasters
1942 Deep Rock Oilers, Tulsa, OK	1952 Briggs Beautyware	1962 Clearwater Bombers

Softball (Cont.)

Year		Year		Year	
1963	Clearwater Bombers	1980	Peterbilt Western, Seattle	1994	Decatur (IL) Pride
1964	Burch Tool, Detroit	1981	Archer Daniels Midland, Decatur, IL	1995	Decatur Pride
1965	Sealmasters			1996	Green Bay All-Car, Green Bay, WI
1966	Clearwater Bombers	1982	Peterbilt Western		
1967	Sealmasters	1983	Franklin Cardinals, Stratford, CA	1997	Tampa Bay Smokers, Tampa Bay, FL
1968	Clearwater Bombers				
1969	Raybestos Cardinals	1984	California Kings, Merced, CA	1998	Meierhoffer-Fleeman, St. Joseph, MO
		1985	Pay'n Pak, Seattle		
1970	Raybestos Cardinals	1986	Pay'n Pak	1999	Decatur Pride
1971	Welty Way, Cedar Rapids, IA	1987	Pay'n Pak		
1972	Raybestos Cardinals	1988	TransAire, Elkhart, IN	2000	Meierhoffer
1973	Clearwater Bombers	1989	Penn Corp, Sioux City, IA	2001	Frontier Players Casino, St. Joseph, MO
1974	Gianella Bros., Santa Rosa, CA				
1975	Rising Sun Hotel, Reading, PA	1990	Penn Corp	2002	Frontier Players Casino
1976	Raybestos Cardinals	1991	Gianella Bros., Rohnert Park, CA	2003	Farm Tavern, Madison, WI
1977	Billard Barbell, Reading, PA				
1978	Billard Barbell	1992	National Health Care, Sioux City, IA		
1979	McArdle Pontiac/Cadillac, Midland, MI	1993	National Health Care		

Super Slow Pitch

Multiple winners: Ritch's/Superior (4); Howard's/Western Steer and Steele's Sports (3); Lighthouse/Worth and Long Haul (2).

Year		Year		Year	
1981	Howard's/Western Steer, Denver, NC	1989	Ritch's Salvage, Harrisburg, NC	1996	Ritch's/Superior
		1990	Steele's Silver Bullets	1997	Ritch's/Superior
1982	Jerry's Catering, Miami	1991	Sun Belt/Worth, Atlanta	1998	Lighthouse/Worth
1983	Howard's/Western Steer	1992	Ritch's/Superior, Windsor Locks, CT	1999	Team Easton, California
1984	Howard's/Western Steer			2000	Team TPS, Louisville, KY
1985	Steele's Sports, Grafton, OH	1993	Ritch's/Superior	2001	Long Haul, Albertville, MN
1986	Steele's Sports	1994	Bellcorp., Tampa	2002	Long Haul
1987	Steele's Sports	1995	Lighthouse/Worth, Stone Mt., GA		
1988	Starpath, Monticello, KY				

Major Slow Pitch

Multiple winners: Gatliff Auto Sales, Riverside Paving and Skip Hogan A.C. (3); Campbell Carpets, Hamilton Tailoring, Howard's Furniture, Long Haul TPS and New Construction (2).

Year		Year		Year	
1953	Shields Construction, Newport, KY	1972	Jiffy Club, Louisville, KY	1990	New Construction, Shelbyville, IN
1954	Waldneck's Tavern, Cincinnati	1973	Howard's Furniture, Denver, NC	1991	Riverside Paving, Louisville
1955	Lang Pet Shop, Covington, KY	1974	Howard's Furniture	1992	Vernon's, Jacksonville, FL
1956	Gatliff Auto Sales, Newport, KY	1975	Pyramid Cafe, Lakewood, OH	1993	Back Porch/Destin (FL) Roofing
1957	Gatliff Auto Sales	1976	Warren Motors, J'ville, FL	1994	Riverside Paving, Louisville
1958	East Side Sports, Detroit	1977	Nelson Painting, Okla. City	1995	Riverside Paving
1959	Yorkshire Restaurant, Newport, KY	1978	Campbell Carpets, Concord, CA	1996	Bell II, Orlando, FL
1960	Hamilton Tailoring, Cincinnati	1979	Nelco Mfg. Co., Okla. City	1997	Long Haul TPS, Albertville, MN
1961	Hamilton Tailoring	1980	Campbell Carpets	1998	Chase Mortgage/Easton, Wilmington, NC
1962	Skip Hogan A.C., Pittsburgh	1981	Elite Coating, Gordon, CA		
1963	Gatliff Auto Sales	1982	Triangle Sports, Minneapolis	1999	Gasoline Heaven/Worth, Commack, NY
1964	Skip Hogan A.C.	1983	No.1 Electric & Heating, Gastonia, NC		
1965	Skip Hogan A.C.			2000	Long Haul TPS
1966	Michael's Lounge, Detroit	1984	Lilly Air Systems, Chicago	2001	New Construction
1967	Jim's Sport Shop, Pittsburgh	1985	Blanton's Fayetteville, NC	2002	Twin States/Worth, Montgomery, AL
1968	County Sports, Levittown, NY	1986	Non-Ferrous Metals, Cleveland		
1969	Copper Hearth, Milwaukee	1987	Stapath, Monticello, KY	2003	New Construction/B&J/Snap-On, Metamora, IL
1970	Little Caesar's, Southgate, MI	1988	Bell Corp/FAF, Tampa, FL		
1971	Pile Drivers, Va. Beach, VA	1989	Ritch's Salvage, Harrisburg, NC		

WOMEN
Major Fast Pitch

Multiple winners: Raybestos/Stratford Brakettes (23); Orange Lionettes (9); Jax Maids (5); California Commotion (4); Arizona Ramblers and Redding Rebels (3); Hi-Ho Brakettes, J.J. Krieg's, National Screw & Manufacturing and Phoenix Storm (2).

Year	Year	Year
1933 Great Northerns, Chicago	1958 Raybestos Brakettes, Stratford, CT	1983 Raybestos Brakettes
1934 Hart Motors, Chicago		1984 Los Angeles Diamonds
1935 Bloomer Girls, Cleveland	1959 Raybestos Brakettes	1985 Hi-Ho Brakettes, Stratford, CT
1936 Nat'l Screw & Mfg., Cleveland	1960 Raybestos Brakettes	1986 So. California Invasion
1937 Nat'l Screw & Mfg.	1961 Gold Sox, Whittier, CA	1987 Orange County Majestics, Anaheim, CA
1938 J.J. Krieg's, Alameda, CA	1962 Orange Lionettes	
1939 J.J. Krieg's	1963 Raybestos Brakettes	1988 Hi-Ho Brakettes
1940 Arizona Ramblers, Phoenix	1964 Erv Lind Florists, Portland, OR	1989 Whittier (CA) Raiders
1941 Higgins Midgets, Tulsa, OK	1965 Orange Lionettes	1990 Raybestos Brakettes
1942 Jax Maids, New Orleans	1966 Raybestos Brakettes	1991 Raybestos Brakettes
1943 Jax Maids	1967 Raybestos Brakettes	1992 Raybestos Brakettes
1944 Lind & Pomeroy, Portland, OR	1968 Raybestos Brakettes	1993 Redding (CA) Rebels
1945 Jax Maids	1969 Orange Lionettes	1994 Redding Rebels
1946 Jax Maids	1970 Orange Lionettes	1995 Redding Rebels
1947 Jax Maids	1971 Raybestos Brakettes	1996 California Commotion, Woodland Hills
1948 Arizona Ramblers	1972 Raybestos Brakettes	
1949 Arizona Ramblers	1973 Raybestos Brakettes	1997 California Commotion
1950 Orange (CA) Lionettes	1974 Raybestos Brakettes	1998 California Commotion
1951 Orange Lionettes	1975 Raybestos Brakettes	1999 California Commotion
1952 Orange Lionettes	1976 Raybestos Brakettes	2000 Phoenix Storm, Phoenix, AZ
1953 Betsy Ross Rockets, Fresno, CA	1977 Raybestos Brakettes	2001 Phoenix Storm
1954 Leach Motor Rockets, Fresno, CA	1978 Raybestos Brakettes	2002 Stratford Brakettes, Stratford, CT
1955 Orange Lionettes	1979 Sun City (AZ) Saints	2003 Stratford Brakettes
1956 Orange Lionettes	1980 Raybestos Brakettes	
1957 Hacienda Rockets, Fresno, CA	1981 Orlando (FL) Rebels	
	1982 Raybestos Brakettes	

Major Slow Pitch

Multiple winners: Spooks (5); Dana Gardens (4); Universal Plastics (3); Cannan's Illusions, Bob Hoffman's Dots, Key Ford Mustangs and Marks Brothers Dots (2).

Year	Year	Year
1959 Pearl Laundry, Richmond, VA	1975 Marks Brothers Dots	1988 Spooks
	1976 Sorrento's Pizza, Cincinnati	1989 Cannan's Illusions, Houston
1960 Carolina Rockets, High Pt., NC	1977 Fox Valley Lassies, St. Charles, IL	
1961 Dairy Cottage, Covington, KY		1990 Spooks
1962 Dana Gardens, Cincinnati	1978 Bob Hoffman's Dots, Miami	1991 Cannan's Illusions, San Antonio
1963 Dana Gardens	1979 Bob Hoffman's Dots	1992 Universal Plastics, Cookeville, TN
1964 Dana Gardens		1993 Universal Plastics
1965 Art's Acres, Omaha, NE	1980 Howard's Rubi-Otts, Graham, NC	1994 Universal Plastics
1966 Dana Gardens		1995 Armed Forces, Sacramento
1967 Ridge Maintenance, Cleveland	1981 Tifton (GA) Tomboys	1996 Spooks
1968 Escue Pontiac, Cincinnati	1982 Richmond (VA) Stompers	1997 Taylor's, Glendale, MD
1969 Converse Dots, Hialeah, FL	1983 Spooks, Anoka, MN	1998 Not held
	1984 Spooks	1999 Lakerettes, Conneaut Lake, PA
1970 Rutenschruder Floral, Cincinnati	1985 Key Ford Mustangs, Pensacola, FL	
1971 Gators, Ft. Lauderdale, FL		2000 Premier Sports, Pittsboro, NC
1972 Riverside Ford, Cincinnati	1986 Sur-Way Tomboys, Tifton, GA	2001 Shooters/Nike, Orlando, FL
1973 Sweeney Chevrolet, Cincinnati	1987 Key Ford Mustangs	2002 Diamond Queens, Nashville, TN
1974 Marks Brothers Dots, Miami		2003 Not held

TRIATHLON
World Championship

Contested since 1989, the Triathlon World Championship consists of a 1.5-kilometer swim, a 40-kilometer bike ride and a 10-kilometer run. The 2003 championship was scheduled for Dec. 7 in Queenstown, New Zealand.

Multiple winners: MEN—Simon Lessing (4); Spencer Smith (2). WOMEN—Emma Carney, Michellie Jones and Karen Smyers (2).

MEN

Year		Time	Year		Time
1989	Mark Allen, United States	1:58:46	1996	Simon Lessing, Great Britain	1:39:50
1990	Greg Welch, Australia	1:51:37	1997	Chris McCormack, Australia	1:48:29
1991	Miles Stewart, Australia	1:48:20	1998	Simon Lessing, Great Britain	1:55:31
1992	Simon Lessing, Great Britain	1:49:04	1999	Dimitry Gaag, Kazakhstan	1:45:25
1993	Spencer Smith, Great Britain	1:51:20	2000	Oliver Marceau, France	1:51:41
1994	Spencer Smith, Great Britain	1:51:04	2001	Peter Robertson, Australia	1:48:01
1995	Simon Lessing, Great Britain	1:48:29	2002	Iván Raña, Spain	1:50:41

WOMEN

Year	Time	Year	Time
1989 Erin Baker, New Zealand	2:10:01	1996 Jackie Gallagher, Australia	1:50:52
1990 Karen Smyers, United States	2:03:33	1997 Emma Carney, Australia	1:59:22
1991 Joanne Ritchie, Canada	2:02:04	1998 Joanne King, Australia	2:07:25
1992 Michellie Jones, Australia	2:02:08	1999 Loretta Harrop, Australia	1:55:28
1993 Michellie Jones, Australia	2:07:41	2000 Nicole Hackett, Australia	1:54:43
1994 Emma Carney, Australia	2:03:19	2001 Siri Lindley, United States	1:58:51
1995 Karen Smyers, USA	2:04:58	2002 Leanda Cave, Wales	2:01:31

Ironman Championship

Contested in Hawaii since 1978, the Ironman Triathlon Championship consists of a 2.4-mile swim, a 112-mile bike ride and 26.2-mile run. The race begins at 7 A.M. and continues all day until the course is closed at midnight.

MEN

Multiple winners: Mark Allen and Dave Scott (6); Peter Reid (3); Tim DeBoom, Luc Van Lierde and Scott Tinley (2).

Year	Date	Winner	Time	Runner-up	Margin	Start	Finish	Location
I	2/18/78	Gordon Haller	11:46	John Dunbar	34:00	15	12	Waikiki Beach
II	1/14/79	Tom Warren	11:15:56	John Dunbar	48:00	15	12	Waikiki Beach
III	1/10/80	Dave Scott	9:24:33	Chuck Neumann	1:08	108	95	Ala Moana Park
IV	2/14/81	John Howard	9:38:29	Tom Warren	26:00	326	299	Kailua-Kona
V	2/6/82	Scott Tinley	9:19:41	Dave Scott	17:16	580	541	Kailua-Kona
VI	10/9/82	Dave Scott	9:08:23	Scott Tinley	20:05	850	775	Kailua-Kona
VII	10/22/83	Dave Scott	9:05:57	Scott Tinley	0:33	964	835	Kailua-Kona
VIII	10/6/84	Dave Scott	8:54:20	Scott Tinley	24:25	1036	903	Kailua-Kona
IX	10/25/85	Scott Tinley	8:50:54	Chris Hinshaw	25:46	1018	965	Kailua-Kona
X	10/18/86	Dave Scott	8:28:37	Mark Allen	9:47	1039	951	Kailua-Kona
XI	10/10/87	Dave Scott	8:34:13	Mark Allen	11:06	1380	1284	Kailua-Kona
XII	10/22/88	Scott Molina	8:31:00	Mike Pigg	2:11	1277	1189	Kailua-Kona
XIII	10/15/89	Mark Allen	8:09:15	Dave Scott	0:58	1285	1231	Kailua-Kona
XIV	10/6/90	Mark Allen	8:28:17	Scott Tinley	9:23	1386	1255	Kailua-Kona
XV	10/19/91	Mark Allen	8:18:32	Greg Welch	6:01	1386	1235	Kailua-Kona
XVI	10/10/92	Mark Allen	8:09:08	Cristian Bustos	7:21	1364	1298	Kailua-Kona
XVII	10/30/93	Mark Allen	8:07:45	Paulli Kiuru	6:37	1438	1353	Kailua-Kona
XVIII	10/15/94	Greg Welch	8:20:27	Dave Scott	4:05	1405	1290	Kailua-Kona
XIX	10/7/95	Mark Allen	8:20:34	Thomas Hellriegel	2:25	1487	1323	Kailua-Kona
XX	10/26/96	Luc Van Lierde	8:04:08	Thomas Hellriegel	1:59	1420	1288	Kailua-Kona
XXI	10/18/97	Thomas Hellriegel	8:33:01	Jurgen Zack	6:17	1534	1365	Kailua-Kona
XXII	10/3/98	Peter Reid	8:24:20	Luc Van Lierde	7:37	1487	1379	Kailua-Kona
XXIII	10/23/99	Luc Van Lierde	8:17:17	Peter Reid	5:37	1471	1419	Kailua-Kona
XXIV	10/14/00	Peter Reid	8:21:01	Tim DeBoom	2:09	1525	1426	Kailua-Kona
XXV	10/6/01	Tim DeBoom	8:31:18	Cameron Brown	14:52	1558	1364	Kailua-Kona
XXVI	10/19/02	Tim DeBoom	8:29:56	Peter Reid	3:10	1540	1457	Kailua-Kona
XXVII	10/18/03	Peter Reid	8:22:35	Rutger Beke	5:51	1647	1569	Kailua-Kona

WOMEN

Multiple winners: Paula Newby-Fraser (8); Natascha Badmann (4); Erin Baker, Lori Bowden and Sylviane Puntous (2).

Year	Winner	Time	Runner-up	Year	Winner	Time	Runner-up
1978	No finishers			1992	Paula Newby-Fraser	8:55:28	Julie Anne White
1979	Lyn Lemaire	12:55.00	None	1993	Paula Newby-Fraser	8:58:23	Erin Baker
				1994	Paula Newby-Fraser	9:20:14	Karen Smyers
1980	Robin Beck	11:21:24	Eve Anderson	1995	Karen Smyers	9:16:46	Isabelle Mouthon
1981	Linda Sweeney	12:00:32	Sally Edwards	1996	Paula Newby-Fraser	9:06:49	Natascha Badmann
1982	Kathleen McCartney	11:09:40	Julie Moss	1997	Heather Fuhr	9:31:43	Lori Bowden
1982	Julie Leach	10:54:08	Joann Dahlkoet-	1998	Natascha Badmann	9:24:16	Lori Bowden
ter				1999	Lori Bowden	9:13:02	Karen Smyers
1983	Sylviane Puntous	10:43:36	Patricia Puntous				
1984	Sylviane Puntous	10:25:13	Patricia Puntous	2000	Natascha Badmann	9:26:17	Lori Bowden
1985	Joanne Ernst	10:25:22	Liz Bulman	2001	Natascha Badmann	9:28:37	Lori Bowden
1986	Paula Newby-Fraser	9:49:14	Sylviane Puntous	2002	Natascha Badmann	9:07:54	Nina Kraft
1987	Erin Baker	9:35:25	Sylviane Puntous	2003	Lori Bowden	9:11:55	Natascha Badmann
1988	Paula Newby-Fraser	9:01:01	Erin Baker				
1989	Paula Newby-Fraser	9:00:56	Sylviane Puntous				
1990	Erin Baker	9:13:42	P. Newby-Fraser				
1991	Paula Newby-Fraser	9:07:52	Erin Baker				

X GAMES

The ESPN Extreme Games, originally envisioned as a biannual showcase for "alternative" sports, were first held June 24-July 1, 1995 in Newport and Providence, R.I. and Mt. Snow, Vt. The success of the inaugural event prompted organizers to make it an annual competition. Newport would again serve as host for the redubbed X Games in 1996. The X Games has evolved rapidly since its inception and have been held in several cities since. New sports and events have been added while others have been dropped.

Summer X Games sites: 1995-Newport/Providence, R.I. (and Mt. Snow, Vt.); 1996-Newport/Providence, R.I.; 1997-San Diego; 1998-San Diego; 1999-San Francisco; 2000-San Francisco; 2001-Philadelphia; 2002-Philadelphia; 2003-Los Angeles.

Winter X Games sites: 1997-Snow Summit Mountain Resort, Big Bear Lake, Calif.; 1998-Crested Butte, Colo.; 1999-Crested Butte, Colo.; 2000- Mt. Snow, Vt.; 2001-Mt. Snow, Vt.; 2002-Aspen, Colo.; 2003-Aspen, Colo.

Summer X Games
Bicycle Stunt

Year	Vert	Year	Dirt	Year	Street/Stunt Park	Year	Flatland
1995	Matt Hoffman	1995	Jay Miron	1996	Dave Mirra	1997	Trevor Meyer
1996	Matt Hoffman	1996	Joey Garcia	1997	Dave Mirra	1998	Trevor Meyer
1997	Dave Mirra	1997	T.J. Lavin	1998	Dave Mirra	1999	Trevor Meyer
1998	Dave Mirra	1998	Brian Foster	1999	Dave Mirra	2000	Martti Kuoppa
1999	Dave Mirra	1999	T.J. Lavin	2000	Dave Mirra	2001	Martti Kuoppa
2000	Jamie Bestwick	2000	Ryan Nyquist	2001	Bruce Crisman	2002	Martti Kuoppa
2001	Dave Mirra	2001	Stephen Murray	2002	Ryan Nyquist	2003	Simon O'Brien
2002	Dave Mirra	2002	Allan Cooke	2003	Ryan Nyquist		
2003	Jamie Bestwick	2003	Ryan Nyquist			**Year**	**Downhill**
						2001	Brandon Meadows
						2002	Robbie Miranda
						2003	Brandon Meadows

Skateboarding

Year	Vert Singles	Year	Vert Doubles	Year	Street/Park	Year	Women's Park
1995	Tony Hawk	1997	Hawk/Macdonald	1995	Chris Senn	2003	Vanessa Torres
1996	Andy Macdonald	1998	Hawk/Macdonald	1996	Rodil de Araujo Jr.	**Year**	**Vert Best Trick**
1997	Tony Hawk	1999	Hawk/Macdonald	1997	Chris Senn	2000	Bob Burnquist
1998	Andy Macdonald	2000	Hawk/Macdonald	1998	Rodil de Araujo Jr.	2001	Matt Dove
1999	Bucky Lasek	2001	Hawk/Macdonald	1999	Chris Senn	2002	Pierre-Luc Gagnon
2000	Bucky Lasek	2002	Hawk/Macdonald	2000	Eric Koston	2003	Tony Hawk
2001	Bob Burnquist	2003	Lasek/Burnquist	2001	Kerry Getz		
2002	Pierre-Luc Gagnon			2002	Rodil de Araujo Jr.	**Year**	**Street Best Trick**
2003	Bucky Lasek			**Year**	**Street**	2001	Kerry Getz
				2003	Eric Koston	2002	Rodil de Araujo Jr.
				Year	**Park**	2003	Chad Muska
				2003	Ryan Sheckler		

Big-Air Snowboarding

Year	Men
1997	Peter Line
1998	Kevin Jones
1999	Peter Line
2000	Event discontinued

Year	Women
1997	Tina Dixon
1998	Janet Matthews
1999	Barrett Christy
2000	Event discontinued

Moto X

Year	Freestyle
1999	Travis Pastrana
2000	Travis Pastrana
2001	Travis Pastrana
2002	Mike Metzger
2003	Travis Pastrana

Year	Step Up
2001	Tommy Clowers
2002	Tommy Clowers
2003	Matt Buyten

Year	Big Air
2001	Kenny Bartman
2002	Mike Metzger
2003	Brian Deegan

Bungee Jumping

Year	
1995	Doug Anderson
1996	Peter Bihun
1997	Event discontinued

Skysurfing

Year	
1995	Fradet/Zipser
1996	Furrer/Scmid
1997	Hartman/Pappadato
1998	Rozov/Burch
1999	Fradet/Iodice
2000	Klaus/Rogers
2001	Event discontinued

Surfing

Year	
2003	East Coast*

*The X Games surfing event was a competition called The Game. It was contested by teams of surfers from the East Coast and the West Coast.

Street Luge

Year	Dual
1995	Bob Pereyra
1996	Shawn Goular
1997	Biker Sherlock
1998	Biker Sherlock
1999	Dennis Derammelaere
2000	Bob Ozman
2001	Event discontinued

Year	Mass
1995	Shawn Gilbert
1996	Biker Sherlock
1997	Biker Sherlock
1998	Rat Sult
1999	Event discontinued

Year	Super Mass
1997	Biker Sherlock
1998	Rat Sult
1999	David Rogers
2000	Bob Pereyra
2001	Brent DeKeyser
2002	Event discontinued

Year	King of the Hill
2001	Dennis Derammelaere
2002	Event discontinued

Sportclimbing

Year	Men's Difficulty
1995	Ian Vickers
1996	Arnaud Petit
1997	Francois Legrand
1998	Christian Core
1999	Chris Sharma
2000	Event discontinued

Year	Women's Difficulty
1995	Robyn Erbersfield
1996	Katie Brown
1997	Katie Brown
1998	Katie Brown
1999	Stephanie Bodet
2000	Event discontinued

Year	Men's Speed
1995	Hans Florine
1996	Hans Florine
1997	Hans Florine
1998	Vladimir Netsvetaev
1999	Aaron Shamy
2000	Vladimir Zakharov
2001	Maxim Stenkovoy
2002	Maxim Stenkovoy
2003	Event discontinued

Year	Women's Speed
1995	Elena Ovtchinnikova
1996	Cecile Le Flem
1997	Elena Ovtchinnikova
1998	Elena Ovtchinnikova
1999	Renata Piszczek
2000	Etti Hendrawati
2001	Elena Repko
2002	Tori Allen
2003	Event discontinued

CrossOver

Year	
1997	Brian Patch
1998	Event discontinued

Skiboarding

Year	
1998	Mike Nick
1999	Chris Hawks
2000	Neal Lyons
2001	Event discontinued

Skiing

Year	Men's Big Air
1999	J.F. Cusson
2000	Candide Thovex
2001	Tanner Hall
2002	Not held

Year	Men's Skier X
1998	Dennis Rey
1999	Enak Gavaggio
2000	Shaun Palmer
2001	Zach Crist
2002	Reggie Crist
2003	Lars Lewen

Year	Women's Skier X
1999	Aleisha Cline
2000	Anik Demers
2001	Aleisha Cline
2002	Aleisha Cline
2003	Aleisha Cline

Year	SuperPipe
2002	Jon Olsson
2003	Candide Thovex

Year	Men's Slopestyle
2002	Tanner Hall

X-Venture Race

Year	
1995	Team Threadbo*
1996	Team Kobeer
1997	Team Presidio
1998	Event discontinued

*In 1995, Team Threadbo won the Eco-Challenge which was held in conjunction with the ESPN Extreme Games.

In-Line Skating

Year	Men's Vert
1995	Tom Fry
1996	Rene Hulgreen
1997	Tim Ward
1998	Cesar Mora
1999	Eito Yasutoko
2000	Eito Yasutoko
2001	Taig Khris
2002	Event discontinued

Year	Women's Vert
1995	Tash Hodgeson
1996	Fabiola da Silva
1997	Fabiola da Silva
1998	Fabiola da Silva
1999	Ayumi Kawasaki
2000	Fabiola da Silva
2001	Fabiola da Silva
2002	Event discontinued

Year	Combined Vert
2002	Takeshi Yasutoko
2003	Eito Yasutoko

Note: In 2002 the men's and women's vert events were combined.

Year	Men's Park
1995	Matt Salerno
1996	Arlo Eisenberg
1997	Arron Feinberg
1998	Jonathan Bergeron
1999	Nicky Adams
2000	Sven Boekhorst
2001	Jaren Grob
2002	Jaren Grob
2003	Bruno Lowe

Year	Women's Park
1997	Sayaka Yabe
1998	Jenny Curry
1999	Sayaka Yabe
2000	Fabiola da Silva
2001	Martina Svobodova
2002	Martina Svobodova
2003	Fabiola da Silva

Year	Vert Triples
1998	Malina/Fogarty/Popa
1999	Khris/Bujanda/Boekhorst
2000	Event discontinued

Year	Men's Downhill
1995	Derek Downing
1996	Dante Muse
1997	Derek Downing
1998	Patrick Naylor
1999	Event discontinued

Year	Women's Downhill
1995	Julie Brandt
1996	Gypsy Tidwell
1997	Gypsy Tidwell
1998	Julie Brandt
1999	Event discontinued

Winter X Games

Ice Climbing

Year	Men's Difficulty
1997	Jaren Ogden
1998	Will Gadd
1999	Will Gadd
2000	Event discontinued

Year	Women's Difficulty
1997	Bird Lew
1998	Kim Csizmazia
1999	Kim Csizmazia
2000	Event discontinued

Year	Men's Speed
1997	Jared Ogden
1998	Will Gadd
1999	Event discontinued

Year	Women's Speed
1997	Bird Lew
1998	Kim Csizmazia
1999	Event discontinued

Snowboarding

Year	Men's Big Air
1997	Jimmy Halopoff
1998	Jason Borgstede
1999	Kevin Sansalone
2000	Peter Line
2001	Jussi Oksanen
2002	Event discontinued

Year	Women's Big Air
1997	Barrett Christy
1998	Tina Basich
1999	Barrett Christy
2000	Tara Dakides
2001	Tara Dakides
2002	Event discontinued

Watersports

Year	Barefoot Waterski Jumping
1995	Justin Seers
1996	Ron Scarpa
1997	Peter Fleck
1998	Peter Fleck
1999	Event discontinued

Year	Men's Wakeboarding
1996	Parks Bonifay
1997	Jeremy Kovak
1998	Darin Shapiro
1999	Parks Bonifay
2000	Darin Shapiro
2001	Danny Harf
2002	Danny Harf
2003	Danny Harf

Year	Women's Wakeboarding
1997	Tara Hamilton
1998	Andrea Gaytan
1999	Meaghan Major
2000	Tara Hamilton
2001	Dallas Friday
2002	Emily Copeland
2003	Dallas Friday

Year	Men's Boarder X
1997	Shaun Palmer
1998	Shaun Palmer
1999	Shaun Palmer
2000	Drew Neilson
2001	Scott Gaffney
2002	Philippe Conte
2003	Ueli Kestenholz

Year	Women's Boarder X
1997	Jennie Waara
1998	Tina Dixon
1999	Maelle Ricker
2000	Leslee Olson
2001	Line Oestvold
2002	Ine Poetzl
2003	Lindsey Jacobellis

Year	Men's Halfpipe
1997	Todd Richards
1998	Ross Powers
1999	Jimi Scott
2000	Todd Richards
2001	Event discontinued

Year	Women's Halfpipe
1997	Shannon Dunn
1998	Cara-Beth Burnside
1999	Michele Taggart
2000	S. Brun Kjeldaas
2001	Event discontinued

Year	Men's Superpipe
2001	Dan Kass
2002	J.J. Thomas
2003	Shaun White

Winter X Games (Cont.)

Snowboarding (cont.)

Year	Women's Slopestyle
2001	Shannon Dunn
2002	Kelly Clark
2003	Gretchen Bleiler

Year	Men's Slopestyle
1997	Daniel Franck
1998	Ross Powers
1999	Peter Line
2000	Kevin Jones
2001	Kevin Jones
2002	Travis Rice
2003	Shaun White

Year	Women's Slopestyle
1997	Barrett Christy
1998	Jennie Waara
1999	Tara Dakides
2000	Tara Dakides
2001	Jaime MacLeod
2002	Tara Dakide
2003	Janna Meyen

Super-modified Shovel Racing

Year	
1997	Don Adkins
1998	Event discontinued

Snow Mountain Bike Racing

Year	Men's Downhill
1997	Shaun Palmer
1998	Andrew Shandro
1999	Event discontinued

Year	Women's Downhill
1997	Missy Giove
1998	Marla Streb
1999	Event discontinued

Year	Men's Speed
1997	Phil Tintsman
1998	Jurgen Beneke
1999	Event discontinued

Year	Women's Speed
1997	Cheri Elliott
1998	Elke Brutsaert
1999	Event discontinued

Year	Men's Biker X
1999	Steve Peat
2000	Myles Rockwell
2001	Not held

Year	Women's Biker X
1999	Tara Llanes
2000	Katrina Miller
2001	Not held

Snomobiling

Year	Snocross
1998	Toni Haikonen
1999	Chris Vincent
2000	Tucker Hibbert
2001	Blair Morgan
2002	Blair Morgan

Year	Hillcross
2001	Carl Kuster
2002	Carl Kuster
2003	T.J. Kullas

Ultracross

Year	
2000	McLain/Lind
2001	Palmer/Takizawa
2002	Wescott/Lind
2003	Delerue/Zackrisson

Moto X

Year	Big Air
2001	Mike Jones
2002	Brian Deegan
2003	Mike Metzger

2003 Great Outdoors Games

Held July 19-22 in Reno-Tahoe, Nev. Winners of each event listed below. Repeat winners in ALL CAPS.

Fishing

Flyfishing, Fish Length: Lance Egan, Sandy, Utah (11-inch trout).

Flyfishing, Flycasting: Mike McFarland, Tyrone, Penn.

Bass Fishing: Shaw Grigsby, Gainsville, Fla. & Gary Klein, Weatherford, Tex.

Target Sports

Rifle: Doug Koenig, Albertis, Pa.

Shotgun: Scott Robertson, Flower Mound, Tex.

Archery: Darren Collins, Galena, Kan.

Sporting Dogs

(owners/handlers listed first)

Retriever Trials: Chris Akin & Boomer (male Black Labrador), Jonesboro, Ark.

Big Air: Terry Casey & Skeeter (female Black Labrador), Parker, Texas.

Superweave (large dogs): Ken Fairchild & Echo (female border collie), N. Sandwich, N.H.

Superweave (small dogs): Jean LaValley & Taz (female Shetland Sheepdog), Murfreesboro, Tenn.

Agility (large dogs): Sherry kluever & Ransom (female border collie), N. Hollywood, Calif.

Agility (small dogs): Christine Frank & Kimie (female schnauzer), Chesterfield Township, Mich.

Timber Events

Women's Endurance: Peg Engasser, Cortland, N.Y.

Men's Endurance: Jason Wynyard, Auckland, New Zealand.

Hot Saw: MIKE SULLIVAN, Winstead, Conn.

Springboard: Dave Bolstad, Taurmarunui, New Zealand.

Men's Boom Run: JAMIE FISCHER, Stillwater, Minn.

Women's Boom Run: Abbie Hoeschler, La Crosse, Wis.

Mixed Doubles Boom Run: Tanya Fischer, Hudson, Wisc. & JAMIE FISCHER, Stillwater, Minn.

Men's Log Rolling: Jamie Fischer, Stillwater, Minn.

Women's Log Rolling: TINA BOSWORTH, Lake Geneva, Wis.

Speed Climbing: BRIAN BARTOW, Grants Pass, Ore.

Tree Topping: Greg Hart, Maple Ridge, British Columbia.

Team Relay: Team Wynyard (Karmyn Wynyard, Massey, Aukland, NZE; Bryan Schulz, Silverdale, Wash.; Ed Smith, Eatonville, Wash.; Justin Beckett, New South Wales, AUS; Steve Rowe, Tasmania, AUS)

YACHTING

The America's Cup

International yacht racing was launched in 1851 when England's Royal Yacht Squadron staged a 60-mile regatta around the Isle of Wight and offered a silver trophy to the winner. The 101-foot schooner *America*, sent over by the New York Yacht Club, won the race and the prize. Originally called the Hundred-Guinea Cup, the trophy was renamed The America's Cup after the winning boat's owners deeded it to the NYYC with instructions to defend it whenever challenged.

From 1870-1980, the NYYC successfully defended the Cup 25 straight times; first in large schooners and J-class boats that measured up to 140 feet in overall length, then in 12-meter boats. A foreign yacht finally won the Cup in 1983 when *Australia II* beat defender *Liberty* in the seventh and deciding race off Newport, R.I. Four years later, the San Diego Yacht Club's *Stars & Stripes* won the Cup back, sweeping the four races of the final series off Fremantle, Australia.

Then in 1988, New Zealand's Mercury Bay Boating Club, unwilling to wait the usual three- to four-year period between Cup defenses, challenged the SDYC to a match race, citing the Cup's 102-year-old Deed of Gift, which clearly stated that every challenge had to be honored. Mercury Bay announced it would race a 133-foot monohull. San Diego countered with a 60-foot catamaran. The resulting best-of-three series (Sept. 7-8) was a mismatch as the SDYC's catamaran *Stars & Stripes* won two straight by margins of better than 18 and 21 minutes. Mercury Bay syndicate leader Michael Fay protested the outcome and took the SDYC to court in New York State (where the Deed of Gift was first filed) claiming San Diego had violated the spirit of the deed by racing a catamaran instead of a monohull. N.Y. State Supreme Court judge Carmen Ciparick agreed and on March 28, 1989, ordered the SDYC to hand the Cup over to Mercury Bay. The SDYC refused, but did consent to the court's appointment of the New York Yacht Club as custodian of the Cup until an appeal was ruled on.

On Sept. 19, 1989, the Appellate Division of the N.Y. Supreme Court overturned Ciparick's decision and awarded the Cup back to the SDYC. An appeal by Mercury Bay was denied by the N.Y. Court of Appeals on April 26, 1990, ending three years of legal wrangling. To avoid the chaos of 1988-90, a new class of boat—75-foot monohulls with 110-foot masts—has been used by all competing countries since 1992. Note that (*) indicates skipper was also owner of the boat.

The America's Cup moved to Europe for the first time when the Swiss Alinghi Team beat Team New Zealand, 5-0, in the best-of-nine series in February and March 2003. The dates and location of the next America's Cup races are to be determined.

Schooners And J-Class Boats

Year	Winner	Skipper	Series	Loser	Skipper
1851	America	Richard Brown	—	—	—
1870	Magic	Andrew Comstock	1-0	Cambria, GBR	J. Tannock
1871	Columbia (2-1)	Nelson Comstock	4-0	Livonia, GBR	J.R. Woods
	& Sappho (2-0)	Sam Greenwood			
1876	Madeleine	Josephus Williams	2-0	Countess of Dufferin, CAN	J.E. Ellsworth
1881	Mischief	Nathanael Clock	2-0	Atalanta, CAN	Alexander Cuthbert*
1885	Puritan	Aubrey Crocker	2-0	Genesta, GBR	John Carter
1886	Mayflower	Martin Stone	2-0	Galatea, GBR	Dan Bradford
1887	Volunteer	Henry Haff	2-0	Thistle, GBR	John Barr
1893	Vigilant	William Hansen	3-0	Valkyrie II, GBR	Wm. Granfield
1895	Defender	Henry Haff	3-0	Valkyrie III, GBR	Wm. Granfield
1899	Columbia	Charles Barr	3-0	Shamrock I, GBR	Archie Hogarth
1901	Columbia	Charles Barr	3-0	Shamrock II, GBR	E.A. Sycamore
1903	Reliance	Charles Barr	3-0	Shamrock III, GBR	Bob Wringe
1920	Resolute	Charles F. Adams	3-2	Shamrock IV, GBR	William Burton
1930	Enterprise	Harold Vanderbilt*	4-0	Shamrock V, GBR	Ned Heard
1934	Rainbow	Harold Vanderbilt*	4-2	Endeavour, GBR	T.O.M. Sopwith
1937	Ranger	Harold Vanderbilt*	4-0	Endeavour II, GBR	T.O.M. Sopwith

12-Meter Boats

Year	Winner	Skipper	Series	Loser	Skipper
1958	Columbia	Briggs Cunningham	4-0	Sceptre, GBR	Graham Mann
1962	Weatherly	Bus Mosbacher	4-1	Gretel, AUS	Jock Sturrock
1964	Constellation	Bob Bavier & Eric Ridder	4-0	Sovereign, AUS	Peter Scott
1967	Intrepid	Bus Mosbacher	4-0	Dame Pattie, AUS	Jock Sturrock
1970	Intrepid	Bill Ficker	4-1	Gretel II, AUS	Jim Hardy
1974	Courageous	Ted Hood	4-0	Southern Cross, AUS	John Cuneo
1977	Courageous	Ted Turner	4-0	Australia	Noel Robins
1980	Freedom	Dennis Conner	4-1	Australia	Jim Hardy
1983	Australia II	John Bertrand	4-3	Liberty, USA	Dennis Conner
1987	Stars & Stripes	Dennis Conner	4-0	Kookaburra III, AUS	Iain Murray

60-ft Catamaran vs 133-ft Monohull

Year	Winner	Skipper	Series	Loser	Skipper
1988	Stars & Stripes	Dennis Conner	2-0	New Zealand, NZE	David Barnes

75-ft International America's Cup Class

Year	Winner	Skipper	Series	Loser	Skipper
1992	America 3	Bill Koch* & Buddy Melges	4-1	Il Moro di Venezia, ITA	Paul Cayard
1995	Black Magic, NZE	Russell Coutts	5-0	Young America, USA	Dennis Conner & Paul Cayard
2000	Black Magic, NZE	Russell Coutts & Dean Barker	5-0	Luna Rossa, ITA	Francesco de Angelis
2003	Alinghi, SWI	Russell Coutts	5-0	New Zealand, NZE	Dean Barker

Deaths

Althea Gibson, who was a trailblazer for African-American tennis players like the Williams sisters, died Sept. 28 at age 76.

Notable deaths in the world of sports from Nov. 1, 2002-Oct. 30, 2003.

Todd Adams, 35; spectator who died when he fell from the right-field wall at Pacific Bell Park during the eighth inning of a San Francisco Giants game; after a fall; in San Francisco; Sept. 17.

Dee Andros, 79; former head coach of Oregon St. football from 1965-75, nicknamed "The Great Pumpkin" for his size and bright orange jacket; also served as Oregon St. AD from 1975-85; won the Bronze Star in WWII; of undisclosed reasons; in Corvallis, Ore.; Oct. 22.

Mark Antenorcruz, 25; baseball fan who was shot dead during a sports argument in the parking lot of Dodger Stadium following a game between the Los Angeles Dodgers and San Francisco Giants; in Los Angeles; Sept. 19.

Roone Arledge, 71; legendary television executive and innovator who ran both ABC News and ABC Sports simultaneously; created prime-time ratings phenomenon with "Monday Night Football" in 1970 the show that made Howard Cosell a household name; also developed the popular "ABC's Wide World of Sports" in 1960; presided over ABC's coverage of 10 Olympic Games from 1964-88; won four Peabody awards and 37 Emmys; of complications from cancer; in New York City; Dec. 5, 2002.

Steve Bechler, 23; pitching prospect with the Baltimore Orioles who fell ill following a spring training workout in the heat and humidity; the 6-foot-2, 239-pound Bechler had reportedly been taking a controversial dietary supplement containing ephedrine; of multi-organ failure due to heatstroke; in Fort Lauderdale; Feb. 17.

Al Blades, 26; former NFL safety who played for the San Francisco 49ers after a four-year career at the University of Miami, earning All-Big East honors with the Hurricanes in 2000; brother to former Miami and NFL players Bennie and Brian Blades; in an automobile accident; in Miami; Mar. 20.

Bobby Bonds, 57; baseball's first power-hitting leadoff hitter; Bonds had the rare combination of power and speed, becoming just the second player to hit 30 homers and steal 30 bases in a season (Willie Mays); finished his career with 332 career home runs and 461 stolen bases with eight different teams; won three gold gloves as an outfielder; three-time All-Star and MVP of 1973 All-Star Game; father of current San Francisco Giants slugger Barry; of cancer, in San Francisco, Aug. 23.

Herb Brooks, 66; coached the 1980 U.S. Olympic Hockey team to a "Miracle on Ice" win over the Soviet Union at Lake Placid Winter Games on its way to an improbable gold medal; returned to coach the 2002 U.S. Olympic team to a silver medal at Salt Lake City; coached University of Minnesota from 1972-79, winning 3 national championships; inducted into U.S. Hockey Hall of Fame in 1990; coached in the NHL with New York Rangers (1981-85), Minnesota (1987-88), New Jersey (1992-93) and Pittsburgh (1999-2000) compiling an NHL career mark of 219-222-66; in a single car accident after apparently falling asleep at the wheel; outside Minneapolis, Minn.; Aug. 11.

Valery Brumel, 60; world and Olympic champion high jump champion; Brumel, a Russian, won the silver medal at the 1960 Summer Olympics in Rome and the gold medal four years later at the Summer Games in Tokyo when he and American John Thomas both cleared 7-feet-1 3/4 inches; Brumel won the gold because he had fewer misses; held the world record from 1961-71 when his mark of 7-feet-5 3/4 inches was surpassed; after a long illness; in Moscow; Jan. 26.

Ron Burton, 67; football running back who was the first overall draft choice of the AFL by the Boston Patriots in 1959; also drafted by the Philadelphia Eagles and Ottawa of the CFL; a two-time All-America halfback at Northwestern and was inducted into the College Football Hall of Fame in 1990; dedicated philanthropist following his pro career, ran the Ron Burton training village, a sports camp for underprivileged, inner-city kids; of bone cancer, Sept. 13.

John Butler, 56; NFL executive who helped build the Buffalo Bills Super Bowl teams on the 1990s; was general manager of the San Diego Chargers at the time of his death; during his tenure in the Bills' front office the team went to the playoffs 10 times and had a record of 140-83; of lymphoma; in San Diego; April 11.

Bill Cayton, 85; boxing manager who was Mike Tyson's co-manager (with Jim Jacobs) early in his career; Cayton was Tyson's manager from 1984-1988 until Tyson sued to end their business relationship after Jacob's death. Cayton also sold his giant collection of famous fight films to Disney Corp. (for ESPN Classic) in 1998; also managed Wilfred Benitez, Edwin Rosario, Tommy Morrison, Vinny Pazienza, Jeremy Williams and Michael Grant; of lung cancer; in Larchmont, N.Y.; Oct. 4.

Clive Charles, 51; Coach for both the men's and women's soccer teams at the University of Portland, amassing a record of 439-144-44 between the two programs; coached Portland's Lady Pilots to the 2002 NCAA College Cup title, earning the first Div. I national championship in the school's history; also served as the coach of the U.S. Men's Olympic (Under-23) team since 1997 and as an assistant to Steve Sampson with the national team at the 1998 World Cup; following a long battle with prostate cancer; in Portland, Ore.; Aug. 26.

Ken Coleman, 78; sports broadcaster who started in Cleveland doing Indians and Browns games, calling every touchdown of Jim Brown's pro career; later had a 20-year stretch as the voice of the Boston Red Sox, broadcasting their games on radio and television; while being treated for complications from bacterial meningitis; in Plymouth, Mass.; Aug. 21.

Bobby Cox, 69; star quarterback for University of Minnesota who appeared on the cover of *Sports Illustrated* in 1957 and was dubbed the "best college quarterback" in the country. Cox, started at the University of Washington before transferring to Minnesota; led the Golden Gophers to the No. 12 spot in the final AP Poll with a 6-1-2 record; drafted in the fourth round of the 1957 NFL draft by the Los Angeles Rams but didn't make the team; played in the CFL and briefly for the AFL's Boston Patriots; of pancreatic cancer; in Plymouth, Minn.; Oct. 3.

Dave DeBusschere, 62; Hall of Fame forward with the NBA's New York Knicks and Detroit Pistons who also played Major League Baseball with the Chicago White Sox (1962-63); DeBusschere was known for his tenacious defense and rebounding and became the youngest coach in NBA history when he was named player-coach of the Pistons in 1964 at age 24; traded to the Knicks in 1968 for Howard Komives and Walt Bellamy and won 2 NBA titles (1970, 1973) with New York; later became commissioner of the NBA rival ABA (1975-76) and general manager of the Knicks in 1982; of a heart attack, in New York City, June 11.

Patrick Dennehy, 21; Six-foot-10 junior Baylor basketball player who was last seen alive June 12 and found dead July 25; Baylor teammate Carlton Dotson was arrested and charged with his murder; in Waco, Tex.; of gunshot wounds; sometime between June 12-July 25.

USA Hockey
Herb Brooks

George Kalinsky/MSG
Dave DeBusschere

AP/Wide World Photos
Larry Doby

Larry Doby, 78; Hall of Fame outfielder who became the first black player in the American League on July 5, 1947 just 11 weeks after Jackie Robinson broke baseball's color barrier; seven-time All-Star in his 13-year career and won a World Series with Cleveland in 1948; led the AL in home runs twice (32 in 1952 and '54) and hit at least 20 homers in eight straight seasons, finishing his career with 253 homers and 969 RBI; Doby was also the first black player in the American Basketball League, a precursor to the NBA; In 1978, he became the just second black manager (Frank Robinson) in the majors, leading the Chicago White Sox; following a long illness; in Montclair, N.J., June 18.

Fred Ebbett, 70; longtime commissioner of the Cape Cod Baseball League; played a role in the amateur summer league's switch to wooden bats in 1985; after complications from surgery; in Fort Myers, Fla.; May 9.

Trevor Ettinger, 23; minor league hockey player with the Columbus Blue Jackets' organization; Ettinger played left wing with Syracuse of the AHL and Dayton in the ECHL; in Upper Kennetcook, Nova Scotia, Canada; an apparent suicide; July 27.

Ferdinand, 19; thoroughbred winner of the 1986 Kentucky Derby as a 17-1 shot; finished second at the Preakness and third in the Belmont Stakes; 1987 Horse of the Year; the horse was not as successful as a stud and was sold to a Japanese buyer in 1994; the horse's former owner Yoshikazu Watanabe announced on July 22, 2003 that he gave the horse to a unidentified breeder friend in 2001 and that the horse was "disposed of during the last year"; under mysterious circumstances, but likely slaughtered; in Japan; sometime in 2002.

Shea Fitzgerald, 19; sophomore offensive tackle for Northern Illinois University football team; was one of 12 people killed when a multi-level outside porch at an apartment building collapsed during a party; in Chicago; June 29.

Marc-Vivien Foe, 28; soccer midfielder for Cameroon's national team; Foe collapsed on the field during Cameroon's 1-0 win over Colombia in a FIFA Confederation's Cup semifinal game; Foe had played professionally in Europe with France's Lens and Lyon as well as England's West Ham United and Manchester City; of a heart attack; in Lyon, France; June 26.

Kim Gallagher, 38; two-time Olympic medallist for the USA in the 800 meters; won silver at the 1984 and bronze with her courageous third-place finish at Seoul in 1988 while battling anemia and infection; following a stroke; in Philadelphia; Nov. 18.

Kid Gavilan, 77; former world welterweight champion (1951-54), the Cuban-born American boxer's real name was Gerardo Gonzalez. He had a professional record of 71-30-6 and was never knocked out despite fighting some of the sport's legends including Sugar Ray Robinson and Carmen Basilio; the speedy fighter, known for his defense and timing, was inducted into the International Boxing Hall of Fame in 1990; Gavilan challenged Carl "Bobo" Olsen for the middleweight crown in 1954 but lost a decision and retired from boxing at age 32 after he lost his welterweight belt to Johnny Saxton; of a heart attack; in Miami, Fla.; Feb. 14.

Diane Geppi-Aikens, 40; head coach of the Loyola College lacrosse team who coached all but one game of the Greyhounds' 2003 Final Four season from her wheelchair after she was left paralyzed during treatment for a brain tumor; she graduated from Loyola where she was a four-year starter at goalie and a two-time captain in lacrosse and volleyball; of cancer; in Baltimore; June 29.

Althea Gibson, 76; Harlem-raised tennis player who broke the color barrier in tennis, becoming the first black player to compete in the U.S. Championships in 1950. The following year she became the first black player to play at Wimbledon; she won the French Open in 1956 and became the first black woman to win Wimbledon and U.S. national titles (the precursor to the U.S. Open) when she won the two tournaments in consecutive years (1957-58) and for the feat she won the Associated Press Female Athlete of the Year award in 1957 and 1958; she was the only black woman to win the U.S. national title and Wimbledon until the Williams sisters captured the the titles in 1999 and 2000, respectively; Gibson also toured with the Harlem Globetrotters, playing exhibition tennis matches before their games. After retiring from tennis, Gibson took up golf in 1960 and continued her trail blazing ways becoming the first black woman on the LPGA Tour in 1962; of respiratory failure following a long illness; in East Orange, N.J.; Sept. 28.

Sid Gillman, 91; hall of fame football coach who helped devise and popularize the West Coast offense; has been called the father of the modern passing game; coached 18 seasons in the AFL and NFL, compiling a record of 123-104-7 with the Los Angeles Rams (1955-59) and the Los Angeles/San Diego Chargers (1960-69, 1971) and Houston Oilers (1973-74); his family operated movie theaters in Minneapolis and Gillman became the first coach to use game film to analyze his opponents; in his sleep; in Los Angeles; Jan. 3.

Al Gionfriddo, 81; outfielder for the Brooklyn Dodgers who made a spectacular catch in left field of a apparent game-tying home run off the bat of the New York Yankees' Joe DiMaggio in Game 6 of the 1947 World Series; Even though the Yankees would go on to win Game 7 and the series, Gionfriddo's catch sealed the win for Brooklyn in Game 6 at Yankee Stadium; played three big league seasons, two with the Pittsburgh Pirates and one with Brooklyn, finishing his career with a .266 batting average; after collapsing while playing golf; in Solvang, Calif.; Mar. 14.

Ennis Haywood, 23; speedy former Iowa State running back who was participating in the Dallas Cowboy three-day mini-camp as an undrafted free agent; Haywood was fifth all-time on the Iowa State career rushing list; from a mixture of drugs and ethanol complicated by asthma; in Arlington, Tex.; May 11.

Greg Hennigar, 18; redshirt freshman walk-on quarterback at Penn State; in a automobile accident; in Philadelphia; May 31

Bobby Joe Hill, 59; basketball player who was the leading scorer on the Texas Western (now UTEP) team that won the 1966 national championship. Texas Western, with five black starters, beat the Adolph Rupp's all-white Kentucky team, 72-65, in the symbolic NCAA tournament final. The game was credited with helping to knock down barriers for black athletes at colleges around the country; of a heart attack; in El Paso, Tex.; Dec. 8, 2002.

Bob Hope, 100; beloved entertainer who started in vaudeville and became internationally famous for his comedic work in television and films; entertained U.S. Troops overseas on his USO tours that spanned the years from World War II to the Gulf War, always holding his trademark prop: a golf club; Hope was also part-owner of the Cleveland Indians and Los Angeles Rams for a time, but it was his connection with the game of golf that was his identifying link to the sports world; The PGA Tour's Bob Hope Desert Classic in Palm Springs, Calif. first carried his name in 1965 and quickly became one of the most popular events on the tour; Hope once said "Golf is my profession. Entertainment is just a sideline. I tell jokes to pay my greens fees."; golfed with celebrities and U.S. Presidents from Eisenhower to Clinton; Hope also announced the AP All-America college football team for decades on his annual Christmas special on NBC; of pneumonia; in Toluca Lake, Calif.; July 27.

Craig Kelly, 36; four-time world champion snowboarder who helped popularize the fast growing sport; known for his smooth style on the slopes and his willingness to mentor younger pro boarders, Kelly, like many in his profession, had a love for back-country riding and was one of seven riders killed in a avalanche while doing just that; in the Selkirk Mountains near Revelstoke, British Columbia; Jan. 20.

Leonard Koppett, 79; noted sportswriter and author; started in New York City with the *New York Herald Tribune* and *New York Post* before moving to California where he became the first West Coast sports correspondent for *The New York Times;* he covered the NBA in its early days and was inducted in the writers' wing of the Baseball Hall of Fame and the Basketball Hall of Fame; of an apparent heart attack; in San Francisco; June 22.

Sam Lacy, 99; longtime sports editor and columnist at Baltimore's *Afro-American* newspaper; championed the inclusion of blacks in major league baseball; of natural causes; in Baltimore; May 8.

Johnny Longden, 96; Hall of Fame jockey who rode Count Fleet to the Triple Crown in 1943; also the only jockey to ride and train a Kentucky Derby winner with Majestic Prince, winner of the 1969 Derby and Preakness. Majestic Prince narrowly missed giving Longden another Triple Crown finishing second in the Belmont Stakes; also the first jockey to win 6,000 races; in Banning, Calif.; Feb. 14.

Hank Luisetti, 86; basketball pioneer who popularized the one-handed shot and thereby changed the game; a high-scoring three-time All-American for Stanford in the mid 1930's, Luisetti's success using the one-handed shot instead of the traditional two-handed set shot, led to others and eventually everyone to adopt it; he became the first college player to score 50 points in a game when Stanford crushed Duquesne 92-27 on New Year's Day 1938; following an unknown ailment; in San Mateo, Calif.; Dec. 17, 2002.

Roman Lyashenko, 24; Russian forward for the New York Rangers; played two seasons for the Dallas Stars before getting traded to New York; he played two games with the Rangers and then Hartford of the AHL in the 2002-03 season; in 139 NHL games, he had 14 goals and nine assists; an apparent suicide; in Antalya, Turkey; July 5.

Max Manning, 84; former Negro Leagues pitcher who contacted the Detroit Tigers in 1937 about a tryout and was offered one before the team discovered he was black and rescinded the offer; nicknamed "Dr. Cyclops" because of his thick eyeglasses, Manning was a 6-foot-4 right-handed side-armer; he played 10 seasons with the Newark Eagles and in 1946 pitched the deciding game of the Negro League World Series as Newark beat the Kansas City Monarchs 3-2; also barnstormed with Satchel Paige in the 1940s; after a long illness; in Pleasantville, N.J.; June 23.

Mark McCormack, 72; ground-breaking sports agent who founded IMG (International Management Group), the management company that represents Tiger Woods, Michael Schumacher, Jaromir Jagr, Jennifer Capriati, Derek Jeter, Sergio Garica and many other stars from sports and entertainment; McCormack, a lawyer who loved golf, pioneered the industry and his career as an agent with Arnold Palmer in 1960 and in 1990 *Sports Illustrated* named his the most powerful man in sports; while in a coma four months after suffering a heart attack; in New York City; May 16.

Will McDonough, 67; legendary hard-nosed sports reporter and columnist who worked for the *Boston Globe* for 41 years and became most famous for his coverage of pro football; one of the first print journalists to appear regularly on television; of a heart attack; in Hingham, Mass.; Jan. 9.

Dave McNally, 60; All-Star pitcher who, with Andy Messersmith, successfully challenged baseball's reserve clause, ushering in the era of free agency; McNally was a four-time 20-game winner with the Baltimore Orioles and pitching the clinching game of the 1966 World Series and later the longest complete game shutout in post-season history, beating Minnesota 1-0 in 11 inns in the 1969 ALCS; part of Orioles' 1971 quartet (with Jim Palmer, Mike Cuellar and Pat Dobson) of 20-game winners; he was traded to Montreal and retiring following a 3-6 start to the 1975 season, the player's union head Marvin Miller approached him to get involved with the case he was building against baseball's team owners, arguing that they couldn't renew their rights to the players in perpetuity; on Dec. 23, 1975 an arbitrator agreed and the owners and union negotiated a deal that allowed players to

NHL
Roger Neilson

AP/Wide World Photos
George Plimpton

Dallas Cowboys
Tex Schramm

become free agents after six seasons in the major leagues; of cancer, in Billings, Mont., Dec. 2, 2002.

Durwood Merrill, 64; former longtime American League umpire who worked the 1988 World Series and three All-Star Games; retired following the 1999 season; of complications from a heart attack; in Texarkana, Tex.; Jan. 11.

Roger Neilson, 69; longtime NHL coach and scout, Neilson was head coach of eight different teams (Toronto 1977-79, Buffalo 1980, Vancouver 1981-84, Los Angeles 1984, New York Rangers 1989-93, Florida 1993-95, Philadelphia 1997-2000, Ottawa 2002) in a pro coaching career that was interrupted by his battle with cancer; career record of 460-381-159; was an assistant with Ottawa when he filled in for head coach Jacques Martin for two games (in order to reach 1,000 games coached in his career, a milestone that only nine coaches have reached); Neilson was dubbed "Captain Video" because he was one of the first coaches to use videotape as a coaching aid; also known for the loud neckwear he wore behind the bench; elected to the NHL Hall of Fame in the Builder category in 2002; of cancer; in Peterborough, Ontario, Canada; June 21.

Don Padgett, 78; former president of the Professional Golfer's Association (1977-78); During his term as PGA president, the Ryder Cup matches expanded to involve players from Europe joining those from Great Britain and Ireland; of cancer; in Pinehurst, N.C.; May 16.

Laszlo Papp, 77; Hungarian middleweight who became the first boxer to win three Olympic gold medals (1948, 1952, 1956); won the European middleweight title as a professional in 1962 but his communist government would not permit to fight for a world title; known for his big left hook; undefeated in the ring with a 26-0-3 record including 15 knockouts; after a long illness; in Budapest, Hungary; Oct. 16.

George Plimpton, 76; journalist and author who penned the famous "Paper Lion" about his momentary in training camp with the Detroit Lions; he also tried his hand in areas of the world of professional sports. Plimpton pitched to Willie Mays and got in the ring with light heavyweight boxing champion Archie Moore, writing about his experiences living out fans' sports fantasies, always with a self-deprecating, comic slant. Plimpton also helped found the widely-regarded Paris Review, and acted in several films, including Reds and Good Will Hunting. Plimpton also created a famous fictional character when he wrote a 1985 article for Sports Illustrated entitled "The Curious Case of Sidd Finch," about a make-believe ballplayer who purportedly threw a 168-mph fastball. The article was an April Fools Day prank, but fooled many of the readers; Plimpton also was a volunteer in Robert Kennedy's 1968 presidential run and was walking in front of the candidate when he assassinated and helped wrestle the gun away from assassin Sirhan Sirhan; in New York City, Sept. 25.

Richie Regan, 72; star guard for Seton Hall who went on to become the university's basketball coach and AD; along with All-American center Walter Dukes, led the Pirates to a 31-2 record, the 1953 National Invitation Tournament championship and a No. 2 ranking in the season's final AP poll; was drafted in the first round in the 1953 NBA draft by the Rochester Royals and played three seasons in the league before returning to Seton Hall as head coach of the Pirates; Regan finished with a record of 112-131 in 10 seasons and was named AD in 1971, helping to create the Big East Conference in 1979; of congestive heart failure; in Neptune, N.J.; Dec. 24.

Tony Renna, 26; Indy Racing League driver killed while running test laps at Indianapolis Motor Speedway; Renna was on Turn 3 of his fourth lap, reaching speeds of 218 m.p.h., when his car jumped sideways and flew into the catch fence and broke in half; had been named to replace Tomas Scheckter on the Target/Ganassi team for the 2004 season; in Indianapolis; Oct. 22.

Leni Riefenstahl, 101; German filmmaker whose Nazi propaganda films made her infamous. Her documentary "Olympia" covered of the 1936 Summer Olympics in Berlin; in Pocking, Germany; Sept. 8.

Brad Rone, 34; heavyweight boxer who was fighting to earn money to travel to his mother's funeral and wound up being buried next to her in matching coffins; Rone, who had lost 26 straight fights, collapsed in the ring following an uneventful first round in his fight with Billy Zumbrun; Rone was a former sparring partner of Mike Tyson and Evander Holyfield; of an apparent heart attack; in Cedar City, Utah, July 18.

Harold Rose, 92; longtime horse trainer in south Florida, saddled three Kentucky Derby entrants: Rexson's Hope (1984) and Hal's Hope (2000); of natural causes; in North Miami, Sept. 8.

Stanley Rosenfeld, 89; photographer of America's Cup races who along with his father Morris took breathtaking photos of the racing yachts; in Miami, Fla.; Dec. 23, 2002.

Rudy Sablo, 84; Hall of Fame American weightlifter who managed the U.S. teams at the 1972 and 1976 Olympics and served on the USOC board; Sablo was also a former New York City firefighter and after the Sept. 11 terrorist attacks he put his experience to use, assisting crews at ground zero; in New York City; Feb. 4.

Tex Schramm, 83; former longtime president and general manager of the Dallas Cowboys known for his marketing savvy and knack for show business; Schramm hired Tom Landry as the expansion franchise's first coach and his innovations included instant replay, the running play clock and the Dallas Cowboy Cheerleaders; Schramm was deeply involved in the AFL-NFL merger and became the first president of the league's competition committee; while with the Los Angeles Rams, Schramm also gave eventual commissioner Pete Rozelle his first job in the NFL as the Rams' publicity director; of natural causes; in Dallas; July 15.

Bill Shoemaker, 72; Hall of Fame jockey who won 8,883 races, the second most in thoroughbred racing history; nicknamed "The Shoe," he rode for 41 years mostly in Southern California a was 3-time Eclipse Award winner as a jockey (1981) and special award recipient (1976,81); won the Belmont Stakes 5 times, Kentucky Derby 4 times and Preakness twice; oldest jockey to win Kentucky Derby (age 54, aboard Ferdinand in 1986); retired in 1990 to become trainer; was paralyzed in 1991 auto accident but he continued to train horses; in his sleep; in San Marino, Calif.; Oct. 12

Wilbur Snapp, 83; minor league baseball organist who was ejected from the ballpark by an umpire after Snapp played "Three Blind Mice" after a questionable call that went against the hometown Clearwater Phillies during a game at Jack Russell Stadium in 1985; Snapp became a minor celebrity in baseball circles as a result of the incident; played the organ at Philadelphia Phillies spring training games and was a dedicated fan, even attending games after Jack Russell Stadium switched to canned music and canned him; of natural causes; in South Pasadena, Fla.; Sept. 6.

Dan Snyder, 25; young center for NHL's Atlanta Thrashers who had 10 goals and 4 assists in 36 games last season; following a high-speed car crash in a Ferrari driven by teammate Dany Heatley; in Atlanta; Oct. 5.

Spectacular Bid, 27; thoroughbred who nearly captured the 1979 Triple Crown; "Bid" won 26 of 30 career starts and won three Eclipse awards: champion 2-year-old colt, champion 3-year-old colt and champion older horse; in 1979 he won as a favorite at the Kentucky Derby and then again at the Preakness; at the Belmont Stakes with the Triple Crown seemingly all but inevitable, he finished a surprising third and following the race it was revealed that a safety pin had been found in his hoof the morning of the race; the ensuing infection threatened the colt's life and put him out to stud permanently; of a heart attack, in Unadilla, N.Y., June 9.

Dick Stuart, 70; big-hitting, poor-fielding first baseman with Pittsburgh Pirates, Boston Red Sox, and four other major league teams in the late 1950s-1960s; hit 228 career home runs, including 42 (and a league-leading 118 RBI) in 1963 with the Red Sox; of cancer; in Redwood City, Calif., Dec. 15, 2002.

Haywood Sullivan, 72; former part-owner of the Boston Red Sox who rose up through the ranks from reserve catcher to general manager to ultimately a minority owner; as a player, Sullivan was a highly touted recruit but his career was stunted due to military service and back troubles; while in the Red Sox front office, Sullivan was credited with helping build three pennant winners (1967, 1975, 1986) of a stroke, in Fort Myers, Fla., Feb. 12.

Leonard Tose, 88; former owner of the NFL's Philadelphia Eagles who gambled away the considerable fortune he made in trucking and forced him to sell the team to Norman Braman in 1985; Tose led the high life, was married five times and was a major force behind charities such as the Ronald McDonald House program; unsuccessfully sued Atlantic City's Sands Hotel & Casino, claiming he was encouraged to drink while gambling, leading him to lose upwards of $10 million; in Philadelphia; April 15.

Jim Wacker, 66; coach who won back-to-back national football titles in NAIA (Texas Lutheran in 1974-75) and NCAA Division II (Southwest Texas in 1981-82) and went on to coach at Texas Christian University and the University of Minnesota; won the 1982 AFCA College Division Coach of the Year Award while at SW Texas (now Texas St.); at TCU Wacker brought to light long-running NCAA violations involving player payment; following his stint at Minnesota, Wacker left coaching with a 160-130-3 career record and worked as a commentator on CBS radio before becoming athletic director at SW Texas in 1998; following a long battle with cancer; in San Marcos, Tex.; Aug. 26.

Harry Watson, 79; big and fast left wing who won the Stanley Cup five times in 14 NHL seasons and was inducted into the hockey hall of fame; Watson, had 206 goals and 207 assists in 809 games with the Detroit Red Wings, Toronto Maple Leafs and Chicago Blackhawks from 1941-57; following an undisclosed illness; in Toronto, Ontario; Nov. 19, 2002.

Ray Wietecha, 74; center for the New York Giants who did not miss a game in his 10-year, 124-game playing career; served as Vince Lombardi's offensive coordinator with the Super Bowl I and II champion Green Bay Packers; of an aneurysm; in Phoenix, Dec. 14, 2002.

David Woodley, 44; strong-armed mobile quarterback who starred at LSU and played with the NFL's Miami Dolphins and Pittsburgh Steelers; in Miami, Woodley replaced future Hall of Famer Bob Griese as the starter in 1980 as a rookie; the following year Woodley split time with Don Strock, a superior passer but inferior runner, and the tandem was labeled "Woodstrock"; in the 1982 strike-shortened season Woodley started the Super Bowl but the Dolphins were beaten 27-17 by the Washington Redskins; in 1983 another rookie was given the starting job, this time it was Dan Marino replacing Woodley as the team's starter in 1983; of liver and kidney failure; in Shreveport, La.; May 4.

Julian Yearwood, 31; arena football fullback/linebacker for the Bakersfield Blitz who collapsed while on the bench at an arenafootball2 game against the Wichita Stealth; of sudden cardiac death due to focally severe coronary artery atherosclerotic disease; in Valley Center, Kan.; July 19.

Many sources were used in the gathering of information for this almanac. Day-to-day material was almost always found in copies of *USA Today, The Boston Globe,* and *The New York Times* or online at various World Wide Web addresses (see below).

Several weekly and bi-weekly periodicals were also used in the past year's pursuit of facts and figures, among them— *Baseball America, Boxing Digest, ESPN the Magazine, FIFA News* (Soccer), *The Hockey News, The NCAA News, Soccer America, Sports Illustrated, The Sporting News, Street & Smith's Sports Business Journal, Track & Field News* and *USA Today Baseball Weekly.*

In addition, the following books provided background material for one or more chapters of the almanac.

Arenas & Ballparks

The Ballparks, by Bill Shannon and George Kalinsky; Hawthorn Books, Inc. (1975); New York.

Diamonds, by Michael Gershman; Houghton Mifflin Co. (1993); Boston.

Green Cathedrals (Revised Edition), by Philip Lowry; Addison-Wesley Publishing Co. (1992); Reading, Mass.

The NFL's Encyclopedic History of Professional Football, Macmillan Publishing Co. (1977); New York.

Take Me Out to the Ballpark, by Lowell Reidenbaugh; The Sporting News Publishing Co. (1983); St. Louis.

24 Seconds to Shoot (An Informal History of the NBA), by Leonard Koppett; Macmillan Publishing Co. (1968); New York.

Auto Racing

Indy: 75 Years of Racing's Greatest Spectacle, by Rich Taylor; St. Martin's Press (1991); New York.

2003 CART FedEx Championship Series Media Guide; Championship Auto Racing Teams; Troy, Mich.

2003 Indy Racing League Media Guide, by IMS Publications; Indianapolis.

2003 NASCAR Winston Cup Series Media Guide, compiled and edited by Sports Marketing Enterprises; NASCAR Winston Cup Series; Winston-Salem, N.C.

Marlboro Grand Prix Guide, 1950-1998 (1999 Edition), compiled by Jacques Deschenaux and Claude Michele Deschenaux; Charles Stewart & Company Ltd; Brentford, England.

NASCAR Online, produced by Turner Sports Interactive, http://www.nascar.com

CART Online, maintained by CART and VFX Digital Solutions, http://www.cart.com

Indy Racing Online, maintained by IRL, http://www.indyracingleague.com

NHRA Online, maintained by NHRA, http://www.nhra.com

Baseball

The All-Star Game (A Pictorial History, 1933 to Present), by Donald Honig; The Sporting News Publishing Co. (1987); St. Louis.

The Baseball Chronology, edited by James Charlton; Macmillian Publishing Co. (1991); New York.

The Baseball Encyclopedia (Ninth Edition), editorial director, Rick Wolff; Macmillan Publishing Co. (1993); New York.

The Complete 2002 Baseball Record Book, edited by Craig Carter; The Sporting News Publishing Co.; St. Louis.

The Scrapbook History of Baseball by Jordan Deutsch, Richard Cohen, Roland Johnson and David Neft; Bobbs-Merrill Company, Inc. (1975); Indianapolis/New York.

2002 Sporting News Official Baseball Guide, edited by Craig Carter and Dave Sloan; The Sporting News Publishing Co.; St. Louis.

2002 Sporting News Official Baseball Register, edited by Jeff Paur, David Walton, John Duxbury; The Sporting News Publishing Co.; St. Louis.

The Sports Encyclopedia: Baseball (1996 Edition), edited by David Neft and Richard Cohen; St. Martin's Press; New York.

Total Baseball (Seventh Edition), edited by John Thorn, Pete Palmer and Michael Gershman; Total Sports Publishing (2001); Kingston, N.Y.

The Official Site of Major League Baseball, produced by Major League Baseball Properties, Inc., http://www.mlb.com

College Basketball

All the Moves (A History of College Basketball), by Neil D. Issacs; J.B. Lippincott Company (1975); New York.

College Basketball, U.S.A. (Since 1892), by John D. McCallum; Stein and Day (1978); New York.

Collegiate Basketball: Facts and Figures on the Cage Sport, by Edwin C. Caudle; The Paragon Press (1960); Montgomery, Ala.

The Encyclopedia of the NCAA Basketball Tournament, written and compiled by Jim Savage; Dell Publishing (1990); New York.

The Final Four (Reliving America's Basketball Classic), compiled by Billy Reed; Host Communications, Inc. (1988); Lexington, Ky.

2000 NCAA Final Four Records Book, compiled by Gary Johnson; edited by Marty Benson; NCAA Books; Indianapolis.

The Modern Encyclopedia of Basketball (Second Revised Edition), edited by Zander Hollander; Dolphins Books (1979); Doubleday & Company, Inc.; Garden City, N.Y.

2000 NCAA Men's Records Book, compiled by Gary Johnson and Sean Straziscar; edited by Marty Benson; NCAA Books; Indianapolis.

2000 NCAA Women's Records Book, compiled by Richard M. Campbell and Jenifer L. Scheibler; edited by Vanessa L. Abell; NCAA Books; Indianapolis.

NCAA Online, produced by National Collegiate Athletic Association, http://www.ncaa.org

Plus many 2001-2002 NCAA Division I conference guides from America East to the WAC.

Pro Basketball

The Official NBA Basketball Encyclopedia (Third Edition), edited by Jan Hubbard; Doubleday (2000); New York.

2002-03 Sporting News Official NBA Guide; edited by Craig Carter and Rob Reheuser; The Sporting News Publishing Co.; St. Louis.

2002-03 Sporting News Official NBA Register, edited by David Walton, John Gardella; The Sporting News Publishing Co.; St. Louis.

NBA Online, produced by NBA Media Ventures, LLC, ESPN Internet Ventures and/or Starwave Corporation, http://www.nba.com

Bowling

1995 Bowlers Journal Annual & Almanac; Luby Publishing; Chicago.

2001 PWBA Guide, Professional Women's Bowling Association; Rockford, Ill.

2002-03 PBA Tour Media Guide; Professional Bowlers Association; Seattle, Wash.

PBA Online, produced by the Pro Bowlers Association, http://www.pba.com

PWBA Online, produced by Professional Women's Bowling Association, http://www.pwba.com

Boxing

The Boxing Record Book (1996 Edition), edited by Phill Marder; Fight Fax Inc.; Sicklerville, N.J.

The Ring 1985 Record Book & Boxing Encyclopedia, edited by Herbert G. Goldman; The Ring Publishing Corp.; New York.

The Ring: Boxing, The 20th Century, Steven Farhood, editor-in-chief; BDD Illustrated Books (1993); New York.

College Sports

1994-95 National Collegiate Championships, edited by Ted Breidenthal; NCAA Books; Overland Park, Kan.
1999-2000 National Directory of College Athletics, edited by Kevin Cleary; Collegiate Directories, Inc.; Cleveland.
NCAA Online, produced by National Collegiate Athletic Association, http://www.ncaa.org
NAIA.org, produced by National Association of Intercollegiate Athletics, http://www.naia.org

College Football

Football: A College History, by Tom Perrin; McFarland & Company, Inc. (1987); Jefferson, N.C.
Football: Facts & Figures, by Dr. L.H. Baker; Farrar & Rinehart, Inc. (1945); New York.
Great College Football Coaches of the Twenties and Thirties, by Tim Cohane; Arlington House (1973); New Rochelle, N.Y.
2000 NCAA College Football Records Book, compiled by Richard M. Campbell, John Painter and Sean Straziscar; edited by Scott Deitch; NCAA Books; Indianapolis.
Saturday Afternoon, by Richard Whittingham; Workman Publishing Co., Inc. (1985); New York.
Saturday's America, by Dan Jenkins; Sports Illustrated Books; Little, Brown & Company (1970); Boston.
Tournament of Roses, The First 100 Years, by Joe Hendrickson; Knapp Press (1989); Los Angeles.
NCAA Online, produced by National Collegiate Athletic Association, http://www.ncaa.org
Plus numerous college football team and conference guides, especially the 2001 guides compiled by the Atlantic Coast Conference, Big Ten, Big 12 and Southeastern Conference.

Pro Football

2000 Canadian Football League Guide, compiled by the CFL Communications Dept.; Toronto.
The Football Encyclopedia (The Complete History of NFL Football from 1892 to the Present), compiled by David Neft and Richard Cohen; St. Martin's Press (1994); New York.
The Official NFL Encyclopedia, by Beau Riffenburgh; New American Library (1986); New York.
Official NFL 1999 Record and Fact Book, compiled by the NFL Communications Dept. and Seymour Siwoff, Elias Sports Bureau; edited by Chris McCloskey and Matt Marini; produced by NFL Properties, Inc.; Los Angeles.
The Scrapbook History of Pro Football, by Richard Cohen, Jordan Deutsch, Roland Johnson and David Neft; Bobbs-Merrill Company, Inc. (1976); Indianapolis/New York.
2002 Sporting News Football Guide, edited by Craig Carter, Terry Shea and Christen Sager; The Sporting News Publishing Co.; St. Louis.
2002 Sporting News Football Register, edited Brendan Roberts; The Sporting News Publishing Co.; St. Louis.
1995 Sporting News Super Bowl Book, edited by Tom Dienhart, Joe Hoppel and Dave Sloan; The Sporting News Publishing Co.; St. Louis.
Total Football II, edited by Bob Carroll, Michael Gershman, David Neft and John Thorn; HarperCollins; New York.
NFL Online, produced by NFL Enterprises http://www.nfl.com
CFL Online, produced by SLAM! Sports, http://www.cfl.ca

Golf

The Encyclopedia of Golf (Revised Edition), compiled by Nevin H. Gibson; A.S. Barnes and Company (1964); New York.
Guinness Golf Records: Facts and Champions, by Donald Steel; Guinness Superlatives Ltd. (1987); Middlesex, England.
The History of the PGA Tour, by Al Barkow; Doubleday (1989); New York.
The Illustrated History of Women's Golf, by Rhonda Glenn, Taylor Publishing Co. (1991); Dallas.

2003 LPGA Player Guide, produced by LPGA Communications Dept.; Ladies Professional Golf Assn. Tour; Daytona Beach, Fla.
2003 PGA Tour Guide, written and edited by Chuck Adams, James Cramer, Nelson Luis and Lee Patterson; Professional Golfers Assn. Tour; Ponte Vedra, Fla.
Official Guide of the PGA Championships; Triumph Books (1994); Chicago.
The PGA World Golf Hall of Fame Book, by Gerald Astor, Prentice Hall Press (1991); New York.
2003 Champions Tour Guide, written and edited by Dave Senko, Phil Stambaugh and Joan Von Thron-Alexander; Professional Golfers Assn. Tour; Ponte Vedra, Fla.
Pro-Golf 2003, PGA European Tour Media Guide, Virginia Water, Surrey, England.
The Random House International Encyclopedia of Golf, by Malcolm Campbell; Random House (1991); New York.
USGA Record Books (1895-1959, 1960-80 and 1981-90); U.S. Golf Association; Far Hills, N.J.
LPGA Online, produced by the LPGA and Ignite Sports Media LLC., http://www.lpga.com
PGA Online, produced by the PGA of America, http://www.pgaonline.com
PGATour Online, produced by PGA Tour Inc., http://www.pgatour.com

Hockey

Canada Cup '87: The Official History, No.1 Publications Ltd.; Toronto.
The Complete Encyclopedia of Hockey; edited by Zander Hollander; Visible Ink Press (1993); Detroit.
The Hockey Encyclopedia, by Stan Fischler and Shirley Walton Fischler; research editor, Bob Duff; Macmillan Publishing Co. (1983); New York.
Hockey Hall of Fame (The Official History of the Game and Its Greatest Stars), by Dan Diamond and Joseph Romain; Doubleday (1988); New York.
The National Hockey League, by Edward F. Dolan Jr.; W H Smith Publishers Inc. (1986); New York.
The Official National Hockey League 75th Anniversary Commemorative Book, edited by Dan Diamond; McClelland & Stewart, Inc. (1991); Toronto.
2003 Official NHL Guide & Record Book, compiled by the NHL Public Relations Dept.; New York/Montreal/Toronto.
2003 Sporting News Hockey Guide, edited by Craig Carter; The Sporting News Publishing Co.; St. Louis.
2003 Sporting News Hockey Register, edited by David Walton; The Sporting News Publishing Co.; St. Louis.
The Stanley Cup, by Joseph Romain and James Duplacey; Gallery Books (1989); New York.
The Trail of the Stanley Cup (Volumes I-III), by Charles L. Coleman; Progressive Publications Inc. (1969); Sherbrooke, Quebec.
Total Hockey (Second Edition), edited by Dan Diamond, et al.; Total Sports Publishing; Kingston, N.Y.
NHL Online, produced by the NHL Interactive Cyber Enterprises, http://www.nhl.com

Horse Racing

1999 NTRA Media Guide, compiled by the National Thoroughbred Racing Association; New York.
1997 American Racing Manual, compiled by the Daily Racing Form; Hightstown, N.J.
1997 Breeders' Cup Statistics; Breeders' Cup Limited; Lexington, Ky.
1996 Directory and Record Book, Thoroughbred Racing Associations of North America Inc.; Elkton, Md.
2001 Trotting and Pacing Guide, compiled and edited by John Pawlak; United States Trotting Association; Columbus, Ohio.
USTA Online, produced by the USTA, http://www.ustrotting.com
NTRA Online, hosted by Equibase Company LLC, http://www.ntra.com
Equibase.com, hosted by Equibase Company LLC, http://www.equibase.com

International Sports

Athletics: A History of Modern Track and Field (1860-1990, Men and Women), by Roberto Quercetani; Vallardi & Associati (1990); Milan, Italy.

1999 International Track & Field Annual, Association of Track & Field Statisticians; edited by Peter Matthews; SportsBooks Ltd.; Surrey, England.

Track & Field News' Little Blue Book; Metric conversion tables; From the editors of *Track & Field News* (1989); Los Altos, Calif.

US Ski Team Online, produced by US Ski Team and SportsLine USA, http://www.usskiteam.com

Miscellaneous

The America's Cup 1851-1987 (Sailing for Supremacy), by Gary Lester and Richard Sleeman; Lester-Townsend Publishing (1986); Sydney, Australia.

The Encyclopedia of Sports (Fifth Revised Edition), by Frank G. Menke; revisions by Suzanne Treat; A.S. Barnes and Co., Inc. (1975); Cranbury, N.J.

ESPN SportsCentury, edited by Michael McCambridge; Hyperion (1999); New York.

The Great American Sports Book, by George Gipe; Doubleday & Company, Inc. (1978); Garden City, N.Y.

1999 Official PRCA Media Guide, edited by Steve Fleming; Professional Rodeo Cowboys Association; Colorado Springs.

The Sail Magazine Book of Sailing, by Peter Johnson; Alfred A. Knopf (1989); New York.

Ten Years of the Ironman, *Triathlete* magazine; October, 1988; Santa Monica, Calif.

The Ultimate Book of Sports Lists, by Mike Meserole; DK Publishing (1999); New York.

Iditarod Online, produced by the Iditarod Trail Committee and GCI, http://www.iditarod.com

PRCA Online, produced by the Pro Rodeo Cowboys Association, http://www.prorodeo.com

Olympics

All That Glitters Is Not Gold (An Irreverent Look at the Olympic Games) by William O. Johnson, Jr.; G.P. Putnam's Sons (1972); New York.

Barcelona/Albertville 1992; edited by Lisa H. Albertson; for U.S. Olympic Committee by Commemorative Publications; Salt Lake City.

Chamonix to Lillehammer (The Glory of the Olympic Winter Games); edited by Lisa H. Albertson; for U.S. Olympic Committee by Commemorative Publication (1994); Salt Lake City.

The Complete Book of the Olympics (1992 Edition); by David Wallechinsky; Little, Brown and Co.; Boston.

The Games Must Go On (Avery Brundage and the Olympic Movement), by Allen Guttmann; Columbia University Press (1984); New York.

The Golden Book of the Olympic Games, edited by Erich Kamper and Bill Mallon; Vallardi & Associati (1992); Milan, Italy.

Hitler's Games (The 1936 Olympics), by Duff Hart-Davis; Harper & Row (1986); New York/London.

An Illustrated History of the Olympics (Third Edition); by Dick Schaap; Alfred A. Knopf (1975); New York.

The Nazi Olympics, by Richard D. Mandell; Souvenir Press (1972); London.

The Official USOC Book of the 1984 Olympic Games (1984), by Dick Schaap; Random House/ABC Sports; New York.

The Olympics: A History of the Games, by William Oscar Johnson; Oxmoor House (1992); Birmingham, Ala.

Pursuit of Excellence (The Olympic Story), by The Associated Press and Grolier; Grolier Enterprises Inc. (1979); Danbury, Conn.

The Story of the Olympic Games (776 B.C. to 1948 A.D.), by John Kieran and Arthur Daley; J.B. Lippincott Company (1948); Philadelphia/New York.

United States Olympic Books (Seven Editions): 1936 and 1948-88; U.S. Olympic Association; New York.

The USA and the Olympic Movement, produced by the USOC Information Dept.; edited by Gayle Plant; U.S. Olympic Committee (1988); Colorado Springs.

Soccer

The American Encyclopedia of Soccer, edited by Zander Hollander; Everest House Publishers (1980); New York.

The European Football Yearbook (1994-95 Edition), edited by Mike Hammond; Sports Projects Ltd; West Midlands, England.

The Guinness Book of Soccer Facts & Feats, by Jack Rollin; Guinness Superlatives Ltd. (1978); Middlesex, England.

History of Soccer's World Cup, by Michael Archer; Chartwell Books, Inc. (1978); Secaucus, N.J.

The Simplest Game, by Paul Gardner; Collier Books (1994); New York.

The Story of the World Cup, by Brian Glanville; Faber and Faber Limited (1993); London/Boston.

2001 MLS Official Media Guide, edited by the MLS Communications staff; Los Angeles.

1991-92 MSL Official Guide, Major (Indoor) Soccer League; Overland Park, Kan.

FIFA Online, produced by FIFA, http://www.fifa.com

MLSnet, produced by Major League Soccer, http://mlsnet.com

Tennis

Bud Collins' Modern Encyclopedia of Tennis, edited by Bud Collins and Zander Hollander; Visible Ink Press (1994); Detroit.

The Illustrated Encyclopedia of World Tennis, by John Haylett and Richard Evans; Exeter Books (1989); New York.

Official Encyclopedia of Tennis, by the staff of the U.S. Lawn Tennis Assn.; Harper & Row (1972); New York.

2003 ATP Tour Player Guide, edited by Greg Sharko; Association of Tennis Professionals Tour Publications; Ponte Vedra Beach, Fla.

2003 WTA Tour Media Guide, compiled by Sanex WTA Public Relations staff; St. Petersburg, Fla.

ATP TourOnline, produced by ATP Tour, Inc., http://www.atptour.com

WTA Tour Online, produced by the WTA Tour, http://www.wtatour.com

Who's Who

The Guinness International Who's Who of Sport, edited by Peter Mathews, Ian Buchanan and Bill Mallon; Guinness Publishing (1993); Middlesex, England.

101 Greatest Athletes of the Century, by Will Grimsley and the Associated Press Sports Staff; Bonanza Books (1987); Crown Publishers, Inc.; New York.

The New York Times Book of Sports Legends, edited by Joseph Vecchione; Simon & Schuster (1991); New York.

Superstars, by Frank Litsky; Vineyard Books, Inc. (1975); Secaucus, N.J.

A Who's Who of Sports Champions (Their Stories and Records), by Ralph Hickok, Houghton Mifflin Co. (1995); Boston.

Other Reference Books/Sites

Facts & Dates of American Sports, by Gorton Carruth & Eugene Ehrlich; Harper & Row, Publishers, Inc. (1988); New York.

Sports Market Place 1997 (January Edition), edited by Kevin J. Myers; Franklin Quest Sports; Phoenix, Ariz.

The World Book Encyclopedia (1988 Edition); World Book, Inc.; Chicago.

The World Book Yearbook (Annual Supplements, 1954-95); World Book, Inc.; Chicago.

ESPN.com, produced by ESPN Internet Ventures., http://espn.com

CBS SportsLine, produced by CBS and SportsLine USA, http://cbs.sportsline.com

Olympics

Winter Games

Year	No.	Host City	Dates
2006	XX	Turin, Italy	Feb. 4-19
2010	XXI	Vancouver, Canada	Feb. 12-28

Summer Games

Year	No.	Host City	Dates
2004	XXVIII	Athens, Greece	Aug. 13-29
2008	XXIX	Beijing, China	July 25-Aug. 10

All-Star Games

Baseball

Year	Site	Date
2004	Minute Maid Park, Houston	July 7
2005	Comerica Park, Detroit	July 6

NBA Basketball

Year	Site	Date
2004	Staples Center, Los Angeles	Feb. 15
2005	Pepsi Center, Denver	Feb. 14

NFL Pro Bowl

Year	Site	Date
2004	Aloha Stadium, Honolulu	Feb. 8
2005	Aloha Stadium, Honolulu	Feb. 13

NHL Hockey

Year	Site	Date
2004	XCel Energy Center, St. Paul, Minn.	Feb. 7
2005	TBA	

Auto Racing

The Daytona 500 stock car race is usually held on the Sunday before the third Monday in February, while the Indianapolis 500 is usually held on the Sunday of Memorial Day weekend in May. The following dates are tentative.

Year	Daytona 500	Indy 500
2004	Feb. 15	May 30
2005	Feb. 20	May 29
2006	Feb. 19	May 28

NCAA Basketball

Men's Final Four

Year	Site	Dates
2004	Alamodome, San Antonio	April 3-5
2005	Edward Jones Dome, St. Louis	April 2-4
2006	RCA Dome, Indianapolis	April 1-3
2007	Georgia Dome, Atlanta	Mar. 31-April 2
2008	Alamodome, San Antonio	TBD

Women's Final Four

Year	Site	Dates
2004	New Orleans Sports Arena	April 4-6
2005	Indianapolis (RCA Dome)	April 3-5
2006	FleetCenter, Boston.	April 2-4
2007	Gund Arena, Cleveland	April 1-3

Horse Racing

Triple Crown

The Kentucky Derby is always held at Churchill Downs in Louisville on the first Saturday in May, followed two weeks later by the Preakness Stakes at Pimlico Race Course in Baltimore and three weeks after that by the Belmont Stakes at Belmont Park in Elmont, N.Y.

Year	Ky Derby	Preakness	Belmont
2004	May 1	May 15	June 5
2005	May 7	May 21	June 11
2006	May 6	May 20	June 10

NFL Football

Super Bowl

No.	Site	Date
XXXVIII	Reliant Stadium, Houston	Feb. 1, 2004
XXXIX	ALLTEL Stadium, Jacksonville	Feb. 6, 2005
XL	Ford Field, Detroit	Feb. 5, 2006

Golf

The Masters

Year	Site	Dates
2004	Augusta (Ga.) National GC	April 8-11
2005	Augusta (Ga.) National GC	April 7-10

U.S. Open

Year	Site	Dates
2004	Shinnecock Hills GC, Southampton, N.Y.	June 17-20
2005	Pinehurst (N.C.) Resort & CC	June 16-19
2006	Winged Foot GC, Mamaroneck, N.Y.	June 15-18
2007	Oakmont CC, Oakmont, Pa.	June 14-17
2008	Torrey Pines GC, La Jolla, Ca.	June 12-15

U.S. Women's Open

Year	Site	Dates
2004	The Orchards GC, South Hadley, Mass.	July 1-4
2005	Cherry Hills CC, Englewood, Colo.	June 23-26

U.S. Senior Open

Year	Site	Dates
2004	Bellerive CC, St. Louis, Mo.	July 29-Aug. 1
2005	NCR CC, Kettering, Ohio	July 28-31

PGA Championship

Year	Site	Dates
2004	Whistling Straits GC, Kohler, Wisc.	Aug. 13-15
2005	Baltusrol GC, Springfield, N.J.	TBA
2006	Medinah CC, Medinah, IL	TBA
2007	Southern Hills CC, Tulsa, OK	TBA
2008	Oakland Hills CC, Bloomfield Hills, Mich	TBA

British Open

Year	Site	Dates
2004	Royal Troon GC, Scotland	July 15-18
2005	St. Andrews, Scotland	July 14-17
2006	Royal Liverpool GC, England	July 20-23

Ryder Cup

Year	Site	Date
2004	Oakland Hills CC, Bloomfield Hills, Mich.	Sept. 17-19
2006	Kildare Hotel and CC, Dublin, IRE	TBA
2008	Valhalla GC, Louisville, Ky.	TBA
2010	Celtic Manor, Wales	TBA

Soccer

World Cup

Year	Site	Dates
2006	Germany	June 9-July 9
2010	Africa, Country TBD	TBD

Women's World Cup

Year	Site	Date
2007	China	TBD

Tennis

U.S. Open

Usually held from the last Monday in August through the second Sunday in Sept., with Labor Day weekend the midway point in the tournament.

Year	Site	Dates
2004	Arthur Ashe Stadium, NYC.	Aug. 30-Sept.12
2005	Arthur Ashe Stadium, NYC	Aug. 29-Sept. 11